COMBAT FLEETS OF THE WORLD
1982/83
Their Ships, Aircraft, and Armament

Edited by
JEAN LABAYLE COUHAT

English language edition prepared by A. D. Baker III

This guide was first published in 1897 by Captain de Balincourt, French Navy. It was continued from 1928 to 1943 by Captain Vincent-Bréchignac, French Navy, and from 1943 to 1974 by Henri Le Masson.

NAVAL INSTITUTE PRESS
Annapolis, Maryland

WORKS BY JEAN LABAYLE COUHAT

- *French Warships of World War I* } Published by Ian Allan, London. Sold in France by Éditions
- *French Warships of World War II* } Maritimes et d'Outre-Mer
- Articles for *"La Revue Maritime," "Marine," "Revue de Défense Nationale,"* and *"Armées d'aujourdhui"*
- Monographs on the French, American, British, and Soviet navies, published by Éditions Ozanne. These works are all out of print.
- *Flottes de Combat 1974* in collaboration with H. Le Masson
- *Flottes de Combat 1976*
- *Flottes de Combat 1978*
- *Flottes de Combat 1980*
- *Combat Fleets of the World 1976/77 Their Ships, Aircraft, and Armament*
- *Combat Fleets of the World 1978/79 Their Ships, Aircraft, and Armament* } Published in the United States, Canada, and Great Britain under the auspices of the U.S Naval Institute
- *Combat Fleets of the World 1980/81 Their Ships, Aircraft, and Armament*

Library of Congress Catalog Card Number: 78-50192
ISBN 0-87021-125-0

All photographs are official, unless otherwise credited, and have been issued by the national authories concerned; new drawings in this edition are by Henri Simoni, unless otherwise credited.

Printed in the United States of America

CONTENTS

PREFACE TO THE ENGLISH LANGUAGE EDITION

The English language edition of *Flottes de Combat* appears several months after its French parent and consequently benefits from later information supplied by M. Labayle Couhat and many other contributors. This edition has been extremely fortunate in receiving great numbers of additional photographs from Gilbert Gyssels, Leo and Linda Van Ginderen, John Jedrlinic, Gerhard Koop, Charles Dragonette, Stefan Terzibaschitsch, and others. There are minor differences in format between the English and French language editions: for example, propulsion power is given in horsepower only, as the dual presentation of horsepower and kilowattage proved too space-consuming. Ship type designations have been brought into line with the current U.S. and NATO system (for the very different Soviet system, meanings are given in the text). Because of the unusual number of developments during 1981, and the length of time it takes to update this volume, an addenda of recent changes, additions, and new photographs has been included.

In addition to those persons listed by M. Labayle Couhat in his preface to the French edition, the following have provided invaluable photographs or information or both used in the compilation of this volume (some persons will find their names mentioned twice, as they have contributed to both editions): Duane Anderson; Christian Beilstein; Larry L. Booda, editor, *Sea Technology*; Stewart A. Carpenter; Peter Dakan, Boeing Marine Services; Charles Dragonette; Ron Elias, Ingalls Shipbuilding Division, Litton Industries; J. E. Frenette; Dr. Norman Friedman, Hudson Institute; George Flynn, United Technologies Corp.; John T. Gilbride, Jr., vice-president and general manager, Todd Pacific Shipyards, Seattle Division; Ross Gillett, editor, *The Navy* (Australia); T. K. Glenn, RCA Government and Commercial Systems, Missile and Surface Radar Division; Gilbert Gyssels; Charles Haberlein, Naval Historical Center; Kohji Ishiwata, editor, *Ships of the World*; John Jedrlinic; Captain Charles Koberger, USCG (Retired); Gerhard Koop; Jürg Kürsener; Daniel London; Roy T. McMillan, Todd Shipyards Corp.; Paul Martineau, Ingalls Shipbuilding Division, Litton Industries; Samuel L. Morison, editor of the U.S. section, *Jane's Fighting Ships*; J. S. Noot; A.E.H. Piranian, General Dynamics, Electric Boat Division; Norman Polmar, editor, *Ships and Aircraft of the U.S. Fleet*; Fred Rainbow, Managing Editor, U.S. Naval Institute *Proceedings*; Dr. Steven B. Roberts, Center for Naval Analyses; Dr. Robert L. Scheina, Historian of the U.S. Coast Guard; Michael Shen, Naval Sea Systems Command; H. M. Stupinski, Bath Iron Works Corp.; Albert T. Tappman; Stefan Terzibaschitsch, editor, *Nachrichten aus der USN*; Dr. Milan Vego; Deborah Walsh, Grumman Aircraft; Christopher C. Wright III, editor, *Warship International*. Many others were of assistance as well.

Particular appreciation must be expressed to Carol Swartz of the Naval Institute Press, who arranged the many hundreds of pages of hand-written interpolations, late notes, sketches, and seeming thousands of photographs into a comprehensible whole; to her colleagues, Pat Solley who proofread the galleys, Beverly S. Baum and Cynthia Taylor, who gave the book its final crisp appearance; and to Thomas F. Epley, Press Director of the Naval Institute Press, who had the courage to stick with this sizable project. Mary Veronica Amoss, who prepared the previous two editions, was so kind as to translate J. Labayle Couhat's introduction and preface. Finally, immense appreciation is due to my wife, Anne-Marie, and daughter, Alexandra, for their patience with my daily sojourn in the "office" and their unfailing support at all times.

Any reference work can only attempt perfection, and readers may discover items on which they have later or better information; they are urged to communicate these to the publisher. Similarly, *Flottes de Combat* and *Combat Fleets* are continually in need of recent, *dated* photographs—both as illustrations and for the invaluable information which only photographs can convey. The next editions are already in preparation.

A.D. Baker III

PREFACE TO THE FRENCH EDITION

This 1982 edition of *Flottes de Combat*, the forty-second since the work was first published in 1897, contains a wealth of new material, particularly on the small navies, which have been given special attention. There are new drawings and a great many new or updated photographs. The characteristics of weapons and equipment have been updated and completed.

This edition owes a large debt to those who have helped me by providing information and photographs. I am particularly grateful to the officers of the General Staff of the Navy in Paris; the naval section of the Office of Public Relations of the Armed Forces; the director of the periodical *Cols Bleus*; the officers of the Navy's office of Public Relations; Flotilla 16F of the Naval Air Service; Captain T.-J. Honiball, South African naval attaché in Paris; Rear Admiral C. Hoffman, defense attaché at the Federal Republic of Germany embassy; Captain Sisson, U.S. naval attaché; Captain C.S. Argles, British naval attaché; Captain A.-J. van der Hout, defense attaché at the Netherlands Embassy; Colonel Lundell, naval air attaché at the Swedish embassy; foreign admiralties that responded to my questions; Mr. Robert A. Carlisle of the U.S. Navy's Still Photos Branch, Information Office, in Washington D.C.; and Mr. John Margetts of the Public Relations Service of the Ministry of Defense in London.

I must also mention the editors of foreign works of this nature: Captain Moore of *Jane's Fighting Ships*; Captain Allan Kunn of the Swedish publication *Marin Kalender*; Mr. Gerhard Albrech of Weyer's *Flottentaschenbuch*; and Mr. Giorgio Giorgerini of the Italian *Almanacco Navale*.

This 1982 edition also owes much to information and photographs generously submitted by the following, most of whom are longtime friends of *Flottes de Combat*: Commander Aldo Fraccaroli, Mr. J.-C. Bellonne, Mr. Carlo Martinelli, Mr. Giorgio Arra, Mr. Gerhard Koop, Colonel Guiglini, Mr. Hannsjorg Kowark, Mr. Norman Polmar (editor of a recent outstanding work on the ships and aircraft of the U.S. Navy), Mr. Peter Voss, and Mr. Stefan Terzibaschitsch.

Most of the photos of Japanese ships were kindly submitted by Mr. Kohji Ishiwata, director of *Ships of the World*. I am equally grateful to Mr. M. J. Goss of Navpictures, Portsmouth, and the well-known firm of Marius Bar in Toulon, which has always been responsive to my requests for photographs. Numerous naval shipyards have provided me with documentation, among them Constructions Mécaniques de Normandie and S.F.C.N. in France, Vosper Thornycroft and Yarrow in Great Britain, and Ingalls and Bath Iron Works in the United States.

Finally, I owe a tribute of gratitude to Mr. Bernard Prezelin, a reserve ensign, who, in spite of numerous other duties, helped me with the demanding job of correcting proof for this work.

J. LC.
9/15/81

INTRODUCTION

U. S. NAVY

Faced with Soviet military expansionism, President Reagan and the new American administration have, as is well known, elected to increase considerably the defense potential of the United States, primarily that of the Navy. During the preceding administration, steps were taken in this direction when Congress authorized funds in the 1980 budget for building a fourth *Nimitz*-class nuclear aircraft carrier, CVN 71. As soon as it came to power, the Reagan administration requested that funds be added to the already approved 1981 budget, to permit, among other things, work to begin on reactivating the 33,000-ton aircraft carrier *Oriskany*, which went into reserve in 1976, and the battleship *New Jersey*, which went into reserve at Bremerton in 1969. Funds for these operations were also requested in the 1982 budget, which was revised upward. This budget provides for beginning construction on two *Los Angeles*-class nuclear attack submarines (SSNs); three 9,100-ton, *Ticonderoga*-class, guided-missile cruisers equipped with the Aegis weapons system; two 3,000-ton, *Oliver Hazard Perry*-class guided-missile frigates; and a number of other ships. It also provides funds for work on the *New Jersey* and for preliminary work on reactivating her sister *Iowa*, but none for the *Oriskany*; it is now quite certain that the old aircraft carrier will not be reactivated. The *New Jersey* is being brought back to service to fill the U.S. Navy's desire to have a ship corresponding to the big nuclear Soviet cruiser, the *Kirov*, which went into service in 1980; by 1987, it is planned to have all four of the *Iowa*-class battleships back in operation—which should greatly exceed the Soviet effort. The Reagan administration requested that the Navy initiate a long-term development plan based on its new American defense policy. At the end of last June, this plan was submitted to Congress by Vice Admiral Walters, Deputy Chief of Naval Operations for Surface Warfare. The plan calls for the Navy to have, in the year 2000, besides its strategic components, 100 nuclear attack submarines, 15 big nuclear or conventional aircraft carriers, 137 guided-missile cruisers and destroyers, 101 frigates, and an amphibious force capable of transporting and landing one and a half Marine Amphibious Forces, consisting of some 30,000 men and their equipment, and capable of maintaining one Marine Air Wing (150 aircraft). This new plan will be the guideline on which future annual new construction will be based and will cover the years 1983 to 1987. This five-year plan, which, like all its predecessors, will be revised each year, foresees the construction of 123 ships and the acquisition of 1,942 aircraft for naval aviation. For the fleet's major operations, the following should be ordered during the 1983–87 plan:

—7 *Ohio*-class SSBNs, which—including those in service, under construction, ordered, and financed—will bring the total of this type to 16;

—18 *Los Angeles*-class SSNs, which, taking into account previous actions, will bring the total number of these submarines to 57;

—2 90,000-ton, *Nimitz*-class nuclear aircraft carriers, CVN 72 and CVN 73, will be added to the four already in service or building. These ships, however, will not be ready until the 1990s;

—18 guided-missile cruisers armed with Aegis, including the long-delayed nuclear cruiser CGN 42. If this program is approved, counting the units already ordered or envisaged, the fleet will have 24 ships equipped with Aegis. An ultimate force of 27 *Ticonderoga*-class cruisers is desired;

—12 of a new version of the *Oliver Hazard Perry*-class frigate, which will bring the total of both versions to 60;

—10 amphibious ships;

—3 big *Spruance*-class destroyers.

We do not know at this writing when this plan will be completed, but it probably will be very carefully scrutinized by Congress, since it calls for a considerable investment. Its magnitude is an indication of the new American administration's determination to meet the Soviet challenge. As far as the completion of earlier plans is concerned, the following large combatants have joined the fleet since publication of the 1980 edition of this work:

—SSBN *Ohio*, very much later than originally estimated;

—9 *Los Angeles*-class SSNs, bringing the number in service at this time to 18;

—the guided-missile cruiser *Arkansas* (CGN 41), the fourth and last unit of the *Virginia* class;

—9 large *Spruance*-class destroyers, bringing the total number of these ships to 30 (this program was to have been completed when DD 997 goes into service in 1983, but up to six more ships are now envisioned);

—15 *Oliver Hazard Perry*-class frigates have joined the prototype of this class, which went into service in 1977;

—the big amphibious assault ship *Peleliu*, last of the class of five.

Further, the Navy has implemented measures for prepositioning material for the Rapid Deployment Force in sensitive areas of the world. The first element, currently consisting of 13 ships, has been constituted and is based at Diego Garcia in the Indian Ocean. Eight 52,000-ton, 33-knot, container ships from Sea Land have been or are about to be bought; the same is true of four 33,900-ton *Maine*-class roll-on/roll-off cargo ships, while a new class of 48,860-ton military cargo ships (T-AKR 14) have been canceled in favor of plans to acquire 12–15 existing merchant ships for conversion.

The most important development in weapons is the ongoing program to install Tomahawk surface-to-surface missiles in large surface ships, as well as in submarines. New vertical launchers are being developed that make it possible to launch surface-to-surface, surface-to-air, or antisubmarine missiles, according to need.

We cannot end this all-too-brief overview of the development of the U.S. Navy without commenting that during last year's events in Afghanistan and Iran, it demonstrated its extraordinary ability to adapt to a sudden crisis. In very short order, a large naval air force, drawn partly from the Sixth Fleet in the Mediterranean and partly from the Seventh Fleet in the Pacific, was present in the Arabian Sea. Based on two big aircraft carriers—the only other facilities being the rather inadequate ones on the distant atoll of Diego Garcia—this deployment provided a vivid demonstration of the superiority of nuclear aircraft carriers over conventional ones. The *Nimitz*, for example, was at sea without interruption from 4 January to 25 May 1980, and the *Eisenhower* set a record by remaining at sea 152 days at a stretch. Today, the Americans still keep two aircraft carriers and their escorts in the Indian Ocean, but the situation there is not the same as it was. The facilities of Diego Garcia have been expanded, and two years after the abrupt collapse of their positions in Iran, the Americans have acquired access to a whole range of facilities in the area that have improved their strategic position considerably: Râs Bânas in Egypt, Riyadh in Saudi Arabia, Berbera in Somaliland, and so on.

SOVIET NAVY

With never-changing tenacity and consistency, the Soviet Navy continues its development and modernization, clearly showing that those in charge understand the impossibility of carrying out a global policy in today's world without a powerful fleet.

The prototype of the new *Typhoon* class of strategic submarines was launched last year at Severodvinsk on the White Sea. This submarine, which has undergone its sea trials, is—with its submerged displacement considerably in excess of 25,000 tons—by far the largest submarine in the world. It carries 20 nuclear missiles with multiple warheads and independent trajectories capable of reaching targets at a range of more than 7,400 km. Besides the *Typhoon* class, with its estimated rate of construction of one unit per year, the Soviet Navy is continuing its program of Delta-III SSBNs, which carry 16 SS-N-18 missiles with a range of 7,000 km. Twelve or more of these boats are now in service, along with the 22 older Delta-Is and Delta-IIs. According to the SALT I accords (which are still in force), the entry into active service of these boats calls for the removal of missiles from the older Yankee-class submarines.

The *Oscar* also made her appearance in 1980; she is the first of a new class of nuclear attack submarines equipped with long-range tactical missiles that can be launched by submerged submarines. This submarine displaces around 13,000 tons submerged, and carries 24 SS-N-19 cruise missiles of the same type as those carried by the guided-missile cruiser *Kirov*. This submarine is obviously intended to supplement the Echo-IIs, which are aging and can only launch their SS-N-3 and SS-N-12 cruise missiles on the surface—a serious handicap.

The handsome nuclear-powered Victor-III-class attack submarines continue building, as do the unique Alfas. Alfa, with a speed of more than 40 knots, is the fastest submarine in the world; it is believed to be able to dive to over 900 meters. With Alfa, Soviet engineers have achieved a submarine that, from certain points of view, is a "first." For example, it employs a titanium alloy pressure hull. But from the points of view of quiet running and vulnerability to detection—particularly passive—Soviet attack submarines are still far behind the latest American and British achievements. It is estimated that at the end of 1981, five Alfas were operational and the annual rate of construction of Victor-IIIs and Alfas together was from three to four.

The Soviet Navy continues to build conventional submarines but apparently not at a rate to replace, one on one, its 60 general-purpose Foxtrot submarines. Indeed, the construction rate for the recent Tango class is only matching the rate of disposal of the even older Zulu class. The newly announced Kilo class may be intended to replace the aged smaller submarines of the Whiskey and Romeo classes, many of which are over a quarter of a century old. While such diesel-powered submarines have limitations of endurance and speed when compared to nuclear-powered boats, they have distinct advantages in quiet operation while submerged, and their lesser cost evidently makes them as attractive to the Soviets as they are to most of the world's major navies.

Turning to the surface fleet, naval experts today agree in thinking that the U.S.S.R., after criticizing the type for a long time, has begun or will soon begin building a big nuclear-propelled aircraft carrier. Some believe that it is being or will be built in the yards at Severodvinsk, others say in those at Nikolayev on the Black Sea. If the latter are correct, the Soviets will have to give the ship some other designation, because the Montreux Convention, which regulates the passage of warships through the straits, does not allow the passage of aircraft carriers. They might well, however, not be concerned about that, since no one protested when the VTOL carrier *Kiev*, designated initially as a "Large Antisubmarine Cruiser" and later as a "Tactical Aircraft-Carrying Cruiser," transited the Dardanelles in 1976 and several times since. The *Kiev* is now attached to the Northern Fleet and her sister ship, the *Minsk*, to the Pacific Fleet. Two other ships of this type, the *Kharkov* and the *Novorossiysk*, are in different stages of completion. The first, which, it is said, has been undertaking her trials, could go into service early in 1982, considerably later than was forecast in the West, perhaps because of modifications to the plans or problems during construction. Most Western experts think that the *Kiev* class is a very mediocre compromise between a real aircraft carrier and a guided-missile cruiser. The fourth unit, still on the ways in Nikolayev, is expected to enter into active service in 1983 or 1984. The *Kharkov* and the *Novorossiysk* may deploy a successor to the Forger, a less than satisfactory vertical take-off and landing aircraft. This new plane would need vertical or short landing and takeoff (V/STOL) capabilities if these ships, like their predecessors, lack catapults and arresting gear.

The guided-missile cruiser *Kirov* went into service in 1981. With a displacement of more than 25,000 tons, she is the world's largest active non-carrier surface combatant and might be best termed a "battle cruiser." Her armament, which includes 20 SS-N-19 long-range surface-to-surface missiles, antiair and ASW missiles, torpedoes, helicopters, and a powerful gun battery, makes her a general-purpose ship without equal. Her new radars, Top Pair and Top Dome, and her very long range antiair missiles give her good area air defense. Her propulsion has been the subject of much speculation in specialty journals, but it is now virtually certain that the steam supplied by her reactor is super-heated by oil-fired superheaters, which allow modern, high-yield turbines to be used for her propulsion when high speeds are required. A second *Kirov*-class cruiser was launched in Leningrad in June 1981 but will not go into service until 1983 at the earliest.

Three cruisers intended as follow-ons to the seven Kara-class cruisers are being built at Nikolayev near the Black Sea. NATO has given them the temporary name BLK-COM-1 (Black Sea Combatant No. 1). It is believed that they will have a displacement of about 12,000 tons and will carry long-range surface-to-surface missiles.

The building of Krivak-class frigates seems to have been halted in favor of two new destroyer classes, *Udaloy* and *Sovremennyy*. The *Udaloy* and *Sovremennyy* classes will give the Soviets, for the first time but far behind Westerners, destroyers with permanently embarked helicopters—although it could be argued that the Kresta-II and Kara classes, which each carry one helicopter, are in fact more "destroyer" than "cruiser" in their capabilities. Displacing nearly 8,000 tons, these classes constitute the Soviet counterparts to the American *Spruance* and *Kidd* destroyer classes. The primary mission of the *Udaloy* is ASW, whereas that of the *Sovremennyy* is surface warfare; their combination thus constitutes a powerful combatant force. The *Udaloy* was delivered to the Northern Fleet in the fall of 1981; at the same time, a sister has commenced trials and four sister ships are building, half of them at Kaliningrad and half at Leningrad. The *Sovremennyy* was delivered to the Black Sea Fleet from the Baltic at the end of 1981; one sister has begun trials, another is afloat, and three or four others are probably on the ways.

With the *Kirov*s, the new cruisers at Nikolayev, the *Udaloy*s, and the *Sovremennyy*s, the Soviets are providing themselves with a new, up-to-date surface fleet. Their smaller combatants, however, lag behind. Of ships of 1,000 tons and more—i.e., the only ones that can operate on the high seas under all conditions—well over half are more than twenty years old with obsolete designs, such as the *Sverdlov*-class cruisers, Skoryy- and Kotlin-class destroyers, and Riga- and Mirka-class frigates.

The large landing ship *Ivan Rogov* recently visited the Baltic while on a deployment from the Pacific Fleet. A second ship of this class has been laid down but work on her must be proceeding slowly, since the first ship completed back in 1978. Her plans may have been changed in light of experience gained by her predecessor, for the *Ivan Rogov* is very complex—and not completely successful.

The powerful Backfire tactical bomber, now numbering at least 70, continues to join the fleet at a consistent rate. With its supersonic speed, great operational radius, and ability to deploy nuclear-warhead missiles, the Backfire constitutes a serious threat to Western fleets and lines of communication. This threat explains the recent American emphasis on ships with air defense and on aircraft carriers, for the hunt at sea is the most efficient way to deal with this menace.

Backfire bombers, the most modern nuclear-powered submarines, and the big new surface ships constitute the spearhead of the Soviet Navy. Its deployment of a very powerful force in the Indian Ocean at the time of the invasion of Afghanistan, and for many long months thereafter, demonstrated clearly that it is now capable of sustaining a long-term effort very far from home. That certainty, however, was achieved only at the expense of its presence in other parts of the world, particularly the Mediterranean where, for several months, the number of ships on station was the smallest it had been for a long time. Wherever Soviet ships are deployed overseas, they do not spend much time under way; most often they anchor just beyond territorial waters, either in open roadsteads or sheltered anchorages. This habit may allow for the training of crews, but it does nothing to help the officers acquire seamanship, that "sense of the sea" so dear to Anglo-Saxon sailors.

To wind up this brief overview of the recent development of the Soviet Navy, it should be noted that the U.S.S.R. is a major purveyor of naval armaments. While it continues to provide many Third World countries with guided-missile patrol boats, it now provides them with much more important and more sophisticated ships. The Indian Navy has received, or is about to receive, the second of three Kashin-class guided-missile destroyers; Foxtrot-class submarines have been transferred to Libya, India, and Cuba; guided-missile corvettes to Algeria, India, and Libya; and Koni-class frigates to Libya, Algeria, Cuba, and Yugoslavia. East Germany, the only Warsaw Pact country that has made a significant effort to modernize its facilities, has received from the U.S.S.R. two 1,900-ton, Koni-class frigates; it has begun to replace its little Hai-class corvettes with much-better-armed, Parchim-class small frigates; and it has completely renovated its amphibious forces through the construction of a dozen *Frosch*-class landing ships. To be sure, Romania has recently completed a number of new units, but their appearances and capabilities have yet to be demonstrated.

ROYAL NAVY

In July 1980, the British government signed a contract with the U.S. government for 100 Trident missiles to be installed in its new generation of strategic nuclear submarines that will, during the 1990s, replace the *Resolution* class now in service. The new class, like the *Resolution* class, will be attached to an Anglo-American force at the disposal of NATO, but the British government will have the explicit right to withdraw it whenever it considers its national interests to be at stake. The cost of this program is estimated at six billion pounds. Five billion will go for the purchase of the missiles and the building of four or five ballistic-missile submarines and one billion for the Chevaline system, which is intended to update the Polaris missiles of the *Resolution* class until such time as the new submarines go into service. Furthermore, since London has decided to proceed with the Royal Air Force's Tornado program at a cost of three billion pounds and since the economy of the United Kingdom makes a decrease in defense spending necessary, the government foresees that it will have to make substantial cuts in appropriations for the armed forces for the next ten years. The surface fleet will be the principal victim of that decision, a development that has brought numerous protests, including that of the Navy minister, who was relieved by Mrs. Thatcher. It will not, however, affect the nuclear-attack-submarine program, which will be continued until the planned seventeen boats have been completed (twelve are already in service). It appears that the building of conventional submarines envisaged last year will go ahead. At least ten of these boats—some sources say fourteen—are supposed to be built, and the first might join the fleet in 1988, which means that it would be laid down about 1984.

The *Ark Royal*, the third *Invincible*-class aircraft carrier, was launched on 2 June 1981 and will be completed. Before that ship joins the fleet in 1984, the old *Hermes*, which has had a "ski jump" takeoff ramp for Sea Harrier installed, will be decommissioned. Two of the *Ivincible*-class carriers will be retained in active service, while the *Invincible* herself has been offered for sale to Australia, to be transferred when the *Ark Royal* is operational.

The program for the *Sheffield*-class guided-missile destroyers (Type 42) will be completed in 1986 when the fourteenth and last ship of the series goes into service. As the *Sheffield*-class destroyers leave the yards and join the fleet, the larger County-class destroyers are being decommissioned, and by 1983 only three of the original eight will be in service; the *Norfolk* is being sold to Chile.

The program for the *Broadsword*-class frigates (Type 22) will be dropped after the seventh of the class, which has just been ordered, is completed. Instead of these big and expensive frigates, the Royal Navy intends to build lighter ships, Type 23, which will not cost more than twenty-four million pounds apiece—or so it is hoped. This comes back to the "small and many" concept held by the Admiralty for a long time. The trend will be toward ships with characteristics that might make them easily sold abroad, if their armament and sensor packages are sufficiently impressive.

Only half of the so-called "broad-beamed" *Leander*-class frigates that were scheduled to be modernized will actually undergo that program. All the pre-*Leander*-class frigates that are still in service will be gradually removed from the lists of the fleet, although some may be assigned to such special tasks as trials, schools, and so forth.

The assault ship *Intrepid* will be laid up next year and her sister, the *Fearless*, in 1984. These two ships will not be replaced, which will make it impossible for the Royal Navy to intervene overseas, except on a very small scale. The Royal Marine commandos, however, are not to be abolished.

The logistics fleet, which used to be the pride of the Royal Navy and gave it great strategic mobility, is being drastically cut. The *Lyness* has been sold to the U.S. Navy and renamed the *Sirius*, and in 1982 the *Tarbatness* will follow suit. All but three large fleet-replenishment oilers have been withdrawn from service, with *Tidepool* sold to Chile in 1982.

The decision reached a few years ago to abandon a permanent naval presence in the Indian Ocean, together with the decision not to build another fleet of aircraft carriers, was the beginning of an inevitable reduction in the British surface fleet; the decision to renew the strategic oceanic fleet has only accelerated that reduction. But in spite of North Sea oil, the slow but continuous erosion of the United Kindgom's economic and political power has primarily led to the decline of the Royal Navy. Such a decline is not as dire as some may have written, but the idea that it *is* pleases incorrigible Anglophobes. There is no doubt that in the near future the Royal Navy will become numerically smaller than it is today, but it will consist of younger ships and the best fleet of nuclear attack submarines in Western Europe. With its composition and superior manning, it will be perfectly competent to fulfill what has become its principal mission: to back up the U.S. Navy in meeting the threat that the Soviet desire for maritime expansion constantly creates in the Atlantic.

FRENCH NAVY

Two defense councils, one in 1978 and one last year, after defining the various missions that would devolve upon the Navy between now and the end of the century, drew up a kind of charter called "Marine 2000" outlining what would be needed to carry these missions out. That sketch sets forth realistically the size and nature of the forces envisaged and what necessary or possible actions they will be able to undertake. The plan was drawn up under severe financial constraints, and its realization will require serious and regular financial effort, but as one great statesman expressed it, "He who speaks of the navy, speaks of consistency, time, and goodwill." This project calls for replacing the two aircraft carriers now in service, the *Clemenceau* and the *Foch*, with two ships of equivalent tonnage but with nuclear propulsion. These carriers will have conventional aircraft embarked. The successor to the *Clemenceau* is supposed to be laid down in 1983 at Brest and go into service in 1990.

The sixth ballistic-missile submarine, the *Inflexible*, was laid down at Cherbourg on 27 March 1980. She will be launched in mid-1982 and will go into service in 1985, by which time the multiple-warhead M–4 missile, which will constitute her armament, will have become operational. Therefore, this weapon will be installed, in turn, in the older ballistic-missile submarines, except for the *Redoutable*, which will by then be too old to undergo such a substantial alteration. This operation will probably be completed in the early 1990s. Taking into account the submarines that will not be given substantial yard work, the Strategic Ocean Force will be seven and a half times as powerful as it is today and will be able to attain the longer-range objectives at the same time as its submarines' area of deployment will increase. But if this "diamond point" of French deterrent forces, as President François Mitterand calls it, is to remain credible, technical and technological advances will constantly have to be taken into account. When he visited Brest on 24 July 1981 to see the naval base and visit the *Terrible*, the president also announced the building of a seventh ballistic-missile submarine; recently, however, it has been announced that this ship will not be laid down until 1989—for completion in 1994.

The *Rubis*, the first of a series of five nuclear-attack submarines, has begun her first sea trials, and the *Saphir* was launched on 1 September last. Obviously, because of their small size, these submarines cannot be compared with the newest American, British, and Soviet boats, but they will give the French Navy's attack-submarine force a new dimension, for which all French submariners are grateful. Besides torpedoes, these attack submarines will carry anti-surface SM–39 missiles, whose development is proceeding well.

As for the surface forces, the modernization of the *Clemenceau* and the *Foch* has now been completed. From now on, the aircraft embarked will be the Super-Étendard, an excellent assault plane that can carry the AM–39 missile, an air-to-surface weapon capable of striking a target at a range of 70 km; it can also carry a nuclear tactical weapon. The fleet's offensive capability will increase even more when, as is foreseen, the Super-Étendard deploys the new Mach 2 ANS missile, which will make it possible to strike targets at a range of 300 km.

In the category of escorts, the three *Tourville*-class guided-missile destroyers have now had the Crotale surface-to-air launcher installed. The *Georges Leygues*, *Dupleix*, and *Montcalm*, C–70-class guided-missile ASW destroyers, are now in service, and the *Jean de Vienne* has been launched; two others have been laid down or authorized, and eight of this very efficient type are expected to be built. The first two antiair versions of the same design have been ordered, but they are not yet on the ways because some of their characteristics are still under discussion; the first is due to be laid down in June 1982.

The "aviso" program, on the other hand, is continuing without a hitch. Ten are in service and seven others are building or ordered. Four of them, attached to the Mediterranean Squadron, have been given the MM 38 Exocet missile, but the others have been arranged so that this system or its higher-performance successor, the MM 40, can be installed very quickly. The last six "avisos" will have one or other of these systems installed at the time of their building. The MM 40 was first installed in the destroyer *Montcalm*, and it will gradually replace the MM 38 in ships that carry it. A "very short range surface-to-air" missile (SATCP) is now under study and should, in a few years' time, be embarked in all surface ships to strengthen their defense. Such a system, which should be as unsophisticated as possible, will be of particular interest to small ships that, because of their size, cannot operate very elaborate antiaircraft systems.

Like all the big navies, the French Navy is becoming increasingly interested in electronic warfare, for victory or defeat tomorrow might depend upon it. Thus, although a subject of strict secrecy, the modern *Dagaie* countermeasures system is gradually being installed in all ships.

Along with its strictly military missions, the French Navy uses its facilities to perform many public services: pollution control, fisheries protection, maritime sur-

veillance, navigation control, rescue, and so on. Few of its facilities are suited to such services, however, particularly when they become a burden. In 1980 a program was initiated to devote eleven ships to public service and to acquire several aircraft for this task between now and 1986. The program got under way this year when a 300-ton patrol boat was delivered and a trawler was bought.

In the area of naval patrol planes, the prototype of the new-generation Atlantic has begun its trials. Although it has the same fuselage, this plane—as much because of its equipment (Iguane radar, computerized tactical data handling, new sensors, etc.) as because of its armament (the AM–39 missile)—represents a considerable improvement over the present Atlantic; it is virtually a new plane. The Navy hopes to acquire 42 of the new Atlantics and expects delivery of the first planes in five years.

France has signed a very substantial contract with Saudi Arabia. Named "Sawari," the progam calls for the building of four 2,000-ton frigates and two replenishment ships and for the procurement of twenty-four helicopters.

The six PR–72 guided-missile corvettes ordered by Peru from the Société Française de Constructions Navales (S.F.C.M.), have been delivered, and a ship of the same type for Senegal is being built. Constructions Mécaniques de Normandie (CMN) has delivered the last three of a series of twelve guided-missile patrol boats ordered by Iran, and has completed 10 such boats for Libya and three for Nigeria. Qatar and Tunisia have each ordered three such boats from the same builder.

FEDERAL GERMAN NAVY

Five of the West Germany Navy's six Type 122 guided-missile frigates are now afloat, and the first, the *Bremen*, was delivered in 10–81. These frigates are very similar to the Dutch *Kortenaer*s, but the former have CODOG propulsion instead of COGOG. The Navy hopes that at least two more of the six others originally planned will be built. The first of the ten 393-ton Type 143A guided-missile patrol boats was launched late in September 1981, and the series is supposed to be completed in 1984; these boats are replacing the *Zobel*-class torpedo boats, which were modernized about ten years ago.

The German shipbuilding industry does a lively export business. There is no space here for details, but it has already delivered to foreign navies twenty-five 1,000-ton, Type 209 submarines, and it has more than fifty ships for foreign customers undergoing trials, building, or on order—among them nine submarines, five destroyers, six corvettes, and thirty-three patrol boats of various types. Furthermore, German shipyards are helping to build boats ordered from them but which the customers want built in their own yards.

BELGIAN AND NETHERLANDS NAVIES

The Belgian Navy's four 1,880-ton, *Wielingen*-class (Type E–71) frigates are now completely operational; one of them is attached to NATO, one to the Belgian high command, and one is undergoing overhaul. The tripartite minehunter program, to which Belgium is a party, is proceeding according to plan; it is designed to bring up to date this small navy's mine warfare component, an area in which it has been a leader. Unfortunately, necessary economies forced the laying up of a significant portion of the mine countermeasures force during 1981.

Five of the 12 *Kortenaer*-class frigates planned for by the Netherlands Navy are in service at this writing. Two of those already launched have been sold to Greece, the *Pieter Floresz* and the *Witte de With*, which have become the *Elli* and the *Lemnos*, respectively. Two modified frigates have been ordered to replace them, but since they will not be in service for four years, completion of the *Kortenaer* program will be later than envisaged. This final pair is to be equipped with U.S. Standard surface-to-air missile systems. The Netherlands has sold to Peru the *Friesland*-class destroyers *Limburg, Amsterdam, Utrecht, Groningen, Drenthe,* and *Rotterdam,* and the Peruvians are expected to buy the *Overijssel,* the last ship of this class. The characteristics of the four 2,650-ton M-class guided-missile frigates, which are intended as replacements for the six 1954-vintage Roofdier-class corvettes, have now been agreed upon and they are programmed to be ordered in 1983. The mid-life refitting of the six *Van Speijk*-class frigates, which are almost exact copies of the British *Leander* class, will be completed in 1982. Two attack submarines, the *Walrus* and the *Zeeleeuw,* have been laid down. They will replace the *Dolfijn* in 1983 and the *Zeehond* in 1984 (these submarines date from 1960 and 1961). The program of building Tripartite minehunters is proceeding on course, and the first two of the fifteen-ship series are expected to join the fleet in 1982.

The Netherlands shipbuilding industry has successfully entered the export business. Three light frigates have been delivered to Indonesia, and a contract with Taiwan for building two *Walrus*-class submarines has recently been signed—over vociferous mainland Chinese protests.

SCANDINAVIAN NAVIES

The *Peter Tordenskjold,* last of the 1,100-ton *Niels Juel*-class corvettes, will be commissioned in 1982, completing the rejuvenation of the Danish Navy's surface forces. The ten *Willimoes*-class guided-missile boats have been or are about to be given their final armament, two twin Harpoon nests. The next project is to replace the aging *Delfinen*-class submarines (one of which was laid up late in 1981 for budgetary reasons). They might be replaced either by Swedish-built or German-Norwegian-built boats, the latter being the more likely.

All fourteen of the Norwegian Navy's 155-ton *Hauk*-class guided-missile patrol boats ordered in 1975 are now in service. The same is true of the three 2,950-ton *Nordkapp*-class ocean patrol ships ordered for the Coast Guard. Originally, seven of these ships were to have been built, but for the time being, the number has been cut back to these three because of lack of funds. While waiting for better times, the Coast Guard has chartered and armed several commercial trawlers to ensure protection of fisheries and offshore oil rigs, and to patrol the 200-nautical-mile economic exclusion zone.

In the Swedish Navy, the *Näcken,* the first of three Type A–14 submarines that were ordered ten years ago, is now in service. Lack of funds has slowed the building of these boats. Four of the *Draken*-class submarines are to be modernized and the other two scrapped. For the future, the Swedish government has commissioned the Kockums Shipyard to study a new type of submarine, the A–17, and expects to build four to six of them. The last active destroyer, the *Halland,* temporarily replaced the stricken *Älvsnabben* as a training ship for cadets during 1981; the *Halland,* in turn, is being placed in reserve and succeeded by the new training ship and minelayer, the *Carlskrona,* which joined the fleet in December 1981.

The sixteen *Hugin*-class guided-missile patrol boats ordered in 1975 from Norwegian shipyards are now all in service, following prolonged trials of the prototype *Jägaren.* They are in many respects counterparts of the Norwegian *Hauk* class. Despite delays in delivery, all will have six Penguin missiles, and later will receive the new Swedish long-range (100-km) missile, the RBS–15, as it becomes available. This latter weapon, which is still under development, is also to be installed in the large *Spica*–1 and *Spica*–II torpedo boats. Two new guided-missile patrol boats of the YA–18 design were

ordered during 1981. Also ordered are the first two of a series of perhaps nine 300-ton, Type M 80 minesweepers-minehunters with plastic and fiberglass hulls.

No longer having any big ships, the Swedish Navy will now have in the Baltic two types of forces: an offensive submarine force capable of operating on the open sea, and a defensive fleet of small high-speed ships well suited to the conditions of the Baltic. Because guided-missile patrol boats and torpedo boats now constitute the framework of the fleet, it is to be hoped that lack of money will not delay the installation of modern weapons aboard them. As it is, the Swedish defense system rests on the mobilization of reservists, and if Swedish neutrality were violated, the fleet's necessary training and teamwork might not have time to develop. Of course, a seaborne attack on Sweden would be no simple thing to mount for geographic reasons. The 1981 "Whiskey on the Rocks" incident, however, has understandably renewed flagging Swedish interest in defense, and in particular *naval* defense. The Soviet Baltic-Fleet, Whiskey-class submarine that went aground almost within sight of Sweden's principal naval base was almost certainly equipped with nuclear-warhead torpedoes.

SPANISH NAVY

The most important program in this navy is that of the aircraft carrier *Canarias,* to which the biggest share of current appropriations seems to be devoted. This 14,700-ton ship, inspired by the U.S. Navy's Sea Control Ship concept of the early 1970s, should, if all goes well, enter active service in 1985. The priority given the *Canarias* has made it necessary to slow the building of the *Oliver Hazard Perry*-class guided-missile frigates, although progress on all three continues. Five of the smallest *Descubierta*-class frigates are now in service; the other three are being completed, but have not received all the weapons and equipment due them, especially their Harpoon missiles and the Meroka antiaircraft/anti-missile, point-defense system. On the debit side, the destroyer *Roger de Lauria* had to be stricken after sustaining severe damage from a terrorist attack.

The construction of four 1,200-ton *Agosta*-class submarines ordered from the Cartagena naval shipyard continues with French technical assistance, and the first boat should at last be completed during 1982.

The Spanish Navy is also working on a program for ten 300-ton patrol boats for surveillance and the protection of the country's maritime interests, and it has a large construction program for small inshore patrol craft. The Spanish naval shipbuilding industry, too, is seeking outlets abroad—and is meeting considerable success. Morocco has ordered a *Descubierta*-class frigate and four large guided-missile patrol boats, and a contract has recently been signed for the building of six, 900-ton, coast-guard vessels for Mexico and five for Argentina.

MEDITERRANEAN NAVIES

In the Italian Navy, the first sections of the helicopter carrier *Garibaldi* were finally laid down last June. This ship which, on paper, seems to be better designed than the British *Invincible* class, will probably not go into service for five or six years. The *Maestrale,* prototype of six 2,500-ton, *Venti*-class frigates, was launched on 2 February 1981 and two sisters followed later in the year. The four 2,200-ton *Lupo*-class frigates are all in service. The first two 1,450-ton, *Sauro*-class submarines, having overcome some problems with their batteries, are now in operation and the other two have conducted trials. The big salvage ship *Anteo* has joined the fleet, as have the first three of five follow-on *Sparviero*-class guided-missile hydrofoils.

Like its German counterpart, the Italian shipbuilding industry is very active. Last February it entered into a contract with Iraq that calls for the building of four *Lupo*-class guided-missile frigates, six 650-ton corvettes, a *Stromboli*-class replenishment oiler, and a floating drydock. The corvettes will be similar to the six that are being built for Ecuador and to the four *Wadi M'ragh* class that have been delivered to Libya. Two *Lupo*-class frigates have been delivered to Peru, and Italian yards are helping the Peruvians with two other greatly delayed units of the same class at Callao. Three of the six *Lupo*-class frigates ordered by Venezuela have been delivered.

In 1980–81 the Algerian Navy acquired a Soviet Koni-class frigate and two Nanuchka-II-class guided-missile corvettes. The transfer of these ships gives this small navy a new dimension. With the Nanuchka-IIs, it is in a position to increase its operating radius considerably and to conduct timely offensive operations quite far from its coasts. The main function of the frigate *Mourad Rais* is to provide prestige.

In Libya, Colonel Qadaffi may have dreams about the exploits of Arudj and his brother Khair ed Din, the famous Khaireddin Barbarossa, and about the wild Barbary pirates who, for several centuries, ransacked the coasts of the Mediterranean. He has great naval ambitions, and since his oil brings in a lot of money, he has bought or has on order abroad some very sophisticated warships. Besides the four Italian-built *Wadi M'ragh*-class guided-missile corvettes that were delivered in 1980 and 1981, the Libyan Navy recently acquired a fourth Soviet Foxtrot submarine and two Soviet Natya-class minesweepers. Ten *Combattante II*-class guided-missile patrol boats are in various shapes of building in the yards of Constructions Mécaniques in Cherbourg; the first of an order for four Nanuchka-II-class guided-missile corvettes has been delivered (see Addenda); and it is said that Libya will also receive two Koni-class frigates. Turkey, too, is benefiting from Libyan orders, and has large programs in progress for landing craft and patrol boats.

The spectacular development of the Libyan Navy has altered the strategic balance in the Mediterranean, but the question is whether, without permanent outside technical assistance, the personnel manning these very complicated ships will have the ability to operate and, above all, maintain them. Meanwhile, both Western and Communist shipyards are prospering.

The Greek Navy, as previously mentioned, has bought from the Netherlands two *Kortenaer*-class frigates, with the first, *Elli*, commissioned in October 1981. Along with its force of aged U.S.-built destroyers and frigates—ships that at least give it an honorable place among the NATO forces—the Greek Navy has a force of modern small ships very well suited to the type of operations that might take place in the Aegean Sea, should Greco-Turkish rivalry over the continental plateau (which is suspected of having considerable oil reserves) take a disastrous turn. This force has eight 1,000-ton German Type 209 submarines and fourteen 290–350-ton guided-missile patrol boats built in France and in Greece; some of these carry French Exocet and others Norwegian Penguin anti-ship missiles.

The Turkish Navy does not have ships as modern as the Greek *Kortenaer*s, but it will presumably buy some abroad in order to reestablish parity with its rival. Its biggest ships are old American ones; its only modern ships comparable to those of the Greeks are four 1,000-ton Type 209 submarines and four FPB–57-class guided-missile patrol boats.

At the other end of the eastern Mediterranean, the Israeli Navy is developing and modernizing in order to maintain its defenses against the Arab navies. It has three small submarines, a dozen *Sa'ar*-class patrol boats, and a considerable force of large *Reshev*-class guided-missile patrol boats, whose building program, with modifications, is still going on. The armament of these ships, the anti-surface Gabriel missile, has been reinforced with the much-longer-ranged American Harpoon. The *Aliyah* and *Geoula* guided-missile patrol boats, which entered service in 1981, have a light helicopter embarked, which allows these patrol boats to target Harpoons from well beyond the surface horizon. The navy yard in Haifa has delivered some patrol boats to South Africa and to South and Central America, and it continues to cooperate with the Taiwanese Navy.

LATIN AMERICAN NAVIES

The navy of Argentina is in a fair way of overtaking Brazil as first in Latin America. Four 3,000-ton MEKO-360 (*Almirante Brown*-class) destroyers are being built in the yard of Blohm & Voss in the Federal Republic of Germany, and two were launched during 1981. Six small MEKO–140 (*Espora*-class) frigates are being built in Argentina with the help of the same yard. Four 1,700-ton and two 1,400-ton submarines of German design are being built. The first three 1,700-tonners are being built in West Germany; the others are being built in Argentina with the help of the Thyssen yard, the designer of the project. The *Granville*, the last of three A-69-class frigates that Argentina bought in France, was delivered in 1981. Five 900-ton coast-guard vessels are being built in Spain. Fourteen Super Étendard attack fighters were ordered last year and will replace the aging American A–4Q Skyhawk embarked in the aircraft carrier *25 de Mayo*; the first five were delivered during December 1981.

The Brazilian Navy is, so to speak, digesting the modern ships it has acquired in the last few years, particularly the six Vosper Thornycroft Mk 10-class frigates, some of which were built in Great Britain and some in Rio de Janeiro. The next modernization of the fleet is to replace the five old, ex-American submarines still in service. Several foreign firms are bidding for this business. A training frigate based on the Mk 10 design was laid down in 1981, and four light frigates were ordered in November, out of a program for an eventual dozen.

The Peruvian Navy has grown substantially. As mentioned above, it has bought from the Netherlands six *Friesland*-class destroyers. The two *Lupo*-class frigates ordered from Italy have been delivered, as have the six big PR72–560-class guided-missile patrol boats built by S.F.C.N., half at Villeneuve-la-Garenne and half at Lorient. The order for six Type 209 submarines from West Germany will be completed when the last unit is delivered in 1982.

Comparted with these three navies, the Chilean Navy is having great difficulty in updating itself, and the gap that separates it from the three big South American navies gets ever wider. To remedy this in part, the British County-class guided-missile *Norfolk* and the fleet replenishment oiler *Tidepool* are being purchased during 1982. Reportedly, the carrier *Hermes* has been offered, for delivery in 1983, but it is unlikely that the offer of this very old ship will be taken up, especially as it would require the purchase of Sea Harrier V/STOL fighters. The Chilean Navy further was able to buy two used *Reshev*-class guided-missile patrol boats from Israel: the *Campa* (ex-Israeli *Romach*) was delivered in 1979 and the *Chipana* (ex-*Keshet*) in 1980. Additional ships of this class may be ordered. Two *Descubierta*-class frigates were ordered from Spain in May of 1981. As far as submarines are concerned, it has signed a contract for two Type 209 boats to be built in West Germany, but the order has to be approved by the German parliament. France is assisting in the construction of two BATRAL-class landing ships, while Brazil is delivering a large series of patrol craft.

INDIAN NAVY

With its sixty-seven warships and a tonnage totaling almost 100,000 tons, the Indian Navy has first place in the Indian Ocean and is, in fact, one of the world's major navies. With Iran, wracked by revolution, out of the running, and with no other navy in that area able to contest its primacy, the Indian Navy intends to take advantage of the situation and play an increasingly significant role.

The Indian Navy consists of two types of fleets, one of Soviet origin and the other of British origin or basic design. The amalgamation of these two fleets should, in time, produce a navy whose inspiration and formation are truly national. That course is well under way. Indeed, in just a few years India has created for itself a naval shipbuilding industry capable of building the most modern warships. For example, the building of six British *Leander*-class frigates, begun fourteen years ago, was completed last July with the delivery of the *Vindhyagiri*. While it took at least seven years to build the first of these ships, the building of the last one took no longer than it would take a Western yard to complete a similar type. This shows what progress the Indians have made.

Three 3,850-ton *Godavari*-class frigates have been laid down. They are the first that will constitute an amalgamation of British and Soviet concepts. They will derive their general shape, their accommodations, and the research of their nautical characteristics from the former, and their major weapon system and sensors from the latter.

Nevertheless, the Indian Navy is still buying material abroad. In 1980 it received the *Rajput*, the first of the three Kashin-class guided-missile destroyers it ordered from the U.S.S.R., and this year it signed a contract with the Federal Republic of Germany for the building of two 1,000-ton Type 209 submarines, with the apparent right to build the four follow-on submarines in India.

THE CHINESE NAVY

On 30 April last, China launched its first nuclear-powered guided-missile submarine and so joined the club of so-called nuclear navies. It is true that it had already built two Han-class nuclear submarines, but they were largely experimental boats that gave Chinese engineers an opportunity to become aware of the innumerable problems attendant on the building of a nuclear-powered submarine.

It now remains to complete this nuclear submarine, to have its trials, to work it up, and to give it its strategic missiles. The perfecting of this missile is not the least difficulty that the Chinese will have to resolve; their apparently successful firings of a ballistic missile last year show that they are capable of building an effective ICBM, but, even so, this first nuclear submarine will certainly not be operational for at least three or four years. And it will still lag a good way behind Western submarines, especially in submarine detection—an area in which the Chinese have no experience whatsoever. Nonetheless, the launching of this strategic submarine shows plainly that China wants to have an oceangoing navy. Its deployment of a large naval force in the southern Pacific in May 1980 when the experimental ICBMs were being launched showed that its navy has made substantial progress in the areas of planning, organization, and logistics, and that China is now capable of showing her presence a long way from her own coasts. Nevertheless, with the vast majority of its ships small and out of date, China will be unable to conduct any military operations on the high seas; the Chinese Navy is a coast-defense force and will remain such for a long time to come.

JAPANESE NAVY

Today, the Japanese Navy follows immediately behind the French Navy in tonnage as well as in the number of its ships. Since our last edition, the helicopter-carrying destroyers *Shirane* and *Kurama* have gone into service, as have the guided-missile destroyer *Asakaze* and the first two *Yushio*-class 2,200-ton attack submarines. The first two of a class of eight 2,900-ton destroyers have been launched; their main missile armament will be the American Harpoon. The *Ishikari*, the prototype of a new class of small frigates, joined the fleet last March, and the minehunter program is on schedule.

One facet of the Japanese Navy that is not given adequate attention is its air arm, which is one of the biggest. Except for a few helicopters embarked on some destroyers, it is land-based, and consists of around 300 aircraft, about sixty of which are helicopters and most of which have ASW missions. It has twice as many patrol planes as the French Navy. This naval patrol force is being rejuvenated and expects to acquire 37 American Orion P–3C aircraft. The first of these was delivered by Lockheed in April 1981, but most of the others will be built under license in Japan. They will all carry the anti-surface Harpoon missile.

The Japanese Navy is very closely linked to the U.S. Navy, because the great majority of its material and equipment are American types built under license. It takes part in frequent exercises with the U.S. Seventh Fleet, which gives it good operational experience and accustoms it to cooperating.

With the Japanese Navy this tour of the world's navies must conclude. Only the significant changes that have taken place in the world's navies since the last edition could be included to indicate the directions toward which the world's fleets are tending. The editor might be reproached for not speaking of the tremendous development of some of the small navies—that, for example, of Nigeria, which is now the most important one in Black Africa. But a glance through this book should satisfy the most exacting reader.

Jean Labayle Couhat

TERMS AND ABBREVIATIONS

Most ships' characteristics are given in the following form:

	Bldr	Laid down	L	In serv.
D 602 SUFFREN	Lorient	12-62	15-5-65	1967

D: 5,090 tons (6,090 fl) **S:** 34 kts

Dim: 157.6 (148.0 pp) × 15.54 × 7.25 (max.)

A: 1/Masurca system (II × 1)—4/MM 38 Exocet—2/100-mm, Model 1953 (I × 2)—4/20-mm AA (I × 4)—1/Malafon system (13 missiles)—2/catapults for L-5 torpedoes (10 torpedoes)

Electron Equipt: Radar: 1/DRBI-23, 1/DRBV-50, 2/DRBR-51, 1/DRBC-32A, 1/DRBN-32

Sonar: 1/DUBV-23, 1/DUBV-43—SENIT-1, 2 Syllex systems

M: 2 Rateau double-reduction GT; 2 props; 72,500 hp

Boilers: 4 multitube, automatic-control; 45 kg/cm²; 450° C

Electric: 3,440 kw (2 × 1,000-kw turbogenerators, 3 × 480-kw diesel alternators)

Range: 2,000/30; 2,400/29; 5,100/18

Man: 23 officers, 164 petty officers, 168 men

Ships' hull numbers and names are in capitals and small capitals. Hull dimensions are in meters, calibers in millimeters, speeds in knots, ranges in nautical miles; speeds and ranges of aircraft are in kilometers/hour and kilometers, unless otherwise indicated.

D: Displacement. In most cases, standard displacement, as defined by the Treaty of Washington (1922), is given. Where possible, full load (fl) is given; otherwise, normal (avg) displacement or trial displacement is given. In the case of most submarines, two displacements are given: the first figure is surfaced displacement; the second is submerged displacement. When available, the figure for standard displacement precedes the surfaced and submerged figures.

S: Speed. This is given in knots and generally refers to maximum speed; in some cases trial speed is given. For submarines, surfaced speed is given first and is followed by submerged speed. Where standard speed is given, it is shown first.

Dim: Hull dimensions are given as follows: length overall × beam × draft (full load, unless otherwise stated). Length between perpendiculars is given as "pp"; length at the waterline as "wl." In cases where two figures are given for one of the dimensions, e.g., the beam of the flight deck and of the hull of an aircraft carrier, the hull measurement is given as "hull."

A: Armament. Number of guns/caliber; or number of torpedo tubes or launchers with caliber. Figures in parentheses show the number of mounts and whether they are single, double, triple, etc.; e.g., (III × 2) indicates two triple mounts.

M: Machinery. Geared turbine is shown as GT; in some cases, the type or manufacturer of turbine is given, e.g., Parsons, etc. COSAG, CODAG/CODOG, COGAG/COGOG are used when such combinations of machinery have to be shown. "Props" indicates propellers. "CP" indicates controllable-pitch.

Boilers: In most cases, number and type are shown. Steam pressure is expressed in kilograms/square centimeter and steam superheat in degrees Centigrade.

Electric: Electric generating power, in kilowatts (kw) or kilovolt-Amperes (kVA).

Armor: Armor protection, thickness given in millimeters.

Range: Cited in nautical miles at a given speed.

Man: Ship's company. Where not broken down into "officers" and "men" (ie, noncommissioned personnel), a total complement figure is given as "tot."

Dates: Dates are given in the following sequence: day-month-year.

A	Armament
AA	Antiaircraft
A & C, At & Ch	Shipbuilding yard (*Atelier & Chantier*)
AAW	Anti-air warfare
AEW	Airborne early warning
ARM	Anti-radiation missile
Ast Nav	Shipyard (*Astilleros Navales*)
ASW	Antisubmarine warfare
Author.	Authorized
avg	Average, normal
BB	Boatbuilding
Bldr	Builder
BPDMS	Base Point Defense Missile System
BW	Boat Works
BY	Boat Yard
Ch, Ch Nav	Builder, shipyard (Chantier, *Chantiers Navals*)
C N, Cant Nav	Naval shipyard (*Cantière Navale*)
COD	Carrier Onboard Delivery
COGAG/CODAG/COSAG/ COGOG/CODOG	Combined propulsive machinery systems, gas turbine, diesel, steam. *CO* means *combined*, *a* means *and*, *o* means *or*. For example, CODOG means *combined diesel or gas turbine*.
CP	Controllable-pitch
D	Displacement
d.c.	Depth charge
d.c.t.	Depth charge thrower
DD, DDM	Dry dock, dry dock company
Dim	Dimensions
DP	Dual-purpose
DSRV	Deep Submergence Rescue Vessel
dwt	Deadweight Tonnage
ECM	Electronic countermeasures
ECCM	Electronic counter-countermeasures
Electron Equipt	Electronic equipment
ELINT	Electronic intelligence
Eng	Engineering
ESM	Electronic support measures
FF, FFG	Frigate, guided-missile frigate
fl	Full load
freq.	Frequency
FR, FRAM	Fleet Rehabilitation and Modernization
fwd	Forward
GE	General Electric Co.
GFCS	Gunfire-control system

GM	General Motors Corp.
grt	Gross registered tons
GT	Geared turbine
HF	High frequency
HMDY	Her Majesty's Dockyard
HSA	Hollandse Signaal Apparaaten
hp	Horsepower
IFF	Identification Friend or Foe
kg	Kilogram
Kon. Mij.	Royal Company
kt	Kiloton
kts	Knots
kVA	Kilovolt-ampere
kw	Kilowatt
L	Launched
LF	Low frequency
loa	Length overall
M	Machinery
MAD	Magnetic (or Anomaly) Detection
Man	Manpower on board ship, crew, ship's company
MAP	Military Assistance Program (U.S. and allies)
MF	Medium frequency
mg	Machine gun
mm	Millimeters
MSC	Military Sealift Command
MTU	Motoren and Turbinen Union
N.B.	New Brunswick
NBC	Nuclear, biological, and chemical
NDY	Naval dockyard
nrt	Net registered tons
N.S.	Nova Scotia
NSY	Naval shipyard
NTDS	Naval Tactical Data System
NY	Navy Yard
oa	Overall
PADLOC	Passive/Active Detection and Location
pp	Between perpendiculars
PUFFS	Passive Underwater Fire-Control System
RDY	Royal dockyard
RL	Rocket launcher
rpm	Revolutions per minute
S	Speed
SAM	Surface-to-air missile
SAR	Search and Rescue
SB	Shipbuilding
S.F.C.N.	Société Française de Construction Navale
SINS	Ship's Inertial Navigation System
SLEP	Service Life Extension Program
SSBN	Nuclear-powered fleet ballistic-missile submarine
SSM	Surface-to-surface missile
STIR	Surveillance Target Indicator Radar
	Separate Track and Illumination Radar
SURTASS	Surface Towed Array Surveillance System
SY	Shipyard
syst	System
TACTASS	Tactical Towed Acoustic Sensor System
TASS	Towed Array Surveillance System
TT	Torpedo tubes/launchers
tot.	Total
VDS	Variable-depth sonar
Wks	Works
wl	Waterline

CONVERSION TABLES

♦ METERS (m.) to FEET (ft.)
based on 1 inch = 25.4 millimeters

m	0	1	2	3	4	5	6	7	8	9
	ft.	ft.	ft.	ft.	ft.	ft.	ft.	ft.	ft.	ft.
—	—	3.28084	6.5617	9.8425	13.1234	16.4042	19.6850	22.9659	26.2467	29.5276
10	32.8084	36.0892	39.3701	42.6509	45.9317	49.2126	52.493	55.774	59.005	62.336
20	65.617	68.898	72.178	75.459	78.740	82.021	85.302	88.583	91.863	95.144
30	98.425	101.706	104.987	108.268	111.549	114.829	118.110	121.391	124.672	127.953
40	131.234	134.514	137.795	141.076	144.357	147.638	150.919	154.199	157.480	160.761
50	164.042	167.323	170.604	173.884	177.165	180.446	183.727	187.008	190.289	193.570
60	196.850	200.131	203.412	206.693	209.974	213.255	216.535	219.816	223.097	226.378
70	229.659	232.940	236.220	239.501	242.782	246.063	249.344	252.625	255.905	259.186
80	262.467	265.748	269.029	272.310	275.590	278.871	282.152	285.433	288.714	291.995
90	295.276	298.556	301.837	305.118	308.399	311.680	314.961	318.241	321.522	324.803
100	328.084	331.365	334.646	337.926	341.207	344.488	347.769	351.050	354.331	357.611
10	360.892	364.173	367.454	370.735	374.016	377.296	380.577	383.858	387.139	390.420
20	393.701	396.982	400.262	403.543	406.824	410.105	413.386	416.667	419.947	423.228
30	426.509	429.790	433.071	436.352	439.632	442.913	446.194	449.475	452.756	456.037
40	459.317	462.598	465.879	469.160	472.441	475.722	479.002	482.283	485.564	488.845
50	492.126	495.407	498.688	501.97	505.25	508.53	511.81	515.09	518.37	521.65
60	524.93	528.22	531.50	534.78	538.06	541.34	544.62	547.90	551.18	554.46
70	557.74	561.02	564.30	567.59	570.87	574.15	577.43	580.71	583.99	587.27
80	590.55	593.83	597.11	600.39	603.67	606.96	610.24	613.52	616.80	620.08
90	623.36	626.64	629.92	633.20	636.48	639.76	643.04	646.33	649.61	652.89
200	656.17	659.45	662.73	666.01	669.29	672.57	675.85	679.13	682.41	685.70
10	688.98	692.26	695.54	698.82	702.10	705.38	708.66	711.94	715.22	718.50
20	721.78	725.07	728.35	731.63	734.91	738.19	741.47	744.75	748.03	751.31
30	754.59	757.87	761.15	764.44	767.72	771.00	774.28	777.56	780.84	784.12
40	747.40	790.68	793.96	797.24	800.52	803.81	807.09	810.37	813.65	816.93
50	820.21	823.49	826.77	830.05	833.33	836.61	839.89	843.18	846.46	849.74
60	853.02	856.30	859.58	862.86	866.14	869.42	872.70	875.98	879.26	882.55
70	885.83	889.11	892.39	895.67	898.95	902.23	905.51	908.79	912.07	915.35
80	918.63	921.92	925.20	928.48	931.76	935.04	938.32	941.60	944.88	948.16
90	951.44	954.72	958.00	961.29	964.57	967.85	971.13	974.41	977.69	980.97
300	984.25	987.53	990.81	994.09	997.38	1000.66	1003.94	1007.22	1010.50	1013.78
10	1017.06	1020.34	1023.62	1026.90	1030.18	1033.46	1036.75	1040.03	1043.31	1046.59
20	1049.87	1053.15	1056.43	1059.71	1062.99	1066.27	1069.55	1072.83	1076.12	1079.40
30	1082.68	1085.96	1089.24	1092.52	1095.80	1099.08	1102.36	1105.64	1108.92	1112.20
40	1115.49	1118.77	1122.05	1125.33	1128.61	1131.89	1135.17	1138.45	1141.73	1145.01
50	1118.29	1151.57	1154.86	1158.14	1161.42	1164.70	1167.98	1171.26	1174.54	1177.82

♦ MILLIMETERS (mm.) to INCHES (in.)
based on 1 inch = 25.4 millimeters

mm	0	1	2	3	4	5	6	7	8	9
	in.	in.	in.	in.	in.	in.	in.	in.	in.	in.
—	—	0.03937	0.07874	0.11811	0.15748	0.19685	0.23622	0.27559	0.31496	0.35433
10	0.39370	0.43307	0.47244	0.51181	0.55118	0.59055	0.62992	0.66929	0.70866	0.74803
20	0.78740	0.82677	0.86614	0.90551	0.94488	0.98425	1.02362	1.06299	1.10236	1.14173
30	1.18110	1.22047	1.25984	1.29921	1.33858	1.37795	1.41732	1.45669	1.49606	1.53543
40	1.57480	1.61417	1.65354	1.69291	1.73228	1.77165	1.81102	1.85039	1.88976	1.92913

mm	0	1	2	3	4	5	6	7	8	9
	in.	in.	in.	in.	in.	in.	in.	in.	in.	in.
50	1.96850	2.00787	2.04724	2.08661	2.12598	2.16535	2.20472	2.24409	2.28346	2.32283
60	2.36220	2.40157	2.44094	2.48031	2.51969	2.55906	2.59843	2.63780	2.67717	2.71654
70	2.75591	2.79528	2.83465	2.87402	2.91339	2.95276	2.99213	3.03150	3.07087	3.11024
80	3.14961	3.18898	3.22835	3.26772	3.30709	3.34646	3.38583	3.42520	3.46457	3.50394
90	3.54331	3.58268	3.62205	3.66142	3.70079	3.74016	3.77953	3.81890	3.85827	3.89764
100	3.93701									

CONVERSION FACTORS

Meter	Yard	Foot	Inch	Centimeter	Millimeter
1	1.093 61	3.280 84	39.370 1	100	1 000
0.914 4	1	3	36	91.44	914.4
0.304 8	0.333 333	1	12	30.48	304.8
0.254	0.027 777 8	0.083 333	1	2.54	25.4 j
0.01	0.010 936 1	0.032 808 4	0.398 701	1	10
0.001	0.001 093 61	0.003 280 84	0.039 370 4	0.1	1

Nautical mile	Statute mile	Meters
1	= 1.151 52	= 1 853.18

♦ Boiler working pressure

Kilogram per square centimeter (atmosphere)   *Pounds per square inch*

1	equivalent →	14.223 3
0.070 307	← equivalent	1

♦ Conversion for Fahrenheit and Centigrade scales

1 degree Centigrade = 1.8 degrees Fahrenheit
1 degree Fahrenheit = 5/9 degree Centigrade
$t\,°F = 5/9(t - 32)°C.$
$t\,°C = (1.8\,t + 32)°F.$

♦ Weights

1 kilogram = 2.204 62 *pounds* (av)
1 *pound* = 0.453 592
1 ton (metric) = 0.984 21 *ton*
1 *ton* = 1.016 05 *metric ton*

♦ Power

1 (CV) = 0.986 32 *horsepower* (HP) 0.735 88 kilowatt (Greenwich) (75 kgm/s)
1 *horsepower* (HP) = 1.013 87 (CV) 0.746 08 kilowatt (Greenwich)

ALBANIA

People's Socialist Republic of Albania

PERSONNEL: 3,000 men

MERCHANT MARINE (1978): 16 ships—43,623 grt

Neither the U.S.S.R. nor China is now supporting Albania, and the material condition of the ships listed below must be suffering. All Soviet equipment transferred prior to 1961.

♦ **3 Soviet Whiskey-class submarines**

D: 1,050/1,350 tons   **S:** 17/13.5 kts   **Dim:** 76.0 × 6.3 × 4.8
A: 6/533-mm TT (4 fwd, 2 aft)—12 torpedoes or 24 mines
Electron Equipt: Radar: 1/Snoop Plate
M: 2/37-D, 2,000-hp diesels, electric motors; 2 props; 2,500 hp
Range: 8,300/8 (snorkel)   **Endurance:** 40-45 days   **Man:** 50 tot.

REMARKS: All reported out of service in 1980.

♦ **4 Soviet Kronshtadt-class patrol boats**

D: 300 tons (330 fl)   **S:** 18 kts   **Dim:** 52.1 × 6.5 × 2.2
A: 1/85-mm DP—2/37-mm AA (I × 2)—6/12.7-mm mg (II × 3)—2/d.c.t.—2/d.c. rack—2/RBU-900 ASW RL—mines
M: 3/9-D diesels; 3 props; 3,300 hp   **Range:** 3,500/14   **Fuel:** 20 tons
Man: 40 tot.

♦ **6 Chinese Shanghai-II-class patrol boats**

D: 122.5 tons (155 fl)   **S:** 28 kts   **Dim:** 38.8 × 5.4 × 1.5
A: 4/37-mm AA (II × 2)—4/25-mm AA (II × 2)
Electron Equipt: Radar: 1/Pot Head
M: 2/1,200-hp diesels, 2/910-hp diesels; 4 props; 4,220-hp   **Man:** 38 tot.

REMARKS: Transferred 1974-75; probably operational.

♦ **35 Chinese Huchwan-class hydrofoil torpedo boats**

Huchwan-class hydrofoil torpedo boat   1976

D: 39 tons (fl)   **S:** 54 kts   **Dim:** 21.8 × 4.9 × 1.0 (hull)
A: 2/533-mm TT—4/14.5-mm mg (II × 2)   **M:** 3 diesels; 3 props; 3,600 hp

REMARKS: Bow foils only; stern planes on surface.

♦ **2 Soviet T-43-class ocean minesweepers**

D: 500 tons (550 fl)   **S:** 14 kts   **Dim:** 58.0 × 8.4 × 2.3
A: 4/37-mm AA (II × 2)—8/12.7-mm mg (II × 4)—2/d.c.t.—mines
M: 2/9-D diesels; 2 props; 2,200 hp   **Range:** 3,200/10

♦ **6 Soviet T-301-class coastal minesweepers**

D: 145.8 tons (160 fl)   **S:** 12.5 kts   **Dim:** 38.0 × 5.1 × 1.6
A: 1/45-mm AA—4/12.7-mm mg (II × 2)—mines
M: 3/6-cyl. diesels; 3 props; 1,440 hp   **Range:** 2,500/8   **Man:** 32 tot.

♦ **1 Soviet Khobi-class small oiler**

D: 1,525 tons (fl)   **S:** 12 kts   **Dim:** 62.0 × 10.0 × 4.4
M: 2 diesels; 2 props; 1,600 hp

REMARKS: Former Soviet *Linda*. 795 grt.

♦ **1 Soviet Toplivo-I-class fuel lighter**

♦ **1 Soviet Sekstan-class degaussing tender** (500 tons)

♦ **1 Soviet Nyryat-I-class diving tender** (50 tons)

♦ **2 Soviet Poluchat-I-class torpedo retrievers**

D: 90 tons (fl)   **S:** 18 kts   **Dim:** 29.6 × 5.8 × 1.5
A: 2/14.5-mm mg (II × 1)   **M:** 2 M50 diesels; 2 props; 2,400 hp
Range: 450/17, 900/10   **Man:** 20 tot.

♦ **2 small personnel transports**

♦ **4 small tugs**

♦ **1 barracks barge**

ALGERIA

Democratic and Popular Republic of Algeria

PERSONNEL (1980): 3,800 men with about 300 to 350 officers, not necessarily on full-time active duty with the navy.

MERCHANT MARINE 1980: 130 ships—1,218,621 grt
(tankers: 22—591,953 grt)

NAVAL AVIATION: The Algerian Air Force uses 11 twin-engine Fokker F-27 (Maritime) patrol aircraft for maritime surveillance.

FRIGATES

♦ **1 Soviet Koni class** Bldr: Zelenodolsk SY

901 Mourad Rais

> **D:** 1,900 tons (fl) **S:** 30 kts **Dim:** 96.0 × 12.0 × 5.0 (4.4 hull)
> **A:** 1/SAN-4 SAM syst. (II × 1; 18 missiles)—4/76.2-mm DP (II × 2)—4/30-mm
>   AA (II × 2)—2/RBU-6000—2/d.c. rack—mines
> **Electron Equipt:** Radar: 1/Strut Curve, 1/Don- 2, 1/Pop Group, 1/Hawk
>   Screech, 1/Drum Tilt
>   Sonar: 1/medium freq., hull-mounted
> **M:** CODAG: 1 gas turbine, 2 diesels; 3 props; 30,000 hp

Remarks: Delivered 20-12-80; a second may follow. Has two chaff launchers, deck-house abaft stack unlike earlier examples.

GUIDED MISSILE CORVETTES

♦ **2 Soviet Nanuchka-II-class** Bldr: Petrovskiy SY, Leningrad

801 Ras Hamidou 802 Salah Rais

Ras Hamidou (801)   French Navy, 1980

> **D:** 780 tons (930 fl) **S:** 30 kts **Dim:** 60.0 × 13.2 × 2.7
> **A:** 4/SS-N-2C (II × 2)—1/SA-N-4 SAM syst. (II × 1; 18 missiles)—2/57-mm AA
>   (II × 1)
> **Electron Equipt:** Radars: 1/Don-2, 1/Square Tie, 1/Pop Group
>   ECM: 1/Bell Tap, 2 chaff launchers
>   IFF: 2/Square Head, 1 High Pole
> **M:** 3 M507 diesels; 3 props; 24,000 hp **Range:** 3,600/15 **Man:** 60 tot.

Remarks: 801 arrived in Algeria 4-7-80, 802 in 2-81. The Square Tie radar antenna is mounted within the Band Stand radome atop the bridge.

GUIDED MISSILE PATROL BOATS

♦ **0+4 new design program** Bldr: ONCN/CNE, Mers-el-Kebir

> **D:**   **S:**   **Dim:** 40.0 × 7.0 × 1.75
> **A:** 2/SSM (Otomat?)-2/76-mm DP OTO Melara Compact (I × 2)
> **M:** 4 MTU diesels; 4 props; 12,000 hp **Man:** 18 tot.

Remarks: Program announced and boats ordered 1979, originally for delivery by 1983, but now delayed. Armament uncertain; most equipment probably Italian.

♦ **8 Soviet Osa-II-class** (transferred 1976-1978)

644 645 646 647 648 649 650 651

Algerian Osa-II (with transfer pendant number)   1977

> **D:** 215 tons (240 fl) **S:** 36 kts **Dim:** 39.0 × 7.7 × 1.9
> **A:** 4/SS-N-2B (I × 4)—4/30-mm AA (II × 2)
> **Electron Equipt:** Radar: 1/Square Tie, 1/Drum Tilt
>   IFF: 2/Square Head, 1/High Pole B
> **M:** 3 M504 diesels; 3 props; 15,000 hp
> **Range:** 430/34, 790/20 **Man:** 30 tot.

♦ **3 Soviet Osa-I class** (transferred 1967)

641 642 643

> **D:** 175 tons (210 fl) **S:** 36 kts **Dim:** 39.0 × 7.7 × 1.8
> **A:** 4/SS-N-2A Styx (I × 4)—4/30-mm AA (II × 2)
> **Electron Equipt:** Radar: 1/Square Tie, 1/Drum Tilt
>   IFF: 2/Square Head, 1/High Pole B
> **M:** 3M503A diesels; 3 props; 12,000 hp **Man:** 30 tot.

♦ **6 Soviet Komar class** (transferred 1966)

671 672 673 674 675 676

> **D:** 71 tons (82 fl) **S:** 40 kts **Dim:** 25.2 × 7.0 × 2.0
> **A:** 2/SS-N-2A Styx (I × 2)—2/25-mm AA (II × 1)
> **Electron Equipt:** Radar: 1/Square Tie—IFF: 1/Dead Duck, 1/High Pole A
> **M:** 4 M-50 F4 diesels; 4 props; 4,800 hp

Remarks: Possibly nonoperational. Wooden construction. The remaining P-6 torpedo boats, which had the same hull and propulsion, have been discarded.

PATROL BOATS

♦ **6 Soviet SO-1 class** (transferred 10-65 to 10-67)

651 652 653 654 655 656

> **D:** 170 tons (215 fl) **S:** 27 kts **Dim:** 42.0 × 6.0 × 1.9
> **A:** 4/25-mm AA (II × 2)—4/RBU-1200 ASW RL—2/d.c. racks—mines
> **Electron Equipt:** Radar: 1/Pot Head
>   IFF: 1/Dead Duck, 1 High Pole
> **M:** 3 40-D diesels; 3 props; 7,500 hp **Man:** 30 tot.

Remarks: Three have 2/533-mm TT, removed from P-6-class torpedo boats.

MINE WARFARE SHIPS

♦ **2 Soviet T-43-class ocean minesweepers** (transferred 1968)

M 521   M 522

    D: 500 tons (550 fl)   **S:** 14 kts   **Dim:** 58.0 × 8.4 × 2.3
    A: 4/37-mm AA (II × 2)—8/12.7-mm mg (II × 4)—2 d.c.t.—mines
    M: 2 9-D diesels; 2 props; 2,200 hp   **Range:** 3,200/10

REMARKS: M 521, in reserve since 1974, is again operational.

AMPHIBIOUS WARFARE SHIPS

♦ **1 Soviet Polnocny-A-class medium landing ship**

555

    D: 900 tons (fl)   **S:** 18 kts   **Dim:** 73.0 × 8.5 × 2.0
    A: 2/30-mm AA (II × 1)—2/140-mm barrage RL (XVIII × 2)
    Electron Equipt: Radar: 1/Don-2, 1/Drum Tilt
                 IFF: 1/Square Head, 1/High Pole A
    M: 2 diesels; 2 props; 5,000 hp   **Man:** 40 tot.

REMARKS: Transferred 9-76.

MISCELLANEOUS

♦ **1 Soviet Sekstan-class degaussing tender**

A 640 MASISA

REMARKS: Transferred 1964, wooden construction, built in Finland ca. 1950. May be hulked.

♦ **1 Soviet Poluchat-1-class torpedo retriever**

A 641

    D: 90 tons (fl)   **S:** 18 kts   **Dim:** 29.6 × 5.8 × 1.5
    M: 2 M50 diesels; 2 props; 2,400 hp   **Man:** 20 tot.

♦ **1 Soviet Nyryat-1-class diving tender** (120 tons)

♦ **1 tug/diving tender** (purchased 1965)

VP 650 YAVDEZAN

♦ **1 survey craft** Bldr: Matsukara, Hirao, Japan
A. . .   El Idrissi (L: 17-4-80) **D:** 250 tons

♦ **2 fisheries protection/customs craft**

DJEBEL ANTAR   DJEBEL HANDA

COAST GUARD

♦ **6 Mangusta-class patrol boats** Bldr: Baglietto, Italy. (In serv. 1977-78)

| 323 OMBRINE | 324 DORADE | 331 REQUIN |
| 332 ESPADON | 333 MARSOUIN | 334 MURÉRIE |

Requin (now renumbered and armed)   C. Martinelli, 1977

    D: 91 tons (fl)   **S:** 32 kts   **Dim:** 30.0 × 5.84 × 2.1
    A: 2/25-mm AA (II × 2)—2/23-mm AA (II × 1)
    Electron Equipt: Radars: 1/3RM 20 SMA
    M: 3 diesels; 3 props; 4,050 hp   **Range:** 800/24, 1,400/12.5
    Man: 3 officers, 11 men

♦ **10 Type 20-GC-class patrol craft** Bldr: Baglietto, Italy (in serv., 8-76 to 12-76)

100   112   113   114   221   222   235   236   237   325

Baglietto —20-GC class   C. Martinelli, 1977

    D: 44 tons (fl)   **S:** 36 kts   **Dim:** 20.4 × 5.2 × 1.7   **A:** 1/20-mm AA
    M: 2 CRM 18DS diesels; 2 props; 2,700 hp   **Range:** 445/20   **Man:** 11 tot.

♦ **several smaller patrol craft**

ANGOLA
People's Republic of Angola

PERSONNEL: 1,500 total

MERCHANT MARINE: (1980): 35 ships—65,667 grt (tankers: 5—3,138 grt)

NAVAL AVIATION: One Fokker F-27 Maritime patrol aircraft was delivered during 1980 for coastal patrol duties.

NOTE: The ex-Portuguese craft were located in Angola in 1975 and were transferred on independence.

TORPEDO BOATS

♦ **6 Soviet Shershen class**

    D: 150 tons (180 fl) **S:** 45 kts **Dim:** 34.0 × 7.2 × 1.5
    A: 4/30-mm AA (II × 2)—4/533-mm TT
    Electron Equipt: Radar: 1/Pot Drum, 1/Drum Tilt
                     IFF: 1/Square Head, 1/High Pole A
    M: 3 M503A diesels; 3 props; 12,000 hp **Range:** 450/34, 700/20

REMARKS: Delivered 12-77 to 11-79. Unlike many recent transfers of this class, all apparently retain torpedo tubes.

PATROL BOATS

♦ **1 Soviet Zhuk class** (transferred 1977)

    D: 50 tons (60 fl) **S:** 30 kts **Dim:** 26.0 × 4.9 × 1.5
    A: 4/14.5-mm mg (II × 2) **M:** 2 M50 diesels; 2 props; 2,400 hp

♦ **2 Soviet Poluchat-1 class** (transferred 12-79)

    D: 90 tons (fl) **S:** 18 kts **Dim:** 29.6 × 5.8 × 1.5
    A: 2/14.5-mm mg (II × 1) **M:** 2 M50 diesels; 2 props 2,400 hp
    Range: 450/17, 900/10 **Man:** 20 tot.

♦ **5 Portuguese Argos class** Bldr: Castelo SY
(P 375, P 1130: Alfeite Navy Yd, Lisbon), In serv. 1963-65

P 361 (ex-*Lira*)	P 375 (ex-*Escorpido*)	P 1130 (ex-*Centauro*)
P 362 (ex-*Orion*)	P 379 (ex-*Pegaso*)	

    D: 180 tons (210 fl) **S:** 18 kts **Dim:** 41.6 × 6.2 × 2.2
    A: 2/40-mm AA (I × 2) **M:** 2 Maybach diesels; 2 props; 2,000 hp
    Fuel: 16 tons **Man:** 24 tot.

REMARKS: Two others, *Argos* and *Dragao*, transferred for cannibalization.

♦ **1 Portuguese Jupiter class** Bldr: Mondego SY (in serv. 1965)

P 1133 (ex-*Venus*)

    D: 32 tons (43.5 fl) **S:** 20 kts **Dim:** 20.7 × 5.0 × 1.3 **A:** 1/20-mm AA
    M: 2 Cummins diesels; 2 props; 1,270 hp

♦ **5 Portuguese Bellatrix class** Bldr: Bayerische Schiffsbaugesellschaft, West Germany (in serv. 1961-62)

P 366 (ex-*Espiga*)	P 368 (ex-*Pollux*)	P 378 (ex-*Rigel*)
P 367 (ex-*Fomelhaut*)	P 377 (ex-*Altair*)	

    D: 23 tons (27.6 fl) **S:** 15 kts **Dim:** 20.5 × 4.6 × 1.2
    A: 1/20-mm AA—1/37-mm RL (atop 20-mm AA)
    M: 2 Cummins diesels; 2 props; 470 hp **Man:** 7 tot.

AMPHIBIOUS WARFARE SHIPS

♦ **3 Soviet Polnocny-B-class medium landing ships** Bldr: Polnocny SY, Gdansk, Poland

    D: 950 tons (fl) **S:** 18 kts **Dim:** 74.0 × 8.5 × 2.0
    A: 2/30-mm AA (II × 1)—2/140-mm barrage RL (XVIII × 2)
    Electron Equipt: Radar: 1/Don 2, 1/Drum Tilt
                      IFF: 1/Square Head
    M: 2 diesels; 2 props; 5,000 hp **Man:** 40 tot.

REMARKS: First transferred in 1977, second in 2-78, third in 1979.

♦ **1 Portuguese Alfange-class medium landing ship** Bldr: Mondego SY (in serv. 1965)

N. . . (ex-*Alfange*)

    D: 500 tons (fl) **S:** 11 kts **Dim:** 57.0 × 11.8 × 1.9 **A:** 2/20-mm AA
    M: 2 diesels; 2 props; 1,000 hp **Range:** 1,500/9 **Man:** 14 tot. + 35 troops

REMARKS: A second unit was not placed in service. Design based on British LCT (4) class of World War II.

♦ **5 Soviet T-4-class LCM** (transferred 1976)

♦ **Up to 9 Portuguese LDM-400-class LCM**

    D: 56 tons (fl) **S:** 9 kts **Dim:** 17.0 × 5.0 × 1.2 **A:** 1/20-mm AA
    M: 2 Cummins diesels; 2 props; 450 hp

ARGENTINA
Argentine Republic

PERSONNEL: 30,430 men, including 2,890 officers and 6,000 Marines

MERCHANT MARINE (1980): 537 ships—2,546,305 grt (tankers: 84—811,465 grt)

NAVAL AVIATION: The air squadron for *25 de Mayo* includes 12 A-4Q Skyhawks, 4 Sikorsky SH-3D helicopters, and 5 S-2A Tracker ASW aircraft. Other seaborne helicopters include 3 WG 13 Lynx, 6 Hughes 500M Cayuse, 2 Sikorsky S-61NR, and 9 Alouette-III helicopters.

    Land-based aircraft included 10 Aeromacchi MB-326GB ground attack/trainers, 5 SP-2E/P-24 Neptune patrol aircraft; 3 Fokker F 28-3000, 1 H.S. 125 Series 400A, 3 Lockheed L-188 Electra, and 5 Short Skyvan transports; 8 Beech Super King Air 200, 5 Beech B80 Queen Air, and 3 Fairchild Porter light transports; 15 Beech T-34 C-1 trainers; and 3 Puma helicopters.

    Fourteen Super Étendard were ordered from France in late 1979 to replace the Skyhawks, while 10 Aeromacchi MB-339 light ground attack jets were ordered in 1980 for delivery beginning at end 1981. Plans call for acquiring at least 8 more WG 13 Lynx helicopters for the MEKO 360 and MEKO 140 classes.

WARSHIPS IN SERVICE OR UNDER CONSTRUCTION AS OF 1 JANUARY 1982

	L	Tons Std.	Main Armament
◆ 4(+6) submarines			
0(+2) GERMAN TR-1400	1980-82	1,450	6/533-mm TT
0(+4) GERMAN TR-1700	1980-82	1,750	6/533-mm TT
2 GERMAN 209	1972-73	980	8/533-mm TT
2 GUPPY IA, II	1944-45	1,517	10/533-mm TT
◆ 1 aircraft carrier			
25 DE MAYO	1943	15,892	9/40-mm AA, 21 aircraft
◆ 1 cruiser			
1 BROOKLYN	1938	10,800	15/152-mm, 2 Sea Cat SAM, 8/127-mm DP
◆ 9(+4) destroyers			
0(+4) MEKO 360	1981-8. . .	2,900	8 Exocet, Albatros, 1/127-mm DP, 2 helicopter
2 SHEFFIELD	1972-74	3,150	2 Exocet, 1 Sea Dart SAM, 1/114-mm DP, 1 ASW helicopter
1 GEARING, FRAM II	1944	2,400	4 Exocet SSM, 6/127-mm DP
3 ALLEN M. SUMNER	1944	2,200	4 Exocet SSM, 6/127-mm DP
3 FLETCHER	1942-43	2,050	4/127-mm DP, 6/76.2-mm DP
◆ 4 (+7) frigates			
0(+6) MEKO 1470	1982-. . .	1,200	4 Exocet, 1/76-mm DP, helicopter
2(+1) A-69	1977-80	1,170	4 Exocet, 1/100-mm DP
2 MURATURE	1943-45	1,000	3/105-mm DP
◆ 7 corvettes			
2 ACHOMAWI	1944-45	1,235	4/40-mm AA
5 SOTOYOMO	1944-45	689	1/40-mm AA
◆ 6 patrol boats			
◆ 6 minesweeper/minehunters			
◆ 5 landing ships			

NOTE: Pendant numbers deleted 1979 during duration of Beagle Islands crisis with Chile.

AIRCRAFT CARRIER

◆ 1 British Colossus-class

	Bldr	Laid down	L	In serv.
25 DE MAYO	Cammell Laird	3-12-42	30-12-43	17-1-45

(ex-*Karel Dorman*, ex-*Venerable*)

D: 15,892 tons (19,896 fl) **S:** 24.5 kts
Dim: 212.67 (192.04 pp) × 24.49 (40.66 flight deck) × 7.5
A: 10/40-mm AA (I × 10)—12 A-4Q Skyhawk, 5 S-2A Tracker, 4 SH-3D helo
Electron Equipt: Radars: Dutch 1/LW-02, 1/SGR-109 (height-finding), 1/SGR-105 (DA-05), 1/SGR-103 (ZW-01), 1/air control—TACAN: URN-20
M: 2 sets Parsons GT; 2 props; 40,000 hp **Electric:** 2,500 kw
Boilers: 4 Admiralty 3-drum type; 30.23 kg/cm² (since refit), 371° C
Fuel: 3,200 tons **Range:** 6,200/23, 12,000/14 **Man:** 1,509 tot.

REMARKS: Purchased by The Netherlands from the British Navy in 1948. Rebuilt from 1955 to 1958 by Wilton-Fijenoord; 165.80 meters angled flight deck, steam catapult, mirror optical landing equipment, new anti-aircraft guns, and new radar equipment of Dutch conception and construction. Modified for service in the tropics. Partially air-conditioned. In 1967 new boilers were installed from the British aircraft carrier *Leviathan*, which was never completed. Purchased in 1968 by Argentina and again refitted, recommissioning 22-8-69. She is equipped with the British C.A.A.I.S. data display system, compatible with the ADAWS 4 data system on the *Sheffield*-class destroyers. 1980 refit enlarged flight deck to permit deck-parking three additional aircraft. To operate to 1990s. New Super Étendard aircraft ordered 1979 to replace Skyhawks.

25 de Mayo—note 1 LWO-01/02 deleted.   R. Scheina, 1980

25 de Mayo—port quarter   R. Scheina, 1980

AIRCRAFT CARRIER *(continued)*

25 de Mayo—island   R. Scheina, 1980

SUBMARINES

♦ **2 TR-1400** Bldr: Tandanor, Buenos Aires

	L		L
N. . .	. . .	N. . .	. . .

D: 1,450 tons (1,650 fl surf.)   **Dim:** 56.20 × 7.30 × 6.30
S: 15/21 kts, 13 with snorkel   **A:** 6/533-mm TT forward, 22 torpedoes
M: Diesel-electric: 2/1100-kw generators; 1 3,700-kw motor; 5,000 hp
Man: 29 tot.

REMARKS: Ordered at same time as the TR-1700 class below. Intended for coastal operations, with less endurance required. Same bow and stern components as TR-1700 class. Half the battery capacity of the TR-1700 design. 300-m diving depth.

♦ **4 TR-1700 class**

	Bldr	Laid down	L	In serv.
S 33 SANTA CRUZ	Thyssen Noordseewerke, Emden	6-12-80	. . .	1983
S 34 SAN JUAN	Thyssen Noordseewerke, Emden	. . .	. . .	. . .
S 35 N. . .	Thyssen Noordseewerke, Emden	. . .	. . .	. . .
S 36 N. . .	Tandanor, Buenos Aires	1982	. . .	. . .

TR 1700 class—artist's rendering   Thyssen/J. Sachse, 1980

D: 1,750 tons (2,050 surf./2,300 sub. fl)
S: 25 kts (sub)—13 snorkel, 15 kts (surf)
Dim: 64.10 × 7.30 × 6.50
Range: 20/25, 50/20, 110/15, 460/6 sub.—15,000/5 surf.
A: 6/533-mm TT, 22 torpedoes
M: Diesel-electric: 4/1,100-kw generators; 1 6,600-kw motor; 1 prop, 8,970 hp
Man: 30 tot.

REMARKS: Ordered 30-11-77. Originally only the first to be built in Germany. Battery has eight groups of 120 cells, 5,858 amp/1 hr. capacity, 11,900 amp/10 hr.

♦ **German Type 209 class**

	Bldr	Laid down	L	In serv.
S 31 SALTA	Howaldtswerke, Kiel	3-4-70	9-11-72	7-3-74
S 32 SAN LUIS	Howaldtswerke, Kiel	1-10-70	3-4-73	24-5-74

D: 980 tons standard, 1,230 submerged   **Dim:** 55.0 × 6.6 × 5.9
S: 21 kts sub.—2 with snorkel   **A:** 8/533-mm TT—14 torpedoes
Fuel: 50 tons
M: 4 MTU type 12V-493-TY60 diesels, Siemens electric motor; 1 prop; 3,600 hp
Man: 5 officers, 26 men

REMARKS: Built in four sections at Kiel and assembled at the Navy Yard in Rio Santiago. Part of the electronic equipment is French. An extension of the German *205/206* class (plans by Professor Ulrich Gabler of IKL); single-hull construction.

SUBMARINES *(continued)*

Salta   1972

♦ **2 ex-U.S. Guppy class** Bldr: Electric Boat Co., Groton

	Laid down	L	In serv.
S 21 SANTA FE	6-1-44	19-11-44	19-3-45
(ex-*Catfish*, SS 339)			
S 22 SANTIAGO DEL ESTERO	21-2-44	14-1-45	28-4-45
(ex-*Chivo*, SS 341)			

Santiago del Estero (S 22)   R. Scheina, 1980

D: 1,517 tons surf, 1,870 normal; 2,340 sub   **S:** 18/14 kts
Range: 10,000/10   **Dim:** 93.6 × 8.4 × 5.25
A: 10/533-mm TT (6 forward, 4 aft)—22 torpedoes
M: 3 (S 22: 4) GM 16-278A diesels, each of 1,625 hp, with 2 electric motors of 2,700 hp each; 2 props
Fuel: 300 tons   **Man:** 9 officers, 76 men

REMARKS: Purchased 7-71. S 21 is a Guppy II; S 22 is a Guppy IA.

CRUISER

♦ **1 U.S. Brooklyn class**

	Bldr	Laid down	L	In serv.
C 4 GENERAL BELGRANO	New York SB Co.	15-4-35	12-3-38	3-10-38
(ex-*17 de Octubre*,				
ex-*Phoenix*, CL 46)				

General Belgrano (C 4)   R. Scheina, 1980

D: 10,800 tons (13,479 fl)   **S:** 25/24 kts   **Dim:** 185.32 × 18.77 × 7.62
A: 15/152-mm (III × 5) 2 Sea Cat SAM Syst. (IV × 2)—8/127-mm DP (I × 8)—20/40-mm AA (IV × 2, II × 6)—10/20-mm AA (II × 10)
Electron Equipt: Radars: 1/navigational 1/SGR-110, 1/SGR-105, 1/SGR-114, 1/RTN-10, 2/Mk 8, 2/Mk 28
      ECM: WLR-1
Armor: Belt,102-mm; Decks, 76-mm; Turret,102-mm; Conning tower,203-mm
M: 4 sets Parsons GT; 4 props; 100,000 hp
Boilers: 8 Babcock & Wilcox Express; 31 kg, 328°C   **Electric:** 2,000 kw
Range: 2,500/30, 9,850/12   **Man:** 980 tot.

REMARKS: Purchased in 12-1-51. Sea Cat systems are controlled by 1 Selenia NA-10 system. Hangar aft can accommodate 2 helicopters. Sister *9 de Julio* (ex-*Boise*, CL 47) hulked 1976 and sold for scrap 1981.

DESTROYERS

♦ **4 MEKO-360 H2 Class** Bldr: Blohm & Voss, Hamburg

	Laid down	L	In Serv.
D 3 ALMIRANTE BROWN	8-9-80	28-3-81	-82
D 4 LA ARGENTINA	31-3-81	. . .	-83
D 5 HEROINA	. . .	. . .	. . .
D 6 SARANDI	. . .	. . .	. . .

DESTROYERS *(continued)*

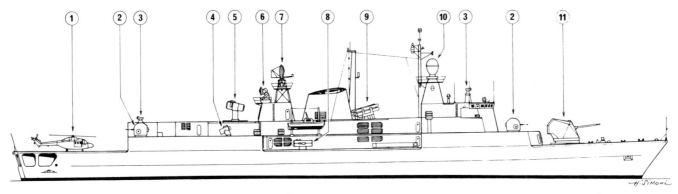

1. WG 13 helicopter 2. 40-mm AA (II × 1) 3. helicopter control radar 4. SCLAR chaff launchers (XX × 1) 5. Albatros launcher
6. STIR radar 7. DA 08 A radar 8. Mk 32 ASW TT (III × 2) 9. MM 40 launchers 10. WM 26 radar 11. 127-mm DP gun

Almirante Brown (D 3)—artist's rendering   Escher Wyss/J. Sachse, 1980

D: 2,900 tons (3,360 fl) **S:** 30.5 kts
Dim: 125.9(119.0 pp) × 15.0 × 4.32(5.80 sonar)
A: 8/MM 40 Exocet SSM (IV × 2)—1 Albatros SAM syst. (VIII × 1; 24 Aspide
  missiles)—1/127-mm OTO Melara DP—8/40-mm Breda AA (II × 4)—6/324-
  mm ASW TT (III × 2; 18 torp.)—2/WG 13 Lynx helicopters (10 ASW
  torp.)
Electron Equipt: Radar: 1/Decca 1226, 1/HSA DA-08A, 1/HSA WM 25 with
      STIR, 2/HSA LIROD
    Sonar: Atlas 80, hull-mounted
    ECM: AEG-Telefunken syst., 2/SCLAR chaff (XX × 2)
M: COGOG: 2 Olympus TM-3B gas turbines, 25,800 hp each; 2 Tyne RM-1C,
  5,100 hp each for cruise; 2 Escher-Wyss CP props; 51,600 hp max.
Electric: 2,600 kw (2/940-kw sets, 2/360 kw) **Range:** 4,500/18
Man: 26 officers, 84 petty officers, 90 men

REMARKS: Ordered 11-12-78 as a class of *six*, four of which were to be built in Argentina, but altered to four when MEKO-140-series frigate program was introduced.
Albatros system will have a 16-missile Aspide SAM rapid-reload magazine nearby.
The two HSA LIROD radar/optronic GFCS each control two twin 40-mm AA, for
which 10,752 rounds will be carried. The MEKO concept calls for modularized weapons and electronics systems, to permit rapid modernization and repair. Nigeria's
Aradu (ex-*Republic*) is very similar.

♦ **2 British Sheffield-class guided-missile destroyers**

	Bldr	Laid down	L	In serv.
D 1 HERCULES	Vickers, Barrow	1971	24-10-72	10-5-76
D 2 SANTISIMA TRINIDAD	Ast. Nav., Rio Santiago	2-72	9-11-74	-81

Hercules—Exocet now atop hangar   G. Arra, 1977

DESTROYERS *(continued)*

D: 3,150 tons (3,600 fl)   **Range:** 4,000/18   **Dim:** 125 (119.5pp) × 14.6 × 5.2
S: 30 kts
A: 2/Exocet MM 38 SSM (I × 2)—1/Sea Dart Mk 30 mod. 2 SAM syst. (II × 1,
   20 missiles)—1/114-mm DP Mk 8—2/20-mm AA—1/WG 13 Lynx ASW and
   anti-ship helicopter—6/324-mm Mk 32 ASW TT (III × 2)
Electron Equipt: Radars: 1/965M,1/992Q, 2/909, 1/1006—ADAWS-4 data syst.
   Sonars: 1/177, 1/174, 1/170B, 1/162
M: COGOG 2 Olympus TM 3B gas turbines, 27,200 hp each for boost; 2 Tyne
   RM 1A gas turbines, 4,100 hp each for cruising; 2 CP, 5-bladed props
Electric: 4,000 kw   **Man:** 270 tot.

REMARKS: Ordered 18-5-70. Normally, the Type 909 control radars for the Sea Dart
system are covered by radomes. D 1 has "Loxton Bends" angled exhausts like HMS
Sheffield. D 2 was sabotaged on 22-8-75 and was delayed, running initial trials on
7-3-80. D 1, refitted 1980, had MM 38 Exocet missiles added atop the hangar; these
were to be relocated lower at a later date.

♦ **1 ex-U.S. Gearing class FRAM II** Bldr: Consolidated Steel, Orange, Texas

	Laid down	L	In serv.
D 27 COMODORO PY (ex-*Perkins*, DD 877)	19-6-44	7-12-44	1-3-45

Comodoro Py (D 27)—Exocet between stacks   R. Scheina, 1980

D: 2,400 tons (3,600 fl)   **S:** 36 kts   **Dim:** 119.17 × 12.45 × 5.8
Range: 2,400/25, 4,800/15
A: 4/MM 38 Exocet—6/127-mm DP 38-cal. (II × 3)—2/Hedgehogs—6/324-mm
   Mk 32 ASW TT (III × 2) for Mk 44 torpedoes—1/Alouette-III helicopter
Electron Equipt: Radars: 1/SPS-40, 1/SPS-10, 1/Mk 25
   Sonar: 1/SQS-23
M: 2 sets Westinghouse GT; 2 props; 60,000 hp
Fuel: 650 tons   **Electric:** 1,200 kw
Boilers: 4 Babcock & Wilcox, 43.3 kg/cm², 454° C   **Man:** 15 officers, 260 men

REMARKS: Transferred 1-73. Had undergone Fram II modernization. Exocet added
1977-78. Mk 37 fire-control system with Mk 25 radar.

♦ **3 ex-U.S. Allen M. Sumner class**

	Bldr	Laid down	L	In serv.
D 25 SEGUI (ex-*Hank*, DD 702)	Federal SB & DD	17-1-44	21-5-44	28-8-44
D 26 HIPOLITO BOUCHARD (ex-*Borie*, DD 704)	Federal SB & DD	29-2-44	4-7-44	20-9-44
D 29 PIEDRABUENA (ex-*Collett*, DD 730)	Bath Iron Works	11-10-43	5-3-44	16-5-44

Segui—Mk 56 fire-control system aft with Mk 35 radar. Four Exocet now mounted
at bridge deck level, abreast forward stack.   1975

Hipolito Bouchard (D 26)   R. Scheina, 1980

D: 2,200 tons (3,300 fl)   **S:** 30 kts   **Dim:** 114.75 × 12.45 × 5.8
A: 4/MM 38 Exocet—6/127-mm DP (II × 3)—D 25: 4/76.2-mm DP (II × 2)
   also—6/324-mm Mk 32 ASW TT (III × 2)—2/Hedgehogs—D 26, D 29: 1/
   Alouette-III helicopter—D 25: 1/d.c. rack
Electron Equipt: Radars: 1/SPS-40, 1/SPS-10, 1/Mk 25 (D 25 also: 1/Mk 35)
   Sonars: 1/SQS-29 or 30
M: 2 sets GT; 2 props, 60,000 hp   **Fuel:** 650 tons   **Electric:** 1,200 kw
Boilers: 4 Babcock & Wilcox; 43.3 kg/cm², 454°C
Range: 1,260/30, 4,600/15   **Man:** 14 officers, 260 men

REMARKS: Two transferred 7-72, and two 4-76. Exocet anti-ship missiles added to all

DESTROYERS *(continued)*

in 1977-78. D 26, D 29 had FRAM II modernization. D 25, not modernized, has SPS-6 radar. *Mansfield* (DD 728), transferred 4-76, was at one time planned for activation as *Espora* (D 31), but she was instead cannibalized. VDS removed from D 26, D 29.

♦ 3 ex-U.S. Fletcher class

	Bldr	Laid down	L	In serv.
D 22 ROSALES (ex-*Stembel*, DD 644)	Bath Iron Works	21-12-42	8-5-43	16-7-43
D 23 ALMIRANTE DOMECQ GARCIA (ex-*Braine*, DD 630)	Bath Iron Works	12-10-42	7-3-43	11-5-43
D 24 ALMIRANTE STORNI (ex-*Cowell*, DD 547)	Bethlehem, San Pedro	7-9-42	18-3-43	23-8-43

D: 2,050 tons (2,850 fl) **S:** 30 kts **Dim:** 114.85 × 12.03 × 5.5
Range: 1,260/30, 4,400/15
A: 4/127-mm DP (I × 4)—6/76.2-mm DP (II × 3)—6/324-mm Mk 32 ASW TT (III × 2)—2/Hedgehogs—1 d.c. rack
Electron Equipt: Radars: 1/SPS-6, 1/SPS-10, 1/Mk 25, 2/Mk 34, 1/Mk 35
Sonar: SQS-4
M: 2 sets GE GT; 2 props; 60,000 hp **Fuel:** 650 tons **Electric:** 580 kw
Boilers: 4 Babcock & Wilcox; 43.3 kg/cm², 454° C
Man: 15 officers, 247 men

REMARKS: Transferred: D 22, 23: 1-8-61; D 24: 17-8-71. Originally on loan, all subsequently purchased. Two others discarded.

FRIGATES

♦ 6 MEKO 140 A16 class Bldr: AFNE, Rio Santiago, Ensenada

	Laid down	L	In serv.
P 4 ESPORAL	3-4-81	...	...
P 5 AZOPARDO	10-81	...	...
P 6 SPIRO	4-82	...	...
P N...	10-82	...	...
P N...	4-83	...	...
P N...	10-83	...	...

D: 1,200 tons (1,470 fl) **S:** 27 kts **Dim:** 91.2 (86.4 pp) × 12.2 × 3.33 (hull)
A: 4/MM 38 Exocet SSM (II × 2)—1/76-mm DP OTO Melara—4/40-mm AA Breda (II × 2), 2/12.7-mm mg (I × 2)—6/324-mm Mk 32 ASW TT (III × 2)—platform for 1/WG 13 Lynx helo
Electron Equipt: Radar: 1/Decca TM 1226, 1/HSA DA-05/2, 1/HSA WM-28, 1/HSA LIROD
Sonar: 1/ADS-4
ECM: RDC-2ABC and RCM-2 systems, DAGAIE chaff
M: 2 SEMT-Pielstick 16 PC2-5V400 diesels; 2/5-bladed props; 22,600 hp
Range: 4,000/18 **Fuel:** 230 tons
Electric: 1,410 kVA (3 × 470 kVA diesel sets)
Man: 11 officers, 46 petty officers, 36 men

REMARKS: Ordered 8-79. Blohm & Voss design, based on Portuguese *João Coutinho* class. Will have fin stabilizers. LIROD radar/electro-optical system controls 40-mm AA. Eight MM 40 Exocet could replace the four larger MM 38 listed. To carry 5 tons aviation fuel, 70 tons fresh water. Also known as MEKO 1470 class.

♦ 3 French A-69 class

	Bldr	L	In serv.
F 701 DRUMMOND (ex-*Good Hope*, F 432)	Lorient DY	5-3-77	10-78
F 702 GUERRICO (ex-*Transvaal*, F 102)	Lorient DY	-9-77	10-78
F 703 GRANVILLE	Lorient DY	28-6-80	22-6-81

Guerrico and Drummond (outboard *Hercules*)　　R. Scheina, 1980

MEKO 140 A16 Class

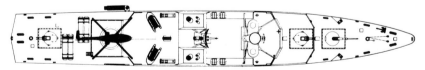

FRIGATES *(continued)*

D: 1,100 tons (1,250 fl) **S:** 24 kts
Dim: 80.5 (76.0 pp) × 10.3 × 3.0 (5.2 sonar)
A: 4/MM 38 Exocet (II × 2)—1/100-mm DP mod. 1968—1/40-mm AA—2/20-mm
   AA (I × 2)—6/324-mm ASW TT (III × 2)
Range: 3,000/18, 4,500/15
Electron Equipt: Radars: 1/DRBV-51A, 1/DRBC-32C, 1/Decca 1226
   Sonar: Diodon
M: 2 SEMT-Pielstick 12 PC 2 diesels; 2 CP props; 11,000 hp **Electric:** 840 kw
Man: 5 officers, 79 men

REMARKS: The first two were originally ordered by South Africa, but delivery was
embargoed. Purchased by Argentina, 25-9-78, to augment fleet in case of war with
Chile. Armament and some electronic gear differ from French Navy version. Third
unit was ordered 10-79.

♦ **2 Murature class**

	Bldr	Laid down	L	In serv.
P 20 MURATURE	Ast. Nav. Rio Santiago	6-38	11-43	11-46
P 21 KING	Ast. Nav. Rio Santiago	3-40	7-43	7-46

King

D: 913 tons, 1,000 normal, 1,032 fl **S:** 16 kts **Dim:** 76.8 × 8.85 × 2.5
A: 3/105-mm DP—4/40-mm AA—4/d.c.t.
M: Werkspoor 4-stroke diesels; 2 props; 2,500 hp **Fuel:** 90 tons
Range: 6,000/12 **Man:** 140 tot.

REMARKS: Both used for training. Marginally seaworthy; due for disposal

CORVETTES

♦ **2 U.S. Achomawi class** Bldr: Charleston SB & DD Co.

	Laid down	L	In serv.
A 1 COMANDANTE GENERAL IRIGOYEN	16-6-44	2-11-44	10-3-45
(ex-*Cahuilla*, ATF 152)			
A 3 FRANCISCO DE CHURRUCA	7-11-44	17-3-45	16-6-45
(ex-*Luiseno*, ATF 156)			

D: 1,235 tons (1,675 fl) **S:** 16.5 kts
Dim: 62.48 (59.44 wl) × 11.73 × 4.67
A: 4/40-mm AA (II × 2, I × 2)—2/20-mm AA (I × 2)
M: 4 GM 12-278A diesels, electric drive; 1 prop; 3,000 hp
Fuel: 363 tons **Electric:** 400 kw **Range:** 7,000/15, 15,000/8 **Man:** 85 tot.

REMARKS: A 1 transferred 1961 as an ocean tug; rerated a patrol ship in 1966. A 3
purchased 1-7-75. Retain tug and salvage facilities. A 3: 2/40-mm AA (II × 1) only.

Comandante General Irigoyen (A 1)   R. Scheina, 1980

♦ **3 U.S. Sotoyomo class** Bldr: Gulfport Boiler & Welding, Port Arthur, Texas
   (A 10: Levingston SB, Orange, Texas)

	Laid down	L	In serv.
A 6 YAMANA	29-5-42	23-10-42	20-1-43
(ex-*Maricopa*, ATA 146)			
A 9 ALFEREZ SOBRAL	5-1-44	15-2-45	18-4-45
(ex-*Catawba*, ATA 210)			
A 10 COMODORO SOMELLERA	29-8-44	29-9-44	7-12-44
(ex-*Salish*, ATA 187)			

Yamana (A 6)   R. Scheina, 1980

CORVETTES (continued)

D: 570 tons (835 fl) **S:** 13 kts **Dim:** 43.59 (41.0 pp) × 10.31 × 4.01
A: 1/40-mm AA—2/20-mm AA (I × 2)
M: 2 GM 12-278A diesels, electric drive; 1 prop; 1,500 hp **Fuel:** 171 tons
Electric: 90 kw **Range:** 16,500/8 **Man:** 49 tot.

REMARKS: Former U.S. auxiliary ocean tugs. A 6 purchased 1947, has two navigational
radars. A 9 and A 10 transferred 10-2-72. Sister *Daiquita* (A 5, ex-ATA 124) sold
commercial, 1979. Two others, unarmed, serve as tugs.

PATROL BOATS

♦ **2 Intrepida class** (Lürssen TNC 45 design)

	Bldr	L	In serv.
ELPR 1 INTREPIDA	Lürssen, Bremen-Vegesack	12-12-74	20-7-74
ELPR 2 INDOMITA	Lürssen, Bremen-Vegesack	8-4-74	12-74

D: 240 tons (265 fl) **S:** 37.8 kts **Dim:** 44.9 × (42.3 pp) × 7.4 × 2.28 (prop.)
A: 1/76-mm DP OTO Melara—2/40-mm wire-guided TT (German T-4 torp.)
Electron Equipt: Radar: 1/Decca 101, 1/HSA M22
M: 4 MTU MD 872 diesels; 4 props; 14,400 hp **Electric:** 330 kw
Range: 640/36, 1,700/16 **Man:** 5 officers, 37 men

REMARKS: Anti-rolling stabilizers. Plans to acquire two more canceled. Have passive
threat-warning ECM.

♦ **4 Israeli Dabur class** Bldr: Israeli Aircraft Industries, Israel (In serv. 1978)

P 61 BARADERO   P 62 BARRANQUERAS   P 63 CLORINDA
P 64 CONCEPCION DEL URUGUAY

D: 26.8 tons (34.2 fl) **S:** 22 kts **Dim:** 19.8 × 5.4 × 1.75
A: 2/20-mm AA (I × 2)—4/12.7-mm mg (II × 2)
Electron Equipt: Radar: Decca 101
M: 2 GM 12V-71T diesels; 2 props; 1,200 hp **Range:** 700/16 **Man:** 8 tot.
Range: 700/16 **Man:** 8 tot.

MINE WARFARE SHIPS

♦ **6 British "Ton" class** Minesweepers/minehunters

	L		L
M 1 NEUQUEN (ex-*Hickleton*)	26-1-55	M 4 TIERRA DEL FUEGO (ex-*Bevington*)	17-3-53
M 2 RIO NEGRO (ex-*Tarlton*)	10-11-54	M 5 CHACO (ex-*Rennington*)	27-11-58
M 3 CHUBUT (ex-*Santon*)	18-8-55	M 6 FORMOSA (ex-*Ilmington*)	8-3-54

D: 370 tons (425 fl) **S:** 15 kts **Dim:** 46.33 (42.68 pp) × 8.76 × 2.50
A: 1/40-mm AA **Electron Equipt:** Radar: Type 978
M: 2 Paxman Deltic 18A-7A diesels; 2 props; 3,000 hp **Fuel:** 45 tons
Range: 2,300/13, 3,000/8 **Man:** 27 tot. (M 5, M 6: 36 tot.)

REMARKS: M5 and M 6 refitted as minehunters in 1968, with Plessey Type 193M sonar.
The others may retain Mirrlees JVSS-12 diesels, totaling 2,,500 hp.

Chaco (M 5)—minehunter   R. Scheina, 1980

AMPHIBIOUS WARFARE SHIPS

♦ **1 ex-U.S. Ashland-class dock landing ship** Bldr: Moore DD, Oakland, Cal.

	Laid down	L	In serv.
Q 43 CANDIDO DE LASALA	28-12-42	1-5-43	10-11-43
(ex-*Gunston Hall*, LSD 5)			

D: 4,032 tons (8,700 fl) **S:** 15 kts
Dim: 139.5 (138.4 wl) × 22.0 × 5.49 **A:** 12/40-mm AA (IV × 2, II × 2)
Electron Equipt: Radar: 1/navigational, 1 SPS-5
M: 2 sets Skinner Uniflow, triple-expansion; 2 props; 7,400 hp
Boilers: 2/2-drum, 17.6 kg/cm² **Electric:** 400 kw **Fuel:** 1,758 tons
Range: 8,000/15 **Man:** . . .

REMARKS: Transferred 24-4-70. Docking well: 119.5 × 13.4. Two 35-ton cranes. Has
been used occasionally as a patrol-craft tender. Four Mk 51 mod. 2 GFCS for 40-
mm AA.

Candido De Lasala (Q 43)—outboard Cabo San Antonio   R. Scheina, 1980

♦ **1 Modified U.S. DeSoto County-class tank landing ship**

	Bldr	L	In serv.
Q 42 Cabo San Antonio	AFNE, Rio Santiago	1968	2-11-78

D: 4,300 tons (8,000 fl) **S:** 16 kts **Dim:** 134.72 (129.8 wl) × 18.9 × 5.5
A: 12/40-mm AA (IV × 3) **Electron Equipt:** Radar: 1 navigational, 1/AWS-1
M: 6 diesels; 2 CP props; 13,700 hp **Electric:** 900 kw **Man:** 124 tot.

REMARKS: Differs from U.S. Navy version primarily in armament and in having a 60-ton Stülcken heavy-lift kingpost set amidships. Carries 4 LCVP. Tank deck 88-m long can stow 23 medium tanks. 700 troops can be carried.

♦ **4 U.S. LCM(6)-class landing craft (6-71)**

EDM 1 EDM 2 EDM 3 EDM 4

D: 24 tons (56 fl) **S:** 10 kts **Dim:** 17.07 × 4.37 × 1.17 (aft)
A: 2/12.7-mm mg **M:** 2 Gray Marine 64 HN9 diesels; 2 props; 330-450 hp
Range: 130/10 **Cargo:** 30 tons

♦ **14 U.S. LCVP-class landing craft**

EDVP 1, 2, 7, 8, 10, 12, 13, 17, 19, 24, 28, 29, 30

D: 13 tons (fl) **S:** 9 kts **Dim:** 10.90 × 3.21 × 1.04 (aft)
M: 1 Gray Marine 64 HN9 diesel; 225 hp **Range:** 110/9

REMARKS: An additional number may have been acquired in 1970. It is not known whether the above list includes the four LCVP carried by *Cabo San Antonio*. Cargo: 36 troops or 3.5 tons.

HYDROGRAPHIC SHIPS

♦ **1 (+1?) Puerto Deseado class**

	Bldr	Laid down	L	In serv.
Q 8 Puerto Deseado	Astarsa, San Fernando	17-3-76	4-12-77	26-2-79 (trials)
Q . . . Alvaro Alberto	Alianza, Avellaneda	. . .	. . .	. . .

D: 2,133 tons **S:** 15 kts **Dim:** 70.81 (67.0 pp) × 13.2 × 4.5
M: 2 Fiat-GMT diesels; 2 props; 2,700 hp **Electric:** 1,280 kVA
Range: 12,000/12 **Man:** 12 officers, 53 men, 9 scientists, 10 technicians

REMARKS: Used for hydrometeorological reporting. Four Hewlett-Packard 2108-A computers for data analysis/storage. Has seismic, gravimetric, and magnetometer equipment. Omega and NAVSAT-equipped. Has geology laboratory. Ice-reinforced.

♦ **1 Comodoro Rivadavia class**

Q 11 Comodoro Rivadavia Bldr: Mestrina, Tigre L: 29-11-73 In serv. 6-12-76

D: 655 tons (830 fl) **S:** 12 kts **Dim:** 52.2 × 8.8 × 2.6
M: 2 Werkspoor Stork RHO-218K diesels; 1,160 hp **Range:** 6,000/12
Man: 27 tot.

Q 15 Cormoran, Coastal survey craft: 82 tons, 13 kts In serv. 1964.
Q . . . Petrel, Coastal survey craft: 52 tons, In serv. 1965.

♦ **1 ex-U.S. Maritime Commission V4-M-A1-class tug** Bldr: Pendleton SY, New Orleans, In serv. 1943

Q 17 Goyena (ex-*Dry Tortugas*)

D: 1,630 tons (1,863 fl) **S:** 11 kts **Dim:** 59.23 × 11.43 × 5.72
A: 2/40-mm AA (II × 1)
M: 2 Enterprise diesels; 2 Kort nozzle props; 2,340 hp **Range:** 19,000/14
Fuel: 566 tons **Man:** 90 tot.

REMARKS: Transferred 1965. Used for antarctic research. Sister *Thompson* (A-4, ex-*Sombrero Key*) discarded.

ICEBREAKER

♦ **1 antarctic support** Bldr: Wärtsilä, Helsinki, Finland

	Laid down	L	In serv.
Q 5 Almirante Irizar	4-7-77	3-2-78	15-12-78

Almirante Irizar (Q 5) Wärtsilä, 1978

D: 11,811 (14,900 fl) **S:** 16.5 kts **Dim:** 119.3 × 25.0 × 9.5
A: 2/40-mm AA (1 × 2)
Electron Equipt: Radar: 1 Plessey AWS-2, 2 navigational
M: Diesel-electric: 4 SEMT-Pielstick 8 PC 2.5 L/400 diesels; 2 Stromberg motors; 2 props; 16,200 hp
Electric: 2,640 kw **Man:** 123 crew plus 100 scientists

REMARKS: Ordered 17-12-75. Canadian RAST helicopter downhaul winch system, 2 helicopters. Sixty-ton towing winch. Two 16-ton cranes. The icebreaker *General San Martin* (Q 4) was stricken in May 1981.

AUXILIARY SHIPS

♦ **1 new construction antarctic supply ship**

	Bldr	Laid down	L	In serv.
B . . . N . . .	Principe & Menghe SY, Maciel Isl.	27-2-79	. . .	. . .

D: 9,200 tons (fl) **S:** 18 kts **Dim:** 130.7 (120.0 pp) × 19.5 × 7.0 **A:** . . .
M: 2 diesels; 2 CP props; 15,000 hp **Fuel:** 300 tons **Man:** 180 tot.

AUXILIARY SHIPS *(continued)*

REMARKS: To carry up to 450 passengers or 150 troops, 3,500m³ dry and 250m³ refrigerated stores. Two helicopters plus hangar. Icebreaking hull form.

♦ **3 "Costa Sur"-class transports** Bldr: Principe & Menghe SY, Maciel Isl.

	Laid down	L	In serv.
B 3 CANAL BEAGLE	10-1-77	14-10-77	28-4-78
B 4 BAHIA SAN BLAS	11-4-77	29-4-78	27-11-78
B 5 CABO DE HORNOS	29-4-78	4-11-78	18-7-79
(ex-*Bahia Camarones*)			

    D: 7,640 tons (fl) **S:** 15 kts **Dim:** 119.9 × 17.5 × 6.4 **A:** None
    M: 2 AFNE-Sulzer diesels; 2 props, 6,400 hp

REMARKS: To supply remote stations. 4,600 grt/5,800 dwt. 9,700 cubic meters cargo. Also carry passengers and cargo in commercial service.

♦ **2 Bahia Aguirre-class transports** Bldr: Canadian Vickers, Halifax

	L	In serv.
B 2 BAHIA AGUIRRE	15-5-49	4-50
B 6 BAHIA BUEN SUCESO	15-6-49	6-50

Bahia Buen Suceso (B 6)   R. Scheina, 1980

    D: 3,100 tons (5,255 fl) **S:** 15 kts **Dim:** 102.0 (95.1 pp) × 14.33 × 7.9
    M: 2 Nordberg diesels; 2 props, 3,750 hp **Fuel:** 442 tons (B 2: 335)
    Man: 100 tot.

REMARKS: Former U.S. Army cargo ship.

♦ **1 fleet replenishment oiler**

	Bldr	L	In serv.
B 18 PUNTA MEDANOS	Swan Hunter	20-2-50	10-50

D: 16,300 tons (fl) **S:** 18 kts **Dim:** 153.0 (143.2 pp) × 18.9 × 8.7
A: 4/40-mm AA (I×4) **Cargo:** 8,250 tons **Range:** 13,700/12
M: 2 sets Parsons GT; 2 props; 9,500 hp **Fuel:** 1,500 tons
Boilers: 2 Babcock & Wilcox; 28 kg/cm², 348°C **Man:** 99 tot.

REMARKS: 2 fueling stations per side, helo deck aft. Also used as a training ship.

♦ **1 U.S. Klickitat-class tanker, former gasoline tanker**

	Bldr	L	In serv.
B 16 PUNTA DELGADA	St. Johns River SB Corp,	7-4-45	1945
(ex-*Sugarland*, ex-*Nanticoke*,	Jacksonville, Fla.		
AOG 66)			

    D: 2,060 tons light (5,970 fl) **S:** 10 kts
    Dim: 99.1 (94.2 pp) × 14.7 × 4.77 **A:** None
    M: 1 Enterprise DNQ-38 diesel; 1 prop; 1,400 hp **Electric:** 540 kw
    Fuel: 145 tons **Range:** 9,000/10 **Man:** 72 tot.

REMARKS: Acquired 1945 after brief commercial service. Used in commercial service as revenue source. Cargo: 4,150 tons

♦ **2 auxiliary ocean tugs** Bldr: Ast. Vicente Forte, Buenos Aires

R 2 QUERANDI (In serv: 22-8-78)   R 3 TEHUELCHE (In serv: 2-11-78)

    D: 370 tons (fl) **S:** 12 kts **Dim:** 33.6 × 8.4 × 3.0
    M: 2 M.A.N. 6V 23.5/33 diesels; 1,200 hp **Range:** 1,200/12 **Man:** 30 tot.

Querandi (R 2)   R. Scheina, 1980

AUXILIARY SHIPS (continued)

♦ 2 U.S. Sotoyomo-class auxiliary ocean tugs

	Bldr	L	In serv.
A 7 CHIRIGUANO (ex-ATA 227)	Levingston SB, Orange, Texas	26-5-45	4-4-46
A 8 SANAVIRON (ex-ATA 228)	Levingston SB, Orange, Texas	9-6-45	25-4-46

REMARKS: Purchased 7-47. Nearly identical to sisters used as corvettes, except no armament, 120-kw generator capacity, and slightly less fuel. Never had names in U.S. service.

♦ 1 sailing training vessel

Q 2 LIBERTAD   Bldr: AFNE, Rio Santiago. L: 30-5-56. In serv.: 1962.

Libertad

D: 3,025 tons (3,625 fl)   **S:** 12 kts   **Dim:** 94.25 (79.9 pp) × 13.75 × 6.75
A: 1/76-mm—4/40-mm—4/47-mm saluting   **M:** Diesels; 2 props; 2,400 hp
Range: 12,000   **Man:** 222 men and 140 cadets

♦ 2 small sail training yachts

ITATI II   Bldr: Cadenazzi SY, 1979   **D:** 80 tons (fl)   **S:** 15 kts
FORTUNA II   Yawl for ocean racing

YARD AND SERVICE CRAFT

♦ 2 Quilmes-class medium harbor tugs Bldr: AFNE, Rio Santiago

	Laid down	L	In serv.
R 32 QUILMES	23-8-56	27-12-58	30-3-60
R 33 GUAYCURU	15-3-56	8-7-57	29-7-60

D: 368 tons (fl)   **S:** 9 kts   **Dim:** 32.7 × 7.4 × 3.8
M: 2 sets Skinner Uniflow triple-expansion, reciprocating; 2 props; 645 hp
Boilers: 2/cyclindrical   **Fuel:** 52 tons   **Range:** 2,200/7   **Man:** 14 tot.

♦ 2 Pehuenche-class medium harbor tugs Bldr: AFNE, Rio Santiago

R 29 PEHUENCHE (1954)   R 30 TONOCOTE (1954)

D: 330 tons (fl)   **S:** 11 kts   **Dim:** 32.0 × 7.5 × 3.8
M: 2 sets triple-expansion, reciprocating; 2 props; 600 hp
Boilers: 2/cylindrical   **Fuel:** 36 tons   **Range:** 1,200/7   **Man:** 13 tot.

♦ 6 U.S. YTL-422-class small harbor tugs (1944-45)

R 5 MOCOVI (ex-YTL 441)	R 6 CALCHAQUI (ex-YTL 445)
R 10 CHULUPI (ex-YTL 426)	R 16 CAPAYAN (ex-YTL 443)
R 18 CHIQUILLAN (ex-YTL 444)	R 19 MORCOYAN (ex-YTL 448)

Bldrs: R 5, 16, 18: Robt. Jacobs, City Isl., NY; R 6,19: H.C. Grebe Co; R 10: Everett Pacific BY, Everett, Wash.

D: 70 tons (80 fl)   **S:** 10 kts   **Dim:** 20.16 × 5.18 × 2.44
M: 1 Hoover-Owens-Rentschler diesel; 300 hp   **Electric:** 40 kw
Fuel: 7 tons   **Man:** 5 tot.

REMARKS: R 16, 18, 19 leased 3-65, others 3-69; purchased outright 16-6-77.

♦ 6 floating dry docks

Y 1 (ex-U.S.ARD 23): 3,500-ton capacity; 149.9 × 24.7 × 1.73 (light) (In serv. 1944)
Y 2: 1,500-ton capacity; 91.5 × 18.3 (In serv. 1913)
Y 3, Y 4: 750-ton capacity; 65.8 × 14
A: 12,000-ton capacity; 172.5 × 26 (In serv. 1958)
B: 2,800-ton capacity; 110.0 × 18.0 (In serv. 1956)
C: 1,000-ton capacity; 75.0 × 15.7

♦ 4 floating cranes

NOTE: The former sail-training ship Presidente Sarmiento (1898) and the sail corvette Uruguay (1874) are maintained by the Navy as museums at Buenos Aires.

COAST GUARD

NOTE: Ships and craft painted white.

PATROL SHIPS AND CRAFT

♦ 5 ocean patrol ships Bldr: Bazan, El Ferrol, Spain

		Laid down	L	In serv.
GC. . .	N . . .	16-2-81	6-81	. . .
GC. . .	N . . .	4-81	8-81	. . .
GC. . .	N . . .	6-81	11-81	. . .
GC. . .	N . . .	9-81	2-82	. . .
GC. . .	N . . .	11-81	4-82	. . .

D: 767 tons normal (900 fl)   **S:** 21.5 kts   **Dim:** 67.0 (63.0 pp) × 10.0 × 3.06
A: 1/40-mm AA Breda-Bofors—1 Alouette-III helo
M: 2 Bazan-MTU 16V 956 TB 91 diesels; 2 props; 9,000 hp (7,500 sust.)
Electron Equipt: Radar: 1 Decca AC 1226   **Electric:** 710 kw
Range: 5,000/18   **Man:** 9 officers/24 men/4 cadets

REMARKS: Ordered 3-79 to patrol 200-nautical-mile economic zone. Endurance 20 days. Same class ordered for Mexico.

ARGENTINA *(continued)*
COAST GUARD *(continued)*

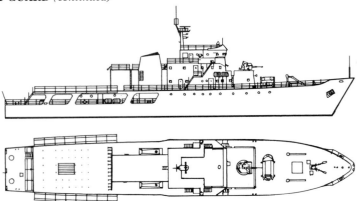

Ocean patrol ship

A.D. Baker III, 9-81

♦ **1 former whaler, used for ocean patrol** (In serv. 1958; purchased 1975)

GC 13 DELFIN

D: 1,000 tons **S:** 15 kts **Dim:** 60.0 × 9.0 × 4.7 **A:** 1/40-mm AA
M: diesel; 2,300 hp **Man:** 32 tot.

♦ **20 Z-28 class** Bldr: Blohm & Voss, Hamburg (All in serv. 9-79/1-80)

GC 64 MARTIN GARCIA	GC 74 N. . .
GC 65 MAR DEL PLATA	GC 75 N. . .
GC 66 RIO LUJEN	GC 76 N. . .
GC 67 N. . .	GC 77 N. . .
GC 68 N. . .	GC 78 N. . .
GC 69 N. . .	GC 79 N. . .
GC 70 N. . .	GC 80 N. . .
GC 71 N. . .	GC 81 N. . .
GC 72 N. . .	GC 82 N. . .
GC 73 N. . .	GC 83 N. . .

D: 81 tons (fl) **S:** 22 kts **Dim:** 27.65 (26.0) × 5.30 × 1.65
A: 2/20-mm AA (I × 2)
M: 2 MTU 8V 331 TC 92 diesels; 2 props; 2,100 hp (1,770 sust.)
Electric: 90 kVA **Range:** 780/18, 1,200/12 **Man:** 15-23 tot.

REMARKS: Ordered 24-11-78. Fin stabilizers fitted.

♦ **3 Lynch-class patrol boats** Bldr: AFNE, Rio Santiago (In serv. 1964-67)

GC LYNCH GC 22 TOLL GC 23 EREZCANO

D: 100 tons (117 fl) **S:** 22 kts **Dim:** 27.44 × 5.80 × 1.85
A: 1/20-mm AA **M:** 2 Maybach diesels; 2 props; 2,700 hp **Man:** 16 tot.

♦ **8 patrol craft** Bldr: Cadenazzi SY, Tigre, 1978-79

D: 13 tons **S:** 25 kts **Dim:** 12.54 × 3.57 × 1.1 **A:** 1 machine gun
M: 2 GM diesels; 2 props; 560 hp

♦ **1 tug** Bldr: Sanym SA, San Fernando, Spain (In serv. 21-10-77)

GC 47 TONINA

D: 200 tons (fl) **S:** 11 kts **Dim:** 25.5 × 3.3 × 2.1 **A:** 1/20-mm AA
M: 1 diesel; 500 hp **Range:** 3,400/10 **Man:** 11 tot.

♦ **Approx. 28 smaller patrol craft for harbor duty**

AUSTRALIA
Commonwealth of Australia

PERSONNEL: approx. 17,000 (2,100 officers/14,900 enlisted)

MERCHANT MARINE (1980): 497 ships—1,642,594 grt (tankers: 18—365,622 grt)

WARSHIPS IN SERVICE OR UNDER CONSTRUCTION AS OF 1 JANUARY 1982

		L	Tons std.	Main armament
♦ **1 aircraft carrier**				
	MELBOURNE	1945	16,000	17 aircraft
♦ **6 submarines**				
	6 OBERON	1965-75	1,610	8/533-mm TT
♦ **4 destroyers**				
	3 CHARLES F. ADAMS	1963-66	3,370	1 Tartar system, 2/127-mm, 2 Ikara
	1 DARING	1956	2,800	6/114-mm
♦ **8 frigates**				
	2(+8) OLIVER HAZARD PERRY	1978-80	2,700	1 Tartar system, 1/76-mm, 2 helo
	6 RIVER	1958-68	2,100	2/114-mm, 1 Ikara
♦ **14 (+23) patrol boats**				
♦ **3 (+8) minesweepers**				
♦ **7 amphibious warfare ship**				

NAVAL AVIATION: Only ship-based and training aircraft belong to the Navy. On 5-12-76 a fire destroyed 12 of the total of 13 S-2E Tracker ASW aircraft. These were replaced by 6 ex-U.S. Navy aircraft and 6 other former USN aircraft already on order. Other than these, the Australian Fleet Air Arm operates: 6 A-4G Skyhawk fighter-bombers and 6 Sea King Mk 50 helicopters for shipboard use, and retains 4 Wessex 31-B helicopters formerly used aboard *Melbourne*. Two Sea King helicopters are on order.

Shore-based patrol aviation is under the direction of the RAAF. Ten P-3C delivered 1978-79; supplemented 11 P-3B, which are to be updated to P-3C standard; all are to carry Harpoon anti-ship missiles. Other land-based navy aircraft include 7 TA-4G Skyhawk and 7 MB-326H for training, 2 HS-748 transports, and 4 Bell UH-1H and 2 Bell 206B helicopters.

WEAPONS AND SYSTEMS: The Australian Navy uses U.S. equipment and systems on its U.S.-built warships and British weapons and systems on its other ships, but some of its air-search and fire-control radars have been purchased in The Netherlands (LWO-2, M-20, etc.). Some 71 U.S. Mk 48 torpedoes have been purchased for use by submarines, with an additional batch ordered in 1980.

Except for the U.S.-built ships, the sonars are of British or Australian (Mulloka) origin. Mulloka is a high-frequency set tailored to Australian coastal water-sound propagation conditions. The Australian Navy has perfected an unusual ASW weapon, the Ikara. Similar in basic concept to the French Malafon, it is a Mk 44 or Mk 46 torpedo coupled with a guided missile and guidance equipment, and has a maximum range of about 20,000 yards.

AIRCRAFT CARRIER

♦ **1 modified U.S. Iwo Jima-class aircraft carrier**

		Bldr	Laid down	L	In serv.
R. . .	N. . .	Ingalls, Pascagoula	. . .	. . .	. . .

D: 19,000 tons (fl) **S:** 25 kts
Dim: 183.79 (180.18 pp) × 31.7 (25.6 wl) × 7.9 **A:** . . .
M: 2 LM-2500 gas turbines; 2 CP props; 50,000 hp

REMARKS: The Litton/Ingalls entry is seen as the most likely candidate for the *Melbourne* replacement, which is planned to be ordered in 1982-88, although the Italcantieri *Garibaldi* and Bazan *Dedalo* (Sea Control Ship) designs are in the running. The aircraft complement has yet to be determined, but it is hoped to employ Harrier-type V/STOL fixed-wing aircraft and ASW helicopters. The original *Iwo Jima* design has been modified by substituting a twin-screw gas turbine plant of twice the power of the original single-screw steam plant.

	Bldr	Laid down	L	In serv.
R 21 MELBOURNE (ex-*Majestic*)	Vickers-Armstrong	15-4-43	28-2-45	28-10-55

Melbourne (R 21)   1980

D: 16,000 tons (20,320 fl) **S:** 23 kts
Dim: 217.7 (198.0 wl) × 24.5 (39.0 max.) × 7.15
A: 12/40-mm AA (II × 4, I × 4)—6 A-4G Skyhawk, 4 S-2E Tracker, 5 Sea King
Electron Equipt: Radar: 1/LWO-2, 1/293, 1/978, 1/SPN-35 CCA—URN-20 TACAN
M: Parsons GT; 2 props; 42,000 hp
Boilers: 4 Admiralty 3-drum, 28 kg/cm², 371°C **Fuel:** 3,200 tons
Range: 6,200/23, 12,000/14 **Man:** 1,335 men, including 347 air group

REMARKS: Steam catapult, 5 ½° angled flight deck, mirror landing equipment, two centerline elevators. Modernized in 1969 to operate ASW aircraft, and again refitted in 1971, 1972-73, and 1978-79, when a flight-deck extension to starboard abaft the island was added to park aircraft. Further refit commenced 1982 to extend operational life to 1986. Carried no A-4G aircraft during late 1980-81 operations, as catapult was inoperable.

SUBMARINES

♦ **6 British Oberon-class** Bldr: Scotts' SB & Eng., Greenock

	Laid down	L	In serv.
S 57 OXLEY	2-7-64	24-9-65	27-3-67
S 59 OTWAY	29-6-65	29-11-66	22-4-68
S 60 ONSLOW	26-5-67	29-8-68	22-12-69
S 61 ORION	6-10-72	16-9-74	15-6-77
S 62 OTAMA	28-5-73	3-12-75	27-4-78
S 70 OVENS	17-6-66	5-12-67	18-4-69

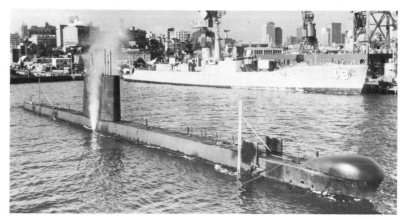

Otway (S 59)—as modernized (*Derwent* in background)   RAN, 1981

D: 1,610/2,196/2,417 tons **S:** 17.5/15 kts
Dim: 89.9 (87.45 pp) × 8.07 × 5.48
A: 6/533-mm TT for Sub-Harpoon and U.S. Mk 48 mod. 3 torpedoes (fwd)—12 reloads
Electron Equipt: Radar: 1/1006—Sonar: 1/187 C, 1/197, 1/2007, "Micro-puffs"
M: Two 3,680-hp Admiralty Standard Range 16 VVS-ASR1 diesel engines; diesel-electric propulsion; 6,000 hp
Man: 6 officers, 57 men

SUBMARINES *(continued)*

Orion—original configuration   G. Arra, 1980

REMARKS: Being modernized in construction sequence, *Oxley* recommissioning 22-2-80 with U.S. Singer/Librascope SFCS Mk 1 digital computer fire-control system with a UYK-20 computer, and a new sonar suit incorporating a Krupp/Atlas CSU-3-41 active/passive system (active transducer in sail, passive array in enlarged dome on bow), U.K. Type 2007 LF passive array, and Type 2004 sound velocity meter. The two short 533-mm torpedo tubes aft are no longer used. All are to receive Sub-Harpoon anti-ship missiles, and U.S. Mk 48 mod. 3 torpedoes have replaced all the Mk 37 type formerly carried. The unmodernized units retain a TCSS Mk 9 fire-control system. All modernizations to complete by 1985.

NOTE: A contract was let in 1980 to Vickers, Cockatoo DY to study the feasibility of constructing future submarines in Australia to replace the *Oberon* class.

DESTROYERS

♦ **3 U.S. Charles F. Adams-class guided-missile destroyers** Bldr: Defoe SB, Bay City, Michigan

	Laid down	L	In serv.
D 38 PERTH (ex-U.S. DDG-25)	21-9-62	26-9-63	17-7-65
D 39 HOBART (ex-U.S. DDG-26)	26-10-62	9-1-64	18-12-65
D 41 BRISBANE (ex-U.S. DDG-27)	15-2-65	5-5-66	16-12-67

D: 3,370 tons (4,618 fl) **S:** 35 kts **Dim:** 134.18 (128.0 pp) × 14.32 × 6.0
A: 1/Mk 13 system for Harpoon SSM and Standard SM-1A SAM (40 missiles)—2/127-mm DP Mk 42 (I × 2)—2/Ikara ASW missile systems—6/324-mm ASW TT Mk 32 (III × 2)
Electron Equipt: Radars: 1/978, 1/SPS-40, 1/SPS-10, 1/SPS-52, 2/SPG-51C, 1/SPG-53A
    Sonar: 1/SQS-23F—TACAN: 1/URN-20
    ECM: WLR-6
M: 2 sets GT; 2 props; 70,000 hp **Fuel:** 900 tons

Brisbane (D 41)   G. Arra, 1980

Hobart (D 39)   G. Arra, 1980

Boilers: 4 Babcock & Wilcox, 84 kg/cm²—superheat 520°C **Electric:** 2,200 kw
Range: 1,600/30, 6,000/14 **Man:** 21 officers, 312 men

REMARKS: D 38 modernized in the U.S. 3-9-74 to 2-1-75 with SM-1A Standard missiles, NTDS, and Mk 42, mod. 10 guns. The other two were refitted to the same standard in Australia. All are schedules to receive Harpoon anti-ship missiles. Missile-fire control is Mk 74, mod. 8, with two radar directors; guns are controlled by one Mk 68 radar director (optical range-finder removed). Further modernization planned.

♦ **1 modified Daring-class destroyer**

	Bldr	Laid down	L	In serv.
D 11 VAMPIRE	Cockatoo D. & Eng. Co.	1-7-52	27-10-56	23-6-59

D: 2,800 tons (3,670 fl) **S:** 30 kts **Dim:** 118.87 (111.55 pp) × 13.1 × 5.1
A: 6/114-mm DP Mk 6 (II × 3)—6/40-mm AA (II × 2, I × 2)—1 Limbo Mk 10 ASW mortar (III × 1)
Electron Equipt: Radars: 1/LW0-2, 1/8GR-301A, 2/HSA M22
    Sonars: 1/162, 1/170, 1/174D
M: Parsons GT; 2 props; 54,000 hp **Boilers:** 2 Foster-Wheeler
Fuel: 584 tons **Range:** 3,700/20 **Man:** 321 tot.

REMARKS: Completed modernization in 1973 with Dutch fire-control and air-search radars. Refit commenced 3-81 for further service as a training ship; some weapons will probably be removed. Sister *Vendetta* (D 08) decommissioned 8-10-79.

FRIGATES

♦ 2 (+8) U.S. Oliver Hazard Perry-class guided-missile frigates

	Bldr	Laid down	L	In serv.
F 01 ADELAIDE (ex-FFG 17)	Todd, Seattle	29-7-77	21-6-78	6-11-80
F 02 CANBERRA (ex-FGG 18)	Todd, Seattle	1-3-78	1-12-78	21-3-81
F 03 SYDNEY (ex-FFG 35)	Todd, Seattle	16-1-80	26-9-80	1-83
F 04 DARWIN (ex-FFG 44)	Todd, Seattle	4-81	3-82	1984
F 05 N. . .	Williamstown DY, Melbourne	. . .	. . .	. . .
F 06 N. . .	Williamstown DY, Melbourne	. . .	. . .	. . .

Adelaide (F 01)   Todd, 1980

Canberra (F 02)   Todd, 1981

D: 2,700 tons light (3,678 fl)   **S:** 30 kts   **Dim:** 135.6 (125.9 wl) × 13.72 × 4.52 (7.47 max.)

A: 1/Mk 13, mod. 4, launcher for Standard SM-1A SAM and Harpoon (40 missiles)—1/76-mm DP OTO Melara Compact (U.S. Mk 75)—6/324-mm ASW TT Mk 32 for Mk 46 torpedoes (III × 2)—2 helicopters

Electron Equipt: Radars: 1/SPS-55, 1/SPS-49, 1/SPG-60, 1/Mk 92 fire control
Sonar: 1/SQS-56—ESM: SLQ-32

M: 2 GE LM 2500 gas turbines; 1 CP prop; 41,000 hp; 2/350 hp aux. propulsors

Electric: 3,000 kw   **Fuel:** 587 tons (plus 64 tons helo fuel)

Range: 4,200/20, 5,000/18   **Man:** 226 tot.

REMARKS: First two ordered 27-2-76 in lieu of Australian DDL design. The third was ordered 23-1-79. The fourth ordered 28-4-80. In 1980 two were authorized for construction in Australia, and it was announced that four more would be ordered later; the Australian six will replace the "River" class. Two drop-down, diesel-electric-driven propellers are located forward beneath the hull for emergency propulsion and maneuvering. No fin stabilizers fitted. Will not have U.S. Vulcan/Phalanx close-defense gun. The type of helicopter to be carried will not be decided until 1983. Crew larger than in U.S. sisters. ECM system not yet aboard first two. F 04 will be 138.8-m overall. Labor problems may delay or relocate construction of F 05 and F 06. See remarks in U.S. section also.

♦ 6 "River"-class frigates

	Bldr	Laid down	L	In serv.
F 45 YARRA	Williamstown Nav. DY	9-4-57	30-9-58	27-7-61
F 46 PARRAMATTA	Cockatoo D. & Eng. Co.	3-1-57	31-1-59	4-7-61
F 48 SUART	Cockatoo D. & Eng. Co.	20-3-59	8-4-61	28-6-63
F 49 DERWENT	Williamstown Nav. DY	16-6-59	17-4-61	30-4-64
F 50 SWAN	Williamstown Nav. DY	18-8-65	16-12-67	20-1-70
F 53 TORRENS	Cockatoo D. & Eng. Co.	18-8-65	28-9-68	19-1-71

D: 2,100 tons (2,750 fl)   **S:** 27 kts   **Dim:** 112.75 (109.75 pp) × 12.5 × 3.9

A: 2/114-mm DP Mk 6 (II × 1)—1/Sea Cat/SAM syst. (IV × 1, 24 missiles)—1/Ikara ASW missile launcher—6/324-mm Mk 32 ASW TT (III × 2; not in F 50, 53)—F 50, 53 only: 1/Limbo Mk 10 ASW Mortar (III × 1)

Electron Equipt: Radars: 1/978, 1/LWO-2, HSA M 22, (1/903 on F 45)
Sonars: 1/162, 1/177, 1/170 (F 50 and F 53 only), Mulloka on F 45, F 46, F 50

M: 2 sets GT; 2 props; 34,000 hp   **Fuel:** 400 tons   **Electric:** 1,140 kw

Torrens (F 53)   G. Arra, 1980

FRIGATES *(continued)*

Swan (F 50)—note recess for Ikara on starboard side   G. Arra, 1980

Yarra (D 45)   G. Arra, 1980

Boilers: 2 Babcock & Wilcox, 38.7 kg/cm², 450°C   **Range:** 4,500/12
Man: 13 officers, 238 men

REMARKS: Improved versions of the British *Rothesay* class. Profiles of the F 50 and F 53 differ from those of other four, resembling more the British *Leander* class. F 45 completed a half-life refit in 12-77. F 46, F 48, and F 49 are being given a more extensive overhaul, receiving two triple Mk 32 ASW torpedo tubes in place of the Limbo mortar, Mulloka sonar in place of part of their original suits, HSA M 22 gunfire-control systems, having their boilers converted to use diesel fuel, and having their accommodations improved. F 46 was due to complete 8-81, F 48 in 9-82, and F 49 was to begin work in mid-1981. F 50 and F 51 are to receive a different modernization later, reportedly to include adding Harpoon missiles. F 45 is not to be modernized and is scheduled to strike in 1986. The Ikara missile carries a U.S. Mk 44 or Mk 46 ASW torpedo as its payload. Variable-depth sonars have been removed, where fitted. F 45 retained cutaway stern and MRS3 GFCS into 1980.

PATROL BOATS

♦ **3 (32) Fremantle class** Bldr: North Queensland Eng. and Agents, Cairns (P 203: Brooke Marine, Lowestoft)

	Laid down	L	In serv.
P 203 FREMANTLE	11-11-77	15-2-79	8-10-79
P 204 WARRNAMBOOL	. . .	25-10-80	-81
P 205 TOWNSVILLE	16-5-81	. . .	. . .
P 206 WOLLONGONG	. . .	. . .	. . .
P 207 LAUNCETON	. . .	. . .	. . .
P 208 WHYALLA	. . .	. . .	. . .
P 209 IPSWICH	. . .	. . .	. . .
P 210 CESSNOCK	. . .	. . .	. . .
P 211 BENDIGO	. . .	. . .	. . .
P 212 GAWLER	. . .	. . .	. . .
P 213 GERALDTON	. . .	. . .	. . .
P 214 DUBBO	. . .	. . .	. . .
P 215 GEELONG	. . .	. . .	. . .
P 216 GLADSTONE	. . .	. . .	. . .
P 217 BUNBURY	. . .	. . .	. . .
P 218 N. . .	. . .	. . .	. . .
P 219 N. . .	. . .	. . .	. . .
P 220 N. . .	. . .	. . .	. . .
P 221 N. . .	. . .	. . .	. . .
P 222 N. . .	. . .	. . .	. . .

Fremantle (P 203)   R. Gillett, 1980

D: 200 tons (230 fl)   **S:** 30 kts   **Dim:** 42.0 × 7.15 × 1.8
A: 1/40-mm AA—1/81-mm mortar—2/12.7-mm mg (II × 2)
Electron Equipt: Radar: 1/Decca 1226
M: 2 MTU MD 16V538 TB 91 diesels; 2 props; 7,200 hp—1 Dorman 12JTM diesel; 1 prop; . . . hp for cruising
Range: 1,450/28, 4,800/8   **Man:** 3 officers/19 men

REMARKS: Brooke Marine PCF-420 design. Ordered 9-77. First 15 in service 12-79 through 1985. Five more authorized 1980, with another five planned for later. The *Fremantle* was built as pattern craft. The 40-mm AA was to be replaced with newer weapons, but will now be retained for reasons of economy. Norwegian Penguin Mk II anti-ship missiles may be fitted later. P 203 26 tons overweight (246 fl), later reduced to 20 tons; all later units will be 10 tons over original 220-ton design fl.

♦ **12 Attack-class coastal-patrol boats**

	Laid down	L	In serv.
P 81 ACUTE	4-67	26-8-67	26-4-68
P 82 ADROIT	8-67	3-2-68	17-8-68

PATROL BOATS (continued)

P 83 ADVANCE	3-67	16-8-67	24-1-68
P 87 ARDENT	10-67	27-4-68	26-10-68
P 89 ASSAIL	8-67	18-11-67	12-7-68
P 90 ATTACK	9-66	8-4-67	17-11-67
P 91 AWARE	7-67	7-10-67	21-6-68
P 97 BARBETTE	11-67	10-4-68	16-8-68
P 98 BARRICADE	12-67	29-6-68	26-10-68
P 99 BOMBARD	4-68	6-7-68	5-11-68
P 100 BUCCANEER	6-68	14-9-68	11-1-69
P 101 BAYONET	10-68	6-11-68	22-2-69

Advance (P 83)   G. Gyssels, 1978

Bldr: Evans Deakin, Ltd. (except P 83, P 97, P 99, P 101: Walkers, Ltd.).

D: 146 tons (fl) **S:** 24/21 kts **Dim:** 32.76 (30.48 pp) × 6.2 × 1.9
A: 1/40-mm AA—2/7.62-mm machine guns **Radar:** 1/Decca RM 916
M: 2 Davey-Paxman Ventura 16 YJCM diesels; 2 props; 3,500 hp
Range: 1,220/13 **Man:** 3 officers, 19 men

REMARKS: Steel hull; light-alloy superstructure; air-conditioned. P 91 is unarmed. Sisters P 84 *Aitape*, P 92 *Lavada*, P 93 *Lae*, P 94 *Madang*, P 85 *Samarai* transferred to Papua New Guinea, in 1974. P 86 *Archer* and P 95 *Bandolier* sold in 1973 to Indonesia and transferred in 1973 and 1974, respectively. P 88 *Arrow* sank 25-12-74 in Typhoon Tracey.

MINE WARFARE SHIPS

♦ **2 (+6) MHCAT-class catamaran minehunters**

N. . .   N. . .

D: 100 tons (160 fl) **S:** 10 kts **Dim:** 31.0 × 9.0 × 1.8
A: 2 machine guns **M:** 2 diesels; 2 props; 530 hp **Range:** 1,200/10

REMARKS: Foam core fiberglass hulls, each 3 meters in beam. For coastal service; will have modularized payloads. First two authorized 1980, ordered late 1981; 6 more planned.

♦ **3 British "Ton"-class coastal minesweepers**

	Bldr	Laid down	L	In serv.
M 1102 SNIPE (ex-*Alcaston*)	John I. Thornycroft	7-51	5-1-53	1953
M 1121 CURLEW (ex-*Chediston*)	Montrose SY	4-53	6-10-53	1954
M 1183 IBIS (ex-*Singleton*)	Montrose SY	10-53	18-11-55	1956

Ibis (M 1183)   RAN, 1977

D: 370 tons (489 fl) **S:** 15 kts **Dim:** 46.33 (42.68 pp) × 8.76 × 2.50
A: 2/40-mm AA (I × 2) **Electron Equipt:** Radar: 1/978
                          Sonar: 193 (not M1183)
M: Napier Deltic 18A-7A diesels; 2 props; 3,000 hp **Fuel:** 45 tons
Range: 2,300/13, 3,500/8 **Man:** 34 to 38 tot.

REMARKS: Bought in 1962 after refitting. Air-conditioned and stabilized. M 1102 and M 1121 are equipped as minehunters, with type 193 sonar and four divers. It is proposed to replace these three survivors of a group of six ex-RN minesweepers with a new class of two oceangoing minehunters in the mid-1980s.

AMPHIBIOUS WARFARE SHIPS

♦ **1 modified British Sir Bedivere class**

	Bldr	Laid down	L	In serv.
L 50 TOBRUK	Carrington Slipways, Tomago	7-2-79	1-3-80	23-4-81

D: 3,400 tons (6,000 fl) **S:** 17 kts **Dim:** 129.5 × 19.6 × 4.3
A: 2/40-mm AA (I × 2)
M: 2 Mirrlees-Blackstone KDM8 diesels; 2 props; 9,600 hp
Man: approx. 18 officers, 50 men

REMARKS: Announced 8-76 as a replacement for the *Sydney*. Can carry Wessex Mk 31B troop helicopters operating from platforms amidships and aft, and can carry 300-500 troops, Leopard tanks, and other military vehicles. Bow and stern ramps fitted. Two LCVP carried. Can carry two LCM 8 on deck. Two 4.5-ton cranes fwd.; 60-ton heavy lift boom before bridge.

♦ **6 Balikpapan-class LCU** Bldr: Walkers Ltd., Maryborough

L 126 BALIKPAPAN (L: 15-8-71)	L 129 TARAKAN (L: 16-3-72)
L 127 BRUNEI (L: 15-10-71)	L 130 WEWAK (L: 18-5-72)
L 128 LABUAN (L: 29-12-71)	L 133 BETANO (L: 5-12-72)

AMPHIBIOUS WARFARE SHIPS *(continued)*

Tobruk (L 50)　　　　　　　　　　RAN, 1981

Balikpapan (L 126)　　　　　　　　　RAN, 1979

D: 316 tons (503 fl)　**S:** 10 kts　**Dim:** 44.5 × 10.1 × 1.9
A: 2/7.62-mm machine guns　**M:** 2 GM 6-71 diesels; 2 props; 675 hp
Range: 3,000/10　**Man:** 2 officers, 11 men

REMARKS: In service 1971-74. The *Salamaua* (L 131) and *Buna* (L 132) were transferred to Papua New Guinea in 1974. Can carry three Leopard tanks. Originally Army-subordinated. Also used in inshore survey work.

♦ The Australian Army operates a number of landing craft, including 11 U.S. LCM-8-class LCMs (AB 1050 to 1053, 1055 to 1061), 4 LCVPs, 2 small tugs for support (*Joe Mann, The Luke*), and 7 workboats.

HYDROGRAPHIC SHIPS

NOTE: A new 54-m. oceanographic ship was authorized in 1980.

♦ **1 improved Moresby class**

	Bldr	Laid down	L	In serv.
A 291 COOK	Williamstown Nav. DY	30-9-74	27-8-77	28-10-80

Cook (A 291)—fitting out　　　　　　　RAN, 1980

D: 1,910 tons (2,550 fl)　**S:** 17 kts　**Dim:** 96.6 (91.2 pp) × 13.41 × 4.6
Electron Equipt: Radar: 1/Decca TM 829
　　　　　　　　Sonar: 1/Simrad SU 2
M: 4 Caterpillar D398TA diesels; 2 props; 3,400 hp　**Fuel:** 640 tons
Range: 11,000/14　**Man:** 137 crew, 13 scientists

REMARKS: Intended for oceanographic research and hydrographic survey. One inshore survey launch. Survey equipment includes Decca Hi-Fix 6, Mini-Ranger MRS3, Atlas DESC-10 echo-sounder, and Harris narrow-beam echo-sounders. Can carry 4/30-mm AA (II × 2)and 4/12.7-mm mg in wartime.

HYDROGRAPHIC SHIPS (continued)

♦ **1 Moresby class**

	Bldr	Laid down	L	In serv.
A 573 MORESBY	State DY, Newcastle, NSW	5-62	7-9-63	3-64

Moresby (A 573)—with heightened stack   RAN, 1977

D: 1,714 tons (2,340 fl)   **S:** 19 kts   **Dim:** 95.7 (86.7 pp) × 12.8 × 4.6
Electron Equipt: Radar: 1/Decca TM 829
              Sonar: 1/Simrad SU-2
M: Diesel-electric propulsion: 3/1,330-hp diesels; 3 CSVM generator sets, each
     1,330 kw/800 rpm; 2 electric motors, 2 props; 5,000 hp
Man: 13 officers, 133 men

REMARKS: A Bell 206B helicopter can be carried. Ship is air-conditioned. 2/40-mm AA removed, stack heightened 1973-74. Two inshore survey launches carried.

♦ **1 Flinders class**

	Bldr	Laid down	L	In serv.
A 312 FLINDERS	Williamstown Nav. DY	11-6-71	29-7-72	27-4-73

D: 765 tons (fl)   **S:** 13.5 kts   **Dim:** 49.1 × 10.05 × 3.7
Electron Equipt: Radar: Decca TM 829—Sonar: Simrad SU 2
M: 2 Paxman Ventura diesels; 2 props; 1,680 hp   **Range:** 5,000/9
Man: 4 officers, 34 men

REMARKS: Similar to the Philippine ship *Atyimba*. Replaces the *Paluma*, stricken in 1974. Operates along Barrier Reef. A sister may be built to replace the *Kimbla*.

♦ **1 former netlayer** Bldr: Walkers, Maryborough

	Laid down	L	In serv.
AGOR 314 KIMBLA	4-11-53	23-3-55	26-3-56

D: 762 tons (1,021 fl)   **S:** 9.5 kts   **Dim:** 54.55 × 9.75 × 3.7
Electron Equipt: Radar: 1/975—Sonar: 1/Simrad SU 2
M: 1 set triple-expansion, reciprocating; 1 prop; 350 hp
Boilers: 2, Scotch type

REMARKS: Converted for oceanographic research in 1959. Will soon be discarded.

♦ **1 inshore survey craft:** LEASH (In serv.: 28-10-80)

Flinders (A 312)   RAN, 1980

Kimbla (AGOR 314)   R. Wright, 1981

AUXILIARIES

♦ **2 modified French Durance-class replenishment oilers**

	Bldr	Laid down	L	In serv.
A. . . SUCCESS	Vickers, Cockatoo DY	9-8-80	3-82	7-83
A. . . N. . .	. . .		3-82	. . . 1985

AUXILIARIES (*continued*)

D: 17,800 tons (fl)   S: 19 kts   Dim: 157.3 (149.0 pp) × 21.2 × 10.8
A: 2/40-mm AA (I × 2)   Fuel: 750 tons
M: 2 SEMT-Pielstick 16PC2-5 diesels; 1 cp prop; 20,000 hp
Range: 9,000/15   Man: 187 tot.

REMARKS: First unit ordered 9-79 from design prepared by DTCN, France. Second authorized 1980. To carry 10,210 tons distillate fuel, 1,110 tons aviation fuel, 120 tons munitions, 170 tons provisions. Will carry 2 stores-handling land craft in davits and will be able to refuel three ships simultaneously.

♦ **1 British "Tide"-class replenishment oiler** Bldr: Harland & Wolff, Belfast

	Laid down	L	In serv.
AO 195 SUPPLY (ex-*Tide Austral*)	5-8-52	1-9-54	3-55

Supply (AO 195)   1980

D: 15,000 tons (26,500 fl)   S: 17 kts   Dim: 177.8 (167.8 pp) × 21.7 × 9.8
A: 2/40-mm AA (I × 2)   Electron Equipt: Radar: 1/Decca RM 916
M: 2 sets double-reduction GT; 2 props; 15,000 hp   Boilers: 2
Range: 8,500/13   Man: 205 tot.

REMARKS: Operated in Royal Navy 1955-62 and in Royal Australian Navy since 8-62. 17,600 dwt. Armament reduced from 6/40-mm, number of replenishment stations halved, new radar fitted 1979. To discard on completion of *Success*.

♦ **1 destroyer tender** Bldr: Cockatoo D & E, Sydney

	Laid down	L	In serv.
AD 215 STALWART	6-64	7-10-66	4-2-68

Stalwart (AD 215)   R. Gillett, 1980

D: 10,000 tons (15,500 fl)   S: 20 kts   Dim: 157.12 (143.25 pp) × 20.57 × 9.0
A: 4/40-mm AA (II × 2)   Electric: 3,200 kw
M: 2 Scott-Sulzer 6 cyl. Mk RD 68 diesels; 2 props; 14,400 hp
Range: 12,000/12   Man: 396 tot.

REMARKS: Helicopter platform and hangar for two Wessex or Sea King. Workshops and foundry (400 m²); boiler shop (100 m²); electric shop; electronic shop (300 m²); mechanical workshop (500 m²); and shops for precision equipment and plastic-boat repairs. Four 3-ton and two 6-ton cranes. Carries spare missiles for destroyers and frigates.

♦ **1 training ship**

	Bldr	Laid down	L	In serv.
AGT 203 JERVIS BAY (ex-*Australian Trader*)	State DY, Newcastle	18-8-67	17-2-69	17-6-69

Jervis Bay (AGT 203)—note vehicle door at stern   1979

D: 8,915 tons (fl)   S: 17 kts
Dim: 135.7 (123.5 pp) × 21.5 × 6.1   A: None
Fuel: 820 tons   Electric: 2,000 kw
M: 2 Crossley-Pielstick 16 PC 2V 400 diesels; 2 props; 13,000 hp
Man: 111 crew plus 40 trainees

REMARKS: A former roll-on/roll-off cargo ferry converted to a training ship to replace the destroyer *Duchess*. Commissioned 25-8-77. Name commemorates an armed merchant cruiser of World War II. Can also serve as a transport and vehicle cargo ship, and has a helicopter platform. Operates with destroyer *Vampire* as a training squadron.

♦ **2 general-purpose tenders** Bldr: Walkers, Ltd, Maryborough

AG 244 BANKS (In serv. 16-2-60)   AG 247 BASS (In serv. 25-5-60)

D: 207 tons (255 fl)   S: 10 kts   Dim: 30.8 (27.5 pp) × 6.7 × 2.5
M: Diesels; 2 props; . . . hp   Man: 2 officers, 12 men

REMARKS: AG 247 was originally equipped as a hydrographic ship and AG 244 for fisheries protection, but both are used primarily for reserve training. AG 247: 260 tons fl.

NOTE: Four new 30-m training craft were proposed in 1978, but none have been ordered. The small launches *Nepean* and *Gayundah* (MRL 253) also train reserves.

AUXILIARIES *(continued)*

Banks (AG 244)   1980

YARD AND SERVICE CRAFT

♦ **2 British "Ham"-class diving tenders, former inshore minesweepers** Bldr: White, Cowes

DTV 1001 SEAL (ex-*Wintringham*)—(L: 24-5-55)
DTV 1002 PORPOISE (ex-*Neasham*)—(L: 14-3-55)

D: 120 tons (159 fl) **S:** 14 kts **Dim:** 32.43 (30.48 pp) × 6.45 × 1.75
M: 2 Paxman YHAXM diesels; 2 props; 1,100 hp **Fuel:** 15 tons
Range: 1,500/12 **Man:** 7 tot.

REMARKS: Transferred in 1966, but not converted until 12-68 (*Seal*) and 1973. Assigned to the school of diving and underwater demolition in Sydney. Can support fourteen divers. Sister *Otter* (Y 299) sold 1974. Large deckhouse replaced sweep winch and cable reel.

♦ **3 501-class harbor tugs** Bldr: Stannard Bros., Sydney (504: Perrin Eng., Brisbane)

HTS 501, 502, 504 (1969, 1972)

D: 47.5 tons **S:** 9 kts **Dim:** 19.4 × 4.6 × . . .
M: 2 GM diesels; 2 props; 340 hp **Man:** 3 tot.

REMARKS: Sister 503 to Papua New Guinea 1974.

HTS 504   R. Gillett, 1980

♦ **2 ex-U.S. Army wooden-hull harbor tugs** (In serv. 1944)

TB 9 SARDIUS   TB 1536

D: 60 tons (fl) **S:** 10 kts **Dim:** 13.7 × . . . × . . .
M: 1 Hercules diesel; 240 hp **Man:** 4 tot.

♦ **3 torpedo-recovery craft** Bldr: Williamstown DY (In serv. 1970-71)

TRV 801   TRV 802   TRV 803

TRV 802   G. Gyssels, 1976

AUSTRALIA *(continued)*
YARD AND SERVICE CRAFT *(continued)*

D: 91.6 tons **S:** 13 kts **Dim:** 27.0 × 6.4 × 1.4
M: 3 GM 6-71 diesels; 3 props; 890 hp **Man:** 1 officer, 8 men

REMARKS: TRV 802 normally used as a diving tender.

◆ 4 water tenders

MRL 253 GAYUNDAH MWL 254 MWL 256 MWL 257

D: 300 tons (600 fl) **S:** 9.5 kts **Dim:** 36.5 × 7.3 × . . .
M: 2 Ruston & Hornsby diesels; 2 props; 440 hp

REMARKS: Built in 1940s. MRL 253 is configured as dry-stores carrier and is used for Reserve Training. Sisters to hydrographic ship *Paluma* scrapped in 1974.

◆ 3 stores lighters

CSL 01 CSL 02 CSL 03

D: . . . **Dim:** 23.7 × 9.8 × 2.0 **M:** 2 GM diesels; 2 props; . . . hp

REMARKS: Built 1972. Catamarans. One 3-ton electric crane. Based on AWL 304 design but with pilothouse aft.

◆ 1 aircraft lighter

AWL 304

REMARKS: Built 1967 to service the *Melbourne*, can carry 2 Skyhawk or 1 Tracker. Similar to CSL 01 class but with A-frame aft and low pilothouse forward.

◆ 1 aircraft-rescue launch

Y 256 AIR SPRITE

D: 23.5 tons **S:** 25 kts **Dim:** 19.2 × 4.7 × 1.0
M: 2 Hall-Scott gasoline engines

REMARKS: Built 1960. Based on U.S. Navy 63-foot AVR design; sisters are in RAAF service. Two 11.6-m Bertram yachts, 38101 and 38102, purchased as rescue launches, are used as yachts. There are also two 24.4-m "Seaward Defense Boats" (SDB 1324, SDB 1325) and the 22.9-m "General Purpose Vessel," GPV 958.

NOTE: There are number of other yard and service craft, including non-self-propelled oil barges, stores lighters, etc., as well as approximately 20 12.2-m motor workboats, and 15 aluminum hulled, 12-ton, 12-m workboats.

AUSTRIA
Republic of Austria

AUSTRIAN ARMY DANUBE FLOTILLA

PERSONNEL: 1 officer, 26 men

MERCHANT MARINE (1980): 13 ships—88,734 grt

◆ 2 patrol craft for the Danube Bldr: Korneuberg

	Laid down	L	In serv.
A 604 NIEDERÖSTERREICH	31-3-69	26-7-69	16-4-70

Niederösterreich

D: 73 tons (fl) **S:** 22 kts **Dim:** 29.67 × 5.41 × 1.1
A: 1/20-mm AA—2/12.7-mm mg—2/7.62-mm mg—1/84-mm mortar
M: 2 MWM V-16 diesels; 1,620 hp **Fuel:** 9.3 tons
Range: 900/. . . **Man:** 1 officer, 11 men

A 601 OBERST BRECHT Bldr: Korneuberg (In serv. 14-1-58)

D: 10 tons **S:** 14 kts **Dim:** 12.30 × 2.51 × 0.75
A: 1/12.7-mm mg—1/84-mm mortar
M: 2 Graf & Stift 6-cyl. diesels; 290 hp
Range: 160/10 **Man:** 5 tot.

10 U.S.-built M-3-class launches (4 in serv. 1965, 6 M-3D in serv. 1976)

D: 2.9-3.2 tons **S:** 18 kts **Dim:** 8.25 × 2.5 × 1.0
M: 2 GM gasoline/diesels; 176 hp **Man:** 3 tot.

◆ several motorized pontoons

D: 8.5 to 40 tons fl **Dim:** 19 × 17 (some: 30) × 0.7

THE BAHAMAS
Commonwealth of the Bahamas

MERCHANT MARINE (1980): 91 ships—87,320 grt (tankers: 4—14,506 grt)

THE BAHAMAS *(continued)*

POLICE MARINE DIVISION

♦ **1 103-foot patrol boat** Bldr: Vosper Thornycroft

	Laid down	L	In serv.
P 01 MARLIN	22-11-76	20-6-77	23-5-78

Marlin (P 01)   Vosper, 1978

D: 100 tons (125 fl)   **S:** 24 kts   **Dim:** 31.5 × 5.9 × 1.6
A: 1/20-mm AA   **M:** 2 Paxman Ventura diesels; 2 props; 2,900 hp
Range: 2,000/13   **Man:** 3 officers, 16 men

REMARKS: Fin stabilizers, steel hulls. Two 50-mm flare launchers. Sister *Flamingo* sunk 11-5-80 by Cuban Mig-21 aircraft.

♦ **7 Keith Nelson patrol craft** Bldr: Vosper-Thornycroft

P 21 ACKLINS	P 23 ELEUTHERA	P 25 EXUMA	P 27 INAGUA
P 22 ANDROS	P 24 SAN SALVADOR	P 26 ABACO	

Andros   1972

First four in serv. 5-3-71, last three 10-12-77

D: 30 tons (37 fl)   **S:** 19.5 kts   **Dim:** 18.29 (17.07 pp) × 5.03 × 1.53
A: Machine guns   **Electron Equipt:** Radar: 1/Decca 110   **Electric:** 29 kVA
M: 2 Caterpillar 3408 TA diesels; 2 props; 950 hp   **Fuel:** 4 tons
Range: 650/16   **Man:** 11 tot.

REMARKS: Fiberglass construction, air-conditioned.

BAHRAIN
State of Bahrain

MERCHANT MARINE (1980): 44 ships—10,248 grt (tankers: 2—913 grt)

♦ **2 TNC 45-class guided-missile boats** Bldr: Lürssen, Vegesack, West Germany

	Laid down	L	In serv.
N. . .	. . .	. . .	1983
N. . .	. . .	. . .	1984

D: 231 tons (259 fl)   **S:** 40.5 kts
Dim: 44.9 (42.3 fl) × 7.3 × 2.31 (props)
A: 4/MM 40 Exocet SSM (II × 2)—1/76-mm OTO Melara DP—2/40-mm Breda AA (II × 1)—2/12.7-mm M3 mg (I × 2)
Electron Equipt: Radar: 1/. . . search radar; 1/PEAB 9 LV223 fcs
          ECM: Decca RDL-2 ABC passive warning, Dagaie chaff RL
M: 4 MTU 16V 538 TB 92 diesels; 4 props; 15,600 hp (13,000 sust.)
Electric: 405 kVA   **Range:** 500/38.5, 1,500/16   **Man:** 5 officers, 27 men

REMARKS: Ordered 1979; very similar to TNC 45 class for the United Arab Emirates. Panda backup director for 40-mm guns. Carry 250 rds 76-mm, 1,800 rds. 40-mm, 6,000 rds. 12.7-mm ammunition.

♦ **2 FPB 38-class patrol boats** Bldr: Lürssen, Vegesack

N. . . (In serv. 1981)   N. . . (In serv. 1981)

D: 188 tons (205 fl)   **S:** 34 kts   **Dim:** 38.5 (36.0 pp) × 7.0 × 2.2 (props)
A: 1/40-mm AA Bofors SAK 40/L70—2/20-mm AA Oerlikon GAM-601 (I × 2)
M: 2 MTU 20V 539 TB 91 diesels; 2 props; 9,000 hp (7,500 sust.)
Electric: 130 kVA   **Range:** 550/31.5, 1,100/16   **Man:** 3 officers, 24 men

REMARKS: Ordered 1979. 2/50-mm rocket flare rails on 40-mm gun, 2/3-pdr. saluting cannon. CSEE Lynx, optical GFCS.

♦ **2 patrol craft** Bldr: Vosper, Singapore (1977)

3 HOWAR   . . . ROUBODH

D: 32 tons (fl)   **S:** 29 kts   **Dim:** 17.1 × 4.9 × 1.5
M: 2 GM 8V TI diesels; 2 props; 900 hp

♦ **3 patrol craft** Bldr: Vosper, Singapore (1977)

. . . AL BAYNEH   . . . JUNNAN   . . . QUAIMAS

D: 6.3 tons (fl)   **S:** 27 kts   **Dim:** 11.1 × 3.3 × 0.9
M: 1 Sabre diesel; 210 hp

♦ **1 Tracker-class patrol craft** Bldr: Fairey Marine, G. B.

1 BAHRAIN

D: 26 tons (fl)   **S:** 28 kts   **Dim:** 19.6 × 4.9 × 1.5   **A:** 1/20-mm AA
M: 2 GM diesels; 2 props; 1,120 hp   **Range:** 500

REMARKS: In service 1975.

BAHRAIN (continued)

♦ **2 Spear-class patrol craft** Bldr: Fairey Marine, G. B.

4 SAHEM   5 KHATAF

> **D:** 4.5 tons (10 fl)   **S:** 26 kts   **Dim:** 9.1 × 2.75 × 0.84
> **A:** 2 machine guns   **M:** 2 Perkins diesels; 2 props; 290 hp
> **Range:** 220   **Man:** 3 tot.

REMARKS: In service 1975.

♦ **3 27-foot patrol craft** Bldr: Cheverton, Cowes, G. B. (1977)

15 NOON   16 ASKAR   17 SUWAD

> **D:** 3.3 tons   **S:** 15 kts   **Dim:** 8.23 × 2.44 × 0.81
> **M:** 2 diesels; 1 prop; 150 hp

♦ **1 50-foot patrol craft** Bldr: Cheverton, Cowes, G. B. (1976)

6 MASHTAN

> **D:** 9 tons   **S:** 22 kts   **Dim:** 15.2 × 4.3 × 1.4
> **M:** 2 GM 8V TI diesels; 2 props; 900 hp   **Range:** 660/12

♦ **1 patrol craft** Bldr: Vosper, Singapore (1976)

2 JIDA

> **D:** 15 tons   **S:** 23 kts   **Dim:** 13.9 × 6.1 × 1.1
> **M:** 2 diesels; 2 props; 1,080 hp

♦ **1 Loadmaster-class landing craft** Bldr: Cheverton, Cowes, G. B. (1976)

7 SAFRA

> **D:** 90 tons (fl)   **S:** 10 kts   **Dim:** 18.23 × 6.1 × 1.0
> **M:** 2 diesels; 2 props; 240 hp

REMARKS: Can carry 40 tons of vehicles or dry cargo, or 60 tons of liquid cargo.

♦ **10 wooden motor dhows for logistics and patrol duties**

♦ **1 utility hovercraft** Bldr: Tropimere, G. B. (1977)

> **D:** 4.23 tons (fl)   **S:** 45 kts   **Dim:** 8.9 × 4.5 × 3.6 high

BANGLADESH
People's Republic of Bangladesh

PERSONNEL: 3,500 men (approx. 200 officers)

MERCHANT MARINE (1980): 179 ships
353,586 grt (tankers: 33—45,504 grt)

♦ **1 British Leopard-class frigate**

	Bldr	Laid down	L	In serv.
F 17 ALI HAIDER (ex-*Jaguar*, F-37)	Wm. Denny, Dumbarton	2-11-53	30-7-57	12-12-59

Ali Haider (F 17)—as the **Jaguar**   G. Arra, 1972

> **D:** 2,300 tons (2,520 fl)   **S:** 23 kts   **Dim:** 103.63 (100.58 pp) × 12.19 × 4.8 (fl)
> **A:** 4/114-mm Mk 6 DP (II × 2)—1/40-mm Mk 9 AA
> **Electron Equipt:** Radars: 1/965, 1/978, 1/993, 1/275 fire-control
> **Electric:** 1,200 kw   **Fuel:** 230 tons
> **M:** 8 Admiralty 16 VVS ASR 1 diesels; 2 CP props; 12,400 hp
> **Range:** 2,300/23, 7,500/16   **Man:** 10 officers, 200 men

REMARKS: Sold 6-7-78; arrived Bangladesh 11-78 after overhaul. Squid ASW mortar and sonars removed while in Royal Navy. Fin stabilizers. 1/Mk 6 GFCS with Type 275 radar for 114-mm guns; 40-mm, local control only. May receive Sea Cat point-defense SAM system.

♦ **1 ex-British Salisbury-class radar-picket frigate**

	Bldr	Laid down	L	In serv.
F 16 UMAR FAROOQ (ex-*Llandaff*, F 61)	Hawthorn Leslie, G. B.	27-8-53	30-11-55	11-4-58

Umar Farooq   1979

BANGLADESH *(continued)*

D: 2,170 tons (2,408 fl)   **S:** 24 kts   **Dim:** 103.6 (100.58 pp) × 12.19 × 4.8
A: 2/114-mm Mk 6 DP (II × 1)—2/40-mm AA (II × 1)—1/Mk 4 Squid ASW
   mortar (III × 1)
Electron Equipt: Radars: 1/985, 1/993, 1/277Q, 1/982, 1/975, 1/275
   Sonars: 1/174, 1/170B
M: 8 Admiralty 16 VVS ASR 1 diesels; 2 props; 12,400 hp
Range: 2,300/24, 7,500/16   **Man:** 14 officers, 223 men

REMARKS: Former aircraft-direction frigate, transferred 10-12-76. Mk 6 GFCS for
114-mm mount. May receive Sea Cat point-defense SAM system.

◆ **6 new-construction patrol boats, 30-m overall, planned.**

◆ **2 ex-Yugoslav Kraljevica-class patrol boats**

P 301 KARNAPHULI (ex-Yugoslav PBR 502)
P 302 TISTNA (ex-Yugoslav PBR 505)

Tistna (P 302)   1976

D: 190 tons (202 fl)   **S:** 18 kts   **Dim:** 41.0 × 6.3 × 2.2
A: 2/40-mm AA (I × 2)—4/20-mm AA (I × 4)—2 Mk 6 depth-charge throwers—
   2 depth-charge racks—2/128-mm RL
Electron Equipt: Radar: 1/Decca 45—Sonar: QCU 2
M: 2 M.A.N. W8V 30/38 diesels; 2 props; 3,300 hp
Range: 1,000/12   **Man:** 4 officers, 40 men

REMARKS: Transferred 6-6-75.

◆ **6 Chinese Shanghai-II-class patrol boats**

P 101   P102   P 103   P 104   P 105   P106

D: 122 tons (150 fl)   **S:** 28.5 kts   **Dim:** 38.8 × 5.4 × 1.5
A: 4/37-mm AA (II × 2)—4/25-mm AA (II × 2)
Electron Equipt: Radar: 1/Pot Head
M: 2 M5OF-4/1,200-hp and 2/910-hp diesels; 4 props; 4,220 hp

REMARKS: First two transferred 1974; four more in 1980.

◆ **1 salvaged Pakistani patrol boat** Bldr: Brooke Marine, Lowestoft, G. B.

P 201 BISHKALI (ex-*Jessore*)—In serv. 20-5-65

D: 115 tons (143 fl)   **S:** 24 kts   **Dim:** 32.62 (30.48 pp) × 6.10 × 1.55
A: 2/40-mm AA (I × 2)
M: 2 MTU 12V538 diesels; 2 props; 3,400 hp   **Man:** 30 tot.

REMARKS: Sunk in 1971 War of Independence; salvaged and repaired, Khulna SY;
recommissioned 23-11-78.

◆ **2 Ajay-class patrol boats** Bldr: Hooghly D & E, Calcutta, 1-62

P 201 PADMA (ex-*Akshay*, P 3136)   P 202 SURMA (ex-*Ajay*, P 3135)

D: 120 tons (151 fl)   **S:** 18 kts   **Dim:** 35.75 (33.52 pp) × 6.1 × 1.9
A: 1/40-mm AA—2/20-mm AA (I × 2)
M: 2 Paxman YHAXM diesels; 2 props; 1,000 hp—1 Foden FD-6 cruise diesel;
   100 hp
Range: 500/12, 1,000/8   **Man:** 3 officers, 32 men

REMARKS: Indian version of British "Ford" class, donated and commissioned 12-4-73
and 26-7-74, respectively.

◆ **5 river patrol boats** Bldr: DEW Narayengonj, Dacca

P 101 PABNA (6-72)   P 103 PATUAKHALI (11-74)   P 105 RANGAMATI (6-77)
P 102 NOAKAHLI (7-72)   P 104 BOGRA (6-77)

D: 69.5 tons (fl)   **S:** 10 kts   **Dim:** 22.9 × 6.1 × 1.9   **A:** 1/40-mm AA
M: 2 Cummins diesels; 2 props   **Range:** 700/8   **Man:** 3 officers, 30 men

REMARKS: Last two differ in configuration, gun forward.

◆ **1 training ship** Bldr: Atlantic SB, Montreal, Canada (1957)

A 601 SHAHEED RUHUL AMIN (ex-*Anticosti*, Canadian merchant)

D: 710 tons (fl)   **S:** 11.5 kts   **Dim:** 47.5 × 11.1 × 3.1   **A:** 1/40-mm AA
M: 1 Caterpillar diesel   **Range:** 4,000/10   **Man:** 8 officers, 72 men

REMARKS: Transferred 1972 from relief agency; recommissioned after conversion,
10-12-74.

◆ **1 floating drydock** Bldr: Tito SY, Trogir, Yugoslavia

A 701 SUNDARBAN (In serv: 15-8-80)
   Lift capacity: 3,500 tons   **Dim:** 117.0 × 27.6 × 0.3 loaded.

REMARKS: Self-docking type with 7 sectional pontoons. 17.6-m between dock walls,
which are 101.4-m long.

BARBADOS

COAST GUARD

PERSONNEL: 61 (4 officers, 57 men)

MERCHANT MARINE (1980): 37 ships—5,257 grt

BARBADOS *(continued)*
COAST GUARD *(continued)*

♦ **1 new-construction patrol boat** Bldr: Brooke Marine, Lowestoft, G. B.

GC. . .   TRIDENT (L: 14-4-81)

   D: 165 tons (200 fl)   **S:** 25 kts   **Dim:** 37.50 × 6.86 × 1.78
   M: 2 Paxman Valenta 12 RP 200 diesels; 2 props; 4,000 hp   **Range:** 3,000/12
   A: 1/40-mm AA—1/20-mm AA   **Man:** 25 tot.

REMARKS: Ordered 21-12-79 for delivery 7-81.

♦ **2 converted shrimp-trawler-design patrol boats**

REMARKS: Converted by Swan-Hunter, Trinidad; re-launched 2-81 and in service 5-81. Wooden hulls.

♦ **1 Halmatic, 20-meter, Guardian-class police patrol craft** Bldr: Aquarius Boat, G. B.

GC 601 GEORGE FERGUSON

   D: 30 tons   **S:** 24 kts   **Dim:** 20.0 × 5.25 × 1.5
   M: 2 GM 12V71 diesels; 1,300 hp   **Range:** 650/12   **Man:** 11 tot.

♦ **3 Halmatic, 12-meter, Guardian-class police patrol craft** Bldr: Aquarius Boat, G. B. (In serv. 12-73 to 2-74)

GC 402 COMMANDER MARSHALL   GC 403 T. T. LEWIS   GC 404 J. T. C. RAMSAY

   D: 11.5 tons   **S:** 21 kts   **Dim:** 12.0 × 3.7 × 1.0
   M: 2 Caterpillar Mk 334 TA diesels; 2 props; 580 hp   **Man:** 4 tot.

BELGIUM
Kingdom of Belgium

PERSONNEL: 4,597, including 300 officers

MERCHANT MARINE (1980): 290 ships—1,809,829 grt (tankers: 18—293,734 grt)

NAVAL AVIATION: Four helicopters (1 Sikorsky S-58 and 3 Alouette IIIB) used for minehunting. One Alouette each may be taken on board *Zinnia* and *Godetia*.

FRIGATES

♦ **4 Wielingen class, Type E 71**

	Bldr	Laid down	L	In serv.
F 910 WIELINGEN	Boëlwerf, Temse	5-3-74	30-3-76	20-1-78
F 911 WESTDIEP	Cockerill, Hoboken	2-9-74	8-12-75	20-1-78
F 912 WANDELAAR	Boëlwerf, Temse	5-3-75	21-6-77	27-10-78
F 913 WESTHINDER	Cockerill, Hoboken	8-12-75	31-1-77	27-10-78

Westdiep (F 911)   G. Gyssels, 1979

Wielingen (F 910)   G. Gyssels, 1981

Westhinder (F 913)   French Navy, 1980

   D: 1,880 tons (2,283 fl)   **S:** 28 kts on gas turbine
   Dim: 106.38 (103 pp) × 12.3 × 5.3 (over sonar)
   A: 4 MM 38 (II × 2) Exocet—1/100-mm DP—1/NATO Sea Sparrow SAM syst (8 missiles)—2/20-mm AA (I × 2)—1/375-mm Bofors sextuple ASW rocket launcher—2 launching racks for L-5 ASW torpedoes

FRIGATES (continued)

Electron Equipt: Radars: 1/DA-05, 1/Raytheon TM 1645/9X navigation, 1/HSA WM-25, SEWACO-IV data system
Sonar: 1/SQS-505A
ESM: Elcos-1—2/Knebworth Corvus 8-tube chaff launchers
Fuel: 250 tons diesel **Electric:** 2,000 kw
M: CODOG: 2 Cockerill CO-240V-12 diesels, each 3,000 hp (1,000 rmp); 1 Rolls-Royce Olympus TM 3B gas turbine of 28,000 hp (5,600 rpm); 2 LIPS CP props
Range: 4,500/18, 6,000/16 **Man:** 15 officers, 145 men

REMARKS: Welded hull, two Vosper Pin stabilizers. 15 knots on one diesel, 20 knots on two; for more than 20 knots the gas turbine is brought on the line. Canadian hull sonar. French 100-mm gun, Model 1968. Belgian-Dutch automatic surface- and air-search radar system, including fire control and an automatic tactical data system with two DMAB optical sights. The ASW rocket launcher carries six 103-mm rocket flare rails.

PATROL CRAFT

♦ **8 Leie-class river gunboats** Bldr: Nitzler, Regensburg

	In serv.		In serv.
P 901 LEIE	16-9-53	P 905 SCHELDE	2-9-53
P 902 LIBERATION	4-8-54	P 906 SEMOIS	28-10-53
P 903 MEUSE	20-8-53	P 907 RUPEL	24-11-54
		(ex-*Tresignies*)	
P 904 SAMBRE	30-9-53	P 908 OURTHE	27-10-54

Leie (P 901)　　　　　　　　　　　　　　　　　G. Gyssels, 1980

D: 25 tons (27.5 fl) **S:** 19 kts **Dim:** 23.25 × 3.8 × 0.9
A: 2/12.7-mm mg (I × 2) **M:** 2 MWM diesels; 2 props; 440 hp
Man: 1 officer, 6 men

REMARKS: Built 1953-54. P 902 is 26 meters in length, 4 meters in beam, 30 tons (fl). P 906 is employed as a diving tender. P 907, 908 loaned to Marine Cadets each summer as V-7, V-8.

MINE WARFARE SHIPS

♦ **10 Tripartite class minehunters** Bldr: Béliard, Ostend and Antwerp

		L			L
M...	N...	...	M...	N...	...
M...	N...	...	M...	N...	...
M...	N...	...	M...	N...	...
M...	N...	...	M...	N...	...
M...	N...	...	M...	N...	...

D: 511 tons (544 fl) **S:** 15 kts **Dim:** 51.6 (47.1 pp) × 8.96 × 2.45
A: 1/20-mm AA
Electron Equipt: Radar: Decca 1229
Sonar: DUBM-21B
M: 1 Brons/Werkspoor A-RUB 215X 12 diesel; 1 CP prop; 1,900 hp (1,200 rpm); 2 maneuvering props (active rudder); bow-thruster
Electric: 750 kw **Range:** 3,000/12 **Man:** 34 tot.

REMARKS: Same as French *Eridan* and Dutch *Alkmaar* classes. Original construction consortium, Polyship, dissolved. Ships reordered 12-2-81 from Béliard; hulls to be launched at Ostend and fitted out by Béliard Mercantile at Antwerp. Three Astazou-IV, 320 kw gas-turbine generators. Two PAP-104 remote-controlled mine locators; automatic pilot; automatic track-plotter; TORAN and Sydelis navigation systems; conventional wire sweep also. Will be of glass-reinforced-plastic construction. To replace MSO and MSC classes.

♦ **7 U.S. Dash-class oceangoing minesweeper/minehunters**

	L	In serv.
M 902 VAN HAVERBEKE (ex-MSO 522)	29-10-59	7-11-60
M 903 A. F. DUFOUR (ex-*Lagen*, ex-MSO 498)	13-8-54	27-9-55
M 904 DE BROUWER (ex-*Nansen*, ex-MSO 499)	15-10-54	1-11-55
M 906 BREYDEL (ex-AM 504)	25-3-55	24-1-56
M 907 ARTEVELDE (ex-AM 503)	19-6-54	12-12-55
M 908 GEORGES TRUFFAUT (ex-AM 515)	1-11-55	21-9-56
M 909 FRANÇOIS BOVESSE (ex-AM 516)	28-2-56	21-12-56

De Brouwer (M 904)　　　　　　　　　　　　　　G. Gyssels, 1980

Bldrs: M 902: Peterson Bldrs, Sturgeon Bay, Wisc.; M 903, 904: Bellingham BY, Bellingham, Wash.; M 906, 907: Tacoma BY, Tacoma, Wash.; M 908,909: Tampa SB, Tampa Fla.

MINE WARFARE SHIPS *(continued)*

D: 720 tons (780 fl) **S:** 14 kts
Dim: 52.42 (50.3 pp) × 10.97 × 4.20 **A:** 2/12.7-mm mg
Electron Equipt: Sonar: SQQ-14 (not in M 907)
M: 4 GM 8-268A diesels; 2 CP props; 1,520 hp **Fuel:** 53 tons diesel
Range: 3,000/10, 2,400/12 **Man:** 5 officers, 67 men

REMARKS: Transferred 1955-60, except M 903 and M 904 transferred from Norway in
1966. M 907 has no sonar and serves as divers' clearance ship, with decompression
chamber. Rest are equipped as minehunters. Wooden hulls. M 907 has 1/40-mm Mk
3 AA.

♦ **5 U.S. Adjutant-class coastal minesweepers**

2 U.S. construction, converted to minehunters

M 934 VERVIERS (ex-AMS 259)   M 935 VEURNE (ex-AMS 260)

Veurne—minehunter version

Bldr: Hodgdon Bros., Maine In serv. 4-6-56, 23-8-56

REMARKS: Converted to minehunters, with Voith-Schneider vertical cycloidal props
and Plessey 193M sonar, in 1972 and 1969, respectively. M 935 used for survey duties
since 1970.

♦ **3 Belgian construction minsweepers** Bldr: Béliard, Ostend

	L	In serv.
M 930 ROCHEFORT	5-6-54	28-11-55
M 932 NIEUPOORT	12-3-55	9-1-56
M 933 KOKSISDE	4-6-55	29-11-55

D: 330 tons (390 fl) **S:** 13.5/12 kts **Dim:** 44.0 (42.1 pp) × 8.3 × 2.6
A: 1/40-mm AA
Electron Equipt: Radar: 1/nav.   Sonar: AN/UQS-1
M: 2 GM 8-268A diesels; 2 props; 880 hp **Fuel:** 40 tons
Range: 2,700/10.5 **Man:** 4 officers, 17 petty officers, 19 men

REMARKS: Minehunters have enclosed bridge, deckhouse aft. *Stavelot* (M 928) stricken
1979. Three other sisters serve as auxiliaries.

Rochefort (M 930)   G. Gyssels, 1980

♦ **14 Herstal-class inshore minsweepers** Bldr: Mercantile Marine Yd., Kruibeke

	L	In serv.		L	In serv.
M 471 HASSELT	5-57	24-4-58	M 478 HERSTAL	6-8-56	14-10-57
M 472 KORTRUK	5-57	13-6-58	M 479 HUY	17-11-56	14-10-57
M 473 LOKEREN	18-5-57	8-8-58	M 480 SERAING	16-3-57	24-3-58
M 474 TURNHOUT	7-9-57	29-9-58	M 482 VISE	7-9-57	11-9-58
M 475 TONGEREN	16-11-57	9-12-58	M 483 OUGRÉE	16-11-57	10-11-58
M 476 MERKSEM	5-4-58	6-2-59	M 484 DINANT	5-4-58	14-1-59
M 477 OUDENAERDE	3-5-58	25-4-59	M 485 ANDENNE	3-5-58	20-4-59

D: 160 tons (190 fl) **S:** 15 kts
Dim: 34.5 (32.5 pp) × 6.7 × 2.1   **A:** 2/12.7-mm mg (II × 1)
M: 2 Fiat-Mercedes Benz MB 820 diesels; 2 props; 1,260 hp
Fuel: 24 tons **Range:** 2,300/10 **Man:** 1 officer, 7 petty officers, 9 men

REMARKS: Wooden hulls. Designed to sweep the Schelde River. Fitted for magnetic,
acoustic, and mechanical sweeping to a depth of 4.50 to 10 m. M 471, 472, 479
designated RDS-Ready Duty Ship, sweep gear removed, deckhouse in place of cable
rail, and pollution cleanup gear, and special cranes added aft. Modified version of
British "-ham" class. M 478 to M 485, built with U.S. funds, are ex-U.S. MSI
90-97.

Seraing (M 480)—minesweeper version   G. Gyssels, 1981

MINE WARFARE SHIPS *(continued)*

Hasselt (M 471)—RDS, pollution control version   G. Gyssels, 1981

AUXILIARIES

♦ **2 "command and logistics support ships" for mine countermeasures**

	Bldr	Laid down	L	In serv.
A 961 ZINNIA	Cockerill (Hoboken)	8-11-66	6-5-67	5-9-67

Zinnia (A 961)—with Alouette-III on deck aft   G. Arra, 1976

D: 1,705 tons (2,685 fl)   **S:** 18 kts (20 on trials)
Dim: 99.5 (94.2 wl) × 14.0 × 3.6   **Range:** 14,000/12.5
A: 3/40-mm AA (I × 3)—1 Alouette IIIB helicopter with telescoping hangar
Fuel: 150 m³ diesel, 300 m³ for supply to minesweepers
M: Cockerill-Ougrée V 12 TR 240 CO diesels; 1 CP; 5,000 hp
Man: 13 officers, 46 petty officers, 64 men

REMARKS: Fin stabilizers, telescoping helicopter hangar.

	Bldr	Laid down	L	In serv.
A 960 GODETIA	Boëlwerf, Temse	15-2-65	7-12-65	23-5-66

D: 1,700 tons (2,500 fl)   **S:** 18 kts   **Dim:** 91.83 (87.85 pp) × 14.0 × 3.5
A: 1/40-mm AA—8/12.7-mm mg (II × 4)
M: 4 ACEC-M.A.N. diesels; 2 CP props; 5,400 hp
Fuel: 294 tons   **Range:** 2,250/15, 8,700/12
Man: 10 officers, 37 petty officers, 48 men

Godetia (A 960)   G. Gyssels, 1980

REMARKS: Used as fishery protection ship. 15 knots on one diesel. Passive tank stabilization. Ship can be protected against radioactive fallout by closed-circuit ventilation. Can accommodate oceanographic research personnel on board and has space for laboratory. Cargo hold with crane to unload supplies or small boats. Minesweeping cables are stowed on reels on the helicopter deck, which has been extended aft to continue to permit one Alouette-III to land. Rearmed during 1979-80 refit.

♦ **1 oceanographic research craft and sail training ship**

A 958 ZENOBE GRAMME

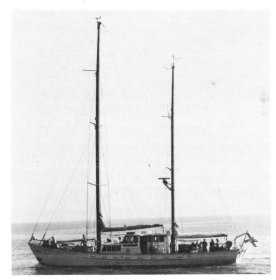

Zenobe Gramme (A 958)   G. Gyssels, 1981

D: 149 tons   **S:** 10 kts   **Dim:** 28.15 (23.10 wl) × 6.85 × 2.64
M: 1 MWM 518A diesel; 232 hp   **Man:** 14 tot.

REMARKS: Fitted out as Bermudian ketch (240m³ sail area).

AUXILIARIES (continued)

♦ **3 U.S. Adjutant-class former minesweepers** Bldr: Boel & Zonen, Temse

		In serv.
A 962 MECHELEN (ex-M 926)—Oceanographic research ship		2-12-54
A 963 SPA (ex-M 927)—Missile/munitions transport for frigates		1-1-56
A 964 HEIST (ex-M 929)—Degaussing/deperming tender		4-4-56

REMARKS: Data as for minesweepers. **A:** A 963: 1/40-mm AA

Mechelen (A 962)   G. Gyssels, 1980

Spa (A 963)   G. Gyssels, 1979

♦ **2 seagoing tugs** Bldr: H. Bodewes, Millengen a/d Ryn (1960)

A 950 VALCKE (ex-*Astronoom*, ex-*Schouwenbank*)
A 998 EKSTER (ex-*Astrodom*, ex-*Steenbank*)

D: 183 tons (fl)   **S:** 13 kts   **Dim:** 30.08 × 7.55 × 2.99
M: 2/4-cycle, single-acting 8-cyl. diesels, electric drive; 1 prop;. . . hp

Valcke (A 950)   G. Gyssels, 1981

REMARKS: Purchased 1980 from A. Smit. Names commemorate former tug *Sub-Lieutenant Valcke* (A 950), stricken 1979, and ammunition transport *Ekster*, stricken 1980.

YARD AND SERVICE CRAFT

♦ **2 Hommel-class small harbor tugs** Bldr: Voith, Heidenheim (1953)

A 951 HOMMEL   A 952 WESP

   D: 22 tons   **M:** 2 diesels; 2 Voith-Schneider vertical cycloidal props; 300 hp

Hommel (A 951)   G. Gyssels, 1980

BELGIUM (*continued*)
YARD AND SERVICE CRAFT (*continued*)

♦ **2 Bij-class small harbor tugs**

	Bldr	In serv.
A 953 Bɪᴊ	Akerboom, Lisse	1959
A 954 Kʀᴇᴋᴇʟ	Rupermonde SY	1961

D: 60 tons (71 fl) **S:** 10 kts **Dim:** 17.65 (16.0) × 5.2 × 2.0
M: 2 MWM RHS 518A diesels; 2 Voith-Schneider vertical cycloidal props; 300 hp

♦ **1 small fireboat tug:** A 959 Mɪᴇʀ Bldr: Liège SY(1962): 12.5 m o.a., 17.5 tons, 90 hp

♦ **3 fuel barges:** FN 4, FN 5, FN 6—300 tons, 32 m. (1957)

♦ **1 diving tender:** ZM 4—8 tons, 10 m. (1954)

♦ **1 personnel launch:** Sᴘɪɴ (1958)—32 tons, 14.6 m., 1 diesel; Voith-Schneider prop; 250 hp; 8 kts—can also be used as a tug.

BELIZE

Pᴇʀsᴏɴɴᴇʟ: approx. 50 men

Mᴇʀᴄʜᴀɴᴛ Mᴀʀɪɴᴇ (1980): 3 ships—620 grt

♦ **2 patrol craft** Bldr: Brooke Marine, Lowestoft, G. B. (1972)

PBM 01 Bᴇʟɪᴢᴇ   PBM 02 Bᴇʟᴍᴏᴘᴀɴ

D: 15 tons (fl) **S:** 22 kts **Dim:** 12.2 × 3.6 × 0.6 **A:** 3 mg (I × 3)
M: 2 Caterpillar diesels; 2 props; 370 hp

BENIN

People's Republic of Benin

Pᴇʀsᴏɴɴᴇʟ: About 100

Mᴇʀᴄʜᴀɴᴛ Mᴀʀɪɴᴇ (1978): 13 ships—4,557 grt

♦ **2 ex-North Korean, Soviet P 4-class torpedo boats** (transferred 1979)

D: 19.3 tons (22.4 fl) **S:** 54 kts **Dim:** 19.3 × 3.7 × 1.0
A: 2/14.5-mm mg (II × 1)—2/450-mm TT
Electron Equipt: Radar: Skin Head **M:** 2 M50 diesels; 2 props; 2,400 hp

Rᴇᴍᴀʀᴋs: Aluminum-construction hydroplanes. May in fact be newer craft of similar design to P 4. Transfer of two ex-Algerian P 6-class torpedo boats, reported in last edition, was either incorrect or the craft have been discarded.

♦ **5 Soviet Zhuk-class patrol craft**

D: 50 tons (fl) **S:** 30 kts **Dim:** 26.0 × 4.9 × 1.5
A: 4/14.5-mm mg (II × 2) **M:** 2 M50 diesels; 2 props; 2,400 hp

Rᴇᴍᴀʀᴋs: Transferred: 2 in 1979, 2 in 5-80, 1 in 9-80.

BOLIVIA

Republic of Bolivia

Pᴇʀsᴏɴɴᴇʟ (1980): 1500

Mᴇʀᴄʜᴀɴᴛ Mᴀʀɪɴᴇ (1980): 2 ships—15,130 grt

♦ **1 seagoing cargo ship**

Lɪʙᴇʀᴀᴛᴀᴅᴏʀ Bᴏʟɪᴠᴀʀ (ex-*Simon Bolivar*, ex-*Ciudad de Barquisimeto*)
Bldr: Fairfield, G. B., 1951

D: 9,000 tons **S:** 14.5 kts **Dim:** 128.3 (120.4 pp) × 16.76 × 6.7
M: 1 Doxford diesel; 4,350 hp **Range:** 7,000/14

Rᴇᴍᴀʀᴋs: Donated by Venezuela, 1977. Home-ported in Argentina. Used to generate revenue and for training in preparation for possible ceding to Bolivia of a "corridor to the sea" between Peru and Chile. 4,214 grt/6,390 dwt/2,352 nrt.

♦ **7 river patrol craft/transports**

MO 1 Aʟᴍɪʀᴀɴᴛᴇ Gʀᴀᴜ, 52 tons	MO 5 Cᴏᴍᴀɴᴅᴀɴᴛᴇ Aʀᴀɴᴅɪᴀ, 82 tons
MO 2 Nɪᴄᴏʟᴀs Sᴜᴀʀᴇᴢ, 26 tons	MO 6 Tᴏᴘᴀᴛᴇʀ
MO 3 Mᴀʀɪsᴄᴀʟ Sᴀɴᴛᴀ Cʀᴜᴢ, 52 tons	MO 8 Cᴏʀᴏɴᴇʟ Eᴅᴜᴀʀᴅᴏ Aᴠᴀʀᴏᴀ, 82 tons
MO 4 Pʀᴇsɪᴅᴇɴᴛᴇ Bᴜsᴄʜ, 52 tons	

Rᴇᴍᴀʀᴋs: Iron-or wooden-hulled, raftlike craft with high superstructures and speeds of 8-10 knots.

♦ **1 or more Brown-class patrol launches**

Aʟᴍɪʀᴀɴᴛᴇ Gᴜɪʟʟᴇʀᴍᴏ Bʀᴏᴡɴ

D: 4 tons **S:** 12 kts **Dim:** 7.0 × 2.3 × 1.0
M: 1 Ford Penta diesel; 116 hp **Man:** 12 tot.

Rᴇᴍᴀʀᴋs: Built 1978-. . .

BOLIVIA *(continued)*

Almirante Grau—used for training

♦ **2 ex-U.S. PBR Mk-II patrol boats**

REMARKS: Transferred 1974.

♦ **24 miscellaneous Lake Titicaca and river service launches** (several oar-propelled)

♦ **2 hospital launches**

JULIAN APAZA   BRUNO RACUA

REMARKS: Launched 1977-78; 17 tons. *Apaza* a gift of the USA.

BRAZIL
Federative Republic of Brazil

PERSONNEL: 3,800 officers, 21,200 men, plus 650 officers and 10,850 men in the Fuzileiros Navais (Marine Corps equivalent)

MERCHANT MARINE (1980): 607 ships—4,533,663 grt (tankers: 61—1,572,737 grt)

NAVAL AVIATION: Established in 1963. Uses 4 U.S. SH-3D Sea King, 9 Westland Wasp, 17 Bell 206B JetRanger II (SAH-11) helicopters, and 9 Westland WG 13 Lynx. Eight SA 530 Écureuil (UH-12). Four more SH-3D are to be ordered. The Air Force makes available to the Navy: 6 RC-130E Hercules, 12 Grumman HU-16A Albatross amphibians, and 18 EMB Bandeirante in a sea-surveillance version. Eight Grumman S-2E Tracker aircraft are available for use on *Minas Gerais*, and 5 S-2A are used for training and transport.

WARSHIPS IN SERVICE OR UNDER CONSTRUCTION AS OF 1 JANUARY 1982

	L	Tons	Main armament
♦ **1 light aircraft carrier (ASW)**			
MINAS GERAIS	1944	15,890	10/40-mm AA, 12 aircraft
♦ **9 submarines**			
3 OBERON	1971-75	1,610	8 TT
2 GUPPY III	1945	1,650	10 TT
3 GUPPY II	1944-45	1,517	10 TT
♦ **10 destroyers**			
2 GEARING, FRAM I	1944-45	2,425	2/127-mm DP, 6 ASW TT AS-ROC
4 ALLEN M. SUMNER, FRAM II	1944	2,200	6/127-mm DP, 6 ASW TT
1 ALLEN M. SUMNER	1944	2,200	6/127-mm DP, 1 Sea Cat SAM, 6 ASW TT
3 FLETCHER	1943-44	2,050	4-5/127-mm DP, 5/533-mm TT
♦ **6 frigates**			
4 NITEROI	1974-75	3,200	1/114-mm DP, 2/40-mm AA, 1 Branik missile launcher, 2 Sea Cat missile launchers, 1 Bofors rocket launcher, 6 ASW TT, 1 helicopter
2 CONSTITUÇÃO	1976-77	3,200	2/114-mm DP, 2/40-mm AA, 4 Exocet missile launchers, 2 Sea Cat missile launchers, 1 Bofors rocket launcher, 6 ASW TT, 1 helicopter
♦ **13 corvettes**			
10 IMPERIAL MARINHEIRO	1954-55	911	1/76.2-mm DP
3 SOTOYOMO	1945	570	2/20-mm AA

♦ **6 patrol boats and craft**

♦ **7 river patrol ships**

♦ **6 mine warfare ships**

♦ **7 amphibious warfare ships**

NOTE: New construction plans for rejuvenating the Brazilian Navy have been hampered by economic conditions and diplomatic problems. A ten-year, new-construction cooperative program with Italy was signed on 10-6-80, but exact details of all the ships programmed have not been announced.

LIGHT AIRCRAFT CARRIER (ASW)

♦ **1 British Colossus class**

	Bldr	Laid down	L	In serv.
A 11 Minas Gerais (ex-*Vengeance*)	Swan Hunter	11-42	23-3-44	1-45

Minas Gerais (A 11)—7 S-2A on deck   1972

Minas Gerais (A 11)—with new radar   1981

D: 15,890 tons (19,890 fl)   **S:** 24 kts
Dim: 211.25 × 36.44 (24.50 hull) × 7.15
A: 10/40-mm AA (IV × 2, II × 1)—4/S-2E aircraft—4/SH-3, 2/SAH-11, 2/UH-12 helicopters
Electron Equipt: Radars: 1/SPS-40B, 1/SPS-8B, 1/SPB-4, 1/Raytheon 1402, 2/SPG-34 fire control
M: Parsons GT; 2 props; 42,000 hp
Boilers: 4 Admiralty 3-drum 28 kg/cm², 371°C   **Fuel:** 3,200 tons
Electric: 2,500 kw   **Range:** 12,000/14, 6,200/23
Man: 1,000 ship's company plus 300 aviation personnel

REMARKS: Purchased from Great Britain in 12-56; refitted in Rotterdam, completing in 1960 with new weapons, steam catapult, angled flight deck (8.5°), mirror optical landing equipment, new radars, and 2 new elevators. GFCS for the 40-mm AA include 2 Mk 63 (with SPG-34 radar on the quadruple mounts) and 1 Mk 51 mod. 2. Hangar 135.6 × 15.8 × 5.3 high; 2 elevators 13.7 × 10.4. Catapult can launch 15-ton aircraft. In refit 1976-81. A data link system for cooperation with the *Niteroi* class has been installed, and U.S. SPS-40B radar has replaced SPS-12. Two V/STOL and helicopter carriers are included in long-range construction plans.

SUBMARINES

♦ **3 new construction** Bldr: Ast. Ilha das Cobras, Rio

REMARKS: An Italian design and the German IKL Type 209 were still in competition at time of writing; see appendix.

♦ **3 British Oberon class**

	Bldr	Laid down	L	In serv.
S 20 Humaitá	Vickers-Barrow	3-11-70	5-10-71	18-6-73
S 21 Tonelero	Vickers-Barrow	18-21-70	22-11-72	8-9-78
S 22 Riachuelo	Vickers-Barrow	26-5-73	6-9-75	12-3-77

Humaita (S 20)   1975

D: 1,610 tons standard, 2,030 surf., 2,400 sub.
S: 17.5/15 kts   **Dim:** 89.9 × 8.07 × 5.48
A: 8/533-mm TT, 6 forward, 2 aft (22 torpedoes)
Electron Equipt: Sonars: 1/187, 1/2007, DUUG-1, AUUD-1
M: 2 Admiralty Standard Range 16VVS-ASR1 diesels; 2 electric generators, each 1,280 kw; 2 electric motors; 2 props; 6,000 hp
Range: 11,000/11 snorkel   **Man:** 5 officers, 57 men

REMARKS: S 21 several years late entering active service due to a fire on board during construction. Batteries made up of 224 elements in two sections, with a 7,240-ampere capacity for five hours. "One-man control" system for immersion and diving. Digital tactical data system. Eighteen torpedoes, British Mk 8 and U.S. Mk 37. Satellite navigation receiver installed.

♦ **2 ex-U.S. GUPPY III class**

	Bldr	Laid down	L	In serv.
S 15 Goiás (ex-*Trumpetfish*, SS 425)	Cramp S.B.	23-8-43	13-5-45	29-1-46
S 16 Amazonas (ex-*Greenfish*, SS 351)	Electric Boat Co.	29-1-44	21-12-45	7-6-46

D: 1,650 tons standard, 1,975 surf., 2,540 sub.   **S:** 20/13-15 kts
Dim: 99.4 × 8.2 × 5.2
A: 10/533-mm TTs, 6 fwd, 4 aft (24 torpedoes)
Electron Equipt: Radar: 1/SS-2A—Sonar: BQG-4 PUFFS, BQR-2B
M: Diesel-electric propulsion; 4 diesel generator sets (6,400 hp); 2 electric motors (5,400 hp)
Range: 12,000/10 surf., 95/5 sub.   **Man:** 86 tot.

REMARKS: S 15 purchased 17-10-73, S 16 on 19-12-73. S 15 converted to GUPPY-II in 1948, lengthened to GUPPY III in 1962; S 16 GUPPY II 1948, GUPPY III in

SUBMARINES *(continued)*

1961. S 15 has Fairbanks-Morse 38D 8⅛-10 diesels, S 16 has GM 16-278A. Two 126-cell batteries.

Goiás (S 15)   1975

◆ 3 ex-U.S. GUPPY II class

	Bldr	Laid down	L	In serv.
S 10 GUANABARA	Electric Boat	22-6-44	27-10-45	29-4-46
(ex-*Dogfish*, SS 350)				
S 12 BAHIA	Portsmouth NSY	7-11-44	2-3-45	11-6-45
(ex-*Sea Leopard*, SS 483)				
S 14 CEARA	Boston NSY	8-2-44	15-12-44	4-3-46
(ex-*Amberjack*, SS 522)				

D: 1,517 tons standard, 1,950 surf., 2,540 sub. **S:** 18/13-15 kts
Dim: 93.8 × 8.2 × 5.2 **A:** 10/533-mm TT, 6 fwd, 4 aft (24 torpedoes)
Electron Equipt: Radar: 1/SS-2A—Sonar: BQR-2B, BQS-4
M: Diesel-electric propulsion; 3 generator groups; 2 electric motors; 2 props;
    4,800/5,400 hp
Fuel: 330 tons diesel **Range:** 10,000/10 surf., 95/5 sub. **Man:** 86 tot.

REMARKS: Purchased 28-7-72, 27-3-73, and 17-10-73. S 10 has GM 16-278A diesels, the others Fairbanks-Morse 38D 8⅛-10; one generator set removed on conversion. Two 126-cell batteries. Converted from fleet submarines 1947-49. S 14 has auxiliary rudder atop hull. Sisters *Rio Grande do Sul* (S 11, ex-*Grampus*, SS 523) and *Rio de Janeiro* (S 13, ex-*Odax*, SS 484) stricken.

DESTROYERS

◆ 2 ex-U.S. Gearing class, FRAM I

	Bldr	Laid down	L	In serv.
D 25 MARCILIO DIAZ	Consolidated Steel Corp	29-5-44	8-11-44	10-3-45
(ex-*Henry W. Tucker*, DDR 875)				
D 26 MARIZ E. BARROS	Consolidated Steel Corp.	20-6-44	26-5-45	1-10-45
(ex-*Brinkley Bass*, DD 887)				

D: 2,425 tons (3,600 fl) **S:** 30 kts
Dim: 119.17 × 12.49 × 4.56 (6.4 over sonar)
A: 4/127-mm (II × 2)—1 ASROC ASW syst. (12 missiles)—6/324-mm ASW TT
    (III × 2) Mk 32 for Mk 44 torpedoes

Marcilia Diaz   1974

Electron Equipt: Radars: 1/SPS-10, 1/SPS-40, 1 Mk 25 fire control
    Sonar: 1/SQS-23—ECM: WLR-1, ULQ-6
M: 2 sets GT; 2 props, 60,000 hp
Boilers: 4 Babcock & Wilcox, 43.3 kg, 454°C **Electric:** 1,200 kw
Fuel: 650 tons **Range:** 2,400/25, 4,800/15 **Man:** 14 officers, 260 men

REMARKS: Purchased 3-12-73 and reached Brazil in 6-74. Sale of *McKean* (DD 784) to Brazil around 10-82 is contemplated. Mk 37 GFCS.

◆ 5 ex-U.S. Allen M. Sumner class

	Bldr	Laid down	L	In serv.
D 34 MATO GROSSO	Federal SB, Kearny	28-3-44	17-9-44	4-11-44
(ex-*Compton*, DD 705)				
D 35 SERGIPE	Bethelem, San Pedro	9-4-44	1-10-44	17-2-45
(ex-*James C. Owens*, DD 776)				
D 36 ALAGAOS	Bethlehem, San Fran.	1-2-44	11-3-44	28-6-46
(ex-*Buck*, DD 761)				
D 37 RIO GRANDE DO NORTE	Bethlehem San Fran.	25-7-43	23-4-44	8-3-45
(ex-*Strong*, DD 758)				
D 38 ESPIRITO SANTO	Bethlehem, San Pedro	1-8-43	6-2-44	28-7-44
(ex-*Lowry*, DD 770)				

D: 2,200 tons (3,320 fl) **S:** 30 kts **Dim:** 114.75 × 12.45 × 5.8
A: 6/127-mm (II × 3)—(D 34 only; 1/quadruple Sea Cat SAM)—2 Hedgehogs—
    6/324-mm ASW TT Mk 32 (III × 2)
Electron Equipt: Radars: 1/SPS-10, 1/SPS-40 (D 34: 1/SPS-6, D 38; 1/SPS-29),
    1 Mk 25 fire-control—ECM: WRL-1
    Sonars: 1/SQS-29-32, D 35 and D 38: VDS also
M: 2 sets GT; 2 props; 60,000 hp
Boilers: 4 Babcock & Wilcox, 43.3 kg/cm², 454°C **Fuel:** 460 tons
Electric: 1,200 kw **Range:** 1,260/30, 4,600/15 **Man:** 15 officers, 260 men

DESTROYERS (continued)

Mato Grosso   1975

Sergipe—note the variable-depth sonar   1975

Rio Grande do Norte   1978

REMARKS: All except D 34 are FRAM II. D 34 transferred 27-9-72, the others in 1973. Mk 37 GFCS. Sea Cat system added in D 34 uses M 20 optical director. D 38 has ULQ-6 jamming gear.

♦ **3 ex-U.S. Fletcher class**

	Bldr	Laid down	L	In serv.
D 29 PARAÑA (ex-*Cushing*, DD 797)	Bethlehem, Staten Isl.	3-5-43	30-9-43	17-1-44
D 30 PERNAMBUCO (ex-*Hailey*, DD 556)	Todd SY, Seattle	1-4-42	9-3-43	30-9-43
D 33 MARANHÃO (ex-*Shields*, DD 596)	Puget Sound B&DD	10-8-44	29-4-44	8-2-45

Maranhão (D 33)   1975

D: 2,050 tons (2,850 fl)   **S:** 30 kts   **Dim:** 114.85 × 12.03 × 5.5
A: D 29, D 33: 5/127-mm DP (I × 5)—10/40-mm AA (IV × 2, II × 2—D 33: none)—D 30: 4/127-mm DB—5/533-mm ASW TT (V × 1)—6/324-mm ASW TT Mk 32 (III × 2)—2 Hedgehog—1/d.c. rack
Electron Equipt: Radar: 1/SPS-10, 1/SPS-6, 1/Mk 25 fire-control
           Sonar: 1/SQS-4, -29, or -32
M: 2 sets GT; 2 props; 60,000 hp   **Electric:** 580 kw
Boilers: 4 Babcock & Wilcox, 43.3 kg/cm², 454°C   **Fuel:** 450 tons
Range: 1,260/30, 4,400/15   **Man:** 15 officers, 247 men

REMARKS: Transferred under Mutual Aid Agreement: D 29 and D 30 in 1961, D 33 in 1972. Four sisters discarded 1977-78. 6/76.2-mm DP removed from D 30. ASW armament and sonar to be deleted in the survivors, which are to be used as 200-nm Economic Zone patrol ships. Mk 37 GFCS for 127-mm, 3 Mk 5/mod. 1 GFCS for 40-mm.

FRIGATES

♦ **1 modified Mk 10 training frigate**

	Bldr	Laid down	L	In serv.
F . . . N . . .	Ast. Ilha das Cobras, Rio	7-81	. . .	. . .

D: 2,333 tons (3,345 fl)   **S:** 19 kts   **Dim:** 131.75 × 13.52 × 4.16 hull
A: 1/76-mm OTO Melara Compact—4/saluting cannon—1 helicopter
Electron Equipt: . . .
M: 2 diesels; 2 props; 8,000 hp
Range: 6,000/15   **Man:** . . .

REMARKS: Uses same hull as *Niteroi* group, but much simpler propulsion plant. To replace *Custódio de Mello* and may be considered an auxiliary on completion.

FRIGATES *(continued)*

♦ 6 British Vosper Thornycroft Mk 10 class

ASW:	Bldr	Laid down	L	In serv.
F 40 NITEROI	Thornycroft, Woolston	8-6-72	8-2-74	20-11-76
F 41 DEFENSORA	Thornycroft, Woolston	14-12-75	27-3-75	5-3-77
F 44 INDEPENDENCIA	Ast. Ilha das Cobras, Rio	11-6-72	2-9-74	3-9-79
F 45 UNIÃO	Ast. Ilha das Cobras, Rio	11-6-72	14-3-75	12-79
General-purpose:				
F 42 CONSTITUÇÃO	Thornycroft, Woolston	13-3-74	15-4-76	31-3-78
F 43 LIBERAL	Thornycroft, Woolston	2-5-75	7-2-77	18-11-78

Constitucão—general-purpose version   Vosper, 1979

D: 3,200 tons (3,800 fl)

S: 30.5 kts (28 cruising on gas turbines, 22 on diesels)

Dim: 129.24 (121.92 pp) × 13.52 × 4.20 (5.94 sonar)

A: ASW type: 1/114-mm Mk 8 Vickers automatic DP—2/40-mm Bofors AA (I × 2)—2/Sea Cat SAM systems (III × 2)—Branik ASW system—1/Bofors 375-mm, twin-barrel ASW system—6/324-mm Mk 32 ASW TT (III × 2)—1/Lynx WG 13 helicopter—1/d.c. rack (5 charges)

General-purpose type: similar but without the Branik system and with a second 114-mm Mk 8 aft and 4 launchers (II × 2) for the MM 38 Exocet SSM system

Electron Equipt: Radars: 1/Plessey AWS-2 with Mk 10 IFF (air search), 1/HSA ZW-06 with RRA, 2/Selenia RTN-10 X fire-control—1/Ikara tracker (not in F 42, 43)

    Sonars: 1/EDO 610 E; ASW ships also have 1/EDO 700 E VDS

M: CODAG: 2 Rolls-Royce Olympus TM3B gas turbines, 28,000 hp each; 4 MTU 16V 956 TB 91 diesels, 3,940 hp each; 2 Escher-Wyss CP props; 56,000 hp max.

Endurance: 45 days   **Electric:** 4,500 kw   **Man:** 21 officers, 180 men

Constitucão (F 42)   Vosper, 1977

REMARKS: Ordered 20-9-70. Fitted with retractable fin stabilizers. Branik is the name of the system devised for handling the Australian Ikara ASW missile in these ships. All have CAAIS action data system (Ferranti 1600B computers) and are equipped with Decca ECM gear. The Brazilian-built units experienced considerable delays in fitting out.

Niteroi—ASW version   Vosper, 1976   **Niteroi (F 40)**   Vosper, 1976

CORVETTES

♦ **12 new-construction program** Bldr: Ast. Ilha das Cobras, Rio

D: 1,600 tons (fl) **S:** 25 kts **Dim:** 88.0 × 11.3 × 3.3
A: proposed: 8/MM 40 Exocet SSM (IV × 2)—1/76-mm DP OTO Melara—1/40-
mm AA—6/324-mm ASW TT Mk 32 (IV × 2)—1/ASW helicopter
M: 4 diesels; 2 props; . . . hp **Range:** . . . **Man:** . . .

REMARKS: Italian design. To be laid down mid-1980s, with completions into 1990s. To
replace *Imperial Marinheiro* class.

♦ **10 Imperial Marinheiro class**

V 15 IMPERIAL MARINHEIRO (24-11-54)	V 20 ANGOSTURA (55)
V 16 IGUATEMI (54)	V 21 BAHIANA (11-54)
V 17 IPIRANGA (29-6-54)	V 22 MEARIM (8-54)
V 18 FORTE DE COIMBRA (11-6-54)	V 23 PURUS (6-11-54)
V 19 CABOCLO (28-8-54)	V 24 SOLIMÕES (24-11-54)

Imperial Marinheiro   1971

D: 911 tons **S:** 15 kts **Dim:** 55.72 × 9.55 × 4.6
A: 1/76.2-mm DP—4/20-mm AA (I × 4)
M: 2 Sulzer diesels; 2 props; 2,160 hp **Fuel:** 135 tons diesel **Man:** 60 tot.

REMARKS: Oceangoing tugs built in Holland. Were intended to be convertible for
minesweeping or minelaying. The V 15 is used as a submarine tender. Officially
designated "corvettes" and used in District patrols and in support of the 200-mile
economic zone.

♦ **3 U.S. Sotoyomo class**—former auxiliary ocean tugs Bldr: Gulfport Boiler &
Welding Works, Port Arthur, Texas

	Laid down	L	In serv.
R 21 TRITÃO (ex-ATA 234)	3-3-45	7-5-45	11-12-45
R 22 TRIDENTE (ex-ATA 235)	21-3-45	19-5-45	3-12-45
R 23 TRIUNFO (ex-ATA 236)	10-4-45	6-6-45	3-12-45

D: 570 tons (835 fl) **S:** 13 kts **Dim:** 43.59 (41.00 pp) × 10.31 × 4.01
A: 2/20-mm AA (I × 2)
M: 2 GM 12-278A diesels, electric drive; 1 prop; 1,500 hp
Electric: 120 kw **Fuel:** 171 tons
Range: 16,500/8 **Man:** 49 tot.

REMARKS: Purchased 16-3-47 (R 23: 22-4-47). Now used to patrol 200-nm economic
zone; armament possibly enhanced.

PATROL BOATS AND CRAFT

♦ **6 Piratini-class patrol boats** Bldr: Ast. Ilha das Cobras, Rio

P 10 PIRANTINI (ex-PGM 109)	30-11-70		P 13 PARATI (ex-PGM 119)	7-71
P 11 PIRAJÁ (ex-PGM 110)	1-71		P 14 PENEDO (ex-PGM 120)	9-71
P 12 PAMPEIRO (ex-PGM 118)	3-71		P 15 POTI (ex-PGM 121)	10-71

Parati   1972

D: 105 tons (fl) **S:** 18.0 kts (15.5 sust.) **Dim:** 28.95 × 6.1 × 1.55
A: 1/81-mm mortar with 12.7-mm mg atop—2/12.7-mm mg (I × 2)
M: 4 Cummins VT-12M diesels; 2 props; 1,100 hp
Electric: 40 kw **Range:** 1,000/15, 1,700/12 **Man:** 2 officers, 14 men

REMARKS: These patrol craft are based on the 95-foot WPBs of the U.S. Coast Guard.

♦ **10 or more U.S. Swift Mk I patrol craft**

R 61, R 62, R 63, R 64, etc.

D: 22.5 tons (fl) **S:** 22 kts **Dim:** 15.3 × 4.55 × 1.1 **A:** 1/12.7-mm mg
M: 2 GM 12V71 TI diesels; 2 props; 850 hp
Range: 400/22 **Man:** 6 tot.

REMARKS: Employed by naval police and port captains. Six ordered 16-1-81 from DM-
Commercio, Importacão & Maintencão de Producto Nauticas. Earlier units built in
U.S., transferred under AID program.

RIVER PATROL SHIPS

♦ **2 new-construction river patrol ships are planned, midway in size between
the Roraima and Pedro Teixeira classes**

♦ **4 Roraima class**—Amazon Flotilla

	Bldr	L	In serv.
P 30 RORAIMA	MacLaren, Niteroi	9-11-72	21-2-75
P 31 RONDÔNIA	MacLaren, Niteroi	10-1-73	3-12-75
P 32 AMAPA	MacLaren, Niteroi	9-3-73	1-76
P 33 N. . .	MacLaren, Niteroi	. . .	. . .

D: 340 tons (365 fl) **S:** 14.5 kts **Dim:** 45.0 × 8.45 × 1.37
A: 1/40-mm AA—6 12.7-mm mg (I × 6)—2/81-mm mortars
Electron Equipt: 3/navigational radars
M: 2 M.A.N. diesels; 2 props; 912 hp
Range: 6,000/11 **Man:** 9 officers, 54 men

REMARKS: In Amazon Flotilla. Carry one LCVP. Fourth unit laid down 1981.

RIVER PATROL SHIPS (continued)

♦ **2 Pedro Teixeira class**—Amazon Flotilla

	Bldr	L	In serv.
P 20 PEDRO TEIXEIRA	Ilha das Cobras, Rio	11-6-72	17-12-73
P 21 RAPOSO TAVARES	Ilha das Cobras, Rio	11-6-72	17-12-73

Raposo Tavares (P 21) 1975

Pedro Teixeira (P 20)—Note hangar offset to starboard 1973

D: 700 tons (fl) **S:** 16 kts **Dim:** 62.0 × 9.35 × 1.65
A: 1/40-mm AA—6/12.7-mm mg (I × 6)—2/81-mm mortars—1/SAH-11 helicopter
Electron Equipt: Radar: 2/navigational
M: 2 MEP-M.A.N. V6V diesels; 2 props; 3,840 hp
Range: 5,500/10 **Man:** . . .

♦ **1 old river monitor**—Mato Grosso Flotilla

	Bldr	Laid down	L	In serv.
U 17 PARNAIBA	Arsenal de Marinha, Rio	11-6-36	2-9-37	11-37

D: 620 tons (720 fl) **S:** 12 kts **Dim:** 55.0 × 10.1 × 1.6
A: 1/76.2-mm DP—2/47-mm—2/40-mm AA (I × 2)—6/20-mm AA (I × 6)
M: 2 sets triple-expansion reciprocating steam; 2 props; 1,300 hp
Boilers: 2/3-drum **Fuel:** 90 tons **Range:** 1,350/10 **Man:** 90 tot.

Parnaiba (U 17) 1976

MINE WARFARE SHIPS

♦ **6 German Schütze-class (Type 340a) patrol minesweepers**

Bldr: Abeking and Rasmussen, German Federal Republic

	L	In serv.		L	In serv.
M 15 ARATU	27-5-70	5-5-71	M 18 ARACATUBA	1971	13-12-72
M 16 ANHATOMIRIM	4-11-70	30-11-71	M 19 ABROLHOS	7-5-74	16-4-75
M 17 ATALAIA	14-4-71	13-12-72	M 20 ALBARDÃO	9-74	21-7-75

Anhatomirim 1972

D: 241 tons (280 fl) **S:** 24 kts **Dim:** 47.44 × 7.16 × 2.4 **A:** 1/40-mm AA
M: 4 Maybach diesels; 2 Escher-Wyss vertical cycloidal props; 4,500 hp
Electric: 120 kw plus 340 kw sweep generator **Fuel:** 22 tons
Range: 710/20 **Man:** 39 tot.

REMARKS: Four ordered 4-69, two 11-73. Fitted for magnetic, mechanical, and acoustic minesweeping. Wooden hulls. A new series of minesweepers is planned.

AMPHIBIOUS WARFARE SHIPS

♦ **1 U.S. Cabildo-class dock landing ship** Bldr: Boston NSY

	Laid down	L	In serv.
G. . . N. . . (ex-Donner, LSD 20)	3-1-45	28-4-45	30-7-45

D: 4,960 tons (9,375 fl) **S:** 15.6 kts **Dim:** 139.52 × 22.00 × 5.49
A: 12/40-mm AA (IV × 2, II × 2) **Radar:** 1/SPS-5
M: 2 sets GT; 2 props; 9,000 hp **Boilers:** 2/30.6 kg/cm², 393°C
Fuel: 1,758 tons **Range:** 8,000/15 **Man:** approx. 325 tot.

REMARKS: To be purchased 1981, along with *Rushmore* (LSD 14), the latter for spares. Modernized under FRAM-II program. Docking well, 119.5 × 13.4, can hold 3 LCU

AMPHIBIOUS WARFARE SHIPS *(continued)*

or 18 LCM(6) and has helicopter platform atop it. LSD 20 was stricken from U.S. Navy 27-4-71 and laid up by MARAD at James River, Va.

♦ **1 U.S. De Soto County-class tank landing ship** Bldr: Avondale, New Orleans

	L	In serv.
G 26 Duque de Caxias (ex-*Grant County*, LST 1174)	12-10-56	8-11-57

Duque de Caxias (G 26)   1975

D: 4,164 tons (7,800 fl)   **S:** 16 kts   **Dim:** 135.7 (129.8 wl) × 18.9 × 5.3
A: 2/76.2-mm DP (II × 1)   **Electron Equipt:** Radar: 1/SPS-21
M: 4 Nordberg diesels; 2 CP props; 13,700 hp
Electric: 900 kw   **Man:** 11 officers, 164 men

Remarks: Transferred 15-1-73; purchased 12-17-78. Can carry 700 men. Air-conditioned. Tank deck 88-m long. Four LCVP in davits; can carry four causeways (pontoon sections). Platform for helicopter. Stülcken 60-ton lift gear reported added forward in place of 4/76.2-mm. Mk 51 mod. 2 GFCS for guns.

♦ **1 U.S. LST 542-class tank landing ship** Bldr: Bethelem, Hingham, Mass.

	Laid down	L	In serv.
G 28 Garcia d'Avila (ex-*Outagamie County*, LST 1073)	20-2-45	22-3-45	17-4-45

Garcia D'Avila (G 28)   1972

D: 1,490 tons light (4,100 fl)   **S:** 11.6 kts   **Dim:** 100.0 × 15.25 × 4.29
A: 8/40-mm AA (II × 2, I × 4)
M: 2 GM 2-278A diesels; 2 props; 1,700 hp   **Electric:** 300 kw

Remarks: Loaned 25-5-71; purchased 1-12-73. Beaching displacement: 2,336 tons. Carries 2 LCVP.

♦ **3 (+1) U.S. LCU 1610-type landing craft** Bldr: Navy Yard, Rio, 1974-78

L 10 Guarapari	L 11 Timbau	L 12 Camboriu	L 13 Tramandai

Guarapari (L 10)   1978

D: 200 tons (396 fl)   **S:** 11 kts   **Dim:** 41.0 × 8.42 × 2.0
A: 3/12.7-mm mg. Typed EDCG-"Embarcaçao de Desembarque de Carga Generales"
M: 2 GM 12V71 diesels; 2 props; 1,000 hp   **Range:** 1,200/8

Remarks: L 13 remains unfinished. Can carry 172 tons cargo.

♦ **28 LCVP** Built in Japan, 1959-60

♦ **15 EDVP** Built in Brazil, 1971

Dim: 11.0 × 3.2 × 0.6 (fwd), 1.0 (aft)   **M:** Brazilian Scania diesel

Remarks: Hulls built of synthetic materials. Can carry 36 men with full pack or one jeep with trailer and 17 men or 1/105-mm howitzer or an anti-tank gun and 18 men.

HYDROGRAPHIC AND OCEANOGRAPHIC SHIPS

♦ **1 U.S. Robert D. Conrad-class oceanographic ship**
Bldr: Marietta Co., Pt. Pleasant, West Virginia

H 41 Almirante Camara (ex-*Sands*, T-AGOR 6)

D: 1,020 tons (1,370 fl)   **S:** 13.5 kts
Dim: 70.0 (63.7 pp) × 11.28 × 6.3 (fl)
Electron Equipt: Radar: 1/RCA CRM-N1A-75
M: 2 Caterpillar D-378 diesels, electric drive; 1 prop; 1,000 hp
Electric: 850 kw (plus 620 kw)   **Fuel:** 211 tons   **Range:** 12,000/12
Man: 8 officers, 18 men, 15 oceanographers

Remarks: Loaned 1-7-74. An auxiliary 620 hp gas turbine powers a small electric maneuvering propeller for stationkeeping purposes at extremely low rpm; also has bow-thruster. Has echo-sounders capable of measuring 11,000-meter depths.

♦ **2 Sirius class**

	Bldr	Laid down	L	In serv.
H 21 Sirius	Ishikawajima	12-56	30-7-57	1-1-58
H 22 Canopus	Ishikawajima	12-56	20-11-57	15-3-58

D: 1,463 tons (1,800 fl)   **S:** 15 kts   **Dim:** 77.9 × 12.03 × 3.7
M: 2 Sulzer diesels; 2 CP props; 2,700 hp   **Range:** 12,000/11
Man: 102 tot.

Remarks: 1 SAH-11 helicopter, 1 LCVP, 3 small survey craft. Fully equipped. Armament removed.

HYDROGRAPHIC AND OCEANOGRAPHIC SHIPS *(continued)*

Almirante Camara (H 41)   1974

Canopus

♦ **6 wooden-hulled hydrographic boats**—Amazon Flotilla
Bldr: Bormann, Rio de Janeiro

	In serv.
H 11 PARAIBANO	10-68
H 12 RIO BRANCO	10-68
H 14 NOGUEIRA DA GAMA (ex-*Jaceguai*)	3-71
H 15 ITACURUSSA	3-71
H 16 CAMOCIM	1971
H 17 CARAVELAS	1971

D: 32 tons (50 fl)   **S:** 11 kts   **Dim:** 16.0 × 4.6 × 1.3
M: 1 GM 6-71 diesel; 165 hp   **Range:** 600/11   **Man:** 2 officers, 9 men

REMARKS: In Amazon Flotilla.

Nogueira da Gama   1971

♦ **1 former sail-training ship**

	Bldr	L	In serv.
H 10 ALMIRANTE SALDANHA	Vickers, Barrow	19-12-33	6-34

Almirante Saldanha (H 10)   1975

REMARKS: Former 4-masted schooner, refit completed in 7-61 as an oceanographic research ship and for training. Refitted again for zooplankton research, completed 6-80; received NAVSAT and Omega navigation systems, new current and salinity meter systems.

♦ **3 Argus-class coastal survey ships**

	Bldr	L	In serv.
H 31 ARGUS	Ars. de Marinha, Rio	6-12-57	29-1-59
H 32 ORION	Ars. de Marinha, Rio	5-2-58	11-6-59
H 33 TAURUS	Ars. de Marinha, Rio	7-1-58	23-4-59

Orion (H 32)

HYDROGRAPHIC AND OCEANOGRAPHIC SHIPS *(continued)*

D: 250 tons (300 fl) **S:** 17 kts (15 cruising)
Dim: 44.8 (42.06 pp) × 6.1 × 2.45 **M:** 2 Caterpillar diesels; 2 props; 1,200 hp
Fuel: 35 tons **Range:** 1,200/15 **Man:** 42 tot.

REMARKS: Based on the Portuguese *Azevia*-class gunboat. H 32 modernized in 1973/
74, with new propulsion machinery, auxiliaries, and electronic equipment. Armament
removed.

♦ **1 fisheries research oceanographic ship** Bldr: INACE, Fortaleza

H. . . SUBOFICIAL OLIVEIRA (In serv. 22-5-81)

D: 120 tons **S:** . . . kts **Dim:** 22.0 × . . . × . . . **M:** diesels **Man:** 8 tot.

REMARKS: For use by the Naval Research Institute in "Capo Frio Project" for shrimp
cultivation. Two more may be built.

AUXILIARY SHIPS

♦ **4 transports**

	Bldr	Laid down	L	In serv.
U 26 CUSTÓDIO DE MELLO	Ishikawajima, Tokyo	12-53	10-6-54	1-12-54
G 16 BARROSO PEREIRA	Ishikawajima, Tokyo	12-53	7-8-54	1-12-54
G 21 ARY PARREIRAS	Ishikawajima, Tokyo	12-55	24-8-56	29-12-56
G 22 SOARES DUTRA	Ishikawajima, Tokyo	12-55	13-12-56	23-3-57

Custódio de Mello   G. Gyssels, 1981.

D: 4,800 tons (8,600 fl) **S:** 16 kts **Dim:** 119.2 (110.4 pp) × 16.0 × 6.1
A: 2/76-mm DP (I × 2)—2/20-mm AA (I × 2)—U 26: 4/76.2-mm DP (I × 4)
M: GT; 2 props; 4,800 hp **Boilers:** 2
Man: 118 tot. Can carry 1,972 troops (497 normal)

REMARKS: 4,200 dwt/4,879 grt. Living spaces mechanically ventilated and partially
air-conditioned. *Custódio de Mello* used as training ship. Others have a helicopter
platform aft, can carry 497 troops, and are occasionally used in commercial service;
all have 425m³ refrigerated cargo space.

♦ **1 U.S. Aristaeus-class small repair ship** Bldr: Maryland DD, Baltimore

	Laid down	L	In serv.
G 24 BELMONTE (ex-*Helios*, ARB 12, ex-LST 1127)	23-11-44	14-2-45	26-2-45

D: 2,030 tons (4,100 fl) **S:** 9 kts **Dim:** 100.0 (96.3 wl) × 15.25 × 3.36
A: 8/40-mm AA (IV × 2)

Belmonte (G 24)

M: 2 GM 12-567A diesels; 2 props; 1,800 hp **Electric:** 600 kw
Fuel: 584 tons **Range:** 6,000/9

REMARKS: Loaned 1-62; purchased 28-12-57. 1/60-ton winch crane, 2/10-ton booms.
Used mainly as a transport.

♦ **1 fleet replenishment oiler** Bldr: Ishikawajima do Brasil, Rio

	Laid down	L	In serv.
G 27 MARAJO	13-12-66	31-1-68	22-10-68

Marajo (G 27)   1977

D: 13,000 tons (fl) **S:** 13.6 kts **Dim:** 137.1 (127.69 pp) × 19.22 × 7.35
M: 1 Sulzer diesel; 8,000 hp **Cargo capacity:** 7,200 tons
Range: 9,200/14.5 **Man:** 80 tot.

REMARKS: 10,500 dwt. Two liquid replenishment stations per side.

♦ **1 river oiler**

G 17 POTENGI Bldr: Papendrecht, Holland (L: 16-3-38)

D: 600 tons (fl) **S:** 10 kts **Dim:** 54.0 × 7.2 × 1.8
M: 1 diesel; 550 hp **Cargo capacity:** 450 tons

REMARKS: In Mato Grosso Flotilla.

♦ **1 U.S. Penguin-class submarine rescue ship**

	Bldr	Laid down	L	In serv.
K 10 GASTÃO MOUTINHO (ex-*Skylark*, ASR 20; ex-*Yustaga*, ATF 165)	Charleston SB&DD	23-7-45	19-3-46	19-7-46

AUXILIARY SHIPS (continued)

Gastão Moutinho (K 10)

D: 1,780 tons (2,140 fl)   **S:** 14.5 kts
Dim: 62.48 (59.44 wl) × 11.96 × 4.72   **A:** 2/20-mm AA (I × 2)
Radar: 1/SPS-5   **M:** 4 GM 12-278A diesels; electric drive; 1 prop; 3,000 hp
Electric: 400 kw   **Fuel:** 301 tons   **Range:** 15,000/8

REMARKS: Begun as an *Achomawi*-class fleet tug. Purchased 30-6-73. Has rescue bell, salvage equipment, pumps, 4 pontoons, etc. Often employed as a hydrographic survey ship and as a diving tender.

♦ **2 U.S. 136-ft. YMS-class Social Action ships, former minesweepers**

	Laid down	L	In serv.
U 18 JAVARI (ex-M 11, ex-*Cardinal*, MSCO 4, ex-YMS 179)	27-10-42	8-5-43	24-8-43
U 19 JURUA (ex-M 13, ex-*Jackdaw*, MSCO 21, ex-YMS 373)	28-12-42	29-1-44	28-4-44

Bldrs: U 18: Henry C. Grebe, Chicago; U 19: Weaver SY, Orange, Texas

D: 270 tons (320 fl)   **S:** 15 kts   **Dim:** 41.45 (39.62 wl) × 7.47 × 3.05   **A:** . . .
M: 2 GM 8-268A diesels; 2 props; 1,000 hp
Fuel: 18 tons   **Electric:** 180kw   **Range:** 2,400/10.8   **Man:** 33 tot.

REMARKS: Transferred 8-60 and 1-63, respectively. Home-ported at Aratu and used to carry medical and dental services to outlying areas. Wooden construction; all minesweeping equipment deleted. Last operational units of some 560 built.

♦ **2 oceangoing tugs** Bldr: Sumitomo Heavy Industries, Japan

R 24 ALMIRANTE GUILHEM (ex-. . .)
R 25 ALMIRANTE GUILLOBEL (ex-. . .)

D: 2,400 tons (fl)   **S:** 14 kts   **Dim:** 63.15 × 13.40 × 4.50   **A:** . . .
M: 2 GM 20-645 ET diesels; 2 CP props; 7,200 hp   **Electric:** 550 kw
Man: 40 tot.

REMARKS: Purchased 1980 from Superpesa Maritime Transport, Ltd.

NOTE: Three U.S. *Sotoyomo*-class tugs are now used as patrol ships.

♦ **1 lighthouse and buoy tender**

	Bldr	Laid down	L	In serv.
H 34 GRAÇA ARANHA	Elbin, Niteroi	end 1970	23-6-74	9-9-76

Graça Aranha   1976

D: 1,253 tons (2,300 fl)   **S:** 13 kts   **Dim:** 75.57 × 13.0 × 3.71
M: Diesel; 1 CP prop; 2,000 hp; 1 bow-thruster   **Man:** 101 tot.

REMARKS: Telescoping helicopter hangar for one SAH-11. Two LCVP carried as supply lighters.

YARD AND SERVICE CRAFT

♦ **1 large yard tug**

R 14 LAURINDO PITTA   Bldr: Vickers, 1910, rebuilt 1969

D: 514 tons   **Dim:** 39.04 × 7.77 × 3.35 (aft)

♦ **6 yard tugs** Bldr: Holland Nautic Yard. In serv. 1953

R 31 AUDAZ	R 33 GUARANI	R 35 PASSO DE PATRIA
R 32 CENTAURO	R 34 LAMEGO	R 36 VOLUNTARIO

D: 130 tons   **S:** 11 kts   **Dim:** 27.6 × 7.2 × 3.1
M: 1 Womag diesel; 765 hp   **Man:** 12 tot.

♦ **3 Isaias de Noronha-class tugs** (1972-74)

R. . . ISAIAS DE NORONHA	R. . . D.N.O.G.
R. . . TENIENTE LAHMEYER	

D: 200 tons (fl)   **Dim:** 47.0 ×. . . ×. . .

♦ **1 personnel and stores transport** Bldr: Embrasa, Itajai, Santa Catarina (L: 29-8-74)

R 47 SARGENTO BORGES

D: 108.5 tons   **S:** 10 kts   **Dim:** 28.0 × 6.5 × 1.5
M: 2 diesels; 2 props; 480 hp   **Cargo:** 106 passengers   **Range:** 400/10

♦ **4 Rio Pardo-class harbor passenger ferries** Bldr: Inconav Niteroi Shipbuilders (In serv. 1975-76)

U 40 RIO PARDO	U 42 RIO CHUI
U 41 RIO NEGRO	U 43 RIO OIAPOQUE

D: 150 tons   **S:** 14 kts   **Dim:** 35.38 × 6.5 × 1.9
M: 2 diesels; 2 props; 548 hp   **Cargo:** 600 passengers

BRAZIL *(continued)*
YARD AND SERVICE CRAFT*(continued)*

♦ **6 Rio Doce-class river transports** Bldr: The Netherlands, 1956

U 20 Rio Doce	U 22 Rio Formoso	U 24 Rio Turvo
U 21 Rio Das Contas	U 23 Rio Real	U 25 Rio Verde

D: 150 tons **S:** 14 kts **Dim:** 35.0 × 6.0 × 2.1
M: 2 Sulzer diesels; 2 props; 450 hp **Cargo:** 600 passenters

♦ **7 Anchova-class personnel launches** Bldr: Brazil (1965-67)

R 54 Anchova	R 55 Arenque	R 56 Atum	R 57 Acará
R 58 Agulha	R 59 Aruana	R 60 Argentina	

D: 11 tons (13 fl) **S:** 25 kts **Dim:** 13.0 × 3.8 × 1.2
M: 2 diesels; 280 hp **Cargo:** 12 passengers **Range:** 400/20 **Man:** 3 tot.

♦ **1 command transport ship**

G 15 Paraguassu (ex-*Guarapuava*)

D: 285 tons **S:** 12 kts **Dim:** 40.0 × 7.0 × 1.2
M: Diesel; 1 prop **Range:** 2,500/10

REMARKS: Former river transport ship, bought in 1971, refitted for the Mato Grosso Flotilla, and used as a river buoy tender and flagship.

♦ **2 small service transports**

Tenente Fabio   Tenente Raul

D: 55 tons **S:** 10 kts **Dim:** 20.28 × 5.1 × 1.2 **M:** Diesel; 135 hp
Cargo capacity: 22 tons **Range:** 350

♦ **5 munitions lighters**

São Francisco Dos Santos (1964), Ubirajara Dos Santos (1968), Operatio Luis Leal (1968), Miguel Dos Santos (1968), Aprendiz Lédio Conceição (1968)

REMARKS: Last two for torpedoes.

♦ **1 yard oiler (purchased 1973)**

R 11 Martins De Oliviera (ex-*Gastão Moutinho*)

D: 588 tons **S:** 10.3 kts **Dim:** 49.4 × 7.0 × 2.4

♦ **1 yard oiler:** Anita Garibaldi—no data

♦ **2 water tankers** (L: 1957)

R 43 Paulo Afonso   R 42 Itapura

D: 485.3 tons **Dim:** 42.8 × 7.0 × 2.5 **M:** 1 diesel **Cargo:** 389 tons

♦ **8 (+3) 130-ton buoy-maintenance ships**

H 13 Mestro Joao Dos Santos	H 30 Faroleiro Nascimento
H 24 Castelhanos	H. . . Cabo Branco
H 27 Faroleiro Areas	H. . . Cabo Callanhar
H 28 Faroleiro Santana	H. . . Cabo Frio

REMARKS: Three additional ordered from Sao João de Nilo SY, Tavares Coutino in 7-80 for delivery 6 through 10-82.

♦ **2 hospital launches for Amazon Flotilla** (Laid down 1981)

♦ **3 Aspirante Nascimento-class training craft** Bldr: Embrassa Itajai, Santa Catarina (In serv. 1981)

U 10 Aspirante Nascimento   U 11 Guarda Marinha Jansen
U 12 Guardia Marinha Brito

D: 130 tons (fl) **S:** . . . **Dim:** . . . × . . . × . . .
A: 2/12.7-mm mg (I × 2) **M:** 2 diesels; 2 props; . . . hp

REMARKS: Used for navigation and seamanship training at the Naval Academy.

FLOATING DRY DOCKS

♦ **1 U.S. AFDL 34 class** Bldr: V.P. Loftis (In serv. 10-44)

G 27 Cidade De Natal (ex-U.S. AFDL 39, ex-ARDC 6)

Lift capacity: 2,800 tons **Dim:** 118.6 × 25.6 × 2.84 (light)

REMARKS: Loaned 10-11-66; purchased 28-12-77. Concrete construction. 17.7-m clear width inside, 105.2-m length on blocks.

♦ **1 U.S. AFDL 1 class** Bldr: Chicago Bridge & Iron, Cal. (In serv. 12-43)

G 26 Almirante Jeronimo Goncalves (ex-*Goiaz*, ex-AFDL 4, ex-AFD 4)

Lift capacity: 1,000 tons **Dim:** 60.96 × 19.51 × 1.04 (light)

REMARKS: Loaned 10-11-66; purchased 28-7-77. Steel construction. 13.7-m clear width inside, 56.4-m length on blocks.

♦ **1 U.S. ARD 12 class** Bldr: Pacific Bridge, Alameda, Cal. (In serv. 11-43)

G 25 Afonso Pena (ex-*Ceara*, ex-ARD 14)

Lift capacity: 3,500 tons **Dim:** 149.86 × 24.69 × 1.73 (light)

REMARKS: Loaned 1963; purchased 28-12-77. Steel construction, pointed ship-type bow. 18.0-m clear with inside, 118.6-m length on blocks.

♦ **1 U.S. dry-dock companion craft** Bldr: Bushell Lyons Ironwks, Tampa, Fla. (In serv. 22-3-45)

. . . (ex-YFN 903)

D: 170 tons (590 fl) **Dim:** 33.53 × 10.36 × 2.74

REMARKS: Converted non-self-propelled cargo barge. Loaned 1963; purchased 28-12-77.

BRUNEI
State of Brunei (British Protected States)

PERSONNEL: (1980): 333 (including 32 officers), plus "Special Boat Squadron" of 91 (including 4 officers) for river duties

MERCHANT MARINE (1980): 2 ships—899 grt

♦ **3 guided-missile patrol boats** Bldr: Vosper Thornycroft, Singapore

	L	In serv.
P 02 WASPADA	3-8-77	7-78
P 03 PEJUANG	3-78	1979
P 04 SETERIA	22-6-78	1979

Waspada (P 02)   G. Arra, 1980

D: 150 tons (fl) **S:** 32 kts **Dim:** 36.88 (33.53 pp) × 7.16 × 1.8
A: 2/MM 38 Exocet SSM—2/30-mm AA (II × 1)—2/7.62-mm mg
Electron Equipt: Radar: Decca AC 1229
M: 2 MTU 20V538 TB91 diesels; 2 props; 9,000 hp (7,500 sust.)
Fuel: 16 tons **Range:** 1,200/14 **Man:** 4 officers, 20 men

REMARKS: P 02 has enclosed upper bridge (open on other two) and facilities for training. All have Sperry Sea Archer fire control and two 50-mm rocket-flare launchers. The 30-mm mount is BMARC/Oerlikon GCM-BOI.

♦ **3 patrol craft** Bldr: Vosper, Singapore

N. . .   N. . .   N. . .

D: 35 tons (fl) **S:** 25 kts **Dim:** 25.24 × 5.8 × 1.60
A: 2/20-mm AA (II × 1)—2/7.62-mm mg
M: 2 diesels; 2 CP props; 3,072 hp (plus 1/200-hp cruise diesel, 8 kts)
Man: 5 officers, 8 men

REMARKS: Built on speculation 1979, purchased 1980. Steel hull, aluminum superstructure. Replace *Masna* (P 11), *Saleha* (P 12), and *Norain* (P 13), discarded 1978-79.

♦ **3 Periwa-class patrol craft**

	Bldr	L	In serv.
P 14 PERIWA	Vosper, Singapore	5-74	9-9-74
P 15 PEMBURU	Vosper, Singapore	30-1-75	17-6-75
P 16 PENYARANG	Vosper, Singapore	20-3-75	24-6-75

Periwa (P 14)   1974

D: 30 tons (38.5 fl) **S:** 32 kts **Dim:** 21.7 × 6.1 × 1.2
A: 2/20-mm AA (I × 2)—2/7.62-mm mg
Electron Equipt: Radar: Decca RM 916 (P 14, 15: Decca 1216A)
M: 2 MTU 12V331 TC 81 diesels; 2,700 hp **Range:** 600/20, 1,000/16

♦ **3 Bendahara-class river patrol craft**

P 21 BENDAHARA   P 23 KEMAINDERA   P 22 MAHARAJALELA

D: 10 tons (fl) **S:** 20 kts **Dim:** 14.1 × 3.6 × 0.9
A: 2/7.62-mm mg **Electron Equipt:** Radar: Decca RM 616
M: 2 6-71 GM diesels; 334 hp **Range:** 200/18 **Man:** 6 tot.

♦ **2 Loadmaster-class landing craft** Bldr: Cheverton, Isle of Wight, G.B.

L 31 DAMUAN (5-76) L 32 PUNI (2-77)

D: 64.3 tons (light) **S:** 8.5 kts **Dim:** 22.86 × 6.1 × 1.07
Electron Equipt: Radar: Decca RM 1216
M: 2 GM 6-71 diesels; 2 props; 348 hp **Cargo:** 30 tons
Range: 300/8.5, 1,000/6 **Man:** 8 tot.

REMARKS: L 31: 19.8-m overall, 60-tons light.

♦ **25 small armed river craft**
A: 1/7.62-mm mg **M:** 100 hp

MARINE POLICE

♦ **4 patrol craft** Bldr: Vosper Thornycroft, Singapore, 1978-80

TENANG   ABADI   N. . .   N. . .

D: 14 tons (fl) **S:** 28 kts **Dim:** 18.0 × 4.88 × 0.79 **A:** Machine guns
M: 2 MTU diesels; 2 water jets

REMARKS: Glass-reinforced plastic hulls. The second pair was ordered early in 1979.

BULGARIA
People's Republic of Bulgaria

PERSONNEL: approx. 4,000 men

MERCHANT MARINE (1980): 192 ships—1,233,303 grt (tankers: 22—352,435 grt)

NAVAL AVIATION: 6 Soviet Mi-4 Hound and 2 Mi-2 helicopters

SUBMARINES

♦ 2 Soviet Romeo class

SLAVA   POBIEDA

D: 1,330/1,700 tons **S:** 15/13 kts **Dim:** 77.0 × 6.7 × 5.0
A: 8/533-mm TT (6 fwd, 2 aft)—14 torpedoes or 24 mines
Electron Equipt: Radar: Snoop Plate **Endurance:** 60 days
M: 2/2,000-hp diesels; electric drive; 3,000 hp **Range:** 14,000/9 surf.

REMARKS: Transferred 1971-72. Replaced two Whiskey class with same names. Can dive to 300 meters.

FRIGATES

♦ 2 Soviet Riga class

DRUZKIY   SMELY

D: 1,000 tons (1,450 fl) **S:** 28 kts **Dim:** 91.0 × 11.0 × 3.4
A: 3/100-mm DP—3/533-mm TT—2/RBU-1200 ASW RL (V × 2)—1/MBU-600 Hedgehog
Electron Equipt: Radars: 1/Slim Net, 1/Neptune, 1/Sun Visor—IFF: 2/Square Head, 1/High Pole—Sonar: 1/MF hull-mounted
M: 2 sets GT; 2 props; 20,000 hp; **Boilers:** 2

REMARKS: Transferred 1957-58.

CORVETTES

♦ 3 Soviet Poti class—Transferred 12-75 (In serv. 1961-68)

D: 500 tons (fl) **S:** 34 kts **Dim:** 60.3 × 8.0 × 3.0
A: 2/57-mm AA (II × 1)—2/RBU-6000 rocket launchers—2/533-mm ASW TT
Electron Equipt: Radars: 1/Spin Trough, 1/Strut Curve, 1/Muff Cob
  IFF: 2/Square Head, 1/High Pole B
  Sonar: 1 high frequency
M: CODAG: 2/M-503A diesels of 4,000 hp each plus 2 gas turbines of 20,000 hp each; 2 props

PATROL BOATS

♦ 6 Soviet SO-1 class—Transferred 1963

41 42 43 44 45 46

D: 190 tons (215 fl) **S:** 28 kts **Dim:** 42.0 × 6.1 × 1.9
A: 4/25-mm AA (II × 2)—4/RBU-1200 ASW RL (V × 4)—2/d.c. rack—mines
Electron Equipt: Radar: 1/Pot Head—IFF: 1/Dead Duck, 1/High Pole
M: 3/40D diesels; 3 props; 7,500 hp

GUIDED-MISSILE PATROL AND TORPEDO BOATS

♦ 1 Soviet Osa-II-class patrol boat—Transferred 1978

20

D: 240 tons (fl) **S:** 36 kts **Dim:** 39.0 × 7.7 × 1.9
A: 4/SS-N-2 Styx—4/30-mm AA (II × 2)
Electron Equipt: Radars: 1/Square Tie, 1/Drum Tilt—IFF: 2/Square Head, 1/High Pole B
M: 3/M-504 diesels; 3 props; 15,000 hp **Range:** 800/25

♦ 3 Soviet Osa-I-class patrol boats—Transferred 1970-71.

21 22 23

D: 175 tons (210 fl) **S:** 36 kts **Dim:** 39.0 × 7.7 × 1.8
A: 4/SS-N-2 Styx—4/30-mm (II × 2)
Electron Equipt: Radars: 1/Square Tie, 1/Drum Tilt—IFF: 2/Square Head, 1/High Pole B
M: 2/M-503A diesels; 3 props; 12,000 hp **Range:** 800/25

♦ 6 Soviet Shershen-class torpedo boats—Transferred 1970

25 26 27 28 29 30

D: 150 tons (180 fl) **S:** 45 kts **Dim:** 34.0 × 7.2 × 1.5
A: 4/533-mm TT—4/30-mm AA (II × 2)
Electron Equipt: Radars: 1/Plot Drum, 1/Drum Tilt
M: 3/M-503A diesels; 3 props; 12,000 hp

MINE WARFARE SHIPS

♦ 4 Soviet Vanya-class minesweepers—Transferred 1971-72

36 37 38 39

D: 220 tons (245 fl) **S:** 18 kts **Dim:** 40.0 × 7.6 × 1.8
A: 2/30-mm AA (II × 1)
Electron Equipt: Radar: 1/Don-2—IFF: 1/Square Head, 1 High Pole B
M: 2 diesels; 2 props; 2,200 hp

♦ 2 Soviet T-43-class minesweepers

48 VUKOV KLANAC 49 N. . .

D: 500 tons (580 fl) **S:** 14 kts **Dim:** 58.0 × 8.4 × 2.3
A: 4/37-mm AA (II × 2)—8/14.5-mm AA (II × 4)—mines
Electron Equipt: Radars: 1/Ball End, 1/Neptune
  IFF: 1/Square Head, 1/High Pole A
M: 2/9D diesels; 2 props; 2,200 hp

REMARKS: Transferred 1953. The two Bulgarian T 43s are early versions of the class with flush bridge faces. They are the only known units of that configuration with tripod, rather than pole, masts.

♦ 1 or more Soviet Yevgenya-class inshore minesweeper—Transferred 1977-

D: 80 tons (90 fl) **S:** 12 kts **Dim:** 26.0 × 6.0 × 1.5
A: 2/14.5-mm AA (II × 1)
Electron Equipt: Radar: 1/Spin Trough
  IFF: 1/High Pole B
M: 2 diesels; 2 props; 600 hp **Man:** 12 tot.

BULGARIA (*continued*)
MINE WARFARE SHIPS (*continued*)

REMARKS: Plastic hull. Equipped with towed television minehunting and marking system effective to 30-meter depths. Probably replaced PO 2 class.

AMPHIBIOUS WARFARE SHIPS

♦ **18 Soviet Vydra-class landing craft**—Transferred 1970-79

D: 425 tons (600 fl) **S:** 11 kts **Dim:** 54.8 × 8.1 × 2.0
Electron Equipt: Radar: 1/Spin Trough **M:** 2 diesels; 2 props; 800 hp

♦ **10 German MFP-D3 class landing craft** Bldr: Bulgaria (1954)

D: 240 tons (410 fl) **S:** 10.3 kts **Dim:** 49.8 × 8.6 × 1.6
A: mg—mines **M:** 3 diesels; 3 props; 600 hp **Range:** 500/9 **Man:** 25 tot.

REMARKS: Patterned on German World War II design. Mine rails on sponson; waterline beam 6.6-m.

AUXILIARIES AND SERVICE CRAFT

♦ **1 "Mesar"-class replenishment oiler** Bldr: Bulgaria (1980)

ANLENE

D: 3,500 (fl) **S:** 20 kts **Dim:** 97.5 × 13.0 × 5.0
A: 4/30-mm AA (II × 2) **M:** 2 diesels; 2 props; . . . hp

REMARKS: Deployed to Mediterranean 1980 with the two Rigas. Over-the-stern underway refueling; also has dry stores cargo.

♦ **1 Soviet Moma-class survey ship/buoy tender** Bldr: Poland (1977)

617

D: 1,260 tons (1,540 fl) **S:** 17 kts **Dim:** 73.3 × 10.8 × 3.8
Electron Equipt: Radar: 2/Don-2
    IFF: 1/High Pole A
M: 2 Sgoda-Sulzer 6 TD 48 diesels; 2 CP props; 3,600 hp
Endurance: 35 days **Range:** 8,700/11 **Man:** 56 tot.

♦ **1 East German Type-700 salvage tug**—Transferred 1964

332 JUPITER—1,800 tons (fl)—12 kts

♦ **2 inshore survey craft:** VLADIMIR ZAIMOU, N. . . (1959)

♦ **2 small degaussing tenders**

♦ **3 yard oilers**

♦ **6 small tugs**

♦ **2 diving tenders**

♦ **6 barracks barges**

BURMA
The Socialist Republic of the Union of Burma

PERSONNEL: approx. 7,000, including reserves and naval infantry

MERCHANT MARINE (1980): 90 ships—87,519 grt (tankers: 13—7,256 grt)

CORVETTES

♦ **1 U.S. PCE 827 class** Bldr: Willamette Iron & Steel, Portland, Ore.

	Laid down	L	In serv.
41 YAN TAING AUNG (ex-*Farmington*, PCE 894)	7-12-42	15-5-43	10-8-44

D: 640 tons (903 fl) **S:** 15 kts **Dim:** 56.24 (54.86 wl) × 10.08 × 2.87 (hull)
A: 1/76.2-mm DP Mk 26—6/40-mm AA (II × 3)—8/20-mm AA (II × 4)—1/Mk
    10 Hedgehog—2/Mk 6 d.c. launcher—2/d.c. rack
Electron Equipt: Radar: 1/SPS-5
    Sonar: 1/QCU-2
M: 2 GM 12-567A diesels; 2 props; 1,800 hp **Electric:** 240 kw
Fuel: 125 tons **Range:** 9,000/10 **Man:** 100 tot.

REMARKS: Transferred 18-6-55.

♦ **1 U.S. Admirable-class former fleet minesweeper** Bldr: Willamette Iron & Steel, Portland, Ore.

	Laid down	L	In serv.
42 YAN GYI AUNG (ex-*Creddock*, MSF 356)	10-11-43	22-7-44	18-12-45

D: 650 tons (905 fl) **S:** 14 kts **Dim:** 56.24 (54.86) × 10.08 × 2.87 (hull)
A: 1/76.2-mm DP Mk 26—2/40-mm AA (II × 1)—4/20-mm AA (II × 2)—1/Mk
    10 Hedgehog—2/Mk 6 d.c. launcher—2/d.c. rack
Electron Equipt: Radar: 1/SPS-5
    Sonar: QCU-2
M: 2 Busch-Sulzer Type 539 diesels; 2 props; 1,710 hp
Electric: 280 kw **Fuel:** 140 tons **Range:** 9,300/10 **Man:** 100 tot.

REMARKS: Minesweeping gear removed prior to transfer 21-3-67.

PATROL BOATS

♦ **6 U.S. PGM 43 class** Bldrs: 401-404: Marinette Marine, Marinette, Wisc.
    405, 406: Peterson Bldrs, Sturgeon Bay, Wisc.

	In serv.		In serv.
401 (ex-PGM 43)	8-59	404 (ex-PGM 46)	9-59
402 (ex-PGM 44)	8-59	405 (ex-PGM 51)	6-61
403 (ex-PGM 45)	9-59	406 (ex-PGM 52)	6-61

D: 100 tons (141 fl) **S:** 17 kts **Dim:** 30.81 × 6.45 × 2.30
A: 1/40-mm AA—4/20-mm AA (II × 2)—2 machine guns

PATROL BOATS *(continued)*

Electron Equipt: Radar: EDO 320 (405, 406: Raytheon 1500)
M: 8 GM 6-71 diesels; 2 props; 2,040 hp   **Fuel:** 16 tons
Range: 1,000/16   **Man:** 17 tot.

♦ **7 U.S. Coast Guard 83-ft. class** Bldr: Rangoon DY (1960-61)

101   102   103   105   106   108   110

D: 49 tons (66 fl)   **S:** 11 kts   **Dim:** 25.0 × 4.85 × 1.6
A: 1/40-mm AA—1/20-mm AA   **M:** 4 GM diesels; 2 props; 800 hp   **Man:** 16 tot.

REMARKS: U.S.C.G. engines from former boats with new hulls, built in Burma, 1960-61. Three or more may have been lost or discarded.

RIVERINE PATROL VESSELS

♦ **2 improved 301 class** Bldr: Similak, Burma, 1967

Y 311   Y 312

D: 250 tons   **S:** 14 kts   **Dim:** 37.0 × 7.3 × 1.1
A: 2/40-mm AA (I × 2)—2/20-mm AA (I × 2)
M: 2 Mercedes-Benz diesels; 2 props; 1,000 hp

♦ **2 Nawarat class** Bldr: Dawbon DY, Rangoon, 1961

NAWARAT   NAGAKYAY

Nawarat

D: 400 tons (450 fl)   **S:** 12 kts   **Dim:** 49.7 × 8.23 × . . .
A: 2/25-pounder guns (Army ordnance)—2/40-mm AA
M: 2 Paxman-Ricardo diesels; 2 props; 1,160 hp   **Man:** 43 tot.

♦ **10 Y 301 class** Bldr: Uljanik, Pula, Yugoslavia, 1957-60

Y 301 to Y 310

Y 301 class

D: 120 tons   **S:** 13 kts   **Dim:** 32.0 × 7.25 × 0.8
A: 2/40-mm AA—2/20-mm AA
M: 2 Mercedes-Benz diesels; 2 props; 1,100 hp   **Man:** 29 tot.

AUXILIARIES

♦ **8 river transports**

SABAN	SEINDA	SETYAHAT	SHWEPAZUN
SAGU	SETKAYA	SHWETHIDA	SINMIN

Armed river transports

D: 98 tons   **S:** 12 kts   **Dim:** 28.8 × 6.7 × 1.4
A: 1/40-mm AA—3/20-mm AA (I × 3)   **M:** 2 Crossley ERL-6 diesels; 160 hp

♦ **10 30-to-40-ton river boats** Bldr: Burma, 1951-52

♦ **25 30-to-40-ton river boats** Bldr: Yugoslavia, 1965

♦ **1 hydrographic survey ship** Bldr: Tito SY, Belgrade, Yugoslavia (1965)

THU TAY THI

D: 1,100 tons (fl)   **S:** . . .   **Dim:** 62.2 × . . . × . . .
M: 2 diesels; 2 props; . . . hp   **Man:** 99 tot.

REMARKS: Helicopter platform. Carries 2 inshore survey craft.

AUXILIARIES (continued)

Thu Tay Thi

♦ **1 inshore survey boat** Bldr: Netherlands (1957)

YAY BO

    D: 108 tons   **Man:** 25 tot.

♦ **4 landing craft** Bldr: Yokohama Yacht, Japan

AIYAR MAUNG   AIYAR MAI
AIYAR MIN THAR   AIYAR MIN THA MEE

    D: 250 tons (fl)   **S:** 10 kts   **Dim:** 38.25 × 9.14 × 1.4
    M: 2 Kubota diesels; 2 props; 560 hp   **Cargo:** 100 tons   **Man:** 10 tot.

REMARKS: Launched 3-69. 200 grt.

♦ **2 landing craft** Bldr: Yokohama Yacht, Japan (1978)

SINDE   HTONBO

    D: 220 tons (fl)   **S:** 10 kts   **Dim:** 29.5 × 6.72 × 1.4
    M: 2 Kubota diesels; 2 props; 300 hp   **Cargo:** 50 tons, 30 passengers

♦ **1 U.S. LCU-1610-class utility landing craft** Bldr: Southern SB, U.S.

AIYAR LULIN (ex-U.S. LCU 1626)

    D: 190 tons (390 fl)   **S:** 11 kts   **Dim:** 41.0 × 9.0 × 2.0
    A: 2/20-mm AA (I × 2)   **M:** 4 GM 6-71 diesels; 2 props; 1,200 hp

REMARKS: Used as a transport. Transferred on completion, 6-67.

♦ **1 diving and repair tender** Bldr: Japan, 1967

YAN LONG AUNG   **D:** 520 tons

REMARKS: Formerly a torpedo retriever and torpedo boat tender.

PEOPLES' PEARL AND FISHERIES MINISTRY

♦ **3 Danish "Osprey"-class fisheries protection ships**

		Bldr	In serv.
FV 388	IN DAW	Frederikshavn SY	5-80
FV. . .		Frederikshavn SY	12-81
FV. . .		Frederikshavn SY	. . .

    D: 320 tons (383 fl)   **S:** 20 kts
    Dim: 49.95 (45.80 pp) × 10.5 (8.8 wl) × 2.75
    A: 2/40-mm AA (II × 1)—1/20-mm AA   **Electric:** 359 kVA
    M: 2 Burmeister & Wain "Alpha" 16V23L-VO diesels; 2 CP props;
        4,640 hp
    Range: 4,500/16   **Man:** 15 or more tot.

REMARKS: Sister to Danish *Havørnen*, armed in Burma. Helicopter hangar and flight deck aft. Rescue launch recessed into inclined ramp at stern.

♦ **3 "Swift"-class fisheries patrol boats** Bldr: Vosper, Singapore (1980-81)

421   422   423

    D: 96 tons (fl)   **S:** 27 kts   **Dim:** 32.3 × 7.2 × . . .
    A: 2/40-mm AA (I × 2)—2-mm AA (I × 2)—2/7.62-mm mg
    M: 2 MTU 12V 331 TC81 diesels; 2 props; . . . hp   **Range:** 1,800/24
    Man: 15 tot.

REMARKS: Origin and date of delivery uncertain.

♦ **6 "Carpentaria"-class fisheries patrol boats** Bldr: deHavilland, Australia (1979-80)

Burmese "Carpentaria"-class patrol boat on trials   G. Gyssels, 1980

    D: 27 tons (fl)   **S:** 27 kts   **Dim:** 16.0 × 5.0 × 1.2
    A: 2/7.62-mm mg (I × 2)   **Electron Equipt:** Radar: 1/Decca 110
    M: 2 GM 12V 71 TI diesels; 2 props; 1,120 hp   **Range:** 700/22
    Man: 8 tot.

REMARKS: Ordered 12-78. Sisters in Indonesian and Solomon Islands forces. Aluminum construction.

CAMEROON
United Republic of Cameroon

PERSONNEL: 300 men

MERCHANT MARINE (1980): 44 ships—62,080 grt

PATROL BOATS

♦ **1 French P 48S class** Bldr: Soc. Française Constructions Navales (SFCN), Ville-neuve-la-Garenne

	Laid down	L	In serv.
N. . .	. . .	. . .	. . .

D: 270 tons **S:** 25 kts **Dim:** 50.0 × 7.15 × . . .
A: 2/40-mm AA (I × 2) **M:** 2 AGO diesels; 2 props; 6,400 hp
Man: 3 officers, 24 men

REMARKS: Ordered 1-81; enlarged version of P 48 class. Two optical sights for 40-mm AA.

♦ **1 French P 48 class** Bldr: SFCN, Villeneuve-la-Garenne

	Laid down	L	In serv.
L'AUDACIEUX	10-2-75	31-10-75	11-5-76

D: 240 tons **S:** 18.5 kts **Dim:** 47.5 (45.5 pp) × 7.1 × 2.5
A: 2/40-mm AA (I × 2) **M:** 2 MGO diesels; 2 props; 2,400 hp
Electric: 100 kw **Range:** 2,000/15 **Man:** 3 officers, 22 men

♦ **2 Chinese Shanghai-II class**—Transferred 7-76

101   102

D: 122 tons (150 fl) **S:** 28.5 kts **Dim:** 38.8 × 5.4 × 1.5
A: 4/37-mm AA (II × 2)—4/25-mm AA (II × 2)
Electron Equipt: Radar: 1/Pot Head
M: 2 M50F diesels of 1,200 hp, 2 12D6 diesels of 910 hp; 4 props; 4,220 hp
Man: 25 tot.

PATROL CRAFT

♦ **3 small coastal surveillance craft**

LE VALEUREUX   Bldr: Chantiers Navals del'Estérel, Nice, 1970

D: 45 tons **S:** 25 kts **Dim:** 26.8 × 4.97 × 1.55 **A:** 2/20-mm AA
M: 2 GM 12V 71 diesels; 2 props; 960 hp **Man:** 1 officer, 8 men

BRIGADIER M'BONGA TOUNDA   Bldr: Ch. Navals del'Estérel, Nice, 1967

D: 20 tons (fl) **S:** 22.5 kts **Dim:** 18.15 (17.03 pp) × 4.03 × 1.1
A: 1/12.7-mm mg **M:** Caterpillar D 333 TA diesels; 2 props; 540 hp
Man: 8 tot.

REMARKS: Customs ship, manned by the Navy. Same characteristics as the Mauritanian *Imrag'Ni* class.

Le Valeureux   Estérel, 1970

QUARTIER MAÎTRE ALFRED MOTTO   Bldr: A.C.R.E., Libreville, Gabon

D: 96 tons (fl) **S:** 15.5 kts **Dim:** 29.1 × 6.2 × 1.85 (aft)
A: 2/20-mm AA—2 mg **M:** 2 Baudoin diesels; 2 props; 1,290 hp
Man: 2 officers, 15 men

AMPHIBIOUS WARFARE CRAFT

♦ **1 LCM** Bldr: Carena, Abidjan, Ivory Coast (1973)

BAKASI

D: 57 tons (fl) **S:** 9 kts **Dim:** 17.5 × 4.28 × 1.3
M: 2 Baudoin diesels; 490 hp

♦ **5 LCVP-type landing craft** Bldr: A.C.R.E., Libreville, Gabon

SOUELLABA   INDEPENDANCE   REUNIFICATION   MANOKA   MACHTIGAL

D: 11 tons **S:** 10 kts

SERVICE CRAFT

♦ **2 10-ton harbor launches**

SANAGA   BIMBIA

♦ **6 FAC 408-class seatrucks** Bldr: Rotork Marine, Poole, G.B. (1978)

D: 2 tons **S:** 10 to 35 kts **Dim:** 7.37 × 2.74 × . . .
M: 1 or 2 inboard/outboard motors

REMARKS: For patrolling rivers and lagoons.

CANADA

The Canadian Armed Forces have been completely unified. Six operational commands have been set up: Mobile Command, Maritime Command, Air Transport Command, Air Defense Command, Training Command, and Material Command. The Maritime Command is in charge of the naval ships, the ship-based aircraft, and all of the units of the former Maritime Air Command (RCAF). Its principal role is ASW, but it can also be called upon to transport men and equipment for the Mobile Command.

PERSONNEL (1980): about 14,200 men

MERCHANT MARINE (1980): 1,324 ships—3,180,126 grt (tankers: 57—295,540 grt)

NAVAL AVIATION: Made up of ship-based helicopters on ASW helicopter destroyers (DDH), maritime patrol aircraft, and ASW aircraft, formerly carrier-based but now maintained at land bases.
  Primary strength as follows:
  —32 ASW CHSS 2 (CH-124) Sea King helicopters (see U.S.A. section). These helicopters are armed with Mk 44 or Mk 46 torpedoes and sensors (AQS-13 sonar, for example) and are used to search for hostile submarines. Upon landing, they are automatically secured and parked in the hangar, thanks to the ingenious Bear Trap recovery system. Several are used in logistics service aboard the replenishment oilers. All are based on the East Coast, at Shearwater, Nova Scotia.
  —16 4-engine CL-28 (CP-121) Argus aircraft.
  The CL-28 Argus is an ASW plane with an extended flight radius. **Wingspan:** 43.50. **Length:** 39.20. **Weight:** 67 tons. **Engines:** 4 Wright, each of 3,700 hp. **Speed:** 250 knots. **Search speed:** 163 knots. **Endurance:** 20 hours. **Range:** 3,900 miles. **Ceiling:** 25,000 feet. Radar dome. Can carry mines, torpedoes, depth charges, and air-to-surface rockets. To be replaced by the CP-140 Aurora.
  As a follow-on for this plane, Canada signed a contract on 25-7-76 with Lockheed for the manufacture of 18 CP-140 Aurora maritime patrol aircraft based on the U.S. Navy's P-3 Orion. The first plane flew on 22-3-79 but underwent tests and was delivered 28-5-80. Thirteen had been delivered by the end of 1980, with the remaining five arriving by 3-81. The Canadian version of the plane differs considerably from the American P-3. It is fitted not only for reconnaissance, ASW, and electronic warfare, but for detecting atmospheric and maritime pollution and for analyzing oil spills at sea. It has a crew of twelve.
  The Aurora will be given the Orion's A-NEW system, based on the miniaturized computer Univac ASQ 114, which can store 65,000 words of 30 bits and has a retrieval time of 4 microseconds. This equipment integrates all the ASW information put into it. It has 36 launching chutes for dropping active and passive sonobuoys and can carry racks for 120 reserve sonobuoys in the rear of the fuselage. It carries ASW torpedoes or depth charges or a combination of these weapons. Other principal systems are: 2 ASN-84 inertial navigation computers; 1 Doppler radar; 1 tactical recorder flight-control director; 1 tactical data link system; 1 FLIR (Forward-Looking Infrared); SLAR (Side-Looking Airborne Radar) antennas; detectors for lasers; a low-light television pod.

CP-140 Aurora, number 140101   1980

—15 CS-2F Tracker former carrier-based ASW aircraft, now used as land-based maritime surveillance aircraft, with additional fuel in the former weapons bay. Omega navigation systems were added during 1979-80, and a wing-mounted camera pod is being installed. Twelve are based at Shearwater, Nova Scotia, while the 3 Pacific Coast units also perform ship target service duties, along with several CT-33A Silver Star jet trainers.

WARSHIPS IN SERVICE AS OF 1 JANUARY 1982

	L	Tons (Surfaced)	Main armament
♦ **3 submarines**			
3 OJIBWA	1964-66	2,070	8/533-mm TT
♦ **4 destroyers**			
4 IROQUOIS	1970-71	3,551	1/127-mm DP, 2 Can. Sea Sparrow, ASW weapons, 2 Sea King helicopters
♦ **16 frigates**			
2 ANNAPOLIS	1961-63	2,400	2/76.2-mm DP, ASW weapons, 1 Sea King helicopter
4 MACKENZIE	1961-62	2,380	4/76.2-mm DP, ASW weapons
4 RESTIGOUCHE	1954-57	2,390	2/76.2-mm DP, ASROC, other ASW weapons
6 ST. LAURENT	1952-56	2,260	2/76.2-mm DP, ASW weapons, 1 Sea King helicopter

WEAPONS AND SYSTEMS

A. MISSILES

♦ **Surface-to-air missiles.** The Canadian Navy has adopted the short-range surface-to-air NATO Sea Sparrow for its four *Iroquois*-class destroyers. The missile is designed to attack aircraft or missiles flying at a low altitude or at a transonic speed. Its characteristics are:

  Length: 3.660 m. **Diameter:** 0.200 m. **Wingspan:** .020 m. **Weight:** 204 kg.
  Speed: Mach 3.5. **Practical antiaircraft range:** 8,000 to 10,000 m.

Its GMLS launching system, designed by Raytheon Canada, is made up of two loaders and two launchers. The launchers are fixed one to port and one to starboard, perpendicular to the axis of the ship. They are retractable, can be trained and elevated, and are housed in the structure forward of the bridge. Each launcher has four missiles ready to be fired. A new Raytheon vertical-launch system for Sea Sparrow underwent trials aboard *Huron* in 2-81 at Roosevelt Roads, Puerto Rico.
  Canada may purchase the U.S. Harpoon missile for use by CP-140 Aurora aircraft, submarines, and surface ships.

B. GUNS

The following guns are currently in use:
76.2-mm Mk 22. Twin DP (U.S. Mk 34 mount) mounted behind a plastic spray shield.
  Length: 50 calibers. **Muzzle velocity:** 822 m/s.
  Maximum firing rate: 50 rounds per minute per barrel. **Arc of elevation:** 15° to +85°.
  Maximum effective antiaircraft range: 4,000 to 5,000 m.
  Fitted on the *St. Laurent, Restigouche, Mackenzie,* and *Annapolis* classes of frigates.

76.2-mm Mk 6. Twin barrel, automatic (British model).
Length: 70 calibers. **Muzzle velocity:**. . . m/s. **Maximum firing rate:** 60 pounds per minute per barrel.
Maximum effective antiaircraft range: 5,000 m.
Installed forward on the *Restigouche* and *Mackenzie* classes of frigates; being replaced by Mk 22.
127-mm OTO-Melara (*see* Italy section)
Installed on the *Iroquois*-class destroyers.

C. ASW WEAPONS

♦ **Depth-charge and torpedo launchers**
—British Mk 10 Limbo triple-barreled mortar on all destroyers and frigates.
—U.S. ASROC on 4 *Restigouche*-class frigates.
—U.S. Mk 32 ASW triple torpedo tubes on all destroyers and most frigates.

♦ **Torpedoes**
—U.S. Mk 44 and 46 ASW torpedoes aboard ships, and on Sea King helicopters and maritime patrol aircraft.
—U.S. Mk 37 aboard submarines.

D. ELECTRONICS

♦ **Radars:**
—SPS-12 long-range air search.
—SPS-501 long-range air search (version of Dutch LWO-3) installed in *Iroquois*-class destroyers. Uses LWO-3 antenna, SPS-12 transmitter.
—SPS-10 and Sperry Mk 2 navigation/surface search.
—SPQ-2D combination search (Italian radar) installed in the *Iroquois* class.

♦ **Sonars:**
—SQS-501 for detection of submarines lying on the sea bottom.
—SQS-503 hull-mounted MF.
—SQS-504 towed MF, Type 503 transducer.
—SQS-505 hull-mounted LF installed in the *Iroquois* class and back-fitting in some frigates.
—SQS-505 towed LF installed in the *Iroquois* class (SQA-502 hoist).

SUBMARINES

♦ **3 British Oberon class**

	Bldr	Laid down	L	In serv.
SS 72 OJIBWA (ex-*Onyx*)	H.M. DY, Chatham	27-9-62	29-2-64	23-9-65
SS 73 ONANDAGA	H.M. DY, Chatham	18-6-64	25-9-65	22-6-67
SS 74 OKANAGAN	H.M. DY, Chatham	25-3-65	17-9-66	22-6-68

D: 1,610/2,070/2,410 tons **S:** 17.5/15 kts
Dim: 89.92(87.45 pp) × 8.07 × 5.48
A: 8/533-mm TT (6 fwd, 2 aft)—22 torpedoes
Electron Equipt: Radar: 1/1006
    Sonar: British: 1/2007, 1/187, 1/197, 1/719
M: 2 Admiralty Standard Range 16VVS-AS21 diesels, diesel-electric drive; 2 props; 6,000 hp

REMARKS: Type 187 is an active attack sonar, Type 197 is a passive intercept system, and Type 719, passive, performs torpedo warning. The *Ojibwa* was begun under the name of *Onyx* for the Royal Navy and transferred while still under construction.

Ojibwa (SS 72)—prior to modernization   1976

The living spaces have been modified for Canadian weather conditions. Being modernized under "SOUP" (Submarine Operational Update Program), beginning in 1980 with SS 72; getting Singer-Librascope Mk 1 mod.0 fire-control system using Sperry UYK-20 computer and new sonar suit to include Krupp-Atlas CSU3-41 active-passive system with enlarged bow dome for the passive array and the active transducer in the sail, as has been done in the Australian units of the class. The Type 2007 long-range passive search array will be retained. Will be able to employ U.S. Mk 48 torpedoes and Sub-Harpoon missiles on completion. SS 72 completes 1982, SS 73 in 1983, and SS 74 in 1984.

DESTROYERS

♦ **4 Iroquois DDH 280 class**

	Bldr	Laid down	L	In serv.
DDH 280 IROQUOIS	Marine Industries, Sorel	15-1-69	28-11-70	29-7-72
DDH 281 HURON	Marine Industries, Sorel	15-1-69	3-4-71	16-12-72
DDH 282 ATHABASCAN	Davie S.B., Lauzon	1-6-69	27-11-70	30-11-72
DDH 283 ALGONQUIN	Davie S.B., Lauzon	1-9-69	23-4-71	30-9-73

Iroquois (DDH 280)—showing "Bear Trap" helo recovery system

DESTROYERS (continued)

Huron (DDH 281)   G. Arra, 1977

Athabascan (DDH 282) with Sea King helicopter   1979

Athabascan (DDH 282)   French Navy, 1980

D: 3,551 tons (4,200 fl)   **S:** 30/29 kts

Dim: 128.92 (121.31 pp) × 15.24 × 4.42

A: 2/Canadian Sea Sparrow SAM syst. (IV × 2; 32 AIM-7E missiles)—
1/127-mm OTO Melara DP—1/Mk 10 Limbo ASW mortar (III × 1)—6/324-
mm Mk 32 TT (III × 2)—2/Sea King ASW helicopters

Electron Equipt: Radars: 1/SPS-501, 1/SPQ-2D; 2/WM-22 directors, URN-20
TACAN

Sonars: 1/SQS-505, 1/SQS-505(VDS), 1/SQS-501

ECM: WLR-1, ULQ-6 jammer—1/6-rail flare and chaff RL—
2/Knebworth-Corvus chaff RL (VIII × 2)

M: COGOG: 2 FT 4A2 Pratt & Whitney gas turbines, 25,000 hp each, 2
Solar Mk FT 12H gas turbines, 3,700 hp each; 2 five-bladed CP props;
50,000 hp

Electric: 2,750 kw   **Range:** 4,500/20   **Man:** 27 officers, 258 men

REMARKS: Two paired stacks, angled to avoid corrosion of the antennas by stack gases.
Bear Trap positive-control helicopter landing system. Passive-tank anti-rolling system fitted to improve stability at low speeds. *Huron* tested the Raytheon vertical-
launch Sea Sparrow SAM system in 2-81.

FRIGATES

♦ **6 new construction** Bldr: . . .

	Laid down	L	In serv.
N. . .	. . .	. . .	1987
N. . .	. . .	. . .	. . .
N. . .	. . .	. . .	. . .
N. . .	. . .	. . .	. . .
N. . .	. . .	. . .	. . .
N. . .	. . .	. . .	1991

D: 3,398 tons (fl)   **S:** 29.2 kts

Dim: 134.0 (125.0 pp) × 14.7 × 4.33 (hull)

A: 8/Harpoon SSM (IV × 2)—1/Sea Sparrow SAM syst. (VIII × 2), vertical
launch; 24 missiles—1/76-mm DP OTO Melara—4/324-mm Mk 32 ASW TT
(fixed, II × 2)—2/Sea King helicopters

Electron Equipt: Radar: 1/Raytheon 1629C navigational, 1/SPS-49 air search, 1/
1031 search, 1/WM-25 fire control

Sonar: SQS-505, U.S. SQR-18A TACTASS

ECM: CANEWS syst., 4/Mk 36 Super-RBOC chaff RL

M: 2 G.E. LM-2500 gas turbines; 2 CP props; 50,000 hp

Electric: 4,000 kw   **Range:** 4,500/20   **Man:** 226 tot.

REMARKS: The Canadian government decided on 22-12-77 to order 6 helicopter-carrying frigates of between 3,500 and 4,000 tons displacement. The ships of this initial
installment of a planned program of 20 ships were to enter service between 1985
and 1989. Lengthy delays resulted, the program being at least two years behind
schedule by 1981. The proposed design above had yet to be formalized and the final
contractor selected.

GENERAL NOTE: Since Canada cannot afford to replace the aging frigate force, as it
nears retirement, with a similar number of ships, a "Destroyer Life Extension
Program" (DELEX) was approved 7-8-80, with a projected cost of $107 million
(Canadian). All frigates are to receive the following: ADLIPS (Automated Data Link
Processing System), hull and machinery overhaul and repairs, new underwater tele-
phones, the Mk 12 IFF system, secure UHF communications, and a new navigational
radar. Additional features will be added to the various ships in proportion to their

FRIGATES (continued)

future value, with $22 million per ship being spent on the 1964-vintage *Annapolis* class, down to only $5 million for the St. Laurent-class ships, which, as the oldest, are the first to be worked on. Individual class DELEX features are listed in the Remarks sections.

◆ 2 Annapolis class

	Bldr	Laid down	L	In serv.
DDE 265 ANNAPOLIS	Halifax Shipyards Ltd	7-60	27-4-63	19-12-64
DDE 266 NIPIGON	Marine Industries, Sorel	4-60	10-12-61	30-5-64

Saskatchewan (DDE 262)—Mk 6, 76.2-mm/70 cal. forward   G. Arra, 1977

Annapolis (DDE 265)—now has TACAN on mast between stacks   1970

D: 2,400 tons (3,000 fl)   **S:** 28 kts   **Dim:** 113.1 × 12.8 × 4.4
A: 2/76.2-mm DP Mk 33 (II × 1)—1/Mk 10 Limbo mortar (III × 2)—6/324-mm
      ASW TT (III × 2) Mk 32—1/Sea King helicopter
Electron Equipt: Radars: 1/SPS-12, 1/SPS-10, 1/Sperry Mk 2, SPG-48 fire
                  control
            Sonars: 1/SQS-503, 1/SQS-504, 1/SQS-501
            ECM: WLR-1—TACAN: URN-20
M: 2 sets English-Electric GT; 2 props; 30,000 hp
Boilers: 2 Babcock & Wilcox; 43.3 kg/cm², 454°C   **Electric:** 1,400 kw
Range: 4,750/14   **Man:** 18 officers, 210 men

REMARKS: Under DELEX will receive new air search radar, ECM, fire-control syst., navigational radar, and vertical-launch Sea Sparrow; SQS-503 sonar will be replaced by SQS-505. Refits scheduled to commence: DDE 265 in 1984, 266 in 1982. Both on East Coast.

◆ 4 Mackenzie-class frigates

	Bldr	Laid down	L	In serv.
DDE 261 MACKENZIE	Canadian-Vickers	15-12-58	25-5-61	6-10-62
DDE 262 SASKATCHEWAN	Victoria Machinery	16-7-59	1-2-61	16-2-63
DDE 263 YUKON	Burrard, Vancouver	25-10-59	27-7-61	25-5-63
DDE 264 QU'APPELLE	Davie S.B., Lauzon	14-1-60	2-5-62	14-19-63

D: 2,380 tons (2,890 fl)   **S:** 28 kts   **Dim:** 111.5 × 12.8 × 4.1
A: 4/76.2-mm DP (II × 2—see remarks)—2/Mk 10 Limbo mortars (III × 2)—
      263, 264: 6/324-mm ASW TT Mk 32 (III × 2)

Qu'appelle (DDE 264)—Mk 33, 76.2-mm/50 cal. forward   1979

Electron Equipt: Radars: 1/SPS-12, 1/SPS-10, 1/Sperry Mk 2, 1/SPG-48,
                  1/SPG-34
            Sonars: 1/SQS-503, 1/SQS-501—ECM: WLR-1
M: 2 sets English-Electric GT; 2 props; 30,000 hp
Boilers: 2 Babcock & Wilcox; 43 kg/cm², 454°C   **Range:** 4,750/14
Man: 11 officers, 199 men

REMARKS: All employed in the Pacific. U.S. Mk 69 gunfire control forward, Mk 63 aft. DDE 263 and 264 have had British Mk 6, 76.2-mm/70-cal. gun mounts replaced by U.S. Mk 34, 76.2-mm/50-cal. mounts. Under DELEX will receive SQS-505 in place of SQS-503 and a new navigational radar in place of Mk 2. Refits scheduled to commence: 264, 1982; 263, 1983; 262, 1984; and 261, 1985. Cost $10 million (Canadian) each.

◆ 4 modified Restigouche-class ASW frigates

	Bldr	Laid down	L	In serv.
DDE 236 GATINEAU	Davie SB, Lauzon	30-4-53	3-6-57	17-2-59
DDE 257 RESTIGOUCHE	Canadian-Vickers	15-7-53	22-11-54	7-6-58
DDE 258 KOOTENAY	Burrard, Vancouver	21-8-52	15-6-54	7-3-59
DDE 259 TERRA NOVA	Victoria Machinery	14-11-52	21-6-55	6-6-59

D: 2,390 tons (2,900 fl)   **S:** 28 kts   **Dim:** 113.1 × 12.8 × 4.3
A: 2/76.2-mm DP Mk 6 (II × 1) fwd—1/ASROC syst. (VIII × 1, 8 reloads)—1/
      Mk 10 Limbo mortar (III × 1)
Electron Equipt: Radars: 1/SPS-12, 1/SPS-10, 1/Sperry Mk 2, 1/SPG-48 fire
                  control
            Sonars: 1/SQS-501, 1/SQS-503, 1/SQS-505(VDS)
            ECM: WLR-1 passive, ULQ-6 jammer, 2 Knebworth-Corvus
            chaff RL (VIII × 2), 1/6-rail chaff and flare RL

FRIGATES (continued)

Restigouche (DDE 257)   G. Arra, 1979

Terra Nova (DDE 259)—note SQS-505 VDS fish   G. Arra, 1979

M: 2 sets English-Electric GT; 2 props; 30,000 hp
Boilers: 2 Babcock & Wilcox, 43.3 kg/cm², 454°C   **Electric:** 1,400 kw
Range: 4,750/14   **Man:** 13 officers, 201 men

REMARKS: All on Pacific Coast. Reconstruction with lengthened hull for VDS and ASROC in place of aft 76.2-mm mount and one Limbo completed 1968-73. U.S. Mk 69 fire-control system. Unmodified sisters *Chaudière*, *Columbia*, and *St. Croix* were reduced to disposal reserve in 1974, although *Columbia* remains in use as a stationary training ship at Esquimault. To receive same DELEX update as *Annapolis* class; cost $20-mil., commencing: DDE 236 in 1983, 258 in 1984, 259 in 1985, and 257 in 1986.

♦ 6 St. Laurent-class helicopter frigates

	Bldr	Laid down	L	In serv.
DDE 206 SAGUENAY	Halifax Shipyards	4-4-51	30-7-53	15-12-56
DDE 207 SKEENA	Burrard, Vancouver	1-6-51	19-8-52	30-3-57
DDE 229 OTTAWA	Canadian-Vickers	8-6-51	29-4-53	10-11-56
DDE 230 MARGAREE	Halifax Shipyards	12-9-51	29-3-56	5-10-57
DDE 233 FRASER	Burrard, Vancouver	11-12-51	19-2-53	28-6-57
DDE 234 ASSINIBOINE	Marine Industries, Sorel	19-5-52	12-2-54	16-8-56

D: 2,260 tons (2,860 fl)   **S:** 28 kts   **Dim:** 111.5 × 12.8 × 4.2
A: 2/76.2-mm DP Mk 33—1/Mk 10 Limbo mortar (III × 1)—6/324-mm Mk 32 ASW TT (III × 2)—1 Sea King helicopter
Electron Equipt: Radars: 1/SPS-12, 1/SPS-10, 1 navigational, 1/SPG-48 f.c.
    Sonars: 1/SQS-503, 1/SQS-501, 1/SQS-504 VDS
    ECM: WLR-1—TACAN: URN-20
M: 2 sets English-Electric GT; 2 props; 30,000 hp
Boilers: 2 Babcock & Wilcox; 43.3 kg/cm², 454°C
Electric: 1,400 kw   **Range:** 4,750/14   **Man:** 18 officers, 210 men

REMARKS: *St. Laurent* (DDE 205) was taken out of service in 1974. *Fraser*, which was completed by Yarrow, Ltd., has a lattice mast between her funnels to support the TACAN dome; the others carry their TACAN atop a pole mast. Nos. 207, 229, and 233 given major overhauls 1977-78. DELEX overhaul performed 1980 on 206, 230, and 234; 1981 on 207, 229, 233; new navigational radar, refit only. Scheduled for retirement 1987-90.

Saguenay (DDE 206)—after DELEX overhaul   G. Gyssels, 1981

Assiniboine (DDE 234)—after DELEX overhaul   G. Gyssels, 1981

FRIGATES (continued)

Fraser (DDE 233)—Sea King above Bear Trap landing rig   1979

SUBMARINE CHASER

♦ 1 experimental hydrofoil

	Bldr	L	Trials
FHE 400 Bras d'Or	Marine Industries, Sorel	7-68	1969

(FHE—Fast Hydrofoil Escort)

D: 237.5 tons (fl) **S:** 50/60 kts in calm seas
Dim: (hull) 46.0 × 6.55 × 5.08 (cruising)
M: Pratt and Whitney Mk FT 4 A gas turbine; 22,000 hp **Man:** 17 tot.

REMARKS: Outboard length of lifting foils: 27.43 m. Draft: hullborne, 7.21, foilborne: 1.32. At 15 knots cruising speed, a Davey-Paxman diesel (2,000 hp) drives 2 controllable-pitch props. After experiments, this ship was placed in reserve in 1971; she remains stored on land. Planned armament of 12 ASWTT (III × 4) was never installed.

OCEANOGRAPHIC AND HYDROGRAPHIC SHIPS

♦ 2 oceanographic research ships

	Bldr	Laid down	L	In serv.
AGOR 172 Quest	Burrard DD, Vancouver	1967	9-7-68	21-8-69

D: 2,130 tons (fl) **S:** 15 kts **Dim:** 77.2 (71.62 pp) × 12.8 × 4.6
Electron Equipt: Radar: 1/Decca 838, 1/Decca 929 **Fuel:** 256 tons
Range: 10,000/12 **Man:** 37 tot.

REMARKS: A modification of the *Endeavour* (AGOR 171) with the same machinery. Can carry a small helicopter. See remarks on the *Endeavour*.

	Bldr	L	In serv.
AGOR 171 Endeavour	Yarrow, Ltd., Victoria	17-8-61	9-3-65

Quest (AGOR 172)   1970

Endeavour (AGOR 171)   1970

D: 1,560 tons (fl) **S:** 16 kts **Dim:** 71.85 (65.53 wl)× 11.73 × 4.0
M: 2 Fairbanks-Morse 38D8 ⅛, 9-cylinder diesels, GE electric drive; 2 props; 2,960 hp
Electron Equipt: Radar: 1/Decca 838, 1/Decca 929 **Fuel:** 256 tons
Range: 10,000/12 **Man:** 37 crew plus 14 scientists

REMARKS: (for both ships): Reinforced hulls for navigation in icefields. Two electro-hydraulic 5- and 9-ton cranes. Bulbous bows. Anti-rolling and anti-pitching devices. Civilian crews.

♦ 1 British "Flower" class, former corvette

	Bldr	Laid down	L	In serv.
AGOR 113 Sackville	St. John DD & SB	28-5-40	15-5-41	29-12-41

D: 1,085 tons (1,350 fl) **S:** 16 kts **Dim:** 62.5 (57.9 pp) × 10.08 × 4.78
M: 1 set 4-cyl. triple-expansion, reciprocating; 1 prop; 2,750 hp (1,750 sust.)
Boilers: 2 Admiralty, single-ended; 15.8 kg/cm² **Fuel:** 230 tons
Range: 3,400/12, 5,000/9

REMARKS: Only active surviving "Flower" of 125 built in Canada and 145 built in Great Britain. Used as a magnetic loop layer postwar and in 1959 designated a cable layer. In 1964 redesignated as an oceanographic research ship. Refit planned 1981-82; ultimately to go to a museum.

OCEANOGRAPHIC AND HYDROGRAPHIC SHIPS *(continued)*

♦ **1 former minelayer**

	Bldr	Laid down	L	In serv.
AGOR 114 BLUETHROAT	Geo. T. Davie, Lauzon	31-10-52	15-9-55	28-11-55

D: 785 tons (870 fl) **S:** 13 kts **Dim:** 47.0 × 9.9 × 3.0
M: 2 diesels; 2 props; 1,200 hp **Man:** 27 tot.

REMARKS: Completed as a mine and magnetic loop layer; redesignated a cable layer in 1959 and as a research ship in 1964.

Bluethroat (AGOR 114) 1969

♦ **1 ex-Royal Canadian Mounted Police patrol boat** Bldr: Canadian SB & Eng. Co.

AGOR 140 FORT STEELE (L: 18-7-59, in serv. 11-59)

D: 85 tons (110 fl) **S:** 18 kts **Dim:** 35.97 × 6.4 × 2.1
M: Paxman Ventura 12 YJCM diesels; 2 CP props; 2,800 hp
Range: 1,200/16 **Man:** 16 tot.

REMARKS: Taken over 1973. Although designated a research ship, primarily acts as training ship for Reserves at Halifax. Originally had Napier Deltic diesels.

DEEP SUBMERGENCE EXPERIMENTAL SHIP

♦ **1 former Italian stern-haul trawler** Bldr: Marelli, Italy (L:. . .)

ASXL 20 CORMORANT (ex-*Aspa Quarto*) (In serv. 10-11-78)

D: 2,350 tons (fl) **S:** 15 kts **Dim:** 74.6 (72.0 pp) × 11.9 × 5.3
Electron Equipt: Radar: 1/Decca TM 1229, 1/RM 1229
M: 3 Marelli-Deutz ACR 12456 CV, 950 hp diesels, electric drive; 1 CP prop; 2,100 hp
Electric: 730 kVA + 250 kw **Range:** 11,800/15, 13,000/12

REMARKS: Ex-Italian stern-haul trawler bought in 1975 and adapted to handle and service the SDL-1 submersible, which can dive to 600 m. A large hangar for SDL-2 and a gallows crane have been built on the stern. The ship can also support conventional and saturation divers and has extensive compressor facilities, decompression chambers, etc. Numerous specialized echo-sounders fitted.

Cormorant (ASXL 20) 1978

REPLENISHMENT OILERS

♦ **2 Protecteur-class multi-purpose underway replenishment ships**

	Bldr	Laid down	L	In serv.
AOR 509 PROTECTEUR	St. John SB & DD (NB)	17-10-67	18-7-68	30-8-69
AOR 510 PRESERVER	St. John SB & DD (NB)	17-10-67	29-5-69	30-7-70

Protecteur (AOR 509) 1980

D: 8,380 tons light (24,700 fl) **S:** 21 kts
Dim: 172.0 (166.42 pp) × 23.16 × 9.15
A: 2/76.2-mm DP Mk 33 (II × 1)—3 Sea King helicopters
Electron Equipt: Radars: 1/Sperry Mk 2, 1/Decca TM 969—TACAN: URN-20
Sonar: 1/SQS-505
M: 1 set Canadian GE GT; 1 prop; 21,000 hp **Boilers:** 2 **Electric:** 3,500 kw

REPLENISHMENT OILERS (continued)

Cargo capacity: 13,250 tons, with 12,000 tons of distillate fuel, 600 tons of diesel oil, 400 tons of jet fuel, frozen and dry foods, spare parts, munitions, etc.

Range: 4,100/20, 7,500/11.5   **Man:** 15 officers, 212 men, 57 passengers

REMARKS: Four replenishment-at-sea stations, one elevator aft of the navigation bridge, two 15-ton cranes on the afterdeck. One bow-thruster. Daily fresh-water distillation capacity is 80 tons. Sea Sparrow SAM was to replace the 76.2-mm, but never fitted. The gun mount is precariously situated in the eyes of the ship and has been washed away several times; fire control is local. Can be used to carry military vehicles and troops for commando purposes. Carry four LCVPs.

♦ **1 Provider-class multi-purpose underway replenishment ship**

	Bldr	Laid down	L	In serv.
AOR 508 PROVIDER	Davie SB, Lauzon	1-5-61	5-7-62	28-9-63

Provider (AOR 508)   1980

D: 7,300 tons (22,000 fl)   **S:** 20 kts
Dim: 168.0 (159.4 pp) × 23.17 × 9.15   **M:** GT; 1 prop; 21,000 hp
Boilers: 2   **Fuel:** 1,200 tons   **Range:** 5,000/20
Electric: 2,140 kw   **Man:** 15 officers, 151 men

REMARKS: Platform and hangar for two Sea King helicopters. Can carry 12,000 tons of distillate fuel, 1,200 tons of diesel, 1,000 tons of aviation gas, 250 tons of provisions, munitions, and various spare parts.

SMALL OILERS

♦ **2 "Dun" class** Bldr: Canadian Bridge Co., Walkerville, Ont.

	Laid down	L	In serv.
AOTL 501 DUNDALK	18-1-43	14-7-43	13-11-43
AOTL 502 DUNDURN	27-1-43	18-9-43	25-11-43

Dundalk (AOTL 501)   1969

D: 950 tons (1,500 fl)   **S:** 10 kts   **Dim:** 54.5 × 9.8 × 3.9
M: 1 Fairbanks-Morse diesel; 1 prop; 700 hp
Cargo: 792 tons fuel/25 tons dry   **Man:** 24 tot.

REPAIR SHIP

♦ **1 "Park"-class dépôt repair ship** Bldr: Burrard DD, Vancouver

	Laid down	L	In serv.
ARE 100 CAPE BRETON	5-7-44	7-10-44	25-4-45
(ex-*Flamborough Head*)			

D: 8,450 tons (11,270 fl)   **S:** 11 kts   **Dim:** 134.6 (129.4) × 17.4 × 6.96
M: 1 set triple-expansion, reciprocating; 2,500 hp
Boilers: 2 Foster-Wheeler 17.6 kg/cm², 316°C   **Fuel:** 709 tons
Range: 5,000/9

REMARKS: Purchased from the Royal Navy in 1951. Used as training ship 1953-58. Refitted 1958-59. Equipped for pierside service at Esquimault and not expected ever to steam again. Sister *Cape Scott* (ARE 101) discarded in 1977.

RESERVE TRAINING SHIPS AND CRAFT

NOTE: In addition to the ships and craft listed below, the four *Mackenzie*-class frigates are used primarily for training, and the research ship *Fort Steele* is used to train Reserves. The units below retain hull numbers associated with their former function.

♦ **6 Bay-class former minesweepers**

	Bldr	Laid down	L	In serv.
PFL 159 FUNDY	Davie S.B., Lauzon	3-55	14-6-56	27-11-56
PFL 160 CHIGNECTO	Davie S.B., Lauzon	10-55	26-2-57	1-8-57
PFL 161 THUNDER	Port Arthur S.B., Ont.	9-55	27-10-56	3-10-57
PFL 162 COWICHAN	Yarrows Ltd., Victoria	7-56	26-2-57	19-12-57
PFL 163 MIRAMICHI	Victoria Machinery	2-56	22-2-57	28-10-57
PFL 164 CHALEUR	Marine Industries, Sorel	2-56	17-11-56	12-9-57

Cowichan   1969

D: 370 tons (415 fl)   **S:** 15 kts   **Dim:** 50.0 (46.05 pp) × 9.21 × 2.8
Electron Equipt: Radar: 1/Sperry Mk 2   **Electric:** 690 kw
M: 2 12-278A GM diesels; 2 props; 2,500 hp
Fuel: 53 tons   **Range:** 4,500/11   **Man:** 3 officers, 35 men

RESERVE TRAINING SHIPS AND CRAFT (continued)

REMARKS: Reclassified as patrol escorts in 1972 and used for training reserve personnel. They took the names of minesweepers transferred to France in 1954. The *Gaspé* (143), *Comox* (146), *Ungava* (148), and *Trinity* (157) were transferred to Turkey in 1958. Hull of composite construction. One 40-mm AA removed.

♦ **5 Porte class** Bldrs: 180, 183: Davie, Lauzon; 184: Victoria Mach. & DD; 185: Burrard DD; 186: Pictou Foundry

	In serv.		In serv.
YMG 180 PORTE ST. JEAN	4-6-52	YMG 185 PORTE QUEBEC	28-8-52
YMG 183 PORTE ST. LOUIS	28-8-52	YMG 186 PORTE DAUPHINE	10-12-52
YMG 184 PORTE DE LA REINE	19-9-52		

Porte Dauphine (YMG 186)—at Esquimault: DDE 261 *Mackenzie* and hulks *Chaudière* and *St. Croix* in background   1980

D: 300 tons (429 fl)   **S:** 12 kts   **Dim:** 38.0 × 8.5 × 3.9
M: 1 Fairbanks-Morse 6-cyl. diesel, electric drive; 1 prop; 600 hp
Fuel: 47 tons   **Range:** 4,100/10   **Man:** 3 officers, 20 men

REMARKS: Launched 1950-52. Trawler-like profile. Built as auxiliary minesweepers and net tenders.

♦ **5 former Mounted Police patrol craft** (In serv. 1957-59)

PB 191 ADVERSUS   PB 193 CAPTOR   PB 195 SIDNEY
PB 192 DETECTOR   PB 194 ACADIAN

D: 48 tons   **S:** 12 kts   **Dim:** 19.8 × 4.6 × 1.2
M: 1 Cummins diesel; 410 hp   **Range:** 1,000/10.5

♦ **1 former Mounted Police patrol craft** Bldr: Smith & Rhulorel, Lunenburg, N.S.

PB 196 NICHOLSON   (In serv. 1968)

D: 85 tons (fl)   **S:** 16 kts   **Dim:** 36.0 × 6.4 × 2.1
M: 2 Paxman YJCM diesels; 2 CP props; 2,800 hp   **Range:** 900/13   **Man:** 18 tot.

♦ **5 Ville-class former tugs** Bldr: Russell Bros., 1944

YTL 582 BURRARD   YTL 587 PLAINSVILLE   YTL 589 LOGANVILLE
YTL 586 QUEENSVILLE YTL 588 YOUVILLE

D: 25 tons   **S:** ...   **Dim:** 12.2 × 3.2 × 1.5   **M:** 1 diesel; 150 hp

♦ **3 miscellaneous reserve training craft**

YAG 116 (18 tons)   YFL 104 (102 tons)   YDT 2 (70 tons)

♦ **1 sailing ketch: QW 3—Oriole: Cadet training**

TUGS

♦ **2 Saint-class oceangoing tugs** Bldr: St. John DD

ATA 531 SAINT ANTHONY   ATA 532 SAINT CHARLES

D: 840 tons (1,017 fl)   **S:** 14 kts   **Dim:** 46.2 (40.7 pp) × 10.0 × 5.2
M: 1 Fairbanks-Morse diesel; 1 prop; 1,920 hp

YARD AND SERVICE CRAFT

♦ **5 Glen-class harbor tugs** (In serv. 1975-77)

Bldrs: 640, 641: Yarrow, Esquimault; others: Georgetown SY, Prince Edward Isl.

YTB 640 GLENDYNE   YTB 642 GLENEVIS   YTB 644 GLENSIDE
YTB 641 GLENDALE   YTB 643 GLENBROOK

D: 255 tons (400 fl)   **S:** 11.5 kts   **Dim:** 28.2 × 8.5 × 4.4
M: 2 Ruston AP-3 diesels; 2 vertical cycloidal props; 1,300 hp   **Man:** 6 tot.

♦ **5 new Ville-class harbor tugs** (In serv. 1974)

YTL 590 LAWRENCEVILLE   YTL 592 LISTERVILLE   YTL 594 MARYSVILLE
YTL 591 PARKSVILLE   YTL 593 MERRICKVILLE

D: 70 tons (fl)   **S:** 9.8 kts   **Dim:** 19.5 × 4.7 × 2.7
M: 1 diesel; 365 hp   **Man:** 3 tot.

♦ **2 Wood-class harbor tugs** (In serv. 1944)

YTL 550 EASTWOOD   YTL 553 WILDWOOD

D: 65 tons (fl)   **S:** 10 kts   **Dim:** 18.3 × 4.9 × 1.5
M: 1 diesel; 250 hp   **Man:** 3 tot.

DIVING TENDERS

♦ **3 steel-hulled** Bldr: Ferguson, Pictou, N.S., 1962-63

YMT 10   YMT 11   YMT 12

YMT 12   1980

DIVING TENDERS (*continued*)

D: 70 tons (132 fl)   **S:** 11 kts   **Dim:** 38.3 × 8.0 × . . .
M: 1 GM 6-71 diesel; 228 hp

♦ **3 wooden-hulled**

YMT 6   YMT 8   YMT 9

D: 70 tons (fl)   **Dim:** 22.9 × 5.6 × . . .   **M:** 2 GM diesels; 2 props; 330 hp

FIREBOATS

♦ **2 130-ton**

YTR 561 FIREBIRD   YTR 562 FIREBRAND

♦ **2 48-ton**

YTR 556 FIRE TUG 1   YTR 557 FIRE TUG

TORPEDO RETRIEVERS

♦ **2 Songhee class** Bldr: Falconer Marine (In serv. 1944)

YPT 1 SONGHEE   YPT 120 NIMPKISH

D: 162 tons (fl)   **Dim:** 22.8 × . . . × . . .   **M:** 2 diesels; 2 props; 400 hp

MISCELLANEOUS SERVICE CRAFT

♦ approximately 12 self-propelled units in the categories of fuel-oil lighter, water tanker, degaussing tender, water tender, floating crane, etc., plus a number of non-self-propelled cargo and fuel barges, power barges, sludge-removal craft, etc.

COAST GUARD

The Canadian Coast Guard is a civilian organization in the Federal Transportation Ministry. It mans some 150 ships, including two weather-station cutters, 20 icebreakers, and about 35 helicopters.

Canadian icebreakers and major service ships are broken down into the following categories:

Type	Designation	Ice-thickness	No. in service
1500	Polar Icebreaker	3-m	0
1400	Sub-Polar Icebreaker	1.6-m	0
1300	Heavy Gulf Icebreaker	1.2-m	1
1200	River Icebreaker	0.7-m	7
1100	Light Icebreaker/Navaids Tender	20-40-ton*	13
1000	Ice-Strengthened Navaids Tender	10-20-ton*	13
900	Small Ice-Strengthened Navaids Tender	5-10-ton*	6
800	Small Navaids Tender	2-5-ton*	6
700	Special River Navaids Tender	5-10-ton*	5
600	Large Search & Rescue Cutter	—	4
500	Intermediate Search & Rescue Cutter	—	7
400	Small Search & Rescue Cutter	—	5
300	Search & Rescue Lifeboat	—	14

*Buoy derrick capacity

AVIATION: The Canadian Coast Guard operates one Douglas DC-3 transport and 34 helicopters: 1 Sikorsky S-61, 3 Alouette III, 4 Bell 212, 21 Bell 206B, and 5 Bell 206L.

♦ **Weather ships for Pacific Ocean service** Bldr: Burrard DD, Vancouver, B.C.

QUADRA (L: 4-7-66)   VANCOUVER (L: 29-6-65)

Quadra   1969

D: 4,720 tons (5,605 fl)   **S:** 18 kts   **Dim:** 123.2 (110.1 pp) × 15.24 × 5.33
Electron Equipt: 1/Decca 838, 1/Decca 939, 1/Sperry SPS-504 weather
M: Turbo-electric propulsion; 2 props; 7,500 hp
Boilers: 2 Babcock & Wilcox; 31.6 kg/cm², 407°C   **Fuel:** 1,333 tons
Electric: 2,610 kw   **Range:** 10,400/14   **Man:** 30 tot.

REMARKS: Passive tank stabilization, 560-hp bow-thruster. Used for meteorological reporting, SAR, and navigation system tending. Telescoping hangar now removed.

SUB-POLAR ICEBREAKER

♦ **1 proposed new-construction sub-polar icebreaker** (Type 1400)

D: 33,000 tons (fl)   **S:** 20 kts   **Dim:** 192.0 × 32.3 × 12.2
M: CODAG: electric drive; 3 props; 90,000 hp   **Range:** 20,000/15
Man: 118 crew plus 56 cadets

REMARKS: This project remains under discussion, but prospects for its construction are dim, due to rising shipbuilding costs. Plans to build an even larger, 42,000-ton full load nuclear-powered icebreaker of 150,000 hp have been shelved.

HEAVY GULF ICEBREAKERS (Type 1300)

♦ **1 programmed new construction**

D: 12 to 16,000 tons (fl)   **S:** . . .   **Dim:** 100.0 to 110.0 × . . . × 9.0
M: CODAG: electric drive; 3 props; 20,100 to 26,800 hp   **Range:** . . .
Man: 90 to 110 tot.

REMARKS: With the cancellation of the nuclear icebreaker program early in 1981, it is now proposed to substitute this much smaller ship for laying down in 1983.

♦ **1 turbo-electric drive**

	Bldr	L	In serv.
LOUIS S. ST. LAURENT	Canadian Vickers, Montreal	3-6-66	8-69

D: 13,300 tons (fl)   **S:** 17.5 kts   **Dim:** 111.7 (101.8 pp) × 24.4 × 9.45
Electron Equipt: Radar: 2/Kelvin-Hughes 14-12, 1/Kelvin-Hughes 14-9
M: 3 sets GT, electric drive; 3 props; 24,000 hp
Electric: 4,300 kw   **Boilers:** 4 Babcock & Wilcox; 42.2 kg/cm², 449°C
Range: 16,000/13   **Man:** 85 tot.

HEAVY GULF ICEBREAKER (continued)

Louis S. St. Laurent   1980

REMARKS: 10,907 grt. Accommodations for 216 total. Two helicopters with hangar below flight deck served by an elevator. Flume passive stabilization tanks. Carries two 15.2-m stores landing craft. Operates off Maritime Provinces.

RIVER ICEBREAKERS (Type 1200)

♦ 3 Pierre Radisson river icebreakers

	Bldr	L	In serv.
PIERRE RADISSON	Burrard DD, Vancouver	3-6-77	1978
FRANKLIN	Burrard DD, Vancouver	10-3-78	1980
N. . .	Port Welland DD, Ont.	. . .	. . .

D: 6,400 tons (8,303 fl)   **S:** 16.5 kts   **Dim:** 98.30 (87.9 pp) × 19.51 × 7.19
Electron Equipt: Radar: 1/TR-611-1, 1/TR-311-S1
M: Diesel-electric: 6 Montreal Loco MLW 251V-16F diesels (17,580 hp total); 6 G.E.C. alternators (11,100 kw); 2 G.E.C. motors; 2 props; 13,600 hp
Fuel: 2,240 tons   **Range:** 15,000/13.5   **Man:** 54 tot.

REMARKS: 5,910 grt/2,820 dwt; 440 m³ cargo capacity. Bow-thruster-equipped. Telescopic hangar and flight deck for one Bell-212 helicopter. Passive-tank stabilization. Used on St. Lawrence River and Great Lakes in winter, in Arctic in summer. Third unit ordered 1981. Seven more proposed.

♦ 2 river icebreakers

NORMAN McLEOD ROGERS   Bldr: Vickers, Montreal (In serv. 6-69)

D: 6,569 tons (fl)   **S:** 16.5 kts   **Dim:** 89.9 (81.1 pp) × 19.0 × 6.2
Electron Equipt: Radar: 2/Kelvin-Hughes 14/12

Pierre Radisson   1980

Norman McLeod Rogers   1980

M: CODAG: 4 Fairbanks-Morse 12-cyl., 2,000-hp diesels; 2 GE W-41G, 4,400-hp gas turbines; electric drive; 2 props; 13,200 hp
Electric: 1,615 kw   **Fuel:** 1,350 tons   **Range:** 12,000/12
Cargo: 900 tons   **Man:** 53 tot.

REMARKS: 4,179 grt/2,320 dwt. Also navigation tender. One helicopter, telescoping hangar.

RIVER ICEBREAKERS (continued)

♦ **1 cable-laying river icebreaker** Bldr: Vickers, Montreal

JOHN CABOT (In serv. 31-5-65)

John Cabot   1969

D: 6,375 tons (fl) **S:** 15 kts **Dim:** 94.0 × 18.0 × 6.45
Electron Equipt: Radar: 1/Decca 969, 1/Decca 2400
M: 4 Fairbanks-Morse 38D8-12 diesels, electric drive; 2 props; 9,000 hp
Electric: 1,060 kw **Fuel:** 705 tons **Range:** 10,000/13 **Man:** 87 tot.

REMARKS: 5,097 grt/2,220 dwt. Carries 400 miles of cable in 3 tanks. Flume passive
stabilization and heeling tanks, telescoping helo hangar.

♦ **1 river icebreaker** Bldr: Davie SB, Lauzon, Que.

JOHN A. MACDONALD (In serv. 9-60)

D: 9,307 tons (fl) **S:** 15.5 kts **Dim:** 96.0 (88.4 pp) × 21.3 × 8.58
M: 9 Fairbanks-Morse 38D8⅛ diesels, electric drive; 3 props; 15,000 hp
Fuel: 2,245 tons **Range:** 20,000/10 **Man:** 76 tot.

REMARKS: 6,186 grt/3,380 dwt. Three helicopters, fixed hangar. 221-m³ cargo space.
Four stores landing craft. Chartered by Dome Petroleum 1978-79.

♦ **1 river icebreaker** Bldr: Marine Ind., Sorel, Que.

	Laid down	L	In serv.
LABRADOR	18-11-49	14-12-51	8-7-54

D: 3,500 tons (7,051 fl) **S:** 16 kts **Dim:** 82.0 (76.2 pp) × 19.4 × 9.3
M: 6 Fairbanks-Morse 38D8⅛ diesels, electric drive; 2 props; 10,000 hp
Fuel: 2,642 tons **Range:** 24,000/12 **Man:** 78 tot.

REMARKS: 3,823 grt. Patterned on U.S. Coast Guard "Wind" class. Transferred from
Canadian Navy 2-58. Heeling tanks, telescoping helicopter hangar.

♦ **1 river icebreaker** Bldr: Davie, Lauzon, Que.

D'IBERVILLE (In serv. 5-53)

D: 10,089 tons (fl) **S:** 15 kts **Dim:** 94.64 × 20.2 × 7.92
Electron Equipt: Radar: 2/Raytheon 1402
M: 2 sets triple-expansion reciprocating; 2 props; 10,800 hp **Boilers:** 2
Fuel: 3,037 tons **Range:** 15,000/10 **Man:** 72 tot.

REMARKS: 5,678 grt. Fixed helicopter hangar. Two 9.1-m landing craft for landing
supplies.

LIGHT ICEBREAKER/NAVIGATIONAL AIDS TENDERS (Type 1100)

♦ GRIFFON Bldr: Davie SB, Lauzon, Que. (In serv. 12-70)

D: 2,960 tons (fl) **S:** 13.5 kts **Dim:** 71.32 × 14.94 × 4.73
Electron Equipt: Radar: 2 Kelvin-Hughes 14-12 **Electric:** 422 kw
M: 4 Fairbanks-Morse 38D8⅛ -8 diesels, electric drive; 2 props; 4,000 hp
Fuel: 345 tons **Range:** 5,500/11 **Man:** 39 tot.

REMARKS: 160-ton cargo capacity. Flume passive tank stabilization. Helicopter landing
platform, no hangar; 10- and 20-ton buoy derricks.

♦ J.E. BERNIER Bldr: Davie SB, Lauzon, Que. (In serv. 8-67)

J.E. Bernier   1969

D: 3,150 tons (fl) **S:** 13.5 kts **Dim:** 70.48 (64.62 pp) × 14.94 × 4.91
Electron Equipt: Radar: Kelvin-Hughes: 1/14-12, 1/14-9
M: 2 diesels, electric drive; 2 props; 4,250 hp **Fuel:** 345 tons
Range: 4,500/11 **Man:** 39 tot.

REMARKS: Similar to *Griffon* and *Montcalm* class, but thinner plating. Has telescoping
helo hangar. Flume passive stabilization tanks.

♦ NARWHAL Bldr: Canadian Vickers, Montreal (In serv. 7-63)

D: 2,258 tons (fl) **S:** 12 kts **Dim:** 76.66 (69.80 pp) × 12.80 × 3.75
M: 2 Cooper-Bessemer direct-drive diesels, fluid couplings; 2 props; 2,000 hp
Electric: 796 kw **Fuel:** 399 tons **Range:** 9,200/11 **Man:** 35 tot.

LIGHT ICEBREAKER/NAVIGATIONAL AIDS TENDERS *(continued)*

Narwhal—with a deck load of navigational buoys   1969

REMARKS: 2,064 grt/697 dwt. Originally typed "Depot Ship/Lighthouse and Buoy Tender" and intended for summer use as an Arctic supply ship carrying 60 stevedores, 20 stores landing craft crew, and 20 administrators. During rest of year, based at Dartmouth, N.S. No helo facilities; has 40-ton buoy derrick.

◆ WOLFE Bldr: Canadian Vickers, Montreal (In serv. 11-59)

Wolfe—note telescoping hangar, stores landing craft   1969

D: 3,043 tons (fl) **S:** 13 kts **Dim:** 76.91 (67.16 pp) × 14.71 × 4.98
M: 2 sets 4-cyclinder, triple-expansion reciprocating steam; 2 props; 4,000 hp
Boilers: 2 Babcock & Wilcox; 16.5 kg/cm², 288°C
Fuel: 621 tons **Range:** 6,000/10 **Man:** 41 tot.

REMARKS: Longer version of *Montcalm*: 2,022 grt. Based at Charlottetown, N.S. Two 9.1-m landing craft, telescoping helo hangar, 25-ton buoy boom.

◆ CAMSELL Bldr: Burrard DD, Vancouver (In serv. 10-59)

D: 3,150 tons (fl) **S:** 13 kts **Dim:** 68.15 (61.53 pp) × 14.63 × 4.88
M: 2 diesels, electric drive; 2 props; 4,250 hp **Fuel:** 536 tons
Range: 12,000/11 **Man:** 42 tot.

REMARKS: 2,022 grt. Based at Vancouver, B.C. Used in lighthouse supply work. Telescoping helicopter hangar.

◆ ALEXANDER HENRY Bldr: Port Arthur SB, Port Arthur, Ont. (In serv. 7-59)

D: 3,196 tons (fl) **S:** 13 kts **Dim:** 64.01 × 13.26 × 5.86
M: Diesels, electric drive; 2 props; 3,550 hp **Fuel:** 387 tons
Range: 6,000/12 **Man:** 34 tot.

REMARKS: 1,674 grt. Based on Lake Ontario at Parry Sound. Has two 9.1-m stores landing craft, helicopter deck but no hangar; 20-ton derrick.

◆ SIR HUMPHREY GILBERT Bldr: Davie SB, Lauzon, Que. (In serv. 6-59)

D: 3,053 tons (fl) **S:** 13 kts **Dim:** 67.06 (61.53 pp) × 14.63 × 4.88
M: 2 diesels, electric drive; 4,250 hp **Fuel:** 552 tons
Range: 10,000/11 **Man:** 40 tot.

REMARKS: 1,931 grt. Home-ported at Quebec City. 25-ton buoy derrick. Telescoping helicopter hangar. No landing craft.

◆ SIR WILLIAM ALEXANDER Bldr: Halifax SY (In serv. 6-59)

Sir William Alexander   1969

D: 3,607 tons **S:** 15 kts **Dim:** 83.06 × 13.73 × 5.33
M: 2 diesels, electric drive; 2 props; 4,250 hp **Fuel:** 563 tons
Range: 12,000/12.5 **Man:** 42 tot.

REMARKS: 2,154 grt/1,610 dwt. Based at Dartmouth, Nova Scotia. Carries two 9.1-m stores landing craft. Helo deck, no hangar. 20-ton buoy boom.

◆ MONTCALM Bldr: Davie SB, Lauzon, Que. (In serv. 7-3-57)

D: 3,043 tons **S:** 13 kts **Dim:** 72.7 × 14.71 × 4.98
M: 2 sets Vickers-Skinner Uniflow 4-cyl., triple-expansion reciprocating steam; 2 props; 4,000 hp
Boilers: 2 Babcock & Wilcox; 16.5 kg/cm², 288°C **Fuel:** 663 tons
Range: 6,000/10 **Man:** 42 tot.

REMARKS: 2,017 grt. Based at Quebec City. Telescoping helicopter hangar, two 9.1-m stores landing craft, 25-ton buoy derrick.

◆ WALTER E. FOSTER Bldr: Canadian Vickers, Montreal (In serv. 12-54)

LIGHT ICEBREAKER/NAVIGATIONAL AIDS TENDERS *(continued)*

Walter E. Foster   1969

D: 2,902 tons (fl) **S:** 12.5 kts **Dim:** 69.85 × 12.95 × 5.03
M: 2 sets Vickers-Skinner Uniflow 4-cyl., triple-expansion reciprocating steam;
2 props; 2,000 hp
Boilers: 2 **Fuel:** 482 tons **Range:** 5,000/11 **Man:** 43 tot.

REMARKS: 1,672 grt. Based at St. John, Newfoundland. No helo facilities.

♦ EDWARD CORNWALLIS Bldr: Canadian Vickers, Montreal (In serv. 12-49)

D: 3,996 tons (fl) **S:** 13.5 kts **Dim:** 78.94 (73.15 pp) × 13.26 × 5.51
M: 2 sets Vickers-Skinner Uniflow 4-cyl., triple-expansion reciprocating; 2
props; 2,800 hp
Boilers: 2, Scotch **Fuel:** 589 tons **Range:** 7,500/12.5 **Man:** 43 tot.

REMARKS: 1,965 grt/1,800 dwt. In reserve at Dartmouth, N.S. since 1969. Only Type
1100 with cargo gear aft. No helo facilities.

ICE-STRENGTHENED NAVIGATIONAL AIDS TENDERS (Type 1000)

♦ **2 Provo Wallis class** Bldr: Marine Industries, Sorel, Que.

PROVO WALLIS (In serv. 10-69) BARTLETT (In serv. 12-69)

D: 1,722 tons (fl) **S:** 12 kts **Dim:** 57.68 × 12.95 × 3.66
Electron Equipt: Radar: 2 Kelvin-Hughes 14-12
M: 2 direct-drive diesels; 2 CP props; 1,760 hp **Fuel:** 102 tons
Range: 3,300/11 **Man:** 29 tot.

REMARKS: 1,313 grt. Carry one 9.1-m landing craft. Have 15-ton derrick. *P. Wallis*
based at St. John's, *Bartlett* at Dartmouth, N.S.

♦ TRACY Bldr: Port Weller DD, Ltd. (In serv. 17-4-68)

D: 1,491 tons (fl) **S:** 13 kts **Dim:** 55.32 (50.29 pp) × 11.58 × 3.66
Electron Equipt: Radar: 1/Kelvin-Hughes 14-12 **Electric:** 402 kw
M: 2 Fairbanks-Morse 38D8⅛-8 diesels, electric drive; 2 props; 2,000 hp
Fuel: 132 tons **Range:** 5,000/10 **Man:** 33 tot.

REMARKS: 960 grt. Based at Sorel, Quebec.

Bartlett   1970

♦ MONTMAGNY Bldr: Russell Bros., Owen Sound, Ont. (In serv. 5-63)

D: 625 tons (fl) **S:** 12 kts **Dim:** 45.11 × 8.84 × 2.59
M: 2 Werkspoor diesels; 2 props; 1,048 hp **Fuel:** 48 tons
Range: 4,000/10 **Man:** 23 tot.

REMARKS: 497 grt. Based at Sorel, Quebec. One 7-ton derrick.

♦ NICOLET Bldr: Collingwood SY, Collingwood, Ont. (In serv. 12-66)

Nicolet—note broad bow at upper deck   1969

ICE-STRENGTHENED NAVIGATIONAL AIDS TENDERS *(continued)*

D: 935 tons (fl) **S:** 13 kts **Dim:** 51.44 × 10.67 × 2.90
Electron Equipt: Radar: 1/Kelvin-Hughes 14-9
M: 2 diesels; 2 props; 1,350 hp **Fuel:** 75 tons **Range:** 3,000/11 **Man:** 26 tot.

REMARKS: 887 grt. Based at Sorel, Que., for use as a soundings ship on the St. Lawrence Ship Channel. An updated *Beauport*.

♦ SIMCOE Bldr: Canadian Vickers, Montreal (In serv. 1962)

D: 1,392 tons (fl) **S:** 13 kts **Dim:** 54.62 × 11.58 × 3.83
M: 2 diesels, electric drive; 2 props; 2,000 hp **Fuel:** 156 tons
Range: 5,000/10 **Man:** 32 tot.

REMARKS: 961 grt. Based on Lake Ontario at Prescott.

♦ THOMAS CARLTON Bldr: St. John's DD (In serv. 1960)

D: 1,491 tons (fl) **S:** 12 kts **Dim:** 50.84 × 12.83 × 4.15
M: 2 diesels, electric drive; 2 props; 2,900 hp **Fuel:** 178 tons
Range: 5,000/11 **Man:** 39 tot.

REMARKS: 1,217 grt. Home-ported at St. John, New Brunswick. Helicopter platform, no hangar; has 20-ton buoy derrick.

♦ BEAUPORT Bldr: Davie SB, Lauzon, Que. (In serv. 1960)

D: 876 tons (fl) **S:** 13 kts **Dim:** 51.05 × 10.36 × 2.74
Electron Equipt: Radar: 1/LN-47 **M:** 2 diesels; 2 props; 1,280 hp
Fuel: 62 tons **Range:** 3,000/11 **Man:** 26 tot.

REMARKS: 813 grt. Based at Sorel, Que., as a soundings ship on the St. Lawrence Ship Channel. 8-ton electric buoy crane.

♦ SIMON FRASER Bldr: Burrard DD, Vancouver (In serv. 2-60)

Simon Fraser—telescoping hangar extended   1969

D: 1,874 tons (fl) **S:** 13.5 kts **Dim:** 62.33 × 12.80 × 4.27
M: 2 diesels, electric drive; 2 props; 2,900 hp **Fuel:** 178 tons
Range: 5,000/10 **Man:** 38 tot.

REMARKS: 1,352 grt. Based at Quebec City. Helicopter deck and telescoping hangar. Very similar to *Tupper*.

♦ TUPPER Bldr: Marine Ind., Sorel, Que. (In serv. 12-59)

D: 1,876 tons (fl) **S:** 13.5 kts **Dim:** 62.26 × 12.80 × 4.23
M: 2 diesels, electric drive; 2 props; 2,900 hp **Fuel:** 206 tons
Range: 5,000/11 **Man:** 37 tot.

REMARKS: 1,358 grt. Based at Charlottetown, Prince Edward Isl. Helicopter deck, no hangar. 15-ton buoy derrick.

♦ MONTMORENCY Bldr: Davie SB, Lauzon, Que. (In serv. 8-57)

Montmorency   1969

D: 980 tons (fl) **S:** 12 kts **Dim:** 50.14 × 9.75 × 3.35
M: 2 diesels; 2 props; 1,200 hp **Fuel:** 142 tons **Range:** 3,500/11 **Man:** 31 tot.

REMARKS: 751 grt. Operates on Lake Huron, from Parry Sound. 12-ton buoy derrick.

♦ **2 Alexander McKenzie class** Bldr: Burrard DD, Vancouver, B.C.

ALEXANDER McKENZIE (In serv. 1950)   SIR JAMES DOUGLAS (In serv. 11-56)

Sir James Douglas—with two 9.1-m stores landing craft   1969

ICE-STRENGTHENED NAVIGATIONAL AIDS TENDERS *(continued)*

D: 768 tons (fl) **S:** 11.5 kts **Dim:** 45.87 × 9.45 × 3.17
M: 2 diesels; 1 prop; 1,000 hp **Fuel:** 85 tons
Range: 6,000/10.5 **Man:** 29 tot.

REMARKS: *McKenzie:* 576 grt—*Douglas:* 564 grt. Based in British Columbia. 10-ton buoy boom.

SMALL ICE-STRENGTHENED NAVIGATIONAL AIDS TENDERS (Type 900)

♦ NAMAO Bldr: Riverton Boatwks, Manitoba (In serv. 1975)

D: 386 tons (fl) **S:** 12 kts **Dim:** 33.53 × 8.53 × 2.13
M: 2 diesels; 2 props; 1,350 hp **Fuel:** 34.5 tons **Range:** 2,000/11
Man: 10 tot.

REMARKS: Employed as buoy tender on Lake Winnepeg.

♦ ROBERT FOULIS Bldr: St. John DD, N.B. (In serv. 24-11-69)

D: 332 tons (fl) **S:** 11 kts **Dim:** 31.70 × 7.62 × 2.44
M: 2 diesels; 2 props; 960 hp **Fuel:** 21 tons **Range:** 1,500/10 **Man:** 12 tot.

REMARKS: 258 grt. Employed on St. John River, New Brunswick.

♦ KENOKI Bldr: Erieu SB (In serv. 5-64)

Kenoki   1969

D: 274 tons (438 fl) **S:** 10.5 kts **Dim:** 33.22 × 9.75 × 1.85
Electron Equipt: Radar: 1/Kelvin-Hughes 14-9 **M:** 2 diesels; 2 props; 800 hp
Fuel: 40 tons **Range:** 1,000/10 **Man:** 12 tot.

REMARKS: 310 grt. Barge-like hull with four hydraulic pilings for precise positioning while working as a shallow-water buoy tender. Two 5-ton cranes. Based at Prescott, Ont.

♦ SKIDEGATE Bldr: Allied SB, Vancouver, B.C. (In serv. 4-64)

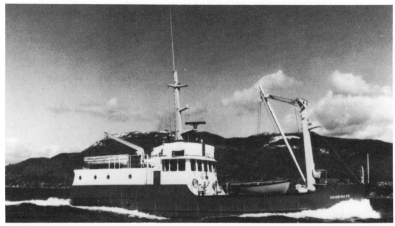

Skidegate   1969

D: 200 tons (fl) **S:** 11.4 kts **Dim:** 30.80 × 8.08 × 2.44
M: 2 Cummins V-12 diesels; 2 props; 680 hp **Fuel:** 23 tons
Range: 2,340/10.5 **Man:** 11 tot.

REMARKS: 136 grt. Based at Prince Rupert, B.C.

♦ VERENDRYE Bldr: Davie SB, Lauzon, Que. (In serv. 10-59)

D: 406 tons (fl) **S:** 10 kts **Dim:** 36.40 × 7.95 × 3.05
M: 2 diesels; 2 props; 760 hp **Fuel:** 28 tons **Range:** 2,000/7.5 **Man:** 20 tot.

REMARKS: 297 grt. Based at Sorel, Que., for use on St. Lawrence Ship Channel. 6-ton electrohydraulic buoy crane.

SMALL NAVIGATIONAL AIDS TENDERS (Type 800)

♦ PARRY SOUND Bldr:. . . (In serv. 1979)

D: . . . tons **S:** 10 kts **Dim:** 20.00 × 6.00 × 1.35
M: diesels; 500 hp **Man:** 4 tot.

♦ F.G. OSBOURNE (In serv. 1974)

D: . . . tons **S:** 8 kts **Dim:** 15.85 × 5.18 × 1.22
M: diesels; . . . hp **Man:** 4 tot.

♦ JEAN BOURDON Bldr: Kingston SY, Ont. (In serv. 5-68)

D: . . . tons **S:** 10 kts **Dim:** 20.60 × 6.10 × 1.71
Electron Equipt: Radar: 1/Raytheon 1405A
M: 2 diesels; 2 props; 340 hp **Electric:** 30 kw **Fuel:** 4 tons
Range: 750/10 **Man:** 4 tot.

REMARKS: 82.2 grt. For hydrographic survey work on the St. Lawrence Ship Channel; based at Sorel, Que.

♦ BARGE 501 (In serv. 1967)

D: . . . tons **S:** 8 kts **Dim:** 15.24 × 4.27 × . . .
M: diesels; . . . hp **Man:** . . . tot.

SMALL NAVIGATIONAL AIDS TENDERS *(continued)*

♦ Nomad V (In serv. 1966)

> **D:** . . . tons **S:** 7 kts **Dim:** 12.80 × 4.27 × 1.22
> **M:** diesels; . . . hp

♦ Nokomis Bldr: Lunenberg Foundry (In serv. 1957)

> **D:** . . . tons **S:** 9.6 kts **Dim:** 20.24 × 5.33 × 2.16
> **M:** 1 diesel; 120 hp **Fuel:** 4.1 tons **Range:** 650/9 **Man:** 4 tot.

REMARKS: 64 grt. Based at Parry Sound, Lake Huron.

SPECIAL RIVER NAVIGATIONAL AIDS TENDERS
(Type 700)

NOTE: All below serve on the Mackenzie River, Northwest Territories.

♦ Dumit Bldr: Allied SB, Vancouver, B.C. (In serv. 7-79)

REMARKS: No data available; replacement for 1958 ship of same name.

♦ Tembah Bldr: Allied SB, Vancouver (In serv. 9-63)

> **D:** 181 tons (fl) **S:** 13 kts **Dim:** 37.51 × 7.92 × 0.91
> **M:** 2 diesels; 2 props; 680 hp **Fuel:** 18 tons **Range:** 1,000/7 **Man:** 9 tot.

♦ Eckaloo Bldr: Allied SB, Vancouver, B.C. (In serv. 1961)

> **D:** 135 tons (fl) **S:** 10 kts **Dim:** 25.26 × 6.71 × 1.22
> **M:** 2 diesels; 2 props; 300 hp **Fuel:** 7 tons **Range:** 600/7 **Man:** 8 tot.

♦ 2 Dumit class Bldr: Allied SB, Vancouver, B.C. (In serv. 1958)

Dumit   Miskanaw

> **D:** 99.6 tons (fl) **S:** 10 kts **Dim:** 19.51 × 5.97 × 1.22
> **M:** 2 diesels; 2 props; 300 hp **Fuel:** 4 tons **Range:** 300/7 **Man:** 8 tot.

LARGE SEARCH AND RESCUE CUTTERS
(Type 600)

♦ 2 former oilfield supply ships Bldr: Bel-Air SY, Vancouver, B.C.

Grenfell (ex-M/V *Baffin Service*, ex-*Nordic V*) (In serv. 8-73)
Jackman (ex-M/V *Hudson Service*, ex-*Nordic IV*)(In serv. 8-73)

> **D:** 2,089 tons (fl) **S:** 13 kts **Dim:** 56.10 (51.94 pp) × 13.72 × 4.42
> **M:** 4 GM 16-565C diesels; 2 props; 6,400 hp **Electric:** 360 kw
> **Fuel:** 587 tons **Range:** 12,000/12 **Man:** . . . tot.

REMARKS: 877 grt/452 dwt. Acquired from Nordic Offshore Services in 1979 and based at Vancouver. Typical oilfield supply tugs with long, low, open cleared fantail. Main engines built 1950, rebuilt in 1972 for shipboard use. Ice-strengthened hulls.

♦ Alert Bldr: Davie SB, Lauzon, Que. (In serv. 20-11-69)

> **D:** 2,025 tons (fl) **S:** 18.7 kts **Dim:** 71.40 × 12.12 × 4.84
> **M:** 2 diesels, electric drive; 2 props; 9,716 hp **Range:** 6,000/14.5
> **Man:** 38 tot.

REMARKS: Was to have been a class of six. Telescoping hangar for helicopter. Operates in Atlantic.

♦ Daring (ex-RCMP *Wood*) Bldr: Davie SB, Lauzon, Que. (In serv. 7-58)

> **D:** 600 tons (676 fl) **S:** 16 kts **Dim:** 54.26 (50.14 pp) × 8.84 × 2.90
> **M:** 2 Fairbanks-Morse 38D8⅛ diesels; 2 props; 2,660 hp
> **Fuel:** . . . tons **Range:** 7,000/15 **Man:** 36 tot.

REMARKS: Ice-reinforced hull, no helicopter. Transferred from Royal Canadian Mounted Police 1971. Based at Halifax.

INTERMEDIATE SEARCH AND RESCUE CUTTERS (Type 500)

♦ 6 R class, based on U.S. Coast Guard 95-ft. design

	Bldr	In serv.
Racer	Yarrow, Esquimault, B.C.	1963
Rally	Davie SB, Lauzon, Que.	1963
Rapid	Ferguson Ind., Pictou, N.S.	1963
Ready	Burrard DD, Vancouver, B.C.	1963
Relay	Kingston SY, Kingston, Ont.	1963
Rider	Victoria Mach Dépôt, Victoria, B.C.	1962

Ready   1963

> **D:** 105 tons (fl) **S:** 20 kts **Dim:** 29.03 (27.34 pp) × 6.10 × 1.96
> **M:** 4 Cummins VT-12-M-700 diesels; 2 props; 2,400 hp
> **Electric:** 76 kw **Fuel:** 12 tons **Range:** 1,050/16, 1,500/12.5 **Man:** 12 tot.

REMARKS: *Relay* is used for traffic control on the St. Lawrence Seaway and is based at Sorel, Que. The others perform SAR duties. *Rider* was taken over from the Bureau of Fisheries in 1969.

♦ Ville Marie Bldr: Russell-Hipwell Eng., Owen Sound, Ont. (In serv. 1960)

> **D:** 518 tons (fl) **S:** 13.5 kts **Dim:** 40.92 × 8.71 × 2.24
> **M:** 2 diesels; 2 props; 1,000 hp **Fuel:** 50 tons **Range:** 1,000/13 **Man:** 23 tot.

REMARKS: 390 grt. Soundings boat for St. Lawrence Ship Channel, based at Sorel, Que.

SMALL SEARCH AND RESCUE CUTTERS (Type 400)

♦ 2 new construction Bldr: Breton Industry & Machinery, Point Hawkesbury, N.S. (In serv. 1981)

N . . .   N . . .

CANADA *(continued)*
SMALL SEARCH AND RESEARCH CUTTERS *(continued)*

D: 77 tons (fl) **S:** 20 kts **Dim:** 21.33 × 5.18 × 1.83
M: 2 MTU 8V 396 TC2 diesels; 2 props; 1,300 hp **Range:** 1,030/12.5
Man: 6 tot.

REMARKS: Proceeded from Nova Scotia to the Pacific Coast under own power. Two more may be built.

◆ **3 S class—for Great Lakes service**

	Bldr	In serv.
SPUME	Grew Ltd., Penatanguishene, Ont.	11-63
SPRAY	J.J. Taylor & Son, Toronto, Ont.	1964
SPINDRIFT	Cliff Richardson BY, Medford, Ont.	1964

Spindrift   1969

D: . . . **S:** 14 kts **Dim:** 21.29 × 5.11 × 1.55 **M:** 2 diesels; 2 props; 1,050 hp
Fuel: 4 tons **Range:** 500/12-13.5 **Man:** 4 tot.

SEARCH AND RESCUE LIFEBOATS (Type 300)

◆ **14 U.S. Coast Guard 44-ft. motor lifeboat class** (In serv. 1967-72)

CG 101 through 109, 114 through 118

D: 16 tons (fl) **S:** 15 kts **Dim:** 13.60 × 3.86 × 0.93
Electron Equipt: Radar: 1/Raytheon 1900
M: 2 GM 6-71 diesels; 2 props; 360 hp (294 hp sust.) **Range:** 150/12
Man: 3 tot.

REMARKS: First unit built U.S.C.G. Yard, Curtis Bay, Md. in 1967, remainder built in Canada. Units on both Atlantic and Pacific coasts.

CAPE VERDE ISLANDS
Republic of Cape Verde

PERSONNEL: . . .

MERCHANT MARINE (1980): 22 ships—11,426 grt (tanker: 1 ship—216 grt)

PATROL BOATS

◆ **3 Soviet Shershen-class former torpedo boats**

D: 180 tons (fl) **S:** 45 kts **Dim:** 34.0 × 7.2 × 1.5
A: 4/30-mm AA (II × 2) **Electron Equipt:** Radar: 1/Pot Head, 1 Drum Tilt
M: 3 M-503A diesels; 3 props; 12,000 hp **Range:** 450/34, 700/20

REMARKS: Transferred 1-, 3-, and 7-79. Torpedo tubes removed prior to transfer.

◆ **2 Soviet Zhuk class—transferred 1980**

D: 50 tons (fl) **S:** 30 kts **Dim:** 22.9 × 4.9 × 1.5 **A:** 4/14.5-mm mg (II × 2)
Electron Equipt: Radar: 1/Spin Trough **M:** 2 M-50 diesels; 2 props; 2,400 hp

CHILE
Republic of Chile

PERSONNEL: 28,000 total (1,995 officers; 23,935 men; 2,680 naval infantry). Civil Service personnel with a more or less military status number about 6,600.

MERCHANT MARINE (1980): 172 ships—614,425 grt (tankers: 6—41,132 grt)

NAVAL AVIATION: Established in 1923, merged in 1939 with the aviation arm of the military, Fuerza Aera de Chile, and reestablished in 1953. However, its growth has been restrained by the Air Force, which retains responsibility for the airspace over the ocean. The naval air arm has 23 aircraft (8 Embraer Bandeirante maritime surveillance aircraft, 6 T-34B Mentor trainers, 3 C-47 transports and 6 Casa 212 Aviocar) and 26 helicopters (10 Alouette-III, 4 Bell 206A JetRanger, 7 Bell 47-G, 3 Bell 47, 2 Bell 47-J). The principal air base is at El Belloto, near Valparaiso.

WARSHIPS IN SERVICE OR UNDER CONSTRUCTION, AS OF 1 JANUARY 1982

	L	Tons (Surfaced)	Main armament
◆ **3 (+2) submarines**			
0 (+2) Type 209	. . .	1,105	8/533-mm TT
2 OBERON	1972-73	2,030	8/533-mm TT
1 BALAO	1944	1,810	10/533-mm TT

	L	Tons	Main armament
◆ **3 cruisers**			
1 TRE KRONOR	1945	8,200	7/152-mm DP, 4/57-mm AA, 6/533-mm TT
2 BROOKLYN	1936-37	10,000	15/152-mm, 8/127-mm DP
◆ **6 destroyers**			
2 ALMIRANTE WILLIAMS	1958	2,730	4/102-mm DP, 2 Exocet SSM
2 ALLEN M. SUMNER	1944	2,200	6/127-mm DP, 2 Exocet SSM
2 FLETCHER	1943-44	2,050	4/127-mm DP, 5/533-mm TT
◆ **3 frigates**			
2 LEANDER	1972-73	2,500	2/114-mm DP, 4 Exocet SSM
1 CHARLES LAWRENCE	1943	1,691	1/127-mm DP
◆ **2 (+?) guided-missile boats**			
	1973-74	415	7 Gabriel, 2/76-mm DP
◆ **4 torpedo boats**	1965-66	134	2/40-mm AA, 4/533-mm TT

WEAPONS AND SYSTEMS

Most of the Chilean Navy's equipment is of U.S. or British origin. Among the most modern weapons are the guns of the cruiser *Almirante Latorre* and the *Almirante Williams*-class destroyers, the French MM-38 Exocet anti-ship missiles on four destroyers and two frigates, and the British Sea Cat point-defense SAM systems on the *Williams* and *Leander* classes.

152-mm Bofors

This gun, which dates from 1942 and is mounted in twin- and triple-barreled turrets, is on the *Almirante Latorre*. Its characteristics are:

Muzzle velocity: 900m/sec
Arc: +70°
Maximum firing rate: 10 rounds/minute/barrel
Projectile: 46 kg
Maximum range, surface target: 26,000 m
Maximum range, surface target (effective): 15,000 m
Maximum range, air target (effective): 10,000 m

102-mm Vickers DP

This single-barreled automatic mount dates from 1955 and is not used by any other navy. It is on the *Almirante Riveros* and the *Almirante Williams*.

Turret weight: about 26 tons
Muzzle velocity: 900m/sec
Arc: +75°
Maximum firing rate: 40 rounds/minute
Projectile: 16 kg
Maximum range, surface target: 18,500 m
Maximum range, surface target (effective): 12,000 m
Maximum range, air target: 12,000 m
Maximum range, air target (effective): 8,000 m

SUBMARINES

◆ **2 German Type 209** Bldr: Howaldtwerke, Kiel

	Laid down	L	In serv.
S. . . ANTOFAGASTA	. . .	. . .	. . .
S. . . N. . .	. . .	. . .	. . .

D: 980 tons/1,230 **S:** 21 kts (for 5 minutes) sub.; 12 kts on snorkel
A: 8/533-mm TT fwd. (6 reserve torpedoes)
M: 4 MTU 12V-493-TY60 diesels, each linked to a 450-kw AEG generator, one Siemens electric motor; 5,000 hp
Fuel: 56 tons **Man:** 5 officers, 26 men

REMARKS: Ordered 12-80, but have encountered considerable political opposition in West Germany, and the arrangement may have to be canceled. These submarines apparently employ components originally intended for the large Iranian order.

◆ **2 British Oberon class**

	Bldr	Laid down	L	In serv.
S 22 O'BRIEN	Scott Lithgow	17-1-71	21-12-72	4-76
S 23 HYATT	Scott Lithgow	16-1-72	26-9-73	27-9-76

O'Brien   G. Arra, 1977

D: 1,610/2,070/2,410 tons **S:** 15/17.5 kts **Dim:** 89.92 (87.45 pp) × 8.07 × 5.48
A: 8/533-mm TT (6 fwd, 2 aft)—22 torpedoes
Electron Equipt: Radar: 1/1006—Sonar: 1/2007, 1/187, 1/197, 1/719
M: 2 Admiralty Standard Range 16 VVS-AS21 diesels, diesel-electric drive; 2 props; 6,000 hp
Man: 65 tot.

REMARKS: Delivery of these submarines was a year late because of a number of malfunctions in the electrical equipment.

◆ **1 U.S. Balao class** Bldr: Mare Island NSY, Cal.

	Laid down	L	In serv.
S 21 SIMPSON (ex-*Spot*, SS 413)	24-8-43	19-5-44	3-8-44

D: 1,526 tons light, 1,810/2,425 tons **S:** 18.5/10 kts
Dim: 95.02 × 8.34 × 5.18
A: 10/533-mm TT (6 fwd, 4 aft—22 torpedoes)—1/127-mm 25-cal. DP WET
M: 4 Fairbanks-Morse 38D81/8 diesels, 5,400 hp, electric drive; 2 props; 4,600 hp
Range: 12,000/13.5, 9,700/6.5 (snorkeling) **Man:** 80 tot.

SUBMARINES *(continued)*

REMARKS: Transferred in 1961, the *Simpson* was decommissioned in 1975 but reactivated in 1977. Four 126-cell batteries. Streamlined, high, Guppy-type sail. Sister *Thompson*, S 20, (ex-*Springer* SS 414) still exists as a training hulk.

CRUISERS

♦ **1 Swedish Tre Kronor class** Bldr: Eriksberg Mekaniska Verkstad, Göteborg

	Laid down	L	In serv.
04 ALMIRANTE LATORRE	27-9-43	17-11-45	15-12-47
(ex-*Göta Lejon*)			

Almirante Latorre (04) 1972

D: 8,200 tons (10,000 fl) **S:** 33 kts **Dim:** 182.0 (174 wl)× 16.5 × 6.5
A: 7.152-mm DP (III × 2, II × 2)—4.57-mm AA—10/40-mm AA (I × 10)—6/533-mm TT (III × 2)—2 d.c. racks—120 mines
Electron Equipt: Radars: 1/LWO-2, 1/277Q and 1/293 (British), 4/SQR 102 fire control, 1/Mk 8 f.c.
M: De Laval GT; 2 props; 100,000 hp **Boilers:** 4 Penhoët; 32 kg/cm², 375°C
Armor: Belt: 80-100-mm—Main deck: 40-60-mm—Turrets: 135-mm fwd, 30-mm sides, 50-mm top
Man: 26 officers, 429 men (peacetime), 30 officers, 618 men (wartime)

REMARKS: Purchased 7-71. Bow 40-mm removed. 103-mm flare launchers on fwd turret, automatic 305-mm flare launcher on stern.

♦ **2 U.S. Brooklyn class**

	Bldr	Laid down	L	In serv.
02 O'HIGGINS	New York NY,	12-3-35	30-11-36	18-7-38
(ex-*Brooklyn*, CL 40)	Brooklyn, N.Y.			
03 PRAT	New York SB Corp,	24-1-35	2-10-37	25-11-38
(ex-*Nashville*, CL 43)	Camden, N.J.			

D: 02: 10,000 tons (13,500 fl) 03: 9,700 tons (13,000 fl)
S: 30/25 kts **Dim:** 185.42 × 21.03 (03: 18.77) × 7.62
A: 15/152-mm (III × 5)—8/127-mm DP (I × 8)—28/40-mm AA (IV × 6, II × 2)—12/20-mm AA (II × 6)—1 SH-57A JetRanger helicopter
Electron Equipt: Radars: 1/SPS-6B, 2/SPS-4, 2 Mk 8, 4 Mk 28
M: 4 sets Westinghouse GT; 4 props; 100,000 hp
Boilers: 8 Babcock & Wilcox; 28 kg/cm², 342°C **Man:** 890/970 tot.
Armor: Belt: 76-127-mm—Main deck: 76-mm—Upper deck: 52-mm—Turrets: 127-mm face **Fuel:** 2,377 tons **Range:** 2,500/30, 9,850/12

REMARKS: Bought 1951, refitted in U.S.A. 1957-58. *O'Higgins*, damaged in collision in 1974 and laid up as an accommodation hulk, was repaired and recommissioned in 1978. Both have two Mk 34 directors for 152-mm guns, two Mk 33 for 127-mm guns, and two Mk 57 and 6 Mk 51 fire-control systems for 40-mm guns. *Prat* has bulges, *O'Higgins* does not. *Prat* placed in reserve 1981.

DESTROYERS

♦ **2 Almirante Williams class**

	Bldr	Laid down	L	In serv.
D 18 ALMIRANTE RIVEROS	Vickers-Armstrong	12-4-57	12-12-58	31-12-60
D 19 ALMIRANTE WILLIAMS	Vickers-Armstrong	20-6-56	5-5-58	26-3-60

Almirante Williams (D 19) 1977

D: 2,730 tons (3,300 fl) **S:** 34.5 kts **Dim:** 122.5 (113.99 pp) × 13.1 × 3.9
A: 2/MM 38 Exocet—2/Sea Cat SAM systems (IV × 2)—4/102-mm DP (I × 4)—4/40-mm AA (I × 4)—6/324-mm Mk 32 ASW TT (III × 2)—2/Squid ASW mortars (III × 2)
Electron Equipt: Radars: 1/Decca 629, 1/Plessey ASW-1, 1/Marconi SNW-10, 1/SWW-20, 2/SGR-102, 2/SNG-20
Sonar: 1/164B—ECM: WLR-1
M: 2 sets Parsons-Pamatreda GT; 2 props; 50,000 hp
Boilers: 4 Babcock & Wilcox; 43.3 kg/cm², 454°C **Range:** 7,800
Man: 17 officers, 249 men

REMARKS: Refitted in Great Britain, D 18 in 1973-75 and D 19 in 1971-74. Dutch M-4 radar directors for Sea Cat. Exocet replaced four 533-mm TT (IV × 1); 2 Exocet removed from each and placed on *Allen M. Sumner* class, 1980.

♦ **2 U.S. Allen M. Sumner FRAM II class**

	Bldr	Laid down	L	In serv.
D 16 MINISTRO ZENTENO	Federal SB & DD,	19-10-43	30-9-44	26-12-44
(ex-*Charles S. Sperry*, DD 697)	Kearny, N.J.			
D 17 MINISTRO PORTALES	Todd Pacific SY,	31-1-44	13-3-44	17-5-44
(ex-*Douglas H. Fox*, DD 779)	Tacoma, Wash.			

D: 2,200 tons (3,300 fl) **S:** 30 kts **Dim:** 114.75 × 12.45 × 5.8 (sonar)
A: 2/MM 38 Exocet—6/127-mm DP 38-cal. (II × 3)—6/324-mm Mk 32 ASW TT (III × 2)—2/Hedgehogs—1 SH-57A helicopter

Ministro Zenteno (D 16) 1977

DESTROYERS (continued)

Ministro Portales (D 17)   1975

   Electron Equipt: Radars: 1/SPS-40 (D-17) or SPS-29 (D-16), 1/SPS-10, 1/Mk 25
               Sonar: 1/SQS-40—ECM: WLR-1
   M: 2 sets GT; 2 props; 60,000 hp
   Boilers: 4 Foster-Wheeler and Babcock & Wilcox; 43.3 kg/cm², 454°C
   Fuel: 650 tons   **Range:** 1,260/30, 4,600/15   **Man:** 14 officers, 260 men

REMARKS: Purchased 8-1-74. VDS removed 1980; 2 Exocet SSM from *Williams* class
mounted on 01 deck between stacks. Mk 37 GFCS.

♦ **2 U.S. Fletcher class**

	Bldr	Laid down	L	In serv.
D 14 BLANCO ENCALADA	Bath Iron Works,	5-4-43	7-8-43	19-10-43
(ex-*Wadleigh*, DD 689)	Bath, Maine			
D 15 COCHRANE	Todd-Pacific SY,	27-10-43	6-6-44	2-9-44
(ex-*Rooks*, DD 804)	Seattle, Wash.			

Blanco Encalada (D 14)   1977

   D: 2,050 tons (2,850 fl)   **S:** 32 kts   **Dim:** 114.85 × 12.03 × 5.5
   A: 4/127-mm DP 38-cal. (I × 4)—6/76.2-mm DP (II × 3)—5/533-mm TT (V ×
      1)—2/Hedgehogs—1 d.c. rack
   Electron Equipt: Radars: 1/SPS-6C, 1/SPS-10, 1/Mk 25, 2/Mk 34, 1/Mk 35
               Sonar: 1/SQS-29—ECM: WLR-1
   M: 2 sets GT; 2 props; 60,000 hp
   Boilers: 4 Babcock & Wilcox; 43.3 kg/cm², 454°C   **Electric:** 660 kw
   Fuel: 512 tons   **Range:** 1,385/32, 3,800/12   **Man:** 15 officers, 247 men

REMARKS: Transferred in 1962. The *Cochrane* refitted and recommissioned 1977-78.
Both were placed in reserve in 1981. One Mk 37, one Mk 56, 2 Mk 63 GFCS.

FRIGATES

♦ **2 Spanish Descubierta class** Bldr: Bazan, el Ferrol or Cartagena

	Laid down	L	In serv.
PF. . . N. . .	. . .	. . .	. . .
PF. . . N. . .	. . .	. . .	. . .

   D: 1,270 tons (1,439 fl)   **S:** 26 kts
   Dim: 88.88 (85.80 pp) × 10.4 × 3.25   **A:** . . .
   Electron Equipt: Radar: . . .
               Sonar: . . .
   M: 4 MTU-Bazan 16MA956 TB91 diesels; 2 CP props; 18,000 hp
   Electric: 1,810 kw   **Fuel:** 197 tons   **Range:** 6,000/18   **Man:** 116 tot.

REMARKS: Ordered early 1981 and described as "antiaircraft frigates," so armament
may differ from sisters in Spanish Navy.

♦ **2 British Leander class**

	Bldr	Laid down	L	In serv.
PF 06 CONDELL	Yarrow & Co	5-6-71	12-6-72	21-12-73
PF 07 LYNCH	Yarrow & Co	6-12-72	6-12-73	25-5-74

Condell (PF 06)   1977

Lynch (PF 07)   1977

   D: 2,500 tons (2,962 fl)   **S:** 27 kts   **Dim:** 113.38 (109.73 pp) × 13.12 × 5.49 (fl)
   A: 4/MM 38 Exocet—2/114-mm Mk VI DP (II × 1)—1/Sea Cat SAM system (IV
      × 1; 16 missiles)—2/20-mm AA—6/324-mm ASW TT Mk 32 (III × 2)—1 heli-
      copter
   Electron Equipt: Radars: 1/965, 1/992 Q, 1/978, 2/903
               Sonars: 1/177, 1/170 B, 1/162
   M: 2 sets GT; 2 props
   Boilers: 2 Babcock & Wilcox; 38.7 kg/cm², 450°C   **Electric:** 2,500 kw
   Fuel: 500 tons   **Range:** 4,500/12   **Man:** 263 tot.

REMARKS: Ordered 14-1-70. GWS 22 FCS for Sea Cat, MRS 3 GFCS for 114-mm.

FRIGATES (continued)

♦ **1 U.S. Charles Lawrence class**

	Bldr	Laid down	L	In serv.
29 VIRGILIO URIBE	Bethlehem, Hingham	7-9-42	25-2-43	9-6-43

(ex-*Daniel Griffin*, APD 38, ex-DE 54)

D: 1,691 tons (2,130 fl) **S:** 23 kts **Dim:** 93.27 × 11.25 × 4.8
A: 1/127-mm DP—6/40-mm AA (II × 3)—2/Hedgehogs—2 d.c. racks
Electron Equipt: 1/SPS-4, 1/SPS-6, 1/navigational
M: Turbo-electric: 2 GE turbines, 2/4,600 kw gen.; 2 props; 12,000 hp
Boilers: 2 Foster-Wheeler; 30.6 kg/cm², 399°C
Electric: 680 kw **Range:** 1,747/23, 4,800/12

REMARKS: Transferred 12-66. Sisters *Serrano* (ex-*Odum*, APD 71) and *Orella* (ex-*Jack C. Robinson*, APD 72) remain as hulks. *Uribe* refitted 1977-78 with SPS-6 atop lattice mast aft, Carries two LCVP.

CORVETTES

♦ **1 U.S. Abnaki-class former fleet tug** Bldr: Charleston SB & DD Co., S.C.

	Laid down	L	In serv.
63 SERGENTE ALDEA (ex-*Arikara*, ATF 98)	28-11-42	22-4-43	15-11-43

Sergente Aldea (63) 1975

D: 1,235 tons (1,675 fl) **S:** 15 kts
Dim: 62.48 (59.44 wl) × 11.73 × 4.67 **A:** 1/76.2-mm DP Mk 26—2/20-mm AA
Electron Equipt: Radar: 1/SPS-5
M: Diesel-electric: 4 Busch-Sulzer BS539 diesels; 1 prop; 3,000 hp
Electric: 400 kw **Fuel:** 363 tons **Range:** 7,000/15, 15,000/8 **Man:** 85 tot.

REMARKS: Transferred 1-7-71 on lease.

♦ **2 U.S. Sotoyomo-class former auxiliary ocean tugs** Bldr: Levington SB, Orange, Texas

	Laid down	L	In serv.
60 LIENTUR (ex-ATA 177)	27-4-44	5-6-44	2-9-44
62 LAUTARO (ex-ATA 122)	19-10-42	27-11-42	10-6-43

D: 534 tons (835 fl) **S:** 13 kts **Dim:** 43.59 (41.00 pp) × 10.31 × 4.01
A: 1/76.2-mm DP Mk 26—2/20-mm AA
M: 2 GM 12-278A diesels, electric drive; 2 props; 1,500 hp
Radar: 1/Decca 505 **Electric:** 90-120 kw **Fuel:** 171 tons
Range: 16,500/18
Man: 46 tot.

REMARKS: Purchased 9-47.

GUIDED-MISSILE BOATS

♦ **2 (+2) Israeli Reshev ("Sa'ar IV") class** Bldr: Israeli SY, Haifa

	L	In serv.
. . . CHASMA (ex-*Romach*)	1-74	3-74
. . . CHIPANA (ex-*Keshet*)	23-8-73	10-73
. . . N . . . (ex-. . .)	. . .	. . .
. . . N . . . (ex-. . .)	. . .	. . .

D: 415 tons (450 fl) **S:** 32 kts **Dim:** 58.10 × 7.60 × 2.40
A: 6/Gabriel SSM (I × 6)—2/76-mm DP OTO Melara (I × 2)—2/20-mm AA (I × 2)—2/12.7-mm mg
Electron Equipt: Radar: 1/Neptune, 1/EL/M-2221 f.c. (Orion)
ECM: passive syst.—4 large/72 small chaff RL
M: 4 MTU MD 871 diesels; 4 props; 14,000 hp **Range:** 1,500/30, 4,000/17
Man: 45 tot.

REMARKS: *Chasma* delivered 12-79, *Chipana* in 1-81. Two additional transfers from Israeli Navy expected. Harpoon SSM removed prior to transfer.

♦ **4 Israeli "Dvora" class** Bldr: Israeli Aircraft Ind. (1979)

N . . . N . . . N . . . N . . .

D: 47 tons (fl) **S:** 36 kts **Dim:** 21.62 × 5.49 × 0.94 (1.82 props)
A: 2/Gabriel SSM—2/20-mm AA (I × 2)—2/12.7-mm mg (I × 2)
Electron Equipt: Radar: 1/Decca 926
M: 2 MTU 12V331 TC81 diesels; 2 props; 2,720 hp **Electric:** 30 kw
Range: 700/32 **Man:** 8-10 tot.

REMARKS: Delivery uncertain, as is whether Gabriel missiles were actually fitted. Aluminum construction.

TORPEDO BOATS

♦ **4 Guacolda (Lürssen 36-m design) class** Bldr: Bazan, Cadiz, Spain (1965-66)

81 FRESIA 82 GUACOLDA 83 QUIDORA 84 TEHUALDA

D: 134 tons (fl) **S:** 30 kts **Dim:** 36.2 (34.0 wl) × 5.6 × 1.68
A: 2/40-mm AA—4/533-mm TT (British Mk IV)
Electron Equipt: Radar: 1/Decca 505
M: 2 Mercedes-Benz MB839Bb diesels; 2 props; 4,800 hp
Electric: 90 kVA **Range:** 1,500/15 **Man:** 20 tot.

TORPEDO BOATS (continued)

Fresia   1970

PATROL BOATS AND CRAFT

♦ **1 (+2) U.S. PC 1638-class submarine chasers** Bldr: ASMAR, Talcahuano

	In serv.
P 36 ABTAO	. . .
P 37 PAPUDO (ex-U.S. PC 1646)	27-11-71
P 38 PISAGUA	. . .

Papudo (P 37)   1977

D: 313 tons (417 fl)   **S:** 20 kts   **Dim:** 52.9 × 7.0 × 3.1
A: 1/40-mm AA—4/20-mm AA (II × 2)—1/trainable Mk 15 Hedgehog—4/Mk 6
d.c. throwers—1 d.c. rack
M: 2 GM-16-567 diesels; 2 props; 2,800 hp   **Fuel:** 60 tons   **Range:** 5,000/10
Man: . . . tot.

♦ **20 "Anchova"-class patrol craft** Bldr: MacLaren, Niteroi, Brazil

		L			L
GC 1801	PILLAN	. . .	GC 18. . .	CORCOVADO	. . .
GC 1802	TRONCADOR	8-8-80	GC 18. . .	CORRAE	. . .
GC 1803	RANO-KAU	25-11-80	GC 18. . .	LLAIMA	. . .
GC 1804	VILLARRICA	25-11-80	GC 18. . .	PUNTA GRUESA	. . .
GC 18. . .	AQUILA	. . .	GC 18. . .	ODORNO	. . .
GC 18. . .	ANTUCO	. . .	GC 18. . .	UNA	. . .
GC 18. . .	ARICA	. . .	GC 18. . .	YAGAN	. . .
GC 18. . .	CALLE CALLE	. . .	GC 18. . .	N. . .	. . .
GC 18. . .	CHOSENCUO	. . .	GC 18. . .	N. . .	. . .
GC 18. . .	COPAHUE	. . .	GC 18. . .	N. . .	. . .

D: 43 tons (fl)   **S:** 30 kts (25 sust.)   **Dim:** 18.6 × 5.35 × 1.65
A: 2/20-mm AA (I × 2)—2/d.c. racks
M: 2 GM 12V71 TI diesels; 2 props; 1,800 hp

REMARKS: First ten ordered 1977. Wooden construction. Named for volcanos ("Anchova" is builder's design name).

♦ **2 small trawlers** Bldr: ASMAR, Talcahuano, 1966-67

PC 75 MARINERO FUENTALBAS   PC 76 CABO ODGER

D: 215 tons   **S:** 9 kts   **Dim:** 24.4 × 6.4 × 2.75   **A:** 1/20-mm
M: 1 Cummins diesel; 340 hp   **Range:** 2,600/9

REMARKS: Purchased 1966. Profile of U.S.-type trawler.

HYDROGRAPHIC SURVEY AND RESEARCH SHIPS

♦ **1 U.S. Cherokee-class former fleet tug** Bldr: Commercial Iron Wks, Portland, Ore.

	Laid down	L	In serv.
AGS 64 YELCHO (ex-USS Tekesta, ATF 93)	7-9-42	20-3-43	16-8-43

Yelcho (AGS 64)   1970

D: 1,235 tons (1,675 fl)   **S:** 15 kts   **Dim:** 62.48 (59.44 wl) × 11.73 × 4.67
A: 1/76.2-mm Mk 26 DP—2/20-mm AA   **Electric:** 260 kw
M: 4 GM 12-278 diesels, electric drive; 1 prop; 3,000 hp
Fuel: 363 tons   **Range:** 7,000/15 15,000/8   **Man:** 5 officers, 59 men

REMARKS: Used for oceanographic research. Loaned 15-5-60. Carries survey launch on fantail.

♦ **1 Antarctic patrol, transport, and research ship**

	Bldr	Laid down	L	In serv.
AP 45 PILOTO PARDO	Haarlemsche Scheepsbouw	1957	1958	8-58

D: 1,250 tons (2,545 fl)   **S:** 14 kts   **Dim:** 83.0 × 11.9 × 7.4 (fl)
M: Diesel-electric propulsion; 1 prop; 2,000 hp   **Range:** 6,000/10
Man: 44 crew, 24 passengers

REMARKS: Armament removed; can carry 2 Bell 47-G helicopters.

HYDROGRAPHIC SURVEY AND RESEARCH SHIPS (continued)

Piloto Pardo (AP 45)   1977

AUXILIARY SHIPS

♦ **2 new construction tankers**

AO 55 N. . .   AO 56 N. . .

 D: approx. 30,000 tons (fl)   **S:** . . .   **Dim:** 176.1 × 25.5 × . . .
 M: Diesels; 18,300 hp

REMARKS: 19,500 tons deadweight. Ordered 1976 from ASMAR, Talcahuano.

♦ **1 replenishment oiler** Bldr: Burmeister & Wain, Copenhagen

	L	In serv.
AO 53 ARAUCANO	21-6-66	10-1-67

Araucano (AO 53)   1977

 D: 23,000 tons (fl)   **S:** 17 kts   **Dim:** 160.93 × 21.95 × 8.8   **A:** Removed
 M: Burmeister & Wain diesel, type 62 VT 2 BF 140, 9-cyl.; 1 prop; 10,800 hp
 Range: 12,000/14.5

REMARKS: Can replenish two ships at sea simultaneously. Carries 21,126 cu. meters liquid and 1,444 cu. meters dry cargo. Can carry 8/40-mm AA (II × 4).

♦ **1 U.S. Patapsco-class former gasoline tanker** Bldr: Cargill, Inc., Savage, Minn.

	Laid down	L	In serv.
AOG 54 BEAGLE (ex-USS Genesee, AOG 8)	22-9-42	23-9-43	27-5-44

 D: 1,850 tons (4,570 fl)   **S:** 14 kts   **Dim:** 94.72 (89.00 pp) × 14.78 × 4.78
 A: 1/76.2-mm DP—4/20-mm AA (II × 2)
 Electron Equipt: Radar: 1/SPS-5, 1/Mk 26   **Electric:** 460 kw
 M: 2 GM 16-278A diesels, electric drive; 2 props; 3,300 hp
 Fuel: 295 tons   **Range:** 6,670/10   **Man:** 46 tot.

Beagle (AOG 54)   1977

REMARKS: Cargo: 2,040 tons. Mk 52 GFCS and Mk 51 for 76.2-mm. Loaned 5-7-72.

♦ **2 French BATRAL class** Bldr: ASMAR, Talcahuano

	Laid down	L	In serv.
AP. . . RANCAGUA	. . .	8-81	1982
AP. . . MAIPO	. . .	12-81	1983

 D: 770 tons (1,330 fl)   **S:** 16 kts
 Dim: 80.0 (68.0 pp) × 13.0 × 3.0 (max.)   **A:** . . .
 M: 2 SACM diesels; 2 props; 1,800 hp   **Range:** 4,500/13   **Man:** 40 tot.

REMARKS: Being constructed with French technical assistance.

♦ **1 transport, former passenger-cargo ship** Bldr: Aalborg Vaerft, 1953

AP 47 AQUILES (ex-Danish *Tjaldur*)

Aquiles (AP 47)   1977

 D: 3,400 tons (fl)   **S:** 16 kts   **Dim:** 87.8 (82.0 pp) × 13.42 × 5.2
 A: 1/40-mm AA   **M:** 1 Burmeister & Wain diesel; 1 prop; 3,600 hp
 Range: 5,500/16   **Man:** 32 crew, 447 troops

REMARKS: Former mixed-cargo ship purchased in 1967. 2,660 grt/1,395 dwt.

♦ **3 U.S. LST 1- and LST 542-class former tank-landing ships**

	Bldr	Laid down	L	In serv.
AP 88 COMANDANTE HEMMERDINGER (ex-New London County, T-LST 1066)	Bethlehem, Hingham, Mass.	18-1-45	21-2-45	20-3-45
AP 89 COMANDANTE ARAYA (ex-Nye County, T-LST 1067)	Bethlehem, Hingham, Mass.	24-1-45	27-2-45	24-3-45
AP 97 COMANDANTE TORO (ex-T-LST 277)	American Bridge, Ambridge, Pa.	31-5-43	5-9-43	1-10-43

AUXILIARY SHIPS *(continued)*

Comandante Hemmerdinger (AP 88)   1977

Comandante Toro (AP 97)   1977

D: 1,620 tons (4,080 fl)   **S:** 11 kts   **Dim:** 99.98 (96.32 wl) × 15.24 × 4.29
A: none   **Electric:** 300 kw   **Range:** 6,000/11
M: 2 GM 12-278A (AP 97: 12-567A) diesels; 2 props; 1,700 hp   **Fuel:** 570 tons

REMARKS: Cargo: 2,100 tons. Former U.S. Military Sealift Command ships; AP 97 transferred in 2-73 and AP 88, 89 in 8-73. AP 91 *Aguila* (ex-*Aventinus*, ARVE 3, ex-LST 1092), a former repair ship used as a transport, was scuttled 17-5-80 after grounding and salvage.

♦ **2 Orompello-class landing ships**

AP 94 OROMPELLO   Bldr: Dade DD Co., Miami, Fla. (In serv. 15-9-64)
AP 95 ELICURA   Bldr: ASMAR, Talcahuano (In serv. 10-12-63)

     D: 290 tons (750 fl)   **S:** 12 kts   **Dim:** 43.9 (42.05 pp) × 10.3 × 6.9
     A: 3/20-mm AA   **Electron Equipt:** Radar: 1 Raytheon 1500B
     Electric: 120 kw   **M:** 2 Cummins VT-17-700M diesels; 2 props; 900 hp
     Fuel: 71 tons   **Range:** 2,900/10.5   **Cargo:** 350 tons   **Man:** 20 tot.

♦ **2 Meteoro-class coastal ferries**

AP 110 METEORO   Bldr: ASMAR, Talcahuano (1967)
AP 112 GRUMETE PEREZ HUEMEL   Bldr: ASMAR, Talcahuano (1975)

     D: 205 tons (fl)   **S:** 8 kts   **Dim:** 24.4 × 6.7 × . . .   **M:** Diesel
     Man: 220 passengers

♦ **1 submarine tender** Bldr: Orenst & Koppel, Germany, 1966

70 ANGAMOS (ex-*Puerto Montt*, ex-Danish *Kobenhavn*)

     D: 3,560 tons   **S:** 16 kts   **Dim:** 93.92 × 16.2 × 4.5
     M: 2 Lind-Pielstick V-8 diesels; 2 props; 6,500 hp

REMARKS: Former car and passenger ferry, purchased 4-77 and in service in 1979. Now fitted with workshops, spare parts stores, ammunition and torpedo magazines. 4,616 grt. Also used as a transport.

♦ **1 sail-training ship**

	Bldr	L	In serv.
BE 43 ESMERALDA (ex-*Don Juan de Austria*)	Bazan, Cadiz	12-5-53	9-54

Esmeralda (BE 43)   1973

     D: 3,673 tons   **S:** 11 kts   **Dim:** 94.1 × 13.1 × 8.7
     A: 4/47-mm saluting   **M:** Fiat diesel; 1,400 hp   **Range:** 8,000/8
     Man: 271 crew, 80 midshipmen

REMARKS: Four-masted schooner, ordered by Spain, sold to Chile in 1953. Similar to the Spanish *Juan Sebastian de Elcano*. Refitted in South Africa, 1977.

♦ **1 hospital craft**

111 CIRUJANO VIDELA   Bldr: ASMAR, Talcahuano, 1964

     D: 140 tons (fl)   **S:** 14 kts   **Dim:** 31.0 × 6.5 × 2.0
     M: 2 Cummins VT-12-700M diesels; 2 props; 700 hp   **Electric:** 60 kw

REMARKS: Modified U.S. PGM 59 design.

♦ **1 buoy tender and lighthouse-servicing ship**

ATA 73 COLO COLO   Bldr: England, 1929

     D: 790 tons   **S:** 11 kts   **Dim:** 41.38 × 8.72 × 4.07
     M: 1 set triple-expansion, reciprocating; 1 prop; 1,050 hp   **Boilers:** 2
     Fuel: 155 tons

♦ **3 tugs**

YT. . . GALVEZ   Bldr: Southern Shipbuilders, G.B., 1975

     D: 112 grt   **S:** . . .   **Dim:** 25.5 × 7.3 × 2.8

YT 120 REYES   YT 128 CORTEZ—no data

♦ **1 10,000-ton capacity floating dry dock, to be purchased in 1981**

CHILE *(continued)*
AUXILIARY SHIPS *(continued)*

♦ **2 U.S. ARD-class floating dry docks** (In serv. 1944)

131 Ingeniero Mery (ex-ARD 25)   132 Mutilla (ex-ARD 32)

    Capacity: 3,500 tons   **Dim:** 149.86 × 24.69 × 1.73 (light)

Remarks: 131 leased 15-12-60; 132 transferred 20-8-73. Both at Talcahuano. Dock inside dimensions: 118.6-m on blocks, 18.0-m clear width, 6.3-m draft over blocks. Bow end pointed.

♦ **1 ex-commercial dry dock** (1924)—Acquired 1-1-78

N. . .

    Capacity: 4,500 tons   **Dim:** 110.2 × 19.5 × . . .

♦ **1 small floating dry dock** (1908)

Manterola

    Capacity: 1,000 tons   **Dim:** 66.0 × 12.8 × . . .

CHINA
People's Republic of China

Personnel: 360,000 men in the following categories:
Regular Naval: 284,000;
Naval air arm: 38,000, Marine Corps: 38,000. There are also about 1,000,000 paramilitary personnel in the Naval Militia.

Merchant Marine (1980): 846 ships 6,336,747 grt

Naval Aviation: The naval air arm, which is under the control of the navy, consists of about 872 aircraft, including 600 Fagot, Fantan-A(50), Farmer(300), and Fresco fighters, 150 Badger, Bat, and Beagle light bombers, and about 60 transports, 6 seaplanes, and 50 Hound helicopters. Its principal mission is defense of the coast and of naval surface forces near the coast. A few of the aircraft are believed to be equipped for minelaying. Control of naval aircraft is integrated with the continental air-defense system.

Warships In Service Or Under Construction As Of 1 January 1982

	L	Tons (Surfaced)	Main armament
♦ **100 submarines**			
2 Han	1971	. . .	TT
1 Soviet Golf	1964	2,300	3 ballistic missiles, 10/533-mm TT
2 Ming	1975	1,500	8/533-mm TT
74 Soviet Romeo	1964 on	1,330	8/533-mm TT
21 Soviet Whiskey	1960-64	1,050	6/533-mm TT

		Tons	
♦ **11 destroyers**			
7 Luta	1970 on	3,960	4/130-mm, 6 Styx
4 Soviet Gordyy	1938-40	1,660	4/130-mm, 4 Styx
♦ **22 (+2) frigates**			
11 (+2) Jianghu	1974 on	1,600	2/100-mm, 4 Styx
2 Jiangdong	1972 on	1,800	4/100-mm, 2 SAM
5 Jiangnan	1966-68	1,400	3/100-mm
4 Soviet Riga	1953-56	1,420	3/100-mm, 2 Styx

♦ **185-215 guided-missile patrol boats**

♦ **285 torpedo boats**

♦ **740+ patrol boats and craft**

♦ **115-120 minesweepers**

♦ **500 amphibious ships and craft**

SUBMARINES

♦ **2 (+1?) Han class, nuclear**

	Bldr	In serv.
N. . .	Luta	1974
	Huludao SY	
N. . .	Luta	1977
	Huludao SY	
N. . .	Huludao SY	. . .

Remarks: Construction and trials on the first took a very long time. Modern hull form, single propeller, one nuclear reactor. During April 1981, a nuclear-powered ballistic missile submarine was reportedly launched at Huludao SY, about 200 kilometers northeast of Peking. No details of its characteristics are available.

♦ **1 Soviet Golf class, ballistic missile**

    D: 2,300/2,700 tons   **S:** 12 kts submerged   **Dim:** 100.0 × 8.5 × 6.6
    A: 3 ballistic missiles—10/533-mm TT (6 fwd, 4 aft)
    M: 3 diesels, electric drive; 3 props; 6,000 hp
    Range: 9,000/5

Remarks: Plans furnished by the Soviet Union at a time when relations between the two countries were good. Medium-range missiles, if any, would be of Chinese origin.

♦ **2 Ming class**

    D: 1,500/1,900 tons   **S:** 17/15 kts   **Dim:** 76.0 ×. . . ×. . .
    A: 8/533-mm TT   **M:** Diesel-electric; 2 props

Remarks: Launched 1975. Evidently a Chinese design derived from the Romeo.

♦ **74 Soviet Romeo class**

    D: 1,330/1,700 tons   **S:** 15/13 kts   **Dim:** 77.0 × 6.7 × 4.95
    A: 8/533-mm TT (6 fwd/2aft)—14 torpedoes or 28 mines
    M: Diesel-electric: 2 diesels, 2,000 hp each; 2 props; 3,000 hp
    Range: 14,000/9 snorkel   **Man:** 56 men

Remarks: Endurance: 45 days. Diving depth: 200 meters. Built at at least three different yards, including one near Canton, Wujiang, and in Shanghai.

SUBMARINES (continued)

Chinese Romeo-class submarine 142   1974

♦ **21 Soviet Whiskey class**

    D: 1,050/1,350 tons **S:** 17/13.5 **Dim:** 76.0 × 6.3 × 4.8
    A: 6/533-mm TT (4 fwd, 2 aft)—12 torpedoes or 24 mines
    M: Diesel-electric: 2 Type 37D diesels; 2,000 hp each; 2,500 hp
    Range: 8,300/8 snorkel

REMARKS: A few were delivered by the U.S.S.R., the others were built in China (1960-64), probably at the Jiangnan Shipyard near Shanghai.

DESTROYERS

♦ **7 (+3)Luta class, guided-missile** Bldr: Luta SY, Kuangchou SY, and. . . SY, Shanghai In serv., 1972-. . .

Luta 132—with 8/57-mm AA   RNZN, 1980

Luta 162—with 8/37-mm AA, no f.c. radars   RNZN, 1980

    D: 3,960 tons (fl) **S:** 32 kts **Dim:** 127.5 × 12.9 × 5.2
    A: 6 SSM (III × 2)—4/130-mm DP (II × 2)—8/57-mm or 37-mm AA (II × 4)—
        4/25-mm AA (II × 2)—2 12-tubed ASW RL—4/d.c. launchers—2/d.c. racks—
        mines
    Electron Equipt: Radar: 1/navigational, 1/short-range air-search, 1/long-range
               air-search, 1/Square Tie, 1/Sun Visor (not on all), 2/for
               57-mm f.c. (not on all)
           Sonar:. . . —ECM: 2/Watch Dog
    M: 2 sets GT; 2 props; 60,000 hp **Boilers:** 4 **Range:** 4,000/15 **Man:** 300 tot.

REMARKS: Superficially resembles Kotlin but is larger and has a flat transom stern, larger superstructure, etc. Some systems of Soviet design; the ASW rocket launchers are derived from the Soviet RBU-1200 design, but have more tubes. Equipment varies greatly from ship to ship, with only a small number having fire-control radar systems, even on the Soviet Wasp Head 130-mm GFCS. Note that 132 and 162 have different long-range air-search radars abaft the second stack. The SSM used is derived from the Soviet SS-N-2 Styx, but is longer. One ship of this class lost 8-78 near Zanjiang through explosion. At least three more were reported building at Luta (Dairen) in 1980. Lutas 105, 106, 107, 131, 132, 160, and 162 participated in a deployment to the Central Pacific (Gilbert and Ellice islands) in May 1980.

♦ **4 Soviet Gordyy class, guided-missile** Bldr: Dalzavod SY, Vladivostok and Komsomolsk SY

ANSHAN   CHI LIN
CHANG CHUN   FU CHUN

    D: 1,657 tons (2,039 fl)
    S: 38 kts when built, certainly much less today
    Dim: 112.86 × 10.20 × 3.8
    A: 4/SSM (II × 2)—4/130-mm (I × 4)—8/37-mm AA (II × 4)—mines
    M: 2 sets GT; 2 props; 48,000 hp **Boilers:** 3 **Fuel:** 500 tons
    Range: 800/38, 2,600/20 **Man:** 197 tot.

REMARKS: Ex-Soviet *Razyashchiy, Reshitelnyy, Retivyy,* and *Reskiy,* all built in the Far East, launched 1938-40, and transferred by the U.S.S.R. in 1955. The SSM, derived from the Soviet SS-N-2 Styx, replaced 6/533-mm TT (III × 2) between 1972 and 1974. No ASW armament.

FRIGATES

♦ **11 (+2) Jianghu class, guided-missile** Bldr: Jiangnan SY, Shanghai (1975-. . .)

Jianghu-class frigate   1978

    D: 1,568 tons (1,900 fl) **S:** 25.5 kts **Dim:** 103.2 × 10.2 × 3.05 (hull)
    A: 4/SSM (II × 2)—2/100-mm DP—8/37-mm AA (II × 4)—2/RBU 1200—2/d.c.
        projectors—2/d.c. racks—mines

FRIGATES *(continued)*

Electron Equipt: Radar: 1/Square Tie, 1/air search, 1/navigational
Sonar: 1/medium freq.
ECM: none
M: 2 Pielstick diesels; 2 props; 16,000 hp **Range:** 4,000/. . . **Man:** 195 tot.

REMARKS: First launched 1975. A variation of the Jiantung class with SSM vice SAM. Has only an optical rangefinder for 100-mm fire control.

♦ **2 Jiangdong class, guided-missile** Bldr: Jiangnan SY, Shanghai

D: 1,568 tons (1,900 fl) **S:** 25.5 kts **Dim:** 103.2 × 10.2 × 3.05 (hull)
A: 2/SAM systems—4/100-mm DP (II × 2)—8/37-mm AA (II × 4)—2/RBU-1200—2/d.c. projectors—2/d.c. racks—mines
M: 2 Pielstick diesels; 2 props; 16,000 hp **Range:** 4,000/. . . **Man:** 195 tot.

REMARKS: Launched 1972 and 1974. SAM system, of Chinese design, not yet operational.

♦ **5 Jiangnan class** Bldr: Jiangnan SY, Shanghai, 1967-69

Jiangnan-class frigate

D: 1,400 tons (fl) **S:** 28 kts **Dim:** 92.0 × 10.2 × 3.0 (hull)
A: 3/100-mm (I × 3, 1 fwd, 2 aft)—8/37-mm AA (II × 4)—4/14.5-mm mg (II × 2)—2/RBU-1200—4/d.c. projectors—2/d.c. racks—mines
M: 2 diesels; 2 props; 16,000 hp

REMARKS: Chinese version of the Soviet Riga class, with diesel propulsion. One built at Canton, 1968

♦ **4 Soviet Riga class** Bldr: Jiangnan SY, Shanghai, 1954-57

Chinese Riga No. 506   1980

D: 1,420 tons (fl) **S:** 28 kts **Dim:** 91.0 × 10.2 × 3.2
A: 2/SSM (II × 1)—3/100-mm DP (I × 3)—4/37-mm AA (II × 2—4/14.5-mm mg (II × 2)—4/d.c. projectors—2/d.c. racks—mines

Electron Equipt: Radars: 1/Neptune, 1/Square Tie, 1/Sun Visor, 1/Slim Net
M: 2 sets GT; 2 props; 20,000 hp **Boilers:** 2: 27 kg/cm², 360°C
Electric: 450 kw **Range:** 550/28, 2,000/13 **Man:** 175 tot.

CORVETTES

NOTE: Some of the following ships, acquired in 1949 following the departure of Kuomintang forces, may have been stricken in recent years.

♦ **1 Japanese Ukuru class** Bldr: Hitachi, Kanagawa

	L	In serv.
HUI AN (ex-*Shisaka*)	31-10-44	7-45

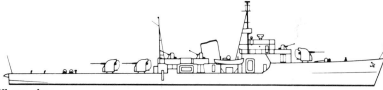

Ukuru class

D: 940 tons (1,020 fl) **S:** 19.5 kts **Dim:** 78.6 × 9.1 × 3.0
A: 3/100-mm DP (I × 3)—4/37-mm AA (I × 4)—mines
M: 2 diesels; 2 props; 4,200 hp **Range:** 5,000/16 **Man:** 150 tot.

REMARKS: Reengined and rearmed with Soviet guns during 1950s. No compound curves to hull plating.

♦ **1 British "Castle" class** Bldr: Blyth DY, G.B.

	L	In serv.
KUANGCHOU (ex-merc. *Wan Lee*, ex-*Ta Lung*, ex-Can. *Coppercliff*, ex-Br. *Hever Castle*)	24-2-44	25-7-44

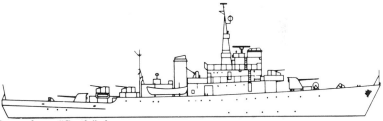

Kuangchou—"Castle" class

D: 1,080 (1,630 fl) **S:** 16.5 kts **Dim:** 76.73 (68.58 pp) × 11.18 × 5.80
A: 2/130-mm (I × 2)—10/37-mm AA (II × 4, I × 2) **Range:** 6,200/15, 9,100/10
M: 1 set 4-cyl. triple-expansion reciprocating steam; 1 prop; 2,750 hp
Boilers: 2 Admiralty 3-drum; 15.5 kg/cm² **Fuel:** 480 tons

♦ **up to 5 Japanese Kaibokan Type D class** Bldrs: . . .

	L	In serv.
WU JANG (ex-14)	1944	5-5-44
JANGSHA (ex-118)	1944	27-12-44
DUNGAN (ex-192)	30-1-45	28-2-45
JIAN (ex-194)	15-2-45	15-3-45
SHIAN (ex-198)	26-2-45	31-3-45

CORVETTES (*continued*)

Japanese Kaibokan Type D in Chinese service

D: 740 tons (940 fl) **S:** 17 kts **Dim:** 69.5 × 8.6 × 3.0
A: 2/100-mm DP (I × 2)—6/37-mm AA (II × 2, I × 2)—mines
M: 1 set GT; 1 prop; 2,500 hp
Boilers: 2 Kampon **Range:** 4,500/14 **Man:** 150 tot.

REMARKS: Some have probably been discarded. Very lightly built. Rearmed in 1950s:
some had 2 U.S. 76.2-mm Mk 26 DP.

♦ **1 Japanese Etorufu class** Bldr: Uraga DY, Tokyo

	L	In serv.
JANGBEI (ex-*Oki*)	20-12-42	31-3-43

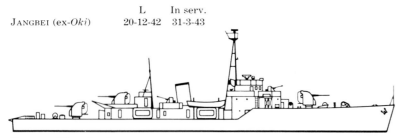

Japanese Etorufu class

D: 860 tons (1,020 fl) **S:** 19 kts **Dim:** 77.7 × 8.8 × 3.0
A: 3/100-mm DP (I × 3)—3/37-mm AA—mines
M: 2 diesels; 2 props; 4,200 hp **Range:** 8,000/16 **Man:** 150 tot.

REMARKS: Rearmed with Soviet weapons during late 1950s.

♦ **1 Australian Bathurst-class former minesweeper** Bldr: Cockatoo DY & Eng.,
Sydney

	Laid down	L	In serv.
LOYANG (ex-*Bendigo*, ex-merc. *Cheung Hing*, ex-Aust.)	12-8-40	1-3-41	10-5-41

D: 733 tons **S:** 15 kts **Dim:** 56.59 × 9.47 × 3.20
A: 2/100-mm DP (I × 2)—5/37-mm AA (I × 5)—2/14.5-mm mg (I × 2)
M: 2 sets triple-expansion reciprocating steam; 2 props; 1,800 hp **Man:** 100 tot.
Boilers: 2/Yarrow 3-drum **Fuel:** 153 tons **Range:** 1,730/14, 2,640/10

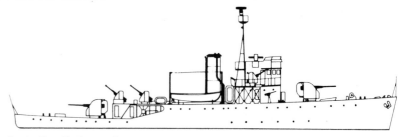

Australian Bathurst class

♦ **1 Japanese Hashidate-class former river gunboat**

	Bldr	L	In serv.
NANJANG (ex-*Uji*)	Sakurajima, Osaka	29-9-40	30-4-41

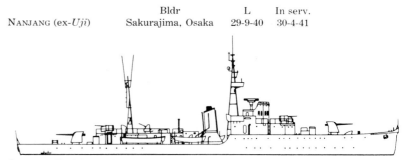

Japanese Hashidate class

D: 999 tons light (1,200 fl) **S:** 19 kts **Dim:** 79.2 × 9.7 × 2.4
A: 2/130-mm (I × 2)—5/37-mm AA (II × 2, I × 1)—mines
M: 2 sets GT; 2 props; 4,600 hp **Boilers:** 2 Kampon
Range: 3,400/14 **Man:** 170 tot.

REMARKS: Sunk twice during World War II. Rearmed with Soviet guns during mid-
1950s; 130-mm guns same as on *Gordyy*-class destroyers.

NOTE: The old (1928) "Customs Cruiser"/river gunboat *Jang Jiang* is now a memorial.

GUIDED-MISSILE PATROL BOATS

♦ **1 Hola class (1970)**

D: 300 tons **S:** . . . kts **Dim:** 43.0 ×. . . ×. . .
A: 2/SSM (I × 2)—2/37-mm AA (II × 2)

REMARKS: An enlarged version of Osa-I, and at one time equipped with a large radome.
Apparently unsuccessful.

♦ **80-100 Soviet Osa-I class** Bldr: Jiangnan SY, Shanghai, 1960-

D: 175 tons (210 fl) **S:** 36 kts **Dim:** 39.0 × 7.7 × 1.8
A: 4/SS-N-2 SSm—4/25-mm AA (II × 2) **Electron Equipt:** Radar: 1/Square Tie
M: 3 M503A diesels; 3 props; 12,000 hp **Man:** 30 tot.

REMARKS: The electronic equipment of these ships is simpler than that of the Soviet
version and different guns are fitted. No fire-control radar. At least four must have
been transferred by the USSR circa 1960 and have 4/30-mm AA (II × 2) but no
Drum Tilt radar.

GUIDED-MISSILE PATROL BOATS (continued)

Chinese-built Osa-I-class guided-missile patrol boats 1978

♦ **100-110 Hoku class**

Hoku-class, guided-missile patrol boat—with Homa hydrofoil variant inboard 1978

D: 68 tons (79 fl) **S:** 38 kts **Dim:** 28.0 × 6.3 × 1.8
A: 2/Styx SSM—2/25-mm AA (II × 1)
Electron Equipt: Radar: 1/Square Tie **M:** 4 M-50 diesels; 4 props; 4,800 hp
Range: 500/25 **Man:** 20 tot.

REMARKS: Steel-hulled improvement on Komar. A slightly longer variant, with hydrofoils and a second 25-mm AA mount aft, is nicknamed "Homa".

♦ **4 Soviet Komar class**

D: 71 tons (82 fl) **S:** 40 kts **Dim:** 25.3 × 7.0 × 2.0
A: 2/Styx SSM—2/25-mm AA (II × 1)
Electron Equipt: Radar: 1/Square Tie **M:** 4 M-50 diesels; 4 props; 4,800 hp

REMARKS: Transferred about 1960. Wooden construction. Possibly scrapped.

TORPEDO BOATS

♦ **140 Huchuan-class hydrofoils** Bldr: Hudong SY, Shanghai

D: 39 tons (fl) **S:** 54 kts **Dim:** 21.8 × 4.9 × 1.0; foilborne: 7.5 × .31
A: 2/533-mm TT—4/14.5-mm machine guns (II × 2)
M: 3 M 50 diesels; 3 props; 3,600 hp

REMARKS: In service since about 1966. Identical to the hydrofoils delivered to Albania, Pakistan, and Tanzania. Also built in Romania.

♦ **80 Soviet P 6-class wooden-hulled** Bldr: China, 1960s

D: 56 tons (66.5 fl) **S:** 43 kts **Dim:** 25.3 × 6.1 × 1.7
A: 2/533-mm TT—4/25-mm AA (II × 2) **Electron Equipt:** Radar: 1/Skin Head
M: 4 M 50 diesels; 4 props; 4,800 hp **Man:** 20 tot.

♦ **65 Soviet P 4-class aluminum-hulled hydroplanes** (1950s)

D: 19.3 tons (22.4 fl) **S:** 55 kts **Dim:** 19.3 × 3.7 × 1.0
A: 2/14.5-mm mg (II × 1)—2/450-mm TT
Electron Equipt: Radar: 1/Skin Head **M:** 2 M50 diesels; 2 props; 2,400 hp

REMARKS: Majority believed to be in reserve.

PATROL BOATS AND CRAFT

♦ **24 Hainan class** (In serv. 1964-. . .)

Hainan-class patrol boat 1980

D: 375 tons (400 fl) **S:** 30.5 kts **Dim:** 58.77 × 7.20 × 2.20 (hull)
A: 4/57-mm AA (II × 2)—4/25-mm AA (II × 2)—4/RBU-1200—2 d.c. projectors—2 d.c. racks—mines
Electron Equipt: Radar: 1/Pot Head **M:** 4 diesels; 4 props; 8,800 hp
Man: 70 tot.

REMARKS: Early units had 2/76.2-mm DP U.S. Mk 26 vice 4/57-mm AA. Two were transferred to Pakistan, 1976, and two more in 1980.

♦ **20 Soviet Kronshstadt class**

D: 300 tons (330 fl) **S:** 18 kts **Dim:** 52.1 × 6.5 × 2.2
A: 1/85-mm DP—2/37-mm AA—6/14.5-mm mg (II × 3)—2 d.c. projectors—2/ d.c. racks. Some: 2/RBU-1200
Electron Equipt: Radar: 1/Ball End **M:** 3 diesels; 3 props; 3,300 hp
Fuel: 20 tons **Range:** 3,500/14 **Man:** 50 tot.

REMARKS: 1956-57. Six could have been delivered by the U.S.S.R., the others built in Shanghai and Canton. Other information indicates that only two were built in China, the balance in the Soviet Union.

PATROL BOATS AND CRAFT *(continued)*

♦ **300-350 Shanghai-II class**

Shanghai II class (early version with squared-off bridge) 1976

   D: 122.5 tons (150 fl) **S:** 28.5 kts **Dim:** 38.78 × 5.41 × 1.49 (hull)
   A: 4/37-mm AA (II × 2)—4/25-mm AA (II × 2)—depth charges—mines. Some:
     2/81-mm recoilless rifles (II × 1)
   Electron Equipt: Radar: Pot Head or Skin Head
   M: 2 M50F-4, 1,200-hp, and 2/12D6, 910-hp diesels; 4 props; 4,220 hp
   Man: 38 tot.

REMARKS: A large number have been transferred to foreign navies. Very unsophisticated and sparsely equipped. Shanghai-I class was smaller and had 2/57-mm (II ×
1) forward.

♦ **50-60 Swatow class**

Swatow class

   D: 80 tons (fl) **S:** 28 kts **Dim:** 25.1 × 6.0 × 1.8
   A: 4/37-mm AA (II × 2)—2/14.5-mm mg (I × 2)—1/81-mm recoilless rifle
   Electron Equipt: Radar: 1/Skin Head **M:** 4 diesels; 4 props; 3,000 hp

REMARKS: 1955-60. Similar to P 6, but broader and with a steel hull. Class nickname
would be "Shantou" under new Pinyin transliteration system.

♦ **30 Beihai-class patrol craft** Bldr:. . . (1960s)

   D: 80 tons (fl) **S:** 18 kts **Dim:** 27.5 × 5.5 × 1.6
   A: 4/25-mm AA (II × 2) **M:** 3 diesels; 3 props; 900 hp

REMARKS: Majority subordinated to Naval Militia of the various "Military Maritime
Districts."

Beihai class

♦ **15 Huangpu-class patrol craft** Bldr:. . . (1970s)

REMARKS: Data as for Beihai class, except A: 4/14.5-mm mg (II × 2). Have low
superstructure fore and aft, providing additional accommodations for police or troops.

♦ **40 Yulin-class patrol craft** Bldr:. . . (In serv. 1964-68)

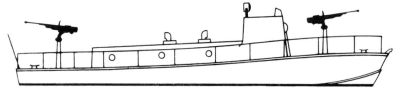

Yulin class

   D: 9.8 tons (fl) **S:** 20 kts **Dim:** 13.0 × 2.9 × 1.1
   A: 2/12.7-mm mg (I × 2) **M:** 1 diesel; 1 prop; 300 hp

REMARKS: Craft of this class also transferred to Kampuchea, Congo, and Tanzania.

♦ **1 or more Yingkou-class patrol craft** Bldr:. . . (In serv. 1960-65)

Yingkou class 1967

   D: 40 tons (fl) **S:** 18 kts **Dim:** 20.0 × . . . × . . . **A:** 2/12.7-mm mg
   M: 2 diesels; 2 props; 600 hp

REMARKS: Subordinated to "Military Maritime District" in South China militia.

♦ **15 Huangpu (formerly "Whampoa") class** (In serv. 1954-58)

   D: 45 tons **S:** 12 kts **Dim:** 27.0 × 4.0 × 1.5
   A: 2/37-mm AA (I × 2)—2/12.7-mm mg **M:** 2 diesels; 2 props; 600 hp

PATROL BOATS AND CRAFT (continued)

♦ **several hundred armed fishing trawlers**

Chinese armed fishing trawler T 710   1973

REMARKS: Many Chinese fishing trawlers are armed with 1 or 2/12.7-mm mg and perform dual service as fisheries patrol craft and fishing trawlers. There are several classes of these Militia-subordinated, steel-hulled, single-screwed craft displacing 200-450 tons (fl).

MINE WARFARE SHIPS

♦ **15-20 Soviet T-43-class fleet minesweepers**

Chinese T-43-class minesweeper 397   1971

D: 500 tons (580 fl) **S:** 14 kts **Dim:** 60.0 × 8.4 × 2.16
A: 4/37-mm AA (II × 2)—4/25-mm AA (II × 2)—4/12.7-mm mg (II × 2)—2/d.c. projectors—mines
Electron Equipt: Radar: 1/Ball End **M:** 2 diesels; 2 props; 2,200 hp

REMARKS: A few shorter-hulled, 58-meter units were transferred from the U.S.S.R.; the majority are long-hulled ships and were built in China. Several were built or converted as surveying ships and civilian research ships. At least one has an 85-mm DP gun forward.

♦ **80 auxiliary minesweepers converted from fishing boats**

♦ **20 Fushun-class coastal minesweepers**—derived from Shanghai II gunboat design

AMPHIBIOUS WARFARE SHIPS

♦ **15 ex-U.S. LST 1- and LST 542-class tank landing ships** (In serv. 1943-45)

D: 1,625 tons (4,080 fl) **S:** 11 kts **Dim:** 99.98 × 15.24 × 4.36
A: 2-3/76.2-mm DP (I)—6-8/37-mm AA (II)
M: 2 GM 12-278A or 12-567A diesels; 2 props; 1,800 hp

REMARKS: Cargo capacity: 2,100 tons. Some are immobile as accommodations ships or tenders for submarines. Most rearmed during late 1950s with U.S. 76.2-mm guns and Soviet twin 37-mm AA.

NOTE: A new class of LST of about 5,000 tons displacement, 120-m o.a. has been reported under construction in China. Armament includes 6/57-mm AA (II × 2), the bow is sharply raked, and there are bow and stern ramps.

♦ **2 Yu Ling class**

REMARKS: 1971-. Design reportedly derived from U.S. LSM class, but larger.

♦ **15 ex-U.S. LSM 1-class medium landing ships** (In serv. 1944-45)

Three ex-U.S. LSM 1 class in the Chinese Navy   1978

D: 743 tons (1,095 fl) **S:** 12.5 kts **Dim:** 62.03 × 10.52 × 2.54
A: 6/37-mm AA (II × 3)—4/25-mm AA (II × 2)—mines
Electron Equipt: Radar: 1/Skin Head
M: 2 Fairbanks-Morse 38D8⅛-10 or GM 16-278A diesels; 2 props; 2,800 hp
Range: 2,500/12

REMARKS: Rearmed with Soviet weapons late 1950s. Most have two mine-laying ports in the stern. Several have superstructure built over the open tank deck.

♦ **2 British LCT(3)-class utility landing craft** (In serv. 1942-43)

D: 350 tons (600 fl) **S:** 10.5 kts **Dim:** 58.5 × 9.7 × 2.0 (max.) **A:** . . .
M: 2 Paxman diesels; 2 props; 1,000 hp **Fuel:** 24 tons
Range: 1,900/10.5, 2,700/9 **Man:** 30 tot.

REMARKS: Acquired 1949. Open stowage for 300 tons cargo.

♦ **6-8 U.S. LCT(6)-class utility landing craft** (In serv. 1943-45)

D: 143 tons (309 fl) **S:** 10 kts **Dim:** 36.3 × 9.6 × 1.2 **A:** . . .
M: 3 GM 6-71 diesels; 3 props; 675 hp **Range:** 1,200/7

REMARKS: Acquired 1949. Cargo: 150 tons. Several LCT(5) of similar design may also survive.

AMPHIBIOUS WARFARE SHIPS *(continued)*

♦ **300 Yunnan-class landing craft** Bldr: Hangzhou SY (In serv. 1968-72)

D: 133.2 tons (fl)   **S:** 10.5 kts   **Dim:** 27.50 (24.07 pp) × 5.40 × 1.40
A: 2-4/14.5-mm mg (I or II × 2)   **M:** 2 diesels; 2 props; 600 hp
Range: 500/10   **Man:** 6 tot.

REMARKS: Cargo: 46 tons (1 tank). Cargo deck 15.0 × 4.0 m.

♦ **approx. 150 copies U.S. LCM(6)-class landing craft** (In serv. 1950s-1960s)

D: 24 tons (56 fl)   **S:** 9 kts   **Dim:** 17.0 × 4.4 × 1.2
A: 2/12.7-mm mg (I × 2)   **M:** 2 diesels; 2 props; 300 hp

♦ **1 Dagu-A-class air-cushion landing craft prototype**

Dagu-A air-cushion vehicle—note bow door   1981

D: 61 tons (fl)   **S:** 55 kts   **Dim:** 27.2 × 13.8 × 9.6 (high)
M: 2 turboprop propulsion engines; 1 gas turbine lift engine geared also to 2
     auxiliary propellers

REMARKS: Cargo: 15 tons. The function of the small airscrews amidships is uncertain; they may aid in maneuvering. Appears to be an engineering prototype rather than an operational combatant.

AUXILIARY SHIPS

There is no comprehensive information on the Chinese fleet's logistic support, but China has designated and built large numbers of auxiliary vessels, reportedly running the spectrum of logistics support, repair, hydrographic survey, and research types, including a great many tugs and small oilers.

ICEBREAKERS

♦ **2 Haiping class** Bldr: Jiu Shin SY, Shanghai

HAIPING 101 (L: 26-12-69)   HAIPING 102 (L: 1972)

D: 3,200 tons   **S:** 16 kts   **Dim:** 84.0 × 15.0 × 5.0
A: 8/37-mm AA (II × 4)—8/25-mm AA (II × 4)
M: 2 diesels; 2 props; 5,200 hp

REMARKS: Differ in details of superstructure. Can also be used as ocean tugs.

♦ **1 Yanheng class**—no data available

HYDROGRAPHIC SURVEY SHIPS

♦ **1 Kanzhu class** (In serv. 1973)

D: 1,000 tons (fl)   **S:** 20 kts   **Dim:** 65.0 × 9.0 × 3.0
A: 4/37-mm AA (II × 2)—4/25-mm AA (II × 2)
M: 4 diesels; 2 props; 4,400 hp   **Man:** 120 tot.

REMARKS: Low, flush-decked hull; resembles a corvette. Operates in South China waters. Prominent raked funnel, well aft.

♦ **3 Yanlai class** (In serv. early 1970s)

D: 1,100 tons (fl)   **S:** 16 kts   **Dim:** 72.0 × 9.8 × 3.0
A: 4/37-mm AA (II × 2)—4/25-mm AA (II × 2)   **M:** 2 diesels; 2 props; 2,200 hp

REMARKS: Funnel amidships; large crane aft.

♦ **2 modified T-43-class minesweepers** (In serv. late 1960s)

D: 550 tons (600 fl)   **S:** 14 kts   **Dim:** 60.0 × 8.4 × 2.16
M: 2 diesels; 2 props; 2,200 hp   **Range:** 3,200/10   **Man:** 80 tot.

♦ **2 Hace-class coastal survey ships** (In serv. 1960s)

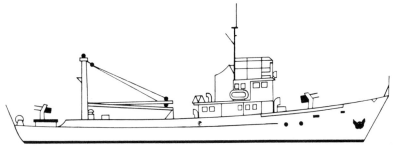

Hace class

D: 400 tons   **S:** 12 kts   **Dim:** 38.0 × 7.6 × 3.4   **A:** 4/14.5-mm mg (II × 2)
M: 1 diesel; 1 prop; 400 hp

REMARKS: Design derived from that of a coastal cargo ship.

♦ **1 British "Flower"-class former corvette**

	Bldr	L	In serv.
N . . . (ex-*Clover*)	Fleming & Ferguson, G.B.	30-1-41	31-5-41

D: 1,060 tons (1,340 fl)   **S:** 16 kts   **Dim:** 62.48 × 10.23 × 4.80   **A:** . . .
M: 1 set 4-cyl., triple-expansion reciprocating steam; 1 prop; 1,750 hp
Boilers: 2 Admiralty 3-drum   **Fuel:** 230 tons   **Range:** 3,100/15, 5,000/10

REMARKS: Used as a corvette until early 1970s; one sister scrapped at that time.

♦ **1 Yanlun class** (In serv. 1965)—no data available

♦ **up to 10 additional naval survey ships**

OCEANOGRAPHIC SURVEY SHIPS

♦ **2 Haiyang class** (In serv. 1972-73)

Haiyang 01   Haiyang 02

OCEANOGRAPHIC SURVEY SHIPS *(continued)*

D: 3,295 tons **S:** 20 kts **Dim:** 104.0 × 13.8 × 5.0
A: 6/37-mm AA (II × 3) **M:** 2 diesels; 2 props; 9,000 hp

REMARKS: Resemble passenger liners; white-painted.

♦ **3 Shukuang class** (In serv. late 1960s)

SHUKUANG 01   SHUKUANG 02   SHUKUANG 03

D: 500 tons (590 fl) **S:** 14 kts **Dim:** 60.0 × 8.4 × 2.15
A: 1/37-mm AA **M:** 2 diesels; 2 props; 2,200 hp **Range:** 3,200/10

REMARKS: Design closely derived from T-43-class minesweeper. White-painted. There
is also *Shukuang* 04, a more modern-appearing ship about the same size.

♦ **2 Shihjian class** (In serv. 1968-69) Bldr: Hutung SY, Shanghai

SHIHJIAN   N. . .

D: 2,955 tons **S:** 16.2 kts **Dim:** 94.73 (87.00 pp) × 14.04 × 4.75
A: 8/14.5-mm mg (II × 4) **Electric:** 1,065 kw
M: 2 Type 6 ESD(2) 48/82 diesels; 2 props; 4,000 hp **Range:** 7,500/14.5

REMARKS: 2,500 grt/1,000 dwt. Enlarged version of *Dong Fang Hong* class.

♦ **2 Dong Fang Hong class** Bldr: Hutung SY, Shanghai (In serv. 1964-66)

N. . .   DONG FANG HONG

Dong Fang Hong   1978

D: 2,900 tons **S:** 14 kts **Dim:** 86.00 × 11.50 × 4.75 **A:** none
M: 2 diesels; 2 props; 4,000 hp

NOTE: There are also large numbers of civilian-agency-subordinated research vessels
for oil exploration, fisheries research, etc.

EXPERIMENTAL SHIPS

♦ **2 Yuanwang-class satellite and missile tracking ships** Bldr: Hutung SY,
Shanghai (In serv. 1980)

YUANWANG 1   YUANWANG 2

D: 17,100 tons (21,000 fl) **S:** 20 kts **Dim:** 190.0 × 22.6 × 7.5
M: 1 diesel; 1 prop; . . . hp

REMARKS: First observed during the 5-80 Chinese ICBM tests in the Central Pacific.
Have one large parabolic tracking antenna, two log-periodic HF ("fish-spine") antennas, several precision theodolite optical tracking stations, and two smaller missile-

Yuanwang 2   RNZN, 1980

Yuanwang 2   RNZN, 1980

tracking radars, as well as positions for later installation of equipment. Large helicopter deck, but no hangar. Have a bow-thruster and retractable fin stabilizers.

The Xiang Yang Hong ("East Is Red"—the title of the Chinese national anthem)—
series ships are mainly disparate in size and characteristics. To date, not all numbers
between 1 and 10 have been sighted, but there probably are 10 ships, all capable of
a variety of experimental duties (including general oceanography), particularly in
support of missile and satellite research and hydrometeorology.

♦ **1 Xiang Yang Hong 10 class** Bldr: Hutung SY, Shanghai (In serv. 1980)

XIANG YANG HONG 10

D: 10,975 tons **S:** 20 kts **Dim:** 156.2 × 20.6 × 6.8
M: 2 diesels; 2 props; . . . hp

REMARKS: Uses same hull and propulsion as the new J 301-class submarine tenders,
but has twin, side-by-side funnels and hangar space for only one French Super Frélon
helicopter; the crane forward is smaller, and the kingposts abaft the stacks and the
heavy foremast support large log-periodic HF antennas. Has retractable fin stabilizers.

EXPERIMENTAL SHIPS (continued)

Xiang Yang Hong 10   RNZN, 1980

♦ **1 Xiang Yang Hong 9 class** Bldr: Hutung SY, Shanghai (In serv. 1979)

XIANG YANG HONG 9

D: 4,400 tons **S:** . . . kts **Dim:** . . . × . . . × . . . **M:** diesels; 4,000 hp
Range: 11,000/. . . **Man:** 145 tot.

♦ **1 Polish Francesco Nullo-class (Type B-41)**—former cargo ship Bldr: Paris
Commune SY, Gdynia, Poland (In serv. 1967)

XIANG YANG HONG 5 (ex-*Chang Niy*)

Xiang Yang Hong 5   RNZN, 1980

D: 14,500 tons (fl) **S:** 16 kts **Dim:** 152.6 (141.6 pp) × 19.5 × 8.75
M: 1 Ciegielski-Sulzer 6RD68 diesel; 1 prop; 7,200 hp **Range:** 15,000/16

REMARKS: Extensively rebuilt as a hydrometeorological-research and radiosonde-bal-
loon tracking ship at Canton in 1970-72, and altered again after 1976, with a two-
level superstructure replacing the after two hatches. Has one large log-periodic HF
antenna forward. One of her four Chinese-operated merchant sisters briefly served
as an unaltered support ship as *Xiang Yang Hong 10* in the late 1970s (not the same
ship as the new unit above).

♦ **1 Xiang Yang Hong 2 class** (In serv. 1971)

XIANG YANG HONG 2

D: 1,000 tons (fl) **S:** . . . kts **Dim:** 72.5 × 8.7 × . . .
M: 2 diesels; 2 props; . . . hp

♦ **3 Xiang Yang Hong 1 class** (In service. 1972-74)

XIANG YANG HONG 1   XIANG YANG HONG 4   XIANG YANG HONG 6

D: approx. 1,000 tons (fl) **S:** . . . kts **Dim:** 67.0 × 10.0 × . . .
A: 2/37-mm AA (II × 1)—8/14.5-mm mg (II × 4)
M: 2 diesels; 2 props; . . . hp

SUBMARINE SUPPORT SHIPS

♦ **2 J 302 class** Bldr: Hutung SY, Shanghai (In serv. 1978-80)

J 302   J 506

J 506—note 2 Super Frélon helicopters   RNZN, 1980

J 302   RNZN, 1980

D: 10,975 tons (fl) **S:** 20 kts **Dim:** 156.2 × 20.6 × 6.8 **A:** none
M: 2 diesels; 2 props; . . . hp

SUBMARINE SUPPORT SHIPS (continued)

REMARKS: Carry two French Super Frélon heavy helicopters in a double hangar. J 301 differs in not having the deep recesses at the stern (evidently intended to permit a 4-point moor). The huge crane forward tends two trainable cradles just forward of the bridge; the cradles are semicircular in section and may be intended to support salvage-and-rescue submersibles. The ships share the hull and propulsion of the research ship *Xiang Yang Hong 10* and probably also have fin stabilizers.

♦ **1 Dazhi class** Bldr: Hutung SY, Shanghai (In serv. mid-1960s)

Dazhi class

D: 5,800 tons (fl) **S:** . . . kts **Dim:** 106.7 × 15.3 × 6.1
A: 4/37-mm AA (II × 2)—8/25-mm AA (II × 4)
M: 1 diesel; 1 prop; . . . hp

♦ **1 Chunghua class** Bldr: Chunghua SY, Shanghai (In serv. 1967)

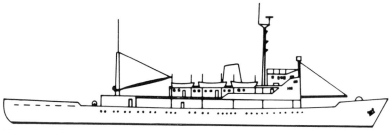

Chunghua class

D: 3,500 tons (fl) **S:** . . . kts **Dim:** 87.0 × 14 × . . . **A:** . . .
M: 2 diesels; 2 props; . . . hp

♦ **1 Hutung class** Bldr: Hutung SY, Shanghai (In serv. 1969)

D: 5,000 tons (fl) **S:** . . . kts **Dim:** 95.0 × 17.0 × 4.5
A: 6/37-mm AA (II × 3) **M:** 1 diesel; 1 prop; . . . hp

REMARKS: Has large gantry over stern for lowering a submarine rescue chamber.

REPAIR SHIPS

♦ **1 Romanian Galati class** Bldr: Galati SY (In serv. early 1970s)

D: 5,200 tons (fl) **S:** 12.5 kts **Dim:** 100.60 (93.70 pp) × 13.92 × 6.60 **A:** . . .
M: 1 Sulzer 5TAD56 diesel; 1 prop; . . . hp **Electric:** 345 kw
Fuel: 250 tons **Range:** 5,000/12.5

REMARKS: Converted from a cargo ship, with minimal external alterations. Of nine sisters purchased by China, two others serve the navy as cargo ships.

♦ **1 U.S. Achelous class** Bldr: Kaiser Co., Vancouver, Wash.

	Laid down	L	In serv.
TAKUSHAN (ex-*Hsing An*, ex-*Achilles*, ARL 41, ex-LST 455)	3-8-42	17-10-42	30-1-43

D: 4,100 tons (fl) **S:** 11 kts **Dim:** 99.98 × 15.24 × 3.40
A: 12/37-mm AA (II × 6) **M:** 2 GM 12-567A diesels; 2 props; 1,800 hp
Electric: 350 kw **Range:** 9,000/9 **Man:** 290 tot.

REMARKS: Acquired 1949. Has 60-ton A-frame gantry, plus several cranes.

CABLE SHIPS

♦ **1 or more . . . class** Bldr: Chunghua SY, Shanghai (In serv. late 1970s)

Chinese cable layer   1980

D: 1,550 tons (fl) **S:** 14 kts (sust.) **Dim:** 71.40 (63.00 pp) × 10.50 × 3.60
A: . . . **M:** 2 Type 8300Z diesels; 2 props; 2,200 hp

REMARKS: Design built for both military and civil use. Cable tank has 187-m³ capacity; ship can lay cable up to 100-mm thick.

REPLENISHMENT OILERS

♦ **2 Fuzhing class** Bldr: . . . (In serv. 1980)

x615   x 950

X 950   RNZN, 1980

REPLENISHMENT OILERS (continued)

X 950   RNZN, 1980

D: 20,000 ton (fl) **S:** 16 kts **Dim:** 166.0 × 20.0 × 8.0 **A:** none
M: 1 diesel; 1 prop;. . . hp

REMARKS: Equipment similar to U.S. Navy transfer systems. Two liquid replenishment stations per side, with constant-tension solid transfer stations each side just forward of the stack. Helo deck, but no hangar. Provision for four AA gun mounts. X 615 has a rounded stack and a higher aft superstructure than X 950. Both have 4 small electric cranes for stores handling.

TRANSPORT OILERS

♦ **1 or more new construction**

D: 4,940 tons (fl) **S:** 14 kts **Dim:** 101.0 (92.0 pp) × 13.8 × 5.5
M: 1 diesel; 1 prop; 2,600 hp **Range:** 2,400/14

REMARKS: 3,318.5 dwt. Cargo: 3,002 tons fuel oil (4,240 m³). For commercial service, but probably also employed by the navy as a follow-on to the Fuzhou class.

♦ **14 or more Fuzhou class** Bldr: Hutung SY, Shanghai (In serv. 1964-70)

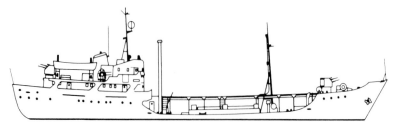

Fuzhou-class transport oiler

D: 1,200 tons (fl) **S:** 10-12 kts **Dim:** 60.0 (55.0 pp) × 9.0 × 3.5
A: 4.25-mm AA (II × 2)—4/14.5-mm mg (II × 2)
M: 1 diesel; 1 prop; 600 hp **Man:** 30 tot.

REMARKS: Five also built in a water-tanker version.

♦ **5 Leizhou class** (In serv. early 1960s)

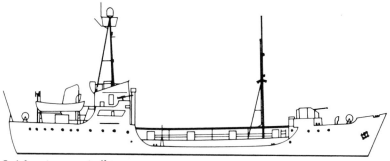

Leizhou transport oiler

D: 900 tons **S:** 10-12 kts **Dim:** 53.0 (48.0 pp) × 9.8 × 3.0
A: 4/37-mm AA (II × 2)—2/12.7-mm mg (I × 2) **M:** 1 diesel; 1 prop; 600 hp
Man: 30 tot.

REMARKS: Four also built in a water-tanker version.

♦ **2 U.S. Mettawee-class former gasoline tankers** (In serv. 1943-44)

D: 700 tons (2,200 fl) **S:** 14 kts **Dim:** 67.21 (64.77 pp) × 11.28 × 3.99
A: . . . **M:** 1 Fairbanks-Morse 37E16 diesel, 1 prop; 800 hp **Fuel:** 29 tons
Electric: 155 kw

♦ **1 Japanese 2 TM class** Bldr: Mitsubishi (In serv. 1944)

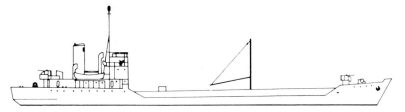

2 TM class

D: 2,935 tons (4,750 fl) **S:** 11.5 kts **Dim:** 98.8 (93.0 pp) × 13.8 × 6.0
A: 4/37-mm AA (II × 2)—4/14.5-mm mg (II × 2)
M: 1 set GT; 1 prop; 1,100 hp **Boilers:** 2 watertube **Range:** 5,000/11

REMARKS: No compound curves to hull. Acquired 1949.

WATER TANKERS

♦ **5 Fuzhou class** Bldr: Hutung SY, Shanghai (In serv. 1964-70)

REMARKS: Data generally as for transport oiler version. Armament distributed differently and lack raised tank top amidships.

♦ **4 Leizhou class** (In serv. early 1960s)

REMARKS: Appearance similar to transport oiler version, but lack raised tank top in well-deck area.

WATER TANKERS *(continued)*

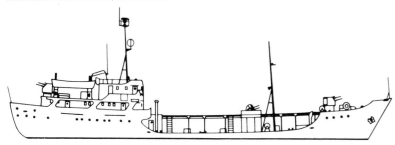

Fuzhou-class water tanker

CARGO SHIPS

♦ **2 Romanian Galati class** (In serv. early 1970s)

REMARKS: Characteristics as for the repair-ship version described earlier.

♦ **1 Zhandou 59 class** (In serv. 1959-65)

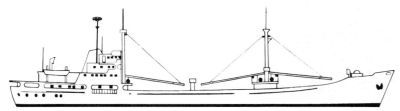

Zhandou 59 class

D: 4,735 tons (fl) **S:** 12.5 kts **Dim:** 99.4 × 13.0 × 5.5 **A:** none
M: 1 diesel; 1 prop;. . . hp **Man:** 50 tot.

REMARKS: 2,798 grt/3,200 dwt. One of a class of 20 built for merchant service; two were combined to produce an oil-drilling platform in the mid-1970s.

♦ **3 Tanlin class** (In serv. mid-1960s)

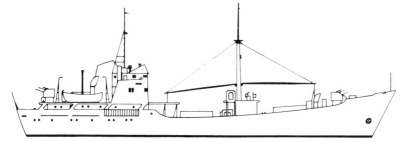

Tanlin class

D: 900 tons (fl) **S:** 10-12 kts **Dim:** 50.0 × 8.8 × 3.0 **A:** 4/25-mm AA
M: 1 diesel; 1 prop; 600 hp

♦ **1 or more U.S. Army FS-331 class** (In serv. 1943-44)

D: 465 tons (935 fl) **S:** 13.5 kts **Dim:** 53-49 (49.99 pp) × 9.75 × 3.05 **A:** . . .
M: 2 GM 6-278A diesels; 2 props; 1,000 hp **Fuel:** 57 tons
Range: 3,000/12.5, 4,300/9.5 **Man:** 30 tot.

REMARKS: Survivor(s) of a group of six or more acquired 1949. Cargo: 595 m³.

♦ **10-12 other cargo ships, types unidentified.**

SALVAGE TUGS

♦ **1 or more new-construction naval seagoing salvage tugs** Bldr: Dalien SY (In serv. . . .)

D: 5,279 tons (fl) **S:** 19 kts **Dim:** 102.2 (92.0 pp) × 16.0 × 6.5
M: 2 Burmeister & Wain/Dalien 8S50LU diesels; 2 CP props; 13,600 hp
Man: 50 tot.

REMARKS: Construction announced 1980; may be intended for civil subordination. 106-ton bollard pull. Equipped with 450-hp bow-thruster, firefighting cannon, pumps, diver's support gear, etc.

♦ **1 or more new-construction, coastal** Bldr . . .

D: 750 tons (fl) **S:** 13.5 kts **Dim:** 49.0 (44.5 pp) × 9.5 × 3.7 **A:** . . .
M: 2 LVP 24 diesels; 2 CP props; 1,800 hp **Fuel:** 135 tons
Electric: 336 kVA **Range:** 2,200/13.5; 1,100/9 (towing)

♦ **2 Tuzhong class** Bldr: Chunghua SY, Shanghai (In serv. late 1970s)

T 164   T 710

Tuzhong class   1980

D: 3,600 tons (fl) **S:** 18.5 kts **Dim:** 84.90 (77.00 pp) × 14.00 × 5.50
A: none **M:** 2/9 ESDZ 43/82B diesels; 2 CP props; 9,000 hp
Range: 18,000/. . .

REMARKS: Powerful salvage tug equipped for firefighting, emergency repairs, and equipped with high-capacity pumps. Has 35-ton-capacity towing winch.

♦ **3 Dinghai class** Bldr: Wuhu SY (In serv. late 1970s)

D: 1,472 tons (fl) **S:** . . . kts **Dim:** 60.22 × 11.60 × 4.44 **A:** . . .
M: 2 diesels; 2 props; 2,640 hp **Range:** 7,200/. . .

SALVAGE TUGS (continued)

REMARKS: Also built for civil use. 980.28 grt. 25-ton-capacity towing winch. Equipped for firefighting.

♦ **3 Yanting class**—D: 450 tons—trawler-type hull

♦ **3 FT 14-class converted trawlers**—D: 400 tons (fl)

CHINA TOWING COMPANY SALVAGE TUGS

♦ **2 De Da class** Bldr: Ishikawajima-Harima Heavy Ind., Chita, Japan

DE DA (In serv. 9-79)   DE YUE (In serv. 12-79)

De Yue   RNZN, 1980

D: 5,700 tons (fl)   **S:** 20.5 kts   **Dim:** 98.0 (90.0 pp) × 15.8 × 6.7   **A:** none
M: 2 IHI-Pielstick 16CS2-5 diesels; 2 CP props with Kort nozzles; 20,800 hp
Fuel: 2,740 tons   **Electric:** 1,980 kw   **Range:** 14,600/19.4

REMARKS: 3,300 grt. World's most powerful salvage tugs. Operated by China Towing Company, which also has 28 other oceangoing tugs, three 5,000-ton barges, and a floating crane of 2,500 tons capacity. *De Yue* accompanied the ICBM test flotilla in May 1980; she and *De Da* have a 200-ton bollard pull and a 320-ton brake capacity towing winch, a 25-ton crane aft and a 10-ton boom forward. The two fire monitors have a capacity of 4,000 liter/min and a range of 100 m. Extensive diver support equipment is aboard. There is a 500-hp bow-thruster.

♦ **2 Sui Jiu 201 class** Bldr: Hitachi, Japan

SUI JIU 201 (In serv. 8-75)   HU JIU (In serv. 15-9-75)

D: 4,100 tons (fl)   **S:** 17.5 kts   **Dim:** 87.0 (80.0 pp) × 14.0 × 6.0
M: 2 diesels; 2 props; 9,000 hp   **Range:** 17,000/17.5

REMARKS: 2,100 grt. 82-ton bollard pull.

♦ **4 De Ping class** Bldr: Wang Tak Eng. & Shbldg, Hong Kong (In serv. 1979)

DE PING   DE AN   DE SHUN   DE LI

D: 2,500 tons (fl)   **S:** 16.5 kts   **Dim:** 66.4 (60.0 pp) × 12.0 × 5.44
M: 2 diesels; 2 props; 6,000 hp   **Range:** 7,500/16.5

REMARKS: 1,186 grt. 60-ton bollard pull.

♦ **3 specialized salvage ships** Bldr: . . .

HU JIU LAO 1   HU JIU LAO 2   HU JIU LAO 3

D: 4,700 tons (fl)   **S:** 17.1 kts   **Dim:** 103.6 × 16.0 × 5.07
M: 2 diesels; 2 props; 5,000 hp   **Range:** 5,000/17

REMARKS: 3,217 grt. Limited towing capability. Have two side-by-side 30-ton electrohydraulic cranes aft, 2/15-ton booms fwd.

♦ **17 coastal salvage tugs** Bldrs: Donghai SY, Wenchong SY, Wuhu SY (in serv. 1975-. . .

HU JIU 1-7   SUI JIU 203, 206   YAN JIU 1-8

D: . . .   **S:** 14 kts   **Dim:** 60.2 (54.0) × 11.6 × 4.44
M: 2 diesels; 2 props; 2,640 hp   **Range:** 7,200/14

REMARKS: 980 grt. 20.8-ton bollard pull. Also in China Towing Co. service are 4,000-hp, 189 grt and 3,000-hp, 192-grt harbor tugs, and 1,900-hp, 603-grt and 1,200-hp, 483-grt coastal tugs, total numbers not available.

TUGS

♦ **16 Soviet Gromovoy class** Bldr: China (early 1960s)

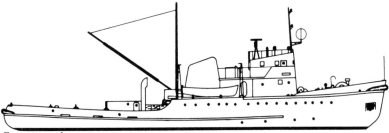

Gromovoy class

D: 900 tons (fl)   **S:** 11 kts   **Dim:** 45.7 (41.5 pp) × 9.45 × 4.6
A: 2/12.7-mm mg (I × 2)   **M:** 2 diesels; 2 props; 1,200 hp

REMARKS: Soviet commercial tug design, built under license.

♦ **4 Soviet Roslavl class** Bldr: See remarks (In serv. 1958-64)

D: 750 tons (fl)   **S:** 11 kts   **Dim:** 44.5 × 9.5 × 3.5
M: 2 diesels, electric drive; 2 props; 1,200 hp

REMARKS: One transferred from the U.S.S.R.; the others built circa 1964-65 in China.

♦ **2 U.S. Sotoyomo class** (In serv. 1943-45)

D: 435 tons (835 fl)   **S:** 13 kts   **Dim:** 43.59 (40.74 wl) × 10.31 × 4.01   **A:** . . .
M: 2 GM 12-278A diesels, electric drive; 1 prop; 1,500 hp
Fuel: 158 tons   **Electric:** 120 kw   **Man:** 50 tot.

REMARKS: Acquired 1949. Former U.S. names unknown.

♦ **2 U.S. Army "149-ft" class**

D: 600 tons (967 fl)   **S:** 12 kts   **Dim:** 45.4 (42.7 pp) × 10.1 × 5.33
M: 1 set Skinner Uniflow 53CYRS triple-expansion reciprocating steam; 1 prop; 1,200 hp
Boilers: 2/14 kg/cm^2 **Fuel:** 325 tons   **Range:** 4,200/8

REMARKS: Acquired 1949. Former U.S. LT numbers unknown. Wooden hulls.

CHINA (*continued*)

YARD AND SERVICE CRAFT

There are a reported 380 units in this category, but the true total number is probably far larger and would include yard oilers, tugs, barges, floating dry docks, dredges, and the like. No details are available.

COLOMBIA

Republic of Colombia

PERSONNEL: (1980): 7,200 total, including 1,500 marines

MERCHANT MARINE (1980): 69 ships—283,457 grt (tankers: 6 ships—30,344 grt)

SUBMARINES

♦ 2 German Type 209

	Bldr	L	In serv.
SS 28 PIJAO	Howaldtswerke, Kiel	10-4-74	17-4-75
SS 29 TAYRONA	Howaldtswerke, Kiel	16-7-74	18-7-75

Pijao or Tayrona 1980

D: 980/1,050/1,230 tons **S:** 14/18 (22 kts for a few minutes)
Dim: 56.0 × 6.2 × 5.9 **A:** 8/533-mm TT fwd—6 reserve torpedoes
M: 4 MTU 12V-493-TY60 diesels, Siemens electric motor; 1 prop; 3,600 hp
Fuel: 50 tons **Endurance:** 30 days **Man:** 5 officers, 26 men

♦ 2 Italian S.X. 506 midget Bldr: Cosmos, Livorno, Italy (1972-74)

SS 20 INTREPIDO   SS 21 INDOMABLE

D: 58/70 tons **S:** 8.5 kts **Dim:** 23.0 × 2.0 × 4.0
Cargo capacity: 2,050 kg of explosives; 8 frogmen fully equipped; 2 submarine vehicles (for the frogmen) supported by a fixed system on lower part of the hull, one on each side.
Range: 1,200/7 **Man:** 5 men

REMARKS: Similar submarines have been bought by the Pakistani and Taiwanese navies. Sisters *Roncador* (SS 23) and *Quita Sueno* (SS 24) are no longer in service.

DESTROYERS

♦ 2 Swedish Hälland class

	Bldr	Laid down	L	In serv.
D 05 VEINTE DE JULIO	Kockums, Malmö	10-55	26-6-56	15-6-58
D 06 SIETE DE AGOSTO (ex-*13 de Junio*)	Götaverken, Göteborg	11-55	19-6-56	31-10-58

Siete de Agosto (D 06)

D: 2,650 tons (3,300 fl) **S:** 25 kts **Dim:** 121.5 × 12.6 × 4.7 (hull)/5.5 max
A: 6/120-mm DP (II × 3)—4/40-mm AA (I × 4)—4/533-mm TT (IV × 1)—2/375-mm Bofors ASW RL (IV × 1)
Electron Equipt: Radars: 1/LWO-3, 1/DA-02, 1/navigational, 6/SGR-102 f.c.
M: De Laval double-reduction GT; 2 props; 55,000 hp
Boilers: 2 Penhoët-Motala **Fuel:** 524 tons **Range:** 450/25, 3,000/18
Man: 21 officers, 227 men

REMARKS: D 05 has been inoperable but maintained in reserve, pending the possibility of a refit. Both made 35 kts on trials. There are six M4-series radar directors, one for each gun mount (the pair flanking the foremast have separate operator positions).

♦ 1 U.S. Allen M. Sumner FRAM II class

	Bldr	Laid down	L	In serv.
D 03 SANTANDER (ex-*Waldron*, DD 699)	Federal SB & DD	16-11-43	26-3-44	8-6-44

D: 2,200 tons (3,300 fl) **S:** 30 kts **Dim:** 114.75 × 12.45 × 5.8
A: 6/127-mm 38-cal. DP (II × 3)—6/324-mm Mk 32 ASW TT (III × 2)
Electron Equipt: Radars: 1/SPS-40, 1/SPS-10, 1/Mk 25 fire-control
Sonar: SQS-30
M: GT; 2 props; 60,000 hp **Boilers:** 4 Babcock & Wilcox; 43.3 kg/cm², 454°C
Fuel: 650 tons **Range:** 4,800/15

REMARKS: Transferred 16-12-73. Has had FRAM II modernization and can handle a small helicopter. VDS and Hedgehogs removed before transfer. Mk 37 GFCS.

FRIGATES

♦ 4 FS 1500 class Bldr: Howaldtswerke, Kiel, W. Germany

	Laid down	L	In serv.
. . . N . . .	1-81	8-81	20-7-82
. . . N . . .	. . .	. . .	. . .
. . . N . . .	. . .	. . .	. . .
. . . N . . .	. . .	. . .	. . .

FRIGATES *(continued)*

D: 1,850 tons (fl) **S:** 28 kts **Dim:** 93.0 (90.0 wl) × 11.0 × 3.5 (hull)
A: 2-4/MM-38 Exocet SSM—1/Albatros SAM system (. . . Aspide missiles)—
1/76-mm OTO Melara DP—2/40-mm Breda AA (II × 1)—4/30-mm Emerlec
AA (II × 2)—6/324-mm Mk 32 ASW TT (III × 2)—1/helicopter
Electron Equipt: Radar: . . . Sonar: Diodon ECM: Phoenix-II, SUSIE
M: 4 MTU 20V 1163 diesels; 2 CP props; 23,000 hp (21,000 sust.) **Fuel:** . . .
Range: 7,000/14 **Man:** 88 tot.

REMARKS: Completion date for first unit is that publicly announced. Engines are a new model, not previously installed in a ship.

♦ 1 U.S. Courtney class

	Bldr	Laid down	L	In serv.
D 07 BOYACA	New York SB	10-55	24-11-56	26-1-57
(ex-*Hartley*, DE 1029)				

D: 1,450 tons (1,914 fl) **S:** 25 kts **Dim:** 95.86 × 11.26 × 4.3/5.3(sonar)
A: 2/76.2-mm DP (II × 1)—6/Mk 32 ASW TT (III × 2)
Electron Equipt: Radars: 1/SPS-6, 1/SPS-10, 1/Mk 34 f.c.
  Sonar: SQS-23 ECM: WLR-1
M: De Laval GT; 1 prop; 20,000 hp **Man:** 11 officers, 150 men
Boilers: 2 Foster-Wheeler; 42 kg/cm², 510°C **Fuel:** 400 tons **Range:** 4,400/11

REMARKS: Transferred by U.S. 8-7-72. Twin rudders. Flight deck and hangar for small helicopter. Mk 63 GFCS. Frigate DT 15 *Cordoba* (ex-*Ruchamkin*, LPR 89) stricken 7-80.

CORVETTES

♦ 4 U.S. Cherokee- and Abnaki-class former fleet tugs Bldr: Charleston SB & DD Co.

	Laid down	L	In serv.
RM . . . N . . . (ex-*Jacarilla*, ATF 104)	25-8-43	25-2-44	26-6-44
RM 72 PEDRO DE HEREDIA (ex-*Choctaw*, ATF 70)	4-4-42	18-10-42	21-4-43
RM 73 SEBASTIAN DE BELALCAZAR (ex-*Carib*, ATF 82)	7-9-42	7-2-43	24-7-43
RM 74 RODRIGO DE BASTEDAS (ex-*Hidatsa*, ATF 102)	8-8-43	29-12-43	25-4-44

D: 1,235 tons (1,675 fl) **S:** 16.5 kts **Dim:** 62.48 × 11.73 × 4.67
A: 1/76.2-mm DP **Electric:** 300 kw **Range:** 15,000/8 **Man:** 75 tot.
M: 4 GM 12-278 diesels (ex-ATF 102, ex-ATF 104: 4 Busch-Sulzer B5-539 diesels, electric drive); 1 prop; 3,000 hp

Pedro de Heredia (RM 72)—prior to arming   1975

REMARKS: RM. . . , 73-74 reactivated from U.S. Maritime Commission reserve fleet and transferred 15-3-79 for use as patrol and rescue ships. RM 72 transferred 1961; purchased 31-3-78. RM 75 may not yet have been reconditioned.

PATROL BOATS

♦ 2 U.S. Asheville class

	Bldr	L	In serv.
. . . N . . . (ex-. . .)	. . .	. . .	. . .
. . . N . . . (ex-. . .)	. . .	. . .	. . .

D: 225 tons (245 fl) **S:** 40 kts (16 cruising) **Dim:** 50.14 (46.94 wl) × 7.28 × 2.9
A: 1/76.2-mm 50 DP Mk 34—4/12.7-mm mg (II × 2)
Electron Equipt: Radar: 1/LN-66, 1/SPG-50 **Electric:** 100 kw
M: CODOG: 1 GE 7LM-1500-PE 102 gas turbines; 13,300 hp (12,500 sust.) 2 Cummins VT 12-875M diesels, 1,650 hp (1,450 sust.); 2 CP props

REMARKS: The U.S. Congress was requested under FY 82 to approve the lease of two out of the following four previously stricken *Asheville*-class ships to Colombia: *Gallup* (PG 85), *Canon* (PG 90), *Beacon* (PG 99), or *Green Bay* (PG 101).

♦ 6 miscellaneous captured drug runners

. . . TURBU, . . . TOLU, . . . SERRANILLA, . . . TENIENTE DE NAVIO JOSE MARIA PALAS, . . . TENIENTE DE NAVIO ALEJANDRO BAL DOMERO SALGADO, . . . TENIENTE PRIMO ALCALA

REMARKS: Characteristics unknown; placed in service 1981 to help combat drug traffic in the Caribbean.

RIVER PATROL BOATS AND CRAFT

♦ 2 Rio Hacha class Bldr: Unial Barranquilla (In serv. 1955)

CF 35 RIO HACHA   CF 37 ARAUCA

D: 170 tons (184 fl) **S:** 13 kts **Dim:** 47.25 × 8.23 × 1.0
A: 2/76.2-mm DP (I × 2)—4/20-mm AA (I × 4)
M: 2 Caterpillar diesels; 2 props; 800 hp **Range:** 1,000/12 **Man:** 27-43 tot.

REMARKS: Sister *Leticia* disarmed and equipped as a hospital boat.

♦ CF 33 Cartagena Bldr: Yarrow & Cl., Glasgow, 1930

D: 142 tons **S:** 15.5 kts **Dim:** 41.9 × 7.16 × 0.8
A: 2/76.2-mm—1/20-mm AA—4/7.7-mm mg **Range:** 2,100/15 **Man:** 39 tot.
M: 2 Gardner diesels; 2 props (in tunnels); 600 hp **Fuel:** 24 tons

REMARKS: Principal parts of the ship protected against small arms.

OCEANOGRAPHIC RESEARCH SHIPS

♦ 2 new construction Bldr: Martin Jansen, Leer, W. Germany

N . . . (In serv. 4-81) N . . . (In serv. 5-81)

D: . . . **S:** 13 kts **Dim:** 50.3 (44.0 pp) × 10.0 × 4.0
M: 1 diesel; 1 prop; 800 hp **Range:** 16,000/11.5 **Man:** 9 officers, 18 men

REMARKS: Delivered 1981 for DIMAR (Direccion General Maritima Portuario), one for geophysical research, one for fisheries. Naval-manned. Prime contractor: Ferrostaal, Kiel.

Arauca (CF 37)

Cartagena (CF 33)

♦ **1 U.S. PCE 821-class former ASW escort** Bldr: Pullman Standard Car Co., Chicago

	Laid down	L	In serv.
BO 151 SAN ANDRES (ex-*Rockville*, PCER 851)	18-10-43	22-2-44	15-5-44

D: 674 tons (858 fl) **S:** 15 kts **Dim:** 56.23 × 10.05 × 3.0 **Electric:** 180 kw
M: 2 GM 12-567A diesels; 2 props; 1,800 hp **Man:** 60 tot.

REMARKS: Purchased 5-6-69 and then converted.

♦ **1 U.S. former refrigerated stores lighter** Bldr: Niagara SB, Buffalo, N.Y.

BO 153 QUINDIO (ex-U.S. YFR 433)   (In serv. 11-11-43)

D: 380 tons (600 fl) **Dim:** 40.4 × 9.10 × 2.5 **M:** 1 Union diesel; 600 hp
Man: 17 tot.

REMARKS: Leased 7-64; purchased 31-3-78.

San Andres (BO 151)   1976

HYDROGRAPHIC SURVEY SHIP

♦ **1 former lighthouse tender** Bldr: Lindigoverken, Sweden (L: 28-5-54)

FB 161 GORGONA

D: 560 tons **S:** 13 kts **Dim:** 41.15 × 9.0 × 2.83
M: 2 Nohab diesels; 2 props; 900 hp

AUXILIARY SHIPS

♦ **1 U.S. Patapsco-class tanker, former gasoline tanker**

	Bldr	Laid down	L	In serv.
BT 67 TUMACO (ex-U.S. *Chewaucan*, AOG 50)	Cargill, Inc. Savage, Minn.	23-12-43	22-7-44	19-2-45

Tumaco (BT 67)   1976

D: 4,570 tons (fl) **S:** 14 kts **Dim:** 94.7 (89.0 pp) × 14.78 × 4.9
A: 2/76.2-mm DP (I × 2) **M:** 2 GM 16-278A diesels; 2 props; 3,300 hp
Range: 8,350/11.5 **Man:** 45 tot.

REMARKS: Purchased 1-7-75. Foremast deleted, small lattice mast stepped for navigational radar. Cargo: 2,575 tons. Retains one Mk 52 radar GFCS (with Mk 26 radar) and one Mk 51 GFCS.

AUXILIARY SHIPS *(continued)*

♦ **1 small transport/cargo ship** Bldr: Sander, Delfzijl, Netherlands (In serv. 1953)

TM 43 CIUDAD DE QUIBO   (ex-M/V *Shamrock*)

    D: 633 tons **S:** 11 kts **Dim:** 50.3 × 7.2 × 2.8
    M: 1 M.A.N. diesel; 1 prop; 390 hp **Fuel:** 32 tons
    Man: 11 tot.

REMARKS: Purchased 1953.

♦ **2 hospital boats**

BD 36 LETICIA   Former river patrol boat, see under *Rio Hacha* class. Has 6 beds, surgery facilities, etc.

BD 33 SOCORRO   Bldr: Cartagena Naval DY, 1956

    D: 70 tons **S:** 9 kts **Dim:** 25.0 × 5.5 × 0.75 **M:** 2 GM diesels; 270 hp
    Man: 10 tot.

REMARKS: Originally fitted to carry 56 troops on the rivers, now used for surgery.

TUGS

♦ **1 U.S. Sotoyomo class auxiliary ocean tug** Bldr: Levingston SY, Orange, Texas

	Laid down	L	In serv.
RM 75 BAHIA UTRIA (ex-*Koka*, ATA 185)	5-8-44	11-9-44	17-11-44

    D: 534 tons (835 fl) **S:** 13 kts **Dim:** 43.6 × 10.3 × 4.0
    A: 1/76.2-mm DP Mk 26 **Electric:** 120 kw
    M: 2 GM 12-278A diesels, electric drive; 1 prop; 1,500 hp **Range:** 8,000/8

REMARKS: Transferred 1-7-71. Sister *Bahia Honda* lost 2-75.

♦ **1 ex-U.S. small harbor tug** Bldr: Henry C. Grebe (In serv. 2-9-43)

RM 73 RICARDO SORZANO (ex-YTL 231)

    D: 70 tons (80 fl) **S:** 9 kts **Dim:** 20.2 × 5.2 × 1.5 **Electric:** 15 kw
    M: 1 Cooper-Bessemer diesel; 240 hp **Fuel:** 7 tons

REMARKS: Loaned 1963; purchased 31-3-78.

♦ **1 old harbor tug** (L: 1928)

RM 71 ANDAGOYA

    D: 117 grt **S:** 12 kts **Dim:** 28.0 × 6.1 × 3.0 **M:** 1 diesel; 400 hp

♦ **6 Capitan Castro class**

RR 81 CAPITAN CASTRO	RR 86 CAPITAN RIGOBERTO GIRALDO
RR 82 CANDIDO LEGUIZAMO	RR 87 CAPITAN VLADIMIR VALEK
RR 84 CAPITAN ALVARO RUIS	RR 88 TENIENTE LUIS BERNAL

    D: 50 tons **S:** 10 kts **Dim:** 20.0 × 4.25 × 0.75 **M:** 2 GM diesels; 260 hp

REMARKS: All for river use.

♦ **1 floating dry dock for river force use**

JAIME ARIAS—D: 700 tons (fl) Capacity: 165 tons

♦ **1 school sailing ship** Bldr: Celaya, Bilbao, Spain (In serv. 7-9-68)

GLORIA

Gloria   A.D. Baker, 1976

    D: 1,300 tons (fl) **S:** 10.5 kts (on diesel) **Dim:** 64.7 × 10.6 × 6.6
    M: 1 diesel; 500 hp **Sail areas:** 1,400 m² (bark-rigged)

CUSTOMS SERVICE

This organization, whose patrol boats had been allowed to deteriorate in recent years, is attempting a resurgence. Astilleros de Colombia is refitting out-of-service units to restore them for anti-drug patrol duties.

PATROL BOATS

♦ **2 Jorge Soto del Corval class** Bldr: Rauma Repola SY, Rauma, Finland (In serv. 1971)

A 208 CARLOS ALBAN   A 209 NITO RESTREPO

    D: 100 tons (130 fl) **S:** 18 kts **Dim:** 34.0 × 6.0 × 1.8 **A:** 1/20-mm AA
    M: 2 MTU diesels; 2 CP props; 2,500 hp

REMARKS: A 208 recommissioned 1980, A 209 in 1981. Sister *J.S. del Corval* hulked.

♦ **1 Pedro Gaul class** Bldr: F. Schürenstedt, Bardenfleth, W. Germany

A 206 CARLOS E. RESTREPO (In serv. 1964)

    D: 85 tons (fl) **S:** 26 kts **Dim:** 34.7 × 5.5 × 1.8 **A:** 1/20-mm AA
    M: 2 Maybach 12-cyl. diesels; 2 props; 2,500 hp

REMARKS: Sisters *Pedro Gaul* (AN 204) and *Estaban Jaramillo* (A 205) hulked. A 206 recommissioned 1981.

COMOROS

Republic of the Comoros

MERCHANT MARINE (1980): 3 ships—1,116 grt (1 tanker—1,139 grt)

♦ **1 British LCT(8)-class tank-landing ship** (In serv. 1945)

N. . .   (ex-Fr. LCT 9061, ex-Br. *Buttress*, LCT(8) 4099)

L 9061   C. Limonier, 1975

D: 657 tons (1,000 fl)   **S:** 12 kts   **Dim:** 70.48 × 11.9 × 1.8
A: 2/20-mm AA (I × 2)—1/120-mm mortar, Army model
M: 4 Paxman diesels; 2 props; 1,840 hp   **Man:** 29 tot.

REMARKS: Bought 7-65 by France, transferred by France, 1976.

CONGO

People's Republic of the Congo

PERSONNEL: 180 men

MERCHANT MARINE (1980): 15 ships—6,784 grt

COASTAL NAVY: The naval forces are divided into coastal navy and the river navy.

♦ **3 Spanish "Pirana"-class patrol boats**

REMARKS: Ordered 1980; no data available.

♦ **1 Soviet Shershen-class former torpedo boat**

D: 150 tons (180 fl)   **S:** 45 kts   **Dim:** 34.0 × 7.2 × 1.5
A: 4/30-mm AA (II × 2)   **Electron Equipt:** Radar: 1/Pot Drum, 1/Drum Tilt
M: 3 M503A diesels; 3 props; 12,000 hp   **Range:** 450/34, 700/20

REMARKS: Transferred 1979; torpedo tubes removed prior to delivery.

♦ **3 ex-Chinese Shanghai-II-class patrol boats**

P 401   P 402   P 403

D: 122.5 tons (150 fl)   **S:** 28.5 kts   **Dim:** 38.78 × 5.41 × 1.49
A: 4/37-mm AA (II × 2)—4/25-mm AA (II × 2)
Electron Equipt: Radar: 1/Pot Head
M: 2 M50F-4, 1,200 hp and 2/12D6 diesels; 4 props; 4,220 hp   **Man:** 38 tot.

REMARKS: Very unsophisticated boats. Delivered in 3-75.

RIVER NAVY:

♦ **4 ex-Chinese Yu Lin-class patrol craft**

D: 9.8 tons (fl)   **S:** 25 kts   **Dim:** 13.0 × 2.9 × 1.1   **A:** 1/12.7-mm mg
M: 1 diesel; 1 prop; 300 hp

REMARKS: Transferred 1966.

♦ **2 locally built small craft**

♦ **10 small craft**

M: 40- to 75-hp Johnson outboards

REMARKS: Probably in poor condition.

COSTA RICA

Republic of Costa Rica

PERSONNEL: 100 men

MERCHANT MARINE (1980): 26 ships—20,333 grt

PATROL BOATS

♦ **1 105-foot** Bldr: Swiftships, Morgan City, Louisiana

FP. . .   (In serv. 1978)

D: 118 tons (fl)   **S:** 36 kts   **Dim:** 31.73 × 7.1 × 2.16   **A:** 2/12.7-mm mg
M: 3 MTU 12V331 diesels; 3 props; . . . hp   **Range:** 1,200/18

♦ **5 65-foot U.S. Swift ships** Bldr: Swiftships, Morgan City, Louisiana (In serv. 1978)

FP 407   FP 408   FP 409   FP 410   FP 411

D: 33 tons (fl)   **S:** 32 kts   **Dim:** 19.77 × 5.56 × 1.98   **A:** 2/12.7 mm mg
M: 2 MTU 8V331 diesels; 2 props; 1,400 hp   **Range:** 1,200/18

CUBA
Republic of Cuba

PERSONNEL: Approx. 9,000 men

MERCHANT MARINE (1980): 405 ships—881,260 grt (tankers: 15—64,505 grt)

SUBMARINES

♦ **2 Soviet Foxtrot class**

D: 1,900/2,400 tons **S:** 16/15.5 kts **Dim:** 91.5 × 7.5 × 6.0
A: 10/533-mm TT (6 fwd, 4 aft)—22 torpedoes or 44 mines
M: 3 diesels, 3 electric motors; 3 props; 5,300 hp **Endurance:** 70 days
Range: 11,000/8 snorkel **Man:** 78 tot.

REMARKS: Transferred 1-79 and 1-80. A nonoperational Whiskey-class submarine was transferred 4-79 for use as a battery-charging barge.

FRIGATES

♦ **1 Soviet Koni class** Bldr: Zelenodolsk SY

MARIEL

D: 1,900 tons (fl) **S:** 30 kts **Dim:** 96.0 × 12.0 × 5.0 (4.4 hull)
A: 1/SAN-4 SAM syst. (II × 1; 18 missiles)—4/76.2-mm DP (II × 2)—4/30-mm
AA (II × 2)—2/RBU-6000—2/d.c. rack—mines
Electron Equipt: Radar: 1/Strut Curve, 1/Don-2, 1/Pop Group, 1/Hawk
Screech, 1/Drum Tilt
Sonar: 1/medium freq., hull-mounted
M: CODAG: 1 gas turbine, 2 diesels; 3 props; 30,000 hp

REMARKS: Delivered 1-8-81.

PATROL BOATS

♦ **4 Soviet Kronshtadt class**

Cuban Kronshtadt   1972

D: 300 tons (330 fl) **S:** 18 kts **Dim:** 52.1 × 6.5 × 2.2
A: 1/85-mm DP—2/37-mm AA (I × 2)—6/14.5-mm machine guns—2/RBU-1200
ASW RL—2 d.c. projectors—2 d.c. racks
Electron Equipt: Radar: 1/Ball End **M:** 3 9D diesels; 3 props; 3,300 hp
Fuel: 20 tons diesel **Range:** 1,500/12 **Man:** 50 tot.

REMARKS: Transferred 2-62. Two additional believed discarded.

♦ **9 Soviet S.O.-1 class**

Cuban S.O.-1   1972

D: 190 tons (215 fl) **S:** 28 kts **Dim:** 42.0 × 6.1 × 1.9
A: 4/25-mm AA (II × 2)—4/RBU-1200 ASW RL—2 d.c. racks (24 d.c.)
Electron Equipt: Radar: 1/Pot Head **M:** 3 diesels; 3 props; 6,000 hp
Man: 30 tot.

REMARKS: Six were transferred in 1964 and six in 1967. Three additional believed discarded.

GUIDED-MISSILE BOATS

♦ **7 Soviet Osa-II class**

D: 215 tons (240 fl) **S:** 36 kts **Dim:** 39.0 × 7.7 × 1.9
A: 4/SS-N-2 Styx (I × 4)—4/30-mm AA (II × 2)
Electron Equipt: Radars: 1/Square Tie, 1/Drum Tilt
M: 3 M504 diesels; 3 props; 15,000 hp **Range:** 800/25 **Man:** 25 men

REMARKS: Transferred 1976-80.

♦ **6 Soviet Osa-I class**

D: 175 tons (210 fl) **S:** 36 kts **Dim:** 39.0 × 7.7 × 1.8
A: 4/SS-N-2 Styx (I × 4)—4/30-mm AA (II × 2)
Electron Equipt: Radars: 1/Square Tie, 1/Drum Tilt
M: 3 M503A diesels; 3 props; 12,000 hp **Range:** 800/25 **Man:** 25 tot.

REMARKS: Two were delivered in 1972, two in 1973, and two in 1974

GUIDED-MISSILE BOATS *(continued)*

♦ **14 Soviet Komar class**

D: 71 tons (82 fl) **S:** 40 kts **Dim:** 25.3 × 7.0 × 2.0
A: 2/SS-N-2 Styx (I × 2)—2/25-mm AA (II × 1)
Electron Equipt: Radar: 1/Square Tie **M:** 4 M50 diesels; 4 props; 4,800 hp
Range: 650/30 **Man:** 19 tot.

REMARKS: Built 1961-63. Twelve were delivered in 1962 and six in 1966. Will probably soon be discarded; 4 deleted 1979.

TORPEDO BOATS

♦ **6 Soviet Turya-class semi-hydrofoils**

Two Turya-class hydrofoils en route to Cuba   1979

D: 240 tons (fl) **S:** 40 kts **Dim:** 39.0 × 7.7 × 2.0
A: 2/57-mm AA aft (II × 1)—2/25-mm AA (II × 1)—4/533-mm TT (I × 4)
Electron Equipt: Radars: 1/Pot Drum, 1/Muff Cob
M: 3 M504 diesels; 3 props; 15,000 hp **Range:** 800/25 **Man:** 16 tot.

REMARKS: First two delivered 2-79, the first foreign transfer of this class; 2 in 2-80, 2 in 1-81. ASW capability omitted. Retractable forward hydrofoils; stern planes on surface. Uses Osa-II hull and propulsion.

♦ **6 Soviet P 6 class**

D: 56 tons (66.5 fl) **S:** 43 kts **Dim:** 25.3 × 6.1 × 1.7
A: 4/25-mm AA (II × 2)—2/533-mm TT—d.c.
Electron Equipt: Radar: 1/Skin Head
M: 4 M50 diesels; 4 props; 4,800 hp **Range:** 450/30 **Man:** 12 tot.

REMARKS: Post-1955. Delivered in 1962. Wooden hulls.

♦ **12 Soviet P 4 class**

Cuban P 4

D: 19.3 tons (22.4 fl) **S:** 55 kts **Dim:** 19.3 × 3.7 × 1.0
A: 2/14.5-mm mg (aft)—2/450-mm TT **Electron Equipt:** Radar: 1/Skin Head
M: 2 M50 diesels; 2 props; 2,400 hp **Man:** 12 tot.

REMARKS: Pre-1955. Delivered 1962-64. Aluminum, stepped-hydroplane hulls. Probably in poor condition.

PATROL CRAFT

♦ **18 Soviet Zhuk class**

D: 50 tons (60 fl) **S:** 30 kts **Dim:** 26.0 × 4.9 × 1.5
A: 4/14.5-mm mg (II × 2) **M:** 2 M50 diesels; 2 props; 2,400 hp

REMARKS: Transferred 1975-80.

MINE WARFARE SHIPS

♦ **2 Soviet Sonya-class coastal minesweepers**

D: 350 tons (400 fl) **S:** 14 kts **Dim:** 48.5 × 8.8 × 2.1
A: 2/30-mm AA (II × 1)—2/25-mm AA (II × 1)
Electron Equipt: Radar: 1/Spin Trough
               IFF: 1/High Pole B, 1/Square Head
M: 2 diesels; 2 props; 2,400 hp **Man:** 43 tot.

REMARKS: Delivered 8-80 and 10-80. Wooden hulls, sheathed in glass-reinforced plastic.

♦ **6 Soviet Yevgenya-class inshore minesweepers**

D: 80 tons (90 fl) **S:** 12 kts **Dim:** 26.0 × 6.0 × 1.5 **A:** 2/25-mm AA (II × 1)
M: 2 diesels; 600 hp **Man:** 12 tot.

REMARKS: Two transferred 1978, two in 1979, and two in 12-80.

MINE WARFARE SHIPS *(continued)*

Cuban Sonya under tow on delivery voyage   1980

HYDROGRAPHIC SURVEY SHIPS

♦ **1 Soviet Biya class** Bldr: Gdansk, Poland (1972-76)

H. . . (ex-GS 186)

    D: 750 tons (fl) **S:** 13 kts **Dim:** 55.0 × 9.2 × 2.6
    Electron Equipt: Radar: 1/Don-2 **M:** 2 diesels; 2 CP props; 1,200 hp
    Range: 4,700/11 **Man:** 25 tot.

REMARKS: Transferred 11-80. Carries one survey launch. Also useful as a buoy tender; one 5-ton crane.

♦ **1 converted trawler**

H 101 SIBONEY **D:** 600 tons

REMARKS: Built in Spain, 1972. Also used for training.

♦ **6 Soviet Nyryat-1 class.**

H 91   H 92   H 93   H 94   H 95   H 96

    D: 120 tons (fl) **S:** 12 kts **Dim:** 29.0 × 5.0 × 1.7
    M: 1 diesel; 2 props; 450 hp **Radar:** 1/Spin Trough **Range:** 1,600/10
    Man: 15 tot.

REMARKS: Date of transfer not known. Known in U.S.S.R. as GPB 480 class. Same class, with different equipment, also used as diving tenders.

AUXILIARIES

♦ **2 lighthouse and buoy tenders**

ENRIQUE COLIAZO Bldr: Great Britain, 1906

    D: 815 tons **Dim:** 64.0 × 10.5 × 2.8 **M:** Triple expansion; 2 props; 680 hp

SF 10 BERTHA

    D: 100 tons **S:** 10 kts **Dim:** 31.5 × 5.75 × 3.4
    M: 2 Gray diesels; 2 props; 450 hp

REMARKS: Dates from 1944.

♦ **7 Soviet T 4-class landing craft (LCM)**

    D: 94 tons (fl) **S:** 9 kts **Dim:** 19.0 × 5.3 × 1.3 **M:** 2 diesels; 2 props; 400 hp

REMARKS: Transferred 1967-74. Used as harbor craft.

♦ **1 yacht**

GRANMA Small cabin cruiser in which Fidel Castro returned to Cuba in 1956. Maintained by the navy as a museum.

♦ **3 small service launches** Bldr: U.S.A., 1949

A 1   A 2   A 3

    D: 58 tons **Dim:** 22.50 × 4.6 × 1.6
    M: 2 Gray Marine diesels; 2 props; 225 hp

♦ **1 Soviet Okhtenskiy-class seagoing tug** (In serv. 1960s)

CARIBE

    D: 700 tons (950 fl) **S:** 13.3 kts **Dim:** 47.3 × 10.3 × 5.5
    M: 2 diesels; 1 prop; 1,500 hp **Range:** 7,800/7 **Man:** 40 tot.

REMARKS: Transferred 1976.

♦ **2 Soviet Yelva-class diving tenders**

    D: 295 tons (fl) **S:** 12.4 kts **Dim:** 40.9 × 8.0 × 2.1
    M: 2 3D12A diesels; 2 props; 600 hp **Radar:** 1/Spin Trough

REMARKS: Transferred 1978. Can support 7 divers to 60-m depths.

COAST GUARD

♦ **7 craft**

GF 528   GF 725   GF 825   GF 720   Similar to 40-foot U.S. Coast Guard small craft

GF 101   GF 102   GF 701   similar to 70-foot U.S. Coast Guard small craft

REMARKS: Assigned to the Department of the Interior. Hull numbers painted in red to distinguish these boats from naval ships.

♦ **1 patrol craft**

GUANABACOA Bldr: Cadiz (L: . . .)
    S: 22 kts

♦ **6 fast launches**

CAMILO CIENFUEGOS   MACEO   MARTI
ESCAMBRAY   CUARTEL MONCADA   FINLAY

    Bldr: Spain, 1971-72

REMARKS: No other information.

CYPRUS
Republic of Cyprus

PERSONNEL: 330 men

MERCHANT MARINE (1980): 688 ships—2,091,089 grt (tankers: 18—111,568 grt)

♦ **2 ex-German R-class minesweepers**

R-class minesweeper in Cypriot service   G. Arra, 1971

    D: 130 tons (fl) **S:** 18 kts **Dim:** 37.8 × 5.8 × 1.4
    A: 1/40-mm AA—2/20-mm AA (I × 2) **M:** 2 M.A.N. diesels; 2 props; 1,800 hp

REMARKS: Date from 1943. Wooden hull; may have been discarded.

♦ **6 Soviet P 4-class torpedo boats**

    D: 19.3 tons (22.4 fl) **S:** 55 kts **Dim:** 19.3 × 3.7 × 1.0
    A: 2/14.5-mm mg (II × 1)—2/450-mm TT
    Electron Equipt: Radar: 1/Skin Head **M:** 2 M50 diesels; 2 props; 2,400 hp
    Man: 12 tot.

REMARKS: Four transferred in 10-64 and two in 2-65. Several may have been discarded.

♦ **10 small former fishing boats**

    D: 50 tons **A:** 1 or 2 machine guns

REMARKS: Several were probably lost during the crisis in July 1974.

DENMARK
Kingdom of Denmark

PERSONNEL: 6,070 men (1,345 officers, 3,345 enlisted, 1,380 conscripts), plus 2,490 civilians. There are 13,640 Naval Reservists and 5,000 members of the Home Guard.

MERCHANT MARINE (1980): 1,253 ships—5,390,365 grt
(tankers: 73 ships—2,807,840 grt)

NAVAL AVIATION: Sixteen helicopters, including 8 Alouette-III and 8 WG 13 Lynx, the first of which was delivered 15-5-80. The Air Force took delivery of three U.S. Gulfstream Maritime Patrol Aircraft during 1981-82.

WARSHIPS IN SERVICE OR UNDER CONSTRUCTION AS OF 1 JANUARY 1982

	L	Tons (Surfaced)	Main armament
♦ **5 submarines**			
2 TYPE 205	1968-69	370	8/533-mm TT
3 DELFINEN	1956-63	595	4/533-mm TT
		Tons	
♦ **5 frigates**			
2 PEDER SKRAM	1965	2,030	8 Harpoon, 1 Sea Sparrow, 2/127-mm DP, 4/40-mm AA
3 NILS JUEL	1978-81	1,320	8 Harpoon, 1 Sea Sparrow, 1/76-mm DP
♦ **5 fisheries protection frigates**			
1 HVIDBJØRNEN, mod.	1975	1,970	1/76.2-mm DP, 1 helicopter
4 HVIDBJØRNEN	1961-62	1,345	1/76.2-mm DP, 1 helicopter
♦ **16 guided-missile and torpedo boats**			
10 WILLIMOES	1974-	250	4 Harpoon—1/76.2-mm DP, 2/533-mm TT
6 SØLØVEN	1963-66	95	2/40-mm AA, 2/533-mm TT
♦ **22 (+1) patrol boats**			
3 (+1)AGDLEK	1974-79	330	2/20-mm AA
9 BARSØ	1969-73	155	2/20-mm AA
2 MAAGEN	1960	175	2/20-mm AA
8 DAPHNE	1960-63	150	1/40-mm AA
♦ **6 minelayers**			
2 LINDORMEN	1977	575	2/20-mm AA, 60 mines
4 FALSTER	1962-63	1,880	4/76.2-mm DP, 400 mines
♦ **8 coastal minesweepers**			

SUBMARINES

NOTE: Denmark is considering the construction of six units of the German/Norwegian Type 210 replacement design to supplant first the *Delfinens* and then the Type 205s.

♦ **2 German Type 205**

	Bldr	Laid down	L	In serv.
S 320 NARHVALEN	RDY Copenhagen	16-2-65	10-9-68	27-2-70
S 321 NORDKAPEREN	RDY Copenhagen	20-1-66	18-12-69	22-12-70

    D: 370/480 tons **S:** 10/17 kts **Dim:** 45.41 × 4.60 × 4.58
    A: 8/533-mm TT, fwd **Man:** 22 tot.
    M: 2/750 hp Mercedes-Benz diesels, electric drive; 1 prop; 1,500 hp

REMARKS: Modeled on the German Type 205 and Norwegian Type 207 (*Kobben* class). S 320 fell off blocks in drydock 21-9-79 but has been salvaged.

SUBMARINES *(continued)*

Narhvalen (S 320)

♦ **4 Delfinen class**

	Bldr	Laid down	L	In serv.
S 326 DELFINEN	RDY Copenhagen	1-7-54	5-5-56	16-9-58
S 327 SPAEKHUGGEREN	RDY Copenhagen	1-12-54	20-2-57	27-6-59
S 328 TUMLEREN	RDY Copenhagen	22-5-56	22-5-58	15-1-60
S 329 SPRINGEREN	RDY Copenhagen	3-1-61	26-4-63	22-10-64

Springeren (S 329) 1970

D: 595/643 tons   **S:** 13/12 kts   **Dim:** 54.0 × 4.7 × 3.8
A: 4/533-mm TT, fwd
M: Burmeister & Wain diesels and motors; 2 props; 1,200 hp
Range: 4,000/8.5   **Man:** 33 tot.

REMARKS: S 329 built with U.S. "Offshore" funds, as U.S. SS 554.

FRIGATES

♦ **2 Peder Skram class**

	Bldr	Laid down	L	In serv.
F 352 PEDER SKRAM	Helsingør Vaerft	25-9-64	20-5-65	30-6-66
F 353 HERLUF TROLLE	Helsingør Vaerft	18-12-64	8-9-65	16-4-67

Peder Skram (F 352) 1980

Herluf Trolle (F 353) 1977

D: 2,030 tons (2,720 fl)   **S:** 28 kts   **Dim:** 112.5 (108.0 pp)· × 12.0 × 3.6
A: 8 Harpoon SSM (IV × 2)—1 NATO Sea Sparrow SAM system (VIII × 1)—
2/127-mm 38-cal. DP, U.S. (II × 1)—4/40-mm AA (I × 4)—4/533-mm TT
(I × 4)—1 d.c. rack
Electron Equipt: Radars: 1 Skanter 009, 1/CWS-2, 1/CWS-3, 3 M-46 fire-
control, 1/Mk 91 mod 1 fire-control (2 radar directors)
Sonar: 1 Plessey MS 26
M: CODOG propulsion: 2 GM 16-567D diesels (4,800 hp); 2 Pratt &Whitney
PWA GG 4A-3 gas turbines (44,000 hp); 2 CP props
Man: 200 tot.

REMARKS: Danish design, built with U.S. "Offshore" funds. Speed with diesels: 16
knots. There are two radar directors for the Mk 91 mod 1 Sea Sparrow system,
which, along with Harpoon, was added 1977-79, as was the CEPLO computerized
tactical data system. The torpedo tubes fire Swedish Type 61 wire-guided torpedoes.

♦ **3 Nils Juel (Type KV 72) class** Bldr: Aalborg Vaerft

	Laid down	L	In serv.
F 354 NILS JUEL	20-10-76	27-9-78	22-8-80
F 355 OLFERT FISCHER	1977	15-1-80	1981
F 356 PETER TORDENSKJOLD	1977	2-81	. . .

Nils Juel (F 354)—with 4 Harpoon aboard   1980

D: 1,320 tons (fl)   **S:** 30 kts (20 on diesel)   **Dim:** 84.0 (80.0 pp) × 10.3 × 3.1
A: 8 Harpoon SSM (IV × 2)—1 NATO Sea Sparrow SAM (VIII × 1)—1/76-mm
  OTO Melara Compact DP—1 d.c. rack
Electron Equipt: Radars: 1/Plessey AWS-5, 2 Skanter 009, 1 Phillips 3-cm, 1
            Phillips 9LV 200 GFCS (with Type 771 low-light t.v.
            tracker), 1/Mk 91 mod 1 MFCS (2 dir.)

            Sonar: . . .
            ECM: Decca-Racal Cutlass
M: CODOG: 1 GE LM-2500 GT (26,600 hp), 1 MTU 20V-956 TB82 diesel (4,800
  hp); 2 CP props
Range: 800/28, 2,500/18   **Man:** 18 officers, 9 CPO, 63 men

REMARKS: Ordered 5-12-75. Planned ASW torpedo system not installed. Two Breda
SCLAR chaff/flare RL not yet added. Only 4 of 8 planned Harpoon carried. NATO
Sea Sparrow system, with no reloads, has two radar directors. DataSAAB CEPLO
data system. F 355 commissioning delayed by fire 5-81.

FISHERIES PROTECTION FRIGATES

♦ **1 modified Hvidbjørnen class** Bldr: Aalborg Vaerft

	Laid down	L	In serv.
F 340 BESKYTERREN	15-12-74	27-5-75	27-2-76

Beskyterren (F 340)—telescoping hangar retracted   1980

D: 1,970 tons (fl)   **S:** 18 kts   **Dim:** 74.4 × 11.8 × 4.5
A: 1/76.2-mm DP—WG 13 Lynx helicopter
Electron Equipt: Radars: 1/CWS-1, 1/Skanter 009
            Sonar: 1/Plessey MS-26
M: 4 Alpha diesels; 1 CP prop; 7,440 hp   **Range:** 6,000/13 (one engine)
Man: 60 tot.

REMARKS: Serves as a fisheries-protection ship. An OTO Melara Compact 76-mm gun
was to have been fitted.

♦ **4 Hvidbjørnen class**

	Bldr	Laid down	L	In serv.
F 348 HVIDBJØRNEN	Aarhus Flydedok	6-61	23-11-61	12-62
F 349 VAEDDEREN	Aalborg SY	10-61	6-4-62	3-63
F 350 INGOLF	Svendborg Skibsvaerft	12-61	27-7-62	6-63
F 351 FYLLA	Aalborg SY	6-62	18-12-62	7-63

Hvidbjørnen (F 348)—with Alouette-III helicopter   1980

D: 1,345 tons (1,650 fl)   **S:** 18 kts   **Dim:** 72.6 × 11.6 × 4.9
A: 1/76.2-mm DP—1/WG 13 Lynx helicopter   **Man:** 10 officers, 60 men
Electron Equipt: Radars: 1/CWS-1, 1/Skanter 009
            Sonar: 1 Plessey MS-46
M: 4 GM 16-567C diesels; 1 CP prop; 6,400 hp   **Range:** 6,000/13

REMARKS: Reinforced bow. F 350, used for hydrographic surveying, has no gun or
helicopter but carries four 13-meter SKA-1-class survey launches on her flight deck.

GUIDED-MISSILE BOATS

♦ **10 Willemoes class** Bldr: Frederikshavn SY

	L	In serv.		L	In serv.
P 540 BILLE	26-3-76	10-76	P 545 NORBY	. . .	22-11-77
P 541 BREDAL	. . .	21-1-77	P 546 RODSTEEN	. . .	16-2-78
P 542 HAMMER	. . .	1-4-77	P 547 SEHESTED	5-5-77	3-78
P 543 HUITFELDT	. . .	15-6-77	P 548 SUENSON	26-8-77	6-78
P 544 KRIEGER	. . .	22-9-77	P 549 WILLEMOES	5-10-74	7-10-76

D: 232 tons (265 fl)   **S:** 40 kts (36 normal)—diesels: 12 kts
Dim: 46.1 (42.4 pp) × 7.4 × 2.1 (2.7 over props)
A: 1/76-mm OTO Melara Compact—4/533-mm TT (or 4 Harpoon—2/533-mm TT)
Electron Equipt: Radars: 1/9GA-208, 1/NWS-3, 1/9LV 200 fire-control
M: CODOG: 3 Rolls-Royce Proteus 52M/544 gas turbines; 2 GM 8V-71 diesels; 3
  Liaan CP props; 12,750/800 hp
Electric: 420 kw   **Range:** 400/36   **Man:** 5 officers, 21 men

GUIDED-MISSILE BOATS *(continued)*

Willemoes (P 549)—with 20 mines in lieu of torpedo tubes   1976

Willemoes (P 549)—with four Harpoon launchers, two torpedo tubes   1979

REMARKS: Based on the Swedish Lürssen-designed Spica class and ordered in 1972. The torpedoes are Swedish Type 61, wire-guided, with a range of 20,000 meters. Endurance is normally 36 hours. Two triple 103-mm flare rocket rails on pilothouse sides. Decca-Racal Cutlass ESM system ordered 1980 for all. Have TORCI torpedo f.c.s and CEPLO tactical data system.

TORPEDO BOATS

♦ **6 Søløven class**

	Bldr	Laid down	L	In serv.
P 510 SØLØVEN	Vosper, Portsmouth	8-62	19-4-63	12-2-65
P 511 SØRIDDEREN	Vosper, Portsmouth	10-62	22-8-63	10-2-65
P 512 SØBJORNEN	RDY Copenhagen	7-63	19-8-64	9-65
P 513 SØHESTEN	RDY Copenhagen	8-63	31-3-65	6-66
P 514 SØHUNDEN	RDY Copenhagen	2-64	12-1-66	1-67
P 515 SØULVEN	RDY Copenhagen	6-64	27-4-66	3-67

D: 95 tons (114 fl)   **S:** 50 kts (10 on diesel)
Dim: 30.26 (27.44 pp) × 7.3 × 2.15   **Man:** 4 officers, 22 men
A: 2/40-mm AA (I × 2)—2/533-mm TT   **Electron Equipt:** Radar: 1/NWS-1
M: Rolls-Royce Marine Proteus gas turbines; 3 props; 10,500 hp (12,750 max); 2 GM 6V-71 diesels, 530 hp, for cruising

REMARKS: A modification of the British Brave class. All in reserve. Two 533-mm TT were removed when the after gun was enclosed. Four 50-mm flare RL on fwd 40-mm shield. P 510 was built as PT 821 with U.S. funds. The *Falken*-class torpedo boats were discarded 1977-78.

Søridderen (P 511)   1970

PATROL BOATS

♦ **4 Agdlek class for fisheries protection** Bldr: Svendborg Vaerft

		In serv.
Y 386	AGDLEK	12-3-74
Y 387	AGPA	14-5-74
Y 388	TULUGAQ	26-6-79
Y 389	N. . .	. . .

Tulugaq (Y 388)   1976

D: 330 tons (fl)   **S:** 12 kts   **Dim:** 31.4 × 7.7 × 3.3   **A:** 2/20-mm AA (I × 2)
Electron Equipt: Radars: 2/Terma 20T48 (NWS-3)
M: 1 Burmeister & Wain Alpha diesel; 800 hp   **Man:** 15 tot.

REMARKS: For fisheries patrol service in Greenland waters. Can carry two survey launches. Y 388 has only one radar, is .3-m longer, and can make 14 kts.

PATROL BOATS *(continued)*

♦ 9 Barsø class Bldr: Svendborg

Y 300 BARSØ	Y 302 ROMSØ	Y 304 THURØ	Y 306 FARØ	Y 308 ROMØ
Y 301 DREJØ	Y 303 SAMSØ	Y 305 VEJRØ	Y 307 LAESØ	

Romø (Y 308)—note trawl boards aft

D: 155 tons (fl) **S:** 11 kts **Dim:** 25.5 × 6.0 × 2.8 **A:** 2/20-mm AA (I × 2)
Electron Equipt: Radar: 1/Terma 20T48 (NWS-3) **M:** 1 diesel; 1 prop; 385 hp

REMARKS: The first six were built in 1969, and the last three 1972-73. For fisheries
protection duties.

♦ 2 Maagen-class fisheries patrol boats Bldr: Helsingør (In serv. 5-60)

Y 384 MAAGEN Y 385 MALLEMUKKEN

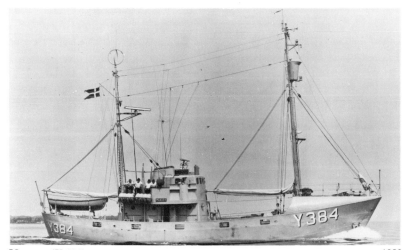

Maagen (Y 384) 1980

D: 175 tons (190 fl) **S:** 10 kts **Dim:** 27.0 × 7.2 × 2.75
A: 2/20-mm AA (I × 2) **M:** Diesel; 1 prop; 350 hp
Electron Equipt: Radar: 1/Terma 20T48 (NWS-3), 1/Skanter 009

REMARKS: Based in Greenland.

♦ 8 Daphne-class antisubmarine patrol boats Bldr: RDY, Copenhagen

	Laid down	L	In serv.
P 530 DAPHNE	4-60	10-11-60	19-12-61
P 531 DRYADEN	7-60	1-3-61	4-4-62
P 533 HAVFRUEN	3-61	4-10-61	20-12-62
P 534 NAJADEN	9-61	20-6-62	26-4-63
P 535 NYMFEN	4-62	1-11-62	4-10-63
P 536 NEPTUN	9-62	29-5-63	18-12-63
P 537 RAN	12-62	10-7-63	15-5-64
P 538 ROTA	6-63	26-11-63	20-1-65

Daphne (P 530) 1979

D: 150 tons (170 fl) **S:** 20 kts **Dim:** 38.0 × 6.75 × 2.0
A: 1/40-mm AA—2 d.c. projectors—2 d.c. racks **Man:** 23 tot.
Electron Equipt: Radar: 1/NWS-3
Sonar: Plessey MS 26
M: 2 Maybach diesels, 1,300 hp, and 1 Foden cruise FD-6 diesel, 100 hp; 3 props

REMARKS: P 530, P 534, and P 536, which were paid for with U.S. "Offshore" funds
as PGM 47, PGM 49, and PGM 50, are now completely disarmed. The *Havmanden*
(P 532) was struck in 1978; others may follow soon.

PATROL CRAFT

♦ 3 Y 377 class Bldr: Botved (In serv. 1975)

Y 377 Y 378 Y 379

D: 9 tons (fl) **S:** 27 kts **Dim:** 9.8 × 3.3 × 0.9
Electron Equipt: Radar 1/NWS-3
M: 2 Volvo Penta inboard/outboard diesels; 2 props; 600 hp

♦ 2 Y 375 class Bldr: Botved (In serv. 1974)

Y 375 Y 376

D: 12 tons (fl) **S:** 26 kts **Dim:** 13.3 × 4.5 × 1.1
Electron Equipt: Radar: 1/NWS-3 **M:** 2 diesels; 2 props; 680 hp

PATROL CRAFT (*continued*)

Y 376   1978

PATROL CRAFT MANNED BY THE HOME GUARD

♦ **5 MHV 20 class** Bldr: Ejvinds, Svendborg (In serv. 1974-81)

MHV 20 MHV 21 MHV 22 MHV 23 MHV 24 MHV 25

MHV 20   1980

D: 60 tons (fl) **S:** 15 kts **Dim:** 16.5 × 4.2 × 2.0 **A:** 1/12.7-mm mg
M: 2 MTU diesels; 2 props; 500 hp **Radar:** 1/NWS-3

REMARKS: Additional units of these craft are intended to replace the older MHV units over the next few years. Glass-reinforced plastic hulls.

♦ **7 MHV-90 class**

MHV 90 MHV 91 MHV 92 MHV 93 MHV 94 MHV 95 MHV 96

MHV 93   1980

D: 85 tons (130 fl) **S:** 10.7 kts **Dim:** 19.8 × 5.7 × 1.6 **A:** 1/20-mm AA
M: 1 Burmeister & Wain diesel; 400 hp **Radar:** 1/NWS-3

REMARKS: In service 1974-75.

♦ **3 MHV 70 class** Bldr: Navy Yard, Copenhagen (In serv. 1958)

MHV 70 MHV 71 MHV 72

MHV 71   1980

D: 78 tons (130 fl) **S:** 10 kts **Dim:** 20.1 × 5.1 × 2.5 **A:** 1/20-mm AA
Electron Equipt: Radar: 1/NWS-3 **M:** 1 diesel; 200 hp

PATROL CRAFT (continued)

♦ **6 MHV 80 class** (In serv. 1941)

MHV 81 Askø	MHV 83 Manø	MHV 85 Hjortø
MHV 82 Enø	MHV 84 Baagø	MHV 86 Lyø

Lyø (MHV 86) 1980

D: 74 tons **S:** 11 kts **Dim:** 24.4 × 4.9 × 1.6 **A:** 1/20-mm AA
Electron Equipt: Radar: 1/NWS-3 **M:** 1 diesel; 350 hp

REMARKS: In Home Guard service 1958. Former inshore minesweepers. Wooden hulls.

♦ **31 smaller craft, including:**

MHV 1, MHV 3 through MHV 15; MHV 51, MHV 52, MHV 54, MHV 56 through 64, MHV 65 through 68, MHV 74, 75. Small, wooden-hulled fishing boat designs. Most have an NWS-3 radar. No fixed armament.

MINE WARFARE SHIPS

♦ 4 Falster-class minelayers

	Bldr	Laid down	L	In serv.
N 80 Falster	Nakskov Skibsvaerft	4-62	19-9-62	7-11-63
N 81 Fyen	Frederikshavn Vaerft	4-62	3-10-62	18-9-63
N 82 Møen	Frederikshavn Vaerft	10-62	6-6-63	20-4-64
N 83 Sjaelland	Nakskov Skibsvaerft	1-63	14-6-63	7-7-64

Falster (N 80) 1980

Møen (N 82) G. Gyssels, 1979

D: 1,880 tons (fl) **S:** 16.5 kts **Dim:** 77.0 (72.5 pp) × 12.8 × 3.4
A: 4/76.2-mm DP U.S. Mk 33 (II × 2)—400 mines (4 minelaying tracks)
Electron Equipt: Radars: 1/CWS-2, 1/NWS-2, 1/NWS-3, 1/M-46
M: 2 GM 16-567D3 diesels; 2 CP props; 4,800 hp **Fuel:** 130 tons
Man: 10 officers, 108 men

REMARKS: NATO design. The Turkish ship *Nusret* identical. N 82 is a training ship for naval cadets. N 83 converted to submarine tender in 1976, to replace *Henrik Gerner* (can still lay mines). N 80 and N 82 built with U.S. "offshore" funds as MMC 14 and MMC 15. Have 2/57-mm multiple chaff launchers.

♦ 2 Lindormen-class coastal minelayers Bldr: Svendborg

	Laid down	L	In serv.
N 43 Lindormen	20-1-77	7-6-77	26-10-77
N 44 Loussen	2-77	9-9-77	30-1-78

Lindormen (N 43) 1980

D: 575 tons (fl) **S:** 14 kts **Dim:** 43.3 (40.0 pp) × 9.0 × 2.65
A: 2/20-mm AA (I × 2)—50 to 60 mines **Electron Equipt:** Radar: 1/NWS-3
M: 2 Wichmann 7AX diesels; 2 props; 4,200 hp **Electric:** 192 kw
Man: 27 tot.

REMARKS: Built to replace the *Lougen* class. 20-mm AA not always mounted. Controlled minefield planters.

MINE WARFARE SHIPS (continued)

♦ **1 Langeland-class coastal minelayer** Bldr: Royal DY, Copenhagen

	Laid down	L	In. serv.
N 42 LANGELAND	1950	17-5-50	1951

Langeland (N 42)   1978

D: 310 tons (342 fl)   **S:** 11.6 kts   **Dim:** 44.0 × 7.2 × 2.1
A: 2/40-mm AA (II × 1)—60 mines   **Electron Equipt:** Radar: 1/NWS-3
M: 2 diesels; 2 props; 770 hp   **Man:** 37 tot.

REMARKS: Controlled minefield planter. In reserve.

♦ **6 ex-U.S. Adjutant- and Redwing*-class coastal minesweepers**

	Bldr	In serv.
M 572 ALSSUND (ex-MSC 128)*	Hiltebrand DD, Kingston, NY	5-4-55
M 573 EGERNSUND (ex-MSC 129)*	Hiltebrand DD, Kingston, NY	3-8-55
M 574 GRØNSUND (ex-MSC 256)	Stephen Bros. SY	21-9-56
M 575 GULDBORGSUND (ex-MSC 257)	Stephen Bros. SY	11-11-56

Aarøsund (M 571)—Redwing class (stricken 1981)   G. Gyssels, 1981

M 577 ULVSUND (ex-MSC 263)	Harbor BY, Terminal Isl., Cal.	20-9-56
M 578 VILSUND (ex-MSC 264)	Harbor BY, Terminal Isl., Cal.	15-11-56

D: 350 tons (376 fl)   **S:** 13 kts (8 sweeping)
Dim: 43.89 (41.50 pp) × 7.95 × 2.55   **A:** 1/40-mm AA
Electron Equipt: Radar: 1/NWS-3—Sonar: 1/UQS-1   **Man:** 38 tot.
M: 2 GM 8-268A diesels; 2 props; 1,000 hp   **Fuel:** 40 tons   **Range:** 2,500/10

REMARKS: Hull entirely of wood. The first two are 405 tons (fl); they have davits abreast the stack to handle noise makers. M 575 has a charthouse between the stack and bridge so that she can act as a survey ship; she still has minesweeping equipment. *Aarøsund* (M 571) and (Omøsund (M 576) stricken 1981.

AUXILIARY SHIPS

♦ **6 inshore survey launches** (In serv. 1958-68)

SKA 3–SKA 8

D: 27 tons   **Dim:** 13.0 × . . . × . . .   **Man:** 6 tot.

REMARKS: Minesweeper *Gulborgsund* and frigate *Ingolf* also used in survey work, the latter being able to transport four of this class.

♦ **2 U.S. YO 65-class coastal oilers** Bldr: Jeffersonville Boat & Machine, Indiana

	Laid down	L	In serv.
A 568 RIMFAXE (ex-YO 226)	21-4-45	20-7-45	22-10-45
A 569 SKINFAXE (ex-YO 229)	25-5-45	28-8-45	7-12-45

Rimfaxe (A 568)   1979

D: 440 tons (1,390 fl)   **S:** 10 kts   **Dim:** 53.0 × 9.75 × 4.0   **A:** 1/20-mm AA
Electron Equipt: Radar: 1/NWS-3   **Electric:** 40 kw   **Man:** 23 tot.
M: 1 GM 8-278A diesel; 1 prop; 640 hp   **Fuel:** 25 tons   **Range:** 2,000/8

REMARKS: Transferred 2-8-62. Cargo: 900 tons.

♦ **1 torpedo transport/retriever**

A 558 SLEIPNER

D: 150 tons (fl)   **S:** 9 kts   **Dim:** 30.0 × . . . × . . .
Electron Equipt: Radar: 1/NWS-3   **M:** 1 diesel; . . . hp

REMARKS: Former coastal cargo ship.

♦ **1 small torpedo retriever**

TO 9 MUNIN—no data available

AUXILIARY SHIPS *(continued)*

Sleipner (A 558)   1980

♦ **1 royal yacht** Bldr: Royal DY, Copenhagen

	L	In serv.
A 540 DANNEBROG	10-10-31	1932

Dannebrog (A 540)   1980

D: 1,130 tons   **S:** 14 kts   **Dim:** 74.9 × 10.4 × 3.7
Electron Equipt: Radar: 1/Skauter 009   **Electric:** 507 kVA
M: 2 Burmeister & Wain Alpha 6 T23L-KVO diesels; 2 CP props; 1,600 hp

REMARKS: Re-engined, new electrical generating plant winter 1980-81. Does not wear pendant number assigned.

MINISTRY OF FISHERIES

♦ **1 "Osprey" FV 710-class fisheries patrol ship** Bldr: Frederikshavn SY

HAVORNEN

D: 320 tons (383 fl)   **S:** 18 kts   **Dim:** 49.98 (45.8 pp) × 10.50 × 2.75   **A:** . . .
Electron Equipt: Radar: 2/Furuno FRM-64

M: 2 Burmeister & Wain Alpha 16V23L-VO diesels; 2 CP props; 4,640 hp
Range: 4,500/16   **Man:** 15 tot.

REMARKS: In service 1979. Has a hangar and flight deck for one Sea Lynx or Alouette-III helicopter and a recessed stern ramp for a 6.5-m rubber inspection dinghy. Built to mercantile specifications, a modified British "Osprey" design.

♦ **1 fisheries oceanographic ship** (In serv. 1960)

SENS VAEVER

D: 280 tons (fl)   **S:** 11.5 kts   **Dim:** 30.53 × 6.35 × 3.15
M: 1 Burmeister & Wain 406 VD diesel; 1 prop; 420 hp   **Fuel:** 20 tons
Range: 2,600/9   **Man:** 10 tot.

♦ **2 Nordsøen-class salvage rescue tugs** Bldr: Frederikshavn DY (In serv. 1968)

NORDYLLAND   NORDSØEN

D: 900 tons (fl)   **S:** 14.5 kts   **Dim:** 52.35 (45.75 pp) × 10.00 × 3.35
M: 2 Burmeister & Wain 8-23MTBF-308G diesels; 1 CP prop; 1,960 hp
Electric: 472 kw   **Man:** 12 tot.

MINISTRY OF TRADE AND SHIPPING

ICEBREAKERS

NOTE: Danish icebreakers all civilian-manned and are subordinate to the Ministry of Trade and Shipping. During summer months they are maintained by the Danish Navy at Frederikshavn.

♦ **1 new construction** Bldr: Svendborg (L: 6-30)

THORBIORN

D: 2,250 tons (fl)   **S:** 16.5 kts   **Dim:** 67.5 × 15.3 × 4.70
M: 4 Burmeister & Wain Alpha diesels, electric drive; 2 props; 6,800 hp

REMARKS: Can be used for hydrographic surveys by the Navy when not needed for icebreaking, and can also act as a tug.

♦ **2 Danbjørn class** Bldr: Lindø Vaerft, Odense

DANBJØRN (In serv. 1965)   ISBJØRN (In serv. 1966)

D: 3,685 tons (fl)   **S:** 14 kts   **Dim:** 76.8 × 16.8 × 6.0
M: diesel-electric; 2 props; 11,880 hp   **Man:** 34 tot.

♦ **1 Elbjørn class** Bldr: Frederikshavn Vaerft (In serv. 1953)

ELBJØRN

D: 898 tons (1,400 fl)   **S:** 12 kts   **Dim:** 47.0 × 12.1 × 4.35
M: diesel electric; 2 props; 3,600 hp

REMARKS: Used by Danish Navy for survey work in the summer.

DJIBOUTI
Republic of Djibouti

On independence, in 1977, a small naval/police force was established and took over one patrol craft formerly operated by the French colonial police at Djibouti.

♦ **1 ex-French fiberglass patrol craft** Bldr: Tecimar (In serv. 1974)

D: 30 tons (fl) **S:** 25 kts **Dim:** 13.3 × 4.1 × 1.1
A: 1/12.7-mm and 1/7.5-mm mg **M:** 2 GM 6V71 diesels; 2 props; 240 hp

---

DOMINICAN REPUBLIC

PERSONNEL: 370 officers and 3,630 men

MERCHANT MARINE (1980): 31 ships—37,659 grt (tanker: 1 ship—674 grt)

FRIGATE

♦ **1 Canadian "River" class**

	Bldr	L	In serv.
451 MELLA (ex-*Presidente Trujillo*, ex-*Carlplace*)	Davie, S.B., Lauzon, Quebec	6-7-44	13-12-44

Mella (F 451) 1980

D: 1,445 tons (2,300 fl) **S:** 19 kts **Dim:** 92.35 × 11.45 × 4.3
A: 1/76.2-mm DP—2/40-mm AA (II × 1)—4/20-mm AA—2/47-mm saluting guns
M: 2 sets triple-expansion; 2 props; 5,500 hp **Boilers:** 2 (3-drum)
Fuel: 645 tons **Range:** 7,700/12 **Man:** 15 officers, 135 men

REMARKS: Bought in 1947. Serves as a training ship; can carry 50 cadets. Two sisters, hulks for many years, *Gregorio Luperon* (F 452) and *Pedro Santana* (F 453), were officially stricken in 1980, as were the hulks of two "Flower"-class corvettes, *Cristobal Colón* (C 401) and *Juan A. Acosta* (C 402).

CORVETTES

♦ **3 ex-U.S. Cohoes-class former net tenders**

	Bldr	L	In serv.
P 207 CAMBIASO (ex-*Etlah*, AN 79)	Marietta Mfg., W.Va.	16-12-44	16-4-45
P 208 SEPARACIÓN (ex-*Passaconaway*, AN 86)	Marine Iron & Ry, Duluth	30-6-44	27-4-45
P 209 CALDERAS (ex-*Passaic*, AN 87)	Leatham B. Smith, Wisc.	29-6-44	6-3-45

D: 650 tons (785 fl) **S:** 12.3 kts **Dim:** 51.36 (44.5 pp)× 10.31 × 3.3
A: 2/76.2-mm DP (I × 2)—3/20-mm AA (I × 3) **Electric:** 120 kw
Electron Equipt: Radar: 1/SPS-64 **Fuel:** 88 tons **Man:** 48 tot.
M: Diesel-electric: 2 Busch-Sulzer B5-539 diesels, 1 motor; 1 prop; 1,200 hp

REMARKS: Recommissioned from the U.S. Maritime Commission's reserve fleet, where they had been laid up since 1963, and transferred 9-76. Despite low speed and general unsuitability, they are employed as patrol ships and tugs. Also used in general support, navigational tender, and hydrographic survey duties. P 207 and P 208 have had the net tender "horns" at the bow removed and a new, curved stem added; they also received a second 76.2-mm gun on the forecastle.

♦ **2 ex-U.S. Admirable-class former minesweepers** Bldr: Associated SB, Seattle, Wash.

	Laid down	L	In serv.
BM 454 PRESTOL BOTELLO (ex-*Separación*, ex-*Skirmish*, MSF 303)	8-4-43	16-8-43	30-6-44
BM 455 TORTUGERO (ex-*Signet*, MSF 302)	8-4-43	16-8-43	20-8-44

Prestol Botello (BM 454) 1976

D: 600 tons (903 fl) **S:** 15 kts **Dim:** 54.24 × 10.06 × 4.4
A: 1/76.2-mm DP—2/40-mm AA (I × 2)—6/20-mm AA (I × 6)
M: 2 Cooper-Bessemer GSB-8 diesels; 2 props; 1,710 hp **Electric:** 240 kw
Fuel: 260 tons **Range:** 5,600/9 **Man:** 100 tot.

REMARKS: Transferred in 1-66. BN 454 renamed 1976. All minesweeping equipment and ASW armament removed from both.

PATROL BOATS AND CRAFT

♦ **1 ex-U.S. PGM 71 class** Bldr: Peterson SB, Sturgeon Bay, Wisc.

GC 102 BETELGEUSE (ex-PGM 77)

PATROL BOATS AND CRAFT *(continued)*

D: 130 tons (145.5 fl) **S:** 16 kts **Dim:** 30.8 (30.2 pp) × 6.4 × 1.85
A: 1/20-mm AA—2/12.7-mm mg (I × 2) **Man:** 20 tot.
M: 2 Caterpillar D-348TA diesels; 2 props; 1,450 hp **Range:** 1,000/12

REMARKS: Transferred 14-1-66. One of many gunboats of this class transferred to smaller navies by the United States. Re-engined and armament reduced, 1980.

♦ 3 ex-U.S. Coast Guard Argo class

	In serv.
P 204 (ex-P 105) INDEPENDENCIA (ex-*Icarus*, WPC 110)	1931
P 205 (ex-P 106) LIBERTAD (ex-*Rafael Atoa*, ex-*Thetis*, WPC 115)	1931
P 206 (ex-P 104, P 203) RESTAURACIÓN (ex-*Galathea*, WPC 108)	1932

D: 235 tons (335 fl) **S:** 14 kts **Dim:** 50.3 × 7.6 × 2.5
A: 1/76.2-mm DP—1/40-mm AA—1/20-mm AA
M: 2 Winton diesels; 2 props; 1,280 hp **Fuel:** 25 tons diesel
Range: 1,300/15 **Man:** 40 tot.

♦ 1 former U.S. Army aircraft-rescue launch

GC 105 CAPITAN ALSINA (L: 1944)

D: 100 tons (fl) **S:** 17 kts **Dim:** 31.5 × 5.8 × 1.75 **A:** 2/20-mm AA (I × 2)
M: 2 GM diesels; 2 props; 1,000 hp **Man:** 20 tot.

REMARKS: Wooden hull. Used as Naval Academy training craft, refitted 1977.

♦ 4 patrol craft Bldr: Sewart Seacraft, Berwick, La.

	In serv.		In serv.
GC 104 ALDEBARÁN	1972	GC 106 BELLATRIX	1967
GC 103 PROCION	1967	GC 107 CAPELLA	1968

D: 60 tons (fl) **S:** 21.7 kts **Dim:** 25.9 × 5.7 × 2.1 **A:** 3/12.7-mm mg (I × 3)
M: 2 GM 16V71N diesels; 2 props; 1,400 hp **Range:** 800/20 **Man:** 9 tot.

♦ 1 former U.S. 63-ft aircraft-rescue launch (In serv. 1953)

GC 101 RIGEL

D: 27 tons (fl) **S:** 18.5 kts **Dim:** 19.3 × 4.7 × 1.2 **A:** 2/12.7-mm mg
M: 2 GM 6V71 diesels; 2 props; 800 hp **Range:** 450/15 **Man:** 9 tot.

♦ 4 small patrol craft Bldr: Dominican NY (In serv. 1975)

BA 3 CARITE   BA 6 ATÓN   BA 9 PICUA   BA 15 JUREL

D: 30 tons (fl) **S:** 12 kts **Dim:** 12.7 × 4.0 × 1.8 **A:** 1/7.62-mm mg
M: 2 GM diesels; 200 hp

REMARKS: Have auxiliary sail power. Sisters *Albacora* and *Bonito* discarded.

AUXILIARY SHIPS

♦ 1 oceanographic research ship, former U.S. Sotoyomo class auxiliary ocean tug Bldr: Levingston Bros. SB, Orange, Tex.

	Laid down	L	In serv.
. . . ENRIQUILLO (ex-*Stallion*, ATA 193)	26-10-44	24-11-44	1-2-45

REMARKS: Leased 30-10-80. Data as for tug version below. Not armed.

♦ 1 converted U.S. LSM-1-class cargo carrier Bldr: Brown Bros., Houston, Tex.

	Laid down	L	In serv.
BDM 301 SIRIO (ex-LSM 483)	17-2-45	10-3-45	13-4-45

D: 734 tons (1,100 fl) **S:** 12 kts **Dim:** 62.8 × 10.4 × 2.1 **Man:** 30 tot.
M: 2 GM 16-278A diesels; 2,800 hp **Electric:** 240 kw **Fuel:** 164 tons

REMARKS: Transferred 3-58. Decked over, bow doors plated up, bridge re-sited on centerline, 1970.

♦ 1 utility landing craft Bldr: Dominican NY (In serv. 1958)

LDM 302 SAMANA

D: 128 tons (310 fl) **S:** 8/7 kts **Dim:** 36.4 × 11.0 × 1.15 **A:** 1/12.7-mm mg
M: 3 GM 64HN9 diesels; 3 props; 450 hp **Fuel:** 80 tons **Man:** 17 tot.

REMARKS: U.S. LCT(5) design, used for logistics duties. Sister *Enriquillo* discarded 1979.

♦ 1 small buoy tender

BA 10 NEPTUNO (ex-*Toro*) Bldr: J. H. Mathis, U.S.A., 1954

D: 72.2 tons (fl) **S:** 10 kts **Dim:** 19.5 × 5.7 × 2.4 **M:** 1 GM diesel; 225 hp
Man: 7 tot.

♦ 1 former U.S. Coast Guard buoy tender

FB 1 CAPOTILLO (ex-FB 101, ex-*Camillia*, WAGL 206) Bldr: U.S.A., 1911

D: 327 tons **S:** 10 kts

REMARKS: Transferred 1949.

♦ 2 small oilers Bldr: Ira S. Bushey, Brooklyn, N.Y.

	Laid down	L	In serv.
BT 4 CAPITAN W. ARVELO (ex-U.S. YO 213)	3-2-45	21-6-45	8-11-45
BT 5 CAPITAN BEOTEGUI (ex-U.S. YO 215)	23-4-45	30-8-45	17-12-45

D: 1,076 tons (fl) **S:** 8 kts **Dim:** 47.6 × 9.3 × 4.0 **A:** 2/20-mm AA (I × 2)
M: 1 Union diesel; 1 prop; 525 hp **Cargo:** 6,071 barrels fuel **Man:** 25 tot.

REMARKS: Both were loaned 4-64; lease extended 31-12-80. Smaller than standard U.S. YO-65-class yard oiler.

♦ 1 small survey ship, converted sport-fishing boat

BA 8 ATLANTIDA

D: . . . tons **S:** . . . hts **Dim:** 12.1 × 3.6 × 1.8
M: 2 GM 4-71 diesels; 2 props; 300 hp

♦ 1 U.S. Cherokee-class fleet tug Bldr: Charleston SB & DD, S. Carolina

	Laid down	L	In serv.
RM 21 MACORIX (ex-*Kiowa*, ATF 72)	22-6-42	5-11-42	7-6-43

D: 1,235 tons (1,675 fl) **S:** 15 kts **Dim:** 62.48 (59.44 wl) × 11.73 × 4.67
A: 1/76.2-mm DP—2/20-mm AA (I × 2) **Electron Equipt:** Radar: 1/SPS-5D
M: 4 GM 12-278 diesels, electric drive; 1 prop; 3,000 hp
Electric: 260 kw **Fuel:** 295 tons **Man:** 85 tot.

REMARKS: Transferred 16-10-72; lease extended 31-12-80. Has what appear to be multiple mg mounts abreast after tripod mast.

DOMINICAN REPUBLIC *(continued)*
AUXILIARY SHIPS *(continued)*

♦ **2 U.S. Sotoyomo-class auxiliary ocean tugs**

	Bldr	Laid down	L	In serv.
RM 18 CAONABO (ex-*Sagamore*, ATA 208)	Gulfport Boiler, Port Arthur, Tex.	27-11-44	19-1-45	19-3-45
RM. . . N. . . (ex-*Samoset*, ATA 190)	Levingston SB, Orange, Tex.	29-9-44	26-10-44	1-1-45

D: 534 tons (860 fl) **S:** 13 kts **Dim:** 43.59 × 10.31 × 3.96
A: 1/76-mm DP—2/20-mm AA (I × 2) **Electron Equipt:** Radar: 1/SPS-5D
M: 2 GM 12-278A diesels, electric drive; 1 prop; 1,500 hp **Electric:** 120 kw
Fuel: 160 tons **Range:** 8,000/8 **Man:** 45 tot.

REMARKS: RM 18 leased 1-2-72, extended 31-12-80. Ex-ATA 190 leased 16-10-78.

♦ **2 Hercules-class harbor tugs** Bldr: Dominican NY (In serv. 1960)

RP 12 HERCULES   RP 13 GUACANAGARIX

D: 200 tons (fl) **S:** . . . kts **Dim:** 21.4 × 4.8 × 2.7
M: 1 Caterpillar diesel; 1 prop; 500 hp **Man:** 8 tot.

♦ **1 former landing craft**

RDM 303 OCOA   Bldr: U.S.A.

D: 50 tons (fl) **S:** 9 kts **Dim:** 17.1 × 4.3 × 1.2
M: 2 GM 6-71 diesels; 2 props; 450 hp **Range:** 130/9

REMARKS: Modified as a tug about 1976. Retains bow ramp.

♦ **3 small harbor tugs**

RP 20 ISABELA   RP 19 CALDERAS   RP 22 PUERTO HERMOSO—no data

♦ **1 U.S. YTL 422-class small tug** Bldr: Robt. Jacob, City Isl., NY

RP 16 BOHECHIO (ex-*Mercedes*, ex-YTL 600)   (In serv. 25-7-45)

D: 70 tons (80 fl) **S:** 10 kts **Dim:** 20.1 × 5.5 × 2.4
M: 1 Hoover-Owens-Rentschler diesel; 1 prop; 375 hp **Fuel:** 7 tons

TRAINING CRAFT

♦ **1 sail-training ship for Naval Academy** (In serv. 1979)

BA 7 NUBE DEL MAR (ex-*Catuan*)

D: 40 tons (fl) **S:** 12 kts **Dim:** 12.8 × 3.6 × . . .
M: 1 Volvo Penta 21A diesel; 1 prop; 75 hp

♦ **1 training launch** (In serv. . . .)

BA. . . DUARTE

D: 60 tons (fl) **S:** . . . kts **Dim:** 22.9 × 5.7 × 2.1
M: 1 GM 6-71 diesel; 1 prop; 325 hp **Man:** 30 tot.

♦ **2 small fishing boats** (In serv. 1979)

BA 11 ALTO VELO   BA 12 SAONA

ECUADOR
Republic of Ecuador

PERSONNEL: 3,800 total

MERCHANT MARINE (1980): 86 ships—275,142 grt (tankers: 17 ships—86,299)

NAVAL AVIATION: A small detachment with three French Alouette-III helicopters, three Israeli Arava light transports, two Cessna T-37, two T-41, one Cessna 320, and one Cessna 177. Three Beech T-34C-1 trainers were delivered in 1980, and one Beech Super King Air light transport in 1981.

NOTE: Ecuadorian pendant numbers change frequently; those listed below are the latest available.

SUBMARINES

♦ **2 German Type 209 (IK 79)**

	Bldr	L	In serv.
S 11 SHYRI	Howaldtswerke, Kiel	8-10-76	16-3-78
S 12 HUANCAVILCA	Howaldtswerke, Kiel	18-3-77	1-6-78

D: 1,100/1,260/1,390 tons **Endurance:** 16 days
S: 21.5 kts (max. sub. for 5 minutes), 12 kts (snorkel)
Dim: 59.5 × 6.6 × 5.9 **A:** 8/533-mm TT, fwd (plus 6 reserve torpedoes)
M: 4 MTU type 12V-493-TY60 diesels; Siemens electric motor; 3,600 hp
Man: 5 officers, 26 men

REMARKS: Ordered in 1974. Two additional units not built.

DESTROYER

♦ **1 U.S. Gearing class, FRAM-I**

	Bldr	Laid down	L	In serv.
DD 01 PRESIDENTE ELOY ALFARO (ex-*Holder*, DD 819)	Consolidated Steel, Orange, Tex.	23-4-45	25-8-45	18-5-46

D: 2,425 tons (3,500 fl) **S:** 30 kts **Dim:** 119.1 × 12.4 × 5.8
A: 4/127-mm DP (II × 2)—6/324-mm Mk 32 ASW TT (III × 2)
Electron Equipt: Radars: 1/LN-66, 1/SPS-10, 1/SPS-40, 1/Mk 25 fire-control
Sonar: SQS-23
ECM: WLR-1
M: 2 sets GT; 2 props; 60,000 hp
Boilers: 4 Babcock & Wilcox; 43.3 kg/cm², 454°C **Electric:** 1,200 kw
Fuel: 650 tons **Range:** 2,400/25, 4,800/15 **Man:** 270 tot.

REMARKS: The *Alfaro* began overhaul in the U.S. 8-78; arrived in Ecuador mid-1980. ASROC deleted. Sale of the USS *Southerland* (DD 743) to Ecuador has been canceled.

DESTROYER (continued)

Presidente Eloy Alfaro (DD 01) J. Jedrlinic, 1980

FRIGATE

♦ **1 U.S. Charles Lawrence class fast transport**

	Bldr	Laid down	L	In serv.
D. . . MORAN VALVERDE (ex-*26 de Julio*, ex-*Enright*, APD 66)	Phila. Navy Yd	22-2-43	29-5-43	21-9-43

Moran Valverde (then D 01) 1974

D: 1,400 tons (2,130 fl) **S:** 23 kts **Dim:** 93.27 × 11.27 × 4.7
A: 1/127-mm DP—6/40-mm AA (II × 3)—2 d.c. racks
Electron Equipt: Radars: 1/SPS-6, 1/navigational
M: GE turbo-electric drive; 2 props; 12,000 hp **Electric:** 680 kw
Boilers: 2 Foster-Wheeler "D" Express; 30.6 kg/cm², 399°C **Fuel:** 350 tons
Range: 2,000/23, 5,000/15 **Man:** 212 tot.

REMARKS: Transferred 7-67. Could carry 162 troops when in U.S. Navy. Davits can handle four LCPR/LCVP. Now has a raised helicopter deck over the stern area, new commercial navigational radar in place of SPS-10.

CORVETTES

♦ **6 Italian modified Wadi M'ragh class**

	Bldr	Laid down	L	In serv.
CM 11 ESMERALDAS	CNR, Muggiano	27-9-79	1-10-80	. . .
CM 12 MANABI	CNR, Ancona	5-11-79	6-2-81	. . .
CM 13 LOS RIOS	CNR, Muggiano	. . .	27-2-81	. . .
CM 14 EL ORO	CNR, Ancona	. . .	6-2-81	. . .
CM 15 GALAPAGOS	CNR, Muggiano	. . .	. . .	. . .
CM 16 LUJA	CNR, Ancona	6-2-81	. . .	. . .

Esmeraldas (CM 11)—at launch C. Martinelli, 1980

D: 605 tons (685 fl) **S:** 37 kts **Dim:** 62.3 (57.8 pp) × 9.3 × 2.8
A: 6/MM 40 Exocet SSM (III × 2)—1 Albatros SAM system (IV × 1; Aspide missiles)—1/76-mm OTO Melara DP—2/40-mm Breda AA (II × 1)—6/324-mm Mk 32 ASW TT (III × 2)—1 small helicopter
Electron Equipt: Radar: 1/SMA 3RM20, 1/RAN-10S, 1/Orion 10X
Sonar: Diodon ECM: Gamma syst., SCLAR chaff RL
M: 4 MTU 20V956 TB92 diesels; 4 props; 24,400 hp (20,400 sust.)
Electric: 650 kw **Fuel:** 126 tons **Range:** 1,200/31, 4,000/18 **Man:** 51 tot.

REMARKS: Ordered 1978 from CNR del Tirreno. More powerful engines than earlier units of class, helicopter platform added. Selenia IPN-10 data system, with NA 21 mod.0 radar f.c.s (Orion 10X radar) and two CO3 directors for guns and SAM system.

NOTE: The two U.S. PCE 821-class corvettes, *Esmeraldas* (ex-*Eunice*, PCE 846) and *Manabi* (ex-*Pascagoula*, PCE 874) have been discarded.

GUIDED-MISSILE PATROL BOATS

♦ **3 Quito class** Bldr: Lürssen, Vegasack, West Germany

	L	In serv.
LM 31 QUITO	20-11-75	13-7-76
LM 32 GUAYAQUIL	5-4-76	22-12-77
LM 33 CUENCA	12-76	17-7-77

Quito (LM 31)   G. Koop, 1976

D: 250 tons (265 fl)   **S:** 35 kts   **Dim:** 47.0 × 7.0 × 2.4
A: 4/MM 38 Exocet SSM (II × 2)—1/76-mm OTO Melara—2/35-mm AA (II × 1)
Electron Equipt: Radar: 1 Triton, 1 Vega f.c., 1 navigational
M: 4 MTU 16V538 diesels; 4 props; 14,000 hp   **Electric:** 330 kw
Fuel: 39 tons   **Range:** 600/30   **Man:** 34 tot.

REMARKS: Carry 250 rounds of 76-mm and 1,100 rounds of 35-mm ammunition.

♦ **3 Manta class** Bldr: Lürssen, Vegasack, W. Germany

LM 24 MANTA (In serv. 11-6-71)   LM 25 TULCAN (In serv. 2-4-71)   LM 26 NUEVA ROCAFUERTE (ex-*Tena*) (In serv. 23-6-71)

D: 119 tons (134 fl)   **S:** 35 kts   **Dim:** 36.2 × 5.8 × 1.7
A: 4/Gabriel II SSM (I × 4)—2/30-mm AA Emerlec (II × 1)
Electron Equipt: Radar: 1/navigational, 1/Orion 10X, 1/Vega
M: 2 Mercedes-Benz diesels; 3 props; 9,000 hp   **Fuel:** 21 tons
Range: 700/30, 1,500/15   **Man:** 19 tot.

REMARKS: Similar to Chilean *Guacolda*, but faster. New guns added 1979; Gabriel missiles replaced 2/533-mm TT 1980/81.

PATROL CRAFT

♦ 3 Port Director class

COMANDANCIA DE BALAO   COMANDANCIA DE SALINAS
COMANDANCIA DE GUYAYQUIL

Bldr: Halter, New Orleans, 1976

D: 34 tons (fl)   **S:** 25 kts   **Dim:** 19.66 × 5.18 × 1.24   **A:** . . .
M: 2 GM 12V71 TI diesels; 2 props; 960 hp

♦ **3 LPI class** Bldr: F. Schürenstedt, Bardenfleth, W. Germany (In serv. 1974-75)

LC 81 BAHA HOYO (ex-*10 de Agosto*)   LC 83 PORTOVIEJO (ex-*3 de Noviembre*)
LC 82 PICHINCHA (ex-*9 de Octubre*)

D: 45 tons (64 fl)   **S:** 20 kts   **Dim:** 23.4 × 4.6 × 1.8   **A:** mg
M: 2 Böhn & Kahler diesels; 2 props; 1,200 hp   **Range:** 556/16   **Man:** 9 tot.

♦ **2 ex-U.S. Coast Guard utility boats**

UT 111 RIO NAPO   UT 112 ISLA PUNA

D: 10.6 tons   **S:** 19 kts   **Dim:** 12.27 × 3.45 × 1.0   **A:** . . .
M: 2 GM diesels; 2 props; 380 hp   **Range:** 280/18   **Man:** 4-5 tot.

REMARKS: Transferred 1971.

AMPHIBIOUS WARFARE SHIPS

♦ **1 ex-U.S. LST 542-class tank landing ship** Bldr: Chicago Bridge & Iron

	Laid down	L	In serv.
T 55 HUALCOPO (ex-*Summit County*, LST 1148)	15-2-45	23-5-45	1-6-45

D: 1,650 tons (4,080 fl)   **S:** 11.6 kts   **Dim:** 100.04 × 15.24 × 4.3
A: 8/40-mm (II × 2, I × 4)   **M:** 2 G.M. 12-567A diesels; 2 props; 1,700 hp
Electric: 300 kw   **Range:** 7,200/10   **Man:** 119 tot.

REMARKS: Bought 2-77. Used as transport; has ice-reinforced waterline.

♦ **2 ex-U.S. LSM 1-class medium landing ships**

	Bldr	Laid down	L	In serv.
T 51 JAMBELLI (ex-LSM 539)	Brown SB, Houston, Tex.	16-6-45	11-8-45	30-11-45
T 52 TARQUI (ex-LSM 555)	Charleston NY, S.C.	3-3-45	22-3-45	24-9-45

D: 513 tons (1,095 fl)   **S:** 12.5 kts   **Dim:** 62.0 × 10.5 × 2.2
A: 2/40-mm AA (II × 1)   **M:** 2 GM 16-278A diesels; 2 props; 2,800 hp
Range: 2,500/12   **Man:** 60 tot.

REMARKS: Built 1945, transferred 11-58. Used as transports.

♦ **6 "Sea Trucks"** Bldr: Rotork, G.B. (In serv. 1979)

LF 91   LF 92   LF 93   LF 94   LF 95   LF 96

D: 5 tons (9 fl)   **S:** 26 kts (light)   **Dim:** 12.65 × 3.20 × . . .
M: 2 Volvo AQD 40A diesels; 2 outdrive props; 240 hp   **Cargo:** 4 tons

AUXILIARY SHIPS

♦ **1 new oceanographic research ship** Bldr: Ishikawajima Harima, Tokyo

O. . . . DOMETER (In serv. 21-10-81)

D: 1,100 grt   **S:** . . . kts   **Dim:** 70.0 × 10.7 × . . .
M: 3 diesels; electric drive (2 motors); 1 prop; . . . hp
Man: 26 crew + 19 scientists

REMARKS: Equipped to conduct physical and biological oceanography, geophysical research, and hydrographic surveys.

NOTE: The former corvette *Esmeraldas* (ex-*Eunice*, PCE 846) was used for oceanographic research from 1979 to 1981.

♦ **1 inshore oceanographic research craft**

O 112 RIGEL   Bldr: Halter Marine, New Orleans (In serv. 1975)

D: 50 tons   **Man:** 10 tot.

AUXILIARY SHIPS (continued)

♦ **1 U.S. Aloe-class hydrographic survey ship, former net tender** Bldr: American SB, Cleveland, Ohio

	Laid down	L	In serv.
HI 101 ORION (ex-*Mulberry*, ex-AN 27)	18-10-40	26-3-41	1-11-41

D: 560 tons (805 fl) **S:** 12.5 kts **Dim:** 49.7 (44.5 pp) × 9.3 × 3.6
M: 2 GM 6-278A diesels; 1 prop; 800 hp **Man:** 20 tot.

REMARKS: Armament removed, replaced by charthouse. Transferred 11-65; purchased 30-8-78.

♦ **1 ex-U.S. Army FS 381-class small cargo ship** Bldr: Higgins, New Orleans (In serv. 1944)

T 12 CALICUCHIMA (ex-FS 525)

D: 650 tons (930 fl) **S:** 11.5 kts **Dim:** 54.86 (52.37 pp) × 9.75 × 3.05
M: 2 GM 6-278A diesels; 2 props; 1,000 hp **Fuel:** 100 tons
Range: 4,000/11 **Man:** 30 tot.

REMARKS: Used to supply the Galápagos Islands. Leased 8-4-63; purchased 30-8-78.

♦ **1 ex-U.S. small water tanker**

T 41 ATALHUAPA (ex-YW 131) Bldr: Leatham D. Smith, Wisc. (In serv. 17-9-45)

D: 440 tons (1,390 fl) **S:** 7 kts **Dim:** 53.1 × 9.8 × 4.6
M: 1 GM diesel; 1 prop; 640 hp **Fuel:** 25 tons **Man:** 20 tot.

REMARKS: Transferred 2-5-63; purchased 1-12-77. Cargo: 930 tons water.

♦ **2 U.S. Abnaki- and Achomawi-class fleet tugs** Bldr: Charleston SB & DD, Charleston, S.C.

	Laid down	L	In serv.
R 101 CAYAMBE (ex-*Los Rios*, ex-*Cusabo*, ex ATF 155)	18-9-44	26-2-45	19-5-45
R 105 CHIMBORAZO (ex-*Chowanoc*, ATF 100)	24-4-43	20-8-43	21-2-44

Cayambe—now new number   1966

D: 1,235 tons (1,675 fl) **S:** 16.5 kts **Dim:** 62.48 (59.44 wl) × 11.73 × 4.67
A: 1/76.2-mm DP—2/40-mm AA (I × 2)—2/20-mm AA (I × 2)
Electron Equipt: Radar: 1/Decca 916
M: 4 GM 12-278A diesels, electric drive; 1 prop; 3,000 hp **Electric:** 400 kw
Fuel: 376 tons **Range:** 16,000/8, 7,000/15 **Man:** 85 tot.

REMARKS: R 105: A: 2/12.7-mm mg; M: 4 Busch-Sulzer B5-539 diesels, pipe vice stack. *Cayambe* leased 2-11-60, purchased 30-8-78. *Chimborazo* purchased 1-10-77.

♦ **1 medium harbor tug** (In serv. 1952)

R 102 SANGAY (ex-*Losa*)

D: 295 tons (390 fl) **S:** 12 kts **Dim:** 32.6 × 7.9 × 4.25
M: 1 Fairbanks-Morse diesel; 1 prop; . . . hp

REMARKS: Bought 1964.

♦ **1 former U.S. Army tug** Bldr: Equitable Bldg. (In serv. 1945)

R 103 COTOPAXI (ex-*R.T. Ellis*)

D: 150 tons **S:** 9 kts **Dim:** 25.0 × 6.62 × 2.9 **M:** Diesel; 1 prop; 650 hp

REMARKS: Bought 1947.

♦ **2 small tugs**

R . . . TUNGURAHUA   R 104 ANTIZANA—no data

♦ **1 sail-training bark** Bldr: Celaya SY, Bilbao, Spain

	L	In serv.
BE 01 GUAYAS	23-9-76	23-7-77

D: 934 grt **S:** 10.5 kts **Dim:** 76.2 × 10.6 × 4.2
M: 1 GM 12V-149 diesel; 1 prop; 700 hp

♦ **1 repair barge**

BT 62 PUTAMAYO (ex-YR 34) Bldr: New York Navy Yard, 1944

D: 520 tons (770 fl) **Dim:** 45.7 × 10.4 × 1.8 **Electric:** 330 kw

REMARKS: Transferred 7-62; purchased 1-12-77.

♦ **1 ex-U.S. auxiliary repair dock** (In serv. 1944)

DF 121 AMAZONAS (ex-ARD 17)
Capacity: 3,500 tons **Dim:** 149.9 × 24.7 × 1.7 (light)

REMARKS: Transferred 7-1-61. Pointed bow. Length over blocks: 118.6 m; 18.0 clear width. Dry dock companion craft YFND 20 leased 2-11-61 to support.

COAST GUARD
Established 1980

♦ **2 U.S. PGM 71-class patrol boats** Bldr: Peterson Bldrs, Sturgeon Bay, Wisc. (In serv. 1965)

VEINTECINCO DE JULIO (ex-*Quito*, ex-PGM 75)
DIEZ DE AGOSTO (ex-*Guayaquil*, ex-PGM 76)

D: 130 tons (147 fl) **S:** 20 kts **Dim:** 30.8 (30.2 pp) × 6.45 × 2.3
A: 1/40-mm AA—4/20-mm AA (II × 2)—2/12.7-mm mg (I × 2)
M: 2 Mercedes-Benz MB 820D diesels; 2 props; 2,200 hp (1,900 sust.)
Electric: 30 kw **Fuel:** 16 tons **Range:** 1,000/12 **Man:** 15 tot.

REMARKS: Transferred to Coast Guard 1980, having been received in 1965.

ECUADOR *(continued)*
AUXILIARY SHIPS *(continued)*

Veinticinco De Julio (old number) 1967

♦ **14 U.S. Baycraft 40-ft. patrol craft** (In serv. 1979-80)

REMARKS: Fiberglass hulls; modified sport-fishing boat design. No other data available.

EGYPT
Arab Republic of Egypt

PERSONNEL: Approx. 17,500 men with more than 1,500 officers

MERCHANT MARINE (1980): 278 ships—555,786 grt
              (tankers: 34 ships—129,025 grt)

COAST DEFENSES: The Navy is responsible for coastal defenses. Fifty Coast Defense, truck-mounted versions of the Otomat missile have been ordered. Targeting will be performed by land-based Sea King helicopters. Some Soviet Samlet coast-defense missiles remain in service also.

SUBMARINES

♦ **6 Soviet Romeo class**

711   722   733   744   755   766

Egyptian Romeo 1977

D: 1,330/1,700 tons **S:** 15/13 kts **Dim:** 77.0 × 6.7 × 4.95
A: 8/533-mm TT (6 fwd, 2 aft)—14 torpedoes or 28 mines
Electron Equipt: Radar: 1/Snoop Tray
                  Sonar: Hercules
M: Diesel-electric, 2 diesels, 2,000 hp each; 2 props; 2,700 hp
Endurance: 45 days **Range:** 7,000/5 (snorkel) **Man:** 60 tot.

REMARKS: Transferred: 5 in 1966, 1 in 1969. To be refitted with European equipment.

♦ **6 Soviet Whiskey class**

415   418   421   432   455   477

D: 1,050/1,350 tons **S:** 17/16 kts **Dim:** 74.0 × 6.6 × 4.8
A: 6/533-mm TT (4 fwd, 2 aft)—12 torpedoes or 28 mines
Electron Equipt: Radar: 1/Snoop Plate
                  Sonar: Hercules, passive array
M: Diesels and electric motors; 2 props; 4,000/2,500 hp **Endurance:** 40-45 days
Range: 6,000/5 **Man:** 60 tot.

REMARKS: Transferred from 6-57 to 8-62. Reported in poor condition. In refit 1978-79; to get British electronic intercept equipment.

DESTROYERS

♦ **4 Soviet Skoryy class**

	Bldr	Transferred
668 6 OCTOBER (ex-*El Nasser*)	U.S.S.R.	11-6-56
822 AL ZAFFER	U.S.S.R.	11-6-56
844 DAMIET	U.S.S.R.	4-67
888 SUEZ	U.S.S.R.	4-67

Damiet (844) 1979

Al Zaffer (822)—with Styx missiles aft 1979

D: 2,240 tons (3,080 fl) **S:** 35 kts **Dim:** 121.5 × 12.5 × 4.6
A: *Suez:* 4/130-mm DP (II × 2)—2/85-mm AA (II × 1)—8/37-mm AA (II × 4)—
      4/25-mm AA (II × 2)—10/533-mm TT (V × 2)—2/d.c. projectors—2/
      d.c. racks—50 mines
    Al Zaffer: 2/SS-N-2A Styx SSM (II × 2)—4/130-mm DP (II × 2)—6/37-mm
        AA (II × 3)—6/25-mm AA (II × 3)—10/533-mm TT (V × 2)—2/
        d.c. projectors—2/d.c. racks—mines

DESTROYERS *(continued)*

6 October, Damiet: 4/130-mm DP (II × 2)—4/57-mm AA (IV × 1)—4/37-mm
AA (II × 2)—4/25-mm AA (II × 2)—10/533-mm TT (V
× 2)—2/RBU-2500—2/d.c. racks—50 mines
Electron Equipt: 668: 1/High Sieve, 1/Top Bow, 1/navigational, 1 Post Lamp
822: 2/navigational, 1/Square Tie, 1/Post Lamp
844,888: 1/navigational, 1/Hawk Screech, 1/Slim Net
M: 2 sets GP; 2 props; 60,000 hp **Boilers:** 4 **Range:** 900/32, 4,000/15
Man: 272 tot.

REMARKS: Two earlier Skoryys were replaced in 1968 by two ships of the same class
and with the same names, which had been modernized by the substitution of 4/57-
mm AA and a Hawk Screech f.c. system for the twin 85-mm AA and its Cylinder
Head director and two twin 37-mm AA. The *Al Zaffer* has had two aft-firing Styx
launchers from a discarded Komar added atop her after deckhouse in place of the
twin 85-mm mount and one twin 37-mm AA. All four carry SA-N-5 Grail shoulder-
launched AA missiles.

NOTE: Transfer of U.S. *Gearing* FRAM I destroyers was canceled 1979 due to the
age and condition of the ships offered.

♦ 1 British Z class

	Bldr	Laid down	L	In serv.
EL FATEH (ex-*Zenith*, ex-*Wessex*)	Wm. Denny, Dumbarton, Scotland	19-5-42	5-6-44	22-12-44

El Fateh   1975

D: 1,730 tons (2,575 fl) **S:** 31 kts **Dim:** 110.6 × 10.9 × 5.2
A: 4/102-mm DP (I × 4)—6/40-mm AA II × 1, I × 4)—8/533-mm TT—4/d.c.
projectors
Electron Equipt: Radar: 1/Decca navigational, 1/Marconi SNW-10, 1/Type 293,
1/Type 275 f.c.
M: 2 sets GT; 2 props; 40,000 hp **Boilers:** 2 Admiralty 3-drum
Fuel: 580 tons **Range:** 2,800/20 **Man:** 250 tot.

REMARKS: Purchased 1955, refitted 1956 and again in 1964.

FRIGATES

♦ 1 British Black Swan class

	Bldr	Laid down	L	In serv.
555 TARIK (ex-*El Malek Farouk*, ex-HMS *Whimbrel*)	Yarrow & Co., Glasgow	31-10-41	25-8-42	13-1-43

Tarik (555)   1980

D: 1,470 tons (1,925 fl) **S:** 19 kts **Dim:** 91.29 × 11.73 × 3.45
A: 6/102-mm DP (II × 3)—4/40-mm AA (II × 2)—4/12.7-mm mg (I × 4)—4/d.c.
projectors—2/d.c. racks
Electron Equipt: Radar: 2/navigational, 1/Type 285 f.c.
M: 2 sets Parsons GT; 2 props; 4,300 hp **Boilers:** 2 Admiralty 3-drum
Fuel: 390 tons **Range:** 5,700/15, 9,200/10 **Man:** 180 tot.

REMARKS: Bought in 12-49.

♦ 1 British "River" class

	Bldr	Laid down	L	In serv.
511 RACHID (ex-*Spey*)	Smith's Dock Co., Ltd.	7-41	18-21-41	3-42

Rachid (511)   1978

D: 1,460 tons (2,175 fl) **S:** 19 kts **Dim:** 91.85 × 11.17 × 4.34 (fl)
A: 1/102-mm—4/40-mm AA (II × 2)—1/SA-N-5 Grail SAM system
M: Triple-expansion; 2 props; 5,500 hp **Boilers:** 2 **Fuel:** 640 tons
Range: 7,700/12, 5,000/16 **Man:** 110 tot.

REMARKS: Bought in 12-49. Used as a submarine tender.

♦ 1 British "Hunt-1" class

	Bldr	Laid down	L	In serv.
PORT SAID (ex-*Mohamed Ali El Kebit*, ex-*Cottesmore*)	Yarrow & Co.	12-12-39	5-9-40	29-12-40

D: 1,000 tons (1,490 fl) **S:** 25 kts **Dim:** 85.35 × 8.84 × 4.19
A: 4/102-mm DP (II × 2)—2/25-mm AA (II × 1)—2/12.7-mm mg (I × 2)
M: 2 sets Parsons GT; 2 props; 19,000 hp **Boilers:** 2 Admiralty 3-drum
Fuel: 240 tons **Range:** 2,000/12, 800/25 **Man:** 146 tot.

REMARKS: Transferred 7-50. Has only one navigational radar, no ASW equipment.

GUIDED-MISSILE PATROL BOATS

♦ **6 Ramadan class** Bldr: Vosper Thornycroft, Portchester, G.B.

	Laid down	L	In serv.
561 RAMADAN	23-11-78	6-9-79	20-7-81
562 N. . .	26-2-79	12-6-80	. . .
563 N. . .	23-4-79	3-80	. . .
564 N. . .	16-5-79	12-6-80	. . .
565 HETTEIN	29-9-79	17-6-81	. . .
566 BADR	3-80	25-11-80	6-82

Ramadan class (561)   Vosper Thornycroft, 1980

D: 262 tons (312 fl)   **S:** 35 kts   **Dim:** 52.0 × 7.6 × 2.3
A: 4/Otomat SSM (II × 2)—1/76-mm DP OTO Melara Compact—2/40-mm AA
   Breda (II × 1)
Electron Equipt: Radar: Marconi: 1/S820, 1/S810, 2/ST802—ECM: Decca-Racal
   Cutlass
M: 4 MTU MD 20V538 TB 91 diesels; 4 props; 16,000 hp   **Fuel:** 43 tons
Electric: 420 kw   **Range:** 2,000/15   **Man:** 31 tot.

REMARKS: Ordered 4-9-77. Has Marconi Sapphire fire control system with two radar/
t.v. directors, two Lawrence Scott optical directors.

♦ **6 6 October class** Bldr: Egypt/Vosper Thornycroft (In serv. 1980-81)

207   208   209   210   211   212

D: 71 tons (82 fl)   **S:** 40 kts   **Dim:** 25.3 × 6.0 × 1.8
A: 2/Otomat SSM—4/30-mm AA Type A32 (II × 2)
Electron Equipt: Radar: Marconi: 1/S810, 1/ST802   **Range:** 400/30
M: 4 CRM 18V-12D/55 YE diesels; 4 props; 5,400 hp   **Man:** 20 tot.

REMARKS: Wooden hulls, built at Alexandria DY, Egypt, 1969 onward. Completed by
Vosper Thornycroft at Portchester, Portsmouth, with Italian-French missiles and
British guns; diesels are Italian. Basic design is that of the Soviet Komar class. An
ESM system is fitted. Uses Marconi Sapphire radar/t.v. fire control system.

♦ **6 ex-Soviet Osa-I class**

D: 175 tons (205 fl)   **S:** 36 kts   **Dim:** 39.0 × 7.7 × 1.8
A: 4/Styx systems (I × 4)—4/30-mm AA (II × 2)
Electron Equipt: Radars: 1/Square Tie, 1/Drum Tilt, 1/Decca 916
M: 3 M503A diesels; 3 props; 12,000 hp   **Range:** 450/34, 700/20

6 October class (210)—Otomat racks empty   Vosper Thornycroft, 1980

REMARKS: Transferred 1966. Reported being refitted with 3 MTU diesels. All carry
SA-N-5, shoulder-launched Grail SAMs.

♦ **4 ex-Soviet Komar class**

393   395   397   399

Soviet-built Egyptian Komar   1976

D: 71 tons (82 fl)   **S:** 40 kts   **Dim:** 25.3 × 7.0 × 2.0
A: 2 Styx systems (I × 2)—2/25-mm AA   **Range:** 450/30
Electron Equipt: Radar: 1/Square Tie   **M:** 4 M50 diesels; 4 props; 4,800 hp

REMARKS: Transferred 1962-66. Wooden hulls. Will probably soon be discarded.

PATROL BOATS

♦ **12 Soviet SO-I class**

> **D:** 190 tons (215 fl) **S:** 28 kts **Dim:** 42.0 × 6.1 × 1.9
> **A:** 4/25-mm AA (II × 2)—4 RBU-1200 RL—2/d.c. racks—mines. Some are
> armed with 2/533-mm TT as well.
> **Electron Equipt:** Radar: 1/Decca 916 **M:** 3 diesels; 3 props; 7,500 hp
> **Man:** 30 tot.

REMARKS: Transferred 1962-63. Also carry SA-N-5 Grail, shoulder-launched SAMs.

TORPEDO BOATS

♦ **6 Soviet Shershen class**

310 321 332 343 354 365

Shershen 343—with 122-mm rocket launchers

> **D:** 150 tons (180 fl) **S:** 45 kts **Dim:** 34.0 × 7.2 × 1.5
> **A:** 4/30-mm AA (II × 2)—4/533-mm TT (I × 4) or 2/122-mm RL (XX × 2)
> **Electron Equipt:** 1/Square Tie, 1/Drum Tilt
> **M:** 3 M-503A diesels; 3 props; 12,000 hp

REMARKS: Transferred 1967-68. Three are armed with two 20-tubed 122-mm artillery
rocket launchers instead of torpedoes. Most carry shoulder-launched SA-N-5 Grail
missiles as well.

♦ **20 ex-Soviet P-6 class**

> **D:** 56 tons (66.5 fl) **S:** 43 kts (cruising) **Dim:** 25.3 × 6.1 × 1.7
> **A:** 4/25-mm AA (II × 2)—2/533-mm TT or 1/122-mm RL (XL × 1)
> **Electron Equipt:** Radar: 1/Decca. . . **M:** 4 M50 diesels; 4 props; 4,800 hp
> **Range:** 450/30 **Man:** 16 tot.

REMARKS: Transferred since 1960. A few are armed with one 40-tubed BM-21 122-
mm rocket launcher, have no TT, and the after 25-mm mount removed. Some of
these boats were built in Egypt. At least two have had 4/533-mm TT.

♦ **4 ex-Soviet P-4 class**

> **D:** 19.3 tons (22.4 fl) **S:** 55 kts **Dim:** 19.3 × 3.7 × 1.0
> **A:** 2/450-mm TT—2/14.5-mm mg (II × 1)—8/122-mm rockets (VIII × 1)
> **M:** 2 M50 diesels; 2 props; 2,400 hp

REMARKS: Transferred from Syria, 1970. Aluminum-hulled hydroplane.

Egyptian P-6 equipped with multiple rocket launcher   1975

P-4 with octuple rocket launcher mounted on bow   1974

MINE WARFARE SHIPS

♦ **4 ex-Soviet Yurka-class minesweepers** (In serv. 1969)

695 ASSUAN 690 GUIZAN 696 QENA 699 SUHAG

> **D:** 460 tons (fl) **S:** 18 kts **Dim:** 52.0 × 8.8 × 2.0
> **A:** 4/30-mm AA (II × 2)—20 mines **Electron Equipt:** Radar: 1/Don-2
> **M:** 2 diesels; 2 props; 4,000 hp

REMARKS: Delivered new 1969. Do not have Drum Tilt radar fire-control system.

♦ **6 ex-Soviet T-43-class minesweepers** (In serv. 1956-59)

> **D:** 500 tons (569 fl) **S:** 14 kts **Dim:** 58.0 × 8.4 × 2.3

MINE WARFARE SHIPS *(continued)*

Egyptian T-43 class   1975

A: 4/37-mm AA (II × 2)—8/12.7-mm mg (II × 4)—2/d.c. throwers—mines
Electron Equipt: Radar: 1/Decca. . .   **M:** 2 diesels; 2 props; 2,200 hp

REMARKS: Five transferred 1956-59; one in 1970.

◆ **2 Soviet T-301-class minesweepers** (In serv. circa 1950)

EL FAYOUD   EL MANUFIEH

D: 145.8 tons (160 fl) **S:** 12.5 kts **Dim:** 38.0 × 5.1 × 1.6
A: 2/45-mm—2/12.7-mm mg **M:** 3 6-cyl. diesels; 3 props; 1,440 hp
Fuel: 20 tons **Range:** 2,500/8

REMARKS: Transferred 1962-63. No radars. Used for harbor clearance.

AMPHIBIOUS WARFARE SHIPS

◆ **3 Soviet Polnocny-class, Type A LSM** Bldr: Polnocny SY, Gdansk, Poland

D: 900 tons (fl) **S:** 18 kts **Dim:** 72.5 × 8.5 × 2.0
A: 2/30-mm AA (II × 1)—2/140-mm multiple RL (XVIII × 2)
Electron Equipt: Radar: 1/Don-2, 1/Drum Tilt **M:** 2 diesels; 2 props; 4,000 hp
Man: 40 tot.

REMARKS: Transferred 1974. Cargo: 3 tanks or 200 tons.

◆ **9 ex-Soviet Vydra-class LCUs**

D: 425 tons (600 fl) **S:** 11 kts **Dim:** 54.8 × 8.1 × 2.0
A: 4/40-mm AA (II × 2)—8/15-tubed artillery RL—see remarks
Electron Equipt: Radar: 1/Spin Trough removed **M:** 2 diesels; 2 props; 800 hp

REMARKS: Transferred 1967-69. Armament now removed. Some had 37-mm AA vice 40-mm.

◆ **5 ex-Soviet SMB-I-class LCUs**

D: 180 tons (335 fl) **S:** 10 kts **Dim:** 48.2 × 6.5 × 2.0
Electron Equipt: Radar: none **M:** 2 diesels; 2 props; 600 hp
Range: 400/8 **Man:** 16 tot.

REMARKS: Transferred 1965. Cargo: 180 tons.

◆ **10 to 12 small landing craft of various origins**

Egyptian Vydra with rocket launchers   1976

AUXILIARY SHIPS

◆ **2 Soviet Toplivo-2-class coastal tankers** Bldr: Egypt

D: 466 tons (1,180 fl) **S:** 10 kts **Dim:** 52.9 (49.4 pp) × 9.5 × 3.4
Electron Equipt: Radar: 1/Spin Trough
M: 1 Russkiy Dizel 6 DR 30/50-5-2 diesel; 1 prop; 440 hp **Electric:** 250 kw
Fuel: 19 tons **Range:** 1,500/10 **Man:** . . . tot.

REMARKS: Part of a series of 26 ordered in Egypt for the U.S.S.R. prior to that country's expulsion. Cargo: 606m³ (500 tons diesel oil).

◆ **4 Soviet Okhtenskiy-class tugs**

AL ISKANDARANI   EL MAKS
EL AGAMI   EL DIKHILA

D: 700 tons (950 fl) **S:** 13.3 kts **Dim:** 47.3 × 10.3 × 5.5
Electron Equipt: Radar: 1/Don-2 or Spin Trough
M: 2 diesels, electric drive; 1 prop; 1,500 hp **Range:** 7,800/7 **Man:** 40 tot.

REMARKS: Two transferred 1966; two assembled in Egypt.

◆ **2 Soviet Nyryat-I-class diving tenders**

D: 120 tons (fl) **S:** 12 kts **Dim:** 29.0 × 5.0 × 1.7
Electron Equipt: Radar: 1/Spin Trough **M:** 1 diesel; 1 prop; 450 hp
Range: 1,600/10 **Man:** 15 tot.

REMARKS: Transferred 1964.

◆ **2 Soviet Poluchat-I-class torpedo retrievers**

D: 80 tons (90 fl) **S:** 18 kts **Dim:** 29.6 × 5.8 × 1.5
Electron Equipt: Radar: 1/Spin Trough
M: 2 M50 diesels; 2 props; 2,400 hp **Range:** 450/17, 900/10 **Man:** 20 tot.

◆ **2 Soviet PO-2-class general-purpose launches**

D: 50 tons (fl) **S:** 9 kts **Dim:** 21.0 × . . . × . . .
M: 1 diesel; 1 prop; 150 hp

EGYPT (*continued*)
AUXILIARY SHIPS (*continued*)

♦ **1 Soviet Sekstan-class degaussing tender**

    D: 800 tons (fl) **S:** 10.5 kts **Dim:** 40.9 × 12.3 × 4.3
    M: 1 diesel; 1 prop; 400 hp

    REMARKS: Wooden construction.

TRAINING SHIPS

♦ **1 former yacht** Bldr: Samuda, Scotland (In serv. 1865)

EL HORRIA (ex-*Mahroussa*)

El Horria   G. Garier, 1976

    D: 4,561 tons (fl) **S:** 16 kts **Dim:** 145.6 (121.9 pp) × 13.0 × 5.3
    A: Several mg **M:** 3 sets GT; 3 props; 5,500 hp

    REMARKS: World's oldest active naval ship; carried President Sadat in naval review,
    12-80. Used as training ship.

♦ **1 navigational training ship for the Naval Academy**

EL KOUSSER **D:** 1,000 tons

♦ **1 former yacht, attached to the Naval Academy**

INTISAR **D:** 500 tons

COAST GUARD

PATROL BOATS

♦ **3 Nisr class** Bldr: de Castro BY, Port Said (In serv. 1963)

NIMR NISR THAR

    D: 110 tons (fl) **S:** . . . **Dim:** . . . × . . . × . . . **A:** 1/20-mm AA
    M: 2 Maybach diesels; 2 props; . . . hp

PATROL CRAFT

♦ **6 (+ 36) MV70 class** Bldr: Crestitalia, Ameglia (La Spezia), Italy

    D: 33 tons (41.5 fl) **S:** 34 kts **Dim:** 21.0 × 5.2 × 0.9
    A: 2/30-mm Oerlikon A32 (II × 1)—1/20-mm AA—2/12.7-mm mg

    M: 2 MTU 12V331 TC92 diesels; 2 props; 2,800 hp **Range:** 500/3

    REMARKS: Fiberglass hulls. An additional 36 may be ordered.

♦ **30 DC-35 class** Bldr: Dawncraft, Wroxham, G.B. (In serv. 1977)

    D: 4 tons (fl) **S:** 25 kts **Dim:** 10.7 × 3.5 × 0.8
    M: 2 Perkins T6-354 diesels; 2 props; 390 hp **Man:** 4 tot.

    REMARKS: Fiberglass hulled. For harbor police duties.

♦ **20 28-ft. "Enforcer" class** Bldr: Bertram Yacht, Miami, Fla. (In serv. 1973)

    D: 8 tons (fl) **S:** 24 kts **Dim:** 8.5 × . . . × . . .
    A: 2/12.7-mm mg (I × 2) **M:** 2 diesels; 2 props; 300 hp

    REMARKS: Formerly naval, had 4/122-mm RL on sides of hull. Fiberglass construction.

    NOTE: The Customs Service received twelve 19.8-m Sea Specter-class patrol craft in
    1980-81.

EL SALVADOR
Republic of El Salvador

PERSONNEL: 130 officers and men

MERCHANT MARINE (1980): 5 ships—2,317 grt

PATROL CRAFT

♦ **3 aluminum-hulled** Bldr: Camcraft, Crown Pt., Louisiana

    In serv.   In serv.   In serv.
    GC 6 (10-75)   GC 7 (12-75)   GC 8 (11-75)

    D: 100 tons (fl) **S:** 25 kts **Dim:** 30.5 × 6.4 × 1.5 **A:** 3/12.7-mm mg
    M: 3 GM 12 V TI diesels; 3 props; 1,200 hp **Range:** 780/24
    Man: 10 tot.

♦ **1 aluminum-hulled** Bldr: Sewart Seacraft, Berwick, Louisiana (In serv. 9-67)

GC 5

    D: 33 tons (fl) **S:** 25 kts **Dim:** 19.8 × 4.9 × 1.5 **A:** 3/12.7-mm mg
    M: 3 GM 8V71 diesels; 3 props; 1,590 hp

♦ **25 small launches with outboard motors**

♦ **1 tug** Bldr: A.C. de la Manche, St. Malo, France (In serv. 2-4-81)

LIBERTAD

    D: 390 tons (fl) **S:** 11.5 kts **Dim:** 26.0 (24.0 pp) × 7.9 × 3.95
    M: 1 Crepelle 8PSN SRR diesel; 1 prop; 1,400 hp

    REMARKS: For government service; bollard pull: 21.45 tons.

EQUATORIAL GUINEA

Republic of Equatorial Guinea

PERSONNEL: 100 men

MERCHANT MARINE (1980): 5 ships—2,317 grt

NOTE: The condition of the craft below (and even their continued existence) is uncertain.

♦ **1 Soviet P-6-class torpedo boat**

 D: 56 tons (66.5 fl) **S:** 43 kts **Dim:** 25.3 × 6.1 × 1.7
 A: 4/25-mm AA (II × 2)—2/533-mm TT (I × 2)
 Electron Equipt: Radar: 1/Skin Head **M:** 4 M50 diesels; 4 props; 4,800 hp
 Range: 400/32, 700/15 **Man:** 12 tot.

REMARKS: Transferred 1974.

♦ **1 Soviet Poluchat-I-class patrol boat**

 D: 80 tons (90 fl) **S:** 18 kts **Dim:** 29.6 × 5.8 × 1.5 **A:** 2/14.5-mm mg
 M: 2 M50 diesels; 2 props; 2,400 hp **Range:** 450/17, 900/10 **Man:** 20 tot.

REMARKS: Transferred 1974.

♦ **2 small patrol craft**

ETHIOPIA

PERSONNEL: 1,200 men including 230 officers

MERCHANT MARINE (1980): 17 ships—23,811 grt (tankers: 1 ship—2,051 grt)

GUIDED-MISSILE PATROL BOATS

♦ **3 Soviet Osa-II class**

 D: 210 tons (240 fl) **S:** 36 kts **Dim:** 39.0 × 7.7 × 1.8
 A: 4/Styx SSM—4/30-mm AA (II × 2)
 Electron Equipt: Radars: 1/Square Tie, 1/Drum Tilt
 IFF: 2/Square Head, 1/High Pole B
 M: 3 M504 diesels; 3 props; 15,000 hp **Range:** 450/34, 700/20 **Man:** 30 tot.

REMARKS: First unit transferred 1978, second 10-80, third 2-81; others expected.

TORPEDO BOATS

♦ **3 Soviet MOL class**

 D: 175 tons (220 fl) **S:** 36 kts **Dim:** 39.0 × 7.7 × 1.8
 A: 4/533-mm TT (I × 4)—4/30-mm AA (II × 2)
 Electron Equipt: Radars: 1/Pot Head, 1/Drum Tilt
 IFF: 1/Square Head, 1/High Pole B
 M: 3 M503A diesels; 3 props; 12,000 hp **Man:** 30 tot.

REMARKS: Transferred 1978. May not carry the torpedo tubes.

PATROL BOATS

♦ **4 aluminum-hulled boats** Bldr: Swiftships, Morgan City, Louisiana

P 201　P 202　P 203　P 204

Aluminum-hulled patrol boat with Emerlec 30-mm AA　　Swiftships, 1977

Aluminum-hulled patrol boat with 23-mm AA　　1978

 D: 118 tons (fl) **S:** 32 kts **Dim:** 31.73 × 7.1 × 2.16
 A: 4/30mm Emerlec AA (II × 2) **Electron Equipt:** Radar: Decca RM 916
 M: 2 MTU MB 16V538 TB90 diesels; 2 props; 7,000 hp
 Range: 1,200/18 **Man:** 21 tot.

REMARKS: Ordered 1976, delivered 4-77; two additional units were canceled by the U.S. arms embargo. P 203 and P 204 have four 23-mm AA (II × 2) and two 12.7-mm machine guns (II × 1).

ETHIOPIA (*continued*)
PATROL BOATS (*continued*)

◆ **4 ex-U.S. Coast Guard Cape design** Bldr: Peterson Bldrs, Sturgeon Bay, Wisc.
PC 12 (ex-CG WPB 95310) (In serv. 1958)   PC 14 (ex-U.S. PGM 54) (In serv. 8-61)
PC 13 (ex-U.S. PGM 53) (In serv. 8-61)   PC 15 (ex-U.S. PGM 58) (In serv. 5-62)

PC 14

D: 80 tons (105 fl)   **S:** 18 kts   **Dim:** 28.95 × 6.1 × 1.55
A: 1/40-mm AA—1/20-mm AA
M: 4 Cummins VT-12M700 diesels; 2 props; 2,200 hp   **Electric:** 40 kw
Fuel: 12 tons   **Range:** 460/20, 1,500/10   **Man:** 15 tot.

REMARKS: PC 11 lost in action, 4-77. All ASW weapons removed. Reportedly, only three are in service. PC 12 built by Coast Guard Yard, Curtis Bay, Md.

◆ **1 ex-Dutch Wildervank-class former minesweeper**

41 (ex-M 829 *Elst*)

D: 373 tons (417 fl)   **S:** 14 kts   **Dim:** 46.62 × 8.75 × 2.28
A: 2/40-mm AA (I × 2)   **Electron Equipt:** Radar: 1/ZW-04
M: 2 Werkspoor diesels; 2 props; 2,500 hp   **Range:** 2,500/10   **Man:** 40 tot.

REMARKS: Launched 21-3-56; bought in 1970. All minesweeping gear removed.

PATROL CRAFT

◆ **4 aluminum-hulled craft** Bldr: Seward Seacraft, Berwick, La. (In serv. 1965-67)

GB 21   GB 22   GB 23   GB 24 (ex-*John*, *Caroline*, *Patrick*, *Jacqueline*)

D: 15 tons (fl)   **S:** 20 kts   **Dim:** 13.1 × 3.9 × 0.9   **A:** 2/12.7-mm mg
M: 2 GM 6-71 diesels; 2 props; 500 hp   **Man:** 7 tot.

AMPHIBIOUS SHIPS

◆ **1 Soviet Polnocny-B class** Bldr: Polnocny SY, Gdansk, Poland

L 1037

D: 950 tons (fl)   **S:** 18 kts   **Dim:** 74.0 × 8.5 × 2.0
A: 4/30-mm AA—2/140-mm RL (XVIII × 2)
Electron Equipt: Radar: 1/Spin Trough, 1/Drum Tilt
       IFF: 1/Square Head, 1/High Pole
M: 2 diesels; 2 props; 4,000 hp   **Man:** 40 tot.

REMARKS: Date of transferral uncertain, probably 1979-80. Cargo: 200 tons.

◆ **2 French EDIC-class LCU** Bldr: SFCN, Villeneuve la Garonne (L: 5-77)

L 1035   L 1036

D: 250 tons (670 fl)   **S:** 8 kts   **Dim:** 59.0 × 11.95 × 1.3
A: 2/20-mm AA (I × 2)   **M:** 2 MGO diesels; 2 props; 1,000 hp
Range: 1,800/8   **Man:** 1 officer, 15 men

REMARKS: Cargo: 11 trucks or 5 light armored vehicles.

◆ **2 ex-U.S. LCM(3)-class landing craft**

◆ **2 ex-U.S. LCVP personnel landing craft**

REMARKS: Two transferred in 1962 and two in 1971.

◆ **4 Soviet T-4-class landing craft**

REMARKS: Transferred 1977-78.

TRAINING SHIP

◆ **1 U.S. Barnegat-class former seaplane tender**

	Bldr	Laid down	L	In serv.
A 01 ETHIOPIA (ex-*Orca*, AVP 49)	Lake Washington SY	13-7-42	4-10-42	23-1-44

D: 1,766 tons (2,800 fl)   **S:** 17 kts   **Dim:** 94.7 (91.5 pp) × 12.52 × 3.65
A: 1/127-mm DP—5/40-mm AA (II × 2, I × 1)
Electron Equipt: Radar: 1/SPS-12, 1/navigational, 1/Mk-26
M: 4 Fairbanks-Morse 38D8 ⅛ × 10 diesels; 2 props; 6,000 hp
Electric: 600 kw   **Range:** 15,000/12   **Man:** 215 tot.

REMARKS: Transferred in 1-62. Probably inoperable due to age, poor condition, and lack of spares. Had Mk 52 radar GFCS for 127-mm gun.

FIJI
Dominion of Fiji

PERSONNEL: (1980) 160 men (20 officers)

MERCHANT MARINE (1980): 43 ships—14,773 grt (1 tanker—254 grt)

PATROL BOATS

◆ **3 ex-U.S. Redwing-class minesweepers** Bldr: Bellingham SY, Washington

	In serv.
204 KIKAU (ex-*Woodpecker*, MSC 209)	3-2-56
205 KULA (ex-*Vireo*, MSC 205)	7-6-55
206 KIRO (ex-*Warbler*, MSC 206)	23-7-55

D: 370 tons (fl)   **S:** 13 kts   **Dim:** 43.9 × 8.5 × 2.6
A: 1/20-mm AA—2/12.7-mm mg
M: 2 GM 8-268A diesels; 2 props; 880 hp   **Range:** 2,500/10   **Man:** 39 tot.

REMARKS: The first two were transferred 10-75, the third 6-76. Most minesweeping gear removed.

FIJI *(continued)*

AUXILIARY SHIPS

♦ **1 survey ship** Bldr: Government SY, Suva, Fiji (In serv. 4-79)

RUVE

D: 100 tons **S:** 10 kts **Dim:** 30.0 × . . . × . . . **M:** 2 diesels **Man:** 14 tot.

♦ **2 logistics support craft** Bldr: Government SY, Suva, Fiji (In serv. 1978)

VASUA

D: . . . **S:** 8 kts **Dim:** 40.0 × . . . × . . . **M:** 2 GM diesels; 2 props; 348 hp
Cargo: 220 tons

REMARKS: Bow-ramped landing craft for logistic support duties.

YAUBULA

D: 500 tons (fl) **S:** 8 kts **Dim:** 42.5 × 9.1 × 1.7
M: 2 GM 12V71 diesels; 2 props; 680 hp **Electric:** 100 kva **Fuel:** 85 tons
Cargo: 200 tons plus 31 passengers **Man:** 17 tot.

REMARKS: Subordinate to the Fiji Marine Department. Landing craft with bow ramp.
343.16 grt/230.99 nrt

FINLAND
Republic of Finland

The naval force, limited by the Treaty of Paris to 10,000 tons and 4,500 men, is a
separate establishment under the orders of the chief of the armed forces. Submarines
and torpedo boats are excluded from the fleet, and there is no naval aviation.

PERSONNEL (1980): about 2,500, including 200 officers

MERCHANT MARINE (1980): 354 ships—2,530,091 grt (tankers: 38 ships—1,201,107 grt)

WEAPONS

The *Turunmaa*-class corvettes and the new minelayer have a single-barrel automatic
Bofors 120-mm gun with the following characteristics:

weight without munitions:	arc of elevation: −10° to +80
28.5 tons	maximum rate of fire:
length: 46 calibers	80 rounds/min
muzzle velocity: 800 m/sec	projectile weight: 35 kg
training speed: 40°/sec	maximum effective range, surface
elevation speed: 30°/sec	fire: 12,000 m

The other major weapons employed are Soviet SS-N-2 Styx missiles, Bofors 40-mm
L70 AA guns, Soviet twin 30-mm AA guns, and 23-mm AA in twin mountings.

FRIGATES

♦ **1 Soviet Riga class**

02 HÄMEENMAA

D: 1,000 (1,420 fl) **S:** 28 kts **Dim:** 91.0 × 10.0 × 3.2
A: 3/100-mm DP (I × 3)—2/40-mm AA (I × 2)—2/30-mm AA (II × 1)—2/20-mm
AA (I × 2)—2 mine rails
Electron Equipt: Radars: 1/Decca navigational, 1/Slim Net, 1/Sun Visor B
M: 2 sets GT, 2 props; 20,000 hp **Boilers:** 2 **Range:** 2,000/10 **Man:** 175 tot.

REMARKS: Transferred in 1964. The twin 30-mm mount is carried at the extreme bow.
Sister *Uusimaa* was discarded early in 1979. *Hämeenmaa* has had all ASW ordnance
removed during a 1979-80 refit and additional minelaying capabilities added.

CORVETTES

♦ **2 Turunmaa class**

	Bldr	Laid down	L	In serv.
03 TURUNMAA	Wärtsilä, Helsinki	3-67	11-7-67	29-8-68
04 KARJALA	Wärtsilä, Helsinki	3-67	16-8-67	21-10-68

Karjala (04)   1978

D: 605 tons (770 fl) **S:** 35 kts **Dim:** 74.1 × 7.8 × 2.83
A: 1/120-mm Bofors DP—2/40-mm AA (I × 2)—2/12.7-mm mg (I × 2)—2/RBU-
1200 ASW RL (V × 2)—2 d.c. racks
Electron Equipt: Radars: 1/HSA M22, 1/navigational
M: CODOG propulsion: 1 Bristol-Siddeley Olympus TM3B, 22,000-hp gas tur-
bine; 3 Mercedes-Benz 1,100-hp diesels; 3 CP props
Electric: 880 kva **Fuel:** 120 tons **Range:** 2,500/14 **Man:** 70 tot.

REMARKS: Flush-deck hull, closed bridge, sharp profile. Cruises on the diesels (3 ×
1,100 hp) at 17 knots. Ka-Me-Wa controllable-pitch propellers. Have Vosper fin
stabilizers. Soviet ASW rocket launchers are behind doors in main-deck superstructure, abreast the mast. Six 103-mm flare RL rails on 120-mm mount. 9LV 200 t.v./
IR director added on mast, 1978.

GUIDED-MISSILE PATROL BOATS

♦ **1 (+7) PB 80 class** Bldr: Wärtsilä, Helsinki

D: 250 tons (300 fl) **S:** 32-33 kts **Dim:** 45.0 × 8.9 × 3.0
A: 2/SSM (I × 2)—1/57-mm Bofors Mk 1 AA—2/23-mm AA (II × 1)
Electron Equipt: Radar: . . .
M: 3 MTU 16V538 diesels; 3 CP props; 12,000 hp

GUIDED-MISSILE PATROL BOATS *(continued)*

REMARKS: Prototype ordered 5-10-78, launched 9-80, in service 6-81. Second through fourth ordered early 1981. Type of antiship missile to be employed uncertain. Has 9LV225 optronic fire control system, 2 Philax chaff RL. Aluminum hull.

♦ **4 Soviet Osa-II class**

11 TUIMA   12 TUISKU   14 TUULI   15 TYRSKY

D: 210 tons (240 fl)   **S:** 36 kts   **Dim:** 39.0 × 7.7 × 1.8
A: 4/SS-N-2 Styx—4/30-mm AA (II × 2)
Electron Equipt: Radars: 1/Square Tie, 1/Drum Tilt, 1/navigational
M: 3 M504 diesels; 3 props; 15,000 hp   **Range:** 450/34, 700/20
Man: 30 tot.

REMARKS: Transferred in 1975. Some Western electronic equipment has been added.

♦ **sea-sled hull type** Bldr: Reposaaren Konepaja, Pori

	Laid down	L	In serv.
16 ISKU	11-68	4-12-69	1970

Isku (16) 1979

D: 115 tons (140 fl)   **S:** 15 kts   **Dim:** 26.35 × 8.70 × 2.00
A: 4/SS-N-2A Styx (I × 4)—2/30-mm AA (II × 1)
Electron Equipt: Radar: 1/navigational, 1/Square Tie
M: 4 Soviet M50-series diesels; 4 props; 4,800 hp   **Man:** 25 tot.

REMARKS: Bargelike hull, designed for more powerful propulsion plant. Used primarily for training.

PATROL BOATS

♦ **1 prototype** Bldr: Fiskar's Turan, Veneveistamo SY/Laivateollisuus

D: . . . tons   **S:** . . . kts   **Dim:** 22.0 × 5.0 × . . .   **A:** . . .
M: diesels; waterjets; . . . hp

REMARKS: Glass-reinforced plastic prototype hull delivered 1-7-80 to Laivateollisuus for fitting out. This class is intended to replace at least seven of the Nuoli class during the 1980s.

♦ **13 Nuoli class** Bldr: Laivateollisuus, Turku (In serv. 1961-66)

	In serv.		In serv.
31 NUOLI 1	14-9-61	38 NUOLI 8	10-10-62
32 NUOLI 2	19-10-61	39 NUOLI 9	27-10-63
33 NUOLI 3	1-11-61	40 NUOLI 10	5-5-64
34 NUOLI 4	21-11-62	41 NUOLI 11	5-5-64
35 NUOLI 5	6-7-62	42 NUOLI 12	30-11-64
36 NUOLI 6	3-8-62	43 NUOLI 13	12-10-66
37 NUOLI 7	22-8-62		

D: 40 tons (64 fl)   **S:** 40 kts   **Dim:** 22.0 × 6.65 × 1.5
A: 1/40-mm AA—1/20-mm AA   **Electron Equipt:** Radar: Decca 707
M: 3 Soviet M50 diesels; 3,600 hp   **Man:** 15 tot.

REMARKS: Date from 1961-63. Six are to be modernized, the other seven discarded. Nuoli 10-13 have a lower superstructure.

♦ **3 Ruissalo class** Bldr: Laivateollisuus, Turku

	L	In serv.
53 RUISSALO	16-6-59	11-8-59
54 RAISIO	2-7-59	12-9-59
55 RÖYTTA	2-6-59	14-10-59

♦ **2 Rihtniemi class** Bldr: Rauma Repola, Rauma

51 RIHTNIEMI	1956	21-2-57
52 RYMATTLYA	1956	20-5-57

D: 110 tons (130 fl)   **S:** 18 kts   **Dim:** 34.0 × 6.0 × 1.8
A: 4/23-mm AA (II × 2)—2/RBU-1200 ASW RL (V × 2)—mines
M: 2 Mercedes-Benz diesels; 2 CP props; 2,500 hp   **Man:** 20 tot.

REMARKS: Former convertible minesweeper/gunboats, modernized 1977-80. 51 and 52 originally only 31 meters overall and are 5.7 meters in beam. All now have bow bulwarks.

MINE WARFARE SHIPS

♦ **1 minelayer/training ship** Bldr: Wärtsilä, Helsinki

	Laid down	L	In serv.
01 POHJANMAA	5-78	28-8-78	8-6-79

D: 1,100 tons (fl)   **S:** 20 kts   **Dim:** 78.3 × 11.6 × 3.0
A: 1/120-mm Bofors DP—2/40-mm AA (I × 2)—8/23-mm AA (II × 4)—2/RBU-1200 ASW RL (II × 2)—mines

Pohjanmaa (01) G. Gyssels, 1981

MINE WARFARE SHIPS *(continued)*

Pohjanmaa (01)   1980

    Electron Equipt: Radar: 1/navigational, 1/air search, 1/fire control, 1/9LV100
                     Sonar: 2 sets
    M: 2 Wärtsilä-Vasa 16V22 diesels; 2 CP prop; 5,800 hp
    Electric: 1,040 kva   **Range:** 3,500/17   **Man:** 80 crew plus 70 cadets

REMARKS: Training facilities fitted in portable containers mounted on the two internal mine rails, easily removable if the ship is required for combat. There is a helicopter pad aft. Bow thruster.

♦ **1 coastal minelayer** Bldr: Valmet Oy, Helsinki (L: 16-3-57)

KEIHASSALMI

    D: 290 tons (360 fl)   **S:** 15 kts   **Dim:** 56.0 × 7.7 × 2.0
    A: 4/30-mm AA (II × 2)—2/20-mm AA (I × 2)—100 mines
    Electron Equipt: Radar: 1/navigational, 1/Drum Tilt
    M: 2 Wärtsilä diesels; 2 props; 2,000 hp   **Man:** 60 tot.

REMARKS: Launched 16-3-57. Given Soviet guns 1972, Drum Tilt f.c. radar 1976.

♦ **6 Kuha-class inshore minesweepers** Bldr: Laivateollisuus, Turku

	In serv.		In serv.		
KUHA 21	28-6-74	KUHA 23	-75	KUHA 25	17-6-75
KUHA 22	-74	KUHA 24	7-3-75	KUHA 26	13-11-75

Kuha 22—now has twin 23-mm AA aft, 12.7-mm mg fwd   1974

    D: 90 tons (fl)   **S:** 12 kts   **Dim:** 26.6 × 6.9 × 2.0
    A: 2/23-mm AA (II × 1)—1/12.7-mm mg   **Man:** 2 officers, 12 men
    M: 2 Cummins NT-380M diesels; 2 outboard-drive props; 600 hp

REMARKS: Plastic hulls. Funds for eight additional were to be provided.

AMPHIBIOUS WARFARE SHIPS

♦ **3 Kampela-class utility landing craft** Bldr: Enso-Gutzeit, Savonlinna

KAMPELA 1 (In serv. 29-7-76)   KAMPELA 2 (In serv. 21-10-76)
KAMPELA 3 (In serv. 23-10-79)

    D: 90 tons (260 fl)   **S:** 9 kts   **Dim:** 32.5 × 8.0 × 1.5   **Man:** 10 tot.
    A: 2/20-mm AA (I × 2)—mines   **M:** 2 Scania diesels; 2 props; 460 hp

REMARKS: *Kampela* 3 built by Finnmekano, Teija.

♦ **6 Kala-class utility landing craft** Bldr: Rauma Repola, Rauma (In serv. 1956-59)

KALA 1—KALA 6

    D: 60 tons (200 fl)   **S:** 9 kts   **Dim:** 27.0 × 8.0 × 1.8   **Man:** 10 tot.
    A: 1/20-mm AA—34 mines   **M:** 2 Valmet diesels; 2 props; 360 hp

♦ **5 Kave-class landing craft** Bldr: Hollming, Rauma (In serv. 1956-60)

KAVE 1   KAVE 2   KAVE 3   KAVE 4   KAVE 6

    D: 27 tons (60 fl)   **S:** 9 kts   **Dim:** 18.0 × 5.0 × 1.3   **A:** 1/20-mm AA
    M: 2 Valmet diesels; 2 props; 360 hp   **Man:** 3 tot.

REMARKS: *Kave* 1 built by Haminen Konepaja Oy.

AUXILIARY SHIPS

♦ **1 missile patrol boat tender** Bldr: Wärtsilä, Helsinki

90 LOUHI (ex-*Sisu*) (L: 24-9-38)

Louhi (90)   1979

    D: 2,075 tons   **S:** 16 kts   **Dim:** 64.1 × 14.2 × 5.1   **A:** 4/37-mm AA (II × 2)
    M: 2 Atlas diesels, electric drive; 2 props; 4,000 hp   **Man:** 100 tot.

REMARKS: Launched 24-9-38. Former icebreaker, converted 1975 as tender to missile boats. Refitted 1979, received AA guns from Riga-class frigate.

AUXILIARY SHIPS *(continued)*

♦ **1 administrative headquarters tender**

KORSHOLM (ex-*Korsholm III*, ex-*Oland*) (In serv. 1931)

D: 650 tons **S:** 11 kts **Dim:** 48.0 × 8.5 × 2.9 **A:** 2/20-mm AA
M: Reciprocating steam; 1 prop; 865 hp

REMARKS: Former car ferry, bought 1967 for use as staff headquarters and small-craft tender.

♦ **1 cable ship** Bldr: Rauma Repola (L: 15-12-65)

PUTSAARI

D: 430 tons (fl) **S:** 10 kts **Dim:** 45.5 × 8.9 × 2.3
M: 1 Wärtsilä diesel; 1 prop; 450 hp **Man:** 20 tot.

♦ **1 salvage tender**

PELLINKI

D: 700 tons **S:** 12 kts **Dim:** . . . × . . . × . . . **M:** Diesels

REMARKS: Purchased 1978. Former rescue tug, has diving and fire-fighting facilities.

♦ **1 modified Valas-class diving tender** Bldr: Hallming SY, Rauma

. . . MERSU(In serv. 10-80)

D: 300 tons (fl) **S:** 12 kts **Dim:** 30.65 × 8.1 × 3.4
A: 2/23-mm AA (II × 1)—1/12.7-mm mg
M: 1 Wärtsilä Vasa 22 diesel; 1 prop; 1,450 hp
Man: 1 officer, 6 crew; 20 divers

REMARKS: Can also be used to transport 300 personnel. Appearance generally as the Valas class.

♦ **4 Valas-class general-service tenders** Bldr: Hollming Oy, Rauma (In serv. 1979-81)

220 VALAS 221 VAHAKARI 222 VAARLEHTI 223 VÄNÖ

Vahakari (221)   1980

D: 100 tons (275 fl) **S:** 12 kts **Dim:** 30.65 × 7.85 × 3.40
A: 2/23-mm AA (II × 1)—1/12.7-mm mg—20 mines
M: 1 Wärtsilä Vasa 22 diesel; 1 prop; 1,300 hp **Man:** 11 tot.

REMARKS: Ordered 1978. Can break .4-meter ice. Carry 30 tons of cargo or 150 passengers. Stern ramp for vehicle-loading or minelaying.

♦ **3 Pirttisaari-class general-service tenders** Bldr: U.S.A., 1943-44

PIRTTISAARI PYHTAA PURHA

D: 150 tons **S:** 8 kts **Dim:** 21.3 × 6.2 × 2.6 **A:** 1/20-mm AA
M: 1 Wärtsilä or Atlas diesel; 1 prop; 400 hp **Man:** 10 tot.

REMARKS: Former U.S. Army tugs used as miscellaneous transports. *Pyhtaa* belongs to the Coast Artillery.

♦ **1 Pukkio-class general-service tender** Bldr: Valmet, Turku

PANSIO (In serv. 25-5-47)

D: 162 tons **S:** 10 kts **Dim:** 28.5 × 6.0 × 2.7
A: 1/40-mm AA—1/20-mm AA—20 mines **M:** 1 Wärtsilä diesel; 1 prop; 300 hp
Man: 10 tot.

REMARKS: Sisters *Porkkala* and *Pukkio* discarded 1980. Used as tug, transport, minelayer, and patrol boat.

♦ **6 Hauki-class personnel transports** Bldr: 1-3: Linnan Telakka, Turku; 4-6: Valmet, Kolka (In serv. 1978-80)

331 HAUKI	333 HAVOURI	335 N. . .
332 HAKUNI	334 HANKONIEMI	336 N. . .

Hankoniemi (334)   1980

D: 46 tons (fl) **S:** 10 kts **Dim:** 14.4 × 4.6 × 2.2
M: 2 Valmet 611 CSM diesels; 1 prop; 280 hp **Man:** 2 tot.

AUXILIARY SHIPS (continued)

REMARKS: Cargo: 45 personnel or 6 tons supplies. Can break .2-meter ice. Operated for the Coast Artillery.

◆ 57 service launches, K, Y, L, YM, and H classes

D: 2 to 34 tons S: 7 to 10 kts

REMARKS: For local transport, primarily in support of Coast Artillery.

COAST GUARD

Operated by the Ministry of the Interior. All ships now have black hull with a red-white-red diagonal stripe, as on U.S. Coast Guard ships. Upperworks are white. AVIATION: Three Soviet Mi-8 helicopters were purchased 12-80 for search-and-rescue duties.

PATROL BOATS ("Outer Sea Patrol Ships")

◆ 1 improved Valpas class Bldr: Laivateollisuus, Turku

TURVA (In serv. 15-12-77)

D: 550 tons S: 16 kts Dim: 48.5 × 8.6 × 3.9 A: 1/20-mm AA
M: 2 Wärtsilä diesels; 1 prop; 2,000 hp

REMARKS: Ordered 24-6-75. An improved *Valpas*, similar in appearance.

◆ 1 Valpas class Bldr: Laivateollisuus, Turku

	Laid down	L	In serv.
VALPAS	20-5-70	22-12-70	21-7-71

Valpas   1974

D: 545 tons S: 15 kts Dim: 48.3 × 8.7 × 4.0 A: 1/20-mm AA
M: 1 Werkspoor TMABS-398 diesel; 1 CP prop; 2,000 hp Man: 22 tot.

REMARKS: Ice-strengthened, equipped with sonar.

◆ 1 Viima class Bldr: Laivateollisuus, Turku

	L	In serv.
VIIMA	20-7-64	12-10-64

D: 135 tons S: 23 kts Dim: 35.7 × 6.6 × 2.0 A: 1/20-mm AA
M: 3 Mercedes-Benz diesels; 3 props; 4,050 hp Man: 12 tot.

◆ 1 Silma class Bldr: Laivateollisuus, Turku

	Laid down	L	In serv.
SILM	30-8-62	23-3-63	19-8-63

D: 530 tons S: 15 kts Dim: 48.3 × 8.3 × 4.3 A: 1/20-mm AA
M: 1 Werkspoor diesel; 1 prop; 1,800 hp Man: 22 tot.

◆ 1 Uisko class Bldr: Valmet, Helsinki (In serv. 1959)

UISKO

Uisko

D: 370 tons S: 15 kts Dim: 43.4 × 7.3 × 3.83 A: 1/20-mm AA
M: 1 Werkspoor diesel; 1 prop; 1,800 hp Man: 20 tot.

◆ 1 (+6) new construction Bldr: Laivateollisuus, Turku

D: 50 tons S: 20 kts Dim: 26.8 × 5.2 × . . . A: . . .
M: MTU 8V396 TC88 diesels; 2 props; 2,000 hp Man: 8 tot.

REMARKS: Aluminum construction. Prototype ordered 17-5-80. To replace *Koskelo* class.

◆ 8 Koskelo class Bldr: Valmet, Helsinki (In serv. 1955-60)

KAAKKURI KIISLA KOSKELO KUIKKA KUOVI KURKI TAVI TELKKA

D: 75 tons (97 fl) S: 23 kts Dim: 29.42 × 5.02 × 1.5 A: 1/20-mm AA
M: Mercedes-Benz diesels; 2 props; 2,700 hp Man: 11 tot.

REMARKS: All but one (to be used as a replacement for the training ship *Eckero*) are to be discarded on completion of units of the new 50-ton class. All modernized and re-engined 1970-74 by Laivateollisuus, Turku.

SERVICE CRAFT

◆ 98 small craft, Series RV, NV, and PV

D: 1.1 to 20 tons S: Most, 9 to 13 kts Dim: 8 to 14 overall

REMARKS: The newest are RV 37 to RV 39, delivered 1978 by Hollming.

D: 20 tons S: 12 kts Dim: 14.3 × 3.5 × . . . M: 1 MTU diesel; 300 hp

FINLAND *(continued)*
SERVICE CRAFT *(continued)*

♦ **1 training ship** Bldr: Kone & Silta, Helsinki (In serv. 1903; rebuilt 1954)

ECKERO

> **D:** 55 tons **S:** 10 kts **Dim:** 40.7 × 7.2 × 4.4
> **M:** 1 Mercedes-Benz diesel; 1 prop; 225 hp

ICEBREAKERS (Under Board of Navigation)

♦ **2 Urho class** Bldr: Wärtsilä, Helsinki

URHO (In serv. 5-3-75)   SISU (In serv. 28-1-76)

Urho   Wärtsilä, 1975

> **D:** 7,960 tons (9,500 fl) **S:** 18 kts **Dim:** 104.6 × 23.8 × 8.3
> **M:** 5 SEMT-Pielstick 5,000-hp diesels, electric drive; 4 props; 22,000 hp

REMARKS: Sisters to Swedish *Atle* class. One helicopter. Two props forward, two aft.

♦ **3 Tarmo class** Bldr: Wärtsilä, Helsinki

TARMO   VARMA   APU

> **D:** 4,890 tons **S:** 17 kts **Dim:** 85.7 × 21.7 × 6.8
> **M:** 4 Sulzer diesels, electric drive; 4 props; 10,000 hp

REMARKS: In service 1963, 1968, and 1970, respectively. Two props forward, two aft.

♦ **3 Karhu class** Bldr: Wärtsilä, Helsinki

KARHU   MURTJALA   SAMPO

> **D:** 3,540 tons **S:** 16 kts **Dim:** 74.2 × 17.4 × 6.4
> **M:** Diesel-electric; 4 props (2 fwd), 7,500 hp

REMARKS: In service 1958, 1959, and 1960, respectively. Sister *Hansa* is owned by West Germany (in serv. 25-11-66), has a Finnish crew and summers in Finnish waters.

♦ **1 Voima class** Bldr: Wärtsilä, Helsinki (In serv. 1954)

VOIMA

Voima—as modernized   1979

> **D:** 4,415 tons **S:** 16.5 kts **Dim:** 83.6 × 19.4 × 6.8
> **M:** 6 Wärtsilä Vasa 16V22 diesels (17,460 hp), electric drive; 4 props; 14,000 hp

REMARKS: Reconstructed and re-engined 1978-79 by Wärtsilä; expected to serve until 1994.

FRANCE

French Republic

For the first time in its history, the Navy is among the most important components in the military might of France and its contribution will become more significant every day.—GENERAL CHARLES DE GAULLE (1965)

PERSONNEL (1981): 67,923 on active duty, including 4,381 officers, 29,306 chief petty officers and petty officers, and 34,071 other enlisted personnel. These figures include 18,000 draftees and career female personnel. The majority of the draftees are aboard the ships of the fleet.

MERCHANT MARINE (1980): 1,241 ships—11,924,557 grt (tankers: 100 ships—7,777,481 grt)

WARSHIPS IN SERVICE OR UNDER CONSTRUCTION AS OF 1 JANUARY 1982

	L	Tons	Main armament
◆ 3 aircraft carriers			
2 CLEMENCEAU (fixed-wing)	1957-60	22,000	8/100-mm DP, 40 aircraft
1 JEANNE D'ARC (helicopter)	1961	10,000	4/100-mm DP, 6/MM 38 Exocet, 8 heavy helicopters
◆ 27 (+6) submarines			
0 (+2) L'INFLEXIBLE (nuclear)	. . .	8,000	16 missiles, 4 TT
5 LE REDOUTABLE (nuclear)	1967-77	8,000	16 missiles, 4 TT
1 GYMNOTE	1964	3,000	2 missiles
1 (+4) RUBIS (nuclear)	1979-. . .	2,265	4 TT
4 AGOSTA	1974-76	1,200	4 TT
9 DAPHNÉ	1959-67	700	12 TT
1 ARÉTHUSE	1957	400	4 TT
6 NARVAL	1954-58	1,320	6 TT
◆ 1 guided-missile cruiser			
1 COLBERT	1956	8,500	1 Masurca, 2/100-mm DP, 12/57-mm AA
◆ 20 (+6) destroyers			
0 (+3) C 70 AA	. . .	4,000	Mk 13 launcher, 8/MM 40, 2/100-mm DP, 2 TT
3 (+3) GEORGES LEYGUES	1975-	3,800	1/100-mm DP, 4/MM 38, 2 TT 2 WG 13 Lynx helicopters
3 TOURVILLE	1972-74	4,800	1 Malafon, 6/MM 38, 1 Crotale, 2/100-mm DP, 2 TT, 2 WG 13 Lynx helicopters
2 SUFFREN	1965-66	5,090	1 Masurca, 2/100-mm DP, 1 Malafon, 4/MM 38
1 ACONIT	1970	3,500	2/100-mm DP, 1 Malafon, ASW mortar, 2 TT
1 LA GALISSONNIÈRE	1960	2,750	2/100-mm DP, 1 Malafon, 1 helicopter
1 DUPERRÉ	1956	2,750	1/100-mm DP, 4/MM 38
5 D'ESTRÉES	1954	2,750	2/100-mm DP, 1 Malafon, ASW weapons
4 KERSAINT	1953-54	2,750	1 SM-1MR, 6/57-mm AA, 1 ASW RL. 6 TT
◆ 20 (+6) frigates			
11 (+6) D'ESTIENNE D'ORVES	1973-80	1,100	1/100-mm DP, 2/MM 38, 1 ASW rocket launcher, 4 TT
1 BALNY	1962	1,750	2/100-mm DP, 1 ASW mortar, 6 TT
8 COMMANDANT RIVIÈRE	1958-63	1,750	4/MM 38, 2/100-mm DP, 1 ASW mortar, 6 TT

◆ 21 (+17) patrol boats and craft			
0 (+6) SUPER PATRA	. . .	320	1/40-mm AA
4 TRIDENT	1976	115	1/40-mm, 6/SS 12 SSM
1 LA COMBATTANTE	1963	180	2/40-mm AA, 4/SS 12 SSM
4 LA LORIENTAISE	1952-53	370	1/40-mm AA
1 MERCURE	1957	365	2/20-mm AA
4 SIRIUS	1954-57	400	1/40-mm AA, 1 or 2/20-mm
6 "HAM"	1954-55	140	1/20-mm AA
0 (+2) SP 2000	. . .	2,040	1/40-mm AA, 2/20-mm AA
0 (+1) trawler type	. . .	3,000	1/40-mm AA
0 (+4) SPN 900	. . .	900	. . .
0 (+4) SP 300	. . .	300	1/20-mm AA
1 STERNE	1979	270	2 mg
◆ 22 (+13) minehunters and minesweepers			
2 (+13) TRIPARTITE (mine-hunters)	1979-. . .	500	1/20-mmAA
5 CIRCÉ (minehunters)	1970-72	460	1/20-mm AA
10 U.S. MSO (5 minehunters)	1953-56	700	1/40-mm AA
5 SIRIUS	1955-56	400	1 or 2/20-mm AA
◆ 19 (+2) amphibious warfare ships			
2 OURAGAN	1963-67	5,800	4/40-mm AA
5 ARGENS	1958-60	1,750	3/40-mm AA
2 (+2) CHAMPLAIN	1973-. . .	750	2/40-mm AA
9 EDIC	1958-69	250	2/20-mm AA

FORCE COMPOSITION OF THE FRENCH NAVY IN 2000

As programmed by Defense Councils held in 1978 and 1980, the wartime and peacetime force compositions of the *Marine Nationale* have been defined. In the "Year 2000," the fleet will consist of:

I—combat and general-purpose force:

—2 nuclear-powered aircraft carriers carrying fixed-wing aircraft
—18 ASW "corvettes" (destroyers)
—9 antiaircraft "corvettes"
—18 "avisos" (ASW escorts)
—10 patrol boats

II—mine countermeasures force:

—40 minehunters and minesweepers

III—transport and logistic support force:

—3 landing-craft transports
—6 light transports
—6 logistic-support ships
—2 multi-purpose repair ships
—3 oceangoing tugs
—4 replenishment oilers

IV—general-purpose submarine force:

—10 nuclear-powered attack submarines
—4 conventionally powered attack submarines

V—seaborne aviation force:

—60 to 70 conventional aircraft
—18 heavy helicopters
—56 light helicopters

VI—maritime patrol aviation force:

—40 to 50 aircraft

VII—public service force:

—11 miscellaneous ships with specialized capabilities

WEAPONS AND SYSTEMS

A. MISSILES

♦ strategic ballistic

M 20

This missile, which has replaced the M 2, has two stages, is aerodynamically unstable and has the following characteristics:

Total height	10.40 m	Launch	compressed air
Height 1st stage	5.20 m	Launch weight	20 tons
Height 2nd stage	2.60 m	Max. range	3,000 km
Diameter	1.50 m		

Solid propulsion system:

fuel mass	10 tons, 1st stage
	6 tons, 2nd stage
thrust	45 tons, 1st stage
	32 tons, 2nd stage
burn duration	50 sec., 1st stage
	52 sec., 2nd stage

The thermonuclear warhead is in the megaton range and has been especially "hardened" to facilitate penetration and countering nuclear anti-missile defenses.

M 4

This missile will enter service in 1985 aboard *L'Inflexible* and will have three stages. Characteristics include:

Total height	11.05 m	Launch	powder charge
Diameter	1.93 m	Launch weight	around 36 tons
		Max. range	4,000 km
		Payload	6 warheads of around 150 KT, of great precision and with improved penetration over the already excellent M 20

Solid propulsion system:

fuel mass	20 tons, 1st stage; 8 tons, 2nd stage; 1.5 tons, 3rd stage
thrust	70 tons, 1st stage; 30 tons, 2nd stage; 7 tons, 3rd stage
burn duration	65 sec., 1st stage; 75 sec., 2nd stage; 45 sec., 3rd stage

The launch interval will be shorter between missiles than with the M 20 and will be capable of being carried out at greater depths. It will commence deployment in 1985 and will be carried by ballistic-missile submarines of the *L'Inflexible* class as completed and be backfitted into all earlier submarines except *Le Redoutable*. To effect installation, it will not be necessary to replace the existing missile tubes.

♦ surface-to-air

Masurca

A medium-range missile (30 nautical-mile range, intercept between 100 ft and 75,000 ft) launched by a solid-propellant booster, which in a few seconds brings it to a speed close to Mach 3; a slower-burning soild propellant maintains this speed throughout the flight. The missile and booster together are 8.6 m long and weigh 2,098 kg. Other characteristics are:

	Missile	Booster
Length	5.38 m	3.32 m
Diameter	0.406 m	0.57 m
Span of fins	—	1.5 m
Weight	950.0 kg	1,148.0 kg
Warhead	100.0 kg	—

Masurca launcher with missiles

MISSILES (continued)

The Mod 2 beam-riding missile is no longer used. Mod 3, a semiactive homing missile, is the only one now in service. It follows a trajectory determined by proportional navigation, keeping its antenna pointed at the target, which is illuminated by the launching ship's radar transmitter.

Masurca, which is installed in the *Suffren*-class guided-missile destroyers and in the guided-missile cruiser *Colbert*, consists of (1) a target-designator and weapon-assignment console, including a computer, which uses the shipboard search radar and the Senit automatic tactical data system, and (2) two guidance systems, each with:

DRBR 51 tracking radar

A director carrying the rear-reference beam and illumination beam for the control system

An illumination beam

A twin launcher

Storage and maintenance facilities, including two horizontal ready-service drums containing 18 missiles in addition to reserve missiles in the magazines

IFF and control equipment

Mascura is scheduled to be modernized between 1981 and 1985. This updating is intended to keep the system up to date to the end of its expected service life (1995).

Standard SM-1 MR

A one-stage missile with solid fuel. Characteristics:

Length: 4.60 m

Diameter: .41 m

Weight: 590 kg

Guidance: semiactive homing, proximity fuze

Range: 50,000 m, max.

Interception altitude: 60 ft to 80,000 ft

The complete system consists of, in addition to the missile:

1 single Mk 13 launcher

1 vertical stowage-loader containing 40 missiles

Various computers

SPS 39B height-finding radar

2 SPG 51C tracking radars

SM-1 MR is mounted on T-47-type destroyers modified for Tartar and will be installed in the C-70 AAW-type destroyers, which will have DRBJ 11 height-finding radar. It has replaced the earlier Tartar ITR and SM-1A in French naval service.

Crotale

A French Air Force missile adapted for naval use. Electronics are by Thomson-CSF and the missile by Matra. Characteristics:

Length: 2.930 m

Diameter: 0.156 m

Span: cruciform (0.54 m with fins extended), antipitching canards forward

Weight: 85.1 kg

Range: 8,000 m

Interception altitudes: 150 ft to 12,000 ft

Warhead: 14 kg

Guidance: beam-riding, then detonation by infrared fuze incorporated in the missile

Launcher: octuple

Crotale is installed on the F 67 and C 70 types of destroyers. It will be used with DRBV 51C radar and will have a special extractor and a Thomson tracking radar in the KU band. Eighteen reload missiles are carried in the magazine. The prototype was installed in the test ship *Ile d'Oléron* in May 1977, while the first operational installation was aboard the *Georges Leygues* in 1978.

Mk 13 launcher—with Standard SM-1MR missile

Crotale launcher—on board the **Georges Leygues** Thomson-CSF, 1979

MISSILES (continued)

SATCP

A contract has been given to Matra to develop a new short-range lightweight surface-to-air missile, the SATCP (*Surface-Air, á Trés Courte Portie*). The system will have an automatic director and IR homing, with proximity and impact fuzing.

Length: 1.80 m   Warhead: 3 kg
Diameter: 0.90 m   Range: under 500 to around 5,000 m
Weight: 17 kg

The missiles will be installed in a multiple launcher. The system should be operational about 1986, in time for installation in the antiaircraft destroyers of the C 70 AAW type and other units of the fleet.

♦ Surface-to-surface

MM 38 Exocet   Manufacturer: S.N.I.A.S.

A homing missile with solid-fuel propulsion. Characteristics:
Weight: 700 kg, approx (explosive charge: more than 150 kg)
Speed: Mach 1
Range: 37 km, min
Length: 5.20 m
Diameter: 0.35 m
Wingspan: 1.00 m
Cylindrical body with a pointed nose, cruciform wings with arrow shape.
The fire-control solution requires a fix on the target provided by the surface radar of the firing ship and uses the necessary equipment for launching the missile and determining the correct range and height bearing of the target.

The missile is launched at a slight elevation (about 15°). After the boost phase, it reaches its flight altitude and is stabilized at between 3 and 15 meters. Altitude is maintained by a radar altimeter.

During the first part of the flight, the missile is automatically guided by an inertial system that has received the azimuth of the target. When within a certain distance

MM 38 launchers—on board the **Tourville**   1975

from the target, an automatic homing radar begins to seek the target, picks it up and directs the missile. Great effort has been made to protect the missile from counter-measures during this phase.

Detonation takes place upon impact or by proximity fuze, according to interception conditions, size of the target ship, and the condition of the sea.

As of 10-81, the MM 38 was mounted on board the *Jeanne d'Arc*, the *Colbert*, the three *Tourville* class, the *Duperré*, eight *Commandant Rivière* class, the *Suffren* and *Duquesne*, A-69-type corvettes, and is planned for installation in the C 70 AA and ASW frigates.

SM 39 Exocet

A submarine torpedo-tube-launched version of the Exocet concept, in trials status in 1981 aboard the *Narval*-class submarine *Requin*.

MM 40 Exocet

An offshoot of the MM 38 and the AM 39 and also built by SNIAS, the MM 40 is an over-the-horizon missile whose range will be adapted to radar performance, but it will be able to use fire-control data relayed by an outside source. Instead of the usual metal launcher, it has a fiberglass, cylindrical one which, because it is lighter and has less fittings, increases firepower by allowing more missiles to be carried.

It has been proposed to equip the future C 70 AA-type guided-missile destroyers with eight launchers each (four per side) for MM 40, and the *Montcalm* will be the first ship to have it. In older ships with box launchers for MM 38 Exocet missiles, the old launchers will be retained, with one MM 40 in each box.

Length: 5.80 m   Weight: 850 kg
Diameter: 0.35 m   Speed: Mach .95
Wingspan: 1.135 m   Range: 65 km

SS 12 M

Wire-guided, solid-fueled missile. Characteristics:
Length: 1.870 m   Weight: 75 kg (upon firing)
Diameter: 0.210 m   Warhead: 30 kg (about)
Wingspan: 0.650   Range: 5,500 m
Mounted only on the missile patrol boat *La Combattante* and on the *Trident* class.

B. AVIATION MISSILES

♦ Air-to-ground

ANS

A new project, succeeding the ASMP project (*Air-Surface á Moyenne Portie*) and intended for use by Super Étendard carrier-based and Tornado land-based aircraft. A surface-to-surface version is projected. Being developed jointly by Aerospatiale and Messerschmidt-Bölkow-Blohm for service introduction in the late 1980s. Intended to have a speed of over Mach 2.

AM 39   Manufacturer: S.N.I.A.S.

This is the air-to-sea version of the MM 38. After being detached by gravity and a retro-firing booster motor, it acquires a trajectory similar to that of the MM 38, whereafter it has the same flight characteristics as the MM 38.
Length: 4.633 m
Diameter: 0.348 m
Wingspan: 1.004 m
Weight: 65 kg (before launching)
Range: 50-70 km, according to altitude and speed at launch
Radar: Active home-seeking head (EMD)

AVIATION MISSILES (continued)

AM 39 is known as a "fire and forget" missile because it permits an aircraft that has fired to renew its attack or to seek a new target. It may be used with the Atlantic patrol aircraft (and the Atlantic's proposed successor) and the Super Étendard aircraft. It is equally suitable for use by such medium-weight helicopters as the Super Frélon.

AS 11   Builder: S.N.I.A.S.
A wire-guided system with optical alignment on the target. Used for training by CM 175 aircraft.

Length: 1.210 m	Wingspan: 0.50 m
Diameter: 0.164 m	Weight: 29.900 kg

AS 12   Builder: S.N.I.A.S.
A wire-guided system with optical alignment on the target. Used by the BR 1150 Atlantic and the BR 1050 Alizé aircraft.

Length: 1.870 m
Diameter: 0.210 m
Wingspan: 0.650 m
Weight: 75 kg
Range: Maximum 7,500 to 8,000 m; minimum 1,500 m

AS 15   Builder: S.N.I.A.S.

Length: 2.16 m	Range: 15 km
Weight: 96 kg	

For use by light helicopters (Dauphine, Lynx).

AS 20   Builder: S.N.I.A.S.

Length: 2.60 m	Weight: 140 kg
Diameter: 0.25 m	Guidance: radio command
Wingspan: 0.80 m	Range: 4,000 m to 8,000 m

Used in firing training of the AS 30 on the Étendard IV M.

AS 30   Builder: S.N.I.A.S.
System developed for firing from a maneuvering aircraft at middle, low, or very low altitude. Used by the Étendard IV M and the Super Étendard.

Length: 3.785 m	Wingspan: 1.000 m
Diameter: 0.342 m	Total weight: 528 kg

Range: maximum 9 to 12,000 m; minimum 1,500 m
Guidance: radio command

AS 37 Martel   Builders: Matra and Hawker Siddeley Dynamics
Two types, television and anti-radar. Only the latter is used in the French Navy.

Length: 4.122 m	Total weight: 531 m
Diameter: 0.40 m	Range: over 20,000 m
Wingspan: 1.192 m	

Passive homing head (EMD); the missile homes on the radar emissions of the enemy vessel. Immediately after being fired, the missile is on its own, permitting the aircraft to depart or evade. Used with BR 1150 Atlantic aircraft.

◆ Air-to-air

R 530   Builder: Matra

There are two versions of this missile: infrared (IR) and radar-homing (EMD).
Length: IR type: 3.198 m; EMD type: 3.284 m
Diameter: 0.263 m
Wingspan: 1.103 m

Weight: IR type: 193.5 kg, EMD type: 192 kg
Range: maximum 10,000 m: minimum 5,000 m
Guidance: Semi-passive-homing (MD) or infrared-homing

Sidewinder

The French Navy uses this air-to-air American missile (see U.S.A. section).

Magic   Builder: Matra

Length: 2.900 m	Weight: 89 kg
Diameter: 0.157 m	Range: 300/8,000 m
Wingspan: 0.660 m	Guidance: Infrared-homing

C. GUNS

100-mm, Models 1953 and 1968

Single-barrel automatic, for use against aircraft, surface vessels, or land targets. Model 1968 is a lighter version of Model 1953. The ammunition is the same. Characteristics of Model 1968:
Weight of mount: 22 tons
Length of barrel: 55 calibers
Range at 40° elevation: 17,000 m
Maximum effective range for surface fire: 15,000 m
Maximum effective range for antiaircraft fire: 8,000 m
Maximum rate of fire: 60 rounds/minute
Arc of elevation: −15° to +80°
Maximum speed: training, 40°/sec, elevation, 25°/sec

Model 1953 uses an analog fire-control system with electro-mechanical and electronic equipment for the fire-control solution. The director can be operated in optical and radar modes.

Model 1968 uses a digital fire-control system, with central units, and memory disks or magnetic tape for data storage. Light radar gun director. Optical direction equipment can be added.

57-mm Model 1951

Twin-barrel automatic:
Length of barrel: 60 calibers
Muzzle velocity: 865 m/sec
Maximum range: 13,000 m
Effective antiaircraft range: 5,000 m
Maximum rate of fire: 60 rounds/min per barrel
Arc of elevation: −8° to 90°
Maximum rate of fire: 60 rounds per minute, per barrel

30-mm

Single-barrel automatic:
Length: 2.440 m
Weight: 4 tons
Muzzle velocity: 1,000 m/sec
Maximum effective range: 2,800 m
Maximum rate of fire: 650 rounds per minute

Also in service are typical **40-mm** guns based on Bofors designs and **20-mm** guns of Oerlikon design.

A new 20-mm mounting has been designed by DCAN for the GIAT CN-MIT-20F2 gun, which has a 650-720 rd/min. firing rate. Two 150-round magazines are carried on the mount.

D. ANTISUBMARINE WEAPONS

Malafon

A glider that carries L-4 torpedoes and is launched with the assistance of a double booster. It is stabilized by automatic pilot and guided by radio command.

Glider: speed, 230 m/sec; range, 12,000 m
Missile: length, 6.15 m; diameter, 0.65 m; span, 3.30 m; weight, including torpedo, 1,500 kg

The Malafon, built by Latécoère in partnership with St. Trôpez, is installed in the two *Suffren*-class destroyers, *La Galissonnière*, the Type T 47 ASW conversions, the *Aconit*, and the *Tourville*-class destroyers.

375-mm Rocket Launchers, Models 1964 or 1972

Sextuple mount. Automatic loading in vertical position. Firing rate, 1 rocket/second. Range: 1,600 m. Time or proximity fuze. Based on Bofors quadruple mounting. Normally has six illumination-flare rocket rails mounted also.

305-mm Mortar

Quadruple mount; automatic loading. ASW projectile weight: 230 kg; range: 400 to 3,000 m. Can also fire a 100-kg projectile against land targets; range: 6,000 m. Normally has four illumination-flare rocket rails mounted on the face of the rotating housing.

E. TORPEDOES

◆ For surface ships

	Weight in kg	Diameter in mm	Speed in kts
L 3	900	550	25
L 4	500	533	30
L 5, mod 1 and mod 4	1,000	533	35

◆ For submarines

Z 13	1,700	550	30
E 12	1,600	550	25
E 14	900	550	25
L 5, mod 3	1,300	533	35
F 17	1,300	533	35

◆ For aircraft

In addition to the U.S. torpedoes, **Mk 44** and **Mk 46,** French naval aircraft use the **L 4** torpedo.

F. SONARS

◆ For surface ships

	Type	Frequency	Average range
DUBA 1	Hull	HF	2,500 m
DUBA 3	Hull	HF	3,000 m
DUBV 24	Hull	LF	6,000 m
DUBV 23	Bow	LF	*see Remarks*
DUBV 43	Towed	LF	*see Remarks*
DUBA 25	Hull	MF	*see Remarks*
DUBA 26	Hull	MF	*see Remarks*
DUBM 20	Hull—on *Circé*-class minehunters		

Automatic-loading 305-mm ASW and bombardment mortar—with flare rails

Automatic-loading, six-barreled, 325-mm ASW rocket launcher—with six flare rails

DUBM 21	Hull—on new Tripartite and modernized MSO minehunters
DUBM 41	Towed—on modernized MSO
ETBF	a towed passive system in development

REMARKS: **DUBV 23** and **DUBV 43** are used simultaneously and, under normal sound-propagation conditions, achieve ranges of 8,000 and 10,000 meters. In certain bathymetric conditions, the range is 20,000 meters. **DUBA 25** is a new sonar designed for the A 69 class. **DUBA 26** is under development.

SONARS *(continued)*

♦ For submarines

Listening devices, active-passive sonars, and underwater telephone equipment, including:
DUUA 1 On the *Narval* and unmodernized *Daphne* classes, and *Argonaute*.
DUUA 2 On modernized *Daphne*, *Agosta*, and *Rubis* classes (DUUA 2B in latter).
DSUV 2 Hydrophone array on *Argonaute*, *Narval*, and *Agosta* classes.
DSUV 22 Hydrophone array on the *Rubis* class.
DUUV 23 Panoramic passive array on the ballistic-missile submarines.
DSUX 21 Multifunction system for *L'Inflexible* and earlier missile submarines.
DUUX 2 Underwater telephone; widely used.

♦ For helicopters

	Frequency	Remark
AQS-13	MF	U.S. sonar
DUAV 1	HF	
DUAV 4	HF	In the WG 13 Lynx

G. COMBAT INFORMATION SYSTEMS

SENIT

This system serves four principal purposes:
It establishes the combat situation from the manual collection of information derived from detection equipment on board and from the automatic or manual collection of information from external sources.
It disseminates the above data to the ship and to other vessels by automatic means (Links 11 and 14).
It assists in decision making.
It transmits to the target-designation console all the information it requires.
The several versions of the SENIT are similar in general concept but differ in construction and programming in order to ensure fulfillment of the various missions assigned to each type of ship.
SENIT 1: A system with one or two computers. Installed in the *Suffren*, the *Duquesne*, and the *Colbert*.
SENIT 2: A single-computer system. Installed in the T 47 type *Kersaint*-class destroyers, as well as in the *Duperré*, which uses a version with two computers.
SENIT 3: A central system consisting of two computers and two memory banks, the entire group designed for the control of various weapons (guns, Malafon ASW system, torpedoes). Installed in the *Aconit*, and the three *Tourville*-class ships.
The above three systems are based on equipment of U.S. origin, some built in France under license.
SENIT 4: A system conceived by the French Navy's programming center and designed around the French Iris N 55 computer. Fitted in the *Georges Leygues* class.
SENIT 5: Also designed by the French Navy's programming center, this system will be fitted on small ships. It uses the French M 15 minicomputer.
SENIT 6: Another system designed by the French Navy's programming center. It will equip the future C 70 AAW version of the *Georges Leygues* class. It combines a number of M 15 computers and a new generation of display devices particularly adapted for command purposes.

H. RADARS

♦ Air search

DRBV 15: Sea Tiger. Commercial design, with pulse-compression

DRBV 20 A: Metric
DRBV 20 C: Metric, long-range. Mounted on aircraft carriers and *Colbert*.
DRBV 22 A: Mounted in T 47 ASW version destroyers, frigates, *Duperré*, *Aconit*, and *La Galissonnière*. L-band (23-cm).
DRBV 22 C: *Ile d'Oléron*
DRBV 22 D: *Jeanne d'Arc*, *Henri Poincaré*
DRBV 23 C: Mounted in *Colbert*
DRBV 26: Jupiter. Mounted in the *Tourville*, *Georges Leygues*, *Rance* and aboard AA destroyers. 150-mm range.
DRBV 13: Doppler-pulse radar, three-dimensional; in the *Aconit*

♦ Height-finding/three-dimensional

DRBI 10: Mounted in aircraft carriers, *Colbert*, *Jeanne d'Arc*, *Ile d'Oléron*. "Nodding"-type antenna with "Robinson" feed.
DRBI 23: Mounted in the *Duquesne* and *Suffren*; monopulse.
SPS-39B: American radar. Mounted on Standard-equipped T 47-class destroyers.
DRBJ 11: Pulse-coded radar for the C 70 AAW-class guided-missile destroyers.

♦ Surface and low-altitude air search

DRBV 50: Mounted on aircraft carriers, *Jeanne d'Arc*, T 47 ASW-class destroyers, the *Rhin*, *Ile d'Oléron*, *Colbert*, and *La Galissonnière*. 16 nm range on aircraft.
DRBV 51: Mounted on A 69 class and the *Duperré*.
DRBV 51B: Mounted on the *Georges Leygues* class.
DRBV 51C: Mounted on the *Tourville* class. Commercial version: Triton II.

♦ Navigational

Decca RM 416
DRBN 31: Mounted on some minesweepers and coastal patrol craft.
DRBV 31: Mounted on the Standard-equipped T 47-class destroyers, and on some frigates. DRBN 32, French Navy designator for Decca 1226.

♦ Fire-control

DRBC 31: For the 100-mm of the *Duperré*. The *Foch* had DRBC 31C and the *Clemenceau* DRBC 31D
DRBC 32A: For 100-mm guns on ASW-modified T 47-class destroyers, some frigates, the *Jeanne d'Arc*, and the *Clemenceau*
DRBC 32B: For 100-mm guns on the *Aconit*
DRBC 32C: Mounted on the *Colbert*, the *Duperré*, and the *Foch*
DRBC 32D: Mounted on the *Tourville* class and the *Georges Leygues* class
DRBC 32E: Mounted on the A 69-class corvettes. Commercial name: Castor. X-band.
SPG 51C: U.S. tracking radar used with the Standard system on the T 47-type AAW destroyers
DRBR 51: Tracking radar for the Masurca on the *Colbert*, *Suffren*, and *Duquesne*. C-band (5-cm) tracker, 7-cm command signal

I. COUNTERMEASURES

The French Navy uses the eight-barreled Syllex chaff launcher (a version of the British Knebworth/Corvus), which will eventually be replaced by the Sagaie, a better system. Smaller ships will receive the Dagaie system. Both Sagaie and Dagaie are fired automatically by the electronic intercept system.

AIRCRAFT CARRIERS

NOTE: The "model" for the French Navy of the year 2000 proposes the construction of two aircraft carriers to carry conventional, fixed-wing aircraft. The ships are to be nuclear-powered. The configuration will be along the lines of the *Clemenceau* class, and the maximum speed will be about 28 knots. There will be an angled deck, two elevators, and two steam catapults. Defensive armament has not yet been determined. The air group will comprise 35 to 40 machines (combat aircraft and a number of ASW helicopters), with stores to permit alternative missions. The first ship is to be laid down at the Brest Naval Arsenal for entry into service in 1990; it will replace the *Clemenceau*. Displacement will be on the order of 32-35,000 tons full load.

♦ **2 Clemenceau class**

	Budget	Bldr	Laid down	L	In serv.
R 98 CLEMENCEAU	1953	Brest Arsenal	11-55	21-12-57	22-11-61
R 99 FOCH	1955	Ch. Atlantique	2-57	28-7-60	15-7-63

D: 22,000 tons (27,307 mean) R 98: 32,780(fl) R 99: 32,185(fl)
S: 32 kts (33 on trials)   **Range** 4,800/24, 7,500/18
Dim: 265.0 (238.0 pp) × 31.72 beam × 51.2 flight deck × 7.5 light draft × 8.5 fl
A: 8/100-mm DP Model 1953 (I × 8)—40 aircraft (*see* Remarks)
Electron Equipt: Radar: 1/DRBV 20C, 1/DRBV 23B, 2/DRBI 10, 1/DRBV 50, 1/DRBC 31, 1/Decca 1226, 1/NRBA (landing aid), 2/DRBC 31C (R 99) or D (R 98), 2/DRBC 32A (R 98) or C (R 99)
Sonar: 1/SQS 505—TACAN: 1/URN-6

M: 2 sets Parsons GT; 2 props; 126,000 hp   **Electric:** 14,000 kw
Boilers: 6; 45 kg/cm², 450°C   **Fuel:** 3,720 tons
Armor: Reinforced flight deck, armored bulkheads in engine room and magazines, reinforced-steel bridge superstructure
Man: Peacetime: As aircraft carriers: 64 officers, 476 petty officers, 798 other enlisted. Total: 1,338 men
As helicopter carriers: 45 officers, 392 petty officers, 547 other enlisted. Total: 984 men.

REMARKS: Flight deck 257 m in length; deck angled at 8°, 165.5 × 29.5; deck forward of the angled deck: 93 × 28; width of the deck abreast the island: 35. Hangar dimensions, 180 × 22 to 24 × 7 (height). Two elevators 16 m long, 11 m in width, one forward on the main flight deck, one slightly abaft the island, able to raise a 15-ton aircraft 8.50 m in 9 seconds. Two 50-meter Mitchell-Brown type BS5 steam catapults, able to launch 15/20-ton aircraft at 110 knots, one forward, another on the angled deck. Optical-mirror landing equipment of French manufacture.

The propulsion machinery was built by the Chantiers de l'Atlantique. Living spaces are air-conditioned. Medium-sized island with three bridges: flag, navigation, aviation. Communication systems, especially with fighter aircraft, are a significant aspect of the ships' capabilities.

The *Foch*, built in a special dry dock at St. Nazaire, was towed to Brest for the installation of her armament.

Aviation fuel: 1,800 m³ of jet fuel and 109 m³ of aviation gasoline carried by the *Foch*; 1,200 m³ of jet fuel and 400 m³ of aviation gasoline by the *Clemenceau*.

Between September 1977 and November 1978, the *Clemenceau* underwent a significant refit in the Toulon dockyard. The work consisted of a general overhaul of her

Clemenceau (R 98)

1979

AIRCRAFT CARRIERS (continued)

Clemenceau (R 98)—island detail   G. Gyssels, 1981

Foch (R 99)—prior to refit   G. Gyssels, 1980

Clemenceau (R 98)   G. Gyssels, 1981

installations and her living spaces, taking into account the new system of naval ranks, modernization of her flight deck, reinforcement of her arresting gear, strengthening of her catapults, and engine overhaul, and the addition of two supplementary boilers. Her electronic systems were modernized, and she was given the SENIT 2 that was removed from the inactivated destroyer *Jaurreguiberry*. On the *Clemenceau*, this system has three main functions: establishment of a situation based on information from external sources (land-based radars, aircraft, ships); dissemination of those data to the ship and to other ships; and assistance in decision making. The ship has been equipped with a closed-circuit television system that displays needed information in interested parts of the ship: flight-deck control, the combat operations center, the ready rooms, the air operations office. To operate the Super Étendard, the *Clemenceau* has been fitted with a central inertial guidance system that transfers information to the inertial guidance system in each plane. Her magazines have been modified to carry AN-52 tactical nuclear weapons. The *Foch* underwent a similar overhaul 15-7-

80 to 15-8-81, receiving SENIT 2 from the inactivated destroyer *Tartu*. As aircraft carriers, the *Clemenceau* class carry an air group that consists of 16 Super Étendard, 3 Étendard IV P, 10 F-8E Corsair, 7 Alizé, and 2 Alouette-III; as helicopter carriers, they can carry 30 to 40 helicopters, depending on their size.

◆ **1 helicopter-carrier and cadet training ship**

	Budget	Bldr	Laid down	L	In serv.
R 97 JEANNE D'ARC (ex-*La Résolue*)	1957	Brest Ars.	7-7-60	30-9-61	30-6-64

D: 10,000 tons (12,365 fl)   **S:** 26.5 kts (cruising)
Dim: 182.0 (172.0 wl) × 24.0 × 22.0 (wl) × 6.6 (7.3 aft)
A: 6/MM 38 Exocet—4/100-mm DP Model 1953 (I × 4)—8 helicopters (*see* Remarks)

AIRCRAFT CARRIERS (continued)

Jeanne d'Arc (R 97)   CECLANT/PREMAR II, 1979

Jeanne d'Arc (R 97)   CECLANT/PREMAR II, 1979

Electron Equipt: Radars: 1/DRBV 22D, 1/DRBV 50, 1/DRBN 32, 1/DRBI 10,
        3/DRBC 32A
        Sonars: SQS-503—2 Syllex countermeasures RL
        TACAN: URN-6
M: 2 sets Rateau-Bretagne GT; 2 props; 40,000 hp   **Electric:** 4,400 kw
Boilers: 4 asymmetric, multitube, 45 kg/cm²—superheat 450°C
Fuel: 1,360 tons   **Range:** 3,000/26.5; 3,750/25; 5,500/20; 6,800/16
Man: Ships company: 31 officers, 182 petty officers, 414 other enlisted

REMARKS: Replaced the former cruiser *Jeanne d'Arc* as a training ship for officer
cadets; when on this mission, she carries only four Super Frélon heavy helicopters.
In wartime, she would be used for ASW missions, amphibious assault, or as a troop
transport. The number of heavy helicopters embarked can be quickly augmented by
simple structural changes.

The landing platform is 62 × 21 m. The hull is welded throughout.

Aviation facilities include: a flight deck aft of the island structure that permits
the simultaneous takeoff of two Super Frélon helicopters, while two machines can
be stationed forward of the takeoff area and two others astern, one on each side of
the elevator. An elevator (12-ton capacity) is located at the after end of the flight
deck.

A hangar deck that, if some of the living quarters used by midshipmen are used,
can accommodate eight helicopters. At the after end of the hangar deck there are
all the machine shops necessary for maintenance and repair, including helicopter
electronic equipment, and an area for inspection. There, also, are the compartments
for handling weapons and ammunition (torpedoes, rockets, etc.).

There are three fire-control directors for the 100-mm guns, each served by three
automatically controlled radar directors. In addition to the navigation bridge, the
superstructure contains a helicopter-control bridge, a modular-type information and
operations center, and a combined control center for amphibious operations. Two
LCVP landing craft are carried.

The engineering spaces are divided into two compartments, each with two boilers
and a turbine, separated by a bulkhead.

The *Jeanne d'Arc* is scheduled for a refit from 1982-83; at that time, the SENIT
2 computerized tactical data handling system is expected to be installed.

NAVAL AVIATION

The Naval Air establishment is made up of combatant flotillas, maintenance squadrons or sections, bases, schools, and the special services necessary to ensure the
efficient operation of the flight components. It is manned by naval personnel.

Administrative problems are handled by the Aeronautical Division of the Naval
General Staff and the Central Service Branch of Naval Air, both headed by flag officers.
Operational and training matters are directed by the Navy Staff, whose various bu-
reaus include aviation officers.

Primary training in fixed-wing planes is provided by the Air Force; helicopter pilots
are given initial training by the Army as well as the Air Force. Specialization of these
pilots in multi-engine aircraft or in carrier-based fixed-wing and rotary aircraft is
provided by Naval Air. The latter also trains navigators and maintenance crews at
the Naval Air School, Rochefort.

The combat flotillas are:

(a) those embarked which, flying from aircraft carriers or helicopter carriers, carry
out intercept, attack, reconnaissance, or CAP missions and engage in antisubmarine
warfare;

(b) maritime patrol flotillas and antisubmarine warfare flotillas that are land-based.

The service support squadrons and sections have various missions: schools, training
exercises, transportation, logistical support for seagoing forces, experimental and
salvage operations.

Authority over embarked flotillas and squadrons is assigned to a rear admiral,
Commander, Aircraft Carriers and seagoing aviation (ALPA).

Maritime patrol squadrons are commanded by a rear admiral (ALPATMAR).

Shore-based flotillas, squadrons, and sections are commanded by the Préfets Maritimes (Naval District Commandants) through the regional aviation commanders.

Bases: Nîmes-Garon, Saint-Mandrier (helicopters), Saint-Raphaël (experimental
station), Hyères, Cuers (maintenance), Ajaccio-Aspretto (training), Lorient-Lann
Bihoué, Lanvéoc-Poulmic (helicopters), Landivisiau.

AIRCRAFT CARRIERS (continued)

Super Étendard 1978

Super Étendard—with AM-39 missile

Super Étendard—landing aboard **Foch** (R 99)

COMBAT ORGANIZATION

Flotilla	Subordination	Bases	Equipment	Missions
4 F	ALPA	Lann-Bihoué	**10 Alizé**	ASW/AEW
6 F	ALPA	Nîmes-Garons	**10 Alizé**[1]	ASW/AEW
11 F	ALPA	Landivisiau	**12 Super Étendard**	Attack
12 F	ALPA	Landivisiau	**15 Crusader (F-8E)**	Interception
14 F	ALPA	Landivisiau	**12 Super Étendard**	Attack
16 F	ALPA	Landivisiau	**7 Étendard IV P**	Reconnaissance
17 F	ALPA	Hyères	**12 Super Étendard**	Attack
21 F	ALPATMAR	Nîmes-Garons	**7 Atlantic**	Maritime patrol
22 F	ALPATMAR	Nîmes-Garons	**7 Atlantic**	Maritime patrol
23 F	ALPATMAR	Lann-Bihoué	**7 Atlantic**	Maritime patrol
24 F	ALPATMAR	Lann-Bihoué	**7 Atlantic**	Maritime patrol
25 F	ALPATMAR	Lann-Bihoué	**12 Neptune (P-2H)**	Maritime patrol
31 F	ALPA	St. Mandrier	**8 WG 13 Lynx**	ASW
32 F	ALPA	Lanvéoc-Poulmic	**10 Super Frélon**	ASW & troop transport
33 F	ALPA	St. Mandrier	**5 Super Frélon**	Troop transport
34 F	ALPA	Lanvéoc-Poulmic	**9 WG 13 Lynx**	ASW
35 F	ALPA	*Jeanne d'Arc* or Lanvéoc-Poulmic[2]	**4 WG 13 Lynx** **3 Alouette-III**	

[1] modernized
[2] from the air complement of *Jeanne d'Arc*

For training, the French Navy uses at its schools Étendard IVM, Alizé, C-47, CM-175, Alouette-II, and Rallye 880 aircraft. Support organizations employ MS 760, Nord 262, Rallye 880, C-47, C-54, CM-175, Falcon 10, and Piper Navajo aircraft and Alouette-II, Alouette-III, Lynx, and Super Frélon helicopters. The Pacific Experimental Center uses P-2H Neptune patrol aircraft and Alouette-III helicopters. Five "Guardian" (Mystère-Falcon), similar to the U.S. Coast Guard's HU-25A, were ordered under the 1981 budget for delivery in 1983-84. A total of 71 Super Étendard attack aircraft have been ordered; all should be operational by 1982. Fourteen additional WG 13 Lynx were ordered in 1980; these will have improvements over those now in service, including 1,120-hp engines and a gross weight of 4,763 kg.

A total of 42 Atlantic MK II patrol aircraft are planned. The prototype was completed in mid-1981 and the first production aircraft is expected to fly in 1985.

1981 aircraft inventories are given with the data tables.

Étendard-IVM

F-8E Crusader

Super Frélon

Alizé

Alouette-III

WG-13 Lynx

WG-13 Lynx

WG-13 Lynx

Atlantic

Altantic

P-2H Neptune

Alouette-III

Atlantic

Alizé—landing on the **Clemenceau**

1981 Total	Type	Mission	Wingspan	Length	Height	Weight (max.) kilos	Engine	Max. speed in Mach or in knots	Maximum ceiling	Range	Weapons	Remarks
	◆ **SHIP-BASED PLANES**											(1) 24 of the 29 Alizé aircraft will be modernized 1980-83 with Iguane radar, Omega radio-navigation equipment, and ARAR 12-A intercept gear.
15	**CRUSADER F8-E (FN)** (Ling-Temco-Vought)	All-weather interceptor	10.72	16.61	4.80	13,000	1 J57 P20 A Pratt & Whitney turbojet with after-burner	Mach 1.8	50,000 ft	1,500 miles 2 hr 30 min	4/20-mm guns, Air-to-air missiles	
36	**Super-Étendard** (Dassault)	Fleet air defense attack, Photo-reconnaissance	9.60	14.35	3.85	11,900	1 8 K 50 SNECMA turbojet developing 5 tons of thrust	Mach 1 at 11,000 m; Mach 0.97 at low altitude			2/30-mm guns, bombs, rockets, combination or AM 39	(2) May be outfitted with a small photo pod for reconnaissance missions. The Atlantic, Mk II, which will enter service in 1985, will have the same airframe, engines, and characteristics as the Mk I but its weapon system will be entirely new, built around a Type 15 M digital tactical computer. It will be able to transport 3 tons of weapons, e.g., 4 Martel under the wings or 2 AM 39 inboard. 42 aircraft will be procured.
14	**Étendard-IVM** (Dassault)	Training	9.60	14.35	3.85	10,200	1 SNECMA Atar 8 turbojet	Mach 1.3	35,000 ft	750 miles 1 hr 45 min or 2 hr 15 min with supplemental reserve tank	2/30-mm guns, air-to-surface missiles (or air-to-air) 68-mm and 100-mm rockets, various bombs of 50 to 400 kg	
7	**Étendard-IVP** (Dassault)	Photo-reconnaissance	9.60	14.50	3.85	10,200	1 SNECMA Atar 8 turbojet	Mach 1.3	35,000 ft	750 miles 1 hr 45 or 2 hr 15 with supplemental reserve tank	100-mm rockets, 68-mm rockets, photo-flash bombs	
29	**Alizé (BR 1050)** (Bréguet)	AEW, ASW (5 for training)	15.60	13.66	5	8,200	1 Rolls-Royce Dart 21 turboprop (1,925 hp + 230 kt of thrust)	240 kts	11,000 ft	685 miles 3 hr 45	Air-to-surface missiles, Mk 44 torpedoes, 100-mm rockets, ASW depth charges, 50 to 250 kg bombs, acoustic buoys, mortar type projectiles	(3) Localization, classification and attack of contacts picked up by an antisubmarine ship. Carries DUAV-4 dipping sonar. (4) Detection, identification, and neutralization of small surface vessels with weak antiaircraft defense. 4 equipped with MAD for ASW.
	◆ **LAND-BASED PLANES**											
12	**P2-H Neptune** (Lockheed)	Patrol, ASW (4 for training)	31.50	31.70	10.80	34,280	2 R 3350 32 Wa Wright engines × 3,250 hp + 2 Westinghouse turbojets type J 34 × 1,540 kg	240 kts	25,000 ft	3,200 miles 16 hr	L 4 or Mk 44 or 46 torpedoes, ASW depth charges, sonobuoys, mortar type projectiles (ASW), photo-flash bombs	
28*	**Atlantic Mk 1** (BR 1150) (Bréguet)	Patrol, ASW (2)	36.30	31.75	11.33	43,500	2 Rolls-Royce Tyne 20 turboprops, 6,000 hp each	300 kts	30,000 ft	4,300 miles 17 hr	Air-to-surface missiles, L 4 or Mk 44 or 46 torpedoes, ASW depth charges, sonobuoys, mortar type projectiles (ASW), photo-flash bombs	
	◆ **HELICOPTERS**											
18	**Super Frélon** (SNIAS)	ASW (2 used as transports)	18.90 (rotor diameter)	23	6.35	13,000	3 C3 Turboméca III turboshafts, each with 1,500 hp	145 kts	10,000 ft	420 miles 3 hr 30 min	Mk 44 and Mk 46 torpedoes, ASW torpedoes	
24	**Lynx (WG 13)** (Westland S.N.I.A.S.)	ASW (3) and surface attack aircraft (4)	12.80 (rotor diameter)	15.2	3.20	4,150	2 BS 360 Rolls-Royce Gem turboshafts, of 900 hp each	150 kts	12,000 ft	1 hr 30, half hovering, half in flight 2 hr 30 min with 3 men and 4 missiles	Mk 44 and Mk 46 torpedoes, air-to-surface missiles	
16	**Alouette-III** (S.N.I.A.S.)	ASW (6)	11.02 (rotor diameter)	12.8	3.0	2,200	1 Turbomeca Astazou turboshaft, 870 hp	110 kts	10,000 ft	325 miles 2 hr 30 min	Mk 44 torpedoes	

*1 lost 10-3-81.

NOTE: Other aircraft in service include 16 Nord 262, 13 PA-31, 5 Falcon 10, 8 MS 760, 7 Rallye 100S, 14 Alouette-II, 21 C-47, 1 C-54, 1 DC-6, 1 Nord 2504, 11 CM 175 Magister, and 6 CAP 10 for training and support duties.

BALLISTIC-MISSILE SUBMARINES

NOTE: The French Navy is studying a new generation of strategic ballistic-missile submarines to be evolved from the *L'Inflexible* and *Le Redoutable* designs. The first will be launched around 1990, according to President Mitterand on 24-7-81. A new missile with a range of 7,000 km may be developed.

♦ 0(+2) L'Inflexible class

	Bldr	Laid down	L	In serv.
S. . . L'INFLEXIBLE	DCAN, Cherbourg	27-3-80	mid-82	1-85
S. . . N. . .	. .	. .		

D: 8,000/9,000 tons   **S:** over 20 kts   **Dim:** 128.0 × 10.6 × 10.0
A: 16/M 4 ballistic missiles—4/533-mm TT fwd (18 torpedoes)
M: 1 nuclear reactor producing pressurized steam for propulsion; 1 prop
Man: 2 crews in rotation, each of 15 officers, 120 men

REMARKS: Ordered 9-78, *L'Inflexible* will have most characteristics in common with the five preceding SSBNs of *Le Redoutable* class but will take advantage of many technological advances in propulsion, sonar systems, navigation systems, etc., and will be able to dive 100 m deeper. The ship will be equipped from the outset with the M4 missile, which will have seven Multiple Independent Re-entry Vehicle (MIRV) warheads, and will have the DSUX 21 sonar. Second unit ordered 1981.

♦ 5 nuclear-powered Le Redoutable class   Bldr: DCAN, Cherbourg

	Laid down	L	Trials	In serv.
S 611 LE REDOUTABLE	11-64	29-3-67	7-69	1-12-71
S 612 LE TERRIBLE	22-6-67	12-12-69	1971	1-1-73
S 610 LE FOUDROYANT	12-12-69	4-12-71	5-73	6-6-74
S 613 L'INDOMITABLE	4-12-71	17-9-74	12-75	23-12-76
S 614 LE TONNANT	10-74	17-9-77	4-79	3-4-80

Le Terrible (S 612)   E.C.P.A., 1978

Le Foudroyant (S 610)   E.C.P.A., 1980

D: 8,000/9,000 tons   **S:** 20 kts, max.   **Dim:** 128.0 × 10.6 × 10.0
A: 16 M 20 ballistic missiles—4/550-mm TT fwd (18 L 5 and F 17 torpedoes)
Electron Equipt: Radar: 1/. . .
          Sonar: 1/DUUV-23, 1/DUUX-2
M: Principal: 1 pressurized water reactor, 2 steam turbines with 1 set turbo reduction gears; 1 prop; 16,000 hp
     Secondary: 1 electric motor driven by batteries powered by 1 SEMT-Pielstick 16 PA4, 850-kw diesel generator set (sufficient fuel for 5,000 nm)
Man: Twin crews of 15 officers and 120 men for each ship, manning in rotation

REMARKS: *Le Redoutable* (authorized in March 1963) and other submarines of this class are the principal elements of the French naval deterrent. They can dive more than 200 meters. All, with the exception of *Le Redoutable*, will be back-fitted to carry the M 4 missile. The substitution will not require replacing the existing missile tubes. The sonar suit will be upgraded by the installation of DSUX-21, and other equipment will be modernized.

♦ 1 experimental ballistic-missile submarine (non-nuclear)

	Bldr	Laid down	L	In serv.
S 655 GYMNOTE	DCAN, Cherbourg	17-3-63	17-3-64	17-10-66

Gymnote   J.-C. Bellonne, 1977

D: 3,000 tons std., 3,250 surfaced (fl)   **S:** 11/10 kts   **Dim:** 84.0 × 10.6 × 7.6
M: 4 sets 620-kw diesel generators; 2 electric motors; 2 props; 2,600 hp
Man: 8 officers, 38 petty officers, 45 other enlisted

REMARKS: Used for testing missiles designed for the SSBNs. Has two vertical missile-launching tubes to port. Bow diving planes do not retract. Noncombatant. Currently involved in M 4 developmental trials. The pressure hull was laid down in 1958 for a nuclear-powered attack submarine that was canceled in 1959.

NUCLEAR-POWERED ATTACK SUBMARINES

♦ 1 (+4) Rubis class, Type SNA 72   Bldr: Cherbourg Arsenal

	Laid down	L	Trials	In serv.
S 601 RUBIS (ex-*Provence*)	11-12-76	7-7-79	1-4-81	7-82
S 602 SAPHIR (ex-*Bretagne*)	1-9-79	1-9-81	1-7-83	7-84

NUCLEAR-POWERED ATTACK SUBMARINES (*continued*)

S 603 N. . . (ex-*Bourgogne*)	9-81	. . .	end-85	7-86
S. . . N. . .	10-82	. . .	end-86	9-87
S. . . N. . .	1984	. . .	end-87	12-88

Rubis (S 601)   1981

Rubis (S 601)   1981

D: 2,265/2,385/2,670 tons (fl)   **S:** 25 kts   **Dim:** 72.10 × 7.60 × 6.90
A: 4/550-mm TT fwd (14 torpedoes, or SM 39 missiles, or mines)
Electron Equipt: Radar: 1/DRUA 33
           Sonar: 1/DSUV 22, 1/DUUA 2B, 1/DUUX 2
M: Principal: 1 48 megawatt pressurized water reactor; two turbo-alternator
     sets; 1 electric motor; 1 prop;. . . hp
     Secondary: 1 electric motor driven by batteries powered by 1 SEMT-Piel-
     stick 16PA4, 85C-kw diesel generator set

Man: 8 officers, 36 chief petty officers, 22 other enlisted

REMARKS: Names changed 11-80. Fire-control, torpedo-launching, and submarine-de-
tection systems are the same as the *Agosta* class. *Rubis* was financed under the
Third Military Equipment Plan. The second through the fifth came under the Fourth
Plan (1977-82). *Saphir* was ordered under the 1977 Budget, the third under the 1979
Budget, and the fourth in 1981. *Rubis's* reactor became operational (went critical)
early 2-81 and trials started 6-81.

ATTACK SUBMARINES

♦ **4 Agosta class** Bldr: Cherbourg Arsenal

	Laid down	L	In serv.
S 620 AGOSTA	10-11-72	19-10-74	28-7-77
S 621 BÉVÉZIERS	17-5-73	14-6-75	27-9-77
S 622 LA PRAYA	1974	15-5-76	9-3-78
S 623 OUESSANT	1974	23-10-76	27-7-78

La Praya (S 622)   1981

Bévéziers (S 621)   G. Gyssels, 1980

D: 1,230/1,490/1,740 tons (fl)   **S:** 12.5 kts/20.5 kts for 5 min., 17.5 kts for 1 hr.
Dim: 67.57 × 6.8 × 5.4
A: 4/550-mm TT fwd—20 L 5 mod. 3 and F 17 torpedoes (rapid loading)
Electron Equipt: Radar: 1/DRUA 33
           Sonar: 1/DUUA 1D, 1/DUUA 2A, 1/DUUA 2D, 1/DSUV 22,
           1/DUUX 2A
           ECM: ARUR, ARUD
M: 2 SEMT-Pielstick 320-16 PA 4 185 diesel generator sets (850 kw each); 1 ×
     3,500-hp propulsion motor; 1 prop; 4,600 hp (1 × 23-hp creep motor)
Fuel: 185 tons   **Endurance:** 45 days   **Man:** 7 officers, 47 men
Range: 7,000/10 (snorkel), 178/3.5 (creep motor), 7,900/. . . surf. (1 engine)

REMARKS: Oceangoing submarines, authorized in the 1970-75 program. Weapons and
equipment similar to the refitted *Daphné* class. Fire control centralized in one
computer bank. Air-conditioned. Retractable deck fittings on hull exterior. Advanced
techniques for quiet operations both inboard and outboard. The torpedo tubes will

ATTACK SUBMARINES (continued)

accept torpedoes of either 550 mm or 533 mm diameter. 320-cell battery with twice the capacity of the *Daphné* class. Diving depth 300 m. Have DLT D3 torpedo fire-control system. To be equipped to fire SM-39 guided missiles. *La Praya* in collision 9-5-80, repaired. Spain has ordered four of this class of submarine, and Pakistan has two—from an embargoed South African order.

◆ 9 Daphné class

	Budget	Bldr	Laid down	L	In serv.
S 641 DAPHNE	1955	Dubigeon, Nantes	3-58	20-6-59	1-6-64
S 642 DIANE	1955	Dubigeon, Nantes	7-58	4-10-60	20-6-64
S 643 DORIS	1955	Cherbourg Ars.	19-58	14-5-60	26-8-64
S 645 FLORE	1956	Cherbourg Ars.	19-58	21-12-60	21-5-64
S 646 GALATEE	1956	Cherbourg Ars.	19-58	22-9-61	25-7-64
S 648 JUNON	1960	Cherbourg Ars.	7-61	11-5-64	25-2-66
S 649 VENUS	1960	Cherbourg Ars.	8-61	24-9-64	1-1-66
S 650 PSYCHE	1964	Brest Arsenal	5-65	28-6-67	1-7-69
S 651 SIRENE	1964	Brest Arsenal	5-65	28-6-67	1-3-70

Psyche (S 650)—old bow sonar dome   G. Gyssels, 1980

Doris (S 643)   1976

Flore (S 645)   J.-C. Bellonne, 1975

D: 700/869/1,043 tons (fl)   **S:** 13.5/16 kts   **Dim:** 57.75 × 6.76 × 4.62
A: 12/550-mm TT, 8 fwd, 4 aft
Electron Equipt: Radar: 1/Calypso II
                  Sonars: DUUA 2A, 1/DUUA-2B, 1/DSUV 2, 1/DUUX-2
M: 2 SEMT-Pielstick/Jeumont-Schneider 450-kw diesel generator sets; 2 × 1,000 hp (1,300 for a brief period) electric motors; 2 props
Range: 4,300/7.5 (snorkel)   **Man:** 6 officers, 39 men

REMARKS: Development of the *Aréthuse* class. Very quiet when submerged. Modernized, beginning in 1971, with special attention given to detection equipment and weapons. S 650 and S 651 were the last modernized, in 1981. Can submerge to 300 meters. No spare torpedoes are carried. This class of submarine has been purchased by the following countries: Portugal, four in 1964; Pakistan, four in 1966; South Africa, three in 1967. Spain has built four with French technical assistance. One Portuguese unit was sold to Pakistan in 1976. Sister *Sirène* lost in 1972, salvaged and scrapped. *Flore* began a second modernization in 1978.

◆ 1 Aréthuse class

	Budget	Bldr	Laid down	L	In serv.
S 636 ARGONAUTE	1953	Cherbourg Ars.	3-55	29-6-57	11-2-59

Argonaute (S 636)   G. Gyssels, 1980

D: 400/543/669 tons (fl)   **S:** 12.5/16 kts   **Dim:** 49.60 × 5.80 × 4.10
A: 4/550-mm TT fwd (8 torpedoes)
Electron Equipt: Radar: 1/. . .
                  Sonar: 1/DUUA 1, 1/DSUV 2, 1/DUUX 2
M: 2 SEMT-Pielstick 12 PA4 diesels, electric drive; 2 props; 1,300 hp
Man: 6 officers, 34 men

REMARKS: Ballast tanks reduced to a minimum; can submerge to more than 200 meters. Quiet, maneuverable submarines. *Aréthuse* (S 635) stricken 4-79; *Amazone* (S 639) in 6-80; and *Ariane* (S 640) in 3-81.

ATTACK SUBMARINES *(continued)*

♦ 6 Narval class

	Budget	Bldr	Laid down	L	In serv.
S 631 NARVAL	1949	Cherbourg Ars.	6-51	11-12-54	1-12-57
S 632 MARSOUIN	1949	Cherbourg Ars.	9-51	21-5-55	1-10-57
S 633 DAUPHIN	1950	Cherbourg Ars.	5-62	17-9-55	1-8-58
S 634 REQUIN	1950	Cherbourg Ars.	6-52	3-12-55	1-8-58
S 637 ESPADON	1954	Cherbourg Ars.	12-55	15-9-58	2-4-60
S 638 MORSE	1954	Seine Maritime	2-56	10-12-58	2-5-60

Requin (S 634)—viewing device on deck forward   J.-C. Bellonne, 1980

Narval (S 631)—swimmer delivery vehicle housing aft   J.-C. Bellonne, 1980

D: 1,320/1,635/1,910 tons   **S:** 15/18 kts   **Dim:** 77.63 × 7.82 × 5.40
A: 6/550-mm TT fwd—20 torpedoes
M: 3 SEMT-Pielstick 12 PA4 motor generator sets; 2 electric motors; 2 props;
3,000 hp (2 × 40-hp creep motors)
Endurance: 45 days   **Range:** 15,000/8 (snorkel)   **Man:** 7 officers, 57 men

REMARKS: Exceptionally strong hull, welded throughout, streamlined sail. Rebuilt from 1966 to 1970 with special attention to the machinery spaces, complete modernization of detection devices and weapons. Separate fixed-pitch bow planes are extended to rise or descend. *Narval* carries a swimmer delivery vehicle in an open-topped container on deck aft. *Requin* modified 1980 for trials with the SM-39 submerged-launch missile.

GUIDED-MISSILE CRUISER

	Budget	Bldr	Laid down	L	In serv.
C 611 COLBERT	1953	Brest	12-53	24-3-56	5-5-59

D: 8,500 tons (11,300 fl)   **S:** 31.5 kts
Dim: 180.00 (175.00 pp) × 19.70 (20.20 max.) × 7.90
A: 4/MM 38 Exocet—1/Masurca syst. (48 missiles)—2/100-mm DP, Model 1968 (I × 2)—12/57-mm AA (II × 6)
Electron Equipt: Radars: 1/Decca RM 416, 1/DRBV 50, 1/DRBV 23C, 1/DRBV 20, 2/DRBR 51, 1/DRBR 32C, 1/DRBC 31, 1/DRBI 10D
ECM: extensive passive intercept arrays, 2/Syllex countermeasures RL   TACAN: URN-20
M: 2 sets C.E.M. Parsons GT; 2 props; 86,000 hp   **Electric:** 4,920 kw
Boilers: 4 asymmetric, multitube; 45 kg/cm², 450°C   **Range:** 4,000/25
Man: 25 officers, 208 petty officers, 329 men
Armor: Deck: 50 mm, Belt: 50 to 80 mm

Colbert (C 611)   1980

Colbert (C 611)   G. Gyssels, 1981

GUIDED-MISSILE CRUISER *(continued)*

REMARKS: Converted into a surface-to-air guided-missile cruiser between 4-70 and 10-72. Together with the guided-missile destroyers *Duquesne* and *Suffren,* this ship, thanks to the Masurca system, provides a high degree of antiaircraft protection to ships at sea at a medium range. The capability of the SENIT 1 tactical data system enables real-time control of the surface and air situation at the center of a widely dispersed formation to be maintained, which makes this an excellent command ship, able as well to coordinate the air defense of the formation. If necessary, the ship can be used as a command post for an interservice operation overseas. During the refit the bridge superstructure was rebuilt, the electronic equipment for command and control was modernized, the electric power increased, and living spaces were improved, including air-conditioning. Four MM 38 Exocet anti-ship missiles have now been installed; racks to support the missile containers are mounted on the deck immediately abaft the upper 100-mm gun mount. In addition to the two DRBR 51 radar directors for the 57-mm AA guns, there are also four lead-computing visual directors. Machinery and boilers are installed in two separate compartments, each with two boilers and a turbine, separated by an 18-meter-long watertight compartment.

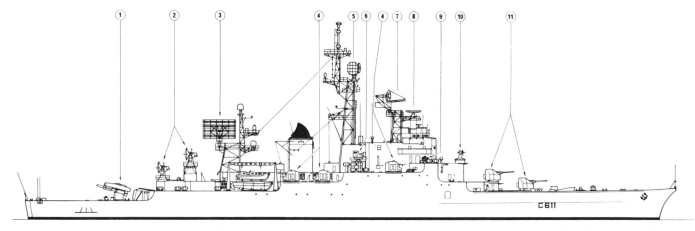

1. Masurca launcher 2. DRBR 51 radars 3. DRBV 20 radar 4. 57-mm mounts 5. DRBI 10D radar 6. 57-mm director (DRBC 31) 7. DRBV 23C radar 8. DRBV 50 radar 9. Syllex systems 10. DRBC 32C radar 11. 100-mm mounts, Model 1968

Colbert (C 611)   G. Gyssels, 1981

GUIDED-MISSILE DESTROYERS

♦ 0 (+3) C 70 class, AA

	Bldr	Laid down	L	In serv.
D. . . N. . .	DCAN, Lorient	. . .	. . .	10-87
D. . . N. . .	DCAN, Lorient	. . .	. . .	5-89
D. . . N. . .	. . .	. . .	. . .	. . .

D: 4,000 tons (4,340 fl) **S:** 29.6 kts **Dim:** 139.00 × 14.00 × 5.50
A: 8/MM40 SSM—1 Mk 13 launcher (40 Standard SM1-MR missiles)—2/100-mm
DP, Model 1968 (I × 2)—2/20-mm AA (I × 2)—2 fixed catapults for Type L-
5 ASW torpedoes (10 torpedoes)
Electron Equipt: Radar: 1/navigational, 1/DRBJ 11, 1/DRBV 26, 2 SPG 51C,
1/DRBC 32D
Sonar: 1/DUBA 25
ECM: 2 Dagaie and 2 Sagaie countermeasures RL
M: 4 SEMT-Pielstick 18 PA 6 BTC diesels; 2 props; 42,300 hp
Electric: 3,400 kw **Fuel:** 600 tons **Range:** 5,000/24, 8,200/17
Man: 12 officers, 124 petty officers, 105 men

REMARKS: 1977-82 program; the first was authorized under the 1978 budget, the second
under the 1979 budget. The launchers for MM 40 Exocet, four per beam, are to be
mounted perpendicular to the ship's centerline in a form of "duck blind" superstructure box (see drawing). There will be a helicopter platform but no facilities for
permanent embarkation. The after 100-mm mount will eventually be replaced by a
launcher for SATCP short-range antiaircraft missiles. Equipped with SENIT 6 data
systems.

The problem of equipment-positioning caused by the amount of space taken up
by the fresh-air intakes and gas exhausts of a CODOG system, such as that installed
in the *George Leygues*, has been overcome in these ships by the adoption of diesels,
which because of double supercharging have a high power-to-weight ratio.

♦ 2 (+4) Georges Leygues C 70 class, ASW Bldr: Brest Arsenal

	Laid down	L	Trials	In serv.
D 640 GEORGES LEYGUES	16-9-74	17-12-76	1977	10-12-79
D 641 DUPLEIX	17-10-75	2-12-78	end-79	16-6-81
D 642 MONTCALM	5-12-75	31-5-80	early-81	3-82
D 643 JEAN DE VIENNE	26-10-79	. . .	late-82	1983
D. . . N. . .	. . .	. . .	10-84	1985
D. . . N. . .	. . .	. . .	10-85	1986

D: 3,830 tons (4,200 fl) **S:** 30 kts (GT), 21 kts (diesels)
Dim: 139.00 (129.00 pp) × 14.00 × 5.50 (hull) 5.73 (props)
A: 4/MM 38 Exocet—1/100-mm DP, Model 1968, with Vega fire-control sys-
tem—1/Crotale system (VIII × 1; 26 missiles)—2/20-mm AA (I × 2)—2 cata-
pults for L-5 ASW torpedoes (10 torpedoes)—2/WG 13 Lynx helicopters
Electron Equipt: Radar: 1/DRBV 26, 1/DRBV 51C, 1/DRBC 32D, 2/Decca 1226
Sonar: 1/DUBV 23, 1/DUBV 43
ECM: ARBR 17 passive arrays—2/Syllex, 2/Dagaie counter-
measures RL
M: CODOG: 2 Rolls-Royce Olympus TM3B gas turbines; 2 SEMT-Pielstick 16
PA 6 CV 280 diesels; 2 CP props; 52,000 hp (gas turbine), 10,400 hp (diesel)
Electric: 3,400 kw (4 × 850-kw alternator sets) **Fuel:** 600 tons distillate

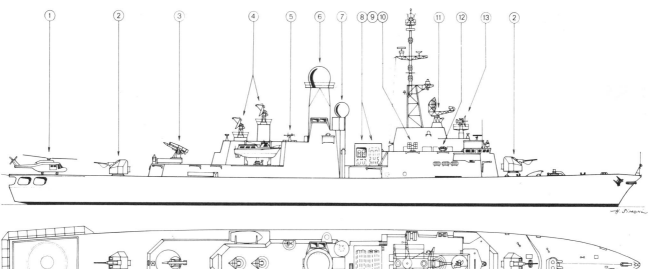

C 70 class: 1. WG-13 Lynx helicopter 2. 100-mm gun mounts 3. Mk 12 launcher for Standard missile 4. SPG-51C missile-control radars 5.
20-mm AA 6. DRBJ 11 radar 7. Satellite communications antenna radomes 8. and 9. MM 40 missile installations 10. Sagaie decoy rocket-
launching system 11. DRBV 26 radar 12. Dagaie decoy rocket-launching system 13. DRBC 32D gunfire-control radar

GUIDED-MISSILE DESTROYERS *(continued)*

Range: 1,000/30, 9,500/17 diesels

Man: Peacetime: 15 officers, 90 petty officers, 111 men (accommodations for 250 total)

REMARKS: Three are under the 1970-75 plan and three under the 1977-82 plan. Two more may be ordered later. The principal mission of these ships is antisubmarine warfare, their secondary mission being anti-ship warfare. Main propulsion and auxiliary equipment is divided among four compartments from forward to aft: forward auxiliary room, turbine room, diesel room with the reduction gears, and after auxiliary room. On diesel power and with the DUBV 43 sonar in the water, maximum speed is 19 knots. Centralized control of the propulsion machinery from the bridge greatly reduces the engineering staff required (3 officers, 23 petty officers, 24 men).

As in the *De Grasse*, much attention has been given to habitability, which caused the addition of 5 meters of length and 150 tons to the original plans. Denny Brown automatic stabilizers fitted. Have SENIT 4 data system. Dagaie rocket launchers to augment Sagaie. *Montcalm* will carry 4/MM 40 SSM initially, but this may later be doubled. Have 1 CSEE Panda optronic backup director for the 100-mm gun. The helicopters can be used for ASW with Mk 46 torpedoes or Mk 54 depth bombs or for anti-ship duties with AS-12 missiles.

Dupleix (D 641) M. Bar, 1980

Montcalm (D 642) CECLANT/PREMAR, 1981

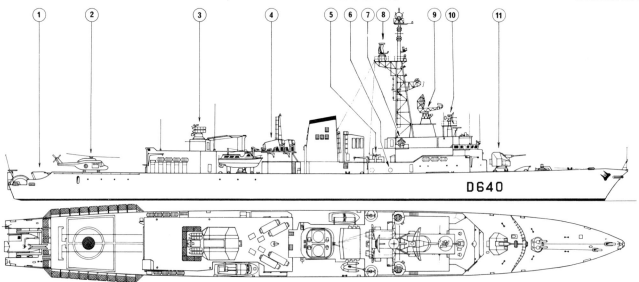

Georges Leygues class: 1. DUBV 43 sonar 2. WG-13 Lynx helicopter 3. Crotale launcher 4. Exocet launchers 5. 20-mm AA 6. ASW torpedo catapults 7. Syllex system 8. DRBV 51C radar 9. DRBV 26 radar 10. DRBC 32D radar 11. 100-mm gun mount, Model 1968

GUIDED-MISSILE DESTROYERS (continued)

Georges Leygues (D 640)   G. Gyssels, 1981

♦ **3 Tourville class, Type F 67, ex-C 67A**   Bldr: Lorient Arsenal

	Budget	Laid down	L	In serv.
D 610 TOURVILLE	1967	3-70	13-5-72	21-6-74
D 611 DUGUAY TROUIN	1967	1-71	1-6-73	17-9-75
D 612 DE GRASSE	1970	1972	30-11-74	1-10-77

D: 4,800 tons (5,800 fl)   **S:** 32 kts
Dim: 152.75 (142.0 pp) × 15.3 × 5.7 (hull) (6.48 props)
A: 6/MM 38 Exocet—1/Crotale syst. (VIII × 1, 26 missiles)—2/100-mm DP,
Model 1968 (I × 2)—2/20-mm AA (I × 2)—1/Malafon ASW syst. (13 mis-
siles)—2/catapults for L-5 antisubmarine torpedoes (10 torpedoes—2/WG 13
Lynx helicopters

Electron Equipt: Radar: 1/DRBV 26, 1/DRBV 51B, 1/DRBV 51C, 1/DRBC
32D, 2/Decca 1226
Sonar: 1/DUBV 23, 1/DUBV 43
ECM: extensive passive array, 2/Syllex countermeasures RL
M: 2 sets Rateau double-reduction GT; 2 props; 54,400 hp
Electric: 4,440 kw (2 × 1,500-kw turbogenerators, 3 × 480-kw diesel alterna-
tors)
Boilers: 4 asymmetric, multitube, automatic-control; 45 kg/cm², 450°C
Range: 1,900/30, 4,500/18   **Man:** 17 officers, 122 petty officers, 143 men

De Grasse (D 612)   1979

Duguay Trouin (D 611)—note bulge added to hull sides 1979-80 in all three ships

16 F, 1980

GUIDED-MISSILE DESTROYERS (continued)

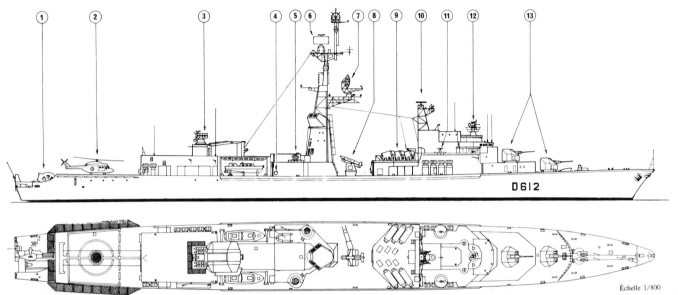

De Grasse: 1. DUBV 43 sonar 2. WG-13 Lynx helicopter 3. Crotale launcher with DRBV 51G radar 4. Torpedo catapults 5. Syllex system 6. DRBV 51B radar 7. DRBV 26 radar 8. Malafon launcher 9. Exocet launchers 10. Decca 1226 navigation radar 11. DRBC 32D radar 12. 100-mm gun mounts, Model 1968

De Grasse (D 612)—with WG-13 Lynx   1979

Tourville (D 610)   CECLANT/PREMAR II, 1980

REMARKS: Built under the 1965-70 plan, these ships were designed for antisubmarine warfare and can operate in a high-air-threat environment. SENIT 3 data system fitted. The *Duguay Trouin* was equipped with the Crotale antiaircraft missile system during 1979, *Tourville* in 1980 and *De Grasse* in 1981. In preparation for Crotale, the third 100-mm gun mount atop the helicopter hangar on *Tourville* and *Duguay Trouin* was removed; it was never carried by *De Grasse*. During her Crotale installation refit, the *Tourville* had her boilers converted to burn distillate fuel, which has been burned by *De Grasse* from the outset. Denny Brown automatic stabilizers are fitted. These ships, particularly *De Grasse*, have a very high standard of habitability and seakeeping qualities on a par with those of the *Suffren* class.

GUIDED-MISSILE DESTROYERS (continued)

◆ 2 Suffren class

	Bldr	Budget	Laid down	L	In serv.
D 602 SUFFREN	Lorient Ars.	1960	12-62	15-5-65	20-7-67
D 603 DUQUESNE	Brest Ars.	1960	11-64	11-2-66	1-4-70

D: 5,090 tons (6,090 fl) **S:** 34 kts
Dim: 157.60 (148.00 pp) × 15.54 × 7.25 (max.)

A: 1/Masurca SAM syst. (II × 1; 48 missiles)—4/MM 38 Exocet SSM—2/100-mm, Model 1953 (I × 2)—4/20-mm AA (I × 4)—1/Malafon ASW syst. (13 missiles)—2/catapults for L-5 torpedoes (10 torpedoes)

Electron Equipt: Radar: 1/DRBI 23, 1/DRBV 50, 2/DRBR 51, 1/DRBC 32A, 1/DRBN 32
Sonar: 1/DUBV 23, 1/DUBV 43
ECM: extensive passive array, 2 Syllex countermeasures RL
TACAN: URN-20

Suffren (D 602) M. Bar, 1980

Suffren (D 602) M. Bar, 1980

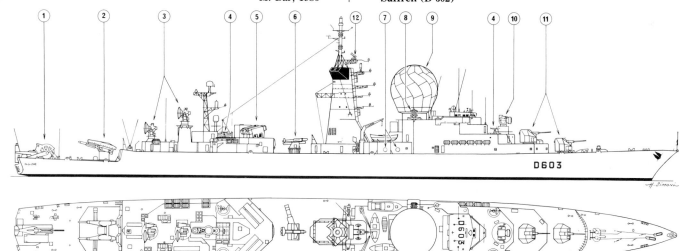

Duquesne: 1. DUBV 43 sonar 2. Masurca launcher 3. DRBR 51 radars 4. 20-mm AA gun mounts 5. Exocet launchers 6. Malafon launcher 7. Catapults for L-5 torpedoes 8. Syllex system 9. DRBI 23 radar 10. 100-mm gun director with DRBC 32A radar 11. 100-mm gun mounts, Model 1953

GUIDED-MISSILE DESTROYERS *(continued)*

Duquesne (D 603) 1977

M: 2 sets Rateau double-reduction GT; 2 props; 72,500 hp
Electric: 3,440 kw (2 × 1,000-kw turbogenerators, 3 × 480-kw diesel alternators)
Boilers: 4 multitube, automatic-control; 45 kg/cm², 450°C
Range: 2,000/30, 2,400/29, 5,100/18
Man: 23 officers, 164 petty officers, 168 men

REMARKS: Built under the 1960-65 plan, these ships are extremely seaworthy; they roll and pitch only slightly and vibrate very little. Three pairs of nonretractable, anti-rolling stabilizers are energized by two central gyros, only one of which is normally in use. Living and operating spaces are air-conditioned. *Suffren* received MM 38 Exocet missile launchers during her 1980 refit. SENIT 1 data system fitted. Two Dagaie countermeasures launchers will replace Syllex.

♦ **1 C 65 class**

	Bldr	Laid down	L	In serv.
D 609 ACONIT	Lorient Ars.	1967	7-3-70	30-3-73

D: 3,500 tons (3,840 fl) **S:** 27 kts **Dim:** 127.0 × 13.4 × 4.05, (5.8 props)
A: 2/100-mm DP, Model 1968 (I × 2)—1/Malafon ASW system (13 missiles)—1/305-mm ASW mortar (IV × 1)—2/catapults for L-5 ASW torpedoes (10 torpedoes)
Electron Equipt: Radars: 1/DRBN 32, 1/DRBV 13, 1/DRBV 22A, 1/DRBC 32B
Sonars: 1/DUBV 23, 1/DUBV 43 VDS
ECM: passive arrays, 2/Syllex countermeasures RL
M: 1 set Rateau double-reduction GT; 1 prop; 28,650 hp (31,500 hp for short periods)

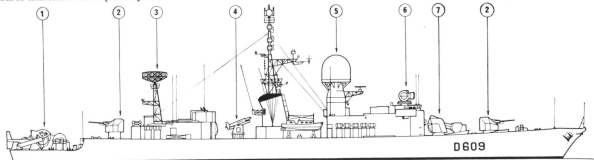

Aconit: 1. DUBV 43 sonar 2. 100-m—gun mounts, Model 1968 3. DRBV 22A radar 4. Malafon launcher 5. DRBV 13 radar 6. 100-mm gun director with DRBC 32B radar 7. quadruple 305-mm mortar

GUIDED-MISSILE DESTROYERS (continued)

Aconit (D 609)—with DUBV 43 VDS streamed   16 F, 1980

Boilers: 2 asymmetric, multitube, automatic-control; 45 kg/cm², 450°C
Electric: 2,960 kw   **Range:** 1,600/27, 5,000/18
Man: 15 officers, 103 petty officers, 114 men

REMARKS: Built under the 1965-70 plan, the *Aconit* is the predecessor of the Type-F-67 destroyer but does not carry a helicopter. One computer controls the SENIT 3 data system functions and the weapons. Propulsion machinery is very compact. Ship is equipped with fin stabilizers. Exocet *not* carried. A major refit is scheduled for 1983. During refit she will receive 4/MM 40 Exocet in place of the 305-mm mortar, and DRBV 15 will replace DRBV 13.

♦ **1 T-56 class, ASW**

	Bldr	Laid down	L	In serv.
D 638 LA GALISSONNIÈRE	Lorient Ars.	11-58	12-3-60	9-7-62

La Galissonnière (D 638)—with hangar closed   J.-C. Bellonne, 1977

La Galissonnière—with hangar open   1979

D: 2,750 tons (3,740 fl)   **S:** 34 kts (32 fl)
Dim: 132.80 × 12.70 × 5.40 (fwd) 5.90 (props)
A: 2/100-mm DP, Model 1953 (I × 2)—1/Malafon ASW syst. (13 missiles)—6/550-mm TT (III × 2) for L-3 torpedoes—1/Alouette-III ASW helicopter
Electron Equipt: Radars: 1/DRBV 22A, 1/DRBV 50, 1/DRBN 32, 1/DRBC 32A
  Sonars: 1/DUBV 23, 1/DUBV 43 VDS
  TACAN: URN 20
M: 2 sets Rateau GT; 2 props; 63,000 hp
Boilers: 4 ACB-Indret; 35 kg/cm², 385°C   **Fuel:** 800 tons
Range: 1,500/30, 5,000/18
Man: Peacetime: 15 officers, 92 petty officers, 165 men

REMARKS: Formerly an experimental vessel for ASW sonar, with two bow-mounted sonars. A quadruple 305-mm ASW mortar and six torpedo tubes (III × 2) have been removed. The hangar unfolds to become the helicopter flightdeck.

♦ **1 modified T-53 class, ASW**

	Bldr	Laid down	L	In serv.
D 633 DUPERRÉ	Lorient Ars.	11-54	23-6-56	8-10-57

GUIDED-MISSILE DESTROYERS (continued)

Duperré (D 633)   16 F, 1980

Duperré (D 633)—with WG-13 Lynx   1980

D: 2,750 tons (3,740 fl) **S:** 34 kts (32 fl) **Dim:** 132.8 × 12.7 × 5.9 (props)

A: 4/MM 38 Exocet—1/100-mm DP, Model 1968—2/20-mm AA (I × 2)—2/catapults for L-5 torpedoes (8 torpedoes)—1/WG-13 Lynx helicopter

Electron Equipt: Radars: 2/Decca 1226, 1/DRBV 22A, 1/DRBV 51, 1/DRBC 32C, 1/DRBC 1/DRBC 31

Sonars: 1/DUBV 23, 1/DUBV 43 VDS

ECM: passive arrays, 2/Syllex countermeasures RL

M: 2 sets Rateau GT; 2 props; 64,000 hp **Electric:** 1,640 kw

Boilers: 4/ACB-Indret; 35 kg/cm², 385°C **Fuel:** 800 tons

Range: 1,500/30, 5,000/18

Man: Peacetime: 15 officers, 102 petty officers, 142 men

REMARKS: From 1967 to 1971, the *Duperré* was unarmed and was used for towed-sonar research, using the huge array now mounted in the auxiliary *Aunis*. Reconverted at Brest from 1972 to 21-5-74, as the final step in the long evolution of the T-47, *Surcouf*-class destroyer design. The hangar is fixed and has maintenance facilities, and the flight deck has a helicopter-recovery system similar to that on the

Tourville and *Georges Leygues* classes. SENIT 2 data system fitted. The ship ran aground 13-4-78 and was badly damaged, but was repaired using components cannibalized from the inactivated *La Bourdonnais*, recommissioning 2-80.

♦ **5 D'Estrées class, converted Type T-47, ASW**

	Bldr	Laid down	L	In serv.
D 627 MAILLE BRÉZÉ	Lorient Ars.	10-53	26-9-54	4-5-57
D 628 VAUQUELIN	Lorient Ars.	3-54	26-9-54	3-11-56
D 629 D'ESTRÉES	Brest Ars.	5-53	27-11-54	19-3-57
D 631 CASABIANCA	F.C. de la Gironde	10-53	13-11-54	4-5-57
D 632 GUÉPRATTE	A.C. de Bretagne	8-53	8-11-54	6-6-57

D'Estrées (D 629)—new TACAN   G. Gyssels, 1981

Casabianca (D 631)—URN 20 TACAN   4 F, 1980

Guépratte (D 632)—new TACAN   J.-C. Bellonne, 1980

GUIDED-MISSILE DESTROYERS (*continued*)

Maille Brézé (D 627) 1977

D: 2,750 tons (3,740 fl) **S:** 32 kts **Dim:** 132.5 × 12.72 × 5.9 (props)
A: 2/100-mm DP, Model 1953 (I × 2)—2/20-mm AA (I × 2)—1/Malafon ASW
syst. (13 missiles)—1/375-mm Bofors ASW RL (VI × 1)—6 TT (III × 2) for
L-3 ASW torpedoes
Electron Equipt: Radars: 1/DRBV 22A, 1/DRBV 50, 1/DRBN 32, 2/DRBC
32A, 2 SPG 51 C
Sonars: 1/DUBV 23, 1/DUBV 43 VDS
TACAN: URN 20 or . . .
M: 2 sets Rateau GT; 2 props; 63,000 hp **Electric:** 1,440 kw
Boilers: 4/ACB-Indret; 35 kg/cm², 385°C **Fuel:** 800 tons
Range: 1,500/30, 5,000/18
Man: Peacetime: 15 officers, 103 petty officers, 151 men

REMARKS: ASW conversions completed between 1-68 and 1-71: weapon system renewed, living spaces air-conditioned, electrical system and safety installations completely redesigned. These ships do not have the SENIT system. The *D'Estrées* has carried the British SCOT satellite-communications system as an experiment. A new, smaller TACAN is fitted in the D 628, D 629, and D 632. DRBV 15 (Sea Tiger) is to replace DRBV 22A.

♦ **4 Kersaint class, converted Type T-47, with Standard SM-MR-1**

	Bldr	Laid down	L	In serv.
D 622 KERSAINT	Lorient Ars.	6-51	3-10-53	20-3-56
D 624 BOUVET	Lorient Ars.	11-51	3-10-53	13-5-56
D 625 DUPETIT THOUARS	Brest Ars.	3-51	4-3-54	15-9-56
D 630 DU CHAYLA	Brest Ars.	7-53	27-11-54	4-6-57

D: 2,750 tons (3,850 fl) **S:** 32 kts (at 3,800 tons)
Dim: 128.50 × 12.96 × 5.00 (6.30 sonar)
A: 1/Mk 13 Standard launcher (40 missiles)—6/57-mm AA (II × 3)—1/375-mm
ASW RL (VI × 1) Model 1954—6/550-mm TT (III × 2) for L-3 ASW torpedoes

Dupetit Thouars (D 625) CECLANT/PREMAR II, 1980

Du Chayla (D 630) G. Gyssels, 1981

Bouvet (D 624) J.-C. Bellonne, 1977

Electron Equipt: Radars: 1/DRBV 22, 1/SPS 39 B, 1/DRBV 31, 2/SPG 51B,
1/DRBC 31
Sonars: 1/DUBA 1, 1/DUBV 24
TACAN: URN 20
M: 2 sets Rateau GT; 2 props; 63,000 hp **Electric:** 1,600 kw
Boilers: 4 ACB-Indret; 35 kg/cm², 385°C
Range: 1,200/32, 3,500/20, 4,100/14
Man: Peacetime: 15 officers, 87 petty officers, 173 men

GUIDED-MISSILE DESTROYERS *(continued)*

REMARKS: Converted to carry U.S. Tartar missile system, 1961-65. DRBV 20 air-search radar replaced by later DRBV 22. Missile systems will be used on new C 70 AA class as these ships are stricken during the 1980s. Have SENIT-2 data system.

NOTE: The training destroyer *Forbin* (D 635), last ship with 127-mm guns in the French Navy, was stricken 5-81.

FRIGATES

♦ **11 (+6) D'Estienne D'Orves class, Type A-69** Bldr: Lorient Arsenal

	Laid down	L	In serv.
F 781 D'ESTIENNE D'ORVES	1-9-72	1-6-73	10-9-76
F 782 AMYOT D'INVILLE	9-73	30-11-74	13-10-76
F 783 DROGOU	10-73	30-11-74	30-9-76
F 784 DÉTROYAT	12-74	31-1-76	4-5-77
F 785 JEAN MOULIN	15-1-75	31-1-76	11-5-77
F 786 QUARTIER-MAÎTRE ANQUETIL	1-8-75	7-8-76	4-2-78
F 787 COMMANDANT DE PIMODAN	1-9-75	7-8-76	20-5-78
F 788 SECOND MAÎTRE LE BIHAN	1-11-76	13-8-77	7-7-79
F 789 LIEUTENANT DE VAISSEAU LE HENAFF	3-77	16-9-78	13-2-80
F 790 LIEUTENANT DE VAISSEAU LAVALLÉE	11-11-77	29-5-79	16-8-80
F 791 COMMANDANT L'HERMINIER	7-5-79	. . .	7-82
F 792 PREMIER MAÎTRE L'HER	15-12-78	28-6-80	1-82
F 793 COMMANDANT BLAISON	15-11-79	. . .	6-82
F 794 ENSEIGNE DE VAISSEAU JACOUBET	4-79	. . .	10-82
F 795 COMMANDANT DUCUING	1-10-80	. . .	1-83
F 796 N. . .	. . .	. . .	11-83
F 797 N. . .	. . .	. . .	5-84

Second Maître le Bihan (F 788)—DRBC 32E dismounted   G. Gyssels, 1981

Lieutenant de Vaisseau Lavallée (F 790)   J.-C. Bellonne, 1980

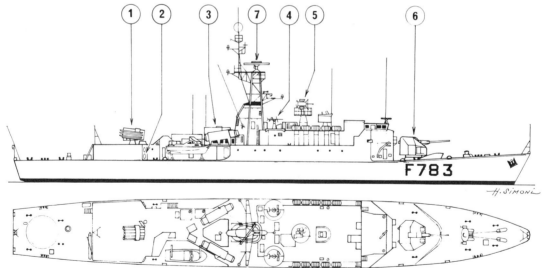

Drogou: 1. Sextuple Bofors ASW rocket launcher, Model 1954 2. ASW torpedo tubes 3. Exocet launchers 4. 20-mm AA gun mounts 5. DRBC 32E fire-control radar 6. 100-mm DP gun mount, Model 1968 7. DRBV 51A search radar

FRIGATES (continued)

Drogou (F 783)—with Exocet and revised funnel/mast   J.-C. Bellonne, 1980

Lieutenant de Vaisseau Henaff (F 789)   1980

Commandant de Pimodan (F 787)   G. Gyssels, 1981

D: 1,100 tons (1,250 fl)   **S:** 24 kts
Dim: 80.0 (76.0 pp) × 10.3 × 3.0 (5.3 sonar)
A: 2/MM 38 Exocet on 5 units—1/100-mm DP, Model 1968—2/20-mm AA (I × 2)—1/375-mm ASW rocket launcher (VI × 1)—4/TT for L-3 and L-5 ASW torpedoes
Electron Equipt: Radars: 1/DRBV 51A, 1/DRBC 32E, 1/DRBN 32 (Decca 1226)
                        Sonars: 1/DUBA 25
                        ECM: 2/Dagaie countermeasures systems
M: 2 SEMT-Pielstick 12 PC 2 diesels; 2 CP props; 11,000 hp
Electric: 840 kw   **Endurance:** 15 days   **Range:** 4,500/15
Man: 7 officers, 42 petty officers, 56 men

REMARKS: Very economical and seaworthy ships designed for coastal antisubmarine warfare but available for scouting missions, instruction, and showing the flag. Can carry a troop detachment of one officer and seventeen men. The control system for the 100-mm gun consists of a DRBC 32E monopulse, X band radar, and a semi-analog, semi-digital computer; it also has an optical sight. F 781, F 783, F 786, and F 787 of the Mediterranean Squadron have 2/MM 38 Exocet. The final six ships will carry 4/MM 40 Exocet. All have fin stabilizers. The 15th ship was ordered in 1979 and the 16th and 17th in 1980. Stacks and masts have been modified from the *Jean Moulin* (F 785) onward. The heightened stack is being backfitted in earlier units. Plans to add a helicopter facility to the *Commandant Blaison* (F 793) and *Enseigne de Vaisseau Jacoubet* (F 794) have been abandoned. The *Commandant L'Herminier* (F 791) has 2 SEMT-Pielstick 12 PA 6 BTC diesels totaling 14,400 hp; later units may get the same plant. As many as seven more may be ordered. The original *Lieutenant de Vaisseau Le Henaff* and *Commandant L'Herminier* were completed to a slightly modified design for South Africa and then sold to Argentina, which also ordered an additional unit.

♦ **1 Balny class**

	Budget	Bldr	Laid down	L	In serv.
F 729 BALNY	1956	Lorient Ars.	3-60	17-3-62	1-2-70

FRIGATES (continued)

Balny (F 729) 1975

    D: 1,750 tons (2,230 fl)   **S:** 26 kts   **Dim:** 102.7 (98.0 pp) × 11.8 × 5.0 (prop)
    A: 2/100-mm DP, Model 1953 (I × 2)—2/30-mm AA (I × 2)—1/305-mm ASW
        mortar (IV × 1)—6/TT for L-3 ASW torpedoes (III × 2)
    Electron Equipt: Radars: 1/DRBV 22A, 1/Decca 1226, 1/DRBC 32C
                  Sonars: 1/DUBA 3, 1/SQS 17
    M: CODAG: 1 Turbomeca M 38 gas turbine (11,500 hp), 2 AGO V-16 diesels
        (3,600 hp each); 1 CP prop; 18,700 hp
    Electric: 1,280 kw   **Range:** 13,000/10
    Man: 9 officers, 67 petty officers, 93 men

REMARKS: In 1964 the *Balny* was allocated for trials with the French Navy's first combined gas-turbine *and* diesel plant (CODAG). The gas turbine is a naval version of the Atar-8 turbojet used in the Étendard fighter, reduced in rate from 15,000 shp to 11,500 hp. Both diesels and the gas turbine can be clutched together to drive the single propeller, which is 3.6 meters in diameter and extends 1 meter beneath the keel. The compactness of the *Balny*'s propulsion plant compared with that of the all-diesel plants in her half-sisters of the *Commandant Rivière* class permits her to carry approximately 100 more tons of fuel, which accounts for her great endurance on diesels alone. Because one of her 100-mm guns is mounted atop the lengthened after superstructure, it has not been possible to install Exocet anti-ship missiles.

♦ **8 Commandant Rivière class** Bldr: Lorient Arsenal

	Budget	Laid down	L	In serv.
F 725 Victor Schoelcher	1956	10-57	11-10-58	15-10-62
F 726 Commandant Bory	1956	3-58	11-10-58	5-3-64
F 727 Amiral Charner	1956	11-58	12-3-60	14-12-62
F 733 Commandant Rivière	1955	4-57	11-10-58	4-12-62
F 728 Doudart De Lagrée	1956	3-60	15-4-61	1-5-63
F 740 Commandant Bourdais	1956	4-59	15-4-61	10-3-63
F 748 Protet	1957	9-61	7-12-62	1-5-64
F 749 Enseigne De Vaisseau Henry	1957	9-62	14-12-63	1-1-65

    D: 1,750 tons (2,070 normal, 2,230 fl)   **S:** 26 kts (26.6 on trials)
    Dim: 102.7 (98.0 pp) × 11.8 × 4.35 (max.)
    A: 4/MM 38 Exocet—2/100-mm DP, Model 1963 (I × 2)—2/30- or 40-mm AA—1/
        305-mm ASW mortar (IV × 1)—6/TT L-3 ASW torpedoes (III × 2)
    Electron Equipt: Radars: 1/DRBV 22A, 1/Decca 1226, 1/DRBC 32C
                  Sonars: 1/DUBA 3, 1/SQS 17
                  ECM: passive array, 1/Dagaie countermeasures RL

Commandant Rivière (F 733) DCAN, 1978

Amiral Charner (F 727) J.-C. Bellonne, 1980

Commandant Bourdais (F 740) C. Martinelli, 1977

    M: 4 SEMT-Pielstick 12 PC-series diesels; 2 props; 16,000 hp
    Electric: 1,280 kw   **Fuel:** 210 tons   **Range:** 2,300/26, 7,500/16.5
    Man: 9 officers, 66 petty officers, 91 men

REMARKS: Designed for escort duty in various climates; air-conditioned; storage for 45 days' provisions. Can embark a flag officer and staff or an 80-man commando

FRIGATES *(continued)*

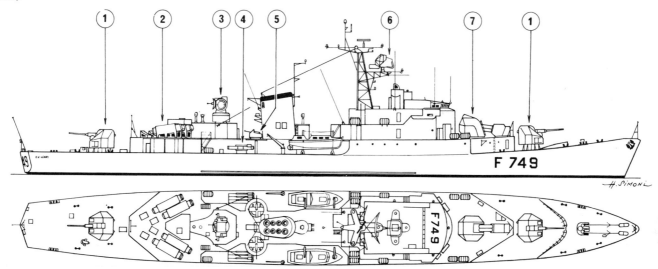

Commandant Rivière class: 1. 100-mm DP gun mounts, Model 1953 2. Exocet launchers 3. Gun-director with DRBC 32C radar 4. ASW torpedo tubes 5. 30-mm or 40-mm AA gun mounts 6. DRBV 22A radar 7. 305-mm quadruple mortar

Enseigne de Vaisseau Henry (F 749)   G. Arra, 1977

unit. These maneuverable ships are very successful. The *Commandant Bory* originally had free-piston generators driving turbines, but these were replaced with a standard diesel plant in 1974-75. Beginning in the mid-1970s, four Exocet missiles replaced a 100-mm gun atop the after superstructure. *Doudart de Lagrée* (F 728) replaced *Forbin* as cadet training ship in 1981. *Commandant Bory* (F 726) was the first ship to carry the Dagaie countermeasures rocket-launching system, with one launcher abaft the Exocet launchers. DRBV 15 (Sea Tiger) radar is to replace DRBV 22A.

NOTE: Of the three frigates of the *L'Alsacien* class, *Le Provençal* (F 777) was stricken 31-10-80, *Le Vendéen* (F 778) was redesignated as an auxiliary in early 1981, and *L'Alsacien* (F 776) was to be stricken 8-81. Of the surviving units of the *Le Normand* class, *L'Agenais* (F 784), removed from the combatant list in 1979, survives as an auxiliary, *Le Savoyard* (F 771) was stricken 29-2-80, and *Le Normand* (F 765) was stricken 1-12-80.

PATROL BOATS

♦ **6 "Super PATRA" class** Bldr: SFCN, Villeneuve-la-Garenne

	L	In serv.		L	In serv.
P . . . N . . .	. . .	1983	P . . . N . . .	. . .	1984
P . . . N . . .	. . .	1983	P . . . N . . .	. . .	1985
P . . . N . . .	. . .	1984	P . . . N . . .	. . .	1985

D: 320 tons **S:** 28.5 kts **Dim:** 50.0 (pp) × 7.0 × 1.9
A: 2/MM 38 Exocet (eventually)—1/40-mm AA—2/20-mm AA (I × 2)
Electron Equipt: Radars: 1/Decca 1226, 1/fire-control (eventually)
M: 2 SEMT-Pielstick 18 PA 4 200 diesels; 2 CP props; 9,000 hp
Electric: 200 kw **Range:** 2,500/15

REMARKS: Projected under the 1977-82 plan. First four ordered in 1980, others 1981.

♦ **4 Trident ("PATRA") class**

	Bldr	L	In serv.
P 670 TRIDENT	Auroux, Arcachon	31-5-76	17-12-76
P 671 GLAIVE	Auroux, Arcachon	25-8-76	3-77
P 672 ÉPÉE	C.N.M. Cherbourg	31-3-76	9-10-76
P 673 PERTUISANE	C.N.M. Cherbourg	2-6-76	20-1-77

PATROL BOATS (continued)

Épée (P 672)   1976

Glaive (P 671)   1980

D: 115 tons (148 fl) **S:** 28 kts **Dim:** 40.70 (38.5 wl) × 5.90 × 1.55
A: 1/40-mm AA—6/SS-12 missiles—1/12.7-mm machine gun
Electron Equipt: Radar: 1/Decca 1226
M: 2 AGO 195 V 12 CZSHR diesels; 2 CP props; 5,000 hp (4,400 sust.)
Electric: 120 kw **Range:** 750/20; 1,500/15; 1,750/10
Man: 2 officers, 5 petty officers, 12 men

REMARKS: Thirty were planned, then fourteen, but only four were initially built. Two sisters have been built for the Ivory Coast. *Epée* and *Trident* are stationed overseas. Carry 500 rounds 40-mm, 2,000 rounds 12.7-mm ammunition.

♦ 1 La Combattante-I class

	Bldr	Laid down	L	In serv.
P 730 LA COMBATTANTE	Const. Méc. de Normandie	4-62	20-6-63	3-64

La Combattante (P 730)   1974

D: 180 tons (202 fl) **S:** 23 kts **Dim:** 45.0 × 7.35 × 2.45 (fl)
A: 4/SS-12 missiles (IV × 1)—2/40-mm AA (I × 2)
M: 2 SEMT-Pielstick 8 PA4 200 VGDS diesels; 2 CP props; 3,600 hp
Electric: 120 kw **Range:** 2,000/12 **Man:** 3 officers, 22 men

REMARKS: Antimagnetic, laminated-wood-and-plastic hull. For a short passage can carry 80 men and their equipment. Re-engined 1978. Based at Tahiti.

♦ 1 Type DB-1 former minesweeper Bldr: Const. Méc. de Normandie, Cherbourg

	Laid down	L	In serv.
P 765 MERCURE	1-55	21-2-57	20-12-58

Mercure (P 765)   1980

D: 365 tons (400 fl) **S:** 15 kts **Dim:** 44.35 (42.0 pp) × 8.27 × 4.04
A: 2/20-mm AA (II × 1) **Electron Equipt:** Radar: 1/Decca 1226
M: 2 MGO diesels; 2 Ka-Me-Wa CP props; 5,000 hp **Range:** 6,200/10
Man: 5 officers, 14 petty officers, 18 men

REMARKS: The *Mercure* was converted to a fisheries-protection ship, re-entering service 22-12-80. Minesweeping equipment removed. Insulated against cold climate. Habitability modernized. Carries two 6-man rubber inspection boats with 20-hp motors. Physician and dentist carried; accommodations for 44 personnel. Former pendant number M 765. Construction financed by U.S. as MSC 254. Six sisters built for West Germany have since been transferred to Turkey.

NOTE: The former submarine chaser *Le Fringant* (P 640), used in fisheries patrol duties, was stricken 8-81.

♦ 4 former Canadian Bay-class coastal minesweepers

	Bldr	L	In serv.
P 652 LA LORIENTAISE (ex-*Miramichi*)	St. John DD, New Brunswick	1953	13-11-54
P 653 LA DUNKERQUOISE (ex-*Fundy*)	St. John DD, New Brunswick	17-7-53	21-5-54
P 655 LA DIEPPOISE (ex-*Chaleur*)	Port Arthur SY	21-6-52	13-11-54
P 657 LA PAIMPOLAISE (ex-*Thunder*)	Can. Vickers, Montreal	7-7-53	21-5-54

PATROL BOATS *(continued)*

La Dieppoise (P 655)   C. Limonier, 1975

D: 370 tons (470 fl) **S:** 15 kts **Dim:** 50.0 (46.05 pp) × 9.21 × 2.8
A: 1/40-mm AA **M:** 2 GM 12-278A diesels; 2 props; 2,400 hp
Electric: 690 kw **Range:** 4,500/11 **Man:** 3 officers, 11 petty officers, 19 men

REMARKS: Wooden hulls with aluminum-alloy frames. All minesweeping gear deleted.
Air-conditioned. All stationed overseas. Transferred to France in 1954 under the
U.S. Military Assistance program.

◆ 4 Sirius-class ex-coastal minesweepers

	Bldr	L	In serv.
P 650 ARCTURUS	C.N. Caen	12-3-54	8-11-54
P 656 ALTAIR	C.M.N., Cherbourg	27-3-56	28-4-58
P 659 CANOPUS	Augustin Normand	31-12-55	17-9-56
P 660 ÉTOILE POLAIRE	Seine Maritime	5-3-57	1-10-58

Altair (P 656)

D: 400 tons (440 fl) **S:** 15 kts **Dim:** 46.4 (42.7 pp) × 8.55 × 2.5
A: 1/40-mm AA—1 or 2/20-mm AA (I or II × 1)
Electron Equipt: Radar: 1/DRBN 31
M: 2 SEMT-Pielstick 16 PA1-175 diesels; 2 props; 2,000 hp
Fuel: 48 tons **Range:** 3,000/10 **Man:** 3 officers, 13 petty officers, 22 men

REMARKS: French-built version of the British "Ton" class. Engines built by S.G.C.M.
Minesweeping equipment removed. All stationed overseas. The *Croix du Sud* (P
658) transferred to the Seychelles in 1979. *Canopus* (P 659) was financed by the
U.S. under the Offshore Procurement Program as MSC 228. *Lyre* (P 759) stricken
6-81.

◆ 6 British "Ham" class ex-minesweepers

		Bldr	In serv.
P 661 JASMIN	(ex-*Stedham*)	Blackmore, Bideford	5-11-55
P 662 PETUNIA	(ex-*Pineham*)	McLean, Renfrew	1956
P 742 PAQUERETTE	(ex-*Kingham*)	J. S. White	14-8-54
P 784 GÉRANIUM	(ex-*Tibenham*)	McGruer	23-7-55
P 787 JONQUILLE	(ex-*Sulham*)	Fairlie Yacht Co.	25-10-55
P 788 VIOLETTE	(ex-*Mersham*)	J. S. White	1955

Petunia (P 662)   1975

D: 140 tons (170 fl) **S:** 14 kts **Dim:** 33.43 × 6.45 × 1.7 **A:** 1/20-mm AA
M: 2 Paxman YHAXM diesels; 2 props; 550 hp **Fuel:** 15 tons
Endurance: 4 days **Man:** 1 officer, 10 petty officers, 2 men

REMARKS: Except for the *Petunia* (P 662), which is used by the Navy as a buoy tender
and patrol boat, all are manned by the Gendarmerie. Built with U.S. Offshore
Procurement funds as USN MSI 86, MSI 87, MSI 82, MSI 84, MSI 83, and MSI 77,
respectively.

PATROL CRAFT

◆ 4 P 778 class (In serv. 1974)

P 778   P 779   P 780 (*Karukera*)   P 781 (*Gugane*)

D: 20 tons (30 fl) **S:** 25 kts **Dim:** 24.9 × 5.3 × . . . **A:** 1/12.2-mm mg
M: 2 diesels; 2 props; . . . hp

REMARKS: *P 778* at Papeete, *P 779* at La Réunion, *P 780* at Cayenne, *P 781* at Pointe
á Pitre. Manned by Gendarmerie Marine.

◆ 3 Volte 43 class Bldr: Tecimar (In serv. 1975)

P 770   P 772   P 774

P 772 and P 774   Tecimar, 1974

PATROL CRAFT *(continued)*

    D: 14 tons **S:** 25 kts **Dim:** 13.3 × 4.1 × 1.1
    A: 1/12.7-mm mg—1/7.5-mm mg **M:** 2 GM 6-71 diesels; 2 props; 670 hp

REMARKS: Hull molded of stratified polyester. Manned by the Gendarmerie, *P 770* at Mayotte, the Comoros, *P 772* and *774* at Brest. *P 771* transferred to Djibouti.

PUBLIC SERVICE SHIPS

As the result of a government decision of 1980, a *Force de Surface á Missions Civiles* (Civil Mission Surface Force) is to be constructed for 200-nautical-mile economic zone patrol, fisheries protection, maritime traffic surveillance, search-and-rescue duties, and pollution control. In addition to the 11 units below, the five Falcon Guardian patrol aircraft ordered in 1981 are to be dedicated to this organization, and about 1,000 men will be added to the Navy by 1985 to man the equipment. The ships are to be built insofar as possible to merchant marine standards.

♦ **0 (+2) SP 2000 Type (Provisional designation)**

	Bldr	Laid down	L	In serv.
N. . .	. . .	. . .	. . .	1985
N. . .	. . .	. . .	. . .	1986

    D: 2,040 tons (fl) **S:** 23 kts **Dim:** 100 × . . . × . . .
    A: 1/40-mm AA—2/20-mm AA (I × 2)—1/Dauphine helicopter
    Electron Equipt: Radar:. . . **M:** 2 diesels; 2 props; . . . hp
    Range: 10,000/15 **Man:** 80 tot. (+ 40 spare)

REMARKS: First to be ordered 1981, second in 1983. Telescopic hangar for the helicopter.

♦ **0 (+1) ex-trawler**

	Bldr	Laid down	L	In serv.
N. . . (ex-*Islande*)	Viareggio	1973	. . .	1983

    D: 3,000 grt **S:** 15 kts **Dim:** 87.00 (77.00 pp) × 13.60 × 5.90
    A: 1/40-mm AA—2/12.7-mm mg (I × 2) **Electron Equipt:** Radar: . . .
    M: 2 Nohab diesels; 1 CP prop; . . . hp **Range:** . . . **Man:** . . .

REMARKS: To be acquired by 1982 for Antarctic area fisheries patrol duties.

♦ **0 (+4) SPN 900 Type (Provisional designation)**

	Bldr	Laid down	L	In serv.
N. . .	. . .	. . .	. . .	. . .
N. . .	. . .	. . .	. . .	. . .
N. . .	. . .	. . .	. . .	. . .
N. . .	. . .	. . .	. . .	. . .

    D: 900 tons (fl) **S:** 16 kts **Dim:** . . . × . . . × . . . **A:** . . .
    Electron Equipt: Radar:. . . **M:** diesels **Range:** . . . **Man:** . . .

REMARKS: To be similar in layout to the *Chamois*-class tenders described under auxiliaries. Intended for pollution control and search-and-rescue duties in home waters. First unit to be ordered 1982.

♦ **0 (+4) SP 300 Type (Provisional designation)**

	Bldr	Laid down	L	In serv.
N. . .	. . .	. . .	. . .	. . .
N. . .	. . .	. . .	. . .	. . .

N. . .	. . .	. . .	. . .	. . .
N. . .	. . .	. . .	. . .	. . .

    D: 300 tons (fl) **S:** 20 kts **Dim:** . . . × . . . × . . . **A:** 1/20-mm AA
    Electron Equipt: Radar:. . . **M:** diesels **Range:** . . . **Man:** 16 tot.

REMARKS: Hull similar to the "Super PATRA"-class patrol boats in the 1977-82 construction plan, and all major data may be similar. Will have one firefighting water monitor and antipollution equipment and will, like *Sterne*, carry two rubber inspection launches. First to be ordered 1982, two in 1983, and last in 1984.

♦ **1 Sterne class** Bldr: A. & C. de la Perrière, Lorient

	Laid down	L	In serv.
P 680 STERNE	18-5-79	31-10-79	18-7-80

Sterne (P 680)   10 F, 1981

    D: 270 tons (380 fl) **S:** 20 kts **Dim:** 49.00 (43.60 pp) × 7.50 × 2.80
    A: 2/12.7-mm mg (I × 2) **Electron Equipt:** Radar: 2/navigational
    M: 2 SACM V12 CZSHR diesels; 2 props; 4,200 hp **Electric:** 160 kw
    Endurance: 15 days **Range:** 1,500/19, 4,900/12
    Man: 16 tot. (accommodations for 23)

REMARKS: Constructed to merchant marine specifications for fisheries patrol duties within the 200-nautical-mile economic zone, including rescue services. Equipped with a large infirmary. Passive tank stabilization system. Can patrol at speeds up to 6.5 knots on an electrohydraulic drive system connected to the starboard propeller. Two rubber inspection dinghies are carried.

MINE WARFARE SHIPS

NOTE: The tender *Loire* (A 615) is, in effect, a mine-countermeasures support ship. However, because she has an auxiliary "A" pendant, and for convenience, she is listed with her *Rhin*-class sisters under Support Tenders.

♦ **0 (+15) Tripartite-class minehunters** Bldr: Lorient Arsenal

	Budget	Laid down	L	In serv.
M 641 ERIDAN	1976	20-12-77	2-2-79	1982
M 642 N. . .	1977	. . .	23-1-80	1982
M. . . N. . .	1977	. . .	. . .	1982
M. . . N. . .	1979	. . .	. . .	1983
M. . . N. . .	1979	. . .	. . .	1984
M. . . N. . .	. . .	. . .	. . .	. . .
M. . . N. . .	. . .	. . .	. . .	. . .
M. . . N. . .	. . .	. . .	. . .	. . .
M. . . N. . .	. . .	. . .	. . .	. . .
M. . . N. . .	. . .	. . .	. . .	. . .
M. . . N. . .	. . .	. . .	. . .	. . .
M. . . N. . .	. . .	. . .	. . .	. . .
M. . . N. . .	. . .	. . .	. . .	. . .
M. . . N. . .	. . .	. . .	. . .	. . .
M. . . N. . .	. . .	. . .	. . .	. . .

D: 500 tons (544 fl) **S:** 15 kts on main engine, 7 kts while hunting
Dim: 51.6 (47.1 pp) × 8.96 × 2.45 (hull) 2.6 (max.)
A: 1/20-mm AA—2/PAP-104 remote-control mine-locators
Electron Equipt: Radar: 1/Decca 1229, 1/automatic track-plotter with numerical calculator, automatic pilot, Toran and Syledis radio navigation systems, Decca HiFix
　　　　　Sonar: DUBM 21B—EVEC 20 automatic plotting table
M: 1 Brons-Werkspoor A-RUB 215 × 12 diesel; 1 CP prop; 1,900 hp 2 electric maneuvering props, 120 hp each; bow-thruster
Electric: 750 kw **Range:** 3,000/12 **Man:** 5 officers, 29 petty officers, 21 men

REMARKS: Hull built of glass and polyester resin. Will have one mechanical drag sweep. France, Belgium, and The Netherlands are cooperating in building these ships for the requirements of the three countries. Second and third ordered 28-4-78, fourth and fifth 25-4-79, sixth and seventh 6-80, and eighth in 1981. Starting with the fifth, deliveries are supposed to come at 9-month intervals.

♦ **5 Circé-class minehunters** Bldr: Const. Méc. de Normandie, Cherbourg

	Laid down	L	In serv.
M 712 CYBELE	15-9-70	2-3-72	28-9-72
M 713 CALLIOPE	4-4-70	20-10-71	28-9-72
M 714 CLIO	4-9-69	10-6-71	18-5-72
M 715 CIRCÉ	30-1-69	15-12-70	18-5-72
M 716 CÉRÈS	2-2-71	10-8-72	8-3-73

Cybele (M 712)　　　　　　　　　　　　　　　　G. Arra, 1976

Clio (M 714)　　　　　　　　　　　　　　　　　　　　1972

D: 460 tons (495 fl) **S:** 15 kts **Dim:** 50.9 (46.5 pp) × 8.9 × 3.6 (max.)
A: 1/20-mm AA—2 PAP-104 remote control mine-locators
Electron Equipt: Radar: Decca 1229—Sonar: DUBM 20 (minehunting)
M: 1 MTU diesel; 1 prop; 1,800 hp
Range: 3,000/12 **Man:** Peacetime: 4 officers, 19 petty officers, 24 men

REMARKS: Designed for the detection and destruction of mines laid as deep as 60 meters. Hull made of laminated wood. Stress is on anti-magnetism and silence. Two independent propulsion systems, one for navigation, the other for minesweeping, both with remote control. Special rudders with small propellers mounted at the base of the rudder's after end and powered by a 260-hp electric motor, giving a speed of 7 knots and permitting exceptional maneuverability. Mines are destroyed either by divers (six in each crew) or by the PAP-104 (*poisson auto-propulsé*) wire-guided sled device, which is 2.7 meters long, 1.1 meters in diameter, weighs 700 kg, is moved by two electric motors that drive it at 6 knots for a distance of up to 500 meters, and has a television camera that displays an image of the mine. It can deposit

MINE WARFARE SHIPS *(continued)*

its explosive charge of 100 kg near the mine. When the sled has been recovered, the charge is detonated by ultrasonic waves. These ships do not have minesweeping gear. *Cérès* carries the prototype EVEC automatic plotting table.

♦ **5 ex-U.S. Agile class, converted to minehunters** Bldr: Bellingham Shipyard, Bellingham, Washington

	In serv.	Converted
M 615 CANTHO (ex-MSO 476)	14-10-55	1-79
M 616 DOMPAIRE (ex-MSO 454)	21-5-55	21-1-78
M 617 GARIGLIANO (ex-MSO 452)	30-10-54	18-9-79
M 618 MYTHO (ex-MSO 475)	21-5-55	7-4-78
M 619 VINH-LONG (ex-MSO 477)	14-10-55	10-4-78

Vinh-Long (M 619)   G. Arra, 1980

Mytho (M 618)   G. Gyssels, 1981

D: 700 tons (780 fl) **S:** 13.5 kts (14 kts on trials) **Dim:** 50.29 × 10.67 × 3.15
A: 1/40-mm AA—2/PAP-104 remote-control mine-locators
Electron Equipt: Radar: 1/Decca 1229
                Sonar: DUBM 21—EVEC 11 automatic plotting table
M: 2 GM 8-278A diesels; 2 CP props; 1,600 hp; bow-thruster
Range: 3,000/10 **Man:** Peacetime: 4 officers, 22 petty officers, 28 men

REMARKS: Mechanical minesweeping capability retained. All have new bridge super-structure.

♦ **5 ex-U.S. Agile-class ocean minesweepers**

	Bldr	In serv.
M 610 OUISTREHAM (ex-MSO 513)	Peterson Bldrs., Sturgeon Bay, Wisc.	8-56
M 612 ALENÇON (ex-MSO 453)	Bellingham SY, Wash.	6-54
M 613 BERNEVAL (ex-MSO 450)	Bellingham SY, Wash.	12-53
M 620 BERLAIMONT (ex-MSO 500)	Bellingham SY, Wash.	1-56
M 623 BACCARAT (ex-MSO 505)	Tacoma Boat, Wash.	3-56

Berlaimont (M 620)   G. Gyssels, 1981

D: 700 tons (780 fl) **S:** 13.5 kts (14 kts on trials) **Dim:** 50.29 × 10.67 × 3.15
A: 1/40-mm AA
Electron Equipt: Radar: Decca 1229
                Sonar: DUBM 41B
M: 2 GM 8-268A diesels; 2 CP props; 1,600 hp **Fuel:** 47 tons **Range:** 3,000/10
Man: 5 officers, 53 men

REMARKS: Budget restrictions have caused the conversion of these five ships to mine-hunters to be abandoned. However, they began receiving the new DUBM 41B sonar in 1978. M 620 recommissioned 3-80, M 613 in 7-80, M 612 in 1-81, and M 610 on 1-7-81. The *Narvik* (M 609) was reclassified A 769 1-1-76 as a trials ship for the AP-4 drag sweep and a new lens-type sonar—*see* Experimental Ships.

♦ **5 Sirius-class coastal minesweepers** Bldr: Const. Méc. de Normandie, Cherbourg

	L	In serv.
M 737 CAPRICORNE	8-8-56	11-7-58
M 749 PHÉNIX	23-5-55	21-12-56
M 755 CAPELLA	6-10-55	1-5-56
M 756 CÉPHÉE	3-1-56	11-6-56
M 757 VERSEAU	26-4-56	10-9-56

D: 400 tons (440 fl) **S:** 15 kts (11.5 kts when sweeping)
Dim: 46.4 (42.7 pp) × 8.55 × 2.5 **A:** 1 or 2/20-mm AA (I × 1 or 2)
Electron Equipt: Radar: 1/DRBN 31
M: 2 SEMT-Pielstick 16 PA1-175 diesels; 2 props; 1,600 hp **Fuel:** 48 tons
Range: 3,000/10 **Man:** 3 officers, 35 men

REMARKS: French-built versions of the British "Ton" class. Engines built by S.G.C.M. Hull is laminated wood and light aluminum alloy. Keel and stem in heavy wood. Have gear for sweeping mechanical, magnetic, and acoustic mines. The *Capricorne* (M 737) has greater degaussing capability than the others. All have one diesel sweep-

MINE WARFARE SHIPS *(continued)*

Céphée (M 756)   G. Gyssels, 1980

generator (500 hp). *Aries* (M 758) was loaned to Morocco in 1975. *Bételgeuse* (A 747) was reclassified 1-5-77 as an experimental ship and used for trials with the DUBM 41 sonar and its computer. Of the other survivors, five were converted to patrol boats. M 749 through M 757 were financed under the U.S. Offshore Procurement program as MSC 232 to MSC 235.

♦ 3 ex-U.S. Adjutant class

	Bldr	In serv.
M 633 PIVOINE (ex-MSC 125)	Stephen Bros.	8-54
M 675 EGLANTINE (ex-MSC 117)	Tacoma Boat, Wash.	30-8-54
M 687 MIMOSA (ex-MSC 99)	Tacoma Boat, Wash.	21-5-55

Muguet (M 688)—stricken late 1981   G. Gyssels, 1981

♦ 6 ex-U.S. Adjutant class for which degaussing/deperming standards are no longer maintained

M 635 RÉSÉDA (ex-MSC 126)	Stephen Bros.	11-54
M 638 ACACIA (ex-MSC 69)	F.L. Sample, Maine	14-6-53
M 668 AZALÉE (ex-MSC 67)	Harbor Boat, Terminal Isl., Cal.	9-10-53
M 674 CYCLAMEN (ex-MSC 119)	National Steel, San Diego	21-5-54
M 679 GLYCINE (ex-MSC 118)	Tacoma Boat, Wash.	30-10-54
M 684 LOBELIA (ex-MSC 96)	Tacoma Boat, Wash.	1-1-55

D: 300 tons (372 fl)   **S:** 13 kts (8 kts when sweeping)
Dim: 43.0 (41.5 pp) × 7.95 × 2.55   **A:** 2/20-mm AA (II × 1)
M: 2 GM 8-268A diesels; 2 props; 1,200 hp   **Fuel:** 40 tons   **Range:** 2,500/10
Man: 3 officers, 9 petty officers, 20 men

REMARKS: These minesweepers are the survivors of a series of 27 transferred 1953-54 under the Military Assistance Program. The hulls are constructed entirely of wood. M 633, M 675, M 668, M 674, and M 684 serve as training ships at the Naval Academy; M 635; M 638, and M 679 serve at the Brest Naval Instruction Center. Most will be replaced by the new *Léopard*-class training ships. Five have been converted to auxiliaries: *Ajonc* as a tender to the diving school, *Liseron, Gardenia,* and *Magnolia* as base ships for mine-demolition divers, and *Jacinthe* as an experimental ship and minelayer. Others have been stricken or transferred abroad: *Coquelicot* and *Marjolaine* to Tunisia, *Marguerite* to Uruguay, and *Pavot* and *Renoncule* to Turkey. *Laurier* (M 681) was stricken 15-4-80, *Camélia* (M 671) on 1-6-80, and *Pervenche* (M 632) on 1-11-80. *Acanthe* (M 639), *Lilas* (M 682), and *Muguet* (M 688) were stricken 9-81.

AMPHIBIOUS WARFARE SHIPS

♦ 2 Ouragan-class dock landing ships

	Budget	Bldr	Laid down	L	In serv.
L 9021 OURAGAN	1960	Brest Ars.	6-62	9-11-63	1-6-65
L 9022 ORAGE	(22-7-65)	Brest Ars.	6-66	22-4-67	1-3-68

Orage—now armed   J.-C. Bellonne, 1973

Ouragan (L 9021)   1979

AMPHIBIOUS WARFARE SHIPS (continued)

Ouragan (L 9021)—Super Frélon on upper helo deck   1979

D: 5,800 tons (8,500 fl) **S:** 17.3 kts
Dim: 149.0 (144.5 pp) × 21.5 × 5.4 (8.7 max.)
A: 4/40-mm AA (I × 4)—2/120-mm mortars (on L 9021 only)
Electron Equipt: Radar: 1/DRBN 32
                    Sonar: 1/SQS 17 on L 9021
M: 2 SEMT-Pielstick diesels; 2 CP props; 8,640 hp **Electric:** 2,650 kw
Range: 4,000/15 **Man:** 10 officers, 66 petty officers, 135 men

REMARKS: Bridge to starboard of permanent helicopter deck. L 9022 is assigned to
the Pacific Test Center and acts as transport to and from France, as well as floating
headquarters, employing a modular structure within the well deck. Both have repair
facilities. Can carry 349 troops, including 14 officers or 470 troops for a short distance.
A 120-meter-long well with a 14-by-5.5-meter stern gate can be submerged by 3
meters. When ships are ballasted down, displacement reaches 14,400 tons. Movement
of the sluices and valves is automatic, using pumps (3,000 m³/h) controlled from a
central position. A removable deck in six sections covers 36 meters of the after part
of the well and allows the landing and takeoff of heavy helicopters. A 90-meter-long
temporary deck in 15 sections can be used to stow cargo or vehicles, but its use
reduces the number of landing craft that can be carried, because the well is then
diminished by half.
  If used as transports, they can embark either two EDIC landing craft for infantry
and tanks, carrying 11 light tanks or trucks, or 18 LCM Mk 6 with tanks or vehicles
and, in addition, heavy helicopters on a landing platform. If used as cargo-carriers,
they can embark 1,500 tons of material. Lifting equipment includes two 35-ton cranes.
A combined command center permits the simultaneous direction of helicopter and
amphibious operations.

♦ **5 Argens-class tank landing ships**

	Bldr	Laid down	L	In serv.
L 9003 ARGENS (BDC-2)	A.C. de Bretagne	10-58	7-4-59	27-6-60
L 9004 BIDASSOA (BDC-5)	Seine Maritime	1-60	30-12-60	7-61
L 9007 TRIEUX (BDC-1)	A.C. de Bretagne	12-58	6-12-58	18-3-60
L 9008 DIVES (BDC-4)	Seine Maritime	5-59	29-6-60	14-4-61
L 9009 BLAVET (BDC-3)	A.C. de Bretagne	4-59	15-1-60	1-1-61

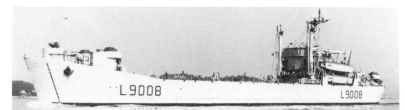

Dives (L 9008)   G. Gyssels, 1981

Argens (L 9003)   G. Gyssels, 1980

D: 1,400 tons, 1,750 (av), 4,225 (fl) **S:** 11 kts
Dim: 102.12 (96.6 pp) × 15.54 × 3.2
A: 3/40-mm AA (I × 3)—1/120-mm mortar mounted fwd
M: 2 SEMT-Pielstick 16 PA1 diesels; 2 props; 2,000 hp **Range:** 18,500/10
Man: 6 officers, 69 men

REMARKS: Design derived from U.S. LST 1 class. Can carry 1,800 tons of cargo, 4
LCVP landing craft, and a maximum of 807 passengers (normally 170 troops).
MacGregor-type loading hatches. *Trieux* and *Blavet* have been modified with a
hangar for two Alouette-III helicopters.

♦ **2 (+2) Champlain-class medium landing ships** Bldrs: L 9030, 9031: Brest Arsenal; others: Constructions de Normandie, Grand-Guerilly

	Laid down	L	In serv.
L 9030 CHAMPLAIN	1973	17-11-73	5-10-74
L 9031 FRANCIS GARNIER	1973	17-11-73	21-6-74
L . . . N . . .	. . .	. . .	1983
L . . . N . . .	. . .	. . .	1983

AMPHIBIOUS WARFARE SHIPS *(continued)*

Champlain (L 9030)   G. Gyssels, 1980

D: 750 tons (1,330 fl) **S:** 16 kts (13 cruising)
Dim: 80.0 (68.0 pp) × 13.0 × 3.0 (max.)
A: 2/40-mm AA (I × 2)—2/81-mm mortars (I × 2)—2/12.7-mm mg
Electron Equipt: Radar: 1/Decca. . .   **Man:** 4 officers, 35 men
M: 2 SACM V-12 diesels; 2 CP props; 1,800 hp   **Range:** 4,500/13

REMARKS: Bow-door design, embarkation ramp and helicopter platform aft. Cargo: 350 tons. Living quarters for a landing team (5 officers, 15 noncommissioned officers, 118 men) and its 12 vehicles, including Leopard armored personnel carriers. The two additional units were authorized under the 1979 budget and ordered 1981; a fifth is planned. The new ships will displace 1,400 tons (fl), have a crew of 47, and be able to transport 180 men; they will have a 40-ton capacity bow ramp, improved accommodations and more electric power. To carry 1 LCVP and 1 LCP landing craft.

♦ **9 EDIC-class tank landing craft**

	L		L		L
L 9091	7-1-58	L 9096	11-10-58	L 9073	1968
L 9093	17-4-58	L 9070	30-3-67	L 9074	22-7-69
L 9094	24-7-58	L 9072	1968	L 9083	1964

L 9093   G. Gyssels, 1980

D: 250 tons (670 fl) **S:** 8 kts **Dim:** 59.0 × 11.95 × 1.3 (1.62 fl)
A: 2/20-mm AA (I × 2) **M:** 2 MGO diesels; 2 props; 1,000 hp
Range: 1,800/8 **Man:** 5 petty officers, 12 men

REMARKS: EDIC = *Engins de débarquement pour infanterie et chars.* L 9082 and L 9083: 310 tons (685 fl). Can carry 11 trucks or 5 LVTs. Two each can be carried aboard the *Ouragan* and the *Orage.* L 9095 transferred to Senegal, 1-7-74. L 9071 stricken 19-4-77, L 9092 and L 9082 stricken 1981. L 9084 reclassified BAME (repair barge).

♦ **16 U.S. LCM (8) class** Bldr: France (In serv. 1966-67)

CTM 1 to CTM 16

D: 56 tons (150 fl) **S:** 9.5 kts **Dim:** 23.8 × 6.35 × 1.17 **Man:** 6 tot.
M: 2 Hispano-HS 103 S diesels; 2 props; 450 hp **Fuel:** 3.4 tons diesel

REMARKS: Cargo: 30 tons.

♦ **10 U.S. LCM (3) class**

LCM 1031	LCM 1035	LCM 1036	LCM 1041	LCM 1045
LCM 1052	LCM 1055	LCM 1056	LCM 1074	LCM 1076

D: 26 tons (52 fl) **S:** 8 kts **Dim:** 15.25 × 4.3 × 1.2
M: 2 Gray Marine 64HN9 diesels; 2 props; 450 hp **Cargo:** 30 tons

EXPERIMENTAL SHIPS

NOTE: For smaller experimental trials tenders (under 300 tons), see Miscellaneous Service Craft entry at end of France section.

♦ **1 missile-range tracking ship** Bldr: Cantieri Riuniti de Adriatico, Monfalcone, Italy

	L	In serv.
A 603 HENRI POINCARÉ (ex-*Maina Morasso*)	10-60	1-3-68

D: 24,000 tons (fl) **S:** 15 kts **Dim:** 180.0 (160.0 pp) × 22.2 × 9.4
A: 2/20-mm AA **Electron Equipt:** Radar: 1/DRBV 22D, 2/Gascogne, 1/Savoie
M: 1 set Parsons GT; 1 prop; 10,000 hp; bow-thruster **Electric:** 7,355 kw
Boilers: 2 Foster-Wheeler; 48 kg/cm², 445°C **Range:** 11,800/13.5
Man: 11 officers, 75 petty officers, 133 men, and several civilian technicians

EXPERIMENTAL SHIPS (continued)

Henri Poincaré (A 603)   DCAN, 1974

REMARKS: Flagship of Group M (the Naval Test and Measurement Group), which makes at-sea tests, takes measurements, and conducts experiments, as requested by the Navy or any other organization, civilian or military. The chief mission of the *Henri Poincaré* is to measure the trajectory of ballistic missiles (MSBS and SSBS) fired from the experimental station at Landes or from missile-carrying nuclear submarines and to compute their flight characteristics, especially from re-entry to impact. Her secondary mission is to assist the flag officer in controlling the naval and air elements in the test area, particularly recovery and security.

A former Italian tanker, the ship was entirely rebuilt by DCAN at Brest between 1964 and 1967, during which time she was given three radars for tracking and trajectory-measuring in ballistic tests and a sonar dome. She also has: an automatic tracking station; celestial position-fixing equipment: a camera-equipped theodolite; infrared equipment; a Transit navigational system; aerological, meterological, and oceanographic equipment; excellent communications equipment; a programming and transcribing center for all experiments and installations; and a platform and hangar for two heavy or five light helicopters. Refitted 1-8-79 to 1-6-80, with 2 Gascogne tracking radars in place of original 2 Bearn, as well as other alterations.

♦ **1 L'Alsacien (E-52B)-class former frigate**

	Bldr	Laid down	L	In serv.
A 778 LE VENDÉEN	F.C. de la Mediterranée	3-57	27-7-57	1-10-60

Le Vendéen (A 778)   G. Gyssels, 1981

D: 1,250 tons (1,700 fl)   **S:** 27 kts
Dim: 99.8 (95.0 pp) × 10.3 × 4.1 (hull), 5.8 (max.)
A: 4/57-mm AA (II × 2)—2/20-mm AA (I × 2)—13/550-mm TT (III × 4, I × 1)—1/305-mm mortar (IV × 1)

Electron Equipt: Radar: 1/DRBV 31, 1/DRBV 22A, 1/DRBC 32
　　　　　　　　　　Sonar: 1/DUBA 1, 1/DUBV 24
M: 2 sets GT; 2 props; 20,000 hp   **Electric:** 790 kw
Boilers: 2 ACB-Indret; 35 kg/cm², 385°C   **Range:** 4,500/15
Man: . . .

REMARKS: Redesignated 5-81 for trials with a 550-mm torpedo tube mounted on the starboard side of the fantail and firing aft (possibly for a wire-guided torpedo). Survivor of a class of three. Original crew: 10 officers, 51 petty officers, 110 men.

♦ **1 Le Normand (E-52A)-class former frigate**

	Bldr	Laid down	L	In serv.
A 784 L'AGENAIS	Lorient Ars.	12-55	23-6-55	14-10-58

L'Agenais (A 784)   G. Gyssels, 1980

D: 1,250 tons (1,700 fl)   **S:** 27 kts   **Dim:** 99.8 (95.0 pp) × 10.3 × 5.8 (max.)
A: 2/57-mm AA (II × 1)—2/20-mm AA (I × 2)—6/550-mm ASW TT (III × 2)
Electron Equipt: Radar: 1/DRBV 31, 1/DRBV 22A, 1/DRBC 32
　　　　　　　　　　Sonar: 1/DUBA 1, 1/DUBV 24
M: 2 sets GT; 2 props; 20,000 hp   **Electric:** 720 kw
Boilers: 2 ACB-Indret; 35 kg/cm², 385°C   **Range:** 4,500/15   **Man:** . . .

REMARKS: Reclassified and partially disarmed 1979. Used for experiments with ETBF towed linear passive hydrophone array, a system similar in concept to the U.S. Navy TACTASS.

♦ **1 guided-missile trials ship** Bldr: A.G. Weser, Bremen

	L	In serv.
A 610 ILE D'OLÉRON (ex-*Lazarettschiff München*, ex-*Sperrbrecher 32*, ex-*Mur*)	1939	29-8-45
		(French Navy)

D: 5,500 tons (6,500 fl)   **S:** 14.5 kts   **Dim:** 115.05 (107.00 pp) × 15.24 × 6.50
A: 1/Crotale syst. (VIII × 1)—. . . /MM 40 Exocet
　　Electron Equipt: Radar: 1/Decca. . . , 1/DRBV 22C, 1/DRBV 50, 1/DRBI 10
M: 2 M.A.N. 6-cyl. diesels; 1 prop; 3,500 hp   **Electric:** 1,240 kw
Fuel: 340 tons   **Range:** 5,900/14; 7,200/19
Man: 9 officers, 46 petty officers, 113 men

REMARKS: Taken from the Germans as a prize of war and used as a transport until converted, 1957-58, to an experimental ship for missiles. Besides the radars listed, she carries guidance radars for the systems under test. She was used for MM 38 Exocet trials and, since 1977, has been used for Crotale. Trials with MM 40 Exocet began 2-80. Helicopter deck aft.

EXPERIMENTAL SHIPS (continued)

Ile d'Oléron (A 610)   G. Gyssels, 1981

♦ **1 Sirius-class mine-countermeasures trials ship**

	Bldr	L	In serv.
A 747 BÉTELGEUSE	CMN, Cherbourg	12-7-54	22-8-55

Bételgeuse (A 747)   G. Gyssels, 1980

REMARKS: For trials with the DUBM 41 minehunting sonar. Retains most minesweeping gear and 1/40-mm AA. Enlarged forward superstructure. For other data, see Sirius-class minesweepers.

♦ **1 electronics experimental ship**

	Bldr	L	In serv.
A 644 BERRY (ex-*Medoc*)	Roland Werft, Bremen	10-9-58	26-11-64

D: 1,150 tons (2,700 fl)   **S:** 15 kts   **Dim:** 86.7 (78.5 pp) × 11.6 × 4.6
A: 2/20-mm AA (I × 2)   **M:** 2 MWM diesels; 2 props; 2,400 hp
Range: 7,000/15

REMARKS: An ex-stores ship, converted 1976-77 at Toulon and recommissioned 2-77. Used for trials with electronic-warfare equipment. Painted white. Former sister *Aunis* is a sonar-trials ship.

♦ **1 ex-U.S. Agile-class ocean minesweeper** Bldr: Peterson Builders, Sturgeon Bay, Wisc. In serv. 3-2-57

A 769 NARVIK (ex-M 609, ex-MSO 512)

Berry (A 644)   J.-C. Bellonne, 1977

REMARKS: Since recommissioning 1-1-76, conducts experiments with the AP-4 drag sweep and a new lens-type sonar. For data, see ex-U.S. *Agile* class under Mine Warfare Ships. Retains 1/40-mm AA.

♦ **1 ex-U.S. Adjutant-class coastal minesweeper** Bldr: Tacoma Boat, Wash.

A 680 JACINTHE (ex-M 680, ex-MSC 115)

REMARKS: In service since 3-54. Equipped as a trials ship and minelayer. For data, see ex-U.S. *Adjutant* class under Mine Warfare Ships.

♦ **1 underwater-research ship**

	Budget	Bldr	Laid down	L	In serv.
A 646 TRITON	1967	Lorient Ars.	1967	7-3-70	20-1-72

Triton (A 646)   G. Gyssels, 1981

D: 1,410 tons (1,510 fl)   **S:** 13 kts   **Dim:** 74.00 (68.00 pp) × 11.85 × 3.65
M: 2 MGO V-12 ASHR diesels, electric drive; aft: 1/Voith-Schneider 30 G cycloidal propeller; 880 hp; forward: 2 electric motors, 1/Voith-Schneider 26 G cycloidal propeller; 530 hp
Electric: 640 kw   **Range:** 4,000/13
Man: Ship's company: 4 officers, 44 men; divers: 5 officers, 12 men

EXPERIMENTAL SHIPS (continued)

REMARKS: Assigned to GISMER (Groupe d'Intervention sous la Mer) for deep-sea diving and observation. Has a decompression chamber, laboratories, television, navigational radar, sonar for deep-water area search, etc. Helicopter platform. Good maneuverability at very slow speeds; capable of remaining positioned above a point 300 meters deep. Can be used in submarine-rescue operations. Her 15-ton crane can lower and raise: (a) a 13.5-ton tethered bell that can be sunk to 250 meters and can carry two four-man diving teams; (b) the two-man submarine *Griffon*, which is capable of diving to 600 meters for underwater exploration; (c) diving devices, sleds (troika, automatically guided). The *Griffon* has a manipulator arm, and other characteristics are:

D: 14.2 to 16.7 tons   **Dim:** 7.8 × 2.3 × 3.1 (height)   **M:** 1 electric motor
Range: 24 hours/4 kts

NOTE: The *Chamois*-class local support tender *Isard* is also subordinated to GISMER and supports the ERIC (Engin de Recherche et d'Intervention par Cable) wireguided submersible. For data, see the *Chamois* class under Miscellaneous Auxiliary Ships.

♦ 1 submersible support ship

	Bldr	In serv.
A 759 GUSTAVE ZEDÉ (ex-*Marcel Le Bihan*, ex-*Grief*)	Stettiner Oderwerke, AG	1-8-37

Gustave Zedé (A 759)   J.-C. Bellonne, 1973

D: 800 tons (1,250 fl)   **S:** 13 kts   **Dim:** 72.0 (69.4 pp) × 10.6 × 3.2
A: 4/20-mm AA (II × 2)
M: 2 GM 16-278A diesels; 2 Voith-Schneider vertical cycloidal props; 2,800 hp
Range: 2,500/13
Man: 3 officers, 47 men, plus accommodations for 22 technicians

REMARKS: An ex-net tender and ex-seaplane tender. Transferred from the U.S. Navy 2-48. Has a 13-ton traveling crane. Formerly tender to the submersible *Archimède* (stricken 1979); subordinated to GISMER (Group d'Intervention sous la Mer). Renamed 1-2-78. Painted white. Refitted 1980-81 to support the surveillance submersible *Licorne* of 13 tons.

♦ 1 sonar-trials ship

	Bldr	L	In serv.
A 643 AUNIS (ex-*Regina Pacis*)	Roland Werft, Bremen	3-7-56	23-11-66

Aunis (A 643)   1978

D: 2,900 tons (fl)   **S:** 12 kts   **Dim:** 94.43 × 11.6 × 4.60
M: 2 M.A.N. diesels; 1 prop; 2,400 hp   **Range:** 4,500/12
Man: 3 officers, 47 men

REMARKS: Former Italian cargo ship purchased as a transport in 1966. Modified at Toulon, 1972-74. Used in the "Cormoran" deep-submerged towed-sonar project in the deep sound channel, using the RAP (Reliable Acoustic Path) equipment formerly carried by the *Duperré* (D 633). To be discarded soon.

OCEANOGRAPHIC RESEARCH SHIPS

♦ 1 Type BH 1 (provisional designation) oceanographic and hydrographic ship

	Bldr	Laid down	L	In serv.
N. . .	. . .	. . .	. . .	1986

D: 2,000 tons (light)   **S:** 15 kts   **Dim:** . . . × . . . × . . .
Electron Equipt: Radar: 1/Decca . . .   **M:** diesels
Endurance: 60 days   **Range:** 12,000/12

REMARKS: Authorized 1981. Intended to operate with one of the two Type BH 2 ships (see under hydrographic survey ships).

♦ 1 expeditionary ship

	Bldr	Laid down	L	In serv.
A 757 D'ENTRECASTEAUX	Brest	7-69	30-5-70	10-10-70

D'Entrecasteaux (A 757)   J.-C. Bellonne, 1979

D: 2,058 tons (2,440 fl)   **S:** 15 kts   **Dim:** 89.0 × 12.0 × 3.9
Electron Equipt: Radar: 1/DRBV 50, 1/DRBN 32

OCEANOGRAPHIC RESEARCH SHIPS *(continued)*

M: 2 diesel engines, electric drive; 2 CP props; 2,720 hp; for extremely slow maneuvering: 2 retractable Schöttel propellers, 1 fwd, 1 aft
Range: 10,000/12
Man: 6 officers, 73 men, up to 38 Hydrographic Service scientists and technicians

REMARKS: For oceanographic research and hydrographic duties. Has a dynamic mooring/manuvering system. Can take soundings and surveys to a depth of 6,000 meters. Two radars, one sonar; helicopter platform and hangar (Alouette-III helicopter). Electrohydraulic oceanographic equipment cranes, one landing craft, three hydrographic launches. Painted white.

♦ **1 U.S. Agile-class former ocean minesweeper**

	Bldr	In serv.
A 640 ORIGNY (ex-M 621, ex-MSO 501)	Bellingham SY, Wash.	2-9-56

Origny (A 640)   C. Martinelli, 1981

D: 700 tons (780 fl)   **S:** 13.5 kts   **Dim:** 50.29 × 10.67 × 3.15
M: 2 GM 8-278A diesels; 2 CP props; 1,600 yp

REMARKS: Converted 1961-62. Wooden hull. Painted white.

♦ **1 underwater archeological research ship**

	Bldr	L
A 789 ARCHÉONAUTE	Auroux, Arcachon	25-8-67

Archéonaute (A 789)   J.-C. Bellonne, 1972

D: 100 tons (120 fl)   **S:** 12 kts   **Dim:** 29.3 × 6.0 × 1.7
M: 2 Baudoin diesels; 2 CP props; 600 hp
Man: 2 officers, 4 men, 3 scientific research personnel, 6 divers

REMARKS: Ordered by the Office of Cultural Affairs, manned by Navy personnel. Laboratory and workshops, decompression chamber, underwater television.

HYDROGRAPHIC SURVEY SHIPS

♦ **2 Type BH 2 (provisional designation)**

	Bldr	Laid down	L	In serv.
N. . .	. . .	. . .	. . .	. . .
N. . .	. . .	. . .	. . .	. . .

D: 800 tons   **S:** 15 kts   **Dim:** . . . × . . . × . . .
Electron Equipt: . . .   **M:** . . .   **Endurance:** 15 days   **Range:** 3,000/12

REMARKS: One intended to operate with the Type BH 1 research ship, the other for coastal hydrographic survey. Authorized 1981.

♦ **2 converted ex-trawlers** Bldr: Gdynia, Poland

	L	In serv. with French Navy
A 756 L'ESPERANCE (ex-*Jacques Coeur*)	1962	12-7-69
A 766 L'ESTAFETTE (ex-*Jacques Cartier*)	1962	16-11-72

L'Estaffette (A 766)   1973

D: 900 tons (1,300 fl)   **S:** 13.5 kts   **Dim:** 63.45 (59.75 pp) × 9.82 × 5.85 (fl)
M: 2 M.A.N. diesels; 1 prop; 1,870 hp   **Range:** 7,500/13
Man: 3 officers, 29 men; 14 Hydrographic Service personnel

REMARKS: Former oceangoing fishing trawlers, purchased 1968-69. Carry one survey launch. Large oceanographic winch on stern, articulated crane amidships. Painted white.

	Bldr	L	In serv.
A 758 LA RECHERCHE (ex-*Guyane*)	Ziegler, Dunkerque	4-51	19-3-62
			(In French Navy)

D: 810 tons (910 fl)   **S:** 13.5 kts   **Dim:** 67.5 (62 pp) × 10.4 × 4.5
M: 1 Werkspoor MABS 398 diesel; 1 prop; 1,535 hp
Range: 3,100/10   **Man:** 2 officers, 10 petty officers, 26 men

REMARKS: Operated for the French Overseas Ministry. Bought in 1960. Hull bulged for improved stability. Carries two inshore survey launches. Painted white.

HYDROGRAPHIC SURVEY SHIPS (continued)

La Recherche (A 758) C. Martinelli, 1981

♦ **2 Astrolabe-class survey ships**

	Bldr	Laid down	L	In serv.
A 780 ASTROLABE	Seine Maritime	1962	27-5-63	7-64
A 781 BOUSSOLE	Seine Maritime	6-62	11-4-63	7-64

Astrolabe (A 780) 1968

D: 330 tons (440 fl) **S:** 12.5 kts **Dim:** 42.7 (36.65 pp) × 8.45 × 2.9
M: 2 Baudoin DV. 8 diesels; 1 CP prop; 800 hp
Range: 4,000/12 **Man:** 1 officer, 32 men

REMARKS: Air-conditioned. Carry two radio-equipped, 4.5-ton survey launches. Painted white. Formerly had "P"-series pendants, and A 780 at one time carried 1/40-mm AA, 2/12.7-mm mg.

♦ **1 inshore survey ship**

	Bldr	L	In serv. (French Navy)
A 794 CORAIL (ex-*Marc Joly*)	Thuin, Belgium	1967	11-4-75

D: 54.78 tons (light) **S:** 10.3 kts **Dim:** 17.8 × 4.92 × 1.83
M: 1 Caterpillar diesel; 1 prop; 250 hp **Man:** 7 tot.

REMARKS: Ex-fishing boat, operates in the Pacific. Painted white.

NOTE: The coastal survey ship *Octant* (A 683) was stricken 1-10-80.

Corail (A 794) 1975

SUPPORT TENDERS

♦ **1 multi-purpose repair ship**

	Budget	Bldr	Laid down	L	In serv.
A 620 JULES VERNE (ex-*Achéron*)	1961	Brest Ars.	1969	30-5-70	1-6-76

Jules Verne (A 620) E.C.P.A., 1976

D: 6,485 tons (10,250 fl) **S:** 18 kts **Dim:** 147.0 × 21.56 × 6.5
A: 2/40-mm AA (I × 2) **M:** 2 SEMT-Pielstick T2 PC diesels; 1 prop; 11,200 hp
Electric: 3,800 kw **Range:** 9,500/18
Man: 16 officers, 150 petty officers, 116 men

REMARKS: Six years after being launched as an ammunition ship, the uncompleted *Jules Verne* was converted to a floating workshop to provide support to a force of from three to six surface warships. Has significant capabilities for both regular maintenance and battle-damage repair: mechanical, engine, electrical, sheet-metal, electronic workshops, etc. She carries a stock of torpedoes and other munitions. Has a platform and hangar for two Alouette-III helicopters. Operates in support of the Indian Ocean Flotilla.

SUPPORT TENDERS (continued)

♦ **5 Rhin class** Bldr: Lorient Arsenal (differences as noted)

	Budget	Purpose	Laid down	L	In serv.
A 615 LOIRE	1962	Minesweepers	9-7-65	1-10-66	10-10-67
A 621 RHIN	1959	Electronics	24-4-61	17-3-62	1-3-64
A 622 RHÔNE	1960	Submarines	23-2-62	8-12-62	1-12-64

Rhin (A 621)—helicopter hangar   J.-C. Bellonne, 1977

Rance (A 618)   J.-C. Bellonne, 1980

Rhône (A 622)—helo deck, no hangar (A 615 similar)   S. Terzibaschitsch, 1980

D: 2,075 tons (2,445 fl) **S:** 16.5 kts **Dim:** 101.05 (92.05 pp) × 13.1 × 3.65
A: 3/40-mm AA (I × 3) **Electron Equipt:** Radar: 1/DRBN 32, 1/DRBV 50
M: 2 SEMT-Pielstick 16 PA 2V diesels; 1 prop; 3,200 hp
Electric: 920 kw **Range:** 13,000/13
Man: A 621, 622: 6 officers, 42 petty officers, 76 men (A 615: 9 officers, 131 men)

	Budget	Purpose	Laid down	L	In serv.
A 618 RANCE	1964	Experimental	8-64	5-5-65	5-2-66

A: None **Electron Equipt:** Radars: 1/DRBV 26, 1/DRBV 50
M: SEMT-Pielstick 12 PA 4 diesels; 3,600 hp
Man: 10 officers, 39 petty officers, 69 men

	Budget	Purpose	Bldr	Laid down	L	In serv.
A 617 GARONNE	1964	Repair	Lorient	11-63	8-8-64	9-65

D: 2,320 tons **S:** 15 kts **Dim:** 101.5 (92.05 pp) × 13.8 × 3.7
A: 1/40-mm AA—2/20-mm AA
M: 2 SEMT-Pielstick 12 PA 4 diesels; 1 prop; 3,600 hp **Range:** 13,000/13
Man: 6 officers, 39 petty officers, 69 men

Garonne (A 617)   J.-C. Bellonne, 1977

REMARKS: *Rhin* has 1,700 m³ of store rooms and 700 m³ of workshops, many air-conditioned. She has a hangar and flight deck for one helicopter, which is equipped to serve minesweepers with spare sweep gear, cable, and repairs. *Rhône* is fitted to service submarines; helicopter deck but no hangar. *Loire* has a helicopter deck but no hangar. All have one 5-ton crane with a 12-meter reach. The profile of the *Rance* is different from that of the other ships of this group; an additional deck has been fitted between her navigating bridge and her stack. She has a laboratory, radioactive decontamination stations, and carries up to three Alouette helicopters. *Garonne* was designed for overseas service. She has metalworking and carpentry shops, an extra deck with lower overhead, and a 30-ton crane mounted in the center of her fantail; no helicopter facilities.

♦ **1 EDIC-class former landing craft**

BAME 9084

REMARKS: Former L 9084, altered as an electronics repair craft and stationed at Mayotte, the Comoros. For data see EDIC class. BAME = *Batiment-Annexe-Électronique.*

FLEET REPLENISHMENT SHIPS

♦ **2 (+2) Durance-class fleet oilers** Bldr: Brest Arsenal

	Laid down	L	In serv.
A 629 DURANCE	10-12-73	6-9-75	1-12-76
A 607 MEUSE	2-6-77	2-12-78	2-8-80
A. . . VAR	12-78	9-5-81	3-83
A. . . N. . .	1981	. . .	1986

Durance (A 629)—tank deck plated in at sides   16 F, 1979

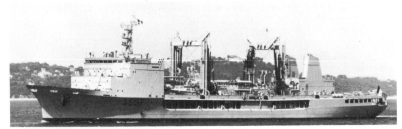

Meuse (A 607)—tank deck open-sided   G. Gyssels, 1981

Durance (A 629)   16 F, 1979

D: 7,600 tons (17,800 fl) **S:** 19 kts (fl)
Dim: 157.3 (149.0 pp) × 21.2 × 8.65 (10.8 fl)
A: 2/40-mm AA (I × 2) (A 607: 1/40-mm AA aft—2/20-mm AA [I × 2] fwd)
M: 2 SEMT-Pielstick 16 PC 2.5 diesels; 2 CP props; 20,000 hp
Electric: 5,400 kw **Fuel:** 750 tons **Range:** 9,000/15
Man: 8 officers, 62 petty officers, 89 men

REMARKS: Two dual solids/liquids underway-replenishment stations per side. Can supply two ships alongside and one astern. *Durance:* 7,500 tons fuel oil, 1,500 tons diesel fuel, 500 tons JP-5, 130 tons distilled water, 170 tons fresh provisions, 150 tons munitions, 50 tons spare parts; *Meuse:* 5,090 tons fuel oil, 4,014 tons diesel, 1,140 tons JP-5, 250 tons distilled water, 180 tons provisions, 122 tons munitions, and 45 tons spare parts. Hangar for one Alouette-III and flight deck for larger helicopters. Superstructure before the bridge one deck higher in *Meuse*. *Var* and the fourth unit are equipped as flagships for a major area commander. The forward superstructure block is extended aft by 8 meters to provide increased staff accommodations, and the two beam-mounted stores cranes immediately abaft the bridge are replaced by a single, centerline crane. A sister is building in Australia for the RAN.

♦ **1 former merchant tanker**

	Bldr	L	In serv.
A 675 ISÈRE (ex-*Caltex Strasbourg*)	A.C. Seine Maritime	22-6-59	6-6-64
			(In French Navy)

Isère (A 675)   J.-C. Bellonne, 1977

D: 7,440 tons light (26,700 fl) **S:** 16 kts
Dim: 170.38 (167.0 pp) × 21.72 × 10.27 (max.)
M: 1 set Parsons GT; 1 prop; 8,260 hp **Boilers:** 2 **Fuel:** 2,126 tons
Man: 6 officers, 41 petty officers, 59 men

REMARKS: Former French merchant tanker. Purchased 1965. She can refuel two ships alongside and one astern. Cargo capacity: 18,200 tons. To be replaced by *Var*.

NOTE: The surviving *La Seine*-class oiler, *La Saône* (A 628) was stricken 30-1-80.

TRANSPORT OILERS

♦ **1 La Charente class, converted for command-ship duties**

	Bldr	L	In serv.
A 626 LA CHARENTE (ex-*Beaufort*)	Haldnes, Tönsberg	1957	6-6-64
			(French Navy)

La Charente (A 626)   1974

TRANSPORT OILERS (continued)

La Charente (A 626)   1974

D: 7,080 tons light (26,000 fl)   **S:** 17.5 kts   **Dim:** 179.0 × 21.9 × 9.25 (10.4 fl)
A: 4/40-mm AA (I × 4)   **M:** 1 set General Electric GT; 1 prop; 12,000 hp
Boilers: 2 Foster-Wheeler; 454°C   **Fuel:** 2,037 tons   **Range:** 9,060/17
Man: 6 officers, 94 men

REMARKS: Fromer Norwegian tanker purchased in 5-64. Completed modification 11-73 to serve as admiral's flagship in the Indian Ocean (staff: 5 officers, 13 petty officers, 5 men). Helicopter platform and hangar on stern. Capability for astern refueling only. Cargo: 16,600 tons.

♦ **2 Punaruu class** Bldr: Trosik Verkstad, Brevek, Norway

	In serv. (French Navy)
A 625 PAPENOO (ex-*Bow Queen*)	9-11-71
A 632 PUNARUU (ex-*Bow Cecil*)	16-11-71

Papenoo (A 625)   1973

D: 1,195 tons light (4,050 fl)   **S:** 13 kts   **Dim:** 83.00 (70.70 pp) × 13.85 × 5.50
Electron Equipt: Radar: 1/Decca RM 316
M: 2 Normo LSMC-8 diesels; 1 CP prop; 2,050 hp   **Electric:** 290 kw
Fuel: 174 tons   **Range:** 8,000/11.5   **Man:** 2 officers, 20 men

REMARKS: 1,119 grt, 2,889 dwt. Former Norwegian solvent tankers purchased at the end of 1969. Highly automated ships. Capacity: 2,554 m³. Ten washable "inox" cargo tanks that can accept any liquid. Astern fueling capability. Bow-thruster equipped (530 kw).

NOTE: The small tanker *Sahel* (A 638) and the U.S. YO 55-class tanker *Lac Tonlé Sap* (A 630) were stricken early in 1981.

LIGHT-FUELS TANKER

	Bldr	Laid down	L	In serv.
A 619 ABER WRACH	C.N.M., Cherbourg	11-62	11-63	27-3-66

Aber Wrach (A 619)   1972

D: 1,220 tons (3,500 fl)   **S:** 12 kts   **Dim:** 86.55 (80.0 pp) × 12.2 × 4.8
A: 1/40-mm AA   **M:** 1 SEMT-Pielstick 6 PL diesel; 1 CP prop; 2,000 hp
Range: 5,000/12   **Man:** 3 officers, 45 men

REMARKS: Cargo capacity: 2,200 tons. Carries diesel oil, jet fuel, and gasoline in point-to-point service. Capable of underway fueling, astern or anchored alongside. Has passive intercept ESM equipment.

NOTE: The refrigerated provisions ship *Saintonge* (A 773) was stricken 28-11-80.

MISCELLANEOUS AUXILIARY SHIPS

♦ **5 Chamois-class local support tenders** Bldr: Ch. de la Perrière, Lorient

	Laid down	L	In serv.
A 767 CHAMOIS	. . .	30-4-76	24-9-76
A 768 ELAN	16-3-77	28-7-77	7-4-78
A 774 CHEVREUIL	15-9-76	8-5-77	7-10-77
A 775 GAZELLE	30-12-76	7-6-77	13-1-78
A 776 ISARD	2-11-77	2-5-78	15-12-78

D: 400 tons   **S:** 14.5 kts   **Dim:** 41.5 (36.96 pp) × 7.5 × 3.18
M: 2 SACM MGO V-16 AFHR diesels; 2 CP props; 2,200 hp
Man: 2 officers, 16 petty officers, 2 men

Élan (A 768)—stern crane dismounted   G. Gyssels, 1981

LIGHT-FUELS TANKER *(continued)*

Chevreuil (A 774)—stern gantry mounted   J.-C. Bellonne, 1980

Isard (A 776)—white-painted divers' support ship   M. Bar, 1979

REMARKS: Except for a 5.6-ton crane, the first four are identical to the 14 merchant FISH class designed for the supply of petroleum platforms. Hydraulic 50-ton stern crane mounted on A 767, A 774. All but A 776 can carry 100 tons dry cargo on deck, or 125 tons fuel and 40 tons water (or 65 tons fuel/125 tons water). A 768 and A 775 primarily used as water tankers. Can be used for coastal towing and cleaning up oil spills. Two rudders and an 80-hp bow-thruster. After winch with 28-ton bollard pull. Can be used as transports for 28 passengers, as minelayers, or as torpedo retrievers. *Isard* is equipped as a divers' support ship and tender for the ERIC wire-guided submersible (2 tons, 4m overall, 600m diving depth). She has a ULISM decompression chamber capable of simulating pressures to a water depth of 150m. She also has a longer aft structure, supporting rubber divers' dinghys and a small helicopter deck; the ship is subordinated to GISMER.

NET TENDERS

♦ 1 seagoing net tender

	Bldr	Laid down	L	In serv.
A 731 TIANÉE	Brest Ars.	1-4-73	1-11-73	8-7-75

Tianée (A 731)   1974

D: 842 tons (905 fl) **S:** 12 kts **Dim:** 54.3 × 10.6 ×. . .
M: 2/480-kw diesel generator sets, 1/880-kw electric motor; 1 prop; 1,200 hp
Range: 5,200/12 **Man:** 1 officer, 12 petty officers, 24 men

REMARKS: Living quarters air-conditioned, transverse bow-thruster. Used primarily as a mooring-buoy tender. Stationed at Papeete.

♦ 5 U.S. AN 93 class

	Bldr	L	In serv.
A 760 CIGALE (ex-AN 98)	A.C. de la Rochelle-Pallice	23-9-54	24-6-55
A 761 CRIQUET (ex-AN 96)	A.C. Seine Maritime	3-6-54	25-3-55
A 762 FOURMI (ex-AN 97)	A.C. Seine Maritime	6-7-54	24-6-55
A 763 GRILLON (ex-AN 95)	Penhoët	18-2-54	25-3-55
A 764 SCARABÉE (ex-AN 94)	Penhoët	21-11-53	15-2-55

D: 770 tons (850 fl) **Dim:** 46.28 (44.5 pp) × 10.2 × 3.2 **Fuel:** 125 m³ diesel oil
A: 1/40-mm AA—4/20-mm AA **Range:** 5,200/12 **Man:** 1 officer, 36 men
M: 2 SEMT-Pielstick PA-1 diesels, electric drive; 1 prop; 1,600 hp

REMARKS: U.S. "Offshore" mutual assistance. One sister built for Spain, two others built in Italy. Used as mooring-buoy and salvage tenders, except A 760, used as a torpedo retriever, with no armament.

♦ 3 La Prudente-class port netlayers

	Bldr	L	In serv.
Y 749 LA PRUDENTE	A.C. de la Manche	13-5-68	27-7-69
Y 750 LA PERSÉVÉRANTE	A.D. de la Rochelle-Pallice	14-5-68	3-3-69
Y 751 LA FIDÈLE	A.C. de la Manche	26-8-68	10-6-69

D: 446 tons (626 fl) **S:** 10 kts **Dim:** 43.5 (42.0 pp) × 10.0 × 2.8
M: 2 Baudoin diesels, electric drive; 1 prop; 620 hp **Electric:** 440 kw
Range: 4,000/10 **Man:** 1 officer, 8 petty officers, 21 men

REMARKS: Used as mooring-buoy tenders. Lifting power via pivoting gantry forward: 25 tons.

NET TENDERS (continued)

Fourmi (A 762)   J.-C. Bellonne, 1980

La Prudente (Y 749)   1976

♦ **1 Tupa class** (In serv. 16-3-74)

Y 667 TUPA

    D: 292 tons light **S:** 6 kts **Dim:** 28.5 × 8.3 × 0.85
    M: 1 diesel; 1 prop; 210 hp

REMARKS: Based at Muraroa.

♦ **1 Calmar class** (In serv. 12-8-70)

Y 698 CALMAR

    D: 270 tons light **S:** 9.5 kts **Dim:** . . . × . . . × . . .
    M: 1 Baudoin diesel; 1 prop;. . . hp

REMARKS: Based at Lorient.

DIVING TENDERS

♦ **1 base tender**

	Bldr	L	In serv.
A 722 POSEIDON	SIGNAV, St.-Malo	5-12-74	14-1-77

Poseidon (A 722)   J.-C. Bellonne, 1977

    D: 200 tons (220 fl) **S:** 13 kts **Dim:** 40.5 (38.5 pp) × 7.2 × . . .
    M: 1 diesel; 600 hp **Endurance:** 8 days **Man:** 42 tot.

REMARKS: Used for training combat frogmen.

♦ **4 ex-U.S. Adjutant-class coastal minesweepers**

	Bldr	In serv.
A 701 AJONC (ex-M 667, ex-MSC 71)	F.L. Sample, Maine	26-2-54
A 711 GARDENIA (ex-M 676, ex-MSC 114)	Tacoma Boat, Wash.	30-8-54
A 723 LISERON (ex-M 683, ex-MSC 98)	Tacoma Boat, Wash.	1-1-55
A 770 MAGNOLIA (ex-M 685, ex-MSC 87)	Stephen Bros.	30-10-54

REMARKS: The *Ajonc* (A 701) is a tender to the French Navy's diving school; the others support mine-demolition divers. A deckhouse has replaced the minesweeping winch, and the forward superstructure has been enlarged. For data, see *Adjutant*-class minesweepers.

♦ **1 British "Ham"-class former minesweeper**

A 710 MYOSOTIS (ex-*Riplingham*)

REMARKS: For details, see "Ham"-class training tender entry.

DIVING TENDERS (continued)

Gardenia (A 711)   J.-C. Bellonne, 1976

TORPEDO RECOVERY SHIPS

NOTE: The net tender *Cigale* (A 760) is also used as a torpedo retriever, and the tenders of the *Chamois* class can be employed as such. The small torpedo retriever *Pétrel* (A 698) was stricken 1-9-80.

◆ 1 former tuna-fishing boat

A 699 PÉLICAN (ex-*Kerfany*) Bldr: Avondale, U.S.A., 1951

Pélican (A 699)   J.-C. Bellonne, 1976

D: 362 tons (425 fl) **S:** 11 kts **Dim:** 37.0 × 8.55 × 4.0
M: 1 Burmeister & Wain diesel; 1 prop; 650 hp **Man:** 5 petty officers, 14 men

REMARKS: Purchased 1965. 550-mm torpedo tube at stern.

◆ 2 small torpedo retrievers for use at the St. Tropez trials center

PÉGASE Bldr: SFCN (in serv. 1975)—880-hp catamaran with one 550-mm torpedo tube aft

SAMBRACITE (In serv. 1974)

COASTAL TRANSPORTS

◆ 9 Ariel class Bldr: A: SFCN, Franco-Belge; B: DCAN, Brest

	Bldr	L		Bldr	L
Y 604 ARIEL	A	27-4-63	Y 700 NÉRÉIDE	B	17-2-77
Y 613 FAUNE	A	8-9-71	Y 701 ONDINE	B	4-10-79
Y 622 DRYADE	A	1973	Y 702 NAIADE	B	4-10-79
Y 661 KORRIGAN	A	6-3-64	Y 741 ELFE	A	14-4-70
Y 696 ALPHÉE	A	10-6-69			

Naiade (Y 702)   J.-C. Bellonne, 1980

D: 195 tons (225 fl) **S:** 15 kts **Dim:** 40.5 × 7.45 × 3.3
M: 2 MGO (1,640 hp) or Poyaud (1,730 hp) diesels; 2 props
Man: 9 tot., 400 passengers (250 seated)

REMARKS: Can carry 400 passengers (250 seated). All based at Brest, except *Ariel* and *Naiade* at Toulon.

◆ 1 small personnel transport: TREBERON (in serv. 26-11-79)—at Brest

NOTE: The personnel transport *Lutin* (Y 664) was stricken 1-7-80.

◆ 3 Merlin class (In serv. 6-68)

Y 735 MERLIN   Y 736 MÉLUSINE   Y 671 MORGANE

Mélusine (Y 736)   G. Gyssels, 1980

COASTAL TRANSPORTS *(continued)*

Bldrs: Y 735 and Y 736: C.N. Franco-Belges; Y 671: A du Mourillon

D: 170 tons **S:** 11 kts **Dim:** 31.5 × 7.06 × 2.4
M: MGO diesels; 2 props; 960 hp **Man:** 400 passengers

REMARKS: All based at Toulon.

♦ **1 Sylphe class** Bldr: C.N. Franco-Belges (In serv. 1960)

Y 710 SYLPHE

Sylphe (Y 710)   1976

D: 142 tons (189 fl) **S:** 12 kts **Dim:** 38.5 (36.75 pp) × 6.9 × 2.5
M: 1 MGO diesel; 1 prop; 425 hp **Man:** 9 tot.

REMARKS: Operates from Toulon.

SALVAGE AND RESCUE TUGS

NOTE: The French government has leased through 1982 four powerful salvage tugs as a result of the *Amoco Cadiz* disaster. All are owned by the PROGEMAR consortium.

♦ **2 Abeille Flandre class** Bldr: Ulstein Hatlo A/S, Ulsteinvick, Norway

ABEILLE FLANDRE (In serv. 1978)   ABEILLE LANGUEDOC (In serv. 1978)
(ex-*Neptun Suecia*)

D: . . . **S:** 17 kts **Dim:** 63.40 (58.60 pp) × 14.74 × 6.90
M: 4/8-cyl. Atlas diesels; 2 CP props; 23,000 hp **Electric:** 1,280 kw
Fuel: 1,450 tons

REMARKS: 1,577 grt. *A. Flandre* at Brest, *A. Languedoc* at Cherbourg. Ice-strengthened; have bow-thrusters.

♦ **2 Abeille Normandie class** Bldr: Beliard-Murdoch, Ostend

ABEILLE NORMANDIE (In serv. 1977)   ABEILLE PROVENCE (In serv. 1978)

D: . . . **S:** 16 kts **Dim:** 66.76 (61.02 pp) × 13.01 × 5.70
M: 2/20-cyl. SACM diesels; 2 CP props; 16,000 hp **Electric:** 1,600 kw
Fuel: 1,079 tons

REMARKS: 1,401 grt. Ice-strengthened, equipped for salvage and firefighting. 120-ton bollard pull. Two 550-hp bow-thrusters. *A. Provence* at Toulon, *A. Normandie* a spare.

Abeille Provence   G. Gyssels, 1980

SEAGOING TUGS

♦ **3 Belier class** Bldr: Cherbourg Arsenal

	L	In serv.
A 695 BELIER	4-12-79	25-7-80
A 696 BUFFLE	18-1-80	19-7-80
A 697 BISON	20-11-80	18-3-81

D: 500 tons (800 fl) **S:** 11 kts **Dim:** 32.0 × 8.8 × . . .
M: 2 diesels, electric drive; 2 Voith-Schneider vertical cycloidal props; 2,600 hp
Man: 1 officer, 7 petty officers, 4 men

REMARKS: Based at Toulon. Bollard pull: 25 tons. Have two firefighting monitors atop bridge.

Bison (A 697)   G. Gyssels, 1981

SEAGOING TUGS *(continued)*

Buffle (A 696)   J.-C. Bellonne, 1980

♦ **3 Tenace class**

		Bldr	L	In serv.
A 664	MALABAR	Oelkers, Hamburg	16-4-75	3-2-76
A 669	TENACE	Oelkers, Hamburg	12-71	15-11-73
A 674	CENTAURE	de la Rochelle-Pallice	8-1-74	15-11-74

D: 970 tons (1,440 fl)   **S:** 13.5 kts   **Dim:** 51.0 × 11.5 × 5.7
M: 2 diesels; 1 prop; 4,600 hp   **Fuel:** 500 tons   **Range:** 9,500/13
Man: 4 officers, 30 petty officers, 24 men

REMARKS: Bollard-pull capacity; 60 tons. Living quarters air-conditioned. All based at Brest. A 664 employed as fisheries protection ship 15-9-80 to 6-11-80.

NOTE: Seagoing tug *Éléphant* (A 666) stricken 1-8-80. Ex-U.S. *Sotoyomo*-class tugs *Rhinocéros* (A 668) and *Hippopotame* (A 660) stricken 1-10-80 and 1981, respectively.

Tenace (A 669)   E.C.P.A., 1975

Malabar (A 664)   J.-C. Bellonne, 1976

Centaure (A 674)   J.-C. Bellonne, 1975

COASTAL TUGS

♦ **11 Actif group**

		Bldr	D: light/fl	In serv.
A 667	HERCULE	Franco-Belges	194/240	21-3-60
A 671	LE FORT	FCG, Bordeaux	248/311	12-7-71
A 672	UTILE	FCG, Bordeaux	226/288	8-4-71
A 673	LUTTEUR	. . .	226/288	19-7-63
A 685	ROBUSTE	Franco-Belges	194/239	4-4-60
A 686	ACTIF	FCM, Le Havre	226/288	11-7-63
A 687	LABORIEUX	FCM, Le Havre	226/287	14-8-63
A 688	VALEUREUX	Franco-Belges	196/247	17-10-60
A 692	TRAVAILLEUR	FCM, Le Havre	226/288	11-7-63
A 693	ACHARNÉ	La Perrière, Lorient	218/293	5-7-74
A 694	EFFICACE	La Perrière, Lorient	230/. . .	17-10-74

COASTAL TUGS (continued)

Lutteur (A 673)   DCAN, 1974

D: see name list   **S:** 11.8 kts   **Dim:** 28.3 (25.3 pp) × 7.9 × 4.3
M: 1 MGO ASHR diesel; 1,100 to 1,450 hp   **Range:** 2,400/1

REMARKS: Bollard-pull: 17 tons. Similar, but not identical, ships. *Courageux* (A 706) stricken 1980.

HARBOR TUGS

◆ **14 pusher tugs** Bldr: La Perrière, Lorient (In serv. 1976-1981)

D: . . .   **S:** 9.2 kts   **Dim:** 11.50 (11.25 wl) × 4.30 × 1.45
M: 2 Poyaud 520V8M diesels; 2 props; 440 hp   **Fuel:** 1.7 tons
Range: 191/9.1, 560/8   **Man:** 2 tot.

REMARKS: For dockyard use. Primarily for pushing, but have 4.1-ton bollard pull. Eleventh delivered 11-80, later units late in 1981. No names or pendant numbers assigned.

NOTE: Two-letter contractions of names used on bows instead of official pendant numbers on tugs listed below.

◆ **2 Bonite class**

Y 634 ROUGET (In serv. 1974)   Y 630 BONITE (In serv. 1975)

Bonite (Y 630)   J.-C. Bellonne, 1975

D: 93 tons (fl)   **S:** 11 kts   **M:** 380 hp

REMARKS: Bollard-pull capacity: 7 tons.

◆ **28 Acajou class** (alphabetical listing; pendant numbers not borne)

Y 601 ACAJOU	Y 618 ÈRABLE	Y 638 MARRONIER	Y 740 PAPAYER
Y 607 BALSA	Y 635 EQUEURDREVILLE	Y 668 MÉLÈZE	Y 688 PEUPLIER
Y 623 CHARME	Y 644 FRÊNE	Y 669 MERISIER	Y 689 PIN
Y 620 CHATAIGNER	Y 654 HÊTRE	Y 739 NOYER	Y 695 PLATANE
Y 624 CHÊNE	Y 655 HEVEA	Y 682 OKOUMÉ	Y 720 SANTAL
Y 629 CORMIER	Y 663 LATANIER	Y 719 OLIVIER	Y 708 SAULE
Y 717 ÉBÈNE	Y 666 MANGUIER	Y 686 PALÉTUVIER	Y 704 SYCOMORE

Manguier (Y 666)   G. Gyssels, 1981

D: 105 tons (fl)   **S:** 11 kts   **Dim:** 21.0 × 6.9 × 3.2   **M:** 1 diesel; 700 hp

REMARKS: Bollard-pull capacity: 10 tons. *Bouleau* (Y 612) stricken 1980.

◆ **29 Oiseau class** (alphabetical listing, pendant numbers not borne)

Y 602 AIGRETTE	Y 723 ENGOULEVENT	Y 725 MARABOUT	Y 691 PINSON
Y 720 ALOUETTE	Y 687 FAUVETTE	Y 675 MARTIN PÊCHEUR	Y 694 PIVERT
Y 730 ARA	Y 748 GELINOTTE	Y 636 MARTINET	Y 724 SARCELLE
Y 611 BENGALI	Y 648 GOELAND	Y 670 MERLE	Y 726 TOUCAN
Y 625 CIGOGNE	Y 728 GRAND DUC	Y 621 MÉSANGE	Y 722 VANNEAU
Y 628 COLIBRI	Y 653 HÉRON	Y 673 MOINEAU	
Y 632 CYGNE	Y 747 LORIOT	Y 617 MOUETTE	
Y 729 EIDER	Y 727 MACREUSE	Y 687 PASSEREAU	

Bengali (Y 611)   DCAN, 1975

D: 200 tons (fl)   **S:** 9 kts   **Dim:** 18.4 × 5.7 × 2.5
M: 1 Poyaud diesel; 250 hp   **Range:** 1,700/9

REMARKS: Bollard-pull capacity: 3.5 tons. *Ibis* (Y 658) on loan to Senegal.

HARBOR TUGS (continued)

Y 680 MURENE

D: 33 tons **S:** 7 kts **M:** 1 diesel; 120 hp

TRAINING SHIPS AND CRAFT

NOTE: In addition to the designated ships and craft below, the French Navy operates a number of other units primarily in training roles. These include the helicopter carrier *Jeanne d'Arc* (R 97), frigate *Doudart de Lagrée* (F 728), nine units of the U.S. *Adjutant* class still listed as minesweeping assets, and the diving tenders *Poseidon* (A 722) and *Ajonc* (A 701).

◆ 0 (+8) Léopard class

	Bldr	Laid down	L	In serv.
A. . . LÉOPARD	de la Manche, St.-Malo	4-81	4-6-81	1982
A. . . JAGUAR	de la Manche, St.-Malo	9-6-81	. . .	1982
A. . . LYNX	de la Manche, St.-Malo	22-7-81	. . .	1982
A. . . N. . .	La Perrière, Lorient	. . .	. . .	1982
A. . . N. . .	de la Manche, St.-Malo	. . .	. . .	1983
A. . . N. . .	de la Manche, St.-Malo	. . .	. . .	1983
A. . . N. . .	La Perrière, Lorient	. . .	. . .	1983
A. . . N. . .	La Perrière, Lorient	. . .	. . .	1983

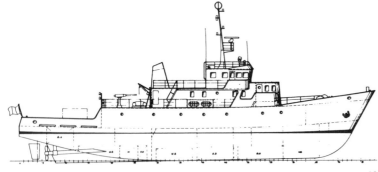

Léopard class   1981

D: 463 tons (fl) **S:** 15 kts **Dim:** 43.00 (40.15 pp) × 8.30 × 3.21
A: 2/20-mm AA (I × 2) **Electron Equipt:** Radar: 1/Decca . . .
M: 2 SACM 75 V16 ASHR diesels; 2 props; 2,200 hp **Range:** 4,100/12
Man: 15 crew, plus 21 trainees and instructors

REMARKS: First four authorized 1980, second group 1981. Intended to replace the minesweepers of the U.S. *Adjutant* class in training duties. Also for patrol use if required.

◆ 2 ex-trawlers

A 772 ENGAGEANTE (ex-*Cayolle*) A 773 VIGILANTE (ex-*Iseran*)

D: 286 tons fl (156 grt) **S:** 11 kts **Dim:** 30.0 (25.0 pp) × 6.7 × 3.8 (aft)
Electron Equipt: Radar: 1/Decca . . . **M:** 1 Deutz diesel; 1 prop; 560 hp

REMARKS: Built 1964; purchased 1975. Used by petty officers' navigation school.

◆ 2 tenders Bldr: Bayonne (In serv. 1971)

Y 706 CHIMÈRE Y 711 FARFADET

D: 100 tons **S:** 11 kts **M:** 1 diesel; 200 hp

REMARKS: Used by the Naval Academy for training in maneuvering. Sail-equipped.

◆ 6 British "Ham"-class former inshore minesweepers

	In serv.
A 735 HIBISCUS (ex-*Sparham*, ex-MSI 85)	9-55
A 736 DAHLIA (ex-*Whippingham*, ex-MSI 88)	9-55
A 737 TULIPE (ex-*Frettenham*, ex-MSI 75)	12-54
A 738 CAPUCINE (ex-*Petersham*, ex-MSI 78)	6-55
A 739 OEILLET (ex-*Isham*, ex-MSI 79)	4-55
A 740 HORTENSIA (ex-*Mileham*, ex-MSI 76)	7-55

Hibiscus (A 735)   G. Gyssels, 1980

D: 140 tons (170 fl) **S:** 14 kts **Dim:** 32.43 × 6.45 × 1.70
A: 1/20-mm AA, or none **Electron Equipt:** Radar: 1/DRBN 32
M: 2 Paxham YHAXM diesels; 2 props; 550 hp **Endurance:** 4 days
Fuel: 15 tons **Range:** 2,350/9 **Man:** 2 officers, 10 men

REMARKS: Wooden-hulled in Great Britain with U.S. Offshore Procurement funds. Used as general-purpose tenders and training craft: *Hibiscus* and *Dahlia* at Cherbourg, *Tulipe* and *Capucine* at the Naval Academy, and *Oeillet* and *Hortensia* at CIN, Brest. The 20-mm gun is usually removed from its mounting. Sister *Myosotis* (A 710) serves as a diving tender, and six others serve as patrol boats.

◆ 2 auxiliary barkentines Bldr: Chantiers de Normandie, Fécamp (In serv. 1932)

A 649 L'ÉTOILE A 650 LA BELLE POULE

D: 225 tons (275 fl) **S:** 6 kts **Dim:** 32.25 × 7.0 × 3.2
M: Sulzer diesel; 125 hp

REMARKS: Assigned to the Naval Academy.

◆ 1 sail-training yawl (L: 1932)

A 653 LA GRANDE HERMINE (ex-*La Route Est Belle*, ex-*Menestrel*)

REMARKS: Fourteen-meter yawl purchased in 1964 for the reserve officers' school. **D:** 7 tons (13 fl).

TRAINING SHIPS AND CRAFT (continued)

La Belle Poule (A 650) 1974

♦ **1 sail training craft** Bldr: C.N. de Vendée (L: 1927)

A 652 MUTIN

 D: 40 tons (55 fl) **S:** . . . **Dim:** 33.0 (22.0 hull) × 6.5 × 3.2 (1.5 fwd)
 M: 1 Baudoin 6-cyl. diesel; 1 prop; 112 hp

REMARKS: Assigned to the Dundee annex of the Seamanship School. 240m³ sail area.

MISCELLANEOUS SERVICE CRAFT

♦ **2 weapons range safety patrol boats** Bldrs: C.N. de L'Esterel

	L	In serv.
A 712 ATHOS	20-11-79	22-11-79
A 713 ARAMIS	9-9-80	22-9-80

 D: 80 tons (99.5 fl) **S:** 28 kts **Dim:** 32.1 × 6.5 × 1.9
 A: 1/20-mm AA **Electron Equipt:** Radar: 1/Decca . . .
 M: 2 SACM diesels; 2 props; 4,640 hp **Range:** 1,500/15
 Man: 1 officer, 6 petty officers, 10-11 men (including 6 divers)

REMARKS: Operate at the Landes Test Center both as range safety craft and for weapons recovery duties. Wooden hulls.

Aramis (A 713) J.-C. Bellonne, 1980

♦ **1 ASW weapons trials support tender**

	Bldr	L	In serv.
A 743 DENTI	DCAN Toulon	7-10-75	15-7-76

Denti (A 743) G. Gyssels, 1980

 D: 170 tons **S:** 12 kts **Dim:** 34.7 × 6.6 × 2.3
 M: 2 Baudoin DP8 diesels; 2 props; 960 hp **Range:** 800/12

REMARKS: A range tender with overhead gantry aft for marker buoy and expended weapons recovery. Carries divers also.

♦ **1 range safety patrol craft**

A 702 GIRELLE

 D: . . . **S:** . . . **M:** . . .

REMARKS: Wooden construction. Operates from St. Raphaël.

♦ **1 range safety patrol boat** Bldr: C.N. de L'Esterel (In serv. 14-2-74)

A 714 TOURMALINE

 D: 37 tons (45 fl) **S:** 15 kts **Dim:** 26.8 × 4.97 × 1.53
 M: 2 diesels; 2 props; 480 hp

REMARKS: Wooden construction. Can carry 1/20-mm AA.

MISCELLANEOUS SERVICE CRAFT (*continued*)

Girelle (A 702)   E.C.P.A., 1976

Tourmaline (A 714)   1974

♦ 6 fireboats

Y 745 Aiguière	Y 618 Cascade	Y 746 Embrun
Y 645 Gave	Y 646 Geyser	Y 684 Oued

    D: 70 tons (85 fl)   **S:** 11.3 kts   **Dim:** 23.8 × 5.3 × 1.7
    M: 2 Poyaud 6 PZM diesels; 2 props; 405 hp

REMARKS: Red hulls, white upperworks.

♦ 1 degaussing (deperming) tender

Y 732

Y 732   DCAN, 1970

    D: 260 tons   **S:** 10 kts   **Dim:** 38.2 × 4.3 × 2.4
    M: 1 diesel; 1 prop; 375 hp   **Man:** 5 tot.

♦ 1 radiological monitoring ship (In serv. 1969)

Y 743 Palangrin

Palangrin (Y 743)   1969

    D: 44 tons   **S:** 9 kts   **M:** 1/220-hp diesel

♦ 16 motor lighters, converted from LCM (3) class landing craft

CHA 1, 6, 7, 8, 9, 13, 14, 15, 16, 17, 18, 19, 22, 23, 24, 25

CHA 13—with four torpedo bodies as cargo   G. Arra, 1972

    D: 20 tons (50 fl)   **S:** 7 kts   **Dim:** 15.2 × 4.4 × 1.6
    M: 1 diesel; 100 hp (CHA 1, CHA 6: 115 hp)

♦ 12 water lighters

1 to 12

    D: . . .   **S:** 9 kts   **Dim:** . . . × . . . × . . .   **M:** 1 diesel; 430 hp

REMARKS: Nos. 5 and 6 in Tahiti, No. 2 at Brest, Nos. 1 and 11 at Toulon, No. 12 at Lorient, the others at the CEP (Centre d'Experimentation Pacifique).

FRANCE (*continued*)
MISCELLANEOUS SERVICE CRAFT (*continued*)

♦ **4 water lighters for SSBNs**

1   2   3   4

D: 44 tons light   **S:** 6 kts   **Dim:** . . . × . . . × . . .   **M:** 1 diesel; 496 hp

REMARKS: Two at Brest, two at Cherbourg.

♦ **1 supply craft/tug** (L: 1971)

Y. . . TAPATAI (ex-*Silver Fish*)

D: 240 tons   **S:** . . .   **Dim:** . . . × . . . × . . .

REMARKS: Purchased at Noumea, 1979, for Pacific Test Center service.

GABON
Gabonese Republic

PERSONNEL (1980): 170 total

MERCHANT MARINE (1980): 14 ships—77,095 grt (tankers: 2 ships—74,471 grt)

PATROL BOATS AND CRAFT

♦ **1 wooden-hulled** Bldr: de l'Esterel, Cannes

GC 05 PRESIDENT EL HADJ OMAR BONGO

President El Hadj Omar Bongo (GC 05)   de l'Esterel, 1977

D: 100 tons (fl)   **S:** 40 kts   **Dim:** 42.0 × 7.8 × 1.9   **Range:** 1,000/18
A: 4/SS-12M SSM (II × 2)—1/40-mm Bofors AA—1/20-mm AA
Electron Equipt: Radar: Decca RM 1226   **Man:** 3 officers, 20 men
M: 3 MTU 16V538TB91 diesels; 2 props; 10,500 hp   **Fuel:** 28.4 tons

REMARKS: Wire-guided, optically aimed antiship missiles.

♦ **1 N'Golo class** Bldr: Intermarine, Sarzana, Italy

GC 04 N'GOLO (In serv. 1981)

D: 65 tons (88 fl)   **S:** 43 kts   **Dim:** 27.3 × 6.8 × 2.1
A: 1/40-mm AA—2/20-mm AA   **Electron Equipt:** Radar: 1/Decca RM 916
M: 2 MTU diesels; 2 props; 7,000 hp   **Man:** 13 tot.

REMARKS: Replaces the original *N'Golo*, which was destroyed by fire 13-3-80. This design uses the largest glass-reinforced plastic hull of any high-speed craft in the world.

♦ **1 U.S. aluminum-hulled design** Bldr: Swiftships, Morgan City (In serv. 2-76)

GC 03 N'GUENE

D: 118 tons (fl)   **S:** 35 kts   **Dim:** 32.17 (29.18 pp) × 2.3 (props)
A: 2/40-mm AA (I × 2)—2/20-mm AA (I × 2)—2/12.7-mm mg (I × 2)
Electron Equipt: Radar: Decca RM 916   **Range:** 825/25   **Man:** 21 tot.
M: 3 GM 16V 149TE diesels; 3 props; 4,800 hp   **Electric:** 80 kw

♦ **1 32-m wooden-hulled** Bldr: de l'Esterel, Cannes (In serv. 3-72)

GC 02 COLONEL DJOUE DABANY (ex-*President Albert Bernard Bongo*)

Colonel Djoué Dabany (GC 02)   de l'Esterel, 1972

D: 80 tons   **S:** 30 kts   **Dim:** 32.0 × 5.8 × 1.5   **A:** 2/20-mm AA (I × 2)
M: 2 MTU diesels; 2,700 hp   **Man:** 17 tot.

♦ **1 Gabonese design** Bldr: Libreville DY, Gabon (L: 16-1-68)

GC 01 PRESIDENT LÉON M'BA

President Léon M'Ba (GC 01)   1968

GABON (*continued*)
PATROL BOATS AND CRAFT (*continued*)

    D: 85 tons **S:** 12.5 kts **Dim:** 28.0 × 6.2 × 1.54
    A: 1/75-mm recoilless rifle—1/12.7-mm mg **Man:** 1 officer, 15 men
    M: 2 Baudoin diesels; 2 props; 540 hp **Range:** 1,000/12

SERVICE CRAFT

♦ **1 transport** Bldr: DCAN, Dakar (In serv. 1976)

GC. . .   Manga

    D: 152 tons **S:** 9 kts **Dim:** 24.0 × 6.4 × 1.3 **A:** 2/12.7-mm mg
    Electron Equipt: Radar: Decca 101
    M: 2 Poyaud V8-520 diesels; 2 props; 480 hp **Man:** 10 tot.

REMARKS: Landing craft design, equipped with bow ramp.

COAST GUARD

♦ **2 harbor patrol craft** Bldr: La Manche, Dieppe (In serv. 24-11-77)

NDJOLE   OMBOUE

    D: . . . **S:** 10 kts **Dim:** 12.4 × 3.7 × 0.9 **M:** 1 diesel; 1 prop; 170 hp

♦ **1 Arcoa 960 launch**—S: 25 kts

♦ **6 Arcoa launches**—S: 15 kts

♦ **1 buoy tender** Bldr: La Manche, Dieppe (In serv. 24-11-77)

N'GOMBE

    D: . . . **S:** 10 kts **Dim:** 17.0 × 4.5 × 1.3
    M: 1 Baudoin DNP-6 diesel; 1 prop; 215 hp

THE GAMBIA
Republic of the Gambia

MERCHANT MARINE (1980): 7 ships—3,907 grt

PATROL CRAFT

♦ **3 Tracker class** Bldr: Fairey Marine, G.B. (In serv. 1977-78)

P 2 JATO   P 3 CHALLENGE   P 4 CHAMPION

    D: 31.5 tons (fl) **S:** 29 kts **Dim:** 19.25 × 4.98 × 1.45
    A: 1/20-mm AA—2/7.62-mm mg **M:** 2 GM 12V-71 TI diesels; 2 props; 990 hp
    Range: 650/20 **Man:** 11 tot.

♦ **1 Lance class** Bldr: Fairey Marine, G. B. (In serv. 28-10-76)

P 1 SEA DOG

    D: 17 tons (fl) **S:** 24 kts **Dim:** 14.81 × 4.76 × 1.3
    A: 1/20-mm AA—3/7.62-mm machine guns (I × 3)
    M: 2 GM 8V-71 TI diesels; 2 props; 850 hp **Range:** 500/15
    Man: 6 crew plus 10-man boarding party

♦ **1 Keith Nelson 75-foot class** Bldr: Camper & Nicholson, G.B. (In serv. 1974)

MANSA KILA IV

    D: 70 tons (fl) **S:** 24.5 kts **Dim:** 22.9 × 6.0 × 1.6 **A:** 2/20-mm AA (I × 2)
    M: 2 diesels; 2 props; 1,840 hp **Range:** 800/20 **Man:** 11 men

GERMANY (EAST)
German Democratic Republic

PERSONNEL: 1,800 officers, 15,200 men (including approx. 3,000 Frontier Guards personnel)

MERCHANT MARINE (1980): 451 ships—1,532,197 grt (tankers: 12 ships—182,754 grt)

NAVAL AVIATION: About 15 Soviet MI-4 Hound helicopters used for ASW and assault operations, and MI-14 helicopters may be in service for ASW.

WEAPONS AND SYSTEMS: Nearly all of Soviet design. *See* U.S.S.R. section for details.

WARSHIPS IN SERVICE OR UNDER CONSTRUCTION AS OF 1 JANUARY 1982

	L	Std. Tons	Main armament
♦ **2 frigates**			
2 KONI	1977-78	1,500	1/SA-N-4, 4/76.2-mm, 4/30-mm, 2 ASW RL
♦ **14 (+ . . .) corvettes**			
12 HAI-III	1962-70	350	4/30-mm AA, 4 ASW RL
2 (+ . . .) PARCHIM	1980-	960	2/57-mm AA, 4 ASW TT, 2 ASW RL
♦ **64-67 missile and torpedo boats**			
15-18 OSA-I	1964-	175	4 Styx 4/30-mm AA
18 SHERSHEN	1966-	150	4/30-mm AA, 4/533-mm TT
31 LIBELLE	1975-79	20	2/533-mm TT
♦ **47 minesweepers**			
47 KONDOR I, II	1968-79	225/310	2 or 6/25-mm AA

WARSHIPS (continued)

♦ 12 landing ships

NOTE: Ships and craft whose hull numbers are preceded by a "G" are operated by the Frontier Guard. Numbers preceded by an "S" are operated by training squadrons. "V" denotes a research or trials unit, while "E" means stores or munitions carrier, and "U" means diving services. Most navigational service and survey ships are operated by the quasi-military, civilian-manned Naval Hydrographic Service, and the ships bear "SHD" on a stripe on their stacks.

FRIGATES

♦ 2 Soviet Koni class Bldr: U.S.S.R.

141 ROSTOCK (In serv. 25-7-78)   142 BERLIN (In serv. 10-5-79)

Rostock (141)—on delivery voyage, wearing old number   1978

D: 1,500 tons (1,900 fl) **S:** 30 kts **Dim:** 96.0 × 12.0 × 3.8 (5.0 max)
A: 1/SA-N-4 SAM system (II × 1)—4/76.2-mm DP (II × 2)—4/30-mm AA (II × 2)—2/RBU-6000 ASW RL (XII × 2)—2 d.c. racks (24 d.c.)—mines
Electron Equipt: Radars: 1/Strut Curve, 1/Don-2, 1/Pop Group, 1/Hawk
        Screech, 1/Drum Tilt
        IFF: 2/Square Head, 1/High Pole A
        ECM: 2/Watch Dog
        Sonar: med.-freq., hull-mounted
M: CODAG: 1 gas turbine; 2 diesels; 3 props; 30,000 hp **Man:** 130 tot.

CORVETTES

♦ 2 (+10) Parchim class Bldr: Peenewerft, Wolgast

17 PARCHIM (In serv. 4-81)   45 N. . .

D: 960 tons (1,200 fl) **S:** 25 kts **Dim:** 72.5 × 9.4 × 3.5 (hull)
A: 2/57-mm AA (II × 1)—2/30-mm AA (II × 1)—2/SA-N-5 SAM systems (IV × 2)—4/400-mm ASW TT (I × 4)—2/RBU-6000 ASW RL (XII × 2)—mines
Electron Equipt: Radar: 1/TSR-333, 1/Strut Curve, 1/Muff Cob
        IFF: 1/High Pole B
        ECM: 2/Watch Dog, 2/chaff RL (XVI × 2)
        Sonar: med.-freq. hull-mounted
M: 2 diesels; 2 props; 12,000 hp **Man:** 60 tot.

Parchim class (45) on trials   1980

REMARKS: Intended to replace the Hai-III class; a total of 12 can therefore be expected. Previously referred to by NATO as the "Bal-Com-4" and by the press as the "Koralle" class.

♦ 12 Hai-III class Bldr: Peenewerft, Wolgast (In serv. 1962-70)

211 GADEBUSCH	241 TETEROW
212 BAD DOBERAN	242 STERNBERG
213 GREVESMÜHLEN	243 LUDWIGSLUST
214 WISMAR	244 BÜTZOW
215 DIRNA	245 PERLEBERG
216 RIBNITZ-DAMGARTEN	246 LÜBZ

Sternberg (242)   G. Koop, 1977

D: 350 tons (400 fl) **S:** 25 kts **Dim:** 56.0 × 5.8 × 3.1
A: 4/30-mm AA (II × 2)—4/RBU-1200 ASW RL (V × 4)—2/d.c. racks (24 d.c.)—mines
Electron Equipt: Radars: 1/Pot Head, 1/Drum Tilt
        Sonar: 1/Tamir-11—IFF: 1/Square Head, 1/High Pole A
M: CODAG: 1/10,000-hp gas turbine; 2 diesels; 4,800 hp each; 3 props; 19,600 hp
Range: 1,000/18 **Man:** 28 tot.

REMARKS: A not very successful design. Will probably be replaced shortly by *Parchim* class.

GUIDED-MISSILE AND TORPEDO PATROL BOATS

♦ **15 Soviet Osa-I-class missile boats** Bldr: U.S.S.R.

S 711 ALBERT GAST	751 PAUL WIEKZOREK
S 712 FRIEDRICH SCHULZE	752 RUDOLF EGELHOFER
S 713 ALBIN KÖBIS	753 RICHARD SORGE
S 714 MAX REICHPIETSCH	754 FRITZ GAST
731 WALTER KRÄMER	. . . HEINRICH DORRENBACH
732 KARL MESEBERG	. . . OTTO TOST
733 AUGUST LÜTTGENS	. . . JOSEPH SCHARES
734 PAUL EISENSCHNEIDER	

August Lüttgens (733)   1970

D: 175 tons (205 fl)   **S:** 35 kts   **Dim:** 39.0 × 7.6 × 1.8
A: 4/Styx (SS-N-2)—4/30-mm AA (II × 2)
Electron Equipt: Radars: 1/Square Tie, 1/Drum Tilt
                IFF: 2/Square Head, 1/High Pole A
M: 3 M503A diesels; 3 props; 12,000 hp   **Range:** 430/34, 700/20   **Man:** 30 tot.

REMARKS: Transferred 1966. Boats with "S" numbers are used for training. Other names reported, *Anton Saefkow, Paul Engelhofer,* indicate that more than 15 may have been delivered.

♦ **18 Soviet Shershen-class torpedo boats** Bldr: U.S.S.R.

811 MAX HOOP	832 ERICH KUTTNER	853 HEINZ BIEMLER
812 WILLI BÄNTSCH	833 ARTUR BECKER	854 HEINZ KAPELLE
813 ARVID HARNACK	834 FRITZ HECKERT	855 ADAM KUCKHOFF
814 BERNHARD BÄSTLEIN	835 ERNST SCHNELLER	. . . RUDOLF BREITSCHEID
815 FRITZ BEHN	851 EDGAR ANDRÉ	. . . ERNST GRUBE
831 WILHELM FLORIN	852 JOSEPH ROEMER	. . . BRUNO KÜHN

D: 150 tons (180 fl)   **S:** 45 kts   **Dim:** 34.0 × 7.2 × 1.5
A: 4/Styx (SS-N-2)—4/30-mm AA (II × 2)
Electron Equipt: Radars: 1/Pot Drum, 1/Drum Tilt
                IFF: 1/Square Head, 1/High Pole A
M: 3 M503A diesels; 3 props; 12,000 hp

REMARKS: Transferred 1968-76. Units without numbers believed to have "S"-series numbers and are employed in training.

Adam Kuckhoff (855)   1976

♦ **31 Libelle-class light torpedo boats** Bldr: East Germany

Libelle class   1976

Libelle class   1975

D: 30 tons (fl)   **S:** 50 kts   **Dim:** 19.6 × 4.5 × 2.0
A: 2/533-mm TT—2/23-mm AA (II × 1)   **Electron Equipt:** Radar: 1/TSR-333
M: 3 M50-F4 diesels; 3 props; 3,600 hp   **Man:** 10 tot.

REMARKS: Hull numbers, 900 series. Completed since 1975. Can quickly convert to commando/frogman carriers. Torpedoes discharged over stern; short tubes on deck may be for smoke generator system. Names reported: *Fritz Globig, Karl Baier.*

PATROL CRAFT

♦ Bremse class

G 30 to G 39

Bremse class—old number

   D: 25 tons **S:** 14 kts **Dim:** 23.0 × 5.0 × 1.1 **A:** Small arms
M: 2 diesels; 2 props; 600 hp

REMARKS: Date from 1971. Also known as KB-123 class. Operated by the Border Guard on rivers and inland waterways. The Border Guard also has a number of smaller craft.

♦ 6 "fishing cutter" class

G 60 to G 65

REMARKS: Wooden-hulled former fishing boats operated by the Border Guard.

MINE WARFARE SHIPS

♦ 26 Kondor-II-class patrol minesweepers Bldr: Peenewerft, Wolgast

(In serv. 1971-78)

311 ALTENBURG	324 RÖBEL	341 EILENSBURG
312 GENTHIN	325 KLÜTZ	342 BOLTENHAGEN
313 ZERBST	326 NEURUPPIN	343 BERNAU
314 BITTERFELD	331 RATHENOW	344 TANGERHÜTTE
315 ROSSLAU	332 TORGAU	345 RIESA
316 DESSAU	333 MEININGEN	346 GUBEN
321 KYRITZ	334 POESSNICK	S 321 SCHÖNEBECK
322 STRASBURG	335 GREIZ	S 322 WITTSTOCK
323 TIMENDORF	336 FREIBERG	

   D: 260 tons (310 fl) **S:** 17 kts **Dim:** 55.0 × 7.0 × 2.4
A: 6/25-mm AA (II × 3)—mines **Electron Equipt:** Radar: 1/TSR-333
M: 2/40D diesels; 2 CP props; 5,000 hp **Man:** 40 tot.

REMARKS: Typed "High Seas Minesweepers" by the East German Navy. Two, with "S" pendants, serve as training ships. Three additional units are trials craft.

Meiningen (333)   1976

Kondor-II class—training squadron hull number (old number)   1976

♦ 21 Kondor-I-class inshore minesweepers Bldr: Peenewerft, Wolgast, 1968-70

G 411 STENDAL	G 422 ZWICKAU	G 443 RERIK
G 412 BERGEN	G 423 PREROW	G 444 WEISSWASSER
G 413 GREIFSWALD	G 424 GRAAL-MÜRITZ	G 445 NEUSTRELITZ
G 414 PASEWALK	G 425 ZINGST	G 446 DEMMIN
G 415 PRENZLAU	G 426 WITTE	S. . . KUHLUNGSBORN
G 416 MEISSEN	G 441 ANKLAM	S. . . WOLGAST
G 421 AHRENSKOOP	G 442 UECKERMÜNDE	S. . . N. . .

Kondor-I class—old number   1976

   D: 225 tons (275 fl) **S:** 17 kts **Dim:** 52.0 × 7.0 × 2.4
A: 2/25-mm AA (II × 1)—mines **Man:** 30 tot.
Electron Equipt: Radar: 1/TSR-333 **M:** 2/40D diesels; 2 CP props; 5,000 hp

MINE WARFARE SHIPS (continued)

REMARKS: Typed "Coastal Minesweeper" by East Germany. Attached to Border Guard as patrol boats but retain minesweeping gear. Three serve as training units, with "S" numbers. Two have been converted as torpedo-recovery craft; two others, the *Komet* and *Meteor*, altered as intelligence collectors; another is the state yacht *Ostseeland;* V 31 is a trials craft; the *Ernst Thaelmann* was converted to a youth-training ship in 1977. Other names reported include *Hettstadt* and *Eisleben*—one of which is probably a training craft and the other now possibly V 31.

AMPHIBIOUS SHIPS AND CRAFT

♦ **12 Frosch-class landing ships** Bldr: Peenewerft, Wolgast, 1976-79

6. . . COTTBUS	6. . . NEUBRANDENBERG
6. . . EBERSWALDE-FINOW	6. . . SCHWERIN
6. . . EISENHÜTTENSTADT	631 SIEGER
6. . . FRANKFURT/ODER	6. . . N . . .
6. . . HOYERSWERDA	6. . . N . . .
6. . . LÜBBEN	6. . . N . . .

Numbers: 611-616, 631-636

Frosch class 615—with two 40-tubed, 122-mm artillery RL   1980

Frosch class 634—without artillery RL   1980

D: 2,000 tons (fl) **S:** 16 kts **Dim:** 98.0 × 12.5 × 2.8
A: 4/57-mm AA (II × 2)—4/30-mm AA (II × 2)—2/122-mm artillery RL (XL × 2)—mines
Electron Equipt: Radars: 1/Strut Curve, 1/Muff Cob, 1/TSR-333
M: 2/40D diesels; 2 props; 5,000 hp

REMARKS: Cargo capacity 400 to 600 tons. Similar in general form to new Soviet Ropucha class, but smaller and with a blunter bow, heavier armament, etc. Two rocket launchers of the type carried by the Soviet ship *Ivan Rogov* are being added forward of the bridge. Two additional units have been completed as Frosch-II-class supply ships—see under Auxiliaries.

NOTE: All units of the Robbe and LABO-100 classes have been stricken.

INTELLIGENCE COLLECTION SHIPS

♦ **2 modified Kondor-I class** Bldr: Peenewerft, Wolgast (In serv. 1968-70)

KOMET (ex-. . .)   METEOR (ex-. . .)

Meteor   G. Koop, 1976

REMARKS: No armament. Collection antennas added; data otherwise as for Kondor-I-class minesweepers.

♦ **1 Soviet Okean-class trawler** (In serv. 1958)

HYDROGRAPH

Hydrograph   1976

D: 1,050 tons (fl) **S:** 11 kts **Dim:** 54.2 × 9.3 × 3.6
M: 1 8NVD48 diesel; 1 prop; 800 hp **Range:** 9,400/11 **Man:** 32 tot.

REMARKS: Former trawler equipped with Sigint collection devices.

HYDROGRAPHIC SURVEY SHIPS

NOTE: All survey ships, buoy tenders, and the cable tender *Dornbusch* are operated under SHD, the Naval Hydrographic Service, and are civilian-manned.

HYDROGRAPHIC SURVEY SHIPS *(continued)*

♦ **1 Soviet Finik class** Bldr: Polnocny SY, Gdansk, Poland (In serv. 12-80)

DORNBUSCH

D: . . . **S:** 13 kts **Dim:** 61.3 × 11.8 × 3.0 **Electron Equipt:** Radar: . . .
M: 2 Sgoda-Sulzer diesels; 2 props; 1,960 hp **Man:** 24 tot.

REMARKS: Replaces German-built ship with same name. Auxiliary electric-drive system gives 6-knot quiet-running speed. Useful as a buoy tender or survey ship.

♦ **1 modified Kondor-II class**

KARL FRIEDRICH GAUSS

REMARKS: Since 1978. No armament; white-painted. Data as for Kondor-II-class minesweepers. Has more extensive superstructure, twin kingposts aft for handling boats, buoys, etc.

♦ **1 Soviet Kamenka class** Bldr: Szczecin SY, Poland, (In serv. 1972)

BUK

D: 703 tons (fl) **S:** 13.7 kts **Dim:** 53.5 × 9.1 × 2.6
M: 2 Zgoda-Sulzer diesels; 2 CP props; 1,765 hp **Range:** 4,000/10

REMARKS: Buoy tender and survey ship; one 5-ton crane.

♦ **3 Arkona class, also buoy tenders**

ARKONA   DARSSER ORT   STUBBENKAMMER

D: 55 tons **S:** 10 kts **M:** Diesel

REMARKS: Built 1965-70.

♦ **8 buoy tenders** (In serv. 1971-72)

BREITLING, ESPER ORT, GOLWITZ, GRASS ORT, LANDTIEFF, PALMER ORT, RAMZOW, ROSEN ORT

D: 158 tons (320 fl) **S:** 11.5 kts **Dim:** 29.6 × 6.2 × 1.9
M: 1 diesel; 1 prop; 580 hp

EXPERIMENTAL SHIPS V = *Versuch* (Research)

♦ **1 ex-civilian research ship** (In serv. late 1950s)

V 84 RÜGEN (ex-V 71, ex-*Meteor*)

D: 700 tons **S:** 10 kts **Dim:** 50.8 × 3.8 × 3.4 **Range:** 7,900/9 **Man:** 30 tot.
Electron Equipt: Radar: 1/TSR-333 **M:** 1 diesel; 1 prop; 540 hp

REMARKS: Built as a fishing boat.

♦ **1 Libelle-class torpedo boat** V 87

NOTE: With the naming of a new corvette *Parchim*, it can be assumed that the Hai-II-class trials unit of the same name has been stricken.

♦ **3 Kondor-II-class minesweeper**

V 381 N. . .   V 382 N. . .   V 383   SCHÖNEBECK

♦ **1 Kondor-I-class minesweeper**

V 85 N. . . (ex-V 31)

Rügen (V 84)—with old number   1976

AMPHIBIOUS WARFARE SUPPORT SHIPS

♦ **2 Frosch-II class** Bldr: Peenewerft, Wolgast (1980)

E 35 NORDPERD   E 36 SÜDPERD

Sudperd (E 36)   1980

Sudperd (E 36)—note 2 twin 25-mm AA at bow   1980

D: 2,000 tons (fl) **S:** 16 kts **Dim:** 98.0 × 12.5 × 2.8
A: 4/57-mm AA (II × 2)—4/25-mm AA (II × 2)—mines

AMPHIBIOUS WARFARE SUPPORT SHIPS *(continued)*

Electron Equipt: Radar: 1/TSR-333, 1/Strut Curve, 1/Muff Cob
IFF: 1/Square Head, 1/High Pole A
M: 2/40D diesels; 2 props; 5,000 hp **Man:** 120 tot.

REMARKS: Differ from Frosch-I in having a large crane amidships and two cargo hatches, and in having 25-mm (mounted right forward to cover the beach) in place of 30-mm AA. Although they have an auxiliary-series pendant number, the bow ramp is retained to permit a beaching capability, and they presumably can be used as assault landing ships if needed. Believed to carry munitions, at least in peacetime.

OILERS

♦ **1 Soviet Baskunchak class** Bldr: Kamysh Buran SY, Kerch (In serv. 1964-68)

C 27 USEDOM

Usedom (C 27)

D: 2,940 tons **S:** 13.2 kts **Dim:** 83.6 (74.0 pp) × 12.0 × 4.6
Electron Equipt: Radar: 1/Don-2
M: 1/8DR43/61 VI diesel; 1 prop; 2,000 hp **Electric:** 325 kw **Fuel:** 124 tons
Range: 5,000/12.6 **Man:** 30 tot.

REMARKS: 1,770 grt/1,660 dwt. Cargo: 1,490 tons (9,993 barrels fuel oil).

♦ **3 Hiddensee class** Bldr: Peenewerft, Wolgast, 1960-61

C 23 POEL   C 37 HIDDENSEE   C 75 RIEMS

Poel (C 23)—before being armed

D: 1,450 tons (fl) **S:** 12 kts **Dim:** 53.7 × 9.0 × 4.5 **A:** 4/25-mm AA (II × 2)
Electron Equipt: Radar: 1/TSR-333 **M:** 2 diesels; 1,400 hp **Man:** 26 tot.

REMARKS: Laid down during World War II. *Sahel* in French Navy was a sister. Cargo: 650 tons.

♦ **2 Kuemo class** Bldr: Matthias Thiesen Werft, Wismar (In serv. 1955-57)

E. . . RUDEN   C. . . VILM

Ruden   1976

D: 585 tons (fl) **S:** 9 kts **Dim:** 36.0 × 7.3 × 2.7
Electron Equipt: Radar: 1/TSR-333 **M:** 1 diesel; 1 prop; 300 hp

REMARKS: *Ruden* is a cargo ship; *Vilm* is an oiler. Sister *Rügen*, a torpedo trials ship, has been discarded.

TRAINING SHIPS   S = *Schulschiff* (Schoolship)

♦ **1 Polish Wodnik class** Bldr: Gdansk SY (In serv. 6-7-76)

S 61 WILHELM PIECK

Wilhelm Pieck (S 61)   1976

D: 2,000 tons (fl) **S:** 17 kts **Dim:** 73.0 × 12.0 × 4.0
A: 4/30-mm AA (II × 2)—4/25-mm AA (II × 2)
Electron Equipt: Radars: 2/TRS-333, 1/Drum Tilt **Man:** 80 tot.
M: 2 Zgoda-Sulzer 6 TD 48 diesels; 2 props; 3,600 hp **Electric:** 530 kw

REMARKS: In service 6-7-76. Sister to *Wodnik* and *Gryf* in Polish Navy and *Oka* and *Luga* in Soviet Navy. Design developed from that of the Soviet Moma-class surveying ships.

NOTE: In addition to the *Wilhelm Pieck,* the following are used for training (data earlier): 3 Osa-I-class missile boats, 3 Shershen-class torpedo boats, 2 Kondor-II-class minesweepers, and 3 Kondor-I-class minesweepers. All have S-series hull numbers.

SALVAGE SHIP

♦ **1 Polish Piast class** Bldr: Gdansk SY, 1977

A 46 OTTO VON GUERICKE

D: 1,560 tons (1,732 fl)   **S:** 16.5 kts   **Dim:** 73.2 × 10.0 × 4.0
M: 2 Zgoda-Sulzer 6TD 48 diesels; 2 props; 3,600 hp   **Range:** 3,000/12

REMARKS: Sister to Polish *Piast* and *Lech.* Can mount 8/25-mm AA (II × 4). Has diving bell. Built on Soviet Moma-class survey-ship hull and propulsion plant.

DIVING TENDER

♦ **1 converted Havel-class fishing trawler** (In serv. 1971)

U 33 HUGO ECKENER

Hugo Eckener (U 33)   1977

D: 450 tons (fl)   **S:** 10.5 kts   **Dim:** 37.7 (33.0 pp) × 8.2 × 3.0
M: 1 type 8 NVD36A diesel; 578 hp   **Electric:** 280 kw   **Man:** 20 tot.

REMARKS: Stern-haul trawler with equipment for mine-clearance divers.

VARIOUS SHIPS

♦ **2 Kondor-I-class torpedo retriever/target ships**

B 73   B 74

REMARKS: Converted Kondor-I-class minesweepers, which they basically resemble. No armament. Ramp at stern for torpedo recovery. Radar reflector array on mast, below TSR-333 radar. See data under minesweepers.

♦ **1 yacht**

OSTSEELAND

REMARKS: Kondor-I minesweeper hull; large, rakish superstructure. Used for head of state.

♦ **several small diving tenders**

♦ **up to 11 Jugend-class barracks barges**

B 74   1976

♦ **1 small cable tender**

FREESENDORF   Built 1963

♦ **1 seagoing tug (also salvage tug)** Bldr: Peenewerft, Wolgast (In serv. 1964)

A 14

D: 800 tons   **S:** 12.8 kts   **Dim:** 44.7 × 10.7 × 3.9
M: 2 diesels; 2 props; 1,100 hp

REMARKS: 505 grt. Sister to Bulgarian *Jupiter.* Bollard pull: 16 tons.

♦ **11 harbor tugs**

♦ **5 Gustav Koenigs-class harbor fuel lighters** Bldr: VEB, Rosslau/Elbe

C 16   C 17   C 25   C 76   C 77

SOCIETY FOR SPORTS AND MECHANICS

The Naval College of this paramilitary youth organization maintains a number of craft for training, the largest of which is the *Ernst Thaelmann.*

♦ **1 converted Kondor-I-class minesweeper**

ERNST THAELMANN

REMARKS: Conversion completed 19-8-77. Superstructure enlarged; carries 10 crew and 28 trainees.

GERMANY (WEST)
Federal Republic of Germany

PERSONNEL: approx. 38,500 men

MERCHANT MARINE (1980): 1,906 ships—8,355,638 grt
(tankers: 107 ships—2,756,863 grt)

SHIPS IN SERVICE, UNDER CONSTRUCTION, OR ORDERED
AS OF 1 JANUARY 1982

	L	Tons	Main armament
♦ 24 submarines			
18 TYPE 206	1972-74	450	8/533-mm TT
6 TYPE 205	1961-68	370	8/533-mm TT
♦ 7 destroyers			
3 CHARLES F. ADAMS	1967-69	3,370	1/Tartar, 2/127-mm DP, 1/ASROC
4 HAMBURG	1960-63	3,400	4/MM 38, 3/100-mm, 8/40-mm AA, 4/ASW TT
♦ 6 (+6) frigates			
0 (+6)TYPE 122	1979-82	2,900	8/Harpoon, 1/Sea Sparrow, 1/76-mm, 4/ASW TT, 2/helicopters
6 KÖLN	1958-62	1,750	2/100-mm DP, 6/40-mm AA, 2/ASW RL, 4/ASW TT
♦ 5 corvettes			
5 THETIS	1960-62	604	2/40-mm AA, 1/ASW RL, 4/ASW TT
♦ 30 (+10) guided-missile boats			
0 (+10) TYPE 143A	1981-83	300	4/MM 38, 1/76-mm DP, 1/RAM system, mines
10 TYPE 143	1973-76	295	4/MM 38, 2/76-mm DP, 2/533-mm TT
20 TYPE 148	1972-75	234	4/MM 38, 1/76-mm DP, 1/40-mm AA
♦ 10 torpedo boats			
10 TYPE 142	1961-63	160	2/40-mm AA, 2/533-mm TT

♦ 64 minesweepers/minehunters

NAVAL AVIATION:
2 groups of Starfighter (F-104 G) all-weather interceptor attack and reconnaissance airplanes (110-120 planes). Characteristics are:
  Length: 16.61 meters
  Wingspan: 6.68 meters
  Takeoff weight: 9,900 kg
  Motor: 1 GE J79 SE 11A turbojet, 7,170 kg thrust
  Max. speed: Mach 2
  Altitude: 50,000 feet

Bréguet Atlantic — 1973

  Range: 250 to 600 nautical miles, depending on equipment
  Weapons: 4,000 kg maximum (bombs, rockets, Bullpup, etc.)
1 squadron of 20 Bréguet Atlantic-1150 aircraft, 5 of which have been modified for electronic warfare. The ASW aircraft are undergoing modernization 1981-83.
1 squadron of 22 Mk 41 Sea King helicopters for search and rescue operations.
On 7-4-76 the German government decided to begin construction of 112 MRCA Tornado variable-geometry fighter-bombers for the Navy. The first entered service in 5-81. Characteristics are:
  Length: 16.70 meters
  Wingspan: 13.90 meters max./8.60 meters min.
  Maximum takeoff weight: 24,500 kg
  Maximum speed: Mach 2.2
Westland/Bréguet WG-13 Lynx ASW helicopters are on order for the new Type 122 frigates. The AQS-13A dipping sonar will be employed. First delivered 15-6-81.
There are also 20 Dornier DO-28 liaison aircraft.

WEAPONS AND SYSTEMS

With few exceptions, West German ships have weapons and systems of foreign origin.

(A)MISSILES

♦ Surface-to-air

Standard Tartar SM-1MR on board the 3 *Charles F. Adams*-class destroyers
In conjunction with the U.S.A., the General Dynamics RAM (Rolling Airframe Missile) is being developed as a close-in defense weapon. It will carry 24 missiles per launcher.

♦ Surface-to-surface

MM 38 Exocet on board *Hamburg*-class destroyers and Types 143 and 148 guided-missile patrol boats; will be carried by the Type 143A also. The U.S. Harpoon (RGM-84A) is carried by the Type 122 frigates and by refitted units of the *Charles F. Adams*-class destroyers.

♦ Air-to-surface

Kormoran missiles, carried by F-104 and Tornado aircraft

WEAPONS AND SYSTEMS *(continued)*

(B) GUNS

Automatic 127-mm U.S. Mk 42 mod. 10 on *Adams*-class destroyers
French Model 1968 100-mm dual-purpose on *Hamburg*-class destroyers, *Koln*-class frigates, 9 *Rhein*-class tenders, and the training ship *Deutschland*
OTO Melara Compact 76-mm guns on board Types 143, 143A, and 148 guided-missile patrol boats
40-mm (70-caliber) Bofors, in single or twin mounts on many types of ships. Replaced by open Breda mountings in combatants
20-mm Oerlikon and Rheinmetall

(C) ANTISUBMARINE WARFARE

♦ Rocket launchers

Quadruple 375-mm Bofors, automatically loaded in a vertical position
The U.S. ASROC system, with an octuple launcher for rockets, with a Mk 46 ASW torpedo payload

♦ Torpedoes

U.S. Mk 37 on submarines
U.S. Mk 44 and Mk 46 on *Charles F. Adams*-class destroyers, Type 122 frigates, and Bréguet Atlantic-1150 ASW patrol aircraft
Wire-guided "Seal" type (20,000 m range) on Type 143 missile boats, Type 142 torpedo boats, and submarines.
Wire-guided "Seeschlange" type on Type 206 submarines.

(D) ELECTRONICS

In addition to the U.S. radars mounted in the *Charles F. Adams*-class destroyers, the West German Navy uses the following Dutch radars (Hollandse Signaal-apparaaten):

LW-02 long-range air search (Band D)
SGR-105 multi-purpose search (Band E-F)
SGR-103 surface search (Band I)
Band X for 100-mm and 40-mm fire control
Type 148 missile patrol boats have a Thomson-CSF Triton target-designation radar and Vega fire-control system with Pollux radar.

Type 143 missile patrol boats carry the AGIS fire-control system combined with Dutch HSA WM 27 M radar. AGIS has two UNIVAC computers, one for fire control and the other for real-time threat-processing. WM 27 has two antennas within its dome, one for search and one for tracking. An automatic data link permits AGIS to relay information with other units of the Type 143, *Charles F. Adams*-class, and with future combatants destined for service with the fleet operating from Glücksberg-Meierwik. The *Adams*-class destroyers are receiving the Lockheed-built Mk 86 gun-fire-control system, with SPQ-9 radar. As a countermeasure system, the Breda SCLAR chaff rocket launcher (20 tubes) has been adopted.

SUBMARINES

♦ . . . Type 210

A 750-ton (submerged) submarine to replace the Norwegian *Kobben* (Type 207) and German 205 classes in the 1980s is under study by IKL Lübeck in conjunction with the Norwegian Navy.

♦ **18 Type 206** Bldrs: (A)—Howaldtswerke-Deutsche Werft, Kiel; (B)—Rheinstahl Nordseewerke, Emden

		Bldr	Laid down	L	In serv.
S 192	U 13	A	24-11-69	28-9-71	19-4-73
S 193	U 14	B	10-9-70	1-2-72	19-4-73
S 194	U 15	A	29-5-70	15-6-72	17-4-74
S 195	U 16	B	22-4-71	29-8-72	9-11-73
S 196	U 17	A	19-10-70	10-10-72	28-11-73
S 197	U 18	B	28-7-71	31-10-72	19-12-73
S 198	U 19	A	14-1-71	15-12-72	9-11-73
S 199	U 20	B	15-2-72	16-1-73	24-5-74
S 170	U 21	A	14-4-71	9-3-73	16-8-74
S 171	U 22	B	3-5-72	27-3-73	26-7-74
S 172	U 23	B	21-8-72	22-5-73	2-5-75
S 173	U 24	B	10-7-72	26-6-73	16-10-74
S 175	U 25	A	6-10-71	23-5-73	14-6-74
S 176	U 26	B	17-11-72	20-11-73	13-3-75
S 177	U 27	A	11-1-72	21-8-73	16-10-74
S 178	U 28	B	26-1-72	22-1-74	18-12-74
S 179	U 29	A	29-2-72	5-11-73	27-11-74
S 130	U 30	B	27-4-73	26-3-74	13-3-75

U 29 (S 179)   1975

U 24 (S 173)   1974

D: 450/500 tons   **S:** 10/17 kts (5 snorkel)   **Dim:** 48.6 × 4.6 × 4.3
A: 8/533-mm TT—(16 torpedoes)—24 mines in external container
Electron Equipt: Sonar: 1/WSU AN 410A4, 1/GHG AN 5039A1, 1/DBQS-21D
                Radar: 1/Calypso

SUBMARINES *(continued)*

M: 2 MTU 820Db diesels; 600 hp each, 2/405-kw generators; 1/2,300-hp electric motor
Range: 4,500/5   **Man:** 22 tot.

REMARKS: *U 13* to *U 24* authorized in 1969, *U 25* to *U 30* in 2-70. An external "mine-belt" container has been developed for these submarines to permit them to carry a full complement of torpedoes plus 24 mines. Range submerged is 200/5. Three batteries, 92 cells each. New fire control systems are to be installed.

♦ **6 Type 205** Bldr: Howaldtswerke-Deutsche Werft, Kiel

	Laid down	L	In serv.
S 180 U 1	1-2-65	17-2-67	6-6-67
S 181 U 2	1-9-64	15-7-66	11-10-66
S 188 U 9	10-12-64	20-10-66	11-4-67
S 189 U 10	15-7-65	5-6-67	28-11-67
S 190 U 11	1-4-66	9-2-68	21-6-68
S 191 U 12	1-9-66	10-9-68	14-1-69

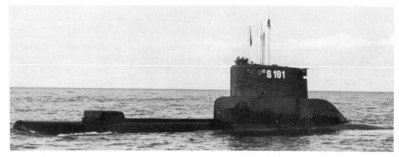

U 2 (S 81)   Marineamt

U 10 (S 189)   Marineamt

D: 419/450 tons   **S:** 10/17 kts   **Dim:** 43.5 × 4.6 × 3.8   **A:** 8/533-mm TT
Electron Equipt: Radar: 1/Thomson-CSF Calypso
Sonar: 1/SRS-M1H, 1/GHG AN5039A1
M: 2 MTU 820Db, 600-hp diesels, 2/405-kw generators, 1/2,300-hp electric motor
Man: 21 tot.

REMARKS: U 10 is 43.8-m overall; U 11, 12: 45.8. The poor quality of the antimagnetic steel used in the first six of this class caused serious pitting, which made it necessary to rebuild the *U 1* and *U 2* (originally launched 21-10-61 and 25-1-62) with regular steel. Beginning with the *U 9*, laid down in 1964, these submarines were built with a new antimagnetic steel. The *U 3* was stricken in 1968, the *U 4* and *U 8* in 1974, the *U 5* in 1975, and the *U 6* and *U 7* in 1974.

NOTE: The Type XXI submarine *Wilhelm Bauer* (ex-*U 2540*) was stricken 28-11-80.

GUIDED-MISSILE DESTROYERS

♦ **3 U.S. Charles F. Adams (Type 103) class** Bldr: Bath Iron Works, Bath, Maine

	Laid down	L	In serv.
D 185 LÜTJENS (ex-DDG 28)	1-3-66	11-8-67	22-3-69
D 186 MÖLDERS (ex-DDG 29)	12-4-66	13-4-68	20-9-69
D 187 ROMMEL (ex-DDG 30)	22-8-67	1-2-69	2-5-70

Mölders (D 186)   G. Arra, 1976

Lütjens (D 185)—prior to modernization   Marineamt

GUIDED-MISSILE DESTROYERS *(continued)*

D: 3,370 tons (4,544 fl) **S:** 35 kts **Dim:** 134.4 (128.1 pp) × 14.38 × 6.4 (max.)
A: 1/Tartar Mk 13 missile launcher (40 SM-1MR and Harpoon missiles)—2/127-mm Mk 42 DP (I × 2)—6/324-mm Mk 32 ASW TT (III × 2)—1/ASROC ASW RL (VIII × 1)
Electron Equipt: Radars: 1/SPS-40, 1/SPS-10, 1/SPS-52, 1/Kelvin-Hughes 14/9, 2/SPG-51C, 1/SPG-53
  Sonar: 1/SQS-23—ECM: Satir-1, WLR-6—TACAN: URN-20
M: GT; 2 props; 70,000 hp **Electric:** 3,000 kw
Boilers: 4 Combustion Engineering, 84 kg/cm² pressure, superheat 500°C
Fuel: 900 tons **Range:** 1600/30, 6,000/14 **Man:** 21 officers, 319 men

REMARKS: Authorized 1964. They differ in several ways, especially in profile, from the *Charles F. Adams* design, on which they are based. Installation of the SM-1MR system and digitalization of some computer equipment has been completed on D 187; the others will complete modernization 1981-82. All being fitted with new Mk 86 gunfire-control system (with SPG-60 and SPQ-9 radars) in place of the Mk 68 GFCS. A U.S. SYS-1 automated data system is being added.

◆ **4 Hamburg class (modified Type 101)** Bldr: H. C. Stülcken, Hamburg

	Laid down	L	In serv.
D 181 HAMBURG	29-1-59	26-3-60	23-3-64
D 182 SCHLESWIG-HOLSTEIN	20-8-59	20-8-60	12-10-64
D 183 BAYERN	14-9-60	14-8-62	6-7-65
D 184 HESSEN	15-2-61	4-5-63	8-10-68

D: 3,500 tons (4,700 fl) **S:** 35 kts **Dim:** 133.7 (128.0 pp) × 13.4 × 5.2 (max.)
A: 4/MM38 Exocet SSM—3/100-mm mod. 1968 DP (I × 3)—8/40-mm Breda AA (II × 4)—4/533-mm ASW TT—2/375-mm Bofors ASW RL (IV × 2)—2/d.c. racks (12 d.c.)—60-80 mines
Electron Equipt: Radars: 1/Kelvin-Hughes 14/9, 1/DA-08, 1/LW-04, 1/SGR-103—3/M45
  Sonar: 1/Atlas ELAC 1BV med. freq.
  ECM: WLR-6, 2/SCLAR chaff RL

Hessen (D 184) 1978

Hamburg (D 181) 1980

Hamburg (D 181) G. Koop, 1981

M: GT; 2 props; 68,000 hp **Electric:** 5,400 kw **Boilers:** 4/59 kg/cm², 465°C
Man: 280 tot.

REMARKS: Between the beginning of 1975 and the end of 1977, refitted with 4/MM38 to replace mount C, in the following order: D 184, D 181, D 182, and D 183. Five fixed antiship torpedo tubes (3 in bows, 2 aft) removed, 40-mm replaced by later model, new air search radar. There are three HSA M4 radar directors for the 100-mm guns. The d.c. racks are bolted to the mine rails. Further modernization is planned.

NOTE: The four remaining "Z" (U.S. *Fletcher*)-class destroyers have been stricken. Z 3, stricken 15-10-80, was transferred to Greece, as was Z 4, stricken 26-2-81. Z 2 and Z 5 were scheduled to strike 9-81, for transfer to Greece.

GUIDED MISSILE FRIGATES

◆ **0 (+6) Bremen (Type 122) class**

	Bldr	Laid down	L	In serv.
F 207 BREMEN	Bremer-Vulkan	9-7-79	27-9-79	3-82
F 208 NIEDERSACHSEN	AG Weser, Bremen	9-11-79	9-6-80	...
F 209 RHEINLAND-PFALZ	Blohm & Voss, Hamburg	25-9-79	3-9-80	...

GUIDED MISSILE FRIGATES (continued)

F 210 EMDEN	Nordseewerke, Emden	24-6-80	17-12-80	. . .
F 211 KÖLN	Blohm & Voss, Hamburg	6-80	29-5-81	. . .
F 212 KARLSRUHE	Howaldtswerke, Kiel	3-81	. . .	. . .

D: 2,900 tons (3,750 fl)   **S:** 30 kts
Dim: 130.0 (121.8 wl) × 14.4 × 4.26 (6.0 sonar)
A: 8/Harpoon SSM (IV × 2)—1/NATO Sea Sparrow SAM system (VIII × 1, Mk 29 launcher, 24 missiles)—1/76-mm OTO Melara DP—4/324-mm Mk 32 ASW TT (I × 4)—2/WG 13 Lynx ASW helicopters
Electron Equipt: Radars: 1/3RM20, 1/LW-08, 1/WM-25, 1/STIR
     Sonar: 1/DSQS-21B(Z) (bow-mounted)
     ECM: FL 1800S intercept array, 4/Mk 36 Super RBOC chaff RL

Bremen on trials   P. Voss, 1981

M: CODOG: 2 GM LM 2500 GT (50,000 hp); 2 MTU 20V956 TB92 diesels (10,400 hp); 2 CP props
Electric: 3,000 kw (4/750-kw diesel sets)   **Range:** 4,000/18
Man: 21 officers, 160 men (plus 6/12 air complement)

REMARKS: Pendant numbers for last four may be F 228-F 231 instead. Germanized version of Dutch *Kortenaar* class. To complete 1982-86. First six ordered 7-77; two additional canceled. The helicopters will be equipped with DAQS-13D dipping sonar. Two RAM point-defense SAM launchers are to be added atop the hangar if and when the system becomes operational. Fin stabilizers fitted. Have SATIR tactical data system. Canadian Bear Trap helicopter landing system fitted.

FRIGATES

♦ **6 Köln class (Type 120)** Bldr: H. C. Stülcken, Hamburg

	Laid down	L	In serv.
F 220 KÖLN	21-12-57	6-12-58	15-4-61
F 221 EMDEN	15-4-58	21-3-59	24-10-61
F 222 AUGSBURG	29-10-58	15-8-59	7-4-62
F 223 KARLSRUHE	15-12-58	24-10-59	15-12-62
F 224 LÜBECK	28-10-59	23-7-60	6-7-63
F 225 BRAUNSCHWEIG	28-7-60	3-2-62	16-6-64

D: 2,425 tons (2,970 fl)   **S:** 30 kts (20 on diesels)
Dim: 109.83 (105.0 pp) × 10.5 × 4.61 (fl)
A: 2/100-mm Mod. 1953 DP (I × 2)—6/40-mm AA (II × 2, I × 2)—2/375-mm Bofors ASW RL (IV × 2)—4/533-mm ASW TT (I × 4)—2/d.c. racks (12 d.c.)—82 mines
Electron Equipt: Radars: 1/DA-02, 1/SGR-103, 1/Kelvin-Hughes 14/9, 2/M 44 fire-control, 1/M-45 fire-control
     Sonar: 1/PAE/CWE hull-mounted M/F

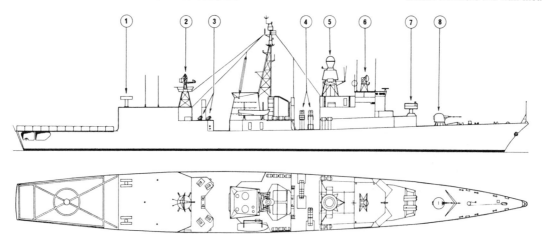

Bremen   H. Simoni
1. RAM system 2. LW-08 radar 3. Super RBOC chaff RL 4. Harpoon launchers 5. WM-25 radar 6. STIR radar 7. NATO Sea Sparrow 8. 76-mm OTO Melara Compact

FRIGATES (continued)

Köln (F 220)   G. Gyssels, 1981

M: CODAG: 4 M.A.N. V-16-cylinder diesels (each 3,000 hp); 2 Brown-Boveri
 gas turbines (each 13,000 hp); 2 CP props; 36,000 hp
Electric: 2,700 kw   **Fuel:** 333 tons   **Range:** 900/30, 2,700/22
Man: 17 officers, 193 men

REMARKS: The rocket-launcher magazines carry 72 projectiles. Two diesels and one
gas turbine on each of the two shafts. Made 33 knots on trials. F 220-F 223 are to
be renamed and retained, converting to 200-nautical-mile economic-zone patrol ships
(probably losing their gas turbine engines).

CORVETTES

♦ **5 Thetis class (Type 420)** Bldr: Roland Werft, Bremen-Hemelingen

	Laid down	L	In serv.
P 6052 THETIS	19-6-59	22-3-60	1-7-61
P 6053 HERMES	8-10-59	9-8-60	16-12-61
P 6054 NAJADE	22-3-60	6-12-60	12-5-62
P 6055 TRITON	15-8-60	5-8-61	10-11-62
P 6056 THESEUS	1-7-61	20-3-62	15-8-63

Hermes (P 6053)

D: 575 tons (658 fl)   **S:** 23.5 kts   **Dim:** 69.78 (65.5 pp) × 8.2 × 2.65
A: 2/40-mm AA (II × 1)—1/Bofors 375-mm ASW RL (IV × 1)—4/533-mm ASW
 TT (I × 4)—2/d.c. racks (12 d.c.)—mines
Electron Equipt: Radars: Kelvin-Hughes 14/9, TRS-N
                   Sonar: ELAC 1BV
M: 2 M.A.N. diesels; 2 props; 6,800 hp   **Electric:** 540 kw
Range: 2,760/15   **Man:** 5 officers, 43 men

REMARKS: Former torpedo-recovery boats, well designed for operations in the Belts
 and the Baltic. May receive OTO Melara 76-mm in place of 40-mm. P 6054 has larger
 forward superstructure. P 6052 is 68.21 meters overall.

NOTE: Former corvette *Hans Bürkner* is now listed under experimental auxiliaries.

GUIDED-MISSILE PATROL BOATS

♦ **10 Type 143A** Bldrs: Lürssen, Vegasack (Kröger, Rendsburg: S 73, 75, 77)

	Laid down	L	In serv.		L	In serv.
P 6121 S 71	7-79	29-9-81	1982	P 6126 S 77	...	...
P 6122 S 72	...	...	...	P 6127 S 78	...	...
P 6123 S 73	15-2-80	...	...	P 6128 S 79	...	...
P 6124 S 74	...	...	...	P 6129 S 80	...	...
P 6125 S 75	...	...	...	P 6130 S 81	...	...

 D: 300 tons (390.6 fl)   **S:** 36 kts (32 fl)
 Dim: 57.6 (54.4 pp) × 7.76 × 2.99 (2.56 hull)
 A: 4/MM38 Exocet—1/RAM ASMD (XXIV × 1)—1/76-mm OTO Melara DP—
  mines
 Electron Equipt: Radars: 1/3RM 20, 1/HSA WM-27
 M: 4 MTU 16V956 TB91 diesels; 4 props; 16,000 hp   **Electric:** 540 kw
 Fuel: 116 tons   **Range:** 600/30, 2,600/16   **Man:** 34 tot.

REMARKS: Ordered 1978. A repeat Type 143 with a point-defense SAM system in place
 of the after 76-mm gun, and mine rails in place of the wire-guided torpedoes, and
 mine rails in place of the torpedo tubes. Wood-planked hull on steel frame. To
 complete 1982-84, will replace the Type-142 class. Will have AGIS integrated data
 system.

♦ **10 Type 143** Bldrs: S 65, S 67, S 69: Kröger, Rendsburg; remainder: Lürssen,
 Vegasack

	L	In serv.		L	In serv.
P 6111 S 61	22-10-73	1-11-76	P 6116 S 66	4-9-75	25-11-76
P 6112 S 62	21-3-74	13-4-76	P 6117 S 67	6-3-75	17-12-76
P 6113 S 63	18-9-74	2-6-76	P 6118 S 68	17-11-75	28-3-77
P 6114 S 64	14-4-75	14-8-76	P 6119 S 69	5-6-75	23-12-77
P 6115 S 65	15-1-74	27-9-76	P 6120 S 70	14-4-76	29-7-77

S 62 (P 6112)   Marineamt, 1976

GUIDED-MISSILE PATROL BOATS *(continued)*

S 64 (P 6114)   Marineamt

D: 300 tons (393 fl)   **S:** 36 kts (32 fl)
Dim: 57.6 (54.4 pp) × 7.76 × 2.82 (2.56 hull)
A: 4/MM38 Exocet—2/76-mm OTO Melara AA (I × 2)—2/533-mm TT (aft-launching, for Seal wire-guided torpedoes)
Electron Equipt: Radars: 1/3RM 20, 1/HSA WM-27
M: 4 MTU 16V956 diesels; 4 props; 16,000 hp   **Electric:** 540 kw
Fuel: 116 tons   **Range:** 600/30, 2,600/16   **Man:** 40-42 tot.

REMARKS: Wood-planked hull on steel frame. To be refitted to Type-143A standard, except that the torpedo tubes will be retained.

♦ **20 Type 148, steel-hulled**

	L	In serv.			L	In serv.
P 6141 S 41	27-9-72	30-10-72		P 6151 S 51	26-4-74	12-6-74
P 6142 S 42	12-12-72	8-1-73		P 6152 S 52	23-3-74	17-7-74
P 6143 S 43	7-3-73	9-4-73		P 6153 S 53	4-7-74	24-9-74
P 6144 S 44	5-5-73	14-7-73		P 6154 S 54	8-7-74	14-11-74
P 6145 S 45	3-7-73	21-8-73		P 6155 S 55	15-11-74	7-1-75
P 6146 S 46	21-5-73	17-10-73		P 6156 S 56	30-10-74	12-2-75
P 6147 S 47	20-9-72	13-11-73		P 6157 S 57	13-2-75	3-4-75
P 6148 S 48	10-9-73	9-1-74		P 6158 S 58	26-2-75	22-5-75
P 6149 S 49	11-1-74	26-2-74		P 6159 S 59	15-5-75	24-6-75
P 6150 S 50	10-12-73	27-3-74		P 6160 S 60	26-5-75	6-8-75

Bldr: Constructions Mécaniques de Normandie, Cherbourg, with Lürssen, Vegasack, who built the boats carrying even-number designations from number P 6146. All were fitted out at Lorient.

D: 234 tons (264 fl)   **S:** 35.8 kts   **Dim:** 47.0 (45.9 pp) × 7.1 × 2.66 (fl)
A: 4/MM38 Exocet—1/76-mm DP OTO Melara (fwd)—1/40-mm Bofors AA (aft)—8 mines in place of the 40-mm AA
Electron Equipt: Radars: 1/3RM 20 navigation, 1/Triton, 1/Pollux
M: 4 MTU MD 872 16-cyl. diesels; 4 props; 14,400 hp (12,000 sust.)

S 49 (P 6149)   G. Koop, 1979

S 59 (P 6159)—without missile cannisters   G. Gyssels, 1981

Electric: 270 kw   **Range:** 570/30, 1,600/15   **Fuel:** 39 tons
Man: 4 officers, 17 petty officers, 9 men

REMARKS: Steel construction. Vega fire-control system with Pollux radar; Triton is used for target designation.

TORPEDO BOATS

♦ **10 Zobel (Type 142) class** Bldr: Lürssen, Vegasack (except *Puma, Hyäne:* Krögerwerft, Rendsburg)

	L	In serv.			L	In serv.
P 6092 ZOBEL	28-1-61	12-12-61		P 6097 PUMA	26-10-61	21-12-62
P 6093 WIESEL	14-3-61	25-6-62		P 6098 GEPARD	14-4-62	18-4-63
P 6094 DACHS	10-6-61	25-9-62		P 6099 HYÄNE	31-3-62	10-5-63
P 6095 HERMELIN	5-8-61	28-11-62		P 6100 FRETTCHEN	20-11-62	26-6-63
P 6096 NERZ	5-9-61	11-1-63		P 6101 OZELOT	4-2-63	25-10-63

Frettchen (P 6100)   G. Gyssels, 1981

TORPEDO BOATS (continued)

Puma (P 6097)   S. Terzibaschitsch, 1980

D: 212 tons (220 fl)   **S:** 38 kts   **Dim:** 42.62 × 7.14 × 2.4
A: 2/40-mm AA (I × 2)—2/533-mm TT (aft-launching for Seal wire-guided torpe-
does)
Electron Equipt: Radars: 1/Kelvin-Hughes 14/9, 1/HSA M 20
M: 4 MTU 20V 538 diesels; 4 props; 12,000 hp   **Range:** 500/38; 1,000/32
Man: 42 tot.

REMARKS: Modernized 1971-72. Wooden hull, light-alloy superstructure. To be stricken
1982-84 on completion of Type 143A class.

MINE WARFARE SHIPS

♦ . . . Type 355 pressure-mine sweepers

REMARKS: A project to design a ship capable of detecting and disposing of the "un-
sweepable" pressure mine. To be built during the mid-1980s—early 1990s.

♦ 10 Type 343 minelayer-minehunters

REMARKS: A design project to begin replacement of the existing Type 340 and 341
minehunters; to be built during the late 1980s. To receive DSQS-11 minehunting
sonar. The Type 331/332 minesweeper-minehunter program has been delayed.

♦ 6 Type 351 drone minesweeper-control ships Bldr: Burmester, Bremen

	L	In serv.	Conversion completed
M 1073 SCHLESWIG	2-10-57	30-10-58	27-5-81
M 1076 PADERBORN	5-12-57	16-12-58	. . .
M 1079 DÜREN	12-6-58	22-4-59	. . .
M 1081 KONSTANZ	30-9-58	23-7-59	. . .
M 1082 WOLFSBURG	10-12-58	8-10-59	. . .
M 1083 ULM	10-2-59	7-11-59	. . .

D: 488 tons (fl)   **S:** 16.5 kts   **Dim:** 47.5 × 8.5 × 2.75   **A:** 1/40-mm AA
Electron Equipt: Radar: 1/TRS-N—Sonar: DSQS-11A
M: 2 MD 871 UM/1D diesels; 2 CP props; 3,300 hp   **Range:** 2,200/16
Man: 44 tot.

REMARKS: Type 320 minesweepers converted in the early 1980s. Each ship controls
three F-1 "Troika" drone magnetic/acoustic/mechanical minesweepers. Also carry
and tow an Oropesa sweep rig.

Schleswig (M 1073)—on trials 6-80   S. Terzibaschitsch, 1980

♦ 18 Type HL 351 "Troika" drones Bldr: MAK, Kiel (In serv. 1980-81)

SEEHOND 1-18

Seehond 1-3 and Schleswig (M 1073)   G. Koop, 1981

D: 91 tons (96.5 fl)   **S:** 9.4 kts   **Dim:** 24.92 × 4.46 × 1.8   **A:** None
M: 1 MWM TRHS 518A diesel; Schöttel prop; 445 hp   **Electric:** 208 kw
Range: 520/8.8   **Man:** 3 tot.

REMARKS: Ordered 1977, to operate three-apiece with the Type-351 control ships.
First three delivered 1-8-80. Essentially remote-controlled, self-propelled magnetic
minesweeping solenoids with all machinery highly shock-protected. Will also be able
to carry two Type SDG-21 Oropesa mechanical minesweeping gear.

♦ 3 HFG F-1 "Troika" trials craft Bldr: Ottenser Eisenwerke, Hamburg

SEEKUH 1 (L:. . .)   SEEKUH 2 (L: 24-3-66)   SEEKUH 3 (L: 24-3-66)

"Seekuh" trials craft   1977

MINE WARFARE SHIPS (continued)

D: 104 tons (181 fl) **S:** . . . kts **Dim:** 27.0 × 3.53 × 2.30 hull/3.01 max.
A: None
M: 2 MWM 8-cyl. diesels, electric drive; 1 Schöttel prop/rudder; 700 hp
Electric: 176 kw **Man:** 3 tot.

REMARKS: Prototypes for "Troika" concept involved in an extraordinarily protracted trial period. *Seekuh 1* (ex-Y 1677) is 23.8 m o.a., 90 tons, 290 hp. Earlier concept trials craft *Walross* (Y 1676) now stricken. All worked with small minesweeper *Niobe*.

♦ **12 Type 331 A* and 331 B minehunters** Bldr: Burmester, Bremen

	L	In serv.		L	In serv.
M 1070 GÖTTINGEN	1-4-57	31-5-58	M 1078 CUXHAVEN	11-3-58	11-3-59
M 1071 KOBLENZ	6-5-57	8-7-58	M 1080 MARBURG	4-8-58	11-6-59
M 1072 LINDAU	16-2-57	24-4-58	M 1084 FLENSBURG*	7-4-59	3-12-59
M 1074 TÜBINGEN	12-8-57	25-9-58	M 1085 MINDEN	9-6-59	22-1-60
M 1075 WETZLAR	24-6-57	20-8-58	M 1086 FULDA*	19-8-59	5-3-60
M 1077 WEILHEIM	4-2-58	28-1-59	M 1087 VÖLKLINGEN	20-10-59	21-5-60

Flensburg (M 1084)—Type 331A G. Koop, 1979

Tübingen (M 1074)—Type 331B G. Gyssels, 1981

D: 388 tons (402 fl) **S:** 17 kts **Dim:** 47.45 × 8.5 × 3.68 (sonar down)
A: 1/40-mm AA
Electron Equipt: Radar: 1/TRS-N or Kelvin-Hughes 14/9
Sonar: DSQS-11 (Type 331A: Plessey 193M Mk 20G)
M: 2 Maybach diesels; 2 CP props; 3,340 hp **Electric:** 220 kw
Range: 1,400/16; 3,950/9 **Man:** 46 tot.

REMARKS: All are conversions from the Type 320, *Lindau*-class, wooden-hulled minesweepers. The Type 331As were converted 1968-71, the Type 331Bs in 1975-80. The earlier Type 331A conversions have German sonar and do not carry the two French PAP-104 minehunting devices fitted to the later Type 331Bs. None have mechanical sweep gear. Minehunting speed is 6 kts, on two 50-kw electric motors. Six divers are carried.

♦ **21 Type 340 and Type 341 patrol minesweepers**

Bldr: Abeking & Rasmussen, Lemwerde (except: Schürenstedt, Bardenfleth: M 1064, 1065, 1092, 1094; Schlichting, Travemünde: M 1067, 1090, 1095)

Type 340:	L	In serv.		L	In serv.
M 1051 CASTOR	12-7-62	11-12-62	M 1064 DENEB	11-9-61	7-12-61
M 1054 POLLUX	15-9-60	28-4-61	M 1065 JUPITER	15-2-61	30-5-61
M 1055 SIRIUS	15-3-61	5-10-61	M 1067 ATAIR	20-4-61	27-9-61
M 1056 RIGEL	2-4-62	19-9-62	M 1069 WEGA	10-10-62	8-4-63
M 1057 REGULUS	18-12-61	20-6-62	M 1090 PERSEUS	22-9-60	16-3-61
M 1058 MARS	1-12-60	18-7-61	M 1092 PLUTO	9-8-60	19-12-60
M 1059 SPICA	25-5-60	10-5-61	M 1093 NEPTUN	9-6-60	29-9-60
M 1060 SKORPION	21-5-63	9-10-63	M 1094 WIDDER	12-3-59	26-9-60
Type 341:			M 1095 HERKULES	25-8-60	9-12-60
M 1062 SCHÜTZE	20-5-58	14-4-59	M 1096 FISCHE	14-7-59	12-1-60
M 1063 WAAGE	9-4-59	19-3-62	M 1097 GEMMA	6-10-59	5-7-60

Mars (M 1058)—Type 340, with mines on deck

Waage—in patrol-boat configuration S. Terzibaschitsch

D: 241 tons (280 fl) **S:** 24.6 kts **Dim:** 47.44 × 7.2 (6.96 wl) × 2.4
A: 1/40-mm AA (*see* Remarks) **Electron Equipt:** Radar: 1/TRS-N
M: Maybach or Mercedes-Benz diesels; 2 Escher-Wyss cycloidal props; 4,000/4,200 hp
Electric: 120 kw plus 340-kw sweep generator **Fuel:** 22 tons
Range: 640/22, 1,000/18 **Man:** 39 tot.

REMARKS: Multi-purpose ships that can be employed as minesweepers, coastal patrol craft (2/40-mm AA), and minelayers (2 mine rails), the minesweeping gear having

MINE WARFARE SHIPS (continued)

been removed in the latter two instances. *Stier* (former M 1061), used as a submarine-rescue ship, has been given a new hull number and disarmed; decompression chamber in new stern deckhouse. Eight with Mercedes-Benz diesels are Type 340; the remainder, with Maybach diesels, are Type 341. Several have been discarded.

♦ **10 Type 394 inshore minesweepers** Bldr: Krögerwerft, Rendsburg

	L	In serv.			L	In serv.
M 2658 Frauenlob	26-2-65	27-9-66	M 2663 Minerva		25-8-66	16-6-67
M 2659 Nautilus	19-5-65	26-10-66	M 2664 Diana		13-12-66	21-9-67
M 2660 Gerion	19-6-65	17-2-67	M 2665 Loreley		14-3-67	29-3-68
M 2661 Medusa	25-1-66	17-2-67	M 2666 Atlantis		20-6-67	29-3-68
M 2662 Undine	16-5-66	20-3-67	M 2667 Acheron		11-10-67	10-2-68

Loreley (Type 394)   1975

D: 238 tons (246 fl) **S:** 14.3 kts **Dim:** 38.01 × 8.03 × 2.1 **A:** 1/40-mm AA
Electron Equipt: Radar: 1/TRS-N **Man:** 4 officers, 20 men
M: 2 Mercedes-Benz MB 820 Db diesels; 2 props; 2,000 hp
Electric: 554 kw **Fuel:** 30 tons **Range:** 648/14, 1,770/7

REMARKS: Wooden construction. Differ from Type 393 in having a 260-kw diesel sweep current generator. Formerly had "Y," and earlier "W," series pendants.

♦ **8 Type 393 inshore minesweepers** Bldr: Krögerwerft, Rendsburg

	L	In serv.			L	In serv.
M 2650 Ariadne	23-4-60	23-10-61	M 2654 Nymphe		20-9-62	8-5-63
M 2651 Freya	25-6-60	6-1-62	M 2655 Nixe		3-12-62	20-6-63
M 2652 Vineta	17-9-60	9-4-62	M 2656 Amazone		27-2-63	4-9-63
M 2653 Herta	18-2-61	7-6-62	M 2657 Gazelle		14-8-63	9-12-63

D: 199-205 tons light (252 fl) **S:** 14.3 kts **Dim:** 38.01 × 8.03 × 1.99
A: 1/40-mm AA **Electron Equipt:** Radar: 1/TRS-N
M: 2 Mercedes-Benz MB 820 Db diesels; 2 props; 2,000 hp **Electric:** 554 kw
Fuel: 30 tons **Range:** 830/12 **Man:** 4 officers, 20 men

REMARKS: Similar to Type 394 but have a 260-kw gas turbine sweep current generator.

NOTE: The Type 390 inshore minesweeper *Holnis* (Y 836) is now listed under intelligence collectors, and the Type 392 minesweeper *Hansa* (Y 806) is listed under training ships.

Amazone (M 2656)   S. Terzibaschitsch, 1980

AMPHIBIOUS WARFARE CRAFT

♦ **22 Type 520 utility landing craft** Bldr: Howaldtswerke, Hamburg, 1965-66 (launch dates in parentheses)

L 760 Flunder (6-1-66)	L 767 Tummler (14-6-66)	L 792 Dorsch (17-3-66)
L 761 Karpfen (5-1-66)	L 768 Wels (15-6-66)	L 793 Felchen (19-4-66)
L 762 Lachs (17-2-66)	L 769 Zander (13-7-66)	L 794 Forelle (20-4-66)
L 763 Plötze (16-2-66)	L 788 Butt (28-3-65)	L 795 Inger (14-7-66)
L 764 Rochen (18-3-66)	L 789 Brasse (28-3-65)	L 796 Makrele (22-8-66)
L 765 Schlei (17-5-66)	L 790 Barbe (26-11-65)	L 797 Muräne (23-8-66)
L 766 Stör (18-5-66)	L 791 Delphin (25-11-65)	L 798 Renke (22-9-66)
		L 799 Salm (23-9-66)

Forelle (L 794)   G. Gyssels, 1981

D: 166 tons (403 fl) **S:** 11 kts **Dim:** 40.04 (36.7 pp) × 8.8 × 1.6 (2.1 max.)
A: 2/20-mm Rheinmetall Rh 202 AA (II × 1)
Electron Equipt: Radar: 1/Kelvin-Hughes 14/9 **Range:** 1,200/11 **Man:** 17 tot.
M: 2 MWM 12-cyl. diesels; 2 props; 1,200 hp **Electric:** 130 kVa

REMARKS: Design based on the American LCU-1646 class. *Renke* (L 798) and *Salm* (L 799) in reserve; *Inger* (L 795) used for reserve training. Cargo: 237 tons max.; 141.6 normal.

♦ **28 Type 521 landing craft** Bldr: Rheinwerft, Walsam (LCM 1, 2: Blohm & Voss, Hamburg)

LCM 1 to LCM 28 (In serv. 1964-67)

AMPHIBIOUS WARFARE CRAFT (continued)

D: 116 tons (168 fl) **S:** 10.6 kts **Dim:** 23.56 × 6.40 × 1.46
M: 2 MWM 8-cyl. diesels; 2 props; 684 hp **Range:** 690/10, 1,430/7
Man: 7 tot.

REMARKS: Design based on U.S. LCM (8). LCM 1 to LCM 8 are in reserve. LCM 11-
20 have a 20-kw diesel generator and a 2-ton cargo boom; they can be used to carry
up to 18 torpedoes. Cargo: 60 tons or 50 troops.

AUXILIARY SHIPS

HYDROGRAPHIC SURVEY SHIP

♦ **1 Type 750** Bldr: Norderwerft, Hamburg

	Laid down	L	In serv.
A 1452 PLANET (ex-Y 843)	30-4-64	23-9-65	15-4-67

Planet—pendant A 1452 not painted on   G. Koop, 1977

D: 1,513 tons (1,943 fl) **S:** 13.9 kts **Dim:** 80.43 (74.0 pp) × 12.60 × 3.97
M: 4 MWM 12-cyl., 850-hp diesels, electric drive; 1 prop; 1,390 hp
Electric: 650 kw **Range:** 9,300/13.4 **Man:** 39 crew plus 22 scientists

REMARKS: Operated for the Ministry of Communications by a civilian crew. Hangar
for one helicopter. Capable of conducting geophysical, meteorological, biological,
chemistry, and hydrographic research. Denny-Brown stabilizers, 125-hp Pleuger
active rudder and bow-thruster fitted. Main engines provide 560 kw of the electrical
power. Painted white, with buff stack.

SUPPORT TENDERS

♦ **11 Rhein-class Types 401, 402, and 403**

(a) Type 401, for missile and torpedo boats

	Bldr	L	In serv.
A 58 RHEIN	Schlieker, Hamburg	10-12-59	6-11-61
A 61 ELBE	Schlieker, Hamburg	5-5-60	17-4-62
A 63 MAIN	Lindenauwerft, Kiel	23-7-60	29-6-63
A 66 NECKAR	Lürssen, Vegasack	26-6-61	7-12-63
A 68 WERRA	Lindenauwerft, Kiel	26-3-63	2-9-64
A 69 DONAU	Schlichting, Travemünde	26-11-60	23-5-64

(b) Type 402, for mine-countermeasures ships

A 54 ISAR	Blohm & Voss, Hamburg	14-7-62	25-1-64
A 65 SAAR	Norderwerft, Hamburg	11-3-61	11-5-63
A 67 MOSEL	Schlieker, Hamburg	15-12-60	8-6-63

(c) Type 403, for submarines

| A 55 LAHN | Flenderwerke, Lübeck | 21-11-61 | 24-3-64 |
| A 56 LECH | Flenderwerke, Lübeck | 4-5-62 | 8-12-64 |

Neckar (A 66)—Type 401   G. Gyssels, 1981

Lech (A 56)—Type 403   1975

Mosel (A 67)—Type 402   S. Terzibaschitsch, 1980

SUPPORT TENDERS *(continued)*

D: (a): 2,370 tons (3,000 fl) (b): 2,330 tons (3,000 fl) (c) 2,400 tons (2,956 fl)

S: 20 kts (trials, 22)   **Dim:** 98.2 × 11.83 × 5.20

A: 2/100-mm AA (I × 2) (not in A 55, A 56)—4/40-mm AA (I × 4, except II × 2 in A 55 and A 56)—mines

Electron Equipt: Radar: 1/Kelvin-Hughes 14/9, 1/SGR-105, 1/SGR-103, 2/Mk 45 fire control; A 55 and A 56: SGR-103 only

M: 6 Maybach diesels (Mercedes-Benz 839Db in A 54-56, 65, 67); 2 props; 11,400 hp

Electric: 2,250 kw   **Fuel:** 334 tons   **Range:** 2,500/16

Man: 98 tot. (space for 40 officers, 40 petty officers, 130 nonrated men)

REMARKS: Slight variations in length: Type 402 are 98.5 m o.a., Type 403 are 98.6 m o.a. Type 401 have one crane to port, Type 402 have two side by side farther aft. A 54, A 55, A 56, A 65, A 67 have electric drive, the others have diesel-reduction drive, CP props. Tenders carry 200 tons of fuel oil, 40 reserve torpedoes; A 55, A 56, and A 58 have an additional 200 tons of stores; A 66, A 68, and A 69 can be used as training ships. *Weser* (A 62) and *Ruhr* (A 64) transferred to the Greek and Turkish navies in 1975 and 1976, respectively. A 54 is in reserve. Two of the combatant-tender version are to be re-equipped to support the new Type-143A missile boats as Type-401 tenders. Type 401 and 402 have two M4 radar GFCS.

UNDERWAY REPLENISHMENT SHIPS

NOTE: These ships are grouped together here because, despite their dissimilar functions, they are variations on the same basic design.

◆ 8 Type 701A and Type 701C multi-purpose supply ships

(a) Type 701A	Bldr	Laid down	L	In serv.
A 1411 LÜNEBURG	Flensburger SY	8-7-64	3-5-65	31-1-66
A 1413 FREIBURG	Blohm & Voss, Hamburg	1965	15-4-66	27-5-68
A 1416 NIENBURG	Flensburger SY	16-11-65	28-7-66	1-8-68
A 1417 OFFENBURG	Blohm & Voss, Hamburg	1966	10-9-66	27-5-68
(b) Type 701C				
A 1412 COBURG	Flensburger SY	9-4-65	15-12-65	9-7-68
A 1414 GLÜCKSBURG	Flensburger SY	18-8-65	3-5-66	9-7-68
A 1415 SAARBURG	Blohm & Voss, Hamburg	1-3-66	15-7-66	30-7-68
A 1418 MEERSBURG	Flensburger SY	5-8-65	22-3-66	25-6-68

D: Type 701A: 3,483 tons (fl); Type 701C: 3,709 tons (fl)   **S:** 17 kts

Dim: 104.18 × 13.2 × 4.2 (Type 701C: 114.9 overall)

Lüneburg (A 1411)—Type 701A　　　　　　　　G. Gyssels, 1979

Coburg (A 1412)—Type 701C　　　　　　　　1980

A: 4/40-mm AA (II × 2) in preservation

M: 2 Maybach MD 872 diesels; 2 CP props; 5,600 hp   **Electric:** 1,935 kw

Range: 3,000/17, 3,200/14   **Man:** 103 tot.

REMARKS: Originally configured to carry more than 1,100 tons of cargo, including 640 tons fuel oil, 200 tons ammunition, 100 tons spare parts (10,000 separate items), and 130 tons fresh water. A 1415 lengthened 11.5 meters in 1974-75 to carry spare Exocet missiles and other supplies for the new Type-143 and Type-148 classes; stowage for spare parts increased to 30,000 items, with inventory management by the Nixdorf computer system. A 1412, A 1414, A 1418 also converted to Type 702C standard, 1975-77. A 1413 converting 1981-82 to support the new Type-122 frigates; will be equipped with helicopter facilities to permit vertical replenishment. A 1412 has a bow-thruster.

◆ 2 Type 760 ammunition ships Bldr: Orenstein & Koppel, Lübeck

	Laid down	L	In serv.
A 1435 WESTERWALD	3-11-65	25-2-66	11-2-67
A 1436 ODENWALD	3-11-65	5-5-66	23-3-67

Westerwald (A 1435)　　　　　　　　1974

D: 3,460 tons (4,014 fl)   **S:** 17 kts   **Dim:** 105.3 × 14.0 × 4.6

A: 4/40-mm AA (II × 2) in preservation

M: 2 Maybach MD 872 diesels; 2 CP props; 5,600 hp   **Electric:** 1,285 kw

Range: 3,500/17   **Man:** 58 tot. (A 1436: 31 tot.)

REMARKS: Similar to Type 701 but carry only ammunition. A 1436 had the forward 40-mm AA mount removed 1981. Cargo: 1,080 tons.

◆ 2 Type 762 mine-supply ships Bldr: Blohm & Voss, Hamburg

	Laid down	L	In serv.
A 1437 SACHSENWALD	1-8-66	10-12-66	20-8-69
A 1438 STEIGERWALD	9-5-66	10-3-67	20-8-69

UNDERWAY REPLENISHMENT SHIPS *(continued)*

Steigerwald (A 1438)   J.-C. Bellonne, 1980

D: 2,962 tons (3,380 fl)   **S:** 17 kts   **Dim:** 110.7 × 13.9 × 3.79
A: 4/40-mm AA (II × 2)—mines
M: 2 Maybach MD 872 diesels; 2 CP props; 5,600 hp   **Electric:** 1,300 kw
Range: 3,500/17   **Man:** 65 tot.

REMARKS: The designation "supply ships" is something of a euphemism, since these ships have four mine ports at the stern and are actually minelayers, capable of carrying 668 to 1,048 mines, depending on type. Construction of a torpedo-transport version was canceled.

REPAIR SHIPS

♦ **2 Type 726, former U.S. Aristaeus class**

	Bldr	L	In serv.
A 512 ODIN (ex-*Ulysses*, ARB 9)	Bethlehem, Hingham	2-12-44	27-12-44
A 513 WOTAN (ex-*Diomedes*, ARB 11)	Chicago Bridge & Iron	11-11-44	23-1-45

Odin (A 512)   G. Koop, 1979

D: 3,435 tons (3,640 fl)   **S:** 11 kts   **Dim:** 101.0 × 15.28 × 3.96
M: 2 GM 12-278A (A 513: 12-567A) diesels; 2 props; 1,800 hp
Fuel: 438 tons   **Range:** 13,200/11   **Man:** 143 tot. (civilian personnel)

REMARKS: Modified former LST 967 and LST 1119, respectively, transferred in 6-61. A 10-ton traveling crane moves on rails between the bridge and the forward sheer.

REPLENISHMENT OILERS

♦ **2 Type 704 former merchant tankers**

	Bldr	L	In serv.
A 1443 RHÖN (ex-*Okene*)	Kröger, Rendsburg	23-8-74	5-9-77
A 1442 SPESSART (ex-*Okapi*)	Kröger, Rendsburg	13-2-75	23-9-77

Rhon (A 1443)   1977

D: 14,260 tons (fl)   6,209 grt/10,950 dwt   **S:** 16 kts   **Dim:** 130.2 × 19.3 × 8.7
M: 1 MAK 12-cyl. diesel; CP prop; 8,000 hp   **Electric:** 2,000 kw   **Man:** 42 tot.

REMARKS: Converted while building. Purchased from Bulk Acid Carriers, Monrovia, in 1976. Fitted with one underway-replenishment station per side. Cargo: 9,500 m³ distillate fuel, 1,650 m³ fuel oil, 400 m³ water.

♦ **4 Type 703** Bldr: Lindenauwerft, Kiel

	Laid down	L	In serv.
A 1424 WALCHENSEE	12-10-64	10-7-65	29-6-66
A 1425 AMMERSEE	28-3-66	9-7-66	2-3-67
A 1426 TEGERNSEE	21-4-66	22-10-66	23-3-67
A 1427 WESTENSEE	28-10-66	8-4-67	6-10-67

Ammersee (A 1425)   1975

D: 2,174 tons (fl)   **S:** 12.5 kts   **Dim:** 71.9 × 11.2 × 4.28
M: 2 MWM 12-cyl. diesels; 1 CP prop; 1,200 hp   **Electric:** 635 kw
Cargo capacity: 1,130 m³   **Range:** 3,250/12   **Man:** 21 tot.

♦ **1 Type 763 former merchant tanker** Bldr: Lindenauwerft, Kiel

	Laid down	L	In serv.
A 1407 WITTENSEE (ex-*Sioux*)	15-2-58	23-9-58	5-12-58

Wittensee (A 1407)   1975

REPLENISHMENT OILERS (continued)

D: 1,237 tons (1,854 fl)   **S:** 12 kts   **Dim:** 67.45 × 9.84 × 4.25
M: 1 MAK 6-cyl. diesel; 1,250 hp   **Electric:** 216 kw   **Cargo:** 1,238 tons
Range: 6,240/12   **Man:** 21 tot. (civilian crew)

REMARKS: Purchased 26-3-59. Sister *Bodensee* transferred to Turkey 8-77.

♦ **1 Type 766 former merchant tanker** Bldr: Norderwerft, Hamburg

	Laid down	L	In serv.
A 1429 EIFEL (ex-*Friedrich Jung*)	5-11-57	2-4-58	26-7-58

Eifel (A 1429)   G. Koop, 1979

D: 6,720 tons (fl)   **S:** 13 kts   **Dim:** 101.76 × 14.43 × 7.1
M: 2 M.A.N. 8-cyl. diesels; 1 prop; 3,360 hp   **Electric:** 760 kVa
Cargo: 4,720 tons   **Range:** 7,300/12   **Man:** 40 tot.

REMARKS: Purchased 1963. Equipped for underway replenishment.

♦ **1 Type 766 former merchant tanker** Bldr: Norderwerft, Hamburg

	Laid down	L	In serv.
A 1428 HARZ (ex-*Claere Jung*)	31-3-53	2-9-53	26-11-53

Harz (A 1428)   G. Koop, 1979

D: 5,380 tons (fl)   **S:** 12 kts   **Dim:** 92.40 × 13.60 × 6.70
M: 2 OEW 8-cyl. diesels; 1 prop; 2,520 hp   **Electric:** 380 kVa
Cargo: 3,525 tons   **Range:** 7,200/11   **Man:** 28 tot.

REMARKS: Purchased 1963. Equipped for underway replenishment, one station per side.

INTELLIGENCE COLLECTORS

♦ **2 Type-442B converted trawlers** Bldr: Unterweser, Bremerhaven

	L	In serv.	Conv.
A 50 ALSTER (ex-*Mellum*)	21-11-60	21-3-61	19-10-71
A 53 OKER (ex-*Hoheweg*)	29-8-60	19-10-60	11-2-72

D: 1,187 tons (1,497 fl)   **S:** 15 kts   **Dim:** 72.83 (68.35 pp) × 10.50 × 5.60
M: 1 Klöckner-Humboldt-Deutz 8-cyl., 1,800-hp diesel, electric drive; 1 KHD 8-cyl. auxiliary propulsion diesel, 400-hp electric drive; 1 prop

REMARKS: Two Type-423 replacements planned.

♦ **1 Type-740 converted inshore minesweeper** Bldr: Abeking & Rasmussen, Lemwerde

	Laid down	L	In serv.
Y 836 HOLNIS	15-8-64	20-5-65	31-3-66

Holnis (Y 836)   G. Koop

D: 150 tons (180 fl)   **S:** 16.5 kts   **Dim:** 36.87 × 7.40 × 1.80
M: 2 Mercedes-Benz MB 820Db diesels; 2 props; 2,000 hp
Electric: 380 kw   **Fuel:** 13 tons   **Man:** 27 tot.

REMARKS: Wooden construction, prototype of a class of 20 Type-390 inshore minesweepers, the other 19 of which were canceled. Altered circa 1968 as an intelligence collector.

♦ **1 Type-422A converted tug** Bldr: Akers Mek., Oslo

	L	In serv.
A 52 OSTE (ex-USN *Puddefjord*, ex-Ger. *Puddefjord*)	21-10-42	1943

Oste (A 52)   G. Koop, 1978

INTELLIGENCE COLLECTORS (continued)

D: 690 tons (940 fl) **S:** 11 kts **Dim:** 49.39 (45.00 pp) × 9.10 × 5.70
M: 2/5-cyl. Akers diesels; 1 prop; 1,600 hp **Electric:** 360 kw **Man:** 45 tot.

REMARKS: Served U.S. Navy 1946-57. Commissioned in German Navy 21-1-57 as a tender (Type 419). Converted for use as an intelligence collector circa 1968.

SEAGOING TUGS

♦ **3 Baltrum (Type 722) class** Bldr: Schichau, Bremerhaven

	Laid down	L	In serv.
A 1451 WANGEROOGE	1-10-65	4-7-66	9-4-68
A 1452 SPIEKEROOGE	20-11-65	26-9-66	14-8-68
A 1455 NORDERNEY	29-5-67	28-2-68	15-10-70

D: 854 tons (1,039 fl) **S:** 13.6 kts **Dim:** 51.78 × 12.11 × 4.2
A: 1/40-mm AA (preserved)
M: 4 MWM 16-cyl. diesels, electric drive; 2 props; 2,400 hp
Electric: 540 kw **Range:** 5,000/10 **Man:** 31 tot.

REMARKS: Also employed as salvage tugs and port icebreakers. Sister *Baltrum* has been used as a diving-training tender since 1974; *Juist* and *Langeoog* were reconfigured for training duties during 1977-78. See page 215 for appearance.

♦ **2 Helgoland (Type 720)-class salvage tugs** Bldr: Schichau, Bremerhaven

	Laid down	L	In serv.
A 1457 HELGOLAND (8-4-65)	24-7-64	9-4-65	8-3-66
A 1458 FEHMARN	23-4-65	25-11-65	1-2-67

Helgoland (A 1457)   G. Koop, 1977

D: 1,304 tons (1,558 fl) **S:** 16.6 kts **Dim:** 67.9 × 12.74 × 4.20
A: None **M:** 4 MWM 12-cyl. diesels, electric drive; 2 props; 3,300 hp
Electric: 1,065 kw **Range:** 6,400/16 **Man:** 34 tot.

REMARKS: Two 40-mm AA (II × 1) removed. *Fehmarn* serves as a tender to the submarine training establishment. Equipped to serve as mine planters, if required.

♦ **2 Eisvogel (Type 721)-class icebreaking tugs** Bldr: Hitzler, Laurenburg

	Laid down	L	In serv.
A 1401 EISVOGEL	10-3-59	28-4-60	11-3-61
A 1402 EISBAR	12-5-59	9-6-60	1-11-61

Eisvogel (A 1401)   G. Koop

D: 496 tons (641 fl) **S:** 13 kts **Dim:** 37.8 × 9.7 × 4.2
Electron Equipt: Radar: 1/Kelvin-Hughes 14/9
M: 2 Maybach 12-cyl. diesels; 2 CP props; 2,400 hp **Electric:** 180 kw
Range: 2,000/12 **Man:** 16 tot.

REMARKS: Provision for 1/40-mm AA aft.

EXPERIMENTAL SHIP

♦ **1 Type-421 former corvette** Bldr: Atlaswerke, Bremen

	Laid down	L	In serv.
A 1449 HANS BÜRKNER	12-10-60	6-6-61	18-5-63

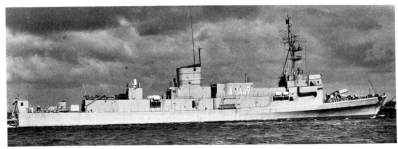

Hans Bürkner (A 1449)   1975

D: 983 tons (1,348 fl) **S:** 24 kts **Dim:** 80.6 × 9.42 × 3.50
A: 1/375-mm Bofors 4-barreled ASW RL (*see* Remarks)
M: 4 M.A.N. 16-cyl. diesels; 2 CP props; 13,600 hp **Electric:** 520 kVa
Range: 2,180/15 **Man:** 50 tot.

REMARKS: Employed as an ASW trials ship. Has recently carried a small variable-depth sonar. Position for two 40-mm AA (II × 1) retained, and has previously carried two 533-mm ASW torpedo tubes. Fitted with mine rails.

TRAINING SHIPS

♦ 1 Type-440 cruiser type

	Bldr	Laid down	L	In serv.
A 59 Deutschland	Nobiskrug, Rendsburg	17-9-59	5-11-60	25-5-63

Deutschland (A 59)

D: 4,880 tons (5,684 fl) **S:** 22 kts (18 cruising) **Range:** 6,000/17
Dim: 138.2 (130.0 pp) × 16.0 × 5.0 **Man:** 33 officers, 521 men (250 cadets)
A: 4/100-mm AA (I × 4)—8/40-mm AA (II × 2, I × 4)—4/533-mm ASW TT—8/
375-mm Bofors ASW RL (IV × 2)
Electron Equipt: Radars: 1/LW-08, 1/SGR-114, 1/SGR-105, 1/SGR-103, 4/M
45 f.c. Sonar: 1/ELAC 1BV (M/F)
M: 4/2,000-hp Maybach diesels; 1 set Wahodag 8,000-hp GT; 3 props (2 CP);
16,000 hp
Boilers: 2 Wahodag, 450°C **Electric:** 1,500 kw **Fuel:** 640 tons

Remarks: Quarters for 7 instructors and 250 cadets. Can be used as a minelayer. Two
Mercedes-Benz diesels replaced by Maybach engines in 1979.

♦ 1 Type-441 sail training ship Bldr: Blohm & Voss, Hamburg

	Laid down	L	In serv.
A 60 Gorch Fock	24-2-58	23-8-58	17-12-58

D: 1,819 tons (2,005 fl) **S:** 10 kts (15 kts under sail)
Dim: 89.32 (81.44 hull, 70.20 pp) × 12.02 × 5.25
M: 1 M.A.N. 6-cyl. diesel; 1 prop; 890 hp **Electric:** 266 kw
Range: 1,100/10 **Man:** 74 tot. plus 200 cadets

Remarks: 1,904 m² sail area. Carries 350 tons permanent ballast. Has made 296
nautical miles progress in one day.

YARD AND SERVICE CRAFT

HARBOR TUGS

♦ 3 Heppens (Type 724)-class tugs Bldr: Schichau, Bremerhaven

	Laid down	L	In serv.
Y 1680 Neuende	29-12-70	2-6-71	27-10-71
Y 1681 Heppens	19-3-71	15-9-71	17-12-71
Y 1682 Ellerbek	29-12-70	2-6-71	26-11-71

D: 232 tons (319 fl) **S:** 12 kts **Dim:** 26.6 × 7.4 × 2.6
M: 1 MWM 8-cyl. diesel; 800 hp **Electric:** 120 kw **Man:** 6 tot.

Gorch Fock—pendant number, A 60, not painted on   G. Gyssels, 1979

Ellerbek (Y 1682)   S. Terzibaschitsch, 1980

♦ 4 Sylt (Type 724)-class tugs Bldr: Schichau, Bremerhaven

	L	In serv.		L	In serv.
Y 820 Sylt	29-4-61	5-7-62	Y 822 Amrum	6-10-61	25-1-63
Y 821 Föhr	13-5-61	11-10-62	Y 823 Neuwerk	12-10-61	5-4-63

D: 266 tons (282 fl) **S:** 12 kts **Dim:** 30.2 × 7.9 × 4.0
M: 1 MAK 8-cyl. diesel; 1,000 hp **Range:** 1,775/12 **Man:** 10 tot.

HARBOR TUGS (continued)

Neuwerk (Y 823)   S. Terzibaschitsch, 1980

♦ **8 Lütje Hörn (Type 723) class**

	L		L
Y 812 LUTJE HÖRN	9-5-58	Y 816 VOGELSAND	12-1-59
Y 813 MELLUM	23-10-58	Y 817 NORDSTRAND	17-4-58
Y 814 KNECHTSAND	3-12-58	Y 818 TRISCHEN	27-2-59
Y 815 SCHARNHORN	9-5-58	Y 819 LANGENESS	7-4-59

Lütje Hörn (Y 812)   G. Koop

D: 52.2 tons (57.5 fl)   **S:** 10 kts   **Dim:** 15.2 × 5.06 × 2.2
M: 2 Deutz 8-cyl. diesels; 2 Voith-Schneider cycloidal props; 340 hp
Range: 550/9   **Man:** 4 tot.

♦ **3 miscellaneous tugs**

Y 886: 41 tons; 24.11 × 4.3 × 1.5; 1/MWM diesel; 320 hp
Y 883, Y 884: 43 tons; 22.1 × 3.8 × 1.5; 1 Deutz diesel; 250 hp

WATER TANKERS

♦ **4 FW 1 (Type 705) class**

	Bldr	Laid down	L	In serv.
Y 864 FW 1	Schichau, Bremerhaven	5-4-63	22-7-63	30-11-63
Y 867 FW 4	Jadewerft, Wilhelmshaven	14-6-63	14-3-64	28-7-64
Y 868 FW 5	Ranke, Hamburg	26-7-63	26-11-63	21-2-64
Y 869 FW 6	Ranke, Hamburg	4-11-63	25-2-64	19-6-64

FW (Y 868)   S. Terzibaschitsch

D: 598 tons (647 fl)   **S:** 9.5 kts   **Dim:** 44.03 (41.1 pp) × 7.80 × 2.63
M: 1 MWM 12-cyl. diesel; 230 hp   **Electric:** 130 kVa   **Fuel:** 15 tons
Range: 2,150/9   **Man:** 12 tot.

REMARKS: Cargo: 343 tons. Sister FW 2 to Turkey in 1975, FW 3 to Greece in 1976.
FW 6 is in reserve.

TORPEDO-RECOVERY BOATS

♦ **9 TF 1 (Type 430) class** Bldrs: Burmester, Bremen & Schweers, Bardenfleth

	L		L		L
Y 851 TF 1	13-10-65	Y 854 TF 4	21-10-65	Y 872 TF 106	10-6-66
Y 852 TF 2	22-9-65	Y 855 TF 5	28-2-66	Y 873 TF 107	13-9-65
Y 853 TF 3	13-10-65	Y 856 TF 6	4-5-66	Y 874 TF 108	22-9-65

TF 5 (Y 855)   1975

TORPEDO-RECOVERY BOATS (continued)

D: 56 tons (63.5 fl) **S:** 17 kts **Dim:** 25.22 × 5.40 × 1.60
M: 1 MWM 12-cyl. diesel; 1 prop; 1,000 hp **Man:** 6 tot.

♦ **1 TF 104 (Type 438) class** Bldr: Kröger, Warnemünde

Y 886 TF 104 (ex-*Suderoog*) (In serv. 1-10-59)

D: 41 tons **S:** . . . kts **Dim:** 24.05 × 4.60 × 1.50
M: 1 MWM 8-cyl. diesel; 320 hp

♦ **2 miscellaneous torpedo-recovery craft:** Y 883, Y 884

AIR-SEA RESCUE CRAFT

♦ **6 KW 15 (Type 369) class**

	Bldr	L
Y 827 KW 15 (ex-BG 1, ex-KW 15, ex-H 15, ex-U.S.N. 57)	Schweers	6-10-52
Y 830 KW 16 (ex-BG 2, ex-KW 16, ex-H 16, ex-U.S.N. 54)	Lürssen	1952
Y 832 KW 18 (ex-H 18, ex-U.S.N. 55)	Abeking & Rasmussen	17-11-51
Y 833 KW 19 (ex-H 19, ex-U.S.N. 59)	Schweers	16-2-53
Y 845 KW 17 (ex-BG 3, ex-KW 17, ex-H 17, ex-U.S.N. 58)	Schürenstedt	27-3-53
Y 846 KW 20 (ex-BG 4, ex-KW 20, ex-H 20, ex-U.S.N. 56)	Lürssen	1953

KW 19 (Y 833) G. Koop

D: 59.5 tons (69.6 fl) **S:** 25.0 **Dim:** 28.90 × 4.70 × 1.42
Electron Equipt: Radar: 1/Kelvin-Hughes 14/9
M: 2 MTU 12-cyl. diesels; 2 props; 2,000 hp **Electric:** 10 kw **Man:** 17 tot.

REMARKS: Built as patrol boats for U.S. Navy, taken over 30-11-56. Served in Border Guard 1963-1969/70.

SUBMARINE RESCUE CRAFT

♦ **1 converted *Schutze*-class former patrol minesweeper**

	Bldr	L	In serv.
Y 849 STIER (ex-M 1092)	Abeking & Rasmussen	30-10-58	28-6-61

REMARKS: Data as for *Schütze* class. Retains 40-mm AA. Converted 1969. Deckhouse with decompression chamber added on fantail; also carries two rubber Gemini dinghies.

EXPERIMENTAL AND TRIALS CRAFT

♦ **1 Type 742 magnetic research ship**

	Bldr	L	In serv.
Y 841 WALTHER VON LEDEBUR	Burmester, Bremen	30-6-66	21-12-67

D: 775 tons (825 fl) **S:** 19 kts **Dim:** 63.2 × 10.6 × 3.0
M: 2 Maybach 16-cyl. diesels; 2 props; 5,200 hp **Electric:** 1,620 kw
Man: 19 crew plus technicians

REMARKS: One of the largest wooden ships built in modern times. Used in mine-warfare research and can be employed as a minesweeper. Two 600-kw sweep current generators.

♦ **2 Type 741 net tenders** Bldr: Schürenstedt K. G., Bardenfleth

	Laid down	L	In serv.
Y 837 SP 1	7-9-65	21-6-66	29-6-67
Y 838 WILHELM PULLWER (ex-SP 2)	4-10-65	16-8-66	22-12-67

SP 1 (Y 837) S. Terzibaschitsch, 1970

D: 132 tons (160 fl) **S:** 12.5 kts **Dim:** 31.54 × 7.5 × 2.2
M: 2 Mercedes-Benz 8-cyl. diesels; 2 Voith-Schneider cycloidal props; 792 hp
Electric: 120 kw **Man:** 17 crew plus trials personnel

REMARKS: Used in experimental trials. Y 838 has a black-painted hull.

♦ **1 Type 740 torpedo-trials ship** Bldr: AG Weser, Bremerhaven

	Laid down	L	In serv.
Y 871 HEINZ ROGGENKAMP (ex-*Greif*)	23-8-52	8-11-52	30-12-52

D: 935 tons (996 fl) **S:** 12 kts **Dim:** 57.19 (51.5 pp) × 9.04 × 3.10
A: 2/533-mm torpedo tubes (1 ASW, on deck; 1 underwater)—3/324-mm Mk 32 ASW TT (III × 1) **Electric:** 192 kw **Man:** 19 crew plus trials personnel
M: 1 Klöckner-Humboldt-Deutz 8-cyl. diesel; 1 prop; 1,145 hp (800 sust.)

REMARKS: Former trawler purchased 1963; commissioned after reconstruction 25-9-64. Civilian crew.

♦ **1 weapons-trials barge**

Y 844 BARBARA Bldr: Howaldtswerke, Kiel (In serv. 26-6-64)

D: 3,500 tons (fl) **Dim:** 62.1 × 24.2 × 3.0 **Electric:** 1,650 kVA

REMARKS: Non-self-propelled. Extensive superstructure. Used to test guns. Civilian crew.

EXPERIMENTAL AND TRIALS CRAFT (continued)

Heinz Roggenkamp (Y 871)   G. Koop, 1973

◆ **1 former fishing cutter**

Y 882 OTTO MEYCKE (ex-*Meteor II*)   **Bldr:** Lürssen, Vegasack (L: 6-47)

   D: 50 tons   **S:** 9 kts   **Dim:** 17.45 (14.95 pp) × 5.0 × 1.9
   M: 1 Modag SRB55 diesel; 1 prop; 150 hp   **Man:** 6 tot.

REMARKS: Wooden craft, purchased 1960; commissioned 5-8-60. Primarily a diving tender. Civilian crew. Pendant number not painted on.

◆ **1 trials tender**   **Bldr:** Nyslands, Oslo

	Laid down	L	In serv.
Y 888 FRIEDRICH VOGE (ex-*Kurefjord*)	5-12-41	16-3-43	1-7-43

Friedrich Voge (Y 888)   1975

   D: 260 tons (298 fl)   **S:** 12 kts   **Dim:** 33.2 × 6.7 × 3.3
   M: 1 M.A.N. 8-cyl. diesel; 550 hp   **Electric:** 120 kw
   Man: 14 tot. plus trials personnel

REMARKS: Launched 16-3-43. Acquired 1959; commissioned 20-12-59.

◆ **2 ex-U.S. YMS-class minesweepers**

	Bldr	Laid down	L	In serv.
Y 881 ADOLF BESTELMEYER (ex-BYMS 2213, ex-YMS 213)	Robt. Jacob, City Isl., N.Y.	13-6-42	13-11-42	17-6-43
Y 889 RUDOLF DIESEL (ex-BYMS 2279, ex-YMS 279)	H.C. Grebe, Chicago, Ill.	23-1-43	29-7-43	15-10-43

Adolf Bestelmeyer (Y 881)   G. Koop, 1978

   D: Y 881: 290 tons (360 fl); Y 889: 280 tons (310 fl)   **S:** 15 kts
   Dim: 42.13 (39.62 pp) × 7.47 × 2.55
   M: 2 GM 8-268A diesels; 2 props; 1,000 hp   **Electric:** 290 kw   **Range:** 2,500/9
   Man: 16 crew plus trials personnel

REMARKS: Operated in British Navy during World War II. Acquired 1957/1960. Wooden hulls. Both employed in mine weapons trials and have two mine rails. Sister OT 2 has been stricken.

◆ **1 ex-U.S. YMS-class minesweeper**   **Bldr:** Weaver Bros., Orange, Texas

	Laid down	L	In serv.
Y 877 HANS CHRISTIAN OERSTED (ex-*Vinstra*, ex-NYMS 247, ex-YMS 247)	27-5-42	14-10-42	13-5-43

H.C. Oersted (Y 877)   S. Terzibaschitsch

EXPERIMENTAL AND TRIALS CRAFT (continued)

D: 260 tons (302 fl) **S:** 16 kts **Dim:** 41.53 (39.62 pp) × 7.52 × 2.40
M: 2 Maybach diesels, electric drive; 2 props; 1,800 hp
Electric: 120 kw (plus 680 kw from main engines)
Man: 16 crew plus trials personnel

REMARKS: Operated in Norwegian Navy from completion to 1959; acquired 1960 and reconstructed and re-engined, recommissioning 12-7-62. Initially used as a degaussing tender, but since 1974 used in research.

DIVING TENDERS

♦ 3 Baltrum (Type 754)-class converted seagoing tugs

Bldr: Schichau, Bremerhaven

	Laid down	L	In serv.
Y 1661 BALTRUM (ex-A 1454)	29-6-66	2-6-67	8-10-68
Y 1664 JUIST (ex-A 1456)	23-9-67	15-8-68	1-10-71
Y 1665 LANGEOOG (ex-A 1453)	12-7-66	2-5-67	14-8-68

Baltrum (Y 1661) S. Terzibaschitsch, 1980

REMARKS: Data as for seagoing tug sisters; can be armed with 1/40-mm AA. Y 1661 converted 1974, others in 1978. Used to train mine-clearance divers.

♦ 1 Type-732 small diving tender Bldr: Burmester, Bremen

Y 1678 TB 1 (In serv. 21-6-72)

D: 70 tons **S:** 14 kts **Dim:** 27.75 × 5.77 × 1.90
M: 1 MWM 12-cyl. diesel; 950 hp **Electric:** 36 kw

REMARKS: Also used for research.

♦ 1 Type-392 former inshore minesweeper Bldr: Kröger, Rendsburg

	Laid down	L	In serv.
Y 806 HANSA (ex-W 22, ex-M 2662)	7-8-57	18-11-57	23-7-58

D: 155 tons (175 fl) **S:** 14 kts **Dim:** 35.18 × 6.84 × 1.95
M: 1 Mercedes-Benz MB 820Db diesel; 1 prop; 1,000 hp **Electric:** 180 kw
Range: 1,500/12 **Man:** 20 tot.

REMARKS: Wooden hull. Converted 1968-69 as a training tender for mine-clearance divers. The torpedo workshop craft *Memmert* (Y 805) was stricken in 1980.

MISCELLANEOUS SERVICE CRAFT

♦ 2 Type-710 tank-cleaning craft Bldr: Deutsche Werft, Hamburg

	Laid down	L	In serv.
Y 1641 FÖRDE	12-1-67	10-3-67	14-12-67
Y 1642 JADE	18-5-67	19-7-67	6-11-67

Jade (Y 1642) G. Koop

D: 1,830 tons (fl) **S:** 8 kts **Dim:** 58.46 × 10.40 × 4.1 (light)
M: 1 MWM 16-cyl. diesel; 1 prop; 390 hp **Range:** 750/8 **Man:** 16 tot.

REMARKS: For steam-cleaning fuel tanks and for sludge removal. Civilian crews.

♦ 2 Type-711 self-propelled floating cranes Bldr: Rheinwerft, Walsum

Y 875 HIEV (In serv. 2-10-62)   Y 876 GRIEP (In serv. 15-5-63)

Griep (Y 876) G. Koop

D: 1,830 tons (1,875 fl) **S:** 6 kts **Dim:** 52.9 × 22.0 × 2.1
M: 3 MWM 600-hp diesels, electric drive; 3 vertical cycloidal props; 1,425 hp
Electric: 358 kVa **Man:** 12 tot.

REMARKS: Electric-crane capacity: 100 tons. Civilian crews.

MISCELLANEOUS SERVICE CRAFT (continued)

◆ **3 Type-718 battery-charging craft** Bldrs: Jadewerft, Wilhelmshaven (LP 2: Oelkers, Hamburg)

LP 1 (In serv. 18-2-64)   LP 2 (In serv. 17-4-64)   LP 3 (In serv. 16-9-74)

LP 2   G. Koop

    D: 192 tons (234 fl)   **S:** 8 kts   **Dim:** 27.6 × 7.0 × 1.6
    M: 1 MTU diesel; 250 hp   **Electric:** 960 kw (LP 3: 1,110 kw)   **Man:** 6 tot.

REMARKS: Each has two 405-kw generators and one (LP 3: two) 150-kw generator for charging submarine batteries. LP 3 is 7.5 m in beam, 1.8 m draft, 267 tons (fl).

TRAINING CRAFT

NOTE: Also included in this category are the three *Baltrum*-class former seagoing tugs and the diving tender *Hansa* listed under diving tenders.

◆ **1 Type-368 ketch, former patrol fishing cutter** (In serv. 1942-44?)

Y 834 NORDWIND (ex-W 43)

    D: 100 tons (110 fl)   **S:** 11 kts   **Dim:** 27.00 (24.00 hull, 21.48 pp) × 6.39 × 2.94
    M: 1 Demag 5-cyl. diesel; 1 prop; 137 hp   **Range:** 1,200/7   **Man:** 10 tot.

REMARKS: Taken over by U.S. Navy 1945; acquired 1-7-56 by German Navy. Wooden hull; 195 m² sail area. Operated for the Mürwik Naval School.

NOTE: There are also 70 smaller sail-training craft, all bearing names. Included are 26 Type-914 class, 5 m long, 10 Type-913 class, 7.64 m long, 25 Type-910 (most 10.46 m o.a.), 6 Type 911, and 1 Type 912.

ACCOMMODATIONS BARGES (Type 130)

◆ **Y 809 Arcona** (ex-*Royal Prince*) Bldr: Ruthoff (In serv. 1943)

    D: 380 tons   **Dim:** 66.40 × 10.00 × 1.60

REMARKS: Accommodations for 81 men, at Kiel. In naval service 16-7-58; former river passenger craft.

◆ **Y 811 Knurrhahn** (ex-U.S.N. *Barge 2*) (In serv. 1916)

    D: 1,250 tons   **Dim:** 58.94 × 11.0 × 2.60

REMARKS: Used by U.S. Navy 1945-55. In German naval service 16-10-55. Accommodations for 300. Also in use for accommodations are the small barges *Siebethsburg*, *Unke*, and *Vesta*.

Knurrhahn (Y 811)—outboard *Arcona*   S. Terzibaschitsch, 1980

NOTE: There are also a number of small personnel launches, generator craft, workboats, and freight barges in service. Some of these have Y-series pendants, while most have alphanumeric pendants denoting their functions.

FLOATING DRY DOCKS

◆ **2 Type 712** Bldr: Krupp, Rheinhausen

HEBEWERK 2 (In serv. 15-3-61)   HEBEWERK A (In serv. 13-1-61)

    D: 1,000 tons   **Dim:** 66.01 × 21.10 × . . .

REMARKS: Serviced by 4 Type-713 "Hebeponton": 500 tons, 56 m by 14.8 m.

◆ **1 Type-714 self-propelled** Bldr: Flenderwerft, Lübeck (In serv. circa 1945)

Y 879 SCHWIMMDOCK B

    D: 4,500 tons   **S:** . . .   **Dim:** 156.00 × 25.00 × 3.50
    M: 4 MWM 16-cyl. diesels, electric drive; 2 Schöttel props; 500 hp

REMARKS: In German naval service 26-10-63 at Kiel. The propellers are at the starboard forward and port aft corners.

◆ **1 Type 715** Bldr: Howaldtswerke, Hamburg (In serv. 1961)

Y 842 SCHWIMMDOCK 3

    D: 8,000 tons   **Dim:** 164.0 × 30.0 × 3.5

REMARKS: Seven pontoon sections.

◆ **1 Type 715** Bldr: Flenderwerke, Lübeck (In serv. 8-9-67)

DRUCKDOCK ("*Dock C*")

    D: . . . tons   **Dim:** 93.0 × 26.5 × 3.6

◆ **1 Type 715 small dock** Bldr: Blohm & Voss, Hamburg (In serv. 1943)

HEBEWERK 1 ("*Dock 1*")

    D: 118 tons   **Dim:** 25.57 × 13.00 × 0.85

COAST GUARD

NOTE: A separate paramilitary force of 1,000 men (Bundesgrenzschutz-See).

PATROL BOATS

◆ **8 Neustadt class** Bldrs: Lürssen, Vegasack, except B-13: Schlichting, Travemünde

PATROL BOATS *(continued)*

BG 11 NEUSTADT	BG 14 DUDERSTADT	BG 17 BAYREUTH
BG 12 BAD BRAMSTEDT	BG 15 ESCHWEGE	BG 18 ROSENHEIM
BG 13 UELTZEN	BG 16 ALSFELD	

D: 140 tons (203 fl) **S:** 30 kts **Dim:** 38.3 × 7.0 × 2.15 **Range:** 450/27
A: 2/40-mm AA (I × 2) **M:** 3 MTU diesels; 3 props; 7,885 hp **Man:** 23 tot.

REMARKS: In service 1969-70. Centerline engine of 685 hp for cruising. Two additional planned were canceled.

♦ **1 tug** Bldr: Mützelbeldt-Werft, Cuxhaven (L: 29-1-76)

BG 5 RETTIN

D: 99.9 grt **S:** 9 kts **Dim:** 22.5 (20.0 pp) × 6.6 × 2.9
M: 2 MWM diesels; 1 prop; 590 hp

FISHERIES PROTECTION

NOTE: Operated by the Ministry of Agriculture and Fisheries.

♦ **7 patrol ships**

SEEFALKE Bldr: Orenstein & Koppel (In serv. 4-8-81)

D: . . . **S:** 20 kts **Dim:** 81.75 × 12.80 × 4.30
M: 2 diesels; 2 CP props; 8,000 hp **Man:** 29 tot.

REMARKS: To operate in East Greenland Sea. A helicopter deck is to be added later. Has fin stabilizers, bow-thruster, 7-bed hospital.

MEERKATZE Bldr: Lürssen, Vegasack (In serv. 1976)

Meerkatze   Lürssen, 1976

D: 2,386 tons **S:** 15 kts **Dim:** 76.5 × 11.8 × 5.5
M: 3 MWM diesels, electric drive; 2 props; 2,300 hp **Man:** 30 tot.

SOLEA Bldr: Sieghold, Bremerhaven (In serv. 1974)

D: 337 grt **S:** 12 kts **Dim:** 33.5 × 9.0 × 3.6 **M:** 1 Deutz diesel; 640 hp
Man: 11 tot.

WALTHER HERWIG Bldr: Schlichting, Travemünde (In serv. 1972)

D: 2,500 tons **S:** 15.5 kts **Dim:** 77.0 × 14.9 × 5.2
M: 2 M.A.N. diesels; 2 props; 3,380 hp **Man:** 35 tot.

FRITHJOF Bldr: Schlichting, Travemünde (In serv. 1967)

D: 2,140 tons **S:** 15 kts **Dim:** 76.0 × 11.8 × 5.2
M: 3 Maybach diesels, electric drive; 2 props; 2,650 hp **Man:** 35 tot.

ANTON DOHRN (ex-*Walther Herwig*) Bldr: Seebeck, Bremerhaven (In serv. 1963)

D: 1,986 grt **S:** 15 kts **Dim:** 83.0 × 12.5 × 5.2
M: Maybach diesels; 2,210 hp **Man:** 38 tot.

POSEIDON Bldr: Mützelfeldt, Cuxhaven (In serv. 1957)

D: 934 grt **S:** 12 kts **Dim:** 58.8 × 10.2 × . . .
M: 1 Verschure diesel; 800 hp **Man:** 20 tot.

GOVERNMENT CIVIL RESEARCH SHIPS

NOTE: Operated by the German Hydrographic Institute, which is subordinate to the Ministry of Transport.

♦ **5 (+1) oceanographic research and survey ships**

N . . . Bldr: Howaldswerke, Kiel (In serv. 11-82)

D: 13,000 tons **S:** 15.5 **Dim:** 117.55 (102.20 pp) × 25.00 × 10.50
M: 4 diesels; 2 Kort-nozzle props; 21,120 hp
Man: 110 tot.

REMARKS: An icebreaking arctic research ship and transport capable of carrying 1,500 tons of liquid cargo and 100 tons of provisions in containers on deck forward; will be able to break 2-m-thick ice. Helicopter and hangar.

GAUSS Bldr: Schlichtingwerft, Travemünde (In serv. 1980)

D: 1,372 tons (1,813 fl) **S:** 13.5 kts **Dim:** 68.7 (61.0 pp) × 13.0 × 4.25
Electron Equipt: Radar: 1 Raytheon 1660/12SR, 1 Raytheon RM1650/9 × R
M: 3 MAK 331 AK 800-hp diesels, electric drive; 1 prop; 1,647 hp
Electric: 220 kVa **Range:** 4,000/13.5 **Man:** 19 crew plus 12 scientists

REMARKS: Has special free-wheeling prop aft of propulsion propeller. Equipped with Becker flap-rudder, Denny-Brown fin stabilizers, and a 725-hp drop-down bow-thruster. Ships service power from main engine generators.

POSEIDON Bldr: Schichau, Unterweser (In serv. 1976)

D: 1,050 grt **S:** 15 kts **Dim:** 58.0 × 11.4 × . . . **M:** MWM diesels; 1,800 hp

KOMET Bldr: Jadewerft, Wilhelmshaven (In serv. 1969)

D: 1,253 grt **S:** 15 kts **Dim:** 68.0 × 11.5 × 4.0
M: 2 Maybach diesels; 1 prop; 2,650 hp **Man:** 42 tot.

METEOR Bldr: Seebeck, Bremerhaven (In serv. 1963)

D: 2,800 tons **S:** 15 kts **Dim:** 81.0 × 13.5 × . . . **M:** Diesel-electric; 765 hp
Man: 57 tot.

ATAIR   WEGA Bldr: Schlichting, Travemünde (In serv. 1962)

D: 157 grt **S:** 10.5 kts **Dim:** 31.7 × 6.5 × 2.3 **M:** 1 Deutz diesel; 205 hp
Man: 13 tot.

GHANA
Republic of Ghana

PERSONNEL (1980): 2,000 men

MERCHANT MARINE 1980: 104 ships—250,428 grt

CORVETTES

◆ 2 Vosper Mk 1 class

	Bldr	L	In serv.
F 17 KROMANTSE	Vosper Ltd	5-9-63	9-64
F 18 KETA	Vickers Ltd	18-1-65	8-65

Keta (F 18)   G. Arra, 1975

D: 435 tons (500 fl)   **S:** 18 kts   **Dim:** 53.95 (49.38 pp) × 8.7 × 3.05
A: 1/102-mm—1/40-mm AA—1/Squid ASW mortar (III × 1)
Electron Equipt: Radar: 1/Type 978 navigational, 1/Plessey AWS-1
                     Sonar: 1/Type 164 (M/F)
M: 2 Bristol Siddeley-Maybach 16-cyl. diesels; 2 props; 5,720 hp
Electric: 360 kw   **Fuel:** 60 tons   **Range:** 1,100/18, 2,900/14
Man: 5 officers, 49 men

REMARKS: Fin stabilizers fitted. Quarters are air-conditioned. Both refitted 1974-75.

PATROL BOATS

◆ 2 FBP 57 class Bldr: Lürssen, Vegasack

	Laid down	L	In serv.
P 28 ACHIMOTA	1978	14-3-79	27-3-81
P 29 YOGAGA	1978	14-3-79	27-3-81

D: 380 tons (410 fl)   **S:** 30 kts   **Dim:** 58.10 × 7.62 × 2.83
A: 1/76-mm OTO Melara DP—1/40-mm Bofors AA
Electron Equipt: Radar: 1/navigational, 1/Thomson-CSF Canopus A
M: 3 MTU 16V 538 TB 91 diesels; 3 props; 10,800 hp   **Man:** 40 tot.

REMARKS: Optronic gun director atop pilothouse. Carry 250 rounds 76-mm, 750 rounds
40-mm. Carry rubber dinghy for air/sea rescue and inspection purposes.

Achimota (P 28)   1980

◆ 2 FPB 45 class Bldr: Lürssen, Vegasack

	Laid down	L	In serv.
P 26 DZATA	1-78	19-9-79	4-12-79
P 27 SEBO	1-78	19-9-79	2-5-80

Sebo (P 27) and Dzata (P 26)—prior to arming   G. Gyssels, 1979

D: 212 tons (252 fl)   **S:** 30 kts   **Dim:** 44.90 (42.25 wl) × 7.00 × 2.50 (props)
A: 1/76-mm OTO Melara DP—1/40-mm Bofors AA
Electron Equipt: Radar: 1/navigational, 1/Thomson-CSF Canopus A
M: 2 MTU 16V 538 TB 91 diesels; 2 props; 7,200 hp (6,000 sust.)
Electric: 408 kVa   **Range:** 1,100/25, 2,000/15   **Man:** 5 officers, 30 men

◆ 2 Sahene class Bldr: Ruthoff, Mainz, Germany (In serv. 1976)

P 24 SAHENE   P 25 DELA

Dela (P 25)   1976

GHANA (*continued*)
PATROL BOATS (*continued*)

> **D:** 160 tons (fl) **S:** 30 kts **Dim:** 35.2 × 6.5 × 1.8
> **A:** 1/40-mm AA (with flare launchers attached)
> **M:** 2 MTU 16V538 TB90 diesels; 2 props; 3,000 hp
> **Range:** 1,000/30 **Man:** 32 tot.

REMARKS: Ordered 1973; builder went bankrupt and four others were not delivered. Designed for rescue and fisheries protection. Rescue equipment aft.

♦ **2 British Ford class** Bldr: Yarrow, Scotstoun

P 13 ELMINA (L: 18-10-62) P 14 KOMENDA (L: 17-5-62)

> **D:** 120 tons (160 fl) **S:** 15 kts **Dim:** 35.7 × 6.2 × 2.1
> **A:** 1/40-mm AA—depth charges
> **M:** 2 Paxman YHAXM diesels; 2 props; 1,100 hp **Fuel:** 23 tons **Man:** 19 tot.

PATROL CRAFT

♦ **2 "Spear" Mk 2 class** Bldr: Fairey Marine, Hamble (In serv. 1978)

> **D:** 4-5 tons (fl) **S:** 29 kts **Dim:** 9.1 × 2.9 × 0.8
> **M:** 2 diesels; 2 props; 360 hp

SERVICE CRAFT

♦ **2 utility landing craft** Bldr: Rotork, Great Britain

> **D:** 5 tons **S:** 25 kts **Dim:** 12.65 × 3.20 × . . .
> **M:** 2 Volvo AQD40A outdrive diesels; 240 hp

REMARKS: One FPB 412 patrol version and one STW 408 utility version.

NOTE: The British "Ton"-class minesweeper *Ejura* (M 16) and the small repair tender *Asuantsi* were stricken 1979-80.

GREAT BRITAIN
United Kingdom of Great Britain and Northern Ireland

PERSONNEL (1981-82): Under the Annual Budget commencing 1-4-81:

Royal Navy	Officers	Non-officers	Total
Men	9,300	53,200	62,500
Women	500	3,400	3,900
Royal Marines			
Men	700	7,200	7,900
Total	10,500	63,800	74,300

In addition, there are about 28,600 (1,000 women) Regular Reservists and 6,800 (900 women) Royal Naval and Royal Marine Reservists. About 85,000 civilians are employed, including those who man the ships and craft of the Royal Fleet Auxiliary Service and the Royal Maritime Auxiliary Service.

MERCHANT MARINE (1980): 3,181 ships—27,135,155 grt (tankers: 434—13,229,642 grt)

NAVAL PROGRAM: There is no publicly announced long-range construction program. However, as of 1 January 1982 there were on order or under construction 6 nuclear-powered attack submarines, 2 small aircraft carriers, 7 guided-missile destroyers, 4 guided-missile frigates, 7 minehunters, and a number of auxiliaries and patrol craft.

WARSHIPS IN SERVICE, UNDER CONSTRUCTION, OR ON ORDER AS OF 1 JANUARY 1982

	L	Tons	Main armament
♦ **2 (+2) aircraft carriers**			
1 (+2) INVINCIBLE	1977-81	16,000	1/Sea Dart, 5/Sea Harrier, 9/Sea King
1 HERMES	1953	23,900	5/Sea Harrier, 9/Sea King
♦ **31 (+7) submarines**			
		Tons (surfaced)	
4 RESOLUTION (nuclear ballistic missile)	1966-68	7,500	16/Polaris A3, 6/533-mm TT
0 (6+. . .) TRAFALGAR (nuclear attack)	1981-	4,200	5/533-mm TT
6 SWIFTSURE (nuclear attack)	1971-79	4,200	5/533-mm TT
5 VALIANT (nuclear attack)	1963-70	4,000	6/533-mm TT
1 DREADNOUGHT	1960	3,500	6/533-mm TT
15 PORPOISE/OBERON	1956-66	2,030	8/533-mm TT
(0+. . .) U (Type 2400)—projected	. . .	2,160	6/533-mm TT
♦ **13 (+7) guided-missile destroyers**			
(5+. . .) MANCHESTER	1980. . .	3,450	1/Sea Dart, 1/114-mm DP, 1/Lynx
8 (+2) SHEFFIELD	1971-82	3,150	1/Sea Dart, 1/114-mm DP, 1/Lynx
1 BRISTOL	1969	6,100	1/Sea Dart, 1/Limbo, 1/Ikara, 1/114-mm DP
4 COUNTY	1964-67	5,440	1/Sea Slug, 2/Sea Cat, 2/114-mm DP, 1/Wessex
♦ **45 (+3) frigates**			
(2+. . .) BOXER	1981-82	3,700	2/Sea Wolf, 2/40-mm AA, 1/Lynx
3 (+1) BROADSWORD	1976-80	3,500	2/Sea Wolf, 2/40-mm AA, 1/Lynx
8 AMAZON	1971-75	2,750	4/MM38 Exocet, 1/Sea Cat, 1/114-mm DP, 1/Lynx or Wasp
26 LEANDER	1961-71	2,450-650	1, 2, or 3/Sea Cat, 2/114-mm and/or 40-mm, 1/Wasp, 1/MM38 Exocet or Ikara in 15, ASW weapons
7 ROTHESAY	1957-60	2,380	2/114-mm DP 1/Sea Cat, 1/Wasp, 1/Limbo
1 WHITBY	1954	2,150	2/114-mm DP, 1/Limbo
♦ **24 (+2) patrol ships, boats, and craft**			

**WARSHIPS IN SERVICE, UNDER CONSTRUCTION,
OR PROJECTED** *(continued)*

Invincible (R 05)   D.J. Houghton, RN, 1980

♦ **33 (+7) mine warfare ships**

♦ **8 amphibious warfare ships**

WEAPONS AND SYSTEMS

A. MISSILES

♦ **strategic ballistic missiles**

Trident 1C-4 (UGM-96A)   Bldr: Lockheed

The Royal Navy is adopting the U.S. Trident missile, but with delivery vehicle and payload of British design and manufacture. Its design will no doubt stem from that of the Chevaline system being incorporated in Britain's Polaris A-3 missiles, but will have an independent trajectory capability (MIRV). The agreement for the acquisition of Trident is comparable to that signed in Nassau in 1962 for the adoption of the Polaris A-3 for the *Resolution* class and is the result of an exchange of letters between the President of the United States and the British Prime Minister on 14-15 July 1980, equally drawn up by the ministers of defense of the two nations. The submarines to carry Trident will not be ready until the 1990s; 80 Trident missiles are to be acquired.

The nuclear-powered ballistic missile submarines of the *Resolution* class employ Polaris A-3 missiles with an ogival payload package containing three 200-kT, non-maneuverable reentry vehicles of British design and manufacture. The payload is to be replaced by a new one named Chevaline, which is composed of six 150-kT warheads with greatly improved penetration aids. The first three trial launchings were carried out at Cape Canaveral in 1978, and the system was scheduled to become operational at the end of 1981. Chevaline employs post-boost guidance to improve accuracy.

MISSILES (continued)

Seaslug Mk 2 launcher aboard Norfolk (D 21)
S. Terzibaschitsch, 1980

♦ **surface-to-air missiles**

Sea Dart (GWS 30) Bldr: British Aerospace Dynamics Group

Medium-range system (25 miles, interception altitudes from 100 to 60,000 ft)
Length: 4,400 m   Diameter: 0.42 m   Wingspan: 0.91 m   Weight: 550 kg
  Propulsion: solid propellant then ramjet
  Guidance: semi-active homing   Fire control: Type 909 radar
Fitted on the *Bristol*, *Sheffield*, and *Invincible* classes
Mk 30 Mod 0 launcher on the *Bristol*; the lighter Mk 30 Mod 2 on the *Sheffield* and *Invincible* classes
A lightweight version of the entire system is in development

Sea Slug Mk 2 Bldr: British Aerospace Dynamics Group

Short-range system (15 miles slant range, 500 to 50,000 ft)
  Length: 5.94 m   Wingspan: 1.420 m (1.600 with fins)
  Diameter: 0.41 m   Weight: 900 kg (2,000 kg with boosters)
  Speed: Mach 1.8
  Propulsion: solid propulsion system with four solid boosters
  Fire control: Type 901, a beam-riding radar
  Fitted on the "County"-class DDGs; the Mk 1 version has been retired. Can also be used against surface targets.

Sea Wolf (GWS 25) Bldr: British Aerospace Dynamics Group

Short-range missile system (5,000 m)
  Length: 1.9 m   Wingspan: 0.45 m
  Diameter: 0.3 m   Weight: 82 kg
  Guidance: radar
  Fire control: Marconi Type 910 pulse-doppler radar, which permits control of 2-missile salvoes
Fitted on *Broadsword*-class frigates; being installed on some *Leander* class
Launcher contains six missiles (total weight with missiles: 3,500 kg)
Target designation is via the combined Type 967-968 radar

Sea Wolf (GWS 40) Bldr: British Aerospace Dynamics Group

Initially intended to replace the Sea Cat systems on the *Amazon*-class frigates as well as for use on smaller warships. GWS 40 is a lightweight system now under development. It will use a quadruple automatically reloadable launcher and will have a new combined warning pulse-doppler pulse-compression control radar system being developed by British Aerospace and HSA of the Netherlands. No longer intended for the *Amazons*, it may be installed in future warships and has been offered for export.

Sea Cat (GWS 20, 22, and 24) Bldr: Short Bros. and Harland

  Length: 1.47 m   Wingspan: 0.65 m
  Diameter: 0.2 m   Weight: 68 kg
  Propulsion: 2-stage solid propellant
  Guidance: GWS 21, GWS 22, or GWS 24, radar or GWS 20 optical system
  Launcher normally carries 4 missiles, although a 3-missile, lightweight launcher has been exported.

♦ **surface-to-surface missiles**

Four Exocet missile launch cannisters aboard Antrim (D 18)—note blast deflector arrangement
G. Arra, 1980

  The Royal Navy has purchased the MM 38 Exocet (*see* section on France) and builds it under license. It is employed on the "County" class, the *Amazon*, *Broadsword*, and some units of the *Leander* class.

  In August 1977, it was announced that the U.S. Harpoon system would be bought for use from all nuclear attack submarines except the elderly *Dreadnought*. The *Churchill* launched six Harpoons in tests Jan.-Feb. 1980 in U.S. waters. 300 have been ordered.

♦ **air-to-surface missiles**

AS 11 (*see* section on France) wire-guided is used from Wasp helicopters on frigates

Sea Skua (CL 834) Bldr: British Aerospace Dynamics Group

Solid propellant
  Length: 2.65 m   Wingspan: 0.6 m
  Diameter: 0.28 m   Weight: 210 kg

MISSILES (*continued*)

    Speed: Mach 0.8   Range: 15,000 m
    Guidance: semi-active   Warhead: 20 kg high explosive
    Developed for use by Lynx helicopters

Sea Eagle (P3T) Bldr: British Aerospace Dynamics Group

Developed from the Anglo-French, television-guided Martel. Sea Eagle is intended for use as an anti-ship weapon by carrier-based Sea Harrier V/STOL aircraft as well as by land-based Tornado GR-1 and Buccaneer attack aircraft. Using active radar guidance, it employs the French Microturbo/Toulouse TRI-60 engine for propulsion. First aerial launchings took place in the spring of 1981. A Mk 2 version is not to be proceeded with.

♦ **air-to-air missiles**

Sidewinder-1B (AIM-9L) Bldr: Philco-Ford

Infrared-homing, solid-fueled, Mach 3.0 lightweight weapon employed with Harrier V/STOL aircraft aboard *Invincible*-class carriers and *Hermes*.
    Range: 18,000 m   Weight: 85 kg

NOTE: Development of the Sky Flash specialized air-to-air missile for Sea Harrier has been canceled.

B. GUNS

114-mm Mk 6

Double-barreled, semi-automatic, dual purpose.
    Muzzle velocity: 850 m/sec
    Maximum effective range in surface fire: 13,000 m
    Maximum effective range in anti-aircraft fire: 6,000 m
    Rate of fire: 10-12 rounds/min/barrel
Installed on some *Leander*, all *Rothesay*, and *Whitby*-class frigates, and on "County"-class destroyers

114-mm Mk 8

Single-barreled, automatic, dual purpose; has a muzzle brake

Vickers, 114-mm Mk 8 gun and Exocet launchers aboard Alacrity (F 174)
                                             G. Arra, 1980

    Length of barrel: 55 calibers
    Maximum effective range in surface fire: 13,000 m
    Maximum effective range in anti-aircraft fire: 6,000 m
    Rate of fire: 25 rounds/min
    Arc of elevation: −10° + 53°
Light gun mount with glass-reinforced plastic housing.
Installed on the *Bristol*, *Sheffield*-class destroyers, and *Amazon*-class frigates

Bofors 40-mm

60-caliber guns are used on single Mk 7 and Mk 9 mounts; all Mk 5 twin mounts have now been discarded

Oerlikon 20-mm

Standard 80-caliber single mountings are used in many classes

C. ANTISUBMARINE WEAPONS

Mk 10 Mortar (Limbo)

Triple-barreled mortar based on the Squid of World War II. Range: 700 to 1,000 m.
Fitted on *Bristol*, some *Leander*, *Rothesay*, and *Whitby* classes.

Ikara

U.S. Mk 46 torpedo below an Australian-designed guided missile launched by a solid-fuel rocket motor
Maximum range: 18,000 m. See Australia section for further details.
Fitted on the *Bristol* and *Leander*-class frigates

Ikara missile and launcher aboard Galatea (F 18)—the magazine is abaft the launcher "gazebo."
                                             G. Arra, 1980

D. TORPEDOES

U.S. Mk 44 and Mk 46 mod ASW torpedoes

The principal torpedoes of British origin are:
    the wire-guided, submarine-launched Mk 23 for ASW
    the wire-guided Mk 24 Tigerfish (ex-Ongar). This torpedo is designed for use by nuclear attack submarines.

TORPEDOES *(continued)*

A new lightweight torpedo designated NST 75 11, Stingray, is scheduled to enter service in the early 1980s; it is intended for launch by helicopters and by the RAF Nimrod ASW aircraft.

Length: 2.597 m   **Speed:** 45 kts
Diameter: 324 mm   **Range:** 7,000 m
Weight: 266 kg   **Depth:** 800 m

Stingray uses seawater-activated batteries powering an electrically driven pump-jet propulsor and employs active/passive acoustic homing.

A new heavyweight submarine torpedo is to be procured to replace the Mk 24 Tigerfish. The British-Marconi MSR 7525 has been chosen; in trials it has achieved over 70 kts in trials.

E. SONARS

◆ On surface ships

No.	Type	Frequency band	Average range (above layer)
162, 162M	Sidelooking classification	High	. . .
170B	Hull, searchlight	High	2,500 m
174	Hull, searchlight	High	2,500 m
177	Hull, 360° scan	Medium	6,000 m
184	Hull, 360° scan	Medium	7,000 m
193, 193M	Minehunting	High	. . .
199	Towed VDS	Medium	7,000 m
2016	Hull, 360° scan	Multiple (5.5-6.5-7.5 kHz)	. . .

199 is the British version of the Canadian SQS-504. VDS has been removed from most *Leander*-class frigates (Ikara *Leanders* retain them); the reason given is that the equipment is not needed in the normal Eastern Atlantic operating area for RN ships. But the real reason is insufficient mastery of VDS employment techniques and a lack of spare parts; additionally, interest is now centering on development of a towed passive line array like the U.S. TACTASS concept, and trials with a system of this type are being carried out in the frigate *Argonaut*.

◆ On submarines

186	Passive	Low	. . .
187	Active-Passive attack	Low-Medium	. . .
2001	Active-Passive	Low	. . .
2007	Passive	Low-Medium	. . .

◆ On helicopters

195, 195 M		Medium	3,000 m

F. DATA SYSTEMS

ADA (Action Data Automation):
ADAWS 1 Aerial defense system. Fitted on "County"-class destroyers
ADAWS 2 Integrated AAW and ASW defense system. Fitted on the *Bristol*
ADAWS 4 Integrated AAW and ASW defense system. Fitted on the *Sheffield*- and *Manchester*-class destroyers
ADAWS 5 Aerial and ASW defense. Fitted on the *Invincible*-class aircraft carriers
CAAIS (Computer Assisted Action Information System)
    In *Amazon*- and *Broadsword*-class frigates for tactical data-handling; linked to WSA 4 fire-control system

G. RADARS

◆ Navigation

978 (3 cm, I band)
1002 (9,650 MHz) for *Porpoise*-class submarines
1003 (. . .) in *Resolution-*, *Swiftsure-* and *Valiant*-class submarines
1006 (9,445 MHz) in newest surface ships and submarines, navalized Kelvin-Hughes 19/9A.

NOTE: Auxiliaries use a number of different commercial navigational radars.

◆ Air-search

965 Metric radar (long range)
965M The **M** is composed of two 965 antennas, one placed on top of the other with the Mk 10 IFF interrogator built in
1022 Dutch LW-08 air search with a Marconi antenna, on *Invincible*-class and later *Sheffield*-class units.

◆ Surface-to-air, low-altitude search (combination)

992, 992 Q, 993 (E-F bands), and **994** (improved 993)
967/968 Pulse doppler: combination of radar bands H, G, and I, found in the Sea Wolf system (GWS 25)
1030 STIR (Surveillance & Target Indicator Radar) to be on the *Manchester* class.

◆ Height-finding

277 (E band)—on County-class destroyers only.

◆ Gun-direction

275 (F band) is used in the older FC system for Mk 6 twin 114-mm gun mounts in the *Whitby*-class frigate, *Torquay*.
903 (I band) is used in all other Mk 6 and Mk 5, 114-mm gun directors (MRS 3).

◆ Missile-guidance

901 Sea Slug system (I band)
903 MRS 3 and GWS 22 fire control for the Sea Cat
909 Sea Dart system (also 114-mm Mk 8 gun in the *Sheffield*-class destroyers)
910 Tracking radar used with the Sea Wolf (GWS 25) system
RTN-10X Used for Sea Cat (GWS 24) and 114-mm gun control in *Amazon*-class frigates. British designation: Type 912.

◆ For aircraft

Sea Spray (. . . band) for helicopters
Blue Fox (. . . band) for Sea Harrier
Sea Searcher (. . . band) for Sea King Mk 5 ASW helicopters, for use in interrogating the LAPADS sonobuoy system.

H. COUNTERMEASURES

A rocket-launched decoy system (chaff) called Knebworth/Corvus is used on major combat units. All ships so equipped now have two eight-tubed launchers. A new chaff rocket is in development for the launcher, with much greater "bloom."

AIRCRAFT CARRIERS

♦ 1 (+2) Invincible class

	Bldr	Laid down	L	In serv.
R 05 INVINCIBLE	Vickers, Barrow	20-7-73	3-5-77	11-7-80
R 06 ILLUSTRIOUS	Swan Hunter, Wallsend	7-10-76	14-12-78	1982
R 07 ARK ROYAL	Swan Hunter, Wallsend	14-12-78	4-6-81	1986

D: 16,256 tons (19,812 fl) **S:** 28 kts

Dim: 206.6 (192.87 wl) × 31.89 (27.5 wl) × 6.4 (mean)

A: 1/Sea Dart GWS 30 system (II × 1; 22 missiles)—Aircraft: 5/Sea Harrier—9/ Sea King Mk 2

Electron Equipt: Radars: 2/1006, 1/992R, 1/1022, 2/909
Sonar: 1/184, 1/762 echo-sounder, 1/185 telephone
Data system: ADAWS-5
ECM: passive; 2/Knebworth/Corvus RL

M: 4 Rolls-Royce Olympus TM3B gas turbines; 2 props; 112,000 hp (94,000 sust.)

Electric: 14,000 kw **Range:** 5,000/18

Man: 131 officers, 869 men (plus 318 aircrew)

Invincible (R 05)   1979

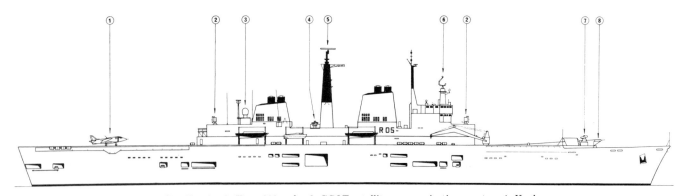

1. Sea Harrier 2. Type 909 radar 3. SCOT satellite communications system 4. Knebworth/Corvus chaff RLs 5. Type 992R radar 6. Type 1022 radar 7. Sea Dart SAM launcher 8. "Ski Jump" ramp

Invincible (R 05)—with four Sea Harrier on deck   1980

AIRCRAFT CARRIERS *(continued)*

◆ **1 improved Centaur class**

	Bldr	Laid down	L	In serv.
R 12 HERMES	Vickers, Barrow	21-6-44	16-2-58	18-11-59

Hermes (R 12)—in final stages of refit with 12-degree "ski jump" 1981

Invincible (R 05) 1979

Hermes (R 12)—as refitted G. Gyssels, 1981

D: 23,900 tons (28,700 fl) **S:** 28 kts
Dim: 226.85 (198.12 pp) × 48.78 (27.43 wl) × 8.8
A: 2/Sea Cat GWS 22 systems (IV × 2)—Aircraft: 5/Sea Harrier—12 Sea King Mk 2,4
Electron Equipt: Radars: 1/965, 1/978, 1/993, 2/903—TACAN
 Sonar: 1/184
 ECM: passive, 2 Knebworth/Corvus RL
M: 2 sets Parsons GT; 2 props; 76,000 hp **Electric:** 9,000 kw
Fuel: 4,200 tons plus 320 tons diesel **Electric:** 4 Admiralty 3-drum
Man: 143 officers, 1,027 men

REMARKS: Redesignated "ASW aircraft carriers" in 1980, previously having been, for political reasons, considered to be a type of cruiser. Although all three are to be completed, only two will be operational at any one time. *Invincible*, ordered 17-4-73 and intended for V/STOL aircraft and helicopters only, has a flight deck 183 meters long with an 8-degree "ski jump" at the forward end to assist Sea Harrier aircraft in making rolling takeoffs at full combat load. The flight deck on *Ark Royal* will be 12 degrees and is 10 to 12 meters longer. The 183-meter long by 13.5-m wide flight deck is slightly angled to port to clear the Sea Dart launcher, which is awkwardly located on the ship's centerline and has been given an elaborate blast shield to protect the aircraft aboard. The single-level hangar has three separate bays, with the amidships bay narrower to permit passage of the gas-turbine exhausts. There are two 9.7 by 16.7-m elevators. The Type 1022 long-range air-search radar uses a Marconi antenna but has the same electronics as the HSA LW-08. Four MM 38 Exocet launchers were deleted from the design. The electrical generating plant consists of 8 General Electric 1,750-kw alternators driven by Paxman Valenta 16-RPM 200A diesels of 2,700 hp each. The MADGE microwave landing system is being installed. Deck symbols: R 05-N, R 06-. . . , R 07-. . . .

NOTE: The previous *Ark Royal* was decommissioned 12-78 and scrapped in 1980.

REMARKS: Converted 1971-73 by the Devonport Naval Dockyard into a helicopter-carrying commando carrier (LPH). Converted again 1976/1-77 as an ASW carrier for Sea King and Wessex helicopters and converted 5-80 to 9-5-81 for operational employment of Sea Harrier V/STOL strike aircraft. She will continue in service until 1983 when *Illustrious* becomes fully operational. *Hermes* retains the ability to em-

AIRCRAFT CARRIERS *(continued)*

bark two commando groups (750 men) and continues to carry four LCVPs in davits. Catapults and arresting gear removed 1971. Flight deck angled 6.5 degrees and strengthened for Harriers, 12-degree "ski jump" takeoff ramp was fitted to her bow, weighing 230 tons and some 45.7-m long by 13.7-m wide by 4.9-m high. In 1978 a Ferranti 1600E computer was added to aid in tactical data handling, and during the 1980-81 overhaul, U.S. satellite communications equipment was added, as was the MADGE microwave landing system and the HAPIS (Horizontal Approach Path Indicator System) for Sea Harrier.

NOTE: The *Centaur*-class carrier *Bulwark*, recommissioned 23-2-79 to serve as an ASW and troop-carrying helicopter carrier, was decommissioned 27-3-81 and placed on the Sales List.

NAVAL AVIATION

Ship-based aviation, the Fleet Air Arm, is the only air component in the Royal Navy. All 12 Phantom and 14 Buccaneer aircraft were handed over to the RAF when the *Ark Royal* was decommissioned in 1978; the remaining eight Gannet early-warning aircraft were discarded.

Except at the level of formation commanders, there is no naval air command. Land-based ASW aircraft belong to the RAF and, since the reorganization of the latter, have constituted the Eighteenth, or Maritime, Group of Strike Command. While the group is part of the RAF as regards personnel and equipment, its employment is determined by the Royal Navy's commander in chief.

The Fleet Air Arm consists of:

First-line squadrons (designation characterized by a group of three figures beginning with an 8) whose missions are: attack, ASW, and helicopter assault. There are about 90 aircraft in this category.

Second line squadrons (designation characterized by a group of three figures beginning with a 7) that are used in schools, tests, and maintenance. There are about 120 aircraft in this category.

RAF MARITIME PATROL SQUADRONS

Squadron	Type	Strength	Base	Remarks
42, 120, 201, 206	Nimrod MR1	18	Kinloss	ASW-equipped
236 OCU[1]	Nimrod MR1	11	St. Mawgan	ASW-equipped

[1] Operational Conversion Unit.

NOTE: There will ultimately be 34 Nimrods in MR 2 configuration.

ACTIVE FLEET AIR ARM ORGANIZATION

AIRCRAFT

Squadrons	Type	Strength	Land Base	Remarks
800	Sea Harrier	5	Yeovilton	In *Hermes*
801	Sea Harrier	5	Yeovilton	In *Invincible*
899	Sea Harrier	5	Yeovilton	Op. Training

NOTE: There are a total of 38 Sea Harrier in service or on order, including four T. Mk 4 two-seat trainers.

HELICOPTERS

Squadrons	Type	Strength	Land Base	Remarks
814	Sea King Mk 2	9	Culdrose	
815	WG 13 Lynx	18	Yeovilton	*Sheffield*, *Broadsword*, *Amazon*, & *Leander* classes
819	Sea King Mk 2	6	Prestwick	Protect *Resolution* class SSBN sorties
820	Sea King Mk 2	4	Culdrose	*Invincible*
824	Sea King Mk 2	8	Culdrose	Logistic support ships
826	Sea King Mk 2	4	Culdrose	*Hermes*
845	Wessex Mk 5	12	Yeovilton	Commando assault
846	Wessex Mk 5	8	Yeovilton	Commando assault
	Sea King Mk 4	6		
702	WG 13 Lynx	5	Yeovilton	Training
703	Wasp	18	Portland	Training
705	Gazelle	18	Culdrose	Elementary training
706	Sea King Mk 2	14	Culdrose	ASW training
707	Wessex Mk 5	. . .	Yeovilton	Training
737	Wessex Mk 3	15	Portland	County class
771	Wessex Mk 5	8	Culdrose	Search and rescue
772	Wessex Mk 5	3	Portland	SAR training

NOTE: In addition, there are 16 Jetstream T2 observer training and liaison aircraft, 4 Heron and 8 Devon liaison aircraft in service; also, a few Canberra and Hunter aircraft are based at Yeovilton for target service duties.

A total of 17 Sea King Mk 5 are in service or on order for ASW duties, with the first two having been delivered in 10-80. Development of the WG 34 helicopter by Westland as a replacement for Sea King has been canceled in favor of a joint venture with Agusta-Bell of Italy; the first prototype is expected to fly in 1985 or 1986.

With the decline in Royal Navy amphibious warfare capabilities, the demise of the County class, and the diminishing number of older frigates in service, the numbers of Wessex and Wasp helicopters in service should decline rapidly in the near future.

ACTIVE FLEET AIR ARM ORGANIZATION (continued)

COMBAT AIRCRAFT

Type and builder	Mission	Wingspan	Length	Height	Weight	Engine	Max. speed in Mach or in knots	Practical maximum ceiling in feet	Range	Weapons	Remarks
◆ **FIXED-WING**											
Sea Harrier (British Aerospace) FRS 1 single seat T Mk 4 2-seat	Attack fighter/ interceptor	7.6	14.5	3.71	10,500	1 Rolls-Royce Pegasus 104 vectored-thrust turbojet with 9,750 kg thrust	Mach 0.96; Mach 1.2 (diving)	50,000 +	VTOL: 50 miles STOL: 250 miles	2,270 kg, max total: 2/AIM-9L Sidewinder, 2/30-mm Aden guns, 454 kg bombs (normal load)	For the *Invincible* class and *Hermes*. To receive Sea Eagle P3T anti-ship missiles. Has Blue Fox navigation/attack radar. Total order: 34 FRS-1, 4 T Mk 4. Despite speed and range limitations, used as an interceptor.
Nimrod MR 1 (British Aerospace) (RAF-operated)	ASW detection and engagement	35.30	38.63	9.08	80,510 to 87,090	4 Rolls-Royce Spey (RB 168-20) Mk 250 jet engines, 5,200 hp thrust each	450 kts	42,000	12 hrs	Bomb bay for 15-m weapons (6 torpedoes + 10 buoys) 2/Martel or 4/AS 12	Can carry nuclear depth charges. Being re-equipped to MR 2 capability. 34 built.
◆ **HELICOPTERS**											
Wasp HAS 1 (Westland)	ASW, antisurface	Rotor diam. 9.82	12.29	3.56	2,495	1 Rolls-Royce Nimbus 503 turboshaft, 710 hp	104 kts 96 kts (cruising)	12,000	234 nm.	1-2/Mk 44 torpedo or 2/AS 11 ASM	On board the *Amazon Rothesay*, and *Leander* frigate classes
WG 13 Lynx HAS 2 (Westland)	ASW, anti-surface	12.80	15.16	3.60	4,763	2 Rolls-Royce Gem BS 360-07-26 turboshafts, 900 hp each	145 kts	12,000	1 hr 30 min. (half hovering, half cruising) (approx. 340 nm.)	2/Mk 44 or Mk 46 torpedoes Sea Skua air-surface missiles	Franco-British helicopter. On board the *Sheffield*, *Amazon*, and *Broadsword* classes. Some to carry AN/ANS-18 dipping sonar. 60 total ordered.
Wessex HAS 3 HU-5 (Westland)	ASW transport assault	17.06	20.03	4.93	Mk 3: 5,700 Mk 5: 5,800 (6,120 max.)	Mk 3: 1 Napier Gazelle 161 NGA 13 turboshaft with 1,650 hp—Mk 5: 2 linked Bristol-Siddeley Gnome H 1400 turboshafts with 1,400 hp each	Mk 3: 120 kts Mk 5: 130 kts	6,000 hovering 14,000 cruising	3 hrs (664 nm normal)	Mk 3: 2/Mk 44 or 46 torpedoes or 4/ depth charges Sonar	Mk 3: on board the County class; has APN-97 radar, Type 194 sonar. Mk 5: now mainly for training and SAR.
Sea King Mk 1 Mk 2 Mk 3 (Westland) Mk 5	ASW ASW troop-carrying ASW	18.9	22.15		9,525	2 Rolls-Royce Gnome H 1400-1 turboshafts, 1,660 hp each driving a 5-bladed rotor and a tail rotor	122 kts	10,000	3 hr 15 min	4/Mk 44 or 46 torpedoes or 4/Mk 11 depth charges. (Mk 4: 4 tons stores or 27 troops)	36 or more Sea King Mk 2 in service with Type 195 sonar, AW 392 radar, and Marconi-Elliot AD580 doppler navigation systems. 15 Mk 4 for troop carrying, no ASW gear. 17 Mk 5 for ASW have Sea Searcher radar (initially: ARI 5955), LI-PADS sonobuoy system. Last to deliver in 1983.

ACTIVE FLEET AIR ARM ORGANIZATION *(continued)*

Sea Harrier FRS 1   1978

Nimrod MR1   1979

Westland WG-13 Lynx HAS 2   1974

Westland Wasp HAS 1

Sea King HAS 2 above U.S. Army submarine   1976

ACTIVE FLEET AIR ARM ORGANIZATION *(continued)*

Sea King HAS 5 aboard Invincible—note enlarged radar dome   1980

Wessex HAS 3 aboard Antrim (D 18)   G. Arra, 1980

Wessex HU-5 troop carrier   1973

First Sea Harrier landing on Invincible (R 05), 20-5-80

NOTE: Royal Navy submarines no longer wear hull numbers. The assigned numbers are included here for reference only.

BALLISTIC-MISSILE SUBMARINES

♦ 4 or 5 new design

At least four new nuclear-powered ballistic-missile submarines, each to carry 16 Trident missiles, are to be built. A decision as to whether to acquire a fifth is to be made in 1983. These submarines are to replace the *Resolution* class, but the first will probably not be ready before 1989-90, and no details of the design (if, indeed, any have been decided) have been released.

♦ 4 Resolution class

	Bldr	Laid down	L	In serv.
S 22 RESOLUTION	Vickers-Armstrong, Barrow	26-2-64	15-9-66	2-10-67
S 23 REPULSE	Vickers-Armstrong, Barrow	12-3-65	4-11-67	28-9-68
S 26 RENOWN	Cammell Laird, Birkenhead	25-6-64	25-2-67	15-11-68
S 27 REVENGE	Cammell Laird, Birkenhead	19-5-65	15-3-68	4-12-69

Resolution (S 22)   1978

BALLISTIC-MISSILE SUBMARINES *(continued)*

Revenge (S 27) 1976

Resolution (S 22)—bow planes hinge at half-span Vickers

D: 7,500/8,400 tons **S:** 25/20 kts **Dim:** 129.54 × 10.05 × 9.15
A: 16/Polaris A3—6/533-mm TT (bow) **Man:** 13 officers, 130 men
Electron Equipt: Radar: 1/1003
  Sonar: 1/2001, 1/2007
M: 1 Rolls-Royce pressurized-water reactor; 1 English-Electric turbine; 1 prop

REMARKS: Characteristics are very similar to those of the U.S. *Lafayette* class, in-cluding the propulsion machinery, the launching and guidance systems, and the inertial navigation system. The A3 missiles with 3 MRV warheads of 200 kilotons each were furnished by the U.S., but the reentry vehicles are of British conception and construction. The warheads are being replaced by the Chevaline system with six 160 kt reentry vehicles and improved "penetration" capability, to guarantee the efficacy of the Polaris A3 system until 1990.

NUCLEAR-PROPELLED ATTACK SUBMARINES

◆ **0 (+6) Trafalgar class** Bldr: Vickers, Barrow

	Laid down	L	In serv.
S 113 TRAFALGAR	25-4-79	7-81	1982
S 114 TURBULENT	8-5-80	1982	1983
S 115 TIRELESS	1981	. . .	1984
S 116 TORBAY	. . .	. . .	1985
S 117 TALENT	. . .	. . .	1986
S 118 TACTICIAN	. . .	. . .	1987

  D: 4,500 tons **S:** 30 submerged **Dim:** 82.9 × 10.1 × 8.2
  A: 5/533-mm TT fwd (20 torpedoes/Sub-Harpoon)
  Electron Equipt: Radar: . . . Sonar: 1/2001, 1/2020
  M: 1 reactor, 1 turbine; 1 prop; . . . hp (1 Paxman 400-hp auxiliary propulsion diesel, electric drive)

REMARKS: An improved version of the *Swiftsure* class; little data released. S 113 ordered 7-4-77, S 114 on 28-7-78, S 115 on 5-7-79, S 116 on 7-80, S 117, 118 on 25-6-81. Will use pump-jet type propeller.

◆ **6 Swiftsure class** Bldr: Vickers, Barrow

	Laid down	L	In serv.
S 104 SCEPTRE	25-10-73	20-11-76	14-2-78
S 108 SOVEREIGN	18-9-70	22-2-73	22-7-74
S 109 SUPERB	16-3-72	30-11-74	13-11-76
S 111 SPARTAN	26-3-76	7-4-78	22-9-79
S 112 SPLENDID (ex-*Severn*)	23-11-77	5-10-79	21-3-81
S 126 SWIFTSURE	6-6-69	7-9-71	17-4-73

NUCLEAR-PROPELLED ATTACK SUBMARINES *(continued)*

Sceptre (S 104)

Superb (S 109)   G. Arra, 1977

Spartan (S111)—note Type 1003 radar mast raised   1979

D: 4,000 light/4,200/4,500 tons   **S:** 20/28 kts   **Dim:** 82.9 × 10.12 × 8.25
A: 5/533-mm bow TT (20 torpedoes/Sub-Harpoon)
Electron Equipt: Radar: 1/1003
              Sonar: 1/2001, 1/2007, 1/197, 1/183

M: 1 reactor; 2 English Electric turbines; 1 prop; 15,000 hp (1 Paxman 400-hp
      auxiliary propulsion diesel, electric drive)
Man: 12 officers, 85 men

REMARKS: High-performance, very quiet submarines with excellent passive sonars.

NUCLEAR-PROPELLED ATTACK SUBMARINES (continued)

Carry the wire-guided Mk 24 Tigerfish torpedo. The forward diving planes are below the surfaced waterline and retract within the outer hull. Torpedo tubes reload in 15 seconds. Will carry the U.S. Sub-Harpoon missile. Intended for ASW defense of surface forces. The refit of *Swiftsure* in 1980 was beset by major labor problems. To receive Type 2020 sonar in place of 2007.

♦ 5 Valiant class

	Bldr	Laid down	L	In serv.
S 46 CHURCHILL	Vickers, Barrow	30-6-67	20-12-68	15-7-70
S 48 CONQUEROR	Cammell Laird	5-12-67	29-8-69	9-11-71
S 50 COURAGEOUS	Vickers, Barrow	15-5-68	7-3-70	16-10-71
S 102 VALIANT	Vickers, Barrow	22-1-62	3-12-63	18-7-66
S 103 WARSPITE	Vickers, Barrow	10-12-63	25-9-65	18-4-67

Churchill (S 46) G. Arra, 1977

D: 3,500/4,200/4,900 tons **S:** 20/28 kts **Dim:** 86.87 × 10.12 × 8.25
A: 6/533-mm TT fwd (26 torpedoes/Sub-Harpoon)
Electron Equipt: Radar: 1/1003
Sonars: 1/2001, 1/2007, 1/197, 1/183
M: 1 pressurized-water reactor; 2 English-Electric GT; 1 prop; 15,000 hp
Man: 13 officers, 90 men

REMARKS: The propulsion plant is of entirely British design and construction. Diving depth: 300 m. Have a 112-cell emergency battery. The hull form of this class is a development of the *Dreadnought*. In 1967 the *Valiant* made a nonstop, submerged cruise from Singapore to Great Britain in 28 days (12,000 miles). S 46 completed trials with Sub-Harpoon missiles in 2-80 and will be in "Long Refit" until late 1982. S 103 completed a "Long Refit" and refuelling 10-81, and S 102 in 2-80.

♦ 1 Dreadnought class

	Bldr	Laid down	L	In serv.
S 101 DREADNOUGHT	Vickers, Barrow	12-6-59	21-10-60	17-4-63

D: 3,000/3,500/4,000 tons **S:** 15/25 kts **Dim:** 81.08 × 9.75 × 7.80
A: 6/533-mm TT fwd

Dreadnought (S 101) Pradignac & Leo, 1971

Electron Equipt: Radar: 1/1003
Sonar: 1/2001, 1/2007, 1/197, 1/183
M: 1 U.S. S5W reactor; GT; 1 prop; 15,000 hp **Man:** 11 officers, 77 men

REMARKS: Authorized in 1956. The first Admiralty studies for the ship were entrusted to the nuclear branch of the Vickers Company, including Rolls-Royce for the reactor, Foster-Wheeler for the heat exchanger, and Vickers for the turbines. Finally, however, a Westinghouse S5W reactor, was furnished by the U.S. in 1958. The hull shape is similar to the U.S. nuclear submarine *Skipjack* except for the forward one-third. Endurance: 70 days. In 1970 the ship made a cruise under the North Pole. Towed to Devonport 10-80 for use as stationary harbor training ship, due to cracks in reactor vessel, but began 2-year refit for further active service in 6-81. Will not receive Sub-Harpoon.

♦ 0 (+6 to 9) "U" class (Type 2400)

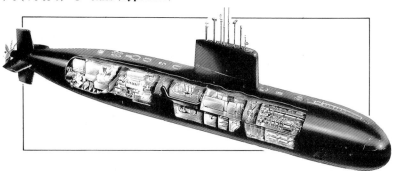

Type 2400 Vickers, 1981

D: 2,160/2,400 tons **S:** 12/20 kts **Dim:** 70.0 × 7.6 × . . .
A: 6/533-mm TT fwd (18 tot. Mk 24 and/or MSR 752S torpedoes, Sub-Harpoon)
Electron Equipt: Radar: . . .
Sonar: . . .
M: 2 Paxman Valenta 16 RPA 200S 16-cyl. diesels, 2,000 hp each, electric drive; 1/6-bladed prop; 3,000 hp
Endurance: over 28 days **Range:** 8,000/8 (snorkel) **Man:** 46 tot.

REMARKS: The "U" class (all to have names beginning with *U*) will be based on the Vickers commercial Type 2400 design and is intended to provide a successor to the

NUCLEAR-PROPELLED ATTACK SUBMARINES *(continued)*

Oberon class. The first units will probably not be ordered before 1983, and the data above are therefore subject to change. Two 240-cell lead-acid batteries. 200-m diving depth. The 28-day endurance is predicated on a patrol radius of 2,500 nm.

TORPEDO ATTACK SUBMARINES

♦ 13 Oberon class

		Bldr	Laid down	L	In serv.
S 09	OBERON	HM Dockyard, Chatham	28-11-57	18-7-59	24-2-61
S 10	ODIN	Cammell Laird	27-4-59	4-11-60	3-5-62
S 11	ORPHEUS	Vickers-Armstrong	16-4-59	17-11-59	25-11-60
S 12	OLYMPUS	Vickers-Armstrong	4-3-60	14-6-61	7-7-62
S 13	OSIRIS	Vickers-Armstrong	26-1-62	29-11-62	11-1-64
S 14	ONSLAUGHT	HM Dockyard, Chatham	8-4-59	24-9-60	14-8-62
S 15	OTTER	Scotts SB, Greenock	14-1-60	15-5-61	20-8-62
S 16	ORACLE	Cammell Laird	26-4-60	26-9-61	14-2-63
S 17	OCELOT	HM Dockyard, Chatham	17-11-60	5-5-62	31-1-64
S 18	OTUS	Scotts SB, Greenock	31-5-61	17-10-62	5-10-63
S 19	OPOSSUM	Cammell Laird	21-12-61	23-5-63	5-6-64
S 20	OPPORTUNE	Scotts SB, Greenock	26-10-62	14-2-64	29-12-64
S 21	ONYX	Cammell Laird	16-11-64	18-8-66	20-11-67

Opportune (S 20)   G. Gyssels, 1980

♦ 2 Porpoise class

		Bldr	Laid down	L	In serv.
S 07	SEA LION	Cammel Laird, Birkenhead	5-6-58	31-12-59	25-7-61
S 08	WALRUS	Scotts SB, Greenock	12-2-53	22-9-59	10-2-61

D: 1,610/2,030/2,400 tons **S:** 17.5/15 kts **Dim:** 89.92 (87.45 pp) × 8.07 × 5.48
A: 6/533-mm TT fwd, 2 aft (22 torpedoes)
Electron Equipt: Radars: 1/1006 (S 07, 08: 1/1002)
                   Sonars: 1/186, 1/187
M: 2/3,680-hp Admiralty Standard Range 16VVS-AS21 diesels, diesel-electric
    drive; 2 props; 6,000 hp
Man: 6 officers, 62 men (S 08: 65 tot.)

REMARKS: Conventional propulsion and hull form. Streamlined sail. Maximum depth: 200 meters. Snorkel. Air-conditioned. Excellent living spaces. Long endurance. Plastics used throughout in the design of the superstructure of the second series (*Oberon, Odin, Onslaught*, for example) as well as light alloys (*Orpheus*). *Oberon* has a higher hull casing and is used in training nuclear submarine crews. The first *Onyx* transferred to Canada (1-64) and renamed the *Ojibwa*; another *Onyx* was built. Canada ordered three ships of this class, Australia six, Chile two, and Brazil three. The *Grampus* (S 04) of the *Porpoise* class was stricken in 1976, *Rorqual* (S 02) in 1976, *Narwhal* (S 03), *Cachelot* (S 06) in 1977, *Finwhale* (S 05) in 1978, and *Porpoise* (S 01) in late 1981. Sale of the *Cachelot* to Egypt was canceled.

Oracle (S 16)   G. Arra, 1978

NOTE: The *Tiger*-class cruiser *Tiger* (C 20), in reserve since 1978, was placed in the Standby Reserve Squadron in 1-80 and on the Sales List in 1-81.

GUIDED-MISSILE DESTROYERS

♦ 0 (0 + 4) Manchester class (Type 42C)

		Bldr	Laid down	L	In serv.
D 95	MANCHESTER	Vickers, Barrow	19-5-79	24-11-80	1984
D 96	GLOUCESTER	Vosper Thornycroft	26-10-79	. . .	. . .
D 97	EDINBURGH	Cammell Laird	9-80	. . .	. . .
D 104	YORK	Swan Hunter	18-1-80	. . .	. . .

D: 3,550 tons (4,500 fl) **S:** 28 kts (18 cruising)
Dim: 141.1 (132.3 wl) × 14.90 × 4.10 (hull)
A: 1/Sea Dart GWS 30 syst. (II × 1, 20 missiles)—1/114-mm Mk 8 DP—2/20-
    mm AA (I × 2)—6/324-mm Mk 32 ASW TT (III × 2)—1/WG 13 Lynx
    helicopter

GUIDED-MISSILE DESTROYERS *(continued)*

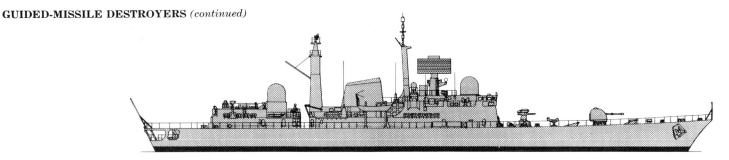

Manchester (D 95)   Vickers, 1980

Electron Equipt: Radar: 1/1006, 1/992Q, 1/1022, 2/909
         Sonar: 1/184, 1/174, 1/170B, 1/162
         ECM: passive array, 2 Knebworth/Corvus chaff RL
M: COGOG: 2 Rolls-Royce Olympus TM3B gas turbines of 25,000 hp each for
     boost, 2 Rolls-Royce Tyne RM1A of 3,800 hp each for cruise; 2/5-bladed CP
     props
Electron Equipt: 4,000 kw (4/1,000-kw diesel sets)   **Range:** . . .
Man: 26 officers, 81 senior petty officers, 194 men

REMARKS: A lengthened version of the *Sheffield* class intended to provide better
seaworthiness, endurance, and habitability but having no change in armament despite the additional 16-m overall length. Will have later radar suit, with later ships
possibly receiving Type 1030 STIR in place of Types 992Q and 1022. D 95 ordered
10-11-78, D 96 on 27-3-79, and D 97 and D 104 on 25-4-79. The fifth unit was to have
been ordered in 7-81. Subsequent units may not be built for economic reasons.

NOTE: The Type 43, a follow-on design, has been canceled as a project and a new
     Type 44 is now in the early planning stages.

♦ **8 (+2) Sheffield class (Type 42)**

	Bldr	Laid down	L	In serv.
D 80 SHEFFIELD	Vickers, Barrow	15-1-70	10-6-71	16-2-75
D 86 BIRMINGHAM	Cammell Laird	28-3-72	30-7-73	3-12-76
D 87 NEWCASTLE	Swan Hunter	21-2-73	24-4-75	23-3-78
D 88 GLASGOW	Swan Hunter	7-3-74	14-4-76	24-5-79
D 89 EXETER	Swan Hunter	22-7-76	25-4-78	19-9-80
D 90 SOUTHAMPTON	Vosper Thornycroft	21-10-76	29-1-79	23-7-81
D 91 NOTTINGHAM	Vosper Thornycroft	6-2-78	12-2-80	-81
D 92 LIVERPOOL	Cammell Laird	5-7-78	25-9-80	. . .
D 108 CARDIFF	Vickers, Barrow	3-11-72	22-2-74	19-10-79
D 118 COVENTRY	Cammell Laird	22-3-73	21-6-74	10-11-78

D: 3,150 tons (4,100 fl)   **S:** 30 kts (18 cruising)
Dim: 125.0 (119.5 pp) × 14.34 × 5.0
A: 1/Sea Dart GWS 30 (II × 1, 20 missiles)—1/114-mm Mk 8 DP—2/20-mm AA
     (I × 2)—6/324-mm Mk 32 ASW TT (III × 2)—1/WG 13 Lynx helicopter
Electron Equipt: Radar: 1/1006, 1/965M (D 89 and later: 1022), 1/992Q, 2/909
         Sonar: 1/184, 1/174, 1/170B, 1/162
         ECM: passive array, 2 Knebworth/Corvus chaff RL
M: COGOG: 2 Rolls-Royce Olympus TM3B gas turbines, 27,200 hp each for high
     speed; 2 Rolls-Royce Tyne RM1A gas turbines, 4,100 hp each for cruising; 2/
     5-bladed CP props

Southampton (D 90)—with Type 1022 radar   Vosper Thornycroft 1981

Cardiff (D 108)   G. Gyssels, 1980

GUIDED-MISSILE DESTROYERS *(continued)*

Electric: 4,000 kw (4/1,000-kw diesel sets)   **Range:** 650/30, 4,500/18
Man: 26 officers, 273 men

REMARKS: D 80 ordered 11-68. Have ADAWS 4 tactical data system. The cruising and high-speed turbines are not linked to each other; each shaft must be driven by one or the other. Mk 30 Mod 2 launcher for the Sea Dart system. The *Sheffield* still did not have any ASW torpedo tubes into 1980; later units do. The *Cardiff*, delayed by labor problems, was completed by Swan Hunter. Completion of the *Glasgow* delayed by fire 9-76. All have two SCOT radomes for Skynet satellite communications system. Very cramped ships. Helicopter is primarily for surveillance and attack (Sea Skua missiles) rather than ASW. Have "Agouti" bubble ejector system for propellers (which rotate inwardly) to reduce cavitation noise.

The prototype, *Sheffield* (shown in the drawing), had an experimental funnel design with the uptakes bent sideways in a form referred to as "Loxton Bends." *Hercules*, the first Argentine unit, has a similar stack. This feature was intended to keep the exhaust gases away from the after part of the ship, but it was found to be unnecessary, and the remainder of the class have reverted to a normal configuration. In D 86 and later units, the Mk 32 torpedo tubes are on the deckhouse at the base of the after mast. D 89 and later have a taller mainmast and Type 1022 radar forward vice Type 965M.

Birmingham (D 86)—tug **Husky** astern   LA (Phot.) Welds, RN, 1980

Coventry (D 118)   G. Arra, 1980

GUIDED-MISSILE DESTROYERS *(continued)*

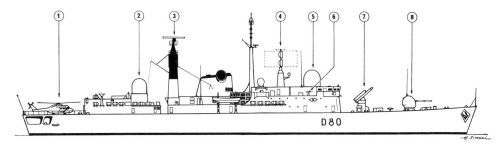

Sheffield Type 42 class
1. WG 13 Lynx helicopter 2. 909 radar 3. 992Q radar 4. 965M radar 5. 909 radar 6. 20-mm AA
7. Sea Dart launcher 8. 114-mm DP mount Mk 8

Sheffield (D 80)—note unique funnel arrangement, lack of ASW TT   1980

♦ **1 Bristol (Type 82) class**

	Bldr	Laid down	L	In serv.
D 23 BRISTOL	Swan Hunter	15-11-67	30-6-69	31-3-73

D: 6,100 tons (7,100 fl)   **S:** 28 kts
Dim: 154.60 (149.90 wl) × 16.77 × 5.20 (6.85 over sonar)
A: 1/Sea Dart GWS 30 (II × 1, 40 missiles)—1/114-mm Mk 8 DP—2/20-mm AA
    (I × 2)—1/Ikara ASW system (32 missiles)—1/Mk 10 Limbo ASW mortar
    (III × 2)
Electron Equipt: Radar: 1/1006, 1/965M, 1/992Q, 2/909, 2/Ikara control
            Sonar: 1/162, 1/170, 1/182, 1/184, 1/185, 1/189
            ECM: passive array, 2 Knebworth/Corvus chaff RL
M: COSAG; 2 A.E.I. GT (15,000 hp each) and 2 Rolls-Royce Olympus TM1A
    gas turbines (22,300 hp each); 2 props; 74,600 hp
Electric: 7,000 kw
Boilers: 2 Babcock & Wilcox, 49.2 kg/cm² pressure, 510°C superheat
Range: 5,000/18   **Man:** 29 officers, 378 men

Bristol (D 23)—with U.S. satellite antenna before bridge   G. Koop, 1980

REMARKS: Designed as an escort for the 50,000-ton aircraft carrier *Furious* when
construction of the latter was being considered. There were to be eight in the class,
but this ship, ordered in 10-66, was the only one built. Fin stabilizers and air-
conditioning. The Sea Dart launcher is Mk 3 Mod 0. Missiles are stowed in a vertical
position. Although nominally commissioned in 1973, she had not been accepted for
active service by the time of her first refit in 1976-78. At that time full military
equipment, including two 20-mm AA and chaff rocket launchers, was fitted; electronic

GUIDED-MISSILE DESTROYERS (continued)

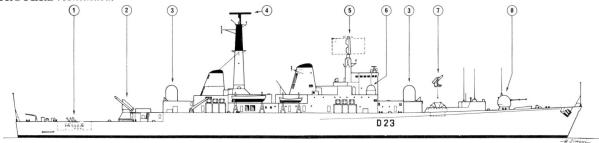

Bristol Type 82 class

1. Limbo mortar 2. Sea Dart launcher 3. 909 radar 4. 992Q radar 5. 965M radar 6. Ikara fire-control radar 7. Ikara ASW launcher 8. 114-mm DP Mk 8 gun

Bristol (D 23)   1980

intercept gear (ECM) and SCOT antennas for the Skynet satellite communications system were fitted even later. As the sole Royal Navy ship equipped with the LINK 11 automated action data communications system, the *Bristol* is the only ship compatible with the U.S. NTDS or French SENIT systems. Equipped with the ADAWS 2 data system. Designated flagship of the Third Flotilla in 1980 and given the U.S. satellite communications equipment from *Hermes*. Can land a helicopter but has no hangar. Only ship with two Ikara ASW missile control systems. Generally considered an expensive failure, but is now Britain's largest non-carrier surface combatant. Refit commenced 12-81.

♦ 4 County class

	Bldr	Laid down	L	In serv.
D 18 ANTRIM	Fairfield SB&E	20-1-66	19-10-67	14-7-70
D 19 GLAMORGAN	Fairfield, SB&E	13-9-62	9-7-64	11-10-66
D 20 FIFE	Vickers-Armstrong	1-6-62	9-7-64	21-6-66
D 21 NORFOLK	Swan Hunter	15-3-66	16-11-67	7-3-70

Glamorgan (D 19)—post refit, with ASW TT   G. Gyssels, 1981

Antrim (D 18)   G. Gyssels, 1981

GUIDED-MISSILE DESTROYERS (continued)

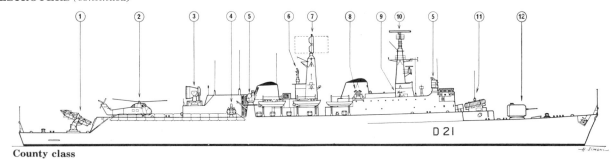

County class

1. Sea Slug launcher 2. Wessex Mk 3 helicopter 3. 901 radar 4. Sea Cat system 5. MRS-3 fire-control radar 6. 278 radar 7. 965M radar 8. Knebworth/Corvus chaff launcher 9. 20-mm AA 10. 992Q radar 11. Exocet launchers 12. 114-mm DP Mk 6 mount

Norfolk (D 21)   S. Terzibaschitsch, 1980

Fife (D 20)   G. Gyssels, 1979

Norfolk (D 21)   1979

D: 5,440 tons (6,200 fl)   **S:** 32.5 kts (30 sust.)
Dim: 158.55 (153.9 pp)× 16.46 × 6.3 (max.)
A: 4/MM38 Exocet—1/Sea Slug Mk 2 system (30 missiles)—2/Sea Cat GWS 22 systems (IV × 2)—2/114-mm Mk 6 DP (II × 1)—2/20-mm AA (I × 2)—1/ Wessex Mk 3 ASW helicopter—D 19 only: 6/324-mm Mk 32 ASW TT (III × 2)
Electron Equipt: Radar: 1/978, 1/965M, 1/992Q, 1/277, 1/901; 1/903, 2/904 fire control
        Sonar: 1/184, 1/170B, 1/174, 1/162
        ECM: active and passive, 2 Knebworth/Corvus chaff RL
M: COSAG; 2 sets A.E.I. GT (15,000 hp each) and 4 linked G 6 gas turbines (7,500 hp each); 2 props; 60,000 hp total
Electric: 4,750 kw
Boilers: 2 Babcock & Wilcox; 49.21 kg/cm^2 pressure, 510°C superheat
Fuel: 600 tons   **Range:** 3,500/28   **Man:** 33 officers, 438 men

REMARKS: Two authorized in 1964-65, and 1965-66. Fin stabilizers. Twin rudders. Air-conditioned. Remote control of the boilers and engines from a command post that is completely protected from radioactive contamination. Sea Slug missile stowage extends to the midships area and is more than 80 meters long; it is inboard, along the centerline of the ship, and contains two parallel rows of 15 missiles, which can also be used against surface targets. All were fitted with four Exocet anti-ship missiles in 1974-76. Of the four earlier Counties with Sea Slug Mk 1, *Hampshire* (D 08) was stricken 4-76, *Devonshire* (D 02) 28-7-78, *Kent* (D 12) was decommissioned 20-4-80 for service as a harbor training hulk, and *London* (D 16) was to decommission late in 1981. Of the Sea Slug Mk 2-equipped ships, *Fife* (D 20), which was inactive

GUIDED-MISSILE DESTROYERS (continued)

from 9-79 as a harbor training ship, entered "Long Refit" in July 1980 and will probably serve for several more years as will *Glamorgan* (D 19), while *Norfolk* (D 21) will probably strike when *Fife* recommissions early in 1982 (for sale to Chile), and *Antrim* (D 18), now active, is scheduled to begin conversion as a Fleet Training Ship and minelayer (sans Sea Slug) in 1984. Other than D 19, which received Mk 32 ASW TT during a "Long Refit" which ended 5-11-80, these ships have virtually no ASW capability in poor weather, as the helicopter can only be flown in calm seas (because of the poor hangar arrangement) and there are no on-board ASW weapons. All have the ADAWS 1 combat data-handling system and two SCOT satellite communications radomes. Each propeller is driven by one general steam turbine and two gas turbines for high speeds, and the steam turbine alone for cruising. There are 3 steam turbo alternators and 3 gas turbine generators.

FRIGATES

♦ **0 (+2) Boxer (Type 22A) class** Bldr: Yarrow, Scotstoun

	Laid down	L	In serv.
F 92 Boxer	5-11-79	17-6-81	1984
F 93 Beaver	20-6-80	. . .	. . .
F 94 N . . .			

D: 3,760 tons (4,650 fl) **S:** 28 kts **Dim:** 143.6 × 14.8 × 4.3 (6.0 sonar)

REMARKS: Other data as for the *Broadsword* (Type 22) class, of which this is a lengthened version to improve seaworthiness, endurance, and habitability. The great cost of these ships ($273 million each) has resulted in a projected third ship not being ordered during 1980, although it was finally ordered 27-8-81. F 92 and F 93 were ordered 25-4-79.

NOTE: A new, less expensive and certainly less combat-worthy design, Type 23, is now in development to supplant Type 22 production and begin replacement of the *Leander* class. The first is to be ordered in 7-84. An earlier Type 24 design, announced for export sales in 1980, failed to find a customer and has been abandoned.

♦ **3 (+1) Broadsword (Type 22) class** Bldr: Yarrow, Scotstoun

	Laid down	L	In serv.
F 88 Broadsword	7-2-75	12-5-76	3-5-79
F 89 Battleaxe	4-2-76	18-5-77	28-3-80
F 90 Brilliant	24-3-77	15-12-78	10-4-81
F 91 Brazen (ex-*Boxer*)	19-8-78	4-3-80	1982

Battleaxe (F 89)—Mk 32 ASW TT not yet aboard   J. Goss, 1980

Battleaxe (F 89)—SCOT radomes not yet fitted   J. Goss, 1980

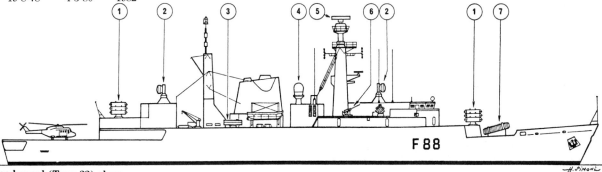

Broadsword (Type 22) class
1. Sea Wolf launchers 2. Type 910 missile fire-control radars 3. Mk 32 triple ASW torpedo tubes 4. radomes for SCOT satellite communications system 5. combined Types 967/968 radars 6. 40-mm Mk 9 AA 7. MM 38 Exocet anti-ship missile launch cannisters

FRIGATES *(continued)*

Brilliant (F 90)   L. & L. Van Ginderen, 1981

Broadsword (F 88)—on trials   1978

Battleaxe (F 89)   Plessey Marine, 1980

D: 3,500 tons (4,400 fl)   **S:** 29 kts (18 cruise)
Dim: 131.2 (125.0 wl) × 14.8 × 4.3 (6.0 sonar)
A: 4/MM 38 Exocet—2/Sea Wolf GWS 25 systems (VI × 2)—2/40-mm AA (I × 2)—6/324-mm Mk 32 ASW TT (III × 2)—1/WG 13 Lynx helicopter
Electron Equipt: Radar: 1/1006, 1/967-968, 2/910 (GWS 25)
                Sonar: 1/2008, 1/2016
                ECM: active and passive, 2 Knebworth/Corvus chaff RL
M: COGOG; 2 Olympus TM3B gas turbines, 27,300 hp each for high speed; 2 Tyne RM1A, 4,100 hp each for cruising; 2 CP props; 54,600 hp max.
Electric: 4,000 kw (4 diesel sets)
Range: 4,500/18 (on Tyne) 1,200/29 (on Olympus)   **Man:** 18 officers, 205 men

REMARKS: Originally to have been a class of 26. Ordered 8-2-74, 4-9-75, 7-9-76, and 21-10-77. Type 2016 is a new multiple-frequency sonar. Have SCOT radomes for the Skynet communications satellite system. The WG 13 Lynx can carry both ASW and anti-ship weapons; two were to have been carried, but only one is aboard each, for economy reasons. Have CAAIS combat data system. The 967-968 radar is a back-to-back array with track-while-scan features.

♦ **8 Amazon (Type 21) class**

	Bldr	Laid down	L	In serv.
F 169 AMAZON	Vosper Thornycroft	6-11-69	26-4-71	11-5-74
F 170 ANTELOPE	Vosper Thornycroft	23-3-71	16-3-72	19-7-75
F 171 ACTIVE	Vosper Thornycroft	23-7-71	23-11-72	17-6-77
F 172 AMBUSCADE	Yarrow, Scotstoun	1-9-71	18-1-73	5-9-75
F 173 ARROW	Yarrow, Scotstoun	28-9-72	5-2-74	29-7-76
F 174 ALACRITY	Yarrow, Scotstoun	5-3-73	18-9-74	2-4-77
F 184 ARDENT	Yarrow, Scotstoun	26-2-74	9-5-75	13-10-77
F 185 AVENGER	Yarrow, Scotstoun	30-10-74	20-11-75	15-4-78

D: 2,750 tons (3,250 fl)   **S:** 32 kts   **Dim:** 117.04 × 12.8 × 4.4 (5.8 over sonar)
A: 4/MM 38 Exocet (not in F 169, 170)—1/Sea Cat GWS 24 system (IV × 1)—1/114-mm Mk 8 DP—2/20-mm AA (I × 2)—1/Wasp or WG 13 Lynx helicopter—6/324-mm Mk 32 ASW TT (III × 2) on F 184, 185 only

FRIGATES (continued)

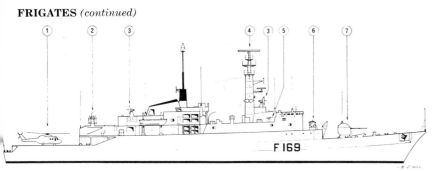

Amazon—as completed
1. WG 13 Lynx helicopter 2. Sea Cat system 3. RTN-10X Sea Cat guidance radar (GWS 22) 4. 992Q radar 5. 20-mm AA 6. Knebworth/Corvus 7. 114-mm Mk 8 mount

Amazon (F 169)—no Exocet missiles   G. Arra, 1977

Active (F 171)—with SCOT radomes fitted   1979

Electron Equipt: Radar: 1/992Q, 1/978, 2/RTN-10X Orion
Sonar: 1/184, 1/170B, 1/174, 1/162M
ECM: passive system, 2 Knebworth/Corvus chaff RL
M: COGOG; 2 Olympus TM3 gas turbines, 25,000 hp each; 2 Tyne RB209 gas turbines, 4,250 hp each; 2 CP props; 50,000 hp max.
Electric: 3,000 kw   **Range:** 4,500/18, 1,200/30   **Man:** 13 officers, 164 men

Arrow (F 173)—still without SCOT radomes   G. Gyssels, 1981

Avenger (F 185) (Type 21)—note ASW TT   L. & L. Van Ginderen, 1981

Antelope (F 170)   G. Arra, 1976

Alacrity (F 174)   G. Arra, 1980

FRIGATES *(continued)*

Alacrity (F 174)—Type 992Q radar and Type 1010 IFF interrogator atop foremast

G. Arra, 1980

REMARKS: Designed jointly by Vosper Thornycroft and Yarrow. The ships have been criticized for fragility, vulnerability, and for being overloaded and top-heavy; permanent ballast had to be added, but none can carry the full originally intended weapon and sensor suit. Sea Wolf GWS 40 is no longer planned for installation. Although the Royal Navy publicly announced satisfaction with the design, they will begin to phase out in the early 1990s without having been modernized and with only 18-20 years service.

Remote control of engine room from the bridge. Supplies on board for 60 days. Ferranti WSA 4 digital system used in fire control, employing two Selenia RTN-10X radar directors for both Sea Cat and the 114-mm gun; there is also a backup optical director for each. The CAAIS combat data system is a separate entity, whose data are automatically transmitted to WSA 4; both use a single FM-1600B computer. The Exocet launchers are paired, toed-in, and forward of the bridge. F 169, F 170, F 172 were completed without Exocet and have not yet had it installed; their Knebworth/Corvus chaff launchers are before the bridge, while on the others they are abaft the bridge, one deck higher. All were to receive two SCOT radomes for the Skynet communications satellite system, but F 184 and 185, the only ships with ASW torpedo tubes, lack the SCOT radomes for stability reasons. Four 750-kw diesel generator sets supply the 450-volt, 3-phase, 60-Hz electrical current.

◆ 26 Leander class

(a) 8 Ikara ASW missile conversions

	Bldr	Laid down	L	In serv.
F 109 LEANDER (ex-*Weymouth*)	Harland & Wolff	10-4-59	28-6-61	27-3-63
F 114 AJAX (ex-*Fowey*)	Cammell Laird	12-10-59	16-8-62	10-12-63
F 104 DIDO (ex-*Hastings*)	Yarrow, Scotstoun	2-12-59	22-12-61	18-9-63
F 10 AURORA	John Brown	1-6-61	28-11-62	9-4-64
F 15 EURYALUS	Scotts SB&E	2-11-61	6-6-63	16-9-64
F 18 GALATEA	Swan Hunter	29-12-61	23-5-63	25-4-64
F 38 ARETHUSA	J. Samuel White	7-9-62	5-11-63	24-11-65
F 39 NAIAD	Yarrow, Scotstoun	30-10-62	4-11-63	15-3-65

Conversions completed: F 109: 12-72; F 114: 9-73; F 18: 9-74; F 39: 7-75; F 15: 3-76; F 10: 3-76; F 38: 4-77; F 104: 10-78.

(b) 7 Exocet anti-ship missile conversions

F 28 CLEOPATRA	HMDY, Devonport	19-6-63	25-3-64	4-1-66
F 45 MINERVA	Vickers-Armstrong	25-7-63	19-12-64	14-5-66
F 42 PHOEBE	Alex. Stephen & Sons	3-6-63	8-7-64	15-4-66
F 40 SIRIUS	HMDY, Portsmouth	9-8-63	22-9-64	15-6-66
F 56 ARGONAUT	Hawthorn Leslie	27-11-64	8-2-66	17-8-67
F 47 DANAE	HMDY, Devonport	16-12-64	31-10-65	7-9-67
F 127 PENELOPE (ex-*Coventry*)	Vickers-Armstrong	14-3-61	17-8-62	31-10-63

Conversions completed: F 28: 11-75; F 42: 4-77; F 40: 10-77; F 45: 3-79; F 56: 2-80; F 47: 9-80; F 127: 5-81.

(c) 2 (+5) Sea Wolf anti-aircraft missile conversions

F 58 HERMIONE	Stephen/Yarrow	6-12-65	26-4-67	11-7-69
F 60 JUPITER	Yarrow, Scotstoun	3-10-66	4-9-67	9-8-69
F 57 ANDROMEDA	HMDY, Portsmouth	25-5-66	24-5-67	2-12-68
F 71 SCYLLA*	HMDY, Devonport	17-5-67	8-8-68	12-2-70

FRIGATES (continued)

F 75 CHARYBDIS	Harland & Wolff	27-1-67	28-2-68	2-6-69
F 70 APOLLO*	Yarrow, Scotstoun	1-5-69	15-10-70	28-5-72
F 72 ARIADNE*	Yarrow, Scotstoun	1-11-69	10-9-71	10-2-73

Conversions completed: F 57: 21-11-80; F 75: 5-82; F 58:. . . ; F 60: . . . .

(d) 3 unmodified "broad-beam" Leander class

F 69 BACCHANTE	Vickers-Armstrong	27-10-66	29-2-68	17-10-69
F 12 ACHILLES	Yarrow, Scotstoun	1-12-67	21-11-68	9-7-70
F 16 DIOMEDE	Yarrow, Scotstoun	30-1-68	15-4-69	2-4-71

(e) 1 navigation and aircraft direction training frigate conversion

F 52 JUNO	Thornycroft, Woolston	16-7-64	24-11-65	18-7-67

Naiad (F 39)　　　　　　　　　　　　　　G. Arra, 1980

Achilles (F 12)—broad-beam **Leander** (note Limbo in well and Wasp, aft)　1975

Andromeda (F 57)　　　　　　　　　　　　　J. Goss, 1981

Andromeda (F 57)—Sea Wolf **Leander**—Type 967/968 radar atop mast; note stern recess

1981

FRIGATES *(continued)*

Galatea (F 18)—Ikara **Leander**　　　　　　　　　G. Arra, 1980

Cleopatra (F 28)—Exocet **Leander** (WG 13 Lynx on deck)　　G. Gyssels, 1981

Cleopatra (F 28)—Exocet **Leander** (SCOT aft. "Abbeyhill" ECM array)　　G. Arra, 1978

D: *(a)* and F 52: 2,450 tons (2,860 fl); *(b)*: 2,650 tons (3,200 fl); *(c)* and *(d)*: 2,500 tons (2,962 fl)

S: 27 kts (30 on trials)

Dim: *(a)*, *(b)*, and F 52: 113.38 (109.73 pp) × 12.5 × 5.49 (sonar); *(c)* and *(d)*: 113.38 (109.73 pp) × 13.12 × 5.49 (sonar)

A: *(a)*: 2/40-mm AA (I × 2)—2/Sea Cat GWS 22 systems (IV × 2)—1/Ikara ASW system—1/Limbo Mk 10 ASW mortar (III × 1)—1/Wasp ASW helicopter

   (b): 4/MM 38 Exocet—2/40-mm AA (I × 2)—3/Sea Cat GWS 22 systems (IV × 3)—6/324-mm Mk 32 ASW TT (III × 2)—1/Wasp or WG 13 Lynx helicopter

   (c): 4/MM 38 Exocet—1/Sea Wolf GWS 25 system (VI × 1)—2/20-mm AA—6/324-mm Mk 32 ASW TT (III × 2)—1/WG 13 Lynx helicopter

   (d): 2/114-mm Mk 6 DP (II × 1)—1/Sea Cat GWS 22 system (IV × 1)—2/20-mm AA (I × 2)—1/Limbo Mk 10 ASW mortar (II × 1)—1/Wasp ASW helicopter

   (e): 2/114-mm Mk 6 DP (II × 1)—2/20-mm AA (I × 2)—1/Limbo Mk 10 ASW mortar (II × 1)

Electron Equipt: Radar: *(a)*: 1/978, 1/993, 1/904, 1/Ikara control
           (b): 1/978, 1/993, 1/965, 2/904
           (c): 1/1006, 1/967-968, 1/910
           (d): 1/978, 1/965, 1/993, 1/903, 1/904
           (e): . . .

FRIGATES (*continued*)

Aurora (F 10)—Ikara **Leander**—Type 1010 IFF interrogator atop after mast

1977

Sonar: *(a):* 1/170B, 1/184, 1/199 VDS
(b): 1/184—*(c):* 1/2016—*(d):* 1/184, 1/170B, 1/162
ECM: passive (and active in some) systems, 2 Knebworth/
Corvus chaff RL
M: 2 sets White-English Electric GT; 2/5-bladed props; 30,000 hp
Electric: *(a)* group plus F 28, F 104: 1,600 kw; *(b)* group and F 52: 1,900 kw;
(c) and *(d)* group: 2,500 kw
Boilers: 2 Babcock & Wilcox 3-drum, 38.7 kg/cm², 450°C superheat
Fuel: 460 tons; *(c)* and *(d)* group: 500 tons   **Range:** approx. 4,500/12
Man: (avg) 17 officers, 245 men

REMARKS: Improvement on the *Rothesay* class. Hull entirely welded; quarters air-conditioned; twin rudders; excellent sea-keeping qualities. Successive improvements to the propulsion and auxiliary machinery. All are gradually being fitted with two SCOT radomes for the Skynet satellite communications system. Many have received the Abbeyhill ECM/ESM system.

In the *(a)* group, or "Ikara *Leander*" class, the Ikara system replaced the 114-mm twin mount, while the number of Sea Cat launchers was doubled and two 40-mm AA were mounted abreast the bridge. These ships have the Ikara guidance radar in a radome atop the bridge and only one GWS 22 director aft for the Sea Cat. All have VDS, and the 965 radar has been removed.

FRIGATES (continued)

The *(b)* group, or "Exocet *Leander*" class, have had the 114-mm mount replaced by four MM 38 Exocet and a Sea Cat launcher. The Limbo mortar was removed and two triple ASW TT were mounted abreast the hangar, which now has two Sea Cat launchers atop it; two GWS 22 directors are carried (one fwd, one aft) and single 40-mm mounts were placed abreast the bridge. The VDS well was plated up. F 127, otherwise disarmed, served as Sea Wolf system-trials ship, with a six-celled launcher on the stern, the 910 radar director atop the deckhouse on the former helicopter deck, and a 967-968 tracking radar atop her after mast; originally scheduled to be an Ikara conversion on completion of the Sea Wolf trials, she was given the Exocet conversion instead. F 42 has carried a WG 13 Lynx helicopter.

The *(d)* group, or "broad-beam *Leander*" class, are 0.61 meters greater in beam to improve seaworthiness, provide larger fuel tanks, and permit installation of a more powerful electrical generator plant. All carried one Sea Cat GWS 22 system as completed—unlike many of the earlier *(a)* and *(b)* groups, which did not get Sea Cat prior to modernization. *Andromeda*, the first, commenced reconstruction 1-78. As refitted, each ship will have a Sea Wolf launcher and four MM 38 Exocet forward, two 20-mm AA, an enlarged hangar and flight deck for WG 13 Lynx, two triple-Mk 32 ASW TT, and new electronics (including Type 2016 sonar); Limbo, the twin 114-mm gun, and Sea Cat were removed. Economies announced in 6-81 will result in termination of the modernization programs, with at least three of the "broad-beam" *Leanders* to go into the Ready Reserve Squadron during 1982-83 instead of undergoing Sea Wolf conversions; three others of the newest *Leanders* may face similar fates. Additionally, at least one "Ikara *Leander*" is to be placed in reserve in 1982. *Juno* (F 52), which was to have been given an "Exocet *Leander*" conversion, was placed in Ready Reserve in 1-81, but is to be converted to replace the training frigate *Torquay*. *Argonaut* (F 56) has been conducting trials with a towed tactical passive hydrophone array since 1980.

NOTE: All frigates of the "Tribal" (Type 81) class have been placed on the sales list: *Ashanti* (F 117) in 12-80, and *Eskimo* (F 119), *Gurkha* (F 122), *Mohawk* (F 125), *Nubian* (F 131), *Tartar* (F 133), and *Zulu* (F 124) in 1-81.

♦ **7 Rothesay class (Type 12)** (one disarmed as trials ship)

	Bldr	Laid down	L	In serv.
F 101 YARMOUTH	John Brown (Clyde-bank)	29-11-57	23-3-59	26-3-60
F 103 LOWESTOFT	Alex Stephen & Sons	9-6-58	23-6-60	18-10-61
F 107 ROTHESAY	Yarrow, Scotstoun	6-11-56	9-12-57	23-4-60
F 108 LONDONDERRY	Thornycroft	15-11-56	20-5-58	22-7-60
F 106 BRIGHTON	Yarrow, Scotstoun	23-7-57	30-10-59	28-9-61
F 126 PLYMOUTH	HMDY, Devonport	1-7-58	20-7-59	11-5-61
F 129 RHYL	HMDY, Portsmouth	29-1-58	23-4-59	31-10-60

Plymouth (F 126)   1978

Londonderry (F 108)—after mast removed   L. & L. Van Ginderen, 1981

D: 2,380 tons (2,800 fl)   **S:** 30 kts (26/25 actual)
Dim: 112.77 (109.73 pp) × 12.5 × 5.3
A: 2/114-mm Mk 6 DP (II × 1)—2/20-mm AA (I × 2)—1/Sea Cat GWS 20 system (IV × 1)—1/Mk 10 Limbo ASW mortar—1/Wasp ASW helicopter (*see* Remarks)
Electron Equipt: Radars: 1/978, 1/993, 1/903 (F 108: 1/978, 1/993)
                              Sonar: 1/174, 1/170, 1/162
                              ECM: passive system, 2 Knebworth/Corvus chaff RL
M: 2 sets English Electric GT; 2 props; 30,000 hp   **Electric:** 1,460 kw
Boilers: 2 Babcock & Wilcox, 38.7 kg/cm², 450°C superheat
Fuel: 400 tons   **Range:** 4,500/12   **Man:** 15 officers, 220 men

REMARKS: Improved version of the *Whitby* class. All modernized 1966-72 with Sea Cat GWS 20 system (no radar) and helicopter facility in place of one Limbo ASW mortar. MRS 3 fire-control system replaced the original Mk 6 director, and new electronics and air-conditioning were installed. F 108 began conversion 11-75 to serve as trials ship for the Admiralty Surface Weapons Establishment; completed 11-10-79. She now has pump-jet propellers and no longer has any armament, but does have a helicopter landing deck. F 103 conducted trials during 1978 with the DA-5 towed passive sonar array and had a deckhouse on her helicopter deck; her Limbo was removed. *Falmouth* (F 115), placed in Standby Reserve 7-80, and *Berwick* (F 115), in reserve since 1-81, were stricken late in 1981. At least three others will probably be decommissioned by the end of 1982. The after pylon mast on F 108 is dismountable.

♦ **1 Whitby class (Type 12) training frigate**

	Bldr	Laid down	L	In serv.
F 43 TORQUAY	Harland & Wolff, Belfast	11-3-53	1-7-54	10-5-56

Torquay (F 43)   G. Arra, 1977

D: 2,150 tons (2,560 fl)   **S:** 26 kts
Dim: 112.77 (109.73 pp) × 12.5 × 5.26 (sonar)
A: 2/114-mm Mk 6 DP (II × 1)—1/Mk 10 Limbo ASW mortar

FRIGATES (continued)

Electron Equipt: Radars: 1/1006, 1/993, 1/275
Sonars: 1/174, 1/170, 1/162
M: 2 sets English-Electric GT; 2 props; 30,000 hp **Electric:** 1,140 kw
Boilers: 2 Babcock & Wilcox, 38.7 kg/cm² pressure, 450°C superheat
Fuel: 370 tons **Range:** 4,500/12

REMARKS: Survivor of a class of six, with two sisters also in Indian Navy. Has CAAIS combat data system for training purposes. The Mk 6 director for the 114-mm mount is the last of its type. Assigned to Navigation and Aircraft Direction Training at Portsmouth. Welded hull, air-conditioned, twin rudders. Cruising turbines for normal underway passage, with automatic shift to high-speed turbines. In trials, 30 knots were attained with 75 per cent of anticipated power. To be replaced by *Juno* (F 52) by 1983. Sister *Eastbourne* (F 73), hulked in 1976, was discarded in 1981.

NOTE: The *Salisbury*-class frigate *Lincoln* (F 99) was placed on the sales list in 3-81, having been in Reserve (except for a brief period in 1979) since 1976. The *Leopard*-class frigate *Lynx* (F 27), active briefly for trials in 1980, was placed on the sales list in 1-81.

CORVETTES

♦ **4 "Castle"-class offshore patrol vessels** Bldr: Hall Russell, Aberdeen

	Laid down	L	In serv.
P 258 LEEDS CASTLE	18-10-79	22-10-80	12-81
P 259 DUMBARTON CASTLE	25-6-80	3-6-81	4-82
P . . . N . . .	. . .	. . .	. . .
P . . . N . . .	. . .	. . .	. . .

D: 1,250 tons (1,450 fl) **S:** 20 kts **Dim:** 81.0 (75.0 pp) × 11.5 × 3.42
A: 1/40-mm AA—2/7.62-mm mg—mines—1 helicopter platform
Electron Equipt: Radar: 1/1006
M: 2 Ruston 12 RK 320CM diesels; 2 CP props; 5,640 hp (4,380 sust.)
Electric: 890 kw **Fuel:** 380 tons **Range:** 10,000/12
Man: 7 officers, 43 men (plus 25 Marine detachment as required)

REMARKS: First pair ordered 8-8-80, *after* both had been laid down; second pair ordered 1981. Will be able to carry acoustic and mechanical minesweeping gear as well as being able to lay mines. The helicopter deck is large enough to accommodate either WG 13 Lynx or a Sea King helicopter. The 40-mm gun is planned to eventually be replaced by an OTO Melara 76-mm Compact gun, controlled by a Sperry Archer Mk 1 electro-optical director. Can carry 19.5 tons helicopter fuel and 30 tons of oil-spill dispersant detergent. To have Decca CANE (Computer-Assisted Navigation Equipt.), NAVSAT, and Omega systems. Two Avon "Searider" rubber rescue/inspection dinghies carried. Have one fire monitor and two oil-dispersant spray booms. Intended for 21-day patrols.

NOTE: The new Hong Kong patrol ships, the first of which was ordered 7-81 from Hall-Russell, Aberdeen, may be additional units of the "Castle" class. Five ships are planned, to replace the wooden-hulled "Ton"-class former minesweepers. Armament is planned to include 1/76-mm OTO Melara gun, with Sea Archer Mk 1 fire control.

♦ **7 Isles-class offshore patrol vessels** Bldr: Hall-Russell, Aberdeen

	L	In serv.
P 277 ANGLESEY	18-10-78	1-6-79
P 278 ALDERNEY	27-2-79	6-10-79

P 295 JERSEY	18-3-76	15-10-76
P 297 GUERNSEY	17-2-77	28-10-77
P 298 SHETLAND	22-11-76	14-7-77
P 299 ORKNEY	29-6-76	25-2-77
P 300 LINDISFARNE	1-6-77	26-1-78

Alderney (P 278) G. Gyssels, 1979

Shetland (P 298) Skyfotos, 1980

D: 1,000 tons (1,280 fl) **S:** 16 kts **Dim:** 59.51 (51.97 pp) × 10.9 × 4.26
A: 1/40-mm AA Mk 3—2/7.62-mm machine guns
Electron Equipt: Radar: 1/1006
Sonar: 1/Simrad SU "sidescan"
M: 2 Ruston 12 RK 3 CM diesels (750 rpm); 1/CP prop; 4,380 hp
Electric: 536 kw **Fuel:** 310 tons **Range:** 7,000/12
Man: 4 officers, 36 men (plus Marine detachment)

REMARKS: Near duplicates of the Scottish Department of Fisheries ships *Jura* and *Westra*. The *Jura* (as P 296) was loaned to the Royal Navy from 1975 to 1-77 for use in patrolling offshore oil rigs and the 200-nautical-mile economic zone, the purpose for which the Isles class was built. First five ordered 11-2-75, other pair 21-10-77. P 277 and P 278 have fin stabilizers.

PATROL BOATS

♦ 5 ex-"Ton"-class converted minesweepers

	Bldr	Laid down	L	In serv.
P 1007 BEACHAMPTON (ex-M 1107)	Goole SB & Repair	2-4-51	29-6-53	30-7-54
P 1055 MONKTON (ex-M 1155)	Herd & MacKenzie	16-12-53	30-11-55	27-2-57
P 1089 WASPERTON (ex-M 1189)	J. Sam'l White & Co.	21-6-54	28-2-56	19-7-57
P 1093 WOLVERTON (ex-M 1193)	Montrose SY	28-9-54	22-10-56	25-3-58
P 1096 YARNTON (ex-M 1196)	Wm. Pickersgill & Son	26-10-54	26-3-56	16-1-57

Beachampton (P 1007)—with Hong Kong Gov't Alouette-III helo   G. Arra

D: 360 tons (425 fl)   **S:** 15 kts   **Dim:** 46.3 (42.7 pp)× 8.8 × 2.5
A: 2/40-mm AA (I × 2)—2/7.62-mm mg (I × 2)   **Electron Equipt:** Radar: 1/978
M: 2 Deltic 18A-7A diesels; 2 props; 3,000 hp   **Fuel:** 45 tons   **Range:** 2,300/13
Man: 5 officers, 25 men

REMARKS: All employed as the 6th Patrol Squadron at Hong Kong. Modified 1971-72. All sweep gear removed, light armor added around bridge. Scheduled to be replaced 1982-83 by new units. Eight minesweepers of this class normally act as Fisheries Protection ships (see under minesweepers).

♦ 1 jetfoil 929-115 class Bldr: Boeing, Seattle

	L	In serv.
P 296 SPEEDY	9-7-79	14-6-80

D: 117 tons (fl)   **S:** 50 kts (43 sust.)
Dim: 27.43 (30.78 with foils up; 23.77 wl) × 9.14 × 1.83 (5.18 with foils down, at rest; 2.4 foiling)
A: 2/7.62-mm mg
M: 2 Allison 501-K20 A gas turbines, driving waterjets; 7,560 hp; 2 GM 8V92 TI diesels; 2 props; 900 hp (for hull-borne cruise)
Fuel: 23 tons   **Range:** 560/43; 1,500/15; 3,500/5   **Man:** 5 officers, 13 men

REMARKS: Ordered 29-6-78 for use in patrolling North Sea fisheries and oil rigs. Fitted out by Vosper Thornycroft 11-79 to 6-80. Aluminum structure. Design evolved from U.S. Navy's *Tucumcari* (PGH 2) through a very successful commercial passenger hydrofoil. Joined Fisheries Protection Squadron at Rosyth 9-80 for six-month evaluation. Plans to order 11 more evidently shelved.

Speedy (P 296)—in service   1980

♦ 4 Kingfisher class Bldr: Richard Dunston, Hessle

	Laid down	L	In serv.
P 260 KINGFISHER	7-73	20-9-74	8-10-75
P 261 CYGNET	10-73	26-10-75	8-7-76
P 262 PETEREL	11-73	14-5-76	7-7-77
P 263 SANDPIPER	12-73	20-1-77	16-9-77

Peterel (P 262)—note lack of hull portholes   S. Terzibaschitsch, 1977

D: 187 tons   **S:** 25 kts   **Dim:** 36.6 (33.8 pp) × 7.0 × 2.0
A: 1/40-mm AA—2/7.62-mm machine guns
M: 2 Paxman 16 YCJM diesels (1,500 rpm); 2 props; 4,000 hp
Range: 2,000/14   **Man:** 4 officers, 10 men

REMARKS: Unsuccessful design based on RAF *Seal*-class air-sea rescue craft. A large number of additional sisters were canceled. P 262 and P 263 are used for naval officer training at Dartmouth; the other two were employed in patrol work in the North

PATROL BOATS (continued)

Sea but have been reassigned as tenders to the mine countermeasures squadron at Rosyth. Have fin stabilizers, but evidently still have stability problems. P 262 and 263 have no hull portholes, the earlier pair do.

♦ **3 Scimitar class** Bldr: Vosper Thornycroft, Portchester

	L	In serv.
P 271 SCIMITAR	4-12-69	19-7-70
P 274 CUTLASS	19-2-70	12-11-70
P 275 SABRE	21-4-70	5-3-71

Scimitar (P 271)—at Hong Kong   G. Arra, 1980

D: 102 tons (fl) **S:** 40 kts **Dim:** 30.5 × 8.1 × 1.95
M: CODOG: 2 Rolls-Royce Proteus gas turbines (9,000 hp); 2 Foden FD 6 diesels (180 hp) for cruising; 2 props
Range: 425/35; 1,500/21.5 **Man:** 2 officers, 10 men

REMARKS: Designed for anti-missile boat training. Hull of laminated and glued wood. A third gas turbine allowed for in design. Can carry two 7.62-mm machine guns if required for patrol duties. P 271 used at Hong Kong, 1980. Placed in land storage early 1981 and unlikely to see further service; replaced as target training craft by a Watercraft P 12 class commercial, 30-knot patrol boat on loan from the builder.

NOTE: The patrol boat *Tenacity* (P 276) was placed on the sales list 30-8-80 because of continual engineering problems. The two "Loyal"-class fleet tenders used for Ulster patrol duties, *Alert* (A 510) and *Vigilant* (A 382), were returned to the RMAS at the end of 1981 and resumed their original names.

MINE WARFARE SHIPS

♦ **12 "Extra Deep Armed Team Sweeps (MSM/EDATS)"**

REMARKS: The first of these adaptions of a commercial stern-haul trawler design were ordered during 1979 for delivery in 1980, with the remainder entering service by 1985, but this has now been considerably delayed, with cancellation of the program perhaps forthcoming. They were intended to sweep deep ocean mines by operating in pairs, with a wire sweep between them. In time of war, additional commercial fishing craft would be acquired for the same duties. The concept is being investigated with *Venturer* and *St. Davids* (see below), and the new ships would have similar characteristics.

♦ **2 (+7) "Hunt"-class minehunters**

	Bldr	Laid down	L	In serv.
M 29 BRECON	Vosper Thornycroft	15-9-75	21-6-78	21-3-80
M 30 LEDBURY	Vosper Thornycroft	5-10-77	5-12-79	-81
M 31 CATTISTOCK	Vosper Thornycroft	20-6-79	22-1-81	. . .
M 32 COTTESMORE	Yarrow, Scotstoun	27-9-79	. . .	. . .
M 33 BROCKLESBY	Vosper Thornycroft	8-5-80	. . .	. . .
M 34 MIDDLETON	Yarrow, Scotstoun	1-7-80	. . .	. . .
M 35 DULVERTON	Vosper Thornycroft	4-81	. . .	. . .
M 36 CHIDDINGFORD	Vosper Thornycroft	. . .	. . .	. . .
M 37 HURWORTH	Vosper Thornycroft	. . .	. . .	. . .

Ledbury (M 30)   1981

D: 625 tons (725 fl) **S:** 17 kts **Dim:** 60.0 (56.6 pp) × 9.85 × 2.2
A: 1/40-mm Mk 9 AA
Electron Equipt: Radar: 1/1006
                          Sonar: 1/193M
M: 2 Ruston-Paxman Deltic 9-59K diesels (1,600 rpm); 2 props; 1,900 hp (1,770 sust.); slow-speed hydraulic drive for hunting (8 kts)
Electric: 1,080 kw (3 Foden FD 12 Mk 7 diesel alternators of 200 kw each for ship's service plus one 480-kw diesel alternator for magnetic mine-sweeping)
Man: 6 officers, 39 men

REMARKS: Equipped for both hunting and sweeping mines. Hull constructed of glass-reinforced plastic. Carry divers and 2 French PAP 104 wire-guided, remote-controlled mine locators. Have Sperry "Osborn" TA 6 acoustic, M.M. Mk 11 magnetic loop and M. Mk 3 mod 2 Orepesa wire sweeping gear as well. Equipped with CAAIS data system and Decca Mk 21 "Hi-Fix" navigation system. M 36 and M 37 may be sold to Australia, although additional units are still planned for the Royal Navy. M 33 laid down *prior* to ordering on 19-6-80.

♦ **2 ex-commercial stern trawlers** Bldr: Cubow Ltd., Woolwich

	L	In serv.
M 07 ST. DAVIDS (ex-*Suffolk Monarch*)	9-73	1973
M 08 VENTURER (ex-*Suffolk Harvester*)	12-72	1973

D: 392 grt **S:** 14 kts **Dim:** 36.64 (34.14 pp) × 8.95 × 3.90
A: None **M:** 2 Mirrlees Blackstone 8-cyl. diesels; 1 CP prop; 2,000 hp
Electric: 240 kw **Man:** . . . tot.

REMARKS: Chartered 11-78, commissioning 9-12-78. Manned by Royal Naval Reserve, M 07 at Cardiff and M 08 at Bristol. Testing concept for "extra deep armed team sweeps." Chartered through 11-82. Have two commercial navigational radars.

MINE WARFARE SHIPS *(continued)*

Venturer (M 08) 1980

◆ **1 prototype glass-reinforced plastic minehunter** Bldr: Vosper Thornycroft

	Ordered	L	In serv.
M 1116 WILTON	11-2-70	18-2-72	25-4-73

Wilton (M 1116) S. Terzibaschitsch, 1977

D: 450 tons (fl) **S:** 15 kts **Dim:** 46.33 × 8.76 × 2.6
A: 1/40-mm AA Mk 7 **M:** As for "Ton" class **Man:** 5 officers, 32 men

REMARKS: First large warship with an all-glass-reinforced plastic hull. Machinery and fittings are from the *Derriton*, scrapped in 1970.

◆ **14 "Ton"-class minehunters**

	Bldr	Laid down	L	In serv.
M 1110 BILDESTON	J.S. Doig, Grimsby	18-5-51	9-6-52	28-4-53
M 1113 BRERETON*	Richard Ironworks	25-9-51	14-5-53	9-7-54
M 1114 BRINTON	Cook, Welton & Gemmell	30-5-51	8-8-52	4-3-54
M 1115 BRONINGTON	Cook, Welton & Gemmell	30-5-51	19-3-53	4-6-54
M 1133 BOSSINGTON	J.I. Thornycroft	1-9-54	2-12-55	11-12-56
M 1140 GAVINTON	J.S. Doig, Grimsby	29-9-52	27-7-53	12-7-54
M 1147 HUBBERSTON	Fleetlands SY, London	29-1-53	14-9-54	14-10-55
M 1151 IVESTON	Philip & Son, Dartmouth	22-10-52	1-6-54	20-6-55
M 1153 KEDLESTON*	Wm. Pickersgill & Son	26-11-52	21-12-53	2-7-55
M 1154 KELLINGTON*	Wm. Pickersgill & Son	5-1-54	12-10-54	4-11-55
M 1157 KIRKLISTON	Harland & Wolff, Belfast	2-2-53	18-2-54	21-8-54
M 1165 MAXTON	Harland & Wolff, Belfast	23-5-55	24-5-56	19-2-57
M 1166 NURTON	Harland & Wolff, Belfast	31-8-55	22-10-56	21-8-57
M 1181 SHERATON	White's SY, Southhampton	23-2-54	20-7-55	24-8-56

* Reserve Training

Nurton (M 1166)—minehunter G. Gyssels, 1981

Bildeston (M 1110)—minehunter G. Gyssels, 1980

◆ **14 "Ton"-class minesweepers**

	Bldr	Laid down	L	In serv.
M 1103 ALFRISTON*	J.I. Thornycroft	16-8-51	29-4-53	16-3-54
M 1109 BICKINGTON†	White's SY, Southhampton	21-9-51	14-5-53	27-5-54
M 1124 CRICHTON†	J.S. Doig, Grimsby	21-4-52	17-3-53	23-4-54
M 1125 CUXTON†	Camper & Nicholson's	23-7-52	4-11-53	13-10-54
M 1146 HODGESTON‡	Fleetlands SY, London	22-9-52	6-4-54	17-12-54
M 1173 POLLINGTON†	Camper & Nicholson's	18-3-55	10-10-54	5-9-58
M 1180 SHAVINGTON†	White's SY, Southampton	30-9-53	25-4-55	1-3-56
M 1187 UPTON‡	J. I. Thornycroft	14-2-55	15-3-56	24-7-56
M 1188 WALKERTON‡	J.I. Thornycroft	4-7-55	21-11-56	10-1-58
M 1195 WOTTON†	Philip & Son, Dartmouth	25-6-54	24-4-56	13-6-57
M 1200 SOBERTON†	Fleetlands SY, Gosport	11-3-55	20-11-56	17-9-57
M 1204 STUBBINGTON†	Camper & Nicholson's	26-10-54	8-8-56	30-7-57
M 1208 LEWISTON‡	Herd & MacKenzie, Banff	19-10-56	3-11-59	16-6-60
M 1216 CROFTON‡	J.I. Thornycroft	3-9-56	7-3-58	26-8-58

* Navigational training ship, Dartmouth Naval College; † Coastal Division, Fisheries Protection Squadron; ‡ Reserve Training

MINE WARFARE SHIPS *(continued)*

Cuxton (M 1125)—Fisheries Protection G. Gyssels, 1979

D: 370 tons (425 fl) **S:** 15 kts (cruising) **Dim:** 46.33 (42.68 pp) × 8.76 × 2.50
A: 1/40-mm AA Mk 7—plus 2/20-mm AA (II × 1) in some sweepers (M 1103, M 1188 disarmed)
Electron Equipt: Radar: 1/978
    Sonar: 1/193 (hunters only)
M: 2 Paxman Deltic 18A-7A diesels; 2 props; 3,000 hp
Fuel: 43 tons (minehunters: 36 tons) **Range:** 3,000/8, 2,300/13
Man: 5 officers, 33 men (sweepers: 24 men)

REMARKS: Survivors of a class of 118 completed 1952-58; five others are equipped as patrol boats. All minehunters are equipped with active rudders for low-speed operations, have a Type 193 sonar, and can carry mine-clearance divers. The mine-hunter conversions were completed 1964-69. M 1125 was first commissioned 10-75, having gone into reserve on completion in 1953. *Shoulton* (M 1182), the prototype minehunter conversion, was stricken 1-80. Of the minesweepers, *Repton* (M 1167) was stricken in 1979, *Glasserton* (M 1141), used in trials, was stricken at end 1980, and *Laleston* (M 1158), most recently used as a patrol boat in Ulster, was discarded in 1981; several more to strike 1982.

All have wooden hulls, most sheathed with nylon below the waterline. Fin stabilizers are fitted. Fisheries Patrol units have a searchlight abaft the stack.

MINE COUNTERMEASURES SUPPORT SHIP

♦ **1 exercise minelayer and tender**

	Bldr	Laid down	L	In serv.
N 21 ABDIEL	Thornycroft, Woolston	23-5-66	22-1-67	17-10-67

D: 1,375 tons (1,460 fl) **S:** 16 kts **Dim:** 80.42 (74.67 pp) × 11.74 × 2.85
A: 44 mines **Electron Equipt:** Radar: 1/978
M: 2 Paxman Ventura 16-YSCM diesels; 2 props; 2,690 hp **Electric:** 1,225 kw
Man: 77 tot.

REMARKS: Carries and repairs spare sweeping equipment and cable.

Abdiel G. Arra, 1976

AMPHIBIOUS WARFARE SHIPS

ASSAULT SHIPS

NOTE: The aircraft carrier *Hermes* can be employed to transport a commando battalion (two over short distances) of Royal Marines, landing them via embarked Wessex Mk 5 or Sea King Mk 4 helicopters. Conversion of the aviation supply ship *Tarbatness* to act as an assault ship was canceled in 1980.

Landing ships and craft subordinated to the Royal Corps of Transport are covered in the Royal Army entry at the conclusion of the Great Britain section, on page 270.

♦ **2 Fearless class**

	Bldr	Laid down	L	In serv.
L 10 FEARLESS	Harland & Wolff	25-7-62	19-12-63	25-11-65
L 11 INTREPID	J. Brown (Clyde)	11-12-62	5-6-64	11-3-67

Intrepid (L 11) 1980

D: 11,060 tons (12,120 fl) (16,950 tons, draft 9.15, with well deck flooded)
S: 21 kts **Dim:** 158.5 (152.4 pp) × 24.38 × 6.2
A: 4/Sea Cat GWS 20 systems (IV × 4)—2/40-mm AA (I × 2)
Electron Equipt: Radar: 1/978, 1/993
    ECM: passive system, 2 Knebworth/Corvus chaff RL

ASSAULT SHIPS *(continued)*

M: English-Electric GT; 2 props; 22,000 hp   **Electric:** 4,000 kw
Boilers: 2 Babcock & Wilcox, 38.66 kg/cm² pressure, 454°C superheat
Range: 5,000/20   **Man:** 36 officers, 520 men, 380-700 troops

REMARKS: Equivalent to U.S. LPD and French TCD types, and have excellent command and communication facilities for amphibious operations. CAAIS combat data system fitted. They can launch four to six Wessex Mk 5 assault helicopters (landing platform but no hangar), and have quarters for troop contingents of various sizes, depending on the duration and distance of operations, but usually a single light infantry battalion and an artillery battery. On board are four LCA landing craft, which can transport 35 men or a half-ton vehicle, and four LCM (9) landing craft carrying two Chieftain or Centurion tanks or four vehicles or 100 tons of supplies; four additional tanks can be carried on the tank deck. The vehicles are divided between the tank deck, a lower deck, and a half-deck reserved for jeeps. The active unit has normally been assigned as officer cadet training ship at the Royal Naval College, Dartmouth, but has been immediately available for amphibious operations as required. *Fearless*, which underwent overhaul 8-80 to 8-81, will operate into 1984; *Intrepid* to be put on the sales list in 1982.

TANK LANDING SHIPS

♦ **6 Sir Bedivere class** (logistic lift ships in peacetime)

	Bldr	Laid down	L	In serv.
L 3004 SIR BEDIVERE	Hawthorn Leslie	10-65	20-7-66	18-5-67
L 3005 SIR GALAHAD	Alexander Stephen	2-65	19-4-66	17-12-66
L 3027 SIR GERAINT	Alexander Stephen	6-65	26-1-67	12-7-67
L 3029 SIR LANCELOT	Fairfield	3-62	25-6-63	16-1-64
L 3036 SIR PERCIVALE	Hawthorn Leslie	4-66	4-10-67	23-3-68
L 3505 SIR TRISTRAM	Hawthorn Leslie	2-66	12-12-66	14-9-67

Sir Galahad (L 3005)   G. Arra, 1980

D: 3,270 tons (5,674 fl)   **S:** 17 kts   **Dim:** 126.45 × 17.7 × 3.8
A: 2/40-mm (not installed)
M: 2 Mirrlees 10-cyl. diesels; 2 props; 9,400 hp (L 3029: 2 Denny-Sulzer diesels; 9,520 hp)
Fuel: 811 tons   **Range:** 8,000/15   **Man:** 18 officers, 51 men

REMARKS: In 1963 the Ministry of Transportation ordered the first of six specially designed LST-type ships for the Army, chartered in peacetime to various private

Sir Geraint (L 3027)—with pontoon and military deckload   1980

maritime firms. In 1970 these ships came under the control of the Royal Fleet Auxiliary Service, which mans them today. Beaching cargo capacity is 340 tons (military lift). Built into the bow and the stern are ramps and doors for the handling of vehicles (roll-on/roll-off system); interior ramps connect the two decks. Quarters are provided in the after superstructure for 402 men. The ships have a helicopter platform and three cranes (two 4.5, one 8.5 tons); landing craft may be carried in cradles normally used for lifeboats. L 3029 has four cranes, and is 5,550 tons full load.

LANDING CRAFT

♦ **14 LCM (9) class** (In serv. 1963-66)

L 700-L 703 (Bldr: Brooke Marine, Lowestoft)
L 704-L 709 (Bldr: Richard Dunston, Thorne)
L 710, L 711 (Bldr: J. Bolson, Poole)
L 3507, L 3508 (Bldr: Vosper)

L 702   G. Arra, 1977

D: 75 tons (176 fl)   **Dim:** 25.7 × 6.5 × 1.7
M: 2 Paxman YHXAM diesels; Kort-nozzle props; 624 hp   **Man:** 6 tot.

REMARKS: Can carry two Centurion tanks or 100 tons of cargo. All naval-manned. Can carry a Type 978 radar. *Fearless* (L 10) and *Intrepid* (L 11) can each carry four of this class.

LANDING CRAFT (*continued*)

♦ **2 LCM (7) class**

L 7037   L 7100

    D: 28 tons (63 fl)   **S:** 9.8 kts   **Dim:** 18.4 × 4.9 × 1.2
    M: 2 Gray Marine diesels; 2 props; 290 hp

REMARKS: Wartime construction, used as stores tenders; survivors of a once-numerous class. Naval-operated.

♦ **1 (+9) new construction LCVP** Bldr: Fairey Allday Marine, Hamble

REMARKS: First ordered 6-2-80 to begin replacement of craft below. Nine more ordered 7-80, with more planned. No details available.

♦ **26 LCVP**

LCVP (1): 102, 112, 118, 120, 123, 127, 128, 134, 136
LCVP (2): 142-149
LCVP (3): 150-158

    D: 8.5 tons (13.5 fl)   **S:** 8-10 kts   **Dim:** 12.7 or 13.1 × 3.1 × 0.8
    M: 2 Foden diesels; 2 props; 130 or 200 hp

REMARKS: Eight of the LCVP (2) could be carried in *Fearless* and *Intrepid*.

♦ **3 LCP(L) (3)**

501, 503, 556

    D: 6.5 tons (10 fl)   **S:** 12 kts   **Dim:** 11.3 × 3.4 × 1.0
    M: 1 diesel; 1 prop; 225 hp

HOVERCRAFT

♦ **1 VT-2 class** Bldr: Vosper (In serv. 1975)

P 234 Bldr: Vosper (In serv. 1975)

P 234—prior to conversion   1979

    D: 62.5 tons (110 max.)   **S:** 60+ kts   **Dim:** 30.17 × 13.3 × 0.86 (at rest)
    M: 2 Rolls-Royce Proteus gas turbines; 2/4.1-m dia. props; 9,000 hp
    Fuel: 10.5 tons

REMARKS: Purchased 3-4-79. Conversion for mine countermeasures logistic support role completed 11-80. Not intended to sweep mines, but rather to bring spare equipment and supplies to "Hunt"-class minehunters on operations. Sliding hatch fitted to cabin roof. Trials 1981. 32 ton payload.

♦ **1 BH-N7 Wellington Mk 4 class** Bldr: British Hovercraft (In serv. 4-70)

P 238 (ex-XW 255)

P 238   G. Arra, 1977

    D: 33 tons (50 max.)   **S:** 60 kts   **Dim:** 23.9 × 13.0 × 1.7 (at rest)
    M: 1 Rolls-Royce Proteus gas turbine; 4,250 hp   **Range:** 464/58   **Man:** 14 tot.

REMARKS: Can carry 60 troops. Has bow hatch.

♦ **3 SR N6 Winchester class** Bldr: British Hovercraft (In serv. 1975)

P 236 (ex-XV 615)   P 237 (ex-XV 617)   P 238 (ex-XV 852)

P 237 at Hong Kong   Sgt. J. Chance, RAF, 1979

HOVERCRAFT (continued)

D: 10 tons **S:** 50 kts **Dim:** 14.8 × 7.0 × 1.3 (at rest)
M: 1 Rolls-Royce Gnome 1301 gas turbine; 900 hp **Range:** 200/50

REMARKS: Two sent to Hong Kong, 1979, for patrol duties.

AUXILIARY SHIPS

Most auxiliary and supply vessels are responsible to the Royal Fleet Auxiliary (RFA), an organization peculiar to the Royal Navy. Built to the specifications of Lloyds of London (compartmentation, security, habitability), they also meet the standards of the Shipping Naval Acts of 1911 and of the Ministry of Transportation. Manned by the Civil Service, they fly the blue ensign of the reserve, rather than the white ensign. In addition, about 40 tugs, salvage vessels, cable-layers, research vessels, etc. are assigned to the Royal Maritime Auxiliary Service (RMAS), whose personnel are also civil servants. The former Port Auxiliary Service (PAS) was absorbed by the RMAS on 1-10-76. Ships not listed below as either RFA or RMAS are manned by the Royal Navy. RMAS ships have black hulls and gray upperworks. They do not normally display hull numbers; pendant numbers are listed hereafter in parentheses for reference only.

HYDROGRAPHIC SHIPS

NOTE: All British survey ships are painted white, with buff-colored stacks and masts.

♦ 1 improved Hecla class

	Bldr	Laid down	L	In serv.
(A 138) HERALD	Robb Caledon	9-11-72	4-10-73	31-10-74

Herald   1976

D: 2,125 tons (2,945 fl) **S:** 14 kts **Dim:** 79.3 × 14.9 × 4.7
M: Diesel-electric propulsion (identical to the *Hecla* class); 1 prop **Man:** 128 tot.

REMARKS: Improved version of the *Hecla* class. Carries one Wasp helicopter. Replaced the *Vidal*, stricken in 1972. Has Type 2034 Sidescan charting sonar.

♦ 3 Hecla class

	Bldr	Laid down	L	In serv.
(A 133) HECLA	Yarrow, Blythswood	6-5-64	21-12-64	9-9-65
(A 137) HECATE	Yarrow, Scotstoun	26-10-64	31-3-65	20-12-65
(A 144) HYDRA	Yarrow, Blythswood	14-5-64	14-7-65	5-5-66

D: 1,915 tons (2,733 fl) **S:** 14 kts **Dim:** 79.25 (71.63 pp) × 14.94 × 4.0
M: diesel-electric propulsion: 3 Paxman Ventura diesels (12 cyl.), each 1,280 hp;
2 electric motors; 1 prop; 2,000 hp
Fuel: 450 tons **Range:** 20,000/9, 12,000/11 **Man:** 14 officers, 104 men

Hecate   G. Arra, 1977

REMARKS: Based on the oceanographic research vessel *Discovery*. Air-conditioned hull, reinforced against ice; bow thruster for navigation in narrow waters. Hangar and platform for one Wasp helicopter. Excellent scientific laboratories; usually carry seven civilian scientists in addition to crew. Two survey launches. Have Type 2034 sidescan charting sonar.

♦ 0 (+4) new construction coastal survey ships Bldr:. . .

N . . .   N . . .   N . . .   N . . .

D: 1,000 tons (fl) **S:** 15 kts **Dim:** . . . × . . . × . . . **M:** diesels

REMARKS: Three new coastal survey ships to begin replacement of the *Echo* class, *Waterwitch* and *Woodlark*, but economics may prevent carrying out the project. A fourth was planned for later. Available data suggest that an updated version of the *Bulldog* class was envisioned. During 1981-82, trials were conducted with a Vosper/Hovermarine HM527 hovercraft as a possible replacement for the *Echo* class: 40 kts max.; range: 400/30; 1 officer, 8 men.

♦ 4 Bulldog-class coastal survey ships Bldr: Brooke Marine, Lowestoft

		L	In serv.
(A 317) BULLDOG	12-7-67	21-3-68
(A 319) BEAGLE (ex-*Barracuda*)	7-9-67	9-5-68
(A 320) FOX	9-11-68	11-7-68
(A 335) FAWN	29-2-68	10-9-68

Bulldog   G. Arra, 1977

HYDROGRAPHIC SHIPS *(continued)*

D: 800 tons (1,088 fl) **S:** 15 kts **Dim:** 60.95 × 11.43 × 3.6
M: 4 Lister-Blackstone ERS-8-M diesels; 2 Ka-Me-Wa CP props; 2,640 hp
Electric: 720 kw **Range:** 4,600/12 **Man:** 5 officers, 34 men

REMARKS: Hulls built to commercial specifications and reinforced against ice damage. Carry one 8.7-meter survey launch. Passive tank stabilization. Decca "Hi-Fix" precision plot. Can be equipped with 2/20-mm AA on bridge wings (I × 2). Carry one 8.7-m survey boat.

♦ 3 Echo-class inshore survey craft

	Bldr	Laid down	L	In serv.
(A 70) ECHO	J. Samuel White, Cowes	9-3-56	1-5-57	12-9-58
(A 71) ENTERPRISE	M. W. Blackmore, Bideford	6-5-57	20-9-58	18-8-59
(A 72) EGERIA	W. Weatherhead, Cockenzie	17-5-57	13-9-58	18-6-59

Enterprise   G. Gyssels, 1981

D: 120 tons (160 fl) **S:** 13/12 kts **Dim:** 32.55 × 6.98 × 2.1
Electron Equipt: Radar: 1/Decca TM 629 **Man:** 2 officers, 16 men
M: 2 Paxman diesels; 2 CP props; 700 hp **Fuel:** 15 tons **Range:** 1,600/10

REMARKS: Built of laminated wood. Quarters for 22. Mount for 1/40-mm. Two echo-sounders; sonar for detecting shipwrecks. Modified version of "Ham"-class minesweeper design.

NOTE: The "Ham"-class inshore survey craft *Waterwitch* was stricken 3-81, and *Woodlark* was to be discarded early in 1982.

EXPERIMENTAL SHIPS

NOTE: The disarmed *Rothesay*-class frigate *Londonderry* (F 108) acts as trials ship for pump-jet propellers and electronics equipment; see under frigates.

♦ 1 sonar-trials ship

	Bldr	Laid down	L	In serv.
A 285 AURICULA	Ferguson Bros.	16-2-79	22-11-79	10-80

D: 1,200 tons (fl) **S:** . . . kts **Dim:** 60.0 (52.0 pp) × 11.0 × . . .
M: 2 Mirrlees-Blackstone ESL-6-MGR diesels; 2 props; 1,300 hp
Man: 7 officers, 15 men, 10 technicians

REMARKS: Ship operated by RMAS. Ordered 5-1-78. "Trials and Experimental Tender" to Admiralty Underwater Weapons Establishment, Portland; replaced *Steady*.

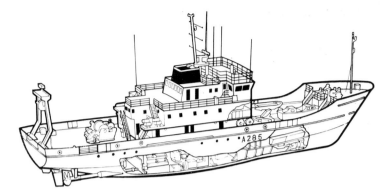

Auricula (A 285)   1980

♦ 1 sonar-research ship

	Bldr	Laid down	L	In serv.
A 367 NEWTON	Scott-Lithgow, Greenock	19-12-73	26-6-75	17-6-76

Newton (A 367)   G. Arra, 1977

D: 3,940 tons (fl) **S:** 15 kts **Dim:** 98.6 (88.7 pp) × 16.15 × 4.7
Electron Equipt: Radar: 1/1006
　　　　　　　　　　Sonar: 1/182, 1/185, 1/2010, 1/2013
M: 3 Mirrlees-Blackstone EWSL-12 MA diesels, electric drive; 1 Kort-nozzle prop; 2,680 hp
Electric: 2,150 kw **Fuel:** 300 tons **Range:** 5,000/13
Man: 61 men (including 12 technicians)

EXPERIMENTAL SHIPS (continued)

REMARKS: Intended for sonar-propagation trials and also fitted to lay cable over the bows. Equipped with bow-thruster and passive tank stabilization system. Propulsion plant extremely quiet, with a 300-hp electric motor for low speeds. Has four laboratories and seven special winches. Can carry and lay 400 tons of undersea cable. Navigation equipment includes SINS, satellite receivers, two optical range-finders, Decca Mk 21, and considerable other equipment. RMAS-operated.

♦ 1 torpedo-research vessel

A 364 WHITEHEAD   Bldr: Scotts SB, Greenock   (L: 5-5-70)

Whitehead (A 364)   1971

D: 3,040 tons (fl)   **S:** 15.5 kts   **Dim:** 97.23 (88.7 pp) × 14.63 × 5.2
A: 1/533-mm TT (bow, submerged)—3/324-mm Mk 32 ASW TT (III × 1)
M: 2 Paxman 12 YLCM diesels; 1 prop; 3,400 hp
Range: 4,000/12   **Man:** 10 officers, 47 men and scientists

REMARKS: Designed not only to launch and recover exercise torpedoes but also to perform precision tracking in three dimensions, using passive hydrophone arrays, and post-firing checkout and maintenance on torpedoes. RMAS-operated.

♦ 1 sonar-research barge

		Bldr	L	In serv.
(RDV 01)	CRYSTAL	HMDY, Devonport	22-3-71	30-11-71

Crystal   G. Arra, 1977

D: 3,040 tons (fl)   **Dim:** 126.0 × 17.0 × 1.7   **Man:** 60 tot.

REMARKS: No propulsion plant. Assigned to test new sonars at Admiralty Underwater Weapons Establishment, Portland. RMAS-operated.

NOTE: The torpedo trials tender *Whimbrel* (A 179) was discarded 1981, while the stabilization systems trials ships *Britannic* and *Steady* were discarded 1979 and 1980, respectively.

REPAIR SHIP

♦ 1 Head class

		Bldr	Laid down	L	In serv.
A 134	RAME HEAD	Burrard, Vancouver	7-44	22-11-44	8-45

Rame Head (A 134)   S. Terzibaschitsch, 1977

D: 9,000 tons (11,270 fl)   **S:** 10 kts   **Dim:** 134.6 (126.8 pp) × 17.5 × 6.9
A: 11/40-mm AA (I × 11)   **M:** Triple-expansion steam; 1 prop; 2,500 hp
Boilers: 2 Foster-Wheeler, 17 kg/cm², 330°C   **Fuel:** 700 tons
Man: 425 tot.

REMARKS: Former escort maintenance ship employed as an accommodations ship at Portsmouth since 6-76. Repair equipment and armament maintained on board in preservation since 1972. Has one 12-ton and two 5-ton cranes. Sister *Berry Head* (A 191), also used as an accommodations ship, was placed on the sales list at the end of 1980.

NOTE: The converted *Colossus*-class repair ship *Triumph*, in reserve since 1970, was placed on the sales list in 11-80.

FLEET-REPLENISHMENT SHIPS

♦ 2 Fort-class ammunition, explosives, food, and stores ships Bldr: Scott-Lithgow, Greenock

		Laid down	L	In serv.
A 385	FORT GRANGE	9-11-73	9-12-76	1978
A 386	FORT AUSTIN	9-12-75	9-3-78	5-79

D: 22,749 tons (fl)   **S:** 20 kts   **Dim:** 183.8 (170.0 pp) × 24.1 × 8.6
Electron Equipt: Radar: Kelvin-Hughes 21/16 P
M: 1 Sulzer 8 RND 90 diesel; 1 prop; 23,200 hp   **Electric:** 4,120 kw
Range: 10,000/20   **Man:** 140 Royal Fleet Auxiliary personnel, plus 45 naval.

Fort Austin (A 386)—MARISAT radome atop bridge   1980

FLEET-REPLENISHMENT SHIPS *(continued)*

Fort Grange (A 385)—note helo platform atop hangar   G. Arra, 1980

REMARKS: Ordered 11-71 and 4-72; 16,009 grt/8,300 dwt/6,729 nrt. In addition to the flight deck on the stern, the roof of the hangar can land helicopters. One Sea King is carried (although four can be accommodated), and the ships will have ASW torpedoes and other ASW stores for use if needed. The design is a combination of features of the *Resource* and *Lyness* classes. Three sliding-stay, constant-tension, alongside-replenishment stations on each beam. Have 2/10-ton and 4/5-ton electric stores cranes. Platforms for two SCOT satellite communications radomes atop superstructure, but received MARISAT commercial system instead. RFA-operated.

◆ 2 Resource-class ammunition, explosives, food, and stores ships

		Bldr	Laid down	L	In serv.
A 480	RESOURCE	Scotts SB, Greenock	6-64	11-2-66	18-5-67
A 486	REGENT	Harland & Wolff, Belfast	9-64	9-3-66	6-6-67

Regent (A 486)   1980

Resource (A 480)   1977

D: 22,890 tons (fl) (18,029 grt)   **S:** 17 kts
Dim: 195.07 (182.88 pp) × 23.47 × 7.95
M: 1 set A.E.I. GT; 1 prop; 20,000 hp   **Boilers:** 2 Foster-Wheeler
Man: 119 Royal Fleet Auxiliary, 52 civilian, plus airgroup

REMARKS: RFA-operated. Three sliding-stay, constant-tension, alongside-replenishment stations per side. Carry two Sea King helicopters.

◆ 1 Lyness-class stores support ship

		Bldr	Laid down	L	In serv.
A 344	STROMNESS	Swan Hunter	10-65	16-9-66	21-3-67

Stromness (A 344)   G. Arra, 1980

D: 9,010 tons, light (16,792 fl)   **S:** 18.5 kts
Dim: 159.76 (149.39 pp) × 21.95 × 6.7
Electron Equipt: Radar: 1 Kelvin-Hughes 14/12, 1 Kelvin-Hughes 14/16
M: Sulzer 8 RD 76 diesel; 1 prop; 11,520 hp (9,970 sust.)   **Electric:** 3,420 kw
Fuel: 1,574 tons   **Range:** 12,500/18, 27,000/12
Man: 28 officers, 82 men, 44 civilians

REMARKS: RFA-operated; 12,359 grt/7,782 dwt/4,744 nrt. Platform for two helicopters. Closed-circuit TV provided to monitor handling of stores. Has 2/5-ton, 2/12.5-ton, and 1/12-ton cranes. Sister *Lyness* (A 339) was leased to the U.S. Navy 12-80, having been placed in reserve after completing an overhaul 1-10-80; she was to be purchased outright in 1982. *Tarbatness* (A 345), which was to have been converted to a commando ship, was placed in reserve at Gibraltar in 1980 and was to be purchased by the U.S. Navy in 1982. *Stromness*, scheduled to be deactivated in 1982, will probably also be purchased by the USN.

NOTE: The armament support ship *Resurgent* (A 280) was discarded 1-80, while the cargo ship *Bacchus* (A 404) was returned to her owners at the end of her 19-year charter in 1981.

FLEET OILERS

◆ 3 Olwen class

		Bldr	L	In serv.
A 122	OLWEN (ex-*Olynthus*)	Hawthorn Leslie	10-7-64	21-6-65
A 123	OLNA	Hawthorn Leslie	28-7-75	1-4-66
A 124	OLMEDA (ex-*Oleander*)	Swan Hunter	19-11-64	18-10-65

D: 10,890 tons light (36,000 fl)   **S:** 20 kts
Dim: 197.51 (185.92 pp) × 25.6 × 10.5
Electron Equipt: Radar: 1 Kelvin-Hughes 14/12, 1 Kelvin-Hughes 14/16
M: 1 set Pamatreda GT; 1 prop; 26,500 hp
Boilers: 2 Babcock & Wilcox, 60 kg/cm², 510°C superheat
Man: 25 officers, 62 men, plus naval air group

FLEET OILERS *(continued)*

Olwen (A 122)   G. Gyssels, 1979

Olna (A 123)   1980

REMARKS: Hull reinforced against ice, living space air-conditioned, advanced auto-mation, excellent facilities for replenishment at sea; 25,000 dwt, 18,600 grt. Heli-copter platform; hangar to port recently enlarged to hold two Sea King helicopters, but normally only one is carried. Can carry 18,400 tons fuel oil, 1,720 tons diesel, 3,730 tons aircraft fuel, and 130 tons lube oil. RFA-operated. Now have MARISAT commercial communications satellite system.

♦ **1 later Tide class** Bldr: Hawthorn Leslie, Hebburn-on-Tyne

	Laid down	L	In serv.
A 76 TIDEPOOL	4-12-61	11-12-62	28-6-63

D: 8,531 tons light (27,400 fl)   **S:** 18.3 kts
Dim: 177.6 (167.65 pp) × 21.64 × 9.75
Electron Equipt: Radar: 1 Kelvin-Hughes 14/12, 1 Kelvin-Hughes 14/16
M: 1 set Pamatreda GT; 1 prop; 15,000 hp
Man: 30 officers, 80 men, plus air group

REMARKS: RFA-operated; 18,900 dwt, 14,130 grt. As built, carried 17,400 tons fuel oil and 700 tons diesel, but with RN dependence on gas-turbine propulsion, propor-tions may have changed. Hangar and flight deck for 1 Wessex 5 helicopter. Sister *Tidespring* (A 75) discarded at end 1981. *Tidepool* to sell to Chile, 1982.

Tidepool (A 76)   C. Dragonette, 1980

SMALL FLEET OILERS

♦ **5 Rover class** Bldr: Swan Hunter, Hebburn-on-Tyne

		L	In serv.
A 268	GREEN ROVER	19-12-68	15-8-69
A 269	GREY ROVER	17-4-69	10-4-70
A 270	BLUE ROVER	11-11-69	15-7-70
A 271	GOLD ROVER	7-3-73	22-3-74
A 273	BLACK ROVER	30-10-73	23-8-74

Grey Rover (A 269)   G. Arra, 1978

Blue Rover (A 270)   G. Arra, 1975

SMALL FLEET OILERS *(continued)*

Black Rover (A 273)   G. Arra, 1976

D: 4,700 tons light (11,522 fl)   **S:** 19.25 kts   **Dim:** 140.5 × 19.2 × 7.3
M: 2 SEMT-Pielstick 16PA 4 diesels; 1 CP prop; 15,300 hp   **Electric:** 2,720 kw
Fuel: 965 tons   **Range:** 15,000/15   **Man:** 16 officers, 31 men

REMARKS: RFA-operated; 6,822 dwt (A 271, A 273: 6,692 dwt), 7,510 grt. Carry 6,600 tons of fuel plus water, dry stores, and provisions. Helicopter deck but no hangar. A 271 is used in training. First three re-engined 1973-74.

SUPPORT OILERS

♦ **2 (+1) Appleleaf class** Bldr: Cammell Laird, Birkenhead

	L	In serv.
A 79 APPLELEAF (ex-*Hudson Cavalier*)	24-7-75	11-79
A 81 BRAMBLELEAF (ex-*Hudson Deep*)	22-1-76	3-80
A. . . N. . . (ex-*Hudson Progress*)	. . .	. . .

Appleleaf (A 79)—in light condition   1980

D: 40,200 tons (fl)   **S:** 16.4 kts   **Dim:** 170.69 (163.51 pp) × 25.94 × 11.56
M: 2 Crossley-Pielstick 14PC2V-400 diesels; 1 CP prop; 14,000 hp
Fuel: 2,498 tons   **Man:** 65 tot.

REMARKS: RFA-operated. A 79 chartered 1978 and refitted 12-78 to 11-79 at Wallsend Dry Docks; stack raised 3.5 m, dry cargo hold added forward, replenishment-at-sea working deck added amidships (but *no* RAS equipment installed), and superstructure enlarged aft. A 81 given similar refit by Cammell Laird after charter in 1979, completing 1980. The third unit was chartered 3-4-81 and was to be similarly altered prior to service. Average 20,440 grt, 33,750 dwt. The fourth ship of this class, typed C 13A by the builders, may be chartered later. There are plans to fit the remaining at-sea-replenishment gear later in all of them.

♦ **2 Leaf-group support oilers**

A 78 PLUMLEAF Bldr: Blyth DD & SB (L: 29-3-60; In serv. 8-60)

Plumleaf (A 78)   1978

D: 26,480 tons (fl)   **S:** 15.5 kts   **Dim:** 170.8 × 22.0 × 9.2
M: 1 6-cyl. Doxford diesel; 1 prop; 9,500-hp   **Fuel:** 684 tons

REMARKS: RFA-operated; 19,430 dwt, 12,459 grt. Chartered 7-60 through 1982. Can refuel at sea alongside (two stations) or astern.

A 77 PEARLEAF Bldr: Blythwood SB, Scotstoun (L: 15-10-59; In serv. 2-60)

Pearleaf (A 77)   S. Terzibaschitsch, 1977

D: 25,790 tons (fl)   **S:** 16 kts   **Dim:** 173.2 (162.7 pp) × 21.9 × 9.2
M: 1 Rowan-Doxford 6-cyl. diesel; 1 prop; 8,800 hp   **Electric:** 700 kw
Fuel: 1,410 tons

REMARKS: RFA-operated; 18,711 dwt, 12,353 grt. Can refuel at sea alongside (two stations) or astern. On charter to RFA to 1983.

NOTE: The surviving "Eddy"-class coastal tanker, *Eddyfirth* (A 261) was stricken 3-81.

MISCELLANEOUS AUXILIARY SHIPS

♦ **1 helicopter training ship**

	Bldr	Laid down	L	In serv.
K 08 ENGADINE	Henry Robb Ltd.	9-8-65	16-9-66	15-12-67

MISCELLANEOUS AUXILIARY SHIPS *(continued)*

Engadine (K 08)   G. Arra, 1976

D: 3,640 tons light (8,690 fl) **S:** 16 kts **Dim:** 129.31 × 17.86 × 6.73
M: 1 Sulzer 5RD68, 5-cyl. diesel; 1 prop; 5,500 hp **Electric:** 1,200 kw
Fuel: 450 tons **Man:** 61 RFA plus 14 RN (and air group: 29 officers, 84 men)

REMARKS: Intended to train flight crews in ASW helicopter procedures at sea. The
hangar can hold either four Wessex or two Sea King and two Wasp. A smaller hangar
atop the superstructure serves a target-drone launch facility. Equipped with Denny-
Brown fin stabilizers and has remote bridge control for all engineering plant. Many
internal compartments are voids. RFA-operated. 6,384 grt, 4,520 dwt.

♦ **1 antarctic patrol ship**

	Bldr	L	In serv.
A 171 ENDURANCE (ex-*Anita Dan*)	Krögerwerft, Rendsburg	25-5-56	12-56

Endurance (A 171)   Skyfotos Ltd., 1978

D: 3,600 tons (fl) **S:** 14.5 kts **Dim:** 93.58 (82.9 pp) × 14.03 × 5.03
A: 2/20-mm AA (I × 2) **Electron Equipt:** Radar: 2/Decca TM 829
M: 1 Burmeister & Wain 550VTBF, 5-cyl. diesel; 1 prop; 3,220 hp (plus a bow-
thruster)
Range: 12,000/14 **Man:** 13 officers, 106 men, up to 12 scientists

REMARKS: Purchased 20-2-67. Hull painted red, superstructure white. Carries two
Wasp helicopters and two survey launches. Converted 1967-68 by Harland & Wolff,
Belfast, to support the British Antarctic Survey and act as guard ship in the Falkland

Islands; 2,641 grt. Large radome added atop hangar 1978 for antenna for MARISAT
satellite communications system. Reportedly, will be discarded during 1982.

♦ **1 royal yacht**

	Bldr	Laid down	L	In serv.
(A 00) BRITANNIA	J. Brown (Clydebank)	7-52	16-4-53	14-1-54

Britannia   G. Arra, 1977

D: 3,990 tons (4,961 fl) **S:** 21 kts **Dim:** 125.9 (115.82 pp) × 16.76 × 4.86
Electron Equipt: Radar: 2/1006 **M:** 2 sets GT; 2 props; 12,000 hp
Boilers: 2 **Fuel:** 510 tons **Range:** 3,100/20 **Man:** 21 officers, 256 men

REMARKS: 5,769 grt. Naval-manned, with a rear admiral as commanding officer in
1981. In wartime, would become a hospital ship (200 beds and 60 medical personnel)
and have a helicopter platform. Gyrofin stabilizers. Reboiled during 1980 refit.

♦ **1 submarine-support ship**

A 236 WAKEFUL (ex-*Dan*, ex-*Herakles*)   Bldr: Cochrane, Selkirk (In serv. 1965)

Wakeful (A 236)   J. Goss, 1980

MISCELLANEOUS AUXILIARY SHIPS (continued)

D: 1,100 tons (fl) **S:** . . . kts **Dim:** 44.43 (38.86 pp) × 10.7 × 4.74
Electron Equipt: Radar: 1/1006 **M:** Ruston & Hornsby 9-cyl. diesels; 1 prop; 4,750 hp
Electric: 380 kw **Man:** 18 tot.

REMARKS: Former commercial tug, 492 grt. Purchased 1974 from Sweden to act as submarine target ship and safety vessel at Faslane; subsequently, also used occasionally on fisheries patrol duties. Naval-manned. Very expensive to operate.

♦ **1 seabed operations tender**

	Bldr	Laid down	L	In serv.
A. . . CHALLENGER	Scotts SB, Govan	25-1-80	19-5-81	. . .

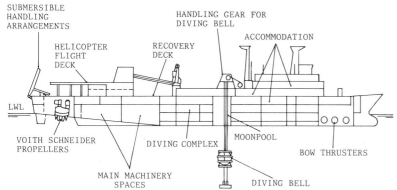

Challenger—The general arrangement of the Seabed Operations Vessel building at Scotts for the Royal Navy.

D: 6,400 tons (7,200 fl) **S:** 15 kts **Dim:** 134.0 (130.5 pp) × 15.0 × . . .
Electron Equipt: Radar: 1/1006
Sonar: 1/2008, 1/2013
M: 5 Ruston 16 RK3CZ diesels (3,430 hp each), electric drive; 2 Voith-Schneider vertical cycloidal props aft; 10,200 hp (three bow-thrusters) **Electric:** 1,500 kw harbor service **Man:** 186 tot.

REMARKS: Ordered 28-9-79 as a replacement for *Reclaim.* To be navy-manned. Will have a dynamic positioning system capable of maintaining a constant location in 50- to 60-kt winds, in a sea state of 5. Will carry a submersible decompression chamber for divers and will be equipped for saturation diving. Twelve divers and their equipment to be handled through a "moon-pool" amidships by a 25-ton crane, while a gallows crane on the stern will handle submersibles. Will have a passive tank stabilization system. The integrated navigational system, with a GEC 4070 computer, to incorporate Decca "Hi-Fix," Omega, navigational satellite reception, and DECCA. The helo platform will accept Sea King.

NOTE: The submarine rescue and salvage ship *Reclaim* (A 231) was stricken 1-80.

♦ **1 offshore support and salvage ship**

. . . SEAFORTH CLANSMAN Bldr: Cochrane, Selby (In serv. 1977)

Seaforth Clansman   J.-C. Bellonne, 1980

D: 3,320 tons (fl) **S:** 14 kts **Dim:** 78.6 (68.7 pp) × 13.7 × 5.01
M: 4 Mirrlees-Blackstone EZSL-12 diesels; 2 CP, Kort-nozzle props; 7,320 hp
Electric: 1,748 kw **Fuel:** 404 tons **Man:** 46 tot. (plus 20-man naval salvage group)

REMARKS: RFA-operated; chartered 1978, extended through 1984. The ship was originally intended for oilfield support duties and for maintaining single-point deep moorings. Has a submersible diver's decompression chamber and a "moonpool" opening through the keel of the ship to ensure smooth waters for diving operations. Both bow and stern thrusters are fitted. Has a four-point mooring system and a 30-ton capacity electrohydraulic crane to port, aft. Four fire monitors atop the forward king post can each deliver 18,500 liters/min. 1,977 grt, 1,180 dwt. Has no pendant number.

♦ **1 cable-layer and repair ship**

	Bldr	L	In serv.
A 259 ST. MARGARETS	Swan Hunter	10-43	3-4-44

St. Margarets (A 259)   J. Goss, 1981

MISCELLANEOUS AUXILIARY SHIPS (continued)

D: 1,300 tons (2,500 fl) **S:** 12 kts **Dim:** 76.8 (69.7 pp) × 10.9 × 4.8
M: Triple-expansion; 2 props; 1,250 hp **Boilers:** 2 Scotch, 17 kg/cm²
Fuel: 261 tons

REMARKS: 1,200 dwt, 1,524 grt. Lays and recovers cables over the bow. Sister *Bullfinch* stricken 1975. RMAS-operated.

MOORING, SALVAGE, AND NET TENDERS

♦ 2 Pochard class

	Bldr	L	In serv.
(A 164) POCHARD (ex-P 197)	Robb Caledon Ltd.	21-6-73	11-12-73
(A 165) GOOSANDER (ex-P 196)	Robb Caledon Ltd.	12-4-73	10-9-73

Goosander (A 165)   Robb Caledon, 1974

D: 750 tons (1,200 fl) **S:** 10 kts **Dim:** 55.4 (48.8 pp) × 12.2 × 5.5
M: 2 Paxman RPHXM 16-cyl. diesels; 550 hp **Range:** 3,250/9.5 **Man:** 26 tot.

REMARKS: RMAS-operated. All mooring, salvage, and boom vessels are multi-purpose and are capable of transporting and servicing moorings, performing salvage duties, and, in wartime, handling harbor-defense nets. Can dead-lift 200 tons over bow horns.

♦ 4 Wild Duck class

	Bldr	L	In serv.
P 192 MANDARIN	Cammell Laird	17-9-63	5-3-64
P 193 PINTAIL	Cammell Laird	3-12-63	3-64
P 194 GARGANEY	Brooke Marine Ltd.	13-12-65	20-9-66
P 195 GOLDENEYE	Brooke Marine Ltd.	31-3-66	21-12-66

Goldeneye (P 195)   G. Gyssels, 1981

D: 850 tons (1,300 fl) (P 192, P 193: 941/1,622 tons) **S:** 10.8 kts
Dim: 57.86 (47.24 pp) × 13.0 × 3.2 (P 192, P 193: 60.23 × 12.22 × 4.21)
M: 2 Davey-Paxman 16-cyl. diesels; 1 CP prop; 550 hp (P 192, P 193: 750 hp)
Electric: P 194, P 195: 640 kw; P 192, P 193: 405 kw **Range:** 3,000/10
Man: 7 officers, 18 men

REMARKS: RMAS-operated. *Pintail* has extra accommodations for divers in deckhouse abaft stack. 200-ton deadlift capacity over bow.

♦ 4 "Kin" class

	Bldr	Laid down	L	In serv.
(A 232) KINGARTH	Alex. Hall, Aberdeen	16-7-43	22-5-44	28-12-44
(A 281) KINBRACE	Alex. Hall, Aberdeen	20-4-44	17-1-45	30-4-45
(A 482) KINLOSS	Alex. Hall, Aberdeen	. . .	. . .	9-7-45
(A 507) UPLIFTER	Smith's Dock Co.	13-2-43	29-11-43	6-4-44

D: 950 tons (1,050 fl) **S:** 9 kts **Dim:** 54.0 × 10.6 × 3.6
M: 1 Atlas Polar M44M diesel; 630 hp **Man:** 34 tot.

REMARKS: RMAS-operated; 200-tons lift. Originally had reciprocating steam engines; diesels fitted 1964-67. 775 grt, 262 dwt.

NOTE: The Insect-class fleet tender *Scarab* is also equipped as a moorings tender (10-ton lift). The "Lay"-class mooring, salvage, and net tender *Laymoor* (P 190) was stricken 1-80.

SEAGOING TUGS

♦ 3 Roysterer class Bldr: C. D. Holmes, Hull

	L	In serv.
A 361 ROYSTERER	20-5-70	25-4-72
A 502 ROLLICKER	29-1-71	2-73
(A 366) ROBUST	7-10-71	6-4-74

Roysterer (A 361)   G. Arra, 1977

D: 1,630 tons (fl) **S:** 15 kts **Dim:** 54.8 (49.4 pp) × 11.6 × 5.5
M: 2 Mirrlees KMR6 diesels; 2 CP props; 4,500 hp
Range: 13,000/12
Man: 10 officers, 21 men (plus 10-man RN salvage party if needed)

REMARKS: RMAS-operated; 50-ton bollard pull. Although designed for long-distance towing, have been used primarily in port service, at Devonport (A 502: the Clyde).

♦ 1 Typhoon class Bldr: H. Robb, Leith

	L	In serv.
A 95 TYPHOON	14-10-58	1960

SEAGOING TUGS *(continued)*

Typhoon (A 95)   G. Arra, 1975

D: 800 tons (1,380 fl) **S:** 17 kts **Dim:** 60.5 × 12.3 × 4.0
M: 2 12-cyl. diesels; 1 CP prop; 2,750 hp

REMARKS: RMAS-operated; 32-ton bollard pull. Based at Portland.

♦ **5 Confiance class** Bldrs: A. & S. Inglis, Glasgow, except A 88: Goole SB Co.

(A 88) AGILE (In serv. 7-59)	(A 289) CONFIANCE (In serv. 3-56)
(A 89) ADVICE (In serv. 10-59)	(A 290) CONFIDENT (In serv. 1-56)
(A 90) ACCORD (In serv. 9-58)	

Agile (A 88)   G. Arra, 1976

D: 760 tons (fl) **S:** 13 kts **Dim:** 47.2 (42.7 pp) × 10.7 × 3.4
M: 4 Paxman HAXM diesels; 2 CP props; 1,800 hp
Man: 29 tot. plus 13 salvage

REMARKS: RMAS-operated. *Agile* only unit with tall mainmast.

SERVICE CRAFT

AMMUNITION TRANSPORTS

♦ **2 Throsk class**

	Bldr	Laid down	L	In serv.
A 378 KINTERBURY	Cleland SB, Wallsend	1980	8-11-80	20-1-81
A 379 THROSK	Cleland SB, Wallsend	25-8-76	31-3-77	20-9-77

Throsk (A 379)   J. Goss, 1980

D: 2,193 tons (fl) **S:** 14 kts **Dim:** 70.57 (64.31 pp) × 11.9 × 4.57
M: 2 Mirrlees-Blackstone diesels; 1 prop; 3,000 hp **Range:** 1,500/14, 5,000/10
Man: 10 officers, 22 men

REMARKS: RMAS-operated. Two holds, two 5-ton cranes; 1,150 dwt. Two cargo holds:
750 m³ total. Can transport 760 tons in holds plus 25 tons of cargo on deck. A 378
has improved accommodations. Sister *St. George* (in serv. 4-81) operated by Army's
Royal Corps of Transport.

DEGAUSSING TENDERS

♦ **2 Magnet class** Bldr: Clelands, Wallsend

	Laid down	L	In serv.
A 114 MAGNET	3-11-78	12-7-79	15-11-79
A 115 LODESTONE	22-12-78	15-11-79	4-80

D: 950 grt **S:** 12 kts **Dim:** 54.8 (50.0 pp) × 11.4 × 3.0
M: 2 Mirrlees-Blackstone ESL-6-MGR diesels, electric drive; 2 props; 1,650 hp
Electric: 245 kw **Fuel:** 40 tons **Range:** 1,750/12 **Man:** 15 tot.

REMARKS: Built to commercial standards. RMAS-operated. Use two 800-cell, 400-V
battery banks and two variable-resistance capacitors to provide 4,000 amps DC for
40 seconds. Can deperm a 60,000-ton ship.

NOTE: The three "Ham"-class degaussing tenders, *Fordham*, *Thatcham*, and *War-
mingham*, were stricken 1980.

DEGAUSSING TENDERS *(continued)*

Lodestone (A 115)   J. Goss, 1981

TORPEDO RETRIEVERS

◆ **4 Tornado class** Bldr: Hall Russell, Aberdeen

	Laid down	L	In serv.
(A 140) TORNADO	2-11-78	24-5-79	15-11-79
(A 141) TORCH	5-12-78	7-8-79	12-2-80
(A 142) TORMENTOR	19-3-79	6-11-79	29-4-80
(A 143) TOREADOR	14-6-79	14-2-80	1-7-80

Tornado (A 140)   J. Goss, 1981

D: 660 tons (698 fl) **S:** 14 kts **Dim:** 47.47 (40.0 pp) × 8.53 × 3.0
M: 2 Lister-Blackstone ESL-8-MGR diesels; 2 props; 2,200 hp
Fuel: 110 tons **Range:** 3,000/. . . **Man:** 17 tot.

REMARKS: RMAS-operated.

◆ **2 Torrent class**

	Bldr	L	In serv.
(A 127) TORRENT	Cleland SB, Wallsend	29-3-71	10-9-71
(A 128) TORRID	Cleland SB, Wallsend	7-9-71	1-72

Torrent (A 127)   1972

D: 468 tons (685 fl) **S:** 11.5 kts **Dim:** 49.55 (44.2 pp) × 9.72 × 3.05
M: Paxman 16 RPHM diesel; 1 prop; 700 hp **Electric:** 300 kw **Fuel:** 49 tons
Range: 1,500/11 **Man:** 19 tot.

REMARKS: Can stow 32 torpedoes in hold and 10 on deck and perform post-firing maintenance. Stern ramp for recovery. RMAS-operated.

◆ **1 converted customs craft**

ENDEAVOR Bldr: R. Dunston, Thorne (In serv. 1966)

D: 88 tons (fl) **S:** 10.5 kts **Dim:** 23.2 × 4.4 × 2.0
M: 1 Lister-Blackstone diesel; 337 hp

REMARKS: RMAS-operated. Resembles a small tug; cannot bring recovered torpedoes aboard. Also used as range safety craft at Portland.

◆ **3 torpedo recovery launches** Bldr: R. Dunston, Thorne (In serv. 1979)

D: 15 tons **S:** 9 kts **Dim:** 13.8 × 2.98 × 0.76
M: 1 Perkins 6-354 diesel; 1 prop; 104 hp **Man:** 4 tot.

◆ **1 ex-RAF RTTL Mk 2-class former target-tow launch**

OSPREY (ex-RAF 2770) (In serv. 1940s)

D: 34.6 tons (fl) **S:** 30 kts **Dim:** 20.7 × 5.8 × 1.8
M: 2 Rolls-Royce Sea Griffon gasoline engines; 2 props; 2,200 hp **Man:** 9 tot.

◆ **1 ex-RAF 1300 series former air-sea rescue launch**

L 72 (ex-RAF. . .) (In serv. 1955-56)

D: 28.3 tons (fl) **S:** 13 kts **Dim:** 19.2 × 4.7 × 1.5
M: 2 Rolls-Royce C8 diesels; 2 props; 190 hp

NOTE: The six "Ham"-class former inshore minesweepers converted to serve as torpedo retrievers were stricken: *Bucklesham, Fritham,* and *Downham* in 1979, *Haversham* and *Everingham* in 1980, and *Lasham* in 1981.

DIVING TENDERS

♦ **5 modified Cartmel class** Bldr: Gregson, Blyth

A 305 ILCHESTER   A 318 IXWORTH
A 309 INSTOW   A . . . N . . .
A 311 IRONBRIDGE (ex-*Invergorden*)

REMARKS: RMAS-operated, except A 308 and A 309, by Navy. All in service 1974, except new unit, ordered 7-80. Details and appearance as for *Cartmel*-class tenders, except for a decompression chamber on deck forward, beneath a stowage platform for a Gemini dinghy. Can be used for harbor mine clearance. Displacement is 150 tons (fl).

♦ **1 Datchet class** Bldr: Vosper, Singapore (In serv. 1968)

DATCHET

Datchet   G. Arra, 1975

D: 70 tons (fl)   **S:** 12 kts   **Dim:** 22.86 × 5.79 × 1.22
M: 2 Gray Marine diesels; 2 props; 500 hp   **Range:** 500/12

REMARKS: RMAS-operated.

TRAINING CRAFT

♦ **4 modified "Loyal" class** Bldr: R. Dunston, Thorne

	Laid down	L	In serv.
(A. . .) MANLY	18-9-80	7-81	1981
(A. . .) MENTOR	20-10-80	9-81	. . .
(A. . .) MILBROOK	30-1-82	. . .	. . .
(A. . .) MESSINA	. . .	. . .	. . .

D: 150 tons (fl)   **S:** 11.5 kts   **Dim:** 24.00 × 6.40 × 2.20
M: 1 Lister-Blackstone ES-8-M diesel; 1 cycloidal prop; 615 hp   **Fuel:** 4.5 tons
Man: 6 tot. (plus trainees)

REMARKS: First three to serve HMS Raleigh training facility; last for Royal Marine training.

♦ **1 "Ham"-class former inshore minesweeper**

M 2793 THORNHAM

D: 120 tons (157 fl)   **S:** 14 kts   **Dim:** 32.47 (30.48 pp) × 6.61 × 1.75
A: 1/20-mm AA   **Electron Equipt:** Radar: 1/978   **Range:** 2,350/9   **Man:** 15 tot.
M: 2 Paxman YHAXM 12-cyl. diesels; 2 props; 1,100 hp   **Fuel:** 15 tons

REMARKS: Attached to Aberdeen University naval training unit. All minesweeping gear removed. Sisters *Dittisham* (M 2621) and *Flintham* stricken 7-81 and 12-81, respectively.

♦ **1 Ley-class former inshore minehunter** Bldr: J. S. White, Cowes

	Laid down	L	In serv.
M 2002 AVELEY	9-10-51	16-2-53	3-2-54

Aveley (M 2002)   G. Arra, 1976

D: 123 tons (140 fl)   **S:** 14 kts   **Dim:** 32.44 (30.48 pp) × 6.1 × 1.68
Electron Equipt: Radar: 1/978
M: 2 Paxman YHAXM 12-cyl. diesels; 2 props; 1,100 hp   **Electric:** 108 kw
Man: 15 tot.

REMARKS: Survivor of 10 built. *Aveley* launched 1953. Had sonars vice magnetic sweep gear; otherwise similar to "Ham" class but with larger superstructure. Sister *Isis* (M 2010) stricken 1981; M 2002, tender at Plymouth, will likely soon follow.

♦ **2 Ford-class former submarine chasers**

	Bldr	In serv.
P 3104 DEE (ex-*Beckford*)	Wm. Simons, Renfrew	1953
P 3113 DROXFORD	Isaac Pimblott, Northwich	1954

D: 115 tons (138 fl)   **S:** 18 kts   **Dim:** 35.76 (33.53 pp) × 6.1 × 1.68
A: Removed   **Electron Equipt:** Radar: 1/978
M: 2 Paxman YHAXM diesels (500 hp each), 1 Foden FD 6 diesel (100 hp); 3 props
Fuel: 23 tons   **Range:** 500/12; 1,000/8 (cruise diesel)   **Man:** 19 tot.

REMARKS: Survivors of a class of 20, some transferred abroad. *Dee* launched 1953; *Droxford* 1954. P 3104 attached to Liverpool University, P 3113 to Glasgow University for naval cadet training.

TRAINING CRAFT *(continued)*

NOTE: General-purpose tenders *Cromarty*, *Clovelly*, and *Froxfield* of the *Cartmel* class and *Alnmouth*, *Bembridge*, and *Aberdovey* of the *Aberdovey* class are also employed in training; *see* under General-purpose Tenders for data.

FUEL LIGHTERS

♦ **6 Oil class** Bldr: Appledore SB (All in serv. 1979)

		L			L
(Y 21)	OILPRESS	10-6-68	(Y 24)	OILFIELD	5-9-68
(Y 22)	OILSTONE	11-7-68	(Y 25)	OILBIRD	21-11-68
(Y 23)	OILWELL	20-1-69	(Y 26)	OILMAN	18-2-69

Oilfield (Y 24) G. Arra, 1977

D: 250 tons (535 fl) **S:** 10 kts **Dim:** 42.26 (39.62 pp) × 7.47 × 2.51
Electron Equipt: Radar: 1/978
M: 1 Lister-Blackstone ES-6-MGR diesel; 405 hp **Electric:** 225 kw
Fuel: 15 tons **Range:** 1,500/10 **Man:** 4 officers, 7 men

REMARKS: First three carry diesel fuel and are 247 tons (527 fl); other three carry fuel oil. RMAS-operated.

WATER LIGHTERS

♦ **7 Water class** Bldr: Drypool, Hull, except A 146: R. Dunston, Hessle

		In serv.			In serv.
(Y 17)	WATERFALL	1967	(Y 30)	WATERCOURSE	1974
(Y 18)	WATERSHED	1967	(Y 31)	WATERFOWL	25-5-74
(Y 19)	WATERSPOUT	1967	A 146	WATERMAN	6-78
(Y 20)	WATERSIDE	1968			

D: 344 tons (fl) **S:** 11 kts **Dim:** 40.02 (37.5 pp) × 7.5 × 2.44
Electron Equipt: Radar: 1/975 or 978
M: 1 Lister-Blackstone ERS-8-MGR diesel; 600 hp **Electric:** 155 kw
Range: 1,500/11 **Man:** 11 tot.

REMARKS: RMAS-operated. Built 1966-73. Carry 150 tons water cargo. Resemble "Oil" class. Y 30, Y 31, and A 146 have deckhouse over after cargo tanks.

NOTE: "Spa"-class water lighter *Spapool* (A 222) stricken 1980; "Fresh"-class water lighters stricken: *Freshlake* in 1980, *Freshspring* in 1978, and *Freshburn* in 1980.

Waterside (Y 20) G. Arra, 1977

TANK-CLEANING CRAFT

♦ **3 Isles-class converted escorts**

		Bldr	Laid down	L	In serv.
(A 332)	CALDY	John Lewis	6-5-43	31-8-43	7-1-44
(A 336)	LUNDY	Cook, Whelton & Gemmell	6-6-42	29-8-42	15-1-43
(A 346)	SWITHA	A. & J. Inglis	31-5-41	3-4-42	15-6-42

D: 560 tons (770 fl) **S:** 12 kts **Dim:** 49.99 (45.72 pp) × 8.43 × 4.9
M: 1 set triple-expansion reciprocating; 1 prop; 850 ihp (510 ihp sust.)
Boilers: 1 Scotch-type; 10.6 kg/cm² **Fuel:** 183 tons coal **Range:** 4,200/8

REMARKS: Survivors of 155 built as ASW trawlers or minesweepers. Converted 1951-57 for cleaning fuel tanks of other ships. All to be stricken 1981-82.

GENERAL-PURPOSE TENDERS

♦ **7 100-foot "Insect" class** Bldr: C.D. Holmes, Beverley (In serv. 1970-73)

(A 216)	BEE	(A 230)	COCKCHAFER	(A 253)	LADYBIRD	(A 272)	SCARAB
(A 229)	CRICKET	(A 239)	GNAT	(A 263)	CICADA		

Bee (A 216) G. Arra, 1977

GENERAL-PURPOSE TENDERS *(continued)*

D: 213 tons (450 fl) **S:** 10.5 kts **Dim:** 34.06 (30.48 pp) × 8.53 × 3.2
Electron Equipt: Radar: 1/978
M: 1 Lister-Blackstone ERS-8-HGR diesel; 660 hp **Man:** 10 tot.

REMARKS: RMAS-operated; 200 tons cargo, one 3-ton crane. *Scarab*, with 5-ton winch and bow horn, is used as a moorings tender; *Gnat* and *Ladybird* transport ammunition.

◆ 9 "Loyal" class Bldr: R. Dunston, Thorne

	In serv.		In serv.
A 157 LOYAL HELPER	1978	A 382 LOYAL FACTOR	1974
A 158 SUPPORTER	1977	(ex-*Vigilant* (P 254),	
(ex-*Loyal Supporter*)		ex-*Loyal Factor*)	
A 159 LOYAL WATCHER	1977	A 510 LOYAL GOVERNOR	1975
A 160 LOYAL VOLUNTEER	1977	(ex-*Alert*, P 252,	
A 220 LOYAL MODERATOR	1973	ex-*Loyal Governor*)	
		A 1770 LOYAL CHANCELLOR	1972
		A 1771 LOYAL PROCTOR	1973

Loyal Proctor (A 1771)   G. Arra, 1977

REMARKS: RMAS-operated. Details as for *Cartmel* class but equipped to carry up to 200 personnel in cargo hold for short distances (except *Loyal Moderator*, RMAS training craft, 12 extra berths instead). A 382 and A 510 operated as patrol craft off Ulster until late 1981/early 1982. A 158 operates as a stores carrier from Belfast. Four very similar craft built as training tenders; *see above*.

◆ 33 Cartmel class Bldrs: (A): Isaac Pimblott & Sons, Northwich;
(B): C.D. Holmes, Beverley;
(C): John Lewis, Aberdeen;
(D): R. Dunston, Thorne;
(E): J. Cook, Wivenhoe

	Bldr	In serv.		Bldr	In serv.
(A 350) CARTMEL	A	1968	(A 365) FULBECK	B	1969
(A 351) CAWSAND	A	1968	(A 392) GLENCOE	A	1971
(A 370) CLOVELLY	A	1971	(A 402) GRASMERE	C	1970
(A 391) CRICCIETH	A	1971	(A 1769) HAMBLEDON	D	1972
(A 381) CRICKLADE	B	1970	(A 1768) HARLECH	D	1972
(A 488) CROMARTY	C	1970	(A 1776) HEADCORN	D	1972
(A 363) DENMEAD	B	1970	(A 1767) HEVER	D	1972
(A 490) DORNOCH	C	1970	(A 1772) HOLMWOOD	D	1973
(A 393) DUNSTER	D	1970	(A 1773) HORNING	D	1973
(A 353) ELKSTONE	E	1969	(A 208) LAMLASH	D	1973
(A 277) ELSING	E	1970	(A 211) LECHLADE	D	1973
(A 355) EPWORTH	E	1970	(A 207) LANDOVERY	D	1973
(A 274) ETTRICK	E	1970	(A. . .) MELTON	D	6-81
(A 348) FELSTED	D	1970	(A. . .) MENAI	D	1981
(A 394) FINTRY	C	1970	(A. . .) MEON	D	1981
(A 341) FOTHERBY	D	1970	(A. . .) MILFORD	D	1982
(A 354) FROXFIELD	D	1970			

Froxfield (A 354)   G. Gyssels, 1979

D: 143 tons (fl) **S:** 10.5 kts **Dim:** 24.38 (22.86 pp) × 6.4 × 1.98
Electron Equipt: Radar: 1/978 (not on all)
M: 1 Lister-Blackstone ERS-4-MGR diesel; 330 hp **Electric:** 106 kw
Range: 700/10 **Man:** 6 tot.

REMARKS: RMAS-operated except *Ettrick* and *Elsing*, which are RN-manned and used for patrol at Gibraltar. Improved version of *Aberdovey* class; 25 tons cargo. First two, 5.49-meter beam. Carry stores, personnel, food. Can tow. *Clovelly*, *Cromarty*, and *Froxfield* are also used for training, and *Dornoch* and *Fotherby* have been used as diving tenders. The four new units were ordered 25-2-80.

◆ 12 Aberdovey class Bldr: (A): Isaac Pimblott & Sons, Northwich;
(B): J. S. Doig, Grimsby

	Bldr	In serv.		Bldr	In serv.
(Y 10) ABERDOVEY	A	1963	(Y 13) ALNMOUTH	A	1966
(Y 11) ABINGER	A	1964	(Y 14) APPLEBY	A	1967
(Y 12) ALNESS	A	1965	(Y 16) ASHCOTT	A	1968

GENERAL-PURPOSE TENDERS *(continued)*

(A 99)	BEAULIEU	B	1966	(A 103)	BIBURY	B	1969
(A 100)	BEDDGELERT	B	1967	(A 104)	BLAKENEY	B	1970
(A 101)	BEMBRIDGE	B	1968	(A 105)	BRODICK	B	1970

Beaulieu (A 99)   G. Arra, 1976

D: 117.5 tons (fl) **S:** 10.5 kts **Dim:** 24.16 (22.86 pp) × 5.79 × 1.68
Electron Equipt: Radar: 1/978
M: 1 Lister-Blackstone ER-4-MGR diesel; 225 hp **Range:** 700/10 **Man:** 6 tot.

REMARKS: RMAS-operated. Carry 25 tons cargo. *Alnmouth* and *Bembridge* used for Sea Cadet Corps training; *Aberdovey* used for training Royal Marines.

♦ **1 converted ex-stern trawler** Bldr: P. K. Harris, Appledore (In serv. 1962)

A 362 DOLWEN (ex-*Hector Gull*)

D: 602 tons (fl) **S:** ... kts **Dim:** 39.65 (36.73 pp) × 9.12 × 4.40
M: 1 National FSSM-6 diesel; 1 CP prop; 1,160 hp

REMARKS: Gallows at stern for laying buoys; used as air bombardment safety range craft. Operated by a private contractor.

♦ **3 "Ham"-class former inshore minesweepers**

(M 2781) PORTISHAM   (M 2726) SHIPHAM   (M 2791) SANDRINGHAM

REMARKS: RMAS-operated. Built 1953-57. Details as for "Ham"-class training craft; no armament, all sweep gear removed. Carry passengers and stores. M 2726 temporarily used as an inshore survey ship, 1978-79. M 2791 has a broad deckhouse extending nearly to the stern and is used as a personnel ferry in the Clyde. Sisters *Pagham*, *Puttenham*, and *Tongham* discarded 1980.

♦ **13 motor fishing vessel tenders**

6 stores carriers: MFV 7 (1943), MFV 15 (1942), MFV 96 (1944), MFV 256 (1944), MFV 740 (1945), MFV 911 (1945)
3 general-purpose: MFV 140 (1946), MFV 175 (1945), MFV 816 (1945)
4 diving tenders: MFV 119 (1944), MFV 642 (1945), MFV 775 (1945), MFV 1077 (1944)

REMARKS: Wooden-hulled fishing boats of varying characteristics. Normally have double-ended hulls, engines and pilothouse aft.

LARGE HARBOR TUGS

♦ **4 Adept-class "Twin-Unit Tractors"** Bldr: R. Dunston, Hessle

		Laid down	L	In serv.
(A 224)	ADEPT	22-7-79	27-8-80	28-10-80
(A 225)	BUSTLER	28-11-79	20-2-80	...
(A 226)	CAPABLE	5-9-80	...	...
(A 227)	CAREFUL	...	...	...

Bustler (A 225)   L. & L. Van Ginderen, 1981

D: 450 tons **S:** 12 kts **Dim:** 39.0 (37.0 pp) × ... × ...
Electron Equipt: Radar: 1/...
M: 2 Lister-Blackstone diesels; 2 Voith-Schneider vertical-cycloidal props; 2,640 hp
Electric: ... **Man:** ... tot.

REMARKS: RMAS-operated. Ordered 22-2-79. 28-ton bollard pull.

♦ **19 Dog class** Bldrs: Various (In serv. 1962-72)

(A 102)	AIREDALE	(A 155)	DEERHOUND	(A 188)	POINTER
(A 106)	ALSATIAN	(A 162)	ELKHOUND	(A 182)	SALUKI
(A 327)	BASSET	(A 326)	FOXHOUND	(A 187)	SEALYHAM
(A 126)	CAIRN		(ex-*Boxer*)	(A 189)	SETTER
(A 328)	COLLIE	(A 169)	HUSKY	(A 250)	SHEEPDOG
(A 330)	CORGI	(A 168)	LABRADOR	(A 201)	SPANIEL
(A 129)	DALMATIAN	(A 180)	MASTIFF		

D: 206 tons (248 fl) **S:** 12 kts **Dim:** 28.65 (25.91 pp) × 7.72 × 3.51
Electron Equipt: Radar: 1/978
M: 2 Lister-Blackstone ERS-86-MGR diesels; 1 prop; 1,320 hp
Electric: 80 kw **Man:** 8 tot.

REMARKS: RMAS-operated. 18.7-ton bollard pull. *Foxhound* renamed 22-10-77.

NOTE: The last *Dexterous* class paddle-tugs have been stricken, *Favourite* (A 87) in 1979, and *Forceful* (A 86) on 21-10-80, the latter after a collision.

LARGE HARBOR TUGS *(continued)*

Setter (A 189)   G. Arra, 1975

MEDIUM HARBOR TUGS

♦ **3 Frances class** Bldr: R. Dunston, Thorne

	Laid down	L	In serv.
(A 147) FRANCES	10-6-79	3-12-79	5-80
(A 149) FLORENCE	26-6-79	28-2-80	8-8-80
(A 150) GENEVIEVE	3-8-79	24-4-80	29-10-80

D: 80 grt **S:** 9 kts **Dim:** 21.5 (20.1 pp) × 6.4 × 2.1
M: 1 Mirrlees-Blackstone ERS-8M diesel; 1 vertical cycloidal prop; 615 hp
Fuel: 12 tons **Range:** 1,800/8 **Man:** 6 tot.

REMARKS: Ordered 13-12-78. RMAS-operated.

♦ **5 Felicity-class water tractors** Bldr: Hancock, Pembroke except *Felicity:* R. Dunston

	In serv.		In serv.
(A 112) FELICITY	1968	(A 196) GWENDOLINE	1974
(A 148) FIONA	1973	(A 198) HELEN	1974
(A 152) GEORGINA	1973		

D: 220 tons (fl) **S:** 10.2 kts **Dim:** 22.25 (20.73 pp) × 6.40 × 2.97
M: 1 Lister-Blackstone ERS-8-MGR diesel; cycloidal prop; 615 hp
Man: 6 tot.

REMARKS: RMAS-operated. 138 grt. 5.9 to 6.1-ton bollard pull.

♦ **8 modified "Girl" class** Bldrs: (A): Isaac Pimblott & Sons, Northwich; (B): R. Dunston, Thorne

	Bldr	In serv.		Bldr	In serv.
(A 210) CHARLOTTE	A	1966	(A 156) DAPHNE	B	1969
(A 217) CHRISTINE	A	1966	(A 252) DORIS	B	1969
(A 218) CLARE	A	1966	(A 173) DOROTHY	B	1969
(A 145) DAISY	B	1968	(A 178) EDITH	B	1969

D: 100 tons (fl) **S:** 10.5 kts **Dim:** 20.57 × 6.25 × 2.9
Electron Equipt: Radar: 1/978
M: 1 Lister-Blackstone ERS-6-MGR diesel; 495 hp
Range: 900/10 **Man:** 4 tot.

REMARKS: RMAS-operated; except *Clare*, used as patrol craft at Hong Kong and manned by Navy. *Celia* (A 206) sold commercially, 1971. 50 grt; 6.5-ton bollard pull.

Fiona (A 148)   G. Arra, 1977

Frances (A 147)   L. & L. Van Ginderen, 7-81

MEDIUM HARBOR TUGS *(continued)*

♦ **8 "Girl" class** Bldrs: (A) P. K. Harris; (B) R. Dunston, Thorne

		Bldr	In serv.			Bldr	In serv.
(A 116)	AGATHA	A	1961	(A 324)	BARBARA	B	1963
(A 121)	AGNES	A	1961	(A 232)	BETTY	B	1963
(A 113)	ALICE	A	1961	(A 335)	BRENDA	B	1963
(A 117)	AUDREY	A	1961	(A 322)	BRIDGET	B	1963

Bridget (A 322) G. Arra

D: 66.5 tons (81 fl) **S:** 10 kts **Dim:** 18.75 (17.3 pp) × 5.11 × 2.36
M: 1 Lister-Blackstone ERS-6-MGR diesel; 495 hp **Range:** 980/9.8
Man: 4 tot.

REMARKS: RMAS-operated. 40 grt; 6.5-tons bollard pull.

SMALL HARBOR TUGS

♦ **12 Triton-class water tractors** Bldr: R. Dunston, Thorne (In serv. 1972-73)

(A 181) IRENE	(A 166) KATHLEEN	(A 175) MARY
(A 183) ISABEL	(A 170) KITTY	(A 199) MYRTLE
(A 190) JOAN	(A 172) LESLEY	(A 202) NANCY
(A 193) JOYCE	(A 174) LILAH	(A 205) NORAH

D: 107.5 tons (fl) **S:** 7.75 kts **Dim:** 17.65 (16.76 pp) × 5.26 × 2.8
M: 1 Lister-Blackstone ERS-4-M diesel; cycloidal prop; 330 hp
Man: 6 tot.

REMARKS: RMAS-operated; 50 grt; 3-ton bollard pull. Voith vertical cycloidal prop to provide instant mobility and full power in any direction.

NOTE: Little information is available on the hundreds of smaller self-propelled service craft or on non-self-propelled units such as cargo, fuel, and water barges in service with the Royal Navy, Royal Dockyards, or the Royal Maritime Auxiliary Service.

Isabel (A 183) G. Arra

ROYAL ARMY
ROYAL CORPS OF TRANSPORT

MEDIUM LANDING SHIPS

♦ **2 Ardennes-class logistic landing craft** Bldr: Brooke Marine, Lowestoft

		Laid down	L	In serv.
L 4001	ARDENNES	27-8-75	29-7-76	1977
L 4003	ARAKAN	16-2-76	23-5-77	9-6-78

Ardennes (L 4001) 1977

D: 870 tons (1,413 fl) **S:** 10.3 kts **Dim:** 73.1 (71.7 pp) × 15.03 × 1.8
M: 2 Mirrlees-Blackstone GWSL 8-MGR 2 diesels; 2 props; 2,000 hp
Fuel: 150 tons **Range:** 4,000/10 **Man:** 4 officers, 31 men

REMARKS: Replacements for the LCT(8) class, operated by the Royal Corps of Transport. Can carry 5 70-ton tanks or 24 standard 20-foot containers (340 dwt) as well as 6 officers and 28 troops. No armament.

LANDING CRAFT

♦ **2 Arromanches class** Bldr: Brooke Marine, Lowestoft

RPL. . . ARROMANCHES (L: 6-1-81)   RPL. . . ANTWERP (L: 9-3-81)

   D: . . . tons **S:** . . . kts **Dim:** 25.0 × . . . × . . .
   M: 2 diesels; 2 props;. . . hp **Man:** . . . tot.

REMARKS: First pair ordered 18-3-80 to begin replacement of the *Avon* class; nine more planned.

♦ **11 Avon class** Bldr: Saunders-Roe, Isle of Wight (In serv. 1961-67)

RPL 01 AVON	RPL 04 DART	RPL 07 GLEN	RPL 11 LODDEN
RPL 02 BUDE	RPL 05 EDEN	RPL 08 HAMBLE	RPL 12 MEDWAY
RPL 03 CLYDE	RPL 06 FORTH	RPL 10 KENNET	

Lodden (RPL 11)   G. Arra, 1977

   D: 61 tons (100 fl) **S:** 8 kts **Dim:** 22.0 × 6.1 × . . .
   M: 2 diesels; 2 props; 870 hp **Man:** 6 tot.

REMARKS: Two-deck superstructure aft. Operated by the Army's Royal Corps of Transport, three in Hong Kong, two at Cyprus, two at Belize, remainder in home waters.

CARGO SHIP

♦ **1 Throsk class** Bldr: Appledore SB

	Laid down	L	In serv.
ST. GEORGE	9-11-80	3-81	1981

   D: 2,193 tons (fl) **S:** 14 kts **Dim:** 70.57 (64.31 pp) × 11.90 × 4.57
   M: 2 Mirrlees-Blackstone diesels; 1 prop; 3,000 hp **Range:** 1,500/14; 5,000/10
   Man: 10 officers, 22 men

REMARKS: Sister to RMAS-operated munitions carriers *Kinterbury* and *Throsk*, with improved accommodations. Two holds, two 5-ton cranes; 1,150 dwt. Ordered 2-10-79.

SERVICE CRAFT

♦ **1 Spitfire-class range safety craft** Bldr: James & Stone, Brightlingsea (In serv. 1978)

ALFRED HERRING, V.C.

   D: 48 tons (60 fl) **S:** 22 kts **Dim:** 23.70 × 5.50 × 1.50
   M: 2 Paxman 8YJCM4 diesels; 2 props; 2,100 hp **Man:** 9 tot.

REMARKS: Sister to RAF target tow launches. Operates in Outer Hebrides at Royal Artillery Range.

♦ **4 Samuel Morley, V.C.-class range safety class** Bldr: A. R. P. Whitstable, except *Morley*, Fairey Marine, Hamble

SAMUEL MORLEY, V.C.	RICHARD MASTERS, V.C.
JAMES DALTON, V.C.	JOSEPH HUGHES, G.C.

   D: 19 tons (fl) **S:** 17 kts **Dim:** 15.0 × 4.6 × 1.6
   M: 2 Rolls-Royce C8M410 diesels; 2 props; 820 hp **Man:** 3 tot.

REMARKS: 12 additional constructing 1980-81 by Fairey-AllDay Marine.

♦ **1 navigational training tender** Bldr: Vosper (In serv. 1964)

TREVOSE

   D: 74 tons **S:** 12 kts **Dim:** 21.9 × . . . × . . .
   M: 2 diesels; 2 props;. . . hp

♦ **1 aviation trials support ship** Bldr: Hall Russell, Aberdeen (In serv. 1966)

COLONEL TEMPLER (ex-*Criscilla*)

   D: . . . **S:** . . . **Dim:** 56.6 × 11.0 × 4.1
   M: 2 diesels; 2 props; . . . hp

REMARKS: 952 grt. Former sternhaul trawler acquired 1980 to support Farnborough aviation research facility.

♦ **1 navigational training craft** Bldr: Richards Ironworks (In serv. 1944)

YARMOUTH NAVIGATOR

   D: 140 tons **S:** 8 kts **Dim:** 29.0 × . . . × . . .

♦ **5 general-purpose workboats** (In serv. 1966-71)

WB 03 BREAM   WB 04 BARBEL   WB 05 ROACH   WB 06 PERCH   WB 07 PIKE

   D: 19 tons (fl) **S:** 8 kts **Dim:** 14.3 × . . . × . . .

♦ **5 command and control craft** (In serv. 1971)

L 01 PETREL   L 02 TERN   L 03 FULMAR   L 04 SKUA   L 05 SHELDUCK

   D: 12 tons (fl) **S:** 15 kts **Dim:** 12.5 × . . . × . . .

♦ **3 general service craft** (In serv. 1944-46)

MARTIN   NEWMAN NOGGS   RADDLE

   D: 20 grt **S:** 8 kts **Dim:** 15.2 × . . . × . . .
   M: 1 diesel; . . . hp

REMARKS: Resemble small fishing boats.

♦ **1 ex-RAF 1300-series general-purpose launch** (In serv. ca. 1960)

HYPERION (ex-1385)

   D: 28.3 tons (fl) **S:** 13 kts **Dim:** 19.2 × 4.7 × 1.5
   M: 2 Rolls-Royce C6 diesels; 2 props; 190 hp **Man:** 5 tot.

SERVICE CRAFT *(continued)*

♦ **1 ex-RAF 1600-series range safety launches** (In serv. 1955-56)

MINORU (ex-1667)

    D: 12 tons (fl) **S:** 16 kts **Dim:** 13.1 × 4.0 × 1.2

ROYAL AIR FORCE

LONG-RANGE RECOVERY AND SUPPORT CRAFT (LRRSC)

♦ **3 Seal class**

	Bldr	In serv.
5000 SEAL	Brooke Marine, Lowestoft	8-67
5001 SEAGULL	Fairmile Const., Berwick-on-Tweed	1970
5002 SEA OTTER	Fairmile Const., Berwick-on-Tweed	1970

Seal (5000)

    D: 159 tons (fl) **S:** 21 kts **Dim:** 36.6 (33.8 pp) × 7.0 × 2.0
Electron Equipt: Radar: 1/978
M: 2 Paxman 16 YJCM diesels; 2 props; 4,000 hp **Electric:** 110 kw
Fuel: 31 tons **Range:** 2,200/12 **Man:** 2 officers, 15 men

REMARKS: Design similar to Royal Navy's *Kingfisher*-class patrol boats. Used for search-and-rescue, target towing, and recovering guided missiles and other air-dropped ordnance.

RESCUE AND TARGET-TOWING LAUNCHES (RTTL)

♦ **9 Spitfire (RTTL Mk 3) class** Bldr: James & Stone, Brightlingsea

		In serv.			In serv.
4000	SPITFIRE	1972	4005	HURRICANE	1980
4001	SUNDERLAND	1976	4006	HARVARD	1980
4002	STIRLING	1976	4007	HUDSON	1980
4003	HALIFAX	1977	4008	WELLINGTON	25-5-81
4004	HAMPDEN	1980			

    D: 48 tons (60 fl) **S:** 22 kts **Dim:** 23.70 (22.15 wl) × 5.50 × 1.50
Electron Equipt: Radar: 1/978
M: 2 Paxman 8YJCM4 diesels; 2 props; 2,000 hp **Electric:** 30 kVa
Fuel: 10 tons **Range:** 500/21; 1,000/15 **Man:** 1 officer, 8 men

REMARKS: *Spitfire* is 20.6-m overall and has two side-by-side stacks; the series-construction units discharge exhaust through ports in the stern.

NOTE: A new series of 8.3-m work boats replaced earlier wooden-hulled service craft during 1980-81.

DEPARTMENT OF AGRICULTURE AND FISHERIES FOR SCOTLAND

FISHERIES PROTECTION SHIPS

♦ **2 new construction**

	Bldr	L	In serv.
SULISKER	Ferguson Brothers, Port Glasgow	8-80	1980
N. . .	Ferguson Brothers, Port Glasgow	1981	9-82

    D: 1,250 tons **S:** 18 kts **Dim:** 71.33 (64.00 pp) × 11.60 × 4.66
M: 2 Ruston 12RKCM diesels; 2 CP props; 5,640 hp **Electric:** 638 kw
Fuel: 198 tons **Range:** 7,000/14 **Man:** 8 officers, 17 men

REMARKS: Equipped with 450-hp bow-thruster, Denny-Brown fin stabilizers, and a platform for a BO 105 light helicopter. 1,177 grt/337 dwt. Equipped for rescue, firefighting, and oil-spill cleanup. Unlike *Jura* class, has long, high forecastle, low superstructure.

♦ **2 Jura class** Bldr: Hall, Russell & Co., Aberdeen

JURA (In serv. 1973) WESTRA (In serv. 1975)

    D: 778 tons (1,285 fl) **S:** 17 kts **Dim:** 59.6 × 10.7 × 4.4
M: 2 British Polar SP112VS-F diesels; 1 prop; 4,200 hp **Man:** 28 tot.

REMARKS: Design (with different engines) employed for Royal Navy's "Isles"-class offshore patrol vessels. *Jura* chartered by Royal Navy 1973-77, had 1/40-mm AA.

GREECE
Hellenic Republic

PERSONNEL: 19,500 men, including 2,500 officers

MERCHANT MARINE (1980): 3,922 ships—39,471,744 grt (tankers: 445 ships—11,780,460 grt)

NAVAL AVIATION: Greek naval aviation began in April 1975, when four Alouette-III ASW helicopters fitted with AS-12 anti-ship, wire-guided missiles went into service. Subsequently, 16 Agusta-Bell AB-212 helicopters were ordered from Italy in 1977; these are based at Eleusis, with the first two having been delivered 19-7-79. The Air Force has 14 HU-16B Grumman Albatross amphibian planes remaining for maritime reconnaissance; these carry mixed Navy/Air Force crews.

NOTE: Greek pendant numbers have been reorganized; see Addenda.

WARSHIPS IN SERVICE OR UNDER CONSTRUCTION AS OF 1 JANUARY 1982

	L	Tons	Main armament
♦ 10 submarines			
8 TYPE 209	1970-79	1100	8/533-mm TT
1 GUPPY III	1945	1;660	10/533-mm TT
1 GUPPY II	1944	1,500	10/533-mm TT
♦ 15 destroyers			
8 GEARING	1944-45	2,425	4-6/127-mm DP, 1/76-mm DP (in 4), ASROC (in 4), 6/ASW TT
1 ALLEN M. SUMNER	1944	2,200	6/127-mm DP, 6/ASW TT
6 FLETCHER	1942-43	2,050	4-5/127-mm DP, 6/76.2-mm DP or 10/40-mm AA, ASW weapons
♦ 6 (+1) frigates			
1 (+1) KORTENAER	1979	3,000	Aspide, 2/76-mm DP, 1 helo
1 RHEIN	1960	2,370	2/100-mm DP, 4/40-mm AA, mines
4 CANNON	1942-43	1,300	3/76.2-mm DP, ASW weapons

♦ **23 guided-missile patrol boats and torpedo boats**

♦ **8 patrol craft**

♦ **17 minesweepers**

♦ **2 minelayers**

♦ **15 amphibious-warfare ships**

SUBMARINES

♦ **8 German Type 209** Bldr: Howaldtswerke, Kiel

	Laid down	L	In serv.
S 110 GLAVKOS	1-9-68	15-9-70	5-11-71
S 111 NEREUS	15-1-69	7-6-71	10-2-72
S 112 TRITON	1-6-69	19-10-71	23-11-72
S 113 PROTEUS	1-10-69	1-2-72	23-11-72
S 116 POSEIDON	15-4-76	21-3-78	22-3-79
S 117 AMFRITITI	16-9-78	14-6-78	14-8-79
S 118 OKEANOS	1-10-76	16-11-78	15-11-79
S 119 PONTOS	15-1-77	22-3-79	29-4-80

Glavkos (S 110)　　　　　　　　1977

Poseidon (S 116)　　　　　　　　1980

D: 980/1,105/1,230　**S:** 21 kts (max. sub. for 5 min.), 12 kts, snorkel
Dim: 55.0 (116-118: 58.0) × 6.6 × 5.9
A: 8/533-mm TT fwd (+ 6 reserve torpedoes)
M: diesel-electric propulsion; 4 MTU 12V 493 TY60 diesels, each linked to an AEG generator of 420 kw; 1 Siemens motor; 1 prop; 5,000 hp
Range: 25/20; 230/8; 400/4 submerged　**Man:** 5 officers, 26 men

REMARKS: Similar to the submarines ordered by Argentina, Peru, and other countries. Diving depth 250 m. The second group of four are 58 m overall, 1,180 tons surfaced/1,300 tons submerged.

SUBMARINES *(continued)*

♦ **1 ex-U.S. GUPPY III class** Bldr: Portsmouth Naval SY, New Hampshire

	Laid down	L	In serv.
S 115 L. KATSONIS (ex-*Remora*, SS 487)	5-3-45	12-7-45	3-1-46

Katsonis (S 115)

D: 1,660/1,975/2,540 tons **S:** 17.2/14.5 kts **Dim:** 99.52 × 8.23 × 5.18
A: 10/533-mm TT (6 fwd, 4 aft; 24 torpedoes)
Electron Equipt: Radar: 1/SS-2A
   Sonar: BQG-4 (PUFFS), BQR-2B
   ECM: WLR-1
M: 4 Fairbanks-Morse 38D 8⅛ 10-cyl. diesels (1,600 hp each),electric drive; 2
   props; 6,400/5,480 hp
Range: 10,000-12,000/10; 95/5 submerged **Man:** 85 tot.

REMARKS: Purchased 29-10-73. GUPPY III conversion completed 1962 at Pearl Harbor
SY.

♦ **1 ex-U.S. Guppy IIA class** Bldr: Manitowoc SB, Wisconsin

	Laid down	L	In serv.
S 114 PAPANIKOLIS (ex-*Hardhead*, SS 365)	7-7-43	12-12-43	18-4-44

D: 1,517/1,870/2,440 tons **S:** 18/13.5 kts **Dim:** 93.6 × 8.2 × 5.2
A: 10/533-mm TT (6 fwd, 4 aft, 24 torpedoes)
Electron Equipt: Radar: 1/SS-2A
   Sonar: BQR-2R
   ECM: WLR-1
M: 3 GM 16-278A diesels (1,600 hp each), 2 electric motors; 2 props; 3,430/5,480
   hp

REMARKS: Purchased 26-7-72. The fourth diesel generator was removed to permit
enlargement of the sonar compartment during Guppy II conversion completed 1953.
Two 126-cell batteries. *Triana* (S 86), ex-*Scabbardfish* (SS 397), is now used for
pierside training.

DESTROYERS

♦ **7 ex-U.S. Gearing FRAM I class**

	Bldr	Laid down	L	In serv.
D 212 KANARIS (ex-*Stickell*, DD 888)	Consolidated Steel	5-1-45	16-6-45	26-9-45
D 213 KONTOURIOTIS (ex-*Rupertus*, DD 851)	Bethlehem, Quincy	2-5-45	21-9-45	8-3-46
D 214 SACHTOURIS (ex-*Arnold J. Isbell*, DD 869)	Bethlehem, Quincy	14-3-45	6-8-45	5-1-46
D 215 TOUMBAZIS (ex-*Gurke*, DD 783)	Todd SY, Seattle	1-7-44	15-4-45	5-12-45
D 216 APOSTOLIS (ex-*Myles C. Fox*, DD 829)	Bath Iron Wks.	14-8-44	13-1-45	20-3-45
D 2 . . . N . . . (ex-*Corry*, DD 817)	Consolidated Steel	5-4-45	28-7-45	26-2-46
D 2 . . . N . . . (ex-*Dyess*, DD 880)	Consolidated Steel	17-8-44	26-1-45	21-5-45

Kanaris (D 212)   J.-C. Bellonne, 1980

Toumbazis (D 215)   G. Gyssels, 1981

D: 2,425 tons (3,500 fl) **S:** 30 kts
Dim: 119.03 × 12.52 × 4.45 (6.40 over sonar)
A: 4/127-mm, 38-cal. (II × 2)—1/76-mm OTO Melara DP—1/ASROC system—1/
   40-mm AA—2/12.7-mm mg—6/324-mm Mk 32 ASW TT (III × 2)—1/d.c. rack
Electron Equipt: Radar: 1/navigational, 1/SPS-10, 1/SPS-40 (SPS-29 on 212,
   215, ex-DD 817, 880), 1/Mk 25, 1/NA 10
   Sonar: SQS-23D—ECM: WLR-1, ULQ-6
M: GT; 2 props; 60,000 hp **Electric:** 1,200 kw
Boilers: 4 Babcock & Wilcox; 43.3 kg/cm², 454°C superheat **Fuel:** 650 tons
Range: 2,400/25, 4,800/15 **Man:** 14 officers, 260 men

DESTROYERS *(continued)*

REMARKS: D 212 transferred 1-7-72; D 213 on 10-7-73 (purchased 11-7-78); D 215 purchased 17-3-77. All have been given an Elsag NA-10 fire-control system aft, 1/ 76-mm OTO Melara Compact on the helicopter deck, and a 40-mm AA before the bridge. D 216, purchased 2-8-80, and ex-DD 817 and DD 880, transferred 8-7-81, will probably receive similar AA improvements. The *Charles P. Cecil* (DD 835) was purchased 2-8-80 for cannibalization. In D 215, which was equipped as Fleet Flagship 1980-81, two of the boilers are Foster-Wheeler. The 1980-81 purchase ships had LN-66 navigational radars.

♦ 1 ex-U.S. Gearing DDR FRAM II class

	Bldr	Laid down	L	In serv.
D 210 THEMISTOCLES (ex-*Frank Knox*, DD 742)	Bath Iron Wks.	8-5-44	17-9-44	11-12-44

Themistocles (D 210)—air-search antenna missing   L. & L. Van Ginderen, 1980

D: 2,425 tons (3,500 fl) **S:** 30 kts
Dim: 119.03 × 12.52 × 4.45 (6.40 over sonar)
A: 6/127-mm DP (II × 3)—4/30-mm AA Emerlec (II × 2)—6/324-mm Mk 32 ASW TT (III × 2)—2 Hedgehog—1 Alouette-III ASW helicopter
Electron Equipt: Radar: 1/navigational, 1/SPS-10, 1/SPS-29, 1/Mk 25
    Sonar: SQS-23, SQA-10 VDS
    ECM: WLR-1   TACAN: URN-6
M: 2 sets GT; 2 props; 60,000 hp **Electric:** 1,200 kw
Boilers: 2 Babcock & Wilcox; 43.3 kg/cm², 454°C superheat
Fuel: 650 tons **Range:** 2,400/25, 4,800/15 **Man:** 16 officers, 253 men

REMARKS: Purchased 30-1-71, having been extensively rebuilt after a grounding in 1966. Radar picket features deleted and helicopter hangar added in Greece by 1978 in place of the after 01 level deckhouse. 30-mm AA substituted for 20-mm single mounts in 1980.

♦ 1 ex-U.S. Allen M. Sumner class Bldr: Federal SB & DD, Kearny, New Jersey

	Laid down	L	In serv.
D 211 MIAOULIS (ex-*Ingraham*, DD 694)	4-4-43	16-1-44	10-3-44

D: 2,200 tons (3,320 fl) **S:** 30 kts
Dim: 114.76 × 12.49 × 4.39 (5.79 over sonar)
A: 6/127-mm, 38-cal. DP (II × 3)—2/40-mm AA (I × 2)—6/20-mm AA (I × 6)—2 Hedgehogs—6/324-mm Mk 32 ASW TT (III × 2)—1/Alouette-III ASW helicopter
Electron Equipt: Radars: 1/navigational, 1/SPS-10, 1/SPS-40, 1/Mk 25
    Sonars: SQS-29, SQA-10 VDS
    ECM: WLR-1

M: 2 sets GT; 2 props; 60,000 hp
Boilers: 4 Babcock & Wilcox; 43.3 kg/cm², 454°C **Fuel:** 495 tons
Range: 2,400/25; 4,800/15 **Man:** 14 officers, 260 men

REMARKS: Transferred 16-7-71. Mk 37 gunfire-control system for 127-mm mounts.

♦ 6 ex-U.S. and West German Fletcher class

	Bldr	Laid down	L	In serv.
D 06 ASPIS (ex-*Conner*, DD 582)	Boston NSY	16-4-42	18-9-42	8-6-43
D 16 VELOS (ex-*Charette*, DD 581)	Boston NSY	20-2-42	3-6-42	18-5-43
D 58 LONCHI (ex-*Hall*, DD 583)	Boston NSY	16-4-42	18-7-42	6-7-43
D 65 NEARCHOS (ex-German Z 3, ex-*Wadsworth*, DD 516)	Bath Iron Wks.	18-8-42	10-1-43	16-3-43
D 85 SPHENDONI (ex-*Aulick*, DD 569)	Consolidated SB	14-5-41	2-3-42	27-10-42
D. . . N. . . (ex-German Z-4, ex-*Claxton*, DD 571)	Consolidated Steel	25-6-41	1-4-42	8-12-42

Velos (D 16)   G. Arra

Nearchos (D 65)—as Z-3 (D 172)   S. Terzabaschitsch, 1980

D: 2,050 tons (2,850 fl) **S:** 32/30 kts **Dim:** 114.85 × 12.03 × 5.5
A: 4/127-mm, 38 cal. (I × 4)—6/76.2-mm DP, 50-cal. (II × 3)—5/533-mm TT (V × 1)—6/324-mm Mk 32 ASW TT (IiI × 2)—2 Hedgehogs—1 d.c. rack *(see remarks)*

DESTROYERS (continued)

Electron Equipt: Radar: 1/SPS-10, 1/SPS-6, 1/Mk 25, 2/Mk 34, 1/Mk 35
         Sonar: SQS-4 or 29 series
M: 2 sets GT; 2 props; 60,000 hp **Electric:** 580 kw
Boilers: 4 Babcock & Wilcox; 43.3 kg/cm², 454° **Fuel:** 650 tons
Range: 1,260/30, 4,400/15 **Man:** 350 tot.

REMARKS: D 06 loaned 15-9-59, D 16 on 15-6-69, D 58 on 9-2-60, and D 85 on 21-8-59; all purchased 25-4-77, along with *Thyella* (D 28, ex-*Bradford*, DD 545), stricken 2-81, and *Navarinon* (D 63, ex-*Brown*, DD 546), stricken 1981. D 65 purchased and transferred from West Germany on 30-10-80, and ex-24 transferred 26-2-80. 22 and 25 were also acquired from West Germany in 9-81 for cannibalization (as had been ex-21 in 1979). The ex-German ships have 2/533-mm ASW TT vice Mk 32 ASW TT and are equipped with mine rails; the after twin 76.2-mm DP mount and Mk 56 GFCS are missing in ex-24.

FRIGATES

♦ **1 (+1) Dutch Kortenaer class** Bldr: de Schelde, Vlissingen

		Laid down	L	In serv.
F 450 ELLI (ex-*Pieter Floresz*)		2-7-77	15-12-79	10-81
F. . . LEMNOS (ex-*Witte de With*)		13-6-78	27-10-79	1982

Elli (F 450)—at Vlissingen, May 1981   G. Gyssels

D: 3,000 tons (3,750 fl) **S:** 30 kts
Dim: 130.2 (121.8 pp) × 14.4 × 4.4 (6.0 props)
A: 1 Mk 29 SAM syst. (VIII × 1; 24 Aspide missiles)—2/76-mm OTO Melara DP—4/324-mm Mk 32 ASW TT (II × 2)—1/AB 212 ASW helicopter
Electron Equipt: Radar: 1/ZW 06, 1/LW 08, 1/WM 25, 1/STIR Sonar: SQS-505
        ECM: Elektronica Sphinx intercept syst., 2 Knebworth/Corvus chaff RL

M: COGOG: 2 Rolls-Royce Tyne RM-1C cruise gas turbines, 4,900 hp each, 2 Rolls-Royce Olympus TM-3B gas turbines, 25,800 hp each; 2 LIPS CP props; 51,600 hp max.
Electric: 3,000 kw (4 SEMT-Pielstick PA4 diesels generator sets)
Range: 4,700/16 (on one Tyne turbine) **Man:** 17 officers, 182 men

REMARKS: *Elli* was officially turned over to Greece on 26-6-81 at the commencement of sea trials, having been ordered 7-81, along with a second unit. Both were taken from production for the Dutch Navy, in order to speed delivery. A third unit may be built later, in Greece. Have Denny-Brown fin stabilizers. *Elli* had been equipped with racks to hold 8 Harpoon SSM containers (IV × 2), but these were removed. Hangar altered to accept Italian-built helicopter vice Lynx used by Dutch Navy. Have SEWACO II combat data system. See also class notes in Netherlands section.

♦ **1 German Rhein-class former tender** Bldr: Elsflether Werft

	Laid down	L	In serv.
215 AEGEON (ex-*Weser*, A 62)	1-8-59	11-6-60	14-7-62

D: 2,370 tons (2,740 fl) **S:** 20.5 kts **Dim:** 98.18 (92.8 pp) × 11.8 × 3.9
A: 2/100-mm DP (I × 2)—4/40-mm AA (I × 4)—70 mines
Electron Equipt: Radars: 1/Kelvin-Hughes 14/9, 1/SGR-105, 1/SGR-103, 2/M 45
M: 6 Maybach 16-cyl. diesels; 2 CP props; 12,600 hp **Electric:** 2,250 kVa
Range: 2,500/16 **Man:** 110 tot.

REMARKS: Transferred 6-7-76. A small combatant tender used by Greece as a frigate. Still can act as a tender. Two M2 GFCS for 100-mm DP.

♦ **4 ex-U.S. Cannon class**

	Bldr	Laid down	L	In serv.
D 01 AETOS (ex-*Ebert*, DE 768)	Tampa Shipbldg	1-4-43	11-5-44	12-7-44
D 31 HIERAX (ex-*Slater*, DE 766)	Tampa Shipbldg	9-3-43	13-2-44	1-5-44
D 54 LEON (ex-*Garfield Thomas*, DE 193)	Federal, Port Newark	23-9-43	12-12-43	24-1-44
D 67 PANTHIR (ex-*Eldridge*, DE 173)	Federal, Port Newark	22-2-43	25-6-43	27-8-43

Leon (D 54)   1977

D: 1,300 tons (1,750 fl) **S:** 19 kts **Dim:** 93.0 (91.5 pp) × 11.17 × 3.25
A: 3/76.2-mm DP—6/40-mm AA (II × 3)—14/20-mm AA (II × 7)—6/324-mm Mk 32 ASW TT (III × 2)—1 Hedgehog—8/d.c. projectors—2/d.c. racks

FRIGATES (continued)

Electron Equipt: Radars: 1/navigational, 1/Mk 26
Sonar: QCU-2
M: 4 GM 16-278A diesels, electric drive; 2 props; 6,000 hp
Electric: 680 kw   **Fuel:** 300 tons   **Range:** 5,500/19, 11,500/11
Man: Peacetime: 150 men Wartime: 185 men

REMARKS: Transferred in 1951. Have Mk 52 GFCS for 76.2-mm guns (plus separate rangefinder), 3 Mk 51 mod. 2 GFCS for 40-mm AA. Obsolete SA radar removed by 1980.

NOTE: The 53-m coastal patrol vessels *Plotarchis Arsanoglou* (P 14) and *Antipliarchos Pezopoulos* (P 70) were stricken by 1979.

GUIDED-MISSILE PATROL BOATS

♦ **10 La Combattante III class** Bldr: (A) Hellenic SY, Skaramanga;
(B) Constr. Méc. de Normandie, Cherbourg

	Bldr	L	In serv.
P 24 SIMAIFOROS KAVALOUTHIS	A	10-11-79	14-7-80
P 25 ANTIPLIARCHOS KOSTAKOS	A	1-3-80	14-7-80
P 26 IPOPLIARCHOS DEYIANNIS	A	14-7-80	12-80
P 27 SIMAIFOROS XENOS	A	8-9-80	31-3-81
P 28 SIMAIFOROS SIMITZOPOULOS	A	12-10-81	. . .
P 29 SIMAIFOROS STARAKIS	A	. . .	. . .
P 50 ANTIPLIARCHOS LASCOS	B	6-7-76	2-4-77
P 51 ANTIPLIARCHOS BLESSAS	B	10-11-76	19-7-77
P 52 ANTIPLIARCHOS TROUPAKIS	B	6-1-77	8-11-77
P 57 ANTIPLIARCHOS MYKONIOS	B	5-5-77	10-2-78

Antipliarchos Lascos (P 50)—First Group   CMN, 1976

Antipliarchos Troupakis (P 52)—First Group   G. Arra, 1977

Simaiforos Kavalouthis (P 24)—Second Group   1981

D: 385 tons (425 fl)   **S:** 36.5 kts (2nd group: 32.6)
Dim: 56.15 (52.50 pp) × 8.00 × 2.50 (props)
A: First four: 4/MM38 Exocet SSM (II × 2)—2/76-mm OTO Melara DP (I × 2)—4/30-mm Emerlec AA (II × 2)—2/533-mm TT (2 SST-4 wire-guided torpedoes
Later six: 6 Penguin SSM (I × 6)—2/76-mm OTO Melara Compact DP (I × 2)—4/30-mm Emerlec AA (II × 2)
Electron Equipt: Radar: First four: Thomson-CSF: 1 Castor, 1 Pollux, 1 Triton
Later six: 1 Decca TM 1226, 1 Thomson-CSF D-1280
M: First four: 4 MTU 20V538 TB92 diesels; 4 props; 18,000 hp
Later six: 4 MTU 20V538 TB91 diesels; 4 props; 15,000 hp (13,400 sust.)
Electric: 450 kw   **Range:** 800/32.5   **Man:** 6 officers, 36 men

REMARKS: First four ordered 22-5-75. Second group, built in Greece, and with less expensive weapon, sensor, and propulsion systems, ordered 22-12-76. Each 76-mm gun has 350 rounds, with 80 in ready service. The Emerlec 30-mm mounts are furnished with 3,200 rounds and fire at 700 rounds/barrel/minute. Ships have excellent habitability; accommodations and operations spaces are air-conditioned. There are 3 Jeumont-Schneider 150-kw generator sets (440v., 3-ph., 60-Hz.).

GUIDED-MISSILE PATROL BOATS (continued)

♦ **4 La Combattante II class** Bldr: Constr. Méc. de Normandie (CMN), Cherbourg

	L	In serv.
P 53 IPOPLIARCHOS KONIDIS (ex-*Kimothoi*)	20-12-71	7-72
P 54 IPOPLIARCHOS BATSIS (ex-*Kalypso*)	26-1-71	12-71
P 55 IPOPLIARCHOS ARLIOTIS (ex-*Evniki*)	26-4-71	4-72
P 56 IPOLIARCHOS ANNINOS (ex-*Navsithoi*)	8-9-71	6-72

Ipopliarchos Konidis (P 53)   1976

Ipopliarchos Batsis (P 54)   1976

D: 234 tons (255 fl) **S:** 36.5 kts **Dim:** 47.0 (44.0 pp) × 7.1 × 2.5 (fl)
A: 4/MM38 Exocet SSM (II × 2)—4/35-mm Oerlikon AA (II × 2)—2/533-mm wire-guided TT aft
Electron Equipt: Radars: Thomson CSF: 1/Castor, 1/Pollux, 1/Triton
M: 4 MTU MD 872 diesels; 4 props; 12,000 hp **Fuel:** 39 tons
Range: 850/25, 2,000/15 **Man:** 4 officers, 36 men

REMARKS: Steel hull, light steel alloy superstructure. Ordered 1969.

NOTE: Transfer of the *Beacon* (PG 99) and *Green Bay* (PG 101) has been under discussion with the U.S. Navy since 1976, but the transfer had not been made as of 1 January 1982, nor had any date been set. They were to have been named *Arsonoglou* and *Pegopoulos*.

♦ **2 Kelefstis Stamou class** Bldr: Chantiers Navales de l'Esterel, Cannes

P 286 KELEFSTIS SAMOU (In serv. 28-7-75)
P 287 DIOPOS ANTONIOU (In serv. 4-12-75)

Kelefstis Stamou—prior to arming and with original pendant number
l'Esterel, 1975

D: 80 tons (115 fl) **S:** 30 kts **Dim:** 32.0 × 5.8 × 1.5
A: 4/SS-12 wire-guided SSM—1/40-mm AA—1/20-mm AA
M: 2 MTU 12V331 TC81 diesels; 2 props; 2,700 hp **Range:** 1,500/15
Man: 17 tot.

REMARKS: These wooden-hulled ships were ordered by Cyprus but acquired by Greece. Pendant numbers were P 28 and P 29 until 1980.

TORPEDO BOATS

♦ **7 ex-German Type 141 class** Bldrs: (A) Lürssen, Vegasack;
(B) Krögerwerft, Rendsburg

	Bldr	Laid down	L	In serv.
P 196 ESPEROS (ex-*Seeadler*)	A	23-9-57	1-2-58	29-8-58
P 197 KATAIGIS (ex-*Falke*)	A	18-3-58	30-8-58	14-4-59
P 198 KENTAUROS (ex-*Habicht*)	B	27-9-58	21-2-59	21-5-59
P 199 KYKLON (ex-*Greif*)	A	5-2-58	28-6-58	3-3-59
P 228 LAIAPS (ex-*Kondor*)	A	2-1-58	17-5-58	24-2-59
P 229 SCORPIOS (ex-*Kormoran*)	B	2-2-59	16-7-59	9-11-59
P 230 TYFON (ex-*Geier*)	A	27-5-58	1-10-58	3-6-59

D: 195 tons (221 fl) **S:** 42.5 kts **Dim:** 42.62 × 7.10 × 2.39
A: 2/40-mm AA (I × 2)—4/533-mm TT (I × 4)
M: 4 Maybach 16-cyl. diesels; 4 props; 14,400 hp **Electric:** 192 kw
Range: 500/39, 1,000/32

REMARKS: Transferred 1976-77. Three others, ex-*Albatros*, ex-*Bussard*, and ex-*Sperber*, were transferred to be cannibalized for spares. Wooden-planked hull skin on metal frame.

PATROL CRAFT

♦ **4 Goulandris class** Bldr: Hellenic SY, Skaramanga (In serv. 1978-80)

P 267 DILOS   P 268 LINDOS   P 269 KNOSSOS   P . . . N . . .

D: 75 tons (86 fl) **S:** 27 kts **Dim:** 29.0 × 6.2 × 1.1
A: 2/20-mm AA (I × 2) **Man:** 15 tot.
M: 2 MTU 12V331 TC92 diesels; 2 props; 2,700 hp **Range:** 1,600/25

PATROL CRAFT (continued)

REMARKS: Designed by Abeking & Rasmussen, West Germany. Used for air-sea rescue. Three each also built for Customs Service and Coast Guard.

♦ **3 Goulandris I class** Bldr: Neozioh SY, Syros

		In serv.			In serv.
P. . .	N.I. GOULANDRIS I	25-6-75	P 290	N.I. GOULANDRIS II	6-6-77
P 61	E. PANAGOPOULOS	23-6-76			

N.I. Goulandris II (P 290)   1981

D: 38.5 tons **S:** 30 kts **Dim:** 24.0 × 6.2 × 1.1 **A:** mg only
M: 2 diesels; 2 props; 2,700 hp **Range:** 1,600/. . .

REMARKS: P 61 pilothouse at extreme stern. All gifts from Greek shipowners.

♦ **1 ex-German KW1 class** Bldr: Burmester, Schwinemünde (In serv. 17-11-44)

P 288 ARCHIKELEFSTIS STASIS (ex-Ger. KW2, ex-H2, ex-W2, ex-*Inger*, ex-*Concordia*,
ex-K 613, ex-M 3253)

D: 112 tons (fl) **S:** 9 kts **Dim:** 22.30 (20.57 pp) × 6.40 × 2.75
A: 1/20-mm AA **M:** 1 Demag 5-cyl. diesel; 1 prop; 150 hp **Electric:** 10 kVa
Range: 1,200/7 **Man:** 16 tot.

REMARKS: Transferred 30-8-75 from West Germany. Wooden-hulled, fishing-cutter
hull, employed in local patrol at Salamis. Sister *Archikelefstis Maliopoulos* (A 476)
is employed as an inshore survey craft.

MINE WARFARE SHIPS

♦ **9 U.S. Falcon (MSC 294)-class coastal minesweepers** Bldr: Peterson Bldrs,
Sturgeon Bay, Wisconsin (except M 246: Tacoma Boatbldg, Tacoma, Washington)

		In serv.			In serv.
M 211	ALKYON (ex-MSC 319)	3-12-68	M 242	KISSA (ex-MSC 309)	1-9-64
M 213	KLIO (ex-*Argo*, ex-MSC 317)	7-8-68	M 246	AIGLI (ex-MSC 299)	4-1-65
M 214	AVRA (ex-MSC 318)	3-10-68	M 247	DAFNI (ex-MSC 307)	23-9-64
M 240	PLEIAS (ex-MSC 314)	22-6-67	M 248	AEDON (ex-MSC 310)	13-10-64
M 241	KICHLI (ex-MSC 308)	14-7-64			

D: 300 tons (394 fl) **S:** 13 kts **Dim:** 44.32 × 8.29 × 2.55
A: 2/20-mm AA (II × 1) **M:** 2 Waukesha L-1616 diesels; 2 props; 1,200 hp
Fuel: 40 tons **Range:** 2,500/10 **Man:** 4 officers, 27 men

Dafni (M 247)   G. Gyssels, 1980

REMARKS: Built for Greece under the Military Aid Program; transferred on completion. Sister *Doris* (A 475, ex-M 245, ex-MSC 298) is employed as a hydrographic
survey ship.

♦ **4 ex-Belgian U.S. Adjutant-class coastal minesweepers**

Bldrs: Consolidated SB, Morris Heights, N.Y. (M 205, M 206: Hodgdon Bros., East
Boothbay, Maine)

	In serv.
M 205 ANTIOPI (ex-*Herve*, ex-MSC 153)	3-54
M 206 PHEDRA (ex-*Malmedy*, ex-MSC 154)	5-54
M 210 THALIA (ex-*Blankenberge*, ex-MSC 170)	5-54
M 254 NIOVI (ex-*Laroche*, ex-MSC 171)	8-54

Antiopi (M 205)   G. Arra, 1973

MINE WARFARE SHIPS (continued)

D: 330 tons (402 fl) **S:** 13 kts (8 sweeping)
Dim: 43.0 (41.50 pp)× 7.95 × 2.55 **A:** 2/20-mm AA (II × 1)
M: 2 GM 8-268A diesels; 2 props; 880/1,000 hp **Fuel:** 40 tons
Range: 2,500/10 **Man:** 4 officers, 27 men

REMARKS: Transferred Belgium on completion; re-transferred to Greece 7-9-69. Sister *Atalanti* (A. . . , ex-M 202, ex-*St. Truiden*, ex-MSC 169) is configured as a hydrographic survey ship.

♦ 4 ex-U.S. 50-ft-class minesweeping launches

D: 21 tons (fl) **S:** 8 kts **Dim:** 15.20 × 4.01 × 1.31
M: 1 Navy DB diesel; 60 hp **Range:** 150/8 **Man:** 6 tot.

REMARKS: Wooden-hulled former personnel launches loaned in 1972 and purchased during 1981.

♦ 2 minelayers, former U.S. LSM 1-class landing ships Bldr: Charleston Naval SY

	Laid down	L	In serv.
N 04 AKTION (ex-LSM 301)	18-10-44	19-11-44	1-1-45
N 05 AMVRAKIA (ex-LSM 303)	8-10-44	14-11-44	6-1-45

Amvrakia (N 05)

D: 720 tons (1,100 fl) **S:** 13 kts **Dim:** 62.0 × 10.5 × 2.4
A: 8/40-mm AA (II × 4)—6/20-mm AA (I × 6)—100 to 300 mines, depending upon type
M: 2 GM 16-278A diesels; 2 props; 2,800 hp **Range:** 3,500/12 **Man:** 65 tot.

REMARKS: Transferred in 1953. Four derricks, two forward and two aft, for handling mines. Two minelaying rails. Four 30-cm searchlights, 1 of 60 cm. Twin rudders. Three of the same class ships were transferred to Turkey and two to Norway, who passed them on to Turkey in 1961.

AMPHIBIOUS WARFARE SHIPS

♦ 1 ex-U.S. Cabildo-class dock landing ship Bldr: Boston Naval SY

	Laid down	L	In serv.
L 153 NAFKRATOUSSA (ex-*Fort Mandan*, LSD 21)	16-12-44	6-4-45	31-10-45

D: 4,790 tons (9,375 fl) **S:** 15 kts **Dim:** 139.5 × 21.9 × 5.49
A: 8/40-mm AA (IV × 2) **Electron Equipt:** Radar: 1/SPS-5, 1/SPS-6
M: 2 sets GT; 2 props; 7,000 hp **Electric:** 600 kw **Man:** 254 tot.
Boilers: 62/30.6 kg/cm², 393°C **Fuel:** 1,758 tons **Range:** 8,000/15

REMARKS: Modernized under the FRAM program and transferred 1-71. Flagship of the amphibious forces. Helicopter deck. Well deck: 103.0 × 13.3. Two 35-ton cranes. Can carry 18 LCMs, each with an LCVP nested in it. SPS-6 air-search radar recently added.

♦ 2 ex-U.S. Suffolk County-class LSTs

	Bldr	Laid down	L	In serv.
L. . . N. . . (ex-*Suffolk County*, LST 1173)	Boston NSY	17-7-56	5-9-56	15-8-57
L. . . N. . . (ex-*Wood County*, LST 1178)	American SB Lorrain, Ohio	1-10-56	14-12-57	5-8-59

D: 3,560 tons (7,800 fl) **S:** 16 kts **Dim:** 135.7 (129.8 wl) × 18.9 × 5.3 (aft)
A: 6/76.2-mm DP (II × 3) **Electron Equipt:** Radar: 1/SPS-21
M: 6 Fairbanks-Morse 38D8⅛ (ex-LST 1178: Cooper-Bessemer) diesels; 2 CP props; 14,000 hp
Electric: 900 kw **Man:** 15 officers, 173 men, 700 troops

REMARKS: Permission to sell to Greece requested FY 81; both in reserve in U.S. since 1972. Special tanks for vehicle fuel. Carry four LCVP. Tank deck, 88-m long, can stow 23 tanks. Helicopter pad amidships.

♦ 2 ex-U.S. Terrebonne Parish-class LSTs

	Bldr	Laid down	L	In serv.
L 104 OINOUSSAI (ex-*Terrell County*, LST 1157)	Bath Iron Wks	3-3-52	6-12-52	19-3-53
L 116 KOS (ex-*Whitfield County*, LST 1169)	Christy Corp.	. . .	22-8-53	14-9-54

D: 2,590 tons (6,225 fl) **S:** 12 kts **Dim:** 112.35 × 16.7 × 3.7
A: 6/76.2-mm AA (II × 3)—4/20-mm AA (I × 4)
Electron Equipt: Radar: 1/SPS-10, 2/Mk 34
M: 4 GM diesels; 2 CP props; 6,000 hp **Man:** 115 crew, 395 troops

REMARKS: Transferred 1976. Two Mk 63 GFCS.

♦ 5 ex-U.S. LST 1 and LST 511-class tank landing ships

	Bldr	Laid down	L	In serv.
L 144 SYROS (ex-LST 325)	Philadelphia NY	10-8-42	27-10-42	1-2-43
L 154 IKARIA (ex-*Potter County*, LST 1086)	American Bridge, Ambridge, Pa.	5-12-44	28-1-45	24-2-45
L 157 RODOS (ex-*Bowman County*, LST 391)	Newport News SB & DD	14-7-42	28-10-42	3-12-42
L 171 KRITI (ex-*Page County*, LST 1076)	Bethlehem Steel, Hingham, Mass.	16-3-45	14-4-45	1-5-45
L 172 LESBOS (ex-*Boone County*, LST 389)	Newport News SB & DD	20-6-42	15-10-42	24-11-42

D: 1,653 tons (4,080 fl) **S:** 11.6 kts **Dim:** 99.98 × 15.24 × 3.4
A: 8/40-mm AA (II × 2, I × 4)
M: 2 GM 12-567A (L 171: 16-278A) diesels; 1,700 hp
Electric: 300 kw **Fuel:** 569 tons **Range:** 15,000/9 **Man:** 125 tot.

REMARKS: L 144 (with reinforced waterline belt for ice operations!) was transferred 29-5-64 after a complete refit and modernization; L 154, L 157, and L 172 transferred 9-8-60; L 171 transferred 3-71 (purchased 11-7-78). All carry 4 LCVP in Welin davits. Cargo: 2,100 tons

AMPHIBIOUS WARFARE SHIPS (continued)

Rodos (L 157)   1975

♦ 5 ex-U.S. LSM 1-class medium landing ships

Bldrs: L 161, 162, 165: Brown Bros SB, Houston; L 163: Dravo Corp, Wilmington, Del.; L 164: Charleston NSY

	Laid down	L	In serv.
L 161 IPOPLIARCHOS GRIGOROPOULOS (ex-LSM 45)	6-6-44	30-6-44	31-7-44
L 162 IPOPLIARCHOS TOURNAS (ex-LSM 102)	23-9-44	14-10-44	9-11-44
L 163 IPOPLIARCHOS DANIOLOS (ex-LSM 227)	17-7-44	9-9-44	5-10-44
L 164 IPOPLIARCHOS ROUSEN (ex-LSM 399)	29-12-44	18-1-45	13-8-45
L 165 IPOPLIARCHOS KRYSTALLIDIS (ex-LSM 541)	7-7-45	18-8-45	7-12-45

D: 1,095 tons (fl)   **S:** 12.5 kts   **Dim:** 62.03 × 10.52 × 2.54
A: 2/40-mm AA (II × 1)—4/20-mm AA (I × 4)
M: 2 Fairbanks-Morse 38D⅛-10 (L 164: GM 16-278A) diesels; 2 props; 2,800 hp
Electric: 240 kw   **Fuel:** 161 tons   **Range:** 4,900/12   **Man:** 60 tot.

REMARKS: Transferred 3-11-58 (L 165: 30-10-58).

♦ 6 ex-U.S. LCU 501-class utility landing craft

Bldrs: L 145, 146, 147: Mare Island NSY, Cal.; L 149; Missouri Valley Bridge & Iron, Leavenworth, Kan.; L 150: Pidgeon-Thomas Iron, Memphis, Tenn.; L 152: Kansas City Steel, Kansas City, Missouri

	In serv.		In serv.
L 145 KASSOS (ex-LCU 1382)	30-11-44	L 149 KYTHNOS (ex-LCU 763)	24-12-43
L 146 KARPATHOS (ex-LCU 1379)	17-11-44	L 150 SIFNOS (ex-LCU 677)	11-3-44
L 147 KIMONOS (ex-LCU 971)	1-2-44	L 152 SKYATOS (ex-LCU 827)	10-4-44

D: 143 tons (309 fl)   **S:** 8 kts   **Dim:** 36.3 × 9.96 × 1.14
A: 2/20-mm AA (I × 2)   **M:** 3 GM 6-71 diesels; 675 hp   **Man:** 13 tot.

REMARKS: Transferred 1959-62.

♦ 13 ex-U.S. LCM(6)-class mechanized landing craft—D: 62 tons (fl)

♦ 34 ex-U.S. LCVP—D: 13 tons (fl)

REMARKS: All carried aboard the LSTs.

♦ 14 LCP

REMARKS: Ordered 1977. No data available.

HYDROGRAPHIC SHIPS

♦ 1 new construction

REMARKS: Ordered 1979. 50-m overall; no other data available.

♦ 1 Naftilos class

	Bldr	L	In serv.
A 478 NAFTILOS	Anastadiades Tsortanides Perama	19-11-75	3-4-76

Naftilos (A 478)   1976

D: 1,480 tons   **S:** 15 kts   **Dim:** 63.1 (56.5 pp) × 11.6 × 4.0
M: 2 Burmeister & Wain SS28LH diesels; 2 props; 2,640 hp   **Man:** 57 tot.

REMARKS: In service 3-4-76. Near sisters *St. Lykoudis* (A 481) and *I. Theophilopoulos Karavoyiannos* (A 485) are lighthouse tenders. Helicopter-landing platform.

♦ 1 modified U.S. Falcon-class coastal minesweeper

	Bldr	In serv.
A 475 DORIS (ex-M 245, ex-MSC 298)	Tacoma Boatbldg.	9-11-64

REMARKS: Transferred on completion; converted late 1970s. Man: 3 officers, 32 men; other details as for minesweeper version.

♦ 1 modified U.S. Adjutant-class coastal minesweeper

	Bldr	In serv.
M 202 ATALANTI (ex-*St. Truiden*, ex-MSC 169)	Consolidated SB	2-54

REMARKS: Retains minesweeping pendant number. Transferred from Belgium 29-7-69. Details as for minesweeper version.

♦ 1 ex-German KW1-class coastal survey ship

A 476 ARCHIKELEFSTIS MALIOPOULOS (ex-KW 8, ex-H 8, ex-W 17)

REMARKS: Characteristics as for patrol boat version; no armament. Construction yard unknown; entered West German service 10-4-52. Transferred 30-8-75 as a patrol boat; later converted to replace sister *Anemos* (A 469), stricken 1977.

NOTE: The ex-U.S. Barnegat-class oceanographic research ship *Hephaistos* (A 413) was stricken in 1976.

AUXILIARY SHIPS

♦ 1 training ship Bldr: Anastiadis Tsortanides, Perama

	Laid down	L	In serv.
A 74 ARIS	10-76	4-10-78	1-81

D: 3,100 tons (4,500 fl)   **S:** 20 kts   **Dim:** 100.0 (95.0 pp) × 11.0 × 4.5
A: 1/76-mm DP OTO Melara—2/40-mm AA (I × 2)—4/20-mm AA (I × 4)—1 Alouette-III helicopter
M: 2 MAK diesels; 2 props; 10,000 hp

REMARKS: Largest naval ship built in Greece. Resembles a small passenger ship and can serve as a hospital ship or transport in wartime. Completion delayed by payment dispute.

AUXILIARY SHIPS (continued)

Aris (A 74)   1981

♦ **1 yacht/training ship, ex-Canadian "River"-class frigate**

	Bldr	Laid down	L	In serv.
A. . . Argo (ex-*Christina*, Can. Vickers, Montreal	23-12-42	12-6-43	14-11-44
ex-*Montreal*,
ex-*Stormont*)

D: 1,526 grt **S:** 20 kts **Dim:** 99.15 (86.59 pp) × 11.13 × 5.33 **A:** . . .
M: 2 sets 4-cyl. triple-expansion steam; 2 props; 5,500 hp **Electric:** 400 kw
Boilers: 2 water-tube, 17.6 kg/cm² **Range:** 7,400/15, 12,000/10
Man: . . .

REMARKS: Donated 12-7-78. Former yacht of Shipowner Aristotle Onassis, converted from a frigate 1951-54 by Howaldtswerke, Kiel. Used as presidential yacht.

♦ **2 personnel ferries** Bldr: Perama SY

A 419 Pandora (In serv. 26-10-73)   A 420 Pandrosos (In serv. 1-12-73)

D: 350 tons (390 fl) **S:** 11 kts **Dim:** 46.8 × 8.3 × 1.9
M: 2 diesels; 2 props;. . . hp

REMARKS: Can carry up to 500 personnel.

♦ **1 netlayer** Bldr: Krögerwerft, Rendsburg

A 307 Thetis (ex-U.S. AN 103) (In serv. 4-60)

D: 560 tons (805 fl) **S:** 13 kts **Dim:** 51.7 (44.5 wl) × 10.3 × 3.6 **Man:** 48 tot.
A: 1/40-mm AA—4/20-mm AA (II × 2) **M:** 2 M.A.N. diesels; 1 prop; 1,400 hp

REMARKS: Launched 1959. Transferred 4-60.

♦ **2 ex-U.S. Patapsco-class oilers** Bldr: Cargill Savage, Minn.

	Laid down	L	In serv.
A 377 Arethousa (ex-*Natchaug*, AOG 54)	15-8-44	6-12-44	11-6-45
A 414 Ariadni (ex-*Tombigbee*, AOG 11)	23-10-42	18-11-43	13-7-44

Ariadne (A 414)

D: 1,850 tons (4,335 fl) **S:** 13 kts **Dim:** 94.72 (89.0 pp) × 14.78 × 4.78
A: A 377: 4/76.2-mm AA (I × 4)—A 414: 2/76.2-mm AA (I × 2)
Electron Equipt: Radar: 1/navigational, 1/SPS-5, 1/Mk 26
M: 2 GM 16-278A diesels; 2 props; 3,300 hp **Electric:** 460 kw
Fuel: 295 tons **Man:** 46 tot.

REMARKS: Former gasoline tankers. Cargo: 2,040 tons. One Mk 52 and one Mk 51 GFCS.

♦ **2 coastal tankers** Bldr: Kynossoura SY, Piraeus

A 416 Ouranos (In serv. 29-1-77)   A 417 Hyperion (In serv. 27-2-77)

D: 1,200 tons (fl) **S:** 13 kts **Dim:** 67.7 × 10.0 × 4.7
M: 1 MWM TPD-484BU diesel; 1,750 hp

♦ **1 small harbor oiler**

A 471 Vivies

REMARKS: Cargo: 187 tons; S: 11 kts.

NOTE: *Kronos* (A 373), built in 1943, still exists as a fuel lighter, unpowered; cargo: 110 tons. *Zeus* (A 372) and *Sirios* (A 345) have been stricken.

♦ **1 ammunition ship** Bldr: Dubigeon, Nantes

	Laid down	L	In serv.
A 415 Evros (ex-German *Schwarzwald*, ex-French	30-6-55	31-1-56	7-6-56
Amalthée)

D: 2,395 tons **S:** 15 kts **Dim:** 80.18 × 11.99 × 4.65
A: 4/40-mm AA (II × 2)
M: 1 Sulzer 6-SD-60 diesel; 3,000 hp **Electric:** 500 kw **Range:** 4,500/15
Man: 32 tot.

REMARKS: Purchased 2-60 by the German Navy and converted for naval use, commissioning 11-10-61; transferred to Greece 2-6-76. 1,667 grt.

GREECE *(continued)*
AUXILIARY SHIPS *(continued)*

♦ **1 ex-German FW 1-class water lighter**

	Bldr	Laid down	L	In serv.
A 433 KERKINI (ex-FW 3)	Jadewerft, Wilhelmshaven	14-6-63	15-10-63	11-5-64

D: 598 tons (624 fl) **S:** 9.5 kts **Dim:** 44.03 (41.10 pp) × 7.80 × 2.63
M: 1 MWM 12-cyl. diesel; 1 prop; 230 hp **Electric:** 83 kw
Range: 2,150/9 **Man:** 12 tot.

REMARKS: Transferred 22-4-76. Cargo: 350 m³.

♦ **5 small water lighters**

A 434 PRESPA (In serv. 10-10-76)—Cargo: 600 tons
A 468 KALLIROI (In serv. 26-10-72)—Cargo: 600 tons
A 470 KASTORIA (In serv. . . .)—Cargo: 520 tons
A. . . DOIRANI (In serv. 1976)—Cargo: 450 tons
A 473 TRICHONIS (In serv. 1980)—Cargo: 650 tons

♦ **1 salvage tug**

A. . . ATLAS

D: . . . tons **S:** . . . kts **Dim:** . . . × . . . × . . .
M: . . . diesels;. . . props; 5,000 hp

REMARKS: Transferred to Navy 1-8-79. Replaced *Sotir* (A 384, ex-British *Salventure*).

♦ **3 Heraklis-class coastal tugs** Bldr: Perama SY

A 423 HERAKLIS (In serv. 6-4-78)   A 425 ODISSEUS (In serv. 28-6-78)
A 424 JASON (In serv. 6-3-78)

D: 345 tons **S:** 12 kts **Dim:** 30.0 × 7.9 × 3.4
M: 1 MWM diesel; 1,200 hp

♦ **10 harbor tugs**

A 407 ANTAIOS (ex-U.S. *Busy*, YTM 2012) (Transferred 1947)—650 hp
A 408 ATLAS (ex-F5, ex-Brit. *Mediator*) (In serv. 28-11-47)—200 hp
A 409 ACCHILEUS (ex-U.S. *Confident*, YTM. . .) (Transferred 1947)
A 410 ATROMITOS ⎱
A 411 ADAMASTOS ⎰ (In serv. 20-6-68)—1,260 hp, D: 310 tons
A 412 AIAS (ex-U.S. *Ankachak*, YTM 767) (Transferred 1972)—650 hp
A 418 ROMALEOS (In serv. 25-3-62)—600 hp
A 421 MINOTAUROS (ex-U.S. Army ST 539) (Transferred 1962)—650 hp
A 431 TITAN (In serv. 1962)—240 hp
A 432 CIGAS (In serv. 26-11-61)—1,200 hp

♦ **2 lighthouse tenders** Bldr: Perama SY

A 481 ST. LYKOUDIS (In serv. 17-3-76)
A 485 I. THEOPHILOPOULOS KARAVOYIANNOS (In serv. 2-1-76)

D: 1,350 tons (1,450 fl) **S:** 15 kts **Dim:** 63.24 × 11.6 × 4.0
M: 1 MWM TBD-500-8UD diesel; 2,400 hp **Man:** 40 tot.

REMARKS: Near sisters to hydrographic survey ship *Naftilos*. Have a helicopter deck.

COAST GUARD
HARBOR CORPS

The Greek Coast Guard has some 4,000 personnel, most of whom are shore-based. There are some 80 small craft, the largest and newest of which are three units of the *Dilos*-class patrol boats, as described above. The Greek Customs Service also operates about 20 boats in its Anti-Smuggling Flotilla.

GRENADA

♦ **1 patrol craft** Bldr: Brooke Marine, Lowestoft (In serv. 1972)

D: 15 tons (fl) **S:** 22 kts **Dim:** 12.2 × 3.7 × 0.6 **A:** 3/7.62-mm mg (I × 3)
M: 2 Caterpillar diesels; 2 props; 740 hp

♦ **3 Spear-class patrol craft** Bldr: Fairey Marine, Hamble, G.B. (In Serv. . . . ?)

GUATEMALA
Republic of Guatemala

PERSONNEL: 535 total: 40 officers, 205 enlisted, plus 5 officers and 285 enlisted marines
MERCHANT MARINE (1980): 6 ships—13,626 grt

PATROL BOATS AND CRAFT

♦ **1 U.S. Broadsword class** Bldr: Halter Marine, New Orleans, La.

P 1051 KUKULKAN (In serv. 4-8-76)

Kukulkan—on trials with the **Bitol** (P 655), **Picuda** (P 361), and **Barracuda** (P 362)
Halter, 1976

GUATEMALA (continued)
PATROL BOATS AND CRAFT (continued)

D: 90.5 tons (fl) **S:** 32 kts **Dim:** 32.0 × 6.3 × 1.9
A: 1/75-mm recoilless rifle—1/81-mm mortar with a 12.7-mm machine gun atop
it—2/12.7-mm mg (I × 2)
M: 2 GM 16V-149TI diesels; 3,200 hp **Electric:** 60 kw **Range:** 1,150/20
Man: 5 officers, 15 men

♦ **2 U.S. 85-foot class** Bldr: Sewart Seacraft, Berwick, La.

P 851 Utatlan (In serv. 5-67) P 852 Subteniente Osorio Saravia (In serv. 1972)

D: 50 tons **S:** 23 kts **Dim:** 25.9 × 5.8 × 1.0
A: 2/12.7-mm machine guns—1/81-mm recoilless rifle
M: 2 GM diesels; 2 props; 2,200 hp **Range:** 780/15
Man: 7 officers, 10 men

♦ **5 U.S. Cutlass class** Bldr: Halter Marine, New Orleans, La. (In serv. 1972-76)

P 651 Tecunuman   P 653 Azumanche   P 655 Bitol
P 652 Kaibilbalan   P 654 Tzacol

D: 34 tons (fl) **S:** 25 kts **Dim:** 19.7 × 5.2 × 0.9
A: 1/12.7-mm machine gun—3/7.6-mm machine guns (I × 3)
M: 2 GM 12V-71 diesels; 2 props; 960 hp **Electric:** 20 kw **Range:** 400/
15 **Man:** 10 tot.

♦ **30 river patrol craft** Bldr: Trabejos Baros SY, Guatemala (In serv. 1979)

D: . . . tons **S:** 19 or 28 kts **Dim:** 9.14 × 3.66 × 0.61
A: 2/7.62-mm mg (I × 2)
M: 1 diesel; 1 prop; 150 or 300 hp **Range:** 400-500 nm

REMARKS: Wooden construction—in two series, with different engines.

AMPHIBIOUS WARFARE CRAFT

♦ **2 U.S. Machete class** Bldr: Halter Marine, New Orleans, La. (In serv. 4-8-76)

P 361 Picuda P 362 Barracuda

D: 6 tons **S:** 36 kts **Dim:** 11.0 × 4.0 × 0.76
M: 2 GM 6V 53PI diesels; 2 water jets

REMARKS: Troop carriers. Square bows, aluminum construction.

♦ **1 ex-U.S. LCM (6) class**

561 Chinaltenango

D: 24 tons (56 fl) **S:** 10 kts **Dim:** 17.07 × 4.37 × 1.17 (aft)
A: 2/12.7-mm mg (I × 2)
M: 2 Gray Marine 64 HN9 diesels; 2 props; 450 hp **Range:** 130/10

REMARKS: Transferred in 12-65. Cargo: 30 tons.

HYDROGRAPHIC SHIP

♦ **1 new construction coastal survey craft** (In serv. 1981)

D: . . . **S:** . . . **Dim:** 19.8 × . . . × . . .

GUINEA
Republic of Guinea

PERSONNEL: 350 total

MERCHANT MARINE (1980): 14 ships—5,648 grt

CORVETTE

♦ **1 ex-Soviet T 58-class minesweeper**

Lamine Sadji Kaba

D: 790 tons (900 fl) **S:** 17 kts **Dim:** 70.0 × 9.0 × 2.4
A: 4/57-mm AA—2/RBU-1200 ASW RL (V × 2)—mines
Electron Equipt: Radar: 1/Don-2, 1/Muff Cob
M: 2 diesels; 2 props; 4,000 hp

REMARKS: Transferred 5-79. Unlike Soviet Navy units that were redesignated patrol
ships, has had *all* mine countermeasures equipment removed, including the sweep
winch.

PATROL BOATS

♦ **6 Chinese Shanghai-II class**

P 733   P 734   P 735   P 736   P 737   P 778

D: 123 tons (150 fl) **S:** 28.5 kts **Dim:** 38.78 × 5.41 × 1.49
A: 4/37-mm AA (II × 2)—4/25-mm AA (II × 2)—depth charges
Electron Equipt: Radar: 1/Pot Head
M: 2 M50F-4 diesels (1,200 hp each), 2 12D6 diesels (910 hp each); 4 props;
4,220 hp
Man: 38 tot.

REMARKS: Four transferred 1973-74, two in 1976.

♦ **3 ex-Soviet Shershen-class former torpedo boats**

D: 150 tons (180 fl) **S:** 45 kts **Dim:** 34.0 × 7.2 × 1.5
A: 4/30-mm AA (II × 2)
Electron Equipt: Radar: 1/Pot Drum, 1/Drum Tilt
IFF: 1/Square Head, 1/High Pole
M: 3 M503A diesels; 3 props; 12,000 hp **Man:** 24 tot.

REMARKS: Two delivered 1978, one in 1979. Torpedo tubes removed prior to transfer.

NOTE: The four ex-Soviet P6-class former torpedo boats have been stricken.

PATROL CRAFT

♦ **1 French 28-m class** Bldr: Chantiers Navals de l'Esterel, Cannes

P 400 Almariy Bocar Biro Barry (In serv. 8-79)

D: 56 tons (fl) **S:** 35 kts **Dim:** 28.0 × 5.2 × 1.6 **A:** 1/20-mm AA
M: 2 MTU 12V331 TC82 diesels; 2 props; 2,600 hp **Range:** 750/15
Man: 12 tot.

GUINEA (*continued*)
PATROL CRAFT (*continued*)

♦ **2 ex-Soviet Poluchat-I class**

D: 70 tons (90 fl) **S:** 18 kts **Dim:** 29.6 × 5.8 × 1.5
A: 2/14.5-mm mg (II × 1)
Electron Equipt: Radar: 1/Spin Trough
　　　　　　　　　IFF: 1/High Pole A
M: 2 M50-series diesels; 2 props; 2,400 hp

GUINEA-BISSAU
Republic of Guinea-Bissau

PERSONNEL: 250 men
MERCHANT MARINE (1980): 3 ship—757 grt

PATROL BOATS AND CRAFT

♦ **1 ex-Soviet Shershen-class former torpedo boat**

D: 150 tons (180 fl) **S:** 45 kts **Dim:** 34.0 × 7.2 × 1.5
A: 4/30-mm AA (II × 2)
Electron Equipt: Radar: 1/Pot Drum, 1 Drum Tilt
　　　　　　　　　IFF: 1/Square Head, 1/High Pole A
M: 3 M503A diesels; 3 props; 12,000 hp **Range:** 450/34; 700/20
Man: 24 tot.

REMARKS: Transferred 12-78. Torpedo tubes removed prior to transfer.

♦ **1 ex-Soviet Poluchat-I class**

D: 70 tons (90 fl) **S:** 18 kts **Dim:** 29.6 × 5.8 × 1.5
A: 2/14.5-mm mg (II × 1) **Electron Equipt:** Radar: 1/Spin Trough
M: 2 M50-series diesels; 2 props; 2,400 hp **Range:** 450/17; 900/10
Man: 20 tot.

REMARKS: Transferred 1978.

♦ **2 French Plascoa-1900 class** (In serv.. . .)

CABO ROXO　ILHA DE POILÃO

D: 30 tons (fl) **S:** 25 kts **Dim:** 19.0 × 5.35 × 1.2
A: 2/12.7-mm mg (I × 2) **M:** 2 GM diesels; 2 props; 1,050 hp
Range: 650/25; 1,500/9

♦ **3 Spanish LVC-1 class** Bldr: Aresa, Barcelona (In serv. 1979)

D: 20.8 tons (fl) **S:** 23.3 kts **Dim:** 16.00 × 4.36 × 1.30
A: 1/12.7-mm mg **M:** 2 Baudouin DNP-8　M1R diesels; 2 props; 700 hp
Range: 400/18 **Man:** 6 tot.

AUXILIARIES AND SERVICE CRAFT

♦ **1 ex-Soviet Biya-class survey ship and buoy tender** Bldr: Gdansk, Poland

D: 750 tons (fl) **S:** 13 kts **Dim:** 55.0 × 9.2 × 2.6
Electron Equipt: Radar: 1/Don-2 **M:** 2 diesels; 2 CP props; 1,200 hp
Range: 4,700/11 **Man:** 25 tot.

REMARKS: Transferred 6-78. One 5-ton buoy crane; one inshore survey launch; one 15-m² oceanographic laboratory.

♦ **2 ex-Soviet T4-class landing craft**

REMARKS: Employed in logistic support duties.

GUYANA
Cooperative Republic of Guyana

PERSONNEL: 150 total
MERCHANT MARINE (1980): 82 ships—18,261 grt (tankers: 3 ships—1,626 grt)

♦ **2 ex-North Korean patrol boats**

D: 35 tons (fl) **S:** 40 kts **Dim:** 18.3 × 3.4 × 1.7 **A:** 2/14.5-mm mg (I × 2)
M: 2 gasoline engines; 2 props; . . . hp **Man:** 9 tot.

REMARKS: Transferred 1980.

♦ **1 103-foot British patrol boat**

	Bldr	L	In serv.
DF 1010 PECCARI	Vosper Thornycroft, Portsmouth	26-3-76	26-1-77

D: 96 tons (109 fl) **S:** 27 kts **Dim:** 31.4 × 6.0 × 1.6 **A:** 2/20-mm AA (I × 2)
M: 2 Paxman Ventura 12-cyl. diesels; 2 props; 3,500 hp
Range: 1,400/14 **Man:** 22 tot.

REMARKS: A second unit was ordered in 1977 but was canceled because of lack of funds.

♦ **3 patrol boats** Bldr: Vosper Thornycroft

JAGUAR (In serv. 28-4-71)　MARGAY (In serv. 21-5-71)　OCELOT (In serv. 22-6-71)

D: 10 tons **S:** 20 kts **Dim:** 14.0 × 3.4 × 2.0 **A:** 1/7.62-mm machine gun
M: 2 Cummins D366A diesels; 2 props; 270 hp **Range:** 150/12 **Man:** 6 tot.

REMARKS: Fiberglass hull; light-alloy superstructure.

♦ **3 45-foot boats, supplied by the U.S.**

CAMOUDIE　LABANA　RATTLER

♦ **2 ex-fishing boats**

EKEREKU　NUMBER 2

NOTE: Guyana also received the ex-U.S. Navy tug YTM 190 and the converted lighter YFN 960, both operated by the Guyana Harbor Board.

HAITI
Republic of Haiti

PERSONNEL: 250 total

MERCHANT MARINE (1980): 4 ships—1,120 grt

COAST GUARD

PATROL BOATS AND CRAFT

♦ **3 U.S. 65-foot Commercial Cruiser class** Bldr: Sewart, Louisiana (In serv. 1976)

MH 21 JEAN CLAUDE DUVALIER   MH 22 N. . .   MH 23 N. . .

   D: 33 tons (fl) **S:** 25 kts **Dim:** 21.3 × 5.2 × 1.0
   A: 1/20-mm AA—2/12.7-mm mg (I × 2)
   M: 3 GM 8V71 diesels; 3 props; 1,590 hp

♦ **9 U.S. 3812-VCF class** Bldr: Monark, Monticello, Arkansas (In serv. 1980-81)

MH 11 LE MAROON   MH 14 CAPOIS   MH 17 CHARLEMAGNE PERRAULT
MH 12 OGE   MH 15 BAUCKMAN   MH 18 N. . .
MH 13 CHAVANNES   MH 16 MAKANDAL   MH 19 N. . .

   D: 8.5 tons (9.0 fl) **S:** . . . kts **Dim:** 12.34 × 4.11 × . . .
   A: 1/12.7-mm mg—2/7.62-mm mg (I × 2)
   M: 2 GM 6V71N diesels; 2 props; 480 hp **Man:** 4 tot.

♦ **1 U.S. Enforcer class** Bldr: Bertram, Miami

MH 6—**Dim:** 9.5 × . . . × . . .   **M:** 2 Caterpillar 3160 diesels; 2 props; 420 hp

AUXILIARIES

♦ **2 U.S. Sotoyomo-class auxiliary ocean tugs**

	Bldr	Laid down	L	In serv.
MH 20 HENRI CHRISTOPHE	Levingston SB,	5-6-44	14-7-44	27-9-44
(ex-*Samoset*, ATA 180)	Orange, Tex.			
MH 21 N. . . (ex-*Keywadin*,	Gulfport Boiler Wks.,	16-2-45	9-4-45	31-5-45
ATA 213)	Port Arthur, Tex.			

   D: 689 tons (835 fl) **S:** 13 kts **Dim:** 43.6 (40.75 pp) × 10.37 × 3.65
   A: MH 20: 1/40-mm AA—2/12.7-mm mg (I × 2)
   M: 2 GM 12-278A diesels, electric drive; 1 prop; 1,500 hp
   Electric: 120 kw **Fuel:** 154 tons **Range:** 16,500/9 **Man:** 40 tot.

REMARKS: MH 20 transferred 18-9-78. MH 21 transferred 28-3-81 for use in oceanographic research.

HONDURAS
Republic of Honduras

PERSONNEL: Approx. 50 total

MERCHANT MARINE (1980): 124 ships—213,421 grt (tankers: 13 ships—16,976 grt)

PATROL BOATS AND CRAFT

♦ **3 U.S. 105-foot class** Bldr: Swiftships, Morgan City, Louisiana

FN 1051 GUAYMURAS (In serv. 4-77)   FN 1053 HIBURES (In serv. 3-80)
FN 1052 HONDURAS (In serv. 3-80)

   D: 103 tons (fl) **S:** 32 kts **Dim:** 31.5 × 6.6 × 2.1 **A:** . . .
   M: 2 MTU diesels; 2 props; 7,000 hp **Range:** 1,200/18 **Man:** 16 tot.

♦ **1 U.S. 85-foot Commercial Cruiser class** Bldr: Swiftships, Morgan City, Louisiana

FN 8502 CHAMELECON (In serv. . . .)

   D: 50 tons **S:** 23 kts **Dim:** 25.9 × 5.8 × 1.0
   A: . . . **M:** 2 GM 12V71 TI diesels; 2 props; 2,200 hp **Range:** 780/15
   Man: 17 tot.

♦ **5 U.S. 65-foot Commercial Cruiser class** Bldr: Swiftships, Morgan City, Louisiana

	In serv.		In serv.
FN 6501 AGUAN (ex-*Gral*)	12-73	FN 6504 ULUA	1980
FN 6502 GOASCORAN (ex-*J.T. Cabanas*)	1-74	FN 6505 CHULUTECA	1980
FN 6503 PETULA	1980		

   D: 33 tons (fl) **S:** 25 kts **Dim:** 21.3 × 5.2
   A: 2/12.7-mm mg (I × 2) **M:** 3 GM 8V71 diesels; 3 props; 1,590 hp
   Range: 2,000/22 **Man:** 5 tot.

REMARKS: First two originally ordered for Haiti and delivered to Honduras in 1977. Others, ordered 1979, have 3 MTU diesels and can make 36 kts.

♦ **2 inshore patrol craft** Bldr: Ampela Marine, Honduras (In serv. 1981-82)

FN 2501 N. . .   FN 2502 N. . .

   D: 3 tons (fl) **S:** 24 kts **Dim:** 7.62 × 2.74 × 0.38
   A: 1/12.7-mm mg—1/7.62-mm mg
   M: 1 Chrysler 6M655 TI diesel, waterjet drive; . . . hp **Range:** 250/18
   Man: 4 tot.

REMARKS: Built of wood and glass-reinforced plastic.

♦ **6 miscellaneous ex-fishing boats for logistics support**

FN 7501 JULIANA   FN 7503 CARMEN   FN 7505 YOSURO
FN 7502 SAN RAFAEL   FN 7504 MAIRY   FN 7506 JOSE GREGORI

HONG KONG
British Crown Colony of Hong Kong

PERSONNEL (1980): 71 officers, 1,220 men

MERCHANT MARINE (1980): 187 ships—1,717,230 grt (tankers: 23 ships—160,836 grt)

NOTE: In addition to the craft listed below, the Royal Navy maintains five converted "-ton"-class minesweepers, a tug, and two hovercraft for patrol at Hong Kong.

ROYAL HONG KONG POLICE FORCE
MARINE DISTRICT

PATROL BOATS

♦ **2 command boats** Bldr: Hong Kong United DY, 1965

PL 1 SEA LION   PL 2 SEA TIGER

D: 222 tons (fl)   **S:** 11.8 kts   **Dim:** 33.9 × 7.3 × 3.2
A: 1/12.7-mm mg   **M:** 2 Cummins diesels; 2 props; 674 hp   **Range:** 5,200/11.8
Man: 29 tot.

♦ **10 Damen-design** Bldr: Chung Wah SB & Eng, Kowloon

	In serv.		In serv.
PL 60 N. . .	2-80	PL 66 DORADO	8-9-80
PL 61 N. . .	2-80	PL 67 N. . .	. . .
PL 62 N. . .	2-80	PL 68 N. . .	. . .
PL 63 N. . .	1980	PL 69 N. . .	. . .
PL 64 N. . .	1980		
PL 65 CETUS	2-9-80		

PL 60

G. Arra, 1980

D: 86 tons (normal)   **S:** 23 kts   **Dim:** 26.2 × 5.9 × 1.80
A: 1/12.7-mm mg   **Electron Equipt:** Radar: 1 Decca 150
M: 2 MTU 12V396 TC 82 diesels (1,300 hp each), 1 MAN D2566 cruise diesel (195 hp); 3 props (Schottel on centerline); 2,600 hp
Range: 1,400/8   **Man:** 1 officer, 13 men

REMARKS: First unit laid down 9-79 to a Dutch design. Cruise engine provides 7-8 kt. max. speeds. Three more ordered 3-81 for logistic support duties, with same engines, but waterjet vice Schottel propeller for cruise; will have restricted patrol range but have a cargo hold.

♦ **7 78-foot craft** Bldr: Vosper Thornycroft, Singapore (In serv. 5-72 to 5-73)

PL 50 SEA CAT	PL 52 SEA LEOPARD	PL 54 SEA HAWK	PL 56 SEA FALCON
PL 51 SEA PUMA	PL 53 SEA EAGLE	PL 55 SEA LYNX	

Sea Eagle (PL 53)

G. Arra, 1980

D: 82 tons (fl)   **S:** 20.7 kts   **Dim:** 23.7 × 5.2 × 1.7   **A:** 1/12.7-mm mg
M: 2 Cummins diesels; 2 props; 1,500 hp   **Range:** 4,000/20   **Man:** 16 tot.

♦ **1 78-foot craft** Bldr: Thornycroft, Singapore (In serv. 1958)

PL 4 SEA HORSE

D: 72 tons (fl)   **S:** 15.5 kts   **Dim:** 23.7 × 4.6 × 1.4
A: Small arms   **M:** 3 diesels; 3 props; 2,070 hp   **Range:** 600/15.5   **Man:** 21 tot.

♦ **9 70-foot craft** Bldrs: 26-28: Hong Kong SY; 29-34: Cheoy Lee SY (In serv. 1954-55)

PL 26 SEA ROVER	PL 29 SEA RIDER	PL 32 SEA RAKER
PL 27 SEA FARER	PL 30 SEA NOMAD	PL 33 SEA RESCUER
PL 28 SEA ROAMER	PL 31 SEA WANDERER	PL 34 SEA RANGER

D: 52 tons (fl)   **S:** 10 kts   **Dim:** 21.3 × 5.2 × 1.6
A: Small arms   **M:** 2 diesels; 2 props; 430 hp   **Range:** 1,600/10   **Man:** 12 tot.

♦ **1 65-foot craft**

PL 6 ISLANDER

D: 48 tons (fl)   **S:** 10.5 kts   **Dim:** 19.8 × 4.4 × 1.6   **A:** Small arms
M: 1 diesel; 152 hp   **Range:** 1,400/9   **Man:** 11 tot.

♦ **8 45-foot converted wooden tugs** Bldr: Australia (In serv. 1944-45)

PL 9 SNIPE	PL 11 WREN	PL 13 GULL	PL 15 CORMORANT
PL 10 PUFFIN	PL 12 MALLARD	PL 14 TERN	PL 16 KESTREL

D: 27.7 tons   **S:** 9 kts   **Dim:** 13.7 × 4.6 × 2.1   **Man:** 5 tot.
A: Small arms   **M:** 1 Gray Marine 64 HN9 diesel   **Range:** 1,700/8

HONG KONG (*continued*)
PATROL BOATS (*continued*)

Sea Farer (PL 27)   G. Arra, 1977

Kestrel (P 16)   G. Arra

♦ **3 40-foot patrol launches** Bldr: Cheoy Lee SY (In serv. 1971)

WJB 20 JETSTREAM   WJB 21 SWIFTSTREAM   WJB 22 TIDESTREAM

    D: 17 tons   **S:** 24 kts   **Dim:** 12.3 × 3.5 × 0.6   **A:** small arms
    M: 2 diesels; 2 props; 740 hp   **Range:** 380/24   **Man:** 5 tot.

♦ **9 30-foot Spear class** Bldr: Fairey AllDay Marine, Hamble (In serv. 1981)

    D: 4.5 tons (fl)   **S:** 28 kts   **Dim:** 9.10 × 2.89 × 0.84
    A: 1/7.62-mm mg   **M:** 2 Perkins T6.3544 diesels; 2 props; 370 hp
    Range: 250/25   **Man:** 4 tot.

REMARKS: Glass-reinforced plastic construction.

MISCELLANEOUS CRAFT

♦ **1 support craft** Bldr: Thornycroft, Singapore (In serv. 1958)

PL 3 PANTHER

    D: 37 tons   **S:** 15 kts   **Dim:** 17.7 × . . . × . . .   **A:** Small arms
    M: 2 diesels; 2 props; . . . hp   **Range:** 240/15   **Man:** 8 tot.

♦ **1 personnel launch** Bldr: Hip Hing Cheung SY (In serv. 1975)

PL 7 DRAGON

    D: 18.5 tons   **S:** 23.5 kts   **Dim:** 16.0 × . . . × . . .
    A: Small arms   **M:** 2 diesels; 2 props; 700 hp   **Range:** 300/20   **Man:** 6 tot.

♦ **11 22-foot personnel launches** Bldr: Cheoy Lee SY, 1970

PMB 35 ARROW	PMB 38 SLINGSHOT	PMB 41 BULLET	PL 44 SWORD
PMB 36 DART	PMB 39 LANCE	PMB 42 SABRE	PL 45 SPEAR
PMB 37 JAVELIN	PMB 40 CROSSBOW	PMB 43 ASSEGAI	

    D: 4.8 tons   **S:** 20 kts   **Dim:** 6.7 × . . . × . . .
    A: Small arms   **M:** 1 diesel; . . . hp   **Range:** 160/20   **Man:** 2 tot.

HUNGARY
Hungarian People's Republic

PERSONNEL: 500 total

MERCHANT MARINE (1980): 22 ships—74,997 grt

HUNGARIAN ARMY MARITIME FORCE

♦ **10 river patrol craft**

    D: 100 tons   **S:** . . .   **Dim:** . . . × . . . × . . .
    A: 1/14.5-mm mg   **M:** 2 diesels

♦ **5 landing craft**

♦ **several small tugs**

♦ **several river transports**

ICELAND
Republic of Iceland

PERSONNEL: 160 men

MERCHANT MARINE (1980): 393 ships—188,215 grt (tankers—4 ships—3,028 grt)

AVIATION: 2 Fokker F-27 Friendship patrol aircraft, 1 Hughes helicopter, 2 Bell 47-G helicopters

COAST GUARD

FISHERIES-PROTECTION SHIPS

♦ **2 Aegir class**

	Bldr	L	In serv.
AEGIR	Aalborg SY, Denmark	1967	1968
TYR	Dannebrog Vaerft, Aarhus, Denmark	10-10-74	15-3-78

Aegir J. Meister, 1971

Tyr 1975

D: 1,150 tons (1,500 fl) **S:** 20 kts **Dim:** 69.65 (62.18 pp) × 10.0 × 4.7
A: 1/57-mm (6-pdr.)
M: 2 M.A.N. R8V 40/54 diesels; 2 Ka Me Wa CP props; 8,600 hp
Electric: 630 kVA **Man:** 22 tot.

REMARKS: Although built ten years apart, these two ships are nearly identical. Helicopter hangar between twin stacks. Three radar sets, fish-finding sonar. 20-ton bollard-pull towing winch, passive rolling tanks. Guns manufactured in 1896!

	Bldr	Laid down	L	In serv.
ODINN	Aalborg SY, Denmark	1-59	9-59	1-60

Odinn—now has a hangar like the **Aegir** J. Meister, 1971

D: 1,000 tons (fl) **S:** 18 kts **Dim:** 63.63 (56.61 pp) × 10.0 × 4.8
A: 1/57-mm (6-pdr.) low-angle
M: 2 Burmeister & Wain diesels; 2 props; 5,050 hp **Man:** 22 tot.

REMARKS: Rebuilt in 1975 with hangar, helicopter deck, and passive antirolling tanks.

THOR Bldr: Aalborg SY, Denmark (In serv. 1951)

Thor 1973

D: 920 tons (fl) **S:** 17 kts **Dim:** 62.8 (55.9 pp) × 9.5 × 4.0
A: 1/57-mm (6-pdr.)—1/47-mm (3-pdr.)
M: 2 MWM diesels; 2 props; 3,200 hp **Man:** 22 tot.

REMARKS: Fixed hangar, flight deck, and passive antirolling tanks added in 1971.

ARVAKUR Bldr: Bodewes, Netherlands (In serv. 1962)

D: 716 tons (fl) **S:** 12 kts **Dim:** 32.3 × 10.0 × 4.0
A: 1/12.7-mm mg **M:** 1 Deutz diesel; 1,000 hp **Man:** 12 tot.

REMARKS: Built as a lighthouse tender. Transferred to the Coast Guard in 1969.

ICELAND (*continued*)
FISHERIES-PROTECTION SHIPS (*continued*)

♦ **1 Nelson 45-foot customs launch** Bldr: W. S. Souter, Cowes, G.B. (In serv. 1978)
   S: 17 kts **M:** 2 Cummins V555M diesels

♦ . . . **21-SS Smuggler-class patrol launches** Bldr: Norway, 1975
   S: 36 kts **M:** Castoldi water jets

INDIA
Republic of India

PERSONNEL: approx. 46,000 men

MERCHANT MARINE (1980): 616 ships—5,911,367 grt (tankers: 42 ships—1,135,010 grt)

NAVAL AVIATION: The Navy has 16 Sea Hawk and 11 Bréguet Alizé fixed-wing planes for the carrier *Vikrant* and 14 Sea King (11 Mk 42, plus 3 Mk 42A delivered 8-80) and 19 Alouette-III helicopters. Three Soviet Ka-25 Hormone-A helicopters are to be delivered for the newly transferred Kashin-class guided-missile destroyers. The Indian Air Force has turned over to the Navy 5 Lockheed Constellations for long-range reconnaissance, while the U.S.S.R. has delivered at least 3 IL-38 May aircraft. Eight Sea Harrier planes, two of which will be T Mk 60 two-seaters and the others FRS Mk 51, have been ordered from Great Britain to replace the *Vikrant*'s Sea Hawk fighters; deliveries will begin in 1983, but plans to purchase a second batch have been dropped. The Harriers will be equipped with French Magic air-to-air missiles. Support aircraft include 2 Devon transports, 4 Hughes 300 helicopters, 4 Vampire T55 jet trainers, and 7 H3T 16 Kiran trainers.

WARSHIPS IN SERVICE, UNDER CONSTRUCTION, OR PROJECTED AS OF 1 JANUARY 1982

	L	Tons	Main armament
♦ **1 aircraft carrier**			
1 GLORY	1945	15,700	15 aircraft
♦ **8 (+6) submarines**			
		Tons (submerged)	
0 (+6) TYPE 209	19. . .	1,150	8/533-mm TT
8 FOXTROT	1965	2,400	10/533-mm TT
♦ **1 (+2) destroyers**			
1 (+2) KASHIN	1963-72	3,500	2 Goa SAM, 4 Styx, 2/76-mm, ASW weapons, 1 helicopter

♦ **22 (+6) frigates**

0 (+6) GODVARI	1980-. . .	3,000	4/SS-N-2C, 1/SA-N-4, 4/57-mm, 2 helicopters
6 LEANDER	1968-77	2,250	2/114-mm, 1 or 2 Sea Cat, 1 helicopter
10 PETYA II	1963	950	4/76.2-mm DP, 3/533-mm TT
3 LEOPARD	1957-59	2,250	2-4/114-mm DP, 1 Squid
2 WHITBY	1958	2,144	3/SS-N-2, 2 Limbo
1 MOD. BLACK SWAN	1943	1,470	4/102-mm DP

♦ **3 corvettes**

3 NANUCHKA	1977-78	600	4/SS-N-2C, 1/SA-N-4, 2/57-mm

♦ **14 guided-missile patrol boats**

♦ **10 minesweepers**

♦ **6 amphibious ships**

AIRCRAFT CARRIER

♦ **1 Glory class** Bldr: Vickers-Armstrong

	Laid down	L	In serv.
R 11 VIKRANT (ex-*Hercules*)	14-10-43	22-9-45	4-3-61

Vikrant (R 11)

D: 15,700 tons (19,500 fl) **S:** 24 kts (fl), 17 kts cruising
Dim: 211.25 (198.0 wl) × 24.29 × 7.15
A: 15/40-mm (II × 4, I × 7)—15 aircraft (max. capacity)
Electron Equipt: Radar: 1/960, 1/278, 1/293, 1/963—TACAN
M: 2 sets Parsons GT; 2 props; 40,000 hp
Boilers: 4 Admiralty; 28 kg/cm²   **Fuel:** 3,200 tons
Range: 6,200/23, 12,000/14 **Man:** Peacetime: 1,075 tot. Wartime: 1,340 tot.

REMARKS: Bought in Great Britain in 1-57 while still incomplete. Air-conditioned. One hangar, two elevators, angled flight deck, steam catapult. Flight deck: 210 × 34. Being modernized 1974-81 with new boilers, engines, and new CIC, and will receive eight Sea Harrier (two 2-seat) to replace obsolete Sea Hawk fighters. The Alizé ASW aircraft are to be refurbished, and the ship will also carry Alouette-III ASW helicopters and possibly Sea King helicopters. A replacement carrier, to be built in India, is being designed.

SUBMARINES

♦ **6 West German Type SSK-1500** Bldr: Howaldtswerke, Hamburg (first two);

India (remainder)

	Laid down	L	In serv.		Laid down	L	In serv.
S. . . N. . .	. . .	. . .	1983	S. . . N. . .	. . .	. . .	. . .
S. . . N. . .	. . .	. . .	. . .	S. . . N. . .	. . .	. . .	. . .
S. . . N. . .	. . .	. . .	. . .	S. . . N. . .	. . .	. . .	. . .

D: 1,150/980/1,440 tons **S:** 11/21.5 kts **Dim:** 61.0 × 6.20 × 5.5
A: 8/533-mm (fwd)—14 torpedoes (tot.)
M: 4 MTU 820Db diesels (600 hp each), 2 motors; 1 prop; 5,000 hp
Fuel: 118 tons **Range:** 8,200/8 (snorkel) **Man:** 32 tot.

REMARKS: Reportedly ordered 10-7-80, but has been denied during 1981 by some
Indian authorities. A variant of the Type 209 design.

♦ **8 Soviet Foxtrot class**

	In serv.		In serv.
S 20 KURSURA	12-70	S 40 VELA	31-8-73
S 21 KARANJ	10-70	S 41 VAGIR	3-11-73
S 22 KANDHERI	1-69	S 42 VAGLI	10-8-74
S 23 KALVARI	16-7-68	S 43 VAGSHEER	26-12-74

Karanj (S 21) G. Arra, 1978

Karanj (S 21) G. Arra, 1978

D: 1,950/2,400 tons **S:** 16/15.5 **Dim:** 91.50 × 7.50 × 6.0
A: 10/533-mm TT (6 fwd, 4 aft)—22 torpedoes or mines
Electron Equipt: Radar: 1/Snoop Tray
Sonar: 1/MF active, passive array
M: 3 diesels (2,000 hp each), 3 motors; 3 props; 5,300 hp
Range: 11,000/8 (snorkel) **Man:** 8 officers, 70 men

REMARKS: Patrol endurance: 70 days

NOTE: The cruiser Mysore (C 60) was decommissioned at the end of 1981.

GUIDED-MISSILE DESTROYERS

♦ **3 Soviet Kashin class** Bldr: Nikolayev SY

	In serv.		In serv.		In serv.
D 51 RAJPUT	10-80	D 52 RANA	1981	D 53 RANJIT	1982

Rajput (D 51) 1980

Rajput (D 51) 1980

GUIDED-MISSILE DESTROYERS (*continued*)

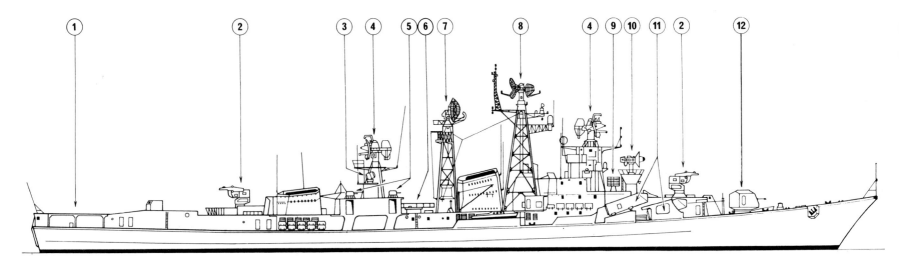

Rajput 1. Helicopter facility 2. SA-N-1 systems 3. Drum Tilt radar GFCS 4. Peel Group radar 5. 30-mm AA guns 6. Torpedo tubes (V + 1) 7. Big Net radar 8. Head Net-C radar 9. RBU 6000 ASW RL 10. Owl Screech radar GFCS 11. SS-N-2C SSM 12. 76.2-mm DP (II × 1)

D: 3,950 tons (4,950 fl) **S:** 35 kts **Dim:** 146.0 × 15.8 × 4.8 (hull)
A: 4/SS-N-2C SSM (I × 4)—2/SA-N-1 SAM syst. (II × 2; 44 Goa Missiles)—
  2/76.2-mm DP (II × 1)—8/30-mm AA (II × 4)—5/533-mm TT (V × 1)—2/
  RBU 6000 ASW RL (XII × 2)—1/Ka-25 Hormone-A ASW helicopter
Electron Equipt: Radar: 2/Don Kay, 1/Big Net, 1/Head Net C, 2/Peel Group,
    1/Owl Screech, 2/Drum Tilt
  IFF: 2/High Pole B
  Sonar: 1/hull-mounted MF, 1/MF VDS
  ECM: 2/Watch Dog, 2 Top Hat A, 2 Top Hat B, 4/chaff RL
    (XVI × 4)
M: 4 gas turbines; 2 props; 96,000 hp **Range:** 900/35; 5,000/18

REMARKS: New construction units, not conversions from former Soviet Navy units.
  In contrast to Soviet Navy "Modified Kashins," the SS-N-2C missiles are mounted
  forward and fire forward, while the after twin 76.2-mm gun mount has been omitted

in favor of a hangar for the helicopter, reached by an inclined elevator/ramp. Have
twin 30-mm vice 30-mm gatling guns.

FRIGATES

♦ **0 (+6) Bldr:** Mazagon Docks, Bombay

	Laid down	L	In serv.
F. . . GODAVARI	6-78	15-5-80	1983
F. . . GANGA	. . .	10-81	. . .
F. . . GOMATI	. . .	. . .	. . .
F. . . N. . .	. . .	. . .	. . .
F. . . N. . .	. . .	. . .	. . .
F. . . N. . .	. . .	. . .	. . .

FRIGATES (continued)

D: 3,000 tons (3,600 fl) **S:** 31 kts **Dim:** 121.0 × 14.1 × 4.3 (hull)
A: 4/SS-N-2C SSM (I × 4)—1/SA-N-4 SAM syst. (II × 1; 18 Gecko missiles)—1/
76-mm DP OTO Melara—8/30-mm AA (II × 4)—6/324-mm Mk 32 ASW TT
(III × 2; A 184 torpedoes)—2 Sea King ASW helicopters
Electron Equipt: Radar: 1/navigational, 1/Head Net C, 1/LW-08, 1/Pop Group,
4/Drum Tilt, 1/WM-25(?)
Sonar: 1 British Type 184
M: 2 sets GT; 2 five-bladed props; 30,000 hp
Boilers: 2 Babcock & Wilcox, 3-drum; 38.7 kg/cm², 450°C

REMARKS: Design derived from the *Leander* class, with the same propulsion plant but
larger hull. The second group of three will use gas turbine propulsion. Electronics
and weapons systems a very diverse selection of Western European and Soviet
systems.

♦ **6 British Leander class** Bldr: Mazagon Docks, Bombay

	Laid down	L	In serv.
F 33 NILGIRI	10-66	23-10-68	3-6-72
F 34 HIMGIRI	1967	6-5-70	23-11-74
F 35 UDAYGIRI	14-9-70	24-10-72	18-2-76
F 36 DUNAGIRI	1-73	9-3-74	5-5-77
F 37 TARAGIRI	1974	25-10-76	16-5-80
F 38 VINDHYAGIRI	1976	12-11-77	8-7-81

Udaygiri (F 35)—VDS well, but no VDS fitted   1977

Taragiri (F 37)—final, improved variant   1979

Himgiri (F 34)—with Wasp helicopter on deck   1973

D: 2,250 tons (2,800 fl) **S:** 30 kts **Dim:** 113.38 × 13.1 × 4.27 (avg.)
A: 2/114-mm DP (II × 1)—F-33: 1/Sea Cat GWS 22; Others; 2/Sea Cat with M-4
directors—1/Limbo Mk 10 ASW mortar (not on F 37 and F 38, which have 1/
375-mm Bofors ASW RL (II × 1))—1 Alouette-III ASW helicopter (Sea
King on F 37 and F 38)—F 37, 38: 6/324-mm Mk 32 ASW TT (III × 2; A-184
torpedoes)
Electron Equipt: Radar: F 33: 1/965, 1/993, 1/978, 2/903
F 35 on: 1/Decca navigational, 1/ZW-06, 1/DA-08,
3/M 45
Sonar: 1/177—1/199 VDS on F 33 and F 34
M: 2 sets GT; 2 five-bladed props; 30,000 hp **Electric:** 2,500 kw
Boilers: 2 Babcock & Wilcox, 3-drum; 38.7 kg/cm², 450°C **Fuel:** 500 tons
Range: approx. 4,500/12

REMARKS: The first two are very similar to British versions of the *Leander* class, but
later units have been progressively improved, using HSA radars and an ever-greater
proportion of Indian-built components. F 37 and F 38 have very large telescoping
hangars situated much nearer the stern and requiring removal of the three-barreled
Limbo ASW mortar (replaced by a twin Bofors ASW RL on the forecastle); the new
hangar will hold a Westland Sea King ASW helicopter. F 37 and F 38 also have
openings in the hull sides beneath the helicopter deck at the stern. F 33 and F 34
received Type 199 variable-depth sonar; later units did not. The single Sea Cat
quadruple SAM launcher in the F 33 has one MRS-3 director; later ships have two
Dutch M-4 directors (with M-45 radar).

♦ **10 Soviet Petya-II class** Bldr: U.S.S.R

P 68 ARNALA	P 74 ANDAMAN	P 78 KADMATH	P 80 KAVARATTI
P 69 ANDROTH	P 75 AMINI	P 79 KILTAN	P 81 KATCHAL
P 73 ANJADIP	P 77 KAMORTA		

Amini (P 75)   1975

FRIGATES (continued)

Andaman (P 74)—with old pendant number

D: 950 tons (1,150 fl) **S:** 28 kts **Dim:** 80.0 (76.2 pp) × 9.8 × 3.0 (hull)
A: 4/76.2-mm DP (II × 2)—4/RBU-2500 ASW RL (XVI × 4)—3/533-mm TT
   (III × 1)—2 d.c. racks—2/mine rails
Electron Equipt: Radars: 1/Don-2, 1/Slim Net, 1/Hawk Screech
               Sonar: 1 Hercules
M: CODOG: 1 diesel (6,000 hp), 2 gas turbines (15,000 hp each); 3 props; 36,000
   hp **Man:** 98 tot.

REMARKS: Transferred in 1969, 1972, and 1975. Considered patrol ships (corvettes)
by India, rather than frigates; hence "P" series pendants. Were new construction,
export-version ships.

◆ 3 British Leopard class

	Bldr	Laid down	L	In serv.
F 31 BRAHMAPUTRA	J. Brown, Clydebank	1956	15-3-57	28-3-58
(ex-*Panther*)				
F 37 BEAS	Vickers-Armstrong	1957	9-10-58	24-5-60
F 38 BETWA	Vickers-Armstrong	1957	15-9-59	8-12-60

Beas (F 137)—prior to removal of 40-mm director aft   1971

D: 2,250 tons (2,515 fl) **S:** 25 kts
Dim: 103.63 (100.58 pp) × 12.19 × 4.80 (hull)
A: 4/114-mm DP Mk 6 (II × 2)—2/40-mm AA Mk 5 (II × 1)—1/Squid ASW
   mortar (III × 1)
Electron Equipt: Radar: 1/293, 1/978, 1/275
              Sonar: 1/177, 1/162, 1/174B
M: 8 Admiralty Standard Range-I diesels; 2 props; 12,380 hp
Electric: 1,200 kw **Range:** 7,500/15 **Man:** 240 tot.

REMARKS: *Brahmaputra*, originally ordered for the British Navy, had the after 114-
mm twin gun mount replaced by an accommodations deckhouse in 1978 and acts as
Cadet Training Ship to replace the "River"-class former frigate, *Tir* (stricken 1979).
The *Beas* was modernized during 1980. 40-mm radar GFCS removed.

◆ 2 British Whitby class

	Bldr	Laid down	L	In serv.
F 40 TALWAR	Cammell Laird	1957	18-7-58	4-60
F 43 TRISHUL	Harland & Wolff	1957	18-6-58	1-60

Talwar (F 40)   1977

D: 2,144 tons (2,560 fl) **S:** 30 kts **Dim:** 112.7 × 12.5 × 5.4 (over sonar)
A: 3/SS-N-2 Styx SSM (I × 3)—4/40-mm AA (II × 1, I × 2)—2/Limbo ASW
   mortars (III × 2)
Electron Equipt: Radars: 1/293, 1/277, 1/978, 1/Square Tie
              Sonars: 1/177, 1/174B, 1/162
M: 2 sets GT; 2 props; 30,000 hp **Electric:** 1,140 kw
Boilers: 2 Babcock & Wilcox; 38.7 kg/cm², 450°C **Fuel:** 370 tons
Range: 4,500/12 **Man:** 11 officers, 220 men

REMARKS: Three SS-N-2 Styx launchers—removed from Osa-I-class, guided-missile
patrol boats—have replaced the twin 114-mm Mk 6 gun mount in these two ships.
Soviet Square Tie radar associated with Styx replaced the gun director, atop the
pilothouse.

FRIGATES (continued)

♦ **1 British Modified "Black Swan" class**

	Bldr	Laid down	L	In serv.
F 46 KISTNA	Yarrow, Scotstoun	14-7-42	22-4-43	26-8-43

D: 1,470 tons (1,925 fl) **S:** 19 kts **Dim:** 91.92 × 11.73 × 3.50 (hull)
A: 4/102-mm DP (II × 2)—2/40-mm AA (I × 2)—2/d.c. projectors
Electron Equipt: Radar: 1/navigational, 1/293
　　　　　　　　　　Sonar: 1/149
M: 2 sets GT; 2 props; 4,300 hp **Boilers:** 2 Admiralty 3-drum
Fuel: 390 tons **Range:** 3,700/17; 5,700/15; 9,200/10 **Man:** 210 tot.

REMARKS: Sole survivor in Indian service of a group of World War II British-built
sloops and frigates. Employed in training and will probably soon be stricken.

GUIDED-MISSILE CORVETTES

♦ **3 Soviet Nanuchka II class** Bldr: Petrovskiy SY, Leningrad

K 71 VIJAYDURG (In serv. 12-76)　K 73 HOSDURG (In serv. 1-78)
K 72 SINDHURDURG (In serv. 5-77)

Sindhurdurg (K 72)　　　　　　　　　　　　　　　　　　　1977

D: 780 tons (930 fl) **S:** 30 kts **Dim:** 60.0 × 13.2 × 2.7
A: 4/SS-N-2C (II × 2)—1/SA-N-4 system—2/57-mm AA (II × 1)
Electron Equipt: Radar: 1/Band Stand, 1/Pop Group, 1/Muff Cob, 1/Don-2
　　　　　　　　　　IFF: 2/Square Head, 1/High Pole
　　　　　　　　　　ECM: passive syst., 2 chaff RL (XVI × 2)
Range: 3,600/15 **Man:** 60 tot.

REMARKS: Arrived in India 3-77, 8-77, and 3-78 respectively. Additional units (if,
indeed, any were ordered) canceled, possibly due to reports that these are poor sea
boats. A new, larger missile corvette to carry SS-N-2C SSM is under design in India.

GUIDED-MISSILE PATROL BOATS

♦ **8 Soviet Osa-II class**

K 90 PRACHAND	K 92 PRABAL	K 94 CHAMAK	K 96 CHAPAK
K 91 PRALAYA	K 93 PRATAP	K 95 CHAPAL	K 97 CHARAG

D: 215 tons (240 fl) **S:** 36 kts **Dim:** 39.0 × 7.7 × 1.8
A: 4/SS-N-2B Styx (I × 4)—4/30-mm AA (II × 2)
Electron Equipt: Radar: 1/Square Tie, 1/Drum Tilt
　　　　　　　　　　IFF: 2/Square Head, 1/Head Pole B
M: 3 M-504 diesels; 3 props; 15,000 hp **Range:** 450/34; 700/20 **Man:** 30 tot.

REMARKS: To be equipped with modern ECM system. First four in service 17-2-76,
second four on 5-11-76.

♦ **6 Soviet Osa-I class** (In serv. 1971)

K 82 VEER	K 85 VINASH	K 88 NIRBHIK
K 83 VIDYUT	K 86 NIPAT	K 89 NIRGHAT

D: 175 tons (210 fl) **S:** 36 kts **Dim:** 39.0 × 7.7 × 1.8
A: 4/SS-N-2A Styx (I × 4)—4/30-mm AA (II × 2)
Electron Equipt: Radar: 1/Square Tie, 1/Drum Tilt
　　　　　　　　　　IFF: 2/Square Head, 1/High Pole B
M: 3 M503A diesels; 3 props; 12,000 hp **Range:** 450/34; 700/20 **Man:** 30 tot.

REMARKS: Transferred 1971. *Vijeta* (K 84) and *Nashat* (K 87) had their missile tubes
removed and three from each placed on the frigates *Talwar* (F 40) and *Trishul* (F
43). Both, however, remain in service as patrol boats.

PATROL BOATS

♦ **2 Soviet OSA-I class** (In serv. 1971)

. . . VIJETA (ex-K 84)　. . . NASHAT (ex-K 87)

REMARKS: Missile tubes removed, as noted above. *Nashat* was converted to carry
frogmen in 1980.

MINE WARFARE SHIPS

♦ **6 Soviet Natya class**

M 61 PONDICHERY	M 63 BEDI	M 65 ALLEPPY
M 62 PORBANDAR	M 64 BHAVNAGAR	M 66 RATNAGIRI

Pondichery (M 61)　　　　　　　　　　　　　　　　　　　1978

D: 650 tons (750 fl) **S:** 18 kts **Dim:** 61.0 × 10.0 × 3.0
A: 4/30-mm AA (II × 2)—4/25-mm AA (II × 2)—2/RBU-1200 ASW RL (V ×
　　2)—mines **M:** 2 diesels; 2 props; 5,000 hp **Man:** 80 tot.
Electron Equipt: Radar: 1/Don-2, 1/Drum Tilt
　　　　　　　　　　IFF: 2/Square Head, 1/High Pole B

REMARKS: Two transferred in 1978, two in 1979, and two in 1980. Differ from the
units in the Soviet Navy in that they do not have a ramp at the stern. Can be used
as ASW escorts.

MINE WARFARE SHIPS *(continued)*

NOTE: The British "Ton"-class minesweepers *Cuddalore* (M 90) and *Kakinada* (M 93) were stricken in 1980 and *Cannamore* (M 91) and *Karwar* (M 92) in 1981.

♦ 4 British "Ham"-class inshore minesweepers

		Bldr	L
M 79	BIMLIPATHAM (ex-*Hildersham*)	Vosper, Portsmouth	5-2-54
M 80	BASSEIN (ex-*Littleham*)	Brooke Marine, Lowestoft	4-5-54
M 81	BHATKAL	Mazagon Docks, Bombay	5-67
M 82	BULSAR	Mazagon Docks, Bombay	17-5-69

Bhatkal (M 81)—old pendant number   1968

D: 120 tons (159 fl)   **S:** 14 kts (9, sweeping)
Dim: 32.43 (30.48 pp) × 6.45 × 1.7   **A:** 1/20-mm AA
Electron Equipt: Radar: 1/978   **Man:** 2 officers, 13 men
M: 2 Paxman YHAXM diesels; 2 props; 1,000 hp   **Fuel:** 25 tons

REMARKS: M 79 and M 80 were transferred in 1955. The Indian-built units have teakwood hulls but are otherwise almost identical.

AMPHIBIOUS WARFARE SHIPS

♦ 4 Soviet Polnocny-C class Bldr: Polnocny SY, Gdansk, Poland

L 14 GHORPAD   L 15 KESARI   L 16 SHARDUL   L 17 SHARABH

D: 1,150 (fl)   **S:** 18 kts   **Dim:** 81.0 × 10.0 × 2.0
A: 4/30-mm AA (II × 2)—2/140-mm rocket launchers (XVIII × 2)
Electron Equipt: Radar: 1/Don-2   **M:** 2 diesels; 2 props; 5,000 hp
Man: 60 tot.

REMARKS: Three transferred in 1975, one in 1976. Do not have a helicopter platform as on other export Polnocny-Cs. Cargo: 350 tons.

♦ 2 Soviet Polnocny-A class Bldr: Polnocny SY, Gdansk, Poland

L 13 GULDAR   L 14 GHARIAL

D: 900 tons (fl)   **S:** 18 kts   **Dim:** 72.5 × 8.5 × 2.0
A: 2/25-mm AA (II × 1)—2/140-mm rocket-launchers (XVIII × 2)
Electron Equipt: Radar: 1/Don-2   **M:** 2 diesels; 2 props; 4,000 hp
Man: 40 tot.

REMARKS: Transferred 1966. Cargo: 200 tons.

Shardul (L 16)   1976

♦ 4 Vasco da Gama-class utility landing craft

		Bldr	L	In serv.
L 34	VASCO DA GAMA	Goa SY, Goa	29-11-78	28-1-80
L 35	N . . .	Goa SY, Goa	13-1-79	1-12-80
L 36	N . . .	Hooghly DY, Calcutta	16-3-80	. . .
L 37	N . . .	Hooghly DY, Calcutta	. . .	. . .

D: 500 tons (fl)   **S:** 9 kts   **Dim:** 55.96 × 7.94 × 1.71 (aft)
A: 2/40-mm AA (I × 2)—mines
M: 3 Kirlasker-M.A.N. W8V 17.5/22 AMAL diesels; 3 Kort-nozzle props; 1,245 hp
Range: 1,000/8

REMARKS: Cargo: 250 tons or 120 men.

HYDROGRAPHIC SURVEY SHIPS

♦ 3 Sandhayak class Bldr: Garden Reach SB & Engineers, Calcutta

		L	In serv.
J . . .	SANDHAYAK	6-4-77	26-2-81
J . . .	NIRDESHAK	16-11-78	1982
J . . .	NIRUPAK	10-7-81	. . .

D: 1,200 tons (1,880 fl)   **S:** 16.75 kts   **Dim:** 85.77 (78.80 pp) × 12.30 × 3.34
A: 2/40-mm AA (I × 2)
Electron Equipt: Radar: 1/Decca TM-series navigational
M: 1 GRSE-M.A.N. G8V 30/45 ATL diesel; 1 prop; 3,920 hp (plus 1 Pleuger 200-hp active rudder; 5 kts)
Fuel: 264 tons   **Range:** 6,000/14   **Man:** 12 officers, 134 men

REMARKS: Intended to replace old *Sutlej*-class ships. 2,050 grt. Telescoping hangar for one Alouette-III helicopter. Four inshore survey launches with "Hydrodist" fixing system. Have 3 precision depth-finders, Decca "Navigator," Decca "Hi-Fix," taut-wire measuring gear and a gravimeter. Carry 169 tons water and 5 tons aviation fuel.

HYDROGRAPHIC SURVEY SHIPS *(continued)*

♦ **1 hydrographic-survey ship**

	Bldr	L	In serv.
J 14 DARSHAK	Hindustan SY, India	2-11-59	28-12-61

Darshak (J 14) 1974

D: 2,790 tons **S:** 16 kts **Dim:** 97.3 × 14.94 × 5.8
A: 1/40-mm AA **M:** 2 diesels, electric drive; 2 props; 3,000 hp **Man:** 150 tot.

REMARKS: Carries one Alouette-III helicopter.

♦ **2 Gaveshani-class small inshore-survey craft**

J . . . GAVESHANI J . . . N . . .

REMARKS: Launched 2-76.

AUXILIARY SHIPS

♦ **1 Soviet Ugra-class submarine tender** Bldr: U.S.S.R. (In serv. 28-12-68)

A 54 AMBA

Amba (A 54) 1968

D: 6,750 tons (9,500 fl) **S:** 20 kts **Dim:** 141.4 × 17.7 × 6.5
A: 4/76.2-mm DP (II × 2)
Electron Equipt: Radars: 1/Don-2, 1/Slim Net, 2/Hawk Screech
M: 4 diesels; 2 props; 8,000 hp **Range:** 10,000/12

REMARKS: Helicopter platform. Quarters for 750 men. Two 6-ton cranes, one 10-ton crane.

♦ **1 Soviet T 58-class submarine-rescue ship**

A 55 NISTAR

D: 725 tons (840 fl) **S:** 18 kts **Dim:** 72.0 × 9.1 × 2.5
Electron Equipt: Radar: 1/Don-2 **M:** 2 diesels; 2 props; 4,000 hp
Man: 60 tot.

REMARKS: Built during late 1950s, transferred 1971. Two rescue chambers, port and starboard sides of the stern. Decompression chamber, diving bells.

NOTE: Two new submarine rescue ships are to be built in India.

♦ **1 repair ship** Bldr: Foundation Maritime, Canada (L: 25-7-44)

A 52 DHARINI (ex-*La Petite Hermine*, ex-*Ketowna Park*)

D: 6,000 tons (fl) **S:** 9 kts **Dim:** 99.0 × 13.9 × 4.0
M: Triple-expansion reciprocating steam; 1 prop; 800 hp **Fuel:** 620 tons

REMARKS: Sold to India for cargo use, 1953; in service in Indian Navy 5-60.

♦ **1 transport** Bldr: Mazagon DY, Bombay

. . . N . . .

D: 1,800 grt **S:** 20 kts **Dim:** 74.0 (pp) × 14.4 × . . .
M: 2 diesels; 2 props; 8,000 hp

REMARKS: Ordered 3-81. No other details available.

♦ **1 hospital ship** Bldr: Hindustan SY

N . . .

D: . . . **S:** 12 kts **Dim:** 52.0 (46.8 pp) × 9.5 × 3.0
M: 2 diesels; 2 props; 900 hp
Man: 19 crew, plus 15 medical staff (90 hospital berths)

REMARKS: Ordered 2-81.

OILERS

♦ **2 Deepak class** Bldr: Bremer Vulkan Schiffbau, Bremen-Vegasack, West Germany

A 50 DEEPAK (In serv. 20-11-72) A 57 SHAKTI (In serv. 21-2-76)

Shakti (A 57) G. Arra, 1978

D: 6,785 tons (22,000 fl) **S:** 20 kts **Dim:** 168.43 (157.5 pp) × 23.0 × 9.14
A: 3/40-mm AA (I × 3)—2/20-mm AA (I × 2) **M:** 1 set GT; 1 prop; 16,500 hp
Boilers: 2 Babcock & Wilcox **Range:** 5,500/18.5 **Man:** 169 tot.

REMARKS: 12,690 grt/15,800 dwt. Two liquid-replenishment stations per side, with British-style rigs. Telescoping hangar and flight deck for one helicopter. Carry 12,624 tons fuel oil, 1,280 tons diesel fuel, 1,495 tons aviation fuel, 812 tons fresh water, and some dry cargo.

NOTE: The tanker *Lok Adhar* was returned to civil control in 1979.

♦ **1 former merchant tanker** Bldr: Japan (In serv. 1959)

DESH DEEP

OILERS (continued)

D: 16,400 tons (fl)   **S:** 13 kts   **Dim:** 145.0 (135.0 pp) × 19.5 × 7.8
M: 2 Sulzer 6-cyl. diesels; 2 props; 8,200 hp   **Electric:** 320 kw
Fuel: 1,056 tons   **Range:** 23,000/13   **Man:** . . . tot.

REMARKS: 8,324 grt, 12,177 dwt. Taken over 1972 and operated as a freighting tanker. Cargo: 11,800 tons (100,048 m³).

TUGS

♦ **2 Gaj-class oceangoing tugs** Bldr: Garden Reach SB & Eng., Calcutta

A 51 GAJ (In serv. 20-9-73)   A. . . MATANGA (L: 29-10-77)

Gaj (A 51)—old pendant number   Garden Reach, 1973

D: 1,465 tons (1,600 fl)   **S:** 15 kts   **Dim:** 66.0 (60.0 pp) × 11.6 × 4.0
A: . . .   **M:** 2 GRSE-M.A.N. G7V diesels; 2 CP props; 3,292 hp
Range: 8,000/12

REMARKS: Fitted for salvage work. 40-ton bollard pull.

YARD AND SERVICE CRAFT

♦ **3 fuel lighters** Bldr: Rajabagan Yd., Bombay

PURAN (In serv. 3-6-77)   PRADHAYAK (In serv. 2-78)
N. . . (In serv. . . .)

D: 376 tons   **S:** 9 kts   **Dim:** 49.7 × . . . × 3.0
M: 1 diesel; 1 prop; 560 hp

♦ **2 fuel lighters** Bldr: Mazagon Dock, Bombay (In serv. 1970)

POSHAK   PURAK

REMARKS: Cargo: 400 tons diesel fuel.

♦ **3 water lighters** Bldr: 1 by Rajabagan, Bombay; others: Mazagon DY, Bombay

D: 200 tons   **S:** 9 kts   **Dim:** 32.0 × . . . × 2.4
M: 1 diesel; 1 prop; . . . hp

♦ **3 torpedo retrievers** Bldr: Goa SY

A 71 N. . . (L: 5-11-80)   A 72 N. . . (L: 5-11-80)

D: 110 tons (fl)   **S:** 11 kts   **Dim:** 28.5 × 6.1 × 1.4
M: 1 Kirlasker-M.A.N. 12-cyl. diesel; 1 prop; 300 hp

♦ **3 diving tenders** Bldr: Cleback SY (In serv. 1979)

♦ **3 large harbor tugs** Bldr: Mazagon Dock, Bombay (In serv. 1973-74)

AJARAL   ARJUN   BALSHIL

♦ **1 sail-training craft** Bldr: Alcock Ashdown, Bhavnagar

VARUNA (In serv. 17-4-81)   **D:** 105 tons   **Man:** 20 cadets

REMARKS: Two-masted brig. Construction of a second sail-training ship has been proposed; to carry 90 cadets.

NOTE: There are undoubtedly a large number of other yard and service craft, for which no names or data are available.

COAST GUARD

The Coast Guard was established 1-2-77 to ensure surveillance of India's 200-nautical-mile economic zone. Commanded by an admiral, it consisted initially of ships and craft transferred from the Indian Navy. The name "Coast Guard" is written in large black letters on the sides of ship hulls, which are painted white.

The Coast Guard has announced that, in addition to the units listed below, it plans to acquire a salvage tug of 1,570 grt, a pollution-control ship, twelve patrol aircraft, and one search-and-rescue aircraft.

PATROL SHIPS

♦ **3 "1,000-ton" new construction** Bldr: Mazagon DY, Bombay

	Laid down	L	In serv.
T. . . VIKRAM	3-81	9-81	. . .
T. . . N. . .	. . .	. . .	. . .
T. . . N. . .	. . .	. . .	. . .

D: 1,040 tons (fl)   **S:** 21 kts   **Dim:** . . . × . . . × . . .   **A:** . . .
M: 2 SEMT-Pielstick 16PA6 diesels; 2 CP props; 12,800 hp   **Man:** . . .

REMARKS: Ordered 1979. Will have a helicopter hangar and flight deck.

♦ **2 British Blackwood class** former ASW frigates

	Bldr	Laid down	L	In serv.
T 31 KIRPAN	Alex. Stephen, Glasgow	1957	19-8-58	7-59
T 32 KUTHAR	Samuel White, Cowes	1957	14-10-58	1960

D: 1,180 tons (1,456 fl)   **S:** 23 kts   **Dim:** 94.5 (91.44 pp) × 10.05 × 4.7
A: 3/40-mm AA (I × 3)—2/Mk-10 Limbo ASW mortars (III × 2)
Electron Equipt: Radar: 1/978
                    Sonars: 1/174, 1/170B, 1/162
M: 1 set GT; 1 prop; 15,000 hp   **Electric:** 1,108 kw
Boilers: 2 Babcock & Wilcox; 38.7 kg/cm²; 450°C   **Range:** 4,500/12

REMARKS: Transferred to the Coast Guard 1-7-77. Sister *Khukri* sunk 9-12-71 by a Pakistani submarine.

INDIA (*continued*)
PATROL SHIPS (*continued*)

Kirpan (T 31)—in naval service
1969

PATROL BOATS

♦ **3 new construction** Bldr: Garden Reach SB & Eng., Calcutta

N . . .   N . . .   N . . .

   D: 200 tons **S:** . . . kts **Dim:** . . .

REMARKS: Ordered 1979; still in design stage as of 1-81.

♦ **7 SDB Mk-2 class** Bldr: Garden Reach SB & Eng., Calcutta

	L	In serv.		L	In serv.
T 51 N . . .	31-12-75	17-11-78	T 55 N . . .	2-81	. . .
T 52 N . . .	. . .	3-9-77	T 56 N . . .	2-81	. . .
T 53 N . . .	. . .	12-4-78	T 57 N . . .	. . .	. . .
T 54 RAJHANS	. . .	1-81			

   D: 160 tons (fl) **S:** 32 kts **Dim:** 37.5 × 7.5 × 1.75
   A: 1/40-mm AA—2/d.c. projectors—2/d.c. racks
   M: 2 Deltic 18-42K diesels; 2 props; 7,000 hp; 1 Cummins NH-220 cruise diesel;
     165 hp
   Electric: 220 kVa **Range:** 1,000/14 **Man:** 4 officers, 26 men

REMARKS: Patterned after the "Ford" class. Construction program far behind schedule.

♦ **5 Soviet Poluchat-I class**

501 PANAJI   502 PANVEL   503 PAMBAN   504 PULI   505 PULICAT

   D: 80 tons (90 fl) **S:** 18 kts **Dim:** 29.57 × 6.1 × 1.9
   A: 2/14.5-mm AA (II × 1) **M:** 2 M-50 diesels; 2 props; 2,400 hp
   Range: 460/17; 900/10 **Man:** 20 tot.

REMARKS: Transferred 1967-69.

♦ **1 British "Ford" class** Bldr: Hooghly Docking & Eng., Calcutta

735 ABHAY (In serv. 13-11-61)

   D: 120 tons (151 fl) **S:** 18 kts **Dim:** 35.76 × 6.1 × 1.7 **A:** 1/40-mm AA
   M: 2 Paxman YHAXM diesels; 2 props; 1,000 hp; 1 Foden FD-6 cruise diesel;
     100 hp **Fuel:** 23 tons **Range:** 500/12, 1,000/8 (cruise engine)

REMARKS: Originally a class of six: two stricken, two to Bangladesh, one to Mauritius.

Indian "Ford" class
1968

INDONESIA

PERSONNEL (1980): 40,000 men, including 5,000 Marines

MERCHANT MARINE (1980): 1,180 ships—1,411,688 grt (tankers: 98 ships—164,341 grt)

NAVAL AVIATION: The Indonesian Navy has a small coastal-surveillance and logistic-support force consisting of 12 Australian Searchmaster N22B maritime surveillance aircraft, 6 C-47 Dakota transports, 3 Aero Commander light transports, 4 BO-105 and 3 Alouette-III helicopters. Six additional Searchmaster aircraft have been ordered. Planned is a "Naval Combat Element" of 12 Northrup F-5E "Tiger-II" jet fighters.

WARSHIPS IN SERVICE OR UNDER CONSTRUCTION AS OF 1 JANUARY 1982

	L	Tons (Surfaced)	Main armament
♦ **3 submarines**			
2 TYPE 209	1980	980	8/533-mm TT
1 WHISKEY	1958	1,050 Tons	6/533-mm TT
♦ **11 frigates**			
1 KAPAL LATIH	1980	1,850	4/Exocet, 1/57-mm DP
3 FATAHILAH	1977-79	1,160	4/Exocet, 1/120-mm DP, 1/40-mm
4 CLAUD JONES	1958-59	1,450	1 or 2/76-mm, 6/Mk-32 TT
2 RIGA	1954-57	1,200	3/100-mm DP, 3/533-mm TT
1 PATTIMURA	1956	950	2/85-mm DP

♦ **4 (+4) guided-missile patrol boats**

♦ **16 patrol boats**

♦ **2 minesweepers**

♦ **9 (+2) amphibious-warfare ships**

NOTE: The names of Indonesian ships are preceded by the designation KRI (*Kapalperang Republik Indonesia*, or Warship of the Republic of Indonesia).

SUBMARINES

♦ **2 West German Type 209** Bldr: Howaldtswerke, Kiel

	Laid down	L	In serv.
401 CAKRA	25-11-77	10-9-80	18-3-81
402 CANDRASA	14-3-78	10-9-80	8-81

D: 980/1,150/1,440 tons   **S:** 11 (snorkel)/21.5 kts
Dim: 61.00 × 6.20 × 5.50   **A:** 8/533-mm TT (fwd)—14 total torpedoes
Electron Equipt: Radar: 1/Thompson CSF Calypso
                     Sonar: . . .
M: 4 MTU 820 Db diesels (600 hp each), 2 electric motors; 5,000 hp
Range: 16/21.5; 25/20; 230/8; 400/4—8,200/11 (snorkel)
Man: 6 officers, 28 men

REMARKS: Ordered 2-4-77. Can dive to 250 m. Originally named *Candrasa*.

♦ **1 Soviet Whiskey class**

410 PASOPATI

Pasopati (410)   1976

D: 1,050/1,350 tons   **S:** 17/16 kts   **Dim:** 76.0 × 6.3 × 5.0
A: 6/533-mm TT (4 fwd, 2 aft)—14 torpedoes or 28 mines
M: 2 diesels (4,000 hp), electric drive; 2 props; 2,500 hp
Endurance: 40 to 45 days   **Range:** 6,000/5 (snorkel)   **Man:** 60 tot.

REMARKS: Sister *Bramastra* (412) stricken 1981, along with *Nagabanda* (403), which had been used for dockside training. *Pasopati* has been given new batteries.

FRIGATES

♦ **1 training frigate** Bldr: Uljanic SY, Yugoslavia

	Laid down	L	In serv.
HAJER DEWARTARU	11-5-79	11-10-80	20-8-81

D: 1,850 tons (fl)   **S:** 27 kts   **Dim:** 96.70 (92.00 wl) × 11.20 × 3.55
A: 4/MM 38 Exocet SSM (II × 2)—1/57-mm Bofors—2/20-mm AA (I × 2)—2/
   ASW TT (2/SUT wire-guided torpedoes)—mines—1 helicopter
Electron Equipt: Radar: 1/Decca 1229, 1/HSA WM 28
                     Sonar: PH-32
                     ECM: SUSIE-I system—2/128-mm flare RL (II × 2)
M: CODOG: 1 Rolls-Royce Olympus TM-3B gas turbine, 27,250 hp; 2 MTU
   16V956 TP 91 diesels, 7,000 hp; 2 CP props
Fuel: 338 tons   **Range:** 1,150/27 (gas turbine); 4,000/20 (diesels)
Man: 92 crew + 100 students

REMARKS: Same Basic design as ship laid down in 1977 for Iraq. Ordered 14-3-78. SEWACO GM 101-41 computerized data system. Fin stabilizers, 114 tons water ballast, 50 tons potable water, 7 tons helo fuel. Carries two LCVP-type landing craft. 1,000 rounds 57-mm, 3,120 rounds 20-mm ammunition. Gas turbine rated at 22,300 hp in tropics.

♦ **3 Fatahilah class** Bldr: Wilton-Fijenoord, Schiedam, The Netherlands

	Laid down	L	In serv.
361 FATAHILAH	31-1-77	22-12-77	16-7-79
362 MALAHAYATI	28-7-77	19-6-78	21-3-80
363 NALA	27-1-78	11-1-79	8-80

D: 1,160 tons (1,450 fl)   **S:** 30 kts (21 diesel)   **Dim:** 83.85 × 11.10 × 3.30
A: 361, 362: 4/MM 38 Exocet SSM (II × 2)—1/120-mm Bofors L-46 DP—1/40-
   mm Bofors L-70—2/20-mm AA (I × 2)—2/375-mm Bofors SR-375A ASW RL
   (II × 1)—6/324-mm Mk 32 ASW TT (III × 2); 363: 4/MM 38 Exocet (II ×
   2)—1/120-mm Bofors L-46 DP—2/40-mm AA (I × 2)—2/20-mm AA (I × 2)—
   1/BO 105 helicopter
Electron Equipt: Radar: 1/Decca AC 1229, 1/DA-05/2, 1/WM-28
                     Sonar: PHS 32
                     ECM: SUSIE-I syst.—2/Knebworth/Corvus chaff RL
M: CODOG: 1 Rolls-Royce Olympus TM-3B gas turbine, 22,360 hp (tropical); 2
   MTU 16V956 TB81 diesels; 8,000 hp; 2 CP props
Electric: 1,350 kw   **Range:** 4,250/16 (diesels)   **Man:** 11 officers, 71 men

Fatahilah (361)   1979

Malahayati (362)   1980

FRIGATES *(continued)*

Nala (363)   1980

Martadinata (342)   1974

D: 1,450 tons (1,750 fl)   **S:** 22 kts
Dim: 95.10 (91.75 wl) × 11.84 × 3.66 (hull)/5.50 (sonar)
A: 1 or 2/76.2-mm DP (I × 1 or 2)—0 or 2/37-mm AA (II × 1)—0 or 2/25-mm
     AA (II × 1)—6/324-mm ASW Mk 32 TT (III × 2)
Electron Equipt: Radars: 1/SPS-10, 1/SPS-6, 1/SPG-52
                  Sonar: SQS-42 series
                  ECM: WLR-1
M: 4 Fairbanks-Morse 38ND8⅛ diesels; 1 prop; 9,240 hp   **Electric:** 600 kw
Fuel: 296 tons   **Range:** 3,590/22; 10,300/9   **Man:** 15 officers, 160 men

REMARKS: No. 341 was transferred on 20-2-73, No. 342 on 31-1-74, Nos. 343 and 344
on 16-12-74. Nos. 341 and 342 have a twin Soviet 37-mm AA in place of one 76.2-
mm on fantail and a twin 25-mm at the forecastle break. ESM domes removed from
No. 341, retained in others. Have Mk 70 Mod. 2 GFCS, Mk 105 ASW FCS.

♦ **2 ex-Soviet Riga class** Bldr: U.S.S.R., 1954-57

351 JOS SUDARSO   357 LAMBUNG MANEGURAT

D: 1,260 tons (1,480 fl)   **S:** 28 kts   **Dim:** 91.0 × 10.2 × 3.2 (hull)
A: 3/100-mm DP—4/37-mm AA (II × 2)—3/533-mm TT (III × 1)—1/MBU 600
     Hedgehog—4/BMB-2 d.c. projectors—2/d.c. racks—50 mines
Electron Equipt: Radar: 1/Neptune, 1/Slim Net, 1/Sun Visor A fire-control
M: 2 sets GT; 2 props; 20,000 hp   **Electric:** 450 kw
Boilers: 2; 27 kg/cm², 360°C   **Range:** 550/28; 2,000/13   **Man:** 175 tot.

REMARKS: Transferred in 1964. Survivors of six. *Nuku* (360) stricken 1981.

♦ **1 Pattimura class**

	Bldr	Laid down	L	In serv.
371 PATTIMURA	Ansaldo, Livorno	1-56	1-7-56	28-1-58

D: 950 tons (1,200 fl)   **S:** 21.5 kts   **Dim:** 82.37 × 10.3 × 2.8
A: 2/85-mm DP—4/25-mm AA (II × 2)—4/14.5-mm AA (II × 2)—2/Hedge-
     hogs—4/d.c. projectors—1/d.c. rack
M: 2 Ansaldo diesels; 2 props; 7,000 hp   **Fuel:** 100 tons diesel
Range: 2,400/18   **Man:** 119 tot.

Nala (363)—detail of hangar/flight deck in folded state   1980

REMARKS: Ordered 8-75. The *Nala* has a new type of helicopter deck that folds around
the helicopter to form a hangar, two single 40-mm AA instead of one, and ASW
torpedo tubes. DAISY computerized data system. Have an NBC warfare citadel.
Living spaces air-conditioned. Fin stabilizers. Ammunition supply: 400 rounds 120-
mm, 3,000 rounds 40-mm, 12 ASW torpedoes, 54 Nelli and Erica ASW rockets, 50
rounds chaff. The GFCS has a t.v./laser/infrared backup director.

NOTE: One or two additional "corvettes" are planned, not necessarily of the *Fatahilah*
class.

♦ **4 ex-U.S. Claud Jones class** Bldrs: 341, 343: Avondale Marine, Westwego, La.;
   342, 344: American SB, Toledo, Ohio

		L	In serv.
341 SAMADIKUN	(ex-*John R. Perry*, DE 1034)	29-7-58	5-5-59
342 MARTADINATA	(ex-*Charles Berry*, DE 1035)	17-3-59	25-11-60
343 MONGINDISI	(ex-*Claud Jones*, DE 1033)	27-5-58	10-2-59
344 NGURAH RAI	(ex-*McMorris*, DE 1036)	26-5-59	4-3-60

FRIGATES (continued)

Pattimura (371)—prior to rearmament   1975

REMARKS: Rearmed 1976-77 with Soviet guns removed from stricken units of the Kronstadt, P 6, and Komar classes. Sister *Sultan Hasanudin* (802) stripped and decommissioned in 1978.

GUIDED-MISSILE PATROL BOATS

♦ **4 (+4) PSK Mk-5 class** Bldr: Korea-Tacoma SY

		In serv.			In serv.
621	MANDAU	7-79	623	BADEK	2-80
622	RENCONG	7-79	624	KERIS	2-80

Rencong (622)   1980

D: 250 tons (290 fl)   **S:** 41 kts   **Dim:** 53.58 × 8.00 × 1.63 (hull)
A: 4/MM 38 Exocet (II × 2)—1/57-mm Bofors AA—1/40-mm Bofors AA—2/20-mm AA (I × 2)
Electron Equipt: Radar: 1/Decca AC 1229, 1/HSA WM-28
M: CODOG: 1 GE-Fiat LM-2500 gas turbine, 25,000 hp; 2 MTU 12V331 TC81 diesels, 1,120 hp each; 2 CP props
Fuel: 65 tons   **Range:** 2,600/14   **Man:** 5 officers, 34 men

REMARKS: First unit laid down 5-77. Modification of U.S. *Asheville*-class design. Four more ordered 1980.

NOTE: All remaining wooden-hulled ex-Soviet Komar-class missile boats were stricken 1979-81. The four remaining German TNC 45-class torpedo boats were stricken in 1980.

PATROL BOATS

♦ **6 Carpentaria class** Bldr: De Havilland Marine, Australia

		In serv.			In serv.
851	SAMADAR	8-76	854	SAWANGI	11-76
852	SASILA	9-76	855	SADARIN	12-76
853	SABOLA	10-76	856	SALMANETI	7-77

Samadar (851)   1981

D: 27 tons (fl)   **S:** 25 kts   **Dim:** 15.7 × 5.0 × 1.3
A: 2/12.7-mm mg (I × 2)   **Electron Equipt:** Radar: 1/Decca 110
M: 2 MTU 8V331 diesels; 2 props; 1,400 hp   **Range:** 950/18   **Man:** 10 tot.

REMARKS: Grant-aid from Australia. Aluminum construction.

♦ **3 Australian Attack class**

847 SIBARU (ex-*Bandolier*)   848 SULIMAN (ex-*Archer*)   849 N. . . (ex-*Barracuda*)

D: 146 tons (fl)   **S:** 21 kts   **Dim:** 32.76 (30.48 pp) × 6.2 × 1.9
A: 1/40-mm AA—2/7.62-mm mg (I × 2)
Electron Equipt: Radar: 1/Decca RM 916
M: 2 Davey-Paxman Ventura 16 YJCM diesels; 3,460 hp   **Fuel:** 20 tons
Range: 1,220/13   **Man:** 3 officers, 19 men

REMARKS: Light-alloys superstructure. Air-conditioned. 847 transferred 16-11-73, 848 in 1974, 849 in late 1981.

♦ **5 ex-Yugoslav PBR-500 class**

819	KAYANG	823	TODAK	830	SEMBILANG
820	LEMADANG	829	TOHOK		

D: 190 tons (202 fl)   **S:** 18 kts   **Dim:** 41.0 × 6.3 × 2.2
A: 1/76.2-mm—1/40-mm AA—6/20-mm AA (II × 3)—2/Mousetrap Mk 22 ASW RL—2 d.c. projectors—2/d.c. racks
Electron Equipt: Radar: 1/Decca 45
                      Sonar: U.S. QCU-2
M: 2 M.A.N. W8V 30/38 diesels; 2 props; 3,300 hp   **Fuel:** 15 tons
Range: 1,000/12   **Man:** 54 tot.

PATROL BOATS (*continued*)

Kayang (819) 1976

REMARKS: Transferred in 1959. *Krapu* (821) and *Dorang* (822) stricken 1980.

♦ **3 Soviet Kronstadt class** Bldr: U.S.S.R., 1951-52

814 PANDRONG   815 SURA   817 BARAKUDA

Sura (815) 1978

D: 300 tons (330 fl)   **S:** 18 kts   **Dim:** 52.1 × 6.5 × 2.2   **Man:** 50 tot.
A: 1/85-mm—2/37-mm AA (I × 2)—6/14.5-mm—2/MBU 1200 ASW RL (V × 2)—2 d.c. projectors—2/d.c. racks—mines
M: 3 9D diesels; 3 props; 3,300 hp   **Fuel:** 20 tons   **Range:** 3,500/14

REMARKS: Transferred 1958-59. A number of others have been stricken, including *Kakap* (816) in 1981.

NOTE: The three patrol boats of the Kelabang class, the three units of the U.S. PGM 53 class and the remaining units of the U.S. 173-ft. class were stricken 1980-81.

MINE WARFARE SHIPS

♦ **2 ex-Soviet T-43-class minesweepers**

701 PULAU RANI   702 PULAU RATEWO

D: 500 tons (570 fl)   **S:** 14 kts   **Dim:** 58.0 × 8.6 × 2.3
A: 4/37-mm AA (II × 2)—8/12.7-mm mg (II × 4)—2/d.c. projectors—2 mine rails
M: 2 9D diesels; 2 props; 2,200 hp   **Fuel:** 70 tons   **Range:** 3,200/10

REMARKS: Transferred 1962-64. Used on patrol duties. *Pulau Roon* (703) lost 1980, *Pulau Rorbas* (704) and *Pulau Radja* (705) stricken 1980-81.

NOTE: The two German Raumboote-class patrol minesweepers were stricken in 1980-81.

AMPHIBIOUS WARFARE SHIPS

♦ **6 Teluk Semangka-class landing ships** Bldr: Hyundai SY, South Korea

		In serv.			In serv.
512	TELUK SEMANGKA	20-1-81	515	TELUK SAMPIT	1981
513	TELUK PENYU	20-1-81	516	TELUK. . .	1982
514	TELUK MANDAR	7-81	517	TELUK. . .	1982

D: 3,770 tons (fl)   **S:** . . . kts   **Dim:** 100.0 × 14.4 × 4.2   **A:** . . .
M: 2 diesels; 2 props;. . . hp   **Man:** 90 tot.

REMARKS: First four ordered 6-79, two more in 6-81. Near duplicates of U.S. LST 1/542-class design. Cargo: 1,800 tons.

♦ **5 ex-U.S. LST 542-class tank landing ships** Bldr: Chicago Bridge & Iron Wks., Seneca, Ill. (except 511: American Bridge, Ambridge, Pa.; 509: unknown)

		Laid down	L	In serv.
501	TELUK LANGSA (ex-LST 1128)	23-11-44	19-2-45	9-3-45
504	TELUK KAU (ex-LST 652)	24-7-44	19-10-44	1-1-45
509	TELUK RATAI (ex-M/V *Inagua Shipper*, ex-LST. . .)	. . .	. . .	. . .
510	TELUK SALEH (ex-*Clarke County*, LST 601)	21-10-43	4-3-44	25-3-44
511	TELUK BONE (ex-*Iredell County*, LST 839)	25-9-44	12-11-44	6-12-44

D: 1,650 tons light (4,080 fl)   **S:** 11.6 kts   **Dim:** 99.98 × 15.24 × 4.29
A: 6 or 7/40-mm or 37-mm AA
M: 2 GM 12-567A diesels; 2 props; 1,800 hp   **Electric:** 300 kw   **Fuel:** 590 tons
Range: 6,000/9 (loaded)   **Man:** 119 crew + 264 passengers

REMARKS: Transferred in 3-60, 1961, and Nos. 510 and 511 in 7-70 under the Military Assistance Program. Can carry 2,100 tons of cargo. Sisters *Teluk Bayer* and *Teluk Tomani* are in the Military Sealift Command, as is the Japanese-built near-sister *Teluk Amboina*.

HYDROGRAPHIC SHIPS

♦ **1 Burudjulasad class** Bldr: Schlichtingwerft, Travemünde (L: 8-65; In serv. 1967)

931 BURUDJULASAD

D: 1,800 tons (2,150 fl)   **S:** 19 kts   **Dim:** 82.0 (78.0 pp) × 11.4 × 3.5
M: 4 M.A.N. V6V 22/30 diesels; 2 CP props; 6,400 hp   **Electric:** 1,008 kw
Fuel: 600 tons   **Range:** 14,500/15.7   **Man:** 13 officers, 88 men, 28 technicians

REMARKS: Launched in 8-65. Can accommodate 28 scientists and can carry one helicopter.

HYDROGRAPHIC SHIPS *(continued)*

Burudjulasad (931)   1981

♦ **1 hydrometeorological and oceanographic research ship**

Bldr: Sasebo Heavy Industries, Japan (In serv. 12-1-63)

1005 JALANIDHI

Jalanidhi (1005)   1972

    D: 740 tons (985 fl)   **S:** 12.7 kts   **Dim:** 53.9 (48.5 pp) × 9.5 × 4.3
    M: 1 M.A.N. G6V 30/42 diesel; 1,000 hp   **Electric:** 261 kw   **Fuel:** 165 tons
    Range: 7,200/10.5

REMARKS: Weather-balloon facility aft.

♦ **1 ex-Soviet PO-2-class inshore survey craft**

1008 ARIES

    D: 56 tons (fl)   **S:** 12 kts   **Dim:** 21.3 × 3.8 × 2.0
    M: 1 3D12 diesel; 300 hp   **Man:** 13 tot.

REMARKS: Transferred in 1964.

♦ **1 hydrographic survey ship** Bldr: De Waal Scheepswerf, Nijmegen (L: 6-9-52; In serv. 7-53)

1002 BURDJAMHAL

    D: 1,200 tons (1,500 fl)   **S:** 13 kts   **Dim:** 64.5 (58.5 pp) × 10.1 × 3.3
    M: 2 Werkspoor TMAB-278 diesels; 2 props; 1,160 hp   **Fuel:** 150 tons
    Man: 90 tot.

AUXILIARY SHIPS

♦ **1 ex-Soviet Don-class submarine tender** Bldr: U.S.S.R., 1960

301 RATULANGI (ex-441)

Ratulangi (ex-441)   1979

    D: 6,700 tons (fl)   **S:** 21 kts   **Dim:** 137.2 × 16.8 × 5.2
    A: 4/100-mm DP (I × 4)—8/57-mm AA (II × 4)—8/25-mm AA (II × 4)
    M: 4 diesels; 2 props; 8,000 hp   **Man:** 300 tot.

REMARKS: Transferred in 1962.

♦ **1 command ship** Bldr: Ishikawajima, Japan (L: 13-6-81)

561 MULTATULI

Multatuli (561)   1979

    D: 4,500 tons (fl)   **S:** 18.5 kts   **Dim:** 111.35 (103.0 pp) × 16.0 × 6.98
    A: 8/37-mm AA (II × 2, I × 4)—4/14.5-mm AA (II × 2)—1 Alouette-III heli-
        copter
    M: 1 Burmeister & Wain diesel; 5,500 hp   **Fuel:** 1,400 tons   **Range:** 6,000/16
    Man: 134 tot.

REMARKS: Built as a submarine-support ship, converted as a fleet command ship in the late 1960s. Has a helicopter platform aft. Construction of two similar ships of about 10,000 tons, to carry fuel, troops, and hospital facilities is planned.

♦ **1 ex-U.S. Achelous-class repair ship** Bldr: Chicago Bridge & Iron, Seneca, Illinois

	Laid down	L	In serv.
921 JAJA WIDJAJA (ex-*Askari*, ARL 30, ex-LST 1131)	8-12-44	2-3-45	15-3-45

    D: 2,130 (3,640 fl)   **S:** 11 kts   **Dim:** 99.98 × 15.24 × 4.25
    A: 8/40-mm AA (IV × 2)   **M:** 2 GM 12-267A diesels; 2 props; 1,800 hp
    Electric: 520 kw   **Fuel:** 590 tons   **Man:** 280 tot.

AUXILIARY SHIPS *(continued)*

REMARKS: Leased 31-8-71; purchased 22-2-79. Cargo capacity: 300 tons. 60-ton lift rig. Converted LST.

♦ **1 new-construction replenishment oiler**

REMARKS: Reported ordered in Japan 1981.

♦ **1 replenishment oiler** Bldr: Yugoslavia, 1965

911 SORONG

Sorong (911)   1979

D: 5,100 (dwt) **S:** 15 kts **Dim:** 112.17 × 15.4 × 6.6
A: 8/12.7-mm machine guns (II × 4) **M:** 1 diesel; 1 prop; . . . hp

REMARKS: Cargo: 3,000 tons fuel/300 tons water. Can conduct underway replenishments.

♦ **1 ex-Soviet Khobi-class oiler**

909 PAKAN BARU

D: 1,525 tons (fl) **S:** 12.7 kts **Dim:** 67.4 (63.7 pp) × 10.0 × 4.4
M: 2 diesels; 2 props; 1,600 hp **Range:** 2,500/10

REMARKS: Cargo: 700 tons fuel oil.

♦ **1 ex-U.S. Cherokee-class fleet tug** Bldr: United Eng., Alameda, California

	Laid down	L	In serv.
922 RAKATA (ex-U.S. *Menominee*, ATF 73)	27-9-41	14-2-42	25-9-42

D: 1,640 tons (fl) **S:** 15 kts **Dim:** 62.5 × 11.7 × 4.7
A: 1/76.2-mm DP—2/40-mm AA (I × 2)—4/25-mm AA (II × 2)
M: 4 GM 12-278A diesels, electric drive; 1 prop; 3,000 hp

REMARKS: Transferred 3-61.

♦ **1 new-construction coastal tug** Bldr: PAL, Surabaja (L: 6-6-79)

D: . . . **S:** 10 kts **Dim:** 24.25 × 6.5 × . . . **M:** diesel; 1 prop; . . . hp
Man: 10 tot.

♦ **1 coastal tug** Bldr: Ishikawajima Harima, Tokyo (L: 4-61)

934 LAMPO BATANG

D: 250 tons **S:** 11 kts **Dim:** 28.1 × 7.6 × 2.6 **Man:** 13 tot.
M: 2 M.A.N. diesels; 2 props; 600 hp **Fuel:** 18 tons **Range:** 1,000/11

♦ **2 Tambora-class coastal tugs** Bldr: Ishikawajima Harima, Tokyo (both L: 6-61)

935 TAMBORA 936 BROMO

D: 250 tons (fl) **S:** 10.5 kts **Dim:** 24.1 × 6.6 × 3.0
M: 2 M.A.N. diesels; 2 props; 600 hp **Fuel:** 9 tons **Range:** 690/10.5
Man: 15 tot.

♦ **1 sail training ship** Bldr: Stülcken, Hamburg (L: 21-1-52)

DEWARUTJI

Dewarutji   1977

D: 810 tons (1,500 fl) **S:** 9 kts **Dim:** 58.3 (41.5 pp) × 9.5 × 4.23
M: 1 M.A.N. diesel; 575 hp **Man:** 110 men, 78 cadets

REMARKS: Sail area: 1,091 m². Will be replaced by the new training frigate.

MILITARY SEALIFT COMMAND (KOLINLAMIL)

Formed in 1978 to coordinate the Indonesian Navy's logistic support for its far-flung bases and outposts in the Indonesian archipelago. Some of the units have been taken over from the Indonesian Army and others from the Navy.

♦ **1 tank landing ship** Bldr: Sasebo Heavy Industries (L: 17-3-61)

9. . . TELUK AMBOINA

D: 4,145 tons (fl) **S:** 13 kts **Dim:** 99.9 × 15.2 × 4.6
A: 4/40-mm AA—1/37-mm AA **Man:** 88 men + 212 passengers
M: 2 M.A.N. V6V 22.30 diesels; 2 props; 3,200 hp (2,850 sust.)
Electric: 135 kw **Fuel:** 1,200 tons **Range:** 4,000/13

REMARKS: Built as reparations. Near duplicate of U.S. LST 542 design. Guns may have been removed. Can carry 654 tons water. Has a 30-ton crane.

♦ **2 ex-U.S. LST 542-class tank landing ships**

	Bldr	Laid down	L	In serv.
9. . . TELUK BAYER (ex-LST 616)	Chicago Bridge & Iron, Seneca, Ill.	12-2-44	12-5-44	29-5-44
9. . . TELUK TOMANI (ex-LST 983)	Boston Navy Yard, Boston, Mass.	22-12-43	10-2-44	25-3-44

MILITARY SEALIFT COMMAND (*continued*)

D: 1,650 tons (4,080 fl)   **S:** 11 kts   **Dim:** 99.98 × 15.24 × 4.29
A: None   **M:** 2 GM 12-567A diesels; 2 props; 1,800 hp
Fuel: 590 tons   **Range:** 6,000/9 (loaded)   **Man:** 119 men + 264 passengers

REMARKS: Bought since 1961. *Teluk Tomani* is used as a cattle-carrier and does not carry passengers.

♦ 3 Krupang-class utility landing craft Bldr: Surabaja DY

9. . . KRUPANG (In serv. 3-11-78)   9. . . DILI (In serv. 27-2-79)   9. . . NUSANTARA (In serv. 1980)

D: 400 tons (fl)   **S:** 11 kts   **Dim:** 42.9 (36.27 pp) × 9.14 × . . .
M: 2 diesels; 2 props; . . . hp   **Range:** 700/11   **Man:** 17 tot.

REMARKS: Based on U.S. LCU 1610 class. Cargo: 200 tons.

♦ 2 Amurang-class landing craft Bldr: Korneuberg SY, Austria (In serv. 1968)

9. . . AMURANG   9. . . DORE

D: 182 tons (275 fl)   **S:** 8 kts   **Dim:** 38.3 × 10.0 × 1.8
M: 2 diesels; 2 props; 420 hp   **Man:** 17 tot.

REMARKS: Sister *Banten* and one other in merchant service. 200 grt.

♦ 1 oiler Bldr: Japan, 1965

901 BALIKPAPAN (ex-*Komado V*)

D: 1,780 dwt   **S:** 11 kts   **Dim:** 69.6 × 9.6 × 4.9
M: 1 diesel; 1,300 hp   **Man:** 26 tot.

REMARKS: Purchased in 1977.

♦ 1 oiler   902 SAMBU   No data available

♦ 6 Hungarian Tisza-class cargo ships Bldr: Angyalfold SY, Budapest

951 TELAUD	953 NATUNA	957 KARIMUNDSA
952 NUSATELU	956 TELUK MENITAWI	960 KARAMAJA

D: 2,000 tons (fl)   **S:** 12 kts   **Dim:** 74.5 (67.4 pp) × 11.3 × 4.6
A: some ships: 4/14.5-mm mg (II × 2)   **M:** 1 Lang 8-cyl. diesel; 1,000 hp
Electric: 746 kw   **Fuel:** 98 tons   **Range:** 4,200/10.7   **Man:** 26 tot.

REMARKS: Transferred 1963-64. Taken over from the Army in 1978. Had originally been naval. 1,296 grt/1,280 dwt. Cargo: 1,100 tons.

♦ 2 transports

931 TANSUNG PANDAN (ex-*Cut Nya Dhien*)   932 TANSUNG OISINA (ex-*Gununjati*)

REMARKS: Purchased in 1978. Large (approx. 6,000-8,000 grt) but elderly passenger-cargo ships.

SEA COMMUNICATIONS AGENCY

Established in 1978 to patrol Indonesia's 200-nautical-mile economic zone and to maintain navigational aids.

PATROL BOATS

♦ 4 Kapak class Bldr: Schlichtingwerft, Harmsdorf, W. Germany

	L	In serv.		L	In serv.
PAT 206 KAPAK	. . .	. . .	PAT 208 N. . .	. . .	. . .
PAT 207 N. . .	. . .	. . .	PAT 209 N. . .	. . .	. . .

D: 200 tons (fl)   **S:** 28 kts   **Dim:** 37.50 × 7.00 × 2.00   **A:** mg   **Man:** 18 tot.
M: 2 MTU 16V652 TB 61 diesels; 2 props; 4,200 hp   **Range:** 1,500/18

REMARKS: Intended for search-and-rescue duties. 120m³/hr. fire pump and water monitor, rescue launch, 8-man sick bay.

♦ 5 Kujang class Bldr: SFCN, Villeneuve-la-Garenne

	L		L
PAT 201 KUJANG	17-10-80	PAT 204 CUNDRIK	10-11-80
PAT 202 PARANG	18-11-80	PAT 205 BELATI	21-5-81
PAT 203 CELURIT	20-2-81		

D: 126 tons (162 fl)   **S:** 28 kts
Dim: 38.32 (35.46 pp) × 6.00 × 1.78 (2.60 props)   **A:** mg   **Range:** 1,500/18
M: 2 S.A.C.M. AGO V12 195 CZ SHR T5; 2 props; 4,400 hp   **Man:** 18 tot.

REMARKS: Intended for search-and-rescue duties.

♦ 6 PAT-01 class patrol craft Bldr: Tanjung Priok SY, 1978-79

PAT 01 to PAT 06

D: 12 tons (fl)   **S:** 14 kts   **Dim:** 12.15 × 4.25 × 1.0
A: mg   **M:** 1 Renault diesel; 260 hp

NAVIGATIONAL AID TENDERS

♦ 2 coastal service Bldr: . . . , Japan (In serv. 1976)

KARAKATA   KUMBA

D: 569 grt/552 dwt   **S:** 13 kts   **Dim:** 50.50 (47.43 pp) × 10.00 × 3.71
M: 2 Niigata diesels; 1 prop; 850 hp

REMARKS: Two more buoy tenders were ordered from Japan in 1978.

♦ 2 seagoing buoy tender/cargo ships Bldr: . . . (In serv. 1963)

MAJANG   MIZAN

D: 2,150 tons (fl)   **S:** 14 kts   **Dim:** 78.0 (71.0 pp) × 13.7 × 4.0
M: 1 set 4-cyl. compound reciprocating steam; 1 prop; 1,800 hp
Boilers: two 16 kg/cm²   **Fuel:** 376 tons   **Man:** 70 tot.

REMARKS: 1,705 grt/1,170 dwt. Resemble small cargo ships, with bridge forward, engine aft, and holds amidships.

♦ 1 seagoing buoy tender and cable layer Bldr: . . . , the Netherlands

BIDUK (L: 30-10-51; In serv. 7-52)

D: 1,250 dwt   **S:** 12 kts   **Dim:** 65.0 × 12.0 × 4.5   **Boilers:** two 16-kg/cm²
M: 1 set triple-expansion reciprocating steam; 1 prop; 1,600 hp   **Man:** 66 tot.

REMARKS: Cable sheaves over bow. Transferred from navy, 1978 (ex-pendant 1003).

CUSTOMS SERVICE

NOTE: The Indonesian Customs Service is currently undergoing an ambitious expansion, with patrol boats and craft constructed in Western Europe and at home.

PATROL BOATS

♦ **8 Lürssen PB 57 design-programmed** Bldr: PAL SY, Indonesia

D: 342 tons (399 fl) **S:** 29.5 kts **Dim:** 58.10 (54.40 wl) × 7.60 × . . .
A: 1/57-mm Bofors AA—1/40-mm AA **Electron Equipt:** Radar:. . .
M: 2 MTU 16V956 TB92 diesels; 2 props; 9,000 hp (7,500 sust.)
Electric: 405 kVa **Range:** 4,200/17 **Man:** 3 officers, 27 men

REMARKS: Program uncertain. Armament may include 76-mm OTO Melara gun vice the 57-mm weapon listed. Additional units may be built for the Indonesian Navy. Prototypes to build in Germany.

♦ **12 (+24)Lürssen FPB 28 class** Bldr: See remarks

	L	In serv.		L	In serv.
BC 4001	14-4-80	4-81	BC 5001	. . .	. . .
BC 4002	. . .	. . .	BC 5002	. . .	. . .
BC 4003	. . .	. . .	BC 5003	. . .	. . .
BC 4004	. . .	. . .	BC 5004	. . .	. . .
BC 4005	. . .	. . .	BC 5005	. . .	. . .
BC 4006	. . .	. . .	BC 5006	. . .	. . .

D: 61 tons (68.5 fl) **S:** 30 kts **Dim:** 28.0 (26.0 wl) × 5.4 × 1.6 **A:** . . .
M: BC 4001-4003: 2 Deutz BA 16M815 diesels; 2 props; 2,720 hp—BC 5001-5003: 2 MTU diesels; 2 props; 2,620 hp
Electric: 36 kVa **Fuel:** 10 tons **Range:** 700/27.5; 1,050/17
Man: 6 officers, 13 men

REMARKS: A collaborative effort by Lürssen with Abeking & Rasmussen of West Germany delivering prefabricated sections to PAL shipyard, Surabaja. BC 5001-5003 rated at 30.6 kts. Twenty-four more building in Belgium (BC 6001, etc.)

♦ **7 BC 2001 class** Bldr: CMN, Cherbourg

	L	In serv.		L	In serv.
BC 2001	27-9-79	8-2-80	BC 2005	19-8-80	5-9-80
BC 2002	20-12-79	8-2-80	BC 2006	14-10-80	7-11-80
BC 2003	4-3-80	3-4-80	BC 2007	9-12-80	10-2-81
BC 2004	14-5-80	9-6-80			

BC 2006 CMN, 1980

D: 58.5 tons (70.3 fl) **S:** 29.7 kts (at 64.4 tons)
Dim: 28.5 (26.5 wl) × 5.4 × 1.3 (1.65 props) **A:** 1/12.7-mm mg
M: 2 MTU 12V331 TC92 diesels; 2 props; 2,440 hp **Man:** . . . tot.

♦ **7 BC 3001 class** Bldr: Chantiers Navals de l'Esterel, Cannes

BC 3001	7-79	BC 3005	1980
BC 3002	1-80	BC 3006	1981
BC 3003	1980	BC 3007	1981
BC 3004	1980		

BC 3003 1980

D: 57 tons (fl) **S:** 34 kts **Dim:** 28.2 × 5.2 × 1.6
A: 1/20-mm AA **M:** 2 MTU 12V331 TC 81 diesels; 2 props; 2,700 hp
Range: 800/15 **Man:** 2 officers, 16 men

REMARKS: Similar design to BC 1001 class; also built of wood.

♦ **3 BC 1001 class** Bldr: Chantiers Navals de l'Esterel, Cannes

BC 1001 (In serv. 4-75)   BC 1002 (In serv. 6-75)   BC 1003 (In serv. 11-75)

BC 1002 l'Esterel, 1975

D: 56 tons (fl) **S:** 34 kts **Dim:** 28.0 (26.6 wl) × 5.3 × 1.6
A: 1/12.7-mm mg **M:** 2 MTU 12V331 TC81 diesels; 2 props; 2,700 hp
Fuel: 10 tons **Range:** 750/15 **Man:** 15 tot.

♦ **16 or more Lürssen FPB 28 class**—original series Bldr: Lürssen, Bremen-Vegasack (In serv. 1962-63)

BC 401 series   BC 501 series   BC 601 series   BC 701 series

REMARKS: Characteristics as for Deutz-engined FPB 28-class units above. To be replaced by the virtually identical units now under construction.

INDONESIA (*continued*)

BC 704   1980

MARITIME POLICE

PATROL BOATS

♦ **9 DKN 908 class** Bldr: Baglietto, Italy; Riva Trigoso, Italy (In serv. 1961-64)

DKN 908   DKN 911   DKN 914
DKN 909   DKN 912   DKN 915
DKN 910   DKN 913   DKN 916

   D: 139 tons (159 fl)   **S:** 21 kts   **Dim:** 42.0 × 6.5 × 1.8
   A: 3/20-mm AA (I × 3)   **M:** 2 Maybach MD655 diesels; 2 props; . . . hp
   Range: 1,500/17   **Man:** 22 tot.

♦ **10 DKN 504 class** Bldrs: DKN 504-508: Ishikawajima Harima, Tokyo; others: Uraga Dockyard, Yokosuka (In serv. 1963-64)

DKN 504   DKN 507   DKN 510   DKN 513
DKN 505   DKN 508   DKN 511
DKN 506   DKN 509   DKN 512

   D: 314 tons light (390 std., 444 fl)   **S:** 15.3 kts
   Dim: 48.1 (44.0 pp) × 7.5 × 2.9   **A:** 1/20-mm AA
   M: 2 M.A.N. W8V 22/30 ALU diesels; 2 props; 1,400 hp   **Electric:** 126 kw
   Fuel: 41 tons   **Range:** 2,700/14   **Man:** 35 tot.

REMARKS: Cargo hold with 75 tons capacity.

♦ **2 DKN 901 class** Bldr: Abeking & Rasmussen, Lemwerder (In serv. 1959)

DKN 905   DKN 906

   D: 150 tons (fl)   **S:** 21 kts   **Dim:** 38.9 (36.0 pp) × 7.0 × 1.9
   A: 1/20-mm AA—2/12.7-mm mg (I × 2)
   M: 2 Maybach MD 655S diesels; 2 props; 3,200 hp
   Range: 1,500/13   **Man:** 21 tot.

REMARKS: Three earlier sisters stricken.

INDONESIAN ARMY (ADRI)

At one time the Indonesian Army operated a great variety of ships, including up to 29 units in the ADRI-I series, most of which were old passenger-cargo ships acquired for use as troop transports. Most of its serviceable ships were turned over to the new Military Sealift Command in 1977 and 1978, but a new series of logistics landing craft is under construction.

♦ **28 utility landing craft** Bldr: Koja SY, Tanjung Priok (In serv. 1978-. . .)

ADRI XXXI to ADRI LVIII

   D: 580 tons (fl)   **S:** 10 kts   **Dim:** 42.0 (38.0 wl) × 10.7 × 1.8
   M: 2 GM 6-71 diesels; 2 props; 680 hp   **Electric:** 100 kw   **Fuel:** 40 tons
   Range: 1,500/10   **Man:** 15 tot.

REMARKS: 300 dwt. Construction continues. Cargo: 122 tons vehicles/stores; 120 tons water. Two 150-dwt landing craft were also completed during 1980.

INDONESIAN AIR FORCE (AURI)

The Indonesian Air Force operates six passenger-cargo logistics ships that were completed in the mid-1960s. Of about 600 dwt, they are intended to beach and are equipped with bow doors.

IRAN
Islamic Republic of Iran

PERSONNEL: 12,500 men, including 1,100 officers (before the revolution)

MERCHANT MARINE (1980): 229 ships—1,283,629 grt (tankers: 27 ships—664,441 grt)

MARITIME AVIATION: On hand before the revolution and war with Iraq were: 7 SH-3D Sea King, 7 AB-212, 5 AB-205A, 14 AB-206A, and 2 Sikorsky RH-53D helicopters, 6 P-3F Orion long-range patrol aircraft, 4 Fokker F-27 Mk 400M. Friendship transports, 4 Falcon 20, and 4 Aero Commander utility transports.

NOTE: Although reporting on the current conflict between Iran and Iraq seems anything but accurate, the following ships appear to have been lost:
♦ 2 U.S. PF 103-class frigates
♦ 2 La Combattante II-class guided-missile patrol boats (including *Peykan*)
♦ 5 patrol boats
♦ 4 mine countermeasures ships
   The two La Combattante II class and one of the PF 103 class were sunk by AM 39 Exocet missiles launched from Super Frelon helicopters.

NOTE: The U.S. *Teng*-class submarine *Kusseh* (ex-*Trout*, SS 566) was abandoned at Norfolk, Virginia in 5-79 and is unlikely to be reacquired.

GUIDED-MISSILE DESTROYERS

♦ **1 ex-British Battle class** Bldr: Cammell Laird, Birkenhead

	Laid down	L	In serv.
51 ARTEMIZ (ex-*Sluys*, D 60)	24-11-43	28-2-45	30-9-46

GUIDED-MISSILE DESTROYERS (continued)

Artemiz (D 51)—wearing old number   Thornycroft, 1969

D: 2,325 tons (3,360 fl) **S:** 31 kts **Dim:** 115.32 (108.2 pp) × 12.95 × 5.2 (fl)

A: 4/Standard SM-1 box launchers (8 missiles)—4/114-mm DP (II × 2, fwd)—4/40-mm AA (I × 4)—1/Sea Cat SAM (IV × 1)—1/Squid ASW mortar (III × 1)

Electron Equipt: Radars: 1/Plessey AWS-1 air-search, 1/Plessey surface-search, 1/Contraves Sea Hunter fire-control
Sonar: Plessey MS-26—ESM: 1 Decca RDL-1

M: 2 sets Parsons GT; 2 props; 50,000 hp **Boilers:** 2 Admiralty 3-drum

Fuel: 680 tons **Range:** 3,200/20 **Man:** 260 tot.

REMARKS: Modernized before transfer on 20-1-67. Anti-ship missiles added after refit in South Africa, 1975-76. Sea Cat system NSCS optical director only. Standard missiles may be SAM version, vice SSM, using Sea Hunter for fire control.

♦ 2 ex-U.S. Allen M. Sumner, FRAM II, class

		Bldr	Laid down	L	In serv.
61	BABR (ex-*Zellars*, DD 777)	Todd, Pacific	24-12-43	19-7-44	25-10-44
62	PALANG (ex-*Stormes*, DD 780)	Federal SB, Kearny	25-2-44	4-11-44	27-1-45

Babr (D 61)   1976

D: 2,200 tons (3,320 fl) **S:** 30 kts **Dim:** 114.75 × 12.45 × 5.6

A: 4/Standard SSM box-launchers (8 missiles)—4/127-mm DP (II × 2)—6/324-mm Mk-32 ASW TT (III × 2)—2/Hedgehogs—1/AB-204 ASW helicopter

Electron Equipt: Radar: 1/SPS-10, 1/SPS-29, 1/Mk 25
Sonar: 1/SQS-29
ECM: WLR-1, ULQ-6

M: 2 sets GT; 2 props; 60,000 hp

Boilers: 4 Babcock & Wilcox; 43.3 kg/cm², 454°C **Fuel:** 650 tons

Range: 1,260/30; 4,600/14 **Man:** 14 officers, 260 men

REMARKS: Purchased in 3-71 and delivered in 10-73 and 1974. The *Bordelon* (DD 881) and the *Kenneth D. Bailey* (DD 713) were transferred for cannibalization. The Standard missiles are on a platform between the stacks and also on the 01 level forward of the bridge. Mk 37 fire-control for the 127-mm guns. VDS now removed from the *Babr*.

FRIGATES

♦ 4 Saam (Vosper Mk 5) class

		Bldr	Laid down	L	In serv.
71	SAAM	Vosper Thornycroft	22-5-67	25-7-68	20-5-71
71	ZAAL	Vickers, Newcastle	3-3-68	25-7-68	1-3-71
73	ROSTAM	Vickers, Barrow	10-12-67	4-3-69	28-2-72
74	FARAMARZ	Vosper Thornycroft	25-7-68	30-7-69	28-2-72

Faramarz (F 74)   1978

Zaal (F 71)   1977

D: 1,100 tons (2,350 fl) **S:** 40/30 kts (17.5 with diesel)

Dim: 94.5 (88.4 pp) × 11.07 × 3.25

A: 1/Sea Killer SSM system (V × 1)—1/Sea Cat SAM system (III × 1) 1/114-mm DP Mk 8—2/35-mm AA (II × 1)—1/Limbo Mk 10 ASW mortar (III × 1)

Electron Equipt: Radars: 1/Plessey AWS-1 air-search, 2/Contraves Sea Hunter fire-control

M: CODOG: 2 Rolls-Royce Olympus TM3A gas turbines; 2 Paxman 16-cyl. Ventura diesels for cruising; 2 CP props; 46,000 hp (turbines), 3,800 hp (diesels)

Fuel: 150 tons (250 with overload) **Range:** 5,000/15 **Man:** 135 tot.

REMARKS: Air-conditioned. Retractable fin stabilizers. All now carry Mk 8 guns in place of original Mk 6.

FRIGATES *(continued)*

♦ **2 U.S. PF 103 class** (see remarks) Bldr: Levingston SB, Orange, Texas

	Laid down	L	In serv.
81 BAYANDOR (ex-PF 103)	20-8-62	7-7-63	18-5-64
82 NAGHDI (ex-PF 104)	12-9-62	10-10-63	22-7-64
83 MILANIAN (ex-PF 105)	1-5-67	4-1-68	13-2-69
84 KAHNAMUIE (ex-PF 106)	12-6-67	4-4-68	13-2-69

Kahnamuie (F 84)   1978

D: 900 tons (1,135 fl)   **S:** 20 kts   **Dim:** 83.82 × 10.06 × 3.05 (4.27 sonar)
A: 2/76.2-mm DP (I × 2)—2/40-mm AA (II × 1)—2/23-mm AA (II × 1)—4/d.c.
    projectors—2/d.c. racks
Electron Equipt: Radars: 1/SPS-6, 1/Raytheon navigational, 1/Mk 34
            Sonar: SQS-17A
M: 4 Fairbanks-Morse 38D81/8-10 diesels; 2 props; 5,300 hp   **Electric:** 750 kw
Fuel: 110 tons   **Range:** 2,400/18; 3,000/15   **Man:** 133 tot.

REMARKS: Transferred under the Military Aid Program. Twin Soviet 23-mm AA have
been added forward of the bridge in place of the single Hedgehog ASW mortar. Mk
63 GFCS for 76.2-mm guns (radar on fwd gunmount); Mk 51 Mod. 2 GFCS for 40-
mm mount. Two, names unknown, reported lost to Iraqi forces.

GUIDED-MISSILE PATROL BOATS

♦ **11 La Combattante-II class** Bldr: Constr. Méc. de Normandie, Cherbourg

	L	In serv.		L	In serv.
P 221 KAMAN	8-1-76	6-77	P 228 GORZ	28-12-77	15-9-78
P 222 ZOUBIN	14-4-76	6-77	P 229 GARDOUNEH	23-2-78	23-10-78
P 223 KHADANG	15-7-76	15-3-78	P 230 KHANJAR	27-4-78	1-8-81
P 225 JOSHAN	21-2-77	31-3-78	P 231 NEYZEH	5-7-78	1-8-81
P 226 FALAKHON	2-6-77	31-3-78	P 232 TABARZIN	15-9-78	1-8-81
P 227 SHAMSHIR	12-9-77	31-3-78			

D: 249 tons (275 fl)   **S:** 36 kts   **Dim:** 47.0 × 7.1 × 1.9   **Fuel:** 41 tons
A: 4/Harpoon SSM (II × 2)—1/76-mm DP OTO Melara—1/40-mm AA
Electron Equipt: Radar: 1/WM 28 fire-control   **Range:** 700/33.7   **Man:** 31 tot.
M: 4 MTU 16V538 TB91 diesels; 4 props; 14,400 hp   **Electric:** 350 kw

Khadang (P 223)—with 4 Harpoon launchers   1978

Zoubin (P 222)   CMN, 1977

REMARKS: Contracted 19-2-74 and 14-10-74. The last three were embargoed at Cherbourg 4-79 and released 22-6-81. P 232 captured off Spain 13-8-80 by anti-Khomeini
forces but abandoned later at Toulon. P 231 and 232 had no Harpoon tubes on
delivery. Two, including *Peykan* (P 224), reported lost to Iraqi forces.

PATROL BOATS

♦ **2 U.S. Coast Guard Cape class** Bldr: U.S. Coast Guard, Curtis Bay, Md. (In
serv. 1956-59)

P 201 KEYVAN   P 202 TIRAN

D: 85 tons (107 fl)   **S:** 20 kts   **Dim:** 29.0 × 6.2 × 2.0
A: 1/40-mm AA—2/Mk 22 Mousetrap ASW RL—2/d.c. racks
Range: 1,500/15   **Man:** 15 tot.
M: 4 Cummins VT-12-M700 diesels; 2 props; 2,200 hp   **Electric:** 40 kw

REMARKS: Sisters *Mehran* (P 203) and *Mahvan* (P 204) lost 1980-81, as were the three
U.S. PGM 71-class patrol boats *Parvin* (P 211), *Bahram* (P 212), and *Nahid* (P 213).

MINE WARFARE SHIPS

♦ **1 ex-U.S. Falcon-class minesweeper** Bldr: Peterson (L: 1958)

301 SHAHROKH (ex-MSC 276)

D: 320 tons (378 fl)   **S:** 12.5 kts (8, sweeping)
Dim: 43.0 (41.5 pp) × 7.95 × 2.55   **A:** 2/20-mm AA (II × 1)
Electron Equipt: Radar: 1/Decca 707   Sonar: UQS-1

MINE WARFARE SHIPS (continued)

M: 2 GM 8-268A diesels; 2 props; 890 hp **Fuel:** 27 tons
Range: 2,500/10 **Man:** 3 officers, 35 men

REMARKS: Sisters *Shabaz* lost through fire in 1975, *Simorgh* (302) and *Karkas* (303) to Iraqi forces 1980-81.

NOTE: The two U.S. *Cape* class inshore minesweepers, *Harischi* (311) and *Riazi* (312) were apparently lost to Iraqi forces 1980-81.

AMPHIBIOUS WARFARE SHIPS

♦ **2 Hengam-class LSTs** Bldr: Yarrow & Co., Scotstoun

	L	In serv.		L	In serv.
511 HENGAM	27-9-73	12-8-74	512 LARAK	7-5-74	12-11-74

Larak (512)—wearing old number   1976

D: 2,540 tons (fl) **S:** 14.5 kts **Dim:** 93.0 (86.8 wl) × 14.95 × 2.21
A: 4/40-mm AA (I × 4) **Electron Equipt:** Radar: 1/Decca 1229
M: 4 Paxman Ventura Mk 2, 12 YJCM diesels; 2 CP props; 5,600 hp
Electric: 1,100 kw **Man:** 80 men + 227 troops

REMARKS: Sisters *Lavan* (513; launched 12-6-78) and *Tonb* (514, launched 6-12-79) laid up incomplete at Yarrows, who are looking for a customer. Two others, ordered 19-7-77, were canceled in 3-79. Flight deck for one helicopter aft. Cargo capacity of 700 tons includes 300 tons of vehicle fuel. Vehicle deck is 42.7 × 9.4 meters and can accommodate 12 Soviet T-55 or 6 British Chieftain tanks. Bow doors and ramp for beaching. Upper deck forward has a 10-ton crane to handle two Uniflote cargo lighters (LCVP) and twelve Z-boat rubber personnel landing craft. Intended for logistics support (when ten 20-ton or thirty 10-ton containers would be carried) or for amphibious assault.

HOVERCRAFT

♦ **6 BH.7 Wellington class** Bldr: British Hovercraft (In serv. 1970-75)

101 to 106

D: 50 to 55 tons (fl) **S:** 65 kts **Dim:** 23.9 × 13.8 × 10.36 (high)
A: several mg **Electron Equipt:** Radar: 1/Decca 914
M: 1 Rolls-Royce Proteus 15M549 gas turbine; 1 6.4-m diameter prop; 4,250 hp
Electric: 110 kVa **Fuel:** 9 tons **Range:** 400/56

REMARKS: Four are of the logistics-support version, with a 14-ton payload. Two are of the Mk 4 version with recess for two SSM, which have not been mounted. The Mk 4 uses the Gnome 15M541 engine of 4,750 hp and can carry 60 troops in side

compartments as well as assault vehicles on its 56-m² cargo deck. Speed in both versions is reduced to 35 kts in a 1.4-meter sea. Probably inoperable due to lack of maintenance and spares support.

♦ **8 SR-N6 Winchester class** Bldr: British Hovercraft (In serv. 1973-75)

01 to 08

D: 10 tons **S:** 52 kts **Dim:** 14.8 × 7.7 × 3.8 (high)
A: 1/7.6-mm mg **M:** 1 Gnome Mk 1050 gas turbine **Range:** 110/30

REMARKS: Probably inoperable.

AUXILIARY SHIPS

♦ **1 large replenishment oiler**

	Bldr	Laid down	L	In serv.
91 KHARG	Swan Hunter, Wallsend	1-76	3-2-77	25-4-80

D: 33,014 tons (fl) **S:** 21.5 kts **Dim:** 207.15 (195.00 pp)× 25.50 × 9.14
A: 1/76-mm OTO Melara AA—4/40-mm Breda AA (II × 2)—3 helicopters
M: 1 set Westinghouse GT; 1 prop; 26,870 hp **Electric:** 7,000 kw
Boilers: 2 Babcock & Wilcox 2-drum **Man:** 248 tot.

REMARKS: Ordered 10-74. 21,100 grt/20,000 dwt. Carries fuel and ammunition. Design is greatly modified version of the Royal Navy's *Olwen* class. Ran initial trials 11-78 but delays in fitting-out made delivery before the revolution impossible. Delivered despite voluntary embargo. Has U.S. URN-20 TACAN equipment.

♦ **2 Bandar Abbas-class small replenishment oilers** Bldr: C. Lühring, Brake, West Germany

422 BANDAR ABBAS (L: 14-8-73)   441 BOOSHEHR (L: 22-3-74)

Booshehr (441)—composite photo   G. Koop, 1974

D: 5,000 tons (fl) **S:** 15 kts **Dim:** 108.0 × 16.6 × 4.5
A: 2/40-mm AA (I × 2)—1/helicopter **M:** 2 M.A.N. diesels; 2 props; 6,000 hp
Man: 60 tot.

REMARKS: 3,250 dwt. Telescoping hangar. Carry fuel, food, ammunition, and spare parts. Armed after delivery.

♦ **1 modified U.S. 174-foot-class yard oiler** Bldr: Nav. Mec. Castellammare (In serv. 2-56)

43 HORMUZ (ex-U.S. YO 247)

AUXILIARY SHIPS (continued)

Hormuz (43)   1974

D: 1,400 tons (fl)   **S:** 9 kts   **Dim:** 54.4 × 9.8 × 4.3
A: 2/20-mm AA (I × 2)   **Electron Equipt:** Radar: 1/Decca 707
M: 1 Ansaldo Q370 diesel; 600 hp   **Fuel:** 25 tons

REMARKS: Built under U.S. Military Aid Program. Cargo: 900 tons.

♦ **2 water tankers** Bldr: Mazagon Dock, Bombay, India

411 KANGAN (L: 4-78)   412 TAHERI (L: 17-9-78)

Kangan (411)   1979

D: 12,000 tons (fl)   **S:** 12 kts   **Dim:** 147.95 (140.0 pp) × 21.5 × 5.0
M: 1 M.A.N. 7L52/55A diesel; 7,385 hp

REMARKS: 9,430 dwt. Intended to supply Arabian Gulf islands. Liquid cargo: 9,000 m³.

♦ **1 U.S. 174-foot-class water tanker** Bldr: Zenith Dredge, Duluth, Minn.

	Laid down	L	In serv.
46 LENGEH (ex-U.S. YW 88)	18-3-43	18-5-43	17-10-43

D: 440 tons light (1,390 fl)   **S:** 10 kts   **Dim:** 53.04 × 10.01 × 4.27
M: 2 Union diesels; 2 props; 580 hp   **Electric:** 80 kw   **Fuel:** 25 tons
Man: 22 tot.

REMARKS: Purchased in 1964. Cargo: 930 tons.

♦ **1 ex-U.S. Amphion-class repair ship** Bldr: Tampa SB, Florida

	Laid down	L	In serv.
CHAH BAHAR (ex-Amphion, AR 13)	20-9-44	15-5-45	30-1-46

D: 8,670 tons light (14,450 fl)   **S:** 16 kts   **Dim:** 150.0 × 21.4 × 8.4
A: 2/76.2-mm DP (I × 2)   **M:** 1 set GT; 1 prop; 8,500 hp   **Electric:** 3,600 kw

Boilers: 2 Foster-Wheeler "D"; 30.6 kg/cm², 382°C   **Fuel:** 1,850 tons
Man: Quarters for 921 men

REMARKS: Transferred in 10-71. Primarily stationary, but can steam.

♦ **1 former imperial yacht for Caspian Sea** Bldr: Boele's SW, Bolnes, The Netherlands

CHAH SEVAR

D: 530 tons   **S:** 15 kts   **Dim:** 53.0 × 7.65 × 3.2
M: 2 Stork diesels; 2 props; 1,300 hp

♦ **1 former Imperial yacht for Arabian Gulf** Bldr: Burmester, W. Germany (In serv. 1970)

KISH

D: 175 tons   **Dim:** 37.0 × 7.6 × 2.2   **M:** 2 MTU diesels; 2 props; 2,920 hp

YARD AND SERVICE CRAFT

♦ **2 barracks ships**

	Bldr	L	In serv.
MICHELANGELO	Ansaldo	9-62	. . .
RAFFAELLO	CRDA, Monfalcone	. . .	7-7-65

D: 42,000 tons (fl)   **S:** 29 kts   **Dim:** 275.8 (244.0 pp) × 31.0 × 9.3
M: 4 sets GT; 4 props; 65,000 hp   **Boilers:** 4 Foster-Wheeler

REMARKS: Former cruise liners, purchased 12-12-76. Arrived July/August 1977 at Bandar Abbas for use as floating barracks for Iranian naval personnel and their families. Retain original names.

♦ **1 ex-U.S. Army tug**

45 BAHMAN SHIR (ex-ST 1002)

D: 150 tons

REMARKS: Transferred in 1962.

♦ **2 ex-German tugs**

1 (ex-Karl)   2 (ex-Ise)

D: 134 tons

REMARKS: Built 1962-63, and transferred 17-6-74.

♦ **2 ammunition lighters** Bldr: Karachi SY & Eng. Wks. (In serv. 1978)

481 N. . .   482 CHIROO

D: 840 grt   **S:** 11 kts   **Dim:** 64.0 × 10.5 × 3.2
M: 2 M.A.N. G6V-23.5/33ATL diesels; 2 props; 1,560 hp

♦ **2 water barges** Bldr: Karachi SY & Eng. Wks. (In serv. 1977-78)

1701   1702

D: 1,410 grt   **Dim:** 65.0 × 13.0 × 2.6

NOTE: In addition to the four units immediately above, Karachi Shipyard and Engineering Works delivered 14 other yard and service craft between 1977 and 7-81. All were designed in Great Britain. A variety of craft were built, all initially numbered

IRAN (*continued*)
YARD AND SERVICR CRAFT (*continued*)

1701 through 1718. Types included a self-propelled dredge (1711), a fuel-oil barge (1706), a pontoon barge (1710), fuel-oil barges (1718, named *Dayere* and a sister), and garbage lighter (120 m³ hopper with compacter). Two cargo lighters were reportedly similar to the ammunition lighters described above.

♦ **1 floating dry dock** Bldr: Pacific Bridge, Alameda, Cal. (In serv. 7-44)

400 (ex-ARD 28)

   D: 3,500 tons lift   **Dim:** 149.8 × 25.6 × 1.7 (light)

REMARKS: Transferred 1-3-77.

COAST GUARD

PATROL CRAFT

♦ **20 + 50 (?) U.S. 64-foot Mk III class** Bldr: Peterson Bldrs., Sturgeon Bay, Wisc. (In serv. 1975-. . .)

   D: 28.6 tons (34.7 fl)   **S:** 30 kts   **Dim:** 19.8 × 5.6 × 2.0
   A: 3/20-mm AA (I × 3)—1/12.7-mm mg
   M: 3 GM 8V71-TI diesels; 3 props; 2,050 hp   **Range:** 500/30   **Man:** 5 tot.

REMARKS: Twenty were ordered in 1973 and up to fifty more in 1976. Some were to be built under license in Iran. Totals are uncertain, and some have probably been lost.

♦ **20 U.S. Swift Mk II class** Bldr: Peterson Bldrs., Sturgeon Bay, Wisc. (In serv. 1976-77)

1201 to 1220

   D: 22 tons (fl)   **S:** 26 kts   **Dim:** 15.3 × 4.8 × 1.9
   A: none   **M:** 2 GM 12V71 diesels; 2 props; 900 hp   **Man:** 6 tot.

REMARKS: Equipped to carry extra personnel and have no fixed armament.

♦ **6 U.S. 40-foot class** Bldr: Sewart Seacraft, Louisiana (In serv. 1963)

MAHMAVI-HAMARAZ   MAHMAVI-VANEDI   MORDARID
MAHMAVI-TAHERI   MARDJAN   SADAF

   D: 10 tons   **S:** 30 kts   **Dim:** 12.2 × 3.4 × 1.1
   A: 2/7.62-mm mg   **M:** 2 GM diesels; 2 props; 600 hp

REMARKS: Four given to Sudan in 1978, two stricken.

♦ **40+ U.S. Bertram Enforcer harbor patrol craft**   **Dim:** 9.5 and 6.1 oa

♦ **10 Medina-class motor lifeboats** Bldr: Fairey Marine, Hamble (In serv. 1978)

1601 to 1610

   D: 15.5 tons (fl)   **S:** 16 kts   **Dim:** 14.0 × 3.7 × 1.1
   M: 2 Ford Sabre Turbo-Plus diesels; 2 props; 500 hp   **Range:** 150/12
   Man: 4 tot. (plus 12 passengers)

IRAQ
Republic of Iraq

PERSONNEL: 3,000 men, including 400 officers

MERCHANT MARINE (1980): 142 ships—1,465, 949 grt (tankers: 30 ships—1,148,487 grt)

NAVAL AVIATION: The Air Force operates eight French-supplied Super Frélon helicopters, armed with AM-39 Exocet anti-ship missiles.

NOTE: Losses to date during the war with Iran reportedly include:
   ♦ 4 Osa II-class guided-missile patrol boats (two to Iranian naval ships and two to aircraft)
   ♦ 6 P-6-class torpedo boats
   ♦ 1 Polnocny C-class landing ship

FRIGATES

♦ **4 Italian Lupo class** Bldr: CNR, Ancona

	Laid down	L	In serv.
N. . .	6-81	. . .	. . .
N. . .	. . .	. . .	. . .
N. . .	. . .	. . .	. . .
N. . .	. . .	. . .	. . .

   D: 2,213 tons (2,525 fl)   **S:** 35 kts (20.5 diesel)
   Dim: 112.8 (106.0 pp) × 11.98 × 3.84
   A: 8/Otomat Mk II SSM (I × 8)—1/Albatros SAM syst. (VIII × 1; no reloads)— 1/127-mm DP OTO Melara—4/40-mm AA Breda Dardo (II × 2)—6/324-mm ASW TT (III × 2)—2/AB 212 ASW helicopters
   Electron Equipt: Radar: 1/3RM20 navigational, 1/RAN-11X surf./air search, 1/ RAN-10S air search, 2/Orion RTN-10XRCT f.c., 2/Orion RTN-20X f.c.
         Sonar: Edo 610E or Raytheon 1160B
         ECM: Lambda F passive syst.—2/SCLAR chaff RL
   M: CODOG: 2 Fiat/G.E. LM-2500 gas turbines (25,000 hp each); 2 GMT A230- 20M diesels (3,900 hp each); 2 CP props
   Electric: 4,000 kVa   **Range:** 900/35; 3,450/20.5   **Man:** 185 tot.

REMARKS: Ordered 2-81. The SSM may possibly be French MM 40 Exocet. 127-mm gun and SAM fire control by two Elsag Mk 10 Mod. 0 systems with NA-10 radar directors; 40-mm f.c. by two Dardo systems. Selenia IPN-10 combat data system. SAM system will use Aspide missiles rather than NATO Sea Sparrow. Fin stabilizers fitted. Fixed hangar, as on Venezuelan and Peruvian units of the class, to which this version will in other ways be similar. U.S. objection to the sale of major components of the LM-2500 gas turbines seems to have been overcome.

♦ **1 training frigate** Bldr: Uljanic SY, Yugoslavia

	Laid down	L	In serv.
507 IBN KHALDUM	1977	1978	21-3-80

   D: 1,850 tons (fl)   **S:** 26 kts   **Dim:** 96.7 × 11.2 × 3.55
   A: 1/57-mm Bofors SAK 57 AA—1/40-mm AA—8/20-mm AA (II × 4)—1 d.c. rack

FRIGATES (continued)

Ibn Khaldum (507)   1980

Electron Equipt: Radar: 2/navigational, 1/surface search, 1/Phillips 9LV200
   Mk II f.c.
   Sonar: . . .
M: CODOG: 1 Rolls-Royce Olympus TM-3B gas turbine, 22,360 hp; 2 MTU
   16V956 TB61 diesels, 7,500 hp; 2 CP props
Range: 4,000/20 (diesels)   **Man:** 93 men + 100 students

REMARKS: Same basic design as the ship laid down in 1979 for Indonesia. To provide
experience in operating larger ships for future expansion of the Iraqi fleet and has
served as a transport during the Iranian war. No helicopter facilities.

GUIDED-MISSILE PATROL BOATS

♦ **6 Italian "650-ton" class** Bldrs: CNR Muggiano and La Spezia

	L	In serv.		L	In serv.
N...	...	...	N...	...	...
N...	...	...	N...	...	...
N...	...	...	N...	...	...

D: 600 tons (675 fl)   **S:** 37.5 kts   **Dim:** 62.3 (57.8 pp) × 9.3 ×. . .
A: 4 units: 6/Otomat Mk II SSM (III × 2)—1/Albatros SAM system (IV × 1;
   Aspide missiles)—1/76-mm DP OTO Melara—2/40-mm AA Breda Dardo (II
   × 1)—2/324-mm ASW TT (I × 2)
   2 units: 4/Otomat Mk II SSM (II × 2)—1/Albatros SAM system (IV × 1;
   Aspide missiles)—1/76-mm DP OTO Melara—2/40-mm AA Breda Dardo (II
   × 1)—6/324-mm ASW TT (III × 2)—1/AB 212 helicopter
Electron Equipt: Radar: 1/3RM 20, 1/RAN-12L/X, 1/Orion 10X
   Sonar: Diodon
   ECM: Elettronica Gamma syst.—1/SCLAR chaff RL
M: 4 MTU 20V956 TB92 diesels; 4 props; 24,400 hp (20,400 sust.)
Electric: 650 kw   **Fuel:** 126 tons   **Range:** 1,200/31; 4,000/18   **Man:** 51 tot.

REMARKS: Ordered 2-81. Two to be generally similar to the helicopter-capable units
built for Ecuador and displacing 685 tons (fl). Four to be of a new "Attack" version.

♦ **4 Soviet Osa-II class**

D: 210 tons (240 fl)   **S:** 36 kts   **Dim:** 39.0 × 7.7 × 1.8
A: 4/SS-N-2B Styx (I × 4)—4/30-mm AA (II × 2)

Electron Equipt: Radars: 1/Square Tie, 1/Drum Tilt
   IFF: 2/Square Head, 1/High Pole A
M: 3 M-504 diesels; 3 props; 15,000 hp   **Range:** 430/34; 700/20   **Man:** 30 tot.

REMARKS: Two transferred in 1974 and two in each year through 1977. Four reported
lost 1980-81.

♦ **4 Soviet Osa-I class**

D: 175 tons (210 fl)   **S:** 36 kts   **Dim:** 39.0 × 7.7 × 1.8
A: 4/SS-N-2 Styx—4/30-mm AA (II × 2)
Electron Equipt: Radars: 1/Square Tie, 1/Drum Tilt
   IFF: 2/Square Head, 1/High Pole A
M: 3 M-503A diesels; 3 props; 12,000 hp   **Range:** 430/34; 700/20   **Man:** 25 tot.

REMARKS: Two transferred 1971-72, two in 1973, and two in 1974. Of these, two have
been "retired from service."

TORPEDO BOATS

♦ **4 ex-Soviet P 6 class**

D: 65 tons (66.5 fl)   **S:** 43 kts   **Dim:** 25.3 × 6.1 × 1.7
A: 4/25-mm AA (II × 2)—2/533-mm TT (I × 2)
Electron Equipt: Radar: Pot Head
   IFF: 1/Dead Duck, 1/High Pole A
M: 4 M50 diesels; 4 props; 4,800 hp   **Range:** 650/26   **Man:** 2 officers, 12 men

REMARKS: Two transferred 1959, four in 11-60 and six in 1-61. Six have reportedly
been lost to Iranian forces, including some to Harpoon missiles.

PATROL BOATS

♦ **3 ex-Soviet S.O.-1 class**

210   211   212

D: 190 tons (215 fl)   **S:** 28 kts   **Dim:** 42.0 × 6.1 × 1.9
A: 4.25-mm AA (II × 2)—4/RBU-1200 ASW RL (V × 4)—2/d.c. racks—mines
Electron Equipt: Radar: 1/Pot Head
   Sonar: high-frequency
M: 3 40D diesels; 3 props; 7,500 hp   **Range:** 1,500/12   **Man:** 3 officers, 27 men

REMARKS: Delivered in 1962.

PATROL CRAFT

♦ **5 Soviet Zhuk class**

D: 50 tons (60 fl)   **S:** 30 kts   **Dim:** 23.0 × 4.9 × 1.5
A: 4/14.5-mm AA (II × 2)   **Electron Equipt:** Radar: 1/Spin Trough
M: 2 M50 diesels; 2 props; 2,400 hp

REMARKS: Transferred in 1975.

♦ **2 Soviet Poluchat-I class**

D: 80 tons (90 fl)   **S:** 18 kts   **Dim:** 29.6 × 6.1 × 1.9
A: 2/14.5-mm AA   **Electron Equipt:** Radar: 1/Spin Trough
M: 2 M50 diesels; 2 props; 2,400 hp   **Man:** 20 tot.

REMARKS: Transferred in 1966. May in fact be torpedo-recovery versions of the Poluchat class.

MINE WARFARE SHIPS

♦ **2 Soviet T-43-class fleet minesweepers**

465 AL YARMOUK   467 AL KADISIA

D: 500 tons (570 fl)   **S:** 14 kts   **Dim:** 58.0 × 8.6 × 2.3
A: 4/37-mm AA (II × 2)—8/12.7-mm mg (II × 4)—2/d.c. projectors—mines
Electron Equipt: Radar: 1/Ball End
                    IFF: 1/Square Head, 1/High Pole A
M: 2 9D diesels; 2 props; 2,200 hp   **Range:** 3,200/10

REMARKS: Transferred in 1969.

♦ **3 Yevgenya-class inshore minesweepers**

D: 80 tons (90 fl)   **S:** 12 kts   **Dim:** 26.0 × 6.0 × 1.5   **A:** 2/25-mm AA (II × 1)
Electron Equipt: Radar: 1/Spin Trough
                    IFF: 1/High Pole A
M: 2 diesels; 2 props; 600 hp

REMARKS: Transferred in 1975 as "oceanographic research craft." Have heavier guns than their Soviet Navy sisters.

♦ **4 Yugoslav Nestin-class river minesweepers** Bldr: Brodotehnika, Belgrade

D: 65 tons   **S:** 15 kts   **Dim:** 27.0 × 6.3 × 1.6
A: 20-mm AA (III × 1, I × 1)—mines   **M:** 2 diesels; 2 props; 520 hp

REMARKS: Transferred 1978-79. Previously mistakenly reported as Kraljevica-class patrol boats.

AMPHIBIOUS WARFARE SHIPS

♦ **3 Soviet Polnocny-C class** Bldr: Poland

D: 1,150 tons (fl)   **S:** 18 kts   **Dim:** 81.3 × 10.1 × 2.0
A: 4/30-mm AA (II × 2)—2/122-mm rocket launchers (XL × 2)
M: 2 40D diesels; 2 props; 5,000 hp

REMARKS: Have a helicopter platform forward of the superstructure. Barrage rocket launchers differ from others of this class, which use 140-mm rockets. Two transferred in 1977, one in 1978, and one in 9-79. Names of first three: *Atika*, *Ganda*, and *Nouh*. One lost to Iranian Harpoon missiles, 1980-81.

AUXILIARY SHIPS AND CRAFT

♦ **1 Italian Stromboli-class replenishment oiler**

	Bldr	Laid down	L	In serv.
N. . .	Castellamare di Stabia, Naples	. . .	. . .	. . .

D: 8,706 tons (fl)   **S:** 19.5 kts   **Dim:** 129.0 (118.5 pp) × 18.0 × 6.5
A: 1/76-mm DP OTO Melara   **Electron Equipt:** Radar: . . .
M: 2 GMT A428SS diesels; 1 CP prop; 11,200 hp   **Electric:** 4,200 kw
Range: 10,000/16   **Man:** 119 tot.

REMARKS: Ordered 2-81. Will probably be modified from the Italian Navy version as to cargo and equipment. Capable of serving two ships alongside while under way.

♦ **1 Yugoslav Spasilac-class salvage ship** Bldr: Tito SY, Belgrade

A 51 AKA (In serv. 1978)

D: 750 tons (fl)   **S:** 16 kts   **Dim:** 61.0 × 11.0 × 3.4
A: 4/14.5-mm mg (II × 2)   **M:** 2 diesels; 2 props; 3,000 hp

♦ **1 presidential yacht** Bldr: Elsinore SB & Eng., Denmark

N. . . (L: 10-80)

Iraq's new presidential yacht—artist's rendering   Elsinore SY 1980

D: 2,000 grt   **S:** 19 kts   **Dim:** 82.0 × 13.0 × . . .
M: 2 MTU diesels; 2 props; . . . hp

♦ **1 presidential barge** Bldr: Elsinore SB & Eng., Denmark

N. . .

D: . . .   **S:** . . .   **Dim:** 67.0 × . . . × 1.2   **M:** . . .

REMARKS: Ordered 1981. Luxurious barge-type yacht for use on the Tigris.

♦ **1 new-construction diving tender** Bldr: . . . , the Netherlands (In serv. 1980)

N. . .

D: 200 tons (fl)   **S:** 12 kts   **Dim:** 28.5 (27.8 pp) × 6.4 × 1.8
M: 2 MTU 8V331 TB82 diesels; 2 props; . . . hp

♦ **4 Soviet Nyryat-2-class diving tenders**

D: 56 tons (fl)   **S:** 12 kts   **Dim:** 21.3 × 3.8 × 2.0   **M:** 1 3D12 diesel; 300 hp

REMARKS: May also be used as tugs.

♦ **1 Soviet Pozharney-I-class fireboat**

D: 180 tons (fl)   **S:** 17 kts   **Dim:** 35.0 × 6.2 × 2.0
M: 2 diesels; 2 props; 1,800 hp

♦ **1 Soviet Prometey-class tug** Bldr: Okhtenskiy SY, Leningrad

D: 319 tons (fl)   **S:** 12 kts   **Dim:** 29.8 (28.2 pp) × 8.3 × 3.2
M: 2 6D30/50-4 diesels; 2 Kort-nozzle props; 1,200 hp   **Electric:** 50 kw
Range: 1,800/12   **Man:** 3 tot.

REMARKS: Delivered mid-1970s. Has firefighting monitor.

♦ **1 new-construction floating dry dock** Bldr: Italcantiere, Trieste

REMARKS: Ordered 2-81. No details available.

CUSTOMS SERVICE

♦ **1 yacht used as a pilot station** (In serv. 1929)

AL THAWRA (ex-*Malike Aliyah*)

IRAQ (continued)
CUSTOMS SERVICE (continued)

D: 746 tons S: 14 kts M: Diesels; 2 props; 1,800 hp

♦ **9 Tana-class pilot launches** Bldr: Kone-Jyraa Oy, Jyvasky, Finland (In serv. 1980-81)

D: . . . S: 33 kts Dim: 9.45 × 2.44 × . . .
M: 2 MTU diesels; 2 props; . . . hp

REMARKS: Delivery delayed by war.

♦ **8 pilot launches** Bldr: Thornycroft, 1961-62

D: 10 tons S: . . . Dim: 11.0 × . . . × . . . M: 1 diesel; 125 hp

♦ **4 pilot launches** Bldr: Thornycroft
Dim: 6.4 × . . . × . . . M: 40 hp

♦ **6 SR. N6-class hovercraft** Bldr: British Hovercraft

REMARKS: Ordered 1981.

IRELAND
Eire

PERSONNEL (1980): 866 total (107 officers, 759 men)

MERCHANT MARINE (1980): ships—212,143 grt (tankers: 5 ships—6,989 grt)

NAVAL AVIATION: The Irish Air Force operates 3 Beech A200 Maritime Patrol Aircraft. Purchase of 2 Dauphine 360 helicopters for the new patrol ships is planned.

FISHERIES-PROTECTION SHIPS

♦ **2 P 31 class** Bldr: Verolme, Cork

	Laid down	L	In serv.
P 31 N. . .	11-81	. . .	1984
P 32 N. . .	1982	. . .	1985

D: 1,760 tons (fl) S: 19 kts Dim: 80.75 × 12.0 × 4.15
A: 1/76-mm DP OTO Melara—1/Dauphine 360 helicopter
M: 2 diesels; 2 CP props; 7,200 hp Range: 7,000/15 Man: 85 tot.

REMARKS: Patterned after the U.S. Coast Guard's 270-ft. *Bear* class. Will have a helicopter hangar.

♦ **3 Emer class** Bldr: Verolme, Cork

	L	In serv.
P 21 EMER	1977	18-1-78
P 22 AOIFE	12-4-79	21-11-79
P 23 AISLING	3-10-79	21-5-80

D: 1,025 tons (fl) S: 18 kts Dim: 65.20 (58.50 pp) × 10.40 × 4.36
A: 1/40-mm AA—2/20-mm AA (I × 2)

Aoife (P 22)   Verolme, 1979

Electron Equipt: Radars: 2/Decca. . . Sonar: Simrad SU side-scan
M: 2 SEMT-Pielstick 6 PA6L-280 diesels; 1 CP prop; 4,800 hp Fuel: 170 tons
Range: 4,500/18, 6,750/12 Man: 5 officers, 41 men

REMARKS: Developed version of the *Deirdre* with raised forecastle instead of bow bulwarks, to improve sea-keeping. Have advanced navigational aids, fin stabilizers. P 22 and P 23 have satellite navigation receivers, a 225 kw bow-thruster, a computerized plotting table, and a new-pattern Ka-Me-Wa propeller. Only P 23 has evaporators.

♦ **1 Dierdre class** Bldr: Verolme, Cork

	L	In serv.
P 20 DEIRDRE	29-12-71	19-6-72

Deirdre (P 20)   Verolme, 1972

IRELAND (*continued*)
FISHERIES-PROTECTION SHIPS (*continued*)

D: 980 tons (fl) **S:** 18 kts (15.5 cruising)
Dim: 62.61 (56.20 pp) × 10.40 × 4.35
A: 1/40-mm AA—2/52-mm flare launchers
M: 2 British Polar SF 112 VS-F diesels; 1 CP prop; 4,200 hp
Fuel: 150 tons **Range:** 3,000/15.5, 5,000/12 **Man:** 5 officers, 41 men

REMARKS: Vosper fin stabilizers. New Ka-Me-Wa propeller fitted 1980.

♦ **2 ex-British "Ton"-class minesweepers**

	Bldr	In serv.
CM 10 GRAINNE (ex-*Oulston*)	Thornycroft	1955
CM 12 FOLA (ex-*Blaxton*)	Thornycroft	1956

Grainne (CM 10)   G. Gyssels, 1979

D: 370 tons (425 fl) **S:** 15 kts **Dim:** 46.33 (42.68 pp) × 8.76 × 2.5
A: 1/40-mm AA—2/20-mm AA (II × 1)
M: 2 Mirrlees or Napier Deltic diesels; 2 props; 2,500-3,000 hp **Fuel:** 45 tons
Range: 2,300/12, 3,000/8 **Man:** 33 tot.

REMARKS: Transferred in 1971. Most portable sweep gear has been landed, but winches, cable reels, and davits remain aboard. Sister *Banba* (CM 11) deactivated 1980.

AUXILIARIES AND SERVICE CRAFT

♦ **1 training ship** Bldr: Liffey, Dublin, 1953

A 15 SETANTA (ex-*Isolde*)

D: 1,173 tons (fl) **S:** 11.5 kts **Dim:** 63.5 × 11.6 × 4.0
A: 2/20-mm AA (I × 2) **M:** Reciprocating steam; 2 props; 1,500 hp
Fuel: 276 tons **Range:** 3,500/10 **Man:** 44 tot.

REMARKS: Taken over in 1976 from the Irish Lighthouse Commission. Now immobilized at Haulbowline, Cork, and used for recruit training.

♦ **1 stores tender** Bldr: R. Dunston, G.B., 1934

JOHN ADAMS

D: 94 grt **S:** 10 kts **Dim:** 25.9 × 5.6 × 2.1 **M:** 1 diesel; 216 hp

REMARKS: The *Ferdia* (A 16), a former Danish trawler for Irish naval service, was returned to her owners in 1978.

♦ **1 inshore survey launch** Bldr: Fairey Marine, Hamble (In serv. 11-78)

HYDRAFIX

REMARKS: No data available.

♦ **1 sail-training craft** Bldr: J. Tyrell, Arklow (In serv. 1981)

N. . .

D: 120 tons (fl) **S:** . . . **Dim:** 25.6 × 6.4 × 2.9
M: 1 diesel; 1 prop; 120 hp/418.2 m² sail area **Man:** 4 crew plus 20 cadets

REMARKS: Sister *Creidne* on lease until new unit is completed. *Tatlye*, a French-built Dufour 10.7-m sailboat, is also in service.

♦ **4 passenger and service launches**

COLLEEN II (In serv. 1972)	RAVEN II (In serv. 1938)
SIR CECIL ROMER (In serv. 1938)	JACKDAW (In serv. 1938)

♦ **1 fuel barge**

CHOWL—**D:** 100 tons **M:** 1 diesel; 50 hp

ISRAEL
State of Israel

PERSONNEL: Active: 3,500, of whom 250 officers and 500 men are especially trained as commandos and frogmen. Reserves: 500 total.

MERCHANT MARINE (1980): 56 ships—450,216 grt (tankers: 2 ships—368 grt)

NAVAL AVIATION: During 1978 the Israeli Navy put into service three IAI Westwind 1124 Sea Scan maritime-reconnaissance aircraft, whose mission is to cooperate with surface forces. Range: 1,350 nm at 270 kts. Carry sonobuoys.

WEAPONS AND SYSTEMS

The Israeli Navy uses foreign equipment such as 76-mm OTO Melara Compact, Breda 40-mm, and Oerlikon guns, and it has perfected the Gabriel anti-ship missile system.

Gabriel is a 400-kg, solid-propellant, surface-to-surface missile. After being fired, it climbs about 100 meters, then, at 7,500 meters from the launcher, descends slowly to an altitude of 20 meters. Optical or radar guidance is provided in azimuth, and a radio altimeter determines altitude. At a distance of 1,200 meters from the target, the missile descends to 3 meters, under either radio command or semiactive homing. The explosive charge is a 75-kg conventional warhead. In the Yom Kippur War of 1973, 85 percent of the Gabriel missiles fired reached their targets.

WEAPONS AND SYSTEMS (continued)

Chaff launchers on a Reshev-class guided-missile patrol boat 1975

The Gabriel II carries a television camera and a transceiver for azimuth and altitude commands. The television is energized when the missile has attained a certain height and sends to the firing ship a picture of the areas that cannot be picked up by shipboard radar. The operator then can send any necessary corrections during the middle and final phases of the missile's flight, and thus find a target that cannot be seen either by the naked eye or on radar. The range of the Gabriel II is about 40,000 meters. The Gabriel III version has a range of 36,000 m and employs active radar guidance.

The U.S. Harpoon was acquired beginning in 1978 and is used on guided-missile patrol boats in a mix with Gabriel.

Triple trainable Gabriel missile launcher

Israeli Aircraft Industries and Oerlikon are cooperative in the development of a twin 30-mm antiaircraft gun mounting, the PCM-30. The system would replace 40-mm AA guns in earlier Israeli missile combatants.

SUBMARINES

♦ **3 German Type 206** Bldr: Vickers, Barrow, G.B.

	Laid down	L	In serv.
GAL	1973	2-12-75	12-76
TANIN	1974	25-10-76	6-77
RAHAV	1975	. . .	12-77

Gal 1977

D: 420/600 tons **Dim:** 17/11 kts **S:** 45.0 × 4.7 × 3.8 **A:** 8/533-mm TT, fwd
M: 2 MTU 12V-493-TY60 diesels (600 hp each); AEG generators; 1 prop; 1,800 hp
Man: 22 tot.

REMARKS: Ordered in 4-72. Carry two spare torpedoes. The first unit ran aground on delivery voyage, but has been repaired. These submarines do *not* carry the Vickers SLAM submarine-launched antiaircraft missile systems.

GUIDED-MISSILE CORVETTES

♦ **0 (+2) Q 9 class** Bldr: Israeli SY, Haifa

D: 850 tons (fl) **S:** 40 kts **Dim:** 77.1 × 9.1 × 3.04
A: 8/Harpoon SSM (IV × 2)—2/76-mm DP OTO Melara (I × 2)—4/30-mm PCM-30 AA (II × 2)—1/short-range SAM system—6/324-mm ASW TT (III × 2)—1 helicopter
M: CODAG: 1 GE LM-2500 gas turbine, 20,000-25,000 hp; 2 MTU diesels, 8,000 hp; 2 props
Range: 4,500/diesels **Man:** 45 tot.

REMARKS: The helicopter would provide over-the-horizon target data for the Harpoon. First unit reportedly laid down early 1981, but no orders have been announced. Maximum speed on diesels: 25 kts.

GUIDED-MISSILE PATROL BOATS

♦ **3 (+3) Aliyah class** Bldr: Israeli SY, Haifa

ALIYAH	10-7-80	8-80
GEOULA	10-80	31-12-80
N ROMAT	1981	10-81
N. . .	1981	. . .
N. . .	. . .	. . .
N. . .	. . .	. . .

Aliyah at launch   10-7-80

D: 500 tons (fl) **S:** 31 kts **Dim:** 61.7 × 7.6 × 2.4
A: 8/Harpoon SSM (IV × 2)—4/Gabriel SSM (I × 4)—*Aliyah:* 1/40-mm AA
Geoula: 2/30-mm PCM-30 AA (II × 1)—2/20-mm AA (I × 2)—4/12.7-mm mg (I × 4)—1 helicopter
Electron Equipt: Radar: 1/TH-D 1040 Neptune, 1/Orion RTN-10X
ECM: MN-53 intercept system—10/multiple chaff RL
M: 4/MTU MD 871 diesels; 4 props, 14,000 hp
Range: 1,500/30; 4,000/17 **Man:** 53 tot.

REMARKS: The helicopters are intended to provide an over-the-horizon targeting capability to utilize fully the range capabilities of the Harpoon missiles, which are mounted athwartships in the gap between the fixed hangar and the bridge superstructure. Each *Aliyah* will lead a group of missile boats. Later units may not have the helicopter facility, mounting instead an OTO Melara 76-mm gun and four additional Gabriel.

♦ **8 Reshev (Sa'ar IV) class** Bldr: Israeli SY, Haifa

	L	In serv.		L	In serv.
RESHEV	19-2-73	4-73	NITZAHON	10-7-78	9-78
KIDON	7-74	9-74	HATZMAAT	3-12-78	2-79
TARSHISH	1-75	3-75	MOLEDET	22-3-79	5-79
YAFO	2-75	4-75	KOMEMIYUT	19-7-79	8-80

A Reshev—with 4 Harpoon, 5 Gabriel, 1/76-mm and 1/40-mm gun   1980

Yafo—with 4 Harpoon, 4 Gabriel, 2 OTO Melara 76-mm guns   1975

D: 415 tons (450 fl) **S:** 32 kts **Dim:** 58.1 × 7.6 × 2.4
A: 4/Harpoon SSM (II × 2 or IV × 1)—4.5 Gabriel SSM (I × 4)—1-2/76-mm OTO Melara Compact (I × 2)—0-1/40-mm AA—2/20-mm AA (I × 2)—6/12.7-mm mg (II × 3)
Electron Equipt: Radar: 1/Thomson CSF Neptune TH-D 1040, 1 Selenia Orion RTN-10X
ECM: Elta MN-53 intercept—4 large and 72 small chaff RL
M: 4 MTU MD871 diesels; 4 props; 14,000 hp
Range: 1,500/30, 4,000/17 **Man:** 45 tot.

REMARKS: Quarters are air conditioned. The *Tarshish* had a temporary helicopter deck in place of the after 76-mm gun for experiment with over-the-horizon targeting for Harpoon in 1979. Original missile armament was seven Gabriel. The Gabriel launchers are fixed. The 76-mm guns have been specially adapted for shore bombardment. The forward 76-mm mount has been temporarily replaced by a 40-mm

GUIDED-MISSILE PATROL BOATS (continued)

AA in *Nitzahon* and *Komemiyut*, pending availability of the PCM-30 twin 30-mm AA to deal with quick-response threats. Sisters *Keshet* and *Romach* were transferred to Chile 1979–80, and a third may follow. Three were built in Israel for South Africa, with others built under license at Durban. The elaborate ECM/ESM system was supplied by the Italian firm Elettronica.

♦ **6 Sa'ar III class** Bldr: Constr. Méc. de Normandie, Cherbourg

	L		L
SA'AR	25-11-69	HEREV	20-6-69
SOUFA	4-2-69	HANIT	1969
GAASCH	24-6-69	HETZ	14-12-69

Sa'ar III—with 2 Harpoon, 3 Gabriel, 1/76-mm gun   1980

♦ **6 Sa'ar II class** Bldr: Constr. Méc. de Normandie, Cherbourg

	L		L
MIVTACH	11-4-67	EILATH	14-6-68
MIZNAG	1967	HAIFA	14-6-68
MISGAV	1967	AKKO	1968

Miznag—Sa'ar II with 5 Gabriel, 2/40-mm AA   1978

D: 220 tons (250 fl)   **S:** 40 kts   **Dim:** 45.0 × 7.0 × 1.8 (2.5 fl)
A: *Sa'ar II*: 5/Gabriel SSM (III × 1, I × 2)—2/40-mm AA Breda (I × 2)—2/
    12.7-mm machine guns—*see* Remarks
    Sa'ar III: 2/Harpoon SSM (I × 2)—3/Gabriel SSM (III ×)—1/76-mm DP
    OTO Melara—2/12.7-mm machine guns
Electron Equipt: Radar: 1/Thomson CSF Neptune TH-D 1040, 1/Selenia Orion
        RTN-10x
        ECM: VHFD/F and intercept gear
M: 4 MTU MD871 diesels; 4 props; 14,000 hp   **Fuel:** 30 tons
Range: 1,000/30, 1,600/20, 2,500/15   **Man:** 5 officers, 30-35 men

REMARKS: Excellent sea qualities and endurance. *Sa'ar I* is the name that was used for these ships in an all-gun configuration. Four units of the *Sa'ar II* variant now carry an EDO 780 variable-depth sonar and 2/324-mm Mk 32 ASW TT (Mk 46 torpedoes) aft and have no missiles. *Sa'ar III* has no ASW capability. Armaments now fairly standardized, but triple Gabriel launchers can be interchanged with the after 40-mm mountings.

GUIDED-MISSILE HYDROFOILS

♦ **0 (+2) Grumman Mk II/M 161 class**

	Bldr	L	In serv.
SHIMRIT	Lantana BY, Lantana, Fla.	26-5-81	. . .
N. . .	Israeli SY, Haifa	. . .	. . .

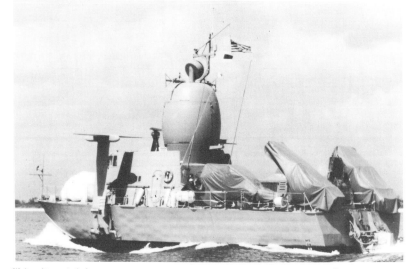

Shimrit on trials   Grumman, 1981

D: 67 tons light (101.6 fl)   **S:** 45 kts
Dim: 31.09 foils retracted (25.60 hull; 23.40 wl) × 12.95 (7.32 hull) × 4.75 at
    rest (1.93 foiling; 1.52 foils retracted)
A: 4/Harpoon SSM (II × 2)—2/Gabriel SSM (I × 2)—2/30-mm AA (II × 1)
M: 1 Allison 501-KF gas turbine; 1 CP, 4-bladed prop; 5,400 hp—2 retractable
    100-hp hydraulic motors for hull-borne maneuvering

GUIDED-MISSILE HYDROFOILS (continued)

Shimrit on trials
Grumman, 1981

Electric: 400 kw (2 Pratt & Whitney ST-6 gas turbines)
Fuel: 22.3 tons **Endurance:** 3 to 5 days **Range:** 1,056/44 foiling
Man: 15 tot.

REMARKS: Ordered 1978 from Grumman, with prototype construction subcontracted to Lantana. Name *Shimrit* means "Guardian." Numerous delays in program. First Israeli unit built simultaneously at Haifa. Aluminum construction. Pineapple-shaped radome conceals elaborate intercept array. Maximum speed on auxiliary system: 10 kts. Turning radius at 45 kts: 200 m.

PATROL CRAFT

♦ **1 Dvora class** Bldr: Israeli Aircraft Industries, 1978

D: 47 tons (fl) **S:** 36 kts **Dim:** 21.62 × 5.49 × 0.94 (1.82 props)
A: 2/20-mm AA (I × 2)—2/12.7-mm mg **Electron Equipt:** Radar: 1/Decca 926
M: 2 MTU 12V331 TC81 diesels; 2 props; 2,720 hp
Electric: 30 kw **Range:** 700/32 **Man:** 8-10 tot.

REMARKS: Privately funded prototype, acquired in 1979 to begin replacing the Coast Guard's four "Wind"-class patrol boats. The design has been offered with two Gabriel SSM and has been exported to Nicaragua, Argentina, and Chile.

♦ **37 Dabur class** Bldrs: 12 by Sewart Seacraft, U.S.A.; others by Israeli Air Industries, 1973–77

Dabur class
1978

D: 25 tons (35 fl) **S:** 25 kts **Dim:** 19.8 × 5.8 × 0.8
A: 2/20-mm (I × 2)—2/12.7-mm machine guns (I × 2)
Electron Equipt: Radar: 1/Decca 101 or 926
M: 2 GM 12V71 TI diesels; 2 props; 960 hp
Electric: 20 kw **Range:** 1,200/17 **Man:** 1 officer, 5 men

REMARKS: Quarters air-conditioned and spacious. Five given to Christian forces in Lebanon in 1976.

♦ **up to 28 Yatush class (U.S. PBR type)**

D: 6.5 tons **S:** 25 kts **Dim:** 9.8 × 3.4 × 0.8
A: 2/7.62-mm mg **M:** 2 diesels; water jets **Man:** 5 tot.

REMARKS: Early units bought in the United States in 1968, later ones built in Israel. Several may be stationed in the Red Sea. Two given to Lebanonese Christians, 1975-76.

AMPHIBIOUS WARFARE SHIPS

♦ BAT SHEVA

Bat Sheva
1969

D: 900 tons (1,150 fl) **S:** 10 kts **Dim:** 95.1 × 11.2 × . . .
A: 4/20-mm—4/12.7-mm mg **M:** Diesels; 2 props **Man:** 26 tot.

REMARKS: Built in Germany in 1967 and bought in South Africa in 1968.

♦ **3 LCT type** Bldr: Israeli SY, Haifa In serv. 1966-67

ASHDOD ASHKELON AHZIV

D: 400 tons (730 fl) **S:** 10.5 kts **Dim:** 62.7 × 10.0 × 1.8
A: 2/20-mm AA (I × 2) **M:** 3 MWM diesels; 3 props; 1,900 hp
Fuel: 37 tons **Man:** 20 tot.

ISRAEL (continued)
AMPHIBIOUS WARFARE SHIPS (continued)

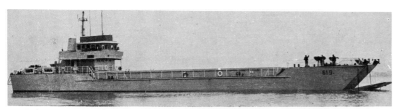

Ashdot 1971

♦ **2 Etzion Gueber class** Bldr: Israeli SY, Haifa (In serv. 1965)

ETZION GUEBER   SHIKMONA   N...

Etzion Gueber

D: 182 tons (230 fl)   **S:** 10 kts   **Dim:** 30.5 × 5.9 × 1.3
A: 2/20-mm AA (I × 2)   **M:** Diesels; 2 props; 1,280 hp   **Man:** 10 tot.

♦ **3 ex-U.S. LSM 1 class**

N...   N...   N...

D: 1,095 tons (fl)   **S:** 12.5 kts   **Dim:** 62.1 × 10.5 × 2.2
A: 1/20-mm AA—several mg
M: 2 GM or Fairbanks-Morse diesels; 2 props; 2,800 hp

REMARKS: Built 1944-45 and bought in 1972 from commercial sources.

VARIOUS SHIPS

♦ **1 training ship**

NOGAH

REMARKS: Former small cargo vessel equipped as a training ship for the merchant marine.

♦ **1 small missile boat tender**

NAHARYA

REMARKS: Base craft for the missile craft stationed at Eilath.

♦ **1 missile boat tender** Bldr: Todd SY, Seattle (In serv. 1976)

MA'OZ

REMARKS: 4,000-ton oilfield-supply type used as a missile-boat tender in the Mediterranean. Acquisition of U.S. 65-D-13, *Casa Grande*, was superseded by the purchase of this ship.

NOTE: The vehicle cargo ship *Bat Yam* was sold 10-80.

ITALY
Italian Republic

PERSONNEL (1980): 42,000, including 5,200 officers

MERCHANT MARINE (1980): 1,739 ships; 11,095,694 grt
(tankers: 273 ships; 4,685,141 grt)

NAVAL AVIATION (Aviazione per la Marina Militare—MARINAVIA): Fixed-wing ASW aircraft belong to the Air Force, which puts them at the disposal of the Navy. For some time, American two-engined S-2 Trackers were the primary planes in use, but following a contract entered into in October 1968, the BR-1150 Atlantic became the principal type, the last 18 units being delivered in 1973. One squadron of eight S-2F Trackers remains in service.

Helicopters, of which there are 82, are under the control of the Navy. They are used mainly for ASW, but can also be used in an anti-ship role; they can carry such missiles as the AS-12. For antisubmarine warfare, the Italian Navy originally favored a light, weapon-carrying helicopter working in combination with another helicopter of the same size equipped with ASW sensors. Because this limits the ships that can participate in ASW operations to those that are fitted to carry both types of helicopter, future orientation in ASW operations appears to be towards the use of a heavier helicopter (SH-3D) that carries both weapons and sensors. These helicopters, 24 of which have been acquired, may be based ashore or on such ships as can handle them (*Giuseppe Garibaldi*, *Vittorio Veneto*, the two *Andrea Doria*-class cruisers, and the two *Audace*-class destroyers). There are 24 AB-204B and 23 AB-212 light ASW helicopters in service; 3 old SH-34 helicopters are also available. Procurement of 30 additional SH-3D Sea Kings is planned, while the total of AB-212 is to be 27.

The Bell AB-204B and AB-212 are built under American license by Agusta in Italy. Principal characteristics are:

AB-204B
Ceiling: 10,800 ft
Range: 2 hr 5 min without torpedoes
1 hr 15 min with torpedoes
Armament: 2 Mk 44 or Mk 46 torpedoes or
4 AS-12
Electronics: ASQ-13 sonar
Crew: 3

Length: 17.4 m
Rotor: 14.6 m
Max. weight: 4,310 kg
Motor: 1 turboshaft, 1,200 hp
Max. Speed: 104 kts
Cruising speed: 90 kts

NAVAL AVIATION *(continued)*

Vittorio Veneto (C 550)   1980

AB-212

Ceiling: 5,000 ft
Range: 4 hr 15 min (360 nm at 100 kts)
Armament: 2 Mk 44 or Mk 46 torpedoes, depth
    charges, or 2 AS-12 ASM
Electronics: ASQ-13B sonar
Crew: 3

Length: 17.4 m
Rotor: 14.6
Max. weight: 5,086 kg; 3,420 light
Motor: 1 turboshaft, 1,290 hp
Max. speed: 130 kts
Cruising speed: 100 kts

NOTE: A new ASW helicopter to succeed the SH-3D in the late 1980s is being jointly
developed by Agusta and Westland, in Great Britain.

WARSHIPS IN SERVICE, UNDER CONSTRUCTION, OR AUTHORIZED AS OF 1 JANUARY 1982

	L	Tons	Main armament
♦ 0 (+1) VTOL carrier			
GIUSEPPE GARIBALDI	1983	10,043	4/Otomat, 2/Albatros, 16/helicopters

♦ 10 submarines

		Tons (surfaced)	
4 NAZARIO SAURO	1976-...	1,456	6/533-mm TT
4 ENRICO TOTI	1967-68	535	4/533-mm TT
2 TANG	1951	2,100	8/533-mm TT

♦ 3 cruisers

		Tons	
1 VITTORIO VENETO	1967	7,500	1/missile launcher, 8/ 76.2-mm, 9/helicopters
2 ANDREA DORIA	1962-63	6,500	1/missile launcher, 8/ 76.2-mm, 4/helicopters

♦ 5 (+2) destroyers

0 (+2) "Improved AUDACE"	...	4,400	1/missile launcher, 2/ 127-mm, ASW weapons
2 AUDACE	1971	3,950	1/missile launcher, 2/ 127-mm, ASW weapons
2 IMPAVIDO	1962	3,201	1/missile launcher, 2/ 127-mm, ASW weapons
1 IMPETUOSO	1955	2,775	4/127-mm, ASW weapons

♦ 21 (+7) frigates and corvettes

1 (+7) MAESTRALE	1981-	3,040	4/Otomat, 1/Sea Sparrow, /127-mm, ASW weapons
4 LUPO	1976-79	2,208	8/Otomat, 1/Sea Sparrow, 1/127-mm, ASW weapons
2 ALPINO	1967	2,000	6/76-mm, ASW weapons
3 CARLO BERGAMINI	1960	1,410	2/76-mm, ASW weapons
3 CANOPO	1954-56	1,807	3/76-mm, ASW weapons
4 PIETRO DE CRISTOFARO	1964-65	850	2/76-mm, ASW weapons
4 ALBATROS	1954	800	2/40-mm, ASW weapons

♦ 8 (+3) missile hydrofoils and torpedo boats

♦ 35 (+9) mine countermeasures ships

♦ 2 amphibious ships

WEAPONS AND SYSTEMS

A. MISSILES

♦ Surface-to-air

American SM1, and **SM1-MR** *(see under U.S.A.)*

Albatros Aspide (Italian version of the Sea Sparrow) Bldr: Selenia

Ceiling: 15 m (min.); 5,000 m (max.)
Length: 3.70 m

MISSILES *(continued)*

Wingspan: 1.02 m
Range: 10,000 m
Diameter: 0.20 m
Weight: 204 kg
Guidance: semiactive homing

This equipment employs an octuple launcher built by OTO Melara and weighing 7 tons; elevation: 5 to +65 degrees. Controlled by NA-30 system.

◆ Surface-to-surface

Otomat Mk 1 Bldr: OTO Melara/Matra

Length: 4,820 m
Wingspan: 1.19 m
Range: 60-80 km
Diameter: 1,060 m (with boosters); 460 m (without boosters)
Weight: 750 kg
Guidance: Thomson/CSF active homing, 3-axis

This missile flies almost at sea level after firing, climbs at a steep angle to a pre-determined height, and strikes its target during descent. For export only; not used by Italian Navy.

Otomat Mk 2 (also known as "Teseo")

This model differs from the Mk 1 in having an Italian (SMA) active radar homing head, instead of a French one. It is also a "sea-skimmer"; that is, it flies close to the water after firing. Its explosive charge is about 200 kg. and its ramjet propulsion system allows it to be used at ranges limited only by its guidance system and its target designation. Range: 150 km; speed: 300 m/sec.

Two additional projects are in development: "Briaero," a Mach 1 weapon with a 200-400-km range, and "Otomach," a Mach 2, turbojet-powered weapon being developed by OTO Melara and Alfa-Romeo.

◆ Air-to-surface

The French S.N.I.A.S. AS-12 wire-guided anti-shipping missile has been adopted for use by helicopters.

B. GUNS

With the exception of some old American guns, such as the 127-mm twin-barreled 38-caliber semi-automatic, the following Italian systems are used:

40-mm Breda/Bofors Compact

Length: 70 calibers
Muzzle velocity: 1,000 m/sec.
Max. effective range, antiaircraft fire: 3,500-4,000 m
Rate of fire: 300 rounds/min/barrel
Projectile weight: 0.96 kg
Number of ready-service rounds: 444 or 736 (depending on installation)
Fire control: Dardo system (Selenia RTN-20X radar)
Impact or proximity fusing

76-mm

Single- or twin-barreled, automatic, for air, surface, and land targets

Length: 62 calibers
Muzzle velocity: 850 m/sec

Max. effective range, surface fire: 8,000 m
Max. effective range, antiaircraft fire: 4,000-5,000 m
Rate of fire: 60 rounds/min/barrel

76-mm OTO Melara Compact

Single-barreled light antiaircraft automatic fire; entirely remote control with muzzle brake and cooling system

Length: 62 calibers
Muzzle velocity: 925 m/sec
Max. effective range, surface fire: 8,000 m
Max. effective range, antiaircraft fire: 4,000-5,000 m
Rate of fire: 85 rounds/min
Weight of mount: 7.35 tons, because of the use of light alloys and fiberglass; 80 ready-service rounds in the drum, which permits at least 1 minute of fire before reloading. There are no personnel in the mount; the ammunition handlers in the magazine have only to feed the drum.

The gun has been purchased by a great many navies.

127-mm OTO Melara Compact

Single-barreled automatic, triple-purpose, remote control

Length: 54 calibers
Muzzle velocity: 807 m/sec
Max. effective range, surface fire: 15,000 m
Max. effective range, antiaircraft fire: 7,000 m
Rate of fire: 45 rounds/min, automatic setting
Weight of the mount: 32 tons because of the use of light alloys and a fiberglass shield. The gun has a muzzle brake; it can automatically fire 66 rounds, thanks to 3 loading drums, each with 22 rounds. Two hoists serve two loading trays with rounds coming from the magazine, and a drum may be loaded even while the gun is firing. An automatic selection system allows a choice of ammunition (antiaircraft, surface target, pyrotechnics, chaff for cluttering radar).

This equipment has also been purchased by the Canadian Navy for its *Iroquois*-class destroyers.

C. ANTISUBMARINE WEAPONS

Menon triple-barreled mortar

The system has a launcher carrying three 320 m, 4.6-m-long barrels. These tubes fire a 160-kg projectile at a fixed elevation of 45 degrees. The range (400 to 900 m) is reached by varying the quantity of gas admitted into the tubes from three powder chambers. The tubes are reloaded at a 90-degree elevation from a drum containing the depth-charge projectiles.

Menon single-barreled mortar

The system has a single barrel with automatic loading. Fire control is usually directed in the underwater battery plot. The mortar is fired at a 45-degree angle with the range fixed by a system similar to that of the triple-barreled Menon; firing 160-kg depth-charges round by round; the gas relief valves have adjustable vents. The weapon is automatically reloaded from the magazine by hoist and a loading drum.

Torpedoes

American Mk 44 and Mk 46 torpedoes are used on ships (using the triple Mk 32 tube mount) and helicopters.

ANTISUBMARINE WEAPONS (continued)

The Whitehead Motofides A-184 wire-guided torpedo is now in use, with a 533-mm carrier torpedo that ejects a Mk 46 passive homing torpedo; range is over 15,000 m. A replacement for Mk 46, A-244, is in development.

D. RADARS

The Italian Navy uses a number of American radars (SPS-6, SPS-12, SPS-52, etc.) but also uses a number of systems developed in Italy, including:

Type	Band	Remarks
Orion RTN-10X	I/J	Gun and missile fire control (Argo system)
Orion RTN-20X	I/J	With Dardo system (40-mm gun)
SPQ-2D	I/J	Combined surveillance
RAN-3L	D	Air search, 3-dimensional
RAN-10S	E/J	Combined surveillance
RAN-20S	E/F	Air search
RTN-30X	I/J	Target acquisition (Albatros system)
3 RM series	I/J	Navigation and surface search

E. SONARS

Most of the newest equipment is American or Dutch.

	Type	Frequency		Type	Frequency
SQS-23	Hull	MF	SQS-4	Hull	MF
SQS-29	Hull	MF	SQA-10	VDS	MF
SQS-11A	Hull	MF	SQS-36	VDS	HF
SQS-10	Hull	MF	SQQ-14	Minehunting	HF
			CWE 610	Hull	LF (Dutch)

F. TACTICAL INFORMATION SYSTEM

The Italian Navy has developed the SADOC system, which is compatible with the American NTDS and the French SENIT. The Breda SCLAR chaff-rocket-launching system is widely used; it employs 20 105-mm rockets in a trainable/elevatable launcher controlled by the computer system.

G. COUNTERMEASURES

A wide variety of intercept arrays, many with stabilized cylindrical radome antennas, are in use. The Breda SCLAR chaff rocket-launching system is used on frigates and larger ships; it has 20 tubes for 105-mm rockets in a trainable elevatable launcher.

HELICOPTER CARRIER

♦ 1 Garibaldi class

	Bldr	Laid down	L	In serv.
C 551 GARIBALDI	Italcantieri, Monfalcone	26-3-81	1983	1985

Garibaldi 1. Twin 40-mm AA 2. Dardo system radar (RTN-20X) 3. Otomat Mk II launchers 4. Albatros SAM launchers 5. RTN-30X radar for Albatros/Aspide 6. RAN-3L 3-dimensional air-search radar 7. RAN-10S surface/air search radar 8. RAN-20S air search radar 9. SCLAR chaff launchers

HELICOPTER CARRIER *(continued)*

Cutaway model of Garibaldi   Italcantieri

D: 10,043 tons (13,370 fl)   **S:** 29 kts
Dim: 180.2 (162.8 pp) × 30.4 (23.8 wl) × 6.7
A: 4/Otomat Mk 2 SSM (I × 4)—2/Albatros SAM (VIII × 2)—6/40-mm AA
     Breda Compact (II × 3) with Dardo control system—6/324-mm Mk 32 ASW
     TT (III × 2)—16/SH-3D Sea King helicopters
Electron Equipt: Radar: 1/RAN-3L, 1/RAN-205, 1/RAN-106, 1/SPS-702 surface
          search, 1/SPS-703 navigational—3/RTN-20X,
          2/RTN-30X
         Sonar: Raytheon DE 1160
         ECM: passive intercept arrays—2/SCLAR chaff RL (XX ×
         2)—TACAN
M: 4 GE/Fiat LM 2500 gas turbines; 2 CP props; 80,000 hp
Electric: 9,360 kw (6 GMT B230-12M diesel alternator sets)
Range: 7,000/20   **Man:** 560 tot. (accommodations for 825)

REMARKS: The *Garibaldi* is essentially an ASW ship for helicopters, although the
design would permit the handling of V/STOL aircraft as well. The flight deck is
173.8 meters long. There are two elevators, one forward of and one abaft the island.
There are six flight deck spaces for flight operations. The hangar (110 × 15 × 6
meters) can accommodate 12 Sea King, or 10 Sea Harrier and 1 Sea King, although
political considerations have precluded acquisition of the "offensive" Sea Harrier for
the present. Steel superstructure and hull. To permit helicopter operations in heavy
weather, much attention was given to stability, and the ship has two pairs of fin
stabilizers. There are five decks: the flight deck; the hangar deck, which is also the
main deck; and two decks and a platform deck below the hangar deck. Thirteen
watertight bulkheads divide the ship into 14 sections. Has IPN-20 computerized
data system, capable of handling 200 threat tracks simultaneously.

SUBMARINES

♦ **4 Nazario Sauro class** Bldr: C.R.D.A., Monfalcone

	Laid down	L	In serv.
S 518 NAZARIO SAURO	15-7-74	9-10-76	1-3-80
S 519 CARLO FECIA DI COSSATO	15-11-75	16-11-77	5-11-79
S 520 LEONARDO DA VINCI	8-6-78	20-10-79	1981
S 521 GUGLIERMO MARCONI	23-10-79	20-9-80	1981

Nazario Sauro (S 518)—on trials   C.R.D.A. Monfalcone, 1978

Nazario Sauro (S 518)   C. Martinelli, 1980

Carlo Fecia di Cossato (S 519)   C. Martinelli, 1981

D: 1,456/1,641 tons   **S:** 12/20 kts   **Dim:** 63.85 × 6.83 × 5.7
A: 6/533-mm TT fwd. (12 torpedoes)
Electron Equipt: Radar: 1/3 RM-20/SMG
                 Sonar: USEA/Selenia IPD-70 system, Velox M5
M: 3 GMT A210 16M diesels (2,160 kw), electric drive; 1 prop; 4,000 hp
Fuel: 144 tons   **Endurance:** 45 days   **Range:** 12,500/4 (snorkel); 7,000/12
Man: 45 tot.

REMARKS: First two authorized 1972. Second pair ordered 12-2-76. Can travel 20 knots
submerged for 1 hour, or 100 hours at 4 knots. Maximum diving depth is 250 meters.
All 12 torpedoes are of the A-184 type. Seven-bladed propeller. Completion of first
pair delayed by need to replace original batteries. Have SISU-1 (IPD-70) fire-control
system.

SUBMARINES *(continued)*

♦ **4 Enrico Toti class** Bldr: C.R.D.A., Monfalcone

	Laid down	L	In serv.
S 505 ATTILIO BAGNOLINI	15-4-65	28-8-67	16-6-68
S 506 ENRICO TOTI	15-4-65	12-3-67	22-1-68
S 513 ENRICO DANDOLO	10-3-67	16-12-67	25-9-68
S 514 LAZZARO MOCENIGO	12-6-67	20-4-68	11-1-69

Enrico Dandolo (S 513)   C. Martinelli, 1976

Enrico Toti (S 506)   1978

D: 535/591 tons **S:** 14/20 kts **Dim:** 46.2 × 4.7 × 3.99
A: 4/533-mm TT (6 torpedoes)
Electron Equipt: Radar: 1/3 RM 20/SMG
              Sonar: Passive and active
M: Diesel-electric propulsion: 2 Fiat/MB 820 diesels; 1 electric motor; 1 prop;
    2,200 hp
Range: 7,500/4.5 **Man:** 4 officers, 22 men

♦ **2 U.S. Tang class** Bldr: Electric Boat, Groton, Connecticut

	Laid down	L	In serv.
S 515 LIVIO PIOMARTA (ex-*Trigger*, SS 564)	24-2-49	14-6-51	31-3-52
S 516 ROMEO ROMEI (ex-*Harder*, SS 568)	30-6-50	3-12-51	19-8-52

Romeo Romei (S 516)   G. Arra, 1976

D: 2,100/2,700 tons **S:** 15.5/16 kts **Dim:** 87.5 × 8.3 × 6.2
A: 8/533-mm TT (6 fwd, 2 aft)
Electron Equipt: Radar: 1/SS-2
              Sonar: BQR-3, BQS-4, BQG-4
M: Diesel-electric propulsion: 3 Fairbanks-Morse 38ND8⅛ diesels; 2 props;
    5,600 hp
Man: 8 officers, 73 men

REMARKS: The S 515 was transferred to Italy on 10-7-73; S 516 on 20-2-74. Both ships have BQG-4 "PUFFS" passive ranging sonar.

NOTE: U.S. Guppy-III-class submarine *Primo Longobardo* (S 501) was stricken 31-1-80; sister *Gianfranco Gazzana Priaroggia* (S 502) stricken 1981.

CRUISERS

♦ **1 Vittorio Veneto class**

	Bldr	Laid down	L	In serv.
C 550 VITTORIO VENETO	Cant. Riuniti Castellammare	10-6-65	5-2-67	12-7-69

D: 7,500 tons (8,870 fl) **S:** 30.5 kts
Dim: 179.6 (170.61 pp) × 19.4 (hull) × 6.0 (hull)
A: 1/Mk 20 Mod 7 Aster launch system (60 ASROC and Standard)—8/76-mm
    OTO Melara DP—6/324-mm Mk 32 ASW TT (III × 2)—9/AB-204B or AB-
    212 or 4 SH-3D ASW helicopters

Vittorio Veneto (C 550)   1980

CRUISERS (continued)

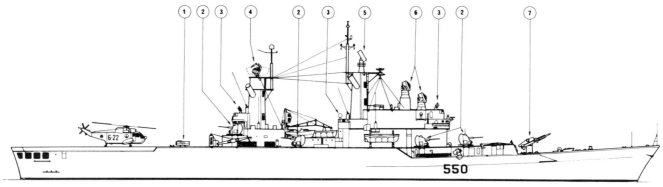

Vittorio Veneto (C 550) 1. Mk 32 ASW TT 2. 76-mm DP 3. Argo fire-control syst. 4. SPS-40 radar 5. SPG-52 radar 6. SPG-55 radar 7. Mk 10 mod 7 missile launcher

Vittorio Veneto (C 550)   1980

    Electron Equipt: Radars: 1/SPS-40, 1/SPS-52B, 1/SPQ-2B, 1/3RM-7, 2/SPG-55B, 4/RTN-10X (Argo systems)
        TACAN: URN-20A
        Sonar: SQS-23
        ECM: passive arrays, 2/SCLAR chaff RL (XX × 2)
  M: 2 sets Tosi GT; 2 props; 73,000 hp   **Electric:** . . .
  Boilers: 4 Foster-Wheeler; 43 kg/cm², 450°C   **Fuel:** 1,200 tons
  Range: 3,000/28, 6,000/20   **Man:** 72 officers, 493 men

REMARKS: The flight deck (40 × 18.5) is served from a hangar immediately below by two elevators (18 × 5.3). The hangar (27.5 × 15.3) is two decks in depth. When carrying SH-3 helicopters, none will fit into the hangar. Very extensive, stabilized intercept arrays. Eight Otomat II SSMs are to be installed on this ship. Two sets anti-rolling fin stabilizers. The Aster system can launch either ASROC ASW or Standard SAM and has a total capacity of 60 missiles on three magazine drums. Beam listed does not include projections around SCLAR launchers fwd or flight deck aft. Has British "Abbeyhill" intercept array on foremast.

♦ **2 Andrea Doria class**

	Bldr	Laid down	L	In serv.
C 553 ANDREA DORIA	C. Nav. Tirreno, Riva Trigoso	11-5-58	27-2-63	23-2-64
C 554 CAIO DUILIO	Navalmeccanica Castellammare	16-5-58	22-12-62	30-11-64

  D: 6,500 tons (7,300 fl)   **S:** 30 kts   **Dim:** 149.3 (144.0 pp) × 17.25 × 4.96 (7.5 fl)
  A: 1/Mk 10 launcher (40 Standard SM-1 ER)—6 or 8/76-mm AA (I × 6 or 8)—6/324-mm Mk 32 ASW TT (III × 2)—4/AB-204B helicopters (C 554:2)
  Electron Equipt: Radar: 1/RAN-20S, 1/SPQ-2D, 1/SPS-52B, 2/SPG-55C, 3 or 4/RTN-10X (Argo system)
        TACAN: URN-20A (not on C 554)   Sonar: SQS-23
        ECM: passive arrays, 2/SCLAR chaff launchers (XX × 2)
  M: 2 sets GT; 2 props; 60,000 hp   **Electric:** 4,700 kw
  Boilers: 4 Foster-Wheeler; 43 kg/cm², 450°C   **Fuel:** 1,100 tons
  Range: 6,000/15   **Man:** 54 officers, 460 men

Andrea Doria (C 553)   1980

CRUISERS (*continued*)

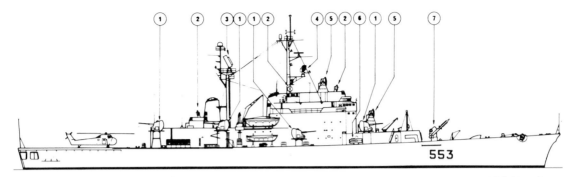

Andrea Doria (C 553) 1. 76-mm DP 2. Argo fire-control syst. 3. SPS-52 radar 4. RAN-3L radar 5. SPG-55 radar 6. Mk 32 ASW TT 7. Mk 10 missilel launcher

Andrea Doria (C 553) 1980

Caio Duilio (C 554)—as training cruiser 1980

Caio Duilio (C 554)—note lengthened hangar structure 1980

REMARKS: The flight deck is 30 × 16 meters on C 553. Hangar on main deck. Fin anti-rolling stabilizers fitted. The engineering spaces are divided into two groups, forward and aft: each has a boiler room with two boilers and a turbine compartment separated by living spaces. In each turbine space are two 1,000-kw turbo-alternators; there are also two 350-kw emergency diesel alternators. The engineering groups are automatic and remote-controlled. Listed beam does not include platforms extending from sides aft. C 554 refitted 1979-80 as training cruiser to replace *San Giorgio* (D 562). The after two 76-mm guns and the aft NA-9 gunfire control system were removed, and the hangar was converted to accommodations and classrooms; a new, lower hangar was built on aft of the old one, reducing the flight deck length and limiting the ship to two helicopters. A British "Abbeyhill" electronic intercept array was added to the foremast (also on C 553), and the TACAN system was deleted. A small navigational radar was added atop the hangar for helicopter control.

Both received Standard SM-1 ER missiles and associated electronics during refits in the latter 1970s. Have four (C 554: 3) Argo NA-9 GFCS.

GUIDED-MISSILE DESTROYERS

♦ 0 (+2) "improved Audace" class

	Bldr	Laid down	L	In serv.
D. . . N. . .	. . .	1982	. . .	. . .
D. . . N. . .	. . .	1982	. . .	. . .

D: . . . tons (5,500 fl) **S:** . . . **Dim:** . . . × . . . × . . .
A: 1/Mk 13 launcher aft (40 Standard SM-1 MR missiles—2/127-mm OTO Melara
Compact DP (I × 2)—4/76-mm OTO Melara Compact DP (I × 4)—6/324-mm
ASW TT (III × 2, Mk 46 torpedoes)—2/AB-212 or 1/SH-3D Sea King heli-
copter
Electron Equipt: Radar: 1/RAN-20S, 1/SPS-52C, 1/surface search, 1/naviga-
tional, 2/SPG-51D, 3/GFCS
Sonar:. . .
ECM: passive arrays, 2/SCLAR chaff RL (XX × 2)
M: 2 sets GT; 2 props; 73,000 hp **Electric:** . . .
Boilers: 4; 43 kg/cm², 450°C **Range:** . . . **Man:** . . .

REMARKS: Authorized 1980; to be laid down 1982. Strongly resemble *Audace* class,
but with Mk 13 launcher base at same height as hangar roof.

♦ 2 Audace class

	Bldr	Laid down	L	In serv.
D 550 ARDITO	Nav. Mec. Castellammare	19-7-68	27-11-71	5-12-73
D 551 AUDACE	C. Nav. del Tirreno	27-4-68	2-10-71	16-11-72

D: 3,950 tons (4,559 fl) **S:** 33 kts **Dim:** 136.60 × 14.23 × 4.60 (avg)
A: 1/Mk 13 missile launcher aft (40 Standard SM-1 MR)—2/127-mm OTO Melara
Compact DP (I × 2)—4/76-mm AA OTO Melara Compact DP (I × 4)—6/324-
mm ASW TT (III × 2)—4/533-mm TT (I × 4, AS-184 wire-guided torpe-
does)—2/AB-204B or AB-212 or 1/SH-3D Sea King ASW helicopter
Electron Equipt: Radar: 1/3 RM 20, 1/RAN-20S, 1/SPQ-2, 1/SPS-52,
2/SPG-51B, 3/RTN-10X (Argo systems)
Sonar: CWE 610
ECM: passive arrays, 2/SCLAR chaff RL (XX × 2)
M: 2 sets GT; 2 props; 73,000 hp
Boilers: 4 Foster-Wheeler; 43 kg/cm², 450°C
Range: 4,000/25 **Man:** 30 officers, 350 men

Ardito (D 550)—note torpedo tubes at stern   1980

Audace (D 551)   1980

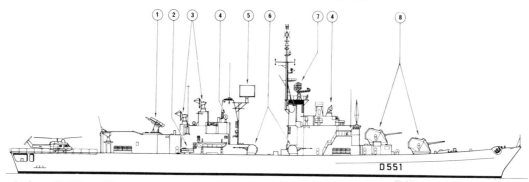

Audace (D 551) 1. Mk 13 launcher 2. Triple ASW TT 3. SPG-51B radars 4. Argo fire-control systems 5. SPS-
52B radar 6. 76-mm DP 7. RAN-20S radar 8. 127-mm DP

GUIDED-MISSILE DESTROYERS *(continued)*

Audace (D 551) 1979

REMARKS: Habitability has been given much attention in the design of these very fine ships. The four single 533-mm torpedo tubes are mounted at the extreme stern, below the fantail, and launch aftward. Both now have RAN-20S air-search radar, replacing SPS-12 (D 550) or RAN-3 (D 551).

♦ 2 Impavido class

	Bldr	Laid down	L	In serv.
D 570 IMPAVIDO	C. N. del Tirreno, Riva Trigoso	10-6-57	25-5-62	16-11-63
D 571 INTREPIDO	Ansaldo, Livorno	16-5-59	21-10-62	28-7-64

Impavido (D 570) 1980

Intrepido (D 571) G. Arra, 1976

D: 3,201 tons (3,990 fl) **S:** 33.5 kts **Dim:** 131.3 × 13.65 × 4.43
A: 1/Mk 13 launcher aft (40 Standard SM-1 MR missiles)—2/127-mm 38-cal. DP (II × 1)fwd—4/76-mm DP (I × 4)—6/324-mm Mk 32 ASW TT (III × 2)
Electron Equipt: Radars: 1/SPS-12, /SPQ-2, 1/SPS-52B, 2/SPG-51B, 3/RTN-10X (Argo systems)
　　　　　　　　　　Sonars: 1/SQS-23
　　　　　　　　　　ECM: passive arrays, 2/SCLAR chaff RL (XX × 2)
M: 2 sets Tosi GT; 2 props; 70,000 hp
Boilers: 4 Foster-Wheeler; 43 kg/cm², 450°C **Fuel:** 650 tons
Range: 3,300/20, 2,900/25, 1,500/30 **Man:** 22 officers, 312 men

REMARKS: Refitted (D 571 in 1974-75, D 570 in 1976-77) with new fire control for guns and new missiles. Have fin stabilizers.

DESTROYERS

♦ 2 Impetuoso class

	Bldr	Laid down	L	In serv.
D 558 IMPETUOSO	C. Nav. del Tirreno, Riva Trigoso	7-5-52	16-9-56	25-1-58
D 559 INDOMITO	Ansaldo, Livorno	24-4-52	9-8-55	23-2-58

Indomito (D·559) G. Gyssels, 1979

DESTROYERS (continued)

Impetuoso (D 558) 1978

D: 2,775 tons (3,811 fl)   **S:** 34 kts   **Dim:** 127.6 (123.4 pp) × 13.15 × 4.5
A: 4/127-mm 38-cal. DP (II × 2)—16/40-mm AA (IV × 2, II × 4)—1/Menon
 ASW mortar (III × 1)—6/324-mm Mk 32 ASW TT (III × 2)
Electron Equipt: Radar: /SPS-6, 1/SPQ-2, 1/Mk-25, 4/SPG-34
 Sonar: 1/SQS-11
 ECM: passive arrays, 2/SCLAR chaff RL (XX × 2)
M: 2 sets GT; 2 props; 60,000 hp   **Electric:** 1,300 kw
Boilers: 4 Foster-Wheeler; 43 kg/cm², 450°C   **Fuel:** 650 tons   **Range:** 3,400/20
Man: 24 officers, 330 men

REMARKS: Both given modest updating during the mid-1970s, but retain obsolescent
U.S. gear. Mk 25 f.c. radar is on the Mk 37 director for the 127-mm guns. The four
SPG-34 are carried two on the quadruple 40-mm AA mounts and on two of the four
twin 40-mm mounts; the radars support four Mk 63 control systems. The SCLAR
rocket launchers each have 3/103-mm illumination flare rocket launch rails on these
ships. D 558 has had the forward superstructure enlarged around the stack. D 559
decommissioned 30-11-80. D 558 to be stricken 1982-83.

GUIDED-MISSILE FRIGATES

♦ **1 (+7) Maestrale class** Bldr: CNR, Riva Trigoso (F 571: CNR, Muggiano)

	Laid down	L	In serv.
F 570 MAESTRALE	5-3-78	2-2-81	-82
F 571 GRECALE	21-3-79	12-9-81	8-82
F 572 LIRECCIO	1-3-80	7-9-81	6-82
F 573 SCIROCCO	1-11-80	1-82	1983
F 574 ALISEO	15-6-81	6-82	1983
F 575 EURO	. . .	82	1984
F 576 ESPERO	. . .	1983	1984
F 577 ZEFFIRO	. . .	1983	1984

Maestrale (F 570)—at launch, 2-2-81 C. Martinelli, 1981

D: 3,040 tons (3,200 fl)   **S:** 30 kts
Dim: 122.73 (116.4 pp) × 12.88 × 4.10 (hull)
A: 4/Otomat Mk 2 SSM (I × 4)—1/Albatros SAM system (VIII × 1, Aspide
 missiles)—1/127-mm DP OTO Melara—4/40-mm AA Breda (II × 2)—2/533-
 mm TT (A-184 torpedoes)—6/324-mm ASW TT (III × 2)—2/AB-212 helicop-
 ters
Electron Equipt: Radars: 1/RAN-10S, 1/SPQ-2F, 1/RTN-30X (NA-30A sys-
 tem), 2/RTN-20X (Dardo system), 1/RTN-10X
 (Argo system)
 Sonars: 1/Raytheon DE 1160B, /Raytheon DE 1164 VDS
 ECM: 2/SCLAR chaff launchers (XX × 2)
M: CODOG: 2 GE/Fiat LM-2500 gas turbines, 50,000 hp; 2 GMT B 230-20 DV
 diesels, 10,146 hp; 2 CP props
Electric: 3,120 kw   **Endurance:** 90 days
Range: 1,500/30, 3,800/22, 6,000/15
Man: 23 officers, 190 men

REMARKS: An enlarged version of *Lupo* with better seaworthiness and two helicopters
at the expense of four anti-ship missiles and about 2.5 knots maximum speed. Have
SADOC-2 (IPN-10) computerized data system. The hull sonar is a commercial version
of the U.S. Navy SQS-56 as used on the *Oliver Hazard Perry* (FFG 7) class. FF
576 and FF 577 ordered 10-80, others 12-76.

GUIDED-MISSILE FRIGATES *(continued)*

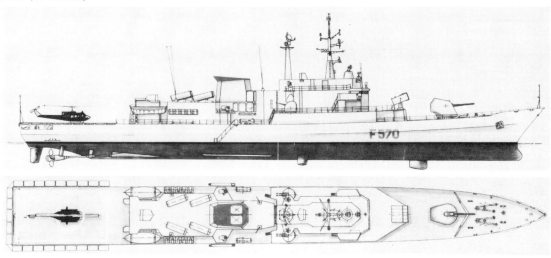

Maestrale class

CNR

♦ **4 Lupo class** Bldr: C. N. Riuniti, Riva Trigoso (F 567: CNR Muggiano)

	Laid down	L	In serv.
F 564 LUPO	8-10-74	29-7-76	20-9-77
F 565 SAGITTARIO	4-2-76	22-6-77	18-11-78
F 566 PERSEO	18-1-76	8-7-78	1-3-80
F 567 ORSA	1-8-77	2-3-79	1-3-80

Lupo (F 564) 1980

D: 2,208 tons (2,340 trials; 2,525 fl)   **Dim:** 112.8 (106.0 pp) × 11.98 × 3.84
S: 35.23 kts (trials, *Lupo*); 32 kts at 80% power; 20.3 kts on 2 diesels
A: 8/Otomat Mk 2 SSM (I × 8)—1/Nato Sea Sparrow system (VIII × 1)—1/127-mm OTO Melara DP—4/40-mm Breda AA (II × 2)—6/324-mm Mk 32 ASW TT (III × 2)—1/AB-212 helicopter
Electron Equipt: Radar: 1/3 RM 20, 1/RAN-10S combined search, 1/SPQ-2F, 1/RAN-11/LX combined search, 1/Orion RTN-10X (NA-10 mod 2 Argo f.c. system), 1/Mk 91 mod 1, 2/Orion RTN-20X (Dardo system)
Sonars: Raytheon 1160B
ECM: active and passive systems, 2/SCLAR chaff RL (XX × 2)
M: CODOG: 2 GE/Fiat LM-2500 gas turbines, 50,000 hp; 2 GMT A230-20M diesels, 7,900 hp; 2 CP props
Electric: 3,120 kw (4 Fiat 236 SS diesel alternator sets
Endurance: 90 days   **Range:** 900/35, 3,450/20 (diesels)
Man: 16 officers, 95 senior enlisted, 75 men

Perseo (F 566)—hangar extended   C. Martinelli, 1980

GUIDED-MISSILE FRIGATES *(continued)*

REMARKS: Fin stabilizers. Telescopic hangar. The Otomat Mk-II launchers are mounted two per side abreast the hangar and two per side on the forward superstructure. The *Lupo* had her radar antennae redistributed 1978-79 and a new mast added at the after end of the stack. The SAM system uses the U.S. Mk 29 launcher and a U.S. director, rather than the later Albatros system with the similar Aspide missiles of the *Maestrale* class. Machinery is mounted in four compartments: auxiliaries, gas turbines, reduction gearing, and diesel alternator sets. Much automation is used. Conditions on board are cramped and spartan. Six ships of the same class were ordered for Venezuela, four for Peru, and four for Iraq.

FRIGATES

♦ **2 Alpino class** Bldr: C. N. del Tirreno, Riva Trigoso

	Laid down	L	In serv.
F 580 ALPINO (ex-*Circe*)	27-2-63	14-6-67	14-1-68
F 581 CARABINIERE (ex-*Climene*)	9-1-65	30-9-67	28-4-68

Carabiniere (F 581)   1978

Alpino (F 580)—with MAD experimental radar atop bridge   1980

D: 2,000 tons (2,700 fl) **S:** 27 kts **Dim:** 113.3 (106.4 pp) × 13.1 × 3.76
A: 6/76-mm 62-cal. DP (I × 6)—1/305-mm Menon ASW mortar (I × 1)—6/324-mm Mk 32 ASW TT (III × 2)—2/AB-204B or AB-212 helicopters

Electron Equipt: Radars: 1/SPS-12, 1/SPQ-2, 1/RTN-30X (NA-30 system), 3/RTN-10X (Argo systems), F 580 also: 1/MAD
Sonars: 1/SQS-43, 1/SQA-10 VDS
ECM: MM/SPR-A intercept, 2/SCLAR chaff RL (XX × 2)
M: CODAG: 4 Tosi OTV-320 diesels, 4,200 hp each; 2 Tosi-Metrovik G6 gas turbines, 7,700 hp each; 2 props; 31,800 hp
Electric: 2,400 kw **Fuel:** 275 tons **Range:** 4,200/17
Man: 20 officers, 244 men

REMARKS: Fin stabilizers. Cruising, 22 knots on diesels. F 580 fitted with experimental MAD gunfire-control radar 1975.

♦ **3 Carlo Bergamini class**

	Bldr	Laid down	L	In serv.
F 593 CARLO BERGAMINI	C.R.D.A., Trieste	19-7-59	16-6-60	23-6-62
F 594 VIRGILIO FASAN	Castellammare	6-3-60	9-10-60	10-10-62
F 595 CARLO MARGOTTINI	Castellammare	26-5-57	12-6-60	5-5-62

Virgilio Fasan (F 594)   A. Molinari, 1972

D: 1,410 tons (1,650 fl) **S:** 25 kts **Dim:** 93.95 (86.51 pp) × 11.35 × 3.1
A: 2/76-mm 62-cal. DP (I × 2)—1/single-barreled Menon ASW mortar—6/324-mm Mk 32 ASW TT (III × 2)—1/AB-204B or AB-212 helicopter
Electron Equipt: Radars: 1/SPS-12, 1/SPQ-2, 1/Orion RTN-10X (OG-3 system)
Sonars: SQS-30
ECM: MM/SPR-A intercept
M: 4 high-speed Fiat 3012 RSS or Tosi diesels; 2 props; 16,000 hp
Electric: 1,200 kw **Range:** 4,500/16, 3,600/18 **Man:** 155 tot.

REMARKS: Equipped with Denny-Brown anti-rolling stabilizers to reduce rolling from 20 degrees to 3 degrees. Enlargement of the helicopter platform between 1968 and 1971 required the removal of the after 76-mm gun. Telescopic hangar. Sister *Luigi Rizzo* (F 596) stricken 30-11-80; others to be decommissioned 1982-83.

♦ **3 Canopo class**

	Bldr	Laid down	L	In serv.
F 551 CANOPO	C. Nav. di Taranto	15-5-52	20-2-55	1-4-58
F 554 CENTAURO	Ansaldo, Livorno	31-5-52	4-4-54	5-5-57
F 555 CIGNO	C. Nav. di Taranto	10-2-54	14-3-55	7-3-57

D: 1,807 tons (2,250 fl) **S:** 26 kts **Dim:** 103.1 (93.3 pp) × 12.0 × 3.8
A: 3/76-mm DP (1 fwd, 2 aft)—1/305-mm Menon ASW mortar (III × 1)—6/324-mm Mk 32 TT (III × 2)

FRIGATES (continued)

Centauro (F 554)   1979

Cigno (F 555)   1978

Electron Equipt: Radars: 1/SPS-6, 1/SPQ-2, 1/Orion RTN-10X (OG-3 system)
Sonars: SQS-11
ECM: Intercept: MM/SPR-A
M: 2 sets Tosi GT; 2 props; 22,000 hp   **Range:** 2,600/20   **Man:** 160 tot.
Boilers: 2 Foster-Wheeler; 43 kg/cm², 450°C   **Fuel:** 400 tons

REMARKS: Originally had four 76-mm (II × 2) guns; reconfigured 1966-73. Refitted
mid-1970s. OG-3 radar director is atop bridge; a U.S. Mk 51 visual-only director is
located aft (on F 551 the OG-3 is aft). Sister *Castore* (F 553) decommissioned 30-11-
80, others to decommission 1982-83.

CORVETTES

♦ 4 Pietro de Cristofaro class

	Bldr	Laid down	L	In serv.
F 540 PIETRO DE CRISTOFARO	C. N. del Tirreno	30-4-63	29-5-65	19-12-65
F 541 UMBERTO GROSSO	Ansaldo, Livorno	21-10-62	12-12-64	25-4-66
F 546 LICIO VISINTINI	C.R.D.A., Monfalcone	30-9-63	30-5-65	25-8-66
F 550 SALVATORE TODARO	Ansaldo, Livorno	21-10-62	24-10-64	25-4-66

D: 850 tons (1,020 fl)   **S:** 22-23 kts   **Dim:** 80.2 (75.0 pp) × 10.0 × 2.5
A: 2/76-mm DP (I × 2)—1/305-mm Menon ASW mortar (I × 1)—6/324-mm Mk
32 ASW TT (III × 2)

Licio Visintini (F 546)   G. Arra, 1976

Electron Equipt: Radar: 1/SPQ-2, 1/Orion RTN-10X (OG-3 system)
Sonar: 2/SQS-36 (1 hull, 1 VDS)
ECM: MM/SPR-A intercept
M: 2 diesels (*see* Remarks); 2 props; 8,400 hp   **Fuel:** 100 tons
Range: 4,600/18   **Man:** 8 officers, 123 men

REMARKS: High-speed diesels: Fiat 3012 RSS on F 540, F 541, and F 550; Tosi on F
546, with reduction gears and Tosi-Vulcan hydraulic linkage. OG-3 gun director
forward, U.S. Mk 51 director aft. The VDS uses an SQA-13 hoist.

♦ 4 Albatros class

	Bldr	Laid down	L	In serv.
F 542 AQUILA (ex-Dutch *Lynx*)	Breda, Marghera, Venice	25-7-53	31-7-54	2-10-56
F 543 ALBATROS	Nav. Mec. Castellammare	1953	18-7-54	1-6-55
F 544 ALCIONE	Nav. Mec. Castellammare	1953	19-9-54	23-10-55
F 545 AIRONE	Nav. Mec. Castellammare	1953	21-11-54	2-10-55

Airone (F 545)   1979

D: 800 tons (950 fl)   **S:** 19 kts   **Dim:** 76.3 (69.49 pp) × 9.65 × 2.8
A: 3/40-mm 70-cal. AA (I × 3)—6/324-mm Mk ASW TT (II × 2)—2/Mk 11
Hedgehogs—1/d.c. rack (F 543: 1/40-mm AA, 2/Mk 11 Hedgehog, no ASW
TT)
Electron Equipt: Radar: 1/SPQ-2   Sonar: QCU-2
M: 2 Fiat M 409 diesels; 2 props; 5,200 hp   **Electric:** 1,200 kw   **Fuel:** 100 tons
Range: 2,988/18   **Man:** 7 officers, 111 men

REMARKS: Ships built with U.S. "Offshore" funds (ex-U.S. PC 1626, PC 1619, PC 1620,
and PC 1921). One similar ship was delivered to The Netherlands (returned to Italy in
10-61) and four to Denmark. Originally had two 76-mm DP, two 40-mm AA (II × 1);
rearmed 1963. F 543 is equipped for minesweeping, having rubber dinghies, 2 para-
vanes, and equipment davits on the stern. All to be decommissioned 1982-83.

GUIDED-MISSILE PATROL BOATS

♦ **7 Sparviero class** Bldr: CNR, Muggiano (P 420: CNR, La Spezia)

	Laid down	L	In serv.
P 420 SPARVIERO	4-71	3-73	15-7-74
P 421 NIBBIO	. . .	. . .	10-11-80
P 422 FALCONE	1-10-77	. . .	1-3-81
P 423 ASTORE	5-1-78	8-80	1-4-81
P 424 GRIFFONE	. . .	10-81	. . .
P 425 GREPPIO	16-5-79	. . .	. . .
P 426 CONDORE	1980	. . .	12-81

Nibbio (P 421)—foils retracted   C. Martinelli, 1980

Sparviero (P 420)—on foil   G. Arra, 1976

D: 64.5 tons (fl)   **S:** 43 kts (heavy sea), 50 kts (calm sea)
Dim: 22.95 (24.56, foils retracted) × 7.01 (12.06 max. over foils) × 1.87 (1.45 over foils at speed, 4.37 over foils at rest)
A: 1/76-mm OTO Melara Compact—2 Otomat Mk-II SSM (I × 2)
Electron Equipt: Radars: 1/3RM7-250, 1/RTN-10X (NA-10 system)
M: CODOG: 1 Rolls-Royce Proteus 15 M-560 gas turbine; 1 waterjet; 4,500 hp; 1 GM 6V-53N diesel; 1 prop; 180 hp
Fuel: 11 tons   **Range:** 1,050/8 (diesels), 400/45   **Man:** 2 officers, 8 men

REMARKS: Prototype studied by the Alinavi Society, which was formed in 1964 by Boeing, U.S.A., the Italian government's I.R.I., and Carlo Rodriguez of Messina, builder of commercial hydrofoils. Six more (of eight planned) were ordered 1977. The three hydrofoils are raised when cruising, and the diesel engine is engaged. All-aluminum construction. Project based on U.S. *Tucumcari*. F 421 onward have a later surface-search radar, incorporating an IFF interrogator.

PATROL BOATS

♦ **2 Freccia class**

	Bldr	Laid down	L	In serv.
P 493 FRECCIA (ex-MC 590)	C. Nav. di Taranto	30-4-63	9-1-65	6-7-65
P 494 SAETTA (ex-MC 591)	C.R.D.A., Monfalcone	11-6-63	11-4-65	25-7-66

Freccia (P 493)—in torpedo-boat rig (now has new director)   G. Arra, 1972

D: 175 tons (205 fl)   **S:** 40 kts   **Dim:** 46.1 × 7.2 × 1.54
A: As patrol boat: 3/40-mm 70-cal. AA (I × 3)
As torpedo boat: 2/40-mm AA (I × 2)—2/533-mm TT
As minelayer: 1/40-mm AA—8 mines
Electron Equipt: Radar: 1/3ST7-250   **Range:** 800/27   **Man:** 4 officers, 33 men
M: CODAG: 2 Fiat diesels, 3,800 hp each; 1 Rolls-Royce Proteus; 1 gas turbine, 4,250 hp; 3 props; 11,860 hp

REMARKS: P 494 served trials with the Sea Killer Mk 1 SSM (V × 1), later removed; she retains a Contraves gun director, with RTN-150 radar, while P 493 has only a Mk 51 lead-computing director.

♦ **2 Lampo class** Bldr: C. Nav. di Taranto

	Laid down	L	In serv.
P 491 LAMPO	4-1-58	22-11-60	7-63
P 492 BALENO	22-11-60	10-5-64	16-7-65

PATROL BOATS *(continued)*

Lampo (P 491)—in torpedo-boat rig   G. Arra, 1972

D: 197 tons (210 fl) **S:** 39 kts **Dim:** 43.0 × 6.3 × 1.5
A: As patrol boat: 3/40-mm 70-cal. AA
   As torpedo boat: 2/40-mm 70-cal. AA—2/533-mm TT
Electron Equipt: Radar: 1/3ST7-250 **Man:** 5 officers, 28 men
M: CODAG: 2 MTU 518D diesels, 3,600 hp each; 1 Metrovik-Nuove Reggiane
   gas turbine, 4,500 hp; 3 props; 11,700 hp

REMARKS: Re-engined with German diesels in 1976. Have one U.S. Mk 51 gun director.

MINE WARFARE SHIPS

♦ **10 Lerici-class minehunter/minesweepers** Bldr: Intermarine, La Spezia

	Laid down	L	In serv.				Laid down	L	In serv.
M 5550 LERICI	...	...	1981	M...		TERMOLI	...	...	...
M 5551 SAPRI	...	...	1982	M...		ALGHERO	...	...	...
M 5552 MILAZZO	...	...	1982	M...		NUMANO	...	...	...
M 5553 VIESTE	...	...	1983	M...		CROTONE	...	...	...
M... GRETA	...	...	...	M...		VIAREGGIO	...	...	...

D: 470 tons (502 fl) **S:** 15 kts **Dim:** 49.98 (45.5 pp) × 9.56 × 2.63
A: 1/20-mm AA **Electric:** 887 kVA **Range:** 2,500/12, 1,500/14 **Man:** 39 tot.
Electron Equipt: Radar: 1/3ST7/DG Sonar: SQQ-14
M: 1 GMT B230-8M diesel; 1 prop; 1,840 hp (2 retractable auxiliary thrusters;
   470 hp)

REMARKS: First four ordered 4-78; six more authorized 1980. Glass-reinforced, shock-resistant plastic construction throughout. Hull material 140-mm thick. To carry two PAP-104 remote-controlled minehunting devices as well as conventional sweep gear. SQQ-14 is a high-frequency minehunting sonar with a retractable transducer. While minehunting, speed is 7 knots, using the two drop-down, shrouded thrusters. Range at 12 knots can be extended to 4,000 nautical miles by using the passive roll stabilization tanks to carry fuel. Four also ordered for Malaysia.

♦ **4 ex-U.S. Agile-class fleet minesweepers**

	Bldr	In serv.
M 5430 SALMONE (ex-MSO 507)	Martinolich, San Diego	15-6-56
M 5431 STORIONE (ex-MSO 506)	Martinolich, San Diego	23-2-56
M 5432 SGOMBRO (ex-MSO 517)	Tampa Marine	12-5-57
M 5433 SQUALO (ex-MSO 518)	Tampa Marine	20-6-57

Sgombro (M 5432)   1978

D: 665 tons (750 fl) **S:** 14 kts **Dim:** 52.27 × 10.71 × 4.0 (fl)
A: 1/40-mm AA
Electron Equipt: Radar: 1/3ST7/DG
   Sonar: UQS-1
M: 2 GM 8-278ANW diesels; 2 CP props; 1,600 hp **Fuel:** 46 tons
Range: 3,000/10 **Man:** 7 officers, 44 men

REMARKS: Scheduled for disposal 1982-83. Wooden construction.

♦ **25 U.S. Adjutant-class minesweepers**

	Bldr	In serv.
M 5504 CASTAGNO (ex-MSC 74)	H. Grebe, New York	7-53
M 5505 CEDRO (ex-MSC 88)*	Berg SY, Wash.	10-53
M 5508 FRASSINO (ex-MSC 89)	Berg SY, Wash.	1-54
M 5509 GELSO (ex-MSC 75)	H. Grebe, New York	2-54
M 5510 LARICE (ex-MSC 82)	Lake Union DD, Wash.	12-53
M 5511 NOCE (ex-MSC 90)	Berg SY, Wash.	5-54
M 5512 OLMO (ex-MSC 133)	Bellingham BY, Wash.	3-54
M 5516 PLATANO (ex-MSC 136)*	Bellingham BY, Wash.	9-54
M 5519 MANDORLO (ex-MSC 280)*	Tacoma BY, Wash.	12-60
M 5521 BAMBU (ex-MSC 214)	CRDA, Monfalcone	11-56
M 5522 EBANO (ex-MSC 215)	CRDA, Monfalcone	11-56
M 5523 MANGO (ex-MSC 216)	CRDA, Monfalcone	12-56
M 5524 MOGANO (ex-MSC 217)	CRDA, Monfalcone	1-57
M 5525 PALMA (ex-MSC 238)	CRDA, Monfalcone	2-57
M 5527 SANDALO (ex-MSC 240)	CRDA, Monfalcone	4-57
M 5531 AGAVE	CRDA, Monfalcone	12-55
M 5532 ALLORO	CRDA, Monfalcone	4-56
M 5533 EDERA	CRDA, Monfalcone	7-56
M 5535 GELSOMINO	Baglietto, Varezze	5-56
M 5536 GIAGGIOLO	Picchiotti, Viareggio	6-56
M 5538 LOTO*	Celli, Venice	9-56
M 5540 TIMO	Costaguta, Voltri	8-56
M 5541 TRIFOGLIO	CN, Taranto	12-55
M 5542 VISCHIO	C. Mediterraneo, Piera	8-56
(minehunters: *)		

MINE WARFARE SHIPS *(continued)*

Castagno (M 5504) C. Martinelli, 1979

Mandorlo (M 5519)—minehunter C. Martinelli, 1977

Noce (M 5511) C. Martinelli, 1977

D: 375 tons (405 fl) **S:** 13.5 kts **Dim:** 43.9 (42.1 pp) × 8.2 × 2.5
A: 2/20-mm AA (II × 1)
Electron Equipt: Radar: 1/3ST7/DG Sonar: UQS-1

M: 2 GM 8-268A diesels; 2 props; 1,200 hp *(see Remarks)* **Fuel:** 40 tons
Range: 2,500/10 **Man:** 5 officers, 33 men

REMARKS: M 5531 to M 5542 were built with "Offshore Procurement" funds and did not receive MSC-series hull numbers; the others were built under the U.S. Military Aid Program. M 5519 is of a later design than the others, with a lower bridge and larger stack; she was converted as a minehunter in 1975, while M 5505, M 5516, and M 5538 have been similarly altered. An additional four were to become minehunters by end 1981. All have wooden hulls and nonmagnetic fittings. M 5521 to M 5527 have Fiat diesels. More units have been scrapped: *Acacia* (M 5502), *Betulla* (M 5503), *Ciciegio* (M 5506), and *Rovere* (M 5526) in 1974; *Abete* (M 5501) in 1977; and *Faggio* (M 5507), *Ontano* (M 5513), *Pino* (M 5514), *Gaggia* (M 5534), and *Glicine* (M 5537) in 1980. *Mirto* (ex-M 5539) and *Pioppo* (ex-M 5515) have been converted to survey ships. *Quercia* (M 5517) stricken 31-10-81; four others (names not available) also discarded late 1981.

♦ 5 Aragosta-class inshore minesweepers

	Bldr	L
M 5450 ARAGOSTA (ex-MSI 55)	CRDA, Monfalcone	8-56
M 5452 ASTICE (ex-MSI 61)	CRDA, Monfalcone	1-57
M 5459 MITILA (ex-MSI 74)	Picchiotti, Viareggio	6-57
M 5463 POLIPO	Costaguta, Voltri	5-57
M 5464 PORPORA (ex-MSI 65)	Costaguta, Voltri	6-57

Porpora (M 5464) G. Arra, 1976

D: 120 tons (188 fl) **S:** 14 kts **Dim:** 32.5 × 6.4 × 1.9 **A:** none
Electron Equipt: Radar: 1/MLN-1A
M: 2 Fiat/MTU MB 820D diesels; 2 props; 1,000 hp **Electric:** 340 kw
Fuel: 15 tons **Range:** 2,000/9 **Man:** 14 tot.

REMARKS: Based on British "Ham"-class design. Originally 20 in class. Built with U.S. Military Assistance Program funds. Wooden construction. Single 20-mm AA fwd removed. M 5450 has a deckhouse in place of the sweep reel and is used in support of frogmen. *Gambero* (M 5457), *Granchio* (M 5458), *Pinna* (M 5462), *Riccio* (M 6465), and *Scampo* (M 5466) stricken 1979-80.

AMPHIBIOUS WARFARE SHIPS

NOTE: A new, large amphibious warfare ship was requested under the 1980 Budget. The design strongly resembles that of the U.S. *Raleigh* (LPD 1) class, but the reported displacement of 6,000 tons is smaller. Intended to relieve *Ciao Duilio* (C 554) as training ship as well as being available for amphibious warfare duties.

AMPHIBIOUS WARFARE SHIPS (continued)

♦ 2 ex-U.S. De Soto County-class LSTs

	Bldr	L
L 9890 GRADO (ex-*De Soto County*, LST 1171)	Boston NSY	28-2-57
L 9891 CAORLE (ex-*York County*, LST 1175)	Newport News SB & DD	5-9-57

Caorle (L 9891)   G. Gyssels, 1980

D: 4,164 tons (7,804 fl)   **S:** 16/15 kts   **Dim:** 134.7 × 18.9 × 5.5
A: 6/76.2-mm 50-cal. DP (II × 3)   **Electron Equipt:** Radar: 1/3 RM-20
M: 6 Fairbanks-Morse 38D8⅛ diesels; 2 CP props; 14,000 hp
Man: 15 officers, 173 men

REMARKS: Quarters for 634 troops, including 30 officers. Three Mk 51 gunfire-control systems, two forward, one aft. Carry four LCVPs each. Leased 17-7-72, purchased outright 1981.

♦ 1 assault transport Bldr: Todd, Tacoma

	Laid down	L	In serv.
L 9871 ANDREA BAFILE (ex-*St. George*, AV 16)	4-8-43	14-2-44	24-7-44

D: 8,510 tons (13,380 fl)   **S:** 17 kts   **Dim:** 149.96 (141.73 pp) × 21.18 × 7.24
A: 2/127-mm DP (I × 2)   **Electron Equipt:** 1/SPS-6, 1/3RM-20
M: 1 set Allis-Chalmers GT; 1 prop; 8,500 hp   **Electric:** 1,500 kw
Boilers: 2 Foster-Wheeler "D"; 32.7 kg/cm², 393°C   **Range:** 13,400/13

REMARKS: Former U.S. seaplane tender transferred 11-12-68 and modified as support ship for special forces. In reserve at Taranto since 1976. Can carry four or more LCVPs.

♦ 18 U.S. LCM(3)-class landing craft

MTM 9901	MTM 9909	MTM 9913	MTM 9918	MTM 9923	MTM 9926
MTM 9902	MTM 9911	MTM 9914	MTM 9919	MTM 9924	MTM 9927
MTM 9905	MTM 9912	MTM 9915	MTM 9920	MTM 9925	MTM 9929

D: 56 tons (fl)   **S:** 9 kts   **Dim:** 15.2 × 4.3 × 1.17
M: 2 Gray Marine 64 HN9 diesels; 2 props; 330 hp   **Range:** 130/9

REMARKS: Transferred 1953. Several are of the 17.1-meter, 62-ton LCM(6) version. MTM 9922 stricken 1980.

♦ 32 U.S. LCVP class

MTP 9703	MTP 9715	MTP 9723	MTP 9728	MTP 9730
MTP 9711	MTP 9720	MTP 9727	MTP 9729	MTP 9732-MTP 9754

D: 7 tons (11 fl)   **S:** 9 kts   **Dim:** 10.9 × 3.2 × 1.03
M: 1 Gray Marine 64 HN9 diesel; 165 hp   **Range:** 110/9

REMARKS: Transferred 1953. MTP 9708, 9714 stricken 1979; MTP 9707, 9710, 9719 stricken 1980.

HYDROGRAPHIC SHIPS

♦ 1 Ammiraglio Magnaghi class Bldr: C. N. del Tirreno, Riva Trigoso

	Laid down	L	In serv.
A 5303 AMMIRAGLIO MAGNAGHI	13-6-73	11-9-74	2-5-75

Ammiraglio Magnaghi (A 5303)   G. Arra, 1976

D: 1,700 tons (fl)   **S:** 16 kts   **Dim:** 82.7 (76.8 pp) × 13.7 × 3.6
A: 1/40-mm—1/AB-212 helicopter   **Electron Equipt:** Radar: 1/2RM-20
M: 2 GMT B306 SS diesels; 1 CP prop; 3,000 hp; 1 electric auxiliary engine; 240 hp (4 kts)
Range: 6,000/12, 4,200/16   **Man:** 10 officers, 125 men, 15 scientists

REMARKS: Equipped for survey and oceanographic studies. Passive tank stabilization. Bow-thruster. Part of 1972 program.

♦ 2 ex-U.S. Adjutant-class minesweepers

	Bldr	In serv.
A 5306 MIRTO (ex-M 5539)	Breda, Marghera	4-8-56
A 5307 PIOPPO (ex-M 5515, ex-MSC 135)	Bellingham SY, Washington	31-7-54

Pioppo (A 5307)   1979

HYDROGRAPHIC SHIPS (continued)

Mirto (A 5306)   G. Arra, 1976

REMARKS: Characteristics generally as for minesweeper version. Superstructure enlarged, stack raised on A 5306; A 5307 less extensively altered. Both can carry two 20-mm AA (II × 1). Man: 4 officers, 36 men.

REPLENISHMENT OILERS

♦ **2 Stromboli-class oilers** Bldr: C. N. del Tirreno, Riva Trigoso

	Laid down	L	In serv.
A 5327 STROMBOLI	1-10-73	20-2-75	20-11-75
A 5329 VESUVIO	1976	4-6-77	25-3-79

Vesuvio (A 5329)   1980

D: 8,706 tons (fl)   **S:** 19.5 kts   **Dim:** 129.0 (118.5 pp) × 18.0 × 6.5
A: 1/76-mm DP
Electron Equipt: Radars: 1/3RM7-250, 1/Orion RTN-10X (Argo system)
M: 2 GMT A428 SS diesels; 1 LIPS 4-bladed CP prop; 11,200 hp
Electric: 2,350 kw   **Range:** 10,000/16   **Man:** 10 officers, 109 men

REMARKS: Cargo: 1,370 tons fuel oil, 2,830 tons diesel, 480 tons aviation fuel, and 200 tons miscellaneous (torpedoes, missiles, projectiles, spare parts). Capable of serving

Stromboli (A 5327)   1978

two units simultaneously alongside while underway with constant-tension fueling rigs, each capable of pumping 650 m³/hr of fuel oil and 480 m³/hr of diesel fuel or aviation fuel. Can also refuel over the stern at the rate of 430 m³/hr. There are also constant-tension cargo transfer rigs on either side, each capable of transferring 1.8-ton loads, as well as two stations for lighter loads. The ships can also replenish via helicopters, although they do not have hangars. Two single 40-mm AA can be added abreast the stack. Twenty repair-party personnel can also be accommodated, and the ships can carry up to 250 passengers.

EXPERIMENTAL SHIPS

♦ **1 ex-landing ship** Bldr: Taranto Naval Base

	Laid down	L	In serv.
A 5314 QUARTO	19-3-66	18-3-67	3-68

Quarto (A 5314)—bow door open   Cdr. A. Fraccaroli, 1980

D: 764 tons (980 fl)   **S:** 13 kts   **Dim:** 69.0 × 9.55 × 1.81
A: 2/Otomat Mk 2 SSM (I × 2)—2/40-mm AA (II × 1)
Electron Equipt: Radars: 1/3ST-7, 1/SPQ-2, 1/tracking radar
M: 3 diesels; 3 props; 2,300 hp   **Range:** 1,300/13

REMARKS: Unsuccessful landing ship used as a trials ship since early 1970s. Blunt bow restricts speed and seaworthiness. Sisters *Marsala* (hull used as a pontoon) and *Caprara* canceled. Retains bow door.

♦ **1 converted fishing boat** Bldr: Castracani, Ancona

A 3315 BARBARA

    D: 195 tons   **S:** 12 kts   **Dim:** 30.0 × 6.3 × 1.5
    M: 2 diesels; 2 props; 600 hp

REMARKS: Purchased 1975. Used for oceanographic research.

SUPPORT TENDERS

♦ **1 supply ship** Bldr: Lake Washington SY, Houghton, Washington

	Laid down	L	In serv.
A 5301 PIETRO CAVEZZALE (ex-*Oyster Bay*, AGP 6, ex-AVP 28)	17-4-42	23-5-43	17-11-43

Pietro Cavezzale (A 5301)   C. Martinelli, 1973

D: 1,766 tons (2,800 fl) **S:** 16 kts **Dim:** 94.6 × 12.58 × 3.7
A: 1/76.2-mm 50-cal. DP—2/40-mm AA (II × 1)
Electron Equipt: Radars: 1/3ST-7, 1/SPS-6C
M: 2 Fairbanks-Morse 38D8⅛ diesels; 2 props; 6,000 hp **Electric:** 600 kw
Fuel: 400 tons **Range:** 10,000/11 **Man:** 210 men

REMARKS: Transferred at the end of 1957. Serves amphibious ships and small boats.

NOTE: The frogman support ship (ex-corvette) *Ape* (A 5328) was stricken late 1979.

SALVAGE SHIPS

♦ **1 salvage ship**

	Bldr	Laid down	L	In serv.
A 5309 ANTEO	C. N. Breda, Mestre	1977	11-11-78	31-7-80

Anteo (A 5309)   C. Martinelli, 1981

D: 2,178 tons (3,070 fl) **S:** 18.3 kts **Dim:** 98.4 (93.0 pp) × 15.8 × 5.18
A: 2/20-mm AA (II × 1)—1/AB-212 helicopter
M: 3 GMT A-230-12V diesels (4,050 hp each), electric drive (2 motors); 1 prop; 5,360 hp
Fuel: 270 tons **Range:** 4,000/14 **Man:** 130 tot.

REMARKS: Ordered 1977. Will carry U.S. Navy-style submarine rescue equipment, including a McCann rescue bell capable to 150 meters, and two decompression chambers. A Type MSM-1/S, 25-ton salvage submersible named *Usel* will be carried also; 9.0 × 2.5 × 2.7 meters, it will submerge to 600 meters and will have 120-hour autonomous endurance with a 4-kt max. speed. The ship will support saturation diving to 350 meters and will have a 27-ton bollard pull at 10 kts. A bow-thruster is fitted to *Anteo*. Replaced *Proteo* (A 5310), stricken 1980.

♦ **1 U.S. AN 93-class former netlayer**

	Bldr	Laid down	L	In serv.
A 5304 ALICUDI (ex-AN 99)	Ansaldo, Livorno	4-54	11-7-54	1955

Alicudi (A 5304)   G. Arra, 1976

D: 680 tons (832 fl) **S:** 13 kts **Dim:** 46.28 × 10.26 × 3.2
A: 1/40-mm AA—4/20-mm AA (I × 4) **Electron Equipt:** Radar: 1/3ST7
M: 2 Maybach MBA 6H/D650/655 diesels, electric drive; 1 prop; 1,200 hp
Fuel: 105 tons

REMARKS: Sister *Filicudi* (A 5305) stricken 1979. Used for salvage work and mooring-buoy laying.

WATER TANKERS

♦ **1 Piave class**

	Bldr	L	In serv.
A 5354 PIAVE	Orlando, Livorno	1971	23-5-73

WATER TANKERS *(continued)*

Piave (A 5354) G. Arra, 1976

D: 4,973 tons **S:** 13.6 kts **Dim:** 86.7 × 13.4 × 5.9 **A:** removed
Electron Equipt: Radar: 1/3RM7 **M:** 2 diesels; 2,560 hp
Cargo capacity: 3,500 tons **Range:** 1,500/12

REMARKS: Sister *Tevere* (A 5355) sold commercially, 1976. Formerly carried 4/40-mm AA (II × 2).

♦ **3 Basento class** Bldr: Inma, La Spezia (In serv. 1970-71)

A 5356 BASENTO A 5357 BRADANO A 5358 BRENTA

Basento (A 5356)

D: 1,914 tons (fl) **S:** 12.5 kts **Dim:** 66.1 × 10.0 × 3.9
A: 2/20-mm AA (I × 2) **Electron Equipt:** Radar: 1/3RM7
M: 2 Fiat LA-230 diesels; 1,730 hp **Cargo Capacity:** 1,200 tons
Range: 1,650/12.5 **Man:** 4 officers, 31 men

♦ **3 ex-U.S. Army 327E class** (In serv. 1943-44)

A 5369 ADIGE (ex-YW 92) A 5376 TANARO (ex-YW 99)
A 5377 TICINO (ex-YW 79)

D: 476 tons (1,517 fl) **S:** 9 kts **Dim:** 55.63 × 9.14 × 4.29
A: 3/20-mm AA (I × 3) **Electron Equipt:** Radar: 1/3RM7
M: 2 Clark MD-4 diesels; 2 props; 700 hp **Cargo Capacity:** 1,000 tons
Fuel: 32 tons **Range:** 2,560/7 **Man:** 23 tot.

Ticino (A 5377) C. Martinelli, 1974

TRAINING SHIPS

NOTE: The training ship, former destroyer *San Giorgio* (D 562) was stricken 31-10-79 and replaced by the cruiser *Ciao Duilio* (C 554).

♦ **1 sail training ship** Bldr: Nav. Mec. Castellammare

	L	In serv.
A 5312 AMERIGO VESPUCCI	22-3-30	15-5-31

Amerigo Vespucci (A 5312) 1979

D: 3,545 tons (4,186 fl) **S:** 10 kts **Dim:** 82.38 (70.72 pp) × 15.54 × 6.7
A: 4/40-mm AA (I × 4)—1/20-mm AA
M: 2 Tosi E6 diesels, electric drive; 1 prop; 1,900 hp
Range: 5,450/6.5 **Man:** 400 men, 150 cadets

REMARKS: Sail area: 2,100 m². Steel construction, including masts. Modernized 1964.

♦ **1 sail training barkentine** Bldr: Dubigeon (In serv. 1920)

A 5311 PALINURO (ex-*Cdt Louis Richard*)

TRAINING SHIPS (continued)

Palinuro (A 5311)

A. Fraccaroli

D: 1,042 tons (1,351 fl) **S:** 7.5 kts **Dim:** 59.0 × 9.7 × 4.8
A: 2/76-mm (saluting battery) **M:** 1 M.A.N. G8V23.5/33 diesel; 450 hp
Range: 5,300/7.5

REMARKS: Former French cod-fishing craft bought in 1951, refitted and recommissioned 1-7-55. Steel hull.

♦ **1 sail training yawl** Bldr: Costaguta, Genoa (In serv. 1960)

A 5316 CORSARO II

D: 41 tons **Dim:** 20.9 × 4.7 **M:** 1 auxiliary engine; 96 hp

♦ **1 RORC-class cruising yacht** Bldr: Sangermani, Chiavari (In serv. 7-10-65)

A 5313 STELLA POLARE

D: 41 tons (47 fl) **S:** . . . kts **Dim:** 20.9 × 4.7 × 2.9
M: 1 Mercedes-Benz diesel; 1 prop; 96 hp **Man:** 8 officers, 6 men

REMARKS: Sail area: 197 m².

SERVICE CRAFT

♦ **7 ex-British LCT(3)-class tenders** (In serv. 1943-44)

A 5331 MOC 1201 A 5335 MOC 1205
A 5332 MOC 1202 A 5337 MOC 1207
A 5333 MOC 1203 A 5338 MOC 1208
A 5334 MOC 1204

D: 640 tons (fl) **S:** 10 kts **Dim:** 58.5 × 9.4 × 2.0
M: 2 Paxman diesels; 1,000 hp **Man:** 3 officers, 21 men

REMARKS: MOC 1201 is used for torpedo trials and torpedo-recovery; MOC 1207 and MOC 1208 are ammunition transports; the remainder serve as repair craft for minesweepers and small combatants. MOC 1201 has one torpedo tube.

MOC 1207 (A 5337)

C. Martinelli, 1977

♦ **1 ex-German MFP-D-class cargo lighter, former landing craft** (In serv. 1942)

MTC 1101

D: 280 tons (fl) **S:** 10 kts **Dim:** 49.8 × 6.6 × 1.34
A: 2/20-mm AA **M:** 3 Deutz diesels; 3 props; 450 hp **Range:** 540/9

REMARKS: Built 1942. Can carry 150 tons cargo; beaching capability retained.

♦ **7 MZ-class cargo lighters** (In serv. 1942)

MTC 1004 MTC 1007 MTC 1010
MTC 1005 MTC 1008
MTC 1006 MTC 1009

D: 350 tons (fl) **S:** 10.5 kts **Dim:** 47.0 × 6.55 × 1.5
A: 2/20-mm AA **M:** 3 Deutz diesels; 3 props; 450 hp

REMARKS: Former landing craft. Similar to MFP-D class but hull has sheer fore and aft. Can carry 1500 tons cargo.

SEAGOING TUGS

♦ **2 Atlante class** Bldr: Visintini Donada (Both in serv. 14-8-75)

A 5317 ATLANTE A 5318 PROMETEO

D: 478 tons (750 fl) **S:** 13.5 kts **Dim:** 38.8 × 9.6 × 4.1
M: 1 Tosi QT 320/8SS diesel; 1 CP prop; 3,000 hp **Man:** 23 tot.

♦ **1 Ciclope class** (In serv. 1948)

A 5319 CICLOPE

D: 1,200 tons (fl) **S:** 8 kts **Dim:** 47.9 × 9.8 × 3.61
M: 1 set triple expansion reciprocating steam; 1,000 hp

REMARKS: Sister *Titano* stricken.

♦ **2 U.S. Army 293-design class**

A 5320 COLOSSO (ex-LT 214) A 5321 FORTE (ex-LT 159)

D: 525 tons (835 fl) **S:** 11 kts **Dim:** 38.6 × 8.53 × 3.89
M: 2 Fairbanks-Morse 38D8⅛ diesels; 2 props; 1,690 hp
Fuel: 112 tons **Range:** 3,800/8

REMARKS: Built during World War II; transferred 1948. Wooden hulls.

SEAGOING TUGS (continued)

Colosso (A 5320)   C. Martinelli, 1980

♦ **1 San Giusto class** Bldr: CNR, Palermo, 1940

A 5326 SAN GIUSTO

    D: 370 tons (486 fl) **S:** 12 kts **Dim:** 38.7 × 8.2 × 3.8
    M: Triple-expansion reciprocating steam; 900 hp

♦ **4 Gagliardo class**

	L		L
A 5322 GAGLIARDO	1938	A 5388 ERCOLE	1971
A 5323 ROBUSTO	1939	A 5394 VIGOROSO	1971

Robusto (A 5323)   C. Martinelli, 1980

    D: 389 tons (506 fl) **S:** 8 kts **Dim:** 33.2 × 7.1 × 3.6
    M: Triple-expansion reciprocating steam; 850 hp

LARGE HARBOR TUGS

♦ **2 Favignana class** (Both L: 1973)

Y 424 FAVIGNANA   Y 488 USTICA

    D: 270 tons **S:** 13 kts **Dim:** 35.0 × 9.0 × 4.0
    M: Triple-expansion reciprocating steam; 1,200 hp

♦ **2 Porto d'Ischia class** Bldr: CNR, Riva Trigoso (In serv. 1969-70)

Y 436 PORTO D'ISCHIA   Y 443 RIVA TRIGOSO

    D: 250 tons (296 fl) **S:** 12 kts **Dim:** 25.5 × 7.1 × 3.3
    M: 1 diesel; 1 CP prop; 850 hp

MEDIUM HARBOR TUGS

♦ **5 Porto group**

	L		L
Y 426 LEVANZO	1973	Y 441 PORTO RICANATI	1937
Y 432 PANTELLERIA	1972	Y 447 TINO	1930
Y 434 PIANOSA	1974		

    D: 226 tons (270 fl) **S:** 9 kts **Dim:** 27.1 × 6.7 × 3.1
    M: Triple-expansion reciprocating steam; 600 hp

REMARKS: Differ from one another in detail. *Caprera* (Y 418), *Porto Pisano* (Y 438), and *Salvore* (Y 445) stricken 1979-80.

♦ **2 U.S. Army 327-E-design class**

Y. . . MISENO (ex-ST 795)   Y. . . MONTE CRISTO (ex-ST 762)

    D: 161 tons (729 fl) **S:** 9.5 kts **Dim:** 26.3 × 7.0 × 2.6
    M: 1 GM 8-567 diesel; 700 hp **Range:** 2,760/9.5

REMARKS: Launched 1943-44; transferred 1948.

NOTE: The older Italian-built tug *Ventimiglia* was stricken 30-9-81.

SMALL HARBOR TUGS

♦ **3 RP 122 class** Bldr: Visitini, Donada (In serv. 8-5-81)

RP 122   RP 123   RP 124

REMARKS: No data available.

♦ **12 RP-101 class** Bldr: CN Visitini-Donado, Rovigo (In serv. 1972-75)

Y 403 RP 101	Y 408 RP 105	Y 456 RP 109
Y 404 RP 102	Y 410 RP 106	Y 458 RP 110
Y 406 RP 103	Y 413 RP 107	Y 460 RP 111
Y 407 RP 104	Y 452 RP 108	Y 462 RP 112

RP 110 (Y 458)   C. Martinelli, 1980

ITALY (*continued*)
SMALL HARBOR TUGS (*continued*)

    D: 36 tons (75 fl) **S:** 12 kts **Dim:** 18.8 × 4.5 × 1.9
    M: 1 diesel; 500 hp

♦ **15 miscellaneous tugs**

	L		L
Y 412 ALBENGA	1973	Y 435 MESCO	1933
Y 414 ARZACHENA	1931	Y 437 NISIDA	1943
Y 417 BOEO	1943	Y 439 PASSERO	1934
Y 419 CARBONARA	1936	Y 440 PLOMBINO	1969
Y 422 POZZI	1912	Y 446 SAN BENEDETTO	1941
Y 430 LINARO	1913	Y 454 SPERONE	1965
Y 433 CIRCEO	1956	Y 469 No. 78	1965
		Y 473 RIZZUTO	1956

IVORY COAST

Republic of the Ivory Coast

PERSONNEL: 500 men (45 officers, 455 enlisted)

MERCHANT MARINE (1978): 65 ships—156,749 grt

GUIDED-MISSILE PATROL BOATS

♦ **2 French Patra class** Bldr: Auroux, Arcachon

	Laid down	L	In serv.
L'ARDENT	15-4-77	21-7-78	6-10-78
L'INTREPIDE	7-7-77	21-7-78	6-10-78

L'Ardent   Auroux, 1978

    D: 125 tons (148 fl) **S:** 26.3 kts **Dim:** 40.70 (38.50 pp) × 5.90 × 1.55
    A: 4/MM 40 Exocet—1/40-mm AA—1/20-mm AA—2/7.62-mm mg
    Electron Equipt: Radar: 1/Decca 1226
    M: 2 AGO 195 V12CZ SHR diesels; 2 CP props; 5,000 hp (4,400 sust.)
    Electric: 120 kw

REMARKS: Ordered 1-77 and 4-77, respectively. Exocet added 1981.

♦ **2 PR-48 class** Bldr: S.F.C.N., Villeneuve-la-Garenne

	Laid down	L	In serv.
VIGILANT	2-67	23-5-67	1968
LE VALEUREUX	28-10-75	8-3-76	25-9-76

    D: 250 tons (fl) **S:** 23 kts **Dim:** 47.5 (45.5 pp) × 7.0 × 2.25
    A: 4/MM 40 Exocet—2/40-mm AA (I × 2)
    M: 2 MGO diesels with Masson reduction gear; 2 props; 4,200 hp
    Range: 2,000/16 **Man:** 4 officers, 30 men

REMARKS: *Vigilant* refitted at Brest, France, 1981. Exocet added 1981.

NOTE: Patrol boat *Perseverance* stricken 1979.

AMPHIBIOUS WARFARE SHIPS

♦ **1 French BATRAL-type medium landing ship** Bldr: Dubigeon, Normandy

	L	In serv.
ÉLÉPHANT	. . .	2-2-77

    D: 750 tons (1,330 fl) **S:** 16 kts **Dim:** 80.0 (68.0 pp) × 13.0 × 3.0 (max.)
    A: 2/40-mm AA (I × 2) **M:** 2 SACM diesels; 2 CP props; 1,800 hp
    Range: 4,500/13 **Man:** 4 officers, 35 men

REMARKS: Ordered 2-8-74. Similar to the French Navy's *Champlain*. Helicopter platform aft. Refitted at Brest, 1981.

♦ **10 Type 412 fast assault boats** Bldr: Rotork, G.B. (In serv. 1979-80)

    D: 5.2 tons (8.9 fl) **S:** 21 kts **Dim:** 12.65 × 3.20 × . . .
    M: 2 Volvo AQD 40A outdrive diesels; 2 props; 240 hp

♦ **1 Barracuda-type launch** Bldr: Halter, New Orleans, U.S.A. (In serv. 1976)

    D: 6 tons (8.35 fl) **S:** 36 kts **Dim:** 11.0 × 3.8 × 0.6
    M: 2 GM 6V-53PI diesels; 2 water jets; 540 hp **Capacity:** 20 men

♦ **2 LCVP** Bldr: Abidjan, 1970

    D: 7 tons (9 fl) **S:** 9 kts **Dim:** 10.9 × 3.2 × 1.0
    M: 1 Mercedes-Benz diesel

SERVICE CRAFT

♦ **4 small craft** **Dim:** 7-10 meters

♦ **1 Arcoa-class small craft**

NOTE: The training ship *Locodjo* was stricken 1979.

JAMAICA

DEFENCE FORCE COAST GUARD

PERSONNEL: 18 officers, 115 men (plus reserves: 16 officers, 30 men)

MERCHANT MARINE (1980): 10 ships—13,307 grt

JAMAICA *(continued)*

PATROL BOAT AND CRAFT

♦ **1 Fort Charles-class boat** Bldr: Teledyne Sewart, Berwick, La., U.S.A., 1974

P 7 FORT CHARLES

    D: 103 tons (fl) **S:** 32 kts **Dim:** 31.5 × 5.7 × 2.1
    A: 1/20-mm AA—2/12.7-mm mg
    M: 2 MTU MB 16V538 TB90 diesels; 2 props; 7,000 hp
    Range: 1,200/18 **Man:** 3 officers, 13 men

REMARKS: Can carry 24 soldiers and serve as a floating hospital. Refitted 1979-80 at Jacksonville, Florida.

♦ **3 85-foot commercial cruisers** Bldr: Sewart Seacraft, Berwick, La., U.S.A., 1966-67

P 4 DISCOVERY BAY P 5 HOLLAND BAY P 6 MANATEE BAY

Discovery Bay (P 4)

    D: 60 tons **S:** 30 kts **Dim:** 25.9 × 5.68 × 1.83
    A: 3/12.7-mm mg (I × 3) **M:** 3 MTU 8V331 TC81 diesels; 3 props; 3,000 hp
    Fuel: 13 tons **Range:** 800/20 **Man:** 2 officers, 9 men

REMARKS: Re-engined twice, most recently from 1975 to 1977, more than quadrupling the original horsepower.

JAPAN

PERSONNEL (1981): 43,092 total, plus approx. 4,300 civilian employees

MERCHANT MARINE (1980):10,568 ships—40,959,683 grt
                (tankers: 1,559 ships—17,671,022 grt)

The Maritime Self-Defense Force (MSDF), or Kaiso Jeitai, was created in 1954. In Article 9 of her constitution, Japan waived the right of belligerence and declared her peaceful intentions. Consequently, her armed forces are designed to carry out purely defensive tasks. The duties of the MSDF involve essentially the protection of coastal traffic and of Japan's sea lines of communication, both of which are vital to the economic survival of one of the world's most industrialized nations. For some years now, however, the MSDF has tended to look more and more like an oceangoing navy, as is evidenced by the construction of more important ships.

In addition to the MSDF, Japan has a large and recently modernized Maritime Safety Agency (Kaijo Hoancho) which, in function, is roughly comparable to the U.S. Coast Guard and which, in time of war, would come under the control of the Navy. Its ships are listed at the end of this section.

CONSTRUCTION PROGRAMS:
1977-78 Budget:
    1 DDG (122 *Hatsayuki*), 1 frigate (226 *Ishikari*), 1 SS (573 *Yushio*), 2 MHC (650 *Ninoshima*, 651 *Miyajima*)
1978-79 Budget:
    1 DDG (170 *Sawakaze*), 1 DDG (123 *Shirayuki*), 1 SS (574 *Mochishio*), 2 MHC (652 *Nenoshima*, 653 *Ukishima*)
1979-80 Budget:
    3 DDG (124. . . , 125. . . , 126. . .), 1 frigate (227 *Yubari*), 1 SS (575 *Setoshio*), 2 MHC (654 *Ohshima*, 655 *Miijima*), 2 LSU, 1 AGS (5103 *Suma*), and 6 service craft
1980-81 Budget:
    2 DDG (127. . . , 128. . .), 1 frigate (228. . .), 1 SS (576. . .), 2 MHC (656. . . , 657. . .), and 3 service craft
1981-82 Budget:
    1 DDG (171. . .), 2 DDG (129. . . , 130. . .), 1 SS (577. . .), 2 MHC (658. . . , 659. . .), 1 ASR (403. . .), and 2 service craft
1982-83 Budget:. . .

The 1980-84 Construction Plan called for the construction of 39 ships, totaling 70,160 tons. These included: 2/3,850-ton DDG, 10/2,900-ton DDG, 4/1,400-ton frigates, modernization of 4 *Takatsuki*-class DD and 2 *Haruna*-class DDH, construction of 5/2,208-ton SS, 11/440-ton MHC, 1/3,600-ton ASR, 2/1,100-ton "ocean surveillance ships," and 1/5,000-ton oiler.

NAVAL AVIATION: Naval air is an integral part of the Navy. The MSDF does not have any aircraft carriers: some 20 helicopters serve on board the destroyers and frigates.
    As of 1 Jan. 1980, the naval air arm consisted of:
        80 P-2J and 7 P-2V7 patrol planes
        21 S-2F1 ASW aircraft (some mothballed)
        19 PS-1 ASW seaplanes
        62 HSS-2 Sea King helicopters
    Naval aviation is divided into two commands:
1. The Fleet Air Force, which consists of 8,000 men and 140 aircraft. Its headquarters are in Atsuegi, and it has twelve bases along the coasts of Japan.
2. The Air Training Command, which has several centers at Shimofusa.
    Over the period 1980 through 1984, it is planned to acquire 37 Lockheed/Kawasaki P-3C long-range ASW aircraft (in addition to the 8 ordered in 1978 for delivery in 1982), 51 more Sikorsky/Mitsubishi HSS-2B Sea King ASW helicopters (26 shipboard, 25 land-based), 6 RH-53E minesweeping helicopters, 2 Shin-Meiwa US-1 rescue amphibians, 18 Beech C-90 King Air trainers, 3 Fuji KM-2 trainers, 6 Hughes/Kawasaki OH-6J training helicopters, and 3 support craft. By 1984, the JMSDF plans to have 14 squadrons of long-range ASW patrol aircraft (P-3C, P-2J). 1 squadron of PS-1 ASW seaplanes, and five squadrons of HSS-2A and HSS-2B Sea King ASW helicopters in service. The first P-3C was delivered from the U.S. in

NAVAL AVIATION (continued)

1981. Two others, plus 5 kits, will be built in the U.S., and the remaining 29 are to be built entirely by Kawasaki. All will be able to carry Harpoon missiles.

It is also planned to acquire 18 aerial-minelaying versions of the C-130 Hercules, beginning in 1984. The 1979-80 budget included 1 PS-1 seaplane (to replace a lost aircraft), 8 HSS-2B ASW helicopters, 2 S-61A SAR helicopters, 3 Fuji KM-2 trainers, and 2 Beech TC-90 instrument trainers. In the 1980-81 Budget, 10 P-3C, 2 HSS-2B, 1 US1, and 2 Beech TC-90 were authorized. In the 1981-82 Budget, 6 HSS-2B, 1 S-61A rescue helicopter, 1 KM-2, and 4 TC-90 were authorized.

WARSHIPS IN SERVICE AND UNDER CONSTRUCTION
AS OF 1 JANUARY 1982

	L	Tons (Surfaced)	Main armament
♦ **13 (+3) submarines**			
2 (+3) YUSHIO	1979-	2,200	6/533-mm TT
7 UZUSHIO	1970-75	1,850	6/533-mm TT
4 ASASHIO	1965-68	1,650	8/533-mm TT
♦ **33 (+10) destroyers**			
		Tons	
0 (+1) 4,500-ton DDG	. . .	4,500	Harpoon, 1/Standard launcher, 1/127-mm, ASROC, ASW TT
2 SHIRANE	1978-	5,200	2/127-mm DP, 3 helicopters
0 (+9) HATSUYUKI	1980-	2,900	Harpoon missiles, Sea Sparrow
3 TACHIKAZE	1974-81	3,850	1/Standard launcher, 2/127-mm, ASROC, 6 TT
2 HARUNA	1971-73	4,700	2/127-mm DP, 6/324-mm TT, AS-ROC, 3 helicopters
6 YAMAGUMO	1965-77	2,100	4/76-mm DP, 4/375-mm TT
3 MINEGUMO	1967-69	2,066	4/76-mm DP, 1 rocket launcher, 6/324-mm TT
4 TAKATSUKI	1966-69	3,200	2/127-mm DP, ASROC
1 AMATSUKAZE	1963	3,050	1/Standard launcher, 4/76-mm DP, ASROC
2 AKIZUKI	1959	2,300	3/127-mm AA, 4/76-mm DP
3 MURASAME	1958-59	1,800	3/127-mm DP, 4/76-mm DP, 6/324-mm TT
7 AYANAMI	1957-60	1,700	6/76-mm DP, 4/533-mm TT
♦ **16 (+2) frigates**			
1 (+2) ISHIKARI/YUBARI	1980-	1,200	Harpoon missiles, 1/76-mm DP
11 CHIKUGO	1970-76	1,470	2/76-mm DP, 2/40-mm AA, AS-ROC
4 ISUZU	1961-63	1,490	4/76-mm DP, ASW weapons
♦ **12 patrol boats**			
3 MIZUTORI	1962-65	440	2/40-mm, 6/ASW TT
♦ **5 torpedo boats**			
♦ **39 (+4) mine warfare ships and craft**			
♦ **8 amphibious warfare ships**			

WEAPONS AND SYSTEMS

Until recently, most weapons and detection gear were of American design, built under license in Japan. However, the latest ships are being equipped with Japanese-designed, long-range, pulse-compression air-search radars and with the 76-mm OTO Melara gun. The latter is built under license. U.S. Vulcan/Phalanx 20-mm CIWS (Close-In Weapon System) and Harpoon anti-ship missiles are being procured in quantity.

In Japan, the U.S. SPS-10 radar is referred to as OPS-1, SPS-6 as OPS-15, and SPS-12 as OPS-16. Similarly, the U.S. SQS-23 sonar, when built in Japan, is referred to as the OQS-3, while the OQS-1 and -2 were license-built SQS-4/29 series equipments. The OQS-4 is an indigenous, low-frequency design, as is OQS-101.

SUBMARINES

♦ 2 (+3) Yushio class

		Bldr	Laid down	L	In serv.
573	YUSHIO	Mitsubishi, Kobe	3-12-76	29-3-79	26-2-80
574	MOCHISHIO	Kawasaki, Kobe	28-4-78	12-3-80	5-3-81
575	SETOSHIO	Kawasaki, Kobe	17-4-79	12-2-81	3-82
576	N. . .	Kawasaki, Kobe	17-4-80	7-82	3-83
577	N. . .	Mitsubishi, Kobe	4-81	. . .	. . .

Yushio (573) *Ships of the World*

D: 2,200 tons (surf.) **S:** 12/20 kts **Dim:** 76.0 × 9.9 × 7.5 **A:** 6/533-mm TT
M: 2 Kawasaki/M.A.N. V8/V24-30 AMTL, 1,700-hp diesel generator sets, electric drive; 1 prop; 7,200 hp
Man: 80 tot.

REMARKS: Deeper-diving than the *Uzushio* class and have more modern electronic equipment; otherwise, similar. This class will be ordered at the rate of one per year, 1980-84.

♦ 7 Uzushio class

		Bldr	Laid down	L	In serv.
566	UZUSHIO	Kawasaki, Kobe	25-9-68	11-3-70	21-1-71
567	MAKISHIO	Mitsubishi, Kobe	21-6-69	27-1-71	2-2-72
568	ISOSHIO	Kawasaki, Kobe	9-7-70	18-3-72	25-11-72
569	NARUSHIO	Mitsubishi, Kobe	8-5-71	22-11-72	28-9-73
570	KUROSHIO	Kawasaki, Kobe	5-7-72	22-2-74	27-11-74
571	TAKASHIO	Kawasaki, Kobe	6-7-73	30-6-75	30-1-76
572	YAESHIO	Kawasaki, Kobe	14-4-75	19-5-77	7-3-78

D: 1,850/3,600 tons **S:** 12/20 kts **Dim:** 72.0 × 9.9 × 7.5 **A:** 6/533-mm TT
M: Diesel-electric propulsion; 2 Kawasaki-M.A.N. V8/V24-30 AMTL, 1,700-hp diesels; 1 prop; 7,200 hp
Man: 10 officers, 70 men

SUBMARINES *(continued)*

Narushio (569)   1974

Makishio (567)   *Ships of the World*

REMARKS: Tear-drop hull. Double-hull construction, bow-sonar array, torpedo tubes amidships, as in modern U.S. Navy submarines. Maximum depth: 200 m.

♦ 4 Asashio class

	Bldr	Laid down	L	In serv.
562 ASASHIO	Kawasaki, Kobe	5-10-64	27-11-65	13-10-66
563 HARUSHIO	Mitsubishi, Kobe	12-10-65	25-2-67	1-12-67
564 MICHISHIO	Kawasaki, Kobe	26-7-66	5-12-67	29-8-68
565 ARASHIO	Mitsubishi, Kobe	5-7-67	27-10-68	25-7-69

Asashio (562)   *Ships of the World*

D: 1,650 tons **S:** 14/18 kts **Dim:** 88.0 × 8.2 × 4.9
A: 8/533-mm TT (6 fwd, 2 aft)
M: 2 Kawasaki diesels, 2,900 hp each; 2 electric motors, 3,150 hp each; 2 props
Man: 80 tot.

REMARKS: *Oshio*, built during the 1961 program, was the prototype for the other four and was considered a separate class. She had a less elaborate sonar array and a more pointed bow; scheduled for disposal 3-82.

HELICOPTER-CARRYING DESTROYERS (DDH)

♦ 2 Shirane class

	Bldr	Laid down	L	In serv.
143 SHIRANE	Ishikawajima, Tokyo	25-2-77	18-9-78	17-3-80
144 KURAMA	Ishikawajima, Tokyo	1977	20-9-79	27-3-81

Shirane (DDH 143)   *Ships of the World*, 1980

Shirane (DDH 143)   *Ships of the World*, 1980

Shirane (DDH 143)   *Ships of the World*, 1980

HELICOPTER-CARRYING DESTROYERS *(continued)*

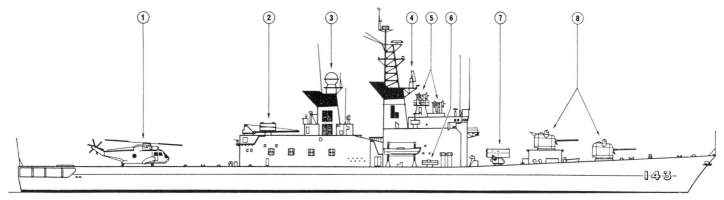

Shirane (DDH 143)   1. HSS-2B Sea King helicopter   2. Sea Sparrow Mk 29   3. WM 25 track-while-scan fire-control radar   4. OPS-12 3-dimensional air-search radar   5. GFCS 1A gun fire-control radar directors   6. Triple Mk 32 ASW torpedo tubes   7. ASROC ASW rocket launcher   8. Mk 42 mod. 10 127-mm dual-purpose guns

Kurama (DDH 144)—with Vulcan/Phalanx mounted   *Ships of the World*, 1981

D: 5,200 tons (6,800 fl)   **S:** 32 kts   **Dim:** 158.8 × 17.5 × 5.3
A: 2/127-mm Mk 42 DP (I × 2)—1/Mk 29 launcher (VIII × 1, Sea Sparrow)—2/20-mm Vulcan/Phalanx AA (I × 2)—1/ASROC—6/324-mm Mk 68 ASW TT (III × 2)—3/HSS-2B ASW helicopters
Electron Equipt: Radar: 1/OPS-12, 1/OPS-28, 1/WM-25 (HSA), 2/GFCS 1A
    TACAN: . . .
    Sonar: 1/OQS-101 (hull), 1/SQS-35 VDS, SQR-18A towed array
M: 2 sets GT; 2 props; 70,000 hp   **Boilers:** 2; 60 kg/cm², 480°C   **Man:** 370 tot.

REMARKS: Modified *Haruna* class. Both received U.S. SQR-18A TACTASS passive towed hydrophone arrays during 1981. Have "Masker" bubble-generating system to reduce radiated noise. WM-25 controls the Sparrow missiles. Will eventually receive Harpoon missiles. Have *two* stacks to one on the *Haruna* class.

Kurama (DDH 144)—note VDS, open hangar   *Ships of the World*, 1981

◆ **2 Haruna class**

	Bldr	Laid down	L	In serv.
141 HARUNA	Mitsubishi, Nagasaki	19-3-70	12-71	22-3-73
142 HIEI	Ishikawajima-Harima	8-3-72	13-8-73	27-12-74

D: 4,700 tons (6,300 fl)   **S:** 32 kts   **Dim:** 153.0 × 17.5 × 5.1
A: 2/127-mm Mk 42 DP (I × 2)—6/324-mm Mk 68 ASW TT (III × 2)—1/ASROC ASW system—3/HSS-2 ASW helicopters
Electron Equipt: Radars: 1/OPS-11, 1/OPS 17, 2/GFCS 1
    Sonar: OQS-3
    TACAN: URN-20A
M: 2 sets GT; 2 props; 70,000 hp   **Boilers:** 2; 60 kg/cm², 480°C
Man: 36 officers, 304 men

HELICOPTER-CARRYING DESTROYERS *(continued)*

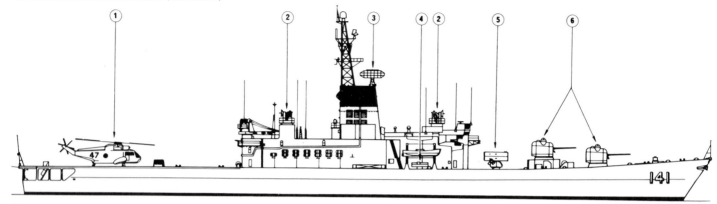

Haruna (DDH 141) 1. HSS-2 Sea King helicopter 2. GFCS-1 gun fire-control system 3. OPS-11 air-search radar 4. Mk 68 ASW TT 5. ASROC ASW rocket launcher 6. 127-mm, 54-caliber, dual-purpose guns, Mk 42, mod. 10

Haruna (DDH 141)   *Ships of the World,* 1973

Hiei (DDH 142)   *Ships of the World,* 1980

REMARKS: Plan to upgrade by installing Sea Sparrow, Vulcan/Phalanx, SQS-35 VDS (for which provision was made in the design), and Harpoon. DDH 142 getting improved sonar, 1981. Have single "mack," offset to port.

GUIDED-MISSILE DESTROYERS

♦ 1 new construction, 1981 program (DDG)

	Bldr	Laid down	L	In serv.
171 N. . .	. . .	. . .	10-84	1986

D: 4,500 tons (. . . fl) **S:** 32 kts **Dim:** . . . × . . . × . . .

A: 1/Mk 13 missile launcher (I × 1, 40 Standard SM-1 MR missiles)—8/Harpoon SSM (IV × 2)—2/127-mm Mk 42 DP (I × 2)—2/20-mm Vulcan/Phalanx AA (I × 2)—1/ASROC ASW RL(VIII × 1)—6/324-mm Mk 68 ASW TT (III × 2)—1/HSS-2B helicopter (no hangar)

Electron Equipt: Radar: 1/SPS-52C, 1/OPS-28, 1/OPS-11, 2/SPG-51C, 1/GFCS-2, 1/. . .

Sonar: OQS-4

ECM: NOLR-1

M: 2 Rolls-Royce Spey SM-1A and 2 Olympus TM-3D gas turbines; 2 CP props; 72,000 hp

Range: . . . **Man:** . . .

REMARKS: Mk 13 missile launcher and one of the two 127-mm guns will be forward. No hangar for helicopter. U.S. Mk 73 missile fire-control system (2/SPG-51C radar directors) for the Standard missile system.

♦ 0 (+9) Hatsuyuki class (DDG)

		Bldr	Laid down	L	In serv.
122	HATSUYUKI	Sumitomo, Uraga	14-3-79	7-11-80	3-82
123	SHIRAYUKI	Hitachi, Maizuru	3-12-79	4-8-81	2-83
124	N. . .	Mitsubishi, Nagasaki	4-81	10-82	3-83
125	N. . .	Ishikawajima-Harima, Tokyo	4-81	8-82	2-83
126	N. . .	Mitsui, Tamano	4-2-81	6-82	2-83
127	N. . .	Ishikawajima-Harima, Tokyo	. . .	. . .	. . .
128	N. . .	Sumitomo, Uraga	. . .	. . .	. . .
129	N. . .	. . .	. . .	. . .	3-86
130	N. . .	. . .	. . .	. . .	3-86

D: 2,950 tons (3,700 fl) **S:** 30 kts **Dim:** 131.7 (126.0 wl) × 13.7 × 4.3

A: 8/Harpoon SSM (IV × 2)—1/Mk 29 missile launcher (VIII × 1, Sea Sparrow missiles)—1/76-mm DP OTO Melara Compact—2/20-mm Vulcan/Phalanx AA (I × 2)—1/ASROC ASW RL (VIII × 1)—6/324-mm Mk 68 ASW TT (III × 2)—1/HSS-2B ASW helicopter

Electron Equipt: Radar: 1/OPS-18, 1/OPS-14B, 1/FCS-2, 1/GFCS-2

Sonar: OQS-4

GUIDED-MISSILE DESTROYERS (continued)

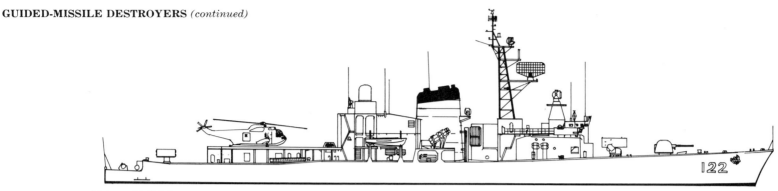

Hatsuyuki (DDG 122)

A.D. Baker III

M: COGOG: 2 Kawasaki-Rolls-Royce Olympus TM-3B gas turbines, 28,390 hp each; 2 Tyne RM-1C gas turbines, 5,340 hp each; 2 CP props

REMARKS: Will have fin stabilizers, DD 122 in 1977 Budget, 123 in 1978, 124-126 in 1979, 129 and 130 in 1981. Later units may be Rolls-Royce Spey vice Tyne cruise engines.

◆ 3 Tachikaze class (DDG)

	Bldr	Laid down	L	In serv.
168 TACHIKAZE	Mitsubishi, Nagasaki	19-6-73	12-12-74	26-3-76
169 ASAKAZE	Mitsubishi, Nagasaki	27-5-76	15-10-77	27-3-79
170 SAWAKAZE	Mitsubishi, Nagasaki	14-9-79	4-6-81	2-82

D: 3,850 tons (4,800 fl) **S:** 32 kts **Dim:** 143.0 × 14.3 × 4.6
A: 1/Mk 13 system (40 Standard SM-1 MR SAM)—2/127-mm Mk 42 DP (I × 2)—1/ASROC ASW RL (VIII × 1)—6/324-mm Mk 32 ASW TT (III × 2)
Electron Equipt: Radars: 1/OPS-11, 1/SPS-52B, 2/SPG-51C, 1/GFCS 2
      Sonar: OQS-3 (170: OQS-4)
      ECM: OLT-3 system, 4/Mk 36 Super RBOC chaff RL
M: 2 sets GT; 2 props; 70,000 hp **Boilers:** 2; 60 kg/cm², 480°C **Man:** 277 tot.

Tachikaze (DDG 168)—prior to installation of OPS-11 radar *Ships of the World,*
1978

REMARKS: U.S. Vulcan/Phalanx Gatling guns are to be added to 168 under 1981 Budget, as well as improvements to SAM system. The SPS-52B acts as the principal air-search radar. The missile-control system is Mk 73 and uses the two SPG-51C radars. The propulsion plant is identical to that of the *Haruna* class. All receiving two SATCOMM antenna radomes atop bridge.

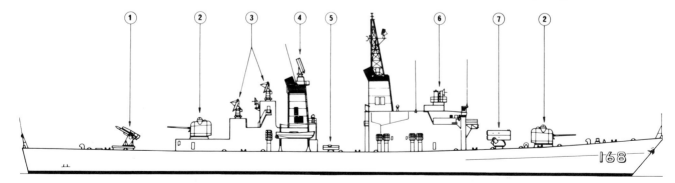

Tachikaze (DDG 168) 1. Mk 13 launcher for Standard SM1-MR missiles 2. 127-mm, 54-caliber, dual-purpose guns, Mk 42, mod. 10 3. SPG-51 missile-control radars 4. SPS-52B 3-D radar 5. Mk 68 ASW TT 6. GFCS-1 gun fire-control system 7. ASROC ASW rocket launcher

GUIDED-MISSILE DESTROYERS *(continued)*

Tachikaze (DDG 168)—with SATCOMM radomes — *Ships of the World*, 1980

♦ **1 Amatsukaze class (DDG)**

	Bldr	Laid down	L	In serv.
163 AMATSUKAZE	Mitsubishi, Nagasaki	29-11-62	5-10-63	15-2-75

Amatsukaze (DDG 163) — *G. Arra*, 1980

D: 3,050 tons (4,000 fl) **S:** 33 kts **Dim:** 131.0 × 13.4 × 4.2
A: 1/Mk 13 system (40 Standard SM-1 MR SAM)—4/76.2-mm 50-cal. DP Mk 33 (II × 2)—1/ASROC ASW RL (VIII × 1)—6/324-mm Mk 32 ASW TT (III × 2)—2/Mk 15 trainable Hedgehog

Electron Equipt: Radars: 1/OPS-17, 1/SPS-29, 1/SPS-52, 2/SPG-51, 2/SPG-34
Sonars: SQS-23
M: 2 sets Ishikawajima-GE GT; 2 props; 60,000 hp **Fuel:** 900 tons
Boilers 2 Ishikawajima-Foster-Wheeler; 38 kg/cm², 438°C **Electric** 2,700 kw
Range: 7,000/18 **Man:** 290 tot.

REMARKS: Refitted in 1967 with ASW TT and SPS-52 radar. The U.S. Mk 63 fire-control systems for 76.2-mm guns, which have SPG-34 radars on the mounts. Guns may be replaced by two OTO Melara 76-mm compact mounts and plans call for replacement of Mk 63 GFCS with GFCS 2 and substitution of NOLR-6 ECM system for present gear. Crane at stern handles boats stowed in a below-decks hangar.

DESTROYERS (DD, DDK)

♦ **4 Takatsuki class (DD)**

	Bldr	Laid down	L	In serv.
164 TAKATSUKI	Ishikawajima, Tokyo	8-10-65	7-1-66	15-3-67
165 KIKIZUKI	Mitsubishi, Nagasaki	15-3-66	25-3-67	27-3-68
166 MOCHIZUKI	Ishikawajima, Tokyo	25-11-66	15-3-69	25-3-69
167 NAGATSUKI	Ishikawajima, Tokyo	2-3-68	19-3-69	12-2-70

D: 3,200 tons (4,500 fl) **S:** 32 kts **Dim:** 136.0 (131.0 pp) × 13.4 × 4.4

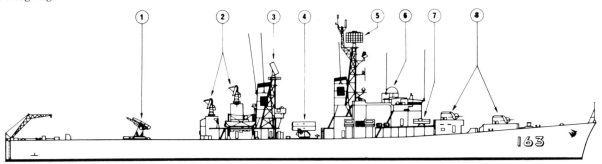

Takatsuki (DD 164)—with URN-20A TACAN — *Ships of the World*

Amatsukaze (DDG 163) 1. Mk 13 missile launcher 2. SPG-51 missile-control radars 3. SPS-52 3-D radar 4. ASROC ASW rocket launcher 5. SPS-29 air-search radar 6. Mk 63 gun fire-control director 7. Mk 32 ASW TT 8. 76.2-mm, 50-caliber, U.S. Mk 33, dual-purpose gun mounts

DESTROYERS (continued)

Mochizuki—now has TACAN

Ships of the World

A: 2/127-mm Mk 42 DP (I × 2)—1/ASROC ASW RL—1/375-mm Bofors ASW
RL (IV × 1)—6/324-mm Mk 32 ASW TT
Electron Equipt: Radar: 1/OPS-11B, 1/OPS-17, 2/Mk 35 (Mk 56 GFCS)
Sonar: DD 164, DD 165: SQS-23; DD 166, DD 167: OQS-3;
SQS-35(J) VDS (not in 166)
ECM: NOLR-1B
TACAN: URN-20 (not on 165)
M: 2 sets Mitsubishi GT; 2 props; 60,000 hp
Boilers: 2 Mitsubishi-Combustion Eng.; 43 kg/cm², 454°C   **Fuel:** 900 tons
Range: 7,000/20   **Man:** 270 tot.

REMARKS: Originally carried three U.S. DASH drone ASW helicopters, removed in
1977 and hangar not now used. DD 166 and 167 have a knuckle in the hull sides
forward; the earlier two do not. DD 165 has fin stabilizers. DD 167 has two Japanese
GFCS gun directors vice two Mk 56 GFCS. DD 164 authorized under 1981 Budget
to receive extensive modernization completing in 1985. The DASH hangar and after
127-mm gun are to be removed. Gained will be a Mk 29 launcher aft for Sea Sparrow,
8 Harpoon missiles (IV × 2), provision for (but *not* installation of) 2 Vulcan/Phalanx
Gatling AA guns, upgrading of the OQS-3 sonar, addition of U.S. SQR-18A TAC-
TASS towed passive hydrophone array, replacement of the two Mk 56 GFCS with
two GFCS-2, substitution of the NOLQ-1 ECM system for the present array, addition
of new digital data link equipment, and installation of the U.S. Mk 36 Super RBOC
chaff launching system. DD 164 received a MARISAT SATCOMM radome atop the
after "mack" in 1981. All are eventually to be modernized to the new DD 164 configuration.

◆ **6 Yamagumo class (DDK)**

		Bldr	Laid down	L	In serv.
113	YAMAGUMO	Mitsui, Tamano	23-3-64	27-2-65	29-1-66
114	MAKIGUMO	Uraga, Yokosuka	10-6-64	26-7-65	19-3-66
115	ASAGUMO	Maizuru, H.I.	24-6-65	25-11-66	29-8-67
119	AOKUMO	Sumitomo, Uraga	2-10-70	30-3-72	25-11-72
120	AKIGUMO	Sumitomo, Uraga	7-7-72	23-10-73	24-7-74
121	YUGUMO	Sumitomo, Uraga	4-2-76	31-5-77	24-3-78

D: 2,100 tons (2,700 fl)   **S:** 27 kts   **Dim:** 114.9 × 11.8 × 4.0
A: 4/76.2-mm 50-cal. DP Mk 33 (II × 2)—1/ASROC ASW RL (VIII × 1)—1/
375-mm Bofors ASW RL (IV × 1)—6/324-mm Mk 32 ASW TT (III × 2)

Aokumo (DDK 119)

Akigumo (DDK 120)

Ships of the World

Electron Equipt: Radars: 1/OPS-11, 1/OPS-17, 2/GFCS 1 (*see* Remarks)
Sonars: DDK 113-115: SQS-23; later: OQS-3; also SQS-35(J)
VDS (not in DDK 115)
M: 6 Mitsubishi 12UEV 30/40N diesels; 2 props; 26,500 hp   **Range:** 7,000/20

REMARKS: Version of the *Minegumo* class completed with ASROC instead of DASH.
May get OTO Melara 76-mm guns in place of U.S. Mk 33 mounts during refits in
the 1980s. DDK 113-115 and 119 were given U.S. Mk 56 gun director forward (Mk
35 radar) and Mk 63 GFCS aft (Mk 34 radar on after gun mount); DDK 120 and 121
got two Japanese GFCS-1 systems instead. DDK 113 has Mitsui diesels. DDK 113
and 114 have raised sterns to house VDS; on DDK 119-121 the VDS was installed
during construction and, therefore, the stern was not raised.

◆ **3 Minegumo class (DDK)**

		Bldr	Laid down	L	In serv.
116	MINEGUMO	Mitsui, Tamano	14-3-67	16-12-67	21-8-68
117	NATSUGUMO	Uraga, Yokosuka	26-6-67	25-7-68	25-4-69
118	MURAKUMO	Maizuru, H.I.	19-10-68	15-11-69	21-8-70

Minegumo (DDK 116)

Ships of the World

DESTROYERS (continued)

Murakumo (DDK 118)—with OTO Melara gun and ASROC aft *Ships of the World,*
1979

D: 2,100 tons (2,750 fl) **S:** 27 kts **Dim:** 114.9 × 11.8 × 3.8

A: DDK 116, 117: 4/76.2-mm 50-cal. DP Mk 32 (II × 2)—1/375-mm Bofors ASW
RL (IV × 1)—6/324-mm Mk 32 ASW TT (III × 2)
DDK 118: 1/76-mm OTO Melara Compact—2/76.2-mm DP (II × 1)—1/AS-
ROC ASW RL—1/375-mm Bofors ASW RL (IV × 2)—6/324-mm Mk 32
ASW TT (III × 2)

Electron Equipt: Radars: 1/OPS-11, 1/OPS-17, 1/Mk 35, 1/SPG-34; DDK 118:
1/GFCS-2, 1/GFCS-1; DDK 117: 1/GFCS-1, 1/SPG-34
Sonars: OQS-3—DDK 118: SQS-35(J) VDS also

M: 6 Mitsubishi 12UEV 30/40 diesels; 2 props; 26,500 hp

Range: 7,000/20 **Man:** 19 officers, 196 men

REMARKS: Originally differed from the *Yamagumo* class in having a DASH drone-
helicopter facility instead of ASROC, but DASH is no longer carried. In 1976, DDK
118 had an OTO Melara 76-mm gun and the prototype GFCS-2 radar director substituted for her after 76.2-mm twin mount and U.S. Mk 63 control system; in 1979,
she received an ASROC launcher on what had been her DASH flight deck. All have
a Mk 56 director forward. DDK 116 and 117 are to receive ASROC, and all three
will eventually carry two OTO Melara guns.

◆ 2 Akizuki class (DD)

	Bldr	Laid down	L	In serv.
161 AKIZUKI	Mitsubishi, Nagasaki	31-7-58	26-6-59	13-2-60
162 TERUZUKI	Shin-Mitsubishi, Kobe	15-8-58	24-6-59	29-2-60

Teruzuki (DD 162) *Ships of the World,* 1979

D: 2,300 tons (3,100 fl) **S:** 32 kts **Dim:** 118.0 (115.0 pp) × 12.0 × 4.02

A: 3/127-mm 54-cal. DP Mk 39 (I × 3)—4/76.2-mm 50-cal. DP Mk 33 (II × 2)—
4/533-mm TT (IV × 1)—1/375-mm Bofors ASW RL (IV × 1)—2/Mk 15 trainable Hedgehogs—6/324-mm Mk ASW TT (III × 2)

Electron Equipt: Radars: 1/OPS-1, 1/OPS-15, 3/Mk 34
Sonars: SQS-23, OQA-1 VDS

M: DD 161: 2 sets Mitsubishi-Escher-Wyss GT; DD 162: 2 sets Westinghouse
GT; 2 props; 45,000 hp

Boilers: 4; 43 kg/cm², 454°C **Man:** 330 tot.

REMARKS: Weapons and ASW sensors modernized, DD 162 in 1976-77 and DD 161 in
1977-78, the Bofors ASW RL replacing a U.S. Mk 108 "Weapon Alfa," VDS being
added, and SQS-23 replacing SQS-29. The 127-mm guns were removed from U.S.
Midway-class carriers. Two U.S. Mk 57 and one Mk 63 gun fire-control systems are
carried. Four reload 533-mm torpedoes can be stowed on deck.

◆ 3 Murasame class (DD)

	Bldr	Laid down	L	In serv.
107 MURASAME	Mitsubishi, Nagasaki	17-12-57	31-7-58	28-2-59
108 YUDACHI	Ishikawajima, Tokyo	16-12-57	29-7-58	25-3-59
109 HARUSAME	Uraga, Yokosuka	17-6-58	18-6-59	15-12-59

Harusame (DD 109) *Ships of the World*

D: 1,800 tons (2,400 fl) **S:** 30 kts **Dim:** 109.73 × 10.97 × 3.7 (light)

A: 3/127-mm 54-cal DP Mk 39 (I × 3)—4/76.2-mm 50-cal. Mk 33 DP (II × 2)—1/
Mk 15 trainable Hedgehog—6/324-mm Mk 32 ASW TT (III × 2)

Electron Equipt: Radars: 1/OPS-15, 1/OPS-1, 3/Mk 34—DD 109: 2/Mk 34,
1/GFCS-0
Sonars: SQS-29 (DD 109: OQA-1 VDS also)

M: DD 107, 108: 2 sets Kampon GT; DD 109: Mitsubishi-Escher-Wyss GT; 2
props; 35,000 hp

Boilers: 2; 43 kg/cm², 454°C **Range:** 6,000/18 **Man:** 250 tot.

REMARKS: Hull and machinery spaces similar to those of the *Ayanami* class. DD 109
has Mitsubishi boilers, DD 107 and 108 have Foster-Wheeler-D boilers. All have
two Mk 57 and one Mk 63 gun-control systems except DD 109. DD 107 and 108 retain
one depth-charge rack, two U.S. Mk 4 torpedo launchers (for Mk 32 ASW torpedoes),
and a Y-gun depth-charge mortar. The 127-mm gun mounts were removed from the
U.S. Navy's *Midway*-class carriers.

◆ 7 Ayanami class (DD)

	Bldr	Laid down	L	In serv.
103 AYANAMI	Mitsubishi, Nagasaki	20-11-56	1-6-57	12-2-58
104 ISONAMI	Mitsubishi, Kobe	14-12-56	30-9-57	14-3-58
105 URANAMI	Kawasaki, Kobe	1-2-57	29-8-57	27-2-58
106 SHIKINAMI	Mitsui, Tamano	24-12-56	25-9-57	15-3-58
110 TAKANAMI	Mitsui, Maizuru	8-11-58	8-8-59	30-1-60
111 ONAMI	Ishikawajima, Tokyo	20-3-59	13-2-60	29-8-60
112 MAKINAMI	Iino, Maizuru	20-3-59	25-4-60	30-10-60

DESTROYERS (continued)

Uranami (DD 105) 1978

Isonami (DD 104)—with classroom in place of torpedo tubes *Ships of the World,* 1979

D: 1,700 tons (2,400 fl) **S:** 32 kts **Dim:** 109.0 × 10.7 × 3.7 (light)
A: 6/76.2-mm DP Mk 33 (II × 3)—4/533-mm TT (IV × 1; not in DD 104, 106)—
2/Mk 15 trainable Hedgehog—6/324-mm Mk 32 ASW TT (III × 2) (except
DD 110 and 111: 2/Mk 4 torpedo launchers for Mk 32 ASW torpedoes)
Electron Equipt: Radar: 1/OPS-15, 1/OPS-1 (DD 103-106: OPS-2), 2/Mk 34
  Sonar: OQS-12 or 14 (DD 103, 104, 110: OQA-1 VDS also)
M: DD 111: Hitachi-GE GT; Others: Mitsubishi-Escher-Wyss GT; 2 props;
35,000 hp
Boilers: 2; 43 kg/cm², 454°C **Range:** 6,000/18 **Man:** 220-230 tot.

REMARKS: The boilers in DD 106 and 110 are Hitachi-Babcock; in the others, Mitsubishi. DD 104 and 106 were fitted as training ships in 1975-76; their trainable torpedo
tubes have been replaced by a classroom. There are two Mk 63 gun-control systems.
OPS-1 radar is the Japanese version of the U.S. SPS-6; OPS-2 = U.S. SPS-12.

NOTE: The two *Harukaze*-class destroyers, *Harukaze* (DD 101) and *Yukikaze* (DD
102) were reclassified as auxiliaries (ASU) on 27-3-81; see later page for data.

GUIDED-MISSILE FRIGATES (DE)

♦ 0 (+2) Yubari class

	Bldr	Laid down	L	In serv.
227 YUBARI	Sumitomo, Uraga	2-81	2-82	3-83
228 N. . .	. . .	. . .	. . .	. . .

D: 1,400 tons (1,690 fl) **S:** 25 kts **Dim:** 91.0 × 10.8 × 3.5
A: 8/Harpoon SSM (IV × 2)—1/76-mm DP OTO Melara—1/20-mm Vulcan/Phal-
anx AA—1/375-mm Bofors ASW RL (IV × 1)—6/324-mm Mk 68 ASW TT
(III × 2)

Electron Equipt: Radar: OPS-28, 1/GFCS-2
  Sonar: . . .
M: CODOG: 1 Kawasaki-Rolls-Royce Olympus TM-3B gas turbine, 28,390 hp; 1
Mitsubishi 6DRV 35/44 diesel, 4,650 hp; 2 CP props
Range: . . . **Man:** 98 tot.

REMARKS: An enlarged version of the *Ishikari* class, presumably as the earlier ship
is too cramped for the mission requirements. Greater length permits addition of a
Vulcan/Phalanx Gatling AA gun at the extreme stern. DE 227 ordered under FY
1979-80 Budget, DE 228 under FY 1980-81. None requested under FY 1981-82, but
one may be in 1982-83 request.

♦ 1 Ishikari class

	Bldr	Laid down	L	In serv.
226 ISHIKARI	Mitsui, Tamano	17-5-79	18-3-80	30-3-81

Ishikari (DE 220)—Harpoon missiles aft *Ships of the World,* 1981

D: 1,200 tons (1,450 fl) **S:** 25 kts **Dim:** 84.5 × 10.0 × 3.5 (mean)
A: 8/Harpoon SSM (IV × 2)—1/76-mm DP OTO Melara—1/375-mm Bofors ASW
RL (IV × 1)—6/324-mm Mk 68 ASW TT
Electron Equipt: Radars: 1/OPS 28, 1/GFCS-2
  Sonar: . . .
  ECM: . . . system, 2/U.S. Mk 36 Super RBOC chaff RL
M: CODOG: 1 Kawasaki-Rolls-Royce Olympus TM-3B gas turbine, 28,390 hp; 1
Mitsubishi 6DRV 35/44 diesel, 4,650 hp; 2 CP props
Man: 90 tot.

REMARKS: Smaller, more lightly armed, faster, and with fewer sensors than the preceding *Chikugo* class. Aluminum superstructure. Either the gas turbine *or* the single
diesel will drive both propellers. Ordered under 1977-78 program. 19 kts max. on
diesel. The Combat Information Center (CIC) is below the waterline. Highly automated ship with very small crew.

FRIGATES (DE)

♦ 11 Chikugo class

		Bldr	Laid down	L	In serv.
215	CHIKUGO	Mitsui, Tamano	9-12-68	13-1-70	31-7-70
216	AYASE	Ishikawajima, Tokyo	5-12-69	16-9-70	20-7-71
217	MIKUMO	Mitsui, Tamano	17-3-70	16-2-71	26-8-71
218	TOKACHI	Mitsui, Tamano	11-12-70	25-11-71	17-5-72
219	IWASE	Mitsui, Tamano	6-8-71	29-6-72	12-12-72
220	CHITOSE	Hitachi, Maizuru	7-10-71	25-1-73	21-8-73
221	NIYODO	Mitsui, Tamano	20-9-72	28-8-73	8-2-74
222	TESHIO	Hitachi, Maizuru	11-7-73	29-5-74	10-1-75
223	YOSHINO	Mitsui, Tamano	28-9-73	22-8-74	6-2-75
224	KUMANO	Hitachi, Maizuru	29-5-74	24-2-75	19-11-75
225	NOSHIRO	Mitsui, Tamano	27-1-76	23-12-76	31-8-77

Ayase (DE 216)   *Ships of the World,* 1977

Noshiro (DE 225)   *Ships of the World,* 1980

D: 1,470–1,530 tons (1,700–1,800 fl)   **S:** 25 kts   **Dim:** 93.0 × 10.8 × 3.5
A: 2/76.2-mm 50-cal. DP Mk 33 (II × 1)—2/40-mm AA (II × 1)—1/ASROC
     ASW RL (VIII × 1)—6/324-mm Mk 68 ASW TT (III × 2)
Electron Equipt: Radars: 1/OPS-16, 1/OPS-14, 1/GFCS-1B
                Sonars: OQS-3, SQS-35(J) (*see* Remarks)
M: 4 Mitsubishi-Burmeister & Wain UEV 30/40 or Mitsui 28VBC-38 diesels; 2
     props; 16,000 hp
Range: 10,700/12; 12,000/9   **Man:** 13 officers, 152 men

REMARKS: SQS-35(J) towed, variable-depth sonar has not yet been mounted in all
units; it is stowed in an open well at the stern, offset to starboard. These are the
smallest ships in any navy to carry ASROC. A Mk 51 director (no radar) controls
the twin 40-mm mounts. DE 215 and 220 are 1,480 tons std., DE 216-219 and 221

are 1,470 tons std.; later units 1,500 tons std. DE 215, 217-219, 221, 223, 225 have
the Mitsubishi diesels.

♦ 4 Isuzu class (DE)

		Bldr	Laid down	L	In serv.
211	ISUZU	Mitsui, Tamano	16-4-60	17-1-61	29-7-61
212	MOGAMI	Mitsubishi, Nagasaki	4-8-60	13-3-61	28-10-61
213	KITAKAMI	Ishikawajima, Tokyo	7-6-62	21-6-63	27-2-64
214	OHI	Maizuru H.I.	10-6-62	15-6-63	22-1-64

Mogami (DE 212)   *Ships of the World,* 1979

Kitakami (DE 213)

D: 1,490 tons (1,790 fl)   **S:** 25 kts   **Dim:** 94.0 × 10.4 × 3.5
A: 2/76.2-mm 50-cal. DP Mk 33 (II × 2)—1/375-mm Bofors ASW RL (IV × 1)—
     DE 213, 214: 6/324-mm Mk 32 ASW TT (III × 2)—1 d.c. projector (not on
     DE 212 and 213)
Electron Equipt: Radars: 1/OPS-1, 1/OPS-16, 2/Mk 34
               Sonars: OQS-12 or -14; DE 212, 213: OQA-1 VDS also
M: Diesels; 2 prop; 16,000 hp   **Man:** 180 tot.

REMARKS: Each has a different diesel propulsion plant: DE 211: 4 Mitsui 35 VBU 45V;
DE 212: 2 Mitsubishi UET 52/65; DE 213: 4 Mitsubishi UEV 30/40; and DE 214: 4
Mitsui 28 VBU 38. DE 212, which has only two main engines, has a smaller stack.
Have two U.S. Mk 63 GFCS (Mk 34 radar on gunmounts) for the guns.

PATROL BOATS (PC)

♦ 3 Mizutori class

	Bldr	Laid down	L	In serv.
316 UMIDORI	Sasebo DY	15-2-62	15-10-62	30-3-63
319 SHIRATORI	Sasebo DY	29-2-64	8-10-64	26-2-65
320 HIYODORI	Sasebo DY	26-2-65	29-9-65	28-2-66

D: 430-440 tons (470-480 fl) **S:** 20 kts **Dim:** 60.0 × 7.1 × 2.35
A: 2/40-mm AA (II × 1)—6/324-mm Mk 32 ASW TT (III × 2)—1/Mk 10 Hedge-
    hog—1/d.c. rack
Electron Equipt: Radars: PC 316: OPS-36; Others: OPS-16; All: 1/Mk 34
    Sonar: SQS-11A
M: 2 Kawasaki-M.A.N. V8V diesels; 2 props; 3,800 hp **Fuel:** 24 tons
Range: 2,000/12 **Man:** 75 tot.

REMARKS: PC 316: 430 tons std (470 fl); others 440/480 tons. For appearance see under
auxiliaries. Five sisters reclassified as auxiliaries 1981-82: *Mizutori* (PC 311) to
ASU. . . , *Yamadori* (PC 312) to ASU 90, and *Kasasagi* (PC 314) to ASU 87 all on
27-3-81; *Otori* (PC 313) to ASU. . . , and *Hatsukari* to ASU. . . prior to 31-3-82.

NOTE: The four *Umitaka*-class patrol boats have been reclassified as auxiliaries (ASU):
Umitaka (PC 309) to ASU 86 during 1980, *Otaka* (PC 310) to ASU 88 on 27-3-81,
and *Wakataka* (PC 317) and *Kumataka* (PC 318) prior to 31-3-82.

TORPEDO BOATS (PT)

♦ 5 PT 11 class Bldr: Mitsubishi

	L	In serv.		L	In serv.
811 PT 11	10-70	23-3-71	814 PT 14	. . .	10-7-73
812 PT 12	7-72	8-72	815 PT 15	. . .	8-1-75
813 PT 13	7-72	12-72			

PT 13 (813)   *Ships of the World*

D: 100 tons (125 fl) **S:** 40 kts **Dim:** 35.0 × 9.2 × 1.2
A: 2/40-mm AA (I × 2)—4/533-mm TT (I × 4)
Electron Equipt: Radar: 1/OPS-13 **Man:** 26 tot.
M: CODAG: 2 Ishikawajima IM-300 gas turbines, 2 Mitsubishi 24 WZ-31MC
    diesels; 3 props; 10,500 hp

PATROL CRAFT (PB)

♦ 9 PB type Bldr: Ishikawajima, Yokohama

PB 19 to PB 27 (PB 19-24 in serv. 31-3-72; others, 29-3-73)

D: 18 tons **S:** 20 kts **Dim:** 17.0 × 4.3 × 0.8 **A:** 1/20-mm AA
Electron Equipt: Radar: 1/OPS-29 **M:** 2 Isuzu 17T-MF RCOR diesels; 760 hp
Man: 5 tot.

REMARKS: Fiberglass hulls. Two additional units delivered 3-79 and 28-3-80 for use
as radio-controlled surface gunnery target-towing craft; 850 hp, 25 kts.

MINE WARFARE SHIPS

♦ 1 minelayer (MMC) Bldr: Hitachi, Maizuru

	Laid down	L	In serv.
951 SOUYA	9-7-70	31-3-71	30-9-71

Souya (MMC 951)   *Ships of the World*, 1972

D: 2,150 tons (3,250 fl) **S:** 18 kts **Dim:** 99.0 × 15.0 × 4.2
A: 2/76.2-mm DP Mk 33 (II × 1)—2/20-mm AA (I × 2)—6/324-mm Mk 32 ASW
    TT (III × 2)—200 mines
Electron Equipt: Radars: 1/OPS-14, 1/OPS-16, 1/GFCS-1
    Sonar: SQS-11A
M: 4 Kawasaki-M.A.N. V6V 22/30 ATL diesels; 2 props; 6,400 hp
Man: 185 tot.

REMARKS: Platform for minesweeping-helicopter, six mine rails, two external, four
through the transom stern.

♦ 1 mine-countermeasures support ship/minelayer (MST)

	Bldr	Laid down	L	In serv.
462 HAYASE	Ishikawajima, Haruna	16-9-70	21-6-71	6-11-71

D: 2,000 tons (3,050 fl) **S:** 18 kts **Dim:** 99.0 × 13.0 × 3.8
A: 2/76-mm 50-cal. DP (II × 1)—2/20-mm AA (I × 2)—6/324-mm Mk 32 ASW
    TT (III × 2)—200 mines
Electron Equipt: Radars: 1/OPS-17, 1/Mk 34
    Sonar: SQS-11A
M: 4 Kawasaki-M.A.N. V6V 22/30 ATL diesels; 2 props; 6,400 hp

REMARKS: The *Hayase* is similar to the *Souya* but has no forecastle, and has five mine
rails existing through the transom stern. Her OPS-14 air-search radar has been
removed. She has a U.S. Mk 63 gun-control system. Fantail cleared as a helicopter
platform.

MINE WARFARE SHIPS (continued)

Hayase (MST 462)—large radar since deleted   *Ships of the World,* 1978

♦ 1 Kasado-class mine-countermeasures support ship (MST)

	Bldr	L	In serv.
474 OTSU (ex-MSC 621)	Nippon Kokan, Tsurumi	5-11-64	24-2-65

Otsu (MST 474)   1981

D: 330 tons (360 fl)   **S:** 14 kts   **Dim:** 45.70 × 8.38 × 2.30   **A:** none
Electron Equipt: Radar: OPS-9
                  Sonar: ZQQ-2
M: 2 Mitsubishi YV10Z-DE diesels; 2 props; 1,200 hp   **Man:** . . .

REMARKS: Reclassified 18-3-81 to replace *Kouzo* (MST 473) of the same class. Former wooden-hulled minesweeper converted to support minesweeping boats.

♦ 7 (+4) Hatsushima-class minehunter/minesweepers (MSC)

	Bldr	Laid down	L	In serv.
649 HATSUSHIMA	Nippon Kokan, Tsurumi	6-12-77	30-10-78	30-3-79
650 NINOSHIMA	Hitachi, Kanagawa	8-5-78	9-8-79	19-12-79
651 MIYAJIMA	Nippon Kokan, Tsurumi	8-11-78	18-9-79	29-1-80
652 NENOSHIMA	Nippon Kokan, Tsurumi	4-10-79	25-7-80	25-12-80
653 UKISHIMA	Hitachi, Kanagawa	15-5-79	11-7-80	27-11-80
654 OSHIMA	Hitachi, Kanagawa	2-6-80	17-6-81	11-81
655 MILJIMA	Nippon Kokan, Tsurumi	4-8-80	2-6-81	11-81
656 N. . .	Hitachi, Kanagawa	. . .	. . .	. . .
657 N. . .	Nippon Kokan, Tsurumi	. . .	. . .	. . .
658 N. . .	. . .	. . .	. . .	. . .
659 N. . .	. . .	. . .	. . .	. . .

Ninoshima (MSC 650)   *Ships of the World,* 1979

D: 440 tons   **S:** 14 kts   **Dim:** 55.0 × 9.4 × 2.4   **A:** 1/20-mm AA
Electron Equipt: Radar: OPS-9
                  Sonar: ZQS-2B
M: 2 Mitsubishi YV12ZC-15/20 diesels; 2 CP props; 1,440 hp   **Man:** 45 tot.

REMARKS: Expansion of the *Takami* design. Will be equipped with Type-54 mobile minehunting devices, which carry and lay their own disposal charges. MSC 653 has a 20-mm Type JM-61-MB Gatling gun AA. Wooden construction. Two more requested under FY 1982-83.

♦ 18 Takami-class minehunter/minesweepers

	Bldr	L	In serv.
630 TAKAMI	Nippon Kokan, Tsurumi	15-7-69	15-12-69
631 IOU	Hitachi, Kanagawa	12-8-69	22-1-70
632 MIYAKE	Nippon Kokan, Tsurumi	3-6-70	19-11-70
633 UTONE	Hitachi, Kanagawa	6-4-70	3-9-70
634 AWAJI	Nippon Kokan, Tsurumi	11-12-70	29-3-71
635 TOUSHI	Hitachi, Kanagawa	13-12-70	18-3-71
636 TEURI	Nippon Kokan, Tsurumi	10-71	10-3-72
637 MUROTSU	Hitachi, Kanagawa	10-71	3-3-72
638 TASHIRO	Nippon Kokan, Tsurumi	2-4-73	30-7-73
640 TAKANE	Nippon Kokan, Tsurumi	8-3-74	28-8-74
641 MUZUKI	Hitachi, Kanagawa	5-4-74	28-8-74

MINE WARFARE SHIPS *(continued)*

642 Yokose	Nippon Kokan, Tsurumi	21-7-75	15-12-75
643 Sakate	Hitachi, Kanagawa	5-8-75	17-12-75
644 Oumi	Nippon Kokan, Tsurumi	28-5-76	18-11-76
645 Fukue	Hitachi, Kanagawa	12-7-76	18-11-76
646 Okitsu	Nippon Kokan, Tsurumi	4-3-77	20-9-77
647 Hashira	Hitachi, Kanagawa	8-11-77	28-3-78
648 Iwai	Nippon Kokan, Tsurumi	8-11-77	28-3-78

Murotsu (MSC 637) 1978

Yokose (MSC 642) *Ships of the World*

D: 380 tons **S:** 14 kts **Dim:** 52.0 × 8.8 × 2.4 **A:** 1/20-mm AA
Electron Equipt: Radar: OPS-9
Sonar: ZQS-2
M: Mitsubishi YV12ZC-15/20 diesels; 2 CP props; 1,440 hp **Man:** 45-47 tot.

Remarks: ZQS-2 sonar is a license-built version of the British Type 193-M minehunting sonar. OPS-9 radar, used in conjunction with a Mk 20 plotter, is a Japanese version of the British Type 978. These ships are of wooden construction, and they carry four divers for mine-clearance. Sister *Miyato* (MSC 639) to be stricken by 31-3-82.

♦ **5 Kasado-class minehunter/minesweepers**

	Bldr	L	In serv.
625 Amami	Nippon Kokan, Tsurumi	31-10-66	6-3-67
626 Urume	Hitachi, Kanagawa	12-11-66	30-1-67
627 Minase	Nippon Kokan, Tsurumi	10-1-67	25-3-67
628 Ibuki	Hitachi, Kanagawa	2-12-67	27-2-68
629 Katsura	Nippon Kokan, Tsurumi	18-9-67	15-2-68

D: 330 tons (360 fl) **S:** 14 kts **Dim:** 45.70 × 8.38 × 2.30
A: 1/20-mm AA
Electron Equipt: Radar: OPS-9
Sonar: ZQS-2
M: 2 Mitsubishi YV10Z-DE diesels; 2 props; 1,200 hp

Remarks: Wooden construction. Twenty-one earlier units of the class (604-624) have been converted to auxiliary duties. In 1980, *Mutsure* (MSC 619) and *Chiburi* (MSC 620) were redesignated YAS 72 and 73 respectively, while *Kudako* (MSC 622) became YAS 74 on 18-3-81. *Otsu* (MSC 621) became MST 474 on 18-3-81. *Rishiri* (MSC 623) and *Rebun* (MSC 624) were to be redesignated ASU by 31-3-82.

♦ **6 inshore minesweepers (MSB)** Bldrs: Odd-numbered craft: Hitachi, Kanagawa; even-numbered craft: Nippon Kokan, Tsurumi

	In serv.		In serv.		In serv.
MSB 707	30-3-73	MSB 709	28-3-74	MSB 711	10-5-75
MSB 708	27-3-73	MSB 710	29-3-74	MSB 712	24-4-75

MSB 709 *Ships of the World*

D: 58 tons (fl) **S:** 10 kts **Dim:** 22.5 × 5.4 × 1.1 **A:** None
M: 2 Mitsubishi 4ZV20 diesels; 2 props; 480 hp **Man:** 10 tot.

Remarks: Wooden construction. Supported by *Otsu* (MST 474). No radar.

AMPHIBIOUS WARFARE SHIPS

♦ **3 Miura-class landing ships (LST)** Bldr: Ishikawajima Harima, Tokyo

	Laid down	L	In serv.
4151 Miura	26-11-73	13-8-74	29-1-75
4152 Ojika	10-6-74	2-9-75	27-3-76
4153 Satsuma	26-5-75	12-5-76	17-2-77

AMPHIBIOUS WARFARE SHIPS (*continued*)

Miura (LST 4151)   *Ships of the World*

D: 2,000 tons (3,200 fl)   **S:** 14 kts   **Dim:** 98.0 (94.0 pp) × 14.0 × 3.0
A: 2/76.2-mm 50-cal. Mk 33 DP—2/40-mm AA (II × 1)
Electron Equipt: Radars: 1/OPS-14, 1/OPS-16, 1/GFCS-1   **Man:** 118 tot.
M: 2 Kawasaki-M.A.N. V8V 22/30 AMTL diesels; 2 props; 4,400 hp

REMARKS: Carry 180 troops, 1,800 tons cargo. LST 4153 has carried prototype OTO
Melara Compact gun at bow. All have two LCVP in davits and two LCM(6) on deck,
the latter served by a traveling gantry with folding rails that can be extended over
the sides. GFCS-1 fwd, controls 76.2-mm guns; U.S. Mk 51 mod. 2 GFCS aft controls
40-mm.

♦ **3 Atsumi class (LSTs)** Bldr: Sasebo Heavy Industries

		Laid down	L	In serv.
4101	ATSUMI	7-12-71	13-6-72	27-11-72
4102	MOTOBU	23-4-73	3-8-73	21-12-73
4103	NEMURO	18-11-76	16-6-77	27-10-77

D: 1,480 tons (2,400 fl)   **S:** 14 kts   **Dim:** 89.0 × 13.0 × 2.7   **Range:** 4,300/12
A: 4/40-mm AA (II × 2)   **Electron Equipt:** Radar: 1/OPS-9   **Man:** 100 tot.
M: 2 Kawasaki-M.A.N. V8V 22/30 AMTL diesels; 2 props; 4,400 hp

REMARKS: Can carry 120 men and 20 vehicles. LST 4102 and 4103 are 1,550 tons
standard. Have U.S. Mk 51 mod. 2 GFCS, two LCVP in davits, and can carry one
LCVP on deck, amidships.

♦ **2 Yura-class utility landing ships (LSU)** Bldr: Sasebo Heavy Industries

		Laid down	L	In serv.			Laid down	L	In serv.
4171	YURA	23-4-80	10-8-80	27-3-81	4172	NOTO	23-4-80	1-11-80	27-3-81

D: 500 tons (590 fl)   **S:** 12 kts   **Dim:** 58.0 × 9.5 × 1.7 (aft)
A: 1/20-mm JM 61-MB Gatling AA
M: 2 Fuji 6L 27.5X diesels; 2 CP props; 3,000 hp   **Man:** 32 tot.

REMARKS: Both in 1979-80 Budget; request for a third in 1981-82 Budget denied. Bow
doors and ramp.

Nemuro (LST 4103)   *Ships of the World*

Noto (LSU 4172)   1981

♦ **15 U.S. LCM(6)-class landing craft**

D: 24 tons (56 fl)   **S:** 10 kts   **Dim:** 17.07 × 4.37 × 1.17 (aft)
M: 2 Yanmar diesels; 2 props; 450 hp

REMARKS: Total includes 6 units carried aboard the *Miura*-class LSTs. Built in Japan.
One ex-U.S. unit exists in reserve as YAC 32.

♦ **22 U.S. LCVP-class landing craft**

D: 13 tons (fl)   **S:** 9 kts   **Dim:** 10.90 × 3.21 × 1.04 (aft)
M: 1 Yanmar diesel; 1 prop; 225 hp

AMPHIBIOUS WARFARE SHIPS (continued)

REMARKS: Japanese-built, most with GRP hulls. Total includes the 12-15 carried by the 6 LSTs.

HYDROGRAPHIC SHIPS

♦ **1 Suma class (AGS)** Bldr: Hitachi Heavy Ind., Maisuru

	Laid down	L	In serv.
5103 SUMA	11-80	1-9-81	3-82

D: 1,100 tons **S:** 15 kts **Dim:** 72.0 × 12.8 × 3.5
A: None **M:** 2 Fuji 6 LS 27.5X diesels; 2 CP props; 3,000 hp **Man:** . . .

REMARKS: Built under 1979-80 Budget to begin replacement of the *Kasado*-class former minesweepers used as coastal survey ships. Will carry one 7.9-m boat and one 11-m inshore survey launch. Passive tank stabilization, bow-thruster fitted.

♦ **1 Futami class (AGS)**

	Bldr	Laid down	L	In serv.
5102 FUTAMI	Mitsubishi, Shimonoseki	20-1-78	9-8-78	27-2-79

Futami (AGS 5102) *Ships of the World*, 1980

D: 2,050 tons **S:** 16 kts **Dim:** 96.8 (90.0 pp) × 15.0 × 4.3
A: None **Electron Equipt:** Radar: 1/OPS-18 **Man:** 105 tot.
M: 2 Kawasaki-M.A.N. V8V 22/30 ATL diesels; 2 CP props; 4,400 hp

REMARKS: Configured for both hydrographic-surveying and cable-laying. Bow-thruster. Has three diesel and one gas-turbine generator sets. Carries one RCV-225 remote-controlled unmanned submersible.

♦ **1 Akashi class (AGS)**

	Bldr	Laid down	L	In serv.
5101 AKASHI	Nippon Kokan, Tsurumi	21-9-68	30-5-69	25-10-69

Akashi (AGS 5101) *Ships of the World*, 1978

D: 1,420 tons **S:** 16 kts **Dim:** 74.0 × 12.9 × 4.3
A: None **Electron Equipt:** Radar: . . .
M: 2 Kawasaki-M.A.N. V8V 22/30 ATL diesels; 2 CP props; 3,800 hp
Range: 16,500/14 **Man:** 70 crew, 10 scientists

REMARKS: Bow-thruster. Two cranes: one 5-ton and one 1-ton. Has extensive electronics intercept arrays, new radar.

♦ **4 Kasado-class converted minesweepers (MSC)** Bldr: Hitachi, Kanagawa

	Laid down	L	In serv.
5112 AGS 2 (ex-*Habuchi*, MSC 608)	25-8-58	19-6-59	30-9-59
5113 AGS 3 (ex-*Tatara*, MSC 610)	30-3-59	14-1-60	31-3-60
5114 AGS 4 (ex-*Hirado*, MSC 614)	14-3-60	3-10-60	17-12-60
5115 AGS 5 (ex-*Hario*, MSC 618)	. . .	. . .	1962

D: 340 tons (355 fl) **S:** 14.5 kts **Dim:** 45.7 × 8.38 × 2.3
A: None **Electron Equipt:** Radar: OPS-4
M: 2 Mitsubishi YV10ZC diesels; 2 props; 1,200 hp **Man:** 30 tot.

REMARKS: Sister AGS 1 (AGS 5111, ex-*Kasado*, MSC 604) stricken by 31-3-82.

EXPERIMENTAL SHIP

♦ **1 Kurihama class (AGE)**

	Bldr	Laid down	L	In serv.
6101 KURIHAMA	Sasebo Heavy Industries	23-3-79	20-9-79	8-4-80

D: 959 tons **S:** 15 kts **Dim:** 68.0 × 11.6 × 3.3
A: Various **Electron Equipt:** Radar: 1/OPS-9B
M: 2 Fuji 6S 30B diesels; 2 props; 2,600 hp (plus 2 electric auxiliary propulsors; 400 hp)
Man: 42 crew + 13 technicians

EXPERIMENTAL SHIP (continued)

Kurihama (AGE 6101)   *Ships of the World*, 1980

REMARKS: For testing mines, torpedoes, and sonars. In 1979-80 Budget. Has Flume-type passive stabilization tanks in superstructure.

CABLE-LAYER

◆ 1 Muroto class (ARC)

	Bldr	Laid down	L	In serv.
482 MUROTO	Mitsubishi, Shimonoseki	28-11-78	25-7-79	27-3-80

Muroto (AGS 482)   *Ships of the World*

D: 4,500 tons **S:** 17 kts **Dim:** 131.0 × 17.4 × 5.7
A: None **Electron Equipt:** Radar: 1/OPS. . .
M: 2 Mitsubishi MTU V8V 22/30 diesels; 2 CP props; 4,400 hp **Man:** 122 tot.

REMARKS: Intended to replace the *Tsugaru* as naval cable layer. Able to lay cable over bow or stern at 2-6 knots. Bow-thruster. Similar to commercial *Kuroshio Maru*. Has extensive facilities for oceanographic research.

NOTE: The former cable-layer *Tsugaru* (ARC 481) was redesignated ASU 7001 in 1979 and is listed under training ships.

SUBMARINE RESCUE SHIPS

◆ 0 (+1) new construction (ASR)

	Bldr	Laid down	L	In serv.
403 N...	...	...	...	...

D: 3,600 tons **S:** 16 kts **Dim:** 107.0 × 18.0 × 8.0
M: 2 diesels; 2 props; . . . hp **Man:** . . .

REMARKS: In 1981-82 Budget, to replace *Chihaya*. Will carry a 40-ton rescue submersible (12.0 × 3.2 × 3.2) capable of 4 kts.

◆ 1 Fushimi class (ASR)

	Bldr	Laid down	L	In serv.
402 FUSHIMI	Sumitomo, Uraga	5-11-68	10-9-69	10-2-70

Fushimi (ASR 402)   *Ships of the World*, 1975

D: 1,430 tons **S:** 16 kts **Dim:** 76.0 × 12.5 × 3.8
Electron Equipt: Radar: OPS-9
                    Sonar: SQS-11A
M: 1 Kawasaki-M.A.N. V6V 22/30 ATL diesel; 1 prop; 3,000 hp **Man:** 102 tot.

REMARKS: Has one rescue bell, two decompression chambers; one 12-ton crane.

◆ 1 Chihaya class (ASR)

	Bldr	Laid down	L	In serv.
401 CHIHAYA	Mitsubishi, Yokohama	15-3-60	4-10-60	15-3-61

Chihaya (ASR 401)   *Ships of the World*

D: 1,340 tons (1,800 fl) **S:** 15 kts **Dim:** 73.0 × 12.0 × 3.9 **Man:** 90 tot.
Electron Equipt: Radar: OPS-4 Sonar: SQS-11A
M: 1 Yokohama-M.A.N. G6Z S170 diesel; 2,700 hp **Range:** 5,000/12

REMARKS: Has a McCann rescue bell for six persons, 12-ton crane, four flotation pontoons, and a 4-point mooring system.

REPLENISHMENT OILERS (AOE/AO)

♦ 1 Sagami class (AOE)

	Bldr	Laid down	L	In serv.
421 SAGAMI	Hitachi, Maizuru	28-9-77	4-9-78	30-3-79

Sagami (AOE 421) — *Ships of the World*, 1979

D: 5,000 tons (11,600 fl) **S:** 22 kts **Dim:** 146.0 (140.0 pp) × 19.0 × 7.3
A: None **Electron Equipt:** Radar: 1/OPS-16
M: 2 Type 12 DRV diesels; 2 props; 18,600 hp **Range:** 9,500/20
Man: 130 tot.

REMARKS: Has three stations per side, two for liquid transfers, one for solid. Large helicopter deck but no hangar. In addition to fuel oil, diesel fuel, and JP-5 aviation fuel, carries food and ammunition. 1975-76 budget.

♦ 1 Hamana class (AO)

	Bldr	Laid down	L	In serv.
411 HAMANA	Uraga DY	17-4-61	24-10-61	10-3-62

Hamana (AO 411) — Uraga

D: 2,900 tons (7,550 fl) **S:** 16 kts **Dim:** 128.0 × 15.7 × 6.3
A: 2/40-mm AA (II × 1) **Electron Equipt:** Radar: OPS-9
M: 1 Yokohama-M.A.N. KGZ 6D/150C diesel; 1 prop; 5,000 hp **Man:** 100 tot.

REMARKS: Refitted, 1978-79, with two fueling positions per side. Mk 51, mod. 2, director for gunmount. Carries only a small cargo of stores for transfer via highline station forward.

TRAINING SHIPS

♦ 1 Katori-class cadet-training ship (TV)

	Bldr	Laid down	L	In serv.
3501 KATORI	Ishikawajima Harima, Tokyo	8-12-67	19-11-68	10-9-69

Katori (TV 3501) — L. & L. Van Ginderen, 1979

D: 3,372 tons (4,100 fl) **S:** 25 kts **Dim:** 127.5 (122.0 pp) × 15.0 × 4.35
A: 4/76.2-mm DP Mk 33 (II × 2)—1/375-mm Bofors ASW RL (IV × 1)—6/324-mm Mk 32 ASW TT (III × 2)
Electron Equipt: Radars: 1/SPS-12, 1/OPS-15, 1/Mk 34
　　　　　　　　　Sonar: OQS-3
M: 2 sets Ishikawajima GT; 2 props; 20,000 hp **Boilers:** 2 **Range:** 7,000/18
Man: 295 crew + 165 cadets

REMARKS: U.S. Mk 63 GFCS system for 76.2-mm guns. After superstructure contains an auditorium. Helicopter deck is also used for ceremonial functions and calisthenics. An Intelset satellite communication system was added in mid-1979.

♦ 1 Azuma-class target service ship (ATS)

	Bldr	Laid down	L	In serv.
4201 AZUMA	Hitachi, Maizuru	15-7-68	14-4-69	26-11-69

Azuma (ATS 4201) — *Ships of the World*, 1976

TRAINING SHIPS (continued)

D: 1,950 tons (2,400 fl) **S:** 18 kts **Dim:** 98.0 (94.0 pp) × 13.0 × 3.8
A: 1/76.2-mm DP Mk 34—2/Mk 4 launchers for Mk 32 ASW torpedoes
Electron Equipt: Radars: 1/OPS-15, 1/SPS-40, 1/tracking radar
          Sonar: SQS-11A
M: 2 Kawasaki-M.A.N. V8V 23/30 ATL diesels; 2 props; 4,000 hp
Electric: 700 kw **Man:** 185 tot.

REMARKS: Has ten KD2R-5 and three BQM-34 drones. Portable catapult on helicopter deck for launching. Hangar is used for drone check-out and storage. Special drone-tracking radar above the bridge. Has the only SPS-40 in Japanese service. Mk 51 mod. 2 director for gun (no radar). Obsolescent ASW torpedo system may have been removed.

♦ **5 target-support craft (ASU)** Bldr: . . .

	Laid down	L	In serv.
ASU 81 (ex-YAS 101)	10-10-67	18-1-68	30-3-68
ASU 82 (ex-YAS 102)	25-9-68	20-12-68	31-3-68
ASU 83 (ex-YAS 103)	2-4-71	24-5-71	30-9-71
ASU 84 (ex-YAS 104)	4-2-72	15-6-73	19-9-73
ASU 85 (ex-YAS 105)	20-2-73	16-7-73	19-9-73

ASU 85—wearing former number   1974

D: 490 tons (543 fl) **S:** 14.5 kts **Dim:** 51.5 × 10.0 × 2.6
Electron Equipt: Radar: OPS-10 (ASU 84: OPS-29; ASU 85: OPS-19)
M: 2 Akasaka UH-527-42 diesels; 2 props; 1,600 hp
Range: 2,500/12 **Man:** 26 men + 14 passengers

REMARKS: ASU 82 is configured as a rescue ship. The others are intended to carry, control, recover, and service up to six KD2R-5 drone target aircraft. ASU 81: 480 tons std.; ASU 85: 500 tons std.

♦ **2 Harukaze-class former destroyers (ASU)**

	Bldr	Laid down	L	In serv.
7002 HARUKAZE (ex-DD 101)	Mitsubishi, Nagasaki	15-12-54	20-9-55	26-4-56
7003 YUKIKAZE (ex-DD 102)	Mitsubishi, Kobe	17-12-54	20-8-55	31-7-56

Harukaze (ASU 7002, ex-DD 101)   *Ships of the World, 1981*

D: 1,700 tons (2,400 fl) **S:** 30 kts **Dim:** 106.3 × 10.5 × 4.4 (hull)
A: ASU 7002: 3/127-mm DP 38-cal. (I × 3)—8/40-mm AA (IV × 2)—2/Hedgehog Mk 10
    ASU 7003: 1/127-mm DP—4/40-mm AA (IV × 1)
Electron Equipt: Radar: 1/SPS-5, 1/SPS-6, 1/Mk 26, 2 (7003: 1) Mk 34
              Sonar: SQS-29 (ASU 7003: towed passive array also)
M: 2 sets Mitsubishi-Escher-Wyss (ASU 7003: Westinghouse) GT; 2 props; 30,000 hp
Boilers: 2; 43 kg/cm², 435°C **Fuel:** 557 tons **Range:** 6,000/18 **Man:** . . .

REMARKS: Redesignated ASU (Auxiliary, Special Use) on 27-3-81 and subordinated to the Fleet Training and Development Command. Since 1976, ASU 7003 has conducted trials with a towed passive hydrophone array, necessitating the removal of the two after 127-mm guns; the ship's forward quadruple 40-mm AA has been replaced by the 127-mm practice loading machine, and she carries a prototype waste-disposal system between the stacks. ASU 7003 has a Mk 52 GFCS (Mk 26 radar) atop the bridge, and both have one Mk 63 GFCS per 40-mm mount, with the Mk 34 radar mounted on the gunmount; ASU 7002 has a Contraves NA 10 GFCS in place of the Mk 52.

♦ **1 Tsugaru class (ASU, ex-ARC)**

	Bldr	Laid down	L	In serv.
7001 TSUGARU (ex-ARC 481)	Yokohama SY	18-12-54	19-7-55	15-12-55

D: 2,150 tons **S:** 13 kts **Dim:** 103.0 × 14.6 × 4.9
A: 2/20-mm AA (I × 2) **Electron Equipt:** Radar: 1/OPS-16
M: 2 Sulzer diesels; 2 props; 3,200 hp **Man:** 103 tot.

TRAINING SHIPS *(continued)*

Tsugaru (ASU 7001, ex-ARC 481) 1971

REMARKS: Originally completed as a minelayer/cable-layer; between 10-7-69 and 30-4-70 she was lengthened and the amidships part of her hull widened by 2.2 meters at Nippon Kokan, Tsurumi. Also, her cable facilities were greatly enlarged. Redesignated ASU (Auxiliary, Special Use) in 1979.

♦ 5 Mizutori-class former patrol boats (ASU)

	Bldr	Laid down	L	In serv.
ASU 87 KASASAGI (ex-PC 314)	Fujinagata, Osaka	18-12-59	31-5-60	31-10-60
ASU 89 MIZUTORI (ex-PC 311)	Kawasaki, Kobe	13-3-59	22-9-59	27-2-60
ASU 90 YAMADORI (ex-PC 312)	Fujinagata, Osaka	13-3-59	22-10-59	15-3-60
ASU . . . OTORI (ex-PC 313)	Kure SY	16-12-59	27-5-60	13-10-60
ASU . . . HATSUKARI (ex-PC 315)	Sasebo DY	25-1-60	24-6-60	15-11-60

Kasasagi (ASU 87, ex-PC 314)—note ESM radome L. & L. Van Ginderen, 1980

D: 420 tons (450 fl) **S:** 20 kts **Dim:** 60.00 × 7.10 × 2.35
A: 2/40-mm AA (II × 1)—2/Mk 4 launchers for Mk 32 ASW torpedoes—1/Mk 10 Hedgehog—1/d.c. rack
Electron Equipt: Radar: 1/OPS-35 or OPS-36, 1/Mk 34
    Sonar: SQS-11A
M: 2 Kawasaki-M.A.N. V8V diesels; 2 props; 3,800 hp **Fuel:** 24 tons
Range: 3,000/12 **Man:** 70 tot.

REMARKS: Reclassified for training duties: ASU 87, 89, and 90 on 27-3-81, and the others prior to 31-3-82. The three units of the class remaining designated PC may be retyped later as well. Mk 63 GFCS for 40-mm AA.

♦ 4 Umitaka-class former patrol boats

	Bldr	Laid down	L	In serv.
ASU 86 UMITAKA (ex-PC 309)	Kawasaki, Kobe	13-3-59	25-7-59	30-11-59
ASU 88 OOTAKA (ex-PC 310)	Kure SY	13-3-59	2-9-59	14-1-60
ASU . . . WAKATAKA (ex-PC 317)	Kure SY	5-3-62	13-11-62	30-3-63
ASU. . . KUMATAKA (ex-PC 318)	Fujinagata, Osaka	20-3-63	21-10-63	25-3-64

Ootaka (ASU 88, ex-PC 310) *Ships of the World*

D: 490 tons (530 fl) **S:** 20 kts **Dim:** 60.0 × 7.1 × 2.4 (hull)
A: 2/40-mm AA (II × 1)—ASU 86, 88: 2/Mk 4 launchers for Mk 32 ASW torpedoes; others: 6/324-mm Mk 32 ASW TT (III × 2)—1/Mk 10 Hedgehog—1/d.c. rack
Electron Equipt: Radar: ASU 86, 88: 1/OPS-35; ex-PC 317: 1/OPS-36; ex-PC 318: 1/OPS-16; all: 1/Mk 34
    Sonar: SQS-11A
M: 2 Mitsui-Burmeister & Wain V8V diesels; 2 props; 4,000 hp **Fuel:** 24 tons
Range: 3,000/12 **Man:** 80 tot.

REMARKS: Reclassified for training duties: ASU 86 in 1980, ASU 88 on 27-3-81, others prior to 31-3-82. Mk 63 GFCS for 40-mm AA.

ICEBREAKERS

♦ 0 (+1) new construction (AGB)

	Bldr	Laid down	L	In serv.
5002 SHIRASE	Nippon Kokan, Tsurumi	3-81	12-81	9-82

Shirase (AGB 5002)—official model *Ships of the World*, 1981

D: 11,660 tons (18,900 fl) **S:** 19 kts **Dim:** 134.0 × 28.0 × 9.2
M: 6 M.A.N.-Mitsui 12V42M diesels, electric drive; 3 props; 30,000 hp
Range: 25,000/15 **Man:** 37 officers, 137 men, plus 60 passengers

ICEBREAKERS (continued)

REMARKS: Built under 1979-80 Budget. Cargo capacity: 1,000 tons. Will have hangar and flight deck for 2 CH-53E and 1 OH-6 helicopters.

♦ **1 icebreaker** Bldr: Nippon Kokan, Tsurumi

	Laid down	L	In serv.
5001 FUJI	28-8-64	18-3-65	15-7-65

Fuji (AGB 5001)   J.-C. Bellonne, 1974

D: 5,299 tons (8,566 fl) **S:** 16.5 kts **Dim:** 100.0 (90.0 pp) × 22.0 × 8.3
Electron Equipt: Radars: 1/OPS-4, 1/OPS-16, 1/weather
                Sonar: SQS-11A
                TACAN: URN-20
M: 4 Mitsubishi-M.A.N. 48V30/42 AL diesels, electric drive; 2 props; 12,000 hp
Fuel: 1,900 tons **Range:** 15,000/15 **Man:** 200 crew + 45 scientists

REMARKS: Carries three large and one small helicopters. Intended for antarctic exploration and support. Cargo capacity in forward hold: 450 tons. Can break 2.5-meter ice. Passive tank roll stabilization. Hull plating up to 45 mm thick.

YACHT

♦ **1 former ASW patrol boat, converted (ASY)**

	Bldr	Laid down	L	In serv.
91 HAYABUSA (ex-PC 308)	Mitsubishi, Nagasaki	23-5-56	20-11-56	10-6-57

D: 400 tons **S:** 13 kts **Dim:** 58.0 × 7.8 × 2.2 **A:** None
M: 2 diesels; 2 props; 1,000 hp **Man:** 35 crew, plus 125 passengers

REMARKS: Unique unit, fitted with 5,000-hp gas turbine on centerline shaft, 1962-70. Rebuilt 20-11-77 to 15-4-78 at Yokohama Yacht Co. as naval yacht, with extensive superstructure added aft, new engines. Painted white.

SERVICE SHIPS AND CRAFT

NOTE: All Japanese Navy service ships and craft are listed below in the alphabetical order of the two- or three-letter designator system employed to define their functions. Self-propelled units have 2-digit hull numbers following the letter designator (as in "YO 01"). Non-self-propelled craft with the same functions have 3-digit numbers starting with "1" (as in "YO 102"). Self-propelled units that have returned to

an original type designation *after* an initial type change receive 3-digit numbers beginning with "2" (as in "YG 202," ex-YO 20, ex-YG 08).

STORAGE CRAFT (HULKS) (YAC)

♦ **2 Ikazuchi-class former frigates**

	Bldr	L	In serv.
YAC 30 IKAZUCHI (ex-DE 202)	Kawasaki, Kobe	6-9-55	29-5-56
YAC 31 INAZUMA (ex-DE 203)	Mitsui, Tamano	4-8-55	5-3-56

D: 1,070 tons **S:** 25 kts **Dim:** 87.50 × 8.70 × 3.10 (hull)
A: 2/76.2-mm DP Mk 34 (I × 2)—2/40-mm AA (II × 1)—1/Mk 10 Hedgehog—8/
    d.c. projectors—2/d.c. racks
Electron Equipt: Radar: 1/SPS-5, 1/SPS-6, 1/Mk 34
                   Sonar: SQS-11A
M: 2 Mitsui 9 UET diesels; 2 props; 12,000 hp **Range:** 6,000/16

REMARKS: Retained in mothballed condition for emergency recommissioning; will probably strike soon. Have 1 U.S. Mk 63 radar GFCS for 76.2-mm guns and 1 Mk 51 mod. 2 for the after 76.2-mm gun and the 40-mm AA. The 76.2-mm guns have been dismounted.

NOTE: YAC 32, a former U.S. LCM(6)-class landing craft, also exists in storage. Sisters YAC 24 through 27 were stricken 1980, as was *Akebono* (YAC 29, ex-DE 201).

MINE TRIALS AND SERVICE CRAFT (YAL)

♦ **1 YAL 01 class**

YAL 01 (In serv. 22-3-76)

D: 240 tons (265 fl) **S:** 12 kts **Dim:** 37.00 × 8.00 × 1.90
A: mine rails **M:** 2 Type 64 H 19-E-4A diesels; 2 props; 800 hp **Man:** 16 tot.

♦ **3 former U.S. LCU 1466-class landing craft**

YAL 02 (L: 23-1-55) YAL 03 (L: 5-1-55) YAL 04 (L: 13-12-54)

D: 180 tons (347 fl) **S:** 9 kts **Dim:** 35.08 × 10.36 × 1.60 (aft)
A: 2/20-mm AA (I × 2)—mines
M: 3 Gray Marine 64YTL diesels; 3 props; 675 hp
Fuel: 11 tons **Range:** 1,200/6 **Man:** . . .

REMARKS: Three of the six-unit LCU 2001 class (ex-U.S. LCU 1602-1607), built in Japan under the Offshore Procurement Program), reconfigured to serve as exercise mine planters.

SPECIAL SERVICE CRAFT (YAS)

♦ **1 explosive-ordnance disposal diving tender**

	Bldr	Laid down	L	In serv.
YAS 69 ERIMO	Uraga DY	1955	12-7-55	28-12-55

D: 630 tons (670 fl) **S:** 18 kts **Dim:** 64.0 × 7.93 × 2.60 (2.95 max.)
A: 2/40-mm AA (II × 1)—2/20-mm AA (I × 2)—1/Mk 10 Hedgehog
M: 2 Sasebo-LKT diesels; 2 props; 2,500 hp **Man:** 74 tot.

REMARKS: Former minelayer (491), converted 1975-76. Retains some ASW ordnance and could still be used as a minelayer.

SPECIAL SERVICE CRAFT (*continued*)

♦ 11 (+2) Kasado-class former coastal minesweepers

	Bldr	L	In serv.
YAS 62 SHISAKA (ex-MSC 605)	Nippon Kokan, Tsurumi	20-3-58	16-8-58
YAS 64 SAKITO (ex-MSC 607)	Nippon Kokan, Tsurumi	22-4-59	31-8-59
YAS 65 KANAWA (ex-MSC 606)	Hitachi, Kanagawa	22-4-59	24-7-59
YAS 66 TSUKUMI (ex-MSC 611)	Nippon Kokan, Tsurumi	12-1-60	30-4-60
YAS 67 MIKURA (ex-MSC 612)	Hitachi, Kanagawa	14-3-60	27-5-60
YAS 68 SHIKINE (ex-MSC 613)	Nippon Kokan, Tsurumi	22-7-60	15-11-60
YAS 70 HOTAKA (ex-MSC 616)	Hitachi, Kanagawa	23-10-61	24-2-62
YAS 71 KARATO (ex-MSC 617)	Nippon Kokan, Tsurumi	11-12-62	23-3-63
YAS 72 MUTSURE (ex-MSC 619)	Nippon Kokan, Tsurumi	16-12-63	24-3-64
YAS 73 CHIBURI (ex-MSC 620)	Hitachi, Kanagawa	29-11-63	25-3-64
YAS 74 KUDAKO (ex-MSC 622)	Hitachi, Kanagawa	8-12-64	24-3-65
YAS. . . RESHIRI (ex-MSC 623)	Nippon Kokan, Tsurumi	22-11-65	5-3-66
YAS. . . REBUN (ex-MSC 624)	Hitachi, Kanagawa	7-12-65	24-3-66

D: 330-340 tons (350-360 fl) **S:** 14 kts **Dim:** 45.7 × 8.38 × 2.30
A: 1/20-mm AA **Electron Equipt:** Radar: 1/OPS-9
M: 2 Mitsubishi YV102-DE diesels; 2 props; 1,200 hp
Range: 2,000/10 **Man:** 40 tot.

REMARKS: Majority converted to serve as mine-disposal divers' support ships. YAS 66 and 67 are tenders to the Gunnery School. Wooden construction. Sister *Koshiki* (YAS 63, ex-MSC 615) stricken 1981; other early units likely to be replaced by the remaining MSC-designated *Kasado*-class minesweepers, including MSC 623, 624 by 31-3-82.

NOTE: Earlier ex-minesweepers *Atada* (YAS 56, ex-MSC 601) and *Yashiro* (YAS 58, ex-MSC 603) stricken 1981.

OIL SLUDGE REMOVAL CRAFT (YB)

♦ 1 YB 01-class lighter (L: 31-3-75)

YB 01

D: 177 tons **S:** 9 kts **Dim:** 27.5 × 5.2 × 1.9
M: 1 diesel; 230 hp **Cargo:** 100 dwt

♦ 4 YB 101-class barges (In serv. 1975-76)

YB 101-104

D: 100 dwt **Dim:** 17.0 × 5.2 × 2.0 **M:** non-self-propelled

SELF-PROPELLED FLOATING CRANES (YC)

♦ 1 YC 09 class

YC 09 (In serv. 25-2-74)

D: 260 tons **S:** 6 kts **Dim:** 26.0 × 14.0 × 0.9 **M:** 2 diesels; 2 props; 280 hp

♦ 3 YC 06 class

YC 06 (In serv. 31-3-69) YC 07 (In serv. 28-2-70) YC 08 (In serv. 29-3-72)

D: 150 tons **S:** 5 kts **Dim:** 24.0 × 10.0 × 0.8 **M:** 2 diesels; 2 props; 240 hp
REMARKS: In service 1969-72.

♦ 1 YC 05 class

YC 05 (In serv. 27-3-67)

D: 110 tons **S:** 5 kts **Dim:** 22.0 × 10.0 × 0.9 **M:** 2 diesels; 180 hp

DOCKYARD SERVICE CRAFT (YD)

YD 01, 02: 0.8 tons, 7.60 × 1.90, rowboats in serv. 25-3-75; YD 03: 1.7 tons, same dimensions, in service 1978; YD 04: 0.5 tons, in serv. 25-12-79

FIREBOAT (YE)

♦ 1 Shobo class Bldr: Azumo, Yokosuka (In serv. 28-2-64)

YE 41 SHOBO 1 (ex-*Kosuko* 6)

D: 45 tons **S:** 19 kts **Dim:** 22.9 × 5.5 × 1.0 **M:** 3 diesels; 3 props; 1,300 hp

REMARKS: Employed as Air/Sea Rescue boat and fireboat at Iwakuni Air Station for seaplanes. Three firefighting monitors. Re-engined 1977; originally made 30 kts on 2,800 hp.

COMMUNICATIONS BOATS (YF)

♦ 67 miscellaneous service boats

YF 1021-1028: ex-U.S. LCVP landing craft (redesignated 1964-1980); YF 2097-YF 2101, 2103-2109 are ex-U.S. LCM(6) landing craft redesignated in Nov.-Dec. 1954.
  The remainder consist of small class of personnel launches, of which the latest unit is typical:
YF 1028 (In serv. 26-3-80)

D: 9 tons **S:** 14 kts **Dim:** 13.00 × 3.80 × 0.60
M: 2 Type E 120 T-MF6RE diesels; 2 props; 280 hp **Cargo:** 73 passengers

Aside from the above, the following are in service:
YF 2060-2096, YF 2110-2122. The majority are of wood or fiberglass construction and displace 8.6 to 13 tons standard.

JET ENGINE FUEL CRAFT (YG)

♦ 2 YG 07-class lighters

YG 07 (In serv. 30-3-73) YG 202 (ex-YO 20, ex-YG 08; In serv. 29-3-77)

D: 270 dwt **S:** 10 kts **Dim:** 36.7 × 6.8 × 2.6
M: 1 diesel; 1 prop; 350 hp

REMARKS: Sister YG 08 reclassified YO 20 in 1979, then again reclassified YG 202 in 1981.

NOTE: Fuel lighters YG 01 to YG 06 reclassified to YO 15-19 in 1979-80.

CARGO CRAFT (YL)

♦ 1 YL 09-class lighter

	Laid down	L	In serv.
YL 09	24-11-79	3-3-80	28-3-80

D: 126 tons (fl) **S:** 9-10 kts **Dim:** 27.00 × 7.00 × 1.04
M: 2 Type E 120 T-MF6 RE diesels; 2 props; 560 hp **Man:** 5 tot.

REMARKS: 50 dwt. Resembles a U.S. LCM(8) and has a bow ramp, two 2-ton stores cranes.

CARGO CRAFT (continued)

YL 09

Ships of the World, 1980

♦ **1 YL 08-class lighter**

YL 08 (In serv. 10-3-67)

   D: 50 dwt **S:** 8 kts **Dim:** 22.40 × 5.10 × 1.20 **M:** 1 diesel; 1 prop; 180 hp

♦ **5 YL 02-class lighters**

YL 03 (In serv. 31-5-54)   YL 05 (In serv. 30-11-54)   YL 07 (In serv. 30-11-54)
YL 04 (In serv. 31-5-54)   YL 06 (In serv. 30-11-54)

   D: 50 dwt **S:** 8 kts **Dim:** 20.00 × 5.10 × 1.20
   M: 1 diesel; 1 prop; 100 hp

NOTE: Sister YL 02 stricken 1979.

♦ **1 YL 01-class lighter**

YL 01 (In serv. 30-5-53)

   D: 50 dwt **S:** 7 kts **Dim:** 20.00 × 5.50 × 1.20
   M: 1 diesel; 1 prop; 90 hp

♦ **1 YL 119-class barge**

YL 119 (In serv. 20-3-71)

   D: 200 dwt **Dim:** 34.00 × 13.00 × 1.00

♦ **3 YL 116-class barges**

YL 116 (In serv. 21-12-63)   YL 117 (In serv. 25-2-64)   YL 118 (In serv. 31-3-66)

   D: 100 dwt **Dim:** 21.50 × 8.40 × 1.00

♦ **2 YL 114-class barges**

YL 114 (In serv. 20-2-63)   YL 115 (In serv. 12-3-63)

   D: 80 dwt **Dim:** 18.40 × 7.40 × 0.90

FUEL LIGHTERS (YO)

NOTE: YO is now applied to all fuel carriers except jet fuel carriers, which are typed YG.

♦ **2 YO 21 class** Bldr: Yoshiura Shipbuilding

	Laid down	L	In serv.
YO 21	. . .	15-3-80	31-3-80
YO 22	11-11-80	26-2-81	28-2-81

   D: 490 tons (694 fl) **S:** 9 kts **Dim:** 45.4 × 7.8 × 2.9
   M: 2 Yanmar 6 MA diesels; 2 props; 460 hp **Cargo:** 520m³

♦ **1 YO 19-class former diesel fuel lighter**

YO 19 (ex-YG 06; In serv. 20-6-63)

   D: 270 dwt **S:** 9 kts **Dim:** 34.4 × 6.8 × 2.8 **M:** 2 diesels; 2 props; 330 hp

REMARKS: Reclassified under FY 1979-80. YO 20 (ex-YG 08) reclassified YG 202 in 1981.

♦ **4 YO 15-class former diesel fuel lighters**

	In serv.		In serv.
YO 15 (ex-YG 01)	20-5-53	YO 17 (ex-YG 03)	28-2-54
YO 16 (ex-YG 02)	15-10-53	YO 18 (ex-YG 04)	10-1-55

   D: 100 dwt **S:** 8 kts **Dim:** 23.0 × 5.0 × 2.0 **M:** 1 diesel; 1 prop; 90 hp

REMARKS: Reclassified 1979-80.

♦ **1 YO 14-class lighter**

YO 14 (In serv. 31-3-76)

   D: 490 dwt **S:** 9 kts **Dim:** 45.0 × 7.8 × 2.9 **M:** 2 diesels; 2 props; 460 hp

♦ **4 YO 10-class lighters**

YO 10 (In serv. 31-3-65)   YO 12 (In serv. 21-3-67)
YO 11 (In serv. 14-3-66)   YO 13 (In serv. 31-3-67)

   D: 290 dwt **S:** 9 kts **Dim:** 36.5 × 6.8 × 2.6 **M:** 2 diesels; 2 props; 360 hp

♦ **3 YO 07-class lighters**

YO 07 (In serv. 28-2-63)   YO 08 (In serv. 29-2-64)   YO 09 (In serv. 15-3-65)

   D: 490 dwt **S:** 9 kts **Dim:** 43.9 × 7.8 × 3.1
   M: 2 diesels; 400 hp

♦ **4 YO 03-class lighters**

YO 03 (In serv. 15-4-55)   YO 05 (In serv. 15-3-56)
YO 04 (In serv. 15-4-55)   YO 06 (In serv. 15-3-56)

   D: 300 dwt **S:** 7 kts **Dim:** 33.0 × 7.0 × 2.6
   M: 2 diesels; 150 hp

NOTE: Fuel lighters YO 01 and YO 02 stricken 1981 and 1979, respectively.

♦ **2 YO 107-class barges**

YO 107 (In serv. 29-6-53)   YO 108 (In serv. 15-3-54)

   D: 100 dwt **Dim:** 17.00 × 5.20 × 2.20

♦ **1 YO 106-class barge**

YO 106 (In serv. 20-5-53)

   D: 250 dwt **Dim:** 23.00 × 7.00 × 2.50

DEBRIS CLEARANCE CRAFT (YS)

♦ 1 catamaran "sweeper boat"

YS 01 (In serv. 30-3-79)

    D: 80 tons **S:** 9 kts **Dim:** 22.0 × 7.80 × 1.40
    M: 2 diesels; 2 props; 460 hp **Man:** 6 tot.

REMARKS: Stationed at Iwakuni Air Station seaplane base; used to clear floating debris in seaplane landing lanes and as a marker buoy tender.

TUGS (YT)

♦ 3 YT 60-class pusher tugs Bldr: Yokohama Yacht

YT 60 (In serv. 31-3-80)   YT 62 (In serv. 16-3-81)
YT 61 (In serv. 26-3-80)

YT 61   *Ships of the World*, 1980

    D: 30 tons (37 fl) **S:** 8.6 kts **Dim:** 15.50 × 4.20 × 1.50 (0.97 hull)
    M: 2 Isuzu E 120-MF64A diesels; 2 cycloidal props; 380 hp

♦ 1 YT 59-class pusher tug

YT 59 (In serv. 16-1-79)

    D: 30 tons **S:** 10 kts **Dim:** 14.50 × 4.00 × 1.00
    M: 2 diesels; 2 props; 320 hp

♦ 1 YT 58-class large harbor tug

YT 58 (In serv. 31-10-78)

    D: 260 tons **S:** 11 kts **Dim:** 28.40 × 8.60 × 2.50
    M: 2 diesels;. . . props; 1,800 hp

♦ 3 YT 55-class large harbor tugs

YT 55 (In serv. 22-8-75)   YT 56 (In serv. 13-7-76)   YT 57 (In serv. 22-8-77)

    D: 200 tons **S:** 10 kts **Dim:** 25.70 × 7.00 × 2.30
    M: 2 diesels; 1 prop; 1,500 hp

♦ 1 YT 50-class former U.S. LCM(6) landing craft

YT 52 (ex-. . . , In serv. 14-10-72)

    D: 26 tons **S:** 10 kts **Dim:** 17.00 × 4.20 × 0.70
    M: 2 Gray Marine 64HN9 diesels; 2 props; 450 hp

REMARKS: Landing craft decked over and converted to a pusher tug. Sister YT 50 discarded.

♦ 8 YT 35-class harbor tugs

YT 35 (In serv. 28-2-63)   YT 41 (In serv. 31-3-66)   YT 46 (In serv. 29-3-67)
YT 37 (In serv. 31-3-65)   YT 44 (In serv. 29-3-67)   YT 48 (In serv. 31-3-68)
YT 40 (In serv. 31-3-66)   YT 45 (In serv. 30-3-67)

YT 35   *Ships of the World*, 1979

    D: 100 tons **S:** 10 kts **Dim:** 23.80 × 5.40 × 1.80
    M: 2 diesels; 2 props; 400 hp

♦ 10 YT 34-class harbor pusher tugs

YT 34 (In serv. 20-3-63)   YT 42 (In serv. 31-3-65)   YT 51 (In serv. 28-2-72)
YT 36 (In serv. 14-3-64)   YT 43 (In serv. 29-3-66)   YT 54 (In serv. 24-3-75)
YT 38 (In serv. 31-3-65)   YT 47 (In serv. 20-1-67)
YT 39 (In serv. 31-3-65)   YT 49 (In serv. 5-3-68)

    D: 28 tons (30 fl) **S:** 9 kts **Dim:** 14.50 × 4.00 × 1.00
    M: 2 diesels; 2 props; 320 hp **Man:** 3 tot.

REMARKS: Conventional tugs. Sisters YT 27 and 33 stricken 1979, and YT 32 during 1981.

TRAINING TENDER (YTE)

♦ 1 navigational training tender Bldr: Ando Iron Works

YTE 11 (In serv. 31-3-73)

    D: 120 tons (170 fl) **S:** 13 kts **Dim:** 33.0 × 7.0 × 1.5
    M: 2 Shinko-Zoki SG175/CM diesels; 2 props; 1,400 hp

REMARKS: Based at Etajima Naval Academy to teach officer cadets ship-handling and navigation. Can carry 25 cadets.

TRAINING TENDER (*continued*)

YTE 11   *Ships of the World*, 1979

SEAPLANE BUOY TENDERS (YV)

♦ **3 YV 01 class**

YV 01 (In serv. 30-3-68)   YV 02 (In serv. 28-3-69)   YV 03 (In serv. 20-3-70)

YV 01   *Ships of the World*

   D: 45 tons   **S:** 10 kts   **Dim:** 20.0 × 4.40 × 1.00
   M: 2 diesels; 2 props; 240 hp

REMARKS: Maintain seaplane fairway marker buoys.

WATER LIGHTERS (YW)

♦ **5 YW 12 class**

YW 12 (In serv. 14-3-64)   YW 15 (In serv. 20-3-67)
YW 13 (In serv. 28-3-66)   YW 16 (In serv. 20-3-67)
YW 14 (In serv. 30-3-66)

   D: 160 dwt   **S:** 8 kts   **Dim:** 30.5 × 5.7 × 2.2
   M: 1 diesel; 180 hp

YW 12 (YO and YG lighters similar)   *Ships of the World*, 1979

♦ **1 YW 11 class**

YW 11 (In serv. 25-3-64)

   D: 310 dwt   **S:** 10 kts   **Dim:** 36.7 × 6.8 × 2.8   **M:** 2 diesels; 2 props; 360 hp

♦ **1 YW 10 class**

YW 10 (In serv. 20-3-63)

   D: 100 dwt   **S:** 8 kts   **Dim:** 23.5 × 5.1 × 1.0   **M:** 1 diesel; 160 hp

♦ **7 YW 03 class**

YW 03 (In serv. 22-3-54)   YW 06 (In serv. 20-12-54)   YW 09 (In serv. 20-12-54)
YW 04 (In serv. 31-3-54)   YW 07 (In serv. 11-12-54)
YW 05 (In serv. 20-12-54)   YW 08 (In serv. 20-12-54)

   D: 150 dwt   **S:** 8 kts   **Dim:** 27.0 × 5.5 × 2.1
   M: 1 diesel; 75 hp

♦ **1 YW 02 class**

YW 02 (In serv. 20-5-53)

   D: 150 dwt   **S:** 9 kts   **Dim:** 27.0 × 5.5 × 2.1   **M:** 1 diesel; 90 hp

MOTOR BOATS (B)

♦ **12 miscellaneous**

B 4005: 15 tons—4.00 × 1.70 × 0.60—8 kts (In serv. 30-3-65)
B 4006: 8 tons—13.00 × 3.20 × 0.50—14 kts (In serv. 16-3-76)
B 4007-4013: 1 ton—5.00 × 2.10 × 0.40—22 kts (All in serv. 26-1-76)
B 4014-4016: 8 tons—13.00 × 3.20 × 0.50—14 kts (In serv. 1978-80)

REMARKS: Wooden or fiberglass hulled. B 4016 capable of 18 kts.

ROWING CRAFT AND SAILBOATS

59 "C" group: C 5108-5112, 5075, 5090-5107, 5113-5147

   D: 1.5 tons   **Dim:** 9.0 × 2.5 × . . .

35 "T" group: T 6033, 6046-6048, 6050-6080

   D: .5 tons   **Dim:** 6.0 × 1.6 × . . .

11 "Y" group sailboats: Y 1010-1020

MARITIME SAFETY AGENCY
(*Kaijo Hoancho*)

PERSONNEL (2-80): 11,793 men (2,506 officers, 9,287 men)

The Maritime Safety Agency, which was organized in 1948, is undergoing a massive expansion, which by 1982 will make it the world's largest and best-equipped coast guard, by far. In peacetime, it is directed by the Department of Transportation and, although most of its ships are armed, they are not considered part of the Navy; they fly only the national colors (a red disk on a white background), not the flag flown by naval ships. In wartime, the ships would be under naval control.

PROGRAMS: The 1981-82 Budget approved funds for construction of one *Tsugaru*-class PL (PL 06), one *Teshio*-class PM (PM 07), one 130-ton PS (PS 102), two 30-m PC (PC 82, 83), six 15-m CL (CL 239-246), and one 2,600-ton HL (HL 02).

AVIATION: In 1981, the MSA operated 19 fixed-wing aircraft (5 YS-11A transports, 2 SC-7 Skyvan, 11 Beech 200T light transports, and 1 Cessna SA 790/185C), and 25 helicopters (17 Bell 212, 4 Bell 206B, and 2 Hughes 369-HS). Under the 1981-82 Budget, 2 Beech 200T transports and 3 Bell 212 helicopters are to be acquired.

HIGH-ENDURANCE CUTTERS (PL)

◆ 3 (+2) Tsugaru class

	Bldr	Laid down	L	In serv.
PL 02 TSUGARU	Ishikawa-Harima, Tokyo	18-4-78	6-12-78	17-4-79
PL 03 OOSUMI	Mitsui, Tamano	1-9-78	1-6-79	18-10-79
PL 04 URAGA	Hitachi, Maizuru	14-3-79	12-10-79	5-3-80
PL 05 ZAOO	Mitsubishi, Nagasaki	23-10-80	-81	3-82
PL 06 N. . .	. . .	. . .	. . .	. . .

Tsugaru (PL 02)   *Ships of the World*, 1979

D: 3,730 tons (4,037 fl)   **S:** 22 kts   **Dim:** 105.4 (100.0 wl) × 14.6 × 4.8
A: 1/40-mm AA—1/20-mm AA (not in PL 03)—PL 05, 06: 1/35-mm AA—1/Bell 212 helicopter
M: 2 Pielstick 12PC2-5V400 diesels; 2 CP props; 16,000 hp (13,260 hp sust.)
Electric: 1,450 kVA   **Fuel:** 650 tons   **Range:** 5,700/18
Man: 21 officers, 7 warrant officers, 28 men, 15 spare

REMARKS: Have bow-thruster, 2 pair fin stabilizers, normal ship bow for operations in ice-free waters. Also have Flume-type passive stabilization tanks in superstructure. Have 3 radars. Engines manufactured by different builders. PL 03, 04 built under 1978-79 program PL 05 under 1979-80 program, PL 06 under 1981-82 program. Up to seven more may be built.

◆ 1 Soya class

	Bldr	Laid down	L	In serv.
PL 01 SOYA	Nippon Kokan, Tsurumi	12-9-77	3-7-78	22-11-78

Soya (PL 01)   *Ships of the World*, 1979

D: 3,562 tons (4,089 fl)   **S:** 21 kts   **Dim:** 98.6 × 15.6 × 5.2
A: 1/40-mm AA—1/20-mm AA—1/Bell 212 helicopter
M: 2 Nippon Kokan-Pielstick 12PC2-5V400 diesels; 2 CP props; 16,000 hp (13,260 hp sust.)
Electric: 1,450 kVA   **Fuel:** 650 tons   **Range:** 5,700/18   **Man:** 71 tot.

REMARKS: The *Soya* was built under the 1977 program. The *Soya* has an icebreaking bow and operates in the north. Passive tank stabilization only, no bow-thruster. Four radars (one aft for helo control).

◆ 26 (+2)Shiretoko class

	Bldr	L	In serv.
PL 101 SHIRETOKO*	Mitsui, Tamano	13-7-78	16-11-78
PL 102 ESAN	Sumitomo, Oshima	8-78	16-11-78
PL 103 WAKASA*	Kawasaki, Kobe	8-78	29-11-78
PL 104 YAHIKO	Mitsubishi, Shimonoseki	8-78	16-11-78
PL 105 MOTOBU	Sasebo Dockyard	8-78	29-11-78
PL 106 RISHIRI	Shikoku DY	27-3-79	8-79
PL 107 MATSUSHIMA*	Tohoku DY	11-4-79	9-79
PL 108 IWAKI*	Hitichi, Usumi	28-3-79	10-8-79
PL 109 SHIKINE	Usugine SY	27-4-79	9-79
PL 110 SURUGA*	Kurushima SY	20-4-79	9-79
PL 111 REBUN*	Narazaki SY	6-79	11-79
PL 112 CHOKAI*	Nihonkai SY	6-79	11-79
PL 113 ASHIZURI*	Sanoyasu SY	6-79	31-10-79
PL 114 OKI	Tsuneishi SY	6-79	11-79
PL 115 NOTO	Miho SY	7-79	11-79
PL 116 YONAKUNI	Hiyashikane	6-79	31-10-79
PL 117 DAISETSU*	Hakodate DY	22-8-79	31-1-80
PL 118 SHIMOKITA	Kakoki	9-79	3-80
PL 119 SUZUKA	Kanazashi	4-10-79	3-80

HIGH-ENDURANCE CUTTERS (continued)

PL 120 KUNASAKI	Kouyo	8-10-79	2-80
PL 121 GENKAI*	Sumitomo, Oshima	9-79	31-1-80
PL 122 GOTO*	Onomichi	10-79	2-80
PL 123 KOSHIKI	Kasado	9-79	25-1-80
PL 124 HATERUMA*	Osaka DY	11-79	3-80
PL 125 KATORI	Tohoku DY	5-80	21-10-80
PL 126 KUNIGAMI	Kanda, Kanagiri	28-3-80	17-10-80
PL 127 ETOMO	Naikai, Taguma	30-9-81	3-82
PL 128 MASHU	Shikoku DY	9-81	3-82

Motobu (PL 105) *Ships of the World, 1979*

D: 974 tons (1,350-1,360 fl) **S:** 20 kts **Dim:** 77.8 (73.6 pp) × 9.6 × 3.42
A: 1/40-mm AA—1/20-mm AA—*see* Remarks
M: 2 Niigata 8MA 40 or Fuji 8540B diesels; 2 props; 7,000 hp
Electric: 625 kVA **Fuel:** 191 tons **Range:** 4,406/17 **Man:** 41 tot.

REMARKS: Program has helped small shipyards to stay in business. Intended to patrol the 200-nautical-mile economic zone. Starred units have Fuji 8540B diesels. PL 106 and later have no 20-mm AA, while PL 118, 122, 124-128 have an Oerlikon 35-mm in place of the 40-mm AA. Carry 153 tons water. Fuel capacities and endurances vary. Last two laid down 11-80.

◆ 2 Izu class

	Bldr	L	In serv.
PL 31 IZU	Hitachi, Mukaishima	1-67	7-67
PL 32 MIURA	Maizuru DY	11-68	3-69

D: 2,081 tons (2,200 fl) **S:** 24.6 kts **Dim:** 95.5 (86.45 pp) × 11.6 × 3.8
A: 1/40-mm AA **M:** 2 SEMT-Pielstick 12PC2V diesels; 2 CP props; 10,400 hp
Electric: 800 kVA **Range:** 5,000/20.5, 14,500/12.7 **Man:** 72 tot.

REMARKS: Large weather radar in dome aft removed in 1978 and gun added forward.

Miura (PL 32) 1972

◆ 4 Erimo class

	Bldr	L	In serv.
PL 13 ERIMO	Hitachi, Mukaishima	14-8-65	30-11-65
PL 14 SATSUMA	Hitachi, Mukaishima	4-66	30-7-66
PL 15 DAIO	Hitachi, Maizuru	19-6-73	28-9-73
PL 16 MUROTO	Naikai, Taguma	5-8-74	30-11-74

Daio (PL 15) 1974

D: 980 tons (1,009 fl) **S:** 19.5 kts **Dim:** 76.6 (73.0 pp) × 9.2 × 3.0
A: 1/76.2-mm Mk 26 DP—1/20-mm AA
M: 2 Burmeister & Wain 635V 2 BU 45 diesels; 2 props; 4,800 hp
Electric: 320 kVA **Range:** 5,000/18 **Man:** 72 tot.

REMARKS: The hull of PL 13 is reinforced against ice. PL 15 and PL 16: **D:** 1,206 tons; **Dim:** beam 9.6, draft, 3.18; **A:** 1/40-mm AA—1/20-mm AA; **M:** 7,000 hp for 20.4 kts; **Electric:** 500 kVA; **Range:** 6,600/18; **Man:** 50 tot.

◆ 2 Nojima class Bldr: Uraga Dock Co., Ltd.

	L	In serv.
PL 11 NOJIMA	12-2-62	30-4-62
PL 12 OJIKA	...	10-6-63

D: 980 tons (1,009 fl) **S:** 18.1 kts **Dim:** 69.0 × 9.18 × 3.2
M: 2 Uraga-Sulzer 6 MD 42 diesels; 2 props; 3,000 hp
Electric: 310 kVA **Range:** 6,000/16.5 **Man:** 73 tot.

REMARKS: Used for meteorological reporting. Passive tank stabilization.

HIGH-ENDURANCE CUTTERS (continued)

Nojima (PL 11)   E. Aoki

♦ **1 Kojima-class training cutter**

	Bldr	In serv.
PL 21 KOJIMA	Kure DY	21-5-64

Kojima (PL 21)   1972

D: 1,066 tons (1,206 fl)   **S:** 17.3 kts   **Dim:** 69.6 × 10.3 × 3.53
A: 1/76.2-mm DP Mk 26—1/40-mm AA—1/20-mm AA
M: 1 Uraga-Sulzer 7 MD 51 diesel; 1 prop; 2,600 hp
Electric: 550 kVA   **Range:** 6,120/13   **Man:** 17 officers, 42 crew, 47 cadets

REMARKS: Used as a training ship at Kure Academy.

MEDIUM-ENDURANCE CUTTERS (PM)

♦ **6 (+1) Teshio (500-ton) class**

	Bldr	L	In serv.
PM 01 TESHIO	Shikoku DY	30-5-80	30-9-80
PM 02 OIRASE	Naikai, Taguma	15-5-80	29-8-80
PM 03 ECHIZEN	Usuki Iron Wks.	2-6-80	30-9-80
PM 04 TOKACHI	Navazaki, Muroran	21-11-80	24-3-81
PM 05 HITACHI	Tohoku, Shiogoma	15-11-80	19-3-81
PM 06 OKITSU	Usuki Iron Wks.	5-12-80	17-3-81
PM 07 N. . .	. . .	. . .	. . .

Teshio (PM 01)   *Ships of the World*, 1981

Oirase (PM 02)   *Ships of the World*, 1980

D: 630 tons (670 fl)   **S:** 18 kts   **Dim:** 67.80 (63.00 pp) × 7.90 × 2.65
A: 1/20-mm JN-61B Gatling AA   **Electron Equipt:** Radar: 2/JMA-159B
M: 2 Fuji 6S 32F diesels; 2 props; 3,000 hp   **Electric:** 240 kVA
Endurance: 15 days   **Range:** 3,200/16   **Man:** 33 tot.

REMARKS: 540 grt. Three built under 1979-80 program, three under 1980-81 program, one under 1981-82 program. Some have Arakata 6 M31 EX diesels.

♦ **2 Takatori (350-ton) class**

	Bldr	L	In serv.
PM 89 TAKATORI	Naikai, Taguma	8-12-77	24-3-78
PM 94 KUMANO	Naikai, Taguma	2-11-78	23-2-79

D: 634 tons normal   **S:** 15.7 kts   **Dim:** 45.70 (44.25 pp) × 9.20 × 3.88
A: None   **M:** 2 Niigata 6M31EX diesels; 1 CP prop; 3,000 hp
Electric: 200 kVA   **Range:** 750/15   **Man:** 34 tot.

REMARKS: 469 grt. Rescue-tug types. Equipped for fire-fighting and salvage duties. Two water cannon (3,000 l./min. each). Carry an 8-m. rescue boat and a 4.6-m. speedboat.

MEDIUM-ENDURANCE CUTTERS (continued)

Takatori (PM 89)   Naikai SY, 1978

♦ **20 Bihoro (350-ton) class**

	Bldr	In serv.
PM 73 Bihoro	Tohoku Zosen	28-2-74
PM 74 Kuma	Usuki	28-2-74
PM 75 Fuji	Usuki	7-2-75
PM 76 Kabashima	Usuki	25-3-75
PM 77 Sado	Tohoku Zosen	1-2-75
PM 78 Ishikari	Tohoku Zosen	13-3-76
PM 79 Abakuma	Tohoku Zosen	30-1-76
PM 80 Isuzu	Nakai, Taguma	10-3-76
PM 81 Kikuchi	Usuki	6-2-76
PM 82 Kuzuryu	Usuki	18-3-76
PM 83 Horobetsu	Tohoku Zosen	21-1-77
PM 84 Shirakami	Tohoku Zosen	3-3-77
PM 85 Sagami	Utsumi	30-11-76
PM 86 Tone	Usuki	30-11-76
PM 87 Yoshino	Usuki	28-1-77
PM 88 Kurobe	Shikoku DY	15-2-77
PM 90 Chikugo	Nakai, Taguma	27-1-78
PM 91 Yamakuni	Usuki	26-1-78
PM 92 Katsura	Shikoku DY	15-2-78
PM 93 Shinano	Tohoku Zosen	23-2-78

D: 636 tons (657 fl)   **S:** 18 kts   **Dim:** 63.35 × 7.80 × 2.53
A: 1/20-mm AA   **Electron Equipt:** Radar: 2 JMA-159B
M: 2 Niigata 6M31EX diesels; 2 CP props; 3,000 hp   **Electric:** 200 kVA
Range: 3,260/16   **Man:** 34 tot.

Sado (PM 77)   1978

Yamakuni (PM 91)   *Ships of the World*, 1978

♦ **7 Kunashiri (350-ton) class**

	Bldr	In serv.
PM 65 Kunashiri	Maizuru DY	28-3-69
PM 66 Minabe	Maizuru DY	28-3-70
PM 67 Sarobetsu	Maizuru DY	30-3-71
PM 68 Kamishima	Usuki Iron Wks.	31-1-72
PM 70 Miyake	Tohoku Zosen	25-1-73
PM 71 Awaji	Usuki Iron Wks.	25-1-73
PM 72 Yaeyama	Usuki Iron Wks.	20-12-72

Yaeyama (PM 72)   1975

D: 498 tons (574 fl)   **S:** 17.5 kts   **Dim:** 58.04 × 7.38 × 2.40
A: 1/20-mm AA   **M:** 2 Niigata 6MF32H diesels; 2 props; 2,600 hp
Electric: 120 kVA   **Range:** 3,040/16   **Man:** 40 tot.

REMARKS: PM 70 to PM 72 have 6M31EX diesels, 3,000 hp. PM 72 has controllable-pitch propellers.

MEDIUM-ENDURANCE CUTTERS *(continued)*

♦ **5 Matsuura (350-ton) class** Bldrs: PM 60, PM 61: Osaka SB; Others: Hitachi

	In serv.		In serv.
PM 60 MATSUURA	18-3-61	PM 63 NATORI	20-1-66
PM 61 SENDAI	14-4-62	PM 64 KARATSU	29-3-67
PM 62 AMAMI	29-3-65		

D: 425 tons **S:** 16.5 kts (PM 64: 18 kts; PM 63: 16.8 kts)
Dim: 55.33 × 7.00 × 2.30 **A:** 1/20-mm AA
M: 2 Ikegai 6MSB31S diesels; 2 props; 1,400 hp (PM 63: 2 Type 6MSB31HS diesels; 1,800 hp—PM 64: 2 Type 6MA31X diesels; 2,600 hp)
Electric: 140 kVA **Range:** 3,500/12-13 **Man:** 37-40 tot.

♦ **6 Yahagi (350-ton) class** Bldrs: Niigata (PM 69: Usuki Iron Wks.)

	In serv.		In serv.
PM 55 SUMIDA	30-6-57	PM 58 YUBARI	15-3-60
PM 56 CHITOSE	30-4-58	PM 59 HORONAI	11-2-61
PM 57 SORACHI	31-3-59	PM 69 OKINAWA	8-10-69

D: 376 tons (430 fl) **S:** 15.5 kts **Dim:** 50.27 × 7.36 × 2.16
A: 1/20-mm AA **M:** 2 Ikegai 6 MSB31S diesels; 2 props; 1,400 hp
Electric: 140 kVA **Range:** 4,350/12 **Man:** 44 tot.

REMARKS: PM 69 was originally built for Okinawa, transferred to MSA in 1972. Sister *Yahagi* (PM 54) stricken 1981.

NOTE: Of the 13 *Rebun*, 4 *Chifuri*, 2 *Tokachi*, and 1 *Teshio*-class "350-ton" cutters listed in the previous edition, all were stricken 1979-80.

PATROL BOATS (PS)

♦ **1(+) Akagi (130-ton) class**

	Bldr	Laid down	L	In serv.
PS 101 AKAGI	Sumidigawa	31-7-79	5-12-79	26-3-80
PS 102 N. . .	. . .	. . .	. . .	. . .

Akagi (PS 101) *Ships of the World*, 1980

D: 127.7 tons normal **S:** 26.5 kts **Dim:** 35.0 (33.0 wl) × 6.3 × 1.3
A: 1/12.7-mm mg **M:** 2 Pielstick 16PA 4V-185 diesels; 2 props; 4,400 hp
Electric: 40 kVA **Range:** 570/20 **Man:** 12 tot.

REMARKS: PS 101 in 1979-80 Budget, PS 102 in 1981-82. PS 101 replaced *Akagi* (PS 40), and PS 102 is replacing *Tsukuba* (PS 31) by 31-3-82. Glass-reinforced plastic hull; 4-day endurance. Carry a 25-man rubber rescue dinghy.

♦ **3 Bizan (130-ton) class**

	Bldr	In serv.
PS 42 BIZAN	Mitsubishi, Shimonoseki	28-3-66
PS 47 ASAMA	Mitsubishi, Shimonoseki	31-1-69
PS 48 SHIRAMINE	Mitsubishi, Shimonoseki	15-12-69

D: 42-48 tons (83-85 fl) **S:** 21.6 kts; PS 48: 25 kts **Dim:** 26.0 × 5.6 × 1.0
A: 1/12.7-mm mg
M: 2 Mitsubishi 12 HD 2 OMTK diesels; 2 props; 1,140 hp; PS 48: 2 MTU diesels; 2,200 hp
Electric: 2 kw **Range:** 400/18; PS 48: 250/25 **Man:** 14 tot.

♦ **14 Hidaka (130-ton) class**

	Bldr	In serv.
PS 32 HIDAKA	Azuma	23-4-62
PS 33 HIYAMA	Hitachi	13-3-63
PS 34 TSURUGI	Mukajima	13-3-63
PS 35 ROKKO	Shikoku	31-1-64
PS 36 TAKANAWA	Hayashikane	27-1-64
PS 37 AKIYOSHI	Hashihama	29-2-64
PS 38 KUNIMI	Hayashikane	15-2-65
PS 39 TAKATSUKI	Kurashima	30-3-65
PS 41 KAMUI	Hayashikane	15-2-66
PS 43 ASHITAKA	Usuki	10-2-67
PS 44 KURAMA	Usuki	28-2-67
PS 45 IBUKI	Usuki	5-3-68
PS 46 TOUMI	Usuki	20-2-68
PS 49 NOBARU	Hitachi	10-12-68

Akiyoshi (PS 37) E. Aoki

D: 169 tons normal **S:** 13.7 kts **Dim:** 31.72 (30.5 wl) × 6.29 × 1.80
A: 1/12.7-mm mg (usually not mounted)
M: 1 6MSB 31S diesel; 1 prop; 700 hp **Electric:** 60 kVA
Range: 1,100/12 **Man:** 17 tot.

COASTAL PATROL BOATS (PC)

♦ **19 (+2) Murakomo (30-meter) class**

	Bldr	In serv.
PC 201 MURAKOMO	Mitsubishi, Shimonoseki	24-3-78
PC 202 KITAGUMO	Hitachi, Kanagawa	17-3-78
PC 203 YUKIGUMO	Hitachi, Kanagawa	27-9-78
PC 204 ASAGUMO	Mitsubishi, Shimonoseki	21-9-78
PC 205 HAYAGUMO	Mitsubishi, Shimonoseki	30-1-79
PC 206 AKIGUMO	Hitachi, Kanagawa	28-2-79
PC 207 YAEGUMO	Mitsubishi, Shimonoseki	16-3-79
PC 208 NATSUGUMO	Hitachi, Kanagawa	22-3-79
PC 209 YAMAGIRI	Hitachi, Kanagawa	29-6-79
PC 210 KAWAGIRI	Hitachi, Kanagawa	27-7-79
PC 211 TERUZUKI	Maizuru Heavy Ind.	26-6-79
PC 212 NATSUZUKI	Maizuru Heavy Ind.	26-7-79
PC 213 MIYAZUKI	Hitachi, Kanagawa	13-3-80
PC 214 NIJIGUMO	Mitsubishi, Shimonoseki	29-1-81
PC 215 TATSUGUMO	Mitsubishi, Shimonoseki	19-3-81
PC 216 HAMAYUKI	Hitachi, Kanagawa	27-2-81
PC 217 ISONAMI	Mitsubishi, Shimonoseki	19-3-81
PC 218 NAGOZUKI	Hitachi, Kanagawa	29-1-81
PC 219 YAEZUKI	Hitachi, Kanagawa	19-3-81
PC 220 N. . .	. . .	. . .
PC 221 N. . .	. . .	. . .

Murakomo (PC 201) *Ships of the World*, 1978

D: 88 tons (125 fl) **S:** 30 kts **Dim:** 31.0 (28.5 pp) × 6.3 × 1.2
A: 1/12.7-mm mg **M:** 2 Ikegai MTU 16V652 TB 81 diesels; 2 props; 4,800 hp
Electric: 40 kVA **Range:** 350/28 **Man:** 11 tot.

REMARKS: PC 201 to PC 204 built under 1977-78 program. PC 205-208 under 1978-79, PC 209-212 under 1978-79 supplementary program, PC 213 under 1979-80 program, PC 214-219 under 1980-81 program, PC 220-221 under 1981-82.

♦ **11 (+2) Akizuki (23-meter) class** Bldr: Mitsubishi, Shimonoseki

	In serv.		In serv.
PC 64 AKIZUKI	28-2-74	PC 78 ISOZUKI	18-3-77
PC 65 SHINONOME	25-2-74	PC 79 SHIMANAMI	23-12-77
PC 72 URAYUKI	31-5-75	PC 80 YUZUKI	22-3-79
PC 73 ISEYUKI	31-7-75	PC 81 HANAYUKI	27-3-81
PC 75 HATAYUKI	19-3-15	PC 82 N. . .	. . .
PC 76 HATAGUMO	21-2-76	PC 83 N. . .	. . .
PC 77 HAMAZUKI	29-11-76		

Hatayuki (PC 75) F. Lauga, 1976

D: 77 tons normal **S:** 22.1 kts **Dim:** 26.00 × 6.30 × 1.12
M: 3 Mitsubishi 12 DM 20 MTK diesels; 3 props; 3,000 hp
Electric: 40 kVA **Range:** 290/21.5 **Man:** 10 tot.

♦ **17 Shikinami (23-meter) class**

	Bldr	In serv.
PC 54 SHIKINAMI	Mitsubishi, Shimonoseki	24-2-71
PC 55 TOMONAMI	Mitsubishi, Shimonoseki	20-3-71
PC 56 WAKANAMI	Mitsubishi, Shimonoseki	30-10-71
PC 57 ISENAMI	Hitachi, Kanagawa	29-2-72
PC 58 TAKANAMI	Mitsubishi, Shimonoseki	30-11-71
PC 59 MUTSUKI	Hitachi, Kanagawa	18-12-72
PC 60 MOCHIZUKI	Hitachi, Kanagawa	18-12-72
PC 61 HARUZUKI	Mitsubishi, Shimonoseki	30-11-72
PC 62 KIYOZUKI	Mitsubishi, Shimonoseki	18-12-72
PC 63 URAZUKI	Mitsubishi, Shimonoseki	30-1-73
PC 66 URANAMI	Hitachi, Kanagawa	22-12-73
PC 67 TAMANAMI	Mitsubishi, Shimonoseki	25-12-73
PC 68 MINEGUMO	Mitsubishi, Shimonoseki	30-11-73
PC 69 KIYONAMI	Mitsubishi, Shimonoseki	30-10-73
PC 70 OKINAMI	Hitachi, Kanagawa	8-2-74
PC 71 WAKAGUMO	Hibachi, Kanagawa	25-3-74
PC 74 ASOYUKI	Hitachi, Kanagawa	16-6-75

D: 46 tons normal **S:** 25.8 kts **Dim:** 21.0 × 5.3 × 1.22
A: 1/12.7-mm mg (usually not mounted)
M: 2 Mercedes-Benz MB820Db diesels; 2 props; 2,200 hp **Electric:** 2 kw
Range: 240/23.8 **Man:** 10 tot.

COASTAL PATROL BOATS (*continued*)

Urazuki (PC 63) 1975

♦ **1 Matsunami (23-meter) class** Bldr: Hitachi, Kanagawa

PC 53 MATSUNAMI (In serv. 30-3-71)

    D: 59 tons normal **S:** 20.7 kts **Dim:** 24.96 × 6.0 × 1.33
    M: 2 Mercedes-Benz MB820Db diesels; 2 props; 2,200 hp; 2 DA640 cruise diesels; 180 hp
    Electric: 3 kw **Range:** 270/18 **Man:** 30 tot.

REMARKS: Especially configured for Emperor Hirohito for oceanographic research. Two cruise diesels can be geared to the props.

♦ **1 Hamanami (23-meter) class** Bldr: Sumidagawa

PC 52 HAMANAMI (In serv. 22-3-71)

    D: 60 tons (fl) **S:** 20.9 kts **Dim:** 21.0 × 5.1 × 1.22
    M: 2 Mercedes-Benz MB820Db diesels; 2 props; 2,200 hp
    Electric: 2 kw **Range:** 290/20.9 **Man:** 10 tot.

♦ **1 Hamagiri (23-meter) class** Bldr: Sumidagawa

PC 48 HAMAGIRI (In serv. 19-3-70)

    D: 51 tons (fl) **S:** 14.6 kts **Dim:** 21.0 × 5.1 × 1.11
    M: 2 Mitsubishi 12DH 20TK diesels; 2 props; 1,140 hp
    Electric: 2 kw **Range:** 270/12.9 **Man:** 10 tot.

♦ **5 Umigiri (23-meter) class** Bldr: Hitachi, Kanagawa

	In serv.		In serv.
PC 46 UMIGIRI	15-3-68	PC 50 SETOGIRI	5-3-70
PC 47 ASAGIRI	15-3-68	PC 51 HAYAGIRI	5-3-70
PC 49 SAGIRI	31-3-70		

    D: 42 tons (59 fl) **S:** 26.9 kts **Dim:** 21.0 × 5.1 × 0.95
    A: 1/12.7-mm mg (usually not mounted)
    M: 2 Mercedes-Benz MB820Db diesels; 2 props; 2,200 hp **Range:** 270/25.9
    Man: 10 tot.

NOTE: The five remaining units of the *Matsuyuki* class were stricken 1979-82.

Sagiri (PC 49) 1975

PATROL CRAFT (CL)

♦ **44 Yamayuri (15-meter) class**

	Bldr	In serv.
CL 201 YAMAYURI	Ishihara, Takasago	1-78
CL 202 TACHIBANA	Ishihara, Takasago	2-78
CL 203 KOMAKUSA	Ishihara, Takasago	1-79
CL 204 SHIRAGIKU	Ishihara, Takasago	2-79
CL 205 YAGURUMA	Sumidigawa, Tokyo	31-7-79
CL 206 HAMANASU	Sumidigawa, Tokyo	29-9-79
CL 207 SUZURAN	Sumidigawa, Tokyo	31-7-79
CL 208 ISOGIKU	Sumidigawa, Tokyo	12-9-79
CL 209 ISEGIKO	Sumidigawa, Tokyo	31-8-79
CL 210 AYAME	Yokohama Yacht	29-10-79
CL 211 AJISAI	Yokohama Yacht	26-9-79
CL 212 HIMAWARI	Yokohama Yacht	29-10-79
CL 213 HAZAKURA	Yokohama Yacht	29-8-79
CL 214 HINAGIKU	Ishihara, Takasago	9-7-79
CL 215 HAMAGIKU	Yokohama Yacht	19-9-79
CL 216 FUYUME	Ishihara, Takasago	30-7-79
CL 217 TSUBAKI	Ishihara, Takasago	10-8-79
CL 218 SAZANKA	Ishihara, Takasago	30-8-79
CL 219 AOI	Sumidigawa, Tokyo	31-10-79
CL 220 SUISEN	Yokohama Yacht	29-10-79
CL 221 YAEZAKURA	Ishihara, Takasago	25-9-79
CL 222 AKEBI	Ishihara, Takasago	29-10-79
CL 223 SHIRAHAGI	Sumidigawa, Tokyo	25-1-80
CL 224 BENIBANA	Sumidigawa, Tokyo	25-1-80
CL 225 MURATSUBAKI	Ishihara, Takasago	20-12-79
CL 226 TSUTSUJI	Sumidigawa, Tokyo	22-2-80
CL 227 ASHIBI	Ishihara, Takasago	20-12-79
CL 228 SATOZAKURA	Ishihara, Takasago	26-2-80
CL 229 YUKITSUBAKI	Ishihara, Takasago	28-2-80
CL 230 SATSUKI	Shinki	22-2-80
CL 231 EZOGIKU	Yokohama Yacht	11-80

PATROL CRAFT (continued)

CL 232 Akashio	Sumidigawa, Tokyo	11-80
CL 233 Kozakura	Yokohama Yacht	11-80
CL 234 Shirame	Ishihara, Takasago	11-80
CL 235 Sarubia	Ishihara, Takasago	11-80
CL 236 Suiren	Shinki	19-12-80
CL 237 Hatsugiku	Ishihara, Takasago	29-1-81
CL 238 Hamayura	Ishihara, Takasago	29-1-80
CL 239 N. . .	. . .	. . .
CL 240 N. . .	. . .	. . .
CL 241 N. . .	. . .	. . .
CL 242 N. . .	. . .	. . .
CL 243 N. . .	. . .	. . .
CL 244 N. . .	. . .	. . .

Yukitsubaki (CL 229) *Ships of the World, 1980*

D: 27 tons normal **S:** 20.7 kts **Dim:** 18.00 × 4.30 × 0.82 (1.10 props)
M: 2 RD10T AO6 diesels; 2 props; 900 hp **Range:** 180/19
Man: 6 tot.

REMARKS: Three water cannon for fire-fighting. CL 239-244 in 1981-82 Budget.

♦ **4 Nogekaze class** Bldr: Sumidagawa, Tokyo

	In serv.		In serv.
CL 99 Nogekaze	10-72	CL 107 Itokaze	11-72
CL 105 Kusukaze	10-72	CL 128 Kawakaze	10-73

D: 22.5 tons normal **S:** 16.6 kts **Dim:** 16.00 × 4.10 × 0.80 (hull)
M: 2 Type UDV816 diesels; 2 props; 500 hp **Electric:** 5 kVA
Range: 160/14.7 **Man:** 6 tot.

♦ **95 Chiyokaze class**

Bldrs: Ishihara, Nobotuka, Yokohama Yacht, Sumidagawa, 1968-76

CL 44 Chiyokaze	CL 89 Kishikaze	CL 125 Tonekaze
CL 50 Suzukaze	CL 90 Mayakaze	CL 126 Shizukaze
CL 51 Urakaze	CL 91 Kikukaze	CL 127 Murokaze
CL 53 Sugikaze	CL 92 Hirokaze	CL 129 Yamakaze
CL 54 Fujikaze	CL 93 Kibikaze	CL 130 Hikokaze
CL 55 Miyakaze	CL 94 Ashikaze	CL 131 Takakaze
CL 57 Chinukaze	CL 95 Otokaze	CL 132 Murakaze
CL 59 Nachikaze	CL 96 Kurikaze	CL 133 Nomokaze
CL 65 Tomakaze	CL 97 Imakaze	CL 134 Kumokaze
CL 66 Hibakaze	CL 98 Terukaze	CL 135 Yanakaze
CL 67 Yurikaze	CL 100 Tokitsukaze	CL 136 Yurakaze
CL 68 Sumikaze	CL 101 Tsukikaze	CL 137 Washikaze
CL 69 Kashima	CL 102 Awakaze	CL 138 Kushikaze
CL 70 Takekaze	CL 104 Miokaze	CL 139 Hoshikaze
CL 71 Kinukaze	CL 106 Kilkaze	CL 140 Gettō
CL 72 Shigikaze	CL 108 Tamatsukaze	CL 141 Iwakaze
CL 73 Uzukaze	CL 109 Miyokaze	CL 142 Matsukaze
CL 74 Akikaze	CL 110 Ayakaze	CL 143 Oitsukaze
CL 75 Setokaze	CL 111 Mitsukaze	CL 144 Arakaze
CL 76 Kurekaze	CL 112 Hatakaze	CL 145 Tanikaze
CL 77 Mojikaze	CL 113 Numakaze	CL 146 Kochikaze
CL 78 Satakaze	CL 114 Soyokaze	CL 147 Okikaze
CL 79 Kirikaze	CL 115 Minekaze	CL 148 Suwakaze
CL 80 Kamikaze	CL 116 Okitsukaze	CL 149 Sachikaze
CL 81 Umikaze	CL 117 Deigo	CL 150 Natsukaze
CL 82 Yumekaze	CL 118 Yuuna	CL 151 Harukaze
CL 83 Makikaze	CL 119 Adan	CL 152 Rindō
CL 84 Hakaze	CL 120 Horokaze	CL 153 Sawakaze
CL 85 Shachikaze	CL 121 Somakaze	CL 154 Kaidō
CL 86 Himekaze	CL 122 Hatsukaze	CL 155 Nadeshiko
CL 87 Isekaze	CL 123 Sasakaze	CL 156 Yamazakura
CL 88 Komakaze	CL 124 Hagikaze	

Takekaze (CL 70) 1975

PATROL CRAFT *(continued)*

D: 19.5 tons normal   **S:** 18.4 kts   **Dim:** 15.00 × 4.10 × 0.76 (hull)
M: 2 Mitsubishi DH24MK diesels; 2 props; 500 hp   **Range:** 180/16.1
Man: 6 tot.

REMARKS: The *Nomakaze* (CL 103) was lost in 1978. CL 69 is named for her home port; CL 117 to CL 119 are home-ported in Okinawa.

♦ **19 Yakaze class** Bldrs: Yokohama Yacht, Sumidagawa, Ishihara (In serv. 1967-70)

CL 38 KUKIKAZE	CL 49 TOKIKAZE
CL 39 SAGIKAZE	CL 52 MUTSUKAZE
CL 40 SHIOKAZE	CL 56 YOSHIKAZE
CL 41 NIKAZE	CL 58 SUKIKAZE
CL 42 TOMOKAZE	CL 60 TATSUKAZE
CL 43 WAKAKAZE	CL 61 UMEKAZE
CL 45 TAMAKAZE	CL 62 YUMIKAZE
CL 46 NADAKAZE	CL 63 MIHOKAZE
CL 47 KUNIKAZE	CL 64 KOSHIKAZE
CL 48 TOYOKAZE	

D: 17.9 tons (24 fl)   **S:** 18.7 kts   **Dim:** 15.0 × 4.1 × 0.74
M: 2 Mitsubishi DH24MK diesels; 2 props; 500 hp
Range: 190/15.5, 320/12   **Man:** 6 tot.

REMARKS: Twelve sisters (CL 26-37) stricken 1980–early 1982. Have one fire-fighting water cannon on the bow.

NOTE: During 1979-81, large numbers of older CL-designated craft have been stricken: All 5 *Yukikaze* class (CL 21-25), *Tamayuki* (CL 305, ex-PC 42), all 5 *Hawakaze* class (CL 306, 311, 312, 314, 317), all 8 *Asashimo* class (CL 304, 307, 308, 313, 315, 316, 318, 319), and *Kiyoshimo* (CL 310). In addition, the remaining 6 CS—small patrol craft of the *Shiragiku* class (CS 107, 108, 120, 122-124)—were discarded.

HYDROGRAPHIC SHIPS

♦ **0 (+1) Takuyo (2,600-ton) replacement class**

	Bldr	Laid down	L	In serv.
HL 02 TAKUYO	. . .	. . .	. . .	. . .

D: 3,000 tons normal   **S:** 16 kts   **Dim:** 96.0 (90.0 wl) × 14.2 × 4.5
M: 2 diesels; 2 CP props; 5,200 hp   **Endurance:** 50 days
Range: 12,000/16   **Man:** 64 tot.

REMARKS: In 1981 program to replace existing *Takuyo*. Will have bow-thruster, side-looking bottom contour mapping sonars, precision echo-sounders, etc.

♦ **1 Shoyo (1,900-ton) class** Bldr: Hitachi, Maizuru

HL 01 SHOYO (In serv. 26-2-72)

Shoyo (HL 01)   *Ships of the World*

D: 2,200 tons normal   **S:** 17.4 kts   **Dim:** 81.70 (78.60 wl) × 12.60 × 4.20
M: 2 Fuji 12VM 32 H2F diesels; 1 prop; 4,800 hp   **Electric:** 1,250 kVA
Range: 12,000/14   **Man:** 73 tot.

REMARKS: 1,900 grt. Has bow-thruster.

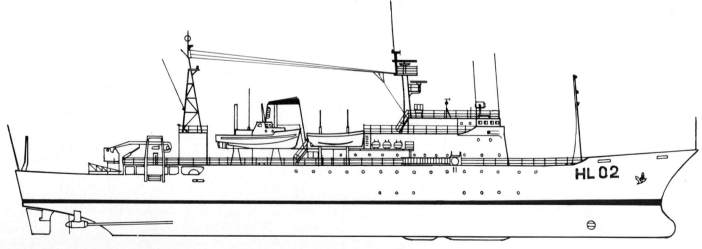

Takuyo (HL 02)   A.D. Baker III, 1981

HYDROGRAPHIC SHIPS (continued)

♦ **1 Meiyo class** Bldr: Nagoya SY

HL 03 MEIYO (In serv. 15-3-63)

Meiyo (HL 03) 1975

D: 486 tons normal **S:** 12 kts **Dim:** 44.80 (40.50 pp) × 8.05 × 2.88
M: 1 Asakasa TR 655 diesel; 1 prop; 700 hp **Electric:** 140 kVA
Range: 5,280/11 **Man:** 40 tot.

♦ **1 Takuyo class** Bldr: Niigata

HL 02 TAKUYO (In serv. 12-3-57)

D: 867 tons (930 fl) **S:** 14 kts **Dim:** 62.4 (58.75 pp) × 9.48 × 3.25
M: 2 MD6 diesels; 2 props; 1,300 hp **Electric:** 160 kw
Range: 9,600/12 **Man:** 50 tot.

REMARKS: Replacement approved 1981-82 Budget.

COASTAL HYDROGRAPHIC SHIPS

♦ **1 Kaiyo class** Bldr: Ishikawajima Harima, Nagoya

HM 06 KAIYO (In serv. 14-5-64)

D: 380 tons normal **S:** 12 kts **Dim:** 44.53 × 8.05 × 2.39
M: 1 Sumiyoshi Tekko S 6 NBS diesel; 1 prop; 450 hp
Electric: 90 kVA **Range:** 3,160/10 **Man:** 31 tot.

♦ **1 Tenyo class** Bldr: Yokohama Yacht

HM 05 TENYO (In serv. 30-3-61)

D: 171 tons normal **S:** 10.5 kts **Dim:** 30.20 (28.00 pp) × 5.80 × 1.96
M: 1 Mitsui MDF5-26 diesel; 1 prop; 230 hp **Electric:** 40 kVA
Range: 3,160/10.1 **Man:** 28 tot.

♦ **1 Heiyo class** Bldr: Shimizu

HM 04 HEIYO (In serv. 22-3-55)

D: 77 tons normal **S:** 10.6 kts **Dim:** 23.30 × 4.40 × 1.45 **Range:** 670/8.6
M: 1 Yanmar 6 MSL diesel; 1 prop; 150 hp **Electric:** 12 kw **Man:** 13 tot.

INSHORE HYDROGRAPHIC CRAFT

♦ **1 Kerama (15-meter) class** Bldr: Ho SB

HS 32 KERAMA (In serv. 28-11-73)

D: 23.2 tons normal **S:** 11 kts **Dim:** 15.0 × 4.0 × 0.86
M: 1 UDV 816 diesel; 250 hp **Range:** 450/10 **Man:** 7 tot.

REMARKS: Glass-reinforced plastic construction.

♦ **4 Akashi (15-meter) class** Bldrs: Various (In serv. 1973-77)

HS 31 AKASHI   HS 33 HAYATOMO   HS 34 KURIHAMA   HS 35 KURUSHIMA

D: 21 tons normal **S:** 10.2 kts **Dim:** 15.0 × 4.0 × 0.84
M: 1 Nissan-MTU UD626 diesel; 180 hp **Range:** 630/9.7 **Man:** 7 tot.

REMARKS: Glass-reinforced plastic hull.

♦ **11 Hamashio class** Bldr: Nichihi (In serv. 1969-72)

HS 01 HAMASHIO	HS 04 UZUSHIO	HS 07 TAKASHIO	HS 10 OYASHIO
HS 02 ISESHIO	HS 05 HAYASHIO	HS 08 WAKASHIO	HS 11 KUROSHIO
HS 03 SETOSHIO	HS 06 ISOSHIO	HS 09 YUKISHIO	

D: 6 tons normal **S:** 8.9-9.3 kts **Dim:** 10.15 × 2.65 × 0.81
M: 1 Nissan-MTU UD326 diesel; 90 hp **Range:** 343/8.5 **Man:** 7 tot.

REMARKS: Glass-reinforced plastic construction.

NAVIGATIONAL AID TENDERS

♦ **1 Tsushima class** Bldr: Mitsui, Tamano

	Laid down	L	In serv.
LL 01 TSUSHIMA	10-6-76	7-4-77	9-9-77

Tsushima (LL 01) *Ships of the World*

D: 1,865 tons normal **S:** 16 kts (17.6 trials)
Dim: 75.00 (70.00 wl) × 12.50 × 4.15
M: 1 Fuji-Sulzer 8S 40C diesel; 1 CP prop; 4,200 hp **Electric:** 900 kVA
Fuel: 477 tons **Range:** 10,000/15 **Man:** 54 tot.

REMARKS: Intended for use as a lighthouse supply ship. Has Flume-type passive
stabilization tanks, bow-thruster.

NAVIGATIONAL AID TENDERS *(continued)*

◆ 3 Hokuto-class buoy tenders

	Bldr	Laid down	L	In serv.
LL 11 Hokuto	Sasebo DY	19-10-78	20-3-79	29-6-79
LL 12 Kaio	Sasebo DY	17-7-79	20-10-79	11-3-80
LL 13 Ginga	Kawasaki, Kobe	13-6-79	16-11-79	18-3-80

Ginga (LL 13)   Kawasaki, 1980

D: 620 tons light (839 fl)   **S:** 13.8 kts   **Dim:** 55.00 (51.00 wl) × 10.60 × 2.65
M: 2 Asakasa MH23 (LL 11: Hanshin 6L 24SH) diesels; 2 props; 1,400 hp
Electric: 300 kVA   **Fuel:** 62 tons   **Range:** 3,460/13
Man: 9 officers, 20 men, 2 technicians

REMARKS: LL 12 replaced old *Kaio* (LL 13), stricken 8-2-80; LL 13 replaced old *Ginga* (LL 12), stricken 8-2-80.

◆ 1 Miyojo-class buoy tender   Bldr: Asano DY

LM 11 Miyojo (In serv. 25-3-74)

Miyojo (LM 11)   F. Lauga, 1976

D: 248 tons (303 normal)   **S:** 11 kts   **Dim:** 27.0 × 12.0 × 2.58
M: 2 Niigata 6MG 16HS diesels; 2 CP props; 600 hp   **Electric:** 135 kVA
Fuel: 15 tons   **Range:** 1,360/10   **Man:** 18 tot.

REMARKS: Has catamaran hull. Replaced a very similar ship with same name and number, which was lost in 4-72.

◆ 2 Hakuun class   Bldr: Sumidagawa, Tokyo

LM 106 Hakuun (In serv. 28-2-78)   LM 107 Toun (In serv. 3-79)

D: 57.6 tons (92.7 fl)   **S:** 15 kts   **Dim:** 24.00 (23.00 pp) × 6.00 × 1.00
Electron Equipt: Radar: 1/FRA-10 Mk III
M: 2 GM 12V71 TI diesels; 2 props; 1,080 hp   **Electric:** 30 kVA
Range: 420/13   **Man:** 10 tot.

REMARKS: Prototypes of a new class intended to replace earlier medium (LM) navigational-aid tenders.

◆ 1 Ayabane class   Bldr: Shimoda

LM 112 Ayabane (In serv. 25-12-72)

D: 187 tons normal   **S:** 12.3 kts   **Dim:** 32.70 × 6.5 × 1.8
M: 1 Hanshin 6 L24SH diesel; 1 prop; 500 hp   **Electric:** 70 kVA
Range: 2,330/11.9   **Man:** 18 tot.

◆ 1 Zuiun class   Bldr: Nihonkai

LM 101 Zuiun (In serv. 21-12-62)

D: 160 tons normal   **S:** 11.4 kts   **Dim:** 32.12 × 5.80 × 1.81
M: 1 Mitsui MD625 diesel; 260 hp   **Man:** 21 tot.

◆ 8 23-meter group   Bldrs: Various

	In serv.		In serv.		In serv.
LM 102 Reiun	11-71	LM 108 Reimei	3-62	LM 110 Seiun	3-68
LM 105 Sekiun	3-70	LM 109 Shoun	3-66	LM 111 Houn	3-70
				LM 113 Genun	3-73

D: 67-74 tons (normal)   **S:** 9.7-10.5 kts   **Dim:** 22.1 × 4.65 × 1.4
M: 1 Yanman or GM diesel; 120-200 hp   **Range:** 760-1,060/9.5
Man: 11-12 tot.

REMARKS: Minor variations but all similar. *Akatsuki* (LM 107) stricken 1979.

◆ 9 17-meter class   Bldr: Yokohama Yacht

	In serv.		In serv.
LS 204 Hatsunikari	3-79	LS 208 N. . .	14-7-79
LS 205 Nahahikari	2-79	LS 209 Kamihikari	17-12-79
LS 206 Matsuhikari	3-79	LS 210 Shimahikari	17-12-79
LS 207 N. . .	14-7-79	LS 211 Akihikari	27-2-81
		LS 218 N. . .	1981

D: 25 tons normal   **S:** 16.3 kts   **Dim:** 17.50 × 4.30 × 0.80
M: 2 E12OT-MF6R diesels; 2 props; 560 hp   **Endurance:** 2 days
Range: 230/14.5   **Man:** 8 tot.

NAVIGATIONAL AID TENDERS *(continued)*

Kamihikari (LS 209) *Ships of the World*, 1980

♦ **3 Himehikari class**

LS 215 WAKAHIKARI (In serv. 3-67)   LS 217 TAMAHIKARI (In serv. 3-69)
LS 216 MIOHIKARI (In serv. 2-68)

   D: 40 tons normal **S:** 9.7 kts **Dim:** 17.00 × 3.90 × . . .
   M: 2 5LD diesels; 2 props; 150 hp **Range:** 380/9 **Man:** 6 tot.

REMARKS: An LS 218, class not available, was laid down 19-6-80 by Yokohama Yacht.

♦ **7 Urahikari (17-meter) class** (In serv. 1969-75)

LS 115 FUSAHIKARI   LS 201 HARUHIKARI
LS 124 URAHIKARI   LS 202 TAKAHIKARI
LS 156 SEKIHIKARI   LS 203 SETOHIKARI
LS 184 TOMOHIKARI

   D: 16 tons (20 fl) **S:** 17.2 kts **Dim:** 17.00 × 3.50 × . . .
   M: 1 MTU UD 626 diesel; 180 hp **Range:** 320/5 **Man:** 10 tot.

♦ **4 12-meter class** Bldr: . . .

	In serv.		In serv.
LS 181 KEIKO	29-6-79	LS 186 TOKO	30-6-79
LS 185 SHITOKO	2-79	LS 187 SANHOKO	30-6-79

   D: 9.4 tons (10 fl) **S:** 15 kts **Dim:** 12.00 × 3.20 × 0.60
   M: 1 diesel; 1 prop; 210 hp **Range:** 120/13.5 **Man:** 6 tot.

♦ **8 Taiko (12-meter) class** (In serv. 1970-73)

LS 122 MEIKO   LS 152 TAIKO   LS 171 MYOKO   LS 218 CHOKO
LS 151 KYOKO   LS 153 SUIKO   LS 183 HAKUKO   LS 219 SAIKO

   D: 8 tons (12 fl) **S:** 14.8 kts **Dim:** 12.0 × 3.2 × . . .
   M: 1 MTU UD 626 diesel; 180 hp **Range:** 130/12.5 **Man:** 6 tot.

♦ **3 No. 1 Kaiko (10-meter) class** Bldr: . . .

LS 144 No. 1 KAIKO (In serv. 5-3-81)   LS 146 No. 3 KAIKO (In serv. 19-3-81)
LS 145 No. 2 KAIKO (In serv. 12-3-81)

   D: 5.2 tons **S:** 13 kts **Dim:** 9.00 × 2.25 × . . .
   M: 2 Nissan FD606 diesels; 1 prop; 230 hp **Range:** 130/12.5 **Man:** 6 tot.

♦ **6 No. 1 Yoko (10-meter) class** (In serv. 1975-79)

LS 114 No. 3 YOKO   LS 182 No. 2 YOKO   LS 142 No. 5 YOKO
LS 180 No. 1 YOKO   LS 141 No. 4 YOKO   LS 143 No. 6 YOKO

   D: 3 tons (5 fl) **S:** 16.2 kts **Dim:** 7.3 × 2.45 × 0.5
   M: 1 GM 3-53N diesel; 112 hp **Range:** 100/12 **Man:** 8 tot.

♦ **16 miscellaneous small navigational aid tenders**

LS 102, LS 103, LS 105, LS 106, LS 112, LS 113, LS 116, LS 117, LS 118, LS 123, LS 125, LS 137, LS 155, LS 163, LS 174, LS 175: 1-3 tons

♦ **16 10-meter class** (In serv. 1966-1972)

LS 104, LS 108, LS 111, LS 132, LS 134, LS 138, LS 140, LS 147, LS 150, LS 159, LS 162, LS 167, LS 179, LS 197, LS 198, LS 199

   D: 6 tons normal **S:** 8.7 kts **Dim:** 9.50 × 2.60 × . . .
   M: 2 MTU UD326 diesels; 1 prop; 180 hp **Range:** 100/8.7 **Man:** 6 tot.

REMARKS: Wooden construction. LS 199: 5 tons, 9.7 kts.

FIREBOATS

NOTE: Most patrol ships, boats, and craft are fitted for fire-fighting.

♦ **5 Hiryu class** Bldr: Asano DY

	In serv.		In serv.
FL 01 HIRYU	4-3-69	FL 04 KAIRYU	18-3-77
FL 02 SHORYU	4-3-70	FL 05 SUIRYU	3-78
FL 03 NANRYU	4-3-71		

Hiryu (FL 01) 1975

FIREBOATS (continued)

D: 199 tons (251 normal) **S:** 13.5 kts **Dim:** 27.5 × 10.4 × 2.1
M: 2 MTU MB820Db diesels; 2 props; 2,200 hp **Electric:** 70 kVA
Range: 400/13 **Man:** 14 tot.

REMARKS: Catamaran hulls. For fighting fires on board supertankers. 14.5m³ tank for fire-fighting chemicals. One 45-meter-range chemical sprayer; seven 60-meter-range water cannon.

♦ 10 Ninobiki class

Bldrs: FM 02, FM 06, FM 08, FM 10: Sumidagawa, Tokyo: Others: Yokohama Yacht

	In serv.		In serv.
FM 01 NINOBIKI	2-74	FM 06 NACHI	2-76
FM 02 YODO	3-75	FM 07 KEGON	1-77
FM 03 OTOWA	12-74	FM 08 MINOO	1-78
FM 04 SHIRAITO	2-75	FM 09 RYUSEI	24-3-80
FM 05 KOTOBIKI	2-76	FM 10 KYOTAKI	25-3-81

Otowa (FM 03)   1975

D: 89 tons (99 normal) **S:** 13.4 kts **Dim:** 23.00 × 6.00 × 1.55
M: 1 MTU MB820Db and 2 Nissan UDV 816 diesels; 3 props; 1,600 hp
Electric: 40 kVA **Range:** 234/13.4 **Man:** 12 tot.

REMARKS: In service 1974-78. Four fire pumps: one of 6,000 l/min., two of 3,000 l/min., and one of 2,000 l/min. Have two 750-liter and one 5000-liter foam tanks.

ENVIRONMENTAL-PRODUCTION CRAFT

♦ 1 Katsuren-class radiation monitoring craft Bldr: Ishihara, Takasago

MS 03 KATSUREN (In serv. 13-12-75)

D: 30 tons (46 fl) **S:** 12.3 kts **Dim:** 16.50 × 5.50 × 1.10
M: 2 UDV 816 diesels; 2 props; 500 hp **Range:** 190/10.8 **Man:** 9 tot.

♦ 2 Kinagusa-class radiation monitoring craft Bldr: Sumidagawa, Tokyo

MS 01 KINAGUSA (In serv. 25-9-70)   MS 02 SAIKAI (In serv. 1-10-70)

D: 16 tons (23 fl) **S:** 8.1 kts **Dim:** 10.50 × 5.00 × 0.63
M: 2 UD 326 diesels; 2 props; 180 hp **Range:** 170/7.6 **Man:** 8 tot.

♦ 32 Orion-class oil spill surveillance craft Bldr: Yokohama Yacht (In serv. 1972-1979)

SS 01 ORION	SS 12 SPICA	SS 23 PERSEUS	SS 33 N. . .
SS 02 PEGASUS	SS 13 SIRIUS	SS 24 CENTAURUS	SS 34 N. . .
SS 04 NEPTUNE	SS 14 VEGA	SS 25 ANDROMEDA	
SS 05 JUPITER	SS 16 PROCYON	SS 26 ALTAIR	
SS 06 VENUS	SS 17 LEO	SS 27 HERCULES	
SS 07 CASSIOPEIA	SS 18 POLARIS	SS 28 GEMINI	
SS 08 PHOENIX	SS 19 RIGEL	SS 29 ERIZU	
SS 09 SERPENS	SS 20 CYGNUS	SS 30 COMET	
SS 10 CARINA	SS 21 DENEB	SS 31 REGULUS	
SS 11 CAPELLA	SS 22 MERCURY	SS 32 N. . .	

D: 2.1 tons (5 fl) **S:** 28.0 kts **Dim:** 5.99 × 2.44 × . . .
M: 1 AQ 200 inboard/outboard motor; 130 hp **Range:** 85/25 **Man:** 6 tot.

REMARKS: Propulsion and speeds vary: 16-28 kts from 130-210 hp.

♦ 1 Antares-class oil spill surveillance craft Bldr: Sajima

SS 15 ANTARES (In serv. 1-7-75)

D: 1.6 tons **S:** 25 kts **Dim:** 5.49 × 2.41 × . . .
M: 1 Yanmar YA-19J2 diesel waterjet; 220 hp **Range:** 170/24 **Man:** 6 tot.

♦ 5 Shirasagi-class oil spill clearance boats Bldr: Sumidagawa, Tokyo (In serv. 1977-79)

OR 01 SHIRASAGI	OR 03 N. . .	OR 05 ISOSHIGI
OR 02 N. . .	OR 04 CHIDORI	

D: 78.5 tons (153 fl) **S:** 6.8 kts **Dim:** 22.0 × 6.4 × 0.9
M: 2 UD 626 diesels; water-jet drive; 390 hp **Range:** 160/6 **Man:** 7 tot.

♦ 3 Uraga-class oil-skimmer boats Bldr: Lockheed, U.S.A. (In serv. 1975-76)

OS 01 TSURUMI (ex-Uraga)   OS 02 BISAN   OS 03 NARUTO

D: 11 tons (fl) **S:** 6 kts **Dim:** 8.26 × 5.00 × 0.70
M: 1 HR-6 diesel; 2 props; 90 hp **Range:** 90/4.5 **Man:** 4 tot.

♦ 19 M-101-class oil-boom-extender barges (In serv. 1974-76)

OX 01 to OX 19 (M 101 to M 119)

D: 48 tons **Dim:** 22.00 × 7.20 × 0.45

M 101 (OX 01)   1975

JORDAN
Hashemite Kingdom of Jordan

COASTAL GUARD

PERSONNEL: 300 men, including those at the base at Aqaba and frogmen

MERCHANT MARINE (1979): 1 ship—496 grt

♦ **4 U.S.-supplied small craft** Bldr: Bertram, Miami

FAYSAL   HAN   HASAYU   MUHAMMED

   D: 8 tons **S:** 25 kts **Dim:** 11.6 × 4.0 × 0.5
   A: 1/12.7-mm mg—2/7.62-mm mg

♦ **2 U.S.-supplied small craft** Bldr: Bertram, Miami

ALI   ABD ALLAH

   D: 6.5 tons **S:** 25 kts **Dim:** 9.26 × 3.26 × 0.46
   A: 1/12.7-mm mg—1/7.62-mm mg **Man:** 8 tot.

KAMPUCHEA
Democratic Kampuchea

MERCHANT MARINE (1980): 3 ships—3,558 grt

NOTE: The composition of Kampuchea's afloat forces, if any, is not known. Most of her large ships and craft fled in 1975, and as of 1979, Vietnam apparently controlled coastal waters. A few small patrol craft, U.S. PBR Mk-I or Mk-II classes, may survive in Khmer Rouge river service.

KENYA
Republic of Kenya

PERSONNEL: 350 total

MERCHANT MARINE (1980): 19 ships—17,371 grt (tankers: 1 ship—1,447 grt)

PATROL BOATS

♦ **3 32-meter class** Bldr: Brooke Marine, Lowestoft, G.B.

	L	In serv.
P 3121 MADARAKA	28-1-75	16-6-75
P 3122 JAMHURI	14-3-75	16-6-75
P 3123 HARAMBEE	2-5-75	28-8-75

Harambee (P 3123)   1975

   D: 120 tons (145 fl) **S:** 25.5 kts **Dim:** 32.6 × 6.1 × 1.7
   A: 4/Gabriel SSM (I × 4)—2/40-mm Mk 7 AA (I × 2)
   M: 2 Paxman 16-cyl. Valenta diesels; 2 props; 5,400 hp
   Range: 2,300/12 **Man:** 3 officers, 18 men

REMARKS: Ordered 10-5-73. P 3121 received Gabriel missiles during 1981, with the other two to follow.

♦ **1 37.5-meter class** Bldr: Brooke Marine, Lowestoft, G.B.

	Laid down	L	In serv.
P 3100 MAMBA	17-2-72	6-11-73	7-2-74

Mamba (P 3100)   1975

   D: 130 tons (160 fl) **S:** 25 kts **Dim:** 37.5 × 6.86 × 1.78
   A: 2/40-mm Mk 7 AA (I × 2)

KENYA (*continued*)
PATROL BOATS (*continued*)

M: 2 Paxman 16-cyl. Valenta diesels; 2 props; 4,000 hp
Range: 3,500/13   **Man:** 3 officers, 22 men

REMARKS: May receive 4 Israeli Gabriel anti-ship missiles.

♦ **3 Vosper 31-meter class** Bldr: Vosper Portsmouth, G.B.

	L	In serv.
P 3110 SIMBA	9-9-65	23-5-66
P 3112 CHUI	25-11-65	7-7-66
P 3117 NDOVU (ex-*Twigg*)	22-12-65	27-7-66

Simba (P 3110)   Vosper, 1966

D: 96 tons (109 fl)   **S:** 24/23 kts   **Dim:** 31.25 (28.95 pp) × 5.95 × 1.65
A: 2/40-mm AA Mk 7 (I × 2)
M: 2 Paxman Ventura 12-cyl. diesels; 2 props; 2,900 hp   **Fuel:** 14 tons
Range: 1,500/16   **Man:** 3 officers, 20 men

♦ **3 port service launches:** no data available

KIRIBATI
(formerly Gilbert Islands)

PATROL CRAFT

♦ **1 17-meter glass-reinforced plastic patrol craft** Bldr: Cheverton, Cowes (In serv. 1980)

D: 22 tons (fl)   **S:** 23.6 kts   **Dim:** 17.0 × 4.5 × 1.2
A: 1/7.62-mm mg   **M:** 2 GM 8V-71 TI diesels; 2 props; 800 hp
Range: 790/18; 1,000/12   **Man:** 7 tot.

KOREA, NORTH
Democratic People's Republic of Korea

PERSONNEL: Approximately 9,000 men

MERCHANT MARINE (1980): 34 ships—230,695 grt (tankers: 5 ships—77,908 grt)

SUBMARINES

♦ **12 Soviet Romeo class**

D: 1,330/1,700 tons   **S:** 15/13 kts   **Dim:** 77.0 × 6.7 × 4.95
A: 8/533-mm TT (6 fwd, 2 aft)—14 torpedoes or 28 mines
Electron Equipt: Radar: 1/Snoop Plate
               Sonar: . . .
M: 2 diesels of 2,000 hp, electric drive; 2 props; 2,500 hp   **Endurance:** 60 days
Range: 7,500/5 snorkel   **Man:** 56 tot.

REMARKS: Seven are of Chinese construction, transferred in 1973 (two), 1974 (two), and 1975 (three). The others were built in North Korea with Chinese assistance; construction may be continuing.

♦ **4 Soviet Whiskey class**

D: 1,050/1,350 tons   **S:** 16/17 kts   **Dim:** 76.0 × 6.3 × 4.8
A: 6/533-mm TT (4 fwd, 2 aft)—12 torpedoes or 24 mines
Electron Equipt: Radar: 1/Snoop Plate
               Sonar: Hercules, passive array
M: 2 Type 37D diesels of 2,000 hp, diesel-electric drive; 2 props; 2,500 hp
Endurance: 60 days   **Range:** 4,000/5 (snorkel)   **Man:** 50 tot.

REMARKS: Transferred from the U.S.S.R. during 1960s.

FRIGATES

♦ **3 Najin class** Bldr: North Korea, 1973, 1975, 1977

D: 1,200 tons   **S:** 25 kts   **Dim:** 100.0 × 10.0 × 2.7
A: 2/100-mm DP (I × 2)—4/57-mm AA (II × 2)—4/25-mm AA (II × 2)—8/14.5-mm mg (II × 4)—3/533-mm TT (III × 1)—4/d.c. projectors—30 mines
Electron Equipt: Radar: 1/Skin Head, 1/Pot Head, 1/Slim Net
               Sonar: . . .
M: 2 diesels; 2 props; 15,000 hp   **Range:** 4,000/14   **Man:** 155 tot.

REMARKS: Very primitive design, crude in finish and appearance.

CORVETTES

♦ **4 Sariwan class** Bldr: North Korea, 1965

D: 475 tons   **S:** 21 kts   **Dim:** 62.1 × 7.3 × 2.4
A: 1/76-mm DP—2/57-mm AA (II × 2)—4/25-mm AA (II × 2)—4/d.c. projectors
M: 2 diesels; 2 props; 3,000 hp

REMARKS: Data dubious. Design based on Soviet *Tral*-class minesweeper.

GUIDED-MISSILE PATROL BOATS

♦ **8 Soviet Osa-I class**

D: 175 tons (210 fl) **S:** 36 kts **Dim:** 39.0 × 7.7 × 1.8
A: 4/SS-N-2A Styx SSM (I × 4)—4/30-mm AA (II × 2)
Electron Equipt: Radar: 1/Square Tie, 1/Drum Tilt
IFF: 2/Square Head, 1/High Pole
M: 3 M503A diesels; 3 props; 12,000 hp **Range:** 450/34, 700/20 **Man:** 30 tot.

♦ **10 Soviet Komar class**

D: 71 tons (82 fl) **S:** 40 kts **Dim:** 25.3 × 7.0 × 1.9
A: 2/SS-N-2A Styx SSM (I × 2)—2/25-mm AA (II × 1)
Electron Equipt: Radar: 1/Square Tie **M:** 4 M50-F4 diesels; 4 props; 4,800 hp
Range: 400/30 **Man:** 18 tot.

REMARKS: Wooden construction; hull same as P 6 torpedo boat.

PATROL BOATS

♦ **6 Taechong class** Bldr: North Korea—no data available

♦ **6 Chinese Hainan class**

D: 360 tons (400 fl) **S:** 30.5 kts **Dim:** 58.77 × 7.20 × 2.20
A: 4/57-mm AA (II × 2)—4/25-mm AA (II × 2)—4/RBU-1200 ASW RL (V × 4)—2/d.c. projectors—2/d.c. racks—mines
Electron Equipt: Radar: 1/Pot Head **M:** 4 Type 9D diesels; 4 props; 8,800 hp
Man: 70 tot.

REMARKS: Two transferred in 1975; two in 1976; and two in 1978.

♦ **60 Chaho class** Bldr: North Korea

D: 80 tons (fl) **S:** 40 kts **Dim:** 27.7 × 6.1 × 1.8
A: 4/14.5-mm AA (II × 2)—1/200-mm artillery RL, (40 tubes)
M: 4 M50 diesels; 4 props; 4,800 hp

REMARKS: Based on P 6 design, but have steel hull.

♦ **30 Chong Jin class** Bldr: North Korea

REMARKS: Data as for Chaho class except armaments include: one 85-mm tank gun and four 14.5-mm anti-aircraft guns (II × 2).

♦ **8 Chinese Shanghai II class**

D: 122.5 tons (150 fl) **S:** 28.5 kts **Dim:** 38.78 × 5.41 × 1.49
A: 4/37-mm AA (II × 2)—4/25-mm AA (II × 2)—d.c.—mines
Electron Equipt: Radar: 1/Pot Head
M: 2 M50-F4, 1,200-hp and 2/12D6, 910-hp diesels; 4 props; 4,220 hp
Man: 38 tot.

REMARKS: Transferred circa 1967-69.

♦ **15 (+. . .) Soviet S.O. 1 class**

D: 190 tons (215 fl) **S:** 28 kts **Dim:** 42.0 × 6.1 × 1.9
A: Soviet version: 4/25-mm AA (II × 2)—4/RBU-1200 ASW RL (V × 4)—2/d.c. racks—mines
North Korean version: 1/85-mm DP—2/37-mm AA (I × 2)—4/14.5-mm mg (II × 2)

Electron Equipt: Radar: 1/Pot Head or Don-2
Sonar: 1/Tamir
M: 3 Type 40D diesels; 3 props; 7,500 hp **Man:** 30-40 tot.

REMARKS: Six transferred from U.S.S.R. in antisubmarine configuration 1957-61; remainder built in Korea for patrol purposes.

♦ **8 Chinese Shantou (Swatow) class**

D: 80 tons (fl) **S:** 28 kts **Dim:** 25.1 × 6.0 × 1.8
A: 4/37-mm AA (II × 2)—2/14.5-mm mg (I × 2)
M: 4 diesels; 4 props; 3,000 hp

♦ **4 Chodo class** Bldr: North Korea

D: 130 tons **S:** 24 kts **Dim:** 42.7 × 5.8 × 2.6
A: 1/76-mm DP—3/37-mm AA (I × 3)—4/25-mm AA (II × 2)
M: Diesels; 2 props; 6,000 hp **Man:** 24 tot.

♦ **4 K-48 class** Bldr: North Korea (In serv. 1951-54)

D: 110 tons (fl) **S:** 24 kts **Dim:** 38.1 × 5.5 × 1.5
A: 1/76-mm DP—3/37-mm AA (I × 3)—4/14.5-mm AA (II × 2)
M: 2 diesels; 2 props; 5,000 hp

♦ **20 Soviet M.O. IV class** (In serv. 1945-47)

D: 56 tons (fl) **S:** 25 kts **Dim:** 27.0 × 4.0 × 1.5
A: 1/37-mm AA—2/14.5-mm AA (I × 2)
M: 2 diesels; 2 props; 2,600 hp **Man:** 20 tot.

REMARKS: Wooden construction. Transferred 1950.

TORPEDO BOATS

♦ **4 Soviet Shershen class**

D: 150 tons (180 fl) **S:** 45 kts **Dim:** 34.0 × 7.2 × 1.5
A: 4/30-mm AA (II × 2)—4/533-mm TT—2/d.c. racks
Electron Equipt: Radar: 1/Pot Drum, 1/Drum Tilt
IFF: 1/Square Head, 1/High Pole A
M: 3 M503A diesels; 3 props; 12,000 hp **Range:** 450/34, 700/20

♦ **64 (+. . .) Soviet P 6/North Korean Sinpo class**

D: 55 tons (66.5 fl) **S:** 43 kts **Dim:** 25.3 × 6.1 × 1.7
A: 4/25-mm AA (II × 2)—2/533-mm TT—d.c.
Electron Equipt: Radar: 1/Skin Head or Pot Head
IFF: 1/Dead Duck, 1/High Pole
M: 4 M50-F4 diesels; 4 props; 4,800 hp **Range:** 450/30

REMARKS: Forty-five transferred by U.S.S.R.; wooden construction. Remainder (Sinpo class) built in Korea, steel construction. Some lack torpedo tubes but have additional AA guns.

♦ **15 Iwon class** Bldr: North Korea (In serv. 1970s)

D: 25 tons (fl) **S:** 45 kts **Dim:** 19.2 × 3.7 × 1.5
A: 2/25-mm AA (II × 2)—2/533-mm TT
M: 3 diesels; 3 props; 3,600 hp

REMARKS: Apparently a Korean version of the P 4 hydroplane design.

KOREA-NORTH (*continued*)
TORPEDO BOATS (*continued*)

♦ **6 An Ju class** Bldr: North Korea

   D: 35 tons (fl) **S:** 50 kts **Dim:** 19.8 × 3.7 × 1.8
   A: 2/25-mm AA (II × 2)—2/533-mm TT
   M: 4 M50 diesels; 4 props; 4,800 hp **Man:** 20 tot.

♦ **60 Sin Hung class** Bldr: North Korea

   D: 25 tons (fl) **S:** . . . **Dim:** 18.3 × 3.4 × 1.7
   A: 2/14.5-mm (II × 1)—2/450-mm TT
   M: 2 diesels; 2 props; 2,400 hp

♦ **12 Soviet P 4 class**

   D: 19.3 tons (22.4 fl) **S:** 55 kts **Dim:** 19.3 × 3.7 × 1.0
   A: 2/14.5-mm mg (II × 1)—2/450-mm TT
   Electron Equipt: Radar: 1/Skin Head
   M: 2 M50 series diesels; 2 props; 2,400 hp

REMARKS: Stepped hydroplanes, transferred 1952-53. Aluminum construction. Possibly stricken, considering age.

AMPHIBIOUS CRAFT

♦ **70 Nampo class assault landing craft** Bldr: North Korea

   D: 70 tons (fl) **S:** 40 kts **Dim:** 27.7 × 6.1 × 1.8
   A: 4/14.5-mm AA (II × 2) **M:** 4 M50 diesels; 4 props; 4,800 hp
   Range: 375/40 **Man:** 19 tot.

REMARKS: A version of the Chaho-class gunboat with a bow ramp and troop accommodations forward.

♦ **9 Hanchon class** Bldr: North Korea: LCU type; no data available

♦ **18 smaller landing craft, LCM type**

KOREA, SOUTH
Republic of Korea

PERSONNEL: Approximately 32,000 men, plus 20,000 Marines

MERCHANT MARINE (1980): 1,426 ships—4,334,144 grt (tankers: 78 ships—1,335,176 grt)

NAVAL AVIATION: Twenty-three land-based U.S. S-2F Tracker aircraft are employed for surveillance and ASW. Ten or more Alouette-III helicopters are available for use on destroyers.

NOTE: Pendant numbers are subject to change at unspecified intervals. The numerals "0" and "4" are considered unlucky and are not used.

DESTROYERS

♦ **5 ex-U.S. Gearing class, FRAM I**

	Bldr	Laid down	L	In serv.
919 TAEJON (ex-*New*, DD 818)	Bath Iron Works	14-4-45	18-8-45	5-4-46
921 KUANG JU (ex-*Richard E. Kraus*, DD 849)	Consolidated Steel, Orange, Tex.	31-7-45	2-3-46	23-5-46
922 KANG WON (ex-*William R. Rush*, DD 714)	Federal SB, Newark, N.J.	19-10-44	8-7-45	21-9-45
923 KYONG KI (ex-*Newman K. Perry*, DD 883)	Consolidated Steel, Orange, Tex.	10-10-44	17-3-45	26-7-45
925 JEONG JU (ex-*Rogers*, DD 876)	Consolidated Steel, Orange, Tex.	3-6-44	20-11-44	26-3-45

Kyong Ki (923)—prior to modification   1981

Kang Won (922)—prior to rearmament   1979

   D: 2,425 tons (3,500 fl) **S:** 30 kts
   Dim: 119.03 (116.74 wl) × 12.52 × 4.45 (6.4 sonar)
   A: 919, 921, 922: 8/Harpoon SSM (IV × 2)—4/127-mm DP (II × 2)—2/40-mm AA (II × 1)—4/20-mm AA (II × 2)—6/324-mm Mk 32 ASW TT (III × 2)—1/Alouette-III ASW helo
      923, 925: 4/127-mm DP (IV × 2)—1/ASROC ASW RL (VIII × 1)—6/324-mm Mk 32 ASW TT
   Electron Equipt: Radar: 1/SPS-10, 1/SPS-29 (919, 921: SPS-40), 1/Mk 25
                  Sonar: SQS-23
                  ECM: WLR-3, ULQ-6, 2/chaff RL on 919-922
   M: 2 sets GT; 2 props; 60,000 hp **Electric:** 1,200 kw
   Boilers: 4 Babcock & Wilcox; 39.8 kg/cm², 454°C **Fuel:** 640 tons
   Range: 4,800/15, 2,400/25 **Man:** 274 tot.

DESTROYERS (continued)

REMARKS: 919, 921 were transferred 25-2-77; 922 on 1-7-79; 923 on 25-7-81; 925 on 11-8-81. Have one Mk 37 director, and 1 Mk 51 mod. 2 for 40-mm; 40-mm AA added fwd, 20-mm AA amidships. Harpoon added 1979.

♦ **2 ex-U.S. Gearing class, FRAM II** Bldr: Bath Iron Works

	Laid down	L	In serv.
915 CHUNG BUK	12-6-44	29-10-44	8-9-44
(ex-*Chevalier*, DDR 805)			
916 JEONG BUK	4-9-44	28-1-45	6-4-45
(ex-*Everett F. Larson*, DDR 830)			

D: 2,400 tons (3,500 fl)   **S:** 30 kts   **Dim:** 119.17 × 12.45 × 5.8
A: 8/Harpoon (IV × 2)—6/127-mm DP (II × 3)—6/324-mm Mk 32 ASW TT (III × 2)—2/Mk 11 Hedgehog—1/Alouette-III helicopter
Electron Equipt: Radars: 1/SPS-10, 1/SPS-40, 1/Mk 25
    Sonar: SQS-29 series
    ECM: WLR-3, ULQ-6
M: 2 sets GT; 2 props; 60,000 hp   **Electric:** 1,200 kw
Boilers: 4 Babcock & Wilcox; 39.8 kg/cm², 454°C   **Fuel:** 640 tons
Range: 4,800/15, 2,400/25   **Man:** 14 officers, 260 men

REMARKS: Transferred on loan 5-7-72 and 30-10-72; sold outright 31-1-77. One Mk 37 director for 127-mm guns.

♦ **2 ex-U.S. Allen M. Sumner class, FRAM II**

	Bldr	Laid down	L	In serv.
917 DAE GU	Federal SB, Kearny, N.J.	19-9-43	14-6-44	8-9-44
(ex-*Wallace L. Lind*, DD 703)				
918 INCHON (ex-*De Haven*, DD 727)	Bath Iron Works	9-8-43	9-1-44	31-3-44

D: 2,350 tons (3,320 fl)   **S:** 34 kts   **Dim:** 114.8 × 12.4 × 5.2
A: 8/Harpoon SSM (IV × 2)—6/127-mm AA (II × 3)—4/40-mm AA (II × 2)—6/324-mm Mk 32 ASW TT (III × 2)—2/Mk 11 Hedgehogs—1/Alouette-III helicopter
Electron Equipt: Radar: 1/SPS-10, 1/SPS-40 (918: SPS-29), 1/Mk 25
    Sonar: SQS-29 series, 1/SQA-10 VDS (917 only)
    ECM: WLR-3
M: 2 sets GE GT; 2 props; 60,000 hp   **Electric:** 1,200 kw
Boilers: 4 Babcock & Wilcox; 39.8 kg/cm², 454°C   **Man:** 235 tot.

REMARKS: Transferred 12-73. Eight Harpoon added 1978-79; helicopter deck and hangar enlarged to accommodate Alouette-III, 1978.

♦ **3 ex-U.S. Fletcher class**

	Bldr	Laid down	L	In serv.
911 CHUNG MU	Bath Iron Works	28-10-42	21-3-43	28-5-43
(ex-*Erben*, DD 631)				
912 SEOUL	Bethlehem, Staten Isl.	4-2-43	30-6-43	25-10-43
(ex-*Halsey Powell*, DD 686)				
913 PUSAN	Federal SB, Kearny, N.J.	12-3-43	4-7-43	10-9-43
(ex-*Hickox*, DD 673)				

D: 2,050 tons (2,850 fl)   **S:** 35 kts   **Dim:** 114.85 (wl) × 12.03 × 5.5
A: 5/127-mm 38-cal. (I × 5)—10/40-mm AA (IV × 2, II × 2, none in 912)—2/Hedgehog—6/324-mm Mk 32 ASW TT (IV × 2)
Electron Equipt: Radar: 1/SPS-10, 1/SPS-6C, 1/Mk 25
    Sonar: 1/SQS-4
    ECM: WLR-1
M: 2 sets GE GT; 2 props; 60,000 hp   **Electric:** 540 kw
Boilers: 4 Babcock & Wilcox; 39.8 kg/cm², 454°C   **Fuel:** 650 tons
Range: 4,500/12, 900/35   **Man:** 303 tot.

REMARKS: The *Chung Mu* transferred 1-5-63, the *Seoul* on 27-4-68, the *Pusan* on 15-11-68; all purchased outright 31-1-77. The *Seoul* may by now have been given 40-mm AA. Have one Mk 37 director for 127-mm mount; one Mk 51 mod. 2 director for each 40-mm mount.

FRIGATES

♦ **1 Ulsan class** Bldr: Hayundai, Ulsan, Korea

	Laid down	L	In serv.
951 ULSAN	1-5-79	8-4-80	1-1-81

D: 1,600 tons (2,880 fl)   **S:** 35 kts   **Dim:** 102.0 × 11.5 × 3.6
A: 8/Harpoon SSM (IV × 2)—2/76-mm DP OTO Melara—8/30-mm AA Emerlec (II × 4)—6/324-mm Mk 32 ASW TT (III × 2)—2/d.c. rack
Electron Equipt: Radar: 1/HSA DA-05, 1/HSA ZW-06, 1/HSA WM 28
    Sonar: 1/PHS-32
M: CODOG: 2 GE LM 2500 gas turbines, 53,600 hp; 2 MTU 12V956 diesels, 7,200 hp; 2 CP props
Range: . . .   **Man:** 123 tot.

REMARKS: Three sisters canceled due to costs. Dutch electronic equipment, including 2 NSA L10D optronic standby gun directors.

♦ **1 ex-U.S. Rudderow class**

	Bldr	L	In serv.
827 CHUNG NAM (ex-*Holt*, DE 706)	Defoe SB	15-12-43	9-6-44

D: 1,650 (2,230 fl)   **S:** 23 kts   **Dim:** 93.3 × 11.8 × 4.3
A: 2/127-mm DP (I × 2)—4/40-mm AA (II × 2)—6/20-mm AA—6/324-mm Mk 32 ASW TT (III × 2)—2/Hedgehog—1/d.c. rack
Electron Equipt: Radar: 1/SPS-5, 1/SPS-6, 1/Mk 26
    Sonar: SQS-11
M: 2 sets GE GT, turbo-electric drive; 2 props; 12,000 hp
Boilers: 2 Foster-Wheeler "D"-Express; 30.6 kg/cm², 399°C   **Fuel:** 360 tons
Range: 5,000/15   **Man:** 210 tot.

REMARKS: Loaned 19-6-63; purchased outright 15-11-74. Mk 52 GFCS for the 127-mm guns, 2 Mk 51 mod. 2 for the 40-mm AA.

♦ **4 ex-U.S. Crosley-class former high-speed transports**

	Bldr	Laid down	L	In serv.
821 KYONG NAM	Defoe SB, Bay City, Mich.	28-3-44	15-6-44	13-3-45
(ex-*Cavallaro*, APD 128)				
823 AH SAN	Bethlehem Steel, Hingham, Mass.	19-1-44	1-3-44	5-6-45
(ex-*Harry L. Corl*, APD 108)				

FRIGATES (continued)

	Bldr	Laid down	L	In serv.
825 Ung Po (ex-*Julius A. Raven*, APD 110)	Bethlehem Steel, Hingham, Mass.	26-1-44	3-3-44	28-6-45
828 Che Ju (ex-*William M.* *Hobby*, APD 95)	Charleston Navy Yard, Charleston, S.C.	15-11-43	11-2-44	4-4-45

D: 1,650 tons (2,130 fl) **S:** 23.6 kts **Dim:** 93.13 × 11.3 × 3.2
A: 2/127-mm DP (I × 2)—6/40-mm AA (II × 3)—2/Mk 6 d.c. projectors—2/d.c.
   racks
Electron Equipt: Radars: 1/SPS-5, 1/SPS-6, 1/Mk 26
                 Sonar: QCU-2
M: 2 sets GE GT, turbo-electric drive; 2 props; 12,000 hp
Boilers: 2 Foster-Wheeler "D"-express; 30.6 kg/cm², 399°C
Range: 4,800/12, 2,300/22 **Man:** 200 tot.

REMARKS: Transferred on loan 10-59, 6-66, 6-66, and 8-67; purchased outright 15-11-74. Second 127-mm gun added aft, as on Taiwanese sisters. Have low bridge compared to ex-*Charles Lawrence* ships, below. Can still carry 160 troops; two LCVPs and two LCPLs stowed beneath quadrantal davits. One Mk 52 director for 127-mm gun; three Mk 51 mod. 2 for 40-mm AA.

♦ **2 ex-U.S. Charles Lawrence-class former high-speed transports**

Bldr: Charleston Navy Yard, Charleston, S.C.

	Laid down	L	In serv.
826 Kyong Puk (ex-*Kephart*, APD 61)	12-5-43	6-9-43	7-1-44
827 Jon Nam (ex-*Hayter*, APD 80)	11-8-43	11-11-43	4-4-45

REMARKS: All data essentially the same as for the *Crosley* class, above. Loaned in 8-67; purchased outright 15-11-74. Have high bridge as compared to the *Crosley* class. All APDs of both classes were laid down originally as DE-destroyer escorts.

CORVETTES

♦ **3 ex-U.S. Auk-class former fleet minesweepers**

	Bldr	Laid down	L	In serv.
PCE 711 Shin Song (ex-*Ptarmigan*, MSF 376)	Savannah Mach., Savannah, Ga.	9-3-44	15-7-44	15-1-45
PCE 712 Sun Chonke (ex-*Speed*, MSF 116)	American SB, Lorain, Ohio	17-11-41	6-6-42	15-10-42
PCE 713 Koje Ho (ex-*Dextrous*, MSF 341)	Gulf SB, Madisonville, Tenn.	8-6-42	17-1-43	8-9-43

D: 890 tons (1,250 fl) **S:** 18 kts **Dim:** 67.2 (65 pp) × 9.75 × 3.3
A: 2/76.2-mm DP (I × 2)—4/40-mm AA (II × 2)—4/20-mm AA (II × 2)—
   1/Hedgehog—3/324-mm Mk 32 ASW TT (III × 1)—2/d.c. racks
Electron Equipt: Radar: 1/SPS-5
                  Sonar: SQS-17A
M: 2 GM 12-278 diesels, electric drive; 2 props; 3,532 hp **Fuel:** 200 tons
Man: 110 tot.

REMARKS: Converted to corvettes before transfer. Minesweeping gear deleted and replaced by additional ASW equipment and second 76.2-mm Mk 26 gun aft. Have 2 Mk 51 mod. 2 GFCS.

GUIDED-MISSILE PATROL BOATS

♦ **8 PSMM-5 class** Bldrs: PGM 352 to PGM 355: Tacoma Boatbuilding Co.; Others: Korea-Tacoma, Chinhae

	Laid down	In serv.
PGM 352 Paek Ku 52	1-75	14-3-75
PGM 353 Paek Ku 53	2-75	14-3-75
PGM 355 Paek Ku 55	. . .	1-2-76
PGM 356 Paek Ku 56	. . .	1-2-76
PGM 357 Paek Ku 57	. . .	1977
PGM 358 Paek Ku 58	. . .	1977
PGM 359 Paek Ku 59	. . .	1977
PGM 361 Paek Ku 61	. . .	1978

D: 240 tons (268 fl) **S:** 40 kts **Dim:** 53.68 (50.30 pp) × 8.00 × 1.63
A: 8/Harpoon SSM (IV × 2)—1/76.2-mm DP—1/40-mm AA—2/12.7-mm mg
Electron Equipt: Radars: 1/LN-66 HP, 1/SPG-50 **Man:** 5 officers, 27 men
M: 6 AVCO TF-35 gas turbines; 2 CP props; 16,800 hp

REMARKS: Korean-built units have Westinghouse M-1200 fire-control systems, using inputs from the LN-66 HP radar and an optical director. Early ships have the U.S. Mk 63 GFCS.

♦ **1 ex-U.S. Asheville class** Bldr: Tacoma Boat, Tacoma, Wash.

	L	In serv.
PGM 351 Paek Ku 51 (ex-*Benicia*, PG 96)	20-12-69	25-4-70

D: 225 tons (249 fl) **S:** 40 kts **Dim:** 50.14 × 7.28 × 2.9
A: 1/76.2-mm Mk 34 DP—1/40-mm AA—4/12.7-mm mg (II × 2)
Electron Equipt: Radar: 1/LN-66, 1/SPG-50
M: CODOG: 1GE LM-1500-PE102 gas turbine, 12,500 hp; 2 Cummins VT12-
   875M diesels; 1,450 hp; 2 CP props
Range: 1,700/16, 390/35 **Man:** 29 tot.

REMARKS: May have eight Harpoon (IV × 2). Mk 63 radar GFCS for 76.2-mm Mk 34 gun. Transferred on loan 15-10-71.

♦ **2 PGF "Sea Dolphin" type** Bldr: Korea SB & Eng. (In serv. 1971-72)

PKM 271 Kilurki 71   PKM 272 Kilurki 72

D: 120 tons (140 fl) **S:** 35 kts **Dim:** 32.9 × 8.0 × 1.1
A: 2/MM 38 Exocet SSM (I × 2)—1/40-mm AA—2/12.7-mm mg—2/barrage RL
   (IV × 2)
M: PKM 271: 2 MTU MB518D diesels; 3 props; 9,960 hp
      PKM 272: 3 MTU 16V538 TB90 diesels; 3 props; 10,800 hp
Range: 1,000/20 **Man:** 28 tot.

PATROL BOATS

♦ **4 "Sea Dolphin" type** Bldr: Korea SB & Eng. (In serv. . . .)

PKM 211 Kilurki 11   PKM 213 Kilurki 13
PKM 212 Kilurki 12   PKM 215 Kilurki 15

D: 113 tons (144 fl) **S:** 38 kts **Dim:** 32.9 × 8.0 × 1.1
A: 1/40-mm AA—2/30-mm Emerlec AA (II × 1)—4/20-mm AA (II × 2)—2/12.7-
   mm mg (I × 2)
M: 3 MTU 16V538 TB90 diesels; 3 props; 10,800 hp (9,000 sust.)
Range: 1,000/20 **Man:** 28 tot.

PATROL BOATS *(continued)*

REMARKS: Gunboat version of the class above.

NOTE: The unsuccessful "CPIC" prototype, PKM 123, has been returned to the U.S. Navy.

♦ **26 PK "Schoolboy" or "Sea Hawk" class** Bldr: Korea SB & Eng.

PK 151 to PK 176   CHEBI 51-76

PK 176   1981

   D: 70 tons (80 fl)   **S:** 40 kts   **Dim:** 25.7 × 5.4 × 1.2
   A: 1/40-mm AA—1/20-mm AA—4/12.7 mm mg (II × 2)—2/7.62-mm mg (I × 2)
   M: 2 MTU 16V538 diesels; 2 props; 5,200 hp   **Range:** 500/20   **Man:** 15 tot.

♦ **8 ex-USCG Cape class** (In serv. 1958-59)

PB 3 (ex-*Cape Rosier*, WPB 95333)   PB 9 (ex-*Cape Falcon*, WPB 95330)
PB 5 (ex-*Cape Sable*, WPB 95334)   PB 10 (ex-*Cape Trinity*, WPB 95331)
PB 6 (ex-*Cape Providence*, WPB 95335) PB 11 (ex-*Cape Darby*, WPB 95323)
PB 8 (ex-*Cape Porpoise*, WPB 95327)   PB 12 (ex-*Cape Kiwanda*, WPB 95329)

   D: 105 tons (fl)   **S:** 18 kts   **Dim:** 28.95 × 5.8 × 1.55
   A: 1/81-mm mortar combined with 12.7-mm mg—2/7.62-mm mg
   M: 4 Cummins VT-12M-700 diesels; 2 props; 2,200 hp   **Electric:** 40 kw
   Fuel: 12 tons   **Range:** 1,500   **Man:** 15 tot.

REMARKS: Transferred 9-68. PB 7 (ex-*Cape Florida*) was lost in 1971.

♦ **9 U.S. 65-foot commercial cruiser class** Bldr: Sewart Seacraft, Berwick, La., 1967

FB 1-3, 5-10

   D: 35 tons (fl)   **S:** 25 kts   **Dim:** 19.8 × 5.5 × 1.5
   A: 2/20-mm AA (I × 2)—3/12.7-mm mg
   M: 3 GM 12V71 diesels; 3 props; 1,590 hp
   Fuel: 7 tons   **Range:** 1,200/17   **Man:** 5 tot.

PATROL CRAFT

♦ **. . . "Sea Snake" class** Bldr: Korea SB & Eng.

   D: 30 tons   **S:** 27 kts   **Dim:** 20.0 × 4.4 × . . .
   A: . . .   **M:** 2 diesels; 2 props; 1,900 hp   **Man:** 8 tot.

MINE WARFARE SHIPS

♦ **5 U.S. MSC-289-class coastal minesweepers** Bldr: Peterson Bldrs., Sturgeon Bay, Wis.

	In serv.
MSC 555 NAM YANG (ex-MSC 295)	8-63
MSC 556 HA DONG (ex-MSC 296)	11-63
MSC 557 SAM KOK (ex-MSC 316)	7-68
MSC 558 YONG DONG (ex-MSC 320)	2-10-75
MSC 559 OK CHEON (ex-MSC 321)	2-10-75

Sam Kok (MSC 557)—old pendant number

   D: 315 tons (380 fl)   **S:** 14 kts   **Dim:** 44.32 × 8.29 × 2.7
   A: 2/20-mm AA (II × 1)   **M:** 4 GM 6-71 diesels; 2 props; 1,020 hp
   Electric: 1,260 kw   **Fuel:** 33 tons   **Man:** 40 tot.

REMARKS: Wooden construction. Built under Military Aid Program. Gas-turbine sweep generator. Lower superstructure than on the MSC 268 class, below.

♦ **3 U.S. MSC-268-class coastal minesweepers** Bldr: Harbor Boat Bldg., Terminal Isl., Cal.

	In serv.
MSC 551 KUM SAN (ex-MSC 284)	6-59
MSC 552 KO HUNG (ex-MSC 285)	8-59
MSC 553 KUM KOK (ex-MSC 286)	10-59

   D: 320 tons (370 fl)   **S:** 14 kts   **Dim:** 43.0 (41.5 pp) × 7.95 × 2.55
   A: 2/20-mm AA (II × 2)
   Electron Equipt: Radar: Decca 45
                        Sonar: UQS-1
   M: 2 GM 8-268A diesels; 2 props; 1,200 hp   **Fuel:** 40 tons
   Range: 2,500/16   **Man:** 40 tot.

REMARKS: Built under Military Aid Program. Wooden hulls.

MINE WARFARE SHIPS (continued)

Kum San (MSC 551)

♦ **1 ex-U.S. minesweeping boat**

MSB 1 Pi Bong (ex-MSB 2)

D: 44 tons (fl) **S:** 12 kts **Dim:** 17.0 × 4.6 × 1.5
M: 2 GM 6-71 diesels; 2 props; 600 hp **Fuel:** 5 tons **Range:** 300/6

REMARKS: Launched 1946; transferred 1-12-61 and purchased 2-7-75. Wooden construction.

AMPHIBIOUS WARFARE SHIPS

♦ **8 ex-U.S. LST 1 and U.S. LST 542-class landing ships**

	Bldr	L	In serv.
LST 671 Un Bong (ex-LST 1010)	Bethlehem, Fore River	29-3-44	25-4-44
LST 672 Tuk Bong (ex-LST 227)	Chicago Bridge, Seneca, Ill.	21-9-43	14-10-43
LST 673 Bi Bong (ex-LST 218)	Chicago Bridge, Seneca, Ill.	20-7-43	12-8-43
LST 675 Kae Bong (ex-LST 288)	American Bridge, Pa.	7-11-43	20-12-43
LST 676 Wee Bong (ex-Johnson County, LST 849)	American Bridge, Pa.	30-12-43	16-1-44
LST 677 Su Yong (ex-Kane County, LST 853)	Chicago Bridge, Seneca, Ill.	17-11-44	11-12-44
LST 678 Buk Han (ex-Linn County, LST 900)	Dravo, Pittsburgh	9-12-44	28-12-44
LST 679 Hwa San (ex-Pender County, LST 1080)	Bethlehem, Hingham, Mass.	2-5-45	29-5-45

Tuk Bong (LST 672)—old pendant number

D: 1,653 tons (4,080 fl) **S:** 10 kts **Dim:** 100.04 × 15.24 × 4.30
A: 8/40-mm AA (II × 2, I × 4)—2/20-mm AA **Electric:** 300 kw
M: 2 GM 12-567A or 12-278A diesels; 2 props; 1,800 hp **Man:** 70 tot.

REMARKS: Transferred 1955-58; all purchased outright 15-11-74. LST 1 class had elevators from upper deck to tank deck; later ships had a ramp.

♦ **11 ex-U.S. LSM 1-class medium landing ships**

Bldr: Brown SB, Houston, Tex. (except: LSM 652: Federal SB, Newark, N.J.; LSM 661: Pullman Standard Car Co., Chicago, Ill.)

	Laid down	L	In serv.
LSM 651 Tae Cho (ex-LSM 546)	14-7-45	25-8-45	16-1-46
LSM 652 Tyo To (ex-LSM 268)	17-5-44	17-7-44	9-8-44
LSM 653 Ka Tok (ex-LSM 462)	13-1-45	3-2-45	3-3-45
LSM 655 Ko Mun (ex-LSM 30)	7-5-44	28-5-44	1-7-44
LSM 656 Pi An (ex-LSM 96)	15-9-44	7-10-44	28-10-44
LSM 657 Wol Mi (ex-LSM 57)	30-6-44	21-7-44	17-8-44
LSM 658 Ki Rin (ex-LSM 19)	24-4-44	14-5-44	14-6-44
LSM 659 Nung Ra (ex-LSM 84)	22-8-44	15-9-44	7-10-44
LSM 661 Sin Mi (ex-LSM 316)	6-4-44	18-6-44	21-7-44
LSM 662 Ul Rung (ex-LSM 17)	10-4-44	7-5-44	12-6-44
LSML. . . Pung To (ex-LSM 54)	22-6-44	14-7-44	16-8-44

D: 520 tons (1,095 fl) **S:** 13 kts **Dim:** 62.0 × 10.52 × 2.53
A: 2/40-mm AA (II × 1)—4/20-mm AA (I × 4) **Fuel:** 160 tons **Man:** 75 tot.
M: 2 Fairbanks-Morse 38D8⅛ × 10 diesels; 2 props; 2,880 hp **Electric:** 240 kw

REMARKS: Pung To has mine rails on the vehicle deck, mine-laying ports through the stern. LSM 652 has GM 16-278A diesels.

♦ **1 ex-U.S. amphibious fire-support ship** Bldr: Brown SB, Houston, Tex.

	Laid down	L	In serv.
. . . Si Hung (ex-St. Joseph River, LSMR 527)	19-5-45	16-6-45	24-8-45

D: 994 tons (1,084 fl) **S:** 14 kts **Dim:** 62.94 × 10.52 × 2.53
A: 1/127-mm DP—2/40-mm AA (II × 2)—4/20-mm AA (II × 2)—8/127-mm Mk 105 RL (II × 8)
M: 2 GM 16-278A diesels; 2 props; 2,800 hp **Electric:** 480 kw
Fuel: 160 tons **Range:** 3,000/12

REMARKS: Transferred 15-9-60; purchased 15-11-74.

AMPHIBIOUS WARFARE SHIPS (continued)

♦ **6 U.S. LCU 1610-class utility landing craft** Bldr: So. Korea (In serv. 1979-81)

D: 190 tons (390 fl)   **S:** 11 kts   **Dim:** 41.07 × 9.07 × 2.08
A: 4/20-mm AA (II × 2)
M: 4 GM 6-71 diesels; 2 Kort-nozzle props; 1,200 hp
Fuel: 13 tons   **Range:** 1,200/11   **Man:** 6 tot.

REMARKS: Cargo capacity: 143 tons; cargo deck 30.5 × 5.5. Copies of U.S. design, built with imported equipment.

♦ **4 LCU 501-class utility landing craft**

MULKAE 71 (ex-U.S. LCU 531)   MULKAE 73
MULKAE 72   MULKAE 74

D: 309 tons (fl)   **S:** 10 kts   **Dim:** 36.3 × 10.0 × 1.14
A: 2/20-mm AA (I × 2)
M: 3 Gray Marine 6-71 diesels; 2 props; 675 hp   **Man:** 12 tot.

REMARKS: *Mulkae 71* transferred 1960; others built shortly thereafter as copies. *Mulkae 71* built by Bison SB, Buffalo, N.Y.; L: 5-9-43.

♦ **10 ex-U.S. Army LCM(8)-class landing craft**

D: 95-115 tons (fl)   **S:** 9-12 kts   **Dim:** 22.7 × 6.4 × 1.4
M: 4 GM 6-71 diesels; 2 props; 600 hp

REMARKS: Transferred 9-78.

AUXILIARIES

♦ **2 ex-U.S. Tonti-class gasoline tankers** Bldr: Todd SB, Houston, Tex.

	L	In serv.
AO 55 N. . . (ex-*Rincon*, T-AOG 77, ex-*Tarland*)	5-1-45	10-45
AO 56 N. . . (ex-*Petaluma*, T-AOG 79, ex-*Raccoon Bend*)	9-8-45	11-45

D: 2,100 tons (6,047 fl)   **S:** 10 kts   **Dim:** 99.1
M: 2 Nordberg diesels; 1 prop; 1,400 hp   **Electric:** 515 kw
Fuel: 154 tons   **Range:** 6,000/10   **Man:** 41 tot.

REMARKS: 3,160 grt/3,933 dwt. Cargo 31,284 bbl. light fuels (diesel, JP-5, gasoline). Acquired from Maritime Commission by U.S. Navy 1-7-50 and 7-9-50, respectively. Scheduled for lease to South Korea in 1982. Will probably be armed.

♦ **1 ex-Norwegian oiler** Bldr: Bergens Mekanske Verksteder, Norway (In serv. 1951)

AO 2 CHUN JI (ex-*Birk*)

D: 1,400 tons (4,160 fl)   **S:** 12 kts   **Dim:** 90.65 (84.0 pp) × 13.56 × 5.35
A: 1/40-mm AA—2/20-mm AA
M: 1 Sulzer 6 TD 48 diesel; 1 prop; 1,800 hp   **Man:** 73 tot.

REMARKS: Bought in 1953. The *Puchon* of the same class was lost 5-71. Can replenish alongside while under way.

♦ **2 ex-U.S. 174-foot class**

	Bldr	L	In serv.
YO 1 KU KYONG (ex-YO 118)	R.T.C. SB, Camden, N.J.	6-5-44	8-8-44
YO 6 N. . . (ex-YO 179)	Smith SY, Pensacola, Fla.	24-11-44	26-5-45

D: 1,400 tons (fl)   **S:** 7 kts   **Dim:** 53.0 × 10.0 × 4.0
M: 1 Union diesel; 1 prop; 560 hp   **Fuel:** 25 tons   **Man:** 36 tot.

REMARKS: YO 1 transferred 1946, YO 6 in 9-71. Cargo: 900 tons.

♦ **1 ex-U.S. YO 55 class** Bldr: R.T.C. SB, Camden, N.J.

	Laid down	L	In serv.
HWA CHON (ex-*Derrick*, YO 59)	15-6-42	21-11-42	2-2-43

D: 800 tons (2,700 fl)   **S:** 10 kts   **Dim:** 71.65 × 11.3 × 4.8
M: 2 Fairbanks-Morse 37E14-5 diesels; 2 props; 1,150 hp   **Electric:** 160 kw
Fuel: 105 tons   **Range:** 4,600/8   **Man:** 46 tot.

REMARKS: Transferred 4-55. Cargo: 1,600 tons.

♦ **2 ex-U.S. Army FS 331-design class** Bldr: Ingalls SB, Decatur, Ala.

	In serv.
AKL 908 KU SAN (ex-*Sharps*, AKL 10, ex-AG 139, ex-Army FS 385)	25-10-44
AKL 909 MA SAN (ex-AKL 35, ex-*Lt. Thomas W. Weigle*, FS 383)	10-44

D: 465 tons (935 fl)   **S:** 13.5 kts   **Dim:** 54.10 (49.99 pp) × 9.75 × 3.05
A: 2/20-mm AA (I × 2)   **M:** 2 GM 6-278A diesels; 2 props; 1,230 hp
Electric: 275 kw   **Fuel:** 57 tons   **Range:** 4,300/9.5, 3,000/12.5   **Man:** 20 tot.

REMARKS: Cargo plus passengers, 595 cubic meters. Transferred: AKL 908 in 4-56; AKL 909 in 9-56. Sisters *In Chon* (AKL 902), *Chi Nam Po* (AKL 905), *Mok Po* (AKL 907), and *Ul San* (AKL 910) stricken 1979-81.

♦ **2 ex-U.S. Diver-class salvage ships** Bldr: Basalt Rock Co., Napa, Cal.

	Laid down	L	In serv.
ARS 5 CHANG WON (ex-*Grasp*, ARS 24)	27-4-43	31-7-43	22-8-44
ARS 6 GUM I (ex-*Deliver*, ARS 23)	2-4-43	25-9-43	18-7-44

D: 1,530 tons (1,970 fl)   **S:** 14.8 kts   **Dim:** 65.1 × 12.5 × 4.0
A: 2/20-mm AA   **Electron Equipt:** Radar: 1/SPS-53
M: 4 Cooper-Bessemer GSB 8 diesels, electric drive; 2 props; 2,440 hp
Electric: 460 kw   **Fuel:** 300 tons   **Range:** 9,000/14, 20,000/7   **Man:** 83 tot.

REMARKS: ARS 5 transferred 31-3-78; ARS 6 on 15-8-79, both by sale. Equipped for salvage, diver support, and towing.

♦ **2 U.S. Sotoyomo-class auxiliary tugs**

	Bldr	Laid down	L	In serv.
ATA 3 DO BANG (ex-*Pinola*, ATA 206)	Gulfport Boiler Wks, Port Arthur, Tex.	26-10-44	14-12-44	10-2-45
ATA 2 YONG MUN (ex-*Keosangua*, ATA 198)	Levingston SB, Orange, Tex.	14-12-44	17-1-45	19-3-45

D: 835 tons (fl)   **S:** 13 kts   **Dim:** 43.6 (40.7 pp) × 10.3 × 4.0
A: 1/76-mm Mk 22 DP—4/20-mm AA (II × 2)
M: 2 GM 12-278A diesels, electric drive; 1 prop; 1,500 hp
Electric: 120 kw   **Fuel:** 158 tons   **Man:** 45 tot.

REMARKS: Transferred 2-62. ATA 3 is used in salvage work. There are also about nine harbor tugs, including YTL 13 (ex-U.S.N. YTL 550), YTL 22 (ex-Army ST 2097), YTL 23 (ex-Army ST 2099), YTL 25 (ex-Army YT 2106), YTL 26 (ex-Army ST 2065), and YTL 30 (ex-Army ST 2101). All transferred 1968-72.

NOTE: There are also about 35 yard and service craft.

KOREA-SOUTH (continued)

KOREAN HYDROGRAPHIC SERVICE
Subordinate to the Ministry of Transport.

♦ **2 ex-Belgian Herstal-class inshore minesweepers**

	L
SURO 5 (ex-*Temse*, ex-*MSI 470*)	6-8-56
SURO 6 (ex-*Tournai*, ex-*MSI 481*)	18-5-57

D: 160 tons (190 fl) **S:** 15 kts **Dim:** 34.5 × 6.6 × 2.1
M: 2 diesels; 2 props; 630 hp **Range:** 2,300/10 **Man:** 10 tot.

REMARKS: Built in Belgium with U.S. funds. Transferred 3-70. Wooden hulls.

♦ **1 ex-U.S. YMS-1-class minesweeper**

SURO 3 (ex-U.S. Coast Geodetic Survey *Hodgson*)

D: 289 tons (fl) **S:** 15 kts **Dim:** 44.6 × 8.1 × 3.0
M: 2 GM 8-268 diesels; 2 props; 1,000 hp

REMARKS: Converted post–World War II as a coastal survey ship. Wooden hull. Launched 1943, transferred 1968.

♦ **3 inshore survey craft**

SURO 7, SURO 8: 30 tons
SURO 2: 145 tons

COAST GUARD

The Republic of Korea Coast Guard operates about 25 seagoing patrol boats and several hundred small craft. Most are very old, including a number of ex-Imperial Japanese Navy tugs and seaplane tenders. Three new classes have been built, in unknown numbers:

♦ **. . . "Sea Whale"-class patrol boats** Bldr: Korea SB & Eng.

D: 500 tons **S:** 25 kts **Dim:** 60.8 × 8.0 ×. . .
A: 1/40-mm AA—2/20-mm AA **M:** 2 MTU diesels; 2 props; 9,600 hp
Range: 7,800/15 **Man:** 35 tot.

REMARKS: Intended for rescue and inspection duties.

♦ **. . . "Sea Shark"-class patrol boats** Bldr: Korea SB & Eng.

D: 250 tons **S:** 25 kts **Dim:** 48.2 × 7.1 ×. . .
A: 2/20-mm AA (I × 2)—2/12.7-mm mg **M:** 2 diesels; 2 props; 7,320 hp
Range: 3,300/15 **Man:** 34 tot.

♦ **. . . "Sea Gull"-class** Bldr: Korea SB & Eng.

D: 80 tons **S:** 30 kts **Dim:** 24.0 × 5.5 ×. . .
A: . . . **M:** 2 diesels; 2 props; 3,920 hp
Range: 950/20 **Man:** 18 tot.

KUWAIT
State of Kuwait

PERSONNEL: 500 men

MERCHANT MARINE (1980): 266 ships—2,529,491 grt
(tankers: 21 ships—1,347,792 grt)

GUIDED-MISSILE PATROL BOATS

♦ **2 FPB 57 class** Bldr: Lürssen, Bremen-Vegasack, West Germany

	Laid down	L	In serv.
P. . . N. . .	. . .	. . .	11-82
P. . . N. . .	. . .	. . .	4-83

D: 353 tons (398 fl) **S:** 36 kts **Dim:** 58.10 (54.40 wl) × 7.62 × 2.83
A: 4/MM 40 Exocet SSM (II × 2)—1/76-mm OTO Melara DP—2/40-mm Breda AA (II × 1)—2/7.62-mm mg
Electron Equipt: Radar: 1/Decca. . ., 1/HSA WM 28
ECM: Decca "Cutlass" syst., 1/Dagaie chaff RL
M: 4 MTU 16V956 TB91 diesels; 4 props; 18,000 hp
Electric: 405 kVA **Range:** 700/35 **Man:** 5 officers, 35 men

REMARKS: Ordered 1980. To function as leaders for the six TNC-45 class below.

♦ **6 TNC-45 class** Bldr: Lürssen, Bremen-Vegasack, West Germany

	Laid down	L	In serv.		Laid down	L	In serv.
P. . . N. . .	1980	. . .	8-82	P. . . N. . .	. . .	. . .	. . .
P. . . N. . .	1980	. . .	. . .	P. . . N. . .	. . .	. . .	. . .
P. . . N. . .	1980	. . .	. . .	P. . . N. . .	. . .	. . .	8-83

D: 231 tons (259 fl) **S:** 41.5 kts **Dim:** 44.90 (42.30 wl) × 7.00 × 2.40
A: 4/MM 40 Exocet—1/76-mm OTO Melara DP—2/40-mm Breda AA (II × 1)—2/7.62-mm AA
Electron Equipt: Radar: 1/Decca. . ., 1/HSA WM 28
ECM: Decca "Cutlass," 1/Dagaie chaff RL
M: 4 MTU 16V538 TB92 diesels; 4 props; 15,600 hp (15,000 sust.)
Electric: 405 kw **Range:** 500/38.5; 1,500/16 **Man:** 5 officers, 27 men

REMARKS: Ordered 1980. To carry 250 rounds 76-mm, 1,800 rounds 40-mm ammunition.

PATROL BOATS

♦ **10 coastal patrol boats** Bldrs: Thornycroft, Woolston, first 2; Vosper Thornycroft, remainder

	L		L
AL SALEMI	30-6-66	MARZOOK	1969
AL MUBARAKI	16-7-66	MASHHOOR	1969
MAYMOON	4-68	MURSHED	1970
AMAN	3-68	WATHAH	1970
AL SHURTI	1972	INTISAR	1972

KUWAIT (*continued*)
PATROL BOATS (*continued*)

Intisar   Vosper, 1972

    D: 40 tons   **S:** 20 kts   **Dim:** 27.78 × 4.73 × 1.38
    Electron Equipt: Radar: Decca 202   **Man:** 5 officers, 7 men
    M: 2 Rolls-Royce 8-cyl. diesels; 2 props; 1,340 hp   **Range:** 700/15

PATROL CRAFT

♦ **5 56-foot boats** Bldr: Vosper Thornycroft Private, Ltd., Singapore

DASTOOR   KASAR   QAHIR   SAGAR   SALAM

    D: 25 tons (fl)   **S:** 29-30 kts   **Dim:** 17.1 × 4.9 × . . .
    A: 2/7.62-mm mg (I × 2)   **M:** 2 MTU 6V331 diesels; 2 props; 1,350 hp
    Range: 320/20   **Man:** 2 officers, 6 men

REMARKS: Steel hull, aluminum superstructure. First two ordered 9-73, in service 6-74; others ordered 1978, in service 1979.

♦ **14 36-foot boats** Bldr: Vosper Thornycroft Private, Ltd., Singapore

ANTAR   AL SALMI II   AL SEBBAH   ISTIQLAL II
QARAH   WARBAH—plus 8 unnamed

    D: 6.8 tons (fl)   **S:** 22 kts   **Dim:** 11.1 × 3.3 × 0.6   **Man:** 4 tot.
    A: 4/7.62-mm mg (II × 2)   **M:** 2 Sabre 210 diesels; 2 props; 420 hp

REMARKS: First four, in service 1972, and second four, in service 5-73, have no names. Wooden construction, nylon sheathed hulls.

♦ **7 Magnum Sedan class** Bldr: Magnum Marine, U.S.A.

    D: . . .   **S:** 60 kts   **Dim:** 8.3 × 2.4 × 0.7   **Range:** 200/. . .
    M: 2 Mercury Mercuiser inboard/outboard motors; 2 props; 660 hp

REMARKS: High-speed craft for inshore work. Three delivered 1977, one in 1978, three in 1979.

♦ **1 46-foot craft** Bldr: Thornycroft Ltd., Singapore (In serv. 1-76)

MAHROOS

    D: 21.5 tons (fl)   **S:** 21.7 kts   **Dim:** 14.1 × 4.5 × . . .   **Man:** 1 officer, 4 men
    A: 2/7.62-mm mg   **M:** 2 Rolls-Royce C8M-410 diesels; 2 props; 780 hp

♦ **7 50-foot craft** Bldr: Thornycroft Ltd., Singapore (In serv. 1957-58)

AUXILIARIES

♦ **3 logistics support landing craft** Bldr: Vosper Private, Ltd., Singapore (In serv. 1979-80)

AL JAHRA   CERIFF   HADIYA

    D: 320 tons (fl)   **S:** 9.5 kts   **Dim:** 32.3 × 7.5 × . . .
    M: 2 Rolls-Royce C8M-410 diesels; 2 props; 750 hp   **Range:** 1,500/9

REMARKS: Unusual in having landing ramp at stern. Have full forecastle bow, low fantail like oilfield supply boats. Cargo: 170 tons, 100m² deck space. Carry 47 tons water ballast.

♦ **3 landing craft** Bldr: Vosper Thornycroft Private Ltd., Singapore

WAHEED (In serv. 5-71)   REGGA (In serv. 5-71)   FAREED (In serv. 11-75)

Regga   Vosper, 1971

    D: 88 tons (170 fl)   **S:** 10 kts   **Dim:** 27.0 × 6.9 × . . .   **M:** 2 Rolls-Royce C8M-410 diesels; 752 hp   **Range:** 1,500/9   **Man:** 8 tot.

REMARKS: Carry 40 tons deck cargo, 24.4 m³ cargo fuel, and 35.6 m³ water.

♦ **1 fireboat** Bldr: Vosper Thornycroft Private, Ltd., Singapore, (In serv. 1978)

WAHEED

    D: 112.6 grt   **S:** 26.6 kts   **Dim:** 26.2 × 5.8 × . . .
    M: 2 diesels; 2 props; 2,200 hp   **Man:** 16 tot.

LEBANON
Republic of Lebanon

PERSONNEL: 200 men

MERCHANT MARINE (1980): 203 ships—267,787 grt
                              (tankers: 2 ships—752 grt)

LEBANON (*continued*)

PATROL BOATS

NOTE: Semi-independent Christian forces have operated five Dabur-class patrol craft, transferred by Israel in 1976; for characteristics, *see* Israel section.

♦ **1 Tarablous class** Bldr: Chantiers Navals de l'Estérel, Cannes (L: 6-59)

TARABLOUS

Tarablous   1959

   D: 105 tons (fl)   **S:** 27 kts   **Dim:** 38.0 × 5.5 × 1.75
   A: 2/40-mm AA (I × 2)   **M:** 2 Mercedes-Benz diesels; 2 props; 2,700 hp
   Range: 1,500   **Man:** 3 officers, 16 men

PATROL CRAFT

♦ **2 Tracker Mk II class** Bldr: Fairey AllDay Marine, Hamble, G.B.

N. . . (In serv. 28-1-80)   N. . . (In serv. 8-2-80)

   D: 31.5 tons (fl)   **S:** 29 kts   **Dim:** 19.25 × 4.98 × 1.45
   A: . . .   **M:** 2 GM 12V71 TI diesels; 2 props; 990 hp
   Range: 650/20   **Man:** 11 tot.

♦ **6 Aztec class** Bldr: Crestitalia, Ameglia, La Spezia, Italy (In serv. 1980)

   D: . . .   **S:** . . .   **Dim:** 9.0 × . . . × . . .
   M: 2 diesels; 2 props; . . . hp

REMARKS: Glass-reinforced plastic construction.

AMPHIBIOUS CRAFT

♦ **1 ex-U.S. LCU-1466-class landing craft**

SOUR (ex-LCU 1474)

   D: 180 tons (347 fl)   **S:** 8 kts   **Dim:** 35.05 × 10.36 × 1.6 (aft)
   A: 2/20-mm AA (I × 2)   **M:** 3 Gray Marine 64YTL diesels; 3 props; 675 hp
   Fuel: 11 tons   **Range:** 1,200/6   **Man:** 6 tot.

REMARKS: Transferred 11-58. Bow ramp. Cargo: 167 tons.

LIBERIA

PERSONNEL: 238 total (13 officers, 225 men)

MERCHANT MARINE (1980): 2,401 ships—80,285,176 grt
                 (tankers: 786 ships—49,897,487 grt)

NAVAL AVIATION: One Cessna 337 is operated by the Coast Guard for surveillance.

COAST GUARD

PATROL CRAFT

♦ **3 CG 27 class** Bldr: Karlskrona Varvet, Sweden

		In serv.
8801 MASTER SERGEANT SAMUEL K. DOE (ex-*Nuah River*)		27-9-80
8802 ALBERT PORTE (ex-. . .)		27-9-80
8803 GENERAL THOMAS QUIWOUKPA (ex-. . .)		27-9-80

Master Sergeant Samuel K. Doe (8801)   1980

   D: 50 tons   **S:** 25 kts   **Dim:** 26.72 × 5.23 × 1.13
   A: 1/12.7-mm mg—2/7.62-mm mg (I × 2)
   Electron Equipt: Radar: 1/Decca 1226C
   M: 2 MTU 8V331 C82 diesels; 2 props; 1,866 hp
   Fuel: 11 tons   **Range:** 1,000/18   **Man:** 8 tot.

REMARKS: Aluminum alloy construction. Names changed due to revolution; all originally named for rivers.

♦ **2 U.S. 65-foot class** Bldr: Swiftships, Morgan City, La. (In serv. 22-7-76)

103 CAVILLA   104 MANO

   D: 38 tons (fl)   **S:** 24 kts   **Dim:** 19.8 × 5.8 × 0.8
   A: 1/81-mm mortar combined with 12.7-mm mg—2/12.7-mm mg (I × 2)
   M: 2 GM 12V71 TI diesels; 2 props; 1,920 hp
   Range: 600/21.5   **Man:** 2 officers, 18 men

LIBERIA (*continued*)
PATROL CRAFT (*continued*)

♦ **1 U.S. 42-foot class** Bldr: Swiftships, Morgan City, La. (In serv. 22-7-76)

101 St. Paul

    D: 11 tons (12 fl) **S:** 20 kts **Dim:** 12.8 × 3.7 × 0.6
    A: 2/12.7-mm mg (I × 2)
    M: 2 GM 8V71 diesels; 2 props; 870 hp **Man:** 4 tot.

NOTE: The U.S. PGM 71-class patrol boat *Alert* has been discarded.

LIBYA
Socialist People's Libyan Arab Jamahiriya

PERSONNEL: Approximately 3,000 men

MERCHANT MARINE (1980): 96 ships—889,908 grt
                    (tankers: 15 ships—795,616 grt)

NAVAL AVIATION: 12 French Alouette-III helicopters are in service for naval use.

NOTE: There are unsubstantiated reports that Libya may receive two *Koni*-class frigates and four *Nanuchka II*-class guided-missile corvettes from the U.S.S.R., beginning late 1981-82. Characteristics for these export model ships can be found in the section on the Algerian Navy. Libya is currently receiving large numbers of ships from both Communist and Free World sources; the ability to man and maintain this extensive armada remains open to question. Some 240 Whitehead A244 ASW torpedoes were ordered from Italy in 1979.

SUBMARINES

♦ **4 (+2) Soviet Foxtrot class** Bldr: Sudomekh SY, Leningrad

311 Al Badr 312 Al Fateh 313 Al Ahad 314 Al Mitraqah
315. . .   316. . .

    D: 1,950/2,400 tons **S:** 18/16 kts **Dim:** 96.0 × 7.5 × 6.0
    A: 10/533-mm TT (6 fwd, 4 aft)—22 torpedoes or 44 mines
    M: 3 diesels, electric motors; 3 props; 5,300 hp **Endurance:** 70 days
    Range: 11,000/8 **Man:** 8 officers, 70 men

REMARKS: One transferred in 12-76, two in 1978, fourth commissioned 30-3-81 at Tripoli. Two more are expected.

Al Ahad (313)   1978

FRIGATE

♦ **1 Vosper Mk 7** Bldr: Vosper Thornycroft, Woolston

	Laid down	L	In serv.
F 211 Dat Assawari	27-9-68	9-69	1-2-73

Dat Assawari (F211)—*prior to modernization*   1976

    D: 1,325 tons (1,650 fl) **S:** 37/17 kts **Dim:** 101.6 (94.5 pp) × 11.08 × 3.36
    A: 4/Otomat Mk II SSM (I × 4)—1/114-mm Mk 8 DP—1/Albatros Mk 2 SAM
        syst. (IV × 1; Aspide missiles)—2/40-mm AA (I × 2)—2/35-mm Oerlikon AA
        (II × 1)—6/324-mm ASW TT (III × 2)
    Electron Equipt: Radar: RAN-10S, 1/navigational, 2/Orion RTN-10X
                      Sonar: 1/Diodon
                      ECM: RDL-1 intercept
    M: CODOG: 2 Rolls-Royce TM 2A Olympus gas turbines, 24,000 hp each; 2 Paxman Ventura diesels, 1,900 hp each; 2 CP props
    Fuel: 300 tons **Range:** 1,000/36; 5,700/17 **Man:** 132 tot.

FRIGATE (continued)

REMARKS: Refitting in Italy, 1979-81; damaged by bomb 29-10-80, delaying refit. Sea Cat SAM and Limbo ASW mortar replaced by 4-cell Albatros launcher and ASW TT for A244 torpedoes. Received Selenia RAN-12L/X (IPN-10) combat data system. Otomat added, new radars, sonar added. Has 2 NA-10 mod. 2 gun/missile f.c.s.

CORVETTES

♦ **4 Wadi M'ragh class** Bldr: CNR, Riva Trigoso, Italy

	L	In serv.
C 412 ASSAD AL. . . (ex-*Wadi M'ragh*)	29-4-77	14-9-79
C 413 ASSAD AL TOUGOUR (ex-*Wadi Majer*)	20-4-78	12-2-80
C 414 ASSAD AL KALIJ (ex-*Wadi Mercit*)	15-12-78	28-3-81
C 415 ASSAD AL HUDUD (ex-*Wadi Megrawa*)	21-6-79	28-3-81

Wadi M'ragh—on trials   CNR, 1979

Wadi M'ragh   CNR, 1979

D: 547 tons (630 fl)   **S:** 34 kts   **Dim:** 61.7 (57.8 pp) × 9.3 × 2.7
A: 4/Otomat Mk I SSM—1/76-mm OTO Melara DP—2/35-mm Oerlikon AA (II × 1)—6/324-mm ASW TT (III × 2)—16 mines
Electron Equipt: Radar: 1/RAN 11 L/X, 1/Decca TM 1226, 1/Orion RTN-10X
          Sonar: Thomson-CSF Diodon
          ECM: Selenia ISN-1 intercept
M: 4 MTU 16V956 TB91 diesels; 4 CP props; 16,400 hp   **Electric:** 650 kw
Fuel: 126 tons   **Range:** 1,400/33; 4,150/18   **Man:** 58 tot.

REMARKS: Ordered in 1974. Completion delayed by prolonged trials. Have fin stabilizers, automatic degaussing system, Selenia IPN-10 combat data system, 1/NA 10 mod. 2 GFCS, with 2C03 optical backup director. Can maintain 31.5 kts sea speed. Four more reported ordered 5-80. Names changed 1981.

♦ **1 Vosper Mk 1B**

	Bldr	L	In serv.
C 411 TOBRUK	Vosper, Ltd., Portsmouth	29-7-65	20-4-66

Tobruk (C 411)   *Shbldg. and Shipping Record*, 1966

D: 440 tons (500 fl)   **S:** 18 kts   **Dim:** 53.95 (48.77 pp) × 8.68 × 4.0
A: 1/102-mm—4/40-mm AA (I × 4)   **Range:** 2,900/14   **Man:** 5 officers, 58 men
M: 2 Paxman Ventura YJCM diesels; 2 props; 3,800 hp   **Fuel:** 60 tons

REMARKS: Launched in 1965. Anti-rolling devices, air-conditioned living spaces. No ASW equipment. Can be used as a yacht. 102-mm gun low-angle only.

GUIDED-MISSILE PATROL BOATS

♦ **10 French La Combattante-II class** Bldr: CMN, Cherbourg

	Laid down	L	In serv.
518 BEIR GRASSA	13-3-78	28-6-79	. . .
519 BEIR GZIR	10-6-78	22-1-80	. . .
520 BEIR GTIFA	30-1-79	20-5-80	. . .
521 BEIR GLULUD	20-10-79	30-9-80	. . .
522 BEIR ALGANDULA	12-9-79	14-1-81	. . .
523 BEIR KTITAT	17-12-79	3-81	. . .
524 BEIR ALKARIM	11-3-80	23-6-81	. . .
525 BEIR ALKARDMEN	9-6-80	23-6-81	. . .
526 BEIR ALKUR	20-10-80	30-11-81	. . .
527 BEIR ALKUESAT	20-1-81	. . .	. . .

D: 258 tons (311 fl)   **S:** 39 kts   **Dim:** 49.0 (46.2 pp) × 7.1 × 2.4 (2.0 hull)
A: 4/Otomat SSM (II × 2)—1/76-mm OTO Melara DP—2/40-mm Breda/Bofors AA
Electron Equipt: Radar: 1/Triton search, 1/Castor track, 1/Vega II fire-control (all Thomson-CSF)
M: 4 MTU 20V538 TB 91 diesels; 4 props; 18,000 hp   **Range:** 1,600/15
Man: 8 officers, 19 men

GUIDED-MISSILE PATROL BOATS (continued)

Beir Grassa (518)—at launch 28-6-79   CMN

REMARKS: Ordered 5-77. The *Beir Grassa* was laid down on 13-3-78 and the second unit on 19-6-78. On 27-2-81 the French government embargoed delivery of these ships, although the first three were ready for delivery.

♦ **12 Soviet Osa-II class**

205 AL KATUM	. . . AL RWAE	. . . AL NARHAA	. . . N . . .
. . . AL OWAKH	. . . AL BAIDA	. . . AL RUHA	. . . N . . .
. . . N . . .	. . . N . . .	. . . N . . .	. . . N . . .

Libyan Osa-II   1978

D: 210 tons (240 fl)   **S:** 36 kts   **Dim:** 39.0 × 7.7 × 1.8
A: 4/SS-N-2 Styx SSM (I × 4)—4/30-mm AA (II × 2)
Electron Equipt: Radar: 1/Square Tie, 1/Drum Tilt
                IFF: 2/Square Head, 1/High Pole
M: 3 M504 diesels; 3 props; 15,000 hp   **Range:** 430/34, 700/20   **Man:** 30 tot.

REMARKS: One transferred in 1976, four in 1977, one in 1978, three in 1979, one in 4-80, one in 5-80, and the twelfth in 7-80. Reportedly, the original order was reduced from twenty-four to twelve.

♦ **3 Sölöven class** Bldr: Vosper, Ltd., Portsmouth

	L	In serv.		L	In serv.
P 512 SUSA	31-8-67	8-68	P 514 SEBHA (ex-*Sokna*)	29-2-68	1-69
P 513 SIRTE	10-1-68	4-68			

Susa (P 512)—firing a wire-guided missile   Vosper, 1968

D: 95 tons (115 fl)   **S:** 50 kts   **Dim:** 30.38 (27.44 pp) × 7.3 × 2.15
A: 8/SS 12 SSM (II × 4)—2/40-mm AA (I × 2)
M: CODOG: 3 Bristol-Siddeley Proteus gas turbines; 3 props; 12,750 hp; 2 GM
      6-71 cruising diesels, 190 hp
Man: 20 tot.

REMARKS: Modeled on the Danish *Sölöven* class. All-wood construction, nylon-sheathed hull. Missiles are wire-guided and are not very accurate, particularly at high speeds. Cruise diesels are on outboard propeller shafts. Refitting in Italy, with new engines, new electronics, and, possibly, new missiles (Otomat?).

PATROL BOATS AND CRAFT

♦ **0 (+14) SAR 33-class patrol boats** Bldr: Taskizak SY, Turkey

D: 150 tons (170 fl)   **S:** 40 kts   **Dim:** 34.5 × 8.60 × 1.85
A: 1/40-mm AA—2/12.7-mm mg (I × 2)
M: 3 SACM AGO V16CSHR; 3 CP props; 12,000 hp   **Electric:** 300 kw
Fuel: 18 tons   **Range:** 400/35; 1,000/. . .   **Man:** 23 tot.

REMARKS: Ordered early 1980 to replace the earlier customs units in service. Wedge-shaped hull of remarkable steadiness at high speeds in heavy seas. Aluminum alloy construction. May be of a lengthened variant, 37.5 m overall. Designed by Abeking & Rasmussen, West Germany.

♦ **2 customs patrol boats** Bldr: Müller, Hameln, West Germany (In serv. 1-78)

JIHAD   SALAM

D: 120 tons (fl)   **S:** 27 kts   **Dim:** 37.0 × 6.2 ×. . .
A: 4/20-mm Hispano-Suiza A32 AA   **M:** MTU diesels; . . . props; . . . hp
Man: . . .

REMARKS: Ordered for Lebanon, but when that country could not pay, sold to Libya 1-78.

PATROL BOATS AND CRAFT (*continued*)

Jihad and Salam (with a third, unidentified craft) at builders   G. Koop, 1977

♦ **4 Brooke type** Bldr: Brooke Marine, Lowestoft, G.B. (In serv. 1968-70)

PC 1 Garian   PC 3 Merawa
PC 2 Khawlan   PC 4 Sabratha

   D: 100 tons (125 fl) **S:** 23.5 kts **Dim:** 36.58 × 7.16 × 1.75
   A: 1/40-mm—1/20-mm AA
   M: 2 Paxman Ventura 10 YJCM diesels; 2 props; 3,600 hp
   Range: 1,800/13 **Man:** 22 tot.

REMARKS: Have the same engines as the *Tobruk* and the *Zeltin*. At least one has a
Soviet BM-21 multiple 122-mm rocket launcher (XX × 1) in place of the 20-mm AA
gun.

♦ **3 security craft** Bldr: Vosper Thornycroft, Portsmouth (In serv. 1967-69)

Benina Misurata Homs

   D: 100 tons **S:** 18-20 kts **Dim:** 30.5 × 6.4 × 1.7
   A: 1/20-mm AA **M:** 3 Rolls-Royce diesels; 1,740 hp
   Range: 1,800/14 **Man:** 15 tot.

REMARKS: Used for customs and fishery protection. Sisters *Ar Rakib*, *Farwa*, and
Akrama ceded to Malta, 1978.

MINE WARFARE SHIPS

NOTE: Libya has laid several minefields, apparently employing the roll-on/roll-off cargo
ship *El Timsah*, with mine rails on the vehicle deck for the purpose.

♦ **2 Soviet Natya-class fleet minesweepers**

111 Ras El Gelais   113 Ras Hadad

   D: 650 tons (750 fl) **S:** 20 kts **Dim:** 61.0 × 10.0 × 3.0
   A: 4/30-mm AA (II × 2)—4/25-mm AA (II × 2)—2/RBU 1200 ASW RL (V ×
   2)—mines

Ras Hadad (113)   1981

   Electron Equipt: Radar: 1/Don-2, 1/Drum Tilt
                  Sonar: . . .
                  IFF: 2/Square Head, 1/High Pole B
   M: 2 diesels; 2 props; 5,000 hp **Man:** 50 tot.

REMARKS: Both delivered 3-81. Names *Ishsaar* and *Tayyar* also reported for these
ships. Like the six built for India, they lack the ramp at the stern found on Soviet
units.

AMPHIBIOUS WARFARE SHIPS

♦ **3 Soviet Polnocny-C class landing ships** Bldr: Poland

112 Ibn Al Hadrani   116 Ibn Omata   118 Ibn El Farat

Polnocny-C class   1979

   D: 1,050 tons (fl) **S:** 18 kts **Dim:** 82.0 × 10.0 × 2.0
   A: 4/30-mm AA (II × 2)—2/122-mm artillery RL (XV × 2)
   Electron Equipt: Radar: 1/Spin Trough, 1/Drum Tilt
   M: 2 diesels; 2 props; 5,000 hp

REMARKS: One transferred in 12-77 and two in 6-79. Like the Iraqi examples of this
Polish-built class of medium landing ships, these export versions have a raised
helicopter deck forward of the superstructure. A fourth Libyan unit, the *Ibn Al
Qyis* (113), was lost on 14 or 15 September 1978 through fire at sea.

AMPHIBIOUS WARFARE SHIPS *(continued)*

♦ **2 Ibn Ouf-class landing ships** Bldr: C.N.I.M., La Seyne

		Laid down	L	In serv.
130	IBN OUF	1-4-76	22-10-76	11-3-77
131	IBN HARISSA	18-4-77	18-10-77	10-3-78

Ibn Ouf (130) J.-C. Bellonne, 1977

D: 2,800 tons (fl) **S:** 15 kts **Dim:** 100.0 × 15.65 × 2.6
A: 6/40-mm Breda AA (II × 3)—1/81-mm mortar
M: 2 SEMT-Pielstick diesels; 2 CP props; 5,340 hp
Range: 4,000/14 **Man:** 35 crew + 240 troops

REMARKS: Cargo: 570 tons, including up to eleven tanks. Helicopter platform aft.

♦ **16 (+. . .) Turkish Ç 107-class large landing craft** Bldr: Taskizak SY, Istanbul, and Gölçük Naval SY

RAS EL HILEL (ex-Turk Ç 132)	EL KOBAYAT (ex-Turk Ç 133)	N. . .
N. . .	N. . .	N. . .

D: 280 tons (600 fl) **S:** 10 kts (8.5 loaded) **Dim:** 56.56 × 11.58 × 1.25
A: 2/20-mm AA (I × 2) **M:** 3 GM 6-71 TI diesels; 3 props; 900 hp
Range: 600/10; 1,100/8 **Man:** 15 tot.

REMARKS: Cargo: Five heavy tanks, up to 100 troops; up to 350 tons. Design follows World War II-era British LCT(4). Cargo deck 28.5 × 7.9 m. Ordered 7-12-79, with first two taken from among ships built for Turkish Navy and delivered 7-12-79. As many as 50 may be acquired, with each Turkish yard building 25. Presumably M. Khadafi has designs on a near-neighbor's territory, as these ships are unsuitable for extended voyages. Sixteen were delivered by 4-81.

AUXILIARY SHIPS

♦ **1 support ship for small combatants**

		Bldr	Laid down	L	In serv.
711	ZELTIN	Vosper Thornycroft, Woolston	1967	29-2-68	23-1-69

D: 2,200 tons (2,470 fl) **S:** 15 kts **Dim:** 98.72 (91.44 wl) × 14.64 × 3.05
A: 2/40-mm AA (I × 2)
M: 2 Paxman Ventura 16 YSCM diesels; 2 props; 3,500 hp **Electric:** 800 kw
Range: 3,000/14 **Man:** 15 officers, 86 men

REMARKS: The well deck, 41 × 12, can receive small craft that draw up to 2.3 m. Hydraulically controlled stern gate. A moveable crane (3-ton loading capacity) is available for the well deck, and a 9-ton crane on the port side supports the workshops.

Zeltin (711) 1968

♦ **1 British LCT(4)-class repair barge, former landing craft**

ZLEITEN (ex-British MRC 1013)

D: 650 tons (900 fl) **S:** 10/11 kts **Dim:** 70.4 × 11.8 × 1.6
A: 4 Paxman diesels; 2 props; 1,840 hp (inoperable)

REMARKS: Former LCT converted to a repair barge while in British service. Bought 5-9-66. Now a hulk.

♦ **1 ex-Italian Expresso-class roll-on/roll-off transport**

EL TIMSAH (ex-. . .)

D: 3,100 tons (fl) **S:** 20 kts **Dim:** 117.5 (108.7 pp) × 17.5 × 4.9
M: 2 Fiat V18 diesels; 2 CP props; 9,000 hp

REMARKS: Has fin stabilizers. Used as military transport and as a minelayer. Purchased 1979.

♦ **3 harbor tugs** Bldr: Jonker & Stans SY, The Netherlands (In serv. 1980)

A 33   A 34   A 35

D: 150 grt **S:** . . . **Dim:** 26.60 × 7.90 × 2.48
M: 2 diesels; 2 Voith-Schneider vertical-cycloidal props; . . . hp

REMARKS: Two 17.00 × 6.25 × 2.75 harbor tugs were delivered at the same time.

♦ **4 Ras El Helal-class tugs** Bldr: Mondego, Foz, Portugal

	In serv.		In serv.
RAS EL HELAL	22-10-77	AL KERIAT	17-2-78
AL SHWEIREF	17-2-78	AL TABKAH	29-7-78

D: 200 grt **S:** 14 kts **Dim:** 34.8 × 9.0 × 4.0 (moulded depth)
M: 2 diesels; 2 props; 2,300 hp

♦ **1 Soviet Yelva-class diving tender**

VM 917 (Soviet number)

D: 295 tons (fl) **S:** 12.4 kts **Dim:** 40.9 × 8.0 × 2.1
Electron Equipt: Radar: 1/Spin Trough
M: 2 Type 3D12 A diesels; 2 props; 600 hp

REMARKS: Transferred 19-12-77. Can support seven hard-hat divers working at 60-m and has a submersible decompression chamber.

MADAGASCAR
Democratic Republic of Madagascar

PERSONNEL: Approximately 600 men

MERCHANT MARINE (1980): 56 ships—91,211 grt (tankers: 6 ships—32,584 grt)

PATROL BOAT AND CRAFT

♦ **1 French PR-48 type coastal patrol boat** Bldr: S.F.C.N., Villeneuve-la-Garenne

	Laid down	L	In serv.
MALAIKA	11-66	22-3-67	12-67

D: 235 tons (250 fl) **S:** 18.5 kts **Dim:** 47.5 (45.5 pp) × 7.1 × 2.25
A: 2/40-mm AA **M:** 2 MGO diesels; 2 props; 2,400 hp
Range: 2,000/15 **Man:** 3 officers, 22 men

REMARKS: Sisters with more powerful propulsion plants in the Senegalese and Tunisian navies.

♦ **4 North Korean Nampo class** (In serv. 1979-80)

D: 70 tons (fl) **S:** 40 kts **Dim:** 27.7 × 6.1 × 1.8
A: 4/14.5-mm mg (II × 2)—1/75-mm recoilless rifle
M: 4 M50-series diesels; 4 props; 4,800 hp
Range: 375/40 **Man:** 19 tot.

REMARKS: Unlike North Korean Navy version, have no bow ramp or troop accommodations, being intended for use strictly as patrol craft. Metal construction.

AMPHIBIOUS WARFARE SHIPS

♦ **1 medium landing ship**

	Bldr	Laid down	L	In serv.
TOKY	Diego Suarez SY	1972	1973	10-74

D: 810 tons (avg) **S:** 13 kts **Dim:** 66.37 (56.0 pp) × 12.5 × 1.9
A: 1/76-mm—2/20-mm AA—1/81-mm mortar
M: 2 MGO diesels; 2 props; 2,400 hp **Electric:** 240 kw **Range:** 3,000/12
Man: 27 tot.

REMARKS: Similar to a French EDIC. Used as a transport and support ship. Forward ramp can be folded upon itself. Transport capacity: 250 tons. Quarters for 30 passengers; 120 soldiers can be carried for short distances. Financed by the French government under the Military Cooperation Pact.

TRAINING SHIP

♦ **1 former trawler**

	Bldr	L
FANANTENANA (ex-*Richelieu*)	A.G. Weser, Bremen	1959

D: 1,040 tons (1,200 fl) **S:** 12 kts **Dim:** 62.9 (56 pp) × 9.15 × 4.52
A: 2/40-mm AA **M:** 2 Deutz diesels ("father-mother" system); 1 prop; 1,060 + 500 hp **Man:** . . .

REMARKS: 691 grt. Bought and modified, 1966-67. Can carry 300 tons of freight and up to 120 military passengers.

MARITIME POLICE

♦ **5 coast surveillance craft** Bldr: Bayerische Schiffbau, West Germany (In serv. 1962)

GC 1 PHILIBERI ISIRANANA	GC 4 FANROSOANA
GC 2 FAHELEOVATENA	GC 5 FAHAFAHANA
GC 3 N. . .	

D: 46 tons **S:** 22 kts **Dim:** 24.0 × . . . × . . .
A: 1/40-mm AA **M:** 2 diesels; 2 props; . . . hp

MALAYSIA

NOTE: Forces specifically assigned to the Malaysian state of Sabah are listed separately.

PERSONNEL: Approximately 6,000 total, plus 800 reserves

MERCHANT MARINE (1980): 221 ships—702,145 grt (tankers: 11 ships—6,203 grt)

NOTE: The names of all Malaysian warships are preceded by "KD" (Kapal Diraja).

FRIGATES

♦ **2 new construction** Bldr: Howaldtswerke, Kiel, West Germany

	Laid down	L	In serv.
F. . . N. . .	. . .	. . .	. . .
F. . . N. . .	. . .	. . .	. . .

D: 1,500 tons (1,850 fl) **S:** 28 rts **Dim:** 93.0 × 11.0 × 3.5 (hull)
A: 4/. . . SSM—1/100-mm DP Compact—2/40-mm Breda AA—4/30-mm Emerlec AA (II × 2)
Electron Equipt: Radar: . . . —Sonar: . . .
M: 4 MTU 20V1163 diesels; 2 CP props; 23,000 hp **Electric:** . . .
Fuel: . . . **Range:** 7,000/14 **Man:** 88 tot.

REMARKS: Ordered 10-6-81. 100-mm gun of French origin. Missiles will probably be MM 38 or MM 40 Exocet.

♦ **1 "Yarrow frigate" class**

	Bldr	Laid down	L	In serv.
F 24 RAHMAT	Yarrow, Scotstoun	2-66	18-12-67	3-71

D: 1,290 tons (1,600 fl) **S:** 27 kts (16.5 on diesels alone)
Dim: 93.97 (pl. 44 pp) × 10.36 × 3.05
A: 1/100-mm DP—2/40-mm Bofors AA (I × 2)—1/Sea Cat SAM system (IV × 1)—1/Mk 10 Limbo ASW mortar (III × 1)
Electron Equipt: Radar: 1/LWO-2, 1/Decca 626, 1/M 22, 1/M 44
Sonar: 1/170B, 1/174
M: CODOG: 1 Rolls-Royce Olympus TM-1B gas turbine, 19,500 hp; 1 Crossley-Pielstick 8PC2V diesel, 3,850 hp; 2 CP props; 22,000 hp
Electric: 2,000 kw **Range:** 1,000/27; 5,200/16.5 **Man:** 120 tot.

FRIGATES (continued)

Rahmat (F 24)—prior to rearmament   1973

REMARKS: Ordered 11-2-66. M 22 fire-control radar atop the mast for the 114-mm gun and M 44 on the stern for the Sea Cat system. The original 114-mm mount was replaced during a 1981-82 refit at Malaysian SY & Eng. The ASW mortar is covered by a hatch that serves as a platform for a light helicopter.

♦ **1 British built** Bldr: Yarrow, Glasgow

	Laid down	L	In serv.
F 76 HANG TUAH (ex-*Mermaid*)	1965	29-12-66	16-5-73

D: 2,300 tons (2,520 fl) **S:** 24/23 kts **Dim:** 103.4 × 12.2 × 4.8
A: 1/100-mm DP Compact—4/30-mm Emerlec AA (II × 2)—2/40-mm AA (I × 2)—1/Mk 10 Limbo ASW mortar (III × 1)
Electron Equipt: Radar: 1/Plessey AWS-1, 1/978
    Sonar: 1/174, 1/170B
M: 8 16-cyl. Admiralty Standard Range-I diesels; 2 props; 14,400 hp
Fuel: 230 tons **Range:** 4,800/15 **Man:** 200-210 tot.

REMARKS: Ordered from Ghana in 1964. Because of the political situation, the ship was not delivered and, at the end of 1971, was purchased by the British government. Transferred to Malaysia in 5-77. Had lead-computing STD Mk 1 sight for the Mk 19 twin 102-mm mount, but no fire-control radar until refit 1981-82 at Singapore SY & Eng., where French 100-mm Compact replaced the 102-mm mount. Helicopter pad.

GUIDED-MISSILE PATROL BOATS

♦ **4 Spica-M class** Bldr: Karlskrona Varvet, Sweden

	Laid down	L	In serv.
P 3511 HANDALAN	24-5-77	...	26-10-79
P 3512 PERKASA	27-6-77	...	26-10-79
P 3513 PENDIKAR	15-7-77	...	26-10-79
P 3514 GEMPITA	21-10-77	...	26-10-79

D: 240 tons (268 fl) **S:** 37.5 kts (34.5 sust.) **Dim:** 43.62 × 7.0 × 2.4 (aft)
A: 4/MM 38 Exocet SSM (II × 2)—1/57-mm Bofors DP—1/40-mm Bofors AA

Hang Tuah (F 76)—prior to rearmament   G. Arra, 1980

Perkasa (P 3512)   J. Jedrlinic, 1981

Electron Equipt: Radar: 1/Decca . . . 9LV200 Mk 2 system (1 tracker, 1 search radar)
    Sonar: Simrad SU
    ECM: M.E.L. SUSIE 1

GUIDED-MISSILE PATROL BOATS (continued)

M: 3 MTU MD 16V538 TB 91 diesels; 3 props; 10,800 hp
Electric: 400 kVA   **Range:** 1,850/14   **Man:** 5 officers, 34 men

REMARKS: Ordered 13-8-76. Given the names of the four *Perkasa*-class torpedo/patrol boats that were stricken in 1977. Have 103-mm rocket flare launchers on the 57-mm mount and 57-mm RFL on the 40-mm mount. Can be equipped with ASW TT if required.

♦ **4 French La Combattante-II 4AL class** Bldr: CMN, Cherbourg

	L	In serv.		L	In serv.
P 3501 PERDANA	31-5-72	31-12-72	P 3503 GANAS	26-10-72	28-2-73
P 3502 SERANG	22-12-71	31-2-73	P 3504 GANYANG	16-3-72	20-3-73

Ganyang (P 3504)   1973

Perdana (P 3501)   1978

D: 234 tons (265 fl)   **S:** 36.5 kts   **Dim:** 47.0 × 7.1 × 2.5 (fl)
A: 2/MM 38 Exocet SSM (I × 2)—1/57-mm Bofors AA—1/40-mm Bofors AA

Electron Equipt: Radar: 1/Decca 1226, 1/Triton, 1/Pollux
M: 4 MTU MB 870 diesels; 4 props; 14,000 hp   **Fuel:** 39 tons
Range: 800/25   **Man:** 5 officers, 30 men

REMARKS: Steel hulls. Superstructure in alloyed metal. Six 103-mm rocket flare launchers on the 57-mm mount, four 57-mm on the 40-mm mount. Thomson C.S.F. Vega fire-control system with Triton search radar, Pollux f.c. radar.

PATROL BOATS

♦ **9 Brooke-Marine 29-m design** Bldr: Penang SY

D: . . . tons   **S:** . . . kts   **Dim:** 29.0 × . . . × . . .
A: . . .   **Electron Equipt:** Radar: . . .
M: 2 Paxman Valenta 16CM diesels; 2 props; 8,000 hp
Range: . . .   **Man:** . . .

REMARKS: Ordered 1980. Not same program as 32-m craft for Customs & Excise or PZ class for Marine Police. Will replace some units of the "103-ft" class.

♦ **6 Jerong class** Bldr: Hong Leong-Lürssen, Butterworth, Malaysia

	L	In serv.		L	In serv.
P 3505 JERONG	28-7-75	23-3-76	P 3508 YU	17-7-76	15-11-76
P 3506 TUDAK	16-3-76	16-6-76	P 3509 BAUNG	5-10-76	11-7-77
P 3507 PAUS	2-6-76	18-8-76	P 3510 PARI	1-77	23-3-77

Baung (P 3509)   J. Jedrlinic, 1981

D: 210 tons (255 fl)   **S:** 34 kts   **Dim:** 44.90 × 7.00 × 2.48 (props)
A: 1/57-mm Bofors AA—1/40-mm Bofors AA
Electron Equipt: Radar: 1/Decca 1226
M: 3 MTU MB 870 diesels; 3 props; 10,800 hp   **Electric:** 384 kVA
Range: 700/31.5; 2,000/15   **Man:** 5 officers, 31 men

REMARKS: Lürssen FPB 45 design. Rocket flare launchers are fitted on both gun mounts. Receiving new C.S.E.E. Naja electro-optical GFCS. Fin stabilizers fitted.

♦ **22 103-foot Vosper type** Bldr: Vosper Ltd., Portsmouth

Ordered in 1965:

	L		L
P 34 KRIS	11-3-66	P 36 SUNDANG	22-5-66
P 37 BADEK	8-5-66	P 38 RENCHONG	22-6-66
P 39 TOMBAK	20-6-66	P 40 LEMBING	22-8-66
P 41 SERAMPANG	15-9-66	P 42 PANAH	10-10-66

PATROL BOATS *(continued)*

	L		L
P 43 KERAMBIT	20-11-66	P 44 BALADAU	11-1-67
P 45 KELEWANG	31-1-67	P 46 RENTAKA	15-3-67
P 47 SRI PERLIS	26-5-67	P 48 SRI JOHORE	21-8-67

Ordered in March 1963:

	L		L
P 3144 SRI SABAH	30-12-63	P 3145 SRI SARAWAK	20-1-64
P 3146 SRI NEGRI SEMBILAN	17-9-64	P 3147 SRI MELAKA	25-2-64

Ordered in September 1961:

	L		L
P 3139 SRI SELANGOR	17-7-62	P 3140 SRI PERAK	30-8-62
P 3142 SRI KELANTAN	8-1-63	P 3143 SRI TRENGGANU	12-12-62

Sri Melaka (P 3147) J. Jedrlinic, 1980

D: 96 tons (109 fl) **S:** 27/23 kts **Dim:** 31.39 (28.95 pp) × 5.95 × 1.65
A: 2/40-mm AA (I × 2)—2 mg **Electron Equipt:** Radar: 1/Decca 1226
M: 2 Bristol-Siddeley or Maybach MD 655/18 diesels; 2 props; 3,550 hp
Range: 1,400/14 **Man:** 3 officers, 19-20 men

REMARKS: Welded hulls. Vosper anti-roll stabilizers. The Malaysian prototype was delivered in February 1963 and was soon followed by many others. The middle group have greater range: 1,660/14. The class prototype, the *Sri Kedah* (P 3138), and the *Sri Pahang* (P 3141) were stricken 1976. Bulwark configurations vary, while early units had hull portholes.

MINE WARFARE SHIPS

♦ **4 Italian Lerici-class minehunters** Bldr: Intermarine, La Spezia

	Laid down	L	In serv.
M . . . N . . .	. . .	. . .	. . .
M . . . N . . .	. . .	. . .	. . .
M . . . N . . .	. . .	. . .	. . .
M . . . N . . .	. . .	. . .	. . .

D: 470 tons (502 fl) **S:** 15 kts **Dim:** 49.98 (45.50 pp) × 9.56 × 2.63
A: 1/20-mm AA
Electron Equipt: Radar: . . .
Sonar: SQQ-14

M: 1 MTU 12V652 TV81 diesel; 1 prop; . . . hp **Electric:** 887 kVA
Range: 1,400/14; 2,500/12 **Man:** 39 tot.

REMARKS: Ordered 2-81. Glass-reinforced plastic construction. Have different main engine than Italian Navy sisters. Two retractable auxiliary props (470 hp) used when minehunting at speeds up to 7 kts. Range at 12 kts can be extended to 4,000 nm by using the passive anti-rolling tanks to carry fuel. Will have two PAP-104 remote-controlled minehunting devices.

♦ **2 ex-British "Ton"-class coastal minesweepers**

	Bldr	L	Trans.
M 1163 TAHAN (ex-*Lullington*)	Harland & Wolff	31-8-55	4-66
M 1172 BRINCHANG (ex-*Thankerton*)	Camper & Nicholson	4-9-56	5-66

Tahan (M 1163) 1980

D: 360 tons (425 fl) **S:** 15 kts **Dim:** 46.33 (42.68 pp) × 8.76 × 2.5
A: 1/40-mm AA—2/20-mm AA (II × 1) **Electron Equipt:** Radar: 1/978
M: 2 Napier Deltic 18A 7A diesels; 2 props; 3,000 hp
Fuel: 43 tons **Range:** 2,300/13; 3,000/8

REMARKS: Refitted 1972-73 by Vosper Thornycroft in Singapore. Wood-planked hulls with aluminum-alloy framing. Sisters *Jerai* (M 1168) stricken in 1977, *Ledang* (M 1143) and *Kinabalu* (M 1134) in 1981, while *Mahamiru* (M 1127) has been expended as a target. The survivors are used primarily for training.

AMPHIBIOUS WARFARE CRAFT

NOTE: In addition to these small craft, the multi-purpose ships of the *Sri Indera Sakti* class, the former U.S. Navy LSTs, and the miscellaneous utility landing craft listed under auxiliaries can be used for amphibious warfare purposes.

♦ **5 U.S. LCM(6)-class vehicle landing craft** Bldr: Australia

LCM 1-5

D: 24 tons (56 fl) **S:** 10 kts **Dim:** 17.07 × 4.37 × 1.17
M: 2 diesels; 2 props; 330 hp **Range:** 130/10

REMARKS: Transferred around 1970 from Australia. Cargo: 30 tons.

♦ **9 RCP-class personnel/vehicle landing craft** Bldr: Hong Leong-Lürssen SY, Butterworth Malaysia (All in serv. 1974)

D: 15 tons (30 fl) **S:** 17 kts **Dim:** 15.0 × 4.4 × . . .
A: 1/20-mm AA **M:** 2 diesels; 2 waterjets; . . . hp

REMARKS: Cargo: 35 troops or one small vehicle.

AMPHIBIOUS WARFARE CRAFT (*continued*)

RCP 2   1974

♦ **15 LCP-class personnel landing craft** Bldr: Australia

LCP 1-15

    D: 19 tons (fl) **S:** 16 kts **Dim:** 14.6 × 4.3 × 1.0
    M: 2 Cummins diesels; 2 props; 400 hp

REMARKS: Transferred 1965-66. Essentially personnel launches with pointed bows; have light armor over pilothouse amidships.

HYDROGRAPHIC SHIP

♦ **1 seagoing oceanographic research and hydrographic survey ship**

	Bldr	In serv.
A 152 MUTIARA	Hong Leong-Lürssen, Butterworth, Malaysia	18-11-77

Mutiara (A 152)   G. Arra, 1980

    D: 1,905 tons (fl) **S:** 16 kts **Dim:** 70.0 (64.0 pp) × 13.0 × 4.0
    A: 2/20-mm AA (I × 2) **M:** 1 Deutz SBA-12M-528 diesel; 1 CP prop; 2,000 hp
    Range: 4,500/16 **Man:** 13 officers, 143 men

REMARKS: Ordered 1975. Carries six small survey launches and has a helicopter deck. White hull, buff stack.

AUXILIARIES

♦ **1 (+2) multi-purpose support ships** Bldr: Bremer Vulcan, West Germany

	Laid down	L	In serv.
A 1503 SRI INDERA SAKTI	15-2-80	1-7-80	24-10-80
A. . . N. . .	. . .	. . .	. . .
A. . . N. . .	. . .	. . .	. . .

Sri Indera Sakti (A 1503)   J. Jedrlinic, 1980

    D: 4,300 tons (fl) **S:** 16.5 kts **Dim:** 100.00 (93.60 pp) × 15.00 × 4.75
    A: 1/40-mm AA **M:** 2 Deutz S/BMV6 540 diesels; 2 props; 5,986 hp
    Electric: 1,200 kw **Endurance:** 60 days **Man:** accommodations for 215 tot.

REMARKS: 1,800 dwt. A 1503 ordered 10-79, two more in 2-81. Intended to perform a variety of tasks, such as: provide support (including up to 1,300 tons of fuel and 200 tons water) to deployed small combatants or mine-countermeasures ships; act as a flagship; perform as a vehicle and troop transport in amphibious operations; and act as a cadet training ship. There is 950m³ of cargo space for spare parts, and ten 20-ft standard cargo containers can be carried on deck amidships. Vehicle holds aft are reached by ramps on either side of the stern, which supports a helicopter deck. Extensive repair facilities and divers' support equipment are provided. Provisions spaces total 300m³, including 100m³ refrigerated stores. Bow-thruster fitted, as is a 15-ton crane amidships.

♦ **3 ex-U.S. LST 542-class tank landing ships, employed as transports**

	Bldr	L	In serv.
A 1500 SRI LANGKAWI (ex-*Hunterdon Co.*, AGP 838, ex-LST 838)	American Bridge, Ambridge, Pa.	8-11-44	4-12-44
A 1501 SRI BANGGI (ex-*Henry County*, LST 824)	Missouri Valley Bridge & Iron Wks.	8-11-44	30-11-44
A 1502 RAJAH JEROM (ex-*Sedgewick Co.*, LST 1123)	Chicago Bridge, Seneca, Ill.	29-1-45	19-2-45

    D: 1,653 tons (4,080 fl) **S:** 11.6 kts **Dim:** 99.98 (96.31 pp) × 15.24 × 4.29
    A: A 1500: 4/40-mm AA (I × 4); others: none
    Electron Equipt: Radar: SPS-53
    M: 2 GM 12-567A diesels; 2 props; 1,700 hp **Electric:** 300 kw
    Fuel: 568 tons **Range:** 6,000/9 (loaded)

AUXILIARIES *(continued)*

Sri Banggi (A 1501)   J. Jedrlinic, 1980

REMARKS: A 1500 was transferred 1-7-71, and the other two, 7-10-76. A 1500 was converted to a small-craft tender while still in U.S. Navy service; part of her tank deck was converted to machine shops and store rooms, and a kingpost and boom were added on her upper deck. The other pair are used as logistics support tenders and have a 2,100-ton cargo capacity. All have a helicopter pad amidships and bow doors. Being re-engined 1981-82.

◆ **2 utility landing craft/transports** Bldr: Penang SY, Pulau Jerejah

	L	In serv.
A. . . Lang Siput	1980	1980
A. . . Lang Tiram	25-9-80	21-10-80

D: 630 grt **S:** 9 kts **Dim:** 48.4 (45.0 pp)× 10.5 ×. . .
M: 2 Caterpillar D3408 diesels; 2 props; 700 hp

◆ **2 Jernih-class utility landing craft/transports** Bldr: Brooke DY, Malaysia

A. . . Jernih (In serv. 1977)   A. . . Terijah (In serv. 1978)

D: 290 (fl) **S:** 8 kts **Dim:** 38.0 (35.2 pp) ×. . . × 1.4
M: 2 Caterpillar D343T diesels; 2 props; 730 hp

REMARKS: Capacity: 170 tons of dry cargo or 240 tons of fresh water. Intended as supply craft for Sarawak.

◆ **1 Meleban-class utility landing craft** Bldr: Brooke DY, Malaysia

A. . . Meleban (L: 15-10-77)

D: . . . **S:** 8 kts **Dim:** 50.0 (43.5 pp) ×. . . × 1.37
M: 2 Caterpillar D343T diesels; 2 props; 730 hp

◆ **1 small cargo ship** (In serv. 1977)

A 301 Enterprise

◆ **1 small tanker** (In serv. 1973)

A 8 Kepah (ex-*Asiatic Supplier*)—432 grt. Purchased 1980.

◆ **1 diving tender**

	Bldr	L	In serv.
A 1109 Duyong	Kall Teck SY, Singapore	18-8-70	5-1-71

D: 140 tons (fl) **S:** 10 kts **Dim:** 33.0 × 6.3 × 1.7
A: 1/20-AA **M:** 2 Cummins diesels; 2 props; 500 hp **Man:** 23 tot.

REMARKS: Used as a support ship for divers. Originally configured as a torpedo-retriever.

◆ **3 Tunda-class harbor tugs** Bldr: Ironwood SY, Malyasia (In serv. 1978-79)

A 1 Tunda 1   A 2 Tunda 2   A 3 Tunda 3

D: 150 tons **S:** . . . **Dim:** 26.0 ×. . . ×. . .
M: 1 Cummins diesel; 1 prop;. . . hp

◆ **1 salvage and fire-fighting tug** (In serv. 1976)

A 4 Penyu (ex-*Salvigilant*)—Purchased 1980; 398 grt.

◆ **2 salvage and fire-fighting tugs**

A 20 Badang I   A 21 Badang II—400 grt

◆ **9 miscellaneous tugs**

A 6 Sotong (ex-*Asiatic Charm*)—233 grt, blt. 1976; purchased 1980.

A 9 Siput	A 10 Teritup	A 11 Belankas
A. . . Mangkasa	A. . . Selar	A. . . Tepuruk
A. . . Kempong	A. . . Patak	

ROYAL MALAYSIAN MARINE POLICE

NOTE: Planned acquisitions include three 40-m patrol boats equipped with helicopter platforms and four 32-m patrol boats.

PATROL BOATS

◆ **12 PZ class** Bldr: Hong Leong-Lürssen, Butterworth, Malaysia

	In serv.		In serv.
P 21 Lang Hitan	12-80	P 27 N. .	. . .
P 22 N. .	. . .	P 28 N. .	. . .
P 23 N. .	. . .	P 29 N. .	. . .
P 24 N. .	. . .	P 30 N. .	. . .
P 25 N. .	. . .	P 31 N. .	. . .
P 26 N. .	. . .	P 32 N. .	. . .

D: 188 tons (205 fl) **S:** 34 kts **Dim:** 38.50 (36.00 wl) × 7.00 × 2.20
A: 1/40-mm AA—1/20-mm AA—2/7.62-mm mg
M: 2 MTU 20V538 TB92 diesels; 2 props; 9,000 hp **Electric:** 130 kVA
Range: 550/31.5; 1,100/16 **Man:** 3 officers, 24 men

REMARKS: Lürssen FPB 38 design. Have 2 rocket flare launchers, carry 1,000 rounds 40-mm, 2,000 rounds 20-mm.

◆ **6 PX 26 class** Bldr: Hong Leong-Lürssen, Butterworth, Malaysia (In serv. 1973-74)

PX 25 N. .	PX 27 Sri Tawau	PX 29 N. .
PX 26 Sri Kudat	PX 28 N. .	PX 30 N. .

MALAYSIA (*continued*)
PATROL BOATS (*continued*)

D: 62.5 tons   **S:** 25 kts   **Dim:** 28.0 × 5.4 × 1.6
A: 1/20-mm AA   **M:** 2 MTU MB820Db diesels; 2 props; 2,460 hp
Range: 1,050/15   **Man:** 19 tot.

♦ **6 improved PX class** Bldr: Vosper Thornycroft Private, Singapore (In serv. 1973-74)

PX 19 ALOR STAR	PX 21 KUALA TRENGGANU	PX 23 SRI MENANTI
PX 20 KOTA BAHRU	PX 22 JOHORE BAHRU	PX 24 KUCHING

D: 92 tons (fl)   **S:** 25 kts   **Dim:** 27.3 × 5.8 × 1.5
A: 2/20-mm AA (I × 2)   **M:** 2 MTU MB820Db diesels; 2 props; 2,460 hp
Range: 750/15   **Man:** 18 tot.

♦ **16 PX class** Bldr: Vosper Thornycroft Private, Singapore, 1963-69

PX 1 MAHKOTA	PX 7 BENTARA	PX 13 PEKAN
PX 2 TEMENGGONG	PX 8 PERWIRA	PX 14 KELANG
PX 3 HULUBALANG	PX 9 PERTANDA	PX 15 KUALA KANGSAR
PX 4 MAHARAJESETIA	PX 10 SHAHBANDAR	PX 16 ARAU
PX 5 MAHARAJELELA	PX 11 SANGSETIA	
PX 6 PAHLAWAN	PX 12 LAKSAMANA	

Shahbandar and Sangsetia (PX 10, PX 11)   1975

D: 85 tons (fl)   **S:** 25 kts   **Dim:** 26.29 × 5.7 × 1.45
A: 2/20-mm AA (I × 2)
M: 2 Mercedes-Benz MB820Db diesels; 2 props; 2,460 hp   **Range:** 700/15
Man: 15 tot.

REMARKS: Sisters *Sri Gumantong* (PX 17) and *Sri Labuan* (PX 18) are operated by the Sabah government.

NOTE: The Royal Malaysian Marine Police operate a large number of smaller patrol and support craft.

MALAYSIAN CUSTOMS AND EXCISE SERVICE

PATROL BOATS

♦ **6 Vosper 103-ft design** Bldr: Malaysian SY & Eng. Co.

D: 100 tons (125 fl)   **S:** 27 kts   **Dim:** 31.29 (28.95 pp) × 6.02 × 1.98
A: . . .   **M:** 2 MTU diesels; 2 props; 4,000 hp   **Range:** 1,500/. . .
Man: 24 tot.

REMARKS: Ordered built under license from Vosper PTY, Singapore. Will generally resemble Malaysian Navy units of this design. The Customs and Excise Service also operates a number of small craft.

MALDIVES
Republic of Maldives

PERSONNEL: Approximately 150 total

MERCHANT MARINE (1980): 41 ships—136,037 grt

PATROL BOATS AND CRAFT

♦ **1 ex-British RTTL Mk-2-class target-towing launch**

D: 34.6 tons (fl)   **S:** 30 kts   **Dim:** 20.7 × 5.8 × 1.8
A: mg   **M:** 2 Rolls-Royce Sea Griffon gasoline engines; 2 props; 1,100 hp
Man: 9 tot.

REMARKS: Transferred in 1976 by the departing Royal Air Force.

♦ **1 ex-British 1300-class tender**

D: 28.3 tons   **S:** 13 kts   **Dim:** 19.2 × 4.9 × 1.5
M: 2 Rolls-Royce C6 diesels; 2 props; 190 hp   **Man:** 5 tot.

REMARKS: Transferred by the departing Royal Air Force. Cargo: 5 tons.

♦ **3 ex-Taiwanese trawlers**

REMARKS: Approximately 600 tons (fl). Fitted with 2/25-mm AA guns (II × 1) by the U.S.S.R. after confiscation for poaching in 1976.

♦ **4 ex-British 19.5-meter landing craft**

REMARKS: Transferred in 1976.

♦ **1 customs launch** Bldr: Fairey Marine, G.B., 1975

MALTA
Republic of Malta

MERCHANT MARINE (1980): 60 ships—132,861 grt (tankers: 2 ships—4,922 grt)

COAST GUARD

PATROL CRAFT

♦ **2 ex-U.S. Swift-class PCF** Bldr: Sewart Seacraft, 1967

C 23 (ex-U.S. C 6823)   C 24 (ex-U.S. C 6824)

D: 22.5 tons (fl)   **S:** 25 kts   **Dim:** 15.6 × 4.12 × 1.5
A: 3/12.7-mm mg (II × 1 and 1 combined with 1/81-mm mortar)
M: 2 GM 12V71T diesels; 2 props; 960 hp   **Endurance:** 24-36 hours
Man: 6-8 tot.

REMARKS: Donated 1-71.

♦ **2 ex-Libyan customs patrol craft** Bldrs: C 31: Vosper Thornycroft, Woolston; C 32: Thornycroft, Woolston

C 31 (ex-*Akrama*)   C 32 (ex-*Ar Rakib*)

D: 100 tons (fl)   **S:** 18 kts   **Dim:** 30.5 × 6.4 × 1.7
A: 1/20-mm AA   **M:** 3 Rolls-Royce diesels; 3 props; 1,740 hp
Range: 1,800/14   **Man:** 15 tot.

REMARKS: Transferred in 1978. C 30 (ex-*Farwa*) sank 1981.

♦ **2 British RAF RTTL Mk 2-class rescue launches**

C 68 (ex-2768)   C 71 (ex-2771)

D: 34.6 tons   **S:** 30 kts   **Dim:** 20.7 × 5.8 × 1.8
M: 2 Rolls-Royce Sea Griffon gasoline engines; 2 props;. . . hp   **Man:** 9 tot.

REMARKS: Transferred early 1970s; wooden construction.

♦ **2 ex-Libyan customs launches** Bldr: Mosir SY, Trogir, Yugoslavia, 1963

C 25   C 26

D: 86.2 tons (100 fl)   **S:** 20 kts   **Dim:** 35.0 × 5.0 × 1.7
A: 1/12.7-mm mg   **M:** 2 MTU 12V493 diesels; 2 props; 1,800 hp
Range: 1,400/12   **Man:** 12 tot.

REMARKS: Transferred 16-1-74.

♦ **1 ex-German customs launch**

C 27 (ex-*Brunsbuttel*)   Bldr: Buschmann, Hamburg, 1953

D: 105 tons (fl)   **S:** 16 kts   **Dim:** 29.5 × 5.2 × 1.6
A: 1/12.7-mm mg   **M:** 2 MWM TRM 134S diesels; 2 props;. . . hp   **Man:** 9 tot.

REMARKS: Purchased in 1974.

NOTE: Old customs launches C 21, C 28, C 29 stricken 1979.

♦ **1 British RAF 1300-series pinnace general-purpose tender**

C. . .

M: 2 Rolls-Royce C6 diesels; 2 props; 190 hp   **Man:** 5 tot.

REMARKS: Also transferred was an RAF 1600-series range safety craft: 12 tons, 13.1 × 4.0 × 1.2, 16 kts.

MAURITANIA
Islamic Republic of Mauritania

PERSONNEL: 200 men

MERCHANT MARINE (1980): 3 ships—874 grt

NAVAL AVIATION: Two Piper Cheyenne II, twin-turboprop aircraft were delivered 1981 for coastal surveillance duties. Capable of 7-hour patrols (1,525 nm), they have a belly-mounted Bendix RDR 1400 radar.

PATROL BOATS AND CRAFT

♦ **2 French PATRA class** Bldr: Auroux SY, Arcachon

	Laid down	L	In serv.
P 674 N RAPIERE	15-2-81	3-6-81	1-11-81
P. . . N. . .	. . .	. . .	. . .

D: 115 tons (148 fl)   **S:** 28 kts   **Dim:** 40.70 (38.50 wl) × 5.90 × 1.55
A: 1/40-mm AA—1/12.7-mm mg   **Electron Equipt:** Radar: 1/Decca 1226
M: 2 AGO 195 V12 CZSHR diesels; 2 CP props; 5,000 hp (4,400 sust.)
Electric: 120 kw   **Range:** 750/20; 1,750/10   **Man:** 2 officers, 17 men

REMARKS: May also carry 6/SS-12M wire-guided missiles.

♦ **3 Spanish Barcelo class** Bldr: Bazán, San Fernando

	In serv.		In serv.		In serv.
P 362 EL VAIZ	12-79	P 363 EL BEG	5-79	P 364 EL KENZ	1981

D: 134 tons (fl)   **S:** 36.5 kts   **Dim:** 36.2 × 5.8 × 1.75
A: 1/40-mm AA—2/20-mm   **Electron Equipt:** Radar: 1/Raytheon 1620
M: 2 MTU MD 16V538 TB90 diesels; 6,000 hp   **Electric:** 330 kVA
Fuel: 18 tons   **Range:** 1,200/17   **Man:** 3 officers, 16 men

REMARKS: Delivery of the first two was greatly delayed when they collided on trials, 12-78. The third unit was ordered in 1979.

♦ **2 French 32-meter craft** Bldr: Chantiers Navals de l'Esterel, Cannes

TICHITT (In serv. 4-69)   DAR EL BARKA (In serv. 9-69)

D: 80 tons (fl)   **S:** 28 kts   **Dim:** 32.0 × 5.75 × 1.7
A: 1/20-mm—1/12.7-mm mg
M: 2 Mercedes-Benz MB820Db/h diesels; 2 props; 2,700 hp
Fuel: 15 tons   **Range:** 1,500/15   **Man:** 17 tot.

MAURITANIA *(continued)*
PATROL BOATS AND CRAFT *(continued)*

Tichitt l'Estérel, 1969

Amar 1976

◆ **2 French 18-m class** Bldr: Chantiers Navals de l'Esterel, Cannes

IMAG'NI (In serv. 11-65) SLOUGHI (In serv. 5-68)

D: 20 tons (fl) **S:** 21 kts (22.7 on trials) **Dim:** 18.15 (17.03 pp) × 4.03 × 1.1
A: 1/12.7-mm mg **M:** 2 GM 6-71 diesels; 2 props; 512 hp
Range: 400/15 **Man:** 8 tot.

◆ **1 service launch: Chinguetti**

NOTE: The two Soviet Mirnyy-class patrol whalers *Idini* and *Boulanouer* and the ex-Spanish trawlers *Tekane* and *Keur Macenf* (ex-*Dar el Barka*) were sold to a ship-broker in the Canary Islands during 1980.

MAURITIUS

MERCHANT MARINE (1978): 18 ships—40,732 grt

PATROL BOAT

◆ **1 ex-Indian Ajay-class patrol boat** Bldr: Garden Reach DY, Calcutta, 1961

AMAR

D: 120 tons (160 fl) **S:** 18 kts **Dim:** 35.7 (33.52 pp) × 6.1 × 1.5
A: 1/40-mm AA
M: 2 Paxman YHAXM diesels; 2 props; 1,000 hp; 1 Foden FD 6 cruise diesel;
100 hp
Fuel: 23 tons **Range:** 1,000/8; 500/12

REMARKS: Retained original name on transfer 4-74. Indian version of British "Ford"-class seaward defense boat.

MEXICO
United Mexican States

PERSONNEL (1981): 20,240 men, including 3,000 Marines

MERCHANT MARINE (1980): 361 ships—925,137 grt
(tankers: 38 ships—445,264 grt)

NAVAL AVIATION: The Mexican Navy operates 15 Grumman HU-16 Albatross amphibious patrol planes, 4 DC-3 transports, and 29 light fixed-wing aircraft, including 1 Learjet 24D and 2 T-34B Mentor trainers. Helicopters include four Alouette-III, five Hughes 269 A, 4 Bell 47G/J, and 2 Bell HU-1H.

DESTROYERS

◆ **2 ex-U.S. Gearing FRAM I class** Bldr: Bethlehem Steel, Staten Island

	Laid down	L	In serv.
IE. . . N. . . (ex-*Vogelgesang*, DD 862)	3-8-44	15-1-45	28-4-45
IE. . . N. . . (ex-*Steinaker*, DD 863)	1-9-44	13-2-45	26-5-45

D: 2,448 tons light (3,528 fl) **S:** 30 kts
Dim: 119.03 × 12.52 × 4.45 (6.4 sonar)
A: 4/127-mm DP (II × 2)—6/324-mm Mk 32 ASW TT (III × 2)
Electron Equipt: Radar: 1/LN-66, 1/SPS-10, 1/SPS-40B (ex-DD 863: SPS-29)
Sonar: SQS-23
ECM: WLR-3
M: 2 sets GE GT; 2 props; 60,000 hp **Electric:** 1,200 kw
Boilers: 4 Babcock & Wilcox; 43.3 kg/cm², 454°C **Fuel:** 650 tons

REMARKS: Both scheduled to be transferred to Mexico 2-82 by sale, as probable replacements for the two *Fletcher*-class destroyers.

DESTROYERS *(continued)*

♦ **2 ex-U.S. Fletcher class** Bldr: Consolidated Steel, Orange, Tex.

	Laid down	L	In serv.
IE-01 CUAUHTEMOC (ex-*Harrison*, DD 573)	25-7-41	7-5-42	9-2-43
IE-02 CUITLAHUAC (ex-*John Rodgers*, DD 574)	25-7-41	7-5-42	25-1-43

D: 2,050 tons (2,850 fl) **S:** 30 kts **Dim:** 114.73 × 12.06 × 5.5
A: 5/127-mm Mk 30 DP (I × 5)—14/40-mm AA (IV × 2, II × 3)
Electron Equipt: Radar: 1/Kelvin-Hughes 14/9, 1/Kelvin-Hughes 17/9, 1/Mk
12/22 f.c.
M: 2 sets GE GT; 2 props; 60,000 hp **Electric:** 590 kw
Boilers: 4 Babcock & Wilcox; 39.8 kg/cm², 454°C **Fuel:** 650 tons
Range: 4,400/15; 1,260/30 **Man:** 197 tot.

REMARKS: Transferred 8-70. All ASW capability, torpedo-tube mount, and obsolete
U.S. electronics systems now deleted. Have one Mk 37 director for 127-mm guns;
five Mk 51 mod. 2 directors for 40-mm guns. Could make 35 kts when new. To be
replaced by U.S. Gearing FRAM I-class destroyers; the name of IE-01 is to be given
to a new sail training ship.

FRIGATES

♦ **1 ex-U.S. Charles Lawrence and 3 Crosley class**

	Bldr	L	In serv.
IB-02 COAHUILA (ex-*Rednour*, APD 102, ex DE 529)	Bethlehem, Hingham, Mass.	12-2-44	30-12-44
IB-05 TEHUANTEPEC (ex-*Joseph M. Auman*, APD 117, ex-DE 674)	Consolidated Steel, Orange, Tex.	5-2-44	25-4-45
IB-06 USUMACINTA (ex-*Don O. Woods*, APD 118, ex-DE 721)	Consolidated Steel, Orange, Tex.	19-2-44	28-5-45
IB-08 CHIHUAHUA (ex-*Barber*, APD 57, ex-DE 161)	Norfolk NY, Va.	20-4-43	10-10-43

D: 1,450 tons (2,130 fl) **S:** 23 kts **Dim:** 93.26 × 11.28 × 3.83
A: 1/127-mm Mk 30 DP—6/40-mm AA (II × 3)
Electron Equipt: Radar: 1/Kelvin-Hughes 14/9
M: 2 sets GE GT, turbo-electric drive; 2 props; 12,000 hp **Electric:** 680 kw
Boilers: 2 "D"-Express; 30.6 kg/cm², 399°C **Fuel:** 350 tons
Range: 5,000/15 **Man:** 204 tot.

REMARKS: Former high-speed transports. IB-05 and IB-06 transferred 12-63; IB-02
and IB-08, 17-2-69. Used primarily as patrol ships; no longer carry the four landing
craft that were once stowed amidships. Converted to APD while being built. IB-08,
with a high bridge and lattice mast aft, is a member of the *Charles Lawrence* class;
the others each have a low bridge and a tripod aft to support the 10-ton capacity
cargo boom. The 127-mm gun has no director, while there are three Mk 51 mod. 2
directors for the 40-mm anti-aircraft. Two others have been lost: *California* (B-3,
ex-*Belet*, APD 109) went aground 16-1-72, and *Papaloapan* (B-4, ex-*Earheart*, APD
113) in 1976.

CORVETTES

♦ **15 new construction** Bldr:. . . , Brazil

REMARKS: Order announced 1980, but no characteristics were given, nor was the
builder mentioned.

♦ **6 Spanish Type 119 class** Bldr: Bazan, San Fernando, Cadiz

	Laid down	L	In serv.		Laid down	L	In serv.
. . .N. . .	. . .	. . .	. . .	. . .N. . .	. . .	. . .	. . .
. . .N. . .	. . .	. . .	. . .	. . .N. . .	. . .	. . .	. . .
. . .N. . .	. . .	. . .	. . .	. . .N. . .	. . .	. . .	. . .

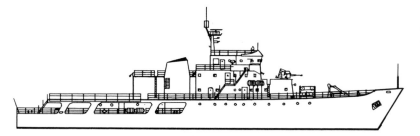

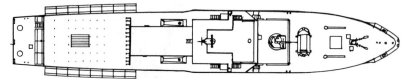

Mexican corvette   A. D. Baker III, 9-81

D: 767 tons (844 fl) **S:** 21.5 kts **Dim:** 67.00 (63.00 pp) × 10.00 × 3.06
A: 1/40-mm AA—1/helicopter **Electron Equipt:** Radar: 1/Decca AC 1226
M: 2 MTU 16V956 TB91 diesels; 2 props; 7,500 hp
Electric: 710 kw **Range:** 5,000/18

REMARKS: Ordered late 1980 for use in patrolling the 200-nautical-mile economic zone.
Have been referred to as the "Puma" class. Generally identical to ships being built
for Argentina. Will probably replace U.S. *Admirable*-class units.

♦ **18 ex-U.S. Auk-class former fleet minesweepers**

	Bldr	L
IG-01 LEANDRO VALLE (ex-*Pioneer*, MSF 105)(1)	A	26-7-42
IG-02 GUILLERMO PRIETO (ex-*Symbol*, MSF 123)(2)	B	2-7-42
IG-03 MARIANO ESCOBEDO (ex-*Champion*, MSF 314)(3)	C	12-12-42
IG-04 PONCIANO ARRIAGA (ex-*Competent*, MSF 316)(3)	C	9-1-43
IG-05 MANUEL DOBLADO (ex-*Defense*, MSF 317)(3)	C	18-2-43
IG-06 SEBASTIAN LEIDO DE TEJADA (ex-*Devastator*, MSF 318)(3)	C	19-4-43
IG-07 SANTOS DEGOLLADO (ex-*Gladiator*, MSF 319)(3)	C	7-5-43
IG-08 IGNACIO DE LA LLAVE (ex-*Spear*, MSF 322)(2)	D	25-2-43
IG-09 JUAN N. ALVAREZ (ex-*Ardent*, MSF 340)(3)	C	22-6-43
IG-10 MELCHIOR OCAMPO (ex-*Roselle*, MSF 379)(4)	E	29-8-45
IG-11 VALENTIN G. FARIAS (ex-*Starling*, MSF 64)(5)	C	15-2-42
IG-12 IGNACIO ALTAMIRANO (ex-*Sway*, MSF 120)(2)	F	29-9-42
IG-13 FRANCISCO ZARCO (ex-*Threat*, MSF 124)(2)	B	15-8-42
IG-14 IGNACIO L. VALLARTA (ex-*Velocity*, MSF 128)(2)	E	19-4-42
IG-15 JÉSUS G. ORTEGA (ex-*Chief*, MSF 315)(3)	C	5-1-43
IG-16 GUTIERREZ ZAMORA (ex-*Scoter*, MSF 381)(4)	E	26-9-45
IG-18 JUAN ALDARMA (ex-*Pilot*, MSF 104)(1)	A	5-7-42
IG-19 HERMENEGILDO GALEANA (ex-*Sage*, MSF 111)(1)	G	21-11-42

CORVETTES (continued)

Ignacio L. Vallarta (IG-14)—bulwarks amidships   1974

Juan Aldarma (IG-18)—no bulwarks   1975

Bldrs: *A*, Pennsylvania Shipyard, Beaumont, Tex.; *B*, Savannah Machine & Foundry Co., Savannah, Ga.; *C*, General Engineering and Drydock Co., Alameda, Cal.; *D*, Associated Shipbuilders; *E*, Gulf Shipbuilding; *F*, J. H. Mathis, Camden, N.J.; *G*, Winslow Marine Railway and Shipbuilding, Seattle, Wash.

D: 890 tons (1,250 fl)   **S:** 17/18 kts   **Dim:** 67.4 (65.5 wl) × 9.8 × 3.28
A: 1/76.2-mm Mk 22 DP—4/40-mm AA (II × 2)
Electron Equipt: Radar: 1/SPS-5 or 1/Kelvin-Hughes 14/9, 1/SO-13
M: 2 diesels, electric drive (*see* Remarks); 2 props; 2,976, 3,118, or 3,532 hp
Electric: 300-360 kw   **Fuel:** 216 tons   **Man:** 9 officers, 96 men

REMARKS: The numbers in parentheses after the ships' names refer to five different diesels used in propulsion plants: (1) Busch-Sulzer 539; (2) GM 12-278; (3) Baldwin VO-8; (4) GM 12-278A; (5) Alco 539. Diesels (1) and (5) produce 3,118 hp, (2) and (4) 3,532 hp, and (3) 2,976 hp.

All transferred in 1973. All minesweeping and ASW equipment removed. One other unit, *Mariano Metamoros* (ex-*Herald*, MSF 101), was converted for use as a surveying ship. Some have a small deckhouse between the stacks; some have no main deck bulwarks. New radars have been added to ships transferred without SPS-5.

♦ **16 ex-U.S. Admirable-class former fleet minesweepers**

	Bldrs	L
ID-01 DM 01 (ex-*Jubilant*, MSF 255)	American SB, Lorain, Oh.	20-2-43
ID-02 DM 02 (ex-*Hilarity*, MSF 241)	Winslow, Seattle, Wash.	30-7-44
ID-03 DM 03 (ex-*Execute*, MSF 232)	Puget Sound, Seattle, Wash.	22-1-44
ID-04 DM 04 (ex-*Specter*, MSF 306)	Associated Shipbldrs.	15-2-44
ID-05 DM 05 (ex-*Scuffle*, MSF 298)	Winslow, Seattle, Wash.	8-8-43
ID-06 DM 06 (ex-*Eager*, MSF 224)	American SB, Lorain, Oh.	10-6-44
ID-10 DM 10 (ex-*Instill*, MSF 252)	Savannah Mach., Ga.	5-3-44
ID-11 DM 11 (ex-*Device*, MSF 220)	Tampa SB, Fla.	21-5-44
ID-12 DM 12 (ex-*Ransom*, MSF 283)	General Eng. & DD	18-9-43
ID-13 DM 13 (ex-*Knave*, MSF 256)	American SB, Lorain, Oh.	13-3-43
ID-14 DM 14 (ex-*Rebel*, MSF 284)	General Eng. & DD	28-10-43
ID-15 DM 15 (ex-*Crag*, MSF 214)	Tampa SB, Fla.	21-3-43
ID-16 DM 16 (ex-*Dour*, MSF 223)	American SB, Lorain, Oh.	25-3-44
ID-17 DM 17 (ex-*Diploma*, MSF 221)	Tampa SB, Fla.	21-5-44
ID-18 DM 18 (ex-*Invade*, MSF 254)	Savannah Mach., Ga.	6-2-44
ID-19 DM 19 (ex-*Intrigue*, MSF 253)	Savannah Mach., Ga.	8-4-44

DM 02 (ID-02)   1975

D: 650 tons (945 fl)   **S:** 15 kts   **Dim:** 56.24 (54.86 wl) × 10.06 × 2.97
A: 1/76.2-mm Mk 22 DP—2/40-mm AA (I × 2)—6/20-mm AA (I × 6)
M: 2 Cooper-Bessemer GSB-8 diesels; 2 props; 1,710 hp
Electric: 240 or 280 kw   **Fuel:** 138 tons   **Man:** 9 officers, 86 men

REMARKS: All minesweeping and ASW equipment deleted. Three more units were scrapped and DM 20 was converted into a hydrographic survey ship. DM 04 was transferred 2-73; all others, 1-10-62.

PATROL BOATS

♦ **31 (+9?) Azteca class**

	Bldr	In serv.
P-01 ANDRES QUINTANA ROO	Ailsa	1-11-74
P-02 MATIAS DE CORDOVA	Scott	22-10-74
P-03 MIGUEL RAMOS ARIZPE	Ailsa	23-12-74
P-04 JOSÉ MARIA IZAZAGO	Ailsa	19-12-74

PATROL BOATS (continued)

	Bldr	In serv.
P-05 JUAN BAUTISTA MORALES	Scott	19-12-74
P-06 IGNACIO LOPEZ RAYON	Ailsa	19-12-74
P-07 MANUEL CRESCENCIO REJON	Ailsa	4-7-75
P-08 ANTONIO DE LA FUENTE	Ailsa	4-7-75
P-09 LEON GUZMAN	Scott	7-4-75
P-10 IGNACIO RAMIREZ	Ailsa	17-7-75
P-11 IGNACIO MARISCAL	Ailsa	23-9-75
P-12 HERIBERTO JARA CORONA	Ailsa	7-11-75
P-13 JOSÉ MARIA MATA	Lamont	13-10-75
P-14 FELIX ROMERO	Scott	25-6-75
P-15 FERNANDO LIZARDI	Ailsa	24-12-75
P-16 FRANCISCO J. MUJICA	Ailsa	21-11-75
P-17 PASTOR ROUAIX JOSÉ MARIA	Scott	7-11-75
P-18 JOSÉ MARIA DEL CASTILLO VELASCO	Lamont	14-1-75
P-19 LUIS MANUEL ROJAS	Lamont	3-4-76
P-20 JOSÉ NATIVIDAD MACIAS	Lamont	2-9-76
P-21 ESTEBAN BACA CALDERON	Lamont	18-6-76
P-22 GENERAL IGNACIO ZARAGOZA	Vera Cruz	1-6-76
P-23 TAMAULIPAS	Vera Cruz	1978
P-24 YUCATAN	Vera Cruz	1978
P-25 TABASCO	Vera Cruz	1-1-79
P-26 VERACRUZ	Vera Cruz	1-1-79
P-27 CAMPECHE	Vera Cruz	1-1-79
P-28 PUEBLA	Vera Cruz	1-1-79
P-29 MARGARITA MAZA DE JUAREZ	Salina Cruz	1-79
P-30 LEONA VICARIO	Salina Cruz	1-79
P-31 JOSEFA ORTIZ DE DOMINGUEZ	Salina Cruz	1-79

Andres Quintana Roo (P-01)—prior to arming   Ailsa Shipbldg., 1975

D: 130 tons   **S:** 24 kts   **Dim:** 34.06 (30.94 pp) × 8.6 × 2.0
A: 1/40-mm AA—1/20-mm AA
M: 2 Ruston-Paxman Ventura 12-cyl. diesels; 7,200 hp   **Electric:** 80 kw
Range: 2,500/12   **Man:** 2 officers, 22 men

REMARKS: Original order for 21 placed 27-3-73 with Associated British Machine Tool Makers, Ltd., which subcontracted the actual construction and assisted with the construction of another 11 in Mexico. Another nine may be built in Mexico, it was announced on 15-10-80.

PATROL CRAFT

♦ **1 (+. . .) Olmeca class** Bldr: Acapulco, Mexico (In serv. 1979-80)

   D: . . .   **S:** 30 kts   **Dim:** 15.0 ×. . . ×. . .
   A: 1/20-mm AA   **M:** 2 Cummins VT-series diesels; 800 hp   **Man:** 7 tot.

REMARKS: Glass-reinforced plastic construction.

♦ **4 Polimar class** Bldrs: Astilleros de Tampico (IF-01, IF-04); Iscacas SY, Guerrero (IF-02, IF-03)

	L		L
IF-01 POLIMAR 1	1962	IF-03 POLIMAR 3	1966
IF-02 POLIMAR 2	1966	IF-04 POLIMAR 4	1968

Polimar 1   1962

   D: 57 tons (fl)   **S:** 16 kts   **Dim:** 20.5 × 4.5 × 1.3
   A: 2/13.2-mm mg (II × 1)   **M:** 2 diesels; 2 props; 450 hp

♦ **2 Azueta class** Bldr: Astilleros de Tampico

	L		L
IF-06 AZUETA	1959	IF-07 VILLAPANDO	1960

   D: 80 tons (85 fl)   **S:** 12 kts   **Dim:** 26.0 × 4.9 × 2.1
   A: 2/13.2-mm mg (II × 1)   **M:** 2 Superior diesels; 2 props; 600 hp

RIVER PATROL CRAFT

♦ **8 AM-1 class** Bldrs: Astilleros de Tampico (4); Vera Cruz SY (4)

AM-1 TO AM-8   (IF-11 to IF-18)

   D: 37 tons (fl)   **S:** 6 kts   **Dim:** 17.7 × 5.0 ×. . .
   A: . . .   **M:** diesels

REMARKS: Launched 1960-62.

AUXILIARIES

HYDROGRAPHIC SURVEY SHIPS

♦ **1 ex-U.S. Robert D. Conrad-class oceanographic research ship**

	Bldr	L	In serv.
H. . . N. . . (ex-*James M. Gillis*, AGOR 4)	Christy Corp., Wisconsin	19-5-62	5-11-62

HYDROGRAPHIC SURVEY SHIPS *(continued)*

D: 1,200 tons (1,380 fl) **S:** 13.5 kts **Dim:** 63.7 × 11.4 × 6.3
Electron Equipt: Radar: 1/Raytheon TM 1600/6X; 1/TM 1660/123
M: 2 Caterpillar D-378 diesels, electric drive; 1 prop; 1,000 hp
Electric: 850 kw **Fuel:** 211 tons **Range:** 12,000/12
Man: 26 crew, 18 scientists

REMARKS: Returned to U.S. Navy by University of Miami in 1980 and laid up, pending lease to Mexico in 1982. The large stack contains a 620-hp gas turbine generator set to drive the main shaft at speeds up to 6.5 kts for experiments requiring "quiet" sea conditions. Also has a retractable electric bow-thruster/propulsor, which can drive the ship to 4.5 kts.

♦ **1 ex-U.S. Admirable-class former minesweeper** Bldr: Willamette Iron & Steel, Ore.

H-2 OCEANOGRAFICO (ex-DM 20, ex-*Harlequin*, MSF 365)

REMARKS: Launched 3-6-44. Data as for corvettes, except for displacement, which is approximately 900 tons (full load); no armament. Converted 1976-78.

♦ **1 ex-U.S. Auk-class former minesweeper** Bldr: General Eng. & DD, Alameda, Cal.

	Laid down	L	In serv.
H-1 MARIANO MATAMOROS (ex-*Herald*, MSF 101)	14-3-42	4-7-42	23-3-43

Mariano Matamoros (H-1)   G. Arra, 1977

REMARKS: Data generally as for corvette version. Has Busch-Sulzer BS539 diesels; 3,118 hp. No armament. Large deckhouse built around after stack with a portable facility for aerological balloon-launching atop it. Oceanographic crane at stern. Radars are one SPS-5 and one Kelvin-Hughes 14/9.

REPAIR SHIP

♦ **1 ex-U.S. Fabius-class former aircraft repair ship**

	Bldr	L	In serv.
IA-05 GENERAL VINCENTE GUERRERO (ex-*Megara*, ARVA 6, ex-LST 1095)	American Bridge, Pa.	25-3-45	27-6-45

D: 4,100 tons (fl) **S:** 11.6 kts **Dim:** 100.0 (96.3 wl) × 15.24 × 3.4
A: 8/40-mm AA (IV × 2) **M:** 2 GM 12-567A diesels; 2 props; 1,700 hp
Electric: 520 kw **Fuel:** 474 tons **Range:** 10,000/10 **Man:** 250 tot.

General Vincente Guerrero (IA-05)   1974

REMARKS: Transferred 1-10-73. Originally intended for repairing aircraft airframes. One 10-ton boom. Two Mk 51 mod. 2 GFCS for the 40-mm AA.

TRANSPORTS

♦ **1 Mexican built** Bldr: Ulua SY, Vera Cruz (In serv. 1959)

B-2 ZACATECAS

D: 780 tons **S:** 10 kts **Dim:** 47.5 × 8.2 × 2.8
A: 1/40-mm AA—2/20-mm AA (I × 2)
M: 1 M.A.N. diesel; 1 prop; 560 hp **Man:** 13 officers, 37 men

♦ **1 ex-U.S. De Soto County-class landing ship**

	Bldr	Laid down	L	In serv.
IA-. . . N. . . (ex-*Lorain County*, LST 1177)	American SB, Lorain, Ohio	9-8-56	22-6-57	3-10-59

Lorain County (LST 1177)—in U.S. Navy service

D: 3,560 tons light (4,164 std., 7,800 fl) **S:** 16 kts
Dim: 135.7 (128.9 wl) × 18.9 × 5.3 **A:** 6/76.2-mm 50-cal. Mk 34 DP (II × 3)
Electron Equipt: Radar: 1/SPS-21 **Man:** 15 officers, 173 men
M: 6 Cooper-Bessemer diesels; 2 CP props; 14,000 hp **Electric:** 900 kw

REMARKS: Scheduled for sale to Mexico 1982; had been in reserve since 1972. Can carry 700 troops. Four LCVP carried in davits. Tank deck 88-m long. Three Mk 51 mod. 2 GFCS for 76.2-mm guns. Helicopter landing pad amidships.

♦ **2 U.S. LST 542-class former landing ships**

	Bldr	L	In serv.
IA-01 RIO PANUCO (ex-*Park Co.*, LST 1077)	Bethlehem Steel, Hingham, Mass.	9-3-44	31-3-44
IA-02 MANZANILLO (ex-*Clearwater Co.*, LST 602)	Chicago Bridge & Iron, Seneca, Ill.	18-4-45	8-5-45

TRANSPORTS (continued)

Rio Panuco (IA-01) 1975

D: 1,625 tons (4,100 fl) **S:** 11.6 kts **Dim:** 100.0 × 96.3 × 15.24 × 3.4
A: 8/40-mm AA (II × 2, I × 4)—IA-02: none **Electric:** 300 kw
Range: 6,000/11 **Man:** 130 men, 170 troops/passengers

REMARKS: Transferred 20-9-71 and 25-5-72. Intended as disaster relief ships. IA-02 had been used in Arctic Supply by the Military Sealift Command and has two cargo kingposts, no armament, and an ice-reinforced waterline forward.

TRAINING SHIPS

♦ **1 frigate type** Bldr:. . . , Norway

REMARKS: Construction of a "training frigate" to be built in Norway was announced 11-10-80, but no other details were forthcoming. Assuming this unit *not* to be the sail training ship listed below, it may be intended as a replacement for *Manuel Azueta.*

♦ **1 sail training ship** Bldr: Celayo, Bilbao, Spain

CUAUHTEMOC

D: 1,200 tons (fl) **S:** 15 kts **Dim:** 90.0 (67.0 pp) × 10.6 × 4.2
M: 1 GM 12V149 diesel; 1 prop; 750 hp **Man:** 90 tot.

REMARKS: Ordered 1980. Apparently a sister to the new Venezuelan *Simon Bolivar.*

♦ **1 ex-U.S. Edsall-class training frigate** Bldr: Brown SB, Houston, Tex.

	Laid down	L	In serv.
IA-06 MANUEL AZUETA (ex-*Hurst*, DE 250)	27-1-43	14-4-43	30-8-43

Manuel Azueta (IA-06) 1980

D: 1,200 tons (1,590 fl) **S:** 21 kts **Dim:** 93.26 × 11.15 × 3.73
A: 3/76.2-mm Mk 22 DP (I × 3)—8/40-mm AA (IV × 1, II × 2)
Electron Equipt: Radar: 1/Kelvin-Hughes 14/9, 1/Kelvin-Hughes 17/9, 1/Mk 26
M: 4 Fairbanks-Morse 38D⅛, 10-cyl. diesels; 2 props; 6,000 hp
Electric: 680 kw **Fuel:** 258 tons **Range:** 13,000/12
Man: 15 officers, 201 men

REMARKS: Transferred 1-10-73. Former destroyer escort. Used as training ship for the Gulf Fleet. Has one Mk 52 radar fire-control director and one Mk 51 range finder for the 76.2-mm guns, and three Mk 51 mod. 2 directors for the 40-mm anti-aircraft.

NOTE: The old frigate *Durango* (IB-1) is employed as a static training hulk for the new-entry sailors.

D: 1,600 tons (2,000 fl) **S:** . . . kts **Dim:** 78.2 × 11.2 × 3.1
A: 2/102-mm (I × 2)—2/57-mm (I × 2)—4/20-mm AA (II × 2)

TUGS

♦ **4 ex-U.S. Abnaki-class fleet tugs** Bldrs: IA-17, United Engineering, Alameda, Cal.; others, Charleston SB & DD, S.C.

	Laid down	L	In serv.
IA-17 OTUMI (ex-*Molala*, ATF 106)	26-7-42	23-12-42	29-9-43
IA-18 YAQUI (ex-*Hitichi*, ATF 103)	24-8-43	29-1-44	27-5-44
IA-19 SERI (ex-*Abnaki*, ATF 96)	28-11-42	22-4-43	15-11-43
IA-20 CORA (ex-*Cocopa*, ATF 101)	23-5-43	5-10-43	25-3-44

D: 1,325 tons (1,675 fl) **S:** 16.5 kts **Dim:** 62.48 × 11.73 × 4.67
A: 1/76.2-mm DP **Electron Equipt:** Radar: 1/LN-66
M: 4 Busch-Sulzer BS539 diesels, electric drive; 1 prop; 3,000 hp
Electric: 400 kw **Fuel:** 304 tons **Range:** 7,000/15; 15,000/8 **Man:** 85 tot.

REMARKS: IA-17 transferred 1-8-78, the others on 30-9-78. Unarmed on delivery. Used on patrol duties and as rescue tugs.

♦ **2 ex-U.S. Maritime Administration V-4 class** Bldr: Pendleton SY, New Orleans (In serv. 1943-44)

IA-12 R-2 (ex-*Montauk*)   IA-13 R-3 (ex-*Point Vicente*)

D: 1,825 tons (fl) **S:** 14 kts **Dim:** 59.23 × 11.43 × 5.72
A: 1/76.2-mm Mk 22 DP—2/20-mm AA
M: 2 Enterprise diesels; 2 Kort-nozzle props; 2,250 hp **Fuel:** 566 tons
Range: 19,000/14 **Man:** 90 tot.

MEXICO (*continued*)
TUGS (*continued*)

REMARKS: Transferred 6-69. Sister R-4 lost in 1973; R-6 discarded in 1970, R-1 in 1978, and R-5 in 1979.

SERVICE CRAFT

♦ 2 ex-U.S. 174-foot-class harbor ships

	Bldr	L	In serv.
IA-03 AGUASCALIENTES (ex-YOG 6)	J. H. Mathis, Camden, N.J.	3-4-43	15-11-43
IA-04 TLAXCALA (ex-YO 107)	G. Lawley, Neponset, Mass.	3-11-43	27-11-43

D: 440 tons (1,480 fl) **S:** 8 kts **Dim:** 53.0 × 9.75 × 2.5
A: 1/20-mm AA **M:** 1 or 2 diesels; 1 prop; 500-600 hp
Man: 5 officers, 21 men

REMARKS: Transferred 8-64. Cargo capacity: 980 tons (6,570 bbl).

♦ 2 yard tugs

PRAGMAR   PATRON

REMARKS: Bought in 1973.

♦ 1 ex-U.S. ARD-12-class floating dry dock

	Bldr	In serv.
N. . . (ex-ARD 15)	Pacific Bridge, Alameda, Cal.	1-44

Lift capacity: 3,500 tons **Dim:** 149.87 × 24.69 × 1.73 (light)

REMARKS: Transferred 4-71 on loan; purchased 1981.

♦ 2 ex-U.S. ARD-2-class floating dry docks Bldr: Pacific Bridge, Alameda, Cal.

N. . . (ex-ARD 2) (In serv. 4-42)   N. . . (ex-ARD 11) (In serv. 10-43)

Lift capacity: 3,500 tons **Dim:** 148.0 × 21.64 × 1.6 (light)

REMARKS: Transferred 8-63 and 6-74.

♦ 1 ex-U.S. small auxiliary floating dry dock Bldr: Doullut & Ewin, Mobile, Ala.

N. . . (ex-AFDL 28) (In serv. 8-44)

Lift capacity: 1,000 tons **Dim:** 60.96 × 19.51 × 1.04 (light)

REMARKS: Transferred 1-73.

♦ 7 ex-U.S. floating cranes

(ex-YD 156)   (ex-YD 179)   (ex-YD 183)   (ex-YD 203)
(ex-YD 157)   (ex-YD 180)   (ex-YD 194)

REMARKS: Transferred 1964-71; purchased 7-78 (except YD 179, 194).

♦ 1 ex-U.S. pile driver

N. . . (ex-YPD 48)

REMARKS: Transferred 8-68.

MOROCCO
Kingdom of Morocco

PERSONNEL: 1,800 men, including 58 officers and 260 petty officers

MERCHANT MARINE (1980): 145 ships—358,659 grt (tankers: 6 ships—113,074 grt)

FRIGATE

♦ 1 Spanish Descubierta class Bldr: Bazán, El Ferrol

	Laid down	L	In serv.
F. . . N. . .	20-3-79	. . .	1982

D: 1,270 tons (1,479 fl) **S:** 26 kts
Dim: 88.88 (85.8 pp) × 10.4 × 3.25 (3.7 fl)
A: 4/MM 38 or 40 Exocet—1/Albatros SAM syst. (24 Aspide missiles)—1/76-mm OTO Melara DP—2/40-mm AA (I × 2)—1/375-mm Bofors ASW RL (II × 1, 24 rockets)—6/324-mm Mk 32 ASW TT (III × 2)
Electron Equipt: Radar: 1/DA-05, 1/ZW-06, 1/WM 25/41
  Sonar: Raytheon DE 1160B
  ECM: ELT 715 intercept/jammer
M: 4 Bazán-MTU 16MA956 TB91 diesels; 2 CP props; 18,000 hp
Electric: 1,810 kw **Fuel:** 150 tons **Range:** 4,000/18 (one engine)
Man: 100 tot.

REMARKS: Ordered 14-6-77. Progress on this unit has been very slow. Carries 600 rds 76-mm. Has fin stabilizers.

PATROL BOATS

♦ 4 Spanish Lazaga class Bldr: Bazán, Cadiz

	L	In serv.		L	In serv.
P 35 AL KHATTABI	1-7-80	30-6-81	N. . .	. . .	2-82
P 36 BOU ABAB	. . .	11-12-81	N. . .	. . .	6-83

D: 303 tons (420 fl) **S:** 29.6 kts **Dim:** 57.40 (54.4 pp) × 7.60 × 2.70
A: 4/Exocet SSM—1/76-mm OTO Melara DP—1/40-mm AA—2/20-mm AA (I × 2)
Electron Equipt: Radar: 1/Raytheon 1620, 1/HSA WM 25
M: 2 Bazán-MTU MA 16V956 TB91 diesels; 2 props; 7,780 hp
Electric: 405 kVA **Range:** 700/27; 3,000/15 **Man:** 41 tot.

REMARKS: Ordered 14-6-77. Carry 300 rds 76-mm, 1,472 rds 40-mm, 3,000 rds 20-mm ammunition.

♦ 2 French PR-72 type Bldr: S.F.C.N., Villeneuve-la-Garenne

	L	In serv.		L	In serv.
OKBA	10-10-75	16-12-76	TRIKI	2-2-76	2-77

D: 370 tons (440 fl) **S:** 28 kts (at 413 tons) **Dim:** 57.0 (54.0 pp) × 7.6 × 2.5
A: 1/76-mm OTO Melara DP—1/40-mm Bofors AA
M: 4 AGO 16ASHR diesels; 2 props; 11,040 hp **Electric:** 360 kw
Range: 2,500/16 **Man:** 5 officers, 48 men

PATROL BOATS (continued)

Okba   S.F.C.N., 1976

REMARKS: Ordered in 6-73 from the Société Française de Construction Navale (ex-C.N. Franco-Belges).

♦ **1 Al Bachir class** Bldr: Constr. Méc. de Normandie (C.M.N.), Cherbourg

	Laid down	L	In serv.
22 AL BACHIR	6-65	25-2-67	4-67

Al Bachir—wearing old number

D: 124.5 tons (light) (153.5 fl)   **S:** 25.5 kts   **Dim:** 40.6 (38.0 pp) × 6.35 × 1.4
A: 2/40-mm—2 mg   **M:** 2 SEMT-Pielstick 12 PA diesels; 2 props; 3,600 hp
Fuel: 21 tons   **Range:** 2,000/15   **Man:** 3 officers, 20 men

♦ **1 French Fougueux class** Bldr: Constr. Méc. de Normandie

	Laid down	L	In serv.
32 LIEUTENANT RIFFI	5-63	1-3-64	5-64

D: 311 tons (374 fl)   **S:** 19 kts   **Dim:** 52.95 (51.82 pp) × 7.04 × 2.01
A: 2/40-mm AA   **M:** 2 SEMT-Pielstick diesels; 2 CP props; 3,600 hp
Range: 2,000/15; 3,000/12   **Man:** 4 officers, 55 men

REMARKS: 1/76.2-mm gun and all ASW ordnance have been removed.

♦ **1 ex-French patrol boat** Bldr: Chantiers Navals de l'Estérel, Cannes

11 EL SABIQ (ex-P 762, VC 12) (L: 13-8-57)

D: 60 tons (80 fl)   **S:** 28 kts   **Dim:** 31.77 × 4.7 × 1.7   **Range:** 1,500/15
A: 2/20-mm AA   **M:** 2 Mercedes-Benz diesels; 2 props; 2,700 hp   **Man:** 17 tot.

REMARKS: Transferred 15-11-60.

PATROL CRAFT

♦ **6 French P 92 type** Bldr: C.M.N., Cherbourg

	L	In serv.		L	In serv.
EL WACIL	12-6-75	9-10-75	EL KHAFIR	21-1-76	16-4-76
EL JAIL	10-10-75	3-12-75	EL HARIS	31-3-76	30-6-76
EL MIKDAM	1-12-75	30-1-76	ESSAHIR	2-6-76	16-7-76

El Wacil   C.M.N., 1975

D: 89 tons   **S:** 28 kts   **Dim:** 32.0 × 4.7 × 1.7
A: 2/20-mm AA (I × 2)   **Electron Equipt:** Radar: 1/Decca
M: 2 MGO 12 V BZSHR diesels; 1,270 hp   **Range:** 1,200/15

REMARKS: Contract, 2-74. Laminated-wood hull.

MINESWEEPER

♦ **1 French Sirius class**

TAWFIC (ex-*Aries*, M 758)

D: 365 tons (440 fl)   **S:** 15 kts   **Dim:** 46.3 × 8.5 × 2.2
A: 1/40-mm AA—1/20-mm AA   **M:** 2 diesels; 2 props; 2,000 hp
Fuel: 48 tons   **Range:** 3,000/10   **Man:** 38 tot.

REMARKS: Loaned by the French Navy 28-11-74 for a period of four years, renewed 1978. Wood-planked hull on aluminum-alloy framing.

AMPHIBIOUS WARFARE SHIPS

♦ **3 French Champlain-class medium landing ships** Bldr: Dubigeon, Normandy

	In serv.
42 DAOUD BEN AICHA	28-5-77
43 AHMED ES SAKALI	9-77
44 ABOU ABDALLAH EL AYACHI	12-78

D: 750 tons (1,305 fl)   **S:** 16 kts   **Dim:** 80.0 (68.0 pp) × 13.0 × 2.4 mean
A: 2/40-mm AA (I × 2)—2/81-mm mortars (I × 2)
M: 2 SACM diesels; 2 CP props; 1,800 hp
Range: 4,500/13   **Man:** 30 officers, 54 men

REMARKS: Can carry 133 troops and about 12 vehicles. Helicopter platform aft.

MOROCCO (*continued*)
AMPHIBIOUS WARFARE SHIPS (*continued*)

Daoud Ben Aicha (42)   G. Gyssels, 1981

♦ **1 French EDIC-class utility landing craft** Bldr: C. N. Franco-Belges (In serv. 1965)

21 LIEUTENANT MALGHAGH

Lieutenant Malghagh—wearing old number   1977

D: 292 tons (642 fl) **S:** 8 kts **Dim:** 59.0 × 11.95 × 1.3 (1.62 fl)
A: 2/20-mm AA (I × 2)—1/120-mm mortar (fwd)
M: 2 MGO diesels; 2 props; 1,000 hp **Range:** 1,800/8 **Man:** 16 tot.

AUXILIARIES

♦ **1 training ship**

ESSAOUIRA

D: 60 tons

REMARKS: Yacht presented by Italy in 1967. Used for training watchstanders.

♦ **2 former Norwegian cargo ships**

ELAIGH (ex-. . .)   AD DAKHLA (ex-. . .)

D: 1,500 grt **S:** . . . **Dim:** . . . × . . . × . . .
A: 2/14.5-mm AA (II × 1) **M:** . . .

REMARKS: Acquired to provide logistic support for operations along the Sahara coast. Four 5-ton cranes.

♦ **1 yacht**

SEQUET EL HAMRA

MOZAMBIQUE
People's Republic of Mozambique

PERSONNEL: 300 total

MERCHANT MARINE (1980): 82 ships—37,887 grt (tankers: 2 ships—6,549 grt)

CORVETTE

♦ **1 ex-British Bangor class** Bldr: North Vancouver Ship Repairs, Canada

N. . . (ex-Portuguese *Almirante Lacerda*, ex-Canadian *Caroquet*)

D: 656 tons (825 fl) **S:** 15.5 kts **Dim:** 54.86 × 8.69 × 2.94
A: 1/76.2-mm Mk 22 DP—2/20-mm AA
M: 2 sets triple-expansion reciprocating steam; 2 props; 2,600 hp
Boilers: 2, three-drum **Range:** 2,600/10 **Man:** 49 tot.

REMARKS: Launched 2-6-41. Purchased by Portugal in 1946 and later converted to a hydrographic survey ship for East African waters, carrying two inshore survey launches. Ceded to Mozambique when it gained its independence, as not worth returning to Portugal.

PATROL CRAFT

♦ **6 Soviet Zhuk class**

D: 50 tons (fl) **S:** 30 kts **Dim:** 26.0 × 4.9 × 1.5
A: 2 or 4/14.5-mm mg (II × 1 or 2) **Electron Equipt:** Radar: 1/Spin Trough
M: 2 M50 diesels; 2 props; 2,400 hp

REMARKS: Transferred: 2 in 79, 2 in 10-80, and 2 in 10-81.

♦ **1 Soviet Poluchat-1 class**

D: 90 tons (fl) **S:** 18 kts **Dim:** 29.6 × 6.1 × 1.9
A: 2/14.5-mm mg (II × 1) **M:** 2 M50 diesels; 2 props; 2,400 hp
Range: 450/17; 900/10 **Man:** 20 tot.

REMARKS: Transferred 1977.

♦ **2 Portuguese Jupiter class**

D: 32 tons (43.5 fl) **S:** 20 kts **Dim:** 21.5 × 5.0 × 1.3
A: 1/20-mm AA **M:** 2 Cummins diesels; 2 props; 1,270 hp **Man:** 8 tot.

REMARKS: Operate on Lake Malawi.

MOZAMBIQUE (continued)
PATROL CRAFT (continued)

◆ **2 Portuguese Bellatrix class**

N. . . (ex-*Sirius*)   N. . . (ex-*Vega*)

D: 23 tons **S:** 15 kts **Dim:** 20.7 × 4.6 × 1.2
A: 1/20-mm AA **Man:** 7 tot.

REMARKS: Operate on Lake Malawi.

AMPHIBIOUS WARFARE CRAFT

◆ **1 Portuguese Alfange-class landing craft**

D: 285 tons (635 fl) **S:** 10 kts **Dim:** 59.0 × 11.91 × 1.6
A: 2/20-mm AA (I × 2) **M:** 2 MTU MD225 diesels; 2 props; 1,000 hp
Range: 1,800/8 **Man:** 20 tot.

◆ **2 Portuguese LDM-100-class landing craft**

D: 50 tons (fl) **S:** 9 kts **Dim:** 15.25 ×. . . ×. . .
M: 2 GM diesels; 2 props; 450 hp

NETHERLANDS
Kingdom of the Netherlands

PERSONNEL: Approximately 16,700 men, including Marines, Naval Air Service, and 411 female personnel; 6,410 civilian employees

MERCHANT MARINE (1980): 1,263 ships—5,723,845 grt (tankers: 76 ships—2,503,367 grt)

NAVAL AVIATION: The Navy's aircraft are divided into four administrative groups: three maritime patrol squadrons at Valkenburg and one helicopter squadron at Dekoog. Principal types include:

13 PH-2S Neptune
7 BR-1050 Atlantique
2 F-27 Maritime
10 AH 12A Wasp helicopters
24 WG-13 Lynx helicopters

The WG-13 Lynx are of the following subtypes: 6 SH-14A search-and-rescue, delivered in 1976; 10 SH-14B with dipping sonar, ordered in 1976; and 8 SH-14C with MAD gear, ordered in 1978. Fifteen more Lynx will be ordered to replace the Wasps.

On 8-12-78, the Dutch Navy announced that 13 Lockheed P-3C Orion would be acquired to replace the PH-2S Neptune. The first two were to be operational in late 1981 and the last of a total of thirteen will be operational in 1984. 2 Fokker F-27 Maritime were delivered 9-81 and 2-82 to replace 3 PH-2S in the Netherlands Antilles at Curaçao.

WARSHIPS IN SERVICE, UNDER CONSTRUCTION OR AUTHORIZED
AS OF 1 JANUARY 1982

	L	Tons (surfaced)	Main armament
◆ **6 (+2) submarines**			
0 (+2) WALRUS	1981-82	2,300	6/533-mm TT
2 ZWAARDVIS	1970-71	2,370	6/533-mm TT
4 DOLFIJN	1959-65	1,494	8/533-mm TT
◆ **3 destroyers**			
		Tons	
2 TROMP	1973-74	3,665	1/Standard, 8/Harpoon, and 1/Sea Sparrow systems, 2/120-mm DP, 6/ASW TT, 1/ASW helicopter
1 FRIESLAND	1956	2,496	4/120-mm DP, ASW weapons
◆ **12 (+11) frigates**			
0 (+5) M CLASS	1984(?)	2,300	8/Harpoon and 1/Sea Sparrow systems, 1/76-mm DP, 6/ASW TT, 1/helicopter
0 (+2) PIETER FLORESZ	1982-83	3,000	1/Standard, 8/Harpoon, 1/Sea Sparrow, 1/76-mm DP, 4/ASW TT
6 (+4) KORTENAER	1976-	3,000	8/Harpoon and 1/Sea Sparrow systems, 1 or 2/76-mm DP, 4/ASW TT, 2/helicopters
6 VAN SPEIJK	1965-67	2,200	2/Sea Cat systems, 2/114-mm or 1/76-mm DP, ASW weapons, 1/helicopter (8 Harpoon being added)
◆ **6 corvettes**			
6 ROOFDIER	1953-54	808	1/76.2-mm DP, 4/40-mm AA
◆ **5 patrol boats**			
◆ **34 (+15) mine warfare ships**			

WEAPONS AND SYSTEMS

A. MISSILES

◆ *surface-to-air*

U.S./SM1-MR on the *Tromp*-class destroyers and to be on the two *Pieter Floresz*-class frigates

U.S. Sea Sparrow on the *Tromp*-class destroyers and *Kortenaer*-class frigates. British Sea Cat on the *Van Speijk*-class frigates.

◆ *surface-to-surface*

U.S. Harpoon on the *Tromp*, *Kortenaer*, and modernized *Van Speijk* classes.

WEAPONS AND SYSTEMS *(continued)*

B. GUNS

120-mm twin-barreled automatic in the *Friesland-* and *Tromp*-class destroyers:
  Weight: 65 tons
  Arc of elevation: 10° to +85°
  Muzzle velocity: 850 m/sec.
  Direction rate: 25°/s in train, 40°/s in elevation
  Rate of fire: 45 rounds/min/barrel
  Maximum effective range in surface fire: 13,000 m
  Maximum effective range in antiaircraft fire: 7,000 m

76-mm OTO Melara Compact on the *Kortenaer* and modernized *Van Speijk*-class frigates.

40-mm Bofors automatic

NOTE: The Dutch Navy is acquiring the "Shortstop" 30-mm Gatling gun, close-in, defense AA gun system (3,200 rounds per minute), which uses a General Electric GAU-8 gun and EX-30 mounting with an HSA "Flycatcher" fire-control radar. The first ship to carry it is *Philips Van Almonde* (F 823).

C. ANTISUBMARINE WEAPONS

375-mm Bofors quadruple rocket launchers aboard *Overijssel*

U.S. Mk 44 and Mk 46 torpedoes on ships and aircraft

U.S. Mk 37 and Mk 48 torpedoes on submarines. Additional Mk 48 torpedoes were ordered in 1980.

D. RADARS

All designed and manufactured by Hollandse Signaal Apparaaten (HSA), a division of Philips:

Name	Type	Band
ZW-06	Navigation/surface search	. . .
LW-02/03	Long-range air-search	D
LW-04	Long-range air-search	D
LW-08	Long-range air-search	D
DA-05, 05A	Combined surveillance	E/F
SPS-01	3-D	F
WM-20/25	Missile- and gunfire-control	. . .
M-44/45	Missile- and gunfire-control	. . .
STIR*	Missile- and gunfire-control	. . .

*U.S. design, built under license

E. SONARS

CWE-610, LF, hull-mounted: On the *Tromp*-class and *Friesland*-class destroyers, and *Van Speijk*-class frigates

SQS-505, MF, Canadian: On the *Kortenaer*-class frigates

Type 184, MF, hull-mounted: On the *Van Speijk*-class frigates

F. DATA-PROCESSING

SEWACO (Sensoren Wapens Commando), built by Hollandse Signaal Apparaaten and centrally directed by a DAISY 1, 2, 3, 4, or 5 digital computer system. It exists in four versions (SEWACO I, II, III, and IV) tailored to the sensors and weapon systems of the ships that carry it.

SUBMARINES

♦ **2 Walrus class** Bldr: Rotterdamse Droogdok Mij, Rotterdam

	Laid down	L	In serv.
S 801 WALRUS	11-10-79	. . .	1985
S 802 ZEELEEUW	24-9-81	. . .	1986

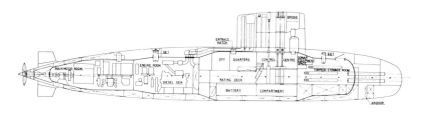

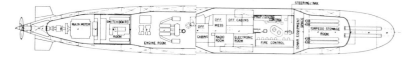

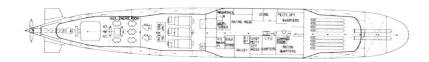

Walrus class   Rhine-Schelde-Verolme, 1980

D: 1,900/2,365/2,700 tons **S:** 12/20 kts **Dim:** 67.0 × 8.4 × 7.0
A: 6/533-mm TT fwd (20 torpedoes)—Sub-Harpoon capability
M: Diesel-electric: 3 SEMT-Pielstick 12 PA4V 185 diesel generator groups; 1 Holec motor; 1 5-bladed prop; 5,500 hp
Fuel: 310 tons **Range:** 10,000/9 (snorkel) **Man:** 7 officers, 42 men

REMARKS: the first ordered 19-6-78, the second in 17-12-79. Design developed from *Zwaardvis* class, with more automation, smaller crew, more modern electronics, and a deeper diving capability. Will have "Gipsy" data system, Sperry Mk 29 mod. 2A inertial navigational system, Thomson-CSF passive sonar array, and a Decca Type 1001 radar. To have 12% reserve buoyancy. Endurance 60 days. Periscope depth 18 m.

SUBMARINES (continued)

♦ **2 Zwaardvis class** Bldr: Rotterdamse Droogdok Mij, Rotterdam

	Laid down	L	In serv.
S 806 Zwaardvis	7-67	2-7-70	18-2-72
S 807 Tijgerhaai	7-67	25-5-71	20-10-72

Tijgerhaai (S 807) 1979

REMARKS: Ordered 24-12-65 and 14-7-66. Based on the U.S. Navy's *Barbel* class, which has a teardrop hull. Use of Dutch equipment necessitated modifications to the original design. The HSA-M8 torpedo-firing system uses a digital computer that permits the simultaneous launching of two torpedoes, one of which may be wire-guided. For silent running, all noise-producing machinery is mounted on a false deck with spring suspension.

♦ **4 Dolfijn/Potvis class**

	Bldr	Laid down	L	In serv.
S 804 Potvis	Wilton-Fijenoord	17-9-62	12-1-65	2-11-65
S 805 Tonijn	Wilton-Fijenoord	26-11-62	14-6-65	24-2-66
S 808 Dolfijn	Rotterdam DDM	30-12-54	20-5-59	16-12-60
S 809 Zeehond	Rotterdam DDM	30-12-54	20-2-60	16-3-61

Potvis (S 804)

Dolfijn (S 808)

Zwaardvis (S 806) 1979

D: 2,408/2,700 tons **S:** 13 kts **Dim:** 66.92 × 8.40 × 6.60
A: 6/533-mm TT fwd—20 torpedoes
Electron Equipt: Radar: 1/Type 1001
                Sonar: . . .
M: Diesel-electric: 3 sets of diesel generators, 960 kw each; 1 3,800-kw motor; 1 5-bladed prop; 5,100 hp
Range: 10,000/9 (snorkel) **Man:** 8 officers, 59 men

D: 1,140/1,510/1,830 tons **S:** 14.5/17 kts **Dim:** 79.50 × 7.84 × 4.95
A: 8/533-mm TT (4 fwd, 4 aft) **Electron Equipt:** Radar: 1/British 1001
M: Diesel-electric: 2 SEMT-Pielstick 12 PA4V185 diesels, 1,400 hp each; 2 electric motors; 2 props; 4,400 hp
Man: 7 officers, 57 men

SUBMARINES *(continued)*

REMARKS: S 804 and S 805 authorized in 1962, S 808 and S 809 in 1949. S 804, 805: D: 1,509/1,831 tons; Dim: 78.25 × 7.80 × 4.95; M: 2 M.A.N. 12-cyl. diesels, 1,550 hp each. The exterior hull has three parallel interior pressure cylinders, one of which is placed on top of a pair of slightly shorter ones. The crew and the armament occupy the top cylinder, and the batteries and diesel engines are mounted in the other two. The *Tonijn* received SEMT-Pielstick diesel generators during 1978; the *Potvis* was given new engines in 1979. The other pair will not be refitted, because they are to be stricken on completion of the *Walrus* class.

GUIDED-MISSILE DESTROYERS

♦ **2 Tromp class** Bldr: Kon. Mij. De Schelde, Flushing

	Laid down	L	In serv.
F 801 TROMP	4-8-71	2-6-73	3-10-75
F 806 DE RUYTER (ex-*Heemskerck*)	22-12-71	9-3-74	3-6-76

Tromp (F 801)   1980

Tromp (F 801)   1980

De Ruyter (F 806)—with Wasp helo on deck   G. Gyssels, 1981

D: 3,665 tons (4,308 fl)   **S:** 28 kts (30 on trials)
Dim: 138.2 (131.0 pp) × 14.8 × 4.6 (6.6 max.)
A: 8/Harpoon missiles (IV × 2)—1 Mk 13 missile launcher (I × 1, 40 SM1-MR missiles)—1/NATO Sea Sparrow system (VII × 1, Mk 29, 60 missiles)—2/120-mm Bofors DP (II × 1)—6/324-mm Mk 32 ASW TT (III × 2)—1/WG-13 Lynx ASW helicopter
Electron Equipt: Radar: 1/SPS-01, 1/ZW-05, 1/WM-25, 2/SPG-51C
              Sonar: 1/CWE-610, 1/162
              ECM: Elettronica passive array, 2/Knebworth Corvus chaff RL (VIII × 2)

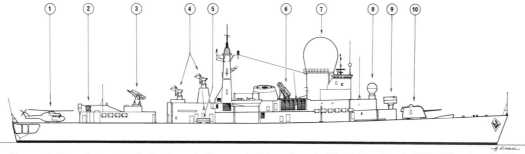

Tromp 1. Lynx helicopter 2. Knebworth Corvus chaff launchers 3. Mk 13 launcher 4. SPG-51C radars 5. Mk 32 torpedo tubes 6. Harpoon launchers 7. SPS-01 3-D radar 8. WM-25 fire-control radar 9. Sea Sparrow system 10. 120-mm gun mount

GUIDED-MISSILE DESTROYERS (continued)

M: COGOG: 2 Rolls-Royce Olympus TM-3B gas turbines, 27,000 hp each; 2
Tyne RM-1C gas turbines, 4,100 hp each, for cruising (18 kts); 2 CP, 4-
bladed props; 54,000 hp
Electric: 4,000 kw   **Fuel:** 600 tons   **Range:** 5,000/18
Man: 34 officers, 271 men

REMARKS: Although the Dutch Navy designates them as frigates, these ships, by
virtue of their armament and size, are more closely related to guided-missile destroyers. They have fin stabilizers and are excellent sea boats. Equipped with an
admiral's cabin and command facilities, they can act as flagships. Berthing for enlisted
men is in 6-, 9-, or 12-man compartments. The propulsion machinery is arranged in
three compartments, forward to aft: 2 Olympus gas turbines, 2 generator sets, and
the auxiliary boilers; 2 Tyne gas turbines; 2 generator sets. The 450-V, 3-phase, 60-
Hz current is produced by four groups of 1,000-kw generators, each driven by a
SMIT/Paxman Valenta RP 200, 12-cylinder diesel; two sets are sufficient for full
combat power. There are three auxiliary boilers for heating. Reduction gears were
made by De Schelde. Fitted with Harpoon 1977/78; normally carry only 4 (II × 2).
SEWACO-I data system. New plastic radomes for SPS-01 radar, 1980, called "Ko-
jack."

DESTROYER

♦ **1 Friesland class, 47-B type**

	Bldr	Laid down	L	In serv.
D 815 OVERIJSSEL	Wilton-Fijenoord	15-10-53	8-7-56	4-10-57

D: 2,496 tons (3,100 fl)   **S:** 36 kts   **Dim:** 116.0 (112.8 pp) × 11.77 × 5.20
A: 4/120-mm DP (II × 2)—4/40-mm AA (I × 4)—2/375-mm Bofors ASW RL (IV
× 2)—1/d.c. rack
Electron Equipt: Radar: 1/LW-02, 1/DA-05, 1/Decca 1229, 1/M-45
Sonar: 1/CWE-610
M: 2 sets Parsons GT; 2 props; 60,000 hp   **Electric:** 1,350 kw
Boilers: 4 Babcock & Wilcox; 39.8 kg/cm², 454°C   **Range:** 4,000/18
Man: 284 tot.

REMARKS: Authorized in 1949. Survivor of a class of eight, will probably strike 1982
on completion of tour as stationship, Netherlands Antilles. Two forward 40-mm AA
were removed around 1965; fire-control radar for the remaining 40-mm AA guns
was removed 1977-78. The sonar was modernized in the early 1970s. The propulsion
plant duplicates that of a U.S. *Gearing*-class destroyer. Sisters stricken: *Friesland*
(D 812) 29-6-79 for scrap; *Groningen* (D 813) to Peru 20-1-81; *Limburg* (D 814) 1-2-
80 (to Peru 27-6-80); *Drenthe* (D 816) to Peru 3-6-81 for probable cannibalization (had
bad fire 12-11-80, not repaired); *Utrecht* (D 817) to Peru 27-8-80; *Rotterdam* (D 818)
to Peru 3-6-81; and *Amsterdam* (D 819) to Peru 5-6-80.

GUIDED-MISSILE FRIGATES

♦ **0 (+5) M class**

	Bldr	Laid down	L	In serv.
F. . . N. . .	. . .	. . .	. . .	. . .
F. . . N. . .	. . .	. . .	. . .	. . .
F. . . N. . .	. . .	. . .	. . .	. . .
F. . . N. . .	. . .	. . .	. . .	. . .
F. . . N. . .	. . .	. . .	. . .	. . .

M-class frigate—artist's impression   1980

D: 1,900 tons light (2,650 fl)   **S:** 28 kts
Dim: 111.8 (105.0 pp) × 13.8 × 4.0 (5.8 props)
A: 8/Harpoon SSM (IV × 2)—1/NATO Sea Sparrow SAM syst. (VIII × 1, 24
missiles)—1/76-mm OTO Melara DP—1/30-mm Shortstop Gatling AA—4/324-
mm Mk 32 ASW TT (II × 2, fixed)—1/WG-13 Lynx helicopter
Electron Equipt: Radar: 1/ZW-06, 1/DA-08, 1/WM-25
Sonar: PHS-36
ECM: Ramses syst., 2/chaff RL
M: CODOG: 1 Rolls-Royce Olympus TM-3B gas turbine, 28,560 hp; 2 SEMT-
Pielstick diesels for cruise, 4,225 hp each; 2 CP props
Electric: 2,400 kw   **Range:** 4,000/19   **Man:** 11 officers, 89 men

REMARKS: Design becoming finalized; plans to order a fifth unit announced 7-81, but
no orders yet placed. Were to have replaced the rapidly aging "Roofdier" class for
fisheries protection, North Sea, and 200-nautical-mile economic zone patrol. Endurance 30 days. Provision made for females in crew, and extra accommodations for 30
Marines. Two diesel and two gas turbine generator sets, 600 kw each. Fin stabilizers.
Four rubber inspection dinghies, no regular boats. DAISY/SEWACO data-handling
system with full LINK 10, 11 capability. Official drawings continue to show 8-cell
Mk 29 Sea Sparrow launcher atop hangar and four vertical Sea Sparrow launchers
on either side of the stack; ships will have one or the other, not both. 21-kt maximum
speed on diesels.

♦ **0 (+2) Pieter Floresz class** Bldr: De Schelde, Vlissingen

	Laid down	L	In serv.
F 812 PIETER FLORESZ	21-1-81	. . .	1984
F 813 WITTE DE WITH	1981	. . .	1985

D: 3,000 tons (3,750 fl)   **S:** 30 kts
Dim: 130.2 (121.8 pp) × 14.4 × 4.4 (6.0 props)
A: 8/Harpoon SSM (IV × 2)—1/Mk 13 missile launcher (I × 1; 40 SM1-MR
Standard missiles)—8/vertical-launch Sea Sparrow—1/76-mm OTO Melara
DP—1/30-mm Shortstop Gatling AA—4/324-mm Mk 32 ASW TT (II × 2,
fixed)
Electron Equipt: Radar: 1/ZW-06, 1/SPS-52(?) or LW-08, 2/SPS-51C, 1/WM-25
Sonar: SQS-505
ECM: Ramses syst.; 2/chaff RL

GUIDED-MISSILE FRIGATES (continued)

REMARKS: Other data as for *Kortenaer* class. Announced 7-81 that these ships, built as replacements for two with the same names and pendant numbers sold to Greece, would have U.S. Standard missile systems in place of the hangar for 2 WG-13 Lynx helicopters and their hangar, although there will be a landing platform aft. Presumably the 30-mm AA gun will be located forward, where the NATO Sea Sparrow launcher is on the earlier ships. No 13th *Kortenaer* hull is now planned for the Dutch Navy.

♦ **6 (+4) Kortenaer class** Bldrs: F 823 and F 824: Wilton-Fijenoord; others: De Schelde

	Laid down	L	In serv.
F 807 KORTENAER	8-3-75	18-12-76	26-10-78
F 808 CALLENBURGH	30-6-75	26-3-77	26-7-79
F 809 VAN KINSBERGEN	2-9-76	16-4-77	24-4-80
F 810 BANCKERT	25-2-76	30-9-78	29-10-80
F 811 PIET HEIN	28-4-77	3-6-78	14-4-81
F 816 ABRAHAM CRIJNSSEN	25-10-78	16-5-81	1982
F 823 PHILIPS VAN ALMONDE	1-10-77	11-8-79	1981
F 824 BLOYS VAN TRESLONG	1-5-78	15-11-80	1982
F 825 JAN VAN BRAKEL	16-11-79	16-5-81	1982
F 826 WILLEM VAN DER ZAAN	15-1-80	1982	1983

Piet Hein (F 811)—40-mm AA aft   S. Terzibaschitsch, 1981

Kortenaer (F 807)—76-mm gun aft   1980

Callenburgh (F 808)—with two Harpoon, 2/76-mm guns   G. Gyssels, 1981

Philips van Almonde (F 823)—on trials   G. Gyssels, 10-81

D: 3,000 tons (3,750 fl)   **S:** 30 kts (20, on 2 Tyne turbines)
Dim: 130.2 (121.8 pp) × 14.4 × 4.4 (6.0 props)
A: 8/Harpoon SSM (IV × 2)—1/NATO Sea Sparrow system (VIII × 1, 24 missiles, Mk 29 launcher)—2/76-mm OTO Melara DP (I × 2), *see* Remarks—4/324-mm Mk 32 ASW TT (II × 2)—2/WG-13 Lynx ASW helicopters
Electron Equipt: Radar: 1/LW-08, 1/ZW-06, 1/WM-25 with STIR
Sonar: 1/SQS-505
ECM: F 807-F 811: Sphinx system; later ships: Ramses system; all: 1/Knebworth Corvus chaff RL (VIII × 2)
M: COGOG: 2 Rolls-Royce Olympus TM-3B gas turbines, 25,800 hp each; 2 Rolls-Royce Tyne RM-1C cruise gas turbines, 4,900 hp each; 2 LIPS CP props; 51,600 hp
Electric: 3,000 kw   **Range:** 4,700/16 (on 1 Tyne turbine)
Man: 18 officers, 182 men

REMARKS: F 807 to F 810 ordered 31-8-74; F 811 to F 816 ordered 28-11-74; F 823-F 826 ordered 29-12-76. The original *Pieter Floresz* (F 812) and *Witte de With* (F 813) were sold to Greece in 1981, and new ships with the same names were begun to a modified design with new armament (*see* above). Initially, F 807 and F 808 have two 76-mm guns. In F 809 to F 816, a single 40-mm Bofors AA is substituted for the after 76-mm mount. In F 824 and later ships, the mount atop the hangar is replaced by a Shortstop 30-mm Gatling AA gun with integral Flycatcher radar. Normally, only two Harpoon SSM (I × 2) are carried. All ships have the Sperry Mk 29 mod. 1 inertial navigation system. Ultimately, all will carry Shortstop aft.

The engineering plant is distributed in four compartments, forward to aft: auxiliaries; Olympus gas turbines; Tyne gas turbines plus reduction gears; auxiliaries. The 450-volt, 3-phase, 60-hertz electric current is supplied by four generators driven

GUIDED-MISSILE FRIGATES *(continued)*

by four SEMT-Pielstick PA4, 750-kw diesels. There are two auxiliary boilers and two evaporators.

The hull is divided by fifteen watertight bulkheads. One pair of Denny-Brown, non-retracting, fin stabilizers is fitted. Officers are berthed in one- or two-man staterooms, while petty officers are in 1-, 2-, or 4-man cabins, and nonrated men are in 6-, 9-, or 12-bunk berthing compartments. Particular attention has been paid to habitability.

♦ 6 Van Speijk class

	Bldr	Laid down	L	In serv.
F 802 Van Speijk	Nederlandsche DSM	1-10-63	5-3-65	14-2-67
F 803 Van Galen	Kon. Mij. De Schelde	25-7-63	19-6-65	1-3-67
F 804 Tjerk Hiddes	Nederlandsche DSM	1-6-64	17-12-65	16-8-67
F 805 Van Nes	Kon. Mij. De Schelde	25-7-63	26-3-66	9-8-67
F 814 Isaac Sweers	Nederlandsche DSM	6-5-65	10-3-67	15-5-68
F 815 Evertsen	Kon. Mij. De Schelde	6-7-65	18-6-66	21-12-67

Van Nes (F 805)—note Abbeyhill ECM array   1980

Van Galen (F 803)—2 Harpoon SSM amidships   1980

Van Speijk (F 802)—HFD/F at masthead   1980

Van Galen (F 803)   1979

D: 2,200 tons (2,835 fl) **S:** 28.5 kts
Dim: 113.42 (109.75 pp) × 12.48 × 4.57 (fl)
A: 4/Harpoon SSM (II × 2)—2/Sea Cat systems (IV × 2)—1/76-mm OTO Melara DP—6/324-mm Mk 32 ASW TT (III × 2)—1/WG-13 Lynx ASW helicopter
Electron Equipt: Radar: 1/DA-05/2, 1/LW-03, 1/Decca 1229, 2/M-44 (for Sea Cat), 1/M-45 (for 76-mm)
Sonar: 1/CWE-610, 1/PDE-700
ECM: Abbeyhill system, 2/Knebworth Corvus chaff RL (VIII × 2)
M: 2 sets Werkspoor-English Electric double-reduction GT; 2 props; 30,000 hp
Electric: 1,900 kw **Boilers:** 2 Babcock & Wilcox; 38.7 kg/cm², 450°C
Range: 4,500/12 **Man:** 180 tot.

REMARKS: Originally similar in general to the British *Leander* class, but with broader bridge and *two* Sea Cat missile systems, each with a director. Major modernizations

GUIDED-MISSILE FRIGATES (continued)

began 1977, during which the twin Mk 6, 114-mm gun mount was replaced by an OTO Melara 76-mm gun; the Limbo ASW mortar was deleted and two triple ASW TT added; the hangar was enlarged and made to telescope to accommodate the SH-14B ASW version of the WG-13 Lynx helicopter; positions for Harpoon SSM canisters (normally only two carried) were added; new radars, sonars, and the SEWACO-II data system were added; and the crew requirement was reduced from 247 to 180 total. All but F 802 (which initially also had the Mk 32 ASW TT one deck higher) have an elaborate passive intercept array at the masthead. Conversion dates: F 802: 24-12-76 to 3-1-78; F 803: 15-7-77 to 30-11-79; F 805: 31-3-78 to 1-8-80; F 804 15-12-78 to 1-6-81; F 815: 18-7-79 to 1-12-81; and F 814: 1-7-80 to 1-8-82.

CORVETTES

♦ **6 Roofdier (ex-U.S. PCE 821) class** Bldrs: F 817, 821, 822: Avondale SY, New Orleans; others: General Shipbldg & Eng, Boston, Mass.

	Laid down	L	In serv.
F 817 Wolf (ex-PCE 1607)	15-11-52	2-1-54	26-3-54
F 818 Fret (ex-PCE 1604)	18-12-52	30-7-53	4-5-54
F 819 Hermelijn (ex-PCE 1605)	2-3-53	6-3-54	5-8-54
F 820 Vos (ex-PCE 1606)	3-8-52	1-5-54	2-12-54
F 821 Panther (ex-PCE 1608)	1-12-52	30-1-54	11-6-54
F 822 Jaguar (ex-PCE 1609)	10-12-52	20-3-54	11-6-54

Fret (F 818) 1980

D: 808 tons (878 fl) **S:** 14 kts **Dim:** 56.27 × 10.29 × 3.96 (max.)
A: 1/76.2-mm Mk 22 DP—4/40-mm AA (II × 2)—2/20-mm AA (I × 2)—1/Mk 10 Hedgehog—2/Mk 6 d.c. projectors—2/d.c. racks (12 d.c. each)
Electron Equipt: Radar: 1/Decca 1229
      Sonar: QCU-2
M: 2 GM 12-567ATL diesels; 2 props; 1,800 hp **Range:** 9,000/10
Man: 80 tot.

REMARKS: Built with U.S. "Offshore" funds. F 817 and F 818 are active in fisheries-protection. Originally had an additional twin 40-mm AA on the stern and up to eight 20-mm AA (II × 4). Intended to be replaced by the new M-class frigates.

PATROL BOATS

♦ **5 Balder class** Bldr: Rijkswerf Willemsoord, Den Helder

	Laid down	L	In serv.
P 802 Balder (ex-SC 1627)	8-53	24-2-54	6-8-54
P 803 Bulgia (ex-SC 1628)	10-53	24-4-54	9-8-54
P 804 Freyr (ex-SC 1629)	2-54	17-7-54	1-12-54
P 805 Hadda (ex-SC 1630)	4-54	2-10-54	3-2-55
P 806 Hefring (ex-SC 1631)	8-54	1-12-54	23-3-55

Hefring (P 806) 1977

D: 150 tons (170 fl) **S:** 15.5 kts **Dim:** 36.35 (35.0 pp) × 6.21 × 1.8
A: 1/40-mm AA—3/20-mm AA (I × 3)—2/d.c. throwers—2/d.c. racks
Electron Equipt: Radar: 1/Kelvin Hughes 14/9 **M:** Diesels; 2 props; 1,050 hp
Range: 1,000/13 **Man:** 3 officers, 24 men

REMARKS: Built with U.S. "offshore" funds. P 805 and P 806 are active; the others, in reserve, may retain two Mousetrap ASW rocket launchers. The 40-mm AA is in a British "Boffin" power mounting.

MINE WARFARE SHIPS

♦ **0 (+15) Alkmaar-class minehunters (Tripartite design)** Bldr: van der Giessen de Noord, Alblasserdam

	L	In serv.		L	In serv.
M 850 Alkmaar	. . .	1982	M 858 Scheveningen	. . .	1986
M 851 Delfzijl	. . .	1982	M 859 Schiedam	. . .	1986
M 852 Dordrecht	. . .	1983	M 860 Urk	. . .	1987
M 853 Haarlem	. . .	1983	M 861 Zieriksee (ex-Veere)	. . .	1987
M 854 Harlingen	. . .	1984	M 862 Vlaardingen	. . .	1988
M 855 Hellevoetsluis	. . .	1984	M 863 Willemstad	. . .	1988
M 856 Makkum	. . .	1985	M 864 Maasluis	. . .	1989
M 857 Middelburg	. . .	1985			

D: 511 tons (544 fl) **S:** 15 kts **Dim:** 51.6 (47.1 pp) × 8.96 × 2.45 (2.6 max.)
A: 1/20-mm AA—2/PAP-104 remote-controlled minehunting devices
Electron Equipt: Radar: 1/Decca 1229
      Sonar: 1/DUBM-21A 1 EVEC 20 plot table, autopilot, Toran and Syledis radio navaids, Decca HiFix precision navigation system

MINE WARFARE SHIPS (continued)

Model of Alkmaar (M 850)   1977

M: 1 Brons-Werkspoor A-RUB 215 × 12 diesel; 1 CP prop; 1,900 hp; bow-thruster; 2 active rudders
Electric: 880 kw   **Range:** 3,000/12   **Man:** 34 tot.

REMARKS: Same design as "Tripartite" minehunters for France and Belgium. Hull made of a compound of glass and polyester resin. M 850 and 851 ordered 6-77; M 850 laid down 15-12-78. M 854 and 855 ordered 31-3-81. The last unit will not be laid down until 1985. These ships can tow a mechanical drag sweep.

♦ 18 Dokkum class

4 Minehunters:

	Bldr	Laid down	L	In serv.
M 801 DOKKUM (ex-MSC 172)	Wilton-Fijenoord, Schiedam	15-6-53	12-10-54	26-7-55
M 818 DRUNEN (ex-MSC 181)	Gusto/F.A. Smulders, Schiedam	8-1-55	24-3-56	30-8-56
M 828 STAPHORST (ex-MSC 185)	Gusto/F.A. Smulders, Schiedam	2-5-55	21-7-56	23-1-57
M 842 VEERE (ex-MSC 188)	L. Smit & Son, Kinderdijk	30-3-55	9-2-56	27-9-56

11 Coastal Minesweepers:

M 802 HOOGEZAND (ex-MSC 173)	Gusto/F.A. Smulders, Schiedam	18-7-53	22-3-55	7-11-55
M 809 NAALDWIJK (ex-MSC 175)	De Noord, Alblasserdam	2-11-53	1-2-55	8-12-55
M 810 ABCOUDE (ex-MSC 176)	Gusto/F.A. Smulders, Schiedam	10-11-53	2-9-55	18-5-56
M 812 DRACHTEN (ex-MSC 177)	Niestern SB, Hellevoetsluis	9-12-53	24-3-55	27-1-56
M 813 OMMEN (ex-MSC 178)	J. & K. Smits, Kinderdijk	22-12-53	5-4-55	19-4-56
M 815 GIETHOORN (ex-MSC 179)	L. Smit & Son, Kinderdijk	22-12-53	30-3-55	29-3-56
M 817 VENLO (ex-MSC 180)	Arnhemse SB, Arnhem	10-2-54	21-5-55	26-4-56
M 823 NAARDEN (ex-MSC 183)	Wilton-Fijenoord, Schiedam	28-10-54	27-1-56	18-5-56
M 827 HOOGEVEEN (ex-MSC 184)	De Noord, Alblasserdam	1-2-55	8-5-56	2-11-56
M 830 SITTARD (ex-MSC 186)	Niestern SB, Hellevoetsluis	10-3-55	26-4-56	19-12-56
M 841 GEMERT (ex-MSC 187)	J. & K. Smits, Kinderdijk	5-4-55	13-3-56	7-9-56

3 Support Ships for Mine-demolition Divers:

M 806 ROERMOND (ex-MSC 174)	Wilton-Fijenoord, Schiedam	19-9-53	13-8-55	29-12-55
M 820 WOERDEN (ex-MSC 182)	Haarlemse SB, Haarlem	10-8-54	28-11-56	24-4-57
M 844 RHENEN (ex-MSC 189)	Arnhemse SB, Arnhem	18-4-55	31-5-56	7-12-56

Staphorst (M 828)—minehunter   L. & L. van Ginderen, 1981

Rhenen (M 844)—mine clearance diver support   G. Gyssels, 1980

MINE WARFARE SHIPS (continued)

Sittard (M 830)—minesweeper   G. Gyssels, 1981

D: 373 tons (453 fl)   **S:** 14 kts   **Dim:** 46.62 × 8.75 × 2.28
A: 2/40-mm AA (I × 2)
Electron Equipt: Radar: 1/Decca 1229 or ZW-04
                     Sonar: 1/193M (hunters only)
M: 2 Fijenoord-M.A.N. diesels; 2 props; 2,500 hp
Range: 2,500/10   **Man:** 38 tot.

REMARKS: Similar to the French *Sirius* and British "Ton" classes. The highly auto-mated minehunters are equipped with the ARNAS system, which displays dropped marker buoys on the radar screen. The after 40-mm AA is mothballed in peacetime. The similar *Wildervank* class had all been scrapped by 1976.

♦ **16 Van Straelen-class inshore minesweepers** Bldrs: (A): De Noord, Alblasser-dam; (B): De Vries-Lentsch, Amsterdam; (C): Arnhemse Scheepsbouw Maatschappij, Arnhem

	Bldr	Laid down	L	In serv.
M 868 ALBLAS (ex-MSI 3)	A	26-2-58	26-9-59	12-3-60
M 869 BUSSEMAKER (ex-MSI 4)	B	28-8-58	27-2-60	19-8-60
M 870 LACOMBLE (ex-MSI 5)	C	24-9-58	6-2-60	22-8-60
M 871 VAN HAMEL (ex-MSI 6)	B	27-4-59	28-5-60	14-10-60
M 872 VAN STRAELEN (ex-MSI 7)	C	28-11-58	17-5-60	20-12-60
M 873 VAN MOPPES (ex-MSI 8)	A	16-4-59	10-5-60	19-12-60
M 874 CHÖMPFF (ex-MSI 9)	A	29-6-59	10-5-60	19-12-60
M 875 VAN WELL GROENEVELD	C	29-12-59	1-10-60	28-4-61
M 876 SCHUILING (ex-MSI 10)	B	26-6-56	30-6-60	5-4-61
M 877 VAN VERSENDAAL	A	27-3-61	4-12-61	11-4-62
M 878 VAN DER WEL	B	30-5-60	3-5-61	6-10-61
M 879 VAN'T HOFF	A	8-6-60	15-3-61	6-10-61
M 880 MAHU	A	8-6-60	15-3-61	6-10-61
M 881 STAVERMAN	B	8-7-60	30-8-61	21-2-62
M 882 HOUTEPEN	C	19-9-60	26-8-61	21-3-62
M 883 ZOMER	C	6-5-60	4-3-61	6-10-61

D: 151 tons (171.3 fl)   **S:** 13 kts   **Dim:** 33.08 × 6.87 × 1.80
A: 1/20-mm AA   **Electron Equipt:** Radar: Decca 12
M: 2 Werkspoor diesels; 2 props; 1,100 hp   **Man:** 14 tot.

Alblas (M 868)

REMARKS: Eight of these ships were built with U.S. "Offshore" funds. Although sim-ilar, the Dutch designs differ from the French and British "Ham" classes. Wooden hulls. Named for officers, petty officers, and nonrated men who died for their country during World War II. Sweep speed: 9 kts.

AMPHIBIOUS WARFARE SHIPS

♦ **10 personnel landing craft (LCA)** Bldrs: L 9510-9513: Rijkswerf Willemsoord, den Helder; L 9514-9517: A. Le Comte, Jutphaas; L 9518-9522: Verolme, Heus-den (In serv. 1962-64)

L 9510   L 9512   L 9514   L 9517   L 9520
L 9511   L 9513   L 9515   L 9518   L 9522

L 9520   G. Gyssels, 1979

D: 8.5 tons (13.6 fl)   **S:** 11.6 kts   **Dim:** 14.45 × 3.82 × 1.3
A: 1/7.62-mm mg   **M:** 1 Rolls-Royce diesel; 1 Schöttel prop; 200 hp
Man: 3 tot.

REMARKS: Polyester plastic hulls. L 9510 is 14.5 × 3.62, and displaces 12.6 tons (fl).

HYDROGRAPHIC SHIPS

♦ **1 Tydeman class** Bldr: B. V. De Merwede, Hardinxveld-Giessendam

	Laid down	L	In serv.
A 906 TYDEMAN	29-4-75	18-12-75	10-11-76

Tydeman (A 906)—white hull, buff stack   1976

D: 3,000 tons (fl) **S:** 15 kts **Dim:** 90.15 × 14.43 × 4.75
M: 3 Stork-Werkspoor 8-FCHD-240 diesels, electric drive; 1 prop; 2,730 hp; 2
bow-thrusters; 1 active rudder
Electric: 1,400 kw **Range:** 10,300/13.5, 15,700/10.3
Man: 59 men, 15 civilians

REMARKS: Assigned to civilian and military research. Hangar and flight deck for one
Wasp helicopter. Eight laboratories. Any two of the three main diesels power the
propulsion motors, the other then provides ship's service power.

♦ **2 Blommendal class** Bldr: Boele S & M, Bolnes

	Laid down	L	In serv.
A 904 BUYSKES	31-1-72	11-7-72	9-3-73
A 905 BLOMMENDAL	1-8-72	21-11-72	22-5-73

Blommendal (A 905)—white hull, buff stack   G. Gyssels, 1980

D: 867 tons (1,050 fl) **S:** 14 kts **Dim:** 59.0 × 11.3 × 3.75
M: 3 700-hp diesels, electric drive; 1 prop; 1,400 hp **Man:** 43 tot.

REMARKS: Carry two survey launches and two chain-clearance drag boats. Automated
data-logging system.

REPLENISHMENT SHIPS

♦ **1 improved Poolster class** Bldr: Verolme, Alblasserdam

	Laid down	L	In serv.
A 832 ZUIDERKRUIS	16-7-43	15-10-74	27-6-75

Zuiderkruis (A 832)   G. Gyssels, 1979

D: 17,357 tons **S:** 21 kts **Dim:** 169.59 (157.0 pp) × 20.3 × 8.4 (max.)
A: 2/20-mm AA (I × 2)
Electron Equipt: Radar: 2/Decca 1226
                     ECM: passive syst., 2/Knebworth Corvus chaff RL
                     (VIII × 2)
M: 2 Werkspoor TM 410 16-cyl. diesels; 2 props; 21,000 hp **Electric:** 3,000 kw
Man: 17 officers, 26 petty officers, 130 men

REMARKS: Cargo capacity: 9,000 tons fuel, 400 tons TR-5, 200 tons fresh water, spare
parts, ammunition. Hangar for three Lynx helicopters. Can carry ASW torpedoes
and other stores to support up to five ASW helicopters. Two fueling stations per
side, amidships, and one sliding-stay, constant-tension, solid transfer station each
side, forward. There are plans to construct a third replenishment oiler, for completion
in 1990.

♦ **1 Poolster class** Bldr: Rotterdamse Droogdok Mij., Rotterdam

	Laid down	L	In serv.
A 835 POOLSTER	18-9-62	16-10-63	10-9-64

Poolster (A 835)   1964

REPLENISHMENT SHIPS *(continued)*

D: 16,836 tons (fl)   **S:** 21 kts   **Dim:** 168.3 (157.0 pp) × 20.3 × 8.2
A: 2/40-mm AA (I × 2)—2/d.c. racks
Electron Equipt: Radars: 1/Kelvin Hughes 14/9, 1/ZW-04
          Sonar: 1/CWE-610
          ECM: passive syst., 2/Knebworth Corvus chaff RL
          (VIII × 2)
M: 2 sets GT; 1 prop; 22,500 hp   **Boilers:** 2   **Man:** 200 tot.

REMARKS: Cargo capacity: 10,300 tons, including 8,000 tons of fuel. Hangar for three Lynx helicopters. Also a combat supply ship capable of participating effectively in antisubmarine warfare with a hunter/killer group, thanks to her ability to handle five ASW helicopters, if required. For short distances, she can carry 300 Marines as well as her own crew.

TENDERS

♦ **3 U.S. Agile-class mine-countermeasures support ships** Bldrs: A 859: Peterson Bldrs., Sturgeon Bay, Wisc.; others: Astoria Marine, Astoria, Ore.

	Laid down	L	In serv.
A 855 ONBEVREESD (ex-M 885, ex-MSO 481)	8-12-52	7-11-53	21-9-54
A 858 ONVERVAARD (ex-M 888, ex-MSO 482)	14-4-52	6-3-54	31-1-55
A 859 ONVERDROTEN (ex-M 889, ex-MSO 485)	17-2-52	22-8-53	22-11-54

Onbevreesd (A 855)   G. Gyssels, 1981

D: 735 tons (790 fl)   **S:** 15.5 kts   **Dim:** 52.7 × 10.75 × 3.7
A: 1/40-mm AA—2/d.c. racks—A 858: mine rails
Electron Equipt: Radar: 1/Kelvin-Hughes 14/9   Sonar: QCU-2
M: 2 GM 8-278A diesels; 2 CP props; 1,600 hp   **Electric:** 560 kw
Fuel: 47 tons   **Range:** 3,000/10   **Man:** 67 tot.

REMARKS: Former ocean minesweepers. A 855 and A 858 are typed "escort ships" and are intended to serve as flagships for the mine-countermeasures force and to lay mines in exercises. A 859 was reclassified 1-1-69 as a mine-countermeasures support ship. A 858 and A 859 are in reserve. Sister *Onversaagd* was stricken in 31-7-79.

♦ **1 U.S. Agile-class torpedo-trials ship** Bldr: Peterson Bldrs., Sturgeon Bay, Wisc.

	Laid down	L	In serv.
A 856 MERCUUR (ex-*Onverschrokken*, M 886, ex-MSO 483)	19-2-52	17-1-53	22-7-54

Mercuur (A 856)

REMARKS: Former ocean minesweeper. Data as for ships above, except no gun. Converted to a torpedo-trials and servicing ship in 1972; scheduled to be replaced by 1985.

♦ **1 torpedo-trials ship** Bldr: Zaanlandse SM, Zaandam

	Laid down	L	In serv.
A 923 VAN BOCHOVE	6-12-61	20-7-62	3-8-62

Van Bochove (A 923)

D: 140.8 tons (fl)   **S:** 8 kts   **Dim:** 29.79 × 5.53 × 1.8
A: 2/533-mm TT (submerged, at bow)
M: 1 Kromhout diesel; 1 Schöttel prop; 140 hp   **Man:** 8 tot.

TUGS

♦ **2 Westgat-class coastal tugs** Bldr: Rijkswerf Willemsoord, Den Helder

	Laid down	L	In serv.
A 872 WESTGAT	3-4-67	22-8-67	10-1-68
A 873 WIELINGEN	28-8-67	6-1-68	31-5-68

D: 206 tons (fl)   **S:** 12 kts   **Dim:** 27.18 × 6.97 × 2.34
A: none   **Electron Equipt:** 1/Kelvin-Hughes 14/9
M: 1 Bolnes diesel; 1 prop; 720 hp   **Man:** 9 tot.

TUGS *(continued)*

Wielingen (A 873)   G. Gyssels, 1979

♦ **1 Wamandai-class coastal tug** Bldr: Rijkswerf Willemsoord, Den Helder

	Laid down	L	In serv.
A 870 WAMANDAI (ex-Y 8035)	27-8-58	28-5-60	1-62

   D: 201 tons (fl) **S:** 11 kts **Dim:** 27.25 × 6.98 × 2.8
   A: None **M:** 1 Werkspoor diesel; 1 prop; 500 hp **Man:** 10 tot.

REMARKS: Can carry 2/20-mm AA (I × 2).

♦ **1 Wambrau-class coastal tug** Bldr: Rijkswerf Willemsoord, Den Helder

	Laid down	L	In serv.
A 871 WAMBRAU (ex-Y 8036)	24-7-56	27-8-56	8-1-57

   D: 179.4 tons (fl) **S:** 10.8 kts **Dim:** 26.38 × 6.6 × 2.45
   A: None **M:** 1 Werkspoor diesel; 1 prop; 500 hp **Man:** 10 tot.

TRAINING SHIPS

♦ **1 former pilot ship**

	Bldr	Laid down	L	In serv.
A 903 ZEEFAKEL	J. & K. Smit, Kinderijk	28-11-49	21-7-50	16-3-51

   D: 303 tons (384 fl) **S:** 12 kts **Dim:** 45.38 × 7.5 × 2.2
   M: 2 Smit-M.A.N. diesels; 2 props; 640 hp **Man:** 26 tot.

REMARKS: Used for seamanship training at Den Helder. Disarmed.

Zeefakel (A 903)   G. Gyssels, 1980

♦ **1 sail training ketch**

	Bldr	L	In serv.
Y 8050 URANIA (ex-*Tromp*)	Haarlemse Scheepsbouw Mij.	1929	23-4-38

   D: 76.4 tons (fl) **S:** 5 kts (10 under sail) **Dim:** 23.94 × 5.29 × 3.15
   M: 1 Kromhout diesel; 1 prop; 65 hp (625m² sail area) **Man:** 17 tot.

♦ **1 former Holland-class destroyer**

	Bldr	Laid down	L	In serv.
D 811 GELDERLAND	Wilton-Fijenoord, Schiedam	10-3-51	19-9-53	17-8-55

   D: 2,215 tons (2,765 fl) **S:** 32 kts **Dim:** 111.3 × 11.33 × 3.88
   A: None **M:** 2 sets Parsons GT; 2 props; 45,000 hp
   Electric: 1,350 kw **Boilers:** 4 Babcock & Wilcox

REMARKS: Since 1973 used for technical training at Rotterdam and for accommodations. Does not get under way. Two twin 120-mm DP guns mounted on destroyers *Tromp* and *De Ruyter*.

NOTE: There are also 25 small sports and training sail yachts under naval control.

ACCOMMODATIONS SHIPS

♦ **1 non-self-propelled** Bldr: Voorwarts SY, Hoogezand

	Laid down	L	In serv.
A 886 CORNELIUS DREBBEL	18-5-70	19-11-70	30-11-71

   D: 775 tons (fl) **Dim:** 63.22 × 11.82 × 1.1 **Man:** 201 tot.

REMARKS: Stationed at Rotterdam to serve ships in overhaul.

ACCOMMODATIONS SHIPS *(continued)*

♦ **1 former radar training ship, former gunboat**

	Bldr	Laid down	L	In serv.
A 891 SOEMBA	Wilton's, Rotterdam	24-12-24	24-8-25	12-4-26

D: 1,457 tons (fl) **Dim:** 75.6 × 11.5 × 3.6

REMARKS: No longer self-propelled. Stationed at Den Oever.

SERVICE CRAFT

♦ **1 fuel lighter** Bldr: H.H. Bodewes, Millingen (In serv. 1963)

Y 8536 PATRIA

D: 827 dwt **S:** . . . **Dim:** 61.6 × 8.1 × . . .
M: 1 Bolnes diesel; 1 prop; . . . hp **Man:** . . . tot.

REMARKS: Purchased 1978. Based at Den Helder. Bow number: 611.

NOTE: Small fuel lighter Y 8535 stricken 1980.

♦ **2 fuel barges:** Y 8335 (In serv. 1952) Y 8538 (In serv. 1955)

♦ **1 small water tanker:** Y 8480 (In serv. 1952)

♦ **1 torpedo lighter:** Y 8512 (In serv. 1950)

♦ **2 small cargo lighters:** Y 8500 (In serv. 1953) Y 8501 (In serv. 1951)

♦ **3 personnel launches:** Y 8216, Y 8217, Y 8220 (In serv. 1951-52)

♦ **3 steam supply craft:** Y 8005 (In serv. 1937), Y 8122 (In serv. 1937) Y 8260 (In serv. 1940)

♦ **1 electrical power supply craft:** Y 8676 (In serv. 1962)

♦ **1 tank-cleaning boat:** Y 8262 (In serv. 1918)

♦ **1 hull-cleaning boat:** Y 8263 (In serv. 1967)

♦ **4 Berkel-class harbor tugs** Bldr: H.H. Bodewes, Millingen

	Laid down	L	In serv.
Y 8037 BERKEL	27-4-56	29-9-56	27-12-57
Y 8038 DINTEL	22-5-56	17-11-56	23-1-57
Y 8039 DOMMEL	29-8-56	22-12-56	27-2-57
Y 8040 IJSSEL	17-9-56	19-1-57	20-3-57

D: 163.4 tons (fl) **S:** 10.6 kts **Dim:** 25.09 × 6.27 × 2.45
M: 1 Werkspoor diesel; 1 Kort-nozzle prop; 500 hp **Man:** 5 tot.

♦ **2 Bambi-class harbor tugs** Bldr: Rijkswerf Willemsoord, Den Helder

Y 8016 BAMBI Y 8017 DOMBO

D: 43 tons (fl) **S:** . . . kts **Dim:** 16.58 × 4.63 × 1.9
M: 1 Bolnes diesel; 1 prop; 200 hp **Man:** 4 tot.

REMARKS: Y 8016 launched 12-5-53; Y 8017, 25-5-57.

IJssel (Y 8040)   1979

♦ **1 small harbor tug** Bldr: Boot, Alphen aan den Rijn (In serv. 1942)

Y 8014 (ex-A 857, ex-RS 17, ex-OZD 4, ex-*Jade*)

D: 75 tons (fl) **S:** . . . kts **Dim:** 20.0 × 5.25 × 1.8
M: 1 diesel; 1 prop; 75 hp **Man:** 3 tot.

♦ **1 small harbor tug** Bldr: Foxhol (In serv. 1938)

Y 8028 (ex-A 868, ex-RS 28, ex-KM 15, ex-*Eems*)

D: 70 tons (fl) **S:** . . . kts **Dim:** 19.5 × 5.1 × 2.3
M: 1 Bolnes diesel; 1 prop; 200 hp **Man:** 7 tot.

REMARKS: Small tug Y 8022 stricken 10-79.

♦ **3 Triton-class diving tenders** Bldr: Rijkswerf Willemsoord, Den Helder

	Laid down	L	In serv.
A 848 TRITON (ex-Y 8125)	3-2-64	27-2-64	5-8-64
A 849 NAUTILUS (ex-Y 8126)	17-3-64	1-5-64	20-4-65
A 850 HYDRA (ex-Y 8127)	21-5-64	1-7-64	20-4-65

D: 69.3 tons (fl) **S:** 9 kts **Dim:** 23.28 × 5.15 × 1.35
M: 1 Volvo Penta diesel; 1 prop; 105 hp **Man:** 8 tot.

♦ **1 training tender for divers** Bldr: Rijkswerf Willemsoord, Den Helder

	Laid down	L	In serv.
A 847 ARGUS (ex-Y 8124, ex-Y 8651, ex-A 950, ex-RD 10, ex-MOD IV, ex-D1)	18-5-38	6-12-38	10-5-39

D: 44.5 tons (fl) **S:** 8 kts **Dim:** 23.0 × 4.68 × 1.05
M: 1 Kromhout diesel; 1 prop; 144 hp **Man:** 8 tot.

♦ **1 floating crane:** Y 8514 (In serv. 1974)

♦ **2 floating dry docks** Y 8678 RW 22 (In serv. 1949) Y 8679 RW 60 (In serv. 1960)

NETHERLANDS (*continued*)
SERVICE CRAFT (*continued*)

♦ **1 torpedo target craft:** Y 8301 (In serv. 1938)

♦ **1 wreck simulation craft:** Y 8690 (In serv. 1969)

♦ **18 dry cargo barges** (In serv. 1900-1965): Y 8299, Y 8321, Y 8322, Y 8324, Y 8325, Y 8327, Y 8328, Y 8330, Y 8331, Y 8332, Y 8333, Y 8334, Y 8337, Y 8338, Y 8339, Y 8340, Y 8341, Y 8403

♦ **2 salvage pontoons:** Y 8594, Y 8595 (In serv. 1956)

♦ **3 submarine salvage pontoons:** Y 8597, Y 8598 (In serv. 1971), Y 8599 (In serv. 1977)

♦ **8 miscellaneous pontoon barges:** Y 8600, Y 8601, Y 8602, Y 8603, Y 8711, Y 8713, Y 8714, Y 8716

♦ **8 miscellaneous floats:** (In serv. 1951-53) Y 8583, Y 8584, Y 8585, Y 8586, Y 8588, Y 8589, Y 8590, Y 8592

NOTE: The Netherlands Pilot Service, carried in the previous edition, was transferred from nominal naval control early in 1980.

NETHERLANDS NATIONAL POLICE FORCE

NOTE: This organization operates a small number of patrol boats and craft, of which only the *De Ruiter* class, listed below, is seagoing. A number of other jurisdictions, including the Customs Service, the Rotterdam City Police, and the Department of Communications, also operate patrol craft.

♦ **3 15-meter class** Bldr: Schöttel, Warmond (Ordered 6-80)

♦ **3 De Ruiter class** Bldr: Schöttel, Warmond

RP 15 DE RUITER (In serv. 5-79)   RP. . . N. . .   RP. . . N. . .

   D: 27 tons (fl)   **S:** 18.5 kts   **Dim:** 19.13 × 4.27 × 1.3
   M: 2 12-cyl. diesels; 2 Schöttel vertical cycloidal props; 680 hp   **Man:** 3-4 tot.

REMARKS: The second and third were ordered 6-80.

♦ **3 RP 17 class** Bldr: Le Comte, Vianen, 1974

RP 17   RP. . . N. . .   RP. . . N. . .

   D: 29 tons   **S:** 15 kts   **Dim:** 15.75 × 3.83 × 1.05
   M: 1 MTU OM403 diesel; 1 Schöttel vertical cycloidal prop; 250 hp

♦ **RP 26 and 6 others** Bldr: Le Comte, Vianen, 1970

   D: 8.5 tons   **S:** 14.5 kts   **Dim:** 10.8 × 3.22 × 1.2
   M: 1 MTU OM346 diesel; 1 Schöttel prop; 165 hp

♦ **RP 10** Bldr: Schuiten, Muiden, 1968

   D: 70 tons (fl)   **S:** 14 kts   **Dim:** 23.0 × . . . × . . .
   M: 1 Bolnes GDNL diesel; 600 hp

♦ **RP 3** Bldr: Koopman, Dordrecht, 1967

   D: 60 tons (fl)   **S:** 12.7 kts   **Dim:** 22.0 × 5.3 × 1.5
   M: 2 GM 12V71 diesels; 2 props; 670 hp

NEW ZEALAND
Dominion of New Zealand

PERSONNEL (1981): 2,840 total (plus 373 reserves)

MERCHANT MARINE (1980): 122 ships—263,543 grt
(tankers: 3 ships—52,309 grt)

NAVAL AVIATION: Wasp helicopters are carried on the two *Leander*-class frigates and on the survey ship *Monowai*. Five Lockheed P3-B Orion patrol planes belong to the Royal New Zealand Air Force; these are being modernized by Boeing over a 41-month period commencing 7-80.

FRIGATES

NOTE: New Zealand is examining the possibility of purchasing two of the recently redundant Royal Navy *Leander*-class frigates, with *Bacchante* (F 69), to be stricken in 1982, intended as a replacement for *Otago*. See addenda.

♦ **2 British Leander class**

	Bldr	Laid down	L	In serv.
F 55 WAIKATO	Harland & Wolff	10-1-65	18-2-65	16-9-66
F 421 CANTERBURY	Yarrow, Scotstoun	12-4-69	6-5-70	22-10-71

Canterbury (F 421)   1978

Waikato (F 55)   G. Gyssels, 1980

   D: F 55: 2,450 tons (2,850 fl); F 421: 2,470 tons (2,990 fl)
   S: F 55: 30 kts; F 421: 28 kts
   Dim: 113.38 (109.73 pp) × 12.5 (F 421: 13.12) × 5.49
   A: 2/114-mm Mk 6 DP (II × 1)—1/Sea Cat system (IV × 1)—2/20-mm AA (I × 2)—6/324-mm Mk 32 ASW TT (III × 2)—1/Wasp ASW helicopter

FRIGATES *(continued)*

Electron Equipt: Radar: 1/965, 1/993, 1/978, 1/903, 1/904
Sonar: 1/177, 1/162B, 1/70
M: 2 sets English-Electric GT; 2 props; 30,000 hp
Electric: F 55: 1,900 kw; F 421: 2,500 kw
Boilers: 2 Babcock & Wilcox; 38.7 kg/cm², 450°C   **Range:** 4,500/12
Fuel: F 55: 460 tons; F 421: 500 tons   **Man:** 14 officers, 229 men

REMARKS: F 55 originally had a Mk 10 Limbo triple ASW mortar and no ASW TT; she was refitted in 1977, when the Type 170B sonar was also removed. F 421 has extensions for her smoke pipes from the top of the stack and is a unit of the final, "broad-beam" version of the class. The Sea Cat system is GWS 22 with a modified MRS-3 radar director.

♦ 2 British Rothesay class

	Bldr	Laid down	L	In serv.
F 111 OTAGO (ex-*Hastings*)	J. Thornycroft	1957	11-12-58	22-6-60
F 148 TARANAKI	J. Samuel White	1957	19-8-59	28-3-61

Otago (F 111)   R. Gillett, 1980

Taranake (F 148)   1980

D: 2,144 (2,557 fl)   **S:** 30 kts   **Dim:** 112.8 (109.7 pp) × 12.5 × 5.3
A: F 111: 2/114-mm Mk 6 DP (II × 1)—1/Sea Cat system (IV × 2)—2/20-mm
   AA (I × 2)—6/324-mm Mk 32 ASW TT (III × 2)
   F 148: 2/114-mm Mk 5 DP (II × 1)—1/40-mm AA (II × 1)—2/20-mm AA (I
   × 2)—6/324-mm Mk 32 ASW TT (III × 2)

Electron Equipt: Radar: 1/993, 1/978, 1/275, 1/262 (F 111 only)
Sonar: 1/177, 1/170B, 1/162B
M: 2 sets English-Electric GT; 2 props; 30,000 hp   **Electric:** 1,460 kw
Boilers: 2 Babcock & Wilcox, 37.5 kg/cm², 450°C   **Fuel:** 400 tons
Range: 4,500/12   **Man:** 31 officers, 227 men (F 148: 140 tot.)

REMARKS: F 148 was recommissioned from ready reserve in 1979 as a combination training ship and patrol ship for the 200-nautical-mile economic zone. Her ASW mortars and Sea Cat SAM system were removed, the latter being replaced by a 40-mm AA. Both ships carried two 40-mm AA (I × 2) from 1968-69 to the early 1970s and were originally fitted with 12 533-mm ASW TT (II × 2, I × 8). The Sea Cat system on F 111 is GWS 21 with a modified MRS-8 director and Type 262 radar; her Type 277 height-finding radar has been removed. F 148 to be re-engined and extensively reconfigured under a contract signed in 1980. Two Rolls-Royce Tyne RM1C gas turbines of 4,250 hp each will replace the steam turbine, employing GEC gearboxes and Franco-Tosi couplings; accommodations will be improved, the endurance will be extended, and a hangar and flight deck for a WG-13 Lynx helicopter will be added. Maximum speed will probably be about 20 kts. See addenda.

PATROL BOATS AND CRAFT

♦ 4 Pukaki-class patrol boats   Bldr: Brooke Marine, Lowestoft, G.B.

	L	In serv.
P 3568 PUKAKI	1-3-74	24-2-75
P 3569 ROTOITI	8-3-74	24-2-75
P 3570 TAUPO	25-7-74	29-7-75
P 3571 HAWEA	9-9-74	29-7-75

Rotoiti (P 3569)   R. Gillett

D: 105 tons (135 fl)   **S:** 22 kts   **Dim:** 32.6 × 6.1 × 1.7
A: 1/81-mm mortar combined with 12.7-mm mg—2/12.7-mm mg (II × 1)
Electron Equipt: Radar: 1/Decca 916
M: 2 Ruston-Paxman 12 YCJM diesels; 2 props; 3,000 hp   **Range:** 2,500/12
Man: 3 officers, 18 men

PATROL BOATS AND CRAFT (continued)

◆ 4 British HDML class patrol craft

	Bldr	In serv.
P 3552 PAEA (ex-Q 1184)	Hadden & Lewis, Sausalito, Cal.	21-12-42
P 3563 KUPARU (ex-Pegasus, ex-Q 1349)	Ackerman Boatyard, Cal.	19-1-44
P 3564 KOURA (ex-Toroa, ex-Q 1350)	Ackerman Boatyard, Cal.	19-1-44
P 3567 MANGA (ex-Q 1185)	Hadden & Lewis, Sausalito, Cal.	21-12-42

Paea (P 3552)

D: 46 tons (54 fl)   **S:** 11-12 kts   **Dim:** 21.95 × 4.83 × 1.45   **A:** None
Electron Equipt: Radar: 1/Decca 45
M: 2 Gray Marine 64HN9 diesels; 2 props; 320 hp   **Range:** 900/10
Man: 9 tot.

REMARKS: The *Paea* and the *Manga* originally had two Hercules diesels; 240 hp. All used for naval reserve training. Six sisters scrapped 1972-77. Two others, the *Takapu* (P 3556) and the *Tarapunga* (P 3566) were used as inshore survey craft until 1979. Wooden hulls.

HYDROGRAPHIC SURVEY SHIPS

◆ 1 converted passenger-cargo ship Bldr: Grangemouth DY (L: 8-60)

A 06 MONOWAI (ex-*Moana Roa*)

D: 4,027 tons (fl)   **S:** 13.5 kts   **Dim:** 90.33 (82.30 pp) × 14.02 × 5.21
A: 2/20-mm AA (I × 2)
M: 2 Clark-Sulzer 7-cyl. diesels; 2 CP props; 3,640 hp—bow-thruster
Fuel: 300 tons   **Range:** 12,000/13   **Man:** 11 officers, 115 men

REMARKS: Taken over from the government-run commercial service in 1974 and converted at Scott-Lithgow, Greenock, Scotland, 9-77 to 4-10-77. Telescoping hangar fitted for one Wasp helicopter. Two 10.36-meter and one 8.84-meter survey craft carried, as well as one Rotork "Sea Truck" workboat. Decca HiFix positioning system and Omega radio navigational aids installed, as well as a navigational satellite receiver. One 4-ton crane. Side-scanning mapping sonar and other sophisticated survey equipment carried. Guns added 1980.

Monowai (A 06)—white hull, buff stack   R. Gillett

◆ 2 inshore survey craft Bldr: Whangarei Eng. Ltd.

A 07 TAKAPU (In serv. 8-7-80)   A 08 TARAPUNGA

Tarapunga (A 08) and Takapu (A 07)—white-painted   1981

D: 90 tons (115 fl)   **S:** 12 kts   **Dim:** 27.0 × 6.1 × 3.0
M: 2 Cummins diesels; 2 props; 730 hp   **Man:** 2 officers, 10 men

REMARKS: Ordered 30-11-77. Similar to diving tender *Manawanui*.
Replaced HDML-class survey craft *Takapu* (P 3556) and *Tarapunga* (P 3566).

NEW ZEALAND (*continued*)

OCEANOGRAPHIC RESEARCH SHIP

♦ **1 ex-U.S. Robert D. Conrad class** Bldr: Christy Corp., Sturgeon Bay, Wis.

	Laid down	L	In serv.
A 02 Tui (ex-*Charles H. Davis*, T-AGOR 5)	15-6-61	30-6-62	25-1-63

Tui (A 02)—white hull, buff stack   1971

D: 1,200 tons (1,380 fl)   **S:** 12 kts   **Dim:** 70.0 (63.7 pp) × 11.4 × 4.7 (6.3 max.)
Electron Equipt: Radar: 1/RCA CRM-N1A-75
M: 2 Caterpillar D-378 diesels, electric; 1 prop; 1,000 hp—175-hp bow-thruster
Electric: 850 kw   **Fuel:** 211 tons   **Range:** 12,000/12
Man: 8 officers, 16 men, 15 scientists

REMARKS: Transferred on loan 28-7-70. Used in acoustics research for the New Zealand Defense Research Establishment, which has modified the ship so that it may be used to lay and tow hydrophone arrays. Has a 620-kw gas turbine generator to drive the prop for quiet running.

SERVICE CRAFT

♦ **1 tug** Bldr: Steel Ships, Ltd., Auckland (L: 1947)

ARATAKI

D: 190 tons   **S:** 10 kts   **Dim:** 22.9 × 5.8 × 2.44
M: 1 Atlas diesel; 1 prop; 320 hp   **Man:** 8 tot.

♦ **1 diving tender**

	Bldr	L	In serv.
MANAWANUI	Whangarei Eng. Ltd.	8-12-78	28-5-79

D: 90 tons (110 fl)   **S:** 12 kts   **Dim:** 27.0 × 6.1 × 3.0
M: 2 Cummins diesels; 2 props; 730 hp   **Man:** 16 tot.

NICARAGUA
Republic of Nicaragua

PERSONNEL: Approximately 200 total

MERCHANT MARINE (1980): 17 ships—15,726 grt
                        (tankers: 2 ships—3,711 grt)

PATROL CRAFT

♦ **4 Israeli Dabur class** Bldr: Israeli Aircraft Industries (In serv. 5-78)

GC 10   GC 11   GC 12   GC 13

D: 25 tons (35 fl)   **S:** 19.6 kts   **Dim:** 19.79 × 5.40 × 1.75
A: 2/20-mm AA (I × 2)   **M:** 2 GM 12V72 diesels; 2 props; 960 hp
Electric: 20 kw   **Range:** 700/16   **Man:** 6 tot.

REMARKS: Two larger *Dvora*-class patrol craft were also ordered from Israel, but their delivery was embargoed in 1979 at the request of the U.S. government.

♦ **1 U.S. 65-foot cruiser class** Bldr: Sewart Seacraft, La. (In serv. 1962)

GC 7 RIO KURINGWAS

D: 60 tons   **S:** 26.5 kts   **Dim:** 25.9 × 5.6 × 1.8
A: 2/20-mm AA (I × 2)   **M:** 3 GM 8V71 diesels; 3 props; 2,000 hp
Range: 1,000/20   **Man:** 10 tot.

♦ **6 U.S. Hatteras-class cabin cruisers**

Dim: 11.6 oa

NIGERIA
Republic of Nigeria

PERSONNEL: 120 officers, 1,700 total

MERCHANT MARINE (1978): 101 ships—324,024 grt
                        (tankers: 8 ships—143,999 grt)

FRIGATES

♦ **1 MEKO 360-H class** Bldr: Blohm & Voss, Hamburg

	Laid down	L	Trials	In serv.
F 89 ARADU (ex-*Republic*)	2-5-79	25-1-80	12-5-81	7-81

D: 3,680 tons (fl)   **S:** 30.5 kts
Dim: 125.9 (119.0 pp) × 15.0 (14.0 wl) × 4.32 (5.8 props)
A: 8/Otomat Mk 1 SSM (I × 8)—1/127-mm OTO Melara DP—1/Albatros SAM syst., Mk 2, mod. 9 (VIII × 1, 24 Aspide missiles)—8/40-mm Breda AA (II × 4)—6/324-mm ASW TT (III × 2, 18 torpedoes)—1/WG-13 Lynx ASW helicopter

FRIGATES (continued)

Aradu (F 89)—on trials   P. Voss, 1981

Electron Equipt: Radar: 1/AWS-5D, 1/Decca 1226, 1/HSA WM-25,
               1/HSA STIR
            Sonar: 1/HSA PHS-32
            ECM: Decca intercept equipt—2/SCLAR 105-mm chaff RL
M: CODOG: 2 Rolls-Royce Olympus TM-3B gas turbines, 50,000 hp; 2 MTU
     20V956 TB92 diesels, 11,070 hp; 2 CP props
Electric: 4,120 kVA   **Fuel:** 440 tons   **Range:** 4,500/18
Man: 26 officers, 169 men, 35 cadets

REMARKS: Ordered 3-11-77; prefabrication began 1-12-78. Similar ships (but with CO-
GOG propulsion, two helicopters, and different electronics) ordered 11-12-78 for
Argentina. Makes use of modular containers for electronics and weapon systems.
Carries 460 rounds of 127-mm ammunition, 10,752 rounds of 40-mm ammunition,
and 120 chaff rounds for the Elsag/Breda chaff rocket launchers. The helicopter is
to be delivered in 1983.

◆ 1 training frigate

	Bldr	Laid down	L	In serv.
F 87 OBUMA (ex-*Nigeria*)	Wilton-Fijenoord, Netherlands	4-64	9-65	9-66

Obuma (F 87)   1966

D: 1,724 tons (2,000 fl)   **S:** 25 kts   **Dim:** 109.85 (104.0 pp) × 11.3 × 3.35
A: 2/102-mm Mk 19 DP (II × 1)—4/40-mm AA (I × 4)—1/Squid ASW mortar
     (III × 1)
Electron Equipt: Radar: 1/293B, 1/navigational   Sonar: 1/162B, 1/177
Range: 3,500/15   **Man:** 216 tot.

REMARKS: Renamed 1981. Helicopter platform. Refit by Cammell Laird, 1970-71, and
again at Schiedam, the Netherlands, in 1977. Only a simple lead-computing director
is fitted for the 102-mm gun mount. To be converted into a training ship.

CORVETTES

◆ 2 Erin'mi class (Mk 9) Bldr: Vosper Thornycroft, Portsmouth

	Laid down	L	In serv.
F 83 ERIN OMI	14-10-75	20-1-77	29-1-80
F 84 ENYMIRI	11-2-77	9-2-78	2-5-80

Enymiri (F 84)   Vosper/M. Lennon, 1980

Enymiri (F 84)   Vosper/M. Lennon, 1980

D: 850 tons (fl)   **S:** 27 kts   **Dim:** 69.0 (64.0 pp) × 9.6 × 3.0 (3.6 max.)
A: 1/76-mm OTO Melara DP—1/Sea Cat system (III × 1; 15 missiles)—1/40-mm
     Bofors AA—2/20-mm AA (I × 2)—1/375-mm Bofors ASW RL (II × 1)

CORVETTES (continued)

Electron Equipt: Radar: 1/AWS-2, 1/Decca TM 1226, 1/HSA WM-24
Sonar: 1/Plessey PMS26—Decca intercept
ECM: Decca "Cutlass" intercept
M: 4 MTU 20V956 TB92 diesels; 2 CP props; 20,512 hp **Endurance:** 10 days
Electric: 889 kw **Range:** 2,200/14 **Man:** 90 tot.

REMARKS: Can sustain 20 kts on two diesels. Uses three MTU 6V51 diesel generator sets of 260 kw each and one 109-kw emergency generator. Carry 750 rounds 76-mm ammunition, 24 rds. ASW rockets. Have 2/50-mm flare launchers. Funnel heightened on F 83 after initial trials. Both names are local words for "hippopotamus."

♦ **2 Dorina class (Mk 3) Bldr:** Vosper Thornycroft, Portsmouth

	Laid down	L	In serv.
F 81 DORINA	26-1-70	16-9-70	6-72
F 82 OTOBO	28-9-70	25-5-71	11-72

Dorina (F 81)   Vosper Thornycroft, 1972

D: 650 tons (fl) **S:** 22 kts **Dim:** 61.57 (55.4 pp) × 7.45 × 3.35
A: 2/102-mm Mk 19 DP (II × 1)—2/40-mm Bofors AA (I × 2)—2/20-mm AA (I × 2)
Electron Equipt: Radar: 1/AWS1, 1/Decca TM 626, 1/HSA M 22
Sonar: Plessey MS 22
M: 2 M.A.N. V8V 24/30-B diesels; 2 props; 4,430 hp (3,400 sust.)
Electric: 600 kw **Fuel:** 68 tons **Range:** 3,500/14
Man: 7 officers, 13 petty officers, 46 men

REMARKS: Can carry a flag officer and his staff. Living spaces air-conditioned. Fin stabilizers. The 102-mm guns are hand-loaded. Twelve watertight compartments. Refitted 1975-76. Have sonar, but no ASW ordnance fitted.

GUIDED-MISSILE PATROL BOATS

♦ **3 La Combattante-IIIB class Bldr:** CMN, Cherbourg, France

	Laid down	L	In serv.
P 181 SIRI	15-5-79	3-6-80	19-2-81
P 182 AYAM	7-9-79	10-11-80	11-6-81
P 183 EKUN	14-11-79	11-2-81	18-9-81

Siri (P 181)   CMN, 1981

D: 376 tons light (430 fl) **S:** 37 kts **Dim:** 56.0 (53.0 pp) × 8.16 (7.61 wl) × 2.15
A: 4/MM 38 Exocet SSM (II × 2)—1/76-mm OTO Melara DP—2/40-mm Breda AA (II × 1)—4/30-mm Emerlec AA (II × 2)
Electron Equipt: Radar: 1/Decca 1226, 1/Thomson-CSF Triton, 1/Thomson-CSF Castor
M: 4 MTU 16V956 TB92 diesels; 4 props; 20,840 hp (17,320 sust.)
Range: 2,000/15 **Man:** 42 tot.

REMARKS: Ordered 1977. Remained at Cherbourg at end 81; final payments not met.

♦ **3 FPB 57 class Bldr:** Lürssen, Vegasack, West Germany

	Laid down	L	Trials	In serv.
P 178 EKPE	. . .	. . .	8-80	4-81
P 179 DAMISA	. . .	. . .	2-81	4-81
P 180 AGU	. . .	7-11-80	2-81	4-81

Ekpe (P 178)—prior to delivery, 30-6-81   G. Gyssels

D: 373 tons (436 fl) **S:** 35 kts **Dim:** 58.1 (54.4 wl) × 7.62 × 2.83 (props)
A: 4/Otomat Mk 1 (I × 4)—1/76-mm OTO Melara DP—2/40-mm Breda-Bofors (II × 1)—4/30-mm Emerlec AA (II × 2)
Electron Equipt: Radar: 1/Decca TM 1226C, 1/HSA WM-28
ECM: Decca RDL intercept
M: 4 MTU 16V956 TB92 diesels; 4 props; 20,840 hp (17,320 sust.)
Electric: 405 kVA **Range:** 1,600/32; 3,000/16 **Man:** 40 tot.

GUIDED-MISSILE PATROL BOATS *(continued)*

REMARKS: Ordered late 1977. Navigation systems include Decca Mk 21 "Navigator" NAVSAT receiver, OMEGA receiver and Marconi "Lodestone" D/F. Made 42 kts on trials.

PATROL BOATS

♦ **4 Makurdi class** Bldr: Brooke Marine Ltd., Lowestoft, G.B.

	In serv.		In serv.
P 167 MAKURDI	14-8-74	P 171 JEBBA	29-4-77
P 168 HADEJIA	14-8-74	P 172 OGUTA	29-4-77

Hadejia (P 168)—prior to rearmament　　　　　　　1975

D: 115 tons (143 fl) **S:** 20.5 kts **Dim:** 32.6 × 6.1 × 3.5
A: 4/30-mm Emerlec AA (II × 2)
M: 2 Ruston-Paxman YJCM diesels; 2 props; 3,000 hp **Fuel:** 18 tons
Range: 2,300/12 **Man:** 4 officers, 20 men

REMARKS: First two refitted by builders, 1981-82, others refitted in Nigeria; rearmed, engines overhauled.

♦ **4 Argundu class** Bldr: Abeking & Rasmussen, West Germany

	L	In serv.		L	In serv.
P 165 ARGUNDU	4-7-73	10-74	P 169 BRAS	12-1-76	3-76
P 166 YOLA	12-6-73	10-74	P 170 EPE	9-2-76	3-76

Argundu (P 165)—prior to rearmament　　　　　　　1975

D: 90 tons **S:** 20 kts **Dim:** 32.0 (29.0 pp) × 6.0 × 1.7
A: 4/30-mm Emerlec AA (II × 2)
M: 2 MTU diesels; 2 props; 2,070 hp **Range:** . . . **Man:** 25 tot.

REMARKS: Being refitted 1981-82 by builders; originally had 1/40-mm AA, 1/20-mm AA.

♦ **1 British "Ford" class** Bldr: J. Samuel White, Cowes, G.B. (In serv. 1953)

P 09 SAPELE (ex-*Dubford*)

D: 120 tons (160 fl) **S:** 15 kts **Dim:** 35.76 × 6.1 × 1.68
A: 1/40-mm AA—2/20-mm AA (I × 2)
M: 2 Davey-Paxman YHAMX diesels; 2 props; 1,000 hp; 1 Foden FD-6 cruise diesel: 100 hp
Fuel: 23 tons **Range:** 500/12, 1,000/8 **Man:** 26 tot.

REMARKS: Transferred in 1968. Survivor of a group of five sisters. Used primarily for training. Sister *Ibadan* lost 1967; *Ibadan II*, *Bonny*, and *Enugu* stricken 1977-78.

AMPHIBIOUS WARFARE SHIPS

♦ **2 West German Type-502 landing ships** Bldr: Howaldtswerke, Hamburg

	Laid down	L	In serv.
L 1312 AMBE	3-3-78	7-7-78	11-5-79
L 1313 OFIOM	15-9-78	7-12-78	7-79

D: 1,190 tons light (1,470 normal, 1,750 fl) **S:** 17 kts
Dim: 86.9 (74.5 pp) × 14.0 × 2.30
A: 1/40-mm AA—2/20-mm AA (I × 2) **Electron Equipt:** Radar: 1/Decca 1226
M: 2 MTU 16V956 TB92 diesels; 4 props; 7,000 hp **Electric:** 900 kw
Range: 5,000/12 **Man:** 6 officers, 53 men, plus 540 troops (1,000 for short distances)

REMARKS: Cargo: 400 tons vehicles plus troops (typically: 5/40-ton tanks or 7/18-ton tanks plus 4/45-ton trucks). Articulated bow ramp, short stern ramp for loading from a pier. Can fit an 81-mm mortar forward. Each engine drives two props.

Ambe (LST 1312)　　　　　　　　　　　　　　　　1980

AMPHIBIOUS WARFARE SHIPS *(continued)*

Ambe (LST 1312)—articulating bow ramp fitted   G. Koop, 1980

♦ **2 French EDIC-class utility landing craft** Bldr: La Manche, Dieppe

	In serv.			In serv.
L. . . N. . .	. . .	L. . . N. . .		. . .

D: 250 tons (670 fl) **S:** 9 kts **Dim:** 60.0 × 12.6 × 1.8 (props)
A: . . .   **M:** 2 diesels; 2 props; 800 hp

REMARKS: Reported ordered 6-77 and laid down 23-9-77 and 17-10-77; fate uncertain.

HYDROGRAPHIC SHIPS

♦ **1 British Bulldog class** Bldr: Brooke Marine Ltd., Lowestoft, G.B.

	Laid down	L	In serv.
A 498 LANA	5-4-74	4-3-76	9-76

Lana (A 498)   G. Arra, 1976

D: 800 tons (1,100 fl) **S:** 15 kts **Dim:** 60.95 (57.8 pp) × 11.43 × 3.7
A: 2/20-mm AA (I × 2)
M: 4 Lister-Blackstone ERS-8M diesels; 2 CP props; 2,000 hp
Electric: 880 kw **Range:** 4,000/12 **Man:** 38 tot.

♦ **1 coastal survey craft**

	Bldr	L	In serv.
MURTULA MUHAMED	Akerboom, Leiden, Netherlands	14-8-76	28-9-76

D: 13 tons **S:** 9 kts **Dim:** 11.75 × 3.5 × 1.0
M: 1 Perkins 6-354M diesel; 1 prop; 75 hp

TRAINING SHIP

♦ **1 training ship** Bldr: Van Lent, Kaag, Netherlands (In serv. 10-5-75)

A 497 RUWAN YARO (ex-*Ogina Bereton*)

Ruwan Yaro (A 497)

D: 400 tons (fl) **S:** 17 kts **Dim:** 50.0 (44.2 pp) × 8.0 × 2.0
A: None   **Electron Equipt:** Radar: 1/Decca TM 626
M: 2 Deutz SBA 12M528 diesels; 1 CP prop; 3,000 hp **Fuel:** 64 tons
Range: 3,000/15 **Man:** 31 + 11 in officers' training

REMARKS: Purchased 1976; originally a yacht, has a glass-reinforced plastic hull and a bow-thruster.

TUGS

♦ **1 harbor tug** Bldr: De Hoop SY, Hardinxveld, Netherlands (L: 15-11-77)

A. . . KAIN JI-DAM—90 grt

♦ **1 coastal tug** Bldr: Oelkers, Hamburg (In serv. 19-5-73)

A 486 RIBADU

D: 147 tons **S:** 12 kts **Dim:** 28.5 × 7.2 × 3.7
M: 1 diesel; 1 prop; 800 hp

NOTE: There are also 48 service launches built by Fairey Marine, Hamble: 2/10-m, 22/7-m, 15/6.7-m, and 5/5.5 m. Four Cheverton 8.2-m launches are also in use.

NIGERIAN COAST GUARD

PATROL CRAFT

♦ **15 glass-reinforced, plastic-hulled** Bldr: Intermarine, Italy (In serv. 1981)

D: 21 tons (fl) **S:** 33 kts **Dim:** 18.2 × 4.5 × 0.85
A: 1/20-mm AA—2/7.62-mm mg **M:** 2 diesels; 2 water jets; 2,000 hp
Range: 300/33

REMARKS: Ordered 10-78.

NIGERIA *(continued)*
PATROL CRAFT *(continued)*

♦ **1 "Tracker" class** Bldr: Fairey Marine, Hamble, G.B. (In serv. 2-78)

D: 31 tons (fl) **S:** 24 kts **Dim:** 19.3 × 5.0 × 1.5
A: 1/20-mm AA **M:** 2 diesels; 2 props; 1,290 hp
Range: 650/20 **Man:** 11 tot.

♦ **2 "Spear" class** Bldr: Fairey Marine, Hamble, G.B. (In serv. 1978)

D: 4.3 tons **S:** 25 kts **Dim:** 9.1 × 2.8 × 0.8

MARINE POLICE

NOTE: For operations on the Niger River and Lake Chad. All craft built of glass-reinforced plastic.

♦ **1 P 1200 class** Bldr: Watercraft, Ltd., Shoreham, G.B. (In serv. 2-81)

D: 9.7 tons (fl) **S:** 27 kts **Dim:** 11.9 × 4.1 × 1.1
M: 2 GM 8V71 TI diesels; 2 props; 480 hp **Range:** 240/25

♦ **5 P 800 class** Bldr: Watercraft, Shoreham, G.B. (In serv. 12-80)

D: 3.2 tons (fl) **S:** 26 kts **Dim:** 8.0 × 2.6 × 0.8
M: 1 Volvo AQAD 40 outdrive diesel; 1 prop; 150 hp **Range:** 104/26

♦ **8 15-ton class** Bldr: Vosper Thornycroft (In serv. 1971-72)

D: 15 tons (fl) **S:** 19 kts **Dim:** 10.4 × 3.1 × 0.9
M: 2 Rolls-Royce diesels; 2 props; 290 hp

♦ **7 Q 26 class** Bldr: Cheverton Workboats, G.B. (In serv. 1980-81)

♦ **19 Q 33 class** Bldr: Cheverton Workboats, G.B. (Ordered 1981)

NORWAY
Kingdom of Norway

PERSONNEL (1980): 8,500 men, 1,600 of whom in the Coast Artillery

MERCHANT MARINE (1980): 2,501 ships—22,007,490 grt
(tankers: 173 ships—12,082,393 grt)

NAVAL AVIATION: The Norwegian Navy does not have an air arm, as such. However, two of the Air Force's formations are assigned to naval missions, usually reconnaissance and ASW patrol: a squadron of 10 SH-3 Sea King and 20 UH-1 search-and-rescue helicopters; a group of 7 P-3B Orion patrol aircraft and 4 De Havilland Twin Otter utility aircraft. The Coast Guard operates 6 WG-13 Lynx helicopters.

WARSHIPS IN SERVICE OR UNDER CONSTRUCTION AS OF 1 JANUARY 1982

	L	Tons (surfaced)	Main armament
♦ **15 submarines**			
15 GERMAN TYPE 207	1964-67	370	8/533-mm TT
♦ **5 frigates**			
5 OSLO	1964-66	1,450	4-6/Penguin SSM, 1/Sea Sparrow system, 4/76.2-mm DP, 1/Terne ASW system, 6/324-mm ASW TT
♦ **3 corvettes**			
2 SLEIPNER	1963-65	600	1/76-mm DP, 1/Terne ASW system, 6/324-mm ASW TT
1 VADSØ	1951	600	1/40-mm AA
♦ **40 missile and torpedo boats**			

WEAPONS AND SYSTEMS

The Norwegian Navy uses mostly British, American, and Swedish weapons and systems, but it has built two systems of its own, the Terne automatic ASW defense system and the Penguin surface-to-surface missile, which are described below. Submarines are equipped with Swedish T 61 (45 kts, 20,000 m) or American Mk 37 (20,000 m) wire-guided torpedoes. Norway has also developed its own radar and electro-optical gun and missile fire-control systems. Sonars are manufactured by the Simrad Co.

Terne Mk III (ASW)

Maximum range: 900 m
1 search sonar (U.S. AN/SQS-36)
1 attack sonar ("Terne Mk 3" for range/depth determination)
1 computer
1 sextuple launcher mount with a rapid-reloading system.

The sextuple launcher mount weighs a little less than 3 tons. Firing is done between 45° and 75° of elevation, the latter for minimum range. Six rounds are ripple-fired at a time. Reloading is done automatically in 40 seconds, as the carriage is returned to a vertical position, in which ready-service racks reload the launchers. The rocket is 1.97 m in length, 0.2 m in diameter, 120 kg in weight (warhead: 48 kg), and has a combination timed and proximity fuse. Employed on the *Oslo* and *Sleipner* classes.

Penguin Mk I (Anti-ship)

Length: 0.95 m	Maximum range: 20,000 m
Wingspan: 1.4 m	Speed: Mach 0.7
Diameter: 0.28	Guidance: infrared homing
Weight: 330 kg	

The missile is protected by a fiberglass container that also serves as a launcher. Penguin Mk II, developed in conjunction with the Swedish Navy, has a range of 30,000 m, a more powerful warhead, and a speed of Mach 8. Penguin Mk III is being developed for air launch by Norwegian Air Force F-16 fighters.

76-mm Bofors gun

Single-barreled automatic gun mounted on the *Storm*-class patrol boats. Not intended for AA. Also used by the Singapore Navy.

WEAPONS AND SYSTEMS *(continued)*

Turret weight (no ammunition): 6.5 tons
Length: 50 calibers
Muzzle velocity: 825 m/sec
Rate of train: 25°/sec
Rate of elevation: 25°/sec
Arc of elevation: −10° to +30°
Rate of fire: 30 rounds/min—100 rounds immediately available in the ready-firing station

Cartridge weight: 11.3 kg
Shell weight: 5.9 kg
Warhead weight: 0.54 kg
Maximum range, surface mode: 8,000 m

SUBMARINES

♦ 0 (+8) German Type 210

REMARKS: Programmed for construction during late 1980s to replace Type 207 submarines. D: 750 tons surfaced/900 sub.; no other data released.

♦ 15 German Type 207 Bldr: Rheinstahl-Nordseewerke, Emden

	L	In serv.		L	In serv.
S 300 ULA	19-12-64	7-5-65	S 308 STORD	2-9-66	9-2-67
S 301 UTSIRA	11-3-65	1-7-65	S 309 SVENNER	27-1-67	1-7-67
S 302 UTSTEIN	19-5-65	9-9-65	S 315 KAURA	16-10-64	5-2-65
S 303 UTVAER	30-6-65	1-12-65	S 316 KINN	30-11-63	8-4-64
S 304 UTHAUG	8-10-65	16-2-66	S 317 KYA	20-2-64	15-6-64
S 305 SKLINNA	21-1-66	17-8-66	S 318 KOBBEN	25-4-64	17-8-64
S 306 SKOLPEN	24-3-66	17-8-66	S 319 KUNNA	16-7-64	1-10-64
S 307 STADT	10-6-66	15-11-66			

Kya (S 317) 1975

D: 370/482 tons **S:** 13.5/17 kts **Dim:** 45.41 (S 309: 46.41) × 4.6 × 4.58
A: 8/533-mm TT, fwd
M: 2 Mercedes-Benz MB 820Db diesels, 2 405-kw generators, 1 1,100-kw motor; 1 prop (2.3 m diameter); 1,700 hp
Man: 17 tot.

REMARKS: Based on the West German Type 205, but deeper-diving. They are fitted with new sensors, new batteries, and wire-guided U.S. Mk 37 torpedoes. MSI-700 torpedo fire-control is used. The *Svenner* is equipped for training, has a second periscope, and is one meter longer than the others.

GUIDED-MISSILE FRIGATES

♦ 5 Oslo class Bldr: Marinens Hovedverft (Naval Dockyard), Horten

	Laid down	L	In serv.
F 300 OSLO	1963	17-1-64	29-1-66
F 301 BERGEN	1963	23-8-65	15-6-67
F 302 TRONDHEIM	1963	4-9-64	2-6-66
F 303 STAVANGER	1964	4-2-66	1-12-67
F 304 NARVIK	1964	8-1-65	30-11-66

Stavanger (F 303) G. Gyssels, 1981

Oslo (F 300) G. Gyssels, 1980

D: 1,450 tons (1,850 fl) **S:** 25 kts **Dim:** 96.62 (93.87 pp) × 11.17 × 4.4
A: 4-6/Penguin SSM—1/NATO Sea Sparrow system (VIII × 1, 24 missiles)—4/76.2-mm DP (II × 2)—1/Terne-III ASW RL (VI × 1)—6/324-mm Mk 32 ASW TT (III × 2)—1/d.c. rack (6 d.c.)
Electron Equipt: Radar: 1/DRBV 22, 1/Decca TM 1226, 1/HSA M 24, 11/U.S. Mk 91 mod. 0
Sonar: 1/Terne Mk 3 attack, 1/SQS-36
M: 1 set de Laval-Ljungstrom PN 20 GT; 1 prop; 20,000 hp
Electric: 1,100 kw **Boilers:** 2 Babcock & Wilcox; 42.18 kg/cm², 454°C
Range: 4,500/15 **Man:** 11 officers, 19 petty officers, 120 men

REMARKS: Based on the U.S. *Dealey*-class destroyer escorts, but with higher freeboard forward and many European subsystems. Rebuilt during the late 1970s with the Penguin anti-ship missile, NATO Sea Sparrow point-defense SAM, and ASW torpedo tubes. In the Sea Sparrow system, the Mk 91 radar director is on a pylon atop the missile-reload magazine; the launcher is a U.S. Mk 29. F 304 conducted trials during 1980 with the Raytheon C-LAS C-band acquisition radar.

CORVETTES

♦ **2 Sleipner class** Bldr: Nylands Verksted, Oslo

	L	In serv.		L	In serv.
F 310 SLEIPNER	9-11-63	29-4-65	F 311 AEGER	24-9-65	31-3-67

Sleipner (F 310)   G. Koop, 1981

D: 600 tons (790 fl)   **S:** 20+ kts   **Dim:** 69.33 × 7.9 × 2.5
A: 1/76.2-mm Mk 34 DP—1/40-mm AA—1/Terne-III ASW RL (VI × 1)—6/324-mm Mk 32 ASW TT (III × 2)—1/d.c. rack (6 d.c.)
Electron Equipt: Radar: 1/Decca 202, 1/Decca TM 1226
                 Sonar: 1/Terne Mk 3 attack, 1/SQS-36
M: 4 Maybach diesels; 2 props; 9,000 hp   **Man:** 61 tot.

REMARKS: From the 1960 program. Now employed primarily for training. U.S. Mk 63 GFCS replaced by 2 Swedish TVT 300 optronic systems.

♦ **1 former whale-catcher** Bldr: Stord Verft (L: 1951)

P 340 VADSØ

D: 600 tons (905 fl)   **S:** 12 kts   **Dim:** 51.0 × 9.0 × 4.1
A: 1/40-mm AA—1/d.c. rack
Electron Equipt: Radar: 2/navigational
                 Sonar: . . .
M: 1 M.A.K. 8M451 diesel; 1 prop; 1,400 hp   **Range:** 15,000/12   **Man:** 22 tot.

REMARKS: Purchased in 1976 and refitted for local patrol duties. The AA gun is mounted on what was the harpoon-gun platform at the extreme bow; the depth-charge rack is on a platform extending aft from the superstructure.

GUIDED-MISSILE PATROL BOATS

♦ **14 Hauk class** Bldrs: (A) Bergens Mekaniske Verksteder; (B) Westamarin, Alta

	Bldr	L	In serv.
P 986 HAUK	A	2-77	17-8-78
P 987 ØRN	A	2-78	19-1-79
P 988 TERNE	A	5-78	13-3-79
P 989 TJELD	A	8-78	25-5-79
P 990 SKARV	A	10-78	17-7-79
P 991 TEIST	A	6-12-78	11-9-79
P 992 JO	A	. . .	1-11-79
P 993 LOM	A	. . .	15-1-80
P 994 STEGG	A	. . .	18-3-80
P 995 FALK	A	. . .	30-4-80
P 996 RAVN	B	. . .	20-5-80
P 997 GRIBB	B	. . .	10-7-80
P 998 GEIR	B	. . .	16-9-80
P 999 ERLE	B	. . .	10-12-80

Skarv (P 990)   S. Terzibaschitsch, 1981

D: 130 tons (155 fl)   **S:** 35 kts   **Dim:** 36.53 × 6.3 × 1.65
A: 2-6/Penguin Mk II SSM (I × 6)—1/40-mm Bofors AA—1/20-mm Rheinmetall AA—2/533-mm TT for T-61 wire-guided torpedoes
Electron Equipt: Radar: 2/Decca TM 1226
                 Sonar: Simrad SQ3D/SF
M: 2 MTU 16V538 TB92 diesels; 2 props; 7,340 hp   **Range:** 440/34
Man: 22 tot.

REMARKS: MSI-80S fire-control system, developed by Kongsberg, uses two Decca radars plus a TVT-300 electro-optical tracker and an Ericsen laser range finder. Have 2/50-mm flare RL.

♦ **6 Snögg class** Bldr: Båtservice Verft, Mandal, 1970-71

P 980 SNÖGG (ex-*Lyr*)	P 982 SNARR	P 984 KVIK
P 981 RAPP	P 983 RASK	P 985 KJAPP

Snarr (P 982)—4 Penguin Mk I aboard   J.-C. Bellonne, 1974

D: 115 tons (140 fl)   **S:** 36 kts   **Dim:** 36.53 × 6.3 × 1.65
A: 2-4/Penguin Mk I SSM (I × 4)—1/40-mm AA—1/533-mm TT for T-61 wire-guided torpedoes—2/d.c. racks
Electron Equipt: Radar: 1/Decca TM 626, 1/PEAB TORI fire control
M: 2 MTU 16V538 TB92 diesels; 2 props; 7,200 hp
Range: 550/36   **Man:** 3 officers, 17 men

GUIDED-MISSILE PATROL BOATS (continued)

♦ **20 Storm class** Bldrs: P 963, P 966, P 969, P 972, P 975, and P 978: Wester-möen, Mandal; Others: Bergens MV

	L		L		L
P 960 STORM	19-3-63	P 967 SKUDD	25-3-66	P 974 BROTT	27-1-67
P 961 BLINK	28-6-65	P 968 ARG	24-5-66	P 975 ODD	7-4-67
P 962 GLIMT	27-9-65	P 969 STEIL	20-9-66	P 976 PIL	29-3-67
P 963 SKJOLD	17-2-66	P 970 BRANN	3-7-66	P 977 BRASK	27-5-67
P 964 TRYGG	25-11-65	P 971 TROSS	29-9-66	P 978 ROKK	1-6-67
P 965 KJEKK	27-1-66	P 972 HVASS	20-12-66	P 979 GNIST	15-8-67
P 966 DJERV	28-4-66	P 973 TRAUST	18-11-66		

Rokk (P 978)—4 Penquin Mk I aft   S. Terzibaschitsch, 1981

D: 100 tons (125 fl) **S:** 37 kts **Dim:** 36.53 × 6.3 × 1.55
A: 4-6/Penguin Mk I SSM (I × 6)—1/76-mm—1/40-mm AA
Electron Equipt: Radar: 1/Decca TM 1226, 1/HSA WM-26 fire-control
M: Maybach MB 872A diesels; 2 props; 7,200 hp **Range:** 550/36
Man: 4 officers, 9 petty officers, 13 men

REMARKS: Being backfitted with TVT-300 electro-optical tracker and laser range finder, in a tub abaft the radar mast. Diesels are essentially the same as those in the *Hauk* and *Snögg* classes above. Two d.c. racks can be carried in lieu of the after two Penguin containers.

NOTE: The surviving eleven torpedo boats of the *Tjeld* class, all in reserve, were put up for sale in 1981.

MINE WARFARE SHIPS

♦ **2 Vidar-class minelayers** Bldr: Mjellem & Karlsen, Bergen

	Laid down	L	In serv.
N 52 VIDAR	1-3-76	18-3-77	21-10-77
N 53 VALE	1-2-76	5-8-77	10-2-78

D: 1,500 tons (1,722 fl) **S:** 15 kts **Dim:** 64.8 (60.0 pp) × 12.0 × 4.0
A: 2/40-mm AA (I × 2)—6/324-mm Mk 32 ASW TT (III × 2)—2/d.c. racks—320 mines
Electron Equipt: Radar: 2/Decca 1226 Sonar: Simrad SQ3D
M: 2 Wichmann 7AX diesels; 2 props; 4,200 hp **Electric:** 1,000 kw
Fuel: 247 tons **Man:** 50 tot.

Vidar (N 52)   1978

REMARKS: Capable of serving as minelayers (mines carried on three decks, automatic hoist, three mine-laying rails), torpedo-recovery ships, personnel and cargo transports, fisheries-protection ships, and ASW escorts. Bow-thruster fitted.

♦ **1 inshore mine-planter**

	Bldr	L
N 51 BORGEN	Marinens Hovedverft, Horten	29-4-60

 D: 282 tons (fl) **S:** 9 kts **Dim:** 31.28 × 8.0 × 3.35
 A: 2/20-mm AA (I × 2)—2 mine rails
 M: 2 GM 3-71 diesels; 2 Voith Schneider cycloidal props; 330 hp

REMARKS: Patterned on the Swedish MUL-12 class. Designed to "plant" mines by crane.

♦ **10 U.S. Falcon-class coastal minesweepers** Bldrs: M 315, M 332, M 334: Båtservice Verft, Mandal; M 316: Skåluren, Rosendal; M 331: Forenede Båtbyggeri, Risör; M 311, M 313, M 314, M 317: Hodgdon Bros., Gowdy & Stevens, Boothbay, Maine; M 312: C. Hiltebrant DD, Kingston, New York

	In serv.
M 311 SAUDA (ex-MSC 102)	25-8-53
M 312 SIRA (ex-MSC 132)	28-11-55
M 313 TANA (ex-*Roeslaere*, ex-MSC 103)	9-53
M 314 ALTA (ex-*Arlon*, ex-MSC 104)	10-53
M 315 OGNA	5-3-55
M 316 VOSSO	16-3-55
M 317 GLOMMA (ex-*Bastogne*, ex-MSC 151)	12-53
M 331 TISTA	27-4-55
M 332 KVINA	12-7-55
M 334 UTLA	15-11-55

 D: 300 tons (372 fl) **S:** 13 kts (8, sweeping) **Dim:** 43.0 × 7.95 × 2.55
 A: 2/20-mm Rheinmetall AA (I × 2)
 Electron Equipt: Radar: 1/Decca 202 or 1226
                    Sonar: 1/UQS-1 (M 313: 1/193 M)
M: 2 GM 8-268A diesels; 2 props; 1,200 hp **Fuel:** 40 tons
Range: 2,500/10 **Man:** 38 tot.

MINE WARFARE SHIPS (continued)

Utla (M 334)   L. & L. van Ginderen, 1981

REMARKS: *Tana*, *Alta*, and *Glomma* were transferred by Belgium in 1966 in exchange for two ocean minesweepers. *Lagen* and *Namsen*. In 1977, *Tana* was converted to a prototype minehunter, with British type 193M sonar, two PAP-104 remote-controlled minehunting devices, and divers' facilities in a large deckhouse aft. She was armed with 2/20-mm Rheinmetall AA guns (I × 2), now being backfitted into the others. At the waterline, across the stern, she has a platform for diver-recovery; this extends her overall length by more than one meter.

AMPHIBIOUS WARFARE SHIPS

♦ **5 Reinøysund-class utility landing craft** Bldr: Mjellem & Karlsen, Bergen (In serv. 1972-73)

L 4502 REINØYSUND	L 4504 MAURSUND	L 4506 BORGSUND
L 4503 SØRØYSUND	L 4505 ROTSUND	

    D: 596 tons (fl) **S:** 11 kts **Dim:** 51.4 × 10.3 × 1.85
    A: 3/20-mm Rheinmetall (I × 3)—4/12.7-mm mg—rails for 120 mines
    M: 2 MTU diesels; 2 props;. . . hp **Man:** 2 officers, 7 men

REMARKS: Double-folding bow ramp door. Cargo capacity: 5 Leopard tanks, 80-180 men. Similar to class below, but superstructure is farther forward.

♦ **2 Kvalsund-class utility landing craft** Bldr: Mjellem & Karlsen, Bergen

L 4500 KVALSUND (In serv. 6-68) L 4501 RAFTSUND (In serv. 3-69)

    D: 590 tons (fl) **S:** 11 kts **Dim:** 50.0 × 10.2 × 1.8
    A: 2/20-mm AA—rails for 120 mines
    M: 2 MTU diesels; 2 props; . . . hp **Man:** 2 officers, 7 men

REMARKS: Cargo capacity: 5 Leopard tanks, 80-180 men.

AUXILIARY SHIPS

♦ **1 logistic-support ship** Bldr: Horten Verft, Horten

	Laid down	L	In serv.
A 530 HORTEN	28-1-77	12-8-77	9-6-78

Horten (A 530)   1978

    D: 2,500 tons (fl) **S:** 16.5 kts **Dim:** 87.0 (82.0 pp) × 13.7 × . . .
    A: 2/40-mm AA (I × 2)—mines
    M: 2 Wichmann 7AX diesels; 2 props; 4,200 hp **Man:** 86 tot.

REMARKS: Used to support submarines and small combatants. Can accommodate up to 190 additional personnel. Helicopter deck. Bow-thruster.

♦ **1 oceanographic-research ship** Bldr: Orens MV, Trondheim (In serv. 1960)

H. U. SVERDRUP (ex-U.S. AGOR 2)

    D: 400 tons (fl) **S:** 11.5 kts **Dim:** 38.89 × 7.62 × 3.30
    M: 1 Wichmann diesel; 1 prop; 600 hp **Electric:** 104 kw
    Fuel: 65 tons **Range:** 5,000/10 **Man:** 10 men + 9 scientists

REMARKS: 295 grt trawler hull. Operates for the Norwegian Defense Research Establishment and has a civilian crew. Purchase and outfitting financed by the U.S.A. under the Offshore Procurement Program.

♦ **1 royal yacht**

	Bldr	L
A 533 NORGE (ex-*Philante*)	Camper & Nicholson's Ltd., Gosport	17-2-37

Norge (A 533)   1971

    D: 1,686 tons **S:** 17 kts **Dim:** 76.27 × 8.53 × 4.65
    M: 2 8-cyl. diesels; 2 props; 3,000 hp **Electric:** 300 kw
    Fuel: 175 tons **Range:** 9,900/17

REMARKS: Built as a yacht, then used by the Royal Navy as an ASW escort from 1940 to 1943, then as a training ship. Purchased by Norway in 1948. Displacement listed is in Thames Yacht Measurement. Can carry 50-passenger royal party.

SERVICE CRAFT

♦ **1 torpedo-recovery and oil-spill cleanup ship** Bldr: Fjellstrand, Hardinger (In serv. 10-78)

VSD 1 Vernøy

D: 150 grt **S:** 12 kts **Dim:** 31.3 × 6.76 × 2.0
M: 2 MWM diesels; 2 Schöttel props; . . . hp

♦ **7 Torpen-class support tenders**

	Bldr	In serv.
VSD 4 Torpen	Båtservice, Mandal	12-77
ØSD 2 Wisting	Voldnes, Fosnavåg	1-78
TSD 5 Tautra	Båtservice, Mandal	2-78
NSD 35 Rotvaer	Båtservice, Mandal	3-78
RSD 23 Fjøløy	Voldnes, Fosnavåg	4-78
HSD 15 Krøttøy	Voldnes, Fosnavag	6-78
TRSD 4 Karlsøy	P. Høivolds, Kristianstad	7-78

D: 215 tons (300 fl) **S:** 11 kts **Dim:** 29.0 × 6.4 × 2.57
A: 1/12.7-mm mg **M:** 1 MWM TBD 601-6K diesel; 1 CP prop; 530 hp
Fuel: 11 tons **Range:** 1,200/11 **Man:** 6 men + 100 passengers

REMARKS: Basically similar craft tailored to a variety of duties, including logistics support, ammunition transport, personnel transport, and divers' support. Cargo: 100 tons.

♦ **2 navigational training craft** Bldr: Fjellstrand, Omastrand (In serv. 1-78)

VSD 2 Marsteinen   VSD 6 Kvarvan

D: 40 tons **S:** 22 kts **Dim:** 23.2 × 5.0 × 1.1 **A:** 1/12.7-mm mg
M: 2 GM 12V71 diesels; 2 props; 1,800 hp **Man:** 5 men + 8 cadets

REMARKS: Aluminum construction. For use at the Naval Academy.

♦ **2 tenders for combat divers** Bldr: Nielsen, Harstad (In serv. 1972)

SKV 10 Draug   SKV 11 Sarpen

D: 250 tons **S:** 12 kts **Dim:** 29.0 × 6.7 × 2.5 **M:** 1 diesel; 1 prop; 530 hp

♦ **1 harbor tug** Bldr: . . . , Germany (In serv. 1938)

VSD 7 Samson

D: 300 tons **S:** 11 kts **Dim:** 26.6 × . . . × . . . **M:** 1 diesel; 1 prop; . . . hp

♦ **1 harbor tug** Bldr: . . . , Germany (In serv. 1938)

VSD 13 Ramnes (ex-German *Robbe*)

D: 101 tons **S:** 11 kts **Dim:** 24.0 × . . . × . . . **M:** 1 diesel; . . . hp

COAST GUARD (KYSTVAKT)

The Norwegian Coast Guard was established in 1976 to perform fisheries-protection duties, patrol the waters in the vicinity of offshore oil rigs, and maintain surveillance over the 200-nautical-mile economic zone. To begin with, six former naval fisheries-protection ships were transferred to it; then seven miscellaneous seagoing trawlers and oilfield-supply ships were leased from their owners. The Coast Guard operates six WG-13 Lynx helicopters.

PATROL SHIPS

♦ **3 Nordkapp (Type 320) class**

	Bldr	L	In serv.
W 320 Nordkapp	Bergens Mek. Verk.	14-5-80	25-4-81
W 321 Senja	Horten Verft	16-3-81	8-3-81
W 322 Andennes	Haugesund Verk.	21-3-81	11-81

Marsteinen (VSD 2)

Nordkapp (W 320)—official model

PATROL SHIPS (continued)

D: 2,165 tons light (2,950 fl) **S:** 23 kts **Dim:** 105.00 (97.50 pp) × 13.85 × 4.55
A: 1/57-mm Bofors AA—4/20-mm Rheinmetall AA (I × 4)—6/324-mm Mk 32
ASW TT (III × 2)—1/d.c. rack (6 d.c.)—1/WG-13 Lynx helicopter
Electron Equipt: Radar: 2/Decca 1226, 1/Decca RM914, 1/Plessey AWS-4,
1/PEAB GLF 218
Sonar: 1/Simrad SS105
M: 4 Wichmann 9-AXAG diesels; 2 CP props; 14,400 hp **Electric:** 1,600 kw
Fuel: 350 tons **Range:** 7,500/15 **Man:** 48 crew + helo crew

REMARKS: Program delayed by design changes and lack of funding; four additional
units deferred. W 322 and W 323 displace 2,854 tons full load and are not ice-
strengthened as is W 320, intended for service in Arctic waters. In time of conflict,
6 Penguin II anti-ship missiles and chaff launchers are to be added. Fin stabilized.
Carry three 300-m³/hr. water cannon for firefighting and have meteorological reporting gear. The NAVKIS data system is fitted. Wartime crew: 75 total.

♦ 1 former stern-haul trawler Bldr: Båtservice, Mandal (In serv. 5-78)

W 319 GRIMSHOLM

D: 1,189 grt **S:** . . . kts **Dim:** 62.71 (54.60 pp) × 11.63 × 6.43
A: 1/40-mm AA **M:** 1 MaK 9-cyl. diesel; 1 prop; 3,400 hp **Electric:** 524 kw

REMARKS: Chartered 1980. Side-thrusters fore and aft.

♦ 1 former stern-haul trawler Bldr: Brødrene Lothes, Haugesund (In serv. 7-78)

W 317 LAFJORD

D: 814 grt **S:** 14.6 kts **Dim:** 55.40 × 9.81 × 6.18
A: 1/40-mm AA **M:** 1 Wichmann 7-cyl. diesel; 1 prop; 2,100 hp
Electric: 419 kw **Fuel:** 220 tons **Range:** 7,700/14.6

REMARKS: Chartered 1980. Side thrusters fore and aft.

♦ 1 former stern-haul trawler Bldr: Smedvik, Tjørråg (In serv. 4-78)
W 315 NORDSJØBAS

D: 814 grt **S:** 13.5 kts **Dim:** 52.04 (44.75 pp) × 10.01 × 6.55
A: 1/40-mm AA **Electric:** 1,088 kw **Range:** 8,300/13.5
M: 1 MaK 6-cyl. diesel; 1 prop; 2,400 hp **Fuel:** 180 tons

REMARKS: Chartered 1980. Side-thrusters fore and aft.

♦ 1 former purse seiner Bldr: Hall-Russell, Aberdeen, Scotland (In serv. 3-51)

W 312 SØRFOLD (ex-*Olafur Jöhannesson*, ex-*Andvan*)

D: 773 grt **S:** 12 kts **Dim:** 61.37 (55.06 pp) × 9.2 × 4.88
A: 1/40-mm AA **M:** 1 Werkspoor 8-cyl. diesel; 1 CP prop; 2,660 hp
Electric: 175 kw **Fuel:** 80 tons **Man:** . . .

REMARKS: Chartered from Oddvar Jöhannesson in 1977. Side-thrusters fore and aft.

♦ 1 former trawler Bldr: Kvina Verft/Flekkefjord MV (In serv. 11-55)

W 313 MØGSTERFJORD

D: 768 grt **S:** 12 kts **Dim:** 60.86 (55.01 pp) × 12.0 × 3.9
A: 1/40-mm AA **M:** 1 Wichmann 9-cyl. diesel; 1 prop; 2,500 hp
Electric: 786 kw **Man:** . . .

REMARKS: Chartered from Kommandittelskapel Møgster in 1977. Bow-thruster.

♦ 1 former purse seiner Bldr: Beliard, Crighton & Cie., France (In serv. 1955)

W 314 STÅLBAS (ex-*Trålbas*, ex-*Cdt. Charcot*, ex-*Jean Charcot*)

D: 498 grt **S:** . . . **Dim:** 58.76 × 9.41 × 4.51
A: 1/40-mm AA **M:** 1 Klöckner-Humboldt-Deutz 8-cyl. diesel; 1 prop; 1,500 hp
Man: . . .

REMARKS: Side-thrusters fitted, fore and aft.

♦ 1 former whale-catcher Bldr: Fredrikstad MV (In serv. 1950)

W 316 VOLSTAD JR. (ex-XIV)

D: 617 grt **S:** . . . **Dim:** 51.39 (45.32 pp) × 9.05 × 5.67
A: 1/40-mm AA
M: 1 Klöckner-Humboldt-Deutz NE-66 8-cyl. diesel; 1 CP prop; 1,200 hp
Electric: 224 kw **Man:** . . .

REMARKS: Chartered from Einar Volstad Partrederi in 1977. Built as a side-haul
trawler, converted to a whaler in 1966, and well deck filled in.

♦ 1 former naval fisheries-protection ship

	Bldr	L
W 300 NORNEN	Mjellem & Karlsen, Bergen	20-8-62

Nornen (W 300)   1978

D: 1,060 tons (fl) **S:** 17 kts **Dim:** 61.5 × 10.0 × 3.8
A: 1/76.2-mm Mk 26 DP **M:** 4 diesels; 1 prop; 3,700 hp **Man:** 32 tot.

REMARKS: Considerably altered, 1976-77: bridge enlarged, stack heightened, mast
moved aft, hull side openings plated up, two new radars added, gun enclosed.

♦ 2 former naval fisheries-protection ships

	Bldr	L
W 301 FARM (ex-A 532)	Ankerlokken Verft, Fredrikstad	22-2-62
W 302 HEIMDAL (ex-A 534)	Bolsones Verft, Molde	7-3-62

D: 600 grt **S:** 16.5 kts **Dim:** 54.28 (49.0 pp) × 8.2 × 3.2
A: 1/40-mm AA **M:** 2 Wichmann 9ACAT diesels; 2 CP props; 2,400 hp
Electric: 150 kVA **Man:** 29 tot.

NORWAY (*continued*)
PATROL SHIPS (*continued*)

REMARKS: Modernized 1979 (W 301) and 1980 (W 302) with completely revised superstructure, new bridge resembling *Nornen*'s, new armament and revised hull sides along the forecastle.

NOTE: The following chartered Coast Guard ships were returned to their owners in 1980 on completion of their charter periods: *Kr. Tønder* (W 311, *Norviking* (W 315), and *Rig Tugger* (W 317).

The old Coast Guard patrol ships *Andenes* (W 303), *Senja* (W 304), and *Nordkapp* (W 305) were stricken from service during 1981.

HYDROGRAPHIC SURVEY SHIP

♦ **1 former Ministry of the Environment ship** Bldr: Mjellem & Karlsen, Bergen

HYDROGRAF (In serv. 12-67)

D: 302 grt **S:** 13 kts **Dim:** 38.95 (35.11 pp) × 7.83 × 2.94
A: 1/40-mm AA **M:** 1 Bergens Mek. Verk. 6-cyl. diesel; 1 prop; 780 hp
Electric: 100 kw **Fuel:** 38 tons **Range:** 3,900/13 **Man:** 3 officers, 15 men

REMARKS: Now operated by the Coast Guard for the Ministry of the Environment. No pendant number.

OMAN
Sultanate of Oman

PERSONNEL (1981): 1,500 total

MERCHANT MARINE (1980): 12 ships—6,953 grt

GUIDED-MISSILE PATROL BOATS

♦ **0 (+3) "Province" class** Bldr: Vosper Thornycroft, Portchester

	Laid down	L	In serv.
DHOFAR	30-9-80	14-10-81	7-82
N . . .	10-81	5-82	11-83
N . . .	12-81	7-82	1-84

Dhofar—artist's rendering　　　　　　Vosper Thornycroft, 1980

D: 311 tons light (363 fl) **S:** 40 kts **Dim:** 56.7 (52.0) × 8.2 × 2.1 (hull)
A: 6/MM 40 Exocet SSM (III × 2)—1/76-mm OTO Melara DP—2/40-mm Breda AA (II × 1)—2/12.7-mm mg (I × 2)
Electron Equipt: Radar: 1/Decca . . . , 1/Plessey AWS-4
M: 4 Paxman Valenta 18RP200 diesels; 4 props; 17,900 hp (15,000 sust.)
Electric: 420 kw **Fuel:** 45.5 tons **Range:** . . . **Man:** 59 tot.

REMARKS: *Dhofar* ordered 1980, others in 1-81. Will have Sperry Sea Archer Mk 2 fire-control system, with two optical trackers. Complement includes trainees.

♦ **2 37.5-m class** Bldr: Brooke Marine, Lowestoft

B 2 AL MANSUR (In serv. 26-3-73)　　B 3 AL NEJAH (In serv. 13-5-73)

Al Mansur (B 2)　　　　　　　　　　　　　　　　1980

D: 162 tons (184 fl) **S:** 25 kts **Dim:** 37.50 × 6.86 × 2.20
A: 2/MM 38 Exocet SSM (I × 2)—2/40-mm Breda AA (II × 1)—2/7.62-mm mg (I × 2)
Electron Equipt: Radar: 1/Decca 1229
M: 2 Paxman Ventura 16RP200 diesels; 2 props; 4,800 hp
Range: 3,250/12 **Man:** 4 officers, 28 men

REMARKS: Equipped with missiles during 11-77 to 11-78 refit by builder. Have Sperry Sea Archer fire-control systems. Sister *Al Bushra* (B 1) lost overboard in Bay of Biscay 11-78 while being transported to Oman after a similar conversion.

PATROL BOATS

♦ **4 37.5-meter class** Bldr: Brooke Marine Ltd., Lowestoft

	In serv.		In serv.
B 4 AL WAFI	24-3-77	B 6 AL AUL	20-7-77
B 5 AL FULK	24-3-77	B 7 AL JABBAR	6-10-77

D: 153 tons (166 fl) **S:** 25 kts **Dim:** 37.50 × 6.86 × 1.78
A: 1/76-mm OTO Melara DP—1/20-mm AA—2/7.62-mm mg (I × 2)
Electron Equipt: Radar: 1/Decca 1226 or 1229
M: 2 Paxman Ventura 16 RP200 diesels; 2 props; 4,800 hp
Range: 3,250/12 **Man:** 3 officers, 24 men

PATROL BOATS *(continued)*

Al Jabbar (B 7)   1980

REMARKS: Carry 130 rounds 76-mm ammunition. Sperry Sea Archer fire-control system, with Lawrence Scott optical director.

PATROL CRAFT

♦ **4 25-meter class** Bldr: Vosper, Singapore (In serv. 15-3-81)

B 20 SEEB   B 21 SHINAS   B 22 SADAH   B 23 KHASAB

D: ...   **S:** 26 kts   **Dim:** 25.0 (23.0 pp) × 5.8 × 1.5
A: 1/20-mm AA   **M:** 2 diesels; 2 props; ... hp
Range: 2,300/8   **Man:** 14 tot.

REMARKS: Ordered 24-4-81. Craft completed 1980 on speculation by builder. Glass reinforced plastic hulls. Pendant numbers B 21 to B 24.

♦ **2 Tyler Vortex class** Bldr: Cheverton, Cowes (In serv. 1981)

D: 12 tons   **S:** 30 kts   **Dim:** 12.1 (11.5 pp) × 4.6 × ...
A: ...   **M:** 2 Sabre 500 diesels; 2 props; 1,000 hp

NOTE: The two Dutch *Wildervank*-class former minesweepers, *Al Nassiri* (P 1) and *Al Salihi* (P 2), were sold during 1980.

AMPHIBIOUS WARFARE SHIPS

♦ **1 for logistic support**

	Bldr	Laid down	L	In serv.
L 1 AL MUNASSIR	Brooke Marine, Lowestoft	4-7-77	25-7-78	3-4-79

D: 2,000 tons (fl)   **S:** 12 kts   **Dim:** 84.0 (81.25 pp)× 15.03 × 2.15 (max.)
A: 1/76-mm OTO Melara DP—2/20-mm AA (I × 2)
Electron Equipt: Radar: 1/Decca TM 1229
M: 2 Mirrlees-Blackstone ESL8MGR diesels; 2 CP props; 2,400 hp
Range: 2,000/12   **Man:** 7 officers, 38 men, 188 troops

REMARKS: Greatly modified version of British *Ardennes* class by same builder. Cargo: 550 tons of stores or 8 heavy tanks. Has bow doors and ramp for beaching. Large helicopter deck aft can accommodate Westland Sea King or Commando helicopters and is spanned by a 16-ton-capacity traveling crane. Unusually bluff-bowed hull form. Sperry Sea Archer optical fire-control director.

Al Munassir (L 1)   1980

♦ **1 utility landing craft** Bldr: Vosper, Singapore (L: 30-6-81)

C 8 SABA AL BAHR

D: 230 tons (fl)   **S:** 8 kts   **Dim:** 30.0 × 8.0 × 1.2
M: 2 Caterpillar 3408 TA diesels; 2 props; ... hp
Range: 1,800/8

REMARKS: Ordered 24-4-81. Cargo: 100 tons vehicles or stores, or 45 tons deck cargo plus 50 tons fresh water (plus 35 tons water ballast).

♦ **1 utility landing craft** Bldr: Lewis Offshore, Stornaway, Scotland (In serv. 1979)

C 7 AL NEEMRAN

D: 85 dwt   **S:** 8 kts   **Dim:** 25.5 × 7.4 × 1.8   **M:** 2 diesels; ... hp

♦ **1 utility landing craft** Bldr: Impala Marine, Twickenham, G.B. (In serv. 1975)

C6 AL DHAIBAH

D: 122 grt (75 dwt)   **S:** 9 kts   **Dim:** 25.6 × 7.6 × 1.5
M: 2 Caterpillar 3406 diesels; 2 props; 520 hp

♦ **2 75-foot Loadmaster-class landing craft** Bldr: Cheverton, Cowes, G.B. (In serv. 1-75)

C 4 AL SANSOOR   C 5 AL DHOGAS (ex-*Kinzeer al Bahr*)

D: 64 tons (130 fl)   **S:** 8.75 kts   **Dim:** 22.86 × 6.1 × 1.07 (max.)
M: 2 diesels; 2 props; 300 hp

♦ **1 45-foot Loadmaster-class landing craft** Bldr: Cheverton, Cowes, G.B. (In serv. 1975)

C 3 SULHAFA AL BAHR

D: 45 tons   **S:** 8.5 kts   **Dim:** 13.7 × 4.6 × 0.9
M: 2 Perkins 4-236 diesels; 2 props; 240 hp

AUXILIARY SHIPS

♦ **1 royal yacht/transport**

	Bldr	L	In serv.
AL SAID	Brooke Marine, Lowestoft	7-4-70	1971

D: 785 tons (930 fl)   **S:** 17 kts   **Dim:** 54.70 × 10.70 × 3.05
A: 2/7.62-mm mg (I × 2)   **Electron Equipt:** Radar: 1/Decca TM 1226
M: 2 Paxman Ventura 12YJCM diesels; 2 props; 3,350 hp
Man: 11 officers, 23 men, 37 passengers

AUXILIARY SHIPS *(continued)*

Al Said 1980

REMARKS: Carries one Fairey "Spear" high-speed launch. Helicopter platform added aft at last refit, when 1/40-mm AA was removed.

♦ **1 supply and training ship**

	Bldr	L	In serv.
A 6 AL SULTANA	Conoship, Groningen, Netherlands	18-5-75	4-6-75

D: 900 tons (1,380 dwt) **S:** 11 kts **Dim:** 65.4 × 10.7 × 4.2
M: 1 Mirrlees-Blackstone diesel; 1,150 hp

REMARKS: Traveling crane serves all holds.

NOTE: The training ship *Dhofar* was sunk as an Exocet target 18-5-80.

♦ **3 inshore survey craft** Bldr: Watercraft, G.B. (In serv. 1981)

H 1 AL RAHMANYAT   H 2 N . . .   H 3 N . . .

D: 23.6 tons (fl) **S:** 13.5 kts **Dim:** 15.5 (14.0 pp) × 4.0 × 1.25
Electron Equipt: Radar: 1/Decca 101
M: 2 Volvo TMD 120A diesels; 2 props; 520 hp
Electric: 25 kVA **Range:** 500/12

REMARKS: H 1 in service 4-81, others later in year. Glass-reinforced plastic construction. Raytheon DE 719B and Kelvin-Hughes MS 48 echo sounders, Decca DMU transponder and Sea Fix receiver, and Hewlitt-Packard 9815A data storage computer fitted.

♦ **1 sail training craft**

S 1 SHABAB OMAN (ex-*Youth of Oman*, ex-*Captain Scott*)

REMARKS: Purchased in 1978.

ROYAL OMAN POLICE

PATROL CRAFT

♦ **2 CG 29 class** Bldr: Karlskrona, Sweden

HARAS 7 (In serv. 6-81)   HARAS 8 (In serv. 1982)

D: 80 tons (fl) **S:** 25 kts **Dim:** 28.7 × 5.2 × 1.1
A: 2/20-mm AA (I × 2) **Electron Equipt:** Radar: 1/Decca 1226C
M: 2 MTU 8V331 IC82 diesels; 2 props; 1,866 hp

REMARKS: Aluminum construction, enlarged version of design built for Liberia. Second unit ordered early 1981.

♦ **1 wooden 45-ft. class** Bldr: Watercraft, G.B. (In serv. 1980)

♦ **1 wooden-hulled** Bldr: Watercraft, Shoreham (In serv. 1980)

HARAS 6

D: 18 tons (fl) **S:** 25 kts **Dim:** 13.9 × 4.1 × 1.18
A: 1/7.62-mm mg **M:** 2 Cummins VTA-903-M diesels; 2 props; 710 hp
Range: 510/22

♦ **5 Haras 1-class fiberglass-hulled** Bldr: Vosper, Singapore (In serv.: 1-4: 22-12-75; 5: 11-78)

HARAS 1   HARAS 2   HARAS 3   HARAS 4   HARAS 5

Haras 1 1980

D: 45 tons (fl) **S:** 24.5 kts **Dim:** 22.9 × 6.0 × 1.5
A: 1/20-mm AA **Electron Equipt:** Radar: 1/Decca 101
M: 2 Caterpillar D348 diesels; 2 props; 1,840 hp
Range: 600/20; 1,000/11 **Man:** 11 tot.

♦ **7 Customs launches** Bldr: Cheverton, Cowes (In serv. 4-75)

W 1 through W 7

D: 3.3 tons (3.5 fl) **S:** 25 kts **Dim:** 8.23 × 2.74 × 0.81
M: 2 diesels; 2 props; 300 hp

PAKISTAN
Islamic Republic of Pakistan

PERSONNEL (1980): 950 officers, 10,050 men

MERCHANT MARINE (1980): 84 ships—478,019 grt

NAVAL AVIATION: The naval arm consists of: 3 Bréguet BR1150 Atlantic patrol aircraft, 6 SH-3 Sea King helicopters armed with AM-39 anti-ship missiles, 4 Alouette-III helicopters, and 2 Cessna liaison aircraft.

WARSHIPS IN SERVICE AND UNDER CONSTRUCTION
AS OF 1 JANUARY 1980

	L	Tons (Surfaced)	Main armament
◆ **6 submarines**			
2 AGOSTA	1977-79	1,490	4/550-mm TT
4 DAPHNÉ	1968-70	869	12/550-mm TT
◆ **1 training cruiser**			
1 MODIFIED DIDO	1942	5,900	8/133.5-mm DP, 6/533-mm TT
◆ **8 destroyers**			
4 GEARING FRAM I	1945	2,425	4/127-mm DP, 6/324-mm ASW TT
1 BATTLE	1945	2,325	4/114-mm DP, 8/533-mm TT
3 C	1944-45	1,710	3/114-mm DP, 4/533-mm TT

◆ **24 patrol and torpedo boats**

◆ **6 minesweepers**

SUBMARINES

◆ **2 French Agosta class** Bldr: Dubigeon, Nantes

	Laid down	L	In serv.
S 135 HASHMAT (ex-*Astrant*)	15-9-76	14-12-77	17-2-79
S 136 HURMAT (ex-*Adventurous*)	. . .	1-12-78	18-2-80

Hurmat (S 136)　　　　　　　　　　　　J.-C. Bellonne, 1980

D: 1,230/1,480/1,725 tons　**S:** 12.5/20.5 kts　**Dim:** 67.90 × 6.80 × 5.40
A: 4/550-mm TT, fwd (20 torpedoes)

Electron Equipt: Radar: 1/DRUA-33
　　　　　　　　Sonar: DUUA-1D, DUUA-2A, DSUV-2H, DUUA-2B, DUUX-2A
　　　　　　　　ECM: ARUR, ARUD
M: 2 SEMT-Pielstick A16 PA4 185 diesels, electric drive (1 3,500-kw motor); 1 prop; 4,600 hp; 1 23-hp cruise motor
Fuel: 200 tons　**Range:** 7,900/10 (snorkel); 178/3.5 (submerged)　**Man:** 55 tot.

REMARKS: Originally ordered for South Africa but sale canceled in 1977 by arms embargo and completion slowed. Sold to Pakistan in 11-78. Very quiet, highly automated submarines. Diving depth: 300 m. Battery capacity twice that of the *Daphné* class.

◆ **4 French Daphné class**

	Bldr	Laid down	L	In serv.
S 131 HANGOR	Arsenal de Brest	1-12-67	30-6-69	12-1-70
S 132 SHUSHUK	C. N. Ciotat, Le Trait	1-12-67	30-7-69	12-1-70
S 133 MANGRO	C. N. Ciotat, Le Trait	8-7-68	7-2-70	8-8-70
S 134 GHAZI (ex-*Cachalote*)	Dubigeon, Normandy	27-10-66	16-2-68	25-1-69

Ghazi (S 134)　　　　　　　　　　　　J.-C. Bellonne, 1977

D: 700/869/1,043 tons　**S:** 13.5/16 kts　**Dim:** 57.75 × 6.75 × 4.56
A: 12/550-mm TT (8 fwd, 4 aft), no reloads
Electron Equipt: Radar: DRUA 31
　　　　　　　　Sonar: DUUA—1 active, DSUV—1 passive
　　　　　　　　ECM: ARUR, ARUD
M: 2 SEMT-Pielstick 450-kw diesel generator sets; 2 1,300 hp (1,000 sust.) electric motors; 2 props
Man: 5 officers, 45 men

REMARKS: S 134 purchased in 12-75 from Portugal. S 131 sank the Indian frigate *Khukri* in 1971.

◆ **5 SX-404-class midget submarines** Bldr: COS.MO.S., Livorno, Italy

D: 40/70 tons　**S:** 11/6.5 kts　**Dim:** 16.0 × 1.8 × . . .
A: 2/533-mm torpedoes or 6-8 mines
Range: 1,200/11 surfaced, 60/6.5 submerged　**Man:** 4 tot.

REMARKS: Used for the transport of up to twelve raiders. A sixth sank 27-12-76 following an accident at sea. A number of 2-man Chariots from the same builder are also in service.

CRUISER

♦ **1 British modified Dido class**

	Bldr	Laid down	L	In serv.
C 84 BABUR (ex-*Diadem*)	Hawthorn, Leslie & Co.	15-11-39	26-8-42	6-1-44

Babur (C 84)   1976

D: 5,900 tons (7,560 fl)   **S:** 20 kts   **Dim:** 165.05 (154.23 pp) × 15.7 × 5.7
A: 8/133.5-mm DP (II × 4)—12/40-mm (II × 3, I × 6)—6/533-mm TT (III × 2)—4/47-mm (saluting battery)
Electron Equipt: Radar: 1/293Q, 1/975, 1/Marconi SNW-10, 1/274, 2/285
M: 4 sets Parsons GT; 4 props; 62,000 hp (when new)
Armor: Belt: 52-76-mm Deck: 52-mm Turrets: 25-mm Bridge: 25-mm
Boilers: 4 Admiralty, three-drum   **Fuel:** 1,100 tons
Range: 3,800/20; 7,400/12   **Man:** Peacetime: 590 tot.

REMARKS: Purchased 29-2-56. Adapted for use as training cruiser during refit in 1961. In poor condition and no longer able to make original speed of 32 kts. Now used primarily as a floating antiaircraft battery.

DESTROYERS

♦ **4 (+2) ex-U.S. Gearing class, FRAM-I** Bldrs: 165, 166: Federal SB & DD Co., Newark, N.J.; 167: Bethlehem, Staten Island; 168: Todd, Seattle

	Laid down	L	In serv.
D 165 TARIQ (ex-*Wiltsie*, DD 716)	13-3-45	31-8-45	12-1-46
D 166 TAIMUR (ex-*Epperson*, DD 719)	20-6-45	29-12-45	19-3-49
D 167 TIPPU SULTAN (ex-*Damato*, DD 871)	10-5-45	21-11-45	27-4-46
D 168 TUGHRIL (ex-*Henderson*, DD 785)	27-10-44	28-5-45	4-8-45

D: 2,425 tons (3,460 fl)   **S:** 30 kts   **Dim:** 119.0 × 12.45 × 5.8 (max.)
A: 4/127-mm DP (II × 2)—1/ASROC ASW RL (VIII × 1; 17 missiles)—6/324-mm Mk 32 ASW TT (III × 2)
Electron Equipt: Radar: 1/LN-66, 1/SPS-10B, 1/SPS-40, 1/Mk 25
        Sonar: SQS-23D
        ECM: WLR-3, ULQ-6
M: 2 sets GE GT; 2 props; 60,000 hp   **Electric:** 1,300 kw
Boilers: 4 Babcock & Wilcox; 39.8 kg/cm², 454°C   **Fuel:** 600 tons

REMARKS: First two sold to Pakistan 29-4-77, then extensively overhauled at Puget Sound Navy Yard, 165 being completed 2-6-78, and 166 on 16-2-78. Second pair transferred 30-9-80. Two more to be purchased 1982-83.

♦ **1 ex-British Battle class**

	Bldr	Laid down	L	In serv.
D 161 BADR (ex-*Gabbard*)	Swan Hunter	2-2-44	16-3-45	10-12-46

Badr (D 161)   1974

D: 2,325 tons (3,360 fl)   **S:** 31 kts   **Dim:** 115.32 (108.2 pp) × 12.95 × 4.1
A: 4/114-mm DP (II × 2)—8/40-mm AA (II × 2, I × 4)—4/533-mm TT (IV × 1)—1/Mk 4 Squid ASW mortar (III × 1)
Electron Equipt: Radar: 1/975, 1/293Q, 1/Marconi SNW-10, 1/275
        Sonar: 1/170, 1/174
M: 2 Parsons GT; 2 props; 50,000 hp   **Boilers:** 2 Admiralty, three-drum
Fuel: 680 tons   **Range:** 3,200/20   **Man:** 300 tot.

REMARKS: Transferred 29-2-56. Sister ship *Khaibar* was sunk during the Indo-Pakistani conflict, 1971.

♦ **3 ex-British C class** Bldrs: D 160, D 162: J. Samuel White, Cowes; D 164: J. I. Thornycroft, Woolston

	Laid down	L	In serv.
D 160 ALAMGIR (ex-*Creole*)	3-8-44	22-11-45	14-10-46
D 162 JAHANGIR (ex-*Crispin*)	1-2-44	23-6-45	10-7-46
D 164 SHAH JAHAN (ex-U.S. DD 962, ex-*Charity*)	9-7-43	30-11-44	19-11-45

Jahangir (D 162)   1971

D: 1,710 tons (2,500 fl)   **S:** 31 kts   **Dim:** 110.55 (106.07 pp) × 10.88 × 3.8
A: 3/114-mm DP (I × 3)—6/40-mm AA (II × 1, I × 4)—4/533-mm TT (IV × 1)—2/Squid ASW mortars (III × 2)
Electron Equipt: Radar: 1/975, 1/293Q, 1/275
        Sonar: 1/174, 1/170
M: 2 sets Parsons GT; 2 props; 40,000 hp   **Boilers:** 2 Admiralty, three-drum
Fuel: 580 tons   **Range:** 1,000/30, 2,800/20   **Man:** 200 tot.

DESTROYERS (continued)

REMARKS: From two groups within the C class, CH and CR. Minor differences. D 164 was purchased by the U.S. from Great Britain in 1958 (hence DD 962 hull number), then turned over to Pakistan in 16-12-58. The other two were turned over directly in 1956 and then modernized with U.S. funds. Mk 6 GFCS for 114-mm guns.

NOTE: The frigate *Tippu Sultan* (260) was stricken 1980, with her stripped hulk being retained as a work platform.

GUIDED-MISSILE PATROL BOATS

♦ 4 Chinese Hoku class

D: 68 tons (80 fl)   **S:** 38 kts   **Dim:** 28.0 × 6.3 × 1.8
A: 2/SS-N-2a Styx SSM (I × 2)—2/25-mm AA (II × 1)
Electron Equipt: Radar: 1/Pot Head
M: 4 M50-F4 diesels; 4 props; 4,800 hp   **Range:** 200/25   **Man:** 20 tot.

REMARKS: Transferred mid-1981.

PATROL BOATS

♦ 4 Hainan class   Bldr: People's Republic of China

P 155 BALUCHISTAN   P 159 SIND   P . . . PUNJAB   P . . . SARHAD

Baluchistan (P 155)   1978

D: 360 tons (400 fl)   **S:** 30.5 kts   **Dim:** 58.77 × 7.20 × 2.20
A: 4/57-mm AA (II × 2)—4/25-mm AA (II × 2)—4/RBU-1200 ASW RL (V × 4)—2/d.c. throwers—2/d.c. racks—mines
Electron Equipt: Radar: 1/Pot Head   Sonar: . . .
M: 4 Type 9D diesels; 4 props; 8,800 hp   **Range:** 1,000/10   **Man:** 60 tot.

REMARKS: First pair transferred in 1976, *Punjab* and *Sarhad* in 4-80. Very primitive ships.

♦ 12 Shanghai-II class   Bldr: People's Republic of China

P 140 LAHORE	P 145 PISHIN	P 154 BANNU
P 141 QUETTA	P 147 SUKKUR	P 156 KALAT
P 143 MARDAN	P 148 SEHWAN	P 159 LARKANA
P 144 GUILGIT	P 149 BAHAWALPUR	P 160 SAHIVAL

D: 122.5 tons (150 fl)   **S:** 28.5 kts   **Dim:** 38.78 × 5.41 × 1.49 (hull)
A: 4/37-mm AA (II × 2)—4/25-mm AA (II × 2)—mines
Electron Equipt: Radar: 1/Pot Head
M: 2 M50-F4, 1,200 hp diesels, 2 12D6, 910 hp diesels; 4 props; 4,220 hp
Man: 38 tot.

Quetta (P 141)   1974

REMARKS: Eight transferred in 1972, four in 1973. Very primitive ships.

TORPEDO BOATS

♦ 4 Huchwan-class hydrofoils   Bldr: People's Republic of China

HDF 01   HDF 02   HDF 03   HDF 04

HDF 03   1973

D: 39 tons   **S:** 54 kts   **Dim:** 21.8 × 4.9 (7.5 over foils) × 1.0 (0.31 foilborne)
A: 4/14.5-mm AA (II × 2)—2/533-mm TT
Electron Equipt: Radar: 1/Skin Head   **M:** 3 M50F diesels; 3 props; 3,600 hp

REMARKS: Maintained in land storage to prevent corrosion.

PATROL CRAFT

♦ 18 MV55 class   Bldr: Crestitalia, Ameglia, Italy (In serv. 1979-80)

P 551-568

D: 22.8 tons (fl)   **S:** 30 kts   **Dim:** 16.5 × 5.2 × 0.88   **Man:** 5 tot.
A: 1/14.5-mm mg   **M:** 2 V-6 diesels; 2 props; 1,600 hp   **Range:** 425/25

REMARKS: Glass-reinforced plastic construction. P 553 named *Vaqar;* others presumably also named.

MINE WARFARE SHIPS

♦ 6 ex-U.S. coastal minesweepers

Ex-MSC 289 class   Bldr: Peterson Bldrs, Sturgeon Bay, Wisconsin

MINE WARFARE SHIPS (continued)

	In serv.		In serv.
M 161 Momin (ex-MSC 293)	7-62	M 167 Moshal (ex-MSC 294)	6-63

Ex-Falcon class: Bldrs: M 160: Quincy Adams Yacht, Quincy, Mass.; M 162, 164: Hodgdon Bros., East Boothbay, Maine; M 165: Bellingham SY, Bellingham, Wash.

	In serv.		In serv.
M 160 Mahmood (ex-MSC 267)	4-57	M 164 Mujahid (ex-MSC 261)	10-56
M 162 Murabak (ex-MSC 262)	1-57	M 165 Mukhtar (ex-MSC 274)	7-59

Mukhtar (M 165) 1974

D: 320 tons (372 fl) **S:** 13 kts (8, sweeping) **Dim:** 43.0 × 7.95 × 2.55
A: 4/23-mm AA ZSU-23 (IV × 1)
Electron Equipt: Radar: 1/Decca 45
Sonar: UQS-1D
M: 2 GM 8-268A diesels; 2 props; 1,200 hp **Range:** 2,500/10 **Man:** 39 tot.

REMARKS: M 161 and 167 have low bridges, the others have high, open bridges. Wooden hulls. All built under the Military Assistance Program. *Munsif* (M 166, ex-MSC 273) stricken 1979.

AUXILIARY SHIPS

♦ **0 (+1) oceanographic research ship** Ordered 15-4-81. No other data available.

♦ **1 hydrographic ship, ex-"River"-class frigate** Bldr: Smith's Dock, G.B.

	Laid down	L	In serv.
F 262 Zulfiquar (ex-Indian *Dhanush*, ex-British *Deveron*)	18-6-42	12-10-42	2-3-43

D: 1,370 tons (2,100 fl) **S:** 19 kts **Dim:** 91.84 × 11.17 × 4.34
A: 1/102-mm DP—2/40-mm AA (I × 2)
M: 2 sets triple-expansion; 2 props; 5,500 hp **Man:** 150 tot.
Boilers: 2 Admiralty, three-drum **Fuel:** 646 tons **Range:** 7,500/15, 11,900/10

REMARKS: Transferred to India during World War II and to Pakistan after the war. Very little altered from frigate configuration; charthouse and 2/40-mm antiaircraft mounts in place of after 102-mm guns.

♦ **0 (+1) U.S. Klondike-class destroyer tender** Bldr: Los Angeles SB

	Laid down	L	In serv.
. . . N . . . (ex-*Everglades*, AD 24)	26-4-44	28-1-45	25-5-51

D: 8,165 tons (14,700 fl) **S:** 18 kts **Dim:** 149.96 (141.73 pp) × 21.25 × 8.30
A: None at transfer **Electron Equipt:** Radar: 1/SPS-10 **Fuel:** 2,415 tons
M: 1 set Westinghouse GT; 1 prop; 8,500 hp **Electric:** 3,600 kw
Boilers: 2 Foster-Wheeler; 30.6 kg/cm², 393°C **Man:** 800-918 tot.

REMARKS: Scheduled for sale to Pakistan during 1982. Has been used as an accommodations ship at Philadelphia for some years, in reserve. Will be used to support Pakistan's growing destroyer force. Has helo deck and small hangar aft.

♦ **1 ex-U.S. T-2-class replenishment oiler** Bldr: Marinship Corp., Sausalito, Calif.

A 41 Dacca (ex-*Mission Santa Clara*, TAO 132) (In serv. 21-6-44)

Dacca (A 41)—with Hangor (S 131) alongside 1975

D: 5,730 tons light (22,380 fl) **S:** 15 kts **Dim:** 159.56 × 20.73 × 9.4
A: 6/40-mm AA (I × 6) **Electron Equipt:** Radar: 1/RCA CRM-NIA-75
M: 1 set GE GT, electric drive; 1 prop; 10,000 hp **Electric:** 1,150 kw
Boilers: 2 Combustion Engineering "D"; 42 kg/cm², 440°C **Fuel:** 1,300 tons
Man: 15 officers, 145 men

REMARKS: Acquired by U.S. Navy 11-5-47. Loaned 17-1-63, after conversion to permit underway replenishment alongside, one station each side. Bought outright 31-5-74. Cargo: 15,300 tons.

♦ **1 ex-U.S. Cherokee-class ocean tug** Bldr: Commercial Iron Works, Portland, Ore.

	Laid down	L	In serv.
A 42 Madadgar (ex-*Yuma*, ATF 94)	13-2-43	17-7-43	31-8-43

D: 1,325 tons (1,675 fl) **S:** 16.5 kts **Dim:** 62.48 (59.44 pp) × 11.73 × 4.67
A: 2/40-mm AA (I × 2)—1/20-mm AA **Electron Equipt:** Radar: 1/Decca 45
M: 4 GM 12-278 diesels, electric drive; 1 prop; 3,000 hp **Electric:** 260 kw
Fuel: 295 tons **Man:** 85 tot.

REMARKS: Employed as a salvage and rescue tug.

♦ **1 large harbor tug** Bldr: Worstd Dutmer, Meppel, Netherlands (L: 29-11-55)

A 43 Rustom

D: 530 tons (fl) **S:** 9.5 kts **Dim:** 32.0 × 9.1 × 3.3
M: 1 Crossley diesel; 1 prop; 1,000 hp **Range:** 3,000/8 **Man:** 21 tot.

♦ **2 small harbor tugs** Bldr: Costaguta-Voltz, Italy (In serv. 9-58)

Gama (ex-U.S. YTL 754) Bholu (ex-U.S. YTL 755)

REMARKS: Built under the U.S. Offshore Procurement Program. 300 hp.

PAKISTAN *(continued)*
AUXILIARY SHIPS *(continued)*

Madadgar (A 42)—note 20-mm AA before bridge   J-C. Bellonne, 1977

◆ **1 harbor oiler** Bldr: Trieste, Italy (In serv. 5-60)

A 40 ATTOCK (ex-U.S. YO 249)

   D: 600 tons (1,225 fl) **S:** 8 kts **Dim:** 54.0 × 9.8 × 4.6
   A: 2/20-mm AA (I × 2) **M:** 2 diesels; 2 props; 800 hp

REMARKS: Built under the U.S. Offshore Procurement Program. Cargo: 6,500 barrels.

◆ **1 water tanker** Bldr: Italy, 1957

A 46 ZUM ZUM

REMARKS: Characteristics very similar to those of small oiler *Attock* above.

◆ **1 degaussing tender** Bldr: Karachi DY (In serv. 1979)

   D: 260 tons (fl) **S:** 10 kts **Dim:** 35.22 (34.0 wl) × 7.00 × 2.4
   M: 1 diesel; 1 prop; 375 hp **Man:** 5 tot.

REMARKS: Built with French technical assistance and very similar in design to French
   Navy's Y 732. Wooden hull.

◆ **1 new-construction floating dry dock** Bldr: Karachi DY (In serv. 1981)

N . . .

   Lift capacity: 2,000 tons

◆ **1 U.S. ARD-2-class floating dry dock** Bldr: Pacific Bridge, Alameda (In serv. 4-
43)

PESHAWAR (ex-ARD 6)

   Dim: 148.03 × 21.64 × 1.6 (light) **Lift capacity:** 3,500 tons

REMARKS: Transferred 6-61.

◆ **1 small floating dry dock** (In serv. 1974)

FD II **Lift capacity:** 1,200 tons

PANAMA

Republic of Panama

MERCHANT MARINE (1980): 4,090 ships—24,190,680 grt (tankers: 371 ships—6,783,133
grt)

NATIONAL GUARD

PATROL BOATS AND CRAFT

◆ **2 103-foot boats** Bldr: Vosper Thornycroft, Portsmouth, G.B. (In serv. 3-71)

GC 10 PANQUIACO (L: 22-7-70) GC 11 LIGIA ELENA (L: 25-8-70)

   D: 96 tons (123 fl) **S:** 24 kts **Dim:** 31.25 × 6.02 × 1.98
   A: 2/20-mm AA (I × 2) **Electron Equipt:** Radar: 1/Decca 916
   M: 2 Paxman Ventura 12-YJCM diesels; 2 props; 2,800 hp **Electric:** 80 kVA
   Man: 23 tot.

◆ **2 ex-U.S. Coast Guard 40-foot Mk 1-class utility boats** (In serv. 1950)

GC 14 MARTI GC 15 JUPITER

   D: 13 tons (fl) **S:** 18 kts **Dim:** 12.3 × 3.4 × 1.0
   A: 1/12.7-mm mg **M:** 2 GM 6-71 diesels; 2 props; 300 hp
   Range: 160/8 **Man:** 4 tot.

REMARKS: Transferred in 1962.

◆ **2 ex-U.S. 63-foot AVR class**

GC 12 AYANASI GC 13 ZARTI

   D: 35 tons (fl) **S:** 22.5 kts **Dim:** 19.3 × 4.7 × 1.0
   A: 2/12.7-mm mg (I × 2) **Electron Equipt:** Radar: 1/Raytheon 1500B
   M: 2 GM 8V-71 diesels; 2 props; 900 hp **Man:** 8 tot.

REMARKS: In service in 1943 and transferred 1965-66.

PANAMA (*continued*)

AUXILIARY SHIPS AND CRAFT

♦ **1 ex-U.S. LSMR-class rocket-assault ship** Bldr: Brown SB Co., Houston

	Laid down	L	In serv.
GC 10 TIBURON (ex-*Smokey Hill River*, LSMR 531)	2-6-45	7-7-45	21-9-45

D: 2,084 tons (fl) **S:** 12 kts **Dim:** 62.87 × 10.52 × 2.18
A: None **M:** 2 GM 16-278A diesels; 2 props; 2,800 hp
Electric: 440 kw **Man:** . . .

REMARKS: Purchased from a commercial source 14-3-75 and used for logistics-support duties. May have had bow doors added, although as completed she had none and had her well deck plated over. Cargo: approximately 400 tons.

♦ **2 logistics-support landing craft** Bldr: France, 1978

GN . . .   GN . . .

D: 60 tons (fl) **S:** 9 kts **Dim:** 12.6 × . . . × . . .
M: 2 SKL 8NVD26 diesels; 2 props; 400 hp

♦ **3 ex-U.S. Army LCM (8)-class landing craft**

GN 1   GN 2   GN 3

D: 115 tons (fl) **S:** 9 kts **Dim:** 22.7 × 6.4 × 1.4
A: None **M:** 4 GM 6-71 diesels; 2 props; 600 hp **Man:** 6 tot.

REMARKS: Transferred 1972. Used for logistics-support duties. Two-level superstructure aft.

♦ **1 ex-U.S. YF-852-class cargo lighter**

	Bldr	Laid down	L	In serv.
N . . . (ex-YF 886)	Defoe SB, Bay City, Michigan	13-4-45	25-5-45	4-8-45

D: 590 tons (fl) **S:** 11 kts **Dim:** 40.23 × 9.1 × 2.7
M: 2 GM 6-71 diesels; 2 props; 600 hp **Man:** 11 tot.

REMARKS: Transferred 5-75. Cargo: 250 tons.

♦ **1 former shrimp boat,** used for logistics support

GN 8

S: 11 kts **Capacity:** 150 passengers

PAPUA NEW GUINEA

MERCHANT MARINE (1980): 27 ships—23,019 grt
(tankers: 4 ships—1,575 grt)

NAVAL AVIATION: The Papua New Guinea Defense Force operates 7 Nomad N.22B light transports and 1 DC-3 transport for coastal patrol and logistics duties.

PATROL BOATS

♦ **4 ex-Australian Attack class**

	Bldr	In serv.
P 85 SAMARAI	Evans Deakin, Queensland	1-3-68
P 92 LADAVA	Walkers Ltd., Maryborough	21-10-68
P 93 LAE	Evans Deakin, Queensland	3-4-68
P 94 MADANG	Evans Deakin, Queensland	28-11-68

D: 146 tons (fl) **S:** 21-24 kts **Dim:** 32.76 (30.48 pp) × 6.2 × 1.9
A: 1/40-mm AA—2/7.62-mm mg (I × 2)
Electron Equipt: Radar: 1/Decca RM916
M: 2 Davey-Paxman Ventura 16-YJCM diesels; 3,500 hp **Fuel:** 20 tons
Range: 1,220/13 **Man:** 18 tot.

REMARKS: Transferred in 1975. *Aitape* (P 84) stricken 1981 for spares.

AMPHIBIOUS WARFARE SHIPS

♦ **2 ex-Australian Balikpapan-class utility landing craft** Bldr: Walkers, Maryborough

31 SALAMAUA   32 BUNA

Salamaua (31)   G. Gyssels, 1980

PAPUA NEW GUINEA *(continued)*
AMPHIBIOUS WARFARE SHIPS *(continued)*

D: 310 tons (503 fl) **S:** 8 kts **Dim:** 44.5 × 12.2 × 1.9
A: 2/12.7-mm mg (I × 2) **M:** 3 GM 12V71 diesels; 3 props; 675 hp
Range: 1,300-2,280/10 depending on load **Man:** 2 officers, 11 men

REMARKS: In service in 1972 and transferred 1975. Cargo: 140-180 tons.

♦ **7 Kokuba-class personnel landing craft** Bldr: Australia (In serv. 1975)

KOKUBA	KUTUBA	KIAIPIT	KANDEP
KUNIAWA	KIUNGA	KUKIPI	

D: 12 tons (fl) **S:** 9 kts **Dim:** 12.0 × 4.0 × 1.0
M: 2 Gardner diesels; 2 props; 150 hp

♦ **1 ex-Australian tug** Bldr: Perrin, Brisbane, 1972

SHT 503 (ex-503)

D: 47.5 tons **S:** 9 kts **Dim:** 15.4 × 4.6 × . . .
M: 2 GM diesels; 2 props; 340 hp **Man:** 3 tot.

REMARKS: Transferred in 1974.

♦ **1 water tanker** Bldr: Australia (In serv. 1945)

MVL 256 (ex-256)

D: 300 tons (600 fl) **S:** 9.5 kts **Dim:** 36.5 × 7.3 × . . .
M: 2 Ruston & Hornsby diesels; 2 props; 440 hp

PARAGUAY
Republic of Paraguay

PERSONNEL (1981): 2,000 total, including 500 Marines

MERCHANT MARINE (1980): 27 ships—23,019 grt
(tankers: 3 ships—2,935 grt)

NAVAL AVIATION: 4 H-13 Sioux helicopters, 2 AT-6 Texan trainers, 3 Cessna U-206 and 1 Cessna 150M light utility aircraft

RIVER GUNBOATS

♦ **3 ex-Argentinian Bouchard-class ocean minesweepers**

	Bldr	L
M. 1 NANAWA (ex-*Bouchard*)	Rio Santiago NY	20-3-36
M. 2 CAPITÁN MEZA (ex-*Parker*)	Sanchez, San Fernando	2-5-37
M. 3 TENIENTE FARINA (ex-*Py*)	Rio Santiago NY	30-3-38

D: 450 tons (650 fl) **S:** 16 kts **Dim:** 59.5 × 7.3 × 2.6
A: 4/40-mm AA (II × 2)—2/12.7-mm mg—mines
M: 2 M.A.N. diesels; 2 props; 2,000 hp **Range:** 3,000/12 **Man:** 70 tot.

REMARKS: Transferred: M. 1 and M. 3 on 5-3-68, M. 2 in 2-64.

♦ **2 Paraguay class** Bldr: Odero, Genoa (In serv. 5-31)

C. 1 PARAGUAY (ex-*Comodoro Meya*) C. 2 HUMAITÁ (ex-*Capitán Cabral*)

Humaitá (C. 2)—in floating dry dock DF. 1   1970

D: 636 tons, 745 avg. (865 fl) **S:** 17.5 kts **Dim:** 70.15 × 10.7 × 1.65
A: 4/120-mm (II × 2)—3/76.2-mm AA (I × 3)—2/40-mm AA (I × 2)—6 mines
M: 2 sets Parsons GT; 2 props; 3,800 hp **Boilers:** 2
Fuel: 170 tons **Range:** 1,700/16 **Man:** 86 tot.

A. 1 CAPITÁN CABRAL (ex-*Adolfo Riquelme*) Bldr: Werf Conrad, Haarlem (In serv. 1908)

D: 206 tons (fl) **S:** 9 kts **Dim:** 30.5 × 7.0 × 2.9
A: 1/76.2-mm—2/37-mm **M:** Reciprocating; 300 hp **Man:** 47 tot.

REMARKS: Wooden hull, former tug, used for riverine patrol on the Upper Paraña River.

PATROL CRAFT

♦ **6 small craft** Bldr: Sewart Seacraft, Berwick, La.

PT. 101 PT. 102 PT. 103 PT. 104 PT. 105 PT. 106

D: 15 tons (fl) **S:** 20 kts **S:** 13.1 × 3.9 × 0.9
A: 2/12.7-mm mg **M:** 2 GM G-71 diesels; 2 props; 500 hp **Man:** 7 tot.

REMARKS: PT. 101 and PT. 102 in service in 12-67; PT. 103, PT. 104, and PT. 105, in 9-70; and PT. 106, in 3-71.

AUXILIARY SHIPS

♦ **1 repair/headquarters ship** Bldr: Brown SB, Houston

	Laid down	L	In serv.
BC. 1 BOQUERON (ex-*Teniente Pratt Gil*, PH. 1, ex-*Corrientes*, ex-LSM 86)	22-8-44	15-9-44	13-10-44

PARAGUAY (*continued*)
AUXILIARY SHIPS (*continued*)

D: 743 tons (1,095 fl)   **S:** 12.6 kts   **Dim:** 61.88 × 10.51 × 2.54
A: 2/40-mm AA (II × 1)
M: 2 Fairbanks-Morse 38D8⅛ × 10 diesels; 2 props; 2,800 hp
Electric: 240 kw   **Man:** . . .

REMARKS: An ex-U.S. LSM-1-class landing ship donated by Argentina on 13-1-72, after conversion to a command and repair ship. Well deck plated over to create a helicopter deck aft; superstructure enlarged and moved to the centerline. Renamed 1980.

♦ **1 cargo and training ship** Bldr: Tomas Ruiz de Velasco, Bilboa, Spain (In serv. 2-68)

GUARANI

D: 714 grt/1,047 dwt   **S:** 12.2 kts   **Dim:** 73.6 × 11.9 × 3.7
M: 1 diesel; 1 prop; 1,300 hp

REMARKS: Purchased and refitted in 1974 to provide seagoing experience for naval cadets and to engage in commercial voyages to raise revenue for running the navy. Cargo: approximately 1,000 tons.

♦ **2 ex-U.S. LCU-501-class landing craft** (In serv. circa 1944-45)

BT. 1 (ex-YFB 82, ex-LCU. . .)   BT. 2 (ex-YFB 86, ex-LCU. . .)

D: 143 tons (309 fl)   **S:** 10 kts   **Dim:** 36.3 × 9.8 × 1.2 (aft)
M: 3 Gray Marine 64YTL diesels; 3 props; 675 hp

REMARKS: Transferred in 6-70. Used for logistics duties. Cargo: 125 tons.

♦ **2 ex-U.S. 64-foot YTL-422-class tugs**

	Bldr	Laid down	L	In serv.
R. 5 (ex-YTL 211)	Robert Jacob, Inc.	26-12-41	20-6-42	21-8-42
R. 6 (ex-YTL 567)	Gunderson Bros.	5-3-45	17-8-45	30-10-45

D: 84 tons   **S:** 9 kts   **Dim:** 20.2 × 5.5 × 2.4   **M:** 1 diesel; 300 hp   **Man:** 5 tot.

REMARKS: Transferred in 3-67 and 4-74.

♦ **1 ex-U.S. floating dry dock** Bldr: Doullut & Ewin, Mobile, Ala. (In serv. 6-44)

N . . . (ex-AFDL 26)

Dim: 60.96 × 19.5 × 1.04 (light)   **Lifting capacity:** 1,000 tons

REMARKS: Transferred in 3-65.

♦ **1 ex-U.S. floating workshop**

	Bldr	Laid down	L	In serv.
N . . . (ex-YR 37)	Mare Island Naval SY	14-12-41	12-1-42	15-5-42

D: 600 tons (fl)   **Dim:** 45.72 × 10.36 × 1.8   **Electric:** 210 kw   **Man:** 47 tot.

REMARKS: Transferred 3-63.

♦ **3 dredges**

D. 1 N . . . (In serv. 1907)—140 tons, 30 crew
D. 2 TENIENTE O CARRERAS SAGUIER (In serv. 1957)—110 tons, 19 crew
RP. 1 N . . . (In serv. 1908)—107 tons, 29 crew

PERU
Republic of Peru

PERSONNEL (1981): 2,000 officers, 18,500 men, plus 1,400 officers and men of the Naval Infantry

MERCHANT MARINE (1980): 698 ships—740,510 grt   (tankers: 15 ships—130,568 grt)

NAVAL AVIATION: The air arm consists of the following helicopters and fixed-wing aircraft: 6 AM-39 Exocet SSM-equipped SH-3D Sea King, 6 Agusta-Bell AB 212, 10 Bell 206 JetRanger, 20 Bell UH-1, 2 Bell 47G, and 2 Alouette-III helicopters; 9 Grumman S-2 Tracker ASW aircraft, 6 C-47 transports, 1 Piper Aztec liaison aircraft, and 2 Beech T-34 trainers. 4 aging HU-16B Albatross patrol amphibians operated by the Air Force were to be replaced by Fokker F-27 Maritime patrol aircraft beginning in 1981.

WARSHIPS IN SERVICE AND UNDER CONSTRUCTION
AS OF 1 JANUARY 1982

	L	Tons (surfaced)	Main armament
♦ **10 (+2) submarines**			
4 (+2) TYPE 209	1973-1982	980-1,000	8/533-mm TT
4 DOS DE MAYO	1953-57	825	6/533-mm TT, 1/127-mm DP (on two units)
2 GUPPY-IA	1944	1,830	10/533-mm TT
♦ **3 cruisers**		(Std)	
1 AGUIRRE	1950	9,850	4/152-mm DP, 6/57-mm AA, 4/40-mm AA, 3 helicopters
1 ALMIRANTE GRAU	1944	9,529	8/152-mm DP, 8/57-mm AA
1 COLONIES	1942	8,781	9/152-mm, 8/102-mm DP
♦ **9 (+1) destroyers**			
2 DARING	1949-52	2,800	8/MM 38 Exocet, 4/114-mm
6 FRIESLAND	1954-56	2,496	4/20-mm DP, 4/40-mm AA
1 HOLLAND	1953	2,215	4/120-mm DP, 1/40-mm AA
♦ **2 (+2) frigates**			
2 (+2) LUPO TYPE	1976-. . .	2,208	8/Otomat, 1/Albatros SAM system, 1/127-mm DP
♦ **6 guided-missile corvettes**			
6 PR 72	1978-79	560	4/MM 38 Exocet, 1/76-mm DP, 2/40-mm AA
6 PR 72	1978-79	560	4/MM 38 Exocet, 1/76-mm DP, 2/40-mm AA

SUBMARINES

♦ **4 (+2) German Type 209** Bldr: Howaldtswerke, Kiel

	L	In serv.		L	In serv.
S 45 ISLAY	11-10-73	23-1-75	S 32 ANTOFAGASTA	19-12-79	14-3-80
S 46 ARICA	5-4-74	4-4-75	S 33 BLUME	. . .	. . .
S 31 CASMA	31-8-79	19-12-80	S 34 PISAGUA	7-8-81	. . .

SUBMARINES (continued)

Antofagasta (S 32)   G. Gyssels, 1981

D: 980/1,230 tons **S:** 21 kts for 5 minutes, submerged, 12 with snorkel
Dim: 55.0 × 6.6 × 5.9 **A:** 8/533-mm TT—6 torpedoes in reserve
M: 4 MTU Type 12V493 TY60 diesels, each linked to a 450-kw AEG generator,
  1 Siemans electric motor; 1 prop; 3,600 hp
Man: 5 officers, 26 men

REMARKS: S 31 and S 32 were ordered 12-8-76, and two more in 3-77. S 31 and later
are 56.0-m overall, 1,000 tons surfaced.

♦ **4 Dos de Mayo class** Bldr: General Dynamics, Groton, Conn.

	Laid down	L	In serv.
S 41 Dos De Mayo (ex-*Lobo*)	12-5-52	6-2-54	14-6-54
S 42 Abtao (ex-*Tiburon*)	12-5-52	27-10-53	20-2-54
S 43 Angamos (ex-*Atun*)	27-10-55	5-2-57	1-7-57
S 44 Iquique (ex-*Merlin*)	27-10-55	5-2-57	1-10-57

Angamos (S 43)

D: 825/1,400 tons **S:** 16/10 kts **Dim:** 74.1 × 6.7 × 4.2
A: S 41, S 42: 1/127-mm DP—6/533-mm TT (4 fwd, 2 aft)
Electron Equipt: Radar: 1/SS-2A Sonar: BQR-3, BQA-1A
M: 2 GM 12-278A diesels, 2 electric motors; 2 props; 2,400 hp
Fuel: 45 tons **Range:** 5,000/10 (snorkel) **Man:** 40 tot.

REMARKS: Patterned after the U.S. *Marlin* class of 1941. These were the last U.S.
submarines to be built for a foreign customer. S 41 and S 42 were refitted in 1965,
S 43 and S 44 in 1968. The 127-mm gun carried by S 41 and S 42 is a 25-caliber U.S.
"Wet" model and is mounted abaft the sail.

♦ **2 ex-U.S. GUPPY-IA class** Bldr: Portsmouth Naval SY, New Hampshire

	Laid down	L	In serv.
S 49 Pedrera (ex-*Sea Poacher*, SS 406)	23-2-44	20-5-44	31-7-44
S 50 Pacocha (ex-*Atule*, SS 403)	2-12-43	6-3-44	21-6-44

D: 1,830/2,440 tons **S:** 17/15 kts **Dim:** 93.57 × 8.23 × 5.18
A: 10/533-mm TT (6 fwd, 4 aft)
Electron Equipt: Radar: 1/SS-2A
  Sonar: BQS-4, BQR-2B
M: 4 Fairbanks-Morse 38D8⅛ diesels, 2 electric motors; 2 props; 4,610 hp
Fuel: 330 tons **Range:** 10,000/10 **Man:** 82 tot.

REMARKS: Purchased in 7-74. Both were converted to GUPPY-IA configuration during
1951. They can maintain 15 kts for half an hour while submerged, 3 kts for thirty-
six hours. Snorkel speed is 7.5 kts. A third submarine of this class, ex-*Tench* (SS-
417), was towed out in 11-76 for cannibalization.

CRUISERS

♦ **1 ex-Dutch guided-missile cruiser** Bldr: Rotterdamse Droogdok Mij., Rotterdam

	Laid down	L	In serv.
84 Aguirre (ex-*De Zeven Provincien*)	19-5-39	22-8-50	17-12-53

Aguirre (84)   1978

D: 9,850 tons (12,250 fl) **S:** 32 kts **Dim:** 185.7 (182.4 pp) × 17.25 × 6.7
A: 4/152-mm DP (II × 2)—6/57-mm AA (II × 3)—4/40-mm AA (I × 4)—3 SH-
  3D Sea King helicopters
Electron Equipt: Radar: 2/Decca . . . , 1/LW-02, 1/SGR-103, 1/DA-02, 1/ZW-03,
  1/M 25, 2/M 45
M: Parsons GT; 2 props; 80,000 hp **Boilers:** 4 Yarrow, three-drum
Armor: Belt: 76-102-mm; decks (2): 20-25-mm **Man:** 856 tot.

REMARKS: Purchased in 8-76. The Terrier missile system was replaced by a hangar
(20.4 × 16.5) and a helicopter platform (35.0 × 17.0) at Rotterdam. Recommissioned
on 31-10-77. The helicopters carry French AM-39 Exocet anti-ship missiles. The
hangar roof is also a helicopter platform.

♦ **1 ex-Dutch cruiser** Bldr: Wilton-Fijenoord, Schiedam

	Laid down	L	In serv.
81 Almirante Grau (ex-*de Ruyter*)	5-9-39	24-12-44	18-11-53

CRUISERS (continued)

Almirante Grau (81)   1977

D: 9,529 tons (11,850 fl)   **S:** 32 kts   **Dim:** 187.32 (182.4 pp) × 17.25 × 6.7
A: 8/152-mm DP (II × 4)—8/57-mm AA (II × 4)—8/40-mm AA (II × 4)
Electron Equipt: Radar: 1/LW-01, 1/LW-02, 1/SGR-105, 1/SGR-103, 1/SGR-104,
      2/M 45, 4/M 44
M: 2 sets Parsons GT; 2 props; 85,000 hp   **Boilers:** 4 Yarrow, three-drum
Armor: Belt: 76-102-mm; Decks (2): 20-25-mm   **Man:** 49 officers, 904 men

REMARKS: Purchased 7-3-73, commissioning 23-5-73.

♦ **1 ex-British Colonies class** Bldr: Alexander Stephen & Sons, Glasgow, Scotland

	Laid down	L	In serv.
82 CORONEL BOLOGNESI (ex-*Ceylon*)	27-4-39	30-7-42	13-7-43

Coronel Bolognesi (82)   1975

D: 8,781 tons (11,110 fl)   **S:** 29 kts   **Dim:** 169.31 × 18.88 × 6.49
A: 9/152-mm (III × 3)—8/102-mm Mk 19 DP (II × 4)—18/40-mm (II × 5, I × 8)
Electron Equipt: Radar: 1/960, 1/277, 1/293, 1/274, /2/Mk 34
M: 4 sets Parsons GT; 4 props; 72,500 hp   **Boilers:** 4 Admiralty, three-drum
Armor: Belt: 76-102   Deck: 52   Turret: 25-52   Conning tower: 102
Fuel: 1,600 tons   **Range:** 2,300/29, 6,800/20, 11,400/12   **Man:** 766 tot.

REMARKS: Modernized 1955-56, and transferred 9-2-60. U.S. Mk 34 fire-control radars
on two of the 102-mm mounts. Can land a small helicopter at the stern. Sister
Capitán Quiñones (ex-*Almirante Grau*, ex-British *Newfoundland*) stricken in 5-
78.

GUIDED-MISSILE DESTROYERS

♦ **2 ex-British Daring class** Bldr: Yarrow, Glasgow, Scotland

	Laid down	L	In serv.
73 PALACIOS (ex-*Diana*)	3-4-47	8-5-52	29-3-54
74 FERRÉ (ex-*Decoy*)	22-9-46	29-3-49	28-4-53

Palacios (73)—after third reconstruction (hangar now gone)   R. Scheina, 1978

D: 2,800 tons (3,700 fl)   **S:** 30 kts   **Dim:** 118.87 (111.55 pp) × 13.1 × 5.5
A: 8/MM 38 Exocet SSM (II × 4)—4/114-mm Mk 6 DP (II × 2)—4/40-mm Breda
      Dardo AA (II × 2)—1/AB-212 ASW helicopter
Electron Equipt: Radar: 1/Plessey AWS-1, 1/Decca 1226, 1/903, 1/RTN-10X, 1/
      Thomson-CSF TMD-1040 Triton
M: 2 sets English-Electric GT; 2 props, 54,000 hp
Boilers: 2 Foster-Wheeler; 45.7 kg/cm², 454°C   **Fuel:** 584 tons
Range: 3,000/20   **Man:** 297 tot.

REMARKS: Purchased 1969. Welded hull. Refit by Cammell Laird completed at the
end of 1973. In 1975 a helicopter deck was added over the stern. In 1977-78, on 73
a telescoping hangar replaced the after 114-mm gun mount, the after stack was
enlarged and heightened, and a Selenia NA-10 radar GFCS was added abaft the
new second stack to control two enclosed, twin automatic Dardo 40-mm mounts,
which replaced the single 40-mm AA abreast the bridge. These lightly built, much-
modified ships now have no ASW capability other than the embarked helicopter;
sonar removed. They carry a complex and unique mixture of British, French, and
Italian electronics and weapons. 74 retains 6/114-mm and has only 6 Exocet.

DESTROYERS

♦ **6 ex-Dutch Friesland class**

	Bldr	Laid down	L	In serv.
71 CASTILLA (ex-*Utrecht*, D 817)	Kon. Mij. De Schelde, Vlissingen	15-2-54	2-6-56	1-10-57
76 CAPITÁN QUIÑONES (ex-*Limburg*, D 814)	Kon. Mij. De Schelde, Vlissingen	28-11-53	5-9-55	31-10-56
77 VILLAR (ex-*Amsterdam*, D 819)	Nederlandse Dok, Amsterdam	26-3-55	25-8-56	10-8-58
78 GALVEZ (ex-*Groningen*, D 813)	Nederlandse Dok, Amsterdam	4-2-52	9-1-54	19-9-56
79 DIEZ CANSECO (ex-*Rotterdam*, D 818)	Rotterdamse DDM, Rotterdam	7-4-54	26-1-56	28-2-57
. . . GUISE (ex-*Drenthe*, D 816)	Nederlandse Dok, Amsterdam	9-1-54	26-3-55	1-8-57

D: 2,496 tons (3,100 fl)   **S:** 36 kts   **Dim:** 116.0 (112.8 pp) × 11.77 × 5.2
A: 4/120-mm DP (II × 2)—4/40-mm AA (I × 4)—2/375-mm Bofors ASW RL (IV
      × 2)—1/d.c. rack
Electron Equipt: Radar: 1/Decca 1229, 1/LW-02, 1/DA-05, 1/ZW-06, 1/M 45
              Sonar: 1/CWE 610, 1/PAE 1N
M: 2 sets Parsons GT; 2 props; 60,000 hp

DESTROYERS (continued)

Galvez (78)—as Groningen, D 813) 1978

Boilers: 4 Babcock & Wilcox; 39.8 kg/cm², 454°C **Electric:** 1,350 kw
Range: 4,000/18 **Man:** 284 tot.

REMARKS: 77 transferred 19-5-80; 76 transferred 27-6-80; 78 purchased 27-8-80 and transferred 2-2-81; 79 transferred 11-7-81; ex-*Drenthe* also purchased 11-7-81 unrepaired after severe boiler-room fire 12-11-80 and recommissioned 12-81. The remaining Dutch unit of the class, *Overijssel* (D 815), may be purchased 1982 on completion of service. Two forward 40-mm AA removed 1965, fire control for remaining 40-mm AA removed 1977-78. Same propulsion plant as U.S. *Gearing* class. Have one 103-mm rocket flare launcher.

◆ **1 ex-Dutch Holland class** Bldr: Rotterdamse Droogdok Mij., Rotterdam

	Laid down	L	In serv.
75 GARCIA Y GARCIA (ex-*Holland*)	21-4-50	11-4-53	31-12-54

Garcia y Garcia—as Holland A. Baker, 1976

D: 2,215 tons (2,765 fl) **S:** 32 kts **Dim:** 111.3 × 11.3 × 4.86
A: 4/120-mm DP (II × 2)—1/40-mm AA—2/375-mm Bofors ASW RL (IV × 2)—1/d.c. rack
Electron Equipt: Radar: 1/LW-02, 1/DA-05, 2/M 45
       Sonar: 1/CWE 10, 1/170B, 1/162
M: 2 sets Parsons GT; 2 props; 45,000 hp
Boilers: 4 Babcock & Wilcox; 39.8 kg/cm², 454°C
Electric: 1,350 **Range:** 4,000/18 **Man:** 247 tot.

REMARKS: Transferred 5-1-78 without refit. Commissioned 21-1-78 in Peruvian Navy.

◆ **1 ex-U.S. Fletcher class** Bldr: Bethlehem Steel, Staten Island

	Laid down	L	In serv.
72 GUISE (ex-*Isherwood*, DD 520)	12-5-42	24-11-42	12-4-43

Guise (72) R. Scheina, 1978

D: 2,050 tons (3,050 fl) **S:** 30 kts
Dim: 114.73 (112.5 wl) × 12.07 × 5.49 (4.27 hull)
A: 4/127-mm DP (I × 4)—6/76.2-mm DP (II × 3)—5/533-mm TT (V × 1)—2/
  Hedgehog—1/light helicopter
Electron Equipt: Radar: 1/SPS-10, 1/SPS-6, 1/Mk 25, 2/Mk 34, 1/Mk 35
      Sonar: SQS-29 series
M: 2 sets GE GT; 2 props; 60,000 hp **Electric:** 580 kw
Boilers: 4 Babcock & Wilcox; 39.8 kg/cm², 454°C
Fuel: 650 tons **Range:** 1,260/30, 4,400/15 **Man:** 15 officers, 260 men

REMARKS: Transferred 1960-61 under MAP. Has one Mk 37 director for 127-mm, two Mk 63 gun fire-control systems for 76.2-mm, and one Mk 56 for either 127-mm or 76.2-mm. Helicopter platform added in 1975. Two sister ships, *La Valette* (DD 448) and *Terry* (DD 513), were transferred in 1974 for cannibalization. Sister *Villar* (71, ex-*Benham*, DD 796), stricken 1980; late note: *Guise* stricken 1981.

GUIDED-MISSILE FRIGATES

◆ **2 (+2) Italian Lupo type** Bldrs: No. 51, No. 52: CNTR, Riva Trigoso; No. 53,
No. 54: CNTR, Callao

	Laid down	L	In serv.
51 MELITON CARVAJAL	8-10-74	17-11-76	5-2-79
52 MANUEL VILLAVICENCIO	6-10-76	7-2-78	25-6-79
53 N. . .	1977	. . .	3-84
54 N. . .	1977	. . .	3-85

D: 2,208 tons (2,500 fl) **S:** 32 kts **Dim:** 108.4 (106.0 pp) × 11.28 × 3.66
A: 8/Otomat Mk 2 (I × 8)—1/127-mm OTO Melara DP—1/Albatros SAM system
  (VIII × 1)—4/40-mm Breda Dardo AA (II × 2)—6/324-mm Mk 32 ASW TT
  (III × 2)—1/AB-212 ASW helicopter
Electron Equipt: Radar: 1/3RM20, 1/RAN-10S air search, 1/RAN-11LX surface
        search, 1/SPS-2F, 1/RTN-10X, 2/RTN-20X, 1/RTN-
        30X
      Sonar: Edo 610E
      ECM: passive intercept, 2/SCLAR chaff RL
M: CODOG: 2 Fiat-GE LM-2500 gas turbines, 25,000 hp each; 2 GMT A230-20M
  diesels, 3,900 hp each; 2 CP props
Electric: 3,120 kw **Range:** 900/35; 3,450/20.5 (diesel)
Man: 20 officers, 165 men

GUIDED-MISSILE FRIGATES (continued)

Manuel Villavicencio (52)   PHC T. McManus, USN, 1980

REMARKS: Italian technicians were to assist in the building of Nos. 53 and 54 at Callao, which were reported only 50% complete in 10-81. Differ from the Italian Navy's version in having a fixed (vice telescoping) hangar and a step down to the hull at the stern; the Dardo 40-mm mounts are one deck higher, and the SAM fire-control system differs. Selenia IPN-IC data system fitted.

GUIDED-MISSILE CORVETTES

♦ **6 French PR-72-560 class**

	Bldr	L	In serv.
P 101 VELARDE	Lorient DY	16-9-78	25-7-80
P 102 SANTILLANA	S.F.C.N.	11-9-79	25-7-80
P 103 DE LOS HEROES	Lorient DY	20-5-79	17-11-80
P 104 HERRERA	S.F.C.N.	16-2-79	26-2-81
P 105 LARREA	Lorient DY	20-5-79	16-6-81
P 106 SANCHEZ CARRION	S.F.C.N.	28-6-79	14-9-81

D: 470 tons light (560 normal, 610 fl)   **S:** 37 kts (34 sust.)
Dim: 64.0 (59.0 pp) × 8.35 × 2.6

Herrera (P 104)—old number   S.F.C.N., 1981

Herrera (P 104)—old number   S.F.C.N., 1981

A: 4/MM 38 Exocet SSM (II × 2)—1/76-mm OTO Melara DP—2/40-mm Breda-Bofors AA (II × 1)
Electron Equipt: Radar: 1/Decca 1226, 1/Thomson-CSF THD 1040 Triton, 1/Castor III fire control
M: 4 SACM AGO 240, V-16 diesels; 4 props; 22,000 hp   **Electric:** 560 kw
Range: 1,200/30; 2,500/16   **Man:** 36 tot.

REMARKS: These ships, designed by S.F.C.N. Villeneuve-la-Garonne, have been given the names of the Vosper patrol boats that were transferred to the Coast Guard.

RIVER GUNBOATS

♦ **2 Marañon class** Bldr: John I. Thornycroft, Woolston, G.B.

	Laid down	L	In serv.
13 MARAÑON	4-50	23-4-51	7-51
14 UCAYALI	4-50	7-3-51	7-51

Marañon (13)   1975

D: 350 tons (365 fl)   **S:** 12 kts   **Dim:** 47.22 × 9.75 × 1.22
A: 2/76.2-mm DP (I × 2)—4/20-mm (II × 2)   **Man:** 4 officers, 36 men
M: 2 British Polar 441 diesels; 2 props; 800 hp   **Range:** 5,000/10

REMARKS: Based at Iquitos and in service on the Upper Amazon. Superstructure of aluminum alloy.

♦ **2 Amazonas class** Bldr: Electric Boat Co., Groton, 1934

11 AMAZONAS   12 LORETO

D: 250 tons   **S:** 15 kts   **Dim:** 46.7 × 6.7 × 1.2
A: 2/76.2-mm DP (I × 2)—2/40-mm AA (I × 2)—1/20-mm AA (I × 2)
M: 2 diesels; 2 props; 750 hp   **Range:** 4,000/10   **Man:** 5 officers, 20 men

RIVER GUNBOATS *(continued)*

Loreto (12)   1975

REMARKS: Based at Iquitos on Upper Amazon.

NOTE: Old river gunboat *America* (15), reported non-operational 1981, may be retained as a hulk or relic.

PATROL CRAFT

♦ **3 Rio Zarumilla class** Bldr: Viareggio, Italy (In serv. 5-9-60)

PL 250 RIO ZARUMILLA   PL 251 RIO TUMBES   PL 252 RIO PIURA

    D: 37 tons (fl)   **S:** 18 kts   **Dim:** 20.27 × 5.25 × 2.75
    A: 2/40-mm AA (I × 2)   **M:** 2 GM diesels; 2 props; 1,200 hp   **Range:** 1,000/14
    Man: . . .

REMARKS: Patrol the Salto River border with Ecuador.

♦ **4 ex-U.S. Coast Guard 40-foot utility boats** (In serv. 1952-55)

PL 230 LA PUNTA   PL 231 RIO CHILLON   PL 232 RIO SANRA   PL 233 RIO MAJES

    D: 16 tons (fl)   **S:** 18 kts   **Dim:** 12.3 × 3.4 × 1.0
    A: 2/12.7-mm mg (I × 2)   **M:** 2 GM 6-71 diesels; 2 props; 300 hp
    Range: 160/18   **Man:** 5 tot.

♦ **4 Rio Ramis class**

PL 290 RIO RAMIS   PL 292 RIO COATA
PL 291 RIO ILLAVE   PL 293 RIO HUANCANÉ

    D: 12-14 tons (fl)   **A:** 1/12.7-mm mg   **Man:** 4 tot.

REMARKS: Serve on Lake Titicaca.

♦ **1 former lake craft** Bldr: Cammel Laird, Birkenhead (In serv. 1870)

306 (ex-*Yapura*)

    D: 500 grt   **S:** 10 kts   **Dim:** 38.1 × . . . × . . .
    M: 2 diesels; 2 props; 480 hp

REMARKS: Served in Peruvian Navy until 1883; re-acquired 1980 for patrol and hospital ship duties on Lake Titicaca.

♦ **1 former lake craft** Bldr: Cammel Laird, Birkenhead (In serv. 1862)

19 (ex-*Yavari*)

    D: 500 grt   **S:** 8 kts   **Dim:** 47.9 × . . . × . . .   **M:** 2 diesels; 2 props; 320 hp

REMARKS: Served in Peruvian Navy 1871-1883; re-acquired as a patrol boat 1980.

AMPHIBIOUS WARFARE SHIPS

♦ **3 ex-U.S. LST 1-class landing ships**

	Bldr	L	In serv.
141 PAITA (ex-*Burnett County*, LST 512)	Chicago B & I	10-12-43	8-1-44
142 CHIMBOTE (ex-*Rawhiti*, ex-LST 283)	American Bridge	10-10-43	18-11-43
143 SALAVERRY (ex-*Iquitos*, ex-*Carelne*, ex-LST. . .)	Dravo Corp.	. . .	. . .

    D: 1,625 tons (4,080 fl)   **S:** 10 kts   **Dim:** 100.0 × 15.24 × 4.29
    A: 141: 6/20-mm AA (I × 6); 142: 2/40-mm AA (I × 2)—8/20-mm (I × 8); 143: none
    M: 2 GM 12-567A diesels; 2 props; 1,700 hp   **Electric:** 300 kw
    Fuel: 600 tons   **Range:** 9,500/9   **Man:** 16 officers, 106 men

REMARKS: No. 142 was purchased in 1947, No. 141 in 1957. The latter is assigned to the Naval Academy; her 01-level superstructure has been extended forward to increase accommodations. Both have helicopter landing positions amidships. *Salaverry*, purchased 1977 from commercial interests, has a raised helicopter deck at the stern.

♦ **2 ex-U.S. LSM 1-class landing ships** Bldr: Charleston Navy Yd., Charleston, S.C.

	Laid down	L	In serv.
36 LOMAS (ex-LSM 396)	13-12-44	2-1-45	24-3-45
37 ATICO (ex-LSM 554)	3-3-45	22-3-45	14-9-45

    D: 513 tons (1,095 fl)   **S:** 12.5 kts   **Dim:** 62.02 × 10.52 × 2.24
    A: 2/40-mm AA (II × 1)—4/20-mm AA (I × 4)
    M: 2 GM 16-278A diesels; 2 props; 2,800 hp   **Electric:** 240 kw
    Fuel: 165 tons   **Range:** 5,000/7

REMARKS: Purchased 7-59. Living spaces for 116 men.

HYDROGRAPHIC SURVEY SHIPS

♦ **1 new construction** Bldr: SIMA, Callao

	Laid down	L	In serv.
HUMBOLDT	3-1-77	13-10-78	1980

    D: 1,200 tons (1,980 fl)   **S:** 14 kts   **Dim:** 76.0 × 12.0 × 4.4
    M: 2 diesels; 2 props; 3,000 hp   **Man:** 48 tot.

♦ **1 ex-U.S. Sotoyomo-class tug** Bldr: Levingston SB, Orange, Tex.

	Laid down	L	In serv.
136 UNANUE (ex-*Wateree*, ATA 174)	5-10-43	18-11-43	20-7-44

    D: 534 tons (835 fl)   **S:** 13 kts   **Dim:** 43.59 × 10.31 × 4.01
    M: 2 GM 12-278A diesels, electric drive; 1 prop; 1,500 hp   **Electric:** 120 kw

REMARKS: Sold to Peru in 11-61.

HYDROGRAPHIC SURVEY SHIPS (continued)

♦ **3 inshore survey craft** (In serv. 1943)

API 171 Cardenas (ex-YP 99)   API 173 N. . . (ex-YP 243)
API 172 N. . . (ex-YP 242)

D: 50 tons (60 fl)   **S:** 12 kts   **Dim:** 22.9 × 5.2 × 1.5
M: 2 Superior diesels; 2 props; 320 hp   **Fuel:** 3 tons   **Man:** 11 tot.

Remarks: Ex-U.S. patrol craft, purchased in 11-58.

♦ **1 river research craft** (In serv. 5-76)

N. . .

Dim: 23.5 × . . . × . . .   **Man:** 16 tot.

Remarks: Operated on the Amazon by the Navy for the Oceanographic Institute.

REPLENISHMENT OILERS

♦ **1 Talara class** Bldr: SIMA, Callao

	Laid down	L	In serv.
152 Talara	1975	9-7-76	3-77

D: 30,000 tons (fl)   **S:** 16.25 kts   **Dim:** 171.18 (161.55 pp) × 25.38 × 9.53
M: 1 Burmeister & Wain 6K 47EF diesel; 1 prop; 11,600 hp
Electric: 1,890 kw

Remarks: 16,633 grt, 25,648 dwt. Cargo: 35,642 m³. Sisters *Trompeteros* and *Bayovar* (transferred 1979) are operated by Petroperu, the state fuel monopoly, which transferred this ship to the Navy upon completion. One underway fueling station per side.

♦ **2 Parinas class** Bldr: SIMA, Callao

	L	In serv.
155 Parinas	12-6-67	13-6-68
156 Pimental	5-4-68	27-6-69

Pimental (156)   1977

D: 13,600 tons (fl)   **S:** 14.25 kts   **Dim:** 134.19 (124,82 pp) × 18.98 × 7.27
M: 1 Burmeister & Wain 7-cyl. diesel; 1 prop; 4,900 hp   **Electric:** 464 kw
Fuel: 610 tons

Remarks: 7,121 grt, 10,140 dwt. Cargo: 13,851 m³. Normally used by Petroperu for commercial purposes, but have naval crews and can refuel ships from one rig on either beam. No. 156 had her commercial certification withdrawn 19-6-77 pending repairs.

♦ **2 Sechura class** Bldr: SIMA, Callao

	Laid down	L	In serv.
158 Zorritos	8-10-55	8-10-58	1959
159 Lobitos	1964	5-65	1966

Lobitos (159)   C. Dragonette, 1979

D: 8,700 tons (fl)   **S:** 12 kts   **Dim:** 116.82 (109.73 pp) × 15.91 × 6.63
M: 1 Burmeister & Wain 562-VTF-115 diesel; 1 prop; 2,400 hp
Electric: 750 kw   **Fuel:** 549 tons

Remarks: 4,297 grt, 5,732 dwt. Cargo: 7,488 m³. Sister *Sechura*, built in England 1952-55 and fully equipped for underway replenishment, was stricken in 1968. Nos. 158 and 159 are used for commercial cargoes for Petroperu, but have one fueling station on either beam.

♦ **1 ex-Danish commercial tanker** Bldr: Hitachi Zosen, Osaka, Japan

151 Mollendo (ex-*Amalienborg*)

D: 6,084 tons light (25,670 fl)   **S:** 15 kts
Dim: 170.69 (163.0 pp) × 22.05 × 9.06
M: 1 Hitachi-B & W 674-VTFS-160 diesel; 1 prop; 7,500 hp
Electric: 540 kw
Fuel: 1,480 tons   **Range:** 19,800/15

Remarks: 12,490 grt, 19,900 dwt. Cargo: 26,073 m³. In service in 9-62. Purchased in 4-67. Used primarily for commercial cargoes for Petroperu, but can refuel under way from one station on each beam.

CARGO SHIPS

♦ **1 Ilo-class transport** Bldr: SIMA, Callao

131 Ilo

D: 18,400 tons (fl)   **S:** 15.6 kts   **Dim:** 153.85 (144.53 pp) × 20.4 × 9.2
M: 1 B & W 6K 47EF diesel; 1 prop; 11,600 hp   **Electric:** 1,140 kw

Remarks: In service 15-12-71. Cargo: 13,000 tons. Sister *Rimac* is in commercial service for the state shipping company. *Ilo* is also used to carry commercial cargo.

CARGO SHIPS (continued)

Ilo (131)   J. Jedrlinic, 1975

♦ **1 ex-U.S. Bellatrix-class attack cargo ship** Bldr: Tampa SB, Tampa, Fla.

	L	In serv.
31 INDEPENDENCIA (ex-*Bellatrix*, AKA 3, ex-*Raven*, AK 20)	16-4-41	16-2-42

Independencia (31)   1974

D: 6,200 tons (14,225 fl) **S:** 15 kts **Dim:** 140.0 × 19.2 × 7.95
A: 1/127-mm DP—4/76.2-mm 50-cal. DP (I × 4)—10/20-mm AA (I × 10)
Electron Equipt: Radar: 1/SPS-6, 1/Decca . . . , 1/Mk 26
M: 1 Nordberg TSM diesel; 1 prop; 6,000 hp **Range:** 18,000/14
Man: 19 officers, 220 men

REMARKS: Former U.S. C2-T-class cargo ship. Refitted in 1954, and transferred under MAP in 20-7-63. Used for training midshipmen as well as for carrying military and commercial cargo (4,500 tons). Has one Mk 52 radar gunfire-control system and three Mk 51 gunfire-control systems. Normally carries two LCVP.

HOSPITAL SHIPS

♦ **3 Morona class** Bldr: SIMAI, Iquitos, 1976-77

302 MORONA   . . . N. . .   . . . N. . .

D: 150 tons (fl) **S:** 12 kts **Dim:** 30.0 × 6.0 × 0.6 **M:** Diesels; . . . hp

REMARKS: Serve on the upper Amazon River.

NOTE: The old river hospital ship *Napo* was stricken 1978.

TUGS

♦ **1 ex-U.S. Cherokee-class ocean tug** Bldr: Cramp SB, Philadelphia, Pa.

	Laid down	L	In serv.
123 GUARDIAN RIOS (ex-*Pinto*, ATF 90)	10-8-42	5-1-43	1-4-43

D: 1,235 tons (1,675 fl) **S:** 16.5 kts **Dim:** 62.48 × 11.73 × 4.67
M: 4 GM 12-278 diesels, electric drive; 1 prop; 3,000 hp **Electric:** 260 kw
Man: 85 tot.

REMARKS: Transferred in 12-60. Unarmed. Used for salvage and rescue.

SERVICE CRAFT

♦ **2 Selendon-class harbor tugs** Bldr: Ruhrorter, Duisburg, W. Germany (In serv. 1967)

128 OLAYA   129 SELENDON

D: 80 grt **S:** 10 kts **Dim:** 61.3 × 20.3 × 2.3 **M:** 1 diesel; 1 prop; 600 hp

♦ **1 river tug** Bldr: SIMAI, Iquitos (In serv. 1973)

CONTRAESTRE NAVARRO

D: 50 tons

♦ **1 ex-U.S. medium tug** Bldr: City Point Iron Works, Boston (In serv. 1892)

124 FRANCO (ex-*Tigre*, ex-*Iwana*, YTM 2)

D: 192 tons (fl) **S:** 9 kts **Dim:** 29.26 × 6.4 × 2.59
M: 1 set single-expansion, reciprocating steam; 1 prop; 400 hp

REMARKS: Transferred in 3-46. The oldest operational tug in any navy. Converted to burn oil. Has push-bar built across bows for handling barges. Operates in the Upper Amazon Flotilla.

♦ **2 ex-U.S. 174-foot-class yard oilers**

	Bldr	Laid down	L	In serv.
N. . . (ex-YO 221)	Jeffersonville Boat & Mach., Ind.	15-1-45	22-5-45	31-8-45
N. . . (ex-YO 171)	RTC Shbldg., Camden, N.J.	18-3-44	20-7-44	15-11-44

D: 1,400 tons (fl) **S:** 10 kts **Dim:** 53.04 × 9.75 × 4.0
M: 2 diesels; 2 prop; 540 hp **Range:** 2,000/8 **Man:** 20 tot.

REMARKS: Ex-YO 221 transferred in 2-75; ex-YO 171 purchased 26-1-81. Cargo: approximately 900 tons (6,570 barrels).

♦ **2 ex-U.S. 174-foot water tankers**

	Bldr	Laid down	L	In serv.
110 MANTILLA (ex-YW 122)	Henry C. Grebe, Chicago, Ill.	29-6-45	22-9-45	17-11-45
. . . N. . . (ex-YW 128)	Leatham D. Smith, Wisc.	9-4-45	22-5-45	28-7-45

D: 440 tons (1,390 fl) **S:** 7 kts **Dim:** 53.04 × 9.75 × 4.0
M: 1 GM diesel; 1 prop; 640 hp **Fuel:** 25 tons **Man:** 23 tot.

REMARKS: No. 110 transferred in 3-63; ex-YW 128 purchased 26-1-81. Cargo: 930 tons.

SERVICE CRAFT *(continued)*

♦ **2 river-service water tankers**

ABA 113   **D:** 330 tons   **Bldr:** SIMAI, Iquitos (In serv. 1972)

ABA 091   Barge with 800-ton capacity   Built: 1972

♦ **1 torpedo-retreiver Bldr:** Lürssen, Bremen-Vegasack (In serv. 5-81)

ART 322

  D: 68 tons (fl)   **S:** 19 kts   **Dim:** 25.35 × 5.62 × . . .   **Range:** 500/15
  M: 2 MTU 8V 396 TC82 diesels; 2 props; 1,960 hp   **Man:** 9 tot.

REMARKS: Stern recovery ramp. Can stow 4 533-mm full-sized torpedoes or 8 ASW torpedoes.

♦ **1 new construction floating dry dock Bldr:** West Germany (In serv. 1979)

AFD 109

  Dim: 195.0 × 42.0 × . . .   **Lift capacity:** 15,000 tons

REMARKS: Ordered 13-2-78; first unit lost en route Peru, 1978. Lift capacity can be increased to 18,000 tons by use of extension sections, bringing total length to 225 meters.

♦ **1 ex-U.S. ARD 2-class floating dry dock Bldr:** Pacific Bridge, Alameda, Cal.

AFD 112 (ex-WY 20, ex-ARD 8) (In serv. 8-43)

  Dim: 148.03 × 21.64 × 1.6 (light)   **Lift capacity:** 3,500 tons

REMARKS: In service in 1943. Transferred in 2-61; purchased outright 1981.

♦ **1 ex-U.S. AFDL 7-class floating dry dock Bldr:** Foundation Co., Kearny, N.J.

AFD 111 (ex-WY 19, ex-AFDL 33) (In serv. 10-44)

  Dim: 87.78 × 19.51 × 0.99 (light)   **Lift capacity:** 1,900 tons

REMARKS: In service in 10-44. Transferred in 7-59.

♦ **1 small floating dry dock Bldr:** Thornycroft, Southampton (In serv. 1951)

AFD 108

  Dim: 59.13 × 18.7 × . . .   **Lift capacity:** 600 tons

REMARKS: Serves the Amazon Flotilla.

♦ **1 ex-U.S. YR 24-class floating workshop Bldr:** DeKom SB, Brooklyn, NY

	Laid down	L	In serv.
RC 105 (ex-YR 59)	3-11-43	22-4-44	24-8-44

  D: 520 tons (770 fl)   **Dim:** 45.72 × 10.36 × 1.8   **Electric:** 220 kw
  Fuel: 75 tons   **Man:** 47 tot.

REMARKS: Transferred 8-8-61.

♦ **1 floating crane**

  Capacity: 120 tons

REMARKS: Serves at Callao.

COAST GUARD

The Peruvian Coast Guard was established in 1975 and is intended to patrol to the extent of the 200-nautical-mile economic zone. The two former U.S. *Auk*-class former minesweepers *Galvez* and *Diez Canseco* were stricken 1981.

PATROL BOATS

♦ **1 Rio Cañete class Bldr:** SIMA, Callao

	L	In serv.
234 RIO CAÑETE	8-10-74	31-3-76

  D: 300 tons (fl)   **S:** 21 kts   **Dim:** 50.62 (49.1 pp) × 7.4 × 1.7
  A: 1/40-mm AA—1/20-mm AA
  M: 4 MTU V-8 diesels; 2 props; 5,640 hp   **Electric:** 170 kw
  Man: 6 officers, 33 men

REMARKS: Intended as the first of a class of six for the Navy. The design was evidently not a success. Endurance: 20 days.

♦ **2 ex-U.S. PGM 71 class**

	Bldr	In serv.
222 RIO SAMA (ex-PGM 78)	Peterson, Sturgeon Bay, Wisc.	9-66
223 RIO CHIRA (ex-PGM 11)	SIMA, Callao	6-72

  D: 130 tons (145 fl)   **S:** 17 kts   **Dim:** 30.8 (30.2 wl) × 6.4 × 1.85
  A: 1/40-mm AA—4/20-mm AA (II × 2)—2/12.7-mm mg (I × 2)
  Electron Equipt: Radar: 1/Raytheon 1500 Pathfinder
  M: 8 GM 6-71 diesels; 2 props; 2,200 hp   **Range:** 1,000/12   **Man:** 27 tot.

REMARKS: Transferred to the Coast Guard in 1975. *Rio Chira* was built with U.S. aid and equipment.

♦ **6 110-foot class Bldr:** Vosper, Portsmouth

	L		L
224 RIO CHICAWA (ex-*De Los Heroes*)	18-11-64	227 RIO LOCUMBA (ex-*Sanchez Carrion*)	18-2-65
225 RIO PATIVILCA (ex-*Herrera*)	26-10-64	228 RIO ICA (ex-*Santillana*)	24-8-64
226 RIO HUAORA (ex-*Larrea*)	18-2-65	229 RIO VITOR (ex-*Velarde*)	10-7-64

  D: 100 tons (130 fl)   **S:** 30 kts   **Dim:** 33.4 (31.46 wl) × 6.4 × 1.7
  A: 2/20-mm AA   **Electron Equipt:** Radar: 1/Decca TM 707
  M: 2 Napier Deltic T38-37 diesels; 2 props; 6,280 hp
  Range: 1,100/15   **Man:** 4 officers, 27 men

REMARKS: All delivered under own power by 10-65. Never fully equipped with armament, although fittings for four 533-mm torpedo tubes were installed in the decks. Air-conditioned. Steel hull, aluminum-alloy superstructure. Transferred to the Coast Guard in 1975 and renamed, their old names going to a new class of naval guided-missile corvettes.

PHILIPPINES

PERSONNEL (1978): 20,000 men, including a brigade of Marines

MERCHANT MARINE (1978)· 577 ships—1,264,995 grt
(tankers: 57 ships—301,522 grt)

NAVAL AVIATION: Ten Philippine-built Brittain-Norman BN-2 Defender light maritime patrol aircraft and 10 MBB BO-105 helicopters are in service. The Air Force purchased 3 Fokker F-27 Maritime patrol aircraft in 1981.

FRIGATES

♦ 1 ex-U.S. Savage class

	Bldr	Laid down	L	In serv.
PS 4 RAJAH LAKANDULA (ex-*Tran Hung Dao*, ex-*Camp*, DER 251)	Brown SB, Houston	27-1-43	16-4-43	16-9-45

Rajah Lakandula (PS 4)—twin 40-mm AA now fwd of bridge   1977

D: 1,590 tons (1,850 fl)   **S:** 19 kts   **Dim:** 93.27 × 11.15 × 4.27
A: 2/76.2-mm DP Mk 34 (I × 2)—2/40-mm AA (II × 1)—4/20-mm AA (II × 2)—1/81-mm mortar combined with 1/12.7-mm mg—2/12.7-mm mg—6/324-mm Mk 32 ASW TT (III × 2)
Electron Equipt: Radar: 1/SPS-10, 1/SPS-28, 1/Mk 34
          Sonar: SQS-31
M: 4 Fairbanks-Morse 38D⅛ × 10 diesels; 2 props; 6,080 hp
Electric: 580 kw   **Fuel:** 300 tons   **Range:** 11,500/11   **Man:** 150 tot.

REMARKS: Transferred to Vietnam 6-1-71; to the Philippines, 5-4-75. Converted to radar picket in the late 1950s, but most electronic warfare gear and ASW ordnance was removed in 1971. Has one Mk 63 and one Mk 51 gunfire-control system.

♦ 4 ex-U.S. Barnegat-class former seaplane tenders Bldr: Lake Washington SY, Houghton, Wash.

	Laid down	L	In serv.
PS 7 ANDRES BONIFACIO (ex-*Ly Thoung Kiet*, ex-*Chincoteague*, WHEC 375, ex-AVP 24)	23-7-41	15-4-42	12-4-43
PS 8 GREGORIO DE PILAR (ex-*Ngo Kuyen*, ex-*McCulloch*, WHEC 386, ex-*Wachapreague*, AGP 8, ex-AVP 56)	1-2-43	10-7-43	17-5-44
PS 9 DIEGO SILANG (ex-*Tran Quang Khai*, ex-*Bering Strait*, WHEC 382, ex-AVP 34)	7-6-43	15-1-44	19-7-44
PS 10 FRANCISCO DAGAHOY (ex-*Tran Binh Trong*, ex-*Castle Rock*, WHEC 383, ex-AVP 35)	12-7-43	11-3-44	8-10-44

Andres Bonifacio (PS 7)   1977

D: 1,766 tons (2,800 fl)   **S:** 17 kts   **Dim:** 95.72 (91.44 wl) × 12.55 × 4.27
A: 1/127-mm DP—4/40-mm AA (II × 1, I × 2)—2/20-mm AA (I × 2)—2/12.7-mm mg—1/BO-105 helicopter
Electron Equipt: Radar: 1/SPS-53, 1/SPS-29, 1/Mk 26
M: 4 Fairbanks-Morse 38D8⅛ × 10 diesels; 2 props; 6,080 hp
Electric: 600 kw   **Fuel:** 400 tons   **Range:** 18,000/15   **Man:** 160 tot.

REMARKS: Transferred to U.S. Coast Guard in 1946-48, PS 8 having served as a motor-torpedo-boat tender and the others as seaplane tenders. Transferred to South Vietnam in 1971-72 after extensive overhauls. Escaped from Vietnam 4-75 to Philippines, to which they were formally sold 5-4-76. Two other escapees, ex-*Yakutat* (WHEC 380) and *Cook Inlet* (WHEC 383) were in too poor condition to refit and have been used for cannibalization spares. PS 7-PS 10 received helicopter decks at the 01 level aft in 1978-79; a twin 40-mm mount was added in a tub projecting over the stern, adding 1 meter to the original length. Have Mk 52 GFCS with Mk 26 radar for the 127-mm gun.

♦ 2 ex-U.S. Cannon class Bldr: Federal SB & DD Co., Newark, N.J.

	Laid down	L	In serv.
PF 5 DATU SIKATUNA (ex-*Asahi*, ex-*Amick*, DE 168)	30-11-42	27-5-43	26-7-43
PF 6 RAJAH HUMABON (ex-*Hatsuhi*, ex-*Atherton*, DE 169)	14-1-43	27-5-43	29-8-43

D: 1,240 tons (1,620 fl)   **S:** 20 kts   **Dim:** 93.27 (91.44 wl) × 11.15 × 3.56 (hull)
A: 3/76-mm DP (I × 3)—6/40-mm AA (II × 3)—2/20-mm AA (I × 2)—6/324-mm Mk 32 ASW TT (III × 2)—1/Hedgehog—1/d.c. rack
Electron Equipt: Radar: 1/SPS-5, 1/SPS-6C, 1/Mk 26
          Sonar: SQS-17B
M: 4 GM 16-278A diesels, electric drive; 2 props; 6,000 hp
Electric: 680 kw   **Fuel:** 260 tons   **Range:** 11,600/11   **Man:** 165 tot.

FRIGATES *(continued)*

REMARKS: Transferred to Japan on 14-6-55 and stricken 6-75, reverting to U.S. ownership; they were sold to the Philippines 23-12-78 but remained laid up in Japan until towed to South Korea for overhaul in 1979. Both recommissioned 27-2-80. Have one Mk 52 radar GFCS and one Mk 41 range finder for 76.2-mm gun control, plus three Mk 51 mod. 2 GFCS for the 40-mm guns. Sister *Datu Kalantiaw* (PS 76, ex-*Booth*, DE 170) was lost aground in a typhoon, 21-9-81.

CORVETTES

♦ 2 ex-U.S. Auk-class former minesweepers

	Bldr	Laid down	L	In serv.
PS 69 RIZAL (ex-*Murrelet*, MSF 372)	Savannah Mach. & Foundry, Ga.	24-8-44	29-12-44	21-8-45
PS 70 QUEZON (ex-*Vigilance*, MSF 324)	Associated SB, Seattle, Wash.	28-11-42	5-4-43	28-2-44

D: 890 tons (1,250 fl) **S:** 18 kts **Dim:** 67.39 (65.53 wl) × 9.8 × 3.28
A: 1/76.2-mm DP—4/40-mm AA (II × 2)—4/20-mm AA (II × 2)—3/324-mm Mk 32 ASW TT (III × 2)—1/Hedgehog—2/Mk 6 d.c. throwers—2/d.c. racks
Electron Equipt: Radar: 1/SPS-5C
Sonar: SQS-17B
M: 2 GM 12-278 (PS 70: 12-278A) diesels, electric drive; 2 props; 3,532 hp
Electric: 360 kw **Fuel:** 216 tons **Man:** 100 tot.

REMARKS: PS 69 transferred 18-6-65, PS 70 on 19-8-67. A small raised helicopter deck has replaced the after 76.2-mm gun.

♦ 7 ex-U.S. PCE 821 and PCER 848 classes

	Bldr	Laid down	L	In serv.
PS 19 MIGUEL MALVAR (ex-*Ngoc Hoi*. ex-*Brattleboro*, EPCER 852)	A	28-10-43	1-3-44	26-5-44
PS 22 SULTAN KUDARAT (ex-*Dong Da II*, ex-*Crestview*, PCE 895)	B	2-12-42	18-5-43	30-10-44
PS 23 DATU MARIKUDO (ex-*Van Kiep II*, ex-*Amherst*, PCER 853)	A	16-11-43	18-3-44	16-6-44
PS 28 CEBU (ex-PCE 881)	C	11-8-43	10-11-43	31-7-44
PS 29 NEGROS OCCIDENTAL (ex-PCE 885)	C	25-2-44	20-6-44	30-4-45
PS 31 PANGASINAN (ex-PCE 891)	B	28-10-42	24-4-43	15-6-44
PS 32 ILOILO (ex-PCE 897)	B	16-12-42	3-8-43	6-1-45

Bldrs: A: Pullman Standard Car Co., Chicago; *B:* Willamette Iron & Steel Corp., Portland, Ore.; *C:* Albina Eng. & Machine Works, Portland, Ore.

D: 903 tons (fl) **S:** 15 kts **Dim:** 56.24 (54.86 wl) × 10.08 × 2.87
A: PS 19-23: 1/76.2-mm DP—2/40-mm AA (I × 2)—8/20-mm AA (II × 1)
PS 28-32: 1/76.2-mm DP—6/40-mm AA (II × 3)—4/20-mm AA (I × 4)
Electron Equipt: Radar: 1/RCA CR 104A
M: 2 GM 12-278A diesels; 2 props; 2,000 hp (PS 19, 28, 31: 2 GM 12-567A diesels; 2 props; 1,800 hp)
Electric: 240-180 kw **Fuel:** 125 tons **Range:** 9,000/10 **Man:** 100 tot.

REMARKS: PS 28 through PS 32 were transferred 7-48; a fifth, *Leyte* (PS 30, ex-PCE 885),was lost by grounding in 1979. PS 19 through 23 were transferred to South Vietnam on 11-7-66, 29-11-61, and 6-70, and escaped Vietnam in 5-75; they were sold to the Philippines 11-75 (PS 23: 5-4-76). All ASW equipment is now deleted from all units. Ex-PCER and EPCER originally had longer forecastles as rescue ships; they were brought to standard PCE configuration before transfer to South Vietnam.

Leyte (PS 30)—lost 1979 G. Arra, 1977

♦ 1 ex-U.S. Admirable-class former minesweeper Bldr: Winslow Marine Railway, Seattle, Wash.

	Laid down	L	In serv.
PS 20 MAGAT SALAMAT (ex-*Chi Lang II*, ex-*Gayety*, MSF 239)	14-11-43	19-3-44	23-9-45

Magat Salamat (PS 20) 1977

D: 650 tons light (905 fl) **S:** 14 kts **Dim:** 56.24 (54.86 wl) × 10.06 × 2.75
A: 1/76-mm DP—2/40-mm (I × 2)—8/20-mm AA (II × 4)
Electron Equipt: Radar: 1/RCA CR 104A **Electric:** 280 kw **Fuel:** 140 tons
M: 2 Cooper-Bessemer GSB-8 diesels; 2 props; 1,710 hp

REMARKS: Transferred to Vietnam and escaped to the Philippines 4-75. Acquired by the latter in 11-75.

GUIDED-MISSILE PATROL BOATS

♦ 0 (+3) South Korean design Bldr: Pusan SB & Eng. Co.

D: 120 tons (150 fl) **S:** 35 kts **Dim:** 36.0 (34.5 wl) × 6.6 × 1.3
A: 2/MM 38 Exocet (I × 2)—2/30-mm Emerlec AA (II × 1)—2/20-mm AA (I × 2)
M: 2 MTU 20V538 TB91 diesels; 2 props; 10,800 hp **Range:** 700/30

REMARKS: Ordered 1980. Additional units may follow.

PATROL BOATS

♦ 2 ex-U.S. PC 461-class former submarine chasers

	Bldr	Laid down	L	In serv.
PS 29 Negros Oriental (ex-E 312, ex-*L'Inconstant*, ex-PC 1171)	L.D. Smith, Sturgeon Bay, Wis.	12-3-43	15-5-43	24-9-43
PS 80 Nueva Viscaya (ex-USAF *Altus*, ex-PC 568)	Brown SB, Houston, Tex.	15-9-41	25-4-42	13-7-42

D: 280 tons (450 fl) **S:** 18 kts **Dim:** 52.93 × 7.01 × 2.31 (hull)
A: 1/76.2-mm DP—1/40-mm AA—3 or 5/20-mm AA (I × 3 or 5)
M: 2 GM 16-278A diesels; 2 props; 2,880 hp
Electric: 120 kw **Fuel:** 62 tons **Man:** 70 tot.

REMARKS: PS 29 escaped from Cambodia to the Philippines and was acquired by the latter in 1976; she had previously been transferred to France in 1951, then to Cambodia in 1956. PS 80 served the U.S. Air Force 1963-68, transferring to the Philippines in 3-68. All originally had different diesels, but now have been standardized. Several others have been stricken, including the *Capiz* (PS 27, ex-PC 1564) and *Batangas* (PS 24, ex-PC 1134) in 1979.

♦ 2 Katapangan class Bldr: W. Müller, Hameln, West Germany

	In serv.		In serv.
P 101 Katapangan	9-2-79	P 102 Bagong Lakas	9-2-79

D: 135 tons (150 fl) **S:** 16 kts **Dim:** 37.0 × 6.2 × 1.7
A: 4/30-mm AA Emerlec (II × 2)
M: 2 MTU MB 820 Db1 diesels; 2 props; 2,050 hp

REMARKS: Designed in West Germany. Prototype delivered for trials 11-10-78. Program to build more at Cavite Navy Yard and at Boseco, Bekan, abandoned due to poor performance.

♦ 1 ex-U.S. PGM 71 class Bldr: Peterson Builders, Sturgeon Bay, Wis.

PG 60 Basilan (ex-*Hon Troc*, ex-PGM 83)

D: 130 tons (145 fl) **S:** 17 kts **Dim:** 30.8 (30.2 wl) × 6.4 × 1.85
A: 1/40-mm AA—4/20-mm AA (II × 2)—4/12.7-mm mg (III × 2)
Electron Equipt: Radar: 1/Raytheon 1500B
M: 8 GM 6-71 diesels; 2 props; 2,200 hp **Range:** 1,000/12 **Man:** 27 tot.

REMARKS: In service 4-67. Escaped from Vietnam 4-75, the only one of her class to do so out of 20 transferred; acquired officially by the Philippines 12-76.

♦ 4 ex-U.S. PGM 39 class Bldr: Tacoma Boat, Tacoma, Wash.

	In serv.		In serv.
PG 61 Agusan (ex-PGM 39)	3-60	PG 63 Romblon (ex-PGM 1)	6-60
PG 62 Catanduanes (ex-PGM 40)	3-60	PG 64 Palawan (ex-PGM 42)	6-60

D: 122 tons **S:** 17 kts **Dim:** 30.6 × 6.4 × 2.1 (props)
A: 2/20-mm AA (I × 2) **Electron Equipt:** Radar: 1/Raytheon 1500
M: 2 MTU MB 820 Db diesels; 2 props; 1,900 hp **Man:** 15 tot.

PATROL CRAFT

♦ 80 fiberglass-hulled Bldr: Marcelo, Manila, 1976-. . .

PSB 411   PSB 414   PSB 417-434   PSB. . .

PSB 411   G. Arra, 1977

D: 21.75 (fl) **S:** 46 kts **Dim:** 14.07 × 4.32 × 1.04 (1.48 props)
A: 4/12.7-mm mg (II × 1, I × 2) **Electron Equipt:** Radar: 1/LN-66
M: 2 MTU 8V-331 TC80 diesels; 2 props; 1,800 hp
Electric: 7.5 kVA **Range:** 200/36 **Man:** 6 tot.

REMARKS: Eighty were ordered 8-75, but of 25 hulls completed during 1975, 15 were destroyed by fire. Twin machine-gun mount is recessed into the forecastle.

♦ 6 Australian fiberglass-hulled Bldr: De Havilland Marine, Sydney

PC 326-331 (In serv. 20-11-74 to 8-2-75)

D: 16.5 tons (fl) **S:** 25 kts **Dim:** 14.0 × 4.6 × 1.0
A: 2/12.7-mm mg **M:** 2 Caterpillar D348 diesels; 2 props; 740 hp
Range: 500/12 **Man:** 8 tot.

♦ 17 (+22) U.S. Swift Mk III class Bldr: Sewart Seacraft, Morgan City, Louisiana

PCF 333, 334, 336-352

PCF 335—with Swift Mk II **PCF 308** in background   G. Arra, 1977

D: 28 tons (36.7 fl) **S:** 30 kts **Dim:** 19.78 × 5.5 × 1.8
A: 2/12.7-mm mg (I × 2)—2/7.6-mm mg (I × 2)
Electron Equipt: Radar: 1/LN-66
M: 3 GM 8V 71 TI diesels; 3 props; 1,950 hp **Range:** 500/30 **Man:** 8 tot.

PATROL CRAFT (continued)

REMARKS: Aluminum construction. Pilothouse offset to starboard. Some or all have served in the Philippine Coast Guard. In service 1972-76. In early 1980, 25 more were ordered.

◆ 3 Abra class

	Bldr	In serv.
FB 83 ABRA	Vosper, Singapore	8-1-70
FB 84 BUKINDON	Cavite NY	1971
FB 85 TABLAS	Cavite NY	1975

D: 40 tons **S:** 25 kts **Dim:** 26.7 × 5.8 × 1.5
A: 2/20-mm AA **M:** 2 MTU diesels; 2 props; 2,400 hp **Man:** 3 officers, 12 men

REMARKS: Wooden hulls, aluminum superstructure. Construction financed by Australia. Have served in the Coast Guard.

◆ 12 U.S. Swift Mk I and II class Bldr: Sewart, Berwick, La.

PCF 300   PCF 301   PCF 306   PCF 307   PCF 309-316

PCF 308—Swift Mk II type (stricken 1979)   G. Arra, 1977

D: 17.5 tons (22.1 fl) **S:** 24 kts **Dim:** 15.66 × 4.55 × 1.8 (props)
A: 2/12.7-mm mg (II × 1) **Electron Equipt:** Radar: 1/Raytheon 1500B
M: 2 GM 12V 71 N diesels; 2 props; 850 hp **Electric:** 6 kw
Range: 400/22 **Man:** 6 tot.

REMARKS: In service 1966-70. PCF 300 and PCF 301, transferred 1966, are *Swift* Mk I class, 15.3 overall and with flush-decked hulls. All-aluminum construction. PCF 303, PCF 324, PCF 325, and PCF 317 (the last of ferro-concrete construction and used as a yacht) were discarded in 1976; PCF 304, PCF 305, and one other were written-off in 1976, and PCF 308 was discarded 1979.

NOTE: The two U.S. *Falcon*-class coastal minesweepers *Zambales* (M 55, ex-MSC 218) and *Zamboanga del Norte* (M 56, ex-MSC 219) were stricken in 1979, leaving the Philippine Navy with no mine-countermeasures capability.

AMPHIBIOUS WARFARE SHIPS

◆ 20 ex-U.S. LST 1 and LST 542-class landing ships

	Bldr	In serv.
LT 54 AGUSAN DEL SUR (ex-*Nha Trang*, ex-*Jerome Cty.*, LST 848)	A	20-1-45
LT 86 CAGAYAN (ex-*Hickman Cty.*, LST 825)	C	8-12-44
LT 87 COTABATO DEL SUR (ex-*Thi Nai* ex-*Cayuga Cty.*, LST 529)	D	29-2-44
LT 93 MINDORO OCCIDENTAL (ex-T-LST 222)	B	10-9-43
LT 94 SURIGAO DEL NORTE (ex-T-LST 488)	E	24-5-43
LT 95 SURIGAO DEL SUR (ex-T-LST 546)	C	27-3-44
LT 97 ILOCOS NORTE (ex-*Madera Cty.*, LST 905)	F	20-1-45
LT 500 TARLAC (ex-T-LST 47)	F	8-11-43
LT 501 LAGUNA (ex-T-LST 230)	B	3-11-43
LT 502 SAMAR ORIENTAL (ex-T-LST 287)	A	15-12-43
LT 503 LANAO DEL SUR (ex-T-LST 491)	C	3-12-43
LT 504 LANAO DEL NORTE (ex-T-LST 566)	C	29-5-44
LT 505 LEYTE DEL SUR (ex-T-LST 607)	B	24-4-44
LT 506 DAVAO ORIENTAL (ex-*Oosumi*, ex-*Daggett Cty.*, LST 689)	D	2-5-44
LT 507 BENGUET (ex-*Davies Cty.*, T-LST 692)	D	10-5-44
LT 508 AURORA (ex-*Harris Cty.*, T-LST 822)	C	23-11-44
LT 509 CAVITE (ex-*Shimokita*, ex-*Hillsdale Cty.*, LST 835)	A	20-11-44
LT 510 SAMAR DEL NORTE (ex-*Shiretoko*, ex-*Nansemond Cty.*, LST 1064)	G	12-3-45
LT 511 COTABATO DEL NORTE (ex-*Orleans Parrish*, T-LST 1069, ex-MCS 6, ex-LST 1069)	G	31-3-45
LT 512 TAWI-TAWI (ex-T-LST 1072)	G	12-4-45

Bldrs: *A*, American Bridge, Ambridge, Pa.; *B*, Chicago Bridge & Iron Co., Seneca, Ill.; *C*, Missouri Valley Bridge & Iron Co., Evansville, Ind.; *D*, Jeffersonville Boat and Machinery Co., Jeffersonville, Ind.; *E*, Kaiser Co., Richmond, Cal.; *F*, Dravo Corp., Pittsburgh, Pa.; *G*, Bethlehem Steel, Hingham, Mass.

Surigao del Sur (LT 95)   G. Arra

D: 1,620 tons (4,080 fl) **S:** 11 kts **Dim:** 99.98 (96.32 wl) × 15.24 × 4.29
A: 7-8/40-mm AA (II × 1 or 2, I × 4-6)—2-4/20-mm AA (ex-T-LST: 6/20-mm AA)
M: 2 GM 12-567A diesels (LT 510, 511, 512: 2 GM 12-278A); 2 props; 1,700 hp
Electric: 300 kw **Fuel:** 570 tons **Man:** 60-100 tot.

REMARKS: LT 54 and LT 87 escaped from Vietnam (to which they had been transferred in 4-70 and 12-63, respectively) in 4-75; they were officially transferred to the Philippines on 17-11-75. LT 86 and LT 97 were transferred in 11-69. LT 93, LT 94, and LT 95 were transferred unarmed in 7-72 but may since have received guns. LT 500-LT 505, LT 507, LT 508, LT 511, and LT 512 were purchased in 1976, having previously been stricken by the USN and laid up in Japan. LT 506, LT 509, and LT 510 had been transferred to Japan 4-61 and stricken in 1975; they were purchased in 1978. All the LT 500 series were refitted and thoroughly overhauled in Japan, recommissioning in 1978-79. Armament: Some ex-T-LSTs carry only four 20-mm AA (I × 4),while others received a single 40-mm forward after transfer, plus several 20-mm AA. LT 87 has four sets of Welin davits for LCVP landing craft, the others only two; ex-T-LSTs do not carry LCVPs.

AMPHIBIOUS WARFARE SHIPS (continued)

◆ 4 ex-U.S. LSM 1-class landing ships

	Bldr	L	In serv.
LP 41 Isabela (ex-LSM 463)	Brown SB, Houston	3-2-45	7-3-45
LP 65 Batanes (ex-Huong Giang, ex-Oceanside, ex-LSM 175)	Charleston Naval SY	3-8-44	25-9-44
LP 66 Western Samar (ex-Hat Giang, ex-9011, ex-LSM 335)	Pullman, Chicago	10-11-44	9-12-44
LP 68 Mindoro Oriental (ex-LSM 320)	Pullman, Chicago	20-7-44	19-8-44

D: 513 tons (1,095 fl) **S:** 12 kts **Dim:** 62.02 × 10.52 × 2.24
A: 2/40-mm AA (II × 1)—4/20-mm AA (I × 4)
M: 2 GM 16-278A (LP 41: Fairbanks-Morse 38D8⅛ × 10) diesels; 2 props; 2,800 hp
Electric: 240 kw **Fuel:** 165 tons **Range:** 5,000/7 **Man:** 39 tot.

REMARKS: LP 41 transferred 3-61, LP 68 in 4-62. LP 65 and LP 66 escaped from Vietnam (to which they had been transferred in 8-61 and 10-55, respectively, LP 65 having served in the French Navy from 1-54 to 10-55) in 4-75 and were officially transferred on 17-11-75. LP 66 was equipped with hospital facilities in a deckhouse filling much of her tank deck while in Vietnamese service, but retained guns. Ex-Han Giang, ex-LSM 110, which also escaped, was transferred also on 17-11-75, but used for cannibalization.

◆ 3 ex-U.S. LSSL 1-class gunfire-support landing ships

Bldr: Lawley & Sons, Neponset, Mass. (LS 49: Albina Eng. & Mach., Portland, Ore.)

	L	In serv.
LF 48 Camarines Sur (ex-Nguyen Duc Bong, ex-LSSL 129)	13-12-44	31-12-44
LF 49 Sulu (ex-Nguyen Ngoc Long, ex-LSSL 96)	6-1-45	24-1-45
LF 50 La Union (ex-Doan Ngoc Tang, ex-Hallebarde, ex-LSSL 9)	17-8-44	6-9-44

D: 250 tons (387 fl) **S:** 14.4 kts **Dim:** 48.15 × 7.21 × 1.73
A: 1/76-mm DP—4/20-mm AA (II × 2)—4/12.7-mm mg (I × 4)
M: 8 GM 6-71 diesels; 2 CP props; 1,320 hp **Electric:** 120 kw **Fuel:** 84 tons
Range: 5,000/12

REMARKS: These are ex-Vietnamese ships (transferred 1965-66) that took refuge in the Philippines and were acquired by the latter 17-11-75. LF 50 had earlier served in the French (1951-55) and Japanese (1956-64) navies. Four additional ex-Japanese sisters were to have been transferred in 1978, but the sale was canceled.

NOTE: The four ships of the U.S. LSIL 351-class have been stricken, Misamis Oriental (LF 53) in 1979, and Marinduque (LF 36), Sorsogon (LF 37), and Camarines Norte (LF 52) in 1980.

◆ 3 ex-U.S. LCU 1466-class utility landing craft Bldr: Japan (In serv. 3-55)

L. . . N. . . (ex-LCU 2002, ex-LCU 1603)
L. . . N. . . (ex-LCU 2003, ex-LCU 1604)
L. . . N. . . (ex-LCU 2005, ex-LCU 1606)

D: 180 tons (347 fl) **S:** 8 kts **Dim:** 35.05 × 10.36 × 1.6 (aft)
A: 2/20-mm AA (I × 2) **M:** 3 GM Gray Marine 64YTL diesels; 3 props; 675 hp
Cargo capacity: 167 tons **Man:** 6 men plus 8 troops

REMARKS: Built in Japan under the Offshore Procurement Plan; in service 3-55, stricken 1975. Purchased 17-11-75 while laid up, then refitted and recommissioned in 1979.

◆ 9 U.S. LCM(8)-class landing craft

LCM 257 LCM 258 LCM 260-LCM 266

D: 118 tons (fl) **S:** 9 kts **Dim:** 22.43 × 6.42 × 1.4 (aft)
M: 4 GM 6-71 diesels; 2 props; 600 hp **Cargo capacity:** 54 tons

REMARKS: Transferred 19-3-75. The similar Bagong Filipino (TK 81) and Dakila (TK 82), built in the Philippines, have been stricken.

◆ 75 ex-U.S. LCM(6)-class landing craft

D: 56 tons (fl) **S:** 10 kts **Dim:** 17.1 × 4.4 × 1.2 (aft)
M: 2 GM Gray Marine 64HN9 diesels; 2 props; 330 hp **Cargo capacity:** 30 tons

REMARKS: Transferred 19-3-75. The similar Bagong Filipino (TK 81) and Dakila (TK the remainder came directly from the U.S. Navy.

AUXILIARY SHIPS

YACHTS

◆ 1 presidential yacht Bldr: Vosper, Singapore (In serv. 12-77)

TP 77 Ang Pinuno

D: 150 tons **S:** 28.5 kts **Dim:** 37.9 × 7.2 × 3.8 **Range:** . . . **Man:** . . .
A: None **M:** 3 MTU 12V538 TB91 diesels; 3 props; 7,500 hp

REMARKS: Used as a "command ship" for the president. White-painted. Sister Bataan is used as a search-and-rescue ship by the Coast Guard.

◆ 1 former transport Bldr: Ishikawajima, Harima, Japan (In serv. 1959)

TP 777 Ang Pangulo (ex-The President, ex-Roxas, ex-Lapu-Lapu)

Ang Pangulo (TP 777) G. Arra, 1977

D: 2,230 tons (2,750 fl) **S:** 18 kts **Dim:** 83.84 × 13.01 × 6.4
A: 2/20-mm AA
M: 2 Mitsui-Burmeister & Wain DE 642 VBF 75 diesels; 2 props; 5,000 hp
Electric: 820 kw **Man:** 81 men plus 48 passengers

REMARKS: Built as war reparations. Can be converted for use as a troop transport.

TENDERS

◆ 3 ex-U.S. Achelous-class repair ships Bldr: Chicago Bridge & Iron Co., Seneca, Ill. (AR 67: Bethlehem Steel, Hingham, Mass.)

TENDERS *(continued)*

	L	In serv.
AE 517 YAKAL (ex-*Satyr*, ARL 23, ex-LST 852)	13-11-44	24-11-44
AR 67 KAMAGONG (ex-*Aklan*, ex-*Romulus*, ARL 22, ex-LST 926)	15-11-44	9-12-44
AR 88 NARRA (ex-*Krishna*, ARL 38, ex-LST 1149)	25-5-45	3-12-45

D: 3,960 tons (fl)   **S:** 11.6 kts   **Dim:** 99.98 (96.32 wl) × 15.24 × 3.71
A: 8/40-mm AA (IV × 2)
M: 2 GM 12-567A diesels (AR 67: GM 12-278A); 2 props; 1,800 hp
Electric: 420 kw   **Fuel:** 620 tons   **Man:** 250 tot.

REMARKS: AE 517, transferred 24-1-77, may be in use as an ammunition transport, based on the hull number, but was equipped for repair duties on delivery. AR 67 was transferred in 11-61 and AR 88 on 31-10-71. All have a 60-ton capacity A-frame lift boom to port and one 10-ton derrick and one 20-ton derrick.

♦ 2 ex-U.S. LST 542-class small craft tenders

	Bldr	In serv.
AL 57 SIERRA MADRE (ex-*Dumagat*, ex-*My Tho*, ex-*Harnett County*, AGP 821, ex-LST 821)	Missouri Valley B & I, Evansville, Ind.	14-11-44
AE 516 APAYAO (ex-*Can Tho*, ex-*Garrett County*, AGP 786, ex-LST 786)	Dravo Corp., Pittsburgh, Pa.	28-8-44

D: 1,620 tons (4,080 fl)   **S:** 11.6 kts
Dim: 99.98 (96.32 wl) × 15.24 × 4.29 (max.)
A: 8/40-mm AA (II × 2, I × 4)—4/20-mm AA (II × 2)
M: 2 GM 12-567A diesels; 2 props; 1,700 hp   **Electric:** 500 kw
Fuel: 370 tons   **Range:** 19,000/10   **Man:** 160 tot.

REMARKS: Converted in the mid-1960s to act as tenders to riverine-warfare craft. Retain bow doors, but much of the tank deck is filled with repair shops and bins for spare parts. Helicopter deck amidships, tripod masts, 10-ton derrick, and enlarged hatch. Transferred to South Vietnam 10-70 and 4-71; both escaped 4-75 and purchased outright on 13-9-77. Different hull numbers (and change of letter-designator and name to AL 57 from AE 57) may indicate new roles.

CARGO TRANSPORTS

♦ 1 ex-U.S. Alamosa class Bldr: Froemming Bros. Inc., Milwaukee, Wis.

TK 90 MACTAN (ex-*Kukui*, WAK 186, ex-*Colquitt*, AK 174)

D: 4,900 tons (7,450 fl)   **S:** 12 kts   **Dim:** 103.18 (97.54 wl) × 15.24 × 6.43
A: 2/20-mm AA   **M:** 1 Nordberg TSM6 diesel; 1 prop; 1,750 hp
Electric: 500 kw   **Fuel:** 350 tons   **Man:** 85 tot.

REMARKS: In service 22-9-45; 6,071 dwt. Built for U.S. Maritime Commission, taken over by the Navy upon completion, then transferred to the U.S. Coast Guard 24-9-45. First platform deck in cargo-hold area converted to personnel accommodations. Transferred to the Philippines 1-3-72 and used as a military transport, supply ship, and lighthouse tender. Purchased outright 1-8-80.

♦ 3 ex-U.S. Army FS 381 class Bldr: Ingalls, Pascagoula, Miss. (In serv. 1943-44)

TK 79 LIMASAWA (ex-*Nettle*, WAK 129, ex-FS 169)
AS 59 BADJAO (ex-*Miho*, ex-FS 524)
AS 71 MANGYAN (ex-*Nasami*, ex-FS 408)

D: 473 tons light (950 fl)   **S:** 13 kts   **Dim:** 53.8 (50.27 pp) × 9.75 × 3.05
A: 2/20-mm AA (I × 2)   **M:** 2 GM 6-278A diesels; 2 props; 1,000 hp
Electric: 225 kw   **Cargo capacity:** 345 tons
Fuel: 67 tons   **Range:** 4,150/10, 3,700/11   **Man:** . . .

REMARKS: The *Limasawa* was loaned in 1-68 and purchased outright 31-8-78. The other two were purchased 24-9-76 after having served in the Japanese Navy as an inshore minesweeper depot ship and a mine-countermeasures support ship; they were to be refitted and were recommissioned during 1979. All were to serve as buoy tenders and lighthouse supply ships.

♦ 2 ex-U.S. Army FS 330 class Bldr: Higgins, Inc., New Orleans (In serv. 1943- 44)

TK 45 LAUIS LEDGE (ex-FS 185)   TK 46 CAPE BOJEADOR (ex-FS 203)

Cape Bojeador (TK 46)—in Coast Guard colors   G. Arra, 1977

D: 420 tons light (742 fl)   **S:** 10 kts   **Dim:** 51.77 (48.77 pp) × 9.75 × 2.43
A: 2/20-mm AA (I × 2)   **M:** 4 Buda-Lanova 6 DHMR-1879 diesels; 2 props; 680 hp   **Cargo Capacity:** 150 tons
Electric: 225 kw   **Fuel:** 18 tons   **Range:** 1,370/10   **Man:** . . .

REMARKS: TK 45 transferred 11-47; TK 46 transferred 2-50. Can carry up to 50 tons of fuel for a range of 3,830/10. Used as navigational buoy tenders and lighthouse supply ships.

♦ 1 ex-Australian motor stores lighter Bldr: Australia (In serv. 1944)

TK. . . PEARL BANK (ex-U.S. Army LO 4, ex-. . .)

D: 140 tons light (345 fl)   **S:** 8 kts   **Dim:** 37.26 × 7.47 × 2.07
A: 2/20-mm AA   **M:** 2 Fairbanks-Morse 35F8¾ diesels; 2 props; 240 hp
Fuel: 20 tons   **Range:** 2,000/6   **Man:** 35 tot.

REMARKS: Transferred 1947. Used as a navigational buoy tender and lighthouse supply ship. Cargo capacity: 170 tons.

CARGO TRANSPORTS *(continued)*

♦ **1 ex-U.S. Admirable-class minesweeper** Bldr: Gulf SB Corp., Madisonville, La.

	Laid down	L	In serv.
TK 21 Mount Samat (ex-*Pagasa*, ex-*Santa Maria*, ex-*Quest*, MSF 281)	24-11-43	16-3-44	25-10-44

Mount Samat (TK 21)   G. Arra, 1977

D: 650 tons (945 fl) **S:** 14.8 kts **Dim:** 58.0 (54.86 wl) × 10.06 × 2.97
A: 2/20-mm AA **M:** 2 Cooper-Bessemer GSB-8 diesels; 2 props; 1,710 hp
Electric: 280 kw **Fuel:** 138 tons **Man:** 60 tot.

REMARKS: Transferred 2-7-48 and then converted to presidential yacht with considerable additions to superstructure and increased rake to bow. Now primarily used as a lighthouse supply ship.

♦ **1 ex-U.S. Coast Guard Balsam-class buoy tender** Bldr: Marine Iron & SB Corp., Duluth, Minn. (In serv. 2-5-44)

TK 89 Kalinga (ex-*Redbud*, WAGL 398, ex-T-AKL 398, ex-AG 398)

Kalinga (TK 89)—in Coast Guard colors   1977

D: 935 tons (1,020 fl) **S:** 13 kts **Dim:** 54.86 × 11.28 × 3.96
A: 1/20-mm AA
M: 2 Cooper-Bessemer GSD-8 diesels, electric drive; 1 prop; 1,200 hp
Range: 3,500/7.5 **Man:** 50 tot.

REMARKS: Built for U.S. Coast Guard, transferred to the U.S. Navy on 25-3-49 as AG 398, to Military Sealift Command on 10-49 as T-AKL 398, and returned 20-11-70 to the U.S. Coast Guard. Transferred to the Philippines 1-3-72. Has helicopter platform and ice-breaking bow—the latter a useful feature in Philippine waters.

SERVICE CRAFT

TANKERS

♦ **2 ex-U.S. 174-foot YO and YOG-class small tankers** Bldr: R.T.C. SB, Camden, N.J. (YO 78: Puget Sound Naval SY, Washington)

	Laid down	L	In serv.
YO 43 Lake Naujan (ex-YO 173)	17-5-44	30-9-44	22-1-45
YO 78 Lake Buhi (ex-YOG 73)	15-12-43	23-2-44	28-11-44

Lake Naujan (YO 43)   G. Arra, 1977

D: 445 tons light (1,420 fl) **S:** 8 kts **Dim:** 53.04 × 10.01 × 4.27
A: 2/20-mm AA (I × 2)
M: 2 Union diesels; 2 props; 560 hp (YO 78: 2 GM 8-278A diesels; 2 props; 640 hp)
Fuel: 25 tons **Man:** 23 tot.

REMARKS: YO 43 was transferred in 7-48, and YO 78 (formerly used as a gasoline tanker) in 7-67. Ex-U.S. YOG 33 and YOG 80, which escaped from Vietnam, were used for cannibalization spares. Cargo capacity: 985 tons. Sister *Lake Mainit* (YO 35) stricken 1979.

♦ **3 ex-U.S. 174-foot YW-class water tankers** Bldr: L. D. Smith SB, Sturgeon Bay, Wis. (YW 111: Marine Iron & SB Co., Duluth, Minn.)

	Laid down	L	In serv.
YW 33 Lake Boluan (ex-YW 111)	30-9-44	16-12-44	1-8-45
YW 34 Lake Paoay (ex-YW 130)	14-5-45	24-6-45	28-8-45
YW 42 Lake Lanao (ex-YW 125)	18-12-44	7-4-45	16-6-45

D: 440 tons light (1,390 fl) **S:** 8 kts **Dim:** 53.04 × 10.01 × 4.0
A: 2/20-mm AA (I × 2) **M:** 2 GM 8-278A diesels; 2 props; 640 hp
Electric: 80 kw **Fuel:** 25 tons **Man:** 23 tot.

REMARKS: Transferred YW 33 and 34 on 16-7-75 and YW 42 in 7-78. Cargo capacity: 930 tons.

TUGS

♦ **1 ex-U.S. Army tug**

YQ 58 TIBOLI (ex-LT 1976)

REMARKS: Transferred, 3-76.

♦ **5 ex-U.S. YTL 442 class** Bldr: Everett-Pacific Co., Everett, Wash. (YQ 222: Winslow Marine Railway & SB, Winslow, Wash.)

YQ 222 IGOROT (ex-YTL 572)   YQ 226 TASADAY (ex-YTL 425)
YQ 223 TAGBANUA (ex-YTL 429)   YQ 271 AGNO RIVER (ex-YAS 3, ex-YTL 750)
YQ 225 ILONGOT (ex-YTL 427)

D: 70 tons (80 fl)   **S:** 9 kts   **Dim:** 20.17 × 5.18 × 1.5
M: 1 Hamilton 685A diesel; 300 hp

REMARKS: Built 1944-45. Transferred 7-48, 5-63, 12-69, 8-71, and 11-75—the last from Japan, which had received her from the U.S. in 1-55. Two others, the *Maranao* (YQ 221, ex-YTL 554) and the *Aeta* (YQ 224, ex-YTL 449) have been scrapped. The ex-Japanese craft was overhauled and arrived in the Philippines during 1979, sister ex-YAS 4 (ex-YTL 748) having been lost overboard en route.

FLOATING DRY DOCKS

♦ **1 ex-U.S. AFDL** Bldr: V.P. Loftis, Wilmington, N.C. (In serv. 11-44)

YD 205 (ex-AFDL 44, ex-ARDC 11)

Lift Capacity: 2,800 tons   **Dim:** 118.6 × 25.6 × 3.1 (light)

REMARKS: Transferred, 9-69. Purchased outright 1-8-80.

♦ **3 ex-U.S. AFDL 1 class**

	Bldr	In serv.	Transferred
YD 200 (ex-AFDL 24)	Doullet & Ewin, Mobile, Ala.	1-44	7-48
YD 204 (ex-AFDL 20)	G.D. Auchter, Jacksonville, Fla.	6-44	10-61
YD. . . (ex-AFDL 10)	Chicago Bridge & Iron	12-43	12-78

Lift Capacity: 1,000 tons   **Dim:** 60.96 × 19.51 × 1.04 (light)

♦ **2 ex-U.S. Army**

	L	Transferred
YD 201 (ex-AFDL 3681)	1943	5-52
YD 203 (ex-AFDL 3682)	1943	8-55

Lift capacity: 150 tons   **Dim:** 30.63 × 15.83 × 1.0 (light)

FLOATING CRANES

♦ **1 ex-U.S. floating crane**

	In serv.	Transferred
YU 206 (ex-YD 163)	12-5-46	1-71

D: 650 tons (fl)   **Dim:** 36.58 × 13.72 × 2.13   **Lift Capacity:** 30 tons

♦ **1 ex-U.S. floating crane**

	In serv.	Transferred
YU 207 (ex-YD 191)	3-52	8-71

D: 920 tons (fl)   **Dim:** 36.58 × 18.24 × 2.13   **Lift Capacity:** 60 tons

FLOATING REPAIR BARGES

♦ **1 ex-U.S. Army 230 class**

	L	Transferred
YD 202 (ex-. . .)	1943	7-49

D: 2,100 tons (fl)   **Dim:** 64.0 × 12.5 × 3.4   **A:** 2/20-mm AA

BARGES

♦ **1 ex-U.S. YCV 3-class former aircraft transport lighter** Bldr: Pearl Harbor Naval SY (In serv. 25-11-43)

YB 206 (ex-YCV 7)

Dim: 33.53 × 9.14 ×. . .   **Cargo Capacity:** 250 tons

REMARKS: Transferred, 5-63.

♦ **2 ex-U.S. Navy barges**

	Transferred
YC 207 (ex-YC 1402)	8-59
YC 301 (ex-YC 1403)	8-71

Dim: 24.38 × 8.73 × 1.22

COAST GUARD

The size of the Philippine Coast Guard has fluctuated widely since its establishment in the early 1970s. At one time it had responsibility for maintaining navigational aids and included many of the tenders now returned to the Navy. The majority of the patrol craft operated by the Coast Guard have been back under naval control since 1977, leaving only a few small craft and the larger ships described below still under Coast Guard control.

♦ **2 Bessang Pass-class search-and-rescue boats** Bldr: Sumidagawa, Tokyo, Japan (In serv. 1976-77)

SAR 99 BESSANG PASS   SAR 100 TIRAD PASS

Bessang Pass (SAR 99)   G. Arra, 1977

D: 275 tons (fl)   **S:** 30 kts   **Dim:** 44.0 × 7.4 × 1.5
A: None   **M:** 2 diesels; 2 props; . . . hp   **Man:** 32 tot.

♦ **1 search-and-rescue boat** Bldr: Vosper, Singapore (In serv. 12-75)

SAR 77 BATAAN

PHILIPPINES *(continued)*
COAST GUARD *(continued)*

    D: 150 tons **S:** 28 kts **Dim:** 37.9 × 7.2 × 3.8
    M: 3 MTU 12V538 TB91 diesels; 3 props; 7,500 hp

REMARKS: Externally identical to presidential yacht *Ang Pinuno* (TP 77) and may, in fact, be the same ship.

COAST AND GEODETIC SURVEY

The ships listed below are subordinate to the Ministry of Defense and are used for hydrographic survey.

♦ **1 survey ship** Bldr: Walkers, Maryborough, Australia (In serv. 1969)

ATYIMBA

Atyimba   G. Arra, 1977

    D: 611 tons (686 fl) **S:** 11 kts **Dim:** 49.08 (44.3 pp) × 10.14 × 2.74
    M: Mirrlees-Blackstone 6-cyl. diesels; 1,620 hp
    Electric: 175 kw **Range:** 5,000/8 **Man:** 54 tot.

♦ **2 Arinya-class coastal survey ships** Bldr: Walkers, Maryborough, Australia

ARINYA (L: 1962) ALUNYA (L: 1964)

    D: 245 tons (fl) **S:** 10 kts **Dim:** 30.64 (27.44 pp) × 6.76 × 2.43
    M: 2 GM 6-71 diesels; 2 props; 336 hp **Man:** 6 officers, 27 men

♦ **1 ex-U.S. Coast & Geodetic Survey ship** Bldr: Lake Washington SY, Houghton, Wash.

	Laid down	In serv.
PATHFINDER (ex-*Pathfinder*, OSS 30, ex-AGS 1)	3-9-42	31-8-43

    D: 2,175 tons (fl) **S:** 14 kts **Dim:** 69.9 (63.8 wl) × 11.89 × 4.88
    M: 2 sets GT; 2 props; 2,000 hp **Electric:** 145 kw
    Boilers: 2 Babcock & Wilcox, 22 kg/cm², 330°C **Fuel:** 340 tons **Man:** 150 tot.

REMARKS: Served in the U.S. Navy during World War II, transferred to the Philippines in the mid-1970s.

POLAND
Polish People's Republic

PERSONNEL (1980): 25,000 men

MERCHANT MARINE (1980): 842 ships-3,639,078 grt (tankers: 31 ships-570,698 grt)

NAVAL AVIATION: About 40 fixed-wing aircraft, including MIG-17 Fresco fighters and IL-28 Beagle bombers, and about 20 Hare and Hound helicopters. All are of Soviet origin and in need of replacement.

SUBMARINES

♦ **4 ex-Soviet Whiskey class**

292 ORZEL 293 SOKOL 294 KONDOR 295 BIELIK

Orzel (292)   Polish Navy

    D: 1,050/1,350 tons **S:** 17/13.5 kts **Dim:** 76.0 × 6.3 × 4.8
    A: 6/533-mm TT (4 fwd, 2 aft; —14 torpedoes or 28 mines)
    Electron Equipt: Radar: 1/Snoop Plate
                             Sonar: 1/Herkules, passive arrays
    M: 2 Type 37D, 2,000-hp diesels, diesel-electric drive; 2 props; 2,500 hp
    Endurance: 40 days **Range:** 6,000/5 snorkel **Man:** 60 tot.

REMARKS: Transferred 1962-65.

GUIDED-MISSILE DESTROYER

♦ **1 ex-Soviet SAM Kotlin class**

275 WARSZAWA (ex-*Spravedlivyy*)

    D: 2,600 tons (3,500 fl) **S:** 36 kts **Dim:** 126.5 × 13.0 × 4.6 (5.6 sonar)
    A: 1/SA-N-1 SAM system (II × 1)—2/130-mm DP (II × 1)—4/45-mm AA (IV × 1)—2/RBU-2500 ASW RL (XVI × 2)—5/533-mm TT (V × 1)
    Electron Equipt: Radar: 1/Head Net A, 1/Don-2, 1/Sun Visor, 1/Hawk Screech, 1/Peel Group
                              Sonar: 1/Herkules or Pegas
    M: 2 sets GT; 2 props; 72,000 hp **Boilers:** 4; 64 kg/cm², 510°C
    Electric: 1,400 kw **Range:** 1050/34; 3,600/18 **Man:** 285 tot.

REMARKS: Built in the U.S.S.R. in 1958 and transferred in 1970, having completed conversion in 1969. Maintained in immaculate condition.

GUIDED-MISSILE DESTROYER *(continued)*

Warszawa (275)   Polish Navy

GUIDED-MISSILE PATROL BOATS

♦ **13 Osa-I class**

Polish Navy Osa-I 424   1980

D: 175 tons (210 fl) **S:** 36 kts **Dim:** 39.0 × 7.7 × 1.8
A: 4/SS-N-2A Styx SSM (I × 4)—4/30-mm AA (II × 2)
Electron Equipt: Radar: 1/Square Tie, 1/Drum Tilt
　　　　　　　　　IFF: 2/Square Head, 1/High Pole B
M: 3 M503A diesels; 3 props; 12,000 hp **Range:** 430/34; 790/20 **Man:** 25 tot.

REMARKS: Built in the U.S.S.R. during the early 1960s, transferred 1966-196. . . .

TORPEDO BOATS

♦ **10 Wisla class** Bldr: Poland, 1970-. . .

D: 68 tons (80 fl) **S:** 50 kts **Dim:** 24.0 × 7.8 × 1.5
A: 2/30-mm AA—4/533-mm TT

Wisla class (496)

Electron Equipt: Radar: 1/Pot Head—IFF: 1/High Pole A
M: 4 M50-F4 diesels; 4 props; 4,800 hp **Range:** 100/50; 500/20 **Man:** 16 tot.

PATROL BOATS

♦ **5 Modified Obluze class** Bldr: Oksywie SY, 1970-72

321-325

Modified Obluze-class 352 (old number)—now has d.c. racks aft   Polish Navy

D: 210 tons (240 fl) **S:** 24 kts **Dim:** 41.0 (39.5 pp) × 6.0 × 2.0 (hull)
A: 4/30-mm AA (II × 2)—4/d.c. racks (2 topside; 2 through stern)
Electron Equipt: Radar: 1/RN-231, 1/Drum Tilt
　　　　　　　　　Sonar: 1/Tamir-11—IFF: 2/Square Head, 1/High Pole
M: 2 Type 40D diesels; 2 props; 5,000 hp **Electric:** 150 kw
Fuel: 25 tons **Man:** 40 tot.

REMARKS: Similar to a larger group in the Polish Border Guard that do *not* have Drum Tilt fire-control radars.

MINE WARFARE SHIPS

♦ **12 Krogulec-class minesweepers** Bldr: Stocznia Gdynska, Gdynia, 1963-67

PELIKAN	KORMORAN	KANIA	ZURAW
KROGULEC	JASTRAB	TUKAN	CZAPLA
ORLIK	ALBATROS	JASKOLKA	CZALDA

MINE WARFARE SHIPS (continued)

Krogulec class—with six 25-mm AA   Polish Navy

Krogulec class—with four 23-mm AA aft   1978

D: 450 tons (484 fl) **S:** 18 kts **Dim:** 60.0 (58.0 pp) × 7.6 × 2.3
A: 6/25-mm AA (II × 3)—2/d.c. racks—mines
M: 2 Fiat A-230S diesels; 2 props; 3,740 hp **Range:** 3,200/12
Electron Equipt: Radar: 1/RN-231 **Fuel:** 55 tons **Man:** 6 officers, 24 men

REMARKS: Some of these ships have four 23-mm rapid-fire AA (II × 2) mounted aft
in place of the original four 25-mm AA. Hull numbers currently 625 and up.

♦ **12 Soviet T 43-type minesweepers** Bldr: Stocznia Gdynska, Gdynia, 1957-62

601 ZUBR	603 LOZ	605 BIZON	607 ROZMAK	609 FOKA	611 RYS
602 TUR	604 DZIK	606 BOBR	608 DELFIN	610 MORS	612 ZBIK

Zbik (612)—long-hulled version   1975

Zubr (601)—short-hulled version   Polish Navy

D: 520 tons (590 fl) **S:** 14 kts **Dim:** 60.0 × 8.6 × 2.3 (3.5 sonar)
A: 4/37-mm AA (II × 2)—4/25-mm AA (II × 2)—4/14.5-mm mg (II × 2)—2/d.c.
projectors—mines
Electron Equipt: Radar: 1/Don-2
Sonar: 1/Tamir-11
IFF: 1/Square Head, 1/High Pole A
M: 2 Type 9D diesels; 2 props; 2,200 hp **Man:** 7 officers, 70 men

REMARKS: *Zubr, Tur, Loz,* and *Dzik,* built in the U.S.S.R., are 2-meters shorter and
displace 569 tons (fl); they have 8/14.5-mm mg, but no 25-mm AA. *Tur* has been
converted into a radar picket, losing the after twin 37-mm AA and all sweep capability
in favor of a quadripod mast to support a large radar antenna.

♦ **1 (+. . .) new construction coastal minesweeper**

D: 160 tons **S:** . . . kts **Dim:** 35.0 ×. . . ×. . .
A: . . . **M:** 2 diesels; 2 props; . . . hp

REMARKS: Glass-reinforced plastic construction. Launched 16-4-81.

MINE WARFARE SHIPS (continued)

◆ **28 K 8-class inshore minesweepers** Bldr: Gdansk SY, Poland (In serv. 1953-60)

Polish Navy K 8-class inshore minesweeper 1977

D: 20 tons (26 fl) **S:** 12 kts **Dim:** 17.0 × 3.2 × 0.8
A: 2/14.5-mm mg (II × 1) **M:** 2 3D6 diesels; 2 props; 600 hp

REMARKS: Wooden hulls; simple wire sweeps only.

AMPHIBIOUS WARFARE SHIPS

◆ **1 Soviet Polnocny-C-class landing ship** Bldr: Polnocny SY, Gdansk (In serv. 1971)

GRUNWALD

D: 1,150 tons (fl) **S:** 18 kts **Dim:** 81.3 × 10.1 × 2.1
A: 4/30-mm AA (II × 2)—2/140-mm RL (XVIII × 2)
Electron Equipt: Radar: 1/Drum Tilt, 1/Don 2
  IFF: 1/Square Head, 1/High Pole A
M: 2 Type 40D diesels; 2 props; 4,000 hp

◆ **22 Polnocny-A and -B-class landing ships** Bldr: Polnocny SY, Gdansk (In serv. 1964-70)

BALAS, BRDA, JANOW, LENINA, NARWIK, POLICHNO, RABLOW, STUDZIANK, WARTA, and 13 others

Polish Navy Polnocny-A 1976

Polish Navy Polnocny-B 1978

D: A: 770 tons (fl); B: 740 tons (800 fl) **S:** 19 kts
Dim: 73.0 (B: 74.0) × 8.6 × 1.9 **A:** 4/30-mm AA—2/140-mm RL (XVIII × 2)
Electron Equipt: Radar: 1/RN-231 or Don-2, 1/Drum Tilt
  IFF: 1/Square Head, 1/High Pole A
M: 2 Type 40D diesels; 2 props; 5,000 hp
Fuel: 36 tons **Range:** 900/18 **Man:** 35 tot.

REMARKS: Polnocny-A has blunt, convex bow form; the "B" version introduced a raked, flared bow to improve seaworthiness. Unlike Soviet Navy units, Polish Polnocnys have a standard armament suit. Cargo: 180 tons vehicles, 130 troops. Now carry hull numbers 801-811 and 888-899. At least one Type A has a high bridge and low-mounted Drum Tilt radar like the "B" version.

◆ **4 Marabut-class landing craft** (In serv. 1975)

Marabut class (872)

D: 60 tons (fl) **S:** 15 kts **Dim:** 21.0 × 4.2 × 1.0
A: 1/14.5-mm mg **M:** 2 diesels; 2 props;... hp

REMARKS: The *Marabut* class has plastic hull and can carry light vehicles.

◆ **12-15 Eichstaden-class personnel landing craft** (In serv. early 1960s)

D: 25 tons (fl) **S:** 18 kts **Dim:** 16.6 × 4.0 × 1.7
A: Small arms **M:** 2 3D6 diesels; 2 props; 300 hp **Man:** 3 tot.

REMARKS: Cargo: 20 troops. Pointed bow, troops exiting cargo compartment via ramps on sides.

HYDROGRAPHIC SHIPS

♦ **3 Fenik class** Bldr: Polnocny SY, Gdansk (In serv. 1981)

ZODIAK   N . . .   N . . .

D: 1,200 tons (fl) **S:** 13 kts **Dim:** 61.30 × 10.80 × 3.27 **Electric:** 675 kVA
Electron Equipt: Radar: 1/RN-231 **Range:** 3,000/10 **Man:** 5 officers, 23 men
M: 2 Cegielski-Sulzer 6 AL 25/30 diesels; 2 CP props; 1,920 hp; 2 150-kw electric auxiliary drive motors

REMARKS: Two will be able to link via chain drag for clearance surveys. Have a bow-thruster, 4 precision echo-sounders. Two or three 3-ton-capacity ramped landing craft workboats, handled by the 7-ton crane forward, aid in the ships' secondary role as a navigation aids/buoy tenders. Sisters in Soviet and East German navies.

♦ **1 Soviet Moma class** Bldr: Polnocny SY, Gdansk (In serv. 1973)

KOPERNIK

Kopernik—crane forward now removed   1976

D: 1,260 tons (1,540 fl) **S:** 17 kts **Dim:** 73.3 × 10.8 × 3.8
Electron Equipt: Radars: 2/RN-231
M: 2 Zgoda-Sulzer 6TD48 diesels; 2 CP props; 3,600 hp
Endurance: 35 days **Range:** 8,700/11 **Man:** 56 tot.

REMARKS: Sisters in Bulgarian and Yugoslav navies. *Piast*-class salvage ships and *Wodnik*-class training ships are very similar. Two others, the *Nawigator* and *Hydrometr*, serve as intelligence collectors. The *Kopernik* has 35 m² of laboratory deck area and has been modified for use in seismic survey, oil exploration work.

AUXILIARY SHIPS

♦ **3 Moskit-class coastal oilers** Bldr: Poland (In serv. 1971-72)

Z 3 KRAB   Z 8 MEDUSA   Z 9 SLIMAK

D: 1,200 tons (fl) **S:** 10 kts **Dim:** 57.7 (54.0 pp) × 9.5 × 3.4
A: 4/25-mm AA (II × 2) **Electron Equipt:** Radar: 1/RN-231
M: 2 Cegielski-Sulzer diesels; 2 CP props; 850 hp **Man:** 12 tot.

REMARKS: Cargo: 800 tons. Guns occasionally removed.

Medusa (Z 8)   1973

♦ **3 Type 5-class coastal oilers** (In serv. early 1960s)

Z 5   Z 6   Z 7

D: 625 tons (fl) **S:** 9 kts **Dim:** 44.2 × 6.5 × 3.0
M: 2 diesels; 2 props; 600 hp **Man:** 16 tot.

REMARKS: Cargo: 280 tons. Can carry 4/25-mm AA (II × 2).

♦ **2 Piast-class salvage ships** Bldr: Polnocny SY, Gdansk

PIAST (In serv. 30-11-74)   LECH (In serv. 1975)

Piast   1974

D: 1,560 tons (1,732 fl) **S:** 16.5 kts **Dim:** 73.2 (67.2 pp) × 10.8 × 4.0
Electron Equipt: Radar: 2/RN-231
M: 2 Cegielski-Sulzer 6TD48 diesels; 2 CP props; 3,600 hp **Range:** 3,000/12

REMARKS: Variation of *Moma* design for salvage and rescue duties. Equipped to mount eight 25-mm AA in wartime (II × 4). Carry submarine rescue bell to port, can tow, and have extensive pump and fire-fighting facilities. Sister *Otto von Guericke* is in the East German Navy.

♦ **3 Mrovka-class degaussing/deperming tenders** (In serv. 1970-71)

SD 11   SD 12   SD 13

AUXILIARY SHIPS *(continued)*

D: 550 tons (fl) **S:** 9 kts **Dim:** 44.6 × 8.2 × 3.0
M: 1 diesel; 1 prop; 300 hp **Man:** 20 tot.

REMARKS: Provision for 2/25-mm AA (II × 2) on forecastle.

INTELLIGENCE COLLECTORS

♦ **2 modified Moma class** Bldr: Polnocny SY, Gdansk (In serv. 1975-76)

HYDROMETR NAWIGATOR

Nawigator   G. Koop, 1978

REMARKS: Data as for hydrographic ship *Kopernik* above. Crane removed, superstructure lengthened, lattice mainmast as on *Piast* class, two large radomes. Euphemistically described as "navigational training ships."

♦ **1 converted B 1-class trawler** Bldr: Gdansk SY (In serv. 1954)

BALTYK

Baltyk   G. Koop, 1978

D: 1,140 tons (fl) **S:** 11 kts **Dim:** 59.2 (53.5 pp) × 9.2 × 4.2
M: 1 set Friedrichstadt triple-expansion reciprocating steam; 1 prop; 1,000 hp
Boilers: 1 Howden-Johnson; 16.5 kg/cm² **Fuel:** 150 tons **Range:** 7,200/10

REMARKS: Built as a fishing trawler, adapted as intelligence collector early 1960s.

TRAINING SHIPS

♦ **2 Wodnik class** Bldr: Polnocny SY, Gdansk

WODNIK (L: 29-11-75)   GRYF (L: 13-3-76)

Wodnik   Polish Navy

D: 1,800 tons (fl) **S:** 16.8 kts **Dim:** 74.0 × 13.0 × 4.2
A: 4/30-mm AA (II × 2)—4/25-mm AA (II × 2)
Electron Equipt: Radar: 2/RN-231, 1/Drum Tilt
M: 2 Cegielski-Sulzer 6TD48 diesels; 2 CP props; 3,600 hp
Range: 7,500/11 **Man:** 60 men + 13 instructors and 87 cadets

REMARKS: Nearly identical to the East German Navy's *Wilhelm Pieck* and similar to the *Luga* and *Oka* in the Soviet Navy. Developed from the *Moma* design. Have latest navigational systems from the West and the U.S.S.R.

♦ **4 Bryza class** Bldr: Wisla SY

	In serv.		In serv.
BRYZA	1965	KADET	19-7-75
ELEW	8-4-76	PODCHORAZY	30-11-74

Podchorazy   1976

TRAINING SHIPS *(continued)*

D: 147 tons (180 fl) **S:** 10 kts **Dim:** 26.8 × 6.8 × 1.8
Electron Equipt: Radar: 2/RN-231 **M:** 2 diesels; 2 props; 300 hp
Electric: 84 kw **Range:** 1,100/10 **Man:** 11 men, 26 midshipmen

REMARKS: *Bryza*, with a less elaborate superstructure, displaces 167 tons (fl). This class also widely employed by Soviet naval schools and Merchant Marine schools for navigation and seamanship training.

MISCELLANEOUS SERVICE CRAFT

♦ **2 Pajak-class torpedo retrievers** Bldr: Gdynia SY (In serv. 1971)

K 8   K 11

D: 130 tons (fl) **S:** 21 kts **Dim:** 38.0 × 6.0 × 1.6
A: 2/25-mm AA (II × 1) **M:** 2 M50-F4 diesels; 2 props; 2,400 hp

♦ **3 Motyl-class tugs** (In serv. 1962-63)

Motyl-class tug H 20   1974

♦ **8 Goliat-class harbor tugs** Bldr: Gdynia SY (In serv. early 1960s)

H 2   H 5   H 13-18

D: 150 tons (fl) **S:** 12 kts **Dim:** 21.4 × 6.1 × 2.6
M: 1 Buckau-Wolff 8 NVD 36 diesel; 1 prop; 300 hp **Range:** 300/9 **Man:** 5 tot.

♦ **7 miscellaneous tugs:** H 1, 3, 4, 6, 7, 8, 11

♦ **2-4 K-15-class mooring buoy tenders**

D: 40 tons (fl) **S:** 10 kts **Dim:** 17.8 (15.2 pp) × 4.2 × 1.5
M: 1 diesel; 1 prop; 150 hp **Man:** 5 tot.

♦ **6 R 34-class mooring buoy tenders**

D: 58.5 tons (64.5 fl) **S:** 11 kts **Dim:** 16.8 × 5.5 × 2.4
M: 2 diesels; 2 props; 300 hp

BORDER GUARD (WOP)

PATROL BOATS

♦ **8 Obluze class** Bldr: Oksywie SY (In serv. 1965-68)

Polish Border Guard Obluze   1977

D: 150 tons (fl) **S:** 24 kts **Dim:** 41.0 × 6.0 × 2.1
A: 4/30-mm AA (II × 2)—4 d.c. racks (2 internal)
Electron Equipt: Radar: 1/RN-231
                    Sonar: Tamir-11
                    IFF: 1/Square Head, 1/High Pole A
M: 2 Type 40D diesels; 2 props; 5,000 hp

REMARKS: Five additional units with Drum Tilt fire-control radars for the 30-mim AA serve in the Polish Navy. Some have no 30-mm AA aft.

♦ **9 Gdansk class** Bldr: Oksywie SY (In serv. 1962-64)

Gdansk class   Polish Navy

D: 180 tons (200 fl) **S:** 18 kts **Dim:** 41.0 × 5.8 × 1.9
A: 2/37-mm AA (I × 2)—2/12.7-mm mg (II × 1)—2 d.c. racks
Electron Equipt: Radar: 1/RN-231
                    Sonar: Tamir-11
M: 2 diesels; 2 props; 2,400 hp

NOTE: The remaining Oksywie-class patrol boats are believed to have been scrapped.

PATROL CRAFT

♦ **8 Pilica class** Bldr: Poland (In serv. 1973-. . .)

KP 162 to KP 169

POLAND *(continued)*
PATROL CRAFT *(continued)*

Pilica—without torpedo tubes (Oksywie class beyond)   1977

Pilica—with 2/533-mm TT   S. Breyer, 1979

D: 100 tons (fl) **S:** 24 kts **Dim:** 29.2 × 6.0 × 1.4
A: 2/25-mm AA (II × 1) **M:** 3 M50-F4 diesels; 3 props; 3,600 hp
Electron Equipt: Radar: 1/RN-231
                            IFF: 1/High Pole A
Man: 15 tot.

REMARKS: The four most recent have had two 533-mm torpedo tubes added.

♦ **12 Wisloka class** Bldr: Poland (In serv. early 1970s)

   D: 70 tons (fl) **S:** 14 kts **Dim:** 22.8 × 5.0 × 1.1
   A: 2/14.5-mm mg (II × 1) **Electron Equipt:** Radar: 1/navigational
   M: 2 diesels; 2 props; 600 hp **Man:** 10 tot.

Wisloka class   S. Breyer, 1979

♦ **21 K-15-class harbor craft** Bldr: Poland (In serv. early 1960s)

   D: 40 tons **S:** . . . kts **Dim:** 17.8 × 4.2 × . . .
   A: Small arms **M:** 2 diesels **Man:** 5 tot.

PORTUGAL
Portuguese Republic

PERSONNEL (1980): Approximately 14,000, including 2,000 Marines

MERCHANT MARINE (1980): 350 ships—1,355,989 grt
                            (tankers: 19 ships—775,050 grt)

NAVAL AVIATION: There is no aviation arm *per se*, but eight Air Force Casa 212
   Aviocar light transports (four with photo equipment) are equipped for maritime
   reconnaissance duties.

WARSHIPS IN OR UNDER CONSTRUCTION AS OF 1 JANUARY 1982

	L	Tons (surfaced)	Main armament
♦ **3 submarines**			
3 DAPHNÉ	1966-68	869	12/550-mm TT
♦ **17 (+3) frigates**		Tons	
0 (+3) KORTENAER	1984-88		
4 BAPTISTE DE ANDRADE	1973-74	1,252	1/100-mm DP, ASW weapons
6 JOÃO COUTINHO	1969-70	1,252	2/76.2-mm DP, ASW weapons
4 COMMANDANT RIVIÈRE	1966-68	1,760	3/100-mm DP, ASW weapons
3 U.S. DEALEY	1963-65	1,450	4/76.2-mm DP, ASW weapons

SUBMARINES

♦ **3 Daphné class** Bldr: Dubigeon, Normandy

	Laid down	L	In serv.
S 163 ALBACORA	6-9-65	15-10-66	1-10-67
S 164 BARRACUDA	19-10-65	24-4-68	4-5-68
S 166 DELFIM	14-5-67	23-9-68	1-10-69

Delfim (S 166)   G. Gyssels, 1981

D: 869/1,043 tons **S:** 13.5/16 kts **Dim:** 57.75 × 6.76 × 4.56
A: 12/550-mm TT (8 fwd, 4 aft, no reloads)
Electron Equipt: Radar: 1/DRUA-31 (with ECM)
          Sonar: DUUA-1 active, DSUV passive
M: Diesel-electric propulsion: SEMT-Pielstick 12PA1 diesels (450 kw); 2 props;
   1,200 hp
Range: 4,300/7.5 snorkel **Man:** 5 officers, 45 men

REMARKS: See remarks on the *Daphné* class in the French section. Sister *Cachalote*
(S 165) was purchased by the Pakistani Navy in 1975.

GUIDED-MISSILE FRIGATES

	Bldr	Laid down	L	In serv.
F . . . N . . .	de Schelde, Vlissingen	. . .	. . .	1985
F . . . N . . .	. . .	. . .	. . .	1987
F . . . N . . .	. . .	. . .	. . .	1989

D: 3,000 tons (3,750 fl) **S:** 30 kts
Dim: 130.2 (121.8 pp) × 14.4 × 4.4 (6.0 props)
A: 8/. . . SSM(?)—1/NATO Sea Sparrow SAM system (VIII × 1; 24 missiles)—
   1/100-mm French DP, Model 1953—1/smaller AA gun installation—4/324-mm
   ASW TT (II × 2, fixed)—1-2/helicopters
Electron Equipt: Radar: 1/ZW-06, 1/LW-08, 1/WM-25 with STIR
          Sonar: SQS-505
          ECM: . . .
M: CODOG: 2 Rolls-Royce Olympus TM-3B gas turbines, 25,800 hp each; 2 die-
   sels; 2 CP props
Electric: 3,000 kw **Range:** . . . **Man:** 18 officers, 182 men

REMARKS: Ordered 9-80. First unit to be built in Netherlands, other pair in Portugal.
Will differ in armament and propulsion from sisters in Greek and Netherlands navies.
See also remarks in Netherlands section entry on this class. 100-mm guns may come
from the *Commandant Rivière* class.

FRIGATES

♦ **4 Baptiste de Andrade class** Bldr: Bazán, Spain

	Laid down	L	In serv.
F 486 BAPTISTE DE ANDRADE	1972	3-73	19-11-74
F 487 JOÃO ROBY	1972	3-6-73	18-3-75
F 488 AFONSO CERQUEIRA	1973	6-10-73	26-6-75
F 489 OLIVEIRA E. CARMO	1973	2-74	2-76

Oliveira E. Carmo (F 489)   Portuguese Navy

Oliveira E. Carmo (F 489)   S. Terzibaschitsch, 1981

D: 1,252 tons (1,348 fl) **S:** 21 kts **Dim:** 84.59 (81.0 pp) × 10.3 × 3.3
A: 1/100-mm DP, French Model 1968—2/40-mm AA (I × 2)—6/324-mm Mk 32
   ASW TT (III × 2)—1/d.c. rack
Electron Equipt: Radar: 1/Decca TM626, 1/Plessey AWS-2, 1/Thomson-
             CSF Pollux
          Sonar: 1/Diodon
M: 2 OEW-Pielstick 12PC2V400 diesels; 2 props; 10,560 hp
Electric: 1,110 kVA **Range:** 5,900/18 **Man:** 113 tot.

REMARKS: Developed version of the *João Coutinho* class with more modern weapons
and electronics. Helicopter platform. Vega GFCS with optical back-up director for
100-mm gun, 2 directors for 40-mm.

FRIGATES *(continued)*

♦ **6 João Coutinho class** Bldrs: F 475 to F 477: Blohm & Voss, Germany; F 484 to F 471: Bazán, Spain

	Laid down	L	In serv.
F 475 João Coutinho	9-68	2-5-69	7-3-70
F 476 Jacinto Candido	4-68	16-6-69	10-6-70
F 477 General Pereira D'eca	10-68	26-7-69	10-10-70
F 484 Augusto Castilho	8-68	5-7-69	14-11-70
F 485 Honorio Barreto	7-68	11-4-70	15-4-71
F 471 Antonio Enes	4-68	1-8-69	18-6-71

Augusto Castilho (F 484)   J. Jedrlinic, 1980

João Coutinho (F 475)   Portuguese Navy

D: 1,252 tons (1,401 fl)   **S:** 24.4 kts   **Dim:** 84.59 (81.0 pp) × 10.30 × 3.30
A: 2/76.2-mm Mk 33 DP (II × 1)—2/40-mm AA (II × 1)—Mk 10 Hedgehog—2/ Mk 6 d.c. projectors—2/Mk 9 d.c. racks
Electron Equipt: Radar: 1/Decca TM 626, 1/MLA-1B, 1/SPG-34
        Sonar: 1/QCU-2
M: 2 OEW-Pielstick 12PC2V280 diesels; 2 props; 10,560 hp
Electric: 900 kw   **Range:** 5,900/18   **Man:** 9 officers, 84 men

REMARKS: The engines for these ships were ordered from Chantiers de l'Atlantique, St.-Nazaire, France, in 1967. The ships can carry 34 Marines, and have Mk 63 mod. 21 GFCS for the 76.2-mm mount, Mk 51, mod. 2, GFCS for the 40-mm. Modernization planned. Carry 1,200 rounds 76.2-mm, 240 Hedgehog projectiles and up to 84 d.c.

♦ **4 French Commandant Rivière class** Bldr: A. C. de Bretagne, Nantes

	Laid down	L	In serv.
F 480 Comandante João Belo	6-9-65	22-3-66	1-7-67
F 481 Comandante Hermegildo Capelo	13-5-66	29-11-66	26-4-68
F 482 Comandante Roberto Ivens	13-12-66	11-8-67	23-11-68
F 483 Comandante Sacadura Cabral	18-8-67	15-3-68	25-11-69

Comandante João Belo (F 480)

D: 1,760 tons (2,250 fl)   **S:** 25 kts (26.6 max.)
Dim: 103.0 (98.0 pp) × 11.5 × 3.8
A: 3/100-mm DP, Model 1953 (I × 3)—2/40-mm AA (I × 2)—1/305-mm ASW mortar (IV × 1)—6/550-mm ASW TT (III × 2)
Electron Equipt: Radar: 1/Decca RM 316, 1/DRBV-22A, 1/DRBV-50,   1/DRBC-31D
           Sonar: 1/DUBA-7, 1/SQS-17A
M: 4 SEMT-Pielstick diesels; 2 props; 16,000 hp   **Electric:** 1,280 kw
Range: 2,300/25; 4,500/15   **Man:** 214 tot.

REMARKS: See Remarks on Commandant Rivière class in French section. Modernization planned, including provision for a helicopter at the expense of one 100-mm.

♦ **3 U.S. Dealey class** Bldrs: F 472 and F 473: Est. Nav. Lisnave, Lisbon; F 474: Est. Nav de Viana do Castelo

	Laid down	L	In serv.
F 472 Almirante Pereira Da Silva	14-6-62	2-12-63	20-12-66
F 473 Almirante Gago Coutinho	2-12-63	13-8-65	29-11-67
F 474 Almirante Magalhaes Correa	30-8-63	26-4-65	4-11-68

Almirante Magalhaes Correa (F 474)   J.-C. Bellonne, 1980

FRIGATES *(continued)*

Almirante Magalhaes Correa (F 474)   G. Gyssels, 1980

D: 1,450 tons (1,950 fl) **S:** 26 kts **Dim:** 95.86 (93.88 wl) × 11.18 × 4.04 (hull)
A: 4/76.2-mm DP (II × 2)—2/375-mm Bofors ASW RL (IV × 2)—6/324-mm Mk
   32 ASW TT (III × 2)
Electron Equipt: Radar: 1/Decca RM 316P, 1/978, 1/MLA-1B, 2/Mk 34
   Sonar: SQS-30-32, DUBA-3A, 1/SQA-10 (VDS)
   ECM: WLR-1
M: 1 set GT; 1 prop; 20,000 hp **Electric:** 700 kw
Boilers: 2 Foster-Wheeler, 42 kg/cm², 510°C **Fuel:** 360 tons
Range: 1,600/25; 4,400/11 **Man:** 11 officers, 154 men

REMARKS: Funded as U.S. DE 1039, DE 1042, and DE 1046, respectively. Two Mk
63 gunfire-control systems. Search sonars are SQS-30, SQS-31, and SQS-32 respectively, to avoid interference. To be modernized.

PATROL BOATS

♦ **10 Cacine class** (Launch dates in parentheses)

P 1140 CACINE (1968)	P 1144 QUANZA (30-5-69)	P 1160 LIMPOPO (9-4-73)
P 1141 CUNENE (1968)	P 1145 GEBA (21-5-69)	P 1161 SAVE (24-10-72)
P 1142 MANDOVI (1968)	P 1146 ZAIRE (28-11-70)	
P 1143 ROVUMA (1968)	P 1147 ZAMBEZE (1971)	

Bldrs: P 1140 to 1143: Arsenal do Alfeite; others: Est. Nav. do Mondego

D: 292 tons (310 fl) **S:** 20 kts **Dim:** 44.0 × 7.67 × 2.2
A: 2/40-mm AA (I × 2)—1/20-mm AA—2/d.c. racks
Electron Equipt: Radar: 1/975 **M:** 2 Maybach 12V538 diesels; 2 props; 4,400 hp
Range: 4,400/12 **Man:** 3 officers, 30 men

Zambeze (P 1147)   L. & L. van Ginderen, 1980

♦ **4 São Roque-class former minsweepers** Bldr: Estaleiros Navais da C.U.F., Lisbon

	In serv.		In serv.
M 401 SÃO ROQUE	6-6-56	M 403 LAGOA	10-8-56
M 402 RIBEIRA GRANDE	8-2-57	M 404 ROSARIO	8-2-56

D: 394 tons (452 fl) **S:** 15 kts **Dim:** 46.33 (42.68 pp) × 8.75 × 2.5
A: 2/20-mm AA (II × 1) **M:** 2 Mirrlees JVSS-12 diesels; 2 props; 2,500 hp
Fuel: 45 tons **Range:** 2,300/13; 3,000/8 **Man:** 4 officers, 43 men

REMARKS: All portable sweep gear offloaded; now used as patrol vessels. Ordered
   early in 1954 and all launched in 1955. M 401 and M 403 built with U.S. "Offshore"
   funds as MSC 241 and MSC 242. Similar in appearance to the British "Ton" class.
   Wooden hulls, fin stabilizers. One 40-mm AA removed in 1972.

♦ **6 Albatroz class** Bldr: Arsenal do Alfeite (In serv. 1974-75)

P 1162 ALBATROZ	P 1164 ANDORHINA	P 1166 CONDOR
P 1163 ACOR	P 1165 AGUIA	P 1167 CISNE

Andorhina (P 1164)   Portuguese Navy

PATROL BOATS (continued)

D: 45 tons (fl)   **S:** 20 kts   **Dim:** 23.6 (21.88 pp) × 5.25 × 1.6
A: 1/20-mm AA—2/12.7-mm mg (I × 2)
Electron Equipt: Radar: 1/Kelvin-Hughes 14/9
M: 2 Cummins diesels; 2 props; 1,100 hp   **Range:** 450/18; 2,500/12   **Man:** 8 tot.

♦ **2 Dom Aleixo class** Bldr: San Jacintho Aveiro

P 1148 Dom Aleixo   P 1149 Dom Jeremias

Dom Aleixo (P 1148)

D: 62.6 tons (67.7 fl)   **S:** 16 kts   **Dim:** 25.0 × 5.2 × 1.6
A: 1/20-mm   **Electron Equipt:** Radar: Decca RM 316P
M: 2 Cummins diesels; 2 props; 1,600 hp   **Man:** 2 officers, 8 men

REMARKS: Both launched in 12-67. P 1149 is used for inshore surveys.

♦ **1 river patrol craft** Bldr: Arsenal do Alfeite (In serv. 1957)

P 1170 Rio Minho

D: 14 tons   **S:** 9 kts   **Dim:** 15.0 × 3.2 × 0.7
A: 2/7.62-mm mg   **M:** 2 Alfa-Romeo diesels; 2 props; 130 hp   **Man:** 7 tot.

AMPHIBIOUS WARFARE CRAFT

♦ **2 Bombarda-class landing craft** Bldr: Mondego SY (In serv. 1969-71)

LDG 201 Bombarda   LDG 202 Alabarda

D: 285 tons (635 fl)   **S:** 11 kts   **Dim:** 59.0 (52.88 pp) × 11.91 × 1.6
M: 2 MTU MD 225 diesels; 2 props; 1,000 hp   **Range:** 1,800/8
Man: 2 officers, 18 men

♦ **7 LDM 400-class landing craft** (In serv. 1967)

LDM 406   LDM 420   LDM 422   LDM 424
LDM 418   LDM 421   LDM 423

D: 56 tons (fl)   **S:** 9 kts   **Dim:** 17.0 × 5.0 × 1.2
A: 1/20-mm   **M:** 2 Cummins diesels; 2 props; 450 hp

♦ **3 LDM 100-class landing craft** Bldr: Mondego SY (In serv. 1965)

LDM 119   LDM 120   LDM 121

D: 50 tons (fl)   **S:** 9 kts   **Dim:** 15.25 × 4.37 × 1.17
M: 2 GM 6-71 diesels; 2 props; 450 hp   **Range:** 130/9

HYDROGRAPHIC SHIPS

♦ **1 new construction** Bldr: Alfeite Navy Yard

	Laid down	L	In serv.
A. . . N. . .	. . .	. . .	. . .

D: 1,140 tons (fl)   **S:** 15 kts   **Dim:** 60.0 × 12.0 × 4.6
M: Diesels; . . . props; 1,700 hp

REMARKS: Intended to replace *Afonso de Albuquerque.*

♦ **1 ex-U.S. Kellar class** Bldr: Marietta SB Co., Pt. Pleasant, W. Va.

	Laid down	L	In serv.
A 527 Almeida Carvalho (ex-*Kellar*, T-AGS 25)	20-11-62	30-7-64	31-1-69

D: 1,200 tons (1,400 fl)   **S:** 13.5 kts   **Dim:** 63.7 (58.0 pp) × 11.4 × 4.7
Electron Equipt: 1/RCA CRM-N2A-30, 1/Decca TM 829
M: 2 Caterpillar D-378 diesels, electric drive; 1 prop; 1,000 hp
Fuel: 211 tons   **Man:** 5 officers, 25 men

REMARKS: Transferred on loan 21-1-72. Similar to U.S. *Robert D. Conrad*-class T-AGOR.

♦ **1 ex-British Bay-class converted frigate** Bldr: Wm. Pickersgill & Sons, Sunderland

	Laid down	L	In serv.
A 526 Afonso De Albuquerque (ex-*Dalrymple*, ex-*Luce Bay*)	8-2-44	12-4-45	10-2-49

Afonso de Albuquerque (A 526)   G. Gyssels, 1977

D: 1,590 tons (2,230 fl)   **S:** 19.5 kts   **Dim:** 93.57 (87.17 pp) × 11.76 × 4.32
Electron Equipt: Radar: 1/975, 1/978
M: 2 sets triple-expansion reciprocating steam; 2 props; 5,500 hp
Boilers: 2 Admiralty, three-drum   **Range:** 7,055/9.1   **Man:** 9 officers, 100 men

REMARKS: Converted while under construction. Purchased in 1966.

PORTUGAL (*continued*)
HYDROGRAPHIC SHIPS (*continued*)

♦ **1 inshore survey craft** (In serv. 1961)

A 5200 MIRA (ex-*Fomalhaut*, ex-*Arrabile*)

D: 23 tons (30 fl) **S:** 15 kts **Dim:** 19.2 (18.9 pp) × 4.6 × 1.2
M: 3 Perkins diesels; 300 hp **Range:** 650/8 **Man:** 16 tot.

REMARKS: The *Dom Aleixo*-class patrol craft *Dom Jeremias* (P 1149) is also used for survey duties.

AUXILIARY SHIPS

♦ **1 replenishment oiler** Bldr: Est. Nav. de Viana do Castelo

	L	In serv.
A 5206 SÃO GABRIEL	1961	3-63

São Gabriel (A 5206)—fueling boom rigged out   Portuguese Navy, 1968

D: 9,000 tons (14,200 fl) **S:** 17 kts **Dim:** 146.0 (138.0 pp) × 18.22 × 8.0
Electron Equipt: Radar: 1/975, 1/MLN-1A **Man:** 9 officers, 93 men
M: 1 set Pamtreda GT; 1 prop; 9,500 hp **Boilers:** 2 **Range:** 6,000/15

REMARKS: Cargo: 9,000 tons. Two liquid- and one solid-store replenishment stations per side. Helicopter platform aft. Former oiler *Sam Bras* is now an accommodations hulk.

♦ **1 lighthouse tender and tug**

	Laid down	L	In serv.
A 54 SCHULTZ XAVIER	2-70	1972	14-7-72

Schultz Xavier (A 54)   J.-C. Bellonne, 1973

D: 900 tons **S:** 14 kts **Dim:** 56.1 × 10.0 × 3.8
M: 2 diesels; 1 prop; 2,400 hp **Range:** 3,000/12.5 **Man:** . . .

REMARKS: Reported to be in reserve.

♦ **1 sail training ship** Bldr: Blohm & Voss, Hamburg

	L	In serv.
A 520 SAGRES (ex-*Guanabara*, ex-*Albert Leo Schlageter*)	30-10-37	1-2-38

D: 1,725 tons (1,784 fl) **S:** 10.5 kts (18 sail)
Dim: 90.0 (75.90 hull, 70.4 pp) × 11.9 × 5.2
M: 2 M.A.N. diesels; 1 prop; 750 hp
Range: 5,450/7.5 (power) **Man:** 10 officers, 143 men

REMARKS: Acquired by U.S. Navy as reparations, 1945; sold to Brazil in 1948 and to Portugal in 1972, commissioning on 2-2-72. Sail area: 2,355 m². Sisters are U.S. Coast Guard *Eagle* and Soviet *Tovarisch*.

SERVICE CRAFT

♦ **1 U.S. 174-foot-class yard oiler** Bldr: Brunswick Marine, Georgia

	Laid down	L	In serv.
BC 3 (ex-YO 194)	14-5-45	25-8-45	30-1-46

D: 440 tons light (1,390 fl) **S:** 11 kts **Dim:** 53.04 × 9.75 × 3.96
M: 1 GM diesel; 1 prop; 800 hp **Electric:** 120 kw
Fuel: 25 tons **Man:** 23 tot.

REMARKS: Transferred in 4-62. Cargo: 900 tons.

♦ **3 Spartacus-class coastal tugs** Bldr: Argibay, Lisbon

SPARTACUS (L: 18-2-77) ULISSES (L: 9-3-77) N. . . (L: 1977)

D: 194 grt **S:** 12 kts **Dim:** 28.65 (25.0 pp) × 8.53 × 2.0
M: 2 Stork-Werkspoor G-FCHD-240 diesels; 2 cycloidal props; 2,400 hp

♦ **2 ex-U.S. Army harbor tugs**

RB 1 (ex-ST 1994) RB 2 (ex-ST 1996)

REMARKS: Transferred in 1961 and 1962.

QATAR
State of Qatar

PERSONNEL (1981): 400 total

MERCHANT MARINE (1980): 36 ships—91,934 grt
(tankers: 3 ships—72,756 grt)

QATAR (*continued*)

GUIDED-MISSILE PATROL BOATS

♦ **3 French La Combattante III class** Bldr: C.M.N., Cherbourg

	Laid down	L	In serv.
Q. . . N. . .	6-5-81	. . .	8-82
Q. . . N. . .	28-8-81	. . .	10-82
Q. . . N. . .	. . .	. . .	1-83

D: 395 tons (430 fl)   **S:** 38.5 kts
Dim: 56.0 (53.0 pp) × 8.16 × 2.15 hull (2.5 max.)
A: 8/MM 40 Exocet SSM—1/76-mm OTO Melara DP—2/40-mm Breda AA (II × 1)—4/30-mm Oerlikon AA (II × 2)
Electron Equipt: Radar: 1/Thomson-CSF Pollux, 1/Thomson-CSF Castor, 1/Decca 1226
M: 4 MTU 20V538 TB93 diesels; 4 props; 19,300 hp   **Range:** 2,000/15

REMARKS: Ordered 10-80. Very similar in appearance and equipment to the three Nigerian units of the class. Two CSEE Panda optical gun directors.

PATROL BOATS AND CRAFT

♦ **6 103-foot boats** Bldr: Vosper Thornycroft

	In serv.		In serv.
Q 11 BARZAN	13-1-75	Q 14 AL WUSSAIL	28-10-75
Q 12 HWAR	30-4-75	Q 15 AL KHATAB	22-1-76
Q 13 THAT ASSUARI	3-10-75	Q 16 TARIQ	1-3-76

D: 120 tons   **S:** 27 kts   **Dim:** 32.4 (31.1 pp) × 6.3 × 1.6
A: 2/30-mm AA (II × 1)—1/20-mm AA
M: 2 Paxman Valenta 16RP200 diesels; 2 props; 6,250 hp   **Man:** 25 tot.

♦ **7 P 1200 class** Bldr: Watercraft, Shoreham (In serv. 1980)

D: 12.7 tons (fl)   **S:** 29 kts   **Dim:** 11.9 × 4.1 × 1.1
A: 2/7.62-mm mg (I × 2)
M: 2 Wizeman-Mercedes WM400 diesels; 2 props; 660 hp   **Man:** 4 tot.

♦ **2 75-foot craft** Bldr: Whittingham & Mitchell, Chertsey (In serv. 1969)

D: 60 tons (fl)   **S:** . . . kts   **Dim:** 22.5 × . . . × . . .
A: 2/20-mm AA (I × 2)   **M:** 2 diesels; 1,420 hp

♦ **2 45-foot craft** Bldr: Vosper

D: 13 tons   **S:** 26 kts   **Dim:** 13.5 × 3.8 × 1.1
A: 1/12.7-mm mg—2/7.62-mm mg (I × 2)
M: 2 Caterpillar diesels; 2 props; 800 hp   **Man:** 6 tot.

♦ **25 Spear-class craft** Bldr: Fairey Marine (In serv. 1974-77)

D: 4.3 tons   **S:** 26 kts   **Dim:** 9.1 × 2.8 × 0.8
A: 3/7.62-mm mg (I × 3)   **M:** 2 diesels; 2 props; 290 hp   **Man:** 4 tot.

ROMANIA
Socialist Republic of Romania

PERSONNEL (1980): 10,000 men, 2,000 of whom are in the Border Guard

MERCHANT MARINE (1980): 317 ships—1,856,292 (tankers: 10 ships—246,927 grt)

CORVETTES

♦ **3 ex-Soviet Poti class**

V 31   V 32   V 33

D: 500 tons (fl)   **S:** 34 kts   **Dim:** 60.3 × 8.0 × 3.0   **Man:** 50 tot.
A: 2/57-mm AA (II × 1)—2/RBU-2500 ASW RL—2/533-mm ASW TT (I × 2)
Electron Equipt: Radar: 1/Don 2, 1/Strut Curve, 1/Muff Cob
　　　　　IFF: 1/High Pole B
M: CODAG: 2 M503A diesels (4,000 hp each); 2 GT (20,000 hp each); 2 props

REMARKS: Transferred 1970. Have simpler systems than the Soviet units: 533-mm vice 400-mm torpedo tubes, RBU-2500 vice RBU-6000 rocket launchers, etc.

GUIDED-MISSILE PATROL BOATS

♦ **5 ex-Soviet Osa-I class**

194   195   196   197   198

Romanian Osa-I 196　　　　　　　　　　　　　　　　1974

D: 175 tons (210 fl)   **S:** 36 kts   **Dim:** 39.0 × 7.7 × 1.8
A: 4/SS-N-2 missile launchers—4/30-mm AA (II × 2)
Electron Equipt: Radar: 1/Square Tie, 1/Drum Tilt
　　　　　IFF: 2/Square Head, 1/High Pole B
M: 3 M503A diesels; 3 props; 12,000 hp   **Range:** 430/34; 790/20

REMARKS: Transferred after 1960.

PATROL BOATS

♦ **19 Shanghai-II class** Bldr: Mangalia SY, Romania (In serv. 197 . . .)

VS 41 to VS 46   VS 52   VP 20 to VP 31

PATROL BOATS (continued)

D: 123 tons (150 fl) **S:** 28.5 kts **Dim:** 38.78 × 5.41 × 1.49
A: VS 41 to VS 44, VS 52: 1/37-mm AA—2/14.5-mm mg (II × 1)—2/RBU-1200
ASW RL (V × 2)
VP 20 to VP 31: 6/14.5-mm mg (II × 3)
Electron Equipt: Radar: 1/Pot Head   **Man:** 30 tot.
M: 2 M50-F4, 4,200-hp diesels, 2 12D6, 910-hp diesels; 4 props; 4,220 hp

REMARKS: Units with VP pendants serve the Border Guard; some, with only two 14.5-
mm machine guns and a large deckhouse aft, serve as search-and-rescue boats.

♦ **3 ex-Soviet Kronshtadt class** Bldr: U.S.S.R. (In serv. early 1950s)

V 1   V 2   V 3

D: 300 tons (330 fl) **S:** 18 kts **Dim:** 52.1 × 6.5 × 2.2
A: 1/85-mm DP—2/37-mm AA **M:** 3 Type 9D diesels; 3 props; 3,300 hp
Fuel: 20 tons **Range:** 3,500/14 **Man:** 40 tot.

TORPEDO BOATS

♦ **8-10 Epitrop class** Bldr: Romania (In serv. 1980-. . .)

D: 200 tons (fl) **S:** 36 kts **Dim:** 39.0 × 7.7 × 1.8
A: 4/30-mm AA (II × 2)—4/533-mm TT (I × 4) **Electron Equipt:** Radar: . . .
M: 3 M503A diesels; 3 props; 12,000 hp

REMARKS: Dimensions and propulsion, based on Osa class, may not be correct. "Epitrop" is the NATO nickname for the class.

♦ **20 Huchuan-class hydrofoils** Bldr: Dobreta SY, Turnu (1973-. . .)

VT 51 to VT 62, VT. . . to VT. . .

Romanian Huchuan VT 53   1974

D: 39 tons (fl) **S:** 54 kts **Dim:** 21.8 × 4.9 × 1.0; foilborne: 7.5 × 0.31
A: 4/14.5-mm AA (II × 2)—2/533-mm TT
M: 3 M50 diesels; 3 props; 3,600 hp **Range:** 500/20

REMARKS: Three built in China, remainder in Romania. Some have had the torpedo
tubes and hydrofoils removed and are used as search-and-rescue craft.

NOTE: The remaining Soviet P 4-class torpedo boats have been discarded.

MINE WARFARE SHIPS

♦ **1 Cosar-class mine countermeasures support ship** Bldr: Romania (In serv.
1980) (Cosar is the NATO class nickname.)

D: 1,500 tons **S:** . . . **Dim:** 80.0 × . . . × . . .
A: 4/30-mm AA (II × 2)—mines **M:** Diesels; . . . props; . . . hp

♦ **4 Democratia-class minesweepers (German M-40 class)** Bldr: Galati (In serv.
1951)

DB 13 DEMOCRATIA   DB 15 DESROBIREA
DB 14 DESCATUSARIA   DB 16 DREPTATEA

D: 643 tons (775 fl) **S:** 17 kts **Dim:** 62.3 × 8.5 × 2.6
A: 6/37-mm AA (II × 3)—2/d.c. projectors—mines
M: 2 triple-expansion engines, each driving an exhaust turbine; 2 props; 2,400
hp
Boilers: 2 three-drum **Fuel:** 152 tons **Range:** 4,000/10 **Man:** 80 tot.

REMARKS: Begun for German Navy as coal burners, launches 1943-44. Converted to
burn fuel oil on completion. Now being modernized with new superstructures, diesel
engines.

♦ **10 ex-Soviet T-301-class minesweepers**

DR 19   DR 21 to 29

D: 145.8 tons (160 fl) **S:** 12.5 kts **Dim:** 38.0 × 5.1 × 1.6
A: 1/45-mm AA—4/12.7-mm mg (II × 2)—mines
M: 3 6-cyl. diesels; 3 props; 1,440 hp
Fuel: 20 tons **Range:** 2,500/8 **Man:** 32 tot.

REMARKS: Transferred 1956-60. Gradually being disposed of.

♦ **8 Polish TR-40-class river minesweepers**

VD 241 to VD 248

D: 70 tons (fl) **S:** 18 kts **Dim:** 27.7 × 4.1 × 0.6
A: 2/25-mm AA (II × 1)—2/14.5-mm AA (II × 1)—mines
M: 2 3D6 diesels; 2 props; 600 hp

REMARKS: Transferred 1956-60.

AUXILIARY SHIPS

♦ **1 oceanographic research ship** Bldr: Romania (In serv. 1980)

GRIGORE ANTIPA

REMARKS: Reportedly similar to the Cosar-class ship above.

♦ **1 Croitor-class small combatant tender** Bldr: Romania (In serv. 1980)

281 N. . .

D: 3,500 tons (fl) **S:** . . . kts **Dim:** 110.0 × . . . × . . .
A: 2/57-mm AA (II × 1)—4/30-mm AA (II × 2)—4/14.5-mm mg (II × 2)
M: Diesels; 2 props; . . . hp

REMARKS: Croitor is the NATO nickname. Resembles a smaller edition of the Soviet
"Don" class. Helicopter hangar and flight deck aft; long forecastle with sharply raked
bow and prominent hull side knuckle. Crane forward of bridge tends magazine for
torpedoes and missiles.

♦ **3 coastal tankers**

♦ **4 Soviet Roslavl-class ocean tugs** Bldr: Galati (In serv. 1953-54)

RM 101 VITEAZUL   RM. . . VOINICUL   RM. . . N. . .   RM. . . N. . .

D: 750 tons (fl) **S:** 11 kts **Dim:** 44.5 × 9.5 × 3.5
M: Diesel-electric; 2 props; 1,200 hp **Man:** 28 tot.

ROMANIA *(continued)*
AUXILIARY SHIPS *(continued)*

◆ **1 sail training ship** Bldr: Blohm & Voss, Hamburg

	Laid down	L	In serv.
Mircea	30-4-38	22-9-38	29-3-39

Mircea French Navy, 1980

D: 1,630 tons (fl)   **S:** 6 kts (10 sail)   **Dim:** 81.78 (73.5 hull) × 12.5 × 5.2
M: 1 M.A.N. diesel; 500 hp   **Sail area:** 1,750 m² **Man:** 20 men + 120 cadets

Remarks: Refitted in Germany, 1966-67.

Note: The training ship *Neptun* serves the Merchant Marine, not the Navy.

◆ **3 ex-French Friponne-class former minesweepers** Bldrs: Lorient and Brest
Dockyards (In serv. 1916-17)

NH 111 Stihi (ex-*Mignonne*)   ND 113 Ghiculescu (ex-*Impatiente*)
NH 112 Dumitrescu (ex-*Friponne*)

D: 330 tons (400 fl)   **S:** 12 kts   **Dim:** 60.9 × 7.0 × 2.5
A: 1/37-mm AA—4/14.5-mm AA (II × 2)
M: 2 Sulzer diesels; 2 props; 1,800 hp
Fuel: 30 tons   **Range:** 3,000/10   **Man:** 50 tot.

Remarks: ND 113 used as a headquarters ship, the others as survey ships. All recently
modernized with streamlined superstructures, new armament, etc.

DANUBE FLOTILLA

◆ **16 monitors** Bldr: Romania (In serv. 1973-. . .)

VB 76 to VB 91

D: 85 tons   **S:** 17 kts   **Dim:** 32.0 × 4.8 × 0.9
A: 1/85-mm—4/14.5-mm AA (II × 2)—2/81-mm mortars (I × 2)
M: 2 diesels; 2 props; 2,400 hp   **Man:** 25 tot.

◆ **10 VG-class patrol craft** Bldr: Galati (In serv. 1954)

VG class, VG 11 1971

D: 40 tons (fl)   **S:** 18 kts   **Dim:** 16.0 × 4.4 × 1.2
A: 1/20-mm AA—1/7.9-mm mg
M: 2 3D12 diesels; 2 props; 600 hp   **Man:** 10 men

◆ **9 SM 165-class patrol/utility craft**

◆ **5 SD 200-class patrol/utility boats**

SABAH
State of Sabah (semi-autonomous Malaysian state)

PATROL BOATS

◆ **2 55-foot boats** Bldr: Cheverton, Isle of Wight (In serv. 2-75)

Sri Semporna   Sri Bangji

D: 50 tons (fl)   **S:** 20 kts   **Dim:** 16.8 × 4.6 × 0.9
A: 1/12.7-mm mg   **M:** 2 diesels; 2 props; 1,200 hp
Range: 300/15   **Man:** 11 tot.

◆ **2 91-foot boats** Bldr: Vosper Thornycroft, Singapore

PX 17 Sri Gumangtong (In serv. 8-4-70)   PX 18 Sri Labuan (In serv. 6-4-70)

D: 85 tons (fl)   **S:** 29 kts   **Dim:** 26.29 × 5.7 × 1.45
A: 2/20-mm AA   **M:** 2 Mercedes-Benz MB820Db diesels; 2 props; 2,700 hp
Range: 700/15   **Man:** 15 tot.

Remarks: On detachment from the Royal Malaysian Marine Police.

◆ **1 yacht** Bldr: Vosper Thornycroft, Singapore (In serv. 11-7-71)

Putri Sabah

D: 117 tons   **S:** 22 kts   **Dim:** 27.3 × 9.5 × 1.65

SABAH (*continued*)

AMPHIBIOUS WARFARE CRAFT

♦ **1 utility landing craft** Bldr: Chung Wah SY, Hong Kong (In serv. 28-1-78)

GAYA 2

    D: 220 grt **S:** 8 kts **Dim:** . . . × . . . × . . .
    M: 2 Caterpillar D3406TA diesels; 2 props; 275 hp

ST. KITTS
State of Saint Christopher-Nevis-Anguilla

MERCHANT MARINE (1980): 1 ship—256 grt

POLICE FORCE

♦ **1 Spear class** Bldr: Fairey Marine, G.B. (In serv. 10-9-74)

    D: 4.3 tons (fl) **S:** 30 kts **Dim:** 9.1 × 2.8 × 0.8
    A: 2/7.62-mm mg (I × 2) **M:** 2 diesels; 2 props; 360 hp **Man:** 2 tot.

ST. LUCIA
State of Saint Lucia

MERCHANT MARINE (1980): 5 ships—2,378 grt

CUSTOMS SERVICE

♦ **1 small craft** Bldr: Brooke Marine Ltd., Lowestoft, G.B.

HELEN

    D: 15 tons (fl) **S:** 22 kts **Dim:** 13.7 × 4.0 × 1.2
    A: 2/7.62-mm mg (I × 2) **M:** 2 Cummins diesels; 2 props; 370 hp

ST. VINCENT
State of Saint Vincent and the Grenadines

MARINE WING, POLICE FORCE

♦ **1 patrol craft** Bldr: Vosper Thornycroft, Portchester (In serv. 3-81)

SGV 05 GEORGE MCINTOSH

George McIntosh (SGV 05)   Vosper Thornycroft, 1981

    D: 70 tons (fl) **S:** 24.5 kts **Dim:** 22.86 × 7.43 × 1.64
    A: 1/20-mm AA **M:** 2 Caterpillar diesels; 2 props; 1,840 hp
    Electric: 24 kw **Range:** 600/21; 1,000/11 **Man:** 3 officers, 8 men

REMARKS: Glass-reinforced Nelson-design plastic hull. Replaced 15-ton *Chatoyer*, which was lost in a hurricane, 1979.

SAUDI ARABIA
Kingdom of Saudi Arabia

PERSONNEL (1980): 2,000 total

MERCHANT MARINE (1980): 214 ships—1,589,868 grt
        (tankers: 64 ships—1,125,539 grt)

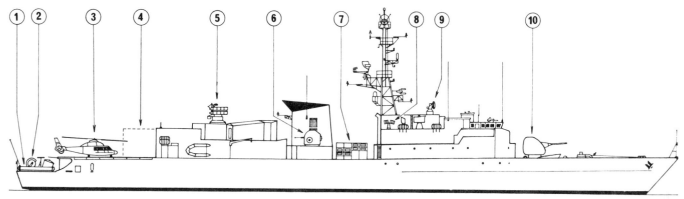

1. Torpedo tubes 2. Sorel variable-depth sonar 3. Dauphin II helicopter 4. Telescoping hangar 5. Crotale SAM launcher 6. Twin 40-mm Breda AA 7. Otomat SSM installation 8. Dagaie chaff launchers 9. Castor fire-control radar 10. 100-mm Compact DP gun

NAVAL AVIATION: The Saudi Navy has ordered 24 helicopters from S.N.I.A.S., France: 20 SA-365 F/AS Dauphin II for ship- and shore-based ASW and ship-attack, and 4 SA-365N Dauphin II configured for search-and-rescue duties.

Dauphin II helicopter:
Rotor diameter: 13.29 m; fuselage length: 11.41 m; height: 4 m; weight: light: 1,850 kg/max.: 3,400-3,800 kg; propulsion: 2 Turbomeca "Ariel" 1C turbines, 565 hp each.

Performance:
Radius of action—100 nautical miles with 4/AS 15; 140 nautical miles with 2/AS 15
Endurance—2 hours with 4/AS 15; 3 hours with 2/AS 15
Armament: 2 or 4 Aerospatiale AS 15 antiship missiles or 2 Mk 46 ASW torpedoes. The AS 15 missile has a range of 15 km, weighs 96 kg, and is 2.16 m long. The helicopter will carry an "Agrion," frequency-agile pulse-doppler radar to provide missile targeting and will permit the helicopter to provide mid-course guidance update information to the ship-launched Otomat Mk 2 ("Erato") missiles.

Otomat Mk 2 Erato antiship missile:
Length: 4.66 m; range: 90 nautical miles; diameter: 0.40 m (0.46 m rear); weight: 780 kg (210 kg warhead); propulsion: Turbomeca "Arbizon" turbojet, 2 rocket boosters.

GUIDED-MISSILE FRIGATES

♦ 0 (+4) of 2,000 tons

	Bldr	Laid down	L	In serv.
N. . .	Arsenal de Lorient	15-10-81	. . .	3-84
N. . .	CNIM, La Seyne	. . .	. . .	. . .
N. . .	CNIM, La Seyne	. . .	. . .	. . .
N. . .	CNIM, La Seyne	. . .	. . .	. . .

D: 2,000 tons (2,250 normal, 2,610 fl) S: 30 kts
Dim: 115.00 (106.50 pp) × 12.50 wl × 3.40 (4.65 over sonar)
A: 8/Otomat Mk 2 "Erato" SSM (IV × 2)—1/Crotale SAM syst. (VIII × 1; 24 total missiles)—1/100-mm Compact DP—4/40-mm Breda AA—4/F17P tubes for wire-guided torpedoes—1/Dauphin II ASW/antiship helicopter

Electron Equipt: Radar: 2/Decca 1226, 1/Sea Tiger (DRBV 15), 1/Castor II, 1/DRBC-32E (on Crotale launcher)
Sonar: Diodon hull-mounted, Sorel VDS
ECM: DR 4000 intercept syst., 2/Dagaie chaff RL
M: 4 SEMT-Pielstick 16 PA 6 BTC diesels; 2 props; 17,600 hp
Electric: 1,600 kw Range: 8,000/15 Man: 15 officers, 179 men

REMARKS: Ordered 10-80 as part of the "Sawari" program under which France has replaced the U.S. Navy as principal naval equipment supplier. Very complex ships, with much new, untried equipment. Will have SENIT VI computer data system. Retractable fin stabilizers fitted.

GUIDED-MISSILE CORVETTES

♦ 2 (+2) U.S. PCG class Bldr: Tacoma Boatbuilding, Tacoma, Wash.

	Laid down	L	In serv.
612 BADR (ex-PCG 1)	30-5-79	26-1-80	9-81
614 AL-YARMOOK (ex-PCG 2)	13-12-79	13-5-80	5-82
616 HITTEN (ex-PCG 3)	19-5-80	5-9-80	10-82
618 TABUK (ex-PCG 4)	22-9-80	18-6-81	12-82

D: 720 tons (815 fl) S: 30 kts gas turbines, 51 kts diesel
Dim: 74.68 × 9.60 × 2.59
A: 8/Harpoon SSM (IV × 2)—1/76-mm U.S. Mk 75 Compact—1/20-mm Vulcan/Phalanx AA—2/20-mm AA (I × 2)—1/81-mm mortar—2/40-mm Mk 19 grenade launchers—6/Mk 32 ASW TT (III × 2)
Electron Equipt: Radar: 1/SPS-55, 1/SPS-40B, 1/Mk 92 fire-control system
Sonar: SQS-56—ECM: SLQ-32
M: CODOG: 1 GE LM-2500 gas turbine (23,000 hp); 2 MTU 12V652 diesels (3,058 hp tot.); 2 CP props
Man: 7 officers, 16 men

REMARKS: Ordered 30-8-77. Have fin stabilizers. Program completed well behind schedule.

GUIDED-MISSILE CORVETTES (continued)

Badr (612) 1981

Badr (612) 1981

GUIDED-MISSILE PATROL BOATS

♦ 5 (+4) U.S. PGG class Bldr: Peterson Builders, Sturgeon Bay, Wisc.

	Laid down	L	In serv.
511 As-Siddiq (ex-PGG 1)	30-9-78	22-9-79	15-12-80
513 Al-Farouq (ex-PGG 2)	12-3-79	17-5-80	22-6-81
515 Abdul-Aziz (ex-PGG 3)	19-10-79	23-8-80	3-9-81
517 Faisal (ex-PGG 4)	4-3-80	15-11-80	11-81
519 Khalid (ex-PGG 5)	27-6-80	28-3-81	12-81
521 Amr (ex-PGG 6)	21-10-80	13-6-81	6-82
523 Tariq (ex-PGG 7)	10-2-81	23-9-81	8-82
525 Oqbah (ex-PGG 8)	8-5-81	12-81	10-82
527 Abu Obaidah (ex-PGG 9)	4-9-81	4-82	12-82

As-Siddiq (511) 1980

As-Siddiq (511) 1980

D: 320 tons (390 fl)   **S:** 38 kts gas turbines, 15.6 kts diesels
Dim: 58.02 × 8.08 × 1.95   **Man:** 5 officers, 33 men
A: 4/Harpoon (II × 2)—1/76-mm U.S. Mk 75 Compact—1/20-mm Vulcan/Phal-
　　anx AA—2/20-mm AA(I × 2)—1/81-mm mortar—2/40-mm Mk 19 grenade
　　launchers
Electron Equipt: Radar: 1/SPS-55, 1/Mk 92 fire-control system
　　　　　　　　ECM: SLQ-32
M: CODOG: 1 GE gas turbine (23,000 hp); 2 MTU 12V652 diesels (3,058 hp tot.)
　　2 CP props
Remarks: Ordered 16-2-77. Fin stabilizers fitted. Program behind schedule.

TORPEDO BOATS

♦ **3 German Jaguar class (Type 141)** Bldr: Lürssen, Vegesack (In serv. 1969)

DAMMAM   KHABAR   MACCAH

Khabar   1975

D: 170 tons (210 fl)   **S:** 40 kts   **Dim:** 42.62 × 7.10 × 2.39
A: 2/40-mm AA (I × 2)—4/533-mm TT   **Man:** 3 officers, 33 men
M: 4 Maybach 16-cyl. diesels; 4 props; 12,000 hp   **Range:** 500/39; 1,000/32

MINE WARFARE SHIPS

♦ **4 U.S. MSC 322 class** Bldr: Peterson Builders, Sturgeon Bay, Wisc.

	Laid down	L	In serv.
412 ADDIRIYAH (ex-MSC 322)	12-5-76	20-12-76	6-7-78
414 AL-QUYSUMAH (ex-MSC 323)	24-8-76	26-5-77	15-8-78
416 AL-WADEEAH (ex-MSC 324)	28-12-76	6-9-77	7-9-78
418 SAFWA (ex-MSC 325)	5-3-77	7-12-77	20-10-78

Al-Quysumah (414)   Peterson Bldrs., 1978

D: 320 tons (407 fl)   **S:** 14 kts   **Dim:** 46.63 × 8.29 × 4.06 max.
A: 2/20-mm AA (II × 1)
Electron Equipt: Radar: SPS-55   Sonar: SQQ-14
M: 2 Waukesha E1616 DSIN diesels; 2 props; 1,200 hp
Electric: 2,150 kw   **Man:** 4 officers, 35 men

REMARKS: Ordered 30-9-75. Longer than standard U.S. export coastal minesweepers. Wooden construction. Have a 1,750-kw sweep current generator.

AMPHIBIOUS WARFARE SHIPS

♦ **4 U.S. LCU 1646 class** Bldr: Newport SY, Rhode Island (In serv. 1976)

212 AL-QIAQ (ex-SA 310)   216 AL-ULA (ex-SA 312)
214 AS-SULAYEL (ex-SA 311)   218 AFIF (ex-SA 313)

D: 173 tons (403 fl)   **S:** 11 kts   **Dim:** 41.07 × 9.07 × 2.08
A: 2/20-mm AA (I × 2)   **Electron Equipt:** Radar: 1/LN-66
M: 4 GM 6-71 diesels; 2 Kort nozzle props; 900 hp   **Cargo:** 168 tons
Electric: 80 kw   **Range:** 1,200/10   **Man:** 2 officers, 12 men, 20 passengers

♦ **8 U.S. LCM(6)-class landing craft** (4 in serv. 7-77, 4 in serv. 7-80)

D: 24 tons (57.5 fl)   **S:** 13 kts   **Dim:** 17.07 × 4.37 × 1.14
A: 2/40-mm Mk 19 grenade launchers
M: 2 GM 6V71 TI diesels; 2 props; 450 hp   **Range:** 130/9 (loaded)   **Man:** 5 tot.

REMARKS: Cargo: 30 tons. Cargo well: 11.9 × 3.7.

AUXILIARIES

♦ **0 (+2) underway replenishment oilers** Bldr: CN la Ciotat, Marseilles

	Laid down	L	In serv.
N. . .	. . .	. . .	. . .
N. . .	. . .	. . .	. . .

D: 10,475 tons   **S:** 20.5 kts   **Dim:** 135.0 × 18.7 × 7.0
A: 4/40-mm AA (II × 2)—2/Dauphin II helicopters
Electron Equipt: Radar: . . .
M: 2 SEMT-Pielstick 16 PA 6 BTC diesels; 2 props; 18,500 hp
Electric: . . . kw   **Range:** 7,000/15   **Man:** 140 tot.

REMARKS: Ordered 10-80 as part of the "Sawari" program. Design a reduced verison of the French *Durance* class. Will carry some trainees.

♦ **1 training ship** Bldr: Bayerische Schiffsbau, Erlenbach, West Germany (In serv. 12-77)

TEBUK

D: 600 tons (fl)   **S:** 19 kts   **Dim:** 60.0 (pp) × 10.0 × 1.8
A: . . .   **M:** 2 MTU diesels; 2 props; 5,260 hp   **Man:** 60 tot.

♦ **1 royal yacht** Bldr: C. Van Lent & Sons, Kaag, Netherlands (In serv. 1-78)

AL RIYADH

D: 670 tons (fl)   **S:** 20 kts   **Dim:** 64.64 (59.22 pp) × 9.7 × 3.0
A: None   **Electron Equipt:** Radar: 1/Decca RM 916
M: 2 MTU 16V956 diesels; 2 props; 5,720 hp   **Electric:** 370 kw
Range: 1,750/18   **Man:** 16 tot.

REMARKS: Fin stabilizers and Schöttel bow-thruster fitted.

494

SAUDI ARABIA *(continued)*
AUXILIARIES *(continued)*

♦ **1 salvage tug** Bldr: Hayashikane, Shimonoseki (In serv. 1978)

13 JEDDAH

    D: 350 tons   **S:** 12 kts   **Dim:** 34.4 × . . . × . . .   **M:** 2 diesels; 800 hp

♦ **2 U.S. YTB 752 class** (In serv. 15-10-75)

EN 111 TUWAIG (ex-YTB 837)   EN 112 DAREEN (ex-YTB 838)

    D: 291 tons (316 fl)   **S:** 12 kts   **Dim:** 33.22 × 9.30 × 4.14
    A: 2/20-mm AA (I × 2)   **Electron Equipt:** Radar: 1/LN-66
    M: 2 diesels; 1 prop; 2,000 hp   **Electric:** 120 kw
    Range: 2,000/10   **Man:** 4 officers, 8 men

REMARKS: 25-ton bollard pull. Intended for target towing, firefighting, torpedo recovery, and local patrol duties.

COAST GUARD

PATROL BOAT

♦ **1 U.S. Coast Guard Cape class**

RIYADH

    D: 102 tons (fl)   **S:** 18 kts   **Dim:** 28.95 × 5.8 × 1.55
    A: 1/40-mm AA   **M:** 4 Cummins VT-12-M-700 diesels; 2 props; 2,324 hp
    Electric: 40 kw   **Range:** 1,500/12   **Man:** 15 tot.

REMARKS: Transferred in 1969.

PATROL CRAFT

♦ **15 Scorpion class** Bldrs: 10 units: Bayerische Schiffsbau; 5 units: Werft Union, West Germany (In serv. 1979)

139-153

    D: 33 tons (fl)   **S:** 25 kts   **Dim:** 17.14 (15.6 pp) × 4.98 × 1.40
    A: 2/7.62-mm mg   **Electron Equipt:** Radar: 1/Decca RM 914
    M: 2 GM 12V-71 TI diesels; 2 props; 1,300 hp (1,050 sust.)
    Range: 200/20   **Man:** 7 tot.

♦ **12 Rapier class** Bldr: Halter Marine, New Orleans, La. (In serv. 1976-77)

127-138

    D: 26 tons (fl)   **S:** 28 kts   **Dim:** 15.24 × 4.57 × 1.35
    A: 2/7.62-mm mg (I × 2)   **M:** 2 GM 12V-71 TI diesels; 2 props; 1,300 hp
    Electric: 20 kw   **Man:** 1 officer, 8 men

♦ **43 C-80 class** Bldr: Northshore Yacht Yard, G.B. (In serv. 1975-77)

    D: 2.8 tons (fl)   **S:** 20 kts   **Dim:** 8.9 × 2.9 × 0.6   **A:** 1/7.62-mm mg
    M: 1 Caterpillar diesel; Castoldi water jet; 210 hp   **Man:** 3 tot.

♦ **10 Huntress class** Bldr: Fairey Marine, Hamble, G.B. (In serv. 1976)

    D: . . .   **S:** 20 kts   **Dim:** 7.1 × 2.7 × 0.8
    A: 1/7.62-mm mg   **M:** 1 diesel; 180 hp   **Range:** 150/20   **Man:** 4 tot.

Rapier class   Halter Marine, 1976

♦ **16 SRN-6-class hovercraft** Bldr: British Hovercraft, 1970 and 1981

    D: 10 tons   **S:** 58 kts   **Dim:** 14.8 × 7.7 × 4.8 (high)   **A:** 1/7.62-mm mg
    M: 1 Rolls-Royce Gnome gas turbine; 900 hp

REMARKS: Eight additional ordered 1980.

♦ **8 harbor patrol craft** Bldr: Yokohama Yacht, Japan, 1972

    D: . . .   **S:** 20 kts   **Dim:** 10.5 × 3.0 × . . .   **M:** 2 diesels, 2 props; 280 hp

NOTE: There are also several hundred small boats: 200 of 5.1-m length with 40-hp engines and 100 of 4.2-m length with a 20-hp engine.

SENEGAL
Republic of Senegal

PERSONNEL: 350 men

MERCHANT MARINE (1980): 87 ships—34,499 grt
        (tankers: 2 ships—1,422 grt)

PATROL BOATS

♦ **1 French PR 72 MS class** Bldr: S.F.C.N., Villeneuve-la Garenne

	Laid down	L	In serv.
P 773 NJAMBUR	5-80	23-12-80	6-81

    D: 381 tons light (451 fl)   **S:** 30 kts   **Dim:** 58.70 (54.0 pp) × 8.22 × 2.18
    A: 2/76-mm OTO Melara Compact (I × 2)—2/20-mm Type F2 AA (I × 2)
    Electron Equipt: Radar: . . .
    M: 4 AGO 195V16 RVR diesels; 4 props; 12,800 hp
    Range: 2,500/16   **Man:** 39 tot. plus 7 passengers

REMARKS: Can be equipped later with 4/Exocet SSM. Two CSEE Naja optical GFCS.

SENEGAL *(continued)*
PATROL BOATS *(continued)*

♦ **3 PR-48 class** Bldr: S.F.C.N., Villeneuve-la-Garenne

	Laid down	L	In serv.
SAINT LOUIS	20-4-70	5-8-70	1-3-71
POPENGUINE	12-73	22-3-74	10-8-74
PODOR	12-75	20-7-76	13-7-77

Saint Louis   1971

D: 240 tons (avg.) **S:** 23 kts **Dim:** 47.5 (45.5 pp) × 7.1 × 2.5
A: 2/40-mm AA (I × 2)—2/7.62-mm mg
M: 2 AGO V12 CZSHR diesels; 2 props; 6,240 hp
Range: 2,000/16 **Man:** 3 officers, 22 men

PATROL CRAFT

♦ **3 fisheries craft** Bldr: Turbec Ltd., St. Catherine, Canada

SENEGAL II SINÉ SALOUM II CASAMANCE II

D: 52 tons (62 fl) **S:** 32 kts **Dim:** 26.5 × 5.81 × . . .
A: 2/20-mm AA (I × 2) **M:** 2 diesels; 2 props; 2,700 hp

REMARKS: In service 2-79, 7-79, and 10-79, respectively.

AMPHIBIOUS WARFARE SHIPS

♦ **1 ex-French EDIC-class landing craft** (L: 11-4-58)

FALEME (ex-EDIC 9095)

D: 250 tons (670 fl) **S:** 8 kts **Dim:** 59.0 × 11.95 × 1.3
A: 2/20-mm AA (I × 2) **M:** 2 MGO diesels; 2 props; 1,000 hp
Range: 1,800/8 **Man:** 16 tot.

REMARKS: Transferred 7-1-74. Can carry eleven trucks or five LVT amphibious personnel carriers.

♦ **2 ex-U.S. LCM-6-class landing craft**

DJOMBOSS DOULOULOU

D: 26 tons (52 fl) **S:** 10 kts **Dim:** 17.1 × 4.4 × 1.2
M: 2 Gray Marine 64 HN9 diesels; 2 props; 330 hp

REMARKS: Transferred in 7-68.

AUXILIARY SHIPS

♦ **1 training ship**

CRAME JEAN (ex-*Raymond Sarr*)

D: 18 tons

REMARKS: A former fishing vessel, acquired 1978.

♦ **1 tug**

IBIS

D: 200 tons (fl) **S:** 9 kts **Dim:** 18.4 × 5.7 × 2.5
M: 1 Poyaud diesel; 250 hp **Range:** 1,700/9

REMARKS: On loan from the French Navy.

SENEGAL POLICE

PATROL CRAFT

♦ **2 new construction** Bldr: Celayo, Bilbao, Spain (In serv. 1981)

D: . . . **S:** . . . **Dim:** 16.0 × 4.6 × . . .
M: 2 GM diesels; 2 props; 870 hp

♦ **4 harbor craft** Bldr: ARESA, Arenys de Mar, Spain (In serv. 1979)

D: 3.5 tons (fl) **S:** 18 kts **Dim:** 8.5 × . . . × . . .

♦ **3 Lance class** Bldr: Fairey Marine, Hamble, G.B. (In serv. 1974-77)

DJIBRILL DJILOR GORÉE

D: 15.7 tons **S:** 24 kts **Dim:** 14.8 × 4.7 × 1.3
A: 2/7.62-mm mg (I × 2) **M:** 2 GM 8V71 TI diesels; 2 props; 850 hp
Man: 7 tot.

♦ **12 45-foot class** Bldr: Vosper Thornycroft

D: 10 tons (fl) **S:** 25 kts **Dim:** 13.7 × 4.0 × 1.1
A: 1/12.7-mm mg—2/7.62-mm mg (I × 2)
M: 2 diesels; 2 props; 920 hp **Man:** 6 tot.

♦ **2 Huntress class** Bldr: Fairey Marine, Hamble, G.B. (In serv. 1974)

D: . . . **S:** 29 kts **Dim:** 7.1 × 2.7 × 0.6
A: 1/7.62-mm mg **M:** 1 diesel; 180 hp **Man:** 2 tot.

SEYCHELLES
Republic of Seychelles

MERCHANT MARINE (1980): 12 ships—3,738 grt

SEYCHELLES *(continued)*

PATROL BOAT

♦ **1 ex-French Sirius-class former minesweeper** Bldr: Seine Maritime (L: 13-6-56)

P. . . TOPAZ (ex-*Croix du Sud*, P 658)

> **D:** 400 tons (440 fl) **S:** 15 kts **Dim:** 46.4 (42.7 pp) × 8.55 × 2.5
> **A:** 1/40-mm AA—1/20-mm AA **M:** 2 SEMT-Pielstick diesels; 2 props; 2,000 hp
> **Fuel:** 48 tons **Range:** 3,000/10 **Man:** 2 officers, 35 men

REMARKS: Transferred 1979. Minesweeping gear removed.

FISHERIES PROTECTION CRAFT

♦ **1 glass-reinforced plastic-hulled** Bldr: Tyler, G.B. (In serv. 4-80)

> **D:** . . . **S:** 26 kts **Dim:** 18.3 × . . . × . . .
> **M:** 2 GM diesels; 2 props; 1,040 hp **Range:** 1,000/22

AUXILIARY SHIP

♦ **1 medium landing ship** Bldr: A.C.de la Perrière, France

	Laid down	L	In serv.
5 JUIN	7-4-78	19-9-78	11-1-79

> **D:** 350 tons (855 fl) **S:** 9 kts **Dim:** 58.2 × 11.37 × 1.9
> **M:** 2 Poyaud A12 150M diesels; 2 props; 880 hp **Range:** 2,000/9

REMARKS: Owned by the government but operated in local commercial service. Bow ramp. Cargo: 272 tons.

SIERRA LEONE
Republic of Sierra Leone

MERCHANT MARINE (1980): 12 ships—3,738 grt

PATROL BOATS AND CRAFT

♦ **3 Chinese Shanghai-II class** (Transferred 6-73)

001 N . . .   002 N . . .   003 N . . .

> **D:** 123 tons (150 fl) **S:** 28.5 kts **Dim:** 38.78 × 5.41 × 1.49
> **A:** 4/37-mm AA (II × 2)—4/25-mm AA (II × 2)—8/d.c.
> **Electron Equipt:** Radar: 1/Pot Head
> **M:** 2 M50-F4, 1,200-hp diesels; 2 12D6 diesels, 910 hp; 4 props; 4,220 hp
> **Man:** 38 tot.

♦ **1 Tracker Mk II class** Bldr: Fairey Allday Marine, Hamble (In serv. 8-81)

> **D:** 31 tons **S:** 25 kts **Dim:** 19.25 × 5.00 × 1.45
> **A:** 1/20-mm AA—2/7.62-mm mg (I × 2) **Man:** 11 tot.
> **M:** 2 GM 12V71 TI diesels; 2 props; 1,300 hp **Range:** 650/25

SINGAPORE
Republic of Singapore

PERSONNEL (1981): 3,000 men

MERCHANT MARINE (1980): 988 ships—7,664,229 grt
(tankers: 151 ships—2,696,860 grt)

GUIDED-MISSILE PATROL BOATS

♦ **6 FPB 45 class**

	In serv.		In serv.		In serv.
P 76 SEA WOLF	1972	P 78 SEA DRAGON	1974	P 80 SEA HAWK	1975
P 77 SEA LION	1972	P 79 SEA TIGER	1974	P 81 SEA SCORPION	1975

Bldrs: P 76, P 77: Lürssen, Vegesack; others: Singapore SB & Eng. Co., Jurong

Sea Dragon (P 78)—without missiles   1979

> **D:** 225 tons (252 fl) **S:** 38 kts **Dim:** 44.90 (42.30 wl) × 7.00 × 2.48
> **A:** 5/Gabriel missiles (III × 1, I × 2)—1/57-mm AA—1/40-mm AA
> **Electron Equipt:** Radar: 1/Decca TM 626, 1/HSA WM 28
> **M:** 4 MTU 16V538 diesels; 4 props; 14,400 hp **Range:** 2,000/15 **Man:** 40 tot.

REMARKS: Ordered in 1970. Frequently seen without missiles. Two multiple 57-mm flare launchers on 57-mm mount. Carry 504 rounds 57-mm, 1,008 rounds 40-mm.

PATROL BOATS AND CRAFT

♦ **3 German FPB 57 class** Bldr: Singapore SB & Eng., Jurong

	Laid down	L	In serv.
P. . . N. . .	6-80	. . .	1982
P. . . N. . .	. . .	. . .	. . .
P. . . N. . .	. . .	. . .	. . .

> **D:** 353 tons normal (398 fl) **S:** 36.5 kts **Dim:** 58.10 (54.40 wl) × 7.62 × 2.83
> **A:** 1/76-mm OTO Melara DP—2/35-mm Oerlikon GDM-A AA (II × 1)
> **Electron Equipt:** Radar: 1/navigational, 1/HSA WM 28-41
>   ECM: SUSIE-1 passive intercept
> **M:** 4 MTU 16V 956 TB91 diesels; 4 props; 18,000 hp
> **Electric:** 405 kVA **Range:** 700/35 **Man:** 5 officers, 33 men

REMARKS: Three to be built for Singapore Navy use and three on speculation, for export. Carry 300 rounds 76-mm, 2,750 rounds 35-mm and can be equipped with anti-ship missiles.

PATROL BOATS AND CRAFT (continued)

♦ 3 110-foot, "Type A"

	Bldr	L	In serv.
P 69 INDEPENDENCE	Vosper Thornycroft, Portsmouth	15-7-69	8-7-70
P 70 FREEDOM	Vosper Thornycroft, Singapore	18-11-69	11-1-71
P 72 JUSTICE	Vosper Thornycroft, Singapore	20-6-70	23-4-71

Independence (P 69)　　　　　　　　　　　　　　　　G. Arra, 1977

D: 100 tons (130 fl)　**S:** 30 kts　**Dim:** 33.4 (31.46 pp) × 6.4 × 1.71
A: 1/40-mm Bofors AA—1/20-mm Oerlikon AA
Electron Equipt: Radar: 1/Decca TM 626
M: 2 MTU 16V538 diesels; 2 props; 7,200 hp
Electric: 100 kw　**Range:** 1,100/15　**Man:** 3 officers, 16 men

REMARKS: Ordered 21-5-68.

♦ 3 110-foot, "Type B"

	Bldr	L	In serv.
P 71 SOVEREIGNTY	Vosper Thornycroft, Portsmouth	25-11-69	2-71
P 73 DARING	Vosper Thornycroft, Singapore	1970	18-9-71
P 74 DAUNTLESS	Vosper Thornycroft, Singapore	6-5-71	7-71

Sovereignty (P 71)　　　　　　　　　　　　　　　　Vosper, 1971

D: 100 tons (130 fl)　**S:** 32 kts　**Dim:** 33.4 × 6.4 × 1.71
A: 1/76.2-mm Bofors—1/20-mm Oerlikon AA
Electron Equipt: Radar: 1/Decca TM 626, 1/HSA M-26
M: 2 MTU 16V538 diesels; 2 props; 7,200 hp
Range: 1,000/15　**Man:** 3 officers, 16 men

REMARKS: Gun and fire-control system as on the Norwegian *Storm* class. The 76.2-mm is for surface-fire only.

♦ 1 British Ford class

	Bldr	L	In serv.
P 48 PANGLIMA	United Engineers, Singapore	14-1-56	5-56

D: 119 tons (131 fl)　**S:** 14 kts　**Dim:** 35.76 × 6.1 × 1.68
A: 1/40-mm AA—1/20-mm AA—2/7.62-mm mg (I × 2)
M: 2 Paxman 12YHAXM diesels; 2 props; 1,000 hp
Fuel: 15 tons　**Man:** 15 tot.

REMARKS: Transferred by Malaysia in 1967 and used for training.

♦ 1 ex-Dutch craft Bldr: Schiffswerf Oberwinter, West Germany (In serv. 1955)

P 75 ENDEAVOR

D: 250 tons (fl)　**S:** 20 kts　**Dim:** 40.9 × 7.6 × 2.4
A: 2/20-mm AA (I × 2)　**M:** 2 Maybach diesels; 2 props; 2,000 hp
Range: 800/8　**Man:** 24 tot.

REMARKS: Purchased on 30-9-70. Low freeboard. Used for training and as a diving tender.

MINE WARFARE SHIPS

♦ 2 ex-U.S. Redwing-class minesweepers Bldr: . . .

	L	In serv.
M 101 JUPITER (ex-*Thrasher*, MSC 203)	6-10-54	16-8-55
M 102 MERCURY (ex-*Whippoorwill*, MSC 207)	13-8-54	20-10-55

D: 300 tons (372 fl)　**S:** 13 kts　**Dim:** 43.0 × 7.95 × 2.55
A: 1/20-mm　**Electron Equipt:** Radar: 1/SPS-5—Sonar: UQS-1D
M: 2 GM 8-268A diesels; 2 props; 1,200 hp　**Fuel:** 40 tons
Range: 2,500/10　**Man:** 39 tot.

REMARKS: Transferred on 5-12-75. Re-armed with new Oerlikon 20-mm AA 1980.

AMPHIBIOUS WARFARE SHIPS

♦ 6 ex-U.S. LST 542 class

	Laid down	L	In serv.
L 201 ENDURANCE (ex-*Holmes County*, LST 836)	11-9-44	29-10-44	25-11-44
L 202 EXCELLENCE (ex-T-LST 629)	13-4-44	8-7-44	28-7-44
L 203 INTREPID (ex-T-LST 579)	4-5-44	22-6-44	21-7-44
L 204 RESOLUTION (ex-T-LST 649)	19-7-44	6-10-44	26-10-44
L 205 PERSISTENCE (ex-T-LST 614)	28-1-44	6-5-44	22-5-44
L 206 PERSEVERANCE (ex-T-LST 623)	13-3-44	12-6-44	21-6-44

Endurance (L 201)　　　　　　　　　　　　　　　　G. Arra, 1977

SINGAPORE *(continued)*
AMPHIBIOUS WARFARE SHIPS *(continued)*

Bldrs: L 201: American Bridge, Pa.; L 202, L 204, L 205, L 206: Chicago Bridge & Iron, Seneca, Ill.: L 203: Missouri Valley Bridge & Iron, Evansville, Ind.

> **D:** 1,653 tons, light (4,080 fl)   **S:** 11.6 kts   **Dim:** 99.98 (96.32 pp) × 15.24 × 4.29
> **A:** 2 or 4/40-mm AA (I × 2 or 4)   **M:** 2 GM 12-567A diesels; 2 props; 1,800 hp
> **Electric:** 300 kw   **Range:** 19,000/9   **Man:** 120 tot.

REMARKS: Originally numbered A 81 to A 86. L 201 loaned 1-7-71 and purchased 5-12-75; chartered in 1976 for commercial service at which time guns were removed. Others purchased 4-6-76. L202 has two 40-mm AA (I × 2) forward and a helicopter deck aft. L 203 is unarmed; both are active. L 204 to 206 in reserve until 1980 when refitting began; all are getting 1/40-mm AA fwd. Three more ex-Military Sealift Command T-LSTs (ex-T-LST 117, ex-T-LST 276, and ex-*Chase County*, T-LST 532) were purchased 4-6-76 but later sold commercially.

♦ **4 Ayer Chawan-class landing craft** Bldr: Vosper Thornycroft, Singapore (In serv. 1968-69)

RPL. . . AYER CHAWAN	RPL . . . N . . .
RPL. . . AYER MERBAN	RPL . . . N . . .

> **D:** 150 tons (fl)   **S:** 10 kts   **Dim:** 27.0 × 6.9 × 1.3
> **M:** 2 diesels; 2 props; 650 hp

♦ **2 Brani-class landing craft** Bldr: Australia (In serv. 1955-56)

RPL. . . BRANI   RPL . . . BERLAYER

> **D:** 56 tons (fl)   **S:** 9 kts   **Dim:** 17.0 × 4.3 × 1.4
> **M:** 2 diesels; 2 props; 460 hp

NOTE: In 5-81 it was announced that a small tanker powered by 2 MWM TBP-6K diesels (2,060 hp) was to be acquired.

MARINE POLICE

PATROL CRAFT

♦ **12 Swift class** Bldr: Singapore SB & Eng., Jurong (In serv. 1980-81)

P 10 SWIFT ARCHER	P 16 SWIFT. . .
P 11 SWIFT WARLORD	P 17 SWIFT. . .
P 12 SWIFT LANCER	P 18 SWIFT. . .
P 13 SWIFT. . .	P 19 SWIFT. . .
P 14 SWIFT. . .	P 20 SWIFT. . .
P 15 SWIFT. . .	P 21 SWIFT. . .

> **D:** 45 tons (fl)   **S:** 34 kts   **Dim:** 22.7 (20.0 pp) × 6.2 × 1.6
> **A:** 1/20-mm AA—1/7.62-mm mg   **M:** 2 Deutz 816 diesels; 2 props; 2,880 hp
> **Range:** 960/20   **Man:** 3 officers, 10 men

REMARKS: Based on Australian De Havilland "Capricornica" design. First unit launched 8-6-80. Used for coastal surveillance and fisheries patrol.

♦ **4 PX class** Bldr: Vosper Thornycroft, Singapore (In serv. 1969)

PX 10   PX 11   PX 12   PX 13

> **D:** 80 tons (fl)   **S:** 29 kts   **Dim:** 26.29 × 5.7 × 1.45
> **A:** 2/20-mm AA   **M:** 2 MTU diesels; 2 props; 2,700 hp
> **Range:** 700/15   **Man:** 15 tot.

♦ **19 new construction** Bldr: Sembawang SY (In serv. 1981)

PX 14-33

> **D:** . . .   **S:** 32 kts   **Dim:** 11.2 × . . . × . . .
> **M:** 2 MTU diesels; 2 props; 770 hp

♦ **20 PC 32 class** Bldr: Vosper Thornycroft, Singapore (In serv. 1978-79)

PC 32 to PC 51

> **D:** 2 tons (fl)   **S:** 35 kts   **Dim:** 6.5 × 2.5 × 0.46
> **A:** Small arms   **M:** 2 Johnson outboards; 280 hp   **Man:** 4 tot.

SOLOMON ISLANDS

MERCHANT MARINE (1980): 12 ships—2,668 grt

PATROL CRAFT

♦ **1 Carpentaria class** Bldr: De Havilland Marine, Homebush Bay, Australia

TULAGI (In serv. 30-3-79)

Tulagi   G. Gyssels, 1980

> **D:** 27 tons (fl)   **S:** 27 kts   **Dim:** 16.0 × 5.0 × 1.2
> **A:** 2/7.62-mm mg (I × 2)   **Electron Equipt:** Radar: 1/Decca 110
> **M:** 2 GM 12V71 TI diesels; 2 props; 1,120 hp   **Range:** 700/22   **Man:** 8 tot.

SOMALIA
Somali Democratic Republic

PERSONNEL (1981): 350 total

MERCHANT MARINE (1980): 22 ships—45,553 grt
(tanker: 1 ship—10,458 grt)

GUIDED-MISSILE PATROL BOATS

♦ **2 ex-Soviet Osa-II class** (transferred 1975-76)

Osa-II class—under tow to Somalia   1976

D: 205 tons (240 fl) **S:** 36 kts **Dim:** 39.0 × 7.7 × 1.9
A: 4/SS-N-2 Styx missile launchers—4/30-mm AA (II × 2)
Electron Equipt: Radar: 1/Square Tie, 1/Drum Tilt
                 IFF: 2/Square Head, 1/High Pole B
M: 3 M504 diesels; 3 props; 15,000 hp **Range:** 450/34, 700/20 **Man:** 30 tot.

TORPEDO BOATS

♦ **4 Soviet Mol class**

D: 170 tons (220 fl) **S:** 36 kts **Dim:** 39.0 × 7.7 × 1.7
A: 4/30-mm AA (II × 2)—4/533-mm TT (I × 4)
Electron Equipt: Radar: 1/Pot Head, 1/Drum Tilt
                 IFF: 1/Square Head, 1/High Pole B
M: 3 M504 diesels; 3 props; 15,000 hp **Range:** 450/34; 700/20 **Man:** 25 tot.

REMARKS: New units transferred in 1976. Two did not have torpedo tubes.

Somali MOL class—without torpedo tubes   1976

Somali Mol class—with torpedo tubes   1976

♦ **4 ex-Soviet P-6 class** (transferred 1968)

D: 56 tons (66.5 fl) **S:** 43 kts **Dim:** 25.3 × 6.1 × 1.7
A: 4/25-mm AA (II × 2)—2/533-mm TT
M: 4 M50-F4 diesels; 4 props; 4,800 hp **Range:** 450/30 **Man:** 20 tot.

PATROL BOATS

♦ **5 ex-Soviet Poluchat class** (transferred 1968-69)

D: 80 tons (90 fl) **S:** 18 kts **Dim:** 29.86 × 5.8 × 1.5
A: 2/14.5-mm AA (II × 1) **M:** 2 M50 diesels; 2 props; 2,400 hp

AMPHIBIOUS WARFARE SHIPS

♦ **1 ex-Soviet Polnocny-A-class landing ship** (transferred 12-76)

D: 770 tons (fl) **S:** 19 kts **Dim:** 73.0 × 8.6 × 1.9
A: 2/25-mm AA (II × 1)—2/140-mm RL (XVIII × 2)
Electron Equipt: Radar: 1/Don-2
M: 2 diesels; 2 props; 4,000 hp **Cargo:** 180 tons **Man:** 35 tot.

♦ **4 ex-Soviet T-4-class landing craft** (transferred 1968-69)

D: 70 tons (fl) **S:** 10 kts **Dim:** 19.0 × 4.3 × 1.0
M: 2 diesels; 2 props; 600 hp

SOUTH AFRICA
Republic of South Africa

PERSONNEL (1981): 6,758, including 693 officers, 4,951 enlisted and 1,574 conscripts

MERCHANT MARINE (1980): 291 ships—728,926 grt
(tankers: 3 ships—37,597 grt)

NAVAL AVIATION: An air force detachment is available to the navy. Seven Shackleton MR3 and 18 Piaggio P166 aircraft are used for patrol, and Wasp helicopters are available to be embarked on the ships.

SUBMARINES

♦ **3 French Daphné class** Bldr: Dubigeon, Nantes

	Laid down	L	In serv.
S 97 MARIA VAN RIEBEECK	14-3-68	18-3-69	22-6-70
S 98 EMILY HOBHOUSE	18-11-68	24-10-69	25-1-71
S 99 JOHANNA VAN DER MERWE	24-4-69	21-7-70	21-7-71

Maria Van Riebeeck (S 97)   S.A.N., 1978

D: 869/1,043 tons   **S:** 13/15.5 kts   **Dim:** 57.75 × 6.75 × 4.5
A: 12/550-mm TT (8 fwd, 4 aft)—no reloads
Electron Equipt: Radar: DRUA-31—Sonar: DUUA-1 active, DSUV passive
M: 2 SEMT-Pielstick 450-kw diesels, electric drive; 2 props; 1,300/1,600 hp
Man: 6 officers, 41 men

REMARKS: See French *Daphné* class. Two embargoed *Agosta*-class submarines ordered from France in 1975 were sold by France to Pakistan.

FRIGATES

♦ **2 British Whitby class** Bldr: Yarrow, Scotstoun

	Laid down	L	In serv.
F 145 PRESIDENT PRETORIUS	21-11-60	28-9-62	4-3-64
F 150 PRESIDENT KRUGER	6-4-59	20-10-60	1-10-62

D: 2,250 tons (2,800 fl)   **S:** 29 kts   **Dim:** 112.77 (100.73 pp) × 12.5 × 5.2 (fl)
A: 2/114-mm Mk 6 DP (II × 1)—2/40-mm AA (I × 2)—6/324-mm Mk 32 ASW
   TT (III × 2)—1/Mk 10 Limbo mortar (III × 1)—1/Wasp helicopter (Mk 44
   torpedoes)
Electron Equipt: Radar: 1/293 M, 1/Thomson-CSF Jupiter, 1/Elsag NA 9C
       fire-control
     Sonar: 1/177, 1/174
M: 2 double-reduction GT; 2 props; 30,000 hp   **Electric:** 1,140 kw

President Kruger (F 150)—now has NA 9 GFCS   S.A.N., 1978

President Pretorius (F 145)   S.A.N., 1978

Boilers: 2 Babcock & Wilcox; 38.7 kg/cm², 454°C   **Fuel:** 370 tons
Range: 2,100/26, 4,500/12   **Man:** 13 officers, 190 men

REMARKS: F 150 modernized at Simonstown, 1969-71; F 145 in 1971-77. F 150 again refitted in 1979 when old fire-control system was replaced. Jupiter is an export version of the French Navy DRBV-23, L-band radar. Sister *President Steyn* (F 147) stricken summer 1981.

GUIDED-MISSILE PATROL BOATS

♦ **6 Israeli Reshev type**

	Bldr	L	In serv.
P 1561 JAN SMUTS	Israeli SY, Haifa	2-77	9-77
P 1562 P.W. BOTHA	Israeli SY, Haifa	9-77	12-77
P 1563 FREDERICK CRESWELL	Israeli SY, Haifa	1-78	6-78
P 1564 JIM FOUCHE	Durban SY	9-78	12-78
P 1565 FRANZ ERASMUS	Durban SY	3-79	7-79
P 1566 OSWALD PIROW	Durban SY	9-79	3-80

D: 415 tons (450 fl)   **S:** 32 kts   **Dim:** 58.1 × 7.6 × 2.4
A: 6/Skorpioen SSM (I × 6)—2/76-mm OTO Melara DP (I × 2)—2/20-mm AA (I
   × 2)—4/12.7-mm mg·(II × 2)
Electron Equipt: Radar: 1/Thomson-CSF THD-1040 Neptune, 1/Selenia RTN-
           10X Orion
    ECM: Elta MN-53 passive intercept, 4 chaff RL
M: 4 MTU MD871 diesels; 4 props; 14,000 hp
Range: 1,500/30; 5,000/15   **Man:** 7 officers, 40 men

REMARKS: Ordered 1974. A further six were reportedly ordered 15-11-77, although they have not yet appeared (the name *Hendrik Mentz* was at one time mentioned in the South African press). Skorpioen is a license-built version of the Israeli Gabriel II anti-ship missile. All named for former Ministers of Defense.

South African Reshev   S.A.N., 1980

GUIDED-MISSILE PATROL BOATS *(continued)*

South African Reshev　　　　　　　　S.A.N., 1980

PATROL BOATS

♦ **1 former yacht** Bldr:. . . , Italy

P . . . ORYX (ex-*Caroline*)

REMARKS: Chartered and refitted 1981 as a patrol ship for duty off the coast of Namibia. No data available.

♦ **5 British "Ford" class**

	Bldr	In serv.
P 3105 GELDERLAND (ex-*Brayford*)	A. & J. Inglis, Glasgow	30-8-54
P 3120 NAUTILUS (ex-*Glassford*)	R. Dunstan, Thorne	23-8-55
P 3125 RIJGER	Vosper, Portsmouth	1958
P 3126 HAERLEM	Vosper, Portsmouth	1959
P 3127 OOSTERLAND	Vosper, Portsmouth	1959

D: 120 tons (160 fl)　**S:** 15 kts　**Dim:** 35.7 × 6.1 × 2.1
A: 1/40-mm AA
M: 2 Paxman YHAXM diesels, 500 hp each, 1 Foden FD-6 diesel, 100 hp; 3 props
Fuel: 23 tons　**Man:** 19 tot.

Rijger (P 3125)　　　　　　　　S.A.N., 1978

Haerlem (P 3126)—white-painted, buff stacks　　　S.A.N., 1978

REMARKS: P 3126 has been fitted as a hydrographic ship and disarmed. P 3125 and P 3127 still carry two depth-charge racks. P 3120 is manned by the Citizens Force.

♦ **4 ex-British "Ton"-class former minesweepers**

	Bldr	L
P 1556 PRETORIA (ex-*Dunkerton*)	Goole SB Co.	8-3-54
P 1557 KAAPSTAD (ex-*Hazelton*)	Cook, Welton & Gemmell	6-2-54
P 1559 WALVISBAAI (ex-*Packington*)	Harland & Wolff	3-7-58
P 1560 DURBAN	Camper & Nicholson	12-6-57

Kaapstad (P 1557)　　　　　　　　S.A.N., 1978

PATROL BOATS (continued)

REMARKS: Data as for minesweepers below, except that P 1556 and P 1557 have 2 Mirrlees JVSS-12 diesels of 1,250 hp each. Manned by Citizens Force, having been redesignated 1977-78. Retain most sweep gear and could be used to sweep moored and mechanical mines. All carry Gemini inspection dinghys.

PATROL CRAFT

♦ **24 Namicura class** Bldr: . . . , South Africa (In serv. 1980-81)

Y 1051-Y 1074

    D: 5 tons (fl)　**S:** 30 kts　**Dim:** 9.0 × . . . × . . .
    A: 1/12.7-mm mg—2/7.62-mm mg　**M:** Diesels　**Man:** 4 tot.

REMARKS: Radar-equipped, glass-reinforced, plastic-hulled harbor craft, which can be land-transported on trailers.

♦ **1 harbor patrol craft** Bldr: South Africa (In serv. 1976)

P 1558 N . . .

    D: . . .　**S:** . . .　**Dim:** . . . × . . . × . . .
    A: 1/40-mm AA—2/20-mm AA (I × 2)　**M:** 2 diesels; 2 props; . . . hp

REMARKS: The first South African-designed warship. Prototype for a new class of local patrol craft, but no further units reported.

MINE WARFARE SHIPS

♦ **6 British "Ton"-class minesweepers and minehunters***

	Bldr	L
M 1207 JOHANNESBURG (ex-*Castleton*)	J.S. White	26-8-58
M 1210 KIMBERLEY (ex-*Stratton*)*	Dorset Yacht	29-7-57
M 1212 PORT ELIZABETH (ex-*Dumbleton*)	Harland & Wolff	8-11-57
M 1213 MOSSELBAAI (ex-*Oakington*)*	Harland & Wolff	10-12-58
M 1215 EAST LONDON (ex-*Chilton*)	Cook, Welton & Gemmell	15-7-57
M 1498 WINDHOEK	Thornycroft	28-6-57

Windhoek (M 1498)

    D: 370 tons (425 fl)　**S:** 15 kts (cruising)　**Dim:** 46.33 (42.68 pp) × 8.76 × 2.5
    A: 1/40-mm AA—2/20-mm AA (II × 1)
    Electron Equipt: Radar: 1/978 (*1/1006)　Sonar: (*only): 1/193M
    M: 2 Paxman Deltic 18A-7A; 2 props; 3,000 hp　**Fuel:** 45 tons
    Range: 2,300/13, 3,000/8　**Man:** 27 tot (*36)

REMARKS: Four have been redesignated as patrol boats, see above. M 1210 and M 1213 have been converted as minehunters, with Type 193M minehunting sonar, Type 1006 radar, two PAP-104 remote-controlled minehunting devices, and mine-disposal diver facilities. All now have enclosed bridges and tripod masts.

AUXILIARY SHIPS

♦ **1 British Hecla-class hydrographic ship**

	Bldr	Laid down	L	In serv.
A 324 PROTEA	Yarrow	20-7-70	14-7-71	23-5-72

Protea (A 324)—white hull, buff stack　　　　　　　S.A.N., 1978

    D: 2,750 tons (fl)　**S:** 15.5 kts　**Dim:** 71.6 × 14.9 × 4.6
    M: 4 Paxman-Ventura diesels; 1 CP prop; 4,800 hp
    Fuel: 500 tons　**Range:** 12,000/11　**Man:** 123 tot.

REMARKS: Ordered 7-11-69. Hull reinforced for navigating in ice. Bow-thruster and anti-roll tanks fitted. Helicopter hangar and flight deck for one Wasp. The "Ford" class patrol boat *Haerlem* (P 3126) is equipped for inshore survey duties; see above.

♦ **1 fleet replenishment ship** Bldr: Nakskovs Skibsvaert, Denmark (L: 20-6-58)

A 243 TAFELBERG (ex-Danish tanker *Annam*)

Tafelberg (A 243)　　　　　　　　　　　　　　S.A.N., 1978

    D: 12,499 grt　**S:** 15 kts　**Dim:** 170.6 × 21.9 × 9.2
    M: 1 B & W diesel; 8,420 hp　**Man:** 100 tot.

REMARKS: Purchased and refitted in Durban, 1965-67. 18,980 dwt. Two refueling stations and one solid-stores transfer station per side.

AUXILIARY SHIPS (continued)

♦ **1 British "Bar"-class net-tender**

	Bldr	Laid down	L	In serv.
P 285 SOMERSET (ex-*Barcross*)	Blyth Dry Dock	15-4-41	21-10-41	14-4-42

Somerset (P 285) — S.A.N., 1976

D: 750 tons (960 fl) **S:** 11.7 kts **Dim:** 52.96 × 9.8 × 4.62 (aft)
M: 1 set triple-expansion reciprocating steam; 1 prop; 850 hp
Boilers: 2 **Fuel:** 214 tons **Range:** 3,100/10

♦ **1 torpedo-recovery and diver-training ship** Bldr: Dorman Long, Durban

P 3148 FLEUR (In serv. 3-12-69)

Fleur (P 3148) — S.A.N., 1978

D: 220 tons (257 fl) **S:** 14 kts **Dim:** 35.0 × 7.5 × 3.4
M: 2 Paxman-Ventura diesels; 2 props; 1,400 hp **Man:** 22 tot.

REMARKS: Ramp at stern for torpedo recovery. Divers' decompression chamber.

♦ **1 training craft** Bldr: Fred Nicholls, Durban (In serv. 1964)

NAVIGATOR

D: 75 tons (fl) **S:** 9.5 kts **Dim:** 19.2 × 6.0 × . . .
M: 2 Foden FD-6 diesels; 2 props; 200 hp

REMARKS: Wooden-hulled fishing cutter type. Serves as tender at Naval College, Gordon's Bay.

♦ **1 seagoing tug**

	Bldr	L	In serv.
DE MIST	Dorman Long, Durban	21-12-78	12-78

D: 275 grt **S:** 12.5 kts **Dim:** 34.3 (32.3 pp) × 7.8 × 3.4
M: 2 Mirrlees-Blackstone ESL-8-MGR diesels; 2 props; 2,440 hp

♦ **1 large harbor tug**

	Bldr	L	In serv.
DE NEYS	Globe Engineering, Capetown	7-69	23-7-69

De Neys — S.A.N., 1978

D: 282 tons (fl) **S:** 11.5 kts **Dim:** 28.6 (27.0 wl) × 8.1 × 3.6
M: 2 Lister-Blackstone ERS-8-M diesels; 2 Voith-Schneider vertical cycloidal props; 1,268 hp
Man: 10 tot.

REMARKS: 14-ton max. bollard pull.

♦ **1 large harbor tug** Bldr: Globe Engineering, Capetown

DE NOORDE (L: 12-61)

D: 170 grt **S:** 9 kts **Dim:** 34.2 × 8.2 × . . .
M: 2 Lister-Blackstone ERS-8-M diesels; 2 Voith-Schneider vertical cycloidal props; 1,268 hp

♦ **1 catamaran trials craft** (In serv. 4-80)

SHIRLEY T.

REMARKS: A 10.8-m prototype for a 50-m fast combatant design concept.

SOUTH AFRICA (*continued*)
AUXILIARY SHIPS (*continued*)

De Noorde   S.A.N., 1978

AIR SEA RESCUE BOATS

♦ **2 Fairey Tracker class** Bldr: Groves & Gutteridge, Cowes, G.B.

P 1554   P 1555

    D: 31 tons (fl)   **S:** 29 kts   **Dim:** 19.25 × 4.98 × 1.45
    M: 2 GM 12V71 TI diesels; 2 props; 1,120 hp   **Range:** 650/20   **Man:** 11 tot.

♦ **2 German-built** Bldr: Krogerwerft, Rendsburg (In serv. 1961–62)

P 1551   P 1552

P 1551   S.A.N., 1978

    D: 67 tons (73 fl)   **S:** 30 kts   **Dim:** 28.8 (27.9 pp) × 5.0 × 1.6
    M: 2 Maybach 12-cyl. diesels; 2 props; 3,000 hp   **Range:** 600/25   **Man:** 8 tot.

DEPARTMENT OF TRANSPORT

♦ **1 Antarctic survey and supply ship**

	Bldr	Laid down	L	In serv.
AGULHAS	Mitsubishi, Shimonoseki	14-6-77	30-9-77	31-1-78

    D: 3,035 dwt   **S:** 14 kts   **Dim:** 109.2 (100.0 pp) × 18.0 × 5.8
    M: 2 Mirrlees-Blackstone K-6 Major diesels; 1 prop; 6,000 hp
    Range: 8,200/14   **Man:** 40 crew + 92 scientists/passengers

REMARKS: Manned by the South African Navy. Twin helicopter hangar. Red hull, white upperworks.

SPAIN
Spanish State

PERSONNEL (1981): 45,000, including 4,750 officers, 40,750 men, plus 650 Naval Infantry officers, and 12,500 Marine enlisted.

MERCHANT MARINE (1980): 2,767 ships—8,112,245 grt
       (tankers: 107 ships—4,812,272 grt)

WARSHIPS IN SERVICE OR UNDER CONSTRUCTION
AS OF 1 JANUARY 1982

	L	Tons	Main armament
♦ **1 (+1) aircraft carrier**			
0 (+1) CANARIAS	. . .	14,500	4/20-mm, 17 aircraft
1 INDEPENDENCE	1943	13,000	22/40-mm, 20 aircraft
		Tons	
♦ **8 (+4) submarines**		(surfaced)	
0 (+4) AGOSTA	1981-82	1,490	4/550-mm TT
4 DAPHNÉ	1972-74	870	12/550-mm TT
3 GUPPY-IIA	1943-44	1,848	10/533-mm TT
1 BALAO	1944	1,827	10/533-mm TT
♦ **13 destroyers**		Tons	
2 ROGER DE LAURIA	1967-68	3,012	6/127-mm DP, ASW weapons
1 ALAVA	1946	1,841	3/76.2-mm DP, ASW weapons
5 GEARING FRAM-I	1945	2,425	4/127-mm, 1/ASROC system
5 FLETCHER	1942-44	2,080	4 or 5/127-mm, 0 or 6/76.2-mm, ASW weapons
♦ **10 (+6) frigates**			
0 (+3) OLIVER HAZARD PERRY	. . .	. . .	1/76-mm, 1 Standard system, 2 helicopters
5 (+3) DESCUBIERTA	1975-80	1,270	1/76-mm, 1/Sea Sparrow

WARSHIPS (continued)

5 Baléares	1970-72	3,015	1/127-mm, 1/ASROC system, 1/Standard system, ASW weapons

♦ **5 corvettes**

1 Pizarro	1945	1,924	2/127-mm, ASW weapons
4 Atrevida	1955-56	977	1/76.2-mm DP, 3/40-mm, ASW weapons

♦ **32 torpedo and patrol boats**

♦ **9 minesweepers**

♦ **6 amphibious warfare ships**

NAVAL AVIATION: Five single-seat AV-8A and two two-seat TAV-8A were delivered in 1976 for service in the *Dedalo;* subsequently, two of the aircraft, named Matador in Spanish service, have been lost. Five more AV-8A were ordered for delivery in 1980-81. Another increment of five may follow.

AV-8A Matador on Dedalo

The Arma Aerea de la Armada also operates 12 Agusta-Bell 212 (with SS-12 missiles), 10 Bell 47G, 15 Sikorsky SH3-D Sea King (with AS-12 missiles), 4 AH-1G Huey, and 11 Hughes 369-HM Cayuse helicopters plus 2 Piper Comanche and 2 Piper Twin Comanche liaison aircraft.

The search-and-rescue service (Servicio de Búsqueda y Salvamento) received 3 Fokker F-27 SAR aircraft in 1979 for coastal surveillance; they carry Litton APS-504V radar.

The Spanish Air Force performs a maritime surveillance role, using two Lockheed P-3A and four P-3C Orion.

WEAPONS AND SYSTEMS

Except for naval guns, which are domestically designed and manufactured, most of the weapon systems in use are of American or French make. However, an advanced antiaircraft/anti-missile point-defense system of Spanish origin is in development. Called Meroka, it consists of two six-barreled, 20-mm Oerlikon guns, whose characteristics are:

Length: 120 calibers
Muzzle velocity: 1,250m/sec
Maximum rate of fire: 3,600 rounds/minute

Maximum effective range: 2,000 m
Fire control: Selenia RAN-12L system with the IPN-10 data system.

Two prototypes are undergoing firing tests, and twenty units may be produced to equip the aircraft carrier *Dedalo,* the *Roger de Lauria*-class destroyers, the *Baléares*-class and *Descubierta*-class frigates, and the programmed new carrier. The planned use of the Lockheed "Sharpshooter" GFCS with Meroka has been canceled.

AIRCRAFT CARRIERS

♦ **1 new construction**

	Bldr	Laid down	L	In serv.
R 11 Canarias	Bazán, el Ferrol	8-10-79	. . .	1985

Canarias (R 11)   X.I. Taibo, 1980

D: 14,500 tons   **S:** 24-26 kts   **Dim:** 195.1 × 24.4 (30.0 flight deck) × 6.7
A: 4/Meroka 20-mm gun systems—11-17 aircraft (3 AV-8A and 8 SH-3D or 14 AB 212, or . . . SH-60B)
Electron Equipt: Radar: 1/SPS-55, 1/SPS-52C, 1 SPN-35A air control
TACAN: URN-22
M: 2 GE LM-2500 gas turbines; 1 prop; 46,400 hp
Range: 7,500/20   **Man:** 750-780 men, including air group

REMARKS: Ordered 29-6-77. Originally to have been named *Almirante Carrero Blanco.* Design is essentially that of the final version of the U.S. Navy's Sea Control Ship concept. The flight deck is 175 × 30 m and is served by two elevators, one at the extreme aft end. Takeoff pattern angled to starboard. A "ski jump" takeoff ramp has been incorporated. Construction of a second, to replace *Dedalo,* is planned.

♦ **1 ex-U.S. Independence-class light aircraft carrier** Bldr: New York SB

	Laid down	L	In serv.
R 01 Dedalo (ex-*Cabot*, AVT 3, ex-CVL 28, ex-*Wilmington*, CL 79)	16-3-42	4-4-43	24-7-43

D: 13,000 tons (16,416 fl)   **S:** 31 kts (trials)
Dim: 188.35 (182.9 wl) × 21.87 (hull) 31.7 (flight deck) × 7.2 (8.1 max.)
A: 22/40-mm AA (IV × 1, II × 9)—about 20 aircraft, 7 of which are Matadors
Electron Equipt: Radar: 1/SPS-10, 1/SPS-40A, 1/SPS-8, 1/SPS-6C, 4/Mk 34 fire-control
TACAN: URN-22
ECM: WLR-1
M: 4 sets GT; 4 props; 100,000 hp
Boilers: 4 Babcock & Wilcox; 39.8 kg/cm², 454°C   **Electric:** 2,400 kw
Fuel: 1,800 tons   **Armor:** Partial belt: 37-127 mm   **Range:** 7,200/15
Man: 51 officers, 1,049 men

AIRCRAFT CARRIERS (*continued*)

Dedalo (R 01)   16F, French Navy, 1980

REMARKS: Ended service in the U.S. Navy as an aviation transport (AVT 3). Transferred on five-year loan on 30-8-67 and purchased in 12-73. Redesignated from PH (portahelicópteros) to PA (portaaviones) on 28-9-76, when AV-8A V/STOL fighters were added to her complement. The flight deck is 166.1 × 32.9 m (max.). Two elevators. Four Mk 63 radar gunfire-control systems and seven Mk 51 mod. 2, optical gunfire control installed. Did not receive SPS-52B radar in place of SPS-8 as planned. Forward quad 40-mm AA now removed. She is supposed to be given the Meroka point-defense gun system. Will probably be retained even after the completion of *Canarias*.

SUBMARINES

♦ **4 Agosta class** Bldr: Bazán, Cartagena

	Laid down	L	In serv.		Laid down	L	In serv.
S 71 GAVERNA	1975	11-81	1982	S 73 MISTRAL	...	1983	1983
S 72 SIROCO	1976	1981	1982	S 74 TRAMONTANA	...	1984	1984

D: 1,230/1,490/1,740 tons   **S:** 20 kts (sub.)   **Dim:** 67.90 × 6.8 × 5.4
A: 4/550-mm TT (rapid reload)—20 torpedoes
Electron Equipt: Radar: 1/DRUA-33
            Sonar: 2/DUUA-1 active, DSUV passive
M: 2 SEMT-Pielstick 16 PA4 185 diesel generator sets, 850 kw each; 4,600-hp main engine; 1/23-kw cruising engine; 1 prop
Fuel: 200 tons   **Range:** 7,000/10 (snorkel)   **Man:** 6 officers, 49 men

REMARKS: See also *Agosta* class in section on France. As with the *Daphné* class, being built with French technical assistance. Agreement signed 6-2-74; first two ordered 9-5-74, second pair 29-6-77.

♦ **4 French Daphné class** Bldr: Bazán, Cartagena

	Laid down	L	In serv.
S 61 DELFIN	13-8-68	25-3-72	3-5-73
S 62 TONINA	1969	3-10-72	10-7-73
S 63 MARSOPA	19-3-71	15-3-74	12-4-75
S 64 NARVAL	1972	14-12-74	22-11-75

Tonina (S 62)—note external TT aft   G. Arra, 1976

Marsopa (S 63)—note small bow dome on Spanish units   Pradignac & Leo, 1976

D: 865/1,042 tons   **S:** 12.5/15.5 kts   **Dim:** 57.78 × 6.75 × 4.60
A: 12/550-mm TT (8 fwd, 4 aft)—no reloads
Electron Equipt: Radar: 1/DRUA-31 (with ECM)
            Sonar: DUUA-1-ABL active, DSUV passive
M: 2 SEMT-Pielstick diesel generators of 450 kw each; 2 props; 2,000 hp
Man: 6 officers, 41 men

REMARKS: Built with French technical assistance; agreement made on 16-7-66. Diving depth: 300 m.

SUBMARINES *(continued)*

♦ **3 ex-U.S. GUPPY-IIA class** Bldrs: S 32, S 34: Portsmouth NSY; S 35: Manitowoc SB, Wisc.

	Laid down	L	In serv.
S 32 ISAAC PERAL (ex-*Ronquil*, SS 396)	9-9-43	27-1-44	22-4-44
S 34 COSME GARCIA (ex-*Bang*, SS 385)	30-4-43	30-8-43	4-12-43
S 35 NARCISO MONTURIOL (ex-*Jallao*, SS-368)	29-9-43	12-3-44	8-7-44

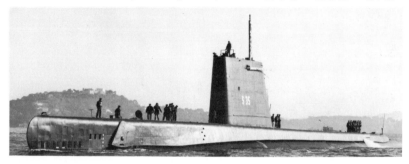

Narciso Monturiol (S 35)   J.-C. Bellonne, 1980

D: 1,525/1,848/2,440 tons   **S:** 15/13.5 kts   **Dim:** 93.57 × 8.23 × 5.18
A: 10/533-mm TT (6 fwd, 4 aft)—22 torpedoes
Electron Equipt: Radar: 1/SS-2
                    Sonar: BQS-2, BQS-3, BQR-2
M: Diesel-electric propulsion: 3 Fairbanks-Morse 38D8⅛ (S 35: GM 16-278A)
     diesels; 2 electric motors; 2 props; 3,430 hp
Fuel: 404 tons (S 35: 472)   **Range:** 10,000/10   **Man:** 74 tot.

REMARKS: S 32 transferred on 1-7-71, S 34 on 1-10-72, and S 35 on 26-6-74. Two 126-cell batteries. Modernized, 1952-53. Diving depth is 137 m. Sister *Narciso Monturiol* (S 33, ex-*Picuda*, SS 382) was stricken on 30-4-77.

♦ **1 ex-U.S. Balao class** Bldr: Manitowoc SB, Manitowoc, Wisc.

	Laid down	L	In serv.
S 31 ALMIRANTE GARCIA DE LOS REYES	14-12-43	30-4-44	8-9-44
(ex-*Kraken*, SS 370)			

Almirante Garcia de los Reyes (S 31)

D: 1,525/1,880/2,400 tons   **S:** 18.5/10 kts   **Dim:** 95.10 × 8.23 × 5.18
A: 10/533-mm TT (6 fwd, 4 aft)—22 torpedoes
Electron Equipt: Radar: 1/SS-2
                    Sonar: BQR-2, BQS-2
M: Diesel-electric propulsion: 4 GM 16-278A diesels; 2 electric motors; 4,610 hp
Fuel: 472 tons   **Range:** 10,000/10   **Man:** 80 tot.

REMARKS: "Fleet Snorkel" conversion, transferred 24-10-59. Complete modernization in Philadelphia, 1965-66. Was to have been stricken in 1975 because of her poor condition, but was refitted as a replacement for the earlier *Narciso Monturiol*.

DESTROYERS

♦ **2 Roger de Lauria class** Bldr: Bazán, el Ferrol, Cartagena

	Laid down	L	Relaunch	In serv.
D 42 ROGER DE LAURIA	4-9-51	12-11-58	22-8-67	30-5-69
D 43 MARQUES DE LA ENSENADA	4-9-51	15-7-59	22-2-68	10-9-70

Roger de Lauria (D 42)   1973

Roger de Lauria (D 42)   1974

D: 3,012 tons (3,785 fl)   **S:** 28 kts (31.5 on trials)
Dim: 116.68 (110.8 pp) × 12.5 × 6.5 (max.)
A: 6/127-mm DP (II × 3)—6/324-mm Mk 32 ASW TT (III × 2)—2/ASW fixed
     Mk 25 TT for Mk 37 torpedoes

DESTROYERS *(continued)*

Electron Equipt: Radar: 1/Decca RM 426, 1/SPS-10B, 1/SPS-40, 1 Mk 25, 1/Mk 35
    Sonar: 1/SQS-32, 1/SQA-10 VDS
    ECM: WLR-1
M: 2 sets Rateau-Bretagne GT; 2 props; 60,000 hp   **Electric:** 1,900 kw
Boilers: 3 three-drum; 35 kg/cm²; 375°C   **Fuel:** 673 tons
Range: 4,500/15   **Man:** 20 officers, 235 men

REMARKS: Widened and lengthened during reconstruction after original launching in order to eliminate defects found in the *Oquendo* prototype; completion consequently delayed. U.S. semiautomatic, 38-caliber guns, 1 Mk 37 and 1 Mk 56 radar gun-control system. *Oquendo* was stricken on 2-11-78. Helicopters not currently carried. To receive Meroka 20-mm AA gun system. Both have had boiler problems.

◆ **1 Alava class** Bldr: Bazán, Cartagena

	Laid down	L	In serv.
D 51 LINIERS	1-1-45	1-5-46	27-1-51

Liniers (D 51)   1969

D: 1,841 tons (2,306 fl)   **S:** 28 kts
Dim: 102.40 (97.52 pp) × 9.65 × 3.10 (5.37 max.)
A: 3/76.2-mm DP (I × 3)—3/40-mm AA (I × 3)—2/Hedgehogs—8/d.c. projectors—2/ASW TT racks (6 Mk 32 torpedoes)—2/d.c. racks
Electron Equipt: Radar: 1/SG-6B, 1/Decca TM 626, 1/MLA-1B, 2/Mk 34
    Sonar: SQS-30
M: 2 sets Parsons GT; 2 props; 31,500 hp   **Boilers:** 4 three-drum Yarrow
Fuel: 540 tons   **Range:** 4,500/14   **Man:** 15 officers, 207 men

REMARKS: Ordered in 1936. Rearmed with U.S. weapons in 1964. Used for training midshipmen at the Naval Academy. Two Mk 63 gunfire-control radars for 76.2-mm guns.

NOTE: The surviving small destroyer of the *Audaz* class, the 1,550-ton (fl) *Intrépido* (D 38) is employed as a stationary enlisted training ship at el Ferrol.

◆ **5 ex-U.S. Gearing FRAM-I class**

	Bldr	Laid down	L	In serv.
D 61 CHURRUCA (ex-*Eugene A. Greene*, DD 711)	Federal SB, Newark	17-8-74	18-3-45	8-6-45
D 62 GRAVINA ex-*Furse*, DD 882)	Consolidated, Orange, Tex.	23-9-44	9-3-45	10-7-45
D 63 MENDEZ NUÑEZ (ex-*O'Hare* DD 889)	Consolidated, Orange, Tex.	27-1-45	22-6-45	29-11-45
D 64 LANGARA (ex-*Leary*, DD 879)	Consolidated, Orange, Tex.	11-8-44	20-1-45	7-5-45
D 65 BLAS DE LEZO (ex-*Noa*, DD 841)	Bath Iron Works	26-3-45	30-7-45	2-11-45

Churruca (D 61)   French Navy, 1980

D: 2,425 tons light (3,520 fl)   **S:** 31 kts
Dim: 119.02 × 12.45 × 6.4 (sonar) 4.45 (hull)
A: 4/127-mm 38-cal. (II × 2)—1/ASROC ASW RL (VIII × 1)—6/324-mm Mk 32 ASW TT (III × 2)
Electron Equipt: Radar: 1/SPS-10, 1/SPS-29 (D 61, D 62: SPS-40), 1/Mk 25
    Sonar: 1/SQS-23
    ECM: WLR-1, ULQ-6
M: GT; 2 props; 60,000 hp   **Electric:** 1,100 kw
Boilers: 4 Babcock & Wilcox; 39.8 kg/cm²; 454°C
Fuel: 650 tons   **Range:** 2,400/25, 4,800/15   **Man:** 17 officers, 257 men

DESTROYERS *(continued)*

REMARKS: D 61 and D 62 were loaned on 31-8-72, and D 63 to D 65 on 31-10-73. All purchased outright on 17-5-78. D 65 has both her 127-mm mounts forward and no ASROC. Mk 37 fire-control system for guns. Carried Hughes 369 manned helicopter in place of original drones, but no longer do so.

♦ 5 ex-U.S. Fletcher class

	Bldr	Laid down	L	In serv.
D 21 LEPANTO (ex-*Capps*, DD 550)	Gulf SB, Chickasaw, Ala.	12-6-41	31-5-42	23-6-43
D 22 ALMIRANTE FERRANDIZ (ex-*David W. Taylor*, DD 551)	Gulf SB, Orange, Texas	12-6-41	4-7-42	18-9-43
D 23 ALMIRANTE VALDES (ex-*Converse*, DD 509)	Bath Iron Works, Me.	23-2-42	30-8-42	20-11-42
D 24 ALCALA GALIANO (ex-*Jarvis*, DD 799)	Todd, Seattle, Wash.	7-6-43	14-2-44	3-6-44
D 25 JORGE JUAN (ex-*McGowan*, DD 678)	Federal SB, Kearny, N.J.	30-6-43	14-11-43	20-12-43

Lepanto (D 21)—5/127-mm guns

Almirante Valdes (D 23)—4/127-mm, 6/76.2-mm guns

D: 2,850 tons (3,050 fl) **S:** 30-32 kts **Dim:** 114.85 × 12.03 × 5.5
A: D 21, D 22: 5/127-mm DP (I × 5)—6/40-mm AA (II × 3)—6/20-mm AA (I × 6)—6/324-mm Mk 32 ASW TT (III × 2)—2/Mk 11 Hedgehogs—6/d.c. mortars—2/d.c. racks
    D 23 to D 25: 4/127-mm DP (I × 4)—6/76.2-mm AA (II × 3)—5/533-mm TT (V × 1)—6/324-mm Mk 32 ASW TT (III × 2)—2/Mk 11 Hedgehogs—1/d.c. rack
Electron Equipt: Radar: 1/SPS-10, 1/SPS-6C, 1/Mk 25; D 23-25 also: 1/Mk 35, 2/Mk 34
    Sonar: SQS-29 series (SQS-4 on D 21, 22)
    ECM: D 23-25: BLR-1
M: 2 sets GE (D 21, 22: Westinghouse) GT; 2 props; 60,000 hp
Electric: 580 kw **Boilers:** 4 Babcock & Wilcox; 39.8 kg/cm², 454°C
Fuel: 650 tons **Range:** 1,260/32; 4,400/15 **Man:** 17 officers, 273 men

REMARKS: D 21 and 22 were transferred on 15-5-57, D 23 on 1-7-59, D 24 on 3-11-60, and D 25 on 1-12-60. D 21, 22, and 23 have high, "early Fletcher" bridges, the others low bridges. All have one Mk 37 gunfire-control system; D23 to D25 also have one Mk 56 and two Mk 63 gunfire-control systems, Mk 5 torpedo director. All five of these very outdated ships are to be retired by 1985.

FRIGATES

♦ 0 (+3) U.S. Oliver Hazard Perry class Bldr: Bazán, el Ferrol

	Laid down	L	In serv.
F 81 NAVARRA	4-81	...	1984
F 82 MURCIA	1981	...	1984
F 83 LEÓN	1982	...	1985

D: 3,537 tons (fl) **S:** 30 kts **Dim:** 135.64 (125.9 wl) × 13.72 × 7.47 (max.)
A: 1/Mk 13, mod. 4 missile launcher (40 Harpoon and Standard SM-1 MR)—1/76-mm OTO Melara DP—1 or 2/Meroka 20-mm AA systems—6/324-mm Mk 32 ASW TT (III × 2)—2/ASW helicopters
Electron Equipt: Radar: 1/SPS-55, 1/SPS-49, 1/Mk 92 fire-control system (with STIR)
    Sonar: Raytheon 1160B
M: 2 GE LM-2500 gas turbines; 1 CP prop; 41,000 hp (2/325-hp electric auxiliary propulsion motors)
Electric: 3,000 kw **Range:** 5,000/18 **Man:** 11 officers, 152 men

REMARKS: Although officially ordered on 29-6-77, little progress has been made on construction, the new carrier *Canarias* taking precedence. Will duplicate U.S. version except for close-defense AA gun system. Sonar essentially the same as the U.S. Navy's SQS-56.

♦ 5 (+3) Descubierta class

	Bldr	Laid down	L	In serv.
F 31 DESCUBIERTA	Bazán, Cartagena	16-11-74	8-7-75	18-11-78
F 32 DIANA	Bazán, Cartagena	8-7-75	26-1-76	30-6-79
F 33 INFANTA ELENA	Bazán, Cartagena	26-1-76	14-9-76	12-4-80
F 34 INFANTA CRISTINA	Bazán, Cartagena	14-9-76	19-4-77	24-11-80
F 35 CAZADORA	Bazán, el Ferrol	14-12-77	17-10-78	20-7-81
F 36 VENCEDORA	Bazán, el Ferrol	5-78	27-4-79	1982
F 37 CENTINELLA	Bazán, el Ferrol	31-10-78	8-10-79	1982
F 38 SERVIOLA	Bazán, el Ferrol	-79	19-2-80	1982

FRIGATES (continued)

Infanta Cristina (F 34)   S. Terzibaschitsch, 1981

Infanta Cristina (F 34)   S. Terzibaschitsch, 1981

D: 1,270 tons (1,479 fl) **S:** 26 kts **Dim:** 88.88 (85.8 pp) × 10.4 × 3.7
A: 1/Sea Sparrow SAM system (VIII × 1; 24 missiles)—1/76-mm OTO Melara—
    2/40-mm AA (I × 2)—1/375-mm Bofors ASW RL (II × 1)—6/324-mm Mk 32
    ASW TT (III × 2)
Electron Equipt: Radar: 1/HSA ZW-06/2, 1/HSA DA-05/2, 1/HSA WM 25 fire-
           control
        Sonar: Raytheon 1160B, Raytheon 1167 (VDS, last four)
        ECM: Elettronica Beta passive system

Descubierta (F 31)   M. Bar, 1980

Descubierta (F 31)   M. Bar, 1980

M: 4 MTU-Bazán 16MA956 TB91 diesels; 2 CP props; 18,000 hp
Electric: 1,810 kw **Fuel:** 250 tons **Range:** 6,100/18
Man: 10 officers, 106 men

REMARKS: Design evolved from the Portuguese Navy's *João Coutinho* class, built by
same yard. The first four were ordered on 7-12-73, the others on 25-5-76. Intended
to receive 8 Harpoon SSM (IV × 2) between bridge superstructure and Y-shaped
stacks, aimed athwartships, but none had been installed by mid-1981. All are scheduled to get 1/20-mm Meroka in place of upper 40-mm, and two chaff launchers. F
35 to F 38 intended to have Raytheon 1167 VDS on completion; others to back-fit.
Have fin stabilization plus U.S. "Prarie/Masker" bubble system to reduce radiated
noise below the waterline. Can accommodate thirty troops. Carry 600 rounds 76-
mm gun ammunition. Have Elettronica SpA Beta ECM suit. Eight improved units
with gas turbine propulsion (described in previous edition) were to follow; they have
been delayed in programming.

♦ **5 Baléares class** Bldr: Bazán, el Ferrol

	Laid down	L	In serv.
F 71 BALÉARES	31-10-68	20-8-70	24-9-73
F 72 ANDALUCIA	2-7-69	30-3-71	23-5-74
F 73 CATALUÑA	20-8-70	3-11-71	16-1-75
F 74 ASTURIAS	30-3-71	13-5-72	2-12-75
F 75 EXTREMADURA	3-11-71	21-11-72	10-11-76

FRIGATES (*continued*)

Baléares (F 71)—new ECM gear aboard   G. Gyssels, 1980

Andalucia (F 72)—note TT and VDS door at stern   French Navy, 1980

D: 3,015 tons (4,177 fl)   **S:** 27/28 kts
Dim: 133.59 (126.5 pp) × 14.33 × 4.6 (7.01 over sonar)
A: 1/Mk 22 guided-missile launcher (16 Standard SM1-MR)—1/127-mm Mk 42
     DP—1/ASROC ASW RL (VIII × 1, plus reloads)—4/324-mm Mk 32 fixed
     ASW TT (I × 4)—2/fixed Mk 25 ASW TT for Mk 37 torpedoes
Electron Equipt: Radar: 1/Decca 1226, 1/SPS-10, 1/SPS-52A, 1/SPG-51C,
                   1/SPG-53B
        Sonar: 1/SQS-23 (hull), 1/SQS-35V (VDS)
        ECM: Elsa passive system
M: 1 set Westinghouse GT; 1 prop; 35,000 hp   **Electric:** 3,000 kw
Boilers: 2 Combustion-Engineering; 84 kg/cm², 510°C
Fuel: 750 tons   **Man:** 15 officers, 241 men

REMARKS: Built with American aid (agreement of 31-5-66) as U.S. DEG 7 to DEG 11.
The Mk 74 missile fire-control system can use both the Mk 73 director (with SPG-

51C radar) and Mk 68 director (with SPG-53B) to control two Standard missiles; the
Mk 68 is also used to control the 127-mm gun. The ships have the Mk 114 digital
ASW computer to control ASROC and ASW-torpedo firing. No less than forty-one
ASW torpedoes of the Mk 44/46 and Mk 37 wire-guided types can be accommodated.
The Mk 32 torpedo tubes are built into the port and starboard sides of the after
superstructure and are oriented to a 45-degree angle outboard of the centerline. The
two Mk 25 tubes are built into the stern, facing aft. The Meroka 20-mm AA gun
system to be installed, and it was planned to install Harpoon SSM abaft stack
("mack") on F 74 in 1980-81, then on one per year thereafter in order: F 75, 71, 72,
73. The ships have non-retractable gyrofin stabilizers. Three 750-kw steam turbogenerators and one 750-kw diesel generator are installed. Have U.S. AN/SRN-15A
TACAN gear, but no helicopter facilities.

CORVETTES

♦ **1 Pizarro class** Bldr: Bazán, el Ferrol

	Laid down	L	In serv.
PA 41 VICENTE YANEZ PINZON	9-44	8-8-45	5-8-49

D: 1,924 tons (2,108 fl)   **S:** 18.5 kts (20 on trials)
Dim: 95.2 (87.54 pp) × 12.15 × 3.4 (4.80 over sonar)
A: 2/127-mm 38-cal. DP (I × 2)—4/40-mm AA (I × 4)—2/fixed ASW torpedo
     launchers (6 Mk 32 torpedoes)—2/Mk 11 Hedgehogs—8/d.c. projectors—2/
     d.c. racks
Electron Equipt: Radar: 1/Decca TM 626, 1/SPS-5B, 1/MLA-1B, 1/Mk 29
                  Sonar: QHB A
M: 2 sets Parsons GT; 2 props; 6,000 hp
Boilers: 2 Yarrow, 25 kg/cm² pressure   **Fuel:** 402 tons (max.), 386 (normal)
Range: 3,000/15   **Man:** 16 officers, 239 men

REMARKS: Exceptionally seaworthy ship, modernized in 1960. Six that were not modernized have been taken out of service since 1965. Although modernized, the *Herman
Cortes* (F 32) and *Sarmiento de Gamboa* (F 36) were stricken in 1971 and 1973, and
the *Legazpi* (F 42) on 4-11-78. Redesignated from frigate to *Patrullero de Altura* in
9-80.

♦ **4 Atrevida class**

	Bldr	Laid down	L	In serv.
PA 61 ATREVIDA	Bazán, Cartegena	26-6-50	2-12-52	25-4-53
PA 62 PRINCESA	Bazán, Cartegena	18-3-53	31-3-55	2-10-59
PA 64 NAUTILUS	Bazán, Cadiz	27-7-53	10-9-56	10-12-59
PA 65 VILLA DE BILBAO	Bazán, Cadiz	18-3-53	19-2-58	2-9-60

D: 977 tons (1,136 fl)   **S:** 16-17 kts
Dim: 75.5 (68.0 pp) × 10.2 × 2.64 (4.08 max.)
A: 1/76.2-mm DP—3/40-mm AA (I × 3)—2/Mk 11 Hedgehogs—8/d.c. projec-
     tors—2/d.c. racks
Electron Equipt: Radar: 1/SPS-5B
                  Sonar: QHB-2
M: 2 Sulzer diesels; 2 props; 3,000 hp
Fuel: 100 tons   **Range:** 8,000/10   **Man:** 9 officers, 123 men

REMARKS: Tandem machinery arrangement. Electronic equipment and weapons modernized with U.S. aid. Can carry twenty mines. *Diana* (F 63) stricken in 1972. F
61 and F 65 were to be stricken in 1979, but all have been refitted and are now
employed in patrolling between Gibraltar and the Canaries. PA = *Patrullero de
Altura*.

CORVETTES (continued)

Princesa (PA 62)—old number   1971

PATROL BOATS

♦ **6 Lazaga class** Bldr: P 01: Lürssen, Vegesack; others: Bazán, La Carraca, Cadiz

	L	In serv.		L	In serv.
PC 01 LAZAGA	30-9-74	14-6-75	PC 04 VILLAMIL	15-5-75	26-4-77
PC 02 ALSEDO	8-1-75	28-2-77	PC 05 BONIFAZ	15-5-75	11-7-77
PC 03 CADARSO	8-1-75	10-7-76	PC 06 RECALDE	16-10-75	15-12-77

Recalde (PC 06)—with old hull number

D: 275 tons (397 fl) **S:** 29.7 kts **Dim:** 57.4 (54.4 pp) × 7.60 × 2.70
A: 1/76-mm OTO Melara DP—1/40-mm Breda-Bofors AA—2/20-mm AA (I × 2)
Electron Equipt: Radar: 1/Raytheon 1620/6, 1/HSA M 22
M: 2 MTU MA-16V956 TB91 diesels; 2 props; 7,780 hp **Electric:** 405 kVA
Fuel: 112 tons **Range:** 2,260/27, 4,200/17 **Man:** 4 officers, 35 men

REMARKS: P 01 and P 03 were commissioned with a U.S. Mk 22, 76-mm instead of an OTO Melara 76-mm. Space reserved for addition of six 324-mm Mk 32 ASW torpedo tubes and a small, high-frequency sonar. Carry 300 rounds of 76-mm, 1,472 rounds of 40-mm, and 3,000 rounds of 20-mm. PC = *Patrulleros Cañaneros*: redesignated 1980.

♦ **6 Barcelo class** Bldrs: P 11 Lürssen; others: Bazán, La Carraca, Cadiz

	L	In serv.		L	In serv.
PC 11 BARCELO	6-10-75	26-3-75	PC 14 ORDONEZ	10-9-76	7-6-77
PC 12 LAYA	16-12-75	23-12-76	PC 15 ACEVEDO	10-9-76	14-7-77
PC 13 JAVIER QUIROGA	16-12-75	1-4-77	PC 16 CANDIDO PEREZ	3-3-77	25-11-77

Barcelo (PC 11)—with old hull number   1976

D: 110 tons (134 fl) **S:** 36.5 kts **Dim:** 36.2 (43.2 pp) × 5.8 × 1.75 (2.15 props)
A: 1/40-mm Bofors AA—1/20-mm AA—2/12.7-mm mg
Electron Equipt: Radar: 1/Raytheon 1620/6
M: 2 MTU 16V538 TB90 diesels; 2 props; 7,320 hp (6,120 sust.)
Electric: 220 kVA **Fuel:** 18 tons **Range:** 600/33.5; 1,200/16
Man: 3 officers, 16 men

REMARKS: Lürssen FPB 36 design. Carry 750 rounds 40-mm, 2,500 rounds 20-mm ammunition.

FISHERIES PATROL BOATS

NOTE: The following units, designated PVZ—*Patrulleros de Vigilancia de Zona* in 9-80—are operated by the Navy in behalf of the Ministry of Commerce for 200-nautical-mile economic zone patrol.

♦ **10 Anaga class** Bldr: Bazán, San Fernando, Cadiz

	L	In serv.		L	In serv.
PVZ 21 ANAGA	14-2-80	30-1-81	PVZ 26 MEDAS	15-12-80	. . .
PVZ 22 TAGOMAGO	14-2-80	30-1-81	PVZ 27 IZARO	15-12-80	. . .
PVZ 23 MAROLA	. . .	13-3-81	PVZ 28 TABARACA	15-12-80	. . .
PVZ 24 MOURO	. . .	. . .	PVZ 29 DEVA	15-12-80	. . .
PVZ 25 GROSA	15-12-80	. . .	PVZ 210 BERGANTIN	15-12-80	. . .

D: 280 tons (350 fl) **S:** 22 kts **Dim:** 44.4 (40.0 pp) × 6.6 × 2.5
A: 1/76.2-mm U.S. Mk 22 DP—1/20-mm AA—2/12.7-mm mg (I × 2)
Electron Equipt: Radar: 1/. . . navigational **Man:** 25 tot.
M: 1 Bazán/MTU 16V956 diesel; 1 prop; 4,800 hp **Range:** 4,000/15

REMARKS: Fisheries protection boats ordered 22-7-78; resemble fishing boats with a long forecastle. PVZ 21 laid down 4-79; last six launched same day.

♦ **4 PVZ 31 class** Bldr: Bazán, San Fernando, Cadiz

	L	In serv.		L	In serv.
PVZ 31 (ex-LVE 1)	. . .	1981	PVZ 33 (ex-LVE 3)	. . .	1981
PVZ 32 (ex-LVE 2)	. . .	1981	PVZ 34 (ex-LVE 4)	. . .	1981

D: 85 tons (fl) **S:** 25 kts **Dim:** 32.15 (30.0 pp) × 5.30 × 1.42
A: 2/20-mm AA (I × 2)
M: 2 Bazán/M.A.N. diesels; 2 props; 2,800 hp **Range:** 1,200/15 **Man:** 12 tot.

REMARKS: Ordered 1978; first two laid down 20-12-79. Aluminum construction.

♦ **5 Carabo class** Bldr: Aresa, Arenys del Mar, Barcelona (1978-80)

PVZ 12 CARABO	PVZ 13 N . . .	PVZ 14 N . . .
PVZ 15 N . . .	PVZ 16 N . . .	

FISHERIES PATROL BOATS (continued)

D: 30.8 tons light (47.7 fl) **S:** 29 kts **Dim:** 22.46 × 5.22 × . . .
A: 1/20-mm AA—1/12.7-mm mg **Electron Equipt:** Radar: 1/Decca 110
M: 2 GM 16V92 TA diesels; 2 props; 1,972 hp **Electric:** 24 kVA
Fuel: 10 tons **Range:** 1,100/18 **Man:** 11 tot.

REMARKS: Formerly operated as customs boats LVE 12-16.

♦ **1 French 32-m class** Bldr: CMN de l'Esterel, Cannes (In serv. 1974)

PVZ. . . AGUILA

D: 80 tons **S:** 30 kts **Dim:** 32.0 × 5.8 × 1.6
A: 2/12.7-mm mg **M:** 2 MTU diesels; 2 props; 2,700 hp **Man:** 16 tot.

REMARKS: Former wooden-hulled customs launch.

♦ **5 U.S. Adjutant and Redwing*-class former minesweepers**

	Bldr	L	In serv.
PVZ 51 NALON	South Coast Co.,	22-11-52	16-2-54
(ex-M 21, ex-MSC 139)	Newport Beach, Cal.		
PVZ 52 ULLA	Adams Yacht,	28-1-56	24-7-58
(ex-M 24, ex-MSC 265)	Quincy, Mass.		
PVZ 53 MIÑO	Adams Yacht,	14-4-56	25-10-56
(ex-M 25, ex-MSC 266)	Quincy, Mass.		
PVZ 54 TURIA	Hiltebrand DD,	14-7-54	1-6-55
(ex-M 27, ex-MSC 130)	Kingston, N.Y.		
PVZ 55 SIL (ex-M 29,	Tampa Marine,	29-4-54	16-6-59
ex-Redwing, MSC 200)*	Tampa, Fla.		

REMARKS: Redesignated 9-80; all portable minesweeping gear removed. Data as for six sisters retained as minesweepers.

♦ **1 U.S. Aggressive-class ex-ocean minesweeper**

	Bldr	L	In serv.
PVZ 41 GUADALETE (ex-M 41,	Colbert Boatworks,	17-12-52	15-12-53
ex-Dynamic, MSO 432)	Stockton, Cal.		

REMARKS: Redesignated 9-80. D: 823 tons (fl). Other data as for three sisters still rated as minesweepers. Portable minesweeping gear removed.

♦ **1 former trawler** Bldr: Juliana, Gijon (In serv. 1948)

PVZ 11 SALVORA (ex-W 32, ex-Virgen de la Almudena, ex-Mendi Eder)

D: 274 tons (fl) **S:** 11 kts **Dim:** 32.58 × 6.22 × 3.77
A: 1/20-mm AA **M:** 1 Sulzer diesel; 1 prop; 400 hp
Fuel: 25 tons **Man:** 31 tot.

REMARKS: Purchased 25-9-54. Redesignated PVZ 11 in 9-80.

♦ **1 ex-smuggling launch** Bldr: . . . , Germany (In serv. 1944)

PVZ 61 GAVIOTA (ex-W 01)

D: 104.2 tons (124 fl) **S:** 12.6 kts **Dim:** 27.5 × 5.2 × 2.1
A: 2/12.7-mm mg **M:** Diesel; . . . hp **Man:** 14 tot.

REMARKS: Captured 1970, commissioned as a fisheries patrol boat 26-11-70. Redesignated PVZ in 9-80.

♦ **1 training boat** Bldr:. . . , Kiel, Germany (L: 1925)

PVZ 01 (ex-V 1, ex-Azor) (In serv. 1-5-47)

D: 112 tons **S:** 12 kts **Dim:** 31.10 × 5.65 × 2.10
A: . . . **M:** Diesels; . . . hp **Man:** 16 tot.

REMARKS: Employed as tender to the Naval Academy at Marín.

NOTE: Two ex-fishing boats, used for fisheries patrol, Nécora (PVZ 71) and Percebe (PVZ 72), were stricken 1981.

PATROL CRAFT

♦ **20 PVC 11 class** Bldr: Aresa, Arenys del Mar, Barcelona (In serv. 1978-80)

PVC 11 through PVC 19, PVC 110 through 120

PVC 11—with old hull number   Aresa, 1978

D: 17.7 tons (22 fl) **S:** 26 kts **Dim:** 15.90 (13.7 pp) × 4.36 × 1.33
A: 1/12.7-mm mg **Electron Equipt:** Radar: 1/Decca 110
M: 2 Baudouin DNP-8 MIR diesels; 2 props; 700 hp **Electric:** 12 kVA
Fuel: 2.2 tons **Range:** 400/18 **Man:** 2 officers, 4 men

REMARKS: Formerly LVC 1-LVC 20. Glass-reinforced plastic construction. PVC = Patrullero Vigilancia Costera.

♦ **30 PVI 11 class** Bldr: Rodman, Vigo (In serv. 1978-80)

PVI 11 through PVI 19, PVI 110 through PVI 130

D: 3 tons (4.2 fl) **S:** 18 kts **Dim:** 9.0 × 3.1 × 0.8 **Range:** 120/18 **Man:** 6 tot.
A: 1/7.62-mm mg **M:** 2 Volvo inboard/outboard diesels; 2 props; 240 hp

REMARKS: Formerly LVI 1-20, redesignated 9-80. PVI = Patrullero de Vigilancia Interior.

♦ **5 PVI 21 class** Bldr: Bazán, La Carraca, Cadiz (In serv. 1963-64)

PVI 21 through PVI 25

D: 17.2 tons (25 fl) **S:** 13 kts **Dim:** 14.04 × 4.57 × 1.0
A: 2/7.62-mm mg (II × 1)
M: 2 Gray Marine 64HN9 diesels; 2 props; 450 hp **Man:** 8 tot.

REMARKS: Copy of U.S. "45-foot picket boat." Formerly LPI 1-5.

PATROL CRAFT (continued)

PVI 129—old hull number   1980

♦ **3 U.S. Coast Guard 83-foot craft** Bldr: Bazán, Cadiz

PAS 11 (In serv. 24-3-65)   PAS 12 (In serv. 21-4-65)   PAS 13 (In serv. 13-9-65)

PAS 11—with old number   1969

 D: 49 tons (63 fl) **S:** 15 kts **Dim:** 25.4 (23.8 pp) × 4.9 × 2.0
 A: 1/20-mm AA—2/13.7-mm mg—2 Mk 20 Mousetrap ASW RL (IV × 2)
 Electron Equipt: Radar: 1/Decca 12
        Sonar: QCU
 M: 2 diesels; 2 props; 800 hp **Man:** 15 tot.

REMARKS: Wooden hull. Based on U.S.C.G. WPB design. PAS = *Patrullero de Antisubmarino.*

♦ **1 river craft** Bldr: Bazán, La Carraca, Cadiz (In serv. 11-1-63)

PVI 01 CABO FRADERA (ex-V 22)

 D: 28 tons **S:** 10 kts **Dim:** 17.80 × 4.20 × 0.82 **A:** 2/mg **M:** Diesel; 280 hp

REMARKS: For use on the Miño River.

♦ **5 miscellaneous patrol craft**

PVC 31 (ex-V 34) Bldr: Aresa, Arenys del Mar, Barcelona (L: 2-1-75)

 D: 14 tons **S:** 24 kts **Dim:** 15.7 × 3.9 × 0.7 **Man:** 7 tot.

PCV 21 (ex-V 33) Bldr: Vindes, Barcelona (L: 24-3-77)

 D: 23 tons **S:** 24 kts **Dim:** 16.06 × 4.30 × 0.97 **Man:** 7 tot.

PVC 01 ALCATRAZ (ex-V 4) Bldr: . . . (L: 10-4-47)

 D: 61 tons **S:** 8 kts **Dim:** 19.3 × 4.5 × 2.3 **Man:** 13 tot.

PVI 31 (ex-V 5) Bldr: Cartagena SY (L: 5-5-69)

 D: 3.1 tons (5 fl) **S:** 7.5 kts **Dim:** 8.3 × 2.7 × 0.8 **Man:** 7 tot.

PVI 32 (ex-V 6) Bldr: Luarca SY (In serv. 10-8-52)

 D: 4.5 tons **S:** 7 kts **Dim:** 8.3 × 3.0 × 1.25 **Man:** 4 tot.

MINE WARFARE SHIPS

♦ **3 ex-U.S. Aggressive-class minesweepers**

	Bldr	L	In serv.
M 42 GUADALMEDINA (ex-*Pivot*, MSO 463)	Wilmington Boatworks, Wilmington, Cal.	9-1-54	12-7-54
M 43 GUADALQUIVIR (ex-*Persistent*, MSO 491)	Tacoma Boat, Tacoma, Wash.	23-4-55	3-2-56
M 44 GUADIANA (ex-*Vigor*, MSO 473)	Burgess Boat, Manitowoc, Wisc.	24-6-53	8-11-54

Guadalmedina (M 42)   1977

 D: 665 tons (780 fl) **S:** 14 kts **Dim:** 52.75 × 10.70 × 3.88 (4.2 max.)
 A: 2/20-mm AA (II × 1)—2/12.7-mm mg (I × 2)
 Electron Equipt: Radar: 1/SPS-5C, 1/Decca TM 626
        Sonar: SQQ-14
 M: 4 Packard diesels; 2 CP props; 2,280 hp
 Range: 2,000/12, 3,000/10 **Man:** 6 officers, 65 men

REMARKS: Modernized 1969-70. Loaned 1-7-71, except M 44 on 4-4-72. All purchased in 8-74. Equipped for mechanical, magnetic, and acoustic sweeping. Sister *Guadelete* (M 41, ex-MSO 432) redesignated PVZ 41 in 9-80.

MINE WARFARE SHIPS *(continued)*

♦ 6 ex-U.S. Adjutant, MSC 268* and Redwing**-class minesweepers

	Bldr	L	In serv.
M 21 JUCAR (ex-M 23, ex-MSC 220)	Bellingham SY, Bellingham, Wash.	24-1-55	22-6-56
M 22 EBRO (ex-M 26, ex-MSC 269)*	Bellingham SY, Bellingham, Wash.	8-11-57	19-12-58
M 23 DUERO (ex-M 28, ex-*Spoonbill*, MSC 202)**	Tampa Marine, Tampa, Fla.	3-8-54	16-6-59
M 24 TAJO (ex-M 30, ex-MSC 287)*	Tampa Marine, Tampa, Fla.	1-5-56	9-7-59
M 25 GENIL (ex-M 31, ex-MSC 279)*	Tacoma Boat, Tacoma, Wash.	8-8-58	11-9-59
M 26 ODIEL (ex-M 32, ex-MSC 288)*	Tampa Marine, Tampa, Fla.	3-9-58	9-10-59

Ebro (M 22)—old number 1977

D: 355 tons (384 fl) **S:** 12 kts **Dim:** 43.0 (41.5 pp) × 7.95 × 2.55
A: 2/20-mm AA (II × 1) **M:** 2 GM 8-268A diesels; 2 props; 1,200 hp
Electron Equipt: Radar: 1/Decca TM 626 or RM 914   Sonar: UQS-1D
Fuel: 40 tons **Range:** 2,500/10 **Man:** 2 officers, 35 men

REMARKS: Originally a group of twelve, transferred under MAP: two in 1954, one in 1955, three in 1956, one in 1958, two in 1959, and three in 1960. The *Llobregat* (M 22, ex-MSC 143) was stricken on 4-7-79 after a fire. M 21 and M 23 have a mast well astern of the stack; the others have only a small davit beside the stack. MSC 268-class ships were 43.9 m overall by 8.51 max. beam and had 4 GM 6-71 diesels; 2 props; 900 hp. Five sisters were redesignated PVZ in 9-80 and had portable sweep gear removed.

AMPHIBIOUS WARFARE SHIPS

♦ 2 ex-U.S. Paul Revere-class transports Bldr: New York SB Corp., Camden, N.J.

	L	In serv.
L 21 CASTILLA (ex-*Paul Revere*, LPA 248, ex-*Diamond Mariner*)	13-2-54	3-9-58
L 22 ARAGÓN (ex-*Francis Marion*, LPA 249, ex-*Prairie Mariner*)	11-4-53	6-7-61

Aragón (L 22) C. Dragonette, 1980

D: 10,704 light (16,838 fl) **S:** 22.5 kts
Dim: 171.80 (160.94 pp) × 23.24 × 7.32 **A:** 8/76.2-mm Mk 33 DP (II × 4)
Electron Equipt: Radar: 1/LN-66, 1/SPS-10, 1/SPS-12 (L 22: SPS-40)
  ECM: WLR-1
  TACAN (L 21 only): URN-20
M: 1 set GE GT; 1 prop; 22,000 hp **Electric:** 2,400 kw
Boilers: 2 Combustion-Eng. (L 22: Foster-Wheeler); 42.3 kg/cm², 467°C
Range: 10,000/22; 17,000/13 **Man:** 28 officers, 424 men + troops: 96 officers, 1,561 men

REMARKS: Mariner-class C4-S-1A merchant ships converted to troop transports. LPA 248 by Todd Shipyard, San Diego, and LPA 249 by Bethlehem Steel, Baltimore. Can carry seven LCM(6) and sixteen LCVP. Four Mk 63 gunfire-control systems removed between 1977 and 1978, but intercept and jamming equipment retained. In recent years had served the Naval Reserve Force. Were sold to Spain: L 21 on 17-1-80, and L 22 on 11-7-80.

♦ 1 ex-U.S. Cabildo-class landing ship, dock Bldr: Philadelphia Navy Yard,

	Laid down	L	In serv.
L 31 GALICIA (ex-*San Marcos*, LSD 25)	1-9-44	10-1-45	15-4-45

Galicia (L 31)—with old number 1978

AMPHIBIOUS WARFARE SHIPS *(continued)*

D: 4,790 tons (9,375 fl) **S:** 15 kts **Dim:** 139.52 × 21.9 × 5.49 max.
A: 12/40-mm AA (IV × 2, II × 2)
Electron Equipt: Radar: 1/Decca TM 626, 1/SPS-10
M: 2 sets GT; 2 props; 7,000 hp **Boilers:** 2 two-drum, 17.6 kg/cm²
Range: 8,000/15 **Man:** 18 officers, 283 men + 137 troops

REMARKS: Loaned 1-7-71 and sold outright 8-74. Well deck is 103.0 × 13.3 m. Platform for three helicopters. Can carry eighteen LCMs with one LCVP nested in each in the well. Cargo capacity: 1,347 tons. Four Mk 51, mod. 2, lead computing GFCS (no radar).

◆ 3 ex-U.S. tank landing ships
Bldrs: L 11 and L 13: Bath Iron Works; L 12: Christy Corp., Sturgeon Bay, Wisc.

	L	In serv.
L 11 VELASCO (ex-*Terrebonne Parish*, LST 1156)	9-8-52	21-11-52
L 12 MARTIN ALVAREZ (ex-*Wahkiakum County*, LST 1162)	. . .	15-6-54
L 13 CONDE DEL VENADITO (ex-*Tom Green County*, LST 1159)	10-7-53	12-9-53

Martin Alvarez (L 12)   1978

D: 2,590 tons (6,225 fl) **S:** 13 kts **Dim:** 117.35 × 16.7 × 3.7
A: 6/76.2-mm Mk 33 AA (II × 3)
Electron Equipt: Radar: 1/Decca TM 626, 1/SPS-10, 2/Mk 34
M: 4 GM diesels; 2 props; 6,000 hp
Fuel: 1,060 tons **Range:** 6,000/9 **Man:** 115 tot.

REMARKS: L 11 and L 12 transferred on 29-10-71, and L 13 on 5-1-72. All purchased outright on 1-11-76. Accommodations for 395 troops. Carry two LCVP to starboard and one LCPL to port. Two Mk 63 radar GFCS.

◆ 3 French EDIC-type utility landing craft Bldr: Bazán, La Carraca, Cadiz

	L	In serv.		L	In serv.
LCT 6	10-11-65	6-12-66	LCT 8	10-11-66	30-12-66
LCT 7	10-2-66	30-12-66			

D: 279 tons (665 fl) **S:** 10.5 kts **Dim:** 56.94 (52.9 pp) × 11.57 × 1.54
A: 2/20-mm AA (I × 2)—2/12.7-mm mg (I × 2)
Electron Equipt: Radar: 1/Decca 404 **M:** 2 MGO diesels; 2 props; 1,040 hp
Electric: 25 kw **Range:** 1,500/9 **Man:** 14 crew + 35 troops

REMARKS: In service in 12-66. Cargo: 300 tons. Formerly BDK 6-8.

LCT 6—with old number   1970

◆ 3 utility landing craft Bldr: Bazán, el Ferrol (All in serv. 15-6-59)
LCT 3 (L: 30-4-59)   LCT 4 (L: 30-4-58)   LCT 5 (L: 31-5-58)

D: 602 tons (925 fl) **S:** 8.5 kts **Dim:** 56.6 × 11.6 × 1.7
A: 2/20-mm AA **M:** 2 MGO V8AS diesels; 2 props; 1,000 hp
Range: 1,000/7 **Man:** 1 officer, 19 men

REMARKS: Cargo: 300 tons. Formerly BDK 3-5.

◆ 1 ex-British LCT(4)-class utility landing craft (In serv. 11-11-48)
LCT 2 (ex-BDK 2, ex-K 2, ex-*Morsa*)

D: 440 tons (722 fl) **S:** 8 kts **Dim:** 56.5 × 11.81 × 1.80
A: 2/20-mm AA (I × 2) **M:** 2 Paxman diesels; 2 props; 920 hp
Man: 1 officer, 19 men

◆ 2 ex-U.S. LCU 1466-class utility landing craft
Bldr: Kingston Dry Dock Const. Co., Kingston, N.Y. (L: 4-55)

LCU 11 (ex-LCU 1471)   LCU 12 (ex-LCU 1491)

D: 180 tons (347 fl) **S:** 8 kts **Dim:** 35.05 × 10.36 × 1.6
A: 2/20-mm AA **M:** 3 Gray Marine 64YTL diesels; 3 props; 675 hp
Man: 6 crew + 8 troops

REMARKS: Transferred in 6-72. Cargo: 160 tons. Formerly LCU 1,2.

◆ 6 U.S. LCM(8)-class landing craft Bldr: Oxnard Boat, Cal. (In serv. 1975)
LCM 81 through LCM 86

LCM 81—with old number   1975

D: 115 tons (fl) **S:** 10 kts **Dim:** 22.7 × 6.55 × 1.83 (aft)
M: 4 GM 6-71 diesels; 2 props; 600 hp **Man:** 5 tot.

REMARKS: Transferred 7 to 9-75. Formerly E 81-86.

AMPHIBIOUS WARFARE SHIPS *(continued)*

♦ **6 ex-U.S. LCM(6)-class landing craft** Bldr: Lukens Steel, Pa.

LCM 61 through LCM 66

D: 24 tons (57 fl) **S:** 10.2 kts **Dim:** 17.07 × 4.37 × 1.52
M: 2 Gray Marine 64HN9 diesels; 2 props; 330 hp

REMARKS: Transferred on 23-12-74. Cargo: 30 tons.

♦ **7 ex-U.S. LCM(3)-class landing craft**

D: 20 tons (50 fl) **S:** 10.2 kts **Dim:** 15.24 × 4.37 × 1.17
M: 2 Gray Marine 64HN9 diesels; 2 props; 330 hp

REMARKS: Transferred in 12-57. Cargo: 25 tons.

♦ **16 ex-U.S. LCP(L)**

D: 10.2 tons (fl) **S:** 19 kts **Dim:** 10.91 × 3.42 × 1.07 (aft)
M: 1 GM 8V71N diesel; 1 prop; 350 hp

REMARKS: Transferred in 10-58 and 1971.

♦ **49 ex-U.S. LCVP**

D: 13 tons (fl) **S:** 5 kts **Dim:** 11.0 × 3.2 × 1.1 (aft)
M: 1 Gray Marine 64HN9 diesel; 1 prop; 225 hp

NOTE: Above totals reflect landing craft on hand before the transfer of LPA 248 and LPA 249, which retained their nine LCM(6) and eleven LCVP each. Most LCP(L) and LCVP are aboard larger ships.

AUXILIARY SHIPS

♦ **4 Castor-class survey ships** Bldr: Bazán, La Carraca, Cadiz

	L	In serv.		L	In serv.
AH 21 CASTOR	5-11-64	1-12-66	AH 23 ANTARES	5-3-73	21-11-74
AH 22 POLLUX	5-11-64	15-12-66	AH 24 RIGEL	5-3-73	21-11-74

Antares (AH 23)—with old hull number   1974

D: 354.5 tons (383.4 fl) **S:** 11.5 kts **Dim:** 38.36 (33.8 pp) × 7.60 × 3.10
Electron Equipt: Radar: 1/Raytheon 1620
M: 1 Echevarria-B & W Alpha 408-26VO diesel; 1 prop; 800 hp
Fuel: 22.5 tons **Range:** 3,000/11.5 **Man:** 38 tot.

REMARKS: Produced in pairs, the later units having full main-deck bulwarks. AH 21 and AH 22 have one Sulzer diesel, one prop, and 720 hp. Have Raydist navigation system, Omega receivers, three echo-sounders, and a Hewlett-Packard 2100A computer. Formerly A 21-24.

♦ **2 Malaspina-class hydrographic ships** Bldr: Bazán, La Carraca, Cadiz

	L	In serv.		L	In serv.
AH 31 MALASPINA	14-8-73	21-2-75	AH 32 TOFIÑO	22-12-73	23-4-75

D: 820 tons (1,090 fl) **S:** 15 kts **Dim:** 57.7 (51.4 pp) × 11.7 × 3.64
A: 2/20-mm AA **Electron Equipt:** Radar: 1/Raytheon 1620
M: 2 San Carlos-MWM TbRHS-345-6I diesels; 2 CP props; 2,700 hp
Electric: 780 kVA **Range:** 3,140/14.5, 4,000/12 **Man:** 63 tot.

REMARKS: Have Magnavox satellite navigation system, Omega, Raydist, three echo-sounders, side-scanning mapping sonar Mk 8, and a Hewlett-Packard 2100AC computer. Formerly A 31–32.

♦ **1 oiler** Bldr: Bazán, Cartagena

	Laid down	L	In serv.
AP 11 TEIDE	11-11-54	20-6-55	20-10-56

Teide (AP 11)

D: 2,750 tons (8,030 fl) **S:** 13.5 kts **Dim:** 117.5 × 14.85 × 7.73
M: 2 diesels; 1 prop; 3,360 hp **Man:** 98 tot.

REMARKS: Fitted for underway refueling, one station each side; can transfer 300 tons/hr. Formerly BP 11. Cargo: 5,350 m³.

♦ **1 netlayer**

	Bldr	L	In serv.
AC 01 (ex-CR 1, ex-G 6)	Penhoët-Loire, Gran-Quecilly	29-9-54	29-7-55

D: 770 tons (831 fl) **S:** 12 kts **Dim:** 50.45 (44.5 pp) × 10.37 × 3.20
A: 1/40-mm AA—4/20-mm AA (I × 4)
M: Diesel-electric propulsion, 2 SEMT-Pielstick diesels; 1 prop; 1,600 hp
Range: 5,200/12 **Man:** 45 tot.

REMARKS: Same characteristics as the French *Scarabée*. Transferred in 1955 under MAP.

AUXILIARY SHIPS *(continued)*

AC 01

♦ **1 submarine rescue, salvage ship, and diving tender** Bldr: Bazán, La Carraca, Cadiz (In serv. 8-8-64)

AS 01 POSEIDÓN (ex BS 1, ex-RA 6)

Poseidón (AS 01)—with old hull number   1977

D: 951 tons (1,107 fl)   **S:** 15 kts   **Dim:** 55.90 (49.80 pp) × 10.00 × 4.80
A: 4/20-mm AA (II × 2)   **Electron Equipt:** Radar: 1/Decca TM 626
M: 2 Sulzer diesels; 1 CP prop; 3,200 hp   **Range:** 4,640/14   **Man:** 60 tot.

REMARKS: Near sister to AR 44 and AR 45. Can support a frogman group and has a 300-meter-depth rescue bell. Equipped for fire-fighting, towing, and has salvage pumps.

♦ **2 AR 44-class ocean tugs** Bldr: Bazán, La Carraca, Cádiz

	L	In serv.
AR 44 (ex-R 4)	20-7-62	25-3-64
AR 45 (ex-R 5)	14-9-62	11-4-64

D: 951 tons (1,069 fl)   **S:** 15 kts   **Dim:** 55.9 (49.8 pp) × 10.0 × 4.0
A: 4/20-mm AA (II × 2)   **Electron Equipt:** Radar: 1/Decca TM 626
M: 2 Sulzer diesels; 1 CP prop; 3,200 hp   **Range:** 4,640/14   **Man:** 49 tot.

REMARKS: Improved version of RA 41 design, similar to AS 01. Can carry and lay twenty-four mines.

♦ **2 AR 41-class ocean tugs** Bldr: Bazán, Cartagena

	L	In serv.
AR 41 (ex-RA 1)	2-9-45	9-7-55
AR 42 (ex-RA 2)	. . .	12-9-55

RA 42

D: 757 tons (1,039 fl)   **S:** 15 kts   **Dim:** 56.1 (49.8 pp) × 10.0 × 4.38
A: 2/20-mm AA (I × 2)   **M:** 2 Sulzer diesels; 1 CP prop; 3,200 hp
Fuel: 142 tons   **Range:** 5,500/15   **Man:** 49 tot.

REMARKS: Can carry and lay twenty-four mines on two rails.

♦ **1 ex-British "Empire"-class ocean tug** Bldr: Clelands Ltd., Wellington, G.B.

AR 33 (ex-RA 3, ex-*Metinda III*, ex-*Empire Jean*)   (In serv. 4-45)

D: 762 tons (1,100 fl)   **S:** 10 kts   **Dim:** 44.02 (41.45 pp) × 10.05 × 4.50
M: Triple-expansion; 1 prop; 3,200 hp   **Boilers:** 2, Scotch type

REMARKS: Purchased on 26-5-61.

♦ **1 royal yacht**

	Bldr	L	In serv.
A 11 AZOR (ex-W 01)	Bazán, el Ferrol	9-6-49	21-7-49

AUXILIARY SHIPS *(continued)*

Azor (A 11)   J. Taibo, 1970

D: 442 tons (486 fl) **S:** 13.3 kts **Dim:** 46.65 × 7.70 × 3.81
Electron Equipt: Radar: 1/Decca TM 626 **M:** 2 diesels; 2 props; 1,200 hp
Range: 4,000/13 **Man:** 47 tot.

♦ **1 sail training ship** Bldr: Ast. Echevarrieta, Cádiz

	Laid down	L	In serv.
A 01 JUAN SEBASTIAN DE ELCANO	24-11-25	5-3-27	17-8-28

Juan Sebastian de Elcano (A 01)   1972

D: 3,420 tons (3,754 fl) **S:** 10 kts **Dim:** 94.11 × 13.6 × 6.95
Electron Equipt: Radar: 2/Decca TM 626 **M:** 1 Sulzer diesel; 1 prop; 1,500 hp
Fuel: 230 tons **Range:** 13,000/8 **Man:** 224 men, 80 cadets

REMARKS: Four-masted schooner, 2,467m² sail area. Carries two 37-mm saluting cannon. To be replaced mid-1980s. Also in use is the 10-m, two-masted *Galatea* (In serv.
1941), purchased 1970.

SERVICE CRAFT

♦ **1 new-construction yard oiler** Bldr: Bazán, Cartagena (In serv. 1980)

YPF 21 (ex-PP 6)

 D: 535 grt **S:** 10.8 kts **Dim:** 34.0 × 7.0 × 3.0
 M: 1 diesel; 1 prop; 600 hp **Cargo:** 300 tons

♦ **4 YPF 3-class yard oilers** Bldr: Bazán, Cartagena (In serv. . . .)

YPF 3 (ex-PP 3)   YPF 4 (ex-PP 4)   YPF 5 (ex-PP 5)   YPF 6 (ex-PP 6)

 D: 510 grt **S:** 10 kts **Dim:** 37.0 × 6.8 × 3.0
 M: 1 diesel; 1 prop;. . . hp

♦ **1 small yard oiler** Bldr: Bazán, Cadiz (In serv. 1979)

YPF 31 (ex-PP 23)

 D: 214 grt **S:** 10.7 kts **Dim:** 24.0 × 5.5 × 2.2
 M: 1 diesel; 1 prop; 400 hp **Cargo:** 100 tons

♦ **8 YPG 01-class small yard oilers** Bldr: Bazán,. . . (In serv. 1960-65)

YPG 01, YPG 02, YPG 03, YPG 21, YPG 22, YPG 31, YPG 41, YPG 51

 D: 200 grt **S:** 10 kts **Dim:** 34.0 × 6.0 × 2.7
 M: 1 diesel; 1 prop; . . . hp **Cargo:** 193 tons

REMARKS: Formerly numbered in the PB-series. Details vary.

♦ **1 old yard oiler** Bldr: Santander (In serv. 1939)

YPF 41

 D: 470 grt **S:** 10 kts **Dim:** 45.0 × 7.6 × 2.9
 M: 1 Deutz diesel; 1 prop; 220 hp **Man:** 12 tot.

♦ **1 new-construction large water tanker** Bldr: Bazán, Cadiz (In serv. 16-10-81)

AA 32 (ex-A 32)

 D: 895 tons (fl) **S:** 10.8 kts **Dim:** 48.8 (42.85 pp) × 8.40 × 3.35
 M: 1 diesel; 1 prop; 700 hp **Cargo:** 600 tons

♦ **1 new-construction large water tanker** Bldr: Bazán, Cadiz (In serv. 1981)

AA 31 (ex-A 31)

 D: 535 tons (fl) **S:** 10.8 kts **Dim:** 34.0 × 7.0 × 3.03
 M: 1 diesel; 1 prop; 600 hp **Cargo:** 300 tons

♦ **3 A-7-class large water tankers** Bldr: Bazán, La Carraca (all in serv. 6-62)

AA 21 (ex-A 9; L: 25-10-58)   AA 22 (ex-A 10; L: 10-10-58)
AA 23 (ex-A 11; L: 5-3-62)

 D: 610 tons (fl) (ex-A-7, A-8: 706 fl) **S:** 9 kts **Dim:** 44.8 × 7.6 × 3.0
 M: 1 diesel; 1 prop; 700 hp **Range:** 1,000/9 **Man:** 16 tot.

REMARKS: Cargo: 300 tons.

♦ **1 large water tanker** Bldr: Bazán, La Carraca (In serv. 29-4-52)

AA 17 (ex-A 7; L: 9-3-51)

 D: 781 tons (fl) **S:** 8 kts **Dim:** 46.70 × 7.50 × 3.36 **M:** Diesel

SERVICE CRAFT (*continued*)

♦ **1 large water tanker** Bldr: Bazán, La Carraca (In serv. ·1-4-51)

AA 06 (ex-A 6)

D: 1,860 tons (fl)   **S:** 8 kts   **Dim:** 64.05 × 9.60 × 4.80   **M:** Diesel

♦ **1 large water tanker** Bldr: Bazán, el Ferrol (In serv. 27-7-33)

AA 02 (ex-A 2; L: 26-12-32)

D: 1,850 tons (fl)   **S:** 9 kts   **Dim:** 60.93 × 9.60 × 4.42   **M:** Diesel

♦ **5 miscellaneous small water tankers**

YA 01 (ex-AB 1)   YA 03 (ex-AB 3)   YA 10 (ex-AB 10)   YA 17 (ex-AB 17)   YA 18 (ex-AB 18)

Cargo: 100 tons

♦ **3 gate craft** (In serv. 1959-60)

YPB 01 (ex-PBP 1)   YPB 02 (ex-PBP 2)   YPB 03 (ex-PBP 3)

D: 140 tons (fl)   **Dim:** 22.3 × 8.7 × 0.8   **M:** Non-self-propelled

♦ **5 netlaying barges** (In serv. 1959-60)

YDS 01 through YDS 05 (ex-PR 1-5)

D: 140 tons   **Dim:** 22.3 × 8.7 × 0.8   **M:** Non-self-propelled

♦ **8 harbor-defense support tugs** (In serv. 1959-60)

YDS 11   YDS 12   YDS 21   YDS 22   YDS. . .   YDS. . .   YDS. . .   YDS. . .

D: . . .   **S:** . . .   **Dim:** 28.0 × 8.5 × 0.7
M: 1 diesel; 1 prop;. . . hp

REMARKS: Handle the YPB-series gate craft and YDS-series netlaying barges.

♦ **2 torpedo-recovery craft/harbor minelayers** (In serv. 1961-63)

YTM 11   YTM 16

D: 60 to 190 tons (fl)   **S:** . . .   **Dim:** . . .

♦ **2 submarine-support torpedo retrievers** (In serv. 1956)

YTM 03 (ex-LRT 3)   YTM 04 (ex-LRT 4)

D: 58.2 tons   **S:** . . .   **Dim:** 17.7 × 2.2 × . . .

REMARKS: Ramp at stern; can stow six torpedoes.

♦ **1 torpedo-tracking launch:** YST 5 (ex-ST 5) **Dim:** 11 m overall

♦ **6 diving tenders**

YBZ 1   YBZ 3   YBZ 11 NEREIDA (BXL 10)   YBZ 21   YBZ 31   YBZ 32

REMARKS: All of 50 tons, self-propelled except YPZ 31, 32. YBZ 21 is a frogman support craft.

♦ **8 floating cranes**

YGR 01 SAMSÓN (100 tons capacity)
YGR 13, 14, 15 (30 tons capacity)
YGR 26, 27, 28, 29 (15 tons capacity)

♦ **2 floating dry docks:** YDF 01   YDF 11

♦ **2 new-construction coastal tugs** Bldr: Bazán, el Ferrol (In serv. 1979)

YRR 71   YRR 72

D: 422 tons (fl)   **S:** 12.4 kts   **Dim:** 28.0 × 8.0 × 3.8
M: 1 diesel; 1 prop; 1,600 hp

♦ **3 YRR-53-class coastal tugs** Bldr: Bazán, Cartagena (In serv. 1967)

YRR 53   YRR 54   YRR 55

D: 227 tons (320 fl)   **S:** 12 kts   **Dim:** 27.8 × 7.0 × 2.6
M: 1 diesel; 1 prop; 1,400 hp   **Man:** 13 tot.

♦ **3 YRR-50-class coastal tugs** Bldr: Bazán, Cartagena (In serv. 1963)

YRR 31 (ex-RR 50)   YRR 32 (ex-RR 51)   YRR 33 (ex-RR 52)

D: 205 tons (300 fl)   **S:** 10 kts   **Dim:** 27.8 × 7.0 × 2.5
M: 1 diesel; 1 prop; 800 hp   **Man:** 13 tot.

♦ **1 coastal tug** Bldr: Bazán, La Carraca (In serv. 26-4-62)

YRR 29 (ex-RR 16)

D: 200 tons   **S:** 10 kts   **Dim:** 27.0 × . . . × . . .
M: 1 diesel; 1 prop;. . . hp

♦ **2 new construction large harbor tugs**

Bldr: Bazán, Cartagena (In serv. 1979)

YRP . . .   YRP . . .

D: 229 tons (fl)   **S:** 11 kts   **Dim:** 28.0 × 7.5 × 3.4
M: 1 diesel; 1 prop; 950 hp

♦ **1 medium harbor tug** (In serv. 27-12-61)

YRP 41 (ex-RP 40)

D: 150 tons (fl)   **S:** . . .   **Dim:** 21.3 × 5.9 × . . .
M: 1 diesel; 1 prop; 600 hp

REMARKS: In service in 12-61.

♦ **12 YRP 01-class small harbor tugs** (In serv. 1965-67)

YRP 01-YRP 09   YRP 10-YRP 12

D: 65 tons (fl)   **S:** . . .   **Dim:** 18.5 × 4.7 × . . .
M: 1 diesel; 1 prop; 200 hp

♦ **3 miscellaneous launch-type small tugs:** YRP 67   YRP 68   YRP 69

♦ **6 personnel launch/yachts**

QF 11 (ex-LVC 79, ex-*Cynosure*)—ex-patrol craft, ex-yacht
QF 01 through QF 05—In serv. 1980-81

♦ **4 pontoon barges**

YCF 01   YCF 02   YCF 11 GALATEA   YCF 21 VULCAN

♦ **38 miscellaneous barges, fuel floats, water barges, etc.**—with hull number prefixes YGC, YGG, YGP, YGT

SPAIN *(continued)*

CUSTOMS SERVICE
(Servicio Especial de Vigilancia Fiscal)

PATROL BOATS

♦ **3 Aguilucho class** Bldr: J. Roberto Rodriguez, Vigo (In serv. 1973-76)

AGUILUCHO GAVILAN-I GAVILAN-II

D: 45 tons (fl) **S:** 30 kts **Dim:** 26.1 × 5.1 × 1.3
A: 1/20-mm AA **M:** 2 MTU 820Db diesels; 2 props; 2,750 hp
Range: 750/30 **Man:** 14 tot.

♦ **3 Albatros class** Bldr: CMN, Cherbourg (In serv. 1968)

ALBATROS-I ALBATROS-II ALBATROS-III

D: 82 tons (fl) **S:** 28 kts **Dim:** 31.8 × 4.7 × 1.7
A: 1/20-mm AA **M:** 2 MTU 820Db diesels; 2 props; 2,750 hp **Man:** 15 tot.

PATROL CRAFT

♦ **4 22-meter patrol craft**

ALCA GERIFALTE MILANO NEBLI-II **S:** 17 kts (*Alca:* 10, *Gerifalte:* 12)

♦ **1 16.5-meter patrol craft:** COLIMBO **S:** 20 kts

♦ **1 14.5-meter patrol craft:** ROQUERO **S:** 14 kts

♦ **6 LVR-class patrol craft:** LVR 1 to LVR 6 **Dim:** 11.4 × . . . × . . . **S:** 14 kts

---

SRI LANKA
Republic of Sri Lanka

PERSONNEL (1980): 2,960 men, including 221 officers; plus 582 tot. Volunteer Naval
Force, including 43 officers, and 131 Naval Reserve, including
37 officers

MERCHANT MARINE (1980): 40 ships—93,471 grt (tankers: 7 ships—21,939 grt)

PATROL BOATS

♦ **1 Soviet Mol class**

SAMUDRA DEVI

D: 170 tons (210 fl) **S:** 40 kts **Dim:** 39.0 × 7.7 × 1.8
A: 4/30-mm AA (II × 2) **Electron Equipt:** Radar: 1/Pot Drum
M: 3 M-504 diesels; 3 props; 15,000 hp **Man:** 25 tot.

REMARKS: Does not have four 533-mm torpedo tubes, Drum Tilt gunfire-control radar,
or IFF gear, as do two Somali units. Hull and propulsion same as Osa-II class missile
boat.

Samudra Devi

♦ **7 Chinese Shanghai-II class**

BALAWITHA   DAKSAYA   JAGATHA   PAKSHAKA
RAMAKAMI   SURAYA   WEERAYA

D: 122.5 tons (150 fl) **S:** 28.5 kts **Dim:** 38.78 × 5.41 × 1.49
A: 4/37-mm AA (II × 2)—4/25-mm AA (II × 2)
Electron Equipt: Radar: 1/Pot Head
M: 2 M50-F4, 1,200-hp diesels; 2 12D6, 910-hp diesels; 4 props; 4,220 hp
Man: 38 tot.

REMARKS: First five transferred in February 1972 and in 1975; *Jagatha* and *Pakshaka*
transferred 1980, commissioning 30-11-80.

PATROL CRAFT

♦ **6 (+5) Pradeepa class** Bldr: Colombo DY, 1976-. . .

P 431 PRADEEPA P 432 N. . . P 433 N. . . P 434 N. . . P. . . N. . . P. . . N. . .

D: 40 tons (44 fl) **S:** 19 kts **Dim:** 19.5 × 4.9 × 1.1
A: 2/20-mm AA (I × 2) **M:** 2 GM 8V 71 TI diesels; 2 props; 800 hp
Range: 1,200/14 **Man:** 10 tot.

REMARKS: Five more with a speed of 22 knots were ordered in 1979; these were to
have 2 GM 12V 71 TI diesels (1,240 hp) and a beam of 5.5 m. Construction has been
slow, with P 433 entering service 30-9-80 and P 434 on 9-10-80.

♦ **3 (+2) craft** Bldr: Colombo DY, 1977-. . .

P 201 P 202 P 203

D: 15 tons **S:** 20 kts **Dim:** 13.7 × 3.6 × 0.9
A: 1/12.7-mm mg **Range:** 250/16 **Man:** 5 tot.

REMARKS: Also employed for customs inspection.

♦ **5 Belikawa class** Bldr: Cheverton, Cowes, G.B.

P 421 BELIKAWA   P 423 KORAWAKKA   P 425 TARAWA
P 422 DIYAKAWA   P 424 SERUWA

D: 22 tons (fl) **S:** 23.6 kts **Dim:** 17.0 × 4.5 × 1.2
A: 3/7.62-mm mg **M:** 2 GM 8V-71 TI diesels; 2 props; 800 hp
Range: 790/18, 1,000/12.2 **Man:** 7 tot.

REMARKS: In service between 4-77 and 10-77. Plastic construction. Originally intended
for customs duties but used as patrol craft.

SRI LANKA *(continued)*
PATROL CRAFT *(continued)*

♦ **11 101 class** Bldr: Thornycroft, Singapore, 1966-68

P 103   P 104   P 105   P 107   P 108   P 109   P 110
P 203   P 206   P 209   P 211

    D: 15 tons (fl)   **S:** 25 kts   **Dim:** 13.86 × 3.65 × 0.92
    A: 1/mg   **M:** 2 GM 6-71 diesels; 2 props; 500 hp   **Man:** 6 tot.

REMARKS: Two are employed as inshore-survey craft. Wooden construction. P 102 was lost in 1979; P 106, 109, 201, 204, 205, 207, 208, 210 stricken 1978-79.

SERVICE CRAFT

♦ **1 lighthouse and navigational aids tender** Bldr: Hawker, G.B.

A 501 PRADEEPA (ex-*Frank Rees*)

    D: 57 tons (fl)   **S:** . . .   **Dim:** 20.0 × 5.5 × 2.0   **M:** 1 diesel

REMARKS: Acquired 1-4-76.

SUDAN
Democratic Republic of the Sudan

PERSONNEL (1981): 600 men

MERCHANT MARINE (1980): 21 ships—104,803 grt

NOTE: Due to operating conditions and the withdrawal of traditional sources of aid, the material condition of the units of the Sudanese fleet is rapidly declining. A number of patrol craft are no longer operable.

PATROL BOATS

♦ **4 El Gihad class** Bldr: Mosor, Yugoslavia (In serv. 1961-62)

PB 1 EL GIHAD   PB 3 EL ISTIQLAL
PB 2 EL HORRIYA   PB 4 EL SHAAB

El Horriya (PB 2)   L.V. Pujo

    D: 86 tons (100 fl)   **S:** 20 kts   **Dim:** 31.4 × 4.9 × 1.45
    A: 2/40-mm AA (I × 2)—2/12.7-mm mg
    M: 2 Mercedes-Benz diesels; 2 props; 1,820 hp   **Range:** 1,200/12   **Man:** 17 tot.

NOTE: The two ex-Yugoslav Kraljevica-class patrol boats, *El Fasher* (522) and *El Khartoum* (523) have been hulked, and the six wooden-hulled "Modified 101"-class patrol boats have been discarded.

♦ **3 ex-Iranian** Bldr: Abeking & Rasmussen, West Germany (In serv. 1970)

SHEKAN (ex-*Gohar*)   KADER (ex-*Shahpar*)   KARARI (ex-*Shahram*)

    D: 80 tons (fl)   **S:** 28 kts   **Dim:** 22.9 × 5.0 × 1.8
    A: 3/20-mm AA (I × 3)   **Electron Equipt:** Radar: 1/Decca 202
    M: 2 MTU diesels; 2 props; 2,200 hp   **Range:** 1,220/21
    Man: 3 officers, 16 men

REMARKS: Built for the Iranian Navy, transferred to the Iranian Coast Guard in 1975 and to Sudan the same year.

PATROL CRAFT

♦ **4 ex-Iranian 40-foot class** Bldr: Sewart, Morgan City, La. (In serv. 1970)

    D: 10 tons (fl)   **S:** 30 kts   **Dim:** 12.2 × 3.4 × 1.1
    A: 1/12.7-mm mg   **M:** 2 GM 6-71 diesels; 2 props; 600 hp

REMARKS: Transferred from the Iranian Coast Guard in 1975.

AUXILIARIES

♦ **2 ex-Yugoslav DTK-221-class utility landing craft**

SOBAT   DINDER

    D: 410 tons   **S:** 10 kts   **Dim:** 49.8 × 6.0 × 2.1
    A: 5/20-mm AA (III × 1, I × 2)—100 mines
    M: 3 Gray Marine 64 MN 9 diesels; 3 props; 495 hp
    Range: 500/9   **Man:** 2 officers, 25 men

REMARKS: Transferred 1970. Copy of German MFP-D3 class. Can carry 200 tons cargo or 250 troops.

♦ **1 small oiler** Bldr: Yugoslavia

FASHODA

    D: 400 tons   **S:** 7 kts   **Dim:** 43.6 × 7.0 × 4.2
    M: 1 Burmeister & Wain diesel; 1 prop; 300 hp   **Cargo:** 250 tons

REMARKS: Transferred in 1969.

♦ **1 water tanker** Bldr: Yugoslavia

BARAKA

    D: 125 dwt   **S:** 7 kts   **Dim:** 32.2 × . . . × . . .
    M: 1 diesel; 1 prop; . . . hp

REMARKS: Transferred in 1969.

♦ **1 survey ship**

TIRHAGA

    D: 240 tons   **S:** . . . kts   **Dim:** 30.0 × . . . × . . .

SURINAM

Republic of Surinam

PERSONNEL (1981): 160 total

MERCHANT MARINE (1980): 25 ships—14,921 grt (tankers: 1 ship—208 grt)

PATROL BOATS AND CRAFT

♦ **3 32-meter** Bldr: De Vries, Aalsmeer, Netherlands

S 401 (In serv. 6-11-76)   S 402 (In serv. 3-5-77)   S 403 (In serv. 1-11-77)

    D: 127 tons (140 fl)   **S:** 17.5 kts   **Dim:** 32.0 × 6.5 × 1.7
    A: 2/40-mm AA (I × 2)—2/7.62-mm mg (I × 2)
    Electron Equipt: Radar: 1/Decca 110
    M: 2 Paxman 12 YHCM diesels; 2 props; 2,110 hp   **Range:** 1,200/13.5
    Man: 15 tot.

♦ **3 22-meter** Bldr: Schottel, Netherlands

C 301 (In serv. 2-76)   C 302 (In serv. 2-76)   C 303 (In serv. 11-76)

    D: 65 tons (70 fl)   **S:** 13.5 kts   **Dim:** 22.0 × 4.7 × . . .
    A: 1/12.7-mm mg—2/7.62-mm mg (I × 2)
    Electron Equipt: Radar: 1/Decca 110
    M: 2 Dorman 8JT diesels; 2 props; 560 hp   **Range:** 650/13.5   **Man:** 8 tot.

♦ **3 12.6-meter river patrol craft** Bldr: Schottel, Netherlands (In serv.1975)

RP 201 BAHADOER   RP 202 FAJABLOW   RP 203 KORANGON

    D: 15 tons (20 fl)   **S:** 14 kts   **Dim:** 12.6 × 3.8 × 1.1
    A: 1/12.7-mm mg   **M:** 1 Dorman 8JT diesel; 280 hp
    Range: 350/10   **Man:** 4 tot.

♦ **1 10-meter river patrol craft** Bldr: Schottel, Netherlands (In serv. 8-75)

    D: 10 tons   **S:** 14 kts   **Dim:** 10.0 × . . . × . . .
    A: . . .   **M:** 1 Dorman 8JT diesel; 280 hp

SWEDEN

Kingdom of Sweden

PERSONNEL (1981): 4,800 men of the regular navy, including officers, petty officers, enlisted men, and civilians with permanent status, plus 7,000 national service men available for immediate service and 3,100 reserves. Additionally, some 8,000 conscripts receive annual naval training.

MERCHANT MARINE (1980): 700 ships—4,233,977 grt
                (tankers: 93 ships—1,871,966 grt)

NAVAL AVIATION: Consists of some 25 helicopters: 5 Alouette-II (HKP-2) for training, 10 Agusta Bell 206-A JetRanger (HKP-6), and 10 Vertol 107 (3 HKP-4B for minesweeping and 7 HKP-4C for rescue).

WARSHIPS IN SERVICE OR UNDER CONSTRUCTION AS OF 1 JANUARY 1982

	L	Tons (surfaced)	Main armament
♦ **12 submarines**			
3 NÄCKEN	1978-79	980	6/533-mm TT
5 SJÖORMEN	1967-68	1,125	4/533-mm TT, 2 ASW TT
4 DRAKEN	1960-61	835	4/533-mm TT
♦ **3 destroyers**		Tons	
1 ÖSTERGÖTLAND	1957	2,150	4/120-mm DP, 1 Sea Cat, 5/533-mm
2 HALLAND	1952	2,650	4/120-mm DP, SSM system
♦ **35 (+2) guided-missile and torpedo patrol boats**			
0 (+2). . .	. . .	. . .	8/RB-15 SSM, 1/57-mm, 1/40-mm
17 HUGIN	1972-81	120	8/RB-15 SSM, 1/57-mm, 6/Penguin Mk 2 SSM
12 SPICA-II	1972-76	230	1/57-mm, 6/533-mm TT
6 SPICA	1966-67	190	1/57-mm, 6/533-mm TT

In peacetime, the fleet is used primarily for training recruits, and not all the ships are manned.

WEAPONS AND SYSTEMS

Most of the electronic equipment in use in the Swedish Navy is of Dutch design (for example, LW-03 air-search radars, HSA fire-control radars), locally manufactured or of wholly Swedish design and construction.

A. Missiles

The Saab 08-A, a surface-to-surface missile based on the CT-30 of the S.N.I.A.S., is in use on both the *Halland*-class destroyers and in the coastal defense batteries.

    Length: 5.7 m   Wingspan: 3.6 m
    Diameter: 0.65 m   Weight: 9,000 kg
    Max range: 30 nautical miles (on destroyers), 70 nautical miles (in coastal batteries)

The infrared homing Norwegian Penguin Mk 2 missile is in use on board the *Hugin*-class patrol boats, where it is called the RB-12. It has a 120-kg warhead.

    Length: 3.0 m   Weight: 340 kg
    Diameter: 280 mm   Speed: Mach 0.7
    Wingspan: 1.4 m   Max. range: 30 km at an altitude of 60-100 m

The Saab RBS-15 is being developed for installation in the *Spica-II* class, becoming operational by 1985. The missile will have a solid rocket booster and a turbojet sustainer. A sea-skimmer, it will have a terminal-homing guidance system.

    Length: 4.35 m   Weight: 595 kg (780 kg with booster)
    Diameter: 0.5 m   Speed: Mach 0.8
    Wingspan: 0.85 m (folded)   Range: 80-100 km at an altitude of 10-20 m
               1.4 (extended)

WEAPONS AND SYSTEMS (continued)

B. Guns

The Swedish Bofors firm furnishes the guns, the principal ones being:

♦ **120-mm twin automatic**

Installed on the *Halland*-class destroyers (also Netherlands, Colombian, and Peruvian navies)

Mount weight: 55 tons
Length of barrel: 46 calibers
Muzzle velocity: 850 m/sec (projectile weight 23.5 kg)
Elevation: +80°
Firing rate: 40 rounds/min/barrel
Max. effective range, surface target: 12,000-13,000 m
Max. effective range, anti-aircraft fire: 7,000-8,000 m

Each barrel can fire 26 rounds, after which the ready-service magazine must be reloaded. Water-cooled. Used with Hollandse Signaal Apparaaten (HSA) LA-01 fire-control radar.

♦ **120-mm twin semi-automatic**

Installed on the destroyer *Hälsingland*

Mount weight:. . . tons   Muzzle velocity: 850 m/sec
Length of barrel: 46 calibers   Elevation: +80°
                                Firing rate: 20 rounds/min/barrel

♦ **57-mm twin automatic**

Installed on the *Halland*-class destroyers (also used by Peruvian Navy)

Mount weight: 20 tons   Max. effective range, surface target: 13,000 m
Muzzle velocity: 850 m/sec   Max. effective range, anti-aircraft fire: 5,000 m
Maximum rate of fire: 120/rounds/barrel

♦ **57-mm single-barrel automatic SAK 57 Mk 1**

Installed on the *Hugin*-class missile boats, the *Spica* and *Spica-II* torpedo boats
Mount weight (without ammunition): 6 tons   Elevation: −10°/+75°
Train speed: 55°/sec   Max. rate of fire: 200 rounds/min
Elevation speed: 20°/sec

♦ **57-mm single-barrel automatic SAK 57 Mk 2**

To enter service aboard the two new *Spica-III*-class fast combatants in 1982/83. Trials with the weapon took place 1981-82 on the *Hugin*-class missile boat *Mjölner*.

Mount weight:. . . tons   Max. rate of fire: 220 rounds/min
Train speed: 55°/sec   Shell weight: AA: 5.8 kg
Elevation: −10°/+85°   Surface fire: 6.1 kg

Will carry 120 rounds ready service within the low, streamlined gunhouse, automatically loading clips of 20 rounds each.

C. Torpedoes

The wire-guided Type 61 is used for anti-surface duties from surface ships and submarines. The weapon entered service in 1977.

Length: 7,025 mm   Weight: 1,765 kg
Diameter: 533.4 mm   Warhead: 250 kg

The Type 42 torpedo is wire-guided and has acoustic homing, for use by submarines, surface ships, and aircraft against submarines. It was developed from the similar Type 41, which is still in service.

Length: 2,600 mm (2,440 mm minus wire-guidance attachment)
Diameter: 400 mm
Weight: 300 kg

The Type 62 is a short homing torpedo for ASW purposes.

D: ASW Weapons

The 375-mm Bofors 4-barreled ASW rocket launcher is used in a quadruple mount on the *Halland*-class destroyers. The British Mk 3 Squid three-barreled ASW mortar is used in the *Östergötland*-class destroyers.

SUBMARINES

♦ **0 (+6) Type A-17 (projected)**

REMARKS: A lengthened, even more highly automated improvement of the Type A-14 (*Näcken*) design is being developed by Karlskrona/Kockums for construction during the mid-1980s. Crew will be 19 men. Exotic forms of propulsion (i.e., Sterling engines, fuel cells, hydrogen peroxide) appear to have been ruled out, and the craft will probably be similar to the A-14.

♦ **3 Näcken (Type A-14) class**

	Bldr	Laid down	L	In serv.
NÄK NÄKEN	Kockums, Malmö	11-72	17-4-78	1-4-79
NAJ NAJAD	Karlskrona	9-73	6-12-78	1980
NEP NEPTUN	Kockums, Malmö	3-74	13-8-79	1981

D: 1,050/980/1,125 tons   **S:** 20/20 kts   **Dim:** 49.5 × 6.1 × 4.1
A: 6/533-mm TT (fwd)—2/400-mm TT (fwd)—12 torpedoes
M: Diesel-electric: 1 MTU 16V 652, 1,800-hp diesel; 1 Jeumont-Schneider generator; 1 5-bladed prop; 1,500 hp
Electric: 150 kw (Scania diesel)   **Man:** 5 officers, 14 men

REMARKS: Ordered at the end of 1972. The 168-cell Tudor electric battery installation is mounted on shock absorbers. Single Kollmorgen periscope. A DataSaab NEDPS central data system furnishes, in addition to tactical information, data on the main engines; it uses 2 Censor 932 computers. Able to lay mines. Stern planes are x-configuration; bow planes on the sail. *Näcken* and *Neptun* were launched by cranes. Diving depth: 300 m (500-m collapse). The 533-mm tubes use Type 61 torpedoes, the 400-mm, Type 42.

Näcken (Näk) with snorkel intake raised   Swedish Navy, 1979

SUBMARINES *(continued)*

Näcken (Näk)   Swedish Navy, 1979

♦ 5 Sjöormen (Type A-11-B) class

		Bldr	Laid down	L	In serv.
SOR	SJÖORMEN	Kockums, Malmö	1965	25-1-67	31-7-67
SLE	SJÖLEJONET	Kockums, Malmö	1966	29-6-67	16-12-68
SHU	SJÖHUNDEN	Kockums, Malmö	1966	21-3-68	25-6-69
SBJ	SJÖBJÖRNEN	Karlskrona	1967	6-8-68	28-2-69
SHÄ	SJÖHÄSTEN	Karlskrona	1966	9-1-68	15-9-69

Sjöormen (Sor)   Swedish Navy, 1972

D: 1,125/1,400 tons   **S:** 15/20 kts   **Dim:** 51.0 × 6.1 × 5.1
A: 4/533-mm TT fwd—2/400-mm TT fwd for Type 42 ASW torpedoes or mines
M: Diesel-electric: 4 Hedemora-Pielstick 12-PA-4 diesel generator groups, 2,100 hp; 1 ASEA electric motor; 1 5-bladed prop; 1,500 hp
Endurance: 21 days   **Man:** 7 officers, 11 men

REMARKS: Maximum diving depth 150 meters (the Baltic Sea is quite shallow). Four battery compartments. Stern planes are x-configuration; bow planes on the sail.

♦ 4 Draken (A-11) class

		Bldr	Laid down	L	In serv.
DEL	DELFINEN	Karlskrona	1959	7-3-61	7-6-62
NOR	NORDKAPAREN	Kockums, Malmö	1959	8-3-60	4-4-62
SPR	SPRINGAREN	Kockums, Malmö	1960	21-8-61	7-11-62
VGN	VARGEN	Kockums, Malmö	1958	20-5-60	15-11-61

Nordkaparen (Nor)   Swedish Navy, 1972

D: 770/835/1,110 tons   **S:** 17/20 kts   **Dim:** 69.0 × 5.1 × 5.0
A: 4/533-mm TT fwd—12 torpedoes
M: Diesel-electric: 2 SEMT-Pielstick diesels, 1,660 bhp; 2 electric motors; 1 prop; 1,500 hp
Man: 36 tot.

REMARKS: Snorkel-equipped; 1 periscope. Sisters *Draken* and *Gripen* stricken 1981; survivors to be modernized. Six similar sisters with two propellers, *Hajen, Sälen, Valen, Bävern, Illern,* and *Uttern,* were stricken in 1978.

♦ 1 URF-class salvage and rescue submersible Bldr: Kockums, Malmö (L: 8-78)

URF 1

D: 50 tons (surfaced)   **S:** 3 kts   **Dim:** 13.5 × 4.3 × 2.9

REMARKS: Has a depth capability of 460 meters and can accommodate up to 25 persons rescued from a bottomed submarine. Based at the Naval Diving Center, Berga. Can be towed at up to 10 kts to the scene of an accident. Lock-out capability to support two divers to 300 meters. Pressure hull of HY 130 steel; collapse depth 900 meters. Two projected sisters not built.

DESTROYERS

♦ 1 Östergötland class

	Bldr	Laid down	L	In serv.
J 23 HÄLSINGLAND	Kockums, Malmö	1-10-55	14-1-57	17-6-59

D: 2,150 tons (2,600 fl)   **S:** 35 kts   **Dim:** 115.8 (112.0 pp) × 11.2 × 3.7
A: 4/120-mm DP (II × 2)—4/40-mm AA (I × 4)—1/Sea Cat SAM system (IV × 1)—5/533-mm TT (V × 1)—1 Squid Mk 3 ASW mortar (III × 1)—60 mines
Electron Equipt: Radar: 1/Thomson-CSF Saturn, 1/Scanter 009, 2/HSA M45, 1/HSA M44
Sonar: 1/search, 1/attack
ECM: passive arrays
M: 2 sets De Laval GT; 2 props; 40,000 hp   **Boilers:** 2 Babcock & Wilcox
Fuel: 330 tons   **Range:** 2,200/20   **Man:** 18 officers, 226 men

REMARKS: Modernized 1968-69. Has one 57-mm and four 103-mm rocket flare launchers. J 23 is in reserve, scheduled to be stricken 1983. Sisters *Östergötland* (J 20), *Södermanland* (J 21), and *Gästrikland* (J 22) were stricken 1979, although they have not yet been scrapped.

♦ 2 Halland class

	Bldr	Laid down	L	In serv.
J 18 HALLAND	Götaverken, Göteborg	1949	16-7-52	8-6-55
J 19 SMALAND	Eriksberg, Göteborg	1949	23-10-52	12-1-56

DESTROYERS (continued)

Halland (J 18)—9LV200 Mk 2 system aft   G. Gyssels, 1981

D: 2,800 tons (3,400 fl)   **S:** 35 kts
Dim: 121.05 (116.0 pp) × 12.6 × 4.7 (5.5 max.)
A: 1/launcher for Saab RB-08A SSM—4/120-mm DP (II × 2)—2/57-mm AA (II × 1)—6/40-mm AA (I × 6)—8/533-mm TT (V × 1, III × 1)—2/375-mm Bofors ASW RL (IV × 2)—mines
Electron Equipt: Radar: 1/Scanter 009, 1/Thomson-CSF Saturn, 1/HSA M22, 1/PEAB 9LV 200 Mk 2 system
Sonar: 1/search, 1/attack
M: 2 sets De Laval double-reduction GT; 2 props; 55,000 hp
Boilers: 2 Penhöet/Motala
Fuel: 524 tons   **Range:** 445/35; 3,000/20   **Man:** 18 officers, 272 men

REMARKS: J 18 acting as cadet training ship since 1980, until new *Carlskrona* is ready (1982); will probably then strike. J 19 in refit 1981. Both now have PEAB 9LV 200 Mk 2 fire-control system aft in place of the LW-03 air-search radar and M 45 fire-control system. Magazine for RB-08A missiles is beneath the after superstructure, and the launcher is atop the after (triple) torpedo tube mount. Two sisters were built for Colombia. Have 6/103-mm flare RL on each 120-mm mount.

NOTE: The frigates *Visby* (F 11) and *Sundsvall* (F 12), both in reserve for a considerable period, were stricken 1981.

GUIDED-MISSILE PATROL BOATS

♦ **0 (+2) YA-81 design** Bldr: Karlskrona

	Laid down	L	In serv.
P...N...	. . .	. . .	1985
P...N...	. . .	. . .	1986

D: 320 tons (fl)   **S:** . . .   **Dim:** 48.0 × . . . × . . .   **M:** . . .
A: 8/RBS-15 SSM (IV × 2)—1/57-mm Bofors SAK 57 Mk 2 DP—1/40-mm Bofors AA—2/533-mm TT—ASW weapons—mines
Electron Equipt: Radar: 1/Ericcson Giraffe—1/PEAB 9LV 200 Mk 2
Sonar: . . .
ECM: Saab-Scania EWS 905

REMARKS: Ordered 25-6-81 in response to Soviet Baltic build-up. Referred to as "Spica-III."

♦ **17 Hugin class** Bldrs: Bergens Mekanske Verksted, Norway (P 154-158 subcontracted to Westermoen, Mandal, Norway)

	L	In serv.
P 150 JÄGEREN	. . .	8-6-72
P 151 HUGIN	3-6-77	3-7-78
P 152 MUNIN	3-10-77	3-7-78
P 153 MAGNE	9-1-78	12-10-78
P 154 MODE	8-8-78	12-1-79
P 155 VALE	3-10-78	26-4-79
P 156 VIDAR	6-3-79	10-8-79
P 157 MJÖLNER	12-6-79	24-10-79
P 158 MYSING	18-9-79	14-2-80
P 159 KAPAREN	8-8-79	5-80
P 160 VÄKTAREN	12-12-79	8-80
P 161 SNAPPHANEN	18-3-80	11-80
P 162 SPEJAREN	13-5-80	2-81
P 163 STYRBJÖRN	8-80	5-81
P 164 STARKODDER	1-81	11-81
P 165 TORDÖN	4-81	1982
P 166 TIRFING	7-81	1982

D: 120 tons (150 fl)   **S:** 35 kts   **Dim:** 36.53 (33.6 pp) × 6.20 × 1.60
A: 6 Penguin Mk 2 (I × 6)—1/57-mm Bofors SAK 57 Mk 1 DP—24 mines or 2/d.c. racks in lieu of missiles
Electron Equipt: Radar: 1/Scanter 009, 1/PEAB 9LV200 Mk 2 system
Sonar: 1/Simrad SQ3D/SF
ECM: Saab-Scania EWS-905
M: 2 MTU 20V672 TB90 diesels; 2 props; 7,200 hp
Electric: 200 kVA   **Range:** 550/35   **Man:** 3 officers, 19 men

REMARKS: Carry 6 Norwegian Penguin Mk 2 (Swedish RB-12) SSM (I × 6), but despite the considerable delay while the system is developed, all will receive RBS-15 missiles when they become available. P 150 briefly carried 6 Penguin Mk 1. Prototype *Jägaren*, renumbered from P 151, has new engines; those in the others came from discarded *Plejad*-class torpedo boats. Carry 103-mm rocket flare launchers on either side of the 57-mm gun mount. The PEAB 9LV200 Mk 2 fire-control system employs

Munin (P 152)   1978

GUIDED-MISSILE PATROL BOATS (continued)

Hugin (P 151) in minelaying configuration   1979

Nortälje (T 133)   G. Gyssels, 1981

Västeras (T 135)   L. & L. van Ginderen, 1980

separate search and tracking radars. P 157 carries the prototype SAK 57 Mk 2 57-mm DP gun, but mounted within the original high gunhouse. Saab-Scania EWS-905 "Doughnut" passive intercept ECM systems are being added, with the toroidal radome mounted just below the search antenna for the 9LV200 system.

♦ **12 Spica-II class** Bldr: Karlskronavarvet and Götaverken

		L	In serv.
T 131	NÖRRKÖPING	16-11-72	5-11-73
T 132	NYNÄSHAMN	24-4-73	8-9-73
T 133	NORTÄLJE	18-9-73	1-8-74
T 134	VARBERG	2-2-74	13-6-74
T 135	VÄSTERAS	15-5-74	25-10-74
T 136	VÄSTERVIK	2-9-74	15-1-75
T 137	UMEA	13-1-75	15-5-75
T 138	PITEA	12-5-73	13-9-75
T 139	LULEA	19-8-75	28-11-75
T 140	HALMSTAD	28-11-75	9-4-76
T 141	STRÖMSTAD	26-4-76	13-9-76
T 142	YSTAD	3-9-76	10-12-76

D: 190 tons (230 fl) **S:** 40.5 kts **Dim:** 43.6 × 7.1 × 1.6 (2.4 props)
A: 1/57-mm AA—6/533-mm TT or 8 RBS-15 SSM (II × 4), 2/533-mm TT
Electron Equipt: Radar: 1/Scanter 009, 1/PEAB 9LV200 Mk 1
M: 3 Rolls-Royce Proteus gas turbines; 3 props; 12,900 hp
Man: 7 officers, 20 men

REMARKS: All are to be re-equipped for the Saab RBS-15 cruise missile during 1982-85. Eight missiles will be carried, plus two 533-mm torpedo tubes for wire-guided Type 61 torpedoes. T 138 received the prototype launchers in 1980-81. The fire-control system is an analog version of the digital system used in the *Hugin* class. The gas turbines exhaust through the transom to provide residual thrust. Mines can be substituted for the torpedo tubes, the forwardmost of which must be swung out several degrees before firing. The L.M. Ericcson "Giraffe" G/H-band radar is to be added, to detect "low-flyers."

♦ **6 Spica class** (In serv. 1966-68)

		Bldr	L
T 121	SPICA	Götaverken	26-4-66
T 122	SIRIUS	Götaverken	26-4-66
T 123	CAPELLA	Götaverken	26-4-66
T 124	CASTOR	Karlskronavaret	7-6-67
T 125	VEGA	Karlskronavarvet	7-6-67
T 126	VIRGO	Karlskronavarvet	7-6-67

D: 190 tons (235 fl) **S:** 40 kts **Dim:** 42.5 × 7.3 × 1.6 (2.6 props)
A: 1/57-mm Bofors DP—6/533-mm TT
Electron Equipt: Radar: 1/Scanter 009, 1/HSA M22
M: 3 Bristol-Siddeley Proteus 1274 gas turbines; 3 Ka-Me-Wa CP props; 12,720 hp
Electric: 120 kw **Man:** 7 officers, 21 men

GUIDED-MISSILE PATROL BOATS *(continued)*

Castor (T 124)   Swedish Navy, 1979

Spica (T 121)—note mine rails and gas turbine exhausts at stern

REMARKS: To be re-equipped with eight RBS-15 missiles (II × 4) by 1985, retaining
the two forward 533-mm torpedo tubes. Carry four 103-mm (I × 4) and six 57-mm
(VI × 1) rocket flare launchers. Mines can be substituted for the torpedo tubes, the
forwardmost of which must be swung out several degrees before firing. There are
two Rover IS90 gas-turbine generators.

PATROL BOATS

♦ **4 (+4) Skanör class** Bldr: Kockums, Malmö, 1956-59

V 01 SKANÖR (ex-T 42)	V 05 N. . . (ex-T 53)
V 02 SMYGE (ex-T 43)	V 06 N. . . (ex-T 54)
V 03 ARILD (ex-T 44)	V 07 N. . . (ex-T 55)
V 04 VIKEN (ex-T 45)	V 08 N. . . (ex-T 56)

    D: 40 tons (44.5 fl)   **S:** 27 kts   **Dim:** 23.0 × 5.9 × 1.2 (1.4 props)
    A: 1/40-mm AA   **Electron Equipt:** Radar: 1/Scanter 009
    M: 2 MTU diesels; 2 props; 1,600 hp

Skänor (V 01)   1978

REMARKS: First four converted at Karlskrona 1976-77 for service as surveillance boats;
original three gasoline engines replaced for safety and economy. The others are
converting 1981-82. Have one six-railed 57-mm rocket flare launcher on the bow.

♦ **4 Hanö-class former minesweepers** Bldr: Karlskrona (All in serv. 1954)

V 52 TÄRNÖ (ex-M 52)	V 54 STURKÖ (ex-M 54)
V 53 TJURKÖ (ex-M 53)	V 55 ORNÖ (ex-M 56)

    D: 270 tons   **S:** 14.5 kts   **Dim:** 42.0 (40.0 pp) × 7.0 × 2.7
    A: 2/40-mm AA (I × 2)
    M: 2 Nohab diesels; 2 props; 910 hp   **Man:** 25 tot.

REMARKS: In service since 1954. Redesignated as patrol craft on 1-1-79. Have steel
hulls. Renumbered with V-series pendants on 1-1-79. Each has one six-railed 57-
mm rocket flare launcher. Two sisters, *Hanö* (V 51) and *Utö* (V 56) stricken 1980.

PATROL BOATS (continued)

Tärnö (V 52) with old number   Swedish Navy, 1972

PATROL CRAFT

♦ **5 SKV 1 class** (In serv. 1944)

SKV 1   SKV 2   SKV 3   SKV 4   SKV 5

  D: 19 tons   **S:** 10 kts   **Dim:** 16.0 × 3.7 × 1.2
  A: 1/20-mm AA   **M:** 1 diesel; 100-135 hp   **Man:** 12 tot.

REMARKS: Maintained for training the Naval Reserve (Sjövarnskarens).

MINE WARFARE SHIPS

♦ **1 fleet minelaying/training ship** Bldr: Karlskrona

	Laid down	L	In serv.
M 04 CARLSKRONA (ex-*Karlskrona*)	1980	28-5-80	10-12-81

  D: 3,130 tons (3,300 fl)   **S:** 20 kts   **Dim:** 105.7 (97.5 pp) × 15.2 × 4.0
  A: 2/57-mm Bofors DP (I × 2)—2/40-mm Bofors AA (I × 2)—105 mines
  Electron Equipt: Radar: 1/Scanter 009, 1/Raytheon . . . , 1/Thomson-CSF
                Saturn, 2/PEAB 9LV200 Mk 2
             Sonar: Simrad SQ3D/SF
  M: 4 Nohab-Polar F212-D825, 12-cyl. diesels; 2 CP props; 10,560 hp
  Electric: 2,570 kVA   **Man:** 186 crew + 136 cadets

REMARKS: Ordered 25-11-77 to replace cadet training ship *Alvsnabben*, which, in the event, expired before her completion. Intended to act as a mine countermeasures ship support tender and submarine torpedo hard target in peacetime, when not conducting the annual Cadet Training Cruise. Hull reinforced below waterline to permit exercise torpedo hits; there are 14 watertight compartments. A bow-thruster is fitted. Has two complete combat information centers (CIC), one duplicating that of a *Hugin* and one duplicating a *Spica-II*. Extensive navigational systems, including Decca NAVIGATOR and Omega receivers. Raised helicopter deck above fantail. Name changed to honor the Swedish king.

♦ **2 Älvsborg-class minelayers** Bldr: Karlskrona

	Laid down	L	In serv.
M 02 ÄLVSBORG	11-68	11-11-69	10-4-71
M 03 VIBORG	16-10-73	22-1-75	6-2-76

Älvsborg (M 02) now has new radars   1971

  D: 2,660 tons (fl) (M 03: 2,450 fl)   **S:** 16 kts   **Dim:** 92.4 (83.3 pp) × 14.7 × 4.0
  A: 3/40-mm AA (I × 3)—300 mines   **Electric:** 1,200 kw   **Man:** 97 tot.
  Electron Equipt: Radar: 1/Scanter 009, 1/Raytheon . . . , 1/HSA M22
                TACAN: . . .
  M: 2 Nohab-Polar 12-cyl. diesels; 1 CP prop; 4,200 hp

REMARKS: M 02 is used as a submarine tender in peacetime and has accommodations for 205 submarine crew members. M 03 is equipped as Flag Ship, Coastal Fleet, and has accommodations for 158 flag staff. Each has a helicopter deck. Radar suit expanded 1977-78.

♦ **1 modified icebreaker** Bldr: Karlskrona

	L	In serv.
M . . . THULE	10-51	1953

  D: 2,200 tons (2,280 fl)   **S:** 14 kts   **Dim:** 57.00 × 16.07 × 5.90
  A: . . .   **M:** 3 diesels, diesel-electric drive; 3 props (1 fwd); 4,800 hp
  Man: 43 tot. (as icebreaker)

REMARKS: Reported 1980 that *Thule* is to be adapted for service as a mine counter-measures support ship; no further details available.

NOTE: The cadet training/minelayer *Älvsnabben* (M 01) was stricken 1980.

♦ **12 Arkö-class coastal minesweepers**

	L	In serv.		L	In serv.
M 57 ARKÖ	21-1-57	1958	M 63 ASPÖ	1962	1962
M 58 SPÅRÖ	1957	1958	M 64 HASSLÖ	1962	1962
M 59 KARLSÖ	1957	1958	M 65 VINÖ	1962	1962
M 60 IGGÖ	1958	1961	M 66 VALLÖ	1962	1963
M 61 STYRSÖ	1961	1962	M 67 NÄMDÖ	1964	1964
M 62 SKAFTÖ	1961	1962	M 68 BLIDÖ	1964	1964

  Bldrs: Odd numbers—Karlskrona; even numbers—Hälsingborg

  D: 285 tons (300 fl)   **S:** 14.5 kts   **Dim:** 44.4 × 7.5 × 2.5 (3.0 prop)
  A: 1/40-mm AA   **M:** 2 MTU 12V493 diesels; 2 props; 1,000 hp   **Man:** 25 tot.

REMARKS: Wooden-hulled construction. M 61 through M 68 have a curved rubbing strake line along the hull side; in earlier ships there are two strakes, paralleling the hull sheer. Each of the twelve ships has one six-railed 57-mm rocket flare launcher. Because of their high magnetic signatures, the six steel-hulled *Hanö* class were redesignated as patrol boats on 1-1-79.

MINE WARFARE SHIPS (continued)

Iggö (M 60)—early version   Swedish Navy, 1972

Aspö (M 63)—late version

♦ **0 (+2 +7) M 80-class inshore minesweepers**

M. . . N. . .   M. . . N. . .

D: 310 tons (fl)   **S:** 14 kts   **Dim:** 45.0 (40.6 pp) × 8.5 × 2.4
A: 1/40-mm AA
Electron Equipt: Radar: 1/. . .
                   Sonar: 1/Thomson-CSF TSM2060
M: 2 diesels; 2 props; 1,120 hp   **Man:** 21 tot.

REMARKS: First two of a planned nine ordered 25-2-81 for delivery in 1984. Glass-reinforced plastic hull design, based on Swedish Coast Guard's Tv 171.

♦ **3 Gåssten-class inshore minesweepers**

	Bldr	L	In serv.
M 31 GÅSSTEN	Knippla SY	11-72	16-11-73
M 32 NORSTEN	Hellevikstrands SY	4-73	12-10-73
M 33 VIKSTEN	Karlskrona	18-4-74	1-7-74

D: 120 tons (M 33: 130 tons)   **S:** 11 kts   **Dim:** 23.0 (M 33: 25.3) × 6.6 × 3.7
A: 1/40-mm AA   **M:** 1 diesel; 1 prop; 460 hp

REMARKS: The hull of M 31 is made of glass-reinforced plastic; she was intended to serve as the prototype for a new class of 300-ton, 43-meter coastal minesweepers, which were not built for lack of funds. The other two are built of wood. These were the latest in a long series of Swedish inshore minesweepers built on fishing-boat designs.

Viksten (M 33)   Swedish Navy, 1975

♦ **7 Hisingen-class inshore minesweepers**

		L			L
M 43 HISINGEN		1960	M 47 GILLÖGA		1964
M 44 BLACKAN		1960	M 48 RÖDLÖGA		1964
M 45 DÄMMAN		1960	M 49 SVARTLÖGA		1964
M 46 GALTEN		1960			

D: 140 tons   **S:** 9 kts   **Dim:** 22.0 × 6.4 × 1.4
A: 1/40-mm AA   **M:** 1 diesel; 1 prop; 380 hp

Gillöga (M 47)—late version   Swedish Navy, 1975

MINE WARFARE SHIPS *(continued)*

Hisingen (M 43)—early version

REMARKS: Wooden-hulled fishing boats. M 47 through M 49 have higher bridges and bluffer bow lines.

♦ **8 M 15-class inshore minesweepers** (All L: 1941)

M 15   M 16   M 21 through M 26

M 15   Swedish Navy, 1975

    D: 70 tons   **S:** 12-13 kts   **Dim:** 27.7 × 5.05 × 1.4 (2.0 props)
    A: 1/20-mm AA   **M:** Diesels; 1 prop; 320-430 hp   **Man:** 10 tot.

REMARKS: Wooden hulls. M 21, M 22, M 25 are used as tenders for mine clearance divers. M 17, M 18, and M 20 are now support tenders.

AUXILIARIES

♦ **0 (+1) intelligence collection ship** Bldr: Karlskrona

               Laid down   L   In serv.
A . . . N . . .   .

    D: 1,400 tons (fl)   **S:** . . .   **Dim:** 60.0 × 10.0 × . . .
    A: None   **M:** Diesels   **Man:** 20 tot.

REMARKS: Ordered 25-6-81. To last 30 years.

♦ **1 coastal tanker** Bldr: D. W. Kremer Sohn, Elmshorn, West Germany (In serv. 1965)

A 228 BRANNAREN (ex-*Indio*)

Brannaren (A 228)   Swedish Navy, 1972

    D: 857 tons (fl)   **S:** 11 kts   **Dim:** 61.71 (56.76 pp) × 8.6 × 3.57
    M: 1 Mak 6 Mu 51 diesel; 1 prop; 800 hp

REMARKS: Eight cargo tanks totaling 1,170 m³. Purchased in 1972.

♦ **1 submarine rescue and salvage ship** Bldr:. . .

                     L   In serv.
A 211 BELOS   15-11-61   29-5-63

Belos (A 211)   Swedish Navy, 1970

    D: 965 tons (fl)   **S:** 13 kts   **Dim:** 62.3 × 11.2 × 4.0
    M: 2 diesels; 2 props; 1,200 hp

REMARKS: Well-equipped for underwater search: decompression chamber, active rudder, underwater television, and a small helicopter deck. Modernized in 1979-80 to support the URF submarine rescue submersible.

SERVICE CRAFT

♦ **1 harbor tanker** Bldr: Asiverken, Åmål (In serv. . . .)

A. . . N. . . (ex-*Brotank*)

D: 231 grt/320 dwt   **S:** 8 kts   **Dim:** 37.3 (34.0 pp) × 6.5 × 2.7
M: 2 Volvo Penta diesels; 1 prop; 300 hp

REMARKS: Purchased 5-81 from commercial service.

♦ **1 water tanker** (L: 1959)

A 217 FRYKEN

D: 307 tons   **S:** 10 kts   **Dim:** 34.4 (32.0 pp) × 6.1 × 2.9
M: 1 diesel; 1 prop; 370 hp

♦ **1 water tanker** (L: 1946)

A 216 UNDEN

D: 540 tons   **S:** 9 kts   **Dim:** 39.8 (36.5 pp) × 7.6 × 3.2
M: 1 set reciprocating triple-expansion steam; 1 prop; 225 hp

♦ **1 provisions lighter** Bldr: Kroger, Rendsburg, West Germany (In serv. 1953)

A 221 FREJA

D: 415 tons (465 fl)   **S:** 11 kts   **Dim:** 49.0 × 8.5 × 3.7
M: 1 diesel; 1 prop; 600 hp

♦ **1 torpedo and missile recovery craft** Bldr: Lundevarv-Ooverkstads AB, Kramfors

	L	In serv.
A 248 PINGVINEN	26-9-73	3-75

D: 191 tons   **S:** 13 kts   **Dim:** 33.0 × 6.1 × 1.8
M: 2 MTU 12V493 diesels; 2 props; 1,040 hp

REMARKS: Similar to A 247 but has superstructure aft, 2 articulated cranes, and bow bulwarks.

♦ **1 torpedo and missile recovery craft** (L: 9-63)

A 247 PELIKANEN

D: 130 tons   **S:** 15 kts   **Dim:** 33.0 × 5.8 × 1.8
M: 2 MTU 12V493 diesels; 2 props; 1,040 hp

♦ **1 torpedo-recovery craft** (L: 1951)

A 246 HÄGERN

D: 50 tons   **S:** 10 kts   **Dim:** 29.0 × 5.4 × 1.6   **M:** 2 diesels; 2 props; 240 hp

♦ **1 trials craft** (L: 1969)

A 241 URD (ex-*Capella*)

D: 63 tons (90 fl)   **S:** 8 kts   **Dim:** 27.0 × 5.6 × 2.8   **M:** 2 diesels; 200 hp

♦ **2 mine-transport lighters**

	L		L
A 236 FÄLLAREN	1941	A 237 MINÖREN	1940

D: 165 tons   **S:** 9 kts   **Dim:** 31.5 × 6.1 × 2.1   **M:** 2 diesels; 1 prop; 240 hp

Pelikanen (A 247)—with RB-08A missile   Swedish Navy, 1974

♦ **1 laundry ship** (L: 1961)

A 256 SIGRUN

Sigrun (A 256)   Swedish Navy, 1974

D: 250 tons   **S:** 11 kts   **Dim:** 32.0 × 6.8 × 3.6   **M:** 1 diesel; 1 prop; 320 hp

REMARKS: Probably the world's only camouflaged laundry, and certainly the fastest.

♦ **3 M 15-class general-purpose tenders, former minesweepers** (L: 1941)

A 231 LOMMEN (ex-M 17)   A 232 SPOVEN (ex-M 18)   A 242 SKULD (ex-M 20)

D: 70 tons   **S:** 13 kts   **Dim:** 26.0 × 5.0 × 1.4
M: 2 diesels; 2 props; 410 hp

REMARKS: Wooden hulls. Used as personnel, mail, and stores transports for mine trials.

SERVICE CRAFT *(continued)*

◆ 5 L 51-class stores lighters (L: 1947-48)

L 51   L 52   L 53   L 54   L 55

D: 32 tons   **S:** 7 kts   **Dim:** 14.0 × 4.8 × 1.0
M: 1 diesel; 140 hp

REMARKS: Steel-hulled former landing craft, bow ramps.

◆ 2 sail training schooners

	L		L
S 01 GLADAN	1947	S 02 FALKEN	1948

Falken (S 02)   G. Gyssels, 1981

D: 220 tons   **S:** . . . kts   **Dim:** 42.5 (28.3 pp) × 7.27 × 4.2
M: 1 diesel auxiliary; 1 prop; 50 hp/Sail area 512 m²

◆ 2 diving tenders Bldr: Storebro Bruks AB (In serv. 1980)

D: . . . tons   **S:** 24 kts   **Dim:** 10.35 × 3.30 × 1.0
Electron Equipt: Radar: 1/Decca 091
M: 2 Volvo Penta TAMD 60 diesels; 2 props; 370 hp

REMARKS: Fold-down door at stern. 1.7-ton useful load.

◆ 2 range safety boats Bldr: Storebro Bruks AB (In serv. 1980)

REMARKS: Data as for diving tender version above.

◆ 3 personnel launches Bldr: Storebro Bruks AB (In serv. 1980)

D: 5.5 tons (fl)   **S:** 24 kts   **Dim:** 9.30 × 3.30 × 1.0
M: 2 Volvo Penta TAMD 60 diesels; 2 props; 370 hp

REMARKS: Builder's Type 31 design; glass-reinforced plastic construction. Can carry 25 men or 6 stretchers.

TUGS

◆ 2 Herkules-class icebreaking tugs

	L		L
A 323 HERKULES	1969	A 324 HERA	1971

D: 127 tons   **S:** 11.5 kts   **Dim:** 21.4 × 6.9 × 3.7
M: Diesels; 615 hp

◆ 2 Achilles-class icebreaking tugs

A 251 ACHILLES   A 252 AJAX

Ajax (A 252)   Swedish Navy, 1974

D: 450 tons   **S:** 12 kts   **Dim:** 35.5 (33.15 pp) × 9.5 × 3.9
M: Diesels; 1,650 hp

REMARKS: *Achilles* launched in 1962.

◆ 3 Hermes-class icebreaking tugs (L: 1953-57)

A 253 HERMES   A 321 HECTOR   A 322 HEROS

D: 185 tons   **S:** 11 kts   **Dim:** 24.5 (23.0 pp) × 6.8 × 3.6   **M:** Diesel; 600 hp

TUGS *(continued)*

♦ **12 harbor tugs**

A 326 HEBE	A 332 MÅRSGARN	A 343 ATB 3
A 327 PASSOP	A 336 VITSGARN	A 345 GRANATEN
A 329 HENRIK	A 341 ATB 1	A 347 EDDA
A 330 ATLAS	A 342 ATB 2	A 349 GERDA

REMARKS: Five new tugs were ordered in 1978 from Lundevarv.

MINISTRY OF TRANSPORT

ICEBREAKERS

NOTE: All Swedish icebreakers are owned by the Ministry of Transport but are manned and administered by the Swedish Navy. Most have provision for arming in wartime.

♦ **3 Finnish Urho class** Bldr: Wärtsilä, Helsinki, Finland

	Laid down	L	In serv.
ATLE	10-5-73	27-11-73	21-10-74
FREJ	. . .	3-6-74	30-9-75
YMER	12-2-76	3-9-76	26-10-77

Frej Wärtsilä, 1975

D: 7,800 tons **S:** 19 kts **Dim:** 104.6 (99.0 pp) × 23.8 × 7.8
M: 5 Wärtsilä-Pielstick 5,000-bhp diesels; diesel-electric drive; 4 props; 22,000 hp
Man: 16 officers, 38 men

REMARKS: Two props forward, two aft. Helicopter platform. All personnel live and normally work above the main deck.

♦ **1 Ale class** Bldr: Wärtsilä, Helsinki, Finland

	L	In serv.
ALE	1-6-73	12-12-73

D: 1,488 tons **S:** 14 kts **Dim:** 46.0 × 13.0 × 5.0
M: Diesels; 2 props; 4,750 hp **Man:** 21 tot.

REMARKS: Built for service on Lake Vänern in central Sweden; also used for surveying in summer.

Ale Wärtsilä, 1973

♦ **1 modified Tor class** Bldr: Wärtsilä, Helsinki, Finland

	L	In serv.
NJORD	2-10-68	10-69

Njord Swedish Navy, 1970

D: 5,150 tons (5,686 fl) **S:** 18 kts **Dim:** 86.45 (79.45 pp) × 21.18 × 6.9
M: Diesel-electric propulsion: 4 Sulzer 9MH-51 diesels; Stromberg electric motors, 2 fwd (3,400 kw each), 2 aft (2,200 kw each); 4 props; 13,620 hp

REMARKS: Can be armed with four 40-mm AA guns (II × 1, I × 2).

ICEBREAKERS (continued)

♦ **1 Tor class** Bldr: Wärtsilä, Turku, Finland

	L	In serv.
TOR	25-5-63	31-1-64

Tor Wärtsilä

D: 4,980 tons (5,290 fl) **S:** 18 kts **Dim:** 84.4 × 20.42 × 6.2

M: Diesel-electric propulsion, 4 Sulzer 9MH-51 diesels; 4 props; 11,200 hp. Same motors as the *Njord*.

REMARKS: The Finnish *Tarmo* is similar. Can be armed with four 40-mm AA guns (II × 1, I × 2). Two propellers fwd, two aft.

♦ **1 Oden class** Bldr: Sandviken, Helsinki, Finland

	L	In serv.
ODEN	16-10-56	1958

D: 4,950 tons (3,370 light) **S:** 17 kts **Dim:** 83.35 (78 pp) × 19.4 × 6.9

M: Diesel-electric; 4 props (2 fwd, 2 aft); 10,500 hp

Fuel: 740 tons **Man:** 75 tot.

REMARKS: Very similar to the Finnish *Voima* and the three Soviet *Kapitan Belousov* class.

NOTE: The older icebreaker *Thule* is reportedly being adapted as a mine counter-measures support ship.

♦ **1 harbor icebreaker/navigational aids tender** Bldr: Åsiverken AB

N. . . (In serv. 1981)

D: . . .   **S:** 13 kts **Dim:** 40.0 (35.5 pp) × 10.5 × 3.3

M: 1 Hedemora V12A/12 diesel; 1 CP prop; 1,350 hp **Man:** 18 tot.

REMARKS: Buoy hold forward served by an 8-ton, telescoping crane. Bow-thruster and Becker flap-rudder fitted. Intended for buoy handling, diving, cable repairs, construction and repair of fixed navigational aids, and harbor icebreaking.

HYDROGRAPHIC SHIPS

NOTE: Swedish hydrographic ships are operated by the Navy but are owned by the Ministry of Transport. The icebreaker *Ale* also performs survey tasks.

♦ **1 seagoing survey ship** Bldr: Falkenbergs Varvet

	Laid down	L	In serv.
JOHAN NORDENANKAR	1977	1-11-79	1-7-80

D: . . .   **S:** 15 kts **Dim:** 73.0 (64.0 pp) × 14.0 × 3.8

Electron Equipt: Radar: 1/Raytheon Raycas, 1/Decca. . .

M: 2 Hedemora V16A/12 diesels; 2 KaMeWa CP props; 3,520 hp

Electric: 2,246 kVA **Man:** 66 tot.

REMARKS: Acts as mother ship for nine small survey craft that act in teams. Data collected by the launches are telemetered to the ship and collected via the Krupp-Atlas computer. There are three sets of davits per side, with 3 additional boats in an internal hangar. Ship very maneuverable, with 700-hp drop-down bow-thruster, which can also drive the ship at 4.5 kts, and a Becker KSV flap-rudder; turning radius 150 m. Navigation equipment includes Decca NAVIGATOR, Magnavox NAV-SAT receiver, Decca Sea Fix, Syledis Ranger, Syledis Miniranger, and 8 echo-sounders. Passive tank stabilization. Helo platform aft. Hull red, superstructure white.

♦ **1 seagoing survey ship** (L: 14-1-66)

JOHAAN MÅNSSON

Johaan Mansson Swedish Navy, 1975

D: 977 tons (1,030 fl) **S:** 15 kts **Dim:** 56.0 × 11.0 × 2.6

M: Nohab-Polar diesel; 3,300 hp **Man:** 85 tot.

REMARKS: Survey boats are stowed in a hangar aft and launched/recovered via a ramp.

♦ **3 coastal survey ships**

RAN (L: 1945)

D: 285 tons **S:** 9 kts **Dim:** 30.0 × 7.0 × 2.6

M: 1 diesel; 1 prop; 260 hp **Man:** 37 tot.

ANDERS BURE (ex-*Rali*)

D: 54 tons **S:** 15 kts **Dim:** 24.6 × 5.9 × 2.0

M: 2 diesels; 2 props; . . . hp **Man:** 11 tot.

REMARKS: Former yacht dating from 1968, bought in 1971.

NILS STRÖMKRONA (L: 1894)

D: 140 tons **S:** 9 kts **Dim:** 26.6 × 5.1 × 2.5

M: 1 diesel; 300 hp **Man:** 14 tot.

REMARKS: Rebuilt in 1952.

NOTE: Survey ship *Gustaf af Klimt* stricken 1980.

COASTAL ARTILLERY SERVICE

PATROL CRAFT

♦ **1 coastal patrol craft** Bldr: Stockholm Naval Dockyard (In serv. 1953)

V 57

    D: 115 tons (135 fl) **S:** 13.5 kts **Dim:** 29.9 × 5.3 × 2.2
    A: 1/20-mm AA—mines **M:** Nohab-Polar diesel; 1 prop; 500 hp **Man:** 12 tot.

♦ **17 61 class**

61 to 77

66   Swedish Navy, 1974

    D: 28 tons (30 fl) **S:** 19 kts **Dim:** 21.1 × 4.6 × 1.3
    A: 1/20-mm AA **M:** 2 diesels; 2 props; . . . hp

REMARKS: Built in two series, nos. 61 to 70 in 1960-61 and nos. 71 to 77 in 1966-67.

MINELAYERS

♦ **8 MUL 12-class mine planters** (In serv. 1952-56)

MUL 12 through MUL 19

MUL 19   1970

    D: 245 tons **S:** 10.5 kts **Dim:** 31.18 (29.0 pp) × 7.62 × 3.1
    A: 1/40-mm AA—. . . mines **M:** 2 Nohab diesels; 2 props; 460 hp

REMARKS: Launched 1952-56. A new coastal mineplanter, MUL-20, is planned. These craft are used for placing and maintaining controlled mine fields.

♦ **1 coastal mine planter** (L: 1946)

MUL 11

    D: 200 tons **S:** 10 kts **Dim:** 30.1 (27.0 pp) × 7.21 × 3.65
    A: . . . mines **M:** 2 Atlas diesels; 1 prop; 300 hp

♦ **36 501-class minelaying launches** (L: 1969-71)

501 through 536

    D: 14 tons (fl) **S:** 14 kts **Dim:** 14.6 × 4.2 × 0.9
    A: 12 mines **Electron Equipt:** Radar: 1/Decca 110
    M: Diesels **Man:** 7 tot.

REMARKS: Nine more are planned.

LANDING CRAFT

♦ **3 Grim-class utility landing craft** Bldr: Åsiverken

BORE   GRIM   HEIMDAL

Bore   Swedish Navy, 1969

    D: 340 tons (fl) **S:** 12 kts **Dim:** 36.0 × 8.5 × 2.6
    A: None **M:** 2 diesels; 2 props; 800 hp

REMARKS: *Grim* was launched in 1962, *Bore* and *Heimdal* in 1967. Car ferry design; bow hinges upward to permit extending ramp.

♦ **2 Sleipner-class utility landing craft**

SKAGUL (L: 1960)   SLEIPNER (L: 1959)

    D: 335 tons **S:** 10 kts **Dim:** 35.0 × 8.5 × 2.9
    A: None **M:** 2 diesels; 2 props; 640 hp

REMARKS: Similar to the *Grim* class.

♦ **4 Ane-class utility landing craft** (L: 1943-45)

324 ANE   325 BALDER   326 LOKE   327 RING

    D: 135 tons **S:** 8.5 kts **Dim:** 28.0 × 8.0 × 1.8
    A: 1/20-mm AA **M:** Diesels

REMARKS: Equipped with a bow ramp.

LANDING CRAFT (continued)

♦ 81 201-series large personnel landing craft

Bldrs: Lundevarv Verkstads and Marinteknik, Oregrund (In serv. 1957-77)

201 through 276   280 through 284

220   Swedish Navy, 1960

D: 31 tons (fl)   **S:** 17 kts   **Dim:** 21.4 × 4.2 × 1.3
A: 2 or 3/6.5-mm mg (II × 1, I × 1)
M: 3 Saab-Scania 6 DS 11 diesels; 3 props; 705 hp   **Man:** 5 crew, 40 troops

REMARKS: 266 through 269 have Volvo Penta diesels. Early units were 20 meters overall and had three 200-hp diesels. Patrol-boat-like bow opens to permit extension of ramp from troop compartment below decks. Twin machine gun to port, plus single-mount aft in some.

♦ 54 personnel landing craft

	L			
337 through 354	1970-73	**D:** 6 tons	**S:** 21 kts	**M:** 225 hp
332 through 336	1967	**D:** 5.4 tons	**S:** 25 kts	**M:** 225 hp
331	1965	**D:** 6 tons	**S:** 20 kts	
301 through 330	1956-59	**D:** 4 tons	**S:** 9.5 kts	**Dim:** 9.5 × 2.5 × 0.9

309   Swedish Navy, 1972

♦ 5 cargo lighters Bldr: Lundevarv

REMARKS: Ordered in 1978.

♦ 3 coastal personnel transports

Bldrs: Farösund Naval SY (2) and Marinteknik, Oregrund (1)

REMARKS: Ordered in 1978.

COAST GUARD

PERSONNEL (1980): 550 total

The Swedish Coast Guard is primarily concerned with rescue and customs services and with anti-pollution patrol and cleanup. In addition to some 130 boats and craft, it also operates 2 Cessna F337G patrol aircraft with side-looking radar (SLAR), one Cessna 402C (a second is planned), and a chartered helicopter. All boat pendants are prefixed "Tv." The Coast Guard is organized into four Regions, with a total of 15 Districts; each District has 2 to 4 stations. All units are painted white and have a narrow red diagonal stripe on each side of the hull. None are armed.

PATROL BOATS AND CRAFT

♦ 1 (+2) Tv 171 class Bldr: Karlskrona

	L	In serv.
Tv 171	11-79	3-9-80
Tv 172	13-9-80	5-82
Tv 173	. . .	. . .

D: . . .   **S:** 20 kts   **Dim:** 49.90 (46.00 pp) × 8.52 × 2.40
Electron Equipt: Radar: 2/Decca navigational
M: 2 Hedemora V16A diesels; 2 KaMeWa CP props; 4,480 hp
Electric: 340 kVA   **Range:** 500/20; 3,000/12   **Man:** 14 tot.

REMARKS: Tv 171 lengthened by 6 m in 1981; others will be longer as completed. Helicopter platform, bow-thruster. Glass-reinforced plastic sandwich hull construction, originally developed for the not-built M 70-class naval minesweeper. Fire monitor can be replaced by a 40-mm AA gun.

♦ 5 Tv 103 class Bldr: Karlskrona, 1969

Tv 103   Tv 104   Tv 105   Tv 106   Tv 107

D: 50 tons (fl)   **S:** 22 kts   **Dim:** 26.7 × 5.2 × 1.1
M: 2 diesels; 2 props; 1,786 hp   **Electric:** 60 kVA
Range: 1,000/15   **Man:** 6 tot.

♦ 8 Tv 271-class aluminum-hulled

Tv 271 through Tv 278

D: 20 tons (fl)   **S:** 20 kts   **Dim:** 19.0 × 4.2 × 1.4
M: 2 diesels; 2 props; 700 hp   **Man:** 5 tot.

♦ 1 Tv 116-class aluminum-hulled

Tv 116   **D:** 36 tons

♦ 3 (+ . . .) Tv 281-class aluminum-hulled

Tv 281   Tv 282   Tv 283

REMARKS: Additional units planned. D: 36 tons.

♦ 20 Tv 236-class aluminum-hulled

Tv 236 through Tv 238, Tv 240 through Tv 250, Tv 255 through Tv 261

D: 17 tons   **S:** . . .   **Dim:** . . . × . . . × . . .

♦ 1 Tv 234 class—D: 15 tons

♦ 4 Tv 251 class: Tv 251 through Tv 254—D: 12 tons

SWEDEN *(continued)*
PATROL BOATS AND CRAFT *(continued)*

♦ **3 Tv 220 class:** Tv 220, Tv 230, Tv 232—D: 12 tons

POLLUTION CONTROL SHIPS AND CRAFT

♦ **2 Class A oil-spill-combating ships** Bldr: Lunde, Ramvik

TV 04 (In serv. 1978)   TV 05 (In serv. 1980)

D: 450 tons (fl) **S:** 12 kts **Dim:** 35.5 × 8.0 × 3.0
M: 2 diesels; 2 props; 1,200 hp **Electric:** 224 kVA **Man:** 10 tot.

REMARKS: Helipad on fantail, 200-hp bow-thruster, 30-kt workboat, 80 m³ oil-containment tanks, 500-m containment boom stowage, oil-spill skimming equipment, firefighting gear.

NOTE: Three other large oil-spill-combating ships are in service: Tv 01, Tv 02, Tv 03.

♦ **5 Class B oil-spill-combating boats** Bldr: Lunde, Ramvik (In serv. 1980-81)

Tv 045   Tv 046   Tv 047   Tv 048   Tv 049

D: 140 tons (200 fl) **S:** 11 kts **Dim:** 28.9 × 6.5 × 1.9
M: 2 Scania DS111 diesels; 2 props; 544 hp **Electric:** 300 kw **Man:** 4 tot.

REMARKS: Resemble landing craft, with bow ramp. 110-m³ tanks for recovered oil. Hydraulic thrusters fore and aft. Stowage for 800-m oil-spill-containment booms, Endless belt-type oil-recovery device.

♦ **4 Type C oil-spill craft:** Tv 011, Tv 012, Tv 014, Tv 015

♦ **4 Class D oil-recovery catamarans**

Tv 020   Tv 021   Tv 022   Tv 023

D: 30 tons **S:** 12 kts **Dim:** 16.5 × 7.6 × . . .

REMARKS: Two types: Tv 020 is Type D1, others D2. Drum-type skimmer mounted fwd between hulls can clean up 40 tons/hour, or a belt-type cleaner can be used at 10-20 tons/hour.

♦ **6 Class G pollution-control craft:** Tv 061 through Tv 064, Tv 068, Tv 069

MISCELLANEOUS SERVICE CRAFT

These include: 24 light patrol craft (Tv 314, Tv 315, Tv 317, Tv 318, Tv 341, Tv 350, Tv 356, Tv 363, Tv 365, Tv 366, Tv 368, Tv 369, Tv 371 through Tv 374, Tv 381 through Tv 385, Tv 388, Tv 389, Tv 391).

♦ **5 Rotork Sea Truck landing craft** (Tv 041 through Tv 044, Tv 059)

♦ **5 iceboats** (Tv 801, Tv 804 through Tv 807), and 27 smaller workboats, rubber dinghies, etc.

SYRIA
Syrian Arab Republic

PERSONNEL (1980): 2,500 total

MERCHANT MARINE (1980): 44 ships—39,255 grt

NAVAL AVIATION: Helicopters: 8 to 10 Kamov Ka-25 Hormone A ASW.

FRIGATES

♦ **2 ex-Soviet Petya class**

12 N. . .   14 N. . .

D: 950 tons (1,100 fl) **S:** 30 kts **Dim:** 82.3 × 9.1 × 3.2
A: 4/76.2-mm DP (II × 2)—4/RBU 2500 ASW RL (XVI × 4)—3/533-mm TT
  (III × 1)—2/d.c. racks—mines
Electron Equipt: 1/Don-2, 1/Strut Curve, 1/Hawk Screech
    IFF: 2/Square Head, 1/High Pole B
    Sonar: Hull-mounted HF
M: CODAG: 2 gas turbines (15,000 hp each); 1 diesel (6,000 hp); 3 props; 36,000 hp
Man: 90 tot.

REMARKS: Transferred: 1975.

GUIDED-MISSILE PATROL BOATS

♦ **6 ex-Soviet Osa-II class**

D: 215 tons (240 fl) **S:** 36 kts **Dim:** 39.0 × 7.7 × 1.9
A: 4/SS-N-2B Styx SSM (I × 4)—4/30-mm AA (II × 2)
Electron Equipt: Radar: 1/Square Tie, 1/Drum Tilt
    IFF: 2/Square Head, 1/High Pole B
M: 3 M504 diesels; 3 props; 15,000 hp **Range:** 430/34, 790/20

REMARKS: Two transferred 1978, four in 1979.

♦ **6 ex-Soviet Osa-II class**

Syrian Osa-I   1976

D: 175 tons (210 fl) **S:** 36 kts **Dim:** 39.0 × 7.7 × 1.8
A: 4/SS-N-2 Styx (I × 4)—4/30-mm AA (II × 2)

SYRIA (continued)
GUIDED-MISSILE PATROL BOATS (continued)

Electron Equipt: Radar: 1/Square Tie, 1/Drum Tilt
IFF: 2/Square Head, 1/High Pole B
M: 3 M503A diesels; 3 props; 12,000 hp **Range:** 430/34, 790/20

REMARKS: Transferred 1966; two were sunk during the Arab-Israeli War, October 1973.

♦ **6 ex-Soviet Komar class**

D: 71 tons (82 fl) **S:** 40 kts **Dim:** 25.3 × 7.0 × 2.0
A: 2/SS-N-2a Styx (I × 2)—2/25-mm AA (II × 1)
Electron Equipt: Radar: 1/Square Tie
M: 4 M50 diesels; 4 props; 4,800 hp **Range:** 400/32, 700/15 **Man:** 20 tot.

REMARKS: Transferred 1963-66. Three others were sunk in the Arab-Israeli War, October 1973. Probably in poor condition due to age. Wooden hulls.

TORPEDO BOATS

♦ **8 ex-Soviet P 4 class**

D: 19.3 tons (22.4 fl) **S:** 55 kts **Dim:** 19.3 × 3.7 × 1.0
A: 2/14.5-mm mg (II × 1)—2/450-mm TT (I × 2)
M: 2 M50 diesels; 2 props; 2,400 hp **Man:** 12 tot.

REMARKS: Survivors of a group of about 17 transferred 1958-60; one was sunk during the Arab-Israeli War, October 1973.

MINE WARFARE AND VARIOUS SHIPS

♦ **1 Soviet T-43-class fleet minesweeper**

504 YARMOUK

D: 500 tons (570 fl) **S:** 14 kts **Dim:** 58.0 × 8.6 × 2.3 (hull)
A: 4/37-mm AA (II × 2)—8/12.7-mm mg (II × 4)—2/d.c. mortars—mines
Electron Equipt: Radar: 1/Ball End **M:** 2 9D diesels; 2 props; 2,200 hp
Fuel: 70 tons **Range:** 3,200/10 **Man:** 75 tot.

REMARKS: Transferred 1962; one sister lost in the October 1973 war.

♦ **2 ex-Soviet Vanya-class coastal minesweepers**

D: 200 tons (245 fl) **S:** 18 kts **Dim:** 39.9 × 7.3 × 1.8
A: 2/30-mm AA (II × 1)—mines **Electron Equipt:** Radar: 1/Don-2
M: 2 diesels; 2 props; 2,200 hp **Man:** 30 tot.

REMARKS: Transferred 12-72.

♦ **1 Soviet Nyryat-1-class diving tender**

D: 120 tons (fl) **S:** 12 kts **Dim:** 29.0 × 5.0 × 1.7
Electron Equipt: Radar: 1/Spin Trough **M:** 1 diesel; 1 prop; 450 hp
Range: 1,600/10 **Man:** 15 tot.

TAIWAN
Republic of China

PERSONNEL (1980): 64,100 total, including 7,100 officers, 28,000 men, plus 3,000 Marine officers and 26,000 Marines

MERCHANT MARINE (1980): 496 ships—2,011,311 grt
(tankers: . . . ships)

NAVAL AVIATION: Nine elderly S-2A/E Tracker ASW aircraft remain in inventory. Twelve Hughes-500 MD/ASW helicopters were ordered during 1979 for use from destroyers.

WARSHIPS IN SERVICE OR UNDER CONSTRUCTION
AS OF 1 JANUARY 1982

	L	Tons (Surfaced)	Main armament
♦ **2 (+2) submarines**			
0 (+2) WALRUS	. . .	2,300	6/533-mm TT
2 GUPPY II	1944-45	1,870	10/533-mm TT
♦ **24 destroyers**		Tons	
10 GEARING FRAM-I	1945-46	2,425	4/127mm, 0-4/40-mm, ASW weapons
2 GEARING FRAM-II	1945	2,425	4-6/127-mm, 4-8/40-mm, ASW weapons
2 ALLEN M. SUMNER FRAM-II	1944	2,350	6/127-mm, ASW weapons
6 ALLEN M. SUMNER	1943-44	2,200	6/127-mm, Gabriel SSM, ASW weapons
4 FLETCHER	1942-43	1,680	4-5/127-mm, Sea Chapparal SAM, ASW weapons
♦ **10 frigates**			
1 RUDDEROW	1943	1,450	2/127-mm, 4/40-mm, ASW weapons
9 CROSLEY/CHARLES LAWRENCE	1943-45	1,680	2/127-mm, 6/40-mm, ASW weapons
♦ **3 corvettes**			
3 AUK	1942-45	890	2/76.2-mm, 4/40-mm, ASW weapons

♦ **4+ guided-missile patrol boats**

♦ **14 minesweepers**

♦ **50 amphibious ships and craft**

NOTE: Almost all ships, weapons, and electronics systems currently in use originated in the United States, the principal exception being the Hsiung Feng anti-ship missile, a copy of the Israeli Aviation Industries' Gabriel II. Although nearly all ships are

WARSHIPS (continued)

ex-U.S. Navy units dating to World War II, maintenance has been superb, and many subsystems have been renewed and updated. At the present time, destroyer gunfire-control systems are being upgraded by U.S. contractors, while a locally designed chaff rocket system has been installed on most larger ships. Hull numbers were altered in 1976 and now are not usually worn. The lastest known numbers are given, but ships are listed in alphabetical order.

SUBMARINES

♦ 0 (+2) Dutch Walrus class Bldr: Rotterdamse Droogdok Mij.

	Laid down	L	In serv.
. . . N. . .	. . .	. . .	. . .
. . . N. . .	. . .	. . .	. . .

D: 1,900/2,365/2,700 tons   **S:** 12/20 tons   **Dim:** 67.0 × 8.4 × 7.0
A: 6/533-mm TT fwd (20 torpedoes)
Electron Equipt: Radar: 1/Decca. . .
         Sonar: Thomson-CSF-supplied
M: 3 SEMT-Pielstick 12PA4V 185, 980-kw diesel generator groups, 1 Holec motor; 1 5-bladed prop; 5,500 hp
Fuel: 310 tons   **Range:** 10,000/9 (snorkel)   **Man:** 49 tot.

REMARKS: Ordered late 1980, over mainland China's protests. May be many years before delivered, as parent program for Dutch Navy will not deliver first ship of class, ordered 6-78, until 1985. Highly automated design. "Gipsy" data system, Sperry Mk 29 mod. 2A inertial navigation system.

♦ 2 ex-U.S. GUPPY II class

	Bldr	Laid down	L	In serv.
736 HAI SHIH	Portsmouth NSY	22-7-44	5-11-44	17-3-45
(ex-*Cutlass*, SS 478)				
794 HAI PAO	Cramp SB, Philadelphia	23-8-43	8-7-45	11-4-46
(ex-*Tusk*, SS 426)				

Hai Pao (794)—as Tusk   1967

D: 1,517/1,870/2,440 tons   **S:** 18/16 kts   **Dim:** 93.57 × 8.33 × 5.18
A: 10/533-mm TT (6 fwd, 4 aft)
Electron Equipt: Radar: 1/SS-2
         Sonar: BQR-2B, BQS-4
M: Diesel-electric propulsion: 4 Fairbanks-Morse 38D8⅛ diesels; 2 electric motors; 4,610/5,200 hp
Range: 10,000/10 surfaced   **Man:** 11 officers, 70 men

REMARKS: Transferred, 12-4-73 and 18-10-73, for ASW training. British Mk 24 Tigerfish torpedoes ordered in 1979 to arm them. Four 126-cell batteries.

DESTROYERS

♦ 10 ex-U.S. Gearing FRAM-I class

	Bldr	Laid down	L	In serv.
921 CHIEN YANG	Todd, Seattle	27-12-44	4-8-45	8-2-46
(ex-*James E. Kyes*, DD 787)				
978 HAN YANG	Bath Iron Wks.	30-10-44	25-3-45	29-5-45
(ex-*Herbert J. Thomas*, DD 833)				
915 KAI YANG	Todd, Seattle	1-12-44	7-7-45	26-10-45
(ex-*Richard B. Anderson*, DD 786)				
981 LAI YANG	Bethlehem, Quincy	8-6-45	4-1-46	28-6-46
(ex-*Leonard F. Mason*, DD 852)				
. . . LAO YANG	Todd, Seattle	31-5-45	8-3-46	21-6-46
(ex-*Shelton*, DD 790)				
938 LIAO YANG	Bath Iron Wks.	7-10-44	11-3-45	11-5-45
(ex-*Hanson*, DD 832)				
932 SHEN YANG	Bath Iron, Wks.	26-2-45	30-6-45	13-9-45
(ex-*Power*, DD 839)				
925 TE YANG	Bath Iron Wks.	15-1-45	27-5-45	31-7-45
(ex-*Sarsfield*, DD 837)				
. . . N. . .	Federal SB Newark, N.J.	5-4-45	24-11-45	11-7-46
(ex-*Hamner*, DD 817)				
. . . N. . .	Consolidated, Orange, Tex.	6-5-45	19-10-45	10-10-46
(ex-*Johnston*, DD 821)				

Te Yang (925)   1977

Han Yang (833)   1977

DESTROYERS *(continued)*

D: 2,425 tons (3,465-3,540 fl) **S:** 32 kts
Dim: 119.03 (116.74 wl) × 12.52 × 4.61 (6.5 over sonar)
A: 4/127-mm DP (II × 2)—*Han Yang, Kai Yang:* 4/40-mm AA (II × 2)—4 or 6/
12.7-mm mg—1/ASROC ASW RL (VIII × 1) (not in *Han Yang, Kai Yang,*
and ex-DD 817, 821)—6/324-mm Mk 32 ASW TT (III × 2)—1/Hughes-500
ASW helicopter
Electron Equipt: Radar: 1/SPS-10, 1/SPS-29 (*Chien Yang, Te Yang:* SPS-40),
1/Mk 25
Sonar: SQS-23
ECM: WLR-1 or WLR-3, ULQ-6 in some, 4/chaff RL
M: 2 sets GE GT; 2 props; 60,000 hp **Electric:** 1,200 kw
Boilers: 4 Babcock & Wilcox; 43.3 kg/cm², 454°C
Fuel: 720 tons   **Range:** 1,500/31; 5,800/12   **Man:** 275 tot.

REMARKS: *Chien Yang, Lao Yang,* and *Liao Yang* transferred 18-4-73; *Han Yang,* 6-
5-74; *Kai Yang,* 10-6-77; *Te Yang, Shen Yang,* 1-10-77; *Lai Yang,* 10-3-78. A ninth
unit, *Chao Yang* (ex-*Rowan,* DD 782) was lost 22-8-77 while on tow to Taiwan. Ex-
DD 817 and 821 purchased (without ASROC) 27-2-81. *Kai Yang* and *Lao Yang* both
have 127-mm twin mounts forward and the Mk 32 ASW torpedo tubes abreast the
after stack. *Han Yang* has extra superstructure, as she was converted for NBC-
warfare defense trials 1963-64; she has an extra gas-turbine generator to run additional air-conditioning systems. She and *Kai Yang* had no ASROC on transfer and
have received two twin 40-mm antiaircraft guns, each with a Mk 51, mod. 2, director
in the ASROC location. All have Mk 37 gunfire-control radars for the 127-mm guns.
New GFCS are to be acquired for all. Hsiung Feng (Israeli Gabriel I) missiles may
be added, and most have four multi-tube chaff RL.

◆ 2 ex-U.S. Gearing FRAM-II class

	Bldr	Laid down	L	In serv.
966 DANG YANG	Bethlehem,	26-3-44	5-10-45	21-3-47
(ex-*Lloyd Thomas,* DD 764)	San Francisco			
963 FU YANG	Bath Iron Works	30-1-45	14-6-45	21-8-45
(ex-*Ernest G. Small,* DD 838)				

Fu Yang (963) 1977

D: 2,425 tons (3,477 fl) **S:** 32 kts
Dim: 119.03 (116.74 wl) × 12.52 × 4.61 (6.54 over sonar)
A: 963: 6/127-mm DP (II × 3)—8/40-mm AA (II × 4)—4/12.7-mm mg (I × 4)—
2/Mk 11 Hedgehog—6/324-mm Mk 32 ASW TT (III × 2)—1/d.c. rack
966: 4/127-mm DP (II × 2)—4/40-mm AA (II × 2)—4/12.7-mm mg (I × 4)—
1/Mk 15 trainable Hedgehog—6/324-mm Mk 32 ASW TT (III × 2)—1/
Hughes-500 ASW helicopter

Electron Equipt: Radar: 963: 1/SPS-10, 1/SPS-37, 1/Mk 25
TACAN: URN-6—ECM: WLR-1
966: 1/SPS-10, 1/SPS-6B, 1/Mk 25
ECM: WLR-1, WLR-3, ULQ-6
Sonar: SQS-23 series (hull); 963 only: SQA 10 (VDS)
M: 2 sets GE GT; 2 props; 60,000 hp **Electric:** 1,200 kw
Boilers: 4 Babcock & Wilcox; 43.3 kg/cm², 454°C
Fuel: 720 tons   **Range:** 1,600/31; 6,100/12   **Man:** 275 tot.

REMARKS: *Dang Yang,* completed as an ASW destroyer (DDE), finished FRAM-I
modernization in 11-61 and was transferred to Taiwan on 12-10-72. *Fu Yang,* transferred in 2-71, completed FRAM-II modernization as a radar picket destroyer in 8-
61; her SPS-30 height-finder was removed before transfer. Both received 40-mm
and 12.7-mm guns in Taiwan. One Mk 37 radar gunfire control for 127-mm, one Mk
51, mod.2, optical gunfire control per 40-mm mount.

◆ 2 ex-U.S. Allen M. Sumner FRAM-II class

	Bldr	Laid down	L	In serv.
949 LO YANG	Bethlehem,	30-8-43	25-1-44	20-5-44
(ex-*Taussig,* DD 746)	Staten I.			
954 NAN YANG	Bethlehem,	21-11-43	30-9-44	11-10-45
(ex-*John W. Thomason,* DD 760)	San Francisco			

D: 2,350 tons (3,220 fl) **S:** 33 kts **Range:** 1,000/32 **Man:** 275 tot.
Dim: 114.63 (112.52 wl) × 12.52 × 4.4 (5.9 over sonar)
A: 6/127-mm DP (II × 3)—4/12.7-mm mg (I × 4)—2/Mk 11 Hedgehogs—6/324-
mm Mk 32 ASW TT (III × 2)—1/Hughes-500 ASW helicopter
Electron Equipt: Radar: 1/SPS-10, 1/SPS-29, 1/Mk 25
Sonar: SQS-29 series, SQA-10 (VDS)
ECM: WLR-1, 4/chaff RL
M: 2 sets GT; 2 props; 60,000 hp **Electric:** 1,200 kw **Fuel:** 500 tons
Boilers: 4 Babcock & Wilcox; 43.3 kg/cm², 454°C

REMARKS: Both transferred on 6-5-74, having completed FRAM-II modernization in
9-62 and 1-60, respectively. Have Mk 37 radar fire control for the 127-mm guns and
Mk 5 target-designation systems.

◆ 6 ex-U.S. Allen M. Sumner class

	Bldr	Laid down	L	In serv.
976 HENG YANG	Bethlehem,	30-9-43	23-2-44	24-6-44
(ex-*Samuel N. Moore,* DD 747)	Staten Isl.			
986 HSIANG YANG	Bethlehem,	30-7-43	28-12-43	17-4-44
(ex-*Brush,* DD 745)	Staten Isl.			
988 HUA YANG	Bethlehem,	5-5-44	29-10-44	17-3-45
(ex-*Bristol,* DD 857)	San Pedro			
972 HUEI YANG	Federal,	19-10-43	27-2-44	4-5-44
(ex-*English,* DD 696)	Kearny			
928 PO YANG	Bath Iron	28-10-43	19-3-44	2-6-44
(ex-*Maddox,* DD 731)	Wks.			
944 YUEN YANG	Federal,	16-12-43	15-4-44	22-6-44
(ex-*Haynsworth,* DD 700)	Kearny			

D: 2,200 tons (3,300 fl) **S:** 33 kts
Dim: 114.63 (112.52 wl) × 12.52 × 4.4 (5.9 over sonar)
A: *Hsiang Yang, Hua Yang, Yuen Yang:* 5/Gabriel SSM (III × 1, II × 1)—6/
127-mm DP (II × 3)—4/40-mm AA (II × 2)—4/12.7-mm mg (I × 4)—2/Mk 11
Hedgehogs—6/324-mm Mk 32 ASW TT (III × 2)—1/d.c. rack

DESTROYERS (continued)

Heng Yang (976)—wearing old number   1972

Heng Yang: 6/127-mm DP (II × 3)—8/40-mm AA (IV × 1, II × 2)—4/12.7-mm mg (I × 4)—2/Mk 11 Hedgehogs—6/324-mm Mk 32 ASW TT (III × 2)—1/d.c. rack

Huei Yang, Po Yang: 6/127-mm DP (II × 3)—4/76.2-mm DP (II × 2)—4/12.7-mm mg—2/Mk 11 Hedgehogs—6/324-mm Mk 32 ASW TT—1/d.c. rack

Electron Equipt: Radar: 1/SPS-10, 1/SPS-6C (*Po Yang:* SPS-40), 1/Mk 25 (*Huei Yang, Po Yang:* 1/Mk 35 also), Gabriel ships: 1/Orion RTN-10X

　　Sonar: SQS-29 series

　　ECM: WLR-1, 4/chaff RL

M: 2 sets GT; 2 props; 60,000 hp   **Electric:** 1,000 kw

Boilers: 4 Babcock & Wilcox; 43.3 kg/cm², 454°C

Fuel: 500 tons   **Range:** 1,000/32; 4,400/11   **Man:** 275 tot.

REMARKS: *Heng Yang* transferred in 2-70; *Hsiang Yang* and *Hua Yang* on 9-12-69; *Huei Yang* in 9-70; *Po Yang* on 6-7-72; *Yuen Yang* on 12-5-70. All unmodified units of the class. *Hsiang Yang* had four 76.2-mm DP before Gabriel conversion. Those that have 40-mm antiaircraft guns had them added in Taiwan; each mount has one associated Mk 51, mod. 2, GFCS. All have Mk 37 radar GFCS for the 127-mm guns; those with 76.2-mm also have one Mk 56 radar GFCS. The Gabriel-equipped units have a Selenia Orion RTN-10X fire-control radar on the after side of the tripod mast. One or more of these ships may be fitted with an Israeli Aviation Industries LPH-292 helicopter hangar/flight deck system to support a helicopter for over-the-horizon missile targeting; it would replace the after 127-mm mount.

♦ 4 ex-U.S. Fletcher class

Bldrs: *An Yang:* Bethlehem Steel, Staten Island; others: Bethlehem, San Francisco

	Laid down	L	In serv.
997 AN YANG (ex-*Kimberly*, DD 521)	27-7-42	4-2-43	24-5-43
947 CHIANG YANG (ex-*Mullany*, DD 528)	15-1-42	12-10-42	23-4-43
934 KUN YANG (ex-*Yarnell*, DD 541)	5-12-42	25-7-43	30-12-43
956 KWEI YANG (ex-*Twining*, DD 540)	21-11-42	11-7-43	1-2-43

D: 2,100 tons (3,036 fl)   **S:** 35 kts

Dim: 114.65 (112.52 wl) × 11.99 × 4.39 (5.38 over sonar)

A: *Chiang Yang:* 4/127-mm DP (I × 4)—6/76.2-mm DP (II × 2)—2/Mk 11 Hedgehogs—6/324-mm Mk 32 ASW TT (III × 2)—1/d.c. rack

Kun Yang: 5/127-mm DP (I × 5)—1/Sea Chaparral SAM system (VI × 1)—4/40-mm AA (II × 2)—5/533-mm TT (V × 1)—2/Mk 11 Hedgehogs—mines

Others: 5/127-mm DP (I × 5)—1/Sea Chaparral system (VI × 1)—4/40-mm AA (II × 2)—2/Mk 11 Hedgehogs—6/324-mm Mk 32 ASW TT (III × 2)—1/d.c. rack

Kun Yang (934)—wearing old number   1970

Electron Equipt: Radar: 1/SPS-10, 1/SPS-6C, 1/Mk 25 (*Chiang Yang:* 1/Mk 35, 2/Mk 34, also)

　　Sonar: SQS-4 or SQS-29 series

　　ECM: BLR-1, 4/chaff RL

M: 2 sets GT; 2 props; 60,000 hp   **Electric:** 880 kw

Boilers: 4 Babcock & Wilcox; 43.3 kg/cm², 454°C   **Fuel:** 512 tons

Range: 860/35; 4,700/13   **Man:** 275 tot.

REMARKS: *An Yang* transferred in 6-67; *Chiang Yang* in 10-71; *Kun Yang* in 6-68; *Kwei Yang* in 10-71. All have Mk 37 radar GFCS for the 127-mm guns, while *Chiang Yang* also has one Mk 56 and two Mk 63 GFCS for her 76.2-mm guns. Sea Chaparral is a manned mounting for launching Redeye, heat-seeking, short-range SAMs; it replaced a twin 40-mm antiaircraft mount in three ships.

FRIGATES

NOTE: A design for an indigenously constructed frigate is being prepared, with Westinghouse, USA, as prime contractor. No details are available.

♦ 1 ex-U.S. Rudderow class Bldr: Bethlehem Steel, Hingham, Mass.

	Laid down	L	In serv.
959 TAI YUAN (ex-*Riley*, DE 579)	20-10-43	29-12-43	13-3-44

Tai Yuan (959)—wearing old number   1968

FRIGATES (continued)

D: 1,450 tons (1,950 fl) **S:** 24 kts **Dim:** 93.27 × 11.24 × 3.43 (4.3 over sonar)
A: 2/127-mm DP (I × 2)—4/40-mm AA (I × 2)—4/20-mm AA (I × 4)—1/Mk 11
　　Hedgehog—6/324-mm Mk 32 ASW TT (III × 2)—2/Mk 9 d.c. racks—mines
Electron Equipt: Radar: 1/SPS-5, 1/SPS-6, 1/Mk 26 fire-control
　　　　　　　　Sonar: . . .
M: 2 sets GE turbo-electric drive; 2 props; 12,000 hp **Electric:** 1,140 kw
Boilers: 2 Foster-Wheeler D-type; 31.7 kg/cm², 399°C
Fuel: 354 tons **Range:** 1,100/24; 5,000/12 **Man:** 200 tot.

REMARKS: Transferred, after modernization, on 10-7-69; purchased outright in 3-74.
Has one Mk 52 radar GFCS and two Mk 51, mod. 2, GFCS. Minelaying capability
added in Taiwan.

♦ 9 former high-speed transports

6 ex-U.S. Crosley class:

	Bldr	Laid down	L	In serv.
838 FU SHAN (ex-*Truxtun*, APD 98, ex-*DE 282*)	Charleston NY	113-12-43	9-3-44	3-7-44
854 HUA SHAN (ex-*Donald W. Wolf*, APD 129, ex-*DE 713*)	Defoe SB, Bay City, Mich.	17-4-44	22-7-44	13-4-45
893 SHOU SHAN (ex-*Kline*, APD 120, ex-*DE 687*)	Bethlehem, Quincy, Mass.	27-5-44	27-6-44	18-10-44
878 TAI SHAN (ex-*Register*, APD 92, ex-*DE 233*)	Charleston NY	27-10-43	20-1-44	11-1-45
615 TIEN SHAN (ex-*Kleinsmith*, APD 134, ex-*DE 718*)	Defoe SB, Bay City, Mich.	30-8-44	27-1-45	12-6-45
. . . YU SHAN (ex-*Kinzer*, APD 91, ex-*DE 232*)	Charleston NY	9-9-43	9-12-43	1-11-44

3 ex-U.S. Charles Lawrence class

	Bldr	Laid down	L	In serv.
845 CHUNG SHAN (ex-*Blessman*, APD 48, ex-*DE 69*)	Bethlehem, Hingham	22-3-43	19-6-43	19-9-43
821 LU SHAN (ex-*Bull*, APD 78, ex-*DE 693*)	Defoe, Bay City	14-12-42	25-3-43	12-8-43
834 WEN SHAN (ex-*Gantner*, APD 42, ex-*DE 60*)	Bethlehem, Hingham	21-12-42	17-4-43	23-7-43

D: 1,680 tons (2,150 fl) **S:** 22 kts **Dim:** 93.27 × 11.24 × 3.96 (hull)
A: 2/127-mm DP (I × 2)—6/40-mm AA (II × 3)—4/20-mm AA (I × 4)—2/Mk 9
　　d.c. racks—*see also* Remarks
Electron Equipt: Radar: 1/SPS-5, 1/Decca 707; some: 1/Mk 26
　　　　　　　　Sonar: . . .
M: 2 sets GE turbo-electric drive; 2 props; 12,000 hp **Electric:** 1,140 kw
Boilers: 2, Babcock & Wilcox, Foster-Wheeler, or Combustion Engineering;
　　31.7 kg/cm², 399°C
Fuel: 346 tons **Range:** 1,800/22; 5,000/13 **Man:** 200 crew + 160 troops

Fu Shan (838)—wearing old number　　　　　　　*Ships of the World*, 1975

REMARKS: *Yu Shan* transferred in 4-62; *Hua Shan* in 5-65; *Fu Shan* and *Shou Shan*
in 3-66; *Wen Shan* in 5-66; *Lu Shan* in 8-66; *Tai Shan* in 10-66; *Tien Shan* in 6-67,
and *Chung Shan* in 8-67. All were sold outright except *Tien Shan* which, because
she was on loan, was not modified by the addition of a second 127-mm mount aft
until after her purchase in 1974; the others all received the second gun in lieu of a
cargo hold and derrick, beginning about 1970. ASW armaments vary, with *Fu Shan*
having two Mk 11 Hedgehogs on her main deck forward and several (but not all)
carrying six 324-mm Mk 32 ASW torpedo tubes (III × 2); all have two Mk 9 depth-
charge racks, and *Hua Shan* has four *twin* 20-mm antiaircraft guns. Most have only
a Mk 51 range-finder for 127-mm fire control forward and a Mk 51 optical gunfire-
control system aft, plus three Mk 51, mod. 2 GFCS for the 40-mm antiaircraft guns.
Welin davits are retained amidships, but only two (vice the original four) landing
craft are carried, to save topweight. The former *Crosley*-class ships have low navigating bridges, the other ships have high ones. Sisters *Heng Shan* (ex-*Raymond
W. Herndon*, APD 121) and *Lung Shan* (ex-*Schmitt*, APD 76) were stricken in 1976,
and *Kang Shan* (ex-*George W. Ingram*, APD 43) was stricken in 1978.

CORVETTES

♦ 3 ex-U.S. Auk-class former minesweepers

Bldrs: *Wu Sheng:* Savannah Machine & Foundry, Ga; others: American SB, Cleveland, O.

	Laid down	L	In serv.
896 CHU YUNG (ex-*Waxwing*, MSF 389)	24-5-44	10-3-45	6-8-45
867 PING JIN (ex-*Steady*, MSF 118)	17-11-41	6-6-42	16-11-42
884 WU SHENG (ex-*Redstart*, MSF 378)	14-6-44	18-10-45	4-4-45

D: 890 tons (1,250 fl) **S:** 18 kts **Dim:** 67.39 (65.53 pp) × 9.8 × 3.3
A: 2/76.2-mm DP (I × 2)—4/40-mm AA (II × 2)—4/20-mm AA (II × 2)—1/Mk
　　11 Hedgehog—3/324-mm Mk 32 ASW TT (III × 1)—2/Mk 9 d.c. racks
Electron Equipt: Radar: 1/SPS-5 Sonar: SQS-17 **Electric:** 360 kw
M: 2 GM 12-278A diesels; 2 props; 3,532 hp **Fuel:** 216 tons **Man:** 80 tot.

REMARKS: After conversion to corvettes, transferred as follows: *Chu Yung* in 11-65,
Ping Jin in 3-68, and *Wu Sheng* in 7-65. *Chu Yung* was fitted with mine rails in
1975.

GUIDED-MISSILE PATROL BOATS

♦ 2 (+. . .) Tzu Chiang class Bldr: China SB, Kaohsiung (In serv. 1980-. . .)

D: 47 tons (fl) **S:** 36 kts **Dim:** 21.62 × 5.49 × 0.94 (1.82 props)
A: 2/Hsiung Feng SSM (I × 2)—1/20-mm AA—2/12.7-mm mg (I × 2)

GUIDED-MISSILE PATROL BOATS (continued)

M: 2 MTU 12V331 TC81 diesels; 2 props; 2,720 hp
Electric: 30 kw **Range:** 700/32 **Man:** 10-12 tot.

REMARKS: Design evidently based closely on the Israeli Dvora class; name means "Seagull." A large number of these aluminum-hulled craft are to be built.

♦ 2 Lung Chiang class

		Bldr	In serv.
581	LUNG CHIANG	Korea Tacoma SY	15-5-78
582	N. . .	China SB, Kaohsiung	1979

D: 218 tons (250 fl) **S:** 40 kts **Dim:** 50.14 (46.94 pp) × 7.25 × 2.26
A: 4/Hsiung Feng SSM—1/76-mm OTO Melara DP—2/30-mm Emerlec AA (II × 1)—2/12.7-mm mg (I × 2)
Electron Equipt: Radar: 1/navigational, 1/RAN 11LX (NA 10 system)
M: CODOG: 3 GM 12V149 TI diesels (3,600 hp), 3 AVCO-Lycoming TF-40A gas turbines; 3 CP props
Range: 700/40 (gas turbines), 1,900/30 (3 diesels), 2,700/12 (1 diesel)
Man: 5 officers, 30 men

REMARKS: Design is a variation of Tacoma Boatbuilding (U.S.) PSMM Mk-5 design. The Hsiung Feng missile is a copy of the Israeli Gabriel I. Prototype built in Korea, with follow-on units to be built in Taiwan.

PATROL CRAFT

♦ 10 or more aluminum-hulled Bldr: China SB, Kaohsiung

D: 12 tons **S:** 25 kts **Dim:** 15.0 × . . . × . . .
A: 1/40-mm AA **M:** 2 diesels; water-jet drive

REMARKS: Date from 1971. There are believed to be a number of other small patrol craft of Taiwanese construction, for which no details are available. The six remaining torpedo boats are believed to have been stricken.

MINE WARFARE SHIPS

♦ 14 ex-U.S. and ex-Belgian Adjutant, MSC 268*, and MCS 289** classes of coastal minesweepers

		Bldr	In serv.
. . . YUNG AN (ex-MSC 123)	. . .		6-55
. . . YUNG CHEN (ex-*Maaseick*, ex-MSC 78)	Adams Yacht, Quincy, Mass.		7-53
. . . YUNG CHI (ex-*Charleroi*, ex-MSC 152)	Hodgdon Bros., Me.		2-54
. . . YUNG CHING (ex-*Eakloo*, ex-MSC 101)	Hodgdon Bros., Me.		5-53
. . . YUNG CHOU (ex-MSC 278)*	Tacoma Boat, Wash.		7-59
. . . YUNG FU (ex-*Diest*, ex-*Macaw*, MSC 77)	Adams Yacht, Quincy, Mass.		5-53
. . . YUNG HSIN (ex-MSC 302)**	Dorchester Bldrs., N.J.		3-65
. . . YUNG JEN (ex-*St. Nicholas*, ex-MSC 64)	H. B. Nevins, N.Y.		2-54
. . . YUNG JU (ex-MSC 300)**	Tacoma Boat, Wash.		3-65
. . . YUNG LO (ex-MSC 306)**	Dorchester Bldrs., N.J.		4-66
. . . YUNG NIEN (ex-MSC 277)*	Tacoma Boat, Wash.		5-59
. . . YUNG PING (ex-MSC 140)	. . .		9-55
. . . YUNG SHAN (ex-*Lier*, ex-MSC 63)	H. B. Nevins, N.Y.		7-53
. . . YUNG SUI (ex-*Diksmude*, ex-MSC 65)	H. B. Nevins, N.Y.		2-54

Yung Chi—Adjutant class, ex-Belgian, wearing old number   1970

Yung Chou—MSC 268 class, wearing old number   1970

Yung Lo—MSC 289 class, wearing old number   1970

MINE WARFARE SHIPS (continued)

D: 320 tons (378 fl) **S:** 12.5 kts **Dim:** 43.0 (41.5 wl) × 7.95 × 2.55
A: 2/20-mm AA (II × 1)
Electron Equipt: Radar: 1/Decca 45 or 707
                    Sonar: UQS-1D
M: 2 GM 8-268A diesels; 2 props; 1,200 hp (MSC 268 class: 4 GM 6-71 diesels; 2
    props; 890 hp)
Fuel: 40 tons **Range:** 2,500/12 **Man:** 40 tot.

REMARKS: Wooden hulls. All transferred on completion except ex-Belgian ships, transferred in 11-69. Have a variety of configurations, the ex-MSC 258 having a different propulsion scheme and the ex-MSC 289 class having a lower bridge and taller stack.

♦ **1 ex-U.S. minesweeping boat**

MSB 12 (ex-U.S. Navy MSB 4, ex-U.S. Army . . .)

D: 39 tons (fl) **S:** 12 kts **Dim:** 17.5 × 4.6 × 1.25
M: 2 Packard diesels; 2 props; 600 hp **Man:** 6 tot.

REMARKS: Built in 1945 and transferred in 12-61. Wooden hull. Sister to South Korean MSB 1.

♦ **8 ex-U.S. minesweeping launches**

MSML 1 MSML 3 MSML 5 MSML 6 MSML 7 MSML 8 MSML 11 MSML 12

D: 24 tons (fl) **S:** 8 kts **Dim:** 15.29 × 3.96 × 1.31
M: 1 diesel; 1 prop; 60 hp **Range:** 800/8 **Man:** 4 tot.

REMARKS: Built between 1943 and 1945, and converted from personnel launches before transfer in 3-61. Wooden hulls.

AMPHIBIOUS WARFARE SHIPS

♦ **1 command ship** Bldr: Dravo Corp., Neville I., Pittsburgh, Pa.

	L	In serv.
663 KAO HSIUNG (ex-*Chung Hai*, LST 229, ex-*Dukes County*, LST 735)	11-3-44	26-4-44

Kao Hsiung (663)—wearing old number   1968

D: 1,650 tons (4,080 fl) **S:** 11 kts **Dim:** 99.98 × 15.24 × 3.4
A: 8/40-mm AA (II × 2, I × 4)—4/20-mm AA (II × 2)
Electron Equipt: Radar: 1/SPS-10, 1/SPS-12
M: 2 GM 12-567A diesels; 2 props; 1,700 hp **Range:** 15,000/9

REMARKS: Transferred in 5-57, converted to command ship in 1964, with additional communications gear and radars. Retains bow doors.

♦ **1 ex-U.S. Cabildo-class dock landing ship** Bldr: Gulf SB, Chickasaw, Ala.

	Laid down	L	In serv.
618 CHEN HAI (ex-*Fort Marion*, LSD 22)	15-9-44	22-5-45	29-1-46

D: 4,790 tons (9,375 fl) **S:** 15.6 kts **Dim:** 139.52 (138.38 wl) × 22.0 × 5.49
A: 12/40-mm AA (IV × 2, II × 2) **Electron Equipt:** Radar: 1/LN-66, 1/SPS-5
M: 2 sets GT; 2 props; 9,000 hp **Boilers:** 2; 30.6 kg/cm², 393°C
Fuel: 1,758 tons **Range:** 8,000/15 **Man:** 326 crew + several hundred troops

REMARKS: Transferred by sale on 15-4-77, having been stricken from the U.S. Navy in 10-74. Modernized under FRAM-II program 12-59 to 4-60. Helicopter platform over 119.5 × 13.4 meter docking well, which can accommodate three LCUs, eighteen LCMs, or thirty-two amphibious armored troop carriers.

♦ **1 ex-U.S. Ashland-class dock landing ship** Bldr: Moore DD Co., Oakland, Cal.

	Laid down	L	In serv.
639 CHUNG CHENG (ex-*Tung Hai*, ex-*White Marsh*, LSD 8)	7-4-43	19-7-43	29-1-44

Chung Cheng (639)—wearing old number

D: 4,032 tons (8,700 fl) **S:** 15 kts **Dim:** 139.52 (138.38 wl) × 22.0 × 5.49
A: 12/40-mm AA (IV × 2, II × 2) **Electron Equipt:** Radar: 1/SPS-5
M: 2 sets Skinner Uniflow reciprocating steam; 2 props; 7,400 hp
Electric: 400 kw **Boilers:** 2, two-drum; 17.6 kg/cm²
Fuel: 1,758 tons **Range:** 8,000/15

REMARKS: Transferred on loan on 17-11-60, purchased in 5-76. Generally similar to *Chen Hai*, above, except for propulsion.

♦ **21 ex-U.S. LST 1 and LST 542-class tank landing ships**

	Bldr	In serv.
. . . CHUNG CHENG (ex-*Lafayette County*, LST 859)	Chicago B & I, Seneca, Ill.	29-12-44
. . . CHUNG CHI (ex-LST 1017)	Bethlehem, Fore River, Mass.	12-4-44
. . . CHUNG CHIANG (ex-*San Bernardino County*, LST 1110)	Missouri Valley B & I, Evansville, Ind.	7-3-45
. . . CHUNG CHIEN (ex-LST 716)	Jeffersonville B & M, Ind.	18-8-44
. . . CHUNG CHIH (ex-*Sagadahoc County*, LST 1091)	American Br., Ambridge, Pa.	6-4-45
. . . CHUNG CHUAN (ex-LST 1030)	Boston Navy Yd.	19-7-44
619 CHUNG FU (ex-*Iron County*, LST 840)	American Br., Ambridge, Pa.	11-12-44
697 CHUNG HAI (ex-LST 755)	American Br., Ambridge, Pa.	29-7-44
. . . CHUNG HSING (ex-LST 557)	Missouri Valley B & I, Evansville, Ind.	5-5-44

AMPHIBIOUS WARFARE SHIPS *(continued)*

. . . CHUNG KUANG (ex-LST 503)	Jeffersonville B & M, Ind.	14-12-43
691 CHUNG LIEN (ex-LST 1050)	Dravo, Pittsburgh, Pa.	3-4-45
. . . CHUNG MING (ex-*Sweetwater County*, LST 1152)	Dravo, Pittsburgh, Pa.	13-4-45
. . . CHUNG PANG (ex-LST 578)	Missouri Valley B & I, Evansville, Ind.	15-7-44
. . . CHUNG SHENG (ex-LST(H) 1033)	Chicago B & I, Seneca, Ill.	. . . -4-44
. . . CHUNG SHU (ex-LST 520)	Chicago B & I, Seneca, Ill.	28-2-44
624 CHUNG SHUN (ex-LST 732)	Dravo, Pittsburgh, Pa.	10-4-44
. . . CHUNG SUO (ex-*Bradley County*, LST 400)	Newport News SB & DD, Va.	7-1-43
. . . CHUNG TING (ex-LST 537)	Missouri Valley B & I, Evansville, Ind.	9-2-44
. . . CHUNG WAN (ex-LST 535)	Missiouri Valley B & I, Evansville, Ind.	4-2-44
. . . CHUNG YEH (ex-*Sublette County*, LST 1144)	Chicago B & I, Seneca, Ill.	28-5-45
. . . CHUNG YUNG (ex-LST 574)	Missouri Valley B & I, Evansville, Ind.	26-6-44

Chung Kuang—wearing old number   1969

D: 1,653 tons (4,080 fl) **S:** 11.6 kts **Dim:** 99.98 × 15.24 × 3.4
A: Several: 2/76.2-mm DP (I × 2)—6-8/40-mm AA (II × 2, or I × 2 or 4)—4-8/ 20-mm AA
M: 2 GM 12-567A diesels; 2 props; 1,700 hp **Electric:** 300 kw
Fuel: 569 tons **Range:** 15,000/9 **Man:** 100-125 tot.

REMARKS: Six transferred in 1946, two in 1947, *Chung Shu* in 1948, seven in 1958, *Chung Yung* in 1959, *Chung Kuang* in 1960, *Chung Yeh* in 1961, and two subsequently. All extensively rebuilt during the late 1960s, in many cases becoming almost new ships; re-engined at the same time. Most have four pairs of Welin davits, while *Chung Chih, Chung Yung, Chung Sheng,* and *Chung Shu* have six, and *Chung Chien* has two; each pair of davits handles one LCVP. Five or more have two 76.2-mm guns. *Chung Chih* (ex-216, ex-LST 279) was stricken in 1978.

♦ **4 ex-U.S. LSM 1-class medium landing ships**

		Bldr	In serv.
637 MEI LO (ex-LSM 362)		Brown SB, Houston, Tex.	11-1-45
659 MEI PING (ex-LSM 471)		Brown SB, Houston, Tex.	23-2-45
694 MEI SUNG (ex-LSM 457)		Western Pipe & Steel, San Pedro, Cal.	28-3-45
649 MEI TSENG (ex-LSM 431)		Dravo, Wilmington, Del.	25-2-45

Mei Tseng (649)—wearing old number   1969

D: 1,095 tons (fl) **S:** 12.5 kts **Dim:** 62.03 (59.89 wl) × 10.52 × 2.54 (max.)
A: 2/40-mm AA—4 or 8/20-mm AA (I or II × 4)—4/12.7-mm mg (I × 4)
M: *Mei Lo, Mei Ping:* 2 Fairbanks-Morse 38D8⅛ × 10 (others: 2 GM 16-278A) diesels; 2 props; 2,800 hp
Electric: 240 kw **Fuel:** 161 tons **Man:** 60 tot.

REMARKS: *Mei Sung* and *Mei Tseng* transferred in 1946, *Mei Ping* in 11-56, and *Mei Lo* in 5-62.

♦ **6 ex-U.S. LCU 1466-class utility landing craft** Bldr: Ishikawajima, Harima, Japan

. . . HO SHAN (ex-LCU 1596)	. . . HO MENG (ex-LCU 1599)
. . . HO CHUAN (ex-LCU 1597)	. . . HO MOU (ex-LCU 1600)
. . . HO SENG (ex-LCU 1598)	. . . HO SHOU (ex-LCU 1601)

Ho Mou—wearing old number   1955

D: 347 tons (fl) **S:** 8 kts **Dim:** 35.08 × 10.36 × 1.6 (max.)
A: 4/20-mm AA (II × 2) **Fuel:** 11 tons **Range:** 1,200/6 **Man:** 14 tot.
M: 3 Gray Marine 64/65YTL diesels; 3 props; 675 hp

REMARKS: Built under Offshore Procurement Program. In service in 3-55. Cargo: 167 tons.

AMPHIBIOUS WARFARE SHIPS *(continued)*

♦ **16 ex-U.S. LCU 501 (LCT (6))-class utility landing craft**

		In serv.			In serv.
. . .	Ho Chang (ex-LCU 512)	7-9-43	. . .	Ho Deng (ex-LCU 1367)	12-10-44
. . .	Ho Chao (ex-LCU 1429)	8-12-44	. . .	Ho Feng (ex-LCU 1397)	26-10-44
. . .	Ho Cheng (ex-LCU 1145)	11-5-44	. . .	Ho Hoei (ex-LCU 1218)	25-8-44
. . .	Ho Chi (ex-LCU 1212)	16-8-44	. . .	Ho Shun (ex-LCU 1225)	4-9-44
. . .	Ho Chie (ex-LCU 700)	18-5-44	. . .	Ho Teng (ex-LCU 1452)	20-10-44
. . .	Ho Chien (ex-LCU 1278)	22-7-44	. . .	Ho Tsung (ex-LCU 1213)	17-8-44
. . .	Ho Chun (ex-LCU 892)	27-7-44	. . .	Ho Yao (ex-LCU 1244)	22-9-44
. . .	Ho Chung (ex-LCU 849)	7-8-44	. . .	Ho Yung (ex-LCU 1271)	19-8-44

D: 143 tons (309 fl) **S:** 10 kts **Dim:** 36.3 (32.0 wl) × 9.96 × 1.14
A: 2/20-mm AA (I × 2)—2/12.7-mm mg
M: 3 GM 6-71 diesels; 3 props; 675 hp **Electric:** 20 kw **Man:** 10 tot.

REMARKS: Six transferred between 1946 and 1948, the others between 1958 and 1959.

♦ **several hundred U.S. LCM (3)- and LCM (6)-class landing craft**

Bldrs: U.S. and Taiwan

D: 62 tons (fl) **S:** 9 kts **Dim:** 17.07 × 4.37 × 1.07
A: 1/20-mm AA or 12.7-mm mg in some
M: 2 Gray Marine 64HN9 diesels; 2 props; 450 hp **Range:** 130/9 **Man:** 5 tot.

REMARKS: LCM (3) are 56 tons (fl), 15.38 m overall. Cargo: LCM (3): 30 tons, LCM (6): 34 tons.

♦ **about 100 U.S. LCVP class**

D: 13 tons (fl) **S:** 9 kts **Dim:** 10.9 × 3.21 × 1.04 **Range:** 110/9 **Man:** 3 tot.
A: 2/7.62-mm mg (I × 2) **M:** 1 Gray Marine 64HN9 diesels; 225 hp

REMARKS: Most attached to LSTs and former APDs. Wooden construction. Cargo: 36 troops or 4 tons.

HYDROGRAPHIC SHIPS

♦ **1 ex-U.S. C1-M-AV1-class former transport** Bldr: Walter Butler SY, Duluth, Minn.

398 Chiu Hua (ex-*Sgt. George D. Keithley*, T-AGS 35, ex-T-APc 117, ex-*Acorn Knot*)

D: 4,100 tons (6,090 fl) **S:** 11.5 kts **Dim:** 103.18 (97.54 wl) × 15.24 × 5.33
A: 1/40-mm AA—2/20-mm AA (I × 2)
M: 1 Nordberg TSM6 diesel; 1 prop; 1,750 hp **Man:** 72 tot.

REMARKS: Completed in 1945 as a Maritime Commission cargo ship and taken over by the U.S. Army as a personnel transport. Transferred to the U.S. Navy in 1950 and converted for hydrographic-survey duties in 1966-67. Loaned to Taiwan on 29-3-72 and extended on 19-5-76; purchased outright 1981.

♦ **1 ex-U.S. Sotoyomo-class former auxiliary tug**

Bldr: Gulfport Boiler & Welding Works, Port Arthur, Tex.

		Laid down	L	In serv.
563	Chiu Lien (ex-*Geronimo*, ATA 207)	10-11-44	4-1-45	1-3-45

D: 835 tons (fl) **S:** 13 kts **Dim:** 43.59 (40.74 wl) × 10.31 × 4.01
A: 1/20-mm AA **M:** 2 GM 12-278A diesels, electric drive; 1 prop; 1,500 hp
Electric: 120 kw **Fuel:** 158 tons **Man:** 45 tot.

REMARKS: Transferred in 2-69. Operated for the Institute of Oceanology and equipped with various oceanographic winches and laboratories.

Chiu Hua (398)—wearing old number   1972

Chiu Lien (563)   1969

♦ **1 ex-U.S. LSIL 351-class former landing craft**

Bldr: Albina Eng. & Mach. Works, Portland, Ore.

		Laid down	L	In serv.
466	Lien Chang (ex-LSIL 1017)	31-1-44	14-3-44	12-4-44

D: 387 tons (fl) **S:** 14.4 kts **Dim:** 48.46 (46.63 wl) × 7.21 × 1.73
A: 1/40-mm AA—4/20-mm AA (I × 4) **M:** 8 GM 6-71 diesels; 2 props; 2,320 hp
Fuel: 113 tons **Man:** 40 tot.

REMARKS: Transferred in 5-58. Retains LSIL appearance.

AUXILIARY SHIPS

♦ **1 offshore-island support tanker**

		Bldr	In serv.
512	Wan Shou	Ujina SB, Hiroshima, Japan	1-11-69

AUXILIARY SHIPS (continued)

Wan Shou (512)   1970

D: 1,049 tons light (4,150 fl) **S:** 13 kts **Dim:** 86.5 × 16.5 × 5.5
A: 2/40-mm AA (I × 2)—2/20-mm AA (I × 2)
M: 1 diesel; 1 prop; 2,100 hp **Fuel:** 230 tons **Man:** 70 tot.

REMARKS: No underway-replenishment capability. Cargo: 2,600 tons.

♦ **3 ex-U.S. Patapsco-class support tankers** Bldr: Cargill Inc., Savage, Minn.

	Laid down	L	In serv.
378 CHANG PEI (ex-Pecatonica, AOG 57)	6-12-44	17-3-45	28-11-45
389 HSIN LUNG (ex-Elkhorn, AOG 7)	7-9-42	15-5-43	12-2-44
342 LUNG CHUAN (ex-Endeavor, ex-Namakagon, AOG 53)	1-8-44	4-11-44	10-5-45

D: 1,850 tons light (4,335 fl) **S:** 14 kts **Dim:** 94.72 (89.0 wl) × 14.78 × 4.78
A: 2/76.2-mm DP (I × 2)—4/20-mm AA (I × 4)
M: 2 GM 16-278A diesels; 2 props; 3,300 hp **Electric:** 460 kw
Fuel: 295 tons **Range:** 6,670/10 **Man:** 124 tot.

REMARKS: Former gasoline tankers. Cargo: 2,040 tons. *Chang Pei* transferred on 24-4-61, *Hsin Lung* on 1-7-72, and *Lung Chuan* on 29-6-71 after serving in the New Zealand Navy as Antarctic supply ship since 5-10-62. All used for supplying offshore islands. All purchased outright 19-5-76.

♦ **1 transport**

	Bldr	L	In serv.
522 LING YUEN	Taiwan SB, Keelung	27-1-75	15-8-75

D: 4,000 tons (fl) **S:** . . . **Dim:** 100.2 × 14.6 × 5.0
A: 2/20-mm AA (I × 2)—2/12.7-mm mg (I × 2)
M: 1 6-cylinder diesel; 1 prop; . . . hp **Man:** 55 tot.

REMARKS: 2,510 dwt/3,040 grt. Can carry 500 troops. There is also a slightly smaller Taiwanese-built transport, name not available.

♦ **1 ex-U.S. Achelous-class transport** Bldr: Kaiser Co., Vancouver, Wash.

	Laid down	L	In serv.
520 WU TAI (ex-Sung Shan, ex-Agenor, ARL 3, ex-LST 490)	24-1-43	3-4-43	20-8-43

D: 4,100 tons (fl) **S:** 11.6 kts **Dim:** 99.98 × 15.24 × 3.4
A: 8/40-mm AA (IV × 2) **M:** 2 GM 12-567A diesels; 2 props; 1,800 hp
Electric: 500 kw **Man:** 100 men + 600 troops

REMARKS: Converted to a repair ship while building. Transferred to France in 1951, then to Taiwan on 15-9-57. Converted to transport, 1973-74.

♦ **1 ex-U.S. Army 427-class small transport** Bldr: Higgins, New Orleans, La. (In serv. 21-12-44)

359 YUNG KANG (ex-*Mark*, AKL 12, ex-AG 143, ex-Army FS 214)

Yung Kang (359)—wearing old number   1971

D: 693 tons (899 fl) **S:** 12 kts **Dim:** 54.86 (52.37 wl) × 9.75 × 3.05
A: 2/20-mm AA (I × 2) **M:** 2 GM 6-278A diesels; 2 props; 1,000 hp
Electric: 225 kw **Fuel:** 100 tons **Range:** 4,000/11 **Man:** 37 tot.

REMARKS: Built as an aircraft maintenance ship for the U.S. Army Air Corps. Transferred to the U.S. Navy on 30-9-47 and to Taiwan on 1-6-71. Sold outright on 19-5-76. Now has intelligence-gathering equipment.

♦ **1 ex-U.S. Amphion-class repair ship** Bldr: Tampa SB, Tampa, Fla.

	Laid down	L	In serv.
358 TU TAI (ex-Cadmus, AR 14)	30-10-44	5-8-45	23-4-46

D: 7,826 tons light (14,490 fl) **S:** 16.5 kts
Dim: 149.96 (141.73 pp) × 21.18 × 8.38
A: 1/127-mm DP—6/40-mm AA (II × 3) **Man:** 920 tot.
M: 1 set Westinghouse GT; 1 prop; 8,500 hp **Electric:** 3,600 kw
Boilers: 2 Foster-Wheeler D-type; 30.6 kg/cm², 399°C **Fuel:** 2,430 tons

REMARKS: Transferred on 15-1-74.

♦ **1 ex-U.S. Diver-class salvage ship** Bldr: Basalt Rock Co., Napa, Cal.

	Laid down	L	In serv.
324 TAI HU (ex-Grapple, ARS 7)	8-9-42	31-12-42	16-12-43

D: 1,530 tons (1,900 fl) **S:** 14.8 kts **Dim:** 65.08 (63.09 wl) × 11.89 × 4.29
A: 2/20-mm AA (I × 2) **Electron Equipt:** Radar: 1/SPS-53
M: 4 Cooper-Bessemer GSB-8 diesels, electric drive; 2 props; 3,060 hp
Electric: 460 kw **Fuel:** 283 tons **Range:** 9,000/14; 20,000/7 **Man:** 85 tot.

REMARKS: Transferred on 1-12-77.

♦ **4 ex-U.S. Cherokee-, Abneki-* and Achomawi-**class fleet tugs**

Bldrs: *Ta Tung, Ta Wan:* United Eng., Alameda, Cal.; others: Charleston SB & DD, Charleston, S.C.

	Laid down	L	In serv.
542 TA HAN (ex-Tawakoni, ATF 114)*	19-5-43	28-10-43	15-9-44
548 TA TUNG (ex-Chickasaw, ATF 83)	14-2-42	23-7-42	4-2-43
550 TA WAN (ex-Apache, ATF 67)	8-11-44	8-5-42	12-12-42
. . .N. . . (ex Shakori, ATF 162)**			

AUXILIARY SHIPS (continued)

D: 1,235 tons (1,675 fl) **S:** 15 kts **Dim:** 62.48 (59.44 wl) × 11.73 × 4.67
A: 1/76.2-mm DP—2/12.7-mm mg
M: 4 GM 12-278 diesels, electric drive; 1 prop; 3,000 hp **Electric:** 260-400 kw
Fuel: 295 tons **Range:** 6,500/16; 15,000/8 **Man:** 85 tot.

REMARKS: *Ta Tung* transferred 1-66 (sold on 19-5-75), *Ta Wan* on 30-6-74, *Ta Han* on 1-6-78, and ex-ATF 162 on 29-8-80. *Ta Han* has Busch-Sulzer BS-539 diesels and only a small exhaust pipe, and ex-ATF 162 has GM 12-278A diesels.

◆ 3 ex-U.S. Sotoyomo-class ocean tugs Bldr: Levingston SB, Orange, Tex.

	Laid down	L	In serv.
395 TA PENG (ex-*Mohopac*, ATA 196)	24-11-44	21-12-44	6-3-45
357 TA SUEH (ex-*Tonkawa*, ATA 176)	30-1-44	1-3-44	19-8-44
367 TA TENG (ex-*Cahokia*, ATA 186)	16-8-44	18-9-44	24-11-44

D: 435 tons (835 fl) **S:** 13 kts **Dim:** 43.59 (40.74 wl) × 10.31 × 4.01
A: 1/76.2-mm DP—2/20-mm AA (I × 2)
M: 2 GM 12-278A diesels, electric drive; 1 prop; 1,500 hp
Electric: 120 kw **Fuel:** 158 tons **Man:** 45 tot.

REMARKS: *Ta Peng* transferred on 1-7-71, *Ta Sueh* in 4-62, and *Ta Teng* on 29-3-72 after serving the U.S. Air Force since 1971. Sister *Chiu Lien* is an oceanographic research ship.

SERVICE CRAFT

◆ 1 ex-U.S. 174-foot yard oiler Bldr: Manitowoc SB, Manitowoc, Wisc.

	Laid down	L	In serv.
504 SZU MING (ex-YO 198)	10-2-45	21-4-45	14-7-45

D: 650 tons (1,595 fl) **S:** 10.5 kts **Dim:** 53.04 × 9.75 × 4.10
A: 1/40-mm AA—5/20-mm AA (I × 5)
M: 1 Union diesel; 1 prop; 560 hp **Man:** 65 tot.

REMARKS: Transferred in 12-49. In reserve.

◆ 6 ex-U.S. Navy YTL 422 class

YTL 8 (ex-ST-2002)	YTL 10 (ex-ST-2008)	YTL 12 (ex-YTL 584)
YTL 9 (ex-ST-2004)	YTL 11 (ex-YTL 454)	YTL 14 (ex-YTL 585)

D: 70 tons (80 fl) **S:** 8 kts **Dim:** 20.3 × 5.18 × 2.4
M: 1 diesel; 1 prop; 375 hp

REMARKS: YTL 8 to YTL 10 transferred in 3-62, YTL 11 in 8-63, YTL 12 and YTL 14 in 7-64. First three are former U.S. Army units, built during World War II.

◆ 1 ex-U.S. ARD 12-class floating dry dock Bldr: Pacific Bridge, Alameda, Cal.

Fo Wu 6 (ex-*Windsor*, ARD 22)

Dim: 149.86 × 24.69 × 1.73 (light) **Capacity:** 3,500 tons

REMARKS: In service 4-44, transferred on 19-5-76; purchased 1981.

◆ 1 ex-U.S. ARD 2-class floating dry dock Bldr: Pacific Bridge, Alameda, Cal.

Fo Wu 5 (ex-ARD 9)

Dim: 148.03 × 21.64 × 1.75 (light) **Capacity:** 3,500 tons

REMARKS: In service 9-43, transferred on 12-1-77; purchased outright 1981.

◆ 2 ex-U.S. floating dry docks Bldr: V. P. Loftis, Wilmington, N.C.

HAY TAN (ex-AFDL 36)   HAN JIH (ex-AFDL 34)

Dim: 73.15 × 19.69 × 1.3 (light) **Capacity:** 1,000 tons

REMARKS: In service 5 and 6-44, transferred in 3-47 and 7-59.

◆ 1 ex-U.S. floating dry dock

KIM MEN (ex-AFDL 5)

Dim: 60.96 × 19.5 × 1.04 **Capacity:** 1,000 tons

REMARKS: Built in 1944, transferred in 1-48.

CUSTOMS SERVICE

Subordinate to the Ministry of Finance

PATROL SHIPS

◆ 2 ex-U.S. Admirable-class former minesweepers

	Bldr	L	In serv.
HUNG HSING (ex-*Embattle*, MSF 226)	American SB, Lorain, O.	17-9-44	25-4-45
N. . . (ex-*Improve*, MSF 247)	Savannah Mach., Ga.	26-9-43	29-2-44

D: 945 tons (fl) **S:** 14.8 kts **Dim:** 56.24 × 10.06 × 2.97
A: 2/20-mm AA **M:** 2 Cooper-Bessemer GSB-8 diesels; 2 props; 1,710 hp

REMARKS: Transferred to Taiwan in late 1940s and handed over to the Customs Service in early 1970s.

◆ 3 ex-U.S. PC 461-class submarine chasers

	Bldr	In serv.
N. . . (ex-*Tung Kiang*, ex-*Placerville*, PC 1087)	G. Lawley, Neponset, Mass.	22-5-44
N. . . (ex-*Hsi Kiang*, ex-*Susanville*, PC 1149)	Defoe, Bay City, Mich.	22-6-44
N. . . (ex-*Pei Kiang*, ex-*Hanford*, PC 1142)	Defoe, Bay City, Mich.	3-6-44

D: 280 tons (450 fl) **S:** 19 kts **Dim:** 52.93 × 7.01 × 2.72
A: 2/20-mm AA (I × 2) **M:** 2 GM 16-278A diesels; 2 props; 2,880 hp
Electric: 120 kw **Fuel:** 62 tons **Range:** 6,000/10

REMARKS: Transferred in 7-57 and turned over to the Customs Service in early 1970s.

PATROL CRAFT

◆ 3 aluminum-hulled Bldr: China SB, Kaohsiung

HAI PING (In serv. 28-2-79)	HAI AN (In serv. 18-3-79)
HAI CHENG (In serv. 1979)	

D: . . . **S:** . . . **Dim:** 26.0 × 5.6 × 2.7
A: . . . **M:** 2 MTU 8V331 TC81 diesels; 2 props; . . . hp

◆ 2 aluminum-hulled Bldr: Halter Marine, New Orleans (In serv. 1977)

D: 70 tons **S:** . . . **Dim:** 23.77 × . . . × . . . **A:** . . .
M: 2 GM diesels; 2 props; . . . hp

TANZANIA
United Republic of Tanzania

PERSONNEL (1980): Approximately 700 men

MERCHANT MARINE (1980): 32 ships—55,916 grt
(4 tankers—3,146 grt)

PATROL BOATS

♦ 4 modified North Korean Nampo class

D: 82 tons (fl) **S:** 40 kts **Dim:** 27.7 × 6.1 × 1.8
A: 4/14.5-mm mg (II × 2) **Electron Equipt:** Radar: 1/Pot Head
M: 4 M50-F diesels; 4 props; 4,800 hp **Range:** 375/40 **Man:** 19 tot.

REMARKS: Transferred 1979-81; lack of the bow ramp employed on the landing craft version used by North Korea.

♦ 7 Chinese Shanghai-II class

JW 9861 through JW 9867

JW 9862   1975

D: 122.5 tons (150 fl) **S:** 28.5 kts **Dim:** 38.78 × 5.41 × 1.49
A: 4/37-mm AA (II × 2)—4/25-mm AA (II × 2)
Electron Equipt: Radar: 1/Pot Head
M: 2 M50-F4, 1,200-hp diesels; 2 12D6, 910-hp diesels; 4 props; 4,220 hp
Man: 38 tot.

REMARKS: Transferred 1970-71.

TORPEDO BOATS

♦ 4 Chinese Huchuan class Bldr: Hudung SY, Shanghai

JW 9841 through JW 9844

D: 39 tons (fl) **S:** 54 kts **Dim:** 21.8 × 4.9 × 1.0
A: 4/14.5-mm mg (II × 2)—2/533-mm TT (I × 2)
Electron Equipt: Radar: 1/Skin Head
M: 3 M50 diesels; 3 props; 3,600 hp

REMARKS: Transferred 1975. Unlike Chinese Navy Huchuans, these craft have no hydrofoils. Gun mounts are fore and aft, while on most units of this class both mounts are aft.

JW 9842   1976

COASTAL PATROL CRAFT

♦ 3 Soviet P 6-class former torpedo boats

D: 62 tons (fl) **S:** 43 kts **Dim:** 25.3 × 6.1 × 1.6
A: 4/25-mm AA (II × 2) **Electron Equipt:** Radar: 1/Pot Head
M: 4 M50 diesels; 4 props; 4,800 hp **Range:** 400/32, 700/15 **Man:** 12 tot.

REMARKS: Transferred from East Germany in 1974-75. Torpedo tubes removed before transfer. Bridges enclosed. Wooden construction.

♦ 2 East German Schwalbe-class former inshore minesweepers

ARAKA   SALAAM

D: 70 tons (fl) **S:** 14 kts **Dim:** 26.0 × 4.5 × 1.4
A: 2/25-mm AA (II × 2) **M:** 2 diesels; 2 props; 600 hp

REMARKS: Transferred in 1-66 and 1-67. Minesweeping gear removed. No radar.

♦ 4 Chinese Yu Lin-class craft

D: 9.8 tons (fl) **S:** 25 kts **Dim:** 13.0 × 2.9 × 1.1
A: 2/12.7-mm mg (I × 2) **M:** 1 diesel; 1 prop; 300 hp

REMARKS: Transferred by the Chinese People's Republic in 11-66. These craft operate on Lake Victoria.

♦ 2 aluminum-hulled craft Bldr: Bayerische Schiffsbau, West Germany, 1967

RAFIKI   UHURU

D: 40 tons (fl) **S:** 14 kts **Dim:** 24.0 × 5.0 × 1.3
A: 1/40-mm AA—2/mg **M:** 2 Caterpillar diesels; 2 props;. . . hp

♦ 1 Soviet Poluchat-1 class

D: 90 tons (fl) **S:** 19 kts **Dim:** 29.6 × 5.8 × 1.6
A: 2/14.5-mm AA **Electron Equipt:** Radar: 1/Skin Head
M: 2 M50 diesels; 2 props; 2,400 hp **Range:** 460/17 **Man:** 15 tot.

REMARKS: May be of the torpedo retriever variant, armed. Transferred sometime in the 1970s.

HYDROGRAPHIC SHIPS

♦ 1 coastal survey craft Bldr: Bayerische Schiffsbau, West Germany (In serv. 1979)

UTAFITI

TANZANIA (*continued*)
HYDROGRAPHIC SHIPS (*continued*)

D: 33 tons (fl)   **S:** 14 kts   **Dim:** 19.05 × . . . × 1.0
Electron Equipt: Radar: 1/Decca 060
M: 2 Caterpillar diesels; 2 props; 456 hp   **Range:** 250/12   **Man:** 6 tot.

REMARKS: Has Atlas DESO 10 echo-sounder. Steel hull, aluminum superstructure.

♦ **2 ex-Chinese landing craft for logistics duties.**

THAILAND
Kingdom of Thailand

PERSONNEL (1981): Navy: approximately 13,000 total—Marines: 7,000 total

MERCHANT MARINE (1980): 153 ships—391,456 grt
(tankers: 47 ships—134,410 grt)

NAVAL AVIATION: Available are: 9 Grumman S-2F land-based ASW aircraft, 2 HU-16 amphibians, 20 C-46 and C-47 transports, 10 Cessna 0-1 Bird Dog observation aircraft, 14 U-17 Skywagon utility aircraft, 2 Lake L-A4 Skimmer training amphibians, and 3 Bell UH-1H and 10 Bell 212 helicopters.

FRIGATES

♦ **1 "Yarrow frigate" class** Bldr: Yarrow, Scotstoun, Glasgow, Scotland

	Laid down	L	In serv.
7 MAKUT RAJAKUMARN	11-1-70	18-11-71	7-5-73

Makut Rajakumarn (7)   Yarrow, 1975

D: 1,650 tons (1,900 fl)   **S:** 26 kts (gas turbine)/18 kts (diesel)
Dim: 97.56 (92.99 pp) × 10.97 × 5.5
A: 2/114-mm DP Mk 8—1/Sea Cat Mk 10 SAM (IV × 1)—2/40-mm AA (I × 2)—1/Limbo ASW mortar (III × 1)—2/d.c. projectors, 1/d.c. rack
Electron Equipt: Radar: 1/Decca 626, 1/HSA LW-04, 1/HSA WM 22, 1/HSA WM 44
Sonar: 1/170B, 1/162, 1/Plessey MS27
M: CODOG: 1 Rolls-Royce Olympus TBM 3B gas turbine (23,125 hp), 1 Crossley-Pielstick 12 PC2 diesel; 2 CP props; 6,000 hp
Electric: 2,200 kw   **Range:** 1,000/25; 4,000/18   **Man:** 16 officers, 124 men

REMARKS: Similar to the Malaysian *Rahmat* but longer and more heavily armed. Highly automated. The WM 22 track-while-scan radar controls the 114-mm guns; the WM 44 system controls the Sea Cat missiles.

♦ **2 ex-U.S. PF 103 class**

	Bldr	Laid down	L	In serv.
5 TAPI (ex-PF 107)	American SB, Toledo, Oh.	1-4-70	17-10-70	1-11-71
6 KHIRIRAT (ex-PF 108)	Norfolk SB & DD, Va.	18-2-72	2-6-73	10-8-74

Tapi (5)   1978

Khirirat (6)   1977

D: 864 tons light (1,143 fl)   **S:** 20 kts   **Dim:** 84.04 × 10.06 × 3.05 (4.27 sonar)
A: 2/76.2-mm DP Mk 34 (I × 2)—2/40-mm AA (II × 1)—2/12.7-mm mg (I × 2)—1/Mk 11 Hedgehog—6/324-mm Mk 32 ASW TT (III × 2)—1/Mk 9 d.c. rack
Electron Equipt: Radar: 1/Raytheon navigational, 1/SPS-6, 1/SPG-34
Sonar: 1/SQS-17A

FRIGATES (continued)

M: 2 Fairbanks-Morse 38D8⅛-10 diesels; 2 props; 5,300 hp   **Electric:** 750 kw
Fuel: 110 tons   **Range:** 2,400/18   **Man:** 15 officers, 135 men

REMARKS: Patterned after the Italian-built *Pattimura* class for Indonesia; four sisters
in the Iranian Navy. Mk 63 radar GFCS forward for 76.2-mm guns (radar on forward
gun mount); Mk 51 mod. 2 GFCS aft for the 40-mm antiaircraft. Transferred on
completion.

♦ **1 ex-U.S. Cannon class** Bldr: Western Pipe and Steel, Los Angeles

	Laid down	L	In serv.
3 PIN KLAO (ex-*Hemminger*, DE 746)	8-5-43	27-12-43	30-5-44

Pin Klao (3)   1980

D: 1,240 tons (fl)   **S:** 20 kts   **Dim:** 93.27 (91.44 wl) × 11.15 × 4.3 (sonar)
A: 3/76.2-mm DP Mk 22 (I × 3)—6/40-mm AA (II × 3)—2/12.7-mm mg (I ×
2)—1/Mk 10 Hedgehog—6/324-mm Mk 32 ASW TT (III × 2)—8/Mk 6 d.c.
projectors—2/Mk 9 d.c. racks
Electron Equipt: Radar: 2/navigational, 1/SC-2, 1/Mk 26, 1/Mk 34
           Sonar: . . .
           ECM: WLR-1
M: 2 GM 16-278A diesels, electric drive; 2 props; 6,000 hp   **Electric:** 680 kw
Fuel: 260 tons   **Range:** 11,500/11   **Man:** 220 tot.

REMARKS: Transferred 7-59; sold outright 6-6-75, at which time the ship underwent
extensive overhaul in Guam. Has Mk 52 radar GFCS for 76.2-mm guns, one Mk 63
radar GFCS and two Mk 51 mod. 2 optical GFCS for the 40-mm guns.

♦ **2 ex-U.S. Tacoma class** Bldr: Consolidated Steel, Los Angeles

	Laid down	L	In serv.
1 TAHCHIN (ex-*Glendale*, PF 36)	6-4-43	28-5-43	1-10-43
2 PRASAE (ex-*Gallup*, PF 47)	18-8-43	17-9-43	29-2-44

Tahchin   1977

D: 1,430 tons (2,100 fl)   **S:** 19 kts   **Dim:** 92.63 (87.02 pp) × 11.43 × 4.17 (hull)
A: 3/76.2-mm DP (I × 3)—2/40-mm AA (I × 2)—9/20-mm AA (I × 9)—1/Mk 10
Hedgehog—2/324-mm Mk 32 ASW TT (I × 2)—8/Mk 6 d.c. projectors—2/Mk
9 d.c. racks
Electron Equipt: Radar: 1/SPS-5, 1/SPS-6   Sonar: QCU
M: 2 sets triple-expansion steam; 2 props; 5,500 hp   **Range:** 5,600/16; 7,800/12
Boilers: 2, 3-drawn Express; 16.9 kg/cm²   **Fuel:** 685 tons   **Man:** 180 tot.

REMARKS: Transferred 29-10-57. Both refitted at Guam in the early 1970s. Last "active" examples of a class that once numbered 100 ships.

GUIDED-MISSILE PATROL BOATS

♦ **3 Ratcharit class** Bldr: Breda, Venice, Italy

	L	In serv.
4 RATCHARIT	30-7-78	10-8-79
5 WITTHAYAKOM	2-9-78	12-11-79
6 UDOMET	28-9-78	21-2-80

Ratcharit (4)   French Navy, 1980

GUIDED-MISSILE PATROL BOATS (*continued*)

D: 235 tons light (270 fl) **S:** 36 kts **Dim:** 49.8 (47.25 pp) × 7.5 × 1.68
A: 4/MM 38 Exocet (II × 2)—1/76-mm DP OTO Melara—1/40-mm AA Breda
Electron Equipt: Radar: 1/navigational, 1/HSA M 25
M: 3 MTU MD20 V538 TB91 diesels; 3 CP props; 13,500 hp
Electric: 440 kw **Range:** 650/36; 2,000/15 **Man:** 7 officers, 38 men

REMARKS: Ordered 23-7-76. Can make 20 kts on two engines.

♦ **3 Prabrarapak class** Bldr: Singapore SB & Eng. Co., Jurong, Singapore

	L	In serv.
1 PRABRARAPAK	29-7-75	28-7-76
2 HANHAK SATTRU	28-10-75	6-11-76
3 SUPHAIRIN	20-2-76	1-2-77

D: 224 tons (260 fl) **S:** 41 kts **Dim:** 44.9 × 7.0 × 2.1 (2.46 props)
A: 5/Gabriel (III × 1, I × 2)—1/57-mm Bofors AA—1/40-mm Bofors AA
Electron Equipt: Radar: 1/Decca TM 626, 1/HSA WM 28
ECM: passive intercept system
M: 4 MTU 16V538 TB92 diesels; 4 props; 14,000 hp **Electric:** 405 kVA
Range: 500/38.5; 1,500/16 **Man:** 40 tot.

REMARKS: Similar to the Singapore Navy's Lürssen-designed boats; built under license. 103-mm rocket flare launch rails are mounted on the 57-mm mount.

PATROL BOATS

♦ **2 MV 400TH design** Bldr: Breda, Venice, Italy

	L	In serv.
. . . N . . .	. . .	6-83
. . . N . . .	. . .	6-85

D: 400 tons (450 fl) **S:** 30 kts **Dim:** 60.40 × 8.80 × 1.95
A: 2/76-mm OTO Melara DP—2/40-mm Breda AA (II × 1)
Electron Equipt: Radar: 1/3RM-series navigational, 1/HSA WM 22/61
ECM: passive intercept, 4/Hycor Mk 135 chaff RL
M: 3 MTU 20V538 diesels; 3 CP props; 15,000 hp (12,600 sust.)
Electric: 800 kw **Range:** 900/29; 3,000/16 **Man:** 7 officers, 38 men

REMARKS: Ordered 11-79, originally for delivery in 1982, but this has reportedly slipped considerably. Will be able to accommodate anti-ship missiles, but none were to be installed at delivery. Steel hull, aluminum-alloy superstructure. Will have LIROD-8 electro-optical GFCS to back up the WM 22/61 system.

♦

♦ **4 T 91 class** Bldr: Royal Thai Naval Dockyard, Bangkok

T 91 (L: 1965) T 92 (L: 1973) T 93 (L: 1973) T 94 (In serv. 16-9-81)

D: 87.5 tons **S:** 25 kts **Dim:** 31.8 × 5.36 × 1.5
A: 2/40-mm AA—1/12.7-mm mg **M:** 2 MTU diesels; 2 props; 3,300 hp
Range: 770/21 **Man:** 21 tot.

REMARKS: T 93 reported 36.0 × 5.7 × 1.7. T 91 has a longer superstructure and no spray strakes on the hull sides forward, and only one 40-mm AA gun. T 94 may differ in detail, having been built so much later than the others.

T 92 G. Arra, 1976

♦ **10 ex-U.S. PGM 71 class** Bldr: Peterson Builders, Sturgeon Bay, Wis.

	L	In serv.		L	In serv.
T 11 (ex-PGM 71)	22-5-65	1-2-66	T 16 (ex-PGM 115)	24-4-69	12-2-70
T 12 (ex-PGM 79)	18-12-65	1967	T 17 (ex-PGM 116)	3-6-69	12-2-70
T 13 (ex-PGM 107)	13-4-67	28-8-67	T 18 (ex-PGM 117)	24-6-69	12-2-70
T 14 (ex-PGM 113)	3-6-69	18-8-69	T 19 (ex-PGM 123)	4-5-70	25-12-70
T 15 (ex-PGM 114)	24-6-69	18-8-69	T 20 (ex-PGM 124)	22-6-70	10-70

T 11 G. Arra, 1967

D: 130 tons (144 fl) **S:** 17 kts **Dim:** 30.81 × 6.45 × 2.3
A: 1/40-mm AA—4/20-mm AA (II × 2)—2/12.7-mm mg (I × 2)
M: 8 GM 6-71 diesels; 2 props; 2,040 hp **Range:** 1,000/12 **Man:** 30 tot.

REMARKS: An over-and-under 81-mm mortar/12.7-mm mounting has replaced the 20-mm AA gun on the fantail in T 14 and several others.

PATROL BOATS (continued)

NOTE: The Thai-built torpedo boat *Sattahip* (8) was stricken in 1979.

♦ **4 ex-U.S.C.G. Cape class** Bldr: U.S. Coast Guard, Curtis Bay, Md. (In serv. 1953)

T 81 (ex-CG 13) T 82 (ex-CG 14) T 83 (ex-CG 15) T 84 (ex-CG 16)

T 84—with old number   1967

  D: 105 tons (fl) **S:** 18 kts **Dim:** 28.95 × 5.8 × 1.55
  A: 1/20-mm AA—2/Mk 20 Mousetrap ASW RL—2/d.c. racks
  Electron Equipt: Radar: 1/SPN-21
                 Sonar: QCU
  M: 4 Cummins VT-12-M-700 diesels; 2 props; 2,200 hp **Electric:** 40 kw
  Fuel: 12 tons **Range:** 2,600/9 **Man:** 15 tot.

REMARKS: Transferred in 1954.

♦ **7 ex-U.S. PC 461 class**

	Bldr	L	In serv.
1 SARASIN (ex-PC 495)	Dravo, Pittsburgh	30-12-41	23-4-42
2 THAYANCHON (ex-PC 575)	Dravo, Pittsburgh	5-5-42	8-8-42
4 PHALI (ex-PC 1185)	Gibbs, Jacksonville, Fla.	27-8-43	24-4-44
5 SUKRIP (ex-PC 1218)	Luders, Stamford, Conn.	24-10-43	29-5-44
6 TONGPLIU (ex-PC 616)	G. Lawley, Neponset, Mass.	4-7-42	19-8-42
7 LIULOM (ex-PC 1253)	Brown, Houston, Tex.	14-10-42	1-4-43
8 LONGLOM (ex-PC 570)	Albina, Portland, Ore.	11-9-41	9-5-42

Tongpliu (6)—outboard **Thayanchon**

  D: 280 tons (450 fl) **S:** 19 kts **Dim:** 52.93 × 7.01 × 2.31 (3.31 sonar)
  A: 1/76.2-mm DP—1/40-mm AA—5/20-mm AA (I × 5)—2/324-mm Mk 32 ASW
    TT (I × 2)—2/Mk 6 d.c. projectors—2 d.c. racks
  M: 2 Hoover, Owens, & Rentschler RB-99DA diesels; 2 props; 2,560 hp
  Electric: 120 kw **Fuel:** 60 tons **Range:** 6,000/10 **Man:** 62-71 tot.

REMARKS: In poor condition. Transferred 1947-52. The *Sarasin* does not have the two fixed ASW torpedo tubes. The *Tongpliu*, the *Liulom*, and the *Longlom* have two Fairbanks-Morse 38D8⅛ diesels; 2,880 hp.

PATROL CRAFT

♦ **12 new construction** Bldr: Ital-Thai Development Co., Bangkok (In serv. 1980-81)

T 213 through T 224

  D: 34 tons (fl) **S:** 22 kts (18 sust.) **Dim:** 19.8 × 5.3 × 1.5
  A: 1/20-mm AA—1/81-mm mortar/12.7-mm mg combination
  M: 2 MTU diesels; 2 props; 1,300 hp **Man:** 1 officer, 7 men

REMARKS: First three in service 29-8-80, last five on 16-9-81. Aluminum construction. Intended for fisheries protection duties.

♦ **12 ex-U.S. Swift Mk II-class inshore patrol craft** Bldr: Swiftships, Morgan City, La.

T 27 through T 35   T 210 through T 212

  D: 22.5 tons (fl) **S:** 25 kts **Dim:** 15.64 × 4.14 × 1.06
  A: 3/12.7-mm mg (II × 1, and 1 combined with an 81-mm mortar)
  Electron Equipt: Radar: 1/Raytheon 1500B
  M: 2 GM 12V71 N diesels; 2 props; 860 hp
  Range: 400/24 **Man:** 1 officer, 7 men

REMARKS: Transferred 1967-75.

♦ **37 ex-U.S. PBR Mk II river patrol boats**

  D: 8 tons (fl) **S:** 24 kts **Dim:** 9.73 × 3.53 × 0.6
  A: 3/12.7-mm mg (II × 1, I × 1)—1/60-mm mortar
  M: 2 Detroit 6V53 N diesels; 2 Jacuzzi waterjets; 430 hp
  Range: 150/23 **Man:** 4 tot.

REMARKS: Transferred: 20 in 1966-67; 10 in 1972; 7 in . . . .

♦ **3 ex-U.S. 36-foot RPC class**

T 21 T 22 T 23

  D: 10.4 tons (13 fl) **S:** 14 kts **Dim:** 10.9 × 3.15 × 1.0
  A: 4/12.7-mm mg (II × 2)—2/7.62-mm mg (I × 2)
  M: 2 Gray Marine 64 HN9 diesels; 2 props; 450 hp **Man:** 6 tot.

REMARKS: Transferred 3-67. Survivors of six. Unsuccessful design, supplanted by PBR in the U.S. Navy.

MINE WARFARE SHIPS

♦ **1 mine countermeasures support ships**

	Bldr	L	In serv.
1 THALANG	Bangkok Naval DY	. . .	25-6-80

MINE WARFARE SHIPS (continued)

D: 1,000 tons (fl) **S:** 12 kts **Dim:** 55.7 × 10.0 × 3.1
A: 1/40-mm AA—2/20-mm AA (I × 2)—2/12.7-mm mg (I × 2)—mines
Electron Equipt: Radar: 1/Decca TM 1226
M: 2 MTU diesels; 2 props; 1,310 hp **Man:** 77 tot.

REMARKS: Replaces *Rang Kwien* (11), stricken 1979. Designed by Ferostaal, Essen, Germany. Has two 3-ton cranes and carries four sets of spare mine countermeasures equipment for transfer to minesweepers.

NOTE: The 1936-vintage minelayers *Bangrachan* (1) and *Nhong Sarhai* (2) were stricken 1980.

♦ 4 ex-U.S. MSC 289-class minesweepers

	Bldr	In serv.
5 LADYA (ex-MSC 297)	Peterson, Sturgeon Bay, Wis.	14-12-63
6 BANGKEO (ex-MSC 303)	Dorchester SB, Camden, N.J.	9-7-65
7 TADINDENG (ex-MSC 301)	Tacoma Boat, Wash.	23-8-65
8 DON CHEDI (ex-MSC 313)	Peterson, Sturgeon Bay, Wis.	17-9-65

Bangkeo (6)   1967

D: 330 tons (362 fl) **S:** 13 kts **Dim:** 44.32 × 8.29 × 2.6
A: 2/20-mm AA (II × 1)
Electron Equipt: Radar: 1/Decca 707
  Sonar: UQS-1D
M: 4 GM 6-71 diesels; 2 props; 1,000 hp (880 sust.)
Range: 2,500/10 **Man:** 7 officers, 36 men

REMARKS: Transferred on completion. Wooden construction. Four new minesweepers are projected.

♦ 5 ex-U.S. 50-foot motor-launch minesweepers

MLMS 6 to MLMS 10

D: 21 tons (fl) **S:** 8 kts **Dim:** 15.29 × 4.01 × 1.31
A: Small arms only **M:** 1 Navy DB diesel; 1 prop; 50 hp
Range: 150/8 **Man:** 6 tot.

REMARKS: Transferred 1963-66. Wooden-hulled former personnel launches, converted before transfer.

NOTE: The smaller MLMS 1 through MLMS 5 were stricken 1980.

AMPHIBIOUS WARFARE SHIPS

♦ 4 ex-U.S. LST 542-class tank-landing ships

	Bldr	L	In serv
2 CHANG (ex-*Lincoln Cty.*, LST 898)	Dravo, Pittsburgh	25-11-44	29-12-44
3 PANGAN (ex-*Stark Cty.*, LST 1134)	Chicago Br. & Iron, Ind.	16-3-45	7-4-45
4 LANTA (ex-*Stone Cty.*, LST 1141)	Chicago Br. & Iron, Ind.	18-4-45	9-5-45
5 PRATHONG (ex-*Dodge Cty.*, LST 722)	Jeffersonville Br. & Mach. Co., Ind.	21-8-44	13-9-44

D: 1,625 tons (4,080 fl) **S:** 11 kts **Dim:** 99.98 × 15.24 × 4.36
A: 8/40-mm AA (II × 2, I × 4) **Cargo Capacity:** 2,100 tons
M: 2 GM 12-567A diesels; 1,700 hp

REMARKS: The *Chang* was transferred in 8-62, the *Pangan* in 5-66, the *Lanta* on 12-3-70, and the *Prathong* on 17-12-75. The *Chang* has a reinforced bow and waterline, originally intended for arctic navigation.

♦ 3 ex-U.S. LSM 1-class medium landing ships

Bldrs: Pullman Standard Car Mfg. Co., Chicago (3: Brown SB, Houston, Tex.)

	Laid down	L	In serv.
1 KUT (ex-LSM 338)	17-8-44	5-12-44	10-1-45
2 PHAI (ex-LSM 333)	13-7-44	27-10-44	25-11-44
3 KRAM (ex-LSM 469)	27-1-45	17-2-45	17-3-45

Kram (3)   1967

D: 743 tons (1,095 fl) **S:** 12.5 kts **Dim:** 62.03 × 10.52 × 2.54
A: 2/40-mm AA (II × 1) (1, 2: 1/40-mm AA)—4/20-mm AA (I × 4)
Electron Equipt: Radar: 1/Raytheon 1500B Pathfinder (3: 1/SPS-5)
M: 2 Fairbanks-Morse 38D8⅛ diesels; 2 props; 2,800 hp
Range: 2,500/12 **Man:** 55 tot.

REMARKS: The *Kut* and the *Phai* were transferred in 10-46, the *Kram* on 25-5-62. The *Kram* has a Mk 51 mod. 2 optical lead-computing director for the 40-mm guns.

♦ 1 ex-U.S. LCI(M) 351-class infantry-landing ship Bldr: Commercial Iron Works, Portland, Ore.

	Laid down	L	In serv.
2 SATAKUT (ex-LSIM 739)	30-1-44	27-2-44	6-3-44

AMPHIBIOUS WARFARE SHIPS (continued)

Satakut (2)　　　　　　　　　　　　　　　　　　G. Arra, 1980

D: 231 tons (381 fl)　**S:** 14 kts　**Dim:** 48.46 × 7.21 × 1.73
A: 1/40-mm AA—4/20-mm AA (I × 4)
Electron Equipt: Radar: 1/Raytheon 1500B
M: 8 GM 6-71 diesels; 2 CP props; 1,320 hp
Electric: 40 kw　**Fuel:** 113 tons　**Man:** 53 tot.

REMARKS: Originally one of 60 LCIL (later LSIL) converted to carry three 107-mm chemical mortars, removed before transfer in 5-47. Now used as personnel-landing craft. Sister *Prab* (ex-LCI(M) 739) exists as a hulk.

◆ **1 ex-U.S. LSSL 1-class support-landing craft** Bldr: Commercial Iron Works, Portland, Ore.

	Laid down	L	In serv
3 NAKHA (ex-*Himiwari*, ex-LSSL 102)	13-1-45	3-2-45	17-2-45

D: 233 tons (387 fl)　**S:** 14 kts　**Dim:** 48.16 × 10.52 × 2.54
A: 1/76.2-mm DP Mk 22—4/40-mm AA (II × 2)—4/20-mm AA (I × 4)—4/12.7-mm mg (I × 4)—4/81-mm mortars (I × 4)
Electron Equipt: Radar: 1/Raytheon 1500B Pathfinder
M: 8 GM 6-71 diesels; 2 CP props; 1,320 hp
Electric: 120 kw　**Fuel:** 84 tons

REMARKS: Transferred to Japan in 7-59 and to Thailand in 10-66 on return to U.S. control. Used mainly as a tender to small patrol craft.

◆ **4 new construction utility landing craft** Bldr: Bangkok Naval DY

. . . .

D: 200 tons (375 fl)　**S:** 12 kts　**Dim:** 41.0 × 8.8 × 1.9
A: 1/20-mm AA—1/12.7-mm mg
M: 2 diesels; 2 props;. . . hp　**Range:** 1,200/10　**Man:** 32 tot.

REMARKS: First unit laid down 1980.

◆ **6 ex-U.S. LCU 501-class utility-landing craft**

	Bldr	L	In serv.
1 MATAPHON (ex-LCU 1260)	Quincy Barge, Ill.	29-7-44	8-9-44
2 RAWI (ex-LCU 800)	Mt. Vernon Br. Co., Oh.	14-6-44	16-6-44
3 ADANG (ex-LCU 861)	Darby, Kansas City, Kans.	15-2-44	22-2-44
4 PHE TRA (ex-LCU 1089)	Quincy Barge, Ill.	10-5-44	20-6-44
5 KOLUM (ex-LCU 904)	Missouri Valley, Kans.	13-5-44	17-5-44
6 TALIBONG (ex-LCU 753)	Quincy Barge, Ill.	30-3-44	10-5-44

Phe Tra (4)　　　　　　　　　　　　　　　　　　G. Arra, 1980

D: 134 tons (309 fl)　**S:** 10 kts　**Dim:** 36.3 × 9.96 × 1.14
A: 4/20-mm AA (II × 2)　**M:** 3 GM 6-71 diesels; 3 props; 675 hp
Fuel: 10.5 tons　**Range:** 1,200/7　**Man:** 10 tot.

REMARKS: Transferred 10-46 to 11-47. Used as logistics transports on the Chao Phraya river. Cargo: 150 tons.

◆ **25 ex-U.S. LCM(6)-class landing craft**

D: 24 tons (56 fl)　**S:** 9 kts　**Dim:** 17.11 × 4.27 × 1.17
M: 2 Gray Marine 64 HN 9 diesels; 2 props; 330 hp
Range: 130/9　**Man:** 5 tot.

REMARKS: Transferred 2-65 to 4-69. Cargo capacity: 34 tons.

◆ **8 ex-U.S. LCVP-class landing craft**

D: 12 tons (fl)　**S:** 9 kts　**Dim:** 10.9 × 3.21 × 1.04
M: 1 Gray Marine 64 HN 9 diesel; 1 prop; 225 hp
Range: 110/9　　**Cargo Capacity:** 39 troops

REMARKS: Transferred 3-63. Eight LCVPs are carried aboard the four Thai LSTs.

◆ **1 personnel-landing craft** Bldr: Royal Thai Navy Dockyard, Bangkok, 11-68

D: 10 tons (fl)　**S:** 25 kts　**Dim:** 12.0 × 3.0 × 1.0
M: 2 Chrysler diesels; 2 Castoldi model 6 waterjets;. . . hp
Cargo Capacity: 35 troops

REMARKS: Built with U.S. aid. Glass-reinforced plastic construction. Additional units may have been constructed.

HYDROGRAPHIC SHIPS

♦ **1 new construction** Bldr: Bangkok Navy DY

	Laid down	L	In serv.
. . . SUK	27-8-79	. . .	16-9-81

D: 1,400 tons **S:** 15 kts **Dim:** 62.9 × . . . × . . .
A: 4/20-mm AA (I × 4) **M:** Diesels **Man:** . . .

♦ **1 navigational buoy tender** Bldr: Royal Thai Naval DY, Bangkok (In serv. 18-1-79)

. . . SURIYA

D: 690 tons light (960 fl) **S:** 12 kts **Dim:** 54.2 (47.3 pp) × 10.0 × 3.0
A: 2/20-mm AA (I × 2) **M:** 2 MTU diesels; 1 prop; 1,310 hp
Electric: 300 kw **Cargo capacity:** 270 tons **Range:** 3,000/12
Man: 14 officers, 46 men

REMARKS: One 10-ton crane.

♦ **1 oceanographic ship** Bldr: C. Melchers, Bremen, W. Germany

	Laid down	L	In serv.
11 CHANDHARA	27-9-60	17-12-60	1961

Chandhara (11) 1966

D: 870 tons (997 fl) **S:** 13 kts **Dim:** 70.0 (61.0 pp) × 10.5 × 3.0
A: 1/40-mm AA—1/20-mm AA **M:** 2 Deutz diesels; 2 props; 1,000 hp
Range: 10,000/12 **Man:** 72 tot.

REMARKS: Built as a training ship.

♦ **2 inshore survey craft** Bldr: Lürssen, Vegesack, West Germany, 1956

D: 96 tons (fl) **S:** 12 kts **Dim:** 29.0 × 5.5 × 1.5
M: 2 diesels; 2 props; . . . hp **Man:** 8 tot.

AUXILIARIES

♦ **1 small underway replenishment oiler**

	Bldr	L	In serv.
2 CHULA	Singapore SY & Eng.	24-9-80	1981

D: 2,000 tons (fl) **S:** 14 kts **Dim:** 67.0 × 9.5 × 4.35
A: . . . **M:** 2 MTU 12V396 TC62 diesels; 2 props; 2,400 hp
Man: 7 officers, 32 men

REMARKS: 960 dwt. Cargo: 800 tons, transferred by means of an electrohydraulic boom supporting the hose.

NOTE: The ex-Japanese tanker *Matra* (3) has been discarded.

♦ **1 personnel and cargo transport** Bldr: Ishikawajima, Harima, Japan

	L	In serv.
1 SICHANG	10-11-37	1-38

Sichang (1) 1978

D: 815 tons (1,369 fl) **S:** 15 kts **Dim:** 48.77 × 8.54 × 4.9
A: 2/40-mm AA (I × 2)—1/20-mm AA
Electron Equipt: Radar: 1/Raytheon 1500B
M: 2 diesels; 2 props; 550 hp **Man:** 66 tot.

TRAINING SHIPS

♦ **1 ex-British Algerine-class former fleet minesweeper**

Bldr: Redfern Const. Co., Toronto, Canada

	Laid down	L	In serv.
1 PHOSAMTON (ex-*Minstrel*)	27-6-44	5-10-44	9-6-45

Phosamton (1) 1981

D: 1,010 tons (1,300 fl) **S:** 16 kts **Dim:** 68.58 × 10.82 × 3.28
A: 1/102-mm DP—1/40-mm AA—6/20-mm AA (II × 2, I × 2)
Electron Equipt: Radar: 1/Raytheon 1500B Pathfinder
M: 2 sets triple-expansion steam; 2 props; 2,400 hp **Boilers:** 2, 3-drum
Fuel: 235 tons **Range:** 10,000/10 **Man:** 103 tot.

REMARKS: Transferred 4-47. Mechanical minesweeping equipment removed, replaced by a deckhouse to increase accommodations.

TRAINING SHIPS *(continued)*

♦ **1 ex-British modified flower-class corvette**

Bldr: Ferguson Bros., Port Glasgow, Scotland

	Laid down	L	In serv.
4 BANGPAKONG (ex-*Burnet*, ex-*Gondwana*)	2-11-42	31-5-43	23-9-43

Bangpakong (4)   1967

D: 980 tons (1,350 fl)   **S:** 16.5 kts   **Dim:** 63.48 × 10.11 × 5.14 (aft)
A: 1/76.2-mm DP—1/40-mm AA—6/20-mm AA (I × 6)—4/d.c. throwers—2/d.c. racks
Electron Equipt: Radar: 1/SG-1
M: 1 set triple-expansion reciprocating steam; 1 prop; 2,750 hp
Boilers: 2, 3-drum   **Fuel:** 337 tons   **Range:** 4,500/14; 7,400/10   **Man:** 100 tot.

REMARKS: Built for the British Navy; loaned to the Indian Navy on completion and returned in 1945; transferred to Thailand 15-5-47. Now mainly immobile.

♦ **1 Tachin-class former frigate** Bldr: Uraga Dockyard, Japan

	Laid down	L	In serv.
4 MAEKLONG	24-7-36	27-11-36	6-37

D: 1,400 tons (2,000 fl)   **S:** 14 kts   **Dim:** 112.5 × 10.5 × 3.2
A: 4/76.2-mm U.S. Mk 22 DP (I × 4)—3/40-mm AA (I × 3)—3/20-mm AA (I × 3)—mines
M: 2 sets triple-expansion reciprocating steam; 2 props; 2,500 hp
Boilers: 2, watertube   **Fuel:** 487 tons   **Range:** 8,000/12   **Man:** 155 tot.

REMARKS: Sister *Tachin* bombed in 1945 and discarded circa 1950. Formerly carried four 102-mm guns (replaced in 1974) and four 450-mm torpedo tubes (II × 2).

♦ **2 Proet-class harbor oilers** Bldr: Royal Thai Navy DY, Bangkok

	In serv.		In serv.
9 PROET	16-1-70	11 SAMED	15-12-70

D: 360 tons (465 fl)   **S:** 9 kts   **Dim:** 39.0 (36.6 pp) × 6.1 × 3.1
A: 2/20-mm AA (I × 2)   **M:** 1 diesel; 500 hp

Samed (11)—while fitting out   1967

♦ **1 provisions transport** Bldr:. . .

7 KLED KEO

Kled Keo (7)   1967

D: 382 tons (450 fl)   **S:** 12 kts   **Dim:** 46.0 × 7.6 × 4.3
A: 3/20-mm AA (I × 3)   **M:** 1 diesel; 600 hp   **Man:** 54 tot.

REMARKS: Former trawler. Acquired in 1967.

♦ **2 Charn-class water tankers** Bldr: Bangkok Naval DY

	L		
6 CHARN	1965	8 CHUANG	14-1-65

D: 355 tons (485 fl)   **S:** 11 kts   **Dim:** 42.0 × 7.5 × 3.1
A: 1/20-mm AA   **M:** 1 GM diesel; 500 hp   **Man:** 29 tot.

REMARKS: Details may apply only to *Charn; Chuang* appears to be smaller and has a cruiser, vice counter, stern.

♦ **2 Rang-class coastal tugs** Bldr: Singapore SB & Eng. (In serv. 9-80)

. . . RANG (L: 6-80)   . . . RIN (L: 6-80)

D: 250 tons (300 fl)   **S:** 12 kts   **Dim:** 32.3 × 9.0 × . . .
M: 1 MWM TBD 441V/12K diesel; 1 prop; 2,100 hp
Electric: 233 kw   **Range:** 1,000/10   **Man:** 16 tot.

REMARKS: Bollard pull: 22 tons.

THAILAND *(continued)*
TRAINING SHIPS *(continued)*

Charn (6)   G. Arra, 1980

♦ **1 ex-British coastal tug** Bldr: Cochrane & Sons, Selby, England (In serv. 1944)

1 SAMAE SAN (ex-*Empire Vincent*)

    D: 274 grt (503 fl)   **S:** 10.5 kts   **Dim:** 34.14 (32.0 pp) × 8.23 × 4.0
    A: . . .   **M:** 1 set triple-expansion reciprocating steam; 1 prop; 850 hp
    Boilers: 2, watertube   **Man:** 27 tot.

REMARKS: Acquired in 1947.

♦ **2 ex-Canadian small harbor tugs** Bldr: Central Bridge Co., Trenton, Ontario
  (In serv. 1943-44)

2 KLUENG BADEN   3 MARIN VICHAI

    D: 63 grt   **S:** 8 kts   **Dim:** 19.8 × 5.0 × 1.8   **M:** 1 diesel; 240 hp

REMARKS: Acquired in 1953. The similar *Rad* (4) was stricken 1980.

ROYAL THAI MARINE POLICE

    This organization performs duties analogous to those of a coast guard and operates
a large number of patrol boats and craft. A number of the newer and larger units are
listed below. Two "offshore" patrol boats were ordered in 1981 from C.N. Breda,
Venice, Italy; no further details announced.

PATROL BOATS AND CRAFT

♦ **8 aluminum-hulled** Bldr: Captain Co., Thailand (In serv. 1978)

    D: 18 tons (fl)   **S:** 22 kts   **Dim:** 16.5 × 3.8 × . . .
    A: 2/12.7-mm mg   **M:** 2 Cummins diesels; 400 hp

♦ **3 U.S. Cutlass class** Bldr: Halter Marine, New Orleans, La. (In serv. 1978)

807 PHRA ONG CHAO KHAMROP   808 PICHARN PHOLAKIT   809 RAM INTHRA

    D: 34 tons (fl)   **S:** 25 kts   **Dim:** 19.66 × 5.18 × 1.12
    A: 2/12.7-mm mg (I × 2)   **M:** 2 GM 12V71 TI diesels; 2 props; 960 hp
    Fuel: 2.7 tons   **Man:** 15 tot.

REMARKS: Up to eight additional units of this size (but not necessarily of this design)
  are programmed.

Phra Ong Chao Khamrop and sisters—with old numbers   Halter, 1978

♦ **1 seagoing patrol boat** Bldr: Yokohama Yacht, Japan (In serv. 1975)

1802 DAMRONG RACHANUPHAT (ex-112)

    D: 200 grt   **S:** 31 kts   **Dim:** 37.0 × 6.5 × . . .
    A: 1/76.2-mm DP—2/20-mm AA   **M:** 4 diesels; 2 props; 2,200 hp

♦ **2 seagoing patrol boats**

102 N. . .   103 N. . .

Police 103   1973

    D: Approx. 400 tons (fl)   **A:** 1/76.2-mm DP—2/20-mm AA
    M: Diesel-powered

NOTE: There are a number of other craft, mostly armed with either one 20-mm antiaircraft or two 12.7-mm machine guns. Most craft are Japanese built.

TOGO
Republic of Togo

PERSONNEL: 100 men

MERCHANT MARINE (1980): 5 ships—25,395 grt

TOGO (*continued*)

PATROL BOATS

♦ **2 wooden-hulled** Bldr: C. N. de l'Estérel, Cannes, France

KARA (L: 18-5-76)   MONO (L: 1976)

Kara   1976

D: 80 tons (fl)   **S:** 30 kts   **Dim:** 32.0 × 5.8 × 1.5
A: 1/40-mm AA—1/20-mm AA   **Electron Equipt:** Radar: 1/Decca 916
M: 2 MTU 12 V 493 diesels; 2,700 hp   **Range:** 1,500/15
Man: 1 officer, 17 men

TONGA
Kingdom of Tonga

MERCHANT MARINE (1980): 16 ships—14,886 grt

MARITIME DEFENSE DIVISION
TONGAN DEFENSE SERVICE

PATROL CRAFT

♦ **2 fiberglass-hulled** Bldr: Brooke Marine, Lowestoft, G.B.

P 101 NGAHAU KOULA (In serv. 10-3-73)   P 102 NGAHAU SILIVA (In serv. 10-5-74)

D: 15 tons (fl)   **S:** 21 kts   **Dim:** 13.7 × 4.0 × 1.2
A: 2/12.7-mm mg (I × 2)   **Electron Equipt:** Radar: 1/Decca 101
M: 2 Cummins KT2300M diesels; 2 props; 700 hp   **Range:** 800/21   **Man:** 7 tot.

AUXILIARIES

♦ **1 utility landing craft** Bldr: Rolandswerft, Bremen, W. Germany

OLOVAHA (L: 24-6-81)

D: 600 grt   **S:** 8 kts   **Dim:** 48.9 (43.5 pp) × 11.0 × 2.4
M: 2 Cummins KT2300M diesels; 2 props; 700 hp

REMARKS: 250 dwt. For logistics support. Bow ramp.

TRINIDAD AND TOBAGO
Republic of Trinidad and Tobago

PERSONNEL (1981): 38 officers, 388 men

MERCHANT MARINE (1980): 41 ships—17,456 grt (1 tanker—1,736 grt)

NAVAL AVIATION: One Cessna 40 light aircraft in service. One Twin Beech maritime surveillance aircraft was ordered during 1981.

PATROL BOATS AND CRAFT

♦ **2 CG 40 class** Bldr: Karlskrona, Sweden (Both In serv. 6-6-80)

CG 5 BARRACUDA   CG 6 CASCADURA

Barracuda (CG 5)   Frency Navy, 1980

D: 200 tons (fl)   **S:** 31 kts   **Dim:** 40.6 × 6.7 × 1.6
A: 1/40-mm Bofors AA—1/20-mm AA
Electron Equipt: Radar: 1/Decca TM 1226
M: 2 Paxman Valenta 16RP200 diesels; 2 props; 8,000 hp
Range: 2,000/15-20   **Man:** 22 tot.

REMARKS: Ordered 8-78. Have an optronic GFCS for the 40-mm AA; rescue dinghy carried on stern. 27 kts sustained speed. Have HF and VHF D/F gear.

♦ **4 103-foot** Bldr: Vosper, Portsmouth

	L	In serv.		L	In serv.
CG 1 TRINITY	14-4-64	20-2-65	CG 3 CHAGUARAMAS	29-3-71	18-3-72
CG 2 COURLAND BAY	20-5-64	20-2-65	CG 4 BUCCO REEF	1971	18-3-72

TRINIDAD AND TOBAGO *(continued)*
PATROL BOATS AND CRAFT *(continued)*

Courland Bay (CG 2) 1968

D: 96-100 tons (123-125 fl) **S:** 23 kts **Dim:** 31.29 (28.95 pp) × 5.94 × 1.68
A: CG 1 and CG 2: 1/40-mm AA; CG 3 and CG 4: 1/20-mm AA
M: 2 Paxman 12 YJCM Ventura diesels; 2 props; 2,900 hp
Fuel: 18 tons **Range:** 1,800/13.5 **Man:** 3 officers, 14 men

REMARKS: Second pair are heavier and have slightly longer range: 2,000/13; their superstructures are broader. All are air-conditioned and have roll-damping fins.

♦ **2 coastal patrol craft** Bldr: Tugs & Lighters, Ltd., Port-of-Spain

CG. . . NAPARIMA (In serv. 15-8-76) CG. . . EL TUCUCHE (In serv. 1977)

D: 20 tons **S:** 20 kts **Dim:** 16.4 × 5.2 × 2.6
M: 2 GM 6V71 diesels; 2 props; 460 hp **Man:** 6 tot.

♦ **1 fiberglass patrol launch** Bldr: Trinidad (In serv. . . .)

CG 9 FORT CHACON

D: . . . **S:** 27 kts **Dim:** 7.0 × . . . × . . .
M: 1 Caterpillar diesel; . . . hp

SERVICE CRAFT

♦ **2 coastal tugs** Bldr: Bodewes, Millengen, Netherlands

	Laid down	L		Laid down	L
SNAPPER	1-9-80	16-1-80	BONITO	23-9-80	1981

D: 291 grt **S:** 15 kts **Dim:** 30.5 (29.0 pp) × 9.8 × . . .
M: 2 Mak diesels; 2 props; 2,600 hp

♦ **1 sail training ketch** Bldr: Trinidad, 1966

HUMMINGBIRD II

REMARKS: 12 meters overall, one 3-cylinder Lister auxiliary diesel.

MARINE POLICE

PATROL CRAFT

♦ **1 fiberglass-hulled** Bldr: Watercraft, Shoreham, G.B. (In serv. 1980)

SEA DRAGON

D: 14.9 tons (fl) **S:** 23.5 kts **Dim:** 13.7 × 4.1 × 1.2
A: 2/7.62-mm mg (I × 2) **Electron Equipt:** Radar: 1/Decca 110
M: 2 GM 8V92 diesels; 2 props; 700 hp **Range:** 360/20 **Man:** 4 tot.

♦ **2 Sword class** Bldr: Fairey Marine, Hamble, G.B.

SEA SPRAY (In serv. 1-78) FOX (In serv. 12-78)

D: 15.2 tons (fl) **S:** 28 kts **Dim:** 13.7 × 4.1 × 1.32
A: 1/7.62-mm mg **M:** 2 GM 8V71 TI diesels; 2 props; 850 hp
Range: 500/. . . **Man:** 6 tot.

TUNISIA

Republic of Tunisia

PERSONNEL (1981): 2,600 men

MERCHANT MARINE (1980): 43 ships—131,079 grt (tankers: 2 ships—27,030 grt)

FRIGATE

♦ **1 ex-U.S. Savage-class former radar picket** Bldr: Consolidated Steel, Orange, Tex.

	Laid down	L	In serv.
E 7 PRESIDENT BOURGUIBA (ex-*Thomas J. Gary*, DER 326, ex-DE 326)	15-6-43	21-8-43	27-11-43

President Bourguiba (E 7) French Navy, 1980

D: 1,590 tons (2,100 fl) **S:** 19 kts **Dim:** 93.27 (91.5 pp) × 11.22 × 4.27
A: 2/76.2-mm DP—2/20-mm AA—6/324-mm ASW TT (III × 2)
Electron Equipt: Radar: 1/SPS-10, 1/SPS-29, 1/Mk 34
Sonar: SQS-29 series
M: 4 Fairbanks-Morse 38D8⅛ diesels; 2 props; 6,080 hp
Range: 11,500/11 **Man:** 160-170 tot.

FRIGATE (continued)

REMARKS: Modified as a radar picket ship in 1957, transferred on 27-10-73. SPS-8 height-finding radar, TACAN, ECM, Hedgehog removed about 1968. Has one Mk 63 radar GFCS and one Mk 51 Mod. 2 GFCS for 76.2-mm guns.

GUIDED-MISSILE PATROL BOATS

♦ **3 La Combattante III class** Bldr: C.M.N., Cherbourg

	Laid down	L	In serv.
P. . . N. . .	8-81	. . .	. . .
P. . . N. . .	. . .	. . .	. . .
P. . . N. . .	. . .	. . .	. . .

D: 385 tons (425 fl)   **S:** 36.5 kts   **Dim:** 56.15 × 8.00 × 2.50 (props)
A: 8/MM 40 Exocet SSM (IV × 2)—1/76-mm OTO Melara DP—2/40-mm Breda AA (II × 2)
Electron Equipt: Radar:. . .
M: 4 MTU 16V538 TB92 diesels; 4 props; 15,600 hp   **Electric:** 405 kVA

REMARKS: Ordered 27-6-81. Will have two CSEE Naja GFCS and a Dagaie chaff rocket launcher.

PATROL BOATS AND CRAFT

♦ **3 French P 48 class** Bldr: SFCN, Villeneuve-la-Garenne

		L	In serv.
P 301	BIZERTE	20-11-69	10-7-70
P 302	HORRIA (ex-*Liberté*)	19-2-70	10-70
P 304	MONASTIR	25-6-74	25-3-75

Horria (P 302)   J.-C. Bellonne, 1973

D: 250 tons (fl)   **S:** 22 kts   **Dim:** 48.0 (45.5 pp) × 7.1 × 2.25
A: 2/40-mm AA (I × 2)—8/SS-12 wire-guided missiles (IV × 2)
Electron Equipt: Radar: 1/DRBN-31
M: 2 MGO MB-839 Db diesels; 2 props; 4,000 hp   **Range:** 2,000/16
Man: 4 officers, 30 men

♦ **1 French Le Fougueux class** Bldr: Dubigeon, Nantes (In serv. 12-3-57)

P 303 SAKIET SIDI YOUSSEF (ex-*UW 12*, ex-*PC 1618*)

Sakiet Sidi Youssef (P 303)   French Navy, 1980

D: 325 tons (402 fl)   **S:** 18.7 kts   **Dim:** 53.1 × 6.4 × 2.1 (3.0 max.)
A: 1/40-mm AA—2/20-mm AA (I × 2)—2/Mk 20 Mousetrap ASW RL—2/Mk 9 d.c. racks
Electron Equipt: Radar: 1/DRBN-31
                     Sonar: DUBA-2
M: 4 SEMT-Pielstick 14 PA17V diesels; 2 CP props; 3,240 hp   **Electric:** 60 kw
Fuel: 45 tons   **Range:** 3,300/15; 6,350/12   **Man:** 4 officers, 59 men

REMARKS: Begun as P 7 for the French Navy, using U.S. "offshore" funds. Transferred to West Germany and used as a training ship at the Underwater Weapons School. Purchased by Tunisia on 16-6-70. Four depth-charge projectors and Hedgehog removed mid-1970s.

♦ **2 ex-U.S. Adjutant-class former coastal minesweepers**

		Bldr	In serv.
P. . .	HANNIBAL (ex-*Coquelicot*, ex-*MSC 48*)	Steven Bros., Cal.	10-53
P. . .	SOUSSE (ex-*Marjolaine*, ex-*MSC 66*)	Harbor Boat, Cal.	4-53

Hannibal   J.-C. Bellonne, 1973

D: 300 tons (372 fl)   **S:** 13 kts   **Dim:** 43.0 (41.5 pp) × 7.95 × 2.55
A: 2/20-mm AA (II × 1)
Electron Equipt: Radar: 1/DRBN-31   Sonar: 1/UQS-1D
M: 2 GM 8-268A diesels; 2 props; 1,200 hp
Fuel: 40 tons   **Range:** 2,500/10   **Man:** 3 officers, 35 men

REMARKS: Loaned in 1973 and 1977. Minesweeping gear removed. Used in fisheries-protection duties.

PATROL BOATS AND CRAFT (*continued*)

♦ **2 103-foot class** Bldr: Vosper Thornycroft, Portchester, G.B.

	L	In serv.
P 205 TAZARKA	19-7-76	27-10-77
P 206 MENZEL BOURGUIBA	19-7-76	27-10-77

Menzel Bourguiba (P 206)   1977

D: 100 tons (125 fl)   **S:** 27 kts   **Dim:** 31.29 (28.95 pp) × 6.02 × 1.98
A: 2/20-mm AA (I × 2)   **Electron Equipt:** Radar: 1/Decca 916
M: 2 MTU diesels; 2 props; 4,000 hp   **Range:** 1,500/14   **Man:** 24 tot.

♦ **2 Chinese Shanghai-II class** (In serv. 2-5-77)

P 305 GAFSA   P 306 AMILCAR

Gafsa (P 305)   1978

D: 122.5 tons (150 fl)   **S:** 28.5 kts   **Dim:** 38.78 × 5.41 × 1.49
A: 4/37-mm AA (II × 2)—4/25-mm AA (II × 2)
Electron Equipt: Radar: 1/Pot Head
M: 2 M50-F4, 1,200-hp diesels, 2 12D6, 910-hp diesels; 4 props; 4,220 hp
Range: 800/17   **Man:** 38 tot.

♦ **4 French 32-meter class** Bldr: CN de l'Estérel, Cannes

	In serv.		In serv.
P 201 ISTIKLAL (ex-French VC 11)	1957	P 203 AL JALA	11-63
P 202 JOUMHOURIA	1-61	P 204 REMADA	7-67

Istiklal (P 201)   1970

D: 60 tons (82 fl)   **S:** 28 kts   **Dim:** 31.45 × 5.75 × 1.7
A: 2/20-mm AA (I × 2)   **M:** 2 MTU 12V493 diesels; 2 props; 2,700 hp
Range: 1,400/15   **Man:** 3 officers, 14 men

REMARKS: Wooden construction. P 201 was launched on 25-5-57 and transferred in 3-59.

♦ **6 French 25-meter class** Bldr: CN de l'Estérel, Cannes (In serv. 1961-63)

V 101 through V 106

V 101 class

D: 38-39 tons   **S:** 23 kts   **Dim:** 25.0 × 4.75 × 1.25   **Man:** 10 tot.
A: 1/20-mm AA   **M:** 2 GM 12V71 TI diesels; 2 props; 940 hp   **Range:** 900/16

REMARKS: V 107 and V 108 were transferred to the Fisheries Administration, disarmed, in 1971, as *Sabeq el Bahr* (T 2) and *Jaouel el Bahr* (T 3).

TUNISIA *(continued)*

AUXILIARY SHIPS

♦ **1 ex-U.S. Sotoyomo-class oceangoing tug**

Bldr: Gulfport Boilers & Welding Works, Port Arthur, Tex.

	Laid down	L	In serv.
. . . RAS ADAR (ex-*Zeeland*, ex-*Pan America*, ex-*Ocean Pride*, ex-*Oriana*, ex-BAT 1)	16-3-42	15-8-42	13-12-42

D: 570 tons (835 fl) **S:** 13 kts **Dim:** 43.59 (41.0 pp) × 10.31 × 4.01
A: None **M:** 2 GM 12-278A diesels, electric drive; 1 prop; 1,500 hp
Electric: 90 kw **Fuel:** 171 tons **Man:** 45 tot.

REMARKS: Built under Lend-Lease, transferred to Great Britain on 22-12-42. Returned and sold commercially in 1946. Purchased for Tunisia from Dutch company in late 1960s. BAT-series had larger superstructure than standard *Sotoyomo* class and were considered to be ocean rescue tugs.

TURKEY
Republic of Turkey

PERSONNEL: 42,000 men

MERCHANT MARINE (1980): 508 ships—1,454,838 grt
(tankers: 58 ships—358,431 grt)

NAVAL AVIATION: A small naval air arm, organized in 1972, consists of 8 S-2A and 12 S-2E Tracker ASW airplanes, 3 AB-204 helicopters, and 9 AB-212 helicopters.

WARSHIPS IN OR UNDER CONSTRUCTION
AS OF 1 JANUARY 1982

	L	Tons (surfaced)	Main armament
♦ **15 (+1) submarines**			
4 (+1) TYPE 209	1974-81	990	8/533-mm TT
1 TANG	1951	2,100	8/533-mm TT
2 GUPPY III	1945	1,975	10/533-mm TT
7 GUPPY II-A	1943-44	1,848	10/533-mm TT
1 GUPPY I-A	1944	1,870	10/533-mm TT
♦ **14 (+3) destroyers**		Tons	
1 (+1) CARPENTER	1945-46	2,425	2/127-mm, 1/ASROC, 6/ASW TT
6 (+2) GEARING FRAM-I	1944-46	2,425	4/127-mm, 1/ASROC, 6/ASW TT
2 GEARING FRAM-II	1945	2,390	4/127-mm, 2/35-mm AA, 1/Hedgehog, 6/ASW TT
1 ALLEN M. SUMNER FRAM-II	1944	2,200	6/127-mm, 6/ASW TT
1 ROBERT H. SMITH	1944	2,250	6/127-mm, mines
3 FLETCHER	1942-43	2,050	4/127-mm, 6/76.2-mm, 6/ASW TT
♦ **2 frigates**			
2 BERK	1971-72	1,450	4/76.2-mm, 6/ASW TT

♦ **48 (+1) patrol and torpedo boats**

♦ **47 (+1) mine warfare ships and craft**

WEAPONS AND SYSTEMS

Most weapons and systems are furnished by the U.S.A., some by West Germany. For characteristics, see the sections on the U.S.A. and Germany, Federal Republic. Twelve Harpoon SSM were ordered in 1981 to supplement existing stocks; Norwegian Penguin Mk 1 missiles are also used.

SUBMARINES

♦ **4 (+1) German Type 209** Bldrs: S 347, S 348, S 349: Howaldtswerke, Kiel; S 350, S 351: Gölcük NSY

	Laid down	L	In serv.
S 347 ATILAY	1-12-72	23-10-74	23-7-75
S 348 SALDIRAY	2-1-73	14-2-75	21-10-75
S 349 BATIRAY	11-6-75	24-10-77	20-7-78
S 350 YILDIRAY	1-5-76	20-7-77	20-7-81
S 351 TITIRAY	21-3-80	1-81	. . .

D: 990/1,290 tons **S:** 10/12 kts **Dim:** 56.03 × 6.25 × 5.9
A: 8/533-mm TT fwd (14 torpedoes)
M: 4 MTU 12V493 TY60 diesels; 1 Siemens electric motor, 3,600 hp
Man: 6 officers, 27 men

REMARKS: Have HSA M8 torpedo-fire control. A total of 12 are planned, with 8 to be built in Turkey.

♦ **1 ex-U.S. Tang class** Bldr: Portsmouth Naval SY, N.H.

	Laid down	L	In serv.
S 343 PIRI REIS (ex-*Tang*, SS 563)	18-4-49	19-6-51	25-10-52

D: 2,100/2,700 tons **S:** 15.5/16 kts **Dim:** 87.5 × 8.3 × 5.7
A: 8/533-mm TT (6 fwd, 2 short aft)
Electron Equipt: Radar: 1/SS-2A
    Sonar: BQS-4, BQG-4 (PUFFS)
M: 3 Fairbanks-Morse 38D8⅛ × 10 diesels, 2 Westinghouse motors; 2 props; 5,600 hp
Man: 11 officers, 75 men

REMARKS: Leased for five years 8-2-80. Has Mk 106, mod. 18, torpedo FCS. Aft tubes can fire Mk 37 torpedoes only.

SUBMARINES *(continued)*

♦ **2 ex-U.S. GUPPY III class** Bldr: Electric Boat Co., Groton, Conn.

	Laid down	L	In serv.
S 333 Ikinci Inonu (ex-*Corporal*, SS 346)	27-4-44	1-4-45	8-8-45
S 341 Canakkale (ex-*Cobbler*, SS 344)	3-4-44	1-4-45	9-11-45

D: 1,975/2,450 tons **S:** 17.2/14.5 kts **Dim:** 99.52 × 8.23 × 5.18
A: 10/533-mm TT (6 fwd, 4 aft)—24 torpedoes
Electron Equipt: Radar: 1/SS-2A—Sonar: BQG-4 (PUFFS), BQR-2B
M: 4 GM 16-278A diesels (1,625 hp each), diesel-electric drive; 2 props; 6,500/5,200 hp
Range: 10,000-12,000/10; 95/5 (sub.) **Man:** 86 tot.

REMARKS: Transferred on 21-11-73. Lengthened by 3.6 meters in 1962 at Philadelphia (S 341) and Charleston (S 333). Two 126-cell batteries. Direct drive on surface.

♦ **7 ex-U.S. GUPPY II-A** Bldrs: S 345: Electric Boat Co., Groton, Conn.; others: Portsmouth NSY

	Laid down	L	In serv.
S 335 Burak Reis (ex-*Sea Fox*, SS 402)	2-11-43	28-3-44	13-6-44
S 336 Murat Reis (ex-*Razorback*, SS 394)	9-9-43	27-1-44	3-4-44
S 337 Oruç Reis (ex-*Pomfret*, SS 391)	17-7-43	27-10-43	19-2-44
S 338 Uluç Ali Reis (ex-*Thornback*, SS 418)	5-4-44	7-7-44	13-10-44
S 340 Cerbe (ex-*Trutta*, SS 421)	22-5-44	18-8-44	16-11-44
S 345 Preveze (ex-*Entemedor*, SS 340)	3-2-44	17-12-44	6-4-45
S 346 Birinci İnönü (ex-*Threadfin*, SS 410)	18-3-44	26-6-44	30-8-44

Murat Reis (S 336)   1976

D: 1,525/1,848/2,440 tons **S:** 17.4/14 kts, 9.4 snorkel
Dim: 93.36 × 8.32 × 5.04
A: 10/533-mm TT (6 fwd, 4 aft)—24 torpedoes or 40 mines
Electron Equipt: Radar: 1/SS-2A
Sonar: BQR-2B, BQS-4
M: 3 Fairbanks-Morse 38D8⅛ (S 345: GM 16-278A) diesels, electric drive; 2 props; 3,430/5,200 hp
Fuel: 330 tons **Range:** 10,000/10; 95/5 (sub.) **Man:** 8-9 officers, 76 men

REMARKS: S 335 was transferred in 12-70, S 336 in 11-70, S 337 on 3-5-72, S 338 and S 345 on 24-8-73, S 340 in 6-72, and S 346 on 15-8-73. S336 and S 338 were at one time while in U.S. service equipped as "hard" targets for ASW training.

♦ **1 ex-U.S. GUPPY I-A class** Bldr: Electric Boat Co., Groton, Conn.

	Laid down	L	In serv.
S 339 Dumlupinar (ex-*Caiman*, SS 323)	1-10-43	30-3-44	17-7-44

D: 1,517/1,870/2,400 tons **S:** 18/15 kts **Dim:** 93.75 × 8.33 × 5.04
A: 10/533-mm TT (6 fwd, 4 aft)—24 torpedoes or 40 mines
Electron Equipt: Radar: 1/SS-2A
Sonar: . . .
M: 4 GM 16-278A diesels, diesel-electric direct drive; 2 props; 4,610/5,200 hp
Fuel: 330 tons **Range:** 16,000/10; 95/5 sub. **Man:** 9 officers, 76 men

REMARKS: Completed GUPPY I-A conversion in 1951. Transferred 24-8-72. Had been relegated to pierside training duties after collision with a Soviet freighter on 1-9-76 and a fire in 1977, but has been refitted and recommissioned during 1980. Two 126-cell batteries.

DESTROYERS

♦ **2 ex-U.S. Carpenter class**

	Bldr	Laid down	L	In serv.
D 347 Anitepe (ex-*Carpenter*, DD 825)	Consolidated Steel, Orange, Tex.	30-7-45	30-12-45	15-12-49
D . . . N . . . (ex-*Robert A. Owens*, DD 827)	Bath Iron Wks. Bath, Maine	29-10-45	15-7-46	5-11-49

Anitepe (D 347)   1981

D: 2,425 tons (3,540 fl) **S:** 34 kts **Dim:** 119.03 × 12.52 × 4.61 (6.4 over sonar)
A: 2/127-mm DP (II × 1)—1/ASROC ASW RL (VIII × 1, 6 reloads)—6/324-mm Mk 32 ASW TT (III × 2)
Electron Equipt: Radar: 1/SPS-10, 1/SPS-40, 1/Mk 35
Sonar: SQS-23
ECM: WLR-1, WLR-3
M: 2 sets GE GT; 2 props; 60,000 hp **Electric:** 1,200 kw
Boilers: 4 Babcock & Wilcox, 43.3 kg/cm², 454°C **Fuel:** 720 tons
Range: 1,500/31; 5,800/12 **Man:** 14 officers, 260 men

REMARKS: D 347 purchased 20-2-81, ex-DD 827 scheduled for purchase 16-2-82. Variant of the *Gearing* design, originally optimized for ASW. Completed FRAM-I modernizations 1962, retaining high bridges. Have Mk 56 radar GFCS, tripod mast aft, larger hangar superstructure than *Gearing* FRAM-I. Will probably have armament augmented in Turkey, as there is considerable space available.

DESTROYERS (continued)

♦ 6 (+2) ex-U.S. Gearing FRAM-I class

	Bldr	Laid down	L	In serv.
D 348 SAVASTEPE (ex-*Meredith*, DD 890)	Consolidated Steel, Orange, Tex.	27-1-45	28-6-45	31-12-45
D 349 KILIÇ ALI PAŞA (ex-*Robert H. McCard*, DD 822)	Consolidated Steel, Orange, Tex.	26-1-45	9-11-45	26-10-46
D 350 PIYALE PAŞA (ex-*Fiske*, DD 842)	Bath Iron Wks., Bath, Maine	9-4-45	8-9-45	28-11-45
D 351 M. FEVZI CAKMAK (ex-*Charles H. Roan*, DD 853)	Bethlehem Steel, Quincy, Mass.	27-9-45	15-3-46	12-9-46
D 352 GAYRET (ex-*Eversole*, DD 789)	Todd SY Seattle, Wash.	28-2-45	8-1-46	10-7-46
D 353 ADATEPE (ex-*Forrest Royal*, DD 872)	Bethlehem, Staten Isl., N.Y.	6-6-45	17-1-46	28-6-46
D . . . N . . . (ex-*Orleck*, DD 886)	Consolidated Steel, Orange, Tex.	28-11-44	12-5-45	15-9-45
D . . . N . . . (ex-*McKean*, DD 784)	Todd SY, Seattle, Wash.	15-9-44	31-3-45	9-6-45

D: 2,425 tons (3,600 fl) **S:** 32 kts

Dim: 119.03 × 12.49 × 4.56 (6.4 over sonar)

A: D 348-350: 4/127-mm DP (II × 2)—1/ASROC ASW RL (VIII × 1, not in D 348)—6/324-mm Mk 32 ASW TT (III × 2)—1/Mk 9 d.c. rack

D 351-353: 4/127-mm 38-cal. AA (II × 2)—2/40-mm AA (I × 2)—2/35-mm Oerlikon AA (II × 1)—6/324-mm Mk 32 ASW TT (III × 2)—1/ASROC ASW RL (VIII × 1)—1/Mk 9 d.c. rack

Piyale Paşa (D 350)—prior to modernization   G. Gyssels, 1981

M. Fevzi Cakmak (D 351)—twin 35-mm mount aft   G. Gyssels, 1981

M. Fevzi Cakmak (D 351)—twin 40-mm AA fwd   French Navy, 1981

Electron Equipt: Radar: 1/SPS-10, 1/SPS-40 (D 348-50: SPS-29), 1/Mk 25 (D 351-353: 1/. . . also)

Sonar: SQS-23

ECM: WLR-1, WLR-3, ULQ-6

M: 2 sets GT; 2 props; 60,000 hp **Electric:** 1,200 kw

Boilers: 4 Foster-Wheeler and/or Babcock & Wilcox, 43.3 kg/cm², 454°C

Fuel: 720 tons **Range:** 2,400/25; 4,800/15 **Man:** 14 officers, 260 men

REMARKS: D 351 was transferred on 29-9-73, D 352 on 11-7-73, and D 353 on 27-3-71. All received a twin 40-mm mount just before the bridge (with Mk 51, mod. 2, optical director) and a twin 35-mm antiaircraft gun on the former DASH drone helicopter deck in the mid-1970s. D 351 has four Babcock & Wilcox boilers, while the other pair have two Babcock & Wilcox and two Foster-Wheeler boilers. All have chaff RL atop former hangar, two saluting guns fwd. GFCS include Mk 37 for 127-mm DP, 1 Mk 51 mod. 2 for the 40-mm mount, and a radar GFCS (antenna atop after mast). D 348 was purchased 20-3-80 for cannibalization but was instead refurbished and recommissioned 20-7-81; she lacks an ASROC launcher. D 349 and D 350 were leased

DESTROYERS *(continued)*

for 5 years 5-6-80 and formally recommissioned 30-7-81. Because of their status they were not drastically altered, although one depth-charge rack was added. Harpoon missiles may be added to all in the near future. *Orleck* (DD 886) is scheduled to transfer to Turkey in 2-82, as is *McKean* (DD 784) later in the year.

♦ 2 ex-U.S. Gearing FRAM-II class

Bldrs: D 354: Bethlehem Steel, San Pedro, Cal.; D 355: Bethlehem Steel, San Francisco, Cal.

	Laid down	L	In serv.
D 354 KOCATEPE (ex-*Norris*, DD 859)	29-8-44	25-2-45	9-6-45
D 355 TINAZTEPE (ex-*Keppler*, DD 765)	23-4-44	24-6-45	23-5-47

Tinaztepe (D 355)   G. Arra, 1976

D: 2,390 tons (3,480 fl)   **S:** 32 kts   **Dim:** 119.03 × 12.49 × 4.6 (6.54 over sonar)
A: 4/127-mm DP (II × 2)—6/40-mm AA (II × 2, I × 2)—1/Mk 15 trainable Hedgehog—6/324-mm Mk 32 ASW TT (III × 2)—1/Mk 9 d.c. rack (D 354: 2/35-mm AA [II × 1] vice 2/40-mm AA aft)
Electron Equipt: Radar: 1/SPS-10, 1/SPS-6B, 1/Mk 25
      Sonar: 1/SQS-23
      ECM: WLR-1
M: 2 sets GT; 2 props; 60,000 hp   **Electric:** 1,200 kw
Boilers: 4 Babcock & Wilcox and/or Foster-Wheeler; 43.3 kg/cm², 454°C
Fuel: 720 tons   **Range:** 2,400/25; 4,800/15   **Man:** 14 officers, 260 men

REMARKS: A previous *Kocatepe* (ex-*Harwood*, DD 861) was lost on 21-7-74 when mistakenly bombed by the Turkish Air Force. She was replaced by the *Norris* (DD 859), which had been transferred on 7-7-74 for cannibalization spares. D 355 was transferred on 30-6-72. Two single 40-mm AA were mounted on former DASH drone

helicopter deck in 1974, and two twin 40-mm AA (with two Mk 51 Mod. 2 directors) added on upper deck between stacks in 1977. Both have Mk 37 radar GFCS. D 354 has Babcock & Wilcox boilers, while D 355 has two Babcock & Wilcox and two Foster-Wheeler. D 354 had a twin Oerlikon 35-mm AA substituted for the two single 40-mm aft in 1980.

♦ 1 ex-U.S. Allen M. Sumner FRAM-II class Bldr: Federal SB, Kearney, N.J.

	Laid down	L	In serv.
D 356 ZAFER (ex-*Hugh Purvis*, DD 709)	23-5-44	17-12-44	1-3-45

Zafer (D 356)   1978

D: 2,200 tons (3,300 fl)   **S:** 33 kts   **Dim:** 114.76 × 12.49 × 4.39 (5.79 over sonar)
A: 6/127-mm DP (II × 3)—6/40-mm AA (II × 2, I × 2)—2/Mk 11 Hedgehogs—6/324-mm Mk 32 ASW TT—1/Mk 9 d.c. rack
Electron Equipt: Radar: 1/SPS-10, 1/SPS-29, 1/Mk 25
      Sonar: SQS-29 series
      ECM: WLR-1, WLR-3, ULQ-6
M: GT; 2 props; 60,000 hp   **Electric:** 1,200 kw
Boilers: 4 Babcock & Wilcox; 43.3 kg/cm², 454°C
Fuel: 650 tons   **Range:** 800/32; 4,300/11   **Man:** 15 officers, 260 men

REMARKS: Transferred on 15-2-72. In 1977 two twin 40-mm AA with two Mk 52, mod. 2, optical GFCS for the twin mounts were added amidships; also has Mk 37 radar GFCS for 127-mm DP.

♦ 1 ex-U.S. Robert H. Smith-class destroyer minelayer Bldr: Bethlehem Steel, San Pedro, Cal.

	Laid down	L	In serv.
D 357 MUAVENET (ex-*Gwin*, MMD 33, ex-DD 772)	31-10-43	9-4-44	30-9-44

D: 2,250 tons (3,375 fl)   **S:** 34 kts   **Dim:** 114.76 × 12.49 × 4.4 (hull)
A: 6/127-mm DP (II × 3)—16/40-mm AA (IV × 3, II × 2)—2/Mk 11 Hedgehogs—1/Mk 9 d.c. rack—80 mines
Electron Equipt: Radar: 1/SPS-10, 1/SPS-6, 1/Mk 25, 2/Mk 34
      Sonar: QCU
      ECM: none
M: 2 sets GT; 2 props; 60,000 hp   **Electric:** 900 kw
Boilers: 4 Babcock & Wilcox; 43.3 kg/cm², 454°C
Fuel: 494 tons   **Range:** 4,600/15   **Man:** 274 tot.

DESTROYERS (continued)

REMARKS: Transferred on 22-10-71 after reactivation and modernization. Fire control includes 1 Mk 37 radar GFCS for 127-mm guns, two Mk 63 radar GFCS, and two Mk 51, mod. 2, optical GFCS for 40-mm AA. Mine rails on either side of main deck of what is basically an *Allen M. Sumner*-class destroyer. Survivor of a class of twelve.

♦ 3 ex-U.S. Fletcher class

Bldrs: D 340: Federal SB, Kearney, N.J.; DD 341: Gulf SB, Chickasaw, Ala.; DD 343, Bethlehem, San Pedro

	Laid down	L	In serv.
D 340 ISTANBUL (ex-*Clarence K. Bronson*, DD 668)	9-12-42	18-4-43	11-6-43
D 341 IZMIR (ex-*Van Valkenburgh*, DD 656)	15-11-42	19-12-43	2-8-44
D 343 ISKENDERUN (ex-*Boyd*, DD 544)	2-4-42	29-10-42	8-5-43

Iskenderun (D 343)

D: 2,050 tons (3,036 fl) **S:** 35 kts **Dim:** 114.74 × 12.09 × 4.29 (5.79 over sonar)
A: 4/127-mm DP (I × 4)—6/76.2-mm DP (II × 3)—2/Mk 11 Hedgehogs—6/324-mm Mk 32 ASW TT (III × 2)—1/Mk 9 d.c. rack
Electron Equipt: Radar: 1/SPS-10, 1/SPS-6C, 1/Mk 25, 1/Mk 35
　　　　　　　　　　Sonar: SQS-29 series
　　　　　　　　　　ECM: WLR-1
M: 2 sets GT; 2 props; 60,000 hp **Electric:** 880 kw
Boilers: 4 Babcock & Wilcox; 43.3 kg/cm², 454°C
Fuel: 530 tons **Range:** 1,260/30; 4,400/15 **Man:** 15 officers, 247 men

REMARKS: D 340 transferred on 14-1-67, D 341 on 28-2-67, D 343 on 1-10-69. All have one Mk 37 and one Mk 56 radar GFCS; two Mk 63 GFCS amidships were removed before transfer. *Izmit* (D 342) was stricken 1980, and *Içel* (D 344) is used as a training hulk, although maintained in good condition.

FRIGATES

♦ 2 Berk class Bldr: Gölcük Naval SY

	Laid down	L	In serv.
D 358 BERK	9-3-67	25-6-71	12-7-72
D 359 PEYK	18-1-68	7-6-72	24-7-75

D: 1,450 tons (1,950 fl) **S:** 25 kts **Dim:** 95.15 × 11.82 × 4.4 (5.5 over sonar)
A: 4/76.2-mm DP (II × 2)—2/Mk 11 Hedgehogs—6/324-mm Mk 32 ASW TT (III × 2)—1/Mk 9 d.c. rack

Berk (D 358)　　　　　　　　　　　　　　　　G. Gyssels, 1980

Electron Equipt: Radar: 1/SPS-10, 1/SPS-40, 2/SPG-34
　　　　　　　　　　Sonar: 1/SQS-11
　　　　　　　　　　ECM: WLR-1
M: 4 Fiat-Tosi 16-cyl., 800 rpm, Type 3-016-RSS diesels; 1 prop; 24,000 hp

REMARKS: Based on the U.S. *Claud Jones* class, but more heavily armed. Can carry a helicopter but have no hangar. Two Mk 63 GFCS with SPG-34 radars mounted on the gun mounts.

GUIDED-MISSILE PATROL BOATS

♦ 4 (+1) German FPB 57 class

Bldrs: P 340: Lürssen, Vegesack, W. Germany; others: Taskizak NDY, Istanbul

	Laid down	L	In serv.
P 340 DOGAN	2-6-75	16-6-76	15-6-77
P 341 MARTI	1-7-75	30-6-77	27-7-78
P 342 TAYFUN	1-12-75	19-7-79	1980
P 343 VOLKAN	. . .	11-8-80	1981
P 344 N. . .	30-7-81	. . .	. . .

Dogan (P 340)　　　　　　　　　　　　　　　French Navy, 1977

GUIDED-MISSILE PATROL BOATS *(continued)*

Dogan (D 340)—note Oerlikon twin 35-mm AA aft
French Navy, 1977

D: 353 tons (398 fl) **S:** 36.5 kts **Dim:** 58.1 (54.4 pp) × 7.62 × 2.83
A: 8/Harpoon SSM (IV × 2)—1/76-mm OTO Melara Compact DP—2/35-mm
  Oerlikon AA (II × 1)—2/7.62-mm mg (I × 2)
Electron Equipt: Radar: 1/Decca 1226, 1/HSA WM28-41
    ECM: SUSIE-1 passive intercept
M: 4 MTU 16V956 TB91 diesels; 4 props; 18,000 hp (16,000 sust.)
Electric: 405 kVA **Range:** 700/35; 1,600/32.5; 3,300/16
Man: 5 officers, 33 men

REMARKS: The 76-mm mount has a local control cupola. Carry 300 rounds 76-mm,
2,750 rounds 35-mm. Steel hulls, aluminum superstructures. Plan continued construction at rate of one per year.

♦ **9 Kartal-class guided-missile and torpedo boats** Bldr: Lürssen, Vegesack (In
  serv. 1967-71)

P 321 DENIZKUSU	P 324 KARTAL	P 327 ALBATROS
P 322 ATMACA	P 325 MELTEN	P 328 SIMSEK
P 323 SAHIN	P 326 PELIKAN	P 329 KARSIGA

Kartal (P 324)
1970

D: 184 tons (210 fl) **S:** 42 kts **Dim:** 42.8 × 7.14 × 2.21
A: 2/40-mm AA (I × 2)—4/533-mm TT (P 325 to P 328: 4/Norwegian Penguin
  missiles and only 2 TT)
M: 2 MTU 16V538 diesels; 4 props; 12,000 hp
Range: 500/39; 1,000/32 **Man:** 39 tot.

REMARKS: Similar to the German *Jaguar* class. Wooden hull; steel and light-metal
  keel and frames; light-metal superstructure. Can be fitted as fast gunboats or minelayers (four mines).

TORPEDO BOATS

♦ **7 ex-German Jaguar class (Type 140)**

  Bldrs: P 330 and P 336: Krögerwerft, Rendsburg; others: Lürssen, Vegesack

	L		L
P 330 FIRTINA (ex-*Pelikan*)	12-12-59	P 334 YILDIZ (ex-*Wolf*)	21-9-57
P 331 TUFAN (ex-*Storch*)	16-11-59	P 335 KALKAN (ex-*Löwe*)	8-11-58
P 332 KILIÇ (ex-*Pinguin*)	4-7-60	P 336 KARAYEL (ex-*Tiger*)	21-4-58
P 333 MIZRAK (ex-*Häher*)	9-1-60		

D: 184 tons (210 fl) **S:** 42 kts **Dim:** 42.62 × 7.1 × 2.21
A: 2/40-mm AA (I × 2)—4/533-mm TT or 2/TT and mines
M: 4 MTU 16V538 diesels; 4 props; 12,000 hp
Range: 500/39; 1,000/32 **Man:** 39 tot.

REMARKS: Transferred 1975-76. The *Alk, Iltis,* and *Reiher* were transferred at the
same time to be cannibalized for the maintenance of the seven in service. Similar to
Kartal class but shorter deckhouse with stepped face.

PATROL BOATS AND CRAFT

♦ **1 German PB 57 class** Bldr: Taskizak Naval DY, Istanbul (In serv. 30-7-76)

P 140 GIRNE

D: 341 tons (399 fl) **S:** 29.5 kts **Dim:** 58.1 (54.4 pp) × 7.6 × 2.8
A: 3/40-mm AA (II × 1, I × 1)—4/Mk 20 Mousetrap ASW RL—2/d.c. projec-
  tors—2/d.c. racks
Electron Equipt: Radar: 1/navigational
M: 2 MTU 16V956 TB91 diesels; 2 props; 9,000 hp **Electric:** 405 kVA
Range: 2,200/28; 4,200/16 **Man:** 3 officers, 27 men

REMARKS: Same basic design as the Spanish *Lazaga*-class patrol boats, but with lighter
armament. Design by Lürssen. Construction program canceled after one unit. IN-
TELSAT satellite-communications antenna mounted on superstructure in 1978. U.S.
Mk 51, mod. 2, optical GFCS for twin 40-mm aft.

♦ **2 ex-U.S. Asheville class** Bldr: Peterson Builders, Sturgeon Bay, Wisc.

	L	In serv.
P 338 YILDIRIM (ex-*Defiance*, PG 95)	24-8-68	17-10-69
P 339 BORA (ex-*Surprise*, PG 97)	15-11-68	24-9-69

D: 225 tons (240 fl) **S:** 40 kts (16 on diesels) **Dim:** 50.14 (46.94 pp) × 7.28 ×
2.9
A: 1/76.2-mm Mk 34 DP—1/40-mm AA—4/12.7-mm mg (II × 2)
Electron Equipt: Radar: 1/LN-66, 1/SPG-50
M: CODAG: 1 LM 1500 Mk 7 gas turbine (12,500 hp); 2 Cummins 875V12 die-
  sels (1,450 hp); 2 props
Fuel: 50 tons **Range:** 325/35; 1,700/16 **Man:** 25 tot.

PATROL BOATS AND CRAFT (continued)

REMARKS: P 338 leased on 11-6-73 and P 339 on 28-2-73. P 338 was formerly P 340. Mk 63 radar GFCS, with SPG-50 on 76.2-mm gunmount.

◆ **11 AB 25 class** Bldrs: Gölçük Naval SY (In serv. 1967-70)

P 1225 AB 25	P 1229 AB 29	P 1232 AB 32
P 1226 AB 26	P 1230 AB 30	P 1233 AB 33
P 1227 AB 27	P 1231 AB 31	P 1234 AB 34
P 1228 AB 28		P 1235 AB 35

AB 26—wearing old number   1969

D: 150 tons (170 fl) **S:** 22 kts **Dim:** 40.24 × 6.4 × 1.65
A: 1/40-mm AA—1/20-mm AA—2/Mk 20 Mousetrap ASW RL—1/d.c. rack
M: SACM-AGO V16CSHR diesels; 2 props; 4,800 hp; 2 cruise diesels; 300 hp

REMARKS: Twenty-three others are assigned to the Gendarmerie. Built with French assistance.

◆ **4 ex-U.S. PGM 71 motor gunboats** Bldr: Peterson Builders, Sturgeon Bay, Wisc.

	L	In serv.
P 1221 AB 21 (ex-PGM 104)	4-5-67	8-67
P 1222 AB 22 (ex-PGM 105)	25-5-67	9-67
P 1223 AB 23 (ex-PGM 106)	7-7-67	10-67
P 1224 AB 24 (ex-PGM 108)	14-9-67	5-68

AB 23—wearing old number   1969

D: 104 tons (144 fl) **S:** 17 kts **Dim:** 30.81 × 6.45 × 1.83
A: 1/40-mm AA—4/20-mm AA (II × 2)—4/12.7-mm mg (II × 2)—2/Mk 22 double Mousetrap ASW RL—2/d.c. racks

Electron Equipt: Radar: 1/Raytheon 1500B   Sonar: SQS-17A
M: 8 GM 6-71 diesels; 2 props; 2,040 hp **Electric:** 30 kw
Fuel: 16 tons **Range:** 1,000/12 **Man:** 30 tot.

◆ **6 ex-U.S. PC 1638 class antisubmarine patrol boats**

Bldrs: P 116: Gölçük Naval SY; others: Gunderson Bros., Portland, Ore.

		L	In serv.
P 111 SULTAN HISAR (ex-PC 1638)		1964	5-64
P 112 DEMIRHISAR (ex-PC 1639)		9-7-64	4-65
P 113 YARHISAR (ex-PC 1640)		14-5-64	9-64
P 114 AKHISAR (ex-PC 1641)		14-5-64	12-64
P 115 SIVRIHISAR (ex-PC 1642)		5-11-64	6-65
P 116 KOCHISAR (ex-PC 1643)		12-64	7-65

Demirhisar (P 112)   1970

D: 325 tons (477 fl) **S:** 19 kts **Dim:** 52.9 × 7.0 × 3.1 (hull)
A: 1/40-mm AA—4/20-mm AA (II × 2)—1/Mk 15 trainable Hedgehog—4/Mk 6 d.c. projectors—1/Mk 9 d.c. rack
Electron Equipt: Radar: 1/Decca 707   Sonar: SQS-17A
M: 2 Alco 16 9 × 10½ T diesels; 2 props; 4,800 hp
Fuel: 60 tons **Range:** 5,000/10 **Man:** 5 officers, 60 men

REMARKS: Based on the PC 471 class of World War II.

◆ **4 ex-U.S. Coast Guard 83-foot class** Bldr: U.S.C.G. Yard, Curtis Bay, Md.

P 1209 LS 9   P 1210 LS 10   P 1211 LS 11   P 1212 LS 12

LS 12—wearing old number   1969

PATROL BOATS AND CRAFT (continued)

D: 63 tons **S:** 18 kts **Dim:** 25.3 × 4.25 × 1.55
A: 1/20-mm AA—2/Mk 20 Mousetrap ASW RL
Electron Equipt: Radar: 1/SO-2
        Sonar: QBE-3
M: 4 GM 6-71 diesels; 2 props; 900 hp **Man:** 15 tot.

REMARKS: Transferred on 25-6-53. Former Turkish hull numbers P 339, P 308, P 309, and P 310. Wooden hulls.

MINE WARFARE SHIPS

NOTE: The destroyer *Muavenet* (D 357) is also a minelayer when required.

♦ **1 Danish Falster-class minelayer** Bldr: Frederikshaven Naval DY, Denmark

	Laid down	L	In serv.
N 110 NUSRET (ex-N 108, ex-MMC 16)	1962	1964	16-9-64

Nusret—wearing old number

D: 1,880 tons **S:** 16.5 kts **Dim:** 77.0 (72.5 pp) × 12.8 × 3.4
A: 4/76.2-mm AA Mk 33 (II × 2)—400 mines
Electron Equipt: Radar: 1/navigational, 1/RAN 7S, 2/SPG-34
M: 2 GM 16-567D3 diesels; 2 CP props; 4,800 hp **Fuel:** 130 tons **Man:** 130 tot.

REMARKS: Paid for by the U.S.A. Two Mk 63 radar GFCS systems.

♦ **1 (+1) Cakabey-class minelayer/landing ship** Bldr: Taskizak NSY, Istanbul

	Laid down	L	In serv.
NL 112 CAKABEY (ex-L 405)	. . .	3-6-77	25-7-80
NL 123 KARAKABEY	25-7-80	30-7-81	. . .

D: 1,600 tons **S:** 14 kts **Dim:** 77.3 (74.3 pp) × 12.0 × 2.3
A: 4/40-mm AA (II × 2)—8/20-mm AA (II × 4)—150 mines
M: 3 diesels; 3 props; 4,500 hp

REMARKS: Redesignated as a minelayer/landing ship in 1980. Originally planned as a class of four; the second unit listed above may be of a different design. As a landing ship, NL 112 can carry 400 troops, 9 U.S. M-48 tanks, and 10 jeeps. Carries two LCVP in davits. Deck cleared forward as a helicopter platform. Ship resembles a U.S. LST.

♦ **2 ex-German, ex-U.S. LST 542-class minelayer/tank landing ships**

Bldrs: L 403: Missouri Valley Bridge & Iron, Evansville, Ind.; L 404: American Bridge Co., Ambridge, Pa.

	Laid down	L	In serv.
NL 120 BAYRAKTAR (ex-L 403, ex-*Bottrop*, ex-*Saline County*, LST 1101)	22-11-44	3-1-45	26-1-45
NL 121 SANCAKTAR (ex-L 404, ex-*Bochum*, ex-*Rice County*, LST 1089)	20-12-44	17-2-45	14-3-45

Bayraktar (NL 120)

D: 3,640 tons (4,140 fl) **S:** 11 kts **Dim:** 101.37 × 15.28 × 3.98 (max.)
A: 6/40-mm AA (II × 2, I × 2)—790 mines
Electron Equipt: Radar: 1/Kelvin-Hughes 14/9
M: 2 GM 16-567A diesels; 2 props; 1,700 hp
Electric: 860 kw **Range:** 15,000/9 **Man:** 60 tot.

REMARKS: NL 120 was transferred to West Germany on 6-2-64 and to Turkey on 13-12-72; NL 121 to West Germany on 23-1-64 and to Turkey on 12-12-72. Converted to minelayers while in German service, with six rails on the upper deck, tapering to two at the stern, and four rails below decks, exiting through a broadened stern. Four two-ton mine-handling cranes added. Bow doors retained. Redesignated as amphibious ships 1974-75, but again placed in mine warfare category 1980.

♦ **5 minelayers** Bldr: Brown SB, Houston, Tex.

	Laid down	L	In serv.
N 101 MORDOGAN (ex-MMC 11, ex-LSM 484)	17-2-45	10-3-45	15-4-45
N 102 MERIC (ex-MMC 12, ex-LSM 481)	17-2-45	10-3-45	8-4-45
N 103 MARMARIS (ex-MMC 10, ex-LSM 490)	3-3-45	24-3-45	28-4-45
N 104 MERSIN (ex-*Vale*, ex-MMC 13, ex-LSM 492)	28-5-44	22-6-44	4-8-44
N 105 MUREFTE (ex-*Vidar*, ex-MMC 14, ex-MSC 493)	10-3-45	30-3-45	4-5-45

Mersin (N 104)

MINE WARFARE SHIPS (continued)

D: 743 tons (1,100 fl)   **S:** 12.5 kts   **Dim:** 62.0 × 10.52 × 2.54
A: 6/40-mm AA (II × 3)—5/20-mm AA (I × 5)—400 mines
Electron Equipt: Radar: 1/SO-8   **M:** 2 GM 16-278A diesels; 2 props; 2,800 hp
Fuel: 60 tons   **Range:** 2,500/12   **Man:** 70 tot.

REMARKS: Ex-U.S. LSM 1-class medium landing ships. In 10-52 after conversion, the first three were transferred to Turkey, the other two to Norway; the latter were returned to the U.S.A. in 1960, then reassigned to Turkey. Four booms, two forward, two aft, for the loading of mines. Two minelaying rails. Originally had four twin 40-mm AA and six 20-mm AA. N 104 has two Fairbanks-Morse 38D8⅛ diesels.

♦ **1 mine-planter** Bldr: Higgins, New Orleans, La. (L: 1958)

N 115 MEHMETCIK (ex-YMP 3)

D: 540 tons (fl)   **S:** 10 kts   **Dim:** 39.62 × 10.67 × 3.05
A: 1/40-mm AA   **Electron Equipt:** Radar: 1/Decca 12
M: 2 diesels; 2 props   **Man:** 22 tot.

REMARKS: Paid for by the U.S. Military Aid Program. Used to place controlled mine-fields. Gun not normally mounted.

♦ **6 ex-German French Mercure-class coastal minesweepers**

Bldr: Amiot (C.M.N.), Cherbourg

	Laid down	L	In serv.
M 520 KARAMÜRSEL (ex-Worms)	19-3-58	30-1-60	30-4-60
M 521 KEREMPE (ex-Detmold)	19-2-58	17-11-59	20-2-60
M 522 KILIMLI (ex-Siegen)	18-4-58	29-3-60	9-7-60
M 523 KOZLU (ex-Hameln)	20-1-58	20-8-59	15-10-59
M 524 KUSADASI (ex-Vegesack)	20-12-57	21-5-59	19-9-59
M 525 KEMER (ex-Passau)	19-5-58	25-6-60	15-10-60

Kilimli (M 522)—with Kozlu (M 523)   French Navy, 1976

D: 366 tons (383 fl)   **S:** 14.5 kts   **Dim:** 44.62 (42.5 pp) × 8.41 × 2.55
A: 2/20-mm AA (II × 1)   **Electric:** 520 kw
Electron Equipt: Radar: 1/Decca 707
M: Mercedes-Benz MB-820 Db diesels; 2 CP props; 4,000 hp   **Man:** 40 tot.

REMARKS: These ships were built for the German Navy, placed in reserve in 1963, and stricken on 31-12-73. Transferred to Turkey between 6-75 and 10-75, except M 525, in 1979. French sister Mercure now a fisheries-protection ship. Wooden construction.

♦ **12 ex-U.S. Adjutant-, MSC 268(*)-, and MSC 289(**)-class coastal minesweepers**

	L	In serv.
M 507 SEYMEN (ex-De Panne, ex-MSC 131)	...	28-10-55
M 508 SELÇUK (ex-Pavot, ex-MSC 124)	...	6-54
M 509 SEYHAN (ex-Renoncule, ex-MSC 142)	...	8-54
M 510 SAMSUN (ex-MSC 268)*	6-9-57	30-9-58
M 511 SINOP (ex-MSC 270)*	4-1-58	2-59
M 512 SÜRMENE (ex-MSC 271)*	1958	27-3-59
M 513 SEDDUL BAHR (ex-MSC 272)*	1958	5-59
M 514 SILIFKE (ex-MSC 304)**	21-11-64	9-65
M 515 SAROS (ex-MSC 305)**	1-5-65	2-66
M 516 SIGAÇIK (ex-MSC 311)**	12-6-64	8-64
M 517 SAPANCA (ex-MSC 312)**	14-9-64	26-7-65
M 518 SARIYER (ex-MSC 315)**	21-4-66	8-9-67

Bldrs: M 507: Hiltebrant DD, Kingston, N.Y.; M 508: Stephen Bros.; M 509: South Coast Co., Newport Beach, Cal.; M 510 to M 513: Bellingham SY, Bellingham, Wash.; M 514, M 515: Dorchester Builders, Dorchester, N.J.; M 516 to M 518: Peterson Builders, Sturgeon Bay, Wisc.

Selçuk (M 508)   J.-C. Bellonne, 1970

D: 300 tons (392 fl)   **S:** 14 kts   **Dim:** 43.0 (41.5 pp) × 7.95 × 2.55
A: 2/20-mm AA (II × 1)   **M:** 2 GM 8-268A diesels; 2 props; 1,200 hp
Range: 2,500/10   **Man:** 4 officers, 34 men

MINE WARFARE SHIPS *(continued)*

REMARKS: M 507 was returned to the U.S.A. by Belgium in 1970, and M 508 and M 509 were returned by France on 23-3-70, then transferred to Turkey. The MSC 268 class have 4 GM 6-71 diesels; 2 props; 880 hp. The MSC 289 class have lower superstructure, taller stacks, and 2 Waukesha L-1616 diesels of 600 hp each; **Dim:** 44.32 × 8.29 × 2.55.

♦ **4 ex-Canadian Bay-class coastal minesweepers** Bldr: Davie SB, Lauzon, Quebec

	L		L
M 530 TRABZON (ex-*Gaspé*)	20-5-73	M 532 TIREBOLU (ex-*Comax*)	24-4-52
M 531 TERME (ex-*Trinity*)	31-7-53	M 533 TEKIRDAG (ex-*Ungava*)	12-11-51

Trabzon (M 530)—wearing old number   1969

D: 390 tons (412 fl) **S:** 16 kts **Dim:** 50.0 (46.05 pp) × 9.21 × 2.8
A: 1/40-mm AA **Electron Equipt:** Radar: 1/Sperry Mk 2
M: 2 GM 12-278A diesels; 2 props; 2,400 hp **Range:** 4,000/10 **Man:** 44 tot.
Electric: 940 kw sweep/plus 690 kw ship's service **Fuel:** 52 tons

REMARKS: Transferred under U.S. Military Aid Program on 19-5-58. Wood-planked skin on steel frame.

♦ **4 ex-U.S. Cape-class inshore minesweepers**

Bldr: Peterson Builders, Sturgeon Bay, Wisc.

	L	In serv.
M 500 FOCA (ex-MSI 15)	23-8-66	8-67
M 501 FETHIYE (ex-MSI 16)	7-12-66	9-67
M 502 FATSA (ex-MSI 17)	11-4-67	10-67
M 503 FINIKE (ex-MSI 18)	11-67	12-67

D: 203 tons (239 fl) **S:** 12.5 kts **Dim:** 34.06 × 7.14 × 2.4
A: 1/12.7-mm mg **M:** 4 GM 6-71 diesels; 2 props; 960 hp
Electric: 120 kw **Fuel:** 20 tons **Range:** 1,000/9 **Man:** 20 tot.

REMARKS: Transferred on completion. Wooden construction.

♦ **2 ex-U.S. 64-foot distribution-box minefield tenders**

Y 1148 SAMANDIRA L 1   Y 1149 SAMANDIRA L 2

D: 72 tons (fl) **S:** 9.5 kts **Dim:** 19.58 × 5.72 × 1.83
M: 1 Gray Marine 64HN9 diesel; 1 prop; 225 hp **Man:** 6 tot.

REMARKS: Transferred in 1959.

Fethiye (M 501)   1970

♦ **9 mine-disposal diving tenders** Bldr: G.B. (In serv. 1942)

P 311 MTB 1	P 314 MTB 4	P 318 MTB 8
P 312 MTB 2	P 316 MTB 6	P 319 MTB 9
P 313 MTB 3	P 317 MTB 7	P 320 MTB 10

D: 70 tons **S:** 20 kts **Dim:** 21.8 × 4.2 × 2.6
M: 2 diesels; 2,000 hp

AMPHIBIOUS WARFARE SHIPS AND CRAFT

NOTE: The *Cakabey* (NL 405), *Bayraktar* (NL 120) and *Sancaktar* (NL 121), formerly listed as landing ships, and now listed as minelayers; they can still be employed in amphibious landings.

♦ **2 ex-U.S. Terrebonne Parish-class tank landing ships**

Bldr: Christy Corp., Sturgeon Bay, Wisc.

	L	In serv.
L 401 ERTUGRUL (ex-*Windham County*, LST 1170)	22-5-54	15-12-54
L 402 SERDAR (ex-*Westchester County*, LST 1167)	18-4-53	10-3-54

D: 2,590 tons (5,786 fl) **S:** 15 kts **Dim:** 117.35 (112.77 pp) × 17.06 × 5.18
A: 6/76.2-mm DP (II × 3) **Electron Equipt:** Radar: 1/SPS-21, 2/Mk 34
M: 4 GM 16-268A diesels; 2 CP props; 6,000 hp **Electric:** 600 kw
Fuel: 874 tons **Man:** 116 crew + 395 troops

REMARKS: L 401 transferred in 6-73 and L 402 in 8-74. Cargo: 2,200 tons. Can carry four LCVPs in Welin davits. Two Mk 63 radar GFCS.

♦ **34 (+ . . .) Ç 107-class utility landing craft** (In serv. 1966-. . .)

Bldrs: Ç 107 through Ç 138: Gölcük Naval SY; Ç 139-141: Taskizak NDY

Ç 107 through Ç 132   Ç 134 through Ç 141

D: 280 tons light (600 fl) **S:** 8.5 kts (Loaded) **Dim:** 56.56 × 11.58 × 1.25 (aft)
A: 2/20-mm AA (I × 2)—2/12.7-mm mg (I × 2)
M: 3 GM 6-71 diesels; 3 props; 900 hp (675 sust.)
Range: 600/10 (light); 1,100/8

AMPHIBIOUS WARFARE SHIPS AND CRAFT *(continued)*

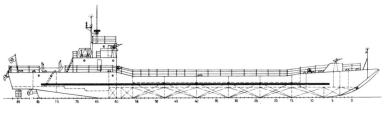

Ç 107 class   Gölçük Naval SY, 1980

REMARKS: Continuing construction program, design based on British LCT(4) design. Also being built for Libya, which received Ç 133 and Ç 134 from Turkish inventory in 12-79. Ç 137 and Ç 138 were launched 21-3-80 and commissioned 20-7-81; Ç 139 through Ç 141 were laid down at Taskizak during 1981. Can carry 100 troops and five M-48 tanks.

♦ 5 ex-British LCT (4)-class utility landing ships

Ç 101   Ç 103   Ç 104   Ç 105   Ç 106

D: 280 tons (600 fl)   **S:** 9.5 kts   **Dim:** 57.07 × 11.79 × 1.3 (aft)
A: 2/20-mm AA (I × 2)   **M:** 2 Paxman diesels; 2 props; 1,000 hp
Range: 500/9.5; 1,100/8   **Man:** 15 tot.

REMARKS: Transferred on 25-9-47. Cargo: 350 tons. Considerably modernized since transfer.

♦ 14 (+. . .) utility landing craft Bldr: Taskizak, Istanbul, 1965-66

Ç 205 through Ç 218

Ç 211   1973

D: 320 tons (405 fl)   **S:** 10 kts   **Dim:** 44.3 (40.3 wl) × 8.5 × 1.7
A: 2/20-mm AA (I × 2)   **M:** 2 GM 6-71 diesels; 3 props; 600 hp (450 sust.)

♦ 4 ex-U.S. LCU 501 (LCT (6))-class utility landing craft

Bldr: Pidgeon-Thomas Iron Co., Memphis, Tenn.

	L	In serv.		L	In serv.
Ç 201 (ex-LCU 588)	8-10-43	13-10-43	Ç 203 (ex-LCU 666)	5-2-44	12-2-44
Ç 202 (ex-LCU 608)	12-12-43	18-12-43	Ç 204 (ex-LCU 667)	9-2-44	16-2-44

Ç 201   1976

D: 143 tons (309 fl)   **S:** 8 kts   **Dim:** 36.68 × 9.75 × 1.22 (aft)
A: 2/20-mm AA (I × 2)   **M:** 3 Gray Marine 64HN9 diesels; 3 props; 675 hp
Electric: 20 kw   **Fuel:** 11 tons   **Range:** 700/7   **Man:** 12 tot.

REMARKS: Transferred in 7-67. Cargo: 150 tons + 8 troops.

♦ 20 U.S. LCM (8)-class landing craft Bldr: Taskizak NDY, Istanbul (In serv. 1965-66)

Ç 301 through Ç 320

D: 56 tons (113 fl)   **S:** 9 kts   **Dim:** 22.43 × 6.42 × 1.6
A: 2/12.7-mm mg   **M:** 4 GM 6-71 diesels; 2 props; 660 hp   **Man:** 5 tot.

HYDROGRAPHIC SHIPS

♦ 2 ex-British Catherine-class former minesweepers

Bldrs: A 593: Assoc. SB, Lake Washington, Wash.; A 594: Gulf SB, Mobile, Ala.

	Laid down	L	In serv.
A 593 ÇANDARLI (ex-*Frolic*, ex-BAM 29)	5-3-43	20-6-43	18-5-44
A 594 ÇARŞAMBA (ex-*Tattoo*, ex-BAM 32)	8-6-42	27-1-43	29-10-43

D: 1,010 tons (1,185 fl)   **S:** 18 kts   **Dim:** 67.31 × 9.75 × 3.2
A: 1/76.2-mm DP—4/20-mm AA   **Electron Equipt:** Radar: 1/Decca 707
M: 4 GM 12-278A diesels, electric drive; 2 props; 3,532 hp   **Electric:** 360 kw
Fuel: 210 tons   **Range:** 3,500/17; 8,500/11   **Man:** 105 tot.

REMARKS: Lend-lease version of the U.S. *Auk* class, transferred to Great Britain on completion. Survivors of a group of seven transferred to Turkey in 3-47. Converted later for service as survey ships. Charthouse added between stacks.

♦ 2 ex-U.S. 52-foot inshore-survey craft (In serv. 1966)

Y 1221 MESAHA 1   Y 1222 MESAHA 2

D: 31.7 tons (37.6 fl)   **S:** 10 kts   **Dim:** 15.9 × 4.45 × 1.3
M: 2 GM 6-71 diesels; 2 props; 330 hp   **Range:** 600/10   **Man:** 10 tot.

HYDROGRAPHIC SHIPS *(continued)*

Çandarli (A 593)   G. Arra, 1972

AUXILIARY SHIPS

♦ **1 transport oiler** Bldr: Gölçük Naval SY, Istanbul (L: 1979)

A 591 N. . .

    D: 9,760 tons (fl) **S:** 13.5 kts **Dim:** 111.1 (108.7 fl) × 16.1 × . . .
    A: . . . **M:** 1 diesel; 1 prop; 4,800 hp

REMARKS: 6,000 dwt. Eighteen cargo tanks. No underway replenishment capability.

♦ **1 Turkish-designed replenishment oiler** Bldr: Taskizak NDY, Istanbul (L: 7-69)

A 573 BİNBAŞI SAADETTIN GÜRCAN

    D: 1,505 tons (4,680 fl) **S:** 16 kts **Dim:** 89.7 × 11.8 × 5.4
    A: 1/40-mm AA—2/20-mm AA (I × 2)
    M: 4 GM 16-567A diesels, electric drive; 2 props; 4,400 hp

REMARKS: One liquid-replenishment station on each side. Primarily a tanker.

♦ **1 Turkish-designed replenishment oiler** Bldr: Gölçük NSY, 1964

A 572 ALBAY HAKKI BURAK

    D: 1,800 tons (3,740 fl) **S:** 16 kts **Dim:** 83.73 × 12.25 × 5.49
    A: 2/40-mm AA (I × 2) **Electron Equipt:** Radar: 1/Decca 707
    M: 4 GM 16-567A diesels, electric drive; 2 props; 4,400 hp **Man:** 88 tot.

REMARKS: One liquid-replenishment station on each side. Primarily a tanker.

♦ **1 ex-West German Bodensee-class replenishment oiler** Bldr: Lindenau-Werft, Kiel

	Laid down	L	In serv.
A 575 ÜNÄBOLU (ex-*Bodensee*, ex-*Unkas*)	24-8-55	19-11-55	11-2-56

    D: 1,237 tons (1,840 fl) **S:** 13.5 kts **Dim:** 67.1 (61.2 pp) × 9.84 × 4.27
    A: . . . **Electron Equipt:** Radar: 1/Kelvin-Hughes 14/9

Ünäbolu (A 575)—as the **Bodensee**   1975

    M: 1 MAK 6-cyl. diesel; 1 prop; 1,050 hp **Electric:** 238 kVA
    Range: 6,240/12 **Man:** 21 tot.

REMARKS: Former merchant tanker acquired on 26-3-59 for the West German Navy; transferred to Turkey on 25-8-77. Cargo: 1,231 tons. One replenishment station.

♦ **1 Turkish-designed replenishment oiler** Bldr: Taskizak NDY, Istanbul

A 571 YUZBASI TOLÜNAY (ex-*Taskizak*)

    D: 2,500 tons (3,500 fl) **S:** 14 kts **Dim:** 79.0 × 12.4 × 5.9
    A: 2/40-mm AA (I × 2) **M:** 2 Atlas-Polar diesels; 2 props; 1,900 hp

REMARKS: Launched on 22-8-50. Has one alongside replenishment station and can replenish over the stern.

♦ **1 ex-U.S. Mettawee-class former gasoline tanker** Bldr: East Coast SY, Bayonne, N.J.

	Laid down	L	In serv.
A 574 AKPINAR (ex-*Chiwaukum*, AOG 26)	2-4-44	5-5-44	22-7-44

    D: 700 tons (2,270 fl) **S:** 14 kts **Dim:** 67.21 (64.77 pp) × 11.28 × 3.99
    A: 1/76.2-mm DP—1/40-mm AA—2/20-mm AA
    M: 1 Fairbanks-Morse 37E16 diesel; 1 prop; 800 hp
    Electric: 155 kw **Fuel:** 29 tons

REMARKS: Transferred in 5-48. Cargo: 1,365 tons. Very low freeboard restricts use to sheltered waters.

NOTE: Former tanker *Akar* (A 570, ex-*Adour*) is used as a fuel storage hulk at Gölçük.

♦ **2 tenders, ex-West German Angeln-class cargo ships**

Bldr: Ateliers et Chantiers de Bretagne, Nantes, France

	Laid down	L	In serv.
A 586 ÜLKÜ (ex-*Angeln*, ex-*Borée*)	17-5-54	9-10-54	20-1-55
A 588 UMERBEY (ex-*Dithmarschen*, ex-*Hebé*)	20-10-54	7-5-55	17-11-55

    D: 2,998 tons (4,089 fl) **S:** 19 kts **Dim:** 90.53 (84.5 pp) × 13.32 × 6.2
    A: 2/20-mm AA (I × 2) **M:** 2 SEMT-Pielstick 6-cyl.diesels; 1 prop; 3,000 hp
    Electric: 335 kw **Range:** 3,660/15 **Man:** 57 tot.

REMARKS: Former French cargo ships acquired for the West German Navy on 27-11-59 and 19-12-59, respectively. A 586 was transferred to Turkey on 28-3-72 and A 588 on 6-10-76. A 586 is used as a patrol-boat tender and A 588 as a submarine tender. A 588's displacement is: 3,098 tons (4,189 fl). Cargo: A 586, 2,665 tons; A 588, 2,670 tons. Six 2.5-ton derricks, three holds.

AUXILIARY SHIPS (continued)

Ülkü (A 586)—as the **Angeln**

♦ **1 ex-U.S. Portunus-class patrol-boat tender** Bldr: Bethlehem Steel, Hingham, Mass.

	Laid down	L	In serv.
A 581 ONARAN (ex-*Alecto*, AGP 14, ex-LST 977)	12-12-44	15-1-45	8-2-45

Onaran (A 581) G. Arra, 1971

D: 4,100 tons (fl) **S:** 11.6 kts **Dim:** 99.98 × 15.24 × 3.4
A: 8/40-mm AA (IV × 2)—8/20-mm AA (II × 4)
M: 2 GM 12-278A diesels; 2 props; 1,800 hp **Electric:** 500 kw
Fuel: 590 tons **Range:** 9,000/9 **Man:** 291 tot.

REMARKS: Transferred in 11-52. Retains bow doors. Superstructure enlarged after transfer.

♦ **1 ex-U.S. Achelous-class submarine tender** Bldr: Bethlehem Steel, Hingham, Mass.

	Laid down	L	In serv.
A 582 BASARAN (ex-*Patroclus*, ARL 19, ex-LST 955)	22-9-44	22-10-44	13-11-44

REMARKS: Former landing-craft repair ship. Data as for *Onaran*, above, except: **Electric:** 420 kw; **Fuel:** 621 tons. Has less superstructure than *Oneran*.

♦ **1 ex-U.S. Aegir-class submarine tender** Bldr: Ingalls, Pascagoula, Miss.

	Laid down	L	In serv.
A 583 DONATAN (ex-*Anthedon*, AS 24)	1943	15-10-43	15-9-44

Donatan (A 583) 1970

D: 16,500 tons (fl) **S:** 18.4 kts (trials)
Dim: 149.96 (141.73 pp) × 21.18 × 8.23
A: 3/76.2-mm DP (I × 3)—8/40-mm AA (II × 1, I × 6)—8/20-mm AA (I × 8)
M: 1 set Westinghouse GT; 1 prop; 8,500 hp
Boilers: 2 Foster-Wheeler "D"; 37.2 kg/cm², 407°C
Electric: 1,200 kw **Fuel:** 3,045 tons **Man:** 1,460 tot.

REMARKS: Transferred on 7-2-69. Had been in U.S. Navy Reserve Fleet since 21-9-46. Unarmed at transfer. A helicopter platform has been added over the stern.

♦ **1 submarine tender** Bldr: Nakskov SY, Nakskov, Denmark

A 599 ERKIN (ex-*Trabzon*, ex-*Imperial*)

Erkin (A 599)—wearing old number G. Arra, 1972

D: 9,900 tons (fl) **S:** 16 kts **Dim:** 134.25 (125.0 pp) × 17.8 × 7.2
A: 2/40-mm AA (II × 1) **Electron Equipt:** Radar: 1/Decca 707, 1/SG-1
M: 1 Fiat B-680-S diesel; 1 prop; 6,560 hp
Electric: 720 kw **Fuel:** 1,380 tons **Range:** 15,950/16 **Man:** 128 tot.

REMARKS: Built as the Chilean passenger-cargo ship *Imperial*; acquired by the U.S. Army on 30-8-43 as a troop transport with same name. Sold to Turkey in 1948 as commercial ship *Trabzon*; taken over by the Turkish Navy for conversion to a submarine-support ship in 1968 and commissioned in 1970. Can carry more than 500 passengers.

♦ **1 ex-U.S. AN 103-class net tender** Bldr: Krögerwerft, Rendsburg, West Germany

	Laid down	L	In serv.
P 305 AG 5 (ex-AN 104)	1960	20-10-60	5-2-61

AUXILIARY SHIPS (continued)

D: 680 tons (960 fl) **S:** 12 kts **Dim:** 52.5 × 10.5 × 4.05
A: 1/40-mm AA—3/20-mm AA (I × 3)
M: 4 M.A.N. 67V 40/60 diesels; 2 props; 1,450 hp
Range: 8,000/12 **Man:** 48 tot.

REMARKS: Sister to the net layer *Thetis* in the Greek Navy. Built with U.S. Offshore Procurement funds.

♦ **1 ex-U.S. AN 93-class net-tender** Bldr: Bethlehem Steel, Staten Island, N.Y.

	L	In serv.
P 306 AG 6 (ex-*Cerberus*, ex-AN 93)	5-52	10-11-52

D: 780 tons (902 fl) **S:** 12.8 kts **Dim:** 50.29 (44.5 pp) × 10.20 × 3.2
A: 1/76.2-mm DP—4/20-mm AA (I × 4)
M: 2 GM 8-268A diesels, electric drive; 1 prop; 1,500 hp
Range: 5,200/12 **Man:** 48 tot.

REMARKS: Prototype of a class also built in France and Italy. Transferred to the Netherlands in 12-52 and returned 17-9-70; transferred to Turkey the same day.

♦ **1 ex-U.S. Aloe-class net tender** Bldr: Marietta Mfg. Co., Pt. Pleasant, W. Va.

	Laid down	L	In serv.
P 304 AG 4 (ex-*Larch*, AN 21, ex-YN 16)	18-10-40	2-7-41	13-12-41

D: 560 tons (805 fl) **S:** 12.5 kts **Dim:** 49.73 (44.5 wl) × 9.3 × 3.56
A: 1/76.2-mm DP—4/20-mm AA (I × 4)
M: 2 Alco 538-6 diesels, electric drive; 1 prop; 620 hp
Electric: 120 kw **Fuel:** 80 tons **Man:** 48 tot.

REMARKS: Transferred in 5-46.

♦ **1 ex-British "Bar"-class net tender** Bldr: Blyth DD & SB Co., G.B.

	Laid down	L	In serv.
P 301 AG 2 (ex-*Barbarian*)	10-6-37	21-10-37	16-4-38

D: 750 tons (1,000 fl) **S:** 11.7 kts **Dim:** 52.96 × 9.8 × 4.62
A: 1/76.2-mm DP **M:** 1 set triple-expansion; 1 prop; 850 hp
Boilers: 2, single-end, three-drum **Fuel:** 214 tons
Range: 3,100/10 **Man:** 32 tot.

REMARKS: Transferred in 1947. Sisters *AG 2* (ex-*Barbette*) and *AG 3* (ex-*Barfair*) were stricken in 1975.

♦ **1 ex-U.S. Bluebird-class submarine-rescue ship**

Bldr: Charleston SB & DD Co., Charleston, S.C.

	Laid down	L	In serv.
A 584 KURTARAN (ex-*Bluebird*, ASR 19, ex-*Yurok*, ATF 164)	23-6-45	15-2-46	28-5-46

D: 1,294 tons (1,760 fl) **S:** 16 kts **Dim:** 62.48 (59.44) × 12.19 × 4.88
A: 1/76.2-mm DP **M:** 4 GM 12-278A diesels, electric drive; 1 prop; 3,000 hp
Electric: 600 kw **Fuel:** 300 tons **Man:** 100 tot.

REMARKS: Begun as an *Achomawi*-class fleet tug but altered while under construction, wooden fenders adding .5 meters to the beam. Carries McCann rescue diving bell and four marker buoys. Transferred on 15-8-50.

Kurtaran (A 584)   1970

♦ **1 ex-U.S. Chanticleer-class submarine-rescue ship**

Bldr: Moore SB & DD Co., Oakland, Cal.

	Laid down	L	In serv.
A 585 AKIN (ex-*Greenlet*, ASR 10)	15-10-41	12-7-42	29-5-43

D: 1,770 tons (2,321 fl) **S:** 15 kts **Dim:** 76.61 (73.15 pp) × 12.8 × 4.52
A: 1/40-mm AA—4/20-mm AA (II × 2) **Electron Equipt:** Radar: 1/SPS-5
M: 4 Alco 539 diesels, electric drive; 1 prop; 3,000 hp
Electric: 460 kw **Fuel:** 235 tons **Man:** 85 tot.

REMARKS: Loaned on 12-6-70 and purchased outright on 15-2-73. Carries McCann rescue diving bell and four marker buoys.

♦ **1 ex-U.S. Diver-class salvage ship** Bldr: Basalt Rock Co., Napa, Cal.

	Laid down	L	In serv.
A 589 ISIN (ex-*Safeguard*, ARS 25)	5-6-43	20-11-43	31-10-44

D: 1,480 tons (1,970 fl) **S:** 14.8 kts **Dim:** 65.08 (63.09 pp) × 12.5 × 4.0
A: 2/20-mm AA (I × 2)
M: 4 Cooper-Bessemer GSB-8 diesels, electric drive; 2 props; 3,000 hp
Electric: 460 kw **Fuel:** 300 tons **Man:** 97 tot.

REMARKS: Purchased on 28-9-79. Wooden fenders add .6 meters to beam.

♦ **1 training ship** Bldr: Schlieker, Hamburg, West Germany

	Laid down	L	In serv.
A 579 CEZAYIRLI GAZI HASAN PAŞA (ex-*Ruhr*)	1959	18-8-60	2-5-64

Cezayirli Gazi Hasan Paşa (A 579)   French Navy, 1979

AUXILIARY SHIPS (continued)

D: 2,370 tons (2,740 fl) **S:** 20 kts **Dim:** 98.18 × 11.8 × 3.9
A: 2/100-mm French Model 1953 DP (I × 2)—4/40-mm AA (I × 4)—2/d.c. racks—
    70 mines
Electron Equipt: Radar: 1/HSA SGR 105, 1/HSA SGR 103, 2/HSA M 45
M: 6 Maybach 16-cyl. diesels; 2 CP props; 11,400 hp
Electric: 2,250 kw **Fuel:** 113 tons **Range:** 1,600/16 **Man:** 120 tot.

REMARKS: Ex-German *Rhein*-class former patrol-boat tender. Transferred on 15-11-76, having served primarily as a training ship in the West German Navy until placed in reserve on 20-12-71. Two radar directors for the 100-mm guns.

◆ **1 training ship** Bldr: Blohm & Voss, Hamburg, West Germany (L: 28-2-31)

A 578 SAVARONA (ex-*Gunes Dil*)

Savarona (A 578)   J.-C. Bellonne, 1973

D: 5,750 tons (fl) **S:** 18 kts **Dim:** 123.0 × 16.1 × 5.6
A: 2/75-mm (I × 2)—2/40-mm AA (I × 2)—2/20-mm (I × 2)
Electron Equipt: Radar: 2/Sperry Mk 2 **M:** 2 sets GT; 2 props; 8,000 hp
Boilers: 4 **Range:** 9,000/15 **Man:** 132 crew, 80 midshipmen

REMARKS: A former state yacht converted to a cadet-training ship in 1952. Pendant number not painted on. White hull, buff stacks. Has 75-mm guns for saluting. Seriously damaged by fire 3-10-79.

◆ **1 ex-U.S. Cherokee-class fleet tug** Bldr: United Eng. Co., Alameda, Cal.

	Laid down	L	In serv.
A 587 GAZAL (ex-*Sioux*, ATF 75)	14-2-42	27-5-42	6-12-42

D: 1,235 tons (1,675 fl) **S:** 16.5 kts **Dim:** 62.48 (59.44 pp) × 11.73 × 4.67
A: 1/76.2-mm DP **M:** 4 GM 12-278 diesels, electric drive; 1 prop; 3,000 hp
Electric: 260 kw **Fuel:** 300 tons **Man:** 85 tot.

REMARKS: Transferred on 30-10-72 and purchased outright on 15-8-73. Can be used for salvage. Similar to submarine-rescue ship *Kurtaran* (A 584).

SERVICE CRAFT

◆ **1 yard oiler** Bldr: Gölcük NSY (L: 4-11-35)

Y 1207 GÖLÇÜK

    D: 1,250 tons **S:** 12.5 kts **Dim:** 56.4 × 9.55 × 3.05
    A: none **M:** 1 Burmeister & Wain diesel; 700 hp

REMARKS: Cargo: 760 tons. Former number A 573.

◆ **3 small yard oilers** Bldr: Taskizak NDY, Istanbul (In serv....)

Y 1233 H 500   Y 1234 H 501   Y 1235 H 503

    D: 300 tons **S:** 11 kts **Dim:** 33.6 × 8.5 × 1.8
    M: 1 GM 6-71 diesel; 1 prop; 225 hp **Cargo:** 150 tons

◆ **1 small water tanker** Bldr: Gölcük Naval DY (L: 1979)

Y 1240

    D: 850 tons (fl) **S:** 10 kts **Dim:** 51.8 (46.8 pp) × 8.1 ×...
    M: 1 diesel; 1 prop; 480 hp **Cargo:** 530 dwt

◆ **2 Van-class water tankers** Bldr: Gölcük NSY, 1969-70

Y 1208 VAN   Y 1209 ULABAT

    D: 900 tons (1,250 fl) **S:** 10 kts **S:** 53.1 × 9.0 × 3.0
    A: 1/20-mm AA **M:** 1 diesel; 1 prop; 650 hp **Cargo:** 700 tons

◆ **1 ex-German FW 1-class water tanker** Bldr: Schichau, Bremerhaven

	Laid down	L	In serv.
Y 1217 SÖGÜT (ex-FW 2)	5-4-63	3-9-63	4-1-64

    D: 598 tons (647 fl) **S:** 9.5 kts **Dim:** 44.03 (41.1 pp) × 7.8 × 2.63
    M: 1 MWM 12-cyl. diesel; 1 prop; 230 hp **Electric:** 130 kVA
    Fuel: 15 tons **Range:** 2,150/9 **Man:** 12 tot.

REMARKS: Transferred on 3-12-75. Cargo: 343 tons of fresh water.

◆ **6 Pinar-class small water tenders** Bldr: Taskizak NDY, Istanbul

Y 1211   Y 1212   Y 1213   Y 1214   Y 1215   Y 1216

    D: 300 tons **S:** 11 kts **Dim:** 33.6 × 8.5 × 1.8
    M: 1 GM 6-71 diesel; 1 prop; 225 hp **Cargo:** 150 tons

◆ **3 Kanarya-class cargo lighters** Bldr: Taskizak NDY, Istanbul (In serv. 1972-74)

Y 1155 KANARYA   Y 1156 SARKÖY   Y 1165 ECEABAD

Kanarya (Y 1155)—at launch   1972

SERVICE CRAFT (continued)

D: 823 tons (fl) **S:** 10 kts **Dim:** 50.7 (47.4 pp) × 8.0 × . . .
A: 1/20-mm AA **M:** 1 diesel; 1 prop; 1,440 hp

REMARKS: 500 dwt. Moulded depth: 3.6 m.

♦ **4 transport ferries** Bldr: Great Britain, 1940-42

Y 1163 LAPSEKI Y 1164 ERDEK Y 1166 KILYA Y 1168 TUZLA

Lapseki (Y 1163)

D: 700 tons (1,012 grt) **S:** 9.5 kts **Dim:** 56.0 × 12.2 × 2.7
A: 1/20-mm AA **M:** 1 set reciprocating steam; 1 prop; 700 hp

REMARKS: Survivors of a class of eleven. Used as personnel and vehicle ferries in the Dardanelles. Ramps at both ends. Can quickly convert to minelayers.

♦ **4 training craft, ex-British HDML-class patrol craft** (In serv. 1943-45)

Y 1223 MESAHA 3 Y 1224 MESAHA 4 Y 1108 Y 1109

D: 46 tons (54 fl) **S:** 11 kts **Dim:** 21.95 × 4.83 × 1.50
M: 2 diesels; 2 props; 320 hp **Range:** 900/10 **Man:** 9 tot.

REMARKS: Y 1223 and Y 1224 formerly used as inshore survey boats. Wooden construction.

♦ **1 training craft, tender to Naval Academy**

Y 1100 TOROS—no further data available

♦ **1 training craft, former minelayer** Bldr: Gölcük NSY (In serv. 1938)

Y 1101 ATAK

D: 350 tons (500 fl) **S:** 13 kts **Dim:** 44.0 × 7.4 × 3.6
M: 1 Atlas-Polar diesel; 1 prop; 1,025 hp

REMARKS: Tender to Naval Academy; resembles a coastal tug.

♦ **3 ex-U.S. non-self-propelled gate craft** Bldr: Weaver SY, Orange, Texas (In serv. 1960-61)

Y 1201 (ex-YNG 45) Y 1202 (ex-YNG 46) Y 1203 (ex-YNG 47)

D: 325 tons (fl) **Dim:** 33.5 × 10.4 × 1.5

♦ **2 ex-U.S. APL 41-class barracks barges**

	Bldr	L
Y 1204 NAŞIT ÖNGEREN (ex-APL 47)	Puget Sound Bridge & Dredge, Seattle, Wash.	5-1-45
Y 1205 BINBAŞI METIN SÜLÜS (ex-APL 53)	Tampa SB, Tampa, Fla.	3-3-45

D: 2,660 tons (fl) **Dim:** 79.6 × 14.99 × 2.59
Electric: 300 kw **Man:** 650 tot.

REMARKS: Y 1204 was leased in 10-72, Y 1205 in 12-74. Lease extended 1982.

♦ **2 Oncü-class coastal tugs** Bldr: Gölcük NSY (In serv. 1953)

Y 1123 ONCÜ Y 1124 ÖNDER

D: 500 tons **S:** 12 kts **Dim:** 40.0 × 9.1 × 4.0 **M:** Diesel

♦ **3 ex-U.S. Army 254-design coastal tugs** Bldr: U.S.A. (In serv. 1943-44)

Y 1118 AKBAS (ex-. . .) Y 1119 KEPEZ (ex-. . .) Y 1120 ONDEV (ex-. . .)

D: 570 tons (967 fl) **S:** 12 kts **Dim:** 45.42 (42.67 pp) × 10.06 × 4.12
M: 1 set Skinner Uniflow reciprocating steam; 1 prop; . . . hp
Electric: 50 kw **Boilers:** 2 **Fuel:** 400 tons **Man:** 28 tot.

REMARKS: Transferred in 1963.

♦ **1 ex-U.S. coastal tug**

Y 1122 KUVVET (ex-. . .)

D: 390 tons **S:** . . . **Dim:** 32.1 × 7.9 × 3.6

REMARKS: Transferred in 2-62.

♦ **1 ex-U.S. Army 320-design small harbor tug**

Y 1134 ERSEN BAYRAK

D: 30 tons **S:** 9 kts **Dim:** 13.8 × 3.9 × 1.6
M: 1 diesel; 1 prop; 175 hp

REMARKS: Transferred in 6-71.

♦ **3 Turkish-designed harbor tugs** Bldr: Denizcilik, Bancusi (In serv. 1976)

Y 1130 GÜVEN Y 1132 ATIL Y 1133 DOĞANARSLAN

D: 300 grt **S:** . . . **Dim:** 32.8 × 8.9 × . . . **M:** Diesels; 250 hp

♦ **2 ex-U.S. small harbor tugs**

Y 1117 SONDUREN (ex-YTL 751) Y 1121 YEDEKCI (ex-YTL 155)

D: 100 tons (120 fl) **S:** 12 kts **Dim:** 21.34 × 5.89 × 2.21
M: 1 Atlas diesel; 1 prop; 500 hp **Fuel:** 18 tons

REMARKS: Transferred in 4-54 and 11-57.

SERVICE CRAFT (continued)

♦ **5 battery-charging craft, ex-U.S. Balao-class submarines** Bldrs: Y 1240, Y 1241: Electric Boat, Groton, Conn.; others: Manitowoc SB, Manitowoc, Wisc.

	Laid down	L	In serv.
Y 1240 CERYAN BOTU I (ex-*Canakkale*, ex-*Bumper*, SS 333)	4-11-43	6-8-44	9-12-44
Y 1241 CERYAN BOTU II (ex-*Inici Inönu*, ex-*Blueback*, SS 326)	29-7-43	7-5-44	28-8-44
Y 1242 CERYAN BOTU III (ex-*Cerbe*, ex-*Hammerhead*, SS 364)	5-5-43	24-10-43	1-3-44
Y 1242 CERYAN BOTU IV (ex-*Preveze*, ex-*Guitarro*, SS 363)	7-4-43	26-9-43	26-1-44
Y 1244 CERYAN BOTU V (ex-*Piri Reis*, ex-*Mapiro*, SS 376)	30-5-44	9-11-44	30-4-45

D: 1,810 tons (fl) **Dim:** 95.0 × 8.31 × 4.65
Electric: 4,700 kw (4 GM 16-278A diesels)

REMARKS: Former fleet submarines relegated to harbor service during the mid-1970s. Also used as accommodations ships and for basic submarine training. All at Gölcük.

♦ **1 ex-U.S. floating crane** Bldr: Odenback SB, Rochester, N.Y. (In serv. 14-8-51)

Y 1023 ALGARNA III (ex-YD 185)

D: 1,200 tons (fl) **Dim:** 36.6 × 13.7 × 2.7

REMARKS: Transferred in 9-63.

♦ **3 miscellaneous floating cranes**—no data available

Y 1021 ALGARNA I   Y 1022 ALGARNA II   Y 1024 TURGUT ALP

♦ **1 dredge**

Y 1029 TARAK—D: 200 tons

♦ **16 miscellaneous service launches**—no data available

Y 1181 through Y 1193, Y 1198, Y 1199 MAVNA 1 through MAVNA 15
Y 1052 TAKIP

♦ **1 ex-U.S. ARD 12-class floating dry dock** Bldr: Pacific Bridge, Alameda, Cal.

Y 1087 (ex-ARD 12)   (In serv. 10-43)

Dim: 149.86 × 24.69 × 1.73 (light)   **Lift capacity:** 3,500 tons

REMARKS: Launched in 1943 and loaned in 11-71.

♦ **7 miscellaneous floating dry docks**

Y 1081 (16,000-ton capacity)	Y 1084 (4,500-ton capacity)
Y 1082 (12,000-ton capacity)	Y 1085 (400-ton capacity)
Y 1083 (2,500-ton capacity)	Y 1086 (3,000-ton capacity)
	Y . . . (4,500-ton capacity)

REMARKS: Y 1083 was built in Turkey in 1958 with U.S. funds; Dim: 116.5 × 26.4 × 9.0 max. These docks are named in sequence *Havuz I* to *Havuz VI*. A new 3-section floating drydock was completed late in 1980.

MARINE POLICE FORCE (GENDARMERIE)

PATROL BOATS

♦ **7 (+7) SAR-33 class**

Bldrs: J 61: Abeking & Rasmussen, Lemwerder, West Germany; others: Taskizak NDY, Istanbul

J 61 through J 71

D: 150 tons (170 fl) **S:** 40 kts   **Dim:** 33.5 (29.0 wl) × 8.6 × 1.85
A: 1/40-mm AA—2/12.7-mm mg (I × 2)
M: 3 SACM-AGO V16CSHR diesels; 3 CP props; 12,000 hp
Electric: 300 kw   **Fuel:** 18 tons   **Range:** 450/35; 1,000/. . .   **Man:** 23 tot.

REMARKS: J 61 was launched on 12-12-77 and J 62 in 7-78; J 65 through J 67 in service 30-7-81; on the same day J 70 and J 71 were laid down. Wedge-shaped hull design of remarkable seaworthiness and steadiness at high speeds in heavy weather. Turkey is also building fourteen units of this class for Libya. The same design can accommodate guns of up to 76-mm bore, missiles, and a propulsion plant of up to twice the power of the above. The 40-mm AA is in a Mk 3 mount. J 65 and later are 37.5 m overall. A larger variant is planned: 370 tons fl, 43.0 × 9.0 × 1.8, capable of 55 kts.

♦ **23 AB 25 class** Bldr: Taskizak NDY, Istanbul, 1972-78

J 21 through J 34   J 41 through J 49

J 28   1976

D: 170 tons (fl) **S:** 22 kts   **Dim:** 40.24 × 6.4 × 1.65
A: 2/40-mm AA (I × 2)—2/12.7-mm mg (I × 2)
M: 2 SACM-AGO V16 CSHR diesels; 2 props; 4,800 hp; 2 cruise diesels; 300 hp

REMARKS: Eleven sisters are operated by the Turkish Navy. Some have one 40-mm AA aft and one 20-mm AA forward. Built with French assistance.

♦ **8 German KW 15 class** Bldr: Schweers, Bardenfleth, West Germany, 1961-62

J 12 through J 16   J 18 through J 20

D: 59.5 tons (69.6 fl) **S:** 25 kts   **Dim:** 28.9 × 4.7 × 1.42
A: 1/40-mm AA—2/20-mm AA (I × 2)
M: 2 MTU 12-cyl. diesels; 2 props; 2,000 hp
Fuel: 8 tons   **Range:** 1,500/19   **Man:** 15 tot.

TURKEY *(continued)*
PATROL BOATS *(continued)*

J 16   1970

U.S.S.R.
Union of Soviet Socialist Republics

PERSONNEL: 443,000, including 185,000 afloat personnel, 59,000 Naval Aviation, 8,000 Coastal Defense, 12,000 Naval Infantry, 54,000 training, and 125,000 shore support, plus approx. 20,000 civilians manning auxiliaries

MERCHANT MARINE (1980): 8,279 ships—23,443,534 grt
(tankers: 503 ships—4,728,079 grt)

WARSHIPS IN SERVICE OR UNDER CONSTRUCTION AS OF 1 JANUARY 1982

	L	Tons	Main armament
♦ **3 (+1) VTOL carriers**			
3 (+1) KIEV	1972-	36,000	Missile launchers, guns, helicopters, VTOL aircraft
		Tons (surfaced)	
♦ **378 (+) submarines**			
90 (+) ballistic-missile:			
1 (+. . .) TYPHOON (nuclear)	. . .	. . .	20/SS-N-20
13 (+. . .) DELTA III (nuclear)	1975-	13,250	16/SS-N-18, 6/TT
		(submerged)	
4 DELTA-II (nuclear)	1975	9,700	16/SS-N-8, 6/TT
18 DELTA-I (nuclear)	1972-75	8,100	12/SS-N-8, 6/TT
1 YANKEE-II (nuclear)	1967?	7,900	16/SS-N-6, 6/TT
26 YANKEE-I (nuclear)	1967-74	7,900	16/SS-N-6, 6/TT
1 HOTEL-III (nuclear)	1965	4,500	3/SS-N-8, 8/TT

Kirov   British MOD, 1980

WARSHIPS IN SERVICE OR UNDER CONSTRUCTION *(continued)*

6 HOTEL-II (nuclear)	1960-63	4,500	3/SS-N-5, 8/TT
1 GOLF-V (diesel)	1958-61	2,300	3/SS-N-. . . , 10/TT
1 GOLF-IV (diesel)	1958-61	2,500	6/SS-N-8, 10/TT
1 GOLF-III (diesel)	1958-61	2,300	3/SS-N-8, 10/TT
12 GOLF-II (diesel)	1958-61	2,300	3/SS-N-5, 10/TT
3 GOLF-I (diesel)	1958-61	2,300	3/SS-N-4, 10/TT

67 (+) cruise-missile attack:

1 (+. . .) OSCAR (nuclear)	1980-	10,000	24/SS-N-19, . . . /TT
1 PAPA (nuclear)	1970	6,700	10/SS-N-9, 8/TT
5 (+. . .) CHARLIE-II (nuclear)	1973-	4,300	8/SS-N-7 or 9, 6/TT
12 CHARLIE-I (nuclear)	1968-72	4,000	8/SS-N-7, 6/TT
29 ECHO-II (nuclear)	1960-68	4,800	8/SS-N-3 or SS-N-12, 10/TT
16 JULIETT (diesel)	1961-68	2,800	4/SS-N-3, 10/TT
3 WHISKEY LONG BIN (diesel)	1961-63	1,200	4/SS-N-3, 4/TT

228 (+. . .) attack:

5 (+. . .) ALFA (nuclear)	1972-	3,900	6/TT
8 (+. . .) VICTOR-III (nuclear)	1978-	4,600	8/TT
7 (+) VICTOR-II (nuclear)	1972-77	4,500	8/TT
16 VICTOR-I (nuclear)	1967-74	4,300	8/TT
7 YANKEE (nuclear)	1967-74	7,900	6/TT
5 ECHO (nuclear)	1960-68	4,600	10/TT
13 NOVEMBER (nuclear)	1958-62	4,000	12/TT
1 (+. . .) KILO (diesel)	1980	2,500	. . . /TT
14 (+. . .) TANGO (diesel)	1972-	3,000	. . . /SS-N-15, 10/TT
60 FOXTROT (diesel)	1957-74	1,950	10/TT
3 MOD GOLF (diesel)	1958-61	2,300	10/TT
10 ROMEO (diesel)	1960	1,330	8/TT
11 ZULU-IV (diesel)	1952-55	1,900	10/TT
60 WHISKEY (diesel)	1949-57	1,050	6/TT
1 WHISKEY CANVAS BAG (diesel)	1949-57	1,080	4/TT
4 QUEBEC (diesel)	1954-57	460	4/TT
2 INDIA (diesel)	1978-79	3,200	. . . /TT
4 BRAVO (diesel)	1968-72	2,400	6/TT

♦ **40 (+4) cruisers**

2 helicopter:

2 MOSKVA	1964-66	14,500	2/SA-N-3, 1/SUW-N-1, 14/helicopters,*

38 (+4) guided-missile:

0 (+3) BLK-COM-1	1979-	10,000	. . . /SS-N-12, . . . /SA-N-6*
1 (+1) KIROV (nuclear)	1977-81	21,000	20/SS-N-19, 2/SS-N-14, 12/SA-N-6, 2/SA-N-4, 2/100-mm DP, 10/TT, 3 helos
7 KARA	1971-78	8,200	8/SS-N-14, 2/SA-N-3, 4/SA-N-4, 4/76.2-mm DP, 10/TT, 1 helo
10 KRESTA-II	1967-76	6,000	8/SS-N-14, 2/SA-N-3, 4/57-mm, 10/TT, 1/helo*
4 KRESTA-I	1965-66	6,000	4/SS-N-3, 2/SA-N-1, 4/57-mm, 10/TT 1/helo*
4 KYNDA	1961-65	4,400	8/SS-N-3, 1/SA-N-1, 4/76.2-mm DP, 6/TT,*
1 MOD. SVERDLOV	1951	12,900	1/SA-N-2, 9/152-mm, 12/100-mm DP, 16/37-mm AA

Minsk

R.N., 1980

WARSHIPS IN SERVICE OR UNDER CONSTRUCTION *(continued)*

11 conventional:

2 MOD. SVERDLOV	1950-54	12,900	1/SA-N-4, 6 or 9/152-mm, 12/100-mm DP
9 SVEROLOV	1950-60	12,900	12/152-mm, 12/100-mm DP

♦ **80 (+. . .) destroyers**

42 guided-missile:

2 (+2. . .) UDALOY	1978-		8/SS-N-14, 8/SA-N. . ., 2/100-mm DP, 4/30-mm AA, 8/533-mm TT, 2/helos, mines*
2 (+2. . .) SOVREMENNYY	1978-	6,700	8/SS-N-. . ., 2/SA-N-7, 4/130-mm DP, 4/30-mm AA, 4/533-mm TT, 1/helo, mines*
6 MOD. KASHIN	1963-72	3,950	4/SS-N-2C, 2/SA-N-1, 4/76.2-mm DP, 5/TT,*
12 KASHIN	1963-72	3,750	2/SA-N-1, 4/76.2-mm DP, 5/TT,*
8 KANIN	1958-60	3,700	1/SA-N-1, 8/57-mm, 10/TT,*
3 MOD. KILDIN	1958	3,100	4/SS-N-2C, 4/76.2-mm DP, 16/45- or 57-mm AA, 4/TT,*
1 KILDIN	1958	2,900	1/SS-N-1, 16/57-mm, 4/TT,*
8 SAM KOTLIN	1955-57	2,850	1/SA-N-1, 2/130-mm DP, 12/45-mm AA, 5/TT,*

38 conventional:

18 KOTLIN AND MOD. KOTLIN	1954-57	2,850	4/130-mm DP, 16/45-mm AA, 4 or 8/25-mm AA, 5 or 10/TT,*
20 SKORY AND MOD. SKORY	1949-54	2,240	4/130-mm DP, 2/85-mm or 5/57-mm AA, 5 or 10/TT,*

♦ **177 (+. . .) frigates**

32 (+. . .) KRIVAK I, II	1970-	3,300	4/SS-N-14, 2/SA-N-4, 2/100-mm or 4/76.2-mm DP, 8/TT,*
1 KONI	1978	1,600	1/SA-N-4, 4/76.2-mm DP,*
20 (+. . .) GRISHA-III	1975-	950	1/SA-N-4, 2/57-mm AA, 4/TT,*
7 GRISHA-II	1974-76	950	4/57-mm AA, 4/TT,*
16 GRISHA-I	1967-73	950	1/SA-N-4, 2/57-mm AA, 4/TT,*
27 PETYA-II	1964-69	950	4/76.2-mm DP, 10/TT,*
8 PETYA-I	1960-63	950	2 or 4/76.2-mm DP, 5/TT,*
18 MIRKA-I, II	1964-66	950	4/76.2-mm DP, 5 or 10/TT,*
37 RIGA	1951-56	1,260	3/100-mm DP, 2 or 3/TT,*

♦ **104 (+. . .) corvettes**

2 (+. . .) TARANTUL	1979-	480	4/SS-N-2C, 1/76.2-mm DP
20 NANUCHKA-I, III	1969-	780	6/SS-N-9, 1/SA-N-4, 1/76.2 DP or 2/57-mm AA
3 (+. . .) PAUK	1979-	480	1/76.2-mm DP, 4/TT,*
62 POTI	1960-67	500	2/57-mm AA, 2-4/TT,*
17 T-58	1956-61	725	4/57-mm AA,*

♦ **175 guided-missile and torpedo boats**

♦ **134 patrol boats and craft**

♦ **over 390 mine warfare ships and craft**

♦ **86 amphibious warfare ships**

* Indicates additional ASW weapons

A note to ship class names: The class names used herein are for the most part those used by NATO. Until 1973, Soviet combatants usually did not display names, and thus NATO devised a series of nicknames based on Russian words (combatants: geographical place names beginning with "K"; small combatants: insects; mine warfare types: diminutives of personal names; amphibious warfare types: reptiles; auxiliaries: rivers). Subsequently, the policy has been to use the actual name of the first ship of a class, as in the West. Often that name is not immediately available, and thus a three-part *interim* nickname is applied. The first syllable denotes the *fleet area* where the class was first identified (BAL = Baltic, BLK = Black, etc.), the second syllable indicates the *type* of ship (COM = combatant, SUB = submarine, AUX = auxiliary, etc.), and the third syllable is a roman numeral indicating the order of discovery within a category. Thus, "BAL-COM-III" would be the third new major combatant discovered under construction in the Baltic. As actual names are learned, they replace the temporary nickname. The Soviet Navy itself uses a series of Project Numbers to identify its ships, as in the West German Navy; these are generally not available.

The Soviet Navy has a number of unique ship type classifications; these are translated, where applicable, in the individual class entries.

WEAPONS AND SYSTEMS

NOTE: All weapon and sensor designations that follow are those assigned by NATO, except where indicated; the Soviet designations are generally unavailable.

A. MISSILES

♦ **ballistic missiles**

NOTE: All have liquid-fuel propulsion, except the SS-N-17, which has solid-fuel propulsion.

SS-N-4 (NATO nickname: Sark)

Range: 300 nautical miles. Nuclear warhead. Fitted in Golf-I diesel-powered fleet ballistic-missile submarines. Can be launched only from the surface. Obsolete.

SS-N-5 (NATO nickname: Serb)

Range: 900 nautical miles. Nuclear warhead of about 800 kilotons. Fitted in Hotel-II nuclear-powered submarines and in Golf-II diesel-powered strategic submarines. Can be launched while submerged. Range has been increased from its original 700 nautical miles. Obsolescent but still significant due to basing of 6 Golf-II in the Baltic.

SS-N-6

Range: Initially, 1,300 nautical miles. Nuclear warhead of about 1 megaton. Fitted in Yankee-I-class nuclear submarines and in the Golf-IV experimental submarine. Can

WEAPONS AND SYSTEMS *(continued)*

be launched while submerged. The current version has a 1,600-nautical-mile range and an MRV-type warhead.

SS-N-8 (NATO nickname: Sawfly)

Range: 4,200 miles. Nuclear warhead of about 1 megaton. Fitted in Delta-I and -II nuclear submarines and in the Golf-II experimental submarine.

SS-N-13

Range: 370 nautical miles. Nuclear warhead. Tactical ballistic missile. Program suspended in 1973 due to inadequate technology, but the concept may yet be revived in a new program.

SS-N-17

Range: 2,000 nautical miles. Nuclear warhead. First ballistic missile with solid-fuel propulsion. Aboard the one Yankee-II-class submarine.

SS-N-18

Two-stage missile with range of 4,000 nautical miles. Triple nuclear MRV-type warhead. Aboard Delta-III submarines. Circular error probable (CEP): 800 m.

SS-NX-20

Three-stage weapon with multiple independent re-entry vehicle (MIRV) payload. Range over 4,000 nautical miles. Presumably has greater payload weight and higher accuracy than the SS-N-18. Expected to enter full operational service aboard the Typhoon class, but has reportedly experienced developmental difficulties.

♦ surface-to-surface cruise missiles

NOTE: Liquid-fuel propulsion, except for SS-N-7 and 9, which have solid-propellant engines.

SS-N-1 (NATO code name: Scrubber)

Range: 25 nautical miles on surface targets, 120 to 130 miles on land targets. Subsonic, with turbojet engine. Radio-directed for initial trajectory, then active automatic radar guidance to the target. Nuclear or conventional warhead. May still be fitted in the remaining Kildin-class destroyer, *Neulovimyy*. No longer produced.

SS-N-2 A and B (NATO code name: Styx)

Maximum range: 25 nautical miles. Practical range: 16 nautical miles. Liquid propulsion. I-band active radar guidance in targeting, with infrared or radar homing in the most recent version, SS-N-2B. Altitude can be preset at 100, 150, 200, 250, or 300 m. 400 to 450 kg conventional warhead. Installed in Osa-I and Osa-II guided-missile boats. The SS-N-2B has folding wings.

SS-N-2C (formerly SS-N-11)

Maximum range: 45 nautical miles. Liquid propulsion. Altitude can be preset at 100, 150, 200, 250, or 300 m. Combined radar and infrared terminal homing. During its final approach to the target, the missile descends to an altitude of 2 to 5 m. In order to employ fully the over-the-horizon maximum range of the SS-N-2C, it is necessary to have a forward observer. The SS-N-2C is carried by the destroyers of the Modified Kashin and Modified Kildin classes, by the Tarantul guided-missile corvettes, and by the exported Nanuchka-II-class guided-missile corvettes.

SS-N-3 (NATO code name: Shaddock)

Maximum range: 220 nautical miles. Inertial guidance with mid-course correction by radio, active radar homing to target. Turbojet propulsion. Conventional or nuclear warhead. Fitted in Kynda (quadruple launcher) and Kresta-I (twin launcher) cruisers, and Whiskey Long Bin, Juliett, and unmodified Echo-II submarines. Launched from the surface by submarines.

SS-N-7

Maximum range: 35 nautical miles. Conventional warhead, can be launched while submerged. Charlie-I-class nuclear-powered attack submarines have eight per ship.

SS-N-9

Maximum range: 30 miles, but can reach 60 miles with an aerial relay (aircraft fitted with a Video Data Link system), inertial guidance, and active radar homing to the target. Conventional or nuclear warhead. Installed in Nanuchka-I and III-class guided-missile corvettes and the Sarancha-class hydrofoil. A submerged-launch version is available for the Charlie I- and II- and Papa-class submarines.

SS-N-12

Maximum range: 300 nautical miles. Conventional or nuclear warhead. Replacing the SS-N-3 on Echo-II-class submarines and is aboard the *Kiev* class and the BLK-COM-1-class cruisers.

SS-N-19

Maximum range: 300 nautical miles. Conventional or nuclear warhead. Evidently has improved performance characteristics over the SS-N-12 and is carried by the *Kirov*-class cruisers and the Oscar-class nuclear-powered submarine (from which it is submerged-launched).

♦ surface-to-air missiles

SA-N-1 (NATO code name: Goa)

Twin-launcher. Range: 20,000 m, interception altitude: 300 to 50,000 feet. Guidance: radar/command. Conventional warhead, 60 kg. Fitted on Kynda and Kresta-I cruisers, as well as on Kashin, Kanin, and Kotlin destroyers. Also has a surface-to-surface capability. Uses Peel Group radar directors.

SA-N-2 (NATO code name: Guideline)

Twin-launcher. Range: 50,000 m, interception altitude: 300 to 90,000 feet. Guidance: radar/command via Fan Song radar director. Conventional warhead, 150 kg. Fitted on the cruiser *Dzerhinskiy* only and has some surface-to-surface capability. Obsolescent.

SA-N-3 (NATO code name: Goblet)

Twin launcher. Range: 30,000 m, interception altitude: 300 to 80,000 feet. Guidance: radar/command via Head Lights-series radar director. Conventional warhead, 60 kg. Fitted on Kresta-II and Kara cruisers as well as the *Moskva*-class helicopter cruisers. An improved version has a range of 55,000 m and is on the *Kiev*. Goblet has an anti-surface target capability.

SA-N-4 (NATO code name: Gecko)

Twin launcher, retracting into a vertical drum. Range: 9,000 m, interception altitude: 30 to 10,000 feet. Guidance: radar/command via Pop Group radar director. Conventional warhead. Fitted in Kara and *Kirov* cruisers, two *Sverdlov* cruisers, Krivak guided-

WEAPONS AND SYSTEMS (continued)

missile frigates, Grisha- and Nanuchka-class corvettes, the Sarancha hydrofoil, the landing ship *Ivan Rogov*, and the replenishment ship *Berezina*. Can be used against surface targets.

SA-N-5

Naval version of SA-7 Grail. Fitted on Pauk- and Tarantul-class corvettes, some Osa-class guided-missile patrol boats, landing ships, some minesweepers, and many auxiliaries. Employs either a 4-missile launch rack with operator, or is shoulder-launched, singly. IR-homing, visually aimed.

SA-N-6

A navalized version of the land-based SA-10. Range 80,000 m or greater. Employs vertical launch from 8-missile rotating magazines and reportedly uses track-via-missile guidance via the Top Dome radar system. Carried by the *Kirov* and BLK-COM-I-class cruisers. Probably also has an anti-ship capability.

SA-N-7

A navalized version of the land-based SA-11, employing single-armed launchers. Mach 3 weapon with 28,000-m range (3,000 minimum) and usable against targets from 100- to 46,000-ft. altitude. Operational on the *Sovremennyy*-class destroyers and the trials destroyer *Provornyy*. Guidance via Front Dome radar tracker/illuminators. Probably has an anti-ship capability.

SA-N-. . .

A new vertically launched, short-ranged system, probably intended as a successor to SA-N-4. To be carried in 2-m diameter launch cylinders aboard the *Udaloy*-class destroyers, although not yet operational, due to lack of radar directors.

◆ air-to-surface missiles

AS 2 (NATO code name: Kipper)

Range: 100 nautical miles. Solid-fuel propulsion. Inertial guidance or automatic pilot with radar homing head. 900-1,000 kg. Conventional or nuclear warhead. Launched from Badger-C aircraft.

AS 4 (NATO code name: Kitchen)

Range: 170 nautical miles. Nuclear warhead. Inertial guidance with radar terminal homing. Mach 3.5. In service on Backfire-B and Blinder-B aircraft.

AS 5 (NATO code name: Kelt)

Range: 100 nautical miles. Solid-fuel propulsion. Inertial or autopilot guidance with radar terminal homing. Conventional and nuclear warheads. In service on Badger-G aircraft.

AS 6 (NATO code name: Kingfish)

Range: over 100 nautical miles. Mach 2.5. Conventional or nuclear warhead. In service on Badger-C and -G aircraft, two on each.

AS 7

Range: 6 nautical miles. Mach 1. Tactical weapon. Solid-fuel propulsion. Pencil-beam radar terminal homing. 100 kg. Conventional warhead. Used on Forger aircraft.

AS 9

Range: 60 nautical miles. Anti-radar missile. Turbojet propulsion; Mach 3.0. Passive homing on electromagnetic radiation. 150 kg. Conventional warhead. In use on Badger, Backfire, and Fitter-C and Fitter-D aircraft.

AS 10

Range: 6 nautical miles. Mach 1.0. Solid propulsion. Electro-optical guidance. Conventional warhead of 100 kg. Carried by Fitter-D.

B. GUNS

152-mm dual-purpose

Fitted in triple turrets on *Sverdlov*-class cruisers. Individual barrels can be loaded and elevated separately. Limited AA capability, using barrage fire.

barrel length: 57 calibers
muzzle velocity: 915 m/sec
altitude arc: −5° to +50°
maximum rate of fire: 4 to 5 rds/min/barrel
maximum range: 27,000 m
effective range: 18,000 m
projectile weight: 50 kg
fire control: optical directors with two 8-m base range finders and associated Top Bow ranging radars or local control using 8-m base range finders in each turret and Egg Cup ranging radars atop upper turrets.

130-mm twin, new model dual purpose

Fully automatic, for surface and aerial targets. Fitted on *Sovremennyy*-class destroyers. May be mechanically triaxially stabilized. Water-cooled.

barrel length: 70 calibers
muzzle velocity: . . .
arc of elevation: −15° to +85°
max. rate of fire: 65 rds./min per mount
max. range: approx. 28,000 m
fire control: Kite Screech radar director or local control by on-mount operator.

130-mm twin dual purpose

Semi-automatic. Fitted on Kotlin and SAM-Kotlin destroyers. Mechanically triaxially stabilized. Twin mount with electric or hydraulic-electric pointing system.

barrel length: 58 calibers
muzzle velocity: 900 m/sec
arc of elevation: −5° to +80°
maximum rate of fire: 10 rounds/min/barrel
maximum range, surface target: 28,000 m
effective range, surface target: 16,000 to 18,000 m
maximum vertical range: 13,000 m
projectile weight: 27 kg
fire control: stabilized Wasp Head director, with Sun Visor tracking radar. Egg Cup ranging radar on each mount (being removed)

130-mm twin dual purpose

Semi-automatic type fitted on *Skoryy*-class destroyers. Obsolescent.

barrel length: 50 calibers
muzzle velocity: 875 m/sec
arc of elevation: −5° to +45°
maximum rate of fire: 10 rounds/min/barrel
maximum range: 24,000 m
effective range: 14,000 to 15,000 m
projectile weight: 27 kg
fire control: Four Eyes optical director and associated Top Bow or Post Lamp radars.

WEAPONS AND SYSTEMS (continued)

Kiev—1. Top Sail 3-D radar   2. Top Knot TACAN radome with High Pole B IFF transponder atop   3. Top Steer 3-D radar   4. Rum Tub ESM antennas   5. Bell Bash jammer antennas   6. Bell Thump jammer radome   7. Tee Plinth electro-optical device with conical Pert Spring radome just below it   8. Side Globe ECM radomes

SUW-N-1 launcher with FRAS-1 missile aboard the helicopter cruiser Moskva

SA-N-3 launcher with Goblet missile aboard Moskva

SS-N-2C launchers (SA-N-1 system at right) on a Modified Kashin-class destroyer

SS-N-2B launcher on an OSA-II-class patrol boat

WEAPONS AND SYSTEMS *(continued)*

RBU-1000, 6-tubed ASW rocket launcher; note swing-away arms on each end of
tube   U.S. Navy

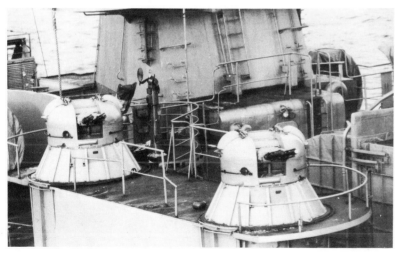

Two twin 30-mm AA and their manual ringsight director on a Kanin-class
destroyer   U.S. Navy

76-mm DP gun on a Nanuchka-III missile corvette   U.S. Navy

Twin 76.2-mm mount and SA-N-4 SAM magazine (with launcher retracted) on a
Kara-class large antisubmarine ship   U.S. Navy

WEAPONS AND SYSTEMS (continued)

SS-N-3 cruise missile tubes in elevated firing position on a Kresta-I missile cruiser
U.S. Navy

100-mm dual-purpose guns on the Krivak-II-class frigate Neukrotimyy. Note upper mount's operator position hatch open.

Head Lights missile-control and tracking radar on a Kara-class cruiser, elevated to about 80 degrees. At left are cupolas for the 30-mm Gatling gun backup directors.

Top Sail (left) and Head Net-C search radars and Side Globe radomes aboard an early Kresta-II class cruiser. Two Gatling guns are visible at lower center, below the tub for their director. Most Kresta-IIs have now been backfitted with two Bass Tilt radar directors to control the 30-mm Gatling guns, but all retain the optical directors for backup.

WEAPONS AND SYSTEMS *(continued)*

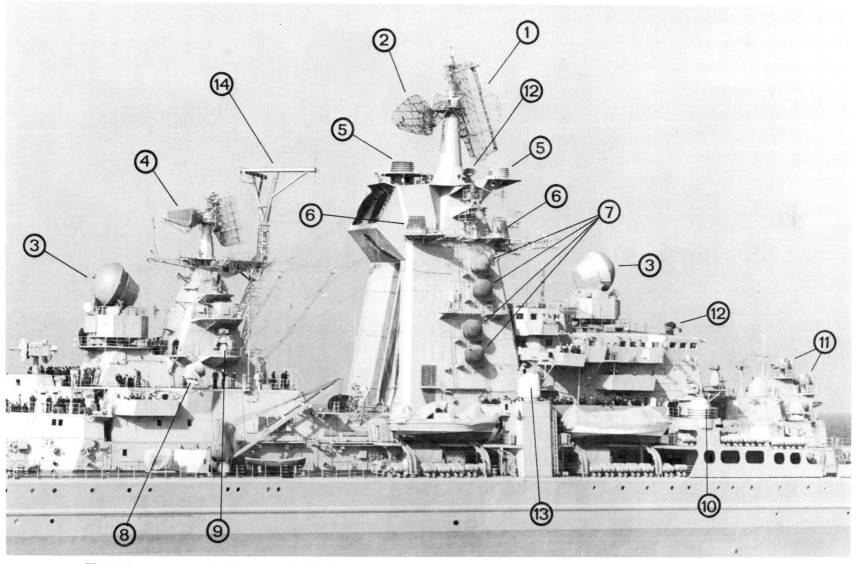

Electronics antennas on the Kirov—1. and 2. Top Pair 3-dimensional long-range air-search radar, comprising Top Sail(1) and Big Net(2) antennas. 3. Top Dome SA-N-6 guidance radar 4. Top Steer 3-dimensional air-search radar 5. Round House helicopter-control/TACAN arrays 6. Rum Tub ECM radomes 7. Side Globe ECM radomes 8. Bass Tilt 30-mm Gatling gun-control radar 9. Possible stabilized t.v./IR tracker 10. Bob Tail (in aluminized rubber protective cover), possible low-light tracking device or radionavigation sextant (with Pop Group radar for SA-N-4 SAM system just above) 11. Eye Bowl control radars for SS-N-14 ASW cruise missiles 12. Palm Frond surface-search radar 13. Punch Bowl satellite communications antenna radome 14. Vee Tube long-range HF communications antenna array

WEAPONS AND SYSTEMS (continued)

Towed variable-depth sonar partially deployed from a Krivak-class frigate; the equipment has, in this instance, suffered a casualty to the hoist system.

Helicopter-type dipping sonar being deployed from a Mirka-II class frigate. Note the circular covers over gas-turbine exhausts and the towed torpedo decoys on deck.

100-mm twin dual purpose

Mechanically triaxially stabilized mounts installed on *Sverdlov*-class cruisers.
barrel length: 50 calibers
weight: approx. 40 tons
muzzle velocity: 900 m/sec
effective range, surface target: 10,000 to 12,000 m
maximum range, AA fire: 15,000 m
effective range, AA fire: 8,000 to 9,000 m
projectile weight: 16 kg
arc of elevation: −15° to 85°
maximum rate of fire: 15 rounds/min/barrel
maximum range, surface target: 20,000 m
fire control: Round Top stabilized director with Sun Visor tracking radar and/or associated Top Bow or Post Lamp radars: Egg Cup ranging radar on each mount (being removed) for local surface control.

100-mm automatic dual purpose

A single-barreled, water-cooled gun in an enclosed mounting found on the cruiser *Kirov*, *Udaloy*-class destroyers, and Krivak-II-class frigates.
rate of fire: 80 rounds/min
maximum theoretical range: 15,000 m
maximum effective range: 8,000 m
fire control: Kite Screech radar director or local, on-mount control

100-mm single dual purpose

Gun mount with a shield. Installed on Riga frigates, and Don-class submarine tenders.

barrel length: 56 calibers
muzzle velocity: 850 m/sec
arc of elevation: −5° to +40°
projectile weight: 13.5 kg
maximum rate of fire: 15 rounds/min
maximum range: 16,000 m
effective range: 10,000 m
fire control: stabilized Wasp Head director fitted with Sun Visor radar

85-mm AA

Twin-barreled gun mount on unmodified *Skoryy* destroyers. Obsolescent.
barrel length: 50 calibers
muzzle velocity: 850 m/sec
arc of elevation: −5° to +70°
maximum rate of fire: 10 rounds/min/barrel
maximum range, surface target: 15,000 m
effective range, surface target: 8,000 to 9,000 m
practical maximum range, AA fire: 6,000 m
fire control: Cylinder Head optical director (no radar).

76.2-mm twin dual purpose

Installed on Kara and Kynda cruisers, Kashin destroyers and Krivak-I, Koni, Petya, and Mirka frigates, *Smol'nyy*-class training ships and *Ivan Susanin*-class icebreakers.

length of barrel: 60 calibers
muzzle velocity: 900 m/sec
maximum rate of fire: 45 rounds/min/barrel
arc of elevation: +80°
maximum range, AA fire: 10,000 m
effective range, AA fire: 6,000 to 7,000 m
projectile weight: 16 kg
fire control: Owl Screech or Hawk Screech radar director.

76.2-mm single dual purpose

Fully automatic, with on-mount crew. Carried by Nanuchka-III, Pauk, and Tarantul-class corvettes, Matka-class guided missile hydrofoils, and the Slepen-class patrol boat.
rate of fire: 120 rounds/min
theoretical maximum range against surface target: 14,000 m
practical range against aerial target: 6,000 to 7,000 m
fire control: Bass Tilt radar director or local, on-mount control

57-mm twin automatic dual purpose

This equipment, which appears to be entirely automatic from the ammunition-handling room to the gun mount, is installed on *Moskva*, Kresta-I, and Kresta-II cruisers, Poti and Grisha corvettes, Nanuchka-I guided-missile corvettes, Turya torpedo boats, Ropucha LSTs, *Ugra* submarine tenders, and the replenishment ship *Berezina*. Now removed from *Boris Chilikin* replenishment ships and *Manych*-class water tankers. Water-cooling system.
length of barrel: 70 calibers
maximum rate of fire: 120 rounds/min/barrel
maximum effective vertical range: 5,000 to 6,000 m
fire control: by Muff Cob or Bass Tilt radar directors

57-mm AA

Single-barrel gun mount (Mod. *Skoryy* destroyers and some Sasha minesweepers), twin-barrel (several classes), and quadruple on Kanin and Kildin destroyers; in the latter case the guns are mounted in superimposed pairs. Has some surface-fire capability.

WEAPONS AND SYSTEMS *(continued)*

length of barrel: 70 calibers
muzzle velocity: 900 to 1,000 m/sec
arc of elevation: 0° to +90°
fire control by Hawk Screech or Muff Cob radar directors

maximum rate of fire: 150 rounds/min/
gun
effective vertical range: 4,500 m

45-mm AA

Quadruple-barreled installations in SAM-Kotlin, Kotlin and one Mod. Kildin destroyers; single on some Sasha minesweepers. The quadruple-mounted guns are arranged in two superimposed pairs.

length of barrel: 85 calibers
muzzle velocity: 900 m/sec
arc of elevation: 0° to +90°

rate of fire: 300 rounds/min/mount
effective maximum vertical range: 4,000
m
fire control: Hawk Screech radar director
(local in Sasha)

37-mm Model 39 AA

Installed in twin-barreled mounts in *Sverdlov* cruisers, *Skoryy* destroyers, Riga frigates, and T-43-class minesweepers.

length of barrel: 60 calibers
muzzle velocity: 900 m/sec
arc of elevation: 0° to +80°?

maximum rate of fire: 160 rounds/min/
gun
fire control: on-mount lead-computing
sights

30-mm Gatling gun AA

This gun is in service on *Kiev*-class carriers, Kara and Kresta-II cruisers, and several other classes. It is installed in mounts similar to those of the 30-mm AA double-barreled automatic guns, and is designed to fire a great number of rounds at an extremely high rate in order to intercept a cruise missile at a comparatively short distance. It has six 30-mm barrels.

minimum rate of fire: 3,000 rounds/min/mount
fire control: Bass Tilt radar director or remote visual director

30-mm twin automatic AA

Installed in a light mount on several classes of ships—cruisers, destroyers, guided-missile boats, supply ships, etc.

length of barrel: 60 calibers
muzzle velocity: 1,000 m/sec
maximum rate of fire: 240 rounds/min/barrel
effective maximum range, AA fire: 2,500 to 3,000 m
fire control: by Drum Tilt radar director or remote optical director.

25-mm twin AA

Found on many ships and made up of two superimposed guns.

length of barrel: 60 calibers
muzzle velocity: 900 m/sec

maximum rate of fire: 150-200 rounds/
min/barrel
fire control: on-mount ring sights

C. ANTISUBMARINE WEAPONS

♦ missiles

SUW-N-1 system

Rocket-propelled weapon, installed on *Kiev*-class carriers and *Moskva*-class helicopter cruisers. Maximum range: 16 miles. Nuclear warhead. Unguided solid-fuel rocket based on land-based FROG-7 artillery rocket and often referred to as FRAS-1.

SS-N-14

A weapon conceptually resembling the French Malafon, using a solid-propelled aerodynamic cruise missile that drops a parachute-retarded homing torpedo. Maximum range: 30 nautical miles (4 nautical miles minimum). Carried by *Kirov*, Kara- and Kresta-II-class cruisers and Krivak-I- and Krivak-II-class frigates. Can also be used against surface ships.

SS-N-15

ASW missile similar to the U.S. Navy's SUBROC. Maximum range: 20 miles. Nuclear warhead. Submerged-launched from submarine torpedo tubes. Carried by Victor I, II, and III and Alfa-class nuclear-powered attack submarines.

SS-N-16

Derived from the SS-N-15 system but using a homing torpedo payload in lieu of the nuclear depth bomb. Maximum range: 50 nautical miles. Would also be useful against surface targets.

♦ rockets

RBU-6000 (Soviet designation)

Formerly MBU-2500 A. Made up of twelve barrels, approximately 1.600 m in length, arranged in a horseshoe and fired in paired sequence. Vertical automatic loading system, barrel by barrel. Range: 6,000 m. Installed in *Kiev*-class carriers, *Kirov*, *Moskva*, Kynda, Kresta-I, and Kresta-II cruisers, *Udaloy*, Kashin, and Kanin guided-missile destroyers, Krivak frigates, the smaller Mirka and Petya frigates, and the Poti and Grisha corvettes.

RBU-2500 (Soviet designation)

Made up of two horizontal rows of eight barrels each, approximately 1.600 m in length, which can be trained and elevated. Manual reloading. Range: 2,500 m. 21-kg warhead. Carried by Kildin and Mod. Kildin, one SAM Kotlin, most Mod. Kotlin, and all *Mod. Skoryy* destroyers, Riga frigates, Petya-I corvettes, and *Smol'nyy* training ships.

RBU-1200 (Soviet designation)

Made up of two horizontal rows of short, superimposed barrels, three on two. Tube diameter: 0.250 m; length: 1.400 m; the 70-kg (34-kg warhead) rocket is somewhat shorter. Range: 1,200 m. Tubes elevate but are fixed in train. Installed in T 58-class corvettes, S.O.-1 patrol boats, and Natya-class minesweepers.

RBU-1000 (Soviet designation)

Made up of six barrels arranged in two vertical rows of three and fired in order, with vertical automatic loading. Trainable. Tube diameter: approx. 0.300 m. Length: approx. 1.800 m. Range: 1,000 m. 90-kg rocket with 55-kg warhead. Installed in Kara, Kresta-I, and Kresta-II cruisers, *Sovremennyy* and Kashin destroyers, and the replenishment ship *Berezina*.

RBU-600 (Soviet designation)

Made up of six barrels, 0.300 m in diameter and 1.500 in length, superimposed in two rows and fired simultaneously. Trainable. Range: 600 m. 90-kg rocket with 55-kg warhead. Used only in Mod. Kotlin destroyers.

WEAPONS AND SYSTEMS (continued)

♦ torpedoes

The Soviet Navy uses 533-mm anti-surface and ASW torpedoes, and short 400-mm ASW homing torpedoes. Nuclear warheads are apparently widely deployed, especially in submarines, as witness their presence aboard the Whiskey-class submarine that ran aground near Karlskrona Naval Base in Sweden during 10-81.

D. RADARS

NOTE: Designations are NATO code names.

♦ navigation

The most widely used are the I-band Neptune, Ball End, various Don types, and Spin Trough. Don-Kay was placed on most large ships in the 1970s, until it was succeeded by the I-band Palm Frond.

♦ surface search

Most common on small surface combatants are Square Tie (also used for cruise-missile target-designation), Pot Head, and Pot Drum. Submarines carry Snoop Tray, Snoop Slab, or Snoop Plate.

♦ long-range air search

Cross Bird, still carried by some *Skoryy*-class destroyers. Copy of British World War II gear.

Head Net-A (C-band)

Head Net-B, consisting of 2 Head Net-A antennas, mounted back-to-back in a horizontal plane (found on *Desna*-class missile range ships).

Head Net-C, consisting of 2 Head Net-A antennas, mounted back-to-back, one in a horizontal plane, the other inclined. Widely used on cruisers and destroyers.

These radars use a band that gives a 60- to 70-mile detection range on an attack bomber flying at high altitude.

Big Net, a large C-band radar fitted on Kresta-I and a few *Sverdlov* cruisers, and some Kashin destroyers. Its detection range on an aircraft is probably over 100 miles.

Slim Net (E-band), early model radar fitted on some cruisers and destroyers.

Hair Net (E-band), early model radar now only on one Riga frigate.

Top Trough (C-band), on some *Sverdlov* cruisers.

Knife Rest (A-band), antenna resembles a large television antenna.

Strut Curve (F-band), mounted on the Petya and Mirka frigates and Poti and Grisha corvettes.

Strut Pair (F-band), mounted on *Udaloy* class and one Mod. Kildin destroyer. Employs pulse-compression. Antenna essentially two Strut Curve reflectors back-to-back.

High Sieve. Carried by some *Sverdlov* cruisers and *Skoryy* destroyers.

♦ Top Pair (C/F-band). Three-dimensional; a Top Sail and a Big Net antenna mounted back-to-back; used on *Kirov.*

Top Sail (C-band), three-dimensional radar installed in *Kiev, Moskva,* Kresta-II, and Kara cruisers.

Top Steer (F-band), three-dimensional radar found with Top Sail on *Kiev.* Possibly for air-controlling.

♦ missile tracking and control

Trap Door, in a retractable mount. Used for SS-N-12 on *Kiev*-class carriers, where it is mounted at the extreme bow; the similar Front Door/Front Piece is used on Echo-II and Juliett submarines for SS-N-3 and SS-N-12.

Peel Group, mounted on Kynda and Kresta-I cruisers as well as Kashin, Kanin, and SAM Kotlin destroyers. Consists of a tracking radar for high altitudes (I-band) and a missile-guidance radar at lower altitudes (E-band). The assembly is made up of two groups of large and small reflectors, in both horizontal and vertical position, with parabolic design. Maximum range approximately 30 to 40 miles. Used for guidance of the Goa missile in the SA-N-1 system.

Head Lights (F-, G-, H-, and D-bands), mounted in *Kiev* carriers and *Moskva,* Kresta-II and Kara cruisers. Similar to the Peel Group with an assembly of tracking radar for the target and guidance radar for the missile. Used for guidance for the Goblet missile of the SA-N-3 system and for the surface-to-underwater missiles of the SS-N-14 system. In several versions, designated "A," "B," and "C".

Scoop Pair (E-band), guidance radar for the Shaddock missile of the SS-N-3 system on board Kynda and Kresta-I cruisers.

Pop Group (F-, H-, and I-bands), missile guidance for the SA-N-4 system.

Eye Bowl (F-band), smaller version of Head Lights, installed in the cruiser *Kirov, Udaloy* destroyers, and Krivak frigates; missile-guidance radar for the SS-N-14 system.

Fan Song E, installed in the *Dzerzhinskiy;* used with the Guideline missile of the SA-N-2 system.

Band Stand, on *Sovremennyy* destroyers, Tarantul-II, and Nanuchka corvettes and the Sarancha hydrofoil, possibly for missile-tracking and control. In large radome.

Top Dome, associated with the SA-N-6 vertically launched SAM system in the cruiser *Kirov.* Employs a 4-m diameter hemispheric radome, fixed in elevation, but mechanically steerable in azimuth. Three smaller dielectric radomes are mounted on the face of its mounting pedestal, and there is also a smaller hemispheric radome below it. Apparently can track multiple targets.

Front Dome, tracker-illuminator associated with the SA-N-7 SAM system in the *Sovremennyy*-class destroyers (with six) and the trials Kashin, *Provornyy* (with eight). Resembles the gun fire-control radar Bass Tilt and is very compact.

Plinth Net, a large parabolic mesh antenna found only in the Kresta-I and Kynda-class cruisers and apparently associated with the SS-N-3 anti-ship missile.

♦ gun fire-control

Half Bow }
Post Lamp } (I-band), mounted on various older classes of ships; also for torpedo fire control.

Top Bow, 152-mm gun.

Sun Visor, 130-mm DP, 100-mm DP guns; mounted on Round Top or Wasp Head directors.

Hawk Screech, 45-mm and 76.2-mm AA guns; always found in conjunction with back-up optical directors.

Owl Screech, 76.2-mm DP; improved version of Hawk Screech.

Kite Screech, 100-mm and new 130-mm twin DP.

Muff Cob (H-Band), for 57-mm AA twin automatic guns. Has t.v. camera attachment.

Egg Cup (E-band), installed in turrets for 152-mm, old twin 130-mm, and old twin 100-mm AA guns.

Drum Tilt (H- and I-bands), installed on Osa missile boats and other ships fitted with 30-mm twin-barrel AA.

Bass Tilt (H-band), used with Gatling gun fitted in *Kiev* carriers, Kara and Kresta-II cruisers, and Mod. Kildin destroyers, as well as in Grisha-III corvettes, where it also controls the twin 57-mm, and on Nanuchka-III corvettes and Matka guided-missile hydrofoils, where it also controls the 76.2-mm gun.

WEAPONS AND SYSTEMS (*continued*)

E. SONARS

Until the early 1960s, the Soviet Navy showed little interest in antisubmarine warfare or, of course, submarine detection. Most of its ships were equipped with high-frequency sonar (Tamir 11, Pegas, Herkules). New or modernized ships appear to have much improved sensors.

Medium-frequency hull sonar, on Kresta-II cruisers, Kanin destroyers, Krivak frigates, and Grisha corvettes.

Medium-frequency, towed, variable-depth sonar, on *Kiev* carriers, *Moskva* and Kara cruisers, Mod. Kashin destroyers, and Krivak frigates.

Low-frequency hull sonar, on *Kiev* carriers and *Moskva* cruisers, the cruiser *Kirov* and the *Udaloy* destroyers.

Helicopter dipping sonar, on Mirka frigates, Stenka and Pchela patrol boats, Turya torpedo boats and others.

Most diesel submarines still have old equipment (active-passive Hercules, passive Feniks), but nuclear submarines have modern low-frequency sonar and extensive passive hydrophone arrays.

While the Soviets may be interested in surface-ship-towed passive sonar arrays, no ships have yet appeared with it.

F. ELECTRONIC WARFARE

The increasing number of radomes of every description that can be seen on Soviet ships, especially on the newest and most important types (helicopter and guided-missile cruisers, for example) is an indication of the attention the Soviet Navy gives to electronic warfare. NATO code names for the antenna arrays for intercept or for jamming radars include: Side Globe, Top Hat A and B, Bell Clout, Bell Shroud, Bell Squat, Cage Pot, Watch Dog, And Rum Tub.

Many of the more modern ships are equipped with twin-tubed chaff rocket launchers (*Kiev*, *Moskva*, Kresta-I and -II, Kara, *Berezina*) or 16-tubed fixed chaff rocket launchers (Mod. Kashin, Krivak-I and -II, Tarantul, Pauk, Nanuchka, Matka, etc.).

IFF (Identification Friend or Foe) is taken care of by High Pole A and B transponders and by Square Head or other interrogators. The modern radars have integral IFF interrogation. TACAN systems included the large Top Knot spherical array on the *Kiev*-class carriers, and various forms of the paired cylindrical Round House array on the *Kirov*, *Udaloy*, and other classes.

VTOL CARRIERS

NOTE: Reports of the building of a nuclear-powered, Western-style, conventional aircraft carrier of 60,000 tons full-load displacement and equipped with catapults and arresting gear continue to appear in the West. Both Severodvinsk and Nikolayev have been mentioned as construction sites, with the latter more likely. Completion in the near future is unlikely, with the late 1980s to 1990 being more probable, using the facilities now devoted to building the *Kiev* class.

♦ 3 (+1) Kiev class

	Bldr	Laid down	L	In serv.
KIEV	Black Sea SY, Nikolayev	9-70	31-12-72	5-75
MINSK	Black Sea SY, Nikolayev	12-72	5-75	2-78
NOVOROSSIYSK	Black Sea SY, Nikolayev	10-75	12-78	1981
KHARKOV	Black Sea SY, Nikolayev	1978	. . .	1983-84

Kiev R.N., 1981

Kiev, showing the pattern of the refractory tiles on the flight deck. Note Hormone helicopters with folded and unfolded rotor blades, deck vehicles parked abaft the blast shield behind the SS-N-12 cruise-missile launchers.

VTOL CARRIERS (continued)

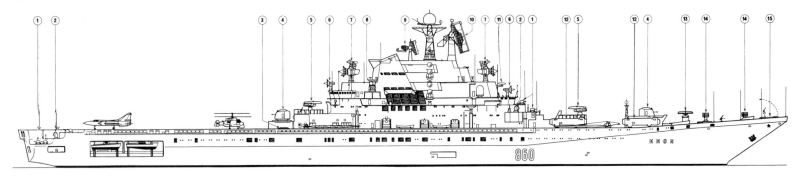

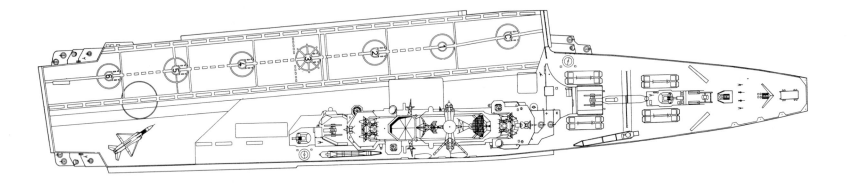

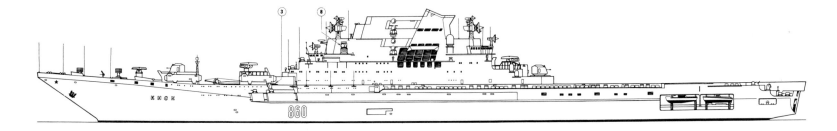

1.—30-mm Gatling guns 2. Bass Tilt radar 3. SA-N-4 system 4. Twin 76.2-mm DP mount 5. SA-N-3 system 6. Owl Screech radar 7. Head Lights radar 8. Pop Group radar 9. Top Steer radar 10. Top Sail radar 11. Don-2 radar 12. Twin launchers for SS-N-12 system 13. SUW-N-1 system 14. RBU-6000 15. Trap Door radar

VTOL CARRIERS (*continued*)

Kiev—From the air, the Kiev class present a spectacular sight, with huge areas of orange-painted deck contrasted with the greenish-gray tones of the tiled portion of the flight deck. Forger aircraft are beetle-green on top and pale green below, while Hormones (aside from the orange and white rescue helo) are a pale gray-green.

D: 36,000 tons (44,000 fl) **S:** 32 kts
Dim: 275.0 (249.5 wl) × 50.0 (38.0 wl) × 9.0
A: 8/SS-N-12 (II × 4)—2/SA-N-3 systems (II × 2; 72 Goblet missiles)—2/launch SA-N-4 systems (II × 2; 36 missiles)—4/76.2-mm DP (II × 2)—8/30-mm Gatling-AA (VI × 8)—10/533-mm TT (V × 2)—1/SUW-N-1 ASW RL (II × 1)—2/RBU-6000 ASW RL (XII × 2)—23/Hormone A and Hormone B helicopters—12/Forger aircraft
Electron Equipt: Radar: 1/Don Kay, 2/Don-2, 1/Top Sail, 1/Top Steer, 2/Head Lights, 2/Pop Group, 2/Owl Screech, 4/Bass Tilt, 1/Trap Door
Sonar: 1/low freq., hull-mounted; 1/med.-freq., towed VDS

ECM: 8/Side Globe, 4/Top Hat A, 4/Top Hat B, 4/Rum Tub, 2/Bell Clout—2/chaff RL (II × 2)
M: 4 sets GT; 4 props; 140,000 hp **Boilers:** . . . **Fuel:** 7,000 tons
Range: 4,000/30; 13,500/18 **Man:** 1,200 tot.

REMARKS: *General:* The Soviet Navy's designation for the *Kiev* class is *Taktycheskiy Avionosnyy Kreyser* (Tactical Aircraft-Carrying Cruiser), and the ships have capabilities for ASW, sea-control, and sea-denial missions. The hull is unusual in having a counter stern that sweeps up several meters above the waterline before meeting the transom. The variable-depth sonar is deployed through doors on the centerline of the transom stern; the black-painted, ribbed recess to port of the VDS housing

VTOL CARRIERS (continued)

Minsk 1979

Minsk's island superstructure, with stores crane swung out forward. Two underway replenishment stations are visible on the sides of the island.

is a spray deflector to prevent spray from entering air intakes of Forger VTOL aircraft while landing. For their size and function, the ships carry very small crews.
Aviation installations: The flight-deck portion of the upper deck is inclined about 4.5° to port of the centerline axis of the ship and is about 185 m long by 20 m wide. To protect against the hot exhaust of the Forger aircraft, it is partially covered with a mosaic of refractory tiles. There are two elevators to the hangar deck: one (19.20 m × 10.35 m) beside the stack; the other (18.50 m × 4.70 m) abaft the island. Five small ammunition elevators are connected by an on-deck rail system.

Minsk—with aft elevator down, five Hormone helicopters and four Forger VTOL fighters on deck

Armament: The SS-N-12 missiles are launched from four twin, non-trainable elevating tubes. In order to use the full over-the-horizon range of the missiles, a forward-located, target-designation observer platform has to be used. On the *Kiev*, that requirement is met by the Hormone-B, which carries a long-range radar giving a range of 100 nautical miles with the helicopter at an altitude of 4,000 feet. The ship may possibly also use target information relayed by a satellite. There are eight missiles in the launch tubes, plus sixteen reloads raised from a below-decks magazine by a centerline elevator between the launch-tube sets and aligned with the launchers for loading by a traversing system.

NAVAL AVIATION

Naval aviation, which dates from 1919, is an integral part of the Soviet Navy in which approximately 65,000 men are involved, but its organization and ranks are the same as those of the air forces. Aircraft are part of the four naval fleets (Northern, Baltic, Black Sea, and Pacific) and are under the direct control of the commanders of those fleets. The air arm has some 1,440 aircraft, including:

Tactical:
   380 strike bombers: Backfire B, Badger C, G
   85 fighters/fighter-bombers: Forger A, Fitter C
Tactical Support:
   70 tankers: Badger A
   180 reconnaissance & electronic warfare: Bear D, Badger H, J
Antisubmarine Warfare:
   190 fixed wing: Bear F, May, Mail
   210 helicopters: Hormone A, Haze A
Utility:
   330 miscellaneous training, transports, etc.
These are divided into the four fleets as follows:

	Northern	Baltic	Black Sea	Pacific	Total
Reconnaissance and electronic warfare	60	15	15	60	150
Bombers	70	90	100	120	380
Attack fighters	15	40	15	15	85
Refueling	15	20	15	20	70
ASW	65	20	25	80	190
Helicopters (all types)	95	45	110	90	340

NOTE: A new ship-borne ASW helicopter, nicknamed "Helix" by NATO, entered service during 1981 aboard the *Udaloy*-class destroyer. Of similar overall dimensions and layout to the Kamov Ka-25 Hormone-series, it is bulkier, has larger engines, and only two vertical stabilizers.

NAVAL AVIATION *(continued)*

Forger-A 1976

Badger-A—tanker 1972

Backfire-B naval bomber 1979

Badger-C—bomber 1972

Hormone-A with dipping sonar deployed 1980

Badger-G—missile carrier

NAVAL AVIATION *(continued)*

Bear-D—reconnaissance   1972

Bear-F—ASW aircraft   1979

Mail—ASW amphibian—MAD boom protruding aft   1979

Blinder A (Tupolev Tu-22)   U.S. Navy

Forger-B two-seat training VTOL aircraft   1981

May—ASW aircraft   1978

Hormone-C air/sea rescue helicopter, on Kiev   1980

NAVAL AVIATION *(continued)*

Haze-A land-based ASW helicopter

Hormone-C reconnaissance helicopter—with long belly pannier and camera pod
1980

COMBAT AIRCRAFT

NATO code name and builder	Mission	Year put in serv.	Weight	Wing-span	Length	Engine	Speed max cruising	Operational radius[1]	Armament	Fitted with	Remarks
♦FIXED-WING											
Backfire TU-22M (Tupolev)	Reconnaissance and ship attack	1975	130 t	34.45 m (26.2 m fully swept)	42 m	2 Kuznetsov NK 144 turbo-jets of 24,000 kg thrust each	Mach 2.2 at 50,000 ft; Mach 1.3 at 3,000 ft	Supersonic: 3,485/2,250 km with/without re-fueling Subsonic: 6,300/5,320 km with/without re-fueling	3/23-mm cannon, 9,000 kg of bombs (nuclear or conven-tional), on external racks, 1-2 AS 6 or AS 9	1 navigation and bomb-ing radar; 1 optical bomb sight; 1 tail ra-dar; IFF.	The naval version of Backfire B has ECM and ECCM equipment. Has variable-geometry swept wing
Blinder-C TU 22 (Tupolev)	Reconnaissance and ship attack	1963	84 t	24 m	38 m	2 turbojets, 20,000-kg thrust each (13,000-kg thrust without using after burners)	Mach 1.6 at 36,000 ft	Supersonic speeds: 1,000 km without refueling; 1,600 km with refueling Subsonic speeds: 1,500 km without refueling, 2,000 km with re-fueling	1/23-mm cannon, 9,000 kg bombs	1 navigation radar; 1 tail radar; IFF; 7 cameras.	The "C" version is especially configured for maritime reconnaissance. The "D" version is a trainer.
Bear-C, -D, -F TU 95 (Tupolev)	Reconnaissance and electronic warfare	1955	165 t	50 m	44 m	4 turboprops of 12,500 hp each; 4 bladed, contrarotating props	500 kts at 25,000 ft 440 kts at sea level	8,000 km without refueling; 9,500 km with	6/23-mm cannon	Radomes and tail radar; well-equipped with electronic counter-measures.	Bear F (TU-142), the ASW version,, has sonobuoys, depth charges, and torpe-does.

COMBAT AIRCRAFT *(continued)*

NATO code name and builder	Mission	Year put in serv.	Weight	Wing-span	Length	Engine	Speed max cruising	Operational radius[1]	Armament	Fitted with	Remarks
Badger-A **TU 16** (Tupolev)	Aerial refuelling	1953	75 t	33 m	35 m	2 RD 3 M tur-bojets, 9,550-kg thrust each	540 kts at 22,000 ft 445 kts at sea level	3,000 km without refueling; 4,500 km with	7/23-mm cannon	1 navigation and bombing radar; 1 tail radar; some electronic warfare equipment.	Wing tip hose dispensers for refuelling. May retain a secondary bombing capability, 9,000 kg bombs.
Badger-C **TU 16** (Tupolev)	Ship attack	. . .	75 t	33 m	35 m	2 RD 3 M tur-bojets, 9,550-kg thrust each	540 kts at 22,000 ft 445 kts at sea level	3,000 km without refueling; 4,500 km with	6/23-mm cannon, 1 AS 2 Kipper or 2 AS 6 Kingfish	1 navigation and bombing radar; 1 Doppler radar; 1 tail radar.	
Badger-G **TU 16** (Tupolev)	Ship attack	. . .	75 t	33 m	35 m	2 RD 3 M tur-bojets, 9,550-kg thrust each	540 kts at 22,000 ft 445 kts at sea level	3,000 km without refueling; 4,500 km with	8/23-mm cannon, 2 AS 5 Kelt or 2 AS 6 Kingfish	1 navigation and bombing radar; 1 Doppler radar; 1 tail radar.	
Badger-D, E, F, J **TU 16** (Tupolev)	Reconnaissance and electronic warfare	. . .	75 t	33 m	35 m	2 RD 3 M tur-bojets 9,550-kg thrust each	540 kts at 22,000 ft 445 kts at sea level	3,000 km without refueling; 4,500 km with	6-7/23-mm cannon	1 navigation and bombing radar; electronic warfare equipment; 1 tail radar; IFF.	Different versions for ELINT, photo reconnaissance, etc.
Forger-A **YAK-36** (Yakovlev)	Attack and reconnaissance	1976	10 t	7 m	15 m	1/7,650 kg thrust main engine; 2/2,520 kg lift engines	Mach 1.1 at 30,000 ft	125 nautical miles low-low-low; 240 n.m. low-high-low	16 or 32 rockets, 2/23-mm cannon, 2/AS-7 or AS-10 missiles	Passive warning system; inertial navigation	Vertical take off and landing, Forger-B, the two-seat training version, is also carried aboard ship. A-version may also carry 2 air-to-air missiles.
Fitter-C, -D **SU-20** (Sukhoi)	Ship attack	1976	18 t	14 m	18 m	1/12,000 kg thrust Turbojet	Mach 2.6 at 50,000 ft	220 nautical miles low-low-low; 435 nm high-low-high	32/57-mm rockets, 2/30-mm cannon, 727 kg bombs, nuclear or conventional	Ranging radar; tail warning radar; laser range finder; automatic control.	Used by Naval Air Force in Baltic area. Can also carry AA-2 Atoll or AA-8 Aphid air-air or AS-7 or AS-10 air-ground-missiles.
May **IL-38** (Ilyushin)	ASW	1969	64 t	37 m	40 m	4 turboprops, 4,000 hp each	380 kts at 30,000 ft 315 kts at sea level	3,000 km endurance: 12 hours	7,000 kg of bombs, depth charges, torpedoes	Radomes, MAD,[2] sonobuoys	
Mail **BE 12** (Beriev)	ASW	1967	38 t	27 m	25 m	2 AI 20 K turbo-props, 4,000 hp each	310 kts at 30,000 ft 240 kts at sea level	1,300 km	Bombs, charges, mines	Radomes, MAD,[2] sonobuoys.	Amphibian
◆**HELICOPTERS**											
Haze-A **MI 14** (Mil)	ASW	1976	12 t	rotor diam. 21.3m	24 m	2 Isotov TV 2 117A turboshafts 1,500 hp each	140 kts 122 kts	305 km endurance: 2.5 hours	Depth bombs and torpedoes: 2,000 kg total	Sonobuoys and dipping sonar.	Land-based; rotors do not fold.
Hormone -A, -B, -C **KA 25** (Kamov)	A: ASW B: Targeting C: Utility	1967	7.3 t	rotor diam. 16 m	10 m	2 GTD 3 F turbo-shafts, 905 hp each	120 kts 105 kts	300 km endurance: 1.5 to 2 hours	Depth charges or torpedoes: 1,000 kg total	Sonobuoys and dipping sonar.	Carried on board *Kiev*, *Moskva*, Kara and Kresta classes. The B version has a Video Data Link system. C version in various utility configurations.

(1) The operational radius is roughly 60% of the radius given by one-half of the range

(2) MAD = Magnetic Anomaly Detection

COMBAT AIRCRAFT *(continued)*

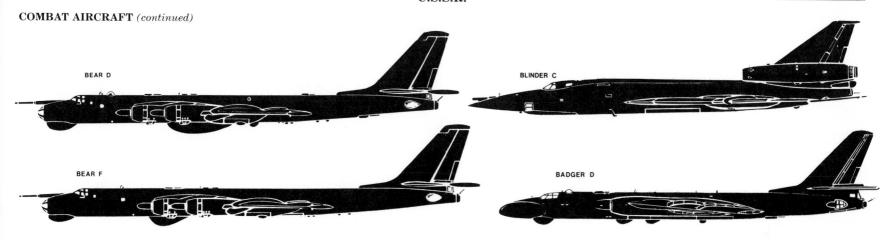

BEAR D

BLINDER C

BEAR F

BADGER D

INTERCEPTION

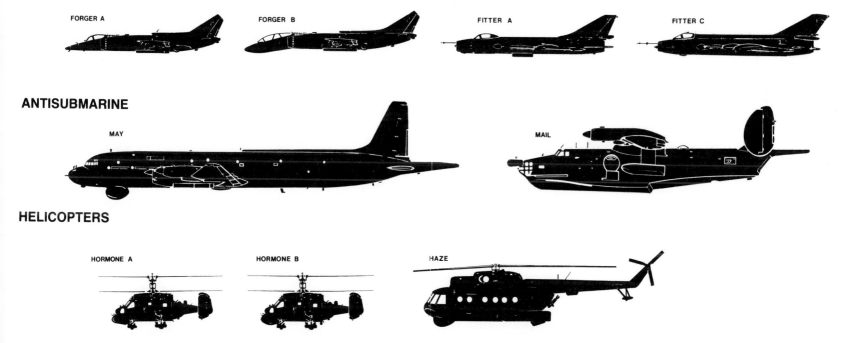

FORGER A

FORGER B

FITTER A

FITTER C

ANTISUBMARINE

MAY

MAIL

HELICOPTERS

HORMONE A

HORMONE B

HAZE

All of the silhouettes are to the same scale. They were furnished through the Commodore, Intelligence (MOD-Royal Navy)

SUBMARINES

Most modern Soviet submarines have an anechoic hull coating that absorbs the echoes of sonars and thus reduces the intensity of reflected echoes.

BALLISTIC-MISSILE SUBMARINES (NUCLEAR-POWERED)

(Soviet Type: PLARB—*Podvodnaya Lodka Atomnaya Raketnaya Ballisticheskaya* = Nuclear-powered Ballistic Missile Submarine.)

NOTE: Nuclear-powered submarines are built or modernized in the Severodvinsk (formerly, Molotovsk) Naval Shipyard on the White Sea, near Arkhangelsk; at Komsomolsk-on-Amur in the Far East; in the Gorkiy Shipyard on the Volga; and at the United Admiralty Shipyard in Leningrad.

♦ **1 Typhoon class** Bldr: Severodvinsk (L: 8-80)

Typhoon—artist's rendering　　　　　　　　　U.S. DOD, 1981

D: 25-30,000 tons (sub.)　**S:** 30 kts (sub.)　**Dim:** 165.0 × 23.0 × . . .
A: 20/SS-N-20 ballistic missiles—. . . /533-mm TT
M: 1 or 2 nuclear reactors; 2 props; . . . hp　**Man:** . . .

REMARKS: World's largest submarine; not expected to be fully operational until missile ready in mid-1980s. Additional units expected.

♦ **13 (+ . . .) Delta-III class** Bldr: Severodvinsk SY

D: 10,500/13,250 tons　**S:** 24 kts　**Dim:** 155.0 × 12.0 × 8.7
A: 16/SS-N-18—6/533-mm TT (12 torpedoes)　**Man:** 120 tot.
Electron Equipt: Radar: 1/Snoop Tray
　　　　　　　　　　Sonar: 1/low frequency
M: 1 nuclear reactor, steam turbines; 2 five-bladed props; 50,000 hp

REMARKS: Two went into service in 1975, four in 1976, two in 1977, two in 1978, and three in 1979-81; construction may be continuing. Has higher "turtle-deck" than Delta-II, to accommodate the longer SS-N-18 tubes.

Delta-III class (stern omitted)　　　　　　　U.S. Navy, 1979

Delta-III

♦ **4 Delta-II** Bldr: Severodvinsk (In serv. 1974-75)

Delta-II

D: 10,000/12,750 tons　**S:** 24 kts　**Dim:** 155.0 × 12.0 × 8.8
A: 16/SS-N-8—6/533-mm TT (18 torpedoes)
Electron Equipt: Radar: 1/Snoop Tray
M: 1 nuclear reactor, steam turbines; 2 5-bladed props　**Man:** 120 tot.

REMARKS: Lengthened version of Delta-I, so as to carry four more SS-N-8.

♦ **18 Delta-I class** Bldrs: Severodvinsk and Komsomolsk, 1973-76

Delta-I class　　　　　　　　　　　　　　　U.S. Navy, 1979

BALLISTIC-MISSILE SUBMARINES (NUCLEAR) *continued*

D: 9,000/11,750 tons **S:** 25 kts **Dim:** 140.0 × 12.0 × 8.7
A: 12/SS-N-8—6/533-mm TT (18 torpedoes)
Electron Equipt: Radar: 1/Snoop Tray
                  Sonar: 1/low freq.
M: 1 nuclear reactor, steam turbines; 2 5-bladed props; 50,000 hp
Man: 120 tot.

REMARKS: One entered service in 1972, four in 1973, six in 1974, two in 1975, two in 1976, and three in 1977. Distinguished from later, longer Delta-II and -III by stepped turtledeck abaft sail.

♦ **1 Yankee-II class** Bldr: . . .

♦ **26 Yankee class** Bldrs: Severodvinsk and Komsomolsk

Yankee-I class

Yankee-II class

Yankee-I class

Yankee class

Yankee-I with angled forward edge to sail, ESM, D/F, and comms masts extended
U.S. Navy

D: 8,000/9,600 tons **S:** 27 kts **Dim:** 130.0 × 12.0 × 8.8
A: Yankee-I: 16/SS-N-6—6/533-mm TT (18 torpedoes)
     Yankee-II: 12/SS-N-17—6/533-mm TT (18 torpedoes)
Electron Equipt: Radar: 1/Snoop Tray
                  Sonar: 1/low freq.
M: 1 nuclear reactor, steam turbines; 2 5-bladed props; 50,000 hp
Man: 120 tot.

REMARKS: In one unit, nicknamed "Yankee-II," SS-N-6 has been replaced by SS-N-17 with twelve tubes. A total of 34 were completed: two in 1967, four in 1968, six in 1969, eight in 1970, six in 1971, five in 1972, two in 1973, and one in 1974. To date, seven have had their missile tubes de-activated, in compliance with the U.S.-Soviet SALT agreements; these "de-fanged" Yankees are listed under attack submarines.

♦ **1 Hotel-III class** Bldr: Severodvinsk (In serv. 1965)

D: 5,500/6,400 tons **S:** 20/25 kts **Dim:** 130.0 × 9.0 × 7.0
A: 3/SS-N-8—6/533-mm TT—2/400-mm TT

BALLISTIC-MISSILE SUBMARINES (NUCLEAR) *continued*

Electron Equipt: Radar: 1/Snoop Tray
Sonar: 1/med. freq.
M: 1 nuclear reactor, steam turbines; 2 6-bladed props; 30,000 hp **Man:** 80 tot.

REMARKS: Used as trial ship for SS-N-8 missiles. Lengthened during conversion.

♦ **6 Hotel-II class** Bldrs: Severodvinsk and Komsomolsk (In serv. 1960-63)

Hotel-II class 1972

Hotel-II class U.S. Navy, 1967

D: 5,000/6,000 tons **S:** 20/25 kts **Dim:** 115.0 × 9.0 × 7.0
A: 3/SS-N-5—6/533-mm TT—2/400-mm TT
Electron Equipt: Radar: 1/Snoop Tray—Sonar: 1/med.-freq.
M: 1 nuclear reactor, steam turbines; 2 6-bladed props; 30,000 hp **Man:** 80 tot.

BALLISTIC-MISSILE SUBMARINES (DIESEL-POWERED)

(Soviet Type: PLRB = *Podvodnaya Lodka Raketnaya Ballisticheskaya* = Ballistic-Missile Submarine)

♦ **1 Golf-V class**

REMARKS: One Golf-II-class submarine has had the original three missile tubes replaced by a single tube for a new missile (possibly SS-N-20) for trials purposes. Other details as for Golf-II class.

♦ **1 Golf-IV class** Bldr: Severodvinsk, 1958-61

D: 3,000/3,400 tons **S:** 12 kts (sub.) **Dim:** 118.0 × 8.5 × 6.6
A: 6/SS-N-6—10/533-mm TT (6 fwd, 4 aft)
Electron Equipt: Radar: 1/Snoop Tray
Sonar: 1/med.-freq., passive array
M: 3 diesels, 2,000 hp each, electric drive; 3 props; 5,300 hp
Endurance: 70 days **Range:** 9,000/5 **Man:** 87 tot.

REMARKS: Around 1970 the sail was lengthened and six missile tubes were installed in order to conduct trials with the SS-N-6 system. Originally a Golf-I. Hull also lengthened.

♦ **1 Golf-III class** Bldr: Severodvinsk (In serv. 1958-61)

Golf-III U.S. Navy

D: 2,900/3,300 tons **S:** 12 kts (sub.) **Dim:** 110.0 × 8.5 × 6.6
A: 6/SS-N-8—10/533-mm TT (6 fwd, 4 aft)
Electron Equipt: Radar: 1/Snoop Tray
Sonar: 1/med. freq., passive array
M: 3 diesels, 2,000 hp each, electric drive; 3 props; 5,300 hp (sub.)
Endurance: 70 days **Range:** 9,000/5 **Man:** 87 tot.

♦ **12 Golf-II class** Bldr: Severodvinsk (In serv. 1958-61)

D: 2,300/2,700 tons **S:** 12 kts (sub.) **Dim:** 100.0 × 8.5 × 6.6
A: 3/SS-N-5—10/533-mm TT (6 fwd, 4 aft)
M: Diesel-electric drive; 3 props; 3 diesels, 2,000 hp
Endurance: 70 days **Range:** 9,000/5 **Man:** 80 tot.

REMARKS: These submarines continue to be active, and a number of them have been stationed in the Baltic. The range of the SS-N-5 has been extended from the original 700 nautical miles to 900. All Golf-IIs are conversions from Golf-I.

♦ **3 Golf-I class** Bldr: Severodvinsk (In serv. 1958-61)

D: 2,300/2,700 tons **S:** 12 kts (sub.) **Dim:** 100.0 × 8.5 × 6.6
A: 3/SS-N-4—10/533-mm TT (6 fwd, 4 aft)
Electron Equipt: Radar: 1/Snoop Tray
Sonar: 1/med. freq., passive arrays
M: 3 diesels of 2,000 hp, electric motors; 3 props; 5,300 hp (sub.)
Endurance: 70 days **Range:** 9,000/5 **Man:** 80 tot.

REMARKS: SS-N-4 can be fired only while the submarine is surfaced. These obsolescent submarines are being retired (see Modified Golf class under Attack Submarines-Diesel-Electric-Powered).

BALLISTIC-MISSILE SUBMARINES (DIESEL) (continued)

Golf-II class—with no communications buoy housing   PH 3 C. Fritz, USN. 1978

Golf-II class—communications buoy housing abaft sail   1976

Golf-II class—version with towed communications buoy housing aft

Golf-I class

CRUISE-MISSILE ATTACK SUBMARINES (NUCLEAR-POWERED)

(Soviet Type: PLARK—*Podvodnaya Lodka Atomnaya Reketnaya Krylataya* = Nuclear-Powered Cruise-Missile Submarine)

♦ **1 Oscar class** Bldr: Severodvinsk SY (L: 4-80)

> **D:** 10,000/13,000 tons **S:** . . . **Dim:** 143.0 × 17.5 × . . .
> **A:** 24/SS-N-19 SSM—. . . /533-mm TT (bow)
> **M:** 1 nuclear reactor; 2 props;. . . hp **Man:** . . .

REMARKS: The missile tubes are mounted in two rows of twelve, fixed in elevation at about 40°, with doors opening through the outer hull, as on the Papa and Charlie-I and -II classes. The missiles are launched while the submarine is submerged, presumably using targeting data from a forward observer.

♦ **1 Papa class** Bldr: Gorkiy SY (In serv. 1970)

Papa class

Papa class   1975

CRUISE-MISSILE ATTACK SUBMARINES (NUCLEAR) *(continued)*

D: 6,700/7,500 tons **S:** 28 kts **Dim:** 109.0 × 12.0 × 8.5
A: 10-SS-N-9—8/533-mm TT
M: 1 nuclear reactor, steam turbines; 2 5-bladed props;. . . hp **Man:** 85 tot.

♦ **5 Charlie-II class** Bldr: Gorkiy SY (In serv. 1973-. . .)

Charlie-II class   U.S. Navy

D: 4,300/5,100 tons **S:** 26 kts (sub.) **Dim:** 103.0 × 10.0 × 8.0
A: 8/SS-N-7 or 9—6/533-mm TT
Electron Equipt: Radar: 1/Snoop Tray
　　　　　　　　　 Sonar: 1/low freq.
　　　　　　　　　 ECM: 1/Stop Light
M: 1 nuclear reactor, steam turbines; 1 5-bladed prop; 30,000 hp **Man:** 85 tot.

REMARKS: One in service in each of the years 1973, 1974, 1977, 1979, and 1980-81.
Construction continues.

♦ **12 Charlie-I class** Bldr: Gorkiy SY (In serv. 1968-72)

D: 4,000/4,900 tons **S:** 27 kts **Dim:** 95.0 × 10.0 × 8.0
A: 8/SS-N-7—6/533-mm TT
Electron Equipt: Radar: 1/Snoop Tray
　　　　　　　　　 Sonar: 1/low freq.
M: 1 nuclear reactor, steam turbines; 1 5-bladed prop; 30,000 hp **Man:** 80 tot.

REMARKS: In service at the rate of about two a year between 1968 and 1973.

Charlie-I class   R.N., 1975

Charlie-I class

LCDR T. Joyner, USN, 1974

CRUISE-MISSILE ATTACK SUBMARINES (NUCLEAR) *(continued)*

Echo-II class

Charlie-I class

Echo-II class

◆ **29 Echo-II class** Bldr: Severodvinsk and Komsomolsk (In serv. 1960-67)

D: 5,000/6,000 tons   **S:** 20/23 kts   **Dim:** 115.0 × 9.0 × 7.5
A: 8/SS-N-3 or SS-N-12—6/533-mm TT (fwd)—4/400-mm TT (aft)
Electron Equipt: Radar: 1/Snoop Tray, 1/Front Piece, 1/Front Door
                    Sonar: 1/low-freq.
M: 1 nuclear reactor, steam turbines; 2 4-bladed props; 25,000 hp   **Man:** 90 tot.

Sail area of SS-N-12-equipped Echo-II   1980

Echo-II with two of the four pairs of SS-N-3 missile tubes elevated   U.S. Navy

REMARKS: Approximately five to date have been modified to launch SS-N-12; they
    have a bulge on either side of the sail and a bulge at the forward ends of the missile
    tubes abreast the sail. The Echo-II must be surfaced to launch, the tubes elevating
    in pairs to fire. The forward part of the sail rotates 180° to expose the Front Door/
    Front Piece guidance radar.

CRUISE-MISSILE ATTACK SUBMARINES (DIESEL-POWERED)

♦ **16 Juliett class** Bldr: Admiralty/Sudomekh, Leningrad (In serv. 1961-63)

(Soviet Type: PLRK—*Podvodnaya Lodka Raketnaya Krylataya* = Cruise-Missile Submarine)

Juliett class—with Snoop Slab radar raised   1978

Juliett class   1978

D: 3,000/3,750 tons   **S:** 16/8 kts   **Dim:** 90.0 × 10.0 × 7.0
A: 4/SS-N-3—6/533-mm TT (fwd)—4/400-mm TT (aft)
Electron Equipt: Radar: 1/Snoop Slab, 1/Front Piece, 1/Front Door
M: 2 diesels, electric drive; 2 props; 5,000 hp
Range: 9,000/7   **Man:** . . .

REMARKS: Missiles are in paired tubes, elevating to fire, as on the Echo-II class.

♦ **3 Whiskey Long Bin class** Bldr: Baltic SY, Leningrad (In serv. 1961-63)

D: 1,200/1,500 tons   **S:** 13.5/8   **Dim:** 83.0 × 6.1 × 5.0
A: 4/SS-N-3—4/533-mm TT (fwd)
Electron Equipt: Radar: 1/Snoop Tray
                 Sonar: 1/med. freq., 1 passive
M: 2 Type 37D 2,000-hp diesels, electric drive; 2 props; 2,700 hp
Endurance: 40 days   **Range:** 6,000/5   **Man:** 60-65 tot.

Whiskey Long Bin class   1968

Whiskey Long Bin class—sail with four inclined missile tubes   1977

REMARKS: Converted from attack submarines by being lengthened and having a section containing four missile tubes inserted in a greatly broadened sail and fixed at elevation of 15°. Stern torpedo tubes removed. All of the less-elaborate Whiskey Twin Cylinder class have been scrapped, and the remaining Long Bin conversions are probably retained for training.

ATTACK SUBMARINES (NUCLEAR-POWERED)

(Soviet Type: PLA—*Podvodnaya Lodka Atomnaya* = Nuclear-Powered Submarine)

♦ **5 Alfa class** Bldr: Sudomekh, Leningrad (In serv. 1972-. . .)

Alfa class   U.S. Navy, 1980

Alfa class

D: 2,800/3,680 tons   **S:** 43-45 kts   **Dim:** 81.4 × 9.5 × 7.0
A: 6/533-mm TT (with SS-N-15 and/or SS-N-16 missiles)
Electron Equipt: Radar: 1/Snoop Tray
                 Sonar: 1/low freq.
M: 1 nuclear reactor, steam turbines; 1 prop; 45,000 hp   **Man:** 45 tot.

REMARKS: The prototype, completed 1972, has been scrapped, but the class has now entered production as the world's fastest and deepest-diving (over 900 m) combatant submarine. The pressure hull is constructed of titanium, and the ships are extremely quiet and highly automated. Construction continues. The second entered active service in 1979.

ATTACK SUBMARINES (NUCLEAR) *(continued)*

◆ **8 Victor-III class** Bldrs: Admiralty SY, Leningrad, and Komsomolsk SY (In serv. 1978-. . .)

Victor-III class

Victor-III   1979

D: 4,600/5,800 tons   **S:** 29 kts (sub.)   **Dim:** 106.0 × 16.0 × 7.0
A: 8/533-mm TT (SS-N-15 and/or SS-N-16 missiles, torpedoes)
Electron Equipt: Radar: 1/Snoop Tray   Sonar: 1/low freq.
M: 1 reactor, steam turbines; 1 5-bladed prop; 30,000 hp   **Man:** 85 tot.

REMARKS: Further lengthened over basic Victor-I; distinguished by large teardrop-shaped pod atop vertical stabilizer. Construction continues.

◆ **7 Victor-II class** Bldr: Admiralty SY, Leningrad (In serv. 1972-78)

Victor-II class   French Navy, 1980

Victor-II class   French Navy, 1980

D: 4,500/5,700 tons   **S:** 28 kts   **Dim:** 100.0 × 10.0 × 7.0
A: 8/533-mm TT (SS-N-15 and/or SS-N-16 missiles, torpedoes)
M: 1 nuclear reactor, steam turbines; 1 5-bladed prop; 30,000 hp   **Man:** 80 tot.

REMARKS: One went into service in each of the years 1972, 1974, and 1975, two in 1976, and one each in 1977 and 1978. Longer than Victor-I, without pronounced hump on forward casing.

◆ **16 Victor-I class** Bldr: Admiralty SY, Leningrad (In serv. 1968-75)

50 LET SSR   13 others

D: 4,300/5,100 tons   **S:** 30 kts   **Dim:** 95.0 × 10.0 × 7.0
A: 8/533-mm TT (SS-N-15 and/or SS-N-16 missiles, torpedoes)

Victor-I class   U.S. Navy, 1974

ATTACK SUBMARINES (NUCLEAR) (continued)

Victor-I class   French Navy, 1980

Electron Equipt: Radar: 1/Snoop Tray
                     Sonar: 1/low freq.
M: 1 nuclear reactor, steam turbines; 1 5-bladed prop; 30,000 hp (2 small, 2-bladed props for slow speeds)
Man: 80 tot.

REMARKS: Completed two per year between 1968 and 1975.

♦ **7 Yankee class** Bldr: Severodvinsk SY and Komsomolsk SY (In serv. 1967-1974)

REMARKS: These are former ballistic-missile submarines that have had their 16 SS-N-6 tubes disabled in compliance with the U.S.-Soviet SALT agreements. As more Delta-III and Typhoon ballistic-missile submarines are built, more Yankees will receive similar treatment in order to keep the number of submarine-launched ballistic-missile tubes at no more than 950. It is believed that, as the Yankees are relatively new, the Soviet Navy will probably adapt them for some other purpose, probably as attack submarines. Characteristics may remain as listed for the Yankee ballistic-missile submarines, although if the missile tube area was removed entirely, the submarines may be considerably shorter overall, and lighter in displacement.

♦ **5 Echo class** Bldr: Komsomolsk (In serv. 1960-62)

D: 4,500/5,500 tons **S:** 20/25 kts **Dim:** 110.0 × 9.0 × 7.5
A: 6/533-mm TT (fwd)—4/400-mm TT (aft)

Echo class   U.S. Navy, 1975

Echo class   1977

Electron Equipt: Radar: 1/Snoop Tray   Sonar: 1/med. freq.
   M: 1 nuclear reactor, steam turbines; 2 5-bladed props; 25,000 hp   **Man:** 75 tot.

REMARKS: Former cruise-missile submarines that carried six SS-N-3. Converted circa 1970-75. One, involved in a casualty 20-8-80, had to be towed to Vladivostok; several men died. All in Pacific Fleet.

♦ **13 November class** Bldr: Severodvinsk SY (In serv. 1958-62)

November class

ATTACK SUBMARINES (NUCLEAR) *(continued)*

D: 4,500/5,300 tons **S:** 30 kts (sub.) **Dim:** 110.0 × 9.0 × 7.7
A: 8/533-mm TT (fwd)—4/400-mm TT (aft)—32 torpedoes or mines
Electron Equipt: Radar: 1/Snoop Tray
　　　　　　　　　 Sonar: 1/med. freq.
M: 1 nuclear reactor, steam turbines; 2 (4 or 6-bladed) props; 30,000 hp
Man: 80 tot.

REMARKS: One of this class was lost off Cape Finisterre in 1970. *Leninskiy Komsomol*, the U.S.S.R.'s first nuclear-powered ship, was commissioned 4-8-58; she later made the Soviet Navy's first trip to the North Pole.

ATTACK SUBMARINES (DIESEL-POWERED)

(Soviet Type: PL—*Podvodnaya Lodka* = Submarine)

♦ 1 (+ . . .) **Kilo class** Bldr: Komsomolsk-na-Amur SY (L: 9-80)

D: 2,500/3,200 tons **S:** . . . **Dim:** 67.0 × 9.0 × . . .
A: . . . /533-mm TT **Electron Equipt:** . . .
M: Diesels, electric drive; . . . props; . . . hp **Man:** . . .

REMARKS: Function uncertain; may be intended to replace Whiskey/Romeo-class submarines in the "medium-range" category, as the "long-range" Tango remains in production.

♦ 14 (+ . . .) **Tango class** Bldr: Gorkiy SY (In serv. 1972-. . .)

Tango class

Tango class

Tango-class sail/upper bridge area

1976

ATTACK SUBMARINES (DIESEL) *(continued)*

Tango class   French Navy, 1976

D: 3,000/3,700 tons   **S:** 20/16 kts   **Dim:** 91.5 × 9.0 × 7.0
A: 10/533-mm TT (6 fwd, 4 aft);. . . /SS-N-15 missiles, torpedoes)
Electron Equipt: Radar: 1/Snoop Tray
                 Sonar: 1/low freq.
M: 3 diesels, electric motors; 3 props; 6,000 hp   **Man:** 72 tot.

REMARKS: Two entered service in 1972, and roughly two per year have been completed since. Construction continues. Hull sheathed in sonar-absorbent rubber compound.

♦ **60 Foxtrot class** Bldr: Admiralty/Sudomekh SY (In serv. 1957-68)

CHELYABINSKIY KOMSOMOLETS	UL'YANOVSKIY KOMSOMOLETS
KOMSOMOLETS KAZAKHSTANA	VLADIMIRSKIY KOMSOMOLETS
KUIBISHEVSKIY KOMSOMOLETS	YAROSLAVSKIY KOMSOMOLETS
MAGNITOGORSKIY KOMSOMOLETS	53 others

D: 1,950/2,400 tons   **S:** 16/15.5 kts   **Dim:** 91.5 × 7.5 × 6.0
A: 10/533-mm TT (6 fwd, 4 aft)—22 torpedoes or 44 mines
Electron Equipt: Radar: 1/Snoop Tray
                 Sonar: 1/med. freq., passive array
M: 3 diesels of 2,000 hp, electric motors; 3 props; 5,300 hp (sub.)
Endurance: 70 days   **Range:** 11,000/8 (snorkel), 350/2 (sub.)
Man: 8 officers, 70 men

Foxtrot class   1978

Foxtrot class   French Navy, 1981

REMARKS: These submarines seem to be strongly built. Eight of the class have also been built for India, four for Libya, and two for Cuba. Two, temporarily named *Sirius* and *Saturn*, have been used in "oceanographic research." Foxtrot is a "long-range" submarine, and the design is a development of that of the Zulu class, with a large bow passive sonar array and a more streamlined sail.

Foxtrot class   1974

ATTACK SUBMARINES (DIESEL) (continued)

♦ **3 Modified Golf class**

Modified Golf class   U.S. Navy, 1978

Modified Golf class   1978

D: 2,300/2,700 tons   **S:** 12 kts (sub.)   **Dim:** 100.0 × 8.5 × 6.6
A: 10/533-mm TT (6 fwd, 4 aft)
Electron Equipt: Radar: 1/Snoop Tray
                  Sonar: 1/med.-freq.; passive array
M: 3 diesels of 2,000 hp, electric motors; 3 props; 5,300 hp (sub.)
Endurance: 70 days   **Range:** 9,500/5 (snorkel)   **Man:** 80 tot.

REMARKS: Three missile tubes removed. Apparently converted in 1978 as submersible command ships. Structure aft supports folding whip antennas; there are similar whips on either side of the sail. Sail extension possibly to house buoy antenna.

♦ **10 Romeo class** Bldr: Baltic SY, Leningrad (In serv. 1957-60)

Romeo class   1980

D: 1,330/1,700 tons   **S:** 15.5/13 kts   **Dim:** 77.0 × 6.7 × 4.9
A: 8/533-mm TT (6 fwd, 2 aft)—14 torpedoes or 28 mines
Electron Equipt: Radar: 1/Snoop Plate
                  Sonar: 1/med.-freq.; passive array
M: 2 diesels of 2,000 hp, electric motors; 2 props; 3,000 hp (sub.)
Endurance: 45 days   **Range:** 7,000/5 (snorkel)   **Man:** 56 tot.

REMARKS: Diving depth: 270-300 meters. Six transferred to Egypt, and two to Bulgaria. Also built in China and North Korea. Intended as Whiskey medium-range successor, but only about 20 built.

♦ **11 Zulu-IV class** Bldr: Sudomekh SY, Leningrad (In serv. 1952-57)

Zulu-IV class   1978

D: 1,900/2,350 tons   **S:** 18/16 kts   **Dim:** 90.0 × 7.5 × 6.0
A: 10/533-mm TT (6 fwd, 4 aft)—22 torpedoes or 44 mines
Electron Equipt: Radar: 1/Snoop Plate
                  Sonar: 1/med.-freq.; small passive array
M: 3 diesels of 2,000 hp, electric drive; 3 props; 5,300 hp (sub.)
Endurance: 70 days   **Range:** 9,500/8 (snorkel)   **Man:** 70 tot.

REMARKS: Between 1956 and 1957, several (since scrapped) were converted as Zulu-V ballistic-missile submarines, the world's first of their type; each had two tubes for surface launch of SS-N-4. Thirteen other Zulu-IVs have been scrapped. Earlier configurations (Zulu-I to Zulu-III) had deck guns, AA guns in the sail, and no snorkel; all later updated to Zulu-IV standard. Most of the survivors are in reserve. Two have served in "oceanographic research" roles as *Vega* and *Lira.*

♦ **60 Whiskey class** Bldrs: Baltic SY, Leningrad; Marti SY, Nikolayev; Gorkiy SY; Komsomolsk-na-Amur SY (In serv. 1949-57)

D: 1,050/1,350 tons   **S:** 17/13.5 kts   **Dim:** 75.0 × 6.3 × 4.8
A: 6/533-mm TT (4 fwd, 2 aft)—12 torpedoes or 24 mines
Electron Equipt: Radar: 1/Snoop Plate
                  Sonar: 1/med.-freq.; small passive array
M: 2 Type 37D, 2,000-hp diesels, electric motors; 2 props; 2,500 hp (sub.)
Endurance: 40-45 days   **Range:** 6,000/5 (snorkel)   **Man:** 50 tot.

ATTACK SUBMARINES (DIESEL) *(continued)*

Whiskey class   1978

REMARKS: Built in prefabricated sections, these strong, uncomplicated boats have proven quite satisfactory. Approximately 236 were built in the U.S.S.R., with China also having built the design. Despite the age, a number remain quite active. Considered to be "medium-range" submarines. Twelve were converted to cruise-missile boats. Four were modified as radar-picket submarines. As many as seventy additional Whiskey-class units are now in reserve. Some have been transferred to Bulgaria, Egypt, Poland, Albania, China, and Indonesia.

♦ **1 Whiskey Canvas Bag class**

   D: 1,080/1,450 tons   **S:** 17/13.5 kts   **Dim:** 76.0 × 6.3 × 4.8
   A: 4/533-mm TT (fwd)—8 torpedoes
   Electron Equipt: Radar: 1/Snoop Plate, 1/Boat Sail
                         Sonar: 1/med.-freq.; passive array
   M: 2 Type 37D, 2,000-hp diesels, electric motors; 2 props; 2,500 hp submerged
   Range: 6,000/5   **Man:** 50 tot.

REMARKS: Four were converted from standard Whiskey class to radar pickets about 1960. One has since had the folding Boat Sail radar removed from the top of the lengthened sail and an unidentified housing built on her stern (re-entering the "standard" Whiskey ranks); two have been scrapped.

♦ **4 Quebec class** Bldr: Sudomekh SY, Leningrad (In serv. 1954-57)

   D: 400/540 tons   **S:** 18/16 kts   **Dim:** 56.0 × 5.1 × 3.8
   A: 4/533-mm TT (fwd)—8 torpedoes or 16 mines
   Electron Equipt: Radar: 1/Snoop Plate
                         Sonar: 1/med.-freq.; passive array
   M: 3 1,000-hp diesels, electric motors; 3 props; 2,200 hp (sub.)   **Man:** 30 tot.

REMARKS: Especially designed for operations in the Baltic and Black Sea. Thirty built, most now stricken; some additional may be in reserve. Some or all had Kreislauf closed-cycle diesel propulsion systems on the centerline prop. Probably used for training.

Whiskey Canvas Bag class—Boat Sail radar unfolded   1965

Quebec class

AUXILIARY SUBMARINES (DIESEL-POWERED)

♦ **1 Lima-class research submarine** Bldr: Admiralty SY, Leningrad (In serv. 1978)

   D: 2,000/2,400 tons   **S:** . . .   **Dim:** 86.0 × 9.5 × 7.4
   A: None   **M:** Diesels, electric drive;. . . props;. . . hp   **Man:** . . .

REMARKS: Function not available. Sail, set well aft on unusually bulky hull, has forward extension housing an active sonar transducer and has fixed radar mast.

♦ **2 India-class salvage submarines** Bldr: Komsomolsk-na-Amur SY (In serv. 1979-80)

   D: 3,200/4,000 tons   **S:** . . .   **Dim:** 106.0 × 10.0 ×. . .
   A: . . ./533-mm TT fwd   **Electron Equipt:** Radar:. . .—Sonar: 1/med.-freq.; passive arrays
   M: . . . diesels, electric motors; 2 props;. . . hp   **Man:** . . .

AUXILIARY SUBMARINES (continued)

India class—with two salvage submersibles   1980

India class in Arctic transfer rig: wells plated up, bow ice protection added   1980

REMARKS: Carry two small salvage/submarine rescue submersibles in wells on after casing. Hull designed for surface cruising. May not have armament, considering function. One unit remains in Pacific, the other transited the Arctic to the Northern Fleet, 1980.

♦ **4 Bravo-class target training submarines** Bldr: Komsomolsk-na-Amur SY (In serv. 1968-70)

Bravo class   U.S. Navy, 1979

Bravo class   1975

D: 2,400/2,900 tons   **S:** 14/16 kts   **Dim:** 73.0 × 9.8 × 7.3
A: 6/533-mm TT (fwd)
Electron Equipt: Radar: 1/Snoop Tray
                Sonar: 1 passive array
M: Diesel-electric drive; 1 prop;. . . hp   **Man:** 65 tot.

REMARKS: Configured as "hard" targets for torpedo firing training, they may also have a training role and, if indeed armed, could be used as attack subs in wartime.

HELICOPTER CRUISERS

♦ **2 Moskva class**

	Bldr	Laid down	L	In serv.
MOSKVA	Black Sea SY, Nikolayev	1962	1964	7-67
LENINGRAD	Black Sea SY, Nikolayev	1964	1966	1968

D: 14,500 tons (19,200 fl)   **S:** 30 kts   **Dim:** 190.0 × 34.0 (flight deck) 26.0 (wl) × 7.6
A: 2/SA-N-3 systems (II × 2 with 44 Goblet missiles)—4/57-mm AA (II × 2)—1/ SUW-N-1 ASW RL—2/RBU 6000 ASW RL—14 Hormone-A helicopters
Electron Equipt: Radar: 3/Don-2, 1/Top Sail, 1/Head Net-C, 2/Head Lights, 2/Muff Cob
                Sonar: 1/low-freq. hull-mounted, 1/med.-freq. towed VDS

Moskva   French Navy, 1979

Leningrad—superstructure detail   French Navy, 1980

HELICOPTER CRUISERS (continued)

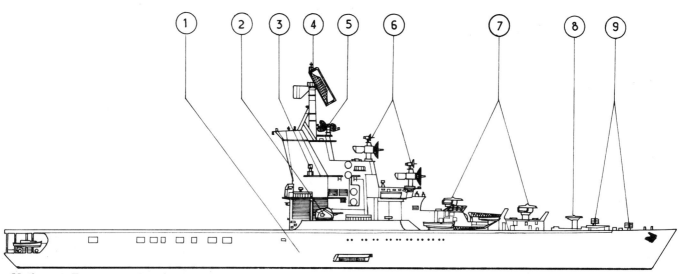

Moskva—1. Former torpedo tube location 2. Twin 57-mm AA 3. Muff Cob radar gunfire-control director 4. Top Sail 3-D air-search radar 5. Head Net-C air-search radar 6. Head Lights SAM control radar directors 7. Twin SA-N-3 missile launchers 8. Twin SUW-N-1 ASW rocket launcher 9. RBU-6000 ASW rocket launchers

H. Simoni

ECM: 8/Side Globe, 2/Top Hat, several Bell series, 2/chaff launchers (II × 2)
IFF: High Pole B
M: 2 sets GT; 2 props; 100,000 hp **Boilers:** 4
Range: 2,500/30; 7,000/15 **Man:** 850 tot.

REMARKS: Soviet type designation: *Protivolodochnyy Kreyser* (Antisubmarine cruiser). Flight deck 86 × 34 m. Hangar beneath flight deck, with small hangar between stack uptakes in superstructure. Two elevators on the flight deck. The *Moskva* was modified for a time to permit the testing of VTOL Forger-A aircraft, which were to go aboard the *Kiev* carriers. Both ships had their ten 533-mm ASW TT removed and the side embrasures plated in during the mid-1970s. Sonar dome is retractable within hull. Fin stabilizers fitted.

GUIDED-MISSILE CRUISERS (NUCLEAR-POWERED)

♦ 1 (+1) **Kirov class** Bldr: Baltic SY, Leningrad

	Laid down	L	In serv.
KIROV	1973	12-77	9-80
N. . .	1-78	6-81	1983

D: 23,400 tons (fl) **S:** 32-34 kts **Dim:** 248.0 (230.0 wl) × 28.0 (24.0 wl) × 7.5

A: 20/SS-N-19 SSM (20 inclined tubes)—12/SA-N-6 vertical SAM launchers (96 missiles)—2/SA-N-4 SAM syst. (II × 2, 36 missiles)—2/100-mm DP (I × 2)—8/30-mm Gatling AA (I × 8)—1/SS-N-14 ASW cruise-missile launcher (II × 1, 14-16 missiles)—8/533-mm TT (IV × 2)—1/RBU-6000 ASW RL (XII × 1)—2/RBU-1000 ASW RL (VI × 2)—3/Hormone-A and/or -B helicopters

Kirov—forward superstructure showing complex array of electronics and optical sensors; the forward Front Dome director is trained aft.

R.N., 1980

GUIDED-MISSILE CRUISERS (NUCLEAR) *(continued)*

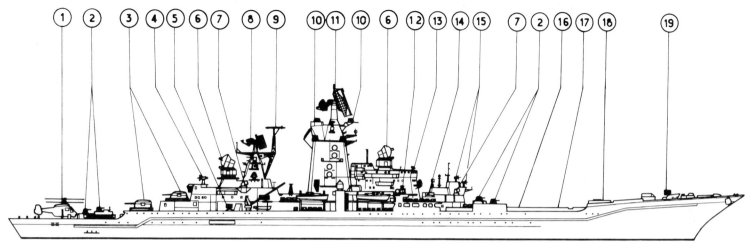

Kirov class—1. Helicopter platform 2. 30-mm Gatling AA guns 3. 100-mm dual-purpose guns 4. Kite Screech radar gunfire-control director 5. RBU-1000 ASW rocket launcher 6. Top Dome radar directors for SA-N-6 7. Bass Tilt radar gunfire-control directors 8. Top Steer 3-D radar 9. Vee Tube HF comms. antenna 10. Round House helo control systems 11. Top Pair 3-D radar 12. Pop Group radar directors for SA-N-4 13. Palm Frond surface-search radars 14. SA-N-4 SAM launchers 15. Eye Bowl radar directors for SS-N-14 16. Location of SS-N-19 cruise-missile tubes 17. Location of vertical launchers for SA-N-6 18. Twin SS-N-14 ASW cruise-missile launcher 19. RBU-6000 ASW rocket launcher   H. Simoni

Kirov foredeck—showing SS-N-19 (left) and SAN-6 launcher hatches, forward Gatling guns, folding replenishment station, and deck rail system   R.N., 1980

Kirov—stern, showing helicopter arrangements (note rope net landing area, control cab in superstructure, 100-mm gun installation and VDS hatch open at left.   R.N., 1980

GUIDED-MISSILE CRUISERS (NUCLEAR) *(continued)*

Kirov   U.S. Navy, 1980

Electron Equipt: Radar: 3/Palm Frond, 1/Top Pair, 1/Top Steer, 2/Top Dome,
2/Pop Group, 2/Eye Bowl, 1/Kite Screech, 4/Bass
Tilt, 1/unidentified landing aid
Sonar: 1/low-freq. bow-mounted, 1/low-freq. VDS
ECM: 8/Side Globe, 4/Rum Tub, 10 Bell-series, 2/chaff RL
(II × 2)
TACAN: 2/Round House
M: 2 nuclear reactors, plus oil-fired superheat boosters; 2 props; 150,000 hp
Range: effectively unlimited   **Man:** approx. 800 tot.

REMARKS:
1. *General:* The *Kirov* is the world's largest "cruiser" and might best be termed a
"battlecruiser." The Soviet type-designation applied has been merely RKR—*Raketnyy Kreyser* (Missile Cruiser). The ship is capable of independent operations, due
to the virtual autonomy conveyed by the nuclear propulsion system, but it would
also make an ideal escort for the expected nuclear-powered carrier.
2. *Hull:* Displacement is provisional; it could be as high as 27,000 tons. The high
forecastle shelters the reloadable SS-N-14 ASW cruise-missile launcher within a
redoubt or cul-de-sac. A long raised strake down either side of the hull covers either
fuel transfer lines (as on U.S. Navy carriers), degaussing cables (although these
would surely be internal?), or is merely meant as an external hull stiffener, as on
smaller Soviet warships. The helicopter hangar is beneath the forward portion of
the fantail, with an elevator delivering the aircraft to the flight deck. The steeply
raked stern has a 9-m broad centerline recess for the VDS installation, whose door
when closed is raked forward past the vertical. The screws appear to be mounted
unusually far forward. Two solid-stores replenishment stations are fitted: one amidships to port, and one folding station forward to port, abreast the SA-N-6 system;
both employ the sliding-stay, constant-tension concept. Oil and water replenishment
is handled at stations on either beam abreast the Kite Screech radar.
3. *Propulsion:* The two circular reactor access hatches can be seen amidships, just
abaft the enormous twin exhaust uptakes for the unusual CONAS (Combined Nuclear and Steam) propulsion system. The steam generated by the reactors is probably lead to oil-fired superheaters that could theoretically boost the energy output
of the steam by 50 to 55% by superheating it; this system would be cut in when

Kirov—aerial stern aspect, showing superheater exhaust trunks on aft face of forward
tower mast   R.N., 1980

maximum speeds were required, and, given the size of the ship, sufficient fuel for
global endurance at maximum speed could be accommodated. One of the stacks
probably serves the superheaters, while the other probably serves to ventilate the
reactor spaces.

GUIDED-MISSILE CRUISERS (NUCLEAR) *(continued)*

Kirov   R.N., 1980

4. *Armament:* The launch tubes for the 20 SS-N-19 anti-ship missiles are buried within the hull at a fixed angle of 40-45-degree elevation, in four rows of five, forward of the superstructure. Before these are the 12 vertical launchers for SA-N-6; each has a door, beneath which is a rotating magazine containing missiles. Targeting data for the SS-N-19, with its 300-nautical-mile maximum range, can come either from Hormone B helicopters embarked on the ship, or from satellites via the Punch Bowl satellite communications antennas on either side of the ship. The SS-N-14 ASW cruise-missile system is the first *reloadable* installation in a Soviet ship, employing a magazine forward of the launcher, buried within the forecastle. The Gatling guns are paired and located so as to cover all four quadrants; each pair is served by a Bass Tilt radar director and a manned, optical backup director.

5. *Electronic equipment:* As might be expected, the communications antenna array is extensive and diverse and includes satellite communications equipment and long-range HF gear. There are four stabilized electro-optical sensors, covering all four quadrants, as well as smaller remote t.v. cameras. Two Bob Tail possible radiometric sextant antennas are housed in spherical enclosures outboard the Pop Group radars. A microwave landing approach radar is mounted on a starboard platform

on the after tower mast. The VDS employs a lens-shaped "fish" about 4 m in diameter to house the transducer and has a twin boom-mounted empennage with horizontal and vertical control surfaces. In addition to a low-frequency bow-mounted sonar, there is probably a medium-frequency set for fire-control purposes (including depth determination) for the RBU-series rocket launchers.

GUIDED-MISSILE CRUISERS

♦ 0 (+3+...) **BLK-COM-1 class** Bldr: 61 Kommuna SY, Nikolayev

	Laid down	L	In serv.
N...	1976	1979	1982
N...	1978	1980	1983
N...	1979	1981	1984

D: 12,000 tons (fl) **S:** 34 kts **Dim:** 183.0 ×...×...
A: .../SS-N-12 SSM—.../SA-N-6 SAM—.../SS-N-14 ASW—.../130-mm DP (II ×...)—etc.
Electron Equipt: Radar: ...
                    Sonar: ...
M: Gas turbines **Range:** ... **Man:** ...

REMARKS: "BLK-COM-1" is a provisional NATO class name meaning "Black Sea Combatant-1." Eight are expected to be built.

♦ 7 **Kara class** Bldr: 61 Kommuna SY, Nikolayev

	Laid down	L	In serv.
NIKOLAYEV	1969	1971	1973
OCHAKOV	1970	1972	1975
KERCH	1971	1973	1976
AZOV	1972	1974	1977
PETROPAVLOVSK	1973	1975	1978
TASHKENT	1975	1976	1979
TALLIN	1976	1977	1980

D: 8,200 tons (10,000 fl) **S:** 34 kts **Dim:** 173.8 × 18.3 × 6.2
A: 8/SS-N-14 (IV × 2, 8 missiles)—2/SA-N-3 systems (II × 2, 44 Goblet missiles)—4/SA-N-4 (II × 2, 36 missiles)—4/76.2-mm DP (II × 2)—4/30-mm Gatling AA (I × 4)—10/533-mm TT (V × 2)—2/RBU-6000 ASW RL (XII × 2)—2/RBU-1000 ASW RL (VI × 2)—1/Hormone-A helicopter
Electron Equipt: Radar: 1/Don-2 or Palm Frond, 2 Don-Kay, 1/Top Sail, 1/Head Net-C, 2/Head Lights, 2/Pop Group, 2/Owl Screech, 2/Bass Tilt
                      Sonar: 1/low freq. hull-mounted, 1/med. freq. VDS

Azov—with Top Dome and SA-N-6 aft   Military Herald, 1979

GUIDED-MISSILE CRUISERS (*continued*)

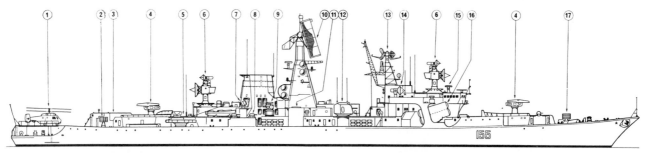

1. Hormone-A 2. RBU-1000 3. Helicopter hangar 4. SA-N-3 5. 533-mm TT 6. Head Lights 7. Bass Tilt 8. Gatling AA guns 9. Pop Group
10. Top Sail 11. SA-N-4 12. 76.2-mm guns 13. Head Net-C 14. Owl Screech 15. Don-Kay 16. SS-N-14 17. RBU-6000

Ochakov   1979

    ECM: 8/Side Globe, 2/Bell Clout, 2/Bell Slam, 2/Bell Tap (or 4
      Rum Tub), 2/chaff RL (II × 2)
    IFF: 1/High Pole B (interrogation by search radars)
  M: 4 gas turbines; 2 props; 120,000 hp
  Range: 2,000/30; 8,000/15 **Man:** 30 officers, 490 men

REMARKS: Soviet type designation: *Bol'shoy Protivolodochnyy Korabl'* (Large Antisubmarine Ship), a type considered to be more in the destroyer than the cruiser
category. *Petropavlovsk* has two cylindrical Round House TACAN abreast the helicopter hangar, which is higher than on the other ships; she has no RBU-1000 rocket

Ochakov   J.-C. Bellonne, 1979

Ochakov   1979

launchers. She and the *Tashkent* joined the Pacific Fleet in 1979. The *Azov* has been
reported as a trials ship for SA-N-6 vertically launched surface-to-air missiles and
has only one SA-N-3 launcher, forward; a Top Dome missile radar director is mounted
aft. The last three built have incomplete ECM/ESM arrays, having been equipped
to take 4 Rum Tub, as on *Petropavlovsk* and *Kerch*. SA-N-3, SA-N-4, and SS-N-14
can also be used against surface targets.

GUIDED-MISSILE CRUISERS *(continued)*

Tashkent

1979

Kerch—with Rum Tub arrays on the tower mast platform

1980

GUIDED-MISSILE CRUISERS *(continued)*

Petropavlovsk—note Round House TACAN antennas flanking the higher-than-standard hangar, no RBU-1000 ASW RL aft, VDS installation beneath flight deck   1979

♦ **10 Kresta-II class** Bldr: Zhdanov SY, Leningrad

	L	In serv.		L	In serv.
KRONSHTADT	1967	1970	ADMIRAL ISACHEN-	1973	1975
ADMIRAL ISAKOV	1968	1971	KOV		
ADMIRAL NAKHIMOV	1969	1972	MARSHAL TIMO-	1974	1976
ADMIRAL MAKAROV	1970	1973	SHENKO		
MARSHAL VOROSHILOV	1971	1973	VASILIY CHAPAEV	1975	1977
ADMIRAL OKTYA-	1972	1974	ADMIRAL	1976	1978
BR'SKIY			YUMASHEV		

D: 6,000 tons (7,600 fl)   **S:** 34 kts   **Dim:** 158.0 × 17.0 × 5.5 (hull)
A: 8/SS-N-14 (IV × 2, 8 missiles)—2/SA-N-3 systems (II × 2, 44 Goblet missiles)—4/57-mm AA (II × 2)—4/30-mm Gatling AA (I × 4)—2/RBU-6000 ASW RL (XII × 2)—2/RBU-1000 ASW RL (VI × 2)—10/533-mm TT (V × 2)—1/Hormone-A helicopter
Electron Equipt: Radar: 1/Don-2, 2/Don-Kay, 1/Top Sail, 1/Head Net-C, 2/Head Lights, 2/Muff Cob, 2/Bass Tilt
     Sonar: 1/med. freq. hull-mounted
     ECM: 8/Side Globe, 1/Bell Clout, 2/Bell Slam, 2/Bell Tap, 2/chaff RL (II × 2)
     IFF: 1/High Pole B (interrogation by search radars)
M: 2 sets GT; 2 props; 100,000 hp   **Boilers:** 4, turbo-pressurized
Fuel: 1,100 tons   **Range:** 1,600/34; 7,000/14   **Man:** 380 tot.

Marshal Timoshenko—with hangar open   French Navy, 1980

Marshal Timoshenko—note enlarged superstructure between bridge and tower mast   French Navy, 1980

GUIDED-MISSILE CRUISERS (continued)

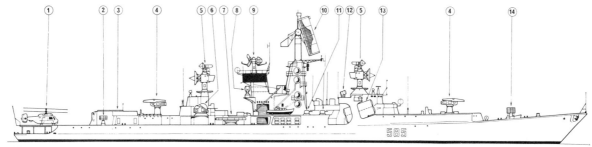

1. Hormone-A 2. RBU-1000 3. Helicopter hangar 4. SA-N-3 5. Head Lights 6. 57-mm AA 7. 533-mm TT 8. Muff Cob 9. Head Net-C 10. Top Sail 11. Gatling AA guns 12. Bass Tilt 13. SS-N-14 14. RBU-6000

Marshal Voroshilov   1979

REMARKS: Soviet type designation: BPK—*Bol'shoy Protivolodochnyy Korabl'* (Large Antisubmarine Ship). The first three units do not have Bass Tilt. Late units have larger forward superstructure, the area between the tower foremast and the bridge being filled in by a two-level deckhouse. *Admiral Makarov* has prototype solid-stores equipment to port and prototype underway refueling equipment to starboard. SA-N-3 and SS-N-14 can also be used against surface targets. Have fin stabilizers.

♦ **4 Kresta-I class** Bldr: Zhdanov SY, Leningrad

	L	In serv.		L	In serv.
VITSE ADMIRAL DROZD	1965	1967	ADMIRAL ZOZULYA	1966	1968
SEVASTOPOL	1965	1967	VLADIVOSTOK	1966	1968

D: 6,000 tons (7,500 fl)   **S:** 34 kts   **Dim:** 155.0 × 17.0 × 5.5 (hull)

Vitse Admiral Drozd   1976

GUIDED-MISSILE CRUISERS *(continued)*

A: 4/SS-N-3 (II × 2)—2/SA-N-1 systems (II × 2, 44 Goa missiles)—4/57-mm AA
(II × 2)—2/RBU-6000 ASW RL (XI × 2)—2/RBU-1000 ASW RL (VI × 2)—
10/533-mm TT (V × 2)—1/Hormone-B helicopter—*Vitse Admiral Drozd:* 4/
30-mm Gatling AA (I × 4)

Electron Equipt: Radar: 2/Don-2, 1/Big Net, 1/Head Net-C, 2/Plinth Net,
      1/Scoop Pair, 2/Peel Group, 2/Muff Cob—
      Vitse Admiral Drozd: 2/Bass Tilt
      Sonar: 1/med.-freq., hull-mounted
      ECM: 8/Side Globe, 1/Bell Clout, 2/Bell Slam, 2/Bell Tap,
      2/chaff RL (II × 2)
      IFF: 2/High Pole B

M: 2 sets GT; 2 props; 100,000 hp **Boilers:** 4, turbo-pressurized
Fuel: 1,150 tons **Range:** 1,600/34; 7,000/14 **Man:** 380 tot.

REMARKS: Soviet type designation: RKR—*Raketnyy Kreyser* (Missile Cruiser). Based
on the Kynda class, but has a better mixture of weapons. The surface-to-surface
launchers, fitted on each side of the superstructure, forward under the bridge wings,
can be elevated, but not trained. No SS-N-3 missile reloads. Installation of Gatling

Sevastopol   1981

Admiral Zozulya—with 2 Palm Frond, 1 Don-Kay navigational radars 1979

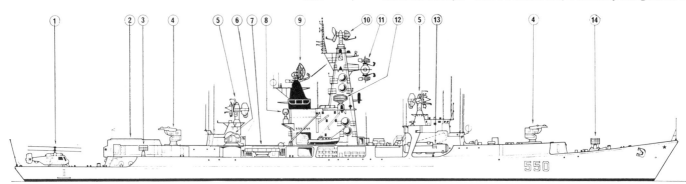

1. Hormone-B 2. Helicopter hangar 3. RBU-1000 4. SA-N-1 5. Peel Group 6. 57-mm AA 7. 533-mm TT 8. Muff Cob 9. Big Net 10. Head Net-C 11. Scoop Pair 12. Plinth Net 13. SS-N-3 14. RBU-6000

GUIDED-MISSILE CRUISERS (continued)

guns abaft the Shaddock launchers and construction of a new deckhouse between the *Vitse Admiral Drozd* (see photos). *Sevastopol* received the new deckhouse, but not the Gatling guns or radar, in 1980.

♦ **4 Kynda class** Bldr: Zhdanov SY, Leningrad

	Laid down	L	In serv.
GROZNYY	6-59	4-62	6-62
ADMIRAL FOKIN	1960	11-61	8-63
ADMIRAL GOLOVKO	1961	1963	7-64
VARYAG	1962	1964	2-65

D: 4,400 tons (5,600 fl) **S:** 34 kts **Dim:** 141.7 × 15.8 × 5.3 (hull)
A: 8/SS-N-3 (IV × 2, 16 missiles)—1/SA-N-1 system (II × 1, 24 Goa missiles)—4/76.2-mm DP (II × 2)—2/RBU-6000 ASW RL (XII × 2)—6/533-mm TT (III × 2)
Electron Equipt: Radar: 2/Don-2, 2/Head Net-A or -C, 2/Scoop Pair, 1/Peel Group, 1/Owl Screech, 2/Plinth Net—*A. Fokin:* 2/Bass Tilt

Admiral Golovko   French Navy, 1978

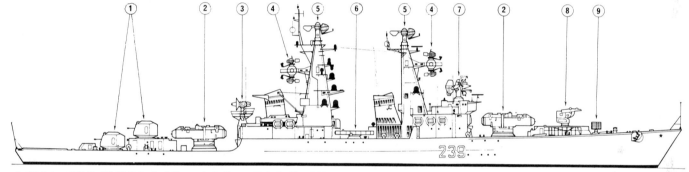

1. 76.2-mm DP 2. SS-N-3 3. Owl Screech 4. Scoop Pair 5. Head Net-A 6. 533-mm TT 7. Peel Group 8. SA-N-1 9. RBU-6000

Admiral Golovko

1979

GUIDED-MISSILE CRUISERS (continued)

Admiral Fokin—Head Net-A fwd, Head Net-C aft   1980

> Sonar: 1/high freq., hull-mounted
> ECM: 1/Bell Clout, 1/Bell Slam, 1/Bell Tap, 4/Top Hat
> IFF: 2/High Pole B

M: 2 sets GT; 2 props; 100,000 hp   **Range:** 1,100/32; 6,800/15   **Man:** 375 tot.

REMARKS: Soviet type designation: RKR—*Raketnyy Kreyser* (Missile Cruiser). Eight Shaddock missiles are loaded in the trainable and elevatable quadruple tubes; reloading from the handling rooms requires some time. *Admiral Fokin* now has one Head Net-A, one Head Net-C, and two Plinth Net; *Groznyy* received two Plinth Net around 1973. *Varyag* received 2 Head Net-C, 2 Plinth Net, 2 Bass Tilt and 4/30-mm Gatling AA in 1981.

♦ 1 Modified Sverdlov class

	Bldr	Laid down	L	In serv.
DZERZHINSKIY	Marti SY, Nikolayev	5-49	1951	11-52

For characteristics of hull and machinery, see *Sverdlov*-class light cruisers

> **A:** 1/SA-N-2 system (II × 1, 10 Guideline missiles)—9/152-mm guns (III × 3)—12/100-mm DP (II × 6)—16/37-mm AA (II × 8)—mines
> **Electron Equipt:** Radar: 1/Neptune, 1/Low Sieve, 1/Big Net, 1/Slim Net, 1/Fan Song-E, 1/Top Brow, 2/Sun Visor, 6/Egg Cup

Man: 1,040 tot.

REMARKS: Soviet type designation: KR—*Kreyser* (Cruiser). In 1961 the *Dzerzhinskiy* completed refit, during which her No. 3 152-mm turret was replaced by an SA-N-2 system (twin launcher aft), making her the only ship to carry the system. Her High Lune height-finding radar was removed in 1976. Experienced casualty in Mediterranean and had to be towed home in 1979.

COMMAND CRUISERS

♦ 2 Modified Sverdlov class

	Bldr	Laid down	L	In serv.
ADMIRAL SENYAVIN	Severodvinsk SY	. . .	. . .	1955
ZHDANOV	Baltic SY, Leningrad	10-49	12-50	1952

Admiral Senyavin—note new satellite comms. radomes   1979

Zhdanov   1973

Dzerzhinskiy   1978

COMMAND CRUISERS (continued)

For characteristics of hull and machinery, see *Sverdlov*-class light cruisers
   A: 6 (*Admiral Senyavin*) or 9/152-mm (III × 2 or 3)—12/100-mm DP (II × 6)—
   1/SA-N-4 system (II × 1)—16/37-mm AA—8 (*Zhdanov*) or 16/30-mm AA (II
   × 4 or 8)
   Electron Equipt: Radar: 2/Top Bow, 1/Top Trough, 2/Sun Visor, 6/Egg Gup, 1/
   Pop Group—*Zhdanov:* 2/Drum Tilt; *Admiral Senyavin:*
   4/Drum Tilt

REMARKS: Soviet type designation: KU—*Korabl' Upravleniy* (Command Ship). Both
completed modernization in 1972. Excellent long-range communications, including a
Vee Cone HF antenna, which can be seen on the after tripod mast. The 30-mm guns
are divided on each side of the forward stack and, on the *Admiral Senyavin*, on
each side of the after deckhouse as well; her two after turrets have been replaced
by a hangar and platform for one Hormone helicopter. Both ships have had their
mine rails removed.

LIGHT CRUISERS

◆ **9 Sverdlov class** Bldr: Baltic SY, Leningrad; Marti SY, Nikolayev; Severodvinsk
SY

	L		L
ADMIRAL LAZAREV	1952	MIKHAIL KUTUZOV	5-54
ADMIRAL USHAKOV	5-52	MURMANSK	1955
ALEXANDR NEVSKIY	7-51	OKTYABRSKAYA REVOLUTSIYA (ex-*Molotovsk*)	1954
ALEXANDR SUVOROV	6-52	SVERDLOV	7-50
DMITRIY POZHARSKIY	1954		

   D: 12,900 tons (17,200 fl)   **S:** 32 kts   **Dim:** 210.0 (199.95 pp) × 21.6 × 7.2
   A: 12/152-mm (III × 4)—12/100-mm DP (II × 6)—32/37-mm AA (II × 16)—140
   mines—*Oktyabrskaya Revolutsiya, Admiral Ushakov, Alexandr Suvorov:*
   16/30-mm AA (II × 8) also

Dmitry Pozharskiy—note enlarged deckhouse below pilothouse   1975

Oktyabrskaya Revolutsiya   1977

Oktyabrskaya Revolutsiya—modernized version with 16/30-mm AA, 4 Drum Tilt   1979

LIGHT CRUISERS (continued)

Electron Equipt: Radar: 1/Neptune or Don-2, 1/Low Sieve or High Sieve, 1/Big
Net or Top Trough, 1/Slim Net, 2/Top Bow,
2/Sun Visor, 8/Egg Cup—Knife Rest in some—
ships with 30-mm AA: 4/Drum Tilt
ECM: 2/Watch Dog—IFF: 1/High Pole
Armor: 152-mm turret; 76-100-mm; Deck: 25-50 and 50-75-mm; 100-mm; gun
shields: 25-mm
M: 2 sets GT; 2 props; 110,000 hp **Boilers:** 6
Fuel: 3,800 tons **Range:** 2,200/32; 8,400/15 **Man:** 70 officers, 940 men

REMARKS: Soviet type designation: KR—*Kreyser*. Based on the *Chapayev* class. Twenty-
four were planned; fourteen put in service between 1951 and 1956; others were laid
down but construction was suspended in 1956 and canceled in 1960. Slight differences
in profile, the merging of the forward stack with the bridge structure being notice-
able. The *Admiral Nakhimov* was scrapped in 1961; the *Ordzhonikidze* was transferred to Indonesia in 1962 and has since been scrapped. By 1961 the *Dzerzhinskiy*
had been converted to a guided-missile cruiser; two others, the *Zhdanov* and *Admiral
Senyavin*, completed conversion to command cruisers in 1972. In 1977 the *Oktyabrskaya Revolutsiya* completed overhaul, during which eight twin 30-mm AA and
four Drum Tilt radars were added, the Egg Cup radars were removed from her 100-
mm mounts, and her bridge was enlarged. Radar suits vary widely. In 1979 the
Admiral Ushakov and *Alexandr Suvorov* appeared with similar alterations; all three
ships have had four of their 37-mm AA (II × 2) removed. The Soviets evidently
intend to continue this class in operation for some time; the ships provide excellent
command facilities and their powerful gunnery batteries give the U.S.S.R. the world's
finest shore-bombardment capability.

NOTE: The last *Chapayev*-class cruiser, *Komsomolets*, was stricken 1980.

GUIDED-MISSILE DESTROYERS

♦ 2 (+2+. . .) **Udaloy class**

	Bldr	Laid down	L	In serv.
UDALOY	Kaliningrad SY	1978	1980	1981
VITSE ADMIRAL KULAKOV	Zhdanov SY, Leningrad	1978	1980	1981
N. . .	Kaliningrad SY	1979	. . .	. . .
N. . .	Zhdanov SY, Leningrad	1979	. . .	. . .

D: 6,200-6,700 tons (8,200 fl) **S:** 32-34 kts
Dim: 162.0 (150.0 wl) × 19.3 (17.8 wl) × 6.2 (hull)
A: 8/. . . vertical SAM launchers (see Remarks)—8/SS-N-14 (IV × 2)—2/100-
mm DP—4/30-mm Gatling AA (I × 4)—2/RBU-6000 ASW RL (XII × 2)—8/
533-mm TT (IV × 2)—mines—2/Helix A ASW helicopters

Udaloy 1980

Udaloy 1980

Udaloy 1980

Udaloy—direct overhead view, with VDS door open 1981

GUIDED-MISSILE DESTROYERS (continued)

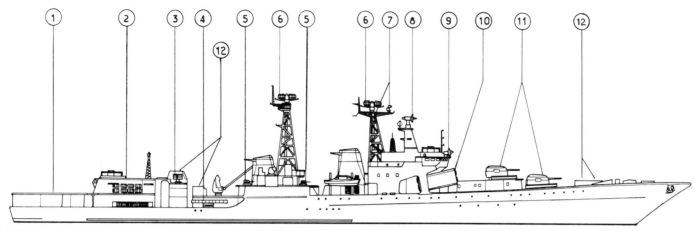

1. Helicopter platform (VDS beneath) 2. Twin helicopter hangars 3. RBU-6000 4. 533-mm TT (IV × 2) 5. 30-mm Gatling AA 6. Strut Pair 7. Palm Frond 8. Kite Screech 9. Eye Bowl 10. SS-N-14 (IV × 2) 11. 100-mm AA guns 12. Vertical-launch SAM positions

H. Simoni

Udaloy—during trials; the device at the bows was later removed

1980

Electron Equipt: Radar: 3/Palm Frond, 2/Strut Pair, 2/Eye Bowl, 1/Kite Screech, 2/Bass Tilt, 1/. . . helo control
Sonar: 1/low freq. bow-mounted, 1/low-freq. VDS
ECM: 2/Bell Shroud, 2/Bell Squat, 2/chaff RL (II × 2)
TACAN: 2/Round House
IFF: . . .
M: 4 gas turbines; 2 CP props; 100-120,000 hp
Electric: . . .   **Range:** . . .   **Man:** 300 tot.

REMARKS: Formerly carried NATO-nickname BAL-COM-3. Soviet type designation probably BPK—*Bol'shoy Protivolodochniy Korabl'* (Large Antisubmarine Ship), as the design is obviously primarily intended for ASW. The design is analogous in size and capability to the U.S. *Spruance* class. Provision has been made for installation of a vertically launched (probably short-ranged) SAM system; there are four 2-meter diameter cover plates on the raised portion of the forecastle, two more disposed athwartships in the small deckhouse between the torpedo tubes, and two arranged fore and aft in the deckhouse between the RBU-6000 ASW RL mounts. Each cylinder

GUIDED-MISSILE DESTROYERS *(continued)*

could hold perhaps 6-8 missiles, for a total of 48-64. There are empty director platforms atop the hangar and atop the bridge. This is the first BPK design to carry two ASW helicopters, which will apparently be of a heavier, successor design to Hormone-A. The two hangars are side by side and use inclined elevator ramps to raise the aircraft to the flight deck; the hangar roofs slide forward in two segmented sections to clear the rotors. Two Round House helicopter-control-system radomes are mounted on yards on the after mast, while the microwave landing-control radar is beside the starboard hangar. The ECM/ESM suit is incomplete, with several empty platforms on the after mast. The sonar suit probably duplicates that of the nuclear-powered cruiser *Kirov.*

♦ **2 (+2+. . .) Sovremennyy class** Bldr: Zhdanov SY, Leningrad

	Laid down	L	In serv.
SOVREMENNYY	1976	11-78	1981
N. . .	1977	8-80	1982
N. . .	1978	1981	. . .
N. . .	1979	. . .	. . .

D: 6,200 tons (7,800 fl)　**S:** 34 kts　**Dim:** 155.6 × 17.0 × 5.6 (hull)
A: 8/SS-N-. . . SSM—2/SA-N-7 SAM systems (I × 2, . . . missiles)—4/130-mm DP (II × 2)—4/30-mm Gatling AA (I × 4)—4/533-mm TT (II × 2)—2/RBU-1000 ASW RL (VI × 2)—mines—1/Hormone-B helicopter

Electron Equipt: Radar: 3/Palm Frond, 1/Top Steer, 6/SA-N-7 fire control,
2/Bass Tilt, 1/Kite Screech
　　　　　　　　Sonar: 1/med.-freq. hull-mounted
　　　　　　　　ECM: 2/Bell Shroud, 2/Bell Squat, 4/. . . , 2/chaff RL
　　　　　　　　　　　(II × 2)
M: 2 sets GT; 2 props; 100,000 hp　**Boilers:** 4, turbo-pressurized
Range: 1,600/34; 7,000/14　**Man:** 380 tot.

Sovremennyy—showing hangar and mine rails　　　　　　　1980

Sovremennyy on initial trials, prior to installation of most armament　1980

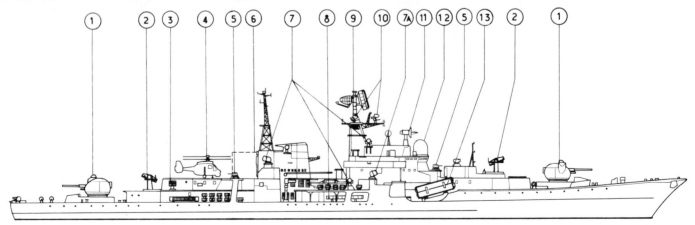

1. Twin 130-mm DP 2. SA-N-7 SAM launchers 3. RBU-1000 4. Hormone-B helicopter 5. 30-mm Gatling AA 6. Telescoping hangar 7. Radar directors for SA-N-7 7A. Bass Tilt 8. Twin 533-mm TT 9. Top Steer 10. Palm Frond 11. Kite Screech 12. Band Stand 13. Quadruple anti-ship missile installation

　　　　　　　　　　　　　　　　　　　　　　　　　　　　H. Simoni

GUIDED-MISSILE DESTROYERS *(continued)*

Sovremennyy

French Navy, 15-2-82

Sovremennyy—bow aspect   1980

REMARKS: Design derived from the Kresta-I and -II series built at the same shipyard; uses same hull form and propulsion. Formerly called the "BAL-COM-2" class by NATO. The class is primarily intended for surface warfare tasks, including anti-ship, shore bombardment, and anti-air defense; the ASW capability is primarily for self-defense. The anti-ship missile system is probably capable of ranges of not more than 100-120 nautical miles, as there are no satellite receiving radomes of the Punch Bowl type; the Hormone-B helicopter can provide targeting data for the missiles, and the ships also have the large Band Stand associated with missile targeting for the SS-N-9 in the Nanuchka class. There are also two small spherical radomes on the sides of the stack that might be missile-associated. The six tracker-illuminators for the SA-N-7 SAM system resemble Bass Tilt radar gun directors. The chaff launchers are at the extreme stern. The 130-mm guns are of a new, fully automatic, water-cooled model, capable of AA or surface fire.

Sovremennyy ran a protracted series of trials beginning in 8-80, appearing at intervals with more and more equipment added; she finally appeared complete by 9-81.

♦ **1 Kashin, converted for missile trials** Bldr: Zhdanov SY, Leningrad (In serv. 1964)

PROVORNYY

Provornyy—SA-N-7 launcher aft, swathed in canvas   1981

D: 3,750 tons (4,750 fl)   **S:** 38 kts   **Dim:** 144.0 × 15.8 × 4.8 (hull)
A: 1/SA-N-7 SAM syst. (I × 1,. . . missiles)—4/76.2-mm DP (II × 2)—5/533-mm TT (V × 1)—2/RBU-6000 (XII × 2)—2/RBU-1000 (VI × 2)—mines
Electron Equipt: Radar: 1/Don-2, 1/Don-Kay, 1/Top Steer, 1/Head Net-C, 2/ Owl Screech, 8/directors for SA-N-7
Sonar: 1/med. freq., hull-mounted
ECM: no intercept arrays, 4/chaff RL (XVI × 4)
M: 4 gas turbines; 2 props; 96,000 hp   **Range:** 900/35; 4,500/18   **Man:** 300 tot.

REMARKS: Converted during the mid-1970s at a Black Sea shipyard as trials ship for the SA-N-7 SAM system. Both SA-N-1 SAM systems were removed and the superstructure reconfigured as on the Modified Kashin class. An SA-N-7 single-armed launcher was emplaced aft, while provision was made for two more to be added forward at a later date. No ECM equipment (other than chaff launchers) is installed, but provision has been made for adding 2 Bell Shroud and 2 Bell Squat. With eight SAM directors, the ship has an unusual antiaircraft capability. Rejoined active fleet late 1981.

GUIDED-MISSILE DESTROYERS (*continued*)

♦ **6 Modified Kashin class** (In serv. 1964-71; conversions 1973-1980)

	Bldr		Bldr
OGNEVOY	Zhdanov SY, Leningrad	SMELYY	Nikolayev
SLAVNYY	Zhdanov SY, Leningrad	SMYSHLENNYY	Nikolayev
SDERZHANNYY	Nikolayev	STROYNYY	Nikolayev

D: 3,950 tons (4,950 fl) **S:** 35 kts **Dim:** 146.0 × 15.8 × 4.8 (hull)
A: 4/SS-N-2C (I × 4)—2/SA-N-1 SAM syst. (II × 2, 44 Goa missiles)—4/76.2-mm DP (II × 2)—4/30-mm Gatling AA (I × 4)—5/533-mm TT (V × 1)—2/RBU-6000 ASW RL (XII × 2)
Electron Equipt: Radar: 2/Don-Kay, 1/Head Net-C (*Ognevoy* only: 2/Head Net-A), 1/Big Net, 2/Peel Group, 2/Owl Screech, 2/Bass Tilt
   Sonar: 1/med.-freq., hull-mounted; 1/med.-freq. VDS

ECM: 2/Bell Squat, 2/Bell Shroud, 4/chaff RL (XVI × 4)
IFF: 1/High Pole B
M: 4 gas turbines, 2 props; 96,000 hp **Range:** 900/35; 5,000/18

REMARKS: Soviet type designation: BPK—*Bol'shoy Protivolodochniy Korabl'* (Large Antisubmarine Ship), having briefly been listed as "Large Missile Ships." Conversions completed from 1973 onward, with *Sderzhannyy* having probably been built to the new configuration. Hull lengthened by 2 meters, helicopter platform raised above new VDS installation, Gatling guns added in place of 2 RBU-1000, new ECM gear (not yet fully fitted in all) and radars; *Ognevoy* retained original air-search radars.

Slavnyy French Navy, 1980

Smelyy—showing VDS door and aft-firing SS-N-2C 1977

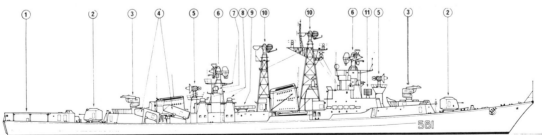

Ognevoy—1. VDS, beneath helo deck 2. 76.2-mm DP 3. SA-N-1 4. SS-N-2C 5. Owl Screech 6. Peel Group 7. Bass Tilt 8. 30-mm Gatling guns 9. 533-mm TT 10. Head Net-A 11. RBU-6000

GUIDED-MISSILE DESTROYERS *(continued)*

Stroynyy—midships portion of the latest of the "Modified Kashin" conversions

French Navy, 1981

Smyshlennyy

Skyfotos, 1979

GUIDED-MISSILE DESTROYERS (continued)

♦ 12 Kashin class

Bldrs: *Obraztsovyy, Odarennyy, Steregushchiy:* Zhdanov, Leningrad (In serv. 1963-66); others: Nikolayev (In serv. 1963-72)

OBRAZTSOVYY	KRASNYY KAVKAZ	SMETLIVVY
ODARENNYY	KRASNYY KRYM	SOOBRAZITELNYY
STEREGUSHCHIY	RESHITELNYY	SPOSOBNYY
KOMSOMOLETS UKRAINYY	SKORYY	STROGIY

Komsomolets Ukrainyy—saluting cannon in tubs abreast foremast   1972

Obraztsovyy—4/Guard Dog radomes   G. Gyssels, 1979

Soobrazitelnyy—radomes on sides of Peel Group pylon   1974

Obraztsovyy—2/Head Net-A   1974

Skoryy—1/Head Net-C, 1/Big Net   1978

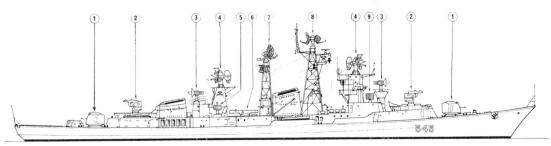

1. 76.2-mm DP 2. SA-N-1 3. Owl Screech 4. Peel Group 5. RBU-1000 6. 533-mm TT 7. Big Net 8. Head Net-C 9. RBU-6000

GUIDED-MISSILE DESTROYERS *(continued)*

Odarennyy—with 2/Head Net-C, 3/Don-2   1980

D: 3,750 tons (4,750 fl)   **S:** 38 kts   **Dim:** 144.0 × 15.8 × 4.8 (hull)
A: 2/SA-N-1 SAM syst. (II × 2, 44 Goa missiles)—4/76.2-mm DP (II × 2)—2/
  RBU-6000 ASW RL (XII × 2)—2/RBU-1000 ASW RL (VI × 2)—5/533-mm
  TT (V × 1)—mines
Electron Equipt: Radar: 2-3/Don-2, 2/Head Net-A or 1/Head Net-C and 1/Big
            Net, 2/Peel Group, 2/Owl Screech (*Odarennyy:*
            2/Head Net-C)
        Sonar: 1/high-freq., hull-mounted
        ECM: 2/Watch Dog
        IFF: 2/High Pole B
M: 4 gas turbines; 2 props; 96,000 hp   **Range:** 900/35; 4,500/18   **Man:** 280 tot.

REMARKS: Soviet type designation: *Bol'shoy Protivolodochnyy Korabl'* (Large Antisubmarine Ship). One of this class, the *Otvazhnyy*, was sunk 31-8-74 following an
explosion: six others have been converted to Modified Kashin configuration and
Provornyy was converted as SA-N-7 SAM trials ship. All have a helicopter pad on
the fantail. The earlier ships carried 2/Head Net-A air-search radars, now apparently
being replaced by Head Net-C. *Obraztsovyy* and *Soobrazitelnyy* have additional
ECM radomes.

♦ 8 Kanin class

Bldrs: Zhdanov SY, Leningrad; Severodvinsk SY; and 61 Kommuna SY, Nikolayev
(In serv. 1958-60)

BOIKIY	GNEVNYY	GREMYASHCHIY	ZHGUCHIY
DERZKIY	GORDYY	UPORNYY	ZORKIY

D: 3,700 tons (4,700 fl)   **S:** 34 kts   **Dim:** 141.0 × 14.6 × 5.0 (hull)
A: 1/SA-N-1 system (II × 1, 22 Goa missiles)—8/57-mm AA (IV × 2)—8/30-mm
  AA (II × 4)—3/RBU-6000 ASW RL (XII × 3)—10/533-mm TT (V × 2)
Electron Equipt: Radar: 2/Don-Kay, 1/Head Net-C, 1/Peel Group, 1/Hawk
            Screech, 2/Drum Tilt
        Sonar: 1 med.-freq., hull-mounted
        ECM: 4/Top Hat, 2/Bell-series
        IFF: 1/High Pole B
M: 2 sets GT; 2 props; 80,000 hp   **Boilers:** 4
Range: 1,000/30; 4,500/18   **Man:** 300 tot.

Zhguchiy   French Navy, 1977

Zhguchiy   French Navy, 1977

REMARKS: Soviet type designation: BPK—*Bol'shoy Protivolodochnyy Korabl'* (Large
Antisubmarine Ship). Helicopter platform. Converted from Krupnyy class SS-N-1-
equipped "Missile Ships" at Zhdanov SY, Leningrad, except for *Gnevnyy* and *Gordyy*
at Vladivostok in the Far East, 1968-77.

♦ 3 Modified Kildin class

	Bldr	L
BEDOVYY	61 Kommuna SY, Nikolayev	1958
NEULOVIMYY	Zhdanov SY, Leningrad	1958
PROZORLIVYY	Zhdanov SY, Leningrad	1958

Bedovyy—with Strut Pair air-search radar   1978

GUIDED-MISSILE DESTROYERS (continued)

Neulovimyy—small stacks, Head Net-C   U.S. Navy, 1978

D: 2,800 tons (3,700 fl) **S:** 36 kts **Dim:** 126.5 × 13.0 × 4.7 (5.7 sonar)
A: 4/SS-N-2C (I × 4)—4/76.2-mm DP (II × 2)—16/57-mm AA (IV × 4) except
Bedovyy: 16/45-mm AA (IV × 4)—2/RBU-2500 ASW RL (XVI × 2)—4/533-
mm TT (II × 2)
Electron Equipt: Radar: 1/Don-2, 1/Head Net-C, 1/Owl Screech, 2/Hawk
Screech
Sonar: 1/high-freq., hull-mounted (Herkules or Pegas)
ECM: 2/Watch Dog
IFF: 1/High Pole B
M: 2 sets GT; 2 props; 72,000 hp **Boilers:** 4; 64 kg/cm², 510°C
Electric: 14,000 kw **Range:** 1,000/34; 3,600/18; 4,700/11 **Man:** 300 tot.

REMARKS: Soviet type designation: BRK—*Bol'shoy Raketnyy Korabl'* (Large Missile
Ship). The *Bedovyy* has broader stacks than her sisters and has Strut Pair radar in
place of Head Net-C. Conversions from Kildin configuration completed at Nikolayev,
1973-75.

♦ **1 Kildin class**

	Bldr	L
NEUDERZHIMYY	Komsomolsk SY	1958

D: 2,600 tons (3,500 fl) **S:** 36 kts **Dim:** 126.5 × 13.0 × 4.6 (5.6 sonar)
A: 1/SS-N-1 (I × 1, 6 Scrubber missiles)—16/57-mm AA (IV × 4)—2/RBU-2500
ASW RL (XVI × 2)—4/533-mm TT (II × 2)
Electron Equipt: Radar: 1/Slim Net, 1/Flat Spin, 1/Top Bow, 2/Hawk Screech
Sonar: 1/high-freq., hull-mounted
ECM: 2/Watch Dog
IFF: 1/High Pole, 2/Square Head
M: 2 sets GT; 2 props; 72,000 hp **Boilers:** 4; 64 kg/cm², 510°C
Electric: 1,400 kw **Range:** 1,000/34; 3,600/18; 4,700/11 **Man:** 285 tot.

Kildin class   1972

REMARKS: Soviet type designation: BRK—*Bol'shoy Raketnyy Korabl'* (Large Missile
Ship). The SS-N-1 launcher and reload hangar are aft. Design modified from that
of the Kotlin class. Unlikely to be converted because of age. In the Pacific Fleet.

♦ **8 SAM Kotlin class** Bldr: Zhdanov SY, Leningrad; 61 Kommuna SY, Nikolayev;
Komsomolsk SY (In serv. 1954-58)

BRAVYY	NASTOCHIVYY	SKROMNYY	SOZNATEL'NYY
NAKHODCHIVYY	NESOKRUSHIMYY	SKRYTNYY	VOZBUZHDENNYY

Bravyy—conversion prototype, with 12/45-mm AA, Head Net-A, RBU-2500

Vozbazhdennyy—with 8/30-mm AA, Head Net-C, RBU-6000   1980

Nesokrushimyy   1980

GUIDED-MISSILE DESTROYERS *(continued)*

Nastochivyy—no Egg Cup radar on 130-mm mount, no 30-mm AA   1974

D: 2,700 tons (3,600 fl)   **S:** 36 kts   **Dim:** 126.5 × 13.0 × 4.6 (avg.)
A: *Bravyy:* 1/SA-N-1 system (II × 1)—2/130-mm DP (II × 1)—12/45-mm AA
(IV × 3)—5/533-mm TT (V × 1)—2/RBU-2500 ASW RL (XVI × 2)
Others: 1/SA-N-1 system (II × 1)—2/130-mm DP (II × 1)—4/45-mm AA (IV
× 1)—5/533-mm TT (V × 1)—2/RBU-6000 ASW RL (XII × 2) (one has
RBU-2500, see Remarks)
Electron Equipt: Radar: 1 or 2/Don-2, 1/Head Net-C, 1/Peel Group, 1/Sun Vi-
sor, 1/Hawk Screech, 1/Egg Cup (see Remarks)
Sonar: 1/high-freq. (Herkules or Pegas)
ECM: 2/Watch Dog
IFF: 1/High Pole B
M: 2 sets GT; 2 props; 72,000 hp   **Boilers:** 4; 64 kg/cm², 510°C
Electric: 1,400 kw   **Range:** 1,000/34; 3,600/18; 4,700/11   **Man:** 300 tot.

REMARKS: Soviet type designation: EM—*Eskhadrennyy Minonosets* (Destroyer). *Nesokrushimyy*, *Skrytnyy*, *Soznatel'nyy*, and *Vozbuzhdennyy* have eight 30-mm AA
(II × 4) in addition to the above, with two Drum Tilt fire-control radars. *Nastochivyy*
has no Egg Cup radar. *Bravyy* has Head Net-A, two extra quadruple 45-mm AA
mounts and, as does the *Skromnyy*, RBU-2500 vice RBU-6000. *Bravyy*, which
served as the SA-N-1 trials ship, completed conversion by 1962, the others 1966-72.
Spravedlivyy was transferred to Poland in 1970.

DESTROYERS

◆ **18 Kotlin and Modified Kotlin* classes** Bldrs: Zhdanov SY, Leningrad; 61 Kommuna SY, Nikolayev (*Dal'nevostochnyy Komsomolets:* Komsomolsk SY (In serv.
1954-58)

BESSLEDNYY	MOSKOVSKIY KOMSOMOLETS*	SVETLYY
BLAGORODNYY*	NAPORISTIY*	VESKIY
BLESTYASHCHIY*	PLAMENNYY*	VDOKHNOVENNYY*
BURLIVYY*	SPESHNYY	VLIYATEL'NYY
BYVALYY*	SPOKOYNYY	VOZMUSHCHYENNYY
DAL'NEVOSTOCHNYY	SVEDUSHCHIY*	VYDERZHANNYY*
KOMSOMOLETS		VYZYVAYUSHCHIY*

D: 2,600 tons (3,500 fl)   **S:** 36 kts   **Dim:** 126.5 × 13.0 × 4.6 (5.6 sonar)
A: Kotlin: 4/130-mm DP (II × 2)—16/45-mm AA (IV × 4)—4/25-mm AA (II ×
2)—10/533-mm TT (V × 2)—6/BMB-2 d.c. projectors—2/d.c. racks—70 mines

Svetlyy—only Kotlin with a helo deck   1977

Modified Kotlin class—with 8/25-mm (II × 4) abreast aft stack   U.S. Navy

Speshnyy   1974

Mod. Kotlin: 4/130-mm DP (II × 2)—16/45-mm AA (IV × 4)—8/25-mm AA
(II × 4)—5/533-mm TT (V × 1)—2/RBU-2500 ASW RL (XVI × 2)—2/RBU-
600 ASW RL (VI × 2)—70 mines
Electron Equipt: Radar: 1/Neptune or 1 or 2 Don-2, 1/Slim Net, 1/Sun Visor, 2/
Hawk Screech, 2/Egg Cup, 1/Post Lamp or Top Bow
Sonar: 1/high-freq. (Herkules)
ECM: 2/Watch Dog
IFF: 1/High Pole, 2/Square Head
M: 2 sets GT; 2 props; 72,000 hp   **Boilers:** 4; 64 kg/cm², 510°C
Electric: 1,400 kw   **Range:** 1,000/34; 3,600/18; 4,700/11
Man: 36 officers, 300 men

DESTROYERS *(continued)*

REMARKS: Soviet type designation: EM—*Eskhadrennyy Minonosets* (Destroyer). Eleven were modified between 1960 and 1962, receiving two RBU-2500 forward and two RBU-600 in place of their depth-charge equipment, the after bank of five 533-mm TT being removed. Later, most of these ships got eight 25-mm AA (II × 4). The *Moskovskiy Komsomolets* got RBU-6000 forward, nothing aft; in 1978 she received a variable-depth sonar on her stern. Most of those that were not modified received four 25-mm AA (II × 2). *Svetlyy* has a helicopter platform in place of depth-charge gear and thus has no ASW armament. Helicopter decks were removed from the other two ships that had them. Many have had their Egg Cup radars removed.

♦ **20 Skoryy and Modified Skoryy classes** (In serv. 1949-54)

Bldrs: Severodvinsk SY; Zhdanov SY, Leningrad; 61 Kommuna SY, Nikolayev; Komsomolsk SY

Modified Skoryy class

Skoryy class—with seven 37-mm AA   1978

Skoryy class—with eight 37-mm AA   1968

D: 2,600 tons (3,130 fl) **S:** 34 kts **Dim:** 121.2 (116.5 pp) × 12.0 × 4.5 (hull)
A: Standard: 4/130-mm DP (II × 2)—2/85-mm AA (II × 1)—7 or 8/37-mm AA (I × 7 or II × 4)—4 or 6/25-mm AA (II × 2 or 3)—10/533-mm TT (V × 2)—2/ d.c. projectors—2/d.c. racks—50 mines
Modified: 4/130-mm DP (II × 2)—5/57-mm AA (I × 5)—2/RBU-2500 ASW

RL (XVI × 2)—5/533-mm TT (V × 1)—50 mines
Electron Equipt: Radar: Standard: 1/High Sieve, 1/Top Bow or Half Bow or Post Lamp, 1/Cross Bird, 1 or 2/Don-2
Modified: 1/Slim Net, 1/Top Bow, 1 or 2 Don-2, 2/Hawk Screech
Sonar: 1/high-freq. (Tamir-5 Pegas)
ECM: 2/Watch Dog
IFF: 2/Square Head, 1/High Pole A
M: 2 sets GT; 2 props; 60,000 hp **Boilers:** 4; 27 kg/cm², 367°C
Electric: 475 kw **Fuel:** 786 tons **Range:** 850/30; 3,000/18
Man: 18 offices, 200 men

REMARKS: Soviet type designation: EM—*Eskhadrennyy Minonosets* (Destroyer). Went into service 1949-54. Survivors of seventy-two built, derived from prewar *Ognevoyy* design. A small number were modernized around 1960 to *Modified Skoryy* configuration. Only those with eight 37-mm AA have been given two or three twin 25-mm AA. Several *Skoryy* class were transferred to Egypt (only four remain), Poland, and Indonesia. Now of little value, with only about seven remaining active.

FRIGATES

♦ **11 Krivak-II class** Bldr: Kaliningrad SY (In serv. 1976-. . .)

BESSMENNYY
GORDELIVYY
GROMKIY
GROZYASHCHIY
NEUKROTIMYY
PITLIVYY
RAZITEL'NYY
REVNOSTNYY
REZKIY
REZVYY
R'YANYY

Neukrotimyy—with VDS deployed   1979

FRIGATES (continued)

R'yanyy   French Navy, 1980

Rezvyy   1980

Gordelivyy   1981

D: 3,575 tons (fl)   **S:** 30.6 kts   **Dim:** 125.0 × 14.3 × 5.0 (hull)
A: 4/SS-N-14 (IV × 1)—2/SA-N-4 systems (II × 2, 36 missiles)—2/100-mm DP
 (I × 2)—2/RBU-6000 ASW RL (XII × 2)—8/533-mm TT (IV × 2)—mines
Electron Equipt: Radar: 1/Palm Frond or Don-Kay, 1/Spin Trough, 1/Head
  Net-C, 2/Eye Bowl, 1/Kite Screech, 2/Pop Group
 Sonar: 1/med.-freq., hull-mounted, 1/med.-freq. VDS
 ECM: 2/Bell Shroud, 2/Bell Squat, 4/chaff launchers
  (XVI × 4)
 IFF: 1/High Pole B
M: CODOG: 2 cruise gas turbines of 12,100 hp each and 2 boost gas turbines of
 24,300 hp each; 2 props; 48,600 hp max.
Range: 700/30; 3,900/20   **Man:** 200 tot.

REMARKS: Soviet type designation: SKR—*Storozhevoy Korabl'* (Patrol Ship), formerly
BPK—Large Antisubmarine Ship. The VDS housing at the stern is somewhat larger
than on the Krivak-Is, but the principal difference is substitution of single 100-mm
for twin 76.2-mm guns. Not all have yet been given ECM gear.

◆ **21 Krivak-I class** Bldrs: Zhdanov SY, Leningrad; Kaliningrad SY; Kamish-Bu-
run SY, Kerch (In serv. 1971-. . .)

BEZUKORIZNENNYY	DRUZHNYY	RAZYASHCHIY
BEZZEVETNIY	LADNYY	RETIVYY
BDITEL'NYY	LENINGRADSKIY KOMSOMOLETS	SIL'NYY
BODRYY	LETUCHIY	STOROZHEVOY
DEYATEL'NYY	PYLKIY	SVIREPYY
DOBLESTNYY	PYTLIVYY	ZADORNYY
DOSTOYNYY	RAZUMNYY	ZHARKYY

D: 3,575 tons (fl)   **S:** 30.6 kts   **Dim:** 125.0 × 14.3 × 5.0 (hull)
A: 4/SS-N-14 (IV × 1)—2/SA-N-4 systems (II × 2, 36 missiles)—4/76.2-mm DP
 (II × 2)—2/RBU-6000 ASW RL (XII × 2)—8/533-mm TT (IV × 2)—mines
Electron Equipt: Radar: 1/Don-2 or Spin Trough, 1/Don-Kay or Palm Frond, 1/
  Head Net-C, 2/Eye Bowl, 1/Owl Screech, 2/Pop Group
 Sonar: 1/hull-mounted, 1/VDS (both med.-freq.)
 ECM: 2/Bell Shroud, 2/Bell Squat, 4/chaff launchers
  (XVI × 4)
 IFF: High Pole B

Razyashchiy   1979

Letuchiy   1980

Letuchiy—with ECM equipment   1980

FRIGATES (continued)

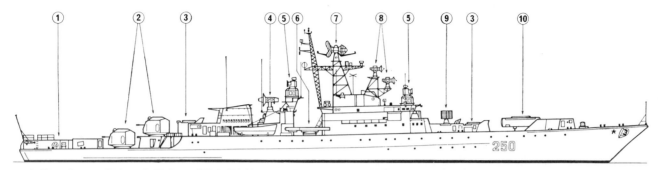

1. Towed sonar fittings 2. 76.2-mm DP 3. SA-N-4 4. Owl Screech 5. Pop Group 6. 533-mm TT 7. Head Net-C 8. Eye Bowl 9. RBU-6000 10. SS-N-14

Bodryy

Skyfotos, 1979

M: CODOG: 2 cruise gas turbines of 12,100 hp each and 2 boost gas turbines of 24,300 hp each; 2 props; 48,600 hp max.
Range: 700/30; 3,900/20 **Man:** 200 tot.

REMARKS: Soviet type designation: SKR—*Storozhevoy Korabl'* (Patrol Ship). Construction began in 1970 and continues. In 1978 Krivak-I and Krivak-II classes were rerated from BPK (*Bol'shoy Protivolodochnyy Korabl'*—large ASW ship) to SKR (*Storozhevoy Korabl'*—patrol ship), a demotion prompted perhaps by their limited endurance at high speeds, speed, and size. Not all units have the ECM gear.

♦ **1 Koni class** Bldr: Zelenodolsk SY (In serv. circa 1978)

TIMOFEY UL'YANTSEV

D: 1,900 tons (fl) **S:** 30 kts **Dim:** 96.0 × 12.0 × 4.4 (5.0 max.)
A: 1/SA-N-4 SAM syst. (II × 1, 18 missiles)—4/76.2-mm DP (II × 2)—4/30-mm AA—2/RBU-6000 ASW RL (XII × 2)—2/d.c. racks—mines
Electron Equipt: Radar: 1/Don-2, 1/Strut Curve, 1/Pop Group, 1/Hawk Screech, 1/Drum Tilt

East German Navy Koni, Rostock—on her delivery voyage 1978

Sonar: 1/med.-freq., hull-mounted
ECM: 2/Watch Dog, 2/chaff RL (XVI × 2)—IFF: 1/High Pole B
M: CODAG: 1 gas turbine of 15,000 hp, 2 diesels of 7,500 hp; 3 props; 30,000 hp

FRIGATES (continued)

REMARKS: One unit of this export SKR—*Storozhevoy Korabl'* (Patrol Ship) design, reportedly with the above name, has been retained, apparently in the Black Sea Fleet. Five sisters have been exported, and the sole Soviet example may be employed for foreign crew training. Only about one Koni per year is built, although the design would seem a natural successor for the Riga class. Have a large teardrop-shaped sonar dome. The d.c. racks are bolted to the mine rails.

♦ **20 Grisha-III class** Bldr:. . . (In serv. 1975-. . .)

Grisha-III class—note differences in stack from unit below   French Navy, 1978

Grisha-III class—Bass Tilt and deckhouse offset to port   1979

Grisha-III class   1979

A: 1/SA-N-4 syst. (II × 1, 18 missiles)—2/57-mm AA (II × 1)—1/30-mm Gatling AA—2/RBU-6000 ASW RL (XII × 2)—4/533-mm TT (II × 2)—2/d.c. racks (12 d.c.) or mines

REMARKS: Soviet type designation: MPK—*Malyy Protivolodochnyy Korabl'* (Small Antisubmarine Ship). Construction continues. Bass Tilt, which is atop a small deck-house to port on the aft superstructure, has been substituted for Muff Cob radar fire control, while a Gatling gun has been mounted in the space occupied by Muff Cob in the Grisha-I and -II. Depth-charge racks can be mounted on the aft end of the mine rails. One may be named *Orlovskiy Komsomolets.*

♦ **7 Grisha-II class** Bldrs:. . . (In serv. 1974-76)

AMETIST	IZUMRUD	SAFFIR	N. . .
BRILLIANT	RUBIN	ZHEMCHUG	

Brilliant—Grisha-II class, 57-mm guns fore and aft

A: 4/57-mm AA (II × 2)—2/RBU-6000 ASW RL (XII × 2)—4/533-mm TT (II × 2)—2/d.c. racks (12 d.c.) or mines

REMARKS: Soviet type designation: PSKR—*Pogranichniy Storozhevoy Korabl'* (Border Patrol Ship). Manned by the KGB Maritime Border Guard. A second twin 57-mm was substituted for SA-N-4 forward, and the Pop Group missile-control radar was not installed.

♦ **16 Grisha-I class** Bldrs:. . . (In serv. 1968-74)

Grisha-I class   1977

FRIGATES (continued)

Grisha-I class 1977

D: 950 tons (1,200 fl) **S:** 34 kts **Dim:** 73.0 × 9.7 × 3.7 (hull)
A: 1/SA-N-4 syst. (II × 1, 18 missiles)—2/57-mm AA (II × 1)—2/RBU-6000
ASW RL (XII × 2)—4/533-mm TT (II × 2)—2/d.c. racks (12 d.c.) or mines
Electron Equipt: Radar: 1/Don-2, 1/Strut Curve, 1/Pop Group, 1/Muff Cob
(Grisha-III: Bass Tilt)
Sonar: 1/med.-freq., 1/dipping
ECM: 2/Watch Dog
IFF: 1/High Pole B
M: CODAG: 4 diesels, 1/15,000-hp gas turbine; 3 props; 31,000 hp
Range: 450/30; 4,000/12 **Man:** 60 tot.

REMARKS: More specialized for ASW than the earlier Petya and Mirka "patrol ships."
Russian type designation: MPK—*Malyy Protivolodochnyy Korabl'* (Small Antisubmarine Ship). A plate has been added forward of the Muff Cob fire-control radar to
protect personnel on the bridge from its radiation.

◆ **1 Modified Petya-II class**

Modified Petya-II class 1978

A: 4/76.2-mm DP—2/RBU-6000 ASW RL (XII × 2)—5/400-mm ASW TT (V × 1)—
mines

REMARKS: Conversion in 1978 similar to Modified Petya-I, but new VDS deckhouse
at stern does not extend to the sides of the ship, which permits retention of mine
rails. One quintuple ASW torpedo-tube mounting and the d.c. racks have been
removed. Apparently experimental, as only one was converted.

◆ **10 Modified Petya-I class** Bldrs: Kaliningrad SY; Komsomolsk SY (In serv.
1961-64)

Modified Petya-I class—standard version 1980

Modified Petya-I class—small deckhouse at stern 1977

A: Standard version (see Remarks): 4/76.2-mm DP (II × 2)—2/RBU-2500 RL—5/400-
mm ASW TT (V × 1)—1/d.c. rack

REMARKS: Conversions began in 1973. Petya-I class altered by the addition of a medium-frequency towed sonar in a new raised stern deckhouse. The designation "Modified Petya I" is also applied to several trials units, one with a very large VDS
exposed at the stern (no raised stern); another with a deckhouse abaft the stack and
a complex towing array, reels, and winch on her stern; still another with a small,
boxlike deckhouse containing a towed sensor at the extreme stern.

◆ **26 Petya-II class** Bldrs: Kaliningrad SY, Komsomolsk SY (1964-69)

◆ **8 Petya-I class** Bldrs: Kaliningrad SY, Komsomolsk SY (In serv. 1961-64)

D: 950 tons (1,100 fl) **S:** 30 kts **Dim:** 82.3 × 9.1 × 3.2 (hull)
A: Petya-I: 4/76.2-mm DP (II × 2)—4/RBU-2500 ASW RL (XVI × 4)—5/400-
mm ASW TT (V × 1)—2/d.c. racks—mines
Petya-II: 4/76.2-mm DP (II × 2)—2/RBU-6000 ASW RL (XII × 2)—10/400-
mm ASW TT (V × 2)—2/d.c. racks—mines
Electron Equipt: Radar: 1/Don-2, 1/Slim Net (Petya-II: Strut Curve), 1/
Hawk Screech

FRIGATES (continued)

Sonar: 1/high-freq. (Herkules), 1/helo dipping sonar
ECM: 2/Watch Dog
IFF: 1/High Pole B
M: CODAG: 2/15,000-hp gas turbines + 1/6,000-hp diesel; 3 props; 36,000 hp
Range: 850/30 (diesel + gas turbine); 4,000/10 (diesel) **Man:** 80-90 tot.

REMARKS: Soviet type designation: SKR—*Storozhevoy Korabl'* (Patrol Ship). Petya-I version is being gradually modernized (see above). Some carry helicopter dipping sonars in temporary installations amidships. Petya-I has two Square Head IFF interrogators. A version with two RBU-2500 rocket launchers and three 533-mm torpedo tubes (III × 1) has been exported to India, Syria, and Vietnam, although a few of that variety have also been in the Soviet Pacific Fleet. The diesel drives the centerline CP prop.

Petya-II 1977

Petya-II—2/RBU-6000, 10/400-mm TT, Strut Curve 1977

Petya-I—4/RBU-2500, 5/400-mm TT, Slim Net

♦ **9 Mirka-I class** Bldr: Kaliningrad SY (In serv. 1964-65)

Mirka-I class—4/RBU-6000, 5/400-mm TT, Slim Net

♦ **9 Mirka-II class** Bldr: Kaliningrad SY (In serv. 1965-66)

Mirka-II class—with Slim Net and dipping sonar 1977

Mirka-II class—with Strut Curve and dipping sonar 1977

D: 950 tons (1,100 fl) **S:** 34 kts **Dim:** 82.3 × 9.1 × 3.2 (hull)
A: Mirka-I: 4/76.2-mm DP (II × 2)—4/RBU-6000 ASW RL (XII × 4)—5/400-mm ASW TT (V × 1)—1/d.c. rack
Mirka-II: 4/76.2-mm DP (II × 2)—2/RBU-6000 ASW RL (XII × 2)—10/400-mm ASW TT (V × 2)

Electron Equipt: Radar: 1/Don-2, 1/Slim Net or Strut Curve, 1/Hawk Screech
Sonar: 1/high-freq. (Herkules or Pegas), Mirka-II also: 1/dipping
ECM: 2/Watch Dog—IFF: 1/High Pole B, 2/Square Head
M: CODAG: 2/15,000-hp gas turbines + 2/6,000-hp diesels; 2 props
Range: 500/30 (gas turbine); 4,000/10 (diesel) **Man:** 98 tot.

REMARKS: Soviet type designation: SKR—*Storozhevoy Korabl'* (Patrol Ship). Propulsion system similar in concept to that of the Poti class. All Mirka-Is have Slim Net, while a few late Mirka-IIs have Strut Curve. The latter have been modernized with a new type of dipping sonar in place of the internal depth-charge rack.

FRIGATES (continued)

♦ **37 Riga class** Bldrs: Various (In serv. 1952-58)

Possible names:

ASTRAKHAN'SKIY KOMSOMOLETS	KOBCHIK	PANTERA
ARKHANGEL'SKIY KOMSOMOLETS	KOMSOMOLETS GRUZIY	RYS ROSOMAKHA
BARS	KOMSOMOLETS LITVIY	SHAKAL
BARSUK	KRASNODARSKIY KOMSOMOLETS	TIGR
BOBR	KUNITSA	TURMAN
BUYVOL	LEOPARD	VOLK
BYK	LEV	VORON
GEPARD	LISA	YAGUAR
GIENA	MEDVED	

D: 1,260 tons (1,480 fl)   **S:** 30 kts   **Dim:** 91.0 × 11.0 × 3.2 (4.4 max.)

A: 3/100-mm DP (I × 3)—4/37-mm AA (II × 2)—4/25-mm AA (II × 2)—2 or 3/ 533-mm ASW TT (II or III × 1)—2/RBU-2500 ASW RL (XVI × 2)—2/d.c. racks—mines

Electron Equipt: Radar: 1/Neptune or Don-2, 1/Slim Net, 1/Sun Visor
                Sonar: 1/high-freq. (Herkules or Pegas)
                ECM: 2/Watch Dog
                IFF: 1/High Pole, 2/Square Head

M: 2 sets GT; 2 props; 20,000 hp   **Boilers:** 2; 27 kg/cm^2, 360°C

Electric: 450 kw   **Range:** 550/28; 2,000/3   **Man:** 175 tot.

Riga class—with flare launcher on the forecastle   1974

Riga class—only one with Bell Series ECM radomes, tall stack cap   1972

Riga class

REMARKS: Soviet type designation: SKR—*Storozhevoy Korabl'* (Patrol Ship). Another eleven units are believed to be maintained in Reserve. One ship has a Hawk Screech radar director forward and the main gun director aft. Some have been transferred to other countries, incuding Indonesia, Finland, Bulgaria, China, and East Germany. A few Soviet examples may retain the original ASW ordnance suit of 1/RBU-600 Hedgehog, 4/BMB-2 d.c. mortars, and 2 d.c. racks.

GUIDED-MISSILE CORVETTES

♦ **2 (+. . .) Tarantul class** Bldr: Petrovskiy SY, Leningrad (In serv. 1979-. . .)

Tarantul class—note turbine exhausts through stern   1980

D: 480 tons (600 fl)   **S:** 35 kts   **Dim:** 56.5 × 10.5 × 2.5

A: 4/SS-N-2C (II × 2)—1/76.2-mm DP—1/SA-N-5 SAM (IV × 1,. . . Grail missiles)—2/30-mm Gatling AA (VI × 2)

Electron Equipt: Radar: 1/Spin Trough, 1/Bass Tilt, 1/. . . targeting
                ECM: 4/passive arrays, 2/chaff RL (XVI × 2)
                IFF: 1/High Pole, 1/Square Head

M: CODAG: 2 gas turbines, 1 cruise diesel; 3 props;. . . hp

REMARKS: The function of this class is uncertain, because in many respects, particularly weapons, it is not as up to date as the Nanuchka class; it may be for export. A version with a Band Stand radome is also reported.

♦ **4 Nanuchka-III class** Bldr: Petrovskiy SY, Leningrad (In serv. 1977-. . .)

D: 780 tons (930 fl)   **S:** 30 kts   **Dim:** 60.3 × 12.2 × 3.1   **Man:** 60 tot.

A: 6/SS-N-9 (III × 2)—1/SA-N-4 system (II × 1, 18 missiles)—1/76.2-mm DP— 1/30-mm Gatling AA (VI × 1)

GUIDED-MISSILE CORVETTES (continued)

Nanuchka-I, and Bass Tilt is situated atop a new deckhouse abaft the mast. The pilothouse is higher and the superstructure is enlarged. The 30-mm Gatling gun is off centerline, to starboard.

Nanuchka class—30-mm Gatling gun, 76.2-mm DP aft   1979

◆ **16 Nanuchka-I class** Bldr: Petrovskiy SY, Leningrad (In serv. 1969-76)

BURUN GRAD MADUGA SHKVAL SHTORM TAFUN TSIKLON ZUB'
7 others

Nanuchka-I class—twin 57-mm AA aft   R.A.F., 1976

Nanuchka-III class—Band Stand on higher pilothouse   1979

    Electron Equipt: Radar: 1/Peel Pair, 1/Band Stand, 1/Bass Tilt
        ECM: 2/passive arrays, 2/chaff RL (XVI × 2)
        IFF: 1/High Pole, 1/Square Head
  M: 3 paired M-504 diesels; 3 props; 30,000 hp **Range:** 4,500/15 (1 engine)

REMARKS: Soviet type designation: MRK—*Malyy Raketnyy Korabl'* (Small Missile Ship). Construction continues. The single 76.2-mm DP was substituted for the twin 57-mm AA aft, the Gatling gun is in the position occupied by Muff Cob in the

Nanuchka-I class—SA-N-4 recessed into forecastle   R.A.F., 1976

  D: 780 tons (930 fl) **S:** 30 kts **Dim:** 60.3 × 12.2 × 3.1
  A: 6/SS-N-9 (II × 3)—1/SA-N-4 system (II × 1, 18 missiles)—2/57-mm AA (II × 1)

GUIDED-MISSILE CORVETTES *(continued)*

Electron Equipt: Radar: 1/Peel Pair, 1/Pop Group, 1/Muff Cob, 1/Band Stand
ECM: 2/passive arrays, 2/chaff RL (XVI × 2)
IFF: 1/High Pole, 1/Square Head

M: 3 paired M-504 diesels; 3 props; 30,000 hp   **Range:** 4,500/15 (1 engine)
Man: 60 tot.

REMARKS: Soviet type designation: MRK—*Malyy Raketnyy Korabl'* (Small Missile Ship). Named for meteorological phenomena. These are reported to be poor sea boats with very unreliable engines (paired M-504 diesels). Three of them, modified with four SS-N-2C missiles, have been sold to India (Nanuchka-II). Band Stand is associated with target designation for the SS-N-9 missiles.

CORVETTES

♦ **3 (+. . .) Pauk class** Bldr:. . . (In serv. 1980-. . .)

Pauk class   1980

Pauk class   1980

D: 480 tons (600 fl)   **S:** 34-36 kts   **Dim:** 58.5 × 10.5 × 2.5
A: 1/76.2-mm DP—1/SA-N-5 SAM syst. (IV × 1,. . . Grail missiles)—1/30-mm Gatling AA—2/RBU-1200 ASW RL (V × 2)—4/400-mm ASW TT (I × 4)—2/ d.c. racks (12 d.c.)
Electron Equipt: Radar: 1/Spin Trough, 1/air-surface search, 1/Bass Tilt
Sonar: 1/med.-freq., hull-mounted, 1/med.-freq. dipping
ECM:. . . passive arrays; 2 chaff RL (XVI × 2)
M: 2 diesels; 2 props; 20,000 hp   **Man:** 40 tot.

REMARKS: Uses same hull as Tarantul-class missile corvette but has ASW armament vice SS-N-2C and an all-diesel propulsion plant vice Tarantul's CODAG/CODOG system. A large housing for a dipping sonar system projects 2 m out from the stern.

Platforms on the mast are intended to carry ECM arrays, while there is a backup optical director for the single Gatling AA gun; Bass Tilt can control both the 76-mm and 30-mm guns. The main engines are probably the same twin diesels as used in the Nanuchka class. Probable Soviet designation MPK—*Malyy Protivolodochnyy Korabl'* (Small Antisubmarine Ship), and apparently intended to replace the Poti class.

♦ **62 Poti class** Bldrs: Various, 1961-67

Poti class   G. Koop, 1977

D: 500 tons (580 fl)   **S:** 36 kts   **Dim:** 61.0 × 7.9 × 2.8
A: 2/57-mm AA (II × 1)—2/RBU-6000 ASW RL (XII × 2)—2 or 4/400-mm TT (I × 2 or 4)
Electron Equipt: Radar: 1/Don-2, 1/Strut Curve, 1/Muff Cob
Sonar: 1/high-freq. (Herkules), 1/Hormone dipping
ECM: 2/Watch Dog—IFF: 1/High Pole B
M: CODAG: 2 M503A diesels (8,000 hp) + 2 gas turbines (40,000 hp); 2 props

REMARKS: Soviet type designation: MPK—*Malyy Protivolodochnyy Korabl'* (Small Antisubmarine Ship). Several have old-style open 57-mm AA mounts and two RBU-2500. This class has been exported to Romania and Bulgaria. The two propellers are mounted in thrust tubes of the same length as the poop, which contains the two turbines; the jets exhaust through ports in the stern and also power air compressors which exhaust into the propeller tubes, producing a thrust-jet effect.

♦ **17 T-58-class ex-minesweepers** (In serv. 1957-61)

DZERZHINSKIY
KALININGRADSKIY KOMSOMOLETS
12 others

KOMSOMOLETS LATVIY
MALAKHIT
SOVETSKIY POGRANICHNIK

T 58 class   1980

D: 725 tons (840 fl)   **S:** 18 kts   **Dim:** 70.0 × 9.1 × 2.5
A: 4/57-mm AA (II × 2)—2/RBU-1200 ASW RL (V × 2)—2/d.c. racks—mines
Electron Equipt: Radar: 1/Spin Trough, 1/Don-2, 1/Muff Cob
Sonar: 1/high-freq., hull mounted

CORVETTES (continued)

ECM: 2/Watch Dog
IFF: 2/Square Head, 1/High Pole A
M: 2 diesels; 2 props; 4,000 hp

REMARKS: Reclassified SKR—*Storozhevoy Korabl'* (Patrol Ship) in 1978 and portable minesweeping gear offloaded. Several are operated by the KGB Border Guard. Most are in the Pacific Fleet, and the class is often deployed to the Indian Ocean. One has been transferred to Guinea, one to Yemen, and others have been converted as radar pickets, with a Big Net radar aft.

GUIDED-MISSILE PATROL BOATS

♦ **8 Matka class** Bldr: Izhora SY, Leningrad (In serv. 1978-. . .)

Matka class at speed, on foils, with new targeting radar

Matka class hull-borne—note low freeboard

D: 225 tons (260 fl) **S:** 40 kts **Dim:** 40.0 × 12.0 (7.7 hull) × 1.9 (hull)
A: 2/SS-N-2C (I × 2)—1/76.2-mm DP—1/30-mm Gatling AA
Electron Equipt: Radar: 1/Cheese Cake, 1/target designation, 1/Bass Tilt
ECM: 2/chaff launchers (XVI × 2)
IFF: 1/High Pole B, 1/Square Head
M: 3 M504 diesels; 3 props; 15,000 hp **Range:** 400/36; 650/20 **Man:** 30 tot.

REMARKS: Essentially, a missile-armed version of the Turya-class hydrofoil torpedo boat, with larger superstructure, 76.2-mm gun forward, and missiles and Gatling gun aft. Construction continues, but slowly. Uses new targeting radar, larger than Square Tie. Appears to be overloaded.

♦ **1 Sarancha class** Bldr: Petrovskiy SY, Leningrad, 1977

Sarancha class

Sarancha class

D: 300 tons (fl) **S:** 50 kts
Dim: 50.6 (45.0 hull) × 23.5 (11.0 hull) × 7.3 (2.8 hull)
A: 4/SS-N-9 (II × 2)—1/SA-N-4 syst. (II × 1)—1/30-mm Gatling AA (VI × 1)

GUIDED-MISSILE PATROL BOATS *(continued)*

Electron Equipt: Radar: 1/Band Stand, 1/Pop Group, 1/Bass Tilt
IFF: 1/Square Head, 1/High Pole B
M: 2 gas turbines; 4 props; 20,000 hp

REMARKS: Too large and complex to be a successor to the Osa class. Essentially a reduced, high-speed Nanuchka. Folding-foil system, with 2 propellers on each of two pods on the after foils. Stepped hydroplane hull bottom.

♦ **40 Osa-II class** (In serv. 1966-70)

AMURSKIY KOMSOMOLETS	TAMBOVSKIY KOMSOMOLETS	KRONSHTADTSKIY
KIROVSKIY KOMSOMOLETS	36 others	KOMSOMOLETS

D: 215 tons (245 fl) **S:** 36 kts **Dim:** 39.0 × 7.7 × 1.9
A: 4/SS-N-2B Styx (I × 4)—4/30-mm AA (II × 2)
Electron Equipt: Radar: 1/Square Tie, 1/Drum Tilt
IFF: 1/High Pole B, 2/Square Head
M: 3 M504 diesels; 3 props; 15,000 hp **Range:** 430/34; 790/20 **Man:** 30 tot.

Osa-II class—with quadruple SA-N-5 Grail launcher   1976

Osa-II class   1976

Osa-II class—export model   1979

REMARKS: Soviet type designation: RKA—*Raketnyy Kater* (Missile Cutter). Some units have been given SA-N-5 systems aft. Widely exported during 1970—present, primarily using new-built units.

♦ **65 Osa-I class** Bldrs: Various (In serv. 1959-66)

D: 175 tons (210 fl) **S:** 36 kts **Dim:** 39.0 × 7.7 × 1.8
A: 4/SS-N-2 Styx (I × 4)—4/30-mm AA (II × 2)
Electron Equipt: Radar: 1/Square Tie, 1/Drum Tilt
IFF: 1/High Pole B, 2/Square Head
M: 3 M503A diesels; 3 props; 12,000 hp **Range:** 430/34; 790/20 **Man:** 30 tot.

REMARKS: Soviet type designation: RKA—*Raketnyy Kater* (Missile Cutter). These small craft can launch their missiles in a Force-4 sea (2-m waves). Many of them have been transferred to other navies. Some have been built as, or converted to, targets. Stenka, Matka, Turya, and Mol (an export torpedo boat, see Somalia and Sri Lanka) all use Osa hulls and propulsion plants. Beginning to diminish in numbers, as some are now well over 20 years old.

Osa-I class

GUIDED-MISSILE PATROL BOATS *(continued)*

Osa-I class

PATROL BOATS

♦ **1 Babochka class** Bldr: . . . , (In serv. 1978)

Babochka class   1978

    D: 400 tons (fl) **S:** 45 kts **Dim:** 50.0 × 13.0 (8.5 hull) × . . .
    A: 8/400-mm ASW TT (IV × 2)—2/30-mm Gatling AA (VI × 2)
    Electron Equipt: Radar: 1/Don-2, 1/new-type surveillance, 1/Bass Tilt
    M: CODOG: 2 cruise diesels, 3 gas turbines; 3 props; 30,000 hp (max.)

REMARKS: A prototype ASW hydrofoil with fixed, fully submerged foils fore and aft.
The torpedo tubes are mounted, two on two, on either side of the forecastle between
the forward Gatling gun and the superstructure.

♦ **1 Slepen class** Bldr: Petrovskiy SY, Leningrad (In serv. circa 1969)

    D: 205 tons (230 fl) **S:** 36 kts **Dim:** 39.0 × 7.7 × 1.8
    A: 1/76.2-mm DP—1/30-mm Gatling gun·
    Electron Equipt: Radar: 1/Don-2, 1/Bass Tilt
                  ECM: 2/passive arrays, 2/chaff RL (XVI × 2)
                  IFF: 1/High Pole B, 2/Square Head
    M: 3 M504 diesels; 3 props; 15,000 hp **Man:** 30 tot.

REMARKS: The Soviet Navy's only high-speed gunboat is a trials craft for systems for
small combatants. Twin 57-mm AA replaced by single 76.2-mm DP forward in 1975.
Resembles a Matka but does not have missiles or hydrofoils.

♦ **100 Stenka class** Bldrs: Various (In serv. 1967-. . .)

Stenka class   S. Breyer

Stenka class

    D: 170 tons (210 fl) **S:** 36 kts **Dim:** 39.5 × 7.7 × 1.8
    A: 4/30-mm AA (II × 2)—4/400-mm ASW TT—2/d.c. racks (12 d.c.)
    Electron Equipt: Radar: 1/Pot Drum, 1/Drum Tilt
                  Sonar: 1/Hormone-helicopter, dipping
                  IFF: 1/High Pole B, 2/Square Head
    M: 3 M503A diesels; 3 props; 12,000 hp **Range:** 450/34; 700/20 **Man:** 22 tot.

REMARKS: Soviet type designation: PSKR—*Pogranichnyy Storozhevoy Korabl'* (Border Patrol Ship). Recent units have a new navigational radar vice Pot Drum. Manned
by the Maritime Border Guard of the KGB.

♦ **30 S.O.-1 class** Bldrs: Various (In serv. 1958-64)

    D: 190 tons (215 fl) **S:** 28 kts **Dim:** 42.0 × 6.1 × 1.9
    A: 4/25-mm AA (II × 2)—4/RBU-1200 ASW RL (V × 4)—2/d.c. racks (24
        d.c.)—mines (Some ships: 2/400-mm ASW TT replacing the 25-mm mount aft)
    Electron Equipt: Radar: 1/Pot Head
                  Sonar: 1/high-freq. (Tamir)
                  IFF: 1/Dead Duck, 1/High Pole A
    M: 3 diesels; 3 props; 7,500 hp **Man:** 3 officers, 27 men

PATROL BOATS (continued)

S.O.-I class—with 400-mm TT aft

REMARKS: Soviet type designation: PKA—*Protivolodochniy Kater* (Antisubmarine Cutter). Units with TT carry short d.c. racks, 12 d.c. Some have helicopter dipping sonar. Poor sea boats. Class being scrapped. Several have been transferred to East Germany, North Vietnam, Algeria, Iraq, Cuba, South Yemen, etc.

HYDROFOIL TORPEDO BOATS

♦ **30 Turya class** Bldr:. . . (In serv. 1974-79)

Turya class at speed, bow raised on foil

Turya class—dipping sonar on starboard quarter

Turya class at low speed, in displacement condition

D: 205 tons (240 fl)   **S:** 42 kts
Dim: 39.0 × 7.7 (12.0 over foils) × 1.8 (without foils)
A: 2/57-mm AA aft (II × 1)—2/25-mm AA (II × 1)—4/533-mm TT (I × 4)
Electron Equipt: Radar: 1/Pot Drum, 1/Muff Cob
    Sonar: 1/Hormone-helicopter, dipping
    IFF: 1/High Pole B, 1/Square Head
M: 3 M504 diesels; 3 props; 15,000 hp
Range: 400/38; 650/20   **Man:** 24 tot.

REMARKS: Fixed hydrofoils forward only; stern planes on water surface. Has Osa-II hull and propulsion. Six of this class, without dipping sonar, have been delivered to Cuba since 1-79.

TORPEDO BOATS

♦ **30 Shershen class** Bldr: . . . (In serv. 1963-70)

Shershen class   Skyfotos, Ltd., 1978

D: 150 tons (180 fl)   **S:** 45 kts   **Dim:** 34.0 × 7.2 × 1.5
A: 4/30-mm AA (II × 2)—4/533-mm TT (I × 4)—2/d.c. racks (12 d.c.)

TORPEDO BOATS (continued)

Electron Equipt: Radar: 1/Pot Drum, 1/Drum Tilt
          IFF: 1/High Pole A, 1-2/Square Head
M: 3 M503A diesels; 3 props; 12,000 hp **Range:** 450/34; 700/20

REMARKS: Contemporaneous with the Osa-I class, and have the same propulsion but a smaller hull. Now being discarded, with some having been exported to Egypt, North Korea, East Germany, Angola, Cape Verde Islands, Guinea, and Vietnam, etc. Yugoslavia built ten under license.

PATROL CRAFT

♦ **30 or more Zhuk class** Bldr: . . . (In serv. 1975-. . .)

D: 50 tons (fl) **S:** 30 kts **Dim:** 22.9 × 4.9 × 1.5
A: 2/14.5-mm mg (II × 1) **Electron Equipt:** Radar: 1/Spin Trough
M: 2 M50 diesels; 2 props; 2,400 hp

REMARKS: Some carry four 14.5-mm AA (II × 2). Probably manned by the KGB Border Guard. A large number have been exported.

♦ **20 Pchela-class hydrofoils** Bldr: . . . (In serv. 1964-65)

Pehela class—with ECM radomes atop bridge

D: 70 tons (83 fl) **S:** 45 kts **Dim:** 25.3 × 5.8 × 1.3 (without foils)
A: 4/14.5-mm AA (II × 2)—4/d.c. racks
Electron Equipt: Radar: 1/Pot Drum
                Sonar: On a few: 1/Hormone-helicopter dipping
M: Diesels; 2 props; 6,000 hp **Man:** 12 tot.

REMARKS: Simple, fixed, surface-piercing hydrofoils. Aircraft-type machine-gun mountings. Manned by the KGB Border Guard.

♦ **34 Poluchat-I class** Bldr:. . . (In serv. 1953-56)

D: 90 tons (fl) **S:** 18 kts **Dim:** 29.6 × 5.8 × 1.5
A: 2/14.5-mm mg (II × 1) **M:** 2 M50 diesels; 2 props; 2,400 hp
Range: 450/17; 900/10 **Man:** 20 tot.

REMARKS: Modified version of a standard Soviet Navy torpedo-retriever, with stern ramp decked over, a boat carried aft, and a twin machine-gun mount. Probably operated by the KGB Border Guard.

Poluchat-I-class torpedo-retriever—patrol version similar

RIVERINE CRAFT

NOTE: The U.S.S.R. maintains a number of river gunboats on the Lower Danube, on the Amur and Ussuri river systems in the Far East, and possibly elsewhere. In addition to gunboats, the riverine forces have a few support craft, including the administrative craft SSV-10 (ex-PS 10) on the Danube (360 tons, 49 m overall).

♦ **5 Yas class**

REMARKS: New design seen in Pacific area; no data available.

♦ **85 Shmel-class patrol gunboats** Bldr: . . . (In serv. 1967-74)

D: 60 tons (fl) **S:** 22 kts **Dim:** 28.3 × 4.6 × 1.0
A: 1/76.2-mm, 48 cal., fwd in a tank turret—2/25-mm AA (II × 1) aft—1/18-tube, 122-mm RL—mines

Shmel class—RL, armored 25-mm mount aft   J. Meister, 1975

RIVERINE CRAFT (continued)

Shmel class—no rocket launcher, unarmored 25-mm mount aft

M: 2 M50 diesels; 2 props; 2,400 hp   **Man:** 15 tot.

REMARKS: Soviet type designation: AKA—*Artilleriyskiy Kater* (Artillery Cutter); earlier classes were BKA—*Bronirovanny Kater* (Armored Cutter). Not all these craft have a rocket launcher. An earlier version has a twin machine-gun mount aft that resembles a tank turret. A few of the older BK-IV-class river monitors may still be in service; similar in size to the Shmel, they had an undulating deckline, were more heavily armed, slower, and carried one 85-mm gun and four 14.5-mm AA (II × 2).

MINE WARFARE SHIPS

♦ **3 Alesha-class minelayers** Bldr:. . . (In serv. 1967-69)

PRIPET   2 others

   D: 2,900 tons (3,500 fl)   **S:** 20 kts   **Dim:** 98.0 × 14.5 × 4.8
   A: 4/57-mm (IV × 1)—400 mines

Alesha class   1969

Alesha class   1969

   Electron Equipt: Radar: 1/Don-2, 1/Strut Curve, 1/Muff Cob
                        IFF: 1/High Pole B
   M: 4 diesels; 2 props; 8,000 hp   **Man:** 190 tot.

REMARKS: Can also be used as netlayers, minesweeper tenders, and command ships.

♦ **35 Natya-class fleet minesweepers** Bldr: Various (In serv. 1970-. . .)

ADMIRAL PERSHIN	SEMEN ROSHAL'	TURBINIST
DMITRIY LYSOV	SNAYPER	ZENITCHIK
KONTRADMIRAL HOROSHKIN	SVYAZIST	27 others

   D: 650 tons (750 fl)   **S:** 18 kts   **Dim:** 61.0 × 9.6 × 2.7
   A: 4/30-mm AA (II × 2)—4/25-mm AA (II × 2)—2/RBU-1200 ASW RL (V × 2)—mines
   Electron Equipt: Radar: 1/Don-2, 1/Drum Tilt
                        Sonar: 1/high-freq.
                        IFF: 1/High Pole B, 2/Square Head
   M: 2 diesels; 2 props; 5,000 hp   **Man:** 50 tot.

REMARKS: Soviet type designation: MT—*Morskoy Tral'shchik* (Seagoing Minesweeper). Equipped to serve as ASW escorts. Early units have rigid davits aft; on later units they are articulated. Six have been built for India and two for Libya. Aluminum alloy hull.

Natya class—late unit with new davits   1978

MINE WARFARE SHIPS (continued)

Natya class—with portable ELINT gear abaft mast, old-style davits French Navy, 1980

♦ **47 Yurka-class fleet minesweepers** Bldr: . . .

GAFEL'   EVGENIY NIKONOV   45 others

Yurka class

    D: 400 tons (460 fl) **S:** 18 kts **Dim:** 52.0 × 9.3 × 2.0 **Man:** 45 tot.
    A: 4/30-mm AA (II × 2)—20 mines **M:** 2 diesels; 2 props; 4,000 hp
    Electron Equipt: Radar: 1/Don-2, 1/Drum Tilt
                   IFF: 1/High Pole B, 2-3/Square Head

REMARKS: Soviet type designation: MT—*Morskoy Tral'shchik* (Seagoing Mine-sweeper). Aluminum-alloy hull. Four transferred to Egypt in 1969, one to Vietnam in 1979.

♦ **40 T-43-class fleet minesweepers** Bldr:. . . (In serv. 1947-57)

IVAN FIOLETOV	KONTRADMIRAL YUROKOVSKIY	NIKOLAY MARKIN
KOMSOMOLETS	KOMSOMOLETS KALMYKIY	SAKHALINSKIY
BYELORUSSIY	LAMINE SADJIKABA	KOMSOMOLETS
KOMSOMOLETS	MEZHADIY AZIZBAKOV	STEPHAN SAUMYAN
ESTONIY		30 others

    D: 500 tons (570 fl) **S:** 14 kts **Dim:** 58.0 × 8.6 × 2.3 (3.5 max.)
    A: 4/37-mm AA (II × 2)—4/25-mm AA (II × 2) or 4-8/14.5-mm or 12.7-mm mg
      (II × 2 or 4)—2/d.c. projectors—mines

T 43 class—long-hull version   1975

T 43 class—with 2/45-mm AA, 4/14.5-mm AA   1974

    Electron Equipt: Radar: 1/Don-2 or Spin Trough, 1/Ball End
                  Sonar: 1/Tamir 11
                  IFF: 1/Square Head, 1/High Pole A
    M: 2/9D diesels; 2 props; 2,200 hp **Electric:** 550 kw
    Fuel: 70 tons **Range:** 3,200/10 **Man:** 65 tot.

REMARKS: Soviet type designation: MT—*Morskoy Tral'shchik* (Seagoing Mine-sweeper). Many of the T-43 class have been transferred to Poland, Egypt, Algeria, China, etc. The version armed with four 25-mm AA amidships is 60 m long and displaces 590 tons (fl). Most Soviet units have no machine guns. A few operated by the KGB Border Guard have two 45-mm AA (I × 2) vice four 37-mm AA. Also built on the T-43 hull were radar pickets, noise-measurement ships, diving tenders, and trials ships. Well over 200 were built. Rapidly being disposed of.

♦ **30-35 Sonya-class coastal minesweepes** Bldr: . . . (In serv. 1973-. . .)

KOMSOMOLETS KIRGIZIY   29-34 others

    D: 350 tons (400 fl) **S:** 14 kts **Dim:** 48.5 × 8.8 × 2.1
    A: 2/30-mm AA (II × 1)—2/25-mm AA (II × 1)

MINE WARFARE SHIPS (*continued*)

Sonya class

Electron Equipt: Radar: 1/Spin Trough
IFF: 1/High Pole B, 2/Square Head
M: 2 diesels; 2 props; 2,400 hp **Man:** 43 tot.

REMARKS: Soviet type designation: BT—*Basovyy Tral'shchik* (Base Minesweeper). Wooden hull with plastic sheathing. Two transferred to Cuba, 1980.

♦ **2 Zhenya-class coastal minesweepers** Bldr: . . . (In serv. 1967-1972)

Zhenya class

D: 220 tons (300 fl) **S:** 18 kts **Dim:** 42.7 × 7.5 × 1.8
A: 2/30-mm AA (II × 1) **Electron Equipt:** Radar: 1/Spin Trough
M: 2 diesels; 2 props; 2,400 hp **Man:** 40 tot.

REMARKS: Soviet type designation: BT—*Basovyy Tral'shchik* (Base Minesweeper). Plastic hull. Apparently not successful, as similar but larger, wooden-hulled Sonya class went into production instead.

♦ **70 Vanya-class coastal minesweepers** Bldr: . . . (In serv. 1961-73)

D: 200 tons (245 fl) **S:** 14 kts **Dim:** 39.9 × 7.3 × 1.8

Vanya class

A: 2/30-mm AA (II × 1)
Electron Equipt: Radar: 1/Don-2
IFF: 1/High Pole B, 1/Dead Duck
M: 2 diesels; 2 props; 2,200 hp **Man:** 30 tot.

REMARKS: Soviet type designation: BT—*Basovyy Tral'shchik* (Base Minesweeper). Wooden construction. At least one was built or has been converted as a minehunter, armed with two 25-mm AA (II × 1)—more accurate than 30-mm for mine-disposal—and with one Don-Kay in place of Don-2; has two boats in davits on the fantail. Some, classed Vanya-II, are one meter longer and have a larger diesel generator exhaust pipe amidships.

♦ **8 Sasha-class coastal minesweepers** Bldr:. . . (In serv. 1954-59)

D: 250 tons (280 fl) **S:** 18 kts **Dim:** 45.7 × 6.2 × 1.8
A: 1/45- or 57-mm AA—4/25-mm AA (II × 2)—mines

Sasha class

MINE WARFARE SHIPS (continued)

Electron Equipt: Radar: 1/Ball End
       IFF: 1/High Pole A, 1/Dead Duck
M: 2 diesels; 2 vertical cycloidal props; 2,200 hp **Man:** 25 tot.

REMARKS: Soviet type designation: RT—*Reydovoy Tral'shchik* (Roadstead Minesweeper). Steel hull. Also used as patrol boats. Ships with 57-mm AA have shorter masts. Class being scrapped.

♦ **40 Yevgenya-class inshore minesweepers** Bldr: . . . (In serv. 1970-. . .)

Yevgenya class   1976

    D: 70 tons (80 fl) **S:** 12 kts **Dim:** 26.1 × 5.8 × 1.2
    A: 2/14.5-mm mg (II × 1) **M:** 2 diesels; 2 props; 600 hp **Man:** 10 tot.
    Electron Equipt: Radar: 1/Spin Trough
                  IFF: 1/High Pole B

REMARKS: Plastic hull. Several transferred abroad. Some foreign ships have two 25-mm AA (II × 1).

♦ **3 Andryusha-class special minesweepers** Bldr: . . . (In serv. 1975-76)

    D: 320 tons (360 fl) **S:** 15 kts **Dim:** 44.9 × 8.2 × 3.0 **A:** None
    Electron Equipt: Radar: 1/Spin Trough
                  IFF: 1/High Pole B
    M: 2 diesels; 2 props; 2,200 hp **Man:** 40 tot.

REMARKS: Wooden or plastic hulls. Large cable ducts running down both sides indicate probable role in sweeping magnetic mines. Prominent stack for gas-turbine generator; diesel engines exhaust through hull sides.

♦ **5 Olya-class minesweeping boats** Bldr: . . . (In serv. 1976-. . .)

    D: 50 tons (70 fl) **S:** 15 kts **Dim:** 25.5 × 4.5 × 1.4
    A: 2/25-mm AA **Electron Equipt:** Radar: 1/Spin Trough
    M: 2 diesels; 2 props; 600 hp **Man:** 15 tot.

♦ **10 Ilyusha-class minesweeping drones** (In serv. 1970-. . .)

    D: 50 tons (70 fl) **S:** 12 kts **Dim:** 24.4 × 4.9 × 1.4 **A:** None
    Electron Equipt: Radar: 1/Spin Trough
                  IFF: 1/High Pole B
    M: 1 diesel; 450 hp **Man:** 10 tot.

REMARKS: Apparently radio-controlled while operating, but can be manned for transit.

♦ **45 K-8-class minesweeping boats** Bldr: Polnocny SY, Gdansk, Poland (In serv. 1954-59)

K-8 class

    D: 19.4 tons (26 fl) **S:** 12 kts **Dim:** 16.9 × 3.2 × 0.8
    A: 2/14.5-mm mg (II × 1) **Electron Equipt:** None
    M: 2 3D6 diesels; 2 props; 300 hp **Range:** 300/9 **Man:** 6 tot.

REMARKS: Wooden construction; being replaced by Yevgenya class.

RADAR PICKET SHIPS

♦ **1 (+. . .) T-58 class** (In serv. 1957-61)

    D: 725 tons (840 fl) **S:** 18 kts **Dim:** 70.0 × 9.1 × 2.5
    A: 2/57-mm AA—2/SA-N-5 SAM syst. (IV × 2,. . . Grail missiles)—4/30-mm
      AA (II × 2)—2/d.c. racks
    Electron Equipt: Radar: 1/Spin Trough, 1/Strut Curve, 1/Big Net, 1/Muff Cob
                  ECM: . . .
                  IFF: . . .
    M: 2 diesels; 2 props; 4,000 hp

REMARKS: Conversion completed 1979 at Izhora SY, Leningrad. Other converted units anticipated, despite age of basic ship.

♦ **6 T-43 class** Bldr: . . . (In serv. 1952-54)

    D: 500 tons (580 fl) **S:** 14 kts **Dim:** 58.0 × 8.6 × 2.3
    A: 4/37-mm AA (II × 2)—2/25-mm AA (II × 1)—2/d.c. projectors—mines
    Electron Equipt: Radar: 1/Don, 1/Big Net or 2/Knife Rest
                  ECM: 2/Watch Dog
    M: 2/9D diesels; 2 props; 2,200 hp **Fuel:** 70 tons **Range:** 3,200/10
    Man: 77 tot.

REMARKS: Configured as radar pickets; otherwise similar to the short-hulled minesweeper version. Not likely to last much longer.

RADAR PICKET SHIPS (continued)

T-43-class radar picket—Big Net radar aft   1966

AMPHIBIOUS-WARFARE SHIPS AND CRAFT

♦ **2 Ivan Rogov-class landing ships** Bldr: Kaliningrad SY

	L	In serv.
IVAN ROGOV	1976	1978
N. . .	. . .	. . .

D: 11,000 tons (13,000 fl) **S:** 20 kts **Dim:** 158.0 × 24.0 × 8.0
A: 1/SA-N-4 SAM syst. (II × 1, 18 missiles)—2/76.2-mm DP (II × 1)—4/30-mm
  Gatling AA (VI × 4)—1/122-mm automatic bombardment RL (XL × 1) for
  BM-21 rockets—4/Hormone helicopters—3/Lebed air-cushion landing craft
Electron Equipt: Radar: 2/Don-Kay, 1/Head Net-C, 1/Owl Screech, 1/Pop
  Group, 2/Bass Tilt

Ivan Rogov   French Navy, 1979

Ivan Rogov—note helo spots, staggered stack locations   1979

Ivan Rogov—showing stern and helicopter hangar doors   French Navy, 1979

  ECM: 2/Bell Shroud, 2/Bell Squat
  IFF: High Pole B
M: 2 gas turbines; 2 props; 20,000 hp
Range: . . . **Man:** 200 crew + 550 troops

REMARKS: Soviet type designation: BDK—*Bol'shoy Desantnyy Korabl'* (Large Landing Ship). The long-awaited second unit has apparently suffered construction delays.
Equipped with bow doors and articulating ramp leading to a vehicle cargo deck in
the forward part of the hull, while a stern door provides access to a floodable docking
well intended to accommodate Lebed air-cushion landing craft. The massive superstructure incorporates a helicopter hangar, with a steep ramp leading downward to
a helicopter pad on the foredeck, and doors aft leading to a second helicopter platform
over the stern. There are also hydraulically raised ramps leading from the upper
deck forward of the superstructure to both the bow doors and the docking well. The
Ivan Rogov is capable of transporting an entire naval infantry battalion and its
vehicles, including 10 tanks, 30 armored personnel carriers, and trucks. Her ability
to use helicopters, to beach, and to deploy air-cushion vehicles gives her a versatility
unmatched by any other amphibious-warfare ship; this is combined with an organic
shore-fire-bombardment capability and very extensive command, control, and surveillance facilities. The hull has a pronounced bulb, or beak, projecting forward
below the waterline.

♦ **11 Ropucha-class tank landing ships** Bldr: Polnocny SY, Gdansk, Poland (In
  serv. 1975-78)

Ropucha class   French Navy

AMPHIBIOUS-WARFARE SHIPS AND CRAFT (continued)

Ropucha class

Ropucha class 1976

D: 2,600 tons (3,600 fl) **S:** 17 kts **Dim:** 113.0 × 14.5 × 3.6 (aft) 2.0 (fwd)
A: 4/57-mm AA (II × 2)
Electron Equipt: Radar: 1/Don-2, 1/Strut Curve, 1/Muff Cob
  IFF: 1/High Pole B
M: 2 diesels; 2 props; 10,000 hp **Man:** 70 crew + 230 troops

REMARKS: Soviet type designation: BDK—*Bol'shoy Desantnyy Korabl'* (Large Landing Ship). Bow and stern doors permit roll-on/roll-off loading. Mounting positions forward for two bombardment rocket launchers. Cargo capacity: 450 tons; usable deck space: 600 m². The later units have angled hances to the corners of the main-deck superstructure and reinforcing gussets around the forward 57-mm AA platform. Several have received 4/SA-N-5 quadruple launchers for Grail SAMs. Although the class was intended to receive two barrage rocket launchers on the forecastle, none have been installed. One unit was transferred to the People's Democratic Republic of Yemen in 1979.

♦ **14 Alligator-class tank landing ships** Bldr: Kaliningrad SY (In serv. 1964-77)

ALEKSANDR TORTSEV	NIKOLAY FIL'CHENKOV	SERGEI LAZO
DONETSKIY SHAKHTER	NIKOLAY VILKOV	TOMSKIY KOMSOMOLETS
KRASNAYA PRESNYA	NIKOLAY OBYEKOV	VORONEZHSKIY KOMSOMOLETS
KRYMSKIY KOMSOMOLETS	PETR IL'ICHYEV	50 LET SHEFSTVA V.L.K.S.M.
2 others		

Alligator class—late unit, no rocket launcher 1969

Alligator class—late unit with 122-mm rocket launcher forward 1976

Alligator class—early unit 1971

AMPHIBIOUS-WARFARE SHIPS AND CRAFT (continued)

D: 3,400 tons (4,500 fl) **S:** 18 kts **Dim:** 114.0 × 15.6 × 4.5 (aft)
A: 2/57-mm AA (II × 1) (See Remarks)
Electron Equipt: Radar: 2/Don-2 and/or Spin Trough
                     IFF: 1/High Pole B
M: 2 diesels; 8,000 hp **Range:** 6,000/16 **Man:** 75 crew + 300 troops

REMARKS: Soviet type designation: BDK—*Bol'shoy Desantnyy Korabl'* (Large Landing Ship). The design evolved continually during the time these ships were built. They have ramps fore and aft. Their hoisting equipment varies (one or two 5-ton cranes, one 15-ton crane), as does their armament: later ships also have a rocket launcher forward for shore bombardment, the last two have four 25-mm AA (II × 2) aft, and some are equipped with 3/SA-N-5 launchers for Grail SAMS (IV × 3).

♦ **55 Polnocny-class medium landing ships** Bldr: Polnocny SY, Gdansk, Poland
(In serv. 1961-73)

A version:

Polnocny-A—with four SA-N-5 quadruple launchers   1977

Polnocny-A—with original low bridge and troughs down sides of hull   1977

D: 770 tons (fl) **S:** 19 kts **Dim:** 73.0 × 8.6 × 1.9 (aft)
A: 2/14.5-mm mg (II × 1) or 2/30-mm AA (II × 1) or none—2/140-mm barrage
     RL (XVIII × 2)—2 or 4/SA-N-5 systems (or none)
Electron Equipt: Radar: 1/Spin Trough
                     IFF: 1/High Pole A; Some: 1/Square Head
M: 2 diesels; 2 props; 4,000 hp **Man:** 35 tot.

B version:

D: 800 tons (fl) **S:** 18 kts **Dim:** 74.0 × 8.6 × 1.9
A: 2 or 4/30-mm AA—2/140-mm barrage RL (XVIII × 2)—4/SA-N-5 systems
Electron Equipt: Radar: 1/Spin Trough, 1/Drum Tilt
                     IFF: 1/Square Head, 1/High Pole B
M: 2 diesels; 2 props; 4,000 hp **Man:** 40 crew + 100 troops

Polnocny-B class—no SA-N-5; note concave bow flare   1979

Polnocny-B—with high stack and 30-mm AA aft, 4/SA-N-5 launchers   1977

C version:

Polnocny-C class—extended after superstructure

Polnocny-C

D: 1,150 tons (fl) **S:** 18 kts **Dim:** 82.0 × 10.0 × 2.1
A: 4/30-mm AA (II × 2)—2/140-mm barrage RL (XVIII × 2)—4/SA-N-5 systems (IV × 2,. . . Grail missiles)
Electron Equipt: Radar: 1/Spin Trough, 1/Drum Tilt
                     IFF: 1/Square Head, 1/High Pole B
M: 2 diesels; 2 props; 5,000 hp **Man:** 40 crew, plus 180 troops

AMPHIBIOUS-WARFARE SHIPS AND CRAFT (continued)

REMARKS: Soviet type designation: SDK—*Srednyy Desantnyy Korabl'* (Medium Landing Ship). Most have now been equipped with two or four SA-N-5 systems. The Polnocny-Bs that have 30-mm aft have heightened stacks. Very few Polnocny-Cs were built. This class delivered to India, Iraq, Indonesia, Egypt, Angola, etc. Few Polnocny-As believed remaining, due to large number transferred aboard. Cargo: about 180 tons in A and B, 250 tons in C.

♦ **15 Vydra-class utility landing craft** Bldr: U.S.S.R. (In serv. 1967-69)

Vydra class

    D: 425 tons (600 fl) **S:** 11 kts **Dim:** 54.8 × 8.1 × 2.0 **A:** None
    Electron Equipt: Radar: 1/Spin Trough
                  IFF: 1/High Pole
    M: 2 diesels; 2 props; 800 hp **Man:** 20 crew, plus 100 troops

♦ **10 Lebed-class surface-effects landing craft**

Lebed class

    D: 85 tons (fl) **S:** 60 kts **Dim:** 24.0 × 12.0 × . . .
    A: 2/14.5-mm mg (II × 1) **M:** 3 gas turbines; 2 props

REMARKS: Broad bow ramp, ducted props, control cab to starboard, gunmount atop. Can carry one or two PT-76 light tanks or 120 troops or about 45 tons of cargo.

♦ **12 Aist-class surface-effects landing craft** (In serv. 1971-. . .)

    D: 220 tons (fl) **S:** 65 kts **Dim:** 47.8 × 17.5 × . . .
    A: 4/30-mm AA (II × 2)
    Electron Equipt: Radar: 1/Spin Trough, 1/Drum Tilt
                  IFF: 1/High Pole B, 1/Square Head
    M: 2 gas turbines; 4 props; 2 lift fans

Aist class—on cushion   1978

REMARKS: Can carry four PT-76 light tanks or one medium tank and 220 troops.

♦ **35 Gus-class surface-effects landing craft**

Gus class   1970

    D: 27 tons (fl) **S:** 57.5 kts **Dim:** 21.3 × 8.2 × . . .
    A: None **M:** 3 gas turbines; 2 props; 1 lift fan; 2,340 hp

REMARKS: Can carry twenty-four troops. A training version with two pilot positions is also in service.

♦ **7 (+ . . .) Ondatra-class landing craft** (In serv. 1978-. . .)

Ondatra class   1979

    D: 90 tons (fl) **S:** 10 kts **Dim:** 24.0 × 6.0 × . . .
    A: None **M:** 2 diesels; 2 props; 600 hp

REMARKS: Apparently intended as successor to the T-4 class. One carried by *Ivan Rogov* as a tug for Lebed-class air-cushion vehicles.

AMPHIBIOUS-WARFARE SHIPS AND CRAFT *(continued)*

♦ . . . **T-4-class landing craft** (In serv. 1954-74)

    D: 70 tons (fl) **S:** 10 kts **Dim:** 19.0 × 4.3 × 1.0
    M: 2 diesels; 2 props; 600 hp **Man:** 5 tot.

REMARKS: Built in two versions; later variant with deeper bow could accommodate a medium tank.

SUBMARINE TENDERS

♦ **6 Ugra-class command tenders** Bldr: Nikolayev (In serv. 1963-72)

IVAN KOLYSHKIN	IVAN VAKHRAMEEV	VOLGA
IVAN KUCHERENKO	TOBOL	N. . .

Volga—Vee Cone communications antenna aft   French Navy, 1980

Ivan Kolyshkin—helicopter hangar aft   1978

Ugra class (no name)—with 2/SA-N-5 atop superstructure   1979

    D: 6,750 tons (9,500 fl) **S:** 20 kts **Dim:** 141.4 × 17.7 × 6.5
    A: 8/57-mm AA (II × 4)

    Electron Equipt: Radar: 1-3/Don-2, 1/Strut Curve, 2/Muff Cob
                    ECM: 4/Watch Dog
                          IFF: 1/High Pole B, 1/High Pole A, 2/Square Head
    M: 4 diesels; 2 props; 8,000 hp **Range:** 10,000/12 **Man:** 450 tot.

REMARKS: Soviet type designation: PB—*Plavuchaya Baza* (Floating Base). One modified version was built for India, as *Amba*. The *Ivan Kolyshkin* has a tall helicopter hangar. The *Volga* has a Vee Cone communications antenna. Can support eight to twelve submarines at sea with supplies, fuel, provisions, water, and spare torpedoes and can offer repair services. Being backfitted with 2/SA-N-5 syst. (IV × 2, . . . Grail missiles). This class and the Don class are frequently used as flagships. One 10-ton and two 6-ton cranes are fitted. Sisters *Gangut* and *Borodino* are configured as training ships for naval officer cadets and do not serve submarines—see Training Ships.

♦ **6 Don-class command tenders** Bldr: Nikolayev (In serv. 1958-61)

DMITRIY GALKIN	KAMCHATSKIY KOMSOMOLETS	MAGOMED GADZIEV
FYODOR VIDYAEV	MAGADANSKIY KOMSOMOLETS	VIKTOR KOTEL'NIKOV

Viktor Kotel'nikov—helicopter platform aft

Dmitriy Galkin—Vee Cone communications antenna aft, 8/25-mm AA   1974

    D: 6,730 tons (9,000 fl) **S:** 21 kts **Dim:** 140.0 × 16.8 × 6.5
    A: 4/100-mm AA (I × 4)—4/57-mm AA (II × 2)
    Electron Equipt: Radar: 1-2/Don-2, 1/Slim Net, 1/Sun Visor, 2/Hawk Screech
                    ECM: 2/Watch Dog
                          IFF: 1/High Pole B, 2/Square Head
    M: 4 diesels; 2 props; 8,000 hp **Man:** 450 tot.

REMARKS: Soviet type designation: PB—*Plavuchaya Baza* (Floating Base). Can serve as logistic support for a flotilla of eight to twelve submarines. The *Viktor Kotel'-*

SUBMARINE TENDERS (continued)

nikov's after 100-mm mounts were replaced by a helicopter platform, while the *Magadanskiy Komsomolets* has always had a very large helicopter platform aft and has never carried any 100-mm guns. The *Dmitriy Galkin* and *Fyedor Vidyaev* have eight 25-mm (II × 4) also, but no Hawk Screech, and have been fitted with a Vee Cone antenna for long-range communications. A bow lift-hook of 100-ton capacity is fitted, as are one 10-ton, two 5-ton, and two 1-ton cranes. All are used as flagships. One other unit was transferred to Indonesia.

♦ **6 Atrek class** Bldr: East Germany (In serv. 1955-57)

ATREK	BAKHMUT	EVGENIY OSIPOV
AYAT	DVINA	MURMAT

Atrek 1970

D: 3,413 tons (5,386 fl) **S:** 13 kts **Dim:** 102.4 × 14.4 × 5.5
M: 1 triple-expansion engine, 1 exhaust turbine; 1 prop; 2,400 hp
Boilers: 2 **Range:** 6,900/13

REMARKS: Soviet type designation: PB—*Plavuchaya Baza* (Floating Base). Modified Kolomna-class cargo ships. Can carry six 37-mm AA (II × 3). Two 5-ton cranes forward.

MISSILE TRANSPORTS

♦ **3 Amga class** Bldr: U.S.S.R.

AMGA (In serv. 1973) VETLUGA (In serv. 1976) DAUGAVA (In serv. 1981)

Amga 1973

D: 4,800 tons (5,800 fl) **S:** 12 kts **Dim:** 102.0 × 18.0 × 4.5
A: 4/25-mm AA (II × 2)
Electron Equipt: Radar: 1/Don-2
　　　　　　　　　　IFF: 1/High Pole B
M: 2 diesels; 2 props; 4,000 hp **Range:** 4,500/12

REMARKS: One 55-ton crane with a reach of 34 meters. Have ice-reinforced hulls. Intended to transport ballistic missiles for Delta-class submarines. The *Vetluga* is 2-m longer than her sister, and *Daugava* is longer still, displacing 6,200 tons (fl), and has a different crane, with solid sides.

♦ **7 Lama class** Bldr: . . . (In serv. 1963-79)

GENERAL RIYABAKOV	PM 44	PM 131	PB 625
VORONEZH	PM 93	PM 150	

General Riyabakov—with 2/57-mm AA fwd, 4/SA-N-5 launchers aft 1980

PM 44—with 8/57-mm AA and two Hawk Screech radars

Lama class—missile-boat tender version (old number), longer missile stowage area

MISSILE TRANSPORTS (continued)

Lama class—with 4/57-mm AA, 1/Muff Cob   French Navy, 1980

D: 6,000 tons (fl) **S:** 14 kts **Dim:** 113.0 × 15.0 × 5.0
A: 4 or 8/57-mm AA (IV × 1 or 2, or II × 2)—*Riyabakov* also: 4/SA-N-5 SAM
  syst. (IV × 4,. . . Grail missiles)
Electron Equipt: Radar: 1/Don-2, 1/Slim Net or Strut Curve, 1 or 2/Hawk
  Screech or 2/Muff Cob
  IFF: 1/High Pole B, 2/Square Head
M: 2 diesels; 1 prop; 4,000 hp

REMARKS: PM—*Plavuchaya Masterskaya* (Floating Workshop) and PB—*Plavuchaya
Baza* (Floating Base). Vary greatly in equipment. Intended to transport cruise
missiles for submarines and surface units. Two have larger missile-stowage areas
and smaller cranes, and carry four 57-mm AA (IV × 1) and four 25-mm AA (II ×
2), but have no fire-control radar. These apparently serve Nanuchka-class corvettes
and Osa-class patrol boats. Two 20-ton (10-ton on missile-boat tenders) precision
cranes.

♦ **2 Modified Andizhan class** Bldr: Neptunwerft, Rostock, East Germany (In
  serv.1960-61)

VENTA   VILYUY

Vilyuy   1978

D: 4,500 tons (fl) **S:** 13.5 kts **Dim:** 104.0 × 14.4 × 5.2 **A:** None
Electron Equipt: Radar: 2/Don-2
  IFF: 1/High Pole B, 1/Square Head
M: 1 diesel; 1,890 hp **Range:** 6,000/13

REMARKS: Converted from cargo ships during the 1970s. Large crane forward, two
small cranes and a helicopter deck aft. Forward holds can accommodate ten SS-N-
9 missiles and twenty SA-N-1 or SA-N-3.

♦ **2 MP 6 class** Bldr: Hungary (In serv. 1959-60)

BUREYA   KHOPER

D: 2,100 tons (fl) **S:** 12 kts **Dim:** 75.0 × 11.3 × 4.4
M: 1 diesel; 1 prop; 1,000 hp

REMARKS: Former medium landing ships, resembling engines-aft coastal freighters.
Bow doors welded shut circa 1960, when they were adapted as cargo vessels. Sub-
sequently modified to transport SS-N-5 ballistic missiles—*Khoper* in the Northern
Fleet and *Bureya* in the Pacific.

REPAIR SHIPS

♦ **21 Amur class** Bldr: A. Warski SY, Szczecin, Poland (In serv. 1968-78,
  1981-. . .)

PM 9	PM 49	PM 64	PM 81	PM 129	PM 140	PM 163
PM 34	PM 52	PM 73	PM 82	PM 138	PM 156	PM 164
PM 40	PM 56	PM 75	PM 94	PM 139	PM 161	PM. . .

PM 82 ("PM" omitted from pendant)   French Navy, 1979

PM 56—servicing a Foxtrot-class submarine   French Navy

REPAIR SHIPS (continued)

D: 5,000 tons (6,500 fl)   **S:** 12 kts   **Dim:** 120.0 × 17.4 × 5.2   **A:** None
Electron Equipt: Radar: 1/Don-2
                              IFF: 1/High Pole B
M: 2 diesels; 1 prop; 4,000 hp   **Man:** . . .

REMARKS: PM—*Plavuchaya Masterskaya* (Floating Workshop). Enlarged version of the Oskol class. Later units have crews of more than 300 men. Two 5-ton cranes. Construction resumed 1980-81.

◆ **12 Oskol class** Bldr: ⌐. Warski SY, Szczecin, Poland (In serv. 1964-67)

PM 20	PM 24	PM 28	PM 68	PM 148	PM. . .
PM 21	PM 26	PM 51	PM 146	PM 447	PM. . .

D: 2,500 tons (3,000 fl)   **S:** 14 kts   **Dim:** 91.4 × 12.2 × 4.0
Electron Equipt: Radar: 1/Don-2
                              IFF: 1/High Pole A
M: 2 diesels; 1 prop; 4,000 hp   **Man:** 60 tot.

REMARKS: PM—*Plavuchaya Masterskaya* (Floating Workshop). Most have a well deck forward of the bridge. PM 24 has two 57-mm AA (II × 1), four 25-mm AA (II × 2); no fire-control radar. All have one or two 3.4-ton cranes.

PM 68—well-deck Oskol class   1977

PM 24—2/57-mm AA (II × 2) fwd, 4/25-mm AA (II × 2) aft   1981

PM 146—flush-decked Oskol class   1970

◆ **5 Dnepr class** Bldr: Nikolayev (In serv. 1960-64)

PM 17	PM 22	PM 30	PM 130	PM 135

PM 17   1960

D: 4,500 tons (5,300 fl)   **S:** 11 kts   **Dim:** 113.3 (100.0 pp) × 16.5 × 4.4
Electron Equipt: Radar: 1/Don or Don-2
                              IFF: 1/High Pole A
M: 1 diesel; 2,000 hp   **Range:** 6,000/8.3   **Man:** 420 tot.

REMARKS: PM—*Plavuchaya Masterskaya* (Floating Workshop). Have one 150-ton bow hoist, one kingpost, and one crane. Equipment varies from ship to ship. PM 130 and 135, the last two units (Modified Dnepr class) are flush-decked. Intended to serve submarines. Can be armed with 2/57-mm AA (II × 1).

GENERATOR SHIPS

◆ **4 Tomba class** Bldr: Szczecin, Poland (In serv. 1974-76)

ENS 244	ENS 254	ENS 348	ENS 357

D: 3,500 tons (4,900 fl)   **S:** 14 kts   **Dim:** 96.5 × 15.5 × 5.0
A: None
Electron Equipt: Radar: 1/Don-2
                              IFF: 1/High Pole B
M: 1 diesel; 1 prop; 4,500 hp   **Man:** 50 tot.

REMARKS: ENS—*Elektrostantsiye Nalivatel'noye Sudno* (Electric Power Station and Steam-Source Ship). Two stacks and a "mack" on the forecastle, all containing diesel-engine exhausts, while the stack amidships also has the uptake from a large boiler. Two 3-ton cranes.

GENERATOR SHIPS (continued)

Tomba class   1974

SUBMARINE-RESCUE SHIPS

♦ **1 Nepa class** Bldr: Nikolayev (In serv. 1970)

KARPATY

Karpaty   1971

    D: 9,500 tons (fl) **S:** 18 kts **Dim:** 130.0 × 19.0 × 6.5 **A:** None
    Electron Equipt: Radar: 2/Don-2
                       IFF: 1/High Pole B
    M: 2-4 diesels; 2 props; 8,000 hp **Man:** 270 tot.

REMARKS: Has a 600-ton lift hook supported by horns extending over the stern, others
beneath the hull. Very large all-purpose salvage ship with submarine-rescue equipment, including several rescue bells and observation chambers.

♦ **9 Prut class** Bldr: U.S.S.R. (In serv. 1960-68)

| ALTAY | VLADIMIR TREFOLEV | SS 21 | SS 26 | SS 83 |
| BESHTAU | ZHIGULI | SS 23 | SS 44 | |

Vladimir Trefolev   1974

SS 26   French Navy, 1979

    D: 2,120 tons (2,640 fl) **S:** 18 kts **Dim:** 86.9 × 13.4 × 4.3
    Electron Equipt: Radar: 1-2/Don-2 and/or Don
    M: 4 diesels; 2 props; 8,000 hp **Man:** 120 tot.

REMARKS: SS—*Spasitel'noye Sudno* (Rescue Ship). One derrick, two or three special
carriers for rescue chambers, submersible decompression chambers for divers, and
salvage observation bells. Four anchor buoys are stowed on inclined racks on the
after deck. One unit was armed for a while with four 57-mm AA (IV × 1) controlled
by a Muff Cob radar director, long since removed.

♦ **13 Modified T-58-class minesweepers** Bldr:. . . (In serv. late 1950s)

GIDROLOG	VALDAY	SS 30	SS 40	SS 48	SS 53
KAZBEK	ZANGEZUR	SS 35	SS 47	SS 50	SS. . .
KHIBINY					

Valday

    D: 725 tons (840 fl) **S:** 18 kts **Dim:** 72.0 × 9.1 × 2.5
    Electron Equipt: Radar: 1/Don-2, 1/Spin Trough
                       Sonar: 1/Tamir
                       IFF: 1/Dead Duck
    M: 2 diesels; 2 props; 4,000 hp **Man:** 60 tot.

SUBMARINE-RESCUE SHIPS (continued)

REMARKS: SS—*Spasitel'noye Sudno* (Rescue Ship). Altered while under construction. Lift rig overhanging the stern to handle divers' gear and submersible decompression chamber. Rescue diving chamber to port, amidships. Can be armed with one 37-mm AA. *Gidrolog* has served as an intelligence-collector. Another was transferred to India.

FLEET REPLENISHMENT SHIPS

Kara-class cruiser Ochakov fueling from the Boris Chilikin   1978

NOTE: In the field of seagoing replenishment, the Soviet Navy has made great progress. With the acquisition of such classes as the *Berezina*, *Boris Chilikin*, and *Dubna* and the modernization of a great many older oilers to enable them to perform alongside fueling under way, the Soviets have made great strides in achieving a large and thoroughly modern afloat logistics force. Furthermore, the navy continues to call on the resources of the Soviet merchant marine, particularly tankers, which still supply a large, if declining, proportion of deployed refuelings. Most of the naval units are now civilian-manned and fly the flag of the Auxiliary Service; for this reason, those that were armed have had their guns and fire-control systems removed or demilitarized.

◆ **1 Berezina class** Bldr: 61 Kommuna SY, Nikolayev (In serv. 1978)

BEREZINA

D: 36,000 tons (fl) **S:** 20-22 kts **Dim:** 208.7 × 24.0 × 11.0

A: 1/SA-N-4 system (II × 1, 18 missiles)—4/57-mm DP (II × 2)—4/30-mm Gatling AA (VI × 4)—2/RBU-1000 ASW RL (VI × 2)—2/Hormone helicopters

Electron Equipt: Radar: 1/Don-2, 2/Don-Kay, 1/Strut Curve, 1/Pop Group, 1/Muff Cob, 2/Bass Tilt

Berezina   1980

Berezina   U.S. Navy, 1979

Berezina   1979

Sonar:. . .

ECM: 2/chaff RL (II × 2)

IFF: 1/High Pole

M: 2 diesels; 2 props; 54,000 hp **Range:** 12,000/18 **Man:** 600 tot.

REMARKS: Soviet type designation: VTR—*Voyenyy Transport* (Military Transport). The largest multipurpose underway replenishment ship yet built for the Soviets and the only one currently to be armed. Can refuel over the stern and from single constant-tension stations on either side, amidships. Solid replenishment is by two sliding-stay, constant-tension transfer rigs on either side. Vertical replenishment is by two specially configured Hormone helicopters hangared in the after superstructure. There are four 10-ton stores-handling cranes to supply ships moored alongside. Cargo: approx. 16,000 tons of fuel oil and diesel fuel, 500 tons fresh water, and 2,000-3,000 tons of provisions, munitions, and combat spares. The very large crew may be accounted for, in part, by a capability to transport crews for spare submarines, for which mooring pockets are provided along the ship's side. No additional units are expected.

◆ **6 Boris Chilikin class** Bldr: Baltic SY, Leningrad (In serv. 1971-78)

BORIS BUTOMA	DNESTR	IVAN BUBNOV
BORIS CHILIKIN	GENRIKH GASANOV	VLADIMIR KOLYACHITSKIY

FLEET REPLENISHMENT SHIPS *(continued)*

Boris Butoma   French Navy, 1979

Dnestr—gunmounts in cylindrical cocoons   French Navy, 1980

D: 8,700 tons light (24,500 fl) **S:** 17 kts **Dim:** 162.3 × 21.4 × 8.9
A: Removed
Electron Equipt: Radar: 2/Don-Kay
           IFF: 1/High Pole B
M: 1 diesel; 9,600 hp **Range:** 10,000/16.6

REMARKS: Soviet type designation: VTR—*Voyenyy Tanker* (Military Tanker). Naval version of the merchant *Velikiy Oktyabr* class. 16,300 dwt. Equipment varies: early units had solid-stores, constant-tension rigs on both sides forward; later units, only to starboard, with liquids to port. All have port and starboard liquid-replenishment stations amidships and can replenish liquids over the stern. Cargo: 13,500 tons liquid (fuel oil, diesel, water); 400 tons ammunition; 400 tons provisions; 400 tons stores. The *Ivan Bubnov* and *Genrikh Gasanov* were completed in merchant colors, without guns, Strut Curve, or Muff Cob; that equipment has now been removed from the other ships, although several retain their gun houses.

♦ **4 Dubna class** Bldr: Rauma-Repola, Rauma, Finland

	In serv.		In serv.
DUBNA	1974	PECHENGA	1978
IRKUT	1975	SVENTA	1979

Sventa   French Navy, 1980

Irkut   1979

D: 4,300 tons light (11,100 fl) **S:** 16 kts **Dim:** 130.1 (126.3 pp) × 20.0 × 7.2
A: None **Electron Equipt:** Radar: 1/Okean
M: 1 Russkiy 8DRPH 23/230, 8-cyl. diesel; 1 prop; 6,000 hp
Electric: 1,485 kVA **Fuel:** 1,056 m³ **Man:** 60 tot.

REMARKS: Soviet type designation: VTR—*Voyenyy Tanker* (Military Tanker). 6,022 grt/6,500 dwt. Cargo: 4,364 m³ heavy fuel oil; 2,646 m³ diesel fuel; 140 m³ cargo water; 537 m³ refrigerated provisions; 810 m³ dry stores. Twenty-seven cargo tanks. Can transfer one-ton loads from constant-tension stations forward. Liquid replenishment from one station on port and starboard, amidships, and over the stern. Additional berths for "turnover crews."

♦ **5 Altay class** Bldr: Rauma-Repola, Rauma, Finland (In serv. 1969-73)

ILIM   IZHORA   KOLA   YEGORLIK   YEL'NYA

D: 2,183 light (2,228 fl) **S:** 14.2 kts **Dim:** 106.0 (97.0 pp) × 15.0 × 6.7
Electron Equipt: Radar: 2/Don-2
           IFF: 1/High Pole A

Izhora   1975

FLEET REPLENISHMENT SHIPS *(continued)*

Ilim 1979

M: 1 Valmet-Burmeister & Wain BM-550 VTBN-110 diesel; 3,250 hp (2,900 sust.)

Electric: 650 kw **Range:** 8,600/12 **Man:** 60 tot.

REMARKS: 3,670 grt/5,045 dwt. All have had an underway replenishment, A-frame kingpost added forward since 1975, permitting them to refuel one ship at a time on either beam. Also able to replenish over stern. Differ in details, heights of masts, etc. More than two dozen sisters in the Soviet merchant marine.

♦ **1 Sofia class** Bldr: U.S.S.R. (In serv. 1969)

AKHTUBA (ex-*Khanoi*)

Akhtuba 1976

D: 62,600 tons (fl) **S:** 17 kts **Dim:** 230.6 × 31.0 × 11.8
M: Steam turbine; 1 prop; 19,000 hp **Boilers:** 2
Range: 20,900/17 **Man:** 70 tot.

REMARKS: 32,840 grt/49,385 dwt. Largest ship in the Soviet Navy. Carries 44,500 tons of liquid cargo. Can refuel over the stern only; primarily used to refuel other tankers, in the Indian Ocean.

♦ **3 Olekhma and Pevek class** Bldr: Rauma-Repola, Rauma, Finland

OLEKHMA   IMAN   ZOLOTOI ROG

D: 6,700 tons (fl) **S:** 14 kts **Dim:** 105.0 × 14.8 × 6.8
Electron Equipt: Radar: 1/Don-2 **M:** 1 Burmeister & Wain diesel; 2,900 hp
Range: 7,900/13.6 **Man:** 40 tot.

REMARKS: The *Zolotoi Rog* belongs to the *Pevek* class. All built in the mid-1960s. 3,300 grt/4,400 dwt. The *Olekhma* was modernized in 1978 with A-frame abaft the

Olekhma—modified for underway replenishment French Navy, 1979

bridge to permit underway fueling of one ship at a time on either beam. The other two may have been similarly upgraded. Predecessor to the *Altay* design but with conventional "three-island" tanker layout. The *Zolotoi Rog* differs very slightly. All can refuel over the stern.

♦ **6 Uda class** Bldr:. . . (In serv. 1962-64)

DUNAY KOIDA LENA SHEKSNA TEREK VISHERA

Lena—with two refueling positions amidships French Navy, 1980

Sheksna—original configuration 1980

FLEET REPLENISHMENT SHIPS *(continued)*

D: 7,100 tons (fl)   **S:** 17 kts   **Dim:** 122.0 × 15.8 × 6.3
A: Removed
Electron Equipt: Radar: 1/Don, 1/Don-2 (or 2/Don-2)
              IFF: High Pole A
M: 2 diesels; 2 props; 8,000 hp   **Man:** 85 tot.

REMARKS: Soviet type designation: VTR—*Voyenyy Tanker* (Military Tanker). Equipped to carry eight 57-mm AA (IV × 2). The *Vishera* and *Lena* have been equipped with a second A-frame kingpost for liquid replenishment, amidships. Three transferred to Indonesia.

♦ 3 Kazbek class

ALATYR'   DESNA   VOLKHOV

Desna   1978

D: 16,250 tons (fl)   **S:** 14 kts   **Dim:** 145.5 × 19.24 × 8.5   **A:** None
Electron Equipt: Radar: 2/Don-2
              IFF: 1/High Pole A
M: 2 Russkiy diesels; 2 props; 4,000 hp   **Range:** 18,000/14   **Man:** 46 tot.

REMARKS: Soviet type designation: VTR—*Voyenyy Tanker* (Military Tanker). Built in the mid-1950s. 8,230 grt/11,800 dwt. Carry 11,600 tons of fuel. The three naval units can be distinguished from their civilian sisters because they have, before the bridge, two tall kingposts and an A-frame kingpost to support fueling hoses and working decks added over the cargo decks before and abaft the bridge. Merchant units of this class are among those most frequently used to support naval forces.

♦ 1 ex-German, ex-Dutch   Bldr: C. van den Giessen, Krimpen, Netherlands

POLYARNIK (ex-*Kärnten*, ex-*Tankboot-I*)

Polyarnik   1975

D: 12,500 tons (fl)   **S:** 17.1 kts   **Dim:** 132.1 (125.0 pp) × 16.15 × 7.6
M: 2 Werkspoor 8-cyl. diesels; 2 props; 7,000 hp   **Man:** 57 tot.

REMARKS: Launched, 3-5-41. War reparations, 30-12-45. Oldest replenishment oiler in any navy. 5,709 grt/6,640 dwt. Liquid cargo 5,600 tons; solid stores and provisions. In the Pacific Fleet.

OILERS

♦ 2 or more Baskunchak class   Bldr: U.S.S.R.

IVAN GOLUBETS   UKHTA

D: 2,940 tons (fl)   **S:** 13.2 kts   **Dim:** 83.6 (74.0 pp) × 12.0 × 4.9
Electron Equipt: Radar: 1/Don-2   **M:** 1 Type 8DR 43/61 VI diesel; 2,000 hp
Electric: 325 kw   **Fuel:** 124 tons   **Range:** 5,000/12.6   **Man:** 30 tot.

REMARKS: 1,768 grt/1,660 dwt. Cargo: 1,490 tons (9,993 bbl.). One sister, *Usedom*, in East German Navy; others in Soviet merchant marine.

♦ 4 Konda class   Bldr: Sweden

KONDA   ROSSOCH'   SOYANA   YAKHROMA

Yakhroma   French Navy, 1981

D: 1,980 tons (fl)   **S:** 12 kts   **Dim:** 69.0 × 10.0 × 4.3
Electron Equipt: Radar: 1-2/Don-2 and/or Spin Trough
M: 1 diesel; 1,600 hp   **Range:** 2,470/10   **Man:** 26 tot.

REMARKS: Built in the mid-1950s. 1,117 grt/1,265 dwt. Can refuel over the stern.

♦ 3 Nercha class   Bldr: Finland (In serv. 1952-55)

KLYAZ'MA   NARVA   NERCHA

Nercha   1967

D: 1,800 tons (fl)   **S:** 11.3 kts   **Dim:** 63.5 × 10.0 × 4.5
Electron Equipt: Radar: 1/Don   **M:** 1 diesel; 1,000 hp

OILERS (continued)

Range: 2,000/10 **Man:** 25 tot.

REMARKS: 1,081 grt/1,127 dwt. Can refuel over the stern.

♦ **17 Khobi class** Bldr: U.S.S.R.

ALAZAN	BAYMAK	CHEREMSHAN	GORYN	INDIGA	KHOBI
LOVAT'	METAN	ORSHA	SASHA	SEIMA	SHELON'
SOS'VA	SYSOLA	TARTU	TITAN	TUNGUSKA	

Lovat' 1978

D: 1,525 tons (fl) **S:** 12 kts **Dim:** 62.0 × 10.0 × 4.4
Electron Equipt: Radar: 1/Don-2, 1/Spin Trough
　　　　　　　　IFF: High Pole A
M: 2 diesels; 2 props; 1,600 hp **Man:** 29 tot.

REMARKS: Built in the early 1950s, now being discarded. 795 grt. Refuel over bows while being towed by receiving ship. *Linda* and one other went to Albania in 1959; others to Indonesia.

♦ **1 ex-German Dora class** Bldr: D. W. Kremer Sohn, Elmshorn (In serv. 1941-43)

IZHMA (ex-. . .)

D: 973 tons (fl) **S:** 12 kts **Dim:** 61.0 (56.5 pp) × 9.0 × 2.75
A: None **Electron Equipt:** Radar: . . .
M: 2 M.W.M. 6-cyl. diesels; 2 props; 900 hp **Fuel:** 17.5 tons
Range: 1,200/12 **Man:** 26 tot.

REMARKS: One of a group of four Luftwaffe aviation-fuel tankers—*Dora, Else, Grete,* and *Hanna*—all of which passed into British hands in 5-45 and went to the U.S.S.R. in 1946. The others may also remain in service. 638 grt. Cargo: 331 tons.

♦ **1 ex-German Usedom class** Bldr: Howaldtswerke, Hamburg (In serv. 5-42)

FEOLENT (ex-*Empire Tegadea*, ex-*Jeverland*) (L: 15-6-38)

D: 5,250 tons (fl) **S:** 15.5 kts **Dim:** 96.16 × 13.8 × 5.56
A: None **Electron Equipt:** Radar: . . .
M: 2 Schichau diesels; 2 props; 3,500 hp **Man:** 64 tot.

REMARKS: Completed by Burmeister & Wain. Turned over to Great Britain in 5-45, later to the U.S.S.R. 2,579 grt. Cargo: 2,600 tons of fuel oil. In Black Sea Fleet.

WATER TANKERS

♦ **2 Manych class** Bldr: Vyborg SY

MANYCH (In serv. 1971) TAYGIL (In serv. 1977)

Manych—when armed 1974

Taygil 1977

D: 6,500 tons (8,600 fl) **S:** 18 kts **Dim:** 115.0 × 15.5 × 7.0
A: Removed **Electron Equipt:** Radar: 2/Don-Kay; *Manych* also: 2/Muff Cob
M: 2 diesels; 2 props; 9,000 hp **Man:** 90 tot.

REMARKS: Originally intended to be small replenishment oilers to carry fuel and solid stores for submarines. Reported in the Soviet press as unsuccessful. *Manych* was assigned as a water tender to support the Mediterranean Squadron. Her four 57-mm guns were removed in 1975. *Taygil* was completed without armament.

♦ **14 Voda class** Bldr:. . . (In serv. 1950s)

ABAKAN	VODOLEY-3	MVT 10	MVT 18	MVT 134
SURA	MVT 6	MVT 16	MVT 20	MVT 138
VODOLEY-2	MVT 9	MVT 17	MVT 21	

WATER TANKERS *(continued)*

Voda class   1972

   D: 2,100 tons (3,100 fl)   **S:** 12 kts   **Dim:** 81.5 × 11.5 × 4.3
   Electron Equipt: Radar: 1/Neptune or Don-2
   M: 2 diesels; 2 props; 1,600 hp   **Man:** 40 tot.

REMARKS: MVT—*Morskoy Vodnyy Tanker* (Seagoing Water Tanker).

SPECIAL-LIQUIDS TANKERS

♦ **1 Ural class** Bldr:. . . (In serv. 1969)

URAL

Ural   1969

   D: 2,000 tons (fl)   **S:** 12 kts   **Dim:** 80.0 × 12.0 × 4.5
   Electron Equipt: Radar: 1/Spin Trough   **M:** 2 diesels; 1 prop; 1,200 hp

REMARKS: Transports liquid nuclear waste. High freeboard, superstructure aft, traveling crane.

♦ **9 Luza class**

ALAMBAY	BARGUZIN	KANA	SASIMA	YENISEY
ARAGUY	DON	OKA	SELENGA	

   D: 1,500 tons (fl)   **S:** 12 kts   **Dim:** 62.0 × 10.5 × 4.2
   Electron Equipt: Radar: 1/Don-2   **M:** 1 diesel; 1,000 hp

Don   1971

REMARKS: Built in the 1960s. Carry volatile liquids, probably missile fuel.

♦ **5 Vala class**

   D: 3,100 tons (fl)   **S:** 14 kts   **Dim:** 76.2 × 12.5 × 5.0
   M: 1 diesel; 1,000 hp   **Range:** 2,000/11

REMARKS: Carry waste liquids from nuclear-propulsion plants.

TRANSPORT

♦ **1 Mikhail Kalinin class**

   Bldr: Mathias Thesen Werft, Wismar, East Germany (In serv. 1963)

KUBAN (ex-*Nadezhda Krupskaya*)

Kuban

TRANSPORT *(continued)*

D: 6,400 tons (fl)   **S:** 18 kts   **Dim:** 122.2 × 16.0 × 5.1
A: None   **Electron Equipt:** Radar: 2/Don-2
M: 2 M.A.N. 6-cyl. diesels; 2 props; 8,000 hp   **Range:** 8,100/17

REMARKS: Former passenger-cargo ship used to rotate crews on ships in the Mediterranean Squadron. 5,260 grt/1,354 dwt. Can carry 340 passengers, 1,000 tons of cargo.

CARGO SHIPS

NOTE: Cargo ships are usually referred to as VTR—*Voyenyy Transport* (Military Transport).

♦ **4 (+. . .) Ivan Antonov class** Bldr:. . . (In serv. 1978-. . .)

IVAN ANTONOV   IVAN ASDNEV   IVAN LEDNEV   IRBIT

D: 5,200 tons (fl)   **S:** 16 kts   **Dim:** 95.0 × 14.7 ×. . .
A: None (see Remarks)   **M:** 1 diesel; 1 prop;. . . hp

REMARKS: Specialized supply ships for remote garrisons of the KGB Border Guard in the Pacific area. Carry a small landing craft aft. Position for a twin 30-mm AA on the forecastle and two twin machine guns amidships.

♦ **1 Amguema class** Bldr: U.S.S.R. (In serv. 1975)

YAUZA

Yauza   1976

D: 15,100 tons (fl)   **S:** 15 kts   **Dim:** 133.1 × 18.9 × 9.1
Electron Equipt: Radar: 2/Don-2
M: 4 1,800-hp diesels, electric drive; 1 prop; 7,200 hp   **Range:** 10,000/15

REMARKS: 7,900 grt/9,045 dwt. Icebreaking passenger-cargo ship. Cargo: 6,600 tons. Numerous merchant sisters.

♦ **4 Yuniy Partizan class** Bldr: Romania (In serv. 1975-78)

PECHORA   PINEGA   TURGAY   UFA

Turgay   1977

D: 3,947 tons (fl)   **S:** 12.9 kts   **Dim:** 88.75 (80.25 pp) × 12.8 × 5.2   **A:** None
Electron Equipt: Radar: 1/Don-2
                    IFF: 1/High Pole A
M: 1 diesel; 2,080 hp   **Range:** 4,000/12   **Man:** 25 tot.

REMARKS: 2,079 grt/2,150 dwt. Small container ships. Three 10-ton cranes, one of which can be rigged to lift 28 tons. Cargo: 3,200 m³. Originally intended to be able to carry fifty-eight standard cargo containers. Twenty sisters are civilian.

♦ **8 Vytegrales class** Bldr: Zhdanov SY, Leningrad (In serv. 1963-66)

APSHERON (ex-*Tosnales*)	DONBASS (ex-*Kirishi*)
BASKUNCHAK (ex-*Vostok-4*)	SEVAN (ex-*Vyborgles*)
DAURIYA (ex-*Suzdal*)	TAMAN' (ex-*Vostok-3*)
DIKSON (ex-*Vagales*)	YAMAL (ex-*Svirles*)

Sevan   1979

CARGO SHIPS (continued)

Yamal—with Hormone helicopter on deck   1979

D: 9,650 tons (fl)   **S:** 16 kts   **Dim:** 121.9 × 16.7 × 7.3   **A:** None
Electron Equipt: Radar: 2/Don-2   IFF: 1/High Pole B   **Range:** 7,380/14.5
M: 1 Burmeister & Wain 950 VTBF 110 diesel; 1 prop; 5,200 hp   **Man:** 90 tot.

REMARKS: Originally built as merchant timber-carriers, then converted as space-event
support ships by the addition of more communications facilities and a helicopter
platform over the stern—consequently losing access to the after hold. They carry
one Hormone helicopter but have no hangar. Now used as fleet supply ships. *Donbass*
has a Big Net air-search radar. All retain three holds forward, except *Dikson*, which
has a deckhouse over hold number three. Seven sisters were converted to serve the
Academy of Sciences as satellite-tracking ships.

♦ **9 Keyla class** Bldr: Hungary (In serv. 1960-66)

MEZEN'	PONOY	TERIBERKA	UNZHA	YERUSLAN
ONEGA	RITSA	TULOMA	USSURI	

D: 2,000 tons (fl)   **S:** 12 kts   **Dim:** 78.5 × 10.5 × 4.6
A: None   **Electron Equipt:** Radar: 1/Don-2 or Spin Trough
M: 1 diesel; 1 prop; 1,000 hp   **Range:** 4,200/10.7   **Man:** 26 tot.

REMARKS: 1,296 grt/1,280 dwt. Carry 1,100 tons of cargo. *Ritsa* has a deckhouse over
her after hatch and numerous communications antennas.

♦ **3 MP-6-class former landing ships** Bldr: Hungary (In serv. 1959-60)

BIRA   IRGIZ   VOLOGDA

D: 2,100 tons (fl)   **S:** 12 kts   **Dim:** 75.0 × 11.3 × 4.4
M: 1 diesel; 1 prop; 1,000 hp

REMARKS: Unsuccessful as landing ships, bow doors welded closed. Sisters *Bureya*
and *Khoper* serve as missile transports.

♦ **3 Andizhan class** Bldr: Neptunwerft, Rostock, East Germany (In serv. 1959-60)

ONDA   POSET   YEMETSK

D: 6,739 tons (fl)   **S:** 13.5 kts   **Dim:** 104.2 × 14.4 × 6.6   **M:** 1 diesel; 1,890 hp
A: None   **Electron Equipt:** Radar: 1/Don-2   **Range:** 6,000/13.5   **Man:** 43 tot.

REMARKS: 3,368 grt/4,324 dwt. Cargo: 3,954 tons. Two naval sisters are now missile
transports; other sisters are in the merchant service.

Bira   1975

♦ **4 Chulym class** Bldr: Szczecin SY, Poland (In serv. 1953-57)

INSAR   KAMCHATKA   LENINSK-KUZNETSKIY   SEVERODONETSK

D: 5,050 tons (fl)   **S:** 12 kts   **Dim:** 101.9 × 14.6 × 6.0
A: None   **Electron Equipt:** Radar: 1/Don-2
M: Reciprocating steam with auxiliary GT; 1 prop; 1,650 hp
Boilers: 2, watertube   **Range:** 5,000/11.5   **Man:** 41 tot.

REMARKS: 2,135 grt/3,120 dwt. 2,240 tons of cargo.

♦ **1 Donbass class** Bldr: Szczecin SY, Poland (In serv. 1955)

SVIR

D: 7,200 tons (fl)   **S:** 12 kts   **Dim:** 108.2 × 14.6 × 7.2
A: None   **Electron Equipt:** Radar: 1/Neptune
M: Reciprocating steam; 1 prop; 2,300 hp   **Boilers:** 2, watertube
Range: 9,800/12

REMARKS: 3,561 grt/4,864 dwt. 3,570 tons of cargo. Originally a coal-burning collier.

♦ **3 Kolomna class** Bldr: Neptunwerft, Rostock (In serv. 1952-54)

KRASNOARMEYSK   MEGRA   SVANETIYA

Svanetiya   1976

D: 6,700 tons (fl)   **S:** 13 kts   **Dim:** 102.3 × 14.4 × 6.6
Electron Equipt: Radar: 1/Don-2, 1/Neptune
                     IFF: 1/High Pole A
M: Reciprocating steam plus GT; 1 prop; 2,450 hp
Range: 6,890/13   **Man:** 44 tot.

CARGO SHIPS (continued)

REMARKS: 3,758 grt/4,355 dwt. Cargo: 3,634 tons. Coal-burners. Six sisters serve as *Atrek*-class submarine tenders. Sister *Kuznetsk* discarded.

♦ **3 Telnovsk class** Bldr: Hungary (In serv. 1949-57)

BUREVESTNIK   LAG   MANOMETR

   D: 1,700 tons (fl) **S:** 11 kts **Dim:** 70.0 × 10.0 × 4.2
   M: 1 diesel; 800 hp **Range:** 3,300/9.7 **Man:** 40 tot.

REMARKS: 1,194 grt/1,133 dwt. Several others serve as survey ships. Being discarded.

♦ **up to 25 Khabarovsk class** Bldr: U.S.S.R. (In serv. 1950s)

   D: 600 tons (fl) **S:** 9.5 kts **Dim:** 46.4 × 8.0 × 3.2
   Electron Equipt: Radar: 1/Neptune or Don **M:** 1 diesel; 600 hp

REMARKS: 402 dwt. Some are civilian, others may be degaussing tenders.

PROVISION SHIPS

♦ **8 Mayak class** Bldr: U.S.S.R. (In serv. 1971-76)

BUZULUK	LAMA	NEMAN	ULMA
ISHIM	MIUS	RIONI	VYTEGRA

Buzuluk   French Navy, 1978

   D: 1,050 tons (fl) **S:** 11 kts **Dim:** 54.3 × 9.3 × 3.6
   A: None **Electron Equipt:** Radar: 1/Spin Trough
   M: 1 diesel; 800 hp **Range:** 9,400/11 **Man:** 29 tot.

REMARKS: 690 grt. Former trawlers. Refrigerated fish holds are used to carry provisions. Other naval sisters operate as intelligence-collectors.

AMMUNITION SHIPS

♦ **9 Muna class**

   D: 680 tons (fl) **S:** 11 kts **Dim:** 51.0 × 8.5 × 2.7
   Electron Equipt: Radar: 1/Spin Trough **IFF:** 1/High Pole A
   M: 1 diesel; 600 hp **Man:** 40 tot.

REMARKS: When deployed, carry VTR—*Voyenyy Transport* (Military Transport) numbers, but in home waters are listed as MBSS—*Morskaya Barzha Samokhodnaya Sukhogruznaya* (Seagoing Self-Propelled Dry-Cargo Lighter). Specialized transports for torpedoes and surface-to-air missiles.

Muna class

MOORING TENDERS

♦ **10 Sura class** Bldr: Neptunwerft, Rostock, East Germany (In serv. 1965-72, 1976-78)

KIL 1	KIL 21	KIL 23	KIL 29	KIL 32
KIL 2	KIL 22	KIL 27	KIL 31	KIL 33

KIL 32   1980

   D: 2,370 tons (3,150 fl) **S:** 13 kts **Dim:** 87.0 (68.0 pp) × 14.8 × 5.0
   A: None **Electron Equipt:** Radar: 2/Don-2
   M: 4 diesels, electric drive; 2 props; 2,240 hp **Range:** 4,000/10

REMARKS: KIL—*Kilektor* (Mooring Tender). 2,366 grt. 890 tons of cargo in hold amidships. Stern rig, which can lift 60 tons, is used for buoy-handling and salvage. Can also carry several hundred tons of cargo fuel.

♦ **14 Neptun class** Bldr: Neptunwerft, Rostock, East Germany (In serv. 1957-60)

KIL 3	KIL 6	KIL 12	KIL 15	KIL 17	KIL. . .	KIL. . .
KIL 5	KIL 9	KIL 14	KIL 16	KIL 18	KIL. . .	KIL. . .

   D: 700 tons (1,240 fl) **S:** 12 kts **Dim:** 57.3 (46.5 pp) × 11.4 × 3.4
   M: 2 triple-expansion; 1,000 hp **Range:** 1,000/11 **Man:** 41 tot.

REMARKS: KIL—*Kilektor* (Mooring Tender). Most burn coal. 80-ton bow lift for buoy-handling and salvage.

MOORING TENDERS *(continued)*

Neptun class

CABLE LAYERS

♦ **3 Emba class** Bldr: Wärtsilä SY, Turku, Finland

EMBA (In serv. 5-80)   NEPRYADVA (L: 24-4-81)   SETUN (L: 29-4-81)

    D: 2,050 tons (fl)   **S:** 11 kts   **Dim:** 75.9 × 12.6 × 3.0
    M: 2 Wärtsilä Vasa 6R22 diesels; 1 prop; 1,360 hp   **Man:** 38 tot.

REMARKS: 1,900 grt. Cargo: 300 tons cable. Intended for use in shallow coastal areas, rivers, and harbors. Intended to replace the Kalar class.

♦ **8 Klazma class** Bldr: Wärtsilä SY, Turku, Finland (In serv. 1962-78)

DONETS	INGURI	TAVDA	YANA
INGUL	KATUN'	TSNA	ZEYA

Klazma class—later unit

    D: 6,920 tons (fl)   **S:** 14 kts   **Dim:** 130.4 (120.0 pp) × 16.0 × 5.75
    Electron Equipt: Radar: 2/Don-2
    M: 5 1,000-hp Wärtsilä 624TS diesels, electric drive; 4,400 hp
    Fuel: 250 tons   **Range:** 12,000/14   **Man:** 110 tot.

REMARKS: 5,760 grt/3,750 dwt. *Ingul* and *Yana*, the first built, have four 2,436-hp diesels, a longer forecastle, and are 5,645 grt/3,400 dwt (6,810 tons fl). All have ice-strengthened hulls. In the later units, the diesel engines drive five 680-kw gener-

ators, which provide power for propulsion and for all auxiliary functions. Soviet type designation: KS—*Kabel'noye Sudno* (Cable Ship). All cable machinery built by Submarine Cables, Ltd., Great Britain. *Katun'* carries 1,850 m³ of cable and displaces 7,885 tons (fl), drawing 5.76 m; she capsized while fitting out. The others have 3 cable tanks totaling 1,600 m³. *Ingul* refitted in Japan 1978, receiving new Dowty paired-wheel cable gear. All have a 500-hp active rudder and a bow-thruster.

♦ **1 Telnovsk class** Bldr: Hungary (In serv. early 1950s)

KS-7

    D: 1,700 tons (fl)   **S:** 11 kts   **Dim:** 73.0 × 10.0 × 4.2
    M: 1 diesel; 1 prop; 800 hp   **Range:** 3,300/9.7

REMARKS: Converted small cargo ship; cable sheaves project 3 m out past bow. In Pacific Fleet.

FLEET TUGS

♦ **3 Goryn class** Bldr: Rauma-Repola, Rauma, Finland (In serv. 1977-78)

MB 105   BAYKALSK   MB 18   BEREZINSK   MB 119   BILBINO

Baykalsh (MB 105)   1978

    D: 2,600 tons (fl)   **S:** 13.5 kts   **Dim:** 63.5 × 14.3 × 5.1
    Electron Equipt: Radar: 2/Don-2
    M: 1 Russkiy 67N diesel; 3,500 hp   **Man:** 40 tot.

REMARKS: Soviet type designation: MB—*Morskoy Buksir* (Seagoing Tug). 1,600 grt. 35-ton pull. For ocean towing, salvage, and fire-fighting. Sister *Bolshevetsk* lost 2-79 off Japan.

♦ **15 (+ . . .) Sorum class** Bldr: U.S.S.R. (In serv. 1974-. . .)

AMUR	PRIMORSK	ZABAYKALYE	MB 115
BREST	PRIMORYE	MB 6	MB 119
KAMCHATKA	SAKHALIN	MB 25	MB 148
LADOGA	YAN BERZIN'	MB 112	

    D: 1,210 tons (1,656 fl)   **S:** 14 kts   **Dim:** 58.3 × 12.6 × 4.6
    A: Named units only: 4/30-mm AA (II × 2)
    Electron Equipt: Radar: 2/Don-2
                        IFF: 1/High Pole B
    M: 2 5-2D42 diesels, electric drive; 1 prop; 1,500 hp
    Fuel: 322 tons   **Range:** 6,720/13   **Man:** 35 tot.

FLEET TUGS *(continued)*

Sakhalin—armed KGB Amur-class seagoing tug   1975

REMARKS: Units with names are manned by the KGB and are typed PSKR—*Pogran-ichnyy Storozhevoy Korabl'* (Border Patrol Ship); MB in naval units means *Morskoy Buksir* (Seagoing Tug).

♦ **51 Okhtenskiy class** Bldr: Okhtenskiy SY, Leningrad (In serv. 1960s)

Okhtenskiy class (MB 173)   1965

    D: 700 tons (950 fl)   **S:** 13.3 kts   **Dim:** 47.3 × 10.3 × 5.5
    Electron Equipt: Radar: 1/Don-2 or Spin Trough   **IFF:** 1/High Pole
    M: 2 diesels; 1 prop; 1,500 hp   **Range:** 7,800/7   **Man:** 40 tot.

REMARKS: Several have two 57-mm AA (II × 1) and are probably manned by the KGB for use as patrol ships. Units with names are civilian; naval units have MB—*Morskoy Buksir* (Seagoing Tug) or SB—*Spastel'noye Buksir* (Rescue Tug) hull numbers; the latter carry an "unsinkable" lifeboat to port.

♦ **18 Roslavl class** Bldr: U.S.S.R. (In serv. 1960s)

MB 94—Roslavl class   1975

    D: 750 tons (fl)   **S:** 11 kts   **Dim:** 44.5 × 9.5 × 3.5
    M: Diesel-electric; 2 props; 1,200 hp   **Man:** 28 tot.

REMARKS: All have MB pendants—*Morskoy Buksir* (Seagoing Tug).

♦ **10-12 Zenit class** Bldr: Finland (In serv. 1948-55)

    D: 800 tons (fl)   **S:** 10 kts   **Dim:** 47.9 × 10.0 × 4.3
    M: Reciprocating steam; 2 props; 800 hp   **Range:** 10,000/8

REMARKS: Well over one hundred of this class were built as war reparations. A number remain in service with the merchant marine, also.

SALVAGE AND RESCUE SHIPS

♦ **2 Pioneer Moskvyy-class salvage ships** Bldr: Vyborg SY

MIKHAIL RUDNITSKIY (In serv. 1979)   GIORGIY KOZMIN (In serv. 1980)

    D: 10,000 tons (fl)   **S:** 15.4 kts   **Dim:** 130.3 (119.0 pp) × 17.3 × 6.93
    A: None   **Electron Equipt:** Radar: 2/Don-2
    M: 1 5DKRN 62/140-3 diesel; 1 prop; 6,100 hp   **Electric:** 1,500 kw
    Man: 120 tot.

REMARKS: Modification of a standard merchant timber-carrier/container ship design, retaining two holds. The after hold has two superstructure levels built over it, and the small hold forward has been plated over. Retains two 40-ton and two 20-ton booms and has had heavy cable fairleads cut in the bulwarks fore and aft and a number of boat booms added to starboard. Carry the ensign of the Naval Salvage and Rescue Service and are named for important developers of research/salvage submersibles.

SALVAGE AND RESCUE SHIPS (continued)

Giorgiy Kozmin—with Prut-class submarine rescue ship alongside   French Navy, 1980

Mikhail Rudnitskiy   1979

♦ **2 Ingul class** Bldr: Admiralty SY, Leningrad (In serv. 1975-77)

PAMIR (In serv. 1975) MASHUK (In serv. 1972)

    D: 3,200 tons (4,050 fl) **S:** 20 kts **Dim:** 92.8 × 15.4 × 5.8
    Electron Equipt: Radar: 2/Don-2
                     IFF: 1/High Pole B, 1/Square Head
    M: 2 type 58D-4R diesels; 2 props; 9,000 hp
    Range: 9,000/18.7 **Man:** 120 tot.

REMARKS: Two sisters, *Yaguar* and *Bars*, are in the Merchant Marine. Very powerful tugs with constant-tension highline personnel rescue system, salvage pumps, fire-fighting equipment, and complete diving gear. Large bulbous bow.

Pamir   1975

♦ **2 Pamir class** Bldr: Gävle, Sweden (In serv. 1958)

AGATAN   ALDAN

Agatan

    D: 1,443 tons (2,240 fl) **S:** 17.5 kts **Dim:** 78.0 × 12.8 × 4.0
    Electron Equipt: Radar: 1-2/Don and/or Don-2
    M: 2 M.A.N. G10V 40/60 diesels; 2 CP props; 4,200 hp **Range:** 15,200/17.5; 21,800/12

REMARKS: 1,443 grt. One 10-ton and two 1.5-ton booms. Carries fixed fire pumps with 2,600 tons/hour capacity and portable pumps with 1,650 tons/hour capacity. Can support divers to a depth of 90 m, and have decompression chambers and powerful air-compressors. Two sisters, the *Gidrograf* and *Peleng*, are intelligence collectors.

♦ **3 Orel class** Bldr: Finland

    D: 1,200 tons (1,760 fl) **S:** 15 kts **Dim:** 61.3 × 11.9 × 4.5
    Electron Equipt: Radar: 1/Don or Don-2
    M: 1 M.A.N. G5Z52/70 diesel; 1,700 hp
    Range: 13,000/13.5 **Man:** 37 tot.

REMARKS: SB—*Spastel'noye Buksir* (Rescue Tug). Built in the late 1950s. Several civilian sisters, including the *Stremitel'nyy*, serve the fishing fleet.

SALVAGE AND RESCUE SHIPS (continued)

SB 43—Orel class 1979

SEAGOING FIRE BOATS

♦ **8 (+. . .) Katun class** Bldr: U.S.S.R. (In serv. 1970-. . .)

| PZHS 64 | PZHS 96 | PZHS 123 | PZHS 124 |
| PZHS 209 | PZHS 282 | PZHS. . . | PZHS. . . |

Katun class

D: 1,016 tons (fl) **S:** 17 kts **Dim:** 62.6 × 10.2 × 3.6
Electron Equipt: Radar: 1/Don-2
                IFF: 1/High Pole B
M: 2 40DM diesels; 2 props; 4,000 hp **Range:** 2,200/16 **Man:** 32 tot.

REMARKS: Originally PDS—*Pozharno-Degazatsionnoye Sudno* (Fire-Fighting and Decontamination Ship); this designation later revised to PZHS—*Pozharnoye Sudno* (Fire-Fighting Ship). Extensive fire-fighting gear, including extendable boom. Powerful pumps. There are several civilian sisters, including the *General Gamidov*. PZHS 64, completed 1981, is the first of a new type, approx. 3 m longer and having an extra level to the superstructure.

HOSPITAL SHIPS

♦ **2 Ob' class** Bldr: A. Warski SY, Szczecin, Poland

OB' (In serv. 1980)   YENESEY (In serv. 1981)

Ob' Skyfotos, Ltd., 1980

Ob' French Navy, 1980

D: 9,000 tons (fl) **S:** 16-18 kts **Dim:** 150.0 (138.0 pp) × 18.5 × 5.7
Electron Equipt: Radar: 3/Don-2 **M:** 2 diesels; 2 props; . . . hp

REMARKS: Have civilian crews but carry uniformed naval medical personnel. Have 100 beds, 7 operating rooms. The hangar aft can accommodate a Hormone-C utility helicopter. Bow-thrusters fitted. *Ob'* left the Baltic for the Pacific Fleet in 9-80; *Yenesey* is in the Black Sea Fleet.

INTELLIGENCE COLLECTORS (AGI)

NOTE: Many of the Soviet ships of this type, often designated ELINT (electronic intelligence) or SIGINT (signal intelligence) collectors, look like trawlers; others, such as the *Primorye* class and the new Bal'zam class are obviously configured for their roles. No pretense is made that the AGIs are anything but intelligence collectors, which detect and analyze radioelectric and electromagnetic signals. Some of them patrol offshore from the home ports of ballistic-missile submarines, others follow Western fleets.

♦ **1 Al'pinist class** Bldr: U.S.S.R. (In serv. 1981)

GS 39

D: 1,202 tons (fl) **S:** 13 kts **Dim:** 53.7 (46.2 pp) × 10.5 × 4.3
Electron Equipt: Radar: 1/Don-2
M: 1 Type 8NVD48-2U diesel; 1 CP prop; 1,320 hp
Fuel: 162 tons **Range:** 7,600/13

INTELLIGENCE COLLECTORS (AGI) *(continued)*

GS 39—Al'pinist class   French Navy, 1981

REMARKS: One of several hundred 322-dwt stern-haul trawlers, in this case modified as an intelligence collector, although there are few identifiable intercept antennas. The 218-m³ former fish hold may provide electronics and/or additional accommodations spaces. Others of the class may be adapted to replace the older Okean-trawler-class collectors.

♦ **1 (+ . . .) Bal'zam class** Bldr: Kaliningrad SY(?) (In serv. 1980-. . .)

SSV 516

    D: 4,500 tons (fl) **S:** 22 kts **Dim:** 105.0 × 15.0 × 6.0
    A: 1/30-mm Gatling AA—2/SA-N-5 syst. (IV × 2,. . . Grail missiles)
    Electron Equipt: Radar: 2/Don-Kay
    M: 2 diesels; 2 props; 9,000 hp **Man:** 200 tot.

SSV 516—Bal'zam class   U.S. Navy, 1980

SSV 516   French Navy, 1980

REMARKS: SSV—*Sudno Svyazyy* (Communications Vessel). Evidently the prototype for a built-for-the-purpose intelligence-collection-and-processing ship design, wholly military in concept. The two spherical radomes probably house satellite transmitting and receiving antennas. There are numerous intercept and direction-finding antenna arrays. Equipped to refuel under way and to transfer solid cargo and personnel via constant-tension rigs on either side of the after mast. There is only a remote "kolonka" pedestal director for the Gatling gun, no radar GFCS.

♦ **6 Primor'ye class**

SSV 591 Kavkaz	SSV 465 Primor'ye	SSV. . . Zakarpat'ye
SSV. . . Krym	SSV 454 Zabaykal'ye	SSV. . . Zaporozh'ye

    D: 2,600 tons (3,700 fl) **S:** 12 kts **Dim:** 84.7 × 14.0 × 5.5
    Electron Equipt: Radar: 2/Don-Kay
    M: 2 diesels; 1 prop; 2,000 hp **Man:** 160 tot.

REMARKS: Although these ships resemble small passenger liners, they are in fact modified versions of *Mayakovsky*-class stern-haul factory trawlers. They have the most extensive arrays and are the newest and largest of the Soviet ELINT/SIGINT ships. All given SSV—*Sudno Svyazyy* (Communications Vessel) pendants, and names obliterated, 1979-81. Carry hand-held Grail SAMs.

Kavkaz (SSV 591)   French Navy, 1979

INTELLIGENCE COLLECTORS (AGI) *(continued)*

Primor'ye (SSV 465)—goal post mast aft deleted   1981

◆ **9 Moma class** Bldr: Polnocny SY, Gdansk, Poland (In serv. 1968–74)

SSV 512 ARKHIPELAG	SSV. . . KIL'DIN	SSV 514 SELIGER
SSV. . . EKVATOR	SSV 506 NAKHODKA	SSV 501 VEGA
GS 117 IL'MEN	SSV. . . PELORUS	SSV. . . YUPITER

D: 1,260 tons (1,540 fl) **S:** 17 kts **Dim:** 73.3 × 10.8 × 3.8
Electron Equipt: Radar: 2/Don-2 **Range:** 8,000/11 **Man:** 80–120 tot.
M: 2 Zgoda-Sulzer 6TD48 diesels; 2 CP props; 3,600 hp

Arkhipelag (SSV 512)—long deckhouse forward   French Navy, 1980

Yupiter—short deckhouse forward   1976

Nakhodka (SSV 506)—deckhouse atop bridge   1980

REMARKS: Ex-survey ships/buoy tenders. The *Yupiter* (see photo) and *Arkhipelag* have new superstructures in the area forward of the bridge and new masts. The others are much less modified, most having only a few canvas-covered antennas atop the bridge and "vans" for support equipment. Several carry 2/SA-N-5 systems (IV × 2,. . . Grail missiles).

◆ **8 Mayak class** Bldr:. . . (In serv. 1967–70)

ANEROYD	KHERSONES	KURSOGRAF	GS 239
GIRORULEVOY (GS 536)	KURS	LADOGA	GS 242

GS 242—poop deck extended   1977

Ladoga—now with 4/14.5-mm mg atop deckhouse fwd, radomes aft   1979

INTELLIGENCE COLLECTORS (AGI) *(continued)*

Girorulevoy (GS 536)—extended superstructure, radome atop bridge

French Navy, 1981

D: 1,050 tons (fl) **S:** 11 kts **Dim:** 54.2 × 9.3 × 3.6
Electron Equipt: Radar: 1-2/Don-2 and/or Spin Trough
M: 1 8NVD48 diesel; 800 hp **Range:** 9,400/11 **Man:** 60 tot.

REMARKS: GS—*Gidrograficheskoye Sudno* (Hydrographic Survey Ship), an interest-
ing euphemism. These ships vary greatly in appearance and equipment carried.
Several carry hand-held SA-7 Grail missiles, and *Ladoga* was given 4/14.5-mm mg
(II × 2) in 1980.

◆ **3 Nikolay Zubov class** Bldr: Poland

SSV 503 KHARITON LAPTEV   SSV. . . GAVRIL SARYCHEV
SSV 469 SEMYEN CHELYUSHKIN

D: 2,200 tons (3,100 fl) **S:** 16.5 kts **Dim:** 90.0 × 13.0 × 4.7
Electron Equipt: Radar: 2/Don-2 (SSV 469 also: 1/Strut Curve
                           IFF: 1/High Pole B
M: 2 Zgoda 85D48 diesels; 2 props; 4,800 hp **Range:** 11,000/14 **Man:** 100 tot.

Semyen Chelyushkin (SSV 469)   1980

Gavril Sarychev (now SSV. . .)   1979

REMARKS: Ex-oceanographic ships. Similar to oceanographic sisters, but have a collection of antenna arrays. The *Gavril Sarychev* has been extensively reconstructed:
her forecastle has been extended to her stern, an extra deck has been added to her
superstructure and 3/SA-N-5 positions (IV × 3) have been added.

◆ **2 Pamir class** Bldr: Gävle, Sweden (In serv. 1958)

SSV 480 GIDROGRAF   SSV 477 PELENG (ex-*Pamir*)

Gidrograf (SSV 840)   1980

D: 1,443 tons (2,300 fl) **S:** 17.5 kts **Dim:** 78.0 × 12.8 × 4.0
A: 3/SA-N-5 syst. (IV × 3,. . . Grail missiles)
Electron Equipt: Radar: 2/Don-2
M: 2 M.A.N. G10V 40/60 diesels; 2 CP props; 4,200 hp
Range: 15,200/17.5; 21,000/12 **Man:** 120 tot.

REMARKS: Ex-rescue tugs. Both heavily modified: extra deckhouse levels, extended
forecastle, numerous collection antenna arrays, etc. Their extremely long endurance
makes them invaluable in the Pacific and Indian oceans. Sisters *Agatan* and *Aldan*
are salvage ships. Redesignated SSV—*Sudno Svyazyy* (Communications Vessel) in
1979-80.

◆ **4 Mirnyy class**

BAKAN   LOTSMAN   VAL   VERTIKAL

INTELLIGENCE COLLECTORS (AGI) *(continued)*

Lotsman   1979

D: 850 tons (1,300 fl)   **S:** 17.5 kts   **Dim:** 63.6 × 9.5 × 4.5
Electron Equipt: Radar: 2/Don-2
M: 4 6-cyl. diesels, electric drive; 1 prop; 4,000 hp   **Range:** 18,700/11
Man: 60 tot.

REMARKS: Ex-whalers. Differ in detail. Very low freeboard amidships. Have two SA-7 Grail hand-launch positions. All received new deckhouse forward during 1970s.

♦ **15 Okean class** Bldr: East Germany (In serv. 1962-1967)

ALIDADA	DEFLEKTOR	LINZA	TEODOLIT
AMPERMETR	EKHOLOT	LOTLIN' (GS 319)	TRAVERS
BAROGRAF	GIDROFON	REDUKTOR	ZOND
BAROMETR	KRENOMETR	REPITER	

D: 700 tons (fl)   **S:** 11 kts   **Dim:** 50.8 × 8.9 × 3.7
Electron Equipt: Radar: 1-2/Don-2   **M:** 1 diesel; 540 hp
Range: 7,900/11   **Man:** 60 tot.

Linza—poop deck extended   1974

Ekholot   R.N., 1980

Barograf—now with 4/14.5-mm mg (II × 2) on forecastle   U.S. Navy, 1976

REMARKS: Ex-trawlers. Appearances vary greatly, many having had their poop deck extended well forward of the bridge superstructure and their port sides plated in (see photo of the *Linza*). *Barograf* has 4/14.5-mm mg (II × 2), and most carry SA-7 Grail missiles.

♦ **2 Dnepr class** Bldr: Ishikawa Hajima Tokyo (In serv. 1959)

IZERMETEL'   PROTRAKTOR

D: 750 tons (fl)   **S:** 11 kts   **Dim:** 52.7 × 9.2 × 3.5
A: 2/14.5-mm mg (II × 1)   **Electron Equipt:** Radar: 2/Don-2
M: 2 Burmeister & Wain diesels; 1 prop; 1,210 hp

REMARKS: Ex-tuna boats.

INTELLIGENCE COLLECTORS (AGI) *(continued)*

Izermetel'   1980

OCEANOGRAPHIC-RESEARCH SHIPS

NOTE: The only units included are those known to be subordinate to the Soviet Navy. There are in addition nearly 300 research ships under the control of civilian agencies, primarily the Ministry of Science and the Ministry of Fisheries. Some of the civilian ships may from time to time perform research in support of military aims, but their purpose is primarily peaceful, and because of their number and variety, they cannot be described here. Such ships include the seven-unit *Akademik Kurchatov* expeditionary ships, the nine *Passat*-class weather ships, and the large and complex *Yuriy Gagarin, Kosmonaut Vladimir Komorov, Akademik Sergey Korolev,* as well as the 20 or more Finnish-built *Dimitriy Ovtsyn* survey ships that operate under the Ministry of Merchant Marine. All naval units are painted white.

♦ **10 Yug class** Bldr: Polnocny SY, Gdansk, Poland (In serv. 1978-79)

GIDROLOG	SENEZH
PEGAS	STRELETS
PERSEY	TAYGA
PLUTON	YUG
SEIMESH	ZODIAK

Pegas   1980

Yug   1979

D: 2,500 tons (fl)   **S:** 15.6 kts   **Dim:** 82.50 (75.80 pp) × 13.50 × 3.97
Electron Equipt: Radar: 2/Don-2
　　　　　　　　IFF: 1/High Pole B
M: 2 Zgoda-Sulzer 8TD48 diesels; 2 CP props; 4,400 hp (3,600 sust.)
Electric: 1,920 kVA   **Fuel:** 343 tons   **Endurance:** 40 days   **Range:** 9,000/12
Man: 8 officers, 38 men, 20 scientists

REMARKS: Deck reinforcements for six 25-mm AA (II × 3). Two 100-kw electric motors for slow-speed operations; 300-hp bow-thruster. Quadrantial davit over stern ramp, with 4-ton lift. Two 5-ton booms and several oceanographic davits. Two Type 727 fiberglass-hulled survey launches. Have 3 echo-sounders, 6 laboratories. Intended to perform all forms of oceanographic research and hydrographic survey duties.

♦ **6 Akademik Krylov class** Bldr: A. Warski SY, Szczecin, Poland
　(In serv. 1974-79)

ADMIRAL VLADIMIRSKY	IVAN KRUZHENSTERN	LEONID SOBELYEV
AKADEMIK KRYLOV	LEONID DEMIN	MIKHAIL KRUSKIY

Leonid Demin—pointed stern   French Navy, 1981

Ivan Kruzhenstern—cropped stern   1976

D: 6,600 tons (9,100 fl)   **S:** 20.4 kts   **Dim:** 147.0 × 18.6 × 6.3
Electron Equipt: Radar: 3/Don-2   IFF: 1/High Pole B
M: 4 diesels; 2 props; 16,000 hp   **Endurance:** 90 days
Range: 23,000/15.4   **Man:** 90 tot.

OCEANOGRAPHIC-RESEARCH SHIPS *(continued)*

REMARKS: The largest ships of their type in any navy. Equipped with helicopter hangar and flight deck, two survey launches, and twenty-six laboratories totaling 900 m². The *Leonid Demin* and *Mikhail Kruskiy* were delivered in 1978 and 1979, respectively, and because they have pointed sterns, are about 1 m longer.

♦ **1 Vladimir Kavrayskiy class** Bldr: Admiralty SY, Leningrad (In serv. 1973)

VLADIMIR KAVRAYSKIY

Vladimir Kavrayskiy 1974

D: 3,900 tons (fl) **S:** 15.4 kts **Dim:** 70.0 × 18.0 × 6.4
M: Type 3 13D100 diesels, electric drive; 2 props; 4,800 hp
Endurance: 60 days **Range:** 13,900/9.4

REMARKS: Greatly modified version of the *Dobrynya Nikitich* icebreaker class for arctic research. Has helicopter deck but no hangar, a survey launch, nine laboratories, totaling 180 m², one 8-ton crane, two 3-ton booms, and a hold capacity of 200 m³. The *Otto Schmidt*, completed in 1979 and subordinate to the Academy of Sciences, differs in appearance but is of similar design. The civilian research icebreakers *Georgiy Sedov* and *Petr Pakhtusov*, also subordinate to the Academy of Science, are units of the *Dobrynya Nikitich* class with very few external alterations.

♦ **4 Abkhaziya class** Bldr: Mathias Thesen Werft, Wismar, East Germany (In serv. 1971-73)

ABKHAZIYA ADZHARIYA BASHKIRIYA MOLDAVIYA

D: 5,460 tons (7,500 fl) **S:** 21 kts **Dim:** 124.7 × 17.0 × 6.4
Electron Equipt: Radar: 3/Don-2
M: 2 M.A.N. K6Z 57/80 diesels; 2 props; 8,000 hp
Endurance: 60 days **Range:** 20,000/16 **Man:** 85 tot.

REMARKS: Military version of the Academy of Science's *Akademik Kurchatov* class, with helicopter deck, telescoping hangar, Vee Cone communications antenna, stern-mounted A-frame lift gear, two survey launches, and twenty-seven laboratories totaling 460 m².

Moldavia 1980

♦ **8 Nikolay Zubov class** Bldr: A. Warski SY, Szczecin, Poland (In serv. 1963-68)

ALEKSEY CHIRIKOV	FYODOR LITKE
ANDREY VIL'KITSKIY	NIKOLAY ZUBOV
BORIS DAVYDOV	SEMEN DEZHNEV
FADDEY BELLINGSGAUZEN	VASILIY GOLOVNIN

Nikolay Zubov—Vee Cone HF communications array aft 1980

Semyen Dezhnev—late unit, with large platform aft 1974

D: 2,200 tons (3,020 fl) **S:** 16.5 kts **Dim:** 90.0 × 13.0 × 4.7
Electron Equipt: Radar: 2/Don-2 **IFF:** 1/High Pole

OCEANOGRAPHIC-RESEARCH SHIPS *(continued)*

M: 2 Zgoda-Sulzer 8TD48 diesels; 4,800 hp
Endurance: 60 days   **Range:** 11,000/14   **Man:** 50 tot.

REMARKS: Considerable variation from ship to ship. Can carry four survey launches but usually have only two. Nine laboratories, totaling 120 m². Two 7-ton and two 5-ton booms, nine .5-1.2-ton oceanographic-equipment davits, 600 m³ capacity total in two holds. The after platform, *not* for helicopters, is larger in the later ships. Three others serve as intelligence collectors.

♦ **1 Nevel'skoy class** Bldr: Nikolayev (In serv. 1962)

NEVEL'SKOY

Nevel'skoy   1979

D: 2,350 tons (fl)   **S:** 18 kts   **Dim:** 83.0 × 15.2 × 3.6   **Man:** 45 tot.
Electron Equipt: Radar: 2/Don-2   **M:** 2 diesels; 2 props; 4,000 hp

REMARKS: The only naval oceanographic-research ship, other than the *Vladimir Kavrayskiy*, built in the Soviet Union; apparently the prototype for the *Nikolay Zubov* design. In the Pacific Fleet.

♦ **3 Polyus class** Bldr: Neptunwerft, Rostock, East Germany (In serv. 1962-64)

BAYKAL   BALKHASH   POLYUS

Baykal

D: 4,560 tons (6,900 fl)   **S:** 14.2 kts   **Dim:** 111.6 × 14.4 × 6.3
Electron Equipt: Radar: 2/Don-2
M: 4 diesels, electric drive; 2 props; 4,000 hp
Endurance: 75 days   **Range:** 25,000/12.3

REMARKS: Seventeen laboratories, totaling 290 m². *Polyus* has less-extensive superstructure, different mast arrangment.

HYDROGRAPHIC-SURVEY SHIPS

NOTE: Ships of the Finik, Moma, Biya, Kamenka, and Samara classes are used as hydrographic-survey ships and as navigation tenders, handling buoys, marking channels, etc. They set and retrieve the 2,000 buoys and 4,000 spar buoys that are taken up for the winter months. Most can carry from two to six navigation buoys. In addition, they are equipped to take basic oceanographic and meteorological samplings. The Soviet Navy's Hydrographic Service has the task not only of surveying Soviet and overseas waters, but of maintaining no less than 600 lighthouses, 150 noise beacons, and 3,000 navigation buoys.

♦ **13 Fenik class** Bldr: Polnocny SY, Gdansk, Poland (In serv. 1979-81)

GS 44   GS 47   GS 270   GS 272   GS 278   GS 280   GS 388
GS 392   GS 397   GS 398   GS 401   GS 402   GS 403

GS 402   French Navy, 1980

GS 272—with landing craft on deck forward   1980

D: 1,200 tons (fl)   **S:** 13 kts   **Dim:** 61.30 × 11.80 (10.80 wl) × 3.27
Electron Equipt: Radar: 2/Don-2—IFF: 1/High Pole B
M: 2 Cegielski-Sulzer diesels; 2 CP props; 1,920 hp (plus two 75-kw electric motors for quiet, 6-kt operations)
Electric: 675 kVA   **Endurance:** 15 days   **Range:** 3,000/13
Man: 5 officers, 23 men

HYDROGRAPHIC-SURVEY SHIPS *(continued)*

REMARKS: GS = *Gidrograficheskoye Sudno* (Hydrographic Vessel). Intended for navigational buoy-tending and survey, for which 4 echo-sounders are fitted. Up to 3 fiberglass 3-dwt utility landing craft can be stowed on the buoy working deck, beneath the 7-ton crane. Bow-thruster of 130 kw fitted. Have hydrological, hydrographic, and cartographic facilities.

♦ **19 Moma class** Bldr: Polnocny SY, Gdansk, Poland (In serv. 1967-74)

AL'TAYR	ARTIKA	KRIL'ON	RYBACHIY (ex-*Odograf*)
ANADYR'	ASKOL'D	LIMAN	SEVER
ANDROMEDA	CHELEKEN	MARS	TAYMRY
ANTARES	EL'TON	MORZHOVETS	ZAPOLAR'E
ANTARTIKA	KOLGUEV	OKEAN	

Cheleken   1977

D: 1,260 tons (1,540 fl) **S:** 17 kts **Dim:** 73.3 × 10.8 × 3.8
Electron Equipt: Radar: 2/Don-2
       IFF: 1/High Pole A
M: 2 Zgoda-Sulzer 6TD48 diesels; 2 CP props; 3,600 hp
Endurance: 35 days **Range:** 8,700/11 **Man:** 56 tot.

REMARKS: Carry one survey launch and a 7-ton crane, and have four laboratories, totaling 35 m². The *Rybachiy* (ex-*Odograf*) has a deckhouse in place of the crane and may be involved in oceanographic research. Sisters in Polish and Yugoslav navies. Nine more serve as intelligence collectors.

♦ **12 Biya class** Bldr: Polnocny SY, Gdansk, Poland (In serv. 1972-76)

GS 193 GS 198 GS 204 GS 208 GS 214 GS 273
GS 194 GS 202 GS 206 GS 210 GS 271 GS 275

D: 750 tons (fl) **S:** 13 kts **Dim:** 55.0 × 9.2 × 2.6
Electron Equipt: Radar: 1/Don-2
M: 2 diesels; 2 CP props; 1,200 hp **Endurance:** 15 days
Range: 4,700/11 **Man:** 25 tot.

GS 186—under tow to Cuba; note crane at forecastle break   1980

REMARKS: GS = *Gidrograficheskoye Sudno* (Hydrographic Survey Ship). Similar to Kamenka class but have longer superstructure and less buoy-handling space; one survey launch; one 5-ton crane. Laboratory space: 15 m². One unit transferred to Guinea-Bissau, another (GS 186) to Cuba in 1980, and one to Cape Verde (1981).

♦ **10 Kamenka class** Bldr: Gdansk, Poland (In serv. 1968-72)

BEL'BEK	VERNIER	GS 74	GS 107	GS 203
SIMA	GS 66	GS 82	GS 108	GS 207

GS 107—note crane in center of working deck   1980

D: 703 tons (fl) **S:** 13.7 kts **Dim:** 53.5 × 9.1 × 2.6
Electron Equipt: Radar: 1/Don-2 **M:** 2 diesels; 2 CP props; 1,765 hp
Range: 4,000/10 **Man:** 40 tot.

REMARKS: GS = *Gidrograficheskoye Sudno* (Hydrographic Survey Ship). Similar to Biya class but have more facilities for stowing and handling buoys. No survey launch. One 5-ton crane. One sister in the East German Navy.

♦ **15 Samara class** Bldr: Polnocny SY, Gdansk, Poland (In serv. 1962-64)

AZIMUT	GLUBOMETR	KOMPAS	TROPIK	VOSTOK
DEVIATOR	GORIZONT	PAMYAT' MERKURIYA	TURA (ex-*Globus*)	GS 275 (ex-*Yug*)
GIGROMETR	GRADUS	RUMB (GS 118)	VAYGACH	ZENIT

D: 1,050 tons (1,276 fl) **S:** 15.5 kts **Dim:** 59.0 × 10.4 × 3.8
Electron Equipt: Radar: 2/Don-2
M: 2 Zgoda 5TD48 diesels; 2 CP props; 3,000 hp **Endurance:** 25 days
Range: 6,200/11 **Man:** 45 tot. (*Tura:* 140 tot.)

HYDROGRAPHIC-SURVEY SHIPS (continued)

Gorizont   1976

Tura—buoy-handling crane removed, forecastle extended   1978

REMARKS: Have one survey launch and 15 m² of laboratory space. The *Tura* (ex-*Globus*) had her forecastle extended to her superstructure in 1978 and her 7-ton crane removed; she may no longer be a survey ship. The *Deviator* served briefly as an intelligence collector. *Vaygach* has a large deckhouse surrounding the base of the buoy crane.

♦ **5 Telnovsk class** Bldr: Hungary (In serv. 1949-57)

AYTODOR   SIRENA   STVOR   SVIYAGA   ULYANA GROMOVA

> **D:** 1,300 tons (1,700 fl)   **S:** 11 kts   **Dim:** 70.0 × 10.0 × 4.2
> **Electron Equipt:** Radar: 1/Neptune, Don, or Don-2
> **M:** 1 Ganz diesel; 800 hp   **Range:** 3,300/9.7   **Man:** 50 tot.

REMARKS: Similar in most respects to cargo-ship version. All carry one launch; 15 m² of laboratory space. The *Stvor* and *Ulyana Gromova* have lengthened poop decks.

♦ **3 Melitopol class** Bldr: U.S.S.R. (In serv. 1952-55)

MAYAK   NIVILER   PRIZMA

> **D:** 1,200 tons (fl)   **S:** 11.3 kts   **Dim:** 57.6 × 9.0 × 4.3
> **Electron Equipt:** Radar: 1/Don
> **M:** 1 Type 6DR30/40 diesel; 600 hp   **Range:** 2,500/10.5

REMARKS: Converted small, two-hatch, cargo ships with few modifications; 673 grt/776 dwt. Carry one survey launch on deck.

♦ **several GPB-480-class inshore-survey craft** Bldr: U.S.S.R. (In serv. 1960s)

GPB 480, etc.

> **D:** 120 tons (fl)   **S:** 12 kts   **Dim:** 29.0 × 5.0 × 1.7
> **Electron Equipt:** Radar: 1/Spin Trough   **M:** 1 diesel; 450 hp
> **Endurance:** 10 days   **Range:** 1,600/10   **Man:** 15 tot.

REMARKS: GPB = *Gidrograficheskoye Pribezhnyy Bot* (Coastal Hydrographic Survey Boat). VM on the diving-tender version stands for *Vodolaznyy Morskoy* (Seagoing Diving Tender). Same hull and propulsion as the Nyryat-I-class diving tenders. The charthouse/laboratory is 6 m² and there are two 1.5-ton derricks. The smaller GPB-710 class is carried aboard the larger survey and oceanographic ships listed above: **D:** 7 tons (fl)   **S:** 10 kts for 150 nautical miles   **Dim:** 11.0 × 3.0 × 0.7.

MISSILE-RANGE INSTRUMENTATION SHIPS

♦ **2 Desna class** Bldr: Poland (In serv. 1963)

CHAZHMA (ex-*Dangera*)   CHUMIKAN (ex-*Dolgeschtchel'ye*)

Chazhma   1978

> **D:** 14,065 tons (fl)   **S:** 15 kts   **Dim:** 139.9 × 18.0 × 7.9
> **Electron Equipt:** Radar: 2/Don-2, 1/Head Net-B, 1/Ship Globe (tracking)
>   ECM: 2/Watch Dog
> **M:** 1 M.A.N. diesel; 5,400 hp   **Range:** 9,000/13

REMARKS: Heavily modified cargo ships. Tracking radar in large dome atop the bridge, with three tracking directors mounted forward. Hormone helicopter with hangar aft. Vee Cone communications antennas atop the stack. Based in the Pacific. Only ships with Head Net-B radar (both reflectors in same plane).

♦ **4 Sibir' class** Bldr: A. Warski SY, Szczecin, Poland (In serv. 1958)

CHUKOTKA   SAKHALIN   SIBIR'   SPASSK (ex-*Suchan*)

MISSILE-RANGE INSTRUMENTATION SHIPS *(continued)*

Sakhalin—now has Head Net-C aft   1976

Chukotka—flush-decked; Hormone-C on deck   1978

D: 7,800 tons (fl)   **S:** 12 kts   **Dim:** 108.2 × 14.6 × 7.2
Electron Equipt: Radar: 2/Don-2, 1/Head Net-C or Big Net, several tracking sets
M: Triple-expansion; 1 prop; 2,300 hp   **Range:** 11,800/12

REMARKS: Converted Donbass-class cargo ships converted circa 1960. Carry Big Net or Head Net-C radar for tracking, and two or three tracking directors forward. *Chukotka* is flush-decked; the others have a well deck forward. All carry one Hormone helicopter, but have no hangar. All are in the Pacific Fleet.

NOISE-MEASUREMENT SHIPS

♦ **3 or more Onega class** Bldr: . . . (In serv. 1973-. . .)

GKS 83   GKS. . .   SFP 95

D: 2,150 tons (2,500 fl)   **S:** 16 kts   **Dim:** 86.0 × 10.5 × 4.5
M: 1 gas turbine; 1 prop; . . . hp   **Man:** 45 tot.

REMARKS: GKS = *Gidroakusticheskoye Kontrol'noye Sudno* (Hydroacoustic Monitoring Ship) and indicates that these ships are successors to the T-43-class noise-monitoring ships. Meaning of "SFP" unknown. Helicopter deck aft, long forecastle, two pylon masts, and a low stack.

♦ **19 Modified T-43 class** Bldr: Various (In serv. mid-1950s)

GKS 11	GKS 15	GKS 19	GKS 23	GKS 42
GKS 12	GKS 16	GKS 20	GKS 24	GKS 45
GKS 13	GKS 17	GKS 21	GKS 25	GKS 46
GKS 14	GKS 18	GKS 22	GKS 26	

GKS 15

D: 500 tons (570 fl)   **S:** 14 kts   **Dim:** 58.0 × 8.6 × 2.3
Electron Equipt: Radar: 1/Neptune or Spin Trough
              IFF: 1/High Pole
M: 2 Type 9D diesels; 2 props; 2,200 hp   **Man:** 77 tot.

REMARKS: GKS = *Gidroakusticheskoye Kontrol'noye Sudno* (Hydroacoustic Monitoring Ship) and indicates that these ships measure the radiated noise of other ships, including submarines, by laying hydrophone arrays via the numerous small davits they carry aft.

DEGAUSSING/DEPERMING SHIPS

♦ **. . . Pelym class** Bldr: . . . (In serv. 1971-. . .)

SB 409   1980

D: 1,200 tons   **S:** 14 kts   **Dim:** . . . × . . . × . . .
M: 2 diesels; 2 props; . . . hp   **Man:** 70 tot.

REMARKS: SR = *Sudno Razmagnichivanya* (Deperming Vessel). Apparently intended to replace the aged Sekstan class.

DEGAUSSING/DEPERMING SHIPS *(continued)*

♦ **1 or more Khabarov class** Bldr: U.S.S.R. (In serv. 1950s)

D: 600 tons (fl) **S:** 9.5 kts **Dim:** 46.4 × 8.0 × 3.2
M: 1 diesel; 1 prop; 600 hp

REMARKS: Version of a steel-hulled coastal cargo ship design, with large deckhouse over forward hold area.

♦ **up to 30 Sekstan class** Bldr: Finland (In serv. 1949-55)

D: 280 tons (345 fl) **S:** 10 kts **Dim:** 40.8 × 12.0 × . . .
M: 1 diesel; 1 prop; 400 hp **Man:** 24 tot.

REMARKS: Wooden-hulled; built as war reparations. Same hull also used for coastal survey ship and cargo ship versions, now discarded.

ICEBREAKERS

NOTE: The Soviet Union has far and away the largest and most powerful icebreaker fleet in the world. Its civilian component includes the atomic-powered *Artika* and *Sibir'*, the most powerful of all (construction of a third unit of this 75,000-hp class, *Rossiya*, began 2-81 at Baltic Shipyard, Leningrad). The two types, patrol and support, that the navy operates are both based on the same civilian design and are among the very few conventionally driven icebreakers in service to be designed and built in the U.S.S.R. All other Soviet icebreakers now in service were built in Finland.

♦ **7 Ivan Susanin-class patrol icebreakers** Bldr: Admiralty SY, Leningrad (In serv. 1974-. . .)

| AYSBERG | IMENI XXV SEZDA K.P.S.S. | NEVA | N. . . |
| DUNAY | IVAN SUSANIN | RUSLAN | |

Imeni XXV Sezda K.P.S.S.   1977

D: 3,400 tons (fl) **S:** 14.5 kts **Dim:** 67.6 × 18.3 × 6.4
A: 2/76-mm DP (II × 1)—2/30-mm Gatling AA (VI × 2)
Electron Equipt: Radar: 2/Don-Kay, 1/Strut Curve, 1/Owl Screech
　　　　　　　　　IFF: 1/High Pole B
M: 3 Type 13D100 diesels, electric drive; 2 props; 5,400 hp
Range: 13,000/9.4 **Man:** 140 tot.

REMARKS: Based on the *Dobrynya Nikitich* and *Vladimir Kavrayskiy* designs. All manned by the KGB Border Guard and typed PSKR—*Pogranichnyy Storozhevoy*

Korabl' (Border Patrol Ship). Helicopter deck aft, but no hangar. Gatling guns do not have Bass Tilt radar directors. The *Dunay* and *Neva* also carry two launch positions for SA-7 Grail short-range AA missiles.

♦ **7 Dobrynya Nikitich-class support icebreakers**

Bldr: Admiralty SY, Leningrad (In serv. 1959-74)

| BURAN | IL'YA MUROMETS | PURGA | VYUGA |
| DOBRYNYA NIKITICH | PERESVET | SADKO | |

Il'ya Muromets   1973

D: 2,940 tons (fl) **S:** 14.5 kts **Dim:** 67.7 × 18.3 × 6.1
A: Four units: 2/57-mm AA (II × 1)—2/25-mm AA (II × 1)
Electron Equipt: Radar: 1-2/Don-2 IFF: 1/High Pole
M: 3 13D100 diesels, electric drive; 3 props (1 fwd); 5,400 hp
Range: 5,500/12 **Man:** 100 tot.

REMARKS: More than twenty of this class were built, the remainder being civilian. The *Peresvet*, *Purga*, *Sadko*, and *Vyuga* are armed. Resemble the *Ivan Susanin* class, but have much less superstructure and an open fantail rigged for ocean towing. Later units do not have a bow propeller but have the same horsepower.

TRAINING SHIPS

♦ **3 Smol'ny class** Bldr: A. Warski SY, Szczecin, Poland (In serv. 1976-78)

| KHASAN | PEREKOP | SMOL'NY |

Smol'ny   J.-C. Bellonne, 1979

TRAINING SHIPS (continued)

Khasan   1978

D: 6,500 tons (fl)   **S:** 20 kts   **Dim:** 137.5 × 16.7 × 6.3
A: 4/76.2-mm DP (II × 2)—4/30-mm AA (II × 2)—RBU-2500 ASW RL (XII × 2)
Electron Equipt: Radar: 4/Don-2, 1/Head Net-C, 1/Owl Screech, 1/Drum Tilt
  Sonar: 1/med.-freq.
  ECM: 2/Watch Dog
  IFF: 1/High Pole B
M: 4 diesels; 2 props; 16,000 hp

REMARKS: Built to relieve the *Sverdlov*-class cruisers that were formerly used for cadet-training. Can carry more than 270 cadets. The *Perekop* substitutes one Don-Kay radar for one of the four Don-2s. Carry six rowboats aft for exercising the cadets.

♦ **2 Ugra class** Bldr: Nikolayev (In serv. 1970-71)

BORODINO   GANGUT

Gangut   1980

D: 6,750 tons (9,500 fl)   **S:** 20 kts   **Dim:** 141.4 × 17.7 × 6.5
A: 8/57-mm AA (II × 4)
Electron Equipt: Radar: 4/Don-2, 1/Strut Curve, 2/Muff Cob
  ECM: 4/Watch Dog
  IFF: 1/High Pole B
M: 4 diesels; 2 props; 8,000 hp   **Man:** 300 crew + 400 cadets

REMARKS: Soviet type designation: *Uchebnoye Sudno* (Training Ship). Similar to the submarine-tender version but have accommodations and training facilities in place of workshops, magazines, storerooms, etc. Enlarged after deckhouse incorporates navigation-training space, including numerous duplicate navigator's positions. No helicopter facilities.

♦ **2 Modified Wodnik class** Bldr: Poland (In serv. 1977)

OKA   LUGA

D: 1,500 tons (1,800 fl)   **S:** 15 kts   **Dim:** 70.0 × 12.0 × 4.0
Electron Equipt: Radar:. . .
M: 2 Zgoda-Sulzer 6TD48 diesels; 2 CP props; 3,600 hp
Range: 8,000/11   **Man:** 58 men + 90 cadets

REMARKS: Used for navigation training. Similar to Polish and East German units of the Wodnik class, but have slightly larger superstructures, pilothouse one deck higher, and are not armed. Based on the Moma design.

TRIALS SHIPS AND CRAFT

♦ **4 or more Potok class** Bldr:. . . (In serv. 1978(?))

OS 100   OS 138   OS 145   OS 225

D: 750 tons (860 fl)   **S:** 18 kts   **Dim:** 71.0 × 9.1 × 2.5
A: 1/533-mm TT, 1/400-mm TT   **Electron Equipt:** Radar: 1/Don-2
M: 2 diesels; 2 props; 4,000 hp

REMARKS: OS = *Opytnoye Sudno* (Experimental Vessel). The design closely resembles the T-58 class, but the forecastle extends well aft. The trainable torpedo tubes are on the bow. A large crane aft is presumably used for retrieval. These ships are probably replacements for Modified T-43-class minesweepers, which had been used in torpedo trials since the 1950s.

♦ **1 or 2 Daldyn class**

Daldyn class   1976

D: 360 tons (fl)   **S:** 9 kts   **Dim:** 31.7 × 7.2 × 2.8
Electron Equipt: Radar: 1/Spin Trough
M: 1 Type 8NVD 36U diesel; 1 prop; 305 hp   **Man:** 15 tot.

REMARKS: Modified Kareliya-class purse-seiner, possibly for use in mine countermeasures trials.

♦ **several T-43-class former minesweepers**

REMARKS: Data as for minesweeper version. Some are disarmed former long-hulled minesweepers, while four or more 58-m versions were built as torpedo trials ships.

TRIALS SHIPS AND CRAFT (continued)

T-43-class trials tender 1976

NOTE: There are probably a number of additional ships of various classes with OS—*Opitnoye Sudno* (Experimental Vessel)—pendants, either built for the purpose or former combatants or auxiliaries adapted for specific trials duties. The largest was OS 24, the former heavy cruiser *Voroshilov*, since scrapped.

TARGET SERVICE CRAFT

♦ 9 Osa-class target-control boats

Osa target controller 1974

REMARKS: Have Osa hull and propulsion. Used to operate craft shown above right by remote control. Carry Square Tie and a High Pole B IFF transponder. Communications antennas have been enhanced to provide for radio-control.

♦ 8 Modified Osa-class missile targets

Kts 594, Osa target 1974

REMARKS: KTs = *Kontrol'naya Tsel'* (Controlled Target). Have Osa hull and propulsion. Crew departs when ship is in operation. Equipped with radar corner reflectors to strengthen target and two heat-generator chimneys to attract infrared homing missiles.

♦ several Shelon-class torpedo-retrievers Bldr:. . . (In serv. 1978-. . .)

Shelon class 1980

    D: 270 tons (fl) **S:** 18-24 kts **Dim:** 41.0 × 6.0 ×. . .
    Electron Equipt: Radar: 1/Spin Trough
                       Sonar: 1/helicopter dipping
                       IFF: 1/High Pole B
    M: 2 diesels; 2 props;. . . hp **Man:** 40 tot.

REMARKS: High-speed hull with a covered torpedo-recovery ramp aft. May be replacing the Poluchat-I class. Can be armed with a twin 25-mm or 30-mm AA.

♦ 60 or more Poluchat-I-class torpedo-retrievers

    D: 90 tons (fl) **S:** 18 kts **Dim:** 29.6 × 6.1 × 1.9
    A: 2/14.5-mm AA (II × 1) in some
    Electron Equipt: Radar: 1/Spin Trough
                       IFF: 1/High Pole A
    M: 2 M50 diesels; 2 props; 2,400 hp
    Range: 450/17; 900/10 **Man:** 20 tot.

REMARKS: Carry numbers in the TL—*Torpedolov* (Torpedo-Retriever)—series. Built in the 1950s. Recovery ramp aft. Some configured as patrol boats. Many exported abroad. See photo in section on Patrol Craft.

U.S.S.R. *(continued)*

DIVING TENDERS

♦ **several Yelva class** (In serv. 1973-. . .)

D: 295 tons (fl) **S:** 12.4 kts **Dim:** 40.9 × 8.0 × 2.1
Electron Equipt: Radar: 1/Spin Trough
M: 2 Type 3D12A diesels; 2 props; 600 hp **Man:** 30 tot.

REMARKS: Can support 7 divers at once to 60 m. Have a decompression chamber; some (but not all) also have a submersible decompression chamber. Replaced T-43 minesweepers built for the role. Several exported.

♦ **several Nyryat-1 class** (In serv. late 1950s-mid 1960s)

D: 120 tons (fl) **S:** 12 kts **Dim:** 29.0 × 5.0 × 1.7
Electron Equipt: Radar: 1/Spin Trough
M: 1 diesel; 1 prop; 450 hp **Endurance:** 10 days
Range: 1,600/10 **Man:** 15 tot.

REMARKS: Carry VM—*Vodolaznyy Morskoy* (Seagoing Diving Tender)—pendants. Same hull used for GPB-480-class inshore survey craft. Many exported.

♦ **several Nyryat-2 class** (In serv. 1950s)

PO 2 class—Nyryat 2 class similar   1975

D: 50 tons **S:** 9 kts **Dim:** 21.0 × 4.5 ×. . .
Electron Equipt: Radar: 1/Spin Trough
M: 1 Type 3D6 diesel; 1 prop; 150 hp **Man:** 10 tot.

REMARKS: Uses same hull as PO-2-class utility launch; distinguishable by bulwarks to hull at bow and stern. Hundreds of PO-2 hulls were built; many were exported.

MISCELLANEOUS SERVICE CRAFT

NOTE: The Soviet Navy operates more than 1,000 service craft in many categories, but space and lack of comprehensive information prohibits their description here.

UNITED ARAB EMIRATES

MERCHANT MARINE (1980): 119 ships—158,210 grt (14 tankers—81,330 grt)

NOTE: Primarily incorporating the former Defense Force Sea Wing of the Abu Dhabi National Defense Force, the UAE Navy was formed on 1 February 1978 as part of the federated forces of Abu Dhabi, Ajman, Dubai, Fujairah, Ras al Khaimah, Sharjah, and Umm al Qaiwan.

GUIDED-MISSILE PATROL BOATS

♦ **6 TNC-45-class guided-missile boats** Bldr: Lürssen, Vegasack

	In serv.		In serv.
P 4501 BANIYAS	11-80	P 4504 SHAHEEN	4-81
P 4502 MARBAN	11-80	P 4505 SAQAR	6-81
P 4503 RODQUM	4-81	P 4506 TARIF	6-81

Rodqum (P 4503)   P. Voss, 1981

D: 231 tons (259 fl) **S:** 41.5 kts **Dim:** 44.9 (42.3 pp) × 7.0 × 2.46 (prop)
A: 4/MM 40 Exocet (II × 2)—1/76-mm OTO Melara DP—2/40-mm Breda AA (II × 1)—2/7.62-mm mg (I × 2)
Electron Equipt: Radar: 1/Decca TM 1226, 1/PEAB 9LV 200 Mk 2, 1/. . .
ECM: Decca Cutlass RDL-2 passive, 1/Dagaie chaff RL
M: 4 MTU 16V538 TB92 diesels; 4 props; 15,600 hp (13,000 sust.)
Electric: 405 kVA **Range:** 500/38.5; 1,600/16 **Man:** 5 officers, 27 men

REMARKS: The CSEE director is equipped with low light-level t.v. and an infrared tracker. There is a CSEE Panda optical back-up director for the 40-mm mount. Carry 350 rds. 76-mm, 1,800 rds. 40-mm, and 6,000 rds. mg ammunition.

PATROL BOATS AND CRAFT

♦ **6 110-foot class** Bldr: Vosper Thornycroft, Portsmouth, G.B.

	L		L
P 1101 ARDHANA	7-3-75	P 1104 AL GHULIAN	16-9-75
P 1102 ZURARA	13-6-75	P 1105 RADOOM	15-12-75
P 1103 MURBAN	15-9-75	P 1106 GHANADHAH	1-3-76

Ardhana and Zurara   1976

D: 110 tons (140 fl)   **S:** 29 kts   **Dim:** 33.5 (31.5 pp) × 6.4 × 1.7
A: 2/30-mm BMARC/Oerlikon A32 AA (II × 1)—1/20-mm AA
Electron Equipt: Radar: 1/Decca RM 916   **Range:** 1,800/14   **Man:** 26 tot.
M: 2 Ruston-Paxman Valenta RP200M diesels; 2 props; 5,400 hp

♦ **3 Kawkab-class patrol craft** Bldr: Keith Nelson, G.B.

	L		L		L
P 561 KAWKAB	1-69	P 562 THOABAN	1-69	P 563 BANIYAS	7-69

Kawkab   Vosper, 1960

D: 25 tons (32 fl)   **Dim:** 17.52 (15.84 pp) × 4.72 × 1.37
A: 2/20-mm AA (I × 2)   **Electron Equipt:** Radar: 1/Decca RM 916
M: 2 Caterpillar diesels; 2 props; 750 hp   **Endurance:** 7 days
Electric: 24 kw   **Man:** 2 officers, 9 men

REMARKS: Fiberglass hull. Used for coastal patrol, hydrographic surveys, and surveillance of petroleum leases. Designed by Keith Nelson, a division of Vosper. Freshwater evaporator provides 900 liters daily.

SERVICE CRAFT

♦ **2 FPB 512-class diving tenders** Bldr: Rotork, G.B. (In serv. 5-81)

D: 8.75 tons (fl)   **S:** 11 kts   **Dim:** 12.7 × 3.2 × 0.45
M: 2 Volvo Penta AQD-40/280 outdrive diesels; 260 hp

REMARKS: Glass-reinforced plastic hull. 250-kg crane to handle divers' stage.

COAST GUARD

NOTE: The Coast Guard operates under the Ministry of the Interior.

PATROL CRAFT

♦ **17 P 1200 class** Bldr: Watercraft, Ltd., G.B. (In serv. 1979-81)

D: 10 tons (fl)   **S:** 29 kts   **Dim:** 11.90 (10.16 wl) × 4.08 × 1.06
A: 2/7.62-mm mg (I × 2)   **M:** 2 MTU diesels; 2 props; 800 hp
Range: 300/20   **Man:** 4 tot.

REMARKS: Glass-reinforced plastic hulls. First ten delivered 1979-80; seven more ordered 1980.

♦ **6 Dhafeer-class patrol craft** Bldr: Keith Nelson, Bembridge, G.B.

	L	In serv.		L	In serv.
P 401 DHAFEER	2-68	1-7-68	P 404 DURGHAM	9-68	7-6-69
P 402 GHADUNFAR	5-68	1-7-68	P 405 TIMSAH	9-68	7-6-69
P 403 HAZZA	5-68	1-7-68	P 406 MURAYJIB	2-70	7-7-70

D: 10 tons   **S:** 19 kts   **Dim:** 12.5 × 3.65 × 1.1
A: 2/7.62-mm mg (I × 2)   **M:** 2 Cummins diesels; 2 props; 370 hp
Range: 15/18; 350/15   **Man:** 1 officer, 5 men

REMARKS: Subordinate to Marine Police. Fiberglass hull.

♦ **6 Spear-class police patrol craft** Bldr: Fairey Marine, Hamble, G.B.

D: 10 tons   **S:** 26 kts   **Dim:** 9.1 × 2.75 × 0.84
A: 2/12.7-mm mg   **M:** 2 Perkins T 6-354 diesels; 2 props; 580 hp   **Man:** 3 tot.

REMARKS: In service in 8-74, 9-74, and 1-75. Fiberglass hull.

♦ **2 motor launches** Bldr: Cheverton, Cowes, G.B. (In serv. 1975)

A 271   A 272

D: 3.3 tons   **S:** 15 kts   **Dim:** 8.2 × 2.7 × 0.8
M: 1 Lister-Blackstone diesel; 150 hp

♦ **10 customs patrol craft**

REMARKS: Ordered in 1978 in the U.S.A. Details not available.

♦ **5 P-77A customs patrol craft** Bldr: Camcraft, New Orleans, La. (In serv. 9-75)

No. 21 through No. 25

D: 70 tons (fl)   **S:** 25 kts   **Dim:** 23.4 × 5.5 × 1.5   **Range:** 750/25
A: 2/20-mm AA (I × 2)   **M:** 2 GM 12V 71T diesels; 2 props; 1,400 hp

UNITED ARAB EMIRATES (*continued*)
PATROL CRAFT (*continued*)

♦ **2 50-foot customs patrol craft** Bldr: Cheverton, Cowes, G.B. (In serv. 2-75)

AL SHAHEEN   AL AQAB

D: 20 tons **S:** 23 kts **Dim:** 15.2 × 4.3 × 1.4
A: 1/7.62-mm mg **M:** 2 GM diesels; 2 props; 850 hp
Range: 1,000/20 **Man:** 8 tot.

U.S.A.

PERSONNEL (1981): 537,456 total: (69,336 officers/468,120 enlisted) plus 188,100 Marines (18,100 officers/170,000 enlisted), 87,000 ready Naval Reserves and 36,653 Marine Reserves

MERCHANT MARINE (1980): 5,579 ships—18,464,271 grt
(tankers: 339 ships—7,887,605 grt)

NAVAL PROGRAM

The table lists new construction programs for fiscal years 1980 through 1987, including the supplemental FY 79 program, as reported to Congress in 1979, and changes reported later in the press. The annual five-year program has fluctuated drastically for many years and, because of changing political pressures, cannot be relied on as an accurate projection of what will actually be proposed, let alone authorized and appropriated by the Congress. It is nonetheless presented here as the best available forecast.

SHIPBUILDING PROGRAMS 1980-87

New Construction:	Authorized			Proposed (Provisional)				
	FY 80	FY 81	FY 82	FY 83	FY 84	FY 85	FY 86	FY 87
SSBN, *Ohio*	1	1	0	2	1	1	1	1
SSN, *Los Angeles*	2	2	2	3	3	4	4	4
CVN, *Roosevelt*	1	—	—	2	—	—	—	—
CGN, CGN 42	—	—	—	—	—	—	—	1
CG, *Ticonderoga*	1	2	3	3	3	3	4	4
DDG, DDG 51	—	—	—	—	—	1	—	3
DD, *Spruance*	—	—	—	—	—	2	1	—
FFG, *O.H. Perry*	5	6	3	—	—	—	—	—
FFG, Mod. *Perry*	—	—	—	2	2	2	3	3

Ohio (SSBN 726)—symbol of a nation's might

General Dynamics, 1981

SHIPBUILDING PROGRAMS (continued)

MSM, *Avenger*	—	—	1	4	4	5	—	—
MSH, MSH 1	—	—	—	—	1	—	5	5
LSD, *Whidbey Isl.*	—	1	1	1	1	2	2	2
LHD, LHDX	—	—	—	—	1	—	—	1
AD	—	—	—	—	—	—	1	1
AE	—	—	—	—	—	1	2	1
T-AGOS, *Stalwart*	1	5	4	—	1	—	2	3
ARC, *Zeus*	—	—	—	—	—	—	1	—
ARS, ARS 50	—	1	2	1	1	—	—	—
AO, T-AO 187	—	—	1	1	3	4	4	6
AOE, AOEX	—	—	—	—	—	1	1	2
Acquisitions:								
BB, *Iowa*	—	—	1	1	1	1	—	—
T-AFS, *Sirius*	—	—	2	—	1(?)	—	—	—
T-AKR, *Maine*	—	—	4	—	—	—	—	—
Conversions:								
CV, CV-SLEP	—	1	—	1	—	1	—	1
T-AGM, . . .	—	—	—	—	—	—	1	—
T-AGS, . . .	—	—	—	—	2	—	—	—
T-AH	—	—	—	1	1	—	—	—
T-AK, *Vega* (C 4)	—	—	—	—	1	—	—	—
T-AKR, *Algol* (SL 7)[1]	—	—	4	4	—	—	—	—

Note[1]: Six purchased with FY 81 funds, two under FY 82; given temporary T-AK numbers; conversion will be to AKR. Source: SECDEF Report to Congress, FY 83.

MARINE CORPS

Created in 1775, the Marine Corps has three missions:
—to seize and/or defend advanced bases as needed for the operations of the fleet
—to furnish security detachments on board ships and at land bases
—to carry out any other operations that the president of the United States may assign.

The third mission permits the corps to be used in operations that are not purely naval (e.g., Belleau Wood in 1918 and Vietnam in the 1960s and 1970s).

Its total strength is about 188,100 men, and they form three divisions (one stationed in Okinawa/Japan, two in the United States), each of 18,000 men and three air wings, organized under two Fleet Marine Forces (FMF). These last also maintain heavy support elements for the divisions. A fourth division-wing team constitutes a reserve cadre.

The Marine Corps has approximately 400 fighter and attack aircraft (A-4M, A-6, AV-8A, F-4), 600 assault and utility helicopters, more than 500 tanks, and some 450 amphibious landing vehicles.

The major operational unit is the Marine Amphibious Force (MAF), which consists of one division, one air wing, and Fleet Marine Forces augmentation, for a total of about 45,600 Marines, plus about 26,300 naval personnel aboard ships, etc.

Amphibious ships currently in service do not permit the rapid overseas deployment of MAFs, but only of two Marine Amphibious Brigades (MAB). An MAB consists of one Regimental Landing Team, a strong unit with two or more battalion landing teams of about 1,500 men each; one mixed air group of fighter, attack fixed-wing aircraft and/or helicopter squadrons; and some augmentation from the Fleet Marine Force, for a total of about 16,500 men.

THE RAPID DEPLOYMENT FORCE

Created by the Carter Administration, the Rapid Deployment Force (RDF) is intended for immediate material support to troops deployed to trouble areas by aircraft. An interim "Near Term" RDF was first deployed to Diego Garcia in 7-80, and it remains there to date. This initial RDF Group has been made up of a mixture of Military Sealift Command vessels and chartered commercial ships, but it is to be replaced by the eight SL-7-class fast container ships acquired in 1981, and later augmented by additional converted merchant cargo ships, plus one oiler. The RDF, which theoretically will eventually be maintained on a ready-to-deploy basis in U.S. home waters when the Mid-East Crisis ends, is intended to supply equipment and supplies for 30 days to three reinforced Marine Amphibious Brigades, i.e., one MAF (Marine Amphibious Force). The current force as of 1-1-82 is listed in the Military Sealift Command section.

THE NAVAL RESERVE FORCE

Naval Reserve Force ships have cadre crews of regular naval personnel, with reserve augmentation personnel constituting up to two-thirds of the total crew assigned. As of 1 January 1982, the Force included: 9 destroyers (1 *Forrest Sherman*, 1 *Carpenter*, and 7 Gearing FRAM-I class), 4 frigates (*Knox* class), 22 ocean minesweepers (2 *Acme*, 4 *Dash*, and 16 *Aggressive* class), 2 tank landing ships (*Newport* class), 4 amphibious cargo ships (*Charleston* class), 1 ammunition ship (*Pyro*), 1 salvage ship (*Preserver*), 5 fleet tugs (*Abnaki* and *Achomawi* class), and a number of small patrol craft. Additional frigates of the *Knox* class and, later, the *Oliver Hazard Perry* class will replace the destroyers.

THE MILITARY SEALIFT COMMAND

The Military Sealift Command (MSC) operates or charters ships in support of the United States Navy. Headed by an active-duty U.S. Navy flag officer, its ships are manned primarily by civilians. The ships of the MSC are listed in a separate section, after naval units.

WARSHIPS IN ACTIVE SERVICE, UNDER CONSTRUCTION, OR APPROPRIATED AS OF 1 JANUARY 1982

	L	Tons	Main armament
♦ **13 (+4) attack carriers**			
0 (+3) THEODORE ROOSEVELT (CVN)	. . .	82,000	90-100 aircraft, 3/Sea Sparrow
2 (+1) NIMITZ (CVN)	1972-80	81,600	90-100 aircraft, 3/Sea Sparrow
1 ENTERPRISE (CVN)	1960	75,700	88-90 aircraft, 3/Sea Sparrow
1 JOHN F. KENNEDY (CV)	1967	61,000	88-90 aircraft, 3/Sea Sparrow
3 KITTY HAWK (CV)	1960-64	60,100	88 aircraft, 2-3/missile launchers

WARSHIPS *(continued)*

| 4 FORRESTAL (CV) | 1954-58 | 59,600 | 88 aircraft, 2/Sea Sparrow |
| 2 MIDWAY (CV) | 1945-46 | 51,000 | 65 aircraft, 0 or 2/Sea Sparrow |

♦ 12 amphibious assault helicopter carriers

| 5 TARAWA (LHA) | 1972-78 | 39,000 (fl) | 3/127-mm DP, 2/Sea Sparrow, 19 or 30 helicopters |
| 7 IWO JIMA (LPH) | 1960-69 | 17,000 | 4/76.2-mm, 2/Sea Sparrow, 28 helicopters |

♦ 32 (+15) nuclear-powered ballistic-missile submarines

		(surfaced)	
1 (+15) OHIO (SSBN)	1979-	15,750	24/Trident, 4/TT
31 LAFAYETTE (SSBN)	1962-66	7,250	16/Poseidon or Trident, 4/TT

♦ 89 (+27) nuclear-powered attack submarines

18 (+27) LOS ANGELES	1973-	6,000	4/TT
1 GLENARD P. LIPSCOMB	1973	5,813	4/TT
37 STURGEON	1966-74	3,640	4/TT
1 NARWHAL	1967	4,550	4/TT
13 PERMIT	1961-66	3,526	4/TT
1 TULLIBEE	1960	2,317	4/TT
5 ETHAN ALLEN	1960-62	6,300	4/TT
3 GEORGE WASHINGTON	1959-60	6,019	6/TT
5 SKIPJACK	1958-60	3,075	6/TT
4 SKATE	1957-58	2,570	8/TT
1 SEAWOLF	1955	3,765	6/TT

♦ 5 diesel/electric-powered submarines

3 BARBEL	1958-59	2,146	6/TT
1 DARTER	1956	1,720	8/TT
1 GRAYBACK	1957	2,670	8/TT

♦ 0 (+4) battleships

| 0 (+4) IOWA | 1942-44 | 46,100 | 32 Tomahawk, 16 Harpoon, 9/406-mm, 12/127-mm DP, 4/20-mm Vulcan/Phalanx AA, 3 SH-60B helicopters |

♦ 27 (+7) cruisers

9 nuclear-powered:

		Tons	
4 VIRGINIA (CGN)	1974-78	10,400	2/missile launchers, 8/ Harpoon, 2/127-mm DP, 2/ASW TT
2 CALIFORNIA (CGN)	1971-72	10,400	2/missile launchers, 8/ Harpoon, 2/127-mm DP, ASROC, 4/ASW TT

1 TRUXTUN (CGN)	1964	8,600	1/missile launcher, 8/ Harpoon, 2/127-mm DP, 4/ASW TT
1 BAINBRIDGE (CGN)	1961	8,600	4/missile launchers, 8/ Harpoon, ASROC, 6/ASW TT
1 LONG BEACH (CGN)	1959	15,500	2/missile launchers, 16/ Harpoon, ASROC, 6/ASW TT

18 (+7) conventional:

0 (+7) TICONDEROGA	1981-	. . .	2/missile launchers, 8 Harpoon, 2/127-mm DP, 6/ASW TT, 2/helicopters
9 BELKNAP (CG)	1963-65	6,570	1/missile launcher, 8/ Harpoon, 1/127-mm DP, 6/ASW TT, 1/helicopter
9 LEAHY (CG)	1961-63	6,070	2/missile launchers, 8/ Harpoon, ASROC, 6/ASW TT

♦ 89 (+2) destroyers

3 (+1) KIDD	1979-80	8,140	2/missile launchers, 2/127- mm DP, 6/ASW TT, 1/ or 2/helicopters
30 (+1) SPRUANCE	1973-81	5,830	1/Sea Sparrow, 8/ Harpoon, 2/127-mm DP, ASROC, 6/ASW TT, 1/helicopter
23 CHARLES F. ADAMS	1959-63	3,370	1/missile launcher, Harpoon, 2/127-mm DP, ASROC, 6/ASW TT
10 COONTZ	1958-60	4,700	1/missile launcher, 8/ Harpoon, 1/127-mm DP, ASROC, 6/ASW TT
4 DECATUR	1955-58	2,850	1/missile launcher, 1/127- mm DP, ASROC, 6/ASW TT
8 MOD. FORREST SHERMAN	1955-58	2,850	2/127-mm DP, ASROC, 6/ASW TT
6 FORREST SHERMAN	1955-58	2,780	3/127-mm DP, 6/ASW TT
4 GEARING	1944-46	2,425	4/127-mm DP, ASROC, 6/ASW TT

♦ 80 (+34) frigates

15 (+34) OLIVER HAZARD PERRY	1976-	2,997	1/missile launcher, Harpoon, 1/76-mm, 6/ASW TT, 2/ helicopters
46 KNOX	1966-73	3,011	0 or 1/Sea Sparrow, Har- poon, 1/127-mm DP, ASROC, 4/ASW TT, 1/helicopter
6 BROOKE	1963-66	2,643	1/missile launcher, 1/127- mm DP, ASROC, 6/ASW TT, 1/helicopter

WARSHIPS *(continued)*

10 GARCIA	1963-65	2,624	2/127-mm DP, ASROC, 6/ASW TT, 1/helicopter
1 GLOVER	1965	2,650	1/127-mm DP, ASROC, 6/ASW TT
2 BRONSTEIN	1962	2,360	2/76.2-mm DP, ASROC, 6/ASW TT

♦ **3 (+3) guided-missile patrol hydrofoils**

♦ **25 mine countermeasures ships**

♦ **54 amphibious warfare ships (plus helicopter carriers above)**

WEAPONS AND SYSTEMS

NOTE: The number of active weapon options available for use by U.S. ships and aircraft is declining. Furthermore, available systems, particularly guns and fire-control systems, are being removed without replacement, while the development of new systems is being stretched out.

A. MISSILES

♦ **fleet ballistic missiles**

NOTE: All are launched from submerged submarines.

Poseidon C-3 (UGM 73A)—Lockheed

Length:	10.4 m
Diameter:	1.8 m
Weight:	29.48 tons at launch
Propulsion:	solid propellant, two stages
Guidance:	inertial
Range:	2,500 or 3,200 nautical miles
Warhead:	14 warheads with independent and controllable trajectory, each of 50 kt (MIRV) to 2,500 nautical miles or 10 of 50 kt to 3,200 nautical miles. Some warheads are currently being "uploaded" to increase destructive force.

Trident-1 C-4 (UGM-96A)—Lockheed

New type missile, operational in 1978 and designed for the *Ohio*-class SSBN, which will carry 24, and for twelve *Lafayette* and *Benjamin Franklin* classes of SSBN, which will carry 16.

Length:	10.4
Weight:	31.75 tons at launch
Propulsion:	solid propellant, three stages
Guidance:	inertial
Range:	4,350 nautical miles
Warhead:	8 MIRV of 100 kt, Mk 4

The Mk 500 Evader MARV (Maneuverable Re-entry Vehicle) with six 100-kt warheads was developed by Lockheed, with procurement commencing in 1980.

Trident-2 D5—Lockheed

In development for deployment in the late 1980s in the Pacific Fleet, and 1992 in the Atlantic.

Length:	13.9 m
Weight:	57.15 at launch
Propulsion:	solid propellant, three stages
Range:	4,000 nautical miles with 122-m circular point of error (CEP)
Warhead:	14 MIRV of 150 kt each or 7 MARV (Maneuverable Re-entry Vehicles) of 300 kt each. Initially will use same Mk 12A re-entry vehicles as the land-based Minuteman III/MX.

♦ **surface-to-surface missiles**

Tomahawk (BGM-109)—General Dynamics

Two versions are projected, strategic and tactical. The anti-ship tactical version will become operational in 1982. Planned procurement is for 3,994 total missiles, with 2,600 potential launchers.

Length:	6.17 m
Diameter:	0.52 m
Weight:	1,542 kg at launch (1,816 kg encapsulated for submarine launch)
Propulsion:	solid booster, turbojet sustainer
Navigation/ Guidance:	TAINS (Tercom-Aided Inertial Navigation System) using preprogrammed data plus TERCOM (Terrain Contour Matching)
Range:	*Strategic version:* 600 nautical miles, operating at an altitude between 15 and 100 meters, at a speed of Mach 0.7. For launching from submarines, the weapon will be fired from torpedo tubes in a special container, jettisoned on leaving the water. *Tactical version:* 350 nautical miles, approximately, thus requiring an external means of target designation. Warhead weight up to 454 kg.

Harpoon (RGM-84A)—McDonnell-Douglas

An all-weather cruise missile that can be launched by aircraft, surface ships, or submarines. A total of 281 surface ships and submarines are programmed to receive it. As of end-1981, there were 108 ships, 34 submarines, and 4 P-3B aircraft equipped to launch Harpoon. By 7-81, 1,848 missiles had been delivered, with plans calling for acquisition of 3,000 for the U.S. Navy, and 2,000 already have been delivered or are on order for foreign navies. Under FY 82, 240 are to be procured.

Length:	4,581 m, including .4-m booster (may add .28-m plug to increase range)
Diameter:	0.343 m—Wingspan: 0.914 m
Weight:	694 kg from canister, 667 kg from SAM or ASROC launcher (with booster)
Propulsion:	turbojet, with a rocket booster added to the ship- and submarine-launched versions
Speed:	Mach 0.85
Guidance:	inertial, then active homing on J band in the final trajectory
Range:	60 nautical miles (being increased to 100 nm by improved JP-10 fuel
Warhead:	227 kg

AGM-84 is the 530-kg, air-dropped version, which does not require a solid rocket booster, and **UGM-84** is the submarine version. The submarine version is shrouded and is launched from the torpedo tubes while submerged. In order to reach the maximum range, it is necessary to use targeting systems external to the launching unit—helicopters, for example. The AGM-84 will be carried by A-6E, P-3B and P-3C aircraft.

MISSILES (continued)

Penguin Mk-II—Norway

The U.S. Navy is testing this weapon for potential use aboard small combatants, presumably for foreign sale as there are no plans to build any craft to carry it for U.S. Navy usage.

♦ **surface-to-air missiles** (Note: Standard and Sea Sparrow can also be used against surface ships)

Thor—Johns Hopkins Applied Physics Laboratory (research)

A conceptual study for a ship-launched SAM with a range of 500-600 nautical miles, to be guided to aerial targets by E-2C or F-14 aircraft. Would use a rocket/ramjet engine. Planned for service in the 1990s.

Standard SM-1 MR (RIM-66B)—General Dynamics

Single-stage missile, replaced Tartar.

Length:	4.3 m
Diameter:	0.36 m
Weight:	590 kg
Guidance:	semi-active homing
Range:	25 nautical miles, 150-60,000 ft

System comprises Mk 11 twin launcher or Mk 13 single launcher with a vertical ready-service magazine containing 40 missiles (on the FFG 1 class, Mk 22 with 16 missiles), a computer, an air-search radar, a three-dimensional SPS-39, SPS-48, or SPS-52 radar, and SPG-51 guidance radars. A series of missiles of approximately the same size as the first RIM 24 Mod. 0 (U.S. military designation) but constantly improved propulsion, miniaturization of components, and improved missile flight profile.

Standard SM-2 MR (RIM-66C)—General Dynamics

Single-stage missile for use with Aegis-equipped ships. Initial procurement of 30 in FY 80.

Length:	4.3 m
Diameter:	0.36 m
Weight:	590 kg
Guidance:	semi-active homing, with mid-course guidance capability, inertial reference, and improved ECCM
Range:	more than 25 nautical miles

Standard SM-1 ER (RIM-67)—General Dynamics

Two-stage missile that replaced the Terrier family. "Block II" series (1,095 ordered under FY 82) to get increased intercept altitude, greater warhead lethality, and improved jam resistance.

Length:	7.9 m
Diameter:	0.36 m
Weight:	1,317 kg
Guidance:	semi-active homing
Range:	30-40 nautical miles

Standard SM-2 ER (RIM-67B)—General Dynamics

Two-stage missile to replace Talos. Will be employed in ships with Mk 10 or Mk 26 launch systems, and later in vertical launches. May have a nuclear warhead option. Initial procurement of 55 in FY 80.

Length:	7.9 m
Diameter:	0.36 m
Weight:	1,317 kg
Guidance:	semi-active homing, with mid-course guidance capability, inertial reference, and improved ECCM
Range:	more than 75 nautical miles

Sea Sparrow (RIM-7)—Raytheon

Known at first as BPDMS (Basic Point Defense Missile System). The 50 initial installations employed RIM-7E-5 fixed-fin missiles launched from the eight-celled Mk 25 launcher and controlled by the Mk 115 radar-equipped fire-control system. These are to be replaced by the Mk 15 Vulcan/Phalanx 20-mm Gatling gun system beginning in 1982. A lightweight launcher, Mk 29, employing eight RIM-7F folding-fin missiles and the Mk 91 radar fire-control system, is now in use. In Europe this later system, IPDMS (Independent Point Defense Missile System), is also known as NATO Sea Sparrow and was first tested in the *Downes* (FF 1070). The RIM-7M version now being procured uses a blast-fragmentation warhead vice the earlier expanding rod variety.

Length:	3.657 m
Weight:	171 kg
Range:	8 nautical miles

Aegis (ex-Advanced Surface Missile-System—ASMS)

Under study since 1964. A fire-control system based on the AN/SPY-1 "billboard" fixed-array radar to provide 360° coverage. It will employ SM-2 ER missiles to repel simultaneously a number of targets under the most adverse electronic countermeasures, including targets at extremely low altitude (sea skimmers). For precise response to threats, the Aegis system will be made of various components permitting the control of all necessary steps from target-acquisition to missile-detonation against the target. Three clusters of four AN/UYK-7 computer systems direct all these functions automatically, especially the detection and tracking of the closing targets, data distribution for target evaluation and designation through pre-programmed information retained in the system, integration of radar and other information sources in the ship, and the selection of missiles and distribution of fire.

The Mk 26 twin launcher, which can also handle the ASW ASROC system and Harpoon surface-to-surface missile, will be used. The various types of missiles are stowed vertically in ready-service magazines below the launcher. The Aegis system has been undergoing trials in the *Norton Sound* since 1974 and will first be operational in CG 47 in 1983. The Martin-Marietta EX-41 vertical launch system is being developed to replace the Mk 26. Trials commenced in late 1981 on *Norton Sound*, with first operational employment to be in CG 52.

RAM (Rolling Airframe Missile) (XRIM-116A)—General Dynamics

A point-defense system intended to replace or supplement Sea Sparrow. Will use a 127-mm missile that employs slow spinning for stability (hence the name). Guidance is by dual-mode infrared homing, and either a new 24-missile launcher, or modified ASROC/Mk 29 Sea Sparrow-type launchers, may be used as the launcher. The 24-missile launcher uses the Phalanx mounting, while the ASROC/Mk 29 version would put 5 missiles each into two cells of the 8-celled ASROC launcher. The missile homes on active radiation from the target until it picks up an infrared target signature and employs the current Stinger seeker in conjunction with Sidewinder fuzes, warheads, and rocket motors. The 24-missile launch installation weighs 5 tons. Target designation will be by the Mk 23 TASS system in U.S. Navy ships. Being developed under a 7-76 agreement by the U.S., Denmark, and West Germany, with introduction now delayed to 1984 or later.

MISSILES (continued)

SIAM (Self-Initiated Antiaircraft Missile)—Ford Aerospace

Trials commenced in 1978 for a short-ranged SAM for use aboard submarines, with underwater launches attempted in 1979, using the AUSEX (Aircraft Undersea Sound-Experimental) towed sonar array for aircraft targeting. Funding denied FY 81 and program currently dormant.

Weight:	45.4 kg	Propulsion:	Solid-fuel rocket
Length:	2.5 m	Range:	. . .
Diameter:	.144-m	Wingspan:	.147 m

♦ antisubmarine warfare missiles

ASROC (RUR-5A)—Honeywell

A solid-fuel rocket used with a parachute-retarded Mk 26 torpedo. Range is regulated by the combustion time of the rocket motor. Rocket-torpedo separation is timed. The Mk 112 launcher carries eight rockets that can be trained together and elevated in pairs. Fire control is made up of a computer linked with an SQS-23, SQS-26, or SQS-53 sonar.

Length:	4.60 m	Range:	9,200 m
Diameter:	0.324 m	Warhead:	Mk 46 mod. 1 torpedo or Mk 17 nuclear depth bomb
Weight:	454 kg		
		Rate of fire:	2 rockets/minute

On some *Knox*-class escorts the launcher was modified to permit the launching of Standard SSM missiles (later, Harpoon also) in place of some ASW weapons. Loading is slow because the rockets have to be manually transferred from the magazines. However, on later *Brooke*- and *Garcia*-class and all *Knox*-class frigates, a hoist transfers the rocket from a magazine below the bridge for semiautomatic loading, while in the *Spruance* class the missiles are reloaded vertically. Some 12,000 ASROC rounds were procured between 1960 and 1970, when production ceased.

ASROC may also be launched from the Mk 10 missile launchers in the CG 26 and CGN 35 classes and from the Mk 26 launchers in the CGN 38 and CG 47 classes.

SUBROC (UUM-44A-2)

Introduced in 1962 as a submarine torpedo tube-launched ASW weapon with a nuclear depth bomb payload, SUBROC is being phased out because of the age of its solid-fueled rocket motors and because its analog fire-control system is incompatible with the Mk 117 Mod. 3 digital fire-control systems now being installed or backfitted in U.S. Navy submarines. It will have disappeared before its successor is ready.

Weight:	1,816 kg	Propulsion:	two-stage solid-fuel rocket
Length:	6.40 m	Range:	30 nautical miles
Diameter:	.533 m	Guidance:	inertial

NOTE: The ASROC replacement ASW Stand-off Weapon (SOW), a developmental contract for which had been given to Boeing, was canceled in 1981 in favor of developing a *single* weapon to replace both the SUBROC in submarines and ASROC in surface ships. It will have a range of up to 106 nautical miles, will fit in conventional 533-mm torpedo tubes, and will be capable of being launched from the EX-41 vertical launch system (which ASROC is not). Operational introduction is planned for the late 1980s.

♦ air-to-surface missiles

Maverick (AGM-65E and AGM 65F)—Hughes

Developed from the Air Force AGM-65D, the AGM-65E is a laser-designated, air-launched missile for the Marine Corps, while the AGM-65F version for the Navy will use infrared homing. Both have the same warhead. Plans call for procuring 7,000 AGM-65F in FY 84, for use by A-7 and A/F-18 aircraft and, later, the A-6E.

Weight:	208.8 kg	Span:	0.71 m
Length:	2.46 m	Propulsion:	solid-fuel rocket
Diameter:	0.30 m	Range:	50 nautical miles

Standard-ARM (AGM-78)—General Dynamics

Air-launched version of Standard that homes on electromagnetic radiation. More versatile than Shrike.

Length:	4.57 m	Warhead:	97.6 kg
Range:	35 nautical miles	Weight:	624.2 kg

Shrike (AGM-45)—Texas Instruments

An anti-radar missile.

Length:	3.048 m	Propulsion:	solid-propellant rocket motor
Diameter:	0.2 m	Range:	12,000 to 16,000 m
Weight:	117 kg	Speed:	Mach 2
		Wingspan:	0.914 m

Walleye I and II (AGM-62)—Martin Marietta/Hughes

Glide bomb guided by television.

Length:	I: 3.5 m; II: 4.0 m	Range:	I: 16 nautical miles; II: 35 nautical miles
Diameter:	0.325 m	Warhead:	conventional—I: 373 kg; II: 908 kg
Weight:	I: 511 kg; II: 1,090 kg	Wingspan:	1.16 m

Harpoon (AGM-84)

See under surface-to-surface missiles.

HARM (AGM-88)—Texas Instruments

HARM (High-Speed Anti-Radiation Missile) is in the final stages of development by the Naval Weapons Center, China Lake, California, with more than 80 missiles built to date. It will be employed by A-7E, A-6E, FA-18, and U.S. Air Force F-4E Wild Weasel aircraft to suppress or destroy ground defenses. Will replace the obsolescent Shrike. Production of 5,000 is scheduled to start in 1982.

Length:	4.17 m	Propulsion:	solid-propellant rocket
Diameter:	0.253 m	Guidance:	homes on electromagnetic radiation
Weight:	361 kg	Range:	. . .
Span:	1.14 m		

TOW (MGM-71)—Hughes

Wire-guided, helicopter- or ground-launched anti-tank weapon that uses optical sight and tube launcher. TOW = Tube-launched, Optically-guided, Wire-controlled.

Length:	1.12 m	Span:	1.14 m
Weight:	19.5	Propulsion:	solid-propellant rocket
Diameter:	.152 m	Warhead:	3.6 kg hollow, shaped-charge
		Range:	2.6 nautical miles

MISSILES (continued)

♦ **air-to-air missiles**

Sparrow III (AIM 7E,F)—Raytheon

Length:	3.65 m	Guidance:	semi-active homing
Diameter:	0.203 m	Speed:	Mach 2.5
Weight:	227 kg	Range:	15,000 m (AIM 7D version), 26,000 m (AIM 7E,F versions)
Propulsion:	solid-fuel rocket	Warhead:	27 kg, proximity fuse

Sidewinder (AIM-9H, L, M)—Raytheon

Over 110,000 Sidewinder missiles have been built. The AIM-9L version uses an active optical fuze and has a guidance system permitting all-angle attacks. The AIM-9M version supplanted the -9L in production in 1981 and has improved capabilities against countermeasures and against targets seen against warm backgrounds.

IA

Length:	2.90 m	Propulsion:	solid-fueled rocket
Diameter:	0.127 m	Guidance:	infrared homing
Wingspan:	0.61 m	Speed:	Mach 2.5
Weight:	84.4 kg	Range:	12 nautical miles

PHOENIX (AIM-54A, C)—Hughes

AIM-54A ceased production in 1980 after only 2,500 had been built for the U.S. and, unfortunately, Iran. The first 30 pilot-production AIM-54C were delivered 10-81, with 60 more to follow. Scheduled to enter service 1983-84, with only 100/yr. to be procured until 1987, when production is scheduled to rise to 500/yr. AIM-54C will be used by the new F-14C Tomcat variant.

Length:	3.96	Weight:	447 kg
Diameter:	0.380 m	Propulsion:	solid-fueled rocket
Wingspan:	0.914 m	Range:	over 80,000 m
		Warhead:	61.3 kg

AMRAAM-. . .

AMRAAM (Advanced Medium-Range Air-to-Air Missile) is intended to replace the AIM-7F Sparrow. In development.

Weight:	91-107 kg	Warhead:	14-23 kg
Guidance:	inertial mid-course, active terminal homing		

B. GUNS

406-mm, Model 1936

Fitted in 1,700-ton triple turrets in *Iowa*-class battleships. Requires a crew of 77 men per mount, plus 30-36 men in the magazine. In 1981, 15,500 high-capacity, 3,200 armor piercing, and 2,300 B, L, & P rounds were available, with 12,500 full-service and 12,600 reduced-charge sets remaining. Armor-piercing rounds can penetrate 9 m of reinforced concrete.
Length: 50 calibers
Muzzle velocity: armor-piercing: 739 m/sec.; high-cap: 902 m/sec.
Rate of fire: 2 rounds/minute/barrel
Maximum range: armor-piercing shell: 36,700 m; high-capacity shell: 38,000 m
Weight of projectile: armor-piercing shell: 1,226 kg; high-capacity shell; 863 kg
Cartridge bags: 6 per charge, 50-kg or 24-kg reduced-charge
Fire control: Mk 38 director with Mk 13 radar

203-mm Mk 16 Mod. 0

Automatic weapon fitted in 451-ton triple turrets on *Des Moines*-class cruisers.
Length: 55 calibers
Muzzle velocity: 900 m/second
Arc of elevation: −5° to +41°
Rate of fire: 10 rounds/minute/barrel
Maximum range: armor-piercing shell: 27,500 m; high-capacity shell: 28,670 m
Weight of projectile: armor-piercing shell: 152 kg; high-capacity shell: 113 kg
Fire control: Mk 54 director with Mk 13 radar

203-mm Mk 71

This model, which has been undergoing tests since the mid-1960s, can fire 75 projectiles in sequence without interference, at a rate of 12 rounds per minute. The evaluation ship was the destroyer *Hull*. The project was canceled on 25-7-78 and the weapon removed in 7-79, but some research is still being pursued in the hope that this extremely effective weapon might be reinstated.

127-mm, twin barrel, Mk 12 Mod. 1

Semiautomatic, dual-purpose gun fitted in the Mk 32 series mounts of the *Iowa*-class battleships and *Des Moines*-class cruisers and in the Mk 38 series mounts of the *Gearing*-class destroyers. 720,000 rounds of 127-mm ammunition for these and the single "5-inch/38" mounts below remained available in 1981.
Length: 38 calibers
Muzzle velocity: 792 m/sec
Elevation: −15° to +85°
Rate of fire: 18 rounds/minute/barrel with a well-trained crew
Maximum range on a surface target: 16,500 m
Maximum effective range on a ship target: 12,000 to 13,000 m
Maximum range in antiaircraft fire: 11,400 m
Maximum effective range in antiaircraft fire: 8,000 m
Weight of projectile: 25 kg
Fire control: Mk 37 director with Mk 25 radar; Mk 56 director with Mk 35 radar in a few ships

127-mm, Mk 24, Mk 30, Mk 37

Single mounting, weighing between 15 and 20.4 tons, in open Mk 24 and Mk 37 series or enclosed Mk 30 series mountings on a few combatants and auxiliaries. Other data as for twin mounting.

127-mm, Mk 42

Single-barrel, dual-purpose gun fitted on ships built in the 1950s and 1960s. Most mounts converted to Mk 42 mod. 10 configuration. An SAL (Semi-Active Laser-guided projectile) is being developed for these and the Mk 45 gun. Trials at sea commenced in *Briscoe* (DD 977) in 1981. The round is 1.548 m long, weighs 47.49 kg, and is similar in concept to the U.S. Army's Copperhead weapon.
Length: 45 calibers
Muzzle velocity: 810 m/second
Mount weight: 65.8 tons, mod. 10: 63.9 tons
Arc of elevation: −5° to +80°
Rate of train: 50°/second
Rate of elevation: 80°/second
Rate of fire: 40 rounds/minute
Weight of projectile: 32 kg
Range: 23,700 m horizontal/14,840 vertical
Fire control: Mk 68 system with SPG-53 radar in most ships

GUNS (continued)

Personnel: 13 men, with 2 in mount

Loading entirely automatic from two ammunition drums in the handling room up to the loading tray by means of a rotating hoist. Each drum contains twenty rounds. The rate of fire can be maintained for only one minute, inasmuch as it is necessary to reload the drums.

127-mm, Mk 45—Northern Ordnance/FMC

Single-barrel mount fitted on *Ticonderoga*-, *California*-, and *Virginia*-class cruisers, *Spruance*-class destroyers, and *Tarawa*-class amphibious assault ships.
Length: 54 calibers
Muzzle velocity: 810 m/second
Mount weight: 21.7 tons
Arc of elevation: −5° to +65°
Rate of fire: 20 rounds/minute
Range: 23,700 m horizontal/14,840 vertical
Fire control: Mk 86 GFCS with SPQ-9 search radar, SPG-60 tracking radar
Personnel: none on mount; 6 in handling room to reload ammunition drums

76.2-mm, Mk 22

Automatic dual-purpose gun in single (Mk 34) or twin (Mk 33) mounts. Mk 27 twin mounts in CA 134 and CA 139. Thoroughly obsolescent.
Length: 50 calibers
Mount weight: 15 tons. Mk 33 open mount
Weight of projectile: 3.2 kg
Rate of fire: 45 rounds/minute/barrel
Maximum range: 12,840 m horizontal/8,950 vertical
Fire control: Mk 56 system with Mk 35 radar or none in active ships

76.2-mm, Mk 21

Single-fire, dual-purpose gun on a few auxiliaries and some Coast Guard ships. Mk 26 mount. Being phased out.
Length: 50 calibers
Mount weight: 4.2 tons
Weight of projectile: 3.2 kg
Rate of fire: 20 rounds/minute
Maximum range: 12,840 horizontal/8,950 vertical
Fire control: ring sight only

76-mm, Mk 75—Northern Ordnance/FMC

Single-barrel, license-built version of OTO Melara Compact, tested in the frigate *Talbot* and used in PHM and FFG 7 classes; to backfit in Coast Guard ships.
Length: 62 calibers
Mount weight: 6.2 tons
Weight of projectile: 6.4 kg
Rate of fire: 85 rounds/minute
Maximum range: 19,200 m horizontal/11,900 m vertical
Fire control: Mk 92 radar system
Personnel: 4 below decks

40-mm, Mk 19

Strictly speaking not a gun, but rather a lightweight rapid-fire grenade launcher in portable tripod-legged mountings. Found aboard auxiliaries and Coast Guard ships.

20-mm Mk 10

Single-barrel, license-built Oerlikon mounting in minesweepers and auxiliaries.
Length: 70 calibers
Mount weight: 318-500 kg
Rate of fire: 450 rounds/minute
Maximum range: 4,390 m horizontal/3,050 m vertical
Fire control: ring sights on mount

20-mm, Mk 16 Mod. 5

Single-barrel Mk 67 or Mk 68 mounting in small combatants, amphibious ships, and auxiliaries.

Length: 80 calibers
Mount weight: . . .
Rate of fire: 800 rounds/minute
Maximum range: 3,000 m horizontal
Fire control: ring sights on mount
Weight of projectile: 0.34 kg

Vulcan/Phalanx, Mk 16 CIWS (Close-In Weapon System)—General Dynamics

"Close-in" system designed to destroy missiles, such as Styx, and sea-skimmer missiles, such as the French Exocet and the Israeli Gabriel. It consists of a multibarrel, M61A1 20-mm gun with a very high rate of fire, which is co-mounted with two radars, one of which follows the target and the other the projectile stream. A computer furnishes necessary corrections for train and elevation so that the two radar targets coincide, bringing heavy fire to bear on the target. 400 units programmed to be fitted to 239 ships. The first production unit completed 9-8-79 and was installed, with two others, in *America* (CV 66) on 17-4-80. An improved "Block II" version with more rounds on-mount and a higher rate of fire will enter service in 1983. Uses Mk 149 rounds with depleted uranium sub-caliber penetrators.
Mount weight: 5.4 tons
Rate of fire: 3,000 rounds/minute
Maximum range: 1,486 m horizontal

C. TORPEDOES

♦ submarine torpedoes

Mk 37 Mod. 2

Electric torpedo with a wire-guided plus active-passive guidance system. Used against surface and submarine targets. About 1,200 remain.
Length: 4.1 m
Diameter: 0.485 m
Weight: 767 kg
Speed: 25 knots
Run duration: 20,000 m

Mk 37 Mod. 3

Similar to the Mk 37 Mod. 0 but is not wire-guided.
Length: 3.4 m
Weight: 649 kg

Mk 48 Mod. 1, Mod. 3, and Mod. 4

Entered service 1972. Can be launched from a submarine against a surface target or a submarine. No surface ships are currently equipped to launch Mk 48, although that capability was originally intended. A total of 3,059 Mk 48s have been procured through 1980, plus 56 for Australia and 92 for the Netherlands; 144 additional for the U.S. Navy were appropriated under FY 80 and again in FY 81.

TORPEDOES *(continued)*

Length: 5.54 m   Speed: 50 kts
Diameter: 0.533 m   Propulsion: 500 hp Otto-cycle swashplate engine
Weight: 1,633 kg

Can be launched with its own active-passive or acoustic homing system or with a wire-guidance system. High speed (40 knots?) and long run duration (50,000 m). An improvement program, ADCAP (Added Capability) is being instituted, with the first twenty-two conversion kits requested under FY 80. The first "Near-Term Update" Mk 48 Mod. 4 torpedo was delivered 12-80.

♦ surface-launched torpedoes

Mk 46 Mod. 1 and Mod. 2

ASW torpedo using solid fuel (Monergol). Active-passive guidance. Launched from Mk 32 ASW torpedo tubes or as payload for the ASROC ASW missile system.
Length: 2.59 m
Diameter: 0.324 m
Weight: 231 kg

The Mk 46 Mod. 1 and Mod. 2 are being upgraded to Mod. 5 NEARTIP (Near-Term Improvement Program) status with improved acoustic homing system and countermeasures resistance. Under FY 80, 576 conversion kits were requested, and 1,128 more will be requested under FY 82; ultimately, some 2,700 torpedoes will be updated. The Mk 46 Mod. 4 is the payload for the Captor mine. 570 *new* Mk 46 Mod. 5 torpedoes were ordered from Honeywell in 1980.

ALWT—Honeywell

The ALWT (Advanced Lightweight Torpedo) is being developed as a replacement for the Mk 46 series and will be supplied in surface-launched and air-droppable configurations. It will be roughly the same weight as the Mk 46 and of the same dimensions, but will be deeper-diving (600 m), faster (40 knots), and have better homing and counter-countermeasures capabilities. Will not be operational before the late 1980s.

♦ aircraft torpedoes

Mk 46 Mod. 0

Similar to the surface-launched weapon, but equipped with a retarding parachute, solid vice liquid propellant, and does not have a straight run-out before commencing helical search. Will be replaced by the ALWT.

D. MINES

Mk 52 Mod. 1, 2, 3, 5, 6

Air-dropped. All 2.75-m long by 338-mm diameter (840 mm over fins). All carry 270 kg HBX explosive. Mod. 1 is an acoustic mine, weight: 542.5 kg. Mod. 2 is a magnetic influence version, weight: 568 kg. Mod. 3 is a dual-pressure/magnetic influence version, weight: 572.5 kg. Mod. 5 is an acoustic/magnetic influence version, weight: 570.7 kg. Mod. 6 is a pressure/acoustic/magnetic influence version, weight: 546 kg. All are bottom mines for depths of up to 47 m (Mod. 2: 183 m) and can be carried by U.S.A.F. B-52D and H bombers as well as Navy aircraft.

Mk 55 Mod. 2, 3, 5, 6, 7

Air-dropped bottom mines. All 2.89 m long by .592 m diameter (1.03 m over fins) and carry 577 kg HBX-1 explosive. Versions: Mod. 2: magnetic influence, weight: 989 kg; Mod. 3: pressure/magnetic influence, weight: 994 kg; Mod. 5: acoustic/magnetic influence, weight: 994 kg; Mod. 6: pressure/acoustic/magnetic, weight: 997 kg.; Mod.

7: dual-channel magnetic influence, weight: 996 kg. All can be laid in 46-m-deep water, except Mod. 2, 7: 183 m.

Mk 56 Mod. 0

Aircraft-dropped moored mine. 996-kg. 3.51 m long by 592-mm diameter (1.06 over fins). Total-field magnetic influence exploder. Carries 577-kg HBX-3 explosive. Depth: 350 m.

Mk 57 Mod. 0

Submarine-laid moored mine. 1012 kg. 3.07 long by 510-mm diameter. Carries 935 kg HBX-3 explosive. Depth: 250 m.

Mk 60 Captor (enCAPsulated TORpedo)

Submarine-laid or aircraft-dropped. Uses Mk 46 Mod. 4 acoustic-homing torpedo payload. Primarily ASW in function. 908 kg. 3.66 m long by 324-mm diameter. 44.5 kg warhead. In development since 1961 but still not fully reliable. 260 requested under FY 80 in first major operational buy, with 660 programmed for FY 81. Moored mine, before torpedo launch.

Mk 67 SLMM (Submarine-Launched Mobile Mine)

Converted Mk 37 Mod. 0 torpedo. 754 kg. 4.09 m long by 483-mm diameter. Bottom mine. Remains in development.

IWD (Intermediate Water-Depth)—General Electric

Formerly PRAM (Propelled Rocket Ascent Mine). Anti-surface and ASW mine for launch by submarines and aircraft. Moored mine. In development, but funding restricted.

DST-36 Quickstrike series (Mods. 0-5)

Aircraft dropped bottom mine. Converted from 500-lb (227 kg) Mk 82 standard aircraft bomb. Magnetic. 87-kg H-6 explosive charge.

DST-40 Quickstrike series (Mods. 0-5)

Aircraft-dropped bottom mine. Converted from 1,000-lb (454-kg) Mk 83 standard aircraft bomb. Magnetic.

DST-41 Quickstrike series (Mods. 0-5)

Aircraft-dropped bottom mine. Converted from 2,000-lb (908-kg) Mk 84 bomb. Magnetic or magnetic/seismic influence. 3.83 m long. Minelaying: no surface ships are capable of minelaying. Naval aircraft of the S-3, P-3, A-6, and A-7 types are capable of laying mines, as are some 80 operational Air Force B-52D bombers. Theoretically, any U.S. Navy submarine can lay mines from its torpedo tubes.

E. RADARS

Radars for active ships are:

♦ surface-search and navigation

SPS-10: C-band, Mods. B through F in service. Primary surface-search set before the introduction of SPS-55.

SPS-53: X-band. Navigational set for large ships and for MSOs, auxiliaries, and Coast Guard ships.

SPS-55: X-band, slotted waveguide antenna. On *Spruance*-class destroyers and FFG 7 frigates, etc.

RADARS (*continued*)

SPS-63: X-band. U.S. version of the Italian 3RM-20N for use on the *Pegasus*-class hydrofoils.

SPS-67: C-band. A solid-state replacement for the SPS-10, using same antenna. Also has an ultra-short pulse mode for navigation. First use on refitted *Long Beach* (CGN 9) in 1982.

Also in use are the small navigational radar sets LN-66, SPS-51, SPS-57, SPS-59, SPS-60, SPS-64, and SPS-66, all X-band and most using slotted-waveguide antennas.

BPS-5, 11, 14, 15: X-band. Submarine search, navigational, and fire-control radars. Mounted on telescoping masts.

◆ two-dimensional air-search

SPS-6: L-band. Obsolescent; used only on *Thomaston* (LSD 28) class.

SPS-12: L-band. On AVT 16, CA 139, and several amphibious warfare ships. Obsolescent.

SPS-29: P-band. On some of the older DDGs and DDs. Same antenna as SPS-37 and SPS-43A.

SPS-37: On CGN 25, some CVs, CGs, and DDGs. **SPS-37A** used long SPS-43A antenna. Pulse-compression version of SPS-29.

SPS-40: B-band. The most widely used air-search radar. Range against medium bombers: 150-180 miles. Earlier "A" models being modernized to SPS-40D. P-band pulse-compression.

SPS-43: SPS-43A with large antenna. Mounted in most aircraft carriers; SPS-43 with small antenna on missile cruisers.

SPS-49: Aboard FFG 7-class and others. Mechanically stabilized antenna.

SPS-58/65: L-band, pulse-doppler. Combined air-surface search radars. SPS-65 uses modified SPS-10 antenna; SPS-58 uses larger, stabilized antenna, otherwise similar.

◆ three-dimensional air search

SPS-39: S-band. Mod. A uses same antenna as SPS-52. In some DDGs: E-band. SPS-52 is a version developed to interface directly with the NTDS data system.

SPS-48A: Mounted on CG classes. Frequency-scanning system.

SPS-48C, E: Electronic frequency scanning in elevation, improved SPS-48A. E version has doubled power, armored antenna; entering service 1982.

SPS-52C: S-band improvement on SPS-39. Electronic frequency scanning in elevation.

SPY-1A: S-band. Aegis system. Obtaining a directional effect by dipole radiation to secure an electronic sweep, it has four fixed aerials that provide instant 360° coverage. Long-range air-search, target-tracking, and missile-guidance. Lighter-weight SPY-1D in development for DDGX program.

◆ fire-control

Mk 13: 3-cm wavelength. Ranging set for Mk 38 director on *Iowa*-class battleships and on Mk 34 director on CA 134 and CA 139.

MK 25: X-band. Mounted on Mk 37 GFCS directors on CA, old DD. Dish antenna.

Mk 35: 3-cm wavelength. Mounted on Mk 56 GFCS director for 127-mm and 76.2-mm guns. On older FFGs and FFs. Removed from auxiliaries. Dish antenna.

Mk 91: Technically, the fire-control *system* for the Sea Sparrow SAM system, used with the Mk 29 lightweight launcher. Either one (Mod. 0) or two (Mod. 1) radar directors per launcher.

Mk 92/94: U.S. Navy adaptation of Dutch H.S.A. (Hollandse Signaal Apparaaten) WM-20 series track-while-scan gun/missile fire-control system. Used in FFG 7, PHM 1, and the Coast Guard's new WMEC classes. Antennas mounted in egg-shaped radome. Combined with STIR (modified SPG-60) antenna in FFG 7 class.

Mk 115: Technically the fire-control *system* for Sea Sparrow when launched from the Mk 25 heavy launcher. Older than Mk 91 and being phased out.

SPQ-9: Special surface-search and weapons-control for use with Mk 86 GFCS. Antenna mounted in spherical radome.

SPG-50: On 76.2-mm gun mount on PG; used with later Mk 63 GFCS. Being phased out. Earlier version, Mk 34/SPG-34, entirely phased out.

SPG-51B, C, D: Standard MR illuminator-tracker; used with Mk 74 missile fire-control system.

SPG-52: Mounted on twin 76.2-mm gun mounts in LPH 2 class only; used with Mk 70 GFCS.

SPG-53: Mounted on Mk 68 GFCS director on CG, DDG, and DD with 127-mm Mk 42 guns.

SPG-55A, B: Standard ER illuminator-tracker; used with Mk 76 missile fire-control system.

SPG-60: Standard MR illuminator-tracker with Mk 74 missile fire-control system in later CGN classes; also illuminates for guns in conjunction with Mk 86 GFCS. STIR version, used on FFG 7 class, is modified for use with Mk 92 Mod. 2 missile/gun control system.

SPG-62: Standard SM-2 illuminator; used with Aegis system, in CG 47 class. Slaved to SPY-1 radar.

TAS/Mk 23: Technically a Target Acquisition System, employing a rapidly rotating, stabilized linear array antenna in conjunction with a UYK-20 computer to counter high- and low-angle aircraft and cruise missile attacks. Range 20 nm on small missiles to 90 nm on aircraft. Mod. 0 on *Downes* (FF 1070) since 1975, Mod. 1 to be added to *Spruance* (DD 963) class, Mod. 2 (with UYA-4 console) on *Sacramento* class, beginning with AOE 3 in 4-80. Can track 54 targets simultaneously.

◆ carrier-controlled approach systems

SPN-6: Formerly installed on aircraft carriers but now limited to AVT 16 and 7 LPH. Antenna in large radome.

SPN-10: Aircraft landing aid, incorporating a radar set to determine aircraft position relative to the carrier. Antennas are two small conical dishes. Being replaced by SPN-42, which is less bulky. Other carrier aircraft landing aid/radar systems include SPN-41, SPN-43, and SPN-44.

F. COUNTERMEASURES SYSTEMS

◆ electronic systems, surface ships

WLR-1: Radar warning array in older ships.

WLR-3: Radar warning and signal collection—also in some submarines.

COUNTERMEASURES SYSTEMS *(continued)*

WLR-8: Radar warning system for carriers.

ULQ-6: Deception repeater/jammer in cruisers, destroyers—being replaced by SLQ-32.

WLR-11: Radar warning system.

SLQ-17: Jammer array in carriers.

SLQ-29: The combined WLR-8/SLQ-17 package—in carriers.

SLQ-32(V)1: Radar warning (H, I, J bands) for auxiliaries and amphibious ships (to be on 113 ships).

SLQ-32(V)2: Radar warning (B-J bands) for newer destroyers and frigates—replaces WLR-3 where fitted (to be on 107 ships).

SLQ-32(V)3: Radar warning (B-J bands) *and* jamming/spoofing (H-J bands) for cruisers, DDG 37 class, and major amphibious ships (to be on 64 ships).

♦ **electronic systems, submarines**

BLQ-3, 4, 5, 8: Acoustic jamming systems.

BLR-1-10, 13-15: Radar warning systems; BLR-14 also launches countermeasures.

WLR-9: Sonar detection system.

WLR-10: Radar warning receiver.

♦ **physical countermeasures systems**

T-Mk 6 Fanfare: Mechanical towed anti-torpedo noisemaker—obsolescent.

SLQ-25 Nixie: Towed torpedo countermeasure/noisemaker, to replace T-Mk 6—180 sets procured.

Chaffroc: Two-celled (8-rocket) launcher for modified Zuni chaff-deploying rockets—obsolescent.

Mk 33 RBOC: Rapid-Blooming Overboard Chaff launcher—replaced by Mk 36.

Mk 36 SRBOC: Super-RBOC—Mod. 1 with two 6-tubed mortars for ships under 140 m; Mod. 2 with four 6-tubed mortars for ships over 140 m. All use Mk 182 chaff-dispensing cartridges, which climb to 244 m. "Torch" infrared decoy being developed for use with Mk 36 SRBOC, and the NATO Sea Gnat rocket chaff dispenser may be adopted.

Mk 70 MOSS: Mobile Submarine Simulator—small torpedo-like device for launch by *Ohio*-class SSBNs.

G. SONARS

♦ **on surface ships**

SQQ-14: High-frequency, minehunting, and classification set in retractable transducer array on MSOs.

SQQ-23: PAIR (Performance and Integration Refit). Modified SQS-23 using two transducer domes (except in CGN 9 and CG 16 classes, one dome); also in DDG 2, DDG 37 classes.

SQQ-30: New minehunting sonar under development by General Electric for use on new-construction mine countermeasures ships.

SQR-15: Developmental passive towed array, in FF 1037 and some FF 1040-class frigates.

SQR-17: Passive classification device for processing data transmitted to CG 26, DD 963, FF 1052, and FFG 7-class ships by LAMPS helicopters from SSQ-53 DIFAR sonobuoys.

SQR-18: TACTAS (Tactical Towed Acoustic Sensor). For use on FF 1052 class equipped with SQS-35 VDS; array attaches to VDS towed body.

SQR-19: Improved TACTAS for use on CG 47, DD 963, and FFG 7 classes; to be deployed through port in stern. Still in development.

SQS-23: Bow- or hull-mounted low-frequency, active-passive. In CV 66, CGN 25, some CG, older DDG, DD 931, and DD 710 classes.

SQS-26: Bow-mounted, low-frequency set, in various versions. In older CGN, CG 26, FFG 1, FF 1037, FF 1040, FF 1052, FF 1098 classes.

SQS-35: Independent, variable-depth, towed, active-passive. In some DD 931 class, most FF 1052 class.

SQS-53: SQS-26 with digital computer interface, for use with Mk 116 UWFCS (Underwater Fire Control System) on DD 963, DDG 993, CG 47 classes.

SQS-56: Raytheon 1160B commercial active-passive, hull-mounted, medium-frequency set; used on FFG 7 class.

SURTASS: SURveillance Towed-Array Sonar System, for use in the *Stalwart* (T-AGOS 1) class. Trails 1,830-m passive hydrophone array at about 3 knots. Still in development.

♦ **on submarines**

BQQ-4: PUFFS (Passive Underwater Fire Control). Three-fin arrays, on SSN 597, SS 574, SS 563 classes.

BQQ-2: Active-passive system on SSN 594 class, SSN 597, SSN 637 class, SSN 671, SSN 685. Incorporates BQR-7 conformed hydrophone array and BQS-6 spherical hydrophone array. Being upgraded to BQQ-5 in most ships.

BQQ-5: Active-passive system on the SSN 688 class; being backfitted in SSN 594 and SSN 637 classes. Incorporates BQS-11, 12, or 13 spherical bow hydrophone array.

BQQ-6: Passive-only version of the BQQ-5 system, for SSBN 626 class.

BQR-15: Towed, passive array for SSN 608, SSN 616 classes. Incorporates BQR-23 signal processor.

BQR-19: Active, short-range, navigational set for SSBNs.

BQR-21: DIMUS (Digital Multi-Beam Steering). Passive array for SSBNs.

BQS-4: Active/passive set in older SSN, SS.

BQS-8, 14, 20: Under-ice and mine-avoidance, high-frequency set, mostly on later SSNs. Part of the BQQ-2, 5, 6 systems.

BQS-15: Under-ice set tailored to the requirements of the SSN 688 class.

♦ **on helicopters**

AQS-13: Dipping sonar used on SH-3 Sea King series.

AQS-14: Mine countermeasures set used by RH-53 helicopters.

H. PROCESSING OF TACTICAL DATA

The system now in use is the NTDS (Naval Tactical Data System). Thanks to its digital calculators (AN/UYK-20 and AN/UYK-7), it instantaneously gives an overall picture of a tactical situation—air, surface, and underwater—and enables the commander to employ the means necessary to oppose the enemy. Excellent automatic data transmission systems (Link-11 and Link-14) permit the exchange of tactical information with similarly equipped ships and aircraft carrying the ATDS (P-3C Orion and S-3A Viking) and amphibious landing forces equipped with NTDS.

By mid-1978, some 427 ships were equipped to receive SATCOMM (Satellite Communications) messages, while 259 could send ultrahigh-frequency messages via satellite and 6 (with another 25 programmed) could send superhigh-frequency messages. The Tactical Flag Command Center (TFCC) is being backfitted into 13 CV/CVN, 2 LCC, and 5 CG. It employs USQ-81(V) computer-generated displays in an integrated 6.2-m × 6.2-m display space.

NUCLEAR-POWERED AIRCRAFT CARRIERS

♦ 0 (+3) improved Nimitz class Bldr: Newport News SB & DD

	Laid down	L	In serv.
CNV 71 THEODORE ROOSEVELT	31-10-81	9-85	1988
CVN 72 N. . .	. . .	. . .	1992-93
CVN 73 N. . .	. . .	. . .	. . .

D: 96,836 tons (fl) **S:** 30+ kts
Dim: 332.84 (317.0 pp) × 40.85 (flight deck: 78.33) × 11.12 **Man:** 5,529 tot.
A: 3/Mk 29 launchers (VIII × 3) for Sea Sparrow—4/Vulcan/Phalanx 20-mm Gatling AA—90+ aircraft, including F-14, F/A-18, EA-6B, A-6E, A-7E, E-2C, 10/S-3A, and 6/SH-3D
Electron Equipt: Radar: 1/SPS-53, 1/SPS-55, 1/SPS-48C, 1/SPS-49, 1/SPS-65, 1/SPN-41, 1/SPN-35A, 1/SPN-44, 3/Mk 91 Mod. 1 (6 directors)
ECM: SLQ-29 (WRL-8+SLQ-17), 4/Mk 36 SRBOC chaff
TACAN: . . .
M: 2 A4W/A1G pressurized-water reactors, 4 sets GT; 4 props; 280,000 hp
Electric: 64,000 kw + 8,000 kw emergency power from 4 diesel sets

REMARKS: CVN 71 appropriated under FY 80; this badly needed ship was repeatedly delayed in favor of conventionally powered designs of inferior capabilities. Won out over both an administration-sponsored 62,427-ton (fl) paper CVV design and a compromise 82,561-ton repeat *John F. Kennedy* (CV 67) design. Will cost in excess of $2.1 billion (1980 dollars), exclusive of aircraft. CVN 72 and 73 requested under FY 83.

The hangar will have 7.6 m clear height. The angled deck will be 237.7 m long and will be equipped with four arrester wires and a barrier, as well as four Mk 13 Mod. 1 catapults (94.5 m long), and four elevators. An aviation payload of some 14,909 tons will be carried, and the aviation ordnance magazines will hold 1,954 tons. Aviation fuel capacity will be more than 9,000 tons. Kevlar armor will be fitted over vital spaces, and hull protection arrangements have been improved.
Other data under the *Nimitz* class will generally apply.

♦ 3 Nimitz class Bldr: Newport News SB & DD

	Laid down	L	In serv.
CVN 68 NIMITZ	22-6-68	13-5-72	3-5-75
CVN 69 DWIGHT D. EISENHOWER	15-8-70	11-10-75	18-10-77
CVN 70 CARL VINSON	11-10-75	25-3-80	13-3-82

Authorized: CVN 68 in FY 67, CVN 69 in FY 71, CVN 70 in FY 74.

Carl Vinson (CVN 70)—note port fwd sponson for fourth Vulcan/Phalanx CIWS
J. Jedrlinic, 10-81

Carl Vinson (CVN 70)—nearly complete, radars, Vulcan/Phalanx, Sea Sparrow launchers installed. Note greater overhang to island than on CVN 68 and CVN 69.

Nimitz (CVN 68)
J. Jedrlinic, 11-80

Dwight D. Eisenhower (CVN 69)
L. & L. Van Ginderen, 9-81

NUCLEAR-POWERED AIRCRAFT CARRIERS (continued)

Nimitz (CVN 68)　　　　　　　　　　PH3 L. Schnell, USN, 1-80

Nimitz (CVN 68)　　　　　　　　　　J. Jedrlinic, 11-80

Dwight D. Eisenhower (CVN 69)　　　L. & L. Van Ginderen, 6-79

D: 81,600 tons (96,351 fl)　**S:** 30+ kts

Dim: 327.0 (over catapult bridle retrieval horns: 332.8, pp: 317.0) × 40.85 (flight deck: 77.11, max.: 89.4) × 11.3

A: 90+ airplanes and helicopters—3/Mk 25 launchers (VIII × 3) for Sea Sparrow

Electron Equipt: Radar: 1/LN-66, 1/SPS-10F, 1/SPS-43A, 1/SPS-48B, 1/SPN-41 (CVN 69, 70 only), 2/SPN-42, 1/SPN-43A, 1/SPN-44, 3/Mk 115

ECM: SLQ-29 (WLR-8 + SLQ-17), 4/Mk 36 SRBOC chaff

TACAN: URN-20

M: 2 A4W/A1G pressurized-water reactors, 4 sets GT; 4 props; 280,000 hp

Electric: 64,000 kw + 8,000 kw emergency power from 4 diesel sets

Man: 6,286 men (569 officers), including aviation personnel (2,626 with 304 officers)

REMARKS: The *Nimitz* cost $685,800,000 to build, while her air wing and equipment cost $710,600,000. The offensive potential of these ships is remarkable; they carry 90% more aviation fuel and 50% more ammunition than the *Forrestal* class. They have an ASCAC (Antisubmarine Classification and Analysis Center), which permits instant sharing of target data between the carrier, its ASW aircraft, and escorting ships.

Electronics: SPS-43A to be replaced by SPS-49. Carry OE-82 satellite communications antennas and have full NTDS installations.

Armament: *Carl Vinson* will be completed with three Mk 29 launchers (VIII × 3) for Sea Sparrow, six directors for the missile (3 Mk 91 Mod. 1 FCS), and four Vulcan/Phalanx Gatling AA guns. The others are to be similarly refitted, but will get only three Vulcan/Phalanx.

Armor: Decks and hull are of extra-strong, high-tensile steel that can limit the impact of semi-armor-piercing bombs. Apart from the longitudinal bulkheads, there are twenty-three watertight transverse bulkheads (more than 2,000 compartments) and ten firewall bulkheads. Foam devices for fire-fighting are very well developed, and pumping equipment is excellent, a 15°-list being correctable in 20 minutes. Thirty damage-control teams are available at all times. *Nimitz*-class ships can withstand three times the severe pounding taken by the *Essex*-class aircraft carriers in 1944-45, and they can take impacts and shock waves in the same proportion. They are to be equipped with Kevlar armor over vital spaces during refits scheduled for 1982, 1987, and 1988 (in order of construction).

Machinery: The cores of these ships are expected to last 13 years in normal usage, for a cruising distance of 800,000 to 1,000,000 miles. The evaporators can produce 1,520 tons of fresh water per day.

Aircraft-handling installations: There are four side elevators: two forward, one aft of the island to starboard, and one on the stern to port. There are also four Mk-C13 Mod. 1 steam catapults, 94.5 m long. CVN 69 and 70 have only the forward starboard bridle retrieval horn, because most aircraft in service do not require the bridle for launching. The 15,134 m³ total aviation magazine spaces can hold 1,954 tons of aviation ordnance, and the total aviation-associated payload is on the order of 15,000 tons. The hangar is 7.8 meters high and can accommodate only 35-40% of the aircaft aboard. The angled part of the flight deck is 237.7 meters long and has four Mk 14 arrester wires and a barrier to halt aircraft (to be changed to 3 wires, 1 net). The aircraft complement normally includes ten S-3A ASW aircraft and six SH-3D ASW helicopters. Other aircraft are a mix of F-14 interceptors, E-2C early-warning, A-7E day and A-6E all-weather attack, and EA-6B electronics aircraft. Sufficient aviation fuel for 16 days' operations is carried.

◆ **1 Enterprise class (SCB 160 type)**

	Bldr	Laid down	L	In serv.
CVN 65 ENTERPRISE	Newport News SB & DD	4-2-58	24-9-60	25-11-61

Authorized: FY 58

D: 73,502 tons (90,970 fl)　**S:** 33 kts

Dim: 335.75 (over catapult bridle horn: 342.3, wl: 317.0) × 40.54 (flight deck: 78.4) × 11.9

A: 88-90 airplanes and helicopters—3/Mk 29 launchers (VIII × 3) for Sea Sparrow—3/Vulcan/Phalanx 20-mm Gatling AA (I × 3)—3/20-mm AA (I × 3, Mk 68)

Electron Equipt: Radar: 1/SPS-65, 1/SPS-48C, 1/SPS-49, 1/SPN-41, 1/SPN-35A, 1/SPN-44, 3/Mk 91 Mod. 1 (6 directors)

ECM: SLQ-29 (WLR-8 + SLQ-17A(V)2), 4/Mk 36 SRBOC chaff

TACAN: URN-26

NUCLEAR-POWERED AIRCRAFT CARRIERS (continued)

Enterprise (CVN 65)—during modernization   U.S. Navy, 2-80

Enterprise (CVN 65)—prior to modernization   L. & L. Van Ginderen, 1978

M: 8 Westinghouse A2W reactors, supplying 32 Foster-Wheeler heat exchangers; 4 sets Westinghouse GT; 4 props; 280,000 hp
Electric: 40,000 kw + 8,000 kw emergency
Man: 462 officers, 5,102 men (including 304/2,323 aviation personnel)

REMARKS: Began what was to have been a two-year overhaul at Puget Sound NSY 15-1-79, during which the radar and other electronics suits were extensively renovated; completed 11-81. The SPS-32 and SPS-33 "billboard" radar arrays were removed, as was the "beehive" dome atop the blockhouse superstructure. A new mast, resembling that on the *Nimitz*, was installed atop the superstructure. SPS-48C and SPS-49 are mounted atop the island. There are four Mk-C13 steam catapults and four elevators—one on the port side of the angled deck, three to starboard—two of which are forward of and one abaft the island. Elevators are steel and alloy and weigh 105 tons; 26 m long, 16 m wide, lift 45 tons. The hangar is 7.62-m high and the flight deck is more than 20,000 m². Carries half again as much aviation fuel as the *Forrestal* class (8,500 tons), which permits 12 days of intensive aerial operations without replenishment. Carries fuel oil to replenish other ships. Has NTDS and ASCAC (Antisubmarine Classification and Analysis Center) and will receive TFCC (Tactical Flag Communications Center).

CONVENTIONAL AIRCRAFT CARRIERS

♦ **1 John F. Kennedy class (SCB 127C type)** Bldr: Newport News SB & DD

	Laid down	L	In serv.
CV 67 JOHN F. KENNEDY	22-10-64	27-5-67	7-9-68

Authorized: FY 63

John F. Kennedy (CV 67)   PH2 R. Wilson, USN, 3-80

John F. Kennedy (CV 67)—note outward-leaning stack PH2 R. Wilson, USN, 3-80

D: 61,000 tons (82,561 fl) **S:** 32 kts
Dim: 320.7 (301.8 wl) × 39.32 (flight deck: 76.9, max.: 81.53) × 11.13
A: 88-90 aircraft—3/Mk 29 launchers (VIII × 3) for Sea Sparrow
Electron Equipt: Radar: 1/SPS-10F, 1/SPS-49, 1/SPS-48C, 1/SPN-35, 2/SPN-42, 1/SPN-43A, 3/Mk 91 Mod. 1 (6 directors)
          ECM: SLQ-29 (WLR-8 + SLQ-17), 4/Mk 36 SRBOC chaff
          TACAN: URN-20
M: 4 sets GE GT; 4 props; 280,000 hp
Boilers: 8 Foster-Wheeler; 83.4 kg/cm², 520°C
Man: 460 officers, 4,917 men (including aviation personnel)

REMARKS: In 1981 carried 24 F-14, 12 A-6E, 24 A-7E, 4 KA-6D, 4 EA-6B, 10 S-3A, 4 E-2C and 6 SH-3H aircraft. Four side elevators, three to starboard (two forward

CONVENTIONAL AIRCRAFT CARRIERS (*continued*)

of and one abaft the island) and one on the port quarter. Completely automatic landing system, permitting all-weather operation. Four arrester wires and a barrier on the 227-m angled flight deck. Three 90-m Mk-C13 and one 94.5-m Mk-C13-1 catapults. Has PLAT, which facilitates the control of launching and recovery operations. Stack angled to starboard. The 11,808-m² aviation-ordnance magazine can accommodate 1,250 tons of ammunition. Carries 5,919 tons of aviation fuel. The Mk 25 Sea Sparrow launchers were replaced by Mk 29 launchers with six radar directors, and three 20-mm Vulcan/Phalanx Gatling AA are still to be added. Equipped to carry SQS-23 sonar in bow dome, but it was not installed. SPS-49 replaced SPS-43A in 1979-80, and SPS-58 was deleted.

♦ **3 Kitty Hawk class (SCB 127A and SCB 127B types)**

	Bldr	Laid down	L	In serv.
CV 63 KITTY HAWK	New York SB	27-12-56	21-5-60	29-4-61
CV 64 CONSTELLATION	Brooklyn NSY	14-9-57	8-10-60	27-10-61
CV 66 AMERICA	Newport News SB	9-1-61	1-2-64	23-1-65

Authorized: CV 63 in FY 56, CV 64 in FY 57, CV 66 in FY 61

D: 60,100 tons (80,300 fl; CV 66: 81,700)   **S:** 33 kts
Dim: 318.8 (CV 66: 319.25) (301.76 pp) × 39.62 (flight deck: 76.81) × 11.2 (CV 66: 11.3)
A: 88 aircraft—2 or 3/Mk 29 launchers (VIII × 2 or 3) for Sea Sparrow
Electron Equipt: Radar: 1/SPS-10F, 1/SPS-43A, 1/SPS-48C, 1/SPN-35, 2/SPN-42, 1/SPN-43A, 2 or 3/Mk 91 Mod. 1
      (4 or 6 directors)
   Sonar: CV 66 only: SQS-23
   ECM: SLQ-29 (WLR-8 + SLQ-17), 4/Mk 36 SRBOC chaff
   TACAN: URN-20

Constellation (CV 64)—still with Mk 10 launchers   G. Arra, 1980

Constellation (CV 64)   PH1 J. Aswegan, USN, 2-80

Kitty Hawk (CV 63)—Mk 29 launcher and 2 radar directors on stbd. sponson aft
G. Arra, 1980

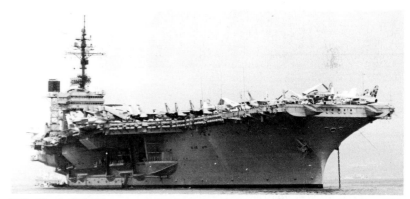

Kitty Hawk (CV 63)   G. Arra, 1980

M: 4 sets Westinghouse GT; 4 props; 280,000 hp   **Fuel:** 7,800 tons
Boilers: 8 Foster-Wheeler; 83.4 kg/cm²; 520°C   **Range:** 4,000/30; 8,000/20
Man: Approx. 5,400: 137 officers, 2,765 men + air group: 290 officers, 2,200 men

REMARKS: Air group composition as on CV 67. These ships are a great improvement over the *Forrestal* class, on which they are based, and have one significant difference: three elevators on the starboard side, two forward of and one abaft the island, and one to port, abaft the angled flight deck. Aircraft can be landed and catapulted simultaneously, a difficult operation on the earlier ships. Four Mk-C13 steam catapults, except on CV 66, on which one is of the longer Mk-C-13-1 type. Carry 5,882 tons of aviation fuel. CV 63 and CV 64 will receive three 20-mm Vulcan/Phalanx; CV 66 was the first ship to receive the weapon, in 4-80. CV 63 has only two Mk 29 launchers for Sea Sparrow. CV 64 retained two Mk 10 twin launchers for Terrier HT missiles and two SPQ-55B radar directors until late 1981. CV 66 was the first to have a special integrated CIC and airborne ASW control center (ASCAC).

♦ **4 Forrestal class (CV 59: SCB 80 type, CV 60 to CV 62: SCB 80M type)**

	Bldr	Laid down	L	In serv.
CV 59 FORRESTAL	Newport News SB & DD	14-7-52	11-12-54	1-10-55
CV 60 SARATOGA	Brooklyn NSY	16-12-52	8-10-55	14-4-56
CV 61 RANGER	Newport News SB & DD	2-8-54	29-9-54	10-8-57
CV 62 INDEPENDENCE	Brooklyn NSY	1-7-55	6-6-58	10-1-59

CONVENTIONAL AIRCRAFT CARRIERS (*continued*)

Saratoga (CV 60)—prior to SLEP modernization   L. & L. Van Ginderen, 5-80

Forrestal (CV 59)   French Navy, 1980

Independence (CV 62)   L. & L. Van Ginderen, 11-79

Ranger (CV 61)   1976

Authorized: CV 59 in FY 52, CV 60 in FY 53, CV 61 IN FY 54, CV 62 in FY 55

D: CV 59: 59,600 tons (79,250 fl); CV 60, CV 61: 60,000 tons (80,250 fl); CV 62: 60,000 tons (79,650 fl)   **S:** 33 kts

Dim: CV 59: 331.0; CV 60: 324.0; CV 61: 326.4; CV 62: 326.1 (319.13 flight deck, 301.8 wl) × 39.47 (CV 59, CV 60: 78.9; CV 61, CV 62: 77.7 flight deck) × 11.2

A: 88 aircraft—CV 59: 2/Mk 25 launchers (VIII × 2) for Sea Sparrow (CV 61, CV 62: 2/Mk 29 launchers)—see Remarks

Electron Equipt: Radar: 1/LN-66, 1/SPS-10, 1/SPS-43A, 1/SPS-48C, 1/SPS-58, 1/SPN-35, 2/SPN-42, 1/SPN-43A, 2/Mk 91 Mod. 1 (2 directors) (CV 59: 2/Mk 115)

ECM: SLQ-29 (WLR-8 + SLQ-17), 4/Mk 36 SRBOC chaff
TACAN: URN-20

M: 4 sets GE or Westinghouse GT; 4 props; CV 59: 260,000 hp, others: 280,000 hp

Boilers: 8 Babcock & Wilcox; CV 59: 41.7 kg/cm², others: 83.4 kg/cm², 520°C

Fuel: 7,800 tons   **Range:** 4,000/30; 8,000/20

Man: Approx. 4,940: 145 officers, 2,645 enlisted + air group: 290 officers, 3,100 enlisted

REMARKS: Aircraft complement as on CV 67. Hangar is 7.6 m high and 234-240 m long. Four side elevators (15.95 × 18.9). Deck angled at 8°. Armored flight deck. Four-cable arresting gear. CV 59 and CV 60 have two Mk-C7 (75 m) and two Mk-C11 (65 m) steam catapults; the others have four Mk-C7. Carry 5,880 tons of aviation fuel. CV 59 has three rudders and four propellers, the two outboard being five-bladed, the two inboard, four-bladed. Deck protection and internal compartmentation are extensive (1,200 watertight compartments). Two longitudinal bulkheads are fitted from keel to waterline from stem to stern; there are transverse bulkheads about every 10 meters.

CV 60 receiving first SLEP (Service Life Extension Program) modernization, beginning 1-10-80 at Philadelphia Navy Yard, for completion 2-83. The others will follow in order of their construction, the yard periods lasting about two years and adding fifteen years to their service lives. All will ultimately be armed with three

CONVENTIONAL AIRCRAFT CARRIERS (*continued*)

Mk 29 Sea Sparrow launchers, each with two directors, and three Mk 15 Vulcan/Phalanx Gatling guns, and will carry SPS-48C and SPS-49 radars. All catapults will be replaced with longer and more powerful Mk-C13s. The ships will get Kevlar armor, improved data systems, the Tactical Flag Command Center, and more habitability. All originally carried eight 127-mm/54, Mk 42 guns. CV 61 relinquished her last two guns in 1977, later than her sisters did, and retains her forward gun sponsons. Stacks raised 3 m in CV 59 and 62.

♦ **2 Midway class** Bldr: Newport News SB & DD

	Laid down	L	In serv.
CV 41 MIDWAY	27-10-43	20-3-45	10-9-45
CV 43 CORAL SEA	10-7-44	2-4-46	1-10-47

D: CV 41: 51,000 tons (64,100 fl)—CV 43: 52,500 tons (63,800 fl) **S:** 33 kts
Dim: 298.38 (293.91 pp) × 41.45 (flight deck: 72.54) × 10.9
A: 65 aircraft—CV 41: 2/Mk 25 launchers (VIII × 2) for Sea Sparrow—both: 3/20-mm Vulcan/Phalanx AA

Midway (CV 41)—modernization completed, stbd. broadside
L. & L. Van Ginderen, 5-81

Midway (CV 41)—partially modernized, port broadside
G. Arra, 1979

Midway (CV 41)—port quarter, showing Mk 25 BPDMS; note large circular antenna on bracket below flight deck amidships
G. Arra, 1979

Coral Sea (CV 43)
PHAN C. Fargo, USN, 2-80

Electron Equipt: Radar: CV 41: 1/LN-66, 1/SPS-10F or SPS-65, 1/SPS-43C, 1/SPS-49, 1/SPS-48C, 1/SPN-35A, 2/SPN-42, 1/SPN-44, 2/Mk 115; CV 43: 1/LN-66, 1/SPS-10, 1/SPS-43C, 1/SPS-30, 1/SPN-43A
    ECM: SLQ-29 (WLR-8 + SLQ-17), 4/Mk 36 SRBOC chaff
    TACAN: URN-20
M: 4 sets Westinghouse GT; 4 props; 212,000 hp
Boilers: 12 Babcock & Wilcox; 41.7 kg/cm², 454°C
Man: CV 41: 338 officers, 4,253 enlisted (including 222/1,724 aviation personnel)
    CV 43: 317 officers, 4,058 enlisted (including 201/2,063 aviation personnel)

REMARKS: CV 43 does not have a regularly assigned air group and is maintained in an operationally contingent status, occasionally being used to train Naval Reserve and student aviators; due to the shortage of carriers, she will be overhauled in FY 84 and retained active into 1989. Sister *Franklin D. Roosevelt* (CV 42) was stricken on 1-10-72. Machinery and ships' bottoms very similar to the *Iowa*-class battleships. Both have now had the last of their Mk 39 127-mm DP guns removed; CV 43 now has no missile armament.

Two side elevators to starboard, one forward of and one abaft the island; one side elevator to port abaft the angled flight deck. The elevator platforms are of alloy construction. CV 41 has a considerably larger flight deck than does CV 43. During her deployment to the Indian Ocean in 11-79, CV 41 carried only 52 aircraft. CV 41 has two Mk-C13 steam catapults (both forward) and three arrester wires on the angled deck. CV 43 retains three C-11-1 catapults.

Refits: From 1954 to 1963, the ships underwent several overhauls: angled flight deck installed; flight deck lengthened; hydraulic catapults replaced with steam ones; side armor removed and "bulges" added; reinforced arresting gear and barriers installed; centerline elevators replaced with side ones; aviation gasoline capacity increased; new jet-fuel bunkers installed. In October 1967 CV 41 began another major overhaul and returned to service in 1-70. Her angled flight deck was extended to port; her three elevators were enlarged; her forward port elevator was moved aft; her catapults were replaced by more powerful ones; and all her electronic equipment was replaced. She can launch the all-weather F-14 Tomcat interceptor. In 1979-80, during short overhauls at Yokosuka, CV 41's radar suit was updated and the Tactical Flag Command Center was added. CV 43 was overhauled 11-78 to 10-79 at Puget Sound NSY, where her catapults were brought up to Mk-C13 capability.

RESERVE AIRCRAFT CARRIERS

♦ **5 Essex,* Intrepid, † and Hancock ‡ class**

	Bldr	Laid down	L	In serv.
CVS 12 HORNET*	Newport News SB	3-8-42	29-8-43	29-11-43
CVS 20 BENNINGTON*	New York NSY	15-12-42	26-2-44	6-8-44
CVA 31 BON HOMME RICHARD‡	New York NSY	1-2-43	29-4-44	26-11-44
CV 34 ORISKANY‡	New York NSY	1-5-44	13-10-45	25-9-50
CVS 38 SHANGRI-LA†	Norfolk NSY	15-1-43	24-2-44	15-9-44

RESERVE AIRCRAFT CARRIERS (continued)

Bennington (CVS 20)   U.S. Navy, 1967

Oriskany (CV 34)   U.S. Navy, 1969

D: Approx. 33,000 tons (40,600 to 41,900 fl) **S:** 30+ kts
Dim: 274.01 (CVS 38: 270.97) (249.9 wl) × 31.39 (CV 34: 32.46) (flight deck: approx. 58.5 × 9.45)
A: 4/127-mm DP (I × 4), except CV 34: 2/127-mm DP (I × 2)
Electron Equipt: Radar: 1/SPS-10, 1/SPS-30, 1/SPS-43A (CVS 11, CV 34: SPS-37), 1/SPN-10, 1/SPN-43, 1-2/Mk 25, 0-4 Mk 35
         Sonar: CVS only; SQS-23 (bow-mounted)
         TACAN: URN-6 or URN-20
M: Westinghouse GT; 4 props; 150,000 hp
Boilers: 8 Babcock & Wilcox; 41.7 kg/cm², 454°C
Fuel: 6,750 tons **Range:** 18,000/12 **Man:** None

REMARKS: All in Category "C" reserve. CV 34, the only unit with sufficiently modern equipment to be worth reactivating, was placed in reserve on 30-9-76. Recommissioning (to cost approx. $510 million), to take 28-34 months, proposed by Reagan Administration for FY 82 but was turned down by Congress on the basis of the cost, age of the ship, and the lack of combat utility; the ship could not have carried modern fighter aircraft, only F-8J fighters retrieved from mothballs and A-4/A-7 light attack aircraft. A new steel flight deck would have been added, and defensive armament would have included Mk 29 Sea Sparrow launchers and Vulcan/Phalanx close-in defense systems. Crew would have been 110 officers and 2,368 men, plus a 150-officer, 1,050-man air group. A study was commissioned in 1980 to convert all to MET (Military Equipment Transports) for the Rapid Deployment Force, but this is apparently not to be done. Sister *Intrepid* (CVS 11) stricken 27-4-81 and transferred to New York City as a memorial. *Lexington* (formerly CVT 16) was redesignated AVT 16 on 1-7-78 and is used for training in deck landing; see entry in auxiliary section. CVS 12 was decommissioned on 15-1-70, CVS 20 on 30-6-69, CVA 31 on 2-7-71, and CVS 38 on 30-7-71. CVS 12 and CVS 20 retain their Mk-H8 hydraulic catapults; the others have C-8 steam catapults. All have three elevators: one on the centerline between the catapults, one at the forward end of the angled deck, and one (vertically stowable) to starboard, abaft the island. Four arrester wires. CV 34 has two Mk 37 gun directors. The others have one Mk 37 and two or three Mk 56 directors.

NAVAL AND MARINE CORPS AVIATION

Aviation is an integral part of the U.S. Navy and Marine Corps. The approximately 4,932 aircraft (FY 1981) assigned include:

1,060 attack planes	1,213 helicopters	43 aerial tankers
714 fighters	952 training aircraft	74 observation
144 ship-based ASW planes	112 early warning	8 target drone control
386 patrol aircraft	173 transports	53 utility

Air squadrons are designated by an alphanumerical system, the letter prefixes for the principal squadron types being:

Navy:

HC	Helicopter Combat Support (UH-46)
HM	Helicopter Mine Countermeasures (RH-53D)
HS	Helicopter Antisubmarine (SH-3)
HSL	Light Helicopter Antisubmarine (SH-2)
HT	Helicopter Training (TH-57A, UH-1E, TH-1L)
VA	Attack (A-4, A-6, A-7)
VAQ	Tactical Electronic Warfare (EA-6B)
VAW	Carrier Airborne Early Warning (E-2C)
VC	Fleet Composite (utility aircraft)
VF	Fighter (F-4, F-14, F-18)
VFP	Light Photographic (RF-8G)
VP	Patrol (P-3)
VQ	Fleet Air Reconnaissance (EP-3, EA-3B), also: Communications Support (EC-130)
VR	Fleet Logistics Support (C-9, C-117D, C-118D, C-130, etc.)
VRC	Fleet Logistics Support-COD (Carrier on-board Delivery) (C-1A, C-2A)
VRF	Aircraft Ferry
VS	Air Antisubmarine (S-3A)
VT	Training (TA-4J, T-28, T-2C, T-39D, T-44A)
VX	Air Test and Evaluation
VXE	Antarctic Development (LC-130F, UH-1)
VXN	Oceanographic Development (RP-3A/D)

Marine Corps:

HMA	Marine Attack Helicopter (AH-1)
HMH	Marine Heavy Helicopter (CH-53)

NAVAL AND MARINE CORPS AVIATION *(continued)*

HML	Marine Light Helicopter (UH-1N)
HMM	Marine Medium Helicopter (CH-46)
VMA	Marine Attack (A-4M, A-6E, AV-8A)
VMAQ	Marine Electronic Warfare (EA-6B)
VMFA	Marine Fighter-Attack (F-4)
VMFP	Marine Photo Reconnaissance (RF-4B)
VMGR	Marine Refueler-Transport (KC-130F)
VMO	Marine Observation (OV-10A/D)

Naval Aviation

The Navy has the following squadrons:

   60 attack and fighter
    1 reconnaissance
    5 helicopter
   23 ASW
   24 patrol
   41 various

The combination of all the aircraft on board an aircraft carrier is called a Carrier Air Wing (CAW), whose composition varies according to the carrier's mission. There are three basic types of air wing: one to project power or support landing operations; one to control the sea, with emphasis on antisubmarine warfare and the protection of ships; and one to perform the two previously mentioned missions at the same time. A typical wing would consist of: 24 all-weather fighters, 34-36 attack planes, 10 ASW aircraft, 6 ASW helicopters, 3 reconnaissance aircraft, 8 electronics-warfare aircraft, and 2 utility aircraft (COD). This combination would be modified according to mission.

Currently, twelve carrier air wings (CVW), twenty-four patrol squadrons (PatRon), and three Marine Corps air wings (MAW) are active, plus others for training and support and in reserve. Aircraft production of about 300 per year is mandatory to sustain the size of the current force, but recent and projected requests for procurement of aircraft have been:

	FY 81	FY 82	FY 83	FY 84	FY 85	FY 86	FY 87	83–87
A-6E (Intruder)	12	12	8	8	12	12	12	52
EA-6B (Prowler)	6	6	6	6	6	6	6	30
F-14A (Tomcat)	30	30	24	30	30	30	30	144
F/A-18A (Hornet)	60	63	84	96	108	132	132	552
AV-8B (Harrier)	—	12	18	30	48	60	60	216
SH-2F (Seasprite)	—	—	18	18	18	18	—	72
CH-53E (Super Stallion)	—	14	11	11	11	14	14	61
SH-60B (Seahawk)	—	—	48	64	74	—	—	186
SH-60 Variant	—	—	—	—	—	64	64	128
AH-1T	—	—	—	22	22	—	—	44
E-2C (Hawkeye)	6	6	6	6	6	6	6	30
UC-12B	—	—	—	—	12	12	37	61
C-2	—	—	8	8	8	8	7	39
T-44A	—	—	—	—	—	15	—	15
HXM	—	—	—	—	—	—	6	6
T-34C	45	60	30	28	28	28	30	144
TH-57	7	—	21	21	—	—	—	42
C-9B (Skytrain II)	2	—	—	2	2	2	2	8
ECX	—	—	—	—	3	3	3	9

	FY 81	FY 82	FY 83	FY 84	FY 85	FY 86	FY 87	83–87
F-5E (Tiger II)	—	—	—	4	4	4	4	16
VTX (Trainer)	—	—	—	—	—	12	24	36
TOTAL: Number of aircraft	168	203	288	359	397	431	442	1,917

Marine Corps Aviation

The Marines operate a considerable air force. Their aircraft are intended to operate principally from amphibious-warfare ships, but their squadrons of attack, reconnaissance, and electronic-warfare aircraft frequently operate from carriers as well. The principal air complement is:

  12 Fighter-Attack Squadrons with 12/F-4 Phantoms each
   5 Attack Squadrons with 16/A-6E Intruders each
   5 Attack Squadrons with 16/A-4M Skyhawks each
   3 Attack Squadrons with 20/AV-8A Harriers each
   3 Attack Helicopter Squadrons with 24/AH-1 Sea Cobras each
   6 Heavy Helicopter Squadrons with 21 CH-53D Sea Stallions each
   9 Medium Helicopter Squadrons with 18/CH-46D/F Sea Knights each
   3 Light Helicopter Squadrons with 24/UH-1N Iroquois (Huey) each
   3 Reconnaissance Squadrons with RF-4B Phantom and EA-6A Intruder
   2 Observation Squadrons with OV-10 Bronco

Aircraft Designations

Besides the name given to an aircraft—Phantom, Intruder, Orion, etc.—each type is designated by a group of letters and figures divided by a hyphen and made up in the following manner:

1. The letter immediately preceding the hyphen indicates the principal mission:

A—attack	P—patrol
B—bomber	S—antisubmarine
C—cargo/transport	T—training
E—airborne early warning	U—utility
F—fighter	V—VTOL/STOL, vertical or short takeoff and landing
K—tanker, inflight refueling	
O—observation	X—research

2. The figure that comes immediately after the hyphen is the design sequence number. When a letter follows this figure, its position in the alphabet indicates that the aircraft is the first, second, third, etc. modification to the original design.

   Example: A-4E = an attack aircraft, the fourth attack plane design, the fifth modification

3. When an aircraft is assigned to duty that is not its principal mission, a second letter precedes the letter of that mission (see para. 1 above):

A—attack	M—missile carrier or mine-countermeasures
C—cargo/transport	Q—drone aircraft
D—direction or control of drones, air-craft, or missiles	R—reconnaissance
E—special electronic installation	S—antisubmarine
H—search and rescue	T—trainer
K—tanker, inflight refueling	U—utility, general sevice
L—cold weather; for arctic regions	V—staff
	W—weather, meteorology

NAVAL AND MARINE CORPS AVIATION (*continued*)

4. A third prefixed letter in front of an aircraft's designation means:

G—permanently grounded   X—experimental
J—temporary special test   Y—prototype
N—permanent special test   Z—planning

F-18A Hornet all-weather fighter—in Marine Corps markings   McDonnell-Douglas, 1981

F-14A Tomcat, all-weather fighter—with 4 Phoenix, 2 Sparrow, and 2 Sidewinder missiles   Grumman, 1981

F-4J over the Mediterranean   U.S. Navy, 1978

Four A-6E Intruder heavy attack aircraft—with Mk 82 bombs   Grumman, 1981

AV-8A Harrier attack aircraft (Marine Corps)   1971

A-4E Skyhawk attack aircraft   1974

RF-4B Phantom, Marine reconnaissance aircraft

NAVAL AND MARINE CORPS AVIATION (continued)

A-7E Corsair light attack aircraft   U.S. Navy, 1975

SH-3A Viking ASW aircraft   French Navy, 1980

RF-8G Crusader reconnaissance aircraft

P-3C Orion patrol aircraft   PH1 W. Wickham, USN, 1980

SH-3G Sea King ASW helicopter   1978

C-2A Greyhound COD (Carrier On-board Delivery) aircraft   1966

SH-2F Sea Sprite LAMPS-I ASW helicopter   PHCS R. Lawson, USN, 1976

NAVAL AND MARINE CORPS AVIATION (continued)

SH-60B Seahawk LAMPS-III ASW helicopter   Sikorsky, 1980

EA-6B Prowler electronics warfare aircraft—low-visibility paint   Grumman, 1981

E-2C Hawkeye early-warning aircraft   Grumman, 1976

EC-130G Hercules TACAMO communications aircraft   PH2 W. Harvey, USN, 1977

CH-53E Super Stallion   Sikorsky, 1978

Three RH-53D minesweeping helicopters (unit at right with tail and rotors folded) aboard *Nashville* (LSD 13); two MSB 5-class minesweeping boats are seen stowed in the ship's docking well, below the flight deck.   L. & L. Van Ginderen, 5-81

NAVAL AND MARINE CORPS AVIATION *(continued)*

PRINCIPAL COMBAT AIRCRAFT

Class, builder	Mission	Wingspan in m	Length in m	Height in m	Weight in kg	Engine	Max speed Mach/knots	Ceiling in feet	1) Ferry range (nautical miles) 2) Combat radius (nautical miles) 3) Range (hours)
SHIP-BASED FIXED WING									
F/A-18 Hornet (McDonnell-Douglas)	Multirole fighter (Navy)	11.43	17.07	4.67	15,247	2 GE F404-GE-400 6,800-kg thrust each	M 1.8	49,400	2,000 460 3

Armament: 5,900 kg of conventional or nuclear bombs; 2/Sidewinder; 4/Sparrow-III; 1/20-mm M61A1 cannon. APG-65 radar; FLIR pod being added.

REMARKS: First aircraft to have a system using a microprocessor to control the various weapons. RF-18 version may be built. A two-seat TF-18 is also being built. Procurement of at least 1,377 planned, with fleet operation commencing in 1984. A-18 version for Marines differs primarily in computer software and provision of bomb racks.

Class, builder	Mission	Wingspan in m	Length in m	Height in m	Weight in kg	Engine	Max speed Mach/knots	Ceiling in feet	
F-14A Tomcat (Grumman)	Two-man, all-weather fighter with variable-geometry wing	19.53/ 11.63	18.85	4.88	32,659 (17,010 empty)	2 P&W TF30-P-414A 9,480-kg thrust each, with afterburners	M 2.34	60,000	2,000 500 2.50 to 3

Armament: 1/20-mm M61A1 Vulcan gun; 2/Phoenix, 2/Sidewinder and 2/Sparrow missiles or 3,856 kg of Sparrow and Sidewinder missiles or bombs, including nuclear bombs. AWG-9 radar.

REMARKS: Primarily an interceptor. Max. landing speed: 120 knots. Thirty planned to be procured each year under FY 80-83. Production now scheduled to continue into FY 95, totaling up to 995. In FY 84 the F-14C with a programmable signal processor, more computer and AIM-54C missiles will enter service. A version with more powerful GE F 101-DFE engines will supplant the present model; the trials aircraft first flew in 1981. Aircraft no. 606 on will be F-14D, with above improvements plus digitized radar.

Class, builder	Mission	Wingspan in m	Length in m	Height in m	Weight in kg	Engine	Max speed Mach/knots	Ceiling in feet	
F-4 Phantom (McDonnell-Douglas)	All-weather fighter (Navy) fighter-bomber (Marine Corps)	11.71	17.75	4.96	24,767 (12,700 empty)	2 GE J79-GE-10 8,120-kg thrust each, with afterburners (RF-4B: G,E,J,79-GE-8)	M 2.2	71,000	2,300 900 2.25

Armament: 4/Sparrow III and 4/Sidewinder missiles (standard weapons) or 6/Sparrow III or 7,258 kg of missiles, rockets, or bombs: 18/340-kg, 15/309-kg, 11/454-kg bombs; 7/smoke bombs; 11/napalm bombs; 4/Bullpup missiles; 15/air-to-surface rocket pods.
REMARKS: Several versions: B, J, G, and RF-4B(reconnaissance). Max. landing speed: 140 knots. The Marines are receiving older Navy F-4B as they are replaced by F14s. 265 F-4B to be upgraded to F-4S with slats, new avionics, etc. RF-4B to get GE J79-GE-10B smokeless engines. EF-4B ELINT version based at Key West.

Class, builder	Mission	Wingspan in m	Length in m	Height in m	Weight in kg	Engine	Max speed Mach/knots	Ceiling in feet	
A-4M Skyhawk (McDonnell-Douglas)	Attack (Navy Reserve and Marine Corps)	8.38	12.50	4.57	11,113 (4,747 empty)	1 P&W J52-P-408A 5,080-kg thrust	580 kts	42,000	2,055 355 2.12

Armament: 2/20-mm Mk 12 guns; 2,950 kg bombs, rockets, or Sidewinder or Bullpup missiles. To be equipped with Maverick missiles.

REMARKS: Nonfolding wings. Very strong; versatile. Can carry a nuclear bomb. Several versions: A-4E & M remain in active Marine squadrons, but Navy use is by Reserves and in support duties. Final units built 1979, after 25 years' production. A-4M has large hump on spine, for electronics. Two-seat TA-4F and J trainers also in use.

Class, builder	Mission	Wingspan in m	Length in m	Height in m	Weight in kg	Engine	Max speed Mach/knots	Ceiling in feet	
A-6E Intruder (Grumman)	All-weather attack (Navy and Marine Corps)	16.15	16.67	4.92	27,397 (11,627 empty)	2 P&W J52-P8A/8B 4,218-kg thrust each	594 kts	44,600	2,400 300 . . .

Armament: 18,000 pounds of conventional or nuclear bombs, rockets, etc. Examples of ordnance: 46/250-pound, 30/450-pound, 15/900-pound, 5/2,000-pound bombs; 13 pods with 247 rockets; 52/Zuni rockets; 4/Sidewinder or 4/Bullpup missiles. Now being equipped for Harpoon, HARM, Maverick, Sidewinder, and Walleye.

REMARKS: Approx. 250 in service, 1981. Now building 12/A-6E, 6/EA-B per year. EA-6B is fitted for electronics warfare and has a four-man crew, a minimum of 30 sensors of various types, and the ALQ-99 jammer; to receiive ALQ-149 to replace ALQ-92 jammers, plus getting UHF bands on ALQ-99. Marines use 2-seat EA-6A with lesser capabilities. Four KA-6D tanker versions are aboard most carriers. KA-6D tanker versions are conversions of A-6As, carry 20,000 lb. fuel for transfer. A-6E getting TRAM (Target Recognition-Attack Multisensor); 45 had it by 1981, all by 1984. Synthetic aperture radar being developed for A-6E.

NAVAL AND MARINE CORPS AVIATION *(continued)*

Class builder	Mission	Wingspan in m	Length in m	Height in m	Weight in kg	Engine	Max speed Mach/knots	Ceiling in feet	1) Ferry range (nautical miles) 2) Combat radius (nautical miles) 3) Range (hours)
A-7E Corsair II (Ling-Temco-Vought)	Attack	11.80	14.06	4.90	19,051 (8,973 empty)	1 Allison TF41-A-2 6,800-kg thrust	599 kts	42,600	2,800 700 2.25

Armament: 1/20-mm M61A1 Vulcan gun; up to 6,800 kg bombs, rockets, or missiles, according to the mission and the target distance. Examples of weapons: 24/113-kg Mk 81 bombs; 4/ Zuni rockets; 28/2.75-inch rockets; 1/Shrike missile and 1/Walleye guided bomb; 12/Snakeye bombs; 2/Shrike missiles; 2/907-kg bombs. Normally carry two Sidewinder AAM for defense. Have APQ-126 attack radar, APR-43 warning syst. (to be replaced by ALR-45F).

REMARKS: A-7E is the only version in use on carriers; earlier A, B, and C models are used by the Reserves. 81 TA-7C two-seat trainers are being converted from single-seat B&C models. A few EA-7C electronics aircraft are in use. A-7E getting capability to launch HARM missiles, plus FLIR sensor being added.

Class builder	Mission	Wingspan in m	Length in m	Height in m	Weight in kg	Engine	Max speed Mach/knots	Ceiling in feet	Range
AV-8A Harrier (McDonnell-Douglas)	Attack (Marine Corps)	7.70	13.87	3.43	VTOL: 7,938 STOL: 9,747	1 Rolls-Royce Pegasus Mk 103 9,750-kg thrust	640 kts	50,000	2,000 VTOL: 160; STOL: 500 1

Armament: 2/30-mm guns; bombs, rockets, etc. to a total of 2,700 kg. Can carry two Sidewinder AAM for defense.

REMARKS: Eight two-seat TAV-8A and 108 single-seat AV-8A have been acquired. High loss rate through accidents. Surviving aircraft being upgraded to AV-8C with ALE-39 chaff/ flare dispensers, APR-43 and ALR-45F threat warning systems.

Class builder	Mission	Wingspan in m	Length in m	Height in m	Weight in kg	Engine	Max speed Mach/knots	Ceiling in feet	Range
AV-8B Harrier (McDonnell-Douglas)	Attack (Marine Corps)	9.22	14.10	3.53	VTOL: 8,558 STOL: 13,416	1 Rolls-Royce Pegasus F402-RR-404 9,761-kg thrust	650 kts	50,000	2,000 VTOL: 100+ STOL: 650 1

Armament: 2/30-mm guns; 2/Sidewinder AAM, and 14/227-kg or 6/454-kg bombs or 4/Maverick ASM. No radar.

REMARKS: Badly needed successor to AV-8A/C, delayed by Dept. of Defense, which has preferred A-18 for Marines. An "AV-8B+" version for the Navy is under consideration, with 10,260-kg thrust engine, APG-65-type attack radar, and improved avionics; to carry Harpoon, Tomahawk, mines, etc. First AV-8B squadron to be operational 1984-85, with first of four AV-8B developmental aircraft flying 10-81. 24 to be requested FY 83.

Class builder	Mission	Wingspan in m	Length in m	Height in m	Weight in kg	Engine	Max speed Mach/knots	Ceiling in feet	Range
S-3A Viking (Lockheed)	ASW	20.93	16.26	6.94	23,853 (12,160 empty)	2 GE TF34-GE-400 4,210-kg thrust each	Max: 440 kts Cruise: 350 kts Patrol: 210 kts	40,000	3,000 2,300 9

Armament: 60/sonobuoys, 4/Mk 32 bombs; 4/Mk 57 depth charges; 4/Mk 53 depth charges or 4/Mk 53 mines or 2/Mk 46 torpedoes. APS-116 radar, ASW-81 magnetic anomaly detector (MAD).

REMARKS: Fitted with a Univac AYK-10 digital computer to apply the information from the sensors on board. Four-man crew. 180 built; one is a US-3A COD aircraft (procurement of more or conversion of S-3A to US-3A has been canceled, as has KS-3A tanker conversion). Some 160 will be updated to S-3B, at the rate of 3/month, beginning 4-87; two trials S-3B to convert beginning 10-83. Will receive WSIP(Weapon & Sensor Improvement Program) with synthetic aperture radar, Harpoon launch capability, new Auxiliary Power Unit(APU).

Class builder	Mission	Wingspan in m	Length in m	Height in m	Weight in kg	Engine	Max speed Mach/knots	Ceiling in feet	Range
RF-8G Crusader (Ling-Temco-Vought)	Photo recon- naissance	10.87	16.61	4.80	12,620 (7,619 empty)	1 P&W J57-P420 8,165-kg thrust with afterburner (5,190 kg without)	854 kts	51,800	. . . 640 2

Armament: None.

REMARKS: 30 RF-8G are retained as the only carrier-operated photo-reconnaissance aircraft owned by the Navy; all are very old, but have been refurbished. To be discarded 1980-81. Carry ALR-45, ALR-50, and ALE-26 countermeasures gear.

NAVAL AND MARINE CORPS AVIATION (*continued*)

Class, builder	Mission	Wingspan in m	Length in m	Height in m	Weight in kg	Engine	Max speed Mach/knots	Ceiling in feet	1) Ferry range (nautical miles) 2) Combat radius (nautical miles) 3) Range (hours)
E-2C Hawkeye (Grumman)	Airborne early warning and air control	24.58	17.56	5.59	23,392 (17,091 empty)	2 Allison T56-A-422 turboprops, 4,591 shp each	326 kts (270 kts, cruise)	30,800	1,525 . . . 6

REMARKS: APS-120 radar in 7.32-m circular, rotating radome. Five-man crew. By 1981 a total of 85 E-2C were available, 6/yr. built. Can track 250 air and surface targets and control 25 simultaneous intercepts; to be improved by TRAC-A (Total Radiation Aperture Control Antenna) radar to reduce side-lobes.

EA-6B Prowler (Grumman)	Electronics warfare	16.15	18.11	4.95	29,536 (15,686 empty)	2 P&W J52-P-408, 5,080-kg thrust each	573 kts (410 kts, cruise)	37,800	2,400 710 . . .

REMARKS: ECM version of A-6 Intruder; four-man crew. Five ALQ-99 jammer pods beneath wings and fuselage. Two-seat Marine EA-6A Intruder carries five ALQ-31B jammer pods and can alternatively be used as an attack aircraft, with up to 8,160 kg of ordnance. Both aircraft are distinguished from the standard A-6E by a large, streamlined electronics-equipment pod atop the vertical stabilizer. See also remarks under A-6E.

EA-3B Skywarrior (McDonnell-Douglas)	Electronics warfare	22.11	23.28	6.94	35,380 (18,685 empty)	2 P&W J57-P-10 5,625-kg thrust each	556 kts (400 kts, cruise)	41,300	5,000 1,100 6

REMARKS: The only type still used on carriers; will remain in service to 1985. EKA-3B is used by the Reserves for both flight refueling and electronics warfare; ERA-3B is used for reconnaissance. Surviving A-3/ERA-3B aircraft are to be modernized, despite great age.

P-3C Orion (Lockheed)	Maritime patrol and ASW	30.37	35.61	10.28	64,411 (27,892 empty)	4 Allison T56-A-14 turboprops, 4,910 hp each	410 kts (205 kts patrol)	28,300	4,500 2,380 patrol 16

Armament: 6/908-kg mines; 2/Mk 101 nuclear depth charges; 4/Mk 46 torpedoes; 87/sonobuoys, 4/Harpoon anti-ship missiles, etc. Weapons vary. Can carry a total of 7,700 kg of disposable ordnance and sensors. APS-115 radar, ASQ-10A magnetic anomaly detector (MAD), ASQ-114 digital computer, etc. P-3C has FLIR gear.

REMARKS: Crews of up to 15 men. The P-C is fitted with an A-NEW central operations module built around the ASQ-114 miniaturized computer and with an Air Tactical Data System. ASQ-10 magnetic anomaly detector (MAD), APS-115 radar, electronics countermeasures carried. EP-3B/E are for electronics warfare, RP-3A/D are for research, and WP-3D perform weather reconnaissance. Twelve P-3C to be procured under FY 80 through FY 83 and for the foreseeable future. P-3C are expected to last 28 years each. Total built for USN through 1981: 157 P-3A, 124 P-3B, 198 P-3C, 1 RP-3D, 2 WP-3D. Also over 70 to date for overseas customers.

C-1A Trader (Grumman)	Carrier Onboard Delivery (COD)	21.23	22.80	4.98	12,247	2 Wright R1820-82 piston; 1,525 hp each	290 kts	22,000	1,200 . . . . . .

REMARKS: Despite advanced obsolescence, 30 retained until more C-2A can be built. Cargo version of out-of-service S-2 Tracker ASW aircraft. Two-man crew plus 9 passengers. Cargo capacity: 1,589 kg. A few EC-1A ECM training variants exist.

C-2A Greyhound (Grumman)	Carrier Onboard Delivery (COD)	24.57	17.27	4.85	24,668 (14,175 empty)	2 Allison T56-A-8A turboshaft; 4,050 shp each	306 kts (257 kts, cruise)	28,800	1,440

REMARKS: Variant of E-2 Hawkeye with large-diameter fuselage. Twelve in service. Three-man crew plus 39 passengers or 20 litter patients or 3,724 kg cargo. Stern ramp for loading, provision for aerial refuelling. Thirty-nine more to be delivered 1984-88, under new proposal.

NAVAL AND MARINE CORPS AVIATION (continued)

Class, builder	Mission	Diameter (rotor)	Length (overall)	Height	Weight in kg	Engine	Max speed in knots	Ceiling in feet	1) Mission range (nautical miles) 2) Ferry range (nautical miles) 3) Endurance (hours)
HELICOPTERS **SH-3A, D, G Sea King** (Sikorsky)	ASW	18.9	22.16 (16.70, fuselage)	5.13	9,300 (5,302 empty)	2 GE T58-GE-10 turboshaft, 1,400 shp each	144 118, cruise	14,700	625 . . . 4.50

Armament: Two Mk 46 torpedoes, sonobuoys.

REMARKS: Four-man crew. On CV aircraft carriers or land-based; can be carried on *Spruance*-class DD. SH-3H is a multipurpose version of the SH-3G utility model. Fitted with AQS-13 dipping sonar, AQS-81 MAD. All 137 SH-3A and G models updating to SH-3H standard, carry APS-24 radar.

SH-2F LAMPS-I (Kaman)	ASW	13.42	16.04 (11.69 fuselage)	4.73	5,800 (3,154 empty)	2 GE T58-GE-8F turboshaft, 1,350 hp each	143 130, cruise	22,500	420 . . . 2.50

Armament: 15/sonobuoys, 2/Mk 46 ASW torpedoes. ASQ-81 MAD (Magnetic Anomaly Detector), LN-66 radar fitted.

REMARKS: Found on FF, DD, and CG types. Approx. 85 in service. All conversions of UH-2 Sea Sprite utility helicopters. Reintroduction into production scheduled, with 18 new aircraft approved in FY 82 to serve in ASW ships not getting SH-60B.

SH-60B LAMPS-III (Sikorsky)	ASW	16.36	19.76 (15.24, fuselage)	5.23	9,435	2 GE T700-GE-400 turboshaft, . . . 1,723 max hp each (1,540 hp cont.)	135 kts	. . .	150 . . . 1.3

Armament: 25/sonobuoys; 2/Mk 46 ASW torpedoes.

REMARKS: To replace SH-2D, F in 1980s. Introduction delayed because of excessive cost. Will carry APS-124 radar, ASQ-81 MAD, SSQ-53 DIFAR sonobuoys, SSQ-50 CASS active sonobuoys. Highly automated; all sensors display on ship, which controls the helicopter. Up to 200 to be procured.

CH-46 A, D, E **Sea Knight** (Boeing Vertol)	Troop-carrying assault (Marine Corps)	15.56	25.72 (13.67 fuselage)	5.08	10,438 (5,947 empty)	2 GE T58-GE-10 turboshaft, 1,450 shp each CH-46E: 2 GE T58-GE10, 1,870 shp each	144	14,000	206 774 . . .

REMARKS: Can carry 18 fully equipped troops. The two cargo versions (UH-46A and 46D) are Navy-subordinated and are usually assigned to vertical-replenishment duties in modern underway replenishment ships. Can carry 1,360 kg of cargo internally or 4,536 kg in a sling beneath. CH-46E is updated (1977) version with automatic navigation system and armored seats; all earlier units will be modernized. Glass-reinforced plastic rotors being substituted and infrared jamming equipment being added.

CH-53 A, D, RH-53D **Sea Stallion** (Sikorsky)	Navy RH-53D: Minesweeping Marine Corps CH-53A, D: Assault transport	22.04	26.92 (20.48, fuselage)	7.59	19,050 (10,718 empty	2 GE T64-GE-413 turboshaft, 3,925 hp each	170 150, cruise	21,000	540 886 3.50

REMARKS: Version A can carry 38 fully equipped troops or 24 occupied stretchers with 4 hospital corpsmen or 4 tons of freight (2 Hawk missiles, for example). The RH-53D version is equipped for aerial minesweeping and has T64-GE-415 engines, 2/12.7-mm machine guns, and points for towing Mk 103 cutters, Mk 104 magnetic minesweeping arrays, Mk 105 hydrofoil sled. MK 106 acoustic sweep array, SPU-1 shallow-water sweep rig, and AQS-14 minehunting sonar. 30 RH-53D were built, but 7 were lost in Iran, and only 16 remained by 1981.

CH-53E Super Stallion (Sikorsky)	Troop-carrying assault (Marines) Heavy lift (Navy)	24.08	30.20 (22.35, fuselage)	8.44	31,638 (14,910 empty)	3 GE T64-GE-415 turboshaft; 4,380b max. shp each (3,695 shp cont.)	170	18,500	50 with 14,500 kg cargo; 1,000 . . .

REMARKS: Can carry 56 troops or 14,500 kg cargo. Three-man crew. Seven-bladed main rotor. One being rebuilt under FY 80 budget as MH-53E minesweeper prototype. Navy use is for cargo, aircraft-recovery, and heavy lift. To acquire 33 total for Marines, 16 for Navy.

NAVAL AND MARINE CORPS AVIATION *(continued)*

Class, builder	Mission	Diameter (rotor)	Length (overall)	Height	Weight in kg	Engine	Max speed in knots	Ceiling in feet	1) Mission range (nautical miles) 2) Ferry range (nautical miles) 3) Endurance (hours)
UH-1E/N Iroquois (Bell)	Assault (Marine Corps)	14.70	17.47 (12.93, fuselage)	4.39	4,763 (2,517 empty)	2 United Aircraft PT6 turboshaft, 900 shp each	110	15,000	250 . . . 2

Armament: 2/7.62-mm machine guns and rockets.

REMARKS: Can carry 16 troops. UH-1N replaced earlier UH-1E, which had 1 Lycoming T53 turboshaft of 1,100 shp. Navy uses UH-1 and TH-1 for utility and training duties.

AH-1G, J, T Sea Cobra (Bell)	Attack (Marine Corps)	13.42	16.27 (13.60, fuselage)	4.17	4,536 3,000 empty	2 United Aircraft T400-CP-400 turboshaft; 1,800 hp each	180	10,500	360 . . . 2

Armament: 1/20-mm XM-197 Gatling gun, plus 76/2.75-in rockets or 2/7.62-mm minigun (AH-1T also: TOW anti-tank missiles).

REMARKS: The initial version, AH-1G, is identical to the Army Huey Cobra and has only 1 Lycoming T53-L5 engine of 1,100 shp; it is being replaced by the AH-1T.

Also in service with Navy and Marine Corps aviation are 23 F-5E/F fighters for "Top Gun" training to simulate Soviet aircraft, OV-10A and OV-10D twin-engine observation/attack aircraft for the Marines, C-4 Gulfstream transports, C-9B transports (military DC-9) for the Marines and Naval Reserve, C-117D Skytrain (military DC-3) transports, C-118B Liftmaster (military DC-6), C-130 Hercules (in C-130, LC-130 arctic, DC-130 drone control, and EC-130 TACAMO communications versions), C-131F, G Samaritan transports, T-2C Buckeye jet trainers, T-28B propeller trainers, T-34B/C student trainers, T-38A Talon jet test-pilot trainers, T-39D Sabreliner flight-officer trainers (and CT-39E/G light transport versions), T-44A Pegasus twin-engine trainers, and TH-57A helicopter trainers.

UH-46 Sea Knight utility helicopter

C-1A Trader COD aircraft PHCS R. Lawson, USN, 1974

AV-8B Advanced Harrier V/STOL fighter-bomber *McDonnell-Douglas, 1978*

NUCLEAR-POWERED BALLISTIC-MISSILE SUBMARINES

♦ **1 (+ 15) Ohio class** (SCB 304, 74 design) Bldr: General Dynamics, Groton, Conn.

	Program	Laid down	L	In serv.
SSBN 726 OHIO	FY 74	10-4-76	7-4-79	11-11-81
SSBN 727 MICHIGAN	FY 75	4-4-77	26-4-80	10-82
SSBN 728 FLORIDA	FY 75	9-6-77	14-11-81	9-83
SSBN 729 GEORGIA	FY 76	7-4-79	11-82	5-84
SSBN 730 RHODE ISLAND	FY 77	7-4-80	7-83	1-85
SSBN 731 ALABAMA	FY 78	. . .	1984	9-85
SSBN 732 N . . .	FY 78	. . .	1984	5-86
SSBN 733 N . . .	FY 80	. . .	1985	1-87
SSBN 734 N . . .	FY 81	. . .	. . .	. . .
SSBN 735 N . . .	FY 83	. . .	. . .	. . .
SSBN 736 N . . .	FY 83	. . .	. . .	. . .
SSBN 737 N . . .	FY 84	. . .	. . .	. . .
SSBN 738 N . . .	FY 85	. . .	. . .	. . .
SSBN 739 N . . .	FY 86	. . .	. . .	. . .
SSBN 740 N . . .	FY 87	. . .	. . .	. . .
SSBN 741 N . . .	FY 88	. . .	. . .	. . .

D: 16,764/18,750 tons   **S:** 25 kts (sub.)   **Dim:** 170.69 × 12.80 × 10.97 (surf.)
A: 24/Trident-1 missiles—4/533-mm Mk 68 TT (fwd)

Ohio (SSBN 726)—on trials   U.S. Navy, 6-81

Ohio (SSBN 726)—on trials   PH2 W. Garlinghouse, USN, 9-81

Electron Equipt: Radar: BPS-15A—ECM: WLR-8(V)
            Sonar: BQQ-6, BQS-13, BQS-15, BQR-15, BQR-19
M: 1 GE S8G natural circulation pressurized-water reactor; turboelectric drive;
     1 prop; 60,000 hp
Endurance: 70 days   **Man:** 14 officers, 137 men (2 crews)

REMARKS: SSBN 726 ran first trials 17-6-81 and was delivered 3 years late. Program continues to experience delays, but is beginning to get on schedule. The availability of this class as a whole is to be 66 percent, using a planned schedule of 70-day patrols, followed by 25-day refit periods, and with a 12-month overhaul every nine years. Each ship has two crews. None ordered under FY 79 because of program delays and cost overruns; the FY 80 unit cost more than $1.1 billion, *without* missiles. Ordering of SSBN 734 was deferred, due to contract disputes between the Navy and General Dynamics.

     Able to submerge to 300 meters. Carry two Mk 2 SINS (Ship's Inertial Navigational System) and have navigational satellite receivers. Mk 98 digital computer missile-fire-control system and Mk 118 torpedo-fire-control system are installed. Under current planning, will begin backfitting with Trident-2 missiles in the late 1980s. SSBN 726 will be based at Bangor, Washington.

♦ **31 Lafayette class** (SCB 216 and SCB 216A types)

	Bldr	Laid down	L	In serv.
SSBN 616 LAFAYETTE	Gen. Dynamics	17-1-61	8-5-62	23-4-63
SSBN 617 ALEXANDER HAMILTON	Gen. Dynamics	26-6-61	18-8-62	27-6-63
SSBN 619 ANDREW JACKSON	Mare Island NSY	26-4-61	15-9-62	3-7-63
SSBN 620 JOHN ADAMS	Portsmouth NSY	19-5-61	12-1-63	12-5-64
SSBN 622 JAMES MONROE	Newport News	31-7-61	4-8-62	7-12-63
SSBN 623 NATHAN HALE	Gen. Dynamics	2-10-61	12-1-63	23-11-63
SSBN 624 WOODROW WILSON	Mare Island NSY	13-9-61	22-2-63	27-12-63
SSBN 625 HENRY CLAY	Newport News	23-10-61	30-11-62	20-2-64
SSBN 626 DANIEL WEBSTER	Gen. Dynamics	23-12-61	27-4-63	9-4-64
SSBN 627 JAMES MADISON*	Newport News	5-3-62	15-3-63	28-7-64
SSBN 628 TECUMSEH	Gen. Dynamics	1-6-62	22-6-63	29-5-64
SSBN 629 DANIEL BOONE*	Mare Island NSY	6-2-62	22-6-63	23-4-64
SSBN 630 JOHN C. CALHOUN*	Newport News	4-6-62	22-6-63	15-9-64

NUCLEAR-POWERED BALLISTIC-MISSILE SUBMARINES *(continued)*

SSBN 631	ULYSSES S. GRANT	Gen. Dynamics	18-8-62	2-11-63	17-7-64
SSBN 632	VON STEUBEN*	Newport News	4-9-62	18-10-63	30-9-64
SSBN 633	CASIMIR PULASKI*	Gen. Dynamics	12-1-63	1-2-64	14-8-64
SSBN 634	STONEWALL JACKSON*	Mare Island NSY	4-7-62	30-11-63	26-8-64
SSBN 635	SAM RAYBURN	Newport News	3-12-62	20-12-63	2-12-64
SSBN 636	NATHANAEL GREENE	Portsmouth NSY	21-5-62	12-5-64	19-12-64
SSBN 640	BENJAMIN FRANKLIN*	Gen. Dynamics	25-5-63	5-12-64	22-10-65
SSBN 641	SIMON BOLIVAR*	Newport News	17-4-63	22-8-64	29-10-65
SSBN 642	KAMEHAMEHA	Mare Island NSY	2-5-63	16-1-65	10-12-65
SSBN 643	GEORGE BANCROFT*	Gen. Dynamics	24-8-63	20-3-65	22-1-66
SSBN 644	LEWIS AND CLARK	Newport News	29-7-63	21-11-64	22-12-65
SSBN 645	JAMES K. POLK	Gen. Dynamics	23-11-63	22-5-65	16-4-66
SSBN 654	GEORGE C. MARSHALL	Newport News	2-3-64	21-5-65	29-4-66
SSBN 655	HENRY L. STIMSON*	Gen. Dynamics	4-4-64	13-11-65	20-8-66
SSBN 656	GEORGE WASHINGTON CARVER	Newport News	24-8-64	14-8-65	15-6-66
SSBN 657	FRANCIS SCOTT KEY*	Gen. Dynamics	5-12-64	23-4-66	3-12-66
SSBN 658	MARIANO G. VALLEJO*	Mare Island NSY	7-7-64	23-10-65	16-12-66
SSBN 659	WILL ROGERS	Gen. Dynamics	20-3-65	21-7-66	1-4-67

Authorized: SSBN 616 to SSBN 626 in FY 61, SSBN 627 to SSBN 636 in FY 62, SSBN 640 to SSBN 645 in FY 63, and SSBN 654 to SSBN 659 in FY 64

Nathan Hale (SSBN 623)   L. & L. Van Ginderen, 6-81

Daniel Webster—note the unique position of the diving planes, on the dome on the bow at the extreme lower right of the photograph   1972

D: 7,250/8,250 tons **S:** 15/25 kts **Dim:** 129.54 × 10.05 × 9.0
A: 16/Poseidon or Trident-1 missiles—4/533-mm TT (fwd)
Electron Equipt: Radar: BPS-11A
         Sonar: BQR-7, BQR-15, BQR-19, BQR-21, BQS-4

M: 1 Westinghouse SW5 pressurized-water reactor; 1 7-bladed prop; 15,000 hp
Endurance: 68 days **Man:** 17 officers, 128 men

REMARKS: All operate in the Atlantic Fleet. The 12 units marked with an asterisk were scheduled to have received Trident-1 missiles by 3-82. SSBN 640 and following units have quieter propulsion machinery and are officially designated the *Benjamin Franklin* class. Three Mk 2 SINS were installed during conversion. Submersion depth for all is more than 300 meters. Mk 88 missile-fire-control system and Mk 113 torpedo-fire-control system fitted. Conversion of both classes from Polaris A-3 to Poseidon missiles was completed between 1970 and 1977. Funds were requested under FY 79 for conversion of the first SSBN and for three each year thereafter through FY 82. SSBN 657 commenced the first Trident-1 operational patrol on 20-10-79. All Trident-1 units are to be home-ported at King's Bay, Georgia, and all ships in both classes belong to the Atlantic Fleet. They operate on a schedule of 68-day patrols, followed by 32-day refit periods; every six years a 16-month yard period is requested, giving an overall force availability of 55 percent. Each ship has two crews. SSBN 641 and two others are now on a nine-year operational/overhaul cycle.

NUCLEAR-POWERED ATTACK SUBMARINES

NOTE: After a prolonged series of studies on the feasibility of constructing a smaller, cheaper nuclear-powered attack submarine (the FA—Fast Attack, or "Fat Albert," so called because of its stubby proportions), the U.S. Navy has decided to continue requesting construction of the *Los Angeles* class indefinitely, albeit in a longer, more capable, and more expensive version.

◆ 18 (+27) Los Angeles class (SCB 303 type)

		Bldr	Laid down	L	In serv.
SSN 688	LOS ANGELES	Newport News	8-1-72	6-4-74	13-11-76
SSN 689	BATON ROUGE	Newport News	18-11-72	18-4-75	25-6-77
SSN 690	PHILADELPHIA	Gen. Dynamics	12-8-72	19-10-74	25-6-77
SSN 691	MEMPHIS	Newport News	23-6-73	3-4-76	17-12-77
SSN 692	OMAHA	Gen. Dynamics	27-1-73	21-2-76	11-3-78
SSN 693	CINCINNATI	Newport News	6-4-74	19-2-76	10-6-78
SSN 694	GROTON	Gen. Dynamics	3-8-73	9-10-76	8-7-78
SSN 695	BIRMINGHAM	Newport News	26-4-75	15-10-77	20-12-78
SSN 696	NEW YORK CITY	Gen. Dynamics	15-12-73	18-6-77	10-3-79
SSN 697	INDIANAPOLIS	Gen. Dynamics	19-10-74	30-7-77	5-1-80
SSN 698	BREMERTON	Gen. Dynamics	8-5-76	22-7-78	28-3-81
SSN 699	JACKSONVILLE	Gen. Dynamics	21-2-76	18-11-78	16-5-81
SSN 700	DALLAS	Gen. Dynamics	9-10-76	28-4-79	18-7-81
SSN 701	LA JOLLA	Gen. Dynamics	16-10-76	11-8-79	24-10-81
SSN 702	PHOENIX	Gen. Dynamics	30-7-77	18-12-79	19-12-81
SSN 703	BOSTON	Gen. Dynamcis	11-8-78	19-4-80	30-1-82
SSN 704	BALTIMORE	Gen. Dynamics	21-5-79	18-12-80	12-82
SSN 705	CORPUS CHRISTI	Gen. Dynamics	4-9-79	25-4-81	4-83
SSN 706	ALBUQUERQUE	Gen. Dynamics	27-12-79	2-82	10-83
SSN 707	PORTSMOUTH	Gen. Dynamics	8-5-80	7-82	2-84
SSN 708	N. . .	Gen. Dynamics	20-1-81	12-82	6-84
SSN 709	N. . .	Gen. Dynamics	23-7-81	11-83	10-84
SSN 710	N. . .	. . .	. . .	83	. . .
SSN 711	SAN FRANCISCO	Newport News	26-5-77	27-10-79	24-4-81
SSN 712	ATLANTA	Newport News	17-8-78	16-8-80	12-81
SSN 713	HOUSTON	Newport News	29-1-79	21-3-81	8-82
SSN 714	NORFOLK	Newport News	1-8-79	31-10-81	1-83
SSN 715	BUFFALO	Newport News	25-1-80	5-82	6-83

NUCLEAR-POWERED ATTACK SUBMARINES *(continued)*

SSN 716 SALT LAKE CITY	Newport News	26-8-80	10-82	11-83
SSN 717 N. . .	Newport News	31-3-81	2-83	4-84
SSN 718 N. . .	Newport News	11-81	5-83	9-84
SSN 719 N. . .	Gen. Dynamics	5-82	4-84	6-85
SSN 720 N. . .	Gen. Dynamics	1-83	9-84	11-85
SSN 721 N. . .	Newport News	82	84	86
SSN 722 N. . .	Newport News	. . .	. . .	87
SSN 723 N. . .	Newport News	. . .	. . .	87
SSN 724 N. . .	. . .	. . .	. . .	. . .
SSN 725 N. . .	. . .	. . .	. . .	. . .
SSN 742 N. . .	. . .	. . .	. . .	. . .
SSN 743 N. . .	. . .	. . .	. . .	. . .
SSN 744 N. . .	. . .	. . .	. . .	. . .
SSN 746 N. . .	. . .	. . .	. . .	. . .
SSN 747 N. . .	. . .	. . .	. . .	. . .
SSN 748 N. . .	. . .	. . .	. . .	. . .
SSN 749 N. . .	. . .	. . .	. . .	. . .
SSN 750 N. . .	. . .	. . .	. . .	. . .

Authorized: SSN 688 to SSN 690 in FY 70, SSN 691 to SSN 694 in FY 71, SSN 695 to SSN 700 in FY 72, SSN 701 to SSN 705 in FY 73, SSN 706 to SSN 710 in FY 74, SSN 711 to SSN 713 in FY 75, SSN 714 and SSN 715 in FY 76, SSN 716 to SSN 718 in FY 77, SSN 719 in FY 78, SSN 720 in FY 79, SSN 721 and SSN 722 in FY 80, SSN 723 and SSN 724 in FY 81, SSN 725 and SSN 742 in FY 82. Proposed: 2 in FY 83, 3 in FY 84, and 4 in FY 85 through FY 87

D: 6,000/6,927 tons **S:** 30+ kts (sub.) **Dim:** 109.73 × 10.06 × 9.75
A: SSN 724 and later: 12/vertical tubes for Tomahawk
   all: 4/533-mm TT (amidships) for Harpoon and Mk 48 torpedoes
Electron Equipt: Radar: 1/BPS-15A—ECM: BRD-7 direction finder, WLR-9A, WLR-12
   Sonar: 1/BQQ-5-A(V)1, BQS-15, BQR-15
M: GE S6G reactor, 2 GT; 1 prop; 35,000 hp

Los Angeles (SSN 688) G. Arra, 1980

REMARKS: SSN 724 and later are to receive twelve vertical launch tubes for Tomahawk cruise missiles, located between the forward end of the pressure hull and the spherical array for the BQQ-5 bow sonar; the submarines may be slightly longer overall. All carry a UYK-7 general-purpose computer and have WSC-3 satellite comms. gear. One Mk 2 optical and one Sperry Mk 18 multi-function periscope fitted. Mk 113 Mod. 10 torpedo-fire-control in SSN 688 to SSN 699, Mk 117 in later units to be backfitted in all. Harpoon began to be carried in 1978. Maximum diving depth is 450 m. Described as the finest ASW platforms now afloat. Bow is of fiberglass as a streamlined cover over the spherical BQQ-5-A(V)1 sonar array. There are two SINS. All have one Fairbanks-Morse 38D8⅛ diesel generator set and batteries for emergency propulsion. Construction program very far behind schedule because of labor problems and lack of shipyard capacity; there have also been problems with quality control at General Dynamics and with the steam turbines. The reactor core is expected to last 10-13 years between refuelings. SSN 694 traveled around the world submerged 4-4-80 to 8-10-80.

Indianapolis (SSN 697)—note bow sonar now fitted and protrusions to the forward edge of the sail G. Arra, 1980

NUCLEAR-POWERED ATTACK SUBMARINES (continued)

♦ 1 Glenard P. Lipscomb class

	Bldr	Laid down	L	In serv.
SSN 685 GLENARD P. LIPSCOMB	Gen. Dynamics	5-6-71	4-8-73	21-12-74

Authorized: FY 68

Glenard P. Lipscomb (SSN 685)　　　　　General Dynamics, 1974

D: 5,813 standard/6,480 tons (sub.)　**S:** 25 kts　**Dim:** 111.3 × 9.7 × 8.8
A: 4/533-mm TT (amidships)
Electron Equipt: Radar: BPS-14—Sonar: BQQ-2

M: 1 Westinghouse S5WA, natural circulation reactor, GE turboelectric drive; 1 prop; . . . hp
Man: 12 officers, 108 men

REMARKS: This TEDS (Turbo-Electric Drive Submarine) was an effort to make an exceptionally quiet submarine at the expense of some speed. Most other equipment is similar to the *Sturgeon* class. During 3-81 to 7-82 overhaul, is to be equipped to launch Harpoon, with BQQ-5 vice BQQ-2 sonar, and Mk 117 torpedo-fire-control vice Mk 113 Mod. 8.

♦ 37 Sturgeon class (SCB 188A and SCB 188M types)

	Bldr	Laid down	L	In serv.
SSN 637 STURGEON	Gen. Dynamics	10-8-63	26-2-66	3-3-67
SSN 638 WHALE	Gen. Dynamics	27-5-64	14-10-66	12-10-68
SSN 639 TAUTOG	Ingalls SB	27-1-64	15-4-67	17-8-68
SSN 646 GRAYLING	Portsmouth NSY	12-5-64	22-6-67	11-10-69
SSN 647 POGY	New York SB	4-5-64	3-6-67	15-5-71
SSN 648 ASPRO	Ingalls SB	23-11-64	29-11-67	20-2-69
SSN 649 SUNFISH	Gen. Dynamics	15-1-65	14-10-66	15-3-69
SSN 650 PARGO	Gen. Dynamics	3-6-64	17-9-66	1-5-68
SSN 651 QUEENFISH	Newport News	11-5-64	25-2-66	6-12-66
SSN 652 PUFFER	Ingalls SB	8-2-65	30-3-68	9-8-69
SSN 653 RAY	Newport News	1-4-65	21-6-66	12-4-67
SSN 660 SANDLANCE	Portsmouth NSY	15-1-65	11-11-69	25-9-71
SSN 661 LAPON	Newport News	26-7-65	16-12-66	14-12-67
SSN 662 GURNARD	Mare Island NSY	22-12-64	20-5-67	6-12-68
SSN 663 HAMMERHEAD	Newport News	29-11-65	14-4-67	28-6-68
SSN 664 SEA DEVIL	Newport News	12-4-66	5-10-67	30-1-69
SSN 665 GUITARRO	Mare Island NSY	9-12-65	27-7-68	9-9-72
SSN 666 HAWKBILL	Mare Island NSY	12-9-66	12-4-69	4-2-71
SSN 667 BERGALL	Gen. Dynamics	16-4-66	17-2-69	13-6-69
SSN 668 SPADEFISH	Newport News	21-12-66	15-5-68	14-8-69
SSN 669 SEA HORSE	Gen. Dynamics	13-8-66	15-6-68	19-9-69
SSN 670 FINBACK	Newport News	26-6-67	7-12-68	4-2-70
SSN 672 PINTADO	Mare Island NSY	27-10-67	16-8-69	11-9-71
SSN 673 FLYING FISH	Gen. Dynamics	30-6-67	17-5-69	29-4-70
SSN 674 TREPANG	Gen. Dynamics	28-10-67	27-9-69	14-8-70
SSN 675 BLUEFISH	Gen. Dynamics	13-3-68	10-1-70	8-1-71
SSN 676 BILLFISH	Gen. Dynamics	20-9-68	1-5-70	12-3-71
SSN 677 DRUM	Mare Island NSY	20-8-68	23-5-70	15-4-72
SSN 678 ARCHERFISH	Gen. Dynamics	19-6-69	16-1-71	24-12-71
SSN 679 SILVERSIDES	Gen. Dynamics	13-12-69	4-6-71	5-5-72
SSN 680 WILLIAM H. BATES (ex-*Redfish*)	Ingalls SB	4-8-69	12-71	5-5-73
SSN 681 BATFISH	Gen. Dynamics	9-2-70	9-10-71	1-9-72
SSN 682 TUNNY	Ingalls SB	22-5-70	10-6-72	26-1-74
SSN 683 PARCHE	Ingalls SB	10-12-70	12-72	17-8-74
SSN 684 CAVALLA	Gen. Dynamics	4-6-70	19-2-72	9-2-73
SSN 686 MENDEL RIVERS	Newport News	26-6-71	2-6-73	1-2-75
SSN 687 RICHARD B. RUSSELL	Newport News	19-10-71	12-1-74	16-8-75

Authorized: SSN 637 to SSN 639 in FY 62, SSN 646 to SSN 653 in FY 63, SSN 660 to SSN 664 in FY 64, SSN 665 to SSN 670 in FY 65, SSN 672 to SSN 677 in FY 66, SSN 678 to SSN 682 in FY 67, SSN 683 and SSN 684 in FY 68, SSN 686 and SSN 687 in FY 69

NUCLEAR-POWERED ATTACK SUBMARINES *(continued)*

D: 3,640/4,640 tons   **S:** 15/30 kts
Dim: 89.0 (SSN 678 and later and 19 refitted units: 92.1) × 9.65 × 8.8
A: 4/533-mm TT (amidships for 15 Mk 48 torpedoes, 4/Harpoon, and 4/SUB-ROC)

Batfish (SSN 681)—note fairing running the length of the hull on the port side for housing the towed sonar array   L. & L. Van Ginderen, 10-81

Archerfish (SSN 678)—note probe/sensor at upper forward edge of sail   G. Gyssels, 5-79

Billfish (SSN 676)   L. & L. Van Ginderen, 9-81

Pintado (SSN 672)—with Mystic (DSRV 1) aboard   PH1 A. Legare, USN, 1977

Electron Equipt: Radar: 1/BPS-14—ECM: WLR-8
        Sonar: BQQ-2 (with BQS-6 active/BQR-7 passive) or BQQ-5,
        BQS-8, (SSN 637 to SSN 664: BQS-12; others: BQS-13
M: 1 Westinghouse S5W2 pressurized-water reactor, 2 GE or de Laval GT; 1
    prop; 20,000 hp
Man: 12 officers, 107 men

REMARKS: The construction contract of SSN 647 with New York Shipbuilding, Camden, N.J., was canceled in 4-67 and completion of the ship was given to Ingalls, Pascagoula, Miss. Completion of SSN 665 was delayed twenty-eight months after ship sank while fitting out. The Mk 113 torpedo-fire-control system is being replaced by Mk 117 to permit Harpoon launching. SSN 678 and later units (SCB 188M) were lengthened to permit installation of BQQ-5 sonar suit, now being backfitted in all; since that extra space is free-flooding it does not materially affect submerged displacement. Diving planes are 11.6 wide. Maximum depth is about 400 m. The 70 megawatt 65W reactor plant operates at 160 kg/cm², has two primary steam loops and two steam generators to supply steam to the two steam turbines. Original core life was 5,000 hours. SSN 666, SSN 672, and others have been modified to carry a DSRV (salvage submarine), which can be launched and recovered while submerged. The after hatch is so constructed that people can be transferred between the two ships while submerged. Since 1978, SSN 687 has an aftward extension to the lower portion of the sail to accommodate a trial towed communications array. Class expected to serve 30 years each.

NUCLEAR-POWERED ATTACK SUBMARINES *(continued)*

♦ 1 Narwhal class (SCB 245)

	Bldr	Laid down	L	In serv.
SSN 671 NARWHAL	Gen. Dynamics	17-1-66	9-9-67	12-7-69

Authorized: FY 64

Narwhal (SSN 671) General Dynamics, 1969

D: 4,550/5,350 tons **S:** 20/25 kts **Dim:** 95.7 × 11.5 × 7.9
A: 4/533-mm TT (amidships)
Electron Equipt: Radar: BPS-14—ECM: WLR-8
Sonar: BQQ-2 (BQS-6 active/BQR-7 passive), BQS-8
M: 1 GE S5G reactor, 2 GT; 1 prop; 17,000 hp **Man:** 12 officers, 108 men

REMARKS: Prototype seagoing reactor designed to study the cooling of the S5G reactor by natural circulation, thus eliminating circulation pumps and their noise. In most other respects, essentially a lengthened *Sturgeon*. Will receive Harpoon Mk 117 torpedo-fire-control system and BQQ-5 sonar suit; currently has Mk 113 Mod. 6 fcs.

♦ 13 Permit class (SSN 594 to SSN 612 and SSN 621 are SCB 188 type, SSN 613 to SSN 615 are SCB 188M type)

	Bldr	Laid down	L	In serv.
SSN 594 PERMIT	Mare Island NSY	16-7-59	1-7-61	29-5-62
SSN 595 PLUNGER	Mare Island NSY	2-3-60	9-12-61	21-11-62
SSN 596 BARB (ex-*Pollack*)	Ingalls SB	9-11-59	12-2-62	24-8-63
SSN 603 POLLACK (ex-*Barb*)	New York SB	14-3-60	17-3-62	26-5-64
SSN 604 HADDO	New York SB	9-9-60	18-8-62	16-12-64
SSN 605 JACK	Portsmouth NSY	16-9-60	24-4-63	31-3-67
SSN 606 TINOSA	Portsmouth NSY	24-11-59	9-12-61	17-10-64
SSN 607 DACE	Ingalls SB	6-6-60	18-8-62	4-4-64
SSN 612 GUARDFISH	New York SB	28-2-61	15-5-65	20-12-66
SSN 613 FLASHER	Gen. Dynamics	14-4-61	22-6-63	22-7-66
SSN 614 GREENLING	Gen. Dynamics	15-8-61	4-4-64	3-11-67
SSN 615 GATO	Gen. Dynamics	15-12-61	14-5-64	25-1-68
SSN 621 HADDOCK	Ingalls SB	24-4-61	21-5-66	22-12-67

Authorized: SSN 594 to SSN 596 in FY 58, SSN 603 to SSN 607 in FY 59, SSN 612 to SSN 615 in FY60, SSN 621 in FY 61

Tinosa (SSN 606)—4.6-meter-high sail 1964

Haddock (SSN 621)—6.1-meter-high sail G. Arra, 7-79

SSN 594 to SSN 604, SSN 606 to SSN 612, and SSN 621:

D: 3,526/4,465 tons **Dim:** 90.11 × 9.65 × 8.80

SSN 606:

D: 3,526/4,465 tons **Dim:** 90.11 × 9.65 × 8.80

SSN 613 to SSN 615:

D: 3,836/4,650 tons **S:** 15/30 kts **Dim:** 89.0 × 9.65 × 8.80
A: 4/533-mm TT (Harpoon) **Man:** 12 officers, 108 men
Electron Equipt: Radar: BPS-11
Sonar: BQQ-2 (BQS-6 active/BQR-7 passive), BQS-14
M: 1 Westinghouse S5W reactor; 2 GE or de Laval GT; 1 prop; 15,000 hp

REMARKS: Sister *Thresher* (SSN 593) was lost 10-4-63. SSN 605 has contrarotating props with a contrarotating turbine and no reduction gearing. SSN 613 to SSN 615 have longer and taller sails (6.1 m vice 4.2 or 4.6 in other ships), heavier machinery, and had safety features built in that were later backfitted in the others. The BQR-7 spherical array is in the bow, necessitating placement of the tubes abreast the sail. These ships are being fitted to carry Harpoon, and are therefore receiving Mk 117 torpedo-fire-control systems in place of Mk 113. SSN 594 conducted Harpoon trials during 1976. All are scheduled to receive the BQQ-5 sonar suit during refits. SSN 621 ran trials in 7-79 for the Sperry PASRAN (passive-ranging) sonar system, which is similar to the exported "Micro Puffs" concept, but with an array of six larger hydrophones.

♦ 5 Ethan Allen class (SCB 180 type) former ballistic-missile submarines

	Bldr	Laid down	L	In serv.
SSN 608 ETHAN ALLEN	Gen. Dynamics	14-9-59	22-11-60	8-8-61
SSN 609 SAM HOUSTON	Newport News	28-12-59	2-2-61	6-3-62
SSN 610 THOMAS A. EDISON	Gen. Dynamics	15-3-60	15-6-61	10-3-62
SSN 611 JOHN MARSHALL	Newport News	4-4-60	15-7-61	21-5-62
SSN 618 THOMAS JEFFERSON	Newport News	3-2-61	24-2-62	4-1-63

Authorized: SSN 608 to SSN 611 in FY 59, SSN 618 in FY 61

NUCLEAR-POWERED ATTACK SUBMARINES (continued)

Ethan Allen (SSN 608)—as SSBN 608 1961

D: 6,300/7,880 tons **S:** 15/20 kts **Dim:** 124.96 × 10.05 × 9.0
A: 4/533-mm TT (fwd)
Electron Equipt: Radar:. . . —Sonar: BQR-7, BQR-15, BQR-19, BQS-4
M: 1 Westinghouse SW5 pressurized-water reactor, GT; 1 7-bladed prop; 15,000 hp
Man: 12 officers, 128 men

REMARKS: First U.S. submarines designed from the outset to launch ballistic missiles. Retained Polaris A-3 missiles until redesignated SSN: SSBN 608 on 1-9-80; SSBN 609 on 10-11-80; SSBN 610 on 6-10-80; SSBN 611 on 1-5-81; and SSBN 618 on 11-3-81 at conclusion of final Polaris cruises. Following redesignation, all are to convert by 1984 for further service as SSNs until the late 1980s. Beginning with SSN 608 in 1-82 and followed by SSN 609 and 610 in FY 83 and the others in FY 84, cement ballast will fill the 16 missile tubes, one of the two Mk 2 Mod. 3 SINS (Ship's Inertial Navigation Systems) will be removed, and the Mk 84 missile-control system will be deleted. Formerly had two complete crews; complement will probably be reduced as SSNs. Deeper-diving (300 m +) than SSN 598 class. All will remain in Pacific Fleet. A plan to install vertical launchers for Tomahawk cruise missiles has apparently been shelved.

♦ **3 George Washington class (SCB 180A type) former ballistic-missile submarines**

	Bldr	Laid down	L	In serv.
SSN 598 GEORGE WASHINGTON	Gen. Dynamics	1-11-57	9-6-59	30-12-59
SSN 599 PATRICK HENRY	Gen. Dynamics	27-5-58	22-9-59	9-4-60
SSN 601 ROBERT E. LEE	Newport News SB	25-8-58	18-12-59	16-9-60

Authorized: SSN 598 and SSN 599 in FY 58, SSN 601 in FY 59

D: 6,019/6,888 tons **S:** 15/20 kts **Dim:** 115.82 × 10.05 × 8.8
A: 6/533-mm Mk 59 TT (fwd)
Electron Equipt: Radar: BPS-9
Sonar: BQS-4, BQR-7, BQR-19
M: 1 Westinghouse S5W pressurized-water reactor, GT; 1 7-bladed prop; 15,000 hp

REMARKS: Conversion of *Skipjack*-class attack submarine design, the first two having been stretched 39.62 m while building, in order to insert new section with sixteen missile tubes. Sisters *Theodore Roosevelt* (SSBN 600) and *Abraham Lincoln* (SSBN

George Washington (SSN 598)—as SSBN 598

602) had the major portion of the 16-tubed missile bay area physically removed, beginning in late 1980; they were officially decommissioned on 28-2-81 at Bremerton, where they remain, still officially on the Navy List, each in two pieces (neither had made a missile patrol since 1978 and both required expensive recorings). The other three, with core life remaining, have been redesignated as SSN and will be altered as with the *Ethan Allen* class above. All are in the Pacific Fleet.

♦ **1 Tullibee class (SCB 178 type)**

	Bldr	Laid down	L	In serv.
SSN 597 TULLIBEE	Gen. Dynamics	26-5-58	27-4-60	9-11-60

Authorized: FY 58

Tullibee (SSN 597) U.S. Navy, 1975

D: 2,490/2,317/2,640 tons **S:** 15/20 kts **Dim:** 83.15 × 7.31 × 6.1
A: 4/533-mm Mk 64 TT (amidships)
Electron Equipt: Radar: 1/BPS-11
ECM: WLR-8
Sonar: BQQ-2 (BQS-6 active/BQR-7 passive), BQG-4 (PUFFS)

NUCLEAR-POWERED ATTACK SUBMARINES (continued)

M: 1 Combustion Engineering S2C reactor, turboelectric propulsion; 1 prop; 2,500 hp
Man: 6 officers, 50 men

REMARKS: The torpedo tubes have a 10° angle from the centerline. PUFFS hydrophones are mounted in three fins along the top of the hull. Mk 112 Mod. 1 torpedo-fire-control system. Active in Atlantic Fleet, but considered to be second-line.

◆ 1 Halibut class (SCB 137A type)

	Bldr	Laid down	L	In serv.
SSN 587 HALIBUT	Mare Island NSY	4-57	9-1-59	4-1-60

Authorized: FY 57

Halibut (SSN 587)—with DSRV aboard aft   1970

D: 3,850/5,000 tons **S:** 15/20 kts **Dim:** 106.7 × 8.85 × 8.8
A: 6/533-mm TT (4 fwd, 2 aft) **Man:** 10 officers, 88 men
Electron Equipt: Radar: BPS-5 Sonar: BQS-4
M: 1 Westinghouse S3W reactor, 2 GT; 2 props; 13,200 hp

REMARKS: Ex-SSGN, redesignated SSN on 25-7-65 and used for research. Placed in reserve on 30-6-76. Forward watertight compartment (where five Regulus-I missiles could be stowed) is 27 m long and 7.6 m high. The missiles and the single, trainable launcher were removed in 1965 when the ship was reclassified as an SSN. Equipped to carry a DSRV. Bow and stern side-thrusters were installed 1970.

◆ 1 Triton class (SCB 132 type)

	Bldr	Laid down	L	In serv.
SSN 586 TRITON	Gen. Dynamics	29-5-56	19-8-58	10-11-59

Authorized: FY 56

Triton (SSN 586)   U.S. Navy, 1959

D: 5,940/7,780 tons **S:** 27/20 kts **Dim:** 136.25 × 11.3 × 7.6
A: 6/533-mm TT (4 fwd, 2 aft) **Electron Equipt:** Sonar: BQS-4
M: 2 GE S4G reactors, 2 GT; 2 props; 34,000 hp **Man:** 14 officers, 156 men

REMARKS: Ex-SSRN. In reserve since 3-5-69 as too unwieldy and uneconomical to operate. First submarine with three decks and only U.S. submarine with two reactors. In 1960 made a round-the-world cruise submerged, sailing 41,519 miles in 84 days at an average speed of 18 knots. Unlike other U.S. nuclear-powered submarines, her speed on the surface was greater than submerged. It was hoped that she would be able to operate as a radar picket with large surface-ship task forces. Reclassified as SSN on 1-3-61. Mk 101 Mod. 11 torpedo-fire-control system.

◆ 5 Skipjack class (SCB 154 type)

	Bldr	Laid down	L	In serv.
SSN 585 SKIPJACK	Gen. Dynamics	29-5-56	26-5-58	15-4-59
SSN 588 SCAMP	Mare Island, NSY	23-1-59	8-10-60	5-6-61
SSN 590 SCULPIN	Ingalls	3-2-58	31-3-60	1-6-61
SSN 591 SHARK	Newport News SB	24-2-56	16-3-60	9-2-61
SSN 592 SNOOK	Ingalls	7-4-58	31-10-60	24-10-61

Authorized: SSN 585 in FY 56, SSN 558 and SSN 590 to SSN 592 in FY 57

Scamp (SSN 588)   G. Arra, 1976

D: 3,075/3,513 tons **S:** 15/30 kts **Dim:** 76.8 × 9.75 × 8.5
A: 6/533-mm TT (fwd) **Man:** 8 officers, 85 men
Electron Equipt: Radar: BPS-11—Sonar: Modified BQS-4
M: 1 Westinghouse S5W reactor; SSN 585: 2 Westinghouse GT, others: 2 GE GT; 1 prop; 15,000 hp

REMARKS: The reactor compartment takes up 6.10 m. Between the reactor and the propeller, all engine fittings are duplicated (two heat exchangers, two pressurized-water coolers; two groups of turbines, two groups of turbo generators). In case of emergency, submerged propulsion can take over by means of two electric motors linked directly on the propeller shaft and feeding off two electric batteries or two small diesel generators. Better hull form than later SSNs. Still considered first-line submarines. Sister *Scorpion* (SSN 589) disappeared in the Atlantic about 27-5-68. Mk 101 Mod. 17 torpedo-fire-control system.

◆ 4 Skate class (SCB 121 type)

	Bldr	Laid down	L	In serv.
SSN 578 SKATE	Gen. Dynamics	21-7-55	16-5-57	23-12-57
SSN 579 SWORDFISH	Portsmouth NSY	25-1-56	27-8-57	15-9-58
SSN 583 SARGO	Mare Island NSY	21-2-56	10-10-57	1-10-58
SSN 584 SEADRAGON	Portsmouth NSY	20-6-56	16-8-58	5-12-59

Authorized: SSN 578 and SSN 579 in FY 55, SSN 583 and SSN 584 in FY 56

NUCLEAR-POWERED ATTACK SUBMARINES (continued)

Swordfish (SSN 579)   G. Arra, 1978

D: 2,570/2,860 tons   **S:** 15/19 kts   **Dim:** 81.4 × 7.62 × 6.1
A: 8/533-mm TT (6 fwd, 2 aft)
Electron Equipt: Radar: BPS-11—Sonar: BQS-4
M: 1 Westinghouse reactor—S3W in SSN 578 and SSN 583, S4W in SSN 579
     and SSN 584; 2 GT; 2 props; 13,200 hp
Man: 11 officers, 76 men

REMARKS: SSN 578 passed under the North Pole twice (8-58), coming to the surface nine times while in ice-capped waters during this cruise. She ran 120,862 miles in 39 months with her first core. Mk 101 Mod. 19 torpedo-fire-control system. Now considered second-line submarines.

♦ **1 Seawolf class (SCB 64A type)**

	Bldr	Laid down	L	In serv.
SSN 575 SEAWOLF	Gen. Dynamics	15-9-53	21-7-55	30-3-57

Authorized: FY 53

Seawolf (SSN 575)—note side-thrusters fore and aft   U.S. Navy, 1977

D: 3,765/4,287 tons   **S:** 20/20 kts   **Dim:** 102.87 × 8.45 × 6.7
A: 6/533-mm TT (fwd)   **Man:** 11 officers, 90 men
M: 1 Westinghouse S2WA reactor; 2 GT; 2 props; 15,000 hp

REMARKS: The original propulsion plant, which was by an S2G reactor with sodium cooling, did not prove satisfactory and was replaced by an S2WA. Four side-thrusters, two forward and two aft, have been added to the casing above the pressure hull for precision maneuvering while submerged, and foundations have been added at the stern to permit a DSRV to be carried and to mate with the after rescue hatch. Mk 101 Mod. 8 torpedo-fire-control system. Now considered a second-line submarine and due to be disposed of during FY 83.

NOTE: The *Nautilus* (SSN 571), the world's first nuclear-powered ship, was placed in technical reserve on 30-9-79 and formally decommissioned 3-3-80. In fact, she was stripped of her reactor plant and will be taken to Groton, Connecticut, where she will serve as a monument to the technical achievements of the U.S. submarine service and ADM H.G. Rickover, her creator.

CONVENTIONAL SUBMARINES

♦ **3 Barbel class (SCB 150 type)**

	Bldr	Laid down	L	In serv.
SS 580 BARBEL	Portsmouth NSY	18-5-56	19-7-58	17-1-59
SS 581 BLUEBACK	Ingalls	15-4-57	16-5-59	15-10-59
SS 582 BONEFISH	New York SB	3-6-57	22-11-58	9-7-59

Authorized: FY 56

Barbel (SS 580)—in dry dock: note bow TT in two rows of three.   1963

Blueback (SS 581)   G. Arra, 9-79

CONVENTIONAL SUBMARINES (continued)

D: 1,740/2,146/2,895 tons **S:** 15/25 kts **Dim:** 66.75 × 8.84 × 5.8
A: 6/533-mm TT (fwd)
Electron Equipt: Radar: BPS-11—Sonar: BQS-4
M: 3 1,600-hp Fairbanks-Morse 38D8⅛ × 10 diesels, 1 Westinghouse electric motor; 1 prop; 3,150 hp
Man: 8 officers, 70 men

REMARKS: Teardrop hull design. Diving planes were moved to the sail structure in 1961-62. Dutch *Zwaardvis* class based on this design. Mk 101 Mod. 20 torpedo-fire-control system. Last conventional submarines built for the U.S. Navy.

♦ 1 Darter class (SCB 116 type)

	Bldr	Laid down	L	In serv.
SS 576 DARTER	Electric Boat Co.	10-11-54	28-5-56	26-10-56

Authorized: FY 54

Darter (SS 576)   G. Arra, 1-80

D: 1,590/1,720/2,388 tons **S:** 20/20 kts **Dim:** 81.68 × 8.23 × 5.8
A: 8/533-mm TT (6 fwd, 2 aft)
Electron Equipt: Radar: 1/BPS-11
  Sonar: BQS-4, BQG-4 (PUFFS)
M: 3 Fairbanks-Morse 38D8⅛ × 10 diesels, 2 Westinghouse motors; 2 props; 5,500 hp
Man: 10 officers, 75 men

REMARKS: Very similar to the ultimate configuration of the *Tang* class. Mk 106 Mod. 11 torpedo-fire-control system. Home-ported at Sasebo, Japan, in 3-79. To have been stricken in 9-79, but has since been retained in service.

♦ 1 Grayback class (SCB 161 type)

	Bldr	Laid down	L	In serv.
SS 574 GRAYBACK	Mare Island NSY	1-7-54	2-7-57	5-58

Authorized: FY 53

Grayback (SS 574)—port hangar open   PH3 B. Halbert, 1975

Grayback (SS 574)—with both hangar doors open   G. Arra, 1978

D: 2,670/3,650 tons **S:** 20/16.7 kts **Dim:** 101.8 × 8.2 × 5.8
A: 8/533-mm TT (6 fwd, 2 aft)
Electron Equipt: Sonar: BQS-4, BQG-4 (PUFFS)
M: 3 Fairbanks-Morse 38D8⅛ × 10 diesels, 2 Elliot motors; 2 props; 5,500 hp
Man: 7 officers, 60 men

REMARKS: Designed as SSG, carrying two Regulus-II surface-to-surface missiles. Conversion to amphibious transport submarine, which took six years, was finished in 9-5-69. Redesignated SS in 1975, but retains capacity for 10 officers and 75 commandoes with their equipment (including swimmer-delivery vehicles) stowed in the former missile hangars. Mk 106 Mod. 12 torpedo-fire-control system. Home-ported at Sasebo, Japan.

NOTE: The guided-missile submarine *Growler* (SSG 577), in reserve since 25-5-64 as a source of spare parts for SS 574, was stricken 1-8-80 for use as a target.

CONVENTIONAL SUBMARINES *(continued)*

♦ 2 Tang class (SCB 2A Type)

	Bldr	Laid down	L	In serv.
SS 565 WAHOO	Portsmouth NSY	24-10-49	16-10-51	30-5-52
SSAG 567 GUDGEON	Portsmouth NSY	20-5-50	11-6-52	21-11-52

Authorized: SS 565 in FY 48, SSAG 567 in FY 49

Gudgeon (SSAG 567) as SS 567—PUFFS fins now gone   PH3 J. Land, USN, 1970

D: 2,100/2,700 tons **S:** 15.5/16 kts **Dim:** 87.48 × 8.33 × 5.80
A: 8/533-mm TT (6 long fwd, 2 short aft)
Electron Equipt: Radar: 1/SS-2—Sonar: BQR-2, BQR-4, BQS-4
M: 3 Fairbanks-Morse 38D8⅛ × 10 diesels, 2 Westinghouse electric motors; 2 props; 5,500 hp
Man: 8 officers, 75 men

REMARKS: SS 565 was halfway through a major overhaul at Philadelphia NSY prior to an intended transfer to Iran when the work was terminated in 1979; she was formally decommissioned to reserve 27-6-80 while partially dismantled, but is being retained on the Navy List pending the faint possibility of transfer (rejected by Egypt in 1980). *Gudgeon* was reclassified SSAG 567 5-11-79 to replace *Tang* (SS 563) as acoustic trials submarine; her BQD-4 PUFFS sonar domes were removed by 1978, but their foundations remained. Noncombatant.

NOTE: The research submarine *Dolphin* (AGSS 575) is described later with auxiliaries.

BATTLESHIPS

♦ 4 Iowa class

	Bldr	Laid down	L	In serv.
BB 61 IOWA	New York NSY	27-6-40	27-8-42	22-2-43
BB 62 NEW JERSEY	Philadelphia NSY	16-9-40	7-12-42	23-5-43
BB 63 MISSOURI	New York NSY	6-1-41	29-1-44	11-6-44
BB 64 WISCONSIN	Philadelphia NSY	25-1-41	7-12-43	16-4-44

D: 46,177 tons light (57,675 fl) **S:** 33 kts (30.5 sust.)
Dim: 270.57 (262.13 pp) × 33.00 × 11.02
A: BB 62 as reactivated: 32/Tomahawk (IV × 8)—16 Harpoon (IV × 4)—9/406-mm (III × 3)—12/127-mm DP (II × 6)—4/20-mm Vulcan/Phalanx AA (I × 4)—4/SH-60B-equivalent helos
  Others: 9/406-MM (III × 3)—20/127-mm (II × 10)—BB 63 also: 80/40-mm AA (IV × 20)
Electron Equipt: BB 62 as reactivated:
  Radar: 1/LN-66, 1/SPS-10F, 1/SPS-49, 2/Mk 13, 4/Mk 25
  TACAN: URN-25
  ECM: SLQ-32(V)3, 8/Mk 36 SRBOC chaff or SPS-4
  Others: Radar: 1/SPS-6C, 1/SPS-10, 2/Mk 13, 4/Mk 25, 1/Mk 27; BB 61 also: 2/Mk 34, 6 Mk 35; BB 63 also: 7/Mk 34
M: 4 sets GE GT; 4 props; 212,000 hp **Electric:** 10,500 kw
Boilers: 8 Babcock & Wilcox; 44.6 kg/cm², 454°C **Fuel:** 8,800 tons

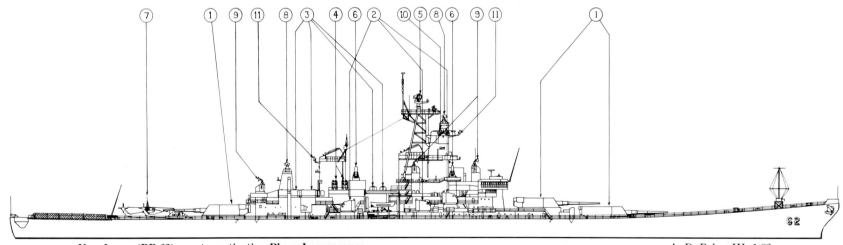

New Jersey (BB 62)—post-reactivation Phase I appearance   A. D. Baker III, 1-82
1. 406-mm triple tureent 2. 127-mm twin DP 3. Tomahawk box-launcher (IV × 1) 4. Harpoon canister launcher (IV × 1) 5. SPS-49 radar 6. Vulcan/Phalanx 20-mm Gatling AA 7. Helicopter parking area 8. Mk 38 GFCS (with Mk 13 radar) 9. Mk 37 GFCS (with Mk 25 radar) 10. SLQ-32 ECM gear 11. Mk 36 SRBOC chaff launchers 12. WSC-3 SATCOMM antennas

BATTLESHIPS (continued)

New Jersey (BB 62)—under tow to Long Beach for reactivation

U.S. Navy, 8-81

New Jersey 1969

Armor: Belt: 307-mm, tapering to 41-mm (343-mm abreast prop shafts)
Main turrets: 432-mm face/184-mm top/305-mm back
Barbettes: 295-mm max.
Decks: 3 armored (152-mm second deck)
Conning tower: 440-mm (184-mm top)
Range: 9,600/25; 16,600/15   **Man:** 74 officers, 1,579 men (after reactivation)

REMARKS: Although the concept has been hotly debated as to its combat value, the reactivation and modernization of all four *Iowa*-class battleships is planned. BB 62, reactivated 6-4-68 for Vietnam service and decommissioned again 17-12-69, was towed from the Bremerton, Washington, mothball facility on 27-7-81, arriving 8-6-81 at Long Beach Naval Shipyard. Congress voted $326-mil. under FY 82 to modernize the ship with new radars and ECM gear, Tomahawk and Harpoon cruise missiles, upgraded communications gear (including the WSC-3 SATCOMM system), seven new 125-ton/hr. air-conditioning plants, provision for Link-11 data link (but not NTDS), and conversion of the boilers to burn distillate fuel (which will cut endurance by approx. 10 percent). Trials are scheduled to commence Sept. 82, with recommissioning scheduled for 15-1-83. Funds were authorized in FY 82 to begin work on BB 61 at an East Coast or Gulf Coast shipyard, with recommissioning scheduled for 1985. Plans call for recommissioning BB 63 in 1986 and BB 64 in 1987.

The work to be done on BB 62 is described as "Phase I." "Phase II" is a more ambitious conversion whose details are not yet fully worked out; the after triple 406-mm will be removed, and increased aviation facilities provided. Some version of the EX-41 VLS (Vertical Launch System) will be added, to provide for some form of air defense ("Phase I" will still leave the ships virtually defenseless against air attack) plus vertical stowage for the cruise missiles. BB 63 and BB 64 may get "Phase II" conversion from the outset, while BB 62 is scheduled to undergo the process during 1987-88.

The helicopter facilities planned for "Phase I" include increased parking area to accommodate up to four SH-60B LAMPS-III-equivalent helicopters, but there will be no hangar; some maintenance facilities, a control cab, fuel tankage, and a glide-path indicator will be added. The Tomahawk missiles will be carried in elevating armored box launchers, while the Harpoons will be placed between the stacks in the standard fixed 4-missile canister arrangement.

The 406-mm guns are controlled by two Mk 38 radar (Mk 13) GFCS and one Mk 40 director, while four Mk 37 GFCS (with Mk 25 radar) will be retained for the 127-mm guns. BB 62's six Mk 56 AA GFCS will be replaced by the Vulcan/Phalanx (Mk 16 CIWS) Gatling guns and the Mk 36 Super RBOC chaff launchers. While in reserve, BB 61 retains 6 Mk 56 and 2 Mk 63 GFCS, and BB 63 has 6 Mk 57 and 2 Mk 63 GFCS; BB 64 had all light AA GFCS removed when decommissioned in 1958. As activated will have WRN-5A NAVSAT, Omega, and other modern navigational systems.

NUCLEAR-POWERED GUIDED-MISSILE CRUISERS

♦ 0 (+3+. . .) **CGN class (projected)**

	Bldr	Laid down	L	In serv.
CGN 42 N. . .	. . .	1987	. . .	1991
CGN 43 N. . .	. . .	1988	. . .	1992
CGN 44 N. . .	. . .	1989	. . .	1993

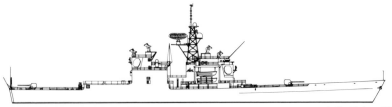

Possible appearance of CGN 42   A.D. Baker III

D: 10,200 tons (12,000 fl)   **S:** 30+ kts   **Dim:** 179.6 × 19.2 × 9.5 (7.3 hull)

A: 8/Tomahawk SSM (IV × 2)—8/Harpoon SSM (IV × 2)—2 vertical launch systems (122 Standard SM-2 MR and ASROC-successor missiles)—2/127-mm Mk 45 DP (I × 2)—2/20-mm Vulcan/Phalanx AA (I × 2)—4/324-mm Mk 32 ASW TT (II × 2)—2/UH-60B LAMPS-III ASW helicopters

Electron Equipt: Radar: 1/SPS-55 or 67, 1/SPS-9A, 1/SPY-1D, 1/Seafire, 1/SPQ-9A, 4/SPG-62

Sonar: SQS-53 series hull-mounted, SQR-19 TACTASS towed array

ECM: SLQ-32(V)3, 4/Mk 36 SRBOC chaff

TACAN: URN-26

M: 2 GE D2G pressurized-water reactors, 2 sets steam turbines; 2 props; 70,000 hp

Man: 52 officers, 582 men

REMARKS: The original CGN 42 concept was intended as a minimum modification of the *Virginia* class to incorporate the Aegis weapons system and was to have been ordered (as CGN 41) under FY 74. The design is now a considerable expansion on the CGN 38, and the hull is longer and has fuller lines aft. Currently intended for request under FY 87, CGN 42 may ultimately differ considerably from the characteristics listed above, which are based on those released for the FY 76 version of the ship, with the incorporation of new weapon and sensors technologies that have since become available. The hull number block CGN 42-46 has been "reserved" for these ships (actually the official explanation for the gap from CGN 41 to CG 47 has more to do with not wishing to renumber the *Ticonderoga* class after they were retyped from destroyers to cruisers). As shipbuilding costs mount, the likelihood of these ships ever being built diminishes.

♦ 4 **Virginia class**

	Bldr	Laid down	L	Inserv.
CGN 38 VIRGINIA	Newport News SB	19-8-72	14-12-74	11-9-76
CGN 39 TEXAS	Newport News SB	18-8-73	9-8-75	10-9-77
CGN 40 MISSISSIPPI	Newport News SB	22-2-75	31-7-76	5-8-78
CGN 41 ARKANSAS	Newport News SB	17-1-77	21-10-78	18-10-80

Authorized: CGN 38 in FY 70, CGN 39 in FY 71, CGN 40 in FY 72, and CGN 41 in FY 75

D: 8,623 tons (10,420 fl)   **S:** 30+ kts

Dim: 177.3 × 19.2 × 9.5 (sonar; 7.3 hull)

Virginia (CGN 38)   G. Arra, 1976

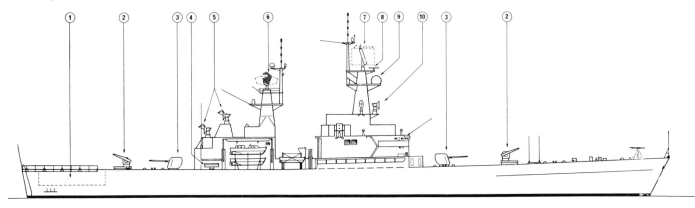

Virginia 1. Helicopter hangar 2. Mk 26 launcher 3. 127-mm Mk 45 mount 4. Mk 32 ASW TT 5. SPG-51D radar 6. SPS-40B radar 7. SPS-48A radar 8. SPS-55 radar 9. SPQ-9A radar 10. SPG-60D radar

NUCLEAR-POWERED GUIDED-MISSILE CRUISERS (continued)

Mississippi (CGN 40)—Harpoon canisters before bridge

PH2 M. Collins, USN, 2-81

Texas (CGN 39)—note elevator just abaft missile launcher   Newport News, 1977

Arkansas (CGN 41)—Harpoon launchers before bridge

Newport News SB/Everton, 9-80

A: 8/Harpoon SSM (IV × 2)—2/Mk 26 launchers (II × 2; Mod. 0 aft, 68 total Standard SM-1 MR surface-to-air or ASROC ASW missiles)—2/127-mm Mk 45 DP (I × 2)—2/324-mm Mk 32 ASW TT (III × 2, Mk 46 torpedoes)—1 or 2/SH-2F LAMPS-II ASW helicopters
Electron Equipt: Radar: 1/navigational, 1/SPS-55, 1/SPS-40B, 1/SPS-48A, 2/SPG-51D, 1/SPQ-9A, 1/SPG-60D
       Sonar: 1/SQS-53A
       TACAN: URN-20
       ECM: SLQ-32(V)3, 4/Mk 36 SRBOC chaff
M: 2 GE D2G reactors; 2 props; 70,000 hp   **Man:** 27 officers, 445 men

REMARKS: These ships are expected to operate for 10 years on one nuclear fueling. The Standard SM-1 MR antiaircraft missiles and ASROC ASW missiles, stowed vertically, will be replaced by SM-2 MR beginning in 1983. Eventually, they will carry eight Tomahawk cruise missiles in two armored box-launchers. It is also planned to add two Vulcan/Phalanx 20-mm Gatling guns on the platforms at the aft end of the forward superstructure. A hangar is fitted beneath the fantail, the helicopter being raised to the main deck by elevator. These ships are no longer scheduled to carry UH-60B LAMPS-III helicopters. CGN 40 and 41 have SPS-48C vice 48A. All have WSC-3 SATCOMM and NTDS data system. The missile-fire-control system is Mk 74; ASW fire-control is Mk 116; and the GFCS is Mk 86 Mod. 5. SQS-53A sonar is a greatly improved version of SQS-26. Kevlar plastic armor will be added over vital topside and magazine spaces during sequential overhauls scheduled from FY 82 to FY 86. Major modernization, possibly including the addition of the Aegis/SPY-1D system, is scheduled to commence under FY 87, beginning with CGN 38.

♦ **2 California class (SCB 241.65 type)**

	Bldr	Laid down	L	In serv.
CGN 36 CALIFORNIA	Newport News SB	23-1-70	22-9-71	16-2-74
CGN 37 SOUTH CAROLINA	Newport News SB	1-12-70	1-7-72	25-1-75

Authorized: CGN 36 in FY 67, CGN 37 in FY 68

D: 8,706 tons light (9,560 fl)   **S:** 30+ kts
Dim: 181.66 × 18.6 × 9.6 (sonar, 7.4 hull)   **Man:** 28 officers, 512 men
A: 2/Mk 13 launchers (I × 2 for 80 Harpoon SM-1 MR missiles)—2/127-mm Mk 45 DP (I × 2) (CGN 36: 2/20-mm Vulcan/Phalanx AA (I × 2)—1/ASROC ASW RL (VIII × 1)—4/324-mm Mk 32 ASW TT (II × 2)
Electron Equipt: Radar: 1/navigational, 1/SPS-10, 1/SPS-40B, 1/SPS-48A, 4/SPG-51D, 1/SPQ-9A, 1/SPG-60
       Sonar: 1/SQS-26CX
       TACAN: URN-20
       ECM: WLR-8, ULQ-6
M: 2 GE D2G pressurized-water reactors, 2 GT; 2 props; 70,000 hp

NUCLEAR-POWERED GUIDED-MISSILE CRUISERS *(continued)*

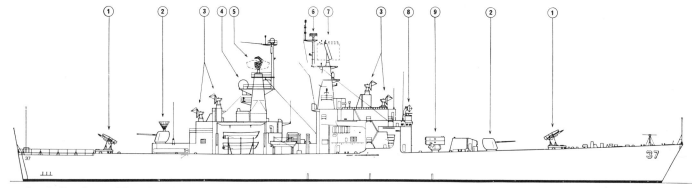

South Carolina 1. Mk 13 launcher 2. 127-mm Mk 45 mount 3. SPG-51D radar 4. SPQ-9A radar 5. SPS-40B radar 6. SPS-10′ radar 7. SPS-48A radar 8. SPG-60D radar 9. ASROC launcher

South Carolina (CGN 37)   PHC T. Ryals, 5-80

California (CGN 36)   J. Jedrlinic, 1980

REMARKS: Each Mk 13 launcher magazine holds 40 vertically stowed missiles (including 4 Harpoon), and the ASROC system includes automatic reloading from a magazine on deck, forward of the launcher. CGN 36 received two Vulcan/Phalanx 20-mm AA in 1980. Both will eventually get Tomahawk, SLQ-32(V)3 ECM/ESM, and four Mk 36 Super RBOC chaff/flare launchers. They have no helicopter hangar. Weapons are controlled by the Mk 11 Mod. 3 direction system, handling two Mk 74 Mod. 2 missile-fire-control systems and Mk 86 Mod. 3 gun-fire-control system. ASW fire is controlled by a Mk 114 system. Both have WSC-3 SATCOMM and NTDS data system. Kevlar plastic armor will be added over vital spaces in overhauls scheduled for 1986 and 1987.

♦ 1 Truxtun class (SCB 222 type)

	Bldr	Laid down	L	In serv.
CGN 35 TRUXTUN	New York SB, Camden, N.J.	17-6-63	19-12-64	27-5-67

Authorized: FY 62

Truxtun (CGN 35)—Harpoon amidships   G. Arra, 3-80

D: 7,800 tons light (8,600 fl) **S:** 30+ kts
Dim: 171.91 × 17.67 × 9.45 (sonar, 7.25 hull)
A: 8/Harpoon (IV × 2)—1/Mk 10 launcher (II × 1, for 40 Standard SM-1 ER and 20 ASROC missiles)—1/127-mm Mk 42, 54-cal. DP—4/324-mm Mk 32 ASW TT (II × 2)—1/SH-2F LAMPS-II ASW helicopter

NUCLEAR-POWERED GUIDED-MISSILE CRUISERS *(continued)*

Electron Equipt: Radar: 1/LN-66, 1/SPS-10, 1/SPS-40, 1/SPS-48, 1/SPG-53F, 2/SPG-55B
Sonar: 1/SQS-26
TACAN: URN-20
ECM: WLR-6, 2/Mk 28 Chaffroc
M: 2 GE D2G pressurized-water reactors, 2 sets GT; 2 props; 70,000 hp
Electric: 14,500 kw **Man:** 36 officers, 465 men

REMARKS: When next overhauled, will receive two Vulcan/Phalanx 20-mm AA. Eight Harpoon SSM (IV × 2) replaced 2/76.2-mm DP in 1980. Two Mk 25 torpedo tubes at stern removed. Eventually will carry the SM-2 ER SAM. The magazine has 3/20-missile horizontal drums. Has flag accommodations for six officers and twelve enlisted in addition to crew. Mk 76 Mod. 6 missile-control system. Mk 68 fire-control system for the 127-mm gun. Has Mk 11 weapon direction system (to be replaced by Mk 14), WSC-3 SATCOMM, and NTDS data system. Mk 114 ASW-fire-control system. The ECM system will be updated with the SLQ-32(V)3 system and four Mk 36 Super RBOC chaff launchers in place of the two Mk 28 Chaffroc. The fixed Mk 32 ASW are mounted within the superstructure, just abaft the Harpoon launchers.

♦ 1 Bainbridge class

	Bldr	Laid down	L	In serv.
CGN 25 BAINBRIDGE	Bethlehem Steel, Quincy	5-59	15-4-61	6-10-62

Authorized: FY 59

Bainbridge (CGN 25)—with Harpoon system   PH2 P. Salesi, USN, 1979

Bainbridge (CGN 25)   G. Arra, 1978

D: 7,800 tons light (8,592 fl) **S:** 30+ kts
Dim: 172.21 (167.65 wl) × 17.57 × 9.45 (sonar, 7.25 hull) **Electric:** 14,500 kw
A: 8/Harpoon SSM (IV × 2)—4/Mk 10 launchers (II × 2; 80 Standard SM-1 ER

missiles)—1/ASROC ASW RL (VIII × 1)—6/324-mm Mk 32 ASW TT (III × 2)

Electron Equipt: Radar: 1/navigational, 1/SPS-10, 1/SPS-48A, 1/SPS-37, 4/SPG-55B
Sonar: 1/SQS-23
TACAN: URN-20
ECM: WLR-6, ULQ-6, 2/Mk 28 Chaffroc
M: 2 GE D2G reactors, 2 GT; 2 props; 70,000 hp **Man:** 34 officers, 436 men

REMARKS: In refit-modernization at Puget Sound NSY from 6-74 to 9-76 to improve AAW; refit completed at San Diego in 4-77. Obsolete 76.2-mm DP removed, temporarily replaced by two 20-mm AA, 1978-79. Two quadruple Harpoon canister launch groups replaced the 20-mm AA during 1979, those to port firing forward and those to starboard firing aft. Two Mk 15 Vulcan/Phalanx 20-mm AA will eventually be added. Large deckhouse added aft to house NTDS data system. SPS-37 radar will be replaced by SPS-49. Still to be fitted with SLQ-32(V)3 ECM/ESM and Mk 36 RBOC chaff-flare system. Helicopter platform but no hangar. Will eventually carry Standard SM-2 ER SAM. Mk 111 ASW-fire-control system, two Mk 76 Mod. 1 missile-fire-control systems. Mk 11 weapons direction system (to be replaced by Mk 14). Has flag accommodations for 6 officers, 12 men.

♦ 1 Long Beach class (SCB 169 type)

	Bldr	Laid down	L	In serv.
CGN 9 LONG BEACH	Bethlehem Steel, (Quincy)	2-12-57	14-7-59	9-9-61

Authorized: FY 57

Long Beach (CGN 9)—post-modernization, artist's rendering   USN/T. Jones, 1979

Long Beach (CGN 9)—interim appearance, Talos deleted   G. Arra, 1980

NUCLEAR-POWERED GUIDED-MISSILE CRUISERS *(continued)*

D: 15,540 tons light (17,525 fl)   **S:** 30.5 kts   **Dim:** 219.75 × 22.35 × 9.45 (over sonar)

A: 16/Harpoon SSM (IV × 4)—1/Mk 10 Mod. 0 and 1/Mk 10 Mod. 1 launcher (II × 2, 120 Standard SM-1 ER missiles—2/127-mm 38-cal. DP (I × 2)—2/20-mm Mk 15 Vulcan/Phalanx AA (I × 2)—1/ASROC ASW RL (VIII × 1)—6/324-mm ASW TT (III × 2)

Electron Equipt: Radar: 1/SPS-10-65, 1/SPS-48C, 1/SPS-49, 4/SPG-55D, 2/Mk 35
Sonar: 1/SQQ-23 PAIR (single-dome)
TACAN: URN-25
ECM: 1/SLQ-32(V)3, 4/Mk 36 SRBOC chaff

M: 2 Westinghouse C1W pressurized-water reactors, 8 Foster-Wheeler heat exchangers, 2 sets GE GT; 2 props; 80,000 hp

Electric: 17,000 kw   **Man:** 79 officers, 1,081 men, + flag group: 10 officers, 58 men

REMARKS: The first U.S. surface ship to have nuclear propulsion. Original number was CLGN 160, then CGN 160. Originally intended to carry Regulus-II cruise missiles and eight Polaris ballistic missiles. Under FY 77, Congress appropriated long-lead funds to equip the ship with Aegis radar/fire-control system, since it is planned to operate the ship into the twenty-first century; the radical modernization plans were, however, canceled in 12-76.

The *Long Beach* entered Puget Sound NSY 6-10-80 for a less extensive two-year modernization period. The equipment and armament listed above will be carried when she emerges in 10-82. The Mk 12 launch system aft for Talos missiles (deactivated in 1978) was stripped out in 1979 and the pedestals on the after superstructure that formerly supported SPG-49B Talos missile-direction radars will carry the two Vulcan/Phalanx Gatling AA guns. Harpoon canister clusters, arranged to fire athwartships, will be situated before and abaft the superstructure, which will be surmounted by a tall lattice mast to support the antenna for the SPS-49 air-search radar. The "billboard" fixed-array antennas on the blockhouse-style forward superstructure will be removed, and the forward superstructure is receiving 44-mm aluminum armor. Radar foundations and waveguides also being armored. SPS-48C will replace SPS-12 on the pole foremast. The obsolescent Mk 30, 127-mm, dual-purpose

guns and their two equally aged Mk 56 directors (Mk 35 radars) will be retained, as will the original ASW weapons and the forward missile-launching arrangements. No helicopter hangar will be provided, only a pad on the stern. The Mk 10 Mod. 0 launcher for Standard missiles has two magazine drums, each holding 20 missiles; the Mk 10 Mod. 1 in the upper position has four magazine drums. Standard SM-2 ER will be substituted for SM-1 ER when available. The *Long Beach* will continue to have flagship facilities (10 officers, 58 men), and extensive satellite-communications facilities will be provided. The Tactical Flag Command Center (TFCC) will be added at her next overhaul (1984-85), as will additional protective armor.

GUIDED-MISSILE CRUISERS

◆ 0 (+7+21) Ticonderoga class

	Bldr	Laid down	L	In serv.
CG 47 TICONDEROGA	Ingalls, Pascagoula	21-1-80	16-5-81	1-83
CG 48 YORKTOWN	Ingalls, Pascagoula	19-10-81	2-83	7-84
CG 49 N. . .	Ingalls, Pascagoula	. . .	. . .	1985
CG 50 N. . .	Ingalls, Pascagoula	. . .	. . .	1986
CG 51 N. . .	. . .	. . .	. . .	. . .
CG 52 N. . .	. . .	. . .	. . .	. . .
CG 53 N. . .	. . .	. . .	. . .	. . .
CG 55 N. . .	. . .	. . .	. . .	. . .
CG 56 N. . .	. . .	. . .	. . .	. . .
CG 57 N. . .	. . .	. . .	. . .	. . .

Authorized: CG 47 in FY 78, CG 48 in FY 80, CG 49-50 in FY 81, CG 51-53 in FY 82. Proposed: CG 55-57 in FY 83, 3/yr. thereafter.

D: 9,100 tons (fl)   **S:** 30+ kts
Dim: 172.5 (16.24 wl) × 16.76 × 6.52 (9.57 over sonar)
A: 2/Mk 26 Mod. 1 launchers (II × 2; 68 Standard SM-2 MR and 20 ASROC missiles)—8/Harpoon SSM (IV × 2)—2/127-mm Mk 45 (I × 2)—2/20-mm Vulcan/Phalanx AA (I × 2)—6/324-mm Mk 32 ASW TT (III × 2)—2/SH-2F LAMPS-I ASW helicopters

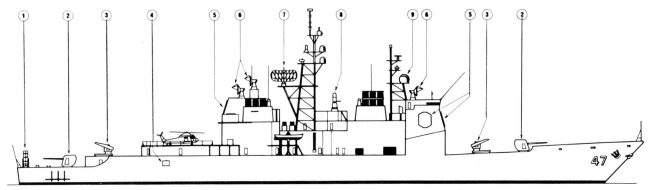

Ticonderoga 1. Quadruple Harpoon launchers, port and starboard 2. 127-mm Mk 45 guns 3. Mk 26 guided-missile launchers 4. Shutters over Mk 32 ASW TT 5. SPY-1A radar antennas 6. SPG-62 illuminators 7. SPS-49 radar 8. Vulcan/Phalanx 20-mm AA 9. SPQ-9A gunfire-control radar

GUIDED-MISSILE CRUISERS (continued)

Ticonderoga (CG 47)—at launch 16-5-81   Ingalls SB, 1981

Ticonderoga (CG 47) model   RCA, 1978

Ticonderoga (CG 47) model   RCA, 1978

Ticonderoga (CG 47)—at launch   Ingalls SB, 1981

Electron Equipt: Radar: 1/SPS-55, 1/SPS-49, 1/SPY-1A, 1/SPQ-9A, 4/SPG-62
Sonar: 1/SQS-53A
TACAN: URN-26
ECM: SLQ-32(V)3, 4/Mk 36 SRBOC chaff
M: 4 GE LM-2500 gas turbines; 2 5-bladed CP props; 80,000 hp
Electric: 7,500 kw   **Fuel:** 2,000 tons
Range: 6,000/20   **Man:** 27 officers, 306 men

REMARKS: Ex-DDG 47 class. Greatly revised version of the *Spruance*-class destroyer, using same hull and propulsion but incorporating the Aegis weapon system (SPY-1A phased-array radar, four missile illuminator radars, Mk 26 missile-launch system, etc.). Designation changed from DDG to CG in late 1979 to reflect size, importance, and combat capability. By FY 83 *each* unit will probably cost more than $1 billion. Plans now call for a total of 28 to be built. CG 47 is scheduled to begin sea trials in 5-82, with acceptance trials beginning in 11-82. The first section of CG 48 was emplaced on 19-10-81. Fabrication for CG 49 was to begin 5-82.

Each Mk 26 Mod. 1 missile-launcher magazine holds 44 missiles, the forward magazine holding the 20 ASROC. The Mk 86 fire-control system for the 127-mm guns provides no AA capability in this class, as no SPG-60 radar is carried. The R.C.A.-built Aegis Mk 7 Mod. 2 system, which uses 12 UYK-7 and 1 UYK-20 computers, uses the four fixed faces of the SPY-1A radar to detect and track up to several hundred targets simultaneously; the four SPG-62 illuminators are slaved to the system and can, through time-share switching, serve more than a dozen missiles in the air at once. The Mk 99 missile fire-control *system* uses 4 Mk 80 *illuminator-directors* with SPG-62 *radars*. The UPX-29 IFF circular antenna array is carried on the mainmast. The Harpoon missiles are in an exposed and vulnerable position at the extreme stern. Bow bulwarks were required to keep decks dry, as draft was increased about one meter over that of the original *Spruance* design. No fin stabilization is fitted. CG 47's "official" launch date is 25-5-81, but the ship was floated on 16-5-81. CG 48's keel was "laid" at Yorktown, Virginia, by President Reagan as part of the ceremonies commemorating the defeat of the British there in 1781; actual structural work commenced 12-81 at Pascagoula, Mississippi.

The class will undergo significant improvements in the course of series production. CG 48 will carry Aegis Mk 7 Mod. 3 and new, lighter-weight missile illuminators. CG 51 will be the first to carry the SH-60B LAMPS-III helicopter from the outset. CG 52 will introduce the EX-41 VLS (Vertical Launch System), containing 122

GUIDED-MISSILE CRUISERS (continued)

vertically stowed Standard SM-2 MR and Harpoon in equal-sized groups located in place of the Mk 26 launchers; the hull may at that point be altered to a flush-decked design, the aft 127-mm DP gun deleted, and an additional 16 vertically launched missiles incorporated (138 total), the displacement rising by some 250 tons. CG 56 and later are to have SQR-19 TACTASS towed passive sonar linear hydrophone arrays, the lighter-weight SQS-53B hull-mounted sonar, and a lighter-weight SPY-1B radar for the Aegis system. A second shipyard may be brought into the program, as these vitally needed ships will otherwise be entering the fleet too slowly; 28 would require well into the late 1990s to build at the present rate.

♦ **9 Belknap class (SCB 212 type)**

	Bldr	Laid down	L	In serv.
CG 26 BELKNAP	Bath Iron Works	5-2-62	20-7-63	7-11-64
CG 27 JOSEPHUS DANIELS	Bath Iron Works	23-4-62	2-12-63	8-5-65
CG 28 WAINWRIGHT	Bath Iron Works	2-7-62	25-4-64	8-1-66
CG 29 JOUETT	Puget Sound NSY	25-9-62	30-6-64	3-12-66
CG 30 HORNE	San Francisco NSY	12-9-62	30-10-64	15-4-67
CG 31 STERRETT	Puget Sound NSY	25-9-62	30-6-64	8-4-67
CG 32 WILLIAM H. STANDLEY	Bath Iron Works	29-7-63	19-12-64	9-7-66
CG 33 FOX	Todd SY, San Pedro	15-1-63	21-11-64	28-5-66
CG 34 BIDDLE	Bath Iron Works	9-12-63	2-7-65	21-1-67

Belknap (CG 26)—as recommissioned, with SPS-48C and SPS-49 radar, SLQ-32(V)2 ECM gear, and Nixie torpedo decoy system (ports through stern). Still to be added here: Harpoon and Vulcan/Phalanx Gatling guns.

GUIDED-MISSILE CRUISERS *(continued)*

Wainwright (CG 28)—with Harpoon aft, SPS-43 on aft mast   French Navy, 1981

Josephus Daniels (CG 27)—with SPS-49, Harpoon, no ULQ-6   J. Jedrlinic, 5-80

Sterrett (CG 31)—with Harpoon, SPS-40, ULQ-6 jammer   G. Arra

Authorized: Three in FY 61 and six in FY 62

D: 5,340 light/6,570 std. tons (8,065 fl; CG 26: 8,575)   **S:** 34 kts
Dim: 166.72 × 16.76 × 5.9 (8.8 over sonar)
A: 8/Harpoon SSM (IV × 2)—1/Mk 10 Mod. 7 launcher (II × 1, 40 Standard

SM-1 ER or SM-2 MR and 20 ASROC missiles)—1/127-mm Mk 42 DP (aft)—
6/324-mm Mk 32 ASW TT (III × 2)—1/SH-2D Sea Sprite LAMPS-I helicopter
Electron Equipt: Radar: 1/LN-66, 1/SPS-10F, 1/SPS-40A (except CG 27 and
CG 30: 1/SPS-49; CG 28: 1/SPS-43), 1/SPS-48A,
2/SPG-55D, 1/SPG-53A
Sonar: 1/SQS-26BX (CG 26: SQS-53A)—TACAN: URN-20
ECM: WLR-6, ULQ-6 (CG 26: SLQ-32(V)2), 2/Mk 28 Chaffroc
or 4/Mk 36 SRBOC
M: 2 sets GT; 2 6-bladed props; 85,000 hp
Boilers: CG 24, CG 28, CG 32, CG 34: 4 Foster-Wheeler; others: 4 Combustion
Engineering; 84 kg/cm², 520°C
Electric: 6,800 kw   **Range:** 2,500/30; 8,000/14
Man: 31 officers, 387 men + flag group: 6 officers, 12 enlisted

REMARKS: Ex-DLG, classified CG on 1-7-75. CG 26, severely damaged in collision with
CV 67 in Mediterranean in November 1975, was out of commission for repairs at
Philadelphia until 10-5-80. She had her 76.2-mm guns replaced by 8 Harpoon SSM,
received SPS-48C and SPS-49 radar, SM-2 MR missiles, the SLQ-25 Nixie towed
torpedo decoy system, improved electronics (including NTDS Mod. 4) and communications gear, and SQS-53A sonar. CG 31 was the first to lose her 76.2-mm, in 1976,
to make way for eight Harpoon ASM (IV × 2), now also carried by the others (firing
forward to port, aft to starboard). All will eventually receive Vulcan/Phalanx, with
CG 29 and 34 getting 2 each in 1980. CG 28 has been used as trials ship for SM-2
MR. SPS-49 will replace SPS-43 in CG 28. The 127-mm gun is controlled by a Mk
68 radar GFCS. Mk 114 (CG 26: Mk 116) ASW-fire-control system, one Mk 11 (CG
26: Mk 14) weapon-direction system, and two Mk 76 missile-fire-control systems,
updated to Mk 76 Mod. 9 in CG 26. CG 33 conducted trials with a twin box-type
launcher for Tomahawk cruise missiles in 1977; all will receive the missile beginning
in 1983. These ships will not receive the SH-60B LAMPS-III ASW helicopter. CG
26, 28, 30, and 31 are scheduled to receive the Tactical Flag Command Center in
1983-85.

♦ **9 Leahy class (SCB 172 type)**

	Bldr	Laid down	L	In serv.
CG 16 LEAHY	Bath Iron Works	3-12-59	1-7-61	4-8-62
CG 17 HARRY E. YARNELL	Bath Iron Works	31-5-60	9-12-61	2-2-63
CG 18 WORDEN	Bath Iron Works	19-9-60	2-6-62	3-8-63
CG 19 DALE	New York SB	6-9-60	28-7-62	23-11-63
CG 20 RICHMOND K. TURNER	New York SB	9-1-61	6-4-63	13-6-64
CG 21 GRIDLEY	Puget Sound SB & DD Co.	15-7-60	31-7-61	25-5-63
CG 22 ENGLAND	Todd SY, Los Angeles	4-10-60	6-3-62	7-12-63
CG 23 HALSEY	San Francisco NSY	26-8-60	15-1-62	20-7-63
CG 24 REEVES	Puget Sound NSY	1-7-60	12-5-62	15-5-64

Authorized: 3 in FY 58, 6 in FY 59

D: 6,070 tons (8,200 fl)   **S:** 34 kts
Dim: 162.46 × 16.15 × 5.9 (7.9 over sonar)
A: 8/Harpoon SSM (IV × 2)—2/Mk 10 launchers (II × 2, 80 Standard SM-1 ER
missiles)—1/ASROC ASW RL (VIII × 2)—6/324-mm Mk 32 ASW TT (III ×
2)
Electron Equipt: Radar: 1/SPS-53, 1/SPS-10F, 1/SPS-43 (CG 19: SPS-49),
1/SPS-48A, 4/SPG-55B

GUIDED-MISSILE CRUISERS *(continued)*

Halsey (CG 23)   J. Jedrlinic, 1980

Halsey (CG 23)   G. Arra, 1980

Richmond K. Turner (CG 20)   French Navy, 1980

Richmond K. Turner (CG 20)   L. & L. Van Ginderen, 9-81

Sonar: 1/SQQ-23B PAIR (single-dome)
TACAN: URN-20
ECM: WLR-6, ULQ-6, 2/Mk 28 Chaffroc or 4/Mk 36 SRBOC chaff
M: CG 16 to CG 19: 2 sets GE, CG 20 to CG 22: 2 sets de Laval, CG 23 and CG 24: 2 sets Allis Chalmers GT; 2 5-bladed props; 85,000 hp
Boilers: CG 16 to CG 20: 4 Babcock & Wilcox; others: 4 Combustion Engineering; 84 kg/cm², 520°C
Electric: 6,800 kw   **Fuel:** 1,800 tons   **Range:** 2,500/30; 8,000/14
Man: 32 officers, 381 men + flag group: 6 officers, 12 men

REMARKS: During overhauls 1967-72, the *Leahy*-class ships received an advanced version of the Mk 76 missile-fire-control system, permitting firing of Standard SM-1 ER missiles. CG 16 was the first to complete this overhaul and returned to active service on 17-8-68. These are former DLGs, classified CG on 1-7-75. All will receive SM-2 ER missiles, commencing with CG 17. Two Vulcan/Phalanx 20-mm Gatling AA will be added. The four 76.2-mm (II × 2) guns have been removed from all, and their gun tubs are used as locations for Harpoon missile launchers. Like CGN 25, these ships are, unfortunately, completely devoid of gun armament. The ASROC system carries no reloads. CG 19 received SPS-49 in place of SPS-43 in 1976; the others may later be similarly re-equipped, and all will get Mk 36 SRBOC chaff/flare rocket launchers and the SLQ-32(V)2 ECM system. Four Mk 76 missile-fire-control systems, with SPG-55B radar trackers/illuminators. Mk 114 ASW-fire-control. Mk 11 Mod. 2 weapons-control system (to be replaced by Mk 14). All have NTDS data system and WSC-3 SATCOMM equipment.

♦ **2 Albany class (SCB 002-26 conversion)**

	Bldr	Laid down	L	In serv.
CG 10 ALBANY (ex-CA 123)	Bethlehem, Quincy	6-3-44	30-6-45	15-6-46
CG 11 CHICAGO (ex-CA 136)	Philadelphia NSY	28-7-43	20-8-44	10-1-45

Albany (CG 10)—in reserve at Norfolk   C. Dragonette, 1981

GUIDED-MISSILE CRUISERS (*continued*)

D: 14,600 tons (19,500 fl) **S:** 32 kts

Dim: 205.25 (202.4 wl) × 21.27 × 7.8 (9.1 fwd)

A: 2/Mk 11 launchers (II × 2; 80 Standard SM-1 MR missiles)—2/127-mm Mk 24 DP (I × 2)—1/ASROC ASW RL (VIII × 1)—6/324-mm Mk 32 ASW TT (III × 2)

Electron Equipt: Radar: 1/LN-66, 1/SPS-10C, 1/SPS-43A, 1/SPS-48, 4/SPG-51C, 2/Mk 35

Sonar: SQS-23

TACAN: URN-20

ECM: WLR-6, 2/Mk 28 Chaffroc

M: 4 sets GE GT; 4 props; 120,000 hp

Boilers: 8 Babcock & Wilcox; 43 kg/cm², 465°C

Armor: Belt: 152-203—Upper Deck: 100   Lower deck: 62

Electric: 3,000 kw **Fuel:** 2,500 tons **Range:** 7,000/15

Man: 72 officers, 1,150 men + flag group: 10 officers, 58 men

REMARKS: CG 10, formerly flagship of the Sixth Fleet, was decommissioned 29-8-80 at Norfolk. CG 11 was decommissioned 1-3-80. Instead of the planned scrapping of these old, overloaded, and worn-out ships, they have been placed in reserve—CG 11 having been towed to Bremerton. CG 11 never received the NTDS data system. The Talos missile systems in both were inactivated in 1978; the two Mk 12 launchers and four SPG-49B radars were left aboard but are not functional. Former *Baltimore*-class heavy cruisers. Reconversion to CG took four years, CG 10 recommissioning on 2-11-62. Alloy superstructure; living spaces entirely air-conditioned. Old masts and stacks replaced by "macks," which allow the stack gases to vent through lateral conduits in the same structures on which the radar antennas are mounted. Two single-barrel 127-mm semiautomatic, 38-caliber, open gun mounts were added in 1963, one on each side; each has a Mk 56 radar GFCS. Sister *Columbus* (CG 12) was decommissioned at Norfolk on 31-1-75 and stricken on 9-8-76. CG 10 and CG 11 were to have been extensively refitted in 1978, and funds were appropriated but used for other purposes. The principal justification for their retention is their extensive communications, including several different satellite systems.

NOTE: The *Galveston*-class guided-missile cruiser *Oklahoma City* (CG 5) was stricken on 15-12-79; her place as flagship of the Seventh Fleet was taken by *Blue Ridge* (LCC 19). However, instead of being scrapped, the partially stripped ship is being retained at Bremerton, with the Talos missile fire-control system (for which there are no missiles) carefully placed in a state of preservation.

HEAVY CRUISERS

♦ 2 Des Moines class

	Bldr	Laid down	L	In serv.
CA 134 DES MOINES	Bethlehem, Fore River	28-5-45	27-9-46	16-11-48
CA 139 SALEM	Bethlehem, Fore River	4-7-45	25-3-47	14-5-49

D: 17,255 tons (21,470 fl) **S:** 32 kts **Dim:** 218.42 (213.36 wl) × 22.96 × 7.5

A: 9/203-mm (III × 3)—12/127-mm DP (II × 6)—20-22/76.2-mm DP (II × 10 or 11)

Electron Equipt: Radar: 1/SG-6, 1/SPS-8, 1/SPS-6C (CA 139: SPS-12), 2/Mk 13, 4/Mk 25, 4/Mk 35 (CA 139: 2/Mk 34 also)

TACAN: URN-6

M: 4 sets GT; 4 props; 120,000 hp

Boilers: 4 Babcock & Wilcox; 43.9 kg/cm², 454°C   **Electric:** 7,700 kw

Des Moines (CA 134)   1960

Armor: Belt: 102-152-mm; Upper deck: 25-mm; Lower deck: 85-mm; Turrets: 203-mm face, 95-mm sides, 102-mm roof; Barbettes: 160-mm; Conning Tower: 102-160-mm; Steering Room: 96-160-mm

Fuel: 2,600 tons   **Range:** 8,000/15   **Man:** 105 officers, 1,745 men (wartime)

REMARKS: CA 139 to reserve on 30-1-59, CA 134 on 14-7-61, both at Philadelphia. Sister *Newport News* (CA 148), in reserve since 27-6-75, was stricken on 30-6-78. The last "gun cruisers" on the Navy List, neither survivor is likely to see further active service; both have thoroughly antiquated sensors and communications systems. CA 134 has ten twin 76.2-mm Mk 34 DP mounts, her sister has eleven. Each has two Mk 54 directors (with Mk 13 radar) for the 203-mm guns, four Mk 37 fire-control systems for the 127-mm guns, and four Mk 56 and Mk 63 fire-control systems for the 76.2-mm guns. Magazines can carry 1,350 rounds 203-mm, 6,060 rounds 127-mm, 12,000 rounds 76.2-mm.

GUIDED-MISSILE DESTROYERS

♦ 0 (+49-59) DDGX class (Planned)

	Bldr	Laid down	L	In serv.
DDG 51 N. . .	. . .	1986	. . .	7-89

D: 8,500 tons (fl) **S:** 30+ kts **Dim:** 146.00× 18.29 ×. . .

A: 1/64-cell and 1/32-cell EX-41 vertical launcher (90 Standard SM-2 MR SAM and Tomahawk SSM missiles)—8/Harpoon SSM (IV × 2)—1/127-mm Mk 45 DP, with guided munitions—2/20-mm Vulcan/Phalanx AA (I × 2)—6/324-mm Mk 32 ASW TT (III × 2)

Electron Equipt: Radar: 1/SPS-55, 1/SPY-1D, 3/SPG-62

Sonar: SQS-53C, provision for SQR-19 TACTASS

ECM: SLQ-32(V)2, 4/Mk 36 SRBOC chaff

TACAN: URN-25

M: 4 GE LM-2500 gas turbines; 2 CP props; 80,000 hp

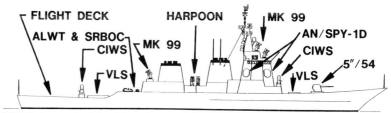

DDGX class—provisional layout   U.S. Navy, 1981

GUIDED-MISSILE DESTROYERS (continued)

DDGX class—artist's rendering   RCA/V. Piecyk, 9-81

Electric: Approx. 7,500 kw **Fuel:** ... **Range:** 6,000/20
Man: 23 officers, 302 men

REMARKS: First unit planned for FY 85 Budget, then 3/yr. or more, beginning FY
87. Design data above is current for 1981, but size and projected costs have risen
(and combat capability has dropped) to a point where a complete recasting may be
required in order to obtain a design smaller and less complex than the current CG
47. Design has unusual, broad-waterplane hull form to improve endurance and seaworthiness. More exotic propulsion plants, such as electric-drive via super-cooled/
super-conducting motors, possibly combined with diesels, had been discussed, but
an improved fuel-consumption development of the current DD 963/CG 47 plant is
the current selection; RACER (Rankine-Cycle Energy Recovery) may be added
later to use waste heat from the four gas turbines to generate steam, which would
then power turbines geared to the two main gearboxes. The superstructure will be
of steel (current USN superstructures are of highly inflammable aluminum) with
twice the shockwave overpressure protection of current ships; over 130 tons of armor
will be carried over vital spaces. For the first time in a USN design, adequate
protection against NBC warfare will be incorporated.

Because the weapons installations are modular, some ships may have a second
32-cell VLS launch group forward in place of the 127-mm 54-cal. gun, which will be
equipped to fire laser-designated or IR-homing, rocket-boosted projectiles. The forward VLS group may be relocated aft, between the torpedo tubes. Although no
hangar will be provided, the ships will be equipped to operate with SH-60B LAMPS-
III helicopters and will have a landing platform at the stern. SLQ-25 Nixie towed
torpedo decoys will be carried.

All four faces of the lightweight Aegis SPY-1D radar system will be mounted on
the forward tower superstructure; unlike CG 47 (with 4), only 3 Mk 99 target illuminators (with SPG-62 or a later, lighter radar) will be fitted. The SM-2 MR Block
II missiles carried will have twice the range of the current version. ASROC does
not fit in the EX-41 VLS cell, and these ships will have to await development of the
new long-range SOW ASW missile in order to have a stand-off ASW weapon. The
Seafire electro-optical GFCS will control the 127-mm gun.

♦ **4 Kidd class** Bldr: Ingalls, Pascagoula

	Laid down	L	In serv.
DDG 993 KIDD (ex-*Kouroush*)	26-6-78	11-8-79	27-6-81
DDG 994 CALLAGHAN (ex-*Daryush*)	23-10-78	1-12-79	29-8-81
DDG 995 SCOTT (ex-*Nader*)	12-2-79	1-3-80	24-10-81
DDG 996 CHANDLER (ex-*Andushirvan*)	7-5-79	24-5-80	3-82

Authorized: FY 79 Supplemental

D: 9,200 tons (fl) **S:** 30+ kts
Dim: 171.7 (161.23 wl) × 16.76 × 6.6 (9.6 over sonar)

Scott (DDG 995)—on trials   Ingalls SB, 1981

Chandler (DDG 996)   Ingalls SB, 1981

GUIDED-MISSILE DESTROYERS *(continued)*

Callaghan (DDG 994)—on trials

Ingalls SB, 1981

GUIDED-MISSILE DESTROYERS (continued)

Kidd (DDG 993)—on trials Ingalls SB, 9-80

Kidd (DDG 993) Ingalls SB, 1980

A: 1/Mk 26 Mod. 0 and 1/Mk 26 Mod. 1 launcher (II × 2, 52 Standard SM-1 MR and 16 ASROC missiles)—2/20-mm Vulcan/Phalanx AA (I × 2)—2/127-mm Mk 45 DP (I × 2)—6/324-mm Mk 32 ASW TT (III × 2)—1/SH-3 Sea King or 2/Sh-2F LAMPS-I ASW helicopters

Electron Equipt: Radar: 1/SPS-53, 1/SPS-55, 1/SPS-48A, 2/SPG-55D, 1/SPG-60, 1/SPQ-9A

Sonar: SPS-53A—TACAN: URN-20

ECM: ULQ-32(V)2, 4/Mk 36 SRBOC

M: 4 GE LM-2500 gas turbines; 2 5-bladed CP props; 86,000 hp (80,000 sust.)

Electric: 6,000 kw **Range:** 3,300/30; 6,000/20 **Man:** 28 officers, 320 men

REMARKS: The original order for these superb ships placed with the U.S. Navy by Iran in 1974 was for six; two were canceled before the order to Ingalls Shipbuilding for the remaining four was issued on 23-3-78. DDG 993 and DDG 994 were canceled by the new Iranian government on 3-2-79, and the other pair shortly thereafter. Their completion for the U.S. Navy was authorized by the U.S. Congress under a Fiscal 1979 Supplementary Appropriation Act. At approximately $510 million each, they represent a considerable bargain. The first two were to be numbered DD 995 and DD 996; the new numbers do not fit in USN hull-numbering sequence for guided-missile destroyers.

Harpoon and Vulcan/Phalanx were not in the weapons suit ordered for Iran and were not fitted when the ships were first commissioned. Standard SM-2 MR missiles will be backfitted at a later date. Two Mk 74 missile-fire-control systems (with SPG-55D radar tracker/illuminators) are carried, as well as the Mk 86 Mod. 5 gun-fire-control system, which uses the SPQ-9A radar for surface fire and the SPG-60 for AA (the latter can also be used as a missile illuminator). There are two IR/TV tracker directors. The ASROC missiles are carried in the larger Mk 26 Mod. 1 missile-launch system's magazine, which is aft; the Mk 116 underwater battery fire-control system is carried. SLQ-25 NIXIE towed anti-torpedo decoys are fitted; the ships were not intended to have the SQR-19A TACTASS towed passive sonar array, but it could be backfitted later. Vulcan/Phalanx added to DDG 993 in 11-81; the others were to receive the weapons during 1982 yard periods at the builders.

These ships were given better air-intake filter systems than the U.S. *Spruance* class, in order to handle the dust and sand prevailing in Iranian operating areas. They also have greater air-conditioning capacity. These features should make them invaluable for duties in the Indian Ocean. The Iranian Navy planned to type them as cruisers. Full load displacement has grown by about 1,000 tons over the original plan, partly as a result of additional Kevlar and aluminum alloy armor being added during the protracted trials period on DDG 993.

♦ 23 Charles F. Adams class (SCB 155 type)

	Bldr	Laid down	L	In serv.
DDG 2 CHARLES F. ADAMS	Bath Iron Works	16-6-58	8-9-59	10-9-60
DDG 3 JOHN KING	Bath Iron Works	25-8-58	30-1-60	4-2-61
DDG 4 LAWRENCE	New York SB	27-10-58	27-2-60	6-1-62
DDG 5 CLAUDE V. RICKETTS (ex-*Biddle*)	New York SB	18-5-59	16-4-60	5-5-62
DDG 6 BARNEY	New York SB	18-8-59	10-12-60	11-8-62
DDG 7 HENRY B. WILSON	Defoe SB	28-2-58	22-4-59	17-12-60
DDG 8 LYNDE McCORMICK	Defoe SB	4-4-58	9-9-60	3-6-61
DDG 9 TOWERS	Todd, Seattle	1-4-58	23-4-59	24-6-61
DDG 10 SAMPSON	Bath Iron Works	2-3-59	9-9-60	24-6-61
DDG 11 SELLERS	Bath Iron Works	3-8-59	9-9-60	28-10-61
DDG 12 ROBISON	Defoe SB	23-4-59	27-4-60	9-12-61
DDG 13 HOEL	Defoe SB	1-6-59	4-8-60	16-6-62
DDG 14 BUCHANAN	Todd, Seattle	23-4-59	11-5-60	7-2-62
DDG 15 BERKELEY	New York SB	1-6-60	29-7-61	15-12-62
DDG 16 JOSEPH STRAUSS	New York SB	27-12-60	9-12-61	20-4-63
DDG 17 CONYNGHAM	New York SB	1-5-61	19-5-62	13-7-63
DDG 18 SEMMES	Avondale SY	18-8-60	20-5-61	10-12-62
DDG 19 TATTNALL	Avondale SY	14-11-60	26-8-61	13-4-63
DDG 20 GOLDSBOROUGH	Puget Sound B & DD	3-1-61	15-12-61	9-11-63
DDG 21 COCHRANE	Puget Sound B & DD	31-7-61	18-7-62	21-3-64
DDG 22 BENJAMIN STODDERT	Puget Sound B & DD	11-6-62	8-1-63	12-9-64

GUIDED-MISSILE DESTROYERS (continued)

DDG 23 RICHARD E. BYRD   Todd, Seattle   12-4-61   6-2-62   7-3-64
DDG 24 WADDELL   Todd, Seattle   6-2-62   26-2-63   28-8-64

Authorized: 8 in FY 57, 5 in FY 58, 5 in FY 59, 3 in FY 60, and 2 in FY 61

D: 3,370 tons (4,600 fl) **S:** 31.5 kts
Dim: 133.19 (128.0 wl) × 14.32 × 6.1 (8.3 over sonar)
A: 1/Mk 11 twin missile launcher or, beginning with DDG 16, 1/Mk 13 single
launcher (4-6 Harpoon and 34-36 Standard SM-1 MR missiles)—2/127-mm Mk
42 DP (I × 2)—1/ASROC ASW RL (VIII × 1)—6/324-mm Mk 32 ASW TT
(III × 2)

Joseph Strauss (DDG 16)—with URN-25 TACAN atop mast   G. Arra, 3-80

Claude V. Ricketts (DDG 5)—Mk 11 launcher, SPS-37 radar
L. & L. Van Ginderen, 3-81

Sampson (DDG 10)   French Navy, 1979

Berkeley (DDG 15)—no ASROC reload magazine   G. Arra, 1980

Electron Equipt: Radar: 1/SPS-10F, 1/SPS-37 (DDG 15 to DDG 24: SPS-40C),
1/SPS-39A, 2/SPG-51C, 1/SPG-53A
Sonar: SQQ-23A or 1/SQS-23A (hull-mounted in DDG 2 to
DDG 19; bow-mounted in DDG 20 to DDG 24)
ECM: WLR-6, ULQ-6
TACAN: URN-20 (DDG 11-16: URN-25)
M: 2 sets GT; 2 props; 70,000 hp **Electric:** 2,200 kw
Boilers: 4; 84 kg/cm², 520°C **Fuel:** 900 tons
Range: 1,600/30; 6,000/14 **Man:** 20-24 officers, 319-330 men

REMARKS: Although they have the lowest hull numbers, these are the newest of the
DDGs. Sisters DDG 25, DDG 26, and DDG 27, built at the Defoe Shipbuilding
Company, Bay City, Michigan, were ordered by Australia; DDG 28, DDG 29, and
DDG 30 were built at Bath Iron Works for the West German Navy. Ships with bow-
mounted sonars have stem-mounted anchors. Some have been backfitted with an
ASROC ASW missile reload magazine (with 4 missiles) beside the forward stack,
to starboard. It was planned to give these ships a badly needed modernization,
beginning with DDG 3 under FY 80. Costs rose enormously, and the program was
cut to ten, permitting them to operate for another fifteen to twenty years. Congressional reluctance to spend $221 million per ship (equal to the cost of a new FFG 7
class frigate) forced cancellation of even the reduced program. Instead, DDG 15
through 24 will be updated during the course of their next two regular overhauls,
requiring about 2 years per ship. Alterations planned include updating the SPS-40
in DDG 15 to DDG 24 to SPS-40C or SPS-40D and replacing the SPS-37 in the
earlier ships with SPS-49. The SPS-10 will be replaced by SPS-65 (which uses the

Goldsborough (DDG 20)—Mk 13 launcher, SPS-40 radar, ASROC reload magazine,
bow anchor   G. Arra, 1978

GUIDED-MISSILE DESTROYERS (continued)

same antenna) and the SPS-39A, 3-D height-finder will be converted to SPS-52B. The Mk 68 gun director will be replaced by Mk 86 (with SPQ-9 in a radome on the mast and SPG-60 atop the bridge), permitting control of three missiles at a time. The missile-fire-control system will thus be upgraded to Mk 74 Mod. 8 status. Harpoon SSM can be carried in the Mk 11 and Mk 13 missile-launcher magazines. The lighter URN-25 TACAN will replace URN-20 (already done in DDG 11). Mk 13 weapons direction is replacing Mk 4, while the CIC will be greatly modernized with the SYS-1 small computerized Tactical Data System, which uses the UYA-4 NTDS. The SLQ-32-(V)2 ECM system will replace existing gear. Mk 36 Super RBOC will be added, engineering and hull systems will be upgraded or overhauled, and generating capacity will be increased to 3,000 kw. The original missile launchers and Mk 42 guns will be retained, and the SQS-23 sonar will be converted to SQQ-23 PAIR with two sonar domes (already done in several ships). Ships with Mk 11 launchers carry 4 Harpoons, the others 6. Several carry small navigational radars.

♦ **10 Coontz class (SCB 142/149 type)**

	Bldr	Laid down	L	In serv.
DDG 37 FARRAGUT (ex-DLG 6)	Bethlehem Steel (Quincy)	3-6-57	18-7-58	12-10-60
DDG 38 LUCE (ex-DLG 7)	Bethlehem Steel (Quincy)	1-10-57	11-12-58	20-5-61
DDG 39 MACDONOUGH (ex-DLG 8)	Bethlehem Steel (Quincy)	15-4-58	9-7-59	4-11-61
DDG 40 COONTZ (ex-DLG 9)	Puget Sound NSY	1-3-57	6-12-58	15-7-60
DDG 41 KING (ex-DLG 10)	Puget Sound NSY	1-3-57	6-12-58	17-11-60
DDG 42 MAHAN (ex-DLG 11)	San Francisco NSY	31-7-57	7-10-59	25-8-60
DDG 43 DAHLGREN (ex-DLG 12)	Philadelphia NSY	1-3-58	16-3-60	8-4-61
DDG 44 WILLIAM V. PRATT (ex-DLG 13)	Philadelphia NSY	1-3-58	16-3-60	4-11-61
DDG 45 DEWEY (ex-DLG 14)	Bath Iron Works	10-8-57	30-11-58	7-12-59
DDG 46 PREBLE (ex-DLG 15)	Bath Iron Works	16-12-57	23-5-59	9-5-60

Authorized: DDG 37 to 42 in FY 57, DDG 43 to 46 in FY 57

D: 4,700 tons (5,700-5,900 fl) **S:** 34 kts **Dim:** 156.21 × 16.0 × 7.6 (max.)
A: 8/Harpoon SSM (IV × 2)—1/Mk 10 Mod. 0 twin launcher (II × 1, 40 Standard SM-1 ER missiles)—1/127-mm Mk 42 automatic DP—1/ASROC ASW RL (VIII × 1)—6/324-mm ASW TT (III × 2)

Farragut (DDG 37)—ASROC reload magazine, taller after mast   J. Jedrlinic, 5-80

Coontz (DDG 40)—with SPS-37 radar aft   1978

Electron Equipt: Radar: 1/SPS-53, 1/SPS-10B, 1/SPS-29C or 37 (DDG 43, 46: SPS-49), 1/SPS-48, 2/SPG-55B, 1/SPG-53A
   Sonar: SQQ-23A PAIR
   TACAN: URN-20
   ECM: WLR-6, ULQ-6, 4/Mk 36 SRBOC chaff
M: DDG 37 to 39, DDG 45: 2 sets de Laval GT; others: 2 sets Allis-Chalmers GT; 2 props; 85,000 hp
Boilers: 4 Foster-Wheeler (Babcock & Wilcox in DDG 40 to DDG 46); 84 kg/cm²; 520°C
Electric: 4,000 kw **Fuel:** 900 tons **Range:** 1,500/30; 6,000/14
Man: 21 officers, 356 men + flag group: 7 officers, 12 men

Preble (DDG 46)—with SPS-49 radar   G. Arra, 3-80

GUIDED-MISSILE DESTROYERS (*continued*)

REMARKS: These are the only *destroyers* with Standard SM-1 ER. Reclassified DDG from DLG 6 to DLG 15 in 1975. All modernized between 1970 and 1977 with Standard SM-1 ER missiles, NTDS (fitted earlier in DDG 40, DDG 41), SPS-48 radar, etc.; four 76.2-mm DP (II × 2) removed and Harpoon launchers installed in their former locations (firing forward to port, aft to starboard). DDG 37, the first to be modernized, received an ASROC reload magazine forward of the bridge and a taller after mast; to save weight and cost, the others were not similarly equipped. Missile fire-control is Mk 76. A Mk 68 fire-control system is carried for the 127-mm gun. DDG 40 carried two Vulcan Gatling guns (*not* Phalanx) in 1975. DDG 41 conducted Vulcan/Phalanx 20-mm Gatling AA sea trials in 1973-74, before she was modernized; however, the ships are no longer scheduled to receive two Vulcan/Phalanx, due to their age, space, and weight problems. All will eventually receive the SLQ-32(V)2 ECM system. SPS-49 will be substituted for the SPS-29C or SPS-37 radars. Mk 111 Mod. 8 ASW fire-control systems and satellite-communications antenna systems in all units. The SQQ-23A PAIR sonar installed uses two separate domes. Helicopter landing pad on stern.

◆ 4 Decatur class (SCB 222-66 type)

	Bldr	Laid down	L	In serv.	After mod.
DDG 31 DECATUR (ex-DD 936)	Bethelehem Steel, Quincy	13-9-54	15-12-55	7-12-56	29-4-67
DDG 32 JOHN PAUL JONES (ex-DD 932)	Charleston NSY	18-1-54	7-5-55	5-4-56	23-9-67
DDG 33 PARSONS (ex-DD 949)	Ingalls, Pascagoula	17-6-57	19-8-58	29-10-59	3-11-67
DDG 34 SOMERS (ex-DD 947)	Bath Iron Works	4-3-57	30-5-58	3-4-59	2-10-68

Decatur (DDG 31)   G. Arra, 1977

Somers (DDG 34)—with SPS-40 forward   G. Arra, 2-79

Parsons (DDG 33)—SPS-29E radar forward, passageway plating removed   G. Arra, 7-80

GUIDED-MISSILE DESTROYERS (*continued*)

D: 2,850 tons (4,200 fl)   **S:** 32.5 kts   **Dim:** 127.4 × 13.7 × 6.1 (fl)

A: 1/Mk 13 launcher (I × 1, 40 Standard SM-1 MR missiles)—1/127-mm Mk 42 DP—1/ASROC ASW RL (VIII × 1)—6/324-mm Mk 32 ASW TT (III × 2)

Electron Equipt: Radar: 1/SPS-10, 1/SPS-29E (DDG 34: SPS-40), 1/SPS-48, 1/SPG-51C, 1/SPG-55B
      Sonar: 1/SQS-23
      TACAN: URN-20
      ECM: WLR-6, ULQ-6

M: DDG 32: 2 sets Westinghouse GT; others: 2 sets GE GT; 2 props; 70,000 hp

Boilers: DDG 31 and DDG 33: 4 Foster-Wheeler; DDG 32 and DDG 34: 4 Babcock & Wilcox; 84 kg/cm², 520°C

Fuel: 750 tons   **Range:** 4,500/20   **Man:** 25 officers, 339 men

REMARKS: Originally *Forrest Sherman*- and *Hull*-class destroyers. Mk 68 Mod. 9 or 10 radar GFCS forward can control gun *or* missiles. DDG 33 and DDG 34 have higher freeboard forward. Alloy superstructure. All to receive Mk 36 SRBOC chaff/flare system. Around 1976 some plating was removed from the covered passageway at the ships' sides amidships, presumably to save top weight; by 1980 the passageways were entirely uncovered.

DESTROYERS

♦ 30 (+1+6) Spruance class (SCN 275 type)

Bldr: Ingalls SB, Pascagoula, Miss. (Litton Industries)

	Laid down	L	In serv.
DD 963 SPRUANCE	17-11-72	10-11-73	20-9-75
DD 964 PAUL F. FOSTER	6-2-73	23-2-74	21-2-76
DD 965 KINKAID	19-4-73	25-5-74	10-7-76
DD 966 HEWITT	23-7-73	24-8-74	25-9-76
DD 967 ELLIOT	15-10-73	19-12-74	22-1-76
DD 968 ARTHUR W. RADFORD	14-1-74	1-3-75	16-4-77
DD 969 PETERSON	29-4-74	21-6-75	9-7-77
DD 970 CARON	1-7-74	24-6-75	1-10-77
DD 971 DAVID R. RAY	23-9-74	23-8-75	19-11-77
DD 972 OLDENDORF	27-12-74	21-10-75	4-3-78
DD 973 JOHN YOUNG	17-2-75	7-2-76	20-5-78
DD 974 COMTE DE GRASSE	4-4-75	26-3-76	5-8-78
DD 975 O'BRIEN	9-5-75	8-7-76	3-12-77
DD 976 MERRILL	16-6-75	1-9-76	11-3-78
DD 977 BRISCOE	21-7-75	15-12-76	3-6-78
DD 978 STUMP	25-8-75	29-1-77	19-8-78
DD 979 CONOLLY	29-9-75	19-2-77	14-10-78
DD 980 MOOSBRUGGER	3-11-75	23-7-77	16-12-78
DD 981 JOHN HANCOCK	16-1-76	29-10-77	10-3-79
DD 982 NICHOLSON	20-2-76	11-11-77	12-5-79
DD 983 JOHN RODGERS	12-8-76	25-2-78	14-7-79
DD 984 LEFTWICH	12-11-76	8-4-78	25-8-79
DD 985 CUSHING	2-2-77	17-6-78	22-9-79
DD 986 HARRY W. HILL	1-4-77	10-8-78	10-11-79
DD 987 O'BANNON	24-6-77	25-9-78	1-12-79
DD 988 THORN	29-8-77	22-11-78	12-1-80
DD 989 DEYO	14-10-77	20-1-79	22-3-80
DD 990 INGERSOLL	5-12-77	10-3-79	12-4-80
DD 991 FIFE	6-3-78	1-5-79	31-5-80
DD 992 FLETCHER	24-4-78	16-6-79	12-7-80
DD 997 HAYLER	20-10-80	9-82	11-83

Authorized: DD 963-965 in FY 70, DD 966-971 in FY 71, DD 972-978 in FY 72, DD 979-985 in FY 74, DD 986-992 in FY 75, DD 997 in FY 78

Fife (DD 991)   Ingalls SB, 1980

Stump (DD 978)—SLQ-32(V)2, Harpoon amidships   French Navy, 1980

DESTROYERS *(continued)*

Fletcher (DD 992)   Ingalls SB, 1980

David R. Ray (DD 971)   G. Arra, 1980

Arthur W. Radford (DD 968)—with WLR-8 ECM suit, Harpoon, SH-2F LAMPS-I helicopter

French Navy, 1979

DESTROYERS (*continued*)

John Hancock (DD 981)—with SLQ-32(V)2 ECM system

L. & L. Van Ginderen, 9-81

Deyo (DD 989)

Ingalls SB, 1980

D: 5,830 tons light (8,040 fl)   **S:** 32.5 kts
Dim: 171.68 (oa) (161.25 pp) × 16.76 × 5.79 (8.84 over sonar)
A: 8/Harpoon SSM (IV × 2)—2/127-mm Mk 45 DP (I × 2)—1/Mk 29 launcher
  (VIII × 1, 24 Sea Sparrow)—1/ASROC ASW RL (VIII × 1, 24)—6/324-mm
  Mk 32 ASW TT (III × 2; 20 Mk 46 torpedoes)—1/SH-3 Sea King or SH-2
  LAMPS-I ASW helicopter
Electron Equipt: Radar: 1/SPS-55, 1/SPS-40, 1/SPQ-9A, 1/SPG-60, 1/Mk 91
              Mod. 0
          Sonar: 1/SQS-53
          TACAN: URN-20
          ECM: WLR-8 or, in later ships, SLQ(V)2, 4/Mk 36 SRBOC
M: 4 GE LM-2500 gas turbines; 2 CP props; 86,000 hp (80,000 sust.)
Electric: 6,000 kw   **Fuel:** 1,650 tons
Range: 3,300/30; 6,000/20   **Man:** 24 officers, 272 men

REMARKS: Largest post–World War II U.S. destroyer program, and the first non-
SAM destroyers ordered since the 1950s. DD 997 intended by Congress to be of an

"air-capable" design, with enlarged hangar for 4 ASW helicopters, but costs rose to
the point that the ship was ordered 29-9-79 as a nearly standard version of the class.
The Navy would like six more of these "simple" ships, which are superbly equipped
for ASW and are also very useful in shore bombardment; current plans call for
ordering two under FY 85 and one in FY 86. The basic *Spruance* hull and propulsion
plant have also served as the basis for the *Kidd* (DDG 993) and *Ticonderoga* (CG
47, ex-DDG 47) designs and may yet be the basis for the planned DDGX class. DD
981 carries her name across the stern in script, duplicating the signature of the first
signer of the Declaration of Independence. Displacements have risen considerably
as equipment has been added; they were originally intended to displace under 7,000
tons full load.

Considerable attention was given to the propulsion machinery from the viewpoint
of silent operation and flexibility. Prarie-Masker bubbler systems are installed to
enhance quietness. On each of the two shafts, two General Electric LM-2500 gas
turbines are coupled to a reduction gear. Each shaft turns a controllable-pitch propeller (5.1 m in diameter, 168 rpm at 30 knots). Electric power is furnished by three
Allison 501-k17 gas turbines, each powering one 2,000-kw alternator and mounted
in separate compartments. Full speed can be reached from 12 knots in only 53
seconds. All propulsion machinery is under the control of a single operator in a
central control station (CCS). 30 knots was considerably exceeded on trials. Endurance can be extended greatly by using one engine on one shaft for cruising. The
plant has been very successful, except for the exhaust-gas auxiliary boilers. The
mean time between overhauls for the LM-2500 gas turbines has been extended to
6,000 hours, due to excellent reliability; one which had run 8,000 hours showed few
signs of wear in 8-80.

The hull form was designed to minimize rolling and pitching; there are no fin
stabilizers. Habitability received particular attention, living spaces being divided by
bulkheads and intended for no more than six men each, with a recreational area and
good sanitary facilities. The crew is small for a ship the size of the *Spruance* class,
because all the machinery and systems have advanced automation.

The armament will be augmented by the installation of two Vulcan/Phalanx systems, accomplished on DD 965 in 1980. All are being equipped with a four-launcher
Mk 36 RBOC chaff-flare rocket system. ASW is handled by a MK 116 fire-control
system. The Mk 32 torpedo tubes are standard triple trainable mountings, fired
through doors in the ships' sides. The Mk 91 Mod. 0 fire-control system for Sea
Sparrow uses a single radar director. The Mk 86 Mod. 3 fire-control system for the
127-mm guns uses the SPG-60 radar for AA and the SPQ-9A for surface fire. Magazines hold 1,200 rounds 127-mm. The ASROC reload missiles are stowed vertically,
directly beneath the launcher. Kevlar plastic armor is to be added over vital spaces,
beginning with four ships under FY 81; the entire class will be equipped by 1986.
All but DD 964 and 965 had received Harpoon by 1-81. Nine ships are currently
scheduled to receive 8 Tomahawk cruise missiles (IV × 2); others may receive the
system, for which box-launcher firing trials were carried out on DD 976 in 1-81 and
later. DD 977 has had the GFCS modified to Mk 86 Mod. 10 (with a UYK-7 computer
in place of the Mk 152 computer, Mk 113 display consoles, new fuze-setters, etc.)
to conduct trials with semi-active laser-guided projectiles. DD 976 was also used in
1981 for trials with the General Electric EX-83, 30-mm Gatling gun system, which
uses a GAU-8 heavy gun and was to carry out trials with an extended-range version
of Sea Sparrow. Planned backfitting of the Mk 71, 203-mm gun in the forward position
was canceled in 1978 when development of that excellent weapon was unfortunately
canceled. Plans for replacing the ASROC and Sea Sparrow launchers with EX-41
VLS (Vertical Launch System) exist, and some ships may convert under FY 84.

All ships of the class are scheduled to receive the Hughes Mk 23 TAS (Target
Acquisition System), which uses a high-rpm radar mounted on an upper foremast
platform to detect low-flying, high-speed missiles and aircraft; the SPS-55 surface-

DESTROYERS *(continued)*

search radar has been moved to a new, higher platform to make way for the Mk 23 TAS. Plans still call for the addition of the SQR-19 TACTASS (Tactical Towed-Array Sonar System), but its introduction has been delayed. Early units were given the WLR-8 ECM system as an interim installation until SLQ-32(V)2 was available.

♦ **14 Forrest Sherman and Hull classes (SCB 240 type):**
  8 ASW refits (1967-71) (SCB 221 modernization, except DD 933: SCB 251):

	Bldr	Laid down	L	In serv.
DD 933 BARRY	Mare Island NSY	15-3-54	1-10-55	31-8-56
DD 937 DAVIS	Bethlehem, Quincy	1-2-55	28-3-56	28-2-57
DD 938 JONAS INGRAM	Bethlehem, Quincy	15-6-55	8-7-56	19-7-57
DD 940 MANLEY	Bath Iron Works	10-2-55	12-4-56	1-2-57
DD 941 DUPONT	Bath Iron Works	11-5-55	8-9-56	1-7-57
DD 943 BLANDY	Bethlehem, Quincy	29-12-55	19-12-56	8-11-57
DD 948 MORTON	Ingalls, Pascagoula	4-3-57	23-5-58	26-5-59
DD 950 RICHARD S. EDWARDS	Puget Sound B & DD	20-12-56	21-9-57	5-2-59

  6 unmodified:

	Bldr	Laid down	L	In serv.
DD 931 FORREST SHERMAN	Boston NSY	27-10-53	5-2-55	9-11-55
DD 942 BIGELOW	Bath Iron Works	6-7-55	2-2-57	8-11-57
DD 944 MULLINIX	Bethlehem, Quincy	5-4-56	18-3-57	7-3-58
DD 945 HULL	Bath Iron Works	12-9-56	10-8-57	3-7-58
DD 946 EDSON	Bath Iron Works	3-12-56	1-1-58	7-11-58
DD 951 TURNER JOY	Puget Sound B & DD	30-9-57	5-5-58	3-8-59

Authorized: DD 931, 933 in FY 55, DD 937, 938 in FY 54, DD 940-944 in FY 55, others in FY 56

Barry (DD 933)—bow sonar, hence greater rake to stem, bow anchor

U.S. Navy, 1971

Morton (DD 948)—SQS-35 VDS aft, SPS-40 radar   G. Arra, 2-79

Jonas Ingram (DD 938)—ASW conversion   S. Terzibaschitsch, 6-81

Turner Joy (DD 951)—3/127-mm DP, SPS-29 radar, TACAN   G. Arra, 1980

D: 2,780-2,850 tons (4,050-4,200 fl)   **S:** 32.5 kts
Dim: 127.51 (DD 933: 129.54; DD 945 to DD 951: 127.4) × 13.7 × 6.1
A: ASW refits: 2/127-mm Mk 42 DP (I × 2)—1 ASROC ASW RL (VIII × 1)—
    6/324-mm Mk 32 ASW TT (III × 2)
    Others: 3/127-mm Mk 42 DP (I × 3)—6/324-mm Mk 32 ASW TT (III × 2)
Electron Equipt: Radar: 1/SPS-10, 1/SPS-40 (DD 933, DD 937, DD 938,
    DD 942, DD 946, DD 951: SPS-29), 1/SPG-53A, 1/Mk 35
    Sonar: SQS-23D; ASW refits: SQS-35 VDS also
    ECM: WLR-2 or WLR-6, ULQ-6
    TACAN: DD 945, 946, 951: URN-20

DESTROYERS *(continued)*

M: 2 sets GE (DD 931, DD 933: Westinghouse) GT; 2 props; 70,000 hp
Boilers: DD 937, DD 938, DD 943, DD 944, DD 948: 4 Foster-Wheeler;
Others: 4 Babcock & Wilcox; 84 kg/cm², 520°C
Fuel: 750 tons **Range:** 4,500/20
Man: ASW refits: 17 officers, 287 men; others: 17 officers, 275 men

REMARKS: DD 946 is assigned to the Naval Reserve Force for reserve training and
as a training ship for the Officer Candidate School, Newport. From DD 937 on, the
bows are somewhat higher than DD 931 and DD 933, while DD 945 and later are
considered a separate class by reason of their different bow design. Four of the same
series were rebuilt as DDGs. From 1974-78 DD 945 was used as the trials ship for
the 203-mm Mk 71 gun mounted forward. All 127-mm Mk 42 guns being modernized
to Mod. 10 configuration. There are two radar gun-fire-control systems, Mk 68
forward and Mk 56 aft (positions reversed in DD 931, DD 937, DD 938, and DD
944). ASW refits have Mk 114 ASW-fire-control systems, the others Mk 105. All
Hedgehog and depth charges removed in early 1970s. Originally had four 76.2-mm
DP (II × 2) but they were removed from all by 1978. There is an ASROC reload
magazine just forward of the launcher.

NOTE: Of the two *Carpenter*-class Naval Reserve Force destroyers, *Carpenter* (DD
825) was sold to Turkey 20-2-81, and *Robert A. Owens* (DD 827) was scheduled to
be sold to Turkey 16-2-82.

♦ 4 Gearing class, FRAM-I

	Bldr	Laid down	L	In serv.
DD 763 WILLIAM C. LAWE	Bethlehem, San Francisco	12-3-44	21-5-45	18-12-46
DD 864 HAROLD J. ELLISON	Bethlehem, Staten Island	3-10-44	14-3-45	23-6-45
DD 866 CONE	Bethlehem, Staten Island	30-11-44	10-5-45	18-8-45
DD 886 ORLECK	Consolidated Steel	28-11-44	12-5-45	15-9-45

William C. Lawe (DD 763)   French Navy, 1978

William G. Lawe (DD 763)   French Navy, 1978

D: 2,448 tons (3,480-3,520 fl) **S:** 30 kts
Dim: 119.03 (116.74 wl) × 12.52 × 4.61 (6.4 over sonar)
A: 4/127-mm 38-cal. DP (II × 2)—1/ASROC ASW RL (VIII × 1)—6/324-mm
Mk 32 ASW TT (III × 2)
Electron Equipt: Radar: 1/SPS-10, 1/SPS-29 (DD 866: SPS-40B), 1/Mk 25
Sonar: SQS-23D
ECM: WLR-3, some also: ULQ-6
M: 2 sets GE GT; 2 props; 60,000 hp **Electric:** 1,200 kw
Boilers: 4 Babcock & Wilcox, 43.3 kg/cm², 454°C **Fuel:** 650 tons
Range: 1,500/30; 2,400/25; 5,800/12
Man: 12 officers, 176 men + Naval Reserve: 7 officers, 112 men

REMARKS: Survivors of some 79 *Gearing*-class destroyers that completed FRAM-I
between 1960 and 1965. All used for Naval Reserve Force training since 1973-75.
The DASH drone ASW helicopter, around which the modernization was designed,
was retired in 1969. DD 763, DD 784, and DD 866, which were to have been stricken
in late 1979, were instead refitted for further service, due to Congressional action.
All have a Mk 37 radar gun-fire-control system and Mk 114 ASW-fire-control system.
Nine ASROC reload missiles can be carried.

The survivors are scheduled to be retained in service through FY 83; all are to
be sold abroad, including two to Pakistan.

Strikings since last edition include: *McKean* (DD 784), stricken and sold to Turkey
1-10-81; *Southerland* (DD 743), stricken and sold to Turkey 26-2-81; *Henderson* (DD
785) sold to Pakistan 1-10-80; *Corry* (DD 817), sold to Greece 5-81 (stricken 27-2-
81); *Johnston* (DD 821), stricken 27-2-81, sold to Taiwan 4-81; *Robert H. McCard*
(DD 822), and *Fiske* (DD 842), sold to Turkey 5-6-80; *Damato* (DD 871), stricken
10-6-79, sold to Pakistan 30-9-80; *Rogers* (DD 876), stricken 19-2-81, sold to South
Korea 7-81; *Dyess* (DD 880), stricken 27-2-81, sold to Greece 5-81; and *Newman K.
Perry* (DD 883), sold to South Korea 27-2-81. *Vogelgesang* (DD 862) and *Steinaker*
(DD 863) were scheduled to be stricken 24-2-82 for sale to Mexico.

GUIDED-MISSILE FRIGATES

♦ 0 (+12+...) Modified Oliver Hazard Perry class—Programmed

	Bldr	Laid down	L	In serv.
FFG 59 N...	...	...	...	...
FFG 60 N...	...	...	...	...
FFG 61 N...	...	...	...	...
FFG 62 N...	...	...	...	...

Programmed: FFG 59-60 in FY 83, FFG 61-62 in FY 84, FFG 63-64 in FY 85, FFG 65-67 in FY 86, FFG 68-70 in FY 87

D: 2,700 tons (3,600 fl) **S:** 30 kts
Dim: 135.64 (125.9 wl) × 13.72 × 4.52 (7.47 max.)
A: 1/Mk 13 launcher (I × 1, 4 Harpoon and 36 Standard SM-1 MR missiles)—1/76-mm Mk 75 DP—1/20-mm Vulcan/Phalanx AA—6/324-mm Mk 32 ASW TT (III × 2)—1 or 2/SH-2F LAMPS-I ASW helicopter
Electron Equipt: Radar: 1/SPS-55, 1/SPS-49, 1/...
    Sonar: SQS-56, SQR-19 TACTASS towed array
    ECM: SLQ-32(V)2, 4/Mk 36 SRBOC chaff
    TACAN: URN-25
M: 2 GE LM-2500 gas turbines; 1 CP prop; 43,000 hp (40,000 sust.)—2 electric drop-down propulsors; 700 hp

REMARKS: Originally it had been proposed to follow the *Oliver Hazard Perry* class with a 2,700 ton "FFX" intended for operation by the Naval Reserve Force. The near-total lack of any combat capability caused Congress in 11-81 to specifically forbid further design-fund spending. The new FFG 59 design will, accordingly, be a simplified version of the *Perry*, incorporating a Sperry-developed 4-faced fixed phased-array radar in place off the Mk 92 Mod. 2 missile-control system. Like their predecessors, they will lack a ship-launched, stand-off ASW weapon.

♦ 15 (+34) Oliver Hazard Perry class (SCN 207/2081 type)

	Bldr	Laid down	L	In serv.
FFG 7 OLIVER HAZARD PERRY	Bath Iron Works	6-12-75	9-25-76	30-11-77
FFG 8 MCINERNEY	Bath Iron Works	16-1-78	4-11-78	15-12-79
FFG 9 WADSWORTH	Todd, San Pedro	13-7-77	29-7-78	28-2-80
FFG 10 DUNCAN	Todd, Seattle	29-4-77	1-3-78	24-5-80
FFG 11 CLARK	Bath Iron Works	17-7-78	24-3-79	17-5-80
FFG 12 GEORGE PHILIP	Todd, San Pedro	14-12-77	16-12-78	18-11-80
FFG 13 SAMUEL ELIOT MORISON	Bath Iron Works	4-12-78	14-7-79	11-10-80
FFG 14 SIDES	Todd, San Pedro	7-8-78	19-5-79	30-5-81
FFG 15 ESTOCIN	Bath Iron Works	2-4-79	3-11-79	10-1-81
FFG 16 CLIFTON SPRAGUE	Bath Iron Works	30-7-79	16-2-80	21-3-81
FFG 19 JOHN A. MOORE	Todd, San Pedro	19-12-78	20-10-79	14-11-81
FFG 20 ANTRIM	Todd, Seattle	21-6-78	27-3-79	26-9-81
FFG 21 FLATLEY	Bath Iron Works	13-11-79	15-5-80	20-6-81
FFG 22 FAHRION	Todd, Seattle	1-12-78	24-8-79	1-82
FFG 23 LEWIS B. PULLER	Todd, San Pedro	23-5-79	15-3-80	1-82
FFG 24 JACK WILLIAMS	Bath Iron Works	25-2-80	30-8-80	19-9-81
FFG 25 COPELAND	Todd, San Pedro	24-10-79	26-7-80	7-82
FFG 26 GALLERY	Bath Iron Works	17-5-80	20-12-80	5-12-81
FFG 27 MAHLON S. TISDALE	Todd, San Pedro	19-3-80	7-2-81	11-82
FFG 28 BOONE	Todd, Seattle	27-3-79	16-1-80	5-82
FFG 29 STEPHEN W. GROVES	Bath Iron Works	16-9-80	4-4-81	3-82
FFG 30 REID	Todd, San Pedro	8-10-80	27-6-81	3-83

	Bldr	Laid down	L	In serv.
FFG 31 STARK	Todd, Seattle	24-8-79	30-5-80	10-82
FFG 32 JOHN L. HALL	Bath Iron Works	5-1-81	24-7-81	6-82
FFG 33 JARRETT	Todd, San Pedro	11-2-81	17-10-81	7-83
FFG 34 AUBREY FITCH	Bath Iron Works	10-4-81	17-10-81	10-82
FFG 36 UNDERWOOD	Bath Iron Works	30-7-81	6-2-82	1-83
FFG 37 CROMMELIN	Todd, Seattle	30-5-80	1-7-81	5-83
FFG 38 CURTS	Todd, San Pedro	1-7-81	3-82	10-83
FFG 39 DOYLE	Bath Iron Works	16-11-81	5-82	5-83
FFG 40 HALYBURTON	Todd, Seattle	26-9-80	13-10-81	9-83
FFG 41 MCCLUSKEY	Todd, San Pedro	21-10-81	6-82	1-84
FFG 42 KLAKRING	Bath Iron Works	3-82	9-82	8-83
FFG 43 THACH	Todd, San Pedro	3-82	11-82	5-84
FFG 45 DERWERT	Bath Iron Works	6-82	12-82	84
FFG 46 RENTZ	Todd, San Pedro	6-82	3-83	84
FFG 47 NICHOLAS	Bath Iron Works	9-82	3-83	84
FFG 48 VANDERGRIFT	Todd, Seattle	13-10-81	7-82	84
FFG 49 ROBERT E. BRADLEY	Bath Iron Works	83	83	84
FFG 50 N...	Bath Iron Works	83	84	84
FFG 51 N...	Todd, San Pedro	82	83	85
FFG 52 CARR	Todd, Seattle	82	83	85
FFG 53 N...	Bath Iron Works	83	84	85
FFG 54 N...	Todd, San Pedro	83	84	85
FFG 55 N...	Bath Iron Works	84	84	85
FFG 56 N...	...	...	...	...
FFG 57 N...	...	...	...	...
FFG 58 N...	...	...	...	...

Authorized: FFG 7 in FY 73, FFG 8-10 in FY 75, FFG 11-16 in FY 76, FFG 19-26 in FY 77, FFG 27-34 in FY 78, FFG 36-43 in FY 79, FFG 45-49 in FY 80, FFG 50-55 in FY 81, FFG 56-58 in FY 82.

McInerney (FFG 8)—as LAMPS-III prototype conversion, with extended stern, RAST system, SLQ-32 and 2 TDS added; SH-60B helicopter on deck

Bath I.W./R. Farr, 9-80

GUIDED-MISSILE FRIGATES (continued)

Oliver Hazard Perry (FFG 7)—SLQ-32 ECM, 2 TDS added, bridge wings enlarged
M. Bar, 10-80

Clark (FFG 11)—short-hull version, as completed   Bath I.W./R. Farr, 5-80

D: 2,647 tons light (3,648 fl); FFG 8, 36-58: 2,709 tons light (3,710 fl)
S: 29 kts (30.6 trials)
Dim: 135.64; FFG 8, 36-58: 138.80 (125.9 wl) × 13.72 × 4.52 (7.47 max.)
A: 1/Mk 13 Mod. 4 launcher (4 Harpoon and 36 Standard SM-1 MR missiles)—1/
76-mm Mk 75 DP—6/324-mm ASW TT (III × 2)—2/SH-2F LAMPS-I (FFG
8, 36-58: 2/SH-60B LAMPS-III) ASW helicopters

Estocin (FFG 15)   Bath I.W./R. Farr, 1980

Electron Equipt: Radar: 1/SPS-55, 1/SPS-49, 1/Mk 92 Mod. 2, 1/STIR (SPG-60
Mod.)
Sonar: 1/SQS-56
TACAN: URN-25
ECM: SLQ-32(V)2, 4/Mk 36 SRBOC
M: 2 GE LM-2500 gas turbines; 1 5.5-m diameter CP, 5-bladed prop; 43,000 hp
(40,000 sust.)—2 drop-down propulsors; 700 hp
Electric: 3,000 kw   **Fuel:** 587 tons + 64 tons helicopter fuel
Range: 4,500/20   **Man:** 12 officers, 180 men

REMARKS: Although these ships were intended to operate the LAMPS-III ASW helicopter, the first twenty-six of them (less FFG 8) lack the equipment necessary to
handle them and are not scheduled to begin receiving LAMPS-III until FY 85.
Beginning with the FY 79 ships (FFG 36 and later), helicopter support equipment
will be aboard on completion; fin stabilizers, RAST (Recovery Assistance, Securing,
and Traversing System), and other systems. The RAST system permits helicopter
launch and recovery with the ship rolling through 28 degrees and pitching 5 degrees.
The equipment was first installed in *McInerney* (FFG 8), which was reconstructed,
completing 12-2-81 at Bath Iron Works, to act as LAMPS-III/SH-60B Sea Hawk
helicopter trials ship; the stern was lengthened by 2.2 m (the extension being slightly
lower than the flight deck, to accommodate mooring equipment) by changing the
rake of the stern. Beginning with FFG 36, SQR-19 TACTASS towed passive hydrophone arrays will be aboard ships when the ships complete; earlier units will be
backfitted. The Mk 16 CIWS (Close-In Weapon System) 20-mm Vulcan/Phalanx will
be backfitted into all units eventually, as will the SLQ-32(V)2 ECM system, the Mk
36 SRBOC chaff system, and two optical target designators (mounted in tubs atop
the pilothouse), which were not fitted to the ships as completed until FFG 27. Thus,
it can be seen that at least the initial units of this class were not well equipped for
most forms of war at sea when they were commissioned; despite this, they are, ton
for ton, the most expensive ships being built for the Navy at this time. FFG 7 was
originally numbered PF 109. Speed on one turbine is 25 knots; the auxiliary power
system uses two retractable pods located well forward and can drive the ships at
up to 6 knots. The Mk 92 Mod. 4 fire-control system controls missile- and 76-mm-
gun fire; it uses a STIR (modified SPG-60) antenna and a U.S.-built version of the
Hollandse Signaal Apparaaten WM-28 radar forward, and can track four separate
targets. The Mk 75 gun is a license-built version of the OTO Melara Compact. A
Mk 13 weapons-direction system is fitted. The only ship-launched ASW ordnance is
the Mk 46 torpedoes in the two triple torpedo tubes. These ships are particularly
well protected against splinter and fragmentation damage, with ¾-inch aluminum-

GUIDED-MISSILE FRIGATES *(continued)*

Samuel Eliot Morison (FFG 13)

Bath I.W./R. Farr, 8-80

alloy armor over magazine spaces, ⅝-in steel over the main engine-control room, and ¾-inch Kevlar plastic armor over vital electronics and command spaces.

Initial plans called for converting FFG 7 and 9-34 to the full FFG 36 standard, beginning about 1985, but this may have to be abandoned due to rising costs. Accordingly, these sub-standard ships may be turned over to the Naval Reserve Force. Original complement was planned at 17 officers, 167 men, which was found to be too many officers but far too few enlisted men to run and maintain the ships. Therefore, FFG 19 and up are being fitted with 30 additional enlisted bunks, with the others to be backfitted.

FFG 17, 18, 35, and 44 of this class were built by Todd, Seattle, for Australia, which plans to build 6 more in-country. Spain is building three.

♦ 6 Brooke class (SCR 199B type)

	Bldr	Laid down	L	In serv.
FFG 1 BROOKE	Lockheed, Seattle	10-12-62	19-7-63	12-3-66
FFG 2 RAMSEY	Lockheed, Seattle	4-2-63	15-10-63	3-6-67
FFG 3 SCHOFIELD	Lockheed, Seattle	15-4-63	7-12-63	11-5-68
FFG 4 TALBOT	Bath Iron Works	4-5-64	6-1-66	2-4-67
FFG 5 RICHARD L. PAGE	Bath Iron Works	4-1-65	4-4-66	5-8-67
FFG 6 JULIUS A. FURER	Bath Iron Works	12-7-65	22-7-66	11-11-67

Authorized: FFG 1-3 in FY 62, FFG 4-6 in FY 63

GUIDED-MISSILE FRIGATES *(continued)*

Brooke (FFG 1)—no ASROC reload magazine   G. Arra, 4-79

Schofield (FFG 3)—showing telescoping hangar   G. Arra, 1-80

D: 2,643 tons (3,425 fl)   **S:** 27.2 kts
Dim: 126.33 (121.9 wl) × 13.47 × 7.9 (over sonar)
A: 1/Mk 22 launcher (I × 1, 16 Standard SM-1 MR missiles)—1/127-mm 38-cal.
   DP—1/ASROC ASW RL (VIII × 1)—6/324-mm Mk 32 ASW TT (III × 2)—
   1/SH-2F LAMPS-I ASW helicopter

Talbot (FFG 4)   S. Terzibaschitsch, 6-81

Electron Equipt: Radar: 1/LN-66, 1/SPS-10F, 1/SPS-52, 1/SPG-51C, 1/Mk 35
   Sonar: 1/SQS-26BX
   ECM: WLR-6, ULQ-6, 4/Mk 36 SRBOC
M: 1 set Westinghouse (FFG 4 to FFG 6: GE) GT; 1 prop; 35,000 hp
Boilers: 2 Foster-Wheeler; 84 kg/cm², 510°C   **Electric:** 2,000 kw
Fuel: . . . tons   **Range:** 4,000/20   **Man:** 17 officers, 231 men

REMARKS: Differ from the *Garcia* class in having their aft 127-mm gun replaced by a
missile launcher. Excellent sea-keeping qualities. Anti-rolling stabilizers. The hangar,
which was enlarged for the SH-2 LAMPS-I helicopter, is telescoping, as on the *Knox*
class. FFG 4 through FFG 6 have an ASROC reload magazine with 8 missiles. FFG
4 was used as an experimental ship for the weapons and systems of the *Oliver Hazard
Perry* (FFG 7) but has now been restored to standard configuration. A Mk 56 Mod.
43 radar gunfire-control system is carried, while the missile system is Mk 74 Mod.
6; Mk 4 Mod. 2 weapons-direction system is fitted, as is the Mk 114 ASW-control
system. These ships are not scheduled to receive Harpoon SSM or the Vulcan/
Phalanx 20-mm Gatling gun.

FRIGATES

♦ **46 Knox class (SCN 199C, 200 and 200-65 types)**

	Bldr	Laid down	L	In serv.
FF 1052 KNOX	Todd, Seattle	5-10-65	19-11-66	12-4-69
FF 1053 ROARK	Todd, Seattle	2-2-66	24-4-67	22-11-69
FF 1054 GRAY	Todd, Seattle	19-11-66	3-10-67	4-4-70
FF 1055 HEPBURN	Todd, San Pedro	1-6-66	25-3-67	3-7-69
FF 1056 CONNOLE	Avondale SY	23-3-67	20-7-68	30-8-69
FF 1057 RATHBURNE	Lockheed, Seattle	8-1-68	2-5-69	16-5-70
FF 1058 MEYERKORD	Todd, San Pedro	1-9-66	15-7-67	28-11-69
FF 1059 WILLIAM S. SIMS	Avondale SY	10-4-67	4-1-69	3-1-70
FF 1060 LANG	Todd, San Pedro	25-3-67	17-2-68	28-3-70
FF 1061 PATTERSON	Avondale SY	12-10-67	3-5-69	14-3-70
FF 1062 WHIPPLE	Todd, Seattle	24-4-67	12-4-68	22-8-70
FF 1063 REASONER	Lockheed, Seattle	6-1-69	1-8-70	31-7-71
FF 1064 LOCKWOOD	Todd, Seattle	3-11-67	5-9-68	5-12-70
FF 1065 STEIN	Lockheed, Seattle	1-6-70	19-12-70	8-1-72
FF 1066 MARVIN SHIELDS	Todd, Seattle	12-4-68	23-10-69	10-4-71
FF 1067 FRANCIS HAMMOND	Todd, San Pedro	15-7-67	11-5-68	25-7-70
FF 1068 VREELAND	Avondale SY	20-3-68	14-6-69	13-6-70
FF 1069 BAGLEY	Lockheed, Seattle	22-9-70	24-4-71	6-5-72
FF 1070 DOWNES	Todd, Seattle	5-9-68	13-12-69	28-8-71
FF 1071 BADGER	Todd, San Pedro	17-2-68	7-12-68	1-12-70

FRIGATES (continued)

FF 1072 BLAKELY	Avondale SY	3-6-68	23-8-69	18-7-70
FF 1073 ROBERT E. PEARY	Lockheed, Seattle	20-12-70	23-6-71	23-9-72
(ex-*Conolly*)				
FF 1074 HAROLD E. HOLT	Todd, San Pedro	11-5-68	3-5-69	26-3-71
FF 1075 TRIPPE	Avondale SY	29-7-68	1-11-69	19-9-70
FF 1076 FANNING	Todd, San Pedro	7-12-68	24-1-70	23-7-71
FF 1077 OUELLET	Avondale SY	15-1-69	17-1-70	12-12-70
FF 1078 JOSEPH HEWES	Avondale SY	15-5-69	7-3-70	24-4-71
FF 1079 BOWEN	Avondale SY	11-7-69	2-5-70	22-5-71
FF 1080 PAUL	Avondale SY	12-9-69	20-6-70	14-8-71
FF 1081 AYLWIN	Avondale SY	13-11-69	29-8-70	18-9-71
FF 1082 ELMER MONTGOMERY	Avondale SY	23-1-70	21-11-70	30-10-71
FF 1083 COOK	Avondale SY	20-3-70	23-1-71	18-12-71
FF 1084 MCCANDLESS	Avondale SY	4-6-70	20-3-71	18-3-72
FF 1085 DONALD B. BEARY	Avondale SY	24-7-70	22-5-71	22-7-72
FF 1086 BREWTON	Avondale SY	2-10-70	24-7-71	8-7-72
FF 1087 KIRK	Avondale SY	4-12-70	25-9-71	9-9-72
FF 1088 BARBEY	Avondale SY	5-2-71	4-12-71	11-11-72
FF 1089 JESSE L. BROWN	Avondale SY	8-4-71	18-3-72	17-2-73
FF 1090 AINSWORTH	Avondale SY	11-6-71	15-4-72	31-3-73
FF 1091 MILLER	Avondale SY	6-8-71	3-6-72	30-6-73
FF 1092 THOMAS C. HART	Avondale SY	8-10-71	12-8-72	28-7-73
FF 1093 CAPODANNO	Avondale SY	12-10-71	21-10-72	17-11-73
FF 1094 PHARRIS	Avondale SY	11-2-72	16-12-72	26-1-74
FF 1095 TRUETT	Avondale SY	27-4-72	3-2-73	1-6-74
FF 1096 VALDEZ	Avondale SY	30-6-72	24-3-73	27-7-74
FF 1097 MOINESTER	Avondale SY	25-8-72	12-7-73	2-11-74

Authorized: 10 in FY 64, 16 in FY 65, 10 in FY 66, 10 in FY 67

Knox (FF 1052)—SH-2D LAMPS-I helicopter on deck   G. Arra, 1980

Donald B. Beary (FF 1085)—WLR-6 and ULQ-6 ECM gear   French Navy, 1980

Lockwood (FF 1064)   G. Arra, 1980

Downes (FF 1070)—with Mk 23 TAS in place of SPS-40, and with the NATO Sea Sparrow system (Mk 29 launcher/Mk 91 Mod. FCS)   French Navy, 1980

Trippe (FF 1075)—with bow bulwarks, SLQ-32 ECM, Mk 25 BPDMS launcher, and SQS-35(V) VDS   L. & L. Van Ginderen, 10-81

FRIGATES (*continued*)

Hepburn (FF 1055)—with telescoping hangar extended

G. Arra, 1980

Ouellet (FF 1077)—bow bulwarks, WLR-6 ECM, no VDS installation G. Arra, 3-80

Moinester (FF 1097)—bow bulwarks, SLQ-32 ECM, no Mk 25 BPDMS launcher
L. & L. Van Ginderen, 10-81

D: 3,066 tons light (4,250 fl) **S:** 27+ kts
Dim: 133.59 (126.5 wl) × 14.33 × 4.60 (7.55 over sonar)—see remarks
A: Harpoon SSM—1/127-mm Mk 42 DP—1/Mk 25 Sea Sparrow on FF 1052 to
FF 1069, FF 1071 to FF 1083 (FF 1070: 1/Mk 29 launcher)—1/ASROC sys-
tem (VIII × 1)—4/324-mm Mk 32 fixed ASW TT—1/SH-2 LAMPS-I ASW
helicopter
Electron Equipt: Radar: 1/SPS-10, 1/SPS-40 (FF 1070: Mk 23 TAS), 1/SPG-53,
1/Mk 115 (FF 1070: Mk 91 Mod. 0)
Sonar: 1/SQS-26CX, SQS-35(V) (except FF 1053 to FF 1055,
FF 1057 to FF 1062, FF 1072, FF 1077), SQR-18A TAC-
TASS on VDS ships

ECM: WLR-6 (some also: ULQ-6) or SLQ-32(V)1, 4/Mk 36 SRBOC
chaff
M: 1 set Westinghouse GT; 1 prop; 35,000 hp **Electric:** 3,000 kw
Boilers: 2 Babcock & Wilcox or Foster-Wheeler; 84 kg/cm², 510°C
Fuel: 750 tons **Range:** 4,300/20 **Man:** 22 officers, 261 men

REMARKS: An additional ten ships of the FY 68 program (FF 1098 to FF 1107) were
canceled. Bow bulwarks and a spray strake are being added forward to reduce deck
wetness, a problem in this class; the addition extends length overall to approx. 134.0

FRIGATES *(continued)*

m. The ASROC system has an automatic reloading magazine beneath the bridge; it is also used to stow Harpoon missiles, which are launched from the port pair of eight launcher cells (FF 1091 first to receive Harpoon, 1976). FF 1084 to FF 1097 did not receive Sea Sparrow. FF 1070 has been used as NATO Sea Sparrow trials ship; she carried a Mk 29 NATO Sea Sparrow launcher and the two-director Mk 91 Mod. 1 fire-control system, since reduced to one director (Mk 91 Mod. 0 system); FF 1070 also carries the Hughes Mk 23 Mod. 0 TAS (Target Acquisition System) in place of the SPS-40 radar. The ASW torpedo tubes are fixed, in the forward end of the hangar superstructure, aimed outboard at an angle of 45°. The Mk 25 BPDMS (Basic Point Defense Missile System) launcher for Sea Sparrow will be *replaced* by a 20-mm Vulcan/Phalanx Gatling AA system, beginning in 1982. FF 1053 to FF 1055, FF 1057 to FF 1062, FF 1072 and FF 1077 do not have SQS-35 independent VDS. Beginning with twelve ships under FY 80, the SQS-35 towed VDS transducer body and hoist was modified to permit towing the SQR-18A TACTASS. FF 1088 also has acted as a trials ship and has a controllable-pitch prop; the large inflatable radome atop her hangar has been removed. All carry a Mk 68 gunfire-control system with SPG-53A, D, or F radar. FF 1083, FF 1084, and others have URN-26 TACAN, to be backfitted in the others. SLQ-32(V)1 (later to be upgraded to (V)2) is replacing WLR-6 as the ECM suit. A few ships retain LN-66 navigational radars and all have two OE-82 satellite-communications antennas for the WSC-3 system. Ships with Sea Sparrow have a single Mk 115 missile-fire-control system (Mk 71 director). All have Mk 114 ASW fire-control system. FF 1078 to FF 1097 have a TEAM (SM-5) computer system for the continual monitoring of ship's electronic equipment. Anti-rolling fin stabilizers fitted in all. Prarie-Masker bubble system fitted to hulls and propellers to reduce radiated noise. All are to receive the ASW TDS (ASW Tactical Data System) beginning FY 83. FF 1054, 1060, and 1091 transferred to the Naval Reserve Force on 15-1-82; FF 1096 scheduled to follow 12-7-82. Eight more will transfer by end FY 84.

◆ 10 Garcia class (SCB 199A type)

	Bldr	Laid down	L	In serv.
FF 1040 GARCIA	Bethlehem, San Francisco	16-10-62	31-10-63	21-12-64
FF 1041 BRADLEY	Bethlehem, San Francisco	17-1-63	26-3-64	15-5-65
FF 1043 EDWARD MCDONNELL	Avondale SY	1-4-63	15-2-64	15-2-65
FF 1044 BRUMBY	Avondale SY	1-8-63	6-6-64	5-8-65
FF 1045 DAVIDSON	Avondale SY	20-9-63	3-10-64	7-12-65
FF 1047 VOGE	Defoe SB, Michigan	21-11-63	4-2-65	25-11-66
FF 1048 SAMPLE	Lockheed, Seattle	19-7-63	28-4-64	23-3-68
FF 1049 KOELSH	Defoe SB, Michigan	19-2-64	8-6-65	10-6-67
FF 1050 ALBERT DAVID	Lockheed, Seattle	29-4-64	19-12-64	19-10-68
FF 1051 O'CALLAHAN	Defoe SB, Michigan	19-2-64	20-10-65	13-7-68

Authorized: 2 in FY 61, 3 in FY 62, 5 in FY 63

D: 2,624 tons (3,403 fl) **S:** 27 kts

Dim: 126.33 (121.9 wl) × 13.47 × 7.9 (over sonar)

A: 2/127-mm 38-cal. DP (I × 2)—1/ASROC ASW RL (VIII × 1)—6/324-mm Mk 32 ASW TT (III × 2)—1/SH-2 LAMPS-I ASW helicopter (except FF 1048 and FF 1050)

Electron Equipt: Radar: 1/LN-66, 1/SPS-10, 1/SPS-40, 1/Mk 35
Sonar: 1/SQS-26; FF 1048 and FF 1050: SQR-15 towed array, also

Albert David (FF 1050)—no LAMPS capability, towed sonar array on deck aft 1975

Bradley (FF 1041)—note restricted firing arc for aft 127-mm gun   G. Arra, 1980

Brumby (FF 1044)—telescoping hangar extended   French Navy, 1978

ECM: WLR-6, ULQ-6

M: 1 set GE GT; 1 prop; 35,000 **Electric:** 2,000 kw

Boilers: 2 Foster-Wheeler; 83.4 kg/cm², 510°C **Range:** 4,000/20

Man: 16 officers, 231 men

REMARKS: Anti-rolling stabilizers fitted. FF 1047 and FF 1049 have a special ASW NTDS. The boilers are vertical and have pressure combustion. Hangar enlarged for SH-2 LAMPS-I helicopter, 1972-75, except for FF 1048 and FF 1050, which conduct trials for towed passive sonar array. Gunfire control is by a Mk 56 radar director and the Mk 114 ASW fire-control system is installed. FF 1047 and later have an ASROC reload magazine beneath the bridge. Twin Mk 25 torpedo tubes at the stern have been removed from the ships that had them. FF 1041 carried Mk 25 Sea Sparrow launcher in 1967-68 for trials. Although these are relatively recent ships, there are no plans to modernize their obsolescent gun systems or to add Harpoon or modern ECM gear. The LAMPS-capable ships are receiving URN-26 TACAN.

FRIGATES (continued)

♦ **1 former experimental escort ship (SCB 198 type)**

	Bldr	Laid down	L	In serv.
FF 1098 GLOVER (ex-AGFF 1, ex-AGDE 1, ex-AG 163)	Bath Iron Works	7-63	17-4-65	11-65

Authorized: FY 61

Glover (FF 1098)   J. Jedrlinic, 5-80

D: 2,643 tons (3,426 fl)   **S:** 27 kts
Dim: 126.33 (121.9 wl) × 13.47 × 7.9 (over sonar)
A: 1/127-mm 38-cal. DP—1/ASROC ASW RL (VIII × 1)—6/324-mm Mk 32
    ASW TT (III × 2)
Electron Equipt: Radar: 1/SPS-10, 1/SPS-40, 1/Mk 35
                Sonar: SQS-26AXD, SQS-35 VDS, SQR-13 PADLOC
                ECM: WLR-6, ULQ-6, 4/Mk 33 RBOC chaff
M: 1 set Westinghouse GT; 1 prop; 35,000 hp   **Electric:** 2,000 kw
Boilers: 2 Foster-Wheeler; 83.4 kg/cm², 510°C   **Man:** 14 officers, 211 men

REMARKS: Redesignated from AGFF on 1-10-79 because she now conducts operational cruises. "FF 1098" was previously used for a later-canceled *Knox*-class frigate; this is the first instance of a previously allocated hull number being reused. Basically a *Garcia*-class ship with identical hull-form, but with a pump-jet propeller and the after 127-mm gun omitted to provide accommodations for civilian technicians. Extreme stern raised during installation of SQS-35 VDS. SQR-13 PADLOC (Passive/Active Detection or Location) sonar is hull-mounted. Scheduled to receive 20-mm Vulcan/Phalanx AA system. No ASROC reload magazine.

♦ **2 Bronstein class**

	Bldr	Laid down	L	In serv.
FF 1037 BRONSTEIN	Avondale SY	16-5-61	31-5-62	16-6-63
FF 1038 McCLOY	Avondale SY	15-9-61	9-6-62	21-10-63

McCloy (FF 1038)   French Navy, 1-79

D: 2,360 tons (2,650 fl)   **S:** 26 kts   **Dim:** 113.23 × 12.34 × 7.0
A: 2/76.2-mm Mk 33 (II × 1)—1/ASROC ASW RL (VIII × 1)—6/324-mm Mk 32
    ASW TT (III × 2)
Electron Equipt: Radar: 1/SPS-10, 1/SPS-40, 1/Mk 35
                Sonar: 1/SQS-26, 1/SQR-15 TASS—ECM: WLR-6, ULQ-6
M: 1 set de Laval GT; 1 prop; 20,000 hp
Boilers: 2 Foster-Wheeler; 83.4 kg/cm², 510°C   **Man:** 16 officers, 180 men

REMARKS: Only remaining U.S. frigates with 76.2-mm guns, controlled by a Mk 56 radar director. Single 76.2-mm aft replaced by TASS towed passive hydrophone array sonar. Have Mk 114 Mod. 7 ASW-fire-control system. No ASROC reload magazine.

GUIDED-MISSILE PATROL BOATS

♦ **3 (+3) PHM (Patrol Hydrofoil Missile) class (SCB 602 type)**

	Bldr	Laid down	L	In serv.
PHM 1 PEGASUS (ex-*Delphinus*)	Boeing, Seattle	10-5-73	9-11-74	9-7-77
PHM 2 HERCULES	Boeing, Seattle	12-9-80	4-82	7-82
PHM 3 TAURUS	Boeing, Seattle	30-1-79	8-5-81	7-10-81
PHM 4 AQUILA	Boeing, Seattle	10-7-79	16-9-81	19-12-81
PHM 5 ARIES	Boeing, Seattle	7-1-80	11-81	4-82
PHM 6 GEMINI	Boeing, Seattle	13-5-80	2-82	5-82

Authorized: 2 in FY 73*, 4 in FY 75

* PHM 2 originally authorized under FY 73 and laid down on 30-5-74; her construction was suspended in 8-75, when 40.9 percent complete, but laid down again 12-9-80 with FY 76 funds.

D: 218 tons (240 fl)   **S:** 48 kts (11 on diesel)
Dim: 40 (45.0 with foils retracted) × 8.6 (14.5 over aft foils) × 7.1 (1.9 with
      foils retracted)/2.7 foilborne
A: 8 Harpoon SSM (IV × 2)—1/76-mm Mk 75 DP (OTO Melara Compact)
Electron Equipt: Radar: 1/SPS-63, 1/Mk 92 Mod. 1 fire-control system
                ECM: SLR-20, 2/Mk 34 SRBOC chaff
M: CODOG: 1 GE LM-2500 PB 102 gas turbine; 1 Aerojet AJW-18800-1 water jet;
      16,000-19, 416 hp; 2 MTU 8V331 TC81 diesels; 2 Aerojet AJW-800-1 water
      jets; 1,340 hp
Electric: 500 kVA   **Range:** 600/40; 1,200 +/11   **Man:** 4 officers, 17 men

REMARKS: Originally projected as a class of thirty, also to be built by or for other NATO nations, but the additional cost over that of conventional missile craft with

GUIDED-MISSILE PATROL BOATS (continued)

Taurus (PHM 3)   Boeing Marine, 1981

Pegasus (PHM 1)   Boeing Marine, 1975

similar capabilities was prohibitive, and the U.S. Navy's interest in the type is minimal. PHM 1 began her protracted trials on 2-25-75. PHM 2 through PHM 6 were canceled on 15-4-77, then reinstated on 14-8-77 at the insistence of Congress, the contract going to Boeing on 20-10-77. No more are likely to be built. PHM 1's gas turbine develops 16,000 hp; on the others 19,416 hp is possible, with the water jet pumping some 341,000 liters/min. at full speed. The Mk 92 Mod. 1 fire-control system is an Americanized version of the Hollandse Signaal Apparaaten M-28 system. SPS-63 is an Americanized version of the Italian SMA 3TM 20-H radar. PHM 1 has the earlier Mk 94 Mod. 1 variant. It was planned at one time to carry eight reload Harpoons, for a total of sixteen. Magazine capacity 330 rds. 76-mm. All are to be based at Key West, Florida.

NOTE: The two final active naval units of the *Asheville* class, *Tacoma* (PG 92) and *Welch* (PG 93) were decommissioned 30-9-81; they were earmarked for lease to Colombia. Four additional ships of the class are in storage, available for foreign transfer.

PATROL CRAFT

♦ **13 PB Mk-III class** Bldr: Peterson Bldrs. (In serv. 1975)

PB Mk-III class with four Penguin Mk II missiles aft   U.S. Navy, 1981

    D: 28 tons (36.7 fl)   **S:** 30 kts   **Dim:** 19.78 × 5.5 × 1.8
    A: 5/12.7-mm mg (II × 1, I × 3)   **Electron Equipt:** Radar: 1/LN-66
    M: 3 GM 8V71 TI diesels; 3 props; 1,950 hp
    Range: 500/30   **Man:** 1 officer, 4 men

REMARKS: For Naval Reserve training. Winner in competition with Mk-I. Sisters were built for Iran and the Philippines. One is being used as trials craft for Norwegian Penguin Mk II missiles, with four missiles mounted on the stern.

♦ **2 PB Mk-I class** Bldr: Sewart Seacraft, Berwick, La. (In serv. 1973)

    D: 27 tons (36.3 fl)   **S:** 25 kts   **Dim:** 19.78 × 5.25 × 1.37
    A: 2/20-mm AA (II × 1)—4/12.7-mm mg—1/81-mm mortar/12.7-mm mg combination
    M: 2 GM 12V71 TI diesels; 2 props; 1,200 hp
    Range: 30/26   **Man:** 2 officers, 6 men

REMARKS: Used for Naval Reserve training.

♦ **5 PCF Mk-I class** Bldr: Swiftships, La. (In serv. 1965-68)

    D: 22.5 tons (fl)   **S:** 22 kts   **Dim:** 15.3 × 4.55 × 1.1
    A: 1/81-mm mortar/12.7-mm mg combination—2/12.7-mm mg
    M: 2 GM 12V71 TI diesels; 2 props; 850 hp
    Range: 400/22   **Man:** 6 tot.

REMARKS: Survivors of some 125 built. Aluminum alloy construction. Used for Naval Reserve training.

PATROL CRAFT (continued)

PCF Mk-I class (PCF 67)

RIVERINE WARFARE CRAFT

♦ **29 PBR (Patrol Boat, Riverine) Mk-II**

PBR Mk-II class   U.S. Navy, 1974

D: 8.9 tons (fl)   **S:** 24 kts   **Dim:** 9.73 × 3.53 × 0.81
A: 3/12.7-mm mg (II × 1, I × 1)—1/60-mm mortar
Electron Equipt: Radar: 1/Raytheon 1900
M: 2 GM 6V53N diesels; 2 Jacuzzi water jets; 430 hp
Range: 150/23   **Man:** 4 tot.

REMARKS: Built 1967-73. Fiberglass hull, plastic armor. Used for Naval Reserve training.

MINE WARFARE SHIPS

NOTE: In addition to the ships and craft listed below, there are also 16 RH-53D minesweeping helicopters in service. Except for MSO 443, MSO 448, and MSO 490, all minesweepers are assigned to the Naval Reserve Force.

♦ **0 (+11+. . .) MSH 1-class coastal minesweeper/minehunters (Planned)**

REMARKS: A new design in preparation 1981-82, with the first unit to be requested in FY 84 and five each in FY 86 and 87, and possibly beyond. To be of about 500 tons (fl) and about 46 m overall, or about the size of the MSC 322 coastal minesweepers delivered by the U.S. to Saudi Arabia in 1978. May be built of glass-reinforced plastic and will probably be powered, like the MCM 1 class below, by Waukesha L-1616 nonmagnetic diesels. No further details yet available.

♦ **0 (+1+13) MCM 1-class oceangoing minesweeper/minehunters**

	Bldr	Laid down	L	In serv.
MCM 1 AVENGER	. . .	. . .	. . .	1984-85

Authorized: MCM 1 in FY 82. Programmed: 4 in FY 83 and FY 84, 5 in FY 85

Avenger (MCM 1)—artist's concept   U.S. Navy, 1980

D: 1,032 tons (fl)   **S:** 14 kts   **Dim:** 64.9 (61.6 wl) × 11.7 × 3.1
A: 2/12.7-mm mg (I × 2)   **M:** 4 Waukesha L-1616 diesels; 2 CP props; 2,400 hp
Electron Equipt: Radar: 1/SPS-55   Sonar: SQQ-30
Electric: . . .   **Range:** . . .   **Man:** 6 officers, 76 men

REMARKS: First unit was to be ordered 1-82. Wooden-hulled expansion of canceled MSO 523 design, with fiberglass superstructure. Will be able to sweep deep-moored mines to 180 m as well as sweeping magnetic and acoustic mines. Will have one MNV (Mine Neutralization Vehicle), a remote-controlled mine-hunting and destruction device. Will carry the SSN-2 precision navigation system. Will have a bow-thruster. Very conservative design, when compared to contemporary European mine countermeasures ship designs.

♦ **2 Acme-class oceangoing minesweepers**

Bldr: Frank L. Sample, Jr., Boothbay Harbor, Maine

	Laid down	L	In serv.
MSO 509 ADROIT	18-11-54	20-8-55	4-3-57
MSO 511 AFFRAY	24-8-55	18-12-56	8-8-58

MINE WARFARE SHIPS (continued)

D: 720 tons (780 fl) **S:** 14 kts **Dim:** 52.73 × 10.97 × 4.3
A: 2/12.7-mm mg (I × 2) **Electron Equipt:** Radar: 1/SPS-53—Sonar: SQQ-14
M: 4 Packard 1D-1700 diesels; 2 CP props; 2,280 hp **Fuel:** 47 tons
Range: 3,000/10 **Man:** 7 officers, 37 men + 4 officers, 33 men Reserves

REMARKS: Similar to *Aggressive* and *Dash* class below, but slightly larger and originally equipped as Mine Division flagships. Not modernized. At 22-23 years of age, they are the U.S. Navy's newest minesweepers.

♦ **23 Aggressive and Dash* class oceangoing minesweepers**

		Bldr	Laid down	L	In serv.
MSO 427	CONSTANT	Fulton SY	16-8-51	14-2-53	8-9-54
MSO 428	DASH*	Astoria Marine	2-7-51	20-9-52	14-8-53
MSO 429	DETECTOR*	Astoria Marine	1-10-51	5-12-52	26-1-54
MSO 430	DIRECT*	C. Hiltebrant DD	2-2-52	27-5-53	9-7-54
MSO 431	DOMINANT*	C. Hiltebrant DD	23-4-52	5-11-53	8-11-54
MSO 433	ENGAGE	Colberg Boat Wks	7-11-51	18-6-53	29-6-54
MSO 437	ENHANCE	Martinolich SB	12-7-52	11-10-52	16-4-55
MSO 438	ESTEEM	Martinolich SB	1-9-52	20-12-52	10-9-55
MSO 439	EXCEL	Higgins, New Orleans	4-2-53	25-9-53	24-2-55
MSO 440	EXPLOIT	Higgins, New Orleans	28-12-51	10-4-53	31-3-54
MSO 441	EXULTANT	Higgins, New Orleans	22-5-52	6-6-53	22-6-54
MSO 442	FEARLESS	Higgins, New Orleans	23-7-52	17-7-53	22-9-54
MSO 443	FIDELITY	Higgins, New Orleans	15-12-52	21-8-53	19-1-55
MSO 446	FORTIFY	Seattle, SB & DD	30-11-51	14-2-53	16-7-54
MSO 448	ILLUSIVE	Martinolich SB	23-10-51	12-7-52	14-11-53
MSO 449	IMPERVIOUS	Martinolich SB	18-11-51	29-8-52	15-7-54
MSO 455	IMPLICIT	Wilmington Boat Wks.	29-10-51	1-8-53	10-3-54
MSO 456	INFLICT	Wilmington Boat Wks.	29-10-51	6-10-53	11-5-54
MSO 464	PLUCK	Wilmington Boat Wks.	31-3-52	6-2-54	11-8-54
MSO 488	CONQUEST	J. M. Martinac	26-3-53	20-5-54	20-7-55
MSO 489	GALLANT	J. M. Martinac	21-5-53	4-6-54	14-9-55
MSO 490	LEADER	J. M. Martinac	22-9-53	15-9-54	16-11-55
MSO 492	PLEDGE	J. M. Martinac	24-6-54	20-7-55	20-4-56

Leader (MSO 490)—regular Navy unit   G. Gyssels, 2-79

Direct (MSO 430)—Dash class   G. Arra, 1976

D: 665 tons light (780-880 fl) **S:** 14 kts **Dim:** 52.42 × 10.97 × 4.2
A: 2/12.7-mm mg (I × 2) **Range:** 2,400/10 (*Dash* class: 3,000/10)
Electron Equipt: Radar: SPS-53E or L Sonar: SQQ-14
M: 4 Waukesha L-1616 diesels; 2 CP props; 2,400 hp; *Dash* class: 2 GM 8-268A diesels; 2 CP props; 1,520 hp
Man: 8 officers, 70 men (Naval Reserve Force ships: 3 officers, 36 men + 3 officers and 44 men Reserves)

REMARKS: Over-aged and badly in need of replacement. Wooden construction; nonmagnetic, stainless-steel machinery. Except for MSO 443, MSO 448, and MSO 490, which are employed in experimental mine-warfare-related duties, all are operated for the Naval Reserve Force. Ninety-three of the MSO 421 to MSO 508 classes were built; many transferred abroad. Hoist machinery for the SQQ-14 minehunting sonar occupies the position of the former 40-mm AA gun. Twelve of the *Aggressive* class were re-engined with Waukesha diesels; the remainder (MSO 427, 439, 440, 455, 464, 489, and 492) retained two Packard 1D1700 diesels, totaling 2,280 hp. *All* the survivors were given very thorough rehabilitations during the early to mid-1970s, receiving semi-enclosed bridges, enlarged superstructures abaft the bridge, SQQ-14 minehunting sonars, new communications gear, and upgraded accommodations.

In 1975 MSO 440 was equipped with the prototype SSN-2 precise-navigation system for the new MCM class, and in 1980 MSO 443 received the prototype SQQ-30 sonar, being developed for the now-canceled MCM class. MSO 428-431, which are slower and have nonstandard propulsion, were to have been decommissioned 30-9-82; instead, for lack of replacements, they will have to be extended in service. In lieu of the MCM class, it is now planned to give these elderly and hard-used ships a second major rehabilitation, through a SLEP (Service Life Extension Program) similar in concept (if not in scope) to that being given *Forrestal*-class aircraft carriers.

MINESWEEPING BOATS

NOTE: A new wooden or glass-reinforced plastic-hulled inshore minesweeper (MSI) design is in the preliminary stages.

♦ **1 MSB 29 class** Bldr: Trumpy, Annapolis (In serv. 1954)

D: 80 tons (fl) **S:** 12 kts **Dim:** 25.0 × 5.8 × 1.7
M: 2 Packard 2D850 diesels; 2 props; 600 hp **Man:** 2 officers, 9 men

REMARKS: Enlarged MSB 5; only one built. Based at Charleston.

MINESWEEPING BOATS *(continued)*

♦ 6 MSB 5 class

MSB 15, MSB 16, MSB 25, MSB 28, MSB 41, MSB 51

MSB 51—minehunting sonar rig over bow   L. & L. Van Ginderen, 5-81

D: 30 tons light (44 fl)   **S:** 12 kts   **Dim:** 17.45 × 4.83 × 1.2
A: 1/12.7-mm mg   **Electron Equipt:** Radar: 1/Raytheon 1900
M: 2 Packard 2D850 diesels; 2 props; 600 hp   **Man:** 6 tot.

REMARKS: Survivors of a class of forty-seven built between 1952 and 1956. Wooden hulls; nonmagnetic machinery. Two Garrett diesel sweep generator sets, except MSB 25: 2 Boeing 502 gas turbine sets. All based at Charleston.

♦ 1 converted shrimp trawler

"MSSB 1" (ex-*Dixie*)

MSSB 1   Captain C. Christensen, USN, 1981

D: . . .   **S:** . . .   **Dim:** 19.2 ×. . . ×. . .
Electron Equipt: Radar: None—Sonar: WQS-1
M: 1 diesel; 1 prop;. . . hp   **Man:** 13 tot.

REMARKS: Wooden-hulled former marijuana-smuggling ex-shrimper captured 2-80 and turned over to the U.S. Navy 9-80 for trial conversion to an "MSSB" (Mine-Sweeping Shrimp Boat), completing 8-81. Re-engined, given a sweep-current diesel generator set and a 100-kw diesel ship's service generator, the craft is operated by Mine Squadron 12 at Charleston, S.C. The shrimp trawl winch is used to handle sweep cables, and a WQS-1 obstacle-avoidance sonar has been mounted for "mine-hunting." A portable 2.4 by 3.0 shack contains display and navigational equipment. About 200 civilian shrimp boats on the U.S. East and Gulf Coasts are to have their crews trained as emergency mine countermeasures forces, should the program continue to prove successful.

AMPHIBIOUS WARFARE SHIPS

♦ 2 Blue Ridge-class amphibious command ships (SCN 400-65 type)

	Bldr	Laid down	L	In serv.
LCC 19 BLUE RIDGE	Philadelphia NSY	27-2-67	4-1-69	14-11-70
LCC 20 MOUNT WHITNEY	Newport News SB & DD	8-1-69	8-1-70	16-1-71

Authorized: FY 65 and FY 66

Blue Ridge (LCC 19)   G. Arra, 1980

Blue Ridge (LCC 19)—note the three satellite communications antennas and ECM array on the after pylon   G. Arra

D: 19,290 tons (fl)   **S:** 21.5 kts
Dim: 189.0 (176.8 wl) × 32.9 (25.0 wl) × 7.5 (8.2 max.)
A: 4/76.2-mm DP (II × 2)—2/Mk 25 launchers for Sea Sparrow (VIII × 2)

AMPHIBIOUS WARFARE SHIPS *(continued)*

Electron Equipt: Radar: 1/SPS-10, 1/SPS-48, 1/SPS-40, 2/Mk 115
　　　ECM: SLQ-29 (WLR-8 + SLQ-17), 4/Mk 36 SRBOC chaff
　　　TACAN: URN-20
M: 1 set GE GT; 1 prop; 22,000 hp
Boilers: 2 Foster-Wheeler; 42.3 kg/cm², 467°C　**Range:** 13,000/16
Man: 40 officers, 680 men + flag group: 200 officers, 500 men

REMARKS: LCC 19 is the flagship of the Seventh Fleet; LCC 20 is the flagship of the Second Fleet. These ships have a good cruising speed (20 knots) and excellent satellite communications and analysis systems: ACIS (Amphibious Command Information System). NIPS (Naval Intelligence Processing System); NTDS and photographic laboratories and document-publication facilities. These LCP, two LCVP landing craft, and one 10-m personnel launch are carried in Welin davits. No helicopter hangar, but they do have a landing pad at the stern. Same machinery and basic hull form as the *Iwo Jima*-class LPH. Air-conditioned; fin stabilizers. Two Mk 56 fire-control systems for the 76.2-mm guns deleted in 1978; two Mk 115 fire-control systems for Sea Sparrow retained. They will eventually receive two Vulcan/Phalanx 20-mm AA. Kevlar plastic armor to be added, as will the Tactical Flag Command Center.

♦ **0 (+2 + . . .) LHDX-class helicopter/dock landing ships (Programmed)**

D: 34,750 tons (fl)　**S:** 24 kts　**Dim:** 232.9 × 32.3 × . . .
A: 28/CH-46 helicopters—. . .　**Man:** . . .

REMARKS: The first LHD was to be requested under the FY 85 budget and the second under FY 87, but $45 mil. in long-lead items for the first were funded under FY 82, indicating accelerated procurement. The ships are intended to combine the features of the LHA and LPD. Some 1,800 troops will be accommodated, and the docking well aft is to hold 12 LCM(6) or 2 LCAC. There will be 3,130 m² of vehicle parking space and 1,700 m³ for cargo. The design is as yet by no means firm but should have many features in common with the LHA. The ships, if built, will no doubt have 2 or more Vulcan/Phalanx 20-mm Gatling AA guns (CIWS Mk 16) and the SLQ-32 series ECM suit.

♦ **5 Tarawa-class amphibious assault ships (SCB 410 type)**

Bldr: Ingalls SB, Litton Ind., Pascagoula, Miss.

	Laid down	L	In serv.
LHA 1 TARAWA	15-11-71	1-12-73	29-5-76
LHA 2 SAIPAN	21-7-72	18-7-74	15-10-77
LHA 3 BELLEAU WOOD (ex-*Philippine Sea*)	5-3-73	11-4-77	23-9-78
LHA 4 NASSAU (ex-*Leyte Gulf*)	13-8-73	21-1-78	28-7-79
LHA 5 PELELIU (ex-*Da Nang*, ex-*Khe Sanh*)	12-11-76	25-11-78	3-5-80

Authorized: 1 in FY 69, 2 in FY 70, 2 in FY 71

D: 39,300 tons (fl)　**S:** 24 kts　**Dim:** 249.94 (237.14 pp) × 32.3 × 8.4
A: 2/Mk 25 Sea Sparrow launchers (VIII × 2)—3/127-mm 54-cal. Mk 45 DP (I × 3)—6/20-mm Mk 67 AA (I × 6)—19/CH-53 or 30/CH-46 helicopters
Electron Equipt: Radar: 1/SPS-53, 1/SPS-10F, 1/SPS-40B, 1/SPS-52B, 1/SPN-35, 1/SPG-60, 1/SPQ-9A, 2/Mk 115
　　　ECM: SLQ-29 (WLR-8 + SLQ-17), 4/Mk 36 SRBOC chaff
　　　TACAN: URN-20
M: 2 sets Westinghouse GT; 2 props; 77,000 hp—900-hp bow-thruster
Electric: 14,600 kw (4 × 2,500 kw, 2 × 2,000 kw, 4 × 150 kw)

Boilers: 2 Combustion Engineering V2M-VS; 49.3 kg/cm², 482°C
Range: 10,000/20　**Man:** 90 officers, 812 men + 172 officers, 1,731 troops

REMARKS: The LHA is a multipurpose assault transport, a combination of LPH and LPD. It has the general profile of an aircraft carrier, with its superstructure to starboard, flight deck, helicopter elevators to port (folding) and aft, and an 80 × 23.4-m well deck for landing craft (up to four LCU 1610 class). Two LCM(6) and

Peleliu (LHA 5)　　　　　　　　　　　　　　　　Ingalls SB, 1980

Saipan (LHA 2)—docking well door open　　　　　J. Jedrlinic, 1980

AMPHIBIOUS WARFARE SHIPS *(continued)*

Tarawa (LHA 1)—20 CH-53, CH-56, UH-1, and AH-1 helos on deck   G. Arra, 1980

Belleau Wood (LHA 3)   J. Jedrlinic, 1981

two LCP are stowed on deck. Vehicle stowage garage forward of docking well totals 3,134 m², and the palletized cargo holds total 3,311 m³. Carry approx. 1,200 tons JP-5 fuel for helicopters. The boilers are the largest ever installed in a U.S. Navy ship; the propulsion plant is highly automated. Communications systems include satellite antennas and a large, long-range, high-frequency, log-periodic array. LHA-4 carried 20 AV-8A Harrier VSTOL attack fighters as well as transport helicopters during a 1981 exercise; may eventually carry one surface-effect landing craft of the LCAC type. Very complete 300-bed hospital and mortuary facilities are fitted. All troops have bunks. Completely air-conditioned. Four additional units were canceled in 1971. The 127-mm guns are aboard primarily to provide shore fire support, but can also be used for AA; they are controlled by a Mk 86 Mod. 4 fire-control system with SPQ-9A radar for surface fire, SPG-60 for AA, and two unmanned electro-optical backup directors. Each Mk 25 Sea Sparrow launcher has an associated Mk 115 radar fire-control system with Mk 71 directors. All scheduled to receive two 20-mm Vulcan/Phalanx Gatling AA in place of the Sea Sparrow launchers and SLQ-32(V)3 in place of the present ECM system. Kevlar plastic armor to be added to all 1982-85.

AMPHIBIOUS ASSAULT HELICOPTER CARRIERS

♦ **7 Iwo Jima class (SCB 157, LPH 12: SCB 401-66)**

	Bldr	Laid down	L	In serv.
LPH 2 Iwo Jima	Puget Sound NSY	2-4-59	17-9-60	26-8-61
LPH 3 Okinawa	Philadelphia NSY	1-4-60	14-8-61	14-4-62
LPH 7 Guadalcanal	Philadelphia NSY	1-9-61	16-3-63	20-7-63
LPH 9 Guam	Philadelphia NSY	15-11-62	22-8-64	16-1-65
LPH 10 Tripoli	Ingalls, Pascagoula	15-6-64	31-7-65	6-8-66
LPH 11 New Orleans	Philadelphia NSY	1-3-66	3-2-68	16-11-68
LPH 12 Inchon	Ingalls, Pascagoula	8-4-68	24-5-69	20-6-70

Authorized: 1 each year in FY 59-63, FY 65, FY 66

Inchon (LPH 12)—LCVP in davits aft, SPN-43, enclosed 76.2-mm mounts fwd.
French Navy, 1979

Guam (LPH 9)—6 AV-8A, 5 CH-53, 8 CH-46, and 2 UH-1 on deck
French Navy, 1977

AMPHIBIOUS ASSAULT HELICOPTER CARRIERS *(continued)*

Tripoli (LPH 10)—no LCVP, SPS-35   G. Arra, 1980

D: 11,000 tons light (17,515-18,300 fl)   **S:** 23 kts
Dim: 183.6 (169.5 wl) × 31.7 (25.5 wl) × 7.9 (hull)
A: 4/76.2-mm DP (II × 2)—2/Mk 25 Sea Sparrow launchers (VIII × 2)—20-24/
    CH-46 helicopters—4/CH-53 heavy helicopters—4/HU-1 utility or AH-1 at-
    tack helicopters
Electron Equipt: Radar: 1/LN-66, 1/SPS-10, 1/SPS-40, 1/SPN-10 or SPN-43
                ECM: WLR-6, ULQ-6, 4/Mk 36 SRBOC chaff
                TACAN: URN-20
M: 1 set GT; 1 prop; 23,000 hp   **Electric:** 6,500
Boilers: 4 Combustion Engineering (LPH 9: Babcock & Wilcox); 42.3 kg/cm²,
         467°C
Man: 47 officers, 605 men + 190 officers, 1,900 troops

REMARKS: LPH 3 conducted V/STOL suitability trials during 1972 and for several
years thereafter operated up to twelve AV-8A Harrier. The ships have also acted
as carriers for RH-53 minesweeping helicopters. One folding side elevator forward,
to port; one to starboard, aft of the island; 70-m hangar. Excellent medical facilities
(300 beds). LPH 9 has an ASCAC (Air-Surface Classification and Analysis Center).
LPH 12, to a slightly different design, carries two LCVP in davits. Two Mk 63
gunfire control being removed. Two 20-m Vulcan/Phalanx AA to be added.

AMPHIBIOUS TRANSPORTS, DOCK

♦ **12 Austin class (SCB 187B type)**

	Bldr	Laid down	L	In serv.
LPD 4 AUSTIN	New York NSY	4-2-63	27-6-64	6-2-55
LPD 5 OGDEN	New York NSY	4-2-63	27-6-64	19-6-65
LPD 6 DULUTH	New York NSY	18-12-63	14-8-65	18-12-65
LPD 7 CLEVELAND	Ingalls, Pascagoula	30-11-64	7-5-66	21-4-67
LPD 8 DUBUQUE	Ingalls, Pascagoula	25-1-65	6-8-66	1-9-67
LPD 9 DENVER	Lockheed SB, Seattle	7-2-64	23-1-65	26-10-68
LPD 10 JUNEAU	Lockheed SB, Seattle	23-1-65	12-2-66	12-7-69
LPD 11 CORONADO	Lockheed SB, Seattle	3-5-65	30-7-66	23-5-70
LPD 12 SHREVEPORT	Lockheed SB, Seattle	27-12-65	25-10-66	12-2-70
LPD 13 NASHVILLE	Lockheed SB, Seattle	14-3-66	7-10-67	14-2-70
LPD 14 TRENTON	Lockheed SB, Seattle	8-8-66	3-8-68	6-3-71
LPD 15 PONCE	Lockheed SB, Seattle	31-10-66	20-5-70	10-7-71

Authorized: 3 in FY 62, 4 in FY 63, 3 in FY 64, 2 in FY 65

D: 11,050 tons (16,550-17,000 fl)   **S:** 21 kts
Dim: 173.4 × 25.6 (hull) × 7.0-7.2
A: 4/76.2-mm DP (II × 2)

Duluth (LPD 6)—non-flagship version, hangar extended   G. Arra, 1978

Nashville (LPD 13)—flagship version, with 4 RH-53D minesweeping helicopters and
two MSB aboard   G. Gyssels, 5-81

Denver (LPD 9)—showing docking well door   G. Arra, 1980

Electron Equipt: Radar: 1/LN-66, 1/SPS-10, 1/SPS-40
                ECM: WLR-1, 2/Mk 28 Chaffroc on LPD 11, 13
                TACAN: URN-20
M: 2 sets de Laval GT; 2 props; 24,000 hp
Boilers: 2 Foster-Wheeler (LPD 5, LPD 12: Babcock & Wilcox), 42.3 kg/cm²,
         467°C
Man: 27 officers, 446 men (+ 90 staff in LPD 7 to LPD 13) + 940 troops (840 in
         LPD 7 to LPD 13)

AMPHIBIOUS TRANSPORTS, DOCK (continued)

REMARKS: Lengthened version of the *Raleigh* class. Combination LSD and assault transports; well deck 120 × 15.24; helicopter platform. Either one LCU and three LCM(6) or nine LCM(6) or four LCM(8) or twenty-eight LVT can be carried in the well deck. Six cranes, one 8.15-ton elevator, two forklifts. Up to six CH-46 helicopters can be carried for brief periods, but the small, telescoping hangar can accommodate only one utility helicopter. LPD 7 to LPD 13 are fitted for flagship duty and have one additional superstructure deck. All have lost their one Mk 56 and two Mk 63 gunfire control, leaving the 76.2-mm guns locally controlled. Two twin 76.2-mm DP removed 1977-78 (port fwd, stbd aft). Two 20-mm Vulcan/Phalanx AA to be added, as well as four Mk 36 SRBOC chaff launchers and the SLQ-32(V)1 ECM system. LPD 11 redesignated AGF 3, *La Salle*, which was undergoing overhaul; reinstated early 1982. Painted white during Persian Gulf tour as Flagship, Commander, Middle East Forces. A follow-on "LPDX" is in the early stages of design.

♦ 2 Raleigh class

	Bldr	Laid down	L	In serv.
LPD 1 RALEIGH	New York NSY	23-6-60	17-3-62	8-9-62
LPD 2 VANCOUVER	New York NSY	19-11-60	15-9-62	11-5-63

Authorized: FY 59 and FY 60

Vancouver (LPD 2)   G. Arra, 2-79

D: 8,040 tons light (13,600 fl)   **S:** 21 kts
Dim: 159.0 (152.4 wl) × 25.60 (hull) × 6.7
A: 6/76.2-mm DP (II × 3)
Electron Equipt: Radar: 1/LN-66, 1/SPS-10, 1/SPS-40
        TACAN: URN-20
        ECM: WLR-1
M: 2 de Laval GT; 2 props; 24,000 hp   **Electric:** 3,600 kw
Boilers: 2 Babcock & Wilcox; 40.8 kg/cm², 467°C
Man: 30 officers, 460 men + 930 troops

REMARKS: Sister *La Salle* (LPD 3), modified as flagship for CoMideastFor in the Indian Ocean and reclassified AGF 3, had an additional superstructure deck like

LPD 7 to LPD 13. Docking well, 51.2 × 15.2 m, is shorter than on *Austin* class. Emphasis in LPD is on personnel capacity, in LSD on dock capacity; the flight deck, which forms the top of the well deck, can handle up to six CH-46 helicopters; there is no hangar. The port, fwd twin 76.2-mm gun mount and all fire-control systems were removed 1977-78.

DOCK LANDING SHIPS

♦ 0 (+2+8) Whidbey Island class

	Bldr	Laid down	L	In serv.
LSD 41 WHIDBEY ISLAND	Lockheed, Seattle	4-8-81	7-83	7-85
LSD 42 N. . .	. . .	. . .	. . .	. . .

Authorized: LSD 41 in FY 81, LSD 42 in FY 82. Programmed: 2 each in FY 84-87.

Whidbey Island (LSD 41)—artist's rendering, with LCAC air-cushion landing craft in foreground   Bell, 1981

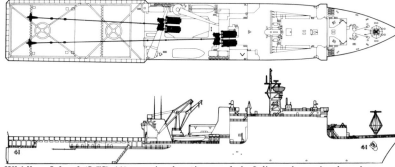

Whidbey Island (LSD 41)—engine locations and shaft lines shown in plan view
        Colt Industries, 1981

D: 11,125 tons (15,726 fl)   **S:** 22 kts   **Dim:** 185.8 (176.8 wl) × 25.6 × 6.0
A: 2/20-mm Vulcan/Phalanx Gatling AA (I × 2)—2/20-mm AA Mk 67
Electron Equipt: Radar: 1/LN-66, 1/SPS-67, 1/SPS-40B
        TACAN: URN-25
        ECM: SLQ(V)1, 4/Mk 36 SRBOC chaff
M: 4 Colt-Pielstick 16 PC2.5V400 diesels; 2 CP props; 41,600 hp (34,000 sust.)
Electric: 3,000 kw   **Man:** 20 officers, 356 men + 440 troops

DOCK LANDING SHIPS (continued)

REMARKS: No long-lead funds for a third unit authorized FY 82, indicating possible congressional displeasure with the design, which is reportedly overloaded. Thus, the planned 8 additional ships may not be built. The design was originally to have been a near-repeat of the LSD 36 class, but a requirement to be able to hold four LCAC (Air-Cushion Landing Craft) in the docking well, which will measure 134.0 × 15.24 m clear necessitated the change. The helicopter deck is raised above the docking well (which can also hold 21 LCM(6) or 3 LCU or 64 LVTP) in order to provide all-around ventilation for the gas turbine-engined LCACs. There will be two landing spots for up to CH-53-sized helicopters, but no hangar facilities. Forward of the docking well will be 1,214 m² of vehicle parking space, while there will be space for 149 m³ of palletized cargo. Will carry one LCM(6), two LCPL Mk-II, and one LCVP on deck, handled by one 20-ton and one 60-ton crane. Originally to have had SPS-65 radar.

◆ 5 Anchorage class (SCN 404-65 and 66 types)

	Bldr	Laid down	L	In serv.
LSD 36 ANCHORAGE	Ingalls, Pascagoula	13-3-67	5-5-68	15-3-69
LSD 37 PORTLAND	Gen'l Dynamics, Quincy	21-9-67	20-12-69	3-10-70
LSD 38 PENSACOLA	Gen'l Dynamics, Quincy	12-3-69	11-7-70	27-3-71
LSD 39 MOUNT VERNON	Gen'l Dynamics, Quincy	29-1-70	17-4-71	13-5-72
LSD 40 FORT FISHER	Gen'l Dynamics, Quincy	15-7-70	22-4-72	12-9-72

Authorized: 1 in FY 65, 3 in FY 66, 1 in FY 67

Mount Vernon (LSD 39)   G. Arra, 1-80

Fort Fisher (LSD 40)   G. Arra, 1980

D: 8,600 tons light (13,600 fl)   **S:** 22 kts
Dim: 168.66 (162.8 wl) × 25.9 × 5.6 (6.1 max.)
A: 6/76.2-mm DP (II × 3)   **Electron Equipt:** Radar: 1/SPS-10, 1/SPS-40

M: 2 sets de Laval GT; 2 props; 24,000 hp
Boilers: 2 Foster-Wheeler (LSD 36: Combustion Engineering); 42.3 kg/cm², 467°C
Man: 21 officers, 376 men + 28 officers, 348 troops

REMARKS: Carry assault landing craft in the well deck (113.28 × 15.24); can accommodate 3 LCU or 15 LCM(6) or 8 LCM(8) or 50 LVT. One or two LCM(6) stowed on deck, handled by the two 50-ton cranes. Have 1,115 m² of vehicle parking space forward of the docking well. The helicopter deck is removable. The starboard forward twin 76.2-mm removed to allow later mounting of two 20-mm Vulcan/Phalanx (one to go aft). Mk 56 and Mk 63 directors removed in 1977. No ECM equipment now, but scheduled to receive SLQ-32(V)1 and 4/Mk 36 SRBOC chaff launchers.

◆ 8 Thomaston class (SCB 75 type) Bldr: Ingalls, Pascagoula, Miss.

	Laid down	L	In serv.
LSD 28 THOMASTON	3-3-53	9-2-54	17-9-54
LSD 29 PLYMOUTH ROCK	5-5-53	7-5-54	29-11-54
LSD 30 FORT SNELLING	17-8-53	16-7-54	24-1-55
LSD 31 POINT DEFIANCE	23-11-53	28-9-54	31-3-55
LSD 32 SPIEGEL GROVE	7-9-54	10-11-55	8-6-56
LSD 33 ALAMO	11-10-54	20-1-56	24-8-56
LSD 34 HERMITAGE	11-4-55	12-6-56	14-12-56
LSD 35 MONTICELLO	6-6-55	10-8-56	29-3-57

Authorized: 4 in FY 52, 2 in FY 54, 2 in FY 55

Thomaston (LSD 28)   G. Arra, 1-80

Spiegel Grove (LSD 32)   L. & L. Van Ginderen, 10-80

D: 6,880 tons (12,150 fl)   **S:** 22.5 kts   **Dim:** 155.45 × 25.6 × 5.4 (5.8 max.)
A: 6/76.2-mm DP (II × 3)   **Electron Equipt:** Radar: 1/SPS-10, 1/SPS-6
M: 2 sets GE GT; 2 props; 24,000 hp   **Range:** 10,000/20

DOCK LANDING SHIPS (continued)

Boilers: 2 Babcock & Wilcox, 40.8 kg/cm² pressure
Man: 21 officers, 379 men + 318 troops

REMARKS: Portable helicopter platform. Can carry 3 LCU, 15 LCM(6), or 9 LCM(8) in 119.2 × 14.6 well deck, with 975 m² of vehicle parking space forward of the docking well. Two 50-ton cranes. Originally had 16 76.2-mm DP (II × 8). Now have one mount forward, to starboard, and two amidships. Two Mk 56 and Mk 63 gunfire-control systems removed in 1977. Last active ships with SPS-6 air-search radar. To be replaced by new LSD 41 class.

TANK LANDING SHIPS

♦ 20 Newport class (SCN 405-66 type)

Bldrs: LST 1179: Philadelphia NSY; others: National Steel SB, San Diego

	Laid down	L	In serv.
LST 1179 NEWPORT	1-11-66	3-2-68	7-6-69
LST 1180 MANITOWOC	1-2-67	4-6-69	24-1-70
LST 1181 SUMTER	14-11-67	13-12-69	20-6-70
LST 1182 FRESNO	16-12-67	28-9-68	22-11-69
LST 1183 PEORIA	22-2-68	23-11-68	21-2-70
LST 1184 FREDERICK	13-4-68	8-3-69	11-4-70
LST 1185 SCHENECTADY	2-8-68	24-5-69	13-6-70
LST 1186 CAYUGA	28-9-68	12-7-69	8-8-70
LST 1187 TUSCALOOSA	23-11-68	6-9-69	24-10-70
LST 1188 SAGINAW	24-5-69	7-2-70	23-1-71
LST 1189 SAN BERNARDINO	12-7-69	28-3-70	27-3-71
LST 1190 BOULDER	6-9-69	22-5-70	4-6-71
LST 1191 RACINE	13-12-69	15-8-70	9-7-71
LST 1192 SPARTANBURG COUNTY	7-2-70	11-11-70	1-9-71
LST 1193 FAIRFAX COUNTY	28-3-70	19-12-70	16-10-71
LST 1194 LA MOURE COUNTY	22-5-70	13-2-71	18-12-71
LST 1195 BARBOUR COUNTY	15-8-70	15-5-71	12-2-72
LST 1196 HARLAN COUNTY	7-11-70	24-7-71	8-4-72
LST 1197 BARNSTABLE COUNTY	19-12-70	2-10-71	27-5-72
LST 1198 BRISTOL COUNTY	13-2-71	4-12-71	5-8-72

Authorized: 1 in FY 65, 8 in FY 66, 11 in FY 67

Sumter (LST 1181)—with pontoon sections   Skyfotos, Ltd., 1978

Barnstable County (LST 1197)   French Navy, 5-79

Barbour County (LST 1195)   G. Arra, 1980

D: 4,164 tons light (8,342-8,450 fl)   **S:** 20 kts
Dim: 159.2 (171.3 over horns) × 21.18 × 5.3 (aft) × 1.80 (fwd)
A: 4/76.2-mm DP (II × 2)   **Electron Equipt:** Radar: 1/LN-66, 1/SPS-10
M: 6 Alco 16-251 (LST 1179 to LST 1181: GM 16-645-E5) diesels; 2 CP props; 16,500 hp
Man: 12 officers, 174 men + 20/411 troops

REMARKS: LST 1190 transferred to the Naval Reserve Force 1-12-80 and LST 1191 on 15-1-81. Can carry 500 tons of cargo on 1,765 m² of deck space, and up to 431 troops (386 normal). A side-thruster propeller forward helps when marrying to a causeway. There is a mobile aluminum ramp forward (34 tons), which is linked to the tank deck by a second ramp. These ramps can carry 75 tons. Aft is a helicopter platform and a stern door for loading and unloading vehicles. Four pontoon causeway sections can be carried on the hull sides. Mk 63 radar gunfire-control systems removed 1977-78; two 20-mm Vulcan/Phalanx AA are intended to replace the 76.2-mm guns.

TANK LANDING SHIPS *(continued)*

NOTE: Of the three surviving *DeSoto County* tank landing ships, all in reserve since 1972, *Suffolk County* (LST 1173) and *Wood County* (LST 1178) were scheduled to transfer to Mexico during 1982, while *Lorain County* (LST 1177) was to go to Greece.

AMPHIBIOUS CARGO SHIPS

♦ 5 Charleston class

	Bldr	Laid down	L	In serv.
LKA 113 CHARLESTON	Newport News	5-12-66	2-12-67	14-12-68
LKA 114 DURHAM	Newport News	10-7-67	29-3-68	24-5-69
LKA 115 MOBILE	Newport News	15-1-68	19-10-68	29-9-69
LKA 116 ST. LOUIS	Newport News	3-4-68	4-1-69	22-11-69
LKA 117 EL PASO	Newport News	22-10-58	17-5-69	17-1-70

Authorized: 4 in FY 65, 1 in FY 66

Durham (LKA 114)   G. Arra, 1980

El Paso (LKA 117)—still with 8/76.2-mm guns   L. & L. Van Ginderen, 10-80

D: 10,000 tons (18,600 fl)   **S:** 20 kts   **Dim:** 175.4 × 18.9 × 7.8
A: 6 (LKA 117: 8)/76.2-mm DP (II × 3)
Electron Equipt: Radar: 1/LN-66, 1/SPS-10
M: 1 set Westinghouse GT; 1 prop; 22,000 hp
Boilers: 2 Combustion Engineering; 42.2 kg/cm² pressure
Man: 24 officers, 310 men + 15 officers, 211 troops

REMARKS: All but LKA 116 transferred to the Naval Reserve Force, LKA 113 on 21-11-79, LKA 114 on 1-10-79, LKA 115 on 1-9-80, and LKA 117 on 1-3-81. Air-conditioned. Machinery control is automatic. Helicopter platform. Fittings include two 70-ton heavy-lift booms, two 40-ton booms, and eight 15-ton booms. Normally carry

four LCM(8), four LCM(6), two LCVP, and two LCP. Two Mk 56 radar gunfire-control systems and one twin 76.2-mm gun mount removed 1977-78; to receive two 20-mm Vulcan/Phalanx AA.

NOTE: The *Mariner*-class amphibious cargo ship *Tulare* (LKA 112) was stricken on 1-8-81 and will be used by the Massachusetts Maritime Academy, renamed *Bay State*.

UTILITY LANDING CRAFT

♦ 54 LCU 1610 class (SCB 149, 149B, and 406 types) Bldrs: Various, 1960-78

LCU 1613	LCU 1621	LCU 1637
LCU 1614	LCU 1623	LCU 1641
LCU 1616	LCU 1624	LCU 1644 to LCU 1651
LCU 1617	LCU 1627 to 1634	LCU 1653 to LCU 1680
LCU 1619		

LCU 1632   G. Arra, 1979

D: 190 tons (390 fl)   **S:** 11 kts   **Dim:** 41.07 × 9.07 × 2.08
A: 2/12.7-mm mg (I × 2)   **Electron Equipt:** Radar: 1/navigational
M: 4 GM 6-71 diesels; 2 Kort-nozzle props; 1,200 hp
Fuel: 13 tons   **Range:** 1,200/11   **Man:** 6 men + 8 troops

REMARKS: LCU 1621 has vertical cycloidal propellers. LCU 1637 is constructed of aluminum, displaces 357 tons (fl), and draws 1.97 m. Cargo capacity is 143 tons; cargo space, 30.5 × 5.5 m. Usually unarmed; can be equipped with an LN-66 or other small navigation radar. Most of the missing hull numbers converted to other functions or transferred to the U.S. Army. Minor differences as construction progressed.

♦ 30 LCU 1466 class (SCB 25 type)

LCU 1466 to LCU 1470	LCU 1487 to LCU 1490	LCU 1547	LCU 1563
LCU 1473	LCU 1492	LCU 1548	LCU 1564
LCU 1477	LCU 1505	LCU 1552	LCU 1578
LCU 1482	LCU 1532	LCU 1554	
LCU 1484	LCU 1535 to LCU 1537	LCU 1558	
LCU 1485	LCU 1539	LCU 1559	

D: 180 tons (347 fl)   **S:** 8 kts   **Dim:** 35.08 × 10.36 × 1.6 (aft)
M: 3 Gray Marine 64YTL diesels; 3 props; 675 hp
Fuel: 11 tons   **Range:** 1,200/6   **Man:** 6 men + 8 troops

REMARKS: Built between 1953 and 1958. Can carry 167 tons. Engines and bridge aft. Improved version of LCU 501 class. Missing numbers have been either transferred, sunk, or converted to service craft (YFU). LCU 1473, LCU 1505, LCU 1532, LCU 1537, LCU 1548, LCU 1552, LCU 1554, LCU 1558, LCU 1563, LCU 1564, and LCU 1578 were reacquired from the U.S. Army in 9-78.

UTILITY LANDING CRAFT *(continued)*

LCU 1468   1969

MINOR LANDING CRAFT

NOTE: Exact totals not available for most types.

♦ **0 (+3+3+101) LCAC class** Bldr: Bell Aerospace/Textron

D: 200 tons (fl)   **S:** 40-50 kts   **Dim:** 29.26 × 14.63
A: . . .   **Electron Equipt:** Radar: 1/navigational
M: 4 Avco TF40 gas turbines (2 for lift); 2 shrouded air propellers; 10,720 hp
Range: 200/50   **Man:** 4 tot.

REMARKS: Based on JEFF-B prototype. First three to order under FY 82 and three in FY 83 for force trials, with no request in FY 84, and then series production of a planned 101 more starting in FY 85. Cargo capacity: 60 tons normal/75 overload. To be carried 4 each aboard LSD 41 class, one of LHA 1 class, also by programmed LHDX class. For appearance, see artist's rendering of LSD 41 on earlier page.

♦ **. . . LCM(8) Mk-2 class**

D: 34 tons light (95 fl)   **S:** 12 kts   **Dim:** 22.7 × 6.41 × 1.37
M: 4 GM 6-71 diesels; 2 props; 590 hp   **Range:** 150/12

REMARKS: Began building in 1969. Aluminum version of LCM(8) Mk-1. Cargo: 58 tons. Some have two GM 12V71 diesels. Ten were to be built under FY 82 for use aboard the new T-AKX maritime prepositioning ships; canceled.

♦ **. . . LCM(8) Mod. 1 and Mod. 2 class**

LCM(8) Mod. 1 class

D: 56 tons light (116 fl)   **S:** 9 kts   **Dim:** 22.43 × 6.42 × 1.57
M: 4 GM 6-71 diesels; 2 props; 620 hp   **Range:** 140/9

REMARKS: Built between 1949 and 1976. Cargo: 54 tons. U.S. Army also uses large numbers of this class, which has now been in production for more than thirty years.

♦ **. . . LCM(6) class**

D: 24 tons (56 fl)   **S:** 10 kts   **Dim:** 17.07 × 4.37 × 1.17 (aft)
M: 2 Gray Marine 64HN9 diesels; 2 props; 330 hp   **Range:** 130/10

REMARKS: Designed during World War II and built between 1952 and 1980. Many used in utility roles. Cargo: 30 tons.

♦ **. . . LCVP class**

D: 13 tons (fl)   **S:** 9 kts   **Dim:** 10.90 × 3.21 × 1.04 (aft)
M: 1 Gray Marine 64HN9 diesel; 225 hp   **Range:** 110/9

REMARKS: 1,552 built, 1950-62. Wooden or plastic hulls. Can carry 36 troops or 3.5 tons cargo.

♦ **. . . LCP(L) Mk-II class**

D: 9.2 tons (fl)   **S:** 17 kts   **Dim:** 10.98 × 3.97 × 1.13
M: 1 GM 6-71 diesel; 270 hp   **Range:** 160/7

REMARKS: Plastic construction. For use as control craft. Carried aboard LHA, LPD, LSD, LST classes, etc. Twenty-two additional authorized in FY 79, 22 in FY 80, 42 in FY 81, and 27 in FY 82. A large number of the older, steel, Mk-4 version remain in service: 10.2 tons; one GM 8V71 diesel; 350 hp for 19 knots.

SPECIAL WARFARE CRAFT

♦ **8 (+10+16) SWCL "Seafox" class** Bldr: Uniflyte, Bellingham, Wash.

D: 11.3 tons (fl)   **S:** 30+ kts   **Dim:** 11.0 × 3.0 × 0.84
A: Small arms   **Electron Equipt:** Radar: 1/LN-66
M: 2 GM 6V92 TA diesels; 2 props; 900 hp   **Man:** 3 tot.

REMARKS: Glass-reinforced plastic construction. SWCL = Special Warfare Craft, Light. Intended for use by SEAL Team commandos; can stow a rubber raft. Have secure voice communications gear, IFF, night vision equipment, and an echo-sounder.

EXPERIMENTAL LANDING CRAFT

NOTE: The best features of the two AALC (Amphibious Assault Landing Craft) designs listed below were to be combined into the new production LCAC air-cushion vehicle.

♦ **JEFF-A** Bldr: Aerojet General

JEFF-A   U.S. Navy, 1977

Weight: 85.8 tons (166 loaded)   **S:** 50 kts   **Dim:** 31.5 × 15.7 × 7.5 (high)
M: 6 Avco T40 gas turbines (2 for lift); 4 shrouded air screws; 11,200 hp
Range: 200/50   **Man:** 6 tot.

EXPERIMENTAL LANDING CRAFT *(continued)*

REMARKS: Actually built at Todd Shipyards, Seattle, and delivered in 2-77. Aluminum construction.

♦ **JEFF-B** Bldr: Bell Aerosystems, New Orleans

JEFF-B   U.S. Navy, 1979

Weight: 93 tons (147 loaded) **S:** 62 kts **Dim:** 26.4 × 14.3 × 7.1 (high)
M: 4 Avco TF40 gas turbines (4 for lift); 2 shrouded propellers; 16,080 hp
Range: 200/50 **Man:** 6 tot.

REMARKS: Delivered in 1976. In this design, all six turbines are interconnected to provide power simultaneously to the two propellers and four lift fans. Vehicle cargo area: 146.5 m², capacity 60 tons (75 overload). Has crossed 3-m-high sand dunes. Design essentially the winner for the LCAC production program.

AUXILIARY SHIPS

NOTE: This section includes only ships that are subordinate to the U.S. Navy proper. Ships assigned to the civilian-manned Military Sealift Command are listed separately in a following section. Below, ships are listed alphabetically by their U.S. Navy type designation i.e., AD, AF, AG, etc.

♦ **4 (+2+3) Samuel Gompers-class destroyer tenders (SCB 244 type)**

Bldrs: AD 37 and AD 38, Puget Sound NSY; AD 41 to AD 44, National Steel, San Diego

	Laid down	L	In serv.
AD 37 SAMUEL GOMPERS	9-7-64	14-5-66	1-7-67
AD 38 PUGET SOUND	15-2-65	16-9-66	27-4-68
AD 41 YELLOWSTONE	27-6-77	27-1-79	28-6-80
AD 42 ACADIA	14-2-78	28-7-79	6-6-81
AD 43 CAPE COD	27-1-79	2-8-80	4-82
AD 44 SHENANDOAH	2-8-80	2-82	83

Authorized: 1 in FY 64, 1 in FY 65, 1 in FY 75, 1 in FY 76, 1 in FY 77, 1 in FY 79

D: 20,500 tons (fl) **S:** 20 kts **Dim:** 196.29 × 25.91 × 6.86
A: AD 37,38: 4/20-mm AA (I × 4); others: 2/20-mm AA (I × 2)
Electron Equipt: Radar: 1/LN-66, 1/SPS-10
M: 1 set de Laval GT; 1 prop; 20,000 hp **Electric:** 12,000 kw
Boilers: 2 Combustion Engineering; 43.6 kg/cm², 462°C
Man: 135 officers, 1,671 men

REMARKS: Similar to *L.Y. Spear*-class submarine tenders; AD 41 and later considered a separate class (SCB 700 type) and have facilities to carry and overhaul LM-2500 gas turbines, being tailored to support DD 963, DDG 993, and FFG 7-class ships. Plan to request AD 45 in FY 86, AD 46 in FY 87. All have helo deck aft, no hangar. Maintenance ships for guided-missile cruisers and destroyers. Two 30-ton cranes; two 3.5-ton traveling cranes. Helicopter deck. Excellent workshops for electronic equipment and surface-to-air-missiles. Originally planned to carry Sea Sparrow in

Puget Sound (AD 38)—as 6th Fleet flagship, with special SATCOMM antenna atop lattice mast, URN-25 TACAN atop foremast   French Navy, 1980

Yellowstone (AD 41)—note rails for traveling crane along upper deck
National Steel/K. Lee, 11-79

AUXILIARY SHIPS (continued)

Prairie (AD 15)   G. Arra, 5-79

M: 2 sets GT; 2 props; 11,000 hp **Electric:** 3,600 kw
Boilers: 4 Babcock & Wilcox; 28.4 kg/cm², 382°C
Fuel: 3,680 tons **Man:** 1,131-1,271 tot.

REMARKS: The design of these support ships goes back to pre-1939 programs, and they are the oldest U.S. Navy ships in service. Modernized under the FRAM program from 1959 to 1963 to serve as maintenance vessels for guided-missile ships, they have workshops, spare parts for missiles, and two 20-ton rotating cranes. Helicopter deck. 127-mm guns removed 1974-75. AD 14 to strike 15-6-82 for sale to Turkey. AD 17 to decommission 30-9-82, probably for disposal.

◆ 7 Kilauea-class ammunition ships (SCB 703 type)

		Bldr	Laid down	L	In serv.
AE 27	BUTTE	Gen. Dynamics	21-7-66	9-8-67	14-12-68
AE 28	SANTA BARBARA	Bethlehem, Sparrows Pt	20-12-66	23-1-68	11-7-70
AE 29	MOUNT HOOD	Bethlehem, Sparrows Pt	8-5-67	17-2-68	1-5-71
AE 32	FLINT	Ingalls, Pascagoula	4-8-69	9-11-70	20-11-71
AE 33	SHASTA	Ingalls, Pascagoula	10-11-69	3-4-71	26-2-72
AE 34	MOUNT BAKER	Ingalls, Pascagoula	10-5-70	23-10-71	22-7-72
AE 35	KISKA	Ingalls, Pascagoula	4-8-71	11-3-72	16-12-72

Authorized: 2 in FY 65, 2 in FY 66, 2 in FY 67, 2 in FY 68

D: 18,088 tons (fl) **S:** 20 kts **Dim:** 171.9 × 24.7 × 8.5
A: 4/76.2-mm DP (II × 2)—2/UH-46 helicopters
Electron Equipt: Radar: 1/SPS-10
M: 1 set GE GT; 1 prop; 22,000 hp
Boilers: 3 Foster-Wheeler; 42.3 kg/cm², 467°C
Man: 28 officers, 373 men

REMARKS: Sister *Kilauea* (AE 26) disarmed and transferred to Military Sealift Command 1-10-80. Sophisticated FAST rapid-replenishment system. Hangar and flight deck aft. Two twin 76.2-mm mounts amidships and both Mk 56 directors removed;

Acadia (AD 42)—on trials   U.S. Navy, 3-81

AD 41 and later. One 127-mm DP removed from AD 38 in 1979. AD 41 and later also carry two 40-mm Mk 19 grenade launchers. AD 38 became 6th Fleet flagship in 7-80, having received an extra mast to support a special SATCOMM antenna (all have the standard WSC-3 SATCOMM installation, with two OE-82 drum-shaped antennas).

◆ 1 Klondike-class destroyer tender

		Bldr	Laid down	L	In serv.
AD 24	EVERGLADES	Los Angeles SB	26-6-44	28-1-45	25-5-51

D: 8,165 tons (14,700 fl) **S:** 18 kts **Dim:** 149.96 (141.73 pp) × 21.25 × 8.3
A: None **Electron Equipt:** Radar: 1/SPS-10
M: 1 set Westinghouse GT; 1 prop; 8,500 hp **Electric:** 3,600 kw
Boilers: 2 Foster-Wheeler; 30.6 kg/cm², 393°C
Fuel: 2,415 tons **Man:** 800-918 tot.

REMARKS: In reserve, used as an accommodations ship at Philadelphia. Built on C-3 cargo hull. Helicopter deck; hangar for DASH. Sister *Bryce Canyon* (AD 36, ex-AV 20) stricken 30-6-81 and earmarked for sale to Pakistan during 1982.

◆ 5 Dixie-class destroyer tenders

		Bldr	Laid down	L	In serv.
AD 14	DIXIE	New York SB	17-3-38	25-5-39	25-4-40
AD 15	PRAIRIE	New York SB	7-12-38	9-12-39	5-8-40
AD 17	PIEDMONT	Tampa SB	1-12-41	7-12-42	5-1-44
AD 18	SIERRA	Tampa SB	31-12-41	23-2-43	20-3-44
AD 19	YOSEMITE	Tampa SB	19-1-42	16-5-43	25-3-44

D: 9,450 tons (17,190 fl) **S:** 18 kts **Dim:** 161.7 × 22.33 × 7.8
A: 4/20-mm AA (I × 4) **Electron Equipt:** Radar: 1/SPS-10

Dixie (AD 14)—oldest active ship in the U.S. Navy   G. Gyssels, 5-80

Mount Baker (AE 34)   U.S. Navy, 1976

AUXILIARY SHIPS (continued)

Butte (AE 27) — French Navy, 1977

two 20-mm Vulcan/Phalanx AA amidships to be added to AE 32-35. Mk 36 SRBOC chaff-flare launchers to be added to all.

♦ **3 Nitro-class ammunition ships (SCB 114A type)** Bldr: Bethlehem Steel Corp., Sparrows Point, Md.

	Laid down	L	In serv.
AE 23 NITRO	20-5-57	26-6-58	1-5-59
AE 24 PYRO	21-10-57	5-11-58	24-7-59
AE 25 HALEAKALA	10-3-58	17-2-59	3-11-59

Nitro (AE 23) — with UH-46 helicopter on deck — G. Arra, 1975

D: 10,000 tons (16,083 fl) **S:** 20 kts **Dim:** 156.1 × 22.0 × 8.8
A: 4/76.2-mm DP (II × 2) **Electron Equipt:** Radar: 1/SPS-10
M: 1 set Bethlehem GT; 1 prop; 16,000 hp
Boilers: 2 Combustion Engineering **Man:** 20 officers, 330 men

REMARKS: All had landing platforms for cargo helicopters added aft during the 1960s. Mk 63 gun directors removed, 1977-78. Mk 36 SRBOC to be added; SPS-6 radar removed. AE 24 transferred to Naval Reserve Force 1-9-80 but is to return to regular Navy 1-6-82.

♦ **2 Suribachi-class ammunition ships (SCB 114 type)** Bldr: Bethelem Steel Corp., Sparrows Point, Md.

	Laid down	L	In serv.
AE 21 SURIBACHI	16-5-55	3-5-56	30-3-57
AE 22 MAUNA KEA	31-1-55	2-11-55	17-11-56

D: 10,000 tons (15,500 fl) **S:** 1 kts **Dim:** 156.1 × 22.0 × 8.8
A: 4/76.2-mm DP (II × 2) **Electron Equipt:** Radar: SPS-10
M: 1 set GT; 1 prop; 16,000 hp **Boilers:** 2 Combustion Engineering
Man: 16 officers, 370 men

Suribachi (AE 21) — note gun arrangement on forecastle — U.S. Navy, 1978

REMARKS: SPS-6 radar removed. Gun mounts superfiring, whereas AE 23 to AE 25 have them side by side. Mk 63 gunfire-control systems removed, 1977-78.

♦ **7 Mars-class combat stores ships (SCB 208 type)** Bldr: National Steel & SB Co., San Diego

	Laid down	L	In serv.
AFS 1 MARS	5-5-62	15-6-63	21-12-63
AFS 2 SYLVANIA	18-8-62	10-8-63	11-7-64
AFS 3 NIAGARA FALLS	22-5-65	25-3-66	29-4-67
AFS 4 WHITE PLAINS	2-10-65	23-7-66	23-11-68
AFS 5 CONCORD	26-3-66	17-12-66	27-11-68
AFS 6 SAN DIEGO	11-3-67	13-4-68	24-5-69
AFS 7 SAN JOSE	8-3-69	13-12-69	23-10-70

Authorized: 1 in FY 61, 1 in FY 62, 1 in FY 64, 2 in FY 65, 1 in FY 66, 1 in FY 67

Sylvania (AFS 2) — French Navy, 1979

D: 16,240 tons (fl) **S:** 20 kts **Dim:** 177.08 (161.54 pp) × 24.08 × 7.32
A: 4/76.2-mm DP (II × 2) — 2/UH-46 helicopters
Electron Equipt: Radar: 1/SPS-10 — TACAN: URN-20 (AFS 1: URN-6)
M: 1 set de Laval (AFS 6: Westinghouse) GT; 1 prop; 22,000 hp
Boilers: 3 Babcock & Wilcox; 40.8 kg/cm² pressure **Man:** 45 officers, 441 men

REMARKS: Helicopter platform and hangar. Four M-shaped cargo masts with constant-tension equipment; transfer from the supply ship to the receiving ship takes 90 seconds. Five holds (1 and 5 for spare parts, 3 and 4 for provisions, 2 for aviation parts) have only two hatches. Eleven hoists, which raise up to 5.5 tons, link the decks; several others feed into the helicopter area. Ten loading areas (five on each side) and palletized cargo help in the control of replenishment. There are four refrigerated compartments, and three for the storage of dried provisions. Some 25,000 types of spare parts are divided between 40,000 bins and racks and are accounted for by five data-processing machines. 16,567 m³ total stores volume. Quarters air-conditioned. Draw 2.7 m more aft than forward. One boiler always in reserve. Three

AUXILIARY SHIPS (continued)

additional units no longer planned. SPS-40 radar Mk 56 fire-control directors and two twin 76.2-mm mounts amidships removed. No longer planned to add Vulcan/Phalanx. Remaining twin gun mounts on the forecastle are enclosed.

◆ **1 former salvage ship** Bldr: Sun Ship, Chester, Pa.

AG 193 N. . . (ex-*Hughes Glomar Explorer*)   (In serv. 7-73)

AG 193—as Hughes Glomar Explorer   U.S. Navy

D: 63,300 tons (fl)   **S:** 10.8 kts   **Dim:** 188.6 (169.8 pp) × 35.3 × 14.3
M: 5 Nordberg 16-cyl. diesels, 6 GE electric motors; 2 props; 13,200 hp—6 side-thrusters
Man: 178 tot.

REMARKS: Built for the Central Intelligence Agency for the sole purpose of recovering a sunken Soviet Golf-class ballistic-missile submarine; given the "cover" role as a deep-sea mining ship (for which she was also useable) by the titular owners, the Summa Corporation. Transferred to Navy ownership in 9-76 and laid up at Suisun Bay, California, was chartered in June 1978 for thirteen months by Global Marine Corporation for deep-water mineral exploration. In late 1979 it was announced that she would be placed at the disposal of the National Science Foundation and would embark on a ten-year research program as a deep-sea drilling ship for the Ocean Marine Drilling Program. When conversion was completed, the ship would have been able to drill to depths of 6,100 meters beneath the sea floor while operating in 4,000-5,500 meters of water. The project was unfortunately not funded, and AG 193 was returned to the Navy 25-4-80 and transferred to the Maritime Administration for mothballing at Suisun Bay, California.

NOTE: *Compass Island* (AG 153), navigations systems trials ship, was decommissioned 1-5-80; on 4-9-80 the ship was transferred to the Maritime Administration for layup at James River, Va. AG 153's place was taken by *Vanguard* (T-AG 194), which is operated by the Military Sealift Command (see later page).

◆ **1 auxilary deep-submergence support ship** Bldr: Maryland SB & DD

	L	In serv.
AGDS 2 POINT LOMA (ex-*Point Barrow*, T-AKD 1)	25-5-57	28-2-58

Point Loma (AGDS 2)—flooded down   1977

Point Loma (AGDS 2)   G. Arra, 7-79

D: 9,415 tons (14,094 fl)   **S:** 18 kts   **Dim:** 150.0 × 23.8 × 6.7
Electron Equipt: Radar: 1/navigational, 1/SPS-10
M: 2 sets Westinghouse GT; 2 props; 6,000 hp   **Boilers:** 2 Foster-Wheeler
Man: 10 officers, 249 men, 8 scientists

REMARKS: Maritime Commission S2-ST·23A design. Built for Arctic supply and configured like a landing ship, dock (LSD). Served in MSC until 28-9-72, when placed in reserve. Transferred to the Navy on 28-2-74, renamed, renumbered, and reactivated as a tender for deep-submergence vehicles, recommissioning 30-4-75. Operates from San Diego for the Naval Ocean Science Center. Carries 275 tons of gasoline as flotation liquid for submersibles. Two traveling cranes. Second stack added for diesel-generator exhausts.

◆ **1 Raleigh-class auxiliary command ship**

	Bldr	Laid down	L	In serv.
AGF 3 LA SALLE (ex-LPD 3)	New York NSY	2-4-62	3-8-63	22-2-64
Authorized: FY 61				

AUXILIARY SHIPS (continued)

La Salle (AGF 3)—white-painted   PH1 R. Green, 1975

D: 8,040 tons (13,900 fl)   **S:** 21 kts   **Dim:** 158.4 (155.4 wl) × 25.6 × 6.4
A: 6/76.2-mm DP (II × 4)—2/20-mm Vulcan/Phalanx Gatling AA (I × 2)
Electron Equipt: Radar: 1/SPS-10, 1/SPS-40—TACAN: URN-20
       ECM: WLR-1, 4/Mk 36 SRBOC chaff
M: 2 sets de Laval GT; 2 props; 24,000 hp
Boilers: 2 Babcock & Wilcox; 42.2 kg/cm^2, 467°C
Man: 25 officers, 415 men + flag staff: 12 officers, 47 men

REMARKS: Ex-landing platform, dock (LPD). Since redesignated 1-7-72 employed as flagship of Commander, Middle East Force. Painted white. Well deck used for ship's boats. Helicopter hangar for one SH-3 built on flight deck, to port, with shelter for ceremonial activities to starboard. One Mk 56 and two Mk 63 gunfire-control systems removed 1977-78; lost one gun mount but gained two 20-mm Vulcan/Phalanx during major overhaul commencing 27-1-81.

NOTE: During *La Salle's* 1981-82 overhaul, she was temporarily relieved by *Coronado* (LPD 11), redesignated AGF 11 for the duration, and also painted white.

♦ 1 Dolphin class (SCB 207 type) research submarine

	Bldr	Laid down	L	In serv.
AGSS 555 DOLPHIN	Portsmouth NSY	9-11-62	8-6-68	17-8-69

Authorized: FY 61

D: 860/950 tons   **S:** 7.5/10 or 15 (see Remarks)   **Dim:** 50.29 × 5.92 × 4.9
Electron Equipt: Sonar: BQS-15, bow passive array, towed array, BQR-2
M: Diesel-electric, 2 GM 12V71 diesels; 1 prop; 1,650 hp
Endurance: 14 days (12 hours sub.)
Man: 3 officers, 26 men, 5 scientists

REMARKS: The pressure hull is a perfect cylinder, 5.49 m in diameter, strongly braced and closed at the forward and after ends by two hemispheric bulkheads. Used for deep-diving tests as well as acoustic and oceanographic experiments. Single torpedo

Dolphin (AGSS 555)   U.S. Navy

tube removed in 1970. Scientific payload of 12 tons. Using two 330-cell, 250-volt, lead-acid batteries, 10 knots can be reached when submerged; when silver-zinc batteries are substituted, the speed is 15 knots. Very quiet machinery. Has four minicomputers for scientific-data processing. Several scientific, passive multihydrophone arrays are fitted at the bow, and acoustic arrays can be towed at up to 4,000 feet behind the craft. Most support is shore-based. Home-ported at San Diego.

NOTE: The high-speed research submarine *Albacore* (AGSS 569), in reserve since 9-72, was stricken 1-5-80 for use as a target. The *Tang*-class submarine *Gudgeon* (SSAG 567, ex-SS 567) is employed for trials purposes; see combatant submarine pages.

♦ 1 hospital ship

	Bldr	Laid down	L	In serv.
AH 17 SANCTUARY	Sun SB & DD	. . .	15-8-44	20-6-45

Sanctuary (AH 17)   U.S. Navy, 1974

D: 11,141 tons (15,400 fl)   **S:** 18.3 kts   **Dim:** 158.5 (151.18 pp) × 21.79 × 7.32
Electron Equipt: Radar: 1/SPS-53, 1/SPS-10B
M: 1 set GE GT; 1 prop; 9,000 hp   **Electric:** 2,400 kw
Boilers: 2 Babcock & Wilcox, 31.7 kg/cm^2, 396°C
Fuel: 2,055 tons   **Man:** 70 officers, 460 men

AUXILIARY SHIPS (continued)

REMARKS: In reserve. Survivor of a class of six; built on C4-S-B2 cargo-ship hull. Converted 15-12-71 to 18-11-72 as a dependent support ship for service at Piraeus, Greece. Has 74-bed hospital that can be expanded to 300. In addition to medical facilities, had stores, entertainment facilities, etc. Could carry 50 officers and 120 enlisted medical personnel. Change in government in Greece canceled plan; decommissioned 28-3-74, having not filled intended purpose.

NOTE: Plans to convert the 33-kt., 38,000-ton former liner *United States* to a hospital and amenities ship to support the Rapid Deployment Force have been canceled, due to Congress having refused to authorize the advanced funds under FY 82. Conversion was to have been requested under FY 83 and would have been extremely expensive. *Sanctuary* (AH 17) is considered to be in too poor condition to recommission, and various smaller laid-up liners in U.S. ports have been examined as substitutes for *United States*. Two merchant ship conversion hospital ships have tentatively been programmed to be requested under the FY 83 and FY 84 budgets, for MSC operation.

♦ 5 (+4) Cimarron-class oilers (SCB 379 type)

	Bldr	Laid down	L	In serv.
AO 177 CIMARRON	Avondale SY	18-5-78	28-4-79	10-1-81
AO 178 MONONGAHELA	Avondale SY	15-8-78	4-8-79	5-9-81
AO 179 MERRIMACK	Avondale SY	16-7-79	17-5-80	14-11-81
AO 180 WILLAMETTE	Avondale SY	4-8-80	18-7-81	7-82
AO 186 PLATTE	Avondale SY	2-2-81	1-82	12-82

D: 26,110 tons (fl) **S:** 20 kts
Dim: 180.29 (167.64 pp) × 25.33 × 10.16 (11.35 prop)
A: 2/20-mm Vulcan/Phalanx AA (I × 2)
Electron Equipt: Radar: 1/LN-66, 1/SPS-55
M: 1 set GT; 1 prop; 24,000 hp **Electric:** 8,250 kw
Boilers: 2 Combustion Engineering; 42.25 kg/cm², 454°C
Man: 11 officers, 124 men

REMARKS: Will carry 72,000 barrels fuel oil, 48,000 barrels JP-5 gas turbine fuel, and will be able to replenish ships while making 15 knots. Mk 36 SRBOC chaff rocket system will be added, and there will be a helicopter platform aft. Four constant-tension replenishment stations to port, three to starboard. Will be able to transfer 408,000 liters of fuel oil and 245,000 liters JP-5 per hour. No additional units planned; subsequent oilers will be under Military Sealift Command control.

Cimarron (AO 177)　　　　　　　　　　　　U.S. Navy, 1981

♦ 3 Ashtabula-class oilers (SCB 244 jumbo type)
Bldr: Bethlehem Steel, Sparrows Point, Md.

	L	In serv.
AO 51 ASHTABULA	22-5-43	7-8-43
AO 98 CALOOSAHATCHEE	6-7-45	3-12-45
AO 99 CANISTEO	2-6-45	10-10-45

Cimarron (AO 177)—without Vulcan/Phalanx　　　　Avondale, 1981

Caloosahatchee (AO 98)　　　　　　　L. & L. Van Ginderen, 1979

AUXILIARY SHIPS (continued)

D: 34,750 tons (fl) **S:** 18 kts **Dim:** 196.3 × 22.9 × 9.6
A: 2/76.2-mm Mk 26 DP (I × 2) **Electron Equipt:** Radar: 1/SPS-10
M: 1 set GT; 2 props; 13,500 hp
Boilers: 4 Foster-Wheeler "K"; 31.7 kg/cm², 399°C **Man:** 13 officers, 287 men

REMARKS: Lengthened 27 m by insertion of new mid-body during 1960s. Two 76.2-mm removed, 1977-78, along with one Mk 52 and two Mk 51 GFCS. Carry 143,000 barrels of fuel, 175 tons of ammunition, and 100 tons of provisions. No helicopter deck. Last World War II-built oilers in regular naval service. AO 51 scheduled to decommission 30-9-82, and the other two will probably follow shortly thereafter.

◆ 4 Sacramento-class fast combat support ships (SCB 196 type)

	Bldr	Laid down	L	In serv.
AOE 1 SACRAMENTO	Puget Sound NSY	30-6-61	14-9-63	14-3-64
AOE 2 CAMDEN	New York SB	17-2-64	29-5-65	1-4-67
AOE 3 SEATTLE	Puget Sound NSY	1-10-65	2-3-68	5-4-69
AOE 4 DETROIT	Puget Sound NSY	29-11-66	21-6-69	28-3-70

Authorized: 1 in FY 61, 1 in FY 63, 1 in FY 65, 1 in FY 66

Camden (AOE 2)   G. Arra, 1980

Seattle (AOE 3)—with Mk 23 TAS on foremast, SLQ-32 ECM C. Dragonette, 1981

D: 19,200 tons light (53,600 fl) **S:** 26 kts **Dim:** 241.4 (215.8 pp) × 32.9 × 11.6
A: 1/Mk 29 launcher for Sea Sparrow (VIII × 1)—4/76.2-mm DP (II × 2)—2/UH-46 helicopters
Electron Equipt: Radar: 1/SPS-10, 1/SPS-53 (AOE 1 and AOE 2: 1/SPS-40 also), 1/Mk 91 Mod. 1
   ECM: WLR-1—TACAN: URN-20
M: GE GT; 2 props; 100,000 hp
Boilers: 4 Combustion Engineering, 42.2 kg/cm², 480°C
Range: 10,000/17 **Man:** 33 officers, 567 men

REMARKS: Sea Sparrow launcher and Mk 91 Mod. 1 control system with two directors replaced two twin 76.2-mm DP; two Mk 56 GFCS removed. The two remaining 76.2-mm gun mounts will be replaced by two 20-mm Vulcan/Phalanx. The gun mounts are enclosed in AOE 4. The SLQ-32 (V)3 ECM will replace WLR-1, and Mk 36 SRBOC chaff rocket system is being added. AOE 3 will be the first to get the Mk 23 TAS Mod. 2 (Target Acquisition System), which in these ships will be a stand-alone system employing the UYA-4 computer. Carry 177,000 barrels fuel plus 2,150 tons ammunition. 750 tons provisions. Helicopter hangar and flight deck for 2-3 UH-46 Sea Knight vertical-replenishment helicopters. Plans to build AOE 5 under FY 68 were canceled in 11-69. Turbines in AOE 1 and AOE 2 are from battleship *Kentucky* (BB 66). SPS-6 radar removed from AOE 3 and AOE 4. These important and very successful ships are scheduled to receive SLEP (Service Life Extension Program) modernization, beginning in FY 84.

NOTE: A new-design AOE is programmed, with the first to be requested under FY 85, one in FY 86, and two more under FY 87.

◆ 7 Wichita-class replenishment oilers (SCB 707 type) Bldr: General Dynamics, Quincy, Mass.

	Laid down	L	In serv.
AOR 1 WICHITA	18-6-66	18-3-68	7-6-69
AOR 2 MILWAUKEE	29-11-66	17-1-69	1-11-69
AOR 3 KANSAS CITY	20-4-68	28-6-69	6-6-70
AOR 4 SAVANNAH	22-1-69	25-4-70	5-12-70
AOR 5 WABASH	21-1-70	6-2-71	20-11-71
AOR 6 KALAMAZOO	28-10-70	11-11-72	11-8-73
AOR 7 ROANOKE	19-1-74	7-12-74	30-10-76

Authorized: 2 in FY 66, 2 in FY 67, 2 in FY 68, 1 in FY 73

Milwaukee (AOR 4)   L. & L. Van Ginderen, 9-81

Wabash (AOR 5)   G. Arra, 1980

AUXILIARY SHIPS (continued)

Kansas City (AOR 3)—Sea Sparrow launcher abaft stack, missile directors atop lattice towers

G. Arra, 1979

D: 37,360 tons (fl) **S:** 20 kts **Dim:** 200.9 × 29.3 × 10.1
A: 1/Mk 29 launcher for Sea Sparrow (VIII); AOR 4: 2/20-mm Vulcan/Phalanx AA (I × 2)—2/UH-46 helicopters
Electron Equipt: Radar: 1/LN-66 or SPS-53, 1/SPS-10, 1/Mk 91 Mod. 1
ECM: WLR-1, 4/Mk 36 SRBOC chaff—TACAN: URN-26
M: GE Gt; 2 props; 32,000 shp **Boilers:** 3 Foster-Wheeler
Range: 6,500/20; 10,000/17 **Man:** 27 officers, 363 men

REMARKS: Carry 175,000 barrels fuel (90,000 distillate fuel), 600 tons ammunition, 575 tons provisions. All except AOR 7 originally had no hangars flanking stack and had 4/76.2-mm DP. Several carried interim armaments of 2 or 4 single 20-mm AA after hangars were added. Still to be added (already done on AOR 4) are two Vulcan/Phalanx Gatling AA. SLQ-32(V)3 will replace WLR-1. As with AOE 1 class, they are to get the Mk 23 Mod. 2 TAS (Target Acquisition System) radar with associated UYA-4 computerized data system. The two Mk 76 radar directors for the Mk 91 Mod. 1 missile fire-control system are mounted atop tall lattice towers just forward of the stack. There are four stations for liquid transfer and two for solid transfer to port, three liquid and two solid to starboard; all have constant-tension devices.

◆ 4 Vulcan-class repair ships

	Bldr	Laid down	L	In serv.
AR 5 VULCAN	New York SB	26-12-39	14-12-40	16-6-41
AR 6 AJAX	Los Angeles SB & DD	7-5-41	22-8-42	30-10-42
AR 7 HECTOR	Los Angeles SB & DD	28-7-41	11-11-42	7-2-44
AR 8 JASON	Los Angeles SB & DD	9-3-42	3-4-43	19-6-44

Vulcan (AR 5)

J. Jedrlinic, 1981

D: 9,140 tons (16,380 fl) **S:** 19.2 kts **Dim:** 161.37 (158.5 pp) × 22.35 × 7.11
A: 4/20-mm AA (I × 4) **Electron Equipt:** Radar: 1/SPS-10, 1/SPS-53
M: 2 sets GT; 2 props; 11,000 hp **Electric:** 4,500 kw
Boilers: 4 Babcock & Wilcox; 28.2 kg/cm², 382°C
Fuel: 3,800 tons **Man:** 63 officers, 1,273 men

REMARKS: Very elaborately equipped repair facilities. Four 127-mm DP (I × 4) removed from all. The *Jason*, typed ARH 1 (heavy hull-repair ship), was redesignated as AR 8 in 1957.

NOTE: The sole surviving converted landing-ship-type small repair ship, *Sphinx* (ARL 24), remains on the Navy List in reserve, earmarked for possible foreign transfer. Sister *Indra* (ARL 37) was stricken on 1-12-77, but has been retained as an accommodations hulk.

◆ 0 (+5) ARS 50-class salvage ships Bldr: Peterson Bldrs., Sturgeon Bay, Wisc.

	Laid down	L	In serv.
ARS 50 N. . .	10-82	. . .	7-1-84
ARS 51 N. . .	2-83	. . .	4-84
ARS 52 N. . .	6-83	. . .	3-85
ARS 53 N. . .	12-83	. . .	7-85
ARS 54 N. . .	4-84	. . .	11-85

Authorized: 1 in FY 81, 2 in FY 82. Programmed: 1 in FY 83, 1 in FY 84

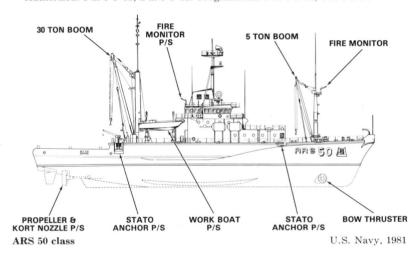

ARS 50 class

U.S. Navy, 1981

D: 2,880 tons (fl) **S:** 14 kts **Dim:** 77.72 (73.15 wl) × 15.24 × 4.72
A: 4/12.7-mm mg (II × 2) **Electron Equipt:** Radar: 1/SPS-55
M: 4 diesels, geared drive; 2 CP Kort-nozzle props; 4,200 hp
Electric: 2,250 kw **Man:** 87 tot.

REMARKS: First unit ordered 1981, with option for four more from same shipyard. Design developed from ARS 38. Will have 54-ton open-ocean bollard pull and, using beach extraction gear, will be able to exert 360-ton pull. Have 500-hp bow-thruster. 30-ton boom aft, 5-ton forward. Able to dead-lift 150 tons over bow or stern. Cargo hold 596 m³. Will be able to support hard-hat divers to 58 m and SCUBA divers; decompression chamber fitted. Up to 25 percent of crew may be women; 12 extra berths to be fitted. Three foam firefighting monitors.

AUXILIARY SHIPS (continued)

♦ **8 Diver- and Bolster-class salvage ships** Bldr: Basalt Rock Co., Napa, Calif.

	Laid down	L	In serv.
ARS 8 Preserver	26-10-42	1-4-43	11-1-44
ARS 21 Curb	1-1-43	24-4-44	12-5-44
ARS 33 Clamp	2-3-42	24-10-42	23-8-43
ARS 34 Gear	2-3-42	24-10-42	24-9-43
ARS 38 Bolster	20-7-44	23-12-44	1-5-45
ARS 39 Conserver	10-8-44	27-1-45	9-6-45
ARS 40 Hoist	13-9-44	31-3-45	21-7-45
ARS 41 Opportune	13-9-44	31-3-45	5-10-45
ARS 42 Reclaimer	11-11-44	25-6-45	20-12-45
ARS 43 Recovery	6-1-45	4-8-45	15-5-46

Recovery (ARS 43)—2 OE-82 SATCOMM antennas above pilothouse

Cellant/Premar II, 1980

D: 1,530 tons (1,970 fl) ARS 38 to ARS 43: 2,050 (fl) **S:** 14.8 kts
Dim: 65.1 × 12.5 × 4.0 (ARS 38 to ARS 43: 13.4 beam)
A: 2/20-mm AA (ARS 21, 33, and 34: none)
Electron Equipt: Radar: 1/LN-66, 1/SPS-53 or SPS-5
M: 4 Cooper-Bessemer GSB-8 diesels, electric drive; 2 props; 3,060 hp (2,440 sust.)
Electric: 460 kw **Fuel:** 300 tons
Range: 9,000/14; 20,000/7 **Man:** 6 officers, 77 men

REMARKS: Equipped for diver support, salvage, and towing. ARS 33 is in the Maritime Administration Reserve Fleet. ARS 34 is operated for the Navy by a private company. ARS 38, ARS 39, and ARS 42 re-engined with Caterpillar diesels. ARS 21 is on loan to a private company but does work for Navy if needed. ARS 8 transferred to Naval Reserve Force 1-11-79. *Escape* (ARS 6) reactivated from Maritime Administration reserve and transferred to Coast Guard 4-12-80.

♦ **5 L. Y. Spear-class submarine tenders (SCB 702 and 737 types)**

	Bldr	Laid down	L	In serv.
AS 36 L. Y. Spear	Gen. Dynamics, Quincy	5-5-66	7-9-67	28-2-70
AS 37 Dixon	Gen. Dynamics, Quincy	7-9-67	20-6-70	7-8-71
AS 39 Emory S. Land	Lockheed SB, Seattle	2-3-76	4-5-77	7-7-79
AS 40 Frank Cable	Lockheed SB, Seattle	2-3-76	14-1-78	5-2-80
AS 41 McKee	Lockheed SB, Seattle	14-1-78	16-2-80	15-8-81

Authorized: 1 in FY 65, 1 in FY 66, 1 in FY 72, 1 in FY 73, 1 in FY 77

Emory S. Land (AS 39)—with service boom extended over a **Los Angeles**-class submarine

J. Jedrlinic, 8-80

Frank Cable (AS 40)

U.S. Navy, 9-79

D: 13,000 tons (AS 36 and AS 37: 22,640 (fl), AS 39 to AS 41: 23,000 (fl)) **S:** 20 kts
Dim: 196.29 × 25.91 × 7.77 **A:** 4/20-mm AA (I × 4)
Electron Equipt: Radar: 1/SPS-10
M: 1 set de Laval GT; 1 prop; 20,000 hp **Electric:** 11,000 kw
Boilers: 2 Combustion Engineering; 43.6 kg/cm², 462°C
Man: AS 36 and AS 37: 96 officers, 1,252 men
AS 39 to AS 41: 50 officers, 1,108 men + flag staff: 75 officers, 44 men

REMARKS: Provide support to up to 12 submarines with up to 4 alongside at once, AS 39 to AS 41 being specifically tailored to the needs of the *Los Angeles* class. One

AUXILIARY SHIPS (continued)

30-ton crane and two 5-ton traveling cranes. Have a total of 53 specialized repair shops. Medical facilities include operating room, 23-bed ward, and dental clinic. AS 39 and later also carry 2/40-mm Mk 19 grenade launchers. Helicopter deck, but no hangar. AS 36 and AS 37 have General Electric turbines and Foster-Wheeler boilers. No longer planned to fit Vulcan/Phalanx or Sea Sparrow in later ships. Two 127-mm DP (I × 2) removed from AS 36 and AS 37. As 38 (FY 69) canceled 27-3-69. No other submarine tenders currently programmed.

♦ 2 Simon Lake-class submarine tenders (SCB 238 type)

	Bldr	Laid down	L	In serv.
AS 33 SIMON LAKE	Puget Sound NSY	7-1-63	8-2-64	7-11-64
AS 34 CANOPUS	Ingalls, Pascagoula	2-3-64	12-2-65	4-11-65

Authorized: 1 in FY 63, 1 in FY 64

Canopus (AS 34)   U.S. Navy, 1966

D: 12,000 tons [AS 33: 19,934 (fl) AS 34: 21,089 (fl)]   **S:** 18 kts
Dim: 196.2 × 25.9 × 8.7   **A:** 4/76.2-mm DP (II × 2)
Electron Equipt: Radar: 1/SPS-10   **M:** de Laval GT; 1 prop; 20,000 hp
Electric: 11,000 kw   **Boilers:** 2 Combustion Engineering; 43.6 kg/cm², 462°C
Man: AS 33: 90 officers, 1,338 men
         AS 34: 95 offices, 1,326 men

REMARKS: Specifically equipped to support nuclear-powered, ballistic-missile submarines, with 16 missiles stowed vertically amidships. Converted to carry Poseidon missiles, 1969-71. Both are to serve Trident-equipped SSBNs; AS 33 converted under FY 78, and AS 34 will convert under FY 84. Sister AS 35 canceled on 3-12-64. Two 30-ton cranes and four 5-ton traveling cranes. Helicopter deck aft, but no hangar. Two Mk 63 fire-control systems for guns removed.

♦ 2 Hunley-class submarine tenders (SCB 194 type)

	Bldr	Laid down	L	In serv.
AS 31 HUNLEY	Newport News SB	28-11-60	28-9-61	16-6-62
AS 32 HOLLAND	Ingalls, Pascagoula	5-3-62	19-1-63	7-9-63

Authorized: 1 in FY 60, 1 in FY 62

D: 10,500 tons (19,300 fl)   **S:** 19 kts   **Dim:** 182.6 × 25.3 × 7.4
A: 4/20-mm AA (I × 4)   **Electron Equipt:** Radar: 1/SPS-10
M: 10 Fairbanks-Morse 38D⅛ diesels, electric drive; 1 prop; 15,000 hp
Electric: 12,000 kw   **Man:** 144 officers, 2,424 men

REMARKS: Intended to support SSBNs; converted to carry Poseidon missiles, 1973-75. Air-conditioned. Helicopter platform. Original 32.5-ton rotating hammerhead gantry crane removed around 1970 and replaced by two 30-ton cranes.

Holland (AS 32)   U.S. Navy, 1971

♦ 1 Proteus-class submarine tender (SCB 190 conversion type) Bldr: Moore SB & DD, Oakland, Cal.

	Laid down	L	In serv.	Conv.
AS 19 PROTEUS	15-9-41	12-11-42	31-1-44	8-7-60

Proteus (AS 19)—prior to removal of 127-mm gun   1965

D: 10,250 tons (19,200 fl)   **S:** 15.4 kts   **Dim:** 175.1 × 27.3 × 8.2
A: 4/20-mm AA (I × 4)   **Electron Equipt:** Radar: 1/SPS-10
M: 8 GM 16-248 diesels, electric drive; 2 props; 11,200 hp
Man: 86 officers, 1,214 men

REMARKS: Lengthened 13.4 m, 1959-60, as the first SSBN tender, carrying Polaris missiles in the new section, handled by an extendable gantry crane. Superstructure enlarged over that of former sisters in the *Fulton* class. Served the *George Washington* and *Ethan Allen* class SSBNs in the Pacific.

♦ 3 Fulton-class submarine tenders

	Bldr	Laid down	L	In serv.
AS 11 FULTON	Mare Island NSY	19-7-39	27-12-40	12-9-41
AS 12 SPERRY	Mare Island NSY	1-2-41	17-12-41	1-5-42
AS 18 ORION	Moore SB, Oakland	31-7-41	14-10-42	30-9-43

D: 9,734 tons (18,000 fl)   **S:** 15.4 kts   **Dim:** 161.4 × 22.3 × 7.8
A: 4/20-mm AA (I × 4)
M: 8 GM 16-248 diesels, electric drive; 2 props; 11,200 hp   **Electric:** 6,700 kw
Fuel: 3,760 tons   **Range:** 15,600/10   **Man:** 1,286 to 1,937 men

REMARKS: All received FRAM-II modernization and can support nuclear submarines. Foundry can cast pieces up to 250 kg. Two 20-ton rotating cranes (as in *Dixie*-class ADs) are fitted. Sisters *Bushnell* (AS 15) stricken 15-11-80, *Howard W. Gilmore*

AUXILIARY SHIPS (continued)

(AS 16) decommissioned 30-9-80 and struck 1-12-80. *Nereus* (AS 17), long in reserve, was to strike by 30-9-82, and *Sperry* (AS 12) is scheduled to decommission 30-9-82, probably for scrapping.

♦ **2 Pigeon-class submarine-rescue ships (SCB 721 type)** Bldr: Alabama DD & SB, Mobile

	Laid down	L	In serv.
ASR 21 Pigeon	17-7-68	13-8-69	28-4-73
ASR 22 Ortolan	22-8-68	10-9-69	14-7-73

Authorized: 1 in FY 67, 1 in FY 68

Pigeon (ASR 21)   PHAN B. Trombecky, 1976

Ortolan (ASR 22)   G. Arra, 7-79

D: 3,411 tons (fl)   **S:** 15 kts   **Dim:** 76.5 × 26.2 × 6.5
A: 2/20-mm AA (I × 2)   **Electron Equipt:** Radar: 1/SPS-53
M: 4 Alco high-speed diesels; 2 props; 6,000 hp   **Range:** 8,500/13
   Man: 6 officers, 109 men + staff: 4 officers, 10 men + DSRV crew: 4 officers, 20 men

REMARKS: The catamaran hulls (7.92-m beam) are separated by 10.36 m. Diving bells and other salvage equipment are lowered between the two hulls by a moving crane. The ships can carry two small DSRV (Deep Submergence Rescue Vehicle) submarines, but as only two DSRV have been built, they normally have only one each—or none. Excellent lowering and handling equipment for up to 60 tons; divers to 260 m. Helicopter platform aft spans both hulls. Not considered to be successful ships, being overly complex and difficult to maneuver.

♦ **4 Chanticleer-class submarine-rescue ships** Bldr: Savannah Machine Foundry
   (ASR 9: Moore SB & DD, Oakland)

	Laid down	L	In serv.
ASR 9 Florikan	30-9-41	14-6-42	5-4-43
ASR 13 Kittiwake	5-1-45	10-7-45	18-7-46
ASR 14 Petrel	26-2-45	29-9-45	24-9-46
ASR 15 Sunbird	2-4-45	3-4-46	28-1-47

Kittiwake (ASR 13)   C. Dragonette, 1979

D: 1,653 tons (2,320 fl)   **S:** 14.9 kts   **Dim:** 76.7 × 13.4 × 4.9
A: 2/20-mm AA (I × 2)
M: 4 GM 12-278A diesels, electric drive; 1 prop; 3,000 hp
Electric: 460 kw   **Man:** 116-221 tot.

REMARKS: Carry a McCann rescue bell aft. All equipped for helium/oxygen diving. ASR 9 has Alco Model 539 diesels.

♦ **5 Abnaki and Achomawi* class fleet ocean tugs**

	Bldr	L	In serv.
ATF 105 Moctabi	Charleston SB & DD	25-3-44	25-7-44
ATF 110 Quapaw	United Eng., Alameda	15-5-43	6-5-44
ATF 113 Takelma	United Eng., Alameda	18-9-43	3-8-44
ATF 159 Paiute*	Charleston SB&DD	4-6-45	27-8-45
ATF 160 Papago*	Charleston SB&DD	21-6-45	3-10-45

D: 1,235 tons (1,640 fl)   **S:** 16.2 kts   **Dim:** 62.48 (59.44 pp) × 11.73 × 4.67
A: None   **M:** 4 diesels, electric drive; 1 prop; 3,000 hp
Electric: 400 kw   **Range:** 6,500/16; 15,000/8
Man: 4 officers, 47 men + Reserves: 3 officers, 33 men

REMARKS: All operated by the Naval Reserve Force. Developed from pre–World War II *Apache* class. ATF 105, ATF 110, and ATF 113 have four Busch-Sulzer BS-539

AUXILIARY SHIPS (continued)

Shakeri (ATF 162)—prior to transfer to Taiwan   G. Arra, 1979

diesels and a small-diameter funnel; the others have GM 12-278A diesels and a large funnel. Available in the Maritime Commission National Defense Reserve Fleet are the *Chippewa* (ATF 69), *Hopi* (ATF 71), *Moreno* (ATF 87), *Narragansett* (ATF 88), *Seneca* (ATF 91), *Tenino* (ATF 115), *Wenatchee* (ATF 118), and *Achomawi* (ATF 148). Five sisters serve in the U.S. Coast Guard, and the class can be found in many of the world's navies. *Shakori* (ATF 162) was decommissioned 15-3-80 and sold to Taiwan 29-8-80.

♦ **3 Edenton-class salvage and rescue ships** Bldr: Brooke Marine, G.B.

Authorized: 1 in FY 66; 2 in FY 67

	Laid down	L	In serv.
ATS 1 EDENTON	1-4-67	15-5-68	23-1-71
ATS 2 BEAUFORT	19-2-68	20-12-68	22-1-72
ATS 3 BRUNSWICK	5-6-68	14-11-69	19-12-72

Brunswick (ATS 3)—now fitted with OE-82 SATCOMM antennas atop pilothouse
G. Arra, 7-79

D: 2,650 tons (2,929 fl)   **S:** 16 kts   **Dim:** 88.0 (80.5 pp) × 1.53 × 4.6
A: 2/20-mm AA (I × 2)   **Electron Equipt:** Radar: 1/SPS-53
M: 4 Paxman 12 YLCM (900 rpm) diesels; 2 Escher-Wyss CP props; 6,000 hp
Man: 9 officers, 91 men

REMARKS: ATS 4 (FY 72) and ATS 5 (FY 73) canceled in favor of *Powhatan* class T-ATF. Can tow ships up to AOE 1-class size. 272-ton dead lift over the bow. 20-ton crane aft; 10-ton boom forward. Can conduct dives to 260 m. Powerful pumps and complete fire-fighting equipment. Equipped with bow-thruster.

♦ **1 Currituck-class guided-missile ship** Bldr: Los Angeles SB & DD Co., San Pedro

	Laid down	L	In serv.
AVM 1 NORTON SOUND (ex-AV 11)	7-9-42	28-11-43	8-1-45

Norton Sound (AVM 1)—showing SPY-1 Aegis radar installation   G. Arra, 7-79

Norton Sound (AVM 1)—Mk 26 launcher on starboard side aft   G. Arra, 7-79

D: 9,106 tons light (15,170 fl)   **S:** 19 kts
Dim: 164.72 (158.5 wl) × 21.11 × 7.16
A: 1/Mk 26 Mod. 0 launcher (II × 1, 24 Standard SM-1/2 MR missiles)—16/EX-41 VLS cells (see Remarks)
Electron Equipt: Radar: 1/SPS-53, 1/SPS-10, 1/SPS-40, 1/SPY-1A, 1/SPG-62—TACAN: URN-20
M: 2 sets Allis-Chalmers GT; 2 props; 12,000 hp
Boilers: 4 Babcock & Wilcox Express; 28.2 kg/cm², 366°C
Fuel: 2,300 tons

REMARKS: Ex-seaplane tender. Has served as a guided-missile trials ship since 1948. The prototype Aegis system was installed in 1975, with only forward, starboard "face" of the SPY-1A phased-array radar operational. SPS-40 replaced the unique, large-antenna SPS-52 variant radar in 1975. Helicopter landing pad between Mk 26 launcher and hangar. Refitted by Ingalls, Pascagoula, 1981, with 16-cell Martin-Marietta EX-41 VLS (Vertical Launching System) recessed into forecastle. Three

AUXILIARY SHIPS *(continued)*

of the cells are required for a telescoping replenishment-at-sea boom, leaving 13 cells for Standard, Harpoon, and Tomahawk missiles. Firing trials were due to begin 12-81.

◆ **1 Intrepid-class auxiliary-training aircraft carrier**

	Bldr	Laid down	L	In serv.
AVT 16 LEXINGTON	Bethlehem, Quincy	16-7-41	25-9-42	17-2-43

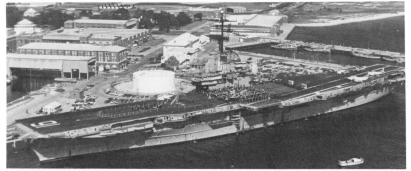

Lexington (AVT 16)   JO1 S. Auld, 1977

D: Approx. 33,000 tons (39,000 fl)   **S:** 30 + kts
Dim: 270.97 (249.94 wl) × 31.39 (58.5 flight deck) × 9.4
A: Removed (no aircraft permanently assigned)
Electron Equipt: Radar: 1/SPS-10, 1/SPS-43, 1/SPN-35, 1/SPN-43
                                 TACAN: URN-20
M: 4 sets Westinghouse GT; 4 props; 150,000 hp
Boilers: 8 Babcock & Wilcox; 41.7 kg/cm², 454°C
Fuel: 6,750 tons   **Range:** 18,000/12   **Man:** 75 officers, 1,365 men

REMARKS: Employed in deck-landing training at Pensacola, Fla. Was to have been stricken in FY 80 and replaced by the *Coral Sea* (CV 43) but has been extended in service through FY 89. On 29-12-68 number changed from CVS 16 to CVT 16; changed to AVT 16 on 15-7-78. Has two Type C11 Mod. 1 steam catapults, three elevators (one centerline forward; one at the forward end of the angled deck; and one to starboard, abaft the island), and four Mk 7 arrester wires. Flight deck composed of 76-mm-thick Douglas fir planking. All guns and fire-control equipment removed. Completed major overhaul 5-80; scheduled to receive a 12-month overhaul in 1984, during which time she will be replaced by *Coral Sea* (CV 41).

UNCLASSIFIED MISCELLANEOUS SHIPS

◆ **1 explosives damage-control barge** Bldr: Norfolk NSY (In serv. 1942)

IX 509 (ex-*Underwater Test Barge No. 1*, ex-YC. . .)

D: 3,000 tons (fl)   **Dim:** 56.1 ×. . . × 3.7

REMARKS: Operated for the Naval Ships Research and Development Center. Reclassified IX 509 on 1-12-79. Has a 60-ton crane.

◆ **1 satellite navigation systems trials craft**

IX 508 (ex-LCU 1618) Bldr: Gunderson Bros., Portland, Ore.

IX 508—as LCU 1618   LCDR J. Strada, 1978

D: 190 tons (390 fl)   **S:** 11 kts   **Dim:** 41.07 × 9.07 × 2.08
M: 4 GM 6-71 diesels; 2 Kort-nozzle props; 1,200 hp
Fuel: 13 tons   **Range:** 1,200/11   **Man:** . . .

REMARKS: Adapted 1978 for Naval Ocean Science Center, San Diego, to conduct trials with NAVSTAR global positioning system. Reclassified IX from LCU 1-12-79.

◆ **2 Admiral W.S. Benson-class barracks ships** Bldr: Bethlehem Steel, Alameda, Cal.

		L	In serv.
IX 507 GENERAL HUGH J. GAFFEY (ex-TAP 121, ex-*Admiral W.L. Capps*, AP 121)		. . .	18-9-44
IX 510 GENERAL WILLIAM O. DARBY (ex-TAP 127, ex-*Admiral W.S. Sims*, AP 127)		4-6-45	27-9-45

General William O. Darby (IX 510)—under tow to Philadelphia   J. Jedrlinic, 10-81

D: 12,657 tons light (22,574 fl)   **S:** 19 kts
Dim: 185.6 (174.65 pp) × 23.01 × 8.05
M: 2 sets GE GT, electric drive; 2 props; 18,000 hp   **Electric:** 2,400 kw
Boilers: 4 Combustion Engineering "D," 42.3 kg/cm², 449°C
Fuel: 3,840 tons   **Man:** Berthing for 499 officers, 1,577 men

REMARKS: Former troop transport transferred to the Army in 1946, reacquired by the Navy on 1-3-50 for MSC (then MSTS). Stricken on 9-1-69 and transferred to Maritime Commission Reserve Fleet. Partially reactivated and redesignated IX 507 on 1-11-78 for service at Bremerton NSY, Washington, as berthing ship for crew of CVN 65, undergoing overhaul. Will be in service into FY 83. IX 510 reclassified 10-81 and towed from James River, Virginia, reserve basin to Philadelphia Navy Yard for rehabilitation to act as barracks ship for *Iowa*-class battleships to be recommissioned. Propulsion plants not reactivated.

UNCLASSIFIED MISCELLANEOUS SHIPS *(continued)*

♦ **1 YFU 71-class trials tender** Bldr: Pacific Coast Eng., Co., Alameda

IX 506 (ex-YFU 82)

> **D:** 400 tons (fl) **S:** 8 kts **Dim:** 38.1 × 10.97 × 2.29
> **M:**. 4 GM 6-71 diesels; 2 props; 1,000 hp

REMARKS: Ex-harbor utility craft. Reclassified on 1-4-78 for service with Naval Ocean Systems Center, San Diego, to replace IX 505 (ex-YTM 759). Can carry 300 tons of cargo. Craft is now permanently attached to former barge YFN 816 as a work platform.

♦ **3 Benewah-class barracks ships** Bldr: Boston NSY

	Laid down	L	In serv.
IX 502 MERCER (ex-APB 39)	25-8-44	17-11-44	19-9-45
IX 503 NUECES (ex-APB 40)	2-1-45	6-5-45	30-11-45
IX 504 ECHOLS (ex-APB 37)	. . .	30-7-45	1-1-47

> **D:** 2,189 tons light (4,080 fl) **S:** 10 kts **Dim:** 100.0 × 15.2 × 3.4
> **M:** 2 GM 12-267 ATL diesels; 2 props; 1,600 hp
> **Man:** (when operational): 13 officers, 180 men + 26 officers, 1,200 troops

REMARKS: IX 502 and IX 503 recommissioned 1968 for service in Vietnam, placed back in reserve 1969-71; activated again in 1-11-75 as barracks ships at Puget Sound NSY. IX 504, in reserve since completion in 1947, activated 1-2-76 as a barracks ship for *Ohio*-class SSBN crews at General Dynamics, Groton. Propulsion plant inactivated. Eight 40-mm AA (IV × 2) removed.

♦ **1 test range support ship (ex-LSMR)** Bldr: Brown SB, Houston

	Laid down	L	In serv.
IX 501 ELK RIVER (ex-LSMR 501)	24-3-45	21-4-45	27-5-45

Elk River (IX 501) 1968

> **D:** 1,785 tons (fl) **S:** 11 kts **Dim:** 70.0 × 15.2 × 2.8
> **Electron Equipt:** Radar: 1/SPS-53
> **M:** 2 GM 16-278A diesels; 2 props; 2,800 hp **Man:** 25 men + 20 technicians

REMARKS: Former fire-support rocket ship converted 1967-68 at Avondale Shipyards, Westwego, Louisiana, to act as support ship at the San Clemente Island Range for the Navy deep-submergence diving program. 2.4-m bulges were added to her hull sides and a center well cut for lowering equipment through the hull. The well is straddled by a 65-ton traveling gantry crane. Thrusters added to allow accurate dynamic mooring. Tests diving procedures, equipment, and small diving vehicles.

♦ **1 sonar test barge**

IX 310 (no name) Actually, two barges moored in Lake Seneca, New York; subordinated to the Naval Underwater Sound Laboratory, Newport, Rhode Island. In service in 1971. IX 309, *Monob I*, is now numbered YAG 61.

♦ **1 U.S. Army FS 381-class torpedo-trials ship**

	Bldr	In serv.
IX 308 NEW BEDFORD (ex-AKL 17, ex-FS 289)	Martinolich SB, San Diego, Cal.	3-45

> **D:** 465 tons light (935 fl) **S:** 13 kts **Dim:** 54.10 (50.29 wl) × 9.75 × 3.05
> **A:** 1/324-mm TT **M:** 2 GM 6-278A diesels; 2 props; 1,000 hp
> **Electric:** 225 kw **Fuel:** 67 tons **Range:** 3,200/11

REMARKS: Operated by the Coast Guard for the Army during World War II; transferred to the Navy as a cargo ship on 1-3-50. Converted as a torpedo-trials ship in 1963. Operated by the Naval Torpedo Station, Keyport, Washington.

♦ **1 explosives-testing instrumentation ship**

IX 307 BRIER (ex-WLI 299)

> **D:** 178 tons (fl) **S:** 8.5 kts **Dim:** 30.5 × 7.3 × 1.6
> **M:** 2 GM diesels, electric drive; 2 props; 600 hp

REMARKS: Former Coast Guard inland buoy tender, built in 1943. Acquired on 10-3-69; redesignated on 29-8-70. Employed at Naval Ordnance Center, Solomons Island, Maryland, explosives-testing facility.

♦ **1 U.S. Army FS 330DC-class torpedo-trials ship**

	Bldr	In serv.
IX 306 (ex-FS 221)	Higgins Industries, New Orleans	1-45

> **D:** 460 tons (906 fl) **S:** 12 kts **Dim:** 54.81 × 9.75 × 4.32
> **A:** 1/533-mm TT **M:** 2 Enterprise diesels; 2 props; 800 hp
> **Electric:** 225 kw **Fuel:** 62 tons

REMARKS: Employed by the Army as a cargo ship until transferred to the Navy on 1-1-69 as a torpedo- and general-experimentation trials ship for the Naval Underwater Weapons Research and Engineering Center, Newport, R.I., at the Atlantic Underwater Test and Evaluation Center (AUTEC) in the Bahamas. Naval and civilian crew. Painted white with blue bow; torpedo-tube exits on starboard bow.

♦ **1 ocean construction platform** Bldr: Missouri Valley Br. & Iron, Ind.

	Laid down	L	In serv.
SEACON (ex-YFNB 33)	16-1-45	22-3-45	25-10-45

> **D:** 2,780 tons (fl) **S:** 7 kts **Dim:** 79.25 × 14.63 × 2.9
> **M:** 1 GM 12-71 diesel, 2 GM 6-71 diesels; 3 Voith-Schneider 14E/87 vertical cycloidal props; 1,020 hp
> **Electric:** 575 kw **Man:** 50 tot.

REMARKS: A large covered barge belonging to the Navy and used by NASA for transporting rockets, the *Seacon* was converted 1974-76 to serve as a seagoing work ship for the Navy Ocean Engineering and Construction Project Office. Intended to be towed at up to 11 knots to work locations and then use own propulsion for precision maneuvering. Can be used to lay cable and has open work deck 40 × 14 aft. Unique in having no ship or yard-craft number.

UNCLASSIFIED MISCELLANEOUS SHIPS *(continued)*

♦ 1 LST 1-class missile range support ship

	Bldr	Laid down	L	In serv.
Ex-LST 399	Newport News SB & DD	28-9-42	23-11-43	4-1-43

D: 1,623 tons light (4,080 fl) **S:** 11.6 kts **Dim:** 99.98 × 15.24 × 4.29
M: 2 GM 12-567A diesels; 2 props; 1,700 hp
Electric: 300 kw **Fuel:** 590 tons **Man:** . . .

REMARKS: Former Military Sealift Command-operated tank landing ship, officially stricken 1-11-73. Re-acquired 25-11-80 to act as support ship for the Pacific Missile Test Range, Point Mugu, Cal.

EXPERIMENTAL CRAFT

♦ 1 BH 110-class Rigid Sidewall Surface Effect Trials craft

	Bldr	L	In serv.
. . . (ex-U.S.C.G. *Dorado*, WSES 1)	Bell-Halter, New Orleans	12-78	2-79

The BH 110 as USCG Dorado (WSES 1)   USCG, 1981

D: 100 tons light (150 fl) **S:** 40 kts **Dim:** 33.53 × 11.89 × 2.36 at rest/1.37 on cushion
A: 2/12.7-mm mg (during 1981 trials) **Electron Equipt:** Radar: 2/navigational
M: 2 GM 16V149 TI diesels for propulsion; 2 props; 3,200 hp, 2 GM 8V92 TI diesels for lift; 2 centrifugal fans; 900 hp
Electric: 60 kw **Range:** 300-500/35 on cushion **Man:** 4 tot.

REMARKS: Designed by Bell Aerospace-Textron and built by Halter Marine in a jointly financed effort. Leased 1-80 for one month by U.S. Coast Guard and then again for a longer trials period in 1981, commencing with a six-month joint USN/USCG operational evaluation from Key West. In early 1982 the ship was to come under U.S. Navy control, be stretched to 47.8 m overall by the builder, be re-engined to achieve 50-60-kt speeds, and have accommodations for 14 additional personnel added. Functions by trapping a fan-generated air bubble between the rigid sidewalls and rubber seals at bow and stern. Not amphibious.

♦ 1 propulsion trials craft

JUPITER II

Jupiter II   U.S. Navy, 9-80

REMARKS: Jupiter II is a 19.8-m workboat operated by the Naval Ships Research and Development Center, Annapolis, Md. On 23-9-80 the gas-turbine-powered craft began trials with a 300-kw superconducting electric propulsion motor, producing 6-7-kt speeds. A 2,250-kw superconducting motor was to be substituted late in 1981.

NOTE: Although it appears that there will not be any construction of large surface effect ships for the U.S. Navy, a small design effort continues to be funded by the Congress, which authorized expenditure of $5.0 million under the FY 82 budget to continue studies on designs of 1,500 tons and larger. The previous 3,000-ton surface effect ship program was terminated in 1979.

♦ 1 Aerojet General prototype surface effect ship

	Bldr	In serv.
SES 100A	Tacoma Boatbuilding	7-72

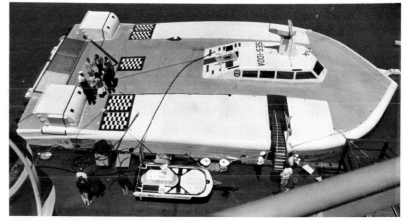

SES 100A—SES 100B model in foreground   A. Baker, 1976

D: 100 tons **S:** 76 kts **Dim:** 25.0 × 12.5 × . . .
M: 4 Avco TF-35 gas turbines (12,000 hp) driving two water jets and 3 lift fans
Man: 1 officer, 3 men, plus 6 technicians

EXPERIMENTAL CRAFT (continued)

REMARKS: A rigid-sidewall design developed in competition with Bell's SES-100B. Can carry 10 tons of test equipment.

♦ **1 Bell Aerospace prototype surface effect ship**

	Bldr	In serv.
SES 100B	Bell, Michoud, Louisiana	2-72

SES 100B at 40 knots   1973

D: 100 tons   **S:** 89 kts   **Dim:** 23.8 × 10.7 × . . .
M: 3 Pratt & Whitney FT-12 gas turbines; 2 props; 13,500 hp (with United Aircraft of Canada ST-6J-70 gas turbines (1,500 hp) driving 8 lift fans)
Man: 1 officer, 3 men, plus 6 technicians

REMARKS: Employed in 1976 in trials with vertically launched Standard-ARM antiship missiles while under way at 80 kts. Reached 89.48 kts on 30-6-76.

♦ **1 SWATH (Small Waterplane Area, Twin Hull) prototype**

SSP 1 KAIMALINO Bldr: U.S. Coast Guard, Curtis Bay, Md. (L: 7-3-73)

Kaimalino (SSP 1)   G. Arra

D: 190 tons (217 fl)   **S:** 25 kts   **Dim:** 27.1 × 13.7 × . . .
M: 2 T-64 gas turbines; 2 props; 5,000 hp

REMARKS: Catamaran hull with cigar-shaped flotation pontoons. Helicopter deck. Operated by the Naval Ocean Systems Center, Hawaii Laboartory. The SWATH concept shows great promise as an economical, high-performance/high endurance ASW ship, but has been hampered in its development by a lack of funding. Reported being lengthened and widened 1981-82, for new displacement of 600 tons.

♦ **3 Asheville-class engineering-trials ships** Bldr: Tacoma Boat building

	In serv.
ATHENA I (ex-*Chehalis*, PG 94)	11-8-69
ATHENA II (ex-*Grand Rapids*, PG 98)	9-5-70
ATHENA III (ex-*Douglas*, PG 100)	6-2-71

D: 225 tons (235 fl)   **S:** 40 kts   **Dim:** 50.14 × 7.28 × 2.9
M: CODOG: 1 GE 7LM-1500-PE 102 LM-1500 gas turbine (12,500 hp), 2 Cummins VT12-875M diesels (1,400 hp); 2 CP props
Electric: 100 kw   **Fuel:** 50 tons   **Range:** 325/37; 1,700/16

REMARKS: These craft are regarded as equipment and therefore do not have USN hull numbers. Operate from Mayport, Florida, for the Naval Ships Research and Development Center, Carderock. Have civilian crews and are disarmed. *Athena I* reclassified on 21-8-75, *Athena II* on 1-10-77, and *Athena III* in 1979. Have a 10-ton instrumentation payload.

♦ **1 gas-turbine engine-trials craft** Bldr: Sewart, Berwick, La.

PTF 25

D: 72 tons (102 fl)   **S:** 40 kts   **Dim:** 28.86 × 7.06 × 2.1
A: Removed   **M:** 2 Garrett GT PF 990 GT; 2 water jets; 6,000 hp
Man: . . .

REMARKS: Built in 1968. New engines, installed in 9-79, replace two Napier Deltic T18-37K diesels. Former fast patrol craft now to be used for propulsion trials for possible future small combatants. Aluminum construction. One 40-mm AA, two 20-mm AA (I × 2), and one 81-mm mortar removed. Sisters PTF 23, PTF 24, and PTF 26, stricken 1979, were to be sold to the Dominican Republic during 1982.

♦ **1 hydrofoil research craft** Bldr: Boeing/Martinac, Tacoma

	Laid down	L	In serv.
HIGH POINT (ex-PCH 1)	27-2-61	17-8-62	15-8-63

High Point (PCH 1)—at rest   Boeing, 1963

EXPERIMENTAL CRAFT (continued)

D: 110 tons (fl) **S:** 48 kts **Dim:** 35.0 × 9.4 × 1.8 (5.2, foils extended)
M: 2 Bristol-Siddeley/Rolls-Royce Proteus gas turbines; 4 props (paired, counter-rotating); 6,200 hp—2 Packard 2D850 diesels; 1 prop; 600 hp for hull-borne drive (12 kts)
Man: 1 officer, 12 men

REMARKS: Officially stricken 30-9-79 but retained as "floating equipment" for experimental purposes at Bremerton, Wash. Foils retract vertically: single forward set is steerable, while after pair each have a nacelle with a propeller at each end. A 40-mm AA and 4/324-mm Mk 32 ASW TT (I × 4, fixed) have been removed. Used for high-speed Harpoon SSM launch trials in 1973-74.

♦ **2 Cove-class former inshore minesweepers** Bldr: Bethlehem SY, Bellingham, Wash.

	Laid down	L	In serv.
MSI 1 COVE	1-2-57	8-2-58	20-11-58
MSI 2 CAPE	1-5-57	5-4-58	27-2-59

Cape (MSI 2) 1959

D: 200 tons (240 fl) **S:** 12 kts **Dim:** 34.1 × 7.1 × 3.0
M: 2 GM diesels; 2 props; 650 hp **Man:** . . . (civilians)

REMARKS: Wooden construction; sweep gear removed. MSI 1 has been operated by the Applied Physics Laboratory of Johns Hopkins University since 31-7-70. MSI 2 serves the Naval Ocean Systems Center, San Diego. Sisters operate as minesweepers in the Iranian and Turkish navies.

DEEP-SUBMERGENCE RESEARCH CRAFT

♦ **1 nuclear research submarine for deep diving**

	Bldr	Laid down	L	In serv.
NR-1	Electric Boat Co.	10-6-67	25-1-69	27-10-69

Authorized: FY 66

D: 400 tons surfaced/700 submerged **Dim:** 42.67 × 3.75 × 4.45
M: 1 pressurized-water reactor, turboelectric drive; 2 props
Man: 2 officers, 3 men, 2 scientists

REMARKS: Project approved 18-4-65. Fitted for all oceanographic missions, military and civilian, and for bottom salvage. Thick cylindrical hull. Wheels for moving on

NR-1 1969

ocean bottom. A very successful vehicle, but cost three times the original estimate. No periscope, uses television cameras. Four ducted maneuvering thrusters.

♦ **2 DSRV class** Bldr: Lockheed Missile & Space Co., Sunnyvale, Calif.

	In serv.	Accepted
DSRV 1 MYSTIC	6-8-71	4-11-77
DSRV 2 AVALON	28-7-72	1-1-78

D: 30.5 tons **S:** 5 kts **Dim:** 15.0 × 2.5 × . . .
M: 1 electric motor; 1 shrouded-pivoting prop; 15 hp **Man:** 3 tot.

REMARKS: The DSRVs are intended to: operate at a maximum depth of 3,500 feet (1,070 m); stand pressure equal to 9,000 feet (2,750 m); dive and rise at 100 feet a minute; make a maximum speed of 5 knots while submerged; remain submerged for 30 hours at 3 knots; maintain station in a 1-knot current; and operate all machinery even while submerged at a 45° angle. DSRVs can bring to the surface as many as 24 men at one time. Motor powered by a silver-zinc battery turns a regular propulsion propeller and two thrusters, one forward and one aft, which can be positioned to permit a close approach to a sunken object. Their size and weight were determined by the possible need to airlift them in an Air Force Starlifter (Lockheed C-141A) cargo plane. Additional equipment, especially a truck transport for the DSRV, would be carried in a second Starlifter. In addition, SSNs have received the equipment necessary to fasten a DSRV to their decks and carry it at 15 knots. The SSN will serve as a base for the DSRV while it awaits the arrival of a *Pigeon*-class rescue ship (ASR). Hull consists of two HY-140 steel spheres surrounded by a fiberglass outer hull.
A cost overrun of nearly 1,500 percent prevented the procurement of any more DSRVs. Twelve were originally planned. Names were assigned in 1977.

♦ **2 Turtle class** Bldr: General Dynamics, Groton, Conn.

DSV 3 TURTLE (ex-*Autec-I*)   DSV 4 SEA CLIFF (ex-*Autec-II*)

Sea Cliff and Turtle—at "launch" 1968

DEEP-SUBMERGENCE RESEARCH CRAFT (continued)

D: 21 tons **S:** 2 kts **Dim:** 7.9 (Sea Cliff: 9.1) × 2.4 (3.7 over thrusters)
M: 1 electric motor; 1 prop; 2 thrusters **Man:** 2 men + 1 scientist

REMARKS: Launched on 11-12-68. Could originally descend to 1,980 m. Spherical pressure hull of HY-100 steel. The *Turtle* was modified in 1979 to descend to 3,660 meters, and the *Sea Cliff* received a titanium pressure sphere in 1981-82, permitting 6,100-m descents. Air transportable. Fitted with external manipulator arms. Eight hours' endurance at 1 knot.

◆ **1 Alvin class** Bldr: General Mills, Minneapolis, Minn. (In serv. 1965)

DSV-2 ALVIN

D: 16 tons **S:** 2 kts **Dim:** 6.9 × 2.4 × . . .
M: Electric motors; 1 prop; 2 thrusters **Man:** 1 man + 2 scientists

REMARKS: Operated by civilian Woods Hole Oceangraphic Institute on contract to the Navy. Sank on 16-10-68 but raised, repaired, and returned to service in 11-72. Single titanium pressure sphere permits descents to 3,600 m. *Trieste* II (DSV 1) was stricken during 1980.

SERVICE CRAFT

NOTE: Few service craft are being built, and the force consists mostly of craft built during World War II. The units currently operational are listed below; those marked with an asterisk are non-self-propelled.

◆ **6 AFDB large auxiliary floating dry docks***

	Bldr	In serv.	Capacity (tons)
AFDB 1 ARTISAN	Pearl Harbor NSY	7-43	45,000
AFDB 2	Mare Island NSY	4-44	30,000
AFDB 3	Mare Island NSY	5-44	81,000
AFDB 4	Mare Island NSY	8-44	55,000
AFDB 5	Mare Island NSY	12-44	55,000
AFDB 7 LOS ALAMOS	Mare Island NSY	3-45	31,000

REMARKS: AFDB 1 and 2 were originally 10-section, 90,000-ton-capacity docks. Sections A, G, H, and I of AFDB 1 were stricken in 1978 and section F on 1-11-81, leaving 4 sections active at Subic Bay, the Philippines. Sections C, D, H, and I of AFDB 2 are active at Subic Bay, with the remainder in reserve at Pearl Harbor. AFDB 3, in Maritime Commission reserve, is a 9 section dock. The others were originally all 7-section docks. AFDB 4 and 5 are in reserve, while sections C, E, and G of ADFB 7 are active at Holy Loch, Scotland, in support of SSBNs; sections A and B are in reserve.

◆ **3 AFDL small auxiliary floating docks***

	Bldr	In serv.	Capacity (tons)
AFDL 1 ENDEAVOR	Chicago Bridge & Iron	9-43	1,000
AFDL 6 DYNAMIC	Chicago Bridge & Iron	3-44	1,000
AFDL 23 ADEPT	G.D. Auchter	12-44	1,900

REMARKS: All one-piece docks. *Diligence* (AFDL 48), built of concrete, and the only postwar unit, was commercially leased 23-3-80. *Reliance* (AFDL 47) had been reacquired 18-1-81 from Maritime Commission reserve but was returned 12-8-81. Twelve additional units (AFDL 8, 9, 12, 15, 16, 19, 21, 22, 25, 29, 40, and 41) are leased to commercial shipbuilders and ship repairers; AFDL 37, 38, and 45, long on lease, were sold outright 1-10-81.

◆ **4 AFDM medium auxiliary floating dry docks*** Bldr: Everett Pacific (AFDN 8: Chicago Bridge & Iron)

	In serv.		In serv.
AFDM 5 RESOURCEFUL	2-43	AFDM 7 SUSTAIN	1-45
AFDM 6 COMPETENT	6-44	AFDM 8 RICHLAND	12-44

REMARKS: All active and of 18,000-ton capacity. 189.6 × 37.8 m.

◆ **16 APL barracks craft***

APL 2, 4, 5, 15, 18, 19, 29, 31, 32, 34, 42, 43, 50, 54, 57, 58

REMARKS: Built 1944-45. All active. 2,660 tons (fl), 79.6 × 15.0 × 2.6.

◆ **2 ARD auxiliary repair dry docks*** Bldr: Pacific Bridge, Alameda, Cal.

ARD 5 WATERFORD (In serv. 6-42) ARD 30 SAN ONOFRE (In serv. 8-44)

REMARKS: Both active, 3,500-ton capacity. Sisters *West Milton* (ARD 7) to Maritime Commission for lay-up 16-7-81, ARD 24 stricken 15-1-80.

◆ **1 new-design submarine support dock** Bldr: Bethlehem Steel, Sparrows Pt., Md.

ARDM 4 SHIPPINGPORT (In serv. 1979)

Capacity: 7,800 tons (8,400 emergency) **Dim:** 150.0 × 29.3 × 16.6 (max.)

REMARKS: First U.S. Navy steel floating dry dock built since World War II. Has 20.7-m clear height inside. Requires shore support. Has 2/25-ton cranes. ARDM = Medium Support Dock.

◆ **3 ARD 12-class submarine support docks** Bldr: Pacific Bridge, Alameda, Cal.

	In serv.
ARDM 1 OAK RIDGE (ex-ARD 19)	3-44
ARDM 2 ALAMAGORDO (ex-ARD 26)	6-44
ARDM 3 ENDURANCE (ex-ARD 18)	2-44

Capacity: 3,500 tons **Dim:** 149.4 × 24.7

REMARKS: Converted from ARD auxiliary repair docks to service nuclear submarines. One end has a pointed, ship-type bow to permit towing.

◆ **1 YAG miscellaneous auxiliary** Bldr: Zenith Dredge Co., Duluth, Minn.

	Laid down	L	In serv.
YAG 61 MONOB (ex-IX 309, ex-YW 87)	1-12-42	3-4-43	11-11-43

D: 1,100 tons (fl) **S:** 7 kts **Dim:** 53.0 × 10.1 × . . .
M: 1 Union diesel; 1 prop; 560 hp

REMARKS: Used as a tender to Naval Mine Defense Laboratory, Panama City, Fla., since 5-69. Redesignated from IX 309 on 1-7-70.

◆ **229 YC open lighters***

REMARKS: Built 1915-77. Three are in reserve. Five new construction requested under FY 80. YC 1517 to YC 1522 built 1976-77, YC 1523-1527 built 1978-79. Three authorized under FY 82 budget. Six stricken 1980-81: YC 1385, 1413, 1456, 1460, 1461, 1462.

◆ **1 YCF car float***

YCF 16 (In serv. 25-1-42)

REMARKS: 45.72 × 10.21; used to transport railroad cars. Active.

SERVICE CRAFT (continued)

♦ 5 YCV aircraft transportation lighters*

YCV 8 (In serv. 4-3-44)   YCV 15 (In serv. 8-8-45)
YCV 10 (In serv. 21-8-44)   YCV 16 (In serv. 29-8-45)
YCV 11 (In serv. 6-10-44)

REMARKS: 28.96 × 9.14; 80-ton capacity. All active. YCV 9 stricken 15-8-80.

♦ 69 YD floating cranes*

REMARKS: Built 1913-70s. Sixty-two are active. YD 171, ex-German, has largest capacity: 350 tons. Most U.S. Navy YD are rectangular barges. Typical data: 1,630 tons (fl), 42.7 × 21.3, 90-100 tons capacity. One new YD authorized FY 82.

♦ 4 YDT diving tenders

YDT 3 (ex-YFNG 1): 205 tons (fl) 29.6 × 6.7 × 2.7; 1 Superior diesel, 400 hp (In serv. 12-41)
YDT 14 PHOEBUS (ex-YF 294), YDT 15 SUITLAND (ex-YF 336): 600 tons, 40.4 × 9.1, 1 Union diesel: 600 hp (In serv. 10-12-42 and 16-6-43, respectively)
YDT 16* TOM O'MALLEY (ex-YFNB 43): 2,000 tons (fl), 79.6 × 14.6

♦ 3 YF covered lighters, YF 852 class

	Bldr	L	In serv.
YF 862	Missouri Valley Bridge & Iron	8-10-45	2-11-45
YF 866 KODIAK	Missouri Valley Bridge & Iron	26-10-45	17-11-45
YF 885 KEYPORT	Defoe SB	19-5-45	4-8-45

D: 300 tons light (650 fl) **S:** 10 kts **Dim:** 40.5 × 9.1 × 2.7
M: 2 GM diesels; 2 props; 1,000 hp
Electric: 120 kw **Fuel:** 40 tons

REMARKS: YF 885 active at Torpedo Testing Station, Keyport, Washington, with **A:** 3/324-mm Mk 32 ASW TT; has "omnithruster" bow-thruster. Others in reserve.

♦ 6 YFB ferryboats

YFB 83

D: 500 tons (fl) **S:** 8.5 kts **Dim:** 49.4 × 17.7
M: 2 diesels **Cargo:** 500 passengers, 38 vehicles

YFB 87

D: 773 tons (fl) **Dim:** 54.9 × 18 **M:** 2 diesels

YFB 88 to YFB 91 (ex-LCU 1636, ex-LCU 1638 to LCU 1640)

D: 390 tons (fl) **S:** 10 kts **Dim:** 41.0 × 9.0
M: 4 GM diesels; 2 props; 1,200 hp

REMARKS: Built 1965-69. Modified 1969-70. All active.

♦ 1 YFD yard floating dry dock* Bldr: Pollock-Stockton SB, Cal. (In serv. 7-45)

YFD 71 **Capacity:** 14,000-tons **Dim:** 182.3 × 36.0

REMARKS: In reserve. Six other YFD on loan to commercial activities (YFD 8, 23, 54, 68-70). YFD 83 (ex-AFDL 31) on loan to Coast Guard since 1-47.

♦ 159(+9) YFN covered lighters*

REMARKS: Built 1940-70s. 151 active. Majority are 685 tons (fl), 33.5 × 9.8. Large rectangular deckhouse. Nine authorized under FY 81. YFN 692 and 902 stricken 1980.

♦ 12 YFNB large covered lighters*

YFNB 5, 8, 25, 30, 31, 32, 34, 36, 37, 39, 41, 42

REMARKS: Built 1945. Ten active. All 831 tons light (2,780 fl), 79.2 × 14.6 × 2.9. Former YFNB 6 and 13, operated by Military Sealift Command, stricken 15-3-81.

♦ 2 YFND dry-dock companion craft*

YFDN 5 (ex-YFN 268; in serv. 3-2-41)   YFND 29 (ex-YFN 974; in serv. 28-8-45)

REMARKS: 170 tons (fl), 33.53 × 9.75, converted YFN. YFND 5 in reserve. YFND 28 stricken 15-7-80.

♦ 14 YFNX special-purpose lighters*

REMARKS: All active. Most converted YFN. Built 1943-45. YFNX 19 (a degaussing barge) stricken 18-6-81; given to Bureau of Indian Affairs. YFNX 34 reclassified YFN, 1981.

♦ 4 YFP floating power barges*

YFP 3   YFP 11   YFP 12

REMARKS: All converted YC, YFN. 33.5 × 9.7-m. YFP 12 in reserve.

YFP 14 INDUCTANCE (ex-Army BD 6235)

REMARKS: Built 1943-45. Transferred 1-10-77.

♦ 1 YFR refrigerated cargo lighter Bldr: Defoe SB (In serv. 28-9-45)

YFR 888 **D:** 650 tons (fl) **Dim:** 40.5 × 9.1 × 2.7 **M:** 2 GM diesels; 1,000 hp

REMARKS: In reserve.

♦ 6 YFRN refrigerated cargo lighters*

YFRN 385, 412, 997, 1235, 1256, 1257

REMARKS: Built 1941-44. Two active. Most 45.7 × 10.4, 340-ton capacity.

♦ 5 YFRT covered lighter range tenders

YFRT 287   YFRT 418   YFRT 451   YFRT 520   YFRT 523

D: 650 tons (fl) **S:** 10 kts **Dim:** 40.5 × 9.1 × 2.7 **M:** 2 GM diesels; 1,000 hp

REMARKS: YF converted for duties on weapon-trials range. YFRT 520 has 3/324-mm Mk 32 ASW TT (III × 1). YFRT 418 in reserve.

♦ 17 YFU harbor utility craft

YFU 50 (ex-LCU 1486): see LCU 1466 class data; in reserve

YFU 71, YFU 72, YFU 74 to YFU 77, YFU 79, YFU 81 (1967-68): Sisters to IX 506 (ex-YFU 82). All in reserve.

YFU 83, YFU 91, YFU 94, YFU 97, YFU 98, YFU 100 to YFU 102: All LCU 1610 class converted, except YFU 83, built for purpose. YFU 94 in reserve. Built 1955-68.

♦ 6 YGN garbage lighters*

YGN 69, 73, 80-83

SERVICE CRAFT *(continued)*

REMARKS: Most approx. 110 tons light (500 fl), 36.6 × 10.7 rectangular barges. Have hopper-type bottoms to permit dumping at sea. YGN 80-83, built 1970-71, are active.

♦ 2 YHLC salvage lift craft, heavy*

YHLC 1 CRILLEY   YHLC 2 CRANDALL

REMARKS: Ex-*Hiev* and ex-*Griep* purchased from Germany for Vietnam War duties. Built in 1940s. Now in the Maritime Commission reserve fleet, but remain Navy property.

♦ 5 YM dredge

YM 17   YM 32   YM 33   YM 35   YM 38

REMARKS: Characteristics vary. YM 32 and YM 33 in reserve. Built 1930s-. YM 37 stricken 15-7-81.

♦ 2 YNG gate craft*

YNG 11   YNG 17   **Dim:** 33.5 × 10.5

REMARKS: Built 1941 to tend harbor-defense nets.

♦ 16 YO fuel-oil lighters

YO 47 CASING HEAD

   D: 2,660 tons (fl)   **Dim:** 71.6 × 11.3 × 4.6
   M: 2 Enterprise diesels; 820 hp. In reserve

YO 106, YO 129, YO 174, YO 200, YO 202, YO 203, YO 220, YO 223 to YO 225, YO 230, YO 241 (ex-YOG 5), YO 251 (ex-YOG 72), YO 264 (ex-YOG 105)

   D: 1,400 tons (fl)   **Dim:** 53.0 × 9.8 × 4.1   **M:** 1-2 diesels; 560-640 hp

YO 153:

   D: 1,076 tons (fl)   **Dim:** 47.6 × 9.3 × 3.6   **M:** 1 diesel, 525 hp

REMARKS: Five in reserve. Built 1941-46. YO 171 sold to Peru 1-11-80.

♦ 7 YOG gasoline lighters

YOG 58, YOG 68, YOG 78, YOG 79, YOG 88, YOG 93, YOG 196 (ex-YO 196)

   D: 1,390 tons (fl)   **Dim:** 53.0 × 9.8 × 4.1   **M:** 1 or 2 diesels; 1 prop; 560-640 hp

REMARKS: Four in reserve. Built 1945-46. Carry aviation fuel. YOG 87 stricken 15-4-80.

♦ 13 YOGN gasoline barges*

REMARKS: Built 1943-71. All active. Carry aviation fuel.

♦ 50 YON fuel-oil barges

REMARKS: Built 1901-76. All active. Typical unit: 1,445 tons (fl); 50.3 × 12.0 × 2.7. Two new YON requested under FY 80. YON 255 and later (30 units) were built 1964-76. Five are ex-U.S. Army. YON 235 is ex-YW 73. YON 305, 306 acquired 9-79 from U.S. Army. Can carry a variety of fuels.

♦ 13 YOS oil-storage barges*

REMARKS: Built 1944-65. All active. Ten: 100 tons light; 24.4 × 10.4; others: 140 tons light; 33.5 × 10.4. YOS 34 (ex-Army OB61-2) acquired 1-9-79.

♦ 22 YP patrol craft

YP 654 to YP 675

   D: 60 tons (71 fl)   **S:** 13.3 kts   **Dim:** 24.51 × 5.72 × 1.6
   M: 2 GM 6-71 diesels; 2 props; 590 hp   **Man:** 2 officers, 8 men, 50 midshipmen

REMARKS: Built 1965-79. Used for navigation and maneuvering training at Naval Academy, Annapolis, and Naval Officer Candidate School, Newport. Not armed. YP 673 to YP 675 completed 1979 by Peterson Builders, Sturgeon Bay, Wisconsin.

♦ 5 YPD floating pile drivers*

YPD 37, 41, 42, 45, 46

REMARKS: Built 1943-65. YPD 42 in reserve. Most built on standard 24.4 × 10.4 barge hulls. YPD 32 stricken 15-10-80.

♦ 23 YR floating workshops*

REMARKS: Built 1941-45. Twenty-one active. Most 520 tons light (770 fl); 46.6 × 10.7 × 1.8. Differ in equipment.

♦ 4 YRB repair and berthing barges*

YRB 1, 2, 22, 25

REMARKS: All 33.5 × 9.1. Built 1940-45. Support submarines.

♦ 22 (+19) YRBM repair, berthing, and messing barges*

YRBM 1-6, 8, 9, 11-15, 20, 23-49

REMARKS: Built 1955-83. All active; support submarines and ships in overhaul. Marinette SB constructing YRBM 31 to YRBM 49 during 1979-83: 688 tons; 44.5 × 14.0 × 1.3; accommodations for 26 officers, 231 men. Have office, workshop, eating, and recreation spaces, 96-seat training theater, galley, etc.

♦ 4 YRDH floating dry dock workshops, hull*

YRDH 1, 2, 6, 7

REMARKS: Built 1946. YRDH 6 active. All converted YR: 770 tons (fl), 46.6 × 10.7 × 1.8.

♦ 4 YRDM floating dry dock workshops, machinery*

YRDM 1, 2, 5, 7

REMARKS: Built 1945-49. YRDM 5 active. All converted YR: 770 tons (fl), 46.6 × 10.7 × 1.8.

♦ 14 YRR radiological repair barges*

REMARKS: Built 1942-46. All active. Most converted YR: 770 tons (fl), 46.6 × 10.7 × 1.8. Before conversion, some served as YRDH/YRDM.

♦ 5 YRST salvage-craft tender*

YRST 1, 2, 3, 5, 6

REMARKS: Built 1942-44. All active. YRST 1 to YRST 3 former YDT, YRST 5 and 6 former YFNX.

♦ 6 YSD seaplane wrecking derricks

YSD 15, 39, 53, 63, 74, 77

SERVICE CRAFT (*continued*)

D: 270 tons (fl) **Dim:** 31.7 × 9.5 × 1.2
M: 2 Superior diesels; 2 props; 320 hp

REMARKS: Built 1941-45. Employed as 10-ton capacity, self-propelled cranes.

♦ **23 YSR sludge-removal barges***

REMARKS: Built 1932-46. Eighteen active. Most either 24.4 × 9.8 or 33.5 × 10.4.

♦ **81 YTB large harbor tugs (SCB 147/147A type)**

YTB 752 EDENSHAW	YTB 783 REDWING	YTB 810 ANOKA
YTB 753 MARIN	YTB 784 KALISPELL	YTB 811 HOUMA
YTB 756 PONTIAC	YTB 785 WINNEMUCCA	YTB 812 ACCOMAC
YTB 757 OSHKOSH	YTB 786 TONKAWA	YTB 813 POUGHKEEPSIE
YTB 758 PADUCAH	YTB 787 KITTANNING	YTB 814 WAXAHATCHIE
YTB 759 BOGALUSA	YTB 788 WAPATO	YTB 815 NEODESHA
YTB 760 NATICK	YTB 789 TOMAHAWK	YTB 816 CAMPTI
YTB 761 OTTUMWA	YTB 790 MENOMINEE	YTB 817 HYANNIS
YTB 762 TUSCUMBIA	YTB 791 MARINETTE	YTB 818 MECOSTA
YTB 763 MUSKEGON	YTB 792 ANTIGO	YTB 819 IUKA
YTB 764 MISHAWAKA	YTB 793 PIQUA	YTB 820 WANAMASSA
YTB 765 OKMULGEE	YTB 794 MANDAN	YTB 821 TONTOGANY
YTB 766 WAPAKONETA	YTB 795 KETCHIKAN	YTB 822 PAWHUSKA
YTB 767 APALACHICOLA	YTB 796 SACO	YTB 823 CANONCHET
YTB 768 ARCATA	YTB 797 TAMAQUA	YTB 824 SANTAQUIN
YTB 769 CHESANING	YTB 798 OPELIKA	YTB 825 WATHENA
YTB 770 DAHLONEGA	YTB 799 NATCHITOCHES	YTB 826 WASHTUENA
YTB 771 KEOKUK	YTB 800 EUFAULA	YTB 827 CHETEK
YTB 774 NASHUA	YTB 801 PALATKA	YTB 828 CATAHECASSA
YTB 775 WAUWATOSA	YTB 802 CHERAW	YTB 829 METACOM
YTB 776 WEEHAWKEN	YTB 803 NANTICOKE	YTB 830 PUSHMATAHA
YTB 777 NOGALES	YTB 804 AHOSKIE	YTB 831 DEKANAWIDA
YTB 778 APOPKA	YTB 805 OCALA	YTB 832 PETALESHARO
YTB 779 MANHATTAN	YTB 806 TUSKEGEE	YTB 833 SHABONEE
YTB 780 SAUGUS	YTB 807 MASSAPEQUA	YTB 834 NEWAGEN
YTB 781 NIANTIC	YTB 808 WENATCHEE	YTB 835 SKENANDOA
YTB 782 MANISTEE	YTB 809 AGAWAN	YTB 836 POKAGON

D: 286 tons (346 fl) **S:** 12.5 kts **Dim:** 33.05 × 9.3 × 4.14
M: 1 diesel; 1 prop; 2,000 hp **Range:** 2,000/12 **Man:** 12 tot.

REMARKS: Built 1959-75. YTB 752 to YTB 759 have a less-streamlined superstructure and are considered a separate class (SCB 147 type). All active. Three also built for Saudi Arabia.

♦ **8 YTL small harbor tugs**

YTL 422 YTL 431 YTL 434 YTL 438 YTL 439
YTL 583 YTL 588 YTL 602

D: 70 tons (80 fl) **S:** 8 kts **Dim:** 20.1 × 5.5 × 2.4
M: 1 Hoover, Owens, Rentschler diesel; 375 hp **Man:** 4 tot.

REMARKS: Built 1944-45. Four in reserve. All will probably soon be disposed of. Survivors of several hundred YTL 422 class; many still in foreign navies.

♦ **53 YTM medium harbor tugs:**

♦ **5 YTM 138 class**

YTM 149 TOKA YTM 151 KONOKA YTM 178 DEKAURY YTM 180 MADOKAWANDO YTM 189

D: 260 tons (310 fl) **S:** 12 kts **Dim:** 30.8 × 8.5 × 3.4
M: 1 Enterprise diesel; 1 prop; 820 hp **Man:** 19 tot.

REMARKS: Built 1943. YTM 178 active; others in reserve.

♦ **6 YTM 174 class**

YTM 252 DEKANISORA	YTM 359 PAWTUCKET	YTM 380 CHANAGI
YTM 381 CHEPANOC	YTM 382 COATOPA	YTM 383 COCHALI

D: 210 tons (320 fl) **S:** 12 kts **Dim:** 31.1 × 7.6 × 3.0
M: 2 GM diesels; 1 prop; 820 hp **Man:** 15 tot.

REMARKS: Built 1942-44. Two active, four in reserve.

♦ **2 YTM 265 class**

YTM 265 HIAWATHA YTM 268 RED CLOUD

D: 230 tons (310 fl) **S:** 12 kts **Dim:** 30.5 × 8.5 × 3.0
M: 1 Enterprise diesel; 1 prop; 820 hp **Man:** 14 tot.

REMARKS: Built 1942-43. Both in reserve.

♦ **15 YTM 364 class**

YTM 364 SASSABA	YTM 397 YANEGUA	YTM 405 CUSSETA
YTM 366 WAUBANSEE	YTM 398 NATAHKI	YTM 406 KITTATON
YTM 391 ITARA	YTM 399 NUMA	YTM 413 PORTOBAGO
YTM 394 WINAMAC	YTM 400 OTOKOMI	YTM 415 SECOTA
YTM 395 WINGINA	YTM 404 COSHECTON	YTM 417 TACONNET

D: 260 tons (310 fl) **S:** 10.5 kts **Dim:** 30.8 × 8.5 × 3.4
M: 2 Fairbanks-Morse diesels; 1 prop; 820 hp **Man:** 14 tot.

REMARKS: Built 1944-45. Nine active. *Ganadoga* (YTM 390) stricken 1-10-79; *Mecosta* (YTM 392) and *Pitamakan* (YTM 403) stricken 1-11-80. Similar YTM 496 (no name) stricken 1-11-81.

♦ **18 YTM 518 class**

YTM 521 NABIGWON	YTM 534 NADLI	YTM 547 YANABA
YTM 522 SAGAWAMICK	YTM 536 NAHOKE	YTM 548 MATUNAK
YTM 523 SENASQUA	YTM 542 CHEGODEGA	YTM 549 MIGADAN
YTM 524 TUTAHACO	YTM 544 YATANOCAS	YTM 701 ACOMA
YTM 526 WAHAKA	YTM 545 ACCOHANOC	YTM 702 ARAWAK
YTM 527 WAHPETON	YTM 546 TAKOS	YTM 704 MORATOC

D: 260 tons (310 fl) **S:** 11 kts **Dim:** 30.8 × 8.5 × 3.3
M: 2 GM diesels; 1 prop; 820 hp **Man:** 8 tot.

REMARKS: Built 1945-46. Sixteen active, two in reserve. *Etawina* (YTM 543) stricken 1-11-80.

♦ **1 ex-U.S. Army tug**

YTM 750 HACKENSACK (ex-Army LT 2089)

D: 470 tons (fl) **S:** 12 kts **Dim:** 32.6 × 8.0 × 4.5
M: 2 diesels; 1 prop; 1,200 hp

REMARKS: Active.

SERVICE CRAFT *(continued)*

◆ 2 YTM 760 class

YTM 760 MASCOUTAH (ex-YTB 772)   YTM 761 MENASHA (ex-YTB 773)

    D: 200 tons (fl)   **S:** 12 kts   **Dim:** 25.9 × 7.3 × 3.4   **Man:** 8 tot.
    M: 2 GM 6-71 diesels; 2 Voith-Schneider vertical cycloidal props; 450 hp

REMARKS: Built 1965-66. The U.S. Navy's only cycloidal-prop tugs. Both active.

◆ 4 YTM 764 class

YTM 768 APOHOLA (ex-YTB 502)   YTM 770 MIMAC (ex-YTB 507)
YTM 776 HIAMONEE (ex-YTB 513)   YTM 779 POCASSET (ex-YTB 516)

    D: 260 tons (350 fl)   **S:** 11 kts   **Dim:** 30.8 × 8.5 × 3.7
    M: 2 Enterprise diesels; 1 prop; 1,270 hp   **Man:** 8 tot.

REMARKS: Built 1945-46. Two active.

◆ 10 YW water barges

YW 83	YW 113
YW 86	YW 119
YW 98	YW 123
YW 101	YW 126
YW 108	YW 127

    D: 1,235 tons (fl)   **S:** 8 kts   **Dim:** 53.0 × 9.7 × 4.6
    M: 2 diesels; 1 prop; 560 hp   **Man:** 22 tot.

REMARKS: Built 1944-45. YW 113, YW 119, YW 123, YW 127 active; others in reserve. Same basic design as YO and YOG classes. YW 128 sold to Peru 1-11-80.

◆ 7 YWN water barges*

YWN 70, 71, 78, 79, 82, 147, 156

REMARKS: Built 1944-45. Five active. Most 220 tons light; 50.3 × 10.7 × 2.4.

NOTE: In addition to the above yard and service craft, all of which have hull numbers and are carried on the Navy List, there are more than 1,000 small craft that are listed as property. Among the larger of these are a class of torpedo retrievers:

    D: 110 tons light (165 fl)   **S:** 18 kts   **Dim:** 31.0 × 6.4 × 2.4
    M: 2 GM 12V-149 diesels; 2 props; 1,350 hp
    Fuel: 7 tons   **Range:** 1,920/10   **Man:** 15 tot.

REMARKS: Design based on PGM 59-class patrol boat. Ramp at stern. Stowage for 17 tons of recovered ordnance. Given unofficial retriever dog names, list unavailable. There are also a number of 19.8-m torpedo retrievers based on a patrol-craft design; the same design has also been built as an air/sea rescue boat.

San Onofre (ARD 30)—YFND 27 alongside   1970

YOG 89—YO and YW nearly identical

YFU 83   Defoe SB, 1971

YP 673   Peterson Builders, 1979

SERVICE CRAFT *(continued)*

Sustain (AFDM 7)—with YD 214 alongside   J. Jedrlinic, 1980

APL 57   J. Jedrlinic, 5-80

Shippingport (ARDM 4)—with special pier facilities   U.S. Navy, 1979

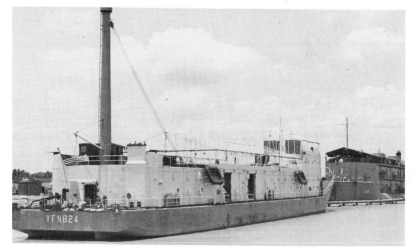

YFNB 24   1969

YRBM 31   Marinette Marine, 10-80

Mascoutah (YTM 760)—with old number   PH3 E. Pichette, 1964

SERVICE CRAFT (continued)

Dahlonega (YTE 770)   C. Dragonette, 1978

Crilley (YHLC 1)—outboard **Crandall (YHLC 2)**   J. Jedrlinic, 1980

YR 26   1969

31.1-m torpedo retriever   Peterson Builders, 1969

MILITARY SEALIFT COMMAND

This quasi-military organization was founded in 1949 as the Military Sea Transportation Service, and given its current name on 1-8-70. It is headed by a flag officer of the U.S. Navy, whose deputy and three area commanders are also flag officers. Its ships, which are not armed, are considered to be noncommissioned, and are manned by civilians, are described below in the order of their hull type numbers. The prefix "T" is appended to the hull numbers of its ships, whose missions are fleet support, transportation of bulk military cargo, and scientific research and survey.

NOTE: MSC ships are painted gray (AGOR/AGS: white) and have blue and gold-yellow stack bands. Fleet support replenishment ships operated by MSC began to carry their hull numbers during late 1979; other MSC ships do *not* display hull numbers. Oceanographic and hydrographic ships usually are painted white.

AMMUNITION SHIP

♦ 1 Kilauea class

	Bldr	Laid down	L	In serv.
T-AE 26 KILAUEA	Gen'l Dynamics, Quincy	10-3-66	9-8-67	10-8-68

Kilauea (T-AE 26)   G. Arra, 1980

AMMUNITION SHIP *(continued)*

D: 18,088 tons (fl) **S:** 20 kts **Dim:** 171.9 × 24.7 × 8.5
Electron Equipt: Radar: 1/navigational, 1/SPS-10
M: 1 set GE GT; 1 prop; 22,000 hp
Boilers: 3 Foster-Wheeler; 42.3 kg/cm², 467°C **Fuel:** 2,612 tons

REMARKS: Transferred to MSC 1-10-80; six sisters remain in Navy. Can carry about 6,500 tons of munitions and has a hangar and flight deck for two UH-46 replenishment helicopters.

STORES SHIPS

♦ **1 Rigel class**

	Bldr	L	In serv.
T-AF 58 RIGEL	Ingalls, Pascagoula	15-3-55	2-9-55

Rigel (T-AF 58)—now carries hull number   C. Martinelli, 1977

D: 7,950 tons (15,540 fl) **S:** 20 kts **Dim:** 153.0 × 22.0 × 8.8
Electron Equipt: Radar: 1/SPS-10, 1/Raytheon 1650/CX
M: 1 set GE GT; 1 prop; 16,000 hp **Boilers:** 2 Combustion Engineering
Range: 11,000/18

REMARKS: 10,781 grt/8,112 dwt. Twelve 10-ton booms. Cargo: 5,975 m³ dry, 5,400 m³ refrigerated. Transferred to MSC 23-6-75 and disarmed. Provides fleet support.

COMBAT STORES SHIPS

♦ **2 (+1) British Lyness-class combat stores ships** Bldrs: Swan Hunter & Wigham Richardson, Wallsend-on-Tyne, G.B.

	Laid down	L	In serv.
T-AFS 8 SIRIUS (ex-*Lyness*)	4-65	7-4-66	22-12-66
T-AFS 9 SPICA (ex-*Tarbatness*)	4-66	22-2-67	10-8-67
T-AFS 10 N. . . (ex-*Stromness*)	10-65	16-9-66	21-3-67

D: 9,010 tons light (16,792 fl) **S:** 19 kts **Dim:** 159.52 (149.35 pp) × 22.0 × 7.77
Electron Equipt: Radar: 1/Kelvin-Hughes 14/9, 1/Kelvin Huges 14/12
M: 1 Sulzer 8RD76 diesel; 1 prop; 12,800 hp **Electric:** 3,575 kw
Fuel: 1,310 tons heavy oil, 264 tons diesel
Range: 11,000/19; 27,500/12 **Man:** 116 civilians, 19 Navy

REMARKS: T-AFS 8 was leased from Great Britain 12-1-81 for one year for use in the Mediterranean and was to be purchased outright 1-82. T-AFS 9, which had been in reserve at Gibraltar, was leased 30-9-81 and is to be purchased 30-9-82. It is planned to purchase the third ship of the class, *Stromness*, which was to be laid up by the

Sirius (T-AFS 8)   G. Kürsener, 7-81

Royal Fleet Auxiliary late in 1981. 12,358 grt/4,744 nrt. Helicopter deck aft 33.5 × 18.3. Have four holds, with 15 levels, 8 stores elevators. Total cargo volume: 12,234 m³ (8,313 m³ dry stores, 3,921 m³ refrigerated/frozen). Cranes: 1/25-ton, 2/12.5-ton, 1/12-ton, and 2/5-ton. Accommodations for 193 total. Very successful, comfortable ships—a useful bargain.

HOSPITAL SHIPS

♦ **0 (+3) converted merchant ships (T-AH)**

REMARKS: Requests for design proposals were made in 1981 to naval architectural firms for conversion of three unnamed merchant ships to provide a total of 2,000 beds and 24 operating suites. Current program for one in FY 83 and one in FY 84.

MISCELLANEOUS RESEARCH SHIPS

♦ **1 Vanguard class** Bldr: Marine Ship Corp., Sausalito, Cal.

	L	In serv.
T-AG 194 VANGUARD (ex-T-AGM 19, ex-*Muscle Shoals*, ex-*Mission San Fernando*, T-AO 122)	23-11-43	21-10-47

REMARKS: For data see under T-AGM 20 on following page. *Vanguard* was converted 1964-66 from a T2-SE-A2-type tanker to a tracking and communications ship to support NASA manned space flights. Reclassified 30-9-80 as T-AG 194 while under conversion to replace *Compass Island* (AG 153) as ballistic-missile submarine navigational system trials ship for the Navy Strategic Systems Project Office. Conversion commenced 1-4-80 at Todd Shipyard, San Pedro, Cal. Appearance similar to *Redstone* (T-AGM 20) but without tracking radars.

♦ **1 Victory class** Bldr: California SB Corp.

	Laid down	L	In serv.
T-AG 164 KINGSPORT (ex-*Kingsport Victory*, AK 239)	1-44	24-5-44	12-7-44

D: 7,190 tons light (10,680 fl) **S:** 16.5 kts **Dim:** 138.7 × 18.9 × 6.7
M: 1 set Westinghouse GT; 1 prop; 8,500 hp
Boilers: 2 Babcock & Wilcox, 37 kg/cm², 399°C **Fuel:** 2,824 tons
Range: 20,000/16.5 **Man:** 13 officers, 42 men, 15 technicians

MISCELLANEOUS RESEARCH SHIPS *(continued)*

Kingsport (T-AG 164)   MSC, 1976

REMARKS: 7,607 grt/6,123 dwt. Acquired by the Navy on 1-3-50 as a cargo ship. Modified 1961-62 as a satellite-communications relay ship; reassigned to hydrographic research in 1966. Operated for Naval Electronics Systems Command. Helicopter deck aft.

RANGE INSTRUMENTATION SHIPS

♦ **1 Mariner class**

	Bldr	L	In serv.
T-AGM 23 OBSERVATION ISLAND (ex-AG 154, ex-YAG 53, ex-*Empire State Mariner*)	New York SB, Camden, N.J.	15-8-53	5-12-58

D: 16,076 tons (fl)   **S:** 20 kts   **Dim:** 171.6 × 23.27 × 9.1
M: 1 set GE GT; 1 prop; 22,000 hp
Boilers: 2 Combustion Engineering, 42.3 kg/cm², 467°C
Fuel: 2,652 tons   **Range:** 17,000/13
Man: 78 civilians + 60-65 technicians

REMARKS: Former ballistic-missile trials ship. Acquired by the Navy on 10-9-56; used for Polaris and Poseidon missile trials until placed in reserve on 29-9-72. Reclassified T-AGM 23 on 1-5-79. Converted between 7-79 and 4-81 to carry Cobra Judy (SPQ-11) missile-tracking, phased-array radar aft. Operated for the U.S. Air Force in the Pacific. Painted white.

Observation Island (T-AGM 23)—Cobra Judy array aft   Raytheon, 1981

♦ **1 converted Haskell-class attack transport** Bldr: Permanente Metals, Richmond, Cal.

	L	In serv.
T-AGM 22 RANGE SENTINEL (ex-*Sherburne*, APA 205)	10-7-44	20-9-44

Range Sentinel (T-AGM 22)   MSC, 1979

D: 11,860 tons (fl)   **S:** 15.5 kts   **Dim:** 138.7 × 18.9 × 8.8
Electron Equipt: Radar: 1/Raytheon TM 1650/9X, 1/Raytheon TM 1660/12S, 1/SPQ-7, 3/other tracking
M: 1 set GT; 1 prop; 8,500 hp
Boilers: 2 Combustion Engineering, 37 kg/cm², 399°C   **Fuel:** 1,197 tons
Range: 10,000/15.5   **Man:** 14 officers, 54 men, 27 technicians

REMARKS: 8,306 grt/5,301 dwt. Converted between 10-69 and 14-10-71 as support ship for the Poseidon (and later, Trident) program. Reclassified T-AGM 22 on 14-10-71. VC2-S-AP 5 Victory-type hull and propulsion.

♦ **1 Vanguard class** Bldr: Marine Ship, Sausalito, Cal.

	In serv.
T-AGM 20 REDSTONE (ex-*Johnstown*, ex-*Mission de Pala*, AO 114)	22-4-44

RANGE INSTRUMENTATION SHIPS (continued)

Redstone (T-AGM 20) MSC, 1980

D: 21,626 tons (fl) **S:** 16 kts **Dim:** 181.4 × 22.9 × 7.6
M: 1 set GE GT, electric drive; 1 prop; 10,000 hp
Boilers: 2 Babcock & Wilcox "D," 42.3 kg/cm², 440°C
Fuel: 3,995 tons **Range:** 27,000/16 **Man:** 20 officers, 71 men, 120 technicians

REMARKS: 16,060 grt/16,255 dwt. Former T2-SE-A2-type tanker converted 1964-66 to serve as tracking and communications ship for NASA manned space flights; 22 meters added amidships. Sister *Mercury* (T-AGM 21) stricken in 1969 after very little use, and sister *Vanguard* (T-AGM 19) redesignated T-AG in 1980. Two tracking radars, two large communications dish antennas.

♦ **2 General H. H. Arnold Class** Bldr: Kaiser, Richmond, Cal.

	In serv.	Conv.
T-AGM 9 GENERAL H. H. ARNOLD (ex-*General R. E. Callan*, T-AP 139)	8-8-44	1963
T-AGM 10 GENERAL HOYT S. VANDENBERG (ex-*General Harry Taylor*, T-AP 145)	8-5-44	1963

General H. H. Arnold (T-AGM 9) J. Jedrlinic, 1981

D: 16,600 tons (fl) **S:** 17 kts **Dim:** 168.5 × 21.8 × 7.9
Electron Equipt: Radar: 1/Raytheon TM 1650/12X, 1/Raytheon 1660/12X, 1/SPQ-7, 1/SPQ-8—TACAN: URN-20
M: 1 set Westinghouse GT; 1 prop; 9,000 hp
Boilers: 2 Babcock & Wilcox, 32.7 kg/cm², 407°C
Fuel: 2,685 tons **Range:** 18,000/17 **Man:** 21 officers, 71 men, 113 technicians

REMARKS: 12,848 grt/3,950 dwt. Converted C4-S-A1-class troop transports, originally under the Air Force but assigned to MSC in 7-64. Hangar and flight deck aft for meteorological balloons, *not* helicopters. Operate in Pacific. To strike soon.

NOTE: *Wheeling* (T-AGM 8) was stricken 31-10-80.

OCEANOGRAPHIC RESEARCH SHIPS

NOTE: *All* naval-owned oceanographic research ships are listed here, for convenience sake; those without "T" before their hull numbers are operated by private organizations, generally on naval-related research programs.

♦ **2 Gyre class (SCB 734 type)** Bldr: Halter Marine, New Orleans

	Laid down	L	In serv.
AGOR 21 GYRE	9-10-72	7-6-73	14-11-73
AGOR 22 MOANA WAVE	9-10-72	23-6-73	16-1-74

Moana Wave (AGOR 22)—temporary laboratory modules on working deck
G. Arra, 7-79

D: 950 tons (1,190 fl) **S:** 12.5 kts **Dim:** 53.14 × 11.05 × 3.05
M: 2 Caterpillar diesels; 2 CP props; 1,700 hp (plus 170-hp retractable maneuvering prop)
Man: 10 men plus 11 scientists

REMARKS: On completion, assigned to Texas A&M University and University of Hawaii, respectively. Modified oil-field supply ships using modular equipment vans on long, open fantail. AGOR 22 has been conducting trials since 1979 with the satellite communications and towed passive sonar equipment for the T-AGOS program, under contract to the Naval Electronics Command (NAVELEX); the SATCOMM antenna is mounted on a platform between the ship's paired stacks.

NOTE: The *Chain* (AGOR 17, ex-ARS 20) was stricken on 30-12-77.

♦ **1 Hayes class (SCB 762 type)** Bldr: Todd SY, Seattle

	Laid down	L	In serv.
T-AGOR 16 HAYES	12-11-69	2-7-70	21-7-71

D: 3,080 tons (fl) **S:** 15 kts **Dim:** 75.1 (67.0 pp) × 22.9 × 6.6
Electron Equipt: Radar: 1/Raytheon TM 1650/6X, 1/Raytheon TM 1660/12S Sonar: 1/3.5 kHz mapping, 1/16 kHz
M: 4 high-speed diesels; 2 CP props; 5,400 hp (plus 2/165-hp diesels for low-speed operations, 2 to 4 kts)
Electric: 850 kw **Fuel:** 368 tons
Range: 6,000/13.5 **Man:** 11 officers, 33 men, 30 scientists

OCEANOGRAPHIC RESEARCH SHIPS *(continued)*

Hayes (T-AGOR 16) 1977

REMARKS: 3,677 grt/393 dwt. Catamaran, each hull 7.3-m beam. Suffered at first from severe pitching problems. Numerous equipment-handling gallows up to 15-ton capacity. Extremely well equipped. Operated under the control of the Oceanographer of the Navy for the Office of Naval Research.

♦ **2 Melville class (SCB 710 type)** Bldr: Defoe SB, Bay City, Mich.

	Laid down	L	In serv.
AGOR 14 MELVILLE	12-7-67	10-7-68	27-8-69
AGOR 15 KNORR	9-8-67	21-8-68	14-1-70

Melville (AGOR 14)—blue hull, white superstructure 1970

D: 1,915 tons (2,080 fl)   **S:** 12.5 kts   **Dim:** 74.7 (67.0 pp) × 14.1 × 4.6
M: 2 Enterprise diesels; Voith-Schneider cycloidal props; 2,500 hp
Range: 10,000/12   **Man:** 9 officers, 16 men, 25 researchers

REMARKS: Operated for the Office of Naval Research, AGOR 14 by Scripps Institute, AGOR 15 by Woods Hole Oceanographic Institution. One vertical cycloidal propeller forward, larger unit aft; intended for precise maneuvering but, because mechanical rather than electric drive was used, have proven troublesome. AGOR 19 and AGOR 20 of this class were therefore canceled. AGOR 14 was placed in reserve 7-79 but reactivated 7-80.

♦ **7 Robert D. Conrad class (SCB 185 and 710* types)**

	Bldr	L	In serv.
AGOR 3 ROBERT D. CONRAD	Gibbs, Jacksonville	26-5-62	29-11-62
AGOR 4 JAMES M. GILLIS	Christy Corp., Wisc.	19-5-62	5-11-62
T-AGOR 7 LYNCH	Marinette, Wisc.	17-3-65	27-3-65
AGOR 9 THOMAS G. THOMPSON	Marinette, Wisc.	18-7-64	24-8-65
AGOR 10 THOMAS WASHINGTON	Marinette, Wisc.	1-8-64	27-9-65
T-AGOR 12 DE STEIGUER*	N.W. Marine, Portland	3-6-66	28-2-69
T-AGOR 13 BARTLETT*	N.W. Marine, Portland	24-5-66	31-3-69

Thomas Washington (AGOR 10)—long forecastle, less superstructure (number no longer carried) 1965

Robert D. Conrad (AGOR 3) 1978

D: 1,200 tons (1,380 fl)   **S:** 13.5 kts   **Dim:** 63.7 × 11.4 × 4.7 (6.3 m max.)
Electron Equipt: Radar: MSC units: 1/Raytheon 1650/SX, 1/Raytheon 1660/12S
M: 2 Caterpillar D-378 (T-AGOR 7-13: Cummins) diesels, electric drive; 1 prop; 1,000 hp
Electric: 850 kw   **Fuel:** 211 tons
Range: 12,000/12   **Man:** 9 officers, 17 men, 18 researchers

OCEANOGRAPHIC RESEARCH SHIPS *(continued)*

REMARKS: All civilian crews; 4 under Navy control, 3 under MSC. Assigned: AGOR 3: Lamont Geophysical Lab., Columbia U.; AGOR 4: in reserve at Beaumont, Texas, 18-3-81 (pending transfer to Mexico); T-AGOR 7: MSC for Oceanographer of the Navy; AGOR 9: U. of Washington for Navy; AGOR 10: Scripps Inst. of Oceanography; T-AGOR 12 and T-AGOR 13: MSC for Oceanographer of the Navy. Vary in details and paint (see photos). *Sands* (T-AGOR 6) on loan to Brazil, *Charles H. Davis* (T-AGOR 5) to New Zealand. Large stack contains 620-hp gas-turbine generator set used to drive main shaft at speed up to 6.5 kts for experiments requiring "quiet" conditions. Also have retractable electric bow-thruster/propulsor, which provides up to 4.5 kts.

♦ **2 Eltanin class** Bldr: Avondale Marine, New Orleans, La.

	L	In serv.
AGOR 8 ELTANIN (ex-*Islas Orcadas*, Q 9, ex-*Eltanin*, T-AGOR 8)	. . .	7-3-58
T-AGOR 11 MIZAR (ex-T-AK 272)	7-10-57	22-11-57

Mizar (T-AGOR 11)—new superstructure amidships, foremast struck

J. Jedrlinic, 4-81

D: 2,040 tons light (4,942 fl) **S:** 13 kts **Dim:** 81.1 × 15.8 × 6.9
Electron Equipt: Radar: T-AGOR 11: Raytheon TM 1650/6X, 1/Raytheon TM 1660/12S
M: 4 Alco diesels, Westinghouse motors; 2 props; 3,200 hp
Fuel: 675 tons **Range:** 14,000/12 **Man:** 11 officers, 30 men, 15 technicians

REMARKS: 2,486 grt/1,850 dwt. Former sisters to *Mirfak* (T-AK 271). Reclassified AGOR on 15-4-64. T-AGOR 11 operates for the Naval Electronics Command. Icebreaker hull; covered well on centerline for lowering equipment. AGOR 8 loaned to Argentina in 12-73 as *Islas Orcadas*, returned 1-8-79 and laid up at James River, Virginia; may be turned over to National Science Foundation or transferred abroad again.

NOTE: Also owned by the U.S. Navy but operated by civilian research organizations are the following small units: *Hoh* and *Onar*, operated by the University of Washington; *Edgerton*, operated by the Massachusetts Institute of Technology; a 16-m former buoy tender operated by the Massachusetts Maritime Academy; a 20-meter workboat operated by the University of Rhode Island; and an LCM(6)-class landing craft, operated by the University of Florida. Also operated on charter through the Military Sealift Command are several small research ships, including *Black Sea II*, *Energy Service I*, *Capt. Sandy II*, and *Empress*.

OCEAN SURVEILLANCE SHIPS

♦ **0 (+8 + 10) Stalwart class** Bldr: Tacoma Boat, Tacoma, Wash.

	Laid down	L	In serv.
T-AGOS 1 STALWART	5-82	12-82	5-83
T-AGOS 2 CONTENDER	9-82	. . .	. . .
T-AGOS 3 VINDICATOR	12-82	. . .	. . .
T-AGOS 4 TRIUMPH	83	. . .	. . .
T-AGOS 5 ASSURANCE	83	. . .	. . .
T-AGOS 6 PERSISTENT	83	. . .	. . .
T-AGOS 7 INDOMITABLE	83	. . .	. . .
T-AGOS 8 PREVAIL	83	. . .	. . .
T-AGOS 9 N. . .	. . .	. . .	. . .
T-AGOS 10 N. . .	. . .	. . .	. . .
T-AGOS 11 N. . .	. . .	. . .	. . .
T-AGOS 12 N. . .	. . .	. . .	. . .
T-AGOS 13 N. . .	. . .	. . .	. . .

Authorized: T-AGOS 1 and 2 in FY 79, T-AGOS 3 in FY 80, T-AGOS 4-8 in FY 81, T-AGOS 9-12 in FY 82. Programmed: T-AGOS 13 in FY 84, T-AGOS 14-15 in FY 86, T-AGOS 16-18 in FY 87.

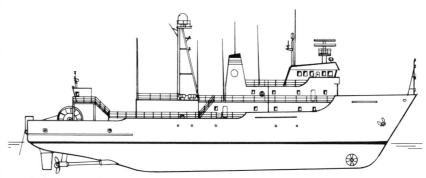

Stalwart (T-AGOS 1) A. D. Baker, 1981

D: 2,400 tons (fl) **S:** 11 kts **Dim:** 67.5 (62.1 wl) × 13.1 × 4.6
Electron Equipt: Radar: 2/navigational—Sonar: SURTASS

OCEAN SURVEILLANCE SHIPS *(continued)*

M: 4 Caterpillar D-348 800-hp diesels, electric drive; 2 props; 2,200 hp
Range: 6,000/11 + 6,400/3 **Man:** 9 officers, 11 men, 10 Navy technicians

REMARKS: Delays have been numerous, and costs have risen. Three were requested for FY 80, but only one was appropriated. The first three T-AGOS were not contracted for until 26-9-80. SURTASS (SURveillance Towed Array Sensor) is an 1,829-m linear, hydrophone array deployed over the ship's stern in a flexible, neutrally buoyant cable; the output from the SURTASS will be instantaneously relayed to shore monitoring stations via satellite communications, and the 10 Navy technicians are primarily for maintenance and backup. Main-engine motor/generator sets also supply ship's-service power; there is a 250-kw emergency generator. Will have passive roll stabilization. Intended to conduct ninety-day patrols and to be at sea 300 days per year, a goal likely not to be attained. FY 84 and later units may be of new design, employing SWATH hull technology.

SURVEYING SHIPS

♦ **0 (+2) converted C3-S-33a cargo ships (Programmed)**

	In serv.	Conv.
T-AGS 39 N. . . (ex-*Pride*, ex-*Mormacpride*)	1960	. . .
T-AGS 40 N. . . (ex-*Scan*, ex-*Mormacscan*)	1961	. . .

REMARKS: General data as for cargo ship sisters on later page. Both currently laid up at James River, Virginia. Programmed under FY 85 to convert both to replace T-AGS 21 and 22 as support survey ships for the SSBN program for sea-floor charting and magnetic mapping.

♦ **1 converted cargo ship (C4-SA type)** Bldr: National Steel, San Diego, Cal.

	L	In serv.
T-AGS 38 H.H. HESS (ex-*Canada Mail*)	3-65	16-1-78

H.H. Hess (T-AGS 38) MSC, 1978

D: 17,874 tons (fl) **S:** 21 kts **Dim:** 171.8 (160.93 pp) × 23.16 × 9.6
Electron Equipt: Radar: 1/Raytheon 1650/6X, 1/Raytheon 1660/12S
M: 1 set GE GT; 1 prop; 19,250 hp **Electric:** 1,400 kw
Boilers: 2 Foster-Wheeler, 43,3 kg/cm², 457°C
Fuel: 3,178 tons **Range:** 14,000/20 **Man:** 48 tot.

REMARKS: Mariner-type passenger-cargo ship acquired from the Maritime Administration on 9-7-76 for conversion to replace the *Michelson* (T-AGS 23) in the SSBN navigational support program. Retains original six cargo holds but most cargo booms removed. Converted National Steel and SB, San Diego, 3-77 to 1-78.

♦ **2 Chauvenet class (SCB 723 type)** Bldr: Upper Clyde SB, Glasgow, G.B.

	Laid down	L	In serv.
T-AGS 29 CHAUVENET	24-5-67	13-5-68	13-11-70
T-AGS 32 HARKNESS	30-6-67	12-6-68	29-1-71

Harkness (T-AGS 32)—twin helicopter hangar Pradignac & Léo, 1972

Chauvenet (T-AGS 29) MSC, 1980

SURVEYING SHIPS (continued)

D: 3,000 tons (4,200 fl) **S:** 15 kts **Dim:** 119.8 (101.8 pp) × 16.5 × 4.9
Electron Equipt: Radar: 1/Raytheon TM 1650/6X, 1/Raytheon TM 1660/12S
M: 2 Alco diesels, Westinghouse motor; 1 CP prop, 3,600 hp
Electric: 1,500 kw **Endurance:** 90 days **Fuel:** 824 tons **Range:** 15,000/12
Man: MSC: 13 officers, 56 men + Navy: 6 officers, 49 men + 12 civilian scientists

REMARKS: 2,890 grt/1,030 dwt. Very complete navigation and communications systems. Can carry four small survey launches; hangar and flight deck for two helicopters. Operated for the Oceanographer of the Navy; some naval personnel aboard. T-AGS 32, placed in reserve in early 1980, reactivated 1-10-80.

◆ 4 Silas Bent class (SCB 226, 725*, and 728† types)

	Bldr	L	In serv.
T-AGS 26 SILAS BENT	American SB, Lorain	16-5-64	23-7-65
T-AGS 27 KANE	Christy, Sturgeon Bay	20-11-65	19-5-67
T-AGS 33 WILKES*	Defoe, Bay City, Mich.	31-7-69	28-6-71
T-AGS 34 WYMAN†	Defoe, Bay City, Mich.	30-10-69	3-11-71

Kane (T-AGS 27)   Pradignac & Léo, 1977

D: 1,935 tons (2,420 to 2,558 fl) **S:** 15 kts **Dim:** 86.9 × 14.6 × 4.6
Electron Equipt: Radar: 1/Raytheon RM 1650/9X, 1/Raytheon TM 1660/12S
M: 2 Alco diesels, Westinghouse or GE motor; 2 CP props; 3,600 hp (plus 350-hp bow-thruster)
Fuel: 461 tons **Range:** 14,000/15 **Man:** 12 officers, 35 men, 30 scientists

REMARKS: Operated for Oceanographer of the Navy. T-AGS 33 has been in Ready Service since shortly after completion. T-AGS 34 is equipped with the Sperry SQN-17 BOTOSS (BOttom TOpography Survey System) for mapping depths to 4,000 m; the system consists of two planar transducer arrays and an HP 2100 computer, which averages the results of four separate passes through an area.

◆ 2 Bowditch class Bldr: Oregon SB, Portland, South Coast Co.

	L	Conv.
T-AGS 21 BOWDITCH (ex-South Bend Victory)	30-6-45	8-10-48
T-AGS 22 DUTTON (ex-Tuskegee Victory)	8-5-45	30-9-58

Dutton (T-AGS 22)

D: 14,512 tons (fl) **S:** 16.5 kts **Dim:** 138.76 (133.05 pp) × 18.98 × 7.62
Electron Equipt: Radar: 1/Raytheon TM 1650/9X, 1/Raytheon TM 1660/12S
M: 1 set GT; 1 prop; 8,500 hp
Boilers: 2 Combustion Engineering; 37 kg/cm², 399°C
Fuel: 2,824 tons **Range:** 20,000/16.5 **Man:** 14 officers, 47 men, 40 technicians

REMARKS: 7,783 grt/8,350 dwt. Victory-class cargo ships converted to support the SSBN program. Used for sea-floor charting and magnetic mapping. Sister Michelson (T-AGS 23) stricken in 1975. To be replaced circa 1986 by two converted C3-S-33a-type cargo ships.

CARGO SHIPS

◆ 14 converted merchant cargo ships (Programmed)

REMARKS: A Carter administration proposal to construct 14 new "Security" class, Maritime Commission C8-M-MA134j-type cargo ships for the Rapid Deployment Force was shelved in late 1981 by the Reagan administration, with the concurrence of Congress. Present plans call for the acquisition and alteration of 12-15 existing merchant cargo ships for the same purpose. The "Security" class would have displaced 48,860 tons (fl) with a cargo capacity of about 28,000 dwt. Dim: 253.4 × 32.2 × 9.1. Propulsion: diesel, 27,000 hp total, for 21 kts. A helicopter pad and stern vehicle ramp were provided, and the ships could have transported 4 powered and 6 unpowered vehicle causeways each. Some of the 12-15 ships to be acquired in their stead will be of the Maine class, described later.

NOTE: Conversion of a LASH (Lighter-Aboard-SHip) barge carrier for the Rapid Deployment Force, for which advanced procurement funds were initially requested under FY 82, is not to be proceeded with; the type was to have been designated T-ALS.

◆ 8 SL-7-class container cargo ships

	Bldr	In serv.	In Navy
T-AK 287 ALGOL (ex-Sea-Land Exchange)	Rotterdamse DDM, Rotterdam	5-73	13-10-81
T-AK 288 BELLATRIX (ex-Sea-Land Trade)	Rheinstahl Nord-seewerke, Emden	1973	13-10-81
T-AK 289 DENEBOLA (ex-Sea-Land Resource)	Rotterdamse DDM, Rotterdam	12-73	27-10-81
T-AK 290 POLLUX (ex-Sea-Land Market)	A.G. Weser, Bremen	9-73	16-11-81
T-AK 291 ALTAIR (ex-Sea-Land Finance)	Rheinstahl Nord-seewerke, Emden	9-73	-81
T-AK 292 REGULUS (ex-Sea-Land Commerce)	A.G. Weser, Bremen	3-73	27-10-81
T-AK 293 CAPELLA (ex-Sea-Land McLean)	Rotterdamse DDM, Rotterdam	10-72	1982
T-AK 294 ANTARES (ex-Sea-Land Galloway)	A.G. Weser, Bremen	9-72	1982

CARGO SHIPS *(continued)*

Sea-Land McLean—now Capella (T-AK 293)   Skyfotos, Ltd., 9-81

D: 51,795 tons (fl)   **S:** 33 kts   **Dim:** 288.38 (268.37 pp) × 32.16 × 10.57
M: 2 sets GE MST-19 GT; 2 props; 120,000 hp   **Electric:** 7,500 kw
Boilers: 2 Foster-Wheeler; 61.6 kg/cm², 507°C   **Fuel:** 5,527 tons
Range: 7,000/23   **Man:** 55 (as merchant ships)

REMARKS: 41,127 grt/28.095 dwt. Six acquired under FY 81 and two under FY 82, with the original intent of extensively converting them to serve as T-AKR, "Roll-on/Roll-off" vehicle cargo ships for the Rapid Deployment Force. Instead, under FY 82 Congress mandated that four be given a "partial" Ro/Ro conversion and the other four be given only a "mini-modification." Since these were non-self-unloading container cargo ships, the four "mini-mod" ships will have little, if any, military value. The ships are rendered even less useful through having been tailored to transport up to 1,086 nonstandard *35-ft.* containers (standard cargo containers are either 20 or 40 feet in length); 4,000 containers were purchased along with the first six ships, but unless the delivery point has specialized unloading equipment, they will be of little use to transport military cargo. These ships have proven expensive to operate for the former merchant owner, and their sophisticated propulsion plants have not been overly reliable. Up to 9,484 tons of salt-water ballast can be carried.

♦ **3 (+2) Northern Light class (C3-S-33a type)** Bldr: Sun SB & DD Co., Chester, Pa. (except ex-*Cape:* Todd SY, San Pedro, Cal.

	In serv.
T-AK 284 NORTHERN LIGHT (ex-*Cove*, ex-*Mormaccove*)	1961
T-AK 285 SOUTHERN CROSS (ex-*Trade*, ex-*Mormactrade*)	1962
T-AK 286 VEGA (ex-*Bay*, ex-*Mormacbay*)	14-10-60
T-AK. . . N. . . (ex-*Lake*, ex-*Mormaclake*)	1961
T-AK. . . N. . . (ex-*Cape*, ex-*Mormaccape*)	1961

D: 16,400 tons (fl)   **S:** 19 kts   **Dim:** 148.15 (139.59 pp) × 20.72 × 8.68
Electron Equipt: Radar: 1/Raytheon TM 1650/6X, 1/Raytheon TM 1660/12S
M: 1 set GE GT; 1 prop; 12,100 hp (15,700 emergency)   **Electric:** 1,275 kw
Boilers: 2 Combustion Engineering; 43.3 kg/cm², 457°C
Fuel: 2,556 tons   **Range:** 14,000/18   **Man:** 67 crew plus 7 naval

REMARKS: Approx. 9,260 grt/12,500 dwt. Former Moore-McCormack cargo liners laid up in the Maritime Administration's National Defense Reserve Fleet since the late 1970s. T-AK 284 acquired 22-4-80 and T-AK 285 on 30-4-80 to replace *Pvt. John R. Towle*, (T-AK 240) and *Pvt. Leonard C. Brostrom* (T-AK 255) as general cargo ships. Have 16,992 m³ bale dry cargo capacity and 1,133 m³ refrigerated cargo capacity.

Northern Light (T-AK 284)   MSC, 1981

Five holds, plus 10 deep tanks for liquid cargo. Have one 75-ton, 8 10-ton, and 10 5-ton cargo booms. Accommodations for 12 passengers.

    T-AK 286 (originally to have been renamed *King's Bay*) acquired 29-4-81 and placed on the Navy List on 15-10-81, is scheduled to recommission 30-10-82 after being converted to transport 16 Trident ballistic missiles in vertical cells in place of No. 3 hold. The *Cape* is expected to receive a similar conversion/activation under FY 85, while *Lake* is to be activated for a purpose not yet determined. Sisters *Pride* (ex-*Mormacpride*) and *Scan* (ex-*Mormacscan*) are scheduled to be converted to T-AGS 39 and T-AGS 40 under FY 84.

♦ **1 Andromeda class** Bldr: Moore DD, Oakland, Calif.

	L	In serv.
T-AK 283 WYANDOT (ex-T-AKA 92)	28-6-44	30-9-44

D: 7,430 tons light (14,200 fl)   **S:** 16.5 kts
Dim: 139.96 (132.59 wl) × 19.2 × 8.03
M: 1 set GE GT; 1 prop; 6,000 hp   **Electric:** 900 kw
Fuel: 1,503 tons   **Range:** 14,000/15.5

REMARKS: 8,895 grt/6,450 dwt. Cargo: 10,734 m³ dry/453 m³ refrigerated. Built as an attack cargo ship. Winterized for Arctic service. Renumbered T-AK 283 on 1-1-69. In Maritime Administration's reserve fleet at Suisun Bay, Cal.

♦ **3 Norwalk class**
    Bldr: Oregon SB, Portland (T-AK 281: Permanente, Richmond, Calif.)

	L	Conv.
T-AK 280 FURMAN (ex-*Furman Victory*)	18-5-45	7-10-64
T-AK 281 VICTORIA (ex-*Ethiopia Victory*)	28-4-44	15-10-65
T-AK 282 MARSHFIELD (ex-*Marshfield Victory*)	15-5-44	28-5-70

D: 6,700 tons light (11,150 fl)   **S:** 16.5 kts
Dim: 138.76 (133.05 pp) × 18.90 × 7.32
Electron Equipt: Radar: 1/Raytheon TM or RM 1650/6X, 1/Raytheon TM 1660/12S
M: 1 set GT; 1 prop; 8,500 hp   **Boilers:** 2; 37 kg/cm², 399°C
Fuel: 2,824 tons   **Range:** 20,000/16.5   **Man:** 80 to 90 tot.

CARGO SHIPS (continued)

Marshfield (T-AK 280)—note circular covers over missile cells on No. 3 hatch cover

U.S. Navy, 1978

REMARKS: 7,491 grt/9,649 dwt. Hold No. 3 accommodates 16 vertically stowed Poseidon or Polaris SLBMs to support SSBN activities. Have MARISAT SATCOMM systems. Carry torpedoes, submarine spares, etc.; also carry 18,000 barrels cargo fuel (7,566 bbl diesel/10,434 bbl fuel oil). 40-ton cargo booms. Small Navy security detachment aboard. *Norwalk* (T-AK 279) stricken 1-8-79. T-AK 280 was to have been stricken 20-9-81, but this was canceled 8-9-81 and the ship has been transferred to the Naval Electronics Command to be used in experimental work. The other two will eventually be replaced by converted C3-S-33a-type cargo ships.

♦ **1 Eltanin-class Arctic service**

	Bldr	L	In serv.
T-AK 271 MIRFAK	Avondale Marine, New Orleans, La.	5-8-57	30-12-57

Mirfak—while active

U.S. Navy, 1970

D: 2,022 tons light (4,800 fl) **S:** 13 kts **Dim:** 81.1 × 15.8 × 7.0
Electron Equipt: Radar: 1/Raytheon TM 1650/6X, 1/Raytheon TM 1660/12S
M: 4 Alco diesels, Westinghouse electric drive; 2 props; 2,700 hp
Fuel: 612 tons **Range:** 14,000/13 **Man:** 48 tot.

REMARKS: 2,486 grt/1,850 dwt. Maritime Administration C1-ME2-13a Type, intended for Arctic operations and having an icebreaker hull form. Cargo: 2,634 m³ dry/227 m³ refrigerated. Deactivated 11-12-79 and transferred to the Maritime Administration; remains Navy property and is laid up at James River, Virginia. Sisters *Eltanin* (AGOR 8, ex-AK 270) and *Mizar* (T-AGOR 11) were converted to serve as oceanographic research ships.

♦ **1 Victory class (VC2-S-AP3 type)** Bldr: Oregon SB, Portland

	Laid down	L	In serv.
T-AK 240 PVT. JOHN R. TOWLE (ex-*Appleton Victory*)	9-12-44	19-1-45	23-3-45

D: 6,700 tons light (12,450 fl) **S:** 17 kts
Dim: 138.76 (133.05 pp) × 18.9 × 8.69
M: 1 set GT; 1 prop; 8,500 hp (T-AK 254: 6,000 hp) **Electric:** 600 kw
Boilers: 2; 37 kg/cm², 399°C **Fuel:** 2,824 tons
Range: 20,000/16.5 **Man:** 49 tot.

REMARKS: 7,607 grt/dwt. Acquired from the Maritime Administration in 1950. Approx. 12,600 m³ dry cargo. T-AK 240 deactivated 25-8-80 and transferred to Maritime Administration; laid up at James River, Virginia. Four Navy-owned sisters, all in Maritime Commission reserve, were stricken 16-1-81: *Greenville Victory* (T-AK 237), *Sgt. Andrew Miller* (T-AK 242), *Sgt. Truman Kimbro* (T-AK 254), and *Lt. James E. Robinson* (T-AK 274).

NOTE: It has been proposed to reactivate 6 Maritime Commission-owned Victory cargo ships under the FY 83 Budget to act as military cargo prepositioning ships for the Southeast Asia area; these ships would presumably be operated by the Military Sealift Command with T-AK hull numbers.

♦ **2 Pvt. Leonard C. Brostrom class (C4-S-B1 type)** Bldr: Sun SB & DD, Chester, Pa.

	Laid down	L	In serv.
T-AK 255 PVT. LEONARD C. BROSTROM (ex-*Marine Eagle*)	5-12-42	10-5-43	18-9-45
T-AK 267 MARINE FIDDLER	15-12-44	15-5-45	31-8-45

Pvt. Leonard C. Brostrom (T-AK 255)

PH2 J. Brown, 3-80

D: 7,526 tons light (22,094 fl) **S:** 15.8 kts
Dim: 158.5 (153.3 pp) × 21.8 × 10.1
Electron Equipt: Radar: 1/Raytheon TM 1650/6X, 1/Raytheon 1660/12S
M: 1 set GE GT; 1 prop; 9,000 hp **Electric:** 900 kw

CARGO SHIPS (continued)

Boilers: 2 Babcock & Wilcox; 32.7 kg/cm², 399°C
Fuel: 2,052 tons   **Range:** 10,000/15.8   **Man:** 14 officers, 43 men

REMARKS: 11,164 grt/13,504 dwt. Cargo: 19,512 m³ dry cargo + 38,000 bbl. fuel oil. T-AK 255, acquired on 9-8-50, was deactivated 29-5-80 and placed in the Maritime Commission Reserve, Suisun Bay, Cal. T-AK 267, acquired on 7-2-52, is in the Maritime Administration's reserve fleet at James River, Va. Both converted 1954 to heavy-lift configuration, with two 150-ton-capacity booms.

NOTE: At any one time, the Military Sealift Command also has approximately 17 breakbulk general cargo ships under charter, operated by their owners. In 1981, two container cargo ships and two bulk cargo carriers were also under charter. The above are not included among the units chartered for the Rapid Deployment Force, listed later.

VEHICLE CARGO SHIPS

NOTE: The proposed 14-unit, T-AKR 14 "Security" (C8-M-MA134j-Type) vehicle cargo ship class was canceled in 9-81 by the Reagan administration, which instead proposes to acquire and convert 12-15 merchant cargo ships for the purpose. In 12-81, the Congress refused to fund conversion of the 8 SL-7 class container ships to full T-AKR configuration, and the ships will retain their T-AK numbers, which were to have been temporary.

♦ **2 (+2) Maine (C7-S-95a-Type) class** Bldr: Bath Iron Wks., Maine

	L	In serv.
T-AKR 10 MERCURY (ex-*Illinois*, ex-*Arizona*)	7-76	1977
T-AKR 11 JUPITER (ex-*Lipscomb Lykes*, ex-*Arizona*)	1-11-75	14-5-76
T-AKR 12 N. . . (ex-*Tyson Lykes*, ex-*Maine*)	24-5-75	27-5-76
T-AKR 13 N. . . (ex-*Charles Lykes*, ex-*Nevada*)	15-5-76	1977

Jupiter (T-AKR 11)   MSC, 1981

D: 33,765 tons (fl)   **S:** 23 kts (sust.)   **Dim:** 208.71 (195.07 pp) × 31.09 × 9.78
Electron Equipt: Radar: 1/Raytheon TM 1650/6X, 1/Raytheon TM 1660/12S
M: 2 sets GE GT; 2 props; 37,000 hp   **Electric:** 4,000 kw
Boilers: 2 Babcock & Wilcox; 77.5 kg/cm²   **Fuel:** 3,394 tons
Range: 10,000/23   **Man:** 55 tot.

REMARKS: 13,156 grt/19,172 dwt. T-AKR 10 acquired 14-4-80 and T-AKR 11 on 7-5-80. Have civilian contract crews, as part of the Rapid Deployment Force. T-AKR 12 is to be acquired under FY 83 and T-AKR 13 under FY 84. Capable of carrying container, as well as vehicle, cargo and can land helicopters amidships on upper deck; can also transport 728 tons liquid cargo. Two 15-ton cranes (paired) forward. A 7.3-m-wide by 24.4-m stern ramp is fitted, and there are two side loading doors also. Total bale cargo volume is 56,640 m³; vehicle cargo deck space is 16,258 m². There are plans to insert a 30.5-m plug in these ships to increase cargo capacity, enlarge the superstructures, and add a raised helicopter deck at the stern.

♦ **1 Meteor class (C4-ST-67a type)** Bldr: Puget Sound Bridge & DD

	Laid down	L	In serv.
T-AKR 9 METEOR (ex-*Sea Lift*, ex-*LSV 9*)	19-5-64	18-4-64	25-5-67

Meteor (T-AKR 9)—note stern ramp and side doors   L. & L. Van Ginderen, 9-81

D: 11,130 tons light (21,700 fl)   **S:** 22 kts   **Dim:** 164.7 × 25.5 × 8.8
Electron Equipt: Radar: 1/Raytheon TM 1650/6X, 1/Raytheon TM 1660/12S
M: 1 set GT; 2 props; 19,400 hp   **Boilers:** 2
Range: 10,000/20   **Man:** 62 tot.

REMARKS: 16,467 grt/12,326 dwt. Cargo: 10,200 tons: 26,819 m³ vehicle parking volume (7,896 m² deck space). Stern and four side ramps for Ro-Ro loading/unloading. Can carry 12 passengers. Authorized as T-AK 278, completed as T-LSV 9, retyped T-AKR 14-8-69. Renamed 12-9-75. Assigned to Rapid Deployment Force 4-80–6-81.

♦ **1 Comet class (C3-ST-14A type)** Bldr: Sun SB & DD, Chester, Pa.

	Laid down	L	In serv.
T-AKR 7 COMET	15-5-56	31-7-57	27-1-58

D: 7,605 tons light (18,150 fl)   **S:** 18 kts   **Dim:** 152.1 × 23.8 × 8.9
Electron Equipt: Radar: 1/Raytheon TM 1650/6X, 1/Raytheon TM 1660/12S
M: 1 set GE GT; 2 props; 13,200 hp   **Boilers:** 2 Babcock & Wilcox
Fuel: 2,423 tons   **Range:** 12,000/18   **Man:** 73 tot.

VEHICLE CARGO SHIPS (continued)

Comet (T-AKR 7)　　　　　　　　　　　　　　J. Jedrlinic, 1979

REMARKS: 13,792 grt/10,111 dwt. Cargo: 7,350 tons: more than 700 military vehicles in holds totaling 19,370 m³ volume (7.525 m² deck space). Side and stern ramps. Denny-Brown fin stabilizers. Authorized as T-AK 269, changed to T-LSV 7 on 1-6-63, then to T-AKR 7 on 1-1-69.

REPLENISHMENT OILERS

♦ 0 (+1+18+ . . .)

	Bldr	Laid down	L	In serv.
T-AO 187 N. . .	. . .	. . .	. . .	4-86
T-AO 188 N. . .	. . .	. . .	. . .	. . .
T-AO 189 N. . .	. . .	. . .	. . .	. . .
T-AO 190 N. . .	. . .	. . .	. . .	. . .
T-AO 191 N. . .	. . .	. . .	. . .	. . .

Authorized: T-AO 187 in FY 82. Programmed: 1 in FY 83, 3 in FY 84, 4 in FY 85, 4 in FY 86, and 6 in FY 87

D: 37,000 tons (fl)　**S:** 20 kts (sust.)　**Dim:** 192.0 × 29.0 × . . .
M: Diesel; 1 prop;. . . hp　**Range:** 6,000/20　**Man:** 96 tot. + 20 Navy

REMARKS: Cargo: 180,000 bbl liquid. Initially intended to be an MSC variant of the *Cimarron* class, designed to merchant standards, but the design has since grown. Will be equipped for underway replenishment of liquids and solids. Helicopter deck aft, no hangar. Design contract (Plans to be delivered in 18 months) to George Sharp, Inc., 11-7-80. A total of 20, to replace all earlier MSC-manned replenishment oilers, is planned.

♦ **6 Neosho class (SCB 82 type)**
Bldr: New York SB, Camden, N.J. (T-AO 143: Bethlehem, Quincy, Mass.)

	L	In serv.	To MSC
T-AO 143 NEOSHO	10-11-53	24-9-54	25-5-78
T-AO 144 MISSISSINEWA	12-6-54	18-1-55	15-11-76
T-AO 145 HASSAYAMPA	12-9-54	19-4-55	17-8-78
T-AO 146 KAWISHWI	11-12-54	6-7-55	1-10-79
T-AO 147 TRUCKEE	10-3-55	23-11-55	30-1-80
T-AO 148 PONCHATOULA	9-7-55	12-1-56	5-9-80

Mississinewa (T-AO 144)　　　　　　　　　　　J. Jedrlinic, 5-80

D: 11,600 tons light (38,000 fl)　**S:** 20 kts　**Dim:** 199.65 (195.07 wl) × 26.21 × 10.67
Electron Equipt: Radar: 1/SPS-10, 1/Raytheon TM 1650/6X or 12X
M: 2 sets GE GT; 2 props; 28,000 hp　**Electric:** 1,500 kw
Boilers: 2 Babcock & Wilcox; 42.2 kg/cm², 357°C
Fuel: 5,000 tons　**Man:** 105-200 tot.

REMARKS: 19,553 grt/36,840 dwt. Carry 180,000 bbl. liquid cargo (approx. 23,600 tons). Helicopter platform aft in all but T-AO 146 and T-AO 148. Operated by MSC as underway-replenishment ships for Navy. Transferred to MSC as a cost-saving measure (Navy crew was 360 total).

♦ **5 Mispillion class (jumboized T3-S2-A3 type)** Bldr: Sun SB, Chester, Pa.

	L	In serv.	To MSC
T-AO 105 MISPILLION	10-8-45	29-12-45	26-7-73
T-AO 106 NAVASOTA	30-8-45	27-2-46	13-8-75
T-AO 107 PASSUMPSIC	31-10-45	1-4-46	24-7-73
T-AO 108 PAWCATUCK	19-2-46	10-5-46	15-7-75
T-AO 109 WACCAMAW	30-3-46	25-6-46	24-2-75

Waccamaw (T-AO 109)—in light load condition　　　J. Jedrlinic, 1980

D: 11,000 tons light (33,750-34,179 fl)　**S:** 16 kts　**Dim:** 196.9 × 22.9 × 10.8
Electron Equipt: Radar: 1/SPS-10, 1/Raytheon TM 1650/6X
M: 2 sets Westinghouse GT; 2 props; 13,500 hp

REPLENISHMENT OILERS (continued)

Boilers: 4 Babcock & Wilcox; 32.7 kg/cm², 393°C
Fuel: 2,205 tons   **Man:** 110 tot.

REMARKS: 19,294 grt/23,250 dwt. Cargo: 107,000 bbl. fuel oil, diesel, etc. plus dry cargo. Fleet support units transferred from the Navy and intended for underway replenishment. Had four single 76.2-mm guns, but now disarmed. Helicopter deck forward. Replenishment station forward of bridge removed around 1980. All lengthened 28.3 m during the mid-1960s. T-AO 105 scheduled to be deactivated FY 81, but was extended.

♦ **2 Cimarron class (T3-S2-A1 type)** Bldr: Bethlehem, Sparrows Point, Md.

	L	In serv.	To MSC
T-AO 57 MARIAS	21-12-43	12-2-44	2-10-73
T-AO 62 TALUGA	10-7-44	25-8-44	4-5-72

Marias (T-AO 57)   1975

D: 24,450 tons (fl)   **S:** 18 kts   **Dim:** 168.56 × 22.86 × 10.1
Electron Equipt: Radar: 1/SPS-10, 1/Raytheon 1650/9X
M: 2 sets GT; 2 props; 13,500 hp   **Electric:** 950 kw
Boilers: 4 Foster-Wheeler; 31.7 kg/cm², 399°C
Fuel: 2,205 tons   **Man:** 107 tot.

REMARKS: 12,000 grt/18,400 dwt. Cargo: 87,000 bbl. fuel oil, diesel, etc. Fleet support ships intended for underway replenishment. Scheduled to strike 30-9-82, probably for foreign sale.

TRANSPORT OILERS

♦ **4 Falcon class** Bldr: Ingalls SB, Pascagoula, Miss.

	L	In serv.	Acquired
T-AOT 182 COLUMBIA (ex-*Falcon Lady*)	12-9-70	11-3-71	15-1-76
T-AOT 183 NECHES (ex-*Falcon Duchess*)	30-1-71	4-8-71	11-2-76
T-AOT 184 HUDSON (ex-*Falcon Princess*)	8-1-72	4-5-72	23-4-76
T-AOT 185 SUSQUEHANNA (ex-*Falcon Countess*)	2-10-71	13-1-72	11-5-76

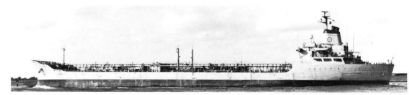

Susquehanna (T-AOT 185)—radome for MARISAT SATCOMM system atop bridge
G. Gyssels, 5-81

D: 45,877 tons (fl)   **S:** 16.5 kts   **Dim:** 204.9 (194.46 pp) × 27.13 × 11.13
Electron Equipt: Radar: 1/Raytheon TM 1650/6X, 1/Raytheon TM 1660/12S
M: 2 Colt-Pielstick 16PC-2V400, 16 cyl. diesels; 1 prop; 15,000 hp
Fuel: 2,620 tons   **Range:** 16,000/16.5   **Man:** 11 officers, 12 men

REMARKS: 20,571 grt/37,267 dwt. Cargo: 310,000 bbl fuels. Bareboat chartered to MSC in 1974, later purchased. Operated by civilian contractor. Redesignated T-AOT on 30-9-78.

♦ **1 Potomac class** Bldr: Ingalls SB, Pascagoula, Miss.

	Laid down	In serv.
T-AOT 181 POTOMAC (ex-*Shenandoah*, ex-*Potomac*, T-AO 150)	9-6-55	1-57/14-12-64

Potomac (T-AOT 181)—with MARISAT radome   J. Jedrlinic, 12-79

D: 35,000 tons (fl)   **S:** 18 kts   **Dim:** 189.0 × 25.5 × 10.4
Electron Equipt: Radar: 1/Raytheon RM 1650/6X, 1/Raytheon 1660/12S
M: 1 set GT; 1 prop; 20,460 hp   **Boilers:** 2
Fuel: 4,321 tons   **Range:** 18,000/18   **Man:** . . .

REMARKS: 15,739 grt/27,467 dwt. Carries 200,000 bbl fuel plus 878 m³ dry cargo. Originally belonging to the *Maumee* class, she was heavily damaged in 1961; only her stern was salvaged. Rebuilt by Sun SB & DD, Chester, Pa., and operated on charter to MSC as the *Shenandoah* from 1964 until purchased on 12-1-76. Operated by a civilian contractor. Reclassified T-AOT on 30-9-78.

TRANSPORT OILERS *(continued)*

♦ **9 Sealift class** Bldrs: First four: Todd, Los Angeles; others: Bath Iron Works

	L	In serv.
T-AOT 168 SEALIFT PACIFIC	13-10-73	14-8-74
T-AOT 169 SEALIFT ARABIAN SEA	26-1-74	6-5-75
T-AOT 170 SEALIFT CHINA SEA	20-4-74	9-5-75
T-AOT 171 SEALIFT INDIAN OCEAN	27-7-74	29-8-74
T-AOT 172 SEALIFT ATLANTIC	26-1-74	26-8-74
T-AOT 173 SEALIFT MEDITERRANEAN	9-3-74	6-11-74
T-AOT 174 SEALIFT CARIBBEAN	8-6-74	10-2-75
T-AOT 175 SEALIFT ARCTIC	31-8-74	22-5-75
T-AOT 176 SEALIFT ANTARCTIC	26-10-74	1-8-75

Sealift Pacific (T-AOT 168)—MARISAT radome atop bridge　　　G. Gyssels, 5-81

D: 33,000 tons (fl)　**S:** 16 kts　**Dim:** 178.92 (170.80 pp) × 25.61 × 10.50
Electron Equipt: Radar: 1/Raytheon TM 1650/6X, 1/Raytheon TM 1660/12S
M: 2 Colt-Pielstick, 14PC-2V400 14-cyl., 520-rpm diesels; 1 CP prop; 14,000 hp
Electric: 2,600 kw　**Fuel:** 3,440 tons
Range: 12,000/16　**Man:** 10 officers, 20 men, 2 cadets

REMARKS: 17,157 grt/27,217 dwt (vary slightly). Cargo: 225,154 barrels fuel oil, diesel, etc. Equipped with bow-thruster. MSC chartered these ships for twenty years and has a commercial contractor operating them. All redesignated T-AOT on 30-9-78. Hulls formerly black, now painted gray. One ship of the class is always attached to the Rapid Deployment Force.

♦ **1 American Explorer class (T5-S-RM2A type)** Bldr: Ingalls SB, Pascagoula, Miss.

	Laid down	L	In serv.
T-AOT 165 AMERICAN EXPLORER	9-7-57	11-5-58	27-10-59

American Explorer (T-AOT 165)—MARISAT radome atop bridge
L. & L. Van Ginderen, 4-81

D: 8,400 tons light (31,300 fl)　**S:** 20 kts　**Dim:** 187.5 × 24.4 × 9.8
Electron Equipt: Radar: 1/Raytheon TM 1650/6X, 1/Raytheon TM 1660/12S
M: 1 set GT; 1 prop; 22,000 hp　**Boilers:** 2 Babcock & Wilcox
Fuel: 3,482 tons　**Range:** 14,000/20　**Man:** 53 tot.

REMARKS: 14,984 grt/24,226 dwt. Cargo: 174,000 bbl fuel oil, diesel, etc. plus 878 m³ dry cargo. Operated by commercial firm. Retyped AOT on 30-9-78.

♦ **3 Maumee class (T5-S-12A type)**

	Bldr	Laid down	L	In serv.
T-AOT 149 MAUMEE	Ingalls SB	8-3-55	16-2-56	12-12-56
T-AOT 151 SHOSHONE	Sun SB, Chester	15-8-55	17-1-57	15-4-57
T-AOT 152 YUKON	Ingalls SB	16-5-55	16-3-56	17-5-57

Shoshone (T-AOT 151)

D: 32,000 tons (fl)　**S:** 18 kts　**Dim:** 189.0 × 25.5 × 9.8
Electron Equipt: Radar: 1/Raytheon TM 1650/6X, 1/Raytheon TM 1660/12S
M: 1 set GT; 1 prop; 20,460 hp　**Boilers:** 2 Combustion Engineering
Fuel: 4,321 tons　**Range:** 18,000/18　**Man:** 62 tot.

REMARKS: 15,626 grt/26,943 dwt. Cargo: 187,000 bbl fuel oil, diesel, etc. plus 878 m³ dry cargo. T-AOT 149 has ice-reinforced bow. Sister *Potomac* (T-AO 150, now T-AOT 181) rebuilt to different design. All retyped T-AOT on 30-9-78.

♦ **1 Mission class (T2-SE-A2 type)** Bldr: Marineship, Sausalito, Calif.

	Laid down	L	In serv.
T-AOT 134 MISSION SANTA YNEZ	9-9-43	19-12-43	13-3-44

D: 5,730 tons light (22,380 fl)　**S:** 16.5 kts　**Dim:** 159.7 (153.3 pp) × 20.7 × 9.4
M: 1 set GE GT, electric drive; 1 prop; 10,000 hp　**Electric:** 1,120 kw
Boilers: 2 Babcock & Wilcox; 42.2 kg/cm², 441°C
Fuel: 1,375 tons　**Range:** 13,000/14.5　**Man:** 52 tot.

REMARKS: 10,461 grt/17,056 dwt. Acquired by the Navy on 22-10-47. Cargo: 16,500 tons liquid (approx. 134,000 bbl). In reserve at Suisun Bay, Cal., since 6-3-75. Retyped T-AOT on 30-9-78.

♦ **5 Suamico class (T2-SE-A1 type)** Bldr: Sun SB & DD, Chester, Pa.

	Laid down	L	In serv.
T-AOT 50 TALLULAH (ex-*Valley Forge*)	. . .	25-6-42	5-9-42
T-AOT 67 CACHE (ex-*Stillwater*)	. . .	7-9-42	3-11-42
T-AOT 73 MILLICOMA (ex-*Conestoga*, ex-*King's Mountain*)	4-8-42	21-1-43	5-3-43
T-AOT 75 SAUGATUCK (ex-*Newton*)	16-9-42	7-7-42	19-2-43
T-AOT 76 SCHUYLKILL (ex-*Louisburg*)	24-9-42	16-2-43	9-4-43

D: 5,782 tons light (21,880 fl)　**S:** 15 kts　**Dim:** 159.7 (153.3 pp) × 20.7 × 9.4
M: 1 set GE GT, electric drive; 1 prop; 8,250 hp (T-AOT 67 and T-AOT 75: 1 set Westinghouse GT, electric drive; 1 prop; 6,600 hp)
Electric: 1,100-1,160 kw　**Boilers:** 2 Babcock & Wilcox, 42.2 kg/cm², 441°C
Fuel: 1,375 tons　**Range:** 13,000/14.5　**Man:** 52 tot.

REMARKS: 10,296 grt/16,500 dwt. Taken over by the Navy while under construction and completed as fleet oilers. Transferred to MSTS (later MSC) in 1949 and operated with civilian crews until placed in the Maritime Administration's reserve fleet be-

TRANSPORT OILERS (continued)

tween 1972 and 1975. Cargo: 141,000 bbl. All reclassified T-AOT on 30-9-78. Sister *Chepachet* (T-AOT 78) loaned to U.S. Department of Energy on 9-11-78 for five years for experiments with the OTEC (Ocean Thermal Energy Conversion) concept for electric-power generation. The ship was extensively altered and is no longer capable of acting as a transport oiler; permanently transferred 1-4-80.

CHARTERED TRANSPORT OILERS

NOTE: The Military Sealift Command charters several tankers for point-to-point transportation of liquid cargoes. These ships are operated by their owners, are not on the Navy List, and have no hull numbers.

♦ **0 (+2) Falcon I class** Bldr: Bath Iron Works, Bath, Maine

N. . . (In serv. 9-83)　N. . . (In serv. 2-84)

D: 28,200 grt/35,000 dwt　**S:** . . .　**Dim:** 203.0 ×. . . ×. . .
M: 2 de Laval Enterprise RV16 diesels; 1 prop; 14,720 hp

REMARKS: Ordered 19-1-81. Being built for Falcon Lines with the intention of long-term charter to MSC. Cargo: 225,000 bbl.

♦ **1 New York Sun class** Bldr: Sun SB, Chester, Pa.

	Laid down	L	In serv.
NEW YORK SUN	23-3-78	22-9-79	1-81

D: 19,000 grt/33,000 dwt　**S:** 15.5 kts
Dim: 186.50 (176.78 pp) × 27.43 × 11.27
M: 1 Mitsubishi-Sulzer, 122rpm 6 RND 76M diesel; 1 prop; 14,200 hp (sust.)
Fuel: 10,213 tons　**Range:** 12,000/15.5

REMARKS: Operated by Sun Transport; chartered 1-81 to MSC for 5 years. Cargo: 247,781 bbl. First U.S. ship to be powered by a low-speed diesel in 50 years. Sister *Philadelphia Sun* completed 17-7-81 but not chartered.

♦ **1 Spirit of Liberty class** Bldr:. . .

SPIRIT OF LIBERTY (In serv. 6-10-68)

D: 20,948 grt/38,238 dwt　**S:** 16.5 kts　**Dim:** 201.1 × 27.4 × 11.3
M: GT　**Fuel:** 2,776 tons　**Range:** 12,000/16.5 kts

REMARKS: Chartered on completion through 4-84 from owners, Charles Kurz & Co. Cargo: 271,400 bbl.

♦ **1 Maritime Commission T2-SE-A1 class** Bldr: Sun SB, Chester, Pa. (L: 11-44)

TEXAS TRADER (ex-*Texaco South Carolina*, ex-*South Carolina*, ex-*Diamond Island*)

D: 15,129 grt/27,500 dwt　**S:** 14.5 kts　**Dim:** 193.2 × 22.6 × 10
M: 1 set GE GT, electric drive; 1 prop; 10,000 hp
Boilers: 2 Combusion Engineering; 42 kg/cm², 440°C
Fuel: 2,017 tons　**Range:** 12,000/14.5

REMARKS: Chartered 11-80 through 11-85 from Ameican Trading Transportation Co. Cargo: 237,000 bbl. Stretched from original 159.6-m length in 1969 by Newport News SB & DD.

NOTE: Other merchant tankers may also be under charter from time to time.

GASOLINE TANKERS

♦ **2 Alatna class (T1-MET-24a type)** Bldr: Bethlehem, Staten I., N.Y.

	L	In serv.
T-AOG 81 ALATNA	1956	7-57
T-AOG 82 CHATTAHOOCHEE	4-12-56	22-10-57

Alatna (T-AOG 81)

D: 5,720 tons (fl)　**S:** 12 kts　**Dim:** 92.0 × 18.6 × 7.0
M: 4 Alco diesels, Westinghouse electric motors; 2 props; 4,000 hp
Fuel: 535 tons　**Range:** 5,760/10　**Man:** 51 tot.

REMARKS: 3,459 grt/4,933 dwt. Icebreaker-type hulls; originally intended as Arctic/Antarctic support ships. Cargo: 30,000 bbls light petroleum products. Both placed in the Maritime Administration's reserve fleet on 8-8-72; reactivation began 28-11-79 at National Steel, San Diego. Both returned to service 3-81 to replace T-AOG 77 and T-AOG 79. Received new diesel engines. Small helicopter deck aft.

♦ **1 Tonti class (T1-M-BT2 type)** Bldr: Todd SY, Houston, Texas

	Laid down	L	In serv.
T-AOG 78 NODAWAY (ex-*Tarcoola*)	19-2-42	15-5-45	11-9-50

D: 2,060 tons light (6,083 fl)　**S:** 10 kts　**Dim:** 99.1 × 14.7 × 5.9
M: 2 Nordberg diesels; 1 prop; 1,400 hp　**Electric:** 515 kw
Fuel: 154 tons　**Range:** 6,000/10　**Man:** 41 tot.

REMARKS: 3,160 grt/3,933 dwt. Cargo: 31,284 bbl light fuels (diesel, JP-5, gasoline). Sisters *Rincon* (T-AOG 77) and *Petaluma* (T-AOG 79) were stricken in 7-81 for foreign transfer and replaced by the reactivated T-AOG 81 and T-AOG 82.

TRANSPORTS

NOTE: The transports listed below are maintained in the Maritime Administration's reserve fleet but remain the Navy's property, earmarked for the MSC, should the requirement arise. Most were placed in reserve in 1969 and 1970.

♦ **1 Barrett class (P2-S1-DN3 type)** Bldr: New York SB, Camden, N.J.

	L	In serv.
AP 198 UPSHUR (ex-*President Hayes*)	19-1-51	20-12-52

TRANSPORTS *(continued)*

D: 6,720 tons light (17,600 fl)   **S:** 19 kts
Dim: 162.69 (153.3 pp) × 22.33 × 8.26
M: 2 sets GE GT; 2 props; 12,500 hp   **Electric:** 2,400 kw
Boilers: 2 Babcock & Wilcox; 43.3 kg/cm², 454°C
Fuel: 3,393 tons   **Range:** 17,000/19   **Man:** 219 tot.

REMARKS: 13,319 grt/6,934 dwt. Cargo: 1,943 passengers plus 2,719 m³ dry cargo. Sister *Barrett* (ex-T-AP 196) stricken in 7-73, and *Geiger* (T-AP 197) loaned to Massachusetts Maritime Academy 12-2-80 as the training ship *Bay State;* she returned 1981 after a major engineering casualty and will probably be scrapped as not worth repairing.

♦ **3 Admiral class (P2-S2-R1 type)** Bldr: Bethlehem, Alameda, Calif.

	L	In serv.
AP 122 GENERAL ALEXANDER M. PATCH	22-4-44	21-11-44
(ex-*Admiral R. E. Coontz*)		
AP 123 GENERAL SIMON B. BUCKNER	14-6-44	24-1-45
(ex-*Admiral E. W. Eberle*)		
AP 126 GENERAL MAURICE ROSE	25-2-45	10-7-45
(ex-*Admiral Hugh Rodman*)		

D: 12.657 tons light (22,574 fl)   **S:** 19 kts
Dim: 185.6 (174.65 wl) × 23.01 × 8.07   **Fuel:** 3,877 tons   **Range:** 15,000/19
M: 2 sets GE GT, electric drive; 2 props; 18,000 hp   **Electric:** 2,000 kw
Boilers: 4 Combustion Engineering "D," 42.2 kg/cm², 449°C   **Man:** 319 tot.

REMARKS: 16,039 grt/9,944 dwt. All operated by the Army Transportation Service until 1-3-50, when transferred to MSTS (later MSC). Active into the late 1960s. Can carry 1,757 troops, 2,889 m³ dry cargo. *Hugh J. Gaffey* (T-AP 121) redesignated IX 507 on 1-11-78 and used as a barracks ship. *General William O. Darby* (AP 127) reactivated as barracks ship (IX 510) in 10-81 (see above). *General Nelson M. Walker* (AP 125) donated 25-1-81 to Life International for conversion as a civilian hospital ship. All could originally carry 5,100 troops. Two others stricken. For appearance, see IX 510.

♦ **3 General class (P2-S2-R2 type)** Bldr: Federal SB & DD, Kearny, N.J.

	L	In serv.
AP 110 GENERAL JOHN POPE	21-3-43	5-8-43
AP 117 GENERAL W. H. GORDON	7-5-44	29-6-44
AP 119 GENERAL WILLIAM WEIGEL (ex-*General C. H. Barth*)	3-9-44	6-1-45

General W.H. Gordon (AP 117)—in Maritime Commission James River reserve fleet
     J. Jedrlinic, 5-80

D: 11,450 tons light (20,700 fl)   **S:** 21 kts   **Dim:** 189.77 × 23.01 × 7.77
M: 2 sets de Laval GT; 2 props; 17,000 hp   **Electric:** 1,600 kw
Boilers: 4 Foster-Wheeler "D," 32.7 kg/cm², 407°C
Fuel: 3,043 tons   **Range:** 11,000/19   **Man:** . . .

REMARKS: T-AP 110: 17,927 grt/7,479 dwt; others vary. Can carry from 2,154 to 3,825 passengers or troops. One sister sold commercially, seven others stricken.

CABLE SHIPS

♦ **1 new construction** Bldr: National Steel, San Diego, Calif.

	Laid down	L	In serv.
T-ARC 7 ZEUS	1-6-81	7-82	12-83

Authorized: FY 79

Zeus (T-ARC 7)   1978

D: 8,370 tons light (14,157 fl)   **S:** 15 kts   **Dim:** 153.2 (138.4 pp) × 22.3 × 7.3
M: 3 diesels, electric drive; 2 props; 10,200 hp   **Electric:** 3,500 kw
Range: 10,000/15   **Man:** 88 tot. MSC: 32 civilians, 6 Navy

REMARKS: Ordered 17-8-79. Cost $107 million. Will replace T-ARC 3. Second unit programmed for FY 86, to replace *Aeolus* (T-ARC 3). Two bow- and stern-thrusters for precision maneuvering. Two 5-ton cranes. Will be able to conduct acoustic, hydrographic, and bathymetric surveys, as well as carrying and laying up to 1,000 miles of cable.

♦ **2 Neptune class (S3-S2-BP1 type)** Bldr: Pusey & Jones, Wilmington, Del.

	L	In serv.
T-ARC 2 NEPTUNE (ex-*Wm. H. G. Bullard*)	1945	1-6-53
T-ARC 6 ALBERT J. MEYER	1945	13-5-63

D: T-ARC 2: 4,960 tons light (7,810 fl); T-ARC 6: 5,030 tons light (7,815 fl)
S: 14 kts   **Dim:** 110.3 (98.1 pp) × 14.3 × 5.5
Electron Equipt: Radar: 1/Raytheon TM 1650/6X, 1/Raytheon TM 1660/12S
M: 2 Skinner Uniflow, 5-cyl. reciprocating steam; 2 props; 4,340 hp
Boilers: 2 Combustion Engineering
Fuel: 1,129 tons (T-ARC 2: 980 tons)   **Range:** 7,400/11.5   **Man:** 74-85 tot.

REMARKS: T-ARC 2: 3,929 grt/2,000 dwt; T-ARC 6: 4,012 grt/4,332 dwt. Differ in detail, with T-ARC 6 being flush-decked. Last reciprocating steam-propelled ships in USN/MSC service. T-ARC 2 to MSC from Navy 8-11-73. T-ARC 6 from U.S. Army in 1953. T-ARC 2 has a helicopter deck aft; T-ARC 6 does not. Both have been given a very extensive modernization. T-ARC 2: 112.8 m overall.

CABLE SHIPS (continued)

Neptune (T-ARC 2)   G. Arra, 1975

Albert J. Meyer (T-ARC 6)—note heavy bow sheaves and OE-82 SATCOMM antennas
MSC, 1980

♦ **1 Aeolus class** Bldr: Walsh Kaiser, Providence, R.I.

	L	In serv.	Conv.
T-ARC 3 Aeolus (ex-*Turandot*, AKA 47)	1945	18-6-45	14-5-55

Aeolus (T-ARC 3)   J. Jedrlinic, 1980

D: 4,283 tons light (7,040 fl)   **S:** 15.5 kts   **Dim:** 133.5 (121.9 pp) × 17.7 × 4.88

Electron Equipt: Radar: 1/Raytheon TM 1650/6X, 1/Raytheon TM 1660/12S
M: 2 sets Westinghouse GT, electric drive; 2 props; 6,000 hp
Boilers: 2 Wickes   **Fuel:** 1,407 tons   **Range:** 9,700/14   **Man:** 86 tot.

REMARKS: 6,063 grt/2,958 dwt. S4-SE2-BE1 attack cargo ship converted by Bethlehem Steel to a cable-layer 1955-56. Sister *Thor* (T-ARC 4) stricken on 17-7-75. Operated for the Naval Electronics Command.

FLEET TUGS

♦ **7 Powhatan class** Bldr: Marinette Marine, Wisc.

	Laid down	L	In serv.
T-ATF 166 POWHATAN	30-9-76	24-6-78	15-6-79
T-ATF 167 NARRAGANSETT	5-5-77	28-11-78	9-11-79
T-ATF 168 CATAWBA	14-12-77	12-5-79	28-5-80
T-ATF 169 NAVAJO	14-12-77	20-12-79	13-6-80
T-ATF 170 MOHAWK	22-3-79	5-4-80	16-10-80
T-ATF 171 SIOUX	22-3-79	30-10-80	12-5-81
T-ATF 172 APACHE	22-3-79	20-12-80	30-7-81

Authorized: 1 in FY 75, 3 in FY 76, 3 in FY 78

D: 2,000 tons (2,260 fl)   **S:** 15 kts   **Dim:** 73.2 (68.88 pp) × 12.8 × 4.6
Electron Equipt: Radar: 1/Raytheon TM 1660/12S
M: 2 GM EMD 20-645X7 diesels, electric drive; 2 Kort-nozzle props; 4,500 hp
Electric: 1,200 kw   **Fuel:** 600 tons   **Range:** 10,000/13
Man: 4 officers, 9-12 men + Navy communications team

REMARKS: Modified oilfield-supply-boat design built to merchant marine specifications. If required, could mount two 20-mm AA (I × 2) and two 12.7-mm machine guns (I × 2). Five were requested under FY 78, three approved. Have a 300-hp bow-thruster and one 10-ton electrohydraulic crane. Can carry the Mk 1 Mod. 1, 90-ton deep-diving support module on the stern and can support a 20-man Navy salvage team. Have a 60-ton bollard-pull capacity. Foam firefighting equipment. Hull has unusual

FLEET TUGS *(continued)*

Narragansett (T-ATF 167)   J. Jedrlinic, 1981

Navajo (T-ATF 169)   PH1 C. Kelly, 8-81

double-chine configuration. Electrohydraulic 10-ton crane. No additional units are planned despite dwindling number of U.S. Navy tugs; consideration has been given to chartering commercial tugs.

NOTE: The two MSC-operated *Cherokee*-class fleet tugs *Ute* (T-ATF 76) and *Lipan* (T-ATF 85) were transferred to the U.S. Coast Guard 30-9-80. The *Achomawi*-class fleet tugs *Atakapa* (T-ATF 149) and *Mosopelia* (T-ATF 158) were deactivated 1-10-81 and transferred to the Maritime Commission for foreign sale.

RAPID DEPLOYMENT FORCE

The Rapid Deployment Force was established in 1980 by the Carter administration. In July, the first ships of the Interim Rapid Deployment Force deployed to Diego Garcia in the Indian Ocean. Aside from the MSC-operated vehicle cargo ships *Mercury* (T-AKR 10), *Jupiter* (T-AKR 11), and one *Sealift*-class transport oiler attached on rotation, which are described in the section on the Military Sealift Command, the ships have all been commercially chartered merchant ships with contract crews. While the composition of the force has changed, the ships described below composed the Force on 1-1-82. They are scheduled to be replaced by a force composed of the four *Maine*-class T-AKRs, the eight SL-7-class ships, and, eventually, some 12-15 purchased and converted merchant ships.

◆ **2 Maritime Commission C4-S-57a-Type cargo ships**

	Bldr	In serv.
AMERICAN CHAMPION	Newport News SB & DD	3-63
AMERICAN COURIER	Bethlehem Steel, Quincy, Mass.	2-63

American Courier   J. Jedrlinic, 1980

D: 21,053 tons (fl)   **S:** 21 kts   **Dim:** 170.85 (161.54 pp) × 22.86 × 9.63
M: 1 set Westinghouse GT; 1 prop; 21,600 hp   **Electric:** 2,500 kw
Boilers: 2 Foster-Wheeler   **Fuel:** 2,570 tons   **Range:** 12,000/21   **Man:** 56 tot.

REMARKS: 11,105 grt/13,563 dwt. Six cargo holds. Can carry 21 cargo containers on deck. Cranes: one 70-ton, eight 15-ton, twelve 10-ton. Leased from U.S. Lines.

◆ **1 Maritime Commission C4-S-69-Type cargo ship**
   Bldr: Avondale SY, Westwego, La.

AMERICAN SPITFIRE (ex-*Idaho*) (In serv. 3-69)

American Spitfire (as Idaho)   J. Jedrlinic, 1980

D: 21,617 tons (fl)   **S:** 23 kts   **Dim:** 176.48 (165.96 pp) × 24.99 × 9.78
M: 1 set GE GT; 1 prop; . . . hp   **Boilers:** 2 Babcock & Wilcox
Electric: 2,000 kw   **Fuel:** 2,658 tons   **Range:** 12,000/23

REMARKS: 13,053 grt/13,074 dwt. Cargo: 21,665 m³ bale dry cargo/1,133 m³ refrigerated. Can be used to carry standard cargo containers and can also carry 7,000 bbl liquid cargo. Chartered 11-81. Seven cargo holds. Cranes: one 70-ton, eight 20-ton, eight 10-ton, eight 5-ton. Can carry 25 containers on deck. Leased from U.S. Lines.

RAPID DEPLOYMENT FORCE (continued)

♦ **2 Maritime Commission C8-S-81b-Type lighter carriers**
Bldr: Avondale SY, Westwego, La.

AUSTRAL LIGHTNING (ex-*Lash España*) (In serv. 4-71)
AUSTRAL RAINBOW (ex-*China Bear*) (In serv. 5-72)

Austral Lightning   MSC, 1981

D: 44,606 tons (fl)   **S:** 22.5 kts   **Dim:** 249.94 (220.68 pp) × 30.48 × 10.70
M: 1 set de Laval GT; 1 prop; 32,000 hp   **Boilers:** 2 Babcock & Wilcox
Electric: 4,500 kw   **Fuel:** 5,500 tons (10,427 max.)   **Range:** 13,000/22.5

REMARKS: 26,456 grt/29,820 dwt. Converted from cargo barge-only carriers to container or barge carriers by owners, prior to lease. Can carry up to 70 cargo barges or 840 (*Austral Rainbow:* 1,004) standard cargo containers, handled by a 30-ton traveling crane. The traveling barge crane can lift 446 tons. Also have two 5-ton cranes. Both are carrying palletized munitions, the largest such explosive cargo ever carried by individual ships.

♦ **1 vehicle cargo ship** Bldr: Howaldtswerke, Kiel, W. Germany

LYRA (ex-*Reichenfels*) (In serv. 30-9-77)

Cygnus—with deck load of M-60 tanks (**Lyra** similar)   L. & L. Van Ginderen, 6-81

D: 9,870 tons (light)   **S:** 21 kts   **Dim:** 193.32 (178.00 pp) × 27.00 × 8.61
Electron Equipt: Radar: 1/Decca RM 1229, 1/Decca TM-S 1230
M: 2 M.A.N. 9L52/55A diesels; 1 CP prop; 18,990 hp (sust.)—2 Lips 1,200-hp
bow-thrusters
Electric: 4,590 kw   **Fuel:** 2,579 tons   **Range:** 27,000/18   **Man:** 49 tot.

REMARKS: 14,189 grt/15,075 dwt. Chartered 19-1-81 for 5 years from Lykes Bros., along with the similar *Cygnus* (ex-*Rabenfels*); both had been purchased from the defunct Hansa Lines. *Cygnus* is *not* part of the Rapid Deployment Force. *Lyra* has a slewing stern ramp capable of supporting 160 tons. Vehicle cargo can also enter via two 4.65 × 4.20 side ports. 316 20-ft. or 156 40-ft. cargo containers can be stowed on deck, while below decks can accommodate the equivalent of 180 40-ft. wheeled

trailers. A portable ramp is used between the first and second vehicle decks, and there are two 80-ton vehicle elevators serving the inner bottom. Can carry up to 6,500 tons of water ballast.

♦ **4 Maritime Commission T6-M-98a-Type tankers** Bldr: Todd SY, San Pedro, Cal.

	In serv.
COURIER (ex-*Zapata Courier*)	1977
PATRIOT (ex-*Zapata Patriot*)	12-75
RANGER (ex-*Zapata Ranger*)	1976
ROVER (ex-*Zapata Rover*)	1977

Ranger   G. Gyssels, 5-81

D: 9,132 tons light (44,503 fl)   **S:** 16 kts   **Dim:** 216.79 (208.66 pp) × 25.60 × 9.75
Electron Equipt: Radar: 1/Raytheon TM 1650/6X, 1/Raytheon TM 1660/12S
M: 2 Colt-Pielstick PC2, 14-cyl. diesels; 1 prop; 14,000 hp
Electric: 2,830 kw   **Fuel:** 3,223 tons   **Range:** 12,000/16   **Man:** 28 tot.

REMARKS: 21,670 grt/35,341 dwt. Cargo: 308,227 bbl. *Patriot* chartered 2-6-80 as a *water* tanker (34,065 m³ capacity) for the Rapid Deployment Force. The other three were chartered 12-81 to carry fuel. All lost the *Zapata* portion of their names 5-81 when sold by Zapata Lines to Ogden Marine, Inc.

NOTE: In addition to the ships listed above for the U.S. Navy and Military Sealift Command, there exist several hundred former naval ships, ranging from aircraft carriers and cruisers to auxiliaries and yard craft, which have been officially stricken but not yet scrapped or otherwise disposed of. Although many might be recalled to service in an emergency, listing them is beyond the scope of this book.

COAST GUARD

PERSONNEL (1981): 7,000 officers and warrant officers, 31,000 enlisted, plus 6,000 civilians, 16,000 Reserves, and 40,000 Coast Guard Auxiliary

GENERAL

The Revenue Marine, which was created in 1790, became the Coast Guard on 28 January 1915 by act of Congress. Until 1 April 1967 the Coast Guard was part of the Department of the Treasury; at that time it was transferred to the Department of Transportation. The act that created the service calls for it to operate in time of crisis under the control of the Navy. The principal responsibilities of the Coast Guard are:
—preparation and training for combat in cooperation with the Navy;
—enforcement of the laws of the sea and the policing of navigation;
—control of territorial waters, suppression of smuggling, and policing and assisting the fishing industry;
—surveillance of the coasts and protection of access to ports and bases;
—search and rescue at sea, including transocean air routes;

COAST GUARD–GENERAL *(continued)*

—manning and maintaining aids to navigation: lighthouses, beacons, buoys, lightships, and Loran stations (46,000 in all);
—control of piloting and the investigation of accidents at sea;
—control of the safety and seaworthiness aspects of shipbuilding;
—international ice patrols (keeping track of drifting icebergs);
—protection of offshore oil installations;
—pollution control and protection of the environment;
—meteorologic, oceanographic, and hydrographic surveying.

ORGANIZATION

The Coast Guard is divided into two main components, one for the Pacific and one for the Atlantic. Each of these area commands is headed by a rear admiral. The Coast Guard is further divided into twelve Coast Guard Districts in order to fulfill its responsibilities along the U.S. coastline (more than 10,000 nautical miles, not including Hawaii).

A four-star admiral heads the Coast Guard. He is appointed for four years and is assisted by a general staff. The Commandant reports to the Secretary of Transportation and not the Joint Chiefs of Staff.

COMPOSITION OF THE FLEET

Coast Guard patrol ships have their names preceded by USCGC (United States Coast Guard Cutter). Cutters and patrol craft are white, icebreakers have red hulls, buoy tenders, black. All ships and craft carry a diagonal red stripe and the USCG shield on the hull.

As of 1-1-82 the in-service, seagoing USCG fleet was composed of the following:

♦ **18 high-endurance cutters** (WHEC):

12 *Hamilton* class, 3,050 tons (fl)
5 Secretary class, 2,656 tons (fl)
1 Casco class, 2,800 tons (fl)

♦ **27 medium-endurance cutters** (WMEC) from 935 to 1,745 tons (fl)

♦ **6 icebreakers** (WAGB)

♦ **79 patrol boats** (WPB), 105 tons (fl) and 66 to 69 tons (fl)

♦ **1 oceanographic research ship** (WAGO)

♦ **45 seagoing buoy tenders** (WLB and WLM)

♦ **42 inland, river, and construction buoy tenders** (WLI, WLR, WLIC)

♦ **31 tugs** (WTGB, WYTM, and WYTL)

♦ **1 officer training ship** (WIX)

♦ **1 reserve training ship** (WTR)

♦ **approximately 2,000 small boats under 20 m length**

AVIATION

As of 1-1-82, the Coast Guard operated 49 fixed-wing aircraft, which included:
 25 HC-130 Hercules long-range search and rescue aircraft (12 HC-130B, 1 HC130E, 12 HC-130H)
 20 HC-131 Samaritan twin-engined turboprop transports transferred in 1977 and 1978 from the U.S. Air Force's reserve stocks for use in patrolling the 200-nautical-mile economic zone (4 maintained in reserve)
 9 HU-16 Albatross amphibians for patrol and rescue duties (3 in storage)
 1 Grumman VC-4A Gulfstream-I as a personnel (VIP) transport
 1 Grumman VC-11A Gulfstream-II as a personnel (VIP) transport
Helicopters in use included:
 37 HH-3F Pelican or rescue duties
 77 HH-52A Sea Guard for rescue duties
The dwindling numbers of HU-16 Albatross and the aged HC-131 are to be replaced by forty-one HU-25A Guardian twin-jet patrol aircraft, ordered in 1-77. A version of the Dassault Mystère-20, the first of these new aircraft was scheduled for delivery in 11-81, but the Coast Guard refused delivery, due to its failure to meet performance guarantees. These aircraft, after considerable delay by the original contractor, are now being assembled by Grumman, and the program is now two and one-half years behind schedule. In 6-79, ninety Aérospatiale SA-366N SRR (Short-Range Recovery) helicopters were ordered from France under the USCG designation HH-65A Dolphin; these will replace the HH-52A helicopters. The first HH-65A Dolphin is to deliver in 9-82, with all 90 to be in service by early 1986. The Coast Guard is to take a 12 percent budget cut in FY 83, probably forcing the closure of five air facilities.

HU-25A Guardian—artist's concept   USCG

USCG HC-131A Samaritan   USCG

PRINCIPAL U.S. COAST GUARD AIRCRAFT

Class, builder	Mission	Wingspan in m	Length in m	Height in m	Weight in kg	Engines	Max speed knots	Ceiling in feet	Radius (nautical miles)
FIXED-WING									
HC-130 B/E/H Hercules (Lockheed)	SAR/cargo/ personnel transport	40.42	30.32	11.66	34,187 empty, 49,780 loaded, 79,380 max.	4 Allison T 56-A-15 turboprops; 4,591 shp (4,061 sust.) each	302 kts (287 cruise)	25,000	3,734 ferry, 2,564 with max. payload
HC-131A Samaritan Convair)	SAR, personnel transport	32.08	24.14	8.53	24,132 loaded	2 Pratt & Whitney R-2800-52W radial piston; 2,500 shp each	274 kts	. . .	2,000
HU-16E Albatross (Grumman) amphibian	SAR, personnel transport	29.48	19.17	7.90	10,444 empty 15,422 water takeoff; 17,010 max.	2 Wright R-1820-76A/B radial piston; 1,425 shp each	177 kts (130 at 10,000 ft; 117 at 1,500 ft)	24,000	1,130 SAR/ 1,090 transport
HU-25 Guardian (Dassault/ Grumman)	SAR	16.30	17.15	5.32	8,618 empty 9,476 loaded; 14,515 max.	2 Garrett AiResearch ATF3-6-2C turbofans; 2,512 kg thrust each	461 kts (40,000 ft); 150 kts (search)	40,000	2,250 SAR
HELICOPTERS:	Mission	Rotor diameter(m)	Length overall (m)	Height in m	Weight in kg	Engines	Max speed in knots	Ceiling in feet	
HH-3F Pelican (Sikorsky)	SAR/ transport	18.90	22.25	5.51	10,000 max.	2GE T58-GE-5 turboshafts; 1,500 shp each	141 kts (109 cruise)	11,400	400
HH-52A Sea Guard (Sikorsky)	SAR	16.17	13.87	4.88	2,306 empty; 3,674 max.	1 GE T58-GE-8B turboshaft; 1,250 shp	95 kts (85 cruise)	11,200	475 ferry, 150 SAR radius
HH-65A Dolphin (Aérospatiale)	SAR	11.68	13.33	3.77	1,900 empty; 3,992 max.	2 Avco Lycoming LTS 101-750A-1 turboshafts; 680 hp each (646 sust.)	175 kts (145 cruise; 128 SAR)	7,510	40 ferry (4.1 hr mission)

USCG HH-52A Sea Guard   USCG

HH-65A Dolphin   USCG

AVIATION (continued)

USCG HG-130 Hercules USCG

USCG HH-3F Pelican USCG

HIGH-ENDURANCE CUTTERS

♦ **12 Hamilton class (378-ft class)** Bldr: Avondale SY, Westwego, La.

	Laid down	L	In serv.
WHEC 715 HAMILTON	1-65	18-12-65	20-2-67
WHEC 716 DALLAS	7-2-66	1-10-66	1-10-67
WHEC 717 MELLON	25-7-66	11-2-67	22-12-67
WHEC 718 CHASE	15-10-66	20-5-67	1-3-68
WHEC 719 BOUTWELL	12-12-66	17-6-67	14-6-68
WHEC 720 SHERMAN	13-2-67	23-9-67	23-8-68
WHEC 721 GALLATIN	17-4-67	18-11-67	20-12-68
WHEC 722 MORGENTHAU	17-7-67	10-2-68	14-2-69
WHEC 723 RUSH	23-10-67	16-11-68	3-7-69
WHEC 724 MUNRO	18-2-70	5-12-70	10-9-71
WHEC 725 JARVIS	9-9-70	24-4-71	30-12-71
WHEC 726 MIDGETT	5-4-71	4-9-71	17-3-72

D: 2,716 tons (3,050 fl) **S:** 29 kts
Dim: 115.37 (106.68 pp) × 13.06 × 4.27 (6.2 over sonar)
A: 1/127-mm 38-cal. DP—2/40-mm Mk 64 grenade launchers (I × 2)—6/324-mm Mk 32 ASW TT (III × 2)

Chase (WHEC 718) L. & L. Van Ginderen, 6-81

Morgenthau (WHEC 722) A. Baker, 1976

Munro (WHEC 724)—with USN SH-2 helicopter USCG, 6-81

Electron Equipt: Radar: 1/SPS-53 navigational, 1/SPS-64 surface-search, 1/SPS-29D air-search, 1/Mk 35
Sonar: SQS-38—ECM: WLR-1

HIGH-ENDURANCE CUTTERS *(continued)*

M: CODOG: 2 Fairbanks-Morse 38TD⅛, 12-cyl. diesels, 3,500 hp each; 2 Pratt & Whitney FT4-A6 gas turbines, 18,000 hp each; 2 CP props; 36,000 hp—350-hp retractable bow propeller
Electric: 1,500 kw **Fuel:** 800 tons
Range: 2,400/29; 9,600/19 (gas turbines); 14,000/11 (diesel)
Man: 15 officers, 149 men

REMARKS: Helicopter platform, 26.82 × 12.2. Living spaces air-conditioned. Laboratories for weather and oceanographic research. Welded hull; aluminum superstructure. Named after early Secretaries of the Treasury and Coast Guard heroes. Thirty-six planned, only twelve built. Mk 56 radar gunfire-control director and Mk 309 ASW fire-control system installed. For FY 85 through FY 88, there are plans to replace the 127-mm gun and Mk 56 gunfire-control system with a 76-mm Mk 75 (OTO Melara Compact) gun and Mk 92 radar gunfire-control system, replace the SPS-29D radar with SPS-40B, replace the WLR-1 ECM system with SLQ-32, and add satellite communications gear; provision will be made to carry the LAMPS-I ASW helicopter, TACTASS towed passive sonar array, and the 20-mm Vulcan/Phalanx Gatling AA gun. The grenade launchers have replaced the 81-mm mortars formerly carried. The helicopter hangars have been blanked off. SQS-38 is a hull-mounted version of the Navy's SQS-35 variable-depth sonar.

♦ 6 Secretary class (327-ft class)

	Bldr	Laid down	L	In serv.
WHEC 31 BIBB	Charleston NSY	15-8-35	14-1-37	19-3-37
WHEC 32 CAMPBELL	Philadelphia NSY	1-5-35	3-6-36	22-10-36
WHEC 33 DUANE	Philadelphia NSY	1-5-35	3-6-36	16-10-36
WHEC 35 INGHAM	Philadelphia NSY	1-5-35	3-6-36	6-11-36
WHEC 37 TANEY	Philadelphia NSY	1-5-35	3-6-36	24-10-36

D: 2,216 tons (2,656 fl) **S:** 19.8 kts **Dim:** 99.67 (93.88 wl) × 12.55 × 4.57
A: 1/127-mm 38-cal. DP—2/40-mm Mk 64 grenade launchers (I × 2)
Electron Equipt: Radar: 1/SPS-53, 1/SPS-64, 1/SPS-29D (not in WHEC 35, 37)
M: 2 sets Westinghouse GT; 2 props; 6,200 hp
Boilers: 2 Babcock & Wilcox; 28.2 kg/cm² **Fuel:** 572 tons
Range: 4,000/19.8; 8,000/10.5 **Man:** 13 officers, 131 men

Taney (WHEC 37)—extra deckhouse atop bridge   French Navy, 6-81

Duane (WHEC 33)—SPS-29D radar antenna atop tripod mast   1979

Ingham (WHEC 35)   G. Gyssels, 6-81

REMARKS: Despite their great age, comfortable and highly reliable ships. WHEC 37 is the last active survivor of the 7-12-41 Pearl Harbor attack. WHEC 36 has been in reserve since 1-2-74; she is used as a stationary engineering training ship at the Coast Guard Yard, Curtis Bay, Md. All have a weather balloon inflation hangar just abaft the stack. All gun fire-control and ASW equipment removed. WSR-S1 weather removed from WHEC 37, SATCOMM antenna radome removed from WHEC 35, both in 1980. *Spencer* (WHEC 36) was sold late 1981.

♦ 2 Owasco class (255-ft class) Bldr: Western Pipe & Steel, San Pedro, Calif.
(WHEC 69 and WHEC 70: Coast Guard, Curtis Bay, Md.)

	Laid down	L	In serv.
WHEC 65 WINONA	8-11-44	22-4-45	15-8-46
WHEC 70 PONTCHARTRAIN (ex-*Okeechobee*)	1-7-43	29-4-44	28-7-45

HIGH-ENDURANCE CUTTERS (continued)

D: 1,563 tons (1,913 fl) **S:** 18.4 kts **Dim:** 77.42 × 13.11 × 5.18 (max.)
A: 1/127-mm 38-cal. DP **Electron Equipt:** Radar: 1/SPS-53, 1/SPS-29D
M: 1 set Westinghouse GT, electric drive; 1 prop; 4,000 hp
Boilers: 2 Foster-Wheeler; 44.7 kg/cm², 399°C
Range: 5,300/18.4; 13,600/11 **Man:** 12 officers, 127 men

REMARKS: In reserve: WHEC 70 at Baltimore, Md., and WHEC 65 at Alameda, Calif. Survivors of a class of thirteen. Not a very successful design and unlikely to see further service. All ASW equipment removed. *Chautauqua* (WHEC 41), *Minnetonka* (WHEC 67), and *Mendota* (WHEC 69) stricken 7-10-80.

♦ **1 Casco class (311-ft class)** Bldr: Associated SB, Seattle

	Laid down	L	In serv.
WHEC 379 Unimak (ex-WTR, ex-WHEC, ex-AVP 31)	12-2-42	27-5-43	31-12-43

Unimak (WHEC 379) L. & L. Van Ginderen, 6-81

D: 1,766 tons (2,800 fl) **S:** 17 kts **Dim:** 94.7 (91.5 pp) × 12.52 × 3.65
A: 1/127-mm 38-cal. DP—2/40-mm Mk 64 grenade launchers (I × 2)
Electron Equipt: Radar: 1/SPS-53, 1/SPS-64
M: 4 Fairbanks-Morse 38D8⅛ diesels; 2 props; 6,080 hp **Electric:** 600 kw
Fuel: 400 tons **Range:** 8,000/17; 20,000/10 **Man:** 13 officers, 137 men

REMARKS: The last of a series of small seaplane tenders (AVP), eighteen of which were transferred to the Coast Guard, 1947-48; seven were given to South Vietnam beginning in 1970, and eight have been taken out of service since 1968. WHEC 379 was a training ship from 11-69 until placed in reserve on 30-5-75. She was recommissioned on 15-8-77 for patrol duties in the 200-nautical-mile economic zone. Gunfire-control and ASW systems have been removed.

MEDIUM-ENDURANCE CUTTERS

♦ **0 (+13+3) Bear class (270-ft class)** Bldr: WMEC 901-904: Tacoma Boatbuilding, Tacoma, Wash.; WMEC 905-913: Robert E. Direcktor, Middletown, Rhode Isl.

	Laid down	L	In serv.
WMEC 901 Bear	23-8-79	25-9-80	5-82
WMEC 902 Tampa	3-4-80	19-3-81	9-82
WMEC 903 Harriet Lane	15-10-80	10-1-82	1-83
WMEC 904 Northland	9-4-81	3-82	3-83
WMEC 905 Spencer (ex-*Seneca*)	. . .	. . .	6-84
WMEC 906 Seneca (ex-*Pickering*)	. . .	. . .	10-84
WMEC 907 Escanaba	. . .	. . .	2-85
WMEC 908 Tahoma (ex-*Legare*)	. . .	. . .	85
WMEC 909 N. . .	. . .	. . .	85
WMEC 910 N. . .	. . .	. . .	86
WMEC 911 N. . .	. . .	. . .	86
WMEC 912 N. . .	. . .	. . .	86
WMEC 913 N. . .	. . .	. . .	87

Authorized: 2 in FY 77, 2 in FY 78, 2 in FY 79, 3 in FY 80, 1 in FY 81 Programmed: 3 in FY 82, 3 or more later

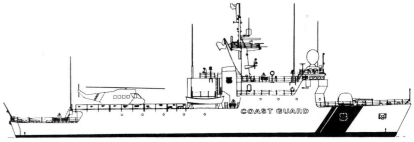

Bear class J.J. Henry Co., 1978

D: 1,722 tons (fl) **S:** 19.7 kts **Dim:** 82.3 × 11.58 × 4.11
A: 1/76-mm Mk 75 DP—2/12.7-mm mg (I × 2)—2/40-mm Mk 19 grenade launchers (I × 2)—1/HH-52A or HH-65A helicopter
Electron Equipt: Radar: 1/SPS-53, 1/SPS-64, 1/Mk 92 fire-control
  Sonar: Provision for SQR-19A TASS
  ECM: SLQ-32(V)1, 4/Mk 36 SRBOC chaff
M: 2 Fairbanks-Morse diesels; 2 CP props; 7,000 hp
Range: 2,500/19; 5,000/10
Man: 15 officers, 94 men

REMARKS: Names have been altered since original listing; others to be used are *Legare*, *Argus*, *Erie*, *McCulloch*, and *Ewing*. Program has suffered numerous delays; first ship was to have completed 31-12-80. WMEC 905-913 originally ordered from Tacoma in 8-80, but lawsuit caused reassignment to R.E. Direcktor, 17-1-81. The latter lacks the facilities to build the ships, and Tacoma is also suing, so the construction schedule for these badly needed ships is very much in doubt. Intended to be able to act as ASW escorts in wartime. No hull-mounted sonar or on-board ASW weapons. Space and weight reserved for Vulcan/Phalanx 20-mm Gatling AA gun and two quadruple Harpoon missile-launch canisters. Satellite-communications system will be carried. Can carry van-mounted towed passive sonar array on fantail. Telescoping hangar, fin stabilization. Will have six light weapons mountings capable of accepting 12.7-mm mg or 40-mm Mk 19 grenade launchers. Two ships of similar design are being built for the Irish Navy at Cork.

MEDIUM-ENDURANCE CUTTERS *(continued)*

♦ **16 Reliance class (210-ft A* and 210-ft B class)**

	Bldr	L	In serv.
WTR 615 RELIANCE*	1	25-5-63	20-6-64
WMEC 616 DILIGENCE*	1	20-7-63	26-8-64
WMEC 617 VIGILANT*	1	24-12-63	3-10-64
WMEC 618 ACTIVE*	2	31-7-65	17-9-66
WMEC 619 CONFIDENCE*	3	8-5-65	19-2-66
WMEC 620 RESOLUTE	3	30-4-66	8-12-66
WMEC 621 VALIANT	4	14-1-67	28-10-67
WMEC 622 COURAGEOUS	4	18-5-67	10-4-68
WMEC 623 STEADFAST	4	24-6-67	25-9-68
WMEC 624 DAUNTLESS	4	21-10-67	10-6-68
WMEC 625 VENTUROUS	4	11-11-67	16-8-68
WMEC 626 DEPENDABLE	4	16-3-68	27-11-68
WMEC 627 VIGOROUS	4	4-5-68	2-5-69
WMEC 628 DURABLE	3	29-4-67	8-12-67
WMEC 629 DECISIVE	3	14-12-67	23-8-68
WMEC 630 ALERT	3	19-10-68	4-8-69

Bldrs: 1. Todd Shipyards—2. Christy Corp., Sturgeon Bay, Wis.—3. Coast Guard SY, Curtis Bay, Md.—4. American SB, Lorain, Ohio.

Courageous (WMEC 622)—with HH-52A Guard helicopter   R. Scheina, 6-80

D: 759 tons (993* or 1,007 fl)   **S:** 18 kts   **Dim:** 64.16 (60.96 pp) × 10.36 × 3.2

A: 1/76.2-mm Mk 22 DP—2/40-mm Mk 64 grenade launchers (I × 2)—1/HH-52A helicopter

Electron Equipt: Radar: 2/SPS-53 or 1/SPS-64   **Endurance:** 15 days

M: 2 Alco 251B 16-cyl. diesels, 2,500 hp each; 2 CP props; (WTR 615 to WMEC 619: CODAG: 2 Solar-Saturn T-1000S gas turbines, 1,000 hp each, and 2 Cooper-Bessemer FVBM12-T diesels, 1,500 hp each; 2 CP props; 5,000 hp

Electric: 500 kw   **Range:** 2,700/18; 6,100/14 (*: 2,100/18; 6,100/13)

Man: 7 officers, 54 men

REMARKS: WTR 615 replaced WHEC 379 as reserve training cutter in 1974; she retains full WMEC capabilities. CODAG propulsion in WTR 615 to WMEC 619; not installed in the others because it provided no speed advantage, despite the extra horsepower, and it cut the endurance; the engines exhaust through the stern. No hangar. Designed to operate up to 500 miles off the coast. High superstructure permits 360-degree visibility. Can two a 10,000-ton ship. Air-conditioned. A plan to replace the obsolescent 76.2-mm single-fire gun by two 20-mm AA (I × 2) has been canceled.

♦ **3 Diver class (213-ft class)** Bldr: Basalt Rock Co., Napa, Calif.

	Laid down	L	In serv.
WMEC 6 ESCAPE (ex-ARS 6)	24-8-42	22-11-42	20-11-43
WMEC 167 ACUSHNET (ex-WAGO 167, ex-WAT 167, ex-*Shackle*, ARS 9)	26-10-42	1-4-43	6-2-44
WMEC 168 YOCONA (ex-WAT 168, ex-*Seize*, ARS 26)	28-9-43	8-4-44	3-11-44

Acushnet (WMEC 167)—oceanographic crane on stern   1975

D: 1,557 tons (1,745 fl)   **S:** 15.5 kts   **Dim:** 65.08 (63.09 wl) × 12.5 × 4.57

A: None   **Electron Equipt:** Radar: 2/SPS-53   **Electric:** 460 kw

M: 4 Cooper-Bessemer GSB-8 diesels, electric drive; 2 props; 3,000 hp

Fuel: 300 tons   **Range:** 9,000/15.5; 20,000/7   **Man:** 7 officers, 65 men

REMARKS: Former salvage ships; WMEC 167, 168 taken over from the Navy in 1946. WMEC 167 served as WAGO 167 from 1968 to 1978, then retyped WMEC. WMEC 168 has a small tripod mast atop the pilothouse and a tall mainmast just forward of the stack. WMEC 6, reactivated from reserve and transferred on loan from U.S. Navy 4-12-80, resembles WMEC 167.

NOTE: Of the two *Sotoyomo* (143-ft.)-class cutters, *Modoc* (WMEC 194) was stricken in 6-79 and *Comanche* (WMEC 202) was stricken 2-80.

♦ **1 Storis class (230-ft class)** Bldr: Toledo SB, Toledo, Ohio

	Laid down	L	In serv.
WMEC 38 STORIS (ex-*Eskimo*)	14-7-41	4-4-42	30-9-42

D: 1,715 tons (1,925 fl)   **S:** 14 kts   **Dim:** 70.1 × 13.1 × 4.6

A: 1/76.2-mm Mk 22 DP   **M:** 2 diesels, electric drive; 1 prop; 1,800 hp

Range: 12,000/14; 22,000/8   **Man:** 10 officers, 96 men

REMARKS: Rated as WAG until 1966, and WAGB until 1-7-72, when she was retyped WMEC. Resembles a *Balsam*-class buoy tender, but is larger. Has an icebreaker hull but is no longer considered capable of acting as such. Based at Kodiak, Alaska.

MEDIUM-ENDURANCE CUTTERS (continued)

Storis (WMEC 38) 1971

♦ **5 Cherokee and Achomawi* class (205-ft class)**

	Bldr	Laid down	L	In serv.
WMEC 76 UTE (ex-T-ATF 76)	United Eng., Alameda	27-2-42	24-6-42	31-12-42
WMEC 85 LIPAN (ex-T-ATF 85)	United Eng., Alameda	30-5-42	17-9-42	29-4-43
WMEC 153 CHILULA* (ex-ATF 153)	Charleston SB	13-7-44	1-12-44	5-4-45
WMEC 165 CHEROKEE (ex-ATF 66)	Bethlehem, Staten I.	23-12-38	10-11-39	26-4-40
WMEC 166 TAMAROA (ex-Zuni, ATF 95)	Commercial Iron Works, Portland, Oregon	8-3-43	13-7-43	9-10-43

D: 1,235 tons (1,731 fl) **S:** 16.2 kts **Dim:** 62.48 (59.44 pp) × 11.73 × 5.18
A: 1/76.2-mm Mk 22 DP **Electron Equipt:** Radar: 2/SPS-53
M: 4 GM 12-278 diesels, electric drive; 1 prop; 3,000 hp **Electric:** 260 kw
Fuel: 315 tons **Range:** 6,500/16.2; 15,000/8 **Man:** 7 officers, 65 men

Lipan (WMEC 85)—in refit. Note rubber dinghies vice motorboats, stockless anchors recessed into bulwarks aft
USCG, 2-81

Tamaroa (WMEC 166) R. Scheina, 1979

REMARKS: WMEC 165 and WMEC 166 were the first and last of their numerous group to be built; WMEC 153 is one of a later version that has similar appearance, but her diesels are GM 12-278A. WMEC 153, 165 and 166 are former U.S. Navy fleet tugs loaned to the Coast Guard in 1946 and transferred outright on 1-6-69; WMEC 76 and 85 were transferred on 30-9-80 and then towed from San Francisco to Curtis Bay, Md., for refits; they are not armed.

♦ **2 Balsam class (180-ft.) former seagoing buoy tenders**

	L
WMEC 292 CLOVER (ex-WLB 292)	1942
WMEC 300 CITRUS (ex-WLB 300)	1943

Clover (WMEC 292)—in new cutter paint scheme
USCG, 1981

MEDIUM-ENDURANCE CUTTERS *(continued)*

REMARKS: WMEC 292 reclassified 6-79 to replace *Modoc* (WMEC 194), and WMEC 300 reclassified 2-80 to replace *Comanche* (WMEC 202). Data as for buoy tender sisters on later page. WMEC 300, stationed at Coos Bay, Oregon, had her hull strengthened for icebreaking. WMEC 292 based at Eureka, Cal. Armament for both is 2/40-mm grenade launchers (I × 2).

ICEBREAKERS

♦ **2 Polar Star class (399-ft class)** Bldr: Lockheed SB, Seattle

	Laid down	L	In serv.
WAGB 10 POLAR STAR	15-5-72	17-11-73	19-1-76
WAGB 11 POLAR SEA	27-11-73	24-6-75	23-2-78

Polar Star (WAGB 10)   1978

Polar Sea (WAGB 11)   USCG, 1981

D: 10,863 tons (12,087 fl)   **S:** 18 kts   **Dim:** 121.91 (102.78 pp) × 25.45 × 1.14
M: CODAG: 6 Alco 16V251 diesels, 3,000 hp each; 3 Pratt & Whitney FT-4A12 gas turbines, 25,000 hp each, down-rated; electric drive; 3 CP props; 66,000 hp
Fuel: 3,555 tons   **Range:** 16,000/18; 28,275/13
Man: 13 officers, 125 men, 10 scientists, 15 helicopter detachment

REMARKS: No additional units planned. Carry two HH-52A helicopters, painted red. Can break 2-meter ice at 3 knots, 6.4-meter ice maximum. Propulsion plant completely cross-connected and automatic. Two 15-ton cranes. Four 20-mm AA (I × 4) and two 40-mm Mk 64 grenade launchers (I × 2) can be installed. Both home-ported at Seattle.

♦ **1 Glacier class (310-ft class)** Bldr: Ingalls SB, Pascagoula, Miss.

	Laid down	L	In serv.
WAGB 4 GLACIER	3-8-53	27-8-54	27-5-55

Glacier (WAGB 4)—SPS-6 radar since removed   1972

D: 5,100 tons (8,449 fl)   **S:** 17.6 kts   **Dim:** 94.5 (88.4 pp) × 22.6 × 8.8
A: 2/40-mm Mk 64 grenade launchers (I × 2)—2/HH-52A helicopters
Electron Equipt: Radar: 1/SPS-53, 1/SPS-64
M: Diesel-electric propulsion; 10 Fairbanks-Morse 38-D8⅛ diesels and 2 Westinghouse electric motor-generators; 21,000 hp
Range: 12,000/17.6; 29,000/12   **Man:** 14 officers, 215 men

REMARKS: Built for the U.S. Navy and transferred to the Coast Guard on 1-7-66. Two 12.5-ton cranes. Based at Long Beach, Cal. Originally had 2/127-mm (I × 2) and 6/76.2-mm (II × 3) guns.

♦ **2 Wind class (269-ft class)** Bldr: Western Pipe & Steel, San Pedro, Calif.

	Laid down	L	In serv.
WAGB 281 WESTWIND (ex-AGB 6, ex-*Severniy Polyus*)	24-8-42	31-3-43	18-9-44
WAGB 282 NORTHWIND	10-7-44	22-2-45	28-7-45

D: 3,500 tons (6,515 fl)   **S:** 16 kts   **Dim:** 81.99 (76.2 pp) × 19.36 × 8.84
Electron Equipt: Radar: 2/SPS-53
M: 4 Enterprise diesels, electric drive; 2 props; 10,000 hp
Electric: 400 kw   **Range:** 16,000/16; 38,000/10.5   **Man:** 135 tot.

ICEBREAKERS (continued)

Westwind (WAGB 281)—telescoping hangar extended   C. Dragonette, 8-80

REMARKS: Can make way in 2.7-m ice. Double hull entirely welded. Telescoping hangar for one HH-52A helicopter. Both reengined 1973-75. Two 12.5-ton cranes. WAGB 281, which was in the Soviet Navy from 31-3-45 to 6-12-51, is on the Great Lakes, based at Milwaukee; WAGB 282 is based at Wilmington, N. Carolina. Five sisters stricken.

♦ **1 Mackinaw class (290-ft class)** Bldr: Toledo SB, Toledo, Ohio

	Laid down	L	In serv.
WAGB 83 MACKINAW (ex-*Manitowoc*)	20-3-43	4-3-44	20-12-44

Mackinaw (WAGB 83)   1971

D: 5,252 tons (fl) **S:** 18.7 kts **Dim:** 88.39 × 22.66 × 5.79
M: 4 Fairbanks-Morse 38D8⅛ diesels, electric drive; 3 props (2 aft, 1 fwd); 10,000 hp
Range: 10,000/18.7; 41,000/9 **Man:** 10 officers, 117 men

REMARKS: Built for use on the Great Lakes. Helicopter platform. Fitted with two 12-ton cranes. Can break 1.2-m solid ice.

PATROL CRAFT

♦ **26 95-ft Cape class** Bldr: Coast Guard Yard, Curtis Bay, Md., 1953-59

WPB 95300 CAPE SMALL	WPB 95313 CAPE MORGAN
WPB 95301 CAPE CORAL	WPB 95314 CAPE FAIRWEATHER
WPB 95302 CAPE HIGGON	WPB 93516 CAPE FOX
WPB 95303 CAPE UPRIGHT	WPB 95317 CAPE JELLISON
WPB 95304 CAPE GULL	WPB 95318 CAPE NEWAGEN
WPB 95305 CAPE HATTERAS	WPB 95319 CAPE ROMAIN
WPB 95306 CAPE GEORGE	WPB 95320 CAPE STARR
WPB 95307 CAPE CURRENT	WPB 95321 CAPE CROSS
WPB 95308 CAPE STRAIT	WPB 95322 CAPE HORN
WPB 95309 CAPE CARTER	WPB 95324 CAPE SHOALWATER
WPB 95310 CAPE WASH	WPB 95326 CAPE CORWIN
WPB 95311 CAPE HEDGE	WPB 95328 CAPE HENLOPEN
WPB 95312 CAPE KNOX	WPB 95332 CAPE YORK

Cape Strait (WPB 95308)   J. Jedrlinic, 1979

D: 105 tons (fl) **S:** 18 kts (cruising, fl) **Dim:** 28.96 × 6.1 × 1.55
A: 2/40-mm Mk 64 grenade launchers (I × 2) **Man:** 1 officer, 13 men
M: 4 Cummins VT-12-M-700 diesels; 2 props; 2,324 hp **Electric:** 40 kw
Range: WPB 95300 to WPB 95311: 460/20; 2,600/9; WPB 95312 to WPB 95320: 460/20; 3,000/9; WPB 95321 to WPB 95332: 500/20; 2,800/9

REMARKS: Two transferred to Haiti (1956), two to Ethiopia (1958), four to Thailand, and one to Saudi Arabia. Nine were given to South Korea (1969-70). Several others have been scrapped. The suvivors have been reengined and rehabilitated, 1977-81, in lieu of building thirty new WPBs.

♦ **53 83-ft Point Class** Bldr: Coast Guard Yard, Curtis Bay, Md. (except WPB 82345 to WPB 83249: J. Martinac SB, Tacoma, Wash.)

In serv: WPB 82302 to WPB 82314: 1960-61; WPB 82318 to WPH 82370: 1961-67; WPB 82371 to WPB 82379: 1970

PATROL CRAFT *(continued)*

WPB 82302 Point Hope	WPB 82354 Point Evans
WPB 82311 Point Verde	WPB 82355 Point Hannon
WPB 82312 Point Swift	WPB 82356 Point Francis
WPB 82314 Point Thatcher	WPB 82357 Point Huron
WPB 82318 Point Herron	WPB 82358 Point Stuart
WPB 82332 Point Roberts	WPB 82359 Point Steele
WPB 82333 Point Highland	WPB 82360 Point Winslow
WPB 82334 Point Ledge	WPB 82361 Point Charles
WPB 82335 Point Countess	WPB 82362 Point Brown
WPB 82336 Point Glass	WPB 82363 Point Nowell
WPB 82337 Point Divide	WPB 82364 Point Whitehorn
WPB 82338 Point Bridge	WPB 82365 Point Turner
WPB 82339 Point Chico	WPB 82366 Point Lobos
WPB 82340 Point Batan	WPB 82367 Point Knoll
WPB 82341 Point Lookout	WPB 82368 Point Warde
WPB 82342 Point Baker	WPB 82369 Point Heyer
WPB 82343 Point Wells	WPB 82370 Point Richmond
WPB 82344 Point Estero	WPB 82371 Point Barnes
WPB 82345 Point Judith	WPB 82372 Point Brower
WPB 82346 Point Arena	WPB 82373 Point Camden
WPB 82347 Point Bonita	WPB 82374 Point Carrew
WPB 82348 Point Barrow	WPB 82375 Point Doran
WPB 82349 Point Spencer	WPB 82376 Point Harris
WPB 82350 Point Franklin	WPB 82377 Point Hobart
WPB 82351 Point Bennett	WPB 82378 Point Jackson
WPB 82352 Point Sal	WPB 82379 Point Martin
WPB 82353 Point Monroe	

Point Verde (WPB 82311)   R. Scheina, 6-80

D: 64 tons (66-69 fl)   **S:** 23.7 kts (see Remarks)   **Dim:** 25.3 × 5.23 × 1.95
A: 2/40-mm Mk 64 grenade launchers (I × 2) or none
M: 2 Cummins VT-12-M diesels; 2 props; 1,600 hp
Range: 460/23.7; 1,400-1,500/8-9   **Man:** 1 officer, 7 men

REMARKS: Hull in mild steel. High-speed diesels controlled from the bridge. The heavier WPB 82371 and later make 22.6 knots, and have a range of 320/22.6; 1,200/8. WPB 82314 had two gas turbines with 1,000 hp (27-knot potential) and controllable-pitch propellers, but was again equipped with diesels. Well-equipped for salvage and towing. Beginning in 6-65, 26 were sent to Vietnam; transferred 1969-70.

♦ 1 experimental surface-effect patrol craft

WSES 1 Dorado

REMARKS: Part of a joint U.S. Navy-U.S. Coast Guard operational evaluation program, *Dorado* was leased from the builders, the consortium of Bell Aerospace-Textron and Halter Marine during 1981. The craft was to be turned over to the Navy in 1982 and is described in the U.S. Navy Experimental Craft section.

OCEANOGRAPHIC CUTTER

♦ 1 Balsam class (180-ft class)

WAGO 295 Evergreen (ex-WLR 295)

Evergreen (WAGO 295)   1973

REMARKS: Data as for *Balsam*-class buoy tenders. Built in 1944. Reconstruction for service as an oceanographic research ship completed in 2-73. Equipped with COG-LAD (Coast Guard Loran Assist Device), which gives a continuous real-time plot of ship's position. Bow-thruster fitted, also enlarged superstructure. Operates on International Ice Patrol when not doing research. Has two 40-mm Mk 64 grenade launchers (I × 2).

TRAINING CUTTER

♦ 1 Horst Wessel class Bldr: Blohm & Voss, Hamburg, Germany

	L	In serv.
WIX 327 Eagle (ex-*Horst Wessel*)	13-6-36	1-46

D: 1,784 tons (fl)   **S:** 18 kts   **Dim:** 89.9 (70.4 wl) × 11.9 × 5.2
Electron Equipt: Radar: 1/Raytheon 1500
M: 1 M.A.N. diesel; 1 prop; 700 hp (10.5 kts); 2,355 m² sail area
Electric: 450 kw   **Range:** 5,450/7.5 (diesel)
Man: 19 officers, 46 men, 180 cadets

REMARKS: Training ship at the Coast Guard Academy, New London. Sisters operate in the Brazilian Navy and Soviet merchant marine.

NOTE: *Reliance* (WTR 615, ex-WMEC 615) acts as training cutter for Coast Guard reserve personnel.

TRAINING CUTTER (continued)

Eagle (WIX 327) 1977

BUOY TENDERS, SEAGOING

♦ **30 Balsam class** Bldrs: WLB 297: Coast Guard Yard; others: Marine Iron SB, Duluth, or Zenith Dredge Co., Duluth, Minn., 1942-44

WLB 277 Cowslip	WLB 308 Papaw	WLB 397 Mariposa
WLB 290 Gentian	WLB 309 Sweetgum	WLB 399 Sagebrush
WLB 291 Laurel	WLB 388 Basswood	WLB 400 Salvia
WLB 296 Sorrel	WLB 389 Bittersweet	WLB 401 Sassafras
WLB 297 Ironwood	WLB 390 Blackhaw	WLB 402 Sedge
WLB 301 Conifer	WLB 392 Bramble	WLB 403 Spar
WLB 302 Madrona	WLB 393 Firebush	WLB 404 Sundew
WLB 305 Mesquite	WLB 394 Hornbeam	WLB 405 Sweetbrier
WLB 306 Buttonwood	WLB 395 Iris	WLB 406 Acacia
WLB 307 Planetree	WLB 396 Mallow	WLB 407 Woodrush

Bittersweet (WLB 389)—with 2/20-mm AA abaft stack USCG, 1981

D: 935 tons (1,025 fl) **S:** 12.8-13 kts **Dim:** 54.9 × 11.3 × 4.0
A: WLB 297, 389, 401, 402, 405: 2/20-mm AA (I × 2)
M: 2 diesels, electric drive; 1 prop; WLB 277 to WLB 302: 1,000 hp; WLB 297, WLB 305 to WLB 407: 1,200 hp; WLB 404: 1,800 hp
Range: Most: 4,600/12-18; 14,000/7.4; WLB 297, WLB 306 to WLB 308, WLB 388, WLB 390, WLB 396, WLB 401: 8,000/13; 23,500/7.5; WLB 305, WLB 392, WLB 406, WLB 407: 10,500/13; 31,000/7.5
Fuel: Varies **Man:** 6 officers, 47 men

Remarks: *Evergreen* (WAGO 295) converted to oceanographic research ship. WLB 296, WLB 390, WLB 392, WLB 402, WLB 403, and WLB 404 have strengthened hulls for icebreaking, but all have icebreaker hull form. All have 20-ton derrick. These ships have been, or are being, modernized, and have rebuilt engines and propulsion motors, improved habitability, hydraulic cargo-handling gear, and bow-thrusters. *Blackthorn* (WLB 391) rammed and sunk 28-1-80, replaced by *Cowslip* (WLB 277), which was previously stricken 23-3-73, sold 1976, repurchased 19-1-81, and recommissioned 9-11-81. WLB 290 and 296 have been in reserve since 1979, awaiting modernization. *Clover* (WLB 292) redesignated WMEC in 2-80, *Citrus* (WLB 300) redesignated WMEC in 6-79. WLB 404 has a maximum speed of 15 knots. Modernized ships have greater endurance.

BUOY TENDERS, COASTAL

♦ **5 Red class (157-ft class)** Bldr: Coast Guard Yard, Curtis Bay, Md.

WLM 685 Red Wood	WLM 687 Red Birch	WLM 689 Red Oak
WLM 686 Red Beech	WLM 688 Red Cedar	

Red Cedar (WLM 688) G. Arra, 1976

D: 471 tons (512 fl) **S:** 12 kts **Dim:** 47.9 × 10.1 × 1.9
M: 2 diesels; 2 CP props; 1,800 hp
Range: 2,248/12.8; 3,055/11.6 **Man:** 4 officers, 27 men

Remarks: WLM 685 and WLM 686 built in 1964, WLM 687 in 1965, WLM 688 in 1970, and WLM 689 in 1971. Can break light ice. Have 10-ton derrick, and a bow-thruster.

♦ **7 White class (133-ft class)**

WLM 540 White Sumac	WLM 545 White Heath
WLM 542 White Bush	WLM 546 White Lupine
WLM 543 White Holly	WLM 547 White Pine
WLM 544 White Sage	

BUOY TENDERS, COASTAL (continued)

White Sage (WLM 544)   1976

D: 435 tons (600 fl)   **S:** 9.8 kts   **Dim:** 40.5 × 9.4 × 2.7
M: 2 Union diesels; 2 props; 600 hp   **Electric:** 90 kw   **Fuel:** 40 tons
Range: 2,100/9.8; 4,500/5.1   **Man:** 1 officer, 20 men

REMARKS: WLM 540 built in 1943, WLM 542 and WLM 543 in 1944; others in 1942.
Former U.S. Navy YF (covered lighter, self-propelled). One 10-ton boom.

♦ 3 Hollyhock class (175-ft class)

WLM 212 FIR   WLM 220 HOLLYHOCK   WLM 252 WALNUT

Fir (WLM 212)   1974

D: 989 tons (fl)   **S:** 12 kts   **Dim:** 53.4 × 10.4 × 3.7
M: 2 diesels; 2 props; 1,350 hp
Range: 6,500/12; 10,000/7.5; WLM 212: 5,650/12; 8,675/7.5
Man: 5 officers, 35 men

REMARKS: WLM 220 built in 1937, others in 1939. WLM 220 and WLM 252, reengined
1958-59, have shorter stacks. All have a 20-ton boom. Redesignated from WLB to
WLM on 1-1-65.

BUOY TENDERS, INLAND

♦ 1 Buckthorn class (In serv. 1963)

WLI 642 BUCKTHORN

D: 200 tons (fl)   **S:** 11.9 kts   **Dim:** 30.5 × 7.3 × 1.2   **Man:** 1 officer, 13 men
M: 2 diesels; 2 props; 600 hp   **Range:** 1,300/11.9; 2,000/7.3

REMARKS: Bow rectangular at main deck. Has one 5-ton boom. Based on the Great
Lakes.

♦ 2 Bayberry class (65400 class) (In serv. 1954)

WLI 65400 BAYBERRY   WLI 65401 ELDERBERRY

D: 68 tons (fl)   **S:** 11.3 kts   **Dim:** 19.8 × 5.2 × 1.2
M: 2 diesels; 2 props; 400 hp   **Range:** 800/11.3; 1,700/6   **Man:** 5 tot.

♦ 2 Blackberry class (65300 class) (In serv. 1946)

WLI 65303 BLACKBERRY   WLI 65304 CHOKEBERRY

D: 68 tons (fl)   **S:** 9 kts   **Dim:** 19.8 × 5.2 × 1.2
M: 1 diesel; 1 prop; 220 hp   **Range:** 700/9; 1,500/5   **Man:** 5 tot.

♦ 1 Cosmos class (100-ft class)

WLI 313 BLUEBELL (In serv. 1945)

D: 178 tons (fl)   **S:** 10.5 kts   **Dim:** 30.5 × 7.3 × 1.5
M: 2 diesels; 2 props; 600 hp   **Range:** 1,400/10.5; 2,700/7

REMARKS: Four sisters retyped WLIC on 1-10-79.

BUOY TENDERS, RIVER

♦ 9 Gasconade class (75-ft class)

	In serv.		In serv.
WLR 75401 GASCONADE	1964	WLR 75406 KICKAPOO	1969
WLR 75402 MUSKINGUM	1965	WLR 75407 KANAWHA	1969
WLR 75403 WYACONDA	1965	WLR 75408 PATOKA	1970
WLR 75404 CHIPPEWA	1965	WLR 75409 CHENA	1970
WLR 75405 CHEYENNE	1966		

D: 141 tons (fl)   **S:** 7.6-8.7 kts   **Dim:** 22.9 × 6.7 × 1.2
M: 2 diesels; 2 props; 600 hp   **Range:** 1,600/7.6; 3,100/6.5   **Man:** 12 tot.

REMARKS: Flat-ended, barge-like hulls. WLR 75401 and WLR 75405 have associated
buoy barges, which they push; they also have slightly larger crews. One 1-ton crane.
All operate on the Mississippi River and its tributaries.

♦ 6 Ouachita class (65-ft class)

WLR 65501 OUACHITA	WLR 65503 OBION	WLR 65505 OSAGE
WLR 65502 CIMARRON	WLR 65504 SCIOTO	WLR 65506 SANGAMON

D: 130-143 tons (fl)   **S:** 10 kts   **Dim:** 20.1 × 6.4 × 1.5
M: 2 diesels; 2 props; 600 hp   **Range:** 1,700/10.5; 3,500/6   **Man:** 10 tot.

BUOY TENDERS, RIVER *(continued)*

REMARKS: WLR 65501 and WLR 65502 built in 1960, others in 1962. WLR 65504 has an associated push-type buoy barge with a 3-ton crane, and a larger crew. All have a 3-ton crane aboard. Operate on the Mississippi River and its tributaries.

◆ **1 Sumac class (115-ft class)** (In serv. 1943)

WLR 311 SUMAC

    D: 404 tons (478 fl) **S:** 10.6 kts **Dim:** 35.1 × 9.1 × 1.8
    M: 3 diesels; 3 props; 2,250 hp
    Range: 5,000/10.6; 11,600/5 **Man:** 1 officer, 22 men

◆ **1 Lantana class (80-ft class)** (In serv. 1943)

WLR 80310 LANTANA

    D: 235 tons (fl) **S:** 10 kts **Dim:** 24.3 × 9.1 × 1.8
    M: 3 diesels; 3 props; 945 hp **Range:** 5,000/10 **Man:** 1 officer, 19 men

◆ **1 Dogwood class (114-ft class)** (In serv. 1940)

WLR 259 DOGWOOD

    D: 230 tons (310 fl) **S:** 11 kts **Dim:** 34.8 × 7.9 × 1.2
    M: 2 diesels; 2 props; 800 hp
    Range: 1,300/11; 2,800/5.5 **Man:** 1 officer, 20 men

CONSTRUCTION TENDERS, INLAND

◆ **4 Pamlico class (160-ft class)** Bldr: Coast Guard Yard, Curtis Bay, Md.

	In serv.		In serv.
WLIC 800 PAMLICO	1966	WLIC 803 KENNEBEC	1977
WLIC 801 HUDSON	1966	WLIC 804 SAGINAW	1977

Pamlico (WLIC 800) 1976

    D: 413 tons (459 fl) **S:** 11.5 kts **Dim:** 49.1 × 9.1 × 1.2
    Electron Equipt: Radar: 1/LN-66
    M: 2 Cummins D379, 8-cyl. diesels; 2 props; 1,000 hp
    Range: 1,400/11; 2,200/6.5 **Man:** 1 officer, 13 men

REMARKS: Design combines capabilities of the *Anvil* class and their associated equipment barges. One 9-ton crane.

◆ **10 Anvil class (75-ft class)** (In serv. 1962-65)

WLIC 75301 ANVIL	WLIC 75305 VISE	WLIC 75308 SPIKE
WLIC 75302 HAMMER	WLIC 75306 CLAMP	WLIC 75309 HATCHET
WLIC 75303 SLEDGE	WLIC 75307 WEDGE	WLIC 75310 AXE
WLIC 75304 MALLET		

    D: 145 tons (fl) **S:** 9.1 kts **Dim:** 22.9 × 6.7 × 1.2
    M: 2 diesels; 2 props; 600 hp **Range:** 2,200/5 **Man:** 0 or 1 officer, 9 men

REMARKS: Most have an associated push-type barge with a 9-ton crane. WLIC 75306 to WLIC 75310 are 23.2 m overall and can make 9.4 knots.

◆ **4 Cosmos class (100-ft class)**

	In serv.		In serv.
WLIC 293 COSMOS	1942	WLIC 315 SMILAX	1944
WLIC 298 RAMBLER	1944	WLIC 316 PRIMROSE	1944

Primrose (WLIC 316) USCG, 5-81

    D: 178 tons (fl) **S:** 10.5 kts **Dim:** 30.5 × 7.3 × 1.5
    Electron Equipt: Radar: 1/LN-66 **M:** 2 diesels; 2 props; 600 hp
    Range: 1,400/10.5; 2,700/7 **Man:** 1 officer, 14 men

REMARKS: Reclassified from WLI on 1-10-79. Sister *Bluebell* remains typed WLI (WLI 313). WLIC 293 and WLIC 298 have associated construction barges, while WLIC 316 has a piledriver on her bow. All have a 5-ton crane.

ICEBREAKING TUGS

◆ **6 (+2+2) Katmai Bay class (140-ft class)** Bldr: Tacoma Boatbuilding, Tacoma, Wash.

ICEBREAKING TUGS (continued)

	Laid down	L	In serv.
WTGB 101 Katmai Bay	7-11-77	8-4-78	8-1-79
WTGB 102 Bristol Bay	13-2-78	22-7-78	5-4-79
WTGB 103 Mobile Bay	13-2-78	11-11-78	6-5-79
WTGB 104 Biscayne Bay	29-8-78	3-2-79	8-12-79
WTGB 105 Neah Bay	6-8-79	. . .	18-8-80
WTGB 106 Morro Bay	6-8-79	. . .	25-1-80
WTGB 107 Penobscot Bay	. . .	. . .	. . .
WTGB 108 Thunder Bay	. . .	. . .	. . .
WTGB 109 Sturgeon Bay	. . .	. . .	. . .
WTGB 110 N. . .	. . .	. . .	. . .

Authorized: 1 in FY 76, 3 in FY 77, 2 in FY 78, 1 in FY 81
Proposed: 1 in FY 82, 1 in FY 83

Neah Bay (WTGB 105) USCG, 8-80

Katmai Bay (WTGB 101)—black hull scheme retained USCG, 1980

D: 662 tons (fl) **S:** 14.7 kts **Dim:** 42.67 (39.62 pp) × 11.43 × 3.66
M: 2 Fairbanks-Morse 38D8⅛ diesels, Westinghouse electric drive; 1 prop; 2,500 hp
Electric: 250 kw **Range:** 1,800/14.7; 4,000/12 **Man:** 3 officers, 14 men

REMARKS: Reclassified from WYTM on 5-2-79; beginning with WGTB 103 have white hulls (the first two will be repainted). Initial units to operate on the Great Lakes. Can break 45-50-mm ice. Have portable bubble-generator system housed in a removeable deckhouse on the fantail. Two firefighting monitors atop the pilothouse, which provides near 360-degree viewing. One 2-ton crane handles a 4.9-m plastic workboat. Initially intended to replace the older WYTMs in service.

HARBOR TUGS, MEDIUM

♦ 10 110-ft class

Bldr: Ira S. Bushey, Brooklyn, N.Y. (WYTM 60 and WYTM 61: Coast Guard Yard, Curtis Bay, Md.)

WYTM 60 Manitou	WYTM 91 Mahoning
WYTM 71 Apalachee	WYTM 93 Raritan
WYTM 72 Yankton	WYTM 96 Chinook
WYTM 73 Mohican	WYTM 98 Snohomish
WYTM 90 Arundel	WYTM 99 Sauk

Chinook (WYTM 96) USCG, 1977

D: 370 tons (384 fl) **S:** 11.2 kts **Dim:** 33.54 × 8.29 × 3.51
Electron Equipt: Radar: 1/LN-66
M: 2 GM or Ingersoll-Rand 8-cyl. diesels, electric drive; 1 prop; 1,000 hp
Range: 1,845/11.2; 4,000/8 **Man:** 1 officer, 19 men

REMARKS: WYTM 90 to WYTM 93 were built in 1939, the others in 1943. *Kaw* (WYTM 61), *Naugatuck* (WYTM 92), were stricken 15-6-79; *Ojibwa* (WYTM 97) stricken 6-5-80. All await disposal.

NOTE: The 85-ft. class tug *Messenger* (WYTM 85009) was reclassified as a "boat" on 25-8-80.

HARBOR TUGS, SMALL

♦ **15 65-ft class** (In serv. 1961-67)

WYTL 65601 Capstan	WYTL 65606 Catenary	WYTL 65611 Line
WYTL 65602 Chock	WYTL 65607 Bridle	WYTL 65612 Wire
WYTL 65603 Swivel	WYTL 65608 Pendant	WYTL 65613 Bitt
WYTL 65604 Tackle	WYTL 65609 Shackle	WYTL 65614 Bollard
WYTL 65605 Towline	WYTL 65610 Hawser	WYTL 65615 Cleat

Capstan (WYTL 65601)   R. Scheina, 1979

D: 72 tons (fl)   **S:** 9.8 (first 6: 10.5)   **Dim:** 19.8 × 5.8 × 2.1
Electron Equipt: Radar: 1/Raytheon 1900   **M:** 1 diesel; 1 prop; 400 hp
Range: 850/9.8; 2,700/5.8 (WYTL 65601 to WYTL 65606: 3,600/6.8; 8,900/10.5
Man: 10 tot.

LIGHTSHIPS

♦ **2 28-ft class** (In serv. 1950)

WLV 604 Lightship Columbia   WLV 612 Lightship Nantucket

D: 607 tons (fl) (WLV 604: 617 tons)   **S:** 11 kts   **Dim:** 39.0 × 9.1 × 3.4
M: 1 diesel; 1 prop; 550 hp   **Range:** 14,000/11; 28,000/4.8

Remarks: All lightships have now been replaced by fixed installations. WLV 604 is assigned to Astoria, Oregon; WLV 612 to Boston, Mass., for the Nantucket Shoals station, both in standby reserve. WLV 604 range: 14,000/10.7; 25,000/6.1.

FERRIES

Note: The following three ships are not commissioned cutters of the U.S. Coast Guard but are under Coast Guard control. Their status is "in service" and they are civilian-manned. Former U.S. Army units, they operate from Governors Island in New York Harbor.

Lt. Samuel S. Cours (In serv. 1956)   Pvt. Nicholas Minue (In serv. 1956)

D: 869 tons   **S:** 12 kts   **Dim:** 54.9 × 18.9 × 3.0
M: Diesel-electric drive;. . . props; 1,000 hp

The Tides (In serv. 1946)

The Tides   J. Jedrlinic, 1981

D: 744 tons (l)   **S:** 12 kts   **Dim:** 56.4 × 16.8 × 2.7
M: Diesel-electric drive;. . . props; 1,350 hp

SMALL CRAFT

The U.S. Coast Guard operates some 2,000 small craft. No central registry of their numbers is maintained, their administration being the responsibility of the stations to which they are attached. All carry five-digit serial numbers, the first two digits of which denote the craft's length in feet. Typical units in several numerically important classes are shown on the following page.

The glass-reinforced, plastic-hulled utility boat series started with number 41300. The design was a replacement for the standard "40-footer" of 1950s construction. No. 41411 carries an LN-66 radar   J. Jedrlinic, 1980

U.S.A. *(continued)*

SMALL CRAFT *(continued)*

Powered by a single GM 6-71 diesel, the 45-ft. buoy-tender class handles small navigational buoys with a hydraulically powered quadrantial derrick over the bow. Number 45312 has a Raytheon 1900 radar.   C. Dragonette, 1980

The 44-ft. motor lifeboat is an "unsinkable" design, built at the U.S. Coast Guard Yard, Curtis Bay, Md. in the 1960s. The 16-ton(fl) craft are powered by two GM 6-71 diesels; 2 props; 360 hp for 15-kt. speeds, and a range of 150/12. Dim: 13.60 × 3.86 × 0.93   USCG

A 20-ft. outdrive-powered, glass-reinforced, plastic-hulled local patrol craft, Number 201511 is a standard Penn Van pleasure craft adapted for Coast Guard requirements.   A. Baker, 7-76

URUGUAY
ORIENTAL REPUBLIC OF URUGUAY

PERSONNEL (1981): 5,200, including 500 officers, 3,700 enlisted, and 1,000 Marines

MERCHANT MARINE (1980): 72 ships—198,478 grt
(tankers: 7 ships—96,616 grt)

NAVAL AVIATION: Fixed-wing aircraft include 3 Grumman S-2A Tracker ASW patrol, 3 Beech SNB-5 (C-45) utility transports, 1 Embraer EMB-110B Bandeirante, 3 North American SNJ (T-6 Texan) trainers, and 1 Beech T-34B Mentor trainer. Helicopters include 2 Bell 47G and 2 Sikorsky SH-34C. 1 Beech King Air Maritime Patrol aircraft with surveillance radar was delivered 15-1-81. In mid-1981, the U.S. agreed to sell Uruguay 3 surplus Grumman S-2G Tracker aircraft.

FRIGATES

♦ **1 ex-U.S. Dealey class** Bldr: Bath Iron Works, Me.

	Laid down	L	In serv.
DE 3 18 DE JULIO (ex-*Dealey*, DE 1006)	15-10-52	8-11-53	3-6-54

D: 1,450 tons (1,914 fl)   **S:** 25 kts   **Dim:** 95.86 × 11.2 × 4.04 (5.27 over sonar)
A: 4/76.2-mm DP (II × 2)—6/324-mm Mk 32 ASW TT—1/d.c. rack
Electron Equipt: Radar: 1/SPS-5D, 1/SPS-6E, 2/SPG-34
                    Sonar: 1/SQS-29 series—ECM: WLR-1
M: 1 set de Laval GT; 1 prop; 20,000 hp
Boilers: 2 Foster-Wheeler "D"; 42 kg/cm², 510°C
Fuel: 360 tons   **Range:** 4,400/11   **Man:** 11 officers, 150 men

REMARKS: First and least-modified of her class. One sister survives in the Colombian Navy. Two Mk 63 GFCS. New superstructure added abreast the stack. Purchased on 28-7-72. Refitted 1979-80 in Argentina.

FRIGATES (continued)

♦ **2 ex-U.S. Cannon class** Bldr: Federal SB & DD, Newark, N.J.

	Laid down	L	In serv.
DE 1 URUGUAY (ex-*Baron*, DE 166)	30-11-42	9-5-43	5-7-43
DE 2 ARTIGAS (ex-*Bronstein*, DE 189)	26-8-43	14-11-43	13-12-43

Artigas (DE 2)

D: 1,240 tons light (1,900 fl) **S:** 19 kts **Dim:** 93.27 × 11.15 × 3.56 (hull)
A: 3/76.2-mm DP (I × 3)—2/40-mm AA (II × 1)—4/20-mm AA (I × 4)—1/Mk 11
  Hedgehog—8/Mk 6 d.c. projectors—1/Mk 9 d.c. rack
Electron Equipt: Radar: 1/SPS-5, 1/SPS-6C (not in DE 1), 1/navigational
  Sonar: SQS-4 series
M: 4 GM 16-278A diesels, electric drive; 2 props; 6,000 hp
Electric: 680 kw **Fuel:** 315 tons **Range:** 8,300/14 **Man:** 160 tot.

REMARKS: DE 1 was transferred in 5-52 and DE 2 in 3-52. Modernized in late 1960s
with new radars. No radar fire control but do have Mk 51 range-finder for 76.2-mm
guns and Mk 51 Mod. 2 lead-computing director for 40-mm AA. DE 1 does not have
stub mainmast and has had the SPS-6C radar removed. Both have had four single
20-mm AA added recently.

CORVETTE

♦ **1 ex-U.S. Auk-class former minesweeper**

Bldr: Defoe Boiler & Machine Works, Bay City, Mich.

	Laid down	L	In serv.
4 COMANDANTE PEDRO CAMPBELL	21-8-41	20-7-42	9-11-42
(ex-MS 31, ex-*Chickadee*, MSF 59)			

D: 890 tons (1,250 fl) **S:** . . . **Dim:** 67.41 (65.53 wl) × 9.78 × 3.28
A: 1/76.2-mm DP—4/40-mm AA (II × 2)—4/20-mm AA (II × 2)
Electron Equipt: Radar: 1/navigational, 1/SO-8
M: 4 Alco 539 diesels, electric drive; 2 props; 3,118 hp
Electric: 300 kw **Man:** 105 tot.

Comandante Pedro Campbell(4)—old number

REMARKS: Transferred on 18-8-66 and purchased on 18-8-76. Retains some minesweeping equipment, but has no ASW capability.

NOTE: The former French, former U.S. MS-33, *Agile*-class ocean minesweeper *Mal-
donado* (ex-*Bir Hakeim*, ex-MSO 451) was stricken 1979; the ship had been considered to be a corvette.

PATROL BOATS

♦ **3 French Vigilante class** Bldr: CMN, Cherbourg

	Laid down	L	In serv.
5 15 DE NOVIEMBRE	6-12-79	16-10-80	25-3-81
6 25 DE AGOSTO	6-2-80	11-2-80	25-3-81
7 COMODORO COE	16-5-80	27-1-81	25-3-81

15 De Noviembre(5)—on trials   CMN, 1981

PATROL BOATS (continued)

D: 166 tons (220 fl) **S:** 28 kts **Dim:** 41.8 (38.9 pp) × 6.7 × 2.5 (1.56 hull)
A: 1/40-mm AA
Electron Equipt: Radar: 1/Decca TM 1226C, 1/Decca 1229
M: 2 MTU 12V538 TB91 diesels; 2 props; 5,400 hp
Range: 2,400/15 **Man:** 5 officers, 22 men

REMARKS: Ordered 1978. CSEE Panda optronic GFCS for the 40-mm gun, which has a fiberglass cover to the mount. All commissioned day of departure under own power to Uruguay from Cherbourg. Twin 20-mm AA planned aft, not mounted.

♦ 1 ex-U.S. Adjutant-class former minesweeper

Bldr: National Steel SB, San Diego, Cal.

	In serv.
13 RIO NEGRO (ex-MS 32, ex-*Marguerite*, ex-MSC 94)	3-54

Rio Negro(13)—old number, most minesweeping gear now removed

D: 300 tons (372 fl) **S:** 13 kts **Dim:** 43.0 (41.5 pp) × 7.95 × 2.95
A: 2/20-mm AA (II × 1)
Electron Equipt: Radar: 1/DRBN-31—Sonar: UQS-1D
M: 2 GM 8-268A diesels; 2 props; 1,200 hp
Range: 2,500/10 **Man:** 38 tot.

REMARKS: On completion, transferred to France, then to Uruguay on 10-11-69. Wooden construction. Most minesweeping equipment, including sweep winch and cable drum, now removed.

PATROL CRAFT

♦ 1 U.S. 85-foot commercial cruiser Bldr: Sewart Seacraft, Morgan City, La.

PR 12 PAYSANDU (L: 11-68)

D: 43.5 tons (54 fl) **S:** 22 kts **Dim:** 25.91 × 5.69 × 2.1
A: 3/12.7-mm mg (I × 3) **Electron Equipt:** Radar: 1/Raytheon 1500B
M: 2 GM 16V71N diesels; 2 props; 1,400 hp **Electric:** 40 kw
Range: 800/21 **Man:** 8 tot.

REMARKS: Built under U.S. Military Assistance Program. Aluminum construction.

♦ 1 ex-German FL-9 class Bldr: Krögerwerft, Rendsburg (In serv. 1955)

PR 11 CARMELO

D: 67 tons (73 fl) **S:** 30 kts **Dim:** 28.8 (27.9 pp) × 5.0 × 1.6
A: 1/20-mm AA **Electron Equipt:** Radar: 1/Decca 12
M: 2 Maybach 12-cyl. diesels; 2 props; 3,000 hp
Range: 600/25 **Man:** 8 tot.

REMARKS: One of five sisters built as air-sea-rescue craft for the British Royal Air Force. Transferred to Uruguay in about 1961. Wooden construction.

♦ 1 ex-U.S. 63-foot AVR class

PR 10 COLONIA (L: 4-7-44)

D: 25 tons (34 fl) **S:** 28 kts **Dim:** 19.3 × 4.67 × 1.22
A: 4/12.7-mm mg (II × 2)
M: 2 Hall-Scott Defender V-12 gasoline engines; 2 props; 1,260 hp
Fuel: 4.3 tons **Range:** 450/25; 600/15 **Man:** 8 tot.

REMARKS: Former air-sea-rescue boat, transferred in about 1945. Wooden construction. No radar.

NOTE: There are a number of small patrol launches with pendant numbers in the PM series.

AMPHIBIOUS WARFARE CRAFT

♦ 2 LD 43-class landing craft Bldr: Naval SY, Montevideo (In serv. 1978-79)

LD 43   LD 44

D: 31.4 tons **S:** 9 kts **Dim:** 14.1 × 3.5 × 0.8
M: 2 GM 6-71 diesels; 2 props; 272 hp

♦ 1 small landing craft Bldr: Mapell S.A. (In serv. . . .)

LD 42

D: 12 tons **S:** 6 kts **Dim:** 12.0 × 3.4 × 1.1
M: 2 British GM Bedford 330 diesels; 2 props; 192 hp

♦ 2 U.S. LCM (6)-class landing craft

LD 40   LD 41

D: 24 tons (57 fl) **S:** 10 kts **Dim:** 17.07 × 4.37 × 1.17
M: 2 Gray Marine 64HN9 diesels; 2 props; 450 hp **Range:** 130/9

REMARKS: LD 41 and LD 42 were leased in 10-72; lease extended 1982. Cargo: 30 tons.

HYDROGRAPHIC SHIPS

♦ 1 Paysandu-class former patrol boat Bldr: CNR, Ancona

14 SALTO (ex-GS 24) (L: 11-8-35)

D: 150 tons (180 fl) **S:** 17 kts **Dim:** 42.1 × 5.8 × 1.58
M: 2 Krupp-Germania diesels; 2 props; 1,000 hp
Range: 4,000/10 **Man:** 26 tot.

REMARKS: Survivor of a class of three, placed on present duties as a survey craft and navigational-buoy tender in 1972.

HYDROGRAPHIC SHIPS *(continued)*

♦ **3 inshore-survey craft**

PS 1   PS 2   PS 3

REMARKS: No data available.

AUXILIARY SHIPS

♦ **1 supertanker** Bldr: Kawasaki, Kobe, Japan, 1975

27 JUAN A. LAVALLEJA (ex-*Solfonn*)

    D: 145,000 tons (fl)   **S:** 15.5 kts   **Dim:** 273.0 × 44.1 × 15.7
    M: 2 sets GT; 1 prop; 24,500 hp   **Boilers:** 2   **Man:** . . .

REMARKS: 131,663 dwt, 68,931 grt. Literally, the world's largest naval ship, by a wide margin. Laid up by Norwegian owner on 13-10-75, when she was completed. Purchased by Uruguay on 13-1-77 for use by ANCAP, the state petroleum monopoly, in commercial service with a naval crew. No underway replenishment capability. Grounded 28-12-80 off Arzew, Algeria; refloated 17-2-81 and repaired in France.

♦ **1 tanker** Bldr: Bazán, Spain, 1971

28 PRESIDENTE RIVERA

    D: 36,000 tons (fl)   **S:** 16.5 kts   **Dim:** 194.0 (191.0 pp) × 25.4 × 9.8
    M: 1 diesel; 1 prop; 15,300 hp   **Man:** 58 tot.

REMARKS: 31,885 dwt, 19,656 grt. Used in commercial service, with a naval crew, by ANCAP, the state petroleum monopoly. Refitted at Durban, South Africa, in 1979.

♦ **1 transport, former merchant cargo ship**

	Bldr	In serv.
29 PRESIDENTE ORIBE (ex-Danish *Catrina*)	Frederikshavn, Denmark	1966

    D: 1,153 tons   **S:** 10 kts   **Dim:** 54.2 × 9.6 × 3.3
    M: 1 Burmeister & Wain diesel; 1 prop; 520 hp

REMARKS: Ran aground while in merchant service 11-78 and salvaged by Uruguayan Navy; purchased from British insurance company and commissioned 19-8-80.

♦ **1 ex-U.S. Cohoes-class salvage ship** Bldr: Commercial Ironworks, Portland, Ore.

	Laid down	L	In serv.
AM 25 HURACAN (ex-*Nahant*, AN 83, ex-YN 102)	31-3-45	30-6-45	24-8-45

    D: 650 tons (855 fl)   **S:** 12.3 kts   **Dim:** 51.36 (44.5 pp) × 10.31 × 3.3
    A: 3/20-mm AA (I × 3)   **Electron Equipt:** Radar: 1/SPS-5
    M: 2 Busch-Sulzer BS539 diesels, electric drive; 1 prop; 1,200 hp   **Man:** 48 tot.

REMARKS: Former netlayer. Transferred in 12-68. A decompression chamber for divers was added in 1974.

♦ **1 ex-U.S. harbor tug** Bldr: Bellingham Iron Works, Bellingham, Wash., 1944

AM 26 VANGUARDIA (ex-YTL 589)

    D: 100 tons   **S:** 12 kts   **Dim:** 20.17 × 5.18 × . . .
    M: 1 Hoover-Owens-Rentschler diesel; 1 prop; 300 hp

REMARKS: Transferred in 9-65.

♦ **1 sail training ship**

	Bldr	In serv.
20 CAPITAN MIRANDA (ex-GS 20)	Soc. Española de Construccion Naval, Matagorda, Cadiz, Spain	1930

Capitan Miranda(20)—number not borne   1980

    D: 516 tons (550 fl)   **S:** 11 kts   **Dim:** 54.6 (61.0 bowsprit/45.0 pp) × 8.4 × 3.2
    Electron Equipt: Radar: 1/Decca TM 1226C
    M: 1 M.A.N. diesel; 1 prop; 500 hp   **Fuel:** 45 tons   **Man:** 49 tot.

REMARKS: Originally built as a 3-masted schooner for use as yacht and cadet training ship; de-rigged during the 1960s and used as a hydrographic survey ship. Refitted and restored to original configuration in 1978.

COAST GUARD

A Uruguayan Coast Guard was established in 1981, with 100 officers and about 1,900 enlisted men. Primarily intended for a shore-based coast watch and port police function, it does operate three 21-m patrol boats, two 9-m patrol craft, and a number of outboard-motor-powered semi-inflatable rubber boats.

VENEZUELA
REPUBLIC OF VENEZUELA

PERSONNEL: 7,500 men, including 4,000 marines

MERCHANT MARINE (1980): 225 ships—848,540 grt
(tankers: 20 ships—324,636 grt)

NAVAL AVIATION: The small naval aviation component operates six Grumman S-2E Tracker ASW patrol aircraft, two Douglas C-47 transports, one Hawker-Siddeley (BAe) HS-748 transport, 2 Beech King Air 98 light transports, and one Cessna 337 liaison aircraft. Twelve Agusta-Bell AB-212 helicopters are on order for the *Lupo*-class frigates; six had been delivered by mid-1981.

SUBMARINES

♦ **2 (+2) German Type 209** Bldr: Howaldtswerke, Kiel

	Laid down	L	In serv.
S 31 SABALO	2-5-73	1-17-75	6-8-76
S 32 CONGRIO	1-8-73	6-11-75	11-3-77
S 33 N. . .	. . .	. . .	. . .
S 34 N. . .	. . .	. . .	. . .

D: 990/1,350 tons **S:** 10/22 kts **Dim:** 55.0 × 6.6 × 5.9
A: 8/533-mm TT—12 torpedoes
M: Diesel-electric propulsion: 4 MTU Type 12V492 Tb90 diesels; Siemens electric motor; 3,600 hp
Man: 5 officers, 26 men

REMARKS: S 31, S 32 ordered 1971; S 33, S 34 ordered 10-3-77. S 31 damaged by fire in 1979, overhauled at Kiel. Progress on second pair unreported.

♦ **1 ex-U.S. Guppy II**

	Bldr	Laid down	L	In serv.
SS 22 PICUDA (ex-*Grenadier*, SS 525)	Boston Naval SY	8-2-44	15-12-44	10-2-51

D: 2,040/2,420 tons **S:** 18/16 kts **Dim:** 93.57 × 8.33 × 5.18
A: 10/533-mm TT (6 fwd, 4 aft)
Electron Equipt: Radar: 1/SS-2—Sonar: BQR-2
M: Fairbanks-Morse 38D8⅛ diesels, electric drive; 2 props; 4,160 hp
Man: 82 tot.

REMARKS: Purchased 15-5-73, having been completed as a Guppy II. Four 126-cell batteries. Sister *Tiburon* (S 21, ex-*Cubora*, SS 347) stricken 1979. S 22 was overhauled at Punta Belgrano Naval SY, Argentina, from 1979 to 7-81.

GUIDED MISSILE FRIGATES

♦ **6 Italian Lupo class** Bldr: CNR, Riva Trigoso, Italy

	Laid down	L	In serv.
F 21 MARISCAL SUCRE	4-10-77	28-9-78	14-7-80
F 22 ALMIRANTE BRION	6-77	22-2-79	7-3-81
F 23 GENERAL URDANETA	23-1-78	23-3-79	8-8-81
F 24 GENERAL SOUBLETTE	26-8-78	4-1-80	1982
F 25 GENERAL SALOM	7-11-78	13-1-80	1982
F 26 JOSÉ FELIX RIBAS	21-8-79	4-10-80	1982

Mariscal Sucre (F 21)—Otomat racks empty   C. Martinelli, 1981

D: 2,213 tons (2,525 fl) **S:** 35 kts (20.5 on diesels)
Dim: 112.8 (106.0 pp) × 11.98 × 3.84 (hull)
A: 8/Otomat Mk II SSM (I × 8)—1/Albatros SAM system (VIII × 1, no reloads)—1/127-mm OTO Melara DP—4/40-mm Breda Dardo AA (II × 2)—6/324-mm Mk 32 ASW TT (III × 2, for A244 torpedoes)—2/AB-212 ASW helicopters
Electron Equipt: Radar: 1/3RM20 navigational, 1/RAN-11/X air and surface search, 1/RAN-10S air search, 2/Orion RTN-10X, 2/Orion RTN-20X—TACAN: SEN-15A
Sonar: Edo 610E—ECM: Lambda-F, 2/SCLAR chaff RL
M: CODOG: 2 Fiat GE LM-2500 gas turbines, 25,000 hp each; 2 GMT A230-2M diesels, 3,900 hp each; 2 CP props
Electric: 3,120 kw **Range:** 900/35; 1,050/31.7; 5,500/16 **Man:** 185 tot.

REMARKS: Ordered 24-10-75. Fin stabilizers fitted. Gun (127-mm) and missile fire control by two Elsag NA-10 Mod. 0 systems. The Albatros system uses Aspide missiles, a re-engineered version of NATO Sea Sparrow. Each twin 40-mm Dardo system antiaircraft mount has an associated RTN-20X radar director. All weapons controlled by a Selenia IPN-10 computerized data system. Fixed, nontelescopic hangar. Near-sisters in the Italian and Peruvian navies, with others on order for Iraq and Egypt.

NOTE: The U.S. *Allen M. Sumner*-class destroyer *Carabobo* (D 21, ex-*Beatty*, DD 756) was stricken in mid-1981, and the *Allen M. Sumner*-class FRAM-II destroyer *Falcon* (D 22, ex-*Robert K. Huntington*, DD 781) was stricken at the end of the year.

FRIGATES

♦ **2 Almirante Clemente class** Bldr: Ansaldo, Livorno

	Laid down	L	In serv.
F 10 General José Trinidad Moran	5-5-54	12-12-54	1956
F 11 Almirante Clemente	5-5-54	12-12-54	1956

D: 1,300 tons (1,500 fl) **S:** 29 kts **Dim:** 97.6 × 10.84 × 2.6
A: 2/76-mm OTO Melara DP (I × 2)—2/40-mm AA (II × 2)—6/324-mm Mk 32 ASW TT (III × 2)
Electron Equipt: Radar: 1/Decca 1226, 1/Plessey AWS-2, 1/Orion RTN-10X
    Sonar: Plessey MS-26
M: 2 sets GT; 2 props; 24,000 hp **Range:** 2,500/18; 4,000/15 **Fuel:** 350 tons
Boilers: 2 Foster-Wheeler, 43.3 kg/cm², 454°C **Man:** 12 officers, 150 men

REMARKS: Survivors of a class of six: *General José de Austria* stricken 1976, *General José Garcia* stricken 1977, and *General Juan José Flores* and *Almirante Brion* stricken 1978. Both were extensively refitted by Cammell Laird, Birkenhead, from 1968 to 1975-76 (much delay caused by financial and labor problems). New radars, sonar, and armament fitted, with OTO Melara Compact mounts replacing the original four 102-mm dual-purpose (II × 2). Have NA-10 GFCS for the 76-mm guns and a lead-computing sight for the 40-mm AA mount. When new, could make 32 knots. Very lightly built with much use of aluminum alloy. Denny-Brown fin stabilizers. Now scheduled to be re-engined with diesels 1982-83 and transferred to the new Coast Guard.

PATROL BOATS

♦ **6 Constitución class** Bldr: Vosper Thornycroft, Portsmouth, G.B.

	Laid down	L	In serv.
P 11 Constitución	1-73	1-6-73	16-8-74
P 12 Federación	8-73	26-2-74	25-3-75
P 13 Independencia	2-73	24-7-73	20-9-74
P 14 Libertad	9-73	5-3-74	12-6-75
P 15 Patria	3-73	27-9-73	9-1-75
P 16 Victoria	3-73	3-9-74	22-9-75

Constitución (P 11)—76-mm gun version   Vosper, 1975

D: 150 tons (170 fl) **S:** 31 kts **Dim:** 36.88 (33.53 wl) × 7.16 × 1.73
A: P 11, P 13, P 15: 1/76-mm OTO Melara Compact
    P 12, P 14, P 16: 2/Otomat Mk I SSM (I × 2)—1/40-mm AA
Electron Equipt: 1/SPQ-2D; P 11, P13, P 15: 1/Orion RTN-10X also
M: 2 MTU MD 16V538 TB90 diesels; 1 prop; 7,000 max. hp/5,900 sust. hp
Electric: 250 kw **Range:** 1,350/16 **Man:** 3 officers, 14 men

REMARKS: Ordered 4-72. All equipped with Vosper fin stabilizers. New hull numbers assigned 1978. Maximum sustained speed is 27 knots. NA-10 Mod. 1 GFCS in 76-mm gun-equipped boats.

AMPHIBIOUS WARFARE SHIP

♦ **1 ex-U.S. Terrebonne Parish-class landing ship**

Bldr: Ingalls, Pascagoula

	Laid down	L	In serv.
T 51 Amazonas (ex-*Vernon County*, LST 1161)	14-4-52	1952	1954

Amazonas (T 51)   1977

D: 2,590 tons (5,786 fl) **S:** 13 kts **Dim:** 117.35 × 16.76 × 5.18
A: 6/76.2-mm DP (II × 3) **Electric:** 600 kw **Man:** 116 tot.
Electron Equipt: 1/Decca navigational, 1/SPS-21, 2/SPG-34
M: 4 GM 16-278A diesels; 2 CP props; 6,000 hp

REMARKS: Loaned 29-6-73, purchased outright 30-12-77. Cargo: 2,200 tons vehicles and stores, 395 troops. Two Mk 63 radar GFCS. Normally carries 2 LCVPs. Went aground 6-8-80 at St. Lucia in a hurricane but was salvaged.

♦ **1 ex-U.S. Achelous-class former repair ship**

Bldr: Chicago Bridge & Iron Co., Seneca, Ill.

	Laid down	L	In serv.
T 31 Guyana (ex-*Quirinus*, ALR 39, ex-LST 1151)	3-3-45	4-6-45	15-6-45

D: 4,100 tons (fl) **S:** 11.6 kts **Dim:** 99.98 × 15.24 × 3.4
A: 8/40-mm AA (IV × 2) **M:** 2 GM 12-567A diesels; 2 props; 1,800 hp
Electric: 420 kw **Man:** 11 officers, 70 men

REMARKS: Loaned 6-62, purchased outright 30-12-77. Repair equipment removed and ship used as a transport. Retains operable bow door.

♦ **1 ex-U.S. LSM 1-class medium landing ship** Bldr: Brown SB Co., Houston, Tex.

	Laid down	L	In serv.
Los Frailes (ex-LSM 544)	7-7-45	18-8-45	4-1-46

D: 1,095 tons (fl) **S:** 12.5 kts **Dim:** 62.03 (59.9 wl) × 10.52 × 2.54
A: 2/40-mm AA (II × 1)—8/20-mm AA (II × 4)
Electron Equipt: Radar: 1/Raytheon 1404

AMPHIBIOUS WARFARE SHIP *(continued)*

M: 2 Fairbanks-Morse 38D8⅛ diesels; 2 props; 2,800 hp
Electric: 240 kw **Fuel:** 165 tons **Range:** 9,000/11 **Man:** 59 tot.

REMARKS: Transferred 1959-60 under Military Aid Program. Beaching displacement at 1.6-meters draft: 743 tons. Cargo: 400 tons. Sisters *Los Monjes* (T 21) and *Los Roques* (T 22) stricken 1979, *Los Testigos* (T 24) in 1980.

♦ **12 U.S. LCVP-class landing craft** Bldr: Dianca, Puerto Cabello, 1976-77

D: 12 tons (fl) **S:** 9 kts **Dim:** 10.9 × 3.2 × 1.0
M: 1 diesel; 1 prop; 225 hp **Range:** 110/9

REMARKS: Follow design of U.S.-built LCVP. Several other LCVP and LCPL transferred with U.S. Navy ships probably survive.

AUXILIARY SHIPS

♦ **1 projected oceanographic research ship**

H. . . FRANCISCO DE MIRANDA

D: Approx. 1,600 (fl) **S:** 14 kts **Dim:** 68.4 × 11.8 × 4.2
M: 2 diesels; 1 prop; 2,180-hp—bow-thruster

REMARKS: Bulbous bow, ramp at stern, two survey launches. Apparently *not* ordered 10-78 from a French yard, as previously reported; remains a project.

♦ **1 ex-U.S. Cohoes-class survey ship** Bldr: Commerical Iron Works, Portland, Ore.

	Laid down	L	In serv.
H 11 PUERTO SANTO (ex-*Marietta*, AN 82, ex-YN 101)	17-2-45	27-4-45	25-6-45

D: 650 tons (855 fl) **S:** 12 kts **Dim:** 48.2 (44.5 wl) × 10.3 × 3.6
A: 3/20-mm AA
M: 2 Busch-Suzler BS 539 diesels, electric drive; 1 prop; 1,500 hp
Electric: 240 kw **Fuel:** 110 tons **Man:** 46 tot.

REMARKS: Ex-net tender. Transferred 1-61 under Military Aid Program; purchased outright 30-12-77. Converted for use as a hydrographic survey ship in 1962 by U.S. Coast Guard Yard, Curtis Bay, Md. Original bow horns removed, reducing overall length from 51.4 meters. Retains 12-ton boom forward. Bridge superstructure raised one deck. Sisters *Puerto Miranda* (ex-*Waxsaw*, AN 91) and *Puerto de Nutrius* (ex-*Tunxis*, AN 90) stricken 1977.

♦ **2 Gabriela-class survey craft**

Bldr: Abeking & Rasmussen, Lemwerder, West Germany

	Laid down	L	In serv.
P 119 GABRIELA	10-3-73	29-11-73	5-2-74
P 121 LELY	28-5-73	12-12-73	7-2-74

D: 90 tons (fl) **S:** 20 kts **Dim:** 27.0 × 5.6 × 1.5
M: 2 MTU diesels; 2 props; 2,300 hp **Man:** 16 tot.

REMARKS: Civilian-manned.

♦ **1 Maracaibo-class cargo ship** Bldr: Canadian Vickers, Montreal (In serv. 1953)

T 42 VALENCIA (ex-*Ciudad de Valencia*)

D: Approx. 8,100 tons (fl) **S:** 15 kts **Dim:** 128.15 × 16.76 × 6.78
M: 1 Nordberg diesel; 1 prop; 4,275 hp **Man:** 7 officers, 50 men

REMARKS: 4,297 grt/5,885 dwt. Transferred from State Shipping Co. in 1977. Five cargo holds. Additional superstructure added on stern to increase accommodations. Sister *Maracaibo* (T 41) stricken 1979.

♦ **1 transport** Bldr: Dubigeon, France (L: 29-12-54)

T 11 LAS AVES (ex-*Dos de Diciembre*)

D: 944 tons (fl) **S:** 15 kts **Dim:** 71.4 (64.5 pp) × 10.2 × 3.0
A: 4/20-mm AA (II × 2) **M:** 2 diesels; 2 props; 1,600 hp
Cargo: 215 tons + troops **Range:** 2,520/14

REMARKS: Also fitted as the presidential yacht.

♦ **3 ex-U.S. Achomawi-class fleet tugs** Bldr: Charleston SB & DD, S.C.

	Laid down	L	In serv.
R 21 FELIPE LARRAZABEL (ex-*Utina*, ATF 163)	6-6-45	31-8-45	30-1-46
R 22 ANTONIO PICARDI (ex-*Nipmuc*, ATF 157)	2-12-44	12-4-45	7-7-45
R 23 MIGUEL RODRIGUEZ (ex-*Salinin*, ATF 161)	13-4-45	20-7-45	11-9-45

Miguel Rodriguez (R 23)   L. & L. Van Ginderen, 5-81

D: 1,235 tons (1,675 fl) **S:** 16.5 kts **Dim:** 62.48 (59.44) × 11.74 × 4.67
A: R 21 only: 1/76.2-mm DP **Electron Equipt:** Radar: 1/SPS-53
M: 4 GM 16-278A diesels, electric drive; 1 prop; 3,000 hp
Electric: 400 kw **Fuel:** 300 tons **Range:** 7,000/15 **Man:** 85 tot.

REMARKS: R 21 loaned 3-9-71; purchased outright 30-12-77. R 22, R 23 purchased 1-9-78.

AUXILIARY SHIPS *(continued)*

♦ **1 sail training ship** Bldr: Ast. Celeya, Bilbao, Spain

	Laid down	L	In serv.
SIMON BOLIVAR	5-6-79	21-9-79	14-8-80

Simon Bolivar   P. Roullet, 1981

D: 1,200 tons (fl)   **S:** 10.5 kts   **Dim:** 82.5 (58.5 pp) × 10.6 × 4.2
M: 1 GM 12V149 diesel; 1 prop; 750 hp
Man: 17 officers, 75 men, 18 instructors, 84 cadets

REMARKS: 934 grt. Sister to Ecuadorian *Guayas*. Three-masted bark; sail area: 1,650 m². Ordered 7-78.

SERVICE CRAFT

♦ **1 large harbor tug** Bldr: Dianca, Puerto Cabello, 1978

C 142

D: . . .   **S:** . . .   **Dim:** . . . × . . . × . . .
M: 2 Werkspoor diesels; 2 props; 1,600 hp

REMARKS: Ordered 1973. Used for Navy by Dianca SY. Three sisters operated by Ministry of Communications: C 139, C 140, C 141.

♦ **1 ex-U.S. medium harbor tug** Bldr: Ramsey & Sons, New Orleans, La.

R 11 FERNANDO GOMEZ (ex-*Dudley*, YTM 744)

D: 161 tons   **S:** 15 kts   **Dim:** 24.5 × 5.8 × 2.4
A: 2/12.7-mm mg (I × 2)   **M:** 1 Clark 6-cyl. diesel; 1 prop; 380 hp   **Man:** 10 tot.

REMARKS: Built 1938. Acquired by U.S. Navy 1-42; sold to Venezuela 1-47.

NOTE: The ex-U.S. Navy large harbor tugs *Fabio Gallipoli* (R 14) and *Diana-III* (R 15) were stricken 1979.

♦ **1 ex-U.S. floating repair barge** Bldr: Mare Isl. NSY, Cal. (L: 30-5-43)

. . . (ex-YR 48)

D: 520 tons (770 fl)   **Dim:** 46.6 × 13.1 × 2.1
Electric: 220 kw   **Fuel:** 75 tons   **Man:** 46 tot.

REMARKS: Leased 7-61; purchased outright 30-12-77.

NOTE: The U.S. ARD 12-class floating drydock *Golfo de Cariaco* (DF 11) was stricken in 1980.

♦ **1 floating crane—Capacity:** 40 tons

♦ **1 small service craft** Bldr: Ast. Lago Maracaibo (In serv. 5-80)

ANGU-01

NATIONAL GUARD

PATROL CRAFT

♦ **4 new construction** Bldr: Robt. E. Direcktor SY, Mamaroneck, N.Y.

N. . .	N. . .
N. . .	N. . .

D: . . .   **S:** . . .   **Dim:** 23.5 × . . . × . . .
A: . . .   **M:** . . .

REMARKS: Ordered 1980. Small helicopter platform aft. Aluminum construction.

♦ **21 Rio Orinoco class** Bldr: C 87-96: INMA, La Spezia; others: Dianca, Puerto Cabello (In serv. 1974-78)

C 87 RIO ORINOCO	C 94 RIO SAN JUAN	C 132 RIO. . .
C 88 RIO VENTUARI	C 95 RIO TUCUYO	C 133 RIO. . .
C 89 RIO CAPARO	C 96 RIO TURBIO	C 134 RIO. . .
C 90 RIO VENAMO	C 128 RIO GUAICAIPURO	C 135 RIO. . .
C 91 RIO TORRES	C 129 RIO TAMANCO	C 136 RIO. . .
C 92 RIO ESCALENTE	C 130 RIO MANAURE	C 137 RIO. . .
C 93 RIO LIMON	C 131 RIO ARA	C 138 RIO. . .

D: 65 tons (fl)   **S:** 25 kts   **Dim:** 28.3 × 4.8 × 1.5
A: 1/12.7-mm mg   **M:** 2 MTU diesels; 2 props; 2,200 hp

REMARKS: Wooden construction.

♦ **12 Rio Meta class** Bldr: N. de l'Estérel, Cannes, France

RIO META	RIO URIBANTE	. . .	. . .	. . .
RIO PORTUGUESA	. . .	. . .	. . .	. . .

D: 45 tons   **S:** 30 kts   **Dim:** 27.0 × 4.9 × 1.5
A: 1/20-mm AA—1/12.7-mm mg   **M:** 2 MTU diesels; 2 props; 3,300 hp
Range: 1,500/15   **Man:** 12 tot.

REMARKS: Six built 1970-71, other six built 1976-77.

♦ **8 Rio Apure class** Bldr: C.N. de l'Estérel, Cannes, France (In serv. 1955)

RIO APURE	RIO CABRALES	RIO GUARICO	RIO NEVERI
RIO ARAUCA	RIO CARONI	RIO NEGRO	RIO TUY

VENEZUELA *(continued)*
PATROL CRAFT *(continued)*

D: 38.5 tons   **S:** 27 kts   **Dim:** 28.0 (25.0 pp) × 4.65 × 1.25
A: 1/12.7-mm mg   **M:** 2 Mercedes-Benz MB820 diesels; 2 props; 1,350 hp
Range: 750/24   **Man:** 12 tot.

REMARKS: Wooden construction, possibly discarded.

♦ **17 U.S. Enforcer class** Bldr: Bertram Yacht, Miami, Fla.

REMARKS: Four of the 11.6-m version delivered 1978, 10 more in 1980. One 14.0-m version and two 13.4-m version delivered 1980. All have outdrive motors and glass-reinforced plastic hulls. **A:** small arms.

COAST GUARD

A Coast Guard was established in 1981, initially operating only two light aircraft transferred from the Navy. The frigates *General José Trinidad Moran* and *Almirante Clemente* may be transferred in 1983, and other, smaller patrol boats are to be acquired.

VIETNAM
SOCIALIST REPUBLIC OF VIETNAM

MERCHANT MARINE (1980): 93 ships—240,895 grt
(tankers: 9 ships—32,032 grt)

NOTE: The following listings include ships known to have been in North Vietnamese service in 1975, those units left behind in South Vietnam that did not escape the communist victory, and a number of ships known to have been turned over to Vietnam by the Soviet Union since 1975. The operability of much of the former U.S. equipment is questionable, but several of the larger units have been seen at sea. New ships names are not known.

NAVAL AVIATION: Three Soviet Beriev Be-12 Mail antisubmarine patrol amphibians were delivered in 1981 for coastal surveillance duties.

FRIGATES

♦ **4 ex-Soviet Petya-II class**

D: 950 tons (1,150 fl)   **S:** 30 kts   **Dim:** 82.3 × 9.1 × 3.2
A: 4/76.2-mm DP (II × 2)—3/533-mm TT (III × 2)—4/RBU-2500 ASW RL (XVI × 4)—2/d.c. racks—mines
Electron Equipt: Radar: 1/Don-2, 1/Strut Curve, 1/Hawk Screech
Sonar: 1/high frequency—ECM: 2/Watch Dog
M: CODAG: 2 gas turbines, 15,000 hp each; 1 diesel, 6,000 hp; 3 props
Range: 4,000/10 (diesel); 500/30 (CODAG)   **Man:** 80-90 tot.

REMARKS: Of the same export version as has been transferred to India and Syria. Two transferred 1978 and two in 4-81.

♦ **1 ex-U.S. Savage-class former radar picket**

Bldr: Consolidated Steel Corp., Orange, Texas

	Laid down	L	In serv.
HQ 03 DAT KY (ex-*Tran Khanh Du*, ex-*Forster*, DER 334)	31-8-43	13-11-43	25-1-44

D: 1,590 (1,850 fl)   **S:** 20 kts   **Dim:** 93.3 (91.4 wl) × 11.2 × 4.3 (hull)
A: 2/76.2-mm DP (I × 2)—6/324-mm Mk 32 ASW TT (III × 2)—1/81-mm mortar—2/127-mm mg (I × 2)
Electron Equipt: Radar: 1/SPS-10, 1/SPS-29, 1/SPG-34
Sonar: SQS-29 series
M: 4 Fairbanks-Morse 38D8⅛ diesels; 2 props; 6,000 hp   **Electric:** 580 kw
Fuel: 310 tons   **Range:** 10,000/15   **Man:** Approx. 170 tot.

REMARKS: Transferred to South Vietnam 25-9-71. Was in overhaul at Saigon in 1975 and has been reactivated by the new government. Mk 63 radar GFCS forward, Mk 51 Mod. 2 optical GFCS aft.

♦ **1 ex-U.S. Barnegat class** Bldr: Lake Washington SY, Houghton, Wash.

	Laid down	L	In serv.
HQ 06 N. . . (ex-*Tham Ngu Lao*, ex-U.S.C.G. *Absecon*, WHEC 374, ex-AVP 23)	23-7-41	8-3-42	28-1-43

D: 1,766 tons (2,800 fl)   **S:** 18 kts   **Dim:** 94.7 (91.4 wl) × 12.5 × 4.1
A: 1/127-mm 38-cal. DP—2/81-mm mortars (I × 2)
Electron Equipt: Radar: 1/SPS-21, 1/SPS-29, 1/Mk 26
M: 4 Fairbanks-Morse 38D8⅛ diesels; 2 props; 6,080 hp   **Electric:** 600 kw
Fuel: 26 tons   **Range:** 20,000/10   **Man:** Approx. 200 tot.

REMARKS: Transferred to South Vietnam in 1971, having served in the U.S. Coast Guard since 1948. Believed to have been made operational by Vietnam. Has probably had 37-mm AA added to armament.

CORVETTES

♦ **2 ex-U.S. Admirable-class former fleet minesweepers**

	Bldr	Laid down	L	In serv.
HQ. . . (ex-*Ky Hoa*, ex-*Sentry*, MSF 299)	Winslow Marine Railway Winslow, Wash.	16-5-43	15-8-43	30-5-44
HQ-07 (ex-*Ha Hoi*, ex-*Prowess*, IX 305, ex-MSF 280)	Gulf SB, Chickasaw, La.	15-9-43	17-2-44	27-9-44

D: 650 tons (945 fl)   **S:** 14.8 kts   **Dim:** 56.2 (54.9 wl) × 10.1 × 3.0
A: 2/57-mm AA (II × 1)—2/37-mm AA (I × 2)—6/23-mm AA (II × 3)
Electron Equipt: Radar: 1/SPS-53
M: 2 Cooper-Bessemer GSB-8 diesels; 1,710 hp   **Electric:** 280 kw
Man: Approx. 80 tot.

REMARKS: Transferred to South Vietnam 8-62 and 6-70, respectively. All minesweeping gear removed before transfer, and antisubmarine warfare gear removed during overhauls in early 1970s. At least one, now numbered HQ 07, is operational, rearmed with Soviet or Chinese weapons.

GUIDED-MISSILE PATROL BOATS

♦ 8 Soviet Osa-II class

D: 210 tons (240 fl) **S:** 36 kts **Dim:** 39.0 × 7.7 × 1.8
A: 4/SS-N-2B Styx (I × 4)—4/30-mm AA (II × 2)
Electron Equipt: Radar: 1/Square Tie, 1/Drum Tilt
IFF: 2/Square Head, 1/High Pole B
M: 3 M-504 diesels; 3 props; 15,000 hp
Range: 430/34; 790/20 **Man:** 30 tot.

REMARKS: Transferred: 2 in 10-79, 2 in 9-80, 2 in 11-80, and 2 in 2-81.

NOTE: The two surviving Komar-class guided-missile patrol boats have apparently been discarded.

TORPEDO BOATS

♦ 8 Soviet Shershen class

D: 180 tons (fl) **S:** 45 kts **Dim:** 34.0 × 7.2 × 1.5
A: 4/30-mm AA (II × 2)—4/533-mm TT—2/d.c. racks
Electron Equipt: Radar: 1/Pot Drum, 1/Drum Tilt
M: 3 M-503A diesels; 2 props; 12,000 hp **Range:** 450/34; 700/20 **Man:** 19 tot.

REMARKS: Transferred: 2 on 16-4-79, 2 on 12-9-79, 2 in 2-80, and 2 in 10-80. The first pair may not have had torpedo tubes.

NOTE: The Shershens apparently replaced 6 worn-out ex-Chinese P 6-class torpedo boats and 4 even older ex-Chinese P 4-class torpedo boats.

PATROL BOATS

♦ 6 Soviet Zhuk class

D: 60 tons (fl) **S:** 34 kts **Dim:** 24.6 × 5.2 × 1.9 **Man:** 18 tot.
A: 4/14.5-mm AA (II × 2) **M:** 2 MSO-F diesels; 2 props; 2,400 hp

REMARKS: Transferred: 3 in 1978 and 3 in 11-79.

♦ up to 17 PGM 59 and PGM 71 class

Bldrs: ex-PGM 59 to ex-PGM 63: J. M. Martinac SB, Seattle, Wash.; ex-PGM 64 to ex-PGM 69: Marinette Marine, Marinette, Wisc.; others: Peterson Bldrs., Sturgeon Bay, Wisc. (In serv. 1963-67)

ex-HQ 600 ex-PHU DU (ex-PGM 64)	ex-HQ 610 ex-DINH HAI (ex-PGM 69)
ex-HQ 601 ex-TIEN MOI (ex-PGM 65)	ex-HQ 611 ex-TRUONG SA (ex-PGM 70)
ex-HQ 602 ex-MINH HOA (ex-PGM 66)	ex-HQ 612 ex-THAI BINH (ex-PGM 72)
ex-HQ 603 ex-KIEN VANG (ex-PGM 67)	ex-HQ 613 ex-THI TU (ex-PGM 73)
ex-HQ 606 ex-MAY RUT (ex-PGM 59)	ex-HQ 614 ex-SONG TU (ex-PGM 74)
ex-HQ 607 ex-NAM DU (ex-PGM 61)	ex-HQ 615 ex-TAT SA (ex-PGM 80)
ex-HQ 608 ex-HOA LU (ex-PGM 62)	ex-HQ 616 ex-HOANG SA (ex-PGM 82)
ex-HQ 609 ex-TO YEN (ex-PGM 63)	ex-HQ 617 ex-PHU QUI (ex-PGM 81)
	ex-HQ 619 ex-THO CHAU (ex-PGM 91)

D: 102 tons light (142 fl) **S:** 17 kts **Dim:** 30.81 × 6.45 × 2.3
A: 1/40-mm AA—4/20-mm AA (II × 2)—4/12.7-mm mg (II × 2)
M: ex-PGM 59 to ex-PGM 70: 2 Mercedes Benz MB 820 Db diesels; 2 props;
1,900 hp
ex-PGM 71 to ex-PGM 91: 8 GM 6-71 diesels; 2 props; 2,040 hp
Electric: 30 kw **Fuel:** 16 tons **Range:** 1,000/17 **Man:** 30 tot.

ex-Dinh Hai (HQ 610)   1967

♦ 4 ex-Soviet S.O.-1 class

D: 190 tons (215 fl) **S:** 28 kts **Dim:** 42.0 × 6.1 × 1.9
A: 4/25-mm AA (II × 2)—4/RBU-1200 ASW RL (V × 4)—2/d.c. racks (24
d.c.)—mines
Electron Equipt: Radar: 1/Pot Head—Sonar: 1/high frequency
M: 3 40D diesels; 3 props; 7,500 hp **Range:** 1,100/13 **Man:** 30 tot.

REMARKS: Transferred: 2 in 3-80, 2 in 9-80, replacing 3 surviving units of a group transferred 1960-66.

♦ 8 ex-Chinese Shanghai-II class

D: 123 tons (150 fl) **S:** 28.5 kts **Dim:** 38.78 × 5.41 × 1.49
A: 4/37-mm AA (II × 2)—4/25-mm AA (II × 2)
Electron Equipt: Radar: Skin Head
M: 2 M50F4, 1,200-hp diesels, 2 12D6, 900-hp diesels; 4 props; 4,220 hp
Man: 38 tot.

REMARKS: Transferred: four in 1966 and four in 1968. Probably in very poor condition. Very unsophisticated craft.

NOTE: The 14 ex-Chinese Shantou (Swatow)-class patrol boats formerly carried have been dropped due to age.

♦ 26 ex-U.S. Coast Guard Point Class Bldr: Coast Guard Yard, Curtis Bay, Md.
(In serv. late 1950s)

ex-HQ 700 ex-LE PHUOC DUI (ex-Pt. Garnet, WPB 82310)
ex-HQ 701 ex-LE VAN NGA (ex-Pt. League, WPB 82304)
ex-HQ 702 ex-HUYNH VAN CU (ex-Pt. Clear, WPB 82315)
ex-HQ 703 ex-NGUYEN DAO (ex-Pt. Gammon, WPB 82328)
ex-HQ 704 ex-DAO THUC (ex-Pt. Comfort, WPB 82317)
ex-HQ 705 ex-LE NGOC THAN (ex-Pt. Ellis, WPB 82330)
ex-HQ 706 ex-NGUYEN NGOC THACH (ex-Pt. Slocum, WPB 82313)
ex-HQ 707 ex-DANG VAN HOANH (ex-Pt. Hudson, WPB 82322)
ex-HQ 708 ex-LE DINH HUNG (ex-Pt. White, WPB 82308)
ex-HQ 709 ex-THUONG TIEN (ex-Pt. Dume, WPB 82325)
ex-HQ 710 ex-PHAM NGOC CHAU (ex-Pt. Arden, WPB 82309)
ex-HQ 711 ex-DAO VAN DANG (ex-Pt. Glover, WPB 82307)
ex-HQ 712 ex-LE DGOC AN (ex-Pt. Jefferson, WPB 82306)
ex-HQ 713 ex-HUYNH VAN NGAN (ex-Pt. Kennedy, WPB 82320)

PATROL BOATS (continued)

ex-HQ 714 ex-Tran Lo (ex-Pt. Young, WPB 82303)
ex-HQ 715 ex-Bui Viet Thanh (ex-Pt. Partridge, WPB 82305)
ex-HQ 716 ex-Nguyen An (ex-Pt. Caution WPB 82301)
ex-HQ 717 ex-Nguyen Han (ex-Pt. Welcome, WPB 82329)
ex-HQ 718 ex-Ngo Van Quyen (ex-Pt. Banks, WPB 82327)
ex-HQ 719 ex-Van Dien (ex-Pt. Lomas, WPB 82321)
ex-HQ 720 ex-Ho Dang La (ex-Pt. Grace, WPB 82323)
ex-HQ 721 ex-Dam Thoaj (ex-Pt. Mast, WPB 82316)
ex-HQ 722 ex-Huynh Bo (ex-Pt. Grey, WPB 82324)
ex-HQ 723 ex-Nguyen Kim Hung (ex-Pt. Orient, WPB 82319)
ex-HQ 724 ex-Ho Duy (ex-Pt. Cypress, WPB 82326)
ex-HQ 725 ex-Troung Ba (ex-Pt. Maromec, WPB 82331)

ex-Ngo Van Quyen (HQ 718)   1969

D: 64 tons (67 fl)   **S:** 23.7 kts   **Dim:** 25.3 × 5.23 × 1.95
A: 1/81-mm mortar combined with 12.7-mm mg—4/12.7-mm mg (I × 4)
M: 2 Cummins VT-12-M-700 diesels; 2 props; 1,600 hp
Range: 460/23.7, 1,400/8   **Man:** 12 tot.

REMARKS: Had been operating in Vietnamese waters with U.S. Coast Guard crews when transferred to South Vietnam in 1969-70. Probably rearmed, if operational.

PATROL CRAFT

♦ **2 ex-Soviet PO 2 class**

   D: 50 tons (fl)   **S:** 9 kts   **Dim:** 22.8 ×. . .×. . .
   A: 1/12.7-mm mg   **M:** 1 diesel; 1 prop; 300 hp

REMARKS: Transferred 2-80. Utility craft also useable as a tug or, with appropriate equipment, a diving tender.

♦ **2 ex-East German Bremse class**

   D: 25 tons   **S:** 14 kts   **Dim:** 23.0 × 5.0 × 1.1
   A: . . .   **M:** 2 diesels; 2 props; 600 hp

REMARKS: Transferred late 1970s. Intended for patrol in sheltered waters and inland waterways.

♦ **up to 107 ex-U.S. Swift Mk-1 and Mk-2 class** Bldr: Swiftships Inc., Morgan City, La. (In serv. 1968-70)

D: 19 tons (fl—Mk-2: 19.2)   **S:** 25 kts
Dim: Mk-1: 15.28 × 3.99 × 1.07; Mk-2: 15.64 × 4.14 × 1.07
A: 1/81-mm mortar combined with 12.7-mm mg—2/12.7-mm mg (II × 1)
M: 2 GM 12V71N diesels; 2 props; 860 hp   **Range:** 400/24   **Man:** 6 tot.

REMARKS: Transferred on completion. Most believed still serviceable.

RIVERINE WARFARE CRAFT

♦ **up to 9 ex-U.S. CCB (command and control boat) class** (In serv. 1969-70)

CCB class   1967

   D: 160 tons light (75.5 fl)   **S:** 8.5 kts   **Dim:** 18.29 × 5.33 × 1.0
   A: 1/20-mm AA—1/12.7-mm mg—2/7.62-mm mg (I × 2)—1/60-mm mortar
   M: 2 Gray Marine 64HN9 diesels; 2 props; 450 hp
   Range: 160/8   **Man:** 11 tot.

REMARKS: Equipped with communications facility in well occupied by 105-mm mortar in otherwise similar LCM monitor class. Can tow disabled craft. Some had three 20-mm AA (I × 3) with an ASPB-type turret forward.

♦ **up to 84 ex-U.S. ASPB (assault support patrol boat) class** (In serv. 1969-70)

   D: 30 tons light (38 fl)   **S:** 14 kts   **Dim:** 15.3 × 5.32 × 1.22
   A: 2/20-mm AA (I × 2)—2/76.2-mm mg (I × 2)—2/40-mm grenade launchers
   M: 2 GM 12V71N diesels; 2 props; 1,050 hp
   Range: 200/10   **Man:** 5 tot.

REMARKS: Two armored turrets with interchangeable armaments of one 20-mm AA, two 12.7-mm mg, or two 40-mm grenade launchers (or a combination thereof). A few had an 81-mm mortar aft in an open well.

♦ **up to 42 ex-U.S. monitor Mk-V class** (In serv. 1969-70)

   D: 60.3 tons light (75.5 fl)   **S:** 8.5 kts   **Dim:** 18.29 × 5.33 × 1.0
   A: 2/20-mm AA (I × 2)—2/12.7-mm mg (I × 2)—4/7.62-mm mg—1/81-mm mortar
   M: 2 Gray Marine 64HN9 diesels; 2 props; 450 hp
   Range: 160/8   **Man:** 11 tot.

REMARKS: Originally built as monitors, rather than converted as the class below. A few had a turret-mounted 105-mm howitzer in place of the bow 20-mm turret and 81-mm mortar in well. All had screen and "venetian-blind-like" bar armor to break up projectiles. Towing rig on stern of most.

RIVERINE WARFARE CRAFT (continued)

Monitor Mk-V class   1967

♦ **up to 22 ex-U.S. converted LCM(6) monitors**

> **D:** 75 tons (fl)   **S:** 8 kts   **Dim:** 18.29 × 5.2 × 1.0
> **A:** 1/40-mm AA (in some)—1/20-mm AA-2/12.7-mm mg (I × 2)—1/81-mm mortar
> (or 2 M10-8 flame throwers)
> **M:** 2 Gray Marine 64HN9 diesels; 2 props; 450 hp   **Man:** 10 tot.

REMARKS: Converted from LCM(6)-class landing craft. Transferred 1964-67.

♦ **up to 100 ex-U.S. ATC (armored troop carriers) class**

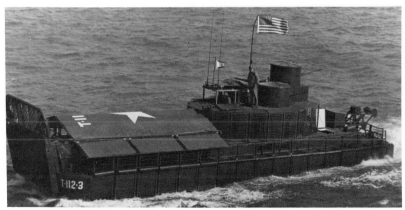

ATC class—note bar armor   1967

> **D:** 55.8 tons light (70 fl)   **S:** 8.5 kts   **Dim:** 17.09 × 5.33 × 3.0
> **A:** 1/20-mm AA—2/12.7-mm mg (I × 2)—2-6/7.62-mm mg (I × 2-6)—2/40-mm
> grenade launchers (I × 2)
> **M:** 2 Gray Marine 64HN9 diesels; 2 props; 450 hp   **Man:** 7 tot.

REMARKS: Transferred 1969. Converted LCM(6)-class landing craft. Can carry up to 40 troops. Bow ramp. Bar armor on hull and superstructure, bullet-proof awning

over troop space. A few had a small helicopter platform in place of awning. Others were configured for refuelling with 4,500-liter tank in the cargo well. Four CSB (combat salvage boat) versions of the LCM(6) design were also left in Vietnam, having been transferred 1969-70.

♦ **up to 293 ex-U.S. PBR (patrol boat, riverine) Mk-II class** Bldr: Uniflyte, Bellingham, Wash. (In serv. 1968-70)

> **D:** 6.7 tons light (8 fl)   **S:** 24 kts   **Dim:** 9.73 × 3.53 × 0.6
> **A:** 3/12.7-mm mg (II × 1, I × 1)—1/60-mm mortar
> **M:** 2 GM 6V53N diesels; 2 Jacuzzi water jets; 430 hp
> **Range:** 150/23   **Man:** 4 tot.

MINE WARFARE SHIPS AND CRAFT

♦ **1 ex-Soviet Yurka-class fleet minesweeper**

> **D:** 400 tons (460 fl)   **S:** 18 kts   **Dim:** 52.0 × 9.3 × 2.0
> **Electron Equipt:** Radar: 1/Don-2, 1/Drum Tilt
>   IFF: 3/Square Head, 1/High Pole B
> **M:** 2 diesels; 2 props; 4,000 hp   **Man:** 45 tot.

REMARKS: Transferred 12-79. Aluminum alloy hull.

♦ **5 ex-Soviet K-8-class minesweeping boats**

> **D:** 26 tons (fl)   **S:** 12 kts   **Dim:** 16.9 × 3.2 × 0.8
> **A:** 2/14.5-mm mg (II × 1)
> **M:** 2 6D12 diesels; 2 props; 300 hp   **Man:** 6 tot.

REMARKS: Transferred 10-80. Wooden construction, built in Poland in the late-1950s. No radar.

♦ **up to 8 ex-U.S. MSB-5-class minesweeping boats** (In serv. 1952-56)

> **D:** 30 tons (42 fl)   **S:** 12 kts   **Dim:** 17.45 × 4.83 × 1.32
> **A:** Several 12.7-mm mg   **M:** 2 Packard 2D850 diesels; 2 props; 600 hp
> **Fuel:** 15.8 tons   **Man:** 6 tot.

REMARKS: Transferred 1970. Wooden construction. Two sweep-current generators; capable of sweeping magnetic, contact, and acoustic mines.

♦ **up to 8 ex-U.S. MSR (minesweeper, riverine) class** (In serv. 1970)

> **D:** 30 tons light (38 fl)   **S:** 14 kts   **Dim:** 15.3 × 5.32 × 1.22
> **A:** 2/12.7-mm mg (II × 1)—1/7.62-mm mg—1/60-mm mortar
> **M:** 2 GM 12V71N diesels; 2 props; 1,050 hp   **Range:** 200/10   **Man:** 5 tot.

REMARKS: A minesweeping version of the ASPB class. Some were equipped with a pipe frame projecting ahead of the craft to explode contact mines. Others had four 88.9-mm rocket launch tubes mounted on the twin machine gun turret on the bow. One or two 40-mm grenade launchers could also be carried.

♦ **up to 8 ex-U.S. MSM (minesweeping monitor) river minesweepers**

> **D:** 70 tons (fl)   **S:** 8.5 kts   **Dim:** 17.09 × 5.33 × 3.1
> **A:** 2/20-mm AA (I × 2)—1/12.7-mm mg—2/40-mm grenade launchers
> **M:** 2 GM 64HN9 diesels; 2 props; 450 hp   **Man:** 5 tot.

REMARKS: Converted LCM(6)-class landing craft, transferred in 1970. Not all had the 20-mm AA. Bar armor fitted to sides. Retained bow ramp. Could sweep mechanical and acoustic mines.

AMPHIBIOUS WARFARE SHIPS

♦ **3 ex-Soviet Polnocny B medium landing ships** Bldr: Polnocny SY, Gdansk, Poland

D: 770 tons (fl) **S:** 18 kts **Dim:** 72.5 × 8.4 × 1.8
A: 2 or 4/30-mm AA (I or II × 2)—2/140-mm barrage RL (XVIII × 2)
Electron Equipt: Radar: 1/Spin Trough, 1/Drum Tilt
M: 2 40D diesels; 2 props; 5,000 hp

REMARKS: Transferred: 1 in 5-79, 1 in 11-79, and 1 in 2-80.

♦ **3 ex-U.S. LST 1- and LST 542-class tank landing ships**

	Bldr	Laid down	L	In serv.
ex-HQ 501 ex-DA NANG	Bethlehem,	12-7-44	15-8-44	9-9-44
(ex-*Maricopa County*, LST 938)	Hingham, Mass.			
ex-HQ 503 ex-VUNG TAU	Chicago B & I,	10-12-43	15-4-44	15-5-44
(ex-*Coconino County*, LST 603)	Seneca, Ill.			
ex-HQ 504 ex-QUI NHON	Jeffersonville	7-10-43	23-11-43	8-1-44
(ex-*Bullock County*, LST 509)	B & M, Ind.			

D: 1,623 tons light (4,080 fl) **S:** 11.6 kts **Dim:** 99.98 × 15.24 × 4.29
Electron Equipt: Radar: 1/SPS-53
M: 2 GM 12-567A (ex-HQ 501: GM 12-278A) diesels; 2 props; 1,700 hp
Electric: 300 kw **Fuel:** 590 tons **Range:** 6,000/9 (loaded) **Man:** Approx. 100 tot.

REMARKS: Transferred to South Vietnam 7-62, 7-69, and 4-70, respectively. All believed to be operational; probably rearmed with Soviet-supplied weapons. Several of the ex-U.S. LSTs may have been transferred to Vietnam by China, at least one configured as a fuel tanker.

♦ **4 ex-U.S. LSM 1-class medium landing ships**

	Bldr	Laid down	L	In serv.
ex-HQ 401 ex-HAN GIANG	Brown SB,	7-10-44	28-10-44	25-11-44
(ex-Fr. LSM 9012, ex-LSM 110)	Houston			
ex-HQ 403 ex-NINH GIANG	Brown SB,	22-8-44	15-9-44	12-10-44
(ex-LSM 85)	Houston			
ex-HQ 405 ex-TIEN GIANG	Pullman Car,	16-3-44	24-5-44	25-6-44
(ex-LSM 313)	Chicago			
ex-HQ 406 ex-HAU GIANG	Federal SB,	11-8-44	20-9-44	16-10-44
(ex-LSM 276)	Newark, N.J.			

D: 520 tons light (1,095 fl) **S:** 12.5 kts **Dim:** 62.03 × 10.52 × 2.54
A: 2/40-mm AA (II × 1)—4 or 5/20-mm AA (I × 4 or 5)—4/12.7-mm mg (I × 4)
M: 2 Fairbanks-Morse 38D8⅛ diesels (ex-HQ 406: GM-278A); 2 props; 2,880 hp
Fuel: 160 tons **Range:** 4,900/12 **Man:** Approx. 70 tot.

REMARKS: Transferred to South Vietnam 10-55 (after service in French Navy), 10-56, 6-62, and 3-63, respectively.

♦ **up to 14 ex-U.S. LCU 1466-class utility landing craft**

ex-LCU 1475	ex-LCU 1485	ex-LCU 1502
ex-LCU 1479	ex-LCU 1493	ex-LCU 1594
ex-LCU 1480	ex-LCU 1494	ex-LCU 1595
ex-LCU 1481	ex-LCU 1498	ex-YFU 90 (ex-LCU 1582)
ex-LCU 1484	ex-LCU 1501	

D: 367 tons (fl) **S:** 8 kts **Dim:** 35.14 × 10.36 × 1.5
A: 4/20-mm AA (II × 2) **M:** 3 Gray Marine 64YTL diesels; 3 props; 675 hp
Fuel: 11 tons **Range:** 1,200/6 **Man:** 14 tot.

REMARKS: Transferred 1954-70 (ex-YFU 90 in 7-71). Cargo: 167 tons.

♦ **1 ex-U.S. LCU 501 (LCT(6)) class untility landing craft** Bldr: Bison SB, Buffalo, N.Y.

ex-LCU 1221 (L: 27-8-44)

D: 143 tons light (309 fl) **S:** 8 kts **Dim:** 36.42 × 9.75 × 1.3
A: 4/20-mm AA (II × 2) **M:** 3 Gray Marine 64HN9 diesels; 3 props; 675 hp
Fuel: 11 tons **Range:** 1,200/7 **Man:** 13 tot.

REMARKS: Transferred to South Vietnam 11-55. Cargo: 150 tons. Three half sisters converted as salvage lift craft were also left behind in 1975; ex-YLLC 1 (ex-LCU 1348), ex-YLLC 3 (ex-YFU 33, ex. LCU 1195), and ex-YLLC 5 (ex-YFU 2, ex-LCU 529).

NOTE: Eighty-four U.S. LCM(6), 38 LCM(8), 40 LCVP, and several LCP-type landing craft were also abandoned; many have probably been returned to service.

♦ **12 ex-Soviet T4-class landing craft**

D: 35 tons (93 fl) **S:** 10 kts **Dim:** 19.9 × 5.6 × 1.4
M: 2 3D6 diesels; 2 props; 600 hp **Range:** 6,500/10

REMARKS: Transferred 1979.

AUXILIARIES AND SERVICE CRAFT

♦ **1 ex-Soviet Kamenka-class hydrographic survey ship/buoy tender**

Bldr: Polnocny SY, Gdansk, Poland

D: 703 tons (fl) **S:** 13.7 kts **Dim:** 53.5 × 9.1 × 2.6
Electron Equipt: Radar: 1/Don-2
M: 2 diesels; 2 CP props; 1,765 hp **Range:** 4,000/10

REMARKS: Transferred 12-79. One 5-ton buoy crane.

♦ **3 ex-U.S. 174-foot-class gasoline tankers**

Bldr: George Lawley & Sons, Neponset, Mass. (ex-YOG 56: R.T.C. SB, Camden, N.J.)

	Laid down	L	In serv.
ex-HQ 472 (ex-YOG 67)	26-1-45	17-3-45	4-5-45
ex-HQ 473 (ex-YOG 71)	11-6-45	24-7-45	27-8-45
ex-HQ 475 (ex-YOG 56)	17-5-44	30-9-44	19-2-45

D: 440 tons light (1,390 fl) **S:** 11 kts **Dim:** 53.04 (51.2 pp) × 9.75 × 3.94
A: 2/20-mm AA (I × 2)
M: 1 GM diesel (ex-YOG 56: Union diesel); 1 prop; 640 hp (ex-YOG 56: 540 hp)
Electric: 80 kw **Fuel:** 25 tons **Cargo:** 860 tons **Man:** 23 tot.

REMARKS: Transferred to South Vietnam in 7-67, 3-70, and 6-72. Employed in transporting diesel fuel.

♦ **1 ex-U.S. 174-foot-class water tanker** Bldr: Nav. Mec. Castellamare, Italy (In serv. 1956)

ex-HQ 9118 (ex-YW 152)

VIETNAM (*continued*)
AUXILIARIES AND SERVICE CRAFT (*continued*)

D: 1,250 tons (fl) **S:** 9 kts **Dim:** 54.4 × 9.8 × 4.3
A: 2/20-mm AA (I × 2)
M: 1 Ansaldo diesel; 1 prop; 600 hp **Man:** 23 tot.

REMARKS: Built with U.S. funds for South Vietnam under the Offshore Procurement Program.

♦ **up to 9 ex-U.S. YTL-type small harbor tugs**

ex-YTL 152	ex-YTL 245	ex-YTL 457
ex-YTL 200	ex-YTL 452	ex-YTL 586
ex-YTL 206	ex-YTL 456	. . .

D: 70 tons (80 fl) **S:** 10 kts **Dim:** 20.16 × 5.18 × 2.44
M: 1 Hoover-Owens-Rentschler diesel; 1 prop; 300 hp
Electric: 40 kw **Fuel:** 7 tons **Man:** 4 tot.

REMARKS: Built 1941-45. Four transferred to South Vietnam in 1955-56, two in 1969, and two in 1971; the original identity of the ninth unit, left behind by the French, is not known.

NOTE: In addition to the ships and craft listed above, the Vietnamese Navy undoubtedly employs many smaller craft ("junks") in patrol and logistics duties. Cargo ships of up to several hundred deadweight tons capacity were built in North Vietnamese shipyards during the Vietnamese War for infiltration purposes; many of these armed craft may still be in military service.

VIRGIN ISLANDS

British Virgin Islands

ROYAL VIRGIN ISLANDS POLICE FORCE

♦ **1 patrol craft** Bldr: Brooke Marine, Lowestoft, G.B. (In serv. 1975)

VIRGIN CLIPPER

D: 15 tons (fl) **S:** 22 kts **Dim:** 12.2 × 3.7 × 0.6
A: 1/7.62-mm mg **Electron Equipt:** Radar: 1/Decca 101
M: 2 Caterpillar diesels; 2 props; 370 hp **Man:** 4 tot.

♦ **2 Sea Eagle-class launches** Bldr: Coloso Boat Co. (In serv. 1980)

D: . . . **S:** . . . **Dim:** 7.0 × . . . × . . .
M: 2 Evinrude outboard engines; 110 hp

YEMEN

People's Democratic Republic of Yemen (South Yemen)

PERSONNEL (1981): Over 750 officers and men

MERCHANT MARINE (1980): 32 ships—12,230 grt (1 tanker: 1 ship—1,886 grt)

CORVETTE

♦ **1 ex-Soviet T-58 class**

D: 790 tons (900 fl) **S:** 18 kts **Dim:** 70.0 × 9.1 × 2.5
A: 4/57-mm AA (II × 2)—2/RBU-1200 ASW RL (V × 2)—mines
Electron Equipt: Radar: 1/Don-2, 1/Muff Cob
　　　　　　　　　Sonar: 1/high frequency
M: 2 diesels; 2 props; 4,000 hp **Man:** Approx. 60 tot.

REMARKS: Former minesweeper. Built in the late 1950s, transferred 1978. Minesweeping equipment entirely deleted.

GUIDED-MISSILE PATROL BOATS

♦ **7 ex-Soviet OSA-II class**

D: 205 tons (245 fl) **S:** 39 kts **Dim:** 39.0 × 7.7 × 1.8
A: 4/SS-N-2B Styx SSM (I × 4)—4/30-mm AA (II × 2)
Electron Equipt: Radar: 1/Square Tie, 1/Drum Tilt
M: 3 M504 diesels; 3 props; 15,000 hp
Range: 450/34; 700/20 **Man:** 30 tot.

REMARKS: Transferred: 2 in 2-4-79, 2 in 1-80, 2 in 12-80, 1 in 1-82.

TORPEDO BOATS

♦ **2 Soviet MOL class**

D: 170 tons (210 fl) **S:** 40 kts **Dim:** 39.0 × 7.6 × 1.8
A: 4/30-mm AA (II × 2)—4/533-mm TT
Electron Equipt: Radar: 1/Pot Drum, 1/Drum Tilt
M: 3 M503 diesels; 3 props; 12,000 hp **Range:** 450/34; 700/20 **Man:** 30 tot.

REMARKS: Transferred 1978. New construction design, based on Osa-class guided-missile patrol boat. Sisters in Somali and Sri Lankan navies.

PATROL BOATS

♦ **2 ex-Soviet Zhuk class**

D: 50 tons (60 fl) **S:** 30 kts **Dim:** 26.0 × 4.9 × 1.5
A: 2/14.5-mm mg (II × 1)
M: 2 M50 diesels; 2 props; 2,400 hp **Man:** 12-14 tot.

REMARKS: Transferred in 2-75.

♦ **2 ex-Soviet S.O.-1 class**

D: 190 tons (215 fl) **S:** 28 kts **Dim:** 42.0 × 6.1 × 1.9
A: 4/25-mm AA (II × 2)—2/RBU-1200 ASW RL (V × 4)—2/d.c. racks (24 d.c.)—mines

YEMEN (SOUTH) *(continued)*
PATROL BOATS *(continued)*

Electron Equipt: Radar: 1/Pot Head—Sonar: 1/high frequency
M: 3 40D diesels; 3 props; 7,500 hp **Range:** 1,100/13 **Man:** 30 tot.

REMARKS: Transferred in 4-72 in bad condition.

♦ **1 ex-Soviet Poluchat-I class**

D: 80 tons (90 fl) **S:** 18 kts **Dim:** 29.6 × 5.8 × 1.5
A: 2/14.5-mm mg (II × 1) **M:** 2 M50F-4 diesels; 2 props; 2,400 hp
Man: 12 tot.

REMARKS: May be a torpedo-retriever vice patrol-boat version. Transferred in the early 1970s.

AMPHIBIOUS WARFARE SHIPS

♦ **1 ex-Soviet Ropucha class** Bldr: Polnocny SY, Gdansk, Poland

South Yemen's Ropucha—note arabic script hull number   1980

D: 2,600 tons (3,600 fl) **S:** 17 kts **Dim:** 113.0 × 14.5 × 3.6 (aft) 2.0 (fwd)
A: 4/57-mm AA (II × 2)
Electron Equipt: Radar: 1/Don-2, 1/Strut Curve, 1/Muff Cob
IFF: 1/High Pole B
M: 2 diesels; 2 props; 10,000 hp **Man:** 70 crew + 230 troops

REMARKS: Transferred 1980. By far the largest unit in South Yemen's service.

♦ **4 ex-Soviet Polnocny-B-class medium landing ships**

Bldr: Polnocny SY, Gdansk, Poland

D: 800 tons (fl) **S:** 18 kts **Dim:** 74.0 × 8.6 × 1.9
A: 2 or 4/30-mm AA (II × 1)—2/140-mm barrage RL (XVIII × 2)—4/SA-N-5 systems
Electron Equipt: Radar: 1/Spin Trough, 1/Drum Tilt
IFF: 1/Square Head, 1/High Pole B
M: 2 diesels; 2 props; 4,000 hp **Man:** 40 crew + 100 troops

REMARKS: Two delivered 8-73, one in 7-77 and one in 1979.

♦ **3 ex-Soviet T-4-class landing craft**

D: 35 tons light (93 fl) **S:** 10 kts **Dim:** 19.9 × 5.6 × 1.4
M: 2 3D6 diesels; 2 props; 600 hp **Range:** 1,500/10

REMARKS: Transferred 11-70. Resemble U.S. LCM(6) class.

MINISTRY OF THE INTERIOR

♦ **5 Tracker-2 class** Bldr: Fairey Marine, G.B.

D: 31 tons (fl) **S:** 29 kts **Dim:** 19.25 × 4.98 × 1.45
A: 1/20-mm AA **M:** 2 MTU 8V331 TC diesels; 2 props; 2,200 hp
Range: 650/25 **Man:** 11 tot.

REMARKS: Ordered 8-77; delivered 1977-78. Used in customs duties.

♦ **4 Spear class** Bldr: Fairey Marine, G.B.

D: 4.5 tons (fl) **S:** 26 kts **Dim:** 9.1 × 2.8 × 0.8
A: 3/7.62-mm mg **M:** 2 diesels; 2 props; 290 hp

REMARKS: Three delivered 20-9-75; fourth during 1978. Used in customs duties. Fiberglass construction.

♦ **1 Interceptor class** Bldr: Fairey Marine, G.B.

REMARKS: Catamaran with two 135-hp outboard motors, can carry eight 25-man life rafts, and intended for rescue duties. Overall: 7.6 meters.

YEMEN
YEMEN ARAB REPUBLIC (North Yemen)

PERSONNEL (1981): Approximately 100 men, plus 250 naval port police
MERCHANT MARINE (1980): 8 ships—2,939 grt

PATROL BOATS

♦ **3 Broadsword class** Bldr: Halter Marine, New Orleans, La. (In serv. 1978)

200 SANA'A   300 13TH JUNE   400 25TH SEPTEMBER

YEMEN (NORTH) *(continued)*
PATROL BOATS *(continued)*

13th June   1978

D: 90 tons (fl)   **S:** 28 kts   **Dim:** 32.0 × 6.3 × 1.9
A: 2/23-mm AA (II × 1)—2/14.5-mm mg (II × 1)—2/12.7-mm mg (I × 2)
Electron Equipt: Radar: 1/Decca 914
M: 3 GM 16V71 TI diesels; 3 props; 1,400 hp   **Electric:** 120 kw
Fuel: 16.3 tons   **Man:** 14 tot.

REMARKS: Ordered 1977. Armament, added after delivery, is of Soviet origin.

♦ **2 Soviet Zhuk class**

D: 60 tons (fl)   **S:** 34 kts   **Dim:** 24.6 × 5.2 × 1.9
A: 4/14.5-mm mg (II × 2)
M: 2/M50-F diesels; 2 props; 2,400 hp   **Man:** 18 tot.

REMARKS: Transferred 1978. Unlike other units of this class, the North Yemeni units have their twin AA in enclosed gun houses with hemispherical covers.

NOTE: The three early 1950s-vintage Soviet P-4-class hydroplane torpedo boats have been removed from service.

SERVICE CRAFT

♦ **2 Soviet T-4-class landing craft**

D: 35 tons light (95 fl)   **S:** 10 kts   **Dim:** 19.9 × 5.6 × 1.4
M: 2 3D6 diesels; 2 props; 600 hp   **Range:** 1,500/10

REMARKS: Transferred around 1970. Resemble U.S. LCM(6) class.

YUGOSLAVIA
SOCIALIST FEDERAL REPUBLIC OF YUGOSLAVIA

PERSONNEL (1981): 2,500 officers, 14,500 men

MERCHANT MARINE (1980): 486 ships—2,466,574 grt
           (tankers: 28 ships—213,015 grt)

NAVAL AVIATION: One squadron of 8 Soviet Ka-25 Hormone ASW helicopters, and two Canadian DHC-2 Beaver STOL light transports. Four Canadian CL 215 amphibians were ordered in 1980, and some of the license-built French SA 341H Gazelle (Partizan) helicopters may enter naval service.

SUBMARINES (P = *Podnornica*)

♦ 2 Sava-class submarines Bldr: Split SY

	Laid down	L	In serv.
P 831 SAVA	1975	1977	1978
P 832 N. . .	1977	. . .	. . .

D: 770/964 tons   **S:** 16 kts (sub.)   **Dim:** 55.8 × 5.05 × . . .
A: 6/533-mm TT—10 torpedoes or 20 mines   **Endurance:** 28 days
M: Diesel-electric; 1 prop; 2,400 hp   **Man:** 35 tot.

REMARKS: Maximum diving depth: 300 meters. Completion of second unit delayed. Resemble the Heroj class, but are smaller.

♦ **3 Heroj class** Bldr: Uljanik SY, Pula

	Laid down	L	In serv.
P 821 HEROJ	1965	18-8-67	1968
P 822 JUNAK	1966	1968	1969
P 823 USKOK	1968	1-70	1970

Heroj (P 821)   1968

D: 1,068/1,170/1,350 tons   **S:** 16/10 kts   **Dim:** 64.0 × 7.2 × 5.0
A: 6/533-mm TT (fwd)   **M:** 2 diesels, electric motors; 1 prop; 2,400 hp
Range: 9,700/8   **Man:** 36 tot.

♦ **2 Sutjeska class** Bldr: Uljanik SY, Pula

	Laid down	L	In serv.
P 811 SUTJESKA	1957	28-9-58	9-60
P 812 NERETVA	1957	1959	1962

SUBMARINES (continued)

Neretva (P 812)—now has bulbous bow   G. Arra, 1969

    D: 700/820/945 tons   **S:** 14/9 kts   **Dim:** 60.0 × 4.8 × 4.8
    A: 6/533-mm TT (4 fwd, 2 aft; 8 torpedoes)
    M: 2 Sulzer diesels, electric motors; 1,800 hp
    Range: 4,400/8.6   **Man:** 38 tot.

REMARKS: First submarines built in Yugoslavia. New bow sonar arrays added during
the early 1970s.

♦ **2 or more Mala-class midget submarines**

    D: . . .   **S:** . . . kts   **Dim:** 8.2 × 1.9 (diameter)
    M: 1 electric motor   **Man:** 2 tot.

FRIGATES (R = *Razarač*)

♦ **0 (+2) new construction** Bldr:. . .

	Laid down	L	In serv.
R. . . N. . .	1981	. . .	. . .
R. . . N. . .	. . .	. . .	. . .

    D: 1,850 tons (fl)   **S:** 27 kts   **Dim:** 96.7 (92.0 wl) × 11.2 × 3.55
    A: . . .   **Electron Equipt:** Radar:. . . —Sonar:. . .
    M: CODAG: 2 SEMT-Pielstick 12 PA6V280 diesels (4,800 hp each), 1 Soviet gas
        turbine (15,000 hp); 3 props (CP outboard); 24,600 hp
    Man: Approx. 90 tot.

REMARKS: These ships will apparently be a modification of the design for two similar
training frigates recently built for Indonesia and Iraq and may have similar armament
(4 anti-ship missiles, 1/57-mm Bofors DP, several 40-mm AA, etc.). The main propulsion diesels were ordered in 6-80 (two to be built under license in Yugoslavia),
and the first was delivered 31-3-81; the propulsion concept duplicates the arrangement in the Koni class.

♦ **1 Soviet Koni class** Bldr: Zelenodolsk SY

R 31 SPLIT (In serv. 4-80)

    D: 1,900 tons (fl)   **S:** 30 kts   **Dim:** 96.0 × 12.0 × 5.0
    A: 1/SA-N-4 SAM syst. (II × 1, 18 Gecko missiles)—4/76.2-mm DP (II × 2)—4/
        30-mm AA (II × 2)—2/RBU-6000 ASW RL (XII × 2)—2/d.c. racks (12
        d.c.)—mines
    Electron Equipt: Radar: 1/Don-2, 1/Strut Curve, 1/Pop Group, 1/Hawk
                  Screech, 1/Drum Tilt
                  Sonar: 1/med. freq., hull-mounted
    M: CODAG: 1 gas turbine, 2 diesels; 3 props; 30,000 hp

Split (R 31)   1980

REMARKS: New-construction unit, transferred 4-80. Took the place of the former destroyer *Split*, which has been discarded. Identical in appearance to the two Koni-
class units transferred to East Germany. Sisters in the Algerian, Cuban, and Soviet
navies also.

CORVETTES (PBR = *Petrolni Brod*)

♦ **2 Mornar class** Bldr: Tito SY, Kraljevica

	Laid down	L	In serv.
PBR 551 MORNAR	1957	1958	10-9-59
PBR 552 BORAC	1964	1965	1965

Borac (PBR 552)   1973

    D: 330 tons (430 fl)   **S:** 24 kts   **Dim:** 51.8 × 6.97 × 3.1 (2.0 hull)
    A: 2/40-mm AA (I × 2)—2/20-mm AA (I × 2)—4/RBU-1200 ASW RL (V × 4)—
        2/Mk 6 d.c. projectors—2/Mk 9 d.c. racks
    Electron Equipt: Radar: 1/Decca 45—Sonar: 1/Tamir-11
    M: 3 Werkspoor diesels; 3 props; 7,500   **Fuel:** 55 tons
    Range: 660/24; 3,000/12   **Man:** 60 tot.

REMARKS: Modernized 1970-73 at Sava Kovacevic Naval Yard, Tivat. Original two
76.2-mm DP guns, two older-model 40-mm AA, and Mousetrap ASW rocket launchers replaced by new Bofors guns and Soviet ASW rocket launchers.

CORVETTES (continued)

♦ **1 French Le Fougueux class** Bldr: F.C. Méditerranée, Le Havre

	Laid down	L	In serv.
PBR 51 UDARNIK (ex-P 6, ex-PC 1615)	1954	21-12-54	1-56

Udarnik (PBR 581)

D: 329 tons (409 fl) **S:** 18.7 kts **Dim:** 53.10 (50.9 wl) × 7.3 × 3.0 (2.1 hull)
A: 2/40-mm AA (I × 2)—2/20-mm AA (I × 2)—1/Mk 11 Hedgehog—4/Mk 6 d.c. projectors—2/Mk 9 d.c. racks
Electron Equipt: Radar: 1/DRBN-30—Sonar: 1/DUBA-2
M: 4 SEMT-Pielstick PA17V diesels; 2 props; 3,240 hp **Electric:** 120 kw
Fuel: 45 tons **Range:** 3,300/15; 6,350/12 **Man:** 62 tot.

REMARKS: Built with U.S. Offshore Procurement Funds as U.S. PC 1615; transferred on completion. One sister in the Tunisian Navy. Engines can produce 3,840 hp for brief periods.

GUIDED-MISSILE PATROL BOATS (RT = *Raketna Topovnjača*)

♦ **6 Rade Končar class** Bldr: Tito SY, Kraljevica

	L	In serv.
RT 401 RADE KONČAR	15-10-76	4-77
RT 402 VLADO ČETKOVIĆ	28-8-77	1977
RT 403 RAMIZ SADIKU	1978	10-9-78
RT 404 HASAN ZAHIROVIĆ LASA	1979	11-79
RT 405 JORDAN NIKOLOV-ORCE	1979	1979
RT 406 ANTE BANINA	1979	12-79

D: 250 tons (fl) **S:** 40 kts **Dim:** 45.0 × 8.4 × 1.8 (3.0 max.)
A: 2/SS-N-2B Styx SSM—2/57-mm Bofors DP (I × 2)
Electron Equipt: 1/Decca 1226—1/9LV200 system
M: CODAG: 2 Rolls-Royce Proteus gas turbines, 5,800 hp each; 2 MTU diesels, 3,600 hp each; 4 CP props; 18,800 hp
Range: 500/35 **Man:** 30 tot.

REMARKS: Of Yugoslav design, using Swedish (Svensk Phillips) fire control and guns and Soviet missiles; RT 40 has 9LV200 Mk I, later ships have 9LV200 Mk II. Have a Soviet Square Head IFF interrogator. Styx missiles chosen over the Exocet originally planned.

Rade Končar (RT 401) 1977

Rade Končar (RT 401) 1977

♦ **10 ex-Soviet Osa-I class** (RC = *Racetni Čamac*)

RC 301 MITAR ACEV	RC 306 NIKOLA MARTINOVIĆ
RC 302 VLADO BAGAT	RC 307 JOSIP MAZAR
RC 303 PETAR DRAPŠIN	RC 308 KARLO ROJC
RC 304 STEVEN FILIPOVIĆ	RC 309 FRANC ROZMAN-STANE
RC 305 VELIMIR ŠKORPIK	RC 310 ZIKACA JOVANOVIĆ-ŠPANAC

D: 175 tons (210 fl) **S:** 36 kts **Dim:** 39.9 × 7.7 × 1.8
A: 4/SS-N-2 Styx SSM—4/30-mm AA (II × 2)
Electron Equipt: Radar: 1/Square Tie, 1/Drum Tilt
IFF: 1/High Pole B, 2/Square Head
M: 3 M503A diesels; 3 props; 12,000 hp **Range:** 450/34; 700/20 **Man:** 25 tot.

REMARKS: Transferred 1965-69.

GUIDED-MISSILE PATROL BOATS *(continued)*

Mitar Acev (RC 301)

TORPEDO BOATS (TČ = *Torpedni Čamac*)

◆ **14 Soviet Shershen class** Bldrs: 4 in USSR; others: Tito SY, Kraljevica (In serv. 1966-71)

TČ 211 to TČ 224

Known names: Biokovac, Crvena Zvijezda, Ivan, Jadran, Kornat, Partizan, Partizan II, Pionir, Pionir II, Proleter, Strjelko, Topčider

Biokovak (TČ 221)   1980

D: 150 tons (180 fl)   **S:** 45 kts   **Dim:** 34.0 × 7.2 × 1.5
A: 4/30-mm AA (II × 2)—4/533-mm TT—mines
Electron Equipt: Radar: 1/Pot Drum, 1/Drum Tilt
                  IFF: 1/High Pole B, 1/Square Head
M: 3 M503A diesels; 3 props; 12,000 hp   **Range:** 450/34; 700/20   **Man:** 22 tot.

REMARKS: Ten built in Yugoslavia under license, after four were transferred in 1965. Unlike Soviet units, have no depth charge racks.

PATROL BOATS (PČ = *Patrolni Čamac*)

◆ **0 (+5) Kobra class** Bldr:. . .

D: . . .   **S:** . . .   **Dim:** . . .
A: 1/76-mm OTO Melara DP—1/40-mm AA—1/375-mm Bofors ASW RL (II × 1)—6/324-mm ASW TT (III × 2)
Electron Equipt: Radar:. . . —Sonar:. . .
M: 2 SEMT-Pielstick 12PA4 200G DS diesels; 2 props; 6,000 hp

REMARKS: Reported laid down 1980; 10 diesels for this class were ordered in 1979, to be built under license in Yugoslavia.

◆ **12 131-type coastal patrol craft** Bldr: Trogir SY (In serv. 1965-68)

PČ 131 to PČ 140:

Bresice	Granica	Kožuf	Rudnik
Cer	Kalnik	Lovćen	Trigeav
Durmitor	Kotor	Romanija	Velibit

Kotor (PČ 135)

D: 85 tons (120 fl)   **S:** 22 kts   **Dim:** 32.0 × 5.5 × 2.5
A: 6/20-mm Hispano Suiza HS831 AA (III × 2)
Electron Equipt: Radar: 1/Kelvin-Hughes 14/9
M: 2 MTU MB820 Db diesels; 2 props; 1,600 hp

REMARKS: May serve in the Maritime Border Brigade, an organization similar to a coast guard.

◆ **5 Kraljevica class** Bldr: Tito SY, Kraljevica (In serv. 1957-59)

PBR 510   PBR 512   PBR 519   PBR 521   PBR 524

D: 190 tons (202 fl)   **S:** 18 kts   **Dim:** 41.0 × 6.3 × 2.2
A: 2/40-mm AA (II × 2)—4/20-mm AA—2/RBU-1200 ASW RL (V × 2)—2/Mk 6 d.c. projectors—2/d.c. racks
Electron Equipt: Radar: 1/Decca 45—Sonar: Tamir-11   **Range:** 1,000/12
M: 2 M.A.N. W8V 30/38 diesels; 2 props; 3,300 hp   **Man:** 44 tot.

PATROL BOATS *(continued)*

REMARKS: Units of this class have been transferred to Sudan, Ethiopia, and Bangladesh. A number have been scrapped. Were produced in two series, some having a U.S. 76.2-mm dual purpose forward and others a U.S. Hedgehog. Survivors all believed to be armed as above; appearance as for units in the Bangladesh Navy.

MINE WARFARE SHIPS (M = *Minolovac*)

◆ 4 French Sirius-class coastal minesweepers

Bldrs: M 161: Mali Losinj SY, Yugoslavia; others: A. Normand, Le Havre, France

	In serv.
M 151 Vukov Klanac (ex-*Hrabri*, ex-MSC 229)	9-57
M 152 Podgora (ex-*Smeli*, ex-MSC 230)	9-57
M 153 Blitvenica (ex-*Slobodni*, ex-MSC 231)	9-57
M 161 Gradac (ex-*Snazhi*)	1960

Blitvenica, Podgora, and Vukov Klanac—with old numbers   1956

D: 400 tons (440 fl)   **S:** 15 kts (sweeping: 11.5)
Dim: 46.4 (42.7 pp) × 8.55 × 2.5
A: 2/20-mm AA (II × 2)   **Electron Equipt:** Radar: 1/DRBN-30
M: 2 SEMT-Pielstick 16 PA1-175 diesels; 2 props; 2,000 hp   **Electric:** 375 kw
Fuel: 48 tons   **Range:** 3,000/10   **Man:** 40 tot.

REMARKS: First three built with U.S. Offshore Procurement funds. M 161 in service 1960. Wooden-planked hulls on metal framing. Being equipped with Plessey 193M minehunting sonar, French PAP-104 remote-controlled minehunting/disposal submersibles, and Decca Hifix precision navigation systems, commencing 1981.

◆ 4 British "Ham"-class minsweepers Bldr: Yugoslavia (In serv. 1964-66)

M 141 N. . . (ex-MSI 98)	M 143 Iz (ex-MSI 100)
M 142 Brsec (ex-MSI 99)	M 144 Olib (ex-MSI 101)

D: 123 tons (164 fl)   **S:** 14 kts   **Dim:** 32.43 × 6.45 × 1.7
A: 1/40-mm   **Electron Equipt:** Radar: 1/Decca 45
M: 2 Paxman YHAXM diesels; 2 props; 1,100 hp   **Fuel:** 15 tons
Range: 1,500/12; 2,000/9   **Man:** 22 tot.

REMARKS: Built under U.S. Offshore Procurement Program. Composite construction: wooden planking over a metal-framed hull.

◆ 6 117-class inshore minesweepers Bldr: Yugoslavia, 1966-68

ML 117	ML 118	ML 119	ML 121	ML 122	ML 123

D: 120 tons (131 fl)   **S:** 12 kts   **Dim:** 30.0 × 5.5 × 1.5
A: 1/20-mm AA—2/12.7-mm mg (I × 2)   **Electron Equipt:** Radar: 1/Decca 45
M: 2 GM diesels; 1,000 hp   **Man:** 25 tot.

REMARKS: Also used for coastal patrol.

◆ 7 (+. . .) Nestin-class river minesweepers Bldr: Brodotehnika, Belgrade (In serv. 1976-. . .)

	L		L
M 331 Nestin	20-12-75	M 335 Vučedol	1979
M 332 Motajica	18-12-76	M 336 Djerdap	. . .
M 333 Belegis	1-77	M 337 Panonsko More	. . .
M 334 Bosut	1978		

Nestin (M 331)   1978

D: 65 tons   **S:** 15 kts   **Dim:** 27.0 × 6.3 × 1.6
A: 5/20-mm AA (III × 1, I × 2)—mines
Electron Equipt: Radar: 1/Decca 101
M: 2 diesels; 2 props; 520 hp

REMARKS: M 331 launched 20-12-75, M 332 launched 18-12-76, and M 333 launched 1-77. Hull of light metal alloy. Additional units may have been completed. Has been offered for export. Very low freeboard. Used on the Danube. Three also built for Iraq.

MINE WARFARE SHIPS (continued)

♦ **up to 14 small river minesweepers** Bldrs: Ivan Cetnic SY, Korcula; Treci Maj SY, Rijeka; and Tito SY, Kraljevica (In serv. 1951-56)

RML 300-313

    D: 38 tons **S:** 14 kts **Dim:** 20.0 × 4.8 × 1.2 **M:** 2 diesels; 2 props; 450 hp
    A: 2/20-mm AA **Electron Equipt:** Radar: 1/Decca 101

REMARKS: RML = *Rečni Miholovac.* Used on the Danube. Being phased out.

AMPHIBIOUS WARFARE SHIPS

NOTE: An LST design of some 2,980 tons, 102.0 × 14.2 × 3.1, has been offered for export, but there are no indications that any are being built for the Yugoslav Navy itself. The ships would have two diesels totaling 6,800 hp, two 40-mm AA (I × 2), and would be able to transport 1,500 tons of cargo.

♦ **24 DTM 211-class landing craft** Bldr: Yugoslavia, 1950s

DTM 21 to DTM 234

    D: 240 tons (410 fl) **S:** 10.3 kts **Dim:** 49.8 × 8.6 × 1.6 (2.1 max.)
    A: 3/20-mm AA (III × 1) **M:** 3 Gray Marine 64HN9 diesels; 3 props; 625 hp
    Range: 500/9.3 **Man:** 27 tot.

REMARKS: DMT = *Desantni Tenkonosac.* Near duplicates of the World War II German MFP-D class. Nearly all have been equipped with 1-m wide hull sponsons extending beam to 8.6 meters and providing space for two mine rails with a total capacity of up to 100 small mines. Bow ramp. Can carry 140 tons of vehicles or 200 men.

♦ **12 601-class landing craft** Bldr: Gleben SY, Vela Luka, Korčula (In serv. 1976-77)

DSC 601 to DSC 612

    D: 35 tons **S:** 22 kts **Dim:** 21.4 × 4.6 × 0.6
    A: 1/20-mm AA **Electron Equipt:** Radar: 1/Decca 101
    M: 2 MTU 12V331 TC 81 diesels; 2 props; 2,250 hp

REMARKS: DSC = *Desantni Jurišni Čamac.* Fiberglass construction. Bow ramp. Can carry 40 troops in 32 m² cargo area. Offered for export also.

AUXILIARY SHIPS

♦ **1 Soviet Moma-class hydrographic ship** Bldr: Gdansk, Poland, 1971

PH 33 ANDRIJA MOHOROVIČIĆ

Andrija Mohorovičič (PH 33)   1971

    D: 1,260 tons (1,540 fl) **S:** 17 kts **Dim:** 73.3 × 10.8 × 3.8
Electron Equipt: Radar: 1/Don-2
M: 2 Zgoda-Sulzer 6TD48 diesels; 2 CP props; 3,600 hp **Range:** 8,700/11
Man: 56 tot.

REMARKS: Transferred in 1972. Carries one survey launch. Five-ton crane for navigational buoy handling. Four laboratories totalling 35 m² deck space. Used for oceanographic research, hydrographic surveys, and buoy tending.

♦ **1 submarine rescue and salvage ship** Bldr: Tito SY, Belgrade (In serv. 10-9-76)

PS 12 SPASILAC

    D: 1,300 tons **S:** 16 kts **Dim:** 61.0 × 11.0 × 3.4
    M: 2 diesels; 2 props; 3,000 hp

REMARKS: In service 10-9-76. Resembles an oilfield supply vessel; low freeboard aft. Sister *Aka* is in the Iraqi Navy.

♦ **1 salvage ship** Bldr: Howaldtswerke, Kiel (In serv. 1929)

PS 11 (ex-*Spasilac*)

    D: 740 tons **S:** 14.5 kts **Dim:** 53.6 × 8.8 × 4.0
    M: 1 set triple-expansion reciprocating steam; 1 prop; 2,000 hp
    Boilers: 2

REMARKS: Not scrapped as previously reported when new *Spasilac* completed in 1976.

♦ **1 presidential yacht** Bldr: C.R.D.A., San Marco, Trieste

	Laid down	L	In serv.
JADRANKA (ex-*Biokovo*, ex-*Beli Orao*, ex-*Zagaria*, ex-*Alba*)	23-12-38	3-6-39	10-39

Jadranka

    D: 567 tons (660 fl) **S:** 17 kts (trials: 18.5) **Dim:** 60.45 × 7.93 × 2.7
    M: 2 Sulzer diesels; 2 props; 1,900 hp

REMARKS: Served in Italian Navy during World War II. Can carry two 40-mm AA (I × 2), two 20-mm AA (I × 2).

AUXILIARY SHIPS *(continued)*

♦ **1 cadet training ship** Bldr: Ansaldo, Genoa (In serv. 1938)

GALEB (ex-*Kuchuk*, ex-*Ramb III*)

Galeb

    D: 5,182 tons (5,700 fl) **S:** 16 kts **Dim:** 121.2 (116.9 pp) × 15.2 × 5.6
    A: 4/40-mm AA (I × 4)—8/20-mm AA (IV × 2)
    M: 2 Burmeister & Wain diesels; 2 props; 7,200 hp **Range:** 20,000/16

REMARKS: Begun as a commercial banana carrier; used as an auxiliary cruiser and minelayer by the Italian Navy during World War II. Ceded to Yugoslavia after the war. Has been used as the presidential yacht, but is mostly used as a cadet training ship. Retains old German quadruple 20-mm AA mounts; may still be useable as a minelayer.

♦ **1 topsail training schooner** Bldr: Blohm & Voss, Hamburg (In serv. 1932)

JADRAN

    D: 720 tons (800 fl) **S:** (14.5 sail/9.5 diesel) kts **Dim:** 60.0 × 8.8 × 4.2
    M: 1 Linke-Hoffman diesel; 375 hp **Sail area:** 933 m²

REMARKS: Accommodations for 100 cadets and 20 instructors.

♦ **1 missile-boat tender and command ship** Bldr:. . . , Yugoslavia (In serv. 1956)

VIS

    D: 510 tons (680 fl) **S:** 17 kts **Dim:** 57.0 × 8.5 × 3.5
    A: 1/40-mm AA—2/20-mm AA (I × 2) **M:** 2 diesels; 2 props; 1,900 hp

REMARKS: Resembles a yacht; primarily an administrative flagship.

♦ **1 river flotilla flagship** Bldr: Linzer Schiffswerft, Austria (In serv. 1940)

KOZARA (ex-U.S. *Oregon*, ex-German *Brünhild*)

    D: 535 tons (693 fl) **S:** 12.4 kts **Dim:** 67.0 × 9.5 × 1.4
    A: 9/20-mm AA (III × 3) **Fuel:** 44 tons
    M: 2 Deutz RV6M545 diesels; 2 props; 800 hp

REMARKS: Taken over by U.S. in immediate postwar period, then turned over to Yugoslavia. Used as a floating hotel until 1960, when taken over by the navy. In 1962 recommissioned as flagship of the Danube River Flotilla. Painted blue and white and home-ported at Bosanka Gradiška.

SERVICE CRAFT

♦ **4 PN 13-class fuel tankers** Bldr: Yugoslavia (In serv. 1955-56)

PN 13   PN 14   PN 15   PN 16

    D: 420 tons (650 fl) **S:** 7 kts **Dim:** 43.2 × 7.0 × 4.2 **Cargo:** 300 tons
    M: 1 Burmeister & Wain diesel; 1 prop; 300 hp **Range:** 1,500/7

REMARKS: Sister PN 17 transferred to Sudan in 1969. PN = *Pomoćni Naftonosac*.

♦ **2 PN 24-class fuel tankers** Bldr: Split SY (In serv. early 1950s)

PN 24   PN 25

    D: 300 tons (430 fl) **S:** 7 kts **Dim:** 46.4 × 7.2 × 3.2
    M: 1 Burmeister & Wain diesel; 1 prop; 300 hp

♦ **4 PT 71-class cargo lighters** Bldr: Split SY (In serv. 1950s)

PT 71   PT 72   PT 73   PT 74

    D: 310 tons (428 fl) **S:** 7 kts **Dim:** 43.1 × 7.2 × 4.85
    M: 1 Burmeister & Wain diesel; 1 prop; 300 hp

REMARKS: PT = *Pomoćni Transporter*.

♦ **6 PT 61-class cargo lighters** Bldr: Pula and Sibenik SYs (In serv. 1951-59)

PT 61   PT62   PT 63   PT 64   PT 65   PT 66

    D: 695 tons (fl) **S:** 7 kts **Dim:** 46.4 × 7.2 × 3.2
    M: 1 Burmeister & Wain diesel; 1 prop; 300 hp

♦ **5 PO 52-class ammunition lighters** Bldr: Split SY, 1950s

PO 52   PO 53   PO 54   PO 55   PO 56

    D: 695 tons (fl) **S:** 7 kts **Dim:** 46.4 × 7.2 × 3.2
    M: 1 Burmeister & Wain diesel; 1 prop; 300 hp

REMARKS: PO = *Pomoćni Oružar*.

♦ **1 water tanker** Bldr: Yugoslavia (In serv. 1950s)

PV 16

    D: 200 tons (600 fl) **S:** 7.5 kts **Dim:** 44.0 × 7.9 × 3.2
    M: 1 diesel; 1 prop; 300 hp **Range:** 1,500/7.5

REMARKS: Cargo: 380 tons. PV = *Pomoćni Vodonosac*.

♦ **4 PR 37-class coastal tugs** (In serv. 1950s)

PR 37   PR 38   PR 39   PR 40

    D: 550 tons (fl) **S:** 11 kts **Dim:** 32.0 × 8.0 × 5.0 **M:** Diesels

REMARKS: Originally reciprocating steam-propelled; recently re-engined with diesels. PR = *Pomorski Remorker*.

♦ **8 LR 67-class harbor tugs** (In serv. 1960s)

LR 67 LR 68 LR 69 LR 70 LR 71 LR 72 LR 73 LR 74

REMARKS: LR = *Lučki Remorker*.

ZAIRE
REPUBLIC OF ZAIRE

PERSONNEL (1980): 900 officers and men, plus 600 marines

MERCHANT MARINE (1980): 33 ships—91,894 grt

TORPEDO BOATS

♦ **3 ex-North Korean-built Soviet P 4 class**

D: 22.5 tons (fl)   **S:** 55 kts   **Dim:** 19.0 × 3.3 × 1.0
A: 2/14.5-mm mg (II × 1)—2/450-mm TT
M: 2 M50F diesels; 2 props; 2,400 hp   **Man:** 12 tot.

REMARKS: Transferred in 1974. May in fact be of a similar, indigenous North Korean design with 533-mm torpedo tubes. The Chinese Huchuan-class torpedo boats previously reported do not seem to have been transferred.

PATROL BOATS

♦ **4 Chinese Shanghai-II class**

101   102   103   104

D: 122.5 tons (150 fl)   **S:** 28.5 kts   **Dim:** 38.78 × 5.41 × 1.49
A: 4/37-mm AA (II × 2)—4/25-mm AA (II × 2)
Electron Equipt: Radar: 1/Pot Head
M: 2 M50F-4, 1,200-hp diesels, 2 12D6 900-hp diesels; 2 props; 4,220 hp
Man: 38 tot.

REMARKS: Transferred: two in 9-76, two in 9-78.

PATROL CRAFT

♦ **29 Arcoa class** Bldr: Arcoa, France (In serv. 1975-81)

REMARKS: Original 12 ordered in 7-74; 14 more delivered by 11-80, another 15 delivered 1981; no other data available. For use on lakes and rivers.

♦ **6 ex-U.S. Swift Mk-II class** Bldr: Swiftships, Morgan City, La. (In serv. 1971)

D: 19.2 tons (fl)   **S:** 25 kts   **Dim:** 15.64 × 4.14 × 1.07
A: 6/12.7-mm mg (II × 1, I × 4)
M: 2 GM 12V71N diesels; 2 props; 860 hp   **Range:** 400/24
Man: 12 tot.

REMARKS: Used on inland lakes. Aluminum construction. One earlier unit of similar design, purchased in 1968, may still exist.

NOTE: There are a number of additional small riverine patrol and logistics support craft.

ZANZIBAR

Although part of the United Republic of Tanzania, Zanzibar has internal autonomy and its own armed forces.

♦ **4 patrol craft** Bldr: Vosper Thornycroft, G.B.

D: 70 tons   **S:** 24.5 kts   **Dim:** 22.9 × 6.0 × 1.5
A: 2/20-mm AA (I × 2)   **M:** 2 diesels; 2 props; 1,840 hp
Range: 800/20   **Man:** 11 tot.

REMARKS: The first two units were delivered 6-7-73, the last two in 1974. Glass-reinforced plastic construction; Keith Nelson design.

INDEX OF SHIPS

All ships are indexed by their full names, e.g., Almirante Domecq Garcia.

ADDENDA
Through 1 February 1982

ALGERIA

One Soviet Zhuk-class patrol craft was transferred 5-81.

The ninth Osa-II-class guided-missile patrol boat was transferred 12-81; two Algerian units of the class were damaged by a missile explosion during 1981.

Vosper Thornycroft of Great Britain has been given a contract to assist in designing the guided-missile patrol boats to be built at Mers-el-Kébir; current concepts include a length of 37.5-m and combined diesel and gas turbine propulsion.

Two medium landing ships of the same class as Oman's *Al Munassir* were reportedly ordered from Brooke Marine, Lowestoft, Great Britain, late in 1981.

Two Soviet Romeo-class submarines are to be transferred or loaned for ASW training during 1982.

ARGENTINA

The first five Super Étendard shipboard fighters were delivered in Argentina on 7-12-81.

TR-1700-class submarine *Santa Cruz* (S 33) was laid down 6-12-80 at Emden, West Germany.

The second MEKO-360-H2-class destroyer, *La Argentina* (D 4), was launched 25-9-81 by Blohm & Voss.

Both *Sheffield*-class guided-missile destroyers now carry 4/MM 38 Exocet (I × 4), two per side in place of the ship's boats on the 01 deckhouse level, abreast the stack.

The third A-69-class frigate, *Granville* (F 703), was commissioned 22-6-81.

The first MEKO-140-class frigate, *Espora* (F 4), was laid down 4-81 by AFNE, Rio Santiago.

The new Antarctic supply ship has been named *Bahia Paraiso* and was completed 11-12-81. Transport *Bahia Aguirre* was stricken late 1981.

The merchant ship *Ciudad de Formosa* was purchased 17-3-81 for use as a naval training ship and renamed *Piloto Alsina*; data: Bldr: Levante, Valencia (In serv. . . .)

D: 3,986 grt **S:** 14 kts **Dim:** 105.0 × 17.4 × . . .
M: 2 diesels; 2 props; . . . hp

The merchant ship *Islas de los Estados* was purchased 22-12-80 for use as a military transport.

D: 3,840 grt **S:** 14 kts **Dim:** 80.0 × . . . × . . .

Names and dates for the five new ocean patrol ships for the Coast Guard are as follows:

	Laid down	L	In serv.
Mantilla	16-2-81	6-81	. . .
Azopardo	4-81	10-81	. . .
N. . .	6-81	12-81	. . .
N. . .	9-81	2-82	. . .
N. . .	11-81	5-82	. . .

AUSTRALIA

At time of closing, no decision had been made on the *Melbourne* replacement carrier, although it appeared more and more likely that the bargain offered through the purchase of HMS *Invincible* when she becomes available (on completion of *Ark Royal*) in 1984 cannot be turned down; this would also necessitate the acquisition of Sea Harrier V/STOL fighters from Britain (or AV-8A or AV-8B Harriers from the U.S.) and the scrapping of the RAN's remaining S-2E Tracker and A-4G Skyhawk fixed-wing aircraft.

"River"-class frigate *Parramatta* (F 46) was recommissioned 26-8-81 after mid-life modernization.

The third *Fremantle*-class patrol boat, *Townsville* (P 205), was launched 16-5-81 and commissioned 18-7-81. The fourth, *Wollongong* (P 206), was launched 17-10-81 and commissioned late in the month.

Attack-class patrol boat *Barricade* (P 98) was stricken and transferred to Indonesia late in 1981.

Landing ship *Tobruk* (L 50) has one Type 1006(3) and one Decca RM 916 navigational radars; the ship's generators produce 1,990 kw.

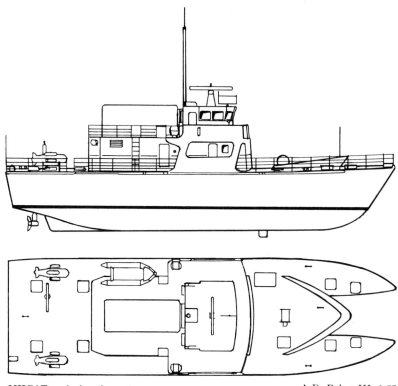

MHCAT—minehunting catamaran

A.D. Baker III, 1-82

BAHRAIN

The two FPB-38-class patrol boats are named *Al Riffa* (10) and *Hawar* (11). *Al Riffa* was launched 4-81 and ran trials 6-81. Both have mine rails and carry the French Dagaie chaff rocket launcher.

Al Riffa (10) and Hawar (11)   L. & L. Van Ginderen, 28-8-81

BANGLADESH

The Shanghai-II-class patrol boats transferred from China in 1980 have been named: P 101 *Shaheed Daulat*, P 102 *Shaheed Farid*, P 103 *Shaheed Mohibullah*, and P 104 *Shaheed Akhtaruddin*.

A 55-m river passenger-cargo transport has been acquired for use as a naval repair ship and named *Shahayak*.

The 11,684-grt merchant ship *Hizbul Bahr* was acquired 12-80 for use as a barracks hulk and renamed *Shaheed Salahuddin*.

BARBADOS

The two 22.8-m former shrimp trawlers have been named:
P 02 ENTERPRISE   P 03 EXCELLENCE

Trident (P 01)   L. & L. Van Ginderen, 21-9-81

BELGIUM

All five U.S. *Adjutant*-class mine countermeasures ships were placed in "Special Reserve" in early 1981, with small caretaker crews.

A third civilian tug has reportedly been purchased.

BRAZIL

Four corvettes were ordered in 11-81 for delivery beginning in 1985 from the Rio de Janeiro Naval Arsenal.

The modified Mk-10-class training frigate laid down 18-9-81 at Rio de Janeiro has been named *Brazil* (U 30). To displace 3,345 tons full load.

Plans to purchase the former U.S. Navy dock landing ship *Donner* (LSD 20) have been canceled due to the ship's poor condition

CANADA

The decision on the winning consortium in the frigate construction program has been delayed into 1982 by the Trudeau government.

CAPE VERDE

A Soviet Kamenka-class survey ship was transferred in 1980 for survey and training duties and named *5th July* (A 450).

CHILE

The British County-class guided-missile destroyer *Norfolk* (D 21) is to be purchased in 1982 when the ship is stricken from the Royal Navy. Also being acquired is the underway-replenishment oiler *Tidepool* (A 76). The V/STOL and helicopter carrier *Hermes* (R 12), due for disposal in 1982, has also been offered.

Corrected launch dates for the French BATRAL-class auxiliary landing ships being built by ASMAR at Talcahuano: *Maipo* launched 26-9-81; *Rancagua* scheduled to launch 3-82.

CHINA

Hull numbers reported in the press for *Luta*-class destroyers include: 105 through 111, 131, 132, and 161 through 165, for a total of 14 built (one lost 1978 through explosion near Canton).

Although reported by the press to have been damaged or lost in August 1981, the Golf-class ballistic-missile submarine has since been sighted unharmed.

COLOMBIA

Santander (03)   Colombian Navy

The U.S. *Asheville*-class patrol boats to be leased to Colombia are now reported to be *Tacoma* (PG 92) and *Welch* (PG 93), both of which were decommissioned by the U.S. Navy on 30-9-81.

The two oceanographic research ships built by Martin Jansen, Leer, West Germany, have been named *Mapelo* (156) and *Providencia* (157); both completed 1981.

COAST GUARD

A new Coast Guard was established in 1981. Its first (and, to date, only) ship is a patrol boat:

♦ **1 U.S. 105-ft. class** Bldr: Swiftships Inc., Berwick, La. (In serv. 16-10-81)
AN 201 OLAYA HERRERA

D: 103 tons (fl)   **S**: 25 kts   **Dim**: 31.5 × 6.6 × 2.1
A: 3/12.7-mm mg (I × 3)   **Electric**: 113 kw   **Man**: 13 tot.
M: 2 MTU 12V331 diesels; 2 props; 7,000 hp   **Range**: 1,600/25; 2,400/15

COMOROS

Two Japanese Maritime Safety Agency *Yamayuri*-class (18-meter) patrol craft were completed 10-81 by Ishihara, Takasago
KASTHALA   NTRINGHUI

D: 27 tons (40.3 fl)   **S**: 20.7 kts   **Dim**: 18.0 × 4.3 × 0.82 (1.1 prop)
M: 2 RD 10T diesels; 2 props; 900 hp   **Man**: 6 tot.

CONGO

The three Spanish "Pirana"-class patrol boats ordered in 1980 are in fact units of the *Barcelo* class, ordered 5-81 from Bazán, Cádiz, with heavier armament than the Spanish Navy version:

D: 116 tons (134 fl)   **S**: 33 kts   **Dim**: 36.2 (34.2 pp) × 5.8 × 1.75 (2.15 prop)
A: 2/40-mm AA (I × 2)—2/12.7-mm mg (I × 2)
M: 2 MTU 16V956 TB90 diesels; 2 props; 7,320 hp (6,120 sust.)
Range: 600/33; 1,200/16   **Fuel**: 15 tons   **Man**: 19 tot.

CUBA

The Soviet-built Koni-class frigate *Mariel* arrived at Havana on 23-9-81 for commissioning, having left the Black Sea under tow in 7-81. The ship has identical characteristics to the unit built for Algeria and, like it, has a deckhouse between the stack and the standard after deckhouse. Two 16-tubed chaff rocket launchers are fitted.

Two additional Osa-II-class missile boats were transferred 11-81, bringing the total to nine.

A Soviet Pelym-class degaussing tender was transferred 2-82.

DENMARK

The *Nils Juel*-class frigate *Olfert Fischer* (F 355) commissioned 16-10-81, having been delayed by repairs made necessary by a fire that took place shortly before the originally scheduled date 25-5-81.

Four of the six *Søløven*-class torpedo boats are to be given life-extension modernizations; the others will be stricken.

The ex-U.S. *Adjutant*-class minesweepers *Aarøsund* (M 571) and *Omøsund* (M 576) were discarded 1981; the six remaining ships of the class are to be given life-extension modernizations.

The small minelayer *Langeland* (N 42) and two of the four *Delfinen*- class submarines may have to be decommissioned during 1982, for budgetary reasons.

DOMINICAN REPUBLIC

The former U.S. Navy fast patrol boats PTF 23, 24, and 26 have been proposed for sale to the Dominican Republic in 1982; all were stricken from the U.S. Navy in 1979.
Bldr: Swiftships, Berwick, La. (In serv. 1967-68)

D: 72 tons (fl)   **S**: 40 kts   **Dim**: 28.86 × 7.06 × 2.10
A: . . .   **Range**: 1,000/35   **Man**: 19 tot
M: 2 Deltic T18 37K diesels; 2 props; 6,200 hp

REMARKS: In U.S. Navy service, carried 1/40-mm Mk 3 AA—2/20-mm AA (I × 2)—1/81-mm mortar/12.7-mm mg combined mounting. Aluminum construction.

ECUADOR

The new oceanographic research ship completed 21-10-81 by Ishikawajima Harima, Tokyo, has been renamed *Orion* (ex-*Dometer*), indicating the probable striking of the

U.S. *Aloe*-class former net tender of the same name. Revised characteristics for the new ship:

D: . . . **S:** 12.6 kts **Dim:** 70.2 × 10.2 × 3.6 (5.4 max.)
Electron Equipt: 2/Decca 1226 **Man:** 6 officers, 25 men, 19 scientists
M: 3 diesels, electric drive; 1 prop; 950 hp **Range:** 6,000/12

EGYPT

Often reported as under negotiation in the past several years, two Italian *Lupo*-class frigates were reportedly ordered late in 9-81.

The *Ramadan*-class guided-missile patrol boat *Khyber* (562) was delivered 15-9-81.

Ramadan (561)—without Otomat missiles   L. & L. Van Ginderen, 17-7-81

The *6 October*-class guided-missile patrol boat 211 was washed overboard in the Bay of Biscay from the merchant ship delivering it to Egypt on 19-12-80; although its wreck was towed into Corunna, Spain, whether the craft is to be repaired has not been reported.

Two Chinese-built Romeo-class submarines were delivered under tow in 3-82.

ETHIOPIA

A Soviet Petya-class frigate was reported to have been scheduled for transfer at the end of 1981.

A Soviet Polnocny-II-class medium landing ship was transferred in 11-81.

FIJI

Two of the three U.S. *Redwing*-class former minesweepers have been equipped with small helicopter landing platforms.

The 359-grt logistics support landing craft *Golea* was launched 13-10-80 by the Government Shipyard, Suva. Powered by 2 GM 8V71 diesels, totaling 500 hp, the craft can achieve 9 kts.

FINLAND

The twin 23-mm AA mounting amidships was restored to the corvette *Turunmaa* in 1981.

The prototype PB-80-class guided-missile patrol boat, named *Helsinki*, was delivered 1-9-81 by Wärtsilä to the Navy for final fitting out.

Salvage tender Pellinki (220)   1978

FINNISH COAST GUARD: The pollution cleanup vessel *Hylje* (99) was delivered 3-6-81 by Laivateollisuus, Turku:

D: . . . **S:** 7 kts **Dim:** 49.9 × 12.5 × 3.0
M: 2 Saab-Scania DSI-14 diesels; 2 retractable, steerable props; 680 hp

REMARKS: Has a bow ramp on a rectangular hull and can be used to transport 100 tons of deck cargo. Storage tanks can hold 550 m³ for recovered seawater/oil slurry and 850 m³ for oil. One 10-m and one 13-m oil-skimming boats are carried.

FRANCE

The Mitterand government has decided that although the seventh nuclear-powered ballistic-missile submarine is to be built, starting construction will be delayed until 1989 and will complete in 1994. Instead of being a sister to *L'Inflexible*, she will be of an entirely new design and will carry a new (as yet undeveloped) missile, the MIRV-ed, M 5, which will have a longer range than the 4,000-km M 4 to enter service in 1985. The delay will cancel the hoped-for achievement of being able to keep three SSBNs at sea at all times.

The antiaircraft version of the C-70-class guided-missile destroyers—the first of which is to be laid down in 6-82 at DCAN, Lorient—will carry a helicopter "shed" on the stern to accommodate one AS 3655 Dauphin surveillance and anti-ship attack helicopter. The helicopters will be able to carry four AS 15 anti-ship missiles each. On either side of the shed will be two SATCP short-range SAM launchers.

The fifth and sixth *Georges Leygues*-class (C 70 ASW) guided-missile destroyers will have ETBF towed passive VLF sonar arrays in addition to their DUBV-23D hull-mounted and DUBV-43B VDS equipment. *Jean de Vienne* (D 643) of this class was launched 7-11-81, and the fifth ship was laid down in her place on 19-11-81.

The *Kersaint*-class guided-missile destroyer *Bouvet* (D 624) was to be stricken 1-1-82.

The *D'Estienne D'Orves*-class (A 69) frigates *Enseigne de Vaisseau Jacoubet* (F 794) and *Commandant Ducuing* (F 795) were launched 26-9-81.

The *Trident*-class "PATRA" patrol boat *Rapière* (P 674), built on speculation by Auroux, Arcachon (Laid down 15-2-81; L: 3-6-81; In serv. 1-11-81), has been sold to Madagascar.

The second *Eridan*-class (Tripartite) minesweeper has been named *Cassiopeé* (M 642) and was launched 26-9-81. The third and fourth units are due to be launched in 5-82.

The third BATRAL-class (*Champlain*) medium landing ship was launched 27-11-81.

The sonar trials ship *Aunis* (A 643) was stricken 1-7-81.

The decommissioning date for the small oiler *Sahel* (A 638) was 24-7-81.

Former frigate *Le Vendéen* (A 778) stricken 1-12-81.

GABON

Two French-designed EDIC-class landing craft have been ordered from Bazan, San Fernando, Spain.

GERMAN DEMOCRATIC REPUBLIC

Koni-class frigate Rostock (141)   1980

The corvette *Parchim* (17) was commissioned 9-4-81; the second ship of the class, N . . . (45), was commissioned 3-9-81.

Libelle-class torpedo boat (914)   1981

Full load displacement for the training ship *Wilhelm Pieck* (S 61) is 1,800 tons.

GERMANY, FEDERAL REPUBLIC

U.S. *Fletcher*-class destroyer Z 5 transferred to Greece 28-2-82.

Type 122 guided-missile frigate *Karlsruhe* (F 231) launched 8-1-82.

The first Type 143A guided-missile patrol boat was launched 29-9-81 and given the name *Gepard* (P 6121), presumably meaning that she is replacing the Type 142-class torpedo boat *Gepard* (P 6098).

Type 143A guided-missile patrol boat *Hermelin* (P 6123) launched 8-12-81 by Krögerwerft.

Type 148 class: the first ten units received the following names at the end of 1981: S 41, *Tiger*; S 42, *Iltis*; S 43, *Luchs*; S 44, *Marder*; S 45, *Leopard*; S 46, *Fuchs*; S 47, *Jaguar*; S 48, *Löwe*; S 49, *Wolf*; S 50, *Panther*.

The Type 351 Seehond control-conversion mine-countermeasures ship *Ulm* (M 1083) recommissioned 10-11-81; sister *Paderborn* (M 1076), recommissioned earlier in the year, was the second ship to complete the conversion.

One Type 520 utility landing craft (identity not available) has been renumbered A 1430.

Type 369 air-sea-rescue boat KW 19 (Y 833) stricken 31-12-81.

Magnetic mine warfare research ship
Walther von Ledebur (Y 841)   L. & L. Van Ginderen, 1981

The new 3,900-ton Arctic research icebreaker being constructed by Howaldtswerke, Kiel, is to be named *Polarstern*.

GREAT BRITAIN

The Marconi NSR 7525 torpedo has been chosen for production over the U.S. Mk 48. It will be able to operate to depths of 914 m at a normal speed of 55 kts and is turbine-driven.

The Type 1030 STIR radar program was canceled in mid-1981. In its place the less-complex Type 996 is being developed.

Invincible (R 05) has been offered for sale to Australia, for transfer on completion of *Ark Royal* (R 07) in late 1984.

Hermes (R 12) has been offered for sale to Chile, for transfer on commissioning of *Illustrious* (R 06) in 1983.

Nuclear attack submarine *Trafalgar* (S 113) was launched 1-7-81; sister *Torbay* (S 116) was ordered 26-6-81 from Vickers. The *Trafalgar*-class submarines are sheathed in anechoic rubber-compound tiles to make them extremely quiet.

The *Manchester*-class guided-missile destroyers will carry Type 966 vice Type 1030 STIR radar.

Sheffield-class (Type 42) guided-missile destroyer *Southampton* (D 90) was commissioned 31-10-81.

Of the County-class guided-missile destroyers, *Norfolk* (D 21) is being sold to Chile during 1982 and *London* (D 16) decommissioned in June 1981.

The third *Boxer*-class (Type 22A) frigate was ordered 27-8-81 from Yarrow, Scotstoun. The Type 22A class will displace 4,200 tons (4,800 fl), will be 145.0 × 14.75 × . . ., and may be propelled by four Rolls-Royce SM-1A Spey gas turbines. Crew will be 320 tot. She is to be fitted with the Type 165 linear towed passive hydrophone array. Presumably Type 966 radar will be fitted.

All *Amazon*-class (Type 21) frigates are being reorganized into a single administrative squadron based at Devonport, with *Avenger* (F 185) as flagship. This class, like the Type 42 and Type 22, will not receive a mid-life modernization.

All "broad-beam" *Leander*-class modernizations not already begun have been canceled. As a result, *Bacchante* (F 69) will be decommissioned in 2-82 and sold to New Zealand, while *Achilles* (F 12) and *Diomede* (F 16) will be placed in Reserve early in 1983, and *Apollo* (F 70) and *Ariadne* (F 72) will follow later as their long refit periods come due. Of the "Ikara" *Leander* group, *Dido* (F 104) will be stricken in 3-83 and sold to New Zealand, while several of the others are to receive Type 165 linear towed passive hydrophone arrays. *Juno* (F 52) commenced conversion as training ship in 8-81; she will recommission in 1984, replacing *Torquay* (F 43).

The five Hong Kong Patrol ships were ordered 2-7-81 from Hall-Russell, Aberdeen, and will be named the *Peacock* class, commemorating World War-II-era *Black Swan*-class sloop names. They are to be of a different design than the "Castle" class, being some 600-700 tons (fl) and capable of 26 kts on two Crossley-Pielstick 18PA6V 280 diesels.

The "Hunt"-class minehunter *Cottesmore* was launched 2-1-82.

The Antarctic patrol ship *Endurance* (A 171) is to be stricken during 1982 and may be sold to Brazil.

The seabed operations tender *Challenger* has been given pendant K 07.

The 622-grt merchant ship *Esquimaux* (ex-*Rangu Aurora*) was chartered 7-81 as an interim training ship to replace the "Ham"-class craft. Built by Brooke Marine, Lowestoft, the ship is 47.24 × 9.75 × 5.63 and is powered by one English Electric diesel, 1 CP prop, 1,270 hp for 11 kts.

Faithful (A 85), the last *Dexterous*-class paddle tug, was stricken 4-9-81.

Adept-class tug *Capable* in service 8-9-81.

The Royal Corps of Transport cargo ship *St. George* bears pendant A 382.

A second unit of the Scottish Fisheries *Sulisker*-class fisheries protection ship class has been ordered from Ferguson Bros., Port Glasgow, for delivery fall 1982.

Leeds Castle (P 258)   L. & L. Van Ginderen, 9-81

Kin-class mooring tender Kingarth (A 232)   L. & L. Van Ginderen, 5-81

Peacock (P 239)—artist's concept   Min. Defense, 10-81

Tender Dolwen (A 362)   L. & L. Van Ginderen, 1980

GREECE

Ex-U.S. *Gearing*-class FRAM-I destroyer *Corry* (DD 817) has been recommissioned and named *Kriezis* (D 217).

Greek Navy small combatant pendants have been changed as follows:

♦ 4 La Combattante III class
P 20 ANTIPLIARCHOS LASCOS (ex-P 50)
P 21 ANTIPLIARCHOS BLESSAS (ex-P 51)
P 22 ANTIPLIARCHOS TROUPAKIS (ex-P 52)
P 23 ANTIPLIARCHOS MYKONIOS (ex-P 53)

♦ 4 La Combattante II class
P 14 IPOPLIARCHOS ARLIOTIS (ex-P 56)
P 15 IPOPLIARCHOS ANNINOS (ex-P 55)
P 16 IPOPLIARCHOS KONIDIS (ex-P 53)
P 17 IPOPLIARCHOS BATSIS (ex-P 54)

♦ 2 Kelefstis Stamou class
P 286 KELEFSTIS STAMOU (ex-P 28)
P 287 DIOPOS ANTONIOU (ex-P 29)

♦ 6 Jaguar class (ex-German Type 141)
P 50 ESPEROS (ex-P 196)   P 54 LAIAPS (ex-P 228)
P 52 KENTAUROS (ex-P 198)   P 55 SCORPIOS (ex-P 229)
P 53 KYKLON (ex-P 199)   P 56 TYFON (ex-P 230)
NOTE: P 51 *Kataigis* (ex-P 197) discarded late 1981.

♦ 1 Goulandris I class
P 289 N. I. GOULANDRIS I (ex-P 22)

West German *Fletcher*-class destroyer Z2 was transferred 18-9-81 and has been named *Kimon* (D 42); *Navarinon* (D 63) stricken.

The ex-Dutch *Kortenaer*-class frigate *Elli* (F 450) commissioned 10-10-81. Her sister ex-*Witte de With* has been named *Lemnos*. Both will carry Italian Aspide missiles in lieu of Sea Sparrow; the hangar has been lengthened by 2.2 m to accommodate *2* AB 212 helicopters.

Elli (F 450)   L. & L. Van Ginderen, 10-81

The five Norwegian *Tjeld*-class torpedo boats were not discarded but remain in service, renumbered:

P 196 ANDROMEDA (ex-P 21)   P 199 PIGASSOS (ex-P 25)
P 197 KASTOR (ex-P 23)   P 228 TOXOTIS (ex-P 26)
P 198 KYKONOS (ex-P 24)

D: 69 tons (76 fl) **S:** 43 kts **Dim:** 24.50 (22.86 pp) × 7.50 × 1.95
A: 2/40-mm AA (I × 2)—4/533-mm TT (I × 4) **Fuel:** 10 tons
M: 2 Napier-Deltic T1827K diesels; 2 props; 6,280 hp **Man:** 22 tot.

REMARKS: Completed 1967 by Båtservice, Mandal. Wooden construction.

The old ex-British LCT(4)-class landing craft L 189 *Milos* (ex-L 261, ex-LCT 1300) and L 185 *Kythera* (ex-L 244, ex-LCT 1198) survive in service.

The ex-German KW1-class patrol boat *Archikelefstis Stasis* (P 288) has been redesignated as a hydrographic service ship and renumbered A 477.

Atalanti (M 202) has been restored to full service as a minesweeper.

GRENADA

♦ 3 Spear-class patrol craft

D: 10 tons **S:** 26 kts **Dim:** 9.10 × 2.75 × 0.84
A: 2/12.7-mm mg (I × 2) **Man:** 3 tot. **M:** 2 diesels; 2 props; 580 hp

GUINEA-BISSAU

A small patrol craft was delivered by Le Comte, the Netherlands, in 5-81 and named *Naga*.

INDIA

The German-Indian submarine program is not yet entirely firm, a dispute having arisen over how many ships might be built in India. The Indian Navy desires to build the second pair in India and is anxious to secure a written spare parts supply agreement; the German builder, Howaldtswerke, wishes to build all units at Kiel. The contract has also come under political fire in India since a Swedish offer for Type A-

14-class submarines would have been considerably cheaper and offered assembly in India as part of the bargain.

All frigates of the *Leopard* class now have a deckhouse (in place of the after twin 114-mm gun mount) for use as training ships.

Vikram, the first of the new, large Coast Guard ships, was launched 26-9-81. The second Coast Guard SDB-Mk II, *Rajtarang*, completed 12-81.

INDONESIA

Four ex-Netherlands Navy Wasp helicopters were turned over to the Indonesian Navy 7-10-81.

Nangala II (402)—ex-*Candrasa*   G. Gyssels, 8-81

A Boeing "Jetfoil" hydrofoil (data similar to the British *Speedy*, except that the craft is in the commercial passenger-carrier configuration, with extra fuel tankage) has been purchased for the Agency for the Development and Application of Technology; it has been named *Bima Sumadera I*, launched 22-10-81, was to be delivered 2-82 for evaluation in naval patrol, logistics support, and civil roles, and was to be operational 3-82.

The "Carpentaria"-class patrol craft *Sasila* (852) and *Sabola* (853) have been transferred to the Sea Police Agency.

The Sea Communications Agency has taken delivery of the hopper suction dredge *Irian*, launched 26-6-81 by Orenstein & Koppel, Lübeck, West Germany. **Dim:** 110.0 × 18.0 × 7.1; **M:** 2 M.W.M. diesels, 7,700 hp = 12 kts.

The Customs Service's FPB 28 new-construction series is more extensive than reported in the text. Apparently 12 (BC 4001-4006, BC 5001-5006) are being built by Lürssen, 6 (BC 6001-6006) by Fulton Marine, and 6 (BC 7001-7006) by Scheepswerven van Gangebrugge, Belgium; the remainder of the total of 48 are to be build by PAL, Surabaja.

BC 7001   L. & L. Van Ginderen, 10-81

The last of the CN de l'Estérel series of customs patrol boats, BC 3007, was delivered 3-4-81.

The PB 57 program includes only 8 units at present, with the first pair to be delivered by Lürssen in 1982 and the remainder to be built by PAL, Surabaja.

The Maritime Police are receiving the following new patrol boat classes:

◆ **4 Kapak class** Bldr: Schlichting Werft, Harmsdorf, West Germany

	In serv.
PAT 206 KAPAK	1-81
PAT 207 N. . .	1982
PAT 208 N. . .	1982
PAT 209 N. . .	1982

D: 200 tons (fl) **S:** 28 kts (25 sust.) **Dim:** 37.5 × 7.0 × 2.0
A: 1/20-mm AA **Range:** 1,500/18 **Man:** 18 tot.
M: 2 MTU 16V652 TB61 diesels; 2 props; 4,200 hp

REMARKS: Equipped for search-and-rescue duties; can carry 8 injured personnel.

◆ **5 Kujang class** Bldr: S.F.C.N., Villeneuve-la-Garenne, France

	Laid down	L	In serv.
PAT 201 KUJANG	5-80	17-10-80	19-8-81
PAT 202 PARANG	7-80	18-11-80	19-8-81
PAT 203 CELURIT	9-80	20-3-81	1981
PAT 204 CUNDRIK	7-9-80	10-11-81	1981
PAT 205 BELATI	2-81	21-5-81	10-81

D: 156 tons **S:** 28 kts **Dim:** 37.7 × 6.0 × 1.8
A: 1/20-mm AA **Range:** 1,500/18 **Man:** 18 tot
M: 2 SACM AGO diesels; 2 props; 4,500 hp

IRAQ

The seagoing presidential yacht has been named *Qadissayat Saddam* and was delivered in 1981. Revised data:

D: 1,660 tons (fl) **S:** 19.3 kts **Dim:** 82.000 × 13.00 × 3.30
M: 2 MTU 12V1163 TB62 diesels; 2 CP props; 6,000 hp **Electric:** 1,095 kVA

REMARKS: 2,282 grt/1,295 dwt. Can carry 56 passengers (plus 74 more on short trips). Sperry folding fin stabilizers, 300 hp bow-thruster. Opulently fitted out; has swimming pool, barbecues. Helicopter deck aft.

The new diving tender listed was delivered 10-80 by Gorter SY, the Netherlands. The propulsion plant should be: 1 MTU 8V396 TC82 diesel; 1 prop; 870 hp for 15 kts.

The floating drydock ordered in 1981 will have a capacity of 6,000 tons and is to be delivered in 1983.

IRELAND

The first P 31-class fisheries-protection ship was laid down 11-81 for delivery in 1984 (i.e., much behind the original schedule). Two 20-mm AA (I × 2) have been added to the armament suit.

ITALY

Two additional *Nazario Sauro*-class submarines were requested in the 1981 Budget.

Maestrale-class frigate *Lireccio* (F 572) was launched 7-9-81.

Adjutant-class minesweeper *Quercia* (M 5517) stricken on 31-10-81.

Harbor tugs RP 122, 123, and 124 were delivered 8-5-81 by Visitini SY, Donada; no data yet available.

JAPAN

The FY 1981, 4,500 ton DDG will reportedly be powered by two Rolls-Royce SM-1A Marine Spey gas turbines and two Rolls-Royce TM-3B Olympus gas turbines in a CODAG arrangement, vice the plant listed.

Hydrographic ship Suma (5103)—artist's concept   *Ships of the World*, 1981

MARITIME SAFETY AGENCY

The Maritime Safety Agency has requested three Lockheed L100 (civil C-130 Hercules) maritime patrol aircraft in its Fiscal Year 1982 Budget and has announced plans to build a new ocean-patrol-ship class; seven of the ships are planned:

♦ **0 (+7) new construction high-endurance cutters**

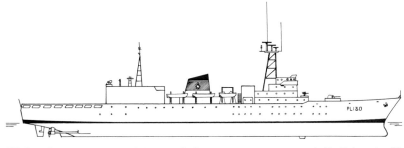

High-endurance cutters—6,600-ton design   A. D. Baker, 1—82

D: 5,900 tons (6,600 fl)   **S:** 22.5 kts   **Dim:** 146.0 (138.0 pp) × 160.0 × 6.0
A: 1/35-mm Oerlikon AA—1/20-mm AA—2/Bell 212 helicopters
M: 2 Pielstick diesels; 2 props; 18,200 hp   **Range:** 14,500/. . .
Endurance: 35 days   **Man:** 212 tot.

KUWAIT

Six SR.N6 Mk 8 hovercraft were ordered from British Hovercraft in 1981.

LIBYA

A fifth Foxtrot-class submarine was delivered 1-82.

The order for two Soviet Koni-class frigates and four Nanuchka-II-class guided-missile corvettes is apparently confirmed by the delivery of the first Nanuchka-II, *Ain Mara* (416), in 10-81. Characteristics data for these classes duplicate those for the examples delivered to Algeria in 1980-81.

Ain Mara (416)   L. & L. Van Ginderen, 10-81

Beir Grassa, the first La Combattante-II missile boat, was commissioned 9-2-81.

MALAYSIA

♦ **4 new construction coastal tugs** Bldr: Penang SY, Pulau Jerejak

	L		L
A. . . N. . .	5-81	A. . . N. . .	. . .
A. . . N. . .	. . .	A. . . N. . .	. . .

D: 300 grt   **S:** 12.5 kts   **Dim:** 29.0 × 7.0 × 2.0
M: 2 diesels; 2 props; 1,800 hp

REMARKS: Design assistance furnished by Brooke Marine, Lowestoft.

One new-construction ammunition ship reported built by Korea—Tacoma SY, South Korea. Has two CSEE Naja optronic gunfire-control systems, so presumably is armed. No further data available.

NEW ZEALAND

Prime Minister Muldoon announced 12-10-81 that the British *Leander*-class frigates *Bacchante* (F 69) and *Dido* (F 104) are to be purchased to replace the *Rothesay*-class frigate *Otago* (F 111) and *Taranaki* (F 148). *Bacchante* is to be transferred in September 1982 and then proceed to Auckland Navy Yard for a major refit. *Dido* will be transferred in mid-1983 and will receive a short refit in Great Britain. See the Great Britain section for characteristics; the ships have differing displacements, beams, and armaments. The major modernization announced for *Taranaki* (which was to have begun in 4-82) will not be proceeded with, and she and *Otago* will be stricken in 1984 when *Bacchante* and *Dido* are fully available.

Four new training craft were ordered late in 1981 from Whangarei Engineering Co., Auckland, to replace the four HDML-class craft; they are to be delivered over a period of three years.

NIGERIA

All three La Combattante-III B class officially commissioned 6-2-82.

Aradu (F 89)—on trials   G. Gyssels, 8-81

MARINE POLICE: Three 14-m patrol craft were ordered from Watercraft, Ltd., Shoreham, in 1981, for delivery in 1982.

♦ **12 glass-reinforced plastic-hulled patrol craft** Bldr: Halmatic, Havant, Great Britain (ordered 8-1-81)

  D: 5.5 tons (6.5 fl)   **S:** 25 kts   **Dim:** 9.8 (8.8 wl) × 3.4 × 0.9
  M: 2 Mermaid diesels; 2 props; 360 hp   **Man:** 4-6 tot.

♦ **13 patrol craft** Bldr: Horne Brothers, Fishbourne, Great Britain (seven in 6-81, six earlier).

  D: . . .   **S:** 30 kts   **Dim:** 7.9 × 2.8 × 0.4
  M: 2 Volvo Penta AQAD-40/280 diesel outdrives; 310 hp   **Man:** 2-4 tot.

♦ **3 landing craft** Bldr: Horne Brothers, Fishbourne (ordered 6-81)

  D: . . .   **S:** 35 kts   **Dim:** 10.0 × 3.5 × 0.75
  A: 2/7.62-mm mg (I × 2)   **Man:** 2 crew plus 24 troops
  M: 2 Sabre 250 diesels; 2 props; 500 hp

OMAN

The Marine Police received three new units during 8-81:

♦ **1 Type PT 1903 Mk III patrol craft** Bldr: Le Comte, Vianen, the Netherlands

HARAS 8

  D: 30 tons (33 fl)   **S:** 30 kts   **Dim:** 19.27 × 4.95 × 1.25
  A: 2/12.7-mm mg (I × 2)   **Range:** 1,650/17; 2,300/12   **Man:** 10 tot.
  M: 2 MTU 8V331 TC 92 diesels; 2 props; 1,770 hp

♦ **1 small patrol craft** Bldr: Watercraft, Shoreham

ZARA 17

  D: 17.25 tons (fl)   **S:** 22 kts   **Dim:** 13.9 (12.6 wl) × 4.3 × 1.1
  M: 2 Cummins VYA-903M diesels; 2 props; 700 hp
  Range: 700/20   **Man:** 6 tot.

♦ **1 landing craft** Bldr: LeComte, Vianen, the Netherlands

ZARA 20

  D: 11 tons (23 fl)   **S:** 20 kts   **Dim:** 18.0 × 3.0 × 0.5
  A: 2/12.7-mm mg (I × 2)   **Range:** . . .   **Man:** 4 tot.
  M: 2 Volvo Penta AQD 70/750 diesel outdrives; 540 hp

PAKISTAN

Tughril (D 167)   L. & L. Van Ginderen

The United States has offered the oiler *Marius* (T-AO 57) and a fleet tug—either *Atakapa* (T-ATF 149) or *Mosopelia* (T-ATF 158)—for sale during 1982, pending congressional approval.

SAUDI ARABIA

Eight SRN6 Mk 8 hovercraft were delivered 1981 by British Hovercraft.

SEYCHELLES

1 Soviet Zhuk-class patrol boat was delivered 14-10-81.
1 41-m, 25-kt patrol boat was ordered from CN, La Spezia, Italy, on 8-10-81.

SINGAPORE

Marine Police: All twelve Capricornica ("Swift")-class patrol boats were formally commissioned 20-10-81; names:

SWIFT ARCHER	SWIFT WARRIOR	SWIFT CHALLENGER
SWIFT WARLORD	SWIFT SWORDSMAN	SWIFT CAVALIER
SWIFT LANCER	SWIFT COMBATANT	SWIFT CENTURION
SWIFT KNIGHT	SWIFT CONQUEROR	SWIFT CHIEFTAIN

SOLOMON ISLANDS

♦ **3 27-m landing craft** Bldr: Carpenter Boatyard, Suva (ordered 1980)
LIGOMO III (L: 24-2-81)   ULUSAGHE (L: 26-3-81) N. . . (L:. . .)

D: 195 grt/105 dwt **S:** 9 kts **Dim:** 27.0 × . . . × . . .
M: 2 diesels; 2 props; . . . hp

SPAIN

Eighteen U.S. SH-60B LAMPS-III ASW helicopters are to be purchased for operations from *Canarias* (PA II) and the three U.S. *Oliver Hazard Perry*-class (FFG 7) frigates, all under construction.
Roger de Lauria-class destroyer *Roger de Lauria* (D 42) was decommissioned 15-1-82. Sister *Marquis de Ensenada* (D 43) was badly damaged by a terrorist explosion on 2-10-81.
Patrol boat *Guadelete* (PVZ 41), a former *Aggressive*-class minesweeper, was again renumbered M 41 in late 1981 and returned to the minesweeper ranks.
The small sailing schooner *Arosa* was purchased in 1-81, refitted and commissioned 1-4-81 as a sail training ship with pendant A 21.

SWEDEN

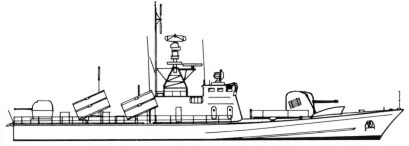

Sweden's new guided-missile/torpedo boat—"Spica-III" design   A. D. Baker, 1-82

A large order for around 150 navigational radar sets was placed with Decca in Great Britain in late 1981. Type RM 1226C sets will be used on Coast Artillery small minelayers, Type RM 914C sets on small support ships, and Type 125 on small craft.

THAILAND

Four PSMM Mk 5-class patrol or guided-missile patrol boats were ordered 9-9-81 from Ital-Thai Shipyard, Bangkok, to be built with aid under license from Korea-Tacoma Shipyard. The first is to deliver in 1983 and the last in 1985. Characteristics will presumably be similar to the four units of the PSMM Mk 5 class delivered from South Korea to Indonesia in 1979-80.

TRINIDAD AND TOBAGO

Six new patrol craft have been ordered from Souter & Sons, Cowes, Great Britain, for delivery in 1982:

♦ **2 aluminum-hulled** (ordered 30-9-81)

D: 32 tons (fl) **S:** 36 kts (30 sust.) **Dim:** 20.0 × 5.0 × 1.5
A: 2/7.62-mm mg (I × 2) **Range:** 300/30 **Man:** 6 tot.
M: 2 GM 16V92 TI diesels; 2 props; 2,400 hp

♦ **4 glass-reinforced plastic-hulled** (ordered 8-81)

D: 19 tons (fl) **S:** 32 kts (28 sust.) **Dim:** 16.75 × 4.20 × 1.40
A: 2/7.62-mm mg **Man:** 6 tot.   **M:** 2 GM 12V92 TI diesels; 2 props; 1,800 hp

TURKEY

U.S. Navy destroyer tender *Dixie* (AD 14) to be purchased in 6-82.

USSR

A salvage-and-rescue ship of some 15-20,000 tons (fl) named *El'brus* exited the Black Sea at the end of 12-81. Equipped with an icebreaker bow and a helicopter hangar and flight deck, the elaborately equipped, low-freeboard ship appears designed to deploy rescue submersibles over the sides by using sophisticated extendable gantry cranes; a large hangar for the submersibles occupies the center portion of a very voluminous superstructure.
The name *Pskovskiy Komsomolets* is applied to a Baltic Fleet Whiskey-class submarine reported in the Soviet press to be the best "Komsomolets"-named submarine in the Soviet Navy.
Additional Nanuchka-class names that have appeared in the Soviet press include *Tsiklon*, *Tayfun*, and *Zyb'*, the last a Black Sea Fleet unit.
The Tarantul-II-class guided-missile corvette is distinguished from the original variant in having a Band Stand radome (as on Nanuchkas), no large target acquisition radar, and a small spherical radome atop a redesigned mast; there are detail design changes in the engine intake and exhaust configuration, and the cruise missiles may be of a new type.

El'brus

French Navy, 1982

El'brus—stern view

French Navy, 12-81

A small inshore or auxiliary minesweeper design has reportedly been created by modifying a Baltika-class stern-haul trawler.

One Kamenka-class hydrographic survey ship was transferred to Cape Verde in 1980.

T-58-class radar picket—former minesweeper

U.S. Navy, 1981

LATE ADDENDA
Through 1 March 1982

AUSTRALIA

On 25-2-82 the Australian Parliament approved purchase of HMS *Invincible*, for acquisition during 1983; will then refit and modify for Australian requirements in Great Britain. Ship will probably be renamed *Australia*. Initially will operate only Sea King Mk 50 ASW helicopters, of which the RAN has six, with two more on order.

The aircraft rescue launch *Sea Sprite* (Y 256) was sunk as a target on 17-5-79.

EGYPT

A new class of Coast Guard patrol boats is being built at Timsah Shipyard on the Suez Canal; *Timsah*, the first, was laid down 1-1-80 and launched 11-81.

D: . . .   **S:** 25 kts   **Dim:** 31.0 × 5.2 × 1.48
A: 1/12.7-mm mg   **M:** 2 MTU diesels; 2 props; 2,960 hp
Range: 600/. . .   **Man:** 13 tot.

GERMANY, FEDERAL REPUBLIC

The full listing of the newly applied names for fast combatants follows; all continue to carry their "S" series numbers as well.

Type 143A	Type 143
P 6021 S 71 GEPARD	P 6111 S 61 ALBATROS
P 6022 S 72 PUMA	P 6112 S 62 FALKE
P 6023 S 73 HERMELIN	P 6113 S 63 GEIER
P 6124 S 74 NERZ	P 6114 S 64 BUSSARD
P 6125 S 75 ZOBEL	P 6115 S 65 SPERBER
P 6126 S 76 FRETTCHEN	P 6116 S 66 GRIEF
P 6127 S 77 DACHS	P 6117 S 67 KONDOR
P 6128 S 78 OZELOT	P 6118 S 68 SEEADLER
P 6129 S 79 WIESEL	P 6119 S 69 HABICHT
P 6130 S 80 HYANE	P 6120 S 70 KORMORAN

Type 148	
P 6141 S 41 TIGER	P 6151 S 51 HÄHER
P 6142 S 42 ILTIS	P 6152 S 52 STORCH
P 6143 S 43 LUCHS	P 6153 S 53 PELIKAN
P 6144 S 44 MARDER	P 6154 S 54 ELSTER
P 6145 S 45 LEOPARD	P 6155 S 55 ALK
P 6146 S 46 FUCHS	P 6156 S 56 DOMMEL
P 6147 S 47 JAGUAR	P 6157 S 57 WEIHE
P 6148 S 48 LÖWE	P 6158 S 58 PINGUIN
P 6149 S 49 WOLF	P 6159 S 59 REIHER
P 6150 S 50 PANTHER	P 6160 S 60 KRANICH

Type 142 torpedo boat *Puma* (P 6097) stricken 17-12-81.

GREAT BRITAIN

In March 1982 it was announced that Great Britain would acquire the Trident II (D-5) submarine-launched ballistic missile, vice the Trident I (C-4) agreed on in July 1981. Fleet introduction will require larger missile tubes than are installed in the current Royal Navy *Resolution*-class submarines; thus, a new class must be built, with deliveries probably not taking place until the early 1990s.

INDONESIA

Indonesian Boeing Jetfoil Bima Samudera I (See Addenda)

Boeing Marine System, 1981

KOREA, SOUTH

USNS *Rincon* (T-AOG 77) and *Petaluma* (T-AOG 79) were leased on 21-2-82.

MEXICO

On 24-2-82 *Vogelgesang* (DD 862) was purchased as *Quetzalcoatl* (IE 03), and *Steinaker* (DD 863) was purchased as *Netzahualcoyotl* (IE 04).

MOROCCO

The Spanish *Descubierta*-class frigate is named *Errhamani* and is to be delivered 12-82.

PAKISTAN

The stricken British "County"-class guided-missile destroyer *London* (D 16) was purchased late 1-82; the obsolete Sea Slug Mk 1 missile system will be removed prior to delivery.

SOUTH AFRICA

The frigate *President Kruger* (F 150) sank 17-2-82 following a collision with the replenishment ship *Tafelberg* (A 243).

SPAIN

The new aircraft carrier (R 11), which was to have been named *Canarias*, will be named *Principe de Asturias* and is due to be launched in May 1982.

USSR

A new Kamov-designed ASW helicopter has entered service with the Soviet Navy aboard the *Udaloy*-class guided-missile destroyers. Although similar in overall dimensions to the KA-25 Hormone, the new helicopter, dubbed "Helix-A" by NATO, is bulkier.

Helix-A ASW helicopter aboard Udaloy   U.S. Navy, 1981

A fourteenth Delta-III-class ballistic-missile submarine has reportedly been launched, probably in 12-81.

The Papa-class nuclear-powered cruise-missile submarine is reported capable of making speeds of 38-39 knots.

The missile fire-control radar director for the SA-N-7 system on the *Sovremennyy*-class guided-missile destroyers and on the Kashin-class trials destroyer *Provornyy* has been nicknamed "Front Dome" by NATO; it is similar in appearance to the Bass Tilt gun fire-control radar.

The cruise missile system in the *Sovremennyy* class reportedly launches sea-skimming anti-ship missiles, indicating a new level of sophisticated development for Soviet naval weapons.

USA

The Military Sealift Command is seeking bids for construction and charter of five new transport tankers (T-AOT) to replace T-AOT 149, 151, 152, 165, and 181. Three are needed by 1-1-86, and the other two by 1-7-86. Although primarily for freighting, they are to be able to transfer their cargoes at sea to a replenishment oiler. Provisional details for the 25–35,000 dwt ships are:

D: . . . S: 16 kts **Dim:** 187.5 × 27.43 × 10.36
M: Steam turbines or diesels **Range:** 12,000/16
Cargo: 200–240,000 bbl

Range Instrumentation Ship *General H.H. Arnold* (T-AGM 9) was stricken 1-3-82

Avenger (MCM 1)   Naval Sea Systems Command, 198

Hayler (DD 997) will have SPS-49 vice the SPS-40 air search radar fitted to earlier units of the *Spruance* class. The ship will have the improvements being backfitted into earlier *Spruances* and will have Kevlar and aluminum armor plating, and the same distillation plate being fitted to the *Ticonderoga* (CG 47) class. Sea trials are scheduled for 11/12-82.

T-AGOS 14 and later are planned to be of a new class, using SWATH (Small Waterplane Area, Twin-Hull) technology developed in the trials craft *Kaimalino* (SSP 1).

Enterprise (CVN 65) entering Puget Sound after successful sea trials

2-7-82

The new nuclear-powered aircraft carrier Carl Vinson (CVN 70) undergoing sea trials off Virginia

PH1 Wm. T. Cline, USN, 26-1-82

A bow-on view of Carl Vinson (CVN 70) during her sea trials

PH 1 Wm. T. Cline, USN, 26-1-82

USSR

Soviet Tarantul II missile gunboat—note Band Stand radome atop pilothouse

1981